**28**

SWEDEN

FINLAND

ESTONIA

LATVIA

RUSSIA

**TO EUROPE AND
COUNTRY INDEX
EAR ENDPAPER**

KAZAKHSTAN

**68**

USTRIA · SLOVAK REP · UKRAINE
SLOK · HUNGARY · MOLDOVA
CROATIA · ROMANIA
BOS) · SERBIA
HERZ · & MONT · BULG.
SRAC

GEORGIA

TURKEY

GREECE

**44**

**46** SYRIA

IRAQ

JORDAN

KUWAIT

QATAR

U.A.E.

OMAN

ARM. AZER · TURKMENISTAN · UZBEKISTAN

**40** AFGHAN.

**42**

PAKISTAN

IRAN

SAUDI
ARABIA

LIBYA

EGYPT

CHAD

SUDAN

ERITREA

YEMEN

DJIBOUTI

ETHIOPIA

SOMALI
REP.

CENTRAL
AFRICAN
REP.

**54**

CONGO

CONGO
(DEM. REP. OF THE)

RWANDA

BURUNDI

UGANDA

KENYA

TANZANIA

MONGOLIA

**34**

**30**

NORTH
KOREA

SOUTH
KOREA

JAPAN

CHINA

KYRGYZSTAN

TAJIK.

NEPAL

BANGLA-
DESH

**38**

BURMA

LAOS

TAIWAN

**36**

**40**

SRI
LANKA

**47**

INDIA

**39**

**39**

**39** MALAYSIA

THAILAND

CAMB.

VIETNAM

PHILIPPINES

INDONESIA

**37**

E. TIMOR

PAPUA
NEW GUINEA

Tropic of Cancer

**PACIFIC
OCEAN**

**64**

Equator

**56**

NAMIBIA

ANGOLA

ZAMBIA

MALAWI

ZIMBABWE

MOZAMBIQUE

BOTSWANA

SWAZILAND

SOUTH
AFRICA

LESOTHO

MADAGASCAR

**60**

**62**

**62**

AUSTRALIA

Tropic of Capricorn

**59**

**59**

**59**

NEW
ZEALAND

International Dateline

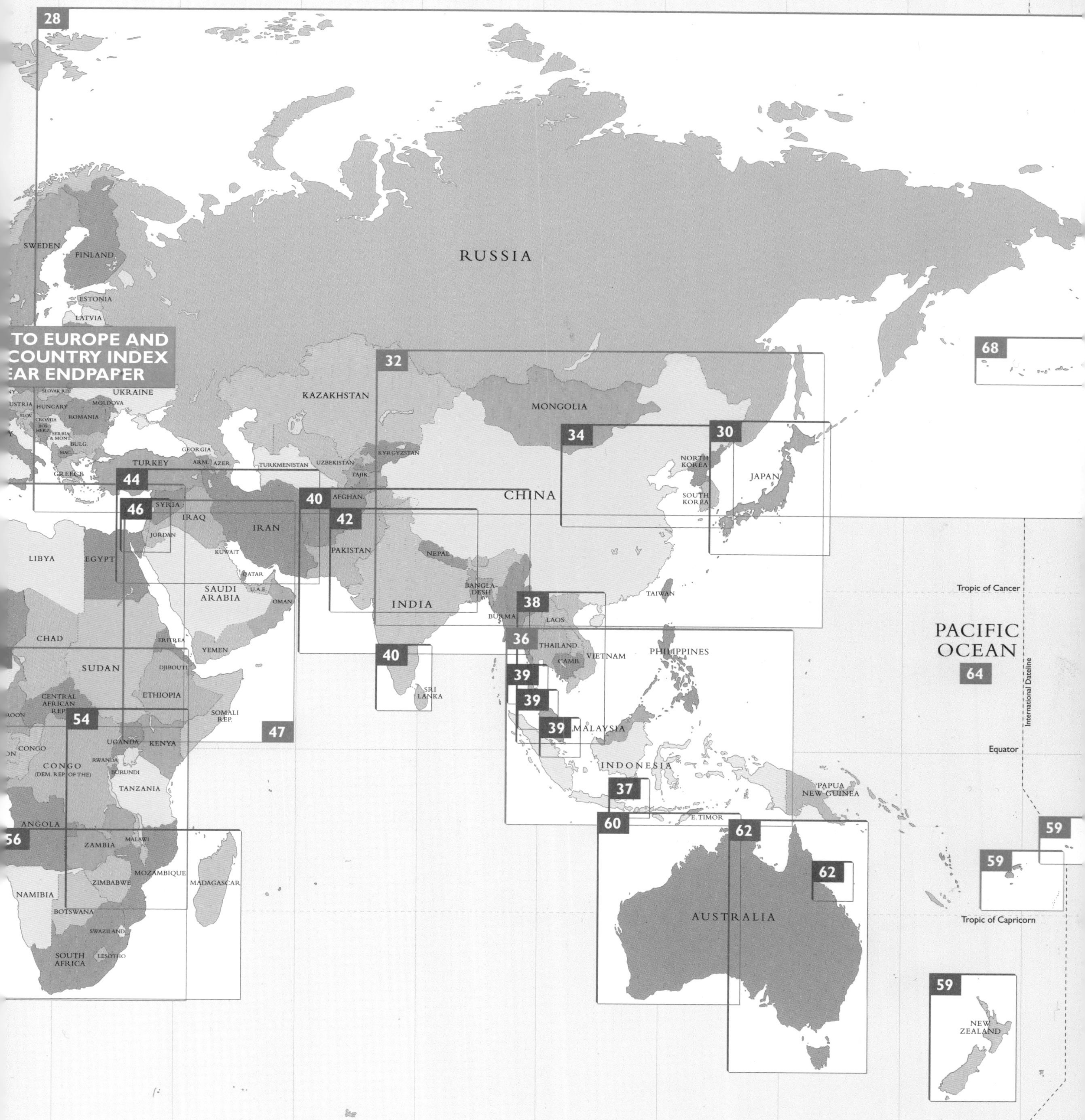

# PHILIP'S

# WORLD ATLAS

## CONSULTANTS

*Philip's* are grateful to the following people for acting as specialist geography consultants on 'The World in Focus' front section:

Professor D. Brunsden, Kings College, University of London, UK
Dr C. Clarke, Oxford University, UK
Dr I. S. Evans, Durham University, UK
Professor P. Haggett, University of Bristol, UK
Professor K. McLachlan, University of London, UK
Professor M. Monmonier, Syracuse University, New York, USA
Professor M-L. Hsu, University of Minnesota, Minnesota, USA
Professor M. J. Tooley, University of St Andrews, UK
Dr T. Unwin, Royal Holloway, University of London, UK

**THE WORLD IN FOCUS**
**Cartography by Philip's**

**Picture Acknowledgements**
**NASA/GSFC** page 14

**Illustrations:** Stefan Chabluk

**WORLD CITIES**
**Cartography by Philip's**

**Page 11, Dublin: The town plan of Dublin is based on Ordnance Survey Ireland by permission of the Government Permit Number 7735. © Ordnance Survey Ireland and Government of Ireland.**

**Page 11, Edinburgh, and page 15, London:**
This product includes mapping data licensed from Ordnance Survey® with the permission of the Controller of Her Majesty's Stationery Office. © Crown copyright 2004. All rights reserved. Licence number 100011710.

**Vector data: Courtesy of Gräfe and Unser Verlag GmbH, München, Germany**
(city centre maps of Bangkok, Beijing, Cape Town, Jerusalem, Mexico City, Moscow, Singapore, Sydney, Tokyo and Washington D.C.)

**All satellite images in this section courtesy of NPA Group Limited, Edenbridge, Kent (www.satmaps.com)**

Published in Great Britain in 2004
by Philip's,
a division of Octopus Publishing Group Limited,
2–4 Heron Quays, London E14 4JP

Copyright © 2004 Philip's

Cartography by Philip's

ISBN-13 978–0–540–08601–6
ISBN-10 0–540–08601–0

A CIP catalogue record for this book is available from the British Library.

Printed in Hong Kong

Details of other Philip's titles and services can be found on our website at: www.philips-maps.co.uk

Philip's World Atlases are published in association with The Royal Geographical Society (with The Institute of British Geographers).

The Society was founded in 1830 and given a Royal Charter in 1859 for 'the advancement of geographical science'. It holds historical collections of national and international importance, many of which relate to the Society's association with and support for scientific exploration and research from the 19th century onwards. It was pivotal in establishing geography as a teaching and research discipline in British universities close to the turn of the century, and has played a key role in geographical and environmental education ever since.

Today the Society is a leading world centre for geographical learning – supporting education, teaching, research and expeditions, and promoting public understanding of the subject.

The Society welcomes those interested in geography as members. For further information, please visit the website at: www.rgs.org

# PHILIP'S

# WORLD ATLAS

IN ASSOCIATION WITH
## THE ROYAL GEOGRAPHICAL SOCIETY
WITH THE INSTITUTE OF BRITISH GEOGRAPHERS

# Contents

## World Statistics

Countries    vi
Physical Dimensions    vii
Philip's World Maps    viii

## The World in Focus

Planet Earth    2–3
Restless Earth    4–5
Landforms    6–7
Oceans    8–9
Climate    10–11
Water and Vegetation    12–13
Environment    14–15
Population    16–17
The Human Family    18–19
Wealth    20–21
Quality of Life    22–23
Energy    24–25
Production    26–27
Trade    28–29
Travel and Tourism    30–31
Index    32

## World Cities

Amsterdam    2
Athens    2
Atlanta    3
Baghdad    3
Bangkok    3
Barcelona    4
Beijing    4
Berlin    5
Boston    6
Brussels    6
Budapest    7
Buenos Aires    7
Cairo    7
Calcutta (Kolkata)    8
Canton (Guangzhou)    8
Cape Town    8
Chicago    9
Copenhagen    10
Delhi    10
Dublin    11
Edinburgh    11
Helsinki    12
Hong Kong    12
Istanbul    12
Jakarta    13
Jerusalem    13
Johannesburg    13
Karachi    14
Lagos    14
Lisbon    14
London    15
Lima    16
Los Angeles    16
Madrid    17
Manila    17
Melbourne    17
Mexico City    18
Miami    18
Milan    18
Montréal    19
Moscow    19
Mumbai (Bombay)    20
Munich    20
New York    21
Osaka    22
Oslo    22
Paris    23
Prague    24
Rio de Janeiro    24
Rome    25
San Francisco    25
St Petersburg    26
Santiago    26
São Paulo    26
Seoul    26
Shanghai    27
Singapore    27
Stockholm    28
Sydney    28
Tokyo    29
Tehran    30
Tianjin    30
Toronto    30
Vienna    31
Warsaw    31
Washington    32
Wellington    32
Index to City Maps    33–39
World Cities Satellite Images    40–48

## World Maps

Map Symbols    1

The World: Political
1:95 000 000    2–3

Arctic Ocean
1:35 000 000    4

Antarctica
1:35 000 000    5

## Europe

Europe: Physical
1:20 000 000    6

Europe: Political
1:20 000 000    7

Scandinavia    1:5 000 000
Iceland    1:5 000 000

8–9

Ireland    1:2 000 000

10

Scotland    1:2 000 000
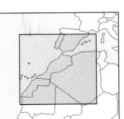
11

England and Wales
1:2 000 000

12–13

British Isles    1:5 000 000
14

Netherlands, Belgium and
Luxembourg    1:2 500 000
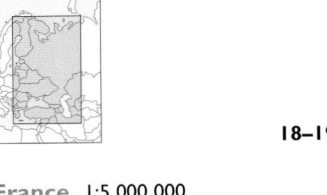
15

Central Europe    1:5 000 000

16–17

Eastern Europe and Turkey
1:10 000 000
18–19

France    1:5 000 000
20

Spain and Portugal
1:5 000 000
21

Italy and the Balkan States
1:5 000 000
22–23

The Balearics, the Canaries and
Madeira    1:1 000 000 / 1:2 000 000
24

Malta, Crete, Corfu, Rhodes
and Cyprus
1:1 000 000 / 1:1 300 000
25

## Asia

Asia: Physical    1:50 000 000    26

Asia: Political    1:50 000 000    27

Russia and Central Asia
1:20 000 000
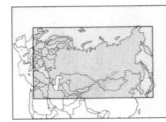
28–29

Japan    1:5 000 000

30–31

China and the Far East
1:15 000 000
Hong Kong and Macau    1:1 000 000

32–33

Northern China and Korea
1:6 000 000
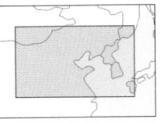
34–35

Indonesia and the Philippines
1:12 500 000
Java and Madura    1:7 500 000
Bali    1:2 000 000

36–37

Mainland South-east Asia
1:6 000 000
Ko Phuket    1:1 000 000
Ko Samui    1:1 000 000
Pinang    1:1 000 000
Singapore    1:1 000 000

38–39

South Asia    1:10 000 000

40–41

**Northern India and Nepal**
1:6 000 000
Jammu and Kashmir 1:6 000 000

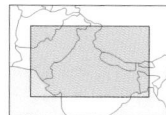

42–43

**The Middle East**
1:7 000 000

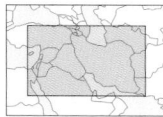

44–45

**The Near East** 1:2 500 000

46

**Arabia and the Horn of Africa** 1:15 000 000

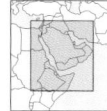

47

## Africa

**Africa: Physical**
1:42 000 000                    48

**Africa: Political**
1:42 000 000                    49

**Northern Africa**
1:15 000 000

50–51

**Central and Southern Africa**
1:15 000 000

52–53

**East Africa** 1:8 000 000

54–55

**Southern Africa**
1:8 000 000
Madagascar 1:8 000 000

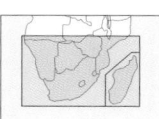

56–57

## Australia and Oceania

**Australia and Oceania: Physical and Political**
1:50 000 000                    58

**New Zealand** 1:6 000 000
Samoan Islands 1:12 000 000
Fiji and Tonga 1:12 000 000

59

**Western Australia**
1:8 000 000

60–61

**Eastern Australia**
1:8 000 000
Whitsunday Islands 1:2 500 000
Tasmania 1:8 000 000

62–63

**Pacific Ocean**
1:54 000 000                    64–65

## North America

**North America: Physical**
1:35 000 000                    66

**North America: Political**
1:35 000 000                    67

**Canada** 1:15 000 000
Alaska 1:30 000 000

68–69

**Western Canada** 1:7 000 000

70–71

**Eastern Canada** 1:7 000 000

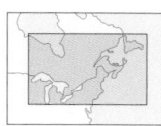

72–73

**United States** 1:12 000 000
Hawaii 1:10 000 000

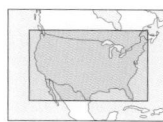

74–75

**Western United States**
1:6 000 000

76–77

**Central and Southern California and Washington**
1:2 500 000

78–79

**Middle United States**
1:6 000 000

80–81

**Eastern United States**
1:6 000 000

82–83

**North-eastern United States**
1:2 500 000

84–85

**Mexico** 1:8 000 000

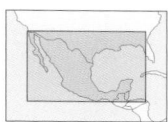

86–87

**Central America and the West Indies** 1:8 000 000
Jamaica 1:3 000 000
Guadeloupe 1:2 000 000
Martinique 1:2 000 000
Puerto Rico 1:3 000 000
Virgin Islands 1:2 000 000
St Lucia 1:2 000 000
Barbados 1:2 000 000

88–89

## South America

**South America: Physical**
1:35 000 000                    90

**South America: Political**
1:35 000 000                    91

**South America – North**
1:16 000 000
Trinidad and Tobago 1:2 500 000

92–93

**Central South America**
1:8 000 000

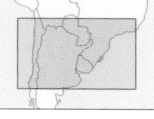

94–95

**South America – South**
1:16 000 000

96

## Index to World Maps
97–176

World: Regions in the News    177

# World Statistics: Countries

This alphabetical list includes the principal countries and territories of the world. If a territory is not completely independent, the country it is associated with is named. The area figures give the total area of land, inland water and ice. The population figures are 2003 estimates where available. The annual income is the Gross Domestic Product per capita† in US dollars. The figures are the latest available, usually 2002 estimates.

| Country/Territory | Area km² Thousands | Area miles² Thousands | Population Thousands | Capital | Annual Income US $ |
|---|---|---|---|---|---|
| Afghanistan | 652 | 252 | 28,717 | Kabul | 700 |
| Albania | 28.7 | 11.1 | 3,582 | Tirana | 4,400 |
| Algeria | 2,382 | 920 | 32,819 | Algiers | 5,400 |
| American Samoa (US) | 0.20 | 0.08 | 70 | Pago Pago | 8,000 |
| Andorra | 0.47 | 0.18 | 69 | Andorra La Vella | 19,000 |
| Angola | 1,247 | 481 | 10,766 | Luanda | 1,700 |
| Anguilla (UK) | 0.10 | 0.04 | 13 | The Valley | 8,600 |
| Antigua & Barbuda | 0.44 | 0.17 | 68 | St John's | 11,000 |
| Argentina | 2,780 | 1,074 | 38,741 | Buenos Aires | 10,500 |
| Armenia | 29.8 | 11.5 | 3,326 | Yerevan | 3,600 |
| Aruba (Netherlands) | 0.19 | 0.07 | 71 | Oranjestad | 28,000 |
| Australia | 7,741 | 2,989 | 19,732 | Canberra | 26,900 |
| Austria | 83.9 | 32.4 | 8,188 | Vienna | 27,900 |
| Azerbaijan | 86.6 | 33.4 | 7,831 | Baku | 3,700 |
| Azores (Portugal) | 2.2 | 0.86 | 236 | Ponta Delgada | 15,000 |
| Bahamas | 13.9 | 5.4 | 297 | Nassau | 15,300 |
| Bahrain | 0.69 | 0.27 | 667 | Manama | 15,100 |
| Bangladesh | 144 | 55.6 | 138,448 | Dhaka | 1,800 |
| Barbados | 0.43 | 0.17 | 277 | Bridgetown | 15,000 |
| Belarus | 208 | 80.2 | 10,322 | Minsk | 8,700 |
| Belgium | 30.5 | 11.8 | 10,289 | Brussels | 29,200 |
| Belize | 23.0 | 8.9 | 266 | Belmopan | 4,900 |
| Benin | 113 | 43.5 | 7,041 | Porto-Novo | 1,100 |
| Bermuda (UK) | 0.05 | 0.02 | 64 | Hamilton | 35,200 |
| Bhutan | 47.0 | 18.1 | 2,140 | Thimphu | 1,300 |
| Bolivia | 1,099 | 424 | 8,586 | La Paz/Sucre | 2,500 |
| Bosnia-Herzegovina | 51.2 | 19.8 | 3,989 | Sarajevo | 1,900 |
| Botswana | 582 | 225 | 1,573 | Gaborone | 8,500 |
| Brazil | 8,514 | 3,287 | 182,033 | Brasília | 7,600 |
| Brunei | 5.8 | 2.2 | 358 | Bandar Seri Begawan | 18,600 |
| Bulgaria | 111 | 42.8 | 7,538 | Sofia | 6,500 |
| Burkina Faso | 274 | 106 | 13,228 | Ouagadougou | 1,100 |
| Burma (= Myanmar) | 677 | 261 | 42,511 | Rangoon | 1,700 |
| Burundi | 27.8 | 10.7 | 6,096 | Bujumbura | 500 |
| Cambodia | 181 | 69.9 | 13,125 | Phnom Penh | 1,600 |
| Cameroon | 475 | 184 | 15,746 | Yaoundé | 1,700 |
| Canada | 9,971 | 3,850 | 32,207 | Ottawa | 29,300 |
| Canary Is. (Spain) | 7.2 | 2.8 | 1,682 | Las Palmas/Santa Cruz | 19,900 |
| Cape Verde Is. | 4.0 | 1.6 | 412 | Praia | 1,400 |
| Cayman Is. (UK) | 0.26 | 0.10 | 42 | George Town | 35,000 |
| Central African Republic | 623 | 241 | 3,684 | Bangui | 1,200 |
| Chad | 1,284 | 496 | 9,253 | Ndjaména | 1,000 |
| Chile | 757 | 292 | 15,665 | Santiago | 10,100 |
| China | 9,597 | 3,705 | 1,286,975 | Beijing | 4,700 |
| Colombia | 1,139 | 440 | 41,662 | Bogotá | 6,100 |
| Comoros | 2.2 | 0.86 | 633 | Moroni | 700 |
| Congo | 342 | 132 | 2,954 | Brazzaville | 900 |
| Congo (Dem. Rep. of the) | 2,345 | 905 | 56,625 | Kinshasa | 600 |
| Cook Is. (NZ) | 0.24 | 0.09 | 21 | Avarua | 5,000 |
| Costa Rica | 51.1 | 19.7 | 3,896 | San José | 8,300 |
| Croatia | 56.5 | 21.8 | 4,422 | Zagreb | 9,800 |
| Cuba | 111 | 42.8 | 11,263 | Havana | 2,700 |
| Cyprus | 9.3 | 3.6 | 772 | Nicosia | 13,200 |
| Czech Republic | 78.9 | 30.5 | 10,249 | Prague | 15,300 |
| Denmark | 43.1 | 16.6 | 5,384 | Copenhagen | 28,900 |
| Djibouti | 23.2 | 9.0 | 457 | Djibouti | 1,300 |
| Dominica | 0.75 | 0.29 | 70 | Roseau | 5,400 |
| Dominican Republic | 48.5 | 18.7 | 8,716 | Santo Domingo | 6,300 |
| East Timor | 14.9 | 5.7 | 998 | Dili | 500 |
| Ecuador | 284 | 109 | 13,710 | Quito | 3,200 |
| Egypt | 1,001 | 387 | 74,719 | Cairo | 4,000 |
| El Salvador | 21.0 | 8.1 | 6,470 | San Salvador | 4,600 |
| Equatorial Guinea | 28.1 | 10.8 | 510 | Malabo | 2,700 |
| Eritrea | 118 | 45.4 | 4,362 | Asmara | 700 |
| Estonia | 45.1 | 17.4 | 1,409 | Tallinn | 11,000 |
| Ethiopia | 1,104 | 426 | 66,558 | Addis Ababa | 700 |
| Faroe Is. (Denmark) | 1.4 | 0.54 | 46 | Tórshavn | 22,000 |
| Fiji Islands | 18.3 | 7.1 | 869 | Suva | 5,600 |
| Finland | 338 | 131 | 5,191 | Helsinki | 25,800 |
| France | 552 | 213 | 60,181 | Paris | 26,000 |
| French Guiana (France) | 90.0 | 34.7 | 187 | Cayenne | 14,400 |
| French Polynesia (France) | 4.0 | 1.5 | 262 | Papeete | 5,000 |
| Gabon | 268 | 103 | 1,322 | Libreville | 6,500 |
| Gambia, The | 11.3 | 4.4 | 1,501 | Banjul | 1,800 |
| Gaza Strip (OPT)* | 0.36 | 0.14 | 1,275 | – | 600 |
| Georgia | 69.7 | 26.9 | 4,934 | Tbilisi | 3,200 |
| Germany | 357 | 138 | 82,398 | Berlin | 26,200 |
| Ghana | 239 | 92.1 | 20,468 | Accra | 2,000 |
| Gibraltar (UK) | 0.006 | 0.002 | 28 | Gibraltar Town | 17,500 |
| Greece | 132 | 50.9 | 10,666 | Athens | 19,100 |
| Greenland (Denmark) | 2,176 | 840 | 56 | Nuuk (Godthåb) | 20,000 |
| Grenada | 0.34 | 0.13 | 89 | St George's | 5,000 |
| Guadeloupe (France) | 1.7 | 0.66 | 440 | Basse-Terre | 9,000 |
| Guam (US) | 0.55 | 0.21 | 164 | Agana | 21,000 |
| Guatemala | 109 | 42.0 | 13,909 | Guatemala City | 3,900 |
| Guinea | 246 | 94.9 | 9,030 | Conakry | 2,100 |
| Guinea-Bissau | 36.1 | 13.9 | 1,361 | Bissau | 700 |
| Guyana | 215 | 83.0 | 702 | Georgetown | 3,800 |
| Haiti | 27.8 | 10.7 | 7,528 | Port-au-Prince | 1,400 |
| Honduras | 112 | 43.3 | 6,670 | Tegucigalpa | 2,500 |
| Hong Kong (China) | 1.1 | 0.42 | 7,394 | – | 27,200 |
| Hungary | 93.0 | 35.9 | 10,045 | Budapest | 13,300 |
| Iceland | 103 | 39.8 | 281 | Reykjavik | 30,200 |
| India | 3,287 | 1,269 | 1,049,700 | New Delhi | 2,600 |
| Indonesia | 1,905 | 735 | 234,893 | Jakarta | 3,100 |
| Iran | 1,648 | 636 | 68,279 | Tehran | 6,800 |
| Iraq | 438 | 169 | 24,683 | Baghdad | 2,400 |
| Ireland | 70.3 | 27.1 | 3,924 | Dublin | 29,300 |
| Israel | 20.6 | 8.0 | 6,117 | Jerusalem | 19,500 |
| Italy | 301 | 116 | 57,998 | Rome | 25,100 |
| Ivory Coast (= Côte d'Ivoire) | 322 | 125 | 16,962 | Yamoussoukro | 1,400 |
| Jamaica | 11.0 | 4.2 | 2,696 | Kingston | 3,800 |
| Japan | 378 | 146 | 127,214 | Tokyo | 28,700 |
| Jordan | 89.3 | 34.5 | 5,460 | Amman | 4,300 |
| Kazakhstan | 2,725 | 1,052 | 16,764 | Astana | 7,200 |
| Kenya | 580 | 224 | 31,639 | Nairobi | 1,100 |
| Kiribati | 0.73 | 0.28 | 99 | Tarawa | 800 |
| Korea, North | 121 | 46.5 | 22,466 | Pyŏngyang | 1,000 |
| Korea, South | 99.3 | 38.3 | 48,289 | Seoul | 19,600 |
| Kuwait | 17.8 | 6.9 | 2,183 | Kuwait City | 17,500 |
| Kyrgyzstan | 200 | 77.2 | 4,893 | Bishkek | 2,900 |
| Laos | 237 | 91.4 | 5,922 | Vientiane | 1,800 |
| Latvia | 64.6 | 24.9 | 2,349 | Riga | 8,900 |
| Lebanon | 10.4 | 4.0 | 3,728 | Beirut | 4,800 |
| Lesotho | 30.4 | 11.7 | 1,862 | Maseru | 2,700 |
| Liberia | 111 | 43.0 | 3,317 | Monrovia | 1,000 |
| Libya | 1,760 | 679 | 5,499 | Tripoli | 6,200 |
| Liechtenstein | 0.16 | 0.06 | 33 | Vaduz | 25,000 |
| Lithuania | 65.2 | 25.2 | 3,593 | Vilnius | 8,400 |
| Luxembourg | 2.6 | 1.0 | 454 | Luxembourg | 48,900 |
| Macau (China) | 0.02 | 0.007 | 470 | – | 18,500 |
| Macedonia (FYROM) | 25.7 | 9.9 | 2,063 | Skopje | 5,100 |
| Madagascar | 587 | 227 | 16,980 | Antananarivo | 800 |
| Madeira (Portugal) | 0.78 | 0.30 | 241 | Funchal | 22,700 |
| Malawi | 118 | 45.7 | 11,651 | Lilongwe | 600 |
| Malaysia | 330 | 127 | 23,093 | Kuala Lumpur/Putrajaya | 8,800 |
| Maldives | 0.30 | 0.12 | 330 | Malé | 3,900 |
| Mali | 1,240 | 479 | 11,626 | Bamako | 900 |
| Malta | 0.32 | 0.12 | 400 | Valletta | 17,200 |
| Marshall Is. | 0.18 | 0.07 | 56 | Majuro | 1,600 |
| Martinique (France) | 1.1 | 0.43 | 426 | Fort-de-France | 10,700 |
| Mauritania | 1,026 | 396 | 2,913 | Nouakchott | 1,700 |
| Mauritius | 2.0 | 0.79 | 1,210 | Port Louis | 10,100 |
| Mayotte (France) | 0.37 | 0.14 | 178 | Mamoundzou | 600 |
| Mexico | 1,958 | 756 | 104,908 | Mexico City | 8,900 |
| Micronesia, Fed. States of | 0.70 | 0.27 | 108 | Palikir | 2,000 |
| Moldova | 33.9 | 13.1 | 4,440 | Chişinău | 2,600 |
| Monaco | 0.001 | 0.0004 | 32 | Monaco | 27,000 |
| Mongolia | 1,567 | 605 | 2,712 | Ulan Bator | 1,900 |
| Montserrat (UK) | 0.10 | 0.04 | 9 | Plymouth | 3,400 |
| Morocco | 447 | 172 | 31,689 | Rabat | 3,900 |
| Mozambique | 802 | 309 | 17,479 | Maputo | 1,100 |
| Namibia | 824 | 318 | 1,927 | Windhoek | 6,900 |
| Nauru | 0.02 | 0.008 | 13 | Yaren District | 5,000 |
| Nepal | 147 | 56.8 | 26,470 | Katmandu | 1,400 |
| Netherlands | 41.5 | 16.0 | 16,151 | Amsterdam/The Hague | 27,200 |
| Netherlands Antilles (Neths) | 0.80 | 0.31 | 216 | Willemstad | 11,400 |
| New Caledonia (France) | 18.6 | 7.2 | 211 | Nouméa | 14,000 |
| New Zealand | 271 | 104 | 3,951 | Wellington | 20,100 |
| Nicaragua | 130 | 50.2 | 5,129 | Managua | 2,200 |
| Niger | 1,267 | 489 | 11,059 | Niamey | 800 |
| Nigeria | 924 | 357 | 133,882 | Abuja | 900 |
| Northern Mariana Is. (US) | 0.46 | 0.18 | 80 | Saipan | 12,500 |
| Norway | 324 | 125 | 4,546 | Oslo | 33,000 |
| Oman | 310 | 119 | 2,807 | Muscat | 8,300 |
| Pakistan | 796 | 307 | 150,695 | Islamabad | 2,000 |
| Palau | 0.46 | 0.18 | 20 | Koror | 9,000 |
| Panama | 75.5 | 29.2 | 2,961 | Panamá | 6,200 |
| Papua New Guinea | 463 | 179 | 5,296 | Port Moresby | 2,100 |
| Paraguay | 407 | 157 | 6,037 | Asunción | 4,300 |
| Peru | 1,285 | 496 | 28,410 | Lima | 5,000 |
| Philippines | 300 | 116 | 84,620 | Manila | 4,600 |
| Poland | 323 | 125 | 38,623 | Warsaw | 9,700 |
| Portugal | 88.8 | 34.3 | 10,102 | Lisbon | 19,400 |
| Puerto Rico (US) | 8.9 | 3.4 | 3,886 | San Juan | 11,100 |
| Qatar | 11.0 | 4.2 | 817 | Doha | 20,100 |
| Réunion (France) | 2.5 | 0.97 | 755 | St-Denis | 5,600 |
| Romania | 238 | 92.0 | 22,272 | Bucharest | 7,600 |
| Russia | 17,075 | 6,593 | 144,526 | Moscow | 9,700 |
| Rwanda | 26.3 | 10.2 | 7,810 | Kigali | 1,200 |
| St Kitts & Nevis | 0.26 | 0.10 | 39 | Basseterre | 8,800 |
| St Lucia | 0.54 | 0.21 | 162 | Castries | 5,400 |
| St Vincent & Grenadines | 0.39 | 0.15 | 117 | Kingstown | 2,900 |
| Samoa | 2.8 | 1.1 | 178 | Apia | 5,600 |
| San Marino | 0.06 | 0.02 | 28 | San Marino | 34,600 |
| São Tomé & Príncipe | 0.96 | 0.37 | 176 | São Tomé | 1,200 |
| Saudi Arabia | 2,150 | 830 | 24,294 | Riyadh | 11,400 |
| Senegal | 197 | 76.0 | 10,580 | Dakar | 1,500 |
| Serbia & Montenegro | 102 | 39.4 | 10,656 | Belgrade | 2,200 |
| Seychelles | 0.46 | 0.18 | 80 | Victoria | 7,800 |
| Sierra Leone | 71.7 | 27.7 | 5,733 | Freetown | 500 |
| Singapore | 0.68 | 0.26 | 4,609 | Singapore | 25,200 |
| Slovak Republic | 49.0 | 18.9 | 5,430 | Bratislava | 12,400 |
| Slovenia | 20.3 | 7.8 | 1,936 | Ljubljana | 19,200 |
| Solomon Is. | 28.9 | 11.2 | 509 | Honiara | 1,700 |
| Somalia | 638 | 246 | 8,025 | Mogadishu | 600 |
| South Africa | 1,221 | 471 | 42,769 | C. Town/Pretoria/Bloem. | 10,000 |
| Spain | 498 | 192 | 40,217 | Madrid | 21,200 |
| Sri Lanka | 65.6 | 25.3 | 19,742 | Colombo | 3,700 |
| Sudan | 2,506 | 967 | 38,114 | Khartoum | 1,400 |
| Suriname | 163 | 63.0 | 435 | Paramaribo | 3,400 |
| Swaziland | 17.4 | 6.7 | 1,161 | Mbabane | 4,800 |
| Sweden | 450 | 174 | 8,878 | Stockholm | 26,000 |
| Switzerland | 41.3 | 15.9 | 7,319 | Bern | 32,000 |
| Syria | 185 | 71.5 | 17,586 | Damascus | 3,700 |
| Taiwan | 36.0 | 13.9 | 22,603 | Taipei | 18,000 |
| Tajikistan | 143 | 55.3 | 6,864 | Dushanbe | 1,300 |
| Tanzania | 945 | 365 | 35,922 | Dodoma | 600 |
| Thailand | 513 | 198 | 64,265 | Bangkok | 7,000 |
| Togo | 56.8 | 21.9 | 5,429 | Lomé | 1,400 |
| Tonga | 0.65 | 0.25 | 108 | Nuku'alofa | 2,200 |
| Trinidad & Tobago | 5.1 | 2.0 | 1,104 | Port of Spain | 10,000 |
| Tunisia | 164 | 63.2 | 9,925 | Tunis | 6,800 |
| Turkey | 775 | 299 | 68,109 | Ankara | 7,300 |
| Turkmenistan | 488 | 188 | 4,776 | Ashkhabad | 6,700 |
| Turks & Caicos Is. (UK) | 0.43 | 0.17 | 19 | Cockburn Town | 9,600 |
| Tuvalu | 0.03 | 0.01 | 11 | Fongafale | 1,100 |
| Uganda | 241 | 93.1 | 25,633 | Kampala | 1,200 |
| Ukraine | 604 | 233 | 48,055 | Kiev | 4,500 |
| United Arab Emirates | 83.6 | 32.3 | 2,485 | Abu Dhabi | 22,100 |
| United Kingdom | 242 | 93.4 | 60,095 | London | 25,500 |
| United States of America | 9,629 | 3,718 | 290,343 | Washington, DC | 36,300 |
| Uruguay | 175 | 67.6 | 3,413 | Montevideo | 7,900 |
| Uzbekistan | 447 | 173 | 25,982 | Tashkent | 2,600 |
| Vanuatu | 12.2 | 4.7 | 199 | Port-Vila | 2,900 |
| Vatican City | 0.0004 | 0.0002 | 1 | Vatican City | N/A |
| Venezuela | 912 | 352 | 24,655 | Caracas | 5,400 |
| Vietnam | 332 | 128 | 81,625 | Hanoi | 2,300 |
| Virgin Is. (UK) | 0.15 | 0.06 | 22 | Road Town | 16,000 |
| Virgin Is. (US) | 0.35 | 0.13 | 125 | Charlotte Amalie | 19,000 |
| Wallis & Futuna Is. (France) | 0.20 | 0.08 | 16 | Mata-Utu | 2,000 |
| West Bank (OPT)* | 5.9 | 2.3 | 2,237 | – | 800 |
| Western Sahara | 266 | 103 | 262 | El Aaiún | N/A |
| Yemen | 528 | 204 | 19,350 | Sana | 800 |
| Zambia | 753 | 291 | 10,307 | Lusaka | 800 |
| Zimbabwe | 391 | 151 | 12,577 | Harare | 2,100 |

*OPT = Occupied Palestinian Territory　　N/A = Not available

† Gross Domestic Product per capita has been measured using the purchasing power parity method. This enables comparisons to be made between countries through their purchasing power (in US dollars), showing real price levels of goods and services.

# World Statistics: Physical Dimensions

Each topic list is divided into continents and within a continent the items are listed in order of size. The bottom part of many of the lists is selective in order to give examples from as many different countries as possible. The order of the continents is the same as in the atlas, beginning with Europe and ending with South America. The figures are rounded as appropriate.

## World, Continents, Oceans

| | km² | miles² | % |
|---|---|---|---|
| The World | 509,450,000 | 196,672,000 | – |
| Land | 149,450,000 | 57,688,000 | 29.3 |
| Water | 360,000,000 | 138,984,000 | 70.7 |
| Asia | 44,500,000 | 17,177,000 | 29.8 |
| Africa | 30,302,000 | 11,697,000 | 20.3 |
| North America | 24,241,000 | 9,357,000 | 16.2 |
| South America | 17,793,000 | 6,868,000 | 11.9 |
| Antarctica | 14,100,000 | 5,443,000 | 9.4 |
| Europe | 9,957,000 | 3,843,000 | 6.7 |
| Australia & Oceania | 8,557,000 | 3,303,000 | 5.7 |
| Pacific Ocean | 179,679,000 | 69,356,000 | 49.9 |
| Atlantic Ocean | 92,373,000 | 35,657,000 | 25.7 |
| Indian Ocean | 73,917,000 | 28,532,000 | 20.5 |
| Arctic Ocean | 14,090,000 | 5,439,000 | 3.9 |

## Ocean Depths

### Atlantic Ocean

| | m | ft |
|---|---|---|
| Puerto Rico (Milwaukee) Deep | 9,220 | 30,249 |
| Cayman Trench | 7,680 | 25,197 |
| Gulf of Mexico | 5,203 | 17,070 |
| Mediterranean Sea | 5,121 | 16,801 |
| Black Sea | 2,211 | 7,254 |
| North Sea | 660 | 2,165 |

### Indian Ocean

| | m | ft |
|---|---|---|
| Java Trench | 7,450 | 24,442 |
| Red Sea | 2,635 | 8,454 |

### Pacific Ocean

| | m | ft |
|---|---|---|
| Mariana Trench | 11,022 | 36,161 |
| Tonga Trench | 10,882 | 35,702 |
| Japan Trench | 10,554 | 34,626 |
| Kuril Trench | 10,542 | 34,587 |

### Arctic Ocean

| | m | ft |
|---|---|---|
| Molloy Deep | 5,608 | 18,399 |

## Mountains

### Europe

| | | m | ft |
|---|---|---|---|
| Elbrus | *Russia* | 5,642 | 18,510 |
| Mont Blanc | *France/Italy* | 4,807 | 15,771 |
| Monte Rosa | *Italy/Switzerland* | 4,634 | 15,203 |
| Dom | *Switzerland* | 4,545 | 14,911 |
| Liskamm | *Switzerland* | 4,527 | 14,852 |
| Weisshorn | *Switzerland* | 4,505 | 14,780 |
| Taschorn | *Switzerland* | 4,490 | 14,730 |
| Matterhorn/Cervino | *Italy/Switzerland* | 4,478 | 14,691 |
| Mont Maudit | *France/Italy* | 4,465 | 14,649 |
| Dent Blanche | *Switzerland* | 4,356 | 14,291 |
| Nadelhorn | *Switzerland* | 4,327 | 14,196 |
| Grandes Jorasses | *France/Italy* | 4,208 | 13,806 |
| Jungfrau | *Switzerland* | 4,158 | 13,642 |
| Grossglockner | *Austria* | 3,797 | 12,457 |
| Mulhacén | *Spain* | 3,478 | 11,411 |
| Zugspitze | *Germany* | 2,962 | 9,718 |
| Olympus | *Greece* | 2,917 | 9,570 |
| Triglav | *Slovenia* | 2,863 | 9,393 |
| Gerlachovka | *Slovak Republic* | 2,655 | 8,711 |
| Galdhöpiggen | *Norway* | 2,468 | 8,100 |
| Kebnekaise | *Sweden* | 2,117 | 6,946 |
| Ben Nevis | *UK* | 1,343 | 4,406 |

### Asia

| | | m | ft |
|---|---|---|---|
| Everest | *China/Nepal* | 8,850 | 29,035 |
| K2 (Godwin Austen) | *China/Kashmir* | 8,611 | 28,251 |
| Kanchenjunga | *India/Nepal* | 8,598 | 28,208 |
| Lhotse | *China/Nepal* | 8,516 | 27,939 |
| Makalu | *China/Nepal* | 8,481 | 27,824 |
| Cho Oyu | *China/Nepal* | 8,201 | 26,906 |
| Dhaulagiri | *Nepal* | 8,172 | 26,811 |
| Manaslu | *Nepal* | 8,156 | 26,758 |
| Nanga Parbat | *Kashmir* | 8,126 | 26,660 |
| Annapurna | *Nepal* | 8,078 | 26,502 |
| Gasherbrum | *China/Kashmir* | 8,068 | 26,469 |
| Broad Peak | *China/Kashmir* | 8,051 | 26,414 |
| Xixabangma | *China* | 8,012 | 26,286 |
| Kangbachen | *India/Nepal* | 7,902 | 25,925 |
| Trivor | *Pakistan* | 7,720 | 25,328 |
| Pik Kommunizma | *Tajikistan* | 7,495 | 24,590 |
| Demavend | *Iran* | 5,604 | 18,386 |
| Ararat | *Turkey* | 5,165 | 16,945 |
| Gunong Kinabalu | *Malaysia (Borneo)* | 4,101 | 13,455 |
| Fuji-San | *Japan* | 3,776 | 12,388 |

### Africa

| | | m | ft |
|---|---|---|---|
| Kilimanjaro | *Tanzania* | 5,895 | 19,340 |
| Mt Kenya | *Kenya* | 5,199 | 17,057 |
| Ruwenzori (Margherita) | *Ug./Congo (D.R.)* | 5,109 | 16,762 |
| Ras Dashan | *Ethiopia* | 4,620 | 15,157 |
| Meru | *Tanzania* | 4,565 | 14,977 |
| Karisimbi | *Rwanda/Congo (D.R.)* | 4,507 | 14,787 |
| Mt Elgon | *Kenya/Uganda* | 4,321 | 14,176 |
| Batu | *Ethiopia* | 4,307 | 14,130 |
| Toubkal | *Morocco* | 4,165 | 13,665 |
| Mt Cameroon | *Cameroon* | 4,070 | 13,353 |

### Oceania

| | | m | ft |
|---|---|---|---|
| Puncak Jaya | *Indonesia* | 5,029 | 16,499 |
| Puncak Trikora | *Indonesia* | 4,750 | 15,584 |
| Puncak Mandala | *Indonesia* | 4,702 | 15,427 |
| Mt Wilhelm | *Papua New Guinea* | 4,508 | 14,790 |
| Mauna Kea | *USA (Hawaii)* | 4,205 | 13,796 |
| Mauna Loa | *USA (Hawaii)* | 4,169 | 13,681 |
| Mt Cook (Aoraki) | *New Zealand* | 3,753 | 12,313 |
| Mt Kosciuszko | *Australia* | 2,230 | 7,316 |

### North America

| | | m | ft |
|---|---|---|---|
| Mt McKinley (Denali) | *USA (Alaska)* | 6,194 | 20,321 |
| Mt Logan | *Canada* | 5,959 | 19,551 |
| Pico de Orizaba | *Mexico* | 5,610 | 18,405 |
| Mt St Elias | *USA/Canada* | 5,489 | 18,008 |
| Popocatepetl | *Mexico* | 5,452 | 17,887 |
| Mt Foraker | *USA (Alaska)* | 5,304 | 17,401 |
| Ixtaccihuatl | *Mexico* | 5,286 | 17,342 |
| Lucania | *Canada* | 5,227 | 17,149 |
| Mt Steele | *Canada* | 5,073 | 16,644 |
| Mt Bona | *USA (Alaska)* | 5,005 | 16,420 |
| Mt Whitney | *USA* | 4,418 | 14,495 |
| Tajumulco | *Guatemala* | 4,220 | 13,845 |
| Chirripó Grande | *Costa Rica* | 3,837 | 12,589 |
| Pico Duarte | *Dominican Rep.* | 3,175 | 10,417 |

### South America

| | | m | ft |
|---|---|---|---|
| Aconcagua | *Argentina* | 6,962 | 22,841 |
| Bonete | *Argentina* | 6,872 | 22,546 |
| Ojos del Salado | *Argentina/Chile* | 6,863 | 22,516 |
| Pissis | *Argentina* | 6,779 | 22,241 |
| Mercedario | *Argentina/Chile* | 6,770 | 22,211 |
| Huascaran | *Peru* | 6,768 | 22,204 |
| Llullaillaco | *Argentina/Chile* | 6,723 | 22,057 |
| Nudo de Cachi | *Argentina* | 6,720 | 22,047 |
| Yerupaja | *Peru* | 6,632 | 21,758 |
| Sajama | *Bolivia* | 6,542 | 21,463 |
| Chimborazo | *Ecuador* | 6,267 | 20,561 |
| Pico Colon | *Colombia* | 5,800 | 19,029 |
| Pico Bolivar | *Venezuela* | 5,007 | 16,427 |

### Antarctica

| | m | ft |
|---|---|---|
| Vinson Massif | 4,897 | 16,066 |
| Mt Kirkpatrick | 4,528 | 14,855 |

## Rivers

### Europe

| | | km | miles |
|---|---|---|---|
| Volga | *Caspian Sea* | 3,700 | 2,300 |
| Danube | *Black Sea* | 2,850 | 1,770 |
| Ural | *Caspian Sea* | 2,535 | 1,575 |
| Dnepr (Dnipro) | *Black Sea* | 2,285 | 1,420 |
| Kama | *Volga* | 2,030 | 1,260 |
| Don | *Black Sea* | 1,990 | 1,240 |
| Petchora | *Arctic Ocean* | 1,790 | 1,110 |
| Oka | *Volga* | 1,480 | 920 |
| Dnister (Dniester) | *Black Sea* | 1,400 | 870 |
| Vyatka | *Kama* | 1,370 | 850 |
| Rhine | *North Sea* | 1,320 | 820 |
| N. Dvina | *Arctic Ocean* | 1,290 | 800 |
| Elbe | *North Sea* | 1,145 | 710 |

### Asia

| | | km | miles |
|---|---|---|---|
| Yangtze | *Pacific Ocean* | 6,380 | 3,960 |
| Yenisey–Angara | *Arctic Ocean* | 5,550 | 3,445 |
| Huang He | *Pacific Ocean* | 5,464 | 3,395 |
| Ob–Irtysh | *Arctic Ocean* | 5,410 | 3,360 |
| Mekong | *Pacific Ocean* | 4,500 | 2,795 |
| Amur | *Pacific Ocean* | 4,400 | 2,730 |
| Lena | *Arctic Ocean* | 4,400 | 2,730 |
| Irtysh | *Ob* | 4,250 | 2,640 |
| Yenisey | *Arctic Ocean* | 4,090 | 2,540 |
| Ob | *Arctic Ocean* | 3,680 | 2,285 |
| Indus | *Indian Ocean* | 3,100 | 1,925 |
| Brahmaputra | *Indian Ocean* | 2,900 | 1,800 |
| Syrdarya | *Aral Sea* | 2,860 | 1,775 |
| Salween | *Indian Ocean* | 2,800 | 1,740 |
| Euphrates | *Indian Ocean* | 2,700 | 1,675 |
| Amudarya | *Aral Sea* | 2,540 | 1,575 |

### Africa

| | | km | miles |
|---|---|---|---|
| Nile | *Mediterranean* | 6,670 | 4,140 |
| Congo | *Atlantic Ocean* | 4,670 | 2,900 |
| Niger | *Atlantic Ocean* | 4,180 | 2,595 |
| Zambezi | *Indian Ocean* | 3,540 | 2,200 |
| Oubangi/Uele | *Congo (D.R.)* | 2,250 | 1,400 |
| Kasai | *Congo (D.R.)* | 1,950 | 1,210 |
| Shaballe | *Indian Ocean* | 1,930 | 1,200 |
| Orange | *Atlantic Ocean* | 1,860 | 1,155 |
| Cubango | *Okavango Delta* | 1,800 | 1,120 |
| Limpopo | *Indian Ocean* | 1,600 | 995 |
| Senegal | *Atlantic Ocean* | 1,600 | 995 |

### Australia

| | | km | miles |
|---|---|---|---|
| Murray–Darling | *Southern Ocean* | 3,750 | 2,330 |
| Darling | *Murray* | 3,070 | 1,905 |
| Murray | *Southern Ocean* | 2,575 | 1,600 |
| Murrumbidgee | *Murray* | 1,690 | 1,050 |

### North America

| | | km | miles |
|---|---|---|---|
| Mississippi–Missouri | *Gulf of Mexico* | 6,020 | 3,740 |
| Mackenzie | *Arctic Ocean* | 4,240 | 2,630 |
| Mississippi | *Gulf of Mexico* | 3,780 | 2,350 |
| Missouri | *Mississippi* | 3,780 | 2,350 |
| Yukon | *Pacific Ocean* | 3,185 | 1,980 |
| Rio Grande | *Gulf of Mexico* | 3,030 | 1,880 |
| Arkansas | *Mississippi* | 2,340 | 1,450 |
| Colorado | *Pacific Ocean* | 2,330 | 1,445 |
| Red | *Mississippi* | 2,040 | 1,270 |
| Columbia | *Pacific Ocean* | 1,950 | 1,210 |
| Saskatchewan | *Lake Winnipeg* | 1,940 | 1,205 |

### South America

| | | km | miles |
|---|---|---|---|
| Amazon | *Atlantic Ocean* | 6,450 | 4,010 |
| Paraná–Plate | *Atlantic Ocean* | 4,500 | 2,800 |
| Purus | *Amazon* | 3,350 | 2,080 |
| Madeira | *Amazon* | 3,200 | 1,990 |
| São Francisco | *Atlantic Ocean* | 2,900 | 1,800 |
| Paraná | *Plate* | 2,800 | 1,740 |
| Tocantins | *Atlantic Ocean* | 2,750 | 1,710 |
| Paraguay | *Paraná* | 2,550 | 1,580 |
| Orinoco | *Atlantic Ocean* | 2,500 | 1,550 |
| Pilcomayo | *Paraná* | 2,500 | 1,550 |
| Araguaia | *Tocantins* | 2,250 | 1,400 |

## Lakes

### Europe

| | | km² | miles² |
|---|---|---|---|
| Lake Ladoga | *Russia* | 17,700 | 6,800 |
| Lake Onega | *Russia* | 9,700 | 3,700 |
| Saimaa system | *Finland* | 8,000 | 3,100 |
| Vänern | *Sweden* | 5,500 | 2,100 |

### Asia

| | | km² | miles² |
|---|---|---|---|
| Caspian Sea | *Asia* | 371,800 | 143,550 |
| Lake Baykal | *Russia* | 30,500 | 11,780 |
| Aral Sea | *Kazakhstan/Uzbekistan* | 28,687 | 11,086 |
| Tonlé Sap | *Cambodia* | 20,000 | 7,700 |
| Lake Balqash | *Kazakhstan* | 18,500 | 7,100 |

### Africa

| | | km² | miles² |
|---|---|---|---|
| Lake Victoria | *East Africa* | 68,000 | 26,000 |
| Lake Tanganyika | *Central Africa* | 33,000 | 13,000 |
| Lake Malawi/Nyasa | *East Africa* | 29,600 | 11,430 |
| Lake Chad | *Central Africa* | 25,000 | 9,700 |
| Lake Turkana | *Ethiopia/Kenya* | 8,500 | 3,300 |
| Lake Volta | *Ghana* | 8,500 | 3,300 |

### Australia

| | | km² | miles² |
|---|---|---|---|
| Lake Eyre | *Australia* | 8,900 | 3,400 |
| Lake Torrens | *Australia* | 5,800 | 2,200 |
| Lake Gairdner | *Australia* | 4,800 | 1,900 |

### North America

| | | km² | miles² |
|---|---|---|---|
| Lake Superior | *Canada/USA* | 82,350 | 31,800 |
| Lake Huron | *Canada/USA* | 59,600 | 23,010 |
| Lake Michigan | *USA* | 58,000 | 22,400 |
| Great Bear Lake | *Canada* | 31,800 | 12,280 |
| Great Slave Lake | *Canada* | 28,500 | 11,000 |
| Lake Erie | *Canada/USA* | 25,700 | 9,900 |
| Lake Winnipeg | *Canada* | 24,400 | 9,400 |
| Lake Ontario | *Canada/USA* | 19,500 | 7,500 |
| Lake Nicaragua | *Nicaragua* | 8,200 | 3,200 |

### South America

| | | km² | miles² |
|---|---|---|---|
| Lake Titicaca | *Bolivia/Peru* | 8,300 | 3,200 |
| Lake Poopo | *Bolivia* | 2,800 | 1,100 |

## Islands

### Europe

| | | km² | miles² |
|---|---|---|---|
| Great Britain | *UK* | 229,880 | 88,700 |
| Iceland | *Atlantic Ocean* | 103,000 | 39,800 |
| Ireland | *Ireland/UK* | 84,400 | 32,600 |
| Novaya Zemlya (N.) | *Russia* | 48,200 | 18,600 |
| Sicily | *Italy* | 25,500 | 9,800 |
| Corsica | *France* | 8,700 | 3,400 |

### Asia

| | | km² | miles² |
|---|---|---|---|
| Borneo | *South-east Asia* | 744,360 | 287,400 |
| Sumatra | *Indonesia* | 473,600 | 182,860 |
| Honshu | *Japan* | 230,500 | 88,980 |
| Sulawesi (Celebes) | *Indonesia* | 189,000 | 73,000 |
| Java | *Indonesia* | 126,700 | 48,900 |
| Luzon | *Philippines* | 104,700 | 40,400 |
| Hokkaido | *Japan* | 78,400 | 30,300 |

### Africa

| | | km² | miles² |
|---|---|---|---|
| Madagascar | *Indian Ocean* | 587,040 | 226,660 |
| Socotra | *Indian Ocean* | 3,600 | 1,400 |
| Réunion | *Indian Ocean* | 2,500 | 965 |

### Oceania

| | | km² | miles² |
|---|---|---|---|
| New Guinea | *Indonesia/Papua NG* | 821,030 | 317,000 |
| New Zealand (S.) | *Pacific Ocean* | 150,500 | 58,100 |
| New Zealand (N.) | *Pacific Ocean* | 114,700 | 44,300 |
| Tasmania | *Australia* | 67,800 | 26,200 |
| Hawaii | *Pacific Ocean* | 10,450 | 4,000 |

### North America

| | | km² | miles² |
|---|---|---|---|
| Greenland | *Atlantic Ocean* | 2,175,600 | 839,800 |
| Baffin Is. | *Canada* | 508,000 | 196,100 |
| Victoria Is. | *Canada* | 212,200 | 81,900 |
| Ellesmere Is. | *Canada* | 212,000 | 81,800 |
| Cuba | *Caribbean Sea* | 110,860 | 42,800 |
| Hispaniola | *Dominican Rep./Haiti* | 76,200 | 29,400 |
| Jamaica | *Caribbean Sea* | 11,400 | 4,400 |
| Puerto Rico | *Atlantic Ocean* | 8,900 | 3,400 |

### South America

| | | km² | miles² |
|---|---|---|---|
| Tierra del Fuego | *Argentina/Chile* | 47,000 | 18,100 |
| Falkland Is. (E.) | *Atlantic Ocean* | 6,800 | 2,600 |

# Philip's World Maps

The reference maps which form the main body of this atlas have been prepared in accordance with the highest standards of international cartography to provide an accurate and detailed representation of the Earth. The scales and projections used have been carefully chosen to give balanced coverage of the world, while emphasizing the most densely populated and economically significant regions. A hallmark of Philip's mapping is the use of hill shading and relief colouring to create a graphic impression of landforms: this makes the maps exceptionally easy to read. However, knowledge of the key features employed in the construction and presentation of the maps will enable the reader to derive the fullest benefit from the atlas.

## Map sequence

The atlas covers the Earth continent by continent: first Europe; then its land neighbour Asia (mapped north before south, in a clockwise sequence), then Africa, Australia and Oceania, North America and South America. This is the classic arrangement adopted by most cartographers since the 16th century. For each continent, there are maps at a variety of scales. First, physical relief and political maps of the whole continent; then a series of larger-scale maps of the regions within the continent, each followed, where required, by still larger-scale maps of the most important or densely populated areas. The governing principle is that by turning the pages of the atlas, the reader moves steadily from north to south through each continent, with each map overlapping its neighbours.

## Map presentation

With very few exceptions (e.g. for the Arctic and Antarctica), the maps are drawn with north at the top, regardless of whether they are presented upright or sideways on the page. In the borders will be found the map title; a locator diagram showing the area covered; continuation arrows showing the page numbers for maps of adjacent areas; the scale; the projection used; the degrees of latitude and longitude; and the letters and figures used in the index for locating place names and geographical features. Physical relief maps also have a height reference panel identifying the colours used for each layer of contouring.

## Map symbols

Each map contains a vast amount of detail which can only be conveyed clearly and accurately by the use of symbols. Points and circles of varying sizes locate and identify the relative importance of towns and cities; different styles of type are employed for administrative, geographical and regional place names. A variety of pictorial symbols denote features such as glaciers and marshes, as well as man-made structures including roads, railways, airports and canals.

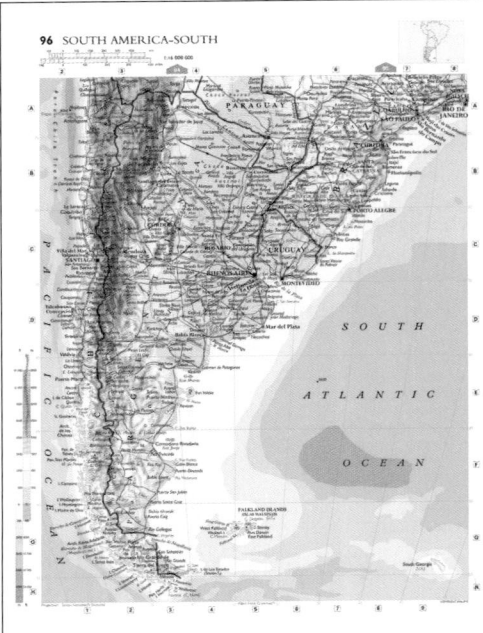

International borders are shown by red lines. Where neighbouring countries are in dispute, for example in the Middle East, the maps show the *de facto* boundary between nations, regardless of the legal or historical situation. The symbols are explained on the first page of the World Maps section of the atlas.

## Map scales

The scale of each map is given in the numerical form known as the 'representative fraction'. The first figure is always one, signifying one unit of distance on the map; the second figure, usually in millions, is the number by which the map unit must be multiplied to give the equivalent distance on the Earth's surface. Calculations can easily be made in centimetres and kilometres, by dividing the Earth units figure by 100 000 (i.e. deleting the last five 0s). Thus 1:1 000 000 means 1 cm = 10 km. The calculation for inches and miles is more laborious, but 1 000 000 divided by 63 360 (the number of inches in a mile) shows that the ratio 1:1 000 000 means approximately 1 inch = 16 miles. The table below provides distance equivalents for scales down to 1:50 000 000.

| LARGE SCALE | | |
|---|---|---|
| 1:1 000 000 | 1 cm = 10 km | 1 inch = 16 miles |
| 1:2 500 000 | 1 cm = 25 km | 1 inch = 39.5 miles |
| 1:5 000 000 | 1 cm = 50 km | 1 inch = 79 miles |
| 1:6 000 000 | 1 cm = 60 km | 1 inch = 95 miles |
| 1:8 000 000 | 1 cm = 80 km | 1 inch = 126 miles |
| 1:10 000 000 | 1 cm = 100 km | 1 inch = 158 miles |
| 1:15 000 000 | 1 cm = 150 km | 1 inch = 237 miles |
| 1:20 000 000 | 1 cm = 200 km | 1 inch = 316 miles |
| 1:50 000 000 | 1 cm = 500 km | 1 inch = 790 miles |
| SMALL SCALE | | |

## Measuring distances

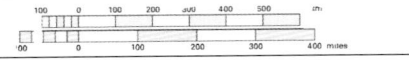

Although each map is accompanied by a scale bar, distances cannot always be measured with confidence because of the distortions involved in portraying the curved surface of the Earth on a flat page. As a general rule, the larger the map scale (i.e. the lower the number of Earth units in the representative fraction), the more accurate and reliable will be the distance measured. On small-scale maps such as those of the world and of entire continents, measurement may only be accurate along the 'standard parallels', or central axes, and should not be attempted without considering the map projection.

## Latitude and longitude

Accurate positioning of individual points on the Earth's surface is made possible by reference to the geometrical system of latitude and longitude. Latitude *parallels* are drawn west–east around the Earth and numbered by degrees north and south of the Equator, which is designated 0° of latitude. Longitude *meridians* are drawn north–south and numbered by degrees east and west of the *prime meridian*, 0° of longitude, which passes through Greenwich in England. By referring to these co-ordinates and their subdivisions of minutes (1/60th of a degree) and seconds (1/60th of a minute), any place on Earth can be located to within a few hundred metres. Latitude and longitude are indicated by blue lines on the maps; they are straight or curved according to the projection employed. Reference to these lines is the easiest way of determining the relative positions of places on different maps, and for plotting compass directions.

## Name forms

For ease of reference, both English and local name forms appear in the atlas. Oceans, seas and countries are shown in English throughout the atlas; country names may be abbreviated to their commonly accepted form (e.g. Germany, not The Federal Republic of Germany). Conventional English forms are also used for place names on the smaller-scale maps of the continents. However, local name forms are used on all large-scale and regional maps, with the English form given in brackets only for important cities – the large-scale map of Russia and Central Asia thus shows Moskva (Moscow). For countries which do not use a Roman script, place names have been transcribed according to the systems adopted by the British and US Geographic Names Authorities. For China, the Pin Yin system has been used, with some more widely known forms appearing in brackets, as with Beijing (Peking). Both English and local names appear in the index, the English form being cross-referenced to the local form.

# THE
# WORLD
# IN FOCUS

| | | | | | |
|---|---|---|---|---|---|
| PLANET EARTH | 2 | WATER & VEGETATION | 12 | QUALITY OF LIFE | 22 |
| RESTLESS EARTH | 4 | ENVIRONMENT | 14 | ENERGY | 24 |
| LANDFORMS | 6 | POPULATION | 16 | PRODUCTION | 26 |
| OCEANS | 8 | THE HUMAN FAMILY | 18 | TRADE | 28 |
| CLIMATE | 10 | WEALTH | 20 | TRAVEL & TOURISM | 30 |

# Planet Earth

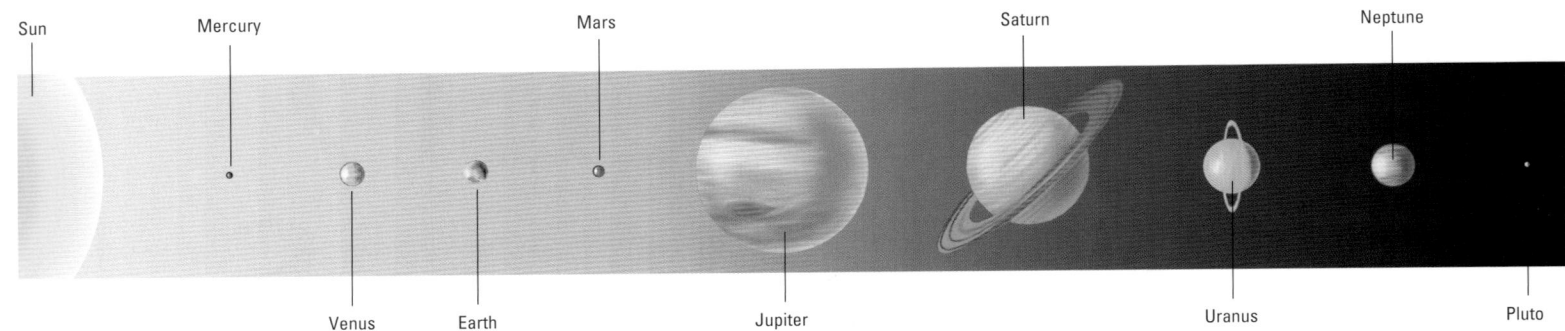

Sun    Mercury    Mars    Saturn    Neptune

Venus    Earth    Jupiter    Uranus    Pluto

## The Solar System

A minute part of one of the billions of galaxies (collections of stars) that comprises the Universe, the Solar System lies some 27,000 light-years from the centre of our own galaxy, the 'Milky Way'. Thought to be about 4,600 million years old, it consists of a central sun with nine planets and their moons revolving around it, attracted by its gravitational pull. The planets orbit the Sun in the same direction – anti-clockwise when viewed from the Northern Heavens – and almost in the same plane. Their orbital paths, however, vary enormously.

The Sun's diameter is 109 times that of Earth, and the temperature at its core – caused by continuous thermonuclear fusions of hydrogen into helium – is estimated to be 15 million degrees Celsius. It is the Solar System's only source of light and heat.

## Profile of the Planets

| | Mean distance from Sun (million km) | Mass (Earth = 1) | Period of orbit (Earth days/years) | Period of rotation (Earth days) | Equatorial diameter (km) | Number of known satellites |
|---|---|---|---|---|---|---|
| Mercury | 57.9 | 0.055 | 87.97 days | 58.67 | 4,878 | 0 |
| Venus | 108.2 | 0.815 | 224.7 days | 243.00 | 12,104 | 0 |
| Earth | 149.6 | 1.0 | 365.3 days | 1.00 | 12,756 | 1 |
| Mars | 227.9 | 0.11 | 687.0 days | 1.028 | 6,794 | 2 |
| Jupiter | 778 | 317.9 | 11.86 years | 0.411 | 143,884 | 63 |
| Saturn | 1,427 | 95.2 | 29.46 years | 0.427 | 120,536 | 31 |
| Uranus | 2,870 | 14.6 | 84.01 years | 0.748 | 51,118 | 27 |
| Neptune | 4,497 | 17.2 | 164.8 years | 0.710 | 50,538 | 13 |
| Pluto | 5,900 | 0.002 | 247.7 years | 6.39 | 2,324 | 1 |

All planetary orbits are elliptical in form, but only Pluto and Mercury follow paths that deviate noticeably from a circular one. Near perihelion – its closest approach to the Sun – Pluto actually passes inside the orbit of Neptune, an event that last occurred in 1983. Pluto did not regain its station as outermost planet until February 1999.

## The Seasons

Seasons occur because the Earth's axis is tilted at an angle of approximately 23½°. When the northern hemisphere is tilted to a maximum extent towards the Sun, on 21 June, the Sun is overhead at the Tropic of Cancer (latitude 23½° North). This is midsummer, or the summer solstice, in the northern hemisphere.

On 22 or 23 September, the Sun is overhead at the Equator, and day and night are of equal length throughout the world. This is the autumn equinox in the northern hemisphere. On 21 or 22 December, the Sun is overhead at the Tropic of Capricorn (23½° South), the winter solstice in the northern hemisphere. The overhead Sun then tracks north until, on 21 March, it is overhead at the Equator. This is the spring (vernal) equinox in the northern hemisphere.

In the southern hemisphere, the seasons are the reverse of those in the north.

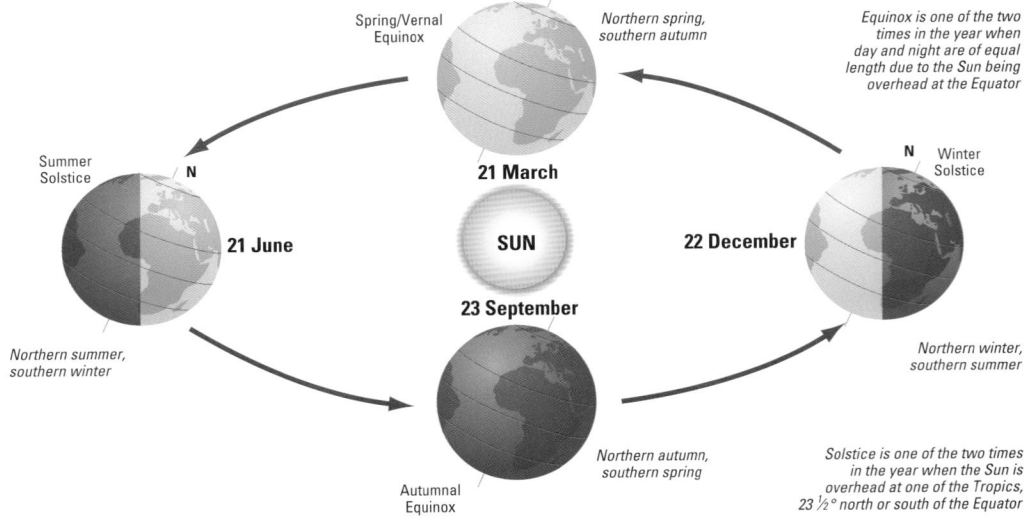

Spring/Vernal Equinox

Northern spring, southern autumn

Equinox is one of the two times in the year when day and night are of equal length due to the Sun being overhead at the Equator

Summer Solstice

21 March

N    Winter Solstice

21 June

SUN

22 December

23 September

Northern summer, southern winter

Northern winter, southern summer

Northern autumn, southern spring

Autumnal Equinox

Solstice is one of the two times in the year when the Sun is overhead at one of the Tropics, 23 ½° north or south of the Equator

## Day and Night

The Sun appears to rise in the east, reach its highest point at noon, and then set in the west, to be followed by night. In reality, it is not the Sun that is moving but the Earth rotating from west to east. The moment when the Sun's upper limb first appears above the horizon is termed sunrise; the moment when the Sun's upper limb disappears below the horizon is sunset.

At the summer solstice in the northern hemisphere (21 June), the Arctic has total daylight and the Antarctic total darkness. The opposite occurs at the winter solstice (21 or 22 December). At the Equator, the length of day and night are almost equal all year.

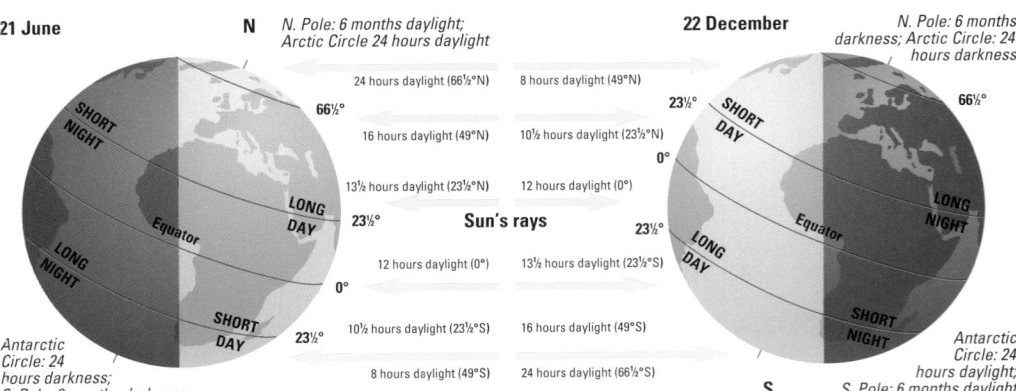

21 June    N    N. Pole: 6 months daylight; Arctic Circle 24 hours daylight

22 December    N. Pole: 6 months darkness; Arctic Circle: 24 hours darkness

24 hours daylight (66½°N)    8 hours daylight (49°N)

66½°    23½°    66½°

16 hours daylight (49°N)    10½ hours daylight (23½°N)

13½ hours daylight (23½°N)    12 hours daylight (0°)

23½°    Sun's rays    23½°

12 hours daylight (0°)    13½ hours daylight (23½°S)

10½ hours daylight (23½°S)    16 hours daylight (49°S)

Antarctic Circle: 24 hours darkness; S. Pole: 6 months darkness

8 hours daylight (49°S)    24 hours daylight (66½°S)

Antarctic Circle: 24 hours daylight; S. Pole: 6 months daylight

## Time

**Year:** The time taken by the Earth to revolve around the Sun, or 365.24 days.

**Leap Year:** A calendar year of 366 days, 29 February being the additional day. It offsets the difference between the calendar and the solar year.

**Month:** The approximate time taken by the Moon to revolve around the Earth. The 12 months of the year in fact vary from 28 (29 in a Leap Year) to 31 days.

**Week:** An artificial period of 7 days, not based on astronomical time.

**Day:** The time taken by the Earth to complete one rotation on its axis.

**Hour:** 24 hours make one day. Usually the day is divided into hours AM (ante meridiem or before noon) and PM (post meridiem or after noon), although most timetables now use the 24-hour system, from midnight to midnight.

## The Moon

The Moon rotates more slowly than the Earth, making one complete turn on its axis in just over 27 days. Since this corresponds to its period of revolution around the Earth, the Moon always presents the same hemisphere or face to us, and we never see 'the dark side'. The interval between one full Moon and the next (and between new Moons) is about 29½ days – a lunar month. The apparent changes in the shape of the Moon are caused by its changing position in relation to the Earth; like the planets, it produces no light of its own and shines only by reflecting the rays of the Sun.

## Phases of the Moon

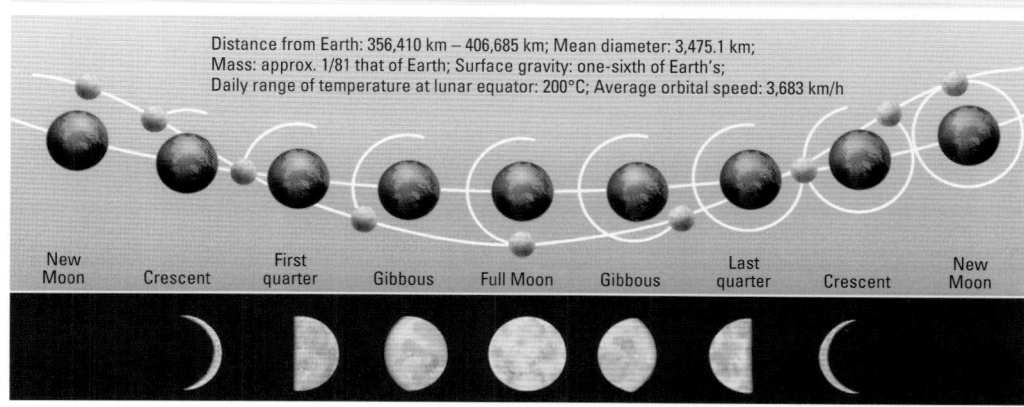

Distance from Earth: 356,410 km – 406,685 km; Mean diameter: 3,475.1 km; Mass: approx. 1/81 that of Earth; Surface gravity: one-sixth of Earth's; Daily range of temperature at lunar equator: 200°C; Average orbital speed: 3,683 km/h

## Eclipses

When the Moon passes between the Sun and the Earth it causes a partial eclipse of the Sun (1) if the Earth passes through the Moon's outer shadow (P), or a total eclipse (2) if the inner cone shadow crosses the Earth's surface. In a lunar eclipse, the Earth's shadow crosses the Moon and, again, provides either a partial or total eclipse.

Eclipses of the Sun and the Moon do not occur every month because of the 5° difference between the plane of the Moon's orbit and the plane in which the Earth moves. In the 1990s only 14 lunar eclipses were possible, for example, seven partial and seven total; each was visible only from certain, and variable, parts of the world. The same period witnessed 13 solar eclipses – six partial (or annular) and seven total.

## Tides

The daily rise and fall of the ocean's tides are the result of the gravitational pull of the Moon and that of the Sun, though the effect of the latter is only 46.6% as strong as that of the Moon. This effect is greatest on the hemisphere facing the Moon and causes a tidal 'bulge'. When the Sun, Earth and Moon are in line, tide-raising forces are at a maximum and Spring tides occur: high tide reaches the highest values, and low tide falls to low levels. When lunar and solar forces are least coincidental with the Sun and Moon at an angle (near the Moon's first and third quarters), Neap tides occur, which have a small tidal range.

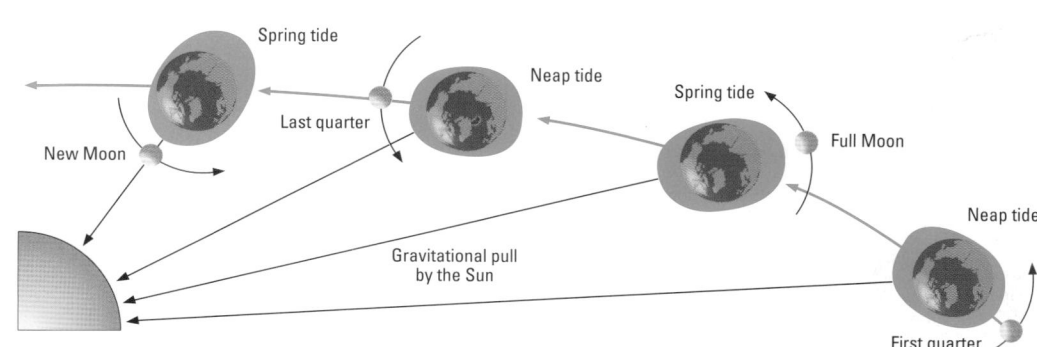

# Restless Earth

## The Earth's Structure

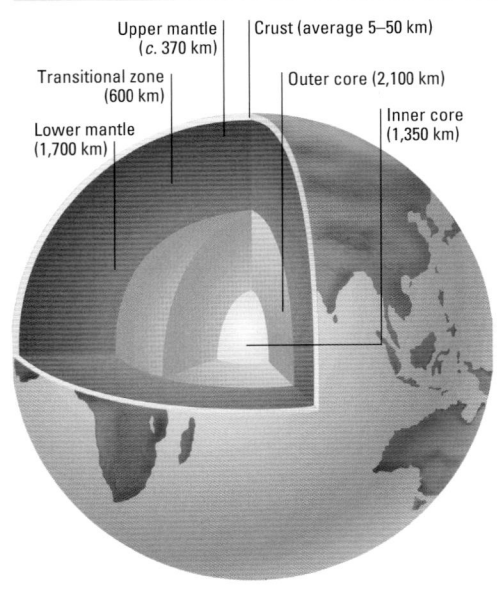

Upper mantle (*c.* 370 km)
Crust (average 5–50 km)
Transitional zone (600 km)
Outer core (2,100 km)
Lower mantle (1,700 km)
Inner core (1,350 km)

## Continental Drift

About 200 million years ago the original Pangaea landmass began to split into two continental groups, which further separated over time to produce the present-day configuration.

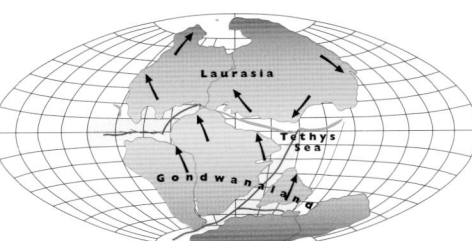

**180 million years ago**

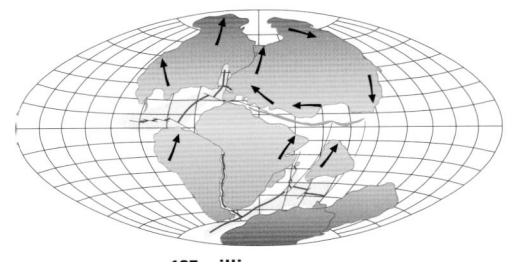

**135 million years ago**

— Trench
— Rift
— New ocean floor
— Zones of slippage

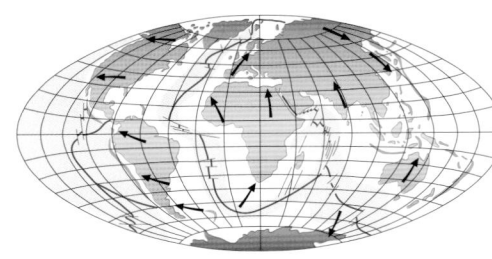

**Present day**

## Notable Earthquakes Since 1900

| Year | Location | Richter Scale | Deaths |
|---|---|---|---|
| 1906 | San Francisco, USA | 8.3 | 3,000 |
| 1906 | Valparaiso, Chile | 8.6 | 22,000 |
| 1908 | Messina, Italy | 7.5 | 83,000 |
| 1915 | Avezzano, Italy | 7.5 | 30,000 |
| 1920 | Gansu (Kansu), China | 8.6 | 180,000 |
| 1923 | Yokohama, Japan | 8.3 | 143,000 |
| 1927 | Nan Shan, China | 8.3 | 200,000 |
| 1932 | Gansu (Kansu), China | 7.6 | 70,000 |
| 1933 | Sanriku, Japan | 8.9 | 2,990 |
| 1934 | Bihar, India/Nepal | 8.4 | 10,700 |
| 1935 | Quetta, India (*now* Pakistan) | 7.5 | 60,000 |
| 1939 | Chillan, Chile | 8.3 | 28,000 |
| 1939 | Erzincan, Turkey | 7.9 | 30,000 |
| 1960 | S. W. Chile | 9.5 | 2,200 |
| 1960 | Agadir, Morocco | 5.8 | 12,000 |
| 1962 | Khorasan, Iran | 7.1 | 12,230 |
| 1964 | Anchorage, USA | 9.2 | 125 |
| 1968 | N. E. Iran | 7.4 | 12,000 |
| 1970 | N. Peru | 7.8 | 70,000 |
| 1972 | Managua, Nicaragua | 6.2 | 5,000 |
| 1974 | N. Pakistan | 6.3 | 5,200 |
| 1976 | Guatemala | 7.5 | 22,500 |
| 1976 | Tangshan, China | 8.2 | 255,000 |
| 1978 | Tabas, Iran | 7.7 | 25,000 |
| 1980 | El Asnam, Algeria | 7.3 | 20,000 |
| 1980 | S. Italy | 7.2 | 4,800 |
| 1985 | Mexico City, Mexico | 8.1 | 4,200 |
| 1988 | N.W. Armenia | 6.8 | 55,000 |
| 1990 | N. Iran | 7.7 | 36,000 |
| 1992 | Flores, Indonesia | 6.8 | 1,895 |
| 1993 | Maharashtra, India | 6.4 | 30,000 |
| 1994 | Los Angeles, USA | 6.6 | 51 |
| 1995 | Kobe, Japan | 7.2 | 5,000 |
| 1995 | Sakhalin Is., Russia | 7.5 | 2,000 |
| 1996 | Yunnan, China | 7.0 | 240 |
| 1997 | N. E. Iran | 7.1 | 2,400 |
| 1998 | Takhar, Afghanistan | 6.1 | 4,200 |
| 1998 | Rostaq, Afghanistan | 7.0 | 5,000 |
| 1999 | Izmit, Turkey | 7.4 | 15,000 |
| 1999 | Taipei, Taiwan | 7.6 | 1,700 |
| 2001 | Gujarat, India | 7.7 | 14,000 |
| 2002 | Afyon, Turkey | 6.5 | 44 |
| 2002 | Baghlan, Afghanistan | 6.1 | 1,000 |
| 2003 | Boumerdes, Algeria | 6.8 | 2,200 |
| 2003 | Bam, Iran | 6.6 | 30,000 |

## Earthquakes

Earthquake magnitude is usually rated according to either the Richter or the Modified Mercalli scale, both devised by seismologists in the 1930s. The Richter scale measures absolute earthquake power with mathematical precision: each step upwards represents a tenfold increase in shockwave amplitude. Theoretically, there is no upper limit, but the largest earthquakes measured have been rated at between 8.8 and 8.9. The 12–point Mercalli scale, based on observed effects, is often more meaningful, ranging from I (earthquakes noticed only by seismographs) to XII (total destruction); intermediate points include V (people awakened at night; unstable objects overturned), VII (collapse of ordinary buildings; chimneys and monuments fall) and IX (conspicuous cracks in ground; serious damage to reservoirs).

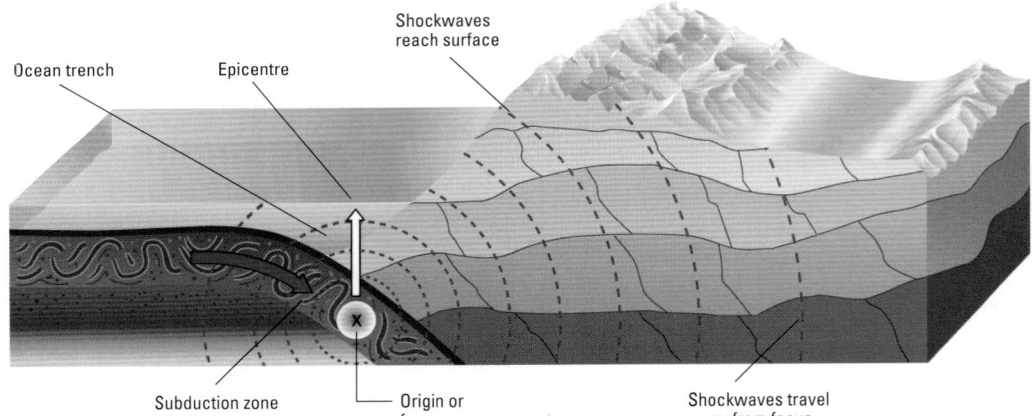

Ocean trench
Epicentre
Shockwaves reach surface
Subduction zone
Origin or focus
Shockwaves travel away from focus

## Structure and Earthquakes

Mobile land areas
Submarine zones of mobile land areas
Stable land platforms
Submarine extensions of stable land platforms
Mid-oceanic volcanic ridges
Oceanic platforms

1976○ Principal earthquakes and dates (since 1900)

Earthquakes are a series of rapid vibrations originating from the slipping or faulting of parts of the Earth's crust when stresses within build up to breaking point. They usually happen at depths varying from 8 km to 30 km. Severe earthquakes cause extensive damage when they take place in populated areas, destroying structures and severing communications. Most initial loss of life occurs due to secondary causes such as falling masonry, fires and flooding.

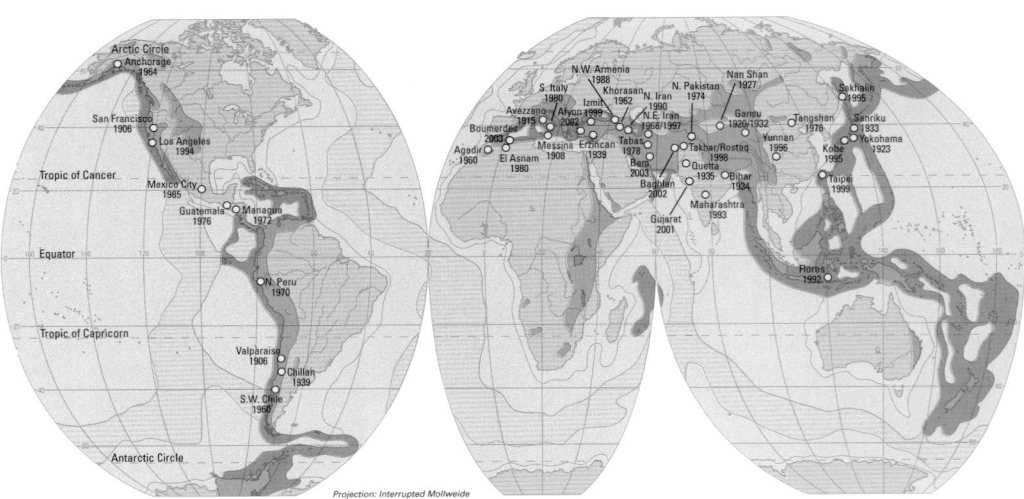

*Projection: Interrupted Mollweide*

# Plate Tectonics

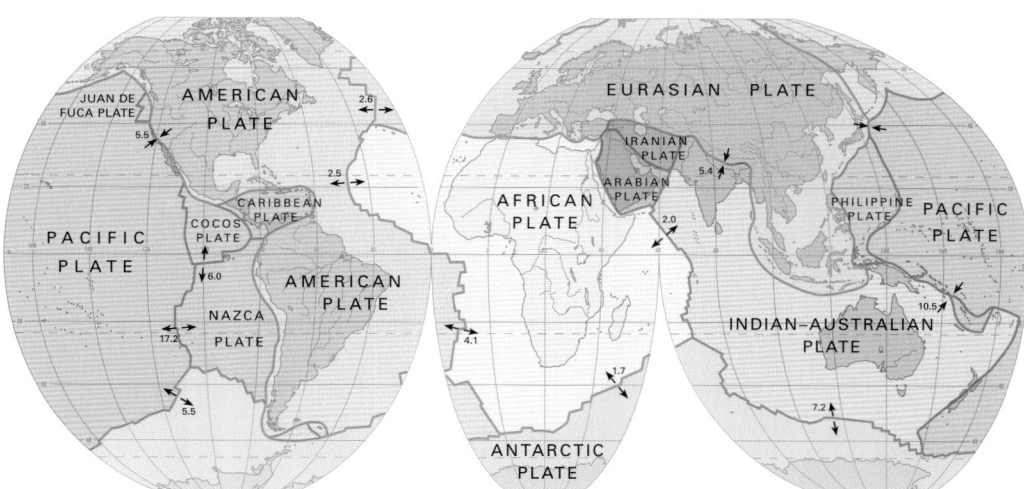

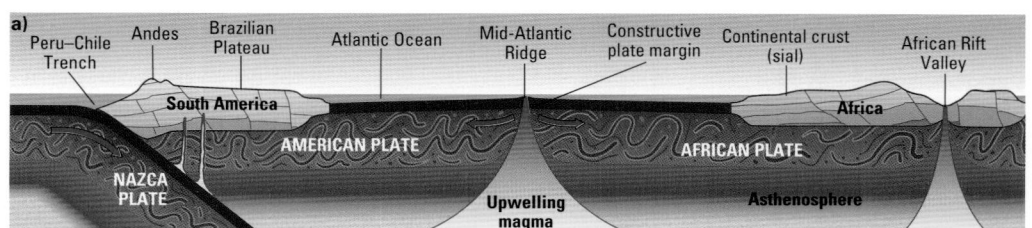

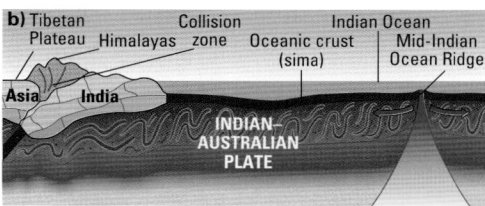

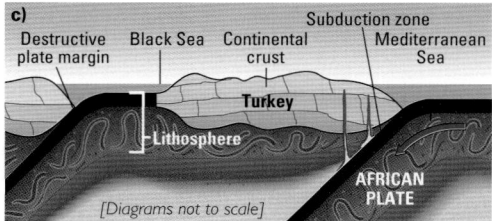

The drifting of the continents is a feature that is unique to Planet Earth. The complementary, almost jigsaw-puzzle fit of the coastlines on each side of the Atlantic Ocean inspired Alfred Wegener's theory of continental drift in 1915. The theory suggested that the ancient super-continent, which Wegener named Pangaea, incorporated all of the Earth's landmasses and gradually split up to form today's continents.

The original debate about continental drift was a prelude to a more radical idea: plate tectonics. The basic theory is that the Earth's crust is made up of a series of rigid plates which float on a soft layer of the mantle and are moved about by continental convection currents within the Earth's interior. These plates diverge and converge along margins marked by seismic activity. Plates diverge from mid-ocean ridges where molten lava pushes upwards and forces the plates apart at rates of up to 40 mm [1.6 in] a year.

The three diagrams, left, give some examples of plate boundaries from around the world. Diagram (a) shows sea-floor spreading at the Mid-Atlantic Ridge as the American and African plates slowly diverge. The same thing is happening in (b) where sea-floor spreading at the Mid-Indian Ocean Ridge is forcing the Indian–Australian plate to collide into the Eurasian plate. In (c) oceanic crust (sima) is being subducted beneath lighter continental crust (sial).

## Volcanoes

Volcanoes occur when hot liquefied rock beneath the Earth's crust is pushed up by pressure to the surface as molten lava. Some volcanoes erupt in an explosive way, throwing out rocks and ash, whilst others are effusive and lava flows out of the vent. There are volcanoes which are both, such as Mount Fuji. An accumulation of lava and cinders creates cones of variable size and shape. As a result of many eruptions over centuries, Mount Etna in Sicily has a circumference of more than 120 km [75 miles].

Climatologists believe that volcanic ash, if ejected high into the atmosphere, can influence temperature and weather for several years afterwards. The 1991 eruption of Mount Pinatubo in the Philippines ejected more than 20 million tonnes of dust and ash 32 km [20 miles] into the atmosphere and is believed to have accelerated ozone depletion over a large part of the globe.

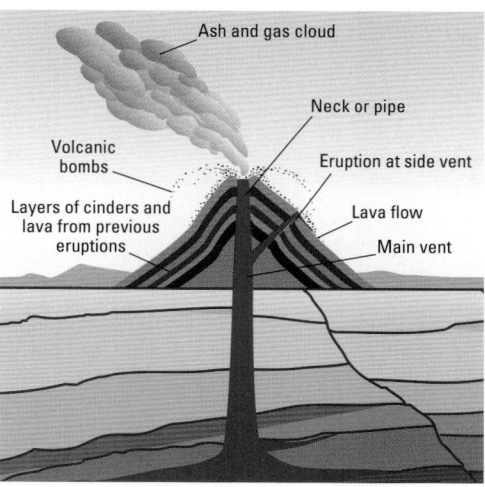

## Distribution of Volcanoes

Volcanoes today may be the subject of considerable scientific study but they remain both dramatic and unpredictable: in 1991 Mount Pinatubo, 100 km [62 miles] north of the Philippines capital Manila, suddenly burst into life after lying dormant for more than six centuries. Most of the world's active volcanoes occur in a belt around the Pacific Ocean, on the edge of the Pacific plate, called the 'ring of fire'. Indonesia has the greatest concentration with 90 volcanoes, 12 of which are active. The most famous, Krakatoa, erupted in 1883 with such force that the resulting tidal wave killed 36,000 people and tremors were felt as far away as Australia.

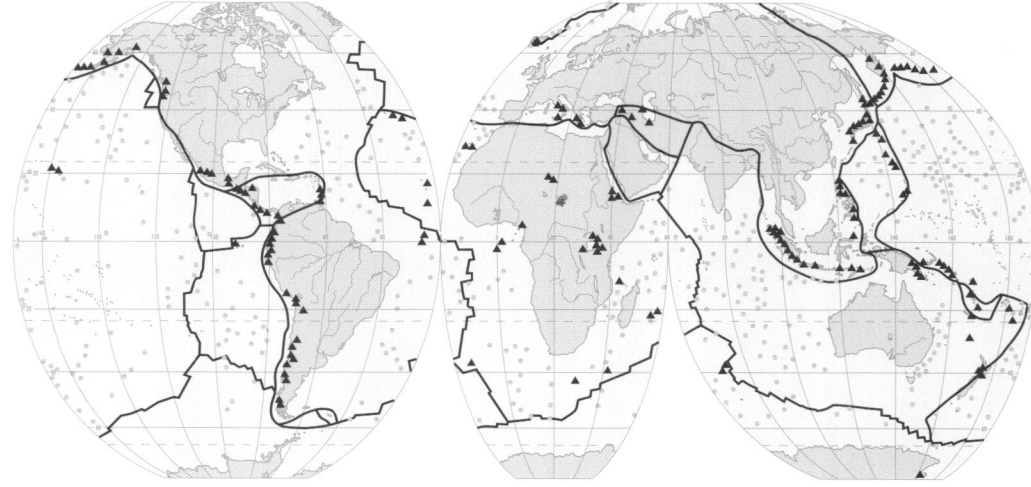

⬤  Submarine volcanoes

▲  Land volcanoes active since 1700

——  Boundaries of tectonic plates

# Landforms

## The Rock Cycle

James Hutton first proposed the rock cycle in the late 1700s after he observed the slow but steady effects of erosion.

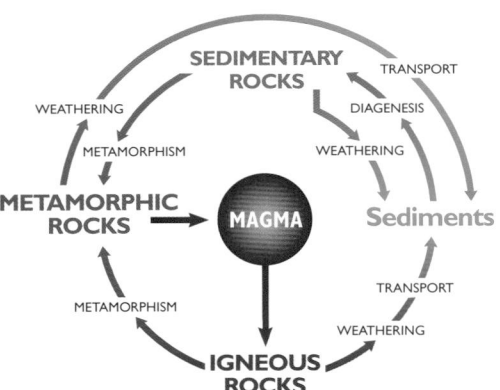

Above and below the surface of the oceans, the features of the Earth's crust are constantly changing. The phenomenal forces generated by convection currents in the molten core of our planet carry the vast segments or 'plates' of the crust across the globe in an endless cycle of creation and destruction. A continent may travel little more than 25 mm [1 in] per year, yet in the vast span of geological time this process throws up giant mountain ranges and creates new land.

Destruction of the landscape, however, begins as soon as it is formed. Wind, water, ice and sea, the main agents of erosion, mount a constant assault that even the most resistant rocks cannot withstand. Mountain peaks may dwindle by as little as a few millimetres each year, but if they are not uplifted by further movements of the crust they will eventually be reduced to rubble and transported away.

Water is the most powerful agent of erosion – it has been estimated that 100 billion tonnes of sediment are washed into the oceans every year. Three Asian rivers account for 20% of this total, the Huang He, in China, and the Brahmaputra and Ganges in Bangladesh.

Rivers and glaciers, like the sea itself, generate much of their effect through abrasion – pounding the land with the debris they carry with them. But as well as destroying they also create new landforms, many of them spectacular: vast deltas like those of the Mississippi and the Nile, or the deep fjords cut by glaciers in British Columbia, Norway and New Zealand.

Geologists once considered that landscapes evolved from 'young', newly uplifted mountainous areas, through a 'mature' hilly stage, to an 'old age' stage when the land was reduced to an almost flat plain, or peneplain. This theory, called the 'cycle of erosion', fell into disuse when it became evident that so many factors, including the effects of plate tectonics and climatic change, constantly interrupt the cycle, which takes no account of the highly complex interactions that shape the surface of our planet.

## Mountain Building

Mountains are formed when pressures on the Earth's crust caused by continental drift become so intense that the surface buckles or cracks. This happens where oceanic crust is subducted by continental crust or, more dramatically, where two tectonic plates collide: the Rockies, Andes, Alps, Urals and Himalayas resulted from such impacts. These are all known as fold mountains because they were formed by the compression of the rocks, forcing the surface to bend and fold like a crumpled rug. The Himalayas are formed from the folded former sediments of the Tethys Sea which was trapped in the collision zone between the Indian and Eurasian plates.

The other main mountain-building process occurs when the crust fractures to create faults, allowing rock to be forced upwards in large blocks; or when the pressure of magma within the crust forces the surface to bulge into a dome, or erupts to form a volcano. Large mountain ranges may reveal a combination of those features; the Alps, for example, have been compressed so violently that the folds are fragmented by numerous faults and intrusions of molten igneous rock.

Over millions of years, even the greatest mountain ranges can be reduced by the agents of erosion (most notably rivers) to a low rugged landscape known as a peneplain.

**Types of faults:** Faults occur where the crust is being stretched or compressed so violently that the rock strata break in a horizontal or vertical movement. They are classified by the direction in which the blocks of rock have moved. A normal fault results when a vertical movement causes the surface to break apart; compression causes a reverse fault. Horizontal movement causes shearing, known as a strike-slip fault. When the rock breaks in two places, the central block may be pushed up in a horst fault, or sink (creating a rift valley) in a graben fault.

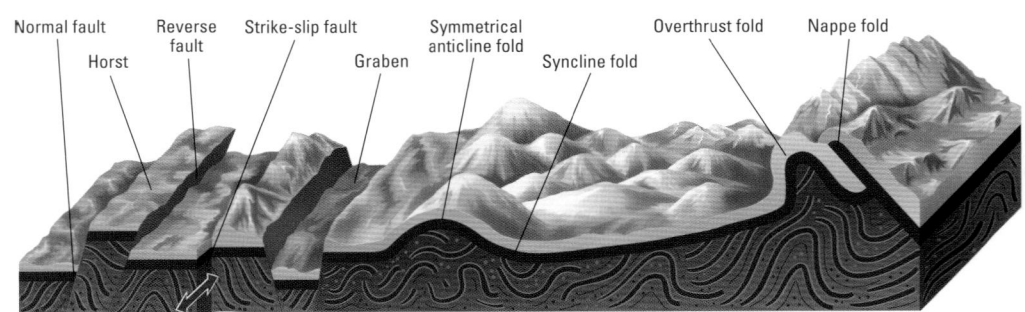

**Types of fold:** Folds occur when rock strata are squeezed and compressed. They are common therefore at destructive plate margins and where plates have collided, forcing the rocks to buckle into mountain ranges. Geographers give different names to the degrees of fold that result from continuing pressure on the rock. A simple fold may be symmetric, with even slopes on either side, but as the pressure builds up, one slope becomes steeper and the fold becomes asymmetric. Later, the ridge or 'anticline' at the top of the fold may slide over the lower ground or 'syncline' to form a recumbent fold. Eventually, the rock strata may break under the pressure to form an overthrust and finally a nappe fold.

## Continental Glaciation

Ice sheets were at their greatest extent about 200,000 years ago. The maximum advance of the last Ice Age was about 18,000 years ago, when ice covered virtually all of Canada and reached as far south as the Bristol Channel in Britain.

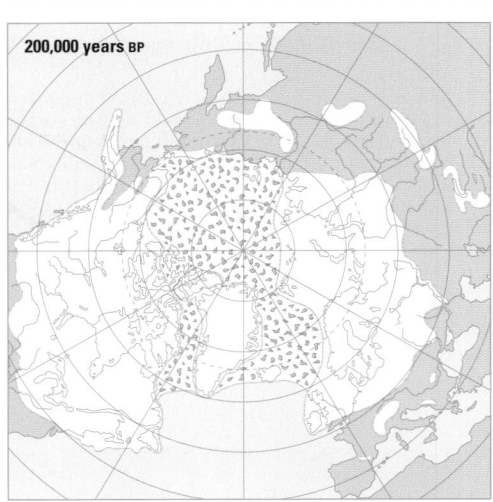

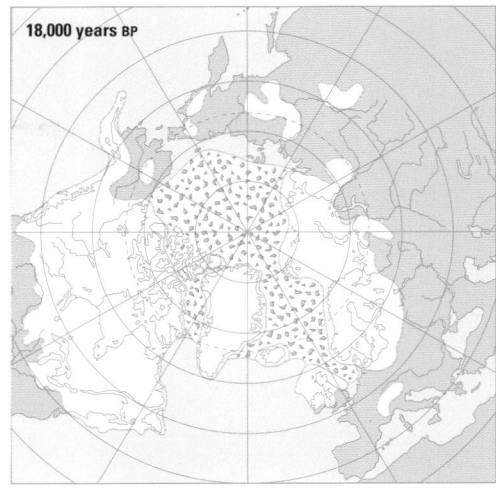

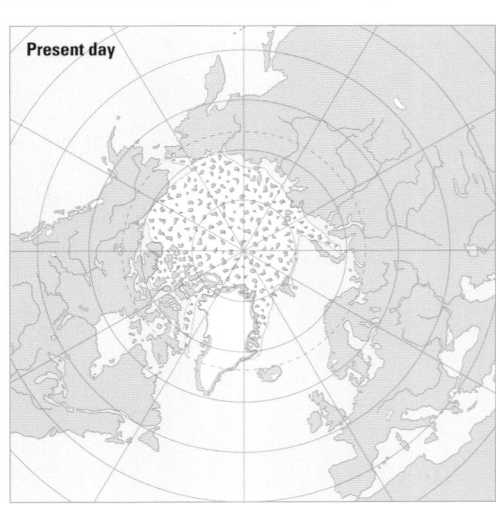

# Natural Landforms

A stylized diagram to show a selection of landforms found in the mid-latitudes.

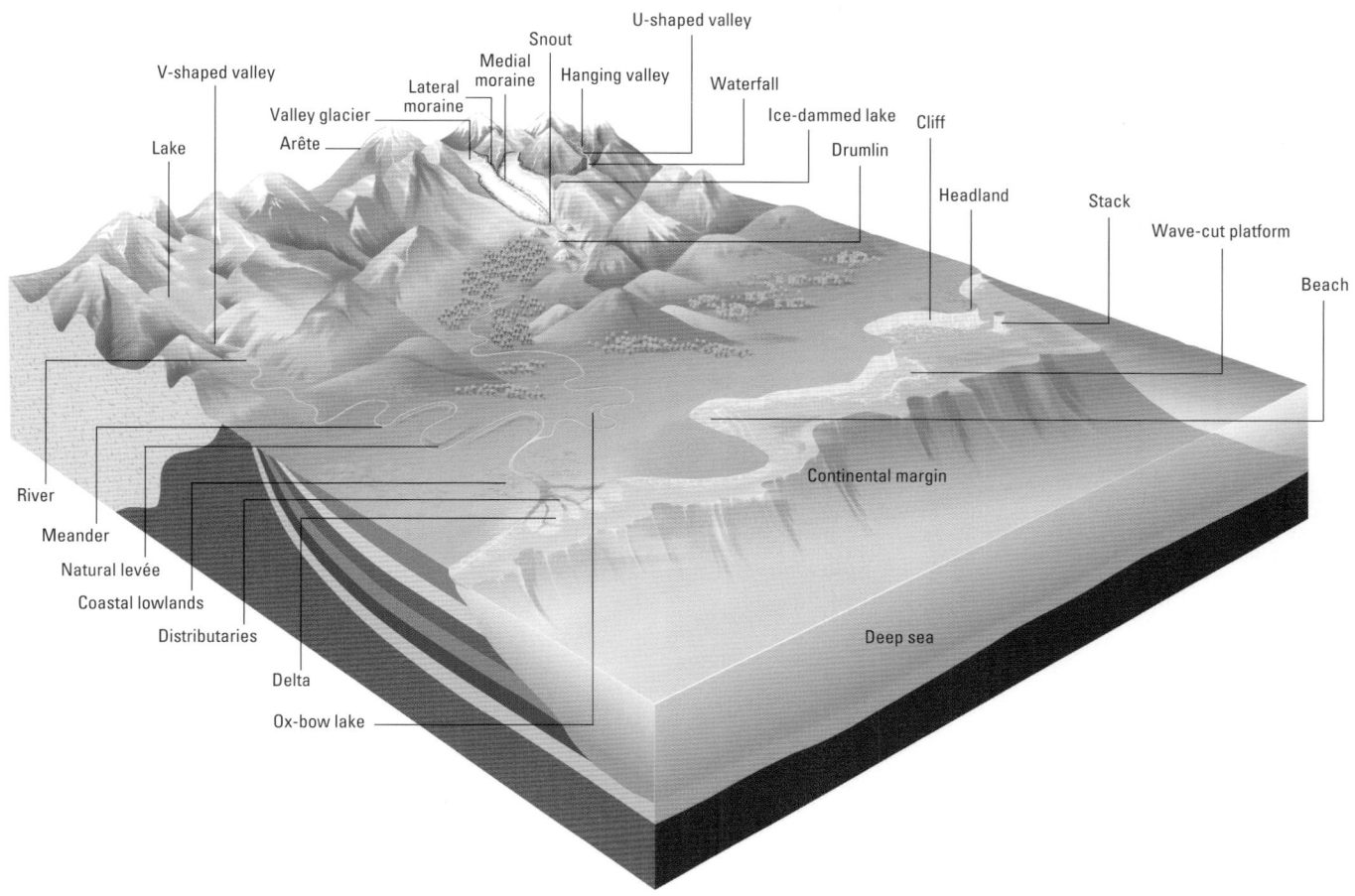

Labels (clockwise): V-shaped valley, Valley glacier, Arête, Lake, Lateral moraine, Medial moraine, Snout, Hanging valley, U-shaped valley, Waterfall, Ice-dammed lake, Drumlin, Cliff, Headland, Stack, Wave-cut platform, Beach, Continental margin, Deep sea, Ox-bow lake, Delta, Distributaries, Coastal lowlands, Natural levée, Meander, River

## Desert Landscapes

The popular image that deserts are all huge expanses of sand is wrong. Despite harsh conditions, deserts contain some of the most varied and interesting landscapes in the world. They are also one of the most extensive environments – the hot and cold deserts together cover almost 40% of the Earth's surface.

The three types of hot desert are known by their Arabic names: sand desert, called *erg*, covers only about one-fifth of the world's desert; the rest is divided between *hammada* (areas of bare rock) and *reg* (broad plains covered by loose gravel or pebbles).

In areas of *erg*, such as the Namib Desert, the shape of the dunes reflects the character of local winds. Where winds are constant in direction, crescent-shaped *barchan* dunes form. In areas of bare rock, wind-blown sand is a major agent of erosion. The erosion is mainly confined to within 2 m [6.5 ft] of the surface, producing characteristic, mushroom-shaped rocks.

Erg

Hammada

Reg

## Surface Processes

Catastrophic changes to natural landforms are periodically caused by such phenomena as avalanches, landslides and volcanic eruptions, but most of the processes that shape the Earth's surface operate extremely slowly in human terms. One estimate, based on a study in the United States, suggested that 1 m [3 ft] of land was removed from the entire surface of the country, on average, every 29,500 years. However, the time-scale varies from 1,300 years to 154,200 years depending on the terrain and climate.

In hot, dry climates, mechanical weathering, a result of rapid temperature changes, causes the outer layers of rock to peel away, while in cold mountainous regions, boulders are prised apart when water freezes in cracks in rocks. Chemical weathering, at its greatest in warm, humid regions, is responsible for hollowing out limestone caves and decomposing granites.

The erosion of soil and rock is greatest on sloping land and the steeper the slope, the greater the tendency for mass wasting – the movement of soil and rock downhill under the influence of gravity. The mechanisms of mass wasting (ranging from very slow to very rapid) vary with the type of material, but the presence of water as a lubricant is usually an important factor.

Running water is the world's leading agent of erosion and transportation. The energy of a river depends on several factors, including its velocity and volume, and its erosive power is at its peak when it is in full flood. Sea waves also exert tremendous erosive power during storms when they hurl pebbles against the shore, undercutting cliffs and hollowing out caves.

Glacier ice forms in mountain hollows and spills out to form valley glaciers, which transport rocks shattered by frost action. As glaciers move, rocks embedded into the ice erode steep-sided, U-shaped valleys. Evidence of glaciation in mountain regions includes cirques, knife-edged ridges, or arêtes, and pyramidal peaks.

# Oceans

## The Great Oceans

**Relative sizes of the world's oceans**

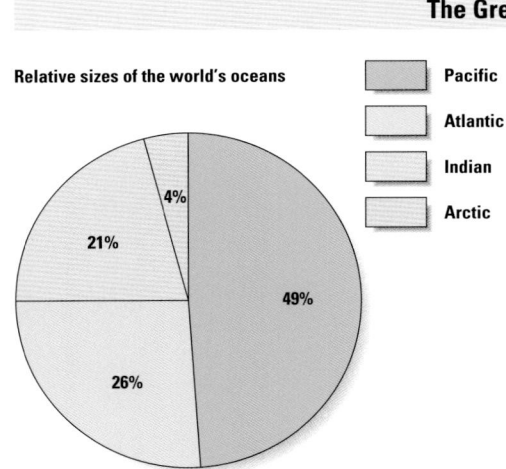

| | |
|---|---|
| ▦ | **Pacific** |
| ▦ | **Atlantic** |
| ▦ | **Indian** |
| ▦ | **Arctic** |

In a strict geographical sense there are only four true oceans – the Atlantic, Indian, Pacific and Arctic. The International Hydrographic Bureau does not recognize the Antarctic Ocean (even less the 'Southern Ocean') as a separate entity. From ancient times to about the 15th century, the legendary 'Seven Seas' comprised the Red Sea, Mediterranean Sea, Persian Gulf, Black Sea, Adriatic Sea, Caspian Sea and Indian Sea.

The Earth is a watery planet: more than 70% of its surface – over 360,000,000 sq km [140,000,000 sq miles] – is covered by the oceans and seas. The mighty Pacific alone accounts for nearly 36% of the total, and 49% of the sea area. Gravity holds in around 1,400 million cu. km [320 million cu. miles] of water, of which over 97% is saline.

The vast underwater world starts in the shallows of the seaside and plunges to depths of more than 11,000 m [36,000 ft]. The continental shelf, part of the landmass, drops gently to around 200 m [650 ft]; here the seabed falls away suddenly at an angle of 3° to 6° – the continental slope. The third stage, called the continental rise, is more gradual with gradients varying from 1 in 100 to 1 in 700. At an average depth of 5,000 m [16,500 ft] there begins the aptly-named abyssal plain – massive submarine depths where sunlight fails to penetrate and few creatures can survive.

From these plains rise volcanoes which, taken from base to top, rival and even surpass the tallest continental mountains in height. Mauna Kea, on Hawaii, reaches a total of 10,203 m [33,400 ft], some 1,355 m [4,500 ft] more than Mount Everest, though scarcely 40% is visible above sea level.

In addition, there are underwater mountain chains up to 1,000 km [600 miles] across, whose peaks sometimes appear above sea level as islands such as Iceland and Tristan da Cunha.

## The Ocean Depths

**Average and maximum depths of the world's great oceans, in metres**

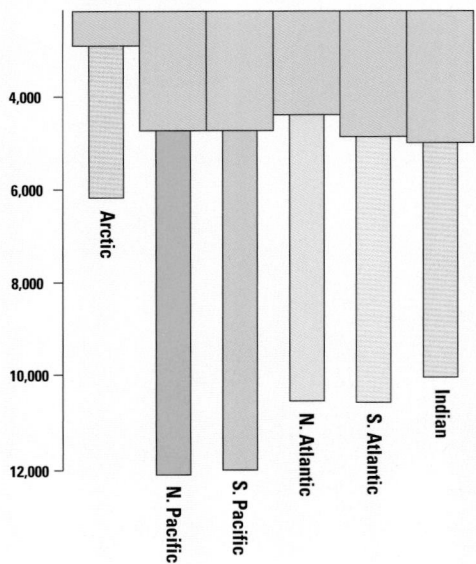

## Ocean Currents

**January ocean currents**

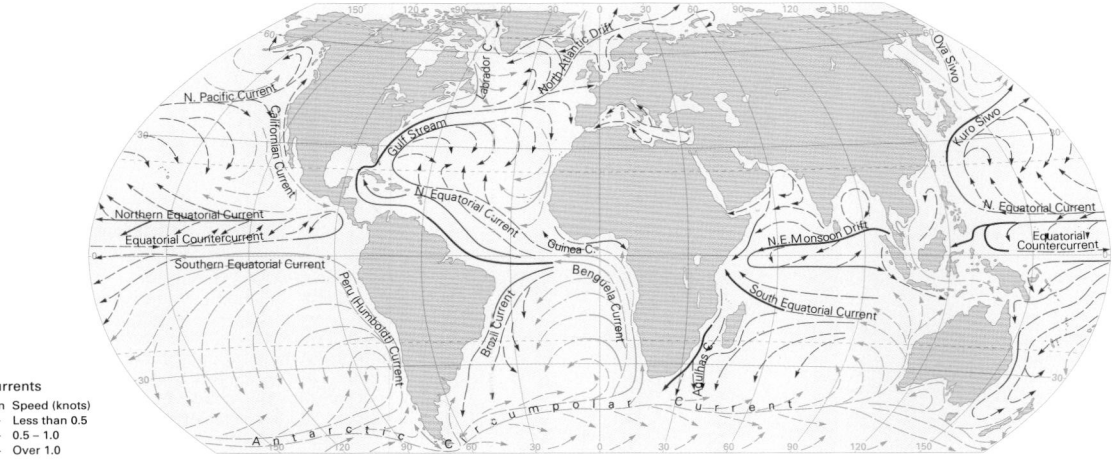

Ocean Currents
Cold Warm Speed (knots)
- Less than 0.5
- 0.5 – 1.0
- Over 1.0

**July ocean currents**

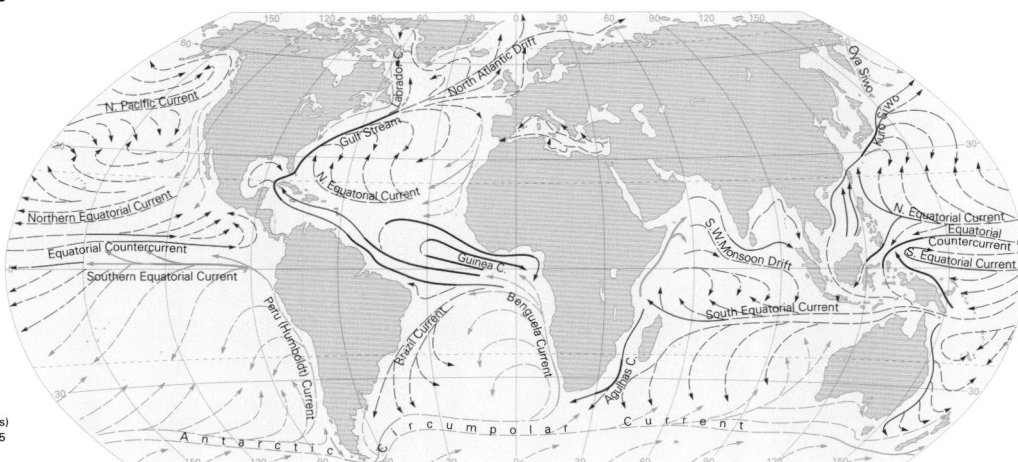

Ocean Currents
Cold Warm Speed (knots)
- Less than 0.5
- 0.5 – 1.0
- Over 1.0

Moving immense quantities of energy as well as billions of tonnes of water every hour, the ocean currents are a vital part of the great heat engine that drives the Earth's climate. They themselves are produced by a twofold mechanism. At the surface, winds push huge masses of water before them; in the deep ocean, below an abrupt temperature gradient that separates the churning surface waters from the still depths, density variations cause slow vertical movements.

The pattern of circulation of the great surface currents is determined by the displacement known as the Coriolis effect. As the Earth turns beneath a moving object – whether it is a tennis ball or a vast mass of water – it appears to be deflected to one side. The deflection is most obvious near the Equator, where the Earth's surface is spinning eastwards at 1,700 km/h [1,050 mph]; currents moving polewards are curved clockwise in the northern hemisphere and anti-clockwise in the southern.

The result is a system of spinning circles known as gyres. The Coriolis effect piles up water on the left of each gyre, creating a narrow, fast-moving stream that is matched by a slower, broader returning current on the right. North and south of the Equator, the fastest currents are located in the west and in the east respectively. In each case, warm water moves from the Equator and cold water returns to it. Cold currents often bring an upwelling of nutrients with them, supporting the world's most economically important fisheries.

Depending on the prevailing winds, some currents on or near the Equator may reverse their direction in the course of the year – a seasonal variation on which Asian monsoon rains depend, and whose occasional failure can bring disaster to millions.

## World Fishing Areas

**Main commercial fishing areas (numbered FAO regions)**

Catch by top marine fishing areas, thousand tonnes (2000)

| | | | | |
|---|---|---|---|---|
| 1. | Pacific, NW | [61] | 23,141 | 24.4% |
| 2. | Pacific, SE | [87] | 15,822 | 16.7% |
| 3. | Atlantic, NE | [27] | 10,920 | 11.5% |
| 4. | Pacific, WC | [71] | 9,899 | 10.4% |
| 5. | Indian, E | [57] | 4,708 | 5.0% |
| 6. | Indian, W | [51] | 3,902 | 4.1% |
| 7. | Atlantic, EC | [34] | 3,523 | 3.7% |
| 8. | Pacific, NE | [67] | 2,518 | 2.7% |
| 9. | Atlantic, NW | [21] | 2,063 | 2.2% |
| 10. | Atlantic, WC | [31] | 1,831 | 1.9% |

Principal fishing areas

**Leading fishing nations**

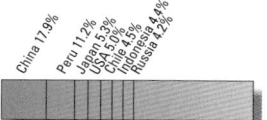

China 17.9%
Peru 11.2%
Japan 5.3%
USA 5.0%
Chile 4.5%
Indonesia 4.4%
Russia 4.2%

World total (2000): 94,849,000 tonnes
(Marine catch 90.7%  Inland catch 9.3%)

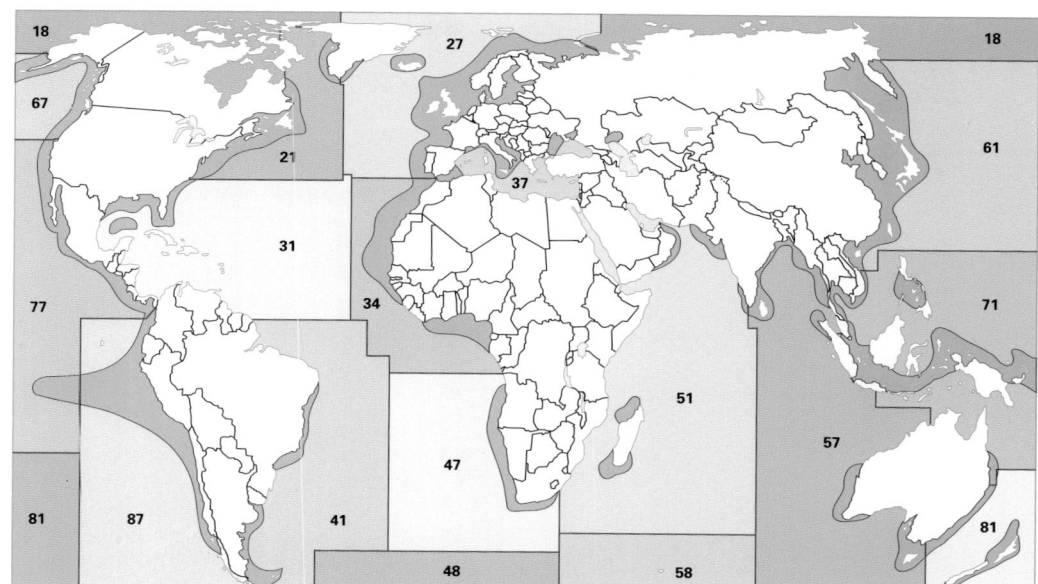

## Marine Pollution

**Sources of marine oil pollution (latest available year)**

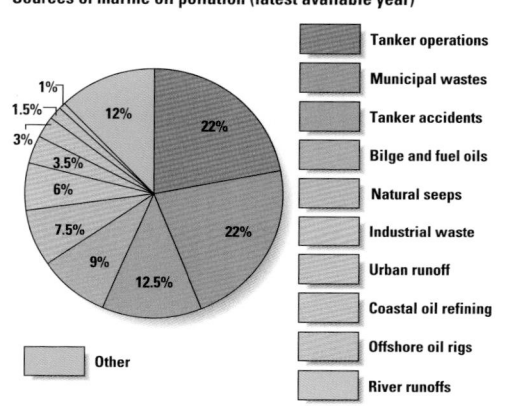

Tanker operations

Municipal wastes

Tanker accidents

Bilge and fuel oils

Natural seeps

Industrial waste

Urban runoff

Coastal oil refining

Offshore oil rigs

River runoffs

Other

## Oil Spills

**Major oil spills from tankers and combined carriers**

| Year | Vessel | Location | Spill (barrels)** | Cause |
|---|---|---|---|---|
| 1979 | Atlantic Empress | West Indies | 1,890,000 | collision |
| 1983 | Castillo De Bellver | South Africa | 1,760,000 | fire |
| 1978 | Amoco Cadiz | France | 1,628,000 | grounding |
| 1991 | Haven | Italy | 1,029,000 | explosion |
| 1988 | Odyssey | Canada | 1,000,000 | fire |
| 1967 | Torrey Canyon | UK | 909,000 | grounding |
| 1972 | Sea Star | Gulf of Oman | 902,250 | collision |
| 1977 | Hawaiian Patriot | Hawaiian Is. | 742,500 | fire |
| 1979 | Independenta | Turkey | 696,350 | collision |
| 1993 | Braer | UK | 625,000 | grounding |
| 1996 | Sea Empress | UK | 515,000 | grounding |

**Other sources of major oil spills**

| | | | | |
|---|---|---|---|---|
| 1983 | Nowruz oilfield | The Gulf | 4,250,000† | war |
| 1979 | Ixtoc 1 oilwell | Gulf of Mexico | 4,200,000 | blow-out |
| 1991 | Kuwait | The Gulf | 2,500,000† | war |

** 1 barrel = 0.136 tonnes/159 lit./35 Imperial gal./42 US gal.  † estimated

## River Pollution

**Sources of river pollution, USA (latest available year)**

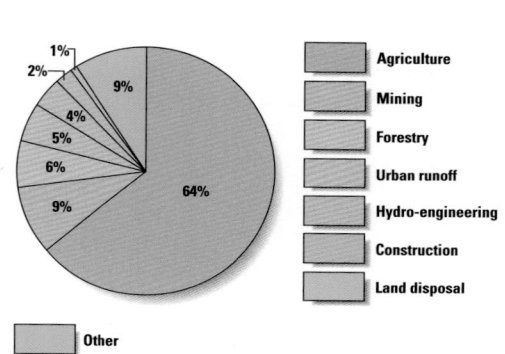

Agriculture

Mining

Forestry

Urban runoff

Hydro-engineering

Construction

Land disposal

Other

## Water Pollution

Severely polluted
sea areas and lakes

Polluted sea
areas and lakes

Areas of frequent oil pollution
by shipping

Major oil tanker spills

Major oil rig blow-outs

Offshore dumpsites for industrial
and municipal waste

Severely polluted
rivers and estuaries

The most notorious tanker spillage of the
1980s occurred when the *Exxon Valdez* ran
aground in Prince William Sound, Alaska,
in 1989, spilling 267,000 barrels of crude oil
close to shore in a sensitive ecological area.
This rates as the world's 28th worst spill in
terms of volume.

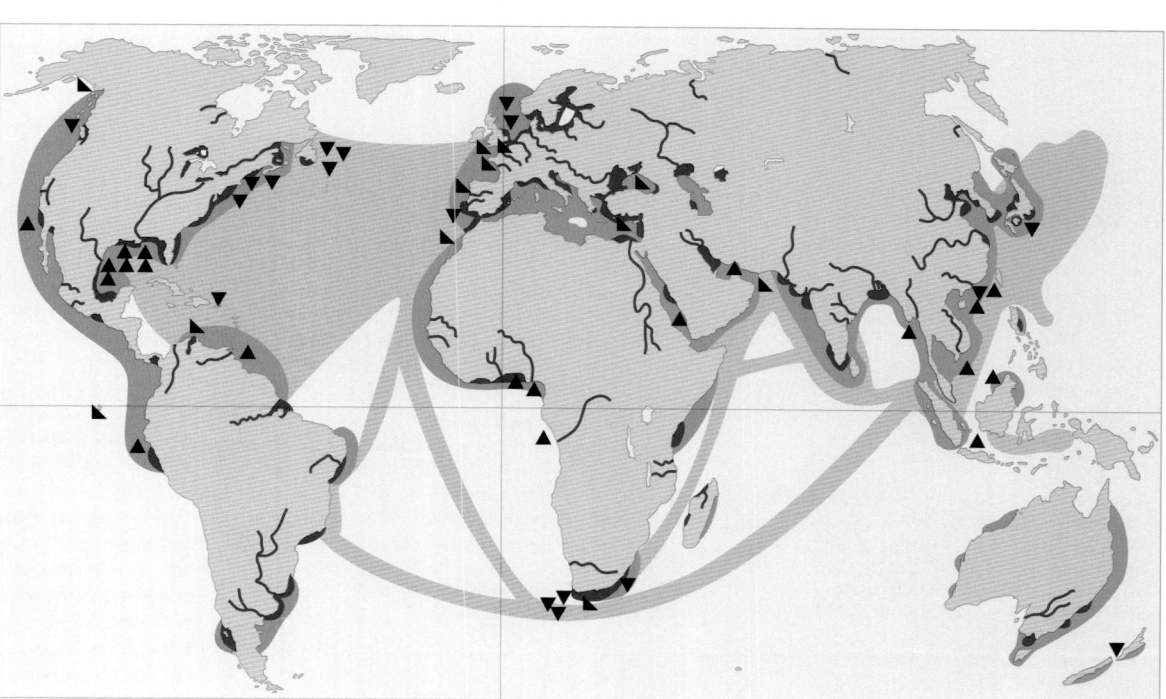

# Climate

## Climatic Regions

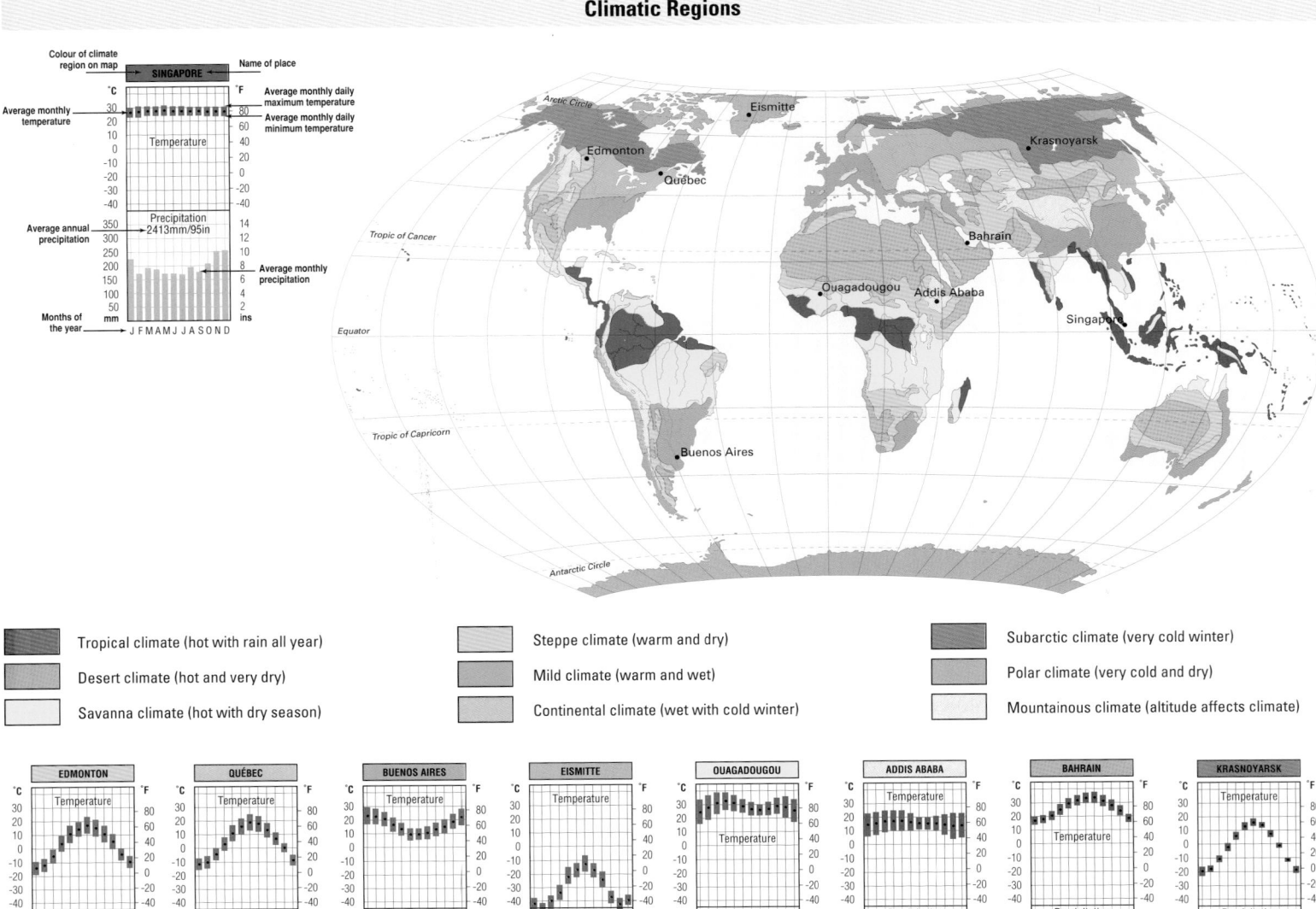

- Tropical climate (hot with rain all year)
- Desert climate (hot and very dry)
- Savanna climate (hot with dry season)
- Steppe climate (warm and dry)
- Mild climate (warm and wet)
- Continental climate (wet with cold winter)
- Subarctic climate (very cold winter)
- Polar climate (very cold and dry)
- Mountainous climate (altitude affects climate)

## Climate Records

### Temperature
Highest recorded shade temperature: Al Aziziyah, Libya, 58°C [136.4°F], 13 September 1922.

Highest mean annual temperature: Dallol, Ethiopia, 34.4°C [94°F], 1960–66.

Longest heatwave: Marble Bar, W. Australia, 162 days over 38°C [100°F], 23 October 1923 to 7 April 1924.

Lowest recorded temperature (outside poles): Verkhoyansk, Siberia, –68°C [–90°F], 6 February 1933.

Lowest mean annual temperature: Plateau Station, Antarctica, –56.6°C [–72.0°F].

### Precipitation
Longest drought: Calama, N. Chile, no recorded rainfall in 400 years to 1971.

Wettest place (12 months): Cherrapunji, Meghalaya, N. E. India, 26,470 mm [1,040 in], August 1860 to August 1861. Cherrapunji also holds the record for the most rainfall in one month: 2,930 mm [115 in], July 1861.

Wettest place (average): Mawsynram, India, mean annual rainfall 11,873 mm [467.4 in].

Wettest place (24 hours): Cilaos, Réunion, Indian Ocean, 1,870 mm [73.6 in], 15–16 March 1952.

Heaviest hailstones: Gopalganj, Bangladesh, up to 1.02 kg [2.25 lb], 14 April 1986 (killed 92 people).

Heaviest snowfall (continuous): Bessans, Savoie, France, 1,730 mm [68 in] in 19 hours, 5–6 April 1969.

Heaviest snowfall (season/year): Paradise Ranger Station, Mt Rainier, Washington, USA, 31,102 mm [1,224.5 in], 19 February 1971 to 18 February 1972.

### Pressure and winds
Highest barometric pressure: Agata, Siberia (at 262 m [862 ft] altitude), 1,083.8 mb, 31 December 1968.

Lowest barometric pressure: Typhoon Tip, Guam, Pacific Ocean, 870 mb, 12 October 1979.

Highest recorded wind speed: Mt Washington, New Hampshire, USA, 371 km/h [231 mph], 12 April 1934. This is three times as strong as hurricane force on the Beaufort Scale.

Windiest place: Commonwealth Bay, Antarctica, where gales frequently reach over 320 km/h [200 mph].

## Climate

Climate is weather in the long term: the seasonal pattern of hot and cold, wet and dry, averaged over time (usually 30 years). At the simplest level, it is caused by the uneven heating of the Earth. Surplus heat at the Equator passes towards the poles, levelling out the energy differential. Its passage is marked by a ceaseless churning of the atmosphere and the oceans, further agitated by the Earth's diurnal spin and the motion it imparts to moving air and water. The heat's means of transport – by winds and ocean currents, by the continual evaporation and recondensation of water molecules – is the weather itself. There are four basic types of climate, each of which can be further subdivided: tropical, desert (dry), temperate and polar.

## Composition of Dry Air

| | | | |
|---|---|---|---|
| Nitrogen | 78.09% | Sulphur dioxide | trace |
| Oxygen | 20.95% | Nitrogen oxide | trace |
| Argon | 0.93% | Methane | trace |
| Water vapour | 0.2–4.0% | Dust | trace |
| Carbon dioxide | 0.03% | Helium | trace |
| Ozone | 0.00006% | Neon | trace |

## El Niño

In a normal year, south-easterly trade winds drive surface waters westwards off the coast of South America, drawing cold, nutrient-rich water up from below. In an El Niño year (which occurs every 2–7 years), warm water from the west Pacific suppresses upwelling in the east, depriving the region of nutrients. The water is warmed by as much as 7°C [12°F], disturbing the tropical atmospheric circulation. During an intense El Niño, the south-east trade winds change direction and become equatorial westerlies, resulting in climatic extremes in many regions of the world, such as drought in parts of Australia and India, and heavy rainfall in south-eastern USA. An intense El Niño occurred in 1997–8, with resultant freak weather conditions across the entire Pacific region.

**Normal year**

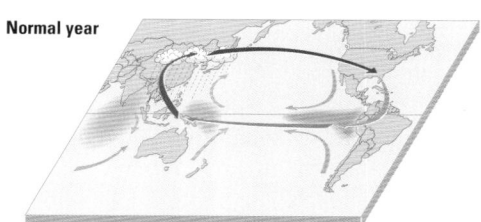

**El Niño event**

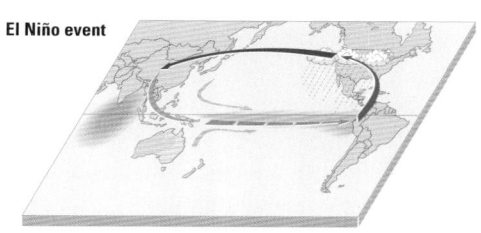

## Beaufort Wind Scale

Named after the 19th-century British naval officer who devised it, the Beaufort Scale assesses wind speed according to its effects. It was originally designed as an aid for sailors, but has since been adapted for use on the land.

| Scale | Wind speed km/h | mph | Effect |
|---|---|---|---|
| 0 | 0–1 | 0–1 | **Calm** Smoke rises vertically |
| 1 | 1–5 | 1–3 | **Light air** Wind direction shown only by smoke drift |
| 2 | 6–11 | 4–7 | **Light breeze** Wind felt on face; leaves rustle; vanes moved by wind |
| 3 | 12–19 | 8–12 | **Gentle breeze** Leaves and small twigs in constant motion; wind extends small flag |
| 4 | 20–28 | 13–18 | **Moderate** Raises dust and loose paper; small branches move |
| 5 | 29–38 | 19–24 | **Fresh** Small trees in leaf sway; wavelets on inland waters |
| 6 | 39–49 | 25–31 | **Strong** Large branches move; difficult to use umbrellas |
| 7 | 50–61 | 32–38 | **Near gale** Whole trees in motion; difficult to walk against wind |
| 8 | 62–74 | 39–46 | **Gale** Twigs break from trees; walking very difficult |
| 9 | 75–88 | 47–54 | **Strong gale** Slight structural damage |
| 10 | 89–102 | 55–63 | **Storm** Trees uprooted; serious structural damage |
| 11 | 103–117 | 64–72 | **Violent storm** Widespread damage |
| 12 | 118+ | 73+ | **Hurricane** |

## Conversions

°C = (°F − 32) × 5/9;  °F = (°C × 9/5) + 32;  0°C = 32°F
1 in = 25.4 mm;  1 mm = 0.0394 in;  100 mm = 3.94 in

## Temperature

**Average temperature in January**

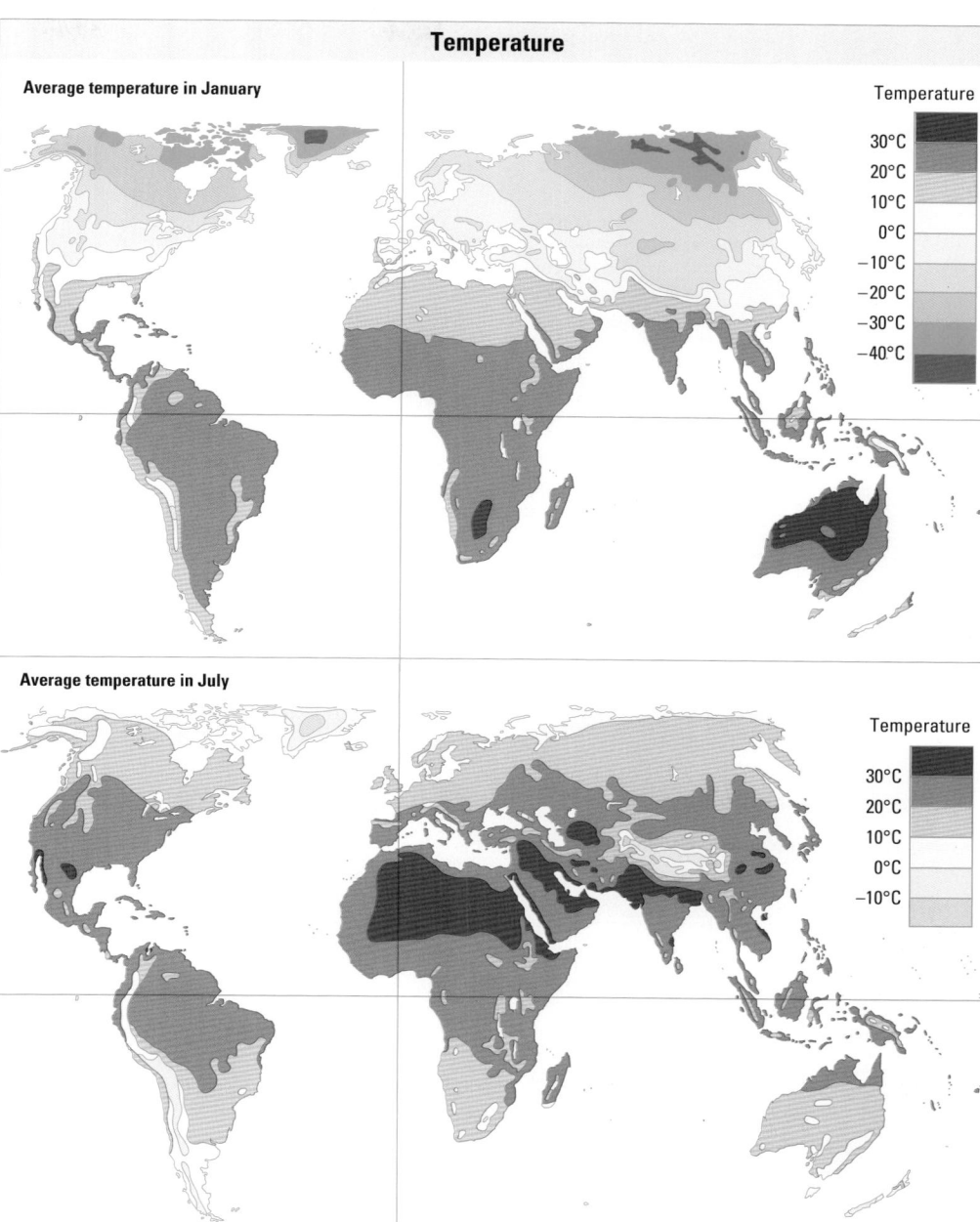

Temperature

30°C
20°C
10°C
0°C
−10°C
−20°C
−30°C
−40°C

**Average temperature in July**

Temperature

30°C
20°C
10°C
0°C
−10°C

## Precipitation

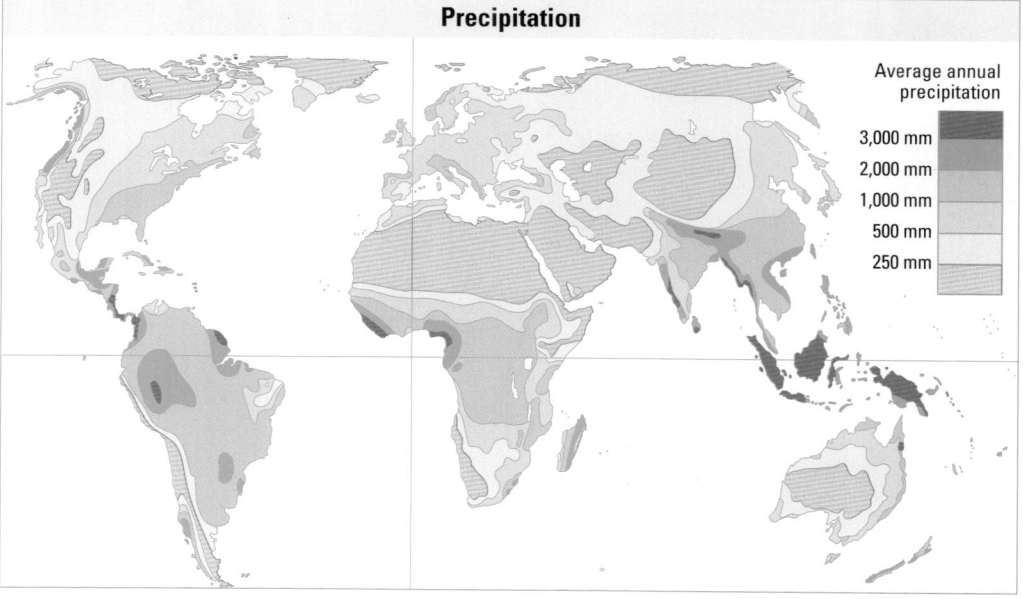

Average annual precipitation

3,000 mm
2,000 mm
1,000 mm
500 mm
250 mm

# Water and Vegetation

## The Hydrological Cycle

The world's water balance is regulated by the constant recycling of water between the oceans, atmosphere and land. The movement of water between these three reservoirs is known as the hydrological cycle. The oceans play a vital role in the hydrological cycle: 74% of the total precipitation falls over the oceans and 84% of the total evaporation comes from the oceans.

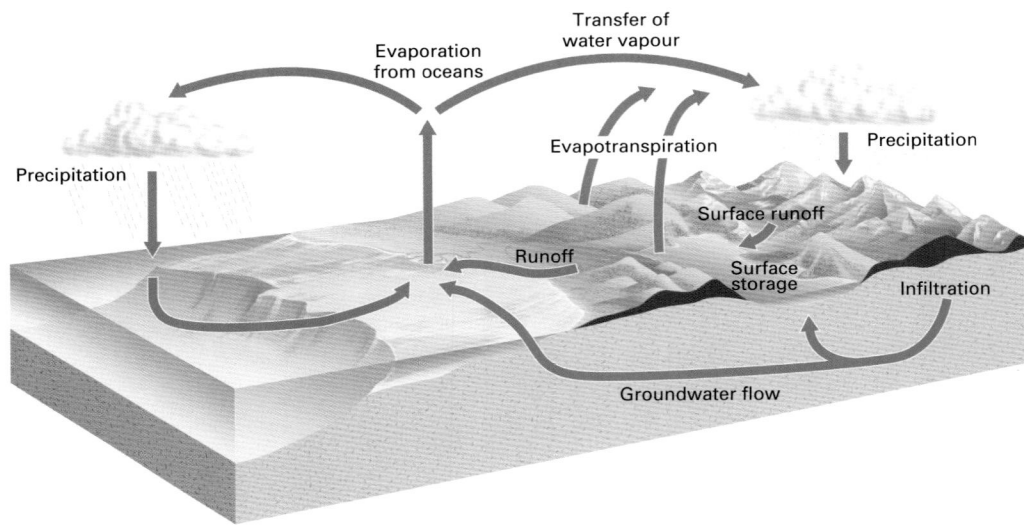

## Water Distribution

The distribution of planetary water, by percentage. Oceans and ice caps together account for more than 99% of the total; the breakdown of the remainder is estimated.

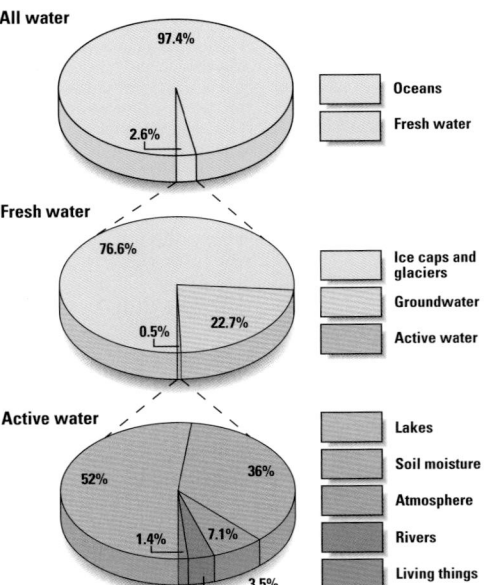

All water — 97.4% / 2.6%
- Oceans
- Fresh water

Fresh water — 76.6% / 0.5% / 22.7%
- Ice caps and glaciers
- Groundwater
- Active water

Active water — 52% / 36% / 1.4% / 7.1% / 3.5%
- Lakes
- Soil moisture
- Atmosphere
- Rivers
- Living things

## Water Utilization

| | Domestic | Industrial | Agriculture |

The percentage breakdown of water usage by sector, selected countries (latest available year)

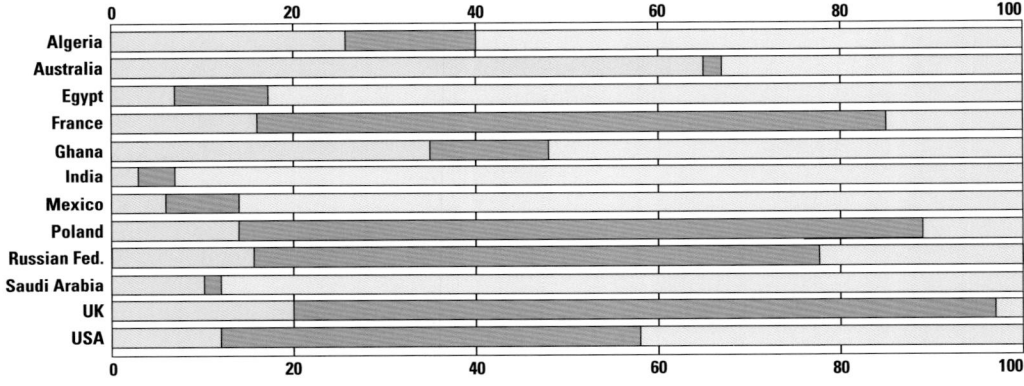

Algeria, Australia, Egypt, France, Ghana, India, Mexico, Poland, Russian Fed., Saudi Arabia, UK, USA

## Water Usage

Almost all the world's water is 3,000 million years old, and all of it cycles endlessly through the hydrosphere, though at different rates. Water vapour circulates over days, even hours, deep ocean water circulates over millennia, and ice-cap water remains solid for millions of years.

Fresh water is essential to all terrestrial life. Humans cannot survive more than a few days without it, and even the hardiest desert plants and animals could not exist without some water. Agriculture requires huge quantities of fresh water: without large-scale irrigation most of the world's people would starve. In the USA, agriculture uses 42% and industry 45% of all water withdrawals.

The United States is one of the heaviest users of water in the world. According to the latest figures the average American uses 380 litres a day and the average household uses 415,000 litres a year. This is two to four times more than in Western Europe.

## Water Supply

Percentage of total population with access to safe drinking water (2000)

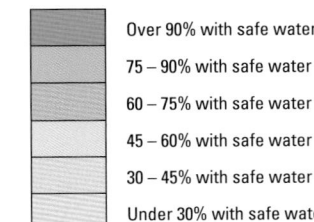

- Over 90% with safe water
- 75 – 90% with safe water
- 60 – 75% with safe water
- 45 – 60% with safe water
- 30 – 45% with safe water
- Under 30% with safe water
- ○ Under 80 litres per person per day domestic water consumption
- ● Over 320 litres per person per day domestic water consumption

*NB: 80 litres of water a day is considered necessary for a reasonable quality of life.*

**Least well-provided countries**

| | | | |
|---|---|---|---|
| Afghanistan | 13% | Sierra Leone | 28% |
| Ethiopia | 24% | Cambodia | 30% |
| Chad | 27% | Mauritania | 37% |

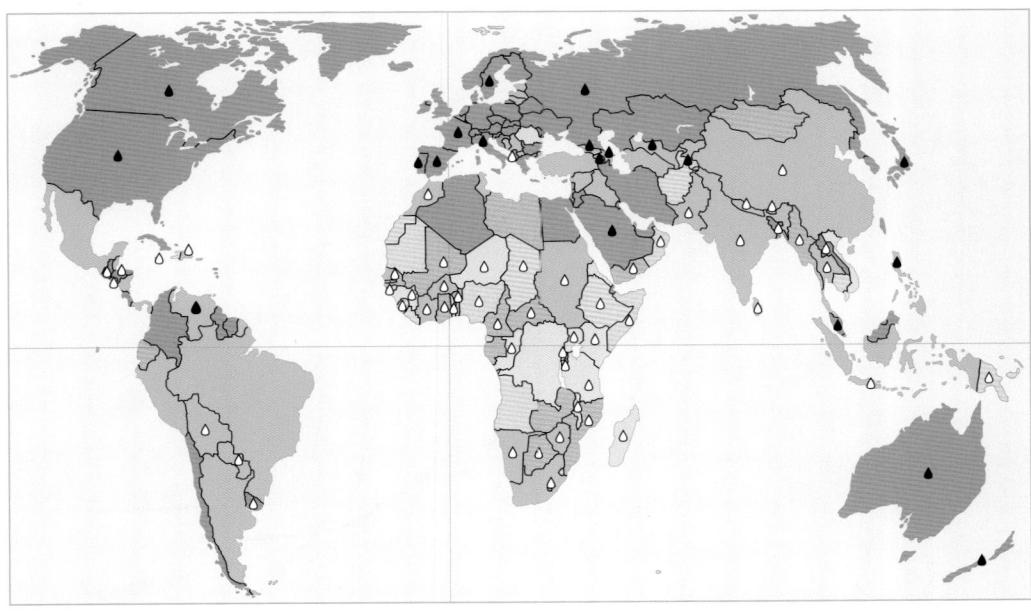

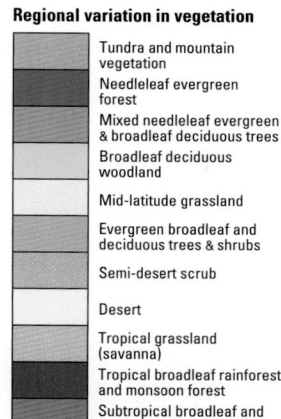

## Natural Vegetation

**Regional variation in vegetation**

- Tundra and mountain vegetation
- Needleleaf evergreen forest
- Mixed needleleaf evergreen & broadleaf deciduous trees
- Broadleaf deciduous woodland
- Mid-latitude grassland
- Evergreen broadleaf and deciduous trees & shrubs
- Semi-desert scrub
- Desert
- Tropical grassland (savanna)
- Tropical broadleaf rainforest and monsoon forest
- Subtropical broadleaf and needleleaf forest

The map shows the natural 'climax vegetation' of regions, as dictated by climate and topography. In most cases, however, agricultural activity has drastically altered the vegetation pattern. Western Europe, for example, lost most of its broadleaf forest many centuries ago, while irrigation has turned some natural semi-desert into productive land.

## Land Use by Continent

- Forest
- Permanent pasture
- Permanent crops
- Arable
- Other

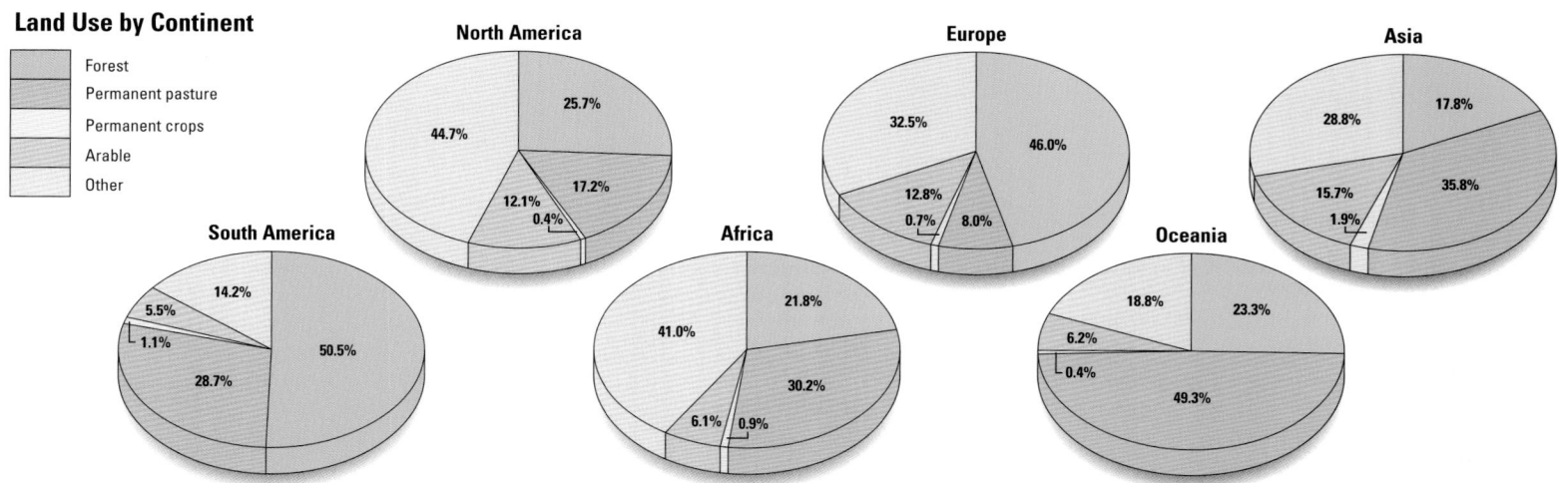

**North America:** 25.7%, 17.2%, 0.4%, 12.1%, 44.7%

**Europe:** 46.0%, 8.0%, 0.7%, 12.8%, 32.5%

**Asia:** 17.8%, 35.8%, 1.9%, 15.7%, 28.8%

**South America:** 50.5%, 28.7%, 1.1%, 5.5%, 14.2%

**Africa:** 21.8%, 30.2%, 0.9%, 6.1%, 41.0%

**Oceania:** 23.3%, 49.3%, 0.4%, 6.2%, 18.8%

## Forestry: Production

| | Forest and woodland (million hectares) | Annual production (2001, million cubic metres) | |
| --- | --- | --- | --- |
| | | Fuelwood | Industrial roundwood* |
| *World* | *3,869.5* | *1,784.3* | *1,543.3* |
| Europe | 1,039.3 | 98.1 | 462.5 |
| S. America | 885.6 | 189.2 | 151.1 |
| Africa | 649.9 | 534.5 | 68.1 |
| N. & C. America | 549.3 | 154.5 | 596.6 |
| Asia | 547.8 | 795.5 | 216.0 |
| Oceania | 197.6 | 12.6 | 48.9 |

**Paper and Board**

| Top producers (2001)** | | Top exporters (2001)** | |
| --- | --- | --- | --- |
| USA | 81,529 | Canada | 14,540 |
| China | 35,529 | Finland | 10,875 |
| Japan | 31,794 | Germany | 8,830 |
| Canada | 19,865 | Sweden | 8,733 |
| Germany | 17,879 | USA | 8,355 |

\* roundwood is timber as it is felled
\*\* in thousand tonnes

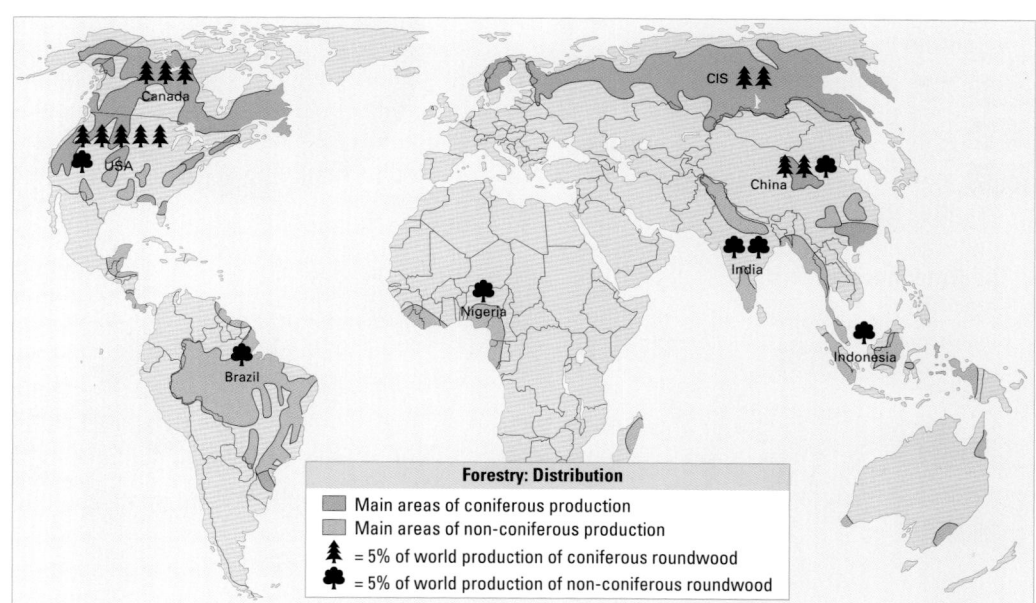

**Forestry: Distribution**

- Main areas of coniferous production
- Main areas of non-coniferous production
- ♠ = 5% of world production of coniferous roundwood
- ♣ = 5% of world production of non-coniferous roundwood

CARTOGRAPHY BY PHILIP'S. COPYRIGHT PHILIP'S

# Environment

Humans have always had a dramatic effect on their environment, at least since the development of agriculture almost 10,000 years ago. Generally, the Earth has accepted human interference without obvious ill effects: the complex systems that regulate the global environment have been able to absorb substantial damage while maintaining a stable and comfortable home for the planet's trillions of lifeforms. But advancing human technology and the rapidly-expanding populations it supports are now threatening to overwhelm the Earth's ability to compensate.

Industrial wastes, acid rainfall, desertification and large-scale deforestation all combine to create environmental change at a rate far faster than the great slow cycles of planetary evolution can accommodate. As a result of overcultivation, overgrazing and overcutting of groundcover for firewood, desertification is affecting as much as 60% of the world's croplands. In addition, with fire and chain-saws, humans are destroying more forest in a day than their ancestors could have done in a century, upsetting the balance between plant and animal, carbon dioxide and oxygen, on which all life ultimately depends.

The fossil fuels that power industrial civilization have pumped enough carbon dioxide and other so-called greenhouse gases into the atmosphere to make climatic change a near-certainty. As a result of the combination of these factors, the Earth's average temperature has risen by approximately 0.5°C [1°F] since the beginning of the 20th century, and it is still rising.

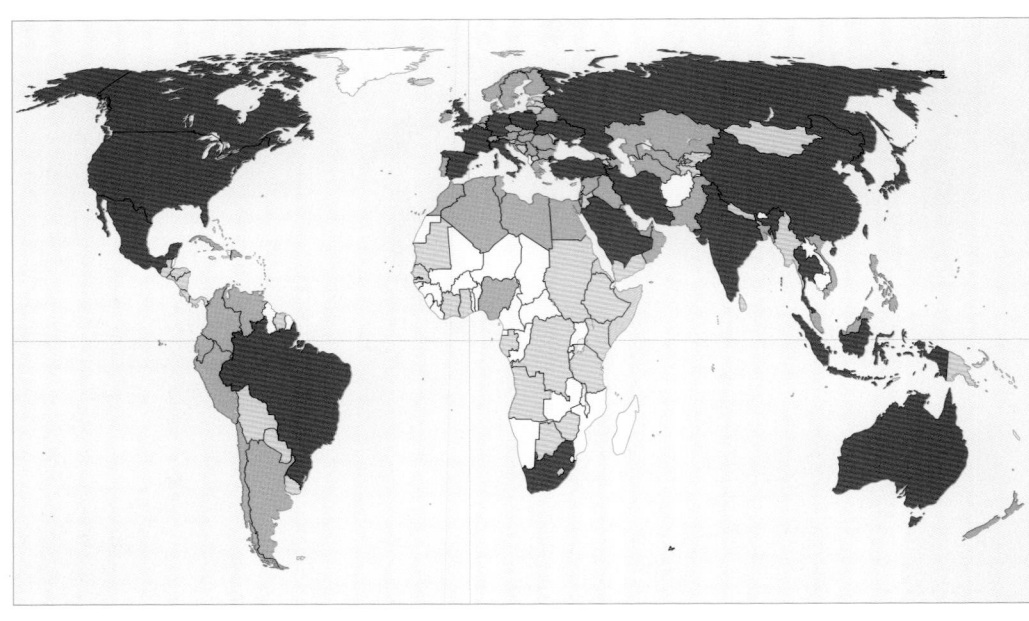

## Global Warming

**Carbon dioxide emissions in tonnes (latest available year)**

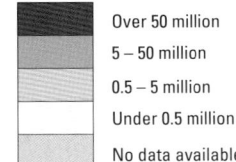

- Over 50 million
- 5 – 50 million
- 0.5 – 5 million
- Under 0.5 million
- No data available

High atmospheric concentrations of heat-absorbing gases appear to be causing a rise in average temperatures worldwide – up to 1.5°C [3°F] by the year 2020, according to some estimates. Global warming is likely to bring about a rise in sea levels that may flood some of the world's densely populated coastal areas.

## Greenhouse Power

**Relative contributions to the Greenhouse Effect by the major heat-absorbing gases in the atmosphere.**

The chart combines greenhouse potency and volume. Carbon dioxide has a greenhouse potential of only 1, but its concentration of 350 parts per million makes it predominant. CFC 12, with 25,000 times the absorption capacity of $CO_2$, is present only as 0.00044 ppm.

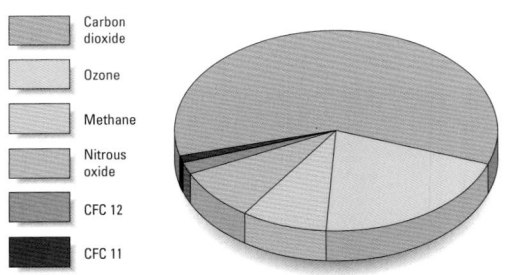

- Carbon dioxide
- Ozone
- Methane
- Nitrous oxide
- CFC 12
- CFC 11

## Ozone Layer

**The ozone 'hole' over the northern hemisphere in March 2000.**

The colours represent Dobson Units (DU). The ozone 'hole' is seen as the dark blue and purple patch in the centre, where ozone values are around 120 DU or lower. Normal levels are around 280 DU. The ozone 'hole' over Antarctica is much larger.

## Carbon Dioxide

**Estimated percentage share of total world $CO_2$ emissions (2000)**

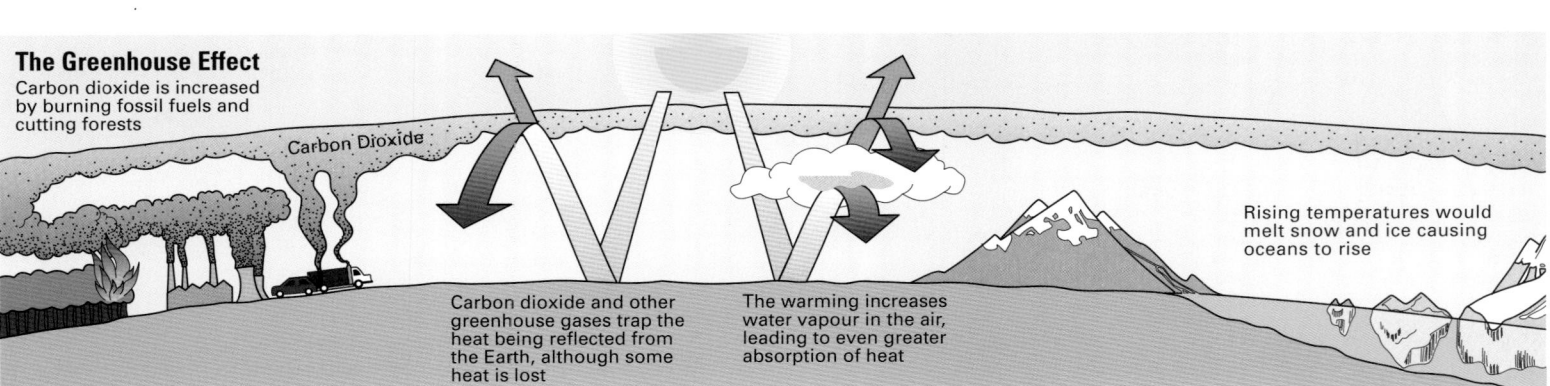

## The Greenhouse Effect

Carbon dioxide is increased by burning fossil fuels and cutting forests

Carbon Dioxide

Carbon dioxide and other greenhouse gases trap the heat being reflected from the Earth, although some heat is lost

The warming increases water vapour in the air, leading to even greater absorption of heat

Rising temperatures would melt snow and ice causing oceans to rise

## Desertification

- Existing deserts
- Areas with a high risk of desertification
- Areas with a moderate risk of desertification
- Former areas of rainforest
- Existing rainforest

## Forest Clearance

**Thousands of hectares of forest cleared annually, tropical countries surveyed 1981–85, 1987–90 and 1990–5. Loss as a percentage of remaining stocks is shown in figures on each column.**

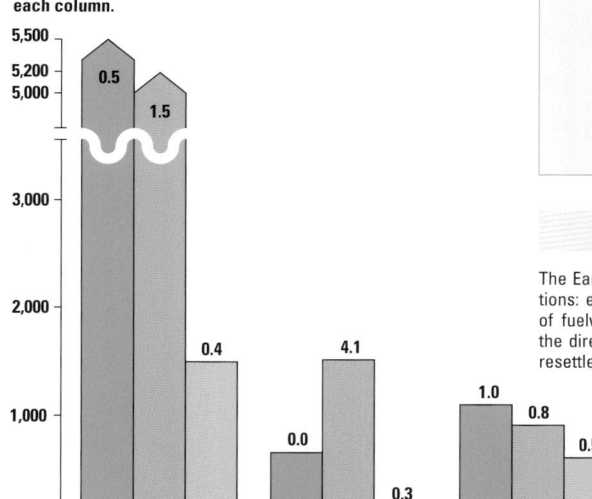

Brazil — 0.5, 1.5, 0.4
India — 0.0, 4.1, 0.3
Indonesia — 1.0, 0.8, 0.5
Burma — 1.4, 2.1, 0.3
Thailand — 2.6, 2.5, 2.4
Vietnam — 1.4, 2.0, 0.7
Philippines — 3.5, 1.5, 1.0
Costa Rica — 3.0, 7.6, 4.0

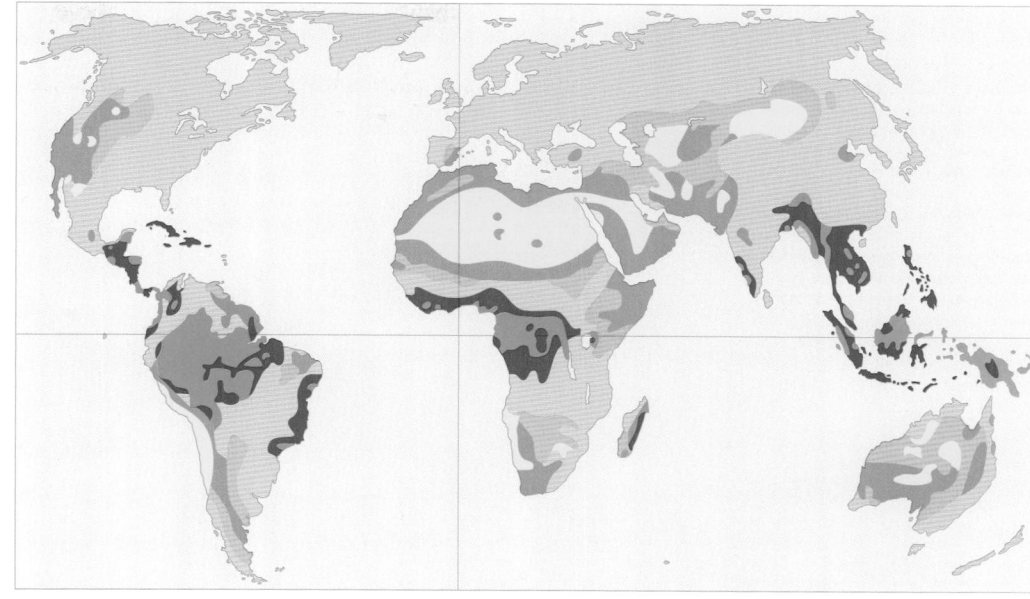

## Deforestation

The Earth's remaining forests are under attack from three directions: expanding agriculture, logging, and growing consumption of fuelwood, often in combination. Sometimes deforestation is the direct result of government policy, as in the efforts made to resettle the urban poor in some parts of Brazil; just as often,

it comes about despite state attempts at conservation. Loggers, licensed or unlicensed, blaze a trail into virgin forest, often destroying twice as many trees as they harvest. Landless farmers follow, burning away most of what remains to plant their crops, completing the destruction.

1990–95 | 1987–90 | 1981–85

## Ozone Depletion

The ozone layer, 25–30 km [15–18 miles] above sea level, acts as a barrier to most of the Sun's harmful ultra-violet radiation, protecting us from the ionizing radiation that can cause skin cancer and cataracts. In recent years, however, two holes in the ozone layer have been observed during winter: one over the Arctic and the other, the size of the USA, over Antarctica. By 1996, ozone had been reduced to around a half of its 1970 amount. The ozone ($O_3$) is broken down by chlorine released into the atmosphere as CFCs (chlorofluorocarbons) – chemicals used in refrigerators, packaging and aerosols.

## Air Pollution

Sulphur dioxide is the main pollutant associated with industrial cities. According to the World Health Organization, at least 600 million people live in urban areas where sulphur dioxide concentrations regularly reach damaging levels. One of the world's most dangerously polluted urban areas is Mexico City, due to a combination of its enclosed valley location, 3 million cars and 60,000 factories. In May 1998, this lethal cocktail was added to by nearby forest fires and the resultant air pollution led to over 20% of the population (3 million people) complaining of respiratory problems.

## Acid Rain

Killing trees, poisoning lakes and rivers and eating away buildings, acid rain is mostly produced by sulphur dioxide emissions from industry and volcanic eruptions. By the mid 1990s, acid rain had sterilized 4,000 or more of Sweden's lakes and left 45% of Switzerland's alpine conifers dead or dying, while the monuments of Greece were dissolving in Athens' smog. Prevailing wind patterns mean that the acids often fall many hundred kilometres from where the original pollutants were discharged. In parts of Europe acid deposition has slightly decreased, following reductions in emissions, but not by enough.

## World Pollution

**Acid rain and sources of acidic emissions (latest available year)**

Acid rain is caused by high levels of sulphur and nitrogen in the atmosphere. They combine with water vapour and oxygen to form acids ($H_2SO_4$ and $HNO_3$) which fall as precipitation.

- Regions where sulphur and nitrogen oxides are released in high concentrations, mainly from fossil fuel combustion
- Major cities with high levels of air pollution (including nitrogen and sulphur emissions)

**Areas of heavy acid deposition**

pH numbers indicate acidity, decreasing from a neutral 7. Normal rain, slightly acid from dissolved carbon dioxide, never exceeds a pH of 5.6.

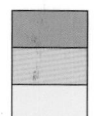

- pH less than 4.0 (most acidic)
- pH 4.0 to 4.5
- pH 4.5 to 5.0
- Areas where acid rain is a potential problem

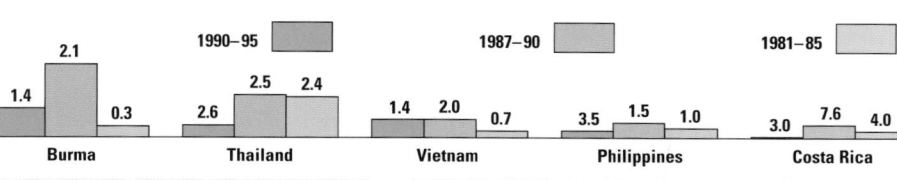

# Population

## Demographic Profiles

Developed nations such as the UK have populations evenly spread across the age groups and, usually, a growing proportion of elderly people. The great majority of the people in developing nations, however, are in the younger age groups, about to enter their most fertile years. In time, these population profiles should resemble the world profile (even Nigeria has made recent progress with reducing its birth rate), but the transition will come about only after a few more generations of rapid population growth.

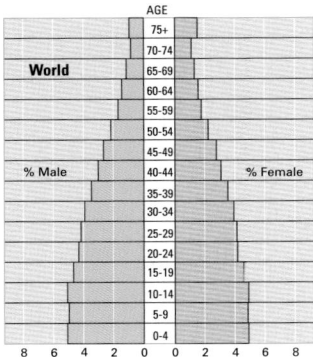

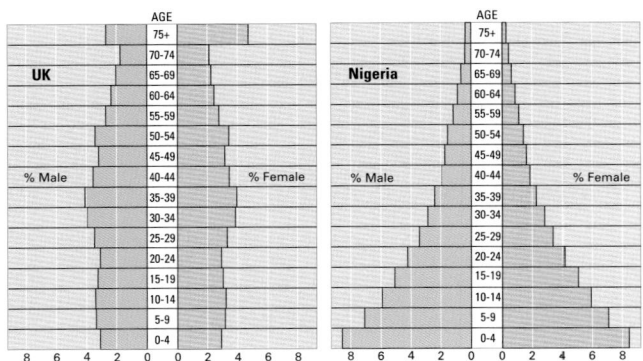

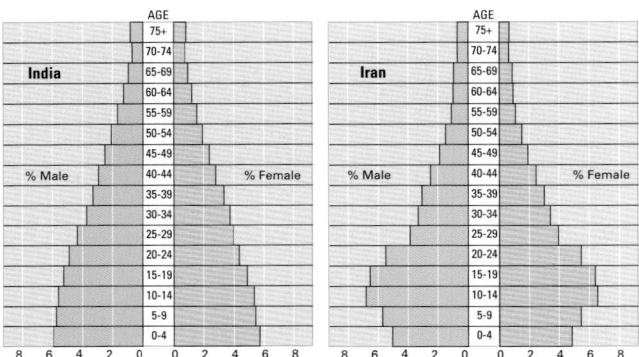

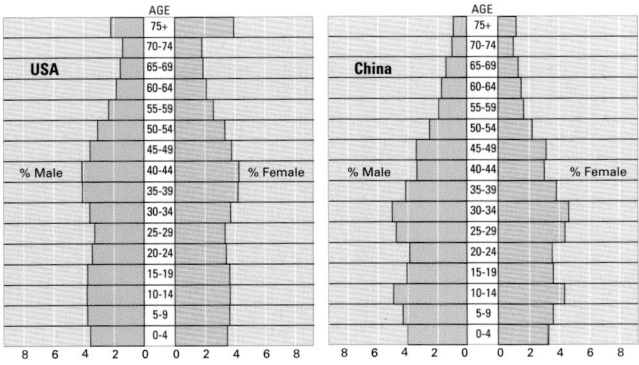

## Most Populous Nations [in millions (2003 estimates)]

| | | | | | | | |
|---|---|---|---|---|---|---|---|
| 1. China | 1,287 | 9. Nigeria | 134 | 17. Turkey | 68 |
| 2. India | 1,050 | 10. Japan | 127 | 18. Ethiopia | 67 |
| 3. USA | 290 | 11. Mexico | 105 | 19. Thailand | 64 |
| 4. Indonesia | 235 | 12. Philippines | 85 | 20. France | 60 |
| 5. Brazil | 182 | 13. Germany | 82 | 21. UK | 60 |
| 6. Pakistan | 151 | 14. Vietnam | 82 | 22. Italy | 58 |
| 7. Russia | 145 | 15. Egypt | 75 | 23. Congo (Dem. Rep.) | 57 |
| 8. Bangladesh | 138 | 16. Iran | 68 | 24. South Korea | 48 |

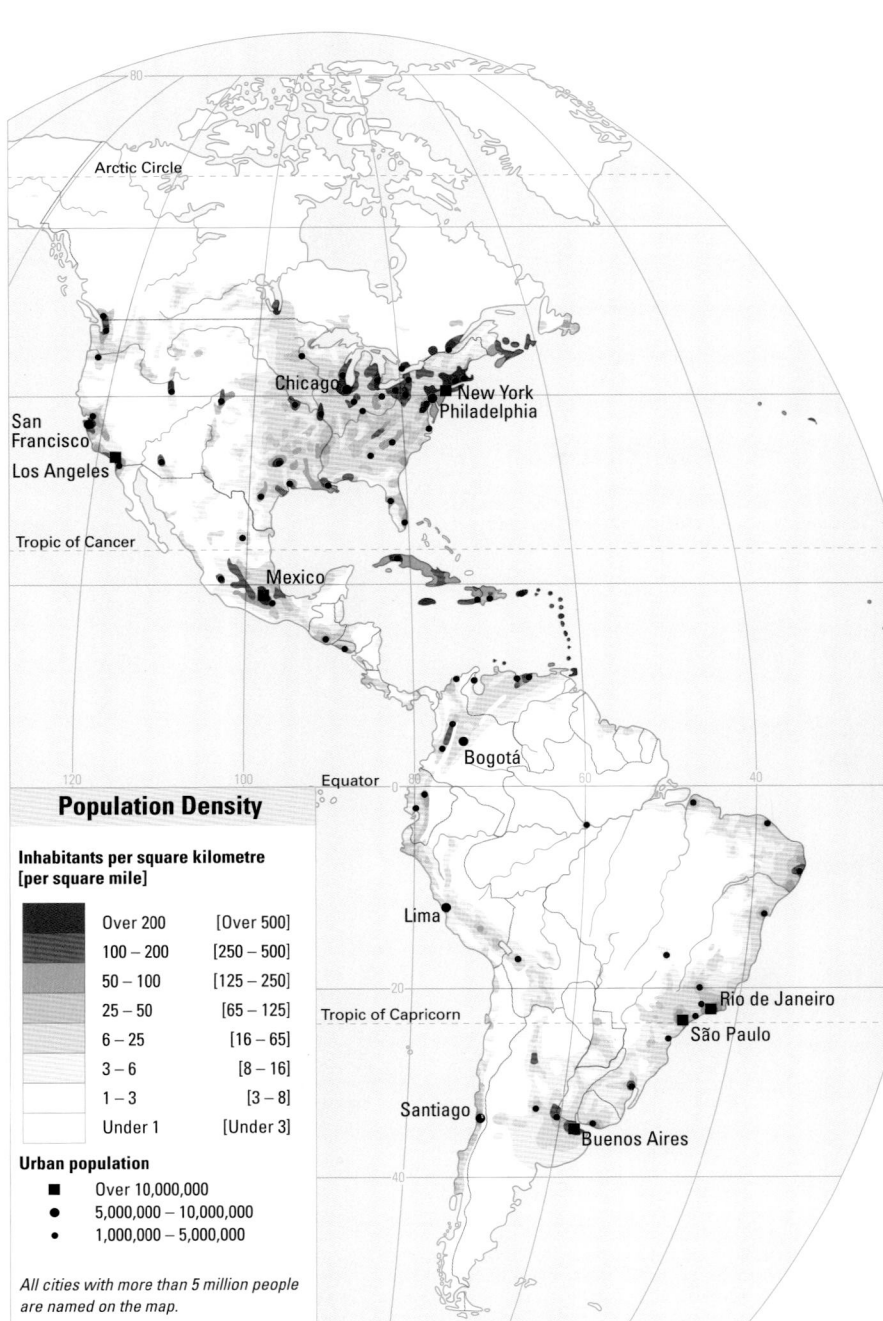

### Population Density

**Inhabitants per square kilometre [per square mile]**

| | |
|---|---|
| Over 200 | [Over 500] |
| 100 – 200 | [250 – 500] |
| 50 – 100 | [125 – 250] |
| 25 – 50 | [65 – 125] |
| 6 – 25 | [16 – 65] |
| 3 – 6 | [8 – 16] |
| 1 – 3 | [3 – 8] |
| Under 1 | [Under 3] |

**Urban population**

■ Over 10,000,000
● 5,000,000 – 10,000,000
• 1,000,000 – 5,000,000

*All cities with more than 5 million people are named on the map.*

## Continental Comparisons

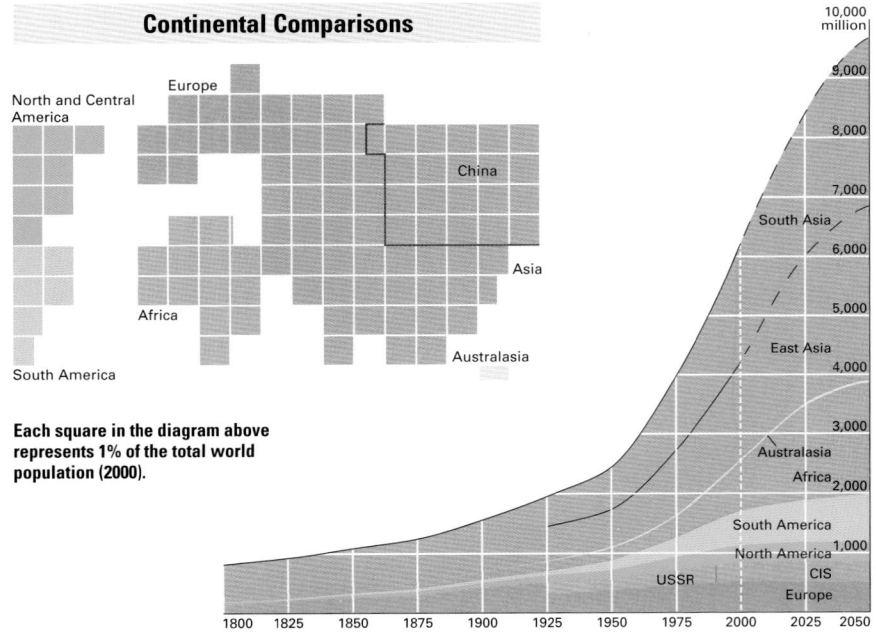

**Each square in the diagram above represents 1% of the total world population (2000).**

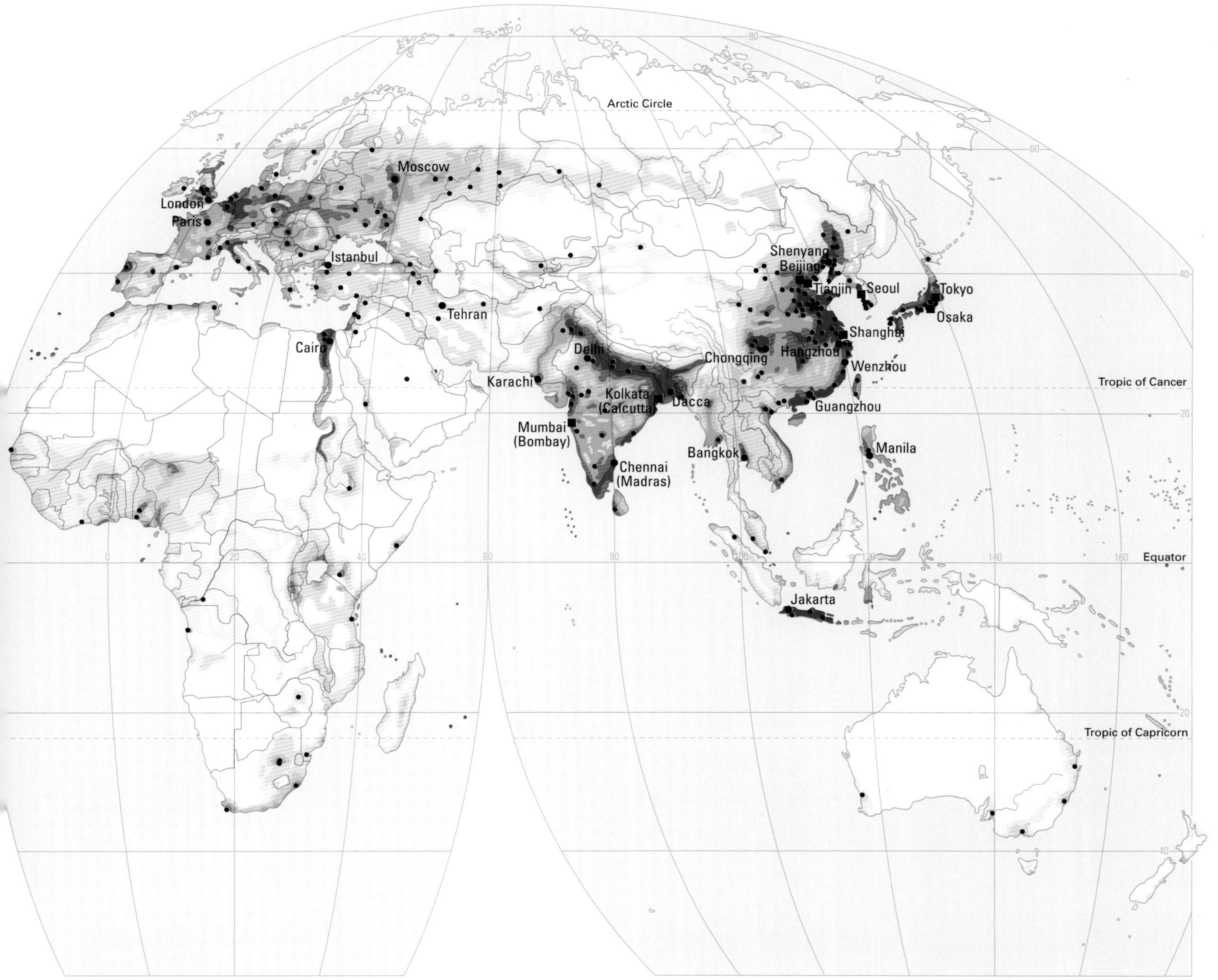

Arctic Circle

Moscow

London
Paris

Istanbul

Tehran

Cairo

Karachi

Delhi

Mumbai
(Bombay)

Kolkata
(Calcutta)

Dacca

Chennai
(Madras)

Bangkok

Shenyang
Beijing
Tianjin    Seoul    Tokyo
Osaka

Shanghai

Chongqing    Hangzhou

Wenzhou

Guangzhou

Manila

Jakarta

Tropic of Cancer

Equator

Tropic of Capricorn

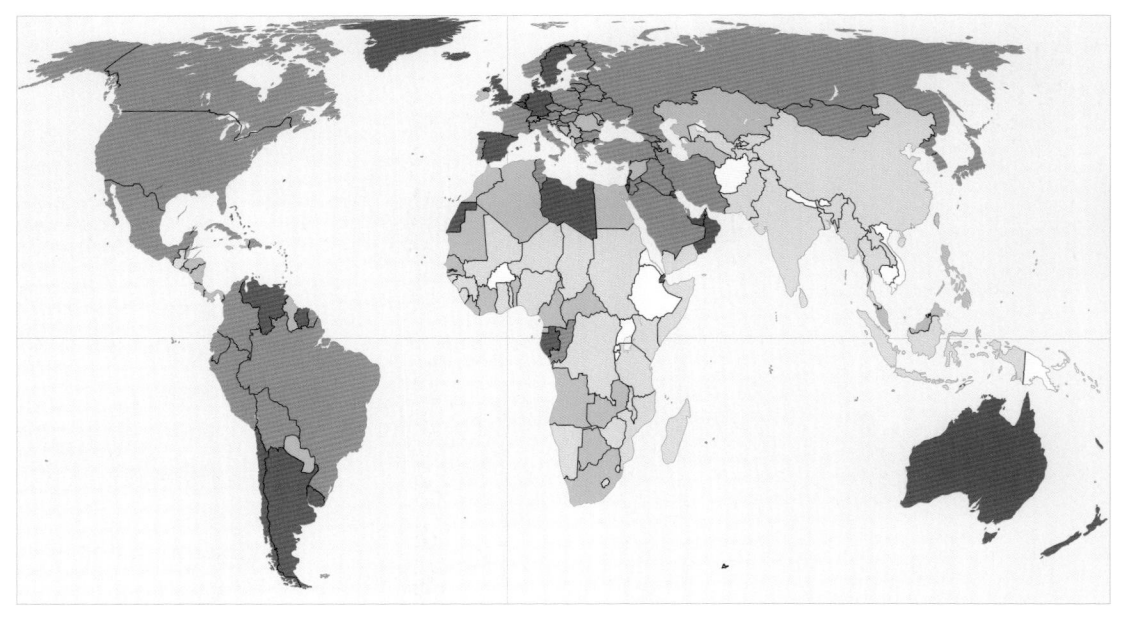

## Urban Population

**Percentage of total population living in towns and cities (2000)**

| | |
|---|---|
| ■ | Over 80% |
| ■ | 60 – 80% |
| ■ | 40 – 60% |
| ■ | 20 – 40% |
| □ | Under 20% |
| ■ | No data available |

**Most urbanized**

Singapore .........100%
Nauru ............100%
Monaco ...........100%
Vatican City .......100%
Belgium .........97.3%

**Least urbanized**

Rwanda ..........6.4%
Bhutan ..........7.3%
East Timor .......7.4%
Burundi ..........9.2%
Nepal ...........10.8%

# The Human Family

## Predominant Languages

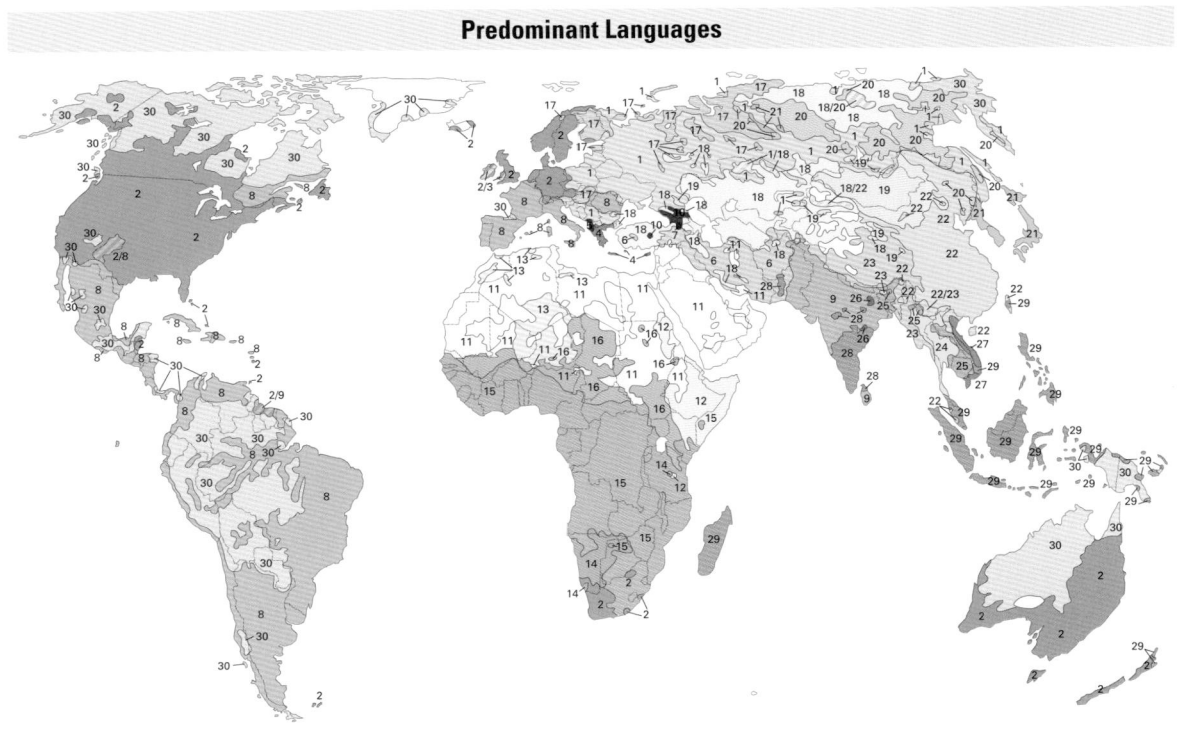

### Languages of the World

Language can be classified by ancestry and structure. For example, the Romance and Germanic groups are both derived from an Indo-European language believed to have been spoken 5,000 years ago.

**First-language speakers, 1999 (in millions)**
Mandarin Chinese 885, Spanish 332, English 322, Bengali 189, Hindi 182, Portuguese 170, Russian 170, Japanese 125, German 98, Wu Chinese 77, Javanese 76, Korean 75, French 72, Vietnamese 68, Yue Chinese 66, Marathi 65, Tamil 63, Turkish 59, Urdu 58.

**Official languages (% of total population)**
English 27%, Chinese 19%, Hindi 13.5%, Spanish 5.4%, Russian 5.2%, French 4.2%, Arabic 3.3%, Portuguese 3%, Malay 3%, Bengali 2.9%, Japanese 2.3%.

### INDO-EUROPEAN FAMILY

1 Balto-Slavic group (incl. Russian, Ukrainian)
2 Germanic group (incl. English, German)
3 Celtic group
4 Greek
5 Albanian
6 Iranian group
7 Armenian
8 Romance group (incl. Spanish, Portuguese, French, Italian)
9 Indo-Aryan group (incl. Hindi, Bengali, Urdu, Punjabi, Marathi)
10 CAUCASIAN FAMILY

### AFRO-ASIATIC FAMILY

11 Semitic group (incl. Arabic)
12 Kushitic group
13 Berber group

14 KHOISAN FAMILY

15 NIGER-CONGO FAMILY

16 NILO-SAHARAN FAMILY

17 URALIC FAMILY

### ALTAIC FAMILY

18 Turkic group (incl. Turkish)
19 Mongolian group
20 Tungus-Manchu group
21 Japanese and Korean

### SINO-TIBETAN FAMILY

22 Sinitic (Chinese) languages (incl. Mandarin, Wu, Yue)
23 Tibetic-Burmic languages

24 TAI FAMILY

### AUSTRO-ASIATIC FAMILY

25 Mon-Khmer group
26 Munda group
27 Vietnamese

28 DRAVIDIAN FAMILY (incl. Telugu, Tamil)

29 AUSTRONESIAN FAMILY (incl. Malay-Indonesian, Javanese)

30 OTHER LANGUAGES

## Predominant Religions

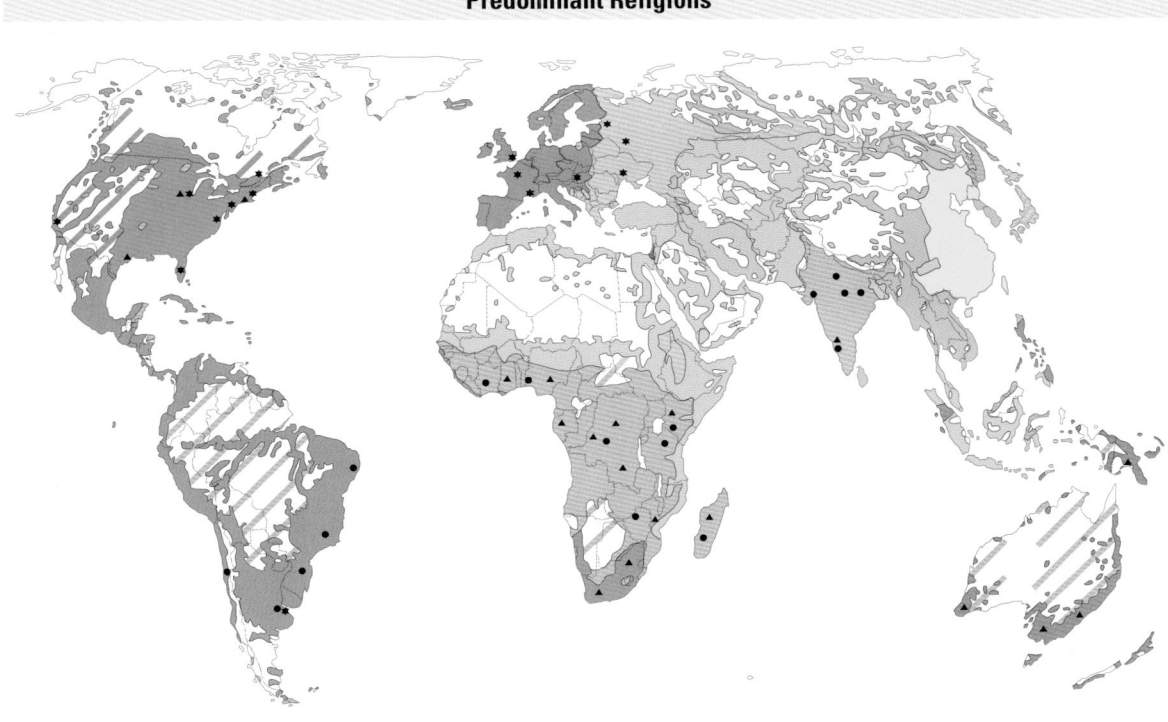

### Religious Adherents

**Religious adherents in millions (2001)**

| | | | |
|---|---|---|---|
| Christianity | 2,019 | Hindu | 820 |
| *Roman Catholic* | *1,067* | Chinese folk | 387 |
| *Protestant* | *346* | Buddhism | 362 |
| *Orthodox* | *216* | Ethnic religions | 242 |
| *Anglican* | *80* | New religions | 103 |
| *Independent* | *392* | Sikhism | 24 |
| *Others* | *139* | Judaism | 14 |
| Islam | 1,207 | Spiritism | 12 |
| *Sunni* | *1,002* | Baha'i | 7 |
| *Shi'ite* | *193* | Confucianism | 6 |
| *Others* | *12* | Jainism | 4 |
| Non-religious/ | | Shintoism | 3 |
| Agnostic/Atheist | 921 | | |

- ▲ Roman Catholicism
- Orthodox and other Eastern Churches
- • Protestantism
- Sunni Islam
- Shi'ite Islam
- Buddhism
- Hinduism
- Confucianism
- ★ Judaism
- Shintoism
- Tribal Religions

## United Nations

Created in 1945 to promote peace and co-operation and based in New York, the United Nations is the world's largest international organization, with 191 members and an annual budget of US $1.3 billion (2002). Each member of the General Assembly has one vote, while the five permanent members of the 15-nation Security Council – China, France, Russia, UK and USA – hold a veto. The Secretariat is the UN's principal administrative arm. The 54 members of the Economic and Social Council are responsible for economic, social, cultural, educational, health and related matters. The UN has 16 specialized agencies – based in Canada, France, Switzerland and Italy, as well as the USA – which help members in fields such as education (UNESCO), agriculture (FAO), medicine (WHO) and finance (IFC). By the end of 1994, all the original 11 trust territories of the Trusteeship Council had become independent.

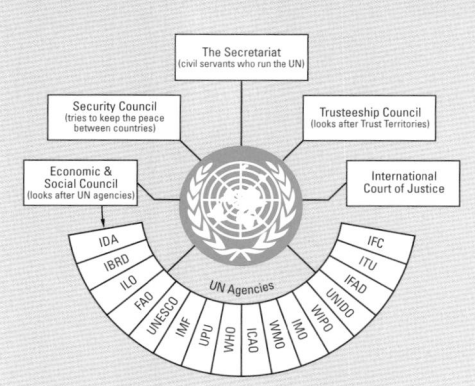

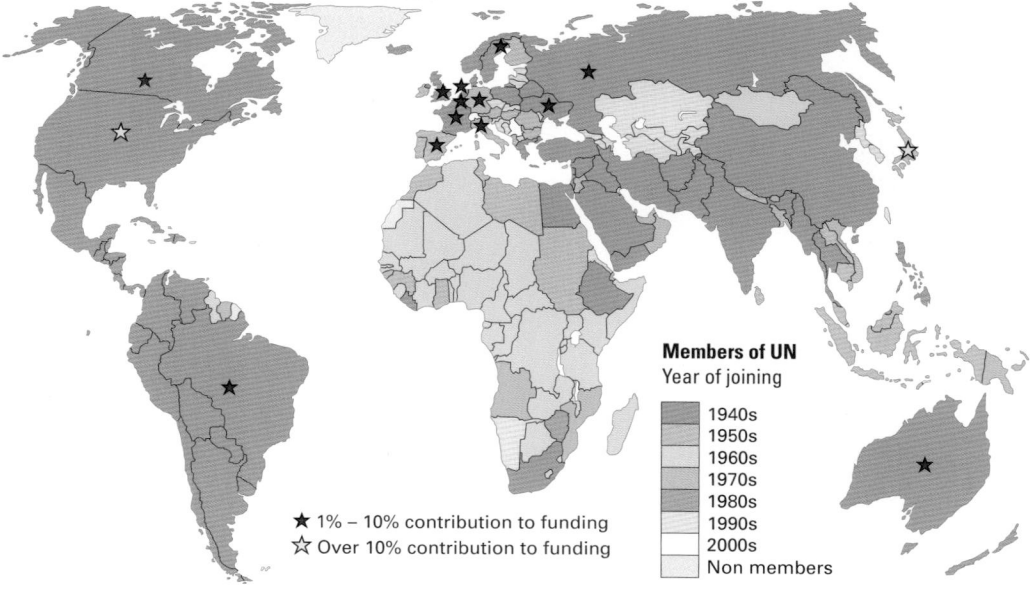

**Members of UN**
Year of joining

- 1940s
- 1950s
- 1960s
- 1970s
- 1980s
- 1990s
- 2000s
- Non members

★ 1% – 10% contribution to funding
☆ Over 10% contribution to funding

**MEMBERSHIP OF THE UN** In 1945 there were 51 members; by the end of 2002 membership had increased to 191 following the admission of East Timor and Switzerland. There are 2 independent states which are not members of the UN – Taiwan and the Vatican City. All the successor states of the former USSR had joined by the end of 1992. The official languages of the UN are Chinese, English, French, Russian, Spanish and Arabic.

**FUNDING** The UN regular budget for 2002 was US $1.3 billion. Contributions are assessed by the members' ability to pay, with the maximum 22% of the total (USA's share), the minimum 0.01%. The European Union pays over 37% of the budget.

**PEACEKEEPING** The UN has been involved in 54 peacekeeping operations worldwide since 1948.

## International Organizations

**ACP** African-Caribbean-Pacific (formed in 1963). Members have economic ties with the EU.
**ARAB LEAGUE** (formed in 1945). The League's aim is to promote economic, social, political and military co-operation. There are 22 member nations.
**ASEAN** Association of South-east Asian Nations (formed in 1967). Cambodia joined in 1999.
**AU** The African Union replaced the Organization of African Unity (formed in 1963) in 2002. Its 53 members represent over 94% of Africa's population. Arabic, French, Portuguese and English are recognized as working languages.
**CIS** The Commonwealth of Independent States (formed in 1991) comprises the countries of the former Soviet Union except for Estonia, Latvia and Lithuania.
**COLOMBO PLAN** (formed in 1951). Its 25 members aim to promote economic and social development in Asia and the Pacific.
**COMMONWEALTH** The Commonwealth of Nations evolved from the British Empire. Pakistan was suspended in 1999, and Zimbabwe in 2002. In response to its continued suspension, Zimbabwe left the Commonwealth in December 2003. It now comprises 16 Queen's realms, 31 republics and 6 indigenous monarchies, giving a total of 53 member states.
**EFTA** European Free Trade Association (formed in 1960). Portugal left the original 'Seven' in 1989 to join what was then the EC, followed by Austria, Finland and Sweden in 1995. Only 4 members remain: Norway, Iceland, Switzerland and Liechtenstein.
**EU** European Union (evolved from the European Community in 1993). Cyprus, the Czech Republic, Estonia, Hungary, Latvia, Lithuania, Malta, Poland, the Slovak Republic and Slovenia joined the EU in May 2004. The other members are Austria, Belgium, Denmark, Finland, France, Germany, Greece, Ireland, Italy, Luxembourg, Netherlands, Portugal, Spain, Sweden and the UK – together these 25 countries aim to integrate economies, co-ordinate social developments and bring about political union. Bulgaria and Romania are expected to join in 2007.
**LAIA** Latin American Integration Association (1980). Its aim is to promote freer regional trade.
**NATO** North Atlantic Treaty Organization (formed in 1949). It continues after 1991 despite the winding up of the Warsaw Pact. Bulgaria, Estonia, Latvia, Lithuania, Romania, the Slovak Republic and Slovenia became members in 2004.

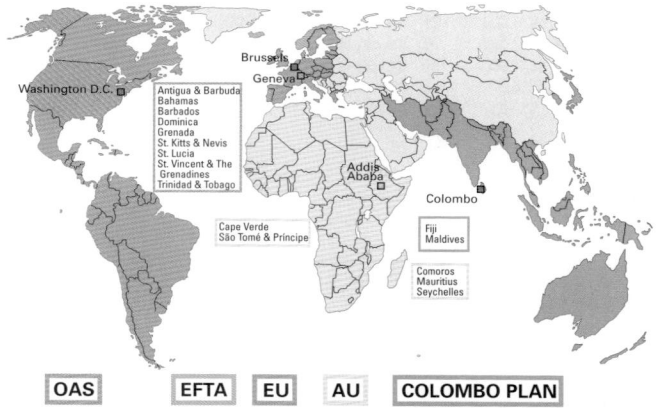

**OAS** Organization of American States (formed in 1948). It aims to promote social and economic co-operation between developed countries of North America and developing nations of Latin America.
**OECD** Organization for Economic Co-operation and Development (formed in 1961). It comprises 30 major free-market economies. Poland, Hungary and South Korea joined in 1996, and the Slovak Republic in 2000. 'G8' is its 'inner group' of leading industrial nations, comprising Canada, France, Germany, Italy, Japan, Russia, UK and USA.
**OPEC** Organization of Petroleum Exporting Countries (formed in 1960). It controls about three-quarters of the world's oil supply. Gabon left the organization in 1996.

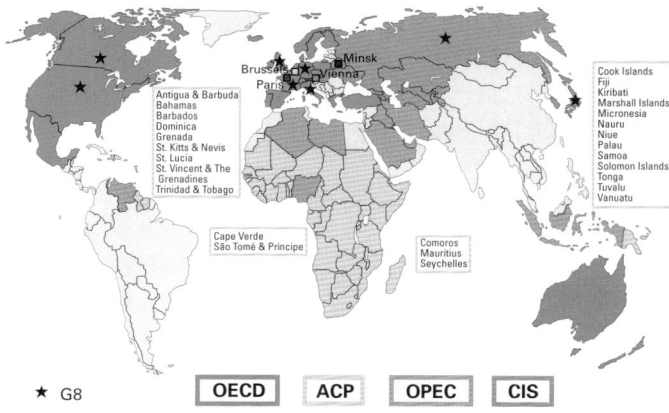

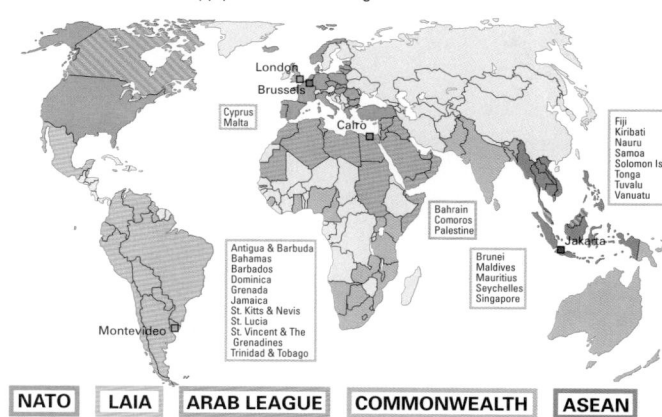

# Wealth

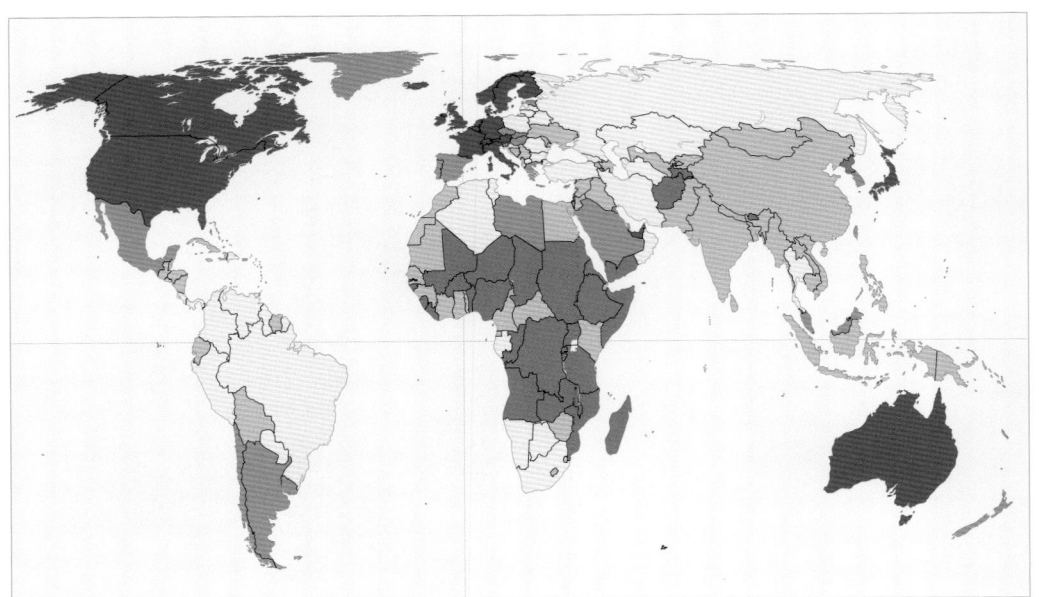

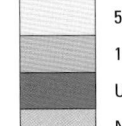
| Highest GDP (US $) | | Lowest GDP (US $) | |
|---|---|---|---|
| Luxembourg | $36,400 | Sierra Leone | $510 |
| USA | $36,200 | Congo (Dem. Rep.) | $600 |
| San Marino | $32,000 | Ethiopia | $600 |
| Switzerland | $28,600 | Somalia | $600 |
| Norway | $27,700 | Eritrea | $710 |

## Wealth Creation

The Gross Domestic Product (GDP) of the world's largest economies, US $ million (2001)

| | | | | | |
|---|---|---|---|---|---|
| 1. | USA | 10,082,000 | 23. | Taiwan | 386,000 |
| 2. | China | 5,560,000 | 24. | Poland | 340,000 |
| 3. | Japan | 3,450,000 | 25. | Philippines | 335,000 |
| 4. | India | 2,500,000 | 26. | Pakistan | 299,000 |
| 5. | Germany | 2,174,000 | 27. | Belgium | 268,000 |
| 6. | France | 1,510,000 | 28. | Egypt | 258,000 |
| 7. | UK | 1,470,000 | 29. | Colombia | 255,000 |
| 8. | Italy | 1,402,000 | 30. | Saudi Arabia | 241,000 |
| 9. | Brazil | 1,340,000 | 31. | Bangladesh | 230,000 |
| 10. | Russia | 1,200,000 | 32. | Switzerland | 226,000 |
| 11. | Mexico | 920,000 | 33. | Austria | 220,000 |
| 12. | Canada | 875,000 | 34. | Sweden | 219,000 |
| 13. | South Korea | 865,000 | 35. | Ukraine | 205,000 |
| 14. | Spain | 757,000 | 36. | Malaysia | 200,000 |
| 15. | Indonesia | 687,000 | 37. | Greece | 190,000 |
| 16. | Australia | 466,000 | 38. | Hong Kong | 180,000 |
| 17. | Argentina | 453,000 | 39. | Algeria | 177,000 |
| 18. | Turkey | 443,000 | 40. | Portugal | 174,000 |
| 19. | Iran | 426,000 | 41. | Vietnam | 168,000 |
| 20. | Netherlands | 413,000 | 42. | Chile | 153,000 |
| 21. | South Africa | 412,000 | 43. | Romania | 153,000 |
| 22. | Thailand | 410,000 | 44. | Denmark | 150,000 |

## The Wealth Gap

The world's richest and poorest countries, by Gross Domestic Product per capita in US $ (2001)

| | | | | | |
|---|---|---|---|---|---|
| 1. | Luxembourg | 43,400 | 1. | Sierra Leone | 500 |
| 2. | USA | 36,300 | 2. | East Timor | 500 |
| 3. | San Marino | 34,600 | 3. | Somalia | 550 |
| 4. | Norway | 31,800 | 4. | Congo (D. Rep.) | 590 |
| 5. | Switzerland | 31,100 | 5. | Burundi | 600 |
| 6. | Denmark | 29,000 | 6. | Tanzania | 610 |
| 7. | Canada | 27,700 | 7. | Malawi | 660 |
| 8. | Ireland | 27,300 | 8. | Ethiopia | 700 |
| 9. | Japan | 27,200 | 9. | Comoros | 710 |
| 10. | Austria | 27,000 | 10. | Eritrea | 740 |
| 11. | Monaco | 27,000 | 11. | Afghanistan | 800 |
| 12. | Finland | 26,200 | 12. | Yemen | 820 |
| 13. | Germany | 26,200 | 13. | Niger | 820 |
| 14. | Belgium | 26,100 | 14. | Nigeria | 840 |
| 15. | Netherlands | 25,800 | 15. | Mali | 840 |
| 16. | France | 25,700 | 16. | Kiribati | 840 |
| 17. | Sweden | 25,400 | 17. | Zambia | 870 |
| 18. | Hong Kong (China) | 25,000 | 18. | Madagascar | 870 |
| 19. | Iceland | 24,800 | 19. | Mozambique | 900 |
| 20. | Singapore | 24,700 | 20. | Guinea-Bissau | 900 |

GDP per capita is calculated by dividing a country's Gross Domestic Product by its total population.

## Continental Shares

Shares of population and of wealth (GNP) by continent

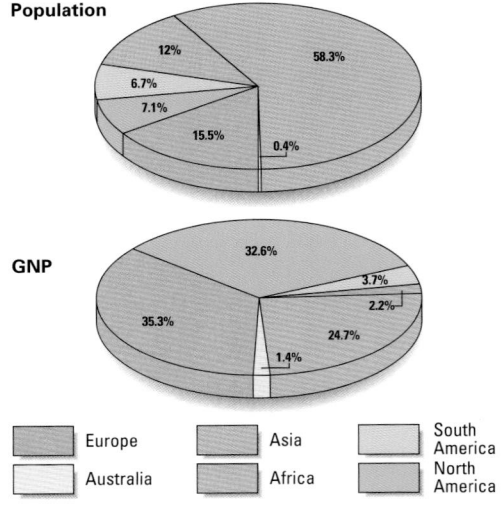

**Population**

**GNP**

| | | | | | |
|---|---|---|---|---|---|
| ■ | Europe | ■ | Asia | | South America |
| | Australia | ■ | Africa | ■ | North America |

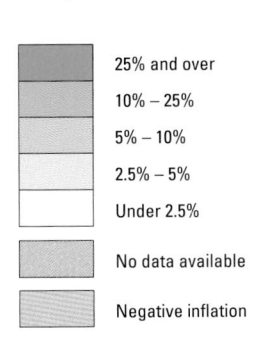

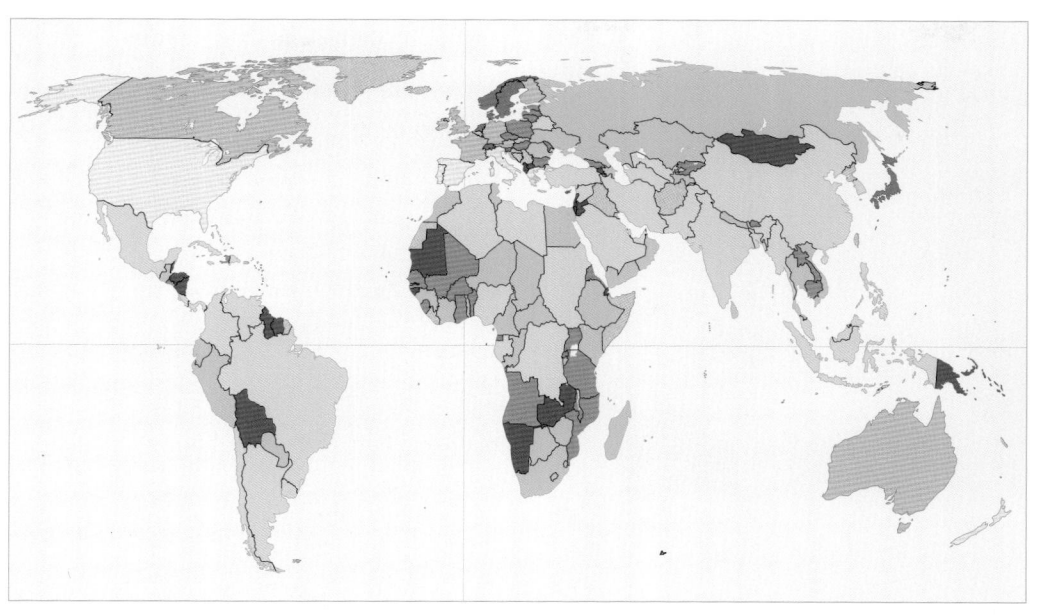

**Official Development Assistance (ODA) provided and received, per capita (2002)**

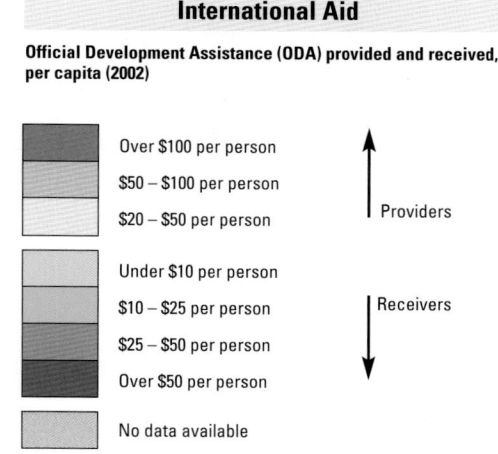

Over $100 per person
$50 – $100 per person
$20 – $50 per person
} Providers

Under $10 per person
$10 – $25 per person
$25 – $50 per person
Over $50 per person
} Receivers

No data available

## Debt and Aid

**International debtors and the aid they receive**

Although aid grants make a vital contribution to many of the world's poorer countries, they are usually dwarfed by the burden of debt that the developing economies are expected to repay. It is estimated that the total debt burden of developing countries is US $410 billion, while the cost of servicing that debt amounts to US $25 billion a year.

Debt, US $ per capita (2000)

Aid, US $ per capita (2000)

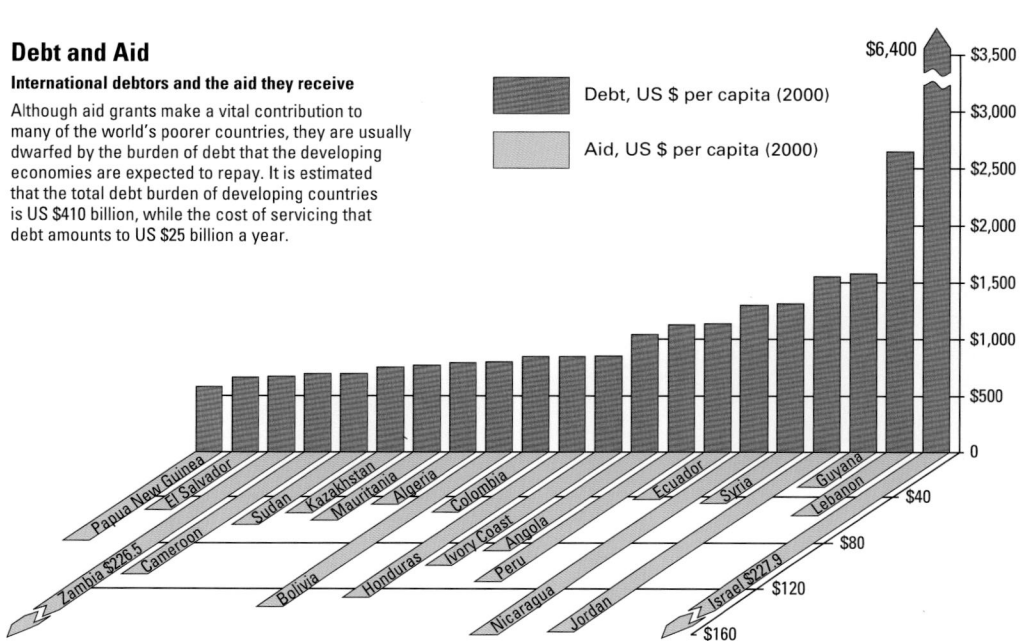

## Distribution of Spending

**Percentage share of household spending, selected countries**

Food
Medicine & Education
Clothing
Transport
Energy & Housing
Other

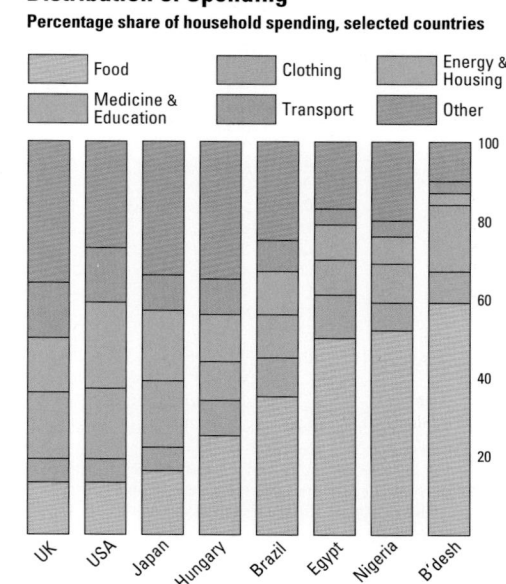

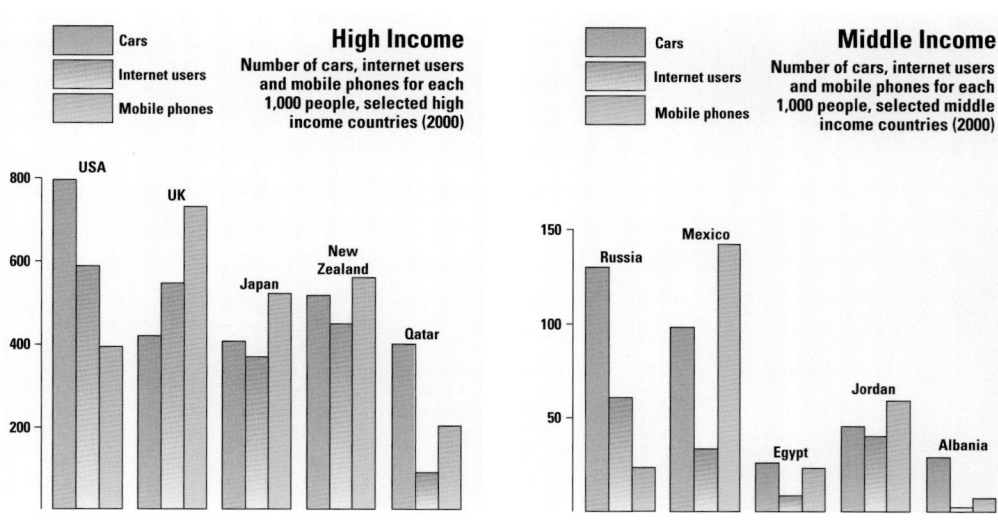

## High Income

Cars
Internet users
Mobile phones

Number of cars, internet users and mobile phones for each 1,000 people, selected high income countries (2000)

## Middle Income

Cars
Internet users
Mobile phones

Number of cars, internet users and mobile phones for each 1,000 people, selected middle income countries (2000)

## Low Income

Cars
Internet users
Mobile phones

Number of cars, internet users and mobile phones for each 1,000 people, selected low income countries (2000)

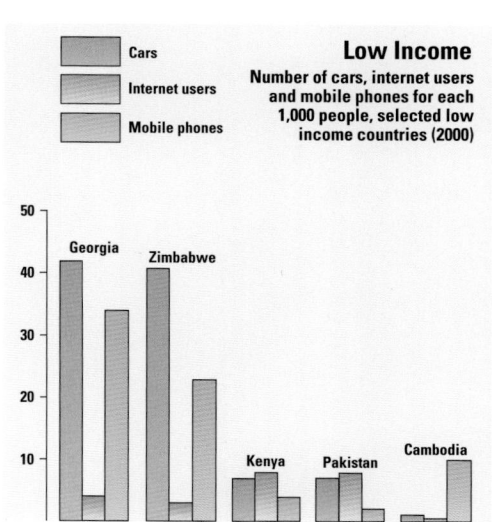

# Quality of Life

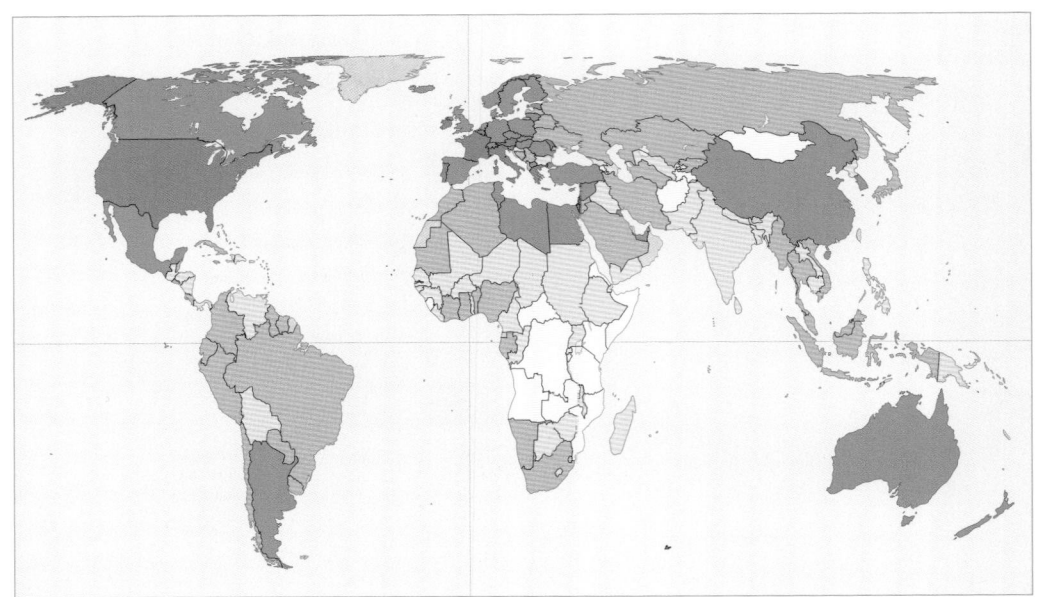

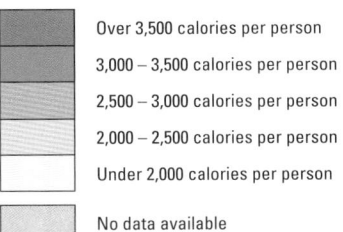
## Hospital Capacity

**Hospital beds available for each 1,000 people (latest available year)**

| Highest capacity | | Lowest capacity | |
|---|---|---|---|
| Switzerland | 20.8 | Benin | 0.2 |
| Japan | 16.2 | Nepal | 0.2 |
| Tajikistan | 16.0 | Afghanistan | 0.3 |
| Norway | 13.5 | Bangladesh | 0.3 |
| Belarus | 12.4 | Ethiopia | 0.3 |
| Kazakhstan | 12.2 | Mali | 0.4 |
| Moldova | 12.2 | Burkina Faso | 0.5 |
| Ukraine | 12.2 | Niger | 0.5 |
| Latvia | 11.9 | Guinea | 0.6 |
| Russia | 11.8 | India | 0.6 |

[UK 4.9] [USA 4.2]

Although the ratio of people to hospital beds gives a good approximation of a country's health provision, it is not an absolute indicator. Raw numbers may mask inefficiency and other weaknesses: the high availability of beds in Kazakhstan, for example, has not prevented infant mortality rates over three times as high as in the United Kingdom and the United States.

## Life Expectancy

**Years of life expectancy at birth, selected countries (2001)**

The chart shows combined data for both sexes. On average, women live longer than men worldwide, even in developing countries with high maternal mortality rates. Overall, life expectancy is steadily rising, though the difference between rich and poor nations remains dramatic.

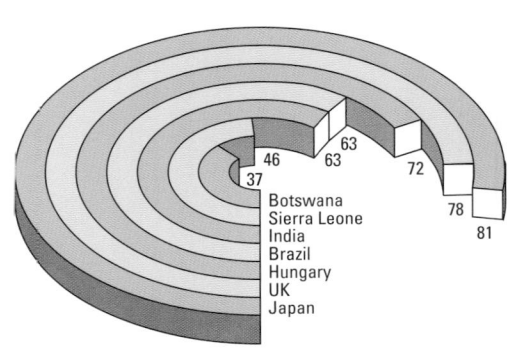

37
46
63
63
72
78
81

Botswana
Sierra Leone
India
Brazil
Hungary
UK
Japan

## Causes of Death

**Causes of death for selected countries by percentage**

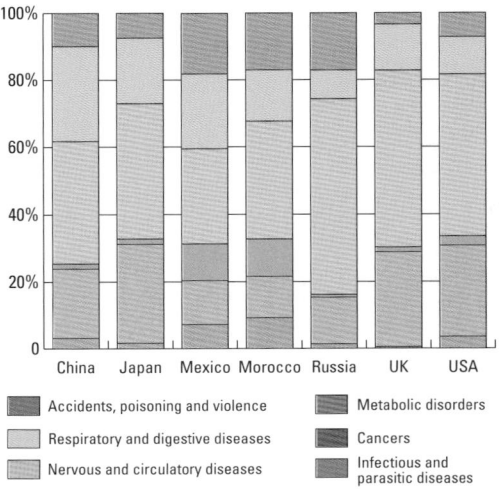

China  Japan  Mexico  Morocco  Russia  UK  USA

Accidents, poisoning and violence

Respiratory and digestive diseases

Nervous and circulatory diseases

Metabolic disorders

Cancers

Infectious and parasitic diseases

## Infant Mortality

**Number of babies who died under the age of one, per 1,000 live births (2001)**

100 deaths and over per 1,000 births

50 – 100 deaths per 1,000 births

25 – 50 deaths per 1,000 births

10 – 25 deaths per 1,000 births

Under 10 deaths per 1,000 births

No data available

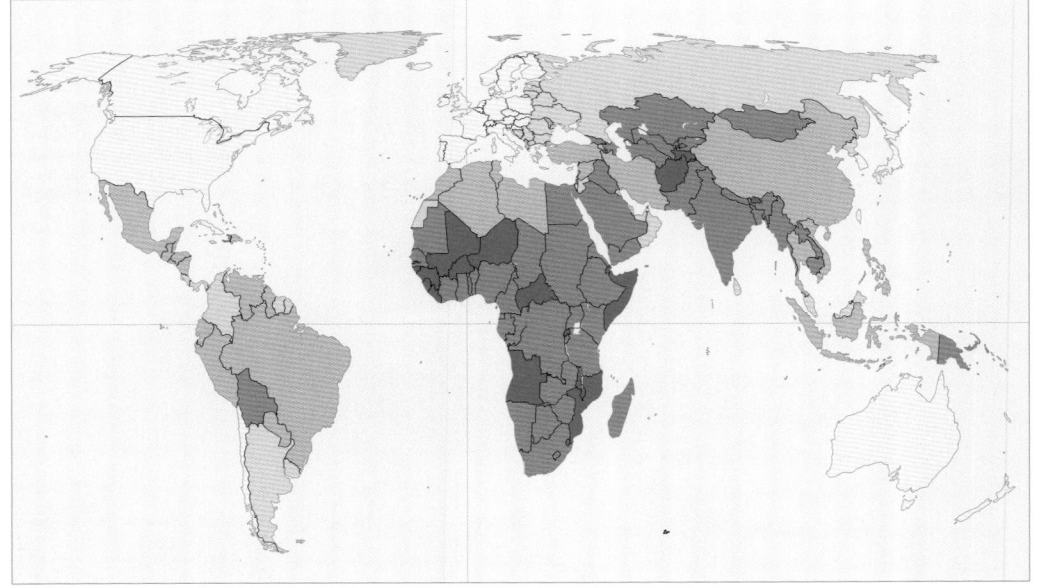

| Highest infant mortality | | Lowest infant mortality | |
|---|---|---|---|
| Angola | 194 deaths | Sweden | 3 deaths |
| Afghanistan | 147 deaths | Iceland | 4 deaths |
| Sierra Leone | 147 deaths | Singapore | 4 deaths |
| Mozambique | 139 deaths | Finland | 4 deaths |
| Liberia | 132 deaths | Japan | 4 deaths |

[UK 6 deaths]

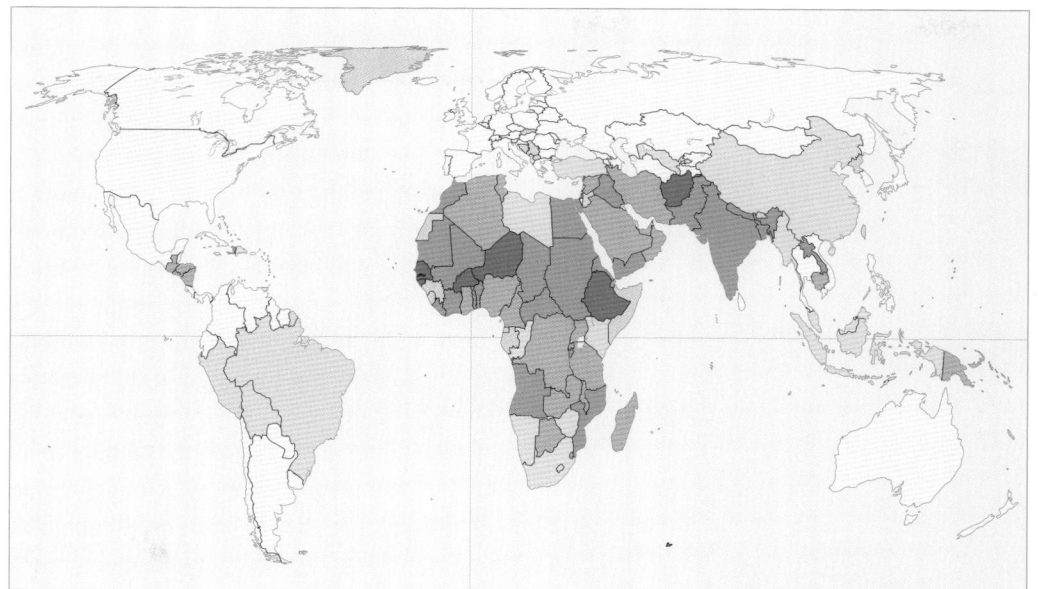

**Percentage of the total adult population unable to read or write (2000)**

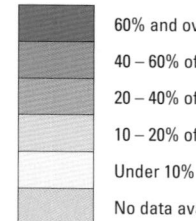

60% and over of population illiterate

40 – 60% of population illiterate

20 – 40% of population illiterate

10 – 20% of population illiterate

Under 10% of population illiterate

No data available

**Countries with the highest and lowest illiteracy rates**

| Highest | | Lowest | |
|---|---|---|---|
| Niger | 84 | Australia | 0 |
| Burkina Faso | 76 | Denmark | 0 |
| Gambia | 63 | Estonia | 0 |
| Afghanistan | 63 | Finland | 0 |
| Senegal | 63 | Luxembourg | 0 |

[UK 1%]

## Fertility and Education

**Fertility rates compared with female education, selected countries (1995–2000)**

 Percentage of females aged 12–17 in secondary education

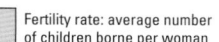 Fertility rate: average number of children borne per woman

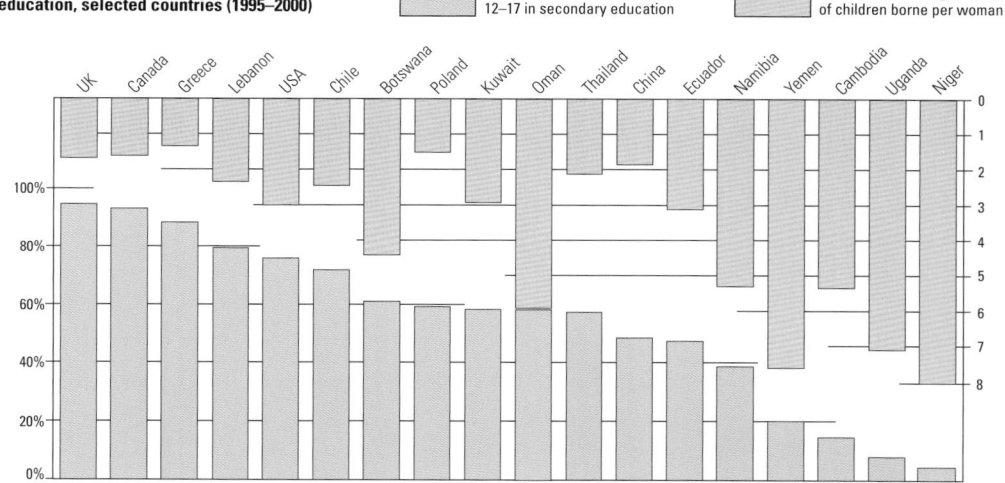

## Living Standards

At first sight, most international contrasts in living standards are swamped by differences in wealth. The rich not only have more money, they have more of everything, including years of life. Those with only a little money are obliged to spend most of it on food and clothing, the basic maintenance costs of their existence; air travel and tourism are unlikely to feature on their expenditure lists. However, poverty and wealth are both relative: slum dwellers living on social security payments in an affluent industrial country have far more resources at their disposal than an average African peasant, but feel their own poverty nonetheless. A middle-class Indian lawyer cannot command a fraction of the earnings of a counterpart living in New York, London or Rome; nevertheless, he rightly sees himself as prosperous.

The rich not only live longer, on average, than the poor, they also die from different causes. Infectious and parasitic diseases, all but eliminated in the developed world, remain a scourge in the developing nations. On the other hand, more than two-thirds of the populations of OECD nations eventually succumb to cancer or circulatory disease.

## Human Development Index

The Human Development Index (HDI), calculated by the UN Development Programme, gives a value to countries using indicators of life expectancy, education and standards of living in 2000. Higher values show more developed countries.

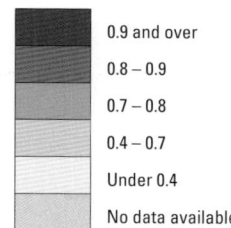

0.9 and over

0.8 – 0.9

0.7 – 0.8

0.4 – 0.7

Under 0.4

No data available

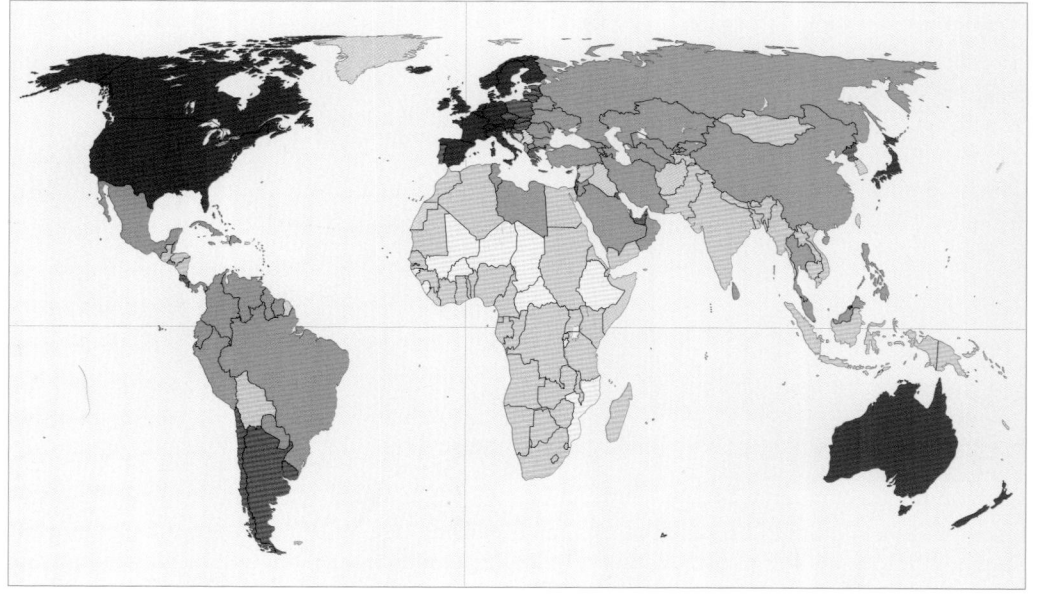

| Highest values | | Lowest values | |
|---|---|---|---|
| Norway | 0.942 | Sierra Leone | 0.275 |
| Sweden | 0.941 | Niger | 0.277 |
| Canada | 0.940 | Burundi | 0.313 |
| USA | 0.939 | Mozambique | 0.322 |
| Belgium | 0.939 | Burkina Faso | 0.325 |

[UK 0.928]

# Energy

## Production

**Each square represents 1% of world energy production (2000)**

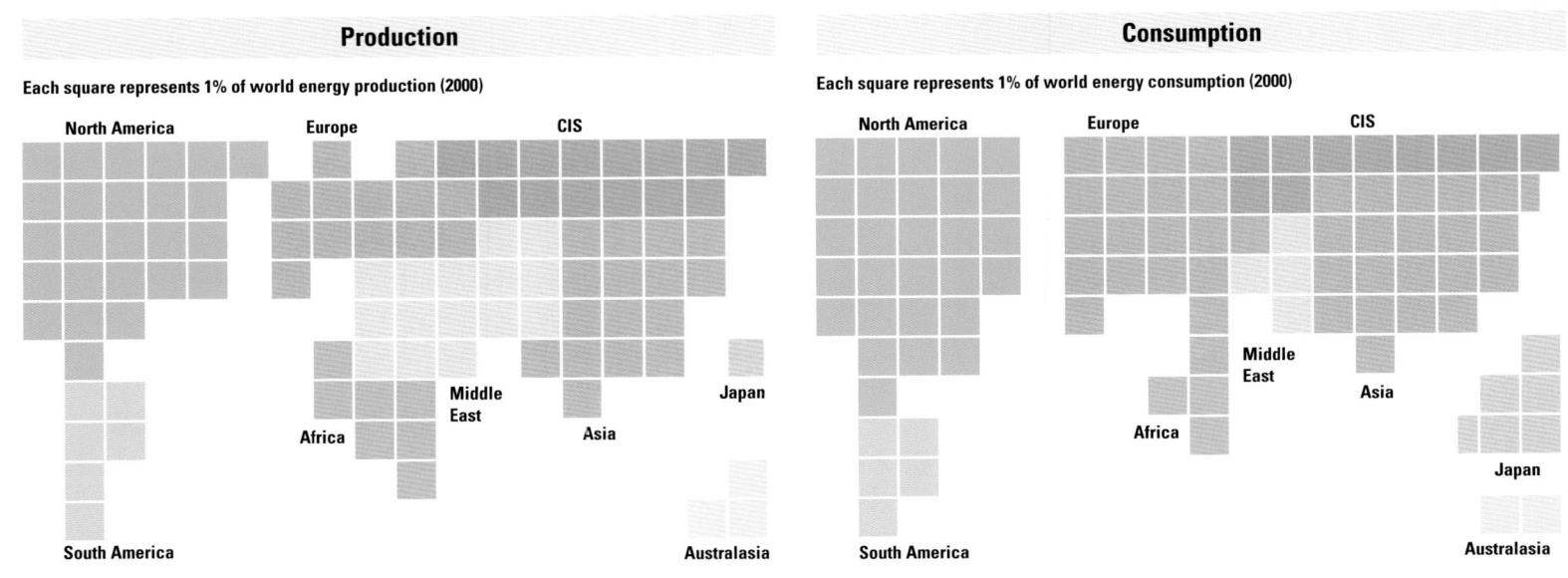

North America    Europe    CIS

Middle East    Japan

Africa    Asia

South America    Australasia

## Consumption

**Each square represents 1% of world energy consumption (2000)**

North America    Europe    CIS

Middle East    Asia

Africa

Japan

South America    Australasia

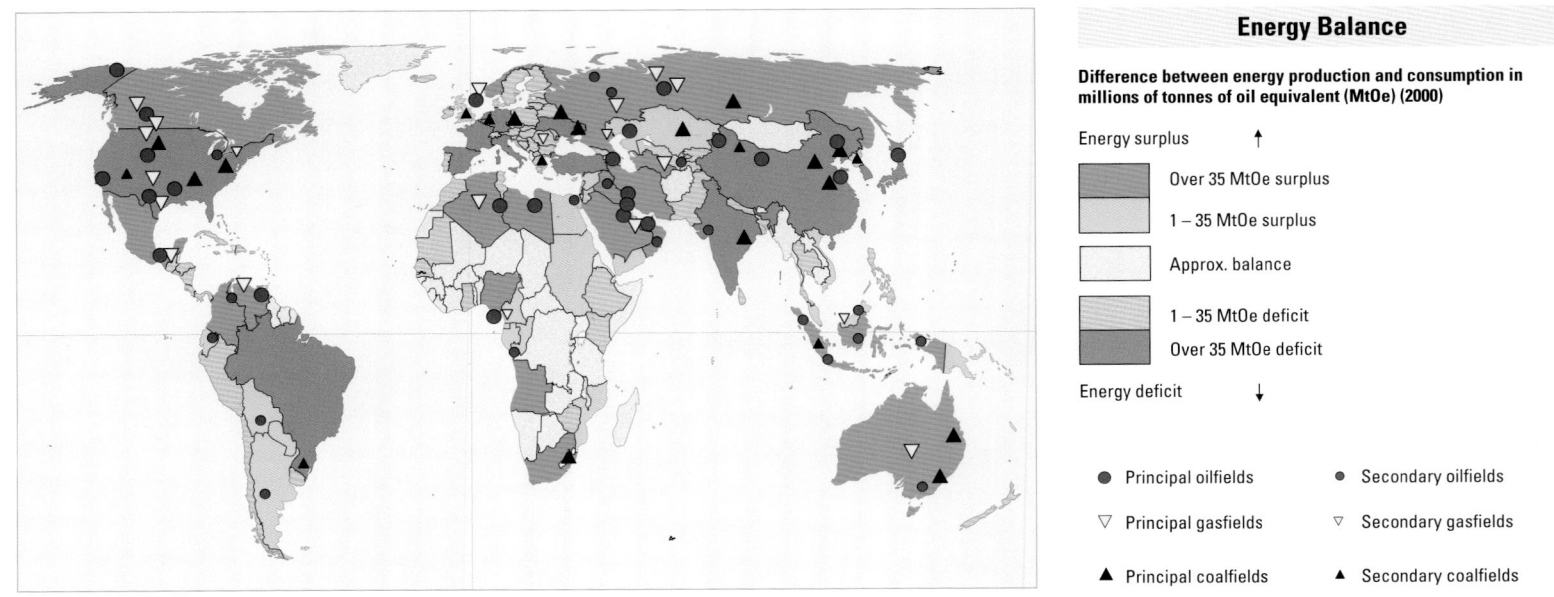

## Energy Balance

**Difference between energy production and consumption in millions of tonnes of oil equivalent (MtOe) (2000)**

Energy surplus ↑

- Over 35 MtOe surplus
- 1 – 35 MtOe surplus
- Approx. balance
- 1 – 35 MtOe deficit
- Over 35 MtOe deficit

Energy deficit ↓

- ● Principal oilfields    ● Secondary oilfields
- ▽ Principal gasfields    ▽ Secondary gasfields
- ▲ Principal coalfields    ▲ Secondary coalfields

## World Energy Consumption

Energy consumed by world regions, measured in million tonnes of oil equivalent in 2001. Total world consumption was 9,125 MtOe. Only energy from oil, gas, coal, nuclear and hydroelectric sources are included. Excluded are fuels such as wood, peat, animal waste, wind, solar and geothermal which, though important in some countries, are unreliably documented in terms of consumption statistics.

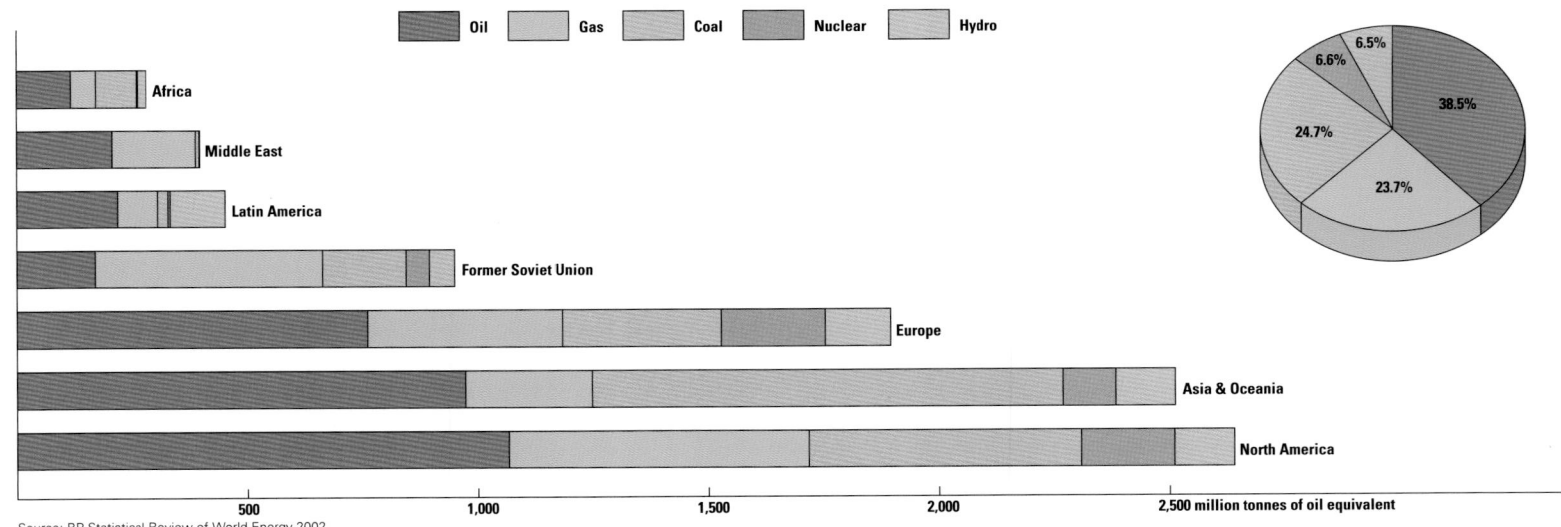

**Oil**    **Gas**    **Coal**    **Nuclear**    **Hydro**

Africa

Middle East

Latin America

Former Soviet Union

Europe

Asia & Oceania

North America

500    1,000    1,500    2,000    2,500 million tonnes of oil equivalent

Pie chart: 38.5%, 23.7%, 24.7%, 6.6%, 6.5%

Source: BP Statistical Review of World Energy 2002

## Energy

Energy is used to keep us warm or cool, fuel our industries and our transport systems, and even feed us; high-intensity agriculture, with its use of fertilizers, pesticides and machinery, is heavily energy-dependent. Although we live in a high-energy society, there are vast discrepancies between rich and poor; for example, a North American consumes 13 times as much energy as a Chinese person. But even developing nations have more power at their disposal than was imaginable a century ago.

The distribution of energy supplies, most importantly fossil fuels (coal, oil and natural gas), is very uneven. In addition, the diagrams and map opposite show that the largest producers of energy are not necessarily the largest consumers. The movement of energy supplies around the world is therefore an important component of international trade. In 1999, total world movements in oil amounted to 2,025 million tonnes.

As the finite reserves of fossil fuels are depleted, renewable energy sources, such as solar, hydro-thermal, wind, tidal and biomass, will become increasingly important around the world.

## Nuclear Power

**Major producers by percentage of world total (2000) and by percentage of domestic electricity generation (1999)**

| Country | % of world total production | Country | % of nuclear as proportion of domestic electricity |
|---------|------|---------|------|
| 1. USA | 30.5% | 1. Lithuania | 76.1% |
| 2. France | 15.7% | 2. France | 75.1% |
| 3. Japan | 12.6% | 3. Belgium | 58.2% |
| 4. Germany | 6.7% | 4. Slovak Rep. | 47.5% |
| 5. Russia | 4.6% | 5. Sweden | 44.2% |
| 6. South Korea | 4.1% | 6. Ukraine | 41.6% |
| 7. UK | 3.8% | 7. Bulgaria | 41.4% |
| 8. Canada | 2.9% | 8. South Korea | 39.1% |
| 9. Ukraine | 2.8% | 9. Hungary | 38.1% |
| = Sweden | 2.8% | 10. Slovenia | 35.9% |

Although the 1980s were a bad time for the nuclear power industry (major projects ran over budget and fears of long-term environmental damage were heavily reinforced by the 1986 disaster at Chernobyl), the industry picked up in the early 1990s. Whilst the number of reactors is still increasing, however, orders for new plants have shrunk. In 1997, the Swedish government began to decommission the country's 12 nuclear power plants.

## Hydroelectricity

**Major producers by percentage of world total (2000) and by percentage of domestic electricity generation (1999)**

| Country | % of world total production | Country | % of hydroelectric as proportion of domestic electricity |
|---------|------|---------|------|
| 1. Canada | 13.1% | 1. Bhutan | 99.9% |
| 2. USA | 12.0% | 2. Paraguay | 99.8% |
| 3. Brazil | 11.1% | = Zambia | 99.8% |
| 4. China | 8.5% | 4. Norway | 99.1% |
| 5. Russia | 6.1% | 5. Ethiopia | 98.1% |
| 6. Norway | 4.6% | 6. Congo (Rep. Dem.) | 97.9% |
| 7. Japan | 3.3% | 7. Tajikistan | 97.8% |
| 8. India | 3.1% | 8. Cameroon | 97.3% |
| 9. France | 2.8% | 9. Albania | 97.2% |
| 10. Sweden | 2.7% | = Laos | 97.2% |

Countries heavily reliant on hydroelectricity are usually small and non-industrial: a high proportion of hydroelectric power more often reflects a modest energy budget than vast hydroelectric resources. The USA, for instance, produces only 8.5% of its power requirements from hydroelectricity; yet that 8.5% amounts to more than three times the hydropower generated by most of Africa.

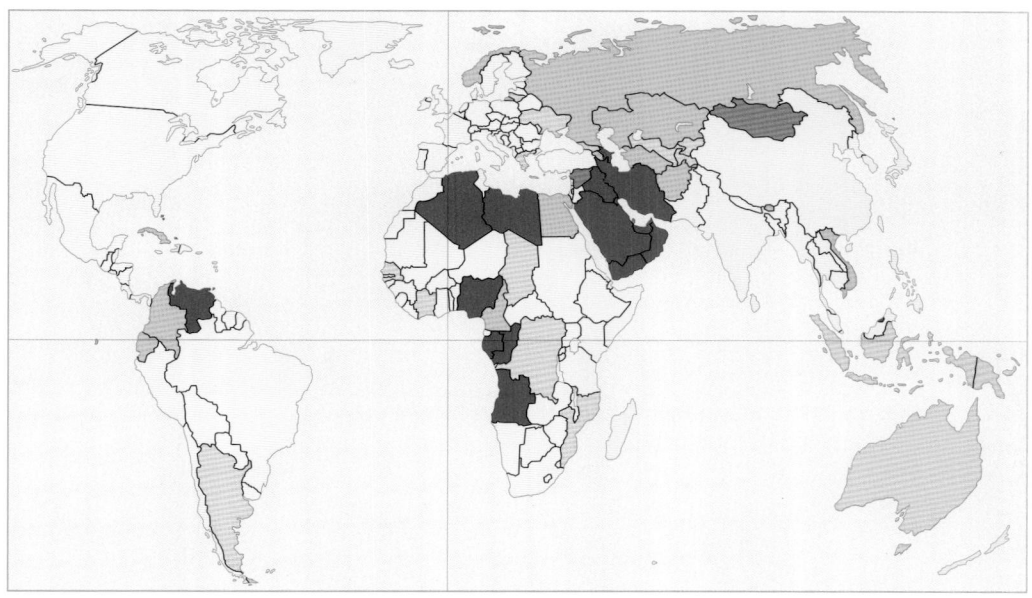

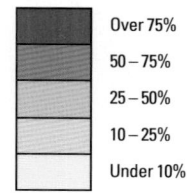

### Measurements
For historical reasons, oil is traded in 'barrels'. The weight and volume equivalents (shown right) are all based on average-density 'Arabian light' crude oil.

The energy equivalents given for a tonne of oil are also somewhat imprecise: oil and coal of different qualities will have varying energy contents, a fact usually reflected in their price on world markets.

## Fuel Exports

**Fuels as a percentage of total value of exports (latest available year)**

- Over 75%
- 50 – 75%
- 25 – 50%
- 10 – 25%
- Under 10%

In the 1970s, oil exports became a political issue when OPEC sought to increase the influence of developing countries in world affairs by raising oil prices and restricting production. But its power was short-lived, following a fall in demand for oil in the 1980s, due to an increase in energy efficiency and development of alternative resources.

### Conversion Rates

**1 barrel** = 0.136 tonnes or 159 litres or 35 Imperial gallons or 42 US gallons

**1 tonne** = 7.33 barrels or 1,185 litres or 256 Imperial gallons or 261 US gallons

**1 tonne oil** = 1.5 tonnes hard coal or 3.0 tonnes lignite or 12,000 kWh

**1 Imperial gallon** = 1.201 US gallons or 4.546 litres or 277.4 cubic inches

## World Coal Reserves

**World coal reserves (including lignite) by region and country, thousand million tonnes (2001)**

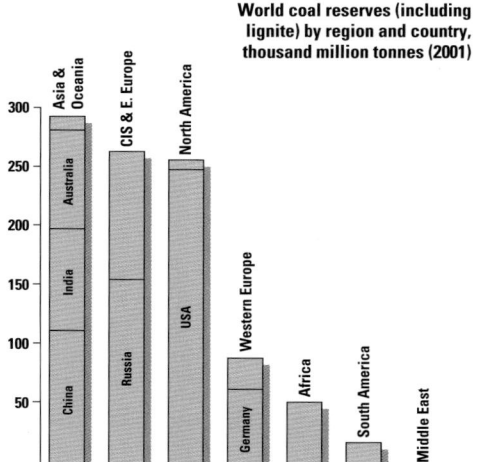

## World Gas Reserves

**World natural gas reserves by region and country, thousand million tonnes of oil equivalent (2001)**

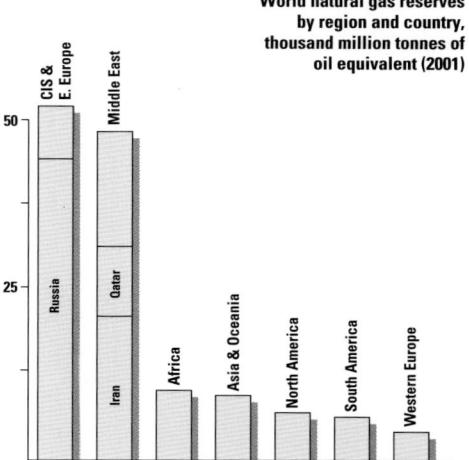

## World Oil Reserves

**World oil reserves by region and country, thousand million tonnes (2001)**

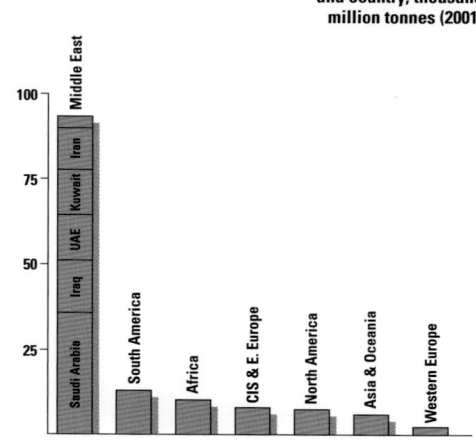

# Production

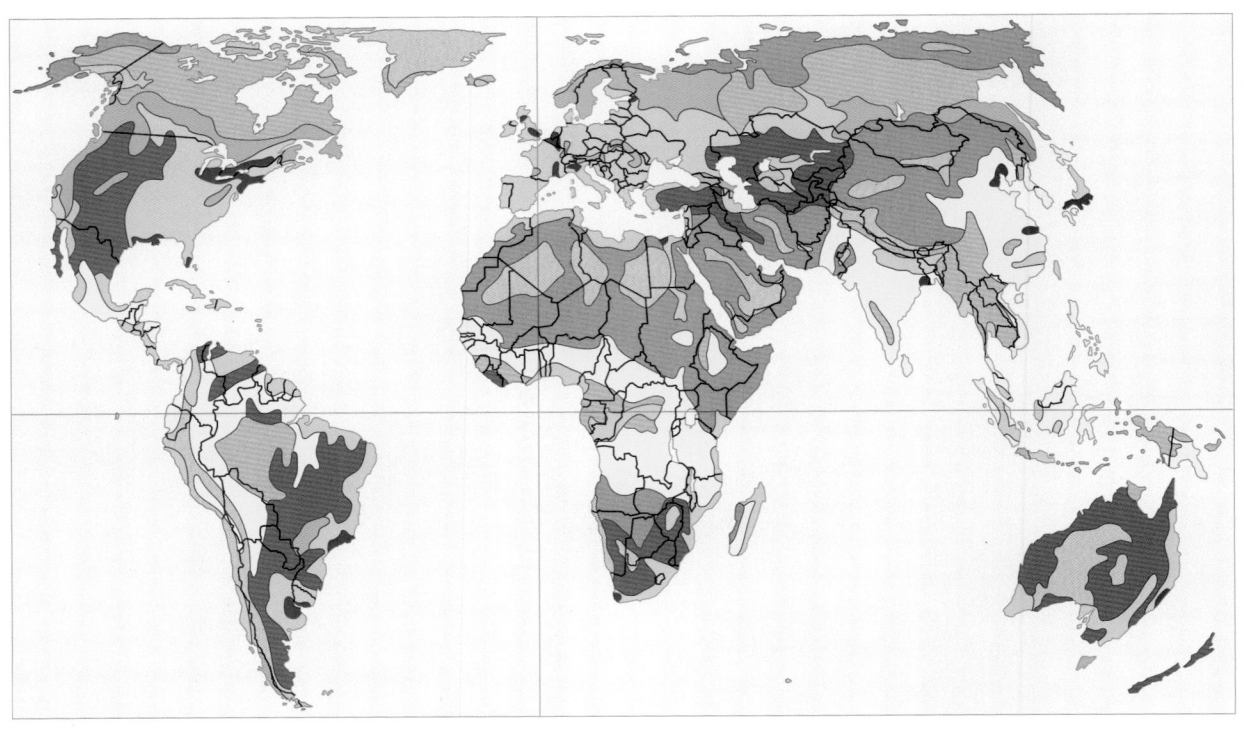

## Agriculture

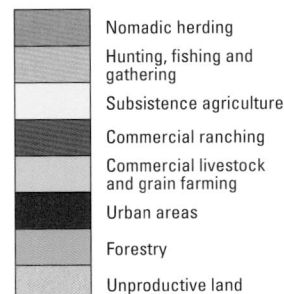

**Predominant type of farming or land use.**

- Nomadic herding
- Hunting, fishing and gathering
- Subsistence agriculture
- Commercial ranching
- Commercial livestock and grain farming
- Urban areas
- Forestry
- Unproductive land

The development of agriculture has transformed human existence more than any other. The whole business of farming is constantly developing: due mainly to the new varieties of rice and wheat, world grain production has increased by over 70% since 1965. New machinery and modern agricultural techniques enable relatively few farmers to produce enough food for the world's 6 billion or so people.

## Staple Crops

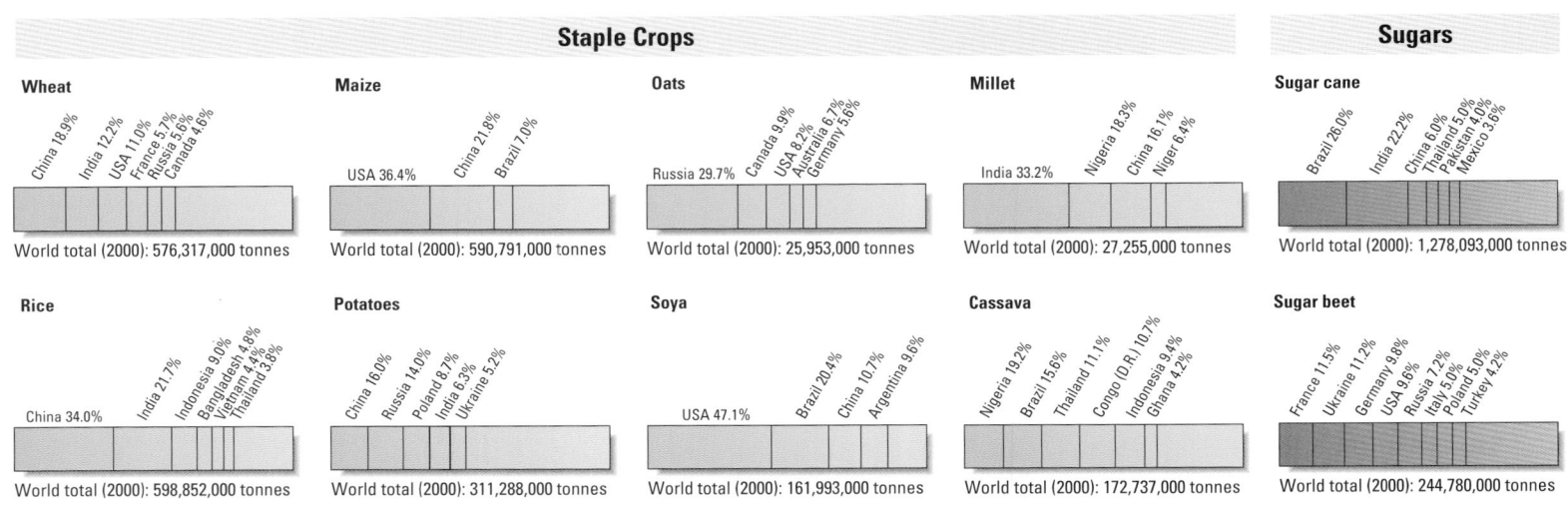

**Wheat**
China 18.9% | India 12.2% | USA 11.0% | France 5.7% | Russia 5.6% | Canada 4.6%
World total (2000): 576,317,000 tonnes

**Maize**
USA 36.4% | China 21.8% | Brazil 7.0%
World total (2000): 590,791,000 tonnes

**Oats**
Russia 29.7% | Canada 9.9% | USA 8.2% | Australia 6.7% | Germany 5.6%
World total (2000): 25,953,000 tonnes

**Millet**
India 33.2% | Nigeria 18.3% | China 16.1% | Niger 6.4%
World total (2000): 27,255,000 tonnes

**Rice**
China 34.0% | India 21.7% | Indonesia 9.0% | Bangladesh 4.8% | Vietnam 4.4% | Thailand 3.8%
World total (2000): 598,852,000 tonnes

**Potatoes**
China 16.0% | Russia 14.0% | Poland 8.7% | India 6.3% | Ukraine 5.2%
World total (2000): 311,288,000 tonnes

**Soya**
USA 47.1% | Brazil 20.4% | China 10.7% | Argentina 9.6%
World total (2000): 161,993,000 tonnes

**Cassava**
Nigeria 19.2% | Brazil 15.6% | Thailand 11.1% | Congo (D.R.) 10.7% | Indonesia 9.4% | Ghana 4.2%
World total (2000): 172,737,000 tonnes

## Sugars

**Sugar cane**
Brazil 26.0% | India 22.2% | China 6.0% | Thailand 5.0% | Pakistan 4.0% | Mexico 3.6%
World total (2000): 1,278,093,000 tonnes

**Sugar beet**
France 11.5% | Ukraine 11.2% | Germany 9.8% | USA 9.6% | Russia 7.2% | Italy 5.0% | Poland 5.0% | Turkey 4.2%
World total (2000): 244,780,000 tonnes

## Employment

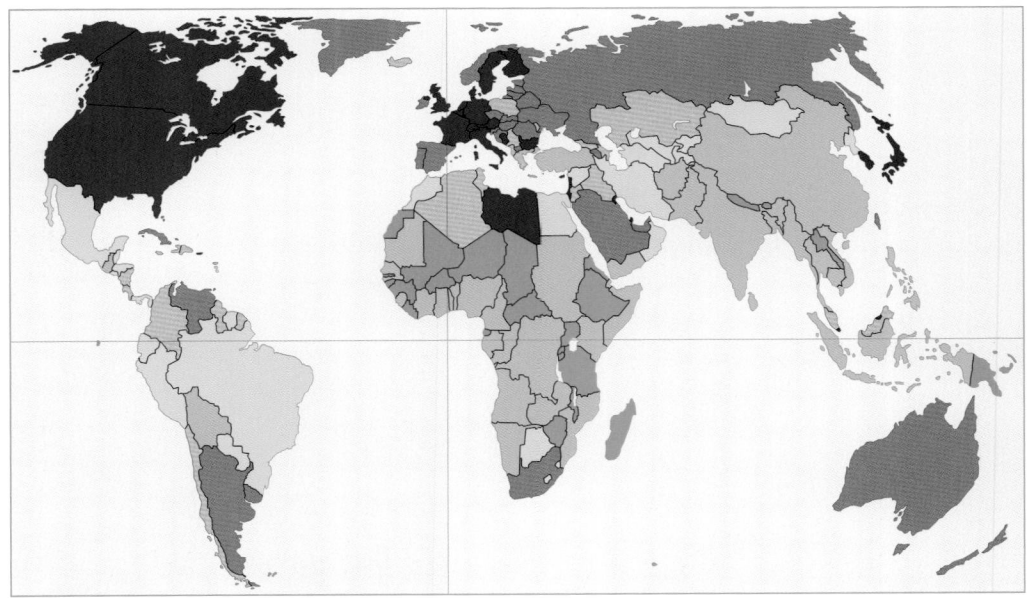

**The number of workers employed in manufacturing for every 100 workers engaged in agriculture (latest available year)**

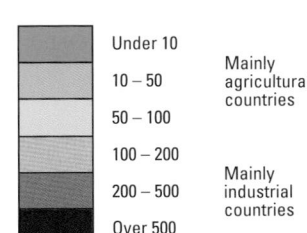

- Under 10 — Mainly agricultural countries
- 10 – 50
- 50 – 100
- 100 – 200
- 200 – 500 — Mainly industrial countries
- Over 500

**Selected countries (latest available year)**

| | | | |
|---|---|---|---|
| Singapore | 8,860 | Germany | 800 |
| Hong Kong | 3,532 | Kuwait | 767 |
| UK | 1,270 | Bahrain | 660 |
| Belgium | 820 | USA | 657 |
| Former Yugoslavia | 809 | Israel | 633 |

# Mineral Production

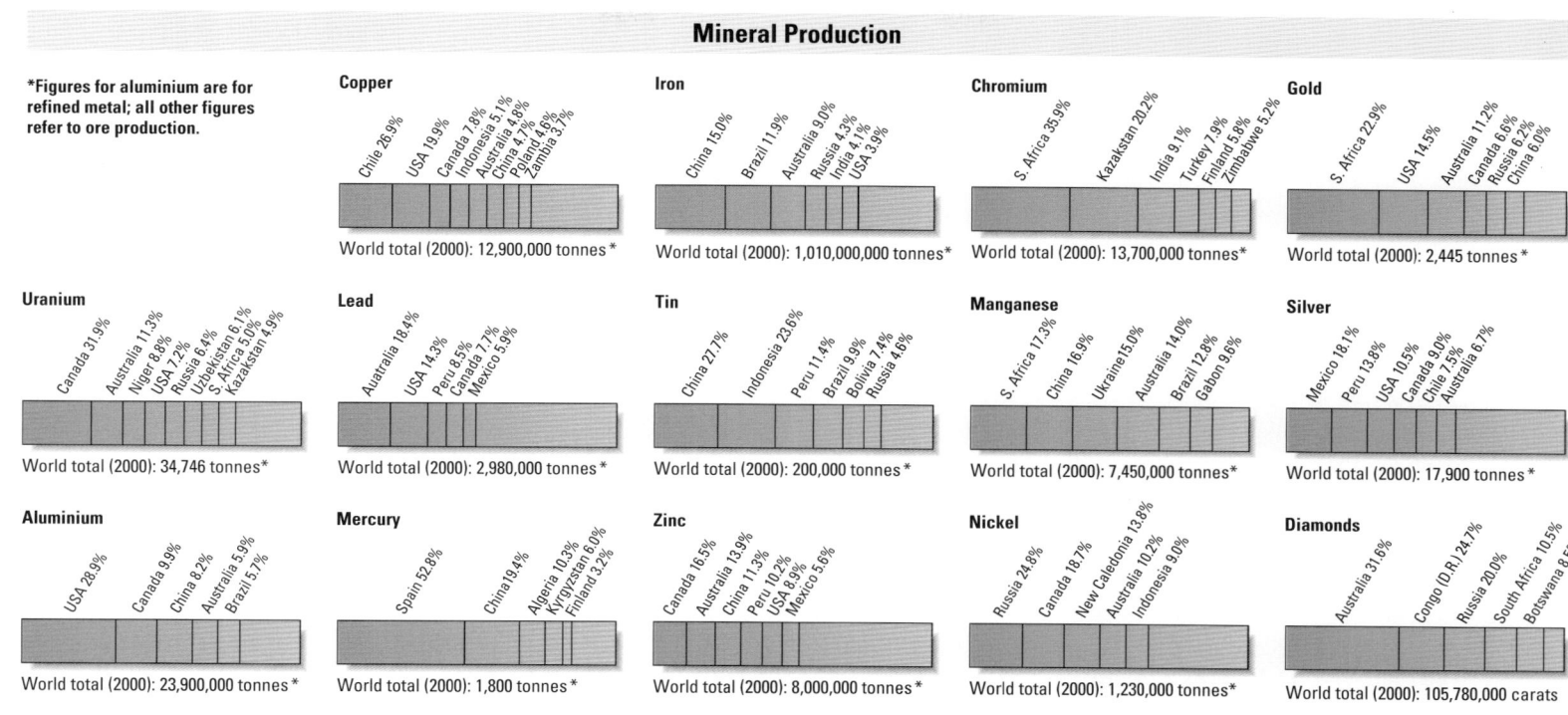

*Figures for aluminium are for refined metal; all other figures refer to ore production.

**Copper**
Chile 26.9% | USA 19.9% | Canada 7.8% | Indonesia 5.1% | Australia 4.8% | China 4.7% | Poland 4.6% | Zambia 3.7%
World total (2000): 12,900,000 tonnes *

**Iron**
China 15.0% | Brazil 11.9% | Australia 9.0% | Russia 4.3% | India 4.1% | USA 3.9%
World total (2000): 1,010,000,000 tonnes*

**Chromium**
S. Africa 35.9% | Kazakstan 20.2% | India 9.1% | Turkey 7.9% | Finland 5.8% | Zimbabwe 5.2%
World total (2000): 13,700,000 tonnes*

**Gold**
S. Africa 22.9% | USA 14.5% | Australia 11.2% | Canada 6.6% | Russia 6.2% | China 6.0%
World total (2000): 2,445 tonnes *

**Uranium**
Canada 31.9% | Australia 11.3% | Niger 8.8% | USA 7.2% | Russia 6.4% | Uzbekistan 6.1% | S. Africa 5.0% | Kazakstan 4.9%
World total (2000): 34,746 tonnes*

**Lead**
Auatralia 18.4% | USA 14.3% | Peru 8.5% | Canada 7.7% | Mexico 5.9%
World total (2000): 2,980,000 tonnes *

**Tin**
China 27.7% | Indonesia 23.6% | Peru 11.4% | Brazil 9.9% | Bolivia 7.4% | Russia 4.6%
World total (2000): 200,000 tonnes *

**Manganese**
S. Africa 17.3% | China 16.9% | Ukraine 15.0% | Australia 14.0% | Brazil 12.8% | Gabon 9.6%
World total (2000): 7,450,000 tonnes *

**Silver**
Mexico 18.1% | Peru 13.8% | USA 10.5% | Canada 9.0% | Chile 7.5% | Australia 6.7%
World total (2000): 17,900 tonnes *

**Aluminium**
USA 28.9% | Canada 9.9% | China 8.2% | Australia 5.9% | Brazil 5.7%
World total (2000): 23,900,000 tonnes *

**Mercury**
Spain 52.8% | China 19.4% | Algeria 10.3% | Kyrgyzstan 6.0% | Finland 3.2%
World total (2000): 1,800 tonnes *

**Zinc**
Canada 16.5% | Australia 13.9% | China 11.3% | Peru 10.2% | USA 8.9% | Mexico 5.6%
World total (2000): 8,000,000 tonnes *

**Nickel**
Russia 24.8% | Canada 18.7% | New Caledonia 13.8% | Australia 10.2% | Indonesia 9.0%
World total (2000): 1,230,000 tonnes*

**Diamonds**
Australia 31.6% | Congo (D.R.) 24.7% | Russia 20.0% | South Africa 10.5% | Botswana 8.5%
World total (2000): 105,780,000 carats

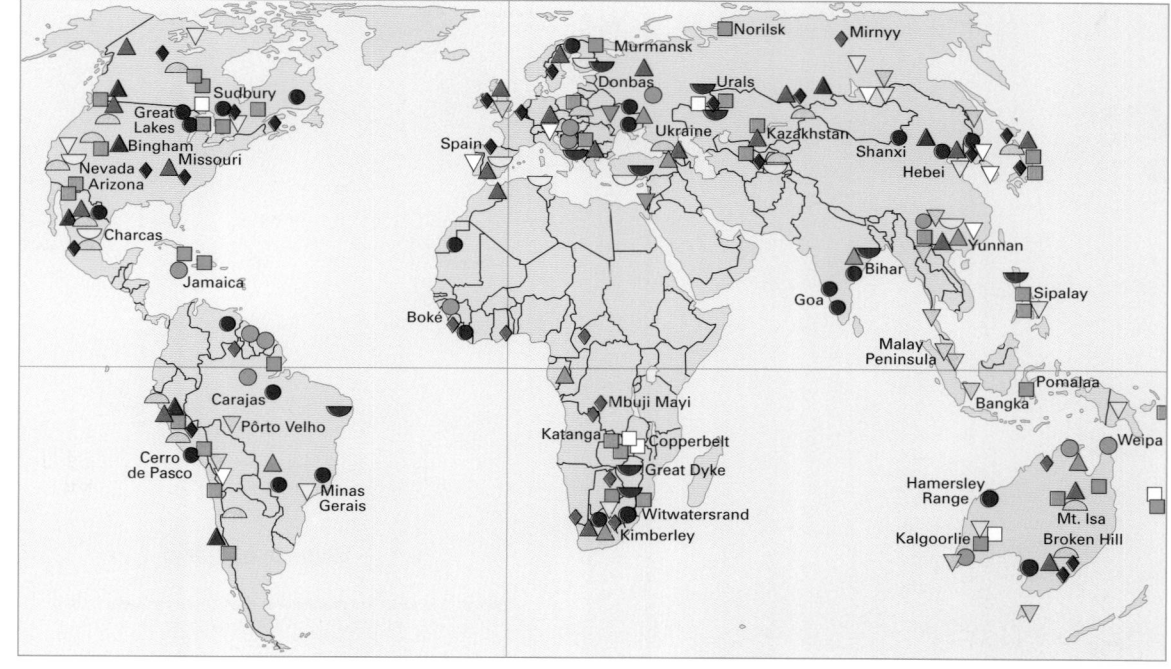

## Mineral Distribution

The map shows the richest sources of the most important minerals. Major mineral locations are named.

- ▽ Gold
- ◗ Silver
- ◆ Diamonds
- ▽ Tungsten
- ● Iron Ore
- ■ Nickel
- ◖ Chrome
- ▲ Manganese
- □ Cobalt
- ▲ Molybdenum
- ■ Copper
- ▲ Lead
- ● Bauxite
- ▽ Tin
- ◆ Zinc
- ◗ Mercury

The map does not show undersea deposits, most of which are considered inaccessible.

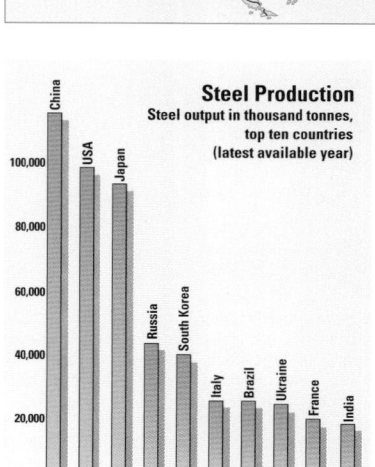

**Steel Production**
Steel output in thousand tonnes, top ten countries (latest available year)

China | USA | Japan | Russia | South Korea | Italy | Brazil | Ukraine | France | India

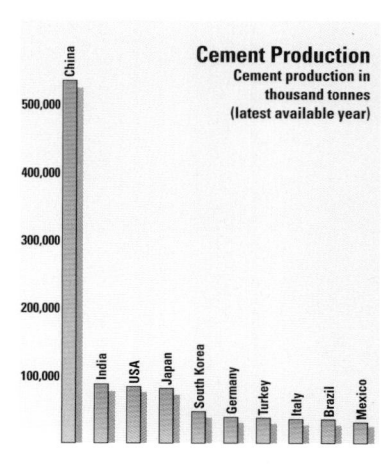

**Cement Production**
Cement production in thousand tonnes (latest available year)

China | India | USA | Japan | South Korea | Germany | Turkey | Italy | Brazil | Mexico

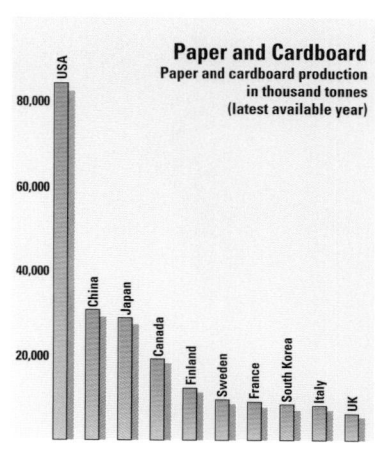

**Paper and Cardboard**
Paper and cardboard production in thousand tonnes (latest available year)

USA | China | Japan | Canada | Finland | Sweden | France | South Korea | Italy | UK

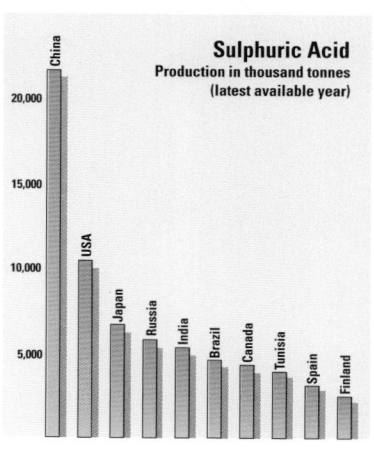

**Sulphuric Acid**
Production in thousand tonnes (latest available year)

China | USA | Japan | Russia | India | Brazil | Canada | Tunisia | Spain | Finland

# Trade

## Share of World Trade

**Percentage share of total world exports by value (2000)**

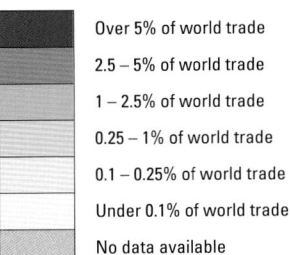

- Over 5% of world trade
- 2.5 – 5% of world trade
- 1 – 2.5% of world trade
- 0.25 – 1% of world trade
- 0.1 – 0.25% of world trade
- Under 0.1% of world trade
- No data available

International trade is dominated by a handful of powerful maritime nations. The members of 'G8', the inner circle of OECD (see page 19), and the top seven countries listed in the diagram below, account for more than half the total. The majority of nations – including all but four in Africa – contribute less than one quarter of 1% to the worldwide total of exports; the EU countries account for 35%, the Pacific Rim nations over 50%.

## The Main Trading Nations

The imports and exports of the top ten trading nations as a percentage of world trade (2001). Each country's trade in manufactured goods is shown in dark blue.

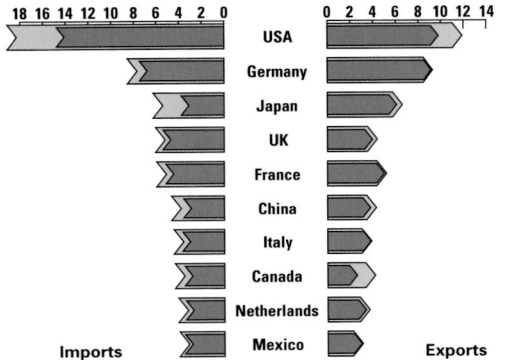

18 16 14 12 10 8 6 4 2 0    0 2 4 6 8 10 12 14

- USA
- Germany
- Japan
- UK
- France
- China
- Italy
- Canada
- Netherlands
- Mexico

Imports    Exports

## Major exports

**Leading manufactured items and their exporters (2000)**

### Motor Vehicles
World total (2000): US$ 299,334 million

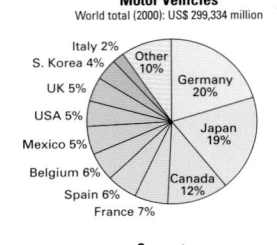

Italy 2%, S. Korea 4%, Other 10%, UK 5%, Germany 20%, USA 5%, Japan 19%, Mexico 5%, Belgium 6%, Canada 12%, Spain 6%, France 7%

### Telecommunications Gear
World total (2000): US$ 214,456 million

USA 12%, UK 8%, Other 39%, Japan 8%, Germany 7%, China 6%, Mexico 5%, France 6%, Canada 5%, Sweden 6%

### Petrol Products
World total (2000): US$ 153,410 million

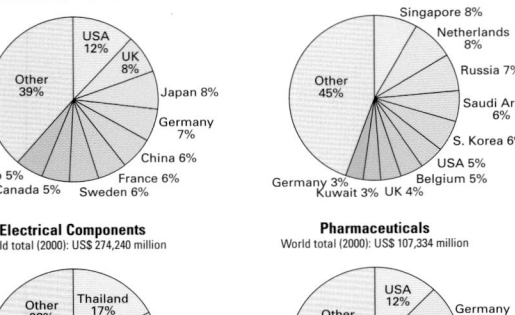

Singapore 8%, Netherlands 8%, Russia 7%, Other 45%, Saudi Arabia 6%, S. Korea 6%, USA 5%, Germany 3%, Belgium 5%, Kuwait 3%, UK 4%

### Computers
World total (2000): US$ 182,866 million

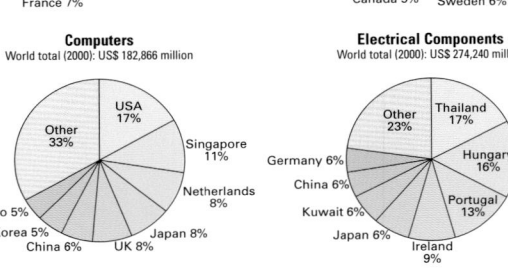

Other 33%, USA 17%, Singapore 11%, Netherlands 8%, Mexico 5%, Japan 8%, S. Korea 5%, UK 8%, China 6%

### Electrical Components
World total (2000): US$ 274,240 million

Other 23%, Thailand 17%, Germany 6%, Hungary 16%, China 6%, Kuwait 6%, Portugal 13%, Japan 6%, Ireland 9%

### Pharmaceuticals
World total (2000): US$ 107,334 million

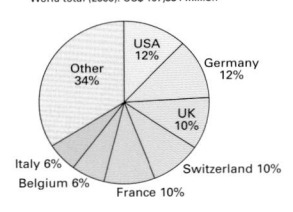

USA 12%, Germany 12%, Other 34%, UK 10%, Switzerland 10%, Italy 6%, France 10%, Belgium 6%

## Balance of Trade

**Value of exports in proportion to the value of imports (2000)**

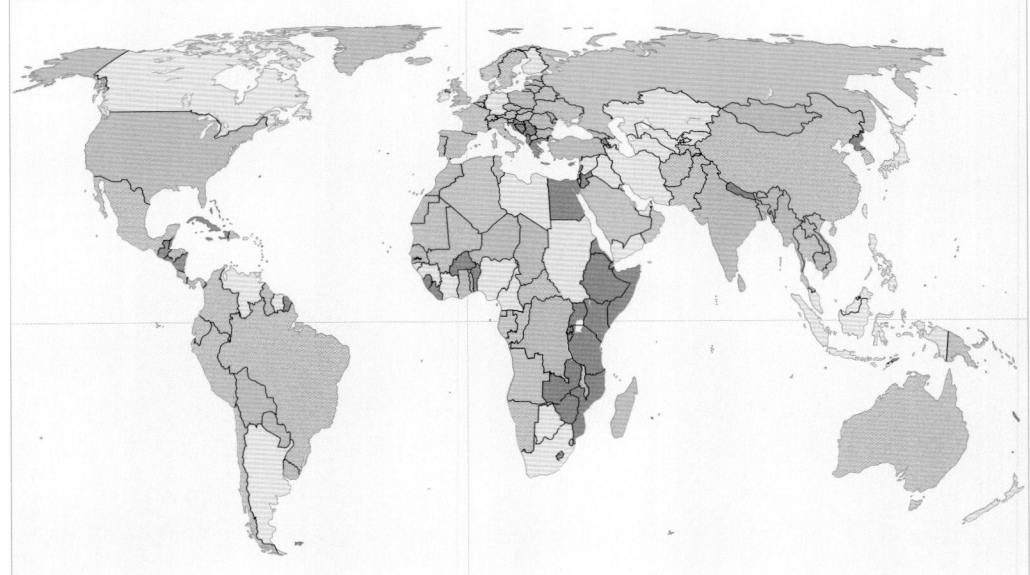

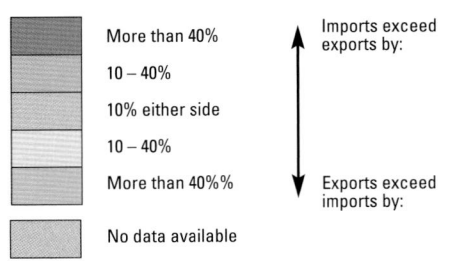

- More than 40%    Imports exceed exports by:
- 10 – 40%
- 10% either side
- 10 – 40%
- More than 40% %    Exports exceed imports by:
- No data available

The total world trade balance should amount to zero, since exports must equal imports on a global scale. In practice, at least $100 billion in exports go unrecorded, leaving the world with an apparent deficit and many countries in a better position than public accounting reveals. However, a favourable trade balance is not necessarily a sign of prosperity: many poorer countries must maintain a high surplus in order to service debts, and do so by restricting imports below the levels needed to sustain successful economies.

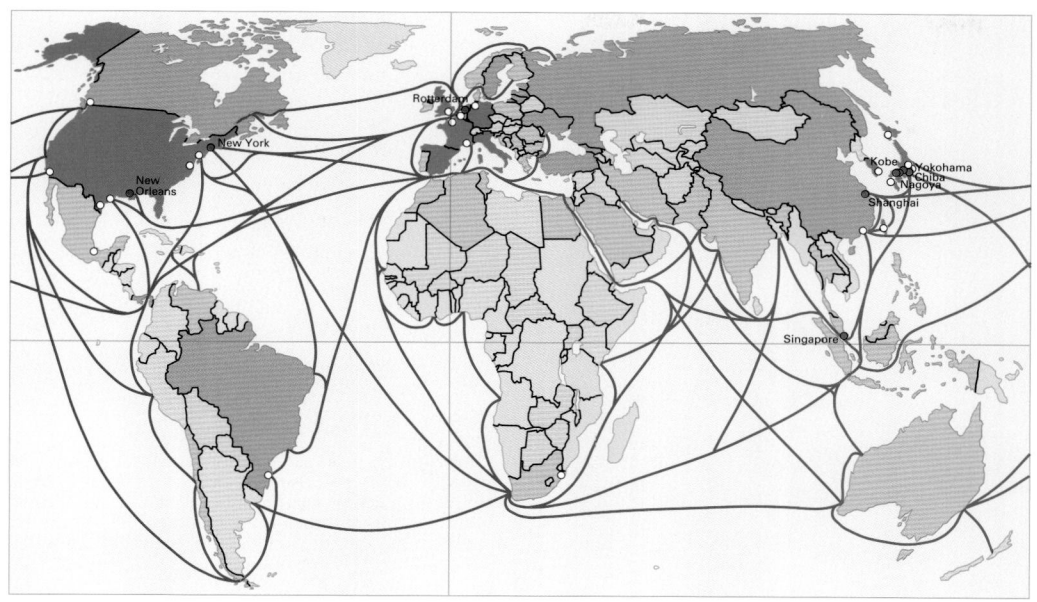

## Seaborne Freight

**Freight unloaded in millions of tonnes (latest available year)**

- Over 100
- 50 – 100
- 10 – 50
- 5 – 10
- Under 5
- Landlocked countries

**Major seaports**

- ● Over 100 million tonnes per year
- ○ 50–100 million tonnes per year
- — Major shipping routes

## Cargoes

**Type of seaborne freight**

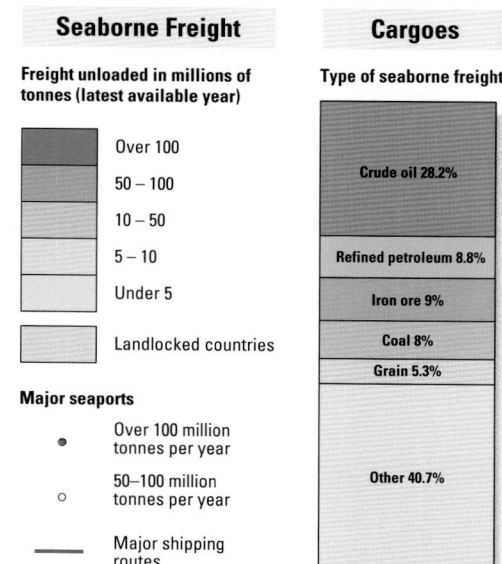

- Crude oil 28.2%
- Refined petroleum 8.8%
- Iron ore 9%
- Coal 8%
- Grain 5.3%
- Other 40.7%

## Merchant Fleets

Merchant fleets in thousand gross registered tonnage (2000). Although a large number of vessels are registered in Liberia and Panama, they are not part of the national fleet.

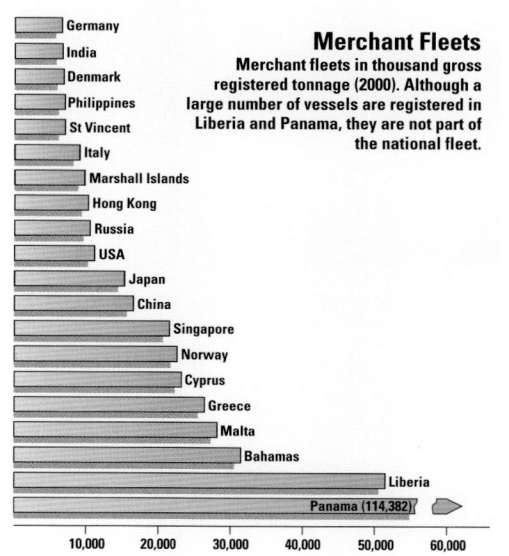

Germany, India, Denmark, Philippines, St Vincent, Italy, Marshall Islands, Hong Kong, Russia, USA, Japan, China, Singapore, Norway, Cyprus, Greece, Malta, Bahamas, Liberia, Panama (114,382)

10,000  20,000  30,000  40,000  50,000  60,000

## The Great Ports

Total cargo traffic, in million tonnes (latest available year)

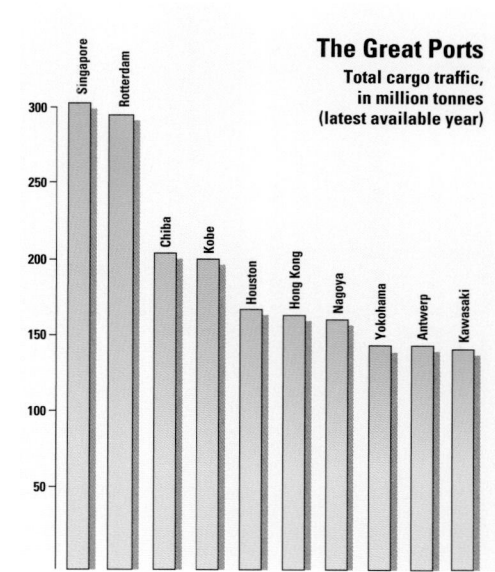

Singapore, Rotterdam, Chiba, Kobe, Houston, Hong Kong, Nagoya, Yokohama, Antwerp, Kawasaki

## World Shipping

World merchant fleet by type of vessel and deadweight tonnage (2000)

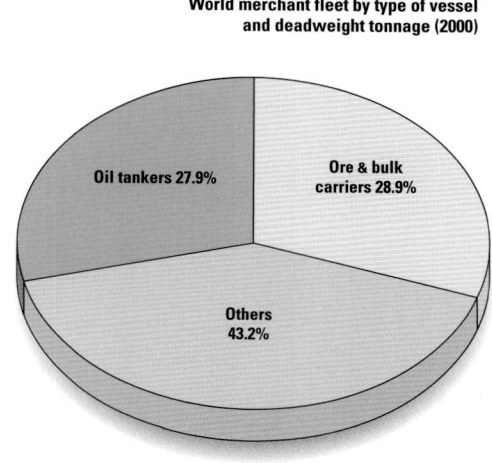

- Oil tankers 27.9%
- Ore & bulk carriers 28.9%
- Others 43.2%

## Exports Per Capita

**Value of exports in US $, divided by total population (2000)**

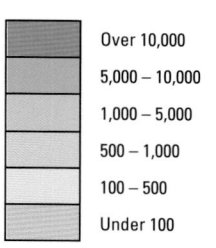

- Over 10,000
- 5,000 – 10,000
- 1,000 – 5,000
- 500 – 1,000
- 100 – 500
- Under 100

[UK 4,728]  [USA 2,791]

**Highest per capita**

| | |
|---|---|
| Kuwait | 113,614 |
| Liechtenstein | 78,848 |
| Singapore | 31,860 |
| Aruba (Neths) | 31,429 |
| Hong Kong (China) | 28,290 |
| Ireland | 19,136 |

# Travel and Tourism

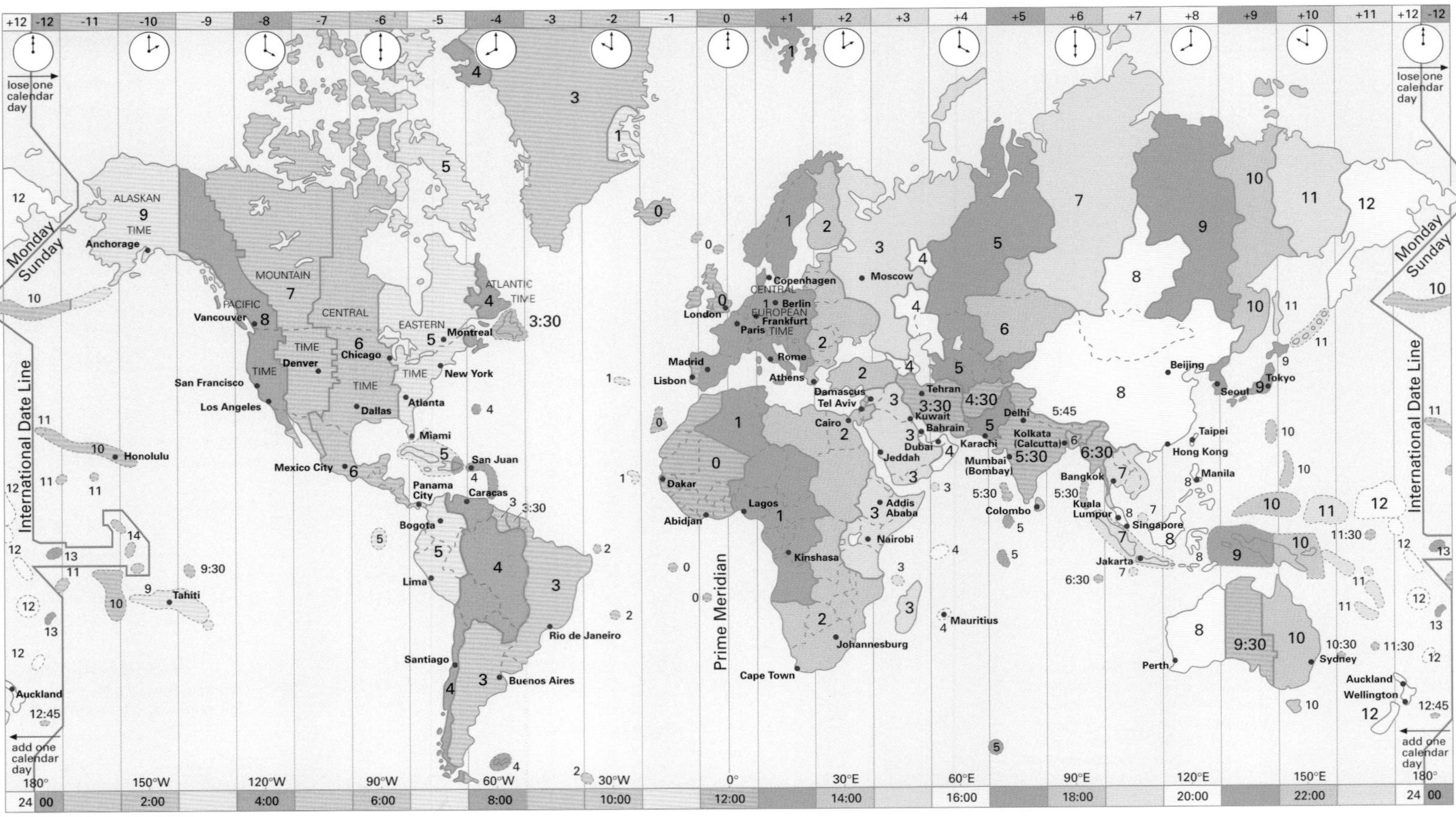

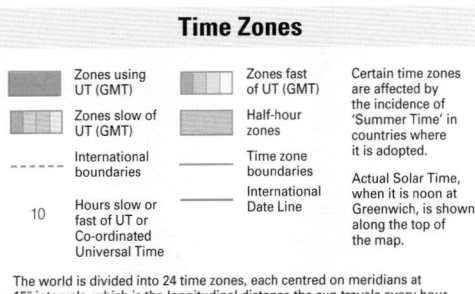

Projection: Mercator

## Time Zones

| | | |
|---|---|---|
| Zones using UT (GMT) | Zones fast of UT (GMT) | Certain time zones are affected by the incidence of 'Summer Time' in countries where it is adopted. |
| Zones slow of UT (GMT) | Half-hour zones | |
| International boundaries | Time zone boundaries | Actual Solar Time, when it is noon at Greenwich, is shown along the top of the map. |
| 10 — Hours slow or fast of UT or Co-ordinated Universal Time | International Date Line | |

The world is divided into 24 time zones, each centred on meridians at 15° intervals, which is the longitudinal distance the sun travels every hour. The meridian running through Greenwich, London, passes through the middle of the first zone.

## Rail and Road: The Leading Nations

| Total rail network ('000 km) | | Passenger km per head per year | | Total road network ('000 km) | | Vehicle km per head per year | | Number of vehicles per km of roads | |
|---|---|---|---|---|---|---|---|---|---|
| 1. USA | 235.7 | Japan | 2,017 | USA | 6,277.9 | USA | 12,505 | Hong Kong | 284 |
| 2. Russia | 87.4 | Belarus | 1,880 | India | 2,962.5 | Luxembourg | 7,989 | Taiwan | 211 |
| 3. India | 62.7 | Russia | 1,826 | Brazil | 1,824.4 | Kuwait | 7,251 | Singapore | 152 |
| 4. China | 54.6 | Switzerland | 1,769 | Japan | 1,130.9 | France | 7,142 | Kuwait | 140 |
| 5. Germany | 41.7 | Ukraine | 1,456 | China | 1,041.1 | Sweden | 6,991 | Brunei | 96 |
| 6. Australia | 35.8 | Austria | 1,168 | Russia | 884.0 | Germany | 6,806 | Italy | 91 |
| 7. Argentina | 34.2 | France | 1,011 | Canada | 849.4 | Denmark | 6,764 | Israel | 87 |
| 8. France | 31.9 | Netherlands | 994 | France | 811.6 | Austria | 6,518 | Thailand | 73 |
| 9. Mexico | 26.5 | Latvia | 918 | Australia | 810.3 | Netherlands | 5,984 | Ukraine | 73 |
| 10. South Africa | 26.3 | Denmark | 884 | Germany | 636.3 | UK | 5,738 | UK | 67 |
| 11. Poland | 24.9 | Slovak Rep. | 862 | Romania | 461.9 | Canada | 5,493 | Netherlands | 66 |
| 12. Ukraine | 22.6 | Romania | 851 | Turkey | 388.1 | Italy | 4,852 | Germany | 62 |

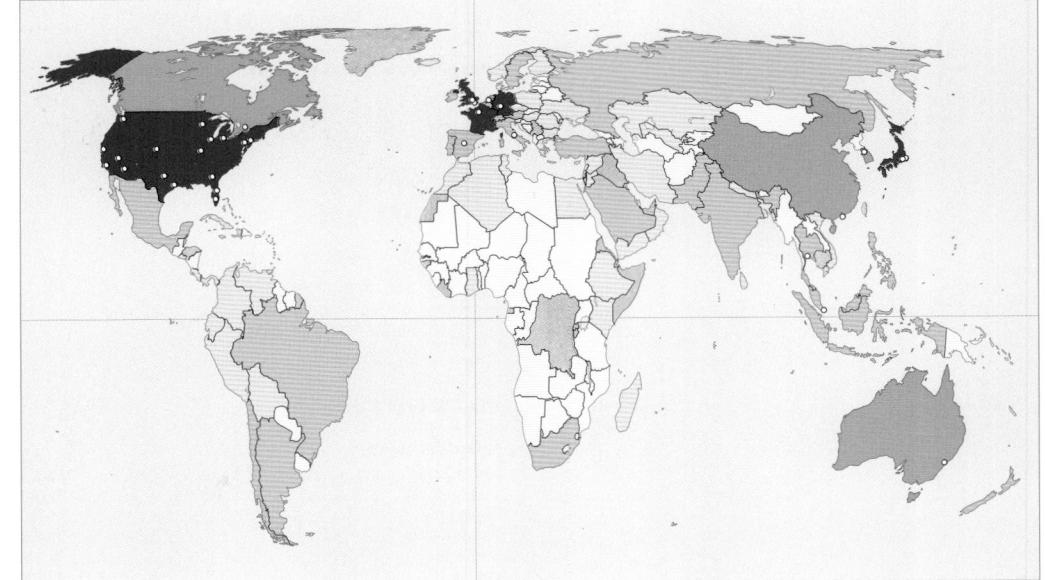

## Air Travel

**Passenger kilometres flown on scheduled flights (the number of passengers in thousands – international and domestic – multiplied by the distance flown from the airport of origin) (1999)**

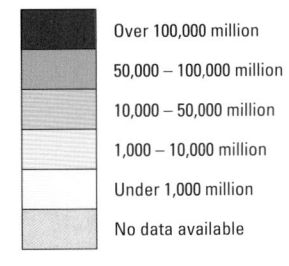

- Over 100,000 million
- 50,000 – 100,000 million
- 10,000 – 50,000 million
- 1,000 – 10,000 million
- Under 1,000 million
- No data available

○ Major airports (handling over 25 million passengers in 2001)

| World's busiest airports (total passengers) | | World's busiest airports (international passengers) | |
|---|---|---|---|
| 1. Atlanta | (Hartsfield) | 1. London | (Heathrow) |
| 2. Chicago | (O'Hare) | 2. Paris | (Charles de Gaulle) |
| 3. Los Angeles | (International) | 3. Frankfurt | (International) |
| 4. London | (Heathrow) | 4. Amsterdam | (Schipol) |
| 5. Tokyo | (Haneda) | 5. Hong Kong | (International) |

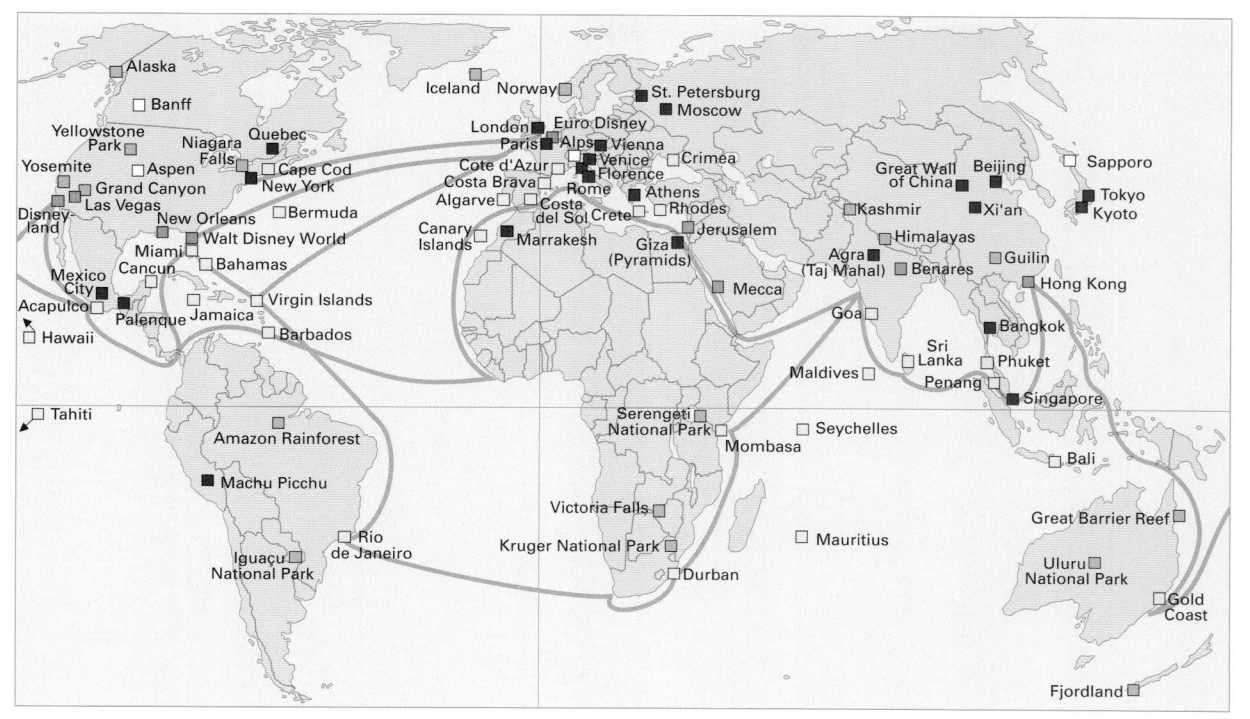

## Destinations

- ■ Cultural and historical centres
- ▢ Coastal resorts
- □ Ski resorts
- ▨ Centres of entertainment
- ▨ Places of pilgrimage
- ▨ Places of great natural beauty
- — Popular holiday cruise routes

### Visitors to the USA

Overseas arrivals to the USA,
in thousands (2000)

1. Canada . . . . . . . . . . . . . . . .14,594
2. Mexico . . . . . . . . . . . . . . . .10,322
3. Japan . . . . . . . . . . . . . . . . .5,061
4. UK . . . . . . . . . . . . . . . . . . .4,703
5. Germany . . . . . . . . . . . . . .1,786
6. France . . . . . . . . . . . . . . . .1,087
7. Brazil . . . . . . . . . . . . . . . . . .737
8. South Korea . . . . . . . . . . . . .662
9. Venezuela . . . . . . . . . . . . . .577
10. Australia . . . . . . . . . . . . . . .540

## Tourist Spending

Countries spending the most
on overseas tourism,
US$ million (2000)

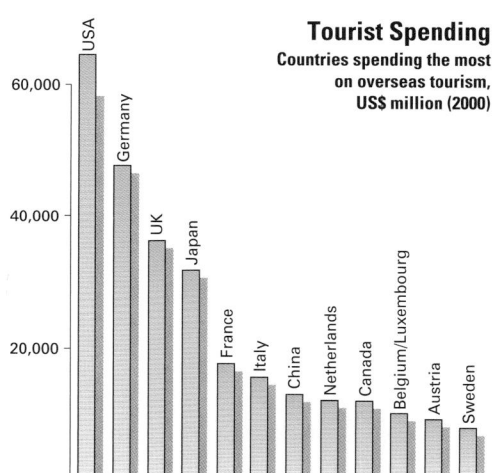

## Importance of Tourism

|  |  | Arrivals from abroad (2001) | % of world total (2001) |
|---|---|---|---|
| 1. | France | 76,500,000 | 11.0% |
| 2. | Spain | 49,500,000 | 7.1% |
| 3. | USA | 45,500,000 | 6.6% |
| 4. | Italy | 39,000,000 | 5.6% |
| 5. | China | 33,200,000 | 4.8% |
| 6. | UK | 23,400,000 | 3.4% |
| 7. | Russia | 21,200,000 | 3.0% |
| 8. | Mexico | 19,800,000 | 2.9% |
| 9. | Canada | 19,700,000 | 2.8% |
| 10. | Austria | 18,200,000 | 2.6% |
| 11. | Germany | 17,900,000 | 2.6% |
| 12. | Hungary | 15,300,000 | 2.2% |

In 2001, there was a 0.6% drop in the number of tourist arrivals
compared to the previous year, to 693 million. This was partly
due to the impact of the terrorist attacks in New York City on
11 September 2001, but was also a result of the weakening
economies of tourism-generating markets worldwide.

## Tourist Earnings

Countries receiving the most
from overseas tourism,
US$ million (2000)

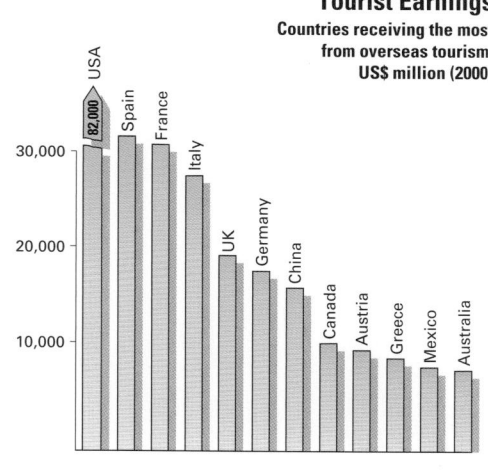

## Tourism

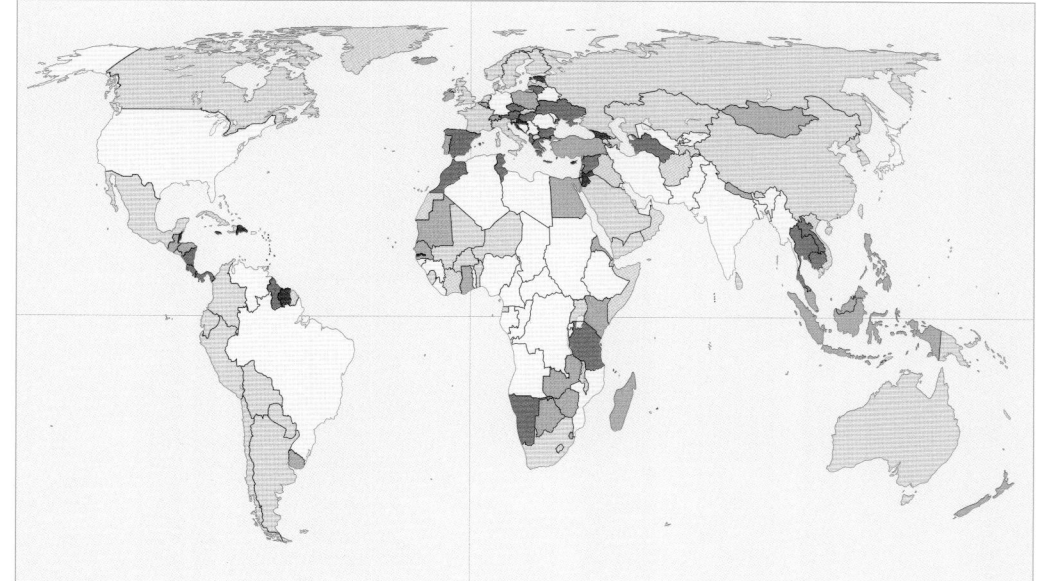

Tourism receipts as a percentage of Gross National Income
(1999)

- ▨ 10% and over
- ▨ 5 – 10%
- ▨ 2.5 – 5%
- ▨ 1 – 2.5%
- □ Under 1%
- ▨ No data available

Percentage change in tourist arrivals from 2000 to 2001
(top six countries in total number of arrivals)

China . . . . . . . . . . . . . . . +6.2%
Spain . . . . . . . . . . . . . . . +3.4%
France . . . . . . . . . . . . . . +1.2%
Italy . . . . . . . . . . . . . . . .–5.3%
UK . . . . . . . . . . . . . . . . .–7.4%
USA . . . . . . . . . . . . . . . –10.6%

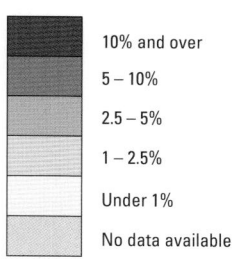
(increase)
(decrease)

# The World In Focus: Index

## A

Acid rain 15
Agriculture 26
Aid 21
Airports 30
Air travel 30

## B

Beaufort Wind Scale 11

## C

Carbon dioxide 10, 14
Cement production 27
Climate regions 10
Coal 25
Continental drift 4
Crops 26
Crust 4–5
Currents 8

## D

Day and night 2
Debt 21
Deforestation 15
Desertification 15

## E

Earth's structure 4
Earthquakes 4
Eclipses 3
Education 23
El Niño 11
Employment 26
Energy balance 24
Epicentre 4
Equinox 2–3

Erosion 7
European Union 19
Exports 28

## F

Faults 6
Female employment 23
Fertility 23
Fishing 9
Folds 6
Food consumption 22
Forestry 13
Fuel exports 25

## G

Geothermal energy 25
Glaciers 7
Global warming 14
Greenhouse effect 14
Gross Domestic Product 29
Gross National Product 20

## H

Holiday destinations 31
Hospital beds 22
Household spending 21
Human Development Index 23
Hydroelectricity 25
Hydrological cycle 12

## I

Illiteracy 23
Imports 28
Infant mortality 22
Infectious diseases 22
Inflation 20

International organizations 19

## L

Land use 13
Language 18
Life expectancy 22

## M

Mantle 4–5
Mercalli Scale 4
Merchant fleets 29
Metals 27
Mid-ocean ridge 5
Minerals 27
Moon 3
Mountain building 6

## N

Nuclear power 25

## O

OECD 19, 28
Oil 24–25
Ozone 14–15

## P

Paper and cardboard 27
Planets 2
Plate tectonics 5
Pollution 9
Population density 16–17
Ports 29
Precipitation 10–12

## R

Railways 30

Rainforest 13, 15
Richter Scale 4
Religions 18
Rivers 7
Roads 30

## S

Sea-floor spreading 5
Seasons 2
Shipping 29
Solar System 2
Subduction zone 6
Sulphuric acid 27

## T

Telecommunications gear 28
Temperature 11
Tides 3
Time zones 30
Tourism 31
Trading nations 28
Transport networks 30

## U

United Nations 19
Urban population 17

## V

Vegetation 13
Vehicles 28, 30
Volcanoes 5

## W

Water 12
Wealth gap 20
Wind power 25

# WORLD CITIES

| | | | | | | | |
|---|---|---|---|---|---|---|---|
| AMSTERDAM | 2 | EDINBURGH | 11 | MOSCOW | 19 | TEHRAN | 30 |
| ATHENS | 2 | HELSINKI | 12 | MUMBAI | 20 | TIANJIN | 30 |
| ATLANTA | 3 | HONG KONG | 12 | MUNICH | 20 | TORONTO | 30 |
| BAGHDAD | 3 | ISTANBUL | 12 | NEW YORK | 21 | VIENNA | 31 |
| BANGKOK | 3 | JAKARTA | 13 | OSAKA | 22 | WARSAW | 31 |
| BARCELONA | 4 | JERUSALEM | 13 | OSLO | 22 | WASHINGTON | 32 |
| BEIJING | 4 | JOHANNESBURG | 13 | PARIS | 23 | WELLINGTON | 32 |
| BERLIN | 5 | KARACHI | 14 | PRAGUE | 24 | INDEX | 33–39 |
| BOSTON | 6 | LAGOS | 14 | RIO DE JANEIRO | 24 | | |
| BRUSSELS | 6 | LISBON | 14 | ROME | 25 | WORLD CITIES | |
| BUDAPEST | 7 | LONDON | 15 | SAN FRANCISCO | 25 | SATELLITE IMAGES | |
| BUENOS AIRES | 7 | LOS ANGELES | 16 | ST PETERSBURG | 26 | CAPE TOWN | 40 |
| CAIRO | 7 | LIMA | 16 | SANTIAGO | 26 | CHICAGO | 41 |
| CALCUTTA (KOLKATA) | 8 | MADRID | 17 | SÃO PAULO | 26 | KARACHI | 42 |
| CANTON | 8 | MANILA | 17 | SEOUL | 26 | LONDON | 43 |
| CAPE TOWN | 8 | MELBOURNE | 17 | SHANGHAI | 27 | NEW YORK | 44 |
| CHICAGO | 9 | MEXICO CITY | 18 | SINGAPORE | 27 | SAN FRANCISCO | 45 |
| COPENHAGEN | 10 | MIAMI | 18 | STOCKHOLM | 28 | SANTIAGO | 46 |
| DELHI | 10 | MILAN | 18 | SYDNEY | 28 | SYDNEY | 47 |
| DUBLIN | 11 | MONTRÉAL | 19 | TOKYO | 29 | TOKYO | 48 |

## CITY MAPS

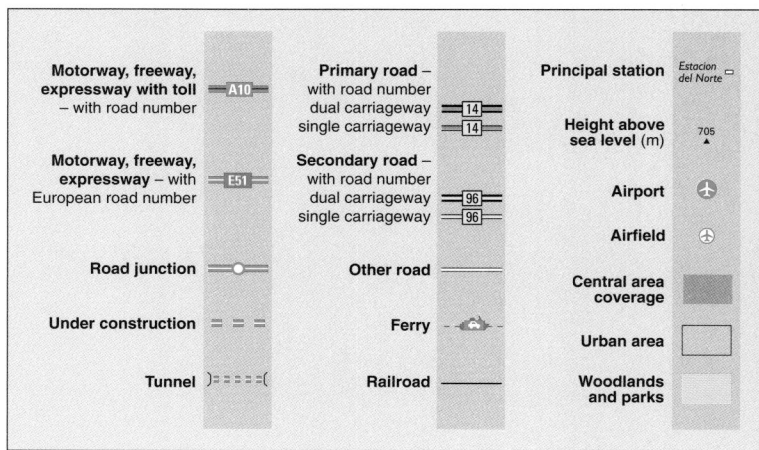

## CENTRAL AREA MAPS

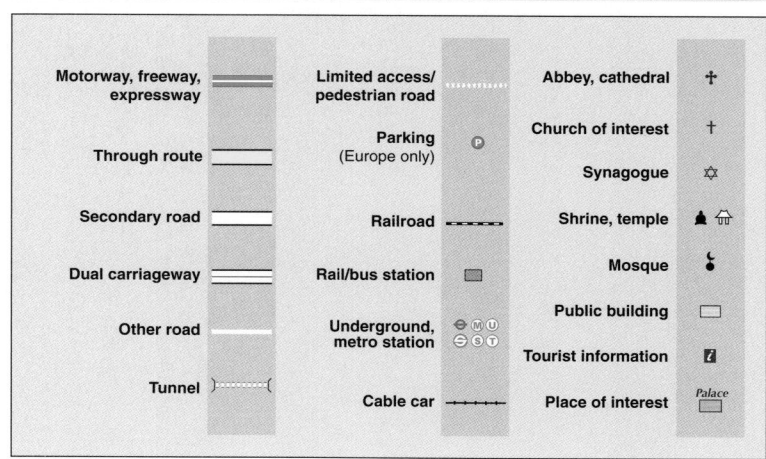

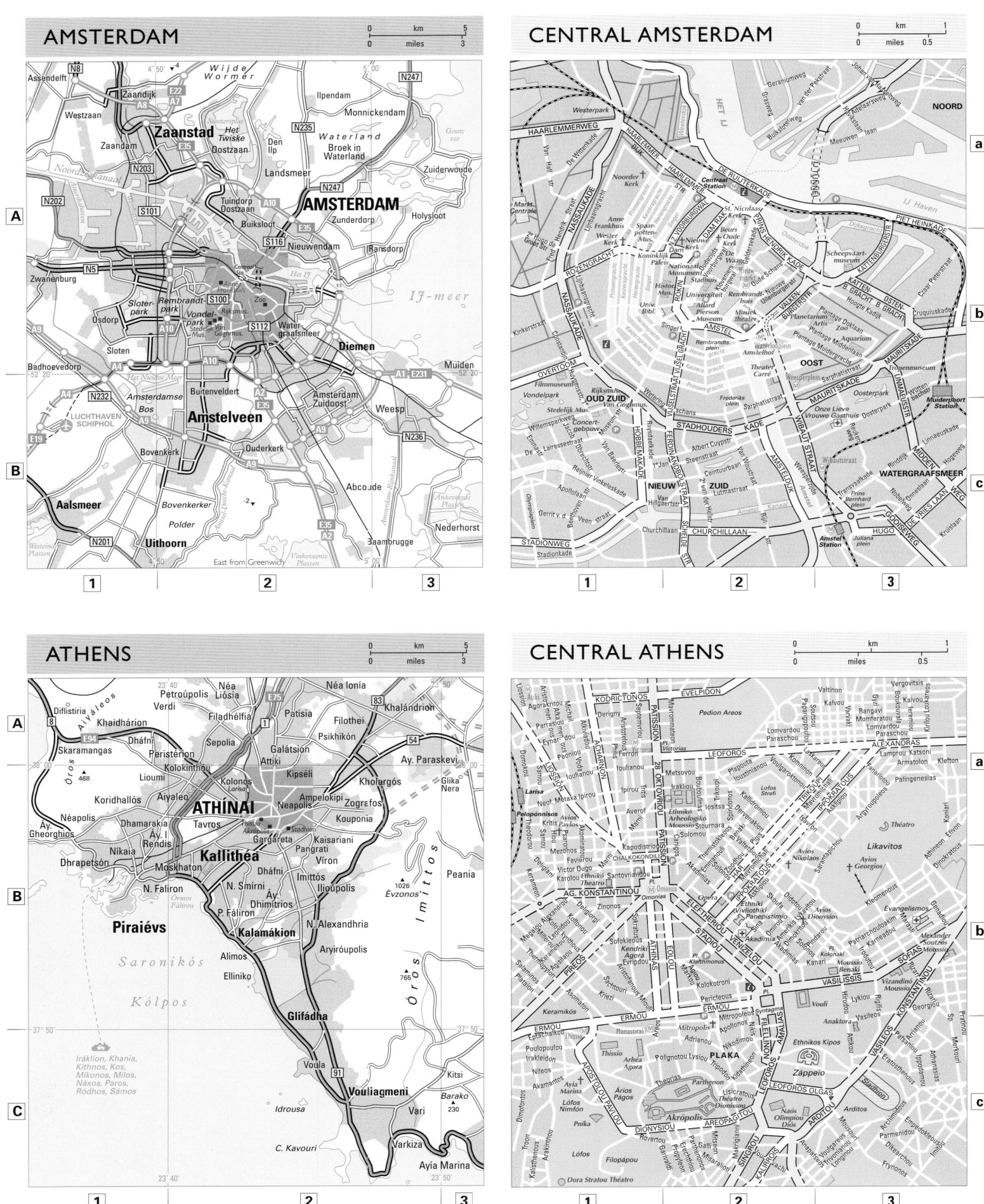

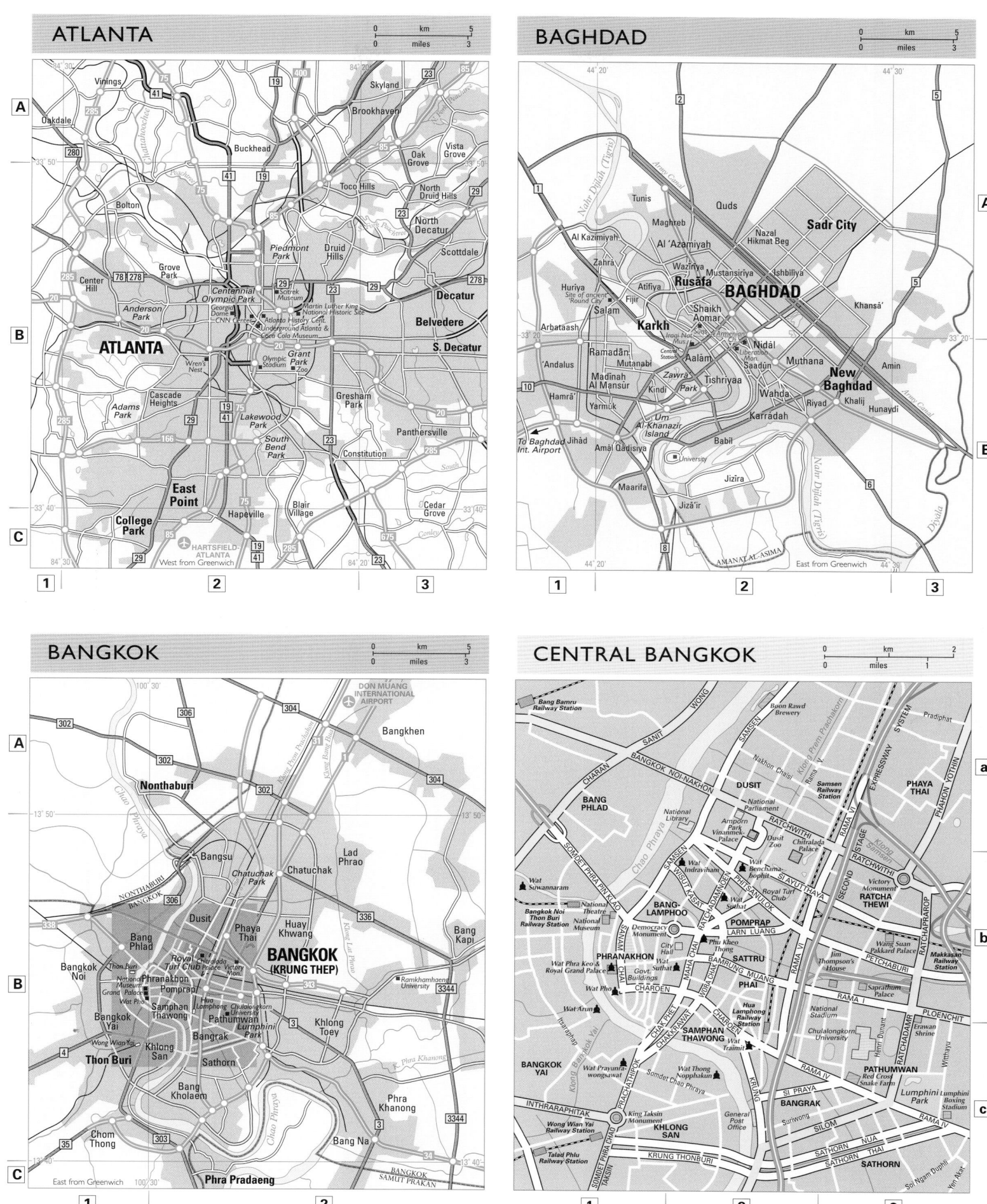

## ATLANTA

km 0 5
miles 0 3

Vinings · Oakdale · Buckhead · Skyland · Brookhaven · Oak Grove · Vista Grove · North Druid Hills · Bolton · Toco Hills · Scottdale · Piedmont Park · Druid Hills · North Decatur · Grove Park · Center Hill · Anderson Park · Centennial Olympic Park · Scitrek Museum · Georgia Dome · CNN Center · Atlanta History Cent. · Martin Luther King National Historic Site · Decatur · Belvedere · S. Decatur · **ATLANTA** · Underground Atlanta & Coca Cola Museum · Wren's Nest · Olympic Stadium · Grant Park Zoo · Gresham Park · Cascade Heights · Adams Park · Lakewood Park · South Bend Park · Panthersville · **East Point** · Hapeville · Blair Village · Constitution · Cedar Grove · **College Park** · HARTSFIELD-ATLANTA · Conley

West from Greenwich

## BAGHDAD

km 0 5
miles 0 3

Tunis · Quds · Maghreb · Al Kazimiyah · Nazal Hikmat Beg · **Sadr City** · Al 'Azamiyah · Zahrā · Mustansiriya · Ishbiliyá · Huriya · Atifiya · **Rusāfa** · Site of ancient Round City · Fijir · Iraqi Nat. Mus. · **BAGHDAD** · Khansá · Salam · Shaikh Aomar · Armenian · Arbataash · Central Station · Liberation Mon. · Nidāl · **Karkh** · Aalām · Saadūn · Muthana · Amin · Ramadān · Mutanabi · Zawrā Park · Tishriyaa · **New Baghdad** · 'Andalus · Kindi · Wahda · Madinah Al Mansūr · Hamrā · Yarmūk · Karradah · Riyad · Khalij · Hunaydi · To Baghdad Jihād Int. Airport · Um Al-Khanazir Island · Amāl Qādisiya · Babil · University · Maarifa · Jizira · Jizā'ir · Nahr Dijlah (Tigris) · Diyala

East from Greenwich

AMANAT AL-ASIMA

## BANGKOK

km 0 5
miles 0 3

DON MUANG INTERNATIONAL AIRPORT · Bangkhen · **Nonthaburi** · Bangsu · Lad Phrao · Bangsu · Chatuchak Park · Chatuchak · Huay Khwang · Bang Kapi · **Dusit** · Phaya Thai · **BANGKOK (KRUNG THEP)** · Royal Turf Club · Parusda Palace · Victory Mon. · National Museum · **Phranakhon** · Hua Lamphong · Chulalongkorn University · Ramkhamhaeng University · Bangkok Noi · Grand Palace · **Pomprap** · Wat Pho · **Samphan Thawong** · Pathumwan · Lumphini Park · **Bangrak** · Khlong Toey · **Bangkok Yai** · Wong Wian Yai · Khlong San · **Sathorn** · **Thon Buri** · Bang Kholaem · Phra Khanong · Phra Khanong · Chom Thong · Bang Na

East from Greenwich

BANGKOK SAMUT PRAKAN · **Phra Pradaeng**

## CENTRAL BANGKOK

km 0 2
miles 0 1

Bang Bamru Railway Station · Boon Rawd Brewery · Pradiphat · Bang Phlad · **DUSIT** · Samsen Railway Station · **PHAYA THAI** · National Library · National Parliament · Amporn Park Vinamnek Palace · Dusit Zoo · Chitralada Palace · **RATCHA THEWI** · Wat Suwannaram · Wat Indraviham · Wat Benchamabophit · Royal Turf Club · Victory Monument · Bangkok Noi Thon Buri Railway Station · National Theatre · National Museum · **BANG LAMPHOO** · Democracy Monument · City Hall · **POMPRAP** · Phu Kheo Thong · Wang Suan Pakkard Palace · Jim Thompson's House · Makkasan Railway Station · **PHRANAKHON** · Wat Phra Keo & Royal Grand Palace · Govt. Buildings · Wat Suthat · **SATTRU** · **PHAI** · Saprathum Palace · Wat Pho · Wat Arun · **BAMRUNG MUANG** · Hua Lamphong Railway Station · National Stadium · Chulalongkorn University · Erawan Shrine · **SAMPHAN THAWONG** · Wat Traimit · **BANGKOK YAI** · Wat Prayumwongsawat · Wat Thong Nopphakun · National Museum · **PATHUMWAN** · Red Cross Snake Farm · King Taksin Monument · General Post Office · **BANGRAK** · Lumphini Park · Lumphini Boxing Stadium · Wong Wian Yai Railway Station · **KHLONG SAN** · **SATHORN** · Talad Phlu Railway Station

## BARCELONA

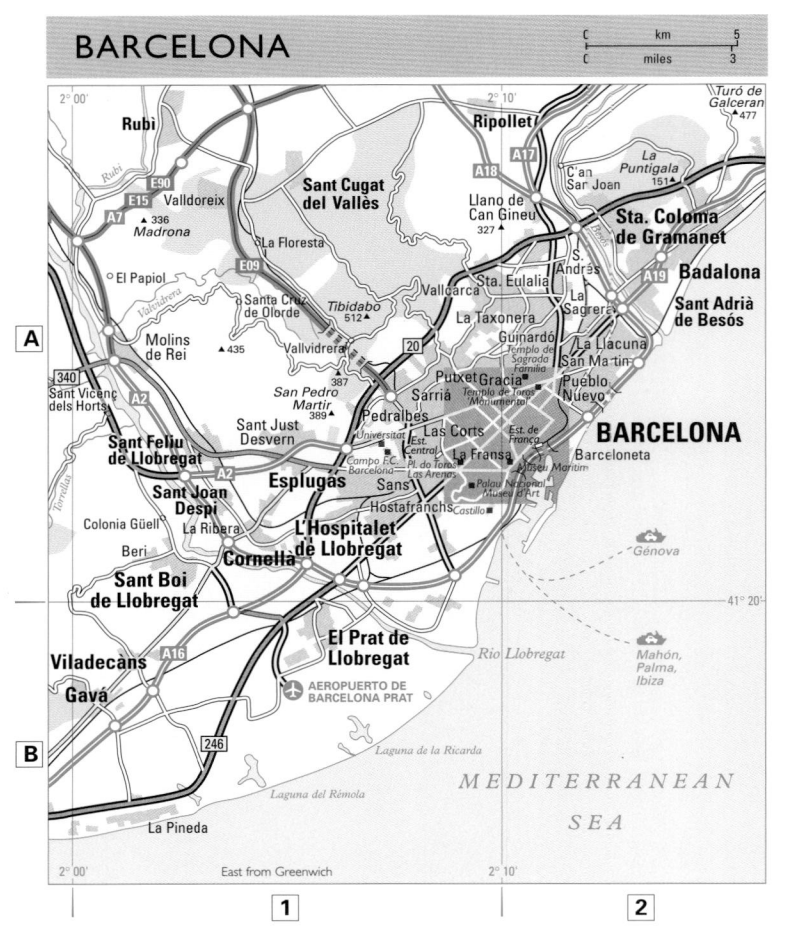

## CENTRAL BARCELONA

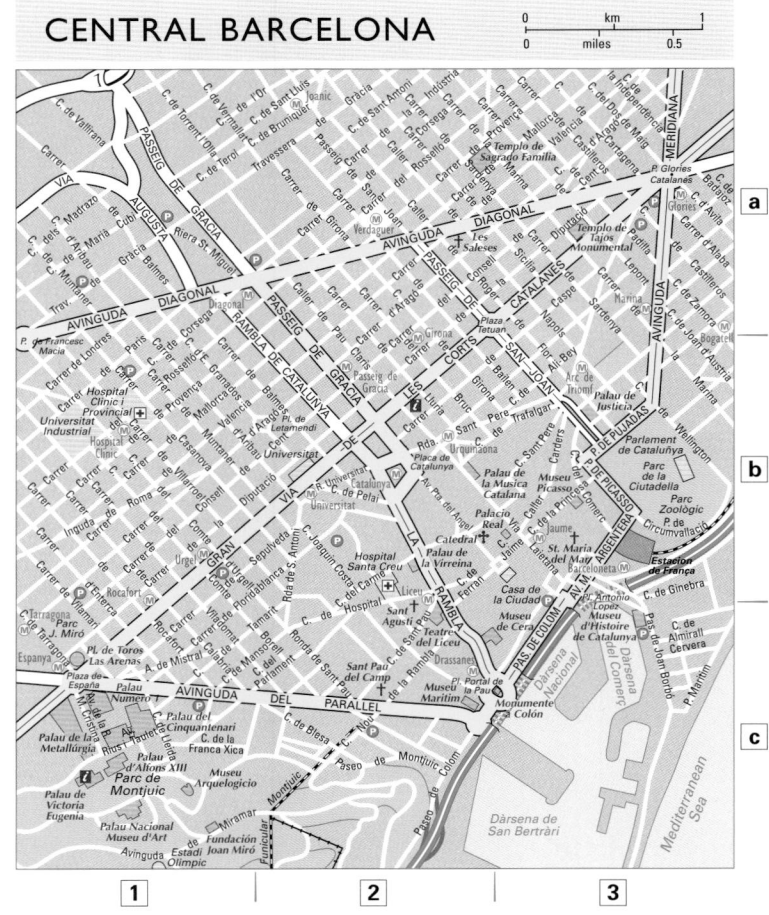

## BEIJING

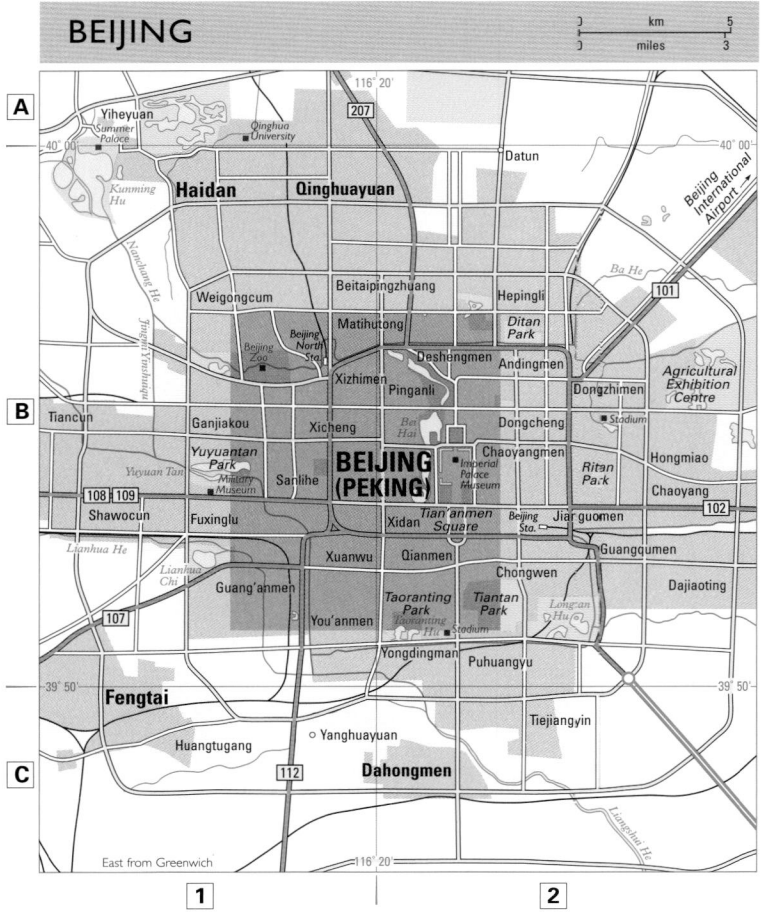

## CENTRAL BEIJING

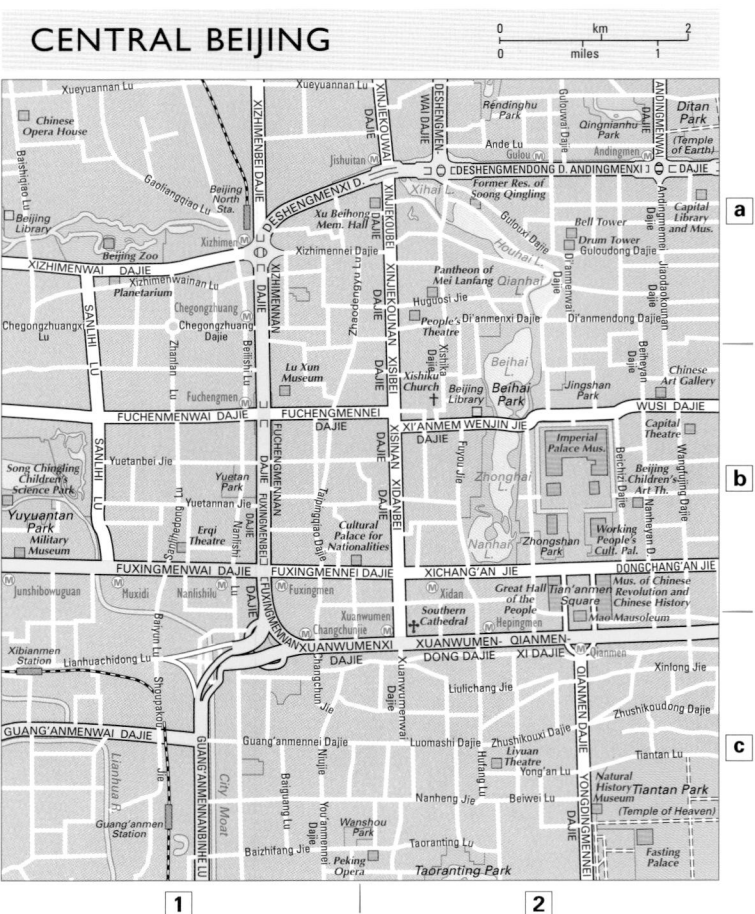

# BERLIN

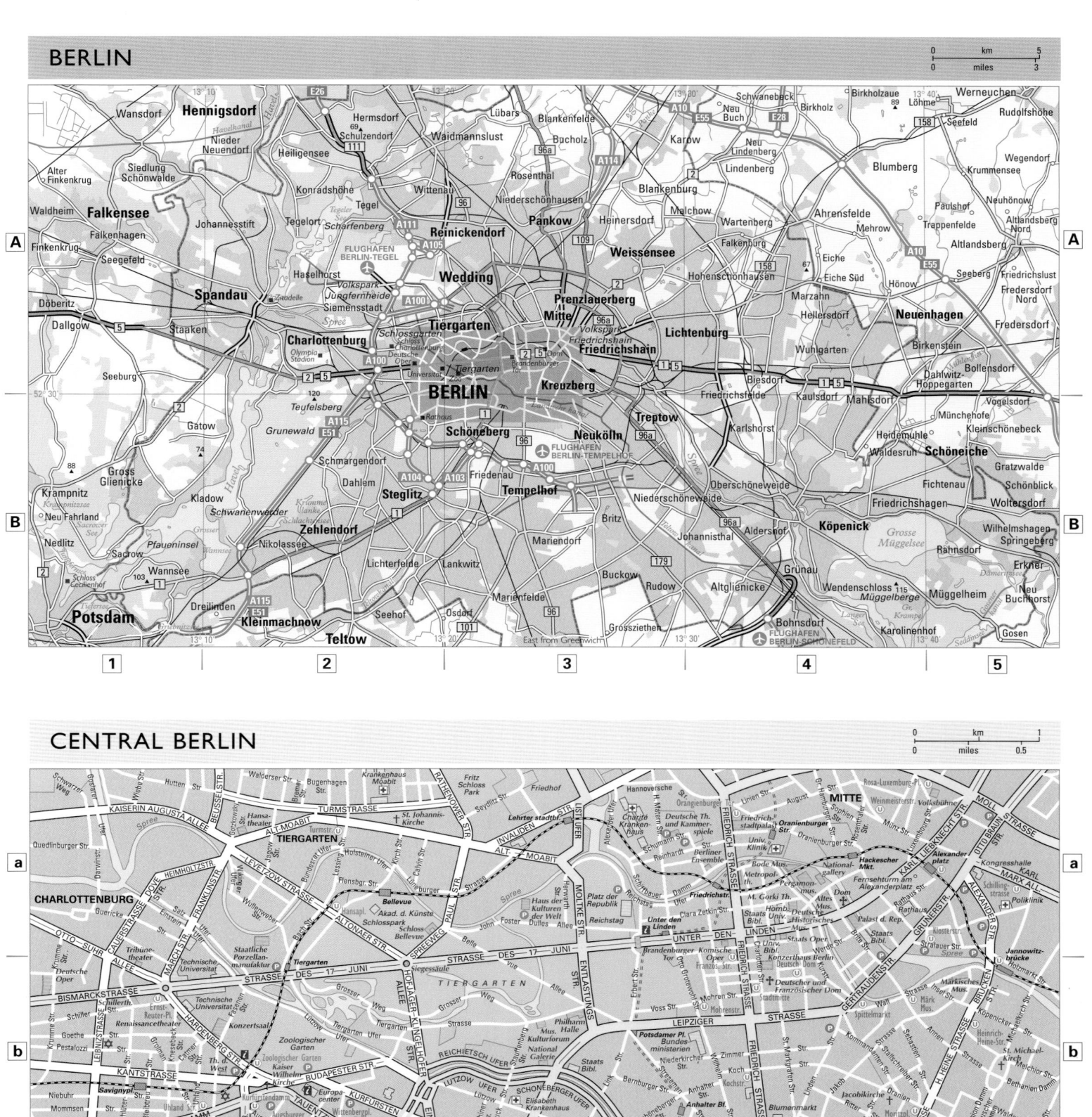

# CENTRAL BERLIN

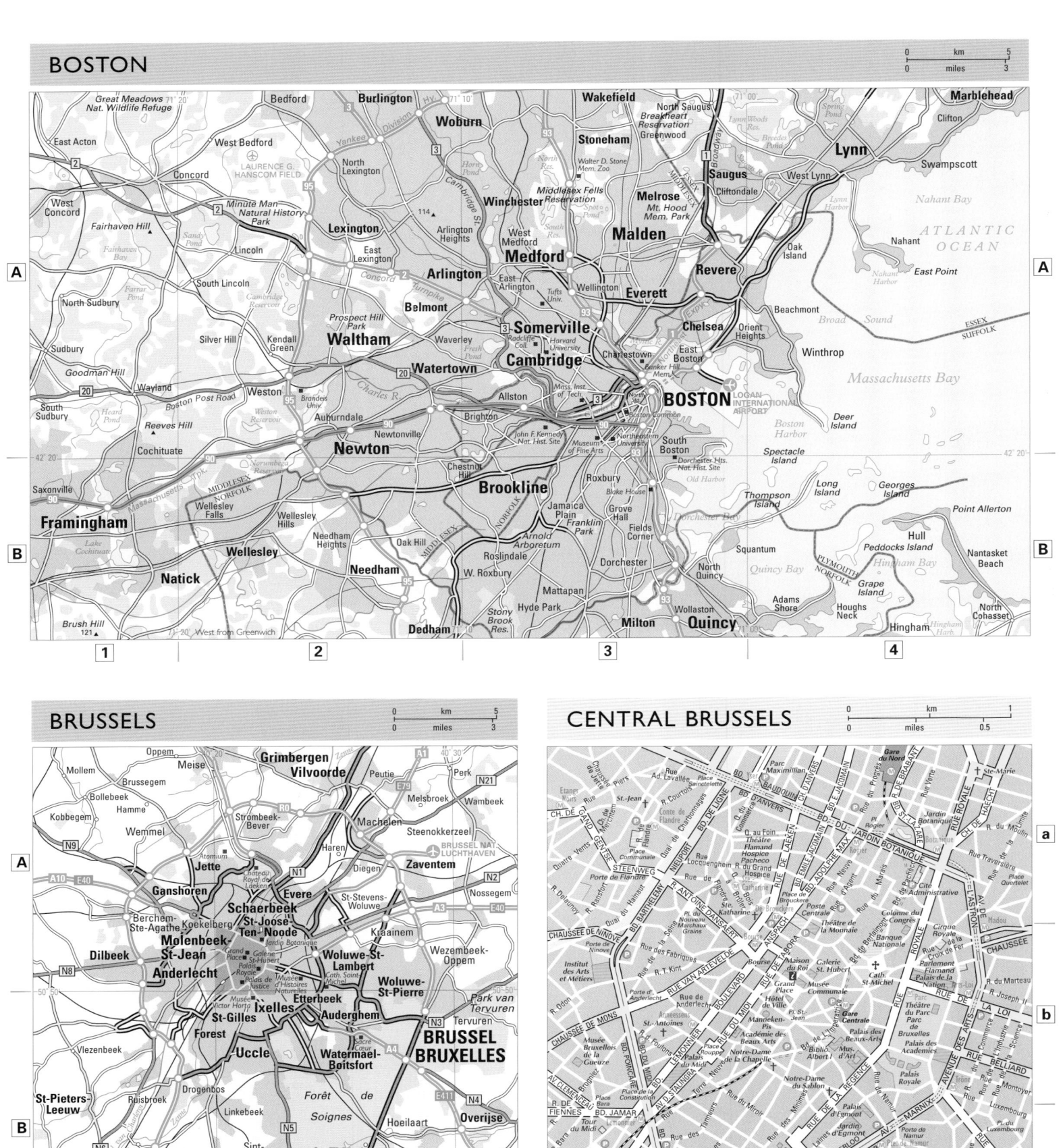

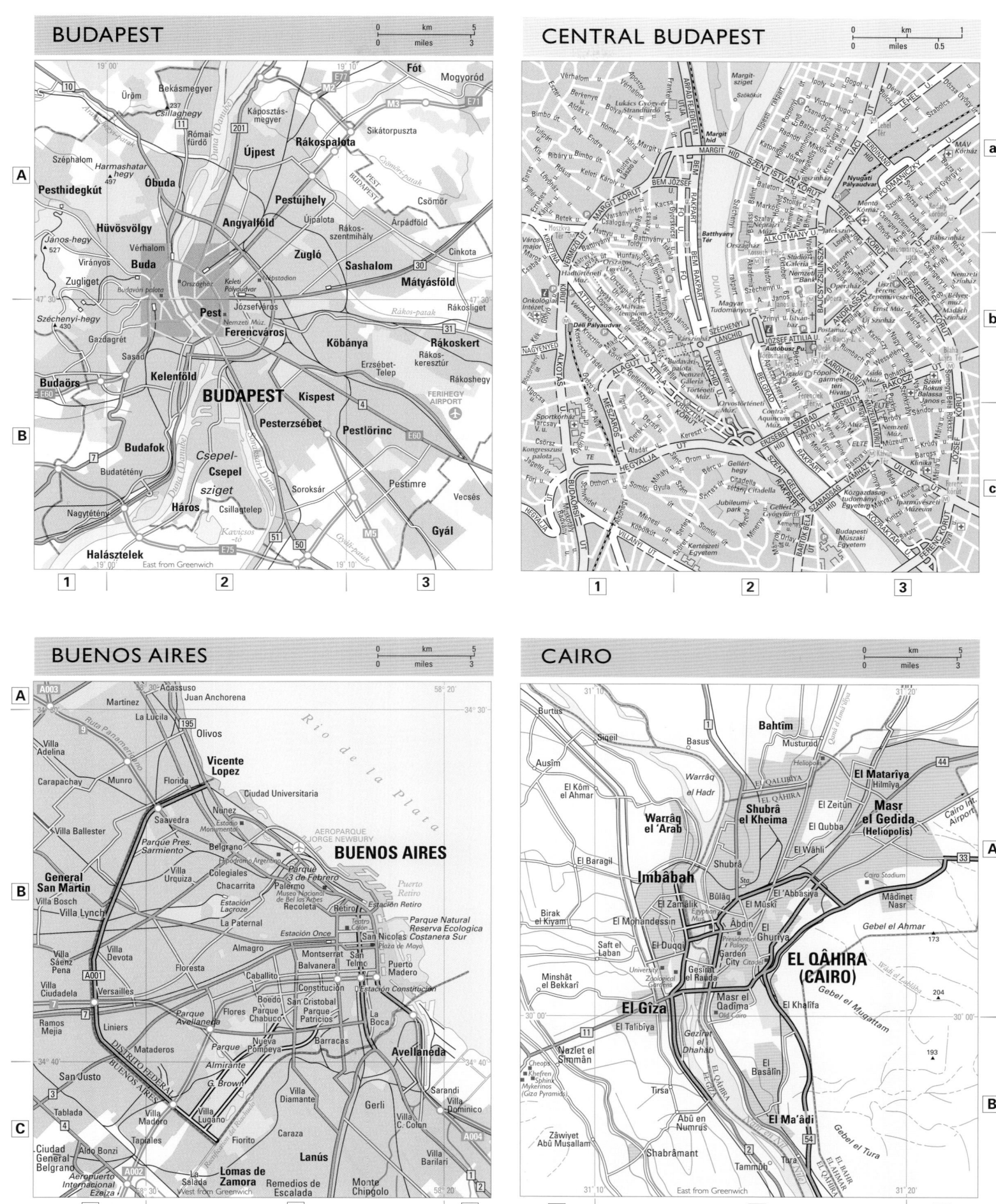

## CALCUTTA (KOLKATA)

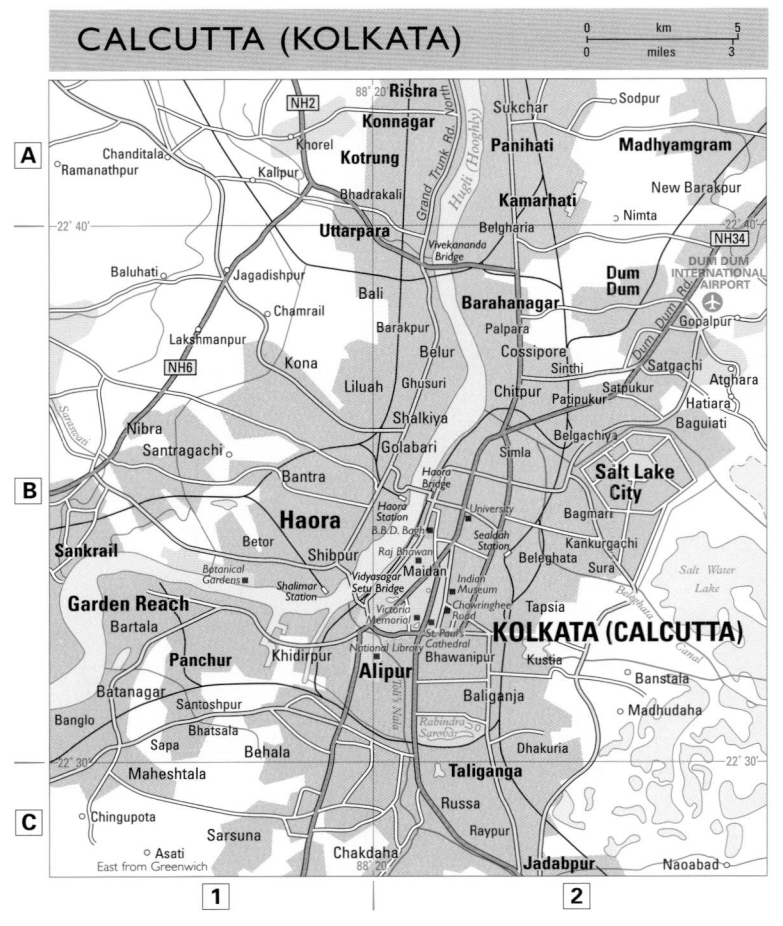

## CANTON

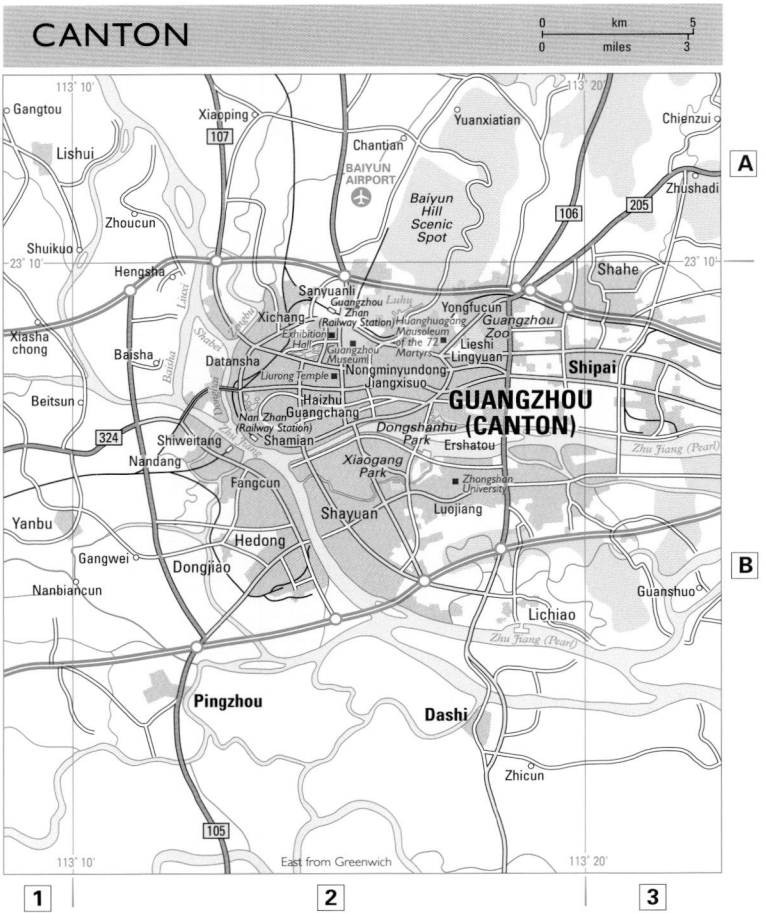

## CAPE TOWN

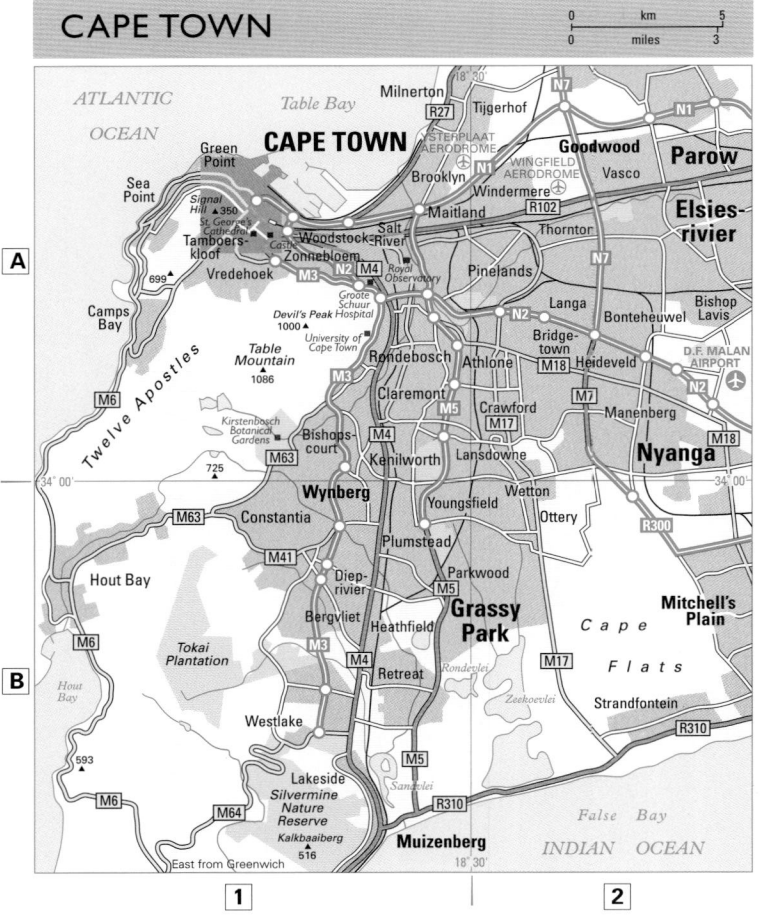

## CENTRAL CAPE TOWN

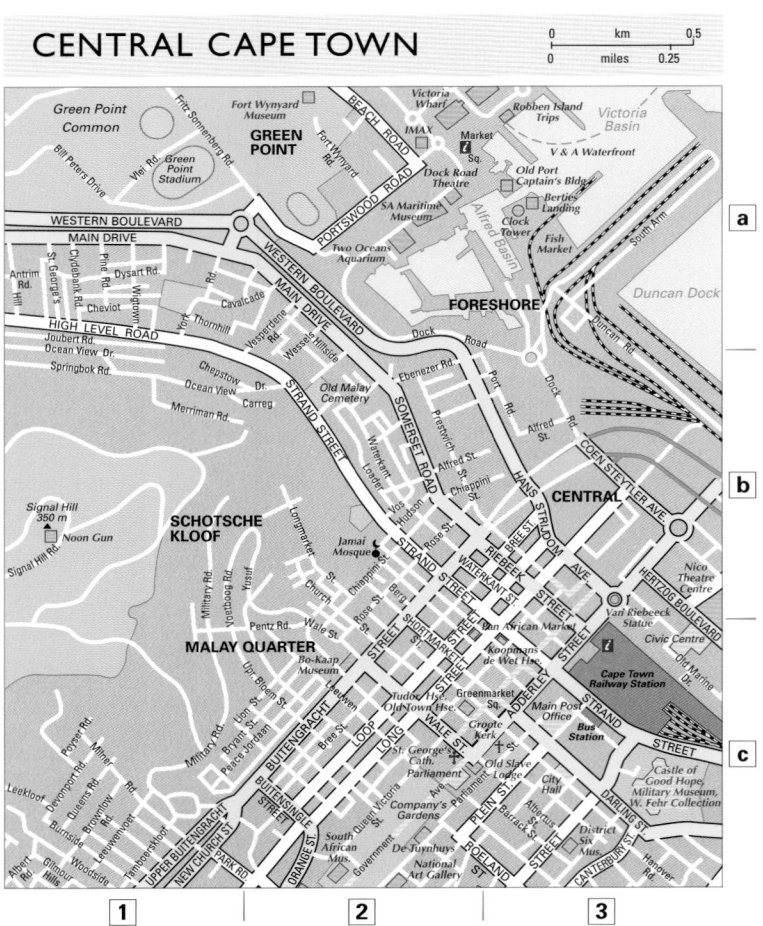

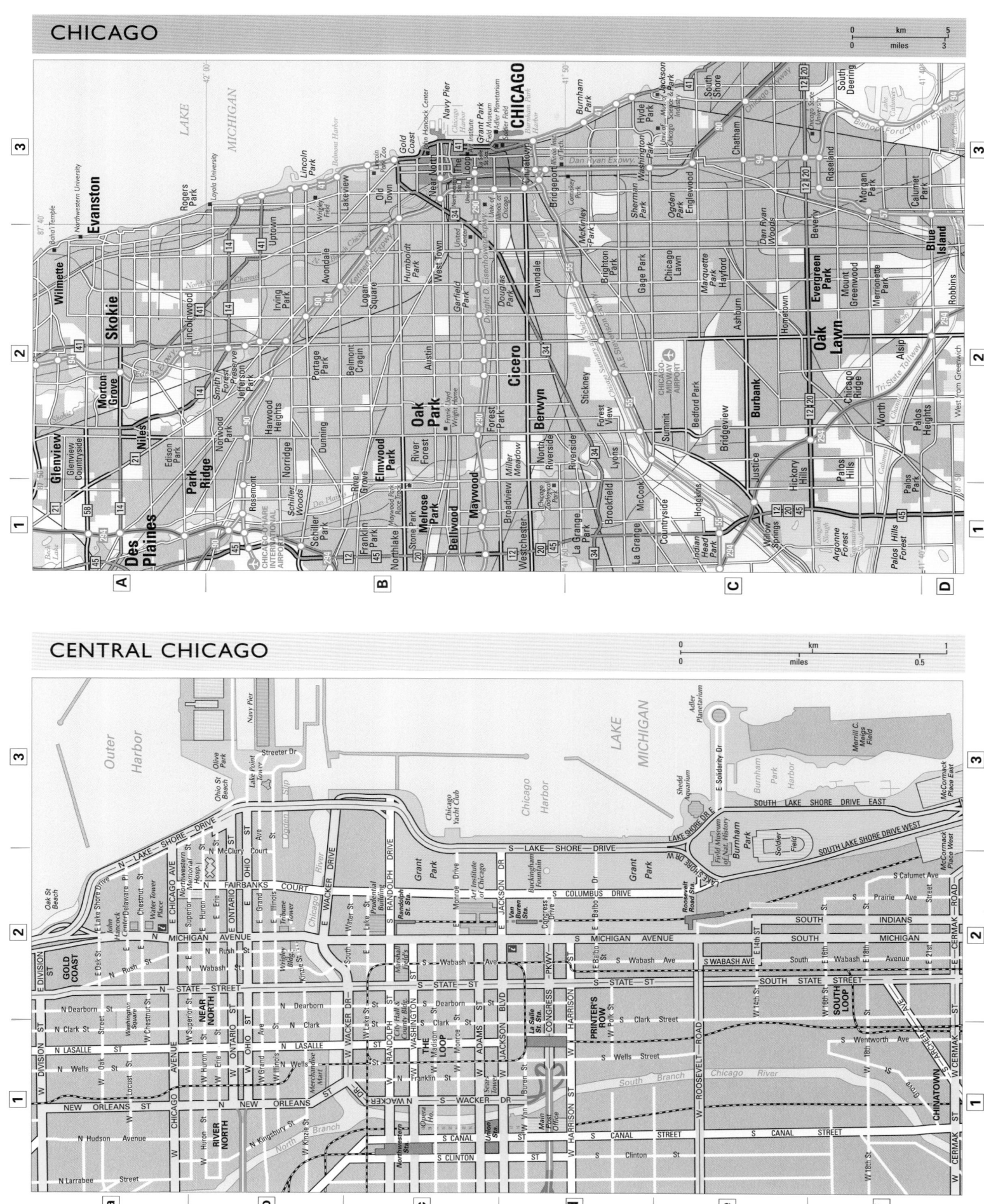

## CHICAGO

0 km 5
0 miles 3

A    B    C    D

## CENTRAL CHICAGO

0 km 1
0 miles 0.5

a    b    c    d    e    f

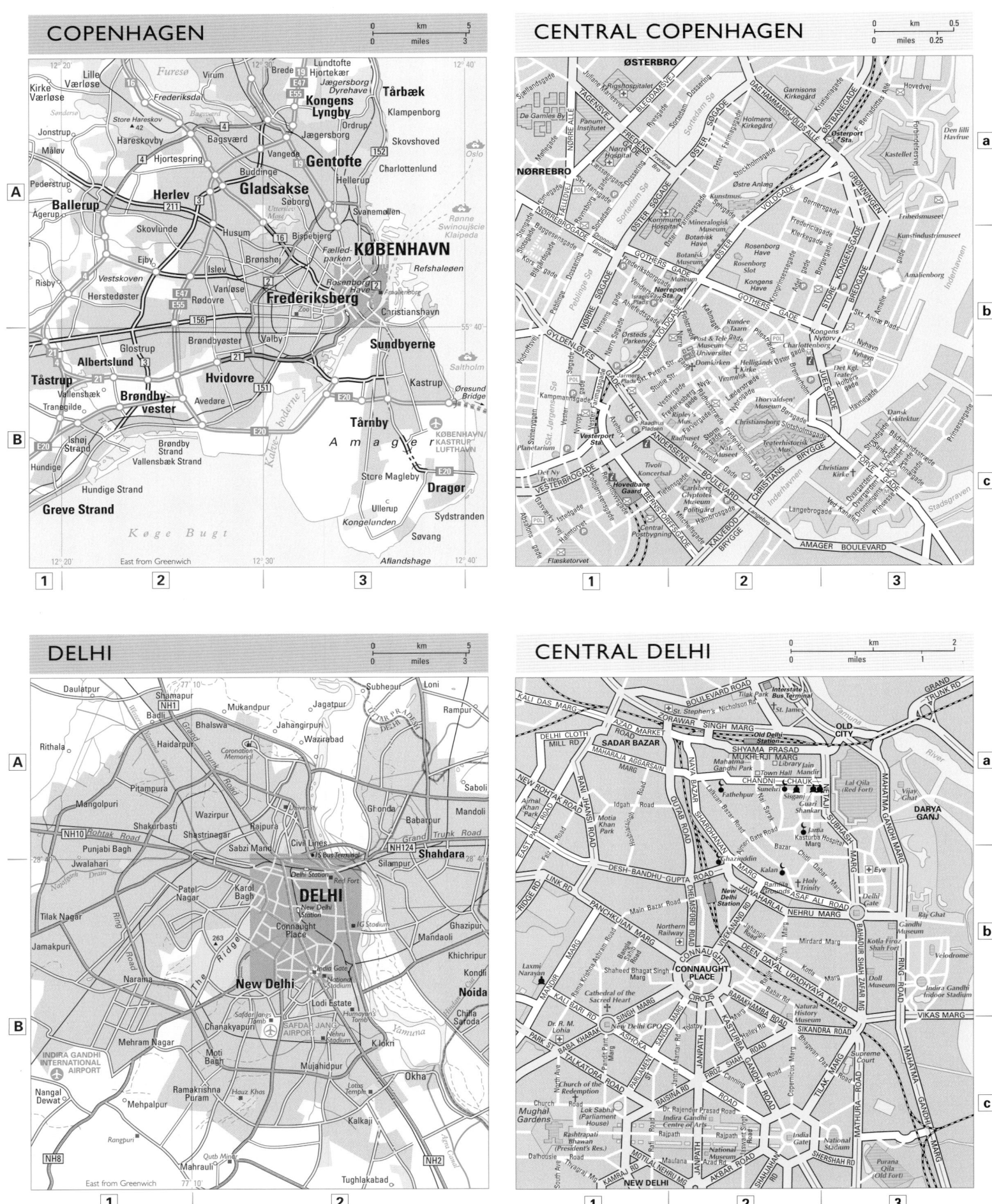

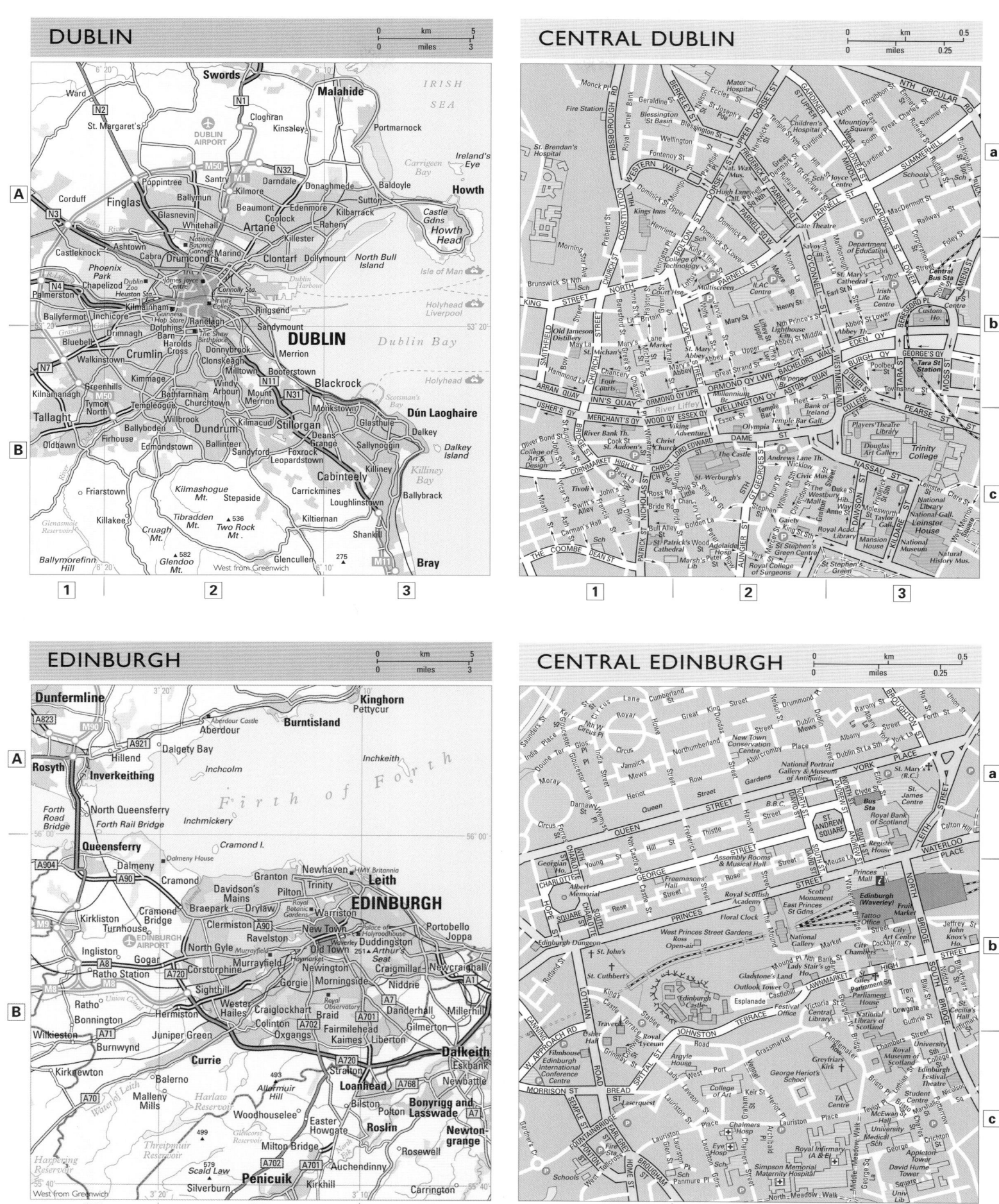

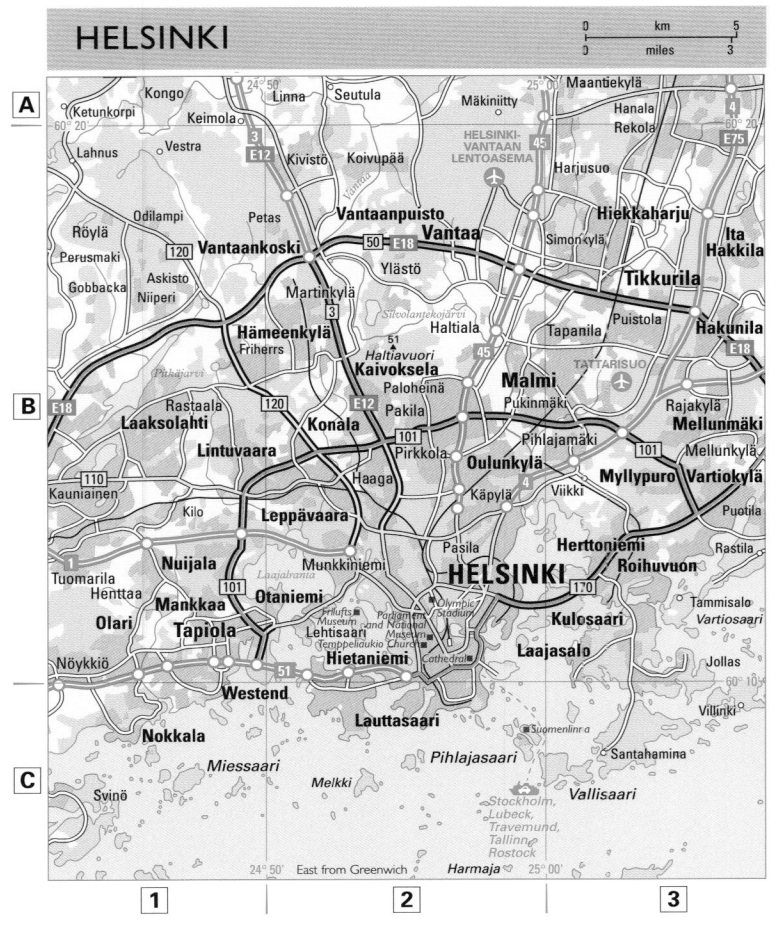

**HELSINKI**

**ISTANBUL**

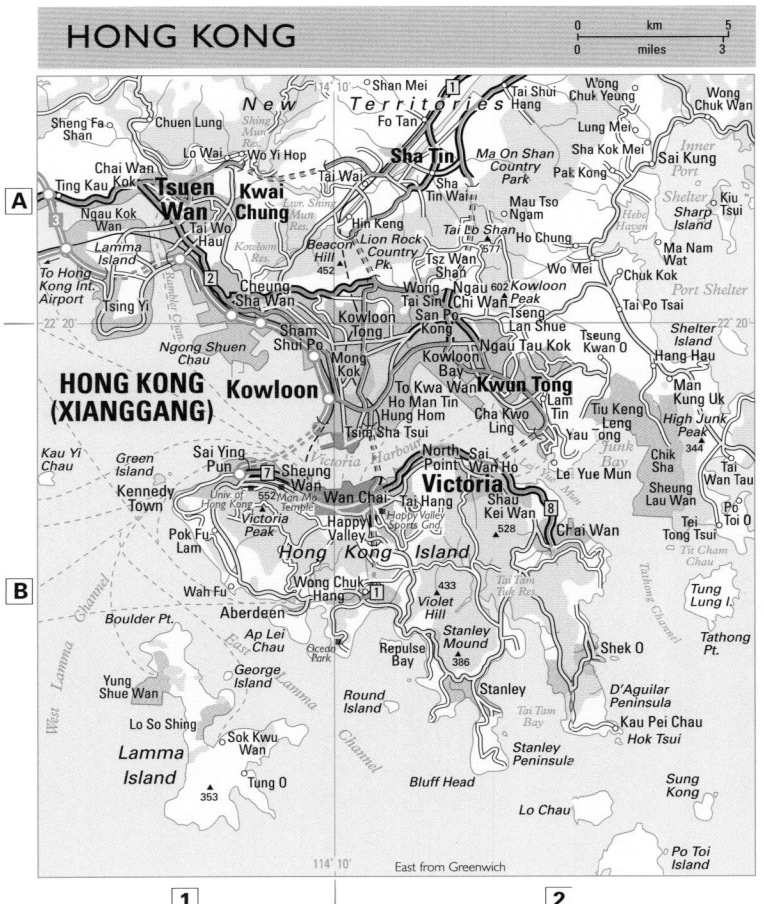

**HONG KONG**

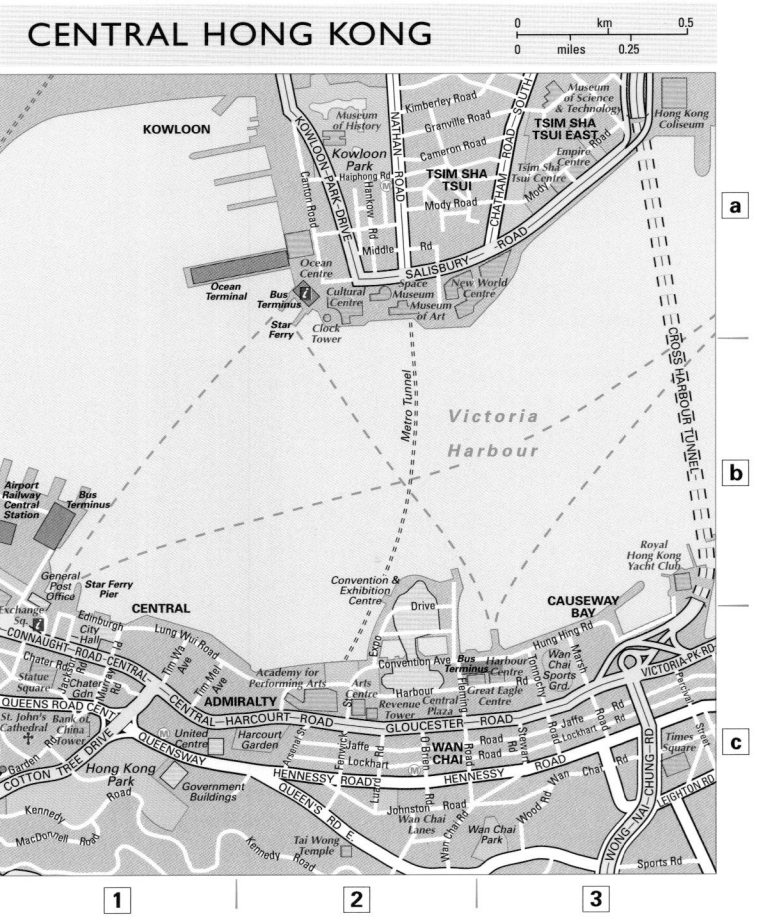

**CENTRAL HONG KONG**

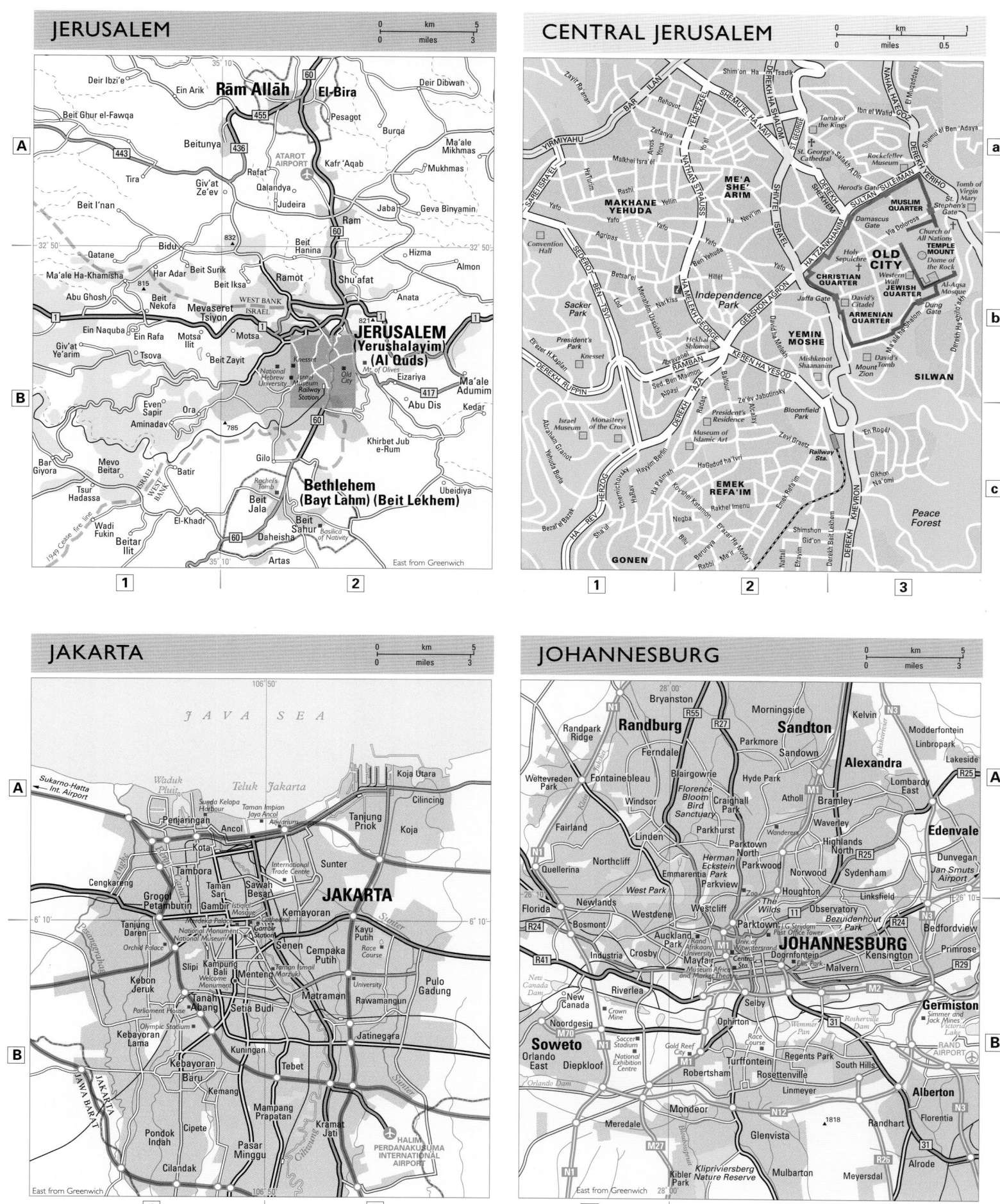

## JERUSALEM

Deir Ibzi'e · Ein Arik · **Rām Allāh** · **El-Bira** · Deir Dibwan

Beit Ghur el-Fawqa · 455 · Pesagot · Burqa

Beitunya · 436 · ATAROT AIRPORT · Kafr 'Aqab · Ma'ale Mikhmas

443 · Tira · Giv'at Ze'ev · Rafat · Qalandya · Mukhmas

Beit I'nan · Judeira · Jaba · Geva Binyamin

Bidu · 832 · Ram · 60

Qatane · Beit Hanina · Hizma · Almon

Ma'ale Ha-Khamisha · Har Adar · Beit Surik · Beit Iksa · Ramot · Shu'afat · Anata

Abu Ghosh · Beit Nekofa · Mevaseret Tsiyon · WEST BANK ISRAEL · Ramot · Anata

Ein Naquba · Ein Rafa · Motsa Ilit · 1

Giv'at Ye'arim · Tsova · Motsa · **JERUSALEM (Yerushalayim) (Al Quds)** · 1

Even Sapir · Ora · Beit Zayit · Knesset · National Hebrew University · Israel Museum Railway Station · Old City · Mt. of Olives · Eizariya · Ma'ale Adumim

Aminadav · 785 · Abu Dis · Kedar · 417

Bar Giyora · Mevo Beitar · Batir · Khirbet Jub e-Rum

Tsur Hadassa · Beit Jala · Gilo · Rachel's Tomb · **Bethlehem (Bayt Lahm) (Beit Lekhem)** · Ubeidiya

Beitar Illit · Wadi Fukin · El-Khadr · Beit Sahur · 60 · Basilica of Nativity

1949 Cease fire line · 60 · Daheisha · Artas

East from Greenwich

## CENTRAL JERUSALEM

MAKHANE YEHUDA · ME'A SHE'ARIM · MUSLIM QUARTER · **OLD CITY** · TEMPLE MOUNT · Dome of the Rock · Al-Aqsa Mosque · CHRISTIAN QUARTER · Holy Sepulchre · ARMENIAN QUARTER · JEWISH QUARTER · Western Wall · David's Citadel · Jaffa Gate · Damascus Gate · Herod's Gate · St. Stephen's Gate · Dung Gate

Tomb of the Kings · St. George's Cathedral · Rockefeller Museum · Tomb of Virgin Mary · Church of All Nations

Convention Hall · Independence Park · Sacker Park · President's Park · Knesset · Hekhal Shlomo · YEMIN MOSHE · Mount Zion · SILWAN

Israel Museum · Monastery of the Cross · President's Residence · Museum of Islamic Art · Bloomfield Park · Railway Sta. · En Rogel

EMEK REFA'IM · Peace Forest

GONEN

## JAKARTA

*J A V A  S E A*

Waduk Pluit · Teluk Jakarta · Koja Utara

Sukarno-Hatta Int. Airport · Penjaringan · Sunda Kelapa Harbour · Taman Impian Jaya Ancol · Aquarium · Cilincing

Ancol · Tanjung Priok · Koja

Kota · Sunter

Cengkareng · Tambora · Taman Sari · Sawah Besar · International Trade Centre · **JAKARTA**

Grogol Petamburin · Gambir · Kemayoran

Tanjung Daren · National Monument National Museum · Istiqlal Mosque · Cathedral · Gambir Station · Kayu Putih · Race Course

Slipi · Kampung I Bali · Senen · Cempaka Putih

Kebon Jeruk · Orchid Palace · Menteng · Taman Ismail Marzuki · Pulo Gadung

Merdeka Palace · Welcome Monument · University · Rawamangun

Tanah Abang · Setia Budi · Matraman

Parliament House · Kebayoran Lama · Olympic Stadium · Kuningan · Tebet · Jatinegara

Kebayoran Baru · Kemang · Mampang Prapatan · Cipete · Kramat Jati

Pondok Indah · Pasar Minggu · HALIM PERDANAKUSUMA INTERNATIONAL AIRPORT

Cilandak

JAWA BARAT

East from Greenwich

## JOHANNESBURG

N1 · Bryanston · R55 · Morningside · Kelvin · N3

Randpark Ridge · **Randburg** · R27 · **Sandton** · Modderfontein · Linbropark

Ferndale · Parkmore · Sandown · Lakeside · R25

Weltevreden Park · Blairgowrie · Hyde Park · **Alexandra** · Lombardy East

Fairland · Windsor · Florence Bloom Bird Sanctuary · Craighall Park · Atholl · Bramley · **Edenvale**

Linden · Parkhurst · Highlands North · Waverley · Dunvegan · Jan Smuts Airport

Quellerina · Northcliff · Parktown North · Herman Eckstein Park · Parkwood · Norwood · Sydenham · Linksfield

West Park · Parkview · Zoo · Houghton · R25

Florida · Newlands · Westdene · Westcliff · The Wilds · Observatory · Bezuidenhout Park · N3 · Bedfordview

Bosmont · Auckland Park · Rand Afrikaans Univ. · Univ. of Witwatersrand · Parktown · Post Office Tower · 11 · R24 · Primrose

Industria · Crosby · Mayfair · **JOHANNESBURG** · Kensington · R29

New Canada · Riverlea · Central Sta. · Museum Africa and Market Theatre · Dogrnfontein · Malvern

Noordgesig · Crown Mine · Selby · M2 · **Germiston** · Simmer and Jack Mines

**Soweto** · Ophirton · Race Course · RAND AIRPORT

Orlando East · Soccer Stadium · Gold Reef City · Turffontein · Regents Park · South Hills · **Alberton**

Diepkloof · National Exhibition Centre · Robertsham · Rosettenville · N3

Linmeyer

Mondeor · 1818 · Glenvista · Randhart · Florentia

Meredale · N12

Klipriviersberg Nature Reserve · Mulbarton · Meyersdal · Alrode

N1 · Kibler Park

East from Greenwich

COPYRIGHT PHILIP'S

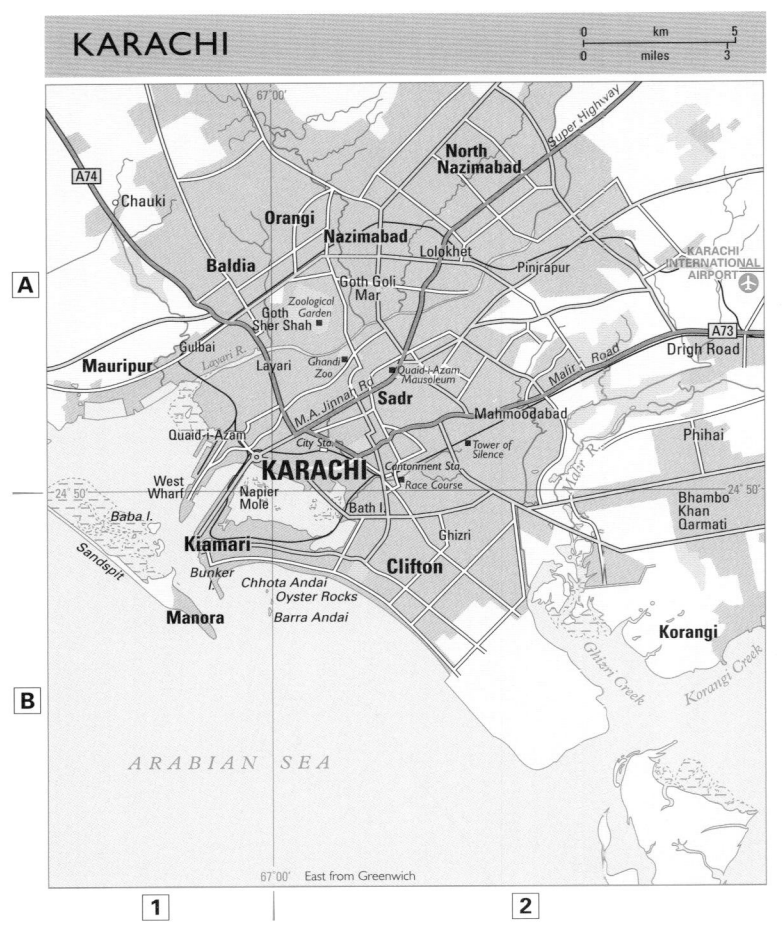

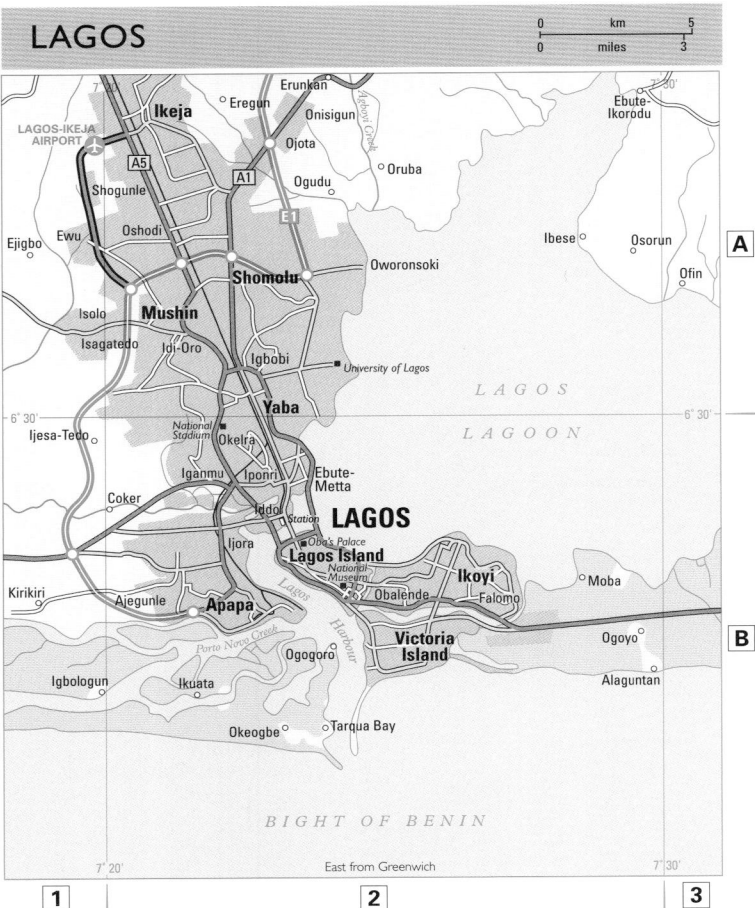

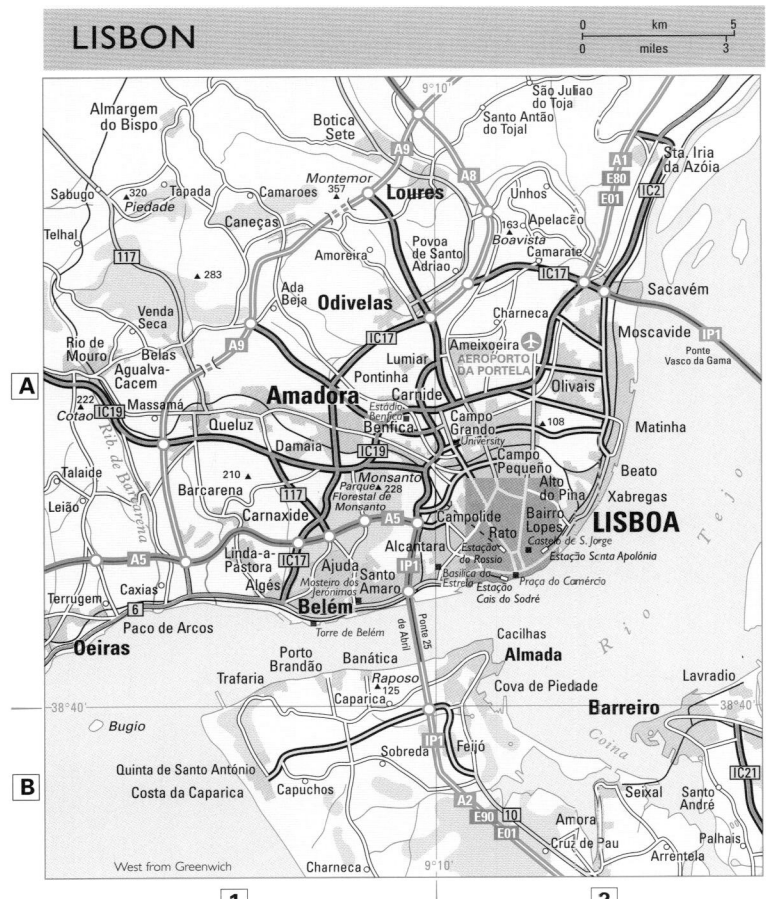

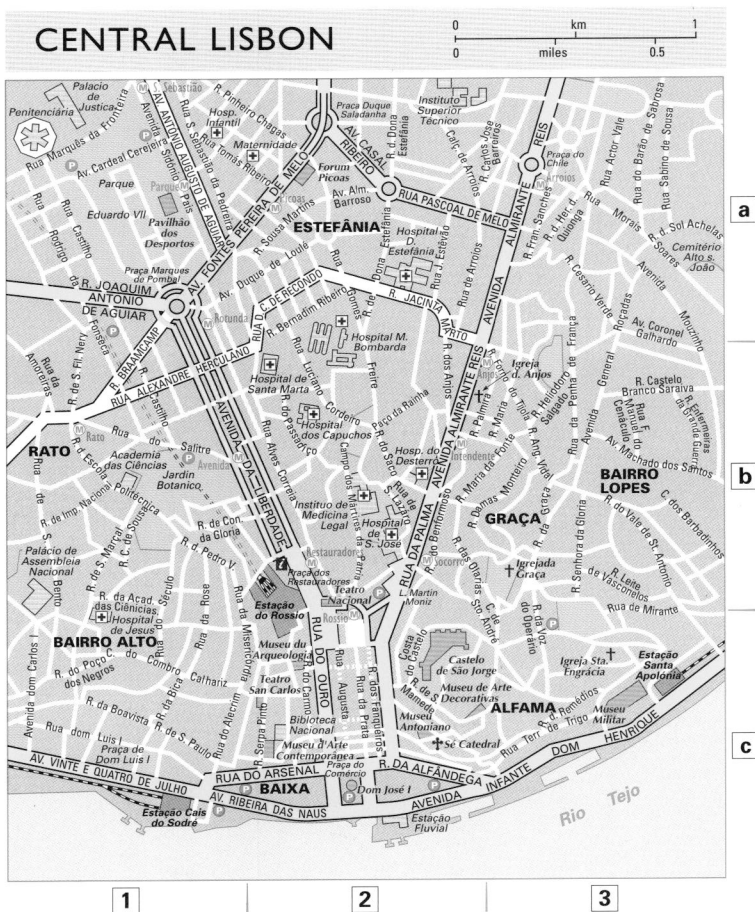

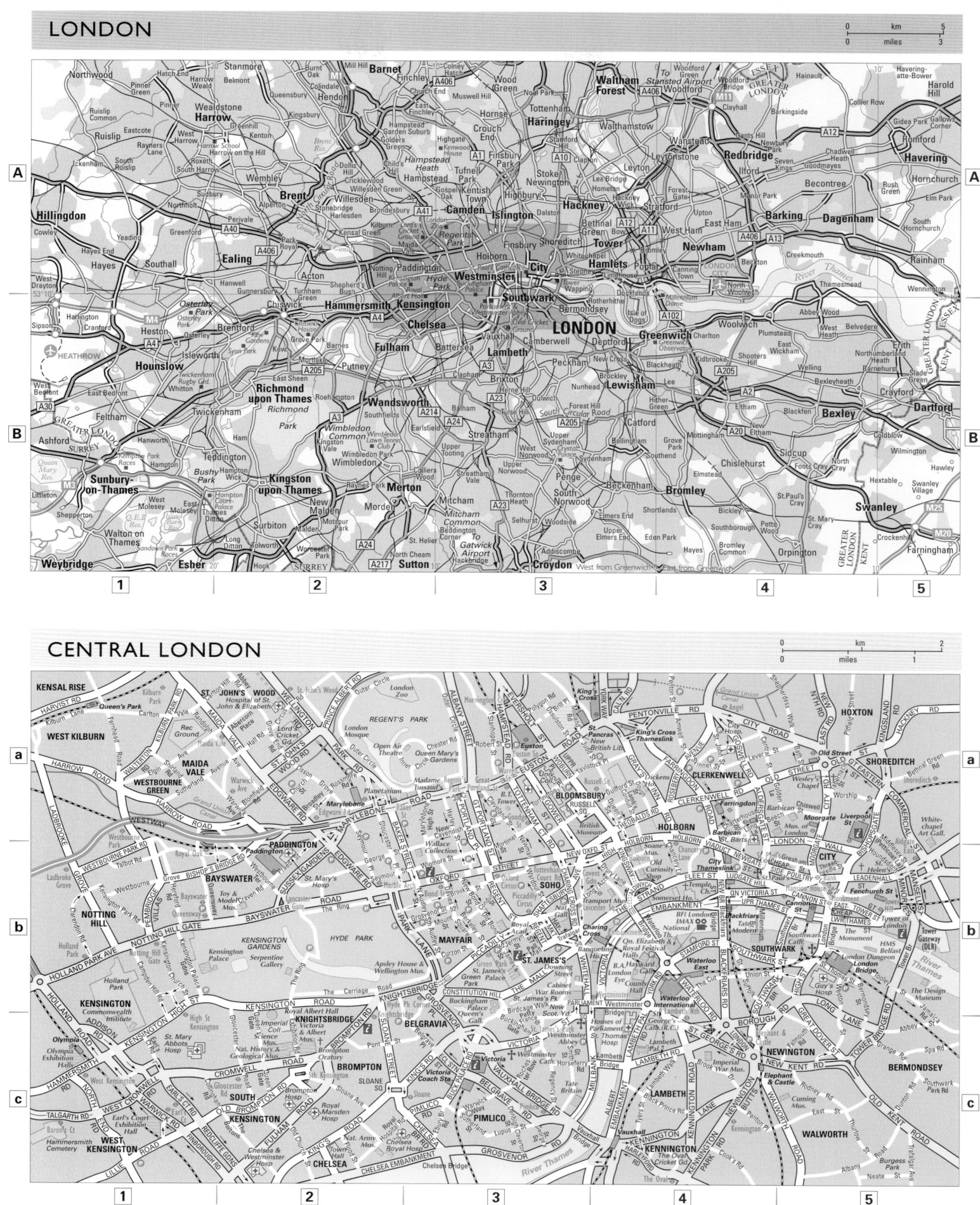

## LONDON

## CENTRAL LONDON

COPYRIGHT PHILIP'S

## LOS ANGELES

km 5
miles 3

Tarzana · 118° 30' · Sepulveda Flood Control Basin · Van Nuys · Burbank · Verdugo Mts. · San Rafael Hills · Altadena · San Gabriel Mts. · 34° 10'

101 · San Fernando Valley · 170 · North Hollywood · Flint Peak 575 · Rose Bowl · 210 · Pasadena · Sierra Madre · Colorado Fwy. · Monrovia

Encino · 216 · Sherman Oaks · Studio City · C.B.S. Fair Studios · 134 · Disney Studios · Warner Bros. Studios · Glendale · Glendale Galleria · 134 · Eagle Rock · California Inst. of Tech. · Arcadia

Encino Reservoir · 405 · Universal Studios · 101 · Cahuenga Peak 555 · Griffith Park · Zoo · 2 · Highland Park · Garvanza · South Pasadena · San Marino · 19 · Temple City

Santa · Monica · Mts. · Stone Canyon Reservoir · Beverly Glen · Franklin Reservoir · 459 · Hollywood Lake · Hollywood Bowl · Mann's Chinese Theatre · Hollywood Blvd. · Sunset Blvd. · Silver Lake Reservoir · Southwest Museum · El Sereno · Pasadena Fwy. · San Gabriel · Rosemead · 10

Bel Air · Beverly Hills · West Hollywood · Santa Monica Blvd. · Paramount Studios · L.A. County Art Museum · 2 · Dodger Stadium · Lincoln Heights · California State Univ. · Alhambra · Monterey Park · South San Gabriel · El Monte · South El Monte

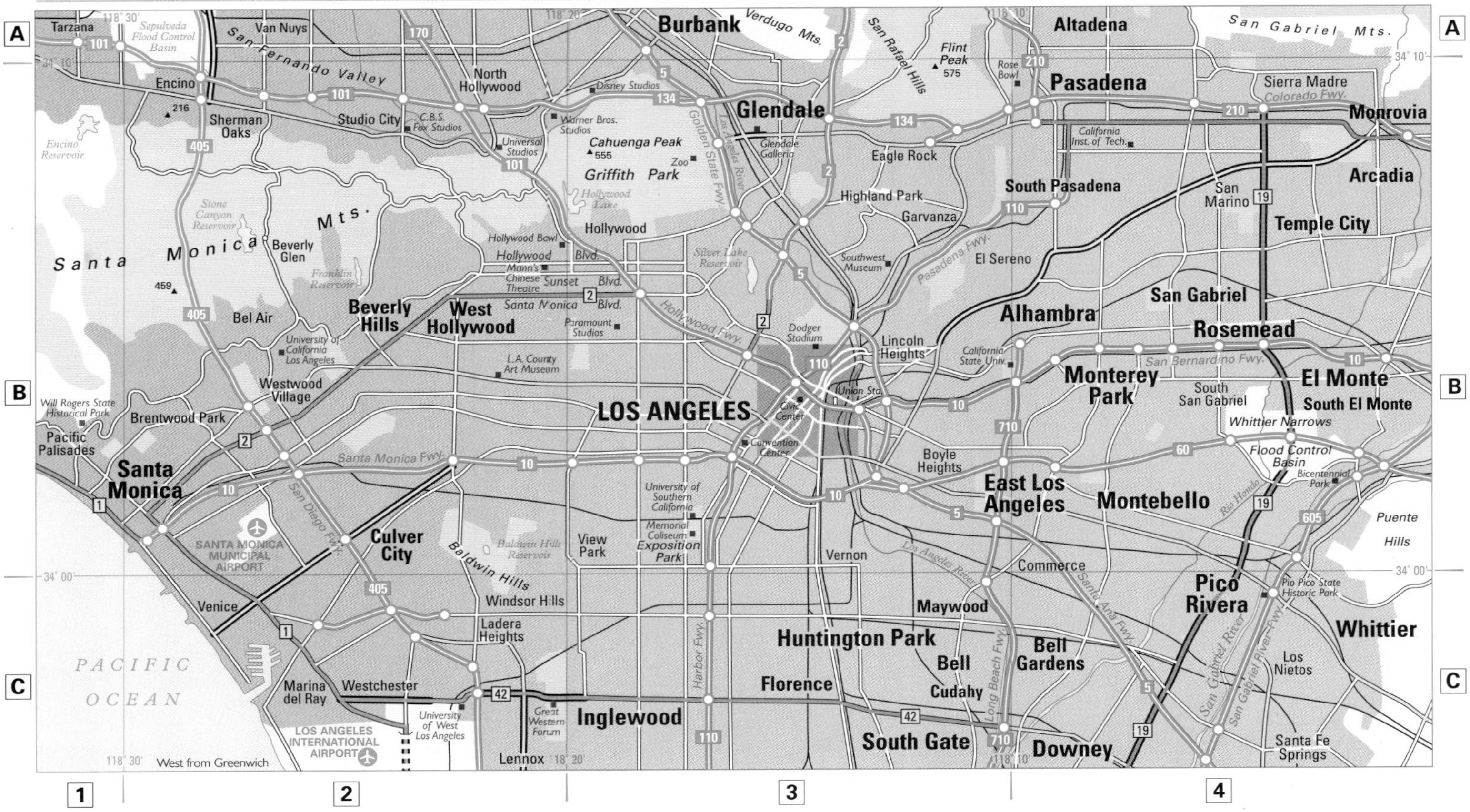

Westwood Village · University of California Los Angeles · Paramount Studios · 110 · LOS ANGELES · Union Sta. · Civic Center · 10 · Whittier Narrows · Flood Control Basin · 60

Wall Rogers State Historical Park · Brentwood Park · 2 · Santa Monica Fwy. · Convention Center · Boyle Heights · East Los Angeles · 710 · Bicentennial Park · Puente Hills

Pacific Palisades · Santa Monica · 10 · San Diego Fwy. · Baldwin Hills Reservoir · View Park · University of Southern California · Memorial Coliseum Exposition Park · Vernon · Montebello · Commerce · Rio Hondo · 605 · 34° 00'

SANTA MONICA MUNICIPAL AIRPORT · Culver City · 405 · Windsor Hills · Harbor Fwy. · Maywood · Commerce · Pico Rivera · Pio Pico State Historic Park

Venice · 1 · Ladera Heights · Huntington Park · Bell · Bell Gardens · Whittier

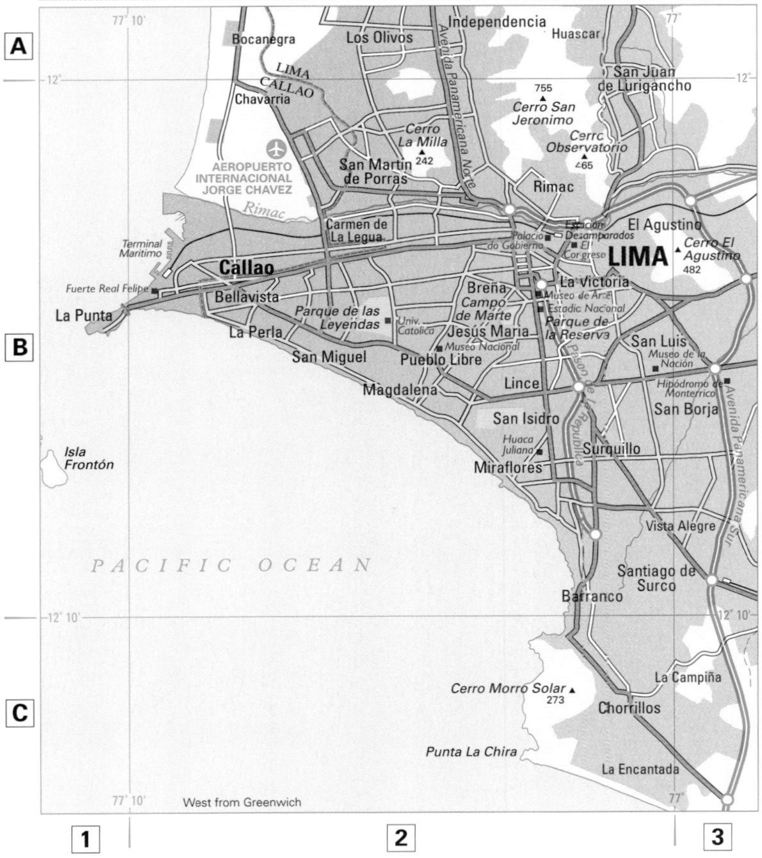

Marina del Ray · Westchester · 42 · Great Western Forum · Inglewood · Florence · Cudahy · Los Nietos · C

PACIFIC OCEAN · LOS ANGELES INTERNATIONAL AIRPORT · University of West Los Angeles · 110 · South Gate · Downey · 710 · 19 · Santa Fe Springs

118° 30' · West from Greenwich · Lennox · 118° 20'

1 · 2 · 3 · 4

---

## LIMA

km 5
miles 3

77° 10' · Bocanegra · Los Olivos · Independencia · Huascar · 77° · 12° · A

LIMA CALLAO · Chavarria · Cerro La Milla · San Juan de Lurigancho · 755 · Cerro San Jeronimo · Cerro Observatorio · 242 · 65

AEROPUERTO INTERNACIONAL JORGE CHAVEZ · San Martín de Porras · Rimac

Terminal Maritimo · Rimac · Carmen de La Legua · Palacio do Gobierno · Estación Desamparados · El Agustino · Cerro El Agustino 482

Fuerte Real Felipe · Callao · Bellavista · Breña · Campo de Marte · Jesús Maria · La Victoria · Museo de Arte · Estadio Nacional · LIMA · B

La Punta · La Perla · Parque de las Leyendas · Univ. Catolica · Museo Nacional · Parque de la Reserva · San Luis · Museo de la Nación

Isla Frontón · San Miguel · Pueblo Libre · Lince · Hipodromo Monterrico · San Borja

Magdalena · San Isidro · Huaca Juliana · Surquillo

PACIFIC OCEAN · Miraflores · Vista Alegre · 12° 10'

Santiago de Surco · Barranco · 77° · C

Cerro Morro Solar 273 · La Campiña · Chorrillos

Punta La Chira · La Encantada

77° 10' · West from Greenwich · 77°

1 · 2 · 3

---

## CENTRAL LOS ANGELES

km 1
miles 0.5

Echo Park Ave · Elysian Park Ave · Dodger Stadium · Elysian Park · a

ECHO PARK · SUNSET BOULEVARD · Stadium Way · BROADWAY · SPRING STREET

HOLLYWOOD FREEWAY · GLENDALE BLVD · Temple Street · PASADENA FREEWAY · CHINA TOWN · NORTH MAIN STREET · ALAMEDA · Cardinal St

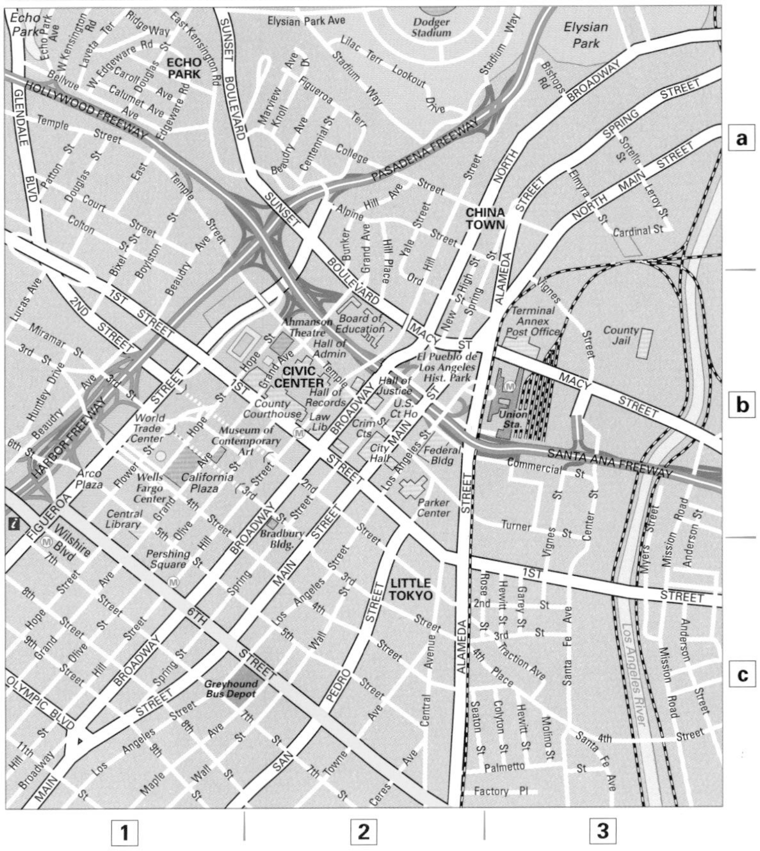

Cotton Street · SUNSET BOULEVARD · Alpine Street · Terminal Annex Post Office · County Jail

2ND STREET · 1ST STREET · Ahmanson Theatre · Board of Education · Hall of Admin · CIVIC CENTER · El Pueblo de Los Angeles Hist. Park · Union Sta. · MACY STREET · b

HARBOR FREEWAY · World Trade Center · County Courthouse · Hall of Records · Museum of Contemporary Art · Hall of Justice · U.S. Ct Ho · Crim Cts · SANTA ANA FREEWAY · Commercial St

FIGUEROA · Arco Plaza · Wells Fargo Center · California Plaza · City Hall · Federal Bldg · Parker Center · MAIN STREET · ALAMEDA · LOS ANGELES RIVER

WILSHIRE BLVD · Central Library · BROADWAY · Bradbury Bldg · Pershing Square · LITTLE TOKYO · 1ST STREET · c

OLYMPIC BLVD · Greyhound Bus Depot · SAN PEDRO · Factory Pl

1 · 2 · 3

## MADRID

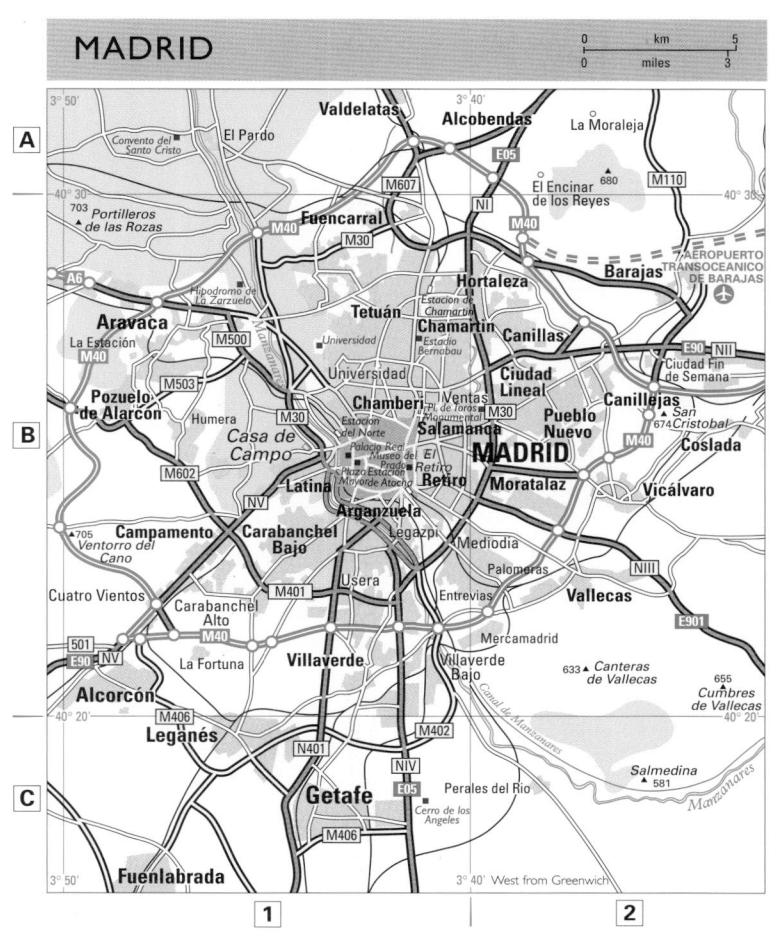

## CENTRAL MADRID

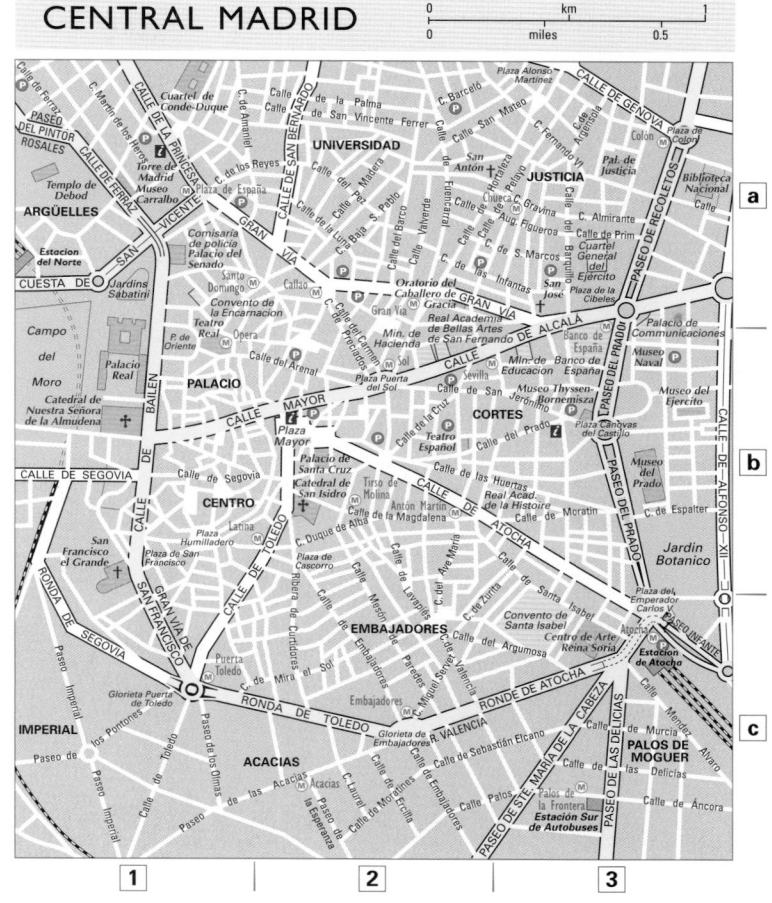

## MANILA

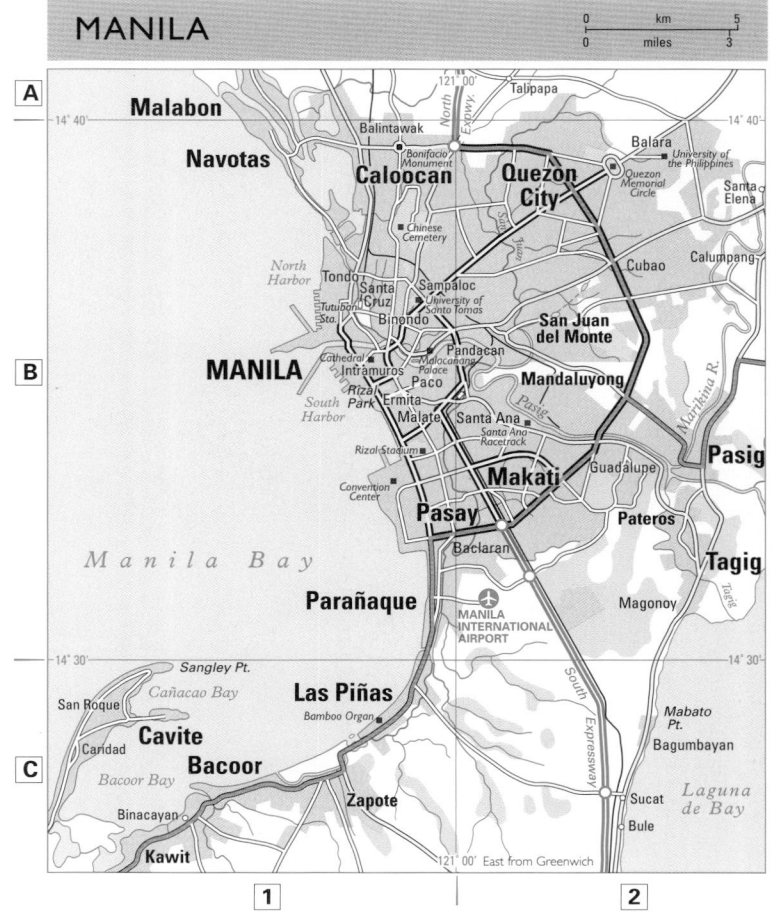

## MELBOURNE

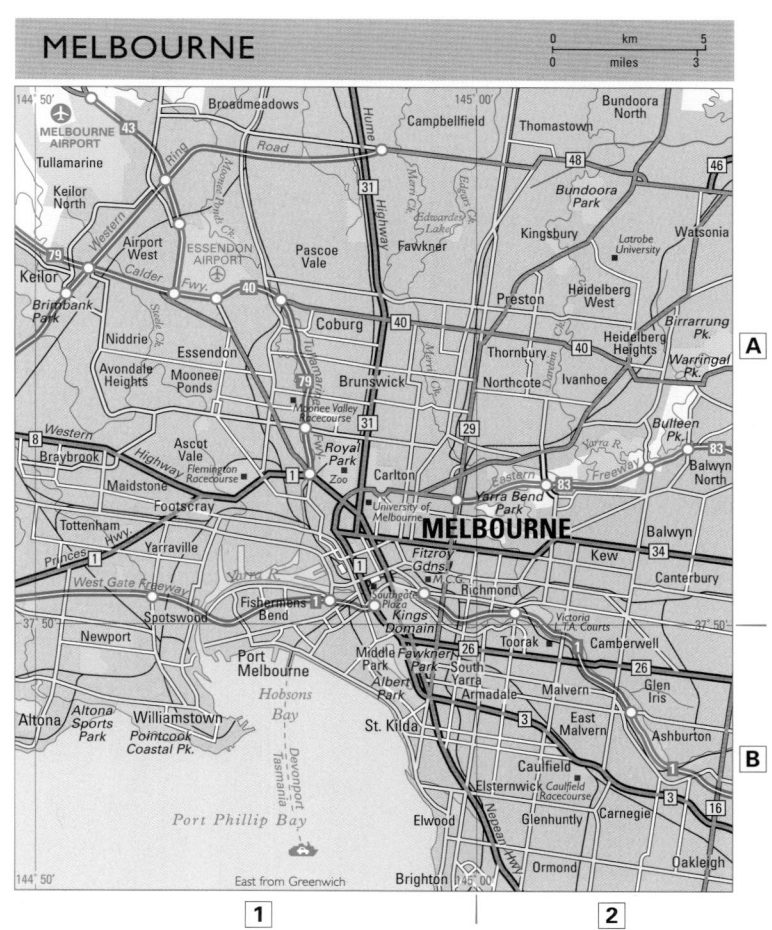

## MEXICO CITY

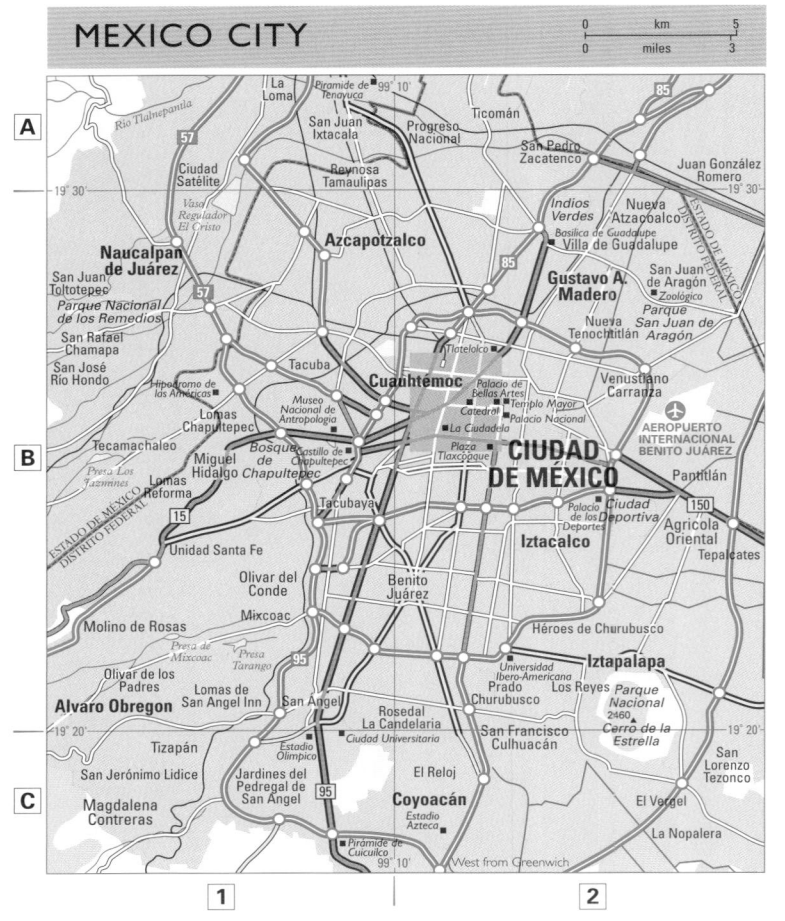

## CENTRAL MEXICO CITY

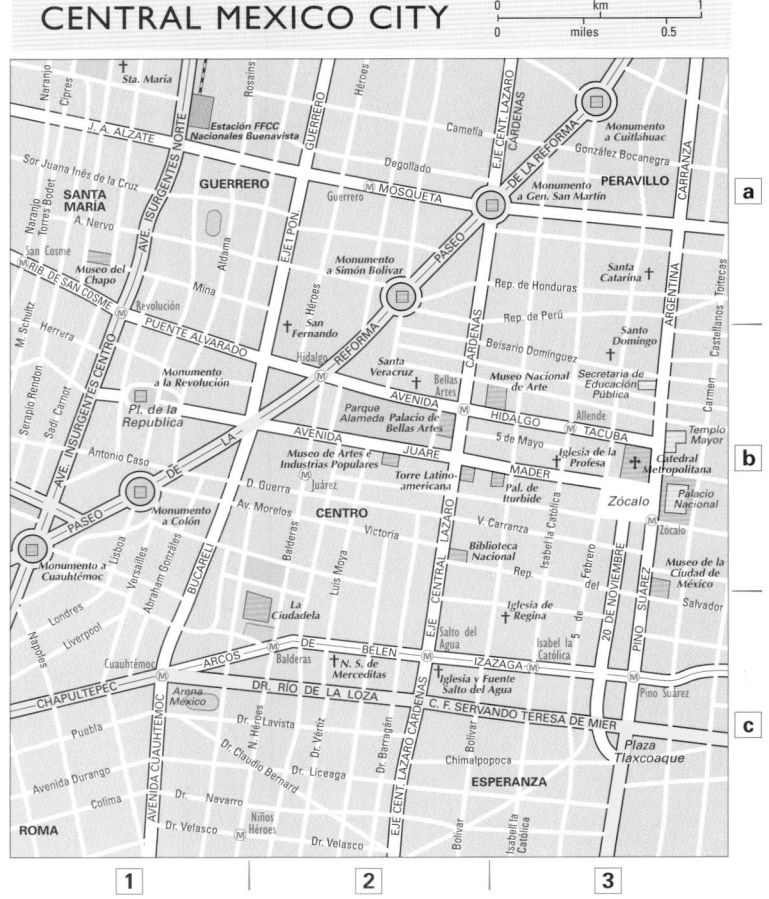

## MIAMI

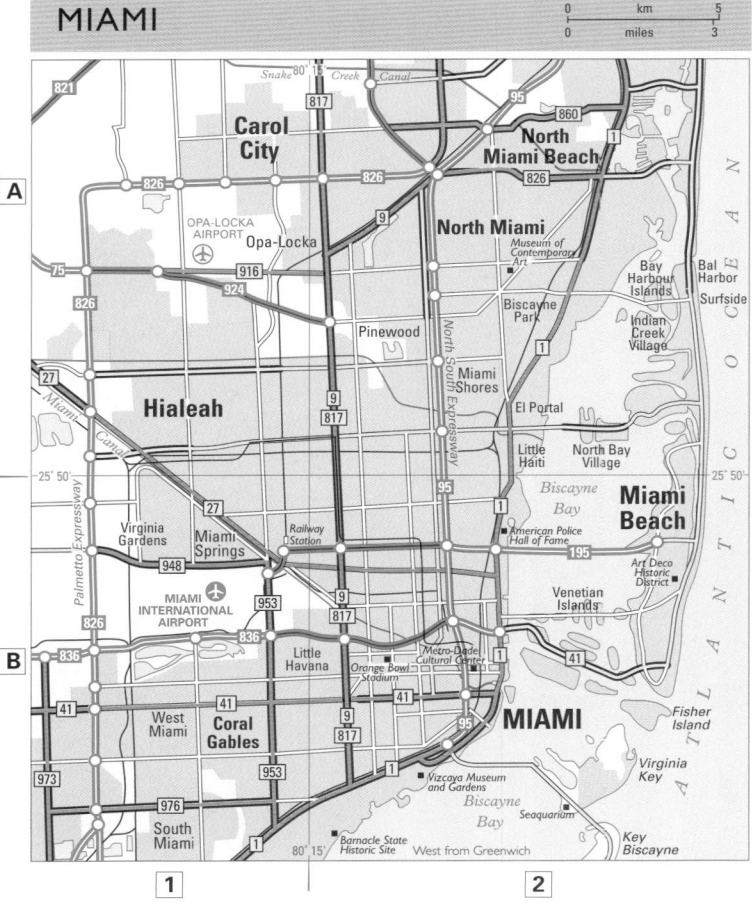

## MILAN

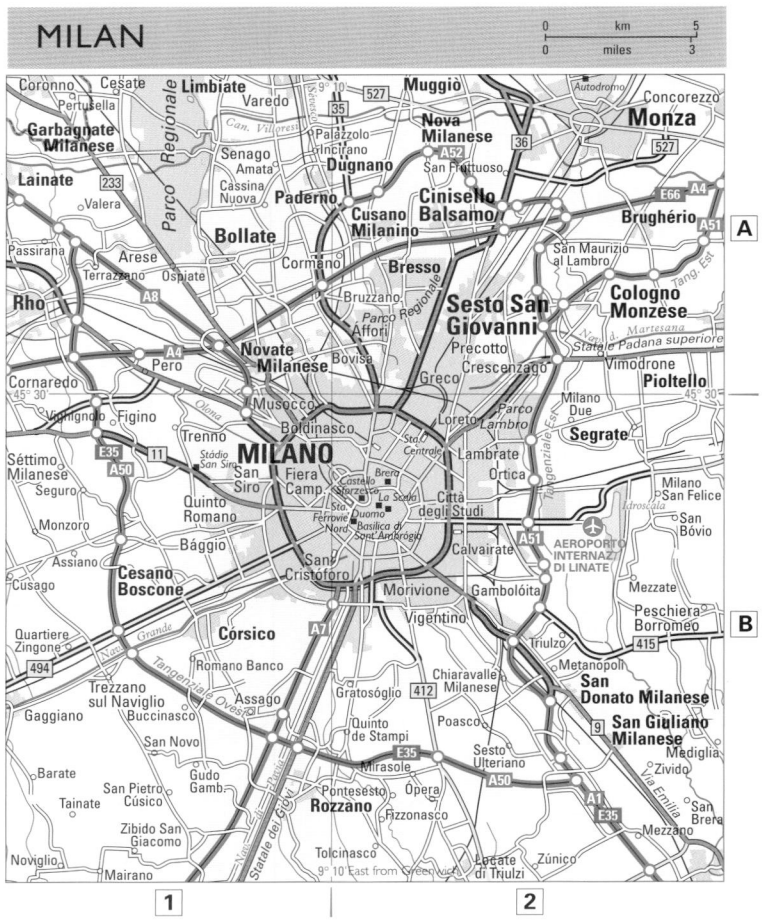

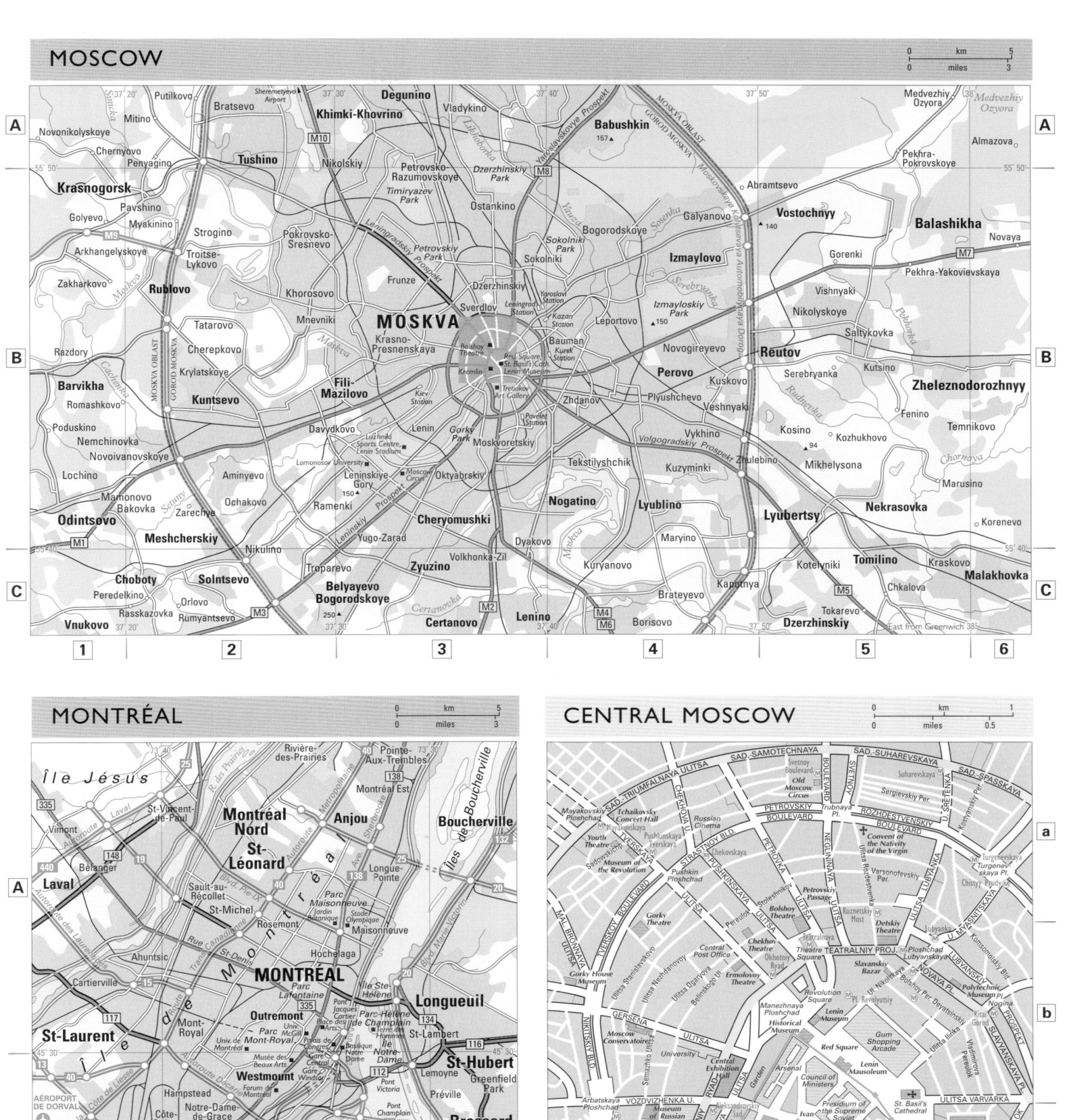

## MOSCOW

0 km 5
0 miles 3

A Novonikolyskoye · Putilkovo · Sheremetyevo Airport · Bratsevo · Degunino · Vladykino · Babushkin · Medvezhiy Ozyora · Medvezhiy Ozyora
Mitino · Khimki-Khovrino · 157▲ · Almazova
Chernyovo · Penyagino · Nikolskiy · Petrovsko-Razumovskoye · Abramtsevo · Pekhra-Pokrovskoye
Krasnogorsk · Tushino · M10 · Dzerzhinskiy Park · M8 · 55° 50'
Pavshino · Timiryazev Park · Vostochnyy
Golyevo · Myakinino · Strogino · Pokrovsko-Sresnevo · Ostankino · Bogorodskoye · Galyanovo · ▲140 · Balashikha
Arkhangelyskoye · M9 · Troitse-Lykovo · Petrovskiy Park · Sokolniki Park · Sokolniki · Izmaylovo · Gorenki · Novaya · M7
Zakharkovo · Leningradskiy Prospekt · Frunze · Dzerzhinskiy · Izmayloskiy Park · Vishnyaki · Pekhra-Yakovievskaya
Rublovo · Dzerzhinskiy · Leningrad Station · Yaroslav Station · 150▲ · Nikolyskoye · Saltykovka
B Tatarovo · Cherepkovo · Khorosovo · MOSKVA · Kazan Station · Leportovo · Novogireyevo · Reutov · Kutsino
Barvikha · Krylatskoye · Krasno-Presnenskaya · Bolshoy Theatre · Red Square · Bauman Kursk Station · Perovo · Kuskovo · Serebryanka · Zheleznodorozhnyy
Romashkovo · Kuntsevo · Fili-Mazilovo · Kremlin · St Basil's Cath · Zhdanov · Plyushchevo · Veshnyaki · Fenino
Poduskino · Nemchinovka · Tretiakov Art Gallery · Pavelet Station · Vykhino · Kosino · Kozhukhovo · Temnikovo
Novoivanovskoye · Davydkovo · Lenin · Gorky Park · Moskvoretskiy · Volgogradskiy Prospekt · Zhulebino · 94▲ · Mikhelysona
Lochino · Aminyevo · Lomonosov University · Leninskiye-Gory · Moscow Circus · Oktyabrskiy · Tekstilyshchik · Kuzyminki · Marusino
Mamonovo · Bakovka · Ochakovo · Zarechye · Ramenki · Leninsky Prospekt · Nogatino · Lyublino · Lyubertsy · Nekrasovka
Odintsovo · Cheryomushki · Dyakovo · Maryino
Meshcherskiy · M1 · Nikulino · Yugo-Zarad · Kuryanovo · Kotelyniki · Tomilino · Kraskovo · 55° 40'
C Choboty · Solntsevo · Troparevo · Zyuzino · Volkhonka-Zil · Kapptnya · Dzerzhinskiy · Malakhovka
Peredelkino · Orlovo · Belyayevo Bogorodskoye · Brateyevo · M5
Vnukovo · Rasskazovka · Rumyantsevo · M3 · 250▲ · Certanovo · Lenino · M2 · M4 · Borisovo · Tokarevo · Chkalova · East from Greenwich 38°

## MONTRÉAL

0 km 5
0 miles 3

Île Jésus · Rivière-des-Prairies · Pointe-Aux-Trembles · Boucherville
Vimont · St-Vincent-de-Paul · Montréal Est · Îles de Boucherville
A Laval · Bélanger · Montréal Nord · St-Léonard · Anjou · Longue-Pointe
Sault-au-Récollet · St-Michel · Parc Maisonneuve · Jardin botanique · Stade Olympique · Maisonneuve
Ahuntsic · Rosemont · Hochelaga
Cartierville · MONTRÉAL · Parc Lafontaine · Île Ste-Hélène · Longueuil
St-Laurent · Outremont · Mont-Royal · Parc du Mont-Royal · Parc Hélène de Champlain · St-Lambert
Hampstead · Westmount · Musée des Beaux Arts · Basilique Notre-Dame · St-Hubert · Greenfield Park
B Côte-St-Luc · Notre-Dame-de-Grace · St-Pierre · Île des Soeurs · Verdun · Préville · Brossard
Lachine · Lasalle · Île aux Herons · La Prairie
Kahnawake · Ste-Catherine · Candiac

## CENTRAL MOSCOW

0 km 1
0 miles 0.5

(Central Moscow map with streets and landmarks including Bolshoy Theatre, Red Square, Kremlin, St Basil's Cathedral, Lenin Mausoleum, Gum Shopping Arcade, Pushkin Fine Arts Museum, Lenin State Library)

## MUMBAI

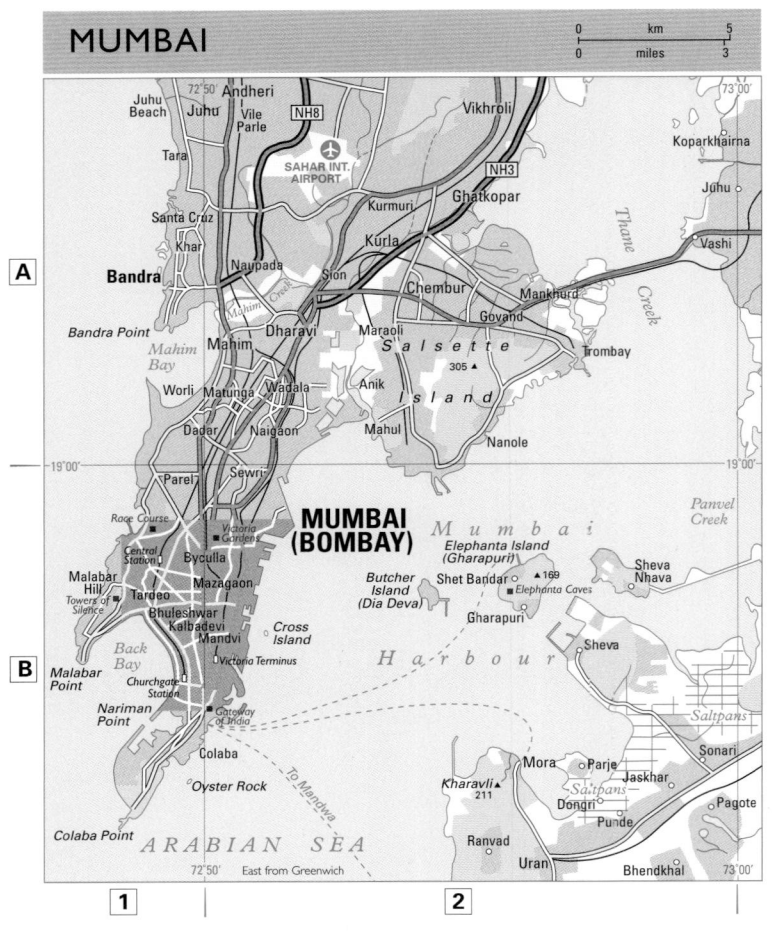

## CENTRAL MUMBAI

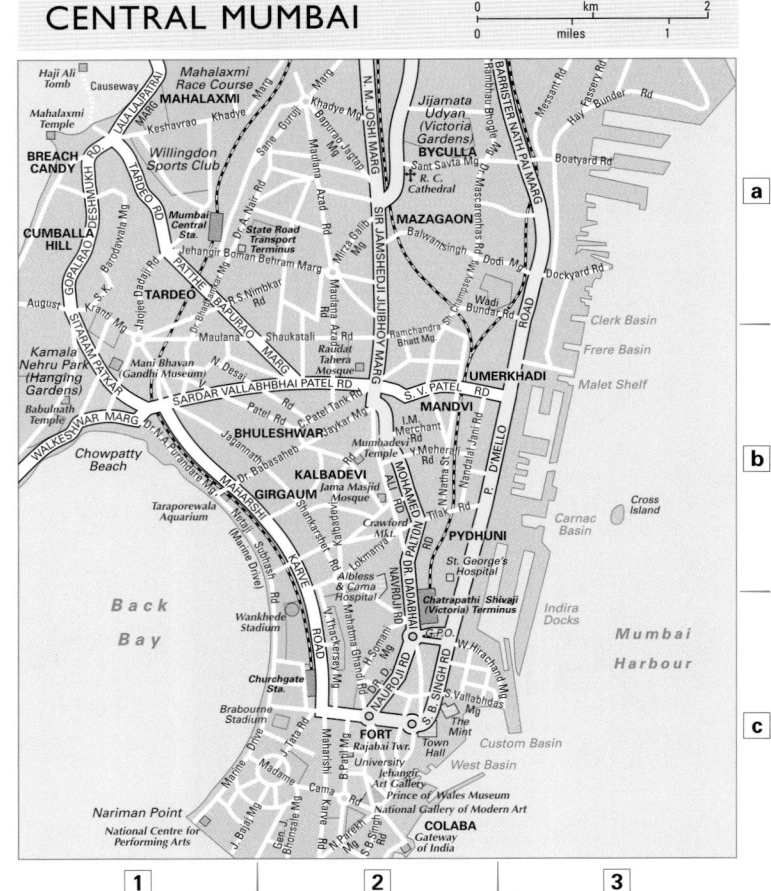

## MUNICH

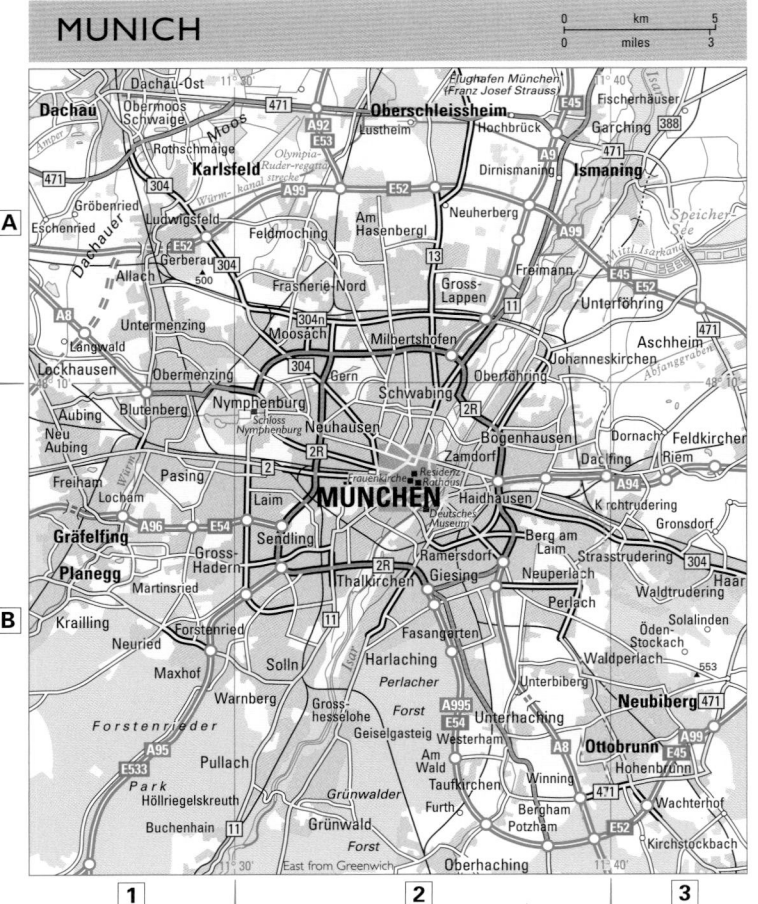

## CENTRAL MUNICH

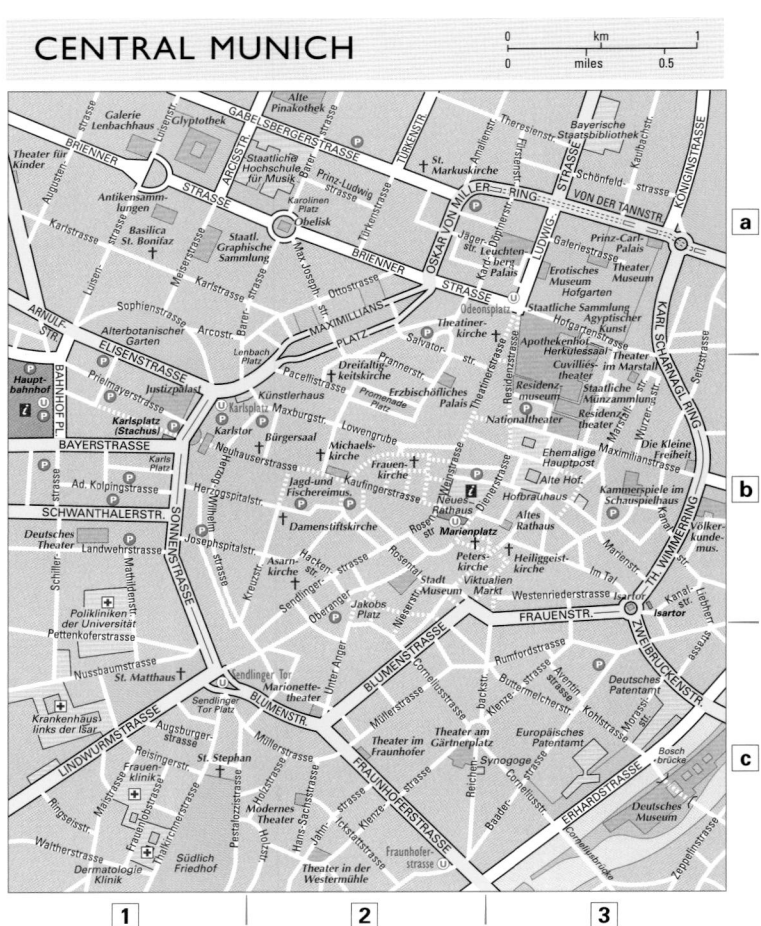

# NEW YORK

km 5
miles 3

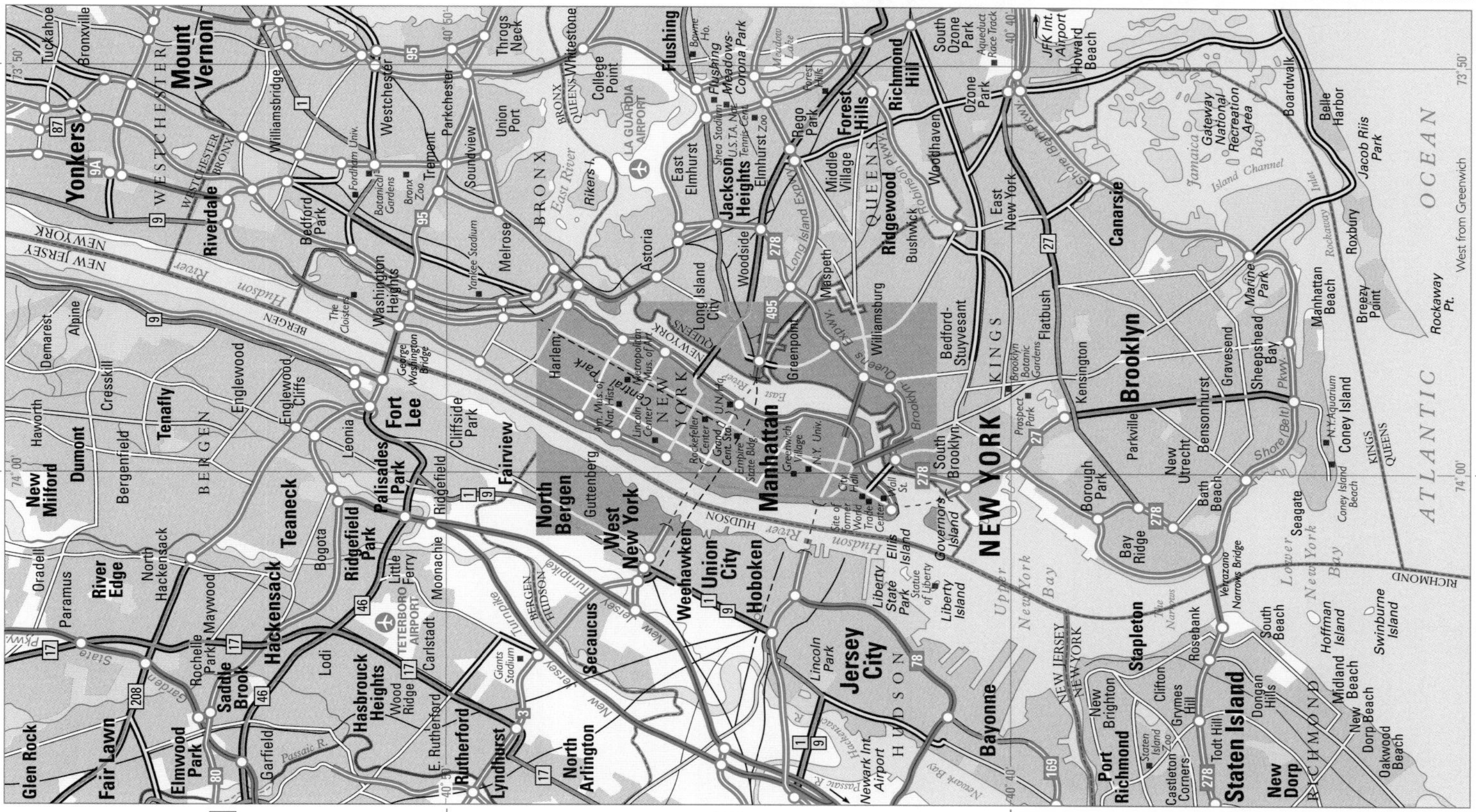

## CENTRAL NEW YORK

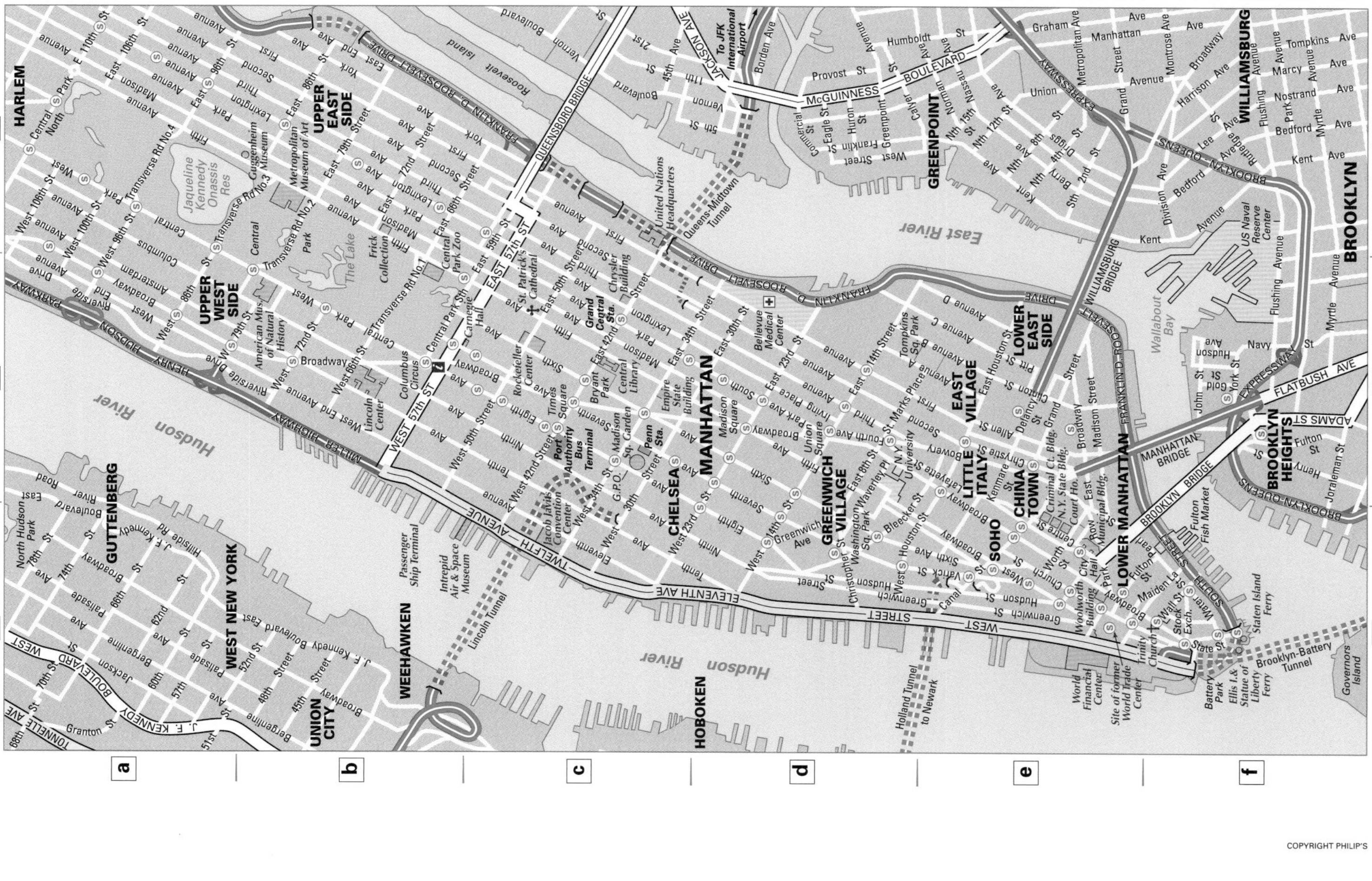

km 2
miles 1

## OSAKA

km 0 5
miles 0 3

509 Arima Funasaka **Takarazuka** Senriyama Yamada **Hirakata**
598 Karato 722 Rokkō-Zan 932 462 Kwansei Gakuin University **Itami** OSAKA INTERNATIONAL AIRPORT **Toyonaka** **Settsu** Kori
Tanigami 428 Iwazono Hirota **Suita** Higashiyodogawa Asahi **Neyagawa**
Obu-tōge 365 Maya-Zan 699 Kōbe University Okamoto **Nishinomiya** Naruo Jūsō Oyodo Miyakojima **Kadoma** Shijonawate
Ōbu 403 Nada Ashiaya **Amagasaki** Umeda **Moriguchi** **Daitō**
Fukiai Higashinada University Fukushima Higashi Jōto Kōnoike
Ikuta Nishiyodogawa Aji Minami Higashinari Ishikiri
**KŌBE** Rokkō Island Konohana Nishi Ikuno 308 **Higashiōsaka**
Suma Nagata Port Island Minato Namiwa **ŌSAKA**
Kōbe Harbour Osaka Aquarium Suntory Museum Taishō Tennōji Zoo Abeno Kyūhōji Kizuri Yamamoto
Nishinari Liberty Osaka Museum **Yao**
Osaka Harbour Higashisumiyoshi Tainaka 25 Onchi
Sakai Harbour Sumiyoshi Shrine Sumiyoshi **YAO AIRPORT**
*Osaka Bay* Ikeuchi **Kashiwara**
26 **Matsubara** Fujidera
**Sakai** East from Greenwich

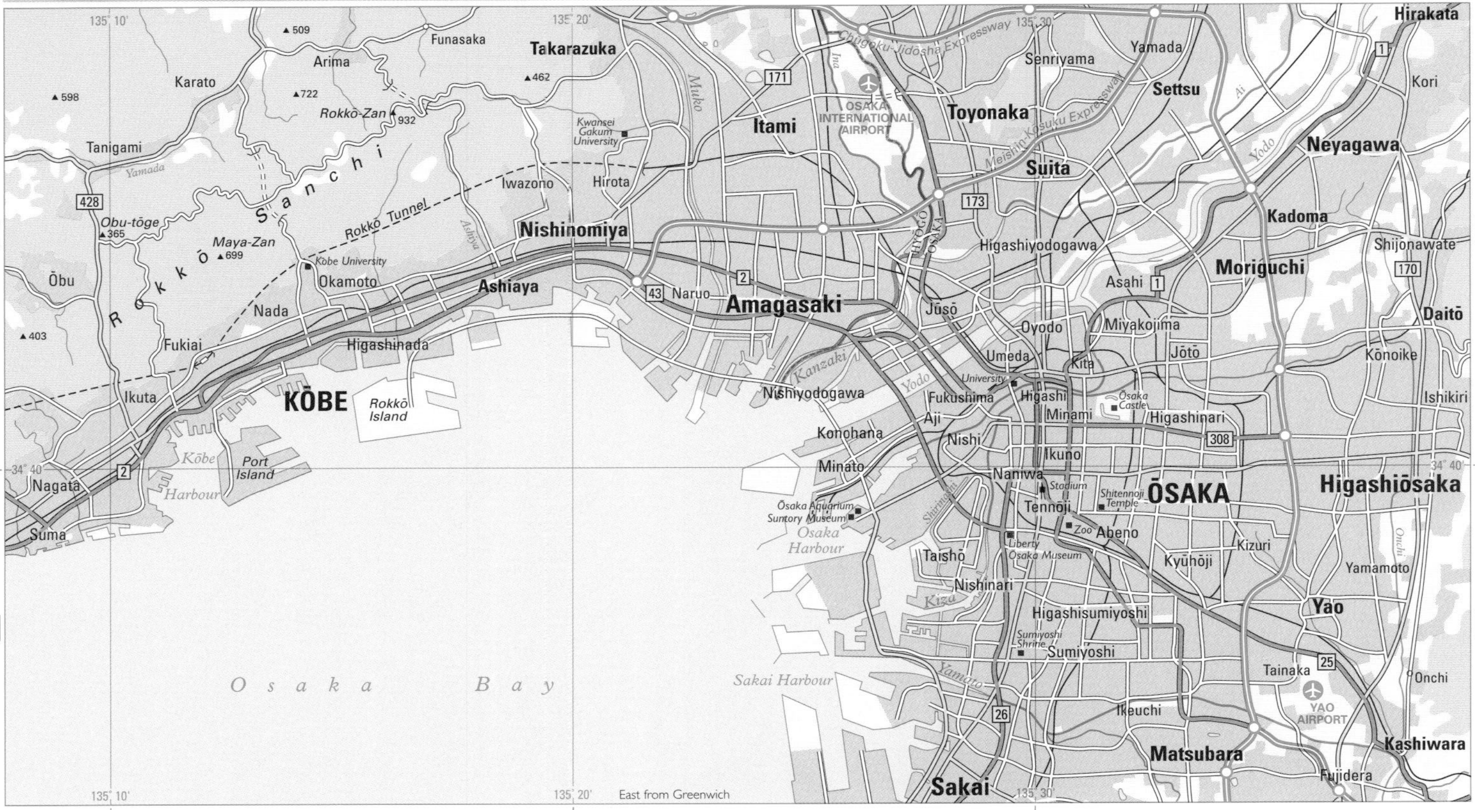

## OSLO

km 0 5
miles 0 3

By Tryvannshøgda 531 Maridalen Maridalsvatnet
OSLO AKERSHUS Bogstadvatn Sognsvatn 418 Alnsjøen Holmenkollen Kjelsås **Gorud** Rødtvet
Ila Røa Ris RING 3 Ullevål 4 163 Rødtvet
Bærums Verk Lijordet 168 **OSLO** RING 2 Sinsen Alna
Bryn 379 Haslum **Ullern** Skøyen Universitet Vestbane stn. Domkirke Tøyen Bryn E6
**Kolsås** Stabekk Lysaker Norsk Folke Museum Akershus Slott Sentralst. Ryen Oppsal
160 **Bærum** Høvik Bygdøy Hovedøya Bøler
Tanum 164 E18 166 Lindøya Bekkelaget Lambertseter Østmark kapellet
Sljependen **Sandvika** Snarøya Fornebu Ormøya Nordstrand
Hvalstad Nesbru Nesøya Ostøya Frederikshavn Helsingborg København Hirtshals, Kiel **Nesoddtangen** Malmøya Ljabru Hauketo 155
**Asker** E18 165 Konglungen Brønnøya Flaskebekk Oksval Skoklefall Klemetsrud
Blåkstad Holmenfjorden 157 215 Torvvik Ingierstrand
167 Vollen Nesodden Nesodden **Kolbotn** E6
Slemmestad Fjellstrand Svestad Hasle Oppgård
Nærsnes Garder Blylaget Oppegård 156 Myrvoll E18 152 **Oppegård**
134 East from Greenwich

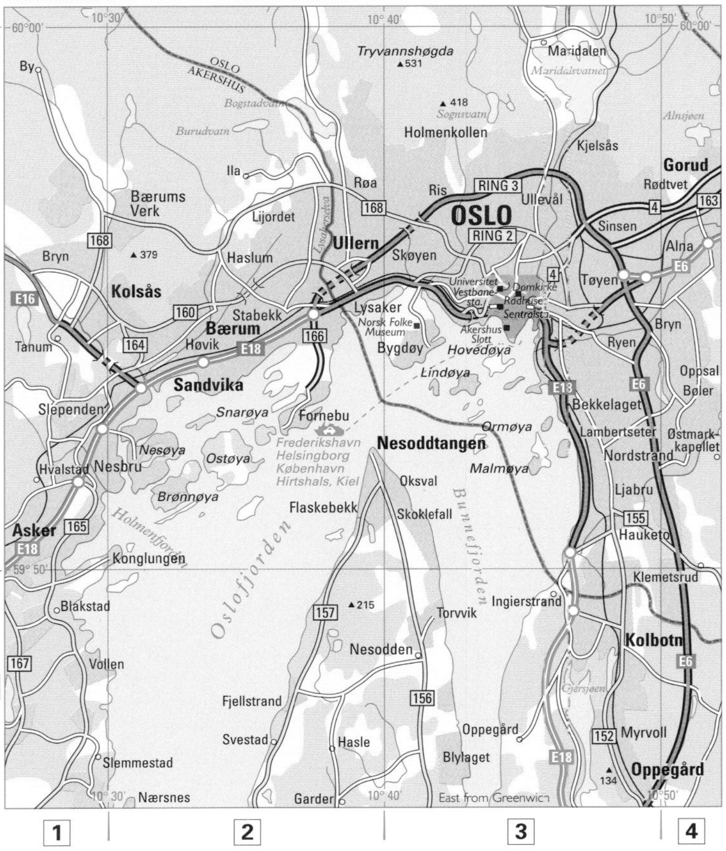

## CENTRAL OSLO

km 0 0.5
miles 0 0.25

Vår Frelsers Gravlund Rikshospitalet Westye Egebergs gate Nordre gate
PARKVEIEN Stens berget Wethayens gate Vor Frue hospitalet Korsgata
Slotts parken ST. OLAVS GATE St. Olavs kirke Kunstindustri mus. Deichmanske biblioteket Akerselva
Det Kongelige Slottet Historisk museum PILESTREDET HAMMERSBORG TUNNELEN Operaen
Dronningparken Universitet Nasjonal galleriet GRENSEN
DRAMMENSVEIEN Ibsen museet National museet National theatret Det Norske Teater Karl Johans gate Stortinget Oslo Spektrum
Stenersen museet Ruseløkka Stortings gata Grensen Biskop Gunnerus gate Grenland
MUNKEDAMSVEIEN Konserthuset Fridtjof Nansens plass Karl Johans gate Jernbane-torget Buss terminalen
Vestbane stasjonen Rådhuset Stortinget Hovedpost kontor Sentralstasjon
Dokkveien Christiania torv OSLOTUNNELEN Rådhusgata Teater museet Børsen NYLANDSVEIEN
*Pipervika* Museet for samtidskunst Arkitekt museet Fred Olsens gate BISPEGATA
Hjemmefront museet Astrup Fearnley museet Myntgata
Akershus Slott og festning Forsvars museet *Bjørvika* *Bispevika*
Frederikshavn, Helsingborg, København

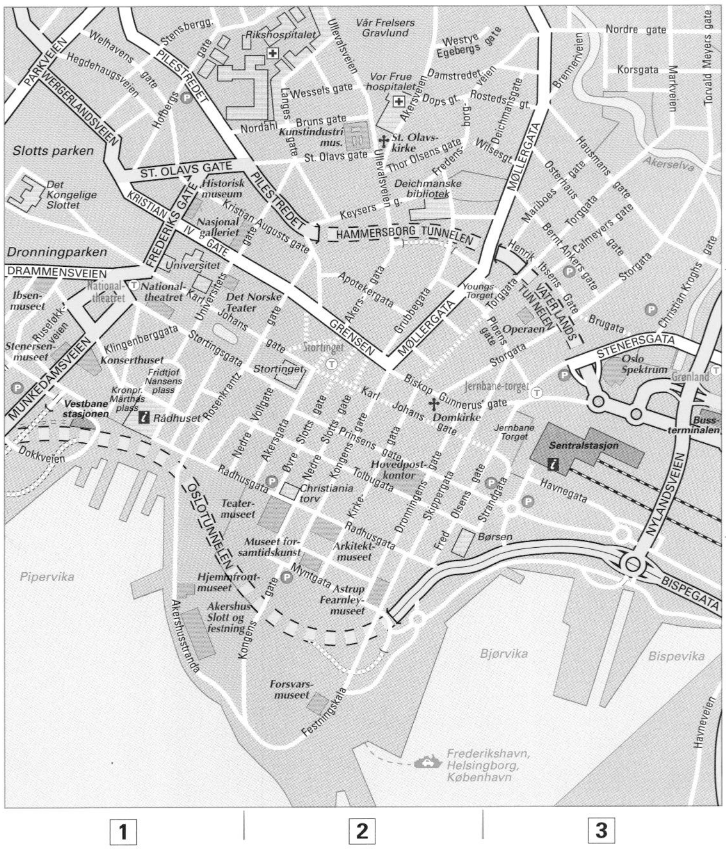

COPYRIGHT PHILIP'S

# PARIS

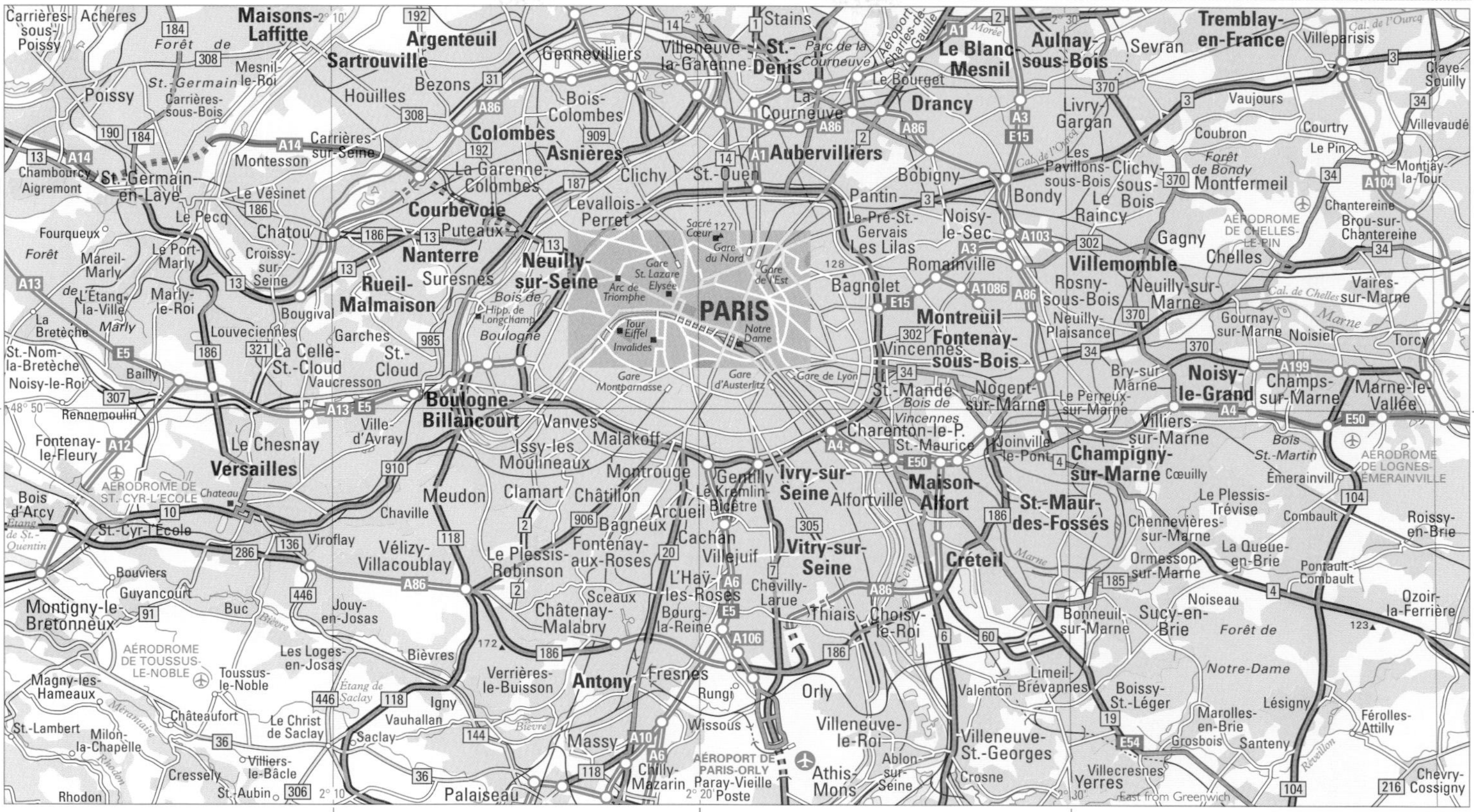

km 5
miles 3

Carrières-sous-Poissy · Achères · Maisons-Laffitte · Sartrouville · Argenteuil · Gennevilliers · Villeneuve-la-Garenne · St.-Denis · Stains · Parc de la Courneuve · Le Blanc-Mesnil · Aulnay-sous-Bois · Tremblay-en-France · Villeparisis · Gal. de l'Ourcq

Poissy · Forêt de St-Germain-le-Roi · Mesnil · Houilles · Bezons · Bois-Colombes · La Courneuve · Le Bourget · Drancy · Livry-Gargan · Coubron · Le Pin · Courtry · Vaujours · Villevaudé

Chambourcy · St-Germain-en-Laye · Aigremont · Montesson · Colombes · Asnières · Clichy · St.-Ouen · Aubervilliers · Bobigny · Bondy · Les Pavillons-sous-Bois · Clichy-sous-Bois · Montfermeil · Aérodrome de Chelles-le-Pin · Chantereine · Brou-sur-Chantereine

Fourqueux · Le Pecq · Châtou · La Garenne-Colombes · Courbevoie · Puteaux · Levallois-Perret · Pantin · Le Pré-St-Gervais · Les Lilas · Romainville · Noisy-le-Sec · Gagny · Chelles · Vaires-sur-Marne

Mareil-Marly · Marly-le-Roi · Bougival · Nanterre · Suresnes · Neuilly-sur-Seine · PARIS · Bagnolet · Villemomble · Rosny-sous-Bois · Neuilly-sur-Marne · Gournay-sur-Marne · Noisiel · Torcy

Rueil-Malmaison · Garches · St.-Cloud · Boulogne · Montreuil · Vincennes · Fontenay-sous-Bois · Le Perreux-sur-Marne · Bry-sur-Marne · Noisy-le-Grand · Champs-sur-Marne · Marne-la-Vallée

Le Chesnay · Versailles · Ville-d'Avray · Boulogne-Billancourt · Vanves · Malakoff · Issy-les-Moulineaux · Montrouge · Gentilly · Le Kremlin-Bicêtre · Charenton-le-P. · St.-Maurice · Joinville-le-Pont · Champigny-sur-Marne · Cœuilly · Émerainville · Aérodrome de Lognes-Émerainville · Roissy-en-Brie

Bois d'Arcy · St-Cyr-l'École · Meudon · Chaville · Clamart · Châtillon · Arcueil · Cachan · Ivry-sur-Seine · Alfortville · Maisons-Alfort · St.-Maur-des-Fossés · Chennevières-sur-Marne · Le Plessis-Trévise · Combault

Viroflay · Vélizy-Villacoublay · Le Plessis-Robinson · Bagneux · Fontenay-aux-Roses · Villejuif · Vitry-sur-Seine · Créteil · Bonneuil-sur-Marne · Sucy-en-Brie · Ozoir-la-Ferrière

Montigny-le-Bretonneux · Bouviers · Guyancourt · Buc · Jouy-en-Josas · Sceaux · Châtenay-Malabry · Bourg-la-Reine · L'Haÿ-les-Roses · Chevilly-Larue · Thiais · Choisy-le-Roi · Limeil-Brévannes · Noiseau · Forêt de Notre-Dame · Boissy-St-Léger · Lésigny · Férolles-Attilly

Magny-les-Hameaux · Les Loges-en-Josas · Bièvres · Verrières-le-Buisson · Antony · Fresnes · Rungis · Orly · Valenton-Brévannes · Marolles-en-Brie · Grosbois · Santeny

Châteaufort · Le Christ de Saclay · Igny · Vauhallan · Saclay · Massy · Chilly-Mazarin · Wissous · Aéroport de Paris-Orly · Villeneuve-le-Roi · Ablon-sur-Seine · Crosne · Villeneuve-St-Georges · Yerres · Villecresnes · Chevry-Cossigny

St-Lambert · Milon-la-Chapelle · Cressely · Rhodon · Villiers-le-Bâcle · Toussus-le-Noble · Palaiseau · St.-Aubin · Athis-Mons

1  2  3  4

# CENTRAL PARIS

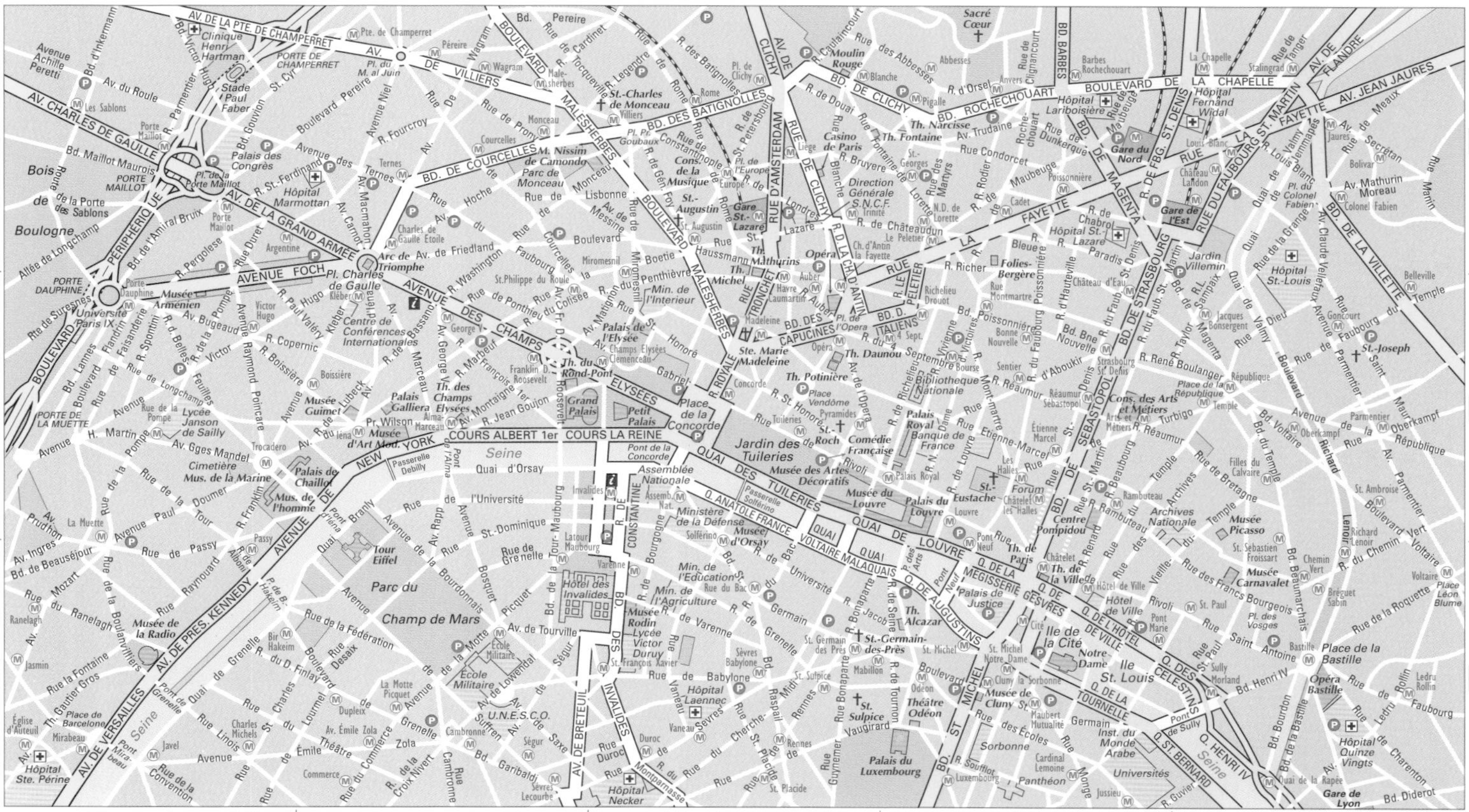

km 1
miles 0.5

Av. de la Pte de Champerret · Sacré Cœur · Bd. des Batignolles · Montmartre · Moulin Rouge · Pigalle · Bd. de Clichy · Gare du Nord · Bd. de la Chapelle · Av. Jean Jaurès

Bois de Boulogne · Porte Maillot · Palais des Congrès · Av. de la Grande Armée · Parc de Monceau · St.-Augustin · Gare St.-Lazare · Opéra · Gare de l'Est · Av. de la Villette

Arc de Triomphe · Pl. Charles de Gaulle · Avenue Foch · Av. des Champs Élysées · Palais de l'Élysée · Bd. Haussmann · Bourse · Bd. de Strasbourg · République

Av. Victor Hugo · Trocadéro · Palais de Chaillot · Tour Eiffel · Place de la Concorde · Jardin des Tuileries · Musée du Louvre · Centre Pompidou · Musée Picasso · Bastille

Champ de Mars · Hôtel des Invalides · Assemblée Nationale · Musée d'Orsay · St-Germain-des-Prés · Île de la Cité · Notre Dame · Île St. Louis · Opéra Bastille

École Militaire · UNESCO · St.-Sulpice · Jardin du Luxembourg · Panthéon · Sorbonne · Gare de Lyon

1  2  3  4  5

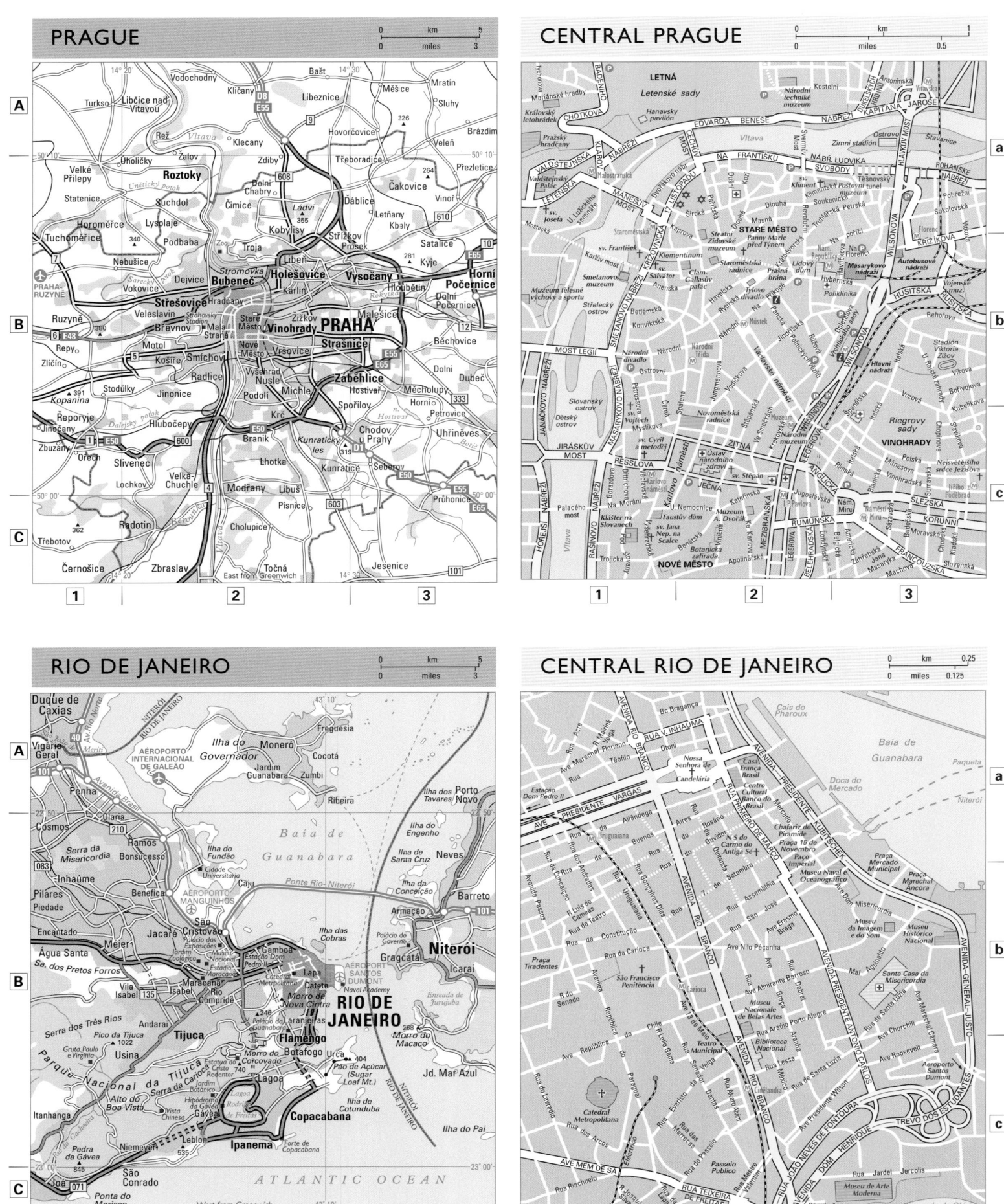

## ROME

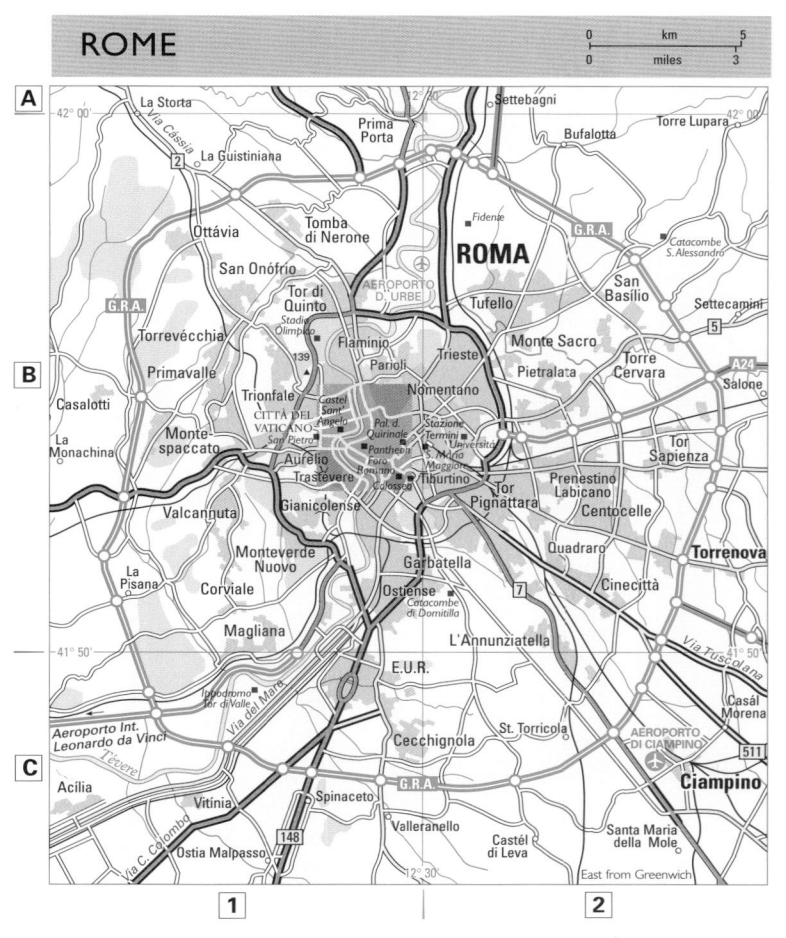

## CENTRAL ROME

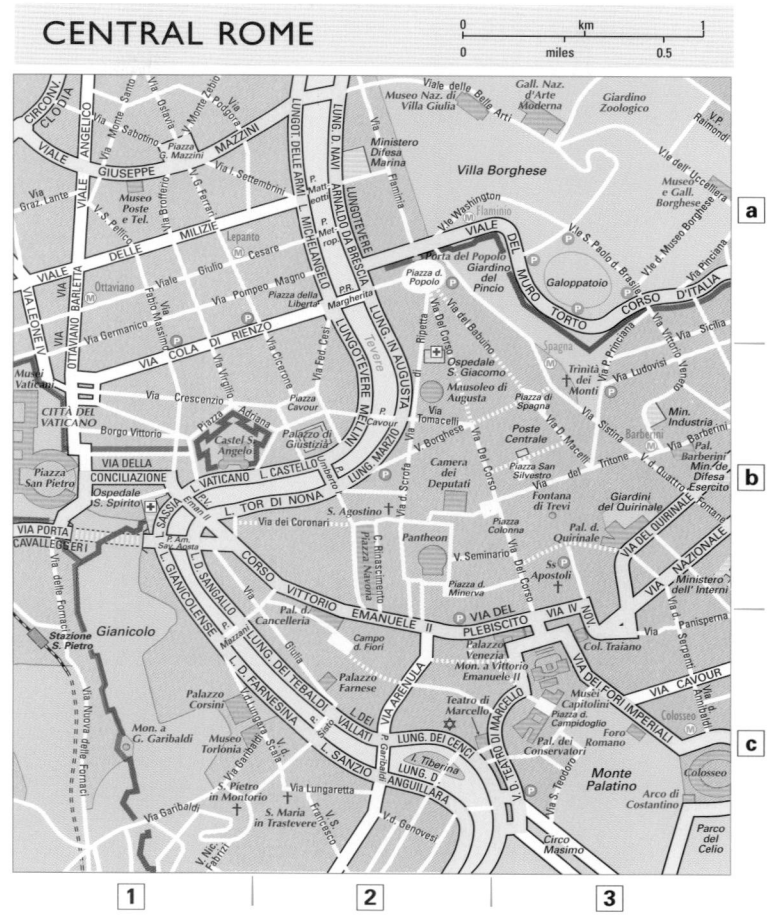

## SAN FRANCISCO

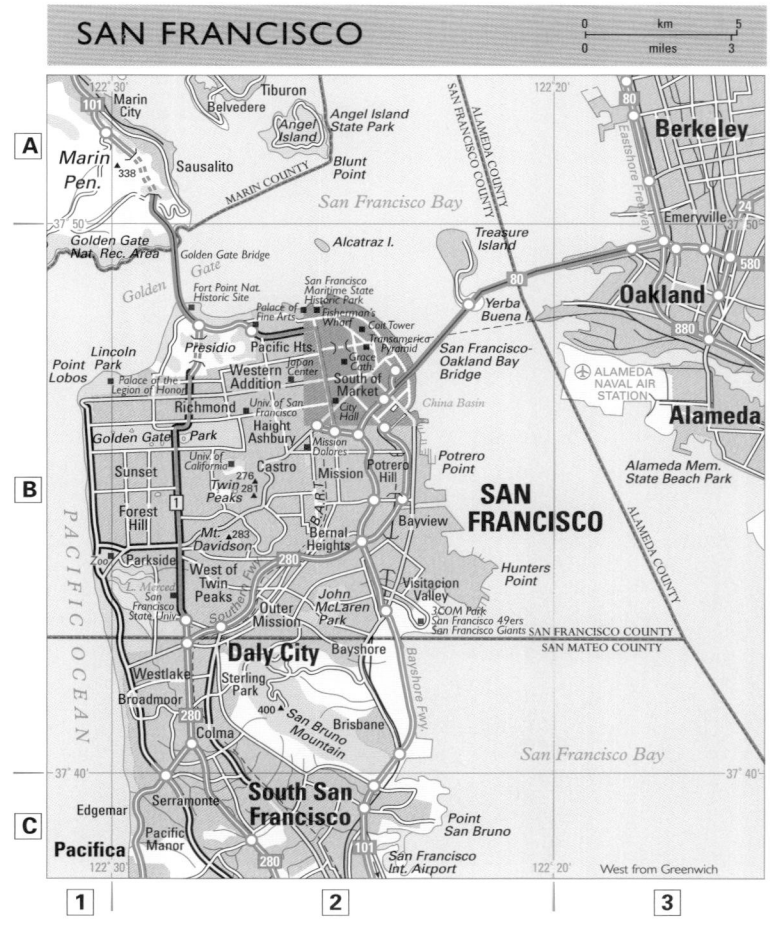

## CENTRAL SAN FRANCISCO

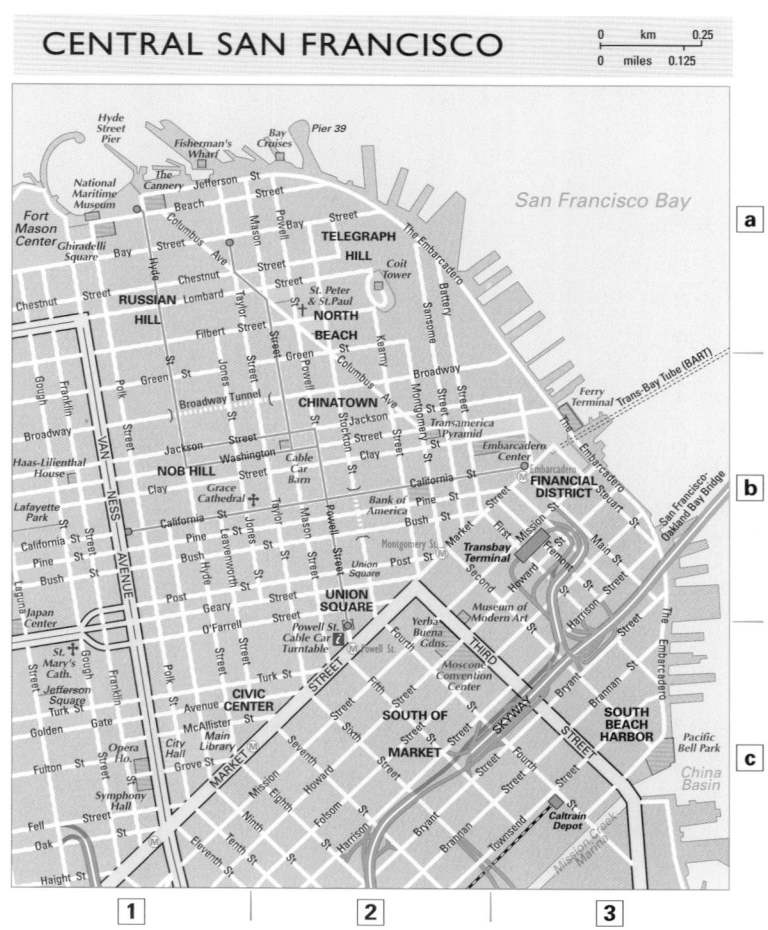

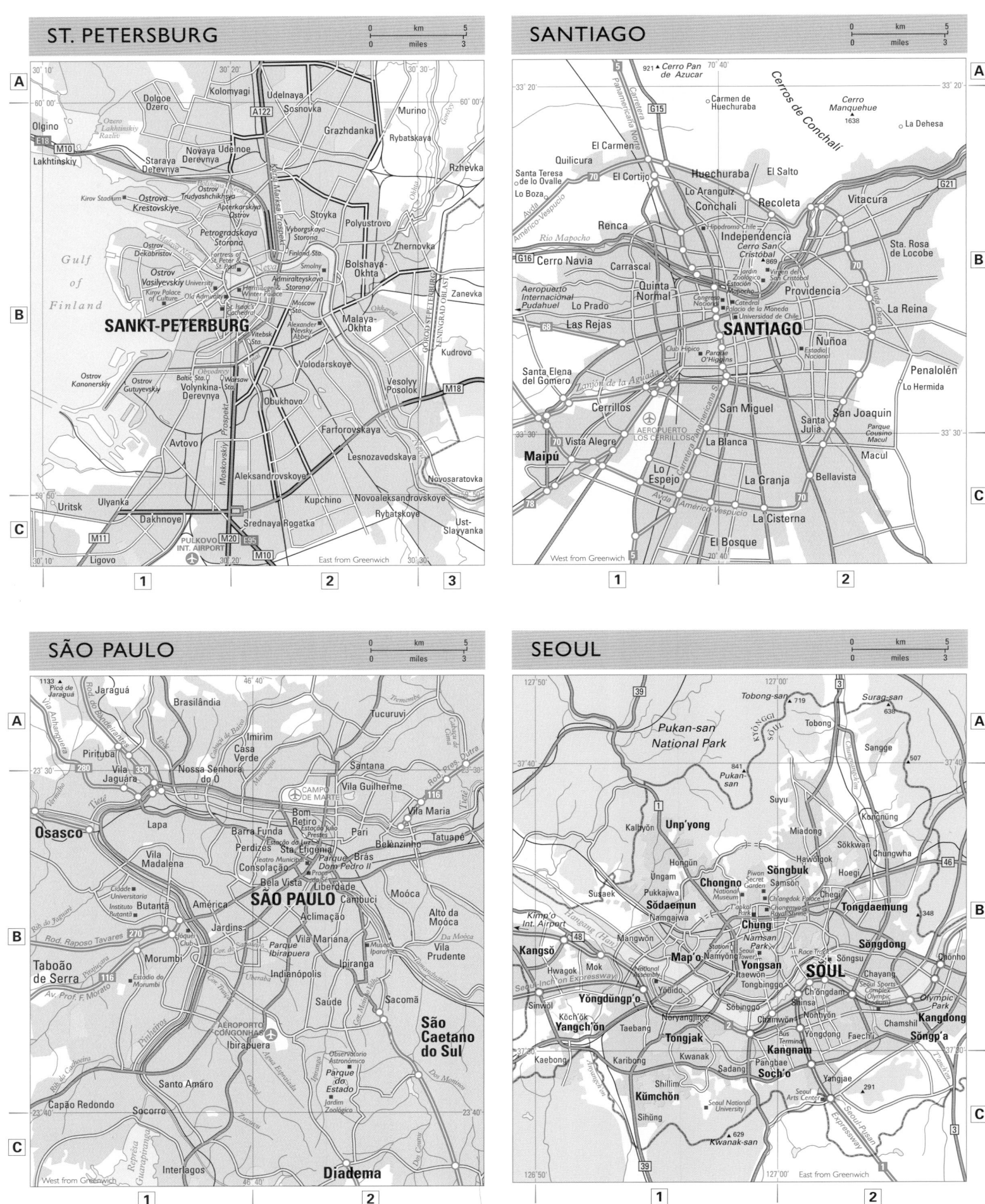

## SHANGHAI

km 0 5
miles 0 3

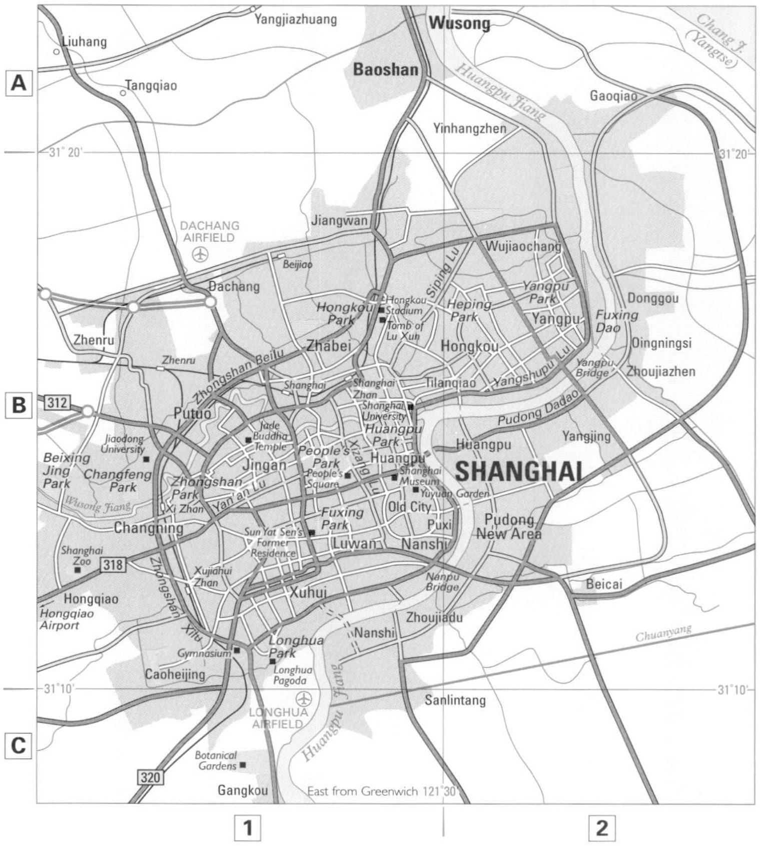

Liuhang
Yangjiazhuang
Wusong
Baoshan
Tangqiao
Gaoqiao
Yinhangzhen
Huangpu Jiang
Chang Ji. (Yangtse)
DACHANG AIRFIELD
Jiangwan
Wujiaochang
Yangpu Park
Yangpu
Fuxing Dao
Qingningsi
Donggou
Beijing
Hongkou Stadium
Heping Park
Hongkou Park
Zhabei
Tomb of Lu Xun
Hongkou
Siping Lu
Zhenru
Jiaodong University
Zhenru
Zhongshan Beilu
Shanghai
Shanghai Zhan
Shanghai University
Tilanqiao
Yangshupu Lu
Yangjing
312
Putuo
Jade Buddha Temple
Huangpu Park
Pudong Dadao
Zhongshan Park
People's Park
Shanghai Museum
Huangpu
Huangpu
Zhoujiazhen
Beixing Jing Park
Changfeng Park
Jingan
People's Square
Yuyuan Garden
Pudong New Area
Zhongshan
Xu Zhan
Yan'an Lu
Puxi
Changning
Fuxing Park
Old City
Nanshi
Sun Yat Sen's Former Residence
Luwan
Shanghai Zoo
318
Xujiahui Zhan
Xuhui
Nanpu Bridge
Zhoujiadu
Beicai
Hongqiao
Honggiao Airport
Gymnasium
Longhua Park
Caoheijing
Longhua Pagoda
Nanshi
Sanlintang
Chuanyang
LONGHUA AIRFIELD
320
Gangkou
East from Greenwich 121°30'
31°20'
31°10'

A  B  C
1  2

## CENTRAL SINGAPORE

km 0 1
miles 0 0.5

CAIRNHILL ROAD
Istana (President's Residence)
BUKIT TIMAH ROAD
Kandang Kerbau Hospital
Zhujiao Centre
Cuff Rd
Upper Wold
BIDEFORD RD
CLEMENCEAU ROAD
CAVENAGH ROAD
Central Park
Edinburgh
Mount Emily
Mackenzie
SERANGOON ROAD
Dunlop
Abdul Gaffoor Mosque
Sim Lim Tower
Thong Sia Building
ORCHARD ROAD
Emerald Hill Rd
Sri Temasek
Sophia
Wilkie Road
Sim Lim Square
ROCHOR
BESAR
Cuppage Centre
Centre point
Orchard Plaza
Faber House
Road
Road
Bus Station
Blanco Court
ORCHARD
Orchard Point
Handy Road
Bencoolen Mosque
MIDDLE ROAD
El Bogis
MARINA ROAD
N2 Somerset
PENANG ROAD
N1 Dhoby Ghaut
Waterloo Street
St. Joseph's Church
COLONIAL DISTRICT
KILLNEY
Lloyd Rd
OXLEY
AVENUE
BRAS BASAH
Singapore Hist. Mus.
Singapore Art Museum
Raffles Hotel
RIVER VALLEY ROAD
Chesed-El Synagogue
BOULEVARD
Sacred Heart Church
Singapore
Battle Box
STAMFORD
Asian Ch. Mus.
Westin Plaza
Sri Thandayuthapani Temple
TANK ROAD
Fort Canning Park
Fort Canning Reserve
CITY CENTRE
b
VICTORIA
War Memorial Park
Hong San See Temple
Van Kleef Aquarium
Singapore Philatelic Mus.
C2 City Hall
St. Andrew's Cathedral
CLEMENCEAU
HILL
Funan Centre
City Hall
CONNAUGHT
Singapore River
Clarke Quay
NORTH
Boat Quay
Supreme Court
Parliament
Esplanade Park
HAVELOCK ROAD
MERCHANT ROAD
North Boat Quay
CANAL
Singapore Cricket Club
Raffles Landing Site
Empress Pl. Museum
Victoria Concert Hall & Theatre
Melaka Mosque
NORTH CANAL ROAD
FULLERTON RD
Merlion Park
Marina Bay
Swee
PICKERING ST
Bus Station
Cheng Bio Temple
CHULIA
OUB Centre
Pearl's Hill CityPark
Pearl's Hill Reservoir
NEW BRIDGE ROAD
SOUTH BRIDGE
Clifford Pier
SENTOSA
CI Raffles Place
People's Park Complex
Pagoda
Jamae Mosque
CHINATOWN
Tak Tak Ch'i Temple
Oriental Theatre
Sri Mariamman Temple

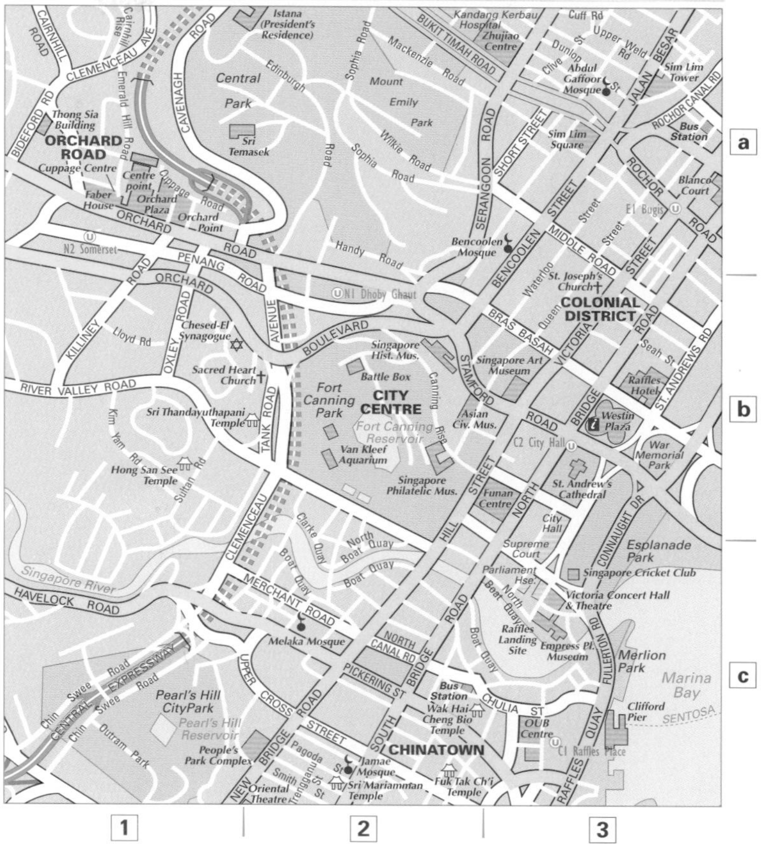

a  b  c
1  2  3

## SINGAPORE

km 0 10
miles 0 6

103°40'
103°50'
104°00'
Johor Baharu
Selat Johor
Sembawang
MALAYSIA / SINGAPORE
Selat Johor
Kranji Ind. Est.
Woodlands New Town
Chong Pang
Pulau Seletar
Selat Tekong
Lim Chu Kang
Seletar Expy.
Yishun New Town
Punggol Point
Pulau Ubin
Pulau Tekong Kechil
Pulau Tekong
Sarimbun Res.
Sungai Kadut Ind. Est.
Zoological Gardens & Seletar Reservoir
Nee Soon
SELETAR AIRPORT
Pulau Serangoon
Tg. Ladang
Sarimbun 85
Ama Keng
Bukit Timah Expy.
Jalan Kayu
Punggol
Serangoon Harbour
Choa Chu Kang
Kranji Expy.
Bukit Panjang Nature Reserve
Seletar Hills
Pasir Ris
Changi
Loyang Ind. Est.
CHANGI INTERNATIONAL AIRPORT
Bulim
132
Bt. Panjang
Bukit Panjang
Upper Peirce Reservoir
Ang Mo Kio
Chia Keng
Yan Kit
Choa Chu Kang 88
Bukit Timah Nature Reserve 162
Serangoon
PAYA LEBAR AIRPORT
Nanyang University
106
Bukit Batok Nature Parks
Air View Park
Raffles Park
MacRitchie Reservoir
Paya Lebar
Bedok Reservoir
Tampines
Simei
Jurong Town
Chinese & Japanese Gardens
Central Expy.
Toa Payoh
Tai Seng
Kg Landang
Tanah Merah Golf Course
Tuas
Jurong
Bt. Peropok 62
Pandan Res.
Clementi
Dunearn
Geylang Serai
Chai Chee
Jurong Industrial Estate
Maryland
Victoria Park
University of Singapore Botanic Gardens
Geylang
Bedok
East Coast Park
Pulau Pesek
Selat Jurong
Holland Village
Katong
Frankel
Pulau Merlimau
Kg Tanjong Penjuru
Pasir Panjang
Queenstown
National Stadium
Kallang Park
East Coast Pkwy.
Pulau Ayer Chawan
Pulau Seraya
Buona Vista Park
Telok Blangah
National Museum
St Andrew's Cathedral
City Hall
Pulau Ayer Merbau
Mt. Fabour
Thian Hock Keng Temple
SINGAPORE
Pulau Sakra
Cable Car
World Trade Centre P. Brani
Selat Pandan
Selat Sinki
Pulau Bukum
Sentosa
Straits of Singapore
East from Greenwich
1°20'N

A  B
1  2  3  4

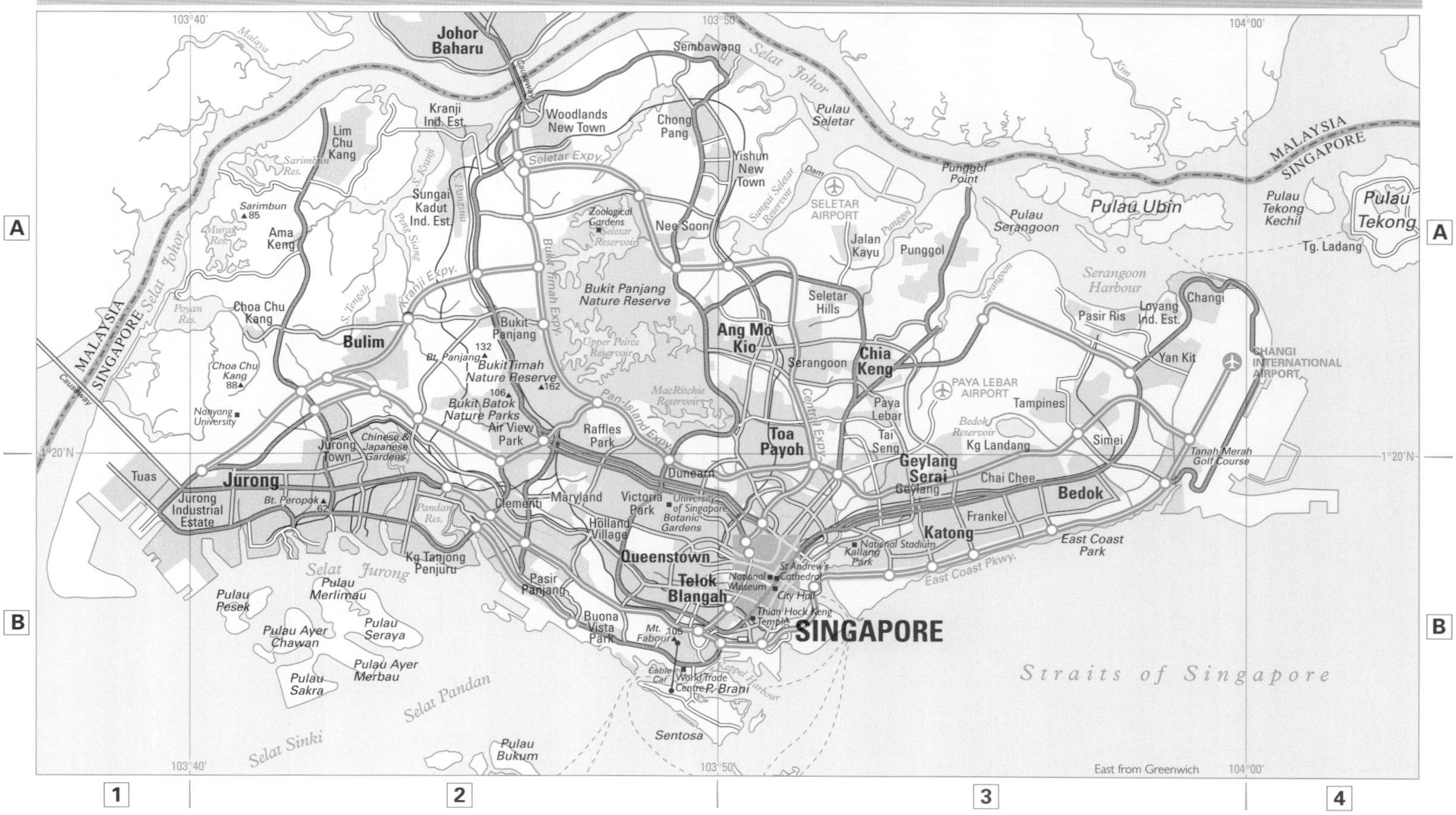

COPYRIGHT PHILIP'S

## STOCKHOLM

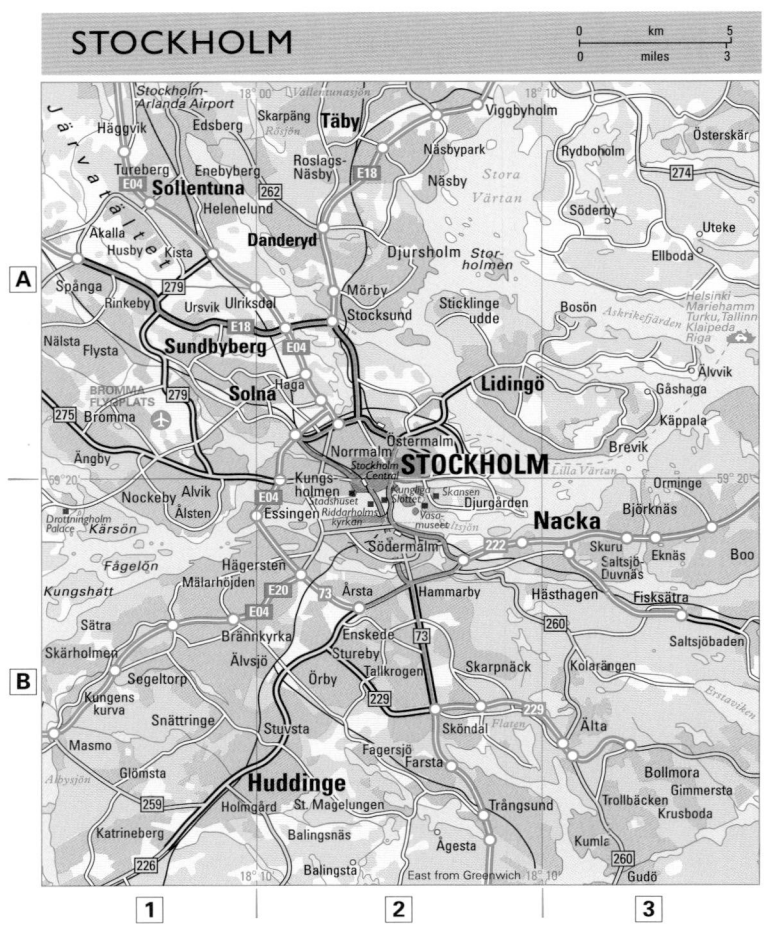

## CENTRAL STOCKHOLM

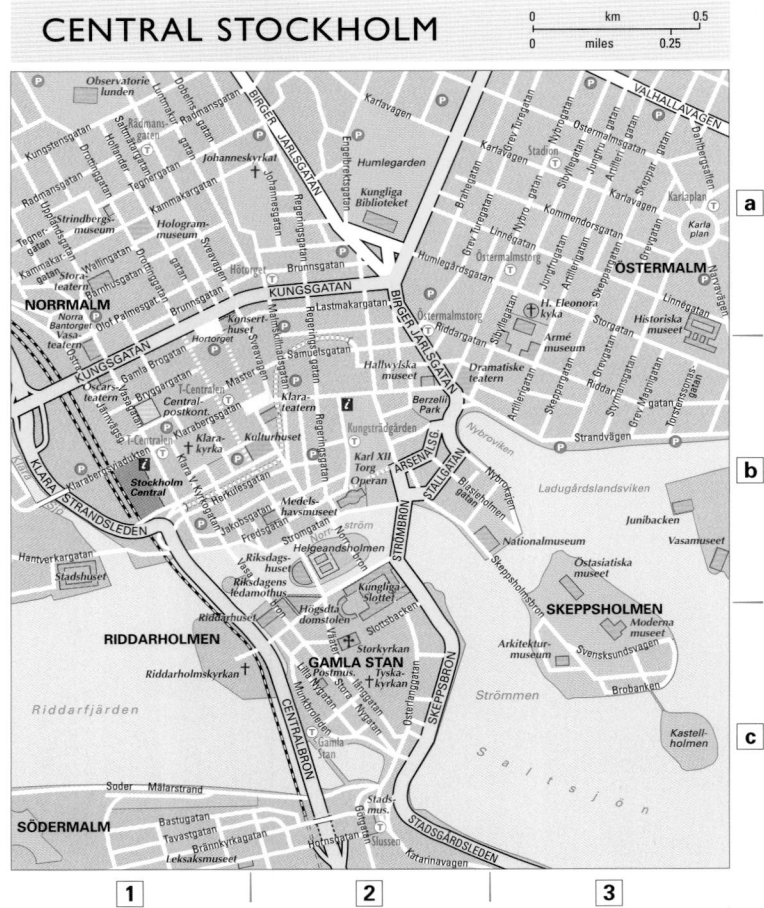

## SYDNEY

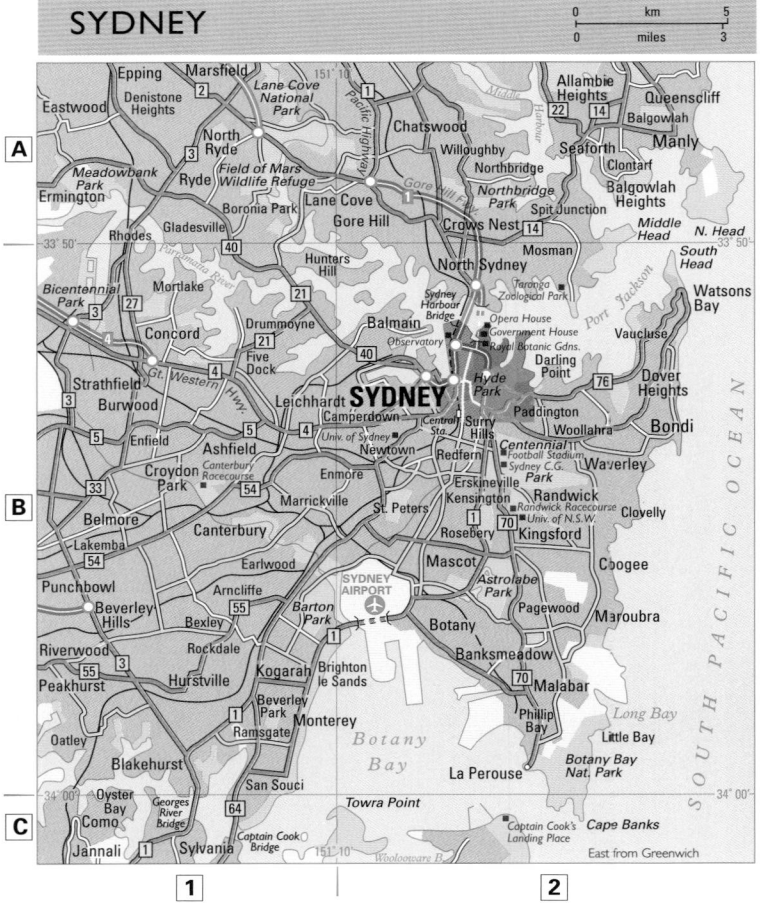

## CENTRAL SYDNEY

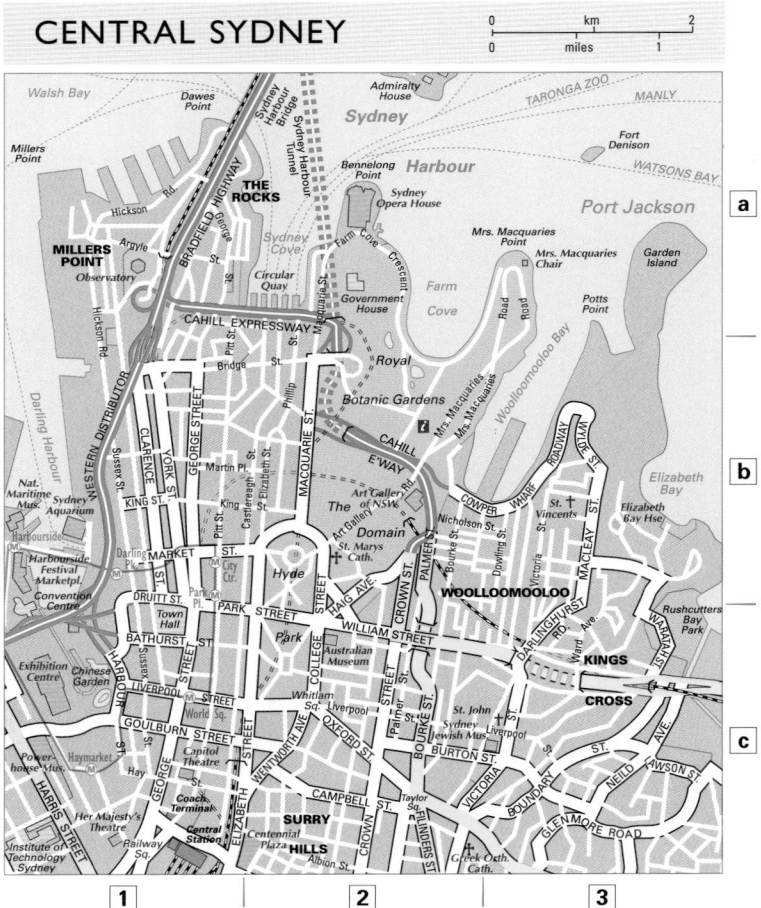

## TOKYO

km 0 — 5
miles 0 — 3

A

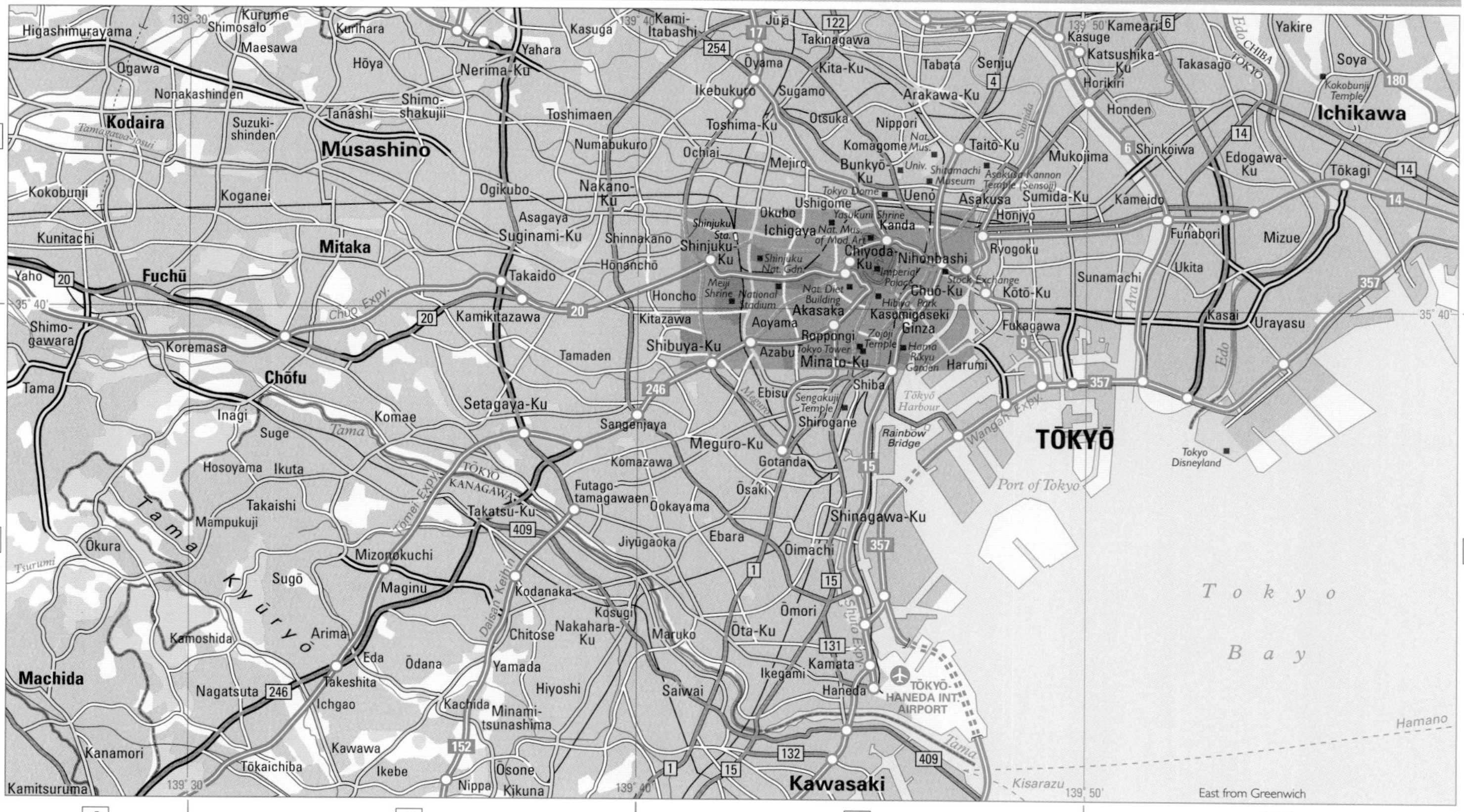

Higashimurayama  Kurume  Shimosato  Kunihara  Kasuga  Kami-Itabashi  Jūjō  Takinogawa  122  Kameari  Yakire
Ōgawa  Shimoshakujii  Maesawa  Yahara  Oyama  17  254  Kita-Ku  Tabata  Senju  Katsushika-Ku  Takasago  Soya
Nonakashinden  Suzuki-shinden  Tanashi  Hōya  Nerima-Ku  Toshimaen  Ikebukuro  Sugamo  Arakawa-Ku  Horikiri  Honden  Shinkoiwa  180
Kodaira  Musashino  Numabukuro  Nakano-Ku  Toshima-Ku  Otsuka  Nippori  Komagome  Taitō-Ku  Mukōjima  Edogawa-Ku  Tōkagi  Ichikawa
Kokubunji  Mitaka  Asagaya  Suginami-Ku  Shinnakano  Honancho  Ushigome  Okubo  Ueno  Asakusa  Sumida-Ku  Kameido  Mizue  14
Kunitachi  Koganei  Ogikubo  Shinjuku-Ku  Ichigaya  Kanda  Nihonbashi  Honjyo  Ryogoku  Funabori  14
Yaho  20  Fuchū  Takaido  Kamikitazawa  20  Honcho  Akasaka  Chiyoda-Ku  Chūō-Ku  Kōtō-Ku  Kasai
Shimogawara  Koremasa  Aoyama  Roppongi  Kasumigaseki  Ginza  Fukagawa  357
Tama  Chōfu  Setagaya-Ku  Shibuya-Ku  Azabu  Minato-Ku  Shiba  TŌKYŌ
Inagi  Suge  Sangenjaya  Ebisu  Harumi  Tokyo Disneyland
Hosoyama  Ikuta  Kōmazawa  Meguro-Ku  Shirogane  Rainbow Bridge  Port of Tokyo

B

Ōkura  Takaishi  Mampukuji  Mizonokuchi  Futago-tamagawaen  Ōokayama  Ōsaki  Shinagawa-Ku  Tokyo Bay
Machida  Sugō  Arima  Eda  Ōdana  Yamada  Kosugi  Jiyūgaoka  Ebara  Ōimachi  15  357
Kamoshida  Takeshita  Ichgao  Nakahara-Ku  Ōmori  131
Nagatsuta  246  Kachida  Hiyoshi  Saiwai  Ikegami  Kamata  Haneda  TOKYO-HANEDA INT AIRPORT
Kanamori  Tōkaichiba  Kawawa  Minami-tsunashima  152  Ōsone  Kisarazu  Hamano
Kamitsuruma  Ōsone  Nippa  Kikuna  1  15  132  Kawasaki  409  East from Greenwich

| 1 | 2 | 3 | 4 |

---

## CENTRAL TOKYO

km 0 — 1
miles 0 — 0.5

a

SHINJUKU-KU  ŌKUBO  OKUBO-DORI  SHOKUAN-DORI  KUDANKITA  AKIHABARA  ASAKUSABASHI
OME-KAIDO  Hanazono-jinja Shrine  ICHIGAYA  Yasukuni-jinja Shrine  JIMBOCHO  KANDA  KODENMACHO
Shinjuku Central Park  Sumitomo Bldg  Shinjuku Sta.  YOTSUYA  SANBANCHO  Fukiage Imperial Garden  MARUNOUCHI
Tokyo City Hall  Minami-shinjuku Station  Shinjuku-National Garden  Yotsuya Sta.  East Garden  NIHONBASHI

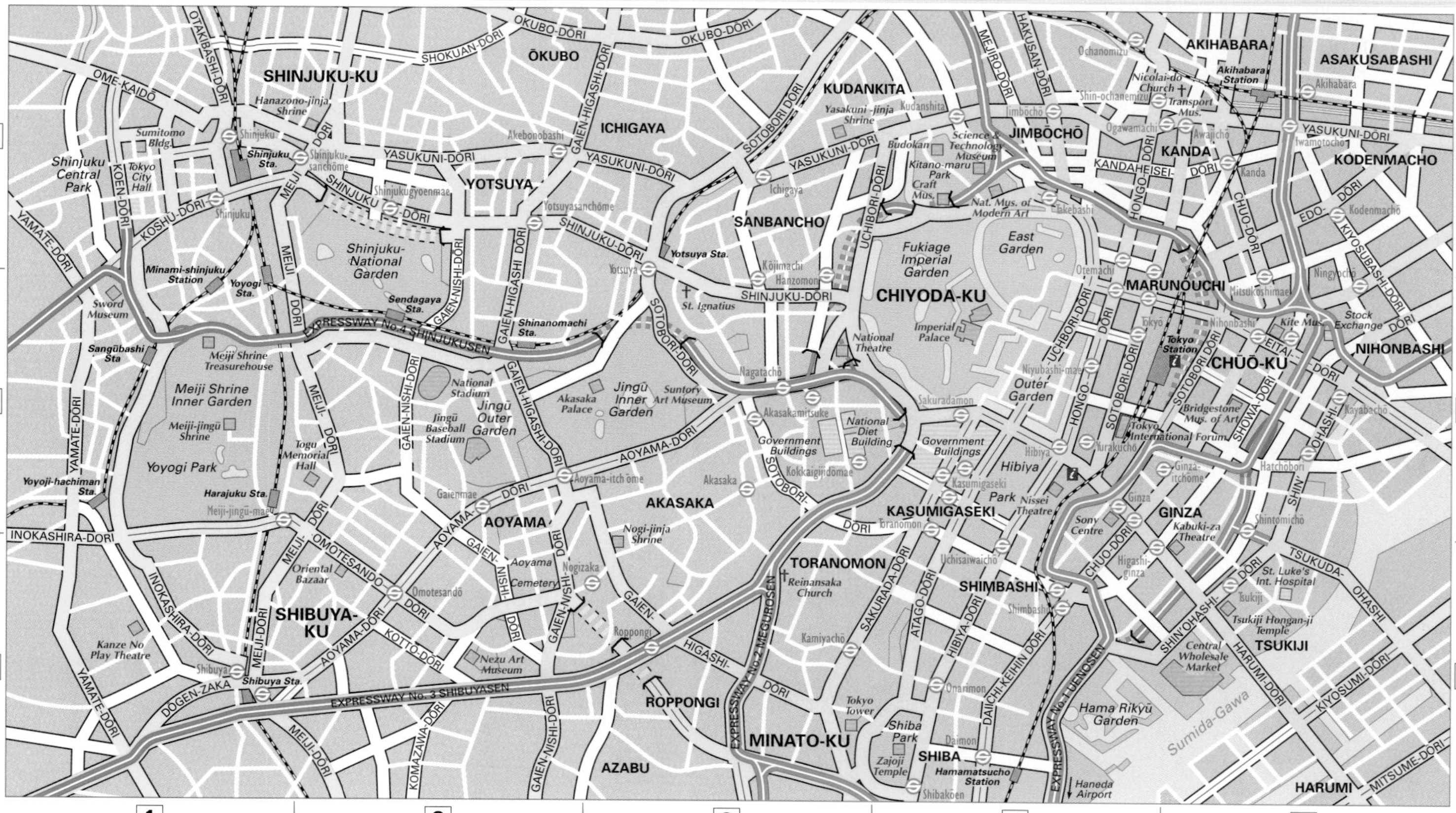

b

Meiji Shrine Treasurehouse  National Stadium  Akasaka Palace  Jingū Inner Garden  National Theatre  CHIYODA-KU  Stock Exchange
Meiji Shrine Inner Garden  Jingū Baseball Stadium  Jingū Outer Garden  Suntory Art Museum  Imperial Palace  Tokyo Station  CHŪŌ-KU
Yoyogi Park  Togu Memorial Hall  Gaienmae  AKASAKA  National Diet Building  Government Buildings  Hibiya  GINZA
Yoyogi-hachiman Sta.  Harajuku Sta.  AOYAMA  Nogi-jinja Shrine  TORANOMON  KASUMIGASEKI  Kabuki-za Theatre

c

Kanze No Play Theatre  Oriental Bazaar  Aoyama Cemetery  SHIMBASHI  Sony Centre  St. Luke's Int. Hospital
SHIBUYA-KU  Omotesando  Nezu Art Museum  ROPPONGI  MINATO-KU  Tokyo Tower  Shiba Park  TSUKIJI
Shibuya Sta.  AZABU  Zōjōji Temple  SHIBA  Hamamatsuchō Station  Hama Rikyū Garden  Central Wholesale Market  HARUMI
EXPRESSWAY NO. 3 SHIBUYASEN  Haneda Airport  Sumida-Gawa

| 1 | 2 | 3 | 4 | 5 |

## TEHRAN

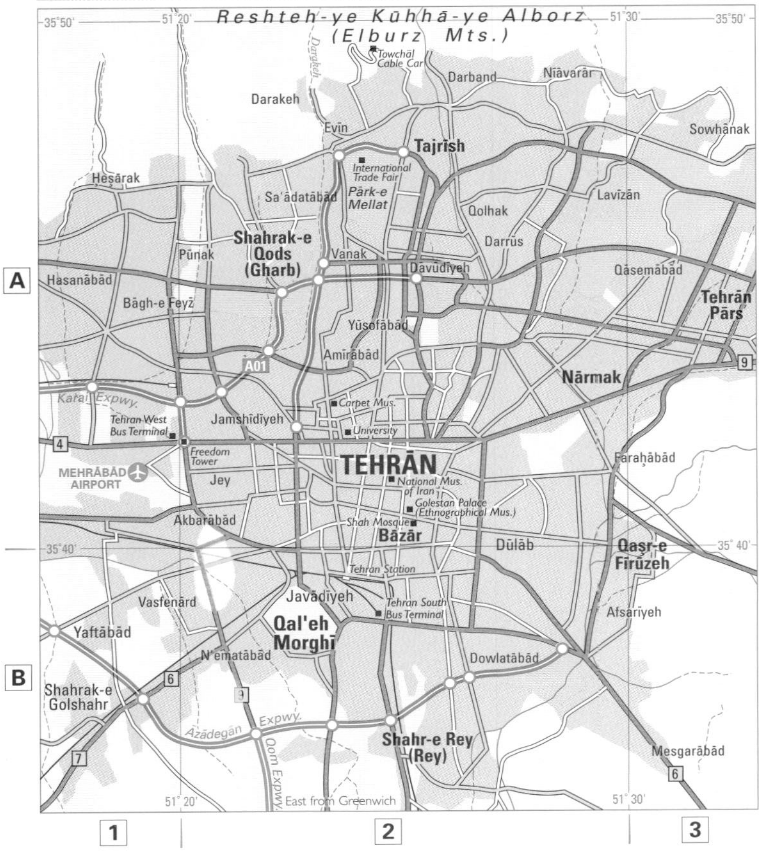
0 km 5
0 miles 3
Reshteh-ye Kūhhā-ye Alborz
(Elburz Mts.)
35°50'
51°20'
51°30'
Towchāl Cable Car
Darakeh
Darband
Niāvarān
Evīn
Sowhānak
Tajrīsh
International Trade Fair
Pārk-e Mellat
Hesārak
Sa'ādatābād
Lavīzān
Qolhak
Pūnak
Shahrak-e Qods (Gharb)
Darrūs
Vanak
Hasanābād
Dāvūdīyeh
Qāsemābād
Bāgh-e Feyz
Tehrān Pārs
Yūsofābād
Amīrābād
A01
Nārmak
Karaj Expwy.
Carpet Mus.
Tehran West Bus Terminal
Jamshīdīyeh
University
Freedom Tower
MEHRĀBĀD AIRPORT
Jey
TEHRĀN
National Mus. of Iran
Farahābād
Golestan Palace (Ethnographical Mus.)
Akbarābād
Shah Mosque
Bāzār
35°40'
Dūlāb
Qasr-e Fīrūzeh
Tehran Station
Vasfenārd
Javādīyeh
Tehran South Bus Terminal
Afsarīyeh
Yaftābād
Qal'eh Morghī
N'ematābād
Dowlatābād
Shahrak-e Golshahr
Āzādegān Expwy.
Shahr-e Rey (Rey)
Dom Expwy.
Mesgarābād
East from Greenwich
A
B
1
2
3

## TIANJIN

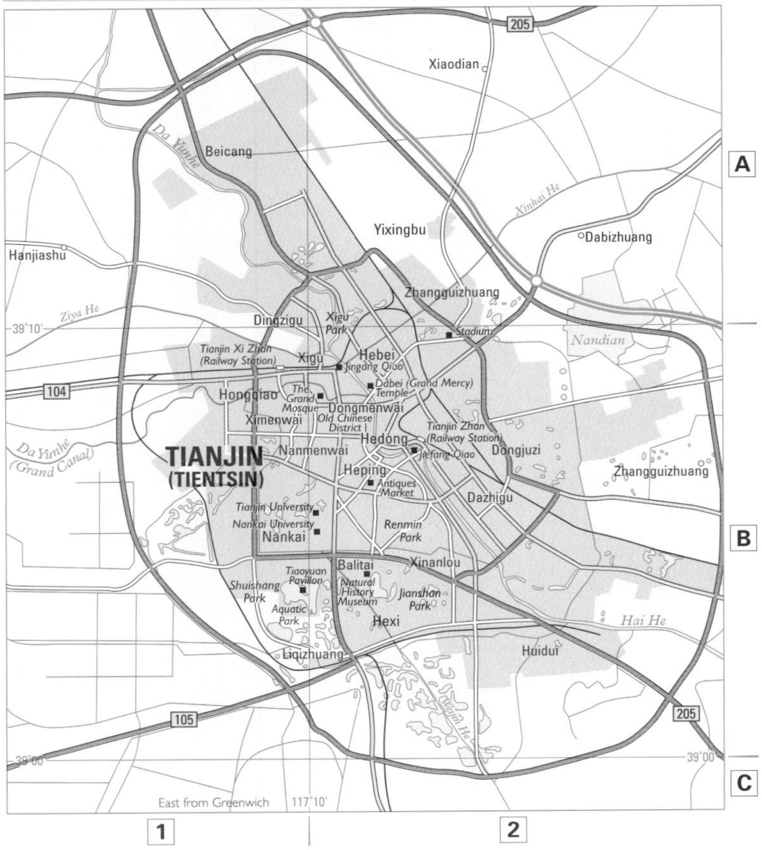
0 km 5
0 miles 3
205
Xiaodian
Da Yunhe
Beicang
A
Xinkai He
Yixingbu
Dabizhuang
Hanjiashu
Zhangguizhuang
39°10'
Ziya He
Dingzigu
Xigu Park
Stadium
Nandian
Tianjin Xi Zhan (Railway Station)
Xigu
Hebei
Jingang Qiao
104
Hongqiao
The Grand Mosque
Dabei (Grand Mercy) Temple
Dongmenwai
Ximenwai
Old Chinese District
Tianjin Zhan (Railway Station)
Da Yunhe (Grand Canal)
TIANJIN (TIENTSIN)
Nanmenwai
Hedong
Jiefang Qiao
Dongjuzi
Heping
Antiques Market
Zhangguizhuang
Tianjin University
Dazhigu
Nankai University
Nankai
Renmin Park
B
Balitai
Xinanlou
Tiaoyuan Pavilion
Shuishang Park
Natural History Museum
Jianshan Park
Aquatic Park
Hexi
Hai He
Liqizhuang
Huidui
205
105
39°00'
C
East from Greenwich
117°10'
1
2

## TORONTO

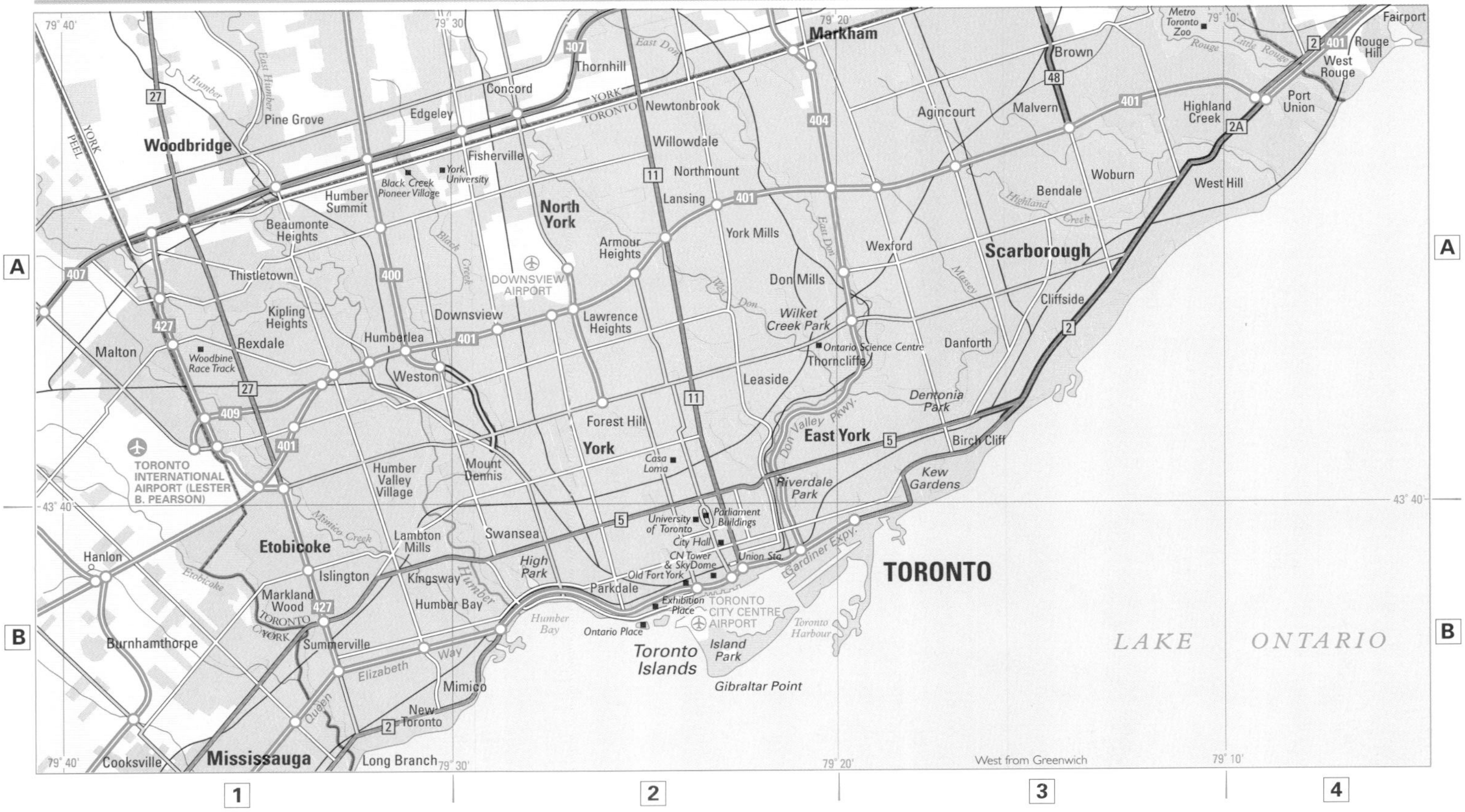
0 km 5
0 miles 3
79°40'
79°30'
79°20'
79°10'
Metro Toronto Zoo
Fairport
Markham
407
East Don
Thornhill
Brown
Rouge Hill
West Rouge
48
27
Humber
East Humber
Concord
YORK TORONTO
Newtonbrook
Agincourt
Malvern
401
Highland Creek
Port Union
2A
Pine Grove
Edgeley
404
Willowdale
PEEL YORK
Woodbridge
Fisherville
York University
Black Creek Pioneer Village
11
Northmount
Bendale
Woburn
West Hill
Humber Summit
Lansing
401
North York
Beaumonte Heights
Armour Heights
York Mills
Wexford
Scarborough
A
407
400
Thistletown
DOWNSVIEW AIRPORT
Don Mills
Cliffside
427
Kipling Heights
Downsview
Lawrence Heights
Wilket Creek Park
Rexdale
Humberlea
401
Ontario Science Centre
Danforth
2
Malton
Woodbine Race Track
Weston
Thorncliffe
Leaside
27
11
Dentonia Park
409
Forest Hill
Don Valley Pkwy.
East York
5
Birch Cliff
TORONTO INTERNATIONAL AIRPORT (LESTER B. PEARSON)
401
York
Casa Loma
Mount Dennis
Humber Valley Village
Riverdale Park
Kew Gardens
43°40'
University of Toronto
Parliament Buildings
5
Mimico Creek
Lambton Mills
Swansea
Hanlon
Etobicoke
City Hall
CN Tower & SkyDome
Union Sta.
Gardiner Expy.
TORONTO
High Park
Islington
Kingsway
Old Fort York
Markland Wood
Parkdale
Etobicoke
TORONTO
427
Humber Bay
Exhibition Place
TORONTO CITY CENTRE AIRPORT
Humber Bay
Ontario Place
Toronto Harbour
LAKE ONTARIO
B
Burnhamthorpe
YORK
Summerville
Toronto Islands
Island Park
Elizabeth Way
Gibraltar Point
Mimico
Queen
New Toronto
2
Cooksville
Mississauga
Long Branch
West from Greenwich
1
2
3
4

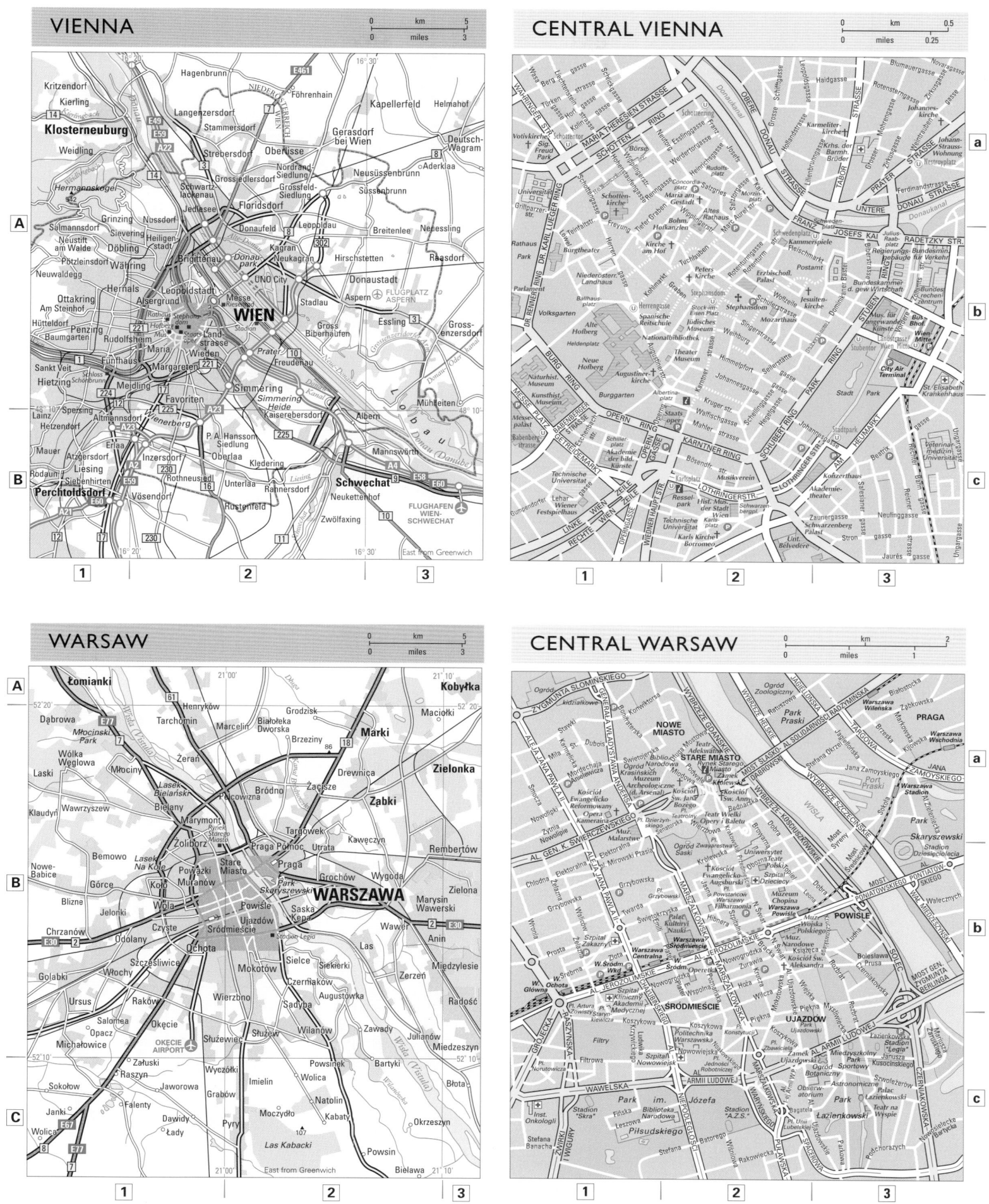

## WASHINGTON

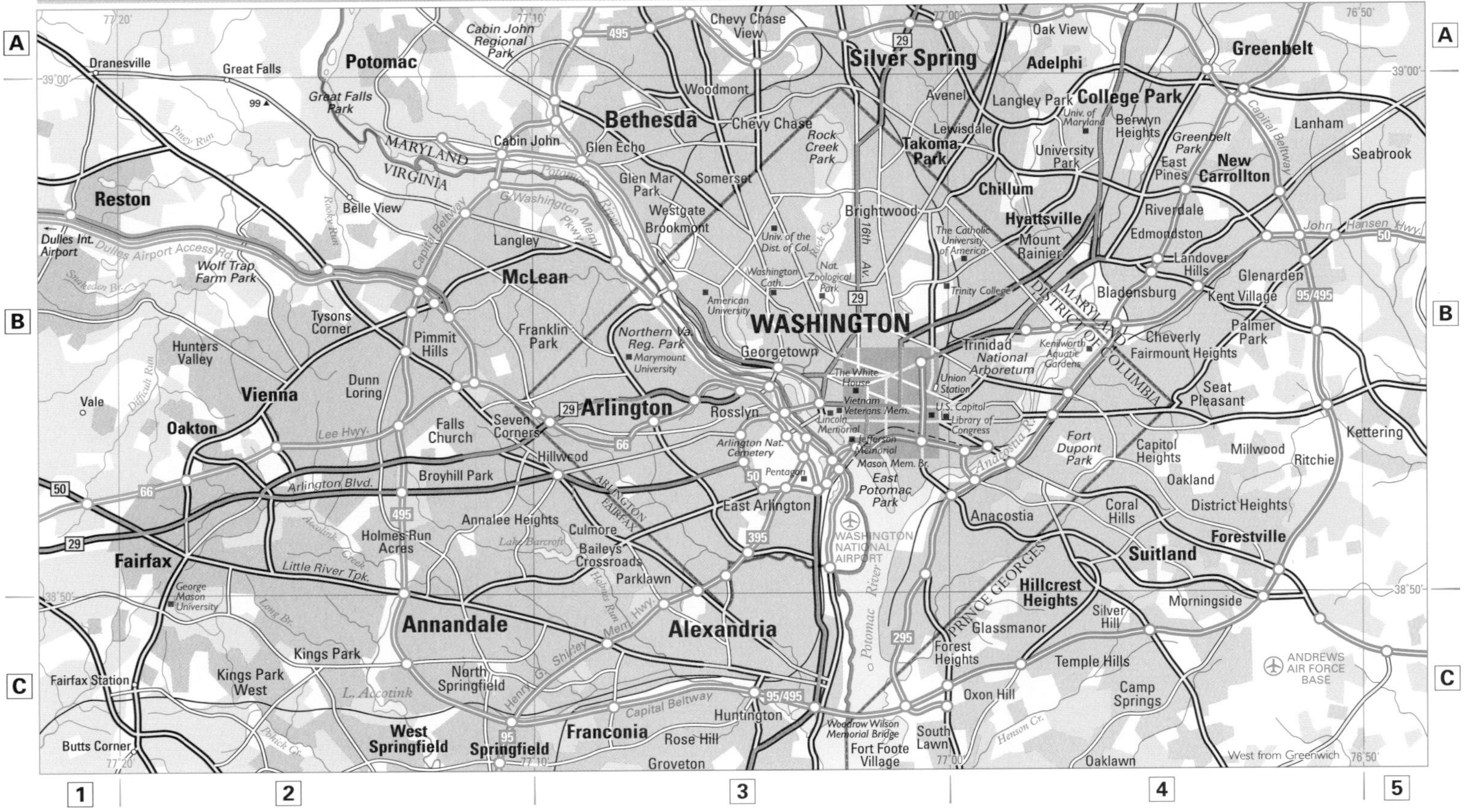

## CENTRAL WASHINGTON

## WELLINGTON

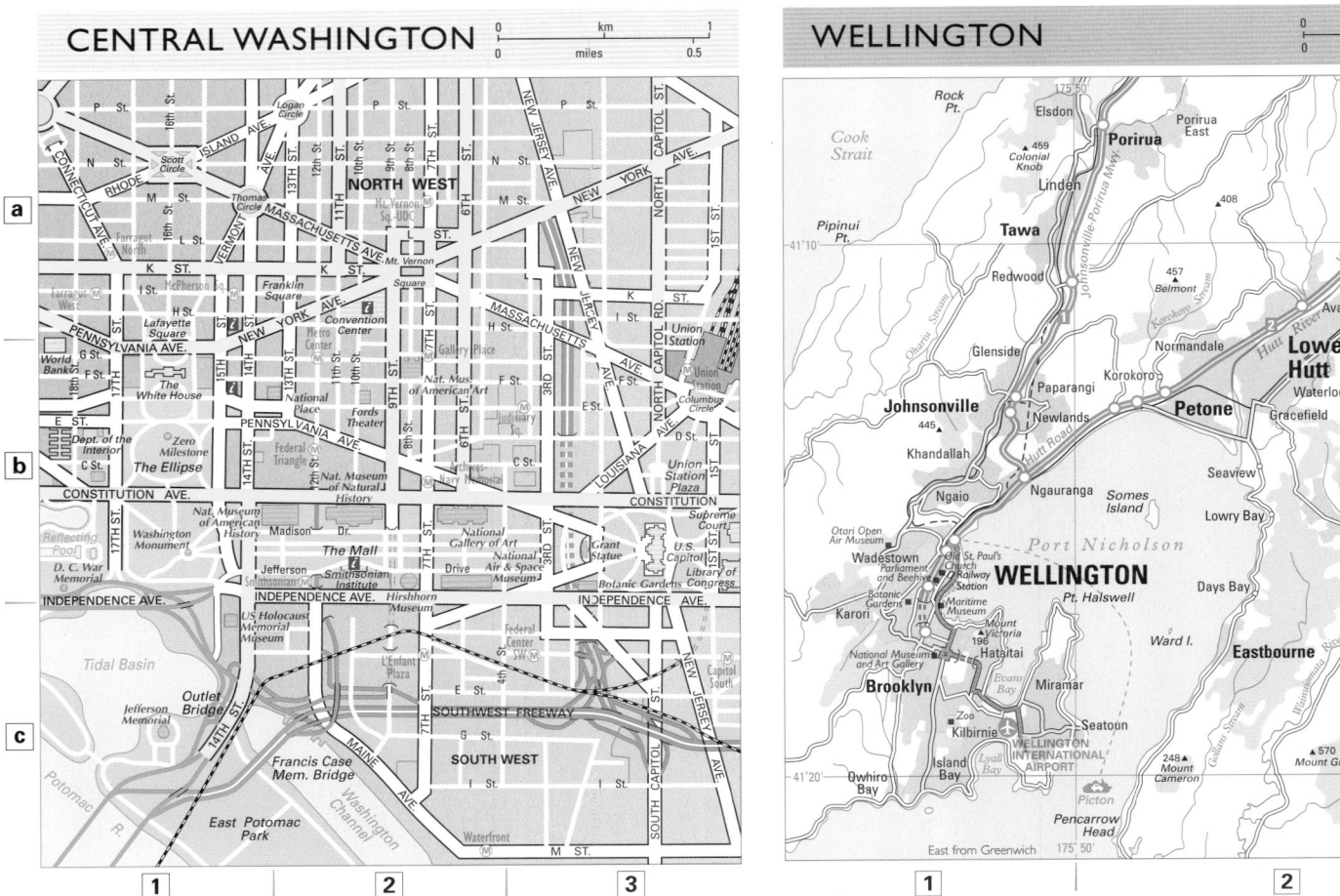

# INDEX TO CITY MAPS

The index contains the names of all the principal places and features shown on the City Maps. Each name is followed by an additional entry in italics giving the name of the City Map within which it is located.

The number in bold type which follows each name refers to the number of the City Map page where that feature or place will be found.

The letter and figure which are immediately after the page number give the grid square on the map within which the feature or place is situated. The letter represents the latitude and the figure the longitude. Upper case letters refer to the City Maps, lower case letters to the Central Area Maps. The full geographic reference is provided in the border of the City Maps.

The location given is the centre of the city, suburb or feature and is not necessarily the name. Rivers, canals and roads are indexed to their name. Rivers carry the symbol → after their name.

An explanation of the alphabetical order rules and a list of the abbreviations used are to be found at the beginning of the World Map Index.

## A


Aalām, *Baghdad* **3** B2
Aalsmeer, *Amsterdam* **2** B1
Abbey Wood, *London* **15** B4
Abcoude, *Amsterdam* **2** B2
Ābdin, *Cairo* **7** A2
Abeno, *Osaka* **22** B4
Aberdeen, *Hong Kong* **12** B2
Aberdour, *Edinburgh* **11** A2
Aberdour Castle, *Edinburgh* **11** A2
Abfanggraben →, *Munich* **20** A3
Ablon-sur-Seine, *Paris* **23** B3
Abramtsevo, *Moscow* **19** B4
Abu Dis, *Jerusalem* **13** B2
Abû en Numrus, *Cairo* **7** B2
Abu Ghosh, *Jerusalem* **13** B1
Acacias, *Madrid* **17** c2
Acassuso, *Buenos Aires* **7** A1
Accotink Cr. →, *Washington* **32** B2
Acheres, *Paris* **23** A1
Acilia, *Rome* **25** C1
Aclimação, *São Paulo* **26** B2
Acton, *London* **15** A2
Açúcar, Pão de, *Rio de Janeiro* **24** B2
Ada Beja, *Lisbon* **14** A1
Adams Park, *Atlanta* **3** B2
Adams Shore, *Boston* **6** B4
Addiscombe, *London* **15** B3
Adelphi, *Washington* **32** A4
Aderklaa, *Vienna* **31** A3
Admiralteyskaya Storona, *St. Petersburg* **26** B2
Áffori, *Milan* **18** A2
Aflandshage, *Copenhagen* **10** B3
Afsarīyeh, *Tehran* **30** B2
Agboyi Cr. →, *Lagos* **14** A2
Agerup, *Copenhagen* **10** A1
Ägesta, *Stockholm* **28** B2
Agincourt, *Toronto* **30** A3
Agora, Arhéa, *Athens* **2** c1
Agra Canal, *Delhi* **10** B2
Agricola Oriental, *Mexico City* **18** B2
Agua Espraiada →, *São Paulo* **26** B2
Agualva-Cacem, *Lisbon* **14** A1
Agustino, Cerro El, *Lima* **16** B2
Ahrensfelde, *Berlin* **5** A4
Ahuntsic, *Montreal* **19** A1
Ai →, *Osaka* **22** A4
Aigremont, *Paris* **23** A1
Air View Park, *Singapore* **27** A2
Airport West, *Melbourne* **17** A1
Aiyaleo, *Athens* **2** B2
Aiyáleos, Óros, *Athens* **2** B1
Ajegunle, *Lagos* **14** B2
Aji, *Osaka* **22** A3
Ajuda, *Lisbon* **14** A1
Akalla, *Stockholm* **28** A1
Akasaka, *Tokyo* **29** b3
Akbarābād, *Tehran* **30** A2
Akershus Slott, *Oslo* **22** A3
Akihabara, *Tokyo* **29** a5
Akrópolis, *Athens* **2** c2
Al 'Azamiyah, *Baghdad* **3** A2
Al Quds = Jerusalem, *Jerusalem* **13** B2
Alaguntan, *Lagos* **14** B2
Alameda, *San Francisco* **25** B3
Alameda, Parque, *Mexico City* **18** b2
Alameda Memorial State Beach Park, *San Francisco* **25** B3
Albern, *Vienna* **31** B2
Albert Park, *Melbourne* **17** B1
Alberton, *Johannesburg* **13** B2
Albertslund, *Copenhagen* **10** B2
Albysjön, *Stockholm* **28** B1
Alcantara, *Lisbon* **14** A1
Alcatraz I., *San Francisco* **25** B2
Alcobendas, *Madrid* **17** A2
Alcorcón, *Madrid* **17** B1
Aldershof, *Berlin* **5** B4
Aldo Bonzi, *Buenos Aires* **7** C1
Aleksandrovskoye, *St. Petersburg* **26** B2
Alexander Nevsky Abbey, *St. Petersburg* **26** B2
Alexander Soutzos Moussío, *Athens* **2** b3
Alexandra, *Johannesburg* **13** A2
Alexandra, *Singapore* **27** B2
Alexandria, *Washington* **32** C3
Alfama, *Lisbon* **14** c3
Alfortville, *Paris* **23** B3
Algés, *Lisbon* **14** A1
Alhambra, *Los Angeles* **16** B4
Alibey →, *Istanbul* **12** B1
Alibey Barajı, *Istanbul* **12** B1
Alibeyköy, *Istanbul* **12** B1
Alimos, *Athens* **2** B2
Alipur, *Calcutta* **8** B1
Allach, *Munich* **20** A1
Allambie Heights, *Sydney* **28** A2
Allard Pierson Museum, *Amsterdam* **2** b2
Allermuir Hill, *Edinburgh* **11** B2
Allerton, Pt., *Boston* **6** B4
Allston, *Boston* **6** A3
Almada, *Lisbon* **14** A2
Almagro, *Buenos Aires* **7** B2
Almargem do Bispo, *Lisbon* **14** A1
Almazovo, *Moscow* **19** A6
Almirante G. Brown, Parque, *Buenos Aires* **7** C2
Almon, *Jerusalem* **13** B2
Almond →, *Edinburgh* **11** B2
Alnabru, *Oslo* **22** A4
Alnsjøen, *Oslo* **22** A4
Alperton, *London* **15** A2
Alpine, *New York* **21** A2
Alrode, *Johannesburg* **13** B2
Alsemerg, *Brussels* **6** B1
Alsergrund, *Vienna* **31** A2
Alsip, *Chicago* **9** C2
Älsten, *Stockholm* **28** B1
Älta, *Stockholm* **28** B2
Altadena, *Los Angeles* **16** A4
Alte-Donau →, *Vienna* **31** A2
Alte Hofburg, *Vienna* **31** b1
Alter Finkenkrug, *Berlin* **5** A1
Altes Rathaus, *Munich* **20** b3
Altglienicke, *Berlin* **5** B4
Altlandsberg, *Berlin* **5** A5
Altlandsberg Nord, *Berlin* **5** A5
Altmannsdorf, *Vienna* **31** B1
Alto da Moóca, *São Paulo* **26** B2
Alto do Pina, *Lisbon* **14** A2
Altona, *Melbourne* **17** B1
Alvaro Obregon, *Mexico City* **18** B1
Alvik, *Stockholm* **28** B1
Älvsjo, *Stockholm* **28** B2
Älvvik, *Stockholm* **28** A3
Am Hasenbergl, *Munich* **20** A2
Am Steinhof, *Vienna* **31** A1
Am Wald, *Munich* **20** B2
Ama Keng, *Singapore* **27** A2
Amadora, *Lisbon* **14** A1
Amagasaki, *Osaka* **22** A3
Amager, *Copenhagen* **10** B3
Amāl Qādisiya, *Baghdad* **3** B2
Amalienborg, *Copenhagen* **10** b3
Amata, *Milan* **18** A1
Ameixoeira, *Lisbon* **14** A2
América, *São Paulo* **26** B1
Amin, *Baghdad* **3** B2
Aminadov, *Jerusalem* **13** B1
Aminyevo, *Moscow* **19** B2
Amirābād, *Tehran* **30** A2
Amora, *Lisbon* **14** B2
Amoreira, *Lisbon* **14** A1
Ampelokipi, *Athens* **2** B2
Amper →, *Munich* **20** A1
Amstel, *Amsterdam* **2** b2
Amstel →, *Amsterdam* **2** c2
Amstel-Drecht-Kanaal, *Amsterdam* **2** B2
Amstel Station, *Amsterdam* **2** c3
Amstelhof, *Amsterdam* **2** b2
Amstelveen, *Amsterdam* **2** B2
Amsterdam, *Amsterdam* **2** A2
Amsterdam-Rijnkanaal, *Amsterdam* **2** B3
Amsterdam Zoo, *Amsterdam* **2** b3
Amsterdam Zuidoost, *Amsterdam* **2** B2
Amsterdamse Bos, *Amsterdam* **2** B1
Anacostia, *Washington* **32** B4
Anadoluhisari, *Istanbul* **12** B2
Anadolukavağı, *Istanbul* **12** A2
Anata, *Jerusalem* **13** B2
Ancol, *Jakarta* **13** A1
'Andalus, *Baghdad* **3** B1
Andarai, *Rio de Janeiro* **24** B1
Anderlecht, *Brussels* **6** A1
Anderson Park, *Atlanta* **3** B2
Andingmen, *Beijing* **4** B2
Andrews Air Force Base, *Washington* **32** C4
Ang Mo Kio, *Singapore* **27** A3
Angby, *Stockholm* **28** A1
Angel I., *San Francisco* **25** A2
Angel Island State Park, *San Francisco* **25** A2
Angke, Kali →, *Jakarta* **13** A1
Angyalföld, *Budapest* **7** A2
Anik, *Mumbai* **20** A2
Anin, *Warsaw* **31** B2
Anjou, *Montreal* **19** A2
Annalee Heights, *Washington* **32** B2
Annandale, *Washington* **32** C2
Anne Frankhuis, *Amsterdam* **2** a1
Antony, *Paris* **23** B2
Anyangch'on, *Seoul* **26** C1
Aoyama, *Tokyo* **29** b2
Ap Lei Chau, *Hong Kong* **12** B1
Apapa, *Lagos* **14** B2
Apelação, *Lisbon* **14** A2
Apterkarskiy Ostrov, *St. Petersburg* **26** B2
Ar Kazimiyah, *Baghdad* **3** B1
Ara →, *Tokyo* **29** A4
Arakawa-Ku, *Tokyo* **29** A3
Arany-hegyi-patak →, *Budapest* **7** A2
Aravaca, *Madrid* **17** B1
Arbataash, *Baghdad* **3** A1
Arc de Triomphe, *Paris* **23** a2
Arcadia, *Los Angeles* **16** B4
Arceuil, *Paris* **23** B2
Arco Plaza, *Los Angeles* **16** b1
Arese, *Milan* **18** A1
Arganzuela, *Madrid* **17** B1
Argenteuil, *Paris* **23** A2
Argonne Forest, *Chicago* **9** C1
Argüelles, *Madrid* **17** a1
Arima, *Osaka* **22** A2
Arima, *Tokyo* **29** B2
Ários Págos, *Athens* **2** c1
Arkhangelyskoye, *Moscow* **19** B1
Arlington, *Boston* **6** A2
Arlington, *Washington* **32** B3
Arlington Heights, *Boston* **6** A2
Arlington Nat. Cemetery, *Washington* **32** B3
Armação, *Rio de Janeiro* **24** B2
Armadale, *Melbourne* **17** B2
Armenian Quarter, *Jerusalem* **13** b3
Armour Heights, *Toronto* **30** A2
Arncliffe, *Sydney* **28** B1
Arnold Arboretum, *Boston* **6** B3
Árpádföld, *Budapest* **7** A3
Arrentela, *Lisbon* **14** B2
Årsta, *Stockholm* **28** B2
Art Institute, *Chicago* **9** c2
Artane, *Dublin* **11** A2
Artas, *Jerusalem* **13** B2
Arthur's Seat, *Edinburgh* **11** B3
Aryiróupolis, *Athens* **2** B2
Asagaya, *Tokyo* **29** A2
Asahi, *Osaka* **22** A4
Asakusa, *Tokyo* **29** A3
Asakusabashi, *Tokyo* **29** a5
Asati, *Calcutta* **8** C1
Aschheim, *Munich* **20** A3
Ascot Vale, *Melbourne* **17** A1
Ashburn, *Chicago* **9** C2
Ashburton, *Melbourne* **17** B2
Ashfield, *Sydney* **28** B1
Ashford, *London* **15** B1
Ashiya, *Osaka* **22** A2
Ashiya →, *Osaka* **22** A2
Ashtown, *Dublin* **11** A2
Askisto, *Helsinki* **12** B1
Askrikefjärden, *Stockholm* **28** A3
Asnières, *Paris* **23** A2
Aspern, *Vienna* **31** A2
Aspern, Flugplatz, *Vienna* **31** A3
Assago, *Milan* **18** B1
Assemblée Nationale, *Paris* **23** b3
Assendelft, *Amsterdam* **2** A1
Assiano, *Milan* **18** B1
Astoria, *New York* **21** B2
Astrolabe Park, *Sydney* **28** B2
Atarot Airport, *Jerusalem* **13** A2
Atghara, *Calcutta* **8** B2
Athens = Athínai, *Athens* **2** B2
Athínai, *Athens* **2** B2
Athis-Mons, *Paris* **23** B3
Athlone, *Cape Town* **8** A2
Atholl, *Johannesburg* **13** A2
Atīfiya, *Baghdad* **3** A2
Atişalen, *Istanbul* **12** B1
Atlanta, *Atlanta* **3** B2
Atlanta History Center, *Atlanta* **3** B2
Atomium, *Brussels* **6** A2
Attiki, *Athens* **2** A2
Atzgersdorf, *Vienna* **31** B1
Aubervilliers, *Paris* **23** A3
Aubing, *Munich* **20** B1
Auburndale, *Boston* **6** A2
Auchendinny, *Edinburgh* **11** B2
Auckland Park, *Johannesburg* **13** B2
Auderghem, *Brussels* **6** B2
Augusta, Mausoleo di, *Rome* **25** b2
Augustówka, *Warsaw* **31** B2
Aulnay-sous-Bois, *Paris* **23** A3
Aurelio, *Rome* **25** B1
Ausīm, *Cairo* **7** A1
Austerlitz, Gare d', *Paris* **23** A3
Austin, *Chicago* **9** B2
Avalon, *Wellington* **32** B2
Avedøre, *Copenhagen* **10** B2
Avellaneda, *Buenos Aires* **7** C2
Avenel, *Washington* **32** B4
Avondale, *Chicago* **9** B2
Avondale Heights, *Melbourne* **17** A1
Avtovo, *St. Petersburg* **26** B1
Ayazağa, *Istanbul* **12** B1
Ayer Chawan, P., *Singapore* **27** B2
Ayer Merbau, P., *Singapore* **27** B2
Ayía Marina, *Athens* **2** C3
Ayía Paraskevi, *Athens* **2** A2
Áyios Dhimitrios, *Athens* **2** B2
Áyios Ioánnis Rendis, *Athens* **2** B1
Azabu, *Tokyo* **29** c3
Azcapotzalco, *Mexico City* **18** B1
Azteca, Estadio, *Mexico City* **18** C2
Azucar, Cerro Pan de, *Santiago* **26** A1


## B


Baambrugge, *Amsterdam* **2** B2
Baba I., *Karachi* **14** B1
Babarpur, *Delhi* **10** A2
Babushkin, *Moscow* **19** A4
Back B., *Mumbai* **20** B1
Baclaran, *Manila* **17** B2
Bacoor, *Manila* **17** C1
Bacoor B., *Manila* **17** C1
Badalona, *Barcelona* **4** A2
Badhoevedorp, *Amsterdam* **2** A1
Badli, *Delhi* **10** A1
Bærum, *Oslo* **22** A2
Bağcılar, *Istanbul* **12** B1
Bággio, *Milan* **18** B1
Bāgh-e-Feyz, *Tehran* **30** A1
Baghdād, *Baghdad* **3** A2
Bagmari, *Calcutta* **8** B2
Bagneux, *Paris* **23** B2
Bagnolet, *Paris* **23** A3
Bagsværd, *Copenhagen* **10** A2
Bagsværd Sø, *Copenhagen* **10** A2
Baguiati, *Calcutta* **8** B2
Bagumbayan, *Manila* **17** C2
Bahçeköy, *Istanbul* **12** A1
Bahtīm, *Cairo* **7** A2
Baileys Crossroads, *Washington* **32** B3
Bailly, *Paris* **23** A1
Bairro Alto, *Lisbon* **14** c1
Bairro Lopes, *Lisbon* **14** b3
Baisha, *Canton* **8** B2
Baisha →, *Canton* **8** B2
Baixa, *Lisbon* **14** c2
Baiyun Airport, *Canton* **8** A2
Baiyun Hill Scenic Spot, *Canton* **8** B2
Bakırköy, *Istanbul* **12** C1
Bakovka, *Moscow* **19** B2
Bal Harbor, *Miami* **18** A2
Balara, *Manila* **17** B2
Balashikha, *Moscow* **19** B5
Baldia, *Karachi* **14** A1
Baldoyle, *Dublin* **11** A3
Baldwin Hills, *Los Angeles* **16** B2
Baldwin Hills Res., *Los Angeles* **16** B2
Balgowlah, *Sydney* **28** A2
Balgowlah Heights, *Sydney* **28** A2
Balham, *London* **15** B3
Bali, *Calcutta* **8** A1
Baliganja, *Calcutta* **8** B2
Balingsnäs, *Stockholm* **28** B2
Balingsta, *Stockholm* **28** B2
Balintawak, *Manila* **17** B1
Balitai, *Tianjin* **30** B2
Ballerup, *Copenhagen* **10** A2
Ballinteer, *Dublin* **11** B2
Ballyboden, *Dublin* **11** B2
Ballybrack, *Dublin* **11** B3
Ballyfermot, *Dublin* **11** A1
Ballymorefinn Hill, *Dublin* **11** B1
Ballymun, *Dublin* **11** A2
Balmain, *Sydney* **28** B2
Baluhati, *Calcutta* **8** B1
Balvanera, *Buenos Aires* **7** B2
Balwyn, *Melbourne* **17** A2
Balwyn North, *Melbourne* **17** A2
Banática, *Lisbon* **14** A1
Banco do Brasil, Centro Cultural, *Rio de Janeiro* **24** a2
Bandra, *Mumbai* **20** A1
Bandra Pt., *Mumbai* **20** A1
Bang Kapi, *Bangkok* **3** B2
Bang Kholaem, *Bangkok* **3** B2
Bang Na, *Bangkok* **3** B2
Bang Phlad, *Bangkok* **3** a1
Bangkhen, *Bangkok* **3** A2
Bangkok = Krung Thep, *Bangkok* **3** B2
Bangkok Noi, *Bangkok* **3** B1
Bangkok Yai, *Bangkok* **3** B1
Banglamphoo, *Bangkok* **3** b2
Banglo, *Calcutta* **8** B1
Bangrak, *Bangkok* **3** B2
Bangsu, *Bangkok* **3** B2
Bank, *London* **15** b5
Bank of America, *San Francisco* **25** b2
Bank of China Tower, *Hong Kong* **12** c1
Banks, C., *Sydney* **28** C2
Banksmeadow, *Sydney* **28** B2
Banstala, *Calcutta* **8** A2
Bantra, *Calcutta* **8** B1
Baoshan, *Shanghai* **27** A1
Bar Giyora, *Jerusalem* **13** B1
Barahanagar, *Calcutta* **8** B2
Barajas, *Madrid* **17** B2
Barajas, Aeropuerto Transoceanico de, *Madrid* **17** B2
Barakpur, *Calcutta* **8** A2
Barberini, Palazzo, *Rome* **25** b3
Barbican, *London* **15** a4
Barcarena, *Lisbon* **14** A1
Barcarena, Rib. de →, *Lisbon* **14** A1
Barcelona, *Barcelona* **4** A2
Barcelona-Prat, Aeropuerta de, *Barcelona* **4** B1
Barceloneta, *Barcelona* **4** A2
Barking, *London* **15** A4
Barkingside, *London* **15** A4
Barnes, *London* **15** B2
Barnet, *London* **15** A2
Barra Andai, *Karachi* **14** B2
Barra Funda, *São Paulo* **26** B2
Barracas, *Buenos Aires* **7** B2
Barranco, *Lima* **16** B2
Barreiro, *Lisbon* **14** B2
Barreto, *Rio de Janeiro* **24** B2
Bartala, *Calcutta* **8** B1
Barton Park, *Sydney* **28** B1
Bartyki, *Warsaw* **31** C2
Barvikha, *Moscow* **19** B1
Bastille, Place de la, *Paris* **23** c5
Basus, *Cairo* **7** A2
Batanagar, *Calcutta* **8** B1
Bath Beach, *New York* **21** C1
Bath I., *Karachi* **14** B2
Batir, *Jerusalem* **13** B1
Batok, Bukit, *Singapore* **27** A2
Battersea, *London* **15** B3
Battery Park, *New York* **21** f1
Bauman, *Moscow* **19** B4
Baumgarten, *Vienna* **31** A1
Bay Harbour Islands, *Miami* **18** A2
Bay Ridge, *New York* **21** C1
Bayonne, *New York* **21** B1
Bayshore, *San Francisco* **25** B3
Bayswater, *London* **15** b2
Bayt Lahm = Bethlehem, *Jerusalem* **13** B2
Bayview, *San Francisco* **25** B2
Bāzār, *Tehran* **30** A2
Beachmont, *Boston* **6** A4
Beacon Hill, *Hong Kong* **12** A2
Beato, *Lisbon* **14** A2
Beaumont, *Dublin* **11** A2
Beaumonte Heights, *Toronto* **30** A1
Bebek, *Istanbul* **12** B2
Běchovice, *Prague* **24** B3
Beck L., *Chicago* **9** A1
Beckenham, *London* **15** B3
Beckton, *London* **15** A4
Becontree, *London* **15** A4
Beddington Corner, *London* **15** B3
Bedford, *Boston* **6** A2
Bedford Park, *Chicago* **9** C2
Bedford Park, *New York* **21** A2
Bedford Stuyvesant, *New York* **21** B2
Bedford View, *Johannesburg* **13** B2
Bedok, *Singapore* **27** B3
Bedok, Res., *Singapore* **27** A3
Beersel, *Brussels* **6** B1
Behala, *Calcutta* **8** B1
Bei Hai, *Beijing* **4** B2
Beicai, *Shanghai* **27** B2
Beicang, *Tianjin* **30** A1
Beihai Park, *Beijing* **4** b2
Beijing, *Beijing* **4** B1
Beit Ghur el-Fawqa, *Jerusalem* **13** A1
Beit Hanina, *Jerusalem* **13** B2
Beit Iksa, *Jerusalem* **13** B2
Beit I'nan, *Jerusalem* **13** A1
Beit Jala, *Jerusalem* **13** B2
Beit Lekhem = Bethlehem, *Jerusalem* **13** B2
Beit Nekofa, *Jerusalem* **13** B1
Beit Sahur, *Jerusalem* **13** B2
Beit Surik, *Jerusalem* **13** B1
Beit Zayit, *Jerusalem* **13** B1
Beitaipingzhuan, *Beijing* **4** B1
Beitar Ilit, *Jerusalem* **13** B1
Beitsun, *Canton* **8** B2
Beitunya, *Jerusalem* **13** A2
Beixing Jing Park, *Shanghai* **27** B1
Békásmegyer, *Budapest* **7** A2
Bekkelaget, *Oslo* **22** A3
Bel Air, *Los Angeles* **16** B2
Bela Vista, *São Paulo* **26** B2
Bélanger, *Montreal* **19** A1
Belas, *Lisbon* **14** A1
Belas Artes, Museu Nacionale de, *Rio de Janeiro* **24** b2
Belghata, *Calcutta* **8** B2
Belém, *Lisbon* **14** A1
Belém, Torre de, *Lisbon* **14** A1
Belénzinho, *São Paulo* **26** B2
Belgachiya, *Calcutta* **8** B2
Belgharia, *Calcutta* **8** B2
Belgrano, *Buenos Aires* **7** B2
Belgravia, *London* **15** c3
Bell, *Los Angeles* **16** C3
Bell Gardens, *Los Angeles* **16** C4
Bell Tower, *Beijing* **4** a2
Bellavista, *Lima* **16** B2
Bellavista, *Santiago* **26** C2
Belle Harbor, *New York* **21** C2
Belle View, *Washington* **32** B2
Bellevue, Schloss, *Berlin* **5** a2
Bellingham, *London* **15** B3
Bellwood, *Chicago* **9** B1
Belmont, *Boston* **6** A2
Belmont, *London* **15** A2
Belmont, *Wellington* **32** B2
Belmont Harbor, *Chicago* **9** B3
Belmore, *Sydney* **28** B1
Belur, *Calcutta* **8** B2
Belvedere, *Atlanta* **3** B3
Belvedere, *London* **15** B4
Belvedere, *San Francisco* **25** A2
Belyayevo Bogorodskoye, *Moscow* **19** C3
Bemowo, *Warsaw* **31** B1
Benaki, Moussío, *Athens* **2** b3
Bendale, *Toronto* **30** A3
Bendkhal, *Mumbai* **20** B2
Benefica, *Rio de Janeiro* **24** B1
Benfica, *Lisbon* **14** A1
Benito Juárez, *Mexico City* **18** B2
Benito Juárez, Aeropuerto Int., *Mexico City* **18** B2
Bensonhurst, *New York* **21** C2
Berchem-Sainte-Agathe, *Brussels* **6** A1
Berg am Laim, *Munich* **20** B2
Bergenfield, *New York* **21** A2
Bergham, *Munich* **20** B2
Bergvliet, *Cape Town* **8** B1
Beri, *Barcelona* **4** A1
Berkeley, *San Francisco* **25** A3
Berlin, *Berlin* **5** A3
Bermondsey, *London* **15** B3
Bernabeu, Estadio, *Madrid* **17** B1
Bernal Heights, *San Francisco* **25** B2
Berwyn, *Chicago* **9** B2
Berwyn Heights, *Washington* **32** B4
Besiktas, *Istanbul* **12** B2
Besós →, *Barcelona* **4** A2
Bethesda, *Washington* **32** B3
Bethlehem, *Jerusalem* **13** B2
Bethnal Green, *London* **15** A3
Betor, *Calcutta* **8** B1
Beurs, *Amsterdam* **2** b2
Beverley Hills, *Sydney* **28** B1
Beverley Park, *Sydney* **28** B1
Beverly, *Chicago* **9** C3
Beverly Glen, *Los Angeles* **16** B2
Beverly Hills, *Los Angeles* **16** B2
Bexley, *London* **15** B4
Bexley, *Sydney* **28** B1
Bexleyheath, *London* **15** B4
Beykoz, *Istanbul* **12** B2
Beylerbeyi, *Istanbul* **12** B2
Beyoğlu, *Istanbul* **12** B1
Bezons, *Paris* **23** A2
Bezuidenhout Park, *Johannesburg* **13** B2
Bhadrakali, *Calcutta* **8** A2
Bhalswa, *Delhi* **10** A2
Bhambo Khan Qarmati, *Karachi* **14** B2
Bhatsala, *Calcutta* **8** B1
Bhawanipur, *Calcutta* **8** B2
Bhuleshwar, *Mumbai* **20** b2
Białołęka Dworska, *Warsaw* **31** B2
Biblioteca Nacional, *Rio de Janeiro* **24** c2
Bicentennial Park, *Sydney* **28** B1
Bickley, *London* **15** B4
Bidu, *Jerusalem* **13** B1
Bielany, *Warsaw* **31** B1
Bielawa, *Warsaw* **31** C2
Biesdorf, *Berlin* **5** A4
Bièvre →, *Paris* **23** B1
Bièvres, *Paris* **23** B2
Bilston, *Edinburgh* **11** B2
Binacayan, *Manila* **17** C1
Binondo, *Manila* **17** B1
Birak el Kiyam, *Cairo* **7** A1
Birch Cliff, *Toronto* **30** A3
Birkenstein, *Berlin* **5** A5
Birkholz, *Berlin* **5** A4
Birkholzaue, *Berlin* **5** A4
Birrarung Park, *Melbourne* **17** A2
Biscayne Bay, *Miami* **18** B2
Biscayne Park, *Miami* **18** A2
Bishop Lavis, *Cape Town* **8** A2
Bishopscourt, *Cape Town* **8** A1
Bispebjerg, *Copenhagen* **10** A3
Biwon Secret Garden, *Seoul* **26** B1
Björknäs, *Stockholm* **28** B3
Black Cr. →, *Toronto* **30** A2
Blackfen, *London* **15** B4
Blackheath, *London* **15** B4
Blackrock, *Dublin* **11** B2
Bladensburg, *Washington* **32** B4
Blair Village, *Atlanta* **3** C2
Blairgowrie, *Johannesburg* **13** A2
Blakehurst, *Sydney* **28** B1
Blakstad, *Oslo* **22** B1
Blankenburg, *Berlin* **5** A3
Blankenfelde, *Berlin* **5** A3
Blizne, *Warsaw* **31** B1
Bloomsbury, *London* **15** a3
Błota, *Warsaw* **31** C3
Blue Island, *Chicago* **9** C2
Bluebell, *Dublin* **11** B1
Bluff Hd., *Hong Kong* **12** B2
Blumberg, *Berlin* **5** A4
Blunt Pt., *San Francisco* **25** A2
Blutenberg, *Munich* **20** B1
Blylaget, *Oslo* **22** B3
Bo-Kaap Museum, *Cape Town* **8** c2
Boa Vista, Alto do, *Rio de Janeiro* **24** B1
Boardwalk, *New York* **21** C3
Boavista, *Lisbon* **14** A2
Bobigny, *Paris* **23** A3
Bocanegra, *Lima* **16** A2
Boedo, *Buenos Aires* **7** B2
Bogenhausen, *Munich* **20** B2
Bogorodskoye, *Moscow* **19** B4
Bogota, *New York* **21** A1
Bogstadvatnet, *Oslo* **22** A2
Bohnsdorf, *Berlin* **5** B4
Bois-Colombes, *Paris* **23** A2
Bois-d'Arcy, *Paris* **23** B1
Boissy-St-Léger, *Paris* **23** B4
Boldinasco, *Milan* **18** B1
Bøler, *Oslo* **22** A4
Bollate, *Milan* **18** A1
Bollebeek, *Brussels* **6** A1
Bollensdorf, *Berlin* **5** A5
Bollmora, *Stockholm* **28** B3
Bolshaya-Okhta, *St. Petersburg* **26** B2
Bolton, *Atlanta* **3** B2
Bom Retiro, *São Paulo* **26** B2
Bombay = Mumbai, *Mumbai* **20** B2
Bondi, *Sydney* **28** B2
Bondy, *Paris* **23** A3
Bondy, Forêt de, *Paris* **23** A4
Bonifacio Monument, *Manila* **17** B1
Bonneuil-sur-Marne, *Paris* **23** B4
Bonnington, *Edinburgh* **11** B1
Bonnyrig and Lasswade, *Edinburgh* **11** B3
Bonsucesso, *Rio de Janeiro* **24** B1
Bonteheuwel, *Cape Town* **8** A2
Boo, *Stockholm* **28** A3
Booterstown, *Dublin* **11** B2
Borisovo, *Moscow* **19** C4
Borle, *Mumbai* **20** A2
Boronia Park, *Sydney* **28** A1
Borough Park, *New York* **21** C2
Bosmont, *Johannesburg* **13** B1
Bosön, *Stockholm* **28** A3
Bosporus = Istanbul Boğazi, *Istanbul* **12** B2
Bostancı, *Istanbul* **12** C2
Boston Harbor, *Boston* **6** A4
Botafogo, *Rio de Janeiro* **24** B1
Botanisk Have, *Copenhagen* **10** b2
Botany, *Sydney* **28** B2
Botany B., *Sydney* **28** B2
Botany Bay Nat. Park, *Sydney* **28** B2
Botič →, *Prague* **24** B3
Botica Sete, *Lisbon* **14** A1
Boucherville, *Montreal* **19** A3
Boucherville, Îs. de, *Montreal* **19** A3
Bougival, *Paris* **23** A1
Boulder Pt., *Hong Kong* **12** B1
Boulogne, Bois de, *Paris* **23** A2
Boulogne-Billancourt, *Paris* **23** A2
Bourg-la-Reine, *Paris* **23** B2
Bouviers, *Paris* **23** B1
Bovenkerk, *Amsterdam* **2** B2
Bovenkerker Polder, *Amsterdam* **2** B2
Bovisa, *Milan* **18** A2
Bow, *London* **15** A3
Bowery, *New York* **21** e2
Boyacıköy, *Istanbul* **12** B2
Boyle Heights, *Los Angeles* **16** B3
Bradbury Building, *Los Angeles* **16** b2
Braepark, *Edinburgh* **11** B2
Braid, *Edinburgh* **11** B2
Bramley, *Johannesburg* **13** A2
Brandenburger Tor, *Berlin* **5** A3
Brani, P., *Singapore* **27** B3
Branik, *Prague* **24** B2
Brännkyrka, *Stockholm* **28** B2
Brás, *São Paulo* **26** B2
Brasilândia, *São Paulo* **26** A1
Brateyevo, *Moscow* **19** C4
Bratsevo, *Moscow* **19** A2
Bray, *Dublin* **11** B3
Braybrook, *Melbourne* **17** A1
Brázdim, *Prague* **24** A3
Breach Candy, *Mumbai* **20** a1
Breakheart Reservation, *Boston* **6** A3
Brede, *Copenhagen* **10** A3
Breeds Pond, *Boston* **6** A4
Breezy Point, *New York* **21** C2
Breitenlee, *Vienna* **31** A3
Breña, *Lima* **16** B2
Brent, *London* **15** A2
Brent Res., *London* **15** A2
Brentford, *London* **15** B2
Brentwood Park, *Los Angeles* **16** B2
Brera, *Milan* **18** B2
Bresso, *Milan* **18** A2
Brevik, *Stockholm* **28** A3
Břevnov, *Prague* **24** B2
Bridgeport, *Chicago* **9** B3
Bridgetown, *Cape Town* **8** A2
Bridgeview, *Chicago* **9** C2
Brighton, *Boston* **6** A3
Brighton, *Melbourne* **17** B1
Brighton le Sands, *Sydney* **28** B1
Brighton Park, *Chicago* **9** C2
Brightwood, *Washington* **32** B3
Brigittenau, *Vienna* **31** A2
Brimbank Park, *Melbourne* **17** A1
Brisbane, *San Francisco* **25** B2
British Museum, *London* **15** a3
Britz, *Berlin* **5** B3
Brixton, *London* **15** B3
Broad Sd., *Boston* **6** A4
Broadmeadows, *Melbourne* **17** A1
Broadmoor, *San Francisco* **25** B2
Broadview, *Chicago* **9** B1
Broadway, *New York* **21** e1
Brockley, *London* **15** B3
Bródno, *Warsaw* **31** B2
Bródnowski, Kanał, *Warsaw* **31** B2
Broek in Waterland, *Amsterdam* **2** A2
Bromley, *London* **15** B4
Bromley Common, *London* **15** B4
Bromma, *Stockholm* **28** A1
Bromma flygplats, *Stockholm* **28** A1
Brompton, *London* **15** c2
Brøndby Strand, *Copenhagen* **10** B2
Brøndbyøster, *Copenhagen* **10** B2
Brøndbyvester, *Copenhagen* **10** B2
Brondesbury, *London* **15** A2
Brønnøya, *Oslo* **22** A2

BRØNSHØJ


Brønshøj, Copenhagen 10 A2
Bronxville, New York 21 A3
Brookfield, Chicago 9 C1
Brookhaven, Atlanta 3 A2
Brookline, Boston 6 B3
Brooklyn, Cape Town 8 A1
Brooklyn, New York 21 C2
Brooklyn, Wellington 32 B1
Brooklyn Bridge, New York 21 f2
Brookmont, Washington 32 B3
Brossard, Montreal 19 B3
Brou-sur-Chantereine, Paris 23 A4
Brown, Toronto 30 A3
Broyhill Park, Washington 32 B2
Brughério, Milan 18 A2
Brunswick, Melbourne 17 A1
Brush Hill, Boston 6 B1
Brussegem, Brussels 6 A1
Brussel Nat. Luchthaven, Brussels 6 A2
Brussels = Bruxelles, Brussels 6 A2
Bruxelles, Brussels 6 A2
Bruzzano, Milan 18 A2
Bry-sur-Marne, Paris 23 A4
Bryanston, Johannesburg 13 A1
Bryn, Oslo 22 A1
Brzeziny, Warsaw 31 B2
Bubeneč, Prague 24 B2
Buc, Paris 23 B1
Buchenhain, Munich 20 B1
Buchholz, Berlin 5 A3
Buckhead, Atlanta 3 A2
Buckingham Palace, London 15 b3
Buckow, Berlin 5 B3
Buda, Budapest 7 A2
Budafok, Budapest 7 A2
Budaörs, Budapest 7 B1
Budapest, Budapest 7 B2
Budatétény, Budapest 7 B2
Budavaripalota, Budapest 7 b2
Buddinge, Copenhagen 10 A3
Budokan, Tokyo 29 a4
Buena Vista, San Francisco 25 B2
Buenos Aires, Buenos Aires 7 B2
Bufalotta, Rome 25 B2
Bugio, Lisbon 14 B1
Buiksloot, Amsterdam 2 A2
Buitenveldert, Amsterdam 2 B2
Buizingen, Brussels 6 B1
Bukit Panjang Nature Reserve, Singapore 27 A2
Bukit Timah Nature Reserve, Singapore 27 A2
Bukum, P., Singapore 27 B2
Būlāq, Cairo 7 A2
Bule, Manila 17 C2
Bulim, Singapore 27 A2
Bullen Park, Melbourne 17 A2
Bundoora North, Melbourne 17 A2
Bundoora Park, Melbourne 17 A2
Bunker I., Karachi 14 B1
Bunkyo-Ku, Tokyo 29 A3
Bunnefjorden, Oslo 22 A3
Buona Vista Park, Singapore 27 B2
Burbank, Chicago 9 C2
Burbank, Los Angeles 16 A3
Burlington, Boston 6 A2
Burnham Park, Chicago 9 c2
Burnham Park Harbor, Chicago 9 B3
Burnhamthorpe, Toronto 30 B1
Burnt Oak, London 15 A2
Burntisland, Edinburgh 11 A2
Burnwynd, Edinburgh 11 B1
Burqa, Jerusalem 13 A2
Burtus, Cairo 7 A1
Burudvatn, Oslo 22 A2
Burwood, Sydney 28 B1
Bushwick, New York 21 B2
Bushy Park, London 15 B1
Butantã, São Paulo 26 B1
Butcher I., Mumbai 20 B2
Butts Corner, Washington 32 C2
Büyükdere, Istanbul 12 B2
Byculla, Mumbai 20 B2
Bygdøy, Oslo 22 A3


# C


C.N. Tower, Toronto 30 B2
Cabaçu de Cima →, São Paulo 26 A2
Caballito, Buenos Aires 7 B2
Cabin John, Washington 32 B2
Cabin John Regional Park, Washington 32 A2
Cabinteely, Dublin 11 B3
Cabra, Dublin 11 A2
Cabuçú de Baixo →, São Paulo 26 A1
Cachan, Paris 23 B2
Cachenka →, Moscow 19 B1
Cachoeira, Rib. da →, São Paulo 26 B1
Cacilhas, Lisbon 14 A2
Cahuenga Pk., Los Angeles 16 B3
Cairo = El Qâhira, Cairo 7 A2
Caju, Rio de Janeiro 24 B1
Čakovice, Prague 24 B3
Calcutta = Kolkata, Calcutta 8 B2
California Inst. of Tech., Los Angeles 16 B4
California Plaza, Los Angeles 16 b1
California State Univ., Los Angeles 16 B3
Callao, Lima 16 B2
Caloocan, Manila 17 B1
Calumet Park, Chicago 9 C3
Calumet Sag Channel →, Chicago 9 C2
Calumpang, Manila 17 B2
Calvairate, Milan 18 B2
Camarate, Lisbon 14 A2
Camaroes, Lisbon 14 A1
Camberwell, London 15 B3
Camberwell, Melbourne 17 B2
Cambridge, Boston 6 A3
Cambridge Res., Boston 6 A2
Cambuci, São Paulo 26 B2
Camden, London 15 A3
Cameron, Mt., Wellington 32 B2
Çamlıca, Istanbul 12 B2
Camp Springs, Washington 32 C4
Campamento, Madrid 17 B1
Campbellfield, Melbourne 17 A1
Camperdown, Sydney 28 B2
Campidoglio, Rome 25 c3
Campo, Casa de, Madrid 17 B1
Campo F.C. Barcelona, Barcelona 4 A1
Campo Grande, Lisbon 14 A2
Campo Pequeño, Lisbon 14 A2
Campolide, Lisbon 14 A2
Camps Bay, Cape Town 8 A1
C'an San Joan, Barcelona 4 A2
Cañacao B., Manila 17 C1
Canarsie, New York 21 C2
Cancelleria, Palazzo dei, Rome 25 c2
Candiac, Montreal 19 B3
Caneças, Lisbon 14 A1
Canillas, Madrid 17 B2
Canillejas, Madrid 17 B2
Canning Town, London 15 A4
Canteras de Vallecas, Madrid 17 B2
Canterbury, Melbourne 17 A2
Canterbury, Sydney 28 B1
Canton = Guangzhou, Canton 8 B2
Caoheijing, Shanghai 27 B1
Capão Redondo, São Paulo 26 B1
Caparica, Lisbon 14 A2
Caparica, Costa da, Lisbon 14 B1
Cape Flats, Cape Town 8 B2
Cape Town, Cape Town 8 A1
Capitol Heights, Washington 32 B4
Capitol Hill, Washington 32 B4
Capitolini, Musei, Rome 25 c3
Captain Cook Bridge, Sydney 28 C1
Captain Cook Landing Place Park, Sydney 28 C2
Capuchos, Lisbon 14 B1
Carabanchel Alto, Madrid 17 B1
Carabanchel Bajo, Madrid 17 B1
Carapachay, Buenos Aires 7 B1
Caraza, Buenos Aires 7 C2
Caridad, Manila 17 C1
Carioca, Sa. da, Rio de Janeiro 24 B1
Carlstadt, New York 21 A1
Carlton, Melbourne 17 A1
Carmen de Huechuraba, Santiago 26 B1
Carmen de la Legua, Lima 16 B2
Carnaxide, Lisbon 14 A1
Carnegie, Melbourne 17 B2
Carnegie Hall, New York 21 c2
Carnide, Lisbon 14 A1
Carol City, Miami 18 A1
Carrascal, Santiago 26 B1
Carrickmines, Dublin 11 B3
Carrières-sous-Bois, Paris 23 A1
Carrières-sous-Poissy, Paris 23 A1
Carrières-sur-Seine, Paris 23 A2
Carrigeen Bay, Dublin 11 A3
Cartierville, Montreal 19 A1
Casa Verde, São Paulo 26 A1
Casal Morena, Rome 25 C2
Casalotti, Rome 25 B1
Cascade Heights, Atlanta 3 B2
Castel di Leva, Rome 25 C2
Castel Sant'Angelo, Rome 25 B1
Castle, Dublin 11 c2
Castle, Edinburgh 11 b2
Castle of Good Hope, Cape Town 8 c3
Castleknock, Dublin 11 A1
Castleton Corners, New York 21 C1
Catedral Metropolitana, Mexico City 18 b3
Catedral Metropolitana, Rio de Janeiro 24 c1
Catete, Rio de Janeiro 24 B1
Catford, London 15 B3
Caulfield, Melbourne 17 B2
Causeway Bay, Hong Kong 12 c3
Cavite, Manila 17 C1
Caxias, Lisbon 14 A1
Cebecci, Istanbul 12 B1
Cecchignola, Rome 25 C2
Cecilienhof, Schloss, Berlin 5 B1
Cedar Grove, Atlanta 3 C3
Cempaka Putih, Jakarta 13 B2
Çengelköy, Istanbul 12 B2
Cengkareng, Jakarta 13 A1
Centennial Park, Sydney 28 B2
Center Hill, Atlanta 3 B2
Centocelle, Rome 25 B2
Centraal Station, Amsterdam 2 a2
Central Park, New York 21 B2
Cerillos, Santiago 26 B1
Cerro de la Estrella, Mexico City 18 B2
Cerro de los Angeles, Madrid 17 C1
Cerro Navia, Santiago 26 B1
Certanovka →, Moscow 19 C3
Certanovo, Moscow 19 C3
Cesano Boscone, Milan 18 B1
Cesate, Milan 18 A1
Cha Kwo Ling, Hong Kong 12 B2
Chacarrita, Buenos Aires 7 B2
Chadwell Heath, London 15 A4
Chai Chee, Singapore 27 B3
Chai Wan, Hong Kong 12 B2
Chai Wan Kok, Hong Kong 12 A1
Chaillot, Palais de, Paris 23 b2
Chakdaha, Calcutta 8 C1
Chamartín, Madrid 17 B1
Chamberi, Madrid 17 B1
Chambourcy, Paris 23 A1
Champ de Mars, Parc du, Paris 23 c2
Champigny-sur-Marne, Paris 23 B4
Champlain, Pont, Montreal 19 B2
Champs Elysées, Avenue des, Paris 23 b2
Champs-sur-Marne, Paris 23 A4
Chamrail, Calcutta 8 B1
Chamshil, Seoul 26 B2
Chamwŏn, Seoul 26 B2
Chanditala, Calcutta 8 A1
Changfeng Park, Shanghai 27 B1
Changi, Singapore 27 A3
Changi Int. Airport, Singapore 27 A3
Changning, Shanghai 27 B1
Chantereine, Paris 23 A4
Chantian, Canton 8 A2
Chao Phraya →, Bangkok 3 B2
Chaoyang, Beijing 4 B2
Chaoyangmen, Beijing 4 B2
Chapelizod, Dublin 11 A1
Chapultepec, Bosque de, Mexico City 18 B1
Chapultepec, Castillo de, Mexico City 18 B1
Charenton-le-Pont, Paris 23 B3
Charing Cross, London 15 b4
Charleroi, Kanal de →, Brussels 6 B1
Charles Bridge, Prague 24 b1
Charles Square, Prague 24 c1
Charlestown, Boston 6 A3
Charlottenburg, Berlin 5 A2
Charlottenburg, Schloss, Berlin 5 A2
Charlottenlund, Copenhagen 10 A3
Charlton, London 15 B4
Charneca, Lisbon 14 A2
Charneca, Lisbon 14 B1
Châteaufort, Paris 23 B1
Châtenay-Malabry, Paris 23 B2
Chatham, Chicago 9 C3
Châtillon, Paris 23 B2
Chatou, Paris 23 A1
Chatpur, Calcutta 8 B2
Chatswood, Sydney 28 A2
Chatuchak, Bangkok 3 B2
Chatuchak Park, Bangkok 3 B2
Chauki, Karachi 14 A1
Chavarria, Lima 16 B2
Chaville, Paris 23 B2
Chayang, Seoul 26 B2
Chegi, Seoul 26 B2
Chelles, Paris 23 A4
Chelles, Canal de, Paris 23 A4
Chells-le-Pin, Aérodrome, Paris 23 A4
Chelsea, Boston 6 A3
Chelsea, London 15 B2
Chelsea, New York 21 c1
Chembur, Mumbai 20 A2
Chennevières-sur-Marne, Paris 23 B4
Cheops, Cairo 7 B1
Cherepkovo, Moscow 19 B2
Chernyovo, Moscow 19 A1
Cheryomushki, Moscow 19 B3
Chestnut Hill, Boston 6 B2
Cheung Sha Wan, Hong Kong 12 A1
Cheverly, Washington 32 B4
Chevilly-Larue, Paris 23 B3
Chevry-Cossigny, Paris 23 B4
Chevy Chase, Washington 32 B3
Chevy Chase View, Washington 32 A3
Chia Keng, Singapore 27 A3
Chiaravalle Milanese, Milan 18 B2
Chicago, Chicago 9 B3
Chicago Harbor, Chicago 9 B3
Chicago Lawn, Chicago 9 C2
Chicago-Midway Airport, Chicago 9 C2
Chicago-O'Hare Int. Airport, Chicago 9 B1
Chicago Ridge, Chicago 9 C2
Chicago Sanitary and Ship Canal, Chicago 9 C2
Chienzui, Canton 8 A3
Chik Sha, Hong Kong 12 B2
Child's Hill, London 15 A2
Chilla Saroda, Delhi 10 B2
Chillum, Washington 32 B4
Chilly-Mazarin, Paris 23 B2
Chinatown, Los Angeles 16 a3
Chinatown, New York 21 e2
Chinatown, San Francisco 25 b2
Chinatown, Singapore 27 c2
Chingupota, Calcutta 8 C1
Chislehurst, London 15 B4
Chiswick, London 15 B2
Chiswick House, London 15 B2
Chitose, Tokyo 29 B2
Chitralada Palace, Bangkok 3 B2
Chiyoda-Ku, Tokyo 29 b4
Chkalova, Moscow 19 C5
Choa Chu Kang, Singapore 27 A2
Choboty, Moscow 19 C2
Chodov u Prahy, Prague 24 B3
Chōfu, Tokyo 29 B2
Choisy-le-Roi, Paris 23 B3
Cholupice, Prague 24 C2
Chom Thong, Bangkok 3 B1
Chong Pang, Singapore 27 A2
Ch'ŏngdam, Seoul 26 B2
Chongmyo Royal Shrine, Seoul 26 B1
Chongno, Seoul 26 B1
Chongwen, Beijing 4 B2
Chŏnho, Seoul 26 B2
Chornaya →, Moscow 19 B6
Chorrillos, Lima 16 C2
Chowpatty Beach, Mumbai 20 b1
Christian Quarter, Jerusalem 13 b3
Christiansborg, Copenhagen 10 c2
Christianshavn, Copenhagen 10 c3
Chrysler Building, New York 21 c2
Chrzanów, Warsaw 31 B1
Chuen Lung, Hong Kong 12 A1
Chuk Kok, Hong Kong 12 A2
Chulalongkom Univ., Bangkok 3 B2
Chung, Seoul 26 B1
Chunghwa, Seoul 26 B2
Chungnangch'on →, Seoul 26 B1
Chūō-Ku, Tokyo 29 b5
Church End, London 15 A2
Churchtown, Dublin 11 B2
Ciampino, Rome 25 C2
Ciampino, Aeroporto di, Rome 25 C2
Cicero, Chicago 9 B2
Cilandak, Jakarta 13 B1
Cilincing, Jakarta 13 A2
Ciliwung →, Jakarta 13 B2
Čimice, Prague 24 B2
Cinecittà, Rome 25 B2
Cinisello Bálsamo, Milan 18 A2
Cinkota, Budapest 7 A3
Cipete, Jakarta 13 B1
Citadella, Budapest 7 c2
Citta degli Studi, Milan 18 B2
Città del Vaticano, Rome 25 B1
City, London 15 A3
City Hall, New York 21 e1
Ciudad Deportiva, Mexico City 18 B2
Ciudad Fin de Semana, Madrid 17 B2
Ciudad General Belgrano, Buenos Aires 7 C1
Ciudad Lineál, Madrid 17 B2
Ciudad Satélite, Mexico City 18 A1
Ciudad Universitaria, Buenos Aires 7 B2
Ciudad Universitaria, Mexico City 18 C1
Ciutadella, Parc de la, Barcelona 4 b3
Civic Center, Los Angeles 16 b2
Clamart, Paris 23 B2
Clapham, London 15 B3
Clapton, London 15 A3
Claremont, Cape Town 8 A1
Clayhall, London 15 A4
Clerkenwell, London 15 a4
Clermiston, Edinburgh 11 B2
Clichy, Paris 23 A2
Clichy-sous-Bois, Paris 23 A4
Cliffside, Toronto 30 A3
Cliffside Park, New York 21 B2
Clifton, Boston 6 A4
Clifton, Karachi 14 B2
Clifton, New York 21 C1
Cliftondale, Boston 6 A3
Cloghran, Dublin 11 A2
Clonskeagh, Dublin 11 B2
Clontarf, Dublin 11 A2
Clontarf, Sydney 28 A2
Clovelly, Sydney 28 B2
Cobras, I. das, Rio de Janeiro 24 B2
Coburg, Melbourne 17 A1
Cochituate, Boston 6 A1
Cochituate, L., Boston 6 B1
Cocotá, Rio de Janeiro 24 A1
Cœuilly, Paris 23 B4
Coina, Lisbon 14 B2
Coit Tower, San Francisco 25 a2
Coker, Lagos 14 B2
Colaba, Mumbai 20 B1
Colaba Pt., Mumbai 20 B1
Colegiales, Buenos Aires 7 B2
Colindale, London 15 A2
Colinton, Edinburgh 11 B2
College Park, Atlanta 3 C2
College Park, Washington 32 B4
College Point, New York 21 B2
Collégien, Paris 23 A4
Collier Row, London 15 A4
Colliers Wood, London 15 B2
Colma, San Francisco 25 B2
Colney Hatch, London 15 A3
Cologno Monzese, Milan 18 A2
Colombes, Paris 23 A2
Colón, Monumento, Barcelona 4 c3
Colon, Plaza de, Madrid 17 a3
Colonia Güell, Barcelona 4 A1
Colonial Knob, Wellington 32 A1
Colosseo, Rome 25 c3
Columbus Circus, New York 21 b2
Combault, Paris 23 B4
Comércio, Praça do, Lisbon 14 A2
Commerce, Los Angeles 16 B4
Como, Sydney 28 C1
Company's Gardens, Cape Town 8 c2
Conceição, I. da, Rio de Janeiro 24 B2
Concertgebouw, Amsterdam 2 c1
Conchali, Santiago 26 B2
Concord, Boston 6 A1
Concord, Sydney 28 B1
Concord, Toronto 30 A2
Concorde, Place de la, Paris 23 b3
Concorezzo, Milan 18 A2
Coney Island, New York 21 C2
Congonhas, Aéroporto, São Paulo 26 B2
Connaught Place, Delhi 10 B2
Conservatori, Palazzo dei, Rome 25 c3
Consolação, São Paulo 26 B2
Constantia, Cape Town 8 B1
Constitución, Buenos Aires 7 B2
Constitution, Atlanta 3 B2
Convention and Exhibition Centre, Hong Kong 12 b2
Coogee, Sydney 28 B2
Cook Str., Wellington 32 A1
Cooksville, Toronto 30 B1
Coolock, Dublin 11 A2
Copacabana, Rio de Janeiro 24 B1
Copenhagen = København, Copenhagen 10 A2
Coral Gables, Miami 18 B2
Coral Hills, Washington 32 B4
Corcovado, Morro do, Rio de Janeiro 24 B1
Corduff, Dublin 11 A1
Cormano, Milan 18 A2
Cornaredo, Milan 18 A1
Corsini, Palazzo, Rome 25 c1
Corviale, Rome 25 B1
Coslada, Madrid 17 B2
Cossigny, Paris 23 B4
Cossipore, Calcutta 8 B2
Costantino, Arco di, Rome 25 c3
Costorphine, Edinburgh 11 B2
Cotao, Lisbon 14 A1
Côte St.-Luc, Montreal 19 B2
Cotunduba, I. de, Rio de Janeiro 24 B2
Coubron, Paris 23 A4
Courbevoie, Paris 23 A2
Courtry, Paris 23 A4
Covent Garden, London 15 b4
Cowgate, Edinburgh 11 b3
Cowley, London 15 A1
Coyoacán, Mexico City 18 B2
Cragin, Chicago 9 B2
Craighall Park, Johannesburg 13 A2
Craiglockhart, Edinburgh 11 B2
Craigmillar, Edinburgh 11 B3
Cramond, Edinburgh 11 B1
Cramond Bridge, Edinburgh 11 B1
Cramond I., Edinburgh 11 B1
Cranford, London 15 B1
Crawford, Cape Town 8 A2
Crayford, London 15 B5
Creekmouth, London 15 A4
Crescenzago, Milan 18 A2
Cressely, Paris 23 B1
Cresskill, New York 21 A2
Creteil, Paris 23 B3
Cricklewood, London 15 A2
Cristo Redentor, Estatua do, Rio de Janeiro 24 B1
Crockenhill, London 15 B4
Croissy-Beaubourg, Paris 23 B4
Croissy-sur-Seine, Paris 23 A1
Crosby, Johannesburg 13 B1
Crosne, Paris 23 B3
Cross I., Mumbai 20 B2
Crouch End, London 15 A3
Crown Mine, Johannesburg 13 B1
Crows Nest, Sydney 28 A2
Croydon, London 15 B3
Croydon Park, Sydney 28 B1
Cruagh Mt., Dublin 11 B2
Crumlin, Dublin 11 B2
Cruz de Pau, Lisbon 14 B2
Crystal Palace, London 15 B3
Csepel, Budapest 7 B2
Csepelsziget, Budapest 7 B2
Csillaghegy, Budapest 7 A2
Csillagtelep, Budapest 7 B2
Csömör, Budapest 7 A3
Csömöri-patak →, Budapest 7 A3
Cuatro Vientos, Madrid 17 B1
Cuauhtémoc, Mexico City 18 B2
Cubao, Manila 17 B2
Çubuklu, Istanbul 12 B2
Cudahy, Los Angeles 16 C3
Cuicuilco, Pirámido de, Mexico City 18 C1
Culver City, Los Angeles 16 B2
Cumballa Hill, Mumbai 20 a1
Cumbres de Vallecas, Madrid 17 B2
Cupecé, São Paulo 26 B1
Currie, Edinburgh 11 B2
Cusago, Milan 18 B1
Cusano Milanino, Milan 18 A2
Custom House, Dublin 11 b3
Çuvuşabaşi →, Istanbul 12 B1
Czerniaków, Warsaw 31 B2
Czyste, Warsaw 31 B1


# D


D.F. Malan Airport, Cape Town 8 A2
Da Moóca →, São Paulo 26 B2
Da Yunhe →, Tianjin 30 A1
Dabizhuang, Tianjin 30 A2
Ďablice, Prague 24 B2
Dąbrowa, Warsaw 31 B1
Dachang, Shanghai 27 B1
Dachang Airfield, Shanghai 27 B1
Dachau-Ost, Munich 20 A1
Dachauer Moos, Munich 20 A1
Dadar, Mumbai 20 A1
Dagenham, London 15 A4
Daglfing, Munich 20 B2
Daheisha, Jerusalem 13 B2
Dahlem, Berlin 5 B2
Dahlwitz-Hoppegarten, Berlin 5 A5
Dahongmen, Beijing 4 C2
Daitō, Osaka 22 A4
Dajiaoting, Beijing 4 B2
Dakhnovo, St. Petersburg 26 C1
Dalejsky potok →, Prague 24 B2
Dalgety Bay, Edinburgh 11 A1
Dalkeith, Edinburgh 11 B3
Dalkey, Dublin 11 B3
Dalkey Island, Dublin 11 B3
Dallgow, Berlin 5 A1
Dalmeny, Edinburgh 11 B1
Dalston, London 15 A3
Daly City, San Francisco 25 B2
Dam, Amsterdam 2 b2
Dam Rak, Amsterdam 2 a2
Damaia, Lisbon 14 A1
Dämeritzsee, Berlin 5 B5
Dan Ryan Woods, Chicago 9 C2
Danderhall, Edinburgh 11 A1
Danderyd, Stockholm 28 A2
Danforth, Toronto 30 A3
Darakeh, Tehran 30 A2
Darband, Tehran 30 A2
Darling Harbour, Sydney 28 b1
Darling Point, Sydney 28 B2
Darndale, Dublin 11 A2
Darrūs, Tehran 30 A2
Dartford, London 15 B5
Darya Ganj, Delhi 1 a3
Dashi, Canton 8 B2
Datansha, Canton 8 B2
Datun, Beijing 4 B2
Daulatpur, Delhi 10 A1
David's Citadel, Jerusalem 13 b3
David's Tomb, Jerusalem 13 b3
Davidson, Mt., San Francisco 25 B2
Davidson's Mains, Edinburgh 11 B2
Dāvūdiyeh, Tehran 30 A2
Davydkovo, Moscow 19 B2
Dawidy, Warsaw 31 C1
Days Bay, Wellington 32 B2
Dazhigu, Tianjin 30 B2
De Waag, Amsterdam 2 b2
Decatur, Atlanta 3 B3
Dedham, Boston 6 B2
Deer I., Boston 6 A4
Degunino, Moscow 19 A3
Deir Dibwan, Jerusalem 13 A2
Deir Ibzi'e, Jerusalem 13 A1
Dejvice, Prague 24 B2
Dekabristov, Ostrov, St. Petersburg 26 B1
Delhi, Delhi 10 B2
Delhi Gate, Delhi 1 b3
Demarest, New York 21 A2
Den Ilp, Amsterdam 2 A2
Denistone Heights, Sydney 28 A1
Dentonia Park, Toronto 30 A3
Deptford, London 15 B3
Depútati, Camera dei, Rome 25 b2
Des Plaines, Chicago 9 A1
Des Plaines →, Chicago 9 B1
Deshengmen, Beijing 4 B2
Deutsch-Wagram, Vienna 31 A3
Deutsche Oper, Berlin 5 A2
Deutscher Museum, Munich 20 B2
Devil's Peak, Cape Town 8 A1
Dhāfni, Athens 2 B2
Dhakuria, Calcutta 8 B2
Dhamarakia, Athens 2 B1
Dharavi, Mumbai 20 A2
Dhrapersón, Athens 2 B1
Diadema, São Paulo 26 C2
Diegem, Brussels 6 A2
Diemen, Amsterdam 2 A2
Diepkloof, Johannesburg 13 B1
Diepriver, Cape Town 8 B1
Difficult Run →, Washington 32 B2
Dilbeek, Brussels 6 A1
Dinzigu, Tianjin 30 A1
Dirnismaning, Munich 20 A2
District Heights, Washington 32 B4
Ditan Park, Beijing 4 B2
Diyāla →, Baghdad 3 B2
Djursholm, Stockholm 28 A2
Döberitz, Berlin 5 A1
Döbling, Vienna 31 A2
Docklands, London 15 A3
Dodder, R. →, Dublin 11 B1
Dodger Stadium, Los Angeles 16 B3
Dolgoe Ozero, St. Petersburg 26 A1
Doll Museum, Delhi 1 b3
Dollis Hill, London 15 A2
Dollymount, Dublin 11 A2
Dolni, Prague 24 B3
Dolni Chabry, Prague 24 B2
Dolni Počernice, Prague 24 B3
Dolphins Barn, Dublin 11 B2
Dom Pedro II, Parque, São Paulo 26 B2
Domain, The, Sydney 28 b2
Dome of the Rock, Jerusalem 13 b3
Don Mills, Toronto 30 A2
Don Muang Int. Airport, Bangkok 3 A2
Donaghmede, Dublin 11 A3
Donau-Oder Kanal, Vienna 31 A3
Donaufeld, Vienna 31 A2
Donaupark, Vienna 31 A2
Donaustadt, Vienna 31 A2
Dongan Hills, New York 21 C1
Dongcheng, Beijing 4 B2
Donggou, Shanghai 27 B2
Dongjiao, Canton 8 B2
Dongjuzi, Tianjin 30 B2
Dongmenwai, Tianjin 30 B2
Dongri, Mumbai 20 B2
Dongshanhu Park, Canton 8 B2
Dongzhimen, Beijing 4 B2
Donnybrook, Dublin 11 B2
Doornfontein, Johannesburg 13 B2
Dorchester, Boston 6 B3
Dorchester B., Boston 6 B3
Dornach, Munich 20 B3
Dorval, Aéroport de, Montreal 19 B1
Dos Couros →, São Paulo 26 C2
Dos Moninos →, São Paulo 26 C2
Douglas Park, Chicago 9 B2
Dover Heights, Sydney 28 B2
Dowlatābād, Tehran 30 B2
Downey, Los Angeles 16 C4
Downsview, Toronto 30 A1
Dragør, Copenhagen 10 B3
Drancy, Paris 23 A3
Dranesville, Washington 32 A1
Dreilinden, Berlin 5 B2
Drewnica, Warsaw 31 B2
Drigh Road, Karachi 14 A2
Drimnagh, Dublin 11 B2
Drogenbos, Brussels 6 B1
Druid Hills, Atlanta 3 B2
Drum Towwer, Beijing 4 a2
Drumcondra, Dublin 11 A2
Drummoyne, Sydney 28 B1
Drylaw, Edinburgh 11 B2
Dubeč, Prague 24 B3
Dublin, Dublin 11 A2
Dublin Airport, Dublin 11 A2
Dublin Bay, Dublin 11 B3
Dublin Harbour, Dublin 11 A2
Duddingston, Edinburgh 11 B3
Dugnano, Milan 18 A2
Dūlāb, Tehran 30 B2
Dulwich, London 15 B3
Dum Dum, Calcutta 8 B2
Dum Dum Int. Airport, Calcutta 8 B2
Dumont, New York 21 A2
Dún Laoghaire, Dublin 11 B3
Duna →, Budapest 7 A2
Duncan Dock, Cape Town 8 a3
Dundrum, Dublin 11 B2
Dunearn, Singapore 27 B2
Dunfermline, Edinburgh 11 A1
Dunn Loring, Washington 32 B2
Dunning, Chicago 9 B2
Dunvegan, Johannesburg 13 A2
Duomo, Milan 18 B2
Duque de Caxias, Rio de Janeiro 24 A1
Dusit, Bangkok 3 B2
Dusit Zoo, Bangkok 3 a2
Dworp, Brussels 6 B1
Dyakovo, Moscow 19 B3
Dzerzhinskiy, Moscow 19 C5
Dzerzhinskiy, Moscow 19 B3
Dzerzhinskiy Park, Moscow 19 B3


# E


Eagle Rock, Los Angeles 16 B3
Ealing, London 15 A2
Earl's Court, London 15 c1
Earlsfield, London 15 B2
Earlwood, Sydney 28 B1
East Acton, Boston 6 A1
East Arlington, Boston 6 A3
East Arlington, Washington 32 B3
East Bedfont, London 15 B1
East Boston, Boston 6 A3
East Don →, Toronto 30 A2
East Elmhurst, New York 21 B2
East Finchley, London 15 A2
East Ham, London 15 A4
East Humber →, Toronto 30 A1
East Lamma Channel, Hong Kong 12 B1
East Lexington, Boston 6 A2
East Los Angeles, Los Angeles 16 B3
East Molesey, London 15 B1
East New York, New York 21 B2
East Pines, Washington 32 B4
East Point, Atlanta 3 B2
East Potomac Park, Washington 32 B3
East Pt., Boston 6 A4
East River →, New York 21 B2
East Rutherford, New York 21 A1
East Sheen, London 15 B2
East Village, New York 21 e2
East Wickham, London 15 B4
East York, Toronto 30 A2
Eastbourne, Wellington 32 B2
Eastcote, London 15 A1
Easter Howgate, Edinburgh 11 B2
Eastwood, Sydney 28 A1
Ebara, Tokyo 29 B3
Ebisu, Tokyo 29 B3
Ebute-Ikorodu, Lagos 14 A2
Ebute-Metta, Lagos 14 B2
Echo Park, Los Angeles 16 a1
Eda, Tokyo 29 B2
Edendale, Johannesburg 13 A2
Edenmore, Dublin 11 A2
Edgars Cr. →, Melbourne 17 A1
Edgeley, Toronto 30 A1
Edgemar, San Francisco 25 C2
Edinburgh, Edinburgh 11 B2
Edison Park, Chicago 9 A2
Edmondston, Washington 32 B4
Edmondstown, Dublin 11 B2
Edo →, Tokyo 29 B4
Edogawa-Ku, Tokyo 29 A4
Edsberg, Stockholm 28 A1
Edwards L., Melbourne 17 A1
Eiche, Berlin 5 A4
Eiche Sud, Berlin 5 A4
Eiffel, Tour, Paris 23 A2
Ein Arik, Jerusalem 13 A1
Ein Naquba, Jerusalem 13 B1
Ein Rafa, Jerusalem 13 B1
Eizariya, Jerusalem 13 B2
Ejby, Copenhagen 10 A2
Ejigbo, Lagos 14 A1
Ekeberg, Oslo 22 A3
Eknäs, Stockholm 28 B3
El 'Abbasiya, Cairo 7 A2
El Agustino, Lima 16 B2
El Baragil, Cairo 7 A2
El Basâtîn, Cairo 7 B2
El-Bira, Jerusalem 13 A2
El Bosque, Santiago 26 C2
El Carmen, Santiago 26 B1
El Cortijo, Santiago 26 B1
El Duqqi, Cairo 7 A2
El Encinar de los Reyes, Madrid 17 A2
El Ghuriya, Cairo 7 A2
El Gîza, Cairo 7 A2
El-Khadr, Jerusalem 13 B1
El Khalifa, Cairo 7 A2
El Kôm el Ahmar, Cairo 7 A2
El Ma'âdi, Cairo 7 B2
El Matariya, Cairo 7 A2
El Mohandessin, Cairo 7 A2
El Monte, Los Angeles 16 B4
El Mûski, Cairo 7 A2
El Pardo, Madrid 17 A1
El Portal, Miami 18 A2
El Prat de Llobregat, Barcelona 4 B1
El Pueblo de L.A. Historic Park, Los Angeles 16 b2
El Qâhira, Cairo 7 A2
El Qubba, Cairo 7 A2
El Reloj, Mexico City 18 C2
El Retiro, Madrid 17 B1
El Salto, Santiago 26 B2
El Sereno, Los Angeles 16 B3
El Talibiya, Cairo 7 B2
El Vergel, Mexico City 18 C2
El Wâhli, Cairo 7 A2
El Zamâlik, Cairo 7 A2
El Zeitûn, Cairo 7 A2
Elephanta Caves, Mumbai 20 B2
Elephanta I., Mumbai 20 B2
Ellboda, Stockholm 28 A3
Ellinikón, Athens 2 B2
Ellis I., New York 21 B1
Elm Park, London 15 A5
Elmers End, London 15 B3
Elmhurst, New York 21 B2
Elmstead, London 15 B4
Elmwood Park, Chicago 9 B2
Elmwood Park, New York 21 A1
Elsdon, Wellington 32 A1
Elsiesrivier, Cape Town 8 A2
Elsternwick, Melbourne 17 B2
Eltham, London 15 B4
Elwood, Melbourne 17 B1
Elysée, Paris 23 A2
Elysian Park, Los Angeles 16 a3
Embajadores, Madrid 17 c2
Embarcadero Center, San Francisco 25 b3
Emek Refa'im, Jerusalem 13 c2
Émerainville, Paris 23 B4
Emeryville, San Francisco 25 A3
Eminönü, Istanbul 12 B1
Emmarentia, Johannesburg 13 A2
Empire State Building, New York 21 c2
Encantado, Rio de Janeiro 24 B1
Encino, Los Angeles 16 B2
Encino Res., Los Angeles 16 B1
Enebyberg, Stockholm 28 A1
Enfield, Sydney 28 B1
Engenho, I. do, Rio de Janeiro 24 B2
Englewood, Chicago 9 C3
Englewood, New York 21 A2
Englewood Cliffs, New York 21 A2
Enmore, Sydney 28 B2
Enskede, Stockholm 28 B2
Entrevias, Madrid 17 B1
Epping, Sydney 28 A1
Erawan Shrine, Bangkok 3 c3
Eregun, Lagos 14 A2
Erenköy, Istanbul 12 C2
Erith, London 15 B5
Erlaa, Vienna 31 B1
Ermington, Sydney 28 A1
Ermita, Manila 17 B1
Ershatou, Canton 8 B2
Erskineville, Sydney 28 B2
Erunkan, Lagos 14 A2
Erzsébet-Telep, Budapest 7 B3
Eschenried, Munich 20 A1
Esenler, Istanbul 12 B1
Esher, London 15 B1
Eskbank, Edinburgh 11 B3
Esperanza, Mexico City 18 c3
Esplanade Park, Singapore 27 c3
Esplugas, Barcelona 4 A1
Esposizione Univ. di Roma (E.U.R.), Rome 25 C1
Essendon, Melbourne 17 A1
Essendon Airport, Melbourne 17 A1
Essingen, Stockholm 28 B1
Essling, Vienna 31 A3
Est, Gare de l', Paris 23 a5
Estadio Maracanã, Rio de Janeiro 24 B1
Estado, Parque do, São Paulo 26 B2
Estefânia, Lisbon 14 a2
Estrela, Basilica da, Lisbon 14 A2
Ethnikó Arheologiko Moussío, Athens 2 a2
Etobicoke, Toronto 30 B1
Etobicoke Cr. →, Toronto 30 B1
Etterbeek, Brussels 6 B2
Euston, London 15 a3
Evanston, Chicago 9 A2
Even Sapir, Jerusalem 13 B1
Evere, Brussels 6 A2
Everett, Boston 6 A3
Evergreen Park, Chicago 9 C2
Evin, Tehran 30 A2
Évzonos, Athens 2 B2
Ewu, Lagos 14 A1
Exchange Square, Hong Kong 12 c1
Exposições, Palácio das, Rio de Janeiro 24 B1
Eyüp, Istanbul 12 B1


# F


Fabour, Mt., Singapore 27 B2
Faechi, Seoul 26 B2
Fælledparken, Copenhagen 10 A3
Fågelön, Stockholm 28 B1
Fagersjö, Stockholm 28 B2
Fair Lawn, New York 21 A1
Fairfax, Washington 32 B2
Fairfax Station, Washington 32 C2
Fairhaven Bay, Boston 6 A1
Fairhaven Hill, Boston 6 A1
Fairland, Johannesburg 13 A1
Fairmilehead, Edinburgh 11 B2
Fairmount Heights, Washington 32 B4
Fairport, Toronto 30 A4
Fairview, New York 21 B1
Falenty, Warsaw 31 C1
Fálirou, Órmos, Athens 2 B2
Falkenburg, Berlin 5 A4
Falkenhagen, Berlin 5 A1
Falkensee, Berlin 5 A1
Falls Church, Washington 32 B3
Falomo, Lagos 14 B2
False Bay, Cape Town 8 B2
Fangcun, Canton 8 B2
Farahābād, Tehran 30 A2
Farforovskaya, St. Petersburg 26 B2
Farningham, London 15 B5
Farrar Pond, Boston 6 A1
Farsta, Stockholm 28 B2
Fasanerie-Nord, Munich 20 A2
Fasangarten, Munich 20 B2
Fasting Palace, Beijing 4 c2
Fatih, Istanbul 12 B1
Favoriten, Vienna 31 B2
Fawkner, Melbourne 17 A1

KAPOTNYA


Fawkner Park, *Melbourne* 17 B1
Feijó, *Lisbon* 14 B2
Feldkirchen, *Munich* 20 B3
Feldmoching, *Munich* 20 A2
Feltham, *London* 15 B1
Fener, *Istanbul* 12 B1
Fenerbahçe, *Istanbul* 12 C2
Fengtai, *Beijing* 4 C1
Fenino, *Moscow* 19 B5
Ferencváros, *Budapest* 7 B2
Ferihegyi Airport, *Budapest* 7 B3
Ferndale, *Johannesburg* 13 A2
Férolles-Attilly, *Paris* 23 B4
Fichtenau, *Berlin* 5 B5
Fields Corner, *Boston* 6 B3
Fiera Camp, *Milan* 18 B1
Fifth Avenue, *New York* 21 b3
Figino, *Milan* 18 B1
Fijir, *Baghdad* 3 A2
Filadhélfia, *Athens* 2 A2
Fili-Mazilovo, *Moscow* 19 B2
Filothei, *Athens* 2 A2
Finchley, *London* 15 A2
Finglas, *Dublin* 11 A2
Finsbury, *London* 15 A3
Finsbury Park, *London* 15 A3
Fiorito, *Buenos Aires* 7 C2
Firhouse, *Dublin* 11 B2
Fischerhäuser, *Munich* 20 A3
Fisher Island, *Miami* 18 B2
Fishermans Bend, *Melbourne* 17 A1
Fisherman's Wharf, *San Francisco* 25 a1
Fisherville, *Toronto* 30 A2
Fisksätra, *Stockholm* 28 B3
Fitzroy Gardens, *Melbourne* 17 A1
Five Dock, *Sydney* 28 B1
Fjellstrand, *Oslo* 22 B2
Flamengo, *Rio de Janeiro* 24 B1
Flaminio, *Rome* 25 B1
Flaskebekk, *Oslo* 22 A2
Flatbush, *New York* 21 C2
Flaten, *Stockholm* 28 B2
Flemington Racecourse, *Melbourne* 17 A1
Flint Pk., *Los Angeles* 16 B3
Florence, *Los Angeles* 16 C3
Florence Bloom Bird Sanctuary, *Johannesburg* 13 A2
Florentia, *Johannesburg* 13 B2
Flores, *Buenos Aires* 7 B2
Floresta, *Buenos Aires* 7 B2
Florida, *Buenos Aires* 7 B2
Florida, *Johannesburg* 13 B1
Floridsdorf, *Vienna* 31 A2
Flushing, *New York* 21 B3
Flushing Meadows Corona Park, *New York* 21 B2
Flysta, *Stockholm* 28 A1
Fo Tan, *Hong Kong* 12 A2
Föhrenhain, *Vienna* 31 A2
Fontainebleau, *Johannesburg* 13 A1
Fontenay-aux-Roses, *Paris* 23 B2
Fontenay-le-Fleury, *Paris* 23 B1
Fontenay-sous-Bois, *Paris* 23 A3
Foots Cray, *London* 15 B4
Footscray, *Melbourne* 17 A1
Foreshore, *Cape Town* 8 a3
Forest, *Brussels* 6 B1
Forest Gate, *London* 15 A4
Forest Heights, *Washington* 32 C3
Forest Hill, *London* 15 B3
Forest Hill, *Toronto* 30 A2
Forest Hills, *New York* 21 B2
Forest Park, *Chicago* 9 B2
Forest View, *Chicago* 9 C2
Forestville, *Washington* 32 B4
Fornebu, *Oslo* 22 A2
Fornebu Airport, *Oslo* 22 A2
Foro Romano, *Rome* 25 c3
Forstenried, *Munich* 20 B1
Forstenrieder Park, *Munich* 20 B1
Fort, *Mumbai* 20 c2
Fort Canning Park, *Singapore* 27 b2
Fort Dupont Park, *Washington* 32 B4
Fort Foote Village, *Washington* 32 C3
Fort Lee, *New York* 21 A2
Fort Mason Center, *San Francisco* 25 a1
Forth, Firth of, *Edinburgh* 11 A2
Forth Rail Bridge, *Edinburgh* 11 A1
Forth Road Bridge, *Edinburgh* 11 A1
Fót, *Budapest* 7 A3
Fourqueux, *Paris* 23 A1
Foxrock, *Dublin* 11 B2
Framingham, *Boston* 6 B1
Franconia, *Washington* 32 C3
Frankel, *Singapore* 27 B3
Franklin Park, *Boston* 6 B3
Franklin Park, *Chicago* 9 B1
Franklin Park, *Washington* 32 B3
Franklin Res., *Los Angeles* 16 B2
Frauenkirche, *Munich* 20 b2
Frederiksberg, *Copenhagen* 10 A3
Frederiksdal, *Copenhagen* 10 A2
Fredersdorf, *Berlin* 5 A5
Freguesia, *Rio de Janeiro* 24 A1
Freidrichshain, Volkspark, *Berlin* 5 A3
Freiham, *Munich* 20 B1
Freimann, *Munich* 20 A2
Fresh Pond, *Boston* 6 A3
Fresnes, *Paris* 23 B2
Freudenau, *Vienna* 31 A2
Friarstown, *Dublin* 11 B1
Frick Collection, *New York* 21 b3
Friedenau, *Berlin* 5 B3
Friedrichsfelde, *Berlin* 5 B4
Friedrichshagen, *Berlin* 5 B4
Friedrichshain, *Berlin* 5 A3
Friedrichslust, *Berlin* 5 A5
Friherrs, *Helsinki* 12 B1
Frontón, I., *Lima* 16 B1
Frunze, *Moscow* 19 B3
Fuchū, *Tokyo* 29 A1
Fuencarral, *Madrid* 17 B1
Fuenlabrada, *Madrid* 17 C1
Fujidera, *Osaka* 22 B4
Fukagawa, *Tokyo* 29 B3
Fukiage Imperial Garden, *Tokyo* 29 a4
Fukiai, *Osaka* 22 A2
Fukushima, *Osaka* 22 A3
Fulham, *London* 15 B2
Funabori, *Tokyo* 29 A4
Funasaka, *Osaka* 22 A2
Fundão, I. do, *Rio de Janeiro* 24 B1
Fünfhaus, *Vienna* 31 A2
Furesø, *Copenhagen* 10 A2
Furth, *Munich* 20 B2
Futago-tamagawaen, *Tokyo* 29 B2
Fuxing Dao, *Shanghai* 27 B2
Fuxing Park, *Shanghai* 27 B1
Fuxinglu, *Beijing* 4 B1


## G


Gage Park, *Chicago* 9 C2
Gagny, *Paris* 23 A4
Galata, *Istanbul* 12 B1
Galátsion, *Athens* 2 A2
Galeão, Aéroporto Int. de, *Rio de Janeiro* 24 A1
Galyanovo, *Moscow* 19 B4
Gambir, *Jakarta* 13 A1
Gamboa, *Rio de Janeiro* 24 B1
Gambolóita, *Milan* 18 B2
Gamla Stan , *Stockholm* 28 c2
Gamlebyen, *Oslo* 22 A3
Gangtou, *Canton* 8 A1
Gangwei, *Canton* 8 B2
Ganjiakou, *Beijing* 4 B1
Ganshoren, *Brussels* 6 A1
Gants Hill, *London* 15 A4
Gaoqiao, *Shanghai* 27 A2
Garbagnate Milanese, *Milan* 18 A1
Garbatella, *Rome* 25 B2
Garches, *Paris* 23 A2
Garching, *Munich* 20 A3
Garden City, *Cairo* 7 A2
Garden Reach, *Calcutta* 8 B1
Garder, *Oslo* 22 B2
Garfield, *New York* 21 A1
Garfield Park, *Chicago* 9 B2
Gargareta, *Athens* 2 B2
Garvanza, *Los Angeles* 16 B3
Gåshaga, *Stockholm* 28 A3
Gateway National Recreation Area, *New York* 21 C2
Gateway of India, *Mumbai* 20 B2
Gatow, *Berlin* 5 B1
Gávea, *Rio de Janeiro* 24 B1
Gávea, Pedra da, *Rio de Janeiro* 24 B1
Gazdagrét, *Budapest* 7 B1
Gebel el Ahmar, *Cairo* 7 A2
Gebel el Muqattam, *Cairo* 7 A2
Gebel el Tura, *Cairo* 7 B2
Geiselgasteig, *Munich* 20 B2
General San Martin, *Buenos Aires* 7 B1
Gennevilliers, *Paris* 23 A2
Gentilly, *Paris* 23 B3
Gentofte, *Copenhagen* 10 A3
Genval, *Brussels* 6 B2
George I., *Hong Kong* 12 B1
Georges I., *Boston* 6 B4
Georges River Bridge, *Sydney* 28 C1
Georgetown, *Washington* 32 B3
Georgia Dome, *Atlanta* 3 B2
Gerasdorf bei Wien, *Vienna* 31 A2
Gerberau, *Munich* 20 A1
Gerli, *Buenos Aires* 7 C2
Germiston, *Johannesburg* 13 B2
Gern, *Munich* 20 B2
Gesîrat el Rauda, *Cairo* 7 A2
Getafe, *Madrid* 17 C1
Geva Binyamin, *Jerusalem* 13 A2
Geylang Serai, *Singapore* 27 B3
Gezîrat el Dhahab, *Cairo* 7 B2
Gharapuri, *Mumbai* 20 B2
Ghatkopar, *Mumbai* 20 A2
Ghazipur, *Delhi* 10 B2
Ghizri, *Karachi* 14 B2
Ghizri Cr. →, *Karachi* 14 B2
Ghonda, *Delhi* 10 A2
Ghusuri, *Calcutta* 8 B2
Gianicolense, *Rome* 25 B1
Gianicolo, *Rome* 25 c1
Gibraltar Pt., *Toronto* 30 B2
Gidea Park, *London* 15 A5
Giesing, *Munich* 20 B2
Gilmerton, *Edinburgh* 11 B3
Gilo, *Jerusalem* 13 B2
Gimmersta, *Stockholm* 28 B3
Ginza, *Tokyo* 29 b5
Girgaum, *Mumbai* 20 b2
Giv'at Ye'arim, *Jerusalem* 13 B1
Giv'at Ze'ev, *Jerusalem* 13 A2
Giza Pyramids = Pyramids, *Cairo* 7 B1
Gjersjøen, *Oslo* 22 B3
Gladesville, *Sydney* 28 B1
Gladsakse, *Copenhagen* 10 A2
Glasnevin, *Dublin* 11 A2
Glassmanor, *Washington* 32 C3
Glasthule, *Dublin* 11 B3
Glen Iris, *Melbourne* 17 B2
Glen Mar Park, *Washington* 32 B3
Glen Rock, *New York* 21 A1
Glenarden, *Washington* 32 B4
Glenasmole Reservoirs, *Dublin* 11 B1
Glencorse Res., *Edinburgh* 11 B2
Glencullen, *Dublin* 11 B2
Glendale, *Los Angeles* 16 B3
Glendoo Mt., *Dublin* 11 B2
Glenhuntly, *Melbourne* 17 B2
Glenside, *Wellington* 32 B1
Glenview, *Chicago* 9 A2
Glenview Countryside, *Chicago* 9 A2
Glenvista, *Johannesburg* 13 B2
Glifádha, *Athens* 2 B2
Glömsta, *Stockholm* 28 B1
Glostrup, *Copenhagen* 10 B2
Gogar, *Edinburgh* 11 B2
Göktürk, *Istanbul* 12 A1
Golabari, *Calcutta* 8 B2
Golabki, *Warsaw* 31 B1
Gold Coast, *Chicago* 9 a2
Golden Gate, *San Francisco* 25 B2
Golden Gate Bridge, *San Francisco* 25 B2
Golden Gate Park, *San Francisco* 25 B2
Golden Horn, *Istanbul* 12 B1
Golders Green, *London* 15 A2
Gollans Stream →, *Wellington* 32 B2
Golyevo, *Moscow* 19 B1
Goodman Hill, *Boston* 6 A1
Goodmayes, *London* 15 A4
Goodwood, *Cape Town* 8 A2
Gopalpur, *Calcutta* 8 B2
Górce, *Warsaw* 31 B1
Gore Hill, *Sydney* 28 A2
Gorelyy →, *St. Petersburg* 26 A3
Gorenki, *Moscow* 19 B5
Gorgie, *Edinburgh* 11 B2
Gorky Park, *Moscow* 19 B3
Gosen, *Berlin* 5 B5
Gosener kanal, *Berlin* 5 B5
Gospel Oak, *London* 15 A3
Gotanda, *Tokyo* 29 B3
Goth Goli Mar, *Karachi* 14 A2
Goth Sher Shah, *Karachi* 14 A1
Gournay-sur-Marne, *Paris* 23 A4
Governador, I. do, *Rio de Janeiro* 24 A1
Governor's I., *New York* 21 B1
Graben, *Vienna* 31 b2
Grabów, *Warsaw* 31 C1
Graça, *Lisbon* 14 b3
Grace, Mt., *Wellington* 32 B2
Grace Cathedral, *San Francisco* 25 b1
Gracefield, *Wellington* 32 B2
Gracia, *Barcelona* 4 A2
Gräfelfing, *Munich* 20 B1
Gragoatá, *Rio de Janeiro* 24 B2
Grand Central Station, *New York* 21 c2
Grand Union Canal, *London* 15 A2
Grande Place, *Brussels* 6 b2
Grant Park, *Atlanta* 3 B2
Grant Park, *Chicago* 9 c2
Granton, *Edinburgh* 11 B2
Grape I., *Boston* 6 B4
Grassy Park, *Cape Town* 8 B2
Gratosóglio, *Milan* 18 B2
Gratzwalde, *Berlin* 5 B5
Gravesend, *New York* 21 C2
Grazhdanka, *St. Petersburg* 26 B2
Great Falls, *Washington* 32 B2
Great Falls Park, *Washington* 32 B2
Great Hall of the People, *Beijing* 4 b2
Great Meadows National Wildlife Refuge, *Boston* 6 A1
Greco, *Milan* 18 A2
Green I., *Hong Kong* 12 B1
Green Point, *Cape Town* 8 A1
Greenbelt, *Washington* 32 A4
Greenbelt Park, *Washington* 32 B4
Greenfield Park, *Montreal* 19 B3
Greenford, *London* 15 A1
Greenhill, *London* 15 A2
Greenhills, *Dublin* 11 B1
Greenmarket Square, *Cape Town* 8 c2
Greenpoint, *New York* 21 B2
Greenwich, *London* 15 B3
Greenwich Observatory, *London* 15 B3
Greenwich Village, *New York* 21 B2
Greenwood, *Boston* 6 A3
Grefsen, *Oslo* 22 A3
Gresham Park, *Atlanta* 3 B2
Greve Strand, *Copenhagen* 10 B1
Greyfriars Kirk, *Edinburgh* 11 c2
Griebnitzsee, *Berlin* 5 B1
Griffen Park, *Los Angeles* 16 B3
Grimbergen, *Brussels* 6 A2
Grinzing, *Vienna* 31 A2
Gröbenried, *Munich* 20 A1
Grochów, *Warsaw* 31 B2
Grodzisk, *Warsaw* 31 B1
Groenendaal, *Brussels* 6 B2
Grogol Petamburin, *Jakarta* 13 A1
Gronsdorf, *Munich* 20 B3
Grorud, *Oslo* 22 A4
Gross Glienicke, *Berlin* 5 B1
Gross-Hadern, *Munich* 20 B1
Gross-Lappen, *Munich* 20 A2
Grosse Krampe, *Berlin* 5 B5
Grosse Müggelsee, *Berlin* 5 B4
Grossenzersdorf, *Vienna* 31 A3
Grossenzersdorfer Arm →, *Vienna* 31 A3
Grosser Biberhaufen, *Vienna* 31 A2
Grosser Wannsee, *Berlin* 5 B2
Grossfeld-Siedlung, *Vienna* 31 A2
Grosshesselohe, *Munich* 20 B2
Grossjedlersdorf, *Vienna* 31 A2
Grossziethen, *Berlin* 5 B3
Grove Hall, *Boston* 6 B3
Grove Park, *Atlanta* 3 B2
Grove Park, *London* 15 B4
Grove Park, *London* 15 B2
Groveton, *Washington* 32 C3
Grünau, *Berlin* 5 B4
Grunewald, *Berlin* 5 B2
Grünwald, *Munich* 20 B2
Grünwalder Forst, *Munich* 20 B2
Grymes Hill, *New York* 21 C1
Guadalupe, *Manila* 17 B2
Guadalupe, Basilica de, *Mexico City* 18 B2
Guanabara, B. de, *Rio de Janeiro* 24 B1
Guanabara, Jardim, *Rio de Janeiro* 24 A1
Guanabara, Palácio da, *Rio de Janeiro* 24 B1
Guang'anmen, *Beijing* 4 B1
Guangqumen, *Beijing* 4 B2
Guangzhou, *Canton* 8 B2
Guanshuo, *Canton* 8 B3
Gudö, *Stockholm* 28 B3
Güell, Parque de, *Barcelona* 4 A2
Guerrero, *Mexico City* 18 a1
Guggenheim Museum, *New York* 21 b3
Guinardó, *Barcelona* 4 A2
Gulbai, *Karachi* 14 A1
Güngören, *Istanbul* 12 B1
Gunnersbury, *London* 15 B2
Gustavo A. Madero, *Mexico City* 18 B2
Guttenberg, *New York* 21 B1
Gutuyevskiy, Ostrov, *St. Petersburg* 26 B1
Guyancourt, *Paris* 23 B1
Gyál, *Budapest* 7 B3
Gyáli-patak →, *Budapest* 7 B2


## H


Haaga, *Helsinki* 12 B2
Haar, *Munich* 20 B3
Hackbridge, *London* 15 B3
Hackensack, *New York* 21 A1
Hackensack →, *New York* 21 B1
Hackney, *London* 15 A3
Hackney Wick, *London* 15 A3
Haga, *Stockholm* 28 A2
Hagenbrunn, *Vienna* 31 A2
Hägersten, *Stockholm* 28 B1
Häggvik, *Stockholm* 28 A1
Hai He →, *Tianjin* 30 B2
Haidan, *Beijing* 4 B1
Haidarpur, *Delhi* 10 A1
Haidhausen, *Munich* 20 B2
Haight-Ashbury, *San Francisco* 25 B2
Hainault, *London* 15 A4
Haizhu Guangchang, *Canton* 8 B2
Hakunila, *Helsinki* 12 B3
Halásztelek, *Budapest* 7 B1
Haliç = Golden Horn, *Istanbul* 12 B1
Halim Perdanakusuma International Airport, *Jakarta* 13 B2
Halle, *Brussels* 6 B1
Haltiala, *Helsinki* 12 B2
Haltiavuori, *Helsinki* 12 B2
Ham, *London* 15 B2
Hämeenkylä, *Helsinki* 12 B1
Hammarby, *Stockholm* 28 B2
Hamme, *Brussels* 6 A1
Hammersmith, *London* 15 B2
Hampstead, *London* 15 A2
Hampstead, *Montreal* 19 B2
Hampstead Garden Suburb, *London* 15 A2
Hampstead Heath, *London* 15 A2
Hampton, *London* 15 B1
Hampton Court Palace, *London* 15 B1
Hampton Wick, *London* 15 B2
Hamrā', *Baghdad* 3 B1
Hanala, *Helsinki* 12 A3
Haneda, *Tokyo* 29 B3
Hang Hau, *Hong Kong* 12 B2
Hanging Gardens, *Mumbai* 20 b1
Hanjiashu, *Tianjin* 30 A1
Hanlon, *Toronto* 30 B1
Hanwell, *London* 15 A1
Hanworth, *London* 15 B1
Haora, *Calcutta* 8 B1
Hapeville, *Atlanta* 3 C2
Happy Valley, *Hong Kong* 12 B2
Har Adar, *Jerusalem* 13 B1
Haren, *Brussels* 6 A2
Hareskovby, *Copenhagen* 10 A2
Haringey, *London* 15 A3
Harjusuo, *Helsinki* 12 B3
Harlaching, *Munich* 20 B2
Harlaw Res., *Edinburgh* 11 B2
Harlem, *New York* 21 B2
Harlesden, *London* 15 A2
Harlington, *London* 15 B1
Harmaja, *Helsinki* 12 C2
Harmashatar hegy, *Budapest* 7 A2
Harolds Cross, *Dublin* 11 B2
Háros, *Budapest* 7 B2
Harperrig Reservoir, *Edinburgh* 11 B1
Harrow, *London* 15 A1
Harrow on the Hill, *London* 15 A1
Harrow School, *London* 15 A1
Harrow Weald, *London* 15 A1
Hartsfield-Atlanta International Airport, *Atlanta* 3 C2
Harumi, *Tokyo* 29 c5
Harvard Univ., *Boston* 6 A3
Harwood Heights, *Chicago* 9 B2
Hasanābād, *Tehran* 30 A1
Hasbrouck Heights, *New York* 21 A1
Haselhorst, *Berlin* 5 A2
Hasköy, *Istanbul* 12 B1
Hasle, *Oslo* 22 B2
Haslum, *Oslo* 22 A2
Hästhagen, *Stockholm* 28 B2
Hataitai, *Wellington* 32 B1
Hatch End, *London* 15 A1
Hatiara, *Calcutta* 8 B2
Hauketo, *Oslo* 22 A3
Havel →, *Berlin* 5 A2
Havelkanal, *Berlin* 5 A2
Havering, *London* 15 A5
Havering-atte-Bower, *London* 15 A5
Hawŏlgok, *Seoul* 26 B2
Haworth, *New York* 21 A2
Hayes, *London* 15 B4
Hayes, *London* 15 A1
Hayes End, *London* 15 A1
Hayford, *Chicago* 9 C2
Haywards, *Wellington* 32 A2
Heard Pond, *Boston* 6 A1
Heathfield, *Cape Town* 8 B1
Heathrow Airport, *London* 15 B1
Hebe Haven, *Hong Kong* 12 A2
Hebei, *Tianjin* 30 B2
Hedong, *Canton* 8 B2
Hedong, *Tianjin* 30 B2
Heidelberg Heights, *Melbourne* 17 A2
Heidelberg West, *Melbourne* 17 A2
Heidemühle, *Berlin* 5 B5
Heideveld, *Cape Town* 8 A2
Heiligensee, *Berlin* 5 A2
Heiligenstadt, *Vienna* 31 A2
Heinersdorf, *Berlin* 5 A3
Heldenplatz, *Vienna* 31 b1
Hélène Champlain, Parc, *Montreal* 19 A2
Helenelund, *Stockholm* 28 A1
Heliopolis = Masr el Gedida, *Cairo* 7 A2
Hellersdorf, *Berlin* 5 A4
Hellerup, *Copenhagen* 10 A3
Helmahof, *Vienna* 31 A3
Helsingfors = Helsinki, *Helsinki* 12 B2
Helsinki, *Helsinki* 12 B2
Helsinki Airport, *Helsinki* 12 B2
Hendon, *London* 15 A2
Hengsha, *Canton* 8 B2
Hennigsdorf, *Berlin* 5 A2
Henryków, *Warsaw* 31 B1
Henson Cr. →, *Washington* 32 C4
Henttaa, *Helsinki* 12 B1
Heping, *Tianjin* 30 B2
Heping Park, *Shanghai* 27 B2
Hepingli, *Beijing* 4 B2
Herlev, *Copenhagen* 10 A2
Herman Eckstein Park, *Johannesburg* 13 A2
Hermannskogel, *Vienna* 31 A1
Hermiston, *Edinburgh* 11 B2
Hermitage and Winter Palace, *St. Petersburg* 26 B1
Hermsdorf, *Berlin* 5 A2
Hernals, *Vienna* 31 A2
Herne Hill, *London* 15 B3
Héroes de Churubusco, *Mexico City* 18 B2
Herons, Î. aux, *Montreal* 19 B2
Herstedøster, *Copenhagen* 10 A2
Herttoniemi, *Helsinki* 12 B3
Heşārak, *Tehran* 30 A1
Heston, *London* 15 B1
Hetzendorf, *Vienna* 31 B1
Hexi, *Tianjin* 30 B2
Hextable, *London* 15 B5
Hialeah, *Miami* 18 A1
Hickory Hills, *Chicago* 9 C2
Hiekkaharju, *Helsinki* 12 B3
Hietaniemi, *Helsinki* 12 B2
Hietzing, *Vienna* 31 A1
Higashi, *Osaka* 22 A4
Higashimurayama, *Tokyo* 29 A1
Higashinada, *Osaka* 22 A2
Higashinari, *Osaka* 22 A4
Higashiōsaka, *Osaka* 22 B4
Higashisumiyoshi, *Osaka* 22 B4
Higashiyodogawa, *Osaka* 22 A3
High Park, *Toronto* 30 B2
Highbury, *London* 15 A3
Highgate, *London* 15 A3
Highland Cr. →, *Toronto* 30 A3
Highland Creek, *Toronto* 30 A3
Highland Park, *Los Angeles* 16 B3
Highlands North, *Johannesburg* 13 A2
Hillcrest Heights, *Washington* 32 C4
Hillend, *Edinburgh* 11 A1
Hillingdon, *London* 15 A1
Hillwood, *Washington* 32 B3
Hilmîya, *Cairo* 7 A2
Hin Keng, *Hong Kong* 12 A2
Hingham, *Boston* 6 B4
Hingham B., *Boston* 6 B4
Hingham Harbor, *Boston* 6 B4
Hirakata, *Osaka* 22 A4
Hirota, *Osaka* 22 A3
Hirschstetten, *Vienna* 31 A2
Histórico Nacional, Museu, *Rio de Janeiro* 24 b3
Hither Green, *London* 15 B3
Hiyoshi, *Tokyo* 29 B2
Hizma, *Jerusalem* 13 B2
Hjortekær, *Copenhagen* 10 A3
Hjortespring, *Copenhagen* 10 A2
Hlubočepy, *Prague* 24 B2
Ho Chung, *Hong Kong* 12 A2
Ho Man Tin, *Hong Kong* 12 B2
Hoboken, *New York* 21 B1
Hobsons B., *Melbourne* 17 B1
Hochbrück, *Munich* 20 A2
Hochelaga, *Montreal* 19 A2
Hodgkins, *Chicago* 9 C1
Hoegi, *Seoul* 26 B2
Hoeilaart, *Brussels* 6 B2
Hofberg, *Vienna* 31 A2
Hoffman I., *New York* 21 C1
Hofgarten, *Munich* 20 a3
Högsdtadomstolen, *Stockholm* 28 c2
Hohenbrunn, *Munich* 20 B3
Hohenschönhausen, *Berlin* 5 A4
Holborn, *London* 15 a4
Holešovice, *Prague* 24 B2
Holland Village, *Singapore* 27 B2
Höllriegelskreuth, *Munich* 20 B1
Hollywood, *Los Angeles* 16 B3
Holmenkollen, *Oslo* 22 A3
Holmes Run Acres, *Washington* 32 B2
Holmgård, *Stockholm* 28 B1
Holysloot, *Amsterdam* 2 A3
Homerton, *London* 15 A3
Hometown, *Chicago* 9 C2
Hōnanchō, *Tokyo* 29 A2
Honcho, *Tokyo* 29 A3
Honden, *Tokyo* 29 A4
Hondo, Rio →, *Los Angeles* 16 B4
Hong Kong, *Hong Kong* 12 B1
Hong Kong, Univ. of, *Hong Kong* 12 B1
Hong Kong I., *Hong Kong* 12 B2
Hong Kong Park, *Hong Kong* 12 c1
Hongkou, *Shanghai* 27 B1
Hongkou Park, *Shanghai* 27 B1
Hongmiao, *Beijing* 4 B2
Hongqiao, *Shanghai* 27 B1
Hongqiao, *Tianjin* 30 B1
Hongqiao Airport, *Shanghai* 27 B1
Hongŭn, *Seoul* 26 B1
Honjyo, *Tokyo* 29 A3
Honoré Mercier, Pont, *Montreal* 19 B1
Hönow, *Berlin* 5 A4
Hooghly = Hugli →, *Calcutta* 8 A2
Hook, *London* 15 B2
Horikiri, *Tokyo* 29 A4
Horn Pond, *Boston* 6 A2
Hornchurch, *London* 15 A5
Horni, *Prague* 24 B3
Horni Počernice, *Prague* 24 B3
Hornsey, *London* 15 A3
Horoměřice, *Prague* 24 B1
Hortaleza, *Madrid* 17 B2
Hosoyama, *Tokyo* 29 B2
Hostafranchs, *Barcelona* 4 A1
Hostivař, *Prague* 24 B3
Hôtel des Invalides, *Paris* 23 c2
Houbětin, *Prague* 24 B3
Houghs Neck, *Boston* 6 B4
Houghton, *Johannesburg* 13 B2
Houilles, *Paris* 23 A2
Hounslow, *London* 15 B1
Houses of Parliament, *London* 15 c3
Hout Bay, *Cape Town* 8 B1
Hove Å →, *Copenhagen* 10 A1
Hovedøya, *Oslo* 22 A3
Høvik, *Oslo* 22 A2
Hovorčovice, *Prague* 24 A3
Howard Beach, *New York* 21 C2
Howth, *Dublin* 11 A3
Howth Head, *Dublin* 11 A3
Hoxton, *London* 15 a5
Hōya, *Tokyo* 29 A2
Hradčany, *Prague* 24 B2
Huanghuagang Mausoleum of the 72 Martyrs, *Canton* 8 B2
Huangpu, *Shanghai* 27 B2
Huangpu Jiang →, *Shanghai* 27 B1
Huangpu Park, *Shanghai* 27 B1
Huangtugang, *Beijing* 4 C1
Huascar, *Lima* 16 A2
Huay Khwang, *Bangkok* 3 B2
Huddinge, *Stockholm* 28 B2
Hudson →, *New York* 21 A2
Huechuraba, *Santiago* 26 B1
Huertas de San Beltran, *Barcelona* 4 A1
Hugli →, *Calcutta* 8 A2
Huidui, *Tianjin* 30 B2
Huizingen, *Brussels* 6 B1
Hull, *Boston* 6 B4
Humber →, *Toronto* 30 A1
Humber B., *Toronto* 30 B2
Humber Bay, *Toronto* 30 B2
Humber Summit, *Toronto* 30 A1
Humber Valley Village, *Toronto* 30 A1
Humberlea, *Toronto* 30 A1
Humboldt Park, *Chicago* 9 B2
Humera, *Madrid* 17 B1
Hunaydī, *Baghdad* 3 B2
Hundige, *Copenhagen* 10 B1
Hundige Strand, *Copenhagen* 10 B2
Hung Hom, *Hong Kong* 12 B2
Hunters Hill, *Sydney* 28 B1
Hunters Pt., *San Francisco* 25 B2
Hunters Valley, *Washington* 32 B2
Huntington, *Washington* 32 C3
Huntington Park, *Los Angeles* 16 C3
Hurīya, *Baghdad* 3 A1
Hurstville, *Sydney* 28 B1
Husby, *Stockholm* 28 A1
Husum, *Copenhagen* 10 A2
Hutt R. →, *Wellington* 32 B2
Hütteldorf, *Vienna* 31 A1
Hüvösvölgy, *Budapest* 7 A2
Hvalstad, *Oslo* 22 A1
Hvalstrand, *Oslo* 22 A2
Hvidovre, *Copenhagen* 10 B2
Hwagok, *Seoul* 26 B1
Hyattsville, *Washington* 32 B4
Hyde Park, *Boston* 6 B3
Hyde Park, *Chicago* 9 C3
Hyde Park, *Johannesburg* 13 A2
Hyde Park, *London* 15 A2
Hyde Park, *Sydney* 28 B2


## I


Ibese, *Lagos* 14 A2
Ibirapuera, *São Paulo* 26 B1
Ibirapuera, Parque, *São Paulo* 26 B2
Icarai, *Rio de Janeiro* 24 B2
Içerenköy, *Istanbul* 12 C2
Ichgao, *Tokyo* 29 B2
Ichigaya, *Tokyo* 29 a3
Ichikawa, *Tokyo* 29 A4
Ickenham, *London* 15 A1
Iddo, *Lagos* 14 B2
Idi-Oro, *Lagos* 14 A2
Iganmu, *Lagos* 14 B2
Igbobi, *Lagos* 14 A2
Igbologun, *Lagos* 14 B1
Igny, *Paris* 23 B2
IJ, Het →, *Amsterdam* 2 A2
IJ-meer, *Amsterdam* 2 A3
Ijesa-Tedo, *Lagos* 14 B1
Ijora, *Lagos* 14 B2
IJtunnel, *Amsterdam* 2 a3
Ikebe, *Tokyo* 29 B2
Ikebukuro, *Tokyo* 29 A3
Ikegami, *Tokyo* 29 B3
Ikeja, *Lagos* 14 A2
Ikeuchi, *Osaka* 22 B4
Ikoyi, *Lagos* 14 B2
Ikuata, *Lagos* 14 B2
Ikuno, *Osaka* 22 A4
Ikuta, *Osaka* 22 A2
Ikuta, *Tokyo* 29 B2
Ila, *Oslo* 22 A2
Ilford, *London* 15 A4
Ilioúpolis, *Athens* 2 B2
Ilpendam, *Amsterdam* 2 A2
Ilsós →, *Athens* 2 B2
Imagem e do Som, Museu da, *Rio de Janeiro* 24 b3
Imbâbah, *Cairo* 7 A2
Imielin, *Warsaw* 31 C2
Imirim, *São Paulo* 26 A2
Imittós, *Athens* 2 B2
Imittoś, Óros, *Athens* 2 B2
Imperial Palace Museum, *Beijing* 4 b2
Inagi, *Tokyo* 29 B2
Inchcolm, *Edinburgh* 11 A2
Inchicore, *Dublin* 11 A1
Inchkeith, *Edinburgh* 11 A3
Inchmickery, *Edinburgh* 11 A2
Incirano, *Milan* 18 A1
Independencia, *Lima* 16 A2
Independencia, *Santiago* 26 B2
India Gate, *Delhi* 1 c2
Indian Creek Village, *Miami* 18 A2
Indian Head Park, *Chicago* 9 C1
Indianópolis, *São Paulo* 26 B2
Indios Verdes, *Mexico City* 18 B2
Indira Gandhi International Airport, *Delhi* 10 B1
Industria, *Johannesburg* 13 B1
Ingierstrand, *Oslo* 22 B3
Inglewood, *Los Angeles* 16 C3
Ingliston, *Edinburgh* 11 B1
Inhaúme, *Rio de Janeiro* 24 B1
Inner Port Shelter, *Hong Kong* 12 A2
Interlagos, *São Paulo* 26 C1
Intramuros, *Manila* 17 B1
Invalides, *Paris* 23 A2
Inverkeithing, *Edinburgh* 11 A1
Inzersdorf, *Vienna* 31 B2
Ipanema, *Rio de Janeiro* 24 B1
Ipiranga, *São Paulo* 26 B2
Ipiranga →, *São Paulo* 26 B2
Iponri, *Lagos* 14 B2
Ireland's Eye, *Dublin* 11 A3
Irving Park, *Chicago* 9 B2
Isabel, *Rio de Janeiro* 24 B1
Isagatedo, *Lagos* 14 A1
Isar →, *Munich* 20 A3
Ishbīlīya, *Baghdad* 3 A2
Ishikiri, *Osaka* 22 A4
Ishøj Strand, *Copenhagen* 10 B2
Island Bay, *Wellington* 32 B1
Island Park, *Toronto* 30 B2
Isle of Dogs, *London* 15 B3
Islev, *Copenhagen* 10 A2
Isleworth, *London* 15 B2
Islington, *London* 15 A3
Islington, *Toronto* 30 B1
Ismaning, *Munich* 20 A3
Ismayloskiy Park, *Moscow* 19 B4
Isolo, *Lagos* 14 A1
Issy-les-Moulineaux, *Paris* 23 B2
Istanbul, *Istanbul* 12 C1
Istanbul Boğazi, *Istanbul* 12 B2
Istinye, *Istanbul* 12 B2
Itä Hakkila, *Helsinki* 12 B3
Itaewŏn, *Seoul* 26 B1
Itahanga, *Rio de Janeiro* 24 B1
Itami, *Osaka* 22 A3
Ivanhoe, *Melbourne* 17 A2
Ivry-sur-Seine, *Paris* 23 B3
Iwazono, *Osaka* 22 A2
Ixelles, *Brussels* 6 B2
Izmaylovo, *Moscow* 19 B4
Iztacalco, *Mexico City* 18 B2
Iztapalapa, *Mexico City* 18 B2


## J


Jaba, *Jerusalem* 13 A2
Jababpur, *Calcutta* 8 C2
Jacaré, *Rio de Janeiro* 24 B1
Jackson Heights, *New York* 21 B2
Jackson Park, *Chicago* 9 C3
Jacques Cartier, *Montreal* 19 A3
Jacques Cartier, Pont, *Montreal* 19 A2
Jade Buddha Temple, *Shanghai* 27 B1
Jægersborg, *Copenhagen* 10 A3
Jægersborg Dyrehave, *Copenhagen* 10 A3
Jagadishpur, *Calcutta* 8 B1
Jagatpur, *Delhi* 10 A2
Jaguaré, Rib. do →, *São Paulo* 26 B1
Jahangirpur, *Delhi* 10 A2
Jakarta, *Jakarta* 13 A2
Jakarta, Teluk, *Jakarta* 13 A1
Jalan Kayu, *Singapore* 27 A3
Jamaica B., *New York* 21 C3
Jamaica Plain, *Boston* 6 B3
Jamakpuri, *Delhi* 10 B1
Jamshīdīyeh, *Tehran* 30 A2
Janki, *Warsaw* 31 C1
Jannali, *Sydney* 28 C1
Japan Center, *San Francisco* 25 c1
Jaraguá, *São Paulo* 26 A1
Jaraguá, Pico de, *São Paulo* 26 A1
Jardim Paulista, *São Paulo* 26 B1
Jardin Botanique, *Brussels* 6 a3
Järvatältet, *Stockholm* 28 A1
Jaskhar, *Mumbai* 20 B2
Jatinegara, *Jakarta* 13 B2
Javādīyeh, *Tehran* 30 B2
Jaworowa, *Warsaw* 31 C1
Jedlesee, *Vienna* 31 A2
Jefferson Memorial, *Washington* 32 c1
Jefferson Park, *Chicago* 9 B2
Jelonki, *Warsaw* 31 B1
Jerónimos, Mosteiro dos, *Lisbon* 14 A1
Jersey City, *New York* 21 B1
Jerusalem, *Jerusalem* 13 B2
Jésus, Î., *Montreal* 19 A1
Jesús Maria, *Lima* 16 B2
Jette, *Brussels* 6 A1
Jewish Quarter, *Jerusalem* 13 b3
Jey, *Tehran* 30 B2
Jianguomen, *Beijing* 4 B2
Jiangwan, *Shanghai* 27 B1
Jianshan Park, *Tianjin* 30 B2
Jihād, *Baghdad* 3 B1
Jim Thompson's House, *Bangkok* 3 b3
Jimbōchō, *Tokyo* 29 a4
Jingan, *Shanghai* 27 B1
Jingu Outer Garden, *Tokyo* 29 b2
Jinočany, *Prague* 24 B1
Jinonice, *Prague* 24 B2
Jiyūgaoka, *Tokyo* 29 B3
Jizā'ir, *Baghdad* 3 B2
Jizīra, *Baghdad* 3 B2
Johannesburg, *Johannesburg* 13 B2
Johanneskirchen, *Munich* 20 A2
Johannesstift, *Berlin* 5 A2
Johannisthal, *Berlin* 5 B4
John Hancock Center, *Chicago* 9 a2
John McLaren Park, *San Francisco* 25 B2
Johnsonville, *Wellington* 32 B1
Joinville-le-Pont, *Paris* 23 B3
Joli-Bois, *Brussels* 6 B2
Jollas, *Helsinki* 12 B3
Jonstrup, *Copenhagen* 10 A2
Joppa, *Edinburgh* 11 B3
Jorge Chavez, Aeropuerto Int., *Lima* 16 B2
Jorge Newbury, Aeroparque, *Buenos Aires* 7 B2
Józefa Piłsudskiego Park, *Warsaw* 31 B1
Jōtō, *Osaka* 22 A4
Jouy-en-Josas, *Paris* 23 B2
Juan Anchorena, *Buenos Aires* 7 A2
Juan González Romero, *Mexico City* 18 A2
Judeira, *Jerusalem* 13 A2
Juhu, *Mumbai* 20 A2
Jūjā, *Tokyo* 29 A3
Jukskeirivier →, *Johannesburg* 13 A2
Julianów, *Warsaw* 31 B2
Jungfernheide, Volkspark, *Berlin* 5 A2
Jungfernsee, *Berlin* 5 B1
Juniper Green, *Edinburgh* 11 B2
Junk B., *Hong Kong* 12 B2
Jurong, *Singapore* 27 B2
Jurong, Selat, *Singapore* 27 B2
Jurong Industrial Estate, *Singapore* 27 B1
Jurujuba, Enseada de, *Rio de Janeiro* 24 B2
Jūsō, *Osaka* 22 A3
Justice, *Chicago* 9 C2
Justicia, *Madrid* 17 a3
Jwalahari, *Delhi* 10 B1


## K


Kabaty, *Warsaw* 31 C2
Kadıköy, *Istanbul* 12 C2
Kadoma, *Osaka* 22 A4
Kaebong, *Seoul* 26 C1
Kafr 'Aqab, *Jerusalem* 13 A2
Kâğıthane, *Istanbul* 12 B1
Kâğıthane →, *Istanbul* 12 B1
Kagran, *Vienna* 31 A2
Kahnawake, *Montreal* 19 B1
Kaimes, *Edinburgh* 11 B2
Kaisariani, *Athens* 2 B2
Kaiser Wilhelm Kirche, *Berlin* 5 b2
Kaiserebersdorf, *Vienna* 31 B2
Kaivoksela, *Helsinki* 12 B2
Kalamákion, *Athens* 2 B2
Kalbadevi, *Mumbai* 20 b2
Kalhyŏn, *Seoul* 26 B1
Kalipur, *Calcutta* 8 A1
Kalkaji, *Delhi* 10 B2
Kallithéa, *Athens* 2 B2
Kalveboderne, *Copenhagen* 10 B3
Kamarhati, *Calcutta* 8 A2
Kamata, *Tokyo* 29 B3
Kameari, *Tokyo* 29 A4
Kameido, *Tokyo* 29 A4
Kami-Itabashi, *Tokyo* 29 A3
Kamikitazawa, *Tokyo* 29 B2
Kamitsuruma, *Tokyo* 29 B1
Kamoshida, *Tokyo* 29 B2
Kampong Landang, *Singapore* 27 A3
Kampong Tanjong Penjuru, *Singapore* 27 B2
Kampung Bali, *Jakarta* 13 B1
Kanamori, *Tokyo* 29 B1
Kanda, *Tokyo* 29 a5
Kandilli, *Istanbul* 12 B2
Kangdong, *Seoul* 26 B2
Kangnam, *Seoul* 26 B1
Kangsŏ, *Seoul* 26 B1
Kankurgachi, *Calcutta* 8 B2
Kanlıca, *Istanbul* 12 B2
Kanonerskiy, Ostrov, *St. Petersburg* 26 B1
Kanzaki →, *Osaka* 22 A3
Kapellerfeld, *Vienna* 31 A2
Káposztásmegyer, *Budapest* 7 A2
Kapotnya, *Moscow* 19 C4

Käppala, Stockholm ..... 28 A3
Käpylä, Helsinki ..... 12 B2
Karachi, Karachi ..... 14 A2
Karachi Int. Airport, Karachi ..... 14 A2
Karato, Osaka ..... 22 A2
Karibong, Seoul ..... 26 C1
Karkh, Baghdad ..... 3 A2
Karlin, Prague ..... 24 A2
Karlsfeld, Munich ..... 20 A1
Karlshorst, Berlin ..... 5 B4
Karlsplatz, Munich ..... 20 b1
Karntner Strasse, Vienna ..... 31 b2
Karol Bagh, Delhi ..... 10 B2
Karolinenhof, Berlin ..... 5 B4
Karori, Wellington ..... 32 B1
Karow, Berlin ..... 5 A3
Karradah, Baghdad ..... 3 B2
Kärson, Stockholm ..... 28 B1
Kasai, Tokyo ..... 29 B4
Kashiwara, Osaka ..... 22 B4
Kastellet, Copenhagen ..... 10 a3
Kastrup, Copenhagen ..... 10 B3
Kastrup Lufthavn, Copenhagen ..... 10 B3
Kasuga, Tokyo ..... 29 A2
Kasuge, Tokyo ..... 29 b4
Kasumigaseki, Tokyo ..... 29 b3
Katong, Singapore ..... 27 B3
Katrineberg, Stockholm ..... 28 B1
Katsushika-Ku, Tokyo ..... 29 A4
Kau Pei Chau, Hong Kong ..... 12 B2
Kau Yi Chau, Hong Kong ..... 12 B1
Kaulsdorf, Berlin ..... 5 B4
Kauniainen, Helsinki ..... 12 B1
Kawasaki, Tokyo ..... 29 B3
Kawawa, Tokyo ..... 29 B2
Kawęczyn, Warsaw ..... 31 B2
Kayu Putih, Jakarta ..... 13 B2
Kbely, Prague ..... 24 A3
Kebayoran Baru, Jakarta ..... 13 B1
Kebayoran Lama, Jakarta ..... 13 B1
Kebon Jeruk, Jakarta ..... 13 B1
Kedar, Jerusalem ..... 23 A2
Keilor, Melbourne ..... 17 A1
Keilor North, Melbourne ..... 17 A1
Keimola, Helsinki ..... 12 B1
Kelenföld, Budapest ..... 7 B2
Kelvin, Johannesburg ..... 13 B1
Kemang, Jakarta ..... 13 B1
Kemayoran, Jakarta ..... 13 B2
Kemerburgaz, Istanbul ..... 12 B1
Kempton Park Races, London ..... 15 B1
Kendall Green, Boston ..... 6 A2
Kenilworth, Cape Town ..... 8 A1
Kennedy Town, Hong Kong ..... 12 B1
Kennington, London ..... 15 c4
Kensal Green, London ..... 15 A2
Kensal Rise, London ..... 15 a1
Kensington, Johannesburg ..... 13 B2
Kensington, London ..... 15 b2
Kensington, New York ..... 21 C2
Kensington, Sydney ..... 28 B2
Kensington Palace, London ..... 15 b2
Kent Village, Washington ..... 32 B4
Kentish Town, London ..... 15 A3
Kenton, London ..... 15 A2
Kenwood House, London ..... 15 A3
Kepa, Warsaw ..... 31 B2
Keppel Harbour, Singapore ..... 27 B2
Keramikos, Athens ..... 2 b1
Kettering, Washington ..... 32 B5
Kew, London ..... 15 B2
Kew, Melbourne ..... 17 A2
Kew Gardens, London ..... 15 B2
Kew Gardens, Toronto ..... 30 B3
Key Biscayne, Miami ..... 18 B2
Khaidhárion, Athens ..... 2 A1
Khalándrion, Athens ..... 2 A2
Khalíj, Baghdad ..... 3 B2
Khandallah, Wellington ..... 32 B1
Khansá', Baghdad ..... 3 A2
Kharavli, Mumbai ..... 20 B2
Khefren, Cairo ..... 7 B1
Khichripur, Delhi ..... 10 B2
Khidirpur, Calcutta ..... 8 B2
Khimki-Khovrino, Moscow ..... 19 A3
Khirbet Jub e-Rum, Jerusalem ..... 13 B2
Khlong San, Bangkok ..... 3 B1
Khlong Toey, Bangkok ..... 3 B2
Kholargós, Athens ..... 2 B2
Khorel, Calcutta ..... 8 A1
Khorosovo, Moscow ..... 19 B2
Kiamari, Karachi ..... 14 A2
Kierling, Vienna ..... 31 A1
Kierlingbach →, Vienna ..... 31 A1
Kifisós →, Athens ..... 2 A1
Kikuna, Tokyo ..... 29 B2
Kilbarrack, Dublin ..... 11 A3
Kilbirnie, Wellington ..... 32 B1
Kilburn, London ..... 15 A2
Kilkee, Dublin ..... 11 B2
Killester, Dublin ..... 11 A2
Killiney, Dublin ..... 11 B3
Killiney Bay, Dublin ..... 11 B3
Kilmacud, Dublin ..... 11 B2
Kilmainham, Dublin ..... 11 A2
Kilmashogue Mt., Dublin ..... 11 B2
Kilmore, Dublin ..... 11 A2
Kilnamanagh, Dublin ..... 11 B1
Kilo, Helsinki ..... 12 B1
Kilokri, Delhi ..... 10 B2
Kiltiernan, Dublin ..... 11 B2
Kinmage, Dublin ..... 11 B2
Kindi, Baghdad ..... 3 B2
Kinghorn, Edinburgh ..... 11 A2
King's Cross, London ..... 15 a4
Kings Cross, Sydney ..... 28 B2
Kings Domain, Melbourne ..... 17 A2
Kings Park, Washington ..... 32 C2
Kings Park West, Washington ..... 32 C2
Kingsbury, London ..... 15 A2
Kingsbury, Washington ..... 32 C2
Kingsford, Sydney ..... 28 B2
Kingston upon Thames, London ..... 15 B2
Kingston Vale, London ..... 15 B2
Kingsway, Toronto ..... 30 B1
Kinsaley, Dublin ..... 11 A2
Kipling Heights, Toronto ..... 30 A1
Kipséli, Athens ..... 2 B2
Kirchstockbach, Munich ..... 20 B3
Kirchtrudering, Munich ..... 20 B3
Kirikiri, Lagos ..... 14 B2
Kirke Værløse, Copenhagen ..... 10 A1
Kirkhill, Edinburgh ..... 11 B3
Kirkliston, Edinburgh ..... 11 B1
Kirknewton, Edinburgh ..... 11 B1
Kirov Palace of Culture, St. Petersburg ..... 26 B1
Kiskli, Istanbul ..... 12 B2
Kispest, Budapest ..... 7 B2
Kista, Stockholm ..... 28 A1
Kita, Osaka ..... 22 A4
Kita-Ku, Osaka ..... 22 A3
Kitazawa, Tokyo ..... 29 B3

Kiu Tsiu, Hong Kong ..... 12 A2
Kivistö, Helsinki ..... 12 B2
Kızıltoprak, Istanbul ..... 12 C2
Kizu →, Osaka ..... 22 B3
Kizuri, Osaka ..... 22 B4
Kjelsås, Oslo ..... 22 A3
Kladow, Berlin ..... 5 B1
Klampenborg, Copenhagen ..... 10 A3
Klarysew, Warsaw ..... 31 B1
Klecany, Prague ..... 24 A2
Kledering, Vienna ..... 31 B2
Klein Jukskei →, Johannesburg ..... 13 A1
Kleinmachnow, Berlin ..... 5 B2
Kleinschönebeck, Berlin ..... 5 B4
Klemetsrud, Oslo ..... 22 A4
Kličany, Prague ..... 24 A2
Klipriviersberg Nature Reserve, Johannesburg ..... 13 B2
Klosterneuburg, Vienna ..... 31 A1
Knesset, Jerusalem ..... 13 b1
Knightsbridge, London ..... 15 c2
Kőbánya, Budapest ..... 7 B2
Kobbegem, Brussels ..... 6 A1
Kobe, Osaka ..... 22 A3
Kōbe Harbour, Osaka ..... 22 B2
Kōbenhavn, Copenhagen ..... 10 A2
Kobylisy, Prague ..... 24 B2
Kobyłka, Warsaw ..... 31 A3
Kōch'ŏk, Seoul ..... 26 B1
Kodaira, Tokyo ..... 29 A1
Kodanaka, Tokyo ..... 29 B2
Kodenmacho, Tokyo ..... 29 a5
Kockelberg, Brussels ..... 6 A1
Koganei, Tokyo ..... 29 A2
Kogarah, Sydney ..... 28 B1
Køge Bugt, Copenhagen ..... 10 B2
Koivupää, Helsinki ..... 12 B2
Koja, Jakarta ..... 13 A2
Kojta Utara, Jakarta ..... 13 A2
Kokobunji, Tokyo ..... 29 A1
Kokobunji-Temple, Tokyo ..... 29 A4
Kolarängen, Stockholm ..... 28 B3
Kolbotn, Oslo ..... 22 B3
Kolkata, Calcutta ..... 8 B2
Koło, Warsaw ..... 31 B1
Kolokinthóu, Athens ..... 2 a1
Kolomyagi, St. Petersburg ..... 26 A1
Kolónos, Athens ..... 2 B2
Kolsås, Oslo ..... 22 A2
Komae, Tokyo ..... 29 B2
Komagome, Tokyo ..... 29 A3
Komazawa, Tokyo ..... 29 B3
Konala, Helsinki ..... 12 B2
Kondli, Delhi ..... 10 B2
Kongelige Slottet, Oslo ..... 22 a1
Kongens Lyngby, Copenhagen ..... 10 A3
Kongnūng, Seoul ..... 26 B2
Kongo, Helsinki ..... 12 A1
Koninklijk Paleis, Amsterdam ..... 2 b2
Konnagar, Calcutta ..... 8 A2
Koohonana, Osaka ..... 22 A3
Konoike, Osaka ..... 22 A4
Konradshöhe, Berlin ..... 5 A2
Kopanina, Prague ..... 24 B1
Koparkhairna, Mumbai ..... 20 A2
Köpenick, Berlin ..... 5 B4
Korangi, Karachi ..... 14 B2
Koremasa, Tokyo ..... 29 B1
Korenevo, Moscow ..... 19 B4
Kori, Osaka ..... 22 A4
Køridhallós, Athens ..... 2 B1
Korokoro, Wellington ..... 32 B2
Korokoro Stream →, Wellington ..... 32 B2
Kosino, Moscow ..... 19 B5
Kosugi, Tokyo ..... 29 B3
Kota, Jakarta ..... 13 A1
Kotelyniki, Moscow ..... 19 C5
Kōtō-Ku, Tokyo ..... 29 A3
Kotrung, Calcutta ..... 8 A2
Koukounariés, Athens ..... 2 B2
Kowloon, Hong Kong ..... 12 B1
Kowloon Park, Hong Kong ..... 12 A2
Kowloon Peak, Hong Kong ..... 12 A2
Kowloon Res., Hong Kong ..... 12 A1
Kowloon Tong, Hong Kong ..... 12 A2
Kozhukhovo, Moscow ..... 19 B5
Kraaimen, Brussels ..... 6 A2
Krailling, Munich ..... 20 B1
Krampnitz, Berlin ..... 5 B1
Krampnitzsee, Berlin ..... 5 B1
Kranji, Sungei →, Singapore ..... 27 A2
Kranji Industrial Estate, Singapore ..... 27 A2
Kraskovo, Moscow ..... 19 C5
Krasno-Presnenskaya, Moscow ..... 19 B3
Krasnogorsk, Moscow ..... 19 B1
Krč, Prague ..... 24 B2
Krestovskiye, Ostrov, St. Petersburg ..... 26 B1
Kreuzberg, Berlin ..... 5 A3
Kritzendorf, Vienna ..... 31 A1
Krumme Lanke, Berlin ..... 5 B2
Krummensee, Berlin ..... 5 A5
Krung Thep, Bangkok ..... 3 B2
Krusboda, Stockholm ..... 28 B3
Krylatskoye, Moscow ..... 19 B2
Küçükköy, Istanbul ..... 12 B1
Kudankita, Tokyo ..... 29 a3
Kudrovo, St. Petersburg ..... 26 B3
Kulosaari, Helsinki ..... 12 B3
Kulturforum, Berlin ..... 5 b3
Kultury i Nauki, Palac, Warsaw ..... 31 b2
Kumch'ŏn, Seoul ..... 26 C1
Kumkapı, Istanbul ..... 12 C1
Kumla, Stockholm ..... 28 B3
Kungens kurva, Stockholm ..... 28 B1
Kungliga Slottet, Stockholm ..... 28 C2
Kungshatt, Stockholm ..... 28 B1
Kungsholmen, Stockholm ..... 28 A2
Kuningan, Jakarta ..... 13 B1
Kunitachi, Tokyo ..... 29 A1
Kunming Hu, Beijing ..... 4 B1
Kunratice, Prague ..... 24 B2
Kunsthistorischesmuseum, Vienna ..... 31 b1
Kuntsevo, Moscow ..... 19 B2
Kupchino, St. Petersburg ..... 26 B2
Kurihara, Tokyo ..... 29 A2
Kurla, Mumbai ..... 20 A2
Kurmuri, Tokyo ..... 29 A2
Kurume, Tokyo ..... 29 A2
Kuryanovo, Moscow ..... 19 C4
Kuskovo, Moscow ..... 19 B4
Kustia, Calcutta ..... 8 B2
Kutsino, Moscow ..... 19 B5
Kuzguncuk, Istanbul ..... 12 B2
Kuzminki, Moscow ..... 19 B4
Kwai Chung, Hong Kong ..... 12 A1
Kwanak-san, Seoul ..... 26 C1
Kypę, Prague ..... 24 B2
Kyūhōji, Osaka ..... 22 B4

## L

La Blanca, Santiago ..... 26 C2
La Boca, Buenos Aires ..... 7 B2
La Bretèche, Paris ..... 23 A1
La Campiña, Lima ..... 16 C2
La Celle-St.-Cloud, Paris ..... 23 A1
La Ciudadela, Mexico City ..... 18 c2
La Courneuve, Paris ..... 23 A3
La Dehesa, Santiago ..... 26 B2
La Encantada, Lima ..... 16 C2
La Estación, Madrid ..... 17 B1
La Floresta, Barcelona ..... 4 A1
La Fortuna, Madrid ..... 17 B1
La Fransa, Barcelona ..... 4 A1
La Garenne-Colombes, Paris ..... 23 A2
La Giustiniana, Rome ..... 25 B1
La Grange, Chicago ..... 9 C1
La Grange Park, Chicago. ..... 9 C1
La Granja, Santiago ..... 26 C2
La Guardia Airport, New York ..... 21 B2
La Hulpe, Brussels ..... 6 B2
La Llacuna, Barcelona ..... 4 A1
La Loma, Mexico City ..... 18 A1
La Lucila, Buenos Aires ..... 7 B2
La Maladrerie, Paris ..... 23 A1
La Milla, Cerro, Lima ..... 16 B2
La Monachina, Rome ..... 25 B1
La Moraleja, Madrid ..... 17 A2
La Nopalera, Mexico City ..... 18 C2
La Paternal, Buenos Aires ..... 7 B2
La Perla, Lima ..... 16 B2
La Perouse, Sydney ..... 28 B2
La Pineda, Barcelona ..... 4 B1
La Pisana, Rome ..... 25 B1
La Prairie, Montreal ..... 19 B3
La Punta, Lima ..... 16 B1
La Puntigala, Barcelona ..... 4 a2
La Queue-en-Brie, Paris ..... 23 B4
La Reina, Santiago ..... 26 B2
La Ribera, Barcelona ..... 4 A1
La Sagrera, Barcelona ..... 4 A2
La Salada, Buenos Aires ..... 7 C2
La Scala, Milan ..... 18 a2
La Storta, Rome ..... 25 A1
La Taxonera, Barcelona ..... 4 A2
La Victoria, Lima ..... 16 B2
Laajalahti, Helsinki ..... 12 B2
Laajasalo, Helsinki ..... 12 B3
Laaksolahti, Helsinki ..... 12 B1
Lablâba, W. el →, Cairo ..... 7 A2
Lac Cisterna, Santiago ..... 26 C2
Lachine, Montreal ..... 19 B1
Lad Phrao, Bangkok ..... 3 B2
Ladera Heights, Los Angeles ..... 16 C2
Ladvi, Prague ..... 24 B2
Łady, Warsaw ..... 31 C1
Lafontaine, Parc, Montreal ..... 19 A2
Lagoa, Rio de Janeiro ..... 24 B1
Lagos, Lagos ..... 14 B2
Lagos Harbour, Lagos ..... 14 B2
Lagos-Ikeja Airport, Lagos ..... 14 A1
Lagos Island, Lagos ..... 14 B2
Lagos Lagoon, Lagos ..... 14 B2
Laguna de B., Manila ..... 17 C2
Laim, Munich ..... 20 B2
Lainate, Milan ..... 18 A1
Lainz, Vienna ..... 31 B1
Lakemba, Sydney ..... 28 B1
Lakeside, Cape Town ..... 8 B1
Lakeside, Johannesburg ..... 13 A2
Lakewood, Chicago ..... 9 B3
Lakewood Park, Atlanta ..... 3 B2
Lakhtinskiy, St. Petersburg ..... 26 B1
Lakhtinskiy Razliv, Oz., St. Petersburg ..... 26 B1
Lakshmanpur, Calcutta ..... 8 B1
Lal Qila, Delhi ..... 1 a3
Lam Tin, Hong Kong ..... 12 B2
Lambert, Oslo ..... 22 A3
Lambeth, London ..... 15 B3
Lambrate, Milan ..... 18 A2
Lambro, Parco, Milan ..... 18 A2
Lambton Mills, Toronto ..... 30 B1
Lamma I., Hong Kong ..... 12 B1
Landover Hills, Washington ..... 32 B4
Landsmeer, Amsterdam ..... 2 A2
Landstrasse, Vienna ..... 31 A2
Landwehr kanal, Berlin ..... 5 B3
Lane Cove, Sydney ..... 28 A1
Lane Cove National Park, Sydney ..... 28 A1
Langa, Cape Town ..... 8 A2
Langenzersdorf, Vienna ..... 31 A2
Langer See, Berlin ..... 5 B4
Langley Park, Washington ..... 32 B4
Langwald, Munich ..... 20 A1
Lanham, Washington ..... 32 B4
Lankwitz, Berlin ..... 5 B3
L'Annunziatella, Rome ..... 25 C2
Lansdowne, Cape Town ..... 8 A2
Lansing, Toronto ..... 30 A2
Lanús, Buenos Aires ..... 7 C2
Lapa, Rio de Janeiro ..... 24 B1
Laranjeiras, Rio de Janeiro ..... 24 B1
Larísa Sta., Athens ..... 2 a1
Las, Warsaw ..... 31 B2
Las Corts, Barcelona ..... 4 A1
Las Kabacki, Warsaw ..... 31 C2
Las Pinas, Manila ..... 17 C1
Las Rejas, Santiago ..... 26 B1
Lasek Bielański, Warsaw ..... 31 B1
Lasek Na Kole, Warsaw ..... 31 B1
Laski, Warsaw ..... 31 B1
Latina, Madrid ..... 17 B1
Laurence G. Hanscom Field, Boston ..... 6 A2
Lauttasaari, Helsinki ..... 12 C2
Laval, Montreal ..... 19 A1
Lavizán, Tehran ..... 30 A2
Lavradio, Lisbon ..... 14 A2
Lawndale, Chicago ..... 9 B2
Lawrence Heights, Toronto ..... 30 A2
Layari, Karachi ..... 14 A2
Layari →, Karachi ..... 14 A1
Lazare, Gare St., Paris ..... 23 a3
Łazienkowski, Palac, Warsaw ..... 31 c3
Łazienkowski Park, Warsaw ..... 31 B2
Le Blanc-Mesnil, Paris ..... 23 A3
Le Bourget, Paris ..... 23 A3
Le Chenoi, Brussels ..... 6 B2
Le Chesnay, Paris ..... 23 A1
Le Christ de Saclay, Paris ..... 23 B2
Le Kremlin-Bicêtre, Paris ..... 23 B3
Le Mesnil-le-Roi, Paris ..... 23 A1
Le Pecq, Paris ..... 23 A1
Le Perreux, Paris ..... 23 A4
Le Pin, Paris ..... 23 A4
Le Plessis-Robinson, Paris ..... 23 B2
Le Plessis-Trévise, Paris ..... 23 B4
Le Pré-St.-Gervais, Paris ..... 23 A3
Le Raincy, Paris ..... 23 A4
Le Vésinet, Paris ..... 23 A1

Lea Bridge, London ..... 15 A3
Leaside, Toronto ..... 30 A2
Leblon, Rio de Janeiro ..... 24 B1
Lee, London ..... 15 B4
Lee, London ..... 15 B4
Leganés, Madrid ..... 17 C1
Legazpi, Madrid ..... 17 B1
Lehtisaari, Helsinki ..... 12 B2
Leião, Lisbon ..... 14 A1
Leicester Square, London ..... 15 b3
Leichhardt, Sydney ..... 28 B1
Leith, Edinburgh ..... 11 B3
Lemoyne, Montreal ..... 19 B3
Lenin, Moscow ..... 19 B3
Leninasy Gory, Moscow ..... 19 C3
Lennox, Los Angeles ..... 16 C2
Leonia, New York ..... 21 A2
Leopardstown, Dublin ..... 11 B2
Leopoldau, Vienna ..... 31 A2
Leopoldstadt, Vienna ..... 31 A2
Leportovo, Moscow ..... 19 B4
Leppävaara, Helsinki ..... 12 B1
Les Lilas, Paris ..... 23 A3
Les Loges-en-Josas, Paris ..... 23 B1
Les Pavillons-sous-Bois, Paris ..... 23 A4
Lésigny, Paris ..... 23 B4
Lesnozavodskaya, St. Petersburg ..... 26 B2
L'Étang-la-Ville, Paris ..... 23 A1
Letná, Prague ..... 24 B3
Letňany, Prague ..... 24 A3
Levallois-Perret, Paris ..... 23 A2
Levent, Istanbul ..... 12 B2
Lewisdale, Washington ..... 32 B4
Lewisham, London ..... 15 B3
Lexington, Boston ..... 6 A2
Leyton, London ..... 15 A3
Leytonstone, London ..... 15 A4
L'Hay-les-Roses, Paris ..... 23 B3
L'Hospitalet de Llobregat, Barcelona ..... 4 A1
Lhotka, Prague ..... 24 B2
Liangshui He →, Beijing ..... 4 C2
Lianhua Chi, Beijing ..... 4 B1
Lianhua He →, Beijing ..... 4 B1
LichBice nad Vitavou, Prague ..... 24 A2
Libeň, Prague ..... 24 B2
Liberdade, São Paulo ..... 26 B2
Liberdade, Ave da, Lisbon ..... 14 b1
Liberton, Edinburgh ..... 11 B3
Liberty I., New York ..... 21 B1
Liberty State Park, New York ..... 21 B1
L'Île-St.-Denis, Paris ..... 23 A2
Limburga, Hong Kong ..... 12 A1
Lim Chu Kang, Singapore ..... 27 A2
Lima, Lima ..... 16 B2
Limbiate, Milan ..... 18 A1
Limehouse, London ..... 15 A3
Limeil-Brévannes, Paris ..... 23 B4
Linate, Aeroporto Internazionale di, Milan ..... 18 B2
Linbropark, Johannesburg ..... 13 A2
Lincoln, Boston ..... 6 A2
Lincoln Center, New York ..... 21 B1
Lincoln Heights, Los Angeles ..... 16 B3
Lincoln Park, Chicago ..... 9 B3
Lincoln Park, New York ..... 21 B1
Lincoln Park, San Francisco ..... 25 B2
Lincolnwood, Chicago ..... 9 A2
Linda-a-Pastora, Lisbon ..... 14 A1
Linden, Johannesburg ..... 13 A2
Linden, Wellington ..... 32 B1
Lindenberg, Berlin ..... 5 A4
Lindøya, Oslo ..... 22 A3
Liniers, Buenos Aires ..... 7 B1
Linkebeek, Brussels ..... 6 B2
Linksfield, Johannesburg ..... 13 B2
Linmeyer, Johannesburg ..... 13 B2
Lintuvaara, Helsinki ..... 12 B1
Lion Rock Country Park, Hong Kong ..... 12 A2
Lioúmi, Athens ..... 2 B2
Liqizhuang, Tianjin ..... 30 B2
Lisboa, Lisbon ..... 14 A2
Lisbon = Lisboa, Lisbon ..... 14 A2
Lishui, Canton ..... 8 A1
Little B., Sydney ..... 28 B2
Little Calumet →, Chicago ..... 9 C3
Little Ferry, New York ..... 21 A1
Little Italy, New York ..... 21 e2
Little Mermaid, Copenhagen ..... 10 a3
Little Rouge →, Toronto ..... 30 A4
Little Tokyo, Los Angeles ..... 16 c2
Liuhang, Shanghai ..... 27 A1
Liurong Temple, Canton ..... 8 B2
Luxi →, Canton ..... 8 A1
Liverpool Street, London ..... 15 a5
Livry-Gargan, Paris ..... 23 A4
Ljan, Oslo ..... 22 A3
Llano de Can Gineu, Barcelona ..... 4 A1
Llobregat →, Barcelona ..... 4 A1
Lo Aranguiz, Santiago ..... 26 B2
Lo Boza, Santiago ..... 26 B1
Lo Chau, Hong Kong ..... 12 B2
Lo Espejo, Santiago ..... 26 C1
Lo Hermida, Santiago ..... 26 B2
Lo Prado, Santiago ..... 26 B1
Lo So Shing, Hong Kong ..... 12 B1
Lo Wai, Hong Kong ..... 12 A2
Loanhead, Edinburgh ..... 11 B3
Lobau, Vienna ..... 31 A3
Lobos, Pt., San Francisco ..... 25 B2
Lochino, Moscow ..... 19 B2
Lochkov, Prague ..... 24 B2
Lockhausen, Munich ..... 20 A2
Lodi, New York ..... 21 A1
Lodi Estate, Delhi ..... 10 B2
Logan Int. Airport, Boston ..... 6 A3
Logan Square, Chicago ..... 9 B2
Lohème, Berlin ..... 5 A4
Lohokhet, Karachi ..... 14 A2
Lomas Chapultepec, Mexico City ..... 18 B1
Lomas de San Angel Inn, Mexico City ..... 18 B1

Lomas de Zamora, Buenos Aires ..... 7 C2
Lombardy East, Johannesburg ..... 13 A2
Lomus Reforma, Mexico City ..... 18 B1
London, London ..... 15 A3
London Bridge, London ..... 15 b5
London City Airport, London ..... 15 A4
London Zoo, London ..... 15 A3
Long B., Sydney ..... 28 B2
Long Branch, Toronto ..... 30 B1
Long Brook →, Washington ..... 32 C2
Long Ditton, London ..... 15 B2
Long I., Boston ..... 6 B4
Long Island City, New York ..... 21 B2
Long Street, Cape Town ..... 8 c2
Longchamp, Hippodrôme de, Paris ..... 23 A2
Longhua Pagoda, Shanghai ..... 27 B1
Longhua Park, Shanghai ..... 27 B1
Longjohn Slough, Chicago ..... 9 C1
Longsha Hu →, Beijing ..... 4 B2
Longue-Pointe, Montreal ..... 19 A2
Longueuil, Montreal ..... 19 A3
Loni, Delhi ..... 10 A2
Loop, The, Chicago ..... 9 c1
Lord's Cricket Ground, London ..... 15 A2
Loreto, Milan ..... 18 B2
Los Angeles Int. Airport, Los Angeles ..... 16 C2
Los Cerrillos, Aeropuerto, Santiago ..... 26 B1
Los Nietos, Los Angeles ..... 16 C4
Los Olivos, Lima ..... 16 A2
Los Reyes, Mexico City ..... 18 B2
Lot, Brussels ..... 6 B1
Loughlinstown, Dublin ..... 11 B3
Loures, Lisbon ..... 14 A1
Louveciennes, Paris ..... 23 A1
Louvre, Musée du, Paris ..... 23 b4
Louvre, Palais du, Paris ..... 23 b4
Lower East Side, New York ..... 21 e2
Lower Hutt, Wellington ..... 32 B2
Lower Manhattan, New York ..... 21 e1
Lower New York B., New York ..... 21 C1
Lower Shing Mun Res., Hong Kong ..... 12 A1
Lowry Bay, Wellington ..... 32 B2
Lu Xun Museum, Beijing ..... 4 b1
Lübars, Berlin ..... 5 A3
Ludwigsfeld, Munich ..... 20 A1
Luhu, Canton ..... 8 B2
Lumiar, Lisbon ..... 14 A2
Lumphini Park, Bangkok ..... 3 B2
Lundtofte, Copenhagen ..... 10 A3
Lung Mei, Hong Kong ..... 12 A2
Luojiang, Canton ..... 8 A2
Lustheim, Munich ..... 20 A2
Luwan, Shanghai ..... 27 B1
Luxembourg, Palais du, Paris ..... 23 c4
Luzhniki Sports Centre, Moscow ..... 19 B3
Lyndhurst, New York ..... 21 B1
Lynn, Boston ..... 6 A4
Lynn Harbor, Boston ..... 6 A4
Lynn Woods Res., Boston ..... 6 A3
Lyon, Gare de, Paris ..... 23 c5
Lyons, Chicago ..... 9 C2
Lysaker, Oslo ..... 22 A2
Lysakerselva →, Oslo ..... 22 A2
Lysolaje, Prague ..... 24 A2
Lyubertsy, Moscow ..... 19 B4
Lyublino, Moscow ..... 19 B4

## M

Ma Nam Wat, Hong Kong ..... 12 A2
Ma On Shan Country Park, Hong Kong ..... 12 A2
Ma'ale Adumim, Jerusalem ..... 13 B2
Ma'ale Ha Khamisha, Jerusalem ..... 13 B1
Ma'ale Mikhmas, Jerusalem ..... 13 A2
Maantiekylä, Helsinki ..... 12 A3
Maarifa, Baghdad ..... 3 A2
Mabato Pt., Manila ..... 17 C2
Macaco, Morro do, Rio de Janeiro ..... 24 B2
McCook, Chicago ..... 9 C2
Machelen, Brussels ..... 6 A2
Machida, Tokyo ..... 29 B1
Maciołki, Warsaw ..... 31 B2
McKerrow, Wellington ..... 32 B2
McKinley Park, Chicago ..... 9 C2
Mclean, Washington ..... 32 B3
Macopocho, R. →, Santiago ..... 26 B2
MacRitchie Res., Singapore ..... 27 A2
Madame Tussaud's, London ..... 15 a3
Madhudaha, Calcutta ..... 8 B2
Madhyamgram, Calcutta ..... 8 A2
Madīnah Al Mansūr, Baghdad ..... 3 B2
Mādinet Nasr, Cairo ..... 7 A2
Madison Avenue, New York ..... 21 d3
Madison Square, New York ..... 21 d2
Madrid, Madrid ..... 17 B1
Madrona, Barcelona ..... 4 A1
Maesawa, Tokyo ..... 29 A2
Magadlena, Lima ..... 16 B2
Magdalena Contreras, Mexico City ..... 18 C1
Maghreb, Baghdad ..... 3 A2
Maginu, Tokyo ..... 29 B2
Magliana, Rome ..... 25 B1
Magny-les-Hameaux, Paris ..... 23 B1
Magomoy, Manila ..... 17 B2
Mahalaxmi, Mumbai ..... 20 a1
Maheshtala, Calcutta ..... 8 C1
Mahim, Mumbai ..... 20 A1
Mahlsdorf, Berlin ..... 5 A5
Mahmoodabad, Karachi ..... 14 B2
Mahrauli, Delhi ..... 10 B1
Mahul, Mumbai ..... 20 A2
Maida Vale, London ..... 15 a1
Maidstone, Melbourne ..... 17 A1
Maipú, Santiago ..... 26 B1
Maisons-Alfort, Paris ..... 23 B3
Maisons-Laffitte, Paris ..... 23 A1
Maitland, Cape Town ..... 8 A1
Makati, Manila ..... 17 B2
Mākiniitty, Helsinki ..... 12 B2
Mala Strana, Prague ..... 24 B2
Malabar, Sydney ..... 28 B2
Malabar Hill, Mumbai ..... 20 B1
Malabar Pt., Mumbai ..... 20 B1

Malabon, Manila ..... 17 B1
Malacañang Palace, Manila ..... 17 B2
Malahide, Dublin ..... 11 A3
Malakhovka, Moscow ..... 19 C6
Malakoff, Paris ..... 23 B2
Mälarhöjden, Stockholm ..... 28 B1
Malate, Manila ..... 17 B1
Malay Quarter, Cape Town ..... 8 c2
Malaya Neva, St. Petersburg ..... 26 B1
Malaya-Okhta, St. Petersburg ..... 26 B2
Malchow, Berlin ..... 5 A3
Malden, Boston ..... 6 A3
Malden, London ..... 15 B2
Maleizen, Brussels ..... 6 B2
Malešice, Prague ..... 24 B3
Malir →, Karachi ..... 14 B2
Mall, The, Washington ..... 32 b2
Malleny Mills, Edinburgh ..... 11 B2
Malmi, Helsinki ..... 12 B3
Malmøya, Oslo ..... 22 A3
Måløv, Copenhagen ..... 10 A2
Malpasso, Ost., Rome ..... 25 B2
Malton, Toronto ..... 30 A1
Malvern, Johannesburg ..... 13 B2
Malvern, Melbourne ..... 17 B2
Malvern, Toronto ..... 30 A3
Mamonovo, Moscow ..... 19 B2
Mampang Prapatan, Jakarta ..... 13 B2
Mampukuji, Tokyo ..... 29 B2
Man Budrukh, Mumbai ..... 20 A2
Man Khurd, Mumbai ..... 20 A2
Mandaluyong, Manila ..... 17 B2
Mandaoli, Delhi ..... 10 B2
Mandoli, Delhi ..... 10 A2
Mandvi, Mumbai ..... 20 B2
Manenberg, Cape Town ..... 8 A2
Mang Kung Uk, Hong Kong ..... 12 B2
Mankkaa, Helsinki ..... 12 B1
Mannsworth, Vienna ..... 31 B3
Manor Park, London ..... 15 A4
Manor Park, Wellington ..... 32 A2
Manora, Karachi ..... 14 B2
Manquehue, Cerro, Santiago ..... 26 B2
Manzanares, Canal de, Madrid ..... 17 C2
Mao Mausoleum, Beijing ..... 4 c2
Map'o, Seoul ..... 26 B1
Maracanã, Rio de Janeiro ..... 24 B1
Maraoli, Mumbai ..... 20 A2
Marblehead, Boston ..... 6 A4
Marcelin, Warsaw ..... 31 B1
Mareil-Marly, Paris ..... 23 A1
Margareten, Vienna ..... 31 A2
Maridalen, Oslo ..... 22 A3
Maridalsvatnet, Oslo ..... 22 A3
Mariendorf, Berlin ..... 5 B3
Marienfelde, Berlin ..... 5 B3
Marienplatz, Munich ..... 20 b2
Marikina →, Manila ..... 17 B2
Marin City, San Francisco ..... 25 A1
Marin Headlands State Park, San Francisco ..... 25 B2
Marin Pen., San Francisco ..... 25 A1
Marina del Rey, Los Angeles ..... 16 C2
Marine Drive, Mumbai ..... 20 B1
Marino, Dublin ..... 11 A2
Maritim, Museu, Barcelona ..... 4 c2
Markham, Toronto ..... 30 A3
Markl, Warsaw ..... 31 A2
Markland Wood, Toronto ..... 30 B1
Marly, Forêt de, Paris ..... 23 A1
Marly-le-Roi, Paris ..... 23 A1
Marne →, Paris ..... 23 B3
Marne-la-Vallée, Paris ..... 23 A4
Marolles-en-Brie, Paris ..... 23 B4
Maroubra, Sydney ..... 28 B2
Marquette Park, Chicago ..... 9 C2
Marrickville, Sydney ..... 28 B1
Marsfield, Sydney ..... 28 A1
Marshall Field's, Chicago ..... 9 c2
Marte, Campo de, São Paulo ..... 26 B2
Martesana, Navíglio della, Milan ..... 18 A2
Martin Luther King National Historic Site, Atlanta ..... 3 B2
Martinez, Buenos Aires ..... 7 A1
Martinkylä, Helsinki ..... 12 B2
Martinsried, Munich ..... 20 B1
Maruko, Tokyo ..... 29 B3
Marunouchi, Tokyo ..... 29 b4
Marusino, Moscow ..... 19 B4
Maryino, Moscow ..... 19 B4
Maryland, Singapore ..... 27 A2
Marylebone, London ..... 15 a3
Marymont, Warsaw ..... 31 B2
Marysin Wawerski, Warsaw ..... 31 B2
Marzahn, Berlin ..... 5 A4
Mascot, Sydney ..... 28 B2
Masmo, Stockholm ..... 28 B2
Maspeth, New York ..... 21 B2
Mas el Gedida, Cairo ..... 7 A2
Mas el Qadīma, Cairo ..... 7 A2
Massachusetts B., Boston ..... 6 A4
Massachusetts' Inst. of Tech., Boston ..... 6 A3
Massamá, Lisbon ..... 14 A1
Massey →, Toronto ..... 30 A3
Massy, Paris ..... 23 B2
Matinha, Lisbon ..... 14 A2
Matinha, Lisbon ..... 14 A2
Matraman, Jakarta ..... 13 B2
Matsubara, Osaka ..... 22 B4
Mattapan, Boston ..... 6 B3
Mátyásföld, Budapest ..... 7 A3
Mátyástemplom, Budapest ..... 7 b1
Mau Tso Ngam, Hong Kong ..... 12 A2
Mauer, Vienna ..... 31 B1
Mauripur, Karachi ..... 14 A1
Maxhof, Munich ..... 20 B1
Mayfair, Johannesburg ..... 13 B2
Mayfair, London ..... 15 b3
Mayor, Plaza, Madrid ..... 17 b2
Maywood, Chicago ..... 9 B1
Maywood, Los Angeles ..... 16 C3
Maywood, New York ..... 21 A1
Mazagão →, Lisbon ..... 14 A1
Me'a She' Arim, Jerusalem ..... 13 a2
Meadowbank, Cape Town ..... 8 A2
Mechelupy, Prague ..... 24 A2
Mèčice, Prague ..... 24 A2
Mecidiyeköy, Istanbul ..... 12 B2
Medford, Boston ..... 6 A3
Mediodia, Madrid ..... 17 B2
Medvezhiy Ozyora, Moscow ..... 19 A5
Meguro →, Tokyo ..... 29 B3
Meguro-Ku, Tokyo ..... 29 B3

Mehrpalpur, Delhi ..... 10 B1
Mehrābād Airport, Tehran ..... 30 A1
Mehram Nagar, Delhi ..... 10 B1
Mehrow, Berlin ..... 5 A4
Mei Lanfang, Beijing ..... 4 a2
Meidling, Vienna ..... 31 A1
Méier, Rio de Janeiro ..... 24 B1
Meiji Shrine, Tokyo ..... 29 b1
Meise, Brussels ..... 6 A1
Mejiro, Tokyo ..... 29 A3
Melbourne, Melbourne ..... 17 A1
Melbourne Airport, Melbourne ..... 17 A1
Melkki, Helsinki ..... 12 C2
Melkniya, Helsinki ..... 12 B3
Mellunmäki, Helsinki ..... 12 B3
Melrose, Boston ..... 6 A3
Melrose, New York ..... 21 B2
Melrose Park, Chicago ..... 9 B1
Melsbroek, Brussels ..... 6 A2
Menteng, Jakarta ..... 13 B1
Mérantaise →, Paris ..... 23 B1
Mercamadrid, Madrid ..... 17 B2
Merced, L., San Francisco ..... 25 B2
Meredale, Johannesburg ..... 13 B1
Merlimau →, Singapore ..... 27 B3
Merri Cr. →, Melbourne ..... 17 A2
Merrion, Dublin ..... 11 B2
Merrionette Park, Chicago ..... 9 C2
Merton, London ..... 15 B2
Mesgarābād, Tehran ..... 30 B2
Meshchersky, Moscow ..... 19 B2
Messe, Vienna ..... 31 A2
Messe-palast, Vienna ..... 31 b1
Metanópoli, Milan ..... 18 B2
Metropolitan Museum of Art, New York ..... 21 b3
Meudon, Paris ..... 23 B2
Mevaseret Tsiyon, Jerusalem ..... 13 B1
Mevo Beitar, Jerusalem ..... 13 B1
México, Ciudad de, Mexico City ..... 18 B1
Meyersdal, Johannesburg ..... 13 B2
Mezzano, Milan ..... 18 A1
Mezzate, Milan ..... 18 B2
Miadong, Seoul ..... 26 B2
Miami, Miami ..... 18 B2
Miami Beach, Miami ..... 18 A1
Miami Int. Airport, Miami ..... 18 B1
Miami Shores, Miami ..... 18 A2
Miami Springs, Miami ..... 18 B1
Miasto, Warsaw ..... 31 B1
Michałowice, Warsaw ..... 31 B1
Michigan Avenue, Chicago ..... 9 b2
Mickle, Prague ..... 24 B2
Middle Harbour, Sydney ..... 28 A2
Middle Hd., Sydney ..... 28 A2
Middle Village, New York ..... 21 B2
Middlesex Fells Reservation, Boston ..... 6 A3
Midi, Gare du, Brussels ..... 6 c1
Midland Beach, New York ..... 21 C1
Miedzeszyn, Warsaw ..... 31 B2
Miedzylesie, Warsaw ..... 31 B3
Miessaari, Helsinki ..... 12 C1
Miguel Hidalgo, Mexico City ..... 18 B1
Mikhelsona, Moscow ..... 19 B5
Milano, Milan ..... 18 A1
Milano Due, Milan ..... 18 B2
Milano San Felice, Milan ..... 18 B2
Milbertshofen, Munich ..... 20 A2
Mill Hill, London ..... 15 A2
Millennium Dome, London ..... 15 A4
Miller Meadow, Chicago ..... 9 B2
Millerhill, Edinburgh ..... 11 B3
Millers Point, Sydney ..... 28 a1
Milltown, Dublin ..... 11 B2
Millwood, Washington ..... 32 B4
Milnerton, Cape Town ..... 8 A1
Milon-la-Chapelle, Paris ..... 23 B1
Milton, Boston ..... 6 B3
Milton Bridge, Edinburgh ..... 11 B3
Mimico, Toronto ..... 30 B2
Minami, Osaka ..... 22 A4
Minamitsunashima, Tokyo ..... 29 B2
Minato, Osaka ..... 22 B3
Minato-Ku, Tokyo ..... 29 c3
Minshāt el Bekkari, Cairo ..... 7 A2
Minute Man Nat. Hist. Park, Boston ..... 6 A2
Miraflores, Lima ..... 16 B2
Miramar, Wellington ..... 32 B1
Misericordia, Sa. da., Rio de Janeiro ..... 24 B1
Mississauga, Toronto ..... 30 B1
Mitaka, Tokyo ..... 29 A2
Mitcham, London ..... 15 B3
Mitcham Common, London ..... 15 B3
Mitchell's Plain, Cape Town ..... 8 B2
Mitino, Moscow ..... 19 A2
Mitte, Berlin ..... 5 A3
Mittel Isarkanal →, Munich ..... 20 A3
Mixcoac, Mexico City ..... 18 B1
Mixcoac, Presa de, Mexico City ..... 18 B1
Miyakojima, Osaka ..... 22 A4
Mizonokuchi, Tokyo ..... 29 B2
Mizue, Tokyo ..... 29 A4
Młocinski Park, Warsaw ..... 31 B1
Młociny, Warsaw ..... 31 B1
Mnevniki, Moscow ..... 19 B2
Moa, Lagos ..... 14 B2
Mocnądo, Warsaw ..... 31 C2
Modderfontein, Johannesburg ..... 13 A2
Modfany, Prague ..... 24 B2
Mogyoród, Budapest ..... 7 A3
Moinho Velho, Cor. →, São Paulo ..... 26 B2
Mok, Seoul ..... 26 B1
Mokotów, Warsaw ..... 31 B2
Molenbeek-Saint-Jean, Brussels ..... 6 A1
Molino de Rosas, Mexico City ..... 18 B1
Mollem, Brussels ..... 6 A1
Mollins de Rey, Barcelona ..... 4 A1
Mondeor, Johannesburg ..... 13 B2
Moneda, Palacio de la, Santiago ..... 26 B2
Mong Kok, Hong Kong ..... 12 A2
Monkstown, Dublin ..... 11 B3
Monkkendam, Amsterdam ..... 2 A3
Monrovia, Los Angeles ..... 16 B4
Monsanto, Lisbon ..... 14 A2
Monsanto, Parque Florestal de, Lisbon ..... 14 A1
Mont-Royal, Montreal ..... 19 A2
Mont-Royal, Parc, Montreal ..... 19 A2
Montana de Montjuïch, Barcelona ..... 4 A1
Monte Chingolo, Buenos Aires ..... 7 C2
Monte Palatino, Rome ..... 25 c3
Montebello, Los Angeles ..... 16 B4
Montemor, Lisbon ..... 14 A1

RÁKOSKERESZTÚR


Monterey Park, *Los Angeles* 16 B4
Montespaccato, *Rome* 25 B1
Montesson, *Paris* 23 A1
Monteverde Nuovo, *Rome* 25 B1
Montfermeil, *Paris* 23 A4
Montigny-le-Bretonneux, *Paris* 23 B1
Montjay-la-Tour, *Paris* 23 A4
Montjuic, Parc de, *Barcelona* 4 c1
Montparnasse, Gare, *Paris* 23 A2
Montréal, *Montreal* 19 A2
Montréal, Î. de, *Montreal* 19 A2
Montréal, Univ. de, *Montreal* 19 B2
Montréal Est, *Montreal* 19 A2
Montréal Nord, *Montreal* 19 A2
Montréal Ouest, *Montreal* 19 B1
Montreuil, *Paris* 23 A3
Montrouge, *Paris* 23 B2
Montserrat, *Buenos Aires* 7 B2
Monza, *Milan* 18 A2
Monzoro, *Milan* 18 B1
Moóca, *São Paulo* 26 B2
Moonachie, *New York* 21 B1
Moonee Ponds, *Melbourne* 17 A1
Moonee Valley Racecourse, *Melbourne* 17 A1
Moosach, *Munich* 20 A2
Mora, *Mumbai* 20 B2
Moratalaz, *Madrid* 17 B2
Mörby, *Stockholm* 28 A2
Morden, *London* 15 B2
Morée →, *Paris* 23 A3
Morgan Park, *Chicago* 9 C3
Moriguchi, *Osaka* 22 A4
Morivione, *Milan* 18 B2
Morningside, *Edinburgh* 11 B2
Morningside, *Johannesburg* 13 A2
Morningside, *Washington* 32 C4
Morro Solar, Cerro, *Lima* 16 C2
Mortlake, *London* 15 B2
Mortlake, *Sydney* 28 B1
Morton Grove, *Chicago* 9 A2
Morumbi, *São Paulo* 26 B1
Moscavide, *Lisbon* 14 A2
Moscow = Moskva, *Moscow* 19 B3
Moskhaton, *Athens* 2 B2
Moskva, *Moscow* 19 B3
Moskva →, *Moscow* 19 B2
Moskvoretskiy, *Moscow* 19 B3
Mosman, *Sydney* 28 A2
Móstoles, *Madrid* 17 C1
Moti Bagh, *Delhi* 10 B2
Motol, *Prague* 24 B1
Motsa, *Jerusalem* 13 B2
Motsa Ilit, *Jerusalem* 13 B1
Motspur Park, *London* 15 B2
Mottingham, *London* 15 B4
Moulin Rouge, *Paris* 23 a3
Mount Dennis, *Toronto* 30 A2
Mount Greenwood, *Chicago* 9 C2
Mount Hood Memorial Park, *Boston* 6 A3
Mount Merrion, *Dublin* 11 B2
Mount Rainier, *Washington* 32 B4
Mount Vernon, *New York* 21 A3
Mount Vernon Square, *Washington* 32 a2
Mount Zion, *Jerusalem* 13 b3
Mozarthaus, *Vienna* 31 b2
Müggelberge, *Berlin* 5 B4
Müggelheim, *Berlin* 5 B5
Muggiò, *Milan* 18 A2
Mughal Gardens, *Delhi* 1 c1
Mühleiten, *Vienna* 31 A3
Mühlenfliess →, *Berlin* 5 A5
Muiden, *Amsterdam* 2 A3
Muiderpoort Station, *Amsterdam* 2 b3
Muizenberg, *Cape Town* 8 B1
Mujahidpur, *Delhi* 10 B2
Mukandpur, *Delhi* 10 A2
Mukhmas, *Jerusalem* 13 A2
Muko →, *Osaka* 22 A3
Mukojima, *Tokyo* 29 A3
Mulbarton, *Johannesburg* 13 B2
Mumbai, *Mumbai* 20 B2
Mumbai Harbour, *Mumbai* 20 B2
Münchehofe, *Berlin* 5 B5
München, *Munich* 20 B2
Munich = München, *Munich* 20 B2
Munkkiniemi, *Helsinki* 12 B2
Munro, *Buenos Aires* 7 B1
Murai Res., *Singapore* 27 A2
Muranów, *Warsaw* 31 B1
Murino, *St. Petersburg* 26 B2
Murrayfield, *Edinburgh* 11 B2
Musashino, *Tokyo* 29 A2
Museu Nacional, *Rio de Janeiro* 24 B1
Mushin, *Lagos* 14 A2
Musiektheater, *Amsterdam* 2 b2
Muslim Quarter, *Jerusalem* 13 a3
Musocco, *Milan* 18 B1
Mustansiriya, *Baghdad* 3 A2
Musturud, *Cairo* 7 A2
Muswell Hill, *London* 15 A3
Mutanabi, *Baghdad* 3 B2
Muthana, *Baghdad* 3 B2
Myakinino, *Moscow* 19 B2
Mykerinos, *Cairo* 7 B1
Myllypuro, *Helsinki* 12 B3


# N


Nacka, *Stockholm* 28 B3
Nada, *Osaka* 22 A2
Naenae, *Wellington* 32 B2
Nærsnes, *Oslo* 22 B1
Nagata, *Osaka* 22 B1
Nagatsuta, *Tokyo* 29 B2
Nagytétény, *Budapest* 7 B1
Nahant, *Boston* 6 A4
Nahant B., *Boston* 6 A4
Nahant Harbor, *Boston* 6 A4
Nahr Dijlah →, *Baghdad* 3 B2
Najafgarh Drain →, *Delhi* 10 B1
Nakahara-Ku, *Tokyo* 29 B2
Nakano-Ku, *Tokyo* 29 A2
Namgajwa, *Seoul* 26 B1
Namsan Park, *Seoul* 26 B1
Namyŏng, *Seoul* 26 B1
Nanbiancun, *Canton* 8 B1
Nanchang He →, *Beijing* 4 B1
Nandang, *Canton* 8 B2
Nandian, *Tianjin* 30 A2
Nangal Dewat, *Delhi* 10 B1
Naniwa, *Osaka* 22 B3
Nankai, *Tianjin* 30 B1
Nanmenwai, *Tianjin* 30 B2
Nanole, *Mumbai* 20 A2
Nanpu Bridge, *Shanghai* 27 B2
Nanshi, *Shanghai* 27 B1
Nantasket Beach, *Boston* 6 B4
Nanterre, *Paris* 23 A2
Naoabad, *Calcutta* 8 C2
Napier Mole, *Karachi* 14 B1
Naraina, *Delhi* 10 B1
Nariman Point, *Mumbai* 20 c1
Nariman Pt., *Mumbai* 20 B1
Nārmak, *Tehran* 30 A2
Naruo, *Osaka* 22 A3
Näsby, *Stockholm* 28 A2
Näsbypark, *Stockholm* 28 A2
Nathan Road, *Hong Kong* 12 a2
Natick, *Boston* 6 B2
National Maritime Museum, *San Francisco* 25 a1
National Museum, *Bangkok* 3 b1
Nationalmuseum, *Stockholm* 28 b2
Natolin, *Warsaw* 31 C2
Naturhistorischesmuseum, *Vienna* 31 b1
Naucalpan de Juárez, *Mexico City* 18 B1
Naupada, *Mumbai* 20 A2
Navíglio di Pavia, *Milan* 18 B1
Navíglio Grande, *Milan* 18 B1
Navona, Piazza, *Rome* 25 b2
Navotas, *Manila* 17 B1
Navy Pier, *Chicago* 9 b3
Nazal Hikmat Beg, *Baghdad* 3 A2
Nazimabad, *Karachi* 14 A2
Nazlet el Simmân, *Cairo* 7 B1
Néa Alexandhria, *Athens* 2 B2
Néa Faliron, *Athens* 2 B1
Néa Ionía, *Athens* 2 A2
Néa Liósia, *Athens* 2 A2
Néa Smírni, *Athens* 2 B2
Neapolis, *Athens* 2 B2
Near North, *Chicago* 9 b2
Nebušice, *Prague* 24 B1
Nederhorst, *Amsterdam* 2 B3
Nedlitz, *Berlin* 5 B1
Nee Soon, *Singapore* 27 A2
Needham Heights, *Boston* 6 B2
Nekrasovka, *Moscow* 19 B5
N'ematābād, *Tehran* 30 B2
Nemchinovka, *Moscow* 19 B1
Nemzeti Muz, *Budapest* 7 c3
Neponsit, *New York* 21 C2
Nerima-Ku, *Tokyo* 29 A3
Nesodden, *Oslo* 22 B3
Nesoddtangen, *Oslo* 22 A3
Nesøya, *Oslo* 22 A2
Neu Aubing, *Munich* 20 B1
Neu Buch, *Berlin* 5 A4
Neu Buchhorst, *Berlin* 5 B5
Neu Fahrland, *Berlin* 5 B1
Neu Lindenberg, *Berlin* 5 A4
Neubiberg, *Munich* 20 B3
Neue Hofburg, *Vienna* 31 b1
Neuenhagen, *Berlin* 5 A4
Neuessling, *Vienna* 31 A3
Neuhausen, *Munich* 20 B2
Neuherberg, *Munich* 20 A2
Neuhönow, *Berlin* 5 A5
Neuilly-Plaisance, *Paris* 23 A4
Neuilly-sur-Marne, *Paris* 23 A4
Neuilly-sur-Seine, *Paris* 23 A2
Neukagran, *Vienna* 31 A2
Neukettenhof, *Vienna* 31 B2
Neukölln, *Berlin* 5 B3
Neuperlach, *Munich* 20 B2
Neuried, *Munich* 20 B1
Neustift am Walde, *Vienna* 31 A1
Neusüssenbrunn, *Vienna* 31 A2
Neuwaldegg, *Vienna* 31 A1
Neva →, *St. Petersburg* 26 B2
Neves, *Rio de Janeiro* 24 B2
New Baghdād, *Baghdad* 3 B2
New Barakpur, *Calcutta* 8 A2
New Brighton, *New York* 21 C1
New Canada, *Johannesburg* 13 B1
New Canada Dam, *Johannesburg* 13 B1
New Carrollton, *Washington* 32 B4
New Cross, *London* 15 B3
New Delhi, *Delhi* 10 B2
New Dorp, *New York* 21 C1
New Dorp Beach, *New York* 21 C1
New Malden, *London* 15 B2
New Milford, *New York* 21 A1
New Territories, *Hong Kong* 12 A1
New Toronto, *Toronto* 30 B1
New Town, *Edinburgh* 11 B2
New Utrecht, *New York* 21 C2
Newark B., *New York* 21 B1
Newbattle, *Edinburgh* 11 B3
Newbury Park, *London* 15 A4
Newcraighall, *Edinburgh* 11 B3
Newham, *London* 15 A4
Newhaven, *Edinburgh* 11 B2
Newington, *Edinburgh* 11 B2
Newington, *London* 15 c5
Newlands, *Johannesburg* 13 B1
Newlands, *Wellington* 32 B1
Newport, *Melbourne* 17 B1
Newton, *Boston* 6 B2
Newtonbrook, *Toronto* 30 A2
Newtongrange, *Edinburgh* 11 B3
Newtonville, *Boston* 6 A2
Newtown, *Sydney* 28 B2
Neyagawa, *Osaka* 22 A4
Ngaio, *Wellington* 32 B1
Ngau Chi Wan, *Hong Kong* 12 A2
Ngau Tau Kok, *Hong Kong* 12 B2
Ngauranga, *Wellington* 32 B1
Ngong Shuen Chau, *Hong Kong* 12 B1
Ngua Kok Wan, *Hong Kong* 12 A1
Nīāvarān, *Tehran* 30 A2
Nibra, *Calcutta* 8 B1
Nidāl, *Baghdad* 3 B2
Niddrie, *Edinburgh* 11 B3
Niddrie, *Melbourne* 17 A1
Nieder Neuendorf, *Berlin* 5 A2
Niederschöneweide, *Berlin* 5 B3
Niederschönhausen, *Berlin* 5 A3
Niemeyer, *Rio de Janeiro* 24 B1
Nieuw Zuid, *Amsterdam* 2 c2
Nieuwe Kerk, *Amsterdam* 2 b2
Nieuwendam, *Amsterdam* 2 A2
Nihonbashi, *Tokyo* 29 b5
Niipperi, *Helsinki* 12 B1
Níkaia, *Athens* 2 B1
Nikolassee, *Berlin* 5 B2
Nikolskiy, *Moscow* 19 B2
Nikolyskoye, *Moscow* 19 B5
Nikulino, *Moscow* 19 B2
Nil, Nahr en →, *Cairo* 7 B2
Nile = Nil, Nahr en →, *Cairo* 7 B2
Niles, *Chicago* 9 A2
Nimta, *Calcutta* 8 A2
Ningyuan, *Tianjin* 30 B2
Nippa, *Tokyo* 29 B2
Nippori, *Tokyo* 29 A3
Nishi, *Osaka* 22 A3
Nishinari, *Osaka* 22 B3
Nishiyodogawa, *Osaka* 22 A3
Niterói, *Rio de Janeiro* 24 B2
Nob Hill, *San Francisco* 25 b1
Nockeby, *Stockholm* 28 B1
Noel Park, *London* 15 A3
Nogatino, *Moscow* 19 B4
Nogent-sur-Marne, *Paris* 23 A3
Noida, *Delhi* 10 B2
Noiseau, *Paris* 23 B4
Noisiel, *Paris* 23 A4
Noisy-le-Grand, *Paris* 23 A4
Noisy-le-Roi, *Paris* 23 A1
Noisy-le-Sec, *Paris* 23 A3
Nokkala, *Helsinki* 12 C1
Nomentano, *Rome* 25 B2
Nonakashinden, *Tokyo* 29 A2
Nongminyundong Jiangxisuo, *Canton* 8 B2
Nonhyŏn, *Seoul* 26 B2
Nonthaburi, *Bangkok* 3 A1
Noon Gun, *Cape Town* 8 b1
Noorder Kerk, *Amsterdam* 2 a1
Noordgesig, *Johannesburg* 13 B1
Noordzeekanaal, *Amsterdam* 2 A1
Nord, Gare du, *Paris* 23 a4
Nordrand-Siedlung, *Vienna* 31 A2
Nordstrand, *Oslo* 22 A3
Normandale, *Wellington* 32 B2
Nørrebro, *Copenhagen* 10 a1
Norridge, *Chicago* 9 B2
Norrmalm, *Stockholm* 28 a1
North Arlington, *New York* 21 B1
North Bay Village, *Miami* 18 A2
North Bergen, *New York* 21 B1
North Branch Chicago River →, *Chicago* 9 B2
North Bull Island, *Dublin* 11 A3
North Cambridge, *Boston* 6 A3
North Cheam, *London* 15 B2
North Cohasset, *Boston* 6 B4
North Cray, *London* 15 B4
North Decatur, *Atlanta* 3 B3
North Druid Hills, *Atlanta* 3 B3
North Esk →, *Edinburgh* 11 B2
North Gyle, *Edinburgh* 11 B2
North Hackensack, *New York* 21 A1
North Harbor, *Manila* 17 B1
North Hd., *Sydney* 28 A2
North Hollywood, *Los Angeles* 16 B2
North Lexington, *Boston* 6 A2
North Miami, *Miami* 18 A2
North Miami Beach, *Miami* 18 A2
North Nazimabad, *Karachi* 14 A2
North Pt., *Hong Kong* 12 B2
North Queensferry, *Edinburgh* 11 A1
North Quincy, *Boston* 6 B3
North Res., *Boston* 6 A3
North Riverside, *Chicago* 9 B2
North Saugus, *Boston* 6 A3
North Shore Channel →, *Chicago* 9 B2
North Springfield, *Washington* 32 C2
North Sudbury, *Boston* 6 A1
North Sydney, *Sydney* 28 B2
North Woolwich, *London* 15 A4
North York, *Toronto* 30 A2
Northbridge, *Sydney* 28 A2
Northbridge Park, *Sydney* 28 A2
Northcliff, *Johannesburg* 13 A1
Northcote, *Melbourne* 17 A2
Northlake, *Chicago* 9 B1
Northmount, *Toronto* 30 A2
Northolt, *London* 15 A1
Northumberland Heath, *London* 15 B5
Northwood, *London* 15 A1
Norumbega Res., *Boston* 6 B2
Norwood, *Johannesburg* 13 A2
Norwood Park, *Chicago* 9 B2
Noryangjin, *Seoul* 26 B1
Nossa Senhora de Candelária, *Rio de Janeiro* 24 a2
Nossa Senhora do Ó, *São Paulo* 26 B1
Nossegem, *Brussels* 6 A3
Notre-Dame, *Paris* 23 c4
Notre-Dame, Bois, *Paris* 23 B4
Notre-Dame-de-Grace, *Montreal* 19 B2
Notting Hill, *London* 15 b1
Nova Milanese, *Milan* 18 A2
Novate Milanese, *Milan* 18 A1
Novaya Derevnya, *St. Petersburg* 26 A1
Nové Město, *Prague* 24 B2
Novoaleksandrovskoye, *St. Petersburg* 26 B2
Novogireyevo, *Moscow* 19 B4
Novoivanovskoye, *Moscow* 19 B1
Novonikolyskoye, *Moscow* 19 A1
Novosaratovka, *St. Petersburg* 26 B3
Nowe-Babice, *Warsaw* 31 B1
Nöykkiö, *Helsinki* 12 B1
Nueva Atzacoalco, *Mexico City* 18 B2
Nueva Pompeya, *Buenos Aires* 7 C2
Nueva Tenochtitlán, *Mexico City* 18 B2
Nuijala, *Helsinki* 12 B1
Numabukuro, *Tokyo* 29 A2
Nunez, *Buenos Aires* 7 B2
Nunhead, *London* 15 B3
Ñuñoa, *Santiago* 26 B2
Nusle, *Prague* 24 B2
Nussdorf, *Vienna* 31 A2
Nyanga, *Cape Town* 8 A2
Nymphenburg, *Munich* 20 B2
Nymphenburg, Schloss, *Munich* 20 B2


# O


Oak Grove, *Atlanta* 3 A3
Oak Island, *Boston* 6 A4
Oak Lawn, *Chicago* 9 C2
Oak Park, *Chicago* 9 B2
Oak View, *Washington* 32 A4
Oakdale, *Atlanta* 3 A2
Oakland, *San Francisco* 25 B3
Oakland, *Washington* 32 B4
Oaklawn, *Washington* 32 C4
Oakleigh, *Melbourne* 17 B2
Oakton, *Washington* 32 B2
Oakwood Beach, *New York* 21 C1
Oatley, *Sydney* 28 B1
Obalende, *Lagos* 14 B2
Oba's Palace, *Lagos* 14 B2
Oberföhring, *Munich* 20 B2
Oberhaching, *Munich* 20 B2
Oberlaa, *Vienna* 31 B2
Oberlisse, *Vienna* 31 A2
Obermenzing, *Munich* 20 A1
Obermoos Schwaige, *Munich* 20 A1
Oberschleissheim, *Munich* 20 A2
Oberschöneweide, *Berlin* 5 B4
Observatory, *Johannesburg* 13 B2
Observatory, *Sydney* 28 a1
Ōbu, *Osaka* 22 A1
Obu-tōge, *Osaka* 22 A1
Óbuda, *Budapest* 7 A2
Obukhovo, *St. Petersburg* 26 B2
Obvodnyy Kanal, *St. Petersburg* 26 B1
Ocean Park, *Hong Kong* 12 B2
Ochakovo, *Moscow* 19 B2
Ochota, *Warsaw* 31 B1
O'Connell Street, *Dublin* 11 b2
Ōdana, *Tokyo* 29 B2
Öden-Stockach, *Munich* 20 B3
Odilampi, *Helsinki* 12 B1
Odintsovo, *Moscow* 19 B1
Odivelas, *Lisbon* 14 A1
Odolany, *Warsaw* 31 B1
Oeiras, *Lisbon* 14 A1
Ofin, *Lagos* 14 A3
Ogawa, *Tokyo* 29 A1
Ogden Park, *Chicago* 9 C2
Ogikubo, *Tokyo* 29 A2
Ogogoro, *Lagos* 14 B2
Ogoyo, *Lagos* 14 B2
Ogudu, *Lagos* 14 A2
Ohariu Stream →, *Wellington* 32 B1
O'Higgins, Parque, *Santiago* 26 B2
Ōimachi, *Tokyo* 29 B3
Ojota, *Lagos* 14 A2
Okamoto, *Osaka* 22 A2
Okęcie, *Warsaw* 31 B1
Okęcie Airport, *Warsaw* 31 B1
Okelra, *Lagos* 14 B2
Okeogbe, *Lagos* 14 B2
Okha, *Delhi* 10 B2
Okhta →, *St. Petersburg* 26 B2
Okkervil →, *St. Petersburg* 26 B2
Okrzeszyn, *Warsaw* 31 C2
Oksval, *Oslo* 22 A3
Oktyabrskiy, *Moscow* 19 B3
Ōkubo, *Tokyo* 29 a2
Ōkura, *Tokyo* 29 B1
Olari, *Helsinki* 12 B1
Olaria, *Rio de Janeiro* 24 B1
Old Admiralty, *St. Petersburg* 26 B1
Old City, *Delhi* 1 a3
Old City, *Jerusalem* 13 b3
Old City, *Shanghai* 27 B1
Old Fort = Purana Qila, *Delhi* 1 c3
Old Harbor, *Boston* 6 B3
Old Town, *Chicago* 9 B3
Old Town, *Edinburgh* 11 B2
Oldbawn, *Dublin* 11 B1
Olgino, *St. Petersburg* 26 A1
Olimpico, Estadio, *Mexico City* 18 C1
Olivais, *Lisbon* 14 A2
Olivar de los Padres, *Mexico City* 18 B1
Olivar del Conde, *Mexico City* 18 B1
Olivos, *Buenos Aires* 7 B2
Olona →, *Milan* 18 B1
Olympia, *London* 15 c1
Olympic Stadium, *Helsinki* 12 B2
Olympique, Stade, *Montreal* 19 A2
Omonias, Pl., *Athens* 2 b1
Ōmori, *Tokyo* 29 B3
Onchi, *Osaka* 22 B4
Onchi →, *Osaka* 22 B4
Onisigun, *Lagos* 14 A2
Ōokayama, *Tokyo* 29 B3
Oosterpark, *Amsterdam* 2 b3
Oostzaan, *Amsterdam* 2 A2
Opa-Locka, *Miami* 18 A1
Opa-Locka Airport, *Miami* 18 A1
Opacz, *Warsaw* 31 B1
Opera House, *Sydney* 28 a2
Ophirton, *Johannesburg* 13 B2
Oppegård, *Oslo* 22 B3
Oppem, *Brussels* 6 A1
Oppsal, *Oslo* 22 A4
Ora, *Jerusalem* 13 B1
Oradell, *New York* 21 A1
Orange Bowl Stadium, *Miami* 18 B2
Orangi, *Karachi* 14 A2
Orchard Road, *Singapore* 27 a1
Ordrup, *Copenhagen* 10 A3
Orech, *Prague* 24 B1
Øresund, *Copenhagen* 10 A3
Orient Heights, *Boston* 6 A4
Orlando Dam, *Johannesburg* 13 B1
Orlando East, *Johannesburg* 13 B1
Orlovo, *Moscow* 19 C2
Orly, *Paris* 23 B3
Ormesson-sur-Marne, *Paris* 23 B4
Ormond, *Melbourne* 17 B2
Ormøya, *Oslo* 22 A3
Orpington, *London* 15 B4
Orsay, Musée d', *Paris* 23 b3
Országház, *Budapest* 7 b2
Országos Levétár, *Budapest* 7 b1
Ortaköy, *Istanbul* 12 B2
Ortica, *Milan* 18 B2
Oruba, *Lagos* 14 A2
Orvostörteneti Múz., *Budapest* 7 c2
Ōsaka, *Osaka* 22 B4
Osaka B., *Osaka* 22 B2
Osaka Castle, *Osaka* 22 A4
Osaka Harbour, *Osaka* 22 B3
Osaka International Airport, *Osaka* 22 A3
Ōsaki, *Tokyo* 29 B3
Osasco, *São Paulo* 26 B1
Osdorf, *Berlin* 5 B3
Osdorp, *Amsterdam* 2 A1
Oshodi, *Lagos* 14 A2
Oslo, *Oslo* 22 A3
Oslofjorden, *Oslo* 22 B2
Ōsone, *Tokyo* 29 B2
Osorun, *Lagos* 14 A2
Ospiate, *Milan* 18 A1
Ostankino, *Moscow* 19 B3
Östasiatiskamuséet, *Stockholm* 28 b3
Österalm, *Stockholm* 28 a3
Østerbro, *Copenhagen* 10 a1
Osterley, *London* 15 B1
Osterley Park, *London* 15 B1
Östermalm, *Stockholm* 28 A2
Österskär, *Stockholm* 28 A3
Ostiense, *Rome* 25 B1
Østmarkkapellet, *Oslo* 22 A4
Ostøya, *Oslo* 22 A2
Østre Aker, *Oslo* 22 A3
Ōta-Ku, *Tokyo* 29 B3
Otaniemi, *Helsinki* 12 B1
Otari Open Air Museum, *Wellington* 32 B1
Otsuka, *Tokyo* 29 A3
Ottakring, *Vienna* 31 A1
Ottávia, *Rome* 25 B1
Ottery, *Cape Town* 8 B2
Ottobrunn, *Munich* 20 B3
Oud Zuid, *Amsterdam* 2 b1
Oude Kerk, *Amsterdam* 2 b2
Ouderkerk, *Amsterdam* 2 B2
Oulunkylä, *Helsinki* 12 B2
Ourcq, Canal de l', *Paris* 23 A3
Outer Mission, *San Francisco* 25 B2
Outremont, *Montreal* 19 A2
Overijse, *Brussels* 6 B3
Owhiro Bay, *Wellington* 32 C1
Oworonsoki, *Lagos* 14 A2
Oxford Street, *London* 15 b3
Oxgangs, *Edinburgh* 11 B2
Oxon Hill, *Washington* 32 C4
Oyodo, *Osaka* 22 A3
Oyster B., *Sydney* 28 C1
Oyster Rock, *Mumbai* 20 B1
Oyster Rocks, *Karachi* 14 B2
Ozoir-la-Ferrière, *Paris* 23 B4
Ozone Park, *New York* 21 B2


# P


Pacific Heights, *San Francisco* 25 B2
Pacific Manor, *San Francisco* 25 C2
Pacific Palisades, *Los Angeles* 16 B1
Pacifica, *San Francisco* 25 C2
Paco, *Manila* 17 B1
Paco de Arcos, *Lisbon* 14 A1
Paco Imperial, *Rio de Janeiro* 24 a2
Paddington, *London* 15 b2
Paddington, *Sydney* 28 B2
Paderno, *Milan* 18 A1
Pagewood, *Sydney* 28 B2
Pagote, *Mumbai* 20 B2
Pai, I. do, *Rio de Janeiro* 24 B2
Pak Kong, *Hong Kong* 12 A2
Pakila, *Helsinki* 12 B2
Palacio de Bellas Artes, *Mexico City* 18 b2
Palacio de Communicaciones, *Madrid* 17 a3
Palacio Nacional, *Mexico City* 18 b3
Palacio Real, *Barcelona* 4 b3
Palacio Real, *Madrid* 17 b1
Palaión Fáliron, *Athens* 2 B2
Palais de Justice, *Brussels* 6 c2
Palais Royal, *Paris* 23 b4
Palais Royale, *Brussels* 6 b3
Palaiseau, *Paris* 23 B2
Palau Nacional Museu d'Art, *Barcelona* 4 c1
Palazzolo, *Milan* 18 A1
Palermo, *Buenos Aires* 7 B2
Palhais, *Lisbon* 14 B2
Palisades Park, *New York* 21 A1
Palmer Park, *Washington* 32 B4
Palmerston, *Dublin* 11 A1
Paloheinä, *Helsinki* 12 B2
Palomeras, *Madrid* 17 B2
Palos Heights, *Chicago* 9 D2
Palos Hills, *Chicago* 9 C2
Palos Hills Forest, *Chicago* 9 C1
Palos Park, *Chicago* 9 C1
Palpara, *Calcutta* 8 B2
Panchur, *Calcutta* 8 B1
Pandacan, *Manila* 17 B2
Pandan, Selat, *Singapore* 27 B2
Pandan Res., *Singapore* 27 B2
Panepistimio, *Athens* 2 b2
Pangbae, *Seoul* 26 C1
Pangrati, *Athens* 2 B2
Pangsua, Sungei →, *Singapore* 27 A2
Panihati, *Calcutta* 8 A2
Panjang, Bukit, *Singapore* 27 A2
Panje, *Mumbai* 20 B2
Panke →, *Berlin* 5 A3
Pankow, *Berlin* 5 A3
Panthéon, *Paris* 23 c4
Pantheon, *Rome* 25 b2
Pantin, *Paris* 23 A3
Pantitlán, *Mexico City* 18 B2
Panvel Cr. →, *Mumbai* 20 B2
Paparangi, *Wellington* 32 B1
Papiol, *Barcelona* 4 A1
Paramus, *New York* 21 A1
Paranaque, *Manila* 17 B1
Paray-Vieille-Poste, *Paris* 23 B3
Parco Regionale, *Milan* 18 A1
Parel, *Mumbai* 20 B1
Pari, *São Paulo* 26 B2
Parioli, *Rome* 25 B1
Paris, *Paris* 23 A3
Paris-Orly, Aéroport de, *Paris* 23 B3
Pārk-e Mellat, *Tehran* 30 A2
Park Ridge, *Chicago* 9 A1
Park Royal, *London* 15 A2
Parkchester, *New York* 21 B2
Parkdale, *Toronto* 30 B2
Parkhurst, *Johannesburg* 13 A2
Parklawn, *Washington* 32 B3
Parkmore, *Johannesburg* 13 A2
Parkside, *San Francisco* 25 B2
Parktown, *Johannesburg* 13 B2
Parktown North, *Johannesburg* 13 A2
Parkview, *Johannesburg* 13 A2
Parkville, *New York* 21 C2
Parkwood, *Cape Town* 8 B1
Parkwood, *Johannesburg* 13 A2
Parow, *Cape Town* 8 A2
Parque Chabuco, *Buenos Aires* 7 B2
Parque Patricios, *Buenos Aires* 7 B2
Parramatta →, *Sydney* 28 A1
Parthenon, *Athens* 2 c2
Paşabahçe, *Istanbul* 12 B2
Pasadena, *Los Angeles* 16 B4
Pasar Minggu, *Jakarta* 13 B1
Pasay, *Manila* 17 B1
Pascoe Vale, *Melbourne* 17 A1
Paseo de la Reforma, *Mexico City* 18 b2
Pasig, *Manila* 17 B2
Pasig →, *Manila* 17 B2
Pasila, *Helsinki* 12 B2
Pasing, *Munich* 20 B1
Pasir Panjang, *Singapore* 27 B2
Pasir Ris, *Singapore* 27 A3
Passaic →, *New York* 21 B1
Passirana, *Milan* 18 A1
Patel Nagar, *Delhi* 10 B1
Pateros, *Manila* 17 B2
Pathersville, *Atlanta* 3 B3
Pathumwan, *Bangkok* 3 B2
Patipukur, *Calcutta* 8 B2
Patisia, *Athens* 2 A2
Paulo E. Virginia, Gruta, *Rio de Janeiro* 24 B1
Paulshof, *Berlin* 5 A5
Pavshino, *Moscow* 19 B1
Paya Lebar, *Singapore* 27 A3
Peachtree →, *Atlanta* 3 B2
Peakhurst, *Sydney* 28 B1
Peania, *Athens* 2 B3
Peckham, *London* 15 B3
Peddocks I., *Boston* 6 B4
Pederstrup, *Copenhagen* 10 A2
Pedralbes, *Barcelona* 4 A1
Pedregal de San Angel, Jardines del, *Mexico City* 18 C1
Pekhorka →, *Moscow* 19 C6
Pekhra-Pokrovskoye, *Moscow* 19 A5
Pekhra-Yakovievskaya, *Moscow* 19 B5
Peking = Beijing, *Beijing* 4 B1
Pelcowizna, *Warsaw* 31 B2
Pelopónnisos Sta., *Athens* 2 a1
Penalolén, *Santiago* 26 B2
Pencarrow Hd., *Wellington* 32 C2
Peng Siang →, *Singapore* 27 A2
Penge, *London* 15 B3
Penha, *Rio de Janeiro* 24 A1
Penicuik, *Edinburgh* 11 B2
Penjaringan, *Jakarta* 13 A1
Penn Station, *New York* 21 c2
Pennsylvania Avenue, *Washington* 32 b1
Pentland Hills, *Edinburgh* 11 B1
Penyagino, *Moscow* 19 A2
Penzing, *Vienna* 31 A1
People's Park, *Shanghai* 27 B1
People's Square, *Shanghai* 27 B1
Perales del Rio, *Madrid* 17 C2
Peravillo, *Mexico City* 18 a3
Perchtoldsdorf, *Vienna* 31 B1
Perdizes, *São Paulo* 26 B2
Peredelkino, *Moscow* 19 C2
Pergamon Museum, *Berlin* 5 a4
Peristérion, *Athens* 2 A2
Perivale, *London* 15 A2
Perk, *Brussels* 6 A2
Perlach, *Munich* 20 B2
Perlacher Forst, *Munich* 20 B2
Pero, *Milan* 18 A1
Peropok, Bukit, *Singapore* 27 B2
Perovo, *Moscow* 19 B4
Pershing Square, *Los Angeles* 16 c1
Pertusella, *Milan* 18 A1
Pesagot, *Jerusalem* 13 A2
Pesanggrahag, Kali →, *Jakarta* 13 B1
Peschiera Borromeo, *Milan* 18 B2
Pesek, P., *Singapore* 27 B2
Pest, *Budapest* 7 B2
Pesterzsébet, *Budapest* 7 B2
Pesthidegkút, *Budapest* 7 A1
Pestimre, *Budapest* 7 B3
Pestlörinc, *Budapest* 7 B3
Pestújhely, *Budapest* 7 A2
Petas, *Helsinki* 12 B2
Petone, *Wellington* 32 B2
Petrogradskaya Storona, *St. Petersburg* 26 B2
Petroúpolis, *Athens* 2 A2
Petrovice, *Prague* 24 B3
Petrovskiy Park, *Moscow* 19 B3
Petrovsko-Razumovskoye, *Moscow* 19 B3
Pettycur, *Edinburgh* 11 A2
Peutie, *Brussels* 6 A2
Pfaueninsel, *Berlin* 5 B1
Phaya Thai, *Bangkok* 3 B2
Phihai, *Karachi* 14 A2
Phillip B., *Sydney* 28 B2
Phoenix Park, *Dublin* 11 A2
Phra Khanong, *Bangkok* 3 B2
Phra Pradaeng, *Bangkok* 3 C2
Phranakhon, *Bangkok* 3 B1
Picasso, Museu, *Barcelona* 4 c2
Piccadilly, *London* 15 b3
Pico Rivera, *Los Angeles* 16 C4
Piedade, *Lisbon* 14 A1
Piedade, *Rio de Janeiro* 24 B1
Piedade, Cova da, *Lisbon* 14 A2
Piedmont Park, *Atlanta* 3 B2
Pietralata, *Rome* 25 B2
Pihlajamäki, *Helsinki* 12 B2
Pihlajasaari, *Helsinki* 12 C2
Pilares, *Rio de Janeiro* 24 B1
Pilton, *Edinburgh* 11 B2
Pimlico, *London* 15 c3
Pimmit Hills, *Washington* 32 B2
Pine Grove, *Toronto* 30 A1
Pinewood, *Miami* 18 A2
Piney Run →, *Washington* 32 B2
Pinganli, *Beijing* 4 B2
Pingzhou, *Canton* 8 B2
Pinheiros →, *São Paulo* 26 B1
Pinjrapur, *Karachi* 14 A2
Pinner, *London* 15 A1
Pinner Green, *London* 15 A1
Pioltello, *Milan* 18 A2
Pipinui Pt., *Wellington* 32 A1
Piraévs, *Athens* 2 B1
Pirajuçara →, *São Paulo* 26 B1
Pirinççi, *Istanbul* 12 B1
Pirituba, *São Paulo* 26 A1
Pirkkola, *Helsinki* 12 B2
Písnice, *Prague* 24 C2
Pitampura, *Delhi* 10 A1
Pitkäjärvi, *Helsinki* 12 B1
Planegg, *Munich* 20 B1
Plumstead, *Cape Town* 8 B1
Plumstead, *London* 15 B4
Plyushchevo, *Moscow* 19 B4
Pníka, *Athens* 2 c1
Po Toi I., *Hong Kong* 12 B2
Po Toi O, *Hong Kong* 12 B2
Poasco, *Milan* 18 B2
Podbaba, *Prague* 24 B2
Podoli, *Prague* 24 B2
Poduskino, *Moscow* 19 B1
Pointe-Aux-Trembles, *Montreal* 19 A2
Poissy, *Paris* 23 A1
Pok Fu Lam, *Hong Kong* 12 B1
Pokrovsko-Sresnevo, *Moscow* 19 B2
Polton, *Edinburgh* 11 B3
Polyustrovo, *St. Petersburg* 26 B2
Pompidou, Centre, *Paris* 23 b4
Pomprap, *Bangkok* 3 B2
Pondok Indah, *Jakarta* 13 B1
Ponta do Marisco, *Rio de Janeiro* 24 C1
Pontault-Combault, *Paris* 23 B4
Pontinha, *Lisbon* 14 A1
Poplar, *London* 15 A3
Popolo, Porta del, *Rome* 25 a2
Poppintree, *Dublin* 11 A2
Porirua, *Wellington* 32 A2
Porirua East, *Wellington* 32 A2
Port I., *Osaka* 22 A2
Port Melbourne, *Melbourne* 17 B1
Port Nicholson, *Wellington* 32 B2
Port Philip Bay, *Melbourne* 17 B1
Port Richmond, *New York* 21 C1
Port Shelter, *Hong Kong* 12 A2
Port Union, *Toronto* 30 A4
Portage Park, *Chicago* 9 B2
Portal de la Pau, Pl., *Barcelona* 4 c2
Portela, Aeroporto da, *Lisbon* 14 A2
Portmarnock, *Dublin* 11 A3
Porto Brandão, *Lisbon* 14 A1
Porto Novo, *Rio de Janeiro* 24 A2
Porto Novo Cr. →, *Lagos* 14 B2
Portobello, *Edinburgh* 11 B3
Portrero, *San Francisco* 25 B3
Potomac, *Washington* 32 A2
Potomac →, *Washington* 32 B3
Potrero Pt., *San Francisco* 25 B2
Potsdam, *Berlin* 5 B1
Potsdamer Platz, *Berlin* 5 b3
Potzham, *Munich* 20 B2
Pötzleinsdorf, *Vienna* 31 A1
Povoa de Santo Adriao, *Lisbon* 14 A2
Powązki, *Warsaw* 31 B1
Powiśle, *Warsaw* 31 B2
Powsin, *Warsaw* 31 C2
Powsinek, *Warsaw* 31 C2
Poyan Res., *Singapore* 27 A2
Pozuelo de Alarcon, *Madrid* 17 B1
Prado, Museo del, *Madrid* 17 b3
Prado Churubusco, *Mexico City* 18 B2
Praga, *Warsaw* 31 B2
Prague = Praha, *Prague* 24 B2
Praha, *Prague* 24 B2
Praha-Ruzyně Airport, *Prague* 24 B1
Praires, R. des →, *Montreal* 19 A2
Prater, *Vienna* 31 A2
Precotto, *Milan* 18 A2
Prenestino Labicano, *Rome* 25 B2
Prenzlauerberg, *Berlin* 5 A3
Preston, *Melbourne* 17 A1
Pretos Forros, Sa. dos, *Rio de Janeiro* 24 B1
Préville, *Montreal* 19 B3
Přezletice, *Prague* 24 B3
Prima Porta, *Rome* 25 B1
Primavalle, *Rome* 25 B1
Primrose, *Johannesburg* 13 B2
Princes Street, *Edinburgh* 11 b2
Printer's Row, *Chicago* 9 d2
Progreso Nacional, *Mexico City* 18 A2
Prosek, *Prague* 24 B3
Prospect Hill Park, *Boston* 6 A2
Providencia, *Santiago* 26 B2
Prudential Building, *Chicago* 9 c2
Průhonice, *Prague* 24 C3
Psikhikón, *Athens* 2 A2
Pudong New Area, *Shanghai* 27 B2
Pueblo Libre, *Lima* 16 B2
Pueblo Nuevo, *Barcelona* 4 A2
Pueblo Nuevo, *Madrid* 17 B2
Puerta del Sol, Plaza, *Madrid* 17 b2
Puerto Madero, *Buenos Aires* 7 B2
Puerto Retiro, *Buenos Aires* 7 B2
Puhuangyu, *Beijing* 4 B2
Puistola, *Helsinki* 12 B3
Pukan-san, *Seoul* 26 B1
Pukinmäki, *Helsinki* 12 B2
Pukkajwa, *Seoul* 26 B1
Pulkovo Int. Airport, *St. Petersburg* 26 C1
Pullach, *Munich* 20 B1
Pulo Gadung, *Jakarta* 13 B2
Pūnak, *Tehran* 30 A2
Punchbowl, *Sydney* 28 B1
Punde, *Mumbai* 20 B2
Punggol, *Singapore* 27 A3
Punggol, Sungei →, *Singapore* 27 A3
Punggol Pt., *Singapore* 27 A3
Punjabi Bagh, *Delhi* 10 A1
Puotila, *Helsinki* 12 B3
Purana Qila, *Delhi* 1 c3
Puteaux, *Paris* 23 A2
Putilkovo, *Moscow* 19 A2
Putney, *London* 15 B2
Putuo, *Shanghai* 27 B1
Putxet, *Barcelona* 4 A1
Puxi, *Shanghai* 27 B1
Pydhuni, *Mumbai* 20 b2
Pyramids, *Cairo* 7 B1
Pyry, *Warsaw* 31 C1


# Q


Qalandya, *Jerusalem* 13 A2
Qal'eh Morghī, *Tehran* 30 B2
Qanâ el Ismâ'ilîya, *Cairo* 7 A2
Qāsemābād, *Tehran* 30 A3
Qasr-e Firūzeh, *Tehran* 30 B3
Qatane, *Jerusalem* 13 B1
Qianmen, *Beijing* 4 B2
Qinghuayuan, *Beijing* 4 B1
Qingningsi, *Shanghai* 27 B2
Qolhak, *Tehran* 30 A2
Quadraro, *Rome* 25 B2
Quaid-i-Azam, *Karachi* 14 A1
Quartiere Zingone, *Milan* 18 B1
Quds, *Baghdad* 3 A2
Queen Mary Res., *London* 15 B1
Queen Street, *Edinburgh* 11 a1
Queensbury, *London* 15 A2
Queenscliffe, *Sydney* 28 A2
Queensferry, *Edinburgh* 11 B1
Queenstown, *Singapore* 27 B2
Quellerina, *Johannesburg* 13 A1
Queluz, *Lisbon* 14 A1
Quezon City, *Manila* 17 B2
Quezon Memorial Circle, *Manila* 17 B2
Quilicura, *Santiago* 26 B1
Quincy, *Boston* 6 B3
Quincy B., *Boston* 6 B4
Quinta Normal, *Santiago* 26 B1
Quinto de Stampi, *Milan* 18 B2
Quinto Romano, *Milan* 18 B1
Quirinale, *Rome* 25 B1
Quirinale, Palazzo dei, *Rome* 25 b3


# R


Raasdorf, *Vienna* 31 A3
Rådhuset, *Oslo* 22 A3
Radlice, *Prague* 24 B2
Radość, *Warsaw* 31 B3
Radotin, *Prague* 24 C2
Rafat, *Jerusalem* 13 A2
Raffles Hotel, *Singapore* 27 b3
Raffles Park, *Singapore* 27 B2
Raheny, *Dublin* 11 A3
Rahnsdorf, *Berlin* 5 B5
Rainham, *London* 15 A5
Raj Ghat, *Delhi* 1 b3
Rajakylä, *Helsinki* 12 B3
Rajpath, *Delhi* 1 c2
Rajpura, *Delhi* 10 A2
Rákos-patak →, *Budapest* 7 B3
Rákoshegy, *Budapest* 7 B3
Rákoskeresztúr, *Budapest* 7 B3

Rákoskert, Budapest ..... 7 B3
Rákosliget, Budapest ..... 7 B3
Rákospalota, Budapest ..... 7 A2
Rákosszentmihály, Budapest 7 A2
Raków, Warsaw ..... 31 B1
Ram, Jerusalem ..... 13 A2
Rām Allāh, Jerusalem ..... 13 A2
Ramadān, Baghdad ..... 3 B2
Ramakrishna Puram, Delhi 10 B1
Ramanathpur, Calcutta ..... 8 A1
Rambla, La, Barcelona ..... 4 b2
Rambler Channel,
  Hong Kong ..... 12 A1
Ramenki, Moscow ..... 19 B2
Ramersdorf, Munich ..... 20 B2
Ramos, Rio de Janeiro ..... 24 B1
Ramos Mejía, Buenos Aires 7 B1
Ramot, Jerusalem ..... 13 B2
Rampur, Delhi ..... 10 A2
Ramsgate, Sydney ..... 28 B1
Rand Afrikaans Univ.,
  Johannesburg ..... 13 B2
Rand Airport, Johannesburg 13 B2
Randburg, Johannesburg ..... 13 A1
Randhart, Johannesburg ..... 13 B2
Randpark Ridge,
  Johannesburg ..... 13 A1
Randwick, Sydney ..... 28 B2
Ranelagh, Dublin ..... 11 A2
Rannersdorf, Vienna ..... 31 B2
Ransbèche, Brussels ..... 6 B3
Ransdorp, Amsterdam ..... 2 A2
Ranvad, Mumbai ..... 20 B2
Raposo, Lisbon ..... 14 A1
Rashtrapati Bhawan, Delhi 10 B2
Rasskazovka, Moscow ..... 19 C2
Rastaala, Helsinki ..... 12 B1
Rastila, Helsinki ..... 12 B3
Raszyn, Warsaw ..... 31 C1
Ratcha Thewi, Bangkok ..... 3 b3
Rathfarnham, Dublin ..... 11 B2
Ratho, Edinburgh ..... 11 B1
Ratho Station, Edinburgh ..... 11 B1
Rato, Lisbon ..... 14 A2
Ravelston, Edinburgh ..... 11 B2
Rawamangun, Jakarta ..... 13 B2
Rayners Lane, London ..... 15 A1
Raynes Park, London ..... 15 B2
Raypur, Calcutta ..... 8 C2
Razdory, Moscow ..... 19 B2
Real Felipe, Fuerte, Lima 16 B2
Recoleta, Buenos Aires ..... 7 B2
Recoleta, Santiago ..... 26 B2
Red Fort = Lal Qila, Delhi 1 A3
Redbridge, London ..... 15 A4
Redfern, Sydney ..... 28 B2
Redwood, Wellington ..... 32 B1
Reeves Hill, Boston ..... 6 A1
Refshaleøen, Copenhagen ..... 10 A3
Regents Park, Johannesburg 13 B2
Regent's Park, London ..... 15 a2
Rego Park, New York ..... 21 B2
Reichstag, Berlin ..... 5 a3
Reina Sofia, Centro de Arte,
  Madrid ..... 17 c3
Reinickendorf, Berlin ..... 5 A3
Rekola, Helsinki ..... 12 B3
Rembertów, Warsaw ..... 31 B2
Rembrandthuis, Amsterdam 2 b2
Rembrandtpark, Amsterdam 2 A2
Rembrandtplein,
  Amsterdam ..... 2 b2
Remedios, Parque Nacional
  de los, Mexico City ..... 18 B1
Remedios de Escalada,
  Buenos Aires ..... 7 C2
Rémola, Laguna del,
  Barcelona ..... 4 B1
Renca, Santiago ..... 26 B1
Renmin Park, Tianjin ..... 30 B2
Rennemculin, Paris ..... 23 A1
Reporyje Prague ..... 24 B1
Republica, Plaza de la,
  Mexico City ..... 18 b1
République, Place de la,
  Paris ..... 23 A3
Repulse Bay, Hong Kong ..... 12 B2
Repy, Prague ..... 24 B1
Residenz, Munich ..... 20 B2
Residenzmuseum, Munich ..... 20 b3
Reston, Washington ..... 32 B2
Retiro, Buenos Aires ..... 7 B2
Retiro, Madrid ..... 17 B1
Retreat, Cape Town ..... 8 B1
Reutov, Moscow ..... 19 B5
Réveillon ➜, Paris ..... 23 B4
Revere, Boston ..... 6 A3
Rexdale, Toronto ..... 30 A1
Reynosa Tamaulipas,
  Mexico City ..... 18 A1
Rho, Milan ..... 18 A1
Rhodes, Sydney ..... 28 B1
Rhodon, Paris ..... 23 B1
Rhodon ➜, Paris ..... 23 B1
Ribeira, Rio de Janeiro ..... 24 A1
Ricarda, Laguna de la,
  Barcelona ..... 4 B1
Richmond, Melbourne ..... 17 A2
Richmond, San Francisco 25 A2
Richmond Hill, New York ..... 21 B2
Richmond Park, London ..... 15 B2
Richmond upon Thames,
  London ..... 15 B2
Riddarholmen, Stockholm ..... 28 c1
Riddarhuset, Stockholm ..... 28 b1
Ridgefield, New York ..... 21 B1
Ridgefield Park, New York ..... 21 A1
Ridgewood, New York ..... 21 B2
Riem, Munich ..... 20 B3
Rijksmuseum, Amsterdam ..... 2 b1
Rikers I., New York ..... 21 B2
Riksdagensledamothus,
  Stockholm ..... 28 b2
Riksdagshuset, Stockholm ..... 28 A2
Rimac, Lima ..... 16 B2
Ringsend, Dublin ..... 11 A2
Rinkeby, Stockholm ..... 28 A1
Rio Compride,
  Rio de Janeiro ..... 24 B1
Rio de Janeiro,
  Rio de Janeiro ..... 24 B1
Rio de la Plata, Buenos Aires 7 B2
Rio de Mouro, Lisbon ..... 14 A1
Ripollet, Barcelona ..... 4 A1
Ris, Oslo ..... 22 A3
Risby, Copenhagen ..... 10 A1
Rishra, Calcutta ..... 8 A2
Ritchie, Washington ..... 32 B4
Rithala, Delhi ..... 10 A1
Rive Sud, Canal de la,
  Montreal ..... 19 B2
River Edge, New York ..... 21 A1
River Forest, Chicago ..... 9 B2
River Grove, Chicago ..... 9 B1
Riverdale, New York ..... 21 A2
Riverdale, Washington ..... 32 B4
Riverdale Park, Toronto ..... 30 A2
Riverlea, Johannesburg ..... 13 B1
Riverside, Chicago ..... 9 C2
Riverwood, Sydney ..... 28 B1

Rivière-des-Praires,
  Montreal ..... 19 A2
Rixensart, Brussels ..... 6 B3
Riyad, Baghdad ..... 3 B2
Rizal Park, Manila ..... 17 B1
Rizal Stadium, Manila ..... 17 B1
Røa, Oslo ..... 22 A2
Robbins, Chicago ..... 9 D2
Robertsham, Johannesburg ..... 13 B2
Rochelle Park, New York ..... 21 A1
Rock Cr. ➜, Washington ..... 32 B3
Rock Creek Park,
  Washington ..... 32 B3
Rock Pt., Wellington ..... 32 A1
Rockaway Pt., New York ..... 21 C2
Rockdale, Sydney ..... 28 B1
Rockefeller Center,
  New York ..... 21 e2
Rodaon, Vienna ..... 31 B1
Rødovre, Copenhagen ..... 10 A2
Rodrigo de Freitas, L.,
  Rio de Janeiro ..... 24 B1
Roehampton, London ..... 15 B2
Rogers Park, Chicago ..... 9 A2
Roihuvuori, Helsinki ..... 12 B3
Roissy-en-Brie, Paris ..... 23 B4
Rokin, Amsterdam ..... 2 b2
Rokkō I., Osaka ..... 22 A2
Rokkō Sanchi, Osaka ..... 22 A2
Rokkō-Zan, Osaka ..... 22 A2
Rokytka ➜, Prague ..... 24 B3
Roma, Rome ..... 25 B1
Romai-Fürdö, Budapest ..... 7 A2
Romainville, Paris ..... 23 A3
Romano Banco, Milan ..... 18 B1
Romashkovo, Moscow ..... 19 B1
Rome = Roma, Rome ..... 25 B1
Romford, London ..... 15 A5
Rondebosch, Cape Town ..... 8 A1
Roppongi, Tokyo ..... 29 c3
Rose Hill, Washington ..... 32 C3
Rosebank, New York ..... 21 C1
Rosebery, Sydney ..... 28 B2
Rosedal La Candelaria,
  Mexico City ..... 18 B2
Roseland, Chicago ..... 9 C3
Rosemead, Los Angeles ..... 16 B4
Rosemont, Montreal ..... 19 A2
Rosenborg Have,
  Copenhagen ..... 10 A3
Rosenthal, Berlin ..... 5 A3
Rosettenville, Johannesburg 13 B2
Rosewell, Edinburgh ..... 11 B3
Rosherville Dam,
  Johannesburg ..... 13 B2
Rösjön, Stockholm ..... 28 A2
Roslags-Näsby, Stockholm 28 A2
Roslin, Edinburgh ..... 11 B3
Roslindale, Boston ..... 6 B3
Rosny-sous-Bois, Paris ..... 23 A4
Rosslyn, Washington ..... 32 B3
Rosyth, Edinburgh ..... 11 A1
Rotherhithe, London ..... 15 B3
Rothneusiedl, Vienna ..... 31 B2
Rothschmaige, Munich ..... 20 A1
Rouge Hill, Toronto ..... 30 A4
Round I., Hong Kong ..... 12 B2
Roxbury, Boston ..... 6 B3
Roxeth, London ..... 15 A1
Royal Botanic Garden,
  Edinburgh ..... 11 B2
Royal Botanic Gardens,
  Sydney ..... 28 b2
Royal Grand Palace,
  Bangkok ..... 3 b1
Royal Observatory,
  Edinburgh ..... 11 B2
Royal Park, Melbourne ..... 17 A1
Royal Turf Club, Bangkok 3 b2
Röylä, Helsinki ..... 12 B1
Rozas, Portilleros de las,
  Madrid ..... 17 B1
Roztoky, Prague ..... 24 B2
Rozzano, Milan ..... 18 B1
Rubi ➜, Barcelona ..... 4 A1
Rublovo, Moscow ..... 19 B2
Rudnevka ➜, Moscow ..... 19 B5
Rudolfsheim, Vienna ..... 31 A2
Rudolfshöhe, Berlin ..... 5 A5
Rudow, Berlin ..... 5 B3
Rueil-Malmaison, Paris ..... 23 A2
Ruisbroek, Brussels ..... 6 B1
Ruislip, London ..... 15 A1
Rumelihisarı, Istanbul ..... 12 B2
Rumyantsevo, Moscow ..... 19 C2
Rungis, Paris ..... 23 B3
Rusafa, Baghdad ..... 3 B2
Rush Green, London ..... 15 A5
Russa, Calcutta ..... 8 C2
Russian Hill, San Francisco 25 a1
Rustenfeld, Vienna ..... 31 B1
Rutherford, New York ..... 21 B1
Ruzyně, Prague ..... 24 B1
Rybatskaya, St. Petersburg 26 B2
Rydboholm, Stockholm ..... 28 A3
Ryde, Sydney ..... 28 A1
Rynek, Warsaw ..... 31 a2
Ryogoku, Tokyo ..... 29 B3
Rzhevka, St. Petersburg ..... 26 B3

## S

Sa'ādatābād, Tehran ..... 30 A2
Saadūn, Baghdad ..... 3 B2
Saavedra, Buenos Aires ..... 7 B2
Saboli, Delhi ..... 10 A2
Sabugo, Lisbon ..... 14 A1
Sabzi Mand, Delhi ..... 10 A2
Sacavém, Lisbon ..... 14 A2
Saclay, Paris ..... 23 B2
Saclay, Étang de, Paris ..... 23 B1
Sacomã, São Paulo ..... 26 B2
Sacré Cœur, Paris ..... 23 a4
Sacrow, Berlin ..... 5 B1
Sacrower See, Berlin ..... 5 B1
Sadang, Seoul ..... 26 C1
Sadar Bazar, Delhi ..... 1 a1
Saddle Brook, New York ..... 21 A1
Sadr, Karachi ..... 14 A2
Sadr City, Baghdad ..... 3 A2
Sadyba, Warsaw ..... 31 B2
Saft el Laban, Cairo ..... 7 A2
Saganashkee Slough,
  Chicago ..... 9 C1
Sagene, Oslo ..... 22 A3
Sagrada Família, Templo de,
  Barcelona ..... 4 A2
Sagrada Família, Templo de,
  Barcelona ..... 4 a2
Sahar Int. Airport, Mumbai 20 A2
Sahar, Hong Kong ..... 12 A2
Sai Kung, Hong Kong ..... 12 A2
Sai Wan Ho, Hong Kong ..... 12 B2
Sai Ying Pun, Hong Kong ..... 12 B1
St.-Aubin, Paris ..... 23 B1
St.-Cloud, Paris ..... 23 A2
St.-Cyr-l'École, Paris ..... 23 B1
St.-Cyr-l'École, Aérodrome
  de, Paris ..... 23 B1

St.-Denis, Paris ..... 23 A3
St.-Germain, Forêt de, Paris 23 A1
St.-Germain-en-Laye, Paris 23 A1
St. Giles Cathedral,
  Edinburgh ..... 11 b2
St-Gilles, Brussels ..... 6 B2
St. Helier, London ..... 15 B2
St.-Hubert, London ..... 15 B2
St. Hubert, Galerie, Brussels 6 b2
St. Isaac's Cathedral,
  St. Petersburg ..... 26 B1
St. Jacques ➜, Montreal ..... 19 B3
St. James's, London ..... 15 b3
St. John's Cathedral,
  Hong Kong ..... 12 c1
St-Joose-Ten-Noode,
  Brussels ..... 6 A2
St. Kilda, Melbourne ..... 17 B1
St. Lambert, Montreal ..... 19 A3
St.-Lambert, Paris ..... 23 B1
St.-Laurent, Montreal ..... 19 A1
St. Lawrence ➜, Montreal ..... 19 A3
St.-Lazare, Gare, Paris ..... 23 A2
St.-Léonard, Montreal ..... 19 A2
St. Magelungen, Stockholm 28 B2
St.-Mandé, Paris ..... 23 A3
St. Margaret's, Dublin ..... 11 A2
St.-Martin, Bois, Paris ..... 23 B4
St. Mary Cray, London ..... 15 B4
St.-Maur-des-Fossés, Paris 23 B3
St.-Maurice, Paris ..... 23 A3
St.-Michel, Montreal ..... 19 A2
St. Nikolaus-Kirken, Prague 24 B2
St.-Ouen, Paris ..... 23 A3
St. Patrick's Cathedral,
  Dublin ..... 11 c1
St. Patrick's Cathedral,
  New York ..... 21 e2
St. Paul's Cathedral, London 15 b4
St. Paul's Cray, London ..... 15 B4
St. Peters, Sydney ..... 28 B2
St. Petersburg = Sankt
  Peterburg, St. Petersburg 26 B1
St.-Pierre, Montreal ..... 19 B2
St-Pieters-Leeuw, Brussels 6 B1
St. Quentin, Étang de, Paris 23 B1
St. Stephen's Green, Dublin 11 c3
St-Stevens-Woluwe, Brussels 6 A2
St.-Vincent-de-Paul,
  Montreal ..... 19 A2
Ste.-Catherine, Montreal ..... 19 A2
Ste.-Hélène, Î., Montreal ..... 19 A2
Saiwai, Tokyo ..... 29 B3
Sakai, Osaka ..... 22 B3
Sakai Harbour, Osaka ..... 22 B3
Sakra, ➜, Singapore ..... 27 B2
Salam, Baghdad ..... 3 A2
Salamanca, Madrid ..... 17 B1
Sällynoggin, Dublin ..... 11 B3
Salmannsdorf, Vienna ..... 31 A1
Salmedina, Madrid ..... 17 C2
Salomea, Warsaw ..... 31 B1
Salsette I., Mumbai ..... 20 A2
Salt Lake City, Calcutta ..... 8 B2
Salt River, Cape Town ..... 8 A1
Salt Water L., Calcutta ..... 8 B2
Saltsjö-Duvnäs, Stockholm 28 B3
Saltykovka, Moscow ..... 19 B5
Samatya, Istanbul ..... 12 C1
Sampaloc, Manila ..... 17 B1
Samphan Thawong,
  Bangkok ..... 3 B2
Samson, Seoul ..... 26 B2
San Andrés, Barcelona ..... 4 A2
San Angel, Mexico City ..... 18 B1
San Angelo, Castel, Rome ..... 25 b1
San Basilio, Rome ..... 25 B2
San Borja, Lima ..... 16 B3
San Bóvio, Milan ..... 18 B2
San Bruno, Pt.,
  San Francisco ..... 25 C2
San Bruno Mt.,
  San Francisco ..... 25 B2
San Cristobal, Buenos Aires 7 B2
San Cristóbal, Madrid ..... 17 B2
San Cristóbal, Cerro,
  Santiago ..... 26 B2
San Cristóforo, Milan ..... 18 B1
San Donato Milanese, Milan 18 B2
San Francisco, San Francisco 25 B2
San Francisco B.,
  San Francisco ..... 25 B3
San Francisco Culhuacán,
  Mexico City ..... 18 C2
San Fruttuoso, Milan ..... 18 A2
San Gabriel, Los Angeles ..... 16 B4
San Giuliano Milanese,
  Milan ..... 18 B2
San Isidro, Lima ..... 16 B2
San Jerónimo Lidice,
  Mexico City ..... 18 C1
San Joaquin, Santiago ..... 26 B2
San José Rio Hondo,
  Mexico City ..... 18 B1
San Juan ➜, Manila ..... 17 B2
San Juan de Aragón,
  Mexico City ..... 18 B2
San Juan de Aragón, Parque,
  Mexico City ..... 18 B2
San Juan de Lurigancho,
  Lima ..... 16 A2
San Juan del Monte, Manila 17 B2
San Juan Ixtacala,
  Mexico City ..... 18 A1
San Juan Toltotepec,
  Mexico City ..... 18 A1
San Just Desvern, Barcelona 4 A1
San Justo, Buenos Aires ..... 7 C1
San Lorenzo Tezonco,
  Mexico City ..... 18 C2
San Luis, Lima ..... 16 B2
San Marino, Los Angeles ..... 16 B4
San Martin, Barcelona ..... 4 A2
San Martin de Porras, Lima 16 B2
San Miguel, Lima ..... 16 B2
San Miguel, Santiago ..... 26 B2
San Nicolas, Buenos Aires ..... 7 B2
San Onófrio, Rome ..... 25 B1
San Pedro Martir, Barcelona 4 A1
San Pedro Zacatenco,
  Mexico City ..... 18 A2
San Pietro, Piazza, Rome ..... 25 b1
San Po Kong, Hong Kong ..... 12 A2
San Rafael Chamapa,
  Mexico City ..... 18 B1
San Rafael Hills,
  Los Angeles ..... 16 A3
San Roque, Manila ..... 17 B2
San Siro, Milan ..... 18 B1
San Souci, Sydney ..... 28 B1
San Telmo, Buenos Aires ..... 7 B2
San Vicenç dels Horts,
  Barcelona ..... 4 A1
Sanbancho, Tokyo ..... 29 a3
Sandown, Johannesburg ..... 13 A2
Sandown Park Races,
  London ..... 15 B1
Sandton, Johannesburg ..... 13 A2
Sandvika, Oslo ..... 22 A2
Sandy Pond, Boston ..... 6 A2
Sandyford, Dublin ..... 11 B2

Sandymount, Dublin ..... 11 B2
Sangenjaya, Tokyo ..... 29 B2
Sangge, Seoul ..... 26 B2
Sangley Pt., Manila ..... 17 C1
Sankrail, Calcutta ..... 8 B1
Sankt Peterburg,
  St. Petersburg ..... 26 B1
Sankt Veit, Vienna ..... 31 A1
Sanlihe, Beijing ..... 4 B1
Sanlintang, Shanghai ..... 27 C1
Sans, Barcelona ..... 4 A1
Sant Agusti, Barcelona ..... 4 c2
Sant Ambrogio, Basilica di,
  Milan ..... 18 B2
Sant Boi de Llobregat,
  Barcelona ..... 4 A1
Sant Cugat, Barcelona ..... 4 A1
Sant Feliu de Llobregat,
  Barcelona ..... 4 A1
Sant Joan Despi, Barcelona 4 A1
Sant Maria del Mar,
  Barcelona ..... 4 b3
Sant Pau del Camp,
  Barcelona ..... 4 c2
Santa Ana, Manila ..... 17 B2
Santa Coloma de Gramanet,
  Barcelona ..... 4 A2
Santa Cruz, Manila ..... 17 B2
Santa Cruz, Mumbai ..... 20 A1
Santa Cruz, I. de,
  Rio de Janeiro ..... 24 B2
Santa Cruz de Olorde,
  Barcelona ..... 4 A1
Santa Efigénia, São Paulo ..... 26 B2
Santa Elena, Manila ..... 17 B2
Santa Elena del Gomero,
  Santiago ..... 26 B1
Santa Eulalia, Barcelona ..... 4 A2
Santa Fe Springs,
  Los Angeles ..... 16 C4
Santa Iria da Azóia, Lisbon 14 A2
Santa Julia, Santiago ..... 26 C2
Santa Maria, Mexico City 18 B1
Santa Monica, Los Angeles 16 B2
Santa Monica Mts.,
  Los Angeles ..... 16 B2
Santa Rosa De Locobe,
  Santiago ..... 26 B2
Santa Teresa de la Ovalle,
  Santiago ..... 26 B1
Santahamina, Helsinki ..... 12 C3
Santana, São Paulo ..... 26 B2
Santeny, Paris ..... 23 B4
Santiago, Santiago ..... 26 B2
Santiago de Surco, Lima ..... 16 B2
Santo Amaro, Lisbon ..... 14 A1
Santo Amaro, São Paulo ..... 26 B2
Santo Andre, Lisbon ..... 14 A1
Santo Antão do Tojal,
  Lisbon ..... 14 A2
Santo António, Qta. de,
  Lisbon ..... 14 A1
Santo Tomas, Univ. of,
  Manila ..... 17 B1
Santos Dumont, Aéroport,
  Rio de Janeiro ..... 24 B1
Santoshpur, Calcutta ..... 8 B1
Santragachi, Calcutta ..... 8 B1
Santry, Dublin ..... 11 A2
Santurtzi, Calcutta ..... 8 B2
São Caetano do Sul,
  São Paulo ..... 26 B2
São Conrado, Rio de Janeiro 24 C1
São Cristovão,
  Rio de Janeiro ..... 24 B1
São Francisco Penitência,
  Rio de Janeiro ..... 24 b1
São Jorge, Castelo de,
  Lisbon ..... 14 A2
São Juliao do Tojal, Lisbon 14 A2
São Paulo, São Paulo ..... 26 B2
Sapa, Calcutta ..... 8 B1
Sapateiro, Cor. do ➜,
  São Paulo ..... 26 B1
Sarandi, Buenos Aires ..... 7 C2
Saraswati ➜, Calcutta ..... 8 A1
Sarecky potok ➜, Prague ..... 24 B2
Sariñdın, Singapore ..... 27 A2
Saribnan Res., Singapore ..... 27 A2
Sariyer, Istanbul ..... 12 A2
Saronikós Kólpos, Athens ..... 2 A1
Sarriá, Barcelona ..... 4 A1
Sarsuna, Calcutta ..... 8 C1
Sartrouville, Paris ..... 23 A2
Sasad, Budapest ..... 7 B2
Sasalumon, Budapest ..... 7 A2
Saska, Warsaw ..... 31 B2
Satalice, Prague ..... 24 B3
Satgachi, Calcutta ..... 8 B2
Sathorn, Bangkok ..... 3 B2
Satpukur, Calcutta ..... 8 B2
Satra, Stockholm ..... 28 B1
Sattru Pha, Bangkok ..... 3 B2
Satde, São Paulo ..... 26 B2
Saugus, Boston ..... 6 A3
Saugus ➜, Boston ..... 6 A3
Sault-au-Récollet, Montreal 19 A2
Sausalito, San Francisco ..... 25 A2
Sawah Besar, Jakarta ..... 13 A1
Saxonville, Boston ..... 6 B1
Scald Law, Edinburgh ..... 11 B2
Scarborough, Toronto ..... 30 A3
Sceaux, Paris ..... 23 B2
Schaerbeek, Brussels ..... 6 A2
Scharfenberg, Berlin ..... 5 A2
Scheepvartmuseum,
  Amsterdam ..... 2 b3
Schiller Park, Chicago ..... 9 B1
Schiller Woods, Chicago ..... 9 B1
Schiphol, Luchthaven,
  Amsterdam ..... 2 B1
Schlachtensee, Berlin ..... 5 B2
Schlossgarten, Berlin ..... 5 B2
Schmargendorf, Berlin ..... 5 B2
Schöbböck, Berlin ..... 5 A5
Schönbrunn, Schloss, Vienna 31 A1
Schöneberg, Berlin ..... 5 B3
Schönefelde, Berlin ..... 5 A1
Schönwalde, Berlin ..... 5 A1
Schotschekloof, Cape Town 8 b1
Schulzendorf, Berlin ..... 5 A2
Schwabing, Munich ..... 20 B2
Schwanebeck, Berlin ..... 5 A4
Schwanenwerder, Berlin ..... 5 B2
Schwarzlackenau, Vienna ..... 31 A2
Schwechat ➜, Vienna ..... 31 B2
Scitrek Museum, Atlanta ..... 3 b2
Scott Monument, Edinburgh 11 b2
Scottdale, Atlanta ..... 3 B3
Sea Point, Cape Town ..... 8 A1
Seaforth, Sydney ..... 28 A2
Seagate, New York ..... 21 C1
Sears Tower, Chicago ..... 9 c1
Seaseal, Johannesburg ..... 13 B2
Seaview, Wellington ..... 32 B2
Seberov, Prague ..... 24 B3
Secaucus, New York ..... 21 B1
Seddinsee, Berlin ..... 5 B5
Seeberg, Berlin ..... 5 A5

Seeburg, Berlin ..... 5 A1
Seefeld, Berlin ..... 5 A5
Seegefeld, Berlin ..... 5 A1
Seehof, Berlin ..... 5 B2
Segeltorp, Stockholm ..... 28 B1
Segrate, Milan ..... 18 B2
Seguro, Milan ..... 18 B1
Seine ➜, Paris ..... 23 A3
Seixal, Lisbon ..... 14 B2
Selby, Johannesburg ..... 13 B2
Selçatar, P., Singapore ..... 27 A3
Sant Agusti, Barcelona ..... ...
Seletar Hills, Singapore ..... 27 A3
Seletar Res., Singapore ..... 27 A2
Selhurst, London ..... 15 B3
Sembawang, Singapore ..... 27 A2
Senago, Milan ..... 18 A1
Sendlinger Tor Platz, Munich 20 c1
Sendling, Munich ..... 20 B2
Senju, Tokyo ..... 29 A3
Senriyama, Osaka ..... 22 A4
Sentosa, P., Singapore ..... 27 B2
Seoul = Sŏul, Seoul ..... 26 B2
Seoul National Univ., Seoul 26 C1
Seoul Tower, Seoul ..... 26 B2
Sepolia, Athens ..... 2 A2
Sepulveda Flood Control
  Basin, Los Angeles ..... 16 A2
Serangoon, Singapore ..... 27 A3
Serangoon, P., Singapore ..... 27 A3
Serangoon, Sungei ➜,
  Singapore ..... 27 A3
Serangoon Harbour,
  Singapore ..... 27 A3
Seraya, P., Singapore ..... 27 B2
Serebryanka, Moscow ..... 19 B5
Serebryanka ➜, Moscow ..... 19 B5
Serramonte, San Francisco 25 C2
Sesto San Giovanni, Milan 18 A2
Sesto Ulteriano, Milan ..... 18 B2
Setagaya-Ku, Tokyo ..... 29 B2
Seter, Oslo ..... 22 A3
Setia Budi, Jakarta ..... 13 B1
Settebagni, Rome ..... 25 A2
Settecamini, Rome ..... 25 B2
Séttimo Milanese, Milan ..... 18 B1
Settsu, Osaka ..... 22 A4
Setuny ➜, Moscow ..... 19 B2
Seutula, Helsinki ..... 12 B2
Seven Corners, Washington 32 B3
Seven Kings, London ..... 15 A4
Séveso ➜, Milan ..... 18 A1
Sevran, Paris ..... 23 A4
Sewri, Mumbai ..... 20 B2
Sforzesco, Castello, Milan ..... 18 B2
Sha Kok Mei, Hong Kong ..... 12 A2
Sha Tin, Hong Kong ..... 12 A1
Sha Tin Wai, Hong Kong ..... 12 A1
Shabrâmant, Cairo ..... 7 B2
Shahdara, Delhi ..... 10 A2
Shahe, Canton ..... 8 B2
Shahr-e Rey, Tehran ..... 30 B2
Shahrak-e Golshahr, Tehran 30 A1
Shahrak-e Qods, Tehran ..... 30 A2
Shaikh Aomar, Baghdad ..... 3 A2
Shakurbasti, Delhi ..... 10 A1
Shalkiya, Calcutta ..... 8 B1
Shamian, Canton ..... 8 B2
Shampur, Delhi ..... 10 A1
Shan Mei, Hong Kong ..... 12 A2
Shanghai, Shanghai ..... 27 B2
Shankill, Dublin ..... 11 B3
Sharp I., Hong Kong ..... 12 A2
Shastrinagar, Delhi ..... 10 A2
Shau Kei Wan, Hong Kong 12 B2
Shawocun, Beijing ..... 4 B1
Shayuan, Canton ..... 8 B2
Sheepshead Bay, New York 21 C2
Shek O, Hong Kong ..... 12 B2
Shelter I., Hong Kong ..... 12 A2
Sheng Fa Shan, Hong Kong 12 A1
Shepherds Bush, London ..... 15 A2
Shepperton, London ..... 15 B1
Sherman Oaks, Los Angeles 16 B2
Sherman Park, Chicago ..... 9 C2
Shet Bandar, Mumbai ..... 20 B2
Sheung Lau Wan,
  Hong Kong ..... 12 B2
Sheung Wan, Hong Kong ..... 12 c1
Sheva, Mumbai ..... 20 B2
Sheva Nhava, Mumbai ..... 20 B2
Shiba, Tokyo ..... 29 c4
Shibpur, Calcutta ..... 8 B1
Shibuya-Ku, Tokyo ..... 29 c1
Shijōnawate, Osaka ..... 22 A4
Shillim, Seoul ..... 26 C1
Shimogawara, Tokyo ..... 29 B1
Shimosalo, Tokyo ..... 29 B2
Shimoshakujii, Tokyo ..... 29 A2
Shinagawa-Ku, Tokyo ..... 29 B3
Shing Mun Res., Hong Kong 12 A1
Shinjuku-Ku, Tokyo ..... 29 a1
Shinjuku National Garden,
  Tokyo ..... 29 a2
Shinkoiwa, Tokyo ..... 29 A4
Shinnakano, Tokyo ..... 29 A2
Shinsa, Seoul ..... 26 B2
Shipai, Canton ..... 8 B3
Shirinashi ➜, Osaka ..... 22 B3
Shirogane ➜, Tokyo ..... 29 c3
Shiweitang, Canton ..... 8 B2
Shogunle, Lagos ..... 14 A2
Shomolu, Lagos ..... 14 A2
Shooters Hill, London ..... 15 B4
Shoreditch, London ..... 15 a5
Shortlands, London ..... 15 B4
Southall, London ..... 15 A1
Southborough, London ..... 15 B4
Southend, London ..... 15 B4
Southfields, London ..... 15 B2
Southwark, London ..... 15 B3
Søvang, Copenhagen ..... 10 B3
Soweto, Johannesburg ..... 13 B1
Sowhānak, Tehran ..... 30 A3
Soya, Tokyo ..... 29 A4
Spånga, Stockholm ..... 28 A1
Spanische Reitschule,
  Vienna ..... 31 b1
Spectacle I., Boston ..... 6 A3
Speicher-See, Munich ..... 20 A3
Speising, Vienna ..... 31 A1
Sphinx, Cairo ..... 7 B2
Spinaceto, Rome ..... 25 C1
Spit Junction, Sydney ..... 28 A2
Spořilov, Prague ..... 24 B3
Spot Pond, Boston ..... 6 A3
Spotswood, Melbourne ..... 17 B1
Spree ➜, Berlin ..... 5 A4
Spring Pond, Boston ..... 6 A3
Springbrae, Berlin ..... 5 B5
Springfield, Johannesburg ..... 13 B2
Spuistraat, Boston ..... 6 A2
Srednaya Rogatka,
  St. Petersburg ..... 26 C2
Śródmieście, Warsaw ..... 31 B2
Staaken, Berlin ..... 5 A1
Stabekk, Oslo ..... 22 A2
Stadhion, Athens ..... 2 b3
Stadhuis, Amsterdam ..... 2 b2

Stadlau, Vienna ..... 31 A2
Stadshuset, Stockholm ..... 28 b1
Stains, Paris ..... 23 A3
Stamford Hill, London ..... 15 A3
Stammersdorf, Vienna ..... 31 A2
Stanley, Hong Kong ..... 12 B2
Stanley Mound, Hong Kong 12 B2
Stanley Pen., Hong Kong ..... 12 B2
Stanmore, London ..... 15 A2
Stapleton, New York ..... 21 C1
Star Ferry, Hong Kong ..... 12 a2
Staraya Derevnya,
  St. Petersburg ..... 26 B1
Stare, Warsaw ..... 31 B1
Staré Město, Prague ..... 24 B2
Starego Miasto, Warsaw ..... 31 a2
Staten Island Zoo, New York 21 C1
Statenice, Prague ..... 24 B1
Statue Square, Hong Kong ..... 12 c1
Stedelijk Museum,
  Amsterdam ..... 2 c1
Steele Creek, Melbourne ..... 17 A1
Steenokkerzeel, Brussels ..... 6 A2
Steglitz, Berlin ..... 5 B3
Stepaside, Dublin ..... 11 B2
Stephansdom, Vienna ..... 31 b2
Stepney, London ..... 15 a5
Sterling Park, San Francisco 25 B2
Sticklinge udde, Stockholm 28 A2
Stickney, Chicago ..... 9 C2
Stillorgan, Dublin ..... 11 B2
Stockholm, Stockholm ..... 28 A2
Stocksund, Stockholm ..... 28 A2
Stoddilky, Prague ..... 24 B1
Stoke Newington, London ..... 15 A3
Stokes Valley, Wellington ..... 32 B2
Stone Canyon Res.,
  Los Angeles ..... 16 B2
Stone Park, Chicago ..... 9 B1
Stonebridge, London ..... 15 A2
Stoneham, Boston ..... 6 A3
Stony Brook Res., Boston ..... 6 B3
Stora Värtan, Stockholm ..... 28 A2
Store Hareskov, Copenhagen 10 A2
Store Magleby, Copenhagen 10 B3
Storholmen, Stockholm ..... 28 A2
Stoyka, St. Petersburg ..... 26 B1
Straiton, Edinburgh ..... 11 B2
Strand, London ..... 15 b4
Strandfontein, Cape Town ..... 8 B2
Strašnice, Prague ..... 24 B2
Strasstrudering, Munich ..... 20 B3
Stratford, London ..... 15 A4
Strathfield, Sydney ..... 28 B1
Streatham, London ..... 15 B3
Streatham Vale, London ..... 15 B3
Streberdorf, Vienna ..... 31 A2
Střešovice, Prague ..... 24 B2
Střížkov, Prague ..... 24 B2
Strogino, Moscow ..... 19 B2
Strombeek-Bever, Brussels 6 A2
Stromovka, Prague ..... 24 B2
Studio City, Los Angeles ..... 16 B2
Stureby, Stockholm ..... 28 B2
Stuvsta, Stockholm ..... 28 B2
Subhepur, Delhi ..... 10 A2
Sucat, Manila ..... 17 C2
Suchdol, Prague ..... 24 B2
Sucy-en-Brie, Paris ..... 23 B4
Sudbury, Boston ..... 6 A1
Sugamo, Tokyo ..... 29 A3
Sugar Loaf Mt. = Açúcar,
  Pão de, Rio de Janeiro ..... 24 B2
Suge, Tokyo ..... 29 B2
Suginami-Ku, Tokyo ..... 29 A2
Sugō, Tokyo ..... 29 B2
Suita, Osaka ..... 22 A4
Suitland, Washington ..... 32 B4
Sukchar, Calcutta ..... 8 A2
Suma, Osaka ..... 22 B1
Sumida ➜, Tokyo ..... 29 A3
Sumida-Ku, Tokyo ..... 29 A3
Sumiyoshi, Osaka ..... 22 B4
Summerville, Toronto ..... 30 A1
Summit, Chicago ..... 9 C2
Sunamachi, Tokyo ..... 29 B4
Sunbury-on-Thames,
  London ..... 15 B1
Sundbyberg, Stockholm ..... 28 A1
Sundbyerne, Copenhagen ..... 10 B3
Sung Kong, Hong Kong ..... 12 B2
Sungei Kadut Industrial
  Estate, Singapore ..... 27 A2
Sungei Selatar Res.,
  Singapore ..... 27 A3
Sunter, Jakarta ..... 13 A2
Sunter, Kali ➜, Jakarta ..... 13 B2
Suomenlinna, Helsinki ..... 12 C2
Supreme Court, Washington 32 b3
Sura, Calcutta ..... 8 B2
Surag-san, Seoul ..... 26 B2
Suresnes, Paris ..... 23 A2
Surfleld, Miami ..... 18 A2
Surquillo, Lima ..... 16 B2
Surrey Hills, Sydney ..... 28 B2
Susaek, Seoul ..... 26 B1
Süssenbrunn, Vienna ..... 31 A2
Sutton, Dublin ..... 11 A3
Sutton, London ..... 15 B2
Suyu, Seoul ..... 26 B2
Suzukishinden, Tokyo ..... 29 A2
Svanemøllen, Copenhagen ..... 10 A3
Sverdlov, Moscow ..... 19 B3
Svestad, Oslo ..... 22 B2
Svinö, Helsinki ..... 12 C1
Swampscott, Boston ..... 6 A4
Swanley, London ..... 15 B4
Swansea, Toronto ..... 30 B2
Swinburne I., New York ..... 21 C1
Swords, Dublin ..... 11 A2
Sydenham, Johannesburg ..... 13 A2
Sydney, Sydney ..... 28 B2
Sydney, Univ. of, Sydney ..... 28 B2
Sydney Airport, Sydney ..... 28 B1
Sydney Harbour Bridge,
  Sydney ..... 28 B2
Sydstranden, Copenhagen ..... 10 B3
Sylvania, Sydney ..... 28 C1
Syntagma, Pl., Athens ..... 2 b3
Syon Park, London ..... 15 B2
Szczęśliwice, Warsaw ..... 31 B1
Széchenyi-hegy, Budapest ..... 7 B1
Szent Istvánbaz, Budapest 7 A1
Széphalom, Budapest ..... 7 A1

## T

Tabata, Tokyo ..... 29 A3
Tablada, Buenos Aires ..... 7 C1
Table Bay, Cape Town ..... 8 A1
Table Mountain, Cape Town 8 A1
Taboão da Serra, São Paulo 26 B1
Täby, Stockholm ..... 28 A2
Tacuba, Mexico City ..... 18 B1
Tacubaya, Mexico City ..... 18 B1
Taebang, Seoul ..... 26 C1
Tagig, Manila ..... 17 B2

Tagig ↠, Manila . . . . . . 17 B2
Tai Hang, Hong Kong . . 12 A2
Tai Lo Shan, Hong Kong 12 A2
Tai Po Tsai, Hong Kong 12 A2
Tai Seng, Singapore . . . 27 A3
Tai Shui Hang, Hong Kong 12 A2
Tai Tam B., Hong Kong . 12 B2
Tai Tam Tuk Res.,
  Hong Kong . . . . . . . 12 B2
Tai Wai, Hong Kong . . . 12 A1
Tai Wan Tau, Hong Kong 12 B2
Tai Wo Hau, Hong Kong 12 A1
Tainaka, Osaka . . . . . . 22 B4
Taishō, Osaka . . . . . . . 22 B3
Taita, Wellington . . . . . 32 A2
Tajrish, Tehran . . . . . . 30 A2
Takaido, Tokyo . . . . . . 29 A1
Takaishi, Tokyo . . . . . . 22 A2
Takarazuka, Osaka . . . . 22 A2
Takasago, Osaka . . . . . 29 A4
Takatsu-Ku, Tokyo . . . . 29 B2
Takeshita, Tokyo . . . . . 29 B2
Takimegawa, Tokyo . . . 29 A3
Takoma Park, Washington 32 B3
Taksim, Istanbul . . . . . 12 B1
Talaide, Lisbon . . . . . . 14 A1
Taliganga, Calcutta . . . 8 B2
Talipapa, Manila . . . . . 17 A2
Talaght, Dublin . . . . . . 11 B1
Tallkrogen, Stockholm . 28 B2
Tama, Tokyo . . . . . . . . 29 B1
Tama ↠, Tokyo . . . . . . 29 B2
Tama Kyūryō, Tokyo . . 29 B2
Tamaden, Tokyo . . . . . 29 B2
Tamagawa-josui ↠, Tokyo 29 A1
Taman Sari, Jakarta . . . 9 A1
Tamanduateí ↠, São Paulo 26 B2
Tamboerskloof, Cape Town 8 A1
Tambora, Jakarta . . . . . 13 A1
Tammisalo, Helsinki . . . 12 B3
Tammūh, Cairo . . . . . . 7 A2
Tampines, Singapore . . . 27 A3
Tanah Abang, Jakarta . . 13 A1
Tanigami, Osaka . . . . . 22 A2
Tanjung Duren, Jakarta . 13 A1
Tanjung Priok, Jakarta . 13 A2
Tanum, Osaka . . . . . . . 22 A1
Taoranting Park, Beijing . 4 c2
Tapada, Lisbon . . . . . . 14 A1
Tapanila, Helsinki . . . . 12 B3
Tapiales, Buenos Aires . 7 C1
Tapiola, Helsinki . . . . . 12 A1
Tapsia, Calcutta . . . . . 8 B2
Tara, Mumbai . . . . . . . 20 A1
Tarabya, Istanbul . . . . 12 B2
Tarango, Presa, Mexico City 18 B1
Tårbæk, Copenhagen . . 10 A3
Tarchomin, Warsaw . . . 31 B1
Tardeo, Mumbai . . . . . 20 B1
Targówek, Warsaw . . . . 31 B2
Tårnby, Copenhagen . . 10 B3
Tarqua Bay, Lagos . . . . 14 B2
Tåstrup, Copenhagen . . 10 B1
Tatarovo, Moscow . . . . 19 B2
Tathong Channel,
  Hong Kong . . . . . . . 12 B2
Tathong Pt., Hong Kong 12 B2
Tatuapé, São Paulo . . . 26 B2
Taufkirchen, Munich . . 20 B2
Tavares, I. dos,
  Rio de Janeiro . . . . 24 A2
Távros, Athens . . . . . . 2 B2
Tawa, Wellington . . . . 32 A1
Teaneck, New York . . . 21 A1
Teatro Municipal,
  Rio de Janeiro . . . . 24 c2
Tebet, Jakarta . . . . . . 13 B2
Tecamachalco, Mexico City 18 B1
Teddington, London . . . 15 B1
Tegel, Berlin . . . . . . . 5 A2
Tegel, Flughafen, Berlin 5 A2
Tegeler See, Berlin . . . 5 A2
Tegelort, Berlin . . . . . 5 A2
Tempelhof, Berlin . . . . 5 B3
Tempelhof, Flughafen,
  Berlin . . . . . . . . . . 5 B3
Temple City, Los Angeles 16 B4
Temple Hills Park,
  Washington . . . . . . 32 C4
Temple Mount, Jerusalem 13 b3
Templeogue, Dublin . . 11 B2
Templo Mayor, Mexico City 18 B2
Tenafly, New York . . . 21 A2
Tenayuca, Piramide de,
  Mexico City . . . . . . 18 A1
Tengah ↠, Singapore . . 27 A2
Tennoji, Osaka . . . . . . 22 B4
Tepalcates, Mexico City 18 B2
Terrazpano, Milan . . . . 18 A1
Terrugem, Lisbon . . . . 14 A1
Tervuren, Brussels . . . 6 B3
Tervuren, Park van, Brussels 6 B3
Tetuán, Madrid . . . . . 17 B1
Teufelsberg, Berlin . . . 5 B2
Tévere ↠, Rome . . . . . 25 B2
Thalkirchen, Munich . . 20 B2
Thames ↠, London . . . 15 A4
Thames Ditton, London 15 B1
Thamesmead, London . 15 A4
Thana Cr. ↠, Mumbai . 20 A2
The Loop, Chicago . . . 9 B3
The Ridge, Delhi . . . . . 10 B2
The Wilds, Johannesburg 13 B2
Theater Carré, Amsterdam 2 b2
Théatro Dionissou, Athens 2 c2
Thiais, Paris . . . . . . . 23 B3
Thissío, Athens . . . . . 2 c1
Thistletown, Toronto . . 30 A1
Thomastown, Melbourne 17 A2
Thompson I., Boston . . 6 B4
Thon Buri, Bangkok . . . 3 B2
Thornbury, Melbourne . 17 A2
Thorncliffe, Toronto . . 30 A2
Thornhill, Toronto . . . 30 A2
Thornton, Cape Town . 8 A2
Thornton Heath, London 15 B3
Threipmuir Res., Edinburgh 11 B3
Throgs Neck, New York 21 B3
Thyssen Bornemisza, Museo,
  Madrid . . . . . . . . . . 17 b3
Tian'anmen Square, Beijing 4 b1
Tiancun, Beijing . . . . . 4 B1
Tianjin, Tianjin . . . . . 30 B1
Tiantan Park, Beijing . . 4 c2
Tibidabo, Barcelona . . 4 A1
Tibradden Mt., Dublin . 11 B2
Tiburon, San Francisco 25 A2
Tiburtino, Rome . . . . . 25 B2
Ticomán, Mexico City . 18 A2
Tiefersee, Berlin . . . . . 5 B1

Tiejiangyin, Beijing . . . 4 C2
Tientsin = Tianjin, Tianjin 30 B1
Tiergarten, Berlin . . . . 5 A3
Tietê ↠, São Paulo . . . 26 B2
Tigerhof, Cape Town . . 8 A2
Tigris = Nahr Dijlah ↠,
  Baghdad . . . . . . . . . 3 B2
Tijuca, Rio de Janeiro . 24 B1
Tijuca, Parque Nacional da,
  Rio de Janeiro . . . . 24 B1
Tijuca, Pico da,
  Rio de Janeiro . . . . 24 B1
Tikkurila, Helsinki . . . 12 B3
Tilak Nagar, Delhi . . . 10 B1
Tilanqiao, Shanghai . . 27 B1
Timah, Bukit, Singapore 27 A2
Times Square, New York 21 c2
Tinshryaa, Baghdad . . 3 B2
Tiu Keng Leng, Hong Kong 12 B2
Tivoli, Copenhagen . . . 10 a3
Tizapán, Mexico City . . 18 B1
Tlalnepantla ↠, Mexico City 18 A1
To Kwai Wan, Hong Kong 12 B2
Toa Payoh, Singapore . 27 A3
Tobong, Seoul . . . . . . 26 B2
Tobong-san, Seoul . . . 26 B2
Točná, Prague . . . . . . 24 C2
Toco Hills, Atlanta . . . 3 B2
Todt Hill, New York . . 21 C1
Tōkagi, Tokyo . . . . . . 29 A4
Tokai Plantation,
  Cape Town . . . . . . . 8 B1
Tōkaichiba, Tokyo . . . 29 B2
Tokarevo, Moscow . . . 19 C5
Tōkyō, Tokyo . . . . . . 29 B3
Tokyo B., Tokyo . . . . . 29 B4
Tokyo-Haneda Int. Airport,
  Tokyo . . . . . . . . . . 29 B3
Tokyo Harbour, Tokyo 29 B3
Tolka ↠, Dublin . . . . . 11 A1
Tolworth, London . . . 15 B2
Tomb of al Xun, Shanghai 27 B1
Tomb of the Kings,
  Jerusalem . . . . . . . . 13 a2
Tomba di Nerone, Rome 25 B1
Tomilino, Moscow . . . 19 C5
Tondo, Manila . . . . . . 17 B1
Tongbinggo, Seoul . . . 26 B1
Tongjak, Seoul . . . . . . 26 B1
Tongnaemeung, Seoul . 26 B2
Tonggiao, Shanghai . . 27 A1
Toorak, Melbourne . . . 17 B2
Topkapı, Istanbul . . . . 12 B1
Tor di Quinto, Rome . . 25 B1
Tor Pignattara, Rome . 25 B2
Tor Sapienza, Rome . . 25 B2
Toranomon, Tokyo . . . 29 c3
Torcy, Paris . . . . . . . 23 A4
Toronto, Toronto . . . . 30 B2
Toronto, Univ. of, Toronto 30 B2
Toronto Harbour, Toronto 30 B2
Toronto I., Toronto . . . 30 B2
Toronto Int. Airport,
  Toronto . . . . . . . . . 30 A1
Toros Las Arenas, Pl. de,
  Barcelona . . . . . . . . 4 c1
Toros Monumental, Templo
  de, Barcelona . . . . . 4 a3
Torre Latino-americana,
  Mexico City . . . . . . 18 b2
Torre Lupara, Rome . . 25 B2
Torre Nova, Rome . . . 25 B2
Torrellas ↠, Barcelona 4 A1
Torrevecchia, Rome . . 25 B1
Toshimae-Ku, Tokyo . 29 A3
Toshimaen, Tokyo . . . 29 A3
Tottenham, London . . 15 A3
Tottenham, Melbourne 17 A1
Tour Eiffel, Paris . . . . 23 c2
Toussus-le-Noble, Paris 23 B3
Toussus-le-Noble,
  Aérodrome de, Paris 23 B1
Tower Bridge, London . 15 b5
Tower Hamlets, London 15 A3
Tower of London, London 15 b5
Towra Pt., Sydney . . . 28 C2
Tøyen, Oslo . . . . . . . 22 A3
Toyonaka, Osaka . . . . 22 A3
Trafalgar Square, London 15 b4
Trafaria, Lisbon . . . . . 14 A1
Traição, Cor. ↠, São Paulo 26 B2
Tranegilde, Copenhagen 10 B2
Trångsund, Stockholm 28 B2
Transamerica Pyramid,
  San Francisco . . . . . 25 b2
Transbay Terminal,
  San Francisco . . . . . 25 b3
Trappenfelde, Berlin . 5 A4
Trastévere, Rome . . . . 25 B1
Treasure I., San Francisco 25 B2
Třebohradice, Prague . 24 C1
Třebotov, Prague . . . . 24 C1
Tremblay-en-France, Paris 23 A4
Tremembe ↠, São Paulo 26 A2
Tremont, New York . . 21 A2
Trenno, Milan . . . . . . 18 A1
Treptow, Berlin . . . . . 5 B3
Trés Rios, Sa. dos,
  Rio de Janeiro . . . . 24 B1
Trevi, Fontana di, Rome 25 b3
Trezzano sul Navíglio, Milan 18 B1
Tribune Tower, Chicago 9 b2
Trieste, Rome . . . . . . 25 B2
Trinidad, Washington . 32 B4
Trinity, Madrid . . . . . 23 B3
Trinity College, Dublin 11 c3
Trionfale, Rome . . . . . 25 B1
Triulzo, Milan . . . . . . 18 B2
Trocadero, Paris . . . . 23 b1
Troitse-Lykovo, Moscow 19 B2
Troja, Prague . . . . . . 24 B2
Trollbäcken, Stockholm 28 B2
Trombay, Mumbai . . . 20 A2
Troparevo, Moscow . . 19 C2
Tropenmuseum, Amsterdam 2 b3
Trudyashchikhsya, Ostrov,
  St. Petersburg . . . . 26 B1
Tryvasshøgda, Oslo . . 22 A2
Tseng Lan Shue, Hong Kong 12 A2
Tsim Sha Tsui, Hong Kong 12 B1
Tsing Yi, Hong Kong . . 12 A1
Tsova, Jerusalem . . . . 13 B1
Tsuchiura, Tokyo . . . . 29 A4
Tsuen Wan, Hong Kong 12 A1
Tsukiji, Tokyo . . . . . . 29 c5
Tsur Hadassa, Jerusalem 13 B2
Tsurumi, Tokyo . . . . . 29 B3
Tsz Wan Shan, Hong Kong 12 A2
Tuas, Singapore . . . . . 27 B1
Tučkomêřice, Prague . 24 B1
Tuckahoe, New York . 21 A3
Tucuruvi, São Paulo . . 26 A2
Tufello, Rome . . . . . . 25 B2
Tufnell Park, London . 15 A3
Tughlakabad, Delhi . . 10 B2
Tuileries, Jardin des, Paris 23 b3
Tuindorp Oostzaan,
  Amsterdam . . . . . . . 2 A2

Tullamarine, Melbourne 17 A1
Tulse Hill, London . . . 15 B3
Tung Lung I., Hong Kong 12 B2
Tung O, Hong Kong . . 12 B1
Tunis, Baghdad . . . . . 3 A2
Tuomarila, Helsinki . . 12 B1
Tugça, Stockholm . . . 28 A1
Turffontein, Johannesburg 13 B2
Turkso, Prague . . . . . 24 B1
Turnham Green, London 15 B2
Turnhouse, Edinburgh 11 B1
Tuscolana, Via, Rome . 25 B2
Tushino, Moscow . . . . 19 A2
Twelve Peaks, Cape Town 8 A1
Twickenham, London . 15 B1
Twickenham Rugby Ground,
  London . . . . . . . . . . 15 B1
Twin Peaks, San Francisco 25 B2
Two Rock Mt., Dublin . 11 B2
Tymon North, Dublin . 11 B1
Tysons Corner, Washington 32 B2

**U**

U.S. Capitol, Washington 32 b3
Ubeidiya, Jerusalem . . 13 B2
Uberaba ↠, São Paulo 26 A1
Ubin, P., Singapore . . . 27 A3
Uccle, Brussels . . . . . 6 B2
Udelnaya, St. Petersburg 26 A2
Udelnoe, St. Petersburg 26 A2
Uddling, Munich . . . . 20 A1
Ueno, Tokyo . . . . . . . 29 b5
Úholičky, Prague . . . . 24 B1
Uhříněves, Prague . . . 24 B3
Üjpalota, Budapest . . . 7 A2
Üjpest, Budapest . . . . 7 A2
Ukita, Tokyo . . . . . . . 29 A4
Ullerup, Copenhagen . 10 B3
Ulleval, Oslo . . . . . . . 22 A3
Ulriksdal, Stockholm . 28 A1
Um Al-Khanazir Island,
  Baghdad . . . . . . . . . 3 B2
Umeda, Osaka . . . . . . 22 A3
Umerkhadi, Mumbai . . 20 B2
Ümraniye, Istanbul . . 12 B2
Underground Atlanta,
  Atlanta . . . . . . . . . 3 B2
Unetický potok ↠, Prague 24 B1
Ongam, Seoul . . . . . . 26 B2
Unhos, Lisbon . . . . . . 14 A2
Unidad Santa Fe,
  Mexico City . . . . . . 18 B1
Union City, New York . 21 B1
Union Port, New York 21 B2
Union Square, New York 21 d2
Union Station, San Francisco 25 B2
United Nations H.Q.,
  New York . . . . . . . . 21 c3
Universidad, Madrid . . 17 B1
Universidad de Chile,
  Santiago . . . . . . . . 26 B2
University Park, Washington 32 B4
Unnye, Seoul . . . . . . 26 B1
Unter den Linden, Berlin 5 a4
Unterbiberg, Munich . 20 B2
Unterföhring, Munich . 20 A3
Unterhaching, Munich . 20 B2
Unterlaa, Vienna . . . . 31 B2
Untermenzing, Munich 20 A1
Upper East Side, New York 21 b3
Upper Elmers End, London 15 B3
Upper New York B.,
  New York . . . . . . . . 21 C1
Upper Norwood, London 15 B3
Upper Peirce Res.,
  Singapore . . . . . . . . 27 A2
Upper Sydenham, London 15 B3
Upper Tooting, London 15 B3
Upper West Side, New York 21 a2
Upton, London . . . . . . 15 A4
Uptown, Chicago . . . . 9 B2
Uran, Mumbai . . . . . . 20 B2
Urayasu, Tokyo . . . . . 29 B4
Urbe, Aeroporto d', Rome 25 B2
Urca, Rio de Janeiro . . 24 B1
Uritsk, St. Petersburg . 26 C1
Örön, Budapest . . . . . 7 A2
Ursus, Warsaw . . . . . 31 B1
Ursvik, Stockholm . . . 28 A1
Usera, Madrid . . . . . . 17 B1
Ushigome, Tokyo . . . . 29 A3
Usina, Rio de Janeiro . 24 B1
Üsküdar, Istanbul . . . . 12 B2
Ust-Slavyanka,
  St. Petersburg . . . . 26 C3
Uteke, Stockholm . . . 28 A1
Utrata, Warsaw . . . . . 31 B2
Uttarpara, Calcutta . . 8 A1
Uttersley Mose, Copenhagen 10 A2

**V**

Vadaul, Mumbai . . . . 20 A2
Vaires-sur-Marne, Paris 23 A4
Valby, Copenhagen . . 10 B3
Valcannuta, Rome . . . 25 B1
Valdelatas, Madrid . . 17 A1
Valdemoro, Madrid . . 25 B1
Valenton, Paris . . . . . 23 B3
Valera, Milan . . . . . . 18 A1
Vallcarca, Barcelona . . 4 A1
Valldoreix, Barcelona . 4 A1
Vallecas, Madrid . . . . 17 B2
Vallensbæk, Copenhagen 10 B2
Vallensbæk Strand,
  Copenhagen . . . . . . 10 B2
Valentunasjön, Stockholm 28 A2
Vällentunsjö, Stockholm 28 A2
Vallisaari, Helsinki . . . 12 C3
Valldvidrera, Barcelona 4 A1
Valvidrera ↠, Barcelona 4 A1
Van Gogh-museum,
  Amsterdam . . . . . . . 2 c1
Vanak, Tehran . . . . . 30 A2
Vanegde, Copenhagen 10 A3
Vanikoy, Istanbul . . . 12 B2
Vantaa ↠, Helsinki . . . 12 B2
Vantaa, Helsinki . . . . 12 B2
Vantaankoski, Helsinki 12 B2
Vantaanpuisto, Helsinki 12 B2
Vanves, Paris . . . . . . 23 B2
Varkiza, Athens . . . . 2 B2
Varsinzhábad, Budapest 7 b2
Vártiosaari, Helsinki . . 12 B3
Vanamuseet, Stockholm 28 B2
Vasco, Cape Town . . . 8 A2
Vasfanárd, Tehran . . . 30 A2
Vashi, Mumbai . . . . . 20 A2

Vasilyevsky, Ostrov,
  St. Petersburg . . . . 26 B1
Vaso Regulador El Cristo,
  Mexico City . . . . . . 18 B1
Vaucluse, Sydney . . . . 28 B2
Vaucresson, Paris . . . 23 A1
Vauhallan, Paris . . . . 23 B2
Vaujours, Paris . . . . . 23 A4
Vauxhall, London . . . 15 c4
Vecsés, Budapest . . . . 7 B3
Veleň, Prague . . . . . . 24 A3
Veleslavin, Prague . . . 24 B2
Vélizy-Villacoublay, Paris 23 B2
Velka-Chuchle, Prague 24 B2
Velké Přílepy, Prague . 24 B1
Venda Seca, Lisbon . . 14 A1
Venetian Islands, Miami 18 B2
Venezia, Palazzo, Rome 25 c2
Venice, Los Angeles . . 16 C2
Ventas, Madrid . . . . . 17 B1
Ventorro del Cano, Madrid 17 B1
Venustiano Carranza,
  Mexico City . . . . . . 18 B2
Verde ↠, São Paulo . . 26 A1
Verdi, Athens . . . . . . 2 A2
Verdun, Montreal . . . 19 B2
Vérhalom, Budapest . 7 A2
Vermelho ↠, São Paulo 26 B1
Vernon, Los Angeles . 16 C3
Verrières-le-Buisson, Paris 23 B2
Versailles, Buenos Aires 7 B1
Versailles, Paris . . . . . 23 B1
Veshnyaki, Moscow . . 19 B4
Vesolyy Posolok,
  St. Petersburg . . . . 26 B2
Vestra, Helsinki . . . . . 12 B1
Vestskoven, Copenhagen 10 A2
Vicálvaro, Madrid . . . 17 B2
Vicente Lopez, Buenos Aires 7 B2
Vigário, Madrid . . . . . 17 B2
Vicenza, Buenos Aires 7 B2
Victoria, London . . . . 15 c3
Victoria, Mt., Wellington 32 B1
Victoria, Pont, Montreal 19 B2
Victoria and Albert
  Waterfront, Cape Town 8 a1
Victoria Gardens, Mumbai 20 B2
Victoria Harbour,
  Hong Kong . . . . . . . 12 B1
Victoria Island, Lagos . 14 B2
Victoria L., Johannesburg 13 B2
Victoria Lawn Tennis
  Courts, Melbourne . 17 B1
Victoria Park, Singapore 27 B2
Victoria Peak, Hong Kong 12 B1
Victoria Wharf, Cape Town 8 a1
Vienna = Wien, Vienna 31 A2
Vienna, Washington . . 32 B2
View Park, Los Angeles 16 B3
Vigário Geral,
  Rio de Janeiro . . . . 24 A1
Vigeyland, Oslo . . . . . 22 A3
Vigghofen, Stockholm 28 A2
Vighignolo, Milan . . . 18 B1
Viikki, Helsinki . . . . . 12 B2
Vikhroli, Mumbai . . . 20 A2
Vila Guilherme, São Paulo 26 B2
Vila Isabel, Rio de Janeiro 24 B1
Vila Jaguára, São Paulo 26 B1
Vila Madalena, São Paulo 26 B1
Vila Mariana, São Paulo 26 B2
Vila Maria, São Paulo . 26 B2
Vila Prudente, São Paulo 26 B2
Viladecans, Barcelona . 4 B1
Vile Parle, Mumbai . . 20 A2
Villa Adelina, Buenos Aires 7 B1
Villa Ballester, Buenos Aires 7 B1
Villa Barilari, Buenos Aires 7 C2
Villa Borghese, Rome . 25 a3
Villa Bosch, Buenos Aires 7 B1
Villa C. Colon, Buenos Aires 7 C2
Villa Ciudadela,
  Buenos Aires . . . . . 7 B1
Villa de Guadalupe,
  Mexico City . . . . . . 18 B2
Villa Devoto, Buenos Aires 7 B1
Villa Diamante,
  Buenos Aires . . . . . 7 C2
Villa Dominico,
  Buenos Aires . . . . . 7 C3
Villa Lugano, Buenos Aires 7 C1
Villa Lynch, Buenos Aires 7 B1
Villa Madero, Buenos Aires 7 C1
Villa Sáenz Pena,
  Buenos Aires . . . . . 7 B1
Villa Urquiza, Buenos Aires 7 B1
Villaverde, Madrid . . . 17 B1
Villaverde Bajo, Madrid 17 B1
Ville-d'Avray, Paris . . 23 B2
Villecresnes, Paris . . . 23 B4
Villejuif, Paris . . . . . 23 B3
Villemomble, Paris . . 23 A4
Villeneuve-la-Garenne, Paris 23 A3
Villeneuve-le-Roi, Paris 23 B3
Villeneuve-St.-Georges,
  Paris . . . . . . . . . . . 23 B3
Villeparisis, Paris . . . 23 A4
Villevaudé, Paris . . . . 23 A4
Villiers-le-Bâcle, Paris 23 B1
Villiers-sur-Marne, Paris 23 B4
Vilinki, Helsinki . . . . 12 C3
Vilrosei, Canale, Milan 18 A1
Vilvoorde, Brussels . . 6 A2
Vimodrone, Milan . . . 18 A2
Vimont, Montreal . . . 19 A1
Vinanmek Palace, Bangkok 3 B2
Vincennes, Paris . . . . 23 A3
Vincennes, Bois de, Paris 23 A3
Vinings, Atlanta . . . . 3 A2
Vinohrady, Prague . . . 24 B2
Vinoř, Prague . . . . . . 24 B3
Violet Hill, Hong Kong 12 B2
Virányos, Budapest . . 7 A1
Virgen del San Cristóbal,
  Santiago . . . . . . . . . 26 B2
Virginia Gardens, Miami 18 B1
Virginia Key, Miami . . 18 B2
Viroflay, Paris . . . . . 23 B2
Viron, Athens . . . . . . 2 B2
Virum, Copenhagen . . 10 A2
Vishnyaki, Moscow . . 19 B5
Visitacion Valley,
  San Francisco . . . . . 25 B2
Vista Alegre, Lima . . . 16 B3
Vista Alegre, Santiago 26 C1
Vista Grove, Atlanta . 3 B2
Vitacura, Santiago . . . 26 B2
Vitinia, Rome . . . . . . 25 C1
Vitry-sur-Seine, Paris 23 B3
Vizandinó, Moussío, Athens 19 A3
Vladykino, Moscow . . 19 A3
Vlezenbeek, Brussels . 6 B1
Vltava ↠, Prague . . . . 24 A2
Vnukovo, Prague . . . . 19 C2
Vokovice, Prague . . . . 24 B1
Vogelsdorf, Berlin . . . 5 B5
Volhonka-Zil, Moscow 19 C3
Vollen, Oslo . . . . . . . 22 B2
Volodarskoye, St. Petersburg 26 B2
Volynkina-Derevnya,
  St. Petersburg . . . . 26 B1
Vondelpark, Amsterdam 2 B2

Vösendorf, Vienna . . . 31 B2
Vostochnyy, Moscow . 19 B5
Voula, Athens . . . . . . 2 C2
Vouliagmeni, Athens . 2 C2
Vredehoek, Cape Town 8 A1
Vršovice, Prague . . . . 24 B2
Vyborgskaya Storona,
  St. Petersburg . . . . 26 B2
Výkhino, Moscow . . . 19 B4
Vyšehrad, Prague . . . 24 B2

**W**

Wachterhof, Munich . 20 B3
Wadala, Mumbai . . . . 20 A2
Wadestown, Wellington 32 B1
Wadi Fukin, Jerusalem 13 B1
Wah Fu, Hong Kong . . 12 B1
Wahda, Baghdad . . . . 3 B2
Währing, Vienna . . . . 31 A2
Waidmannslust, Berlin 5 A3
Wainuiomata, Wellington 32 B2
Wainuiomata R. ↠,
  Wellington . . . . . . . 32 B2
Wakefield, Boston . . . 6 A3
Waldesruh, Berlin . . . 5 B4
Waldperlach, Munich . 20 B3
Waldtrudering, Munich 20 B3
Waldstown, Dublin . . 11 B1
Wall Street, New York 21 f1
Waltham, Boston . . . . 6 A2
Waltham Forest, London 15 A3
Walthamstow, London 15 A3
Walton on Thames, London 15 B1
Wambeek, Brussels . . 6 A1
Wan Chai, Hong Kong 12 B2
Wan Chai Lanes,
  Hong Kong . . . . . . . 12 c2
Wandsworth, London 15 B2
Wankhede Stadium,
  Mumbai . . . . . . . . . 20 c2
Wannsee, Berlin . . . . 5 B1
Wansdorf, Berlin . . . . 5 A1
Wapping, London . . . 15 A3
Ward, Dublin . . . . . . 11 A1
Ward I., Wellington . . 32 B1
Warnberg, Munich . . . 20 B2
Warrāq el 'Arab, Cairo 7 A2
Warrāq el Hadr, Cairo 7 A2
Warrington Park, Melbourne 17 A1
Warrisoew, Edinburgh 11 B2
Warsaw = Warszawa,
  Warsaw . . . . . . . . . 31 B2
Warszawa, Warsaw . . 31 B2
Wartenberg, Berlin . . 5 A4
Washington, Washington 32 B3
Washington Heights,
  New York . . . . . . . . 21 A2
Washington Monument,
  Washington . . . . . . 32 b1
Washington Nat. Airport,
  Washington . . . . . . 32 B3
Washington Park, Chicago 9 C3
Wat Arun, Bangkok . . 3 B2
Wat Pho, Bangkok . . . 3 b1
Wat Phra Keo, Bangkok 3 b1
Wat Traimit, Bangkok . 3 c2
Water of Leith, Edinburgh 11 B1
Water Tower Place, Chicago 9 a2
Watergraafsmeer,
  Amsterdam . . . . . . . 2 B2
Waterland, Amsterdam 2 A2
Waterloo, Brussels . . . 6 B2
Waterloo, Wellington . 32 B2
Waterloo International,
  London . . . . . . . . . . 15 b4
Watermael-Boitsfort,
  Brussels . . . . . . . . . 6 B2
Watertown, Boston . . 6 A2
Watsonia, Melbourne . 17 A2
Waverley, Boston . . . . 6 A2
Waverley, Johannesburg 13 A2
Waverley, Sydney . . . 28 B2
Waverley Station, Edinburgh 11 b3
Wawer, Warsaw . . . . 31 B2
Wawrzyszew, Warsaw 31 B1
Wayland, Boston . . . . 6 A1
Wazirabad, Delhi . . . . 10 A2
Wazir'pur, Delhi . . . . 10 A2
Wealdstone, London . 15 A1
Wedding, Berlin . . . . 5 A3
Weehawken, New York 21 B1
Weesp, Amsterdam . . 2 B3
Weidling, Vienna . . . . 31 A1
Weidlingbach, Vienna 31 A1
Weigongcun, Beijing . 4 B1
Weijin He ↠, Tianjin . 30 B2
Weissensee, Berlin . . . 5 A3
Welkom, Johannesburg 13 A1
Wellesley, Boston . . . 6 B2
Wellesley Falls, Boston 6 B2
Wellesley Hills, Boston 6 B2
Welling, London . . . . 15 B4
Wellington, London . . 15 B4
Wellington, Wellington 32 B1
Wells Fargo Center,
  Los Angeles . . . . . . 16 b1
Weltevreden Park,
  Johannesburg . . . . . 13 A1
Wembley, London . . . 15 A2
Wemmel, Brussels . . . 6 A1
Wemmer Pan, Johannesburg 13 B2
Wenceslas Square, Prague 24 b2
Wenchengshan, Berlin 5 A4
Wenhangong, Tianjin . 30 B2
Wennington, London . 15 A5
Wenshan, Shanghai . . 27 B1
West Bedford, Boston 6 A1
West Concord, Boston 6 A1
West Don ↠, Toronto . 30 A2
West Drayton, London 15 B1
West Ham, London . . 15 A4
West Harrow, London 15 A2
West Heath, London . 15 B4
West Hill, Toronto . . . 30 A3
West Hollywood,
  Los Angeles . . . . . . 16 B2
West Kensington, London 15 c1
West Lamma Channel,
  Hong Kong . . . . . . . 12 B1
West Lynn, Boston . . 6 A4
West Medford, Boston 6 A3
West Miami, Miami . . 18 B1
West Molesey, London 15 B1
West New York, New York 21 B1
West of Twin Peaks,
  San Francisco . . . . . 25 B2
West Park, Johannesburg 13 A1
West Rouge, Toronto . 30 A4
West Roxbury, Boston 6 B3
West Springfield,
  Washington . . . . . . 32 C2
West Town, Chicago . 9 B2
West Wharf, Karachi . 14 B1
Westbourne Green, London 15 b1
Westchester, Washington 32 B2

Westchester, Los Angeles 16 C2
Westcliff, Johannesburg 13 B2
Westdene, Johannesburg 13 B2
Westend, Helsinki . . . 12 C1
Western Addition,
  San Francisco . . . . . 25 B2
Western Wall, Jerusalem 13 b3
Westgate, Washington 32 B3
Westlake, Cape Town 8 B1
Westlake, San Francisco 25 B2
Westminster, London 15 A3
Westmount, Montreal 19 B2
Weston, Boston . . . . . 6 A1
Weston, Toronto . . . . 30 A1
Weston Res., Boston . 6 A2
Westwood Village,
  Los Angeles . . . . . . 16 B2
Westzaan, Amsterdam 2 A1
Wetton, Cape Town . . 8 B2
Wexford, Toronto . . . 30 A3
Weybridge, London . . 15 B1
Wezembeek-Oppem,
  Brussels . . . . . . . . . 6 A2
White House, The,
  Washington . . . . . . 32 b1
Whitechapel, London 15 A3
Whitehall, Dublin . . . 11 A2
Whitehall, London . . . 15 b4
Whittier, Los Angeles 16 C4
Whitton, London . . . . 15 B1
Wieden, Vienna . . . . 31 B2
Wien, Vienna . . . . . . 31 A2
Wien-Schwechat, Flughafen,
  Vienna . . . . . . . . . . 31 B3
Wienerberg, Vienna . . 31 B2
Wierzbno, Warsaw . . 31 B2
Wijde Wormer, Amsterdam 2 A2
Wilanów, Warsaw . . . 31 B2
Wilanówka ↠, Warsaw 31 C2
Wilhelmshagen, Berlin 5 B5
Wilket Creek Park, Toronto 30 A2
Wilkiesdon, Toronto . 30 A2
Willesden, London . . . 15 A2
Willesden Green, London 15 A2
Williamsbridge, New York 21 A3
Williamsburg, New York 21 B2
Williamstown, Melbourne 17 B1
Willoughby, Sydney . . 28 A2
Willow Springs, Chicago 9 C1
Willowdale, Toronto . 30 A2
Willmersdorf, Berlin . 9 c1
Wilmette, Chicago . . . 9 A2
Wilmington, London . 15 B5
Wilshire Boulevard,
  Los Angeles . . . . . . 16 c1
Wimbledon, London . 15 B2
Wimbledon Common,
  London . . . . . . . . . . 15 B2
Wimbledon Park, London 15 B2
Wimbledon Tennis Ground,
  London . . . . . . . . . . 15 B2
Winchester, Boston . . 6 A3
Windermere, Cape Town 8 A3
Windsor, Johannesburg 13 A1
Windsor Hills, Los Angeles 16 C2
Windy Arbour, Dublin 11 B2
Winning, Munich . . . . 20 B2
Winthrop, Boston . . . 6 A4
Wissous, Paris . . . . . 23 B3
Wittenau, Berlin . . . . 5 A2
Witwatersrand, Univ. of,
  Johannesburg . . . . . 13 B2
Włochy, Warsaw . . . . 31 B1
Wo Mei, Hong Kong . 12 A2
Wo Yi Hop, Hong Kong 12 A1
Woburn, Boston . . . . 6 A3
Woburn, Toronto . . . 30 A3
Woduk Pluit, Jakarta . 13 A1
Wola, Warsaw . . . . . . 31 B1
Wolf Trap Farm Park,
  Washington . . . . . . 32 B2
Wolica, Warsaw . . . . . 31 C1
Wolica, Warsaw . . . . . 31 B2
Wólka Węglowa, Warsaw 31 B1
Wollaston, Boston . . . 6 B4
Woltersdorf, Berlin . . 5 B5
Woluwe-Saint-Lambert,
  Brussels . . . . . . . . . 6 A2
Woluwe-Saint-Pierre,
  Brussels . . . . . . . . . 6 A2
Wong Chuk Hang,
  Hong Kong . . . . . . . 12 B2
Wong Chuk Wan,
  Hong Kong . . . . . . . 12 A2
Wong Chuk Yeung,
  Hong Kong . . . . . . . 12 A2
Wong Tai Sin, Hong Kong 12 A2
Wood Green, London 15 A3
Wood Ridge, New York 21 A1
Woodbridge, Toronto . 30 A1
Woodford, Boston . . . 6 A4
Woodford Bridge, London 15 A4
Woodford Green, London 15 A4
Woodhaven, New York 21 B2
Woodhouselee, Edinburgh 11 B2
Woodlands New York,
  New York . . . . . . . . 21 e1
Woodmont, Washington 32 B3
Woodside, London . . . 15 B3
Woodside, New York 21 B2
Woodstock, Cape Town 8 A1
Woollahra, Sydney . . . 28 B2
Woolloomooloo, Sydney 28 b2
Woolooware B., Sydney 28 C2
Woolooware New York, 18 B4
Woolworth Building,
  New York . . . . . . . . 21 e1
World Trade Center, site of
  former, New York . . 21 e1
Worli, Mumbai . . . . . 20 A1
Worth, Chicago . . . . . 9 C2
Wren's Nest, Atlanta . 3 C2
Wrightington, Berlin . 5 B3
Wujiaochang, Shanghai 27 B2
Würm ↠, Munich . . . 20 A1
Würm-kanal, Munich . 20 A1
Wusong, Shanghai . . . 27 A2
Wyczółki, Warsaw . . . 31 C1
Wygoda, Warsaw . . . . 31 B2
Wynberg, Cape Town 8 B1

**X**

Xabregas, Lisbon . . . . 14 A2
Xiangang = Hong Kong,
  Hong Kong . . . . . . . 12 B1
Xiaodian, Tianjin . . . . 30 A2
Xiaogang Park, Canton 8 B2
Xiaoping, Canton . . . . 8 B2
Xiasha chong, Canton . 8 B2
Xichang, Canton . . . . 8 B2
Xicheng, Beijing . . . . 4 B1
Xidan, Beijing . . . . . . 4 B1

Xigu Park, Tianjin . . . 30 A2
Xigucun, Tianjin . . . . 30 A2
Ximenwai, Tianjin . . . 30 B1
Xinanlou, Tianjin . . . 30 B2
Xinkai He ↠, Tianjin . 30 B2
Xizhimen, Beijing . . . 4 B1
Xu Beihong Mem. Hall,
  Beijing . . . . . . . . . . 4 a1
Xuanwu, Beijing . . . . 4 B1
Xuhui, Shanghai . . . . 27 B1

**Y**

Yaba, Lagos . . . . . . . 14 A2
Yaftābād, Tehran . . . 30 B2
Yahara, Tokyo . . . . . 29 A2
Yaho, Tokyo . . . . . . 29 A1
Yakire, Tokyo . . . . . 29 A4
Yamada, Osaka . . . . 22 A3
Yamada, Tokyo . . . . 29 B2
Yamamoto, Osaka . . 22 B4
Yamato ↠, Osaka . . 22 B4
Yamuna ↠, Delhi . . . 10 B2
Yan Kit, Singapore . . 27 A3
Yanbu, Canton . . . . 8 B1
Yangch'ŏn, Seoul . . . 26 B1
Yanghuayuan, Beijing 4 C1
Yangjae, Seoul . . . . . 26 C1
Yangjizhuang, Shanghai 27 A1
Yangpu, Shanghai . . 27 B2
Yangpu Park, Shanghai 27 B2
Yao, Osaka . . . . . . . 22 B4
Yao Airport, Osaka . . 22 B4
Yarmūk, Baghdad . . 3 B1
Yarra ↠, Melbourne . 17 A2
Yarra Bend Park, Melbourne 17 A2
Yarraville, Melbourne 17 A1
Yau Tong, Hong Kong 12 A2
Yauza ↠, Moscow . . 19 A4
Yeading, London . . . 15 A1
Yedikule, Istanbul . . 12 C1
Yemin Moshe, Jerusalem 13 b2
Yenikapı, Istanbul . . 12 C1
Yenıköy, Istanbul . . . 12 B2
Yerba Buena Gardens,
  San Francisco . . . . 25 c2
Yerba Buena I.,
  San Francisco . . . . 25 B2
Yerres, Paris . . . . . . 23 B4
Yerushalayim = Jerusalem,
  Jerusalem . . . . . . . 13 B2
Yiheyuan, Beijing . . . 4 A1
Yinhangzhen, Shanghai 27 A2
Yishun New Town,
  Singapore . . . . . . . . 27 A3
Yixingbu, Tianjin . . . 30 A2
Ylästö, Helsinki . . . . 12 B2
Yodo ↠, Osaka . . . . 22 A3
Yongdingman, Beijing 4 B2
Yongdeng, Seoul . . . 26 B2
Yŏngdŭngp'o, Seoul . 26 B1
Yongfucun, Canton . . 8 B2
Yongjing, Shanghai . 27 B2
Yongsan, Seoul . . . . 26 B1
Yonkers, New York . 21 A2
York, Toronto . . . . . 30 A2
York Mills, Toronto . 30 A2
Yotsuya, Tokyo . . . . 29 b4
Yo'annem, Beijing . . 4 B1
Yŏŭido, Seoul . . . . . 26 B1
Youndsfield, Cape Town 8 B1
Yuanxiatian, Canton . 8 B2
Yugo-Zarad, Moscow 19 B3
Yung Shue Wan, Hong Kong 12 B1
Yūsofābād, Tehran . . 30 A2
Yuyuantan Park, Beijing 4 b2

**Z**

Zaandam, Amsterdam 2 A1
Zaandijk, Amsterdam 2 A1
Zaanstad, Amsterdam 2 A1
Zábehlice, Prague . . . 24 B2
Zacisze, Warsaw . . . . 31 B2
Zahrā, Baghdad . . . . 3 A1
Zahrakovo, Moscow . 19 B1
Zalov, Prague . . . . . . 24 A1
Zabuski, Warsaw . . . 31 C1
Zamdorf, Munich . . . 20 B2
Zamek Królewski, Warsaw 31 a2
Zamek Ujazdowski, Warsaw 31 c3
Zanevka, St. Petersburg 26 B2
Záppeio, Athens . . . . 2 c2
Zarechye, Moscow . . 19 B2
Zaventem, Brussels . . 6 A2
Zawady, Warsaw . . . . 31 B2
Zāwiyat Abū Musallam,
  Cairo . . . . . . . . . . . 7 B1
Zawrā' Park, Baghdad 3 B2
Zbraslav, Prague . . . . 24 C2
Zbuzany, Prague . . . . 24 B1
Zdiby, Prague . . . . . . 24 A2
Zehlendorf, Berlin . . . 5 B2
Zenne ↠, Brussels . . 6 B1
Zerań, Warsaw . . . . . 31 B2
Zerzeń, Warsaw . . . . 31 B2
Zeytinburnu, Istanbul 12 C1
Zhabei, Shanghai . . . 27 B1
Zhangguizhuang, Tianjin 30 B2
Zhdanov, Moscow . . 19 B6
Zhelznodorozhnyy,
  Moscow . . . . . . . . . 19 B6
Zhenru, Shanghai . . . 27 B1
Zhernovka, St. Petersburg 26 B2
Zhicun, Canton . . . . 8 B2
Zhongshan Park, Shanghai 27 B1
Zhongshan Park, Shanghai 27 b1
Zhoujiadu, Shanghai . 27 B2
Zhoujiazhen, Shanghai 27 A1
Zhu Jiang ↠, Canton . 8 B2
Zhulebino, Moscow . 19 B5
Zhuoshadi, Canton . . 8 A3
Zielona, Warsaw . . . . 31 B1
Ziya He ↠, Tianjin . . 30 A1
Žižkov, Prague . . . . . 24 B2
Zócalo, Mexico City . 18 b3
Zografos, Athens . . . 2 B2
Zoliborz, Warsaw . . . 31 B1
Zonnebloem, Cape Town 8 a1
Zoo, London . . . . . . . 4 a1
Zugliget, Budapest . . 7 A2
Zugló, Budapest . . . . 7 A2
Zundert, . . .
Zwanenburg, Amsterdam 2 A2
Zwölfaxing, Vienna . . 31 B3
Zyuzino, Moscow . . . 19 C3

# WORLD
# MAPS

---

## SETTLEMENTS

■ **PARIS**    ◉ **Rotterdam**    ⊚ **Livorno**    ⊚ Brugge    ⊙ Exeter    ∘ *Torremolinos*    ∘ *Oberammergau*    ∘ *Thira*

Settlement symbols and type styles vary according to the scale of each map and indicate the importance
of towns on the map rather than specific population figures

| ● *Vaduz* Capital cities have red infills | ∴ Ruins or archaeological sites |
|---|---|
| ⬠ Urban agglomerations | ˅ Wells in desert |

## ADMINISTRATION

| ——— International boundaries | ········· Internal boundaries | **PERU** Country names |
|---|---|---|
| – – – · International boundaries (undefined or disputed) | ⬡ National parks | KENT Administrative area names |

International boundaries show the *de facto* situation where there are rival claims to territory

## COMMUNICATIONS

| Motorways, freeways and expressways | —— Principal railways | ᴸᴴᴿ ✈ Principal airports |
|---|---|---|
| ——— Principal roads | – – – Railways under construction | ✈ Other airports |
| —— Other roads | —— Other railways | ········· Principal canals |
| +--+ Road tunnels | +--+ Railway tunnels | ≍ Passes |

## PHYSICAL FEATURES

| ～ Perennial streams | ◌ Intermittent lakes | ▲ 8850 Elevations in metres |
|---|---|---|
| – – Intermittent streams | ◌ Swamps and marshes | ▾ 8500 Sea depths in metres |
| ◯ Perennial lakes | ▨ Permanent ice and glaciers | *1134* Height of lake surface above sea level in metres |

## ELEVATION AND DEPTH TINTS

Height of land above sea level        Land below sea level        Depth of sea

| in metres | 6000 | 4000 | 3000 | 2000 | 1500 | 1000 | 400 | 200 | 0 | | | | | | in feet |
| in feet | 18 000 | 12 000 | 9000 | 6000 | 4500 | 3000 | 1200 | 600 | | 6000 | 12 000 | 15 000 | 18 000 | 24 000 | in feet |
| | | | | | | | | | 0 | 200 | 2000 | 4000 | 5000 | 6000 | 8000 | in metres |

Some of the maps have different contours to highlight and clarify the principal relief features

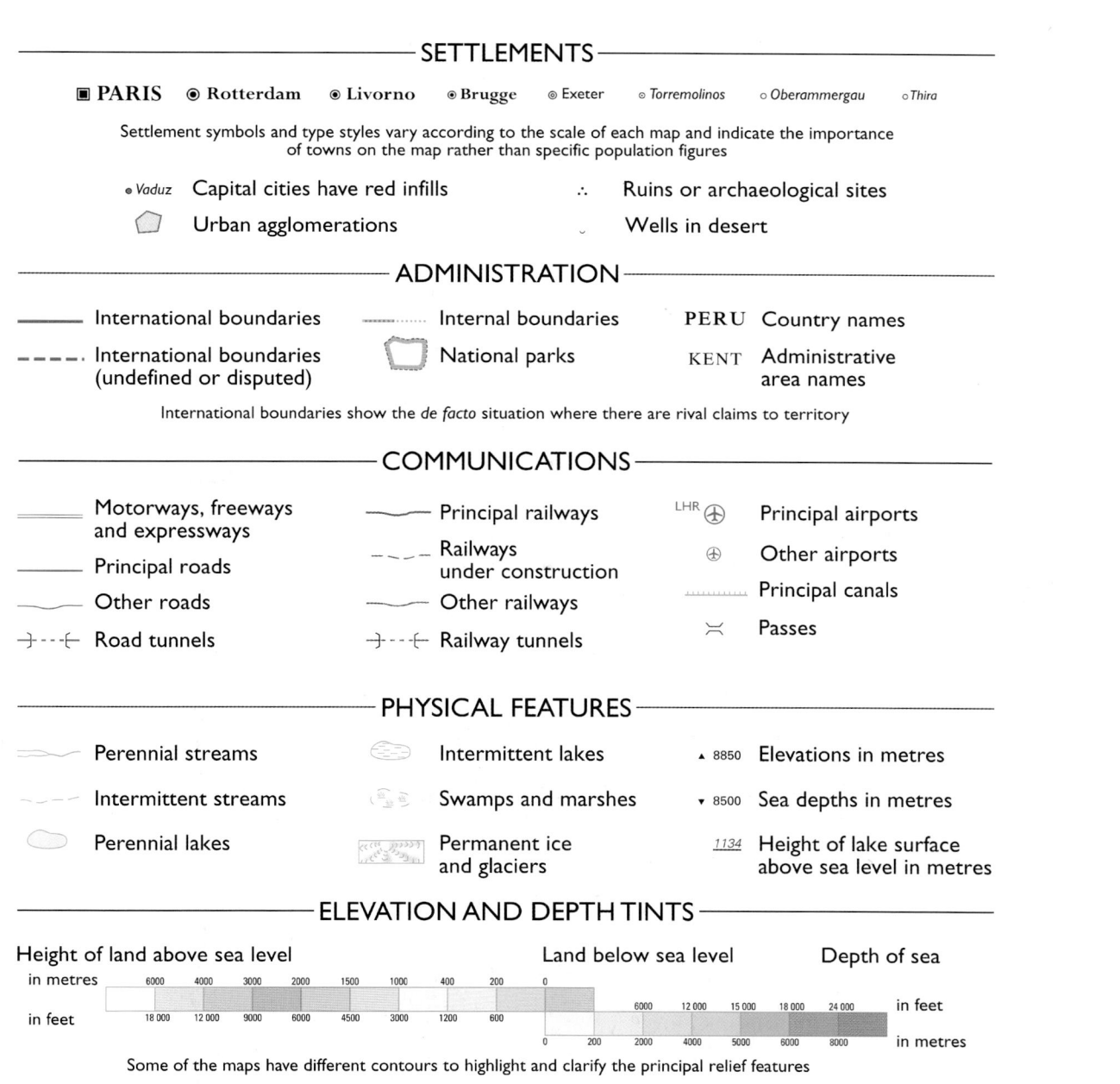

Projection : Hammer Equal Area

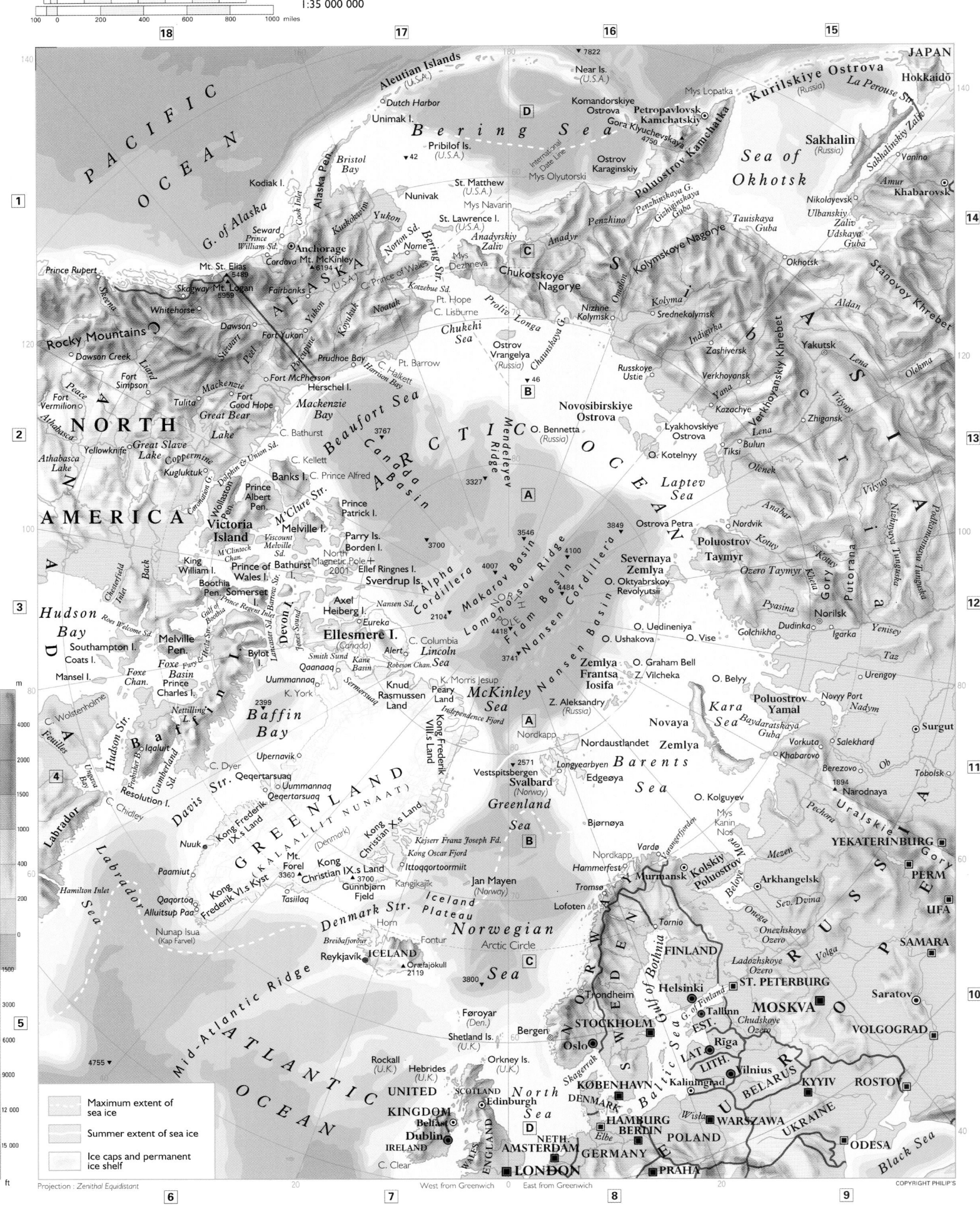

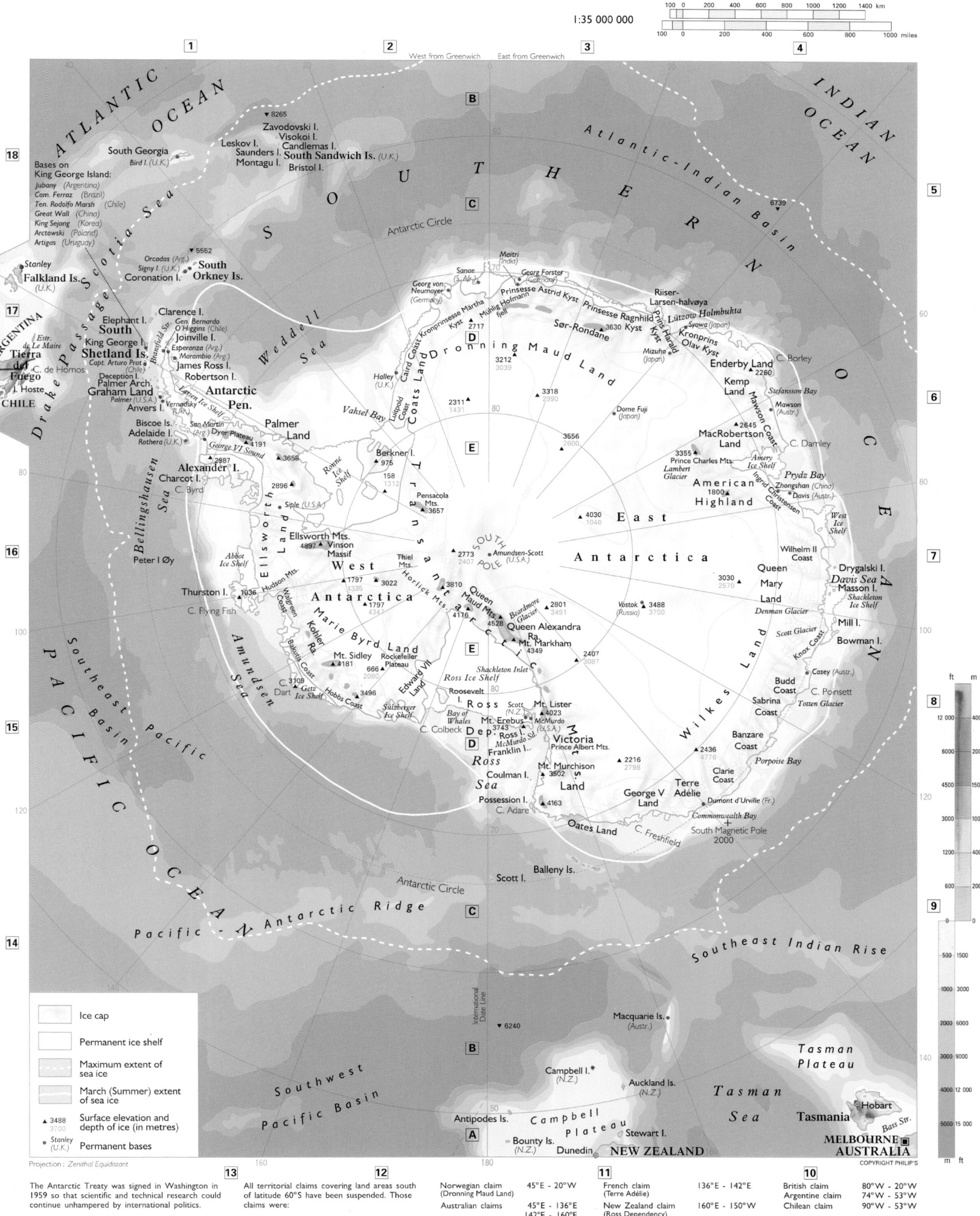

1:35 000 000

100 0 200 400 600 800 1000 1200 1400 km
100 0 200 400 600 800 1000 miles

1 2 West from Greenwich | East from Greenwich 3 4

**ATLANTIC OCEAN**

**INDIAN OCEAN**

18

Bases on
King George Island:
Jubany (Argentina)
Com. Ferraz (Brazil)
Ten. Rodolfo Marsh (Chile)
Great Wall (China)
King Sejong (Korea)
Arctowski (Poland)
Artigas (Uruguay)

Atlantic-Indian Basin

▲ 8265

Zavodovski I.
Visokoi I.
Leskov I.  Candlemas I.
Saunders I.  **South Sandwich Is.** (U.K.)
Montagu I.  Bristol I.

▲ 6739

5

South Georgia
Bird I. (U.K.)

B

C

**S O U T H E R N**

Antarctic Circle

▼ 5552

17

Stanley
**Falkland Is.**
(U.K.)

Orcadas (Arg.)
Signy I. (U.K.)  **South**
Coronation I.  **Orkney Is.**

Sanae
(S. Afr.)  Maitri
(India)  Georg Forster
(Germany)

Riiser-
Larsen-halvøya

ARGENTINA

Clarence I.
Elephant I.
**South**  Gen. Bernardo
**Shetland Is.**  O'Higgins (Chile)
King George I.
Joinville I.
Esperanza (Arg.)
Capt. Arturo Prat (Chile)  Marambio (Arg.)
James Ross I.
Robertson I.

Georg von
Neumayer
(Germany)  Prinsesse Astrid Kyst
Kronprinsesse Märtha
Kyst  Prinsesse Ragnhild
Kyst  Lützow Holmbukta
Syowa (Japan)
Kronprins
Olav Kyst

C. Borley

6

Tierra
del
Fuego
I. Hoste
CHILE

C. de Hornos

Mühlig
Hofmann
Fjell  2717

**Dronning Maud Land**  3630
Prins Harald
Kyst  Mizuho
(Japan)

Enderby Land  C. Borley
Kemp
Land  Stefansson Bay

**Antarctic
Pen.**
Graham Land
Palmer (U.S.A.)
Anvers I.
Vernadsky (U.K.)

**Weddell
Sea**

Halley
(U.K.)

Coats Land

Caird Coast

3212
3039

Dome Fuji
(Japan)

3318
2990

3556
2600

MacRobertson
Land  Mawson
(Austr.)  ▲ 2645

Prince Charles Mts.  ▲ 3355
Lambert
Glacier  Amery
Ice Shelf

16

Biscoe Is.
Adelaide I.
Rothera (U.K.)

San Martín
(Arg.)  Dyer Plateau

**Palmer
Land**  4191

Vahsel Bay  2311
1431

American
Highland  1800
Davis (Austr.)  Prydz Bay
Zhongshan (China)
Ingrid
Christensen
Coast

West
Ice
Shelf

**Bellingshausen
Sea**

Alexander I.
Charcot I.  C. Byrd

2987
3658

**Ronne
Ice Shelf**

Berkner I.  975
158  1312

4030
1040  **East**

**Antarctica**

Queen
Mary
Land  Drygalski I.
Davis Sea
Masson I.  Wilhelm II
Coast

2896

Pensacola
Mts.
3657

Transantarctic

3030
2570

Shackleton
Ice Shelf

7

Peter I Øy

**Ellsworth
Land**

Ellsworth Mts.
4897  Vinson
Massif

2773
2407  South
Pole  Amundsen-Scott
(U.S.A.)

Vostok ▲ 3488
(Russia)  3700

Mill I.

Thurston I.  1036

**West**
1797  3022
**Antarctica**  4335

Thiel
Mts.  3810

Queen  Horlick Mts.
Maud Mts.
4176  4528  Beardmore
Glacier  2801
3491

2407
3087

Knox Coast  Bowman I.

C. Flying Fish

Hudson Mts.

Marie Byrd Land

Kohler
Ra.

Mt. Sidley
4181  Rockefeller
Plateau  666
2080

Queen Alexandra
Ra.  ▲ Mt. Markham
4349

Budd
Coast  Casey (Austr.)

Sabrina
Coast  C. Poinsett
Totten Glacier

15

**Amundsen
Sea**

Walgreen
Coast  Getz
Ice Shelf  C. 3109
Dart  Sulzberger
Ice Shelf  Edward VII
Land  3496  Roosevelt
I.

**Ross Ice Shelf**

Shackleton Inlet

Scott  Mt. Lister
4023  Mt. Erebus
3743  McMurdo
(U.S.A.)

2216
2798

Porpoise Bay

**Banzare
Coast**  2436
4776

Clarie
Coast

**Southeast
Pacific
Basin**

Bakutis Coast

Hobbs Coast  Bay of
Whales  Ross
I.  McMurdo Sd.
Franklin I.

Victoria
Prince Albert Mts.
Mt. Murchison
3502

George V
Land  Terre
Adélie  Dumont d'Urville (Fr.)

**Ross
Sea**

C. Colbeck  **Dep.**

Coulman I.

Land  Commonwealth Bay
+  South Magnetic Pole
2000

**PACIFIC
OCEAN**

Possession I.
C. Adare  4163

Oates Land  C. Freshfield

8

Pacific - Antarctic Ridge

Antarctic Circle

Scott I.

Balleny Is.

9

**Southeast Indian Rise**

14

Pacific
Basin

International Date Line

▼ 6240

Macquarie Is.
(Austr.)

**Tasman
Plateau**

**Southwest
Pacific Basin**

Campbell I.
(N.Z.)  Auckland Is.
(N.Z.)

**Tasman**

**Sea**  **Tasmania**  Hobart

Projection: Zenithal Equidistant

Antipodes Is.  Campbell
Plateau  Stewart I.

Bounty Is.
(N.Z.)  Dunedin  **NEW ZEALAND**

**MELBOURNE
AUSTRALIA**

COPYRIGHT PHILIP'S

**Legend:**

Ice cap

Permanent ice shelf

Maximum extent of
sea ice

March (Summer) extent
of sea ice

▲ 3488
3700  Surface elevation and
depth of ice (in metres)

•  Stanley
(U.K.)  Permanent bases

ft  m

12 000  4000

3000

4500  1500

9000  2000

3000  1000

1200  400

600  200

0  0

500  1500

1000  3000

2000  6000

3000  9000

4000  12 000

5000  15 000

m  ft

The Antarctic Treaty was signed in Washington in
1959 so that scientific and technical research could
continue unhampered by international politics.

All territorial claims covering land areas south
of latitude 60°S have been suspended. Those
claims were:

Norwegian claim  45°E - 20°W
(Dronning Maud Land)

Australian claims  45°E - 136°E
142°E - 160°E

French claim  136°E - 142°E
(Terre Adélie)

New Zealand claim  160°E - 150°W
(Ross Dependency)

British claim  80°W - 20°W

Argentine claim  74°W - 53°W

Chilean claim  90°W - 53°W

100   0   100  200  300  400  500  600  700  800 km

1:20 000 000

100   0   100   200   300   400   500 miles

COPYRIGHT PHILIP'S

Ural Mountains

Ob

Caspian Sea

Caspian Depression

Obtschi Syrt

Ural

Kara

Elbruz
5642

Caucasus

Aras

L. Urmia

L. Van

Tigris

Mesopotamia

Euphrates

Pechora

Kama

Volga

Volga Hts.

Volga

Terek

Kizlyar

Pontine Mts.

Ararat
5165

Küçük Dağı
3770

Kurdistan

N. Dvina

Mezen

Don

Donets
Basin

Tsimlyansk
Res.

Donets

Manych

Sea of
Azov

Str. of Kerch

Armenia

Keyal Irmak

Taurus Mts.

Anatolia
(Asia Minor)

Pechora

Kanin
Pen.

Kola
Pen.

White
Sea

Onega

L. Onega

Rybinsk
Res.

Volga

Oka

Central Russian Uplands

Dnieper

Ukraine

Bug

Crimea

Black Sea
2211

Danube

Bosporus

Sea of
Marmara

Mt. Ida
1766

Dardanelles

Cyprus

North Cape

Nordkinn

Lapland

Imari

Torne

Ume

Indals

Kebnekaise
2117

Scandinavia

Vesterålen

Lofoten

Glittertind
2469

Scandinavia

Finland

L. Ladoga

European
Plain

Shield

W. Dvina

Pripet

Dniester

Prut

Carpathians

Transylvanian Alps

Wallachia

Balkans

Rhodope

Olympus
2917

Aegean
Sea

Rhodes

Crete

L. Tuz

Norwegian
Sea

Aland

G. of Finland

Baltic

Sea

Gotland

Öland

Bornholm

Niemen

Oder

Sudeten

Tatra
2665

Plain of
Hungary

Tisza

Danube Gorge

Drava

Sava

Dinaric Alps

Pindus

Str. of Otranto

Ionian Is.

Morea

C. Matapan

Ionian
Sea

4070

North
Sea

Vänern

Vättern

Mälaren

Kattegat

Skagerrak

Jutland

Elbe

Harz

Bohemian Forest

Moravian
Hts.

Erzgebirge

Adriatic Sea

Apennines

Gran Sasso
2914

d'Italia

Vesuvius

Tyrrhenian
Sea

Str. of Messina

Etna
3340

Sicily

Malta

Mediterranean
Sea

SOUTH UTSIRE

NORTH UTSIRE

VIKING

FISHER

GERMAN
BIGHT

Heligoland

Weser

Jura

Black Forest

Rhine

Vosges

Hunsrück

Ardennes

Meuse

Rhône

Mont Blanc
4807

Alps

St. Gotthard

Po

Tiber

Ligurian
Sea

Corsica

Str. of Bonifacio

Sardinia

C. Bon

Pantelleria

FORTIES

DOGGER
15

HUMBER

THAMES

TYNE

CROMARTY

FORTH

DOVER

WIGHT

Shetland Is.

FAIR ISLE

Orkney

HEBRIDES

Hebrides

Great Britain

Thames

Seine

Loire

Massif

Central

Cévennes

G. of Lions

Pyrenees

Pic de Aneto
3404

New
Castile

Balearic Is.

Minorca

Majorca

Ibiza

Andalusia

Sierra Morena

Plateau of the Shotts

Africa

FITZROY

BAILEY

Arctic Circle

Iceland

Hekla
1491

Öraefajökull
2119

SOUTH EAST
ICELAND

Faeroe Is.

FAEROES

FAIR ISLE

Bear Nevis
1343

Snowdon
1086

SOLE

LUNDY

PLYMOUTH

FASTNET

British
Isles

Ireland

Irish Sea

Celtic
Sea

Land's End

English Channel

Channel Is.

Ushant

Brittany

Garonne

Gironde

Ebro

Old
Castile

Cantabrian Mts.

Iberian

Peninsula

Pico de Aneto

Duero

Serra da Estrela

Tagus

Guadalquivir

Guadiana

Sierra Nevada
3478

Str. of Gibraltar

C. de São
Vicente

C. da
Roca

C. Finisterre

Bay of
Biscay

BISCAY

ATLANTIC

OCEAN

Rockall

C. Clear

SHANNON

ROCKALL

2061

Norwegian
Sea

West from Greenwich   East from Greenwich

Projection Bonne

m
5000
4000
3000
2000
1000
400
200
0

ft
15 000
12 000
6000
3000
1200
600
0
200 - 600

ft
12 000
6000
3000
1000
0

m
4000
2000
1000

1:20 000 000

100  0  100  200  300  400  500  600  700  800 km
100  0  100  200  300  400  500 miles

COPYRIGHT PHILIP'S

Projection: Bonne

■ LONDON  Capital Cities
■ MALTA (Tas)

ATLANTIC OCEAN

Norwegian Sea

White Sea

ICELAND
Reykjavik

Arctic Circle

NORWAY
SWEDEN
FINLAND
Gulf of Bothnia
Baltic Sea

Murmansk
Hammerfest
Tromsø
Narvik
Kiruna
Bergen
Stavanger
Trondheim
Oslo
Bodø
Luleå
Vaasa
Tampere
Turku
Helsinki
Uppsala
Stockholm
Örebro
Göteborg
Jönköping
Gävle
Malmö
Gotland

L. Ladoga
L. Onega
N. Dvina

RUSSIA
Moscow
St. Petersburg
Arkhangelsk
Vologda
Yaroslavl
Nizhniy Novgorod
Kazan
Samara
Saratov
Penza
Tula
Orel
Kursk
Voronezh
Tambov
Simbirsk
Kostroma
Ivanovo
Kirov
Smolensk
Volgograd
Astrakhan
Rostov
Krasnodar
Stavropol
Sevastopol
Ob
Ural
Volga
Don

KAZAKHSTAN
Caspian Sea
Makhachkala
Baku
AZERBAIJAN
ARMENIA
Yerevan
GEORGIA
Tbilisi

ESTONIA
Tallinn
LATVIA
Riga
LITHUANIA
Vilnius
Kaunas
Kaliningrad

BELARUS
Minsk
Vitebsk
Mahilyow
Homel
Brest

UKRAINE
Kiev
Kharkov
Donetsk
Dnepropetrovsk
Zaporozhye
Odessa
Lvov
Chernobyl
Zhytomyr
Nikolayev
Kherson
Dniepr
Crimea

POLAND
Warsaw
Gdańsk
Szczecin
Poznań
Łódź
Wrocław
Kraków
Katowice
Bydgoszcz
Białystok
Lublin
Vistula
Oder

DENMARK
Copenhagen
Århus
Ålborg
Kattegat
Skagerrak
Kiel

GERMANY
Berlin
Hamburg
Bremen
Hannover
Cologne
Dortmund
Essen
Frankfurt am Main
Munich
Stuttgart
Leipzig
Dresden
Magdeburg
Nuremberg
Chemnitz
Halle
Bonn
Elbe
Rhine

NETHERLANDS
Amsterdam
The Hague
Rotterdam
BELGIUM
Brussels
Antwerp
LUX.
Luxembourg

UNITED KINGDOM
ENGLAND
London
Birmingham
Manchester
Liverpool
Leeds
Sheffield
Newcastle-upon-Tyne
Bristol
Southampton
Plymouth
SCOTLAND
Edinburgh
Glasgow
Aberdeen
Dundee
WALES
Cardiff
IRELAND
Dublin
Belfast
Cork
Shetland Is.
Orkney Is.
Hebrides
Faroe Is. (Den.)

English Channel
North Sea
Bay of Biscay

FRANCE
Paris
Lyons
Marseilles
Bordeaux
Toulouse
Nantes
Strasbourg
Nice
Lille
Rouen
Le Havre
Dijon
Brest
Rennes
St-Étienne
Grenoble
Toulon
Limoges
Loire
Seine
Rhône
Garonne
MONACO

SWITZERLAND
Zürich
Geneva
Bern
LIECH.
AUSTRIA
Vienna
Linz
Salzburg
Innsbruck
Graz

CZECH REP.
Prague
SLOVAK REP.
Bratislava
HUNGARY
Budapest
Debrecen
Miskolc

SLOVENIA
Ljubljana
CROATIA
Zagreb
BOSNIA-HERZ.
Sarajevo
SERBIA & MONTENEGRO
Belgrade
Niš
MACEDONIA
Skopje
ALBANIA
Tirana

ROMANIA
Bucharest
Cluj-Napoca
Timişoara
Braşov
Galaţi
Ploieşti
Constanţa
MOLDOVA
Kishinev
Danube

BULGARIA
Sofia
Plovdiv
Varna

GREECE
Athens
Thessaloníki
Pátrai
Corfu
Crete
Rhodes
Aegean Sea
Ionian Sea

ITALY
Rome
Milan
Naples
Turin
Genoa
Florence
Bologna
Venice
Palermo
Messina
Catania
Bari
Taranto
Cagliari
Sardinia
Sicily
Corsica
SAN MARINO
Tiber
Adriatic Sea
Tyrrhenian Sea
MALTA
Valletta

SPAIN
Madrid
Barcelona
Valencia
Sevilla
Zaragoza
Málaga
Murcia
Bilbao
Valladolid
Córdoba
Granada
Alicante
La Coruña
Vigo
Gibraltar (U.K.)
Ceuta
Melilla
Balearic Is.
Minorca
Majorca
Ibiza
Ebro
Guadiana
ANDORRA
Andorra-la-Vella

PORTUGAL
Lisbon
Porto
Tagus
Douro

Mediterranean Sea

Africa
MOROCCO
ALGERIA
TUNISIA
Tangier
Oran
Algiers
Annaba
Constantine
Tunis
Pantelleria

TURKEY
Istanbul
Ankara
İzmir
Bursa
Konya
Antalya
Adana
Kayseri
Samsun
Erzurum
Diyarbakır
Bosporus

SYRIA
Aleppo
IRAQ
Baghdad
Tigris
Euphrates

IRAN
Tabriz

CYPRUS
Nicosia

Black Sea

East from Greenwich
West from Greenwich

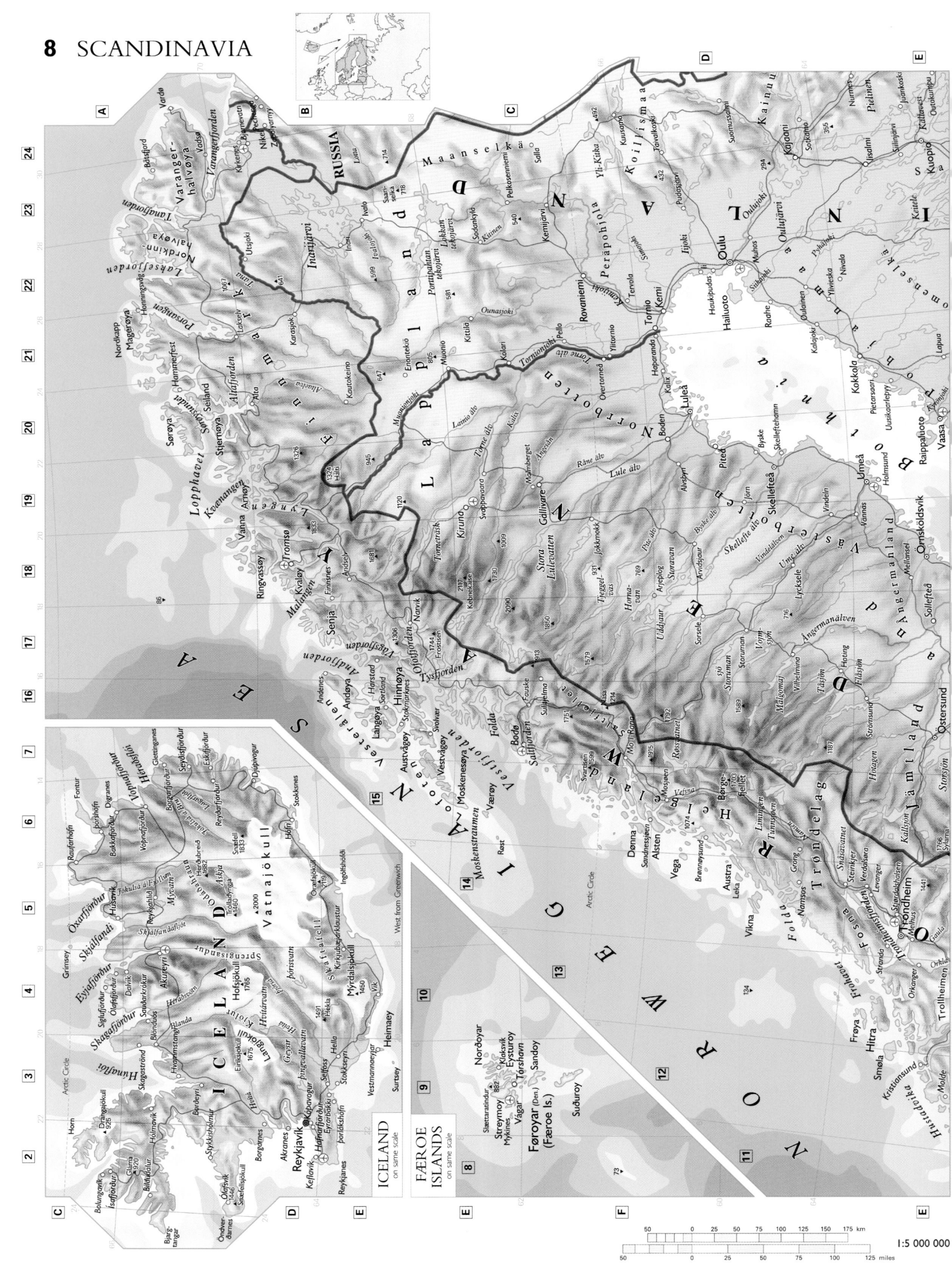

ICELAND
on same scale

FAEROE
ISLANDS
on same scale

1:5 000 000

East from Greenwich

Projection: Conical with two standard parallels

1:2 000 000

10 0 10 20 30 40 50 60 70 80 km
10 0 10 20 30 40 50 miles

**ATLANTIC OCEAN**

**SCOTLAND**
Mull of Oa
Kintyre
Brodick
Arran
Firth of Clyde
Campbeltown
Mull of Kintyre
Ailsa Craig
Cairnryan
Stranraer
L. Ryan
Portpatrick

Inishtrahull
Malin Hd.
Malin Pen.
Tory I.
Horn Hd.
Sheep Haven
Mulroy B.
Fanad Hd.
Lough Swilly
Carndonagh
Moville
Inishowen Pen.
Giants Causeway
Rathlin I.
Fair Hd.
Ballycastle
Bloody Foreland
Gweedore
Errigal 752
Derryveagh Mts.
The Rosses
GLENVEAGH
Rathmelton
Buncrana
Portstewart
Portrush
Mts. of Antrim
Coleraine
L. Foyle
Limavady
Ballymoney 554
GLENARIFF
Trostan
Garron Pt.
North Channel

Aran I.
Inishfree B.
Crohy Hd.
883
Letterkenny
DONEGAL
Glenties
Lifford
Strabane
Sion Mills
Newtownstewart
Sawel Mt. 683
Sperrin Mts.
Magherafelt
Moneymore
Cookstown
Randalstown
Ballyclare
ANTRIM
Larne
269
Carrickfergus
Roe
Bann
Dawros Hd.
Loughros More B.
Gweebarra B.
Rossan Pt.
601
Killybegs
Slieve League
St. John's Pt.
Donegal
676
Lavagh More
Castlederg
ULSTER
TYRONE
Omagh
Coalisland
Dungannon
Aughnacloy
Lough Neagh
Antrim
Belfast L.
Belfast
Comber
Bangor
Donaghadee
Newtownards
Ards Pen.
Strangford L.

Downpatrick Hd.
Killala B.
Ballyshannon
Bundoran
Erne
Lower L. Erne
Enniskillen
Irvinestown
Dromore
FERMANAGH
Upper Erne
Clones
MONAGHAN
Monaghan
Keady
Middletown
ARMAGH
Armagh
Portadown
Lagan
Banbridge
Tandragee
Lurgan
Craigavon
DOWN
Ballynahinch
Downpatrick
Ballyquintin Pt.
St. John's Pt.
Dundrum B.
Newcastle
852 Slieve Donard
Mourne Mts.
577 Slieve Gullion
Warrenpoint
Kilkeel
Greenore
Carlingford L.

Donegal Bay
Sligo Bay
Sligo
Dromore West
544
Colloney
SLIGO
L. Arrow
LEITRIM
Leitrim
L. Allen
Belturbet
Annalee
Cootehill
Clones
Newry
Mourne
380
Erris Hd.
Mullet Pen.
Inishkea North
Inishkea South
Blacksod Bay
Broad Haven
Belmullet
Ballina
Killala
Moy
Slieve Gamph
Ballymote
Charlestown
Boyle
Carrick-on-Shannon
CAVAN
L. Gowna
L. Sheelin
Cavan
Carrickmacross
Kingscourt
Ceanannus Mor (Kells)
Oldcastle
Blackwater
LOUTH
Louth
Ardee
Dunleer
Clogher Hd.
Dundalk Bay
Dundalk

Achill Hd.
672
Achill I.
Corraun Pen.
Nephin 806
L. Conn
Newport
Clew Bay
Clare I.
Westport
765 Croagh Patrick
819 Mweelrea
Inishturk
Killary Harbour
Inishbofin
Inishshark
Castlebar
MAYO
Swinford
Knock
Ballyhaunis
Claremorris
Ballinrobe
ROSCOMMON
Castlerea
Ballaghaderreen
Castlepollard
LONGFORD
Longford
Roscommon
Granard
Mullingar
MEATH
Trim
An Uaimh (Navan)
Boyne
Athboy
Drogheda
Balbriggan
Rush
Lambay I.

CONNACHT
Connemara
CONNEMARA
Clifden
Slyne Hd.
Bertraghboy B.
Kilkieran B.
Lough Mask
Lough Corrib
Tuam
Oughterard
GALWAY
Galway
Athenry
Loughrea
Ballinasloe
Suck
Athlone
Clara
WESTMEATH
Moate
Tullamore
OFFALY
Edenderry
Grand Canal
Daingean
Bog of Allen
KILDARE
Kildare
Naas
Maynooth
Royal Canal
LEINSTER
Liffey
Swords
Malahide
DUBLIN
Dublin
Dun Laoghaire
Howth Hd.

**IRELAND**
Lough Ree
Lough Derg
Slieve Aughty
368
Gort
Portumna
Shannon
Birr
Roscrea
Slieve Bloom
529 Arderin
Mountmellick
Portarlington
Port Laoise
Mountrath
LAOIS
Abbeyleix
Monasterevin
Droichead Nua
Kippure 754
Poulaphouca Res.
WICKLOW
Wicklow Mts.
926 Lugnaquillia
Rathdrum
Wicklow Hd.
Bray
Greystones
Clondalkin
123

Galway Bay
Aran Is.
Inishmore
Inishmaan
Inisheer
Black Hd.
Cliffs of Moher
BURREN
Hags Hd.
Liscannor Bay
Ennistimon
Mal Bay
Mutton I.
Milltown Malbay
CLARE
Ennis
Tulla
Sixmilebridge
Killaloe
Nenagh
Templemore
Thurles
Durrow
Carlow
Tullow
Muine Bheag
Shillelagh
Arklow
Aughrim
Avoca
Gorey
Mizen Hd.

Loop Hd.
Kilkee
Kilrush
Shannon Airport
Limerick
LIMERICK
Foynes
694 Keeper Hill
TIPPERARY
Golden Vale
Tipperary
KILKENNY
Kilkenny
Callan
796 Mt. Leinster
WEXFORD
Enniscorthy
Cahore Pt.

Mouth of the Shannon
Ballybunion
Kerry Hd.
Listowel
Newcastle West
Rathkeale
Kilfinnane
Rath Luirc
Galtymore 920
Galty Mts.
Cashel
Caher
Slievenaman 722
Clonmel
Carrick-on-Suir
Nore
Suir
Barrow
New Ross
Wexford Harbour
Rosslare
Rosslare Harbour
Greenore Pt.
Carnsore Pt.

Tralee B.
Brandon B.
Smerwick Harbour
953 Brandon Mt.
Slieve Mish 853
Dingle
Tralee
Maine
Newmarket
Kanturk
Buttevant
Mitchelstown
Fermoy
Blackwater
Knockmealdown Mts. 795
Comeragh Mts. 792
WATERFORD
Lismore
Dungarvan
Waterford
Tramore
Waterford Harbour
Hook Hd.
Tramore B.
Dungarvan Harbour

Great Blasket I.
Dunmore Hd.
Inishvickillane
Dingle Bay
KERRY
Killorglin
Killarney
Lough Leane
1041 Carrauntoohill
MACGILLYCUDDY'S REEKS
Macgillycuddy's Reeks
707 Caha Mts.
Kenmare
KILLARNEY
Boggeragh Mts. 646
CORK
Macroom
Blarney
Mallow
Cork
Midleton
Cobh
Crosshaven
Cork Harbour
Youghal
Youghal B.

Valencia I.
Puffin I.
Great Skellig
Ballinskelligs B.
Cahirciveen
Kenmare River
Glengarriff
Bantry
Scariff I.
Dursey I.
Crow Hd.
Castletown Bearhaven
Bear I.
686 Caha Mts.
Bantry Bay
Dunmanway
Bandon
Clonakilty
Kinsale
Old Head of Kinsale
Lee
Passage West
Skull
Baltimore
Sherkin I.
Skibbereen
Clonakilty B.
Galley Hd.
Dunmanus B.
Mizen Hd.
Long I.
C. Clear
Clear I.
Fastnet Rock

**CELTIC SEA**

**IRISH SEA**

**St. George's Channel**

**WALES**
St. David's Hd.
St. David's
St. Brides Bay
115

ft m
1500 500
600 200
300 100
0 0
50 150
100 300
200 600
500 1500
1000 3000
2000 6000
m ft

Projection: Lambert's Conformal Conic
West from Greenwich
COPYRIGHT PHILIP'S

☐ National Parks

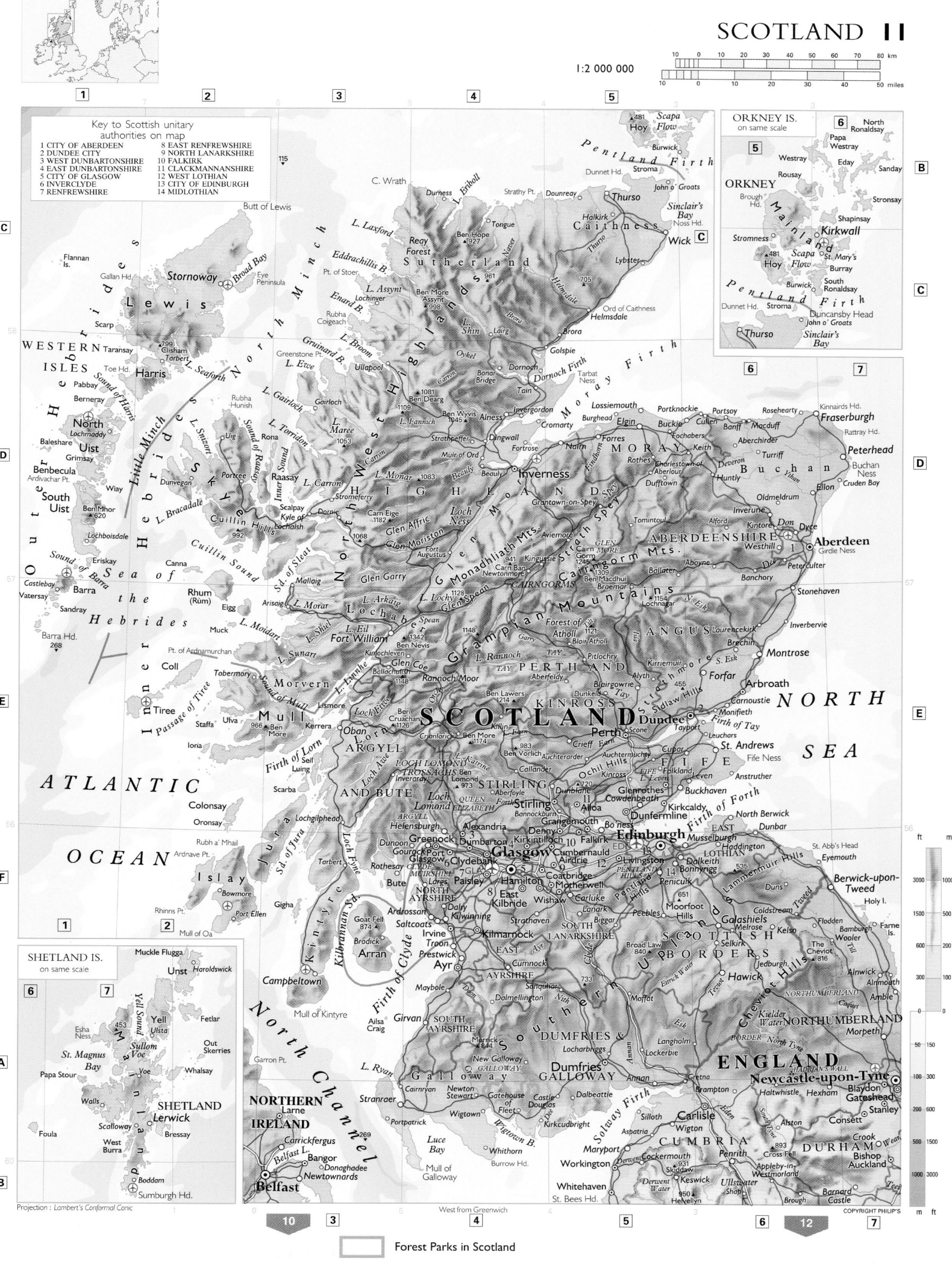

1:2 000 000

Key to Scottish unitary authorities on map
1 CITY OF ABERDEEN
2 DUNDEE CITY
3 WEST DUNBARTONSHIRE
4 EAST DUNBARTONSHIRE
5 CITY OF GLASGOW
6 INVERCLYDE
7 RENFREWSHIRE
8 EAST RENFREWSHIRE
9 NORTH LANARKSHIRE
10 FALKIRK
11 CLACKMANNANSHIRE
12 WEST LOTHIAN
13 CITY OF EDINBURGH
14 MIDLOTHIAN

ORKNEY IS.
on same scale

SHETLAND IS.
on same scale

Projection : Lambert's Conformal Conic

West from Greenwich

COPYRIGHT PHILIP'S

Forest Parks in Scotland

# ENGLAND AND WALES

10 0 10 20 30 40 50 60 70 80 km

10 0 10 20 30 40 50 miles

1:2 000 000

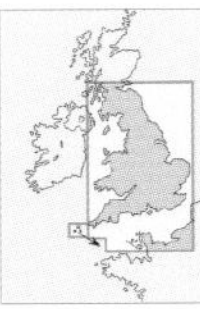

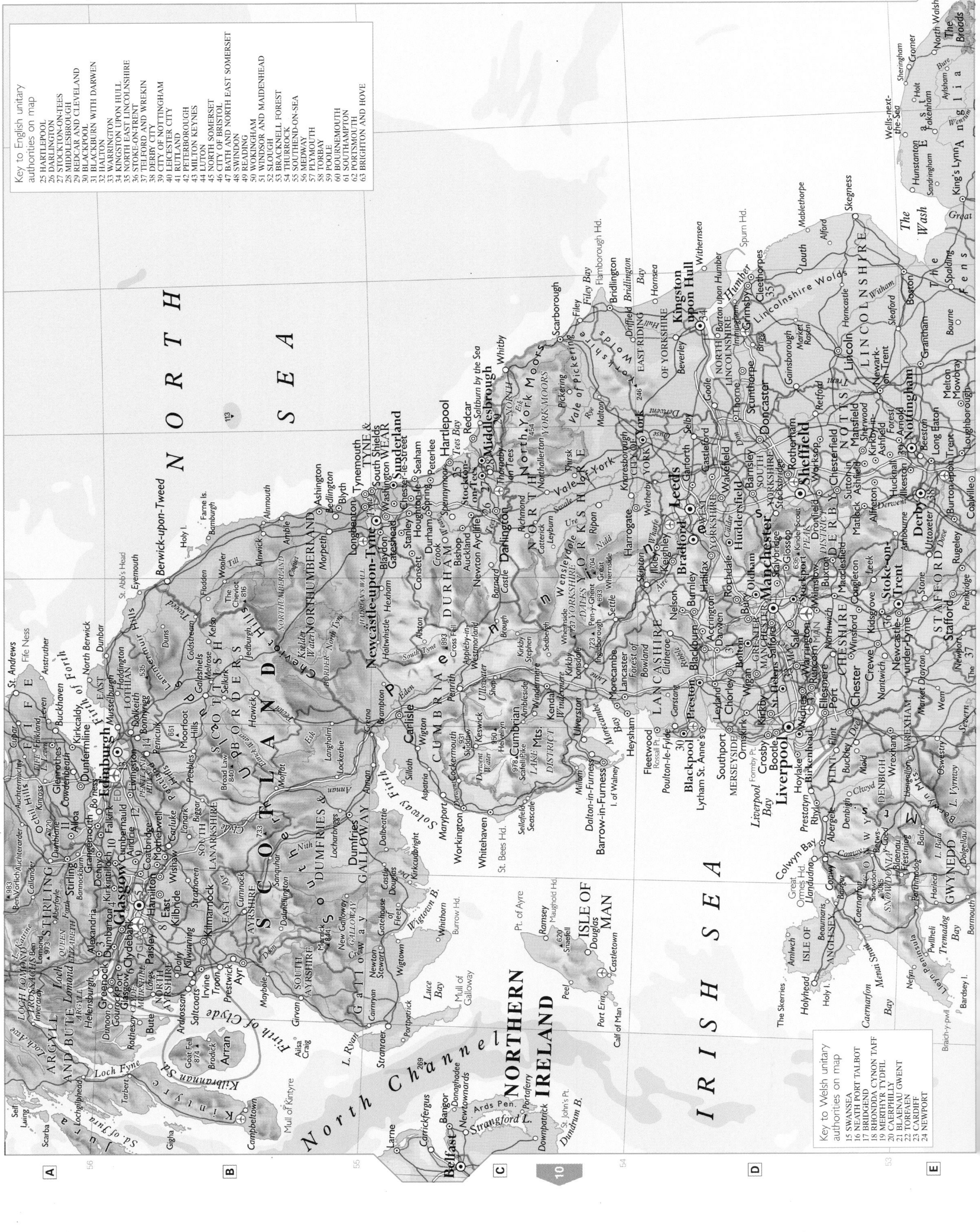
Key to English unitary authorities on map
25 HARTLEPOOL
26 DARLINGTON
27 STOCKTON-ON-TEES
28 MIDDLESBROUGH
29 REDCAR AND CLEVELAND
30 BLACKPOOL
31 BLACKBURN WITH DARWEN
32 HALTON
33 WARRINGTON
34 KINGSTON UPON HULL
35 NORTH EAST LINCOLNSHIRE
36 STOKE-ON-TRENT
37 TELFORD AND WREKIN
38 DERBY CITY
39 CITY OF NOTTINGHAM
40 LEICESTER CITY
41 RUTLAND
42 PETERBOROUGH
43 MILTON KEYNES
44 LUTON
45 NORTH SOMERSET
46 CITY OF BRISTOL
47 BATH AND NORTH EAST SOMERSET
48 SWINDON
49 READING
50 WOKINGHAM
51 WINDSOR AND MAIDENHEAD
52 SLOUGH
53 BRACKNELL FOREST
54 THURROCK
55 SOUTHEND-ON-SEA
56 MEDWAY
57 PLYMOUTH
58 TORBAY
59 POOLE
60 BOURNEMOUTH
61 SOUTHAMPTON
62 PORTSMOUTH
63 BRIGHTON AND HOVE
Key to Welsh unitary authorities on map
15 SWANSEA
16 NEATH PORT TALBOT
17 BRIDGEND
18 RHONDDA CYNON TAFF
19 MERTHYR TYDFIL
20 CAERPHILLY
21 BLAENAU GWENT
22 TORFAEN
23 CARDIFF
24 NEWPORT
NORTH SEA
IRISH SEA
North Channel
NORTHERN IRELAND
ISLE OF MAN
SCOTLAND
Newcastle-upon-Tyne
Sunderland
Middlesbrough
Leeds
Bradford
Sheffield
Manchester
Liverpool
Kingston upon Hull
Nottingham
Derby
Stoke-on-Trent
Edinburgh
Glasgow
Belfast
Blackpool
Preston
York
Carlisle
Lincoln

Projection: Lambert's Conformal Conic

ISLES OF SCILLY
on same scale

National Parks in England and Wales

Forest Parks in Scotland

1:5 000 000

50 0 25 50 75 100 125 150 175 km
50 0 25 50 75 100 125 miles

1 2 3 4 5 6 7 8 9

ATLANTIC OCEAN

NORWAY

Askøy
Bergen
Osøyro
Stord
Bømlo
Leirvik
Haugesund
Åkrahamn
Kopervik
Boknafjorden
Stavanger
Sandnes
Bryne
Nærbø

Shetland Is.
Yell
Unst
Fetlar
Mainland
Lerwick
Foula
Fair Isle

Orkney Is.
Westray
Sanday
Stronsay
Mainland
Hoy
Kirkwall
South Ronaldsay

Pentland Firth
C. Wrath
Thurso
Wick

NORTH SEA

Lewis
Stornoway
Harris
St. Kilda
789
North Uist
Benbecula
South Uist
Barra

Outer Hebrides
North Minch
Ullapool
Lairg
Golspie
Helmsdale

North West Highlands
Tain
Invergordon
Dingwall
Nairn
Elgin
Buckie
Banff
Fraserburgh
Peterhead
Moray Firth

Inner Hebrides
Skye
Portree
Mallaig
Rhum
Eigg
Coll
Tobermory
Tiree
Mull
Oban
Colonsay

L. Ness
Inverness
1182
Aviemore
Spey
Huntly
Inverurie
Aberdeen
1311
Dee
Don
Stonehaven

SCOTLAND
Grampian Mts.
Ben Nevis
1342
Fort William
1214
Ballater
Forfar
Montrose
Arbroath
973
Perth
Dundee
St. Andrews

Jura
Islay
Arran
Campbeltown

Greenock
Paisley
Glasgow
Hamilton
East Kilbride
Irvine
Kilmarnock
Ayr
Girvan

Stirling
Dunfermline
Kirkcaldy
Glenrothes
Edinburgh
Dunbar

Southern Uplands
Berwick-upon-Tweed
Galashiels
840
Jedburgh
Hawick
816
Cheviot Hills

Malin Hd.
Buncrana
Letterkenny
Coleraine
Ballymena
Larne

Aran I.
Donegal
Lifford
Londonderry
Antrim
Bangor

NORTHERN IRELAND
Ulster
Omagh
Lough Neagh
Lisburn
Lurgan
Belfast
Newry

Dumfries
Annan
Carlisle
Workington
Whitehaven
Kirkcudbright
Stranraer
Mull of Galloway

Newcastle-upon-Tyne
South Shields
Sunderland
Gateshead
Hexham
Durham
Hartlepool
Redcar
893
Darlington
Middlesbrough
Stockton-on-Tees
Scarborough

UNITED KINGDOM

Ballina
Sligo
Leitrim
Cavan
Castleblayney
Dundalk
Drogheda

Douglas
I. of Man
Cumbrian Mts.
978
Barrow-in-Furness
Lancaster
Harrogate
Bridlington
Beverley

IRELAND
Lough Mask
Lough Conn
Connemara
Westport
Roscommon
Longford
Athlone
Lough Ree
Mullingar
Ballinasloe
Lough Corrib
Ceanannus Mor
Boyne

IRISH SEA

Blackpool
Preston
Blackburn
Bolton
636
Burnley
Halifax
Huddersfield
Barnsley
Doncaster
Grimsby
Manchester
Oldham
Warrington
Stockport
Sheffield
Rotherham
Lincoln
Louth
Skegness

Leeds
Bradford
Keighley
York
Kingston upon Hull
Scunthorpe
Humber

Galway B.
Galway
Aran Is.
Ennis
Lough Derg
Nenagh
Limerick
Kilrush
Listowel
Tralee
953
Dingle
Carrauntoohill 1041
Killarney
Valencia
Macgillycuddy's Reeks

Ceanannus Mor
Tullamore
Liffey
Dublin
Dun Laoghaire
Bray
Holyhead
Anglesey
Bangor
Colwyn Bay
Chester
Crewe
Stoke-on-Trent
1085
Snowdon
Wrexham
Derby
Stafford
Nottingham
Mansfield
Chesterfield
Trent
Grantham

Port Laoise
Athy
Carlow
Kilkenny
Leinster
926
Wicklow Mts.
Arklow
Pwllheli
Cardigan Bay
Aberystwyth
Cambrian Mts.
Welshpool
Shrewsbury
Telford
Nuneaton
Leicester
Corby
Peterborough
ENGLAND
Great Yarmouth
Lowestoft
Norwich
Thetford

Shannon
Tipperary
Thurles
Clonmel
Carrick-on-Suir
Waterford
Dungarvan
Youghal

Wexford
Rosslare
St. George's Channel
Fishguard
Haverfordwest
Milford Haven
Pembroke
Carmarthen
WALES
Llanelli
Swansea
Neath
Port Talbot

886
Brecon
Merthyr Tydfil
Rhondda
Cwmbran
Newport
Cardiff
Barry

Worcester
Hereford
Royal Leamington Spa
Rugby
Northampton
Bedford
Cambridge
Ely
Bury St. Edmunds
Ipswich
Felixstowe
Harwich
Colchester
Chelmsford
BIRMINGHAM
Redditch
Coventry

Cork
Cobh
Bandon
Kinsale
C. Clear
Mallow
Blackwater
99

Gloucester
Cheltenham
Gloucestershire
Cotswold Hills
Oxford
Milton Keynes
Hemel Hempstead
Luton
Stevenage
Harlow
Basildon
Southend-on-Sea
Margate

Bristol Channel
Barnstaple
Exmoor
Taunton
Bude
618
Dartmoor
Exeter
Exmouth
Torbay

Weston-super-Mare
Bath
Bristol
Swindon
Newbury
Reading
Slough
Watford
High Wycombe
Thames
LONDON
Chatham
Canterbury
Dover

Newquay
Truro
St. Austell
Plymouth
Land's End
Penzance
Falmouth
Isles of Scilly

Yeovil
Salisbury
Winchester
Basingstoke
Guildford
Reigate
Maidstone
Ashford
Folkestone
Str. of Dover

Bournemouth
Poole
Weymouth
Dorchester
Southampton
Fareham
Portsmouth
Havant
Newport
Isle of Wight
Portsmouth
Worthing
Brighton
Eastbourne
Hastings

CELTIC SEA

ENGLISH CHANNEL

NETHERLANDS
Texel
Den Helder
Alkmaar
Haarlem
's-Gravenhage (Den Haag)
Hoek van Holland
ROTTERDAM
Dordrecht
Vlissingen

BELGIUM
BRUSSELS (Bruxelles)
Zeebrugge
Oostende
Antwerpen
Brugge
Gent
Mechelen
Tournai
Lille
Roubaix
Tourcoing
Villeneuve d'Ascq

Dunkerque
Calais
Gris-Nez
Boulogne-sur-Mer
St. Omer
Béthune
Bruay-la-Buissière
Lens
Valenciennes

Le Touquet-Paris-Plage
33
Le Tréport
Abbeville
Dieppe
Fécamp
Amiens
St-Quentin
Picardie
Cambrai

FRANCE
Alderney
C. de la Hague
Pte. de Barfleur
Cherbourg
Valognes
Le Havre
Bolbec
Rouen
Seine
Elbeuf
Bayeux
Trouville-sur-Mer
Caen
Lisieux
Guernsey
St. Peter Port
Sark
Cotentin
St. Helier
Jersey
Channel Is. (U.K.)
Pays de Caux

East from Greenwich
West from Greenwich
COPYRIGHT PHILIP'S

9
16
20

60
58
56
54
52
50

Projection: Conical with two standard parallels

ft m
3000 1000
1500 500
600 200
0 0
150 50
300 100
600 200
1500 500
3000 1000
6000 2000
m ft

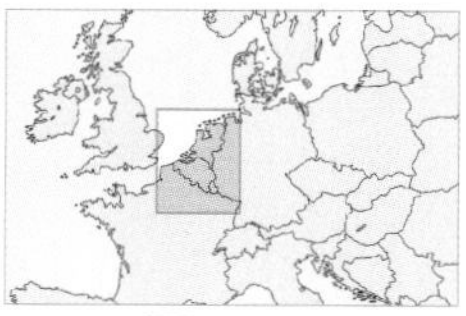

1:2 500 000

NORTH SEA

UNITED KINGDOM
THE BROADS

Cromer
North Walsham
Norwich
Bungay
Beccles
Lowestoft
Southwold
Saxmundham
Aldeburgh
Woodbridge
Orford Ness
Felixstowe
Margate
North Foreland
Ramsgate
Deal
Dover
Calais

**NETHERLANDS**

Helgoland
Düne
Ostfriesische Inseln
Scharhörn
Neuwerk
Spiekeroog Wangerooge
Langeoog
Baltrum
Juist Norderney
NIEDERSÄCHSISCHES WATTENMEER
Borkum
Bremerhaven
Nordenham
Wilhelmshaven
Emden
Ostfriesland
Oldenburg

Waddeneilanden
Schiermonnikoog
Ameland
Terschelling
West-Terschelling
Vlieland
Texel
Den Burg
Den Helder
Den Oever
Leeuwarden
Franeker
Harlingen
GRONINGEN
Groningen
FRIESLAND
Dokkum
Kollum
Zuidhorn
Heerenveen
Drachten
Sneek
Bolsward
Workum
Staveren
Assen
DRENTHE
Emmen
Coevorden
Meppel
Hoogeveen
Steenwijk
Emmeloord
Urk
Kampen
Zwolle
OVERIJSSEL
Almelo
Hengelo
Enschede
Deventer
Apeldoorn
Amersfoort
GELDERLAND
Arnhem
Nijmegen
Utrecht
UTRECHT
Amsterdam
Haarlem
Zaanstad
Hilversum
Almere-Stad
Lelystad
FLEVOLAND
Leiden
's-Gravenhage (Den Haag)
ZUID-HOLLAND
Delft
Rotterdam
Schiedam
Vlaardingen
Hoek van Holland
Dordrecht
Gorinchem
's-Hertogenbosch
Tilburg
Breda
Eindhoven
ZEELAND
Middelburg
Vlissingen
Bergen op Zoom
Roosendaal
Helmond
Venlo
LIMBURG
Roermond
Weert
Maastricht
Heerlen

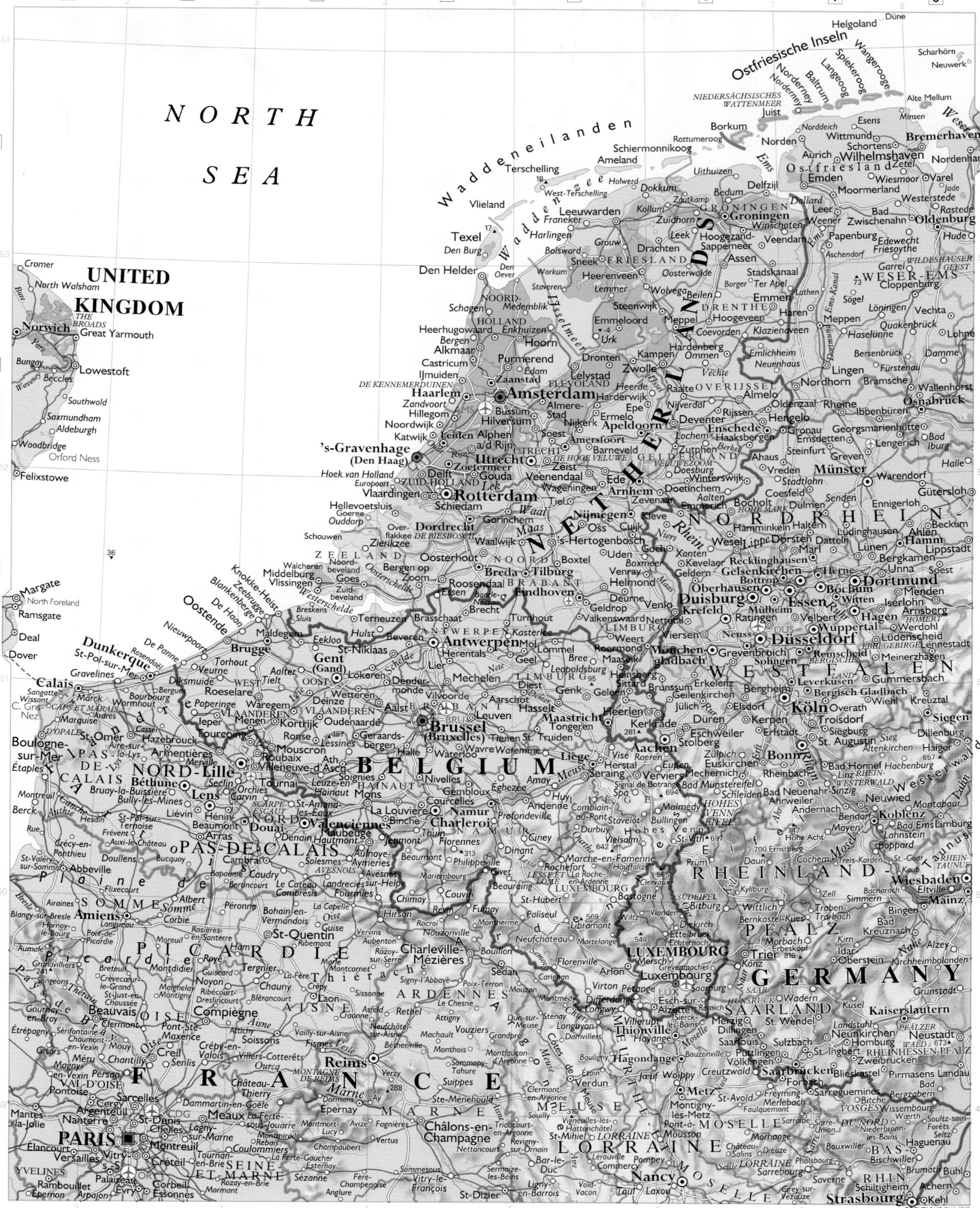

**NORDRHEIN WESTFALEN**
Münster
Osnabrück
Gütersloh
Dortmund
Bochum
Essen
Duisburg
Düsseldorf
Mönchengladbach
Köln
Bonn
Aachen
Krefeld
Wuppertal
Solingen
Leverkusen
Siegen

**BELGIUM**
Antwerpen
Gent (Gand)
Brugge
Oostende
Brussel (Bruxelles)
Leuven
Mechelen
Hasselt
Genk
Tongeren
Liège
Namur
Charleroi
Mons
La Louvière
Kortrijk
Roeselare
Tournai
VLAANDEREN
HAINAUT
Dinant
Bastogne
ARDENNES

**LUXEMBOURG**
Luxembourg
Esch-sur-Alzette
Diekirch
Ettelbruck
Arlon

**FRANCE**
Dunkerque
Lille
NORD
PAS-DE-CALAIS
Boulogne-sur-Mer
Étaples
Béthune
Lens
Douai
Valenciennes
Maubeuge
Cambrai
Arras
St-Omer
Hazebrouck
Armentières
Roubaix
Tourcoing
Amiens
SOMME
Abbeville
PICARDIE
Beauvais
OISE
Compiègne
Creil
St-Quentin
Laon
AISNE
Soissons
Reims
MARNE
Châlons-en-Champagne
Épernay
Charleville-Mézières
ARDENNES
Sedan
MEUSE
Verdun
LORRAINE
Metz
MOSELLE
Thionville
Nancy
MEURTHE-ET-MOSELLE
Longwy
Paris
SEINE-ET-MARNE
Meaux
Versailles

**GERMANY**
**RHEINLAND-PFALZ**
Koblenz
Mainz
Wiesbaden
Bonn
Trier
SAARLAND
Saarbrücken
Neunkirchen
Kaiserslautern
Homburg
Pirmasens
Landau
Bitburg
EIFEL
HUNSRÜCK
WESTERWALD
VOGESEN
BAS-RHIN
Strasbourg
Kehl

National Parks

Underlined towns give their name to the administrative area in which they stand.

COPYRIGHT PHILIP'S

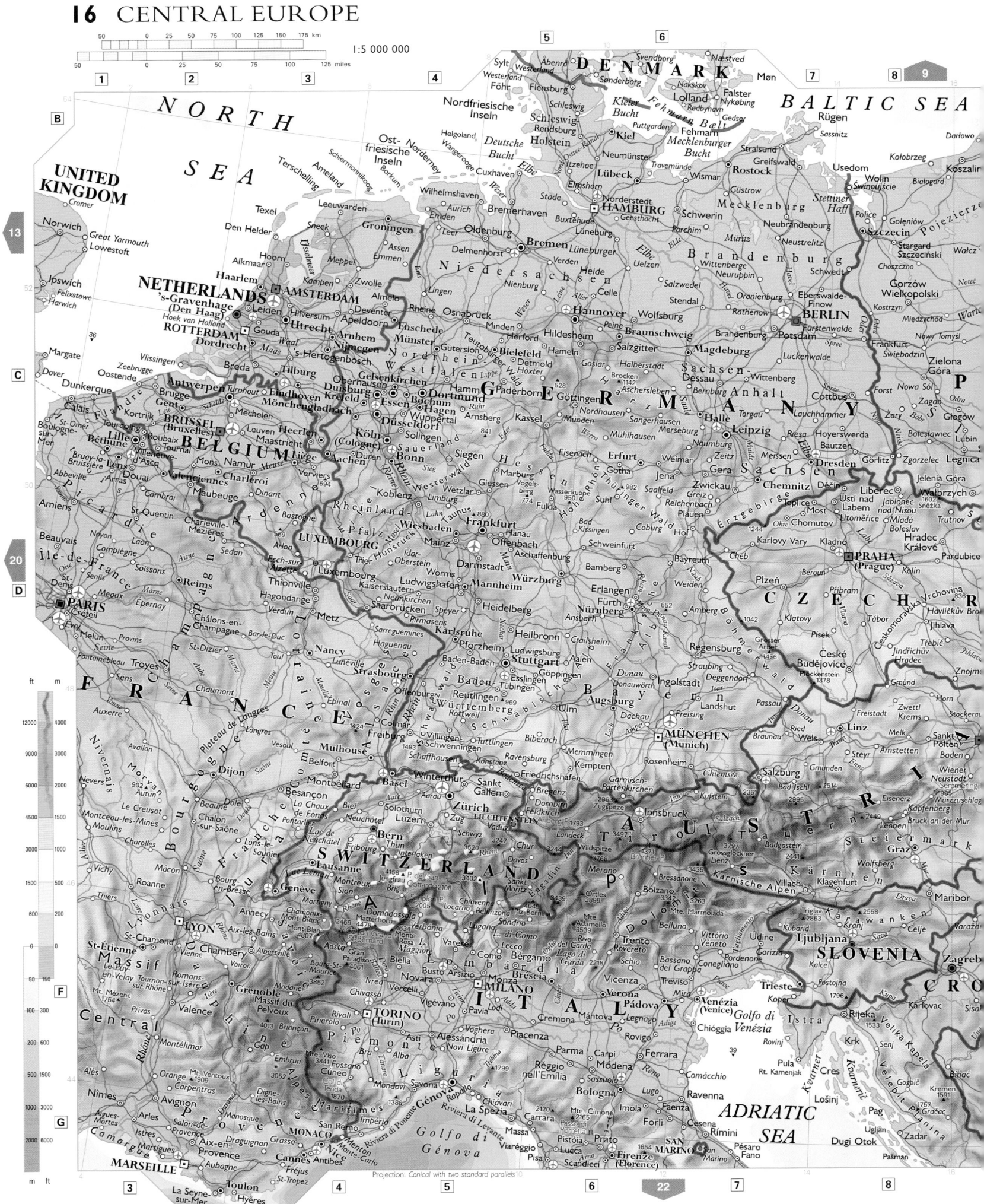

Projection: Conical with two standard parallels

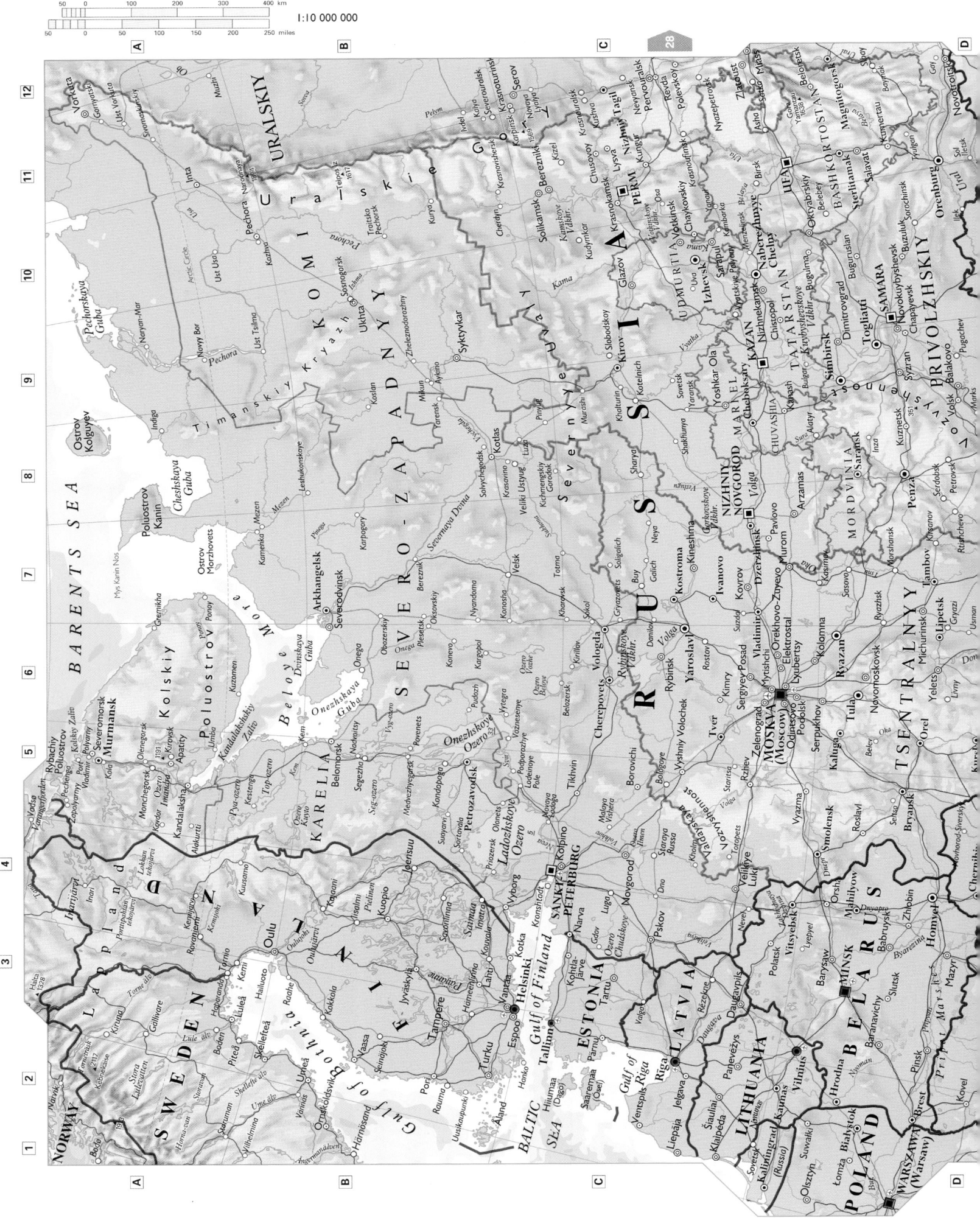

1:10 000 000

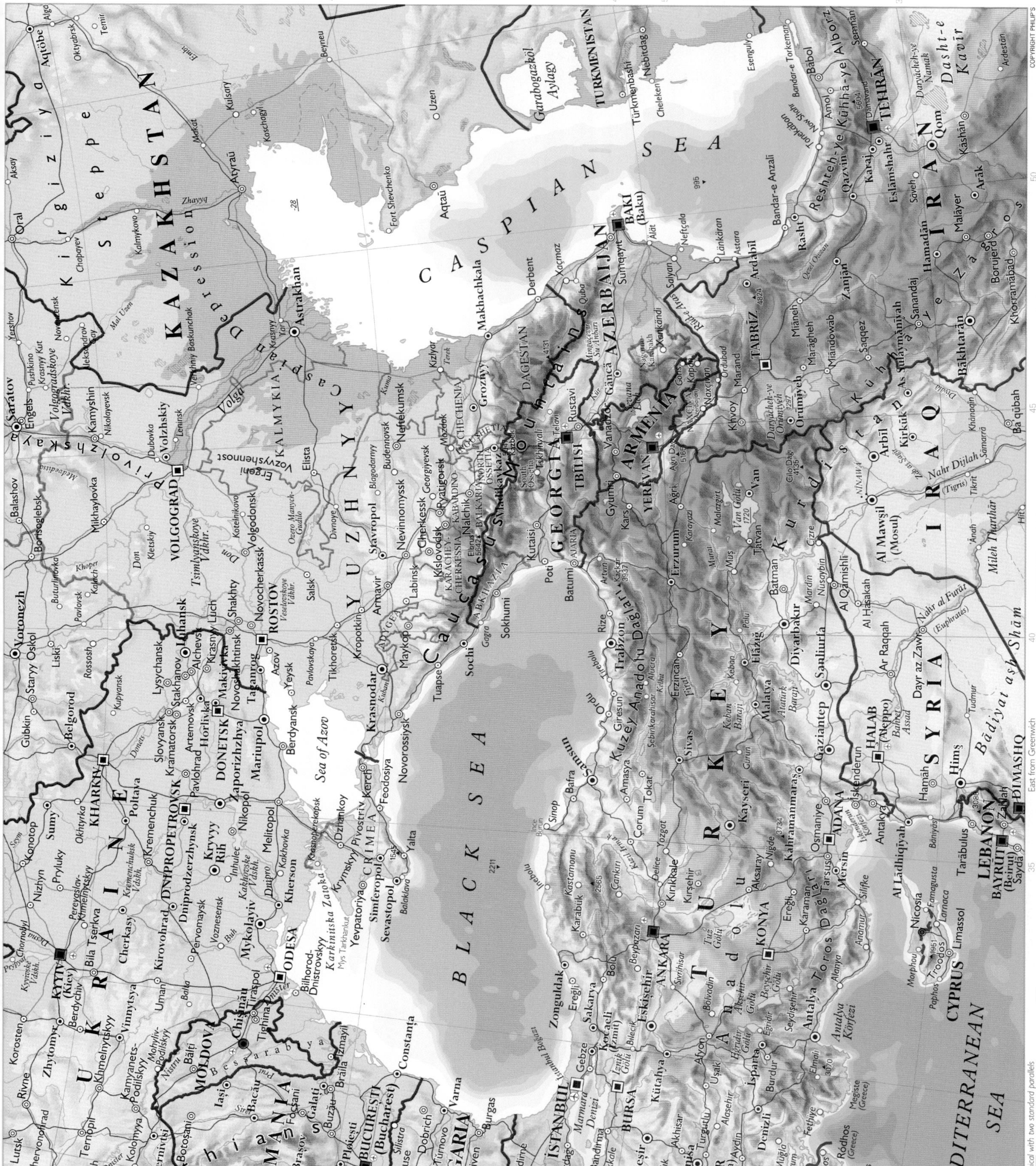

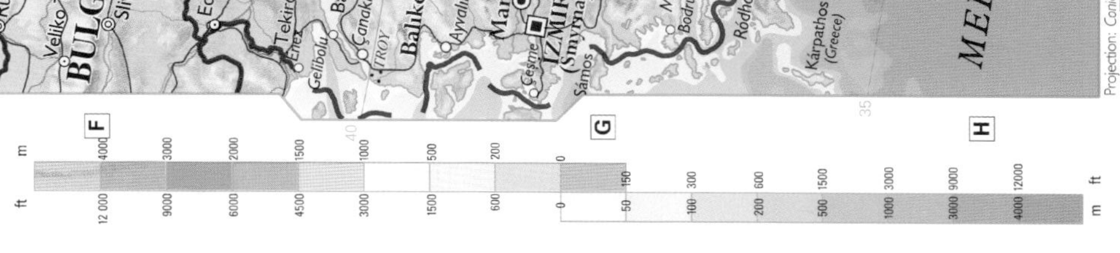

1:5 000 000

50 0 25 50 75 100 125 150 175 km
50 0 25 50 75 100 125 miles

Corse (Corsica)

Projection: Conical with two standard parallels

East from Greenwich / West from Greenwich

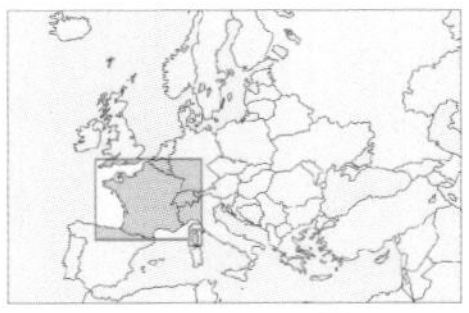

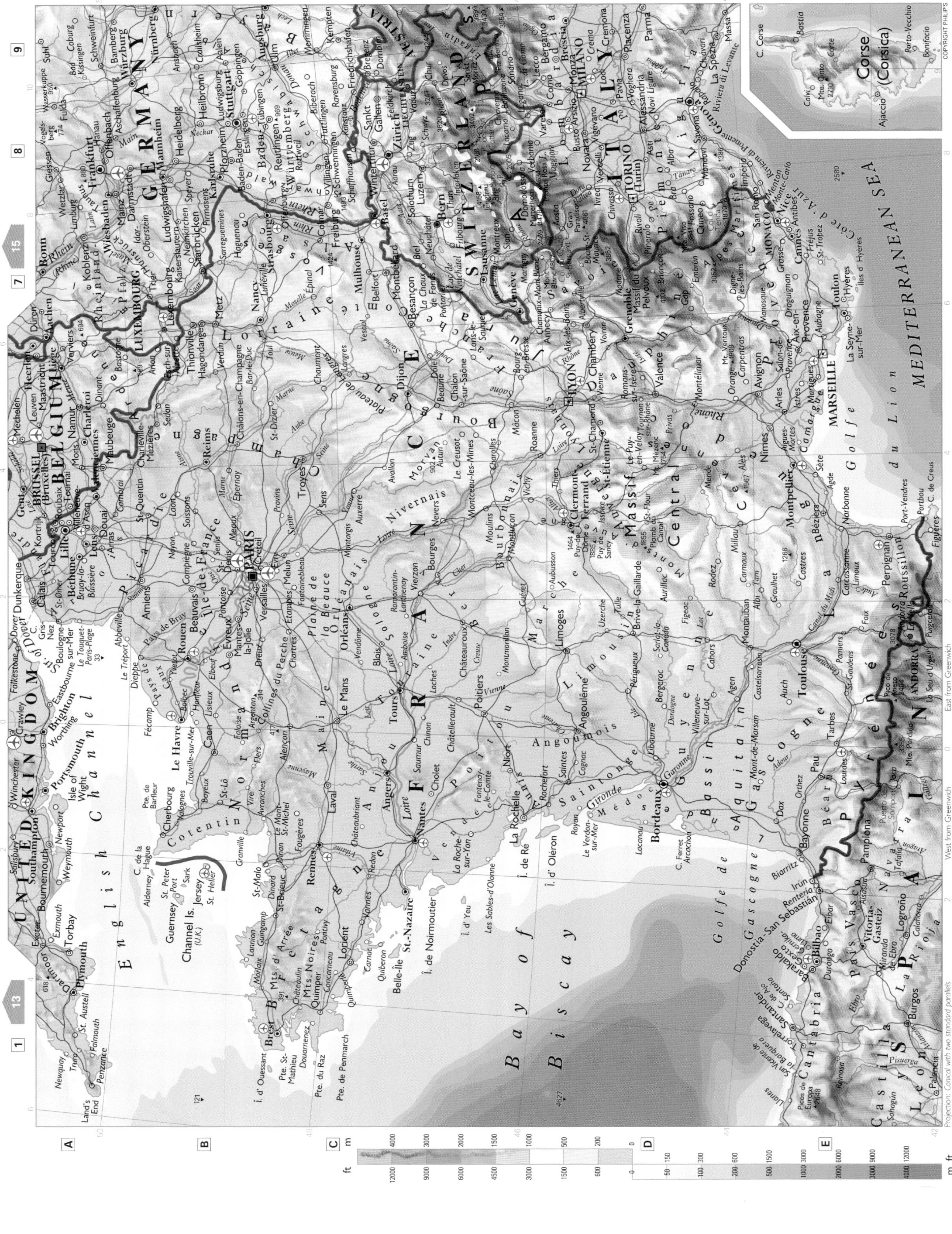

MEDITERRANEAN SEA

Bay of Biscay

English Channel

UNITED KINGDOM

BELGIUM

LUXEMBOURG

GERMANY

SWITZERLAND

AUSTRIA

ITALY

SPAIN

ANDORRA

FRANCE

PARIS

MARSEILLE

ft m
12000 4000
9000 3000
6000 2000
4500 1500
3000 1000
1500 500
600 200
150 50
0 0
m ft

COPYRIGHT PHILIP'S

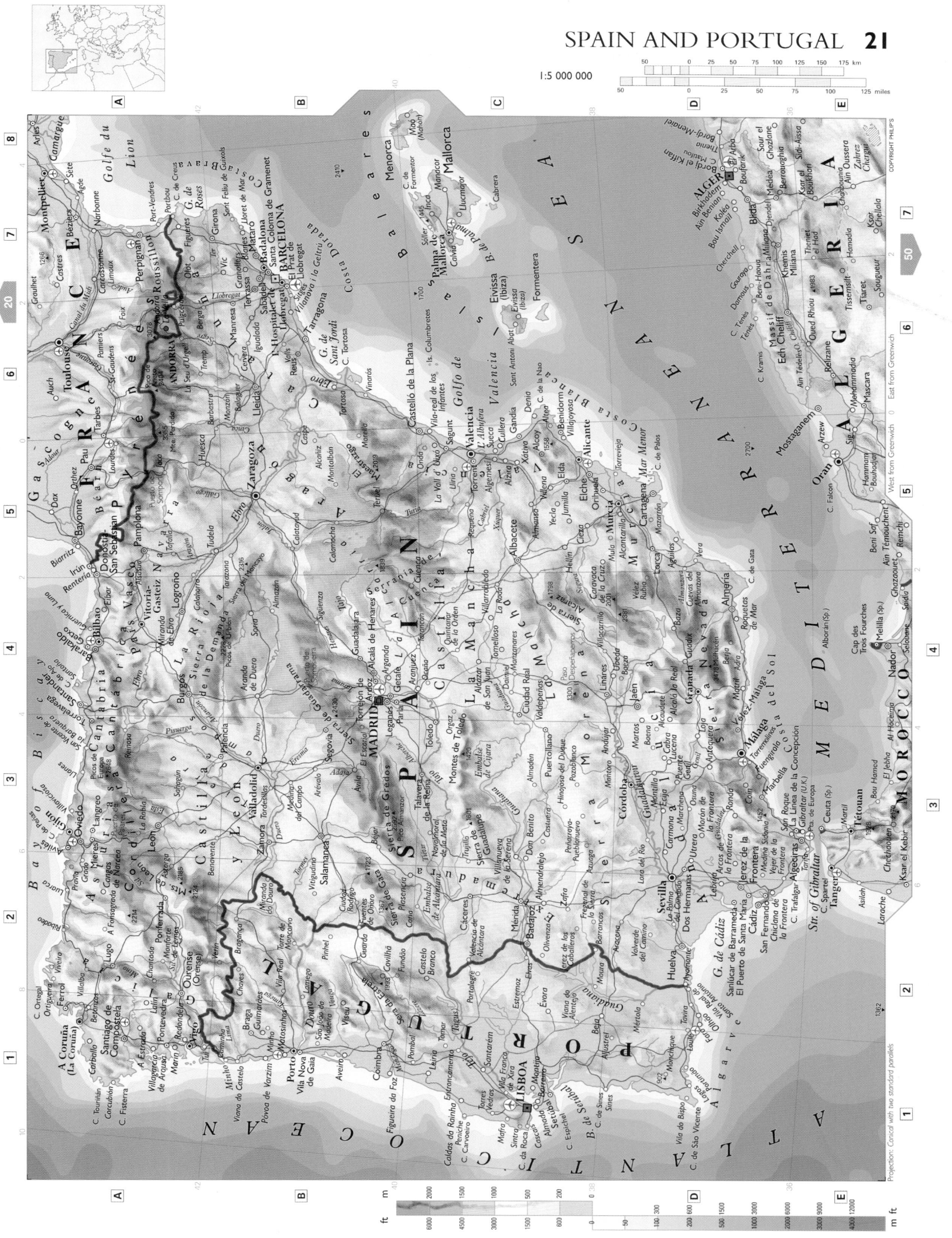

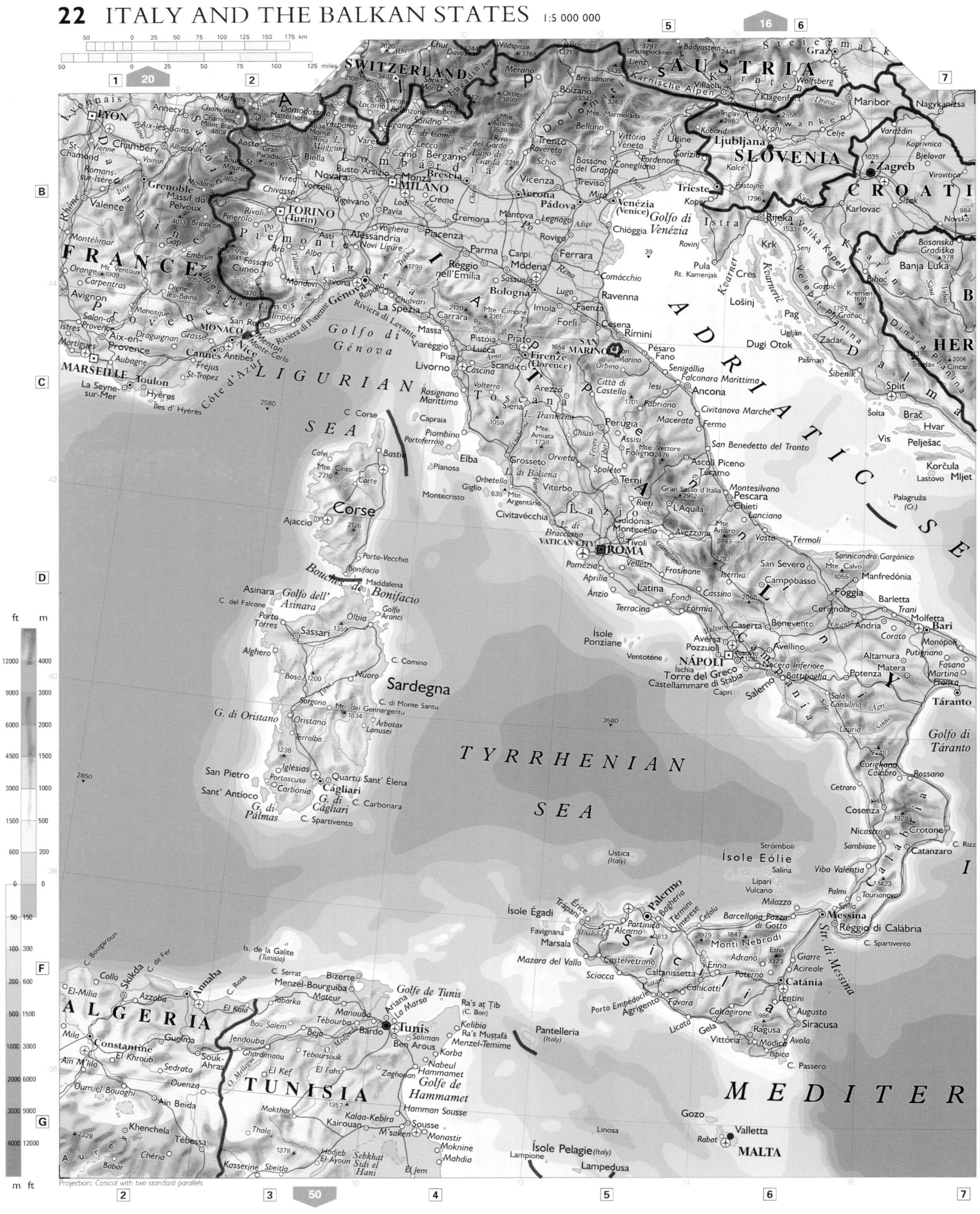

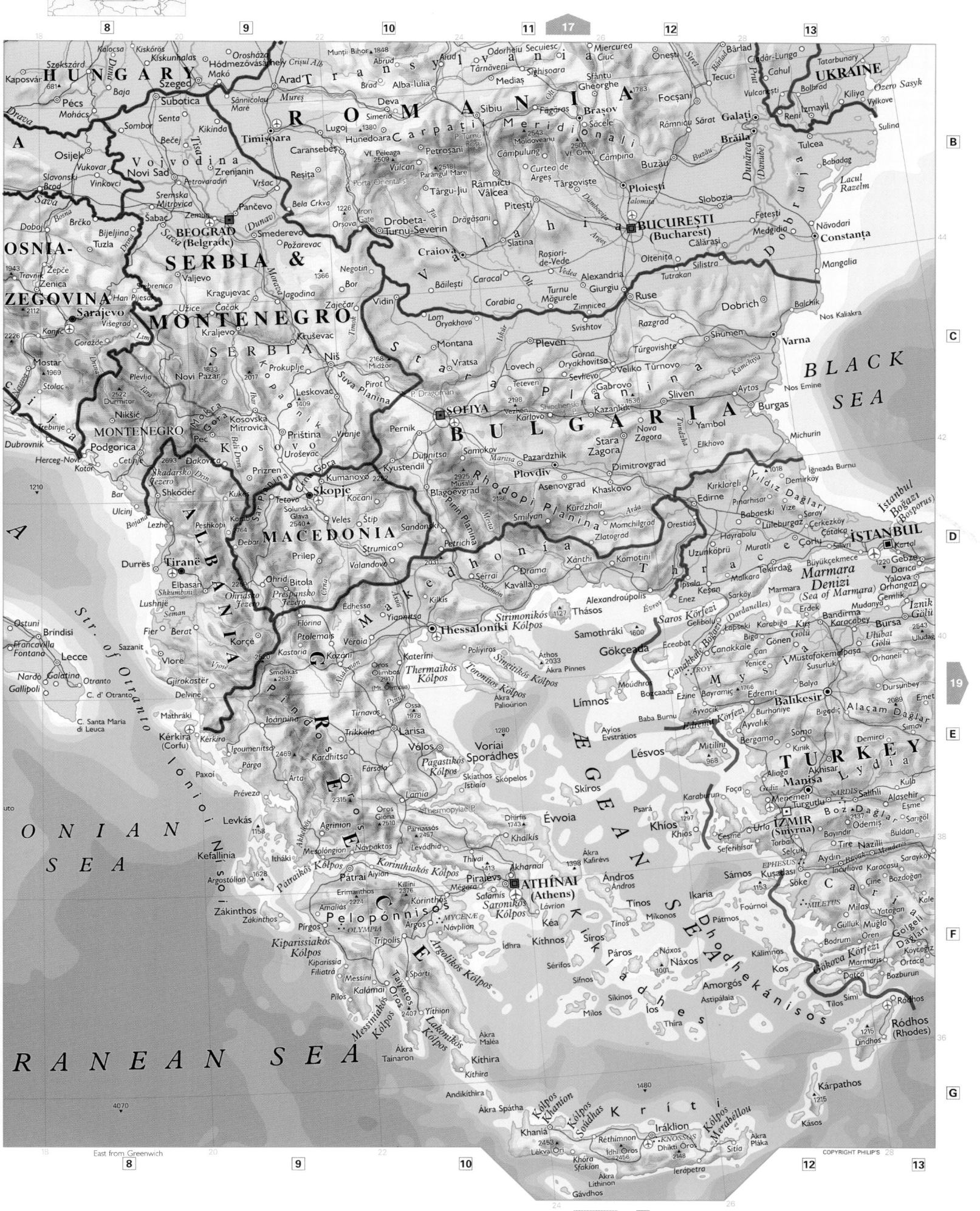

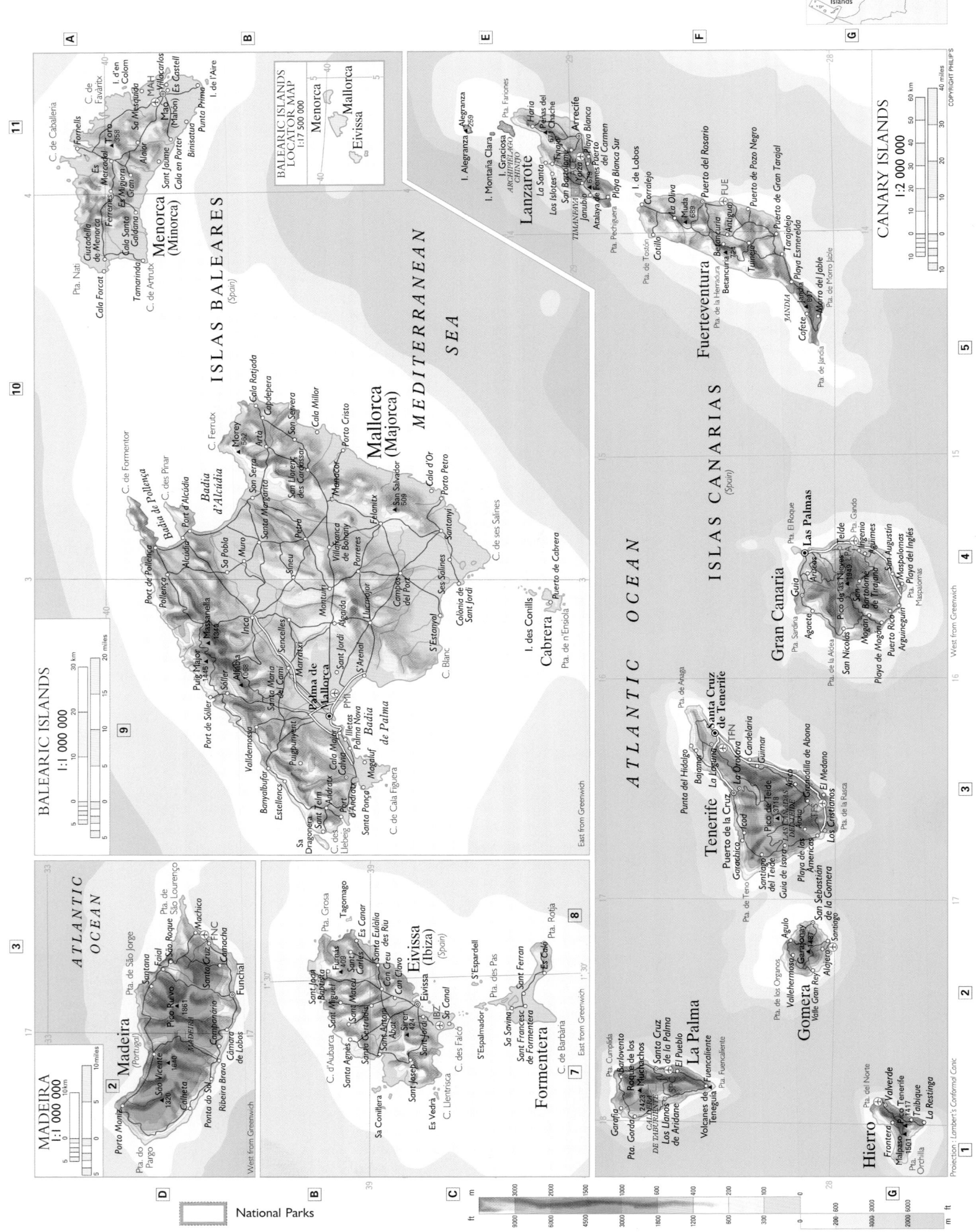

**A** **B** **E** **F** **G**

ISLAS BALEARES *(Spain)*

Menorca (Minorca)

**BALEARIC ISLANDS LOCATOR MAP** 1:17 500 000

Menorca
Mallorca
Eivissa

C. de Caballeria
Fornells
Pta. Nati
Ciutadella de Menorca
Cala Santa Galdana
Ferreries
Cala Forcat
Tamarinda
C. de Artrutx
Pta. de s'Aire

Es Mercadal
Toro 358
Alaior
Sant Jaume
Cala en Porter
Binisafua
Maó (Mahón)
Villacarlos Es Castell
I. de l'Aire
I. d'en Colom
C. de Favàritx
Punta Prima

**MEDITERRANEAN SEA**

Mallorca (Majorca)

C. de Formentor
C. de Pollença
Port de Pollença
Badia de Pollença
Pollença
Port d'Alcúdia
C. des Pinar
Badia d'Alcúdia
Alcúdia
Sa Pobla
Muro
Santa Margarita
Cala Ratjada
Capdepera
Artà
Morey 562
Son Serra
Cala Millor
Son Servera
Porto Cristo
Cala d'Or
Porto Petro
San Salvador 509
Porto Colom
Felanitx
Santanyí
C. de ses Salines
Ses Salines
Colònia de Sant Jordi
Campos del Port
C. Blanc
Llucmajor
S'Arenal
Palma de Mallorca
PM
Badia de Palma
Illetas
Palma Nova
Calvià
Magaluf
Santa Ponça
C. de Cala Figuera
Andratx
Port d'Andratx
Sa Dragonera
Estellencs
Banyalbufar
Valldemossa
Puigpunyent
Santa Maria del Camí
Marratxí
Sant Jordi
Sencelles
Sineu
Inca
Alaró
Alfàbia 1068
Sóller
Port de Sóller
Puig Major 1445
Massanella 1348
Lluc
Son Serra
Son Llorenç des Cardassar
Sant Llorenç des Cardassar
Manacor
Montuïri
Vilafranca de Bonany
Porreres
C. Ferrutx

Badia d'Alcúdia

**BALEARIC ISLANDS** 1:1 000 000

**ATLANTIC OCEAN**

Madeira *(Portugal)*

Porto Moniz
Pta. do Pargo
Seixal
São Vicente 1320
Santana
Faial
São Roque
Machico
Pico Ruivo 1861
Santo Cruz
Caniço
Camacha
Funchal
Ponta do Sol
Câmara de Lobos
Calheta
Ribeira Brava
Campanário
Pico Grande 1648
Pta. de São Jorge
Pta. de São Lourenço
FNC
33

**MADEIRA** 1:1 000 000

Eivissa (Ibiza) *(Spain)*

Pta. Grossa
Tagomago
Portinatx
Sant Joan Baptista
Sant Miquel
Santa Eulàlia
Es Canar
Santa Agnès
Sant Mateu
Sant Antoni
Sant Carles
Sant Rafel
Eivissa
IBZ
Sant Josep
Sant Jordi
Ses Salines
Es Vedrà
C. Llentrisca
Sa Conillera
C. d'Aubarca
Es Canar
Can Clavo
Con Creu des Riu
424
Furnàs 409

Formentera

Sa Savina
Sant Francesc de Formentera
Sant Ferran
Es Caló
C. de Barbària
Pta. Rotja
Pta. de ses Portes
S'Espalmador
S'Espardell
Es Canal
C. des Falcó

La Palma

Garafía
Pta. Gorda
Barlovento
Roque de los Muchachos 2423
Santa Cruz de la Palma
CALDERA DE TABURIENTE
Los Llanos de Aridane
El Pueblo
Fuencaliente
Volcanes de Teneguía
Pta. Cumplida
Pta. Fuencaliente

Hierro

Frontera
Valverde
Malpaso 1501
Tabibga
La Restinga
Orchilla
Pta. del Norte
Pico de Tenerife 1417
Pta. de Orchilla

Gomera

Vallehermoso
Agulo
San Sebastián de la Gomera
Hermigua
Alojera
Valle Gran Rey
Playa de Santiago
Pta. de los Órganos

**ISLAS CANARIAS** *(Spain)*

Tenerife

Punta del Hidalgo
La Laguna
Santa Cruz de Tenerife
TFN
Bajamar
Tacoronte
La Orotava
Puerto de la Cruz
Icod
Garachico
Pico de Teide 3718
Guía de Isora
Santiago del Teide
Adeje
TFS
Playa de las Américas
Los Cristianos
Arona
Granadilla de Abona
El Médano
Güímar
Candelaria
Pta. de Teno
Pta. de la Rasca

**ATLANTIC OCEAN**

Gran Canaria

Las Palmas
Telde
Ingenio
Agüimes
San Bartolomé
San Agustín
Maspalomas
Playa del Inglés
Pico de las Nieves 1949
San Mateo
Tejeda
Mogán
Puerto Rico
Arguineguín
Agaete
Guía
Arucas
Gáldar
San Nicolás
Pta. Sardina
Pta. El Roque
Pta. de Gando
Pta. de la Aldea

**CANARY ISLANDS** 1:2 000 000

Lanzarote

I. Alegranza
Alegranza 289
I. Montaña Clara
I. Graciosa
La Santa
Los Islotes
Arrecife
Haría
Peñas del Chache
Tinajo
TIMANFAYA
Yaiza
Playa Blanca
Puerto del Carmen
I. de Lobos
Corralejo
Pta. de Tostón
Cotillo

Fuerteventura

La Oliva
Puerto del Rosario
FUE
La Muda 689
Betancuria
Tuineje
Antigua
Gran Tarajal
Tarajalejo
Pájara
Playa Esmeralda
JANDÍA
Cofete
Morro del Jable
Pta. de Jandía
Pta. de Pedro Jable
Pta. de la Herradura

**ISLAS CANARIAS** *(Spain)*

Cabrera
I. des Conills
Puerto de Cabrera
I. de n'Ensiola

**National Parks**

Projection: Lambert's Conformal Conic

COPYRIGHT PHILIP'S

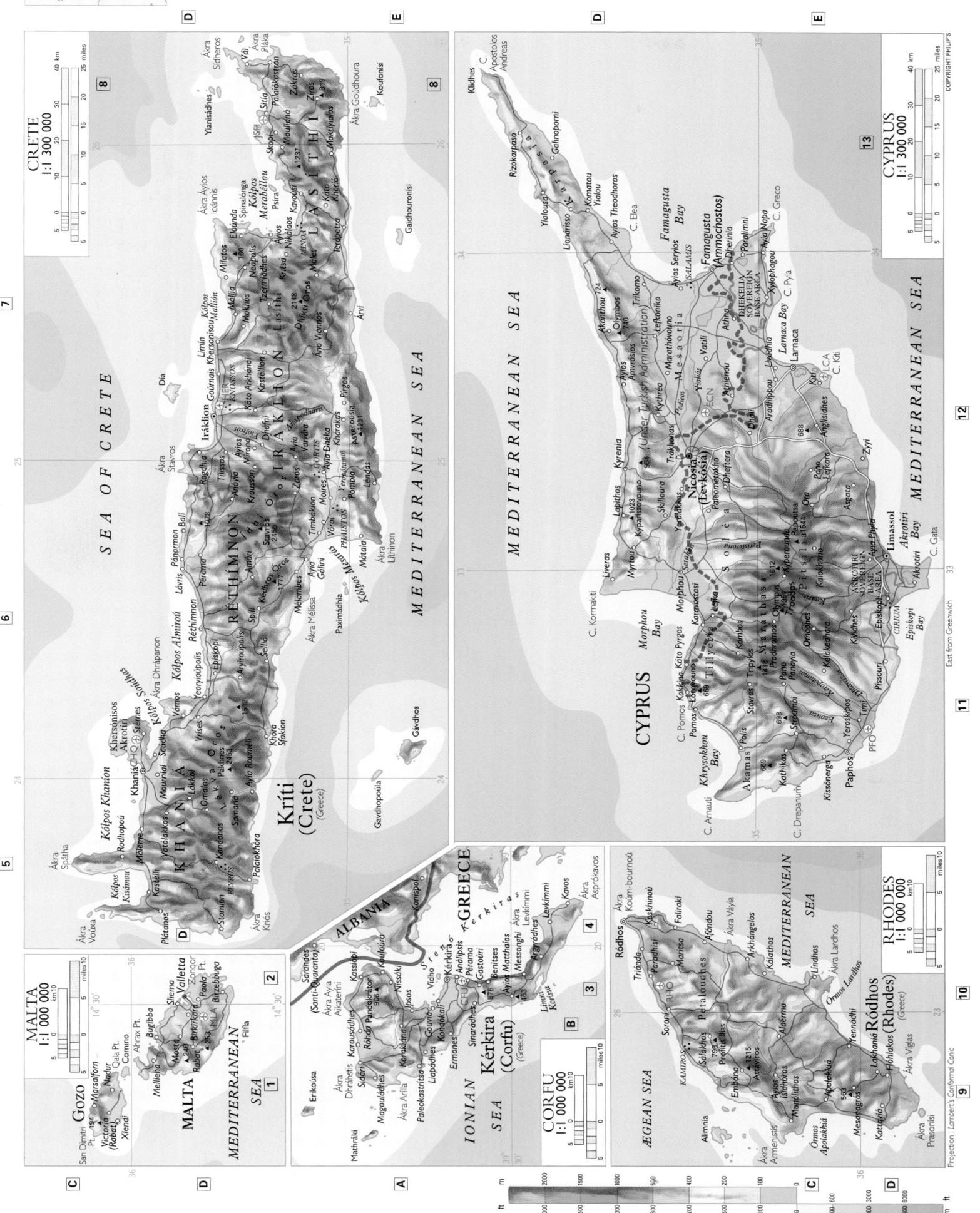

CRETE
1:1 300 000

MALTA
1:1 000 000

CORFU
1:1 000 000

CYPRUS
1:1 300 000

RHODES
1:1 000 000

SEA OF CRETE

MEDITERRANEAN SEA

MEDITERRANEAN SEA

MEDITERRANEAN SEA

IONIAN SEA

AEGEAN SEA

Kríti (Crete) (Greece)

Kérkira (Corfu) (Greece)

Ródhos (Rhodes) (Greece)

CYPRUS

GREECE

ALBANIA

Projection: Lambert's Conformal Conic

East from Greenwich

1:50 000 000

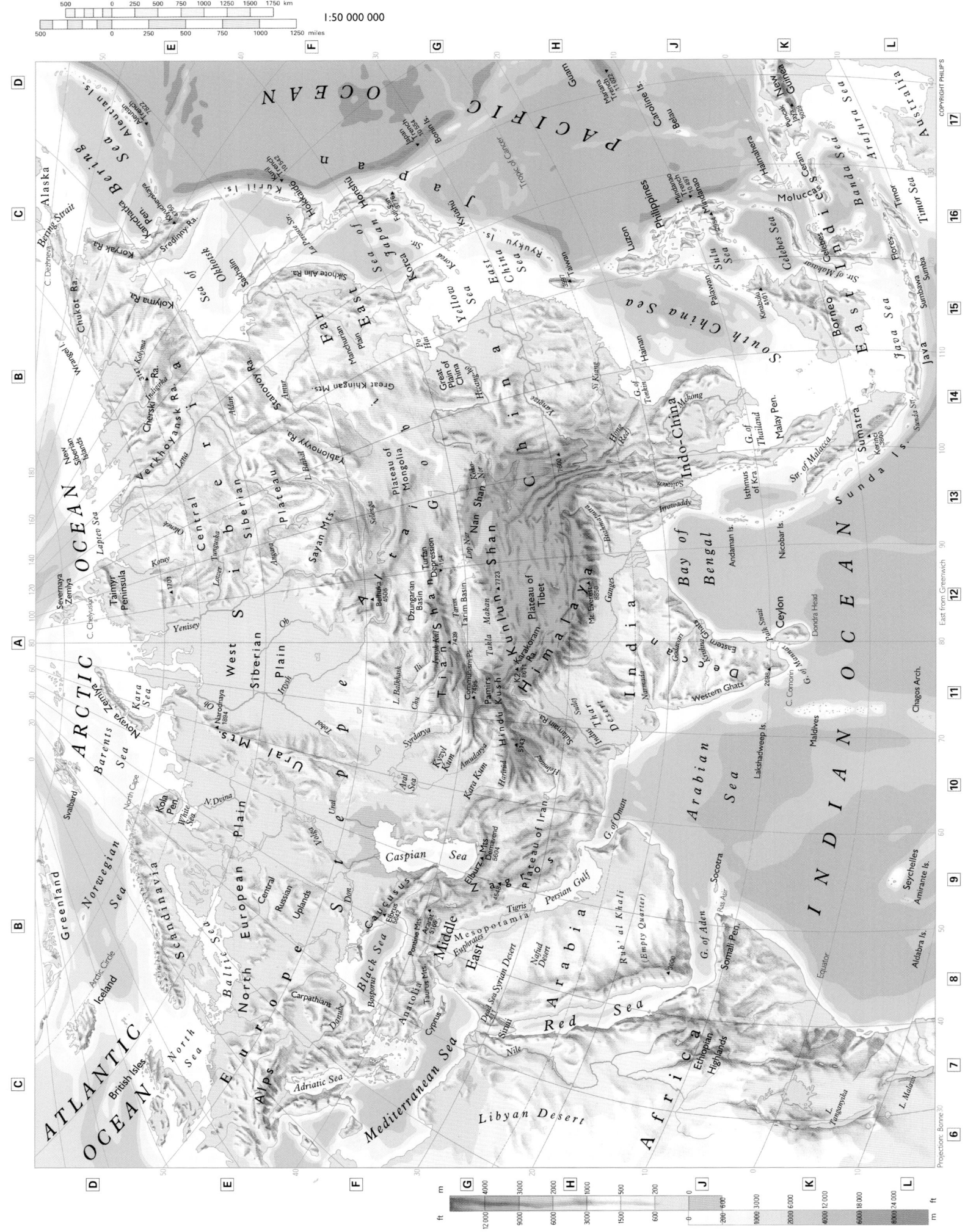

Projection: Bonne 30

East from Greenwich

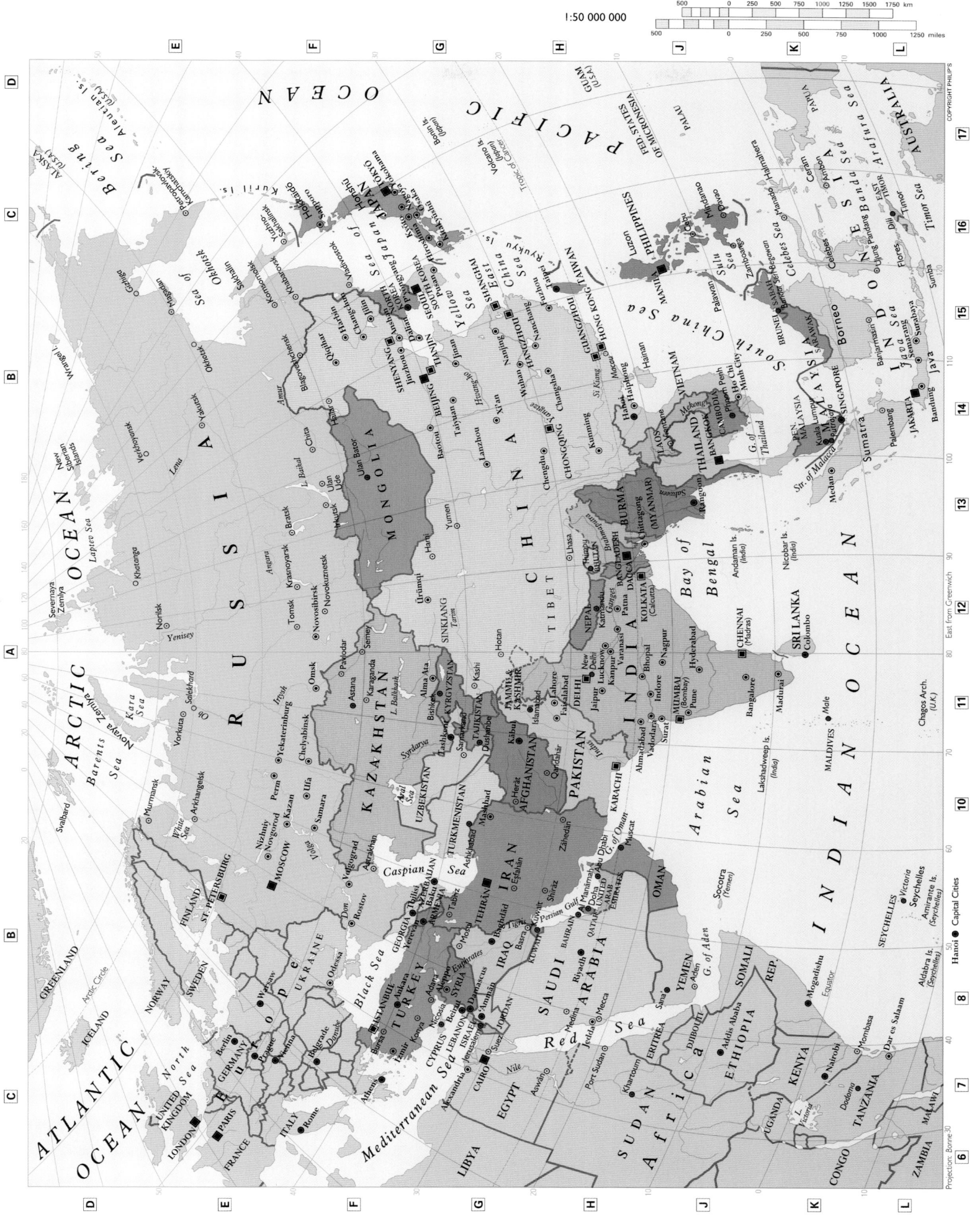

1:50 000 000

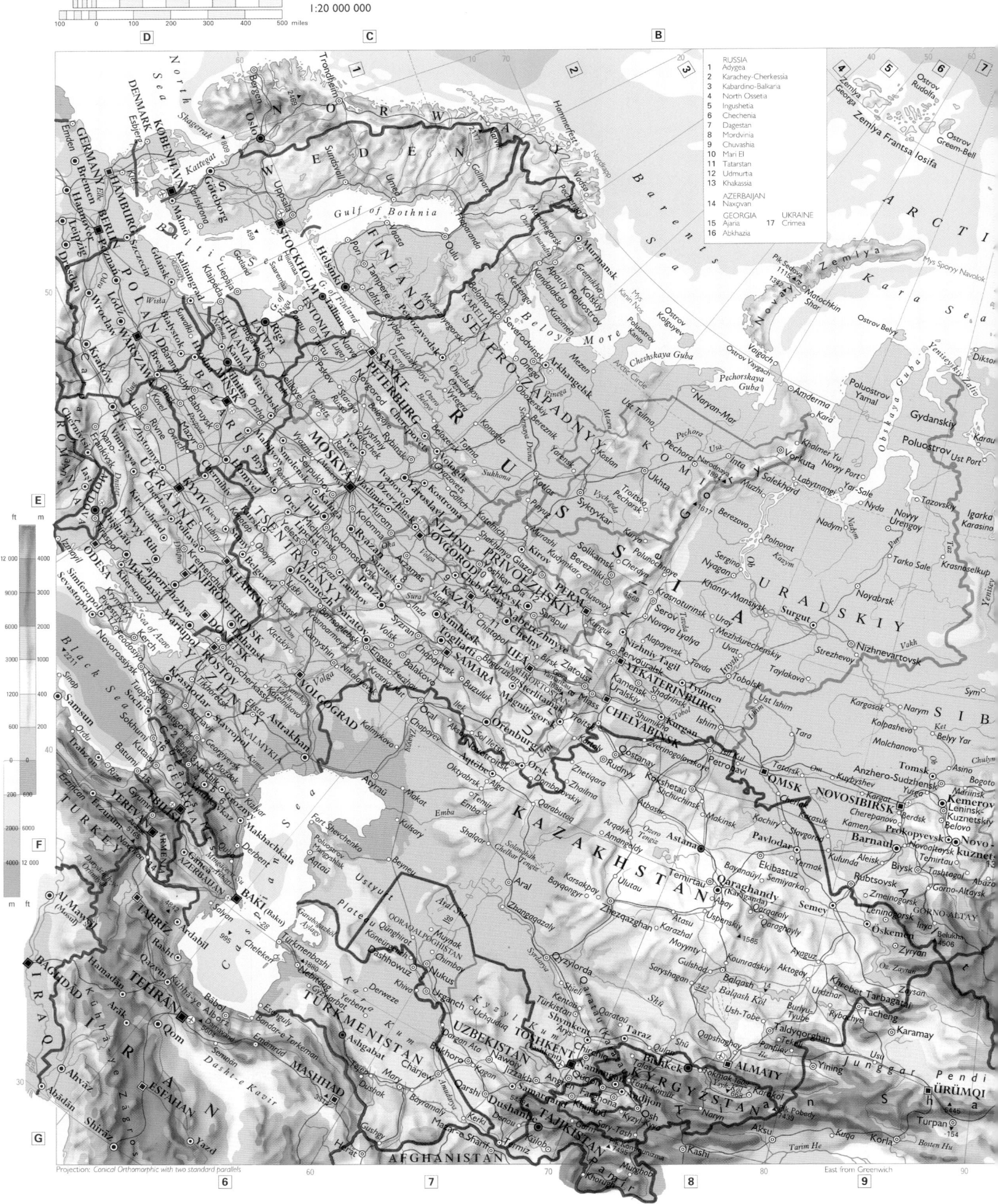

100 0 100 200 300 400 500 600 700 800 km
100 0 100 200 300 400 500 miles

1:20 000 000

Projection: Conical Orthomorphic with two standard parallels

East from Greenwich

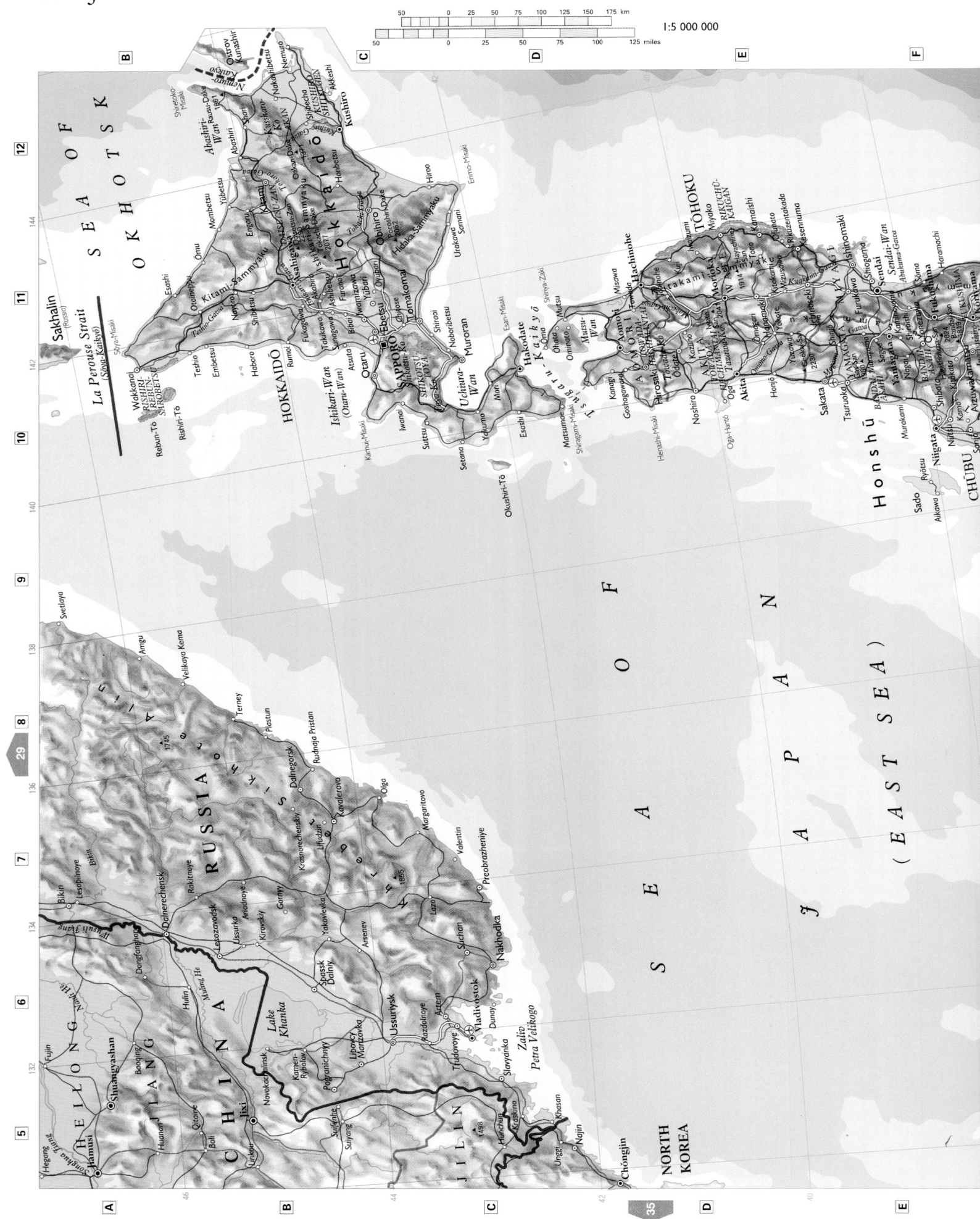

1:5 000 000

**SEA OF OKHOTSK**

**HOKKAIDŌ**

Sakhalin *(Russia)*

*La Perouse Strait (Sōya-Kaikyō)*

SAPPORO

Hakodate

**HOKKAIDO**

**HONSHŪ**

**TŌHOKU**

Sendai

**RUSSIA**

**CHINA**

**HEILONGJIANG**

**JILIN**

**NORTH KOREA**

Vladivostok

Nakhodka

Chŏngjin

**SEA OF JAPAN (EAST SEA)**

Lake Khanka

*Zaliv Petra Velikogo*

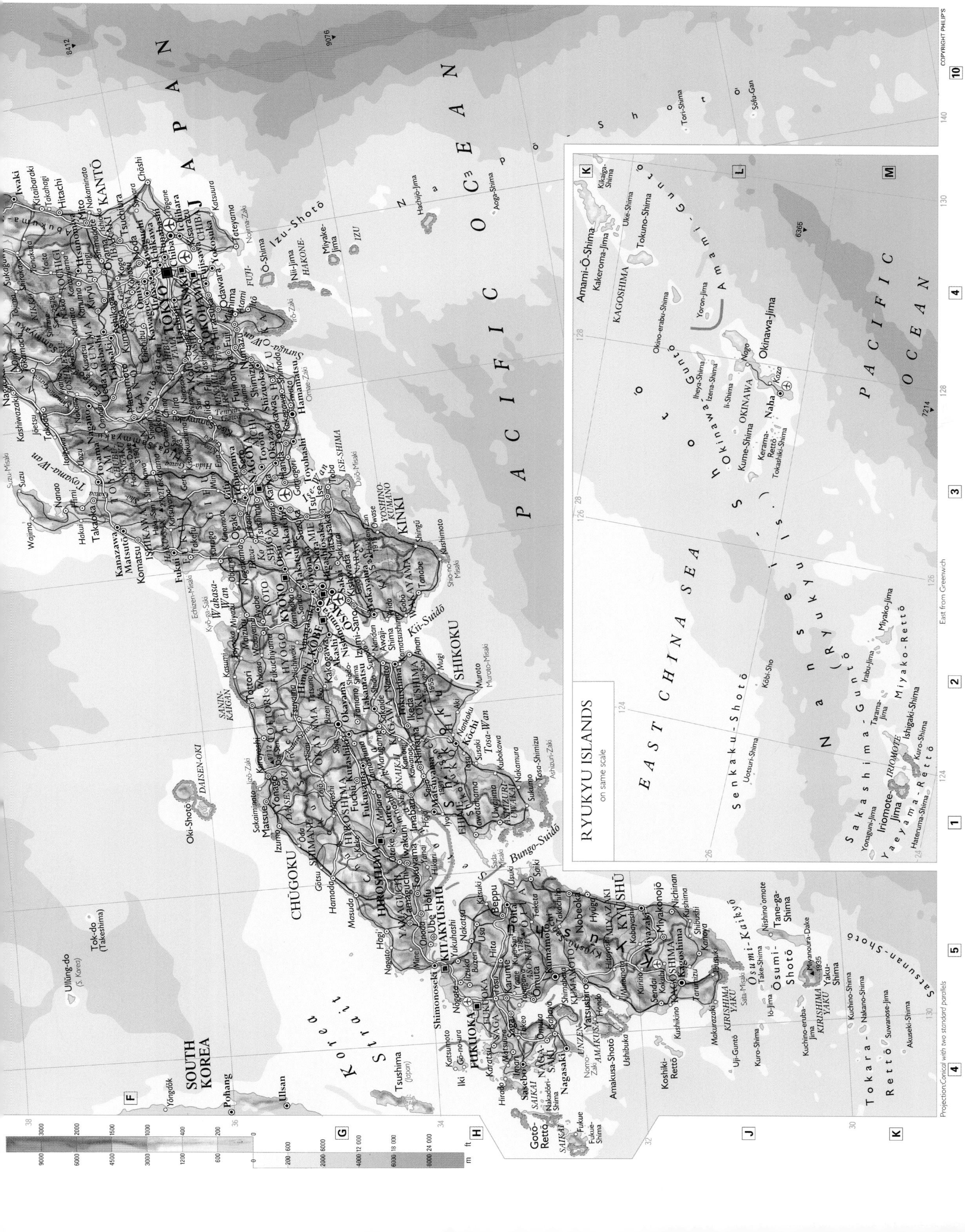

RYUKYU ISLANDS
on same scale

COPYRIGHT PHILIP'S

1:15 000 000

Projection: Bonne

East from Greenwich

**HONG KONG AND MACAU**
1:1 000 000

COPYRIGHT PHILIP'S

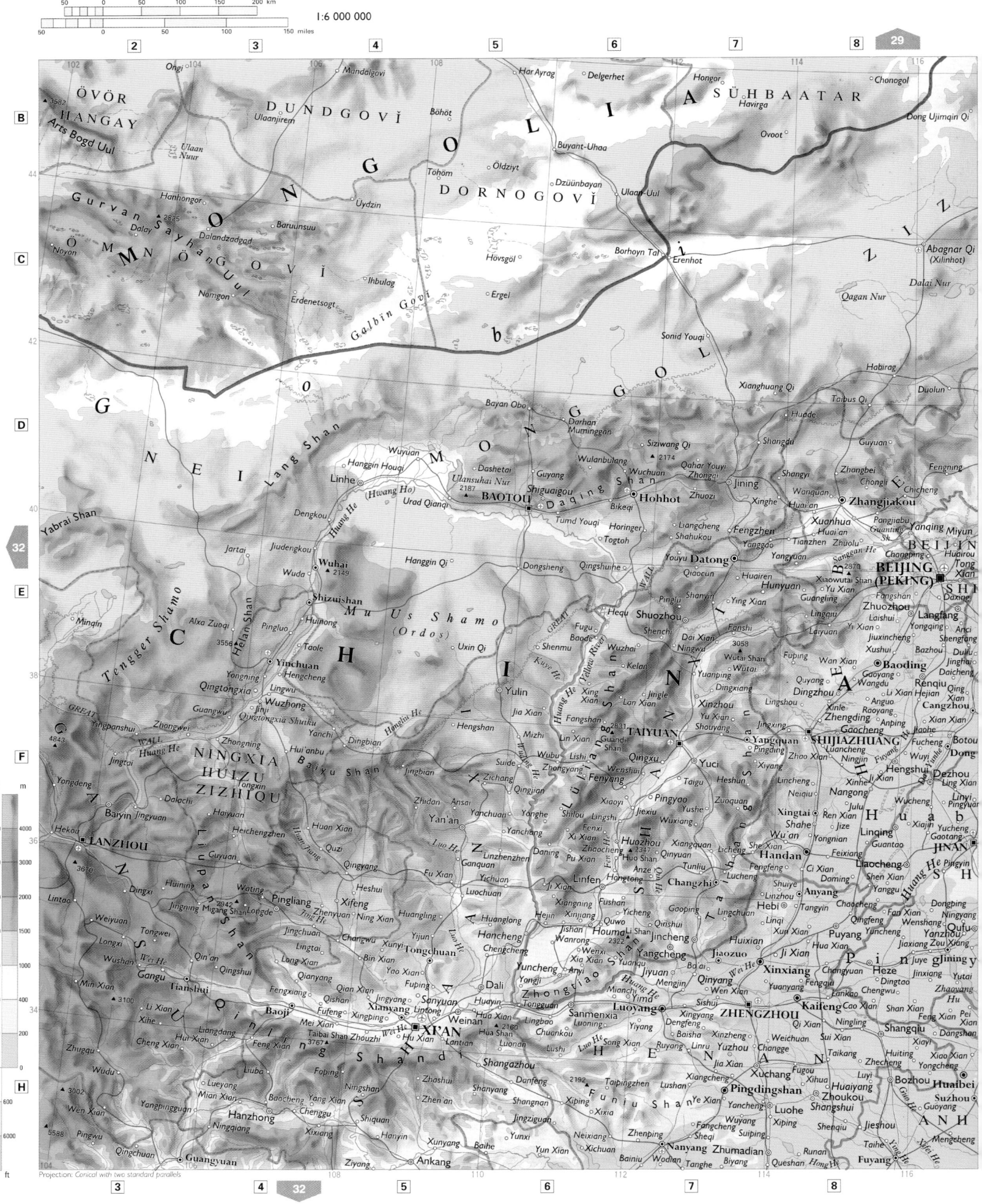

29

32

ft  m

12 000  4000

9000  3000

6000  2000

4500  1500

3000  1000

1200  400

600  200

0  0

200  600

2000  6000

m ft

Projection: Conical with two standard parallels

1:12 500 000

100   0   100   200   300   400   500 km
100   0   50   100   150   200   250   300   350 miles

**BURMA**
Letpadan
Insein
Tharrawaddy
Thoen
**RANGOON (YANGON)**
Ma-ubin
Thaton
Pyapon
G. of Martaban
Moulmein
Kyaikkami

**(MYANMAR)**
Yé
Tavoy
Moscos Is.
2075

**THAILAND**
Phitsanulok
Sawankhalok
Sukhothai
Nong Khai
**Wentiane (Changchun)**
Udon Thani
Nakhon Phanom
Muang Khammouan
Sakon Nakhon
Ba Don
Dong Hoi

Nam Tok
Phra Nakhon Si Ayutthaya
Saraburi
Phetchabun
Khon Kaen
Roi Et
Nakhon Sawan
Chaiyaphum
Ubon Ratchathani
Sisaket
Thakhek
Savannakhet
2701
Quang Tri
**Hue**

Kanchanaburi
**BANGKOK**
Samut Songkhram
Chon Buri
Nakhon Ratchasima
Buriram
Mun
Khu Khan
**Pakxe**
Attapu
2598
Saravan
**VIETNAM**
Chau O
Quang Ngai

**Da Nang**

**CAMBODIA**

**PENINSULAR MALAYSIA**

**KUALA LUMPUR**

**SINGAPORE**

**MALAYSIA**

**BRUNEI**
**Bandar Seri Begawan**

**SARAWAK**

**JAKARTA**
**Bandung**
**SURABAYA**

**INDIAN OCEAN**

**SOUTH CHINA SEA**

**ANDAMAN SEA**

**Projection:** Mercator

East from Greenwich

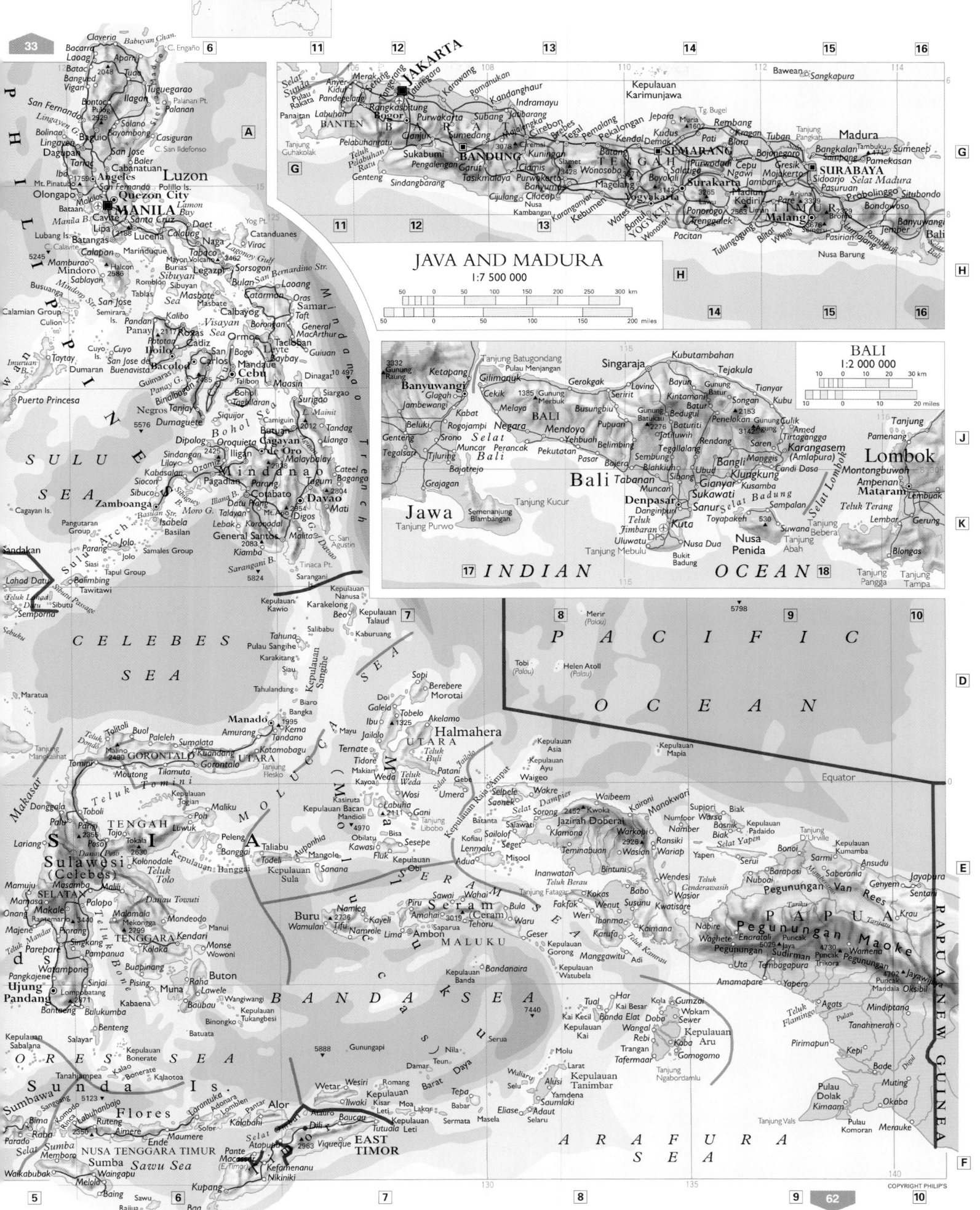

1:6 000 000

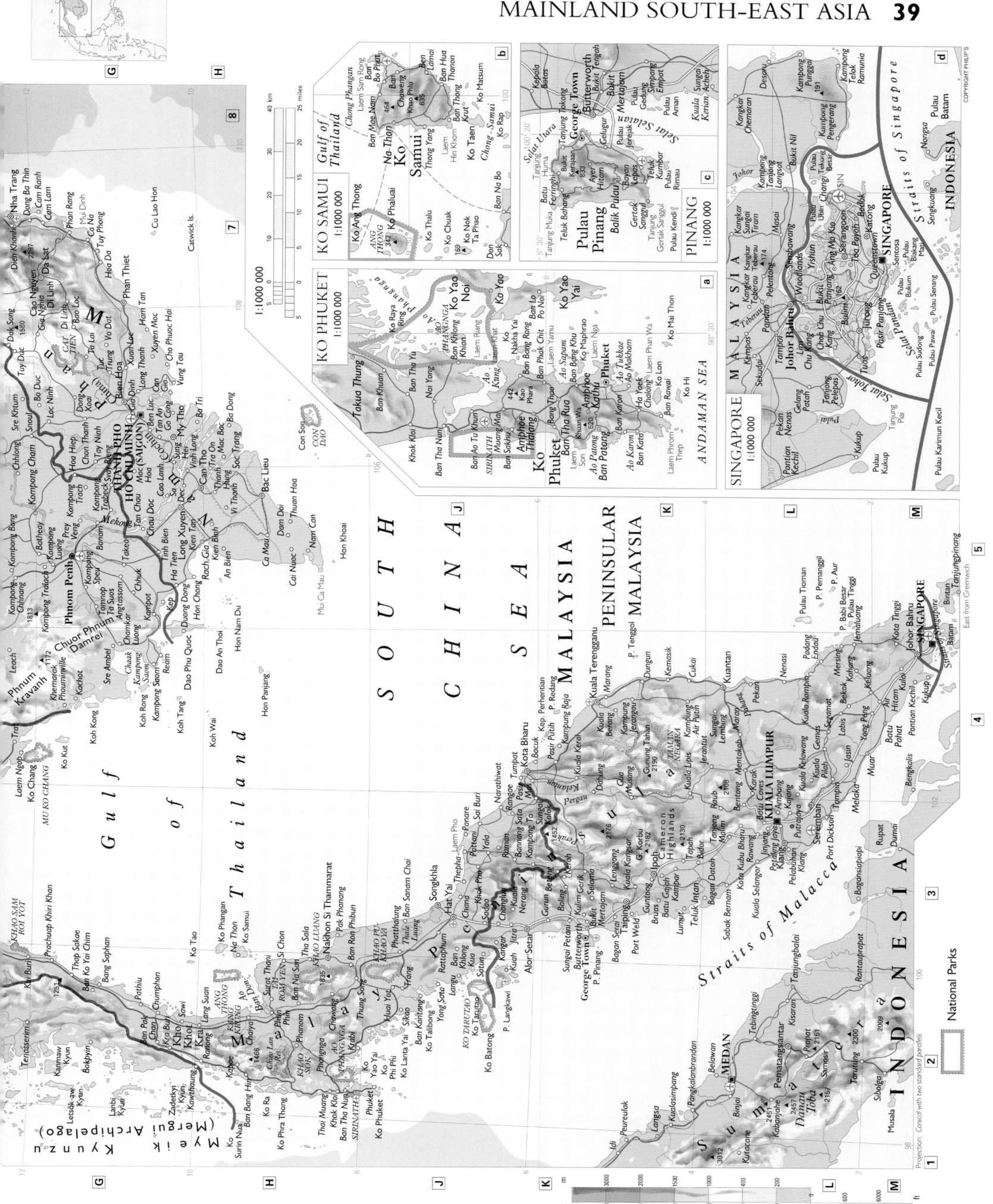

COPYRIGHT PHILIP'S

**KO SAMUI**
1:1 000 000

*Chong Phangan*

*Gulf of Thailand*

Ko Samui

**KO PHUKET**
1:1 000 000

**KO ANG THONG**
1:1 000 000

**PINANG**
Pulau Pinang
1:1 000 000

**SINGAPORE**
1:1 000 000

Gulf
of
Thailand

SOUTH
CHINA
SEA

MALAYSIA

PENINSULAR
MALAYSIA

KUALA LUMPUR

Straits of Malacca

INDONESIA

*Myeik*
*(Mergui Archipelago)*

*Kyunzu*

ANDAMAN SEA

National Parks

Projection: Conical with two standard parallels

East from Greenwich

BAY OF BENGAL

INDIAN OCEAN

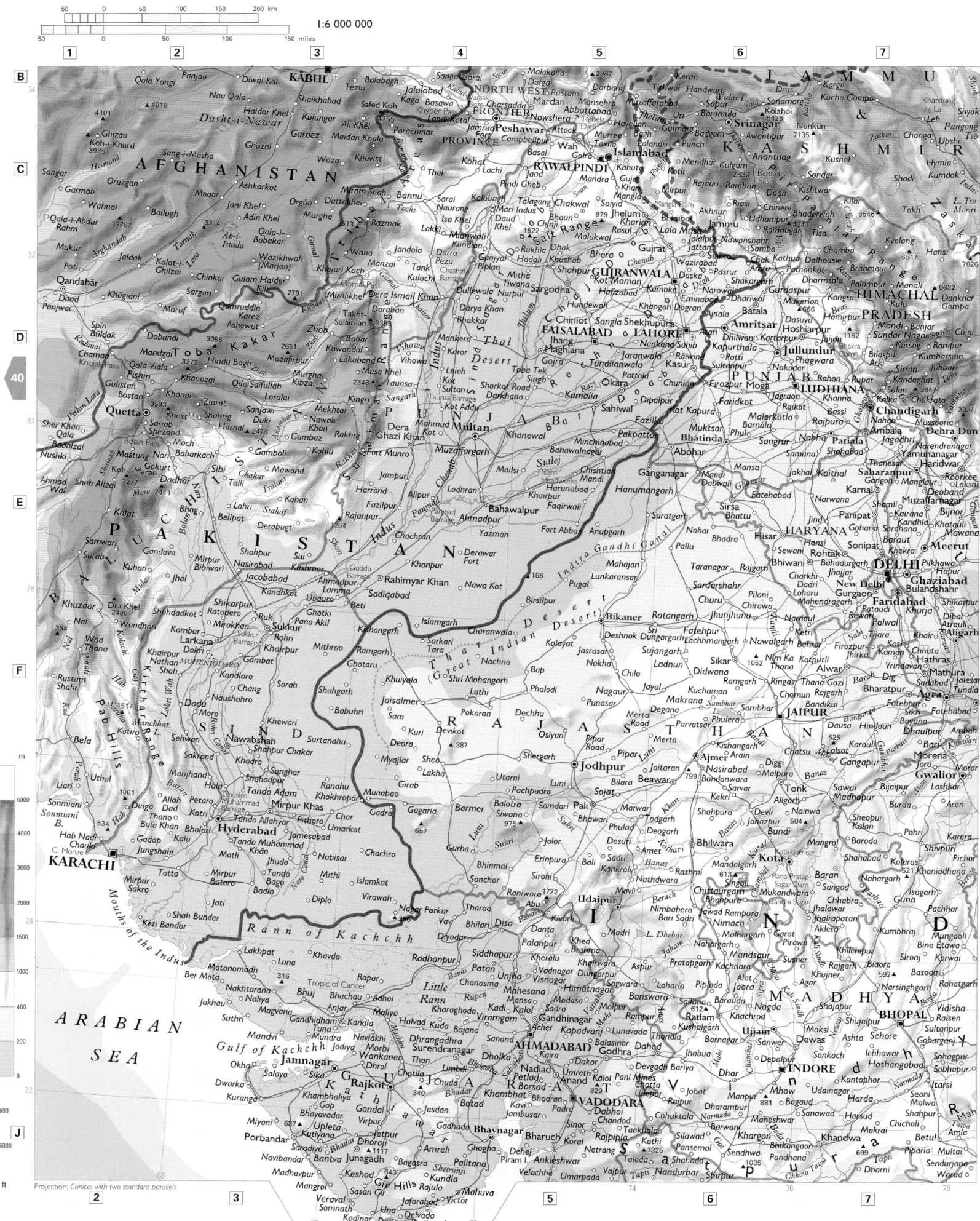

Projection: Conical with two standard parallels

JAMMU AND KASHMIR
on same scale

1:7 000 000

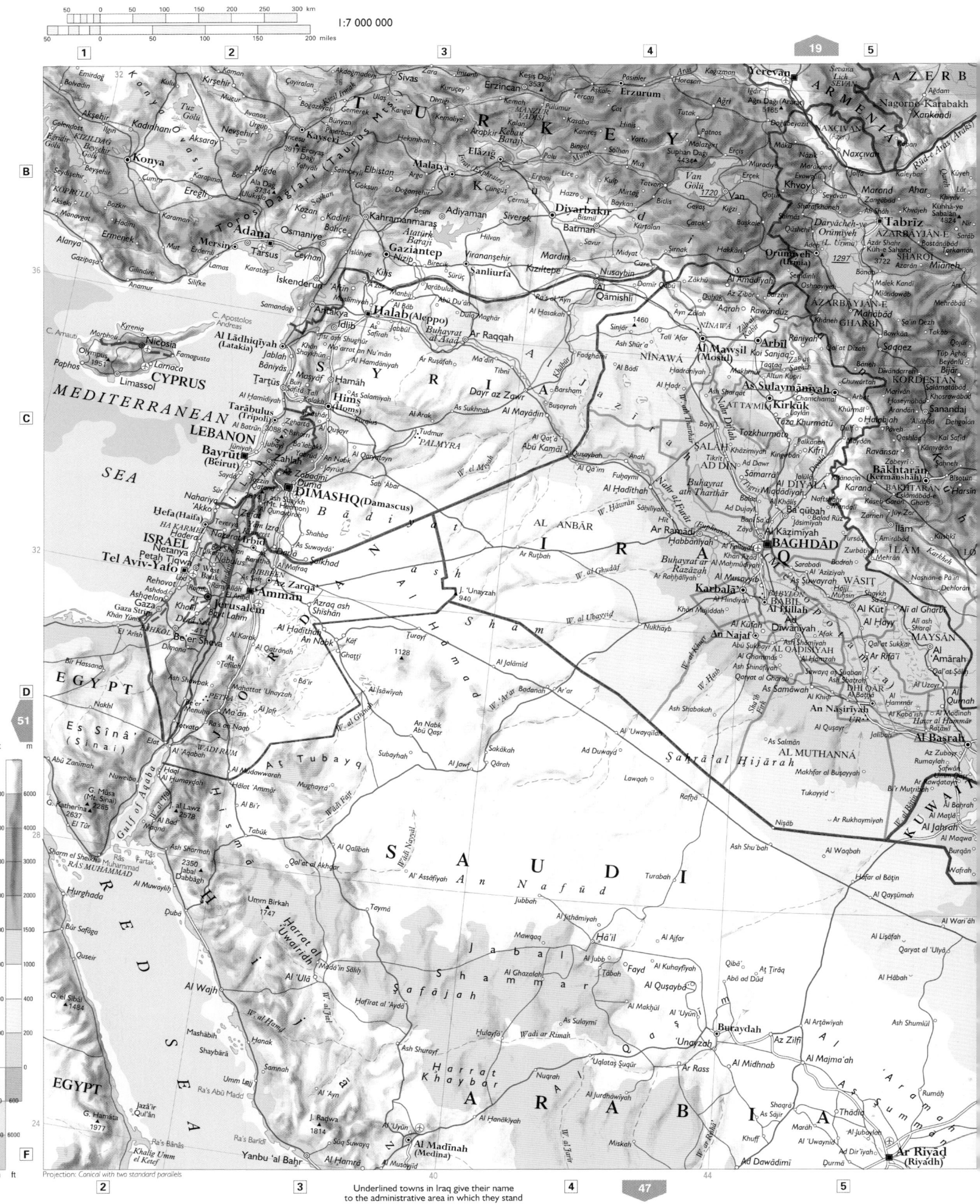

Projection: Conical with two standard parallels

Underlined towns in Iraq give their name
to the administrative area in which they stand

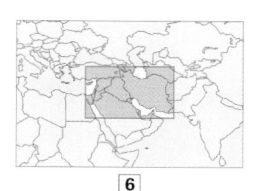

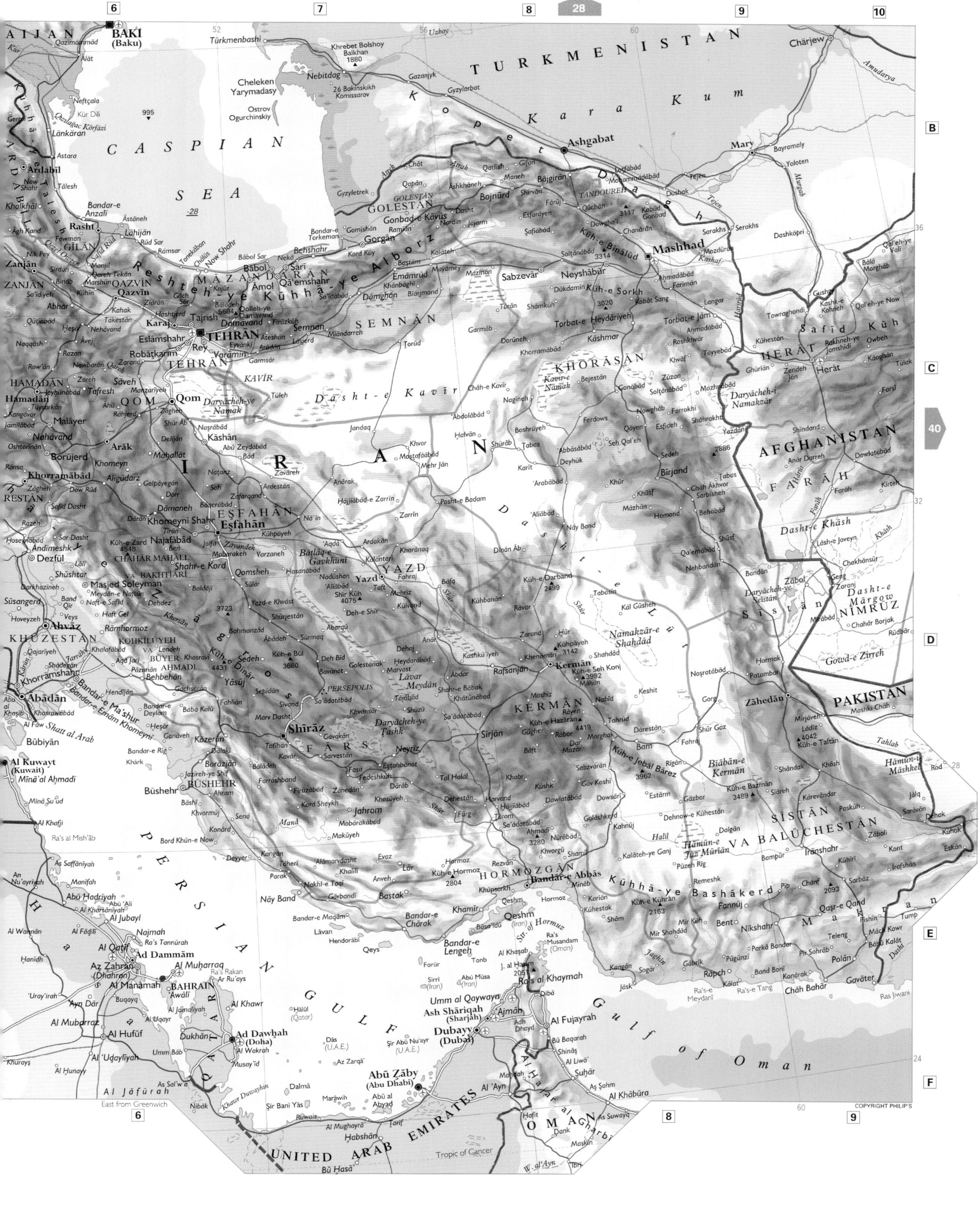

10 0 10 20 30 40 50 60 70 80 100 km

1:2 500 000

10 0 10 20 30 40 50 60 miles

| 1 | 2 | 3 | 4 | 44 | 5 | 6 |

**CYPRUS**

Paphos
Episkopi
Episkopi Bay
Limassol
Akrotiri
Akrotiri Bay
C. Gata

**M E D I T E R R A N E A N**

**S E A**

Al Ḥamidīyah
Ḥims (Homs)
Tall Kalakh
Shinshār
Furqlus

Al Minā'
ASH SHAMĀL
Halbā
Al Qusayr
Al Ḥirmil
HIMS

Tarābulus (Tripoli)
Zgharta
Qurnat as Sawdā' 3088
Al Qaryatayn

Al Batrūn
Bsharri
Al Burayj
2464

Jubayl
Qartaba
AL BIQĀ
An Nabk
Bi'r Ghadīr

Ibrāhīm
Al Labwah
2616

Jūniyah
J. Sannin 2628
Ba'labakk
Yabrūd

**BAYRŪT (Beirut)**
Bikfayyā
Zahlah
Sirghāyā
Al Qutayfah
**SYRIA**

Ash Shuwayfāt
Alayh
AD DĀM
Ḥawsh Mussá
Khān Abū Shāmat

Ad Dāmūr
JABAL LUBNĀN
1942
Az Zabadānī
Dumayr

**LEBANON**
al Bāruk
Jezzîn
Darayyā
**DIMASHQ (Damascus)**
Dūma

Saydā (Sidon)
J'ash Shaykh (Mt Hermon) 2814
Qatana
A'waj

An Nabatīyah at Tahta
Marj 'Uyūn
Al Khiyam
Al Kiswah
Al Ḥājānah

AL JANŪB
Ḥgolan Heights
Al Qunayṭirah
As Sanamayn
Burāq

Sūr (Tyre)
Qiryat Shemona
1197
Mas'ada
Ar Rafid
DAR'Ā
Shahbā
J. al Druz

Naharriyya
Me'ona
Fiq
Shaykh Miskin
Izra
AS SUWAYDĀ'

'Akko (Acre)
Hagalil
Zefat
Yam Kinneret
Sahm al Jawlān
As Suwaydā' 1600

Mifraz Hefa
Qiryat Karmi'el
HAZAFON
Teverya (Tiberias) -210
Dar'ā
Salāh

**Hefa (Haifa)**
Qiryat Ata
Nazerat (Nazareth)
Yarmūk
IRBID
Al Ramthā
Malah

Dāliyat el Karmel
HA KARMEL
Afula
Ta'iba
**Irbid**
Bustā ash Shām
Salkhad

TEL MEGIDDO
Umm el Fahm
Bet She'an
AJLŪN
Umm al Qittayn
AL MAFRAQ

CAESAREA
Pardes
Hanna-Karkur
AJLŪN 1247
Umm ad Danāj
Al Mafraq

**ISRAEL**
Shōmrōn
Tulkarm
Tūbās
JARASH
JARASH

Ḥadera
SAMARIA
N. az Zarqā
Umm al Qittayn

Netanya
HAMERKAZ
Nābulus
AL BALQĀ
Az Zarqā

Herzliyya
Kefar Sava
SHILO
As Salt
Azraq ash Shishān

Benē Beraq
Petaḥ Tiqwa
Wadi as Sīr
**AMMĀN**

**Tel Aviv-Yafo**
Ramat Gan
AZ ZARQĀ

Bat Yam
Lod
Rām Allāh
Karama
AMM

Rishon le Ziyyon
Ramla
El Arīḥā (Jericho)
Na'ūr

Yavne
Rehovot
At Tunayb
'AMMĀN

Ashdod
Qiryat Mal'akhi
**Jerusalem (Yerushalayim) (Al Quds)**
Ma'daba
MA'DĀBA

Ashqelon
Qiryat Gat
Bet Shemesh
Bayt Laḥm (Bethlehem)
Al Ḥaydān

**Gaza Strip**
Gaza
N. Shiqma
Al Khalīl (Hebron)
Dhibān

Khān Yūnis
Sederot
Az Ẓāhirīyah
W. al Mawjib
Al Hadithah

Rafah
ESHKOL
Be'er Sheva (Beersheba)
Arad
Al Qatrānah

**Bûr Sa'îd (Port Said)**
Bûr Fu'ad
El Daheir
Bor Mashash
Sedom
Al Karak
AL KARAK

Khalig el Tîna
Râs Burûn
Sabkhet el Bardawîl
Dimona -333
Al Mazār
W. Bā'ir

El 'Arîsh
HADAROM
1305
JORDAN

Râmâni
Bîr el 'Abd
Bîr el Garârât
Bîr Lahfân
Qezi'ot
Sedé Boqér
W. al Ḥasā
Bā'ir

El Qantara
Bîr Qaṭia
Bîr Kaseiba
-121
At Ṭafīlah
Mahattat 'Unayzah
J. ash Shawmari 1072

Wâhid
Bîr el Duweidar
Bîr el Jafir
Muweilih
Mizpe Ramon
AT ṬAFĪLAH

**Ismâ'ilîya**
Bîr el Mâlḥi
El Quṣeima
**Hanegev**
Nijil
Al Jafr

Ṭalâta
ISMĀ'ILĪYA
Khamsa
Bîr Hasana
Bîr Beiḍa
Rujm Tālān al Jamā'ā 1736
Qa'el Jafr

El Buheirat el Murrat el Kubra (Bitter Lakes)
G.Yi 'Allâq 1094
N. Paran
PETRA
Wādi Mūsā
Ma'ān
MA'ĀN

Gineifa
Bîr el Thamâda
W. Qiraiya
N. Hiwyon
Bi'r al Mārī

**E G Y P T**
Mamarr Mitlā
W. el Brûk
El 'Agrûd
En 'Avrona
Ra's an Naqb

El Suweis (Suez)
Bûr Taufîq
Bîr Gebeil Hisn
W. Maḥashm
Al 'AQABAH
Mahattat ash Shidīyah

Adabiya
ES SÎnâ' (Sinai)
W. El Tamarani
Ra's an Naqb 1435
SAUDI

Uyûn Mûsa
Aîn Sudr
Nakhl
W. El 'Aqaba
W. El Aqaba
WADI RUM 1593
Baṭn al Ghūl
ARABIA

948 G. el Kabrît
El Thamad
1754
Rum

Khalîg el Bûs
Gebel el Tîh
Bîr Abu Muḥammad
Bi'r al Qattār

Ghubbet el Bûs
El Wabeira
Bîr el Biârât
Bîr Ṭâba

Râs Matarma
J A N Û B
S Î N Î
Bîr el Heisi
Gulf of Aqaba
At Tubayq

1272
EL SUWEIS
W. Abu Ga'da
Bîr Wuseit
1165
Ḥaqi
Al Mudawwarah

**Projection:** Polyconic

East from Greenwich

COPYRIGHT PHILIP'S

- - - 1974 Cease Fire Lines

National Parks

| ft | m |
|---|---|
| 9000 | 3000 |
| 6000 | 2000 |
| 4500 | 1500 |
| 3000 | 1000 |
| 1200 | 400 |
| 600 | 200 |
| 0 | 0 |
| 200 | 600 |
| 2000 | 6000 |

m ft

1:15 000 000

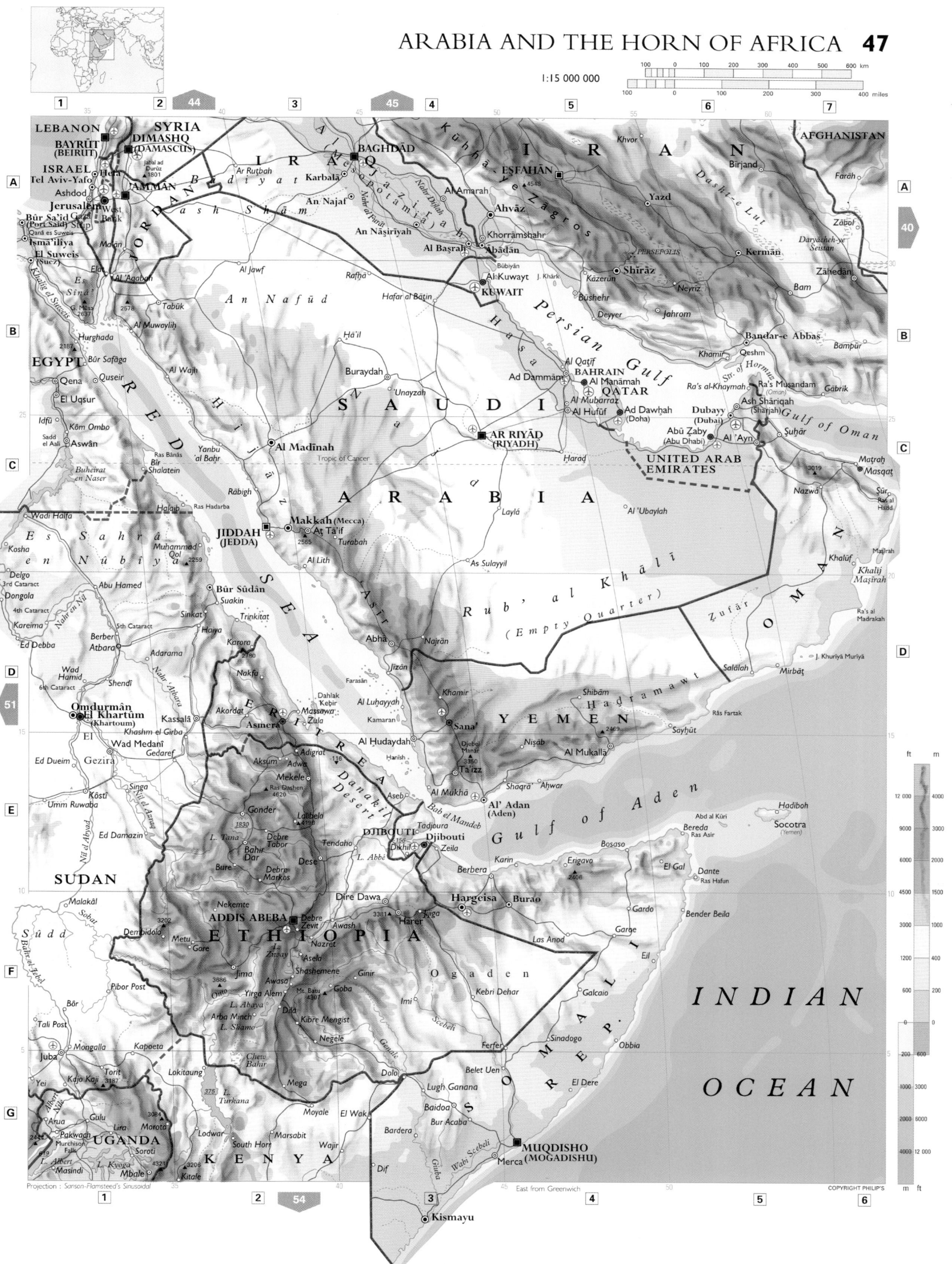

1:42 000 000

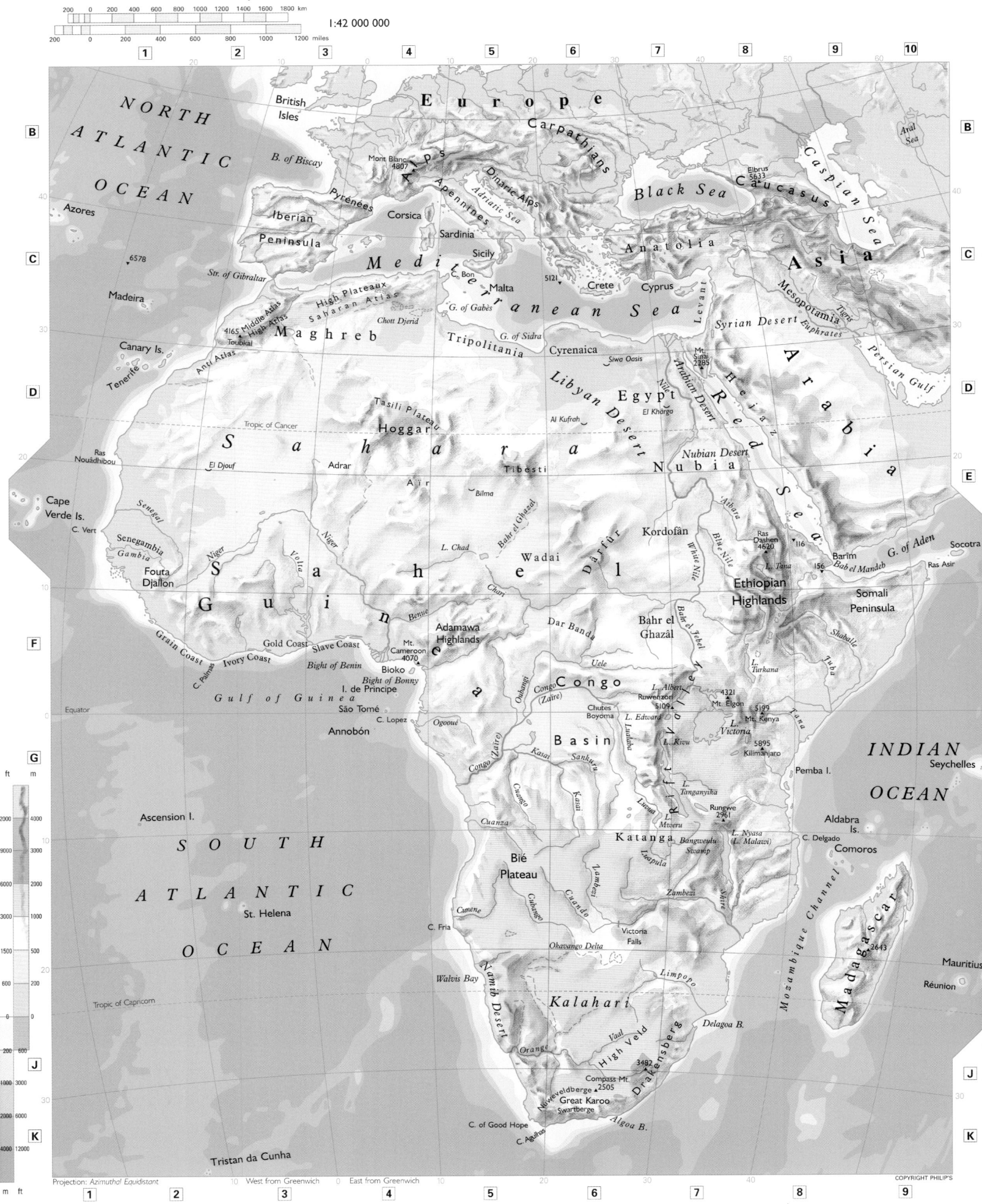

Projection: Azimuthal Equidistant

COPYRIGHT PHILIP'S

1:42 000 000

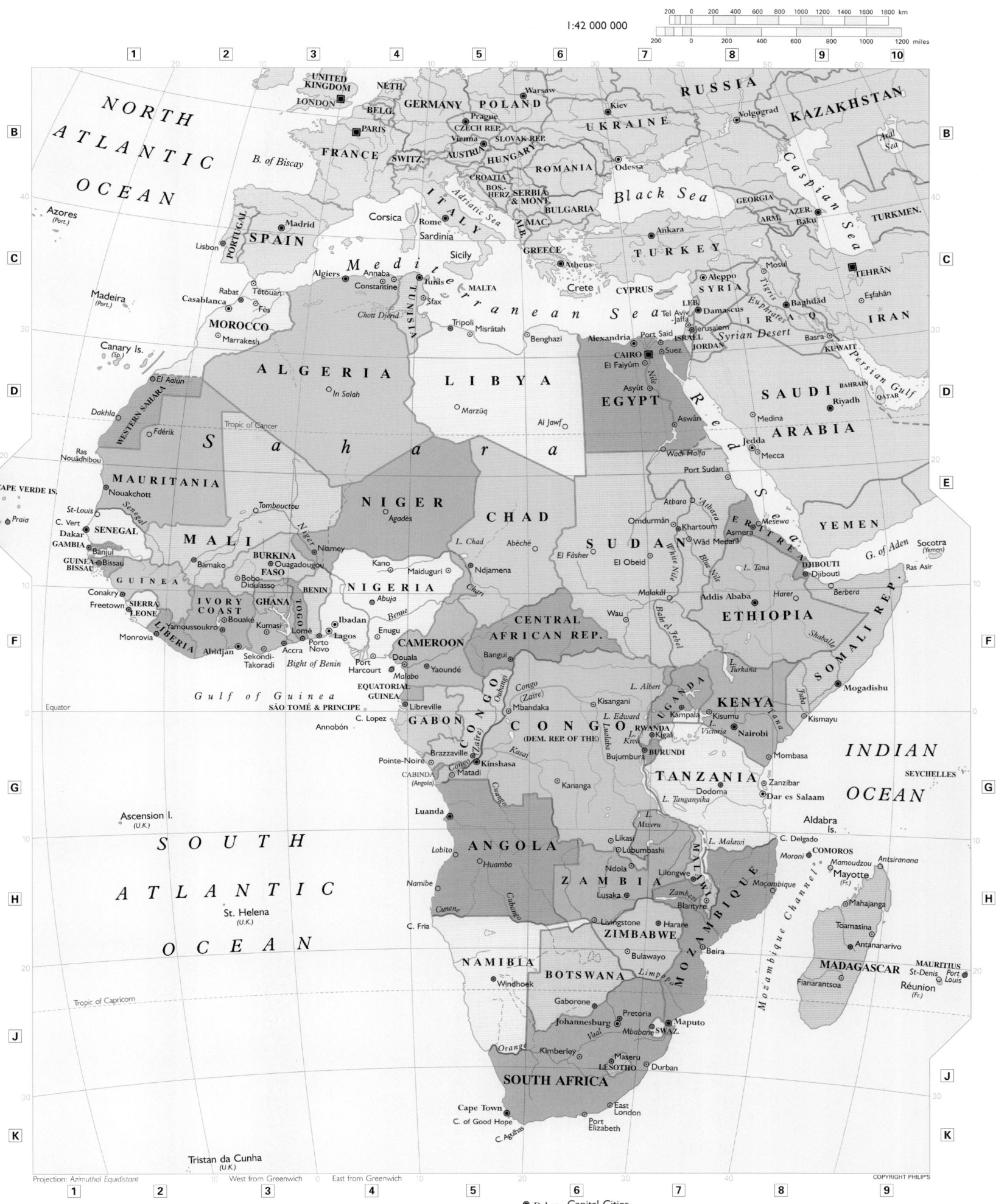

Projection: Azimuthal Equidistant

West from Greenwich   East from Greenwich

COPYRIGHT PHILIP'S

● Dakar   Capital Cities

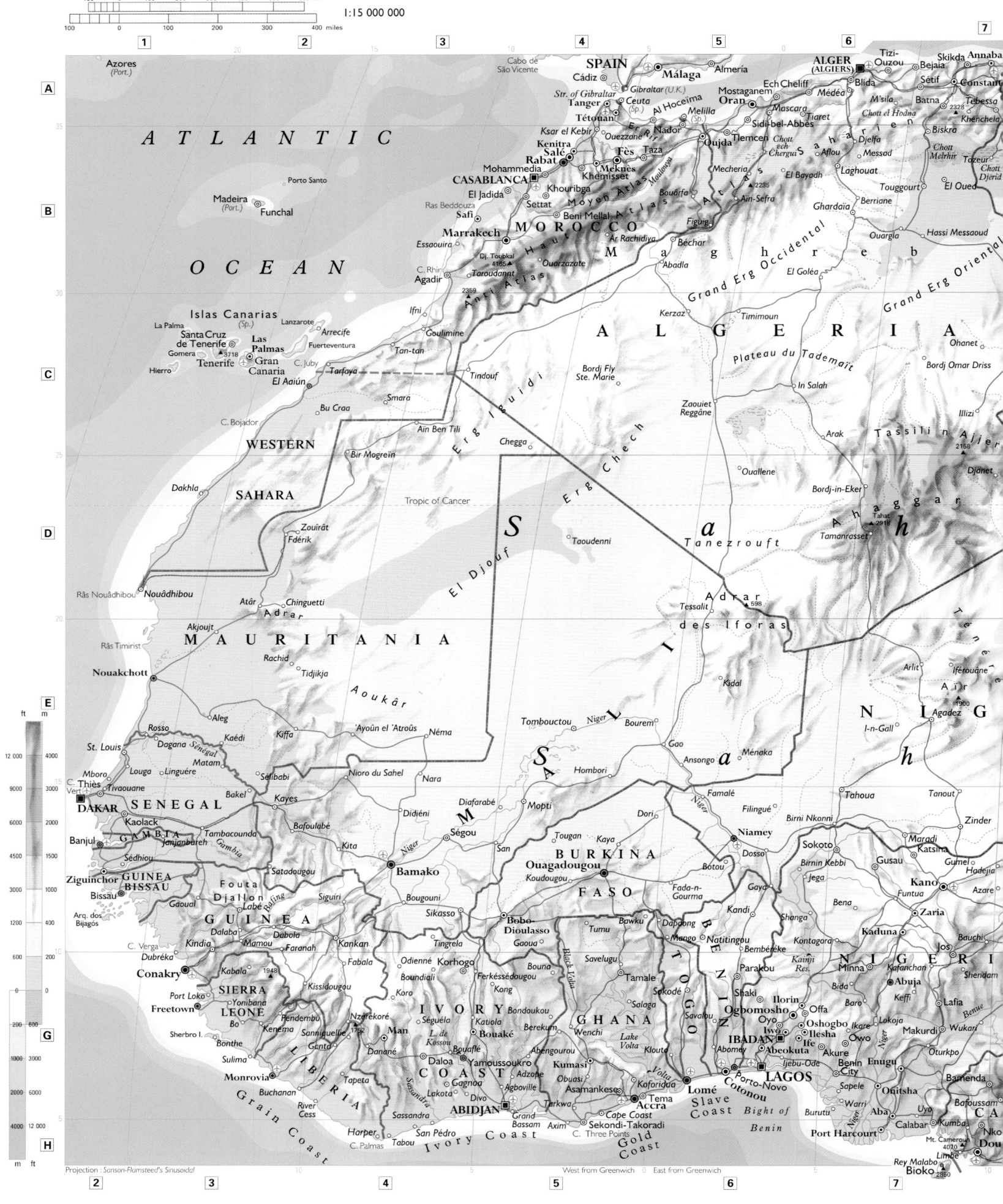

100   0   100   200   300   400   500   600 km

100   0   100   200   300   400 miles

1:15 000 000

Projection : Sanson-Flamsteed's Sinusoidal

West from Greenwich   0   East from Greenwich

1:15 000 000

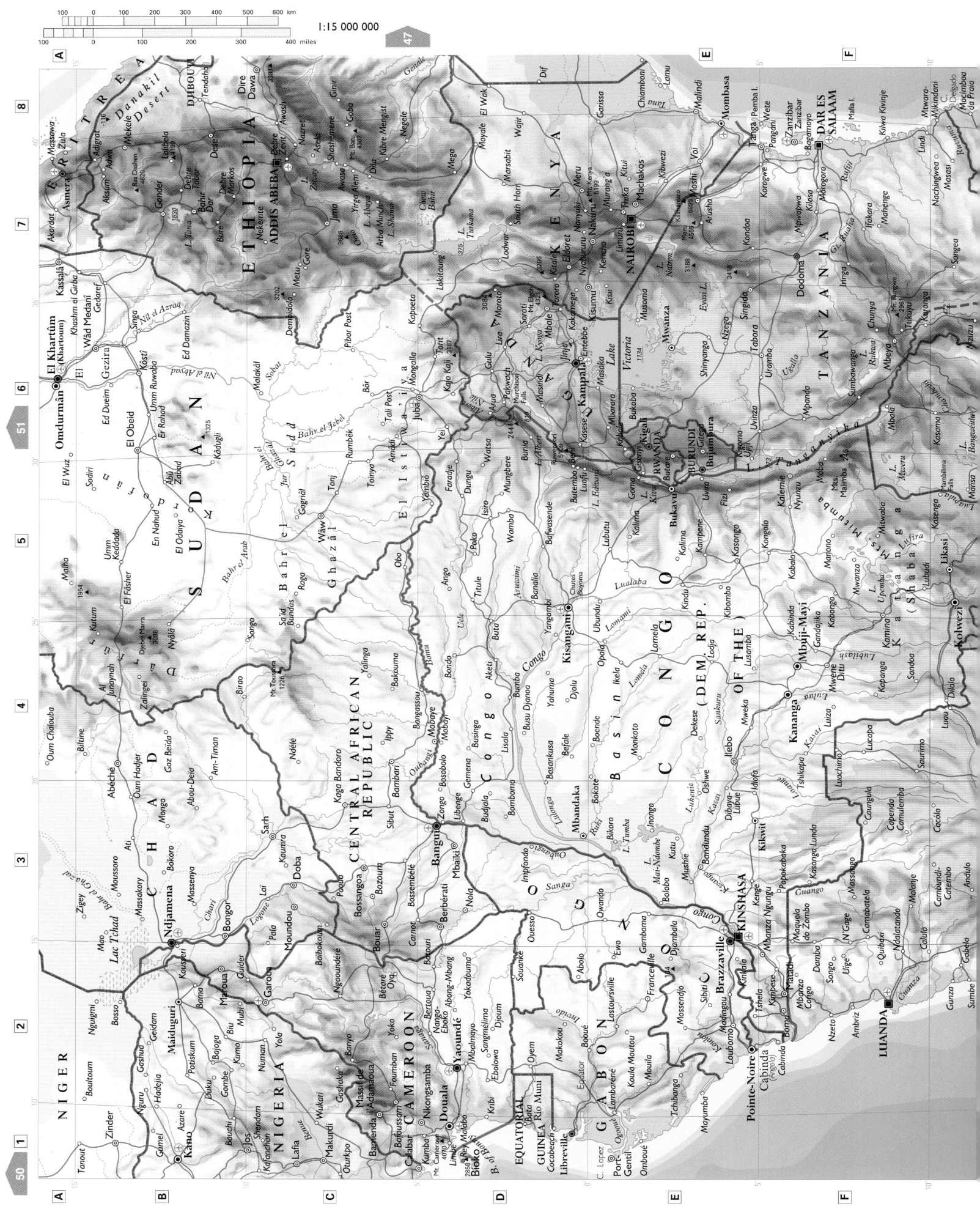

INDIAN OCEAN

INDIAN OCEAN

ATLANTIC OCEAN

ANGOLA

ZAMBIA

NAMIBIA

BOTSWANA

ZIMBABWE

SOUTH AFRICA

MOZAMBIQUE

MADAGASCAR
on same scale

Kalahari

Namib Desert

Skeleton Coast

Tropic of Capricorn

CAPE TOWN
Cape of Good Hope

JOHANNESBURG
PRETORIA

MAPUTO

HARARE

Lusaka

Lubumbashi

Antananarivo

DURBAN

Port Elizabeth

Bulawayo

Windhoek

Gaborone

Beira

L. Nyasa
(L. Malawi)

MALAWI

SWAZI-
LAND

LESOTHO

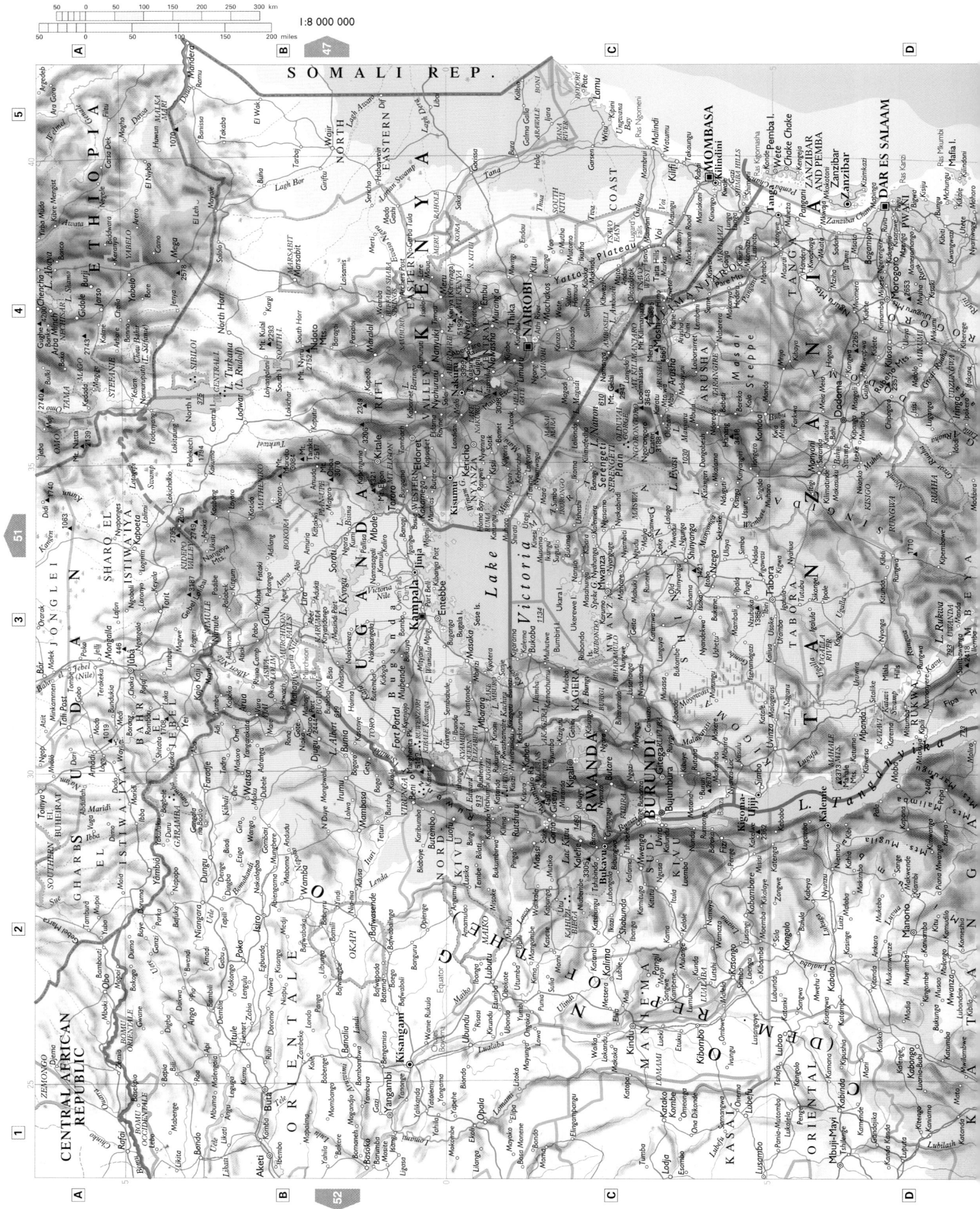

1:8 000 000

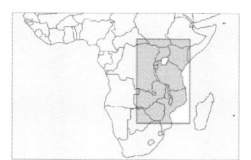

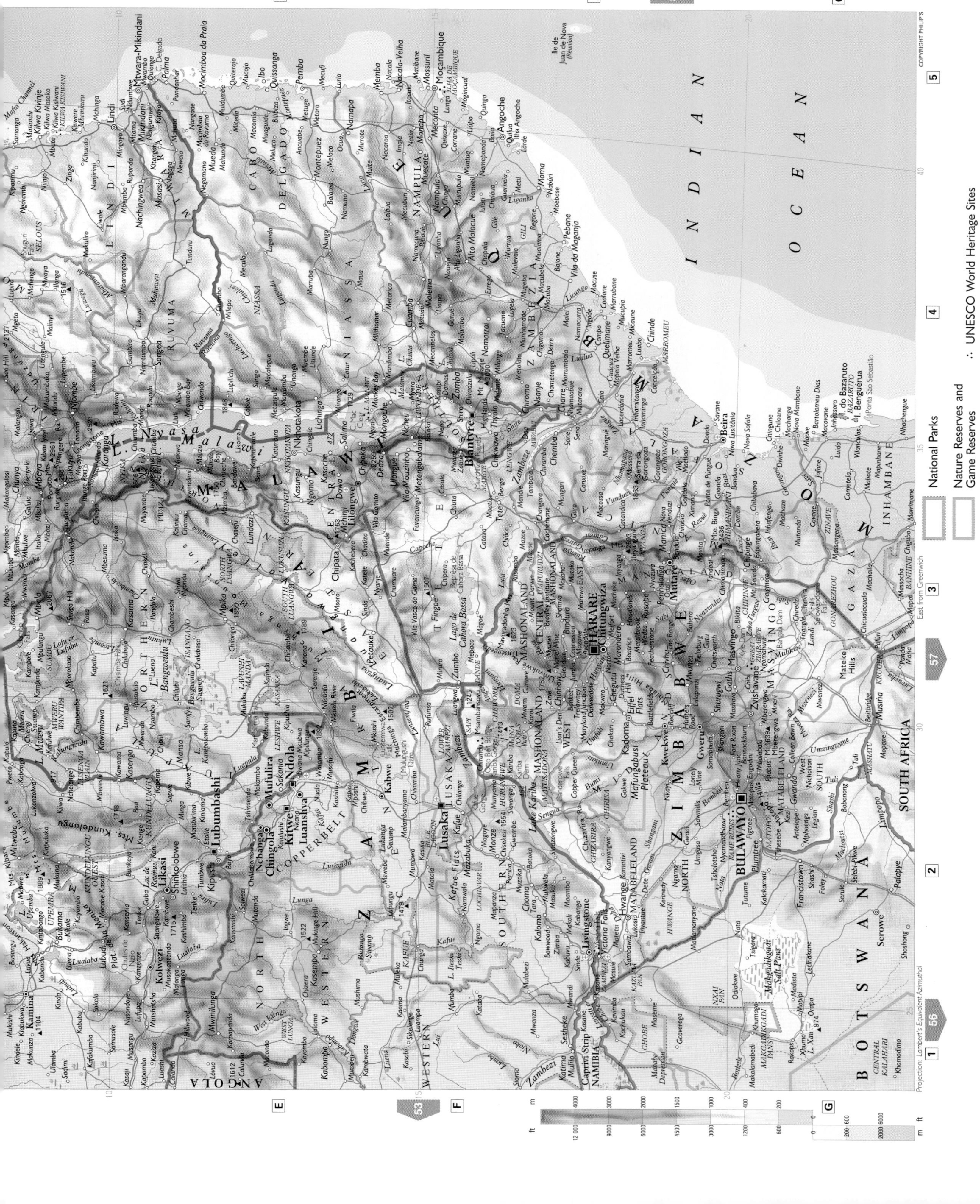

INDIAN OCEAN
ZAMBIA
MALAWI
MOZAMBIQUE
ZIMBABWE
BOTSWANA
NAMIBIA
SOUTH AFRICA
ANGOLA
L. Nyasa / L. Malawi
Lake Kariba
Zambezi
Lusaka
Harare
Lilongwe
Blantyre
Beira
Bulawayo
Lubumbashi
Ndola
Kitwe
Chingola
Livingstone
Victoria Falls
Mutare
Masvingo
Quelimane
Nampula
Moçambique
Pemba
Lindi
Mtwara-Mikindani
Tete
Chipata
Kasama
Mbeya
Francistown
Serowe
Palapye
Kamina
Kolwezi
Likasi
Ile de Juan de Nova (Réunion)
National Parks
Nature Reserves and Game Reserves
∴ UNESCO World Heritage Sites
Projection: Lambert's Equivalent Azimuthal
East from Greenwich
COPYRIGHT PHILIP'S
m 4000 3000 2000 1500 1000 400 200 0
ft 12 000 9000 6000 4500 3000 1200 600 0
0 200 600 2000 6000
53 56 57

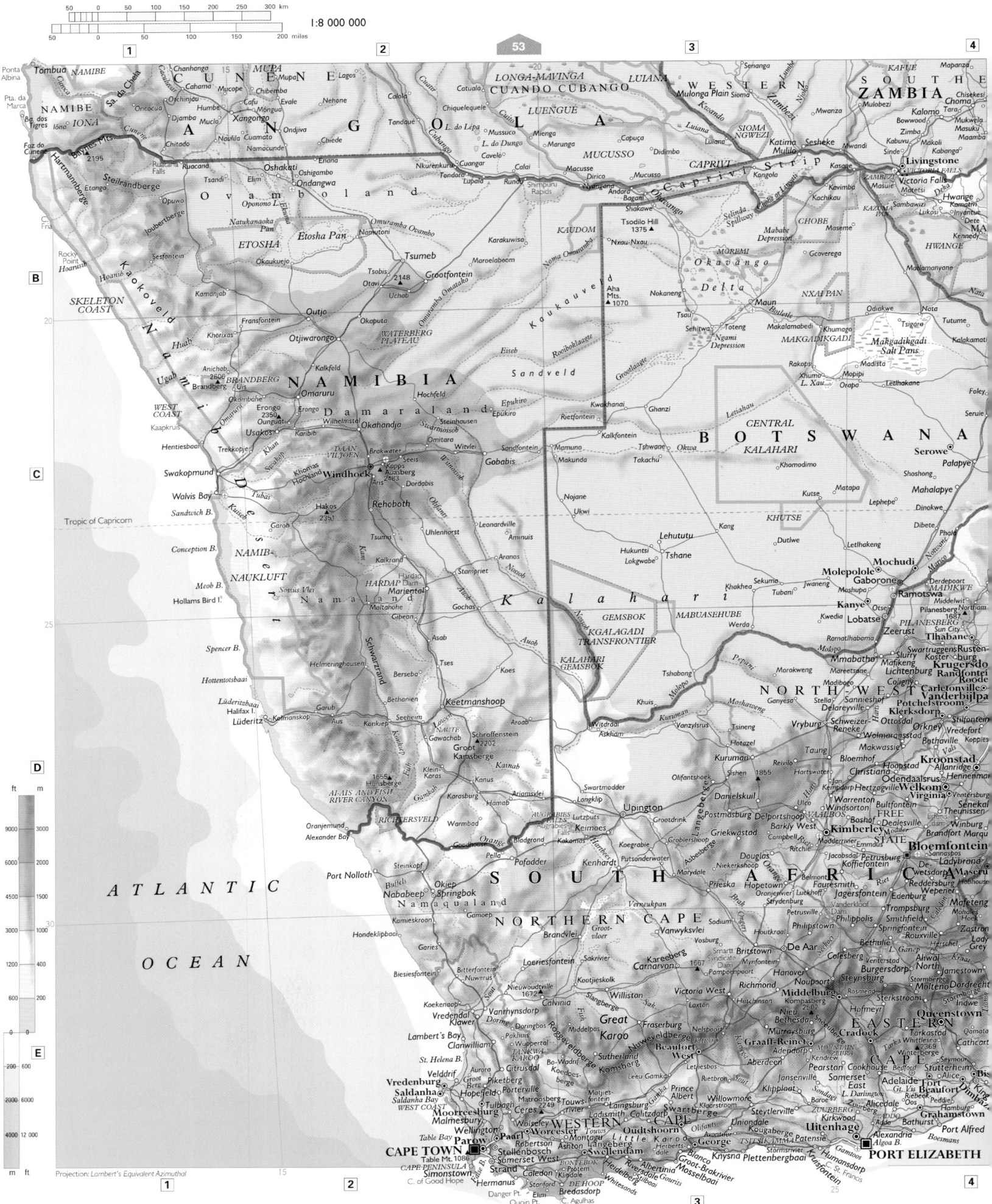

Projection: Lambert's Equivalent Azimuthal

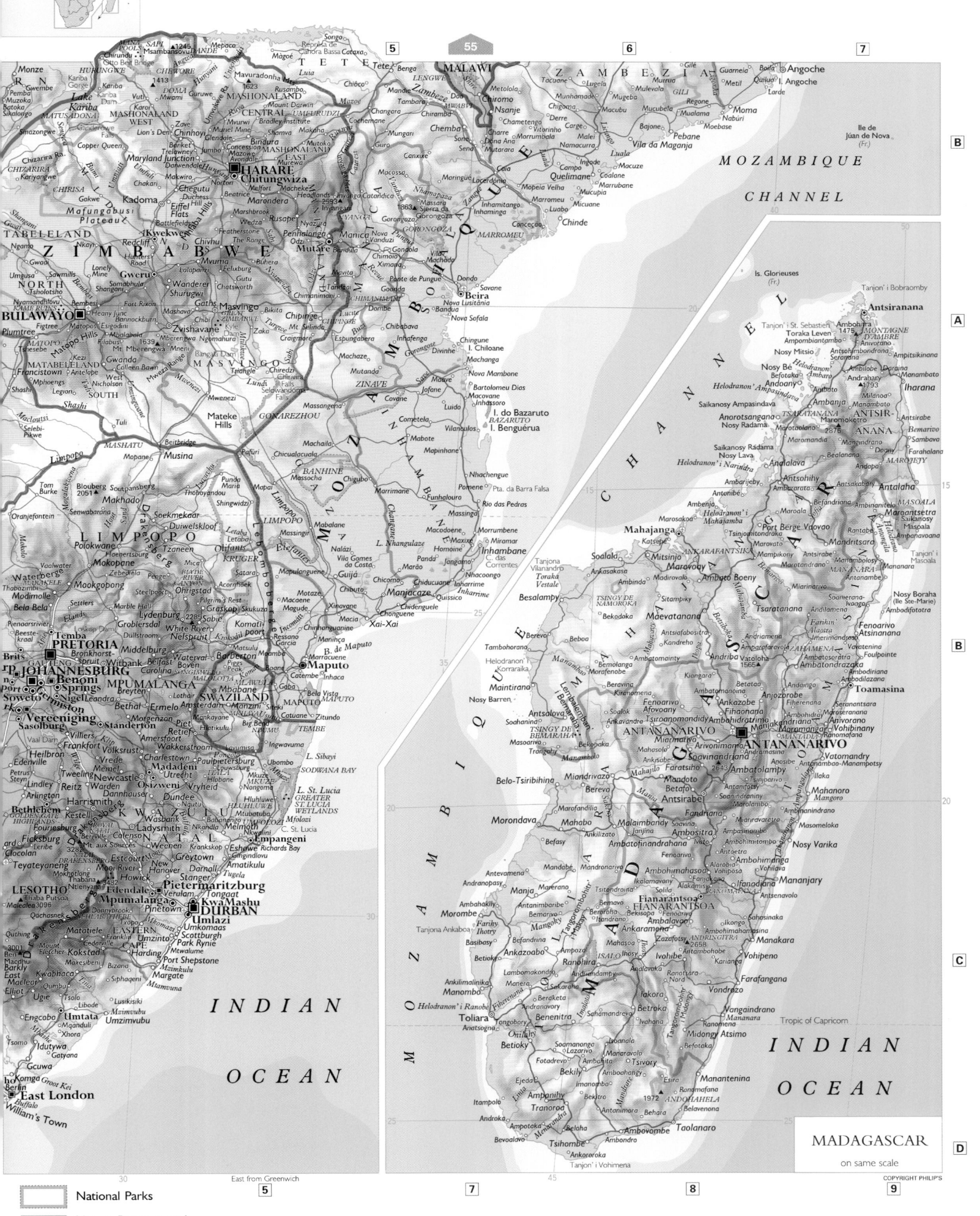

MADAGASCAR

on same scale

National Parks

Nature Reserves and
Game Reserves

∴ UNESCO World Heritage Sites

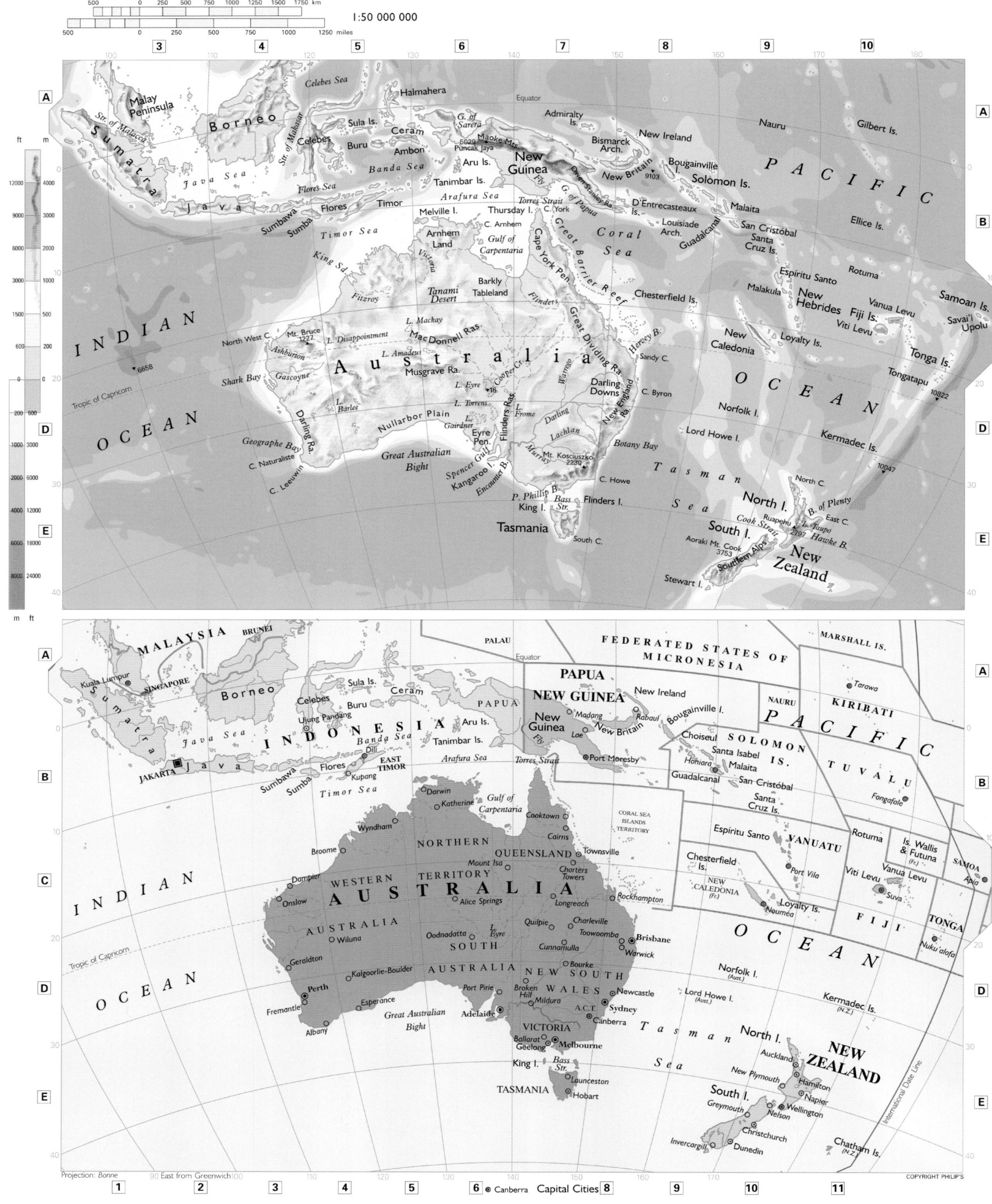

1:6 000 000

50 0 50 100 150 200 km
50 0 50 100 150 miles

**North Island**

C. Reinga
C. Maria van Diemen
North C.
Houhora Heads
Rangaunu B.
Doubtless B.
Mongonui
Whangaroa Harb.
Ahipara B.
Kaitaia
Okaihau
Waitangi
B. of Islands
C. Brett
Tauroa Pt.
Opua
Rawene
Kaikohe
Hokianga Harbour
Hikurangi
Whangarei
Whangarei Harb.
Waipoua Forest
Bream Hd.
Bream B.
Dargaville
Waipu
Little Barrier I.
Warkworth
C. Rodney
Great Barrier I.
Kaipara Harbour
C. Colville
Cuvier I.
Helensville
Hauraki Gulf
Coromandel
Whitianga
Takapuna
Manukau
AUCKLAND
Papakura
Thames
Whangamata
Waiuku
Pukekohe
Mercer
Waihi
Tauranga Harb.
Waikato
Paeroa
Whangamata
Mayor I.
Whakatane
Runaway
Huntly
Te Aroha
Waihi
Whakaari (White I.)
Morrinsville
Tauranga
Te Puke
Raglan
Hamilton
Cambridge
Whakatane
Kawerau
Bay of Plenty
East C.
Te Awamutu
Raukumara Ra.
Kawhia
Kawhia Harbour
Otorohanga
Rotorua
Hikurangi 1753
Waitomo Caves
Te Kuiti
Kinleith
L. Tarawera
Murupara
Waipiro
Mokau
Tokoroa
L. Taratora
UREWERA
Motu
Tolaga Bay
Mokau
Ongarue
Wairakei
Taupo
Waikaremoana
Ormond
North Taranaki Bight
Taumarunui
L. Taupo
Gisborne
Waitara
Turangi
Rangitikei Mts.
Nuhaka
Waikokopu
New Plymouth
WHANGANUI
Whangamomona
Tarawera
Poverty Bay
Inglewood
Kaimanawa Mts.
Waikaremoana
Mahia Pen.
Mt. Taranaki or Mt. Egmont 2518
EGMONT
Ruapehu 2797
Wairoa
C. Egmont
Stratford
Ohakune
TONGARIRO
Bay View
Hawke Bay
Opunake
Eltham
Raethi
Waiouru
Napier
Kaponga
RUAHINE Ra.
C. Kidnappers
Hawera
South Taranaki Bight
Waverley
Mangaweka
Taihape
Hastings
Patea
Hunterville
Waipawa
Wanganui
Marton
Halcombe
Waipukurau
Bulls
Feilding
Dannevirke
Palmerston North
Woodville
Foxton
Levin
Pahiatua
C. Turnagain
Shannon
Eketahuna
Paraparaumu
Otaki
Kapiti I.
Masterton
Carterton
Upper Hutt
Featherston
Greytown
Petone
Martinborough
Lower Hutt
Wellington
Rimutaka Ra.
Eastbourne
Blenheim
Cook Strait

**South Island**

C. Farewell
Golden B.
D'Urville I.
Collingwood
ABEL TASMAN
KAHURANGI
Takaka
Tasman B.
Karamea
Tasman Mts.
Motueka
Pelorus
Karamea Bight
Nelson
Havelock
Picton
Seddonville
Tadmor
Matiri Ra.
Richmond
Blenheim
Granity
Lyell
Wakefield
Seddon
Westport
Murchison
NELSON LAKES
Ward
Inangahua
Rotoroa
2885 Tapuae-o-Uenuku
PAPAROA
Mt. Travers 2338
Clarence
Punakaiki
Spenser Mts.
Reefton
Hanmer Springs
Kaikoura
Blackball
Stillwater
Waiau
Kaikoura
Runanga
L. Brunner
Wau
Greymouth
ARTHUR'S PASS
Waikari
Hurunui
Kumara
L. Jacksons
Culverden
Amberley
Hokitika
Arthur's Pass
Waipara
Oxford
Pegasus Bay
Ross
Waikari
Rangiora
Kaiapoi
Abut Hd.
WESTLAND
Springfield
New Brighton
Christchurch
WESTLAND
Aoraki Mt. Cook 3753
Whitecliffs
Riccarton
Lyttelton
Methven
Lincoln
Banks Pen.
Jackson B.
Mount Cook
Staveley
Akaroa
SOUTHERN ALPS (Tiritiri o te Moana)
Little River
MT. COOK
Okuru
Haast
Tekapo
L. Ellesmere
Southbridge
Rakaia
Rangitata
MOUNT ASPIRING
Mt. Aspiring 3027
Fairlie
Pukaki
Ashburton Bight
Milford Sd.
Earnslaw 2818
L. Wanaka
Ohau
Geraldine
Canterbury Plains
Sutherland Falls
Bligh Sound
Milford Sound
Wanaka
Hawea
Tekapo
Temuka
George Sound
Arrowtown
Cromwell
Timaru
Dunstan Mts.
Kurow
St. Andrews
Queenstown
Clyde
Waitaki
Waimate
Alexandra
Ngapara
Secretary I.
Eyre Mts.
Naseby
Oamaru
Doubtful Sd.
Garvie Mts.
Ranfurly
Maheno
FIORDLAND
Manapouri
Roxburgh
Hampden
Breaksea Sd.
L. Manapouri
Otago
Waikouaiti
Danback
Resolution I.
Umbrella Mts.
Palmerston
Dusky Sd.
Lumsden
Ohai
Waipori
Port Chalmers
Chalky Inlet
Mossburn
Ediēvale
Otago Harbour
Preservation Inlet
Nightcaps
Kelso
Mahinerangi
C. Saunders
Te Waewae B.
Clifden
Tapanui
Lawrence
Dunedin
Orepuki
Winton
Clinton
Milton
Solander I.
Tuatapere
Hedgehope
Mataura
Balclutha
Riverton
Gore
Kaitangata
Invercargill
Wyndham
Owaka
Nugget Pt.
South Invercargill
Tokanui
Tahakopa
Bluff
Ruapuke I.
Foveaux Str.
Halfmoon Bay
Stewart I. (Rakiura)
RAKIURA
Port Pegasus
South West C.

TASMAN SEA
Westland Bight
PACIFIC OCEAN

Projection : Conical with two standard parallels
East from Greenwich

---

**SAMOAN ISLANDS**
1:12 000 000

SAMOA
AMERICAN SAMOA
Savai'i
Apia
Upolu
Pago Pago
Tutuila
West from Greenwich

Futuna
Wallis & Futuna (Fr.)

Niuafo'ou (Tonga)

Thikombia
Labasa
Vanua Levu
Yasawa Group
Vanua Balavu
Taveuni
Koro
FIJI
Lautoka
Levuka
1323
Ovalau
Nandi
Viti Levu
Gau
Lau Group
Vava'u
Suva
Koro Sea
Lakeba
Moala
PACIFIC OCEAN
Kandavu
Vatoa
Tofua
**FIJI AND TONGA**
1:12 000 000
TONGA (Friendly Is.)
Tongatapu
Nuku'alofa

50 0 50 100 150 200 km
50 0 50 100 150 miles

East from Greenwich
West from Greenwich

National Parks

ft m
9000 3000
6000 2000
3000 1000
1200 400
600 200
0 0
200 600
2000 6000
4000 12000
6000 18000
m ft

1:8 000 000

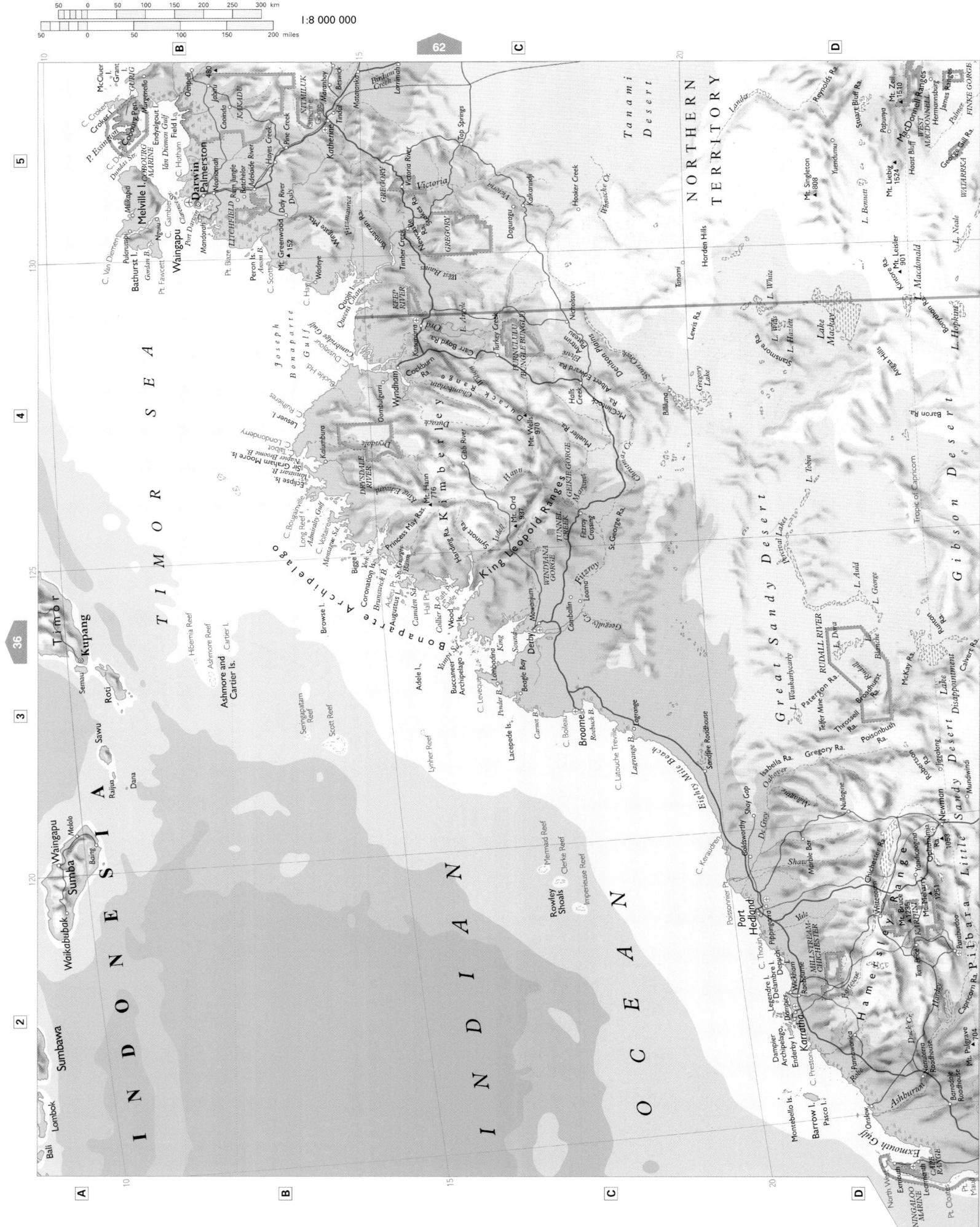

50   0   50   100   150   200   250   300 km

50   0   50   100   150   200 miles

62

10

B

15

C

20

D

5

130

4

125

36

3

2

120

NORTHERN     TERRITORY

T I M O R     S E A

I N D O N E S I A

I N D I A N

O C E A N

Tanami
Desert

Great   Sandy   Desert

Gibson Desert

Little   Sandy   Desert

King Leopold Ranges

Kimberley

Bonaparte   Archipelago

Joseph
Bonaparte
Gulf

Pilbara

Hamersley Range

MacDonnell Ranges

Darwin
Palmerston

Katherine

Wyndham

Derby

Broome

Port
Hedland

Eighty Mile Beach

Karratha

Kupang

Timor

Sumba

Sumbawa

Lombok

Bali

A

10

B

15

C

20

D

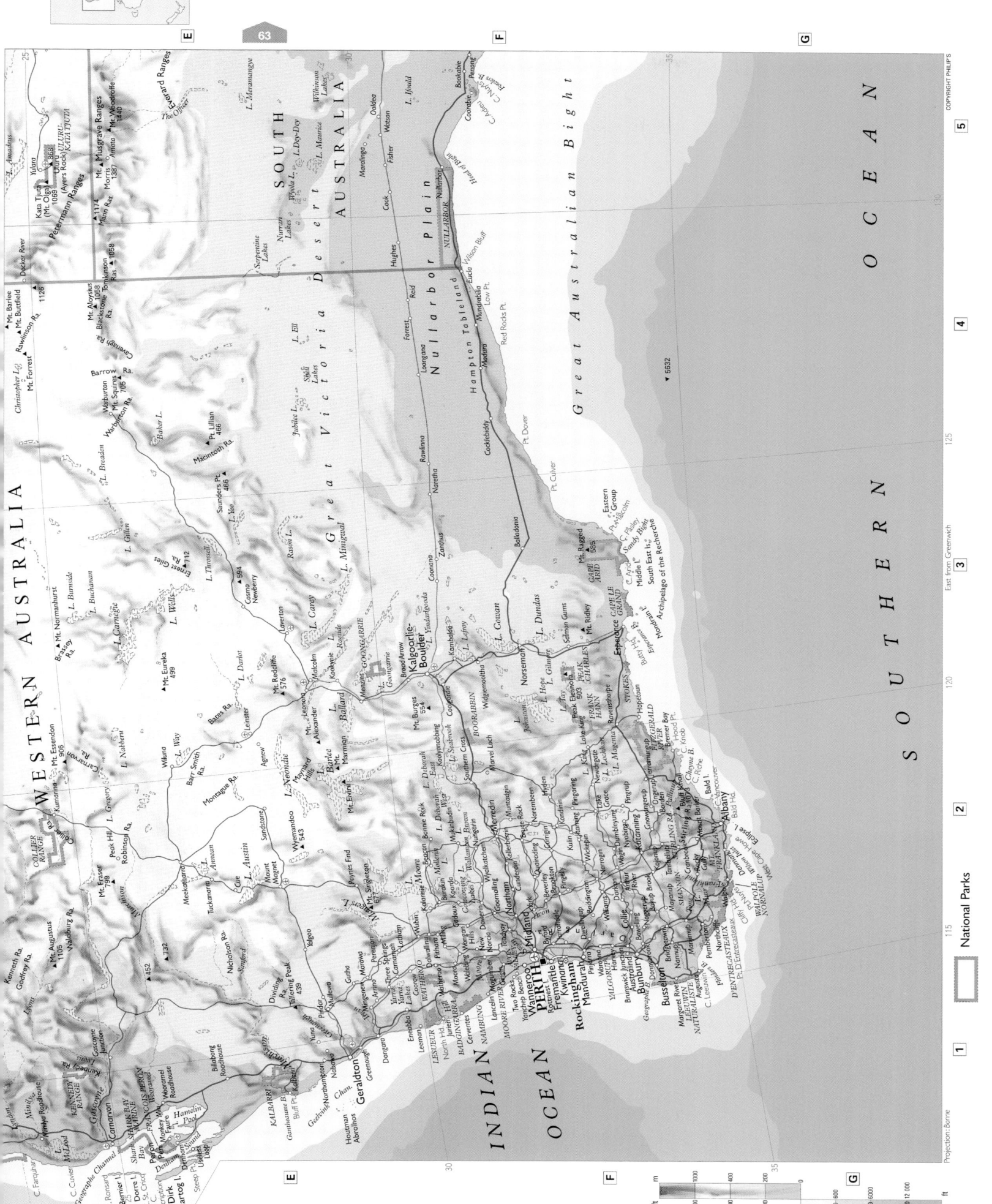

National Parks

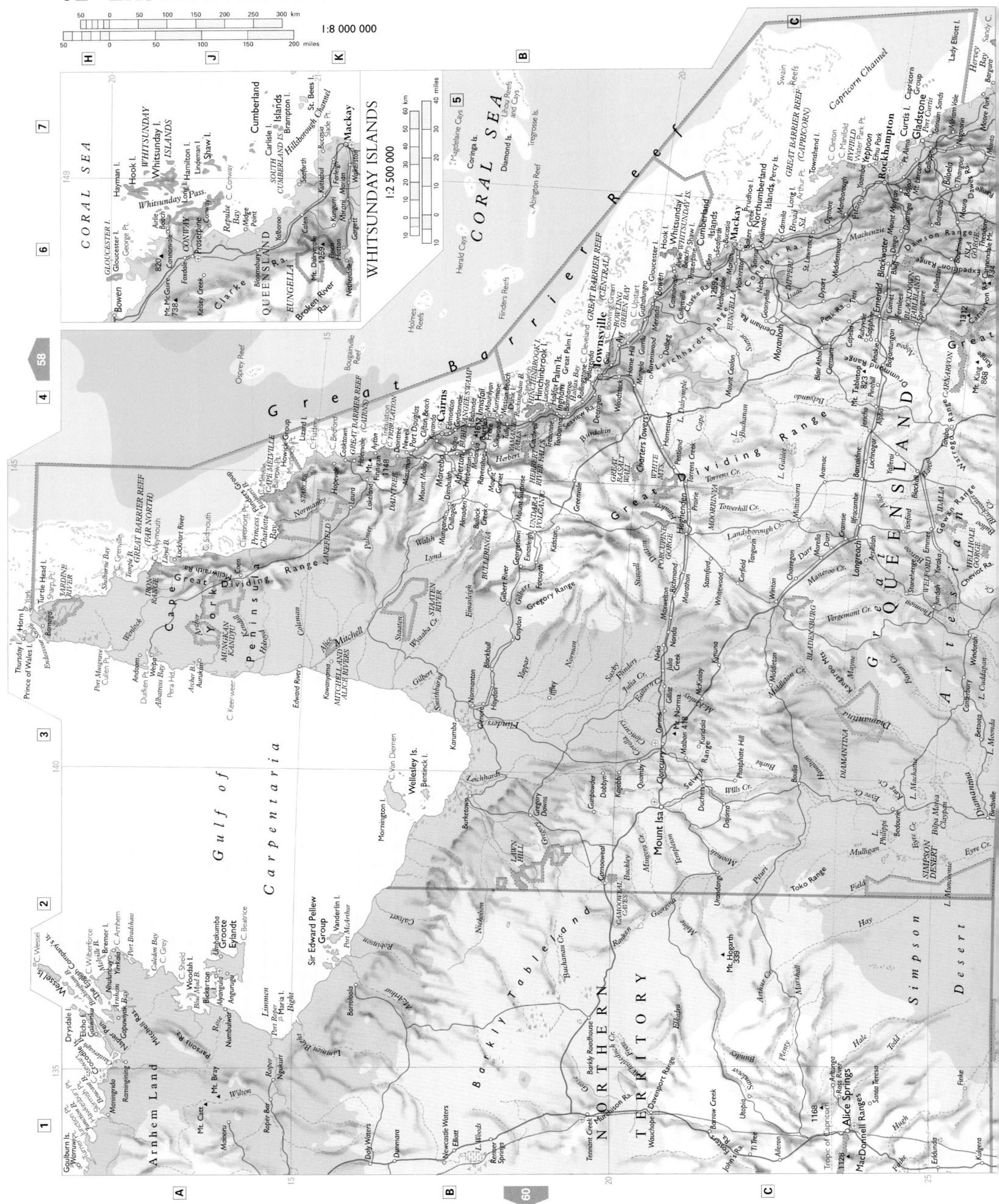

50  0  50  100  150  200  250  300 km

50  0  50  100  150

200 miles

1:8 000 000

**WHITSUNDAY ISLANDS**

1:2 500 000

10  0  10  20  30  40 km

0  10  20  30  40 miles

CORAL SEA

Gulf of Carpentaria

Arnhem Land

NORTHERN TERRITORY

QUEENSLAND

Great Dividing Range

Cape York Peninsula

Great Barrier Reef

Great Artesian Basin

Simpson Desert

Alice Springs

Mount Isa

Townsville

Cairns

Mackay

Rockhampton

Gladstone

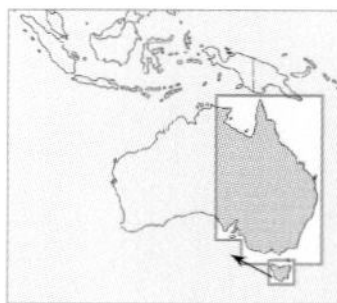

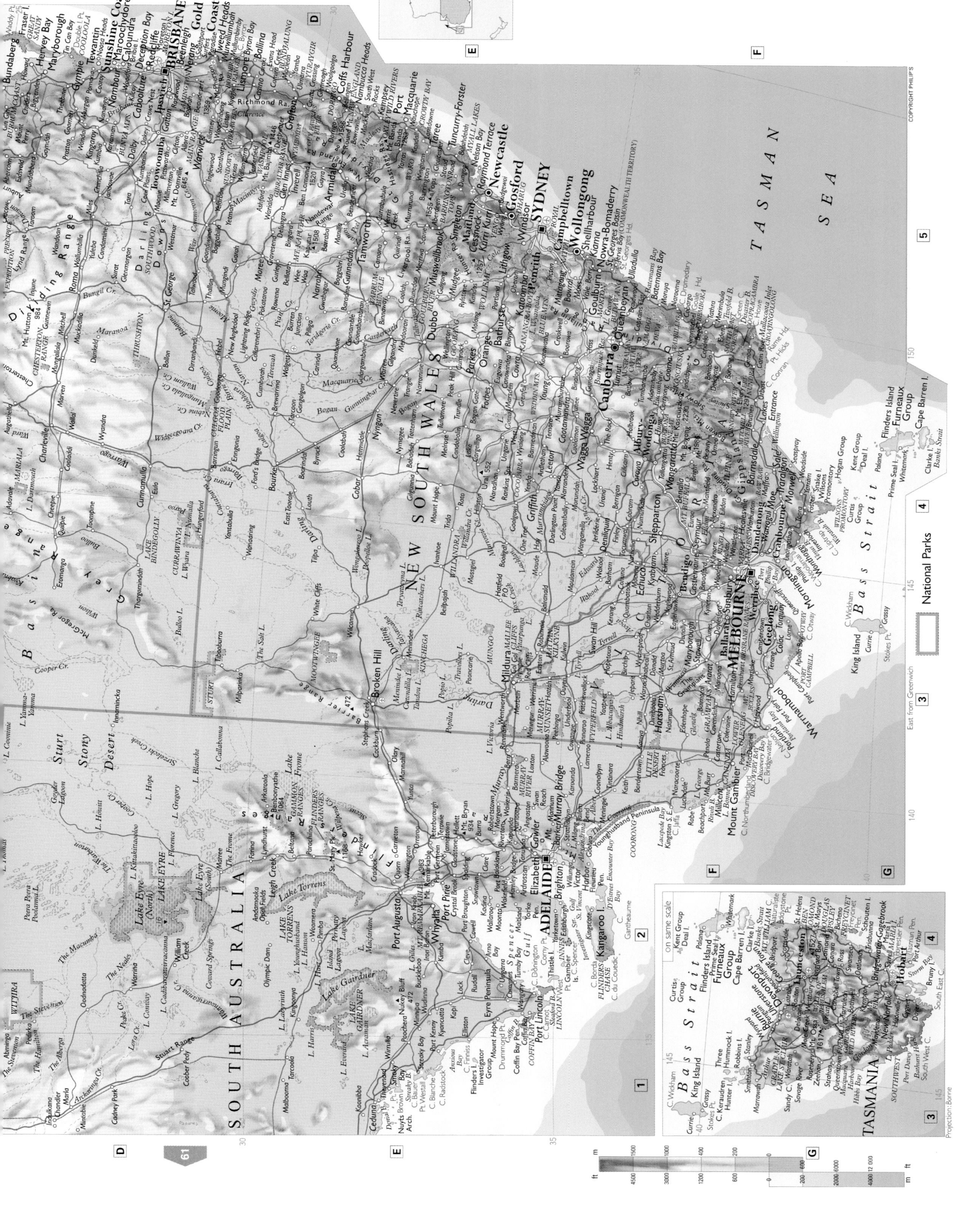

TASMAN SEA

NEW SOUTH WALES

SOUTH AUSTRALIA

QUEENSLAND

VICTORIA

TASMANIA

BRISBANE
Gold Coast
Sunshine Coast
SYDNEY
Newcastle
Gosford
Wollongong
Canberra
Campbelltown
ADELAIDE
MELBOURNE
Geelong
Ballarat
Bendigo
Hobart
Launceston
Devonport
Broken Hill
Port Augusta
Whyalla
Warrnambool
Mount Gambier

Darling R.
Murray R.
Lake Eyre
Lake Torrens
Lake Gairdner
Lake Frome
Flinders Ranges
Great Dividing Range
Darling Downs

Bass Strait
King Island
Flinders Island
Furneaux Group
Cape Barren I.

National Parks

East from Greenwich

COPYRIGHT PHILIP'S

Projection: Bonne

RUSSIA

Yekaterinburg
MOSKVA
Volga
Tomsk
Novosibirsk
Astana (Aqmola)
Semey
Irkutsk
Oz. Baykal
Chita
Lena
Ob'
Amur
Blagoveshchensk
Khabarovsk
Sea of Okhotsk
Okhotsk
Poluostrov Kamchatka
Komandorskiye Ostrova (Russia)
Petropavlovsk-Kamchatskiy
Bering Sea
Near Is. (U.S.A.)
Andreanof Is. (U.S.A.)
Aleutian
Aleutian Trench
7822

KAZAKHSTAN
Aral Sea
Balqash Köl
Almaty
Toshkent
KYRGYZSTAN
TAJIKISTAN
AFGHANISTAN
Kabul
PAKISTAN
Srinagar
Lahore
DELHI
Kanpur
Ganga
INDIA
Hyderabad
Kolkata (Calcutta)
DHAKA
BANGLADESH
Brahmaputra
Ulaanbaatar
MONGOLIA
Altai
Ürümqi
CHINA
Kunlun Shan
XIZANG
Lhasa
Himalaya
Everest 8850?
NEPAL
Irrawaddy
Mandalay
BURMA
Rangoon
Bay of Bengal
CHENNAI (Madras)
Andaman Is. (India)
SRI LANKA
Colombo
Nicobar Is. (India)
Salween
Lanzhou
Xi'an
CHONGQING
Chang J.
Changsha
Kunming
LAOS
Hanoi
THAILAND
BANGKOK
CAMBODIA
Phnom Penh
VIETNAM
Mekong
Thanh Pho Ho Chi Minh
G. of Thailand
MALAYSIA
Kuala Lumpur
PEN. MALAYSIA
SINGAPORE
Changchun
SHENYANG
Harbin
BEIJING
TIANJIN
Taiyuan
Huang He
Dalian
Qingdao
Nanjing
Wuhan
Yellow Sea
SHANGHAI
HANGZHOU
Fuzhou
GUANGZHOU
HONG KONG
Macau
Taipei
TAIWAN
Ryukyu-rettō (Japan)
Hainan
C. Engano
Luzon
Paracel Is.
MANILA
Mindoro
Samar
Palawan
PHILIPPINES
South China Sea
Sulu Sea
Mindanao
Mindanao Trench
410?
SABAH
BRUNEI
SARAWAK
Celebes Sea
East China Sea
NORTH KOREA
SOUTH KOREA
SŎUL
Dalian
Sapporo
Vladivostok
Hakodate
Sea of Japan
Sendai
TOKYO
Yokohama
Nagoya
Kyōto
Osaka
JAPAN
Kitakyūshū
Shikoku
Kyūshū
Fuji-San 3776
10,554
Japan Trench
Ogasawara Gunto (Japan)
Minami-Tori-Shima (Japan)
Kazan-Rettō (Japan)
Marcus Ridge
South Honshu Ridge
Kuril Trench
10,542
Kurilskiye Ostrova (Russia)
La Perouse Str.
Sakhalin
Emperor Seamount Chain
Midway Is. (U.S.A.)
Lisianski I. (U.S.A.)
Howland
Necker Ridge
Wake I. (U.S.A.)
International Dateline
PA
PA
NORTHERN MARIANAS (U.S.A.)
Saipan
GUAM (U.S.A.) 11,022
Mariana Trench
Yap
Koror
PALAU
Caroline Is.
Micronesia
Truk
Pohnpei
Palikir
FEDERATED STATES OF MICRONESIA
Jaluit I.
MARSHALL IS.
Enewetak Atoll
Bikini Atoll
Dalap-Uliga-Darrit
Butaritari
Tarawa
Banaba
Gilbert Is.
NAURU
Melanesia
Howland I. (U.S.A)
Baker I. (U.S.A)
Phoenix Is.
Abariringa
Enderbury
KIR
O
KIR

INDONESIA
Sumatera
Sunda Islands
Palembang
Java Sea
JAKARTA
Jawa
Surabaya
Bali
Selat Sunda
Java Trench
Borneo
Ujung Pandang
Sulawesi
Flores Sea
Flores
Sumbawa
Sumba
Halmahera
Buru
Seram
Maluku
Banda Sea
Timor
East Timor
7440
PAPUA
Puncak Jaya 5029?
New Guinea
PAPUA NEW GUINEA
Admiralty Is.
Bismarck Arch.
Lae
New Britain
Rabaul
New Ireland
Bougainville
Port Moresby
SOLOMON IS.
Honiara
Guadalcanal
Santa Cruz Is. 9165?
Louisiade Arch.
Espíritu Santo
VANUATU
Port Vila
Is. Chesterfield
Vanua Levu
Viti Levu
Suva
FIJI
Rotuma
Fongafale
TUVALU
Is. Wallis & Futuna (Fr.)
SAMOA
Apia
Nuku'alofa
TONGA
Tokelau Is. (N.Z.)

INDIAN OCEAN
Cocos Is. (Austral.)
Christmas I. (Austral.)
Arafura Sea
C. Arnhem
Darwin
Gulf of Carpentaria
Broome
North West C.
Torres Strait
C. York
Coral Sea
Cairns
Townsville
Great Barrier Reef
Great Dividing Ra.
NEW CALEDONIA (Fr.)
Nouméa
Is. Loyauté
7570
AUSTRALIA
Mount Isa
Alice Springs
L. Eyre
Rockhampton
Brisbane
Darling
Geraldton
Great Australian Bight
Perth
Albany
Adelaide
Murray
Sydney
Canberra
Mt. Kosciuszko 2230
Melbourne
Bass Str.
Tasmania
Hobart
Norfolk I. (Austral.)
Lord Howe I. (Austral.)
Kermadec Is. (N.Z.)
Kermadec Trench 10,047
Tonga Trench 10,822
Tasman Sea
NEW ZEALAND
Auckland
Wellington
Cook Strait
Christchurch
Chatham Is. (N.Z.)
Aoraki Mt. Cook 3753
Dunedin
Invercargill
Bounty Is. (N.Z.)
Antipodes Is. (N.Z.)
Auckland Is. (N.Z.)
Campbell I. (N.Z.)
Macquarie Is. (Austral.)
Nouvelle Amsterdam (Fr.)
I. St. Paul (Fr.)
Mid-Indian Ridge
Is. Crozet (Fr.)
Kerguelen (Fr.)
Heard I. (Austral.)

ft  m
12 000  4000
9000  3000
6000  2000
3000  1000
1500  500
600  200
0  0
200  600
1000  3000
2000  6000
4000  12 000
6000  18 000
8000  24 000
m  ft

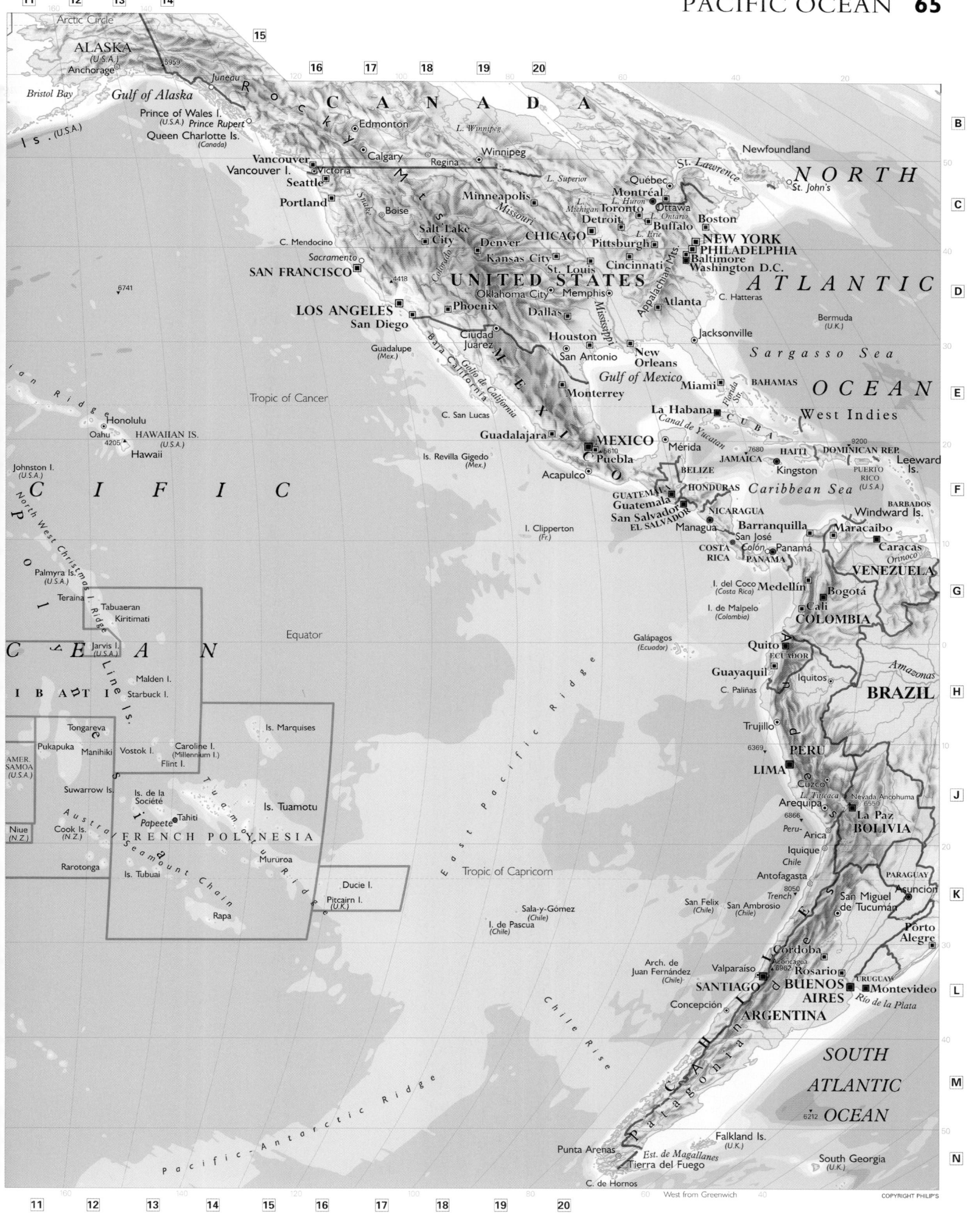

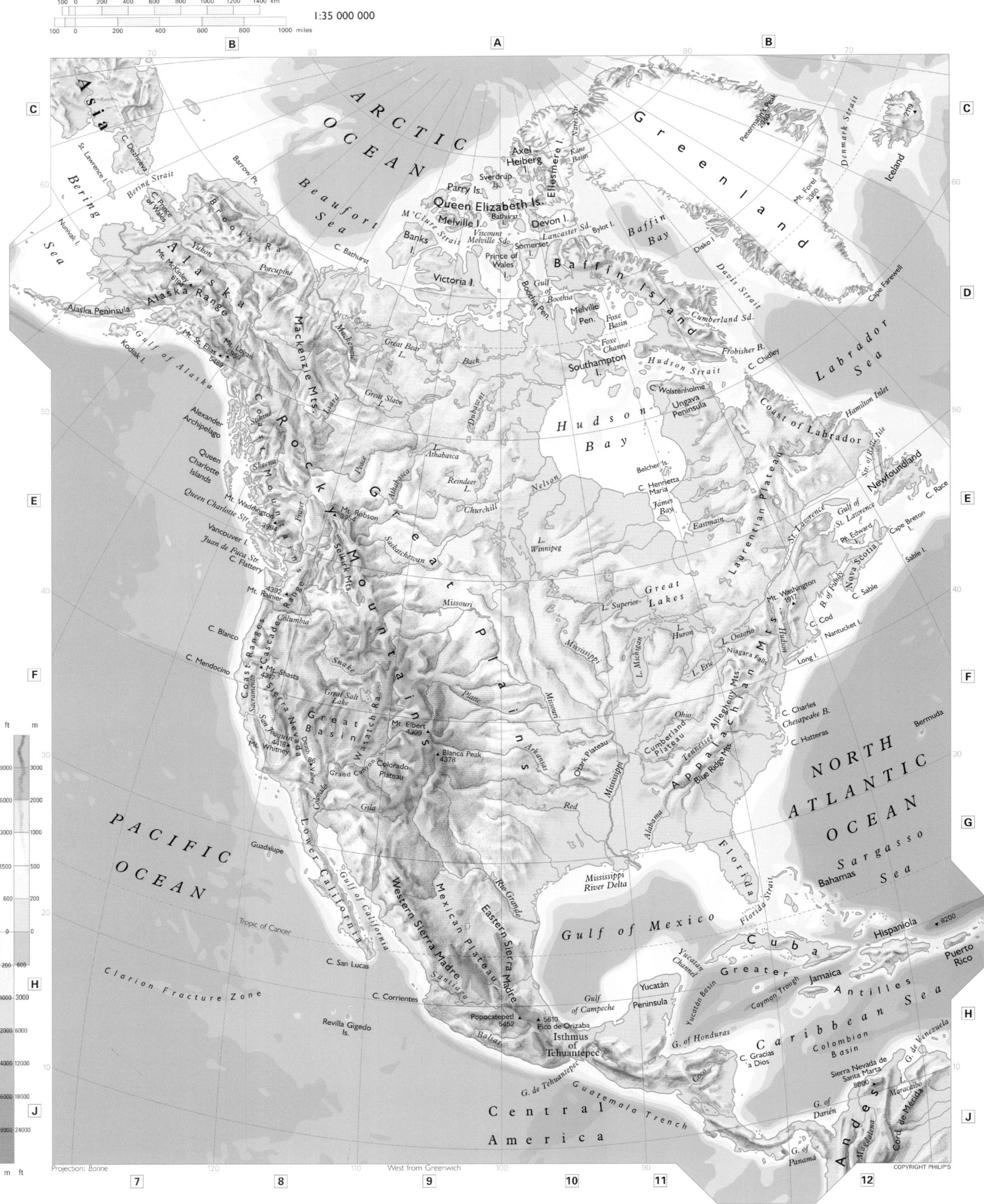

100  0   200  400  600  800  1000  1200  1400 km

1:35 000 000

100  0   200  400  600  800  1000 miles

Projection: Bonne

West from Greenwich

COPYRIGHT PHILIP'S

1:35 000 000

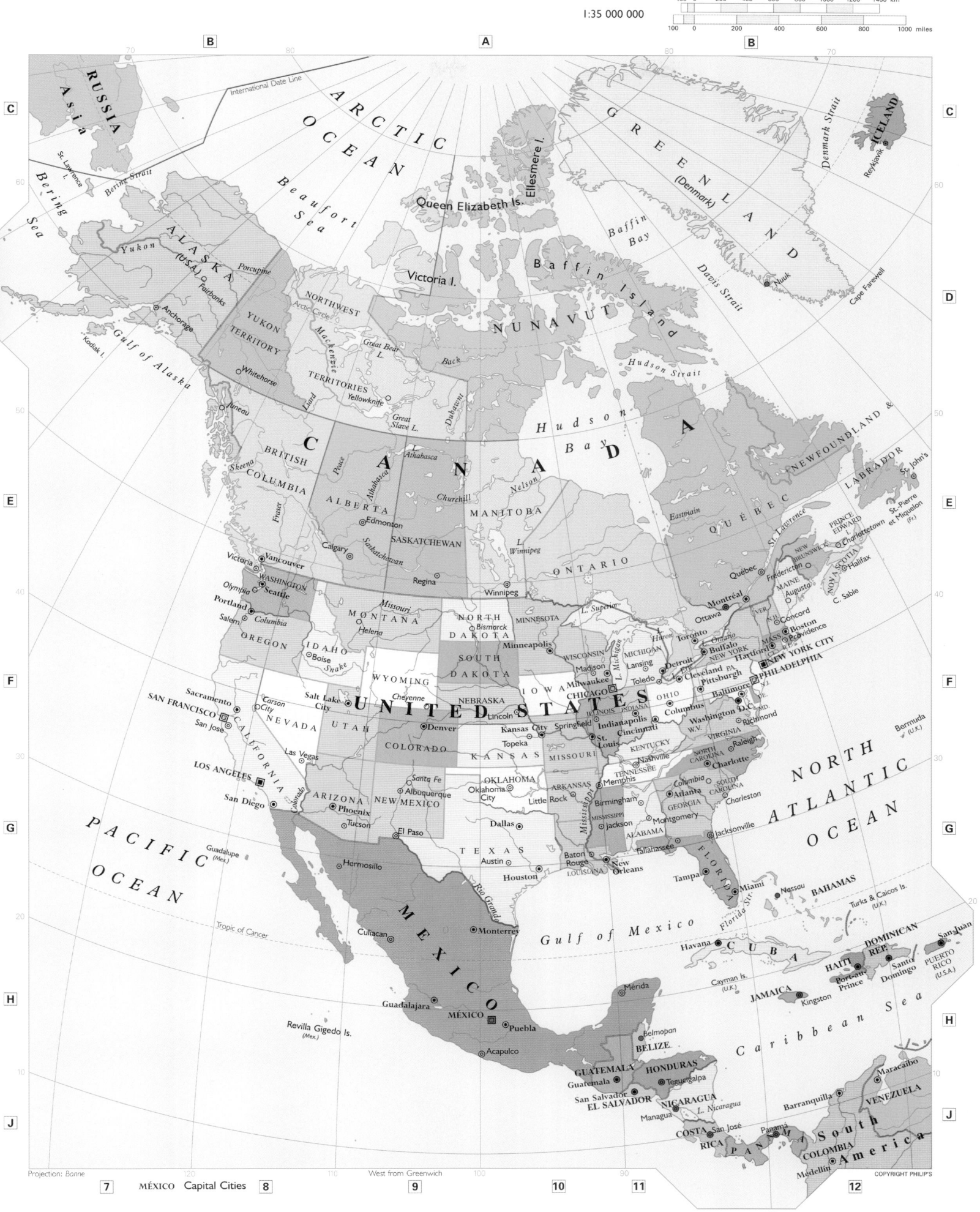

1:15 000 000

Projection: Bonne

ALASKA
1:30 000 000

West from Greenwich

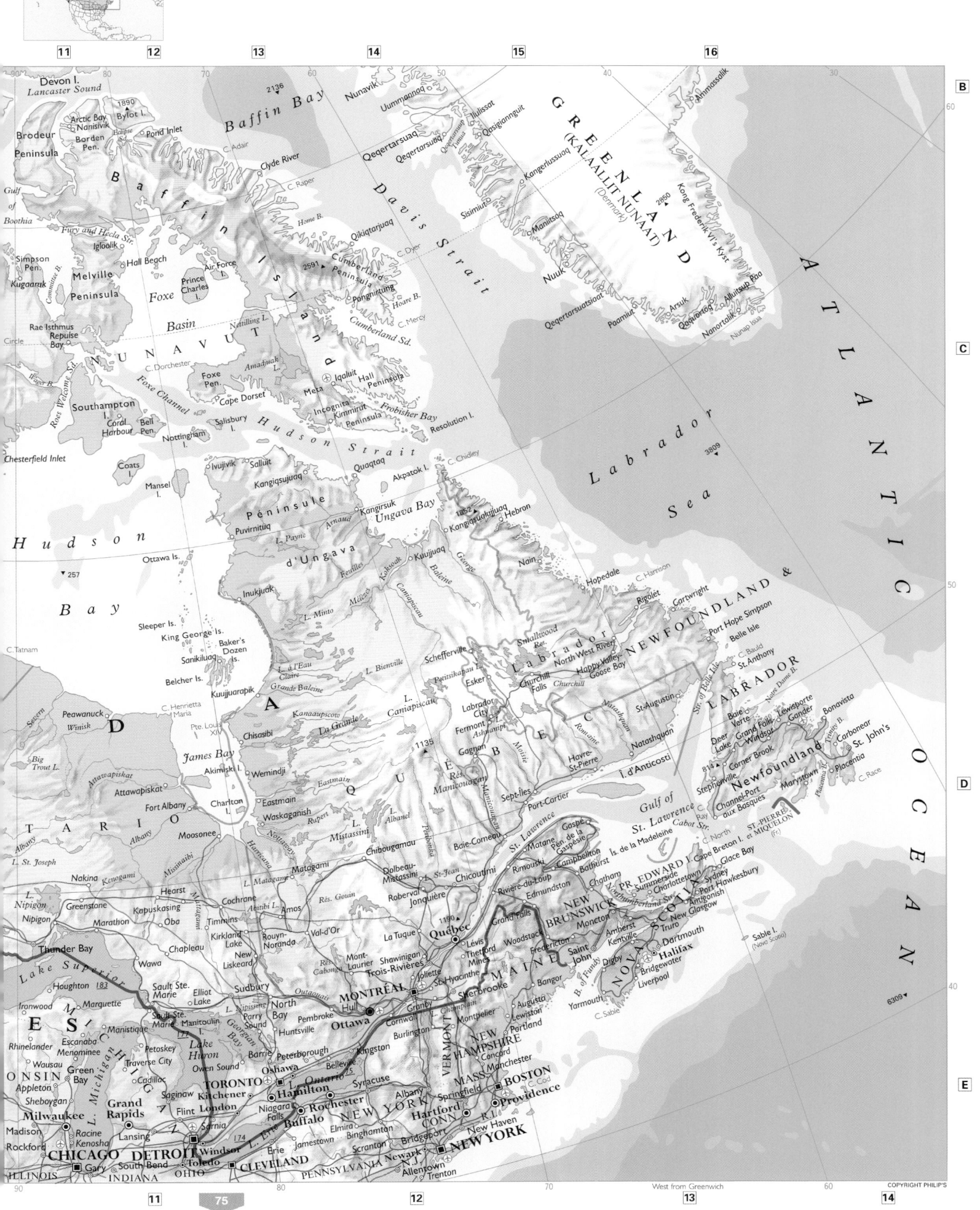

West from Greenwich

COPYRIGHT PHILIP'S

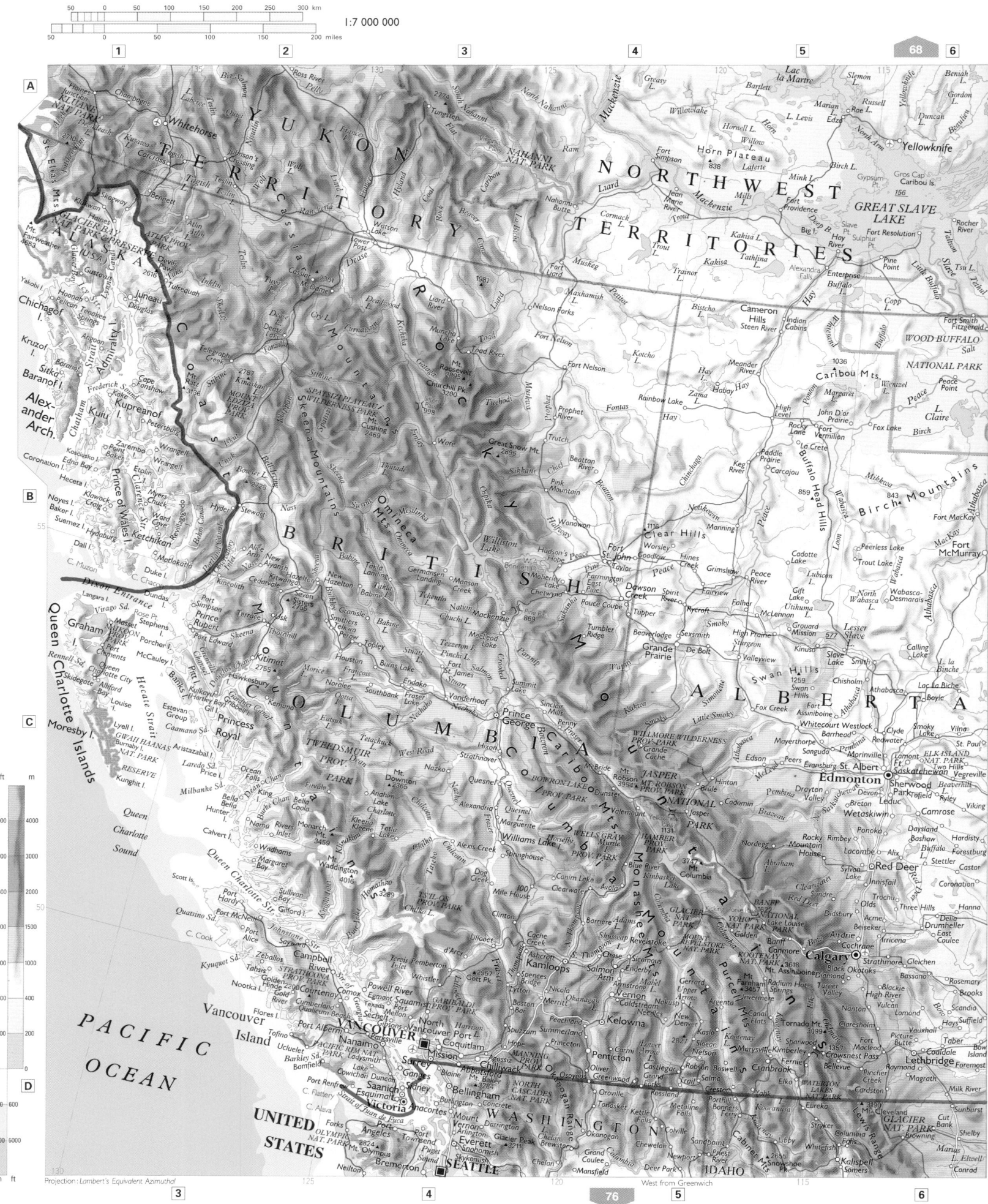

1:7 000 000

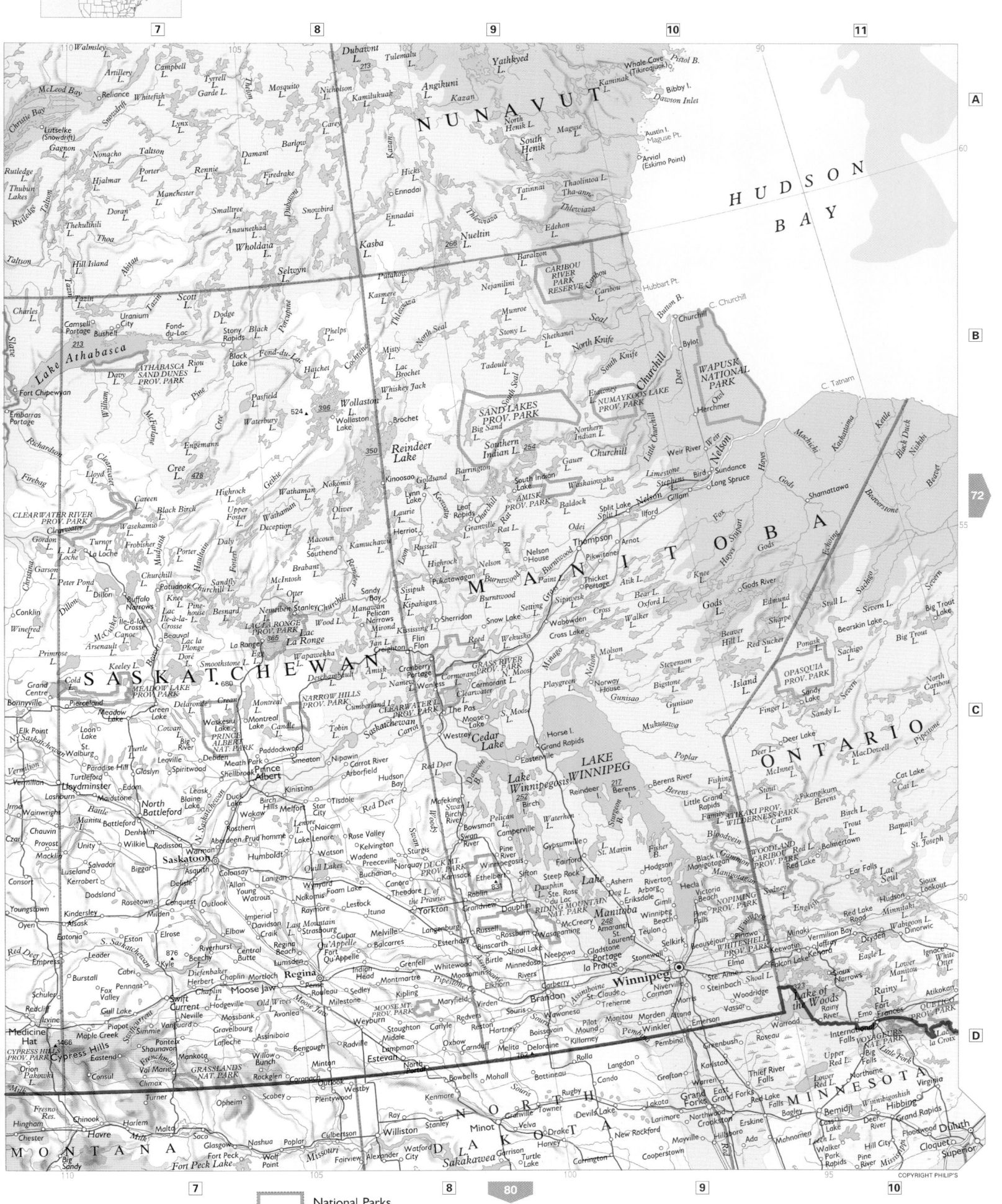

National Parks

COPYRIGHT PHILIP'S

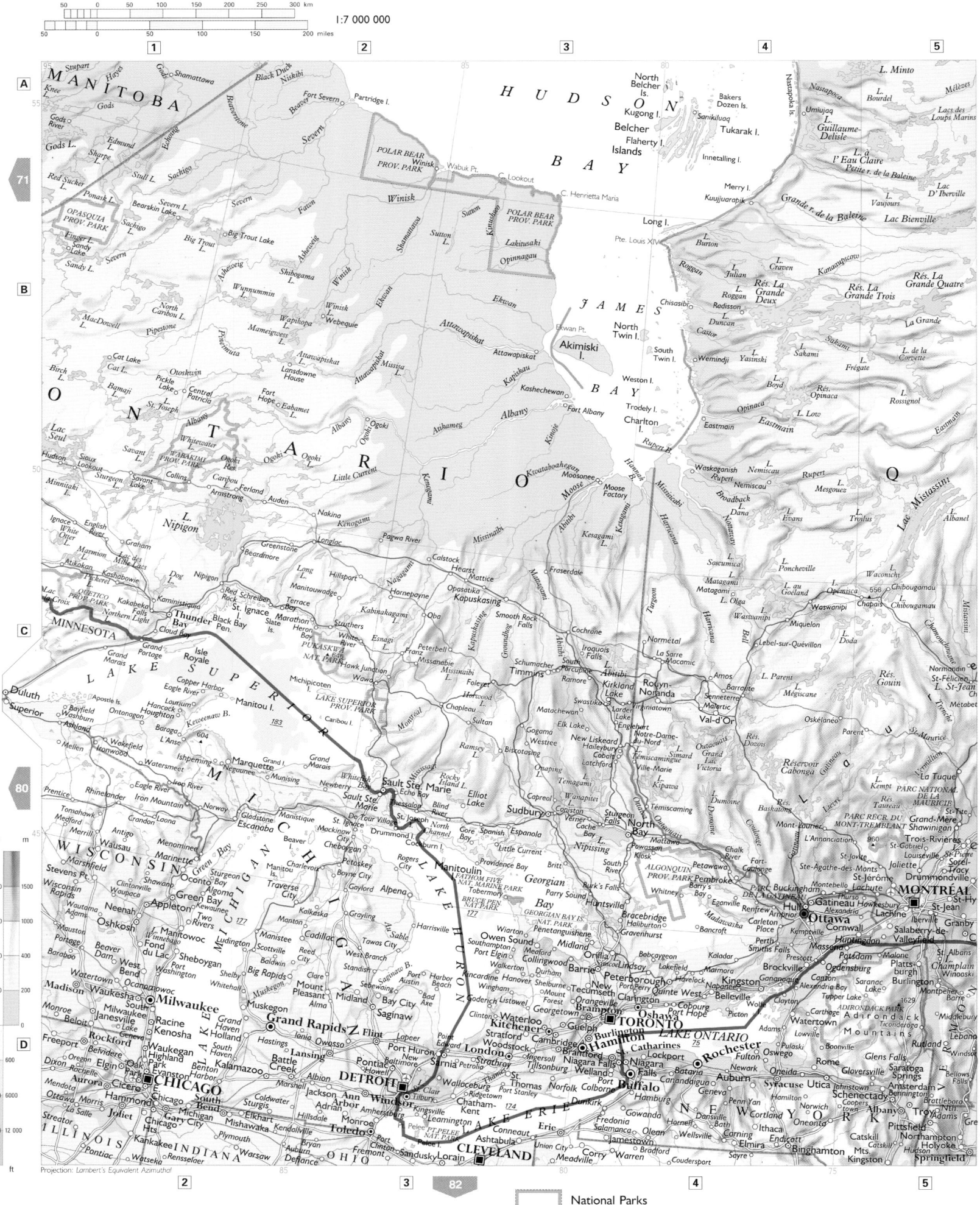

50   0   50   100   150   200   250   300 km

1:7 000 000

50   0   50   100   150   200 miles

Projection: Lambert's Equivalent Azimuthal

National Parks

**6** 69 **7** **8** **9**

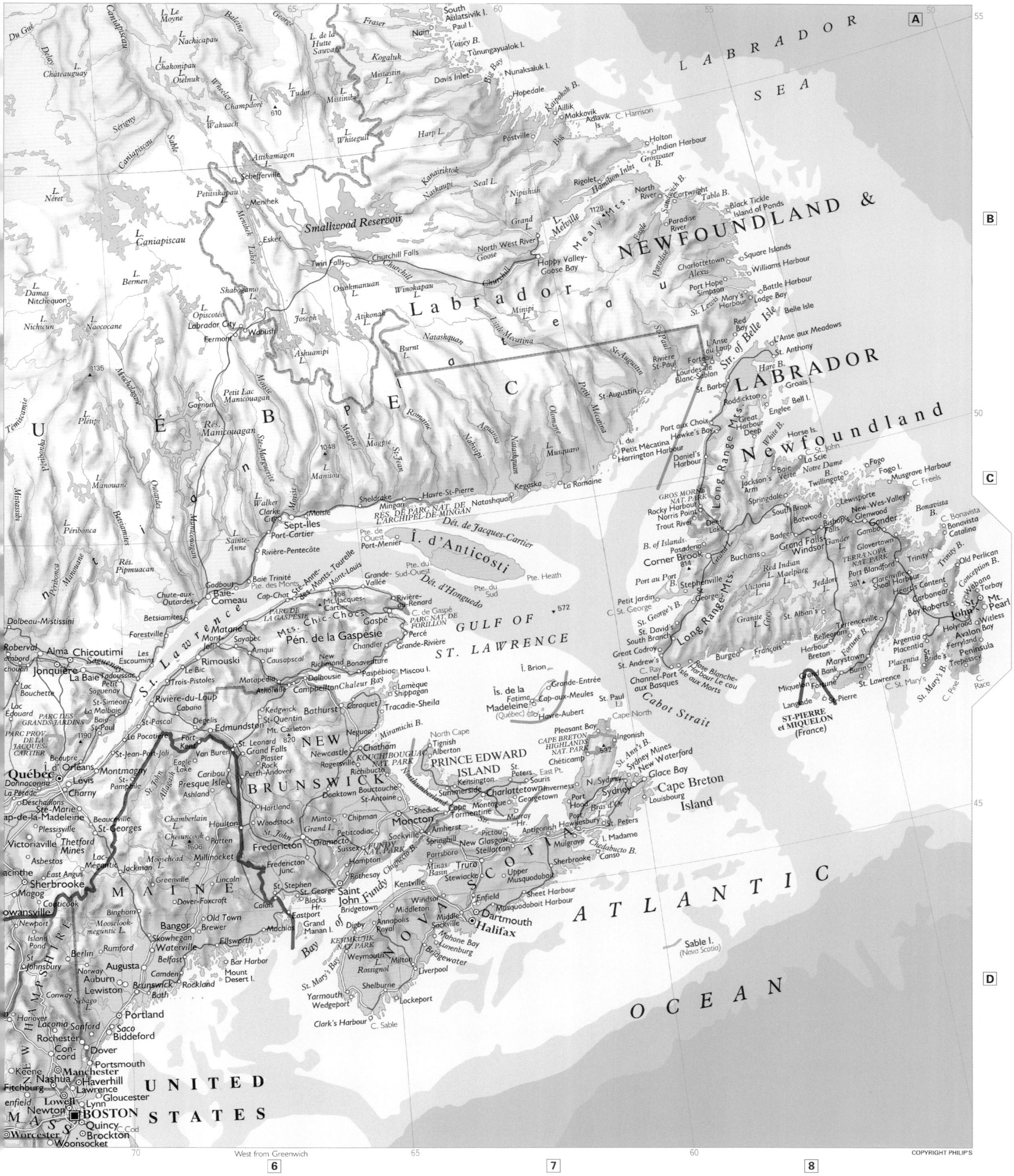

**A**

L A B R A D O R

S E A

**B**

NEWFOUNDLAND &

Labrador

Smallwood Reservoir

Churchill Falls

Happy Valley-
Goose Bay

Labrador City
Wabush
Fermont

LABRADOR

Str. of Belle Isle

L'Anse aux Meadows

St. Anthony

**C**

Newfoundland

GROS MORNE
NAT. PARK

Corner Brook

Long Range Mts.

Gander
Grand Falls
Windsor

TERRA NOVA
NAT. PARK

St. John's
Mt. Pearl

Sept-Îles
Port-Cartier

Î. d'Anticosti

GULF OF
ST. LAWRENCE

ST-PIERRE
et MIQUELON
(France)

**D**

Québec

Pén. de la Gaspésie

Chic-Chocs

Gaspé

Îs. de la
Madeleine
(Québec)

Cabot Strait

Sherbrooke

NEW

BRUNSWICK

PRINCE EDWARD
ISLAND

CAPE BRETON
HIGHLANDS
NAT. PARK

Cape Breton
Island

Sydney

MAINE

Fredericton

Saint
John

Moncton

Charlottetown

NOVA SCOTIA

Truro

Dartmouth
Halifax

A T L A N T I C

Bay of Fundy

KEJIMKUJIK
NAT. PARK

Sable I.
(Nova Scotia)

O C E A N

Portland

U N I T E D

S T A T E S

BOSTON

MASS.

1:12 000 000

Projection: Albers' Equal Area with two standard parallels

HAWAII
1:10 000 000

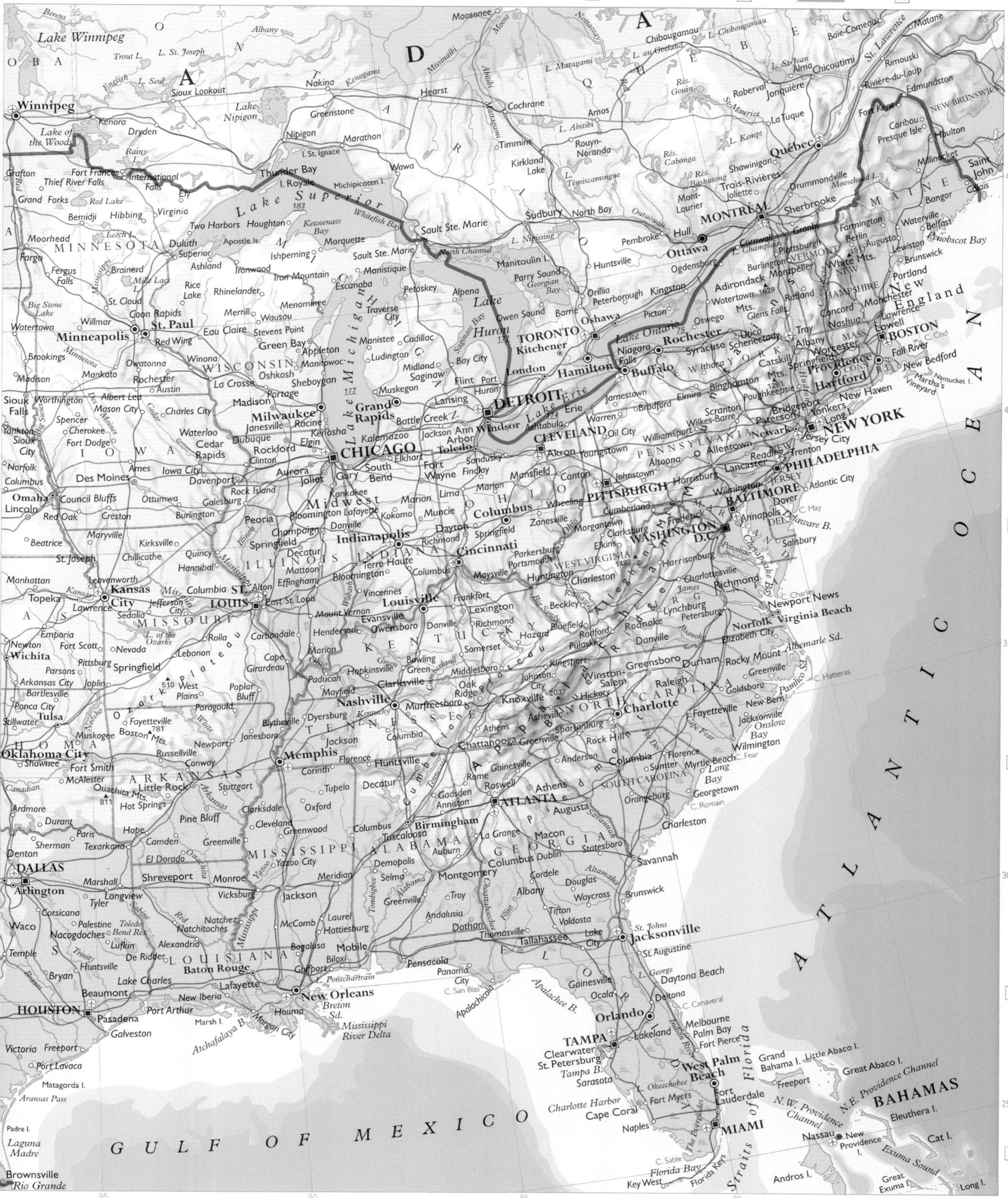

1:6 000 000

50 0 50 100 150 200 km
50 0 50 100 150 miles

80
70

A B C D E F

WESTERN UNITED STATES

SASKATCHEWAN
ALBERTA
BRITISH COLUMBIA
MONTANA
WYOMING
IDAHO
WASHINGTON
OREGON
NEVADA
UTAH
CALIFORNIA

VANCOUVER
SEATTLE
PORTLAND
Salt Lake City
Sacramento
Spokane
Boise
Great Falls
Helena
Butte
Missoula
Billings
Casper
Ogden
Provo
Carson City
Reno
Eugene
Salem
Tacoma
Olympia
Everett
Victoria
Nanaimo

Rocky Mountains
Bighorn Mountains
Absaroka Range
Wind River Range
Bitterroot Mountains
Salmon River Mountains
Sawtooth Range
Blue Mountains
Wallowa Mts.
Cascade Range
Olympic Mts.
Lewis Range
Cabinet Mountains
Medicine Bow Mts.
Park Range
Uinta Mountains
Columbia Basin
Columbia Plateau
Great Salt Lake
Great Salt Lake Desert
Harney Basin
Warner Mts.
Coast Ranges
Sierra Nevada
Ruby Mts.

Pacific Rim Nat. Park
Strait of Juan de Fuca
Puget Sound
Columbia River
Snake River
Missouri River
Yellowstone L.
Grand Teton Nat. Park
Yellowstone National Park
Glacier National Park
Crater Lake Nat. Park
Lake Tahoe

Mt. Rainier
Mt. St. Helens
Mt. Hood
Mt. Shasta
Mt. Baker

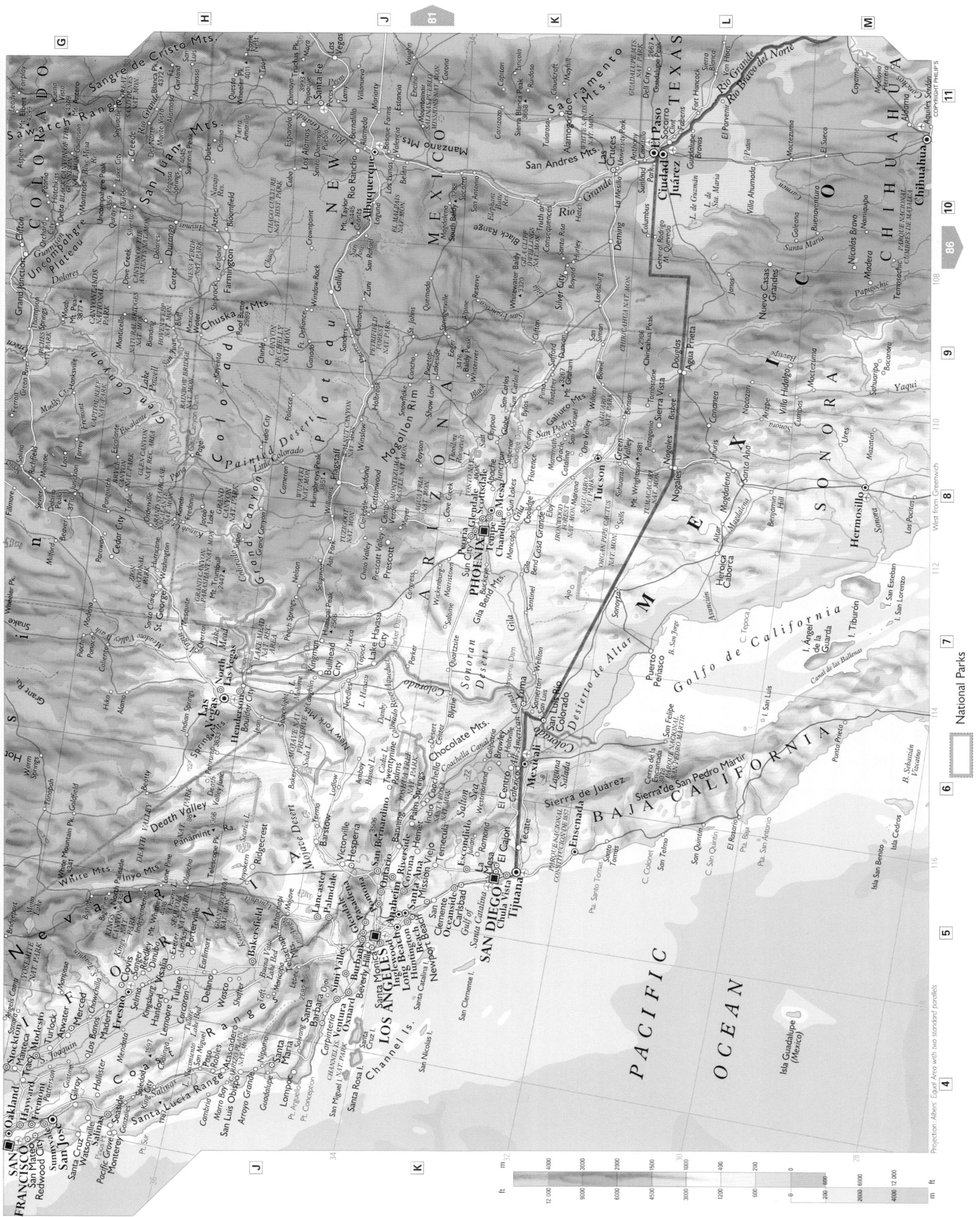

National Parks

1:2 500 000

WESTERN WASHINGTON REGION
on same scale

PACIFIC OCEAN

BRITISH COLUMBIA

Vancouver Island

Strait of Georgia

Strait of Juan de Fuca

WASHINGTON

OREGON

SEATTLE

Tacoma

PORTLAND

OLYMPIC NATIONAL PARK

Olympic Mountains

CALIFORNIA

San Joaquin Valley

Sacramento Valley

Sierra Nevada

SACRAMENTO

SAN FRANCISCO

Oakland

San Jose

Fresno

Lake Tahoe

YOSEMITE NATIONAL PARK

KINGS CANYON NATIONAL PARK

SEQUOIA NATIONAL PARK

Inyo Mts.

White Mts.

Santa Lucia Range

Diablo Range

Monterey Bay

Reno

Sparks

Pahute Mesa

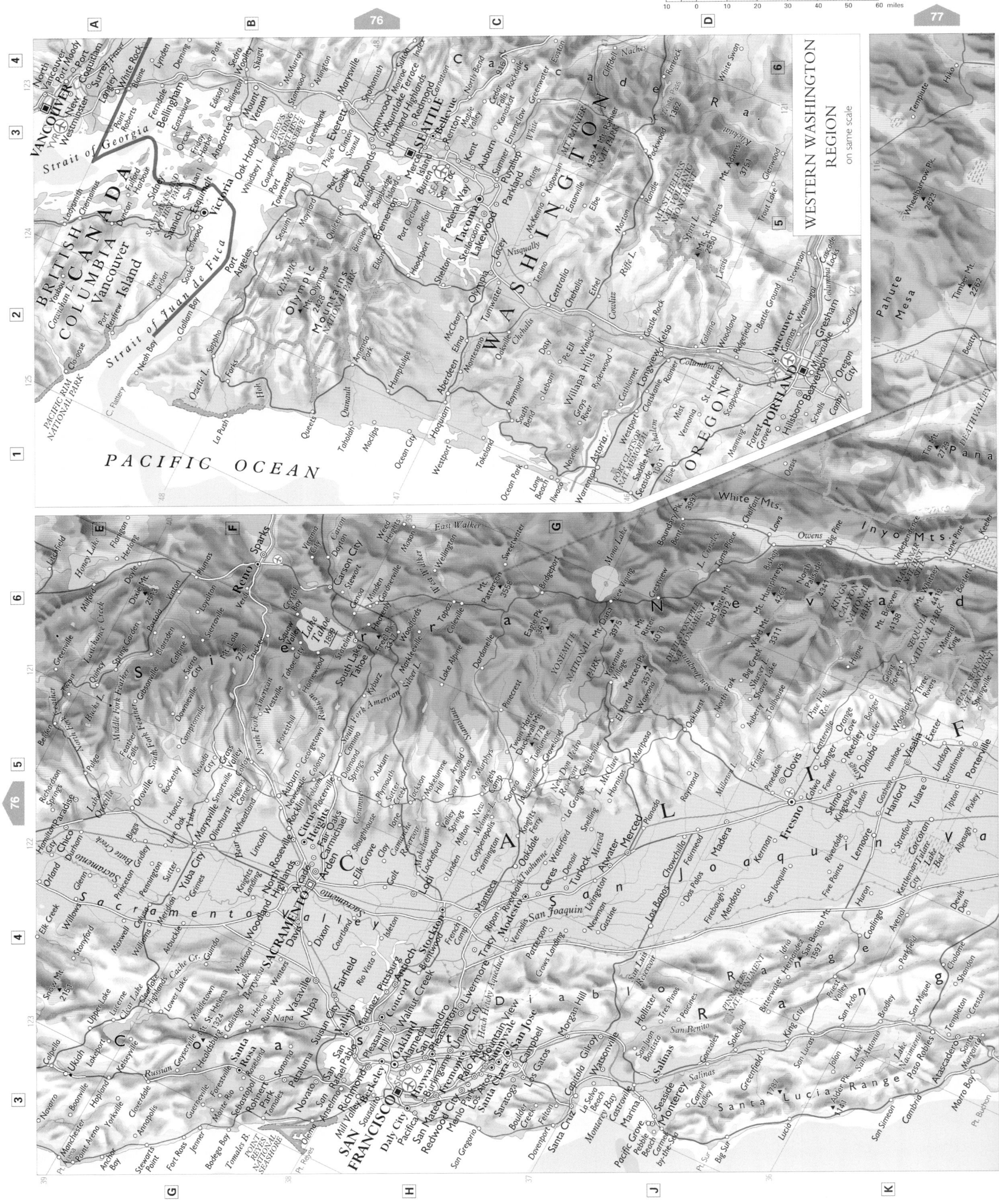

National Parks

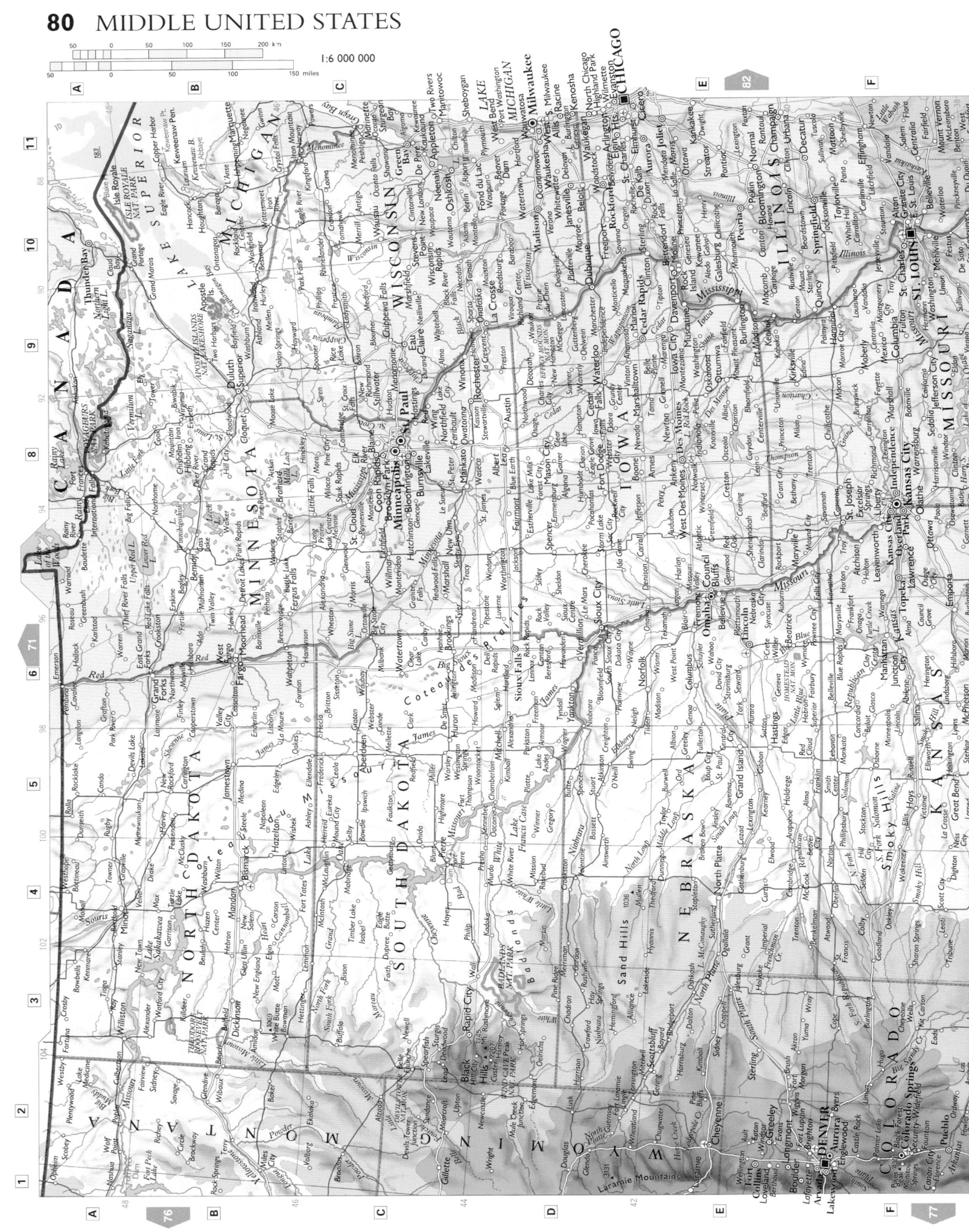

National Parks

continuation
southwards
on same scale

COPYRIGHT PHILIP'S

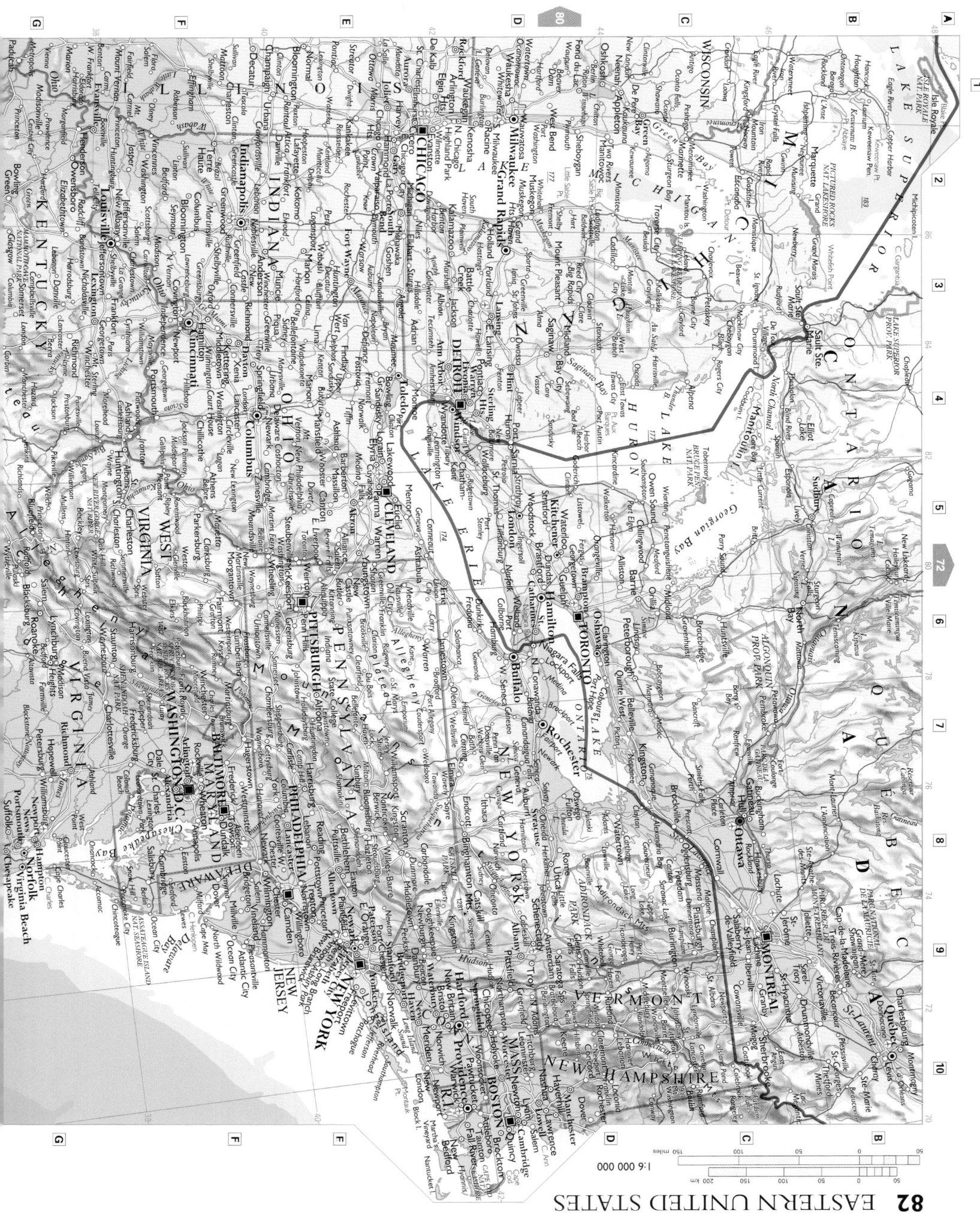

GULF OF MEXICO

ATLANTIC OCEAN

MISSISSIPPI

TENNESSEE

ALABAMA

GEORGIA

FLORIDA

SOUTH CAROLINA

NORTH CAROLINA

CANADA

BAHAMAS

NEW HAMPSHIRE

MAINE

National Parks

continuation eastwards on same scale

Projection: Albers' Equal Area with two standard parallels

West from Greenwich

COPYRIGHT PHILIP'S

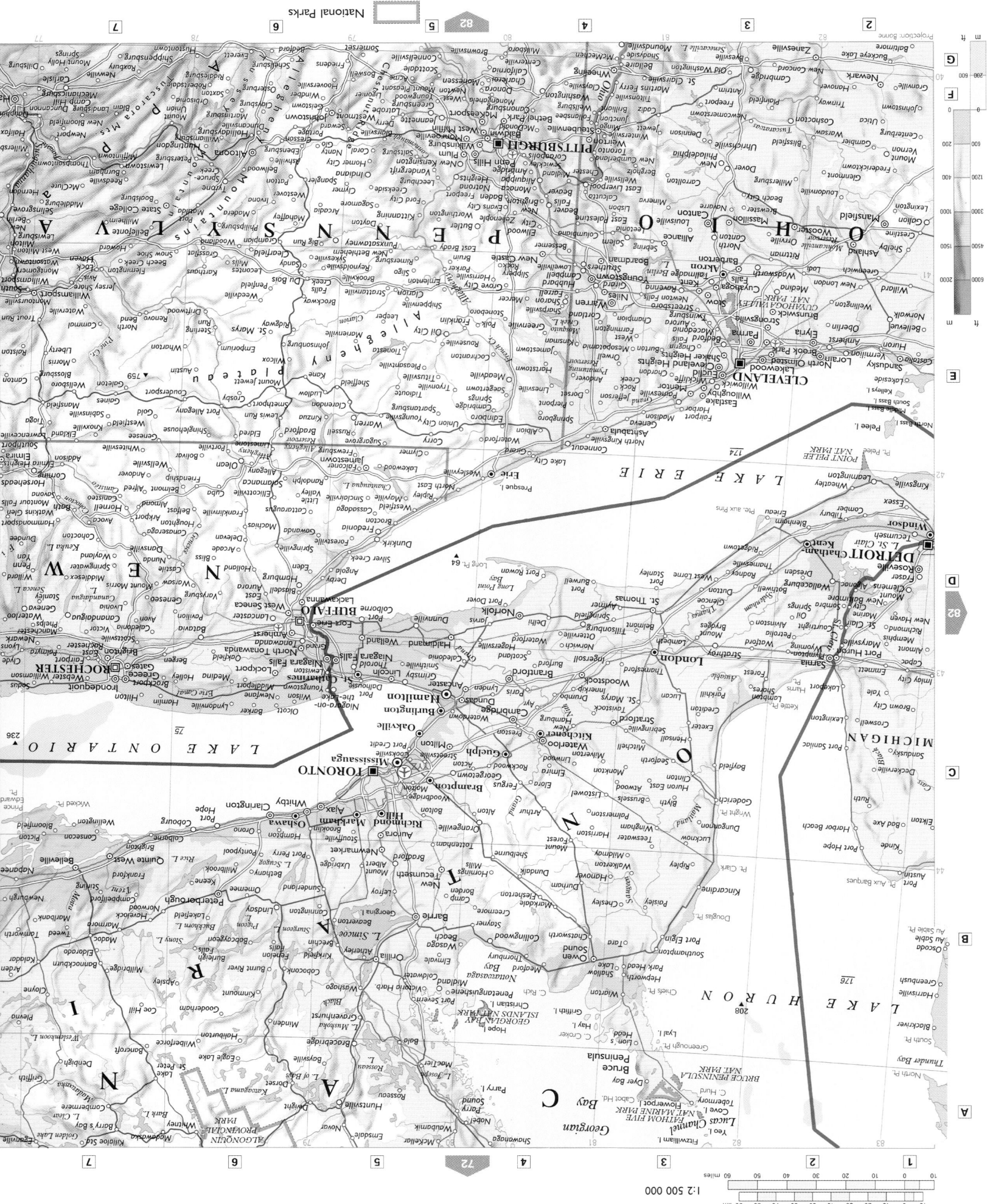

1:2 500 000

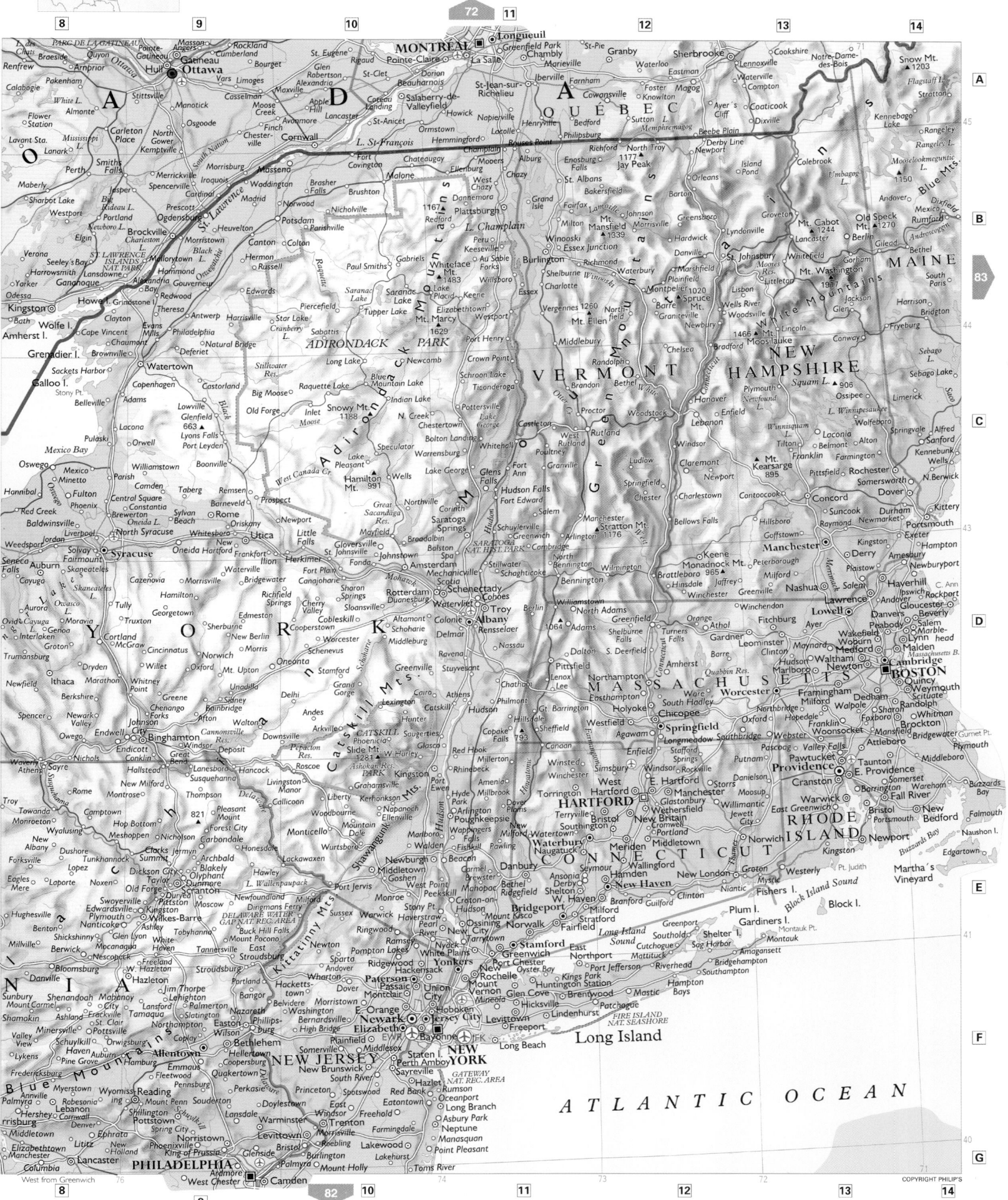

50 0 50 100 150 200 250 300 km

1:8 000 000

50 0 50 100 150 200 miles

77

Projection: Bi-polar oblique Conical Orthomorphic

West from Greenwich

National Parks

State names in Central Mexico

1 DISTRITO FEDERAL    5 MÉXICO
2 AGUASCALIENTES    6 MORELOS
3 GUANAJUATO    7 QUERÉTARO
4 HIDALGO    8 TLAXCALA

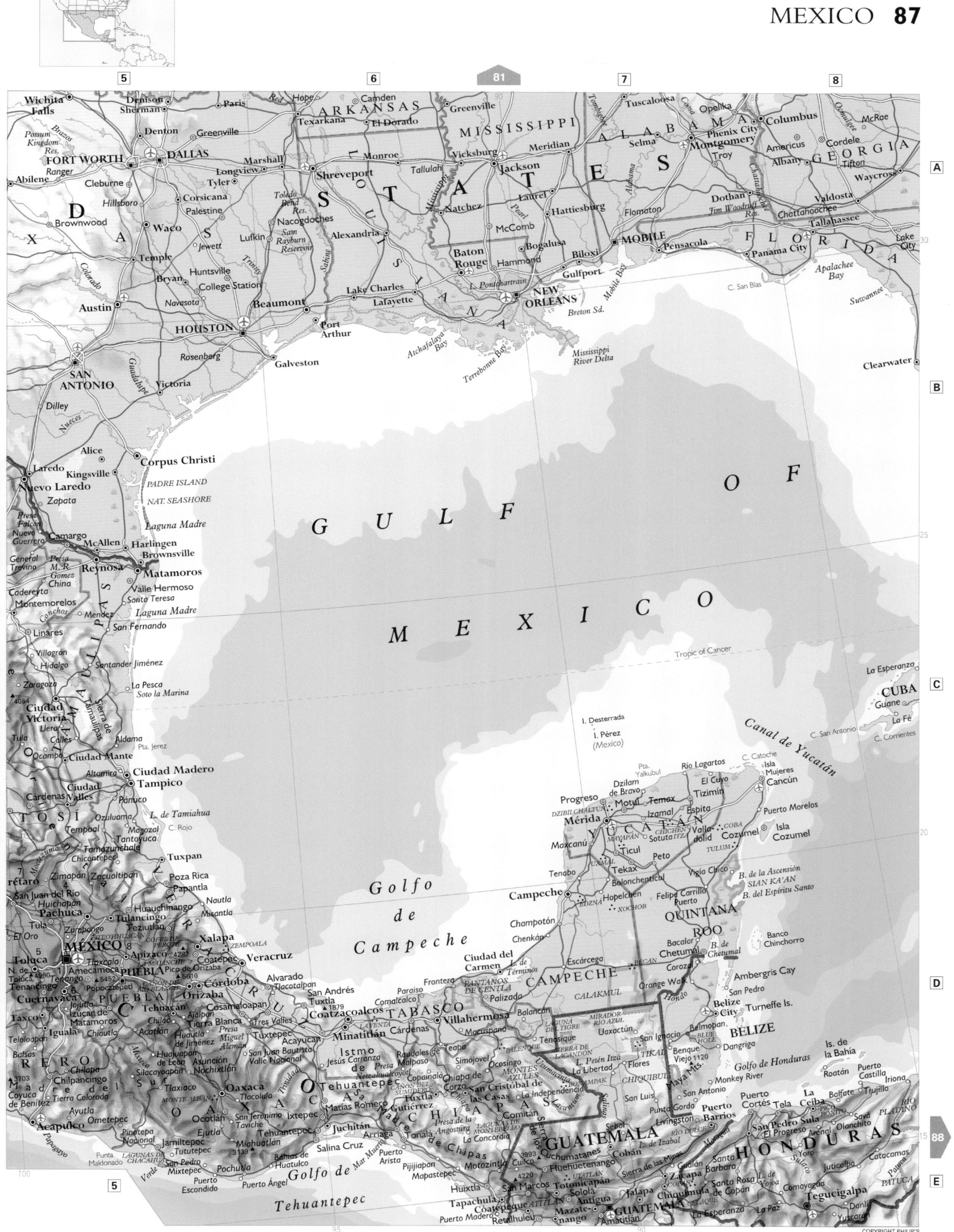

GULF OF MEXICO

M E X I C O

Golfo de Campeche

Tropic of Cancer

CUBA

BELIZE

GUATEMALA

HONDURAS

*Tehuantepec*

*Golfo de Tehuantepec*

COPYRIGHT PHILIP'S

1:8 000 000

**JAMAICA**
1:3 000 000

**GUADELOUPE AND MARTINIQUE**
1:2 000 000

Projection: Bi-polar oblique Conical Orthomorphic

**5**

AMAS

*ATLANTIC OCEAN*

A

Arthur's Town
The Bight
Cat I.
San Salvador I.
Conception I.
Rum Cay
Long I.
Tropic of Cancer
Sandy Cay
Clarence Town
Samana Cay
Crooked I. Passage
Crooked I.
Plana Cays
Albert Town
Snug Corner
Mayaguana I.
Cay Verde
Acklins I.
Mira por vos Cay
Caicos Passage
Turks & Caicos (U.K.)
Cay Santa Domingo
Hogsty Reef
Little Inagua I.
Caicos Is.
Cockburn Town
Turks Is.
Banes
Lake Rose
Great Inagua I.
INAGUA
Turks Island Passage
Antilla
Matthew Town
Mayari
Moa
Baracoa
Guantánamo
GUANTANAMO BAY (U.S.A.)
Pta. de Maisí
Île de la Tortue
Cap-Haïtien
Monte Cristi
LA ISABELA
Puerto Plata
Santiago de los Caballeros
San Francisco de Macorís
Milwaukee Deep 9200 ▼
*Puerto Rico Trench*

ATLANTIC OCEAN
PUERTO RICO
PUERTO RICO (U.S.A.)
1:3 000 000
d
Pta. Agujereada
Isabela
Barceloneta
Aguadilla
Arecibo
Manati
Vega Baja
SAN JUAN
Mayagüez
San Sebastian
Utuado
Bayamón
Carolina
Río Grande
Fajardo
Dewey
Adjuntas
Cordillera Central
Caguas
Sierra de Luquillo
Pta. Culebra
San German
Uroyan Mts.
Cerro 1338 de Punta
Cayey
Naguabo
Yabucoa
Esperanza
Yauco
Coamo
Ponce
Guayama
Pta. Aguila
Guanica
I. Caja de Muertos

VIRGIN ISLANDS
1:2 000 000
e
Virgin Islands (U.K.)
Ruffing Pt.
Anegada
The Settlement
East Pt.
Jost Van Dyke I.
Great Camanoe
Virgin Is. (U.S.A.)
Lollik I.
Guana I.
Virgin Gorda
Tortola
Beef I.
Spanish Town
Charlotte Amalie
Cruz Bay
Road Town
Peter I.
St. Thomas I.
St. John I.

ST. LUCIA
1:2 000 000
f
Cap Point
Pte. Hardy
Gros Islet
Esperance Bay
Castries
Marquis
Babonneau
L'Anse la Raye
Canaries
Millet
Dennery
Soufrière
Mt. Gimie 950
Soufrière Bay
Petit Piton 750
Micoud
Gros Piton Pt. 796
Vierge Pt.
Choiseul
Laborie
Vieux Fort
C. Moule à Chique
ST. LUCIA

BARBADOS
ATLANTIC OCEAN
Crabhill
North Point
Spring Hall
Fustic
Boscobelle
Portland
Belleplaine
245
Speightstown
Bathsheba
Hillcrest
Westmoreland
Alleynes Bay
Mt. Hillaby 340
Martin's Bay
Holetown
Jackson
Bridgefield
Massiah Street
Black Rock
Ellerton
Ragged Pt.
Bridgetown
Edey
Six Cross Roads
Carlisle Bay
Oistins
The Crane
Worthing
Oistins Bay
St. Martins
South Point
Chancery Lane
BGI
BARBADOS
1:2 000 000
g

**6**
B

**7**

B

HAITI
PORT-AU-PRINCE
DOMINICAN REP.
SANTO DOMINGO
Navassa I. (U.S.A.)
Jérémie
Île de la Gonâve
Dame Marie
Massif de la Hotte
C. Carcasse
Les Cayes
Aquin
Goave
Jacmel
Pointe-à-Gravois
Î. à Vache
Pedernales
Barahona
San Cristóbal
Bani
Azua de Compostela
San Juan
L. Enriquillo
SIERRA DE BAHORUCO
I. Beata
C. Beata
*Hispaniola*
*Antilles*
Jean Rabel
Port-de-Paix
Cap-à-Foux
G. de la Gonâve
Gonaïves
St-Marc
Hinche
Central
3175
Pico Duarte
La Vega
Sánchez
Sabana de la Mar
Hato Mayor
Higüey
C. Engaño
La Romana
San Pedro de Macorís
B. de Yuma
I. Saona
Isla Mona (U.S.A.)
Mona Passage
Aguadilla
Mayagüez
Bayamón
Arecibo
SAN JUAN
Carolina
Fajardo
Ponce
Caguas
Guayama
PUERTO RICO (U.S.A.)
Virgin Gorda
Virgin Is. (U.K.)
Tortola
Road Town
Anegada Virgin Is.
Anegada Passage
Sombrero (U.K.)
Anguilla (U.K.)
St. Thomas
Charlotte Amalie
Virgin Is. (U.S.A.)
St-Martin (Fr.)
St-Barthélemy (Fr.)
Christiansted
Saba (Neth.)
St. Croix
Frederiksted
St. Maarten (Neth.)
St. Eustatius (Neth.)
St. KITTS & NEVIS
Basseterre
Nevis
Redonda
Montserrat (U.K.)
Barbuda
ANTIGUA & BARBUDA
St. John's
Antigua
Ste-Rose
Moule
La Désirade
GUADELOUPE (Fr.) 1467
Pointe-à-Pitre
Basse-Terre
Marie-Galante (Fr.)
I. des Saintes (Fr.)
Grand-Bourg
Dominica Passage
Portsmouth
DOMINICA 1447
MORNE TROIS PITONS
Roseau
I. de Aves (Venezuela)
Martinique Passage
Mt. Pelée 1397
Ste-Marie
Fort-de-France
Le François
Rivière-Pilote
MARTINIQUE (Fr.)
St. Lucia Channel
Castries
950
ST. LUCIA
Soufrière
St. Vincent Passage
Soufrière 1234
St. Vincent
Speightstown
Kingstown
Bridgetown
BARBADOS
ST. VINCENT & THE GRENADINES
Hillsborough
St. George's
GRENADA

*Leeward Islands*
*Lesser*
*Windward Islands*
*Antilles*

*BEAN SEA*
C
D

**7**

*Lesser Antilles*
Oranjestad
Aruba (Neth.)
Curaçao
Bonaire
Willemstad
NETH. ANTILLES
Pta. Gallinas
MACUIRA
C. San Román
ARG. LOS ROQUES
I. Orchila (Ven.)
I. las Aves (Ven.)
Is. Los Roques (Ven.)
I. Blanquilla (Ven.)
I. Los Hermanos (Ven.)
NUEVA ESPARTA
I. de Margarita (Ven.)
I. La Tortuga (Ven.)
Is. Los Testigos (Ven.)
Tobago
Scarborough
Port of Spain
Galera Pt.
Arima
TRINIDAD & TOBAGO
Rio Claro
TRINIDAD
San Fernando
Serpent's Mouth
Dragon's Mouth
G. de Paria
Pen. de Paria
Güiria
Carúpano
Caribe
SUCRE
Cariaco
Cumaná
Guasipati
Tumeremo
El Callao
Upata
Guasdualito
Ciudad Bolívar
Ciudad Guayana
El Pao
Sierra Imataca
AMACURO
MARIUSA
DELTA
Tucupita
Los Barrancos

COLOMBIA
Santa Marta
Ríohacha
Uribia
BARRAN-QUILLA
Baranoa
Soledad
ATLÁNTICO
Sabanalarga
Fundación
Calamar
MAGDALENA
El Carmen
Plato
Zambrano
Ariona
CESAR
Santa Marta 5800
SIERRA NEVADA DE STA. MARTA
GUAJIRA
Pen. de la Guajira
Golfo de Venezuela
Punta Cardón
Maracaibo
Lago de Maracaibo
ZULIA
Valledupar
Agustín Codazzi
Machiques
San Carlos del Zulia
Encontrados
CATATUMBO-BARI
El Banco
Mompós
NORTE DE SANTANDER
Ocaña
Cúcuta
San Cristóbal
TÁCHIRA
MÉRIDA
SA. NEVADA
Pico Bolívar
Barinas
BARINAS
Santa Bárbara
Achaguas
San Fernando de Apure
Apure
Bruzual
San Carlos
COJEDES
El Baúl
GUÁRICO
Calabozo
Valle de la Pascua
El Sombrero
Chaguaramas
ANZOÁTEGUI
El Tigre
Pariaguán
Soledad
Ciudad Bolívar
VENEZUELA
Orinoco
Cabimas
La Concepción
Santa Rita
Ciudad Ojeda
TRUJILLO
Valera
Betijoque
PORTUGUESA
Guanare
Acarigua
Araure
Barquisimeto
LARA
Carora
Yaritagua
San Felipe
YARACUY
Valencia
CARABOBO
Villa de Cura
Maracay
ARAGUA
La Victoria
MIRANDA
Los Teques
CARACAS
VARGAS
La Guaira
Maiquetía
Ocumare del Tuy
Río Chico
Higuerote
Puerto La Cruz
Barcelona
Anaco
Cantaura
Maturín
MONAGAS
Caripito
Caigua
San Juan de los Morros
Altagracia de Orituco
Falcón
FALCÓN
Coro
La Vela de Coro
Puerto Cumarebo
MÉDANOS DE CORO
Punta Fijo
Pen. de Paraguaná
Tucacas
Puerto Cabello
Mene de Mauroa
Tocuyo
Baragua
Dabajuro

*West from Greenwich*
m 4000 3000 2000 1500 1000 400 200 0
ft 12 000 9000 6000 4500 3000 1200 600
National Parks
COPYRIGHT PHILIP'S

100 0 200 400 600 800 1000 1200 1400 km
100 0 200 400 600 800 1000 miles

1:35 000 000

Projection: Lambert's Azimuthal Equal Area

80 West from Greenwich 50

COPYRIGHT PHILIP'S

1:35 000 000

Projection: Lambert's Azimuthal Equal Area

COPYRIGHT PHILIP'S

■ LIMA  Capital Cities

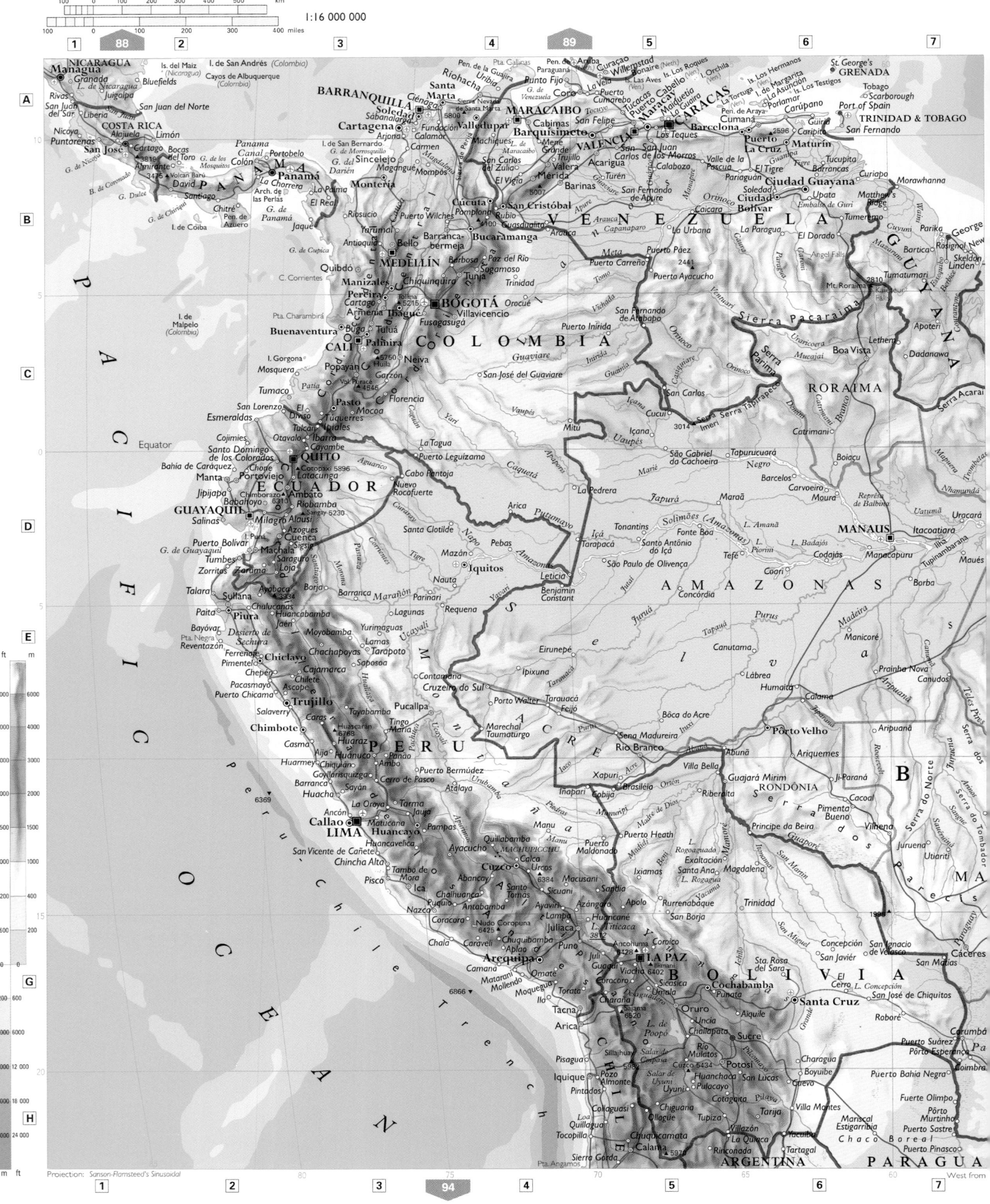

Projection: Sanson-Flamsteed's Sinusoidal

1:16 000 000

**TRINIDAD AND TOBAGO**
1:2 500 000

10  0  10  20  30  40  50 km
10  0  10  20  30 miles

*Tobago*
Charlotteville North Pt.
Castara Little
Plymouth 565 ▲ Roxborough Tobago
Buccoo Reef Scarborough
Crown Pt. Rockly Bay

**VENEZUELA**
Pen. de Paria
Macuro
Güiria
Corozal Pt.
Maraval
Blanchisseuse
Chupara Pt.
La Vache Pt.
Marocos Bay
Sans Souci
Matelot
Toco
Galera Pt.
Redhead
Salibea
Northern Range
936 ▲ 940 ▲ Mt. Aripo
Tunapuna Valencia
Matura Bay
**Port of Spain**
San Juan Arima
Chaguanas
Guaico
Sangre Grande
Upper Manzanilla
Carapichaima Couva
Narva Swamp
Cocos Bay
**Trinidad**
Point Lisas
Otaheite Bay
Talparo
San Fernando
Brighton
Guapo Bay La Brea
Gasparillo
Rio Claro
Pierreville
Mayaro Bay
Point Fortin
Pitch Lake
Penal
Basse Terre
Guayaguayare
Cedros Bay
Bonasse
Palo Seco
Siparia
304 ▲
Galeota Pt.
Icacos Pt.
Erin Pt.
La Lune Moruga
Trinity Hills
*Serpent's Mouth*
**VENEZUELA**
Pta. Bombedor
West from Greenwich

**ATLANTIC OCEAN**

*A T L A N T I C*

*O C E A N*

National Parks

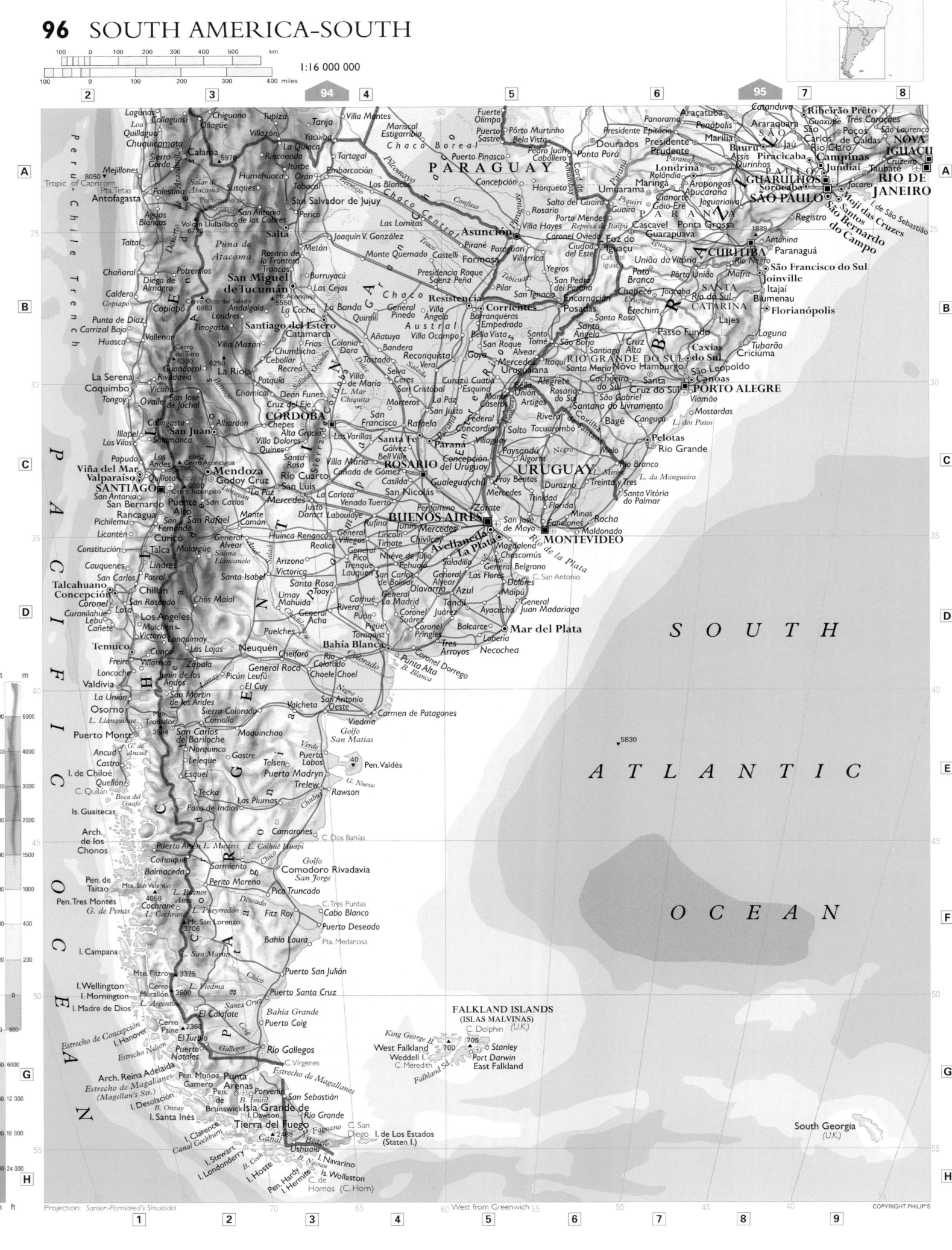

1:16 000 000

# INDEX TO WORLD MAPS

The index contains the names of all the principal places and features shown on the World Maps. Each name is followed by an additional entry in italics giving the country or region within which it is located. The alphabetical order of names composed of two or more words is governed primarily by the first word and then by the second. This is an example of the rule:

| | | | | |
|---|---|---|---|---|
| Mīr Kūh, *Iran* | . . . . . . . . . . . . . . . | **45 E8** | 26 22N | 58 55 E |
| Mīr Shahdād, *Iran* | . . . . . . . . . . . | **45 E8** | 26 15N | 58 29 E |
| Mira, *Italy* | . . . . . . . . . . . . . . . . . | **22 B5** | 45 26N | 12  8 E |
| Mira por vos Cay, *Bahamas* | . . . . | **89 B5** | 22  9N | 74 30W |
| Mirador-Río Azul △, *Guatemala* | . | **88 C2** | 17 45N | 89 50W |
| Miraj, *India* | . . . . . . . . . . . . . . . . | **40 L9** | 16 50N | 74 45 E |

Physical features composed of a proper name (Erie) and a description (Lake) are positioned alphabetically by the proper name. The description is positioned after the proper name and is usually abbreviated:

| | | | | |
|---|---|---|---|---|
| Erie, L., *N. Amer.* | . . . . . . . . . . . . . | **84 D4** | 42 15N | 81  0W |

Where a description forms part of a settlement or administrative name however, it is always written in full and put in its true alphabetic position:

| | | | | |
|---|---|---|---|---|
| Mount Morris, *U.S.A.* | . . . . . . . . | **84 D7** | 42 44N | 77 52W |

Names beginning with M' and Mc are indexed as if they were spelled Mac. Names beginning St. are alphabetized under Saint, but Sankt, Sint, Sant', Santa and San are all spelt in full and are alphabetized accordingly. If the same place name occurs two or more times in the index and all are in the same country, each is followed by the name of the administrative subdivision in which it is located.

The number in bold type which follows each name in the index refers to the number of the map page where that feature or place will be found. This is usually the largest scale at which the place or feature appears.

The letter and figure which are in bold type immediately after the page number give the grid square on the map page, within which the feature is situated. The letter represents the latitude and the figure the longitude. A lower case letter immediately after the page number refers to an inset map on that page.

In some cases the feature itself may fall within the specified square, while the name is outside. This is usually the case only with features which are larger than a grid square.

The geographical co-ordinates which follow the letter-figure references give the latitude and longitude of each place. The first co-ordinate indicates latitude – the distance north of the Equator. The second co-ordinate indicates longitude – the distance east or west of the Greenwich Meridian. Both latitude and longitude are measured in degrees and minutes (there are 60 minutes in a degree).

The latitude is followed by N(orth) or S(outh) and the longitude by E(ast) or W(est).

Rivers are indexed to their mouths or confluences, and carry the symbol ➔ after their names. The following symbols are also used in the index: ■ country, ☑ overseas territory or dependency, ☐ first order administrative area, △ national park, ⌓ other park (provincial park, nature reserve or game reserve), ✕ (LHR) principal airport (and location identifier).

## Abbreviations used in the index

*A.C.T.* – Australian Capital Territory
*A.R.* – Autonomous Region
*Afghan.* – Afghanistan
*Afr.* – Africa
*Ala.* – Alabama
*Alta.* – Alberta
*Amer.* – America(n)
*Arch.* – Archipelago
*Ariz.* – Arizona
*Ark.* – Arkansas
*Atl. Oc.* – Atlantic Ocean
*B.* – Baie, Bahía, Bay, Bucht, Bugt
*B.C.* – British Columbia
*Bangla.* – Bangladesh
*Barr.* – Barrage
*Bos.-H.* – Bosnia-Herzegovina
*C.* – Cabo, Cap, Cape, Coast
*C.A.R.* – Central African Republic
*C. Prov.* – Cape Province
*Calif.* – California
*Cat.* – Catarata
*Cent.* – Central
*Chan.* – Channel
*Colo.* – Colorado
*Conn.* – Connecticut
*Cord.* – Cordillera
*Cr.* – Creek
*Czech.* – Czech Republic
*D.C.* – District of Columbia
*Del.* – Delaware
*Dem.* – Democratic
*Dep.* – Dependency
*Des.* – Desert
*Dét.* – Détroit
*Dist.* – District
*Dj.* – Djebel
*Domin.* – Dominica
*Dom. Rep.* – Dominican Republic

*E.* – East
*E. Salv.* – El Salvador
*Eq. Guin.* – Equatorial Guinea
*Est.* – Estrecho
*Falk. Is.* – Falkland Is.
*Fd.* – Fjord
*Fla.* – Florida
*Fr.* – French
*G.* – Golfe, Golfo, Gulf, Guba, Gebel
*Ga.* – Georgia
*Gt.* – Great, Greater
*Guinea-Biss.* – Guinea-Bissau
*H.K.* – Hong Kong
*H.P.* – Himachal Pradesh
*Hants.* – Hampshire
*Harb.* – Harbor, Harbour
*Hd.* – Head
*Hts.* – Heights
*I.(s).* – Île, Ilha, Insel, Isla, Island, Isle
*Ill.* – Illinois
*Ind.* – Indiana
*Ind. Oc.* – Indian Ocean
*Ivory C.* – Ivory Coast
*J.* – Jabal, Jebel
*Jaz.* – Jazīrah
*Junc.* – Junction
*K.* – Kap, Kapp
*Kans.* – Kansas
*Kep.* – Kepulauan
*Ky.* – Kentucky
*L.* – Lac, Lacul, Lago, Lagoa, Lake, Limni, Loch, Lough
*La.* – Louisiana
*Ld.* – Land
*Liech.* – Liechtenstein
*Lux.* – Luxembourg
*Mad. P.* – Madhya Pradesh
*Madag.* – Madagascar
*Man.* – Manitoba
*Mass.* – Massachusetts

*Md.* – Maryland
*Me.* – Maine
*Medit. S.* – Mediterranean Sea
*Mich.* – Michigan
*Minn.* – Minnesota
*Miss.* – Mississippi
*Mo.* – Missouri
*Mont.* – Montana
*Mozam.* – Mozambique
*Mt.(s)* – Mont, Montaña, Mountain
*Mte.* – Monte
*Mti.* – Monti
*N.* – Nord, Norte, North, Northern, Nouveau
*N.B.* – New Brunswick
*N.C.* – North Carolina
*N. Cal.* – New Caledonia
*N. Dak.* – North Dakota
*N.H.* – New Hampshire
*N.I.* – North Island
*N.J.* – New Jersey
*N. Mex.* – New Mexico
*N.S.* – Nova Scotia
*N.S.W.* – New South Wales
*N.W.T.* – North West Territory
*N.Y.* – New York
*N.Z.* – New Zealand
*Nac.* – Nacional
*Nat.* – National
*Nebr.* – Nebraska
*Neths.* – Netherlands
*Nev.* – Nevada
*Nfld. & L.* – Newfoundland and Labrador
*Nic.* – Nicaragua
*O.* – Oued, Ouadi
*Occ.* – Occidentale
*Okla.* – Oklahoma
*Ont.* – Ontario
*Or.* – Orientale

*Oreg.* – Oregon
*Os.* – Ostrov
*Oz.* – Ozero
*P.* – Pass, Passo, Pasul, Pulau
*P.E.I.* – Prince Edward Island
*Pa.* – Pennsylvania
*Pac. Oc.* – Pacific Ocean
*Papua N.G.* – Papua New Guinea
*Pass.* – Passage
*Peg.* – Pegunungan
*Pen.* – Peninsula, Péninsule
*Phil.* – Philippines
*Pk.* – Peak
*Plat.* – Plateau
*Prov.* – Province, Provincial
*Pt.* – Point
*Pta.* – Ponta, Punta
*Pte.* – Pointe
*Qué.* – Québec
*Queens.* – Queensland
*R.* – Rio, River
*R.I.* – Rhode Island
*Ra.* – Range
*Raj.* – Rajasthan
*Recr.* – Recreational, Récréatif
*Reg.* – Region
*Rep.* – Republic
*Res.* – Reserve, Reservoir
*Rhld-Pfz.* – Rheinland-Pfalz
*S.* – South, Southern, Sur
*Si. Arabia* – Saudi Arabia
*S.C.* – South Carolina
*S. Dak.* – South Dakota
*S.I.* – South Island
*S. Leone* – Sierra Leone
*Sa.* – Serra, Sierra
*Sask.* – Saskatchewan
*Scot.* – Scotland
*Sd.* – Sound
*Sev.* – Severnaya
*Sib.* – Siberia

*Sprs.* – Springs
*St.* – Saint
*Sta.* – Santa
*Ste.* – Sainte
*Sto.* – Santo
*Str.* – Strait, Stretto
*Switz.* – Switzerland
*Tas.* – Tasmania
*Tenn.* – Tennessee
*Terr.* – Territory, Territoire
*Tex.* – Texas
*Tg.* – Tanjung
*Trin. & Tob.* – Trinidad & Tobago
*U.A.E.* – United Arab Emirates
*U.K.* – United Kingdom
*U.S.A.* – United States of America
*Ut. P.* – Uttar Pradesh
*Va.* – Virginia
*Vdkhr.* – Vodokhranilishche
*Vdskh.* – Vodoskhovyshche
*Vf.* – Vírful
*Vic.* – Victoria
*Vol.* – Volcano
*Vt.* – Vermont
*W.* – Wadi, West
*W. Va.* – West Virginia
*Wall. & F. Is.* – Wallis and Futuna Is.
*Wash.* – Washington
*Wis.* – Wisconsin
*Wlkp.* – Wielkopolski
*Wyo.* – Wyoming
*Yorks.* – Yorkshire

## A

A Coruña, Spain ............ 21 A1 43 20N 8 25W
A Estrada, Spain ............ 21 A1 42 43N 8 27W
A Fonsagrada, Spain ........ 21 A2 43 8N 7 4W
Aachen, Germany ........... 16 C4 50 45N 6 6 E
Aalborg = Ålborg, Denmark . 9 H13 57 2N 9 54 E
Aalen, Germany ............ 16 D6 48 51N 10 6 E
Aalst, Belgium ............. 15 D4 50 56N 4 2 E
Aalten, Neths. ............. 15 C6 51 56N 6 35 E
Aalter, Belgium ............ 15 C3 51 5N 3 28 E
Äänekoski, Finland ......... 9 E21 62 36N 25 44 E
Aarau, Switz. .............. 20 C8 47 23N 8 4 E
Aare →, Switz. ............. 20 C8 47 33N 8 14 E
Aarhus = Århus, Denmark .. 9 H14 56 8N 10 11 E
Aarschot, Belgium .......... 15 D4 50 59N 4 49 E
Aba, Dem. Rep. of the Congo 54 B3 3 58N 30 17 E
Aba, Nigeria ............... 50 G7 5 10N 7 19 E
Abaco I., Bahamas .......... 88 A4 26 25N 77 10W
Ābādān, Iran .............. 45 D6 30 22N 48 20 E
Ābādeh, Iran ............... 45 D7 31 8N 52 40 E
Abadla, Algeria ............ 50 B5 31 2N 2 45W
Abaetetuba, Brazil .......... 93 D9 1 40S 48 50W
Abagnar Qi, China .......... 34 C9 43 52N 116 2 E
Abah, Tanjung, Indonesia ... 37 K18 8 46S 115 38 E
Abai, Paraguay ............. 95 B4 25 58S 55 54W
Abakan, Russia ............. 29 D10 53 40N 91 10 E
Abancay, Peru ............. 92 F4 13 35S 72 55W
Abariringa, Kiribati ........ 64 H10 2 50S 171 40W
Abarqū, Iran .............. 45 D7 31 10N 53 20 E
Abashiri, Japan ............ 30 B12 44 0N 144 15 E
Abashiri-Wan, Japan ....... 30 C12 44 0N 144 30 E
Ābay = Nîl el Azraq →, Sudan 51 E12 15 38N 32 31 E
Abay, Kazakhstan .......... 28 E8 49 38N 72 53 E
Abaya, L., Ethiopia ......... 47 F2 6 30N 37 50 E
Abaza, Russia ............. 28 D9 52 39N 90 6 E
'Abbāsābād, Iran .......... 45 C8 33 34N 58 23 E
Abbay = Nîl el Azraq →, Sudan 51 E12 15 38N 32 31 E
Abbaye, Pt., U.S.A. ........ 82 B1 46 58N 88 8W
Abbé, L., Ethiopia ......... 47 E3 11 8N 41 47 E
Abbeville, France .......... 20 A4 50 6N 1 49 E
Abbeville, Ala., U.S.A. ..... 83 K3 31 34N 85 15W
Abbeville, La., U.S.A. ...... 81 L8 29 58N 92 8W
Abbeville, S.C., U.S.A. ..... 83 H4 34 11N 82 23W
Abbot Ice Shelf, Antarctica . 5 D16 73 0S 92 0W
Abbottabad, Pakistan ....... 42 B5 34 10N 73 15 E
Abd al Kūri, Yemen ........ 47 E5 12 5N 52 20 E
Ābdar, Iran ............... 45 D7 30 16N 55 19 E
'Abdolābād, Iran .......... 45 C8 34 12N 56 30 E
Abdulpur, Bangla. ......... 43 G13 24 15N 88 59 E
Abéché, Chad ............. 51 F10 13 50N 20 35 E
Abel Tasman △, N.Z. ...... 59 J4 40 59S 173 3 E
Abengourou, Ivory C. ...... 50 G5 6 42N 3 27W
Åbenrå, Denmark .......... 9 J13 55 3N 9 25 E
Abeokuta, Nigeria ......... 50 G6 7 3N 3 19 E
Aber, Uganda ............. 54 B3 2 12N 32 25 E
Aberaeron, U.K. .......... 13 E3 52 15N 4 15W
Aberayron = Aberaeron, U.K. 13 E3 52 15N 4 15W
Aberchirder, U.K. ......... 11 D6 57 34N 2 37W
Abercorn, Australia ....... 63 D5 25 12S 151 5 E
Aberdare, U.K. ........... 13 F4 51 43N 3 27W
Aberdare △, Kenya ........ 54 C4 0 22S 36 44 E
Aberdare Ra., Kenya ...... 54 C4 0 15S 36 50 E
Aberdeen, Australia ....... 63 E5 32 9S 150 56 E
Aberdeen, Canada ......... 71 C7 52 20N 106 8W
Aberdeen, China .......... 33 G11 22 15N 114 9 E
Aberdeen, S. Africa ....... 56 E3 32 28S 24 2 E
Aberdeen, U.K. ........... 11 D6 57 9N 2 5W
Aberdeen, Ala., U.S.A. ..... 83 J1 33 49N 88 33W
Aberdeen, Idaho, U.S.A. .... 76 E7 42 57N 112 50W
Aberdeen, Md., U.S.A. ..... 82 F7 39 31N 76 10W
Aberdeen, S. Dak., U.S.A. .. 80 C5 45 28N 98 29W
Aberdeen, Wash., U.S.A. ... 78 D3 46 59N 123 50W
Aberdeen, City of □, U.K. .. 11 D6 57 10N 2 10W
Aberdeenshire □, U.K. ..... 11 D6 57 17N 2 36W
Aberdovey = Aberdyfi, U.K. . 13 E3 52 33N 4 3W
Aberdyfi, U.K. ............ 13 E3 52 33N 4 3W
Aberfeldy, U.K. ........... 11 E5 56 37N 3 51W
Aberfoyle, U.K. ........... 11 E4 56 11N 4 23W
Abergavenny, U.K. ........ 13 F4 51 49N 3 1W
Abergele, U.K. ............ 12 D4 53 17N 3 35W
Abernathy, U.S.A. ......... 81 J4 33 50N 101 51W
Abert, L., U.S.A. .......... 76 E3 42 38N 120 14W
Aberystwyth, U.K. ......... 13 E3 52 25N 4 5W
Abhā, Si. Arabia .......... 47 D3 18 0N 42 34 E
Abhar, Iran .............. 45 B6 36 9N 49 13 E
Abhayapuri, India ......... 43 F14 26 24N 90 38 E
Abidjan, Ivory C. ......... 50 G5 5 26N 3 58W
Abilene, Kans., U.S.A. ..... 80 F6 38 55N 97 13W
Abilene, Tex., U.S.A. ...... 81 J5 32 28N 99 43W
Abingdon, U.K. ........... 13 F6 51 40N 1 17W
Abingdon, U.S.A. ......... 83 G5 36 43N 81 59W
Abington Reef, Australia ... 62 B4 18 0S 149 35 E
Abitau →, Canada ......... 71 B7 59 53N 109 3W
Abitibi →, Canada ........ 72 B3 51 3N 80 55W
Abitibi, L., Canada ........ 72 C4 48 40N 79 40W
Abkhaz Republic = Abkhazia □,
Georgia ................. 19 F7 43 12N 41 5 E
Abkhazia □, Georgia ...... 19 F7 43 12N 41 5 E
Abminga, Australia ........ 63 D1 26 8S 134 51 E
Åbo = Turku, Finland ...... 9 F20 60 30N 22 19 E
Abohar, India ............. 42 D6 30 10N 74 10 E
Abomey, Benin ........... 50 G6 7 10N 2 5 E
Abong-Mbang, Cameroon ... 52 D2 4 0N 13 8 E
Abou-Deïa, Chad .......... 51 F9 11 20N 19 20 E
Aboyne, U.K. ............. 11 D6 57 4N 2 47W
Abra Pampa, Argentina .... 94 A2 22 43S 65 42W
Abraham L., Canada ....... 70 C5 52 15N 116 55W
Abreojos, Pta., Mexico ..... 86 B2 26 50N 113 40W
Abrolhos, Banka, Brazil .... 90 E7 18 0S 38 0W
Abrud, Romania .......... 17 E12 46 19N 23 5 E
Absaroka Range, U.S.A. .... 76 D9 44 45N 109 50W
Abu, India ............... 42 G5 24 41N 72 50 E
Abū al Abyaḍ, U.A.E. ..... 45 E7 24 11N 53 50 E
Abū al Khaṣīb, Iraq ....... 45 D6 30 25N 48 0 E
Abū 'Alī, Si. Arabia ....... 45 E6 27 20N 49 27 E
Abū 'Alī →, Lebanon ...... 46 A4 34 25N 35 50 E
Abu Dhabi = Abū Ẓāby, U.A.E. 45 E7 24 28N 54 22 E
Abū Du'ān, Syria ......... 44 B3 36 25N 38 15 E
Abū el Gairi, W. →, Egypt .. 46 F2 29 35N 33 30 E
Abu Ga'da, W. →, Egypt ... 46 F2 29 15N 33 20 E
Abū Ḥadrīyah, Si. Arabia .. 45 E6 27 20N 48 58 E
Abu Hamed, Sudan ........ 51 E12 19 32N 33 13 E
Abū Kamāl, Syria ......... 44 C4 34 30N 41 0 E
Abū Madd, Ra's, Si. Arabia . 44 E3 24 50N 37 7 E
Abū Mūsā, U.A.E. ........ 45 E7 25 52N 55 3 E
Abū Qaşr, Si. Arabia ...... 44 D3 30 21N 38 34 E

Abu Simbel, Egypt ......... 51 D12 22 18N 31 40 E
Abū Şukhayr, Iraq ......... 44 D5 31 54N 44 30 E
Abū Zabad, Sudan ......... 51 F11 12 25N 29 10 E
Abū Ẓāby, U.A.E. ......... 45 E7 24 28N 54 22 E
Abū Zeydābād, Iran ....... 45 C6 33 54N 51 45 E
Abuja, Nigeria ............ 50 G7 9 5N 7 32 E
Abukuma-Gawa →, Japan .. 30 E10 38 6N 140 52 E
Abukuma-Sammyaku, Japan . 30 F10 37 30N 140 45 E
Abunã, Brazil ............. 92 E5 9 40S 65 20W
Abunã →, Brazil .......... 92 E5 9 41S 65 20W
Aburo, Dem. Rep. of the Congo 54 B3 2 4N 30 53 E
Abut Hd., N.Z. ........... 59 K3 43 7S 170 15 E
Acadia △, U.S.A. ......... 83 C11 44 20N 68 13W
Açailândia, Brazil ......... 93 D9 4 57S 47 0W
Acajutla, El Salv. ......... 88 D2 13 36N 89 50W
Acámbaro, Mexico ........ 86 D4 20 0N 100 40W
Acaponeta, Mexico ........ 86 C3 22 30N 105 20W
Acapulco, Mexico ......... 87 D5 16 51N 99 56W
Acarai, Serra, Brazil ...... 92 C7 1 50N 57 50W
Acarigua, Venezuela ...... 92 B5 9 33N 69 12W
Acatlán, Mexico .......... 87 D5 18 10N 98 3W
Acayucan, Mexico ........ 87 D6 17 59N 94 58W
Accomac, U.S.A. ......... 82 G8 37 43N 75 40W
Accra, Ghana ............. 50 G5 5 35N 0 6W
Accrington, U.K. ......... 12 D5 53 45N 2 22W
Acebal, Argentina ......... 94 C3 33 20S 60 50W
Aceh □, Indonesia ........ 36 D1 4 15N 97 30 E
Achalpur, India .......... 40 J10 21 22N 77 32 E
Acheng, China ........... 35 B14 45 30N 126 58 E
Acher, India ............. 42 H5 23 10N 72 32 E
Achill Hd., Ireland ........ 10 C1 53 58N 10 15W
Achill I., Ireland ......... 10 C1 53 58N 10 1W
Achinsk, Russia .......... 29 D10 56 20N 90 20 E
Acireale, Italy ........... 22 F6 37 37N 15 10 E
Ackerman, U.S.A. ........ 81 J10 33 19N 89 11W
Acklins I., Bahamas ....... 89 B5 22 30N 74 0W
Acme, Canada ............ 70 C6 51 33N 113 30W
Acme, U.S.A. ............ 84 F6 40 8N 79 26W
Aconcagua, Cerro, Argentina 94 C2 32 39S 70 0W
Aconquija, Mt., Argentina . 94 B2 27 0S 66 0W
Açores, Is. dos, Atl. Oc. ... 50 A1 38 0N 27 0W
Acornhoek, S. Africa ...... 57 C5 24 37S 31 2 E
Acraman, L., Australia .... 63 E2 32 2S 135 23 E
Acre = 'Akko, Israel ...... 46 C4 32 55N 35 4 E
Acre □, Brazil ............ 92 E4 9 1S 71 0W
Acre →, Brazil ........... 92 E5 8 45S 67 22W
Acton, Canada ........... 84 C4 43 38N 80 3W
Acuña, Mexico ........... 86 B4 29 18N 100 55W
Ad Dammām, Si. Arabia ... 45 E6 26 20N 50 5 E
Ad Dāmūr, Lebanon ....... 46 B4 33 44N 35 27 E
Ad Dawādimī, Si. Arabia ... 44 E5 24 35N 44 15 E
Ad Dawḥah, Qatar ........ 45 E6 25 15N 51 35 E
Ad Dawr, Iraq ........... 44 C4 34 27N 43 47 E
Ad Dir'īyah, Si. Arabia .... 44 E5 24 44N 46 35 E
Ad Dīwānīyah, Iraq ....... 44 D5 32 0N 45 0 E
Ad Dujayl, Iraq .......... 44 C5 33 51N 44 14 E
Ad Duwayd, Si. Arabia .... 44 D4 30 15N 42 17 E
Ada, Minn., U.S.A. ....... 80 B6 47 18N 96 31W
Ada, Okla., U.S.A. ........ 81 H6 34 46N 96 41W
Adabiya, Egypt .......... 46 F1 29 53N 32 28 E
Adair, C., Canada ........ 69 A12 71 30N 71 34W
Adaja →, Spain .......... 21 B3 41 32N 4 52W
Adak I., U.S.A. .......... 68 C2 51 45N 176 45W
Adamaoua, Massif de l',
Cameroon .............. 51 G7 7 20N 12 20 E
Adamawa Highlands =
Adamaoua, Massif de l',
Cameroon .............. 51 G7 7 20N 12 20 E
Adamello, Mte., Italy ..... 20 C9 46 9N 10 30 E
Adaminaby, Australia ..... 63 F4 36 0S 148 45 E
Adams, Mass., U.S.A. ..... 85 D11 42 38N 73 7W
Adams, N.Y., U.S.A. ...... 85 C8 43 49N 76 1W
Adams, Wis., U.S.A. ...... 80 D10 43 57N 89 49W
Adams, Mt., U.S.A. ....... 78 D5 46 12N 121 30W
Adam's Bridge, Sri Lanka .. 40 Q11 9 15N 79 40 E
Adams L., Canada ......... 70 C5 51 10N 119 40W
Adam's Peak, Sri Lanka .... 40 R12 6 48N 80 30 E
Adana, Turkey ........... 19 G6 37 0N 35 16 E
Adapazarı = Sakarya, Turkey 19 F5 40 48N 30 25 E
Adarama, Sudan .......... 51 E12 17 10N 34 52 E
Adare, C., Antarctica ..... 5 D11 71 0S 171 0 E
Adaut, Indonesia ......... 37 F8 8 8S 131 7 E
Adavale, Australia ........ 63 D3 25 52S 144 32 E
Adda →, Italy ........... 20 D8 45 8N 9 53 E
Addis Ababa = Addis Abeba,
Ethiopia ............... 47 F2 9 2N 38 42 E
Addis Abeba, Ethiopia ..... 47 F2 9 2N 38 42 E
Addison, U.S.A. .......... 84 D7 42 1N 77 14W
Addo, S. Africa .......... 56 E4 33 32S 25 45 E
Addo □, S. Africa ........ 56 E4 33 30S 25 50 E
Ādeh, Iran .............. 44 B5 37 42N 45 11 E
Adel, U.S.A. ............. 83 K4 31 8N 83 25W
Adelaide, Australia ....... 63 E2 34 52S 138 30 E
Adelaide, S. Africa ....... 56 E4 32 42S 26 20 E
Adelaide I., Antarctica .... 5 C17 67 15S 68 30W
Adelaide Pen., Canada .... 68 B10 68 15N 97 30W
Adelaide River, Australia .. 60 B5 13 15S 131 7 E
Adelaide Village, Bahamas . 88 A4 25 0N 77 31W
Adelanto, U.S.A. ......... 79 L9 34 35N 117 22W
Adele I., Australia ........ 60 C3 15 32S 123 9 E
Adélie, Terre, Antarctica .. 5 C10 68 0S 140 0 E
Adélie Land = Adélie, Terre,
Antarctica ............. 5 C10 68 0S 140 0 E
Aden = Al 'Adan, Yemen ... 47 E4 12 45N 45 0 E
Aden, G. of, Asia ......... 47 E4 12 30N 47 30 E
Adendorp, S. Africa ...... 56 E3 32 15S 24 30 E
Adh Dhayd, U.A.E. ....... 45 E7 25 17N 55 53 E
Adhoi, India ............. 42 H4 23 26N 70 32 E
Adi, Indonesia ........... 37 E8 4 15S 133 30 E
Adieu, C., Australia ....... 61 F5 32 0S 132 10 E
Adieu Pt., Australia ....... 60 C3 15 14S 124 35 E
Adige →, Italy ........... 22 B5 45 9N 12 20 E
Adigrat, Ethiopia ......... 47 E2 14 20N 39 26 E
Adilabad, India .......... 40 K11 19 33N 78 20 E
Adirondack △, U.S.A. ..... 85 C10 44 0N 74 20W
Adirondack Mts., U.S.A. ... 85 C10 44 0N 74 0W
Adis Abeba = Addis Abeba,
Ethiopia ............... 47 F2 9 2N 38 42 E
Adjumani, Uganda ........ 54 B3 3 20N 31 50 E
Adjuntas, Puerto Rico ..... 89 d 18 10N 66 43W
Adlavik Is., Canada ....... 73 B8 55 0N 58 40W
Admiralty G., Australia .... 60 B4 14 20S 125 55 E
Admiralty I., U.S.A. ...... 70 B2 57 30N 134 30W
Admiralty Is., Papua N. G. . 64 H6 2 0S 147 0 E
Adonara, Indonesia ....... 37 F6 8 15S 123 5 E
Adoni, India ............. 40 M10 15 33N 77 18 E
Adour →, France ......... 20 E3 43 32N 1 32W
Adra, India .............. 43 H12 23 30N 86 42 E

Adra, Spain .............. 21 D4 36 43N 3 3W
Adrano, Italy ............ 22 F6 37 40N 14 50 E
Adrar, Mauritania ........ 50 D3 20 30N 7 30 E
Adrar des Iforas, Algeria .. 50 C5 27 51N 0 11 E
Adrian, Mich., U.S.A. ..... 82 E3 41 54N 84 2W
Adrian, Tex., U.S.A. ...... 81 H3 35 16N 102 40W
Adriatic Sea, Medit. S. .... 22 C6 43 0N 16 0 E
Adua, Indonesia .......... 37 E7 1 45S 129 50 E
Adwa, Ethiopia .......... 47 E2 14 15N 38 52 E
Adygea □, Russia ........ 19 F7 45 0N 40 0 E
Adzhar Republic = Ajaria □,
Georgia ............... 19 F7 41 30N 42 0 E
Adzopé, Ivory C. ......... 50 G5 6 7N 3 49W
Ægean Sea, Medit. S. ..... 23 E11 38 30N 25 0 E
Aerhtai Shan, Mongolia ... 32 B4 46 40N 92 45 E
'Afak, Iraq .............. 44 C5 32 4N 45 15 E
Afándou, Greece ......... 25 C10 36 18N 28 12 E
Afghanistan ■, Asia ...... 40 C4 33 0N 65 0 E
Aflou, Algeria ........... 50 B6 34 7N 2 3 E
Africa ................... 48 E6 10 0N 20 0 E
'Afrin, Syria ............. 44 B3 36 32N 36 50 E
Afton, N.Y., U.S.A. ....... 85 D9 42 14N 75 32W
Afton, Wyo., U.S.A. ...... 76 E8 42 44N 110 56W
Afuá, Brazil ............. 93 D8 0 15S 50 20W
'Afula, Israel ............ 46 C4 32 37N 35 17 E
Afyon, Turkey ........... 19 G5 38 45N 30 33 E
Afyonkarahisar = Afyon, Turkey 19 G5 38 45N 30 33 E
Agadès = Agadez, Niger ... 50 E7 16 58N 7 59 E
Agadez, Niger ........... 50 E7 16 58N 7 59 E
Agadir, Morocco ......... 50 B4 30 28N 9 55W
Agaete, Canary Is. ....... 24 F4 28 6N 15 43W
Agalega Is., Mauritius ..... 3 E12 11 0S 57 0 E
Agar, India .............. 42 H7 23 40N 76 2 E
Agartala, India .......... 41 H17 23 50N 91 23 E
Agassiz, Canada ......... 70 D4 49 14N 121 46W
Agats, Indonesia ......... 37 F9 5 33S 138 0 E
Agawam, U.S.A. ......... 85 D12 42 5N 72 37W
Agboville, Ivory C. ....... 50 G5 5 55N 4 15W
Ağdam, Azerbaijan ....... 44 B5 40 0N 46 58 E
Agde, France ............ 20 E5 43 19N 3 28 E
Agen, France ............ 20 D4 44 12N 0 38 E
Āgh Bābā, Iran .......... 45 B6 37 15N 48 4 E
Aginskoye, Russia ........ 29 D12 51 6N 114 32 E
Agnew, Australia ......... 61 E3 28 1S 120 31 E
Agori, India ............. 43 G10 24 33N 82 57 E
Agra, India .............. 42 F7 27 17N 77 58 E
Ağri, Turkey ............ 19 G7 39 44N 43 3 E
Agri →, Italy ........... 22 D7 40 13N 16 44 E
Ağri Daği, Turkey ........ 19 G7 39 50N 44 15 E
Ağri Karakose = Ağri, Turkey 19 G7 39 44N 43 3 E
Agrigento, Italy .......... 22 F5 37 19N 13 34 E
Agrinion, Greece ......... 23 E9 38 37N 21 27 E
Agua Caliente, Baja Calif.,
Mexico ................ 79 N10 32 29N 116 59W
Agua Caliente, Sinaloa, Mexico 86 B3 26 30N 108 20W
Agua Caliente Springs, U.S.A. 79 N10 32 56N 116 19W
Água Clara, Brazil ........ 93 H8 20 25S 52 45W
Agua Fria △, U.S.A. ...... 77 J8 34 14N 112 0W
Agua Hechicero, Mexico ... 79 N10 32 26N 116 14W
Agua Prieta, Mexico ...... 86 A3 31 20N 109 32W
Aguada, Puerto Rico ...... 89 d 18 26N 67 10W
Aguadilla, Puerto Rico .... 88 E3 18 5N 80 32W
Aguadulce, Panama ....... 79 M10 33 27N 116 51W
Aguanga, U.S.A. ......... 73 B7 50 14N 62 0W
Aguanus →, Canada ...... 73 B7 50 13N 62 5W
Aguapey →, Argentina .... 94 B4 29 7S 56 36W
Aguaray Guazú →, Paraguay 94 A4 24 47S 57 19W
Aguarico →, Ecuador ..... 92 D3 0 59S 75 11W
Aguaro-Guariquito △, Venezuela 89 E6 8 20N 66 35W
Aguas Blancas, Chile ...... 94 A2 24 15S 69 55W
Aguascalientes, Mexico .... 86 C4 21 53N 102 12W
Aguascalientes □, Mexico .. 86 C4 22 0N 102 20W
Aguila, Punta, Puerto Rico . 89 d 17 57N 67 13W
Aguilares, Argentina ...... 94 B2 27 26S 65 35W
Águilas, Spain ........... 21 D5 37 23N 1 35W
Agüimes, Canary Is. ...... 24 G4 27 58N 15 27W
Aguja, C. de la, Colombia .. 90 B3 11 18N 74 12W
Agujereada, Pta., Puerto Rico 89 d 18 30N 67 8W
Agulhas, C., S. Africa ..... 56 E3 34 52S 20 0 E
Agulo, Canary Is. ........ 24 F2 28 11N 17 12W
Agung, Gunung, Indonesia . 36 F5 8 20S 115 28 E
Agur, Uganda ........... 54 B3 2 28N 32 55 E
Agusan →, Phil. ......... 37 C7 9 0N 125 30 E
Aha Mts., Botswana ...... 56 B3 19 45S 21 0 E
Ahaggar, Algeria ......... 50 D7 23 0N 6 30 E
Ahar, Iran .............. 44 B5 38 35N 47 0 E
Ahipara B., N.Z. ......... 59 F4 35 5S 173 5 E
Ahiri, India ............. 40 K12 19 30N 80 0 E
Ahmad Wal, Pakistan ..... 42 E1 29 18N 65 58 E
Ahmadabad, India ....... 42 H5 23 0N 72 40 E
Aḥmadābād, Khorāsān, Iran 45 C9 35 3N 60 50 E
Aḥmadābād, Khorāsān, Iran 45 C8 35 49N 59 42 E
Aḥmadī, Iran ............ 45 E8 27 56N 56 42 E
Ahmadnagar, India ....... 40 K9 19 7N 74 46 E
Ahmadpur, Pakistan ...... 42 E4 29 12N 71 10 E
Ahmadpur Lamma, Pakistan 42 E4 28 19N 70 3 E
Ahmedabad = Ahmadabad, India 42 H5 23 0N 72 40 E
Ahmednagar = Ahmadnagar,
India .................. 40 K9 19 7N 74 46 E
Ahome, Mexico .......... 86 B3 25 55N 109 11W
Ahoskie, U.S.A. ......... 83 G7 36 17N 76 59W
Ahram, Iran ............. 45 D6 28 52N 51 16 E
Ahrax Pt., Malta ......... 25 D1 36 0N 14 22 E
Āhū, Iran ............... 45 C6 34 33N 50 2 E
Ahuachapán, El Salv. ..... 88 D2 13 54N 89 52W
Ahvāz, Iran ............. 45 D6 31 20N 48 40 E
Ahvenanmaa, Finland ..... 9 F19 60 15N 20 0 E
Aḥwar, Yemen ........... 47 E4 13 30N 46 40 E
Ai →, India ............. 43 F14 26 26N 90 44 E
Ai-Ais, Namibia ......... 56 D2 27 54S 17 59 E
Ai-Ais and Fish River Canyon △,
Namibia ............... 56 C2 24 45S 17 15 E
Aichi □, Japan .......... 31 G8 35 0N 137 15 E
Aigua, Uruguay .......... 95 C5 34 13S 54 46W
Aigues-Mortes, France .... 20 E6 43 35N 4 12 E
Aihui, China ............ 33 A7 50 10N 127 30 E
Aija, Peru .............. 92 E3 9 50S 77 45W
Aikawa, Japan .......... 30 E9 38 2N 138 15 E
Aiken, U.S.A. ........... 83 J5 33 34N 81 43W
Aileron, Australia ........ 62 C1 22 39S 133 20 E
Aillik, Canada ........... 73 A8 55 11N 59 18W
Ailsa Craig, U.K. ........ 11 F3 55 15N 5 6W
Aim, Russia ............. 29 D14 59 0N 133 55 E
Aimere, Indonesia ........ 37 F6 8 45S 121 3 E
Aimogasta, Argentina ..... 94 B2 28 33S 66 50W
Aïn Ben Tili, Mauritania .. 50 C4 25 59N 9 27W

Aïn Sefra, Algeria ........ 50 B5 32 47N 0 37W
Ain Sudr, Egypt .......... 46 F2 29 50N 33 6 E
Ainaži, Latvia ........... 9 H21 57 50N 24 24 E
Ainsworth, U.S.A. ........ 80 D5 42 33N 99 52W
Aiquile, Bolivia .......... 92 G5 18 10S 65 10W
Aïr, Niger .............. 50 E7 18 30N 8 0 E
Air Force I., Canada ...... 69 B12 67 58N 74 5W
Air Hitam, Malaysia ...... 39 M4 1 55N 103 11 E
Airdrie, Canada ......... 70 C6 51 18N 114 2W
Airdrie, U.K. ............ 11 F5 55 52N 3 57W
Aire, I. de l', Spain ...... 24 B11 39 48N 4 16 E
Airlie Beach, Australia .... 62 J6 20 16S 148 43 E
Aisne →, France ......... 20 B5 49 26N 2 50 E
Ait, India .............. 43 G8 25 54N 79 14 E
Aitkin, U.S.A. ........... 80 B8 46 32N 93 42W
Aiud, Romania .......... 17 E12 46 19N 23 44 E
Aix-en-Provence, France ... 20 E6 43 32N 5 27 E
Aix-la-Chapelle = Aachen,
Germany .............. 16 C4 50 45N 6 6 E
Aix-les-Bains, France ..... 20 D6 45 41N 5 53 E
Aiyion, Greece .......... 23 E10 38 15N 22 5 E
Aizawl, India ............ 41 H18 23 40N 92 44 E
Aizkraukle, Latvia ....... 9 H21 56 36N 25 11 E
Aizpute, Latvia .......... 9 H19 56 43N 21 40 E
Aizuwakamatsu, Japan .... 30 F9 37 30N 139 56 E
Ajaccio, France .......... 20 F8 41 55N 8 40 E
Ajai →, Uganda ......... 54 B3 2 52N 31 16 E
Ajaigarh, India .......... 43 G9 24 52N 80 16 E
Ajalpan, Mexico ......... 87 D5 18 22N 97 15W
Ajanta Ra., India ........ 40 J9 20 28N 75 50 E
Ajari Rep. = Ajaria □, Georgia 19 F7 41 30N 42 0 E
Ajaria □, Georgia ........ 19 F7 41 30N 42 0 E
Ajax, Canada ........... 84 C5 43 50N 79 1W
Ajdābiyā, Libya ......... 51 B10 30 54N 20 4 E
Ajka, Hungary ........... 17 E9 47 4N 17 31 E
'Ajlūn, Jordan ........... 46 C4 32 18N 35 47 E
'Ajlūn □, Jordan ......... 46 C4 32 18N 35 47 E
'Ajmān, U.A.E. .......... 45 E7 25 25N 55 30 E
Ajmer, India ............ 42 F6 26 28N 74 37 E
Ajnala, India ............ 42 D6 31 50N 74 48 E
Ajo, U.S.A. ............. 77 K7 32 22N 112 52W
Ajo, C. de, Spain ........ 21 A4 43 31N 3 35W
Akabira, Japan .......... 30 C11 43 33N 142 5 E
Akamas, Cyprus ......... 25 D11 35 3N 32 18 E
Akan △, Japan ........... 30 C12 43 20N 144 20 E
Akanthou, Cyprus ........ 25 D12 35 22N 33 45 E
Akaroa, N.Z. ............ 59 K4 43 49S 172 59 E
Akashi, Japan ........... 31 G7 34 45N 134 58 E
Akbarpur, Bihar, India .... 43 G10 24 39N 83 58 E
Akbarpur, Ut. P., India .... 43 F10 26 25N 82 32 E
Akçaabat, Turkey ........ 19 F6 41 3N 39 36 E
Akelamo, Indonesia ...... 37 D7 1 35N 129 40 E
Aketi, Dem. Rep. of the Congo 52 D4 2 38N 23 47 E
Akharnaí, Greece ........ 23 E10 38 5N 23 44 E
Akhelóös →, Greece ...... 23 E9 38 19N 21 7 E
Akhisar, Turkey ......... 23 E12 38 56N 27 48 E
Akhnur, India ........... 43 C6 32 52N 74 45 E
Akhtyrka = Okhtyrka, Ukraine 19 D5 50 25N 35 0 E
Aki, Japan .............. 31 H6 33 30N 133 54 E
Akimiski I., Canada ...... 72 B3 52 50N 81 30W
Akita, Japan ............ 30 E10 39 45N 140 7 E
Akita □, Japan .......... 30 E10 39 40N 140 30 E
Akjoujt, Mauritania ...... 50 E3 19 45N 14 15W
Akkeshi, Japan .......... 30 C12 43 2N 144 51 E
'Akko, Israel ............ 46 C4 32 55N 35 4 E
Aklavik, Canada ......... 68 B6 68 12N 135 0W
Aklera, India ............ 42 G7 24 26N 76 32 E
Akō, Japan ............. 31 G7 34 45N 134 24 E
Akola, India ............ 40 J10 20 42N 77 2 E
Akordat, Eritrea ......... 47 D2 15 30N 37 40 E
Akpatok I., Canada ....... 69 B13 60 25N 68 8W
Åkrahamn, Norway ....... 9 G11 59 15N 5 10 E
Akranes, Iceland ......... 8 D2 64 19N 22 5W
Akron, Colo., U.S.A. ..... 80 E3 40 10N 103 13W
Akron, Ohio, U.S.A. ...... 84 E3 41 5N 81 31W
Akrotiri, Cyprus ......... 25 E11 34 36N 32 57 E
Akrotiri Bay, Cyprus ..... 25 E12 34 35N 33 10 E
Aksai Chin, China ....... 43 B8 35 15N 79 55 E
Aksaray, Turkey ......... 19 G5 38 25N 34 2 E
Aksay, Kazakhstan ....... 19 D9 51 11N 53 0 E
Akşehir, Turkey ......... 44 B1 38 18N 31 30 E
Akşehir Gölü, Turkey ..... 19 G5 38 30N 31 25 E
Aksu, China ............ 32 B3 41 5N 80 10 E
Aksum, Ethiopia ......... 47 E2 14 5N 38 40 E
Aktogay, Kazakhstan ..... 28 E8 46 57N 79 40 E
Aktsyabrski, Belarus ..... 17 B15 52 38N 28 53 E
Aktyubinsk = Aqtöbe, Kazakhstan 19 D10 50 17N 57 10 E
Akure, Nigeria .......... 50 G7 7 15N 5 5 E
Akureyri, Iceland ........ 8 D4 65 40N 18 6W
Akyab = Sittwe, Burma .... 41 J18 20 18N 92 45 E
Al 'Adan, Yemen ......... 47 E4 12 45N 45 0 E
Al Aḩsā = Hasa □, Si. Arabia 45 E6 25 50N 49 0 E
Al Ajfar, Si. Arabia ...... 44 E4 27 26N 43 0 E
Al Amādīyah, Iraq ....... 44 B4 37 5N 43 30 E
Al 'Amārah, Iraq ........ 44 D5 31 55N 47 15 E
Al 'Aqabah, Jordan ...... 46 F4 29 31N 35 0 E
Al 'Aqabah □, Jordan ..... 46 F4 29 30N 35 20 E
Al Arak, Syria ........... 44 C3 34 38N 38 35 E
Al 'Aramah, Si. Arabia .... 44 E5 25 30N 46 0 E
Al 'Arţāwīyah, Si. Arabia .. 44 E5 26 31N 45 20 E
Al 'Azamīyah = 'Ammān □, Jordan 46 D5 31 40N 36 30 E
Al 'Assāfiyah, Si. Arabia ... 44 D3 28 17N 38 59 E
Al 'Ayn, Si. Arabia ....... 44 E3 25 4N 38 6 E
Al 'Ayn, U.A.E. .......... 45 E7 24 15N 55 45 E
Al 'Azīzīyah, Iraq ....... 44 C5 32 54N 45 4 E
Al Bāb, Syria ........... 44 B3 36 23N 37 29 E
Al Bad', Si. Arabia ....... 44 D2 28 28N 35 1 E
Al Bādī, Iraq ............ 44 C4 35 56N 41 32 E
Al Baḩrah, Kuwait ....... 44 D5 29 40N 47 52 E
Al Baḩral Mayyit = Dead Sea,
Asia .................. 46 D4 31 30N 35 30 E
Al Balqā' □, Jordan ...... 46 C4 32 5N 35 45 E
Al Bārūk, J., Lebanon ..... 46 B4 33 39N 35 40 E
Al Başrah, Iraq .......... 44 D5 30 30N 47 50 E
Al Baṭḩā, Iraq .......... 44 D5 31 6N 45 53 E
Al Batrūn, Lebanon ...... 46 A4 34 15N 35 40 E
Al Bayḑā, Libya ......... 51 B10 32 50N 21 44 E
Al Biqā, Lebanon ........ 46 A5 34 10N 36 10 E
Al Bi'r, Si. Arabia ....... 44 D3 28 51N 36 16 E
Al Burayj, Syria ......... 46 A5 34 15N 36 46 E
Al Faḑilī, Si. Arabia ...... 45 E6 26 58N 49 10 E
Al Fallūjah, Iraq ......... 44 C4 33 20N 43 55 E
Al Fāw, Iraq ............ 45 D6 30 0N 48 30 E
Al Fujayrah, U.A.E. ...... 45 E8 25 7N 56 18 E
Al Ghadaf, W. →, Jordan .. 46 D5 31 26N 36 43 E
Al Ghammās, Iraq ........ 44 D5 31 45N 44 37 E

Al Ghazālah, Si. Arabia ........ 44 E4 26 48N 41 19 E
Al Ḥadīthah, Iraq ............ 44 C4 34 0N 41 13 E
Al Ḥadīthah, Si. Arabia ...... 46 D6 31 28N 37 8 E
Al Ḥaḍr, Iraq ................ 44 C4 35 35N 42 44 E
Al Ḥājānah, Syria ............ 46 B5 33 20N 36 33 E
Al Ḥajar al Gharbī, Oman .... 45 E8 24 10N 56 15 E
Al Ḥāmad, Si. Arabia ........ 44 D3 31 30N 39 30 E
Al Hamdāniyah, Syria ........ 44 C3 35 25N 36 50 E
Al Ḥamīdīyah, Syria ........ 46 A4 34 42N 35 57 E
Al Ḥammār, Iraq ............ 44 D5 30 57N 46 51 E
Al Ḥamrā', Si. Arabia ........ 44 E3 24 2N 38 55 E
Al Ḥamzah, Iraq ............ 44 D5 31 43N 44 58 E
Al Ḥanākīyah, Si. Arabia .... 44 E4 24 51N 40 31 E
Al Ḥarīr, W. →, Syria ........ 46 C4 32 44N 35 59 E
Al Ḥaṣā, W. →, Jordan ...... 46 D4 31 4N 35 29 E
Al Ḥasakah, Syria ............ 44 B4 36 35N 40 45 E
Al Ḥaydān, W. →, Jordan .... 46 D4 31 29N 35 34 E
Al Ḥayy, Iraq ................ 44 C5 32 5N 46 5 E
Al Ḥijarah, Asia ............ 44 D4 30 0N 44 0 E
Al Ḥillah, Iraq .............. 44 C5 32 30N 44 25 E
Al Ḥillah, Si. Arabia ........ 47 B4 23 35N 46 50 E
Al Hindīyah, Iraq ............ 44 C5 32 30N 44 10 E
Al Hirmil, Lebanon .......... 46 A5 34 26N 36 24 E
Al Hoceïma, Morocco ........ 50 A5 35 8N 3 58W
Al Ḥudaydah, Yemen ........ 47 E3 14 50N 43 0 E
Al Hufūf, Si. Arabia .......... 45 E6 25 25N 49 45 E
Al Ḥumayḍah, Si. Arabia .... 44 D2 29 14N 34 56 E
Al Ḥunayy, Si. Arabia ...... 45 E6 25 58N 48 45 E
Al Isāwiyah, Si. Arabia ...... 44 D3 30 43N 37 59 E
Al Jafr, Jordan .............. 46 E5 30 18N 36 14 E
Al Jāfūrah, Si. Arabia ........ 45 E7 25 0N 50 15 E
Al Jaghbūb, Libya ............ 51 C10 29 42N 24 38 E
Al Jahrah, Kuwait .......... 44 D5 29 25N 47 40 E
Al Jalāmīd, Si. Arabia ...... 44 D3 31 20N 40 6 E
Al Jamalīyah, Qatar .......... 45 E6 25 37N 51 5 E
Al Janūb □, Lebanon ........ 46 B4 33 20N 35 20 E
Al Jawf, Libya .............. 51 D10 24 10N 23 24 E
Al Jawf, Si. Arabia .......... 44 D3 29 55N 39 40 E
Al Jazirah, Iraq ............ 44 C5 33 30N 44 0 E
Al Jithāmīyah, Si. Arabia .... 44 E4 27 41N 41 43 E
Al Jubayl, Si. Arabia ........ 45 E6 27 0N 49 50 E
Al Jubaylah, Si. Arabia ...... 44 E5 24 55N 46 25 E
Al Jubb, Si. Arabia .......... 44 E4 27 11N 42 17 E
Al Junaynah, Sudan .......... 51 F10 13 27N 22 45 E
Al Kabā'ish, Iraq ............ 44 D5 30 58N 47 0 E
Al Karak, Jordan ............ 46 D4 31 11N 35 42 E
Al Karak □, Jordan .......... 46 E5 31 0N 36 0 E
Al Kāẓimīyah, Iraq .......... 44 C5 33 22N 44 18 E
Al Khābūra, Oman .......... 45 F8 23 57N 57 5 E
Al Khafjī, Si. Arabia ........ 45 E6 28 24N 48 29 E
Al Khalīl, West Bank ........ 46 D4 31 32N 35 6 E
Al Khāliṣ, Iraq .............. 44 C5 33 49N 44 32 E
Al Kharsānīyah, Si. Arabia .. 45 E6 27 13N 49 18 E
Al Khaṣab, Oman ............ 45 E8 26 14N 56 15 E
Al Khawr, Qatar ............ 45 E6 25 41N 51 30 E
Al Khiḍr, Iraq .............. 44 D5 31 12N 45 33 E
Al Khiyām, Lebanon ........ 46 B4 33 20N 35 36 E
Al Khums, Libya ............ 51 B8 32 40N 14 17 E
Al Kiswah, Syria ............ 46 B5 33 23N 36 14 E
Al Kūfah, Iraq .............. 44 C5 32 2N 44 24 E
Al Kufrah, Libya ............ 51 D10 24 17N 23 15 E
Al Kuhayfiyah, Si. Arabia .... 44 E4 27 12N 43 3 E
Al Kūt, Iraq ................ 44 C5 32 30N 46 0 E
Al Kuwayt, Kuwait .......... 44 D5 29 30N 48 0 E
Al Labwah, Lebanon ........ 46 A5 34 11N 36 20 E
Al Lidhiqīyah, Syria ........ 44 C2 35 30N 35 45 E
Al Līth, Si. Arabia .......... 47 C3 20 9N 40 15 E
Al Liwā', Oman .............. 45 E8 24 31N 56 36 E
Al Luḥayyah, Yemen ........ 47 D3 15 45N 42 40 E
Al Madīnah, Iraq ............ 44 D5 30 57N 47 16 E
Al Madīnah, Si. Arabia ...... 44 E3 24 35N 39 52 E
Al Mafraq, Jordan .......... 46 C5 32 17N 36 14 E
Al Mafraq □, Jordan ........ 46 C5 32 17N 36 15 E
Al Maḥmūdīyah, Iraq ........ 44 C5 33 3N 44 21 E
Al Majma'ah, Si. Arabia .... 44 E5 25 57N 45 22 E
Al Makhruq, W. →, Jordan .. 46 D6 31 28N 37 0 E
Al Makhūl, Si. Arabia ...... 44 E4 26 37N 42 39 E
Al Manāmah, Bahrain ........ 45 E6 26 10N 50 30 E
Al Maqwa', Kuwait .......... 44 D5 29 10N 47 59 E
Al Marj, Libya .............. 51 B10 32 25N 20 30 E
Al Maṭlā, Kuwait ............ 44 D5 29 24N 47 40 E
Al Mawjib, W. →, Jordan .... 46 D4 31 28N 35 36 E
Al Mawṣil, Iraq ............ 44 B4 36 15N 43 5 E
Al Mayādin, Syria .......... 44 C4 35 1N 40 27 E
Al Mazār, Jordan ............ 46 D4 31 4N 35 41 E
Al Midhnab, Si. Arabia ...... 44 E5 25 50N 44 18 E
Al Minā', Lebanon .......... 46 A4 34 24N 35 49 E
Al Miqdādīyah, Iraq ........ 44 C5 34 0N 45 0 E
Al Mubarraz, Si. Arabia ...... 45 E6 25 30N 49 40 E
Al Mudawwarah, Jordan .... 46 F5 29 19N 36 0 E
Al Mughayrā', U.A.E. ...... 45 E7 24 5N 53 32 E
Al Muḥarraq, Bahrain ........ 45 E6 26 15N 50 40 E
Al Mukallā, Yemen .......... 47 E4 14 33N 49 2 E
Al Mukhā, Yemen .......... 47 E3 13 18N 43 15 E
Al Musayjid, Si. Arabia ...... 44 E3 24 5N 39 5 E
Al Musayyib, Iraq ............ 44 C5 32 49N 44 20 E
Al Muthannā □, Iraq ........ 44 D5 30 30N 45 15 E
Al Muwaylih, Si. Arabia .... 44 E2 27 40N 35 30 E
Al Qādisīyah □, Iraq ........ 44 D5 32 0N 45 0 E
Al Qā'im, Iraq .............. 44 C4 34 21N 41 7 E
Al Qalībah, Si. Arabia ...... 44 D3 28 24N 37 42 E
Al Qāmishlī, Syria .......... 44 B4 37 2N 41 14 E
Al Qaryatayn, Syria ........ 44 A6 34 12N 37 13 E
Al Qaṣim, Si. Arabia ........ 44 E4 26 0N 43 0 E
Al Qaṭ'ā, Syria ............ 44 C4 34 40N 40 48 E
Al Qaṭīf, Si. Arabia ........ 45 E6 26 35N 50 0 E
Al Qaṭrānah, Jordan ........ 46 D5 31 12N 36 6 E
Al Qaṭrūn, Libya ............ 51 D9 24 56N 15 3 E
Al Qayṣūmah, Si. Arabia .... 44 D5 28 20N 46 7 E
Al Quds = Jerusalem, Israel .. 46 D4 31 47N 35 10 E
Al Qunayṭirah, Syria ........ 46 C3 35 45N 35 45 E
Al Qurnah, Iraq ............ 44 D5 31 1N 47 25 E
Al Quṣayr, Iraq ............ 44 D5 30 39N 45 50 E
Al Quṭayfah, Syria .......... 44 B5 33 44N 36 36 E
Al 'Ubaylah, Si. Arabia ...... 47 C5 21 59N 50 57 E
Al 'Uḍaylīyah, Si. Arabia .... 45 E6 25 8N 49 18 E
Al 'Ulā, Si. Arabia .......... 44 E3 26 35N 38 0 E
Al 'Uqayr, Si. Arabia ........ 45 E6 25 40N 50 15 E
Al 'Uwayniḍ, Si. Arabia ...... 44 D4 30 30N 42 10 E
Al 'Uwayqilah, Si. Arabia .... 44 D4 30 30N 42 10 E
Al 'Uyūn, Ḥijāz, Si. Arabia .. 44 E3 24 33N 39 35 E
Al 'Uyūn, Najd, Si. Arabia .. 44 E4 26 30N 43 50 E
Al 'Uzayr, Iraq ............ 44 D5 31 19N 47 25 E
Al Wajh, Si. Arabia .......... 44 E3 26 10N 36 30 E
Al Wakrah, Qatar .......... 45 E6 25 10N 51 40 E
Al Waqbah, Si. Arabia ...... 44 D5 28 48N 45 33 E
Al Wari'āh, Si. Arabia ...... 44 E5 27 51N 47 25 E

Ala Dağ, Turkey ............ 44 B2 37 44N 35 9 E
Ala Tau Shankou = Dzungarian
Gates, Asia ................ 32 B3 45 0N 82 0 E
Alabama □, U.S.A. ........ 83 J2 33 0N 87 0W
Alabama →, U.S.A. ........ 83 K2 31 8N 87 57W
Alabaster, U.S.A. .......... 83 J2 33 15N 86 49W
Alaçam Dağları, Turkey .... 23 E13 39 18N 28 49 E
Alachua, U.S.A. ............ 83 L4 29 47N 82 30W
Alaérma, Greece ............ 25 C9 36 9N 27 57 E
Alagoa Grande, Brazil ...... 93 E11 7 3S 35 35W
Alagoas □, Brazil .......... 93 E11 9 0S 36 0W
Alagoinhas, Brazil .......... 93 F11 12 7S 38 20W
Alaior, Spain .............. 24 B11 39 57N 4 8 E
Alajero, Canary Is. ........ 24 F2 28 3N 17 13W
Alajuela, Costa Rica ........ 88 D3 10 2N 84 8W
Alakamisy, Madag. ........ 57 C8 21 19S 47 14 E
Alaknanda →, India ........ 43 D8 30 8N 78 36 E
Alakurtti, Russia .......... 18 A5 66 58N 30 25 E
Alamarvdasht, Iran ........ 45 E7 27 37N 52 59 E
Alameda, Calif., U.S.A. .... 78 H4 37 46N 122 15W
Alameda, N. Mex., U.S.A. .. 77 J10 35 11N 106 37W
Alamo, U.S.A. ............ 79 J11 37 22N 115 10W
Alamo Crossing, U.S.A. .... 79 L13 34 16N 113 33W
Alamogordo, U.S.A. ........ 77 K11 32 54N 105 57W
Alamos, Mexico ............ 86 B3 27 0N 109 0W
Alamosa, U.S.A. ............ 77 H11 37 28N 105 52W
Åland = Ahvenanmaa, Finland 9 F19 60 15N 20 0 E
Ålands hav, Europe ........ 9 F18 60 0N 19 30 E
Alania = North Ossetia □, Russia 19 F7 43 30N 44 30 E
Alania, Turkey ............ 19 G5 36 38N 32 0 E
Alaotra, Farihin', Madag. .. 57 B8 17 30S 48 30 E
Alappuzha = Alleppey, India 40 Q10 9 30N 76 28 E
Alarobia-Vohiposa, Madag. .. 57 C8 20 59S 47 9 E
Alaşehir, Turkey ............ 23 E13 38 23N 28 30 E
Alaska □, U.S.A. .......... 68 B5 64 0N 154 0W
Alaska, G. of, Pac. Oc. .... 68 C5 58 0N 145 0W
Alaska Peninsula, U.S.A. .... 68 C4 56 0N 159 0W
Alaska Range, U.S.A. ...... 68 B4 62 50N 151 0W
Älät, Azerbaijan .......... 19 G8 39 58N 49 25 E
Alatyr, Russia .............. 18 D8 54 55N 46 35 E
Alausi, Ecuador ............ 92 D3 2 0S 78 50W
Alava, C., U.S.A. .......... 76 B1 48 10N 124 44W
Alavo = Alavus, Finland .... 9 E20 62 35N 23 36 E
Alavus, Finland ............ 9 E20 62 35N 23 36 E
Alawoona, Australia ........ 63 E3 34 45S 140 30 E
Alba, Italy ................ 20 D8 44 42N 8 2 E
Alba-Iulia, Romania ........ 17 E12 46 8N 23 39 E
Albacete, Spain ............ 21 C5 39 0N 1 50W
Albacutya, L., Australia .... 63 F3 35 45S 141 58 E
Albanel, L., Canada ........ 72 B5 50 55N 73 12W
Albania ■, Europe .......... 23 D9 41 0N 20 0 E
Albany, Australia .......... 61 G2 35 1S 117 58 E
Albany, Ga., U.S.A. ........ 83 K3 31 35N 84 10W
Albany, N.Y., U.S.A. ...... 85 D11 42 39N 73 45W
Albany, Oreg., U.S.A. ...... 76 D2 44 38N 123 6W
Albany, Tex., U.S.A. ...... 81 J5 32 44N 99 18W
Albany →, Canada .......... 72 B3 52 17N 81 31W
Albardón, Argentina ........ 94 C2 31 20S 68 30W
Albatross B., Australia ...... 62 A3 12 45S 141 30 E
Albemarle, U.S.A. .......... 83 H5 35 21N 80 11W
Albemarle Sd., U.S.A. ...... 83 H7 36 5N 76 0W
Alberche →, Spain .......... 21 C3 39 58N 4 46W
Alberdi, Paraguay .......... 94 B4 26 14S 58 20W
Alberga, The →, Australia .. 63 D2 27 6S 135 33 E
Albert, L., Africa .......... 54 B3 1 30N 31 0 E
Albert, L., Australia ........ 63 F2 35 30S 139 10 E
Albert Edward Ra., Australia 60 C4 18 17S 127 57 E
Albert Lea, U.S.A. ........ 80 D8 43 39N 93 22W
Albert Nile →, Uganda ...... 54 B3 3 36N 32 2 E
Albert Town, Bahamas ...... 89 B5 22 37N 74 33W
Alberta □, Canada .......... 70 C6 54 40N 115 0W
Alberti, Argentina .......... 94 D3 35 1S 60 16W
Albertinia, S. Africa ........ 56 E3 34 11S 21 34 E
Alberton, Canada .......... 73 C7 46 50N 64 0W
Albertville, France ........ 20 D7 45 40N 6 22 E
Albertville, U.S.A. .......... 83 H2 34 16N 86 13W
Albi, France ................ 20 E5 43 56N 2 9 E
Albia, U.S.A. .............. 80 E8 41 2N 92 48W
Albina, Suriname .......... 93 B8 5 37N 54 15W
Albina, Ponta, Angola ...... 56 B1 15 52S 11 44 E
Albion, Mich., U.S.A. ...... 82 D3 42 15N 84 45W
Albion, Nebr., U.S.A. ...... 80 E6 41 42N 98 0W
Albion, Pa., U.S.A. ........ 84 E4 41 53N 80 22W
Alborán, Medit. S. ........ 21 E4 35 57N 3 0W
Ålborg, Denmark .......... 9 H13 57 2N 9 54 E
Alborz, Reshteh-ye Kūhhā-ye,
Iran ...................... 45 C7 36 0N 52 0 E
Albuquerque, U.S.A. ........ 77 J10 35 5N 106 39W
Albuquerque, Cayos de,
Caribbean ................ 88 D3 12 10N 81 50W
Alburg, U.S.A. ............ 85 B11 44 59N 73 18W
Albury = Albury-Wodonga,
Australia ................ 63 F4 36 3S 146 56 E
Albury-Wodonga, Australia .. 63 F4 36 3S 146 56 E
Alcalá de Henares, Spain .... 21 B4 40 28N 3 22W
Alcalá la Real, Spain ...... 21 D4 37 27N 3 57W
Álcamo, Italy .............. 22 F5 37 59N 12 55 E
Alcaníz, Spain ............ 21 B5 41 2N 0 8W
Alcântara, Brazil .......... 93 D10 2 20S 44 30W
Alcántara, Embalse de, Spain 21 C2 39 44N 6 50W
Alcantarilla, Spain ........ 21 D5 37 59N 1 12W
Alcaraz, Sierra de, Spain .. 21 C4 38 40N 2 20W
Alcaudete, Spain .......... 21 D3 37 35N 4 5W
Alcázar de San Juan, Spain .. 21 C4 39 24N 3 12W
Alchevsk, Ukraine .......... 19 E6 48 30N 38 45 E
Alcira = Alzira, Spain ...... 21 C5 39 9N 0 30W
Alcova, U.S.A. ............ 76 E10 42 34N 106 43W
Alcoy, Spain .............. 21 C5 38 43N 0 30W
Alcúdia, Spain ............ 24 B10 39 51N 3 7 E
Alcúdia, B. d', Spain ...... 24 B10 39 47N 3 15 E
Aldabra Is., Seychelles ...... 49 G8 9 22S 46 28 E
Aldama, Mexico ............ 87 C5 23 0N 98 4W
Aldan, Russia .............. 29 D13 58 40N 125 30 E
Aldan →, Russia .......... 29 C13 63 28N 129 35 E
Aldeburgh, U.K. .......... 13 E9 52 10N 1 37 E
Alder Pk., U.S.A. .......... 78 K5 35 53N 121 22W
Aldershot, U.K. ............ 13 F7 51 15N 0 44W
Aledo, U.S.A. ............ 80 E9 41 12N 90 45W
Aleg, Mauritania .......... 50 E3 17 3N 13 55W
Alegranza, Canary Is. ...... 24 E6 29 23N 13 32W
Alegranza, I., Canary Is. .. 24 E6 29 23N 13 32W
Alegre, Brazil .............. 95 A7 20 50S 41 30W
Alegrete, Brazil ............ 95 B4 29 40S 56 0W

Aleisk, Russia .............. 28 D9 52 40N 83 0 E
Aleksandriya = Oleksandriya,
Ukraine .................. 17 C14 50 37N 26 19 E
Aleksandrov Gay, Russia .... 19 D8 50 9N 48 34 E
Aleksandrovsk-Sakhalinskiy,
Russia .................... 29 D15 50 50N 142 20 E
Aleksandry, Z., Russia ...... 4 A10 80 25N 48 0 E
Além Paraíba, Brazil ........ 95 A7 21 52S 42 41W
Alemania, Argentina ........ 94 B2 25 40S 65 30W
Alemania, Chile ............ 94 B2 25 10S 69 55W
Alençon, France ............ 20 B4 48 27N 0 4 E
Alenquer, Brazil ............ 93 D8 1 56S 54 46W
Alenuihaha Channel, U.S.A. 74 H17 20 30N 156 0W
Aleppo = Ḥalab, Syria ...... 44 B3 36 10N 37 15 E
Alert, Canada .............. 4 A4 83 2N 60 0W
Alès, France .............. 20 D6 44 9N 4 5 E
Alessándria, Italy .......... 20 D8 44 54N 8 37 E
Ålesund, Norway .......... 9 E12 62 28N 6 12 E
Aleutian Is., Pac. Oc. ...... 68 C2 52 0N 175 0W
Aleutian Trench, Pac. Oc. .. 64 C10 48 0N 180 0 E
Alexander, U.S.A. .......... 80 B3 47 51N 103 39W
Alexander Arch., U.S.A. .... 68 C6 56 0N 136 0W
Alexander Bay, S. Africa .... 56 D2 28 40S 16 30 E
Alexander City, U.S.A. ...... 83 J3 32 56N 85 58W
Alexander I., Antarctica .... 5 C17 69 0S 70 0W
Alexandra, Australia ........ 63 F4 37 8S 145 40 E
Alexandra, N.Z. ............ 59 L2 45 14S 169 25 E
Alexandra Falls, Canada .... 70 A5 60 29N 116 18W
Alexandria = El Iskandarîya,
Egypt .................... 51 B11 31 13N 29 58 E
Alexandria, B.C., Canada .... 70 C4 52 35N 122 27W
Alexandria, Ont., Canada .. 85 A10 45 19N 74 38W
Alexandria, Romania ........ 17 G13 43 57N 25 24 E
Alexandria, S. Africa ...... 56 E4 33 38S 26 28 E
Alexandria, U.K. .......... 11 F4 55 59N 4 35W
Alexandria, La., U.S.A. .... 81 K8 31 18N 92 27W
Alexandria, Minn., U.S.A. .. 80 C7 45 53N 95 22W
Alexandria, S. Dak., U.S.A. 80 D6 43 39N 97 47W
Alexandria Bay, U.S.A. .... 85 B9 44 20N 75 55W
Alexandrina, L., Australia .. 63 F2 35 25S 139 10 E
Alexandroúpolis, Greece .... 23 D11 40 50N 25 54 E
Alexis →, Canada .......... 73 B8 52 33N 56 8W
Alexis Creek, Canada ...... 70 C4 52 10N 123 20W
Alfabia, Spain ............ 24 B9 39 44N 2 44 E
Alford, Aberds., U.K. ...... 11 D6 57 14N 2 41W
Alford, Lincs., U.K. ........ 12 D8 53 15N 0 10 E
Alfred, Maine, U.S.A. ...... 85 C14 43 29N 70 43W
Alfred, N.Y., U.S.A. ........ 84 D7 42 16N 77 48W
Alfreton, U.K. ............ 12 D6 53 6N 1 24W
Alga, Kazakhstan .......... 19 E10 49 53N 57 20 E
Algaida, Spain ............ 24 B9 39 33N 2 53 E
Ålgård, Norway ............ 9 G11 58 46N 5 53 E
Algarve, Portugal .......... 21 D1 36 58N 8 20W
Algeciras, Spain .......... 21 D3 36 9N 5 28W
Algemesí, Spain ............ 21 C5 39 11N 0 27W
Alger, Algeria ............ 50 A6 36 42N 3 8 E
Algeria ■, Africa .......... 50 C6 28 30N 2 0 E
Alghero, Italy .............. 22 D3 40 33N 8 19 E
Algiers = Alger, Algeria .... 50 A6 36 42N 3 8 E
Algoa B., S. Africa ........ 56 E4 33 50S 25 45 E
Algoma, U.S.A. ............ 82 C2 44 36N 87 26W
Algona, U.S.A. ............ 80 D7 43 4N 94 14W
Algonac, U.S.A. ............ 84 D2 42 37N 82 32W
Algonquin ∩, Canada ...... 72 C4 45 50N 78 30W
Algorta, Uruguay .......... 96 C5 32 25S 57 23W
Alhambra, U.S.A. .......... 79 L8 34 8N 118 6W
Alhucemas = Al Hoceïma,
Morocco .................. 50 A5 35 8N 3 58W
'Alī al Gharbī, Iraq ........ 44 C5 32 30N 46 45 E
'Alī ash Sharqī, Iraq ...... 44 C5 32 7N 46 44 E
'Alī Khēl, Afghan. .......... 42 C3 33 57N 69 43 E
Alī Shāh, Iran ............ 44 B5 38 9N 45 50 E
'Alīābād, Khorāsān, Iran .. 45 C8 32 30N 57 30 E
'Alīābād, Kordestān, Iran .. 44 C5 35 4N 46 58 E
'Alīābād, Yazd, Iran ...... 45 D7 31 41N 53 49 E
Aliağa, Turkey ............ 23 E12 38 47N 26 59 E
Aliákmon →, Greece ........ 23 D10 40 30N 22 36 E
Alicante, Spain ............ 21 C5 38 23N 0 30W
Alice, S. Africa ............ 56 E4 32 48S 26 55 E
Alice, U.S.A. .............. 81 M5 27 45N 98 5W
Alice →, Queens., Australia .. 62 C3 24 2S 144 50 E
Alice →, Queens., Australia .. 62 B3 15 35S 142 20 E
Alice Arm, Canada ........ 70 B3 55 29N 129 31W
Alice Springs, Australia .... 62 C1 23 40S 133 50 E
Alicedale, S. Africa ........ 56 E4 33 15S 26 4 E
Aliceville, U.S.A. .......... 83 J1 33 8N 88 9W
Aliganj, India ............ 43 F8 27 30N 79 10 E
Aligarh, Raj., India ........ 42 G7 25 55N 76 15 E
Aligarh, Ut. P., India ...... 42 F8 27 55N 78 10 E
Alīgūdarz, Iran ............ 45 C6 33 25N 49 45 E
Alimnia, Greece ............ 25 C9 36 16N 27 43 E
Alingsås, Sweden .......... 9 H15 57 56N 12 31 E
Alipur, Pakistan .......... 42 E4 29 25N 70 55 E
Alipur Duar, India ........ 41 F16 26 30N 89 35 E
Aliquippa, U.S.A. .......... 84 F4 40 37N 80 15W
Alitus = Alytus, Lithuania .. 9 J21 54 24N 24 3 E
Aliwal North, S. Africa .... 56 E4 30 45S 26 45 E
Alix, Canada .............. 70 C6 52 24N 113 11W
Aljustrel, Portugal ........ 21 D1 37 55N 8 10W
Alkmaar, Neths. .......... 15 B4 52 37N 4 45 E
All American Canal, U.S.A. 77 K6 32 45N 115 15W
Allah Dad, Pakistan ........ 42 G2 25 38N 67 34 E
Allahabad, India .......... 43 G9 25 25N 81 58 E
Allan, Canada ............ 71 C7 51 53N 106 4W
Allanridge, S. Africa ...... 56 D4 27 45S 26 40 E
Allegany, U.S.A. .......... 84 D6 42 6N 78 30W
Allegheny →, U.S.A. ...... 84 F5 40 27N 80 1W
Allegheny Mts., U.S.A. .... 82 G6 38 15N 80 10W
Allegheny Reservoir, U.S.A. 84 E6 41 50N 79 0W
Allègre, Pte., Guadeloupe .. 88 b 16 22N 61 46W
Allen, Bog of, Ireland ...... 10 C5 53 15N 7 0W
Allen, L., Ireland .......... 10 B3 54 8N 8 4W
Allende, Mexico .......... 86 B4 28 20N 100 50W
Allentown, U.S.A. ........ 85 F9 40 37N 75 29W
Alleppey, India ............ 40 Q10 9 30N 76 28 E
Aller →, Germany .......... 16 B5 52 56N 9 12 E
Alleynes B., Barbados ...... 89 g 13 13N 59 39W
Alliance, Ohio, U.S.A. ...... 84 F3 40 55N 81 6W
Allier →, France .......... 20 C5 46 57N 3 4 E
Alliford Bay, Canada ...... 70 C2 53 12N 131 58W
Alligator Pond, Jamaica .... 88 a 17 52N 77 34W
Alliston = New Tecumseth,
Canada .................. 84 B5 44 9N 79 52W

Alloa, U.K. ................ 11 E5 56 7N 3 47W
Allora, Australia .......... 63 D5 28 2S 152 0 E
Alluitsup Paa, Greenland .. 69 B15 60 30N 45 35W
Alma, Canada .............. 73 C5 48 35N 71 40W
Alma, Ga., U.S.A. .......... 83 K4 31 33N 82 28W
Alma, Kans., U.S.A. ........ 80 F6 39 1N 96 17W
Alma, Mich., U.S.A. ........ 82 D3 43 23N 84 39W
Alma, Nebr., U.S.A. ........ 80 E5 40 6N 99 22W
Alma Ata = Almaty, Kazakhstan 28 E8 43 15N 76 57 E
Almada, Portugal .......... 21 C1 38 40N 9 9W
Almaden, Australia ........ 62 B3 17 22S 144 40 E
Almadén, Spain ............ 21 C3 38 49N 4 52W
Almanor, L., U.S.A. ........ 76 F3 40 14N 121 9W
Almansa, Spain ............ 21 C5 38 51N 1 5W
Almanzor, Pico, Spain .... 21 B3 40 15N 5 18W
Almanzora →, Spain ...... 21 D5 37 14N 1 46W
Almaty, Kazakhstan ........ 28 E8 43 15N 76 57 E
Almazán, Spain ............ 21 B4 41 30N 2 30W
Almeirim, Brazil .......... 93 D8 1 30S 52 34W
Almelo, Neths. ............ 15 B6 52 22N 6 42 E
Almendralejo, Spain ........ 21 C2 38 41N 6 26W
Almere-Stad, Neths. ...... 15 B5 52 20N 5 15 E
Almería, Spain ............ 21 D4 36 52N 2 27W
Almirante, Panama ........ 88 E3 9 10N 82 30W
Almiroú, Kólpos, Greece .... 25 D6 35 23N 24 20 E
Almond, U.S.A. ............ 84 D7 42 19N 77 44W
Almont, U.S.A. ............ 84 D1 42 55N 83 3W
Almonte, Canada .......... 85 A8 45 14N 76 12W
Almora, India ............ 43 E8 29 38N 79 40 E
Alness, U.K. .............. 11 D4 57 41N 4 16W
Alnmouth, U.K. ............ 12 B6 55 24N 1 37W
Alnwick, U.K. ............ 12 B6 55 24N 1 42W
Aloi, Uganda .............. 54 B3 2 16N 33 10 E
Alon, Burma .............. 41 H19 22 12N 95 5 E
Alor, Indonesia ............ 37 F6 8 15S 124 30 E
Alor Setar, Malaysia ...... 39 J3 6 7N 100 22 E
Alot, India ................ 42 H6 23 56N 75 40 E
Aloysius, Mt., Australia .... 61 E4 26 0S 128 38 E
Alpaugh, U.S.A. .......... 78 K7 35 53N 119 29W
Alpena, U.S.A. ............ 82 C4 45 4N 83 27W
Alpha, Australia .......... 62 C4 23 39S 146 37 E
Alpha Cordillera, Arctic .... 4 A2 84 0N 118 0W
Alphen aan den Rijn, Neths. 15 B4 52 7N 4 40 E
Alpine, Ariz., U.S.A. ...... 77 K9 33 51N 109 9W
Alpine, Calif., U.S.A. ...... 79 N10 32 50N 116 46W
Alpine, Tex., U.S.A. ...... 81 K3 30 22N 103 40W
Alps, Europe .............. 20 C8 46 30N 9 30 E
Alsace □, France .......... 20 B7 48 15N 7 25 E
Alsask, Canada ............ 71 C7 51 21N 109 59W
Alsasua, Spain ............ 21 A4 42 54N 2 10W
Alsek →, U.S.A. .......... 70 B1 59 10N 138 12W
Alsten, Norway ............ 8 D15 65 58N 12 40 E
Alston, U.K. .............. 12 C5 54 49N 2 25W
Alta, Norway .............. 8 B20 69 57N 23 10 E
Alta Gracia, Argentina .... 94 C3 31 40S 64 30W
Alta Sierra, U.S.A. ........ 79 K8 35 42N 118 33W
Altaelva →, Norway ...... 8 B20 69 54N 23 17 E
Altafjorden, Norway ...... 8 A20 70 5N 23 5 E
Altai = Aerhtai Shan, Mongolia 32 B4 46 40N 92 45 E
Altamaha →, U.S.A. ...... 83 K5 31 20N 81 20W
Altamira, Brazil .......... 93 D8 3 12S 52 10W
Altamira, Chile ............ 94 B2 25 47S 69 51W
Altamira, Mexico .......... 87 C5 22 24N 97 55W
Altamont, U.S.A. .......... 85 D10 42 43N 74 3W
Altamura, Italy ............ 22 D7 40 49N 16 33 E
Altanbulag, Mongolia ...... 32 A5 50 16N 106 30 E
Altar, Mexico .............. 86 A2 30 40N 111 50W
Altar, Desierto de, Mexico .. 86 B2 30 10N 112 0W
Altata, Mexico ............ 86 C3 24 30N 108 0W
Altavista, U.S.A. .......... 82 G6 37 6N 79 17W
Altay, China .............. 32 B3 47 48N 88 10 E
Altea, Spain .............. 21 C5 38 38N 0 2W
Altiplano, Bolivia .......... 90 E4 17 0S 68 0W
Alto Araguaia, Brazil ...... 93 G8 17 15S 53 20W
Alto Cuchumatanes =
Cuchumatanes, Sierra de los,
Guatemala ................ 88 C1 15 35N 91 25W
Alto del Carmen, Chile .... 94 B1 28 46S 70 30W
Alto del Inca, Chile ........ 94 A2 24 10S 68 10W
Alto Ligonha, Mozam. ...... 55 F4 15 30S 38 11 E
Alto Molocue, Mozam. .... 55 F4 15 50S 37 35 E
Alto Paraguai □, Paraguay .. 94 A4 21 0S 58 30W
Alto Paraná □, Paraguay .. 95 B5 25 30S 54 50W
Alton, Canada ............ 84 C4 43 54N 80 5W
Alton, U.K. .............. 13 F7 51 9N 0 59W
Alton, Ill., U.S.A. .......... 80 F9 38 53N 90 11W
Alton, N.H., U.S.A. ........ 85 C13 43 27N 71 13W
Altona, Canada .......... 71 D9 49 6N 97 33W
Altoona, U.S.A. .......... 84 F6 40 31N 78 24W
Altun Kupri, Iraq .......... 44 C5 35 45N 44 9 E
Altun Shan, China ........ 32 C3 38 30N 88 0 E
Alturas, U.S.A. ............ 76 F3 41 29N 120 32W
Altus, U.S.A. .............. 81 H5 34 38N 99 20W
Alucra, Turkey ............ 19 F6 40 22N 38 47 E
Alunite, U.S.A. ............ 79 K12 35 59N 114 55W
Alusi, Indonesia .......... 37 F8 7 35S 131 40 E
Alva, U.S.A. .............. 81 G5 36 48N 98 40W
Alvarado, Mexico .......... 87 D5 18 40N 95 50W
Alvarado, U.S.A. .......... 81 J6 32 24N 97 13W
Alvaro Obregón, Presa, Mexico 87 C5 27 55N 109 52W
Alvear, Argentina .......... 94 B4 29 5S 56 30W
Alvesta, Sweden .......... 9 H16 56 54N 14 35 E
Alvin, U.S.A. .............. 81 L7 29 26N 95 15W
Alvinston, Canada ........ 84 D3 42 49N 81 52W
Älvkarleby, Sweden ........ 9 F17 60 34N 17 26 E
Alvord Desert, U.S.A. ...... 76 E4 42 30N 118 25W
Älvsbyn, Sweden .......... 8 D19 65 40N 21 0 E
Alwar, India .............. 42 F7 27 38N 76 34 E
Alxa Zuoqi, China ........ 34 E3 38 50N 105 40 E
Alyangula, Australia ...... 62 A2 13 55S 136 30 E
Alyata = Älät, Azerbaijan .. 19 G8 39 58N 49 25 E
Alyth, U.K. ................ 11 E5 56 38N 3 13W
Alytus, Lithuania .......... 9 J21 54 24N 24 3 E
Alzada, U.S.A. ............ 80 C2 45 2N 104 25W
Alzira, Spain .............. 21 C5 39 9N 0 30W
Am Timan, Chad .......... 51 F10 11 0N 20 10 E
Amadeus, L., Australia .... 61 D5 24 54S 131 0 E
Amadi, Dem. Rep. of the Congo 54 B2 3 40N 26 40 E
Amâdî, Sudan ............ 51 G12 5 29N 30 25 E
Amadjuak L., Canada ...... 69 B12 65 0N 71 8W
Amagansett, U.S.A. ........ 85 F12 40 59N 72 9W
Amagasaki, Japan .......... 31 G7 34 42N 135 20 E
Amahai, Indonesia ........ 37 E7 3 20S 128 55 E
Amakusa-Shotō, Japan .... 31 H5 32 15N 130 10 E
Åmål, Sweden ............ 9 G15 59 3N 12 42 E
Amaliás, Greece .......... 23 F9 37 47N 21 22 E
Amalner, India ............ 40 J9 21 5N 75 5 E

Amamapare, Indonesia . . . . . . . . 37 E9   4 53S 136 38 E
Amambaí, Brazil . . . . . . . . . . . . . 95 A4   23  5S  55 13W
Amambaí →, Brazil . . . . . . . . . . . 95 A5   23 22S  53 56W
Amambay □, Paraguay . . . . . . . . 95 A4   23  0S  56  0W
Amambay, Cordillera de,
  S. Amer. . . . . . . . . . . . . . . . . . 95 A4   23  0S  55 45W
Amami-Guntō, Japan . . . . . . . . . 31 L4   27 16N 129 21 E
Amami-Ō-Shima, Japan . . . . . . . 31 L4   28  0N 129  0 E
Aman, Pulau, Malaysia . . . . . . . . 39 c    5 16N 100 24 E
Amaná, L., Brazil . . . . . . . . . . . . 92 D6   2 35S  64 40W
Amanat →, India . . . . . . . . . . . . 43 G11  24  7N  84  4 E
Amanda Park, U.S.A. . . . . . . . . . 78 C3   47 28N 123 55W
Amangeldy, Kazakhstan . . . . . . . 28 D7   50 10N  65 10 E
Amapá, Brazil . . . . . . . . . . . . . . 93 C8    2  5N  50 50W
Amapá □, Brazil . . . . . . . . . . . . 93 C8    1 40N  52  0W
Amarante, Brazil . . . . . . . . . . . . 93 E10   6 14S  42 50W
Amaranth, Canada . . . . . . . . . . . 71 C9   50 36N  98 43W
Amargosa →, U.S.A. . . . . . . . . . 79 J10  36 14N 116 51W
Amargosa Range, U.S.A. . . . . . . 79 J10  36 20N 116 45W
Amári, Greece . . . . . . . . . . . . . . 25 D6   35 13N  24 40 E
Amarillo, U.S.A. . . . . . . . . . . . . . 81 H4   35 13N 101 50W
Amarkantak, India . . . . . . . . . . . 43 H9   22 40N  81 45 E
Amaro, Mte., Italy . . . . . . . . . . . 22 C6   42  5N  14  5 E
Amarpur, India . . . . . . . . . . . . . . 43 G12  25  5N  87  0 E
Amarwara, India . . . . . . . . . . . . 43 H8   22 18N  79 10 E
Amasya, Turkey . . . . . . . . . . . . . 19 F6   40 40N  35 50 E
Amata, Australia . . . . . . . . . . . . 61 E5   26  9S 131  9 E
Amatikulu, S. Africa . . . . . . . . . . 57 D5   29  3S  31 33 E
Amatitlán, Guatemala . . . . . . . . . 88 D1   14 29N  90 38W
Amay, Belgium . . . . . . . . . . . . . 15 D5   50 33N   5 19 E
Amazon = Amazonas →,
  S. Amer. . . . . . . . . . . . . . . . . . 93 D9    0  5S  50  0W
Amazonas □, Brazil . . . . . . . . . . 92 E6    5  0S  65  0W
Amazonas →, S. Amer. . . . . . . . 93 D9    0  5S  50  0W
Ambah, India . . . . . . . . . . . . . . . 42 F8   26 43N  78 13 E
Ambahakily, Madag. . . . . . . . . . . 57 C7   21 36S  43 41 E
Ambahita, Madag. . . . . . . . . . . . 57 C8   24  1S  45 16 E
Ambala, India . . . . . . . . . . . . . . 42 D7   30 23N  76 56 E
Ambalavao, Madag. . . . . . . . . . . 57 C8   21 50S  46 56 E
Ambanja, Madag. . . . . . . . . . . . 57 A8   13 40S  48 27 E
Ambararata, Madag. . . . . . . . . . . 57 B8   15  3S  48 33 E
Ambarchik, Russia . . . . . . . . . . . 29 C17  69 40N 162 20 E
Ambarijeby, Madag. . . . . . . . . . . 57 A8   14 56S  47 41 E
Ambaro, Helodran’, Madag. . . . . . 57 A8   13 23S  48 38 E
Ambato, Ecuador . . . . . . . . . . . . 92 D3    1  5S  78 42W
Ambato, Madag. . . . . . . . . . . . . 57 A8   13 24S  48 29 E
Ambato, Sierra de, Argentina . . . 94 B2   28 25S  66 10W
Ambato Boeny, Madag. . . . . . . . 57 B8   16 28S  46 43 E
Ambatofinandrahana, Madag. . . . 57 C8   20 33S  46 48 E
Ambatolampy, Madag. . . . . . . . . 57 B8   19 20S  47 35 E
Ambatomainty, Madag. . . . . . . . . 57 B8   17 41S  45 40 E
Ambatomanoina, Madag. . . . . . . 57 B8   18 18S  47 37 E
Ambatondrazaka, Madag. . . . . . . 57 B8   17 55S  48 28 E
Ambatosoratra, Madag. . . . . . . . 57 B8   17 37S  48 31 E
Ambenja, Madag. . . . . . . . . . . . . 57 B8   16 25S  46 58 E
Amberg, Germany . . . . . . . . . . . 16 D6   49 26N  11 52 E
Ambergris Cay, Belize . . . . . . . . 87 D7   18  0N  87 55W
Amberley, N.Z. . . . . . . . . . . . . . 59 K4   43  9S 172 44 E
Ambikapur, India . . . . . . . . . . . . 43 H10  23 15N  83 15 E
Ambilobé, Madag. . . . . . . . . . . . 57 A8   13 10S  49  3 E
Ambinanindrano, Madag. . . . . . . 57 C8   20  5S  48 23 E
Ambinanitelo, Madag. . . . . . . . . 57 B8   15 21S  49 35 E
Ambinda, Madag. . . . . . . . . . . . . 57 B8   16 25S  45 52 E
Amble, U.K. . . . . . . . . . . . . . . . . 12 B6   55 20N   1 36W
Ambleside, U.K. . . . . . . . . . . . . . 12 C5   54 26N   2 58W
Ambo, Peru . . . . . . . . . . . . . . . . 92 F3   10  5S  76 10W
Amboahangy, Madag. . . . . . . . . 57 C8   24 15S  46 22 E
Ambodifototra, Madag. . . . . . . . . 57 B8   16 59S  49 52 E
Ambodilazana, Madag. . . . . . . . . 57 B8   18  6S  49 10 E
Ambodiriana, Madag. . . . . . . . . . 57 B8   17 55S  49 18 E
Ambohidratrimo, Madag. . . . . . . 57 B8   18 50S  47 26 E
Ambohidray, Madag. . . . . . . . . . 57 B8   18 36S  48 18 E
Ambohimahamasina, Madag. . . . 57 C8   21 56S  47 11 E
Ambohimahasoa, Madag. . . . . . . 57 C8   21  7S  47 13 E
Ambohimanga, Madag. . . . . . . . 57 C8   20 52S  47 36 E
Ambohimitombo, Madag. . . . . . . 57 C8   20 43S  47 26 E
Ambohitra, Madag. . . . . . . . . . . 57 A8   12 30S  49 10 E
Amboise, France . . . . . . . . . . . . 20 C4   47 24N   1  2 E
Ambon, Indonesia . . . . . . . . . . . 37 E7    3 43S 128 12 E
Ambondro, Madag. . . . . . . . . . . 57 D8   25 13S  45 44 E
Amboseli △, Kenya . . . . . . . . . . 54 C4    2 37S  37 13 E
Amboseli, L., Kenya . . . . . . . . . . 54 C4    2 40S  37 10 E
Ambositra, Madag. . . . . . . . . . . 57 C8   20 31S  47 25 E
Ambovombe, Madag. . . . . . . . . . 57 D8   25 11S  46  5 E
Amboy, U.S.A. . . . . . . . . . . . . . . 79 L11  34 33N 115 45W
Amboyna Cay, S. China Sea . . . . 36 C4    7 50N 112 50 E
Ambridge, U.S.A. . . . . . . . . . . . . 84 F4   40 36N  80 14W
Ambriz, Angola . . . . . . . . . . . . . 52 F2    7 48S  13  8 E
Amchitka I., U.S.A. . . . . . . . . . . 68 C1   51 32N 179  0 E
Amderma, Russia . . . . . . . . . . . . 28 C7   69 45N 61 30 E
Amdhi, India . . . . . . . . . . . . . . . 43 H9   23 51N  81 27 E
Ameca, Mexico . . . . . . . . . . . . . 86 C4   20 30N 104  0W
Ameca →, Mexico . . . . . . . . . . . 86 C3   20 40N 105 15W
Amecameca, Mexico . . . . . . . . . 87 D5   19  7N  98 46W
Ameland, Neths. . . . . . . . . . . . . 15 A5   53 27N   5 45 E
Amenia, U.S.A. . . . . . . . . . . . . . 85 E11  41 51N  73 33W
American Falls, U.S.A. . . . . . . . . 76 E7   42 47N 112 51W
American Falls Reservoir, U.S.A. . 76 E7   42 47N 112 52W
American Fork, U.S.A. . . . . . . . . 76 F8   40 23N 111 48W
American Highland, Antarctica . . . 5 D6   73  0S  75  0 E
American Samoa ☑, Pac. Oc. . . . 59 B13  14 20S 170 40W
Americana, Brazil . . . . . . . . . . . 95 A6   22 45S  47 20W
Americus, U.S.A. . . . . . . . . . . . . 83 K3   32  4N  84 14W
Amersfoort, Neths. . . . . . . . . . . . 15 B5   52  9N   5 23 E
Amersfoort, S. Africa . . . . . . . . . 57 D4   26 59S  29 53 E
Amery Ice Shelf, Antarctica . . . . . 5 C6   69 30S  72  0 E
Ames, U.S.A. . . . . . . . . . . . . . . . 80 E8   42  2N  93 37W
Amesbury, U.S.A. . . . . . . . . . . . 85 D14  42 51N  70 56W
Amet, India . . . . . . . . . . . . . . . . 42 G5   25 18N  73 56 E
Amga, Russia . . . . . . . . . . . . . . 29 C14  60 50N 132  0 E
Amga →, Russia . . . . . . . . . . . . 29 C14  62 38N 134 32 E
Amgu, Russia . . . . . . . . . . . . . . 29 E14  45 45N 137 15 E
Amgun →, Russia . . . . . . . . . . . 29 D14  52 56N 139 38 E
Amherst, Canada . . . . . . . . . . . . 73 C7   45 48N  64  8W
Amherst, Mass., U.S.A. . . . . . . . 85 D12  42 23N  72 31W
Amherst, N.Y., U.S.A. . . . . . . . . 84 D6   42 59N  78 48W
Amherst, Ohio, U.S.A. . . . . . . . . 84 E2   41 24N  82 14W
Amherst I., Canada . . . . . . . . . . 85 B8   44  8N  76 43W
Amherstburg, Canada . . . . . . . . 72 D3   42  6N  83  6W
Amiata, Mte., Italy . . . . . . . . . . . 22 C4   42 53N  11 37 E
Amidon, U.S.A. . . . . . . . . . . . . . 80 B3   46 29N 103 19W
Amiens, France . . . . . . . . . . . . . 20 B5   49 54N   2 16 E
Aminuis, Namibia . . . . . . . . . . . . 56 C2   23 43S  19 21 E
Amīrābād, Iran . . . . . . . . . . . . . 44 C5   33 20N  46 16 E
Amirante Is., Seychelles . . . . . . . 26 K9    6  0S  53  0 E
Amisk △, Canada . . . . . . . . . . . 71 B9   54 35N 102  0W
Amisk L., Canada . . . . . . . . . . . 71 C8   54 35N 102 15W
Amistad △, U.S.A. . . . . . . . . . . . 81 L4   29 32N 101 12W

Amistad, Presa de la, Mexico . . . 86 B4   29 24N 101  0W
Amite, U.S.A. . . . . . . . . . . . . . . . 81 K9   30 44N  90 30W
Amla, India . . . . . . . . . . . . . . . . 42 J8   21 56N  78  7 E
Amlapura = Karangasem,
  Indonesia . . . . . . . . . . . . . . . . 37 J18   8 27S 115 37 E
Amlia I., U.S.A. . . . . . . . . . . . . . 68 C2   52  4N 173 30W
Amlwch, U.K. . . . . . . . . . . . . . . . 12 D3   53 24N   4 20W
’Ammān, Jordan . . . . . . . . . . . . . 46 D4   31 57N  35 52 E
’Ammān □, Jordan . . . . . . . . . . . 46 D5   31 40N  36 30 E
’Ammān ✈ (AMM), Jordan . . . . . 46 D5   31 45N  36  2 E
Ammanford, U.K. . . . . . . . . . . . . 13 F4   51 48N   3 59W
Ammassalik = Tasiilaq,
  Greenland . . . . . . . . . . . . . . . 4 C6   65 40N  37 20W
Ammochostos = Famagusta,
  Cyprus . . . . . . . . . . . . . . . . . . 25 D12  35  8N  33 55 E
Ammon, U.S.A. . . . . . . . . . . . . . 76 E8   43 28N 111 58W
Amnat Charoen, Thailand . . . . . . 38 E5   15 51N 104 38 E
Amnura, Bangla. . . . . . . . . . . . . . 43 G13  24 37N  88 25 E
Āmol, Iran . . . . . . . . . . . . . . . . . 45 B7   36 23N  52 20 E
Amorgós, Greece . . . . . . . . . . . . 23 F11  36 50N  25 57 E
Amory, U.S.A. . . . . . . . . . . . . . . 83 J1   33 59N  88 29W
Amos, Canada . . . . . . . . . . . . . . 72 C4   48 35N  78  5W
Åmot, Norway . . . . . . . . . . . . . . 9 G13  59 57N   9 54 E
Amoy = Xiamen, China . . . . . . . . 33 D6   24 25N 118  4 E
Ampanavoana, Madag. . . . . . . . . 57 B9   15 41S  50 22 E
Ampang, Malaysia . . . . . . . . . . . 39 L3    3  8N 101 45 E
Ampangalana, Lakandranon’,
  Madag. . . . . . . . . . . . . . . . . . . 57 C8   22 48S  47 50 E
Ampanihy, Madag. . . . . . . . . . . . 57 C7   24 40S  44 45 E
Amparafaravola, Madag. . . . . . . . 57 B8   17 35S  48 13 E
Ampasinambo, Madag. . . . . . . . . 57 C8   20 31S  48  0 E
Ampasindava, Helodranon’,
  Madag. . . . . . . . . . . . . . . . . . . 57 A8   13 40S  48 15 E
Ampasindava, Saikanosy,
  Madag. . . . . . . . . . . . . . . . . . . 57 A8   13 42S  47 55 E
Ampenan, Indonesia . . . . . . . . . 36 F5    8 34S 116  4 E
Amper →, Germany . . . . . . . . . . 16 D6   48 29N  11 55 E
Amphoe Kathu, Thailand . . . . . . 39 a    7 54N  98 21 E
Amphoe Thalang, Thailand . . . . . 39 a    8  1N  98 20 E
Ampitsikinana, Réunion . . . . . . . 57 A8   12 57S  49 49 E
Ampombiantambo, Madag. . . . . . 57 A8   12 42S  48 57 E
Ampotaka, Madag. . . . . . . . . . . . 57 D7   25  3S  44 41 E
Ampoza, Madag. . . . . . . . . . . . . 57 C7   22 20S  44 44 E
Amqui, Canada . . . . . . . . . . . . . 73 C6   48 28N  67 27W
Amravati, India . . . . . . . . . . . . . 40 J10  20 55N  77 45 E
Amreli, India . . . . . . . . . . . . . . . 42 J4   21 35N  71 17 E
Amritsar, India . . . . . . . . . . . . . . 42 D6   31 35N  74 57 E
Amroha, India . . . . . . . . . . . . . . 43 E8   28 53N  78 30 E
Amsterdam, Neths. . . . . . . . . . . . 15 B4   52 23N   4 54 E
Amsterdam, U.S.A. . . . . . . . . . . 85 D10  42 56N  74 11W
Amsterdam ✈ (AMS), Neths. . . . 15 B4   52 18N   4  45 E
Amsterdam, Î., Ind. Oc. . . . . . . . 3 F13  38 30S  77 30 E
Amstetten, Austria . . . . . . . . . . . 16 D8   48  7N  14 51 E
Amudarya →, Uzbekistan . . . . . . 28 E6   43 58N  59 34 E
Amundsen Gulf, Canada . . . . . . . 68 A7   71  0N 124  0W
Amundsen-Scott, Antarctica . . . . 5 E    90  0S 166  0 E
Amundsen Sea, Antarctica . . . . . 5 D15  72  0S 115  0W
Amuntai, Indonesia . . . . . . . . . . 36 E5    2 28S 115 25 E
Amur →, Russia . . . . . . . . . . . . 29 D15  52 56N 141 10 E
Amurang, Indonesia . . . . . . . . . . 37 D6    1 5N 124 40 E
Amursk, Russia . . . . . . . . . . . . . 29 D14  50 14N 136 54 E
Amyderya = Amudarya →,
  Uzbekistan . . . . . . . . . . . . . . . 28 E6   43 58N  59 34 E
An Anbār □, Iraq . . . . . . . . . . . . 44 C4   33 25N  42  0 E
An Bien, Vietnam . . . . . . . . . . . . 39 H5    9 45N 105  0 E
An Hoa, Vietnam . . . . . . . . . . . . 38 E7   15 40N 108  5 E
An Nabatīyah at Tahta, Lebanon . 46 B4   33 23N  35 27 E
An Nabk, Si. Arabia . . . . . . . . . . 44 D3   31 20N  37 20 E
An Nabk, Syria . . . . . . . . . . . . . . 46 A5   34  2N  36 44 E
An Nafūd, Si. Arabia . . . . . . . . . . 44 D4   28 15N  41  0 E
An Najaf, Iraq . . . . . . . . . . . . . . 44 C5   32  3N  44 15 E
An Nāşiriyah, Iraq . . . . . . . . . . . 44 D5   31  0N  46 15 E
An Nhon, Vietnam . . . . . . . . . . . 38 F7   13 55N 109  7 E
An Nu’ayrīyah, Si. Arabia . . . . . . 45 E6   27 30N  48 30 E
An Nuwayb’ī, W. →, Si. Arabia . . 46 F3   29 18N  34 57 E
An Thoi, Dao, Vietnam . . . . . . . . 39 H4    9 58N 104  0 E
An Uaimh, Ireland . . . . . . . . . . . 10 C5   53 39N   6 41W
Anabar →, Russia . . . . . . . . . . . 29 B12  73  8N 113 36 E
’Anabtā, West Bank . . . . . . . . . . 46 C4   32 19N  35  7 E
Anaconda, U.S.A. . . . . . . . . . . . 76 C7   46  8N 112 57W
Anacortes, U.S.A. . . . . . . . . . . . 78 B4   48 30N 122 37W
Anadarko, U.S.A. . . . . . . . . . . . . 81 H5   35  4N  98 15W
Anadolu, Turkey . . . . . . . . . . . . . 19 G5   39  0N  30  0 E
Anadyr, Russia . . . . . . . . . . . . . 29 C18  64 35N 177 20 E
Anadyr →, Russia . . . . . . . . . . . 29 C18  64 55N 176  5 E
Anadyrskiy Zaliv, Russia . . . . . . . 29 C19  64  0N 180  0 E
Anaga, Pta. de, Canary Is. . . . . . 24 F3   28 34N  16  9W
’Ānah, Iraq . . . . . . . . . . . . . . . . 44 C4   34 25N  42  0 E
Anaheim, U.S.A. . . . . . . . . . . . . 79 M9   33 50N 117 55W
Anahim Lake, Canada . . . . . . . . 70 C3   52 28N 125 18W
Anáhuac, Mexico . . . . . . . . . . . . 86 B4   27 14N 100  9W
Anakapalle, India . . . . . . . . . . . . 41 L13  17 42N  83  6 E
Anakie, Australia . . . . . . . . . . . . 62 C4   23 32S 147 45 E
Analalava, Madag. . . . . . . . . . . . 57 A8   14 35S  48  0 E
Analavoka, Madag. . . . . . . . . . . 57 C8   22 23S  46 30 E
Análipsis, Greece . . . . . . . . . . . . 25 A3   39 36N  19 55 E
Anambar →, Pakistan . . . . . . . . 42 D3   30 15N  68 50 E
Anambas, Kepulauan, Indonesia . 36 D3    3 20N 106 30 E
Anambas Is. = Anambas,
  Kepulauan, Indonesia . . . . . . . 36 D3    3 20N 106 30 E
Anamosa, U.S.A. . . . . . . . . . . . . 80 D9   42  7N  91 17W
Anamur, Turkey . . . . . . . . . . . . . 19 G5   36 8N  32 58 E
Anan, Japan . . . . . . . . . . . . . . . 31 H7   33 54N 134 40 E
Anand, India . . . . . . . . . . . . . . . 42 H5   22 32N  72 59 E
Anantapur, India . . . . . . . . . . . . 40 M10 14 39N  77 42 E
Anantnag, India . . . . . . . . . . . . . 43 C6   33 45N  75 10 E
Ananyiv, Ukraine . . . . . . . . . . . . 17 E15  47 44N  29 58 E
Anapodháris →, Greece . . . . . . . 25 E7   34 59N  25 20 E
Anápolis, Brazil . . . . . . . . . . . . . 93 G9   16 15S  48 50W
Anapu →, Brazil . . . . . . . . . . . . 93 D8    1 53S  50 53W
Anār, Iran . . . . . . . . . . . . . . . . . 45 D7   30 55N  55 13 E
Anārak, Iran . . . . . . . . . . . . . . . 45 C7   33 25N  53 40 E
Anas →, India . . . . . . . . . . . . . . 42 H5   23 26N  74  0 E
Anatolia = Anadolu, Turkey . . . . . 19 G5   39  0N  30  0 E
Anatsogno, Madag. . . . . . . . . . . 57 C7   23 33S  43 46 E
Añatuya, Argentina . . . . . . . . . . . 94 B3   28 20S  62 50W
Anaunethad L., Canada . . . . . . . 71 A8   60 55N 104 25W
Anbyŏn, N. Korea . . . . . . . . . . . . 35 E14  39  1N 127 35 E
Ancaster, Canada . . . . . . . . . . . 84 C5   43  13N  79 59W
Anchor Bay, U.S.A. . . . . . . . . . . 78 G3   38 48N 123 34W
Anchorage, U.S.A. . . . . . . . . . . . 68 B5   61 13N 149 54W
Anci, China . . . . . . . . . . . . . . . . 34 E9   39 20N 116 40 E
Anchuma, Nevado, Bolivia . . . . . 92 G5   16 0S  68 50W
Ancón, Peru . . . . . . . . . . . . . . . . 92 F3   11 50S  77 10W
Ancona, Italy . . . . . . . . . . . . . . . 22 C5   43 38N  13 30 E
Ancud, Chile . . . . . . . . . . . . . . . 96 E2   42  0S  73 50W
Ancud, G. de, Chile . . . . . . . . . . 96 E2   42  0S  73  0W

Anda, China . . . . . . . . . . . . . . . . 33 B7   46 24N 125 19 E
Andacollo, Argentina . . . . . . . . . 94 D1   37 10S  70 42W
Andacollo, Chile . . . . . . . . . . . . . 94 C1   30 14S  71  6W
Andaingo, Madag. . . . . . . . . . . . 57 B8   18 12S  48 17 E
Andalgalá, Argentina . . . . . . . . . 94 B2   27 40S  66 30W
Åndalsnes, Norway . . . . . . . . . . 9 E12  62 35N   7 43 E
Andalucía □, Spain . . . . . . . . . . 21 D3   37 35N   5  0W
Andalucia = Andalucía □, Spain . 21 D3   37 35N   5  0W
Andalusia, U.S.A. . . . . . . . . . . . . 83 K2   31 18N  86 29W
Andaman Is., Ind. Oc. . . . . . . . . 27 H13  12 30N  92 45 E
Andaman Sea, Ind. Oc. . . . . . . . 36 B1   13  0N  96  0 E
Andamooka Opal Fields,
  Australia . . . . . . . . . . . . . . . . . 63 E2   30 27S 137  9 E
Andapa, Madag. . . . . . . . . . . . . 57 A8   14 39S  49 39 E
Andara, Namibia . . . . . . . . . . . . 56 B3   18  2S  21  9 E
Andenes, Norway . . . . . . . . . . . . 8 B17  69 19N  16 18 E
Andenne, Belgium . . . . . . . . . . . 15 D5   50 28N   5  5 E
Anderson, Alaska, U.S.A. . . . . . . 68 B5   64 25N 149 15W
Anderson, Calif., U.S.A. . . . . . . . 76 F2   40 27N 122 18W
Anderson, Ind., U.S.A. . . . . . . . . 82 E3   40 10N  85 41W
Anderson, Mo., U.S.A. . . . . . . . . 81 G7   36 39N  94 27W
Anderson, S.C., U.S.A. . . . . . . . . 83 H4   34 31N  82 39W
Anderson →, Canada . . . . . . . . 68 B7   69 42N 129  0W
Andes, U.S.A. . . . . . . . . . . . . . . 85 D10  42 12N  74 47W
Andes, Cord. de los, S. Amer. . . . 92 H5   20  0S  68  0W
Andfjorden, Norway . . . . . . . . . . 8 B17  69 10N  16 20 E
Andhra Pradesh □, India . . . . . . 40 L11  18  0N  79  0 E
Andijon, Uzbekistan . . . . . . . . . . 28 E8   41 10N  72 15 E
Andikíthira, Greece . . . . . . . . . . 23 G10  35 52N  23 15 E
Andilamena, Madag. . . . . . . . . . 57 B8   17  1S  48 35 E
Andīmeshk, Iran . . . . . . . . . . . . 45 C6   32 27N  48 21 E
Andizhan = Andijon, Uzbekistan . 28 E8   41 10N  72 15 E
Andoany, Madag. . . . . . . . . . . . . 57 A8   13 25S  48 16 E
Andohar_A, Madag. . . . . . . . . . . 57 C8   24  4S  46 44 E
Andong, S. Korea . . . . . . . . . . . . 35 F15  36 40N 128 43 E
Andongwei, China . . . . . . . . . . . 35 G10  35  6N 119 20 E
Andoom, Australia . . . . . . . . . . . 62 A3   12 25S 141 53 E
Andorra ■, Europe . . . . . . . . . . . 20 E4   42 30N   1 30 E
Andorra La Vella, Andorra . . . . . . 20 E4   42 31N   1 32 E
Andover, U.K. . . . . . . . . . . . . . . 13 F6   51 12N   1 29W
Andover, Maine, U.S.A. . . . . . . . 85 B14  44 38N  70 45W
Andover, Mass., U.S.A. . . . . . . . 85 D13  42 40N  71  8W
Andover, N.J., U.S.A. . . . . . . . . . 85 F10  40 59N  74 45W
Andover, N.Y., U.S.A. . . . . . . . . . 84 D7   42 10N  77 48W
Andover, Ohio, U.S.A. . . . . . . . . 84 E4   41 36N  80 34W
Andøya, Norway . . . . . . . . . . . . . 8 B16  69 10N  15 50 E
Andradina, Brazil . . . . . . . . . . . . 93 H8   20 54S  51 23W
Andrahary, Mt., Madag. . . . . . . . 57 A8   13 37S  49 17 E
Andramasina, Madag. . . . . . . . . 57 B8   19 11S  47 35 E
Andranopasy, Madag. . . . . . . . . 57 C7   21 17S  43 44 E
Andranovory, Madag. . . . . . . . . . 57 C7   23  8S  44 10 E
Andratx, Spain . . . . . . . . . . . . . . 24 B9   39 39N   2 25 E
Andreanof Is., U.S.A. . . . . . . . . . 68 C2   51 30N 176  0W
Andrews, S.C., U.S.A. . . . . . . . . 83 J6   33 27N  79 34W
Andrews, Tex., U.S.A. . . . . . . . . 81 J3   32 19N 102 33W
Ándria, Italy . . . . . . . . . . . . . . . . 22 D7   41 13N  16 17 E
Andriamena, Madag. . . . . . . . . . 57 B8   17 26S  47 30 E
Andriandampy, Madag. . . . . . . . 57 C8   22 45S  45 41 E
Andriba, Madag. . . . . . . . . . . . . 57 B8   17 30S  46 58 E
Andringitra △, Madag. . . . . . . . . 57 C8   22 13S  46  5 E
Androka, Madag. . . . . . . . . . . . . 57 C7   24 58S  44  2 E
Ándros, Greece . . . . . . . . . . . . . 23 F11  37 50N  24 57 E
Andros I., Bahamas . . . . . . . . . . 88 B4   24 30N  78  0W
Andros Town, Bahamas . . . . . . . 88 B4   24 43N  77 47W
Androscoggin →, U.S.A. . . . . . . 85 C14  43 58N  70  0W
Andselv, Norway . . . . . . . . . . . . 8 B18  69  4N  18 34 E
Andújar, Spain . . . . . . . . . . . . . . 21 C3   38  3N   4  5W
Andulo, Angola . . . . . . . . . . . . . 52 G3   11 25S  16 45 E
Anegada, Br. Virgin Is. . . . . . . . . 89 e   18 45N  64 20W
Anegada Passage, W. Indies . . . 89 C7   18 15N  63 45W
Aneto, Pico de, Spain . . . . . . . . 21 A6   42 37N   0 40 E
Ang Mo Kio, Singapore . . . . . . . 39 d    1 23N 103 50 E
Ang Thong, Thailand . . . . . . . . . 38 E3   14 35N 100 31 E
Ang Thong →, Thailand . . . . . . . 39 H2    9 40N  99 43 E
Ang Thong, Ko, Thailand . . . . . . 39 b    9 37N  99 41 E
Angamos, Punta, Chile . . . . . . . . 94 A1   23  1S  70 32W
Angara →, Russia . . . . . . . . . . . 29 D10  58  5N  94 20 E
Angarsk, Russia . . . . . . . . . . . . . 29 D11  52 30N 104  0 E
Angas Hills, Australia . . . . . . . . . 60 D4   23  0S 127 50 E
Angaston, Australia . . . . . . . . . . 63 E2   34 30S 139  8 E
Ånge, Sweden . . . . . . . . . . . . . . 9 E16  62 31N  15 35 E
Ángel, Salto = Angel Falls,
  Venezuela . . . . . . . . . . . . . . . . 92 B6    5 57N  62 30W
Ángel de la Guarda, I., Mexico . . 86 B2   29 30N 113 30W
Angel Falls, Venezuela . . . . . . . . 92 B6    5 57N  62 30W
Angeles, Phil. . . . . . . . . . . . . . . 37 A6   15  9N 120 33 E
Ängelholm, Sweden . . . . . . . . . . 9 H15  56 15N  12 58 E
Angels Camp, U.S.A. . . . . . . . . . 78 G6   38  4N 120 32W
Ångermanälven →, Sweden . . . . 8 E17  62 40N  18  0 E
Ångermanland, Sweden . . . . . . . 8 E18  63 36N  17 45 E
Angers, Canada . . . . . . . . . . . . . 85 A9   45 31N  75 29W
Angers, France . . . . . . . . . . . . . 20 C3   47 30N   0 35W
Ängesån →, Sweden . . . . . . . . . 8 C20  66 16N  22 47 E
Angikuni L., Canada . . . . . . . . . . 71 A9   62 12N  99 59W
Angkor, Cambodia . . . . . . . . . . . 38 F4   13 22N 103 50 E
Anglesey, Isle of □, U.K. . . . . . . 12 D3   53 16N   4 18W
Angleton, U.S.A. . . . . . . . . . . . . 81 L7   29 10N  95 26W
Anglisidhes, Cyprus . . . . . . . . . . 25 E12  34 51N  33 27 E
Angmagssalik = Tasiilaq,
  Greenland . . . . . . . . . . . . . . . . 4 C6   65 40N  37 20W
Ango, Dem. Rep. of the Congo . . 54 B2    4  10N  26  5 E
Angoche, Mozam. . . . . . . . . . . . 55 F4   16  8S  39 55 E
Angoche, I., Mozam. . . . . . . . . . 55 F4   16 20S  39 50 E
Angol, Chile . . . . . . . . . . . . . . . . 94 D1   37 56S  72 45W
Angola, Ind., U.S.A. . . . . . . . . . . 82 E3   41 38N  85  0W
Angola, N.Y., U.S.A. . . . . . . . . . . 84 D5   42 38N  79  2W
Angola ■, Africa . . . . . . . . . . . . . 53 G3   12  0S  18  0 E
Angoulême, France . . . . . . . . . . 20 D4   45 39N   0 10 E
Angoumois, France . . . . . . . . . . 20 D3   45 50N   0 25 E
Angra dos Reis, Brazil . . . . . . . . 95 A7   23  0S  44 10W
Angren, Uzbekistan . . . . . . . . . . 28 E8   41  1N  70 12 E
Angtassom, Cambodia . . . . . . . . 39 G5   11  1N 104 41 E
Angu, Dem. Rep. of the Congo . . 54 B1    3 23N  24 21 E
Anguang, China . . . . . . . . . . . . . 35 B12  45 15N 123 45 E
Anguilla ☑, W. Indies . . . . . . . . . 89 C7   18 14N  63  5W
Anguo, China . . . . . . . . . . . . . . . 34 E8   38 28N 115 15 E
Angurugu, Australia . . . . . . . . . . 62 A2   14  0S 136 25 E
Angus □, U.K. . . . . . . . . . . . . . . 11 E6   56 46N   2 56W
Angwa →, Zimbabwe . . . . . . . . 57 B5   16  0S  30 23 E
Anhandui →, Brazil . . . . . . . . . . 95 A5   21 46S  52 9W
Anholt, Denmark . . . . . . . . . . . . 9 H14  56 42N  11 33 E
Anhui □, China . . . . . . . . . . . . . . 33 C6   32  0N 117  0 E
Anhwei = Anhui □, China . . . . . . 33 C6   32  0N 117  0 E
Anichab, Namibia . . . . . . . . . . . . 56 C1   21  0S  14 46 E
Animas →, U.S.A. . . . . . . . . . . . 77 H9   36 43N 108 13W
Anivorano, Madag. . . . . . . . . . . . 57 B8   18 44S  48 58 E
Anjalankoski, Finland . . . . . . . . . 9 F22  60 45N  26 51 E
Anjar, India . . . . . . . . . . . . . . . . 42 H4   23  6N  70 10 E

Anjou, France . . . . . . . . . . . . . . 20 C3   47 20N   0 15W
Anjozorobe, Madag. . . . . . . . . . . 57 B8   18 22S  47 52 E
Anju, N. Korea . . . . . . . . . . . . . . 35 E13  39 36N 125 40 E
Ankaboa, Tanjona, Madag. . . . . . 57 C7   21 58S  43 20 E
Ankang, China . . . . . . . . . . . . . . 34 H5   32 40N 109  1 E
Ankara, Turkey . . . . . . . . . . . . . . 19 G5   39 57N  32 54 E
Ankaramena, Madag. . . . . . . . . . 57 C8   21 57S  46 39 E
Ankaratra, Madag. . . . . . . . . . . . 53 H9   19 25S  47 12 E
Ankasakasa, Madag. . . . . . . . . . 57 B7   16 21S  44 52 E
Ankavandra, Madag. . . . . . . . . . 57 B8   18 46S  45 18 E
Ankazoabo, Madag. . . . . . . . . . . 57 C7   22 18S  44 31 E
Ankazobe, Madag. . . . . . . . . . . . 57 B8   18 20S  47 10 E
Ankeny, U.S.A. . . . . . . . . . . . . . 80 E8   41 44N  93 36W
Ankilimalinika, Madag. . . . . . . . . 57 C7   22 58S  43 45 E
Ankilizato, Madag. . . . . . . . . . . . 57 C8   20 25S  45  1 E
Ankisabe, Madag. . . . . . . . . . . . 57 B8   19 17S  46 29 E
Ankoro, Dem. Rep. of the Congo . 54 D2    6 45S  26 55 E
Ankororoka, Madag. . . . . . . . . . . 57 D8   25 30S  45 11 E
Anmyŏn-do, S. Korea . . . . . . . . . 35 F14  36 25N 126 25 E
Ann, C., U.S.A. . . . . . . . . . . . . . 85 D14  42 38N  70 35W
Ann Arbor, U.S.A. . . . . . . . . . . . 82 D4   42 17N  83 45W
Anna, U.S.A. . . . . . . . . . . . . . . . 81 G10  37 28N  89 15W
Annaba, Algeria . . . . . . . . . . . . . 50 A7   36 50N   7 46 E
Annalee →, Ireland . . . . . . . . . . 10 B4   54  2N   7 24W
Annam, Vietnam . . . . . . . . . . . . 38 E7   16  0N 108  0 E
Annamitique, Chaîne, Asia . . . . . 38 D6   17  0N 106  0 E
Annan, U.K. . . . . . . . . . . . . . . . . 11 G5   54 59N   3 16W
Annan →, U.K. . . . . . . . . . . . . . 11 G5   54 58N   3 16W
Annapolis, U.S.A. . . . . . . . . . . . . 82 F7   38 59N  76 30W
Annapolis Royal, Canada . . . . . . 73 D6   44 44N  65 32W
Annapurna, Nepal . . . . . . . . . . . 43 E10  28 34N  83 50 E
Annean, L., Australia . . . . . . . . . 61 E2   26 54S 118 14 E
Annecy, France . . . . . . . . . . . . . 20 D7   45 55N   6  8 E
Anning, China . . . . . . . . . . . . . . 32 D5   24 55N 102 26 E
Anniston, U.S.A. . . . . . . . . . . . . 83 J3   33 39N  85 50W
Annobón, Atl. Oc. . . . . . . . . . . . . 49 G4    1 25S   5 36 E
Annotto B., Jamaica . . . . . . . . . . 88 a   18 17N  76 45W
Annville, U.S.A. . . . . . . . . . . . . . 85 F8   40 20N  76 31W
Áno Viánnos, Greece . . . . . . . . . 25 D7   35  2N  25 21 E
Anorotsangana, Madag. . . . . . . . 57 A8   13 56S  47 55 E
Anosibe, Madag. . . . . . . . . . . . . 57 B8   19 26S  48 13 E
Anóyia, Greece . . . . . . . . . . . . . 25 D6   35 16N  24 52 E
Anping, Hebei, China . . . . . . . . . 34 E8   38 15N 115 30 E
Anping, Liaoning, China . . . . . . . 35 D12  41  5N 123 30 E
Anqing, China . . . . . . . . . . . . . . 33 C6   30 30N 117  3 E
Anqiu, China . . . . . . . . . . . . . . . 35 F10  36 25N 119 10 E
Ansai, China . . . . . . . . . . . . . . . 34 F5   36 50N 109 20 E
Ansbach, Germany . . . . . . . . . . . 16 D6   49 28N  10 34 E
Anse la Raye, St. Lucia . . . . . . . 89 f   13 55N  61 3W
Anshan, China . . . . . . . . . . . . . . 35 D12  41  5N 122 58 E
Anshun, China . . . . . . . . . . . . . . 32 D5   26 18N 105 57 E
Ansley, U.S.A. . . . . . . . . . . . . . . 80 E5   41 18N  99 23W
Anson, U.S.A. . . . . . . . . . . . . . . 81 J5   32 45N  99 54W
Anson B., Australia . . . . . . . . . . 60 B5   13 20S 130  6 E
Ansongo, Mali . . . . . . . . . . . . . . 50 E6   15 25N   0 35 E
Ansonia, U.S.A. . . . . . . . . . . . . . 85 E11  41 21N  73  5W
Anstruther, U.K. . . . . . . . . . . . . . 11 E6   56 14N   2 41W
Ansudu, Indonesia . . . . . . . . . . . 37 E9    2 11S 139 22 E
Antabamba, Peru . . . . . . . . . . . . 92 F4   14 40S  73  0W
Antakya, Turkey . . . . . . . . . . . . . 19 G6   36 14N  36 10 E
Antalaha, Madag. . . . . . . . . . . . . 57 A9   14 57S  50 20 E
Antalya, Turkey . . . . . . . . . . . . . 19 G5   36 52N  30 45 E
Antalya Körfezi, Turkey . . . . . . . . 19 G5   36 15N  31 30 E
Antambohobe, Madag. . . . . . . . . 57 C8   22 20S  46 47 E
Antanambao-Manampotsy,
  Madag. . . . . . . . . . . . . . . . . . . 57 B8   19 29S  48 34 E
Antanambe, Madag. . . . . . . . . . . 57 B8   16 26S  49 52 E
Antananarivo, Madag. . . . . . . . . 57 B8   18 55S  47 31 E
Antananarivo □, Madag. . . . . . . . 57 B8   19  0S  47  0 E
Antanifotsy, Madag. . . . . . . . . . . 57 B8   19 39S  47 19 E
Antanimbaribe, Madag. . . . . . . . 57 C7   21 30S  44 48 E
Antanimora, Madag. . . . . . . . . . . 57 C8   24 49S  45 40 E
Antarctic Pen., Antarctica . . . . . . 5 C18  67  0S  60  0W
Antarctica . . . . . . . . . . . . . . . . . 5 E   90  0S   0  0 E
Antelope, Zimbabwe . . . . . . . . . 55 G2   21  2S  28 31 E
Antequera, Paraguay . . . . . . . . . 94 A4   24  8S  57  7W
Antequera, Spain . . . . . . . . . . . . 21 D3   37  5N   4 33W
Antero, Mt., U.S.A. . . . . . . . . . . 77 G10  38 41N 106 15W
Antevamena, Madag. . . . . . . . . . 57 C7   21  2S  44  8 E
Anthony, Kans., U.S.A. . . . . . . . . 81 G5   37  9N  98  2W
Anthony, N. Mex., U.S.A. . . . . . . 77 K10  32  0N 106 36W
Anti Atlas, Morocco . . . . . . . . . . 50 C4   30  0N   8 30W
Anti-Lebanon = Ash Sharqi, Al
  Jabal, Lebanon . . . . . . . . . . . . 46 B5   33 40N  36 10 E
Antibes, France . . . . . . . . . . . . . 20 E7   43 34N   7  6 E
Anticosti, Î. d’, Canada . . . . . . . . 73 C7   49 30N  63  0W
Antigo, U.S.A. . . . . . . . . . . . . . . 80 C10  45  9N  89  9W
Antigonish, Canada . . . . . . . . . . 73 C7   45 38N  61 58W
Antigua, Canary Is. . . . . . . . . . . 24 F5   28 24N  14  1W
Antigua, Guatemala . . . . . . . . . . 88 D1   14 34N  90 41W
Antigua, W. Indies . . . . . . . . . . . 89 C7   17  0N  61 50W
Antigua & Barbuda ■, W. Indies . 89 C7   17 20N  61 48W
Antilla, Cuba . . . . . . . . . . . . . . . 88 B4   20 40N  75 50W
Antilles = West Indies,
  Cent. Amer. . . . . . . . . . . . . . . . 89 D7   15  0N  65  0W
Antioch, U.S.A. . . . . . . . . . . . . . 78 G5   38  1N 121 48W
Antioquia, Colombia . . . . . . . . . . 92 B3    6 40N  75 55W
Antipodes Is., Pac. Oc. . . . . . . . . 64 M9   49 45S 178 40 E
Antlers, U.S.A. . . . . . . . . . . . . . . 81 H7   34 14N  95 37W
Antoetra, Madag. . . . . . . . . . . . . 57 C8   20 46S  47 20 E
Antofagasta, Chile . . . . . . . . . . . 94 A1   23 50S  70 30W
Antofagasta □, Chile . . . . . . . . . 94 A2   24  0S  69  0W
Antofagasta de la Sierra,
  Argentina . . . . . . . . . . . . . . . . 94 B2   26  5S  67 20W
Antofalla, Argentina . . . . . . . . . . 94 B2   25 30S  68  5W
Antofalla, Salar de, Argentina . . . 94 B2   25 40S  67 45W
Anton, U.S.A. . . . . . . . . . . . . . . . 81 J3   33 49N 102 10W
Antongila, Helodrano, Madag. . . . 57 B8   15 30S  49 50 E
Antonibé, Madag. . . . . . . . . . . . . 57 B8   15  7S  47 24 E
Antonibé, Presqu’île d’, Madag. . . 57 A8   14 55S  47 20 E
Antonina, Brazil . . . . . . . . . . . . . 95 B6   25 26S  48 42W
Antrim, U.K. . . . . . . . . . . . . . . . . 10 B5   54 43N   6 14W
Antrim, U.S.A. . . . . . . . . . . . . . . 84 F3   40  7N  81 21W
Antrim □, U.K. . . . . . . . . . . . . . . 10 B5   54 56N   6 25W
Antrim, Mts. of, U.K. . . . . . . . . . 10 A5   55  3N   6 14W
Antrim Plateau, Australia . . . . . . 60 C4   18  8S 128 20 E
Antsakabary, Madag. . . . . . . . . . 57 B8   15  3S  48 56 E
Antsalova, Madag. . . . . . . . . . . . 57 B7   18 40S  44 37 E
Antsenavolo, Madag. . . . . . . . . . 57 C8   21 24S  48  3 E
Antsiafabositra, Madag. . . . . . . . 57 B8   17 18S  46 57 E
Antsirabe, Antananarivo, Madag. . 57 B8   19 55S  47  2 E
Antsirabe, Antsiranana, Madag. . . 57 A8   14  0S  49 59 E
Antsirabe, Mahajanga, Madag. . . 57 B8   15 57S  48 58 E
Antsiranana □, Madag. . . . . . . . . 57 A8   12 16S  49 17 E
Antsohihy, Madag. . . . . . . . . . . . 57 A8   14 50S  47 59 E
Antsohimbondrona Seranana,
  Madag. . . . . . . . . . . . . . . . . . . 57 A8   13  7S  48 48 E

Antu, China ............... 35 C15 42 30N 128 20 E
Antwerp = Antwerpen, Belgium 15 C4 51 13N 4 25 E
Antwerp, U.S.A. .......... 85 B9 44 12N 75 37W
Antwerpen, Belgium ....... 15 C4 51 13N 4 25 E
Antwerpen □, Belgium ..... 15 C4 51 15N 4 40 E
Anupgarh, India .......... 42 E5 29 10N 73 10 E
Anuppur, India ........... 43 H9 23 6N 81 41 E
Anuradhapura, Sri Lanka .. 40 Q12 8 22N 80 28 E
Anveh, Iran .............. 45 E7 27 23N 54 11 E
Anvers = Antwerpen, Belgium 15 C4 51 13N 4 25 E
Anvers I., Antarctica .... 5 C17 64 30S 63 40W
Anxi, China .............. 32 B4 40 30N 95 43 E
Anxious B., Australia .... 63 E1 33 24S 134 45 E
Anyang, China ............ 34 F8 36 5N 114 21 E
Anyer-Kidul, Indonesia ... 37 G11 6 4S 105 53 E
Anyi, China .............. 34 G6 35 2N 111 2 E
Anza, U.S.A. ............. 79 M10 33 35N 116 39W
Anze, China .............. 34 F7 36 10N 112 12 E
Anzhero-Sudzhensk, Russia 28 D9 56 10N 86 0 E
Ânzio, Italy ............. 22 D5 41 27N 12 37 E
Ao Makham, Thailand ...... 39 a 7 50N 98 24 E
Ao Phangnga △, Thailand .. 39 a 8 10N 98 32 E
Aoga-Shima, Japan ........ 31 H9 32 28N 139 46 E
Aomen = Macau, China ..... 33 G10 22 12N 113 33 E
Aomori, Japan ............ 30 D10 40 45N 140 45 E
Aomori □, Japan .......... 30 D10 40 45N 140 40 E
Aonla, India ............. 43 E8 28 16N 79 11 E
Aoraki Mount Cook, N.Z. .. 59 K3 43 36S 170 9 E
Aosta, Italy ............. 20 D7 45 45N 7 20 E
Aotearoa = New Zealand ■,
  Oceania ................ 59 J6 40 0S 176 0 E
Aoukâr, Mauritania ....... 50 E4 17 40N 10 0W
Aozou, Couloir d', Chad .. 51 D9 22 0N 19 0 E
Apa →, S. Amer. .......... 94 A4 22 6S 58 2W
Apache, U.S.A. ........... 81 H5 34 54N 98 22W
Apache Junction, U.S.A. .. 77 K8 33 25N 111 33W
Apalachee B., U.S.A. ..... 83 L4 30 0N 84 0W
Apalachicola, U.S.A. ..... 83 L3 29 43N 84 59W
Apalachicola →, U.S.A. ... 83 L3 29 43N 84 58W
Apaporis →, Colombia ..... 92 D5 1 23S 69 25W
Aparados da Serra △, Brazil 95 B5 29 10S 50 8W
Aparri, Phil. ............ 37 A6 18 22N 121 38 E
Apatity, Russia .......... 18 A5 67 34N 33 22 E
Apatzingán, Mexico ....... 86 D4 19 0N 102 20W
Apeldoorn, Neths. ........ 15 B5 52 13N 5 57 E
Apennines = Appennini, Italy 22 B4 44 30N 10 0 E
Apia, Samoa .............. 59 A13 13 50S 171 50W
Apiacás, Serra dos, Brazil 92 E7 9 50S 57 0W
Apies →, S. Africa ....... 57 D4 25 15S 27 59 E
Apizaco, Mexico .......... 87 D5 19 26N 98 9W
Aplao, Peru .............. 92 G4 16 0S 72 40W
Apo, Mt., Phil. .......... 37 C7 6 53N 125 14 E
Apolakkiá, Greece ........ 25 C9 36 5N 27 48 E
Apolakkiá, Órmos, Greece . 25 C9 36 5N 27 45 E
Apolo, Bolivia ........... 92 F5 14 30S 68 30W
Aporé →, Brazil .......... 93 G8 19 27S 50 57W
Apostle Is., U.S.A. ...... 80 B9 47 0N 90 40W
Apostle Islands ○, U.S.A. 80 B9 46 57N 90 53W
Apóstoles, Argentina ..... 95 B4 28 0S 56 0W
Apostolos Andreas, C., Cyprus 25 D13 35 42N 34 35 E
Apoteri, Guyana .......... 92 C7 4 2N 58 32W
Appalachian Mts., U.S.A. . 82 G6 38 0N 80 0W
Appennini, Italy ......... 22 B4 44 30N 10 0 E
Apple Hill, Canada ....... 85 A10 45 13N 74 46W
Apple Valley, U.S.A. ..... 79 L9 34 32N 117 14W
Appleby-in-Westmorland, U.K. 12 C5 54 35N 2 29W
Appledore, U.K. .......... 13 F3 51 3N 4 13W
Appleton, U.S.A. ......... 82 C1 44 16N 88 25W
Approuague →, Fr. Guiana . 93 C8 4 30N 51 57W
Aprília, Italy ........... 22 D5 41 36N 12 39 E
Apsley, Canada ........... 84 B6 44 45N 78 6W
Apucarana, Brazil ........ 95 A5 23 55S 51 33W
Apure →, Venezuela ....... 92 B5 7 37N 66 25W
Apurímac →, Peru ......... 92 F4 12 17S 73 56W
Āqā Jarī, Iran ........... 45 D6 30 42N 49 50 E
Aqaba = Al 'Aqabah, Jordan 46 F4 29 31N 35 0 E
Aqaba, G. of, Red Sea .... 44 D2 29 0N 34 40 E
'Aqabah, Khalīj al = Aqaba, G. of,
  Red Sea ................ 44 D2 28 15N 33 20 E
'Aqdā, Iran .............. 45 C7 32 26N 53 37 E
'Aqrah, Iraq ............. 44 B4 36 46N 43 45 E
Aqtaū, Kazakhstan ........ 28 E6 43 39N 51 12 E
Aquidauana, Brazil ....... 93 H7 20 30S 55 50W
Aquiles Serdán, Mexico ... 86 B3 28 37N 105 54W
Aquin, Haiti ............. 89 C5 18 16N 73 24W
Aquitain, Bassin, France . 20 D3 44 0N 0 30W
Ar Rachidiya = Er Rachidia,
  Morocco ................ 50 B5 31 58N 4 20W
Ar Rafid, Syria .......... 46 C4 32 57N 35 52 E
Ar Raḥḥālīyah, Iraq ...... 44 C4 32 44N 43 23 E
Ar Ramādī, Iraq .......... 44 C4 33 25N 43 20 E
Ar Ramthā, Jordan ........ 46 C5 32 34N 36 0 E
Ar Raqqah, Syria ......... 44 C3 35 59N 39 8 E
Ar Rass, Si. Arabia ...... 44 E4 25 50N 43 40 E
Ar Rifā'ī, Iraq .......... 44 D5 31 50N 46 10 E
Ar Riyāḍ, Si. Arabia ..... 44 E5 24 41N 46 42 E
Ar Ru'ays, Qatar ......... 45 E6 26 8N 51 12 E
Ar Rukhaymiyah, Iraq ..... 44 D5 29 22N 45 38 E
Ar Ruṣāfah, Syria ........ 44 C3 35 45N 38 49 E
Ar Ruṭbah, Iraq .......... 44 C4 33 0N 40 15 E
Ara, India ............... 43 G11 25 35N 84 32 E
Ara →, Brazil ............ 83 H2 34 19N 86 30W
'Arab, Bahr el →, Sudan .. 51 G11 9 0N 29 30 E
Arab, Shatt al →, Asia ... 45 D6 30 0N 48 31 E
'Arabābād, Iran .......... 45 C8 33 2N 57 41 E
Arabia, Asia ............. 26 G8 25 0N 45 0 E
Arabian Desert = Es Sahrâ' Esh
  Sharqîya, Egypt ........ 51 C12 27 30N 32 30 E
Arabian Gulf = Persian Gulf, Asia 45 E6 27 0N 50 0 E
Arabian Sea, Ind. Oc. .... 27 H10 16 0N 65 0 E
Aracaju, Brazil .......... 93 F11 10 55S 37 4W
Aracati, Brazil .......... 93 D11 4 30S 37 44W
Araçatuba, Brazil ........ 95 A5 21 10S 50 30W
Aracena, Spain ........... 21 D2 37 53N 6 38W
Araçuaí, Brazil .......... 93 G10 16 52S 42 4W
'Arad, Israel ............ 46 D4 31 15N 35 12 E
Arad, Romania ............ 17 E11 46 10N 21 20 E
Arādān, Iran ............. 45 C7 35 21N 52 30 E
Aradhippou, Cyprus ....... 25 E12 34 57N 33 36 E
Arafura Sea, E. Indies ... 26 K17 9 0S 135 0 E
Aragón □, Spain .......... 21 B5 41 25N 0 40W
Aragón →, Spain .......... 21 A5 42 13N 1 44W
Araguacema, Brazil ....... 93 E9 8 50S 49 20W
Araguaia →, Brazil ....... 93 E9 5 21S 48 41W
Araguaína, Brazil ........ 93 E9 7 12S 48 12W
Araguari, Brazil ......... 93 G9 18 38S 48 11W
Araguari →, Brazil ....... 93 C9 1 15N 49 55W

Arain, India ............. 42 F6 26 27N 75 2 E
Arak, Algeria ............ 50 C6 25 20N 3 45 E
Arāk, Iran ............... 45 C6 34 0N 49 40 E
Arakan Coast, Burma ...... 41 K19 19 0N 94 0 E
Arakan Yoma, Burma ....... 41 K19 20 0N 94 40 E
Araks = Aras, Rūd-e →, Asia 44 B5 40 5N 48 29 E
Aral, Kazakhstan ......... 28 E7 46 41N 61 45 E
Aral Tengizi = Aral Sea, Asia 28 E7 44 30N 60 0 E
Aralsk = Aral, Kazakhstan 28 E7 46 41N 61 45 E
Aralskoye More = Aral Sea, Asia 28 E7 44 30N 60 0 E
Aramac, Australia ........ 62 C4 22 58S 145 14 E
Aran I., Ireland ......... 10 A3 55 0N 8 30W
Aran Is., Ireland ........ 10 C2 53 6N 9 38W
Aranda de Duero, Spain ... 21 B4 41 39N 3 42W
Arandān, Iran ............ 44 C5 35 23N 46 55 E
Aranjuez, Spain .......... 21 B4 40 1N 3 40W
Aranos, Namibia .......... 56 C2 24 9S 19 7 E
Aransas Pass, U.S.A. ..... 81 M6 27 55N 97 9W
Aranyaprathet, Thailand .. 38 F4 13 41N 102 30 E
Arapahoe, U.S.A. ......... 80 E5 40 18N 99 54W
Arapey Grande →, Uruguay . 94 C4 30 55S 57 49W
Arapgir, Turkey .......... 44 B3 39 5N 38 30 E
Arapiraca, Brazil ........ 93 E11 9 45S 36 39W
Arapongas, Brazil ........ 95 A5 23 29S 51 28W
Ar'ar, Si. Arabia ........ 44 D4 30 59N 41 2 E
Araranguá, Brazil ........ 95 B6 29 0S 49 30W
Araraquara, Brazil ....... 93 H9 21 50S 48 0W
Ararás, Serra das, Brazil 95 B5 25 0S 53 10W
Ararat, Australia ........ 63 F3 37 16S 143 0 E
Ararat, Mt. = Ağrı Dağı, Turkey 19 G7 39 50N 44 15 E
Araria, India ............ 43 F12 26 9N 87 33 E
Araripe, Chapada do, Brazil 93 E11 7 20S 40 0W
Araruama, L. de, Brazil .. 95 A7 22 53S 42 12W
Aras, Rūd-e →, Asia ...... 44 B5 40 5N 48 29 E
Arauca, Colombia ......... 92 B4 7 0N 70 40W
Arauca →, Venezuela ...... 92 B5 7 24N 66 35W
Arauco, Chile ............ 94 D1 37 16S 73 25W
Arawale ○, Kenya ......... 54 C5 1 24S 40 9 E
Araxá, Brazil ............ 93 G9 19 35S 46 55W
Araya, Pen. de, Venezuela 92 A6 10 40N 64 0W
Arba Minch, Ethiopia ..... 47 F2 6 0N 37 30 E
Arbat, Iraq .............. 44 C5 35 25N 45 35 E
Árbatax, Italy ........... 22 E3 39 56N 9 42 E
Arbīl, Iraq .............. 44 B5 36 15N 44 5 E
Arborfield, Canada ....... 71 C8 53 6N 103 39W
Arborg, Canada ........... 71 C9 50 54N 97 13W
Arbroath, U.K. ........... 11 E6 56 34N 2 35W
Arbuckle, U.S.A. ......... 78 F4 39 1N 122 3W
Arcachon, France ......... 20 D3 44 40N 1 10W
Arcade, Calif., U.S.A. ... 79 L8 34 2N 118 15W
Arcade, N.Y., U.S.A. ..... 84 D6 42 32N 78 25W
Arcadia, Fla., U.S.A. .... 83 M5 27 13N 81 52W
Arcadia, La., U.S.A. ..... 81 J8 32 33N 92 55W
Arcadia, Pa., U.S.A. ..... 84 F6 40 47N 78 51W
Arcata, U.S.A. ........... 76 F1 40 52N 124 5W
Archangel = Arkhangelsk, Russia 18 B7 64 38N 40 36 E
Archbald, U.S.A. ......... 85 E9 41 30N 75 32W
Archer →, Australia ...... 62 A3 13 28S 141 41 E
Archer B., Australia ..... 62 A3 13 20S 141 30 E
Archer Bend = Mungkan
  Kandju △, Australia .... 62 A3 13 35S 142 52 E
Archers Post, Kenya ...... 54 B4 0 35N 37 35 E
Arches △, U.S.A. ......... 77 G9 38 45N 109 25W
Archipel-de-Mingan △, Canada . 73 B7 50 13N 63 10W
Archipiélago Chinijo △,
  Canary Is. ............. 24 E6 29 20N 13 30W
Archipiélago Los Roques △,
  Venezuela .............. 89 D6 11 50N 66 44W
Arckaringa Cr. →, Australia 63 D2 28 10S 135 22 E
Arco, U.S.A. ............. 76 E7 43 38N 113 18W
Arcos de la Frontera, Spain 21 D3 36 45N 5 49W
Arcot, India ............. 40 N11 12 53N 79 20 E
Arctic Bay, Canada ....... 69 A11 73 1N 85 7W
Arctic Ocean, Arctic ..... 4 B18 78 0N 160 0W
Arctic Red River = Tsiigehtchic,
  Canada ................. 68 B6 67 15N 134 0W
Arctowski, Antarctica .... 5 C18 62 30S 58 0W
Arda →, Bulgaria ......... 23 D12 41 40N 26 30 E
Ardabīl, Iran ............ 45 B6 38 15N 48 18 E
Ardabīl □, Iran .......... 45 B6 38 15N 48 20 E
Ardakān = Sepīdān, Iran .. 45 D7 30 20N 52 5 E
Ardakān, Iran ............ 45 C7 32 19N 53 59 E
Ardee, Ireland ........... 10 C5 53 52N 6 33W
Arden, Canada ............ 84 B8 44 43N 76 56W
Arden, Calif., U.S.A. .... 78 G5 38 36N 121 33W
Arden, Nev., U.S.A. ...... 79 J11 36 1N 115 14W
Ardenne, Belgium ......... 15 E5 49 50N 5 5 E
Ardennes = Ardenne, Belgium 15 E5 49 50N 5 5 E
Arderin, Ireland ......... 10 C4 53 2N 7 39W
Ardestān, Iran ........... 45 C7 33 20N 52 25 E
Ardivachar Pt., U.K. ..... 11 D1 57 23N 7 26W
Ardlethan, Australia ..... 63 E4 34 22S 146 53 E
Ardmore, Okla., U.S.A. ... 81 H6 34 10N 97 8W
Ardmore, Pa., U.S.A. ..... 85 G9 39 58N 75 18W
Ardnamurchan, Pt. of, U.K. 11 E2 56 43N 6 14W
Ardnave Pt., U.K. ........ 11 F2 55 53N 6 20W
Ardrossan, Australia ..... 63 E2 34 26S 137 53 E
Ardrossan, U.K. .......... 11 F4 55 39N 4 49W
Ards Pen., U.K. .......... 10 B6 54 33N 5 34W
Arecibo, Puerto Rico ..... 89 d 18 29N 66 43W
Areia Branca, Brazil ..... 93 E11 5 0S 37 0W
Arena, Pt., U.S.A. ....... 78 G3 38 57N 123 44W
Arenal, Honduras ......... 88 C2 15 21N 86 50W
Arendal, Norway .......... 9 G13 58 28N 8 46 E
Arequipa, Peru ........... 92 G4 16 20S 71 30W
Arévalo, Spain ........... 21 B3 41 3N 4 43W
Arezzo, Italy ............ 22 C4 43 25N 11 53 E
Arga, Turkey ............. 44 B3 38 21N 37 59 E
Arganda, Spain ........... 21 B4 40 19N 3 26W
Argenta, Canada .......... 70 C5 50 11N 116 56W
Argentan, France ......... 20 B3 48 45N 0 1W
Argentário, Mte., Italy .. 22 C4 42 24N 11 9 E
Argentia, Canada ......... 73 C9 47 18N 53 58W
Argentina ■, S. Amer. .... 96 D3 35 0S 66 0W
Argentine Basin, S. Amer. 90 H5 45 0S 58 0W
Argentino, L., Argentina . 96 G2 50 10S 73 0W
Argeş →, Romania ......... 17 F14 44 5N 26 38 E
Arghandab →, Afghan. ..... 42 D1 31 30N 64 15 E
Argolikós Kólpos, Greece . 23 F10 37 20N 22 52 E
Árgos, Greece ............ 23 F10 37 40N 22 43 E
Argostóli, Greece ........ 23 E9 38 11N 20 29 E
Arguello, Pt., U.S.A. .... 79 L6 34 35N 120 39W
Arguineguín, Canary Is. .. 24 G4 27 46N 15 41W
Argun →, Russia .......... 29 D13 53 20N 121 28 E
Argus, Pk., U.S.A. ....... 79 K9 35 52N 117 26W
Argyle, L., Australia .... 60 C4 16 20S 128 40 E
Argyll ○, U.K. ........... 11 E4 56 6N 5 0W

Argyll & Bute □, U.K. .... 11 E3 56 13N 5 28W
Århus, Denmark ........... 9 H14 56 8N 10 11 E
Ariadnoye, Russia ........ 30 B7 45 8N 134 25 E
Ariamsvlei, Namibia ...... 56 D2 28 9S 19 51 E
Arica, Chile ............. 92 G4 18 32S 70 20W
Arica, Colombia .......... 92 D4 2 0S 71 50W
Arico, Canary Is. ........ 24 F3 28 9N 16 29W
Arid, C., Australia ...... 61 F3 34 1S 123 10 E
Arida, Japan ............. 31 G7 34 5N 135 8 E
Arılla, Ákra, Greece ..... 25 A3 39 43N 19 39 E
Arima, Trin. & Tob. ...... 89 D7 10 38N 61 17W
Arinos →, Brazil ......... 92 F7 10 25S 58 20W
Ario de Rosales, Mexico .. 86 D4 19 12N 102 0W
Aripo, Mt., Trin. & Tob. . 93 K15 10 45N 61 15W
Aripuanã, Brazil ......... 92 E6 9 25S 60 30W
Aripuanã →, Brazil ....... 92 E6 5 7S 60 25W
Ariquemes, Brazil ........ 92 E6 9 55S 63 6W
Arisaig, U.K. ............ 11 E3 56 55N 5 51W
Aristazabal I., Canada ... 70 C3 52 40N 129 10W
Arivonimamo, Madag. ...... 57 B8 19 1S 47 11 E
Arizaro, Salar de, Argentina 94 A2 24 40S 67 50W
Arizona, Argentina ....... 94 D2 35 45S 65 25W
Arizona □, U.S.A. ........ 77 J8 34 0N 112 0W
Arizpe, Mexico ........... 86 A2 30 20N 110 11W
Arjeplog, Sweden ......... 8 D18 66 3N 17 54 E
Arjepluovve = Arjeplog, Sweden 8 D18 66 3N 17 54 E
Arjona, Colombia ......... 92 A3 10 14N 75 22W
Arjuna, Indonesia ........ 37 G15 7 49S 112 34 E
Arka, Russia ............. 29 C15 60 15N 142 0 E
Arkadelphia, U.S.A. ...... 81 H8 34 7N 93 4W
Arkaig, L., U.K. ......... 11 E3 56 59N 5 10W
Arkalyk = Arqalyk, Kazakhstan 28 D7 50 13N 66 50 E
Arkansas □, U.S.A. ....... 81 H8 35 0N 92 30W
Arkansas →, U.S.A. ....... 81 J9 33 47N 91 4W
Arkansas City, U.S.A. .... 81 G6 37 4N 97 2W
Arkaroola, Australia ..... 63 E2 30 20S 139 22 E
Arkhángelos, Greece ...... 25 C10 36 13N 28 7 E
Arkhangelsk, Russia ...... 18 B7 64 38N 40 36 E
Arki, India .............. 42 D7 31 9N 76 58 E
Arklow, Ireland .......... 10 D5 52 48N 6 10W
Arkport, U.S.A. .......... 84 D7 42 24N 77 42W
Arkticheskiy, Mys, Russia 29 A10 81 10N 95 0 E
Arkville, U.S.A. ......... 85 D10 42 9N 74 37W
Arlanzón →, Spain ........ 21 A3 42 3N 4 17W
Arlberpass, Austria ...... 16 E6 47 9N 10 12 E
Arles, France ............ 20 E6 43 41N 4 40 E
Arlington, S. Africa ..... 57 D4 28 1S 27 53 E
Arlington, N.Y., U.S.A. .. 85 E11 41 42N 73 54W
Arlington, Oreg., U.S.A. . 76 D3 45 43N 120 12W
Arlington, S. Dak., U.S.A. 80 C6 44 22N 97 8W
Arlington, Tex., U.S.A. .. 81 J6 32 44N 97 7W
Arlington, Va., U.S.A. ... 82 F7 38 53N 77 7W
Arlington, Vt., U.S.A. ... 85 C11 43 5N 73 9W
Arlington, Wash., U.S.A. . 78 B4 48 12N 122 8W
Arlington Heights, U.S.A. 82 D2 42 5N 87 59W
Arlon, Belgium ........... 15 E5 49 42N 5 49 E
Arltunga, Australia ...... 62 C1 23 26S 134 41 E
Armagh, U.K. ............. 10 B5 54 21N 6 39W
Armagh □, U.K. ........... 10 B5 54 18N 6 37W
Armando Bermudez △,
  Dom. Rep. .............. 89 C5 19 3N 71 0W
Armavir, Russia .......... 19 E7 45 2N 41 7 E
Armenia, Colombia ........ 92 C3 4 35N 75 45W
Armenia ■, Asia .......... 19 F7 40 20N 45 0 E
Armenistis, Ákra, Greece . 25 C9 36 8N 27 42 E
Armidale, Australia ...... 63 E5 30 30S 151 40 E
Armour, U.S.A. ........... 80 D5 43 19N 98 21W
Armstrong, B.C., Canada .. 70 C5 50 25N 119 10W
Armstrong, Ont., Canada .. 72 B2 50 18N 89 4W
Arnarfjörður, Iceland .... 8 D2 65 48N 23 40W
Arnaud →, Canada ......... 69 B12 59 59N 69 46W
Arnauti, C., Cyprus ...... 25 D11 35 6N 32 17 E
Arnett, U.S.A. ........... 81 G5 36 8N 99 46W
Arnhem, Neths. ........... 15 C5 51 58N 5 55 E
Arnhem, C., Australia .... 62 A2 12 20S 137 30 E
Arnhem B., Australia ..... 62 A2 12 20S 136 10 E
Arnhem Land, Australia ... 62 A1 13 10S 134 30 E
Arno →, Italy ............ 22 C4 43 41N 10 17 E
Arno Bay, Australia ...... 63 E2 33 54S 136 34 E
Arnold, U.K. ............. 12 D6 53 1N 1 7W
Arnold, U.S.A. ........... 78 G6 38 15N 120 20W
Arnot, Canada ............ 71 B9 55 56N 96 41W
Arnøy, Norway ............ 8 A19 70 9N 20 40 E
Arnprior, Canada ......... 85 A8 45 26N 76 21W
Arnsberg, Germany ........ 16 C5 51 24N 8 5 E
Aroab, Namibia ........... 56 D2 26 41S 19 39 E
Aron, India .............. 42 G6 25 57N 77 56 E
Arona, Canary Is. ........ 24 F3 28 6N 16 40W
Arqalyk, Kazakhstan ...... 28 D7 50 13N 66 50 E
Arrah = Ara, India ....... 43 G11 25 35N 84 32 E
Arran, U.K. .............. 11 F3 55 34N 5 12W
Arras, France ............ 20 A5 50 17N 2 46 E
Arrecife, Canary Is. ..... 24 F6 28 57N 13 37W
Arrecifes, Argentina ..... 94 C3 34 6S 60 9W
Arrée, Mts. d', France ... 20 B2 48 26N 3 55W
Arriaga, Chiapas, Mexico . 87 D6 16 15N 93 52W
Arriaga, San Luis Potosí, Mexico 86 C4 21 55N 101 23W
Arrilalah, Australia ..... 62 C3 23 43S 143 54 E
Arrino, Australia ........ 61 E2 29 30S 115 40 E
Arrow, L., Ireland ....... 10 B3 54 3N 8 19W
Arrowtown, N.Z. .......... 59 L2 44 57S 168 50 E
Arroyo Grande, U.S.A. .... 79 K6 35 7N 120 35W
Ars, Iran ................ 44 B5 37 9N 45 52 E
Arsenault L., Canada ..... 71 B7 55 6N 108 32W
Arsenev, Russia .......... 30 B6 44 10N 133 15 E
Árta, Greece ............. 23 E9 39 8N 21 2 E
Artà, Spain .............. 24 B10 39 41N 3 21 E
Arteaga, Mexico .......... 86 D4 18 50N 102 20W
Artem, Russia ............ 30 C6 43 22N 132 13 E
Artemovsk, Russia ........ 29 D10 54 45N 93 35 E
Artemovsk, Ukraine ....... 19 E6 48 35N 38 0 E
Artesia = Mosomane, Botswana 56 C4 24 2S 26 19 E
Artesia, U.S.A. .......... 81 J2 32 51N 104 24W
Arthur, Canada ........... 84 C4 43 50N 80 32W
Arthur →, Australia ...... 63 G3 41 2S 144 40 E
Arthur Cr. →, Australia .. 62 C2 22 30S 136 25 E
Arthur Pt., Australia .... 62 C5 22 7S 150 3 E
Arthur River, Australia .. 61 F2 33 20S 117 2 E
Arthur's Pass, N.Z. ...... 59 K3 42 54S 171 35 E
Arthur's Pass △, N.Z. .... 59 K3 42 53S 171 42 E
Arthur's Town, Bahamas ... 89 B4 24 38N 75 42W
Artigas, Antarctica ...... 5 C18 62 30S 58 0W
Artigas, Uruguay ......... 94 C4 30 20S 56 30W
Artillery L., Canada ..... 71 A7 63 9N 107 52W
Artois, France ........... 20 A5 50 20N 2 30 E
Artrutx, C. de, Spain .... 24 B10 39 55N 3 49 E

Artsyz, Ukraine .......... 17 E15 46 4N 29 26 E
Artvin, Turkey ........... 19 F7 41 14N 41 44 E
Aru, Kepulauan, Indonesia 37 F8 6 0S 134 30 E
Aru Is. = Aru, Kepulauan,
  Indonesia .............. 37 F8 6 0S 134 30 E
Arua, Uganda ............. 54 B3 3 1N 30 58 E
Aruanã, Brazil ........... 93 F8 14 54S 51 10W
Aruba ☒, W. Indies ....... 89 D6 12 30N 70 0W
Arucas, Canary Is. ....... 24 F4 28 7N 15 32W
Arun →, Nepal ............ 43 F12 26 55N 87 10 E
Arun →, U.K. ............. 13 G7 50 49N 0 33W
Arunachal Pradesh □, India 41 F19 28 0N 95 0 E
Arusha, Tanzania ......... 54 C4 3 20S 36 40 E
Arusha □, Tanzania ....... 54 C4 4 0S 36 30 E
Arusha △, Tanzania ....... 54 C4 3 16S 36 47 E
Arusha Chini, Tanzania ... 54 C4 3 32S 37 20 E
Aruwimi →, Dem. Rep. of
  the Congo .............. 54 B1 1 13N 23 36 E
Arvada, Colo., U.S.A. .... 80 F2 39 48N 105 5W
Arvada, Wyo., U.S.A. ..... 76 D10 44 39N 106 8W
Árvi, Greece ............. 25 E7 34 59N 25 28 E
Arviat, Canada ........... 71 A10 61 6N 93 59W
Arvidsjaur, Sweden ....... 8 D18 65 35N 19 10 E
Arvika, Sweden ........... 9 G15 59 40N 12 36 E
Arvin, U.S.A. ............ 79 K8 35 12N 118 50W
Arwal, India ............. 43 G11 25 15N 84 41 E
Arxan, China ............. 33 B6 47 11N 119 57 E
Aryirádhes, Greece ....... 25 B3 39 27N 19 58 E
Aryiroúpolis, Greece ..... 25 D6 35 17N 24 20 E
Arys, Kazakhstan ......... 28 E7 42 26N 68 48 E
Arzamas, Russia .......... 18 C7 55 27N 43 55 E
Aş Şafā, Syria ........... 46 B6 33 10N 37 0 E
Aş Saffānīyah, Si. Arabia 45 E6 27 55N 48 50 E
Aş Safīrah, Syria ........ 44 B3 36 5N 37 21 E
Aş Şahm, Oman ............ 45 E8 24 10N 56 53 E
Aş Sājir, Si. Arabia ..... 44 E5 25 11N 44 36 E
Aş Salamīyah, Syria ...... 44 C3 35 1N 37 2 E
Aş Salmān, Iraq .......... 44 D5 30 30N 44 32 E
Aş Salt, Jordan .......... 46 C4 32 2N 35 43 E
Aş Sal'w'a, Qatar ........ 45 E6 24 23N 50 50 E
Aş Samāwah, Iraq ......... 44 D5 31 15N 45 15 E
Aş Sanamayn, Syria ....... 46 B5 33 3N 36 10 E
Aş Sohar = Şuḥār, Oman ... 45 E8 24 20N 56 40 E
Aş Sukhnah, Syria ........ 44 C3 34 52N 38 52 E
Aş Sulaymānīyah, Iraq .... 44 C5 35 35N 45 29 E
Aş Sulaymī, Si. Arabia ... 44 E4 26 17N 41 21 E
Aş Sulayyil, Si. Arabia .. 47 C4 20 27N 45 34 E
Aş Summān, Si. Arabia .... 44 E5 25 0N 47 0 E
Aş Suwaydā', Syria ....... 46 C5 32 40N 36 30 E
Aş Suwaydā' □, Syria ..... 46 C5 32 45N 36 45 E
Aş Suwayq, Oman .......... 45 F8 23 51N 57 26 E
Aş Şuwayrah, Iraq ........ 44 C5 32 55N 45 0 E
Asab, Namibia ............ 56 D2 25 30S 18 0 E
Asad, Buḥayrat al, Syria . 44 C3 36 0N 38 15 E
Asahi-Gawa →, Japan ...... 31 G6 34 36N 133 58 E
Asahigawa, Japan ......... 30 C11 43 46N 142 22 E
Asamankese, Ghana ........ 50 G5 5 50N 0 40W
Asan →, India ............ 43 F8 26 37N 78 24 E
Asansol, India ........... 43 H12 23 40N 87 1 E
Asbesberge, S. Africa .... 56 D3 29 0S 23 0 E
Asbestos, Canada ......... 73 C5 45 47N 71 58W
Asbury Park, U.S.A. ...... 85 F10 40 13N 74 1W
Ascensión, Mexico ........ 86 A3 31 6N 107 59W
Ascensión, B. de la, Mexico 87 D7 19 50N 87 20W
Ascension I., Atl. Oc. ... 49 G2 7 57S 14 23W
Aschaffenburg, Germany ... 16 D5 49 58N 9 6 E
Aschersleben, Germany .... 16 C6 51 45N 11 29 E
Áscoli Piceno, Italy ..... 22 C5 42 51N 13 34 E
Ascope, Peru ............. 92 E3 7 46S 79 8W
Ascotán, Chile ........... 94 A2 21 45S 68 17W
Aseb, Eritrea ............ 47 E3 13 0N 42 40 E
Asela, Ethiopia .......... 47 F2 8 0N 39 0 E
Asenovgrad, Bulgaria ..... 23 C11 42 1N 24 51 E
Aserradero, Mexico ....... 86 C3 23 40N 105 43W
Asgata, Cyprus ........... 25 E12 34 46N 33 15 E
Ash Fork, U.S.A. ......... 77 J7 35 13N 112 29W
Ash Grove, U.S.A. ........ 81 G8 37 19N 93 35W
Ash Shabakah, Iraq ....... 44 D4 30 49N 43 39 E
Ash Shamāl □, Lebanon .... 46 A5 34 25N 36 0 E
Ash Shāmiyah, Iraq ....... 44 D5 31 55N 44 35 E
Ash Shāriqah, U.A.E. ..... 45 E7 25 23N 55 26 E
Ash Sharmah, Si. Arabia .. 44 D2 28 1N 35 16 E
Ash Sharqāt, Iraq ........ 44 C4 35 27N 43 16 E
Ash Sharqi, Al Jabal, Lebanon 46 B5 33 40N 36 10 E
Ash Shaṭrah, Iraq ........ 44 D5 31 30N 46 10 E
Ash Shawbak, Jordan ...... 44 D2 30 32N 35 34 E
Ash Shawmari, J., Jordan . 46 E5 30 35N 36 35 E
Ash Shinafiyah, Iraq ..... 44 D5 31 35N 44 39 E
Ash Shu'bah, Si. Arabia .. 44 D5 28 54N 44 44 E
Ash Shumlūl, Si. Arabia .. 44 E5 26 31N 47 20 E
Ash Shūr'ā, Iraq ......... 44 C4 35 58N 43 13 E
Ash Shuwayfāt, Lebanon ... 46 B4 33 45N 35 30 E
Asha, Russia ............. 18 D10 55 0N 57 16 E
Ashau, Vietnam ........... 38 D6 16 6N 107 22 E
Ashbourne, U.K. .......... 12 D6 53 2N 1 43W
Ashburn, U.S.A. .......... 83 K4 31 43N 83 39W
Ashburton, N.Z. .......... 59 K3 43 53S 171 48 E
Ashburton →, Australia ... 60 D1 21 40S 114 56 E
Ashcroft, Canada ......... 70 C4 50 40N 121 20W
Ashdod, Israel ........... 46 D3 31 49N 34 35 E
Ashdown, U.S.A. .......... 81 J7 33 40N 94 8W
Asheboro, U.S.A. ......... 83 H6 35 43N 79 49W
Ashern, Canada ........... 71 C9 51 11N 98 21W
Asherton, U.S.A. ......... 81 L5 28 27N 99 46W
Asheville, U.S.A. ........ 83 H4 35 36N 82 33W
Ashewat, Pakistan ........ 42 D3 31 22N 68 32 E
Asheweig →, Canada ....... 72 B2 54 17N 87 12W
Ashford, Australia ....... 63 D5 29 15S 151 3 E
Ashford, U.K. ............ 13 F8 51 8N 0 53 E
Ashgabat, Turkmenistan ... 28 F6 38 0N 57 50 E
Ashibetsu, Japan ......... 30 C11 43 31N 142 11 E
Ashikaga, Japan .......... 31 F9 36 28N 139 29 E
Ashington, U.K. .......... 12 B6 55 11N 1 33W
Ashizuri-Ukwai △, Japan .. 31 H6 32 56N 132 32 E
Ashizuri-Zaki, Japan ..... 31 H6 32 44N 133 0 E
Ashkarkot, Afghan. ....... 42 C2 33 3N 67 58 E
Ashkhabad = Ashgabat,
  Turkmenistan ........... 28 F6 38 0N 57 50 E
Âshkhâneh, Iran .......... 45 B8 37 26N 56 55 E
Ashland, Kans., U.S.A. ... 81 G5 37 11N 99 46W
Ashland, Ky., U.S.A. ..... 82 F4 38 28N 82 38W
Ashland, Mont., U.S.A. ... 76 D10 45 36N 106 16W
Ashland, Ohio, U.S.A. .... 84 F2 40 52N 82 19W
Ashland, Oreg., U.S.A. ... 76 E2 42 12N 122 43W
Ashland, Pa., U.S.A. ..... 85 F8 40 45N 76 22W
Ashland, Va., U.S.A. ..... 82 G7 37 46N 77 29W
Ashland, Wis., U.S.A. .... 80 B9 46 35N 90 53W

Ashley, N. Dak., U.S.A. ...... 80 B5  46  2N  99 22W
Ashley, Pa., U.S.A. .......... 85 E9  41 12N  75 55W
Ashmore and Cartier Is., Ind. Oc. 60 B3  12 15S 123  0 E
Ashmore Reef, Australia ..... 60 B3  12 14S 123  5 E
Ashmyany, Belarus ......... 9 J21 54 26N  25 52 E
Ashokan Reservoir, U.S.A. .... 85 E10 41 56N  74 13W
Ashqelon, Israel .......... 46 D3  31 42N  34 35 E
Ashta, India ............. 42 H7  23  1N  76 43 E
Ashtabula, U.S.A. ......... 84 E4  41 52N  80 47W
Ashton, S. Africa ......... 56 E3  33 50S  20  5 E
Ashton, U.S.A. ........... 76 D8  44  4N 111 27W
Ashuanipi, L., Canada ....... 73 B6  52 45N  66 15W
Ashuapmushuan →, Canada ... 72 C5  48 37N  72 20W
Ashville, U.S.A. .......... 84 F6  40 34N  78 33W
Asia .................. 26 E11 45  0N  75  0 E
Asia, Kepulauan, Indonesia ... 37 D8   1  0N 131 13 E
Asifabad, India .......... 40 K11 19 20N  79 24 E
Asinara, Italy ........... 22 D3  41  4N   8 16 E
Asinara, G. dell', Italy ...... 22 D3  41  0N   8 30 E
Asino, Russia ........... 28 D9  57  0N  86  0 E
Asipovichy, Belarus ....... 17 B15 53 19N  28 33 E
'Asir □, Si. Arabia ........ 47 D3  18 40N  42 30 E
Asir, Ras, Somali Rep. ...... 47 E5  11 55N  51 10 E
Askersund, Sweden ........ 9 G16 58 53N  14 55 E
Askham, S. Africa ........ 56 D3  26 59S  20 47 E
Askim, Norway .......... 9 G14 59 35N  11 10 E
Askja, Iceland ........... 8 D5  65  3N  16 48W
Askøy, Norway .......... 9 F11 60 29N   5 10 E
Asmara = Asmera, Eritrea .... 47 D2  15  19N  38 55 E
Asmera, Eritrea .......... 47 D2  15 19N  38 55 E
Åsnen, Sweden .......... 9 H16 56 37N  14 45 E
Aso Kuju △, Japan ........ 31 H5  32 53N 131  6 E
Aspatria, U.K. .......... 12 C4  54 47N   3 19W
Aspen, U.S.A. ........... 77 G10 39 11N 106 49W
Aspermont, U.S.A. ........ 81 J4  33  8N 100 14W
Aspiring, Mt., N.Z. ........ 59 L2  44 23S 168 46 E
Asprókavos, Ákra, Greece .... 25 B4  39 21N  20  6 E
Aspur, India ............ 42 H6  23 58N  74  7 E
Asquith, Canada ......... 71 C7  52  8N 107 13W
Assab = Aseb, Eritrea ...... 47 E3  13  0N  42 40 E
Assam □, India .......... 41 G18 26  0N  93  0 E
Assateague Island △, U.S.A. .. 82 F8  38 15N  75 10W
Asse, Belgium ........... 15 D4  50 24N   4 10 E
Assen, Neths. ........... 15 A6  53  0N   6 35 E
Assiniboia, Canada ....... 71 D7  49 40N 105 59W
Assiniboine →, Canada ..... 71 D9  49 53N  97 8W
Assiniboine, Mt., Canada .... 70 C5  50 52N 115 39W
Assis, Brazil ............ 95 A5  22 40S  50 20W
Assisi, Italy ............ 22 C5  43  4N  12 37 E
Assynt, L., U.K. ......... 11 C3  58 10N   5  3W
Astana, Kazakhstan ....... 28 D8  51 10N  71 30 E
Āstāneh, Iran ........... 45 B6  37 17N  49 59 E
Astara, Azerbaijan ........ 19 G8  38 30N  48 50 E
Asteroúsia, Greece ........ 25 E7  34 59N  25  3 E
Asti, Italy ............. 20 D8  44 54N   8 12 E
Astipálaia, Greece ........ 23 F12 36 32N  26 22 E
Astorga, Spain .......... 21 A2  42 29N   6  8W
Astoria, U.S.A. .......... 78 D3  46 11N 123 50W
Astrakhan, Russia ........ 19 E8  46 25N  48  5 E
Asturias □, Spain ........ 21 A3  43 15N   6  0W
Asunción, Paraguay ....... 94 B4  25 10S  57 30W
Asunción Nochixtlán, Mexico .. 87 D5  17 28N  97 14W
Aswa →, Uganda ........ 54 B3  3 43N  31 55 E
Aswa-Lolim △, Uganda ..... 54 B3  2 43N  31 35 E
Aswân, Egypt ........... 51 D12 24  4N  32 57 E
Aswan Dam = Sadd el Aali, Egypt 51 D12 23 54N  32 54 E
Asyût, Egypt ........... 51 C12 27 11N  31  4 E
At Ţafilah, Jordan ........ 46 E4  30 45N  35 30 E
At Ţafilah □, Jordan ...... 46 E4  30 45N  35 30 E
Aţ Ţā'if, Si. Arabia ....... 47 C3  21  5N  40 27 E
At Ta'mim □, Iraq ........ 44 C5  35 30N  44 20 E
Aţ Ţirāq, Si. Arabia ...... 44 E5  27 19N  44 33 E
Aţ Ţubayq, Si. Arabia ..... 44 D3  29 30N  37  0 E
Atacama □, Chile ........ 94 B2  27 30S  70  0W
Atacama, Desierto de, Chile .. 94 A2  24  0S  69 20W
Atacama, Salar de, Chile .... 94 A2  23 30S  68 20W
Atalaya, Peru ........... 92 F4  10 45S  73 50W
Atalaya de Femes, Canary Is. .. 24 F6  28 56N   13 47W
Atami, Japan ........... 31 G9  35  5N 139  4 E
Atapupu, E. Timor ........ 37 F6  9  0S 124 51 E
Atâr, Mauritania ......... 50 D3  20 30N  13  5W
Atari, Pakistan .......... 42 D6  30 56N  74  2 E
Atascadero, U.S.A. ....... 78 K6  35 29N 120 40W
Atasu, Kazakhstan ........ 28 E8  48 30N  71  0 E
Atatürk Barajı, Turkey ..... 19 G6  37 28N  38 30 E
Atauro, E. Timor ......... 37 F7  8 10S 125 30 E
'Atbara, Sudan .......... 51 E12 17 42N  33 59 E
'Atbara, Nahr →, Sudan .... 51 E12 17 40N  33 56 E
Atbasar, Kazakhstan ...... 28 D7  51 48N  68 20 E
Atchafalaya B., U.S.A. ..... 81 L9  29 25N  91 25W
Atchison, U.S.A. ......... 80 F7  39 34N  95  7W
Āteshān, Iran ........... 45 C7  35 35N  52 37 E
Ath, Belgium ........... 15 D3  50 38N   3 47 E
Athabasca, Canada ....... 70 C6  54 45N 113 20W
Athabasca →, Canada ..... 71 B6  58 40N 110 50W
Athabasca, L., Canada ..... 71 B7  59 15N 109 15W
Athabasca Sand Dunes △,
  Canada .............. 71 B7  59  4N 108 43W
Athboy, Ireland ......... 10 C5  53 37N   6 56W
Athenry, Ireland ......... 10 C3  53 18N   8 44W
Athens = Athínai, Greece .... 23 F10 37 58N  23 46 E
Athens, Ala., U.S.A. ...... 83 H2  34 48N  86 58W
Athens, Ga., U.S.A. ...... 83 J4  33 57N  83 23W
Athens, N.Y., U.S.A. ...... 85 D11 42 16N  73 49W
Athens, Ohio, U.S.A. ...... 82 F4  39 20N  82  6W
Athens, Pa., U.S.A. ...... 85 E8  41 57N  76 31W
Athens, Tenn., U.S.A. ..... 83 H3  35 27N  84 36W
Athens, Tex., U.S.A. ...... 81 J7  32 12N  95 51W
Atherley, Canada ........ 84 B5  44 37N  79 20W
Atherton, Australia ....... 62 B4  17 17S 145 30 E
Athienou, Cyprus ........ 25 D12 35  3N  33 32 E
Athínai, Greece ......... 23 F10 37 58N  23 46 E
Athlone, Ireland ......... 10 C4  53 25N   7 56W
Athna, Cyprus .......... 25 D12 35  3N  33 47 E
Athol, U.S.A. ........... 85 D12 42 36N  72 14W
Atholl, Forest of, U.K. ..... 11 E5  56 51N   3 50W
Atholville, Canada ....... 73 C6  47 59N  66 43W
Áthos, Greece .......... 23 D11 40  9N  24 22 E
Athy, Ireland ........... 10 C5  53  0N   7  0W
Ati, Chad ............. 51 F9  13 13N  18 20 E
Atiak, Uganda .......... 54 B3  3 12N  32  2 E
Atik L., Canada ......... 71 B9  55 15N  96  0W
Atikaki △, Canada ....... 71 C9  51 30N  95 31W
Atikameg →, Canada ...... 72 B3  52 30N  82 46W
Atikokan, Canada ........ 72 C1  48 45N  91 37W
Atikonak L., Canada ...... 73 B7  52 40N  64 32W
Atitlán △, Cent. Amer. ..... 87 E6  14 38N  91 10W
Atka, Russia ........... 29 C16 60 50N 151 48 E

Atka I., U.S.A. .......... 68 C2  52  7N 174 30W
Atkinson, U.S.A. ......... 80 D5  42 32N  98 59W
Atlanta, Ga., U.S.A. ...... 83 J3  33 45N  84 23W
Atlanta, Tex., U.S.A. ...... 81 J7  33  7N  94 10W
Atlantic, U.S.A. ......... 80 E7  41 24N  95  1W
Atlantic City, U.S.A. ...... 82 F8  39 21N  74 27W
Atlantic-Indian Basin, Antarctica  5 B4  60  0S  30  0 E
Atlantic-Indian Ridge, Atl. Oc.  5 B3  53  0S   5  0W
Atlantic Ocean .......... 2 E9   0  0  20  0W
Atlas Mts. = Haut Atlas, Morocco 50 B4  32 30N   5  0W
Atlin, Canada .......... 70 B2  59 31N 133 41W
Atlin →, Canada ........ 70 B2  59 10N 134 30W
Atlin, L., Canada ........ 70 B2  59 26N 133 45W
Atmore, U.S.A. ......... 83 K2  31  2N  87 29W
Atoka, U.S.A. .......... 81 H6  34 23N  96 8W
Atolia, U.S.A. .......... 79 K9  35 19N 117 37W
Atrai →, Bangla. ........ 43 G13 24  7N  89 22 E
Atrak = Atrek →, Turkmenistan 45 B8  37 35N  53 58 E
Atrauli, India .......... 42 E8  28  2N  78 20 E
Atrek →, Turkmenistan .... 45 B8  37 35N  53 58 E
Atsuta, Japan .......... 30 C10 43 24N 141 26 E
Attalla, U.S.A. ......... 83 H2  34  1N  86  6W
Attapu, Laos ........... 38 E6  14 48N 106 50 E
Attáviros, Greece ........ 25 C9  36 12N  27 50 E
Attawapiskat, Canada ..... 72 B3  52 56N  82 24W
Attawapiskat →, Canada ... 72 B3  52 57N  82 18W
Attawapiskat L., Canada ... 72 B2  52 18N  87 54W
Attica, Ind., U.S.A. ...... 82 E2  40 18N  87 15W
Attica, Ohio, U.S.A. ...... 84 E2  41  4N  82 53W
Attikamagen L., Canada .... 73 B6  55  0N  66 30W
Attleboro, U.S.A. ........ 85 E13 41 57N  71 17W
Attock, Pakistan ........ 42 C5  33 52N  72 20 E
Attopeu = Attapu, Laos ..... 38 E6  14 48N 106 50 E
Attu I., U.S.A. ......... 68 C1  52 55N 172 55 E
Attur, India ........... 40 P11 11 35N  78 30 E
Atuel →, Argentina ....... 94 D2  36 17S  66 50W
Åtvidaberg, Sweden ....... 9 G17 58 12N  16  0 E
Atwater, U.S.A. ......... 78 H6  37 21N 120 37W
Atwood, Canada ......... 84 C3  43 40N  81  1W
Atwood, U.S.A. ......... 80 F4  39 48N 101  3W
Atyraü, Kazakhstan ...... 19 E9  47  5N  52  0 E
Au Sable →, U.S.A. ...... 84 B1  44 25N  83 20W
Au Sable →, U.S.A. ...... 82 C4  44 25N  83 20W
Au Sable Forks, U.S.A. .... 85 B11 44 27N  73 41W
Au Sable Pt., U.S.A. ...... 84 B1  44 20N  83 20W
Aubagne, France ........ 20 E6  43 17N   5 37 E
Aubarca, C. d', Spain ..... 24 B7  39  4N   1 22 E
Aube →, France ........ 20 B5  48 34N   3 43 E
Auberry, U.S.A. ........ 78 H7  37  7N 119 29W
Auburn, Ala., U.S.A. ..... 83 J3  32 36N  85 29W
Auburn, Calif., U.S.A. .... 78 G5  38 54N 121  4W
Auburn, Ind., U.S.A. ..... 82 E3  41 22N  85  4W
Auburn, Maine, U.S.A. .... 83 C10 44  6N  70 14W
Auburn, N.Y., U.S.A. ..... 85 D8  42 56N  76 34W
Auburn, Nebr., U.S.A. .... 80 E7  40 23N  95 51W
Auburn, Pa., U.S.A. ..... 85 F8  40 36N  76  6W
Auburn, Wash., U.S.A. .... 78 C4  47 18N 122 14W
Auburndale, U.S.A. ...... 83 L5  28  4N  81 48W
Auburn Ra., Australia ..... 63 D5  25 15S 150 30 E
Aubusson, France ....... 20 D5  45 57N   2 11 E
Auch, France .......... 20 E4  43 39N   0 36 E
Auchterarder, U.K. ...... 11 E5  56 18N   3 41W
Auchtermuchty, U.K. ..... 11 E5  56 18N   3 14W
Auckland, N.Z. ......... 59 G5  36 52S 174 46 E
Auckland Is., Pac. Oc. .... 64 N8  50 40S 166  5 E
Aude →, France ........ 20 E5  43 13N   3 14 E
Auden, Canada ......... 72 B2  50 14N  87 53W
Audubon, U.S.A. ........ 80 E7  41 43N  94 56W
Augathella, Australia ..... 63 D4  25 48S 146 35 E
Aughnacloy, U.K. ....... 10 B5  54 25N   6 59W
Augrabies Falls, S. Africa ... 56 D3  28 35S  20  20 E
Augrabies Falls △, S. Africa .. 56 D3  28 40S  20  22 E
Augsburg, Germany ...... 16 D6  48 25N  10 52 E
Augusta, Australia ....... 61 F2  34 19S 115  9 E
Augusta, Italy ......... 22 F6  37 13N  15 13 E
Augusta, Ark., U.S.A. .... 81 H9  35 17N  91 22W
Augusta, Ga., U.S.A. ..... 83 J5  33 28N  81 58W
Augusta, Kans., U.S.A. .... 81 G6  37 41N  96 59W
Augusta, Maine, U.S.A. ... 69 D13 44 19N  69 47W
Augusta, Mont., U.S.A. ... 76 C7  47 30N 112 24W
Augustów, Poland ....... 17 B12 53 51N  23  0 E
Augustus, Mt., Australia ... 61 D2  24 20S 116 50 E
Augustus I., Australia .... 60 C3  15 20S 124 30 E
Aukum, U.S.A. ........ 78 G6  38 34N 120 43W
Auld, L., Australia ...... 60 D3  22 25S 123 50 E
Ault, U.S.A. .......... 80 E2  40 35N 104 44W
Aunis, France ......... 20 C3  46  5N   0 50W
Auponhia, Indonesia ..... 37 E7   1 58S 125 27 E
Aur, Pulau, Malaysia .... 39 L5   2 35N 104 10 E
Auraiya, India ........ 43 F8  26 28N  79 33 E
Aurangabad, Bihar, India .. 43 G11 24 45N  84 18 E
Aurangabad, Maharashtra, India 40 K9  19 50N  75 23 E
Aurich, Germany ....... 16 B4  53 28N   7 28 E
Aurillac, France ....... 20 D5  44 55N   2 26 E
Aurora, Canada ........ 84 C5  44  0N  79 28W
Aurora, S. Africa ...... 56 E2  39 44N 104 52W
Aurora, Colo., U.S.A. ... 80 F2  39 44N 104 52W
Aurora, Ill., U.S.A. .... 82 E1  41 45N  88 19W
Aurora, Mo., U.S.A. .... 81 G8  36 58N  93 43W
Aurora, N.Y., U.S.A. ... 85 D8  42 45N  76 42W
Aurora, Nebr., U.S.A. ... 80 E6  40 52N  98  0W
Aurora, Ohio, U.S.A. .... 84 E3  41 21N  81 20W
Aurukun, Australia ...... 62 A3  13 20S 141 45 E
Aus, Namibia .......... 56 D2  26 35S  16 12 E
Ausable →, Canada ..... 84 C3  43 19N  81 46W
Auschwitz = Oświęcim, Poland 17 C10 50  2N  19 11 E
Austin, Minn., U.S.A. .... 80 D8  43 40N  92 58W
Austin, Nev., U.S.A. .... 76 G5  39 30N 117  4W
Austin, Pa., U.S.A. ..... 84 E6  41 38N  78  6W
Austin, Tex., U.S.A. .... 81 K6  30 17N  97 45W
Austin, L., Australia ..... 61 E2  27 40S 118  0 E
Austin I., Canada ...... 71 A10 61 10N  94  0W
Austra, Norway ....... 8 D14 65  8N  11 55 E
Austral Is. = Tubuai Is.,
  French Polynesia ...... 65 K13 25  0S 150  0W
Austral Seamount Chain,
  Pac. Oc. ........... 65 K13 24  0S 150  0W
Australia ■, Oceania .... 64 K5  23  0S 135  0 E
Australian Capital Territory □,
  Australia .......... 63 F4  35 30S 149  0 E
Australind, Australia .... 61 F2  33 17S 115 42 E
Austria ■, Europe ...... 16 E8  47  0N  14 0 E
Austvågøy, Norway ..... 8 B16 68 20N  14 40 E
Autlán, Mexico ....... 86 D4  19 40N 104 30W
Autun, France ....... 20 C6  46 58N   4 17 E
Auvergne □, France .... 20 D5  45 20N   3 15 E
Auvergne, Mts. d', France .. 20 D5  45 20N   2 55 E
Auxerre, France ....... 20 C5  47 48N   3 32 E

Ava, U.S.A. ........... 81 G8  36 57N  92 40W
Avallon, France ........ 20 C5  47 30N   3 53 E
Avalon, U.S.A. ......... 79 M8  33 21N 118 20W
Avalon Pen., Canada ..... 73 C9  47 30N  53 20W
Avanos, Turkey ........ 44 B2  38 43N  34 51 E
Avaré, Brazil .......... 95 A6  23  4S  48 58W
Avawatz Mts., U.S.A. .... 79 K10 35 40N 116 30W
Aveiro, Brazil ......... 93 D7  3 10S  55  5W
Aveiro, Portugal ....... 21 B1  40 37N   8 38W
Āvej, Iran ........... 45 C6  35 40N  49 15 E
Avellaneda, Argentina .... 94 C4  34 50S  58 10W
Avellino, Italy ........ 22 D6  40 54N  14 47 E
Avenal, U.S.A. ........ 78 K6  36  0N 120  8W
Aversa, Italy ......... 22 D6  40 58N  14 12 E
Avery, U.S.A. ......... 76 C6  47 15N 115 49W
Aves, I. de, W. Indies .... 89 C7  15 45N  63 55W
Aves, Is. las, Venezuela ... 89 D6  12  0N  67 30W
Avesta, Sweden ........ 9 F17 60  9N  16 10 E
Avezzano, Italy ........ 22 C5  42  2N  13 25 E
Aviá Terai, Argentina .... 94 B3  26 45S  60 50W
Aviemore, U.K. ........ 11 D5  57 12N   3 50W
Avignon, France ....... 20 E6  43 57N   4 50 E
Avila, Spain .......... 21 B3  40 39N   4 43W
Avila Beach, U.S.A. ..... 79 K6  35 11N 120 44W
Avilés, Spain ......... 21 A3  43 35N   5 57W
Avis, U.S.A. .......... 84 E7  41 11N  77 19W
Avoca, U.S.A. ......... 63 F3  35 40S 143 43 E
Avoca →, Ireland ...... 10 D5  52 48N   6 10W
Avola, Canada ......... 70 C5  51 45N 119 19W
Avola, Italy .......... 22 F6  36 56N  15  7 E
Avon, U.S.A. .......... 84 D7  42 55N  77 45W
Avon →, Australia ...... 61 F2  31 40S 116  7 E
Avon →, Bristol, U.K. .... 13 F5  51 29N   2 41W
Avon →, Dorset, U.K. .... 13 G6  50 44N   1 46W
Avon →, Warks., U.K. .... 13 E5  52  0N   2  8W
Avon Park, U.S.A. ...... 83 M5  27 36N  81 31W
Avondale, Zimbabwe ..... 55 F3  17 43S  30 58 E
Avonlea, Canada ....... 71 D8  50  0N 105  0W
Avonmore, Canada ...... 85 A10 45 10N  74 58W
Avonmouth, U.K. ....... 13 F5  51 30N   2 42W
Avranches, France ...... 20 B3  48 40N   1 20W
A'waj →, Syria ........ 46 B5  33 23N  36 20 E
Awaji-Shima, Japan ..... 31 G7  34 30N 134 50 E
'Awālī, Bahrain ........ 45 E6  26  0N  50 30 E
Awantipur, India ....... 43 C6  33 55N  75  3 E
Awasa, Ethiopia ....... 47 F2   7  2N  38 28 E
Awash, Ethiopia ....... 47 F3   9  1N  40 10 E
Awatere →, N.Z. ....... 59 J5  41 37S 174 10 E
Awbārī, Libya ......... 51 C8  26 46N  12 57 E
Awbārī, Idehan, Libya ... 51 C8  27 10N  11 30 E
Awe, L., U.K. ......... 11 E3  56 17N   5 16W
Awjilah, Libya ........ 51 C10 29  8N  21  7 E
Axe →, U.K. .......... 13 F5  50 42N   3  4W
Axel Heiberg I., Canada ... 4 B3  80  0N  90  0W
Axim, Ghana ......... 50 H5   4 51N   2 15W
Axiós →, Greece ....... 23 D10 40 57N  22 35 E
Axminster, U.K. ....... 13 G4  50 46N   3  0W
Ayabaca, Peru ........ 92 D3   4 40S  79 53W
Ayabe, Japan ......... 31 G7  35 20N 135 20 E
Ayacucho, Argentina .... 94 D4  37  5S  58 20W
Ayacucho, Peru ....... 92 F4  13  0S  74  0W
Ayaguz, Kazakhstan ..... 28 E9  48 10N  80 10 E
Ayamonte, Spain ...... 21 D2  37 12N   7 24W
Ayan, Russia ......... 29 D14 56 30N 138 16 E
Ayaviri, Peru ........ 92 F4  14 50S  70 35W
Aydın, Turkey ........ 23 F12 37 51N  27 51 E
Ayer, U.S.A. ......... 85 D13 42 34N  71 35W
Ayer Hitam, Malaysia .... 39 c   5 24N 100 16 E
Ayer's Cliff, Canada .... 85 A12 45 10N  72  3W
Ayers Rock, Australia .... 61 E5  25 23S 131  5 E
Ayia Aikaterini, Ákra, Greece 25 A3  39 50N  19 50 E
Ayia Dhéka, Greece ..... 25 D6  35  3N  24 58 E
Ayia Gálini, Greece ..... 25 D6  35  6N  24 41 E
Ayia Napa, Cyprus ..... 25 E13 34 59N  34  0 E
Ayia Phyla, Cyprus ..... 25 E12 34 43N  33  1 E
Ayia Varvára, Greece .... 25 D7  35  8N  25  1 E
Áyios Amvrósios, Cyprus .. 25 D12 35 20N  33 35 E
Áyios Evstrátios, Greece .. 23 E11 39 34N  24 58 E
Áyios Ioánnis, Ákra, Greece 25 D7  35 20N  25 40 E
Áyios Isídhoros, Greece ... 25 C9  36  9N  27 51 E
Áyios Matthaíos, Greece .. 25 B3  39 30N  19 47 E
Áyios Nikólaos, Greece ... 25 D7  35 11N  25 41 E
Áyios Seryios, Cyprus ... 25 D12 35 12N  33 53 E
Áyios Theodhoros, Cyprus . 25 D13 35 22N  34  1 E
Aykino, Russia ........ 18 B8  62 15N  49 56 E
Aylesbury, U.K. ....... 13 F7  51 49N   0 49W
Aylmer, Canada ....... 84 D4  42 46N  80 59W
Aylmer, L., Canada ..... 68 B8  64  0N 110  8W
'Ayn, Wādī al, Oman .... 45 F7  22 15S  55 28 E
Ayn Dār, Si. Arabia .... 45 E7  25 55N  49 10 E
Ayn Zālah, Iraq ....... 44 B4  36 45N  42 35 E
Ayolas, Paraguay ...... 94 B4  27 10S  56 59W
Ayon, Ostrov, Russia .... 29 C17 69 50N 169  0 E
'Ayoûn el 'Atroûs, Mauritania 50 E4  16 38N   9 37W
Ayr, Australia ........ 62 B4  19 35S 147 25 E
Ayr, Canada ......... 84 C4  43 17N  80 27W
Ayr, U.K. ........... 11 F4  55 28N   4 38W
Ayr →, U.K. ......... 11 F4  55 28N   4 38W
Ayre, Pt. of, I. of Man ... 12 C3  54 25N   4 21W
Aytos, Bulgaria ....... 23 C12 42 42N  27 16 E
Ayu, Kepulauan, Indonesia .. 37 D8   0 35N 131  5 E
Ayutla, Guatemala ..... 88 D1  14 40N  92 10W
Ayutla, Mexico ....... 87 D5  16 58N  99 17W
Ayvacık, Turkey ...... 23 E12 39 36N  26 24 E
Ayvalık, Turkey ...... 23 E12 39 20N  26 46 E
Az Zabadānī, Syria .... 46 B5  33 43N  36  5 E
Az Ẓāhirīyah, West Bank .. 46 D3  31 25N  34 58 E
Aẓ Ẓahrān, Si. Arabia ... 45 E6  26 10N  50  7 E
Az Zarqā, Jordan ...... 46 C5  32  5N  36  4 E
Az Zarqā □, Jordan .... 46 C5  32  5N  36  4 E
Az Zarqā, U.A.E. ...... 45 E7  24 53N  53  4 E
Az Zāwiyah, Libya ..... 51 B8  32 52N  12 56 E
Az Zilfī, Si. Arabia .... 44 E5  26 12N  44  52 E
Az Zubayr, Iraq ....... 44 D5  30 26N  47 40 E
Azamgarh, India ...... 43 F10 26  5N  83 13 E
Azángaro, Peru ....... 92 F4  14 55S  70 13W
Āzar Shahr, Iran ...... 44 B5  37 45N  45 59 E
Āzarbāyjān = Azerbaijan ■, Asia 19 F8  40 20N  48  0 E
Āzarbāyjān-e Gharbī □, Iran 44 B5  37  0N  44 30 E
Āzarbāyjān-e Sharqī □, Iran 44 B5  37 20N  47  0 E
A'zāz, Syria ......... 44 B3  36 36N  37  4 E
Azbine = Aïr, Niger .... 50 E7  18 30N   8  0 E

Azerbaijan ■, Asia ...... 19 F8  40 20N  48  0 E
Azerbaijchan = Azerbaijan ■,
  Asia .............. 19 F8  40 20N  48  0 E
Azimganj, India ....... 43 G13 24 14N  88 16 E
Azogues, Ecuador ...... 92 D3   2 35S  78  0W
Azores = Açores, Is. dos, Atl. Oc. 50 A1  38  0N  27  0W
Azov, Russia ......... 19 E6  47  3N  39 25 E
Azov, Sea of, Europe .... 19 E6  46  0N  36 30 E
Azovskoye More = Azov, Sea of,
  Europe ............ 19 E6  46  0N  36 30 E
Azraq ash Shīshān, Jordan . 46 D5  31 50N  36  49 E
Aztec, U.S.A. ......... 77 H10 36 49N 107 59W
Azúa de Compostela, Dom. Rep. 89 C5  18 25N  70 44W
Azuero, Pen. de, Panama .. 88 E3   7 30N  80 30W
Azul, Argentina ....... 94 D4  36 42S  59 43W
Azusa, U.S.A. ........ 79 L9  34  8N 117 52W

## B

Ba Be △, Vietnam ...... 38 A5  22 25N 105 37 E
Ba Don, Vietnam ...... 38 D6  17 45N 106 26 E
Ba Dong, Vietnam ..... 39 H6   9 40N 106 33 E
Ba Ngoi = Cam Lam, Vietnam 39 G7  11 54N 109 10 E
Ba Tri, Vietnam ....... 39 G6  10  2N 106 36 E
Ba Vì △, Vietnam ...... 38 B5  21  1N 105 22 E
Ba Xian = Bazhou, China .. 34 E9  39  8N 116 22 E
Baa, Indonesia ....... 37 F6  10 50S 123  0 E
Baardeere = Bardera,
  Somali Rep. ........ 47 G3   2  20N  42 27 E
Baarle-Nassau, Belgium ... 15 C4  51 27N   4 56 E
Bab el Mandeb, Red Sea ... 47 E3  12 35N  43 25 E
Bābā, Koh-i-, Afghan. .... 40 B5  34 30N  67  0 E
Baba Burnu, Turkey ..... 23 E12 39 29N  26  2 E
Bābā Kalū, Iran ....... 45 D6  30  7N  50 49 E
Babadag, Romania ...... 17 F15 44 53N  28 44 E
Babaeski, Turkey ...... 23 D12 41 26N  27  6 E
Babahoyo, Ecuador ..... 92 D3   1 40S  79 30W
Babai = Sarju →, India ... 43 F9  27 21N  81 23 E
Babar, Indonesia ...... 37 F7   8  0S 129 30 E
Babar, Pakistan ....... 42 D3  31  7N  69 32 E
Babarkach, Pakistan .... 42 E3  29 45N  68  0 E
Babb, U.S.A. ......... 76 B7  48 51N 113 27W
Baberu, India ........ 43 G9  25 33N  80 43 E
Babi Besar, Pulau, Malaysia . 39 L4   2 25N 103 59 E
Babil □, iraq ......... 44 C5  32 30N  44 30 E
Babinda, Australia ..... 62 B4  17 20S 145 56 E
Babine, Canada ....... 70 B3  55 22N 126 37W
Babine →, Canada ..... 70 B3  55 45N 127 44W
Babine L., Canada ..... 70 C3  54 48N 126  0W
Babo, Indonesia ...... 37 E8   2 30S 133 30 E
Bābol, Iran ......... 45 B7  36 40N  52 50 E
Bābol Sar, Iran ....... 45 B7  36 45N  52 45 E
Babruysk, Belarus ..... 17 B15 53 10N  29 15 E
Babuhri, India ....... 42 F3  26 49N  69 43 E
Babusar Pass, Pakistan ... 43 B5  35 12N  73 59 E
Babuyan Chan., Phil. .... 37 A6  18 40N 121 30 E
Babylon, Iraq ........ 44 C5  32 34N  44 22 E
Bac Can, Vietnam ..... 38 A5  22  8N 105 49 E
Bac Giang, Vietnam .... 38 B6  21 16N 106 11 E
Bac Lieu, Vietnam ..... 39 H5   9 17N 105 43 E
Bac Ninh, Vietnam .... 38 B6  21 13N 106  4 E
Bac Phan, Vietnam .... 38 B5  22  0N 105  0 E
Bac Quang, Vietnam .... 38 A5  22 30N 104 48 E
Bacabal, Brazil ...... 93 D10  4 15S  44 45W
Bacalar, Mexico ...... 87 D7  18 50N  87 27W
Bacan, Kepulauan, Indonesia 37 E7   0 35S 127 30 E
Bacarra, Phil. ....... 37 A6  18 15N 120 37 E
Bacău, Romania ...... 17 E14 46 35N  26 55 E
Bacerac, Mexico ...... 86 A3  30 18N 108 50W
Bach Long Vi, Dao, Vietnam 38 B6  20 10N 107 40 E
Bach Ma △, Vietnam ... 38 D6  16 11N 107 49 E
Bachhwara, India ..... 43 G11 25 35N  85 54 E
Back →, Canada ..... 68 B9  65 10N 104  0W
Bacolod, Phil. ....... 37 B6  10 40N 122 57 E
Bacuk, Malaysia ...... 39 J4   6  4N 102 25 E
Bād, Iran .......... 45 C7  33 41N  52  1 E
Bad Axe, U.S.A. ...... 84 C2  43 48N  83  0W
Bad Ischl, Austria .... 16 E7  47 44N  13 38 E
Bad Kissingen, Germany .. 16 C6  50 11N  10  4 E
Bad Lands, U.S.A. .... 80 D3  43 40N 102 10W
Bada Barabil, India .... 43 H11 22  7N  85 24 E
Badagara, India ...... 40 P9  11 35N  75 40 E
Badajós, L., Brazil .... 92 D6   3 15S  62 50W
Badajoz, Spain ...... 21 C2  38 50N   6 59W
Badakhshān □, Afghan. .. 40 A7  36 30N  71  0 E
Badalona, Spain ...... 21 B7  41 26N   2 15 E
Badalzai, Afghan. ..... 42 E1  29 50N  65 35 E
Badampahar, India .... 41 H15 22 10N  86 10 E
Badanah, Si. Arabia .... 44 D4  30 58N  41 30 E
Badarinath, India ..... 43 D8  30 45N  79 30 E
Badas, Kepulauan, Indonesia 36 D3   0 45N 107  5 E
Baddo →, Pakistan .... 40 F4  28  0N 64 20 E
Bade, Indonesia ...... 37 F9   7 10S 139 35 E
Baden, Austria ...... 16 D9  48  1N  16 13 E
Baden, U.S.A. ....... 84 F4  40 38N  80 14W
Baden-Baden, Germany .. 16 D5  48 44N   8 13 E
Baden-Württemberg □, Germany 16 D5  48 20N   8 40 E
Badgastein, Austria ... 16 E7  47  7N  13  9 E
Badger, Canada ...... 73 C8  49  0N  56  4W
Badger, U.S.A. ...... 78 J7  36 38N 119  1W
Bādghīs □, Afghan. ... 40 B3  35  0N  63  0 E
Badgingarra △, Australia .. 61 F2  30 23S 115 22 E
Badgom, India ...... 43 B6  34  1N  74 45 E
Badin, Pakistan ..... 42 G3  24 38N  68 54 E
Badlands △, U.S.A. .... 80 D3  43 38N 102 56W
Badrah, Iraq ........ 44 C5  33  6N  45 58 E
Badrinath, India ..... 43 D8  30 45N  79 29 E
Badulla, Sri Lanka .... 40 R12  7  1N  81  7 E
Baduria, Selat, Indonesia .. 37 K18  8 40S 115 22 E
Baena, Spain ....... 21 D3  37 37N   4 20W
Baeza, Spain ....... 21 D4  37 57N   3 25W
Baffin B., Canada .... 69 A13 72  0N  64  0W
Baffin I., Canada .... 69 B12 68  0N  75  0W
Bafing →, Mali ..... 50 F3  13 49N  10 50W
Bafliyūn, Syria ..... 44 B3  36 37N  36 59 E
Bafoulabé, Mali .... 50 F3  13 50N  10 55W
Bafoussam, Cameroon .. 52 C2  5 28N  10 25 E
Bāfq, Iran ........ 45 D7  31 40N  55 25 E
Bafra, Turkey ...... 19 F5  41 34N  35 54 E
Bāft, Iran ........ 45 D8  29 15N  56 38 E
Bafwasende, Dem. Rep. of
  the Congo ........ 54 B2   1  3N  27  5 E
Bagamoyo, Tanzania .. 54 D4   6 28S  38 55 E

Bagan Datoh, Malaysia ... 39 L3 3 59N 100 47 E
Bagan Serai, Malaysia ... 39 K3 5 1N 100 32 E
Baganga, Phil. ... 37 C7 7 34N 126 33 E
Bagani, Namibia ... 56 B3 18 7S 21 41 E
Bagansiapiapi, Indonesia ... 36 D2 2 12N 100 50 E
Bagasra, India ... 42 J4 21 30N 71 0 E
Bagaud, India ... 42 H6 22 19N 75 53 E
Bagdad, U.S.A. ... 79 L11 34 35N 115 53W
Bagdarin, Russia ... 29 D12 54 26N 113 36 E
Bagé, Brazil ... 95 C5 31 20S 54 15W
Bagenalstown = Muine Bheag, Ireland ... 10 D5 52 42N 6 58W
Baggs, U.S.A. ... 76 F10 41 2N 107 39W
Bagh, Pakistan ... 43 C5 33 59N 73 45 E
Baghain →, India ... 43 G9 25 32N 81 1 E
Baghdād, Iraq ... 44 C5 33 20N 44 30 E
Bagheria, Italy ... 22 E5 38 5N 13 30 E
Baghlān, Afghan. ... 40 A6 32 12N 68 46 E
Baghlān □, Afghan. ... 40 B6 36 0N 68 30 E
Bagley, U.S.A. ... 80 B7 47 32N 95 24W
Bago = Pegu, Burma ... 41 L20 17 20N 96 29 E
Bagodar, India ... 43 G11 24 5N 85 52 E
Bagrationovsk, Russia ... 9 J19 54 23N 20 39 E
Baguio, Phil. ... 37 A6 16 26N 120 34 E
Bah, India ... 43 F8 26 53N 78 36 E
Bahadurganj, India ... 43 F12 26 16N 87 49 E
Bahadurgarh, India ... 42 E7 28 40N 76 57 E
Bahama, Canal Viejo de, W. Indies ... 88 B4 22 10N 77 30W
Bahamas ■, N. Amer. ... 89 B5 24 0N 75 0W
Baharampur, India ... 43 G13 24 2N 88 27 E
Baharu Pandan = Pandan, Malaysia ... 39 d 1 32N 103 46 E
Bahawalnagar, Pakistan ... 42 E5 30 0N 73 15 E
Bahawalpur, Pakistan ... 42 E4 29 24N 71 40 E
Baheri, India ... 43 E8 28 45N 79 34 E
Bahgul →, India ... 43 F8 27 45N 79 36 E
Bahi, Tanzania ... 54 D4 5 58S 35 21 E
Bahi Swamp, Tanzania ... 54 D4 6 10S 35 0 E
Bahía = Salvador, Brazil ... 93 F11 13 0S 38 30W
Bahía □, Brazil ... 93 F10 12 0S 42 0W
Bahía, Is. de la, Honduras ... 88 C2 16 45N 86 15W
Bahía Blanca, Argentina ... 94 D3 38 35S 62 13W
Bahía de Caráquez, Ecuador ... 92 D2 0 40S 80 27W
Bahía Honda, Cuba ... 88 B3 22 54N 83 10W
Bahía Laura, Argentina ... 96 F3 48 10S 66 30W
Bahía Negra, Paraguay ... 92 H7 20 5S 58 5W
Bahir Dar, Ethiopia ... 47 E2 11 37N 37 10 E
Bahmanzād, Iran ... 45 D6 31 15N 51 47 E
Bahr el Ghazâl □, Sudan ... 51 G11 7 0N 28 0 E
Bahraich, India ... 43 F9 27 38N 81 37 E
Bahrain ■, Asia ... 45 E6 26 0N 50 35 E
Bahror, India ... 42 F7 27 51N 76 20 E
Bāhū Kalāt, Iran ... 45 E9 25 43N 61 25 E
Bai Bung, Mui = Ca Mau, Mui, Vietnam ... 39 H5 8 38N 104 44 E
Bai Duc, Vietnam ... 38 C5 18 3N 105 49 E
Bai Thuong, Vietnam ... 38 C5 19 54N 105 23 E
Baia Mare, Romania ... 17 E12 47 40N 23 35 E
Baião, Brazil ... 93 D9 2 40S 49 40W
Baïbokoum, Chad ... 51 G9 7 46N 15 43 E
Baicheng, China ... 35 B12 45 38N 122 42 E
Baidoa, Somali Rep. ... 47 G3 3 8N 43 30 E
Baie-Comeau, Canada ... 73 C6 49 12N 68 10W
Baie-St-Paul, Canada ... 73 C5 47 28N 70 32W
Baie-Trinité, Canada ... 73 C6 49 25N 67 20W
Baie Verte, Canada ... 73 C8 49 55N 56 12W
Baihar, India ... 43 H9 22 6N 80 33 E
Baihe, China ... 34 H6 32 50N 110 5 E
Baijnath, India ... 43 E8 29 55N 79 37 E
Baikal, L. = Baykal, Oz., Russia ... 29 D11 53 0N 108 0 E
Baikunthpur, India ... 43 H10 23 15N 82 33 E
Baile Atha Cliath = Dublin, Ireland ... 10 C5 53 21N 6 15W
Băileşti, Romania ... 17 F12 44 1N 23 20 E
Bainbridge, Ga., U.S.A. ... 83 K3 30 55N 84 35W
Bainbridge, N.Y., U.S.A. ... 85 D9 42 18N 75 29W
Baing, Indonesia ... 37 F6 10 14S 120 34 E
Bainiu, China ... 34 H7 32 50N 112 15 E
Bā'ir, Jordan ... 46 E5 30 45N 36 55 E
Bairiki = Tarawa, Kiribati ... 64 G9 1 30N 173 0 E
Bairin Youqi, China ... 35 C10 43 30N 118 35 E
Bairin Zuoqi, China ... 35 C10 43 58N 119 15 E
Bairnsdale, Australia ... 63 F4 37 48S 147 36 E
Baisha, China ... 34 G7 34 20N 112 32 E
Baitadi, Nepal ... 43 E9 29 35N 80 25 E
Baiyin, China ... 34 F3 36 45N 104 14 E
Baiyu Shan, China ... 34 F4 37 15N 107 30 E
Baj Baj, India ... 43 H13 22 30N 88 5 E
Baja, Hungary ... 17 E10 46 12N 18 59 E
Baja, Pta., Mexico ... 86 B1 29 50N 116 0W
Baja California, Mexico ... 86 A1 31 10N 115 12W
Baja California □, Mexico ... 86 B2 30 0N 115 0W
Baja California Sur □, Mexico ... 86 B2 25 50N 111 50W
Bajag, India ... 43 H9 22 40N 81 21 E
Bajamar, Canary Is. ... 24 F3 28 33N 16 20W
Bajana, India ... 42 H4 23 7N 71 49 E
Bajatrejo, Indonesia ... 37 J17 8 29S 114 19 E
Bajera, Indonesia ... 37 J18 8 31S 115 2 E
Bajgīrān, Iran ... 45 B8 37 36N 58 24 E
Bajimba, Mt., Australia ... 63 D5 29 17S 152 6 E
Bajo Nuevo, Caribbean ... 88 C4 15 40N 78 50W
Bajoga, Nigeria ... 51 F8 10 57N 11 20 E
Bajool, Australia ... 62 C5 23 40S 150 35 E
Bakel, Senegal ... 50 F3 14 56N 12 20W
Baker, Calif., U.S.A. ... 79 K10 35 16N 116 4W
Baker, Mont., U.S.A. ... 80 B2 46 22N 104 17W
Baker, L., Canada ... 68 B10 64 0N 96 0W
Baker, Mt., U.S.A. ... 76 B3 48 50N 121 49W
Baker City, U.S.A. ... 76 D5 44 47N 117 50W
Baker I., Pac. Oc. ... 64 G10 0 10N 176 35W
Baker I., U.S.A. ... 70 B2 55 20N 133 40W
Baker L., Australia ... 61 E4 26 54S 126 5 E
Baker Lake, Canada ... 68 B10 64 20N 96 3W
Bakers Creek, Australia ... 62 C4 21 13S 149 7 E
Bakers Dozen Is., Canada ... 72 A4 56 45N 78 45W
Bakersfield, Calif., U.S.A. ... 79 K8 35 23N 119 1W
Bakersfield, Vt., U.S.A. ... 85 B12 44 45N 72 48W
Bākhtarān, Iran ... 44 C5 34 23N 47 0 E
Bakı, Azerbaijan ... 19 F8 40 29N 49 56 E
Bakkafjörður, Iceland ... 8 C6 66 2N 14 48W
Bakony, Hungary ... 17 E9 47 10N 17 30 E
Bakony Forest = Bakony, Hungary ... 17 E9 47 10N 17 30 E
Bakouma, C.A.R. ... 52 C4 5 40N 22 56 E
Bakswaho, India ... 43 G8 24 15N 79 18 E
Baku = Bakı, Azerbaijan ... 19 F8 40 29N 49 56 E

Bakutis Coast, Antarctica ... 5 D15 74 0S 120 0W
Baky = Bakı, Azerbaijan ... 19 F8 40 29N 49 56 E
Bala, Canada ... 84 A5 45 1N 79 37W
Bala, U.K. ... 12 E4 52 54N 3 36W
Bala, L., U.K. ... 12 E4 52 53N 3 37W
Balabac I., Phil. ... 36 C5 8 0N 117 0 E
Balabac Str., E. Indies ... 36 C5 7 53N 117 5 E
Balabagh, Afghan. ... 42 B4 34 25N 70 12 E
Ba'labakk, Lebanon ... 46 B5 34 0N 36 10 E
Balabalangan, Kepulauan, Indonesia ... 36 E5 2 20S 117 30 E
Balad, Iraq ... 44 C5 34 1N 44 9 E
Balad Rūz, Iraq ... 44 C5 33 42N 45 5 E
Bālādeh, Fārs, Iran ... 45 D6 29 17N 51 56 E
Bālādeh, Māzandaran, Iran ... 45 B6 36 12N 51 48 E
Balaghat, India ... 40 J12 21 49N 80 12 E
Balaghat Ra., India ... 40 K10 18 50N 76 30 E
Balaguer, Spain ... 21 B6 41 50N 0 50 E
Balaklava, Ukraine ... 19 F5 44 30N 33 30 E
Balakovo, Russia ... 18 D8 52 4N 47 55 E
Balamau, India ... 43 F9 27 10N 80 21 E
Balancán, Mexico ... 87 D6 17 48N 91 32W
Balashov, Russia ... 19 D7 51 30N 43 10 E
Balasinor, India ... 42 H5 22 57N 73 23 E
Balasore = Baleshwar, India ... 41 J15 21 35N 87 3 E
Balaton, Hungary ... 17 E9 46 50N 17 40 E
Balbina, Reprêsa de, Brazil ... 92 D7 2 0S 59 30W
Balboa, Panama ... 88 E4 8 57N 79 34W
Balbriggan, Ireland ... 10 C5 53 37N 6 11W
Balcarce, Argentina ... 94 D4 38 0S 58 10W
Balcarres, Canada ... 71 C8 50 50N 103 35W
Balchik, Bulgaria ... 23 C13 43 28N 28 11 E
Balclutha, N.Z. ... 59 M2 46 15S 169 45 E
Balcones Escarpment, U.S.A. ... 81 L5 29 30N 99 15W
Bald Hd., Australia ... 61 G2 35 6S 118 1 E
Bald I., Australia ... 61 F2 34 57S 118 27 E
Bald Knob, U.S.A. ... 81 H9 35 19N 91 34W
Baldock L., Canada ... 71 B9 56 33N 97 57W
Baldwin, Mich., U.S.A. ... 82 D3 43 54N 85 51W
Baldwin, Pa., U.S.A. ... 84 F5 40 23N 79 59W
Baldwinsville, U.S.A. ... 85 C8 43 10N 76 20W
Baldy Mt., U.S.A. ... 76 B9 48 9N 109 39W
Baldy Peak, U.S.A. ... 77 K9 33 54N 109 34W
Baleares, Is., Spain ... 24 B10 39 30N 3 0 E
Balearic Is. = Baleares, Is., Spain ... 24 B10 39 30N 3 0 E
Baleine = Whale →, Canada ... 73 A6 58 15N 67 40W
Baleine, Petite R. de la →, Canada ... 72 A4 56 0N 76 45W
Baler, Phil. ... 37 A6 15 46N 121 34 E
Baleshare, U.K. ... 11 D1 57 31N 7 22W
Baleshwar, India ... 41 J15 21 35N 87 3 E
Balfate, Honduras ... 88 C2 15 48N 86 25W
Bali, Greece ... 25 D6 35 25N 24 47 E
Bali, India ... 42 G5 25 11N 73 17 E
Bali, Indonesia ... 36 F4 8 20S 115 0 E
Bali □, Indonesia ... 36 F5 8 20S 115 0 E
Bali, Selat, Indonesia ... 37 J17 8 18S 114 25 E
Bali Sea, Indonesia ... 37 J17 8 0S 115 0 E
Baliapal, India ... 43 J12 21 40N 87 17 E
Balik Pulau, Malaysia ... 39 c 5 21N 100 14 E
Balikeşir, Turkey ... 23 E12 39 39N 27 53 E
Balikpapan, Indonesia ... 36 E5 1 10S 116 55 E
Balimbing, Phil. ... 37 C5 5 5N 119 58 E
Baling, Malaysia ... 39 K3 5 41N 100 55 E
Balipara, India ... 41 F18 26 50N 92 45 E
Balkan Mts. = Stara Planina, Bulgaria ... 23 C10 43 15N 23 0 E
Balkhash = Balqash, Kazakhstan ... 28 E8 46 50N 74 50 E
Balkhash, Ozero = Balqash Köl, Kazakhstan ... 28 E8 46 0N 74 50 E
Balla, Bangla. ... 41 G17 24 10N 91 35 E
Ballachulish, U.K. ... 11 E3 56 41N 5 8W
Balladonia, Australia ... 61 F3 32 27S 123 51 E
Ballaghaderreen, Ireland ... 10 C3 53 55N 8 34W
Ballarat, Australia ... 63 F3 37 33S 143 50 E
Ballard, L., Australia ... 61 E3 29 20S 120 40 E
Ballater, U.K. ... 11 D5 57 3N 3 3W
Ballena Gris = Ojo de Liebre □, Mexico ... 86 B2 27 50N 114 0W
Ballenas, Canal de, Mexico ... 86 B2 29 10N 113 45W
Balleny Is., Antarctica ... 5 C11 66 30S 163 0 E
Ballia, India ... 43 G11 25 46N 84 12 E
Ballina, Australia ... 63 D5 28 50S 153 31 E
Ballina, Ireland ... 10 B2 54 7N 9 9W
Ballinasloe, Ireland ... 10 C3 53 20N 8 13W
Ballinger, U.S.A. ... 81 K5 31 45N 99 57W
Ballinrobe, Ireland ... 10 C2 53 38N 9 13W
Ballinskelligs B., Ireland ... 10 E1 51 48N 10 13W
Ballston Spa, U.S.A. ... 85 D11 43 0N 73 51W
Ballybunion, Ireland ... 10 D2 52 31N 9 40W
Ballycastle, U.K. ... 10 A5 55 12N 6 15W
Ballyclare, U.K. ... 10 B5 54 46N 6 0W
Ballyhaunis, Ireland ... 10 C3 53 46N 8 46W
Ballymena, U.K. ... 10 B5 54 52N 6 17W
Ballymoney, U.K. ... 10 B5 55 5N 6 31W
Ballymote, Ireland ... 10 B3 54 5N 8 31W
Ballynahinch, U.K. ... 10 B6 54 24N 5 54W
Ballyquintin Pt., U.K. ... 10 B6 54 20N 5 30W
Ballyshannon, Ireland ... 10 B3 54 30N 8 11W
Balmaceda, Chile ... 96 F2 46 0S 71 50W
Balmertown, Canada ... 71 C10 51 4N 93 41W
Balmoral, Australia ... 63 F3 37 15S 141 48 E
Balmorhea, U.S.A. ... 81 K3 30 59N 103 45W
Balochistan = Baluchistan □, Pakistan ... 40 F4 27 30N 65 0 E
Balonne →, Australia ... 63 D4 28 47S 147 56 E
Balotra, India ... 42 G5 25 50N 72 14 E
Balqash, Kazakhstan ... 28 E8 46 50N 74 50 E
Balqash Köl, Kazakhstan ... 28 E8 46 0N 74 50 E
Balrampur, India ... 43 F10 27 30N 82 20 E
Balranald, Australia ... 63 E3 34 38S 143 33 E
Balsas, Mexico ... 87 D5 18 0N 99 40W
Balsas →, Brazil ... 93 E9 7 15S 44 35W
Balsas →, Mexico ... 86 D4 17 55N 102 10W
Balta, Ukraine ... 17 D15 48 2N 29 45 E
Bălți, Moldova ... 17 E14 47 48N 27 58 E
Baltic Sea, Europe ... 9 H18 57 0N 19 0 E
Baltimore, Ireland ... 10 E2 51 29N 9 22W
Baltimore, Md., U.S.A. ... 82 F7 39 17N 76 37W
Baltimore, Ohio, U.S.A. ... 84 G2 39 51N 82 36W
Baltit, Pakistan ... 43 A6 36 15N 74 40 E
Baltiysk, Russia ... 9 J18 54 41N 19 58 E
Baluchistan □, Pakistan ... 40 F4 27 30N 65 0 E
Balurghat, India ... 43 G13 25 15N 88 44 E
Balvi, Latvia ... 9 H22 57 8N 27 15 E
Balya, Turkey ... 23 E12 39 44N 27 35 E
Bam, Iran ... 45 D8 29 7N 58 14 E

Bama, Nigeria ... 51 F8 11 33N 13 41 E
Bamaga, Australia ... 62 A3 10 50S 142 25 E
Bamaji L., Canada ... 72 B1 51 9N 91 25W
Bamako, Mali ... 50 F4 12 34N 7 55W
Bambari, C.A.R. ... 52 C4 5 40N 20 35 E
Bambaroo, Australia ... 62 B4 18 50S 146 10 E
Bamberg, Germany ... 16 D6 49 54N 10 54 E
Bamberg, U.S.A. ... 83 J5 33 18N 81 2W
Bambili, Dem. Rep. of the Congo ... 54 B2 3 40N 26 0 E
Bamburgh, U.K. ... 12 B6 55 37N 1 43W
Bamenda, Cameroon ... 52 C2 5 57N 10 11 E
Bamfield, Canada ... 70 D3 48 45N 125 10W
Bāmiān □, Afghan. ... 40 B5 35 0N 67 0 E
Bamiancheng, China ... 35 C13 43 15N 124 2 E
Bampūr, Iran ... 45 E9 27 15N 60 21 E
Ban Ao Tu Khun, Thailand ... 39 a 8 9N 98 20 E
Ban Ban, Laos ... 38 C4 19 31N 103 30 E
Ban Bang Hin, Thailand ... 39 H2 9 32N 98 35 E
Ban Bang Khu, Thailand ... 39 a 7 57N 98 23 E
Ban Bang Rong, Thailand ... 39 a 8 3N 98 25 E
Ban Bo Phut, Thailand ... 39 b 9 33N 100 2 E
Ban Chaweng, Thailand ... 39 b 9 32N 100 3 E
Ban Chiang Klang, Thailand ... 38 C3 19 25N 100 55 E
Ban Chik, Laos ... 38 D4 17 15N 102 22 E
Ban Choho, Thailand ... 38 E4 15 2N 102 9 E
Ban Dan Lan Hoi, Thailand ... 38 D2 17 0N 99 35 E
Ban Don = Surat Thani, Thailand ... 39 H2 9 6N 99 20 E
Ban Don, Vietnam ... 38 F6 12 53N 107 48 E
Ban Don, Ao →, Thailand ... 39 H2 9 20N 99 25 E
Ban Dong, Thailand ... 38 C3 19 30N 100 59 E
Ban Hong, Thailand ... 38 C2 18 18N 98 50 E
Ban Hua Thanon, Thailand ... 39 b 9 26N 100 1 E
Ban Kaeng, Thailand ... 38 D3 17 29N 100 7 E
Ban Kantang, Thailand ... 39 J2 7 25N 99 31 E
Ban Karon, Thailand ... 39 a 7 51N 98 18 E
Ban Kata, Thailand ... 39 a 7 50N 98 18 E
Ban Keun, Laos ... 38 C4 18 22N 102 35 E
Ban Khai, Thailand ... 38 F3 12 46N 101 18 E
Ban Kheun, Laos ... 38 B3 20 13N 101 7 E
Ban Khlong Khian, Thailand ... 39 a 8 10N 98 26 E
Ban Khlong Kua, Thailand ... 39 J3 6 57N 100 8 E
Ban Khuan Mao, Thailand ... 39 J2 7 50N 99 37 E
Ban Ko Yai Chim, Thailand ... 39 G2 11 17N 99 26 E
Ban Kok, Thailand ... 38 D4 16 40N 103 40 E
Ban Laem, Thailand ... 38 F2 13 13N 99 59 E
Ban Lamai, Thailand ... 39 b 9 28N 100 3 E
Ban Lao Ngam, Laos ... 38 E6 15 28N 106 10 E
Ban Le Kathe, Thailand ... 38 E2 15 49N 98 53 E
Ban Lo Po Noi, Thailand ... 39 a 8 1N 98 34 E
Ban Mae Chedi, Thailand ... 38 C2 19 11N 99 31 E
Ban Mae Laeng, Thailand ... 38 B2 20 1N 99 17 E
Ban Mae Nam, Thailand ... 39 b 9 34N 100 0 E
Ban Mae Sariang, Thailand ... 38 C1 18 10N 97 56 E
Ban Mê Thuôt = Buon Ma Thuot, Vietnam ... 38 F7 12 40N 108 3 E
Ban Mi, Thailand ... 38 E3 15 3N 100 32 E
Ban Muong Mo, Laos ... 38 C4 19 4N 103 58 E
Ban Na Bo, Thailand ... 39 b 9 19N 99 41 E
Ban Na Mo, Laos ... 38 D5 17 7N 105 40 E
Ban Na San, Thailand ... 39 H2 8 53N 99 52 E
Ban Na Tong, Thailand ... 38 B3 20 56N 101 47 E
Ban Nam Bac, Laos ... 38 B4 20 38N 102 20 E
Ban Nam Ma, Laos ... 38 A3 22 2N 101 37 E
Ban Ngang, Laos ... 38 E6 15 59N 106 11 E
Ban Nong Bok, Laos ... 38 D5 17 5N 104 48 E
Ban Nong Boua, Laos ... 38 E6 15 40N 106 33 E
Ban Nong Pling, Thailand ... 38 E3 15 40N 100 10 E
Ban Pak Chan, Thailand ... 39 G2 10 32N 98 51 E
Ban Patong, Thailand ... 39 a 7 54N 98 18 E
Ban Phai, Thailand ... 38 D4 16 4N 102 44 E
Ban Phak Chit, Thailand ... 39 a 8 0N 98 24 E
Ban Pong, Thailand ... 38 F2 13 50N 99 55 E
Ban Ron Phibun, Thailand ... 39 H2 8 9N 99 51 E
Ban Rawai, Thailand ... 39 a 7 47N 98 20 E
Ban Sakhu, Thailand ... 39 a 8 4N 98 18 E
Ban Sanam Chai, Thailand ... 39 J3 7 33N 100 25 E
Ban Sangka, Thailand ... 38 E4 14 37N 103 52 E
Ban Tak, Thailand ... 38 D2 17 2N 99 4 E
Ban Tako, Thailand ... 38 E4 14 5N 102 40 E
Ban Tha Dua, Thailand ... 38 D2 17 59N 98 39 E
Ban Tha Li, Thailand ... 38 D3 17 37N 101 25 E
Ban Tha Nun, Thailand ... 39 a 8 12N 98 18 E
Ban Tha Rua, Thailand ... 39 a 7 59N 98 22 E
Ban Tha Yu, Thailand ... 39 a 8 17N 98 22 E
Ban Thahine, Laos ... 38 E5 14 12N 105 33 E
Ban Thong Krut, Thailand ... 39 b 9 25N 99 57 E
Ban Xien Kok, Laos ... 38 B3 20 54N 100 39 E
Ban Yen Nhan, Vietnam ... 38 B6 20 57N 106 2 E
Banaba, Kiribati ... 64 H8 0 45S 169 50 E
Banalia, Dem. Rep. of the Congo ... 54 B2 1 32N 25 5 E
Banam, Cambodia ... 39 G5 11 20N 105 17 E
Bananal, I. do, Brazil ... 93 F8 11 30S 50 30W
Banaras = Varanasi, India ... 43 G10 25 22N 83 0 E
Banas →, Gujarat, India ... 42 H4 23 45N 71 25 E
Banas →, Mad. P., India ... 43 G9 24 15N 81 30 E
Bânâs, Ras, Egypt ... 51 D13 23 57N 35 59 E
Banbridge, U.K. ... 10 B5 54 22N 6 16W
Banbury, U.K. ... 13 E6 52 4N 1 20W
Banchory, U.K. ... 11 D6 57 3N 2 29W
Bancroft, Canada ... 84 A7 45 3N 77 51W
Band Boni, Iran ... 45 E8 25 30N 59 33 E
Band Qīr, Iran ... 45 D6 31 39N 48 53 E
Banda, Mad. P., India ... 43 G8 24 3N 78 57 E
Banda, Ut. P., India ... 43 G9 25 30N 80 26 E
Banda, Kepulauan, Indonesia ... 37 E7 4 37S 129 50 E
Banda Aceh, Indonesia ... 36 C1 5 35N 95 20 E
Banda Banda, Mt., Australia ... 63 E5 31 10S 152 28 E
Banda Elat, Indonesia ... 37 F8 5 40S 133 5 E
Banda Is. = Banda, Kepulauan, Indonesia ... 37 E7 4 37S 129 50 E
Banda Sea, Indonesia ... 37 F7 6 0S 130 0 E
Bandai-Asahi △, Japan ... 30 F10 37 38N 140 4 E
Bandai-San, Japan ... 30 F10 37 36N 140 4 E
Bandanaira, Indonesia ... 37 E7 4 32S 129 54 E
Bandanwara, India ... 42 F6 26 9N 74 38 E
Bandar = Machilipatnam, India ... 41 L12 16 12N 81 8 E
Bandar = Abbās, Iran ... 45 E8 27 15N 56 15 E
Bandar-e Anzalī, Iran ... 45 B6 37 30N 49 30 E
Bandar-e Bushehr = Büshehr, Iran ... 45 D6 28 55N 50 55 E
Bandar-e Chārak, Iran ... 45 E7 26 45N 54 20 E
Bandar-e Deylam, Iran ... 45 D6 30 30N 49 5 E
Bandar-e Emām Khomeynī, Iran ... 45 D6 30 30N 49 5 E
Bandar-e Lengeh, Iran ... 45 E7 26 56N 53 29 E
Bandar-e Ma'shur, Iran ... 45 D6 30 35N 49 10 E

Bandar-e Rīg, Iran ... 45 D6 29 29N 50 38 E
Bandar-e Torkeman, Iran ... 45 B7 37 0N 54 10 E
Bandar Lampung = Tanjungkarang Telukbetung, Indonesia ... 36 F3 5 20S 105 10 E
Bandar Maharani = Muar, Malaysia ... 39 L4 2 3N 102 34 E
Bandar Penggaram = Batu Pahat, Malaysia ... 39 M4 1 50N 102 56 E
Bandar Seri Begawan, Brunei ... 36 C4 4 52N 115 0 E
Bandar Sri Aman, Malaysia ... 36 D4 1 15N 111 32 E
Bandawe, Malawi ... 55 E3 11 58S 34 5 E
Bandeira, Pico da, Brazil ... 95 A7 20 26S 41 47W
Bandera, Argentina ... 94 B3 28 55S 62 20W
Banderas, B. de, Mexico ... 86 C3 20 40N 105 30W
Bandhogarh, India ... 43 H9 23 40N 81 2 E
Bandi →, India ... 42 F6 26 12N 75 47 E
Bandikui, India ... 42 F7 27 3N 76 34 E
Bandırma, Turkey ... 23 D13 40 20N 28 0 E
Bandjarmasin = Banjarmasin, Indonesia ... 36 E4 3 20S 114 35 E
Bandon, Ireland ... 10 E3 51 44N 8 44W
Bandon →, Ireland ... 10 E3 51 43N 8 37W
Bandula, Mozam. ... 55 F3 19 0S 33 7 E
Bandundu, Dem. Rep. of the Congo ... 52 E3 3 15S 17 22 E
Bandung, Indonesia ... 36 F3 6 54S 107 36 E
Bâneh, Iran ... 44 C5 35 59N 45 53 E
Banes, Cuba ... 89 B4 21 0N 75 42W
Banff, Canada ... 70 C5 51 10N 115 34W
Banff, U.K. ... 11 D6 57 40N 2 33W
Banff △, Canada ... 70 C5 51 30N 116 15W
Bang Fai →, Laos ... 38 D5 16 57N 104 45 E
Bang Hieng →, Laos ... 38 D5 16 10N 105 10 E
Bang Krathum, Thailand ... 38 D3 16 34N 100 18 E
Bang Lamung, Thailand ... 38 F3 13 3N 100 56 E
Bang Mun Nak, Thailand ... 38 D3 16 2N 100 23 E
Bang Pa In, Thailand ... 38 E3 14 14N 100 31 E
Bang Rakam, Thailand ... 38 D3 16 45N 100 7 E
Bang Saphan, Thailand ... 39 G2 11 14N 99 28 E
Bang Thao, Thailand ... 39 a 7 59N 98 18 E
Bangaduni I., India ... 43 J13 21 34N 88 52 E
Bangala Dam, Zimbabwe ... 55 G3 21 7S 31 25 E
Bangalore, India ... 40 N10 12 59N 77 40 E
Banganga →, India ... 42 F6 27 6N 77 25 E
Bangaon, India ... 43 H13 23 0N 88 47 E
Bangassou, C.A.R. ... 52 D4 4 55N 23 7 E
Banggai, Indonesia ... 37 E6 1 34S 123 30 E
Banggai, Kepulauan, Indonesia ... 37 E6 1 40S 123 30 E
Banggai Arch. = Banggai, Kepulauan, Indonesia ... 37 E6 1 40S 123 30 E
Banggi, Malaysia ... 36 C5 7 17N 117 12 E
Banghāzī, Libya ... 51 B10 32 11N 20 3 E
Bangka, Sulawesi, Indonesia ... 37 D7 1 50N 125 5 E
Bangka, Sumatera, Indonesia ... 36 E3 2 0S 105 50 E
Bangka, Selat, Indonesia ... 36 E3 2 30S 105 30 E
Bangka-Belitung □, Indonesia ... 36 E3 2 30S 107 0 E
Bangkalan, Indonesia ... 37 G15 7 2S 112 46 E
Bangkinang, Indonesia ... 36 D2 0 18N 101 5 E
Bangko, Indonesia ... 36 E2 2 5S 102 9 E
Bangkok, Thailand ... 38 F3 13 45N 100 35 E
Bangladesh ■, Asia ... 41 H17 24 0N 90 0 E
Bangli, Indonesia ... 37 J18 8 27S 115 21 E
Bangong Co, India ... 43 B8 35 50N 79 20 E
Bangor, Down, U.K. ... 10 B6 54 40N 5 40W
Bangor, Gwynedd, U.K. ... 12 D3 53 14N 4 8W
Bangor, Maine, U.S.A. ... 69 D13 44 48N 68 46W
Bangor, Pa., U.S.A. ... 85 F9 40 52N 75 13W
Bangued, Phil. ... 37 A6 17 40N 120 37 E
Bangui, C.A.R. ... 52 D3 4 23N 18 35 E
Banguru, Dem. Rep. of the Congo ... 54 B2 0 30N 27 10 E
Bangweulu, L., Zambia ... 55 E3 11 0S 30 0 E
Bangweulu Swamp, Zambia ... 55 E3 11 20S 30 15 E
Banhine △, Mozam. ... 57 C5 22 40S 32 55 E
Bani, Dom. Rep. ... 89 C5 18 16N 70 22W
Bani Sa'd, Iraq ... 44 C5 33 34N 44 32 E
Banihal Pass, India ... 43 C6 33 30N 75 12 E
Bāniyās, Syria ... 44 C3 35 10N 36 0 E
Banja Luka, Bos.-H. ... 22 B7 44 49N 17 11 E
Banjar, India ... 42 D7 31 38N 77 21 E
Banjar →, India ... 43 H9 22 36N 80 22 E
Banjarmasin, Indonesia ... 36 E4 3 20S 114 35 E
Banjul, Gambia ... 50 F2 13 28N 16 40W
Banka, India ... 43 G12 24 53N 86 55 E
Banket, Zimbabwe ... 55 F3 17 27S 30 19 E
Bankipore, India ... 41 G14 25 35N 85 10 E
Banks I., B.C., Canada ... 70 C3 53 20N 130 0W
Banks I., N.W.T., Canada ... 68 A7 73 15N 121 30W
Banks Pen., N.Z. ... 59 K4 43 45S 173 15 E
Banks Str., Australia ... 63 G4 40 40S 148 10 E
Bankura, India ... 43 H12 23 11N 87 18 E
Banmankhi, India ... 43 G12 25 53N 87 11 E
Bann →, Arm., U.K. ... 10 B5 54 30N 6 31W
Bann →, L'derry., U.K. ... 10 A5 55 8N 6 41W
Bannang Sata, Thailand ... 39 J3 6 16N 101 16 E
Banning, U.S.A. ... 79 M10 33 56N 116 53W
Bannockburn, Canada ... 84 B7 44 39N 77 33W
Bannockburn, U.K. ... 11 E5 56 5N 3 55W
Bannockburn, Zimbabwe ... 55 G2 20 17S 29 48 E
Bannu, Pakistan ... 40 C7 33 0N 70 18 E
Bano, India ... 43 H11 22 40N 84 55 E
Bansgaon, India ... 43 F10 26 33N 83 21 E
Banská Bystrica, Slovak Rep. ... 17 D10 48 46N 19 14 E
Banswara, India ... 42 H6 23 32N 74 24 E
Bantaeng, Indonesia ... 37 F5 5 32S 119 56 E
Banten □, Indonesia ... 37 G11 6 30S 106 0 E
Bantry, Ireland ... 10 E2 51 41N 9 27W
Bantry B., Ireland ... 10 E2 51 37N 9 44W
Bantul, Indonesia ... 37 G14 7 55S 110 19 E
Bantva, India ... 42 J4 21 29N 70 12 E
Banyak, Kepulauan, Indonesia ... 36 D1 2 10N 97 10 E
Banyalbufar, Spain ... 24 B9 39 42N 2 31 E
Banyo, Cameroon ... 52 C2 6 52N 11 45 E
Banyumas, Indonesia ... 37 G13 7 32S 109 18 E
Banyuwangi, Indonesia ... 37 J17 8 13S 114 21 E
Banzare Coast, Antarctica ... 5 C9 68 0S 125 0 E
Bao Ha, Vietnam ... 38 A5 22 11N 104 21 E
Bao Lac, Vietnam ... 38 A5 22 57N 105 40 E
Bao Loc, Vietnam ... 39 G6 11 32N 107 48 E
Bao'an = Shenzhen, China ... 33 F10 22 32N 114 5 E
Baocheng, China ... 34 H4 33 12N 106 56 E
Baode, China ... 34 E6 39 1N 111 5 E
Baodi, China ... 35 E9 39 38N 117 20 E
Baoding, China ... 34 E8 38 50N 115 28 E
Baoji, China ... 34 G4 34 20N 107 5 E
Baoshan, China ... 32 D4 25 10N 99 5 E
Baotou, China ... 34 D6 40 32N 110 2 E

Baoying, *China* ... 35 H10 33 17N 119 20 E
Bap, *India* ... 42 F5 27 23N 72 18 E
Bapatla, *India* ... 41 M12 15 55N 80 30 E
Bāqerābād, *Iran* ... 45 C6 33 2N 51 58 E
Ba'qūbah, *Iraq* ... 44 C5 33 45N 44 50 E
Baquedano, *Chile* ... 94 A2 23 20S 69 52W
Bar, *Serbia & M.* ... 23 C8 42 8N 19 6 E
Bar, *Ukraine* ... 17 D14 49 4N 27 40 E
Bar Bigha, *India* ... 43 G11 25 21N 85 47 E
Bar Harbor, *U.S.A.* ... 83 C11 44 23N 68 13W
Bar-le-Duc, *France* ... 20 B6 48 47N 5 10 E
Bara, *India* ... 43 G9 25 16N 81 43 E
Bara Banki, *India* ... 43 F9 26 55N 81 12 E
Barabai, *Indonesia* ... 36 E5 2 32S 115 34 E
Baraboo, *U.S.A.* ... 80 D10 43 28N 89 45W
Baracoa, *Cuba* ... 89 B5 20 20N 74 30W
Baradā →, *Syria* ... 46 B5 33 33N 36 34 E
Baradero, *Argentina* ... 94 C4 33 52S 59 29W
Baraga, *U.S.A.* ... 80 B10 46 47N 88 30W
Barah →, *India* ... 42 F6 27 42N 77 5 E
Barahona, *Dom. Rep.* ... 89 C5 18 13N 71 7W
Barail Range, *India* ... 41 G18 25 15N 93 20 E
Barakaldo, *Spain* ... 21 A4 43 18N 2 59W
Barakar →, *India* ... 43 G12 24 7N 86 14 E
Barakhola, *India* ... 41 G18 25 0N 92 45 E
Barakot, *India* ... 43 J11 21 33N 84 59 E
Barakpur, *India* ... 43 H13 22 44N 88 30 E
Baralaba, *Australia* ... 62 C4 24 13S 149 50 E
Baralzon L., *Canada* ... 71 B9 60 0N 98 3W
Baramula, *India* ... 43 B6 34 15N 74 20 E
Baran, *India* ... 42 G7 25 9N 76 40 E
Baran →, *Pakistan* ... 42 G3 25 13N 68 17 E
Baranavichy, *Belarus* ... 17 B14 53 10N 26 0 E
Baranof, *U.S.A.* ... 70 B2 57 5N 134 50W
Baranof I., *U.S.A.* ... 68 C6 57 0N 135 0W
Barapasi, *Indonesia* ... 37 E9 2 15S 137 5 E
Barasat, *India* ... 43 H13 22 46N 88 31 E
Barat Daya, Kepulauan, *Indonesia* ... 37 F7 7 30S 128 0 E
Barataria B., *U.S.A.* ... 81 L10 29 20N 89 55W
Barauda, *India* ... 42 H6 23 33N 75 15 E
Baraut, *India* ... 42 E7 29 13N 77 7 E
Barbacena, *Brazil* ... 95 A7 21 15S 43 56W
Barbados ■, *W. Indies* ... 89 g 13 10N 59 30W
Barbària, C. de, *Spain* ... 24 C7 38 39N 1 24 E
Barbastro, *Spain* ... 21 A6 42 2N 0 5 E
Barberton, *S. Africa* ... 57 D5 25 42S 31 2 E
Barberton, *U.S.A.* ... 84 E3 41 0N 81 39W
Barbosa, *Colombia* ... 92 B4 5 57N 73 37W
Barbourville, *U.S.A.* ... 83 G4 36 52N 83 53W
Barbuda, *W. Indies* ... 89 C7 17 30N 61 40W
Barcaldine, *Australia* ... 62 C4 23 43S 145 6 E
Barcellona Pozzo di Gotto, *Italy* ... 22 E6 38 9N 15 13 E
Barcelona, *Spain* ... 21 B7 41 21N 2 10 E
Barcelona, *Venezuela* ... 92 A6 10 10N 64 40W
Barceloneta, *Puerto Rico* ... 89 d 18 27N 66 32W
Barcelos, *Brazil* ... 92 D6 1 0S 63 0W
Barcoo →, *Australia* ... 62 D3 25 30S 142 50 E
Bardaï, *Chad* ... 51 D9 21 25N 17 0 E
Bardas Blancas, *Argentina* ... 94 D2 35 49S 69 45W
Bardawîl, Sabkhet el, *Egypt* ... 46 D2 31 10N 33 15 E
Barddhaman, *India* ... 43 H12 23 14N 87 39 E
Bardejov, *Slovak Rep.* ... 17 D11 49 18N 21 15 E
Bardera, *Somali Rep.* ... 47 G3 2 20N 42 27 E
Bardīyah, *Libya* ... 51 B10 31 45N 25 5 E
Bardsey I., *U.K.* ... 12 E3 52 45N 4 47W
Bardstown, *U.S.A.* ... 82 G3 37 49N 85 28W
Bareilly, *India* ... 43 E8 28 22N 79 27 E
Barela, *India* ... 43 H9 23 6N 80 3 E
Barents Sea, *Arctic* ... 4 B9 73 0N 39 0 E
Barfleur, Pte. de, *France* ... 20 B3 49 42N 1 16W
Bargara, *Australia* ... 62 C5 24 50S 152 25 E
Barguzin, *Russia* ... 29 D11 53 37N 109 37 E
Barh, *India* ... 43 G11 25 29N 85 46 E
Barhaj, *India* ... 43 F10 26 18N 83 44 E
Barharwa, *India* ... 43 G12 24 52N 87 47 E
Barhi, *India* ... 43 G11 24 15N 85 25 E
Bari, *India* ... 42 F7 26 39N 77 39 E
Bari, *Italy* ... 22 D7 41 8N 16 51 E
Bari Doab, *Pakistan* ... 42 D5 30 20N 73 0 E
Bari Sadri, *India* ... 42 G6 24 28N 74 30 E
Barīdī, Ra's, *Si. Arabia* ... 44 E3 24 17N 37 31 E
Barīm, *Yemen* ... 48 E8 12 39N 43 25 E
Barinas, *Venezuela* ... 92 B4 8 36N 70 15W
Baring, C., *Canada* ... 68 B8 70 0N 117 30W
Baringo, L., *Kenya* ... 54 B4 0 47N 36 16 E
Barisal, *Bangla.* ... 41 H17 22 45N 90 20 E
Barisal □, *Bangla.* ... 41 H17 22 40N 90 20 E
Barisan, Bukit, *Indonesia* ... 36 E2 3 30S 102 15 E
Barito →, *Indonesia* ... 36 E4 4 0S 114 50 E
Baritú △, *Argentina* ... 94 A3 23 43S 64 40W
Bark L., *Canada* ... 84 A7 45 27N 77 51W
Barkakana, *India* ... 43 H11 23 37N 85 29 E
Barker, *U.S.A.* ... 84 C6 43 20N 78 33W
Barkley, L., *U.S.A.* ... 83 G2 37 1N 88 14W
Barkley Sound, *Canada* ... 70 D3 48 50N 125 10W
Barkly East, *S. Africa* ... 56 E4 30 58S 27 33 E
Barkly Roadhouse, *Australia* ... 62 B2 19 52S 135 50 E
Barkly Tableland, *Australia* ... 62 B2 17 50S 136 40 E
Barkly West, *S. Africa* ... 56 D3 28 5S 24 31 E
Barkol Kazak Zizhixian, *China* ... 32 B4 43 37N 93 2 E
Bârlad, *Romania* ... 17 E14 46 15N 27 38 E
Bârlad →, *Romania* ... 17 F14 45 38N 27 32 E
Barlee, L., *Australia* ... 61 E2 29 15S 119 30 E
Barlee, Mt., *Australia* ... 61 D4 24 38S 128 13 E
Barletta, *Italy* ... 22 D7 41 19N 16 17 E
Barlovento, *Canary Is.* ... 24 F2 28 48N 17 48W
Barlow L., *Canada* ... 71 A8 62 0N 103 0W
Barmedman, *Australia* ... 63 E4 34 9S 147 21 E
Barmer, *India* ... 42 G4 25 45N 71 20 E
Barmera, *Australia* ... 63 E3 34 15S 140 28 E
Barmouth, *U.K.* ... 12 E3 52 44N 4 4W
Barna →, *India* ... 43 G10 25 21N 83 3 E
Barnagar, *India* ... 42 H6 23 7N 75 19 E
Barnala, *India* ... 42 D6 30 23N 75 33 E
Barnard Castle, *U.K.* ... 12 C6 54 33N 1 55W
Barnaul, *Russia* ... 28 D9 53 20N 83 40 E
Barnesville, *U.S.A.* ... 83 J3 33 3N 84 9W
Barnet □, *U.K.* ... 13 F7 51 38N 0 9W
Barneveld, *Neths.* ... 15 B5 52 7N 5 36 E
Barneveld, *U.S.A.* ... 85 C9 43 16N 75 14W
Barnhart, *U.S.A.* ... 81 K4 31 8N 101 10W
Barnsley, *U.K.* ... 12 D6 53 34N 1 27W
Barnstaple, *U.K.* ... 13 F3 51 5N 4 4W
Barnstaple Bay = Bideford Bay, *U.K.* ... 13 F3 51 5N 4 20W
Barnsville, *U.S.A.* ... 80 B6 46 43N 96 28W
Barnwell, *U.S.A.* ... 83 J5 33 15N 81 23W

Baro, *Nigeria* ... 50 G7 8 35N 6 18 E
Baroda = Vadodara, *India* ... 42 H5 22 20N 73 10 E
Baroda, *India* ... 42 G7 25 29N 76 35 E
Baroe, *S. Africa* ... 56 E3 33 13S 24 33 E
Baron Ra., *Australia* ... 60 D4 23 30S 127 45 E
Barpeta, *India* ... 41 F17 26 20N 91 10 E
Barques, Pt. Aux, *U.S.A.* ... 84 B2 44 4N 82 58W
Barquisimeto, *Venezuela* ... 92 A5 10 4N 69 19W
Barr Smith Range, *Australia* ... 61 E3 27 4S 120 20 E
Barra, *Brazil* ... 93 F10 11 5S 43 10W
Barra, *U.K.* ... 11 E1 57 0N 7 29W
Barra, Sd. of, *U.K.* ... 11 D1 57 4N 7 25W
Barra de Navidad, *Mexico* ... 86 D4 19 12N 104 41W
Barra do Corda, *Brazil* ... 93 E9 5 30S 45 10W
Barra do Piraí, *Brazil* ... 95 A7 22 30S 43 50W
Barra Falsa, Pta. da, *Mozam.* ... 57 C6 22 58S 35 37 E
Barra Hd., *U.K.* ... 11 E1 56 47N 7 40W
Barra Mansa, *Brazil* ... 95 A7 22 35S 44 12W
Barraba, *Australia* ... 63 E5 30 21S 150 35 E
Barrackpur = Barakpur, *India* ... 43 H13 22 44N 88 30 E
Barradale Roadhouse, *Australia* ... 60 D1 22 42S 114 58 E
Barraigh = Barra, *U.K.* ... 11 E1 57 0N 7 29W
Barranca, Lima, *Peru* ... 92 F3 10 45S 77 50W
Barranca, Loreto, *Peru* ... 92 D3 4 50S 76 50W
Barranca del Cobre △, *Mexico* ... 86 B3 27 18N 107 40W
Barrancabermeja, *Colombia* ... 92 B4 7 0N 73 50W
Barrancas, *Venezuela* ... 92 B6 8 55N 62 5W
Barrancos, *Portugal* ... 21 C2 38 10N 6 58W
Barranqueras, *Argentina* ... 94 B4 27 30S 59 0W
Barranquilla, *Colombia* ... 92 A4 11 0N 74 50W
Barraute, *Canada* ... 72 C4 48 26N 77 38W
Barre, Mass., *U.S.A.* ... 85 D12 42 25N 72 6W
Barre, Vt., *U.S.A.* ... 85 B12 44 12N 72 30W
Barreal, *Argentina* ... 94 C2 31 33S 69 28W
Barreiras, *Brazil* ... 93 F10 12 8S 45 0W
Barreirinhas, *Brazil* ... 93 D10 2 30S 42 50W
Barreiro, *Portugal* ... 21 C1 38 40N 9 6W
Barretos, *Brazil* ... 93 H9 20 30S 48 35W
Barrhead, *Canada* ... 70 C6 54 10N 114 24W
Barrie, *Canada* ... 84 B5 44 24N 79 40W
Barrier Ra., *Australia* ... 63 E3 31 0S 141 30 E
Barrière, *Canada* ... 70 C4 51 12N 120 7W
Barrington, *U.S.A.* ... 85 E13 41 44N 71 18W
Barrington L., *Canada* ... 71 B8 56 55N 100 15W
Barrington Tops, *Australia* ... 63 E5 32 6S 151 28 E
Barringun, *Australia* ... 63 D4 29 1S 145 41 E
Barro do Garças, *Brazil* ... 93 G8 15 54S 52 16W
Barron, *U.S.A.* ... 80 C9 45 24N 91 51W
Barrow, *U.S.A.* ... 68 A4 71 18N 156 47W
Barrow →, *Ireland* ... 10 D5 52 25N 6 58W
Barrow Creek, *Australia* ... 62 C1 21 30S 133 55 E
Barrow I., *Australia* ... 60 D2 20 45S 115 20 E
Barrow-in-Furness, *U.K.* ... 12 C4 54 7N 3 14W
Barrow Pt., *Australia* ... 62 A3 14 20S 144 40 E
Barrow Pt., *U.S.A.* ... 66 B4 71 10N 156 20W
Barrow Ra., *Australia* ... 61 E4 26 0S 127 40 E
Barrow Str., *Canada* ... 4 B3 74 20N 95 0W
Barry, *U.K.* ... 13 F4 51 24N 3 16W
Barry's Bay, *Canada* ... 84 A7 45 29N 77 41W
Barsat, *Pakistan* ... 43 A5 36 10N 72 45 E
Barsham, *Syria* ... 44 C4 35 21N 40 33 E
Barsi, *India* ... 40 K9 18 10N 75 50 E
Barsoi, *India* ... 41 G15 25 48N 87 57 E
Barstow, *U.S.A.* ... 79 L9 34 54N 117 1W
Barthélemy, Col, *Vietnam* ... 38 C5 19 26N 104 6 E
Bartica, *Guyana* ... 92 B7 6 25N 58 40W
Bartle Frere, *Australia* ... 62 B4 17 27S 145 50 E
Bartlesville, *U.S.A.* ... 81 G7 36 45N 95 59W
Bartlett, *U.S.A.* ... 78 J8 36 29N 118 2W
Bartlett, L., *Canada* ... 70 A5 63 5N 118 20W
Bartolomeu Dias, *Mozam.* ... 55 G4 21 10S 35 8 E
Barton, *U.S.A.* ... 85 B12 44 45N 72 11W
Barton upon Humber, *U.K.* ... 12 D7 53 41N 0 25W
Bartow, *U.S.A.* ... 83 M5 27 54N 81 50W
Barú, Volcan, *Panama* ... 88 E3 8 55N 82 35W
Barumba, *Dem. Rep. of the Congo* ... 54 B1 1 3N 23 37 E
Baruunsuu, *Mongolia* ... 34 C3 43 43N 105 35 E
Barwani, *India* ... 42 H6 22 2N 74 57 E
Barysaw, *Belarus* ... 17 A15 54 17N 28 28 E
Barzān, *Iraq* ... 44 B5 36 55N 44 3 E
Bāsa'idū, *Iran* ... 45 E7 26 35N 55 20 E
Basal, *Pakistan* ... 42 C5 33 33N 72 13 E
Basankusa, *Dem. Rep. of the Congo* ... 52 D3 1 5N 19 50 E
Basarabeasca, *Moldova* ... 17 E15 46 21N 28 58 E
Basarabia = Bessarabiya, *Moldova* ... 17 E15 47 0N 28 10 E
Basawa, *Afghan.* ... 42 B4 34 15N 70 50 E
Bascuñán, C., *Chile* ... 94 B1 28 52S 71 35W
Basel, *Switz.* ... 20 C7 47 35N 7 35 E
Bashäkerd, Kühhä-ye, *Iran* ... 45 E8 26 42N 58 35 E
Bashaw, *Canada* ... 70 C6 52 35N 112 58W
Bāshī, *Iran* ... 45 D6 28 41N 51 4 E
Bashkir Republic = Bashkortostan □, *Russia* ... 18 D10 54 0N 57 0 E
Bashkortostan □, *Russia* ... 18 D10 54 0N 57 0 E
Basibasy, *Madag.* ... 57 C7 22 10S 43 40 E
Basilan I., *Phil.* ... 37 C6 6 35N 122 0 E
Basilan Str., *Phil.* ... 37 C6 6 50N 122 0 E
Basildon, *U.K.* ... 13 F8 51 34N 0 28 E
Basim = Washim, *India* ... 40 J10 20 3N 77 0 E
Basin, *U.S.A.* ... 76 D9 44 23N 108 2W
Basingstoke, *U.K.* ... 13 F6 51 15N 1 5W
Baskatong, Rés., *Canada* ... 72 C4 46 46N 75 50W
Basle = Basel, *Switz.* ... 20 C7 47 35N 7 35 E
Basoda, *India* ... 42 H7 23 52N 77 54 E
Basoko, *Dem. Rep. of the Congo* ... 54 B1 1 16N 23 40 E
Basque Provinces = País Vasco □, *Spain* ... 21 A4 42 50N 2 45W
Basra = Al Başrah, *Iraq* ... 44 D5 30 30N 47 50 E
Bass Str., *Australia* ... 63 F4 39 15S 146 30 E
Bassano, *Canada* ... 70 C6 50 48N 112 20W
Bassano del Grappa, *Italy* ... 22 B4 45 46N 11 44 E
Bassas da India, *Ind. Oc.* ... 53 J7 22 0S 39 0 E
Basse-Pointe, *Martinique* ... 88 c 14 52N 61 8W
Basse-Terre, *Guadeloupe* ... 88 b 16 0N 61 44W
Basse Terre, *Trin. & Tob.* ... 93 K15 10 7N 61 19W
Bassein, *Burma* ... 41 L19 16 45N 94 30 E
Basses, Pte. des, *Guadeloupe* ... 88 b 15 52N 61 17W
Basseterre, *St. Kitts & Nevis* ... 89 C7 17 17N 62 43W
Bassett, *U.S.A.* ... 80 D5 42 35N 99 32W
Bassi, *India* ... 42 D7 30 44N 76 21 E
Bastak, *Iran* ... 45 E7 27 15N 54 25 E
Baştām, *Iran* ... 45 B7 36 29N 55 4 E
Bastar, *India* ... 41 K12 19 15N 81 40 E

Basti, *India* ... 43 F10 26 52N 82 55 E
Bastia, *France* ... 20 E8 42 40N 9 30 E
Bastogne, *Belgium* ... 15 D5 50 1N 5 43 E
Bastrop, La., *U.S.A.* ... 81 J9 32 47N 91 55W
Bastrop, Tex., *U.S.A.* ... 81 K6 30 7N 97 19W
Bat Yam, *Israel* ... 46 C3 32 2N 34 44 E
Bataan □, *Phil.* ... 37 B6 14 40N 120 25 E
Batabanó, *Cuba* ... 88 B3 22 41N 82 18W
Batabanó, G. de, *Cuba* ... 88 B3 22 30N 82 30W
Batac, *Phil.* ... 37 A6 18 3N 120 34 E
Batagai, *Russia* ... 29 C14 67 38N 134 38 E
Batala, *India* ... 42 D6 31 48N 75 12 E
Batama, *Dem. Rep. of the Congo* ... 54 B2 0 58N 26 33 E
Batamay, *Russia* ... 29 C13 63 30N 129 15 E
Batang, *Indonesia* ... 37 G13 6 55S 109 45 E
Batangas, *Phil.* ... 37 B6 13 35N 121 10 E
Batanta, *Indonesia* ... 37 E8 0 55S 130 40 E
Batatais, *Brazil* ... 95 A6 20 54S 47 37W
Batchelor, *Australia* ... 60 B5 13 4S 131 1 E
Batdambang, *Cambodia* ... 38 F4 13 7N 103 12 E
Batemans B., *Australia* ... 63 F5 35 40S 150 12 E
Batemans Bay, *Australia* ... 63 F5 35 44S 150 11 E
Bates Ra., *Australia* ... 61 E3 27 27S 121 5 E
Batesburg-Leesville, *U.S.A.* ... 83 J5 33 54N 81 33W
Batesville, Ark., *U.S.A.* ... 81 H9 35 46N 91 39W
Batesville, Miss., *U.S.A.* ... 81 H10 34 19N 89 57W
Batesville, Tex., *U.S.A.* ... 81 L5 28 58N 99 37W
Bath, *Canada* ... 85 B8 44 11N 76 47W
Bath, *U.K.* ... 13 F5 51 23N 2 22W
Bath, Maine, *U.S.A.* ... 83 D11 43 55N 69 49W
Bath, N.Y., *U.S.A.* ... 84 D7 42 20N 77 19W
Bath & North East Somerset □, *U.K.* ... 13 F5 51 21N 2 27W
Batheay, *Cambodia* ... 39 G5 11 59N 104 57 E
Bathsheba, *Barbados* ... 89 g 13 13N 59 32W
Bathurst, *Australia* ... 63 E4 33 25S 149 31 E
Bathurst, *Canada* ... 73 C6 47 37N 65 43W
Bathurst, *S. Africa* ... 56 E4 33 30S 26 50 E
Bathurst, C., *Canada* ... 68 A7 70 34N 128 0W
Bathurst B., *Australia* ... 62 A3 14 16S 144 25 E
Bathurst Harb., *Australia* ... 63 G4 43 15S 146 10 E
Bathurst I., *Australia* ... 60 B5 11 30S 130 10 E
Bathurst I., *Canada* ... 4 B2 76 0N 100 30W
Bathurst Inlet, *Canada* ... 68 B9 66 50N 108 1W
Batlow, *Australia* ... 63 F4 35 31S 148 9 E
Batman, *Turkey* ... 19 G7 37 55N 41 5 E
Batna, *Algeria* ... 50 A7 35 34N 6 15 E
Batoka, *Zambia* ... 55 F2 16 45S 27 15 E
Baton Rouge, *U.S.A.* ... 81 K9 30 27N 91 11W
Batong, Ko, *Thailand* ... 39 J2 6 32N 99 12 E
Batopilas, *Mexico* ... 86 B3 27 0N 107 45W
Batouri, *Cameroon* ... 52 D2 4 30N 14 25 E
Båtsfjord, *Norway* ... 8 A23 70 38N 29 39 E
Battambang = Batdambang, *Cambodia* ... 38 F4 13 7N 103 12 E
Batticaloa, *Sri Lanka* ... 40 R12 7 43N 81 45 E
Battipáglia, *Italy* ... 22 D6 40 37N 14 58 E
Battle, *U.K.* ... 13 G8 50 55N 0 30 E
Battle →, *Canada* ... 71 C7 52 43N 108 15W
Battle Creek, *U.S.A.* ... 82 D3 42 19N 85 11W
Battle Ground, *U.S.A.* ... 78 E4 45 47N 122 32W
Battle Harbour, *Canada* ... 73 B8 52 16N 55 35W
Battle Lake, *U.S.A.* ... 80 B7 46 17N 95 43W
Battle Mountain, *U.S.A.* ... 76 F5 40 38N 116 56W
Battlefields, *Zimbabwe* ... 55 F2 18 37S 29 47 E
Battleford, *Canada* ... 71 C7 52 45N 108 15W
Batu, *Ethiopia* ... 47 F2 6 55N 39 45 E
Batu, Kepulauan, *Indonesia* ... 36 E1 0 30S 98 25 E
Batu Caves, *Malaysia* ... 39 L3 3 15N 101 40 E
Batu Ferringhi, *Malaysia* ... 39 c 5 28N 100 15 E
Batu Gajah, *Malaysia* ... 39 K3 4 28N 101 3 E
Batu Is. = Batu, Kepulauan, *Indonesia* ... 36 E1 0 30S 98 25 E
Batu Pahat, *Malaysia* ... 39 M4 1 50N 102 56 E
Batuata, *Indonesia* ... 37 F6 6 12S 122 42 E
Batugondang, Tanjung, *Indonesia* ... 37 J17 8 6S 114 29 E
Batukau, Gunung, *Indonesia* ... 37 J18 8 20S 115 5 E
Batumi, *Georgia* ... 19 F7 41 39N 41 44 E
Batur, *Indonesia* ... 37 J18 8 15S 115 20 E
Batur, Gunung, *Indonesia* ... 37 J18 8 14S 115 23 E
Baturaja, *Indonesia* ... 36 E2 4 11S 104 15 E
Baturité, *Brazil* ... 93 D11 4 28S 38 45W
Baturiti, *Indonesia* ... 37 J18 8 19S 115 11 E
Bau, *Malaysia* ... 36 D4 1 25N 110 9 E
Baubau, *Indonesia* ... 37 F6 5 25S 122 38 E
Baucau, *E. Timor* ... 37 F7 8 27S 126 27 E
Bauchi, *Nigeria* ... 50 F7 10 22N 9 48 E
Baudette, *U.S.A.* ... 80 A7 48 43N 94 36W
Bauer, C., *Australia* ... 63 E1 32 44S 134 4 E
Bauhinia, *Australia* ... 62 C4 24 35S 149 18 E
Baukau = Baucau, *E. Timor* ... 37 F7 8 27S 126 27 E
Bauld, C., *Canada* ... 69 C14 51 38N 55 26W
Bauru, *Brazil* ... 95 A6 22 10S 49 0W
Bausi, *India* ... 43 G12 24 48N 87 1 E
Bauska, *Latvia* ... 9 H21 56 24N 24 15 E
Bautzen, *Germany* ... 16 C8 51 10N 14 26 E
Bavānāt, *Iran* ... 45 D7 30 28N 53 27 E
Bavaria = Bayern □, *Germany* ... 16 D6 48 50N 12 0 E
Bavispe →, *Mexico* ... 86 B3 29 30N 109 11W
Bawdwin, *Burma* ... 41 H20 23 5N 97 20 E
Bawean, *Indonesia* ... 36 F4 5 46S 112 35 E
Bawku, *Ghana* ... 50 F5 11 3N 0 19W
Bawlake, *Burma* ... 41 K20 19 11N 97 21 E
Baxley, *U.S.A.* ... 83 K4 31 47N 82 21W
Baxter, *U.S.A.* ... 80 B7 46 21N 94 17W
Baxter Springs, *U.S.A.* ... 81 G7 37 2N 94 44W
Baxter State △, *U.S.A.* ... 83 B11 46 5N 68 57W
Bay City, Mich., *U.S.A.* ... 82 D4 43 36N 83 54W
Bay City, Tex., *U.S.A.* ... 81 L7 28 59N 95 58W
Bay Minette, *U.S.A.* ... 83 K2 30 53N 87 46W
Bay Roberts, *Canada* ... 73 C9 47 36N 53 16W
Bay St. Louis, *U.S.A.* ... 81 K10 30 19N 89 20W
Bay Springs, *U.S.A.* ... 81 K10 31 59N 89 17W
Bay View, *N.Z.* ... 59 H6 39 25S 176 50 E
Baya, *Dem. Rep. of the Congo* ... 55 E2 11 53S 27 25 E
Bayamo, *Cuba* ... 88 B4 20 20N 76 40W
Bayamón, *Puerto Rico* ... 89 d 18 24N 66 9W
Bayan Har Shan, *China* ... 32 C4 34 0N 98 0 E
Bayan Hot = Alxa Zuoqi, *China* ... 34 E3 38 50N 105 40 E
Bayan Lepas, *Malaysia* ... 39 c 5 17N 100 15 E
Bayan Obo, *China* ... 34 D5 41 52N 109 59 E
Bayan-Ovoo = Erdenetsogt, *Mongolia* ... 34 C4 42 55N 106 5 E
Bayana, *India* ... 42 F7 26 55N 77 18 E

Bayanaūyl, *Kazakhstan* ... 28 D8 50 45N 75 45 E
Bayandalay, *Mongolia* ... 34 C2 43 30N 103 29 E
Bayanhongor, *Mongolia* ... 32 B5 46 8N 102 43 E
Bayard, N. Mex., *U.S.A.* ... 77 K9 32 46N 108 8W
Bayard, Nebr., *U.S.A.* ... 80 E3 41 45N 103 20W
Baybay, *Phil.* ... 37 B6 10 40N 124 55 E
Baydhabo = Baidoa, *Somali Rep.* ... 47 G3 3 8N 43 30 E
Bayern □, *Germany* ... 16 D6 48 50N 12 0 E
Bayeux, *France* ... 20 B3 49 17N 0 42W
Bayfield, *Canada* ... 84 C3 43 34N 81 42W
Bayfield, *U.S.A.* ... 80 B9 46 49N 90 49W
Bayındır, *Turkey* ... 23 E12 38 13N 27 39 E
Bayji, *Iraq* ... 44 C4 35 0N 43 30 E
Baykal, Oz., *Russia* ... 29 D11 53 0N 108 0 E
Baykan, *Turkey* ... 44 B4 38 7N 41 44 E
Baykonur = Bayqongyr, *Kazakhstan* ... 28 E7 47 48N 65 50 E
Baymak, *Russia* ... 18 D10 52 36N 58 19 E
Baynes Mts., *Namibia* ... 56 B1 17 15S 13 0 E
Bayombong, *Phil.* ... 37 A6 16 30N 121 10 E
Bayonne, *France* ... 20 E3 43 30N 1 28W
Bayonne, *U.S.A.* ... 85 F10 40 40N 74 7W
Bayovar, *Peru* ... 92 E2 5 50S 81 0W
Bayqongyr, *Kazakhstan* ... 28 E7 47 48N 65 50 E
Bayram-Ali = Bayramaly, *Turkmenistan* ... 28 F7 37 37N 62 10 E
Bayramaly, *Turkmenistan* ... 28 F7 37 37N 62 10 E
Bayramiç, *Turkey* ... 23 E12 39 48N 26 36 E
Bayreuth, *Germany* ... 16 D6 49 56N 11 35 E
Bayrūt, *Lebanon* ... 46 B4 33 53N 35 31 E
Bays, L. of, *Canada* ... 84 A5 45 15N 79 4W
Baysville, *Canada* ... 84 A5 45 9N 79 7W
Bayt Lahm, *West Bank* ... 46 D4 31 43N 35 12 E
Baytown, *U.S.A.* ... 81 L7 29 43N 94 59W
Bayun, *Indonesia* ... 37 J18 8 11S 115 16 E
Baza, *Spain* ... 21 D4 37 30N 2 47W
Bazaruto △, *Mozam.* ... 57 C6 21 42S 35 26 E
Bazaruto, I. do, *Mozam.* ... 57 C6 21 40S 35 28 E
Bazhou, *China* ... 34 E9 39 8N 116 22 E
Bazmān, Kūh-e, *Iran* ... 45 D9 28 4N 60 1 E
Beach, *U.S.A.* ... 80 B3 46 58N 104 0W
Beach City, *U.S.A.* ... 84 F3 40 39N 81 35W
Beachport, *Australia* ... 63 F3 37 29S 140 0 E
Beachy Hd., *U.K.* ... 13 G8 50 44N 0 15 E
Beacon, *Australia* ... 61 F2 30 26S 117 52 E
Beacon, *U.S.A.* ... 85 E11 41 30N 73 58W
Beaconsfield, *Australia* ... 63 G4 41 11S 146 48 E
Beagle, Canal, *S. Amer.* ... 96 H3 55 0S 68 30W
Beagle Bay, *Australia* ... 60 C3 16 58S 122 40 E
Bealanana, *Madag.* ... 57 A8 14 33S 48 44 E
Beals Cr. →, *U.S.A.* ... 81 J4 32 10N 100 51W
Beamsville, *Canada* ... 84 C5 43 12N 79 28W
Bear →, Calif., *U.S.A.* ... 78 G5 38 56N 121 36W
Bear →, Utah, *U.S.A.* ... 74 B4 41 30N 112 8W
Bear I., *Ireland* ... 10 E2 51 38N 9 50W
Bear L., *Canada* ... 71 B9 55 8N 96 0W
Bear L., *U.S.A.* ... 76 F8 41 59N 111 21W
Beardmore, *Canada* ... 72 C2 49 36N 87 57W
Beardmore Glacier, *Antarctica* ... 5 E11 84 30S 170 0 E
Beardstown, *U.S.A.* ... 80 F9 40 1N 90 26W
Bearma →, *India* ... 43 G8 24 20N 79 51 E
Béarn, *France* ... 20 E3 43 20N 0 30W
Bearpaw Mts., *U.S.A.* ... 76 B9 48 12N 109 30W
Bearskin Lake, *Canada* ... 72 B1 53 58N 91 2W
Beas →, *India* ... 42 D6 31 10N 74 59 E
Beata, C., *Dom. Rep.* ... 89 C5 17 40N 71 30W
Beata, I., *Dom. Rep.* ... 89 C5 17 34N 71 31W
Beatrice, *U.S.A.* ... 80 E6 40 16N 96 45W
Beatrice, *Zimbabwe* ... 55 F3 18 15S 30 55 E
Beatrice, C., *Australia* ... 62 A2 14 20S 136 55 E
Beatton →, *Canada* ... 70 B4 56 15N 120 45W
Beatton River, *Canada* ... 70 B4 57 26N 121 20W
Beatty, *U.S.A.* ... 78 J10 36 54N 116 46W
Beauce, Plaine de la, *France* ... 20 B4 48 10N 1 45 E
Beauceville, *Canada* ... 73 C5 46 13N 70 46W
Beaudesert, *Australia* ... 63 D5 27 59S 153 0 E
Beaufort, *Malaysia* ... 36 C5 5 30N 115 40 E
Beaufort, N.C., *U.S.A.* ... 83 H7 34 43N 76 40W
Beaufort, S.C., *U.S.A.* ... 83 J5 32 26N 80 40W
Beaufort Sea, *Arctic* ... 4 B1 72 0N 140 0W
Beaufort West, *S. Africa* ... 56 E3 32 18S 22 36 E
Beauharnois, *Canada* ... 85 A11 45 20N 73 52W
Beaulieu →, *Canada* ... 70 A6 62 3N 113 11W
Beauly, *U.K.* ... 11 D4 57 30N 4 28W
Beauly →, *U.K.* ... 11 D4 57 29N 4 27W
Beaumaris, *U.K.* ... 12 D3 53 16N 4 6W
Beaumont, *Belgium* ... 15 D4 50 15N 4 14 E
Beaumont, *U.S.A.* ... 81 K7 30 5N 94 6W
Beaune, *France* ... 20 C6 47 2N 4 50 E
Beaupré, *Canada* ... 73 C5 47 3N 70 54W
Beauraing, *Belgium* ... 15 D4 50 7N 4 57 E
Beausejour, *Canada* ... 71 C9 50 5N 96 35W
Beauvais, *France* ... 20 B5 49 25N 2 8 E
Beauval, *Canada* ... 71 B7 55 9N 107 37W
Beaver, Okla., *U.S.A.* ... 81 G4 36 49N 100 31W
Beaver, Pa., *U.S.A.* ... 84 F4 40 42N 80 19W
Beaver, Utah, *U.S.A.* ... 77 G7 38 17N 112 38W
Beaver →, B.C., *Canada* ... 70 B4 59 52N 124 20W
Beaver →, Ont., *Canada* ... 72 A2 55 55N 87 48W
Beaver →, Sask., *Canada* ... 71 B7 55 26N 107 45W
Beaver City, *U.S.A.* ... 80 E5 40 8N 99 50W
Beaver Creek, *Canada* ... 68 B5 63 0N 141 0W
Beaver Dam, *U.S.A.* ... 80 D10 43 28N 88 50W
Beaver Falls, *U.S.A.* ... 84 F4 40 46N 80 20W
Beaver Hill L., *Canada* ... 71 C10 54 5N 94 50W
Beaver I., *U.S.A.* ... 82 C3 45 40N 85 33W
Beaverhill L., *Canada* ... 70 C6 53 27N 112 32W
Beaverlodge, *Canada* ... 70 B5 55 11N 119 29W
Beaverstone →, *Canada* ... 72 B2 54 59N 89 25W
Beaverton, *Canada* ... 84 B5 44 26N 79 9W
Beaverton, *U.S.A.* ... 78 E4 45 29N 122 48W
Beawar, *India* ... 42 F6 26 3N 74 18 E
Bebedouro, *Brazil* ... 95 A6 21 0S 48 25W
Becan, *Mexico* ... 87 D7 18 31N 89 28W
Beccles, *U.K.* ... 13 E9 52 27N 1 35 E
Bečej, *Serbia & M.* ... 23 B9 45 36N 20 3 E
Béchar, *Algeria* ... 50 B5 31 38N 2 18W
Beckley, *U.S.A.* ... 82 G5 37 47N 81 11W
Beddouza, Ras, *Morocco* ... 50 B4 32 33N 9 9W
Bedford, *Canada* ... 85 A12 45 7N 72 59W
Bedford, *S. Africa* ... 56 E4 32 40S 26 10 E
Bedford, *U.K.* ... 13 E7 52 8N 0 28W
Bedford, Ind., *U.S.A.* ... 82 F2 38 52N 86 29W
Bedford, Iowa, *U.S.A.* ... 80 E7 40 40N 94 44W
Bedford, Ohio, *U.S.A.* ... 84 E3 41 23N 81 32W

Bedford, Pa., U.S.A. .... 84 F6 40 1N 78 30W
Bedford, Va., U.S.A. .... 82 G6 37 20N 79 31W
Bedford, C., Australia .... 62 B4 15 14S 145 21 E
Bedfordshire □, U.K. .... 13 E7 52 4N 0 28W
Bedok, Singapore .... 39 d 1 19N 103 56 E
Bedourie, Australia .... 62 C2 24 30S 139 30 E
Bedum, Neths. .... 15 A6 53 18N 6 36 E
Beebe Plain, Canada .... 85 A12 45 1N 72 9W
Beech Creek, U.S.A. .... 84 E7 41 5N 77 36W
Beef I., Br. Virgin Is. .... 89 e 18 26N 64 30W
Beenleigh, Australia .... 63 D5 27 43S 153 10 E
Be'er Menuḥa, Israel .... 44 D2 30 19N 35 8 E
Be'er Sheva, Israel .... 46 D3 31 15N 34 48 E
Beersheba = Be'er Sheva, Israel .... 46 D3 31 15N 34 48 E
Beeston, U.K. .... 12 E6 52 56N 1 14W
Beeville, U.S.A. .... 81 L6 28 24N 97 45W
Befale, Dem. Rep. of the Congo 52 D4 0 25N 20 45 E
Befandriana, Mahajanga, Madag. 57 B8 15 16S 48 32 E
Befandriana, Toliara, Madag. 57 C7 21 55S 44 0 E
Befasy, Madag. .... 57 C7 20 33S 44 23 E
Befotaka, Antsiranana, Madag. 57 A8 13 15S 48 16 E
Befotaka, Fianarantsoa, Madag. 57 C8 23 49S 47 0 E
Bega, Australia .... 63 F4 36 41S 149 51 E
Begusarai, India .... 43 G12 25 24N 86 9 E
Behābād, Iran .... 45 C8 32 24N 59 47 E
Behala, India .... 43 H13 22 30N 88 20 E
Behara, Madag. .... 57 C8 24 55S 46 20 E
Behbehān, Iran .... 45 D6 30 30N 50 15 E
Behm Canal, U.S.A. .... 70 B2 55 10N 131 0W
Behshahr, Iran .... 45 B7 36 45N 53 35 E
Bei Jiang →, China .... 33 D6 23 2N 112 58 E
Bei'an, China .... 33 B7 48 10N 126 20 E
Beihai, China .... 33 D5 21 28N 109 6 E
Beijing, China .... 34 E9 39 55N 116 20 E
Beijing □, China .... 34 E9 39 55N 116 20 E
Beilen, Neths. .... 15 B6 52 52N 6 27 E
Beilpajah, Australia .... 63 E3 32 54S 143 52 E
Beinn na Faoghla = Benbecula, U.K. .... 11 D1 57 26N 7 21W
Beipiao, China .... 35 D11 41 52N 120 32 E
Beira, Mozam. .... 55 F3 19 50S 34 52 E
Beirut = Bayrūt, Lebanon .... 46 B4 33 53N 35 31 E
Beiseker, Canada .... 70 C6 51 23N 113 32W
Beitaolaizhao, China .... 35 B13 44 58N 125 58 E
Beitbridge, Zimbabwe .... 55 G3 22 12S 30 0 E
Beizhen = Binzhou, China .... 35 F10 37 20N 118 2 E
Beizhen, China .... 35 D11 41 38N 121 54 E
Beizhengzhen, China .... 35 B12 44 31N 123 30 E
Beja, Portugal .... 21 C2 38 2N 7 53W
Béja, Tunisia .... 51 A7 36 43N 9 12 E
Bejaïa, Algeria .... 50 A7 36 42N 5 2 E
Béjar, Spain .... 21 B3 40 23N 5 46W
Bejestān, Iran .... 45 C8 34 30N 58 5 E
Bekaa Valley = Al Biqā, Lebanon 46 A5 34 10N 36 10 E
Békéscsaba, Hungary .... 17 E11 46 40N 21 5 E
Bekily, Madag. .... 57 C8 24 13S 45 19 E
Bekisopa, Madag. .... 57 C8 21 40S 45 54 E
Bekitro, Madag. .... 57 C8 24 33S 45 18 E
Bekodoka, Madag. .... 57 B8 16 58S 45 7 E
Bekok, Malaysia .... 39 L4 2 20N 103 7 E
Bekopaka, Madag. .... 57 B7 19 9S 44 48 E
Bekuli, Indonesia .... 37 J17 8 22S 114 13 E
Bela, India .... 43 G10 25 50N 82 0 E
Bela, Pakistan .... 42 F2 26 12N 66 20 E
Bela Bela, S. Africa .... 57 C4 24 51S 28 19 E
Bela Crkva, Serbia & M. .... 23 B9 44 55N 21 27 E
Bela Vista, Brazil .... 94 A4 22 12S 56 20W
Bela Vista, Mozam. .... 57 D5 26 10S 32 44 E
Belan →, India .... 43 G9 24 2N 81 45 E
Belarus ■, Europe .... 17 B14 53 30N 27 0 E
Belau = Palau ■, Pac. Oc. .... 26 J17 7 30N 134 30 E
Belavenona, Madag. .... 57 C8 24 50S 47 4 E
Belawan, Indonesia .... 36 D1 3 33N 98 32 E
Belaya →, Russia .... 18 C9 54 40N 56 0 E
Belaya Tserkov = Bila Tserkva, Ukraine .... 17 D16 49 45N 30 10 E
Belcher Is., Canada .... 72 A3 56 15N 78 45W
Belden, U.S.A. .... 78 E5 40 2N 121 17W
Belebey, Russia .... 18 D9 54 7N 54 7 E
Beled Weyne = Belet Uen, Somali Rep. .... 47 G4 4 30N 45 5 E
Belém, Brazil .... 93 D9 1 20S 48 30W
Belén, Argentina .... 94 B2 27 40S 67 5W
Belén, Paraguay .... 94 A4 23 30S 57 6W
Belen, U.S.A. .... 77 J10 34 40N 106 46W
Belet Uen, Somali Rep. .... 47 G4 4 30N 45 5 E
Belev, Russia .... 18 D6 53 50N 36 5 E
Belfair, U.S.A. .... 78 C4 47 27N 122 50W
Belfast, S. Africa .... 57 D5 25 42S 30 2 E
Belfast, U.K. .... 10 B6 54 37N 5 56W
Belfast, Maine, U.S.A. .... 83 C11 44 26N 69 1W
Belfast, N.Y., U.S.A. .... 84 D6 42 21N 78 7W
Belfast L., U.K. .... 10 B6 54 40N 5 50W
Belfield, U.S.A. .... 80 B3 46 53N 103 12W
Belfort, France .... 20 C7 47 38N 6 50 E
Belfry, U.S.A. .... 76 D9 45 9N 109 1W
Belgaum, India .... 40 M9 15 55N 74 35 E
Belgium ■, Europe .... 15 D4 50 30N 5 0 E
Belgorod, Russia .... 19 D6 50 35N 36 35 E
Belgorod-Dnestrovskiy = Bilhorod-Dnistrovskyy, Ukraine 19 E5 46 11N 30 23 E
Belgrade = Beograd, Serbia & M. 23 B9 44 50N 20 37 E
Belgrade, U.S.A. .... 76 D8 45 47N 111 11W
Belhaven, U.S.A. .... 83 H7 35 33N 76 37W
Beli Drim →, Europe .... 23 C9 42 6N 20 25 E
Belimbing, Indonesia .... 37 J18 8 24S 115 2 E
Belinyu, Indonesia .... 36 E3 1 35S 105 50 E
Beliton Is. = Belitung, Indonesia 36 E3 3 10S 107 50 E
Belitung, Indonesia .... 36 E3 3 10S 107 50 E
Belize ■, Cent. Amer. .... 87 D7 17 0N 88 30W
Belize City, Belize .... 87 D7 17 25N 88 10W
Belkovskiy, Ostrov, Russia .... 29 B14 75 32N 135 44 E
Bell →, Canada .... 72 C4 49 48N 77 38W
Bell I., Canada .... 73 B8 50 46N 55 35W
Bell-Irving →, Canada .... 70 B3 56 12N 129 5W
Bell Peninsula, Canada .... 69 B11 63 50N 82 0W
Bell Ville, Argentina .... 94 C3 32 40S 62 40W
Bella Bella, Canada .... 70 C3 52 10N 128 10W
Bella Coola, Canada .... 70 C3 52 25N 126 40W
Bella Unión, Uruguay .... 94 C4 30 15S 57 40W
Bella Vista, Corrientes, Argentina 94 B4 28 33S 59 0W
Bella Vista, Tucuman, Argentina 94 B2 27 10S 65 25W
Bellaire, U.S.A. .... 84 F4 40 1N 80 44W
Bellata, Australia .... 63 D4 29 53S 149 46 E
Belle-Chasse, U.S.A. .... 81 L10 29 51N 89 59W
Belle Fourche, U.S.A. .... 80 C3 44 40N 103 51W

Belle Fourche →, U.S.A. .... 80 C3 44 26N 102 18W
Belle Glade, U.S.A. .... 83 M5 26 41N 80 40W
Belle-Île, France .... 20 C2 47 20N 3 10W
Belle Isle, Canada .... 73 B8 51 57N 55 25W
Belle Isle, Str. of, Canada .... 73 B8 51 30N 56 30W
Belle Plaine, U.S.A. .... 80 E8 41 54N 92 17W
Bellefontaine, U.S.A. .... 82 E4 40 22N 83 46W
Bellefonte, U.S.A. .... 84 F7 40 55N 77 47W
Belleoram, Canada .... 73 C8 47 31N 55 25W
Belleplaine, Barbados .... 89 g 13 15N 59 34W
Belleville, Canada .... 84 B7 44 10N 77 23W
Belleville, Ill., U.S.A. .... 80 F10 38 31N 89 59W
Belleville, Kans., U.S.A. .... 80 F6 39 50N 97 38W
Belleville, N.Y., U.S.A. .... 85 C8 43 46N 76 10W
Bellevue, Canada .... 70 D6 49 35N 114 22W
Bellevue, Idaho, U.S.A. .... 76 E6 43 28N 114 16W
Bellevue, Nebr., U.S.A. .... 80 E7 41 8N 95 53W
Bellevue, Ohio, U.S.A. .... 84 E2 41 17N 82 51W
Bellevue, Wash., U.S.A. .... 78 C4 47 37N 122 12W
Bellin = Kangirsuk, Canada .... 69 B13 60 0N 70 0W
Bellingen, Australia .... 63 E5 30 25S 152 50 E
Bellingham, U.S.A. .... 68 D7 48 46N 122 29W
Bellingshausen Sea, Antarctica . 5 C17 66 0S 80 0W
Bellinzona, Switz. .... 20 C8 46 11N 9 1 E
Bello, Colombia .... 92 B3 6 20N 75 33W
Bellows Falls, U.S.A. .... 85 C12 43 8N 72 27W
Bellpat, Pakistan .... 42 E3 29 0N 68 5 E
Belluno, Italy .... 22 A5 46 9N 12 13 E
Bellwood, U.S.A. .... 84 F6 40 36N 78 20W
Belmont, Canada .... 84 D3 42 53N 81 5W
Belmont, S. Africa .... 56 D3 29 28S 24 22 E
Belmont, U.S.A. .... 84 D6 42 14N 78 2W
Belmonte, Brazil .... 93 G11 16 0S 39 0W
Belmopan, Belize .... 87 D7 17 18N 88 30W
Belmullet, Ireland .... 10 B2 54 14N 9 58W
Belo Horizonte, Brazil .... 93 G10 19 55S 43 56W
Belo-sur-Mer, Madag. .... 57 C7 20 42S 44 0 E
Belo-Tsiribihina, Madag. .... 57 B7 19 40S 44 30 E
Belogorsk, Russia .... 29 D13 51 0N 128 20 E
Beloha, Madag. .... 57 D8 25 10S 45 3 E
Beloit, Kans., U.S.A. .... 80 F5 39 28N 98 6W
Beloit, Wis., U.S.A. .... 80 D10 42 31N 89 2W
Belokorovichi, Ukraine .... 17 C15 51 7N 28 2 E
Belomorsk, Russia .... 18 B5 64 35N 34 54 E
Belonia, India .... 41 H17 23 15N 91 30 E
Beloretsk, Russia .... 18 D10 53 58N 58 24 E
Belorussia = Belarus ■, Europe . 17 B14 53 30N 27 0 E
Belovo, Russia .... 28 D9 54 30N 86 0 E
Beloye, Ozero, Russia .... 18 B6 60 10N 37 35 E
Beloye More, Russia .... 18 A6 66 30N 38 0 E
Belozersk, Russia .... 18 B6 60 1N 37 45 E
Belpre, U.S.A. .... 82 F5 39 17N 81 34W
Belrain, India .... 43 E9 28 23N 80 55 E
Belt, U.S.A. .... 76 C8 47 23N 110 55W
Beltana, Australia .... 63 E2 30 48S 138 25 E
Belterra, Brazil .... 93 D8 2 45S 55 0W
Belton, U.S.A. .... 81 K6 31 3N 97 28W
Belton L., U.S.A. .... 81 K6 31 8N 97 32W
Beltsy = Bălţi, Moldova .... 17 E14 47 48N 27 58 E
Belturbet, Ireland .... 10 B4 54 6N 7 26W
Belukha, Russia .... 28 E9 49 50N 86 50 E
Beluran, Malaysia .... 36 C5 5 48N 117 35 E
Belvidere, Ill., U.S.A. .... 80 D10 42 15N 88 50W
Belvidere, N.J., U.S.A. .... 85 F9 40 50N 75 5W
Belyando →, Australia .... 62 C4 21 38S 146 50 E
Belyy, Ostrov, Russia .... 28 B8 73 30N 71 0 E
Belyy Yar, Russia .... 28 D9 58 26N 84 39 E
Belzoni, U.S.A. .... 81 J9 33 11N 90 29W
Bemaraha, Lembalemban' i, Madag. .... 57 B7 18 40S 44 45 E
Bemarivo, Madag. .... 57 C7 21 45S 44 45 E
Bemarivo →, Antsiranana, Madag. .... 57 A9 14 9S 50 9 E
Bemarivo →, Mahajanga, Madag. .... 57 B8 15 27S 47 40 E
Bemavo, Madag. .... 57 C8 21 33S 45 25 E
Bembéréke, Benin .... 50 F6 10 11N 2 43 E
Bembesi, Zimbabwe .... 55 G2 20 0S 28 58 E
Bembesi →, Zimbabwe .... 55 F2 18 57S 27 47 E
Bemetara, India .... 43 J9 21 42N 81 32 E
Bemidji, U.S.A. .... 80 B7 47 28N 94 53W
Bemolanga, Madag. .... 57 B8 17 44S 45 6 E
Ben, Iran .... 45 C6 32 32N 50 45 E
Ben Cruachan, U.K. .... 11 E3 56 26N 5 8W
Ben Dearg, U.K. .... 11 D4 57 47N 4 56W
Ben En →, Vietnam .... 38 C5 19 37N 105 30 E
Ben Hope, U.K. .... 11 C4 58 25N 4 36W
Ben Lawers, U.K. .... 11 E4 56 32N 4 14W
Ben Lomond, N.S.W., Australia . 63 E5 30 1S 151 43 E
Ben Lomond, Tas., Australia .... 63 G4 41 38S 147 42 E
Ben Lomond, U.K. .... 11 E4 56 11N 4 38W
Ben Lomond △, Australia .... 63 G4 41 33S 147 39 E
Ben Luc, Vietnam .... 39 G6 10 39N 106 29 E
Ben Macdhui, U.K. .... 11 D5 57 4N 3 40W
Ben Mhor, U.K. .... 11 D1 57 15N 7 18W
Ben More, Arg. & Bute, U.K. .... 11 E2 56 26N 6 1W
Ben More, Stirl., U.K. .... 11 E4 56 23N 4 32W
Ben More Assynt, U.K. .... 11 C4 58 8N 4 52W
Ben Nevis, U.K. .... 11 E3 56 48N 5 1W
Ben Quang, Vietnam .... 38 D6 17 3N 106 55 E
Ben Vorlich, U.K. .... 11 E4 56 21N 4 14W
Ben Wyvis, U.K. .... 11 D4 57 40N 4 35W
Bena, Nigeria .... 50 F7 11 20N 5 50 E
Benalla, Australia .... 63 F4 36 30S 146 0 E
Benares = Varanasi, India .... 43 G10 25 22N 83 0 E
Benavente, Spain .... 21 A3 42 2N 5 43W
Benavides, U.S.A. .... 81 M5 27 36N 98 25W
Benbecula, U.K. .... 11 D1 57 26N 7 21W
Benbonyathe, Australia .... 63 E2 30 25S 139 11 E
Bend, U.S.A. .... 76 D3 44 4N 121 19W
Bender Beila, Somali Rep. .... 47 F5 9 30N 50 48 E
Bendery = Tighina, Moldova .... 17 E15 46 50N 29 30 E
Bendigo, Australia .... 63 F3 36 40S 144 15 E
Benē Beraq, Israel .... 46 C3 32 6N 34 51 E
Benenitra, Madag. .... 57 C8 23 27S 45 5 E
Benevento, Italy .... 22 D6 41 8N 14 45 E
Benga, Mozam. .... 55 F3 16 11S 33 40 E
Bengal, Bay of, Ind. Oc. .... 41 M17 15 0N 90 0 E
Bengalūru = Bangalore, India . 40 N10 12 59N 77 40 E
Bengbu, China .... 35 H9 32 58N 117 20 E
Benghazi = Banghāzī, Libya .... 51 B10 32 11N 20 3 E
Bengkalis, Indonesia .... 36 D2 1 30N 102 10 E
Bengkulu, Indonesia .... 36 E2 3 50S 102 12 E
Bengkulu □, Indonesia .... 36 E2 3 48S 102 16 E
Bengough, Canada .... 71 D7 49 25N 105 10W
Benguela, Angola .... 53 G2 12 37S 13 25 E
Benguérua, I., Mozam. .... 57 C6 21 58S 35 28 E
Beni, Dem. Rep. of the Congo .... 54 B2 0 30N 29 27 E

Beni →, Bolivia .... 92 F5 10 23S 65 24W
Beni Mellal, Morocco .... 50 B4 32 21N 6 21W
Beni Suef, Egypt .... 51 C12 29 5N 31 6 E
Beniah L., Canada .... 70 A6 63 23N 112 17W
Benicia, U.S.A. .... 78 G4 38 3N 122 9W
Benidorm, Spain .... 21 C5 38 33N 0 9W
Benin ■, Africa .... 50 G6 10 0N 2 0 E
Benin, Bight of, W. Afr. .... 50 H6 5 0N 3 0 E
Benin City, Nigeria .... 50 G7 6 20N 5 31 E
Benitses, Greece .... 25 A3 39 32N 19 55 E
Benjamin Aceval, Paraguay .... 94 A4 24 58S 57 34W
Benjamin Constant, Brazil .... 92 D4 4 40S 70 15W
Benjamin Hill, Mexico .... 86 A2 30 10N 111 10W
Benkelman, U.S.A. .... 80 E4 40 3N 101 32W
Bennett, Canada .... 70 B2 59 56N 134 53W
Bennett, L., Australia .... 60 D5 22 50S 131 2 E
Bennetta, Ostrov, Russia .... 29 B15 76 21N 148 56 E
Bennettsville, U.S.A. .... 83 H6 34 37N 79 41W
Bennington, N.H., U.S.A. .... 85 D11 43 0N 71 55W
Bennington, Vt., U.S.A. .... 85 D11 42 53N 73 12W
Benoni, S. Africa .... 57 D4 26 11S 28 18 E
Benque Viejo del Carmen, Belize 87 D7 17 5N 89 8W
Benson, Ariz., U.S.A. .... 77 L8 31 58N 110 18W
Benson, Minn., U.S.A. .... 80 C7 45 19N 95 36W
Bent, Iran .... 45 E8 26 20N 59 31 E
Benteng, Indonesia .... 37 F6 6 10S 120 30 E
Bentinck I., Australia .... 62 B2 17 3S 139 35 E
Bento Gonçalves, Brazil .... 95 B5 29 10S 51 31W
Benton, Ark., U.S.A. .... 81 H8 34 34N 92 35W
Benton, Calif., U.S.A. .... 78 H8 37 48N 118 32W
Benton, Ill., U.S.A. .... 80 G10 38 0N 88 55W
Benton, Pa., U.S.A. .... 85 E8 41 12N 76 23W
Benton Harbor, U.S.A. .... 82 D2 42 6N 86 27W
Bentonville, U.S.A. .... 81 G7 36 22N 94 13W
Benue →, Nigeria .... 50 G7 7 48N 6 46 E
Benxi, China .... 35 D12 41 20N 123 48 E
Beo, Indonesia .... 37 D7 4 25N 126 50 E
Beograd, Serbia & M. .... 23 B9 44 50N 20 37 E
Beppu, Japan .... 31 H5 33 15N 131 30 E
Beqaa Valley = Al Biqā, Lebanon 46 A5 34 10N 36 10 E
Ber Mota, India .... 42 H3 23 27N 68 34 E
Berach →, India .... 42 G6 25 15N 75 2 E
Beraketa, Madag. .... 57 C7 23 7S 44 25 E
Berat, Albania .... 23 D8 40 43N 19 59 E
Berau, Teluk, Indonesia .... 37 E8 2 30S 132 30 E
Beravina, Madag. .... 57 B8 18 10S 45 14 E
Berber, Sudan .... 51 E12 18 0N 34 0 E
Berbera, Somali Rep. .... 47 E4 10 30N 45 2 E
Berbérati, C.A.R. .... 52 D3 4 15N 15 40 E
Berbice →, Guyana .... 92 B7 6 20N 57 32W
Berdichev = Berdychiv, Ukraine 17 D15 49 57N 28 30 E
Berdsk, Russia .... 28 D9 54 47N 83 2 E
Berdyansk, Ukraine .... 19 E6 46 45N 36 50 E
Berdychiv, Ukraine .... 17 D15 49 57N 28 30 E
Berea, U.S.A. .... 82 G3 37 34N 84 17W
Berebere, Indonesia .... 37 D7 2 25N 128 45 E
Bereda, Somali Rep. .... 47 E5 11 45N 51 0 E
Berehove, Ukraine .... 17 D12 48 15N 22 35 E
Berekum, Ghana .... 50 G5 7 29N 2 34W
Berens →, Canada .... 71 C9 52 25N 97 2W
Berens I., Canada .... 71 C9 52 18N 97 18W
Berens River, Canada .... 71 C9 52 25N 97 0W
Beresford, U.S.A. .... 80 D6 43 5N 96 47W
Berestechko, Ukraine .... 17 C13 50 22N 25 5 E
Berevo, Mahajanga, Madag. .... 57 B7 17 14S 44 17 E
Berevo, Toliara, Madag. .... 57 B7 19 44S 44 58 E
Berezhany, Ukraine .... 17 D13 49 26N 24 58 E
Berezina = Byarezina →, Belarus 17 B16 52 33N 30 14 E
Bereznik, Russia .... 18 B7 62 51N 42 40 E
Berezniki, Russia .... 18 C10 59 24N 56 46 E
Berezovo, Russia .... 28 C7 64 0N 65 0 E
Berga, Spain .... 21 A6 42 6N 1 48 E
Bergama, Turkey .... 23 E12 39 8N 27 11 E
Bérgamo, Italy .... 20 D8 45 41N 9 43 E
Bergen, Neths. .... 15 B4 52 40N 4 43 E
Bergen, Norway .... 9 F11 60 20N 5 20 E
Bergen, U.S.A. .... 84 C7 43 5N 77 57W
Bergen op Zoom, Neths. .... 15 C4 51 28N 4 18 E
Bergerac, France .... 20 D4 44 51N 0 30 E
Bergholz, U.S.A. .... 84 F4 40 31N 80 53W
Bergisch Gladbach, Germany . 15 D7 50 59N 7 8 E
Bergville, S. Africa .... 57 D4 28 52S 29 18 E
Berhala, Selat, Indonesia .... 36 E2 1 0S 104 15 E
Berhampore = Baharampur, India 43 G13 24 2N 88 27 E
Berhampur = Brahmapur, India . 41 K14 19 15N 84 54 E
Bering Sea, Pac. Oc. .... 66 C1 58 0N 171 0 E
Bering Strait, Pac. Oc. .... 66 B3 65 30N 169 0W
Beringovskiy, Russia .... 29 C18 63 3N 179 19 E
Berisso, Argentina .... 94 C4 34 56S 57 50W
Berja, Spain .... 21 D4 36 50N 2 56W
Berkeley, U.S.A. .... 78 H4 37 52N 122 16W
Berkner I., Antarctica .... 5 D18 79 30S 50 0W
Berkshire, U.S.A. .... 85 D8 42 19N 76 11W
Berkshire Downs, U.K. .... 13 F6 51 33N 1 29W
Berlin, Germany .... 16 B7 52 30N 13 25 E
Berlin, Md., U.S.A. .... 82 F8 38 20N 75 13W
Berlin, N.H., U.S.A. .... 85 B13 44 28N 71 11W
Berlin, N.Y., U.S.A. .... 85 D11 42 42N 73 23W
Berlin, Wis., U.S.A. .... 82 D1 43 58N 88 57W
Berlin L., U.S.A. .... 84 E4 41 3N 81 0W
Bermejo →, Formosa, Argentina 94 B4 26 51S 58 23W
Bermejo →, San Juan, Argentina 94 C2 32 30S 67 30W
Bermen, L., Canada .... 73 B6 53 35N 68 55W
Bermuda ☒, Atl. Oc. .... 99 A6 32 45N 65 0W
Bern, Switz. .... 20 C7 46 57N 7 28 E
Bernalillo, U.S.A. .... 77 J10 35 18N 106 33W
Bernardo de Irigoyen, Argentina 95 B5 26 15S 53 40W
Bernardo O'Higgins □, Chile .... 94 C1 34 15S 70 45W
Bernardsville, U.S.A. .... 85 F10 40 43N 74 34W
Bernasconi, Argentina .... 94 D3 37 55S 63 44W
Bernburg, Germany .... 16 C6 51 47N 11 44 E
Berne = Bern, Switz. .... 20 C7 46 57N 7 28 E
Berneray, U.K. .... 11 D1 57 43N 7 11W
Bernier I., Australia .... 61 D1 24 50S 113 12 E
Bernina, Piz, Switz. .... 20 C8 46 20N 9 54 E
Beroroha, Madag. .... 57 C8 21 40S 45 10 E
Beroun, Czech Rep. .... 16 D8 49 57N 14 5 E
Berri, Australia .... 63 E3 34 14S 140 35 E
Berriane, Algeria .... 50 B6 32 50N 3 46 E
Berry, Australia .... 63 E5 34 46S 150 43 E
Berry, France .... 20 C5 46 50N 2 0 E
Berry Is., Bahamas .... 88 A4 25 40N 77 50W
Berryville, U.S.A. .... 81 G8 36 22N 93 34W
Bershad, Ukraine .... 17 D15 48 22N 29 31 E
Berthold, U.S.A. .... 80 A4 48 19N 101 44W

Berthoud, U.S.A. .... 80 E2 40 19N 105 5W
Bertoua, Cameroon .... 52 D2 4 30N 13 45 E
Bertraghboy B., Ireland .... 10 C2 53 22N 9 54W
Berwick, U.S.A. .... 85 E8 41 3N 76 14W
Berwick-upon-Tweed, U.K. .... 12 B6 55 46N 2 0W
Berwyn Mts., U.K. .... 12 E4 52 54N 3 26W
Besal, Pakistan .... 43 B5 35 4N 73 56 E
Besalampy, Madag. .... 57 B7 16 43S 44 29 E
Besançon, France .... 20 C7 47 15N 6 2 E
Besar, Indonesia .... 36 E5 2 40S 116 0 E
Besnard L., Canada .... 71 B7 55 25N 106 0W
Besni, Turkey .... 44 B3 37 41N 37 52 E
Besor, N. →, Egypt .... 46 D3 31 28N 34 22 E
Bessarabiya, Moldova .... 17 E15 47 0N 28 10 E
Bessarabka = Basarabeasca, Moldova .... 17 E15 46 21N 28 58 E
Bessemer, Ala., U.S.A. .... 83 J2 33 24N 86 58W
Bessemer, Mich., U.S.A. .... 80 B9 46 29N 90 3W
Bessemer, Pa., U.S.A. .... 84 F4 40 59N 80 30W
Beswick, Australia .... 60 B5 14 34S 132 53 E
Bet She'an, Israel .... 46 C4 32 30N 35 30 E
Bet Shemesh, Israel .... 46 D4 31 44N 35 0 E
Betafo, Madag. .... 57 B8 19 50S 46 51 E
Betancuria, Canary Is. .... 24 F5 28 25N 14 3W
Betanzos, Spain .... 21 A1 43 15N 8 12W
Bétaré Oya, Cameroon .... 52 C2 5 40N 14 5 E
Betatao, Madag. .... 57 B8 18 11S 47 52 E
Bethal, S. Africa .... 57 D4 26 27S 29 28 E
Bethanien, Namibia .... 56 D2 26 31S 17 8 E
Bethany, Canada .... 84 B6 44 11N 78 34W
Bethany, U.S.A. .... 80 E7 40 16N 94 2W
Bethel, Alaska, U.S.A. .... 68 B3 60 48N 161 45W
Bethel, Conn., U.S.A. .... 85 E11 41 22N 73 25W
Bethel, Maine, U.S.A. .... 85 B14 44 25N 70 47W
Bethel, Vt., U.S.A. .... 85 C12 43 50N 72 38W
Bethel Park, U.S.A. .... 84 F4 40 20N 80 1W
Bethlehem = Bayt Laḥm, West Bank .... 46 D4 31 43N 35 12 E
Bethlehem, S. Africa .... 57 D4 28 14S 28 18 E
Bethlehem, U.S.A. .... 85 F9 40 37N 75 23W
Bethulie, S. Africa .... 56 E4 30 30S 25 59 E
Béthune, France .... 20 A5 50 30N 2 38 E
Betioky, Madag. .... 57 C7 23 48S 44 20 E
Betong, Thailand .... 39 K3 5 45N 101 5 E
Betoota, Australia .... 62 D3 25 45S 140 42 E
Betroka, Madag. .... 57 C8 23 16S 46 0 E
Betsiamites, Canada .... 73 C6 48 56N 68 40W
Betsiamites →, Canada .... 73 C6 48 56N 68 38W
Betsiboka →, Madag. .... 57 B8 16 3S 46 36 E
Bettendorf, U.S.A. .... 80 E9 41 32N 90 30W
Bettiah, India .... 43 F11 26 48N 84 33 E
Betul, India .... 40 J10 21 58N 77 59 E
Betung, Malaysia .... 36 D4 1 24N 111 31 E
Betws-y-Coed, U.K. .... 12 D4 53 5N 3 48W
Beulah, Mich., U.S.A. .... 82 C2 44 38N 86 6W
Beulah, N. Dak., U.S.A. .... 80 B4 47 16N 101 47W
Beveren, Belgium .... 15 C4 51 12N 4 16 E
Beverley, Australia .... 61 F2 32 9S 116 56 E
Beverley, U.K. .... 12 D7 53 51N 0 26W
Beverly Hills, U.S.A. .... 83 L4 28 56N 82 28W
Beverly, U.S.A. .... 85 D14 42 33N 70 53W
Beverly Hills, U.S.A. .... 79 L8 34 4N 118 25W
Bevoalavo, Madag. .... 57 D7 25 13S 45 26 E
Bewas →, India .... 43 H8 23 59N 79 21 E
Bexhill, U.K. .... 13 G8 50 51N 0 29 E
Beyānlū, Iran .... 44 C5 36 0N 47 51 E
Beyneu, Kazakhstan .... 19 E10 45 18N 55 9 E
Beypazarı, Turkey .... 19 F5 40 10N 31 56 E
Beyşehir Gölü, Turkey .... 19 G5 37 41N 31 33 E
Béziers, France .... 20 E5 43 20N 3 12 E
Bezwada = Vijayawada, India . 41 L12 16 31N 80 39 E
Bhabua, India .... 43 G10 25 3N 83 37 E
Bhachau, India .... 40 H7 23 20N 70 16 E
Bhadar →, Gujarat, India .... 42 H5 22 17N 72 20 E
Bhadar →, Gujarat, India .... 42 J3 21 27N 69 47 E
Bhadarwah, India .... 43 C6 32 58N 75 46 E
Bhadgaon = Bhaktapur, Nepal . 43 F11 27 38N 85 24 E
Bhadohi, India .... 43 G10 25 25N 82 34 E
Bhadra, India .... 42 E6 29 8N 75 14 E
Bhadrak, India .... 41 J15 21 10N 86 30 E
Bhadran, India .... 42 H5 22 19N 72 6 E
Bhadravati, India .... 40 N9 13 49N 75 40 E
Bhag, Pakistan .... 42 E2 29 2N 67 49 E
Bhagalpur, India .... 43 G12 25 10N 87 0 E
Bhagirathi →, Uttaranchal, India 43 D8 30 8N 78 35 E
Bhagirathi →, W. Bengal, India . 43 H13 23 25N 88 23 E
Bhakkar, Pakistan .... 42 D4 31 40N 71 5 E
Bhakra Dam, India .... 42 D7 31 30N 76 45 E
Bhaktapur, Nepal .... 43 F11 27 38N 85 24 E
Bhamo, Burma .... 41 G20 24 15N 97 15 E
Bhandara, India .... 40 J11 21 5N 79 42 E
Bhanpura, India .... 42 G6 24 31N 75 44 E
Bhanrer Ra., India .... 43 H8 23 40N 79 45 E
Bhaptiahi, India .... 43 F12 26 19N 86 44 E
Bharat = India ■, Asia .... 40 K11 20 0N 78 0 E
Bharatpur, Chhattisgarh, India . 43 H9 23 44N 81 46 E
Bharatpur, Raj., India .... 42 F7 27 15N 77 30 E
Bharno, India .... 43 H11 23 14N 84 53 E
Bharuch, India .... 40 J8 21 47N 73 0 E
Bhatinda, India .... 42 D6 30 15N 74 57 E
Bhatpara, India .... 43 H13 22 50N 88 25 E
Bhattu, India .... 42 E6 29 36N 75 19 E
Bhaun, Pakistan .... 42 C5 32 55N 72 40 E
Bhaunagar = Bhavnagar, India . 40 J8 21 45N 72 10 E
Bhavnagar, India .... 40 J8 21 45N 72 10 E
Bhawari, India .... 42 G5 25 42N 73 4 E
Bhayavadar, India .... 42 J4 21 51N 70 15 E
Bhera, Pakistan .... 42 C5 32 29N 72 57 E
Bhikangaon, India .... 42 J6 21 52N 75 57 E
Bhilai = Bhilainagar-Durg, India 41 J12 21 13N 81 26 E
Bhilsa = Vidisha, India .... 42 H7 23 28N 77 53 E
Bhilwara, India .... 42 G6 25 25N 74 38 E
Bhima →, India .... 40 L10 16 25N 77 17 E
Bhimbar, Pakistan .... 43 C6 32 59N 74 3 E
Bhind, India .... 43 F8 26 30N 78 46 E
Bhinga, India .... 43 F9 27 43N 81 56 E
Bhinmal, India .... 42 G5 25 0N 72 15 E
Bhiwandi, India .... 40 K8 19 20N 73 0 E
Bhiwani, India .... 42 E7 28 50N 76 9 E
Bhogava →, India .... 42 H5 22 26N 72 20 E
Bhola, Bangla. .... 41 H17 22 45N 90 35 E
Bholari, Pakistan .... 42 G3 25 19N 68 13 E
Bhopal, India .... 42 H7 23 20N 77 30 E
Bhubaneshwar, India .... 41 J14 20 15N 85 50 E
Bhuj, India .... 42 H3 23 15N 69 49 E
Bhumiphol Res., Thailand .... 38 D2 17 0N 99 0 E
Bhusawal, India .... 40 J9 21 3N 75 46 E
Bhutan ■, Asia .... 41 F17 27 25N 90 30 E
Biafra, B. of = Bonny, Bight of, Africa .... 52 D1 3 30N 9 20 E

Biak, Indonesia . . . . . . . . . . . 37 E9    1 10S 136  6 E
Biała Podlaska, Poland . . . . . 17 B12 52  4N  23  6 E
Białogard, Poland . . . . . . . . . 16 A8  54  2N  15 58 E
Białystok, Poland . . . . . . . . . 17 B12 53 10N  23 10 E
Biaora, India . . . . . . . . . . . . . 42 H7  23 56N  76 56 E
Biärjmand, Iran . . . . . . . . . . . 45 B7  36  6N  55 53 E
Biaro, Indonesia . . . . . . . . . . 37 D7   2  5N 125 26 E
Biarritz, France . . . . . . . . . . . 20 E3  43 29N   1 33W
Bias, Indonesia . . . . . . . . . . . 37 J18  8 24S 115 36 E
Bibai, Japan . . . . . . . . . . . . . 30 C10 43 19N 141 52 E
Bibby I., Canada . . . . . . . . . . 71 A10 61 55N  93  0W
Biberach, Germany . . . . . . . . 16 D5  48  5N   9 47 E
Bibungwa, Dem. Rep. of
  the Congo . . . . . . . . . . . . . 54 C2   2 40S  28 15 E
Bicester, U.K. . . . . . . . . . . . . 13 F6  51 54N   1  9W
Bicheno, Australia . . . . . . . . . 63 G4  41 52S 148 18 E
Bichia, India . . . . . . . . . . . . . 43 H9  22 27N  80 42 E
Bickerton I., Australia . . . . . . 62 A2  13 45S 136 10 E
Bida, Nigeria . . . . . . . . . . . . . 50 G7   9  3N   5 58 E
Bidar, India . . . . . . . . . . . . . . 40 L10 17 55N  77 35 E
Biddeford, U.S.A. . . . . . . . . . 83 D10 43 30N  70 28W
Bideford, U.K. . . . . . . . . . . . . 13 F3  51  1N   4 13W
Bideford Bay, U.K. . . . . . . . . 13 F3  51  5N   4 20W
Bidhuna, India . . . . . . . . . . . . 43 F8  26 49N  79 31 E
Bidor, Malaysia . . . . . . . . . . . 39 K3   4  6N 101 15 E
Bié, Planalto de, Angola . . . . 53 G3  12  0S  16  0 E
Bieber, U.S.A. . . . . . . . . . . . . 76 F3  41  7N 121  8W
Biel, Switz. . . . . . . . . . . . . . . . 20 C7  47  8N   7 14 E
Bielefeld, Germany . . . . . . . . 16 B5  52  1N   8 33 E
Biella, Italy . . . . . . . . . . . . . . 20 D8  45 34N   8  3 E
Bielsk Podlaski, Poland . . . . 17 B12 52 47N  23 12 E
Bielsko-Biała, Poland . . . . . . 17 D10 49 50N  19  2 E
Bien Hoa, Vietnam . . . . . . . . 39 G6  10 57N 106 49 E
Bienne = Biel, Switz. . . . . . . . 20 C7  47  8N   7 14 E
Bienville, L., Canada . . . . . . 72 A5  55  5N  72 40W
Biesiesfontein, S. Africa . . . . 56 E2  30 57S  17 58 E
Big →, Canada . . . . . . . . . . . 73 B8  54 50N  58 55W
Big B., Canada . . . . . . . . . . . 73 A7  55 43N  60 35W
Big Bear City, U.S.A. . . . . . . 79 L10 34 16N 116 51W
Big Bear Lake, U.S.A. . . . . . . 79 L10 34 15N 116 56W
Big Belt Mts., U.S.A. . . . . . . 76 C8  46 30N 111 25W
Big Bend, Swaziland . . . . . . . 57 D5  26 50S  31 58 E
Big Bend △, U.S.A. . . . . . . . . 81 L3  29 20N 103  5W
Big Black →, U.S.A. . . . . . . . 81 K9  32  3N  91  4W
Big Blue →, U.S.A. . . . . . . . . 80 F6  39 35N  96 34W
Big Creek, U.S.A. . . . . . . . . . 78 H7  37 11N 119 14W
Big Cypress △, U.S.A. . . . . . 83 M5  26 10N  81 10W
Big Cypress Swamp, U.S.A. . 83 M5  26 15N  81 30W
Big Falls, U.S.A. . . . . . . . . . . 80 A8  48 12N  93 48W
Big Fork →, U.S.A. . . . . . . . . 80 A8  48 31N  93 43W
Big Horn Mts. = Bighorn Mts.,
  U.S.A. . . . . . . . . . . . . . . . . 76 D10 44 30N 107 30W
Big I., Canada . . . . . . . . . . . . 70 A5  61  7N 116 45W
Big Lake, U.S.A. . . . . . . . . . . 81 K4  31 12N 101 28W
Big Moose, U.S.A. . . . . . . . . 85 C10 43 49N  74 58W
Big Muddy Cr. →, U.S.A. . . . 80 A2  48  8N 104 36W
Big Pine, U.S.A. . . . . . . . . . . 78 H8  37 10N 118 17W
Big Piney, U.S.A. . . . . . . . . . 76 E8  42 32N 110  7W
Big Rapids, U.S.A. . . . . . . . . 82 D3  43 42N  85 29W
Big Rideau L., Canada . . . . . 85 B8  44 40N  76 15W
Big River, Canada . . . . . . . . . 71 C7  53 50N 107  0W
Big Run, U.S.A. . . . . . . . . . . . 84 F6  40 57N  78 55W
Big Sable Pt., U.S.A. . . . . . . . 82 C2  44  3N  86  1W
Big Salmon →, Canada . . . . . 70 A2  61 52N 134 55W
Big Sand L., Canada . . . . . . . 71 B9  57 45N  99 45W
Big Sandy, U.S.A. . . . . . . . . . 76 B8  48 11N 110  7W
Big Sandy →, U.S.A. . . . . . . 82 F4  38 25N  82 36W
Big Sandy Cr. →, U.S.A. . . . 80 F3  38  7N 102 29W
Big Sioux →, U.S.A. . . . . . . . 80 D6  42 29N  96 27W
Big South Fork △, U.S.A. . . . 83 G3  36 27N  84 47W
Big Spring, U.S.A. . . . . . . . . . 81 J4  32 15N 101 28W
Big Stone City, U.S.A. . . . . . 80 C6  45 18N  96 28W
Big Stone Gap, U.S.A. . . . . . 83 G4  36 52N  82 47W
Big Stone L., U.S.A. . . . . . . . 80 C6  45 30N  96 35W
Big Sur, U.S.A. . . . . . . . . . . . 78 J5  36 15N 121 48W
Big Timber, U.S.A. . . . . . . . . 76 D9  45 50N 109 57W
Big Trout L., Canada . . . . . . . 72 B2  53 40N  90  0W
Big Trout Lake, Canada . . . . . 72 B2  53 45N  90  0W
Biğa, Turkey . . . . . . . . . . . . . 23 D12 40 13N  27 14 E
Bigadiç, Turkey . . . . . . . . . . . 23 E13 39 22N   28  7 E
Biggar, Canada . . . . . . . . . . . 71 C7  52  4N 108  0W
Biggar, U.K. . . . . . . . . . . . . . 11 F5  55 38N   3 32W
Bigge I., Australia . . . . . . . . . 60 B4  14 35S 125 10 E
Biggenden, Australia . . . . . . . 63 D5  25 31S 152  4 E
Biggleswade, U.K. . . . . . . . . . 13 E7  52  5N   0 14W
Biggs, U.S.A. . . . . . . . . . . . . 78 F5  39 25N 121 43W
Bighorn, U.S.A. . . . . . . . . . . . 76 C10 46 10N 107 27W
Bighorn →, U.S.A. . . . . . . . . 76 D9  46 10N 107 28W
Bighorn Canyon △, U.S.A. . . 76 D9  45 10N 108  0W
Bighorn L., U.S.A. . . . . . . . . . 76 D9  44 55N 108 15W
Bighorn Mts., U.S.A. . . . . . . . 76 D10 44 30N 107 30W
Bigstone L., Canada . . . . . . . 71 C9  53 42N  95 44W
Bigwa, Tanzania . . . . . . . . . . 54 D4   7 10S  39 10 E
Bihać, Bos.-H. . . . . . . . . . . . . 16 F8  44 49N  15 57 E
Bihar, India . . . . . . . . . . . . . . 43 G11 25 5N  85 40 E
Bihar □, India . . . . . . . . . . . . 43 G12 25  0N  86  0 E
Biharamulo, Tanzania . . . . . . 54 C3   2 25S  31 25 E
Biharamulo △, Tanzania . . . . 54 C3   2 24S  31 26 E
Biharganj, India . . . . . . . . . . . 43 G12 25 44N  86 59 E
Bihor, Munții, Romania . . . . . 17 E12 46 29N  22 47 E
Bijagós, Arquipélago dos,
  Guinea-Biss. . . . . . . . . . . . 50 F2  11 15N  16 10W
Bijaipur, India . . . . . . . . . . . . 42 F7  26  2N  77 20 E
Bijapur, Chhattisgarh, India . 41 K12 18 50N  80 50 E
Bijapur, Karnataka, India . . . . 40 L9  16 50N  75 55 E
Bijär, Iran . . . . . . . . . . . . . . . . 44 C5  35 52N  47 35 E
Bijawar, India . . . . . . . . . . . . 43 G8  24 38N  79 30 E
Bijeljina, Bos.-H. . . . . . . . . . . 23 B8  44 46N  19 14 E
Bijnor, India . . . . . . . . . . . . . . 42 E8  29 27N  78 11 E
Bikaner, India . . . . . . . . . . . . 42 E5  28  2N  73 18 E
Bikapur, India . . . . . . . . . . . . 43 F10 26 30N  82  7 E
Bikeqi, China . . . . . . . . . . . . . 34 D6  40 43N 111 20 E
Bikfayyā, Lebanon . . . . . . . . 46 B4  33 55N  35 41 E
Bikin, Russia . . . . . . . . . . . . . 29 E14 46 50N 134 20 E
Bikin →, Russia . . . . . . . . . . . 30 A7  46 51N 134  2 E
Bikini Atoll, Marshall Is. . . . . 64 F8  12  0N 167 30 E
Bikita, Zimbabwe . . . . . . . . . 57 C5  20  6S  31 41 E
Bila Tserkva, Ukraine . . . . . . 17 D16 49 45N  30 10 E
Bilara, India . . . . . . . . . . . . . . 42 F5  26 14N  73 53 E
Bilaspur, Chhattisgarh, India 43 H10 22  2N  82 15 E
Bilaspur, Punjab, India . . . . . 42 D7  31 19N  76 50 E
Bilauk Taungdan, Thailand . . 38 F2  13  0N  99  0 E
Bilbao, Spain . . . . . . . . . . . . 21 A4  43 16N   2 56W
Bilbo = Bilbao, Spain . . . . . . 21 A4  43 16N   2 56W
Bildudalur, Iceland . . . . . . . . 8 D2  65 41N  23 36W
Bílé Karpaty, Europe . . . . . . . 17 D9  48  5N  18  0 E
Bilecik, Turkey . . . . . . . . . . . 19 F5  40  5N  30  5 E
Bilgram, India . . . . . . . . . . . . 43 F9  27 11N  80  2 E

Bilhaur, India . . . . . . . . . . . . . 43 F9  26 51N  80  5 E
Bilhorod-Dnistrovskyy, Ukraine 19 E5  46 11N  30 23 E
Bilibino, Russia . . . . . . . . . . . 29 C17 68  3N 166 20 E
Bilibiza, Mozam. . . . . . . . . . . 55 E5  12 30S  40 20 E
Billabong Roadhouse, Australia 61 E2  27 25S 115 49 E
Billiluna, Australia . . . . . . . . . 60 C4  19 37S 127 41 E
Billings, U.S.A. . . . . . . . . . . . 76 D9  45 47N 108 30W
Billiton Is. = Belitung, Indonesia 36 E3   3 10S 107 50 E
Bilma, Niger . . . . . . . . . . . . . 51 E8  18 50N  13 30 E
Biloela, Australia . . . . . . . . . . 62 C5  24 24S 150 31 E
Biloxi, U.S.A. . . . . . . . . . . . . . 81 K10 30 24N  88 53W
Bilpa Morea Claypan, Australia 62 D3  25  0S 140  0 E
Biltine, Chad . . . . . . . . . . . . . 51 F10 14 40N  20 50 E
Bima, Indonesia . . . . . . . . . . 37 F5   8 22S 118 49 E
Bimini Is., Bahamas . . . . . . . 88 A4  25 42N  79 25W
Bin Xian, Heilongjiang, China 35 B14 45 42N 127 32 E
Bin Xian, Shaanxi, China . . . . 34 G5  35  2N 108  4 E
Bina-Etawah, India . . . . . . . . 42 G8  24 13N  78 14 E
Bināb, Iran . . . . . . . . . . . . . . 45 B6  36 35N  48 41 E
Binalbagan, Phil. . . . . . . . . . . 37 B6  10 12N 122 50 E
Binalong, Australia . . . . . . . . 63 E4  34 40S 148 39 E
Binālud, Kūh-e, Iran . . . . . . . 45 B8  36 30N  58 30 E
Binatang = Bintangor, Malaysia 36 D4  2 10N 111 40 E
Binche, Belgium . . . . . . . . . . 15 D4  50 26N   4 10 E
Bindki, India . . . . . . . . . . . . . 43 F9  26  2N  80 36 E
Bindura, Zimbabwe . . . . . . . . 55 F3  17 18S  31 18 E
Bingara, Australia . . . . . . . . . 63 D5  29 52S 150 36 E
Bingham, U.S.A. . . . . . . . . . . 83 C11 45  3N  69 53W
Binghamton, U.S.A. . . . . . . . 85 D9  42  6N  75 55W
Bingöl, Turkey . . . . . . . . . . . . 44 B4  38 53N  40 29 E
Binh Dinh = An Nhon, Vietnam 38 F7  13 55N 109  7 E
Binh Khe, Vietnam . . . . . . . . 38 F7  13 57N 108 51 E
Binh Son, Vietnam . . . . . . . . 38 E7  15 20N 108 40 E
Binhai, China . . . . . . . . . . . . . 35 G10 34  2N 119 49 E
Binisatua, Spain . . . . . . . . . . 24 B11 39 50N   4 11 E
Binjai, Indonesia . . . . . . . . . . 36 D3   3 20N  98 30 E
Binnaway, Australia . . . . . . . . 63 E4  31 28S 149 24 E
Binongko, Indonesia . . . . . . . 37 F6   5 57S 124  2 E
Binscarth, Canada . . . . . . . . . 71 C8  50 37N 101 17W
Bintan, Indonesia . . . . . . . . . 36 D2   1  0N 104  0 E
Bintangor, Malaysia . . . . . . . . 36 D4   2 10N 111 40 E
Bintulu, Malaysia . . . . . . . . . . 36 D4   3 10N 113  0 E
Bintuni, Indonesia . . . . . . . . . 37 E8   2  7S 133 32 E
Binzert = Bizerte, Tunisia . . . . 51 A7  37 15N   9 50 E
Binzhou, China . . . . . . . . . . . 35 F10 37 20N 118  2 E
Bío Bío □, Chile . . . . . . . . . . 94 D1  37 35S  72  0W
Bioko, Eq. Guin. . . . . . . . . . . 52 D1   3 30N   8 40 E
Bir, India . . . . . . . . . . . . . . . . 40 K9  19  4N  75 46 E
Bîr Abu Muḩammad, Egypt . . 46 F3  29 44N  34 14 E
Bi'r ad Dabbāghāt, Jordan . . 46 E4  30 26N  35 32 E
Bi'r al Butayyihāt, Jordan . . . 46 F4  29 47N  35 20 E
Bi'r al Mārī, Jordan . . . . . . . . 46 E4  30  4N  35 33 E
Bi'r al Qattār, Jordan . . . . . . . 46 F4  29 47N  35 32 E
Bîr Atrun, Sudan . . . . . . . . . . 51 E11 18 15N  26 40 E
Bîr Beiḑa, Egypt . . . . . . . . . . 46 E3  30 25N  34 29 E
Bîr el 'Abd, Egypt . . . . . . . . . 46 D2  31  2N  33  0 E
Bîr el Biarât, Egypt . . . . . . . . 46 F3  29 30N  34 43 E
Bîr el Duweidar, Egypt . . . . . 46 E1  30 56N  32 32 E
Bîr el Garârât, Egypt . . . . . . . 46 D2  31  3N  33 34 E
Bîr el Heisi, Egypt . . . . . . . . . 46 F3  29 22N  34 36 E
Bîr el Jafir, Egypt . . . . . . . . . 46 E2  30 50N  32 41 E
Bîr el Mâlhi, Egypt . . . . . . . . 46 E2  30 38N  33 19 E
Bîr el Thamâda, Egypt . . . . . 46 E2  30 12N  33 27 E
Bîr Gebeil Ḩişn, Egypt . . . . . 46 E2  30  2N  33 18 E
Bi'r Ghaḑîr, Syria . . . . . . . . . 46 A6  34 6N   37  3 E
Bîr Ḩasana, Egypt . . . . . . . . . 46 E2  30 29N  33 46 E
Bîr Kaseiba, Egypt . . . . . . . . 46 E2  31  0N  33 17 E
Bîr Lahfân, Egypt . . . . . . . . . 46 E2  31  0N  33 51 E
Bîr Madkûr, Egypt . . . . . . . . . 46 E1  30 44N  32 33 E
Bîr Mogreïn, Mauritania . . . . 50 C3  25 10N  11 25W
Bi'r Muţribah, Kuwait . . . . . . 44 D5  29 54N  47 17 E
Bîr Qaţia, Egypt . . . . . . . . . . 46 E1  30 58N  32 45 E
Bîr Shalatein, Egypt . . . . . . . 51 D13 23  5N  35 25 E
Biratnagar, Nepal . . . . . . . . . 43 F12 26 27N  87 17 E
Birawa, Dem. Rep. of the Congo 54 C2  2 20S  28 48 E
Birch →, Canada . . . . . . . . . . 70 B6  58 28N 112 17W
Birch Hills, Canada . . . . . . . . 71 C7  52 59N 105 25W
Birch I., Canada . . . . . . . . . . . 71 C9  52 26N  99 54W
Birch L., N.W.T., Canada . . . . 70 A5  62  4N 116 33W
Birch L., Ont., Canada . . . . . . 72 B1  51 23N  92 18W
Birch Mts., Canada . . . . . . . . 70 B6  57 30N 113 10W
Birch River, Canada . . . . . . . 71 C8  52 24N 101  6W
Birchip, Australia . . . . . . . . . . 63 F3  35 56S 142 55 E
Bird, Canada . . . . . . . . . . . . . 71 B10 56 30N  94 13W
Bird I. = Aves, I. de, W. Indies 89 C7  15 45N  63 55W
Bird I., Antarctica . . . . . . . . . 5 B1  54  0S  38  0W
Birdsville, Australia . . . . . . . . 62 D2  25 51S 139 20 E
Birdum Cr. →, Australia . . . . 60 C5  15 14S 133  0 E
Birecik, Turkey . . . . . . . . . . . 44 B3  37  2N  38  0 E
Birein, Israel . . . . . . . . . . . . . 46 E3  30 50N  34 28 E
Bireuen, Indonesia . . . . . . . . 36 C1   5 14N  96 39 E
Birigui, Brazil . . . . . . . . . . . . . 95 A5  21 18S  50 16W
Birjand, Iran . . . . . . . . . . . . . 45 C8  32 53N  59 13 E
Birkenhead, U.K. . . . . . . . . . . 12 D4  53 23N   3  2W
Bîrlad = Bârlad, Romania . . . 17 E14 46 15N  27 38 E
Birmingham, U.K. . . . . . . . . . 13 E6  52 29N   1 52W
Birmingham, U.S.A. . . . . . . . . 83 J2  33 31N  86 48W
Birmingham International ✈
  (BHX), U.K. . . . . . . . . . . . . 13 E6  52 26N   1 45W
Birmitrapur, India . . . . . . . . . 41 H14 22 24N  84 46 E
Birni Nkonni, Niger . . . . . . . . 50 F7  13 55N   5 15 E
Birnin Kebbi, Nigeria . . . . . . 50 F6  12 32N   4 12 E
Birobidzhan, Russia . . . . . . . 29 E14 48 50N 132 50 E
Birr, Ireland . . . . . . . . . . . . . . 10 C4  53  6N   7 54W
Birrie →, Australia . . . . . . . . . 63 D4  29 43S 146 37 E
Birsilpur, India . . . . . . . . . . . . 42 E5  28 11N  72 15 E
Birsk, Russia . . . . . . . . . . . . . 18 C10 55 25N  55 30 E
Birtle, Canada . . . . . . . . . . . . 71 C8  50 30N 101  5W
Birur, India . . . . . . . . . . . . . . . 40 N9  13 30N  75 55 E
Biržai, Lithuania . . . . . . . . . . . 9 H21 56 11N  24 45 E
Birzebbugga, Malta . . . . . . . . 25 D2  35 50N  14 32 E
Bisa, Indonesia . . . . . . . . . . . 37 E7   1 15S 127 28 E
Bisalpur, India . . . . . . . . . . . . 43 E8  28 14N  79 48 E
Bisbee, U.S.A. . . . . . . . . . . . . 77 L9  31 27N 109 55W
Biscay, B. of, Atl. Oc. . . . . . . 20 D1  45  0N   2  0W
Biscayne B., U.S.A. . . . . . . . . 83 N5  25 40N  80 12W
Biscoe Is., Antarctica . . . . . . 5 C17  66  0S  67  0W
Biscotasing, Canada . . . . . . . 72 C3  47 18N  82  9W
Bishkek, Kyrgyzstan . . . . . . . 28 E8  42 54N  74 46 E
Bishnupur, India . . . . . . . . . . 43 H12 23  8N  87 20 E
Bisho, S. Africa . . . . . . . . . . . 57 E4  32 50S  27 23 E
Bishop, Calif., U.S.A. . . . . . . 78 H8  37 22N 118 24W
Bishop, Tex., U.S.A. . . . . . . . 81 M6  27 35N  97 48W
Bishop Auckland, U.K. . . . . . 12 C6  54 39N   1 40W
Bishop's Falls, Canada . . . . . 73 C8  49  2N  55 30W
Bishop's Stortford, U.K. . . . . 13 F8  51 52N   0 10 E
Bisina, L., Uganda . . . . . . . . 54 B3   1 38N  33 56 E
Biskra, Algeria . . . . . . . . . . . . 50 B7  34 50N   5 44 E

Bismarck, U.S.A. . . . . . . . . . . 80 B4  46 48N 100 47W
Bismarck Arch., Papua N. G. . 64 H7   2 30S 150  0 E
Biso, Uganda . . . . . . . . . . . . . 54 B3   1 44N  31 26 E
Bison, U.S.A. . . . . . . . . . . . . . 80 C3  45 31N 102 28W
Bisotūn, Iran . . . . . . . . . . . . . 44 C5  34 23N  47 26 E
Bissagos = Bijagós, Arquipélago
  dos, Guinea-Biss. . . . . . . . 50 F2  11 15N  16 10W
Bissau, Guinea-Biss. . . . . . . . 50 F2  11 45N  15 45W
Bistcho L., Canada . . . . . . . . 70 B5  59 45N 118 50W
Bistriţa, Romania . . . . . . . . . . 17 E13 47  9N  24 35 E
Bistriţa →, Romania . . . . . . . 17 E14 46 30N  26 57 E
Biswan, India . . . . . . . . . . . . . 43 F9  27 29N  81  2 E
Bitlis, Turkey . . . . . . . . . . . . . 44 B4  38 20N  42  3 E
Bitola, Macedonia . . . . . . . . . 23 D9  41  1N  21 20 E
Bitolj = Bitola, Macedonia . . . 23 D9  41  1N  21 20 E
Bitter Creek, U.S.A. . . . . . . . 76 F9  41 33N 108 33W
Bitterfontein, S. Africa . . . . . . 56 E2  31  1S  18 32 E
Bitterroot →, U.S.A. . . . . . . . 76 C6  46 52N 114  7W
Bitterroot Range, U.S.A. . . . . 76 D6  46  0N 114 20W
Bitterwater, U.S.A. . . . . . . . . 78 J6  36 23N 121  0W
Biu, Nigeria . . . . . . . . . . . . . . 51 F8  10 40N  12  3 E
Biwa-Ko, Japan . . . . . . . . . . . 31 G8  35 15N 136 10 E
Biwabik, U.S.A. . . . . . . . . . . . 80 B8  47 32N  92 21W
Bixby, U.S.A. . . . . . . . . . . . . . 81 H7  35 57N  95 53W
Biyang, China . . . . . . . . . . . . 34 H7  32 38N 113 21 E
Biysk, Russia . . . . . . . . . . . . . 28 D9  52 40N  85  0 E
Bizana, S. Africa . . . . . . . . . . 57 E4  30 50S  29 52 E
Bizen, Japan . . . . . . . . . . . . . 31 G7  34 43N 134  8 E
Bizerte, Tunisia . . . . . . . . . . . 51 A7  37 15N   9 50 E
Bjargtangar, Iceland . . . . . . . 8 D1  65 30N  24 30W
Bjelovar, Croatia . . . . . . . . . . 22 B7  45 56N  16 49 E
Björneborg = Pori, Finland . . 9 F19  61 29N  21 48 E
Bjørnevatn, Norway . . . . . . . . 8 B23  69 40N  30  0 E
Bjørnøya, Arctic . . . . . . . . . . . 4 B8  74 30N  19  0 E
Black = Da →, Vietnam . . . . . 38 B5  21 15N 105 20 E
Black →, Canada . . . . . . . . . . 84 B5  44 42N  79 19W
Black →, Ariz., U.S.A. . . . . . . 77 K8  33 44N 110 13W
Black →, Ark., U.S.A. . . . . . . 81 H9  35 38N  91 20W
Black →, Mich., U.S.A. . . . . . 84 D2  42 59N  82 27W
Black →, N.Y., U.S.A. . . . . . . 85 C8  43 59N  76  4W
Black →, Wis., U.S.A. . . . . . . 80 D9  43 57N  91 22W
Black Bay Pen., Canada . . . . 72 C2  48 38N  88 21W
Black Birch L., Canada . . . . . 71 B7  56 53N 107 45W
Black Canyon of the Gunnison △,
  U.S.A. . . . . . . . . . . . . . . . . 77 G10 38 40N 107 35W
Black Diamond, Canada . . . . 70 C6  50 45N 114 14W
Black Duck →, Canada . . . . . 72 A2  56 51N  89  2W
Black Forest = Schwarzwald,
  Germany . . . . . . . . . . . . . . 16 D5  48 30N   8 20 E
Black Forest, U.S.A. . . . . . . . 80 F2  39  0N 104 43W
Black Hd., Ireland . . . . . . . . . 10 C2  53  9N   9 16W
Black Hills, U.S.A. . . . . . . . . . 80 D3  44  0N 103 45W
Black I., Canada . . . . . . . . . . 71 C9  51 12N  96 30W
Black L., Mich., U.S.A. . . . . . 82 C3  45 28N  84 16W
Black L., N.Y., U.S.A. . . . . . . 85 B9  44 31N  75 36W
Black L., Canada . . . . . . . . . . 71 B7  59 11N 105 20W
Black Mesa, U.S.A. . . . . . . . . 81 G3  36 58N 102 58W
Black Mt. = Mynydd Du, U.K. . 13 F4  51 52N   3 50W
Black Mts., U.K. . . . . . . . . . . 13 F4  51 55N   3  7W
Black Range, U.S.A. . . . . . . . 77 K10 33 15N 107 50W
Black River, Jamaica . . . . . . . 88 a  18  0N  77 50W
Black River Falls, U.S.A. . . . . 80 C9  44 18N  90 51W
Black Rock, Barbados . . . . . . 89 g  13  7N  59 37W
Black Sea, Eurasia . . . . . . . . 19 F6  43 30N  35  0 E
Black Tickle, Canada . . . . . . . 73 B8  53 28N  55 45W
Black Volta →, Africa . . . . . . 50 G5  8 41N   1 33W
Black Warrior →, U.S.A. . . . . 83 J2  32 32N  87 51W
Blackall, Australia . . . . . . . . . 62 C4  24 25S 145 45 E
Blackball, N.Z. . . . . . . . . . . . . 59 K3  42 22S 171 26 E
Blackbull, Australia . . . . . . . . 62 B3  17 55S 141 45 E
Blackburn, U.K. . . . . . . . . . . . 12 D5  53 45N   2 29W
Blackburn with Darwen □, U.K. 12 D5  53 45N   2 29W
Blackdown Tableland △,
  Australia . . . . . . . . . . . . . . 62 C4  23 52S 149  8 E
Blackfoot, U.S.A. . . . . . . . . . . 76 E7  43 11N 112 21W
Blackfoot →, U.S.A. . . . . . . . 76 C7  46 52N 113 53W
Blackfoot River Reservoir, U.S.A. 76 E8  43  0N 111 43W
Blackpool, U.K. . . . . . . . . . . . 12 D4  53 49N   3  3W
Blackpool □, U.K. . . . . . . . . . 12 D4  53 49N   3  3W
Blackriver, U.S.A. . . . . . . . . . 84 B1  44 46N  83 17W
Blacks Harbour, Canada . . . . 73 C6  45  3N  66 49W
Blacksburg, U.S.A. . . . . . . . . 82 G5  37 14N  80 25W
Blacksod B., Ireland . . . . . . . 10 B1  54  6N  10  0W
Blackstone, U.S.A. . . . . . . . . 82 G7  37  4N  78  0W
Blackstone Ra., Australia . . . . 61 E4  26  0S 128 30 E
Blackwater = West Road →,
  Canada . . . . . . . . . . . . . . . 70 C4  53 18N 122 53W
Blackwater, Australia . . . . . . . 62 C4  23 35S 148 53 E
Blackwater →, Meath, Ireland 10 C4  53 39N   6 41W
Blackwater →, Waterford, Ireland 10 D4  52  4N   7 52W
Blackwater →, U.K. . . . . . . . . 10 B5  54 31N   6 35W
Blackwell, U.S.A. . . . . . . . . . . 81 G6  36 48N  97 17W
Blackwells Corner, U.S.A. . . . 79 K7  35 37N 119 47W
Bladensburg △, Australia . . . 62 C3  22 30S 142 59 E
Blaenau Ffestiniog, U.K. . . . . 12 E4  53  0N   3 56W
Blaenau Gwent □, U.K. . . . . . 13 F4  51 48N   3 12W
Blagodarnoye = Blagodarnyy,
  Russia . . . . . . . . . . . . . . . . 19 E7  45  7N  43 37 E
Blagodarnyy, Russia . . . . . . . 19 E7  45  7N  43 37 E
Blagoevgrad, Bulgaria . . . . . . 23 C10 42  2N  23  5 E
Blagoveshchensk, Russia . . . 29 D13 50 20N 127 30 E
Blahkiuh, Indonesia . . . . . . . . 37 J18  8 31S 115 12 E
Blain, U.S.A. . . . . . . . . . . . . . 84 F7  40 20N  77 31W
Blaine, Minn., U.S.A. . . . . . . . 80 C8  45 10N  93  13W
Blaine, Wash., U.S.A. . . . . . . 78 B4  48 59N 122 45W
Blaine Lake, Canada . . . . . . . 71 C7  52 51N 106 52W
Blair, U.S.A. . . . . . . . . . . . . . 80 E6  41 33N  96  8W
Blair Athol, Australia . . . . . . . 62 C4  22 42S 147 31 E
Blair Atholl, U.K. . . . . . . . . . . 11 E5  56 46N   3 50W
Blairgowrie, U.K. . . . . . . . . . . 11 E5  56 35N   3 21W
Blairsden, U.S.A. . . . . . . . . . . 78 F6  39 47N 120 37W
Blairsville, U.S.A. . . . . . . . . . 84 F5  40 26N  79 16W
Blakang Mati, Pulau, Singapore 39 d   1 15N 103 50 E
Blake Pt., U.S.A. . . . . . . . . . . 80 A10 48 11N  88 25W
Blakely, Ga., U.S.A. . . . . . . . 83 K3  31 23N  84 56W
Blakely, Pa., U.S.A. . . . . . . . . 85 E9  41 28N  75 37W
Blanc, C., Spain . . . . . . . . . . 24 B9  39 21N   2 51 E
Blanc, Mont, Europe . . . . . . . 20 D7  45 48N   6 50 E
Blanc-Sablon, Canada . . . . . 73 B8  51 24N  57 12W
Blanca, B., Argentina . . . . . . 96 D4  39 10S  61 30W
Blanca Peak, U.S.A. . . . . . . . 77 H11 37 35N 105 29W
Blanche, C., Australia . . . . . . 63 E1  33  1S 134  9 E
Blanche, L., S. Austral., Australia 63 D2  29 15S 139 40 E
Blanche, L., W. Austral., Australia 60 D3  22 25S 123 17 E
Blanchisseuse, Trin. & Tob. . . 93 K15 10 48N  61 18W
Blanco, S. Africa . . . . . . . . . . 56 E3  33 55S  22 23 E
Blanco, U.S.A. . . . . . . . . . . . . 81 K5  30  6N  98 25W

Blanco →, Argentina . . . . . . . 94 C2  30 20S  68 42W
Blanco, C., Costa Rica . . . . . 88 E2   9 34N  85  8W
Blanco, C., U.S.A. . . . . . . . . . 76 E1  42 51N 124 34W
Blanda →, Iceland . . . . . . . . . 8 D3  65 37N  20  9W
Blandford Forum, U.K. . . . . . . 13 G5  50 51N   2  9W
Blanding, U.S.A. . . . . . . . . . . 77 H9  37 37N 109 29W
Blanes, Spain . . . . . . . . . . . . 21 B7  41 40N   2 48 E
Blankenberge, Belgium . . . . . 15 C3  51 20N   3  9 E
Blanquillo, Uruguay . . . . . . . . 95 C4  32 53S  55 37W
Blantyre, Malawi . . . . . . . . . . 55 F4  15 45S  35  0 E
Blarney, Ireland . . . . . . . . . . . 10 E3  51 56N   8 33W
Blasdell, U.S.A. . . . . . . . . . . . 84 D6  42 48N  78 50W
Blåvands Huk, Denmark . . . . 9 J13  55 33N   8  4 E
Blaydon, U.K. . . . . . . . . . . . . 12 C6  54 58N   1 42W
Blayney, Australia . . . . . . . . . 63 E4  33 32S 149 14 E
Blaze, Pt., Australia . . . . . . . . 60 B5  12 56S 130 11 E
Blekinge, Sweden . . . . . . . . . 9 H16 56 25N  15 20 E
Blenheim, Canada . . . . . . . . . 84 D3  42 20N  82  0W
Blenheim, N.Z. . . . . . . . . . . . . 59 J4  41 38S 173 57 E
Bletchley, U.K. . . . . . . . . . . . . 13 F7  51 59N   0 44W
Blida, Algeria . . . . . . . . . . . . . 50 A6  36 30N   2 49 E
Bligh Sound, N.Z. . . . . . . . . . 59 L1  44 47S 167 32 E
Blind River, Canada . . . . . . . . 72 C3  46 10N  82 58W
Bliss, Idaho, U.S.A. . . . . . . . . 76 E6  42 56N 114 57W
Bliss, N.Y., U.S.A. . . . . . . . . . 84 D6  42 34N  78 15W
Blissfield, U.S.A. . . . . . . . . . . 84 F3  40 24N  81 58W
Blitar, Indonesia . . . . . . . . . . 37 H15  8  5S 112 11 E
Block I., U.S.A. . . . . . . . . . . . 85 E13 41 11N  71 35W
Block Island Sd., U.S.A. . . . . 85 E13 41 15N  71 40W
Bloemfontein, S. Africa . . . . . 56 D4  29  6S  26  7 E
Bloemhof, S. Africa . . . . . . . . 56 D4  27 38S  25 32 E
Blois, France . . . . . . . . . . . . . 20 C4  47 35N   1 20 E
Blönduós, Iceland . . . . . . . . . 8 D3  65 40N  20 12W
Blongas, Indonesia . . . . . . . . 37 K19  8 53S 116  2 E
Bloodvein →, Canada . . . . . . 71 C9  51 47N  96 43W
Bloody Foreland, Ireland . . . . 10 A3  55 10N   8 17W
Bloomer, U.S.A. . . . . . . . . . . . 80 C9  45  6N  91 29W
Bloomfield, Canada . . . . . . . . 84 C7  43 59N  77 14W
Bloomfield, Iowa, U.S.A. . . . . 80 E8  40 45N  92 25W
Bloomfield, N. Mex., U.S.A. . . 77 H10 36 43N 107 59W
Bloomfield, Nebr., U.S.A. . . . 80 D6  42 36N  97 39W
Bloomington, Ill., U.S.A. . . . . 80 E10 40 28N  89  0W
Bloomington, Ind., U.S.A. . . . 82 F2  39 10N  86 32W
Bloomington, Minn., U.S.A. . . 80 C8  44 50N  93 17W
Bloomsburg, U.S.A. . . . . . . . . 85 F8  41  0N  76 27W
Bloomsbury, Australia . . . . . . 62 J6  20 48S 148 38 E
Blora, Indonesia . . . . . . . . . . 37 G14  6 57S 111 25 E
Blossburg, U.S.A. . . . . . . . . . 84 E7  41 41N  77  4W
Blouberg, S. Africa . . . . . . . . 57 C4  23  8S  28 59 E
Blountstown, U.S.A. . . . . . . . 83 K3  30 27N  85  3W
Blue Earth, U.S.A. . . . . . . . . . 80 D8  43 38N  94  6W
Blue Hole △, Belize . . . . . . . . 88 C2  17 24N  88 30W
Blue Lagoon △, Zambia . . . . 55 F2  15 28S  27 26 E
Blue Mesa Reservoir, U.S.A. . 77 G10 38 28N 107 20W
Blue Mountain Lake, U.S.A. . 85 C10 43 52N  74 30W
Blue Mountain Pk., Jamaica . 88 a  18  3N  76 36W
Blue Mts., Jamaica . . . . . . . . 88 a  18  3N  76 36W
Blue Mts., Maine, U.S.A. . . . . 85 B14 44 50N  70 35W
Blue Mts., Oreg., U.S.A. . . . . 76 D4  45 15N 119  0W
Blue Mts., Pa., U.S.A. . . . . . . 85 F8  40 30N  76 30W
Blue Mud B., Australia . . . . . . 62 A2  13 30S 136  0 E
Blue Nile = Nîl el Azraq →,
  Sudan . . . . . . . . . . . . . . . . 51 E12 15 38N  32 31 E
Blue Rapids, U.S.A. . . . . . . . . 80 F6  39 41N  96 39W
Blue Ridge Mts., U.S.A. . . . . 83 G5  36 30N  80 15W
Blue River, Canada . . . . . . . . 70 C5  52  6N 119 18W
Bluefield, U.S.A. . . . . . . . . . . 82 G5  37 15N  81 17W
Bluefields, Nic. . . . . . . . . . . . 88 D3  12 20N  83 50W
Bluff, Australia . . . . . . . . . . . . 62 C4  23 35S 149  4 E
Bluff, N.Z. . . . . . . . . . . . . . . . 59 M2  46 37S 168 20 E
Bluff, U.S.A. . . . . . . . . . . . . . . 77 H9  37 17N 109 33W
Bluff Knoll, Australia . . . . . . . 61 F2  34 24S 118 15 E
Bluff Pt., Australia . . . . . . . . . 61 E1  27 50S 114  5 E
Bluffton, U.S.A. . . . . . . . . . . . 82 E3  40 44N  85 11W
Blumenau, Brazil . . . . . . . . . . 95 B6  27  0S  49  0W
Blunt, U.S.A. . . . . . . . . . . . . . 80 C5  44 31N  99 59W
Bly, U.S.A. . . . . . . . . . . . . . . . 76 E3  42 24N 121  3W
Blyde River Canyon △, S. Africa 57 C5  24 37S  31  2 E
Blyth, Canada . . . . . . . . . . . . 84 C3  43 44N  81 26W
Blyth, U.K. . . . . . . . . . . . . . . . 12 B6  55  8N   1 31W
Blythe, U.S.A. . . . . . . . . . . . . 79 M12 33 37N 114 36W
Blytheville, U.S.A. . . . . . . . . . 81 H10 35 56N  89 55W
Bo, S. Leone . . . . . . . . . . . . . 50 G3   7 55N  11 50W
Bo Duc, Vietnam . . . . . . . . . . 39 G6  11 58N 106 50 E
Bo Hai, China . . . . . . . . . . . . 35 E10 39  0N 119  0 E
Bo Xian = Bozhou, China . . . 34 H8  33 55N 115 41 E
Boa Vista, Brazil . . . . . . . . . . 92 C6   2 48N  60 30W
Boaco, Nic. . . . . . . . . . . . . . . 88 D2  12 29N  85 35W
Bo'ai, China . . . . . . . . . . . . . . 34 G7  35 10N 113  3 E
Boalsburg, U.S.A. . . . . . . . . . 84 F7  40 46N  77 47W
Boane, Mozam. . . . . . . . . . . . 57 D5  26  6S  32 19 E
Boardman, U.S.A. . . . . . . . . . 84 E4  41  2N  80 40W
Bobadah, Australia . . . . . . . . 63 E4  32 19S 146 41 E
Bobbili, India . . . . . . . . . . . . . 41 K13 18 35N  83 30 E
Bobcaygeon, Canada . . . . . . 84 B6  44 33N  78 33W
Bobo-Dioulasso, Burkina Faso 50 F5  11  8N   4  3W
Bóbr →, Poland . . . . . . . . . . . 16 B8  52  4N  15  4 E
Bobraomby, Tanjon' i, Madag. 57 A8  12 40S  49 10 E
Bobruysk = Babruysk, Belarus 17 B15 53 10N  29 15 E
Boby, Pic, Madag. . . . . . . . . . 53 J9  22 12S  46 55 E
Boca de Drago, Venezuela . . 93 K15 11  0N  61 50W
Bôca do Acre, Brazil . . . . . . . 92 E5   8 50S  67 27W
Boca Raton, U.S.A. . . . . . . . . 83 M5  26 21N  80  5W
Bocas del Toro, Panama . . . . 88 E3   9 15N  82 20W
Bochnia, Poland . . . . . . . . . . 17 D11 49 58N  20 27 E
Bochum, Germany . . . . . . . . . 16 C4  51 28N   7 13 E
Bocoyna, Mexico . . . . . . . . . . 86 B3  27 52N 107 35W
Bodaybo, Russia . . . . . . . . . . 29 D12 57 50N 114  0 E
Boddam, U.K. . . . . . . . . . . . . 11 B7  59 56N   1 17W
Boddington, Australia . . . . . . 61 F2  32 50S 116 30 E
Bodega Bay, U.S.A. . . . . . . . . 78 G3  38 20N 123  3W
Boden, Sweden . . . . . . . . . . . 8 D19 65 50N  21 42 E
Bodensee, Europe . . . . . . . . . 20 C8  47 35N   9 25 E
Bodhan, India . . . . . . . . . . . . 40 K10 18 40N  77 44 E
Bodmin, U.K. . . . . . . . . . . . . . 13 G3  50 28N   4 43W
Bodmin Moor, U.K. . . . . . . . . 13 G3  50 33N   4 36W
Bodø, Norway . . . . . . . . . . . . 8 C16 67 17N  14 24 E
Bodrog →, Hungary . . . . . . . . 17 D11 48 11N  21 22 E
Bodrum, Turkey . . . . . . . . . . . 23 F12 37  3N  27 30 E
Boende, Dem. Rep. of the Congo 52 E4  0 24S  21  0 E
Boerne, U.S.A. . . . . . . . . . . . . 81 L5  29 47N  98 44W
Boesmans →, S. Africa . . . . . 56 E4  33 42S  26 39 E
Bogalusa, U.S.A. . . . . . . . . . . 81 K10 30 47N  89 52W
Bogan →, Australia . . . . . . . . 63 E4  29 59S 146 17 E
Bogan Gate, Australia . . . . . . 63 E4  33  7S 147 49 E
Bogantungan, Australia . . . . . 62 C4  23 41S 147 17 E
Bogata, U.S.A. . . . . . . . . . . . . 81 J7  33 28N  95 13W
Boggabilla, Australia . . . . . . . 63 D5  28 36S 150 24 E

Boggabri, Australia .......... 63 E5 30 45S 150 5 E
Boggeragh Mts., Ireland ...... 10 D3 52 2N 8 55W
Boglan = Solhan, Turkey ...... 44 B4 38 57N 41 3 E
Bognor Regis, U.K. .......... 13 G7 50 47N 0 40W
Bogo, Phil. ................. 37 B6 11 3N 124 0 E
Bogong, Mt., Australia ....... 63 F4 36 47S 147 17 E
Bogor, Indonesia ............ 36 F3 6 36S 106 48 E
Bogotá, Colombia ............ 92 C4 4 34N 74 0W
Bogotol, Russia ............. 28 D9 56 15N 89 50 E
Bogra, Bangla. .............. 41 G16 24 51N 89 22 E
Boguchany, Russia ........... 29 D10 58 40N 97 30 E
Bohemian Forest = Böhmerwald,
    Germany ................. 16 D7 49 8N 13 14 E
Böhmerwald, Germany ......... 16 D7 49 8N 13 14 E
Bohol □, Phil. .............. 37 C6 9 50N 124 10 E
Bohol Sea, Phil. ............ 37 C6 9 0N 124 0 E
Bohuslän, Sweden ............ 9 G14 58 25N 12 0 E
Boi, Pta. de, Brazil ......... 95 A6 23 55S 45 15W
Boiaçu, Brazil .............. 92 D6 0 27S 61 46W
Boileau, C., Australia ....... 60 C3 17 40S 122 7 E
Boise, U.S.A. ............... 76 E5 43 37N 116 13W
Boise City, U.S.A. ........... 81 G3 36 44N 102 31W
Boissevain, Canada .......... 71 D8 49 15N 100 5W
Bojador, C., W. Sahara ....... 50 C3 26 0N 14 30W
Bojana →, Albania ........... 23 D8 41 52N 19 22 E
Bojnūrd, Iran ............... 45 B8 37 30N 57 20 E
Bojonegoro, Indonesia ....... 37 G14 7 11S 111 54 E
Bokaro, India ............... 43 H11 23 46N 85 55 E
Bokhara →, Australia ........ 63 D4 29 55S 146 42 E
Boknafjorden, Norway ........ 9 G11 59 14N 5 40 E
Bokora △, Uganda ........... 54 B3 2 12N 31 32 E
Bokoro, Chad ............... 51 F9 12 25N 17 14 E
Bokpyin, Burma .............. 39 G2 11 18N 98 42 E
Bolan →, Pakistan ........... 42 E2 28 38N 67 42 E
Bolan Pass, Pakistan ......... 40 E5 29 50N 67 20 E
Bolaños →, Mexico ........... 86 C4 21 14N 104 8W
Bolbec, France .............. 20 B4 49 30N 0 30 E
Boldājī, Iran ............... 45 D6 31 56N 51 3 E
Bole, China ................ 32 B3 45 11N 81 37 E
Bolekhiv, Ukraine ........... 17 D12 49 0N 23 57 E
Bolesławiec, Poland ......... 16 C8 51 17N 15 37 E
Bolgrad = Bolhrad, Ukraine ... 17 F15 45 40N 28 32 E
Bolhrad, Ukraine ............ 17 F15 45 40N 28 32 E
Bolívar, Argentina .......... 94 D3 36 15S 60 53W
Bolivar, Mo., U.S.A. ......... 81 G8 37 37N 93 25W
Bolivar, N.Y., U.S.A. ........ 84 D6 42 4N 78 10W
Bolivar, Tenn., U.S.A. ....... 81 H10 35 12N 89 0W
Bolivia ■, S. Amer. .......... 92 G6 17 6S 64 0W
Bolivian Plateau = Altiplano,
    Bolivia ................. 90 E4 17 0S 68 0W
Bollnäs, Sweden ............. 9 F17 61 21N 16 24 E
Bollon, Australia ........... 63 D4 28 2S 147 29 E
Bolmen, Sweden ............. 9 H15 56 55N 13 40 E
Bolobo, Dem. Rep. of the Congo 52 E3 2 6S 16 20 E
Bologna, Italy .............. 22 B4 44 29N 11 20 E
Bologoye, Russia ............ 18 C5 57 55N 34 5 E
Bolonchenticul, Mexico ...... 87 D7 20 0N 89 49W
Boloven, Cao Nguyen, Laos ... 38 E6 15 10N 106 30 E
Bolpur, India ............... 43 H12 23 40N 87 45 E
Bolsena, L. di, Italy ........ 22 C4 42 36N 11 56 E
Bolshevik, Ostrov, Russia ... 29 B11 78 30N 102 0 E
Bolshoy Anyuy →, Russia .... 29 C17 68 30N 160 49 E
Bolshoy Begichev, Ostrov,
    Russia ................. 29 B12 74 20N 112 30 E
Bolshoy Kavkaz = Caucasus
    Mountains, Eurasia ...... 19 F7 42 50N 44 0 E
Bolshoy Lyakhovskiy, Ostrov,
    Russia ................. 29 B15 73 35N 142 0 E
Bolshoy Tyuters, Ostrov, Russia 9 G22 59 51N 27 13 E
Bolsward, Neths. ............ 15 A5 53 3N 5 32 E
Bolt Head, U.K. ............. 13 G4 50 12N 3 48W
Bolton, Canada ............. 84 C5 43 54N 79 45W
Bolton, U.K. ................ 12 D5 53 35N 2 26W
Bolton Landing, U.S.A. ...... 85 C11 43 32N 73 35W
Bolu, Turkey ............... 19 F5 40 45N 31 35 E
Bolungavík, Iceland ......... 8 C2 66 9N 23 15W
Bolvadin, Turkey ............ 19 G5 38 45N 31 4 E
Bolzano, Italy .............. 22 A4 46 31N 11 22 E
Bom Jesus da Lapa, Brazil ... 93 F10 13 15S 43 25W
Boma, Dem. Rep. of the Congo 52 F2 5 50S 13 4 E
Bombala, Australia .......... 63 F4 36 56S 149 15 E
Bombay = Mumbai, India ...... 40 K8 18 55N 72 50 E
Bombedor, Pta., Venezuela ... 93 L15 9 53N 61 37W
Bomboma, Dem. Rep. of
    the Congo ............... 52 D3 2 25N 18 55 E
Bombombwa, Dem. Rep. of
    the Congo ............... 54 B2 1 40N 25 40 E
Bomili, Dem. Rep. of the Congo 54 B2 1 45N 27 5 E
Bømlo, Norway .............. 9 G11 59 37N 5 13 E
Bomokandi →, Dem. Rep. of
    the Congo ............... 54 B2 3 39N 26 8 E
Bomu →, C.A.R. ............. 52 D4 4 40N 22 30 E
Bon, C., Tunisia ............ 48 C5 37 1N 11 2 E
Bon Sar Pa, Vietnam ........ 38 F6 12 24N 107 35 E
Bonaigarh, India ........... 43 J11 21 50N 84 57 E
Bonaire, Neth. Ant. ......... 89 D6 12 10N 68 15W
Bonampak, Mexico ........... 87 D6 16 44N 91 5W
Bonang, Australia ........... 63 F4 37 11S 148 41 E
Bonanza, Nic. .............. 88 D3 13 54N 84 35W
Bonaparte Arch., Australia ... 60 B3 14 0S 124 30 E
Bonar Bridge, U.K. .......... 11 D4 57 54N 4 20W
Bonasse, Trin. & Tob. ........ 93 K15 10 5N 61 54W
Bonaventure, Canada ........ 73 C6 48 5N 65 32W
Bonavista, Canada .......... 73 C9 48 40N 53 5W
Bonavista, C., Canada ....... 73 C9 48 42N 53 5W
Bonavista B., Canada ........ 73 C9 48 45N 53 25W
Bondo, Dem. Rep. of the Congo 54 B1 3 55N 23 53 E
Bondoukou, Ivory C. ......... 50 G5 8 2N 2 47W
Bondowoso, Indonesia ....... 37 G15 7 55S 113 49 E
Bone, Teluk, Indonesia ...... 37 E6 4 10S 120 50 E
Bonerate, Indonesia ......... 37 F6 7 25S 121 5 E
Bonerate, Kepulauan, Indonesia 37 F6 6 30S 121 10 E
Bo'ness, U.K. .............. 11 E5 56 1N 3 37W
Bonete, Cerro, Argentina ..... 94 B2 27 55S 68 40W
Bong Son = Hoai Nhon, Vietnam 38 E7 14 28N 109 1 E
Bongor, Chad ............... 51 F9 10 35N 15 20 E
Bonham, U.S.A. ............. 81 J6 33 35N 96 11W
Boni △, Kenya .............. 54 C5 1 35N 41 18 E
Bonifacio, France ........... 20 F8 41 24N 9 10 E
Bonifacio, Bouches de, Medit. S. 20 F8 41 12N 9 15 E
Bonin Is. = Ogasawara Gunto,
    Pac. Oc. ................ 26 G18 27 0N 142 0 E
Bonn, Germany .............. 16 C4 50 46N 7 6 E
Bonne Terre, U.S.A. ......... 81 G9 37 55N 90 33W
Bonners Ferry, U.S.A. ........ 76 B5 48 42N 116 19W
Bonney, L., Australia ........ 63 F3 37 50S 140 20 E
Bonnie Rock, Australia ....... 61 F2 30 29S 118 22 E
Bonny, Bight of, Africa ...... 52 D1 3 30N 9 20 E

Bonnyrigg, U.K. ............. 11 F5 55 53N 3 6W
Bonnyville, Canada .......... 71 C6 54 20N 110 45W
Bonoi, Indonesia ............ 37 E9 1 45S 137 41 E
Bonsall, U.S.A. ............. 79 M9 33 16N 117 14W
Bontang, Indonesia .......... 36 D5 0 10N 117 30 E
Bontebok △, S. Africa ....... 56 E3 34 5S 20 28 E
Bonthe, S. Leone ........... 50 G3 7 30N 12 33W
Bontoc, Phil. ............... 37 A6 17 7N 120 58 E
Bonython Ra., Australia ...... 60 D4 23 40S 128 45 E
Bookabie, Australia ......... 61 F5 31 50S 132 41 E
Booker, U.S.A. .............. 81 G4 36 27N 100 32W
Booligal, Australia .......... 63 E3 33 58S 144 53 E
Boonah, Australia ........... 63 D5 27 58S 152 41 E
Boone, Iowa, U.S.A. ......... 80 D8 42 4N 93 53W
Boone, N.C., U.S.A. ......... 83 G5 36 13N 81 41W
Booneville, Ark., U.S.A. ...... 81 H8 35 8N 93 55W
Booneville, Miss., U.S.A. ..... 83 H1 34 39N 88 34W
Boonville, Calif., U.S.A. ...... 78 F3 39 1N 123 22W
Boonville, Ind., U.S.A. ....... 82 F2 38 3N 87 16W
Boonville, Mo., U.S.A. ....... 80 F8 38 58N 92 44W
Boonville, N.Y., U.S.A. ....... 85 C9 43 29N 75 20W
Boorabbin △, Australia ...... 61 F4 31 0S 129 57 E
Boorindal, Australia ......... 63 E4 30 22S 146 11 E
Boorowa, Australia .......... 63 E4 34 28S 148 44 E
Boosaaso = Bosaso, Somali Rep. 47 E4 11 12N 49 18 E
Boothia, Gulf of, Canada ..... 69 A11 71 0N 90 0W
Boothia Pen., Canada ........ 68 A10 71 0N 94 0W
Bootle, U.K. ................ 12 D4 53 28N 3 1W
Booué, Gabon ............... 52 E2 0 5S 11 55 E
Boquete, Panama ............ 88 E3 8 46N 82 27W
Boquilla, Presa de la, Mexico . 86 B3 27 40N 105 30W
Boquillas del Carmen, Mexico . 86 B4 29 17N 102 53W
Bor, Serbia & M. ............ 23 B10 44 5N 22 7 E
Bôr, Sudan ................. 51 G12 6 10N 31 40 E
Bor Mashash, Israel ......... 46 D3 31 7N 34 50 E
Borah Peak, U.S.A. .......... 76 D7 44 8N 113 47W
Borås, Sweden .............. 9 H15 57 43N 12 56 E
Borāzjān, Iran .............. 45 D6 29 22N 51 10 E
Borba, Brazil ............... 92 D7 4 12S 59 34W
Borborema, Planalto da, Brazil 90 D7 7 0S 37 0W
Bord Khūn-e Now, Iran ....... 45 D6 28 3N 51 28 E
Borda, C., Australia ......... 63 F2 35 45S 136 34 E
Bordeaux, France ........... 20 D3 44 50N 0 36W
Borden, Australia ........... 61 F2 34 3S 118 12 E
Borden-Carleton, Canada ..... 73 C7 46 18N 63 47W
Borden I., Canada .......... 4 B2 78 30N 111 30W
Borden Pen., Canada ........ 69 A11 73 0N 83 0W
Border Ranges △, Australia ... 63 D5 28 24S 152 56 E
Borders = Scottish Borders □,
    U.K. ................... 11 F6 55 35N 2 50W
Bordertown, Australia ....... 63 F3 36 19S 140 45 E
Borðeyri, Iceland ........... 8 D3 65 12N 21 6W
Bordj Fly Ste. Marie, Algeria .. 50 C5 27 19N 2 32W
Bordj-in-Eker, Algeria ........ 50 D7 24 9N 5 3 E
Bordj Omar Driss, Algeria ..... 50 C7 28 10N 6 40 E
Borehamwood, U.K. .......... 13 F7 51 40N 0 15W
Borgå = Porvoo, Finland ...... 9 F21 60 24N 25 40 E
Borgarfjörður, Iceland ....... 8 D7 65 31N 13 49W
Borgarnes, Iceland .......... 8 D3 64 32N 21 55W
Børgefjellet, Norway ........ 8 D15 65 20N 13 45 E
Borger, Neths. .............. 15 B6 52 54N 6 44 E
Borger, U.S.A. .............. 81 H4 35 39N 101 24W
Borgholm, Sweden ........... 9 H17 56 52N 16 39 E
Borhoyn Tal, Mongolia ....... 34 C6 43 50N 111 58 E
Borikhane, Laos ............. 38 C4 18 33N 103 43 E
Borisoglebsk, Russia ........ 19 D7 51 27N 42 5 E
Borisov = Barysaw, Belarus ... 17 A15 54 17N 28 28 E
Borja, Peru ................. 92 D3 4 20S 77 40W
Borkou, Chad ............... 51 E9 18 15N 18 50 E
Borkum, Germany ........... 16 B4 53 34N 6 40 E
Borlänge, Sweden ........... 9 F16 60 29N 15 26 E
Borley, C., Antarctica ........ 5 C5 66 15S 52 30 E
Borneo, E. Indies ........... 36 D5 1 0N 115 0 E
Bornholm, Denmark .......... 9 J16 55 10N 15 0 E
Borogontsy, Russia .......... 29 C14 62 42N 131 8 E
Boron, U.S.A. ............... 79 L9 35 0N 117 39W
Borongan, Phil. ............. 37 B7 11 37N 125 26 E
Borovichi, Russia ........... 18 C5 58 25N 33 55 E
Borrego Springs, U.S.A. ...... 79 M10 33 15N 116 23W
Borroloola, Australia ........ 62 B2 16 4S 136 17 E
Borşa, Romania ............. 17 E13 47 41N 24 50 E
Borsad, India ............... 42 H5 22 25N 72 54 E
Borth, U.K. ................. 13 E3 52 29N 4 2W
Borüjerd, Iran .............. 45 C6 33 55N 48 50 E
Boryslav, Ukraine ........... 17 D12 49 18N 23 28 E
Borzya, Russia .............. 29 D12 50 24N 116 31 E
Bosa, Italy ................. 22 D3 40 18N 8 30 E
Bosanska Gradiška, Bos.-H. ... 22 B7 45 10N 17 15 E
Bosaso, Somali Rep. ......... 47 E4 11 12N 49 18 E
Boscastle, U.K. ............. 13 G3 50 41N 4 42W
Boscobelle, Barbados ........ 89 g 13 17N 59 35W
Boshan, China .............. 35 F9 36 28N 117 49 E
Boshof, S. Africa ........... 56 D4 28 31S 25 13 E
Boshrūyeh, Iran ............ 45 C8 33 50N 57 30 E
Bosna →, Bos.-H. ........... 23 B8 45 4N 18 29 E
Bosna i Hercegovina = Bosnia-
    Herzegovina ■, Europe .... 22 B7 44 0N 18 0 E
Bosnia-Herzegovina ■, Europe . 22 B7 44 0N 18 0 E
Bosnik, Indonesia ........... 37 E9 1 5S 136 10 E
Bosobolo, Dem. Rep. of
    the Congo ............... 52 D3 4 15N 19 50 E
Bosporus = İstanbul Boğazı,
    Turkey ................. 23 D13 41 10N 29 10 E
Bosque Farms, U.S.A. ........ 77 J10 34 53N 106 40W
Bossangoa, C.A.R. ........... 52 C3 6 35N 17 30 E
Bossier City, U.S.A. ......... 81 J8 32 31N 93 44W
Bosso, Niger ............... 51 F8 13 43N 13 19 E
Bostan, Pakistan ........... 42 D2 30 26N 67 2 E
Bostānābād, Iran ............ 44 B5 37 50N 46 50 E
Bosten Hu, China ........... 32 B3 41 55N 87 40 E
Boston, U.K. ............... 12 E7 52 59N 0 2W
Boston, U.S.A. ............. 85 D13 42 22N 71 4W
Boston Bar, Canada ......... 70 D4 49 52N 121 30W
Boston Mts., U.S.A. ......... 81 H8 35 42N 93 15W
Boswell, Canada ............ 70 D5 49 28N 116 45W
Boswell, U.S.A. ............. 84 F5 40 10N 79 2W
Botad, India ............... 42 H4 22 15N 71 40 E

Botucatu, Brazil ............ 95 A6 22 55S 48 30W
Botwood, Canada ........... 73 C8 49 6N 55 23W
Bouaflé, Ivory C. ........... 50 G4 7 1N 5 47W
Bouaké, Ivory C. ........... 50 G4 7 40N 5 2W
Bouar, C.A.R. ............... 52 C3 6 0N 15 40 E
Bouârfa, Morocco ........... 50 B5 32 32N 1 58W
Boucaut B., Australia ........ 62 A1 12 0S 134 25 E
Bouctouche, Canada ......... 73 C7 46 30N 64 45W
Bougainville, C., Australia .... 60 B4 13 57S 126 4 E
Bougainville I., Papua N. G. ... 64 H7 6 0S 155 0 E
Bougainville Reef, Australia ... 62 B4 15 30S 147 5 E
Bougie = Bejaïa, Algeria ...... 50 A7 36 42N 5 2 E
Bougouni, Mali ............. 50 F4 11 30N 7 20W
Bouillon, Belgium ........... 15 E5 49 44N 5 3 E
Boulder, Colo., U.S.A. ........ 80 E2 40 1N 105 17W
Boulder, Mont., U.S.A. ....... 76 C7 46 14N 112 7W
Boulder City, U.S.A. ......... 79 K12 35 59N 114 50W
Boulder Creek, U.S.A. ........ 78 H4 37 7N 122 7W
Boulder Dam = Hoover Dam,
    U.S.A. .................. 79 K12 36 1N 114 44W
Boulia, Australia ........... 62 C2 22 52S 139 51 E
Boulogne-sur-Mer, France ..... 20 A4 50 42N 1 36 E
Boultoum, Niger ............ 51 F8 14 45N 10 25 E
Boun Neua, Laos ........... 38 B3 21 38N 101 54 E
Boun Tai, Laos ............. 38 B3 21 23N 101 58 E
Bouna, Ivory C. ............ 50 G5 9 10N 3 0W
Boundary Peak, U.S.A. ....... 78 H8 37 51N 118 21W
Boundiali, Ivory C. .......... 50 G4 9 30N 6 20W
Bountiful, U.S.A. ........... 76 F8 40 53N 111 53W
Bounty Is., Pac. Oc. .......... 64 M9 48 0S 178 30 E
Bourbonnais, France ......... 20 C5 46 28N 3 0 E
Bourbonne-les-Bains, France .. 20 C6 46 13N 5 12 E
Bourdel L., Canada .......... 72 A5 56 43N 74 10W
Bourem, Mali ............... 50 E5 17 0N 0 24W
Bourg-en-Bresse, France ...... 20 C6 46 13N 5 12 E
Bourg-St-Maurice, France ..... 20 D7 45 35N 6 46 E
Bourges, France ............ 20 C5 47 9N 2 25 E
Bourget, Canada ............ 85 A9 45 26N 75 9W
Bourgogne □, France ........ 20 C6 47 0N 4 50 E
Bourke, Australia ........... 63 E4 30 8S 145 55 E
Bourne, U.K. ............... 12 E7 52 47N 0 22W
Bournemouth, U.K. .......... 13 G6 50 43N 1 52W
Bournemouth □, U.K. ........ 13 G6 50 43N 1 52W
Bouse, U.S.A. .............. 79 M13 33 56N 114 0W
Bouvet I. = Bouvetøya, Antarctica 3 G10 54 26S 3 24 E
Bouvetøya, Antarctica ....... 3 G10 54 26S 3 24 E
Bovill, U.S.A. .............. 76 C5 46 51N 116 24W
Bovril, Argentina ........... 94 C4 31 21S 59 26W
Bow →, Canada ............. 70 C6 49 57N 111 41W
Bow Island, Canada ......... 70 D6 49 50N 111 23W
Bowbells, U.S.A. ............ 80 A3 48 48N 102 15W
Bowdle, U.S.A. ............. 80 C5 45 27N 99 39W
Bowelling, Australia ......... 61 F2 33 25S 116 30 E
Bowen, Argentina ........... 94 D2 35 0S 67 31W
Bowen, Australia ........... 62 J6 20 0S 148 16 E
Bowen Mts., Australia ....... 63 F4 37 0S 147 50 E
Bowie, Ariz., U.S.A. ......... 77 K9 32 19N 109 29W
Bowie, Tex., U.S.A. .......... 81 J6 33 34N 97 51W
Bowkän, Iran .............. 44 B5 36 31N 46 12 E
Bowland, Forest of, U.K. ..... 12 D5 54 0N 2 30W
Bowling Green, Ky., U.S.A. .... 82 G2 36 59N 86 27W
Bowling Green, Ohio, U.S.A. ... 82 E4 41 23N 83 39W
Bowling Green, C., Australia ... 62 B4 19 19S 147 25 E
Bowling Green Bay △, Australia 62 B4 19 26S 146 57 E
Bowman, U.S.A. ............ 80 B3 46 11N 103 24W
Bowman I., Antarctica ....... 5 C8 65 0S 104 0 E
Bowmanville = Clarington,
    Canada ................. 84 C6 43 55N 78 41W
Bowmore, U.K. ............. 11 F2 55 45N 6 17W
Bowral, Australia ........... 63 E5 34 26S 150 27 E
Bowraville, Australia ........ 63 E5 30 37S 152 52 E
Bowron →, Canada .......... 70 C4 54 3N 121 50W
Bowron Lake △, Canada ..... 70 C4 53 10N 121 5W
Bowser L., Canada .......... 70 B3 56 30N 129 30W
Bowsman, Canada .......... 71 C8 52 14N 101 12W
Bowwood, Zambia .......... 55 F2 17 5S 26 20 E
Box Cr. →, Australia ........ 63 E3 34 10S 143 50 E
Boxmeer, Neths. ............ 15 C5 51 38N 5 56 E
Boxtel, Neths. .............. 15 C5 51 36N 5 20 E
Boyce, U.S.A. .............. 81 K8 31 23N 92 40W
Boyd L., Canada ............ 72 B4 52 46N 76 42W
Boyle, Canada .............. 70 C6 54 35N 112 49W
Boyle, Ireland ............. 10 C3 53 59N 8 18W
Boyne →, Ireland .......... 10 C5 53 43N 6 15W
Boyne City, U.S.A. .......... 82 C3 45 13N 85 1W
Boynton Beach, U.S.A. ....... 83 M5 26 32N 80 4W
Boyolali, Indonesia ......... 37 G14 7 32S 110 35 E
Boyoma, Chutes, Dem. Rep. of
    the Congo ............... 54 B2 0 35N 25 23 E
Boysen Reservoir, U.S.A. ..... 76 E9 43 25N 108 11W
Boyuibe, Bolivia ............ 92 G6 20 25S 63 17W
Boyup Brook, Australia ....... 61 F2 33 50S 116 23 E
Boz Dağları, Turkey ......... 23 E13 38 20N 28 0 E
Bozburun, Turkey ........... 23 F13 36 43N 28 4 E
Bozcaada, Turkey ........... 23 E12 39 49N 26 3 E
Bozdoğan, Turkey ........... 23 F13 37 40N 28 17 E
Bozeman, U.S.A. ............ 76 D8 45 41N 111 2W
Bozen = Bolzano, Italy ....... 22 A4 46 31N 11 22 E
Bozhou, China ............. 34 H8 33 55N 115 41 E
Bozoum, C.A.R. ............. 52 C3 6 25N 16 35 E
Bra, Italy ................. 20 D7 44 42N 7 51 E
Brabant □, Belgium ......... 15 D4 50 46N 4 30 E
Brabant L., Canada ......... 71 B8 55 58N 103 43W
Brač, Croatia .............. 22 C7 43 20N 16 40 E
Bracadale, L., U.K. .......... 11 D2 57 20N 6 30W
Bracciano, L. di, Italy ....... 22 C5 42 7N 12 14 E
Bracebridge, Canada ......... 84 A5 45 2N 79 19W
Brach, Libya ............... 51 C8 27 31N 14 20 E
Bräcke, Sweden ............ 9 E16 62 45N 15 26 E
Brackettville, U.S.A. ........ 81 L4 29 19N 100 25W
Bracknell, U.K. ............. 13 F7 51 25N 0 43W
Bracknell Forest □, U.K. ..... 13 F7 51 25N 0 44W
Brad, Romania ............. 17 E12 46 10N 22 50 E
Bradenton, U.S.A. ........... 83 M4 27 30N 82 34W
Bradford, Canada ........... 84 B5 44 7N 79 34W
Bradford, U.K. ............. 12 D6 53 47N 1 45W
Bradford, Pa., U.S.A. ........ 84 E6 41 58N 78 38W
Bradford, Vt., U.S.A. ........ 85 C12 43 59N 72 9W
Bradley, Calif., U.S.A. ....... 78 K6 35 52N 120 48W
Bradley, Ark., U.S.A. ......... 81 J8 33 6N 93 39W
Bradley Institute, Zimbabwe ... 55 F3 17 7S 31 25 E
Brady, U.S.A. .............. 81 K5 31 9N 99 20W
Braeside, U.S.A. ............ 85 A8 45 28N 76 24W
Braga, Portugal ............ 21 B1 41 35N 8 25W
Bragança, Brazil ........... 93 D9 1 0S 47 2W
Bragança, Portugal ......... 21 B2 41 48N 6 50W
Bragança Paulista, Brazil .... 95 A6 22 55S 46 32W
Brahestad = Raahe, Finland ... 8 D21 64 40N 24 28 E

Brahmanbaria, Bangla. ....... 41 H17 23 58N 91 15 E
Brahmani →, India .......... 41 J15 20 39N 86 46 E
Brahmapur, India .......... 41 K14 19 15N 84 54 E
Brahmaputra →, Asia ....... 32 D3 23 40N 90 35 E
Braich-y-pwll, U.K. ......... 12 E3 52 47N 4 46W
Braidwood, Australia ........ 63 F4 35 27S 149 49 E
Brăila, Romania ............ 17 F14 45 19N 27 59 E
Brainerd, U.S.A. ............ 80 B7 46 22N 94 12W
Braintree, U.K. ............. 13 F8 51 53N 0 34 E
Braintree, U.S.A. ........... 85 D14 42 13N 71 0W
Brak →, S. Africa ........... 56 D3 29 35S 22 55 E
Brakwater, Namibia ......... 56 C2 22 28S 17 3 E
Brampton, Canada .......... 84 C5 43 45N 79 45W
Brampton, U.K. ............. 12 C5 54 57N 2 44W
Bramton I., Australia ........ 62 J7 20 50S 149 17 E
Branco →, Brazil ........... 92 D6 1 20S 61 50W
Brandberg, Namibia ......... 56 C1 21 10S 14 33 E
Brandberg △, Namibia ....... 56 C1 21 10S 14 30 E
Brandenburg = Neubrandenburg,
    Germany ................. 16 B7 53 33N 13 15 E
Brandenburg, Germany ....... 16 B7 52 25N 12 33 E
Brandenburg □, Germany ..... 16 B6 52 50N 13 0 E
Brandfort, S. Africa ......... 56 D4 28 40S 26 30 E
Brandon, Canada ........... 71 D9 49 50N 99 57W
Brandon, U.S.A. ............ 85 C11 43 48N 73 4W
Brandon B., Ireland ......... 10 D1 52 17N 10 8W
Brandon Mt., Ireland ........ 10 D1 52 15N 10 15W
Brandsen, Argentina ........ 94 D4 35 10S 58 15W
Brandvlei, S. Africa ......... 56 E3 30 25S 20 30 E
Branford, U.S.A. ............ 85 E12 41 17N 72 49W
Braniewo, Poland ........... 17 A10 54 25N 19 50 E
Bransfield Str., Antarctica .... 5 C18 63 0S 59 0W
Branson, U.S.A. ............ 81 G8 36 39N 93 13W
Brantford, Canada .......... 84 C4 43 10N 80 15W
Bras d'Or L., Canada ........ 73 C7 45 50N 60 50W
Brasher Falls, U.S.A. ........ 85 B10 44 49N 74 47W
Brasil, Planalto, Brazil ...... 90 E6 18 0S 46 30W
Brasiléia, Brazil ........... 92 F5 11 0S 68 45W
Brasília, Brazil ............. 93 G9 15 47S 47 55W
Brasília Legal, Brazil ........ 93 D7 3 49S 55 36W
Braslaw, Belarus ........... 9 J22 55 38N 27 0 E
Braşov, Romania ........... 17 F13 45 38N 25 35 E
Brasschaat, Belgium ........ 15 C4 51 19N 4 27 E
Brassey, Banjaran, Malaysia ... 36 D5 5 0N 117 15 E
Brassey Ra., Australia ....... 61 E3 25 8S 122 15 E
Brasstown Bald, U.S.A. ...... 83 H4 34 53N 83 49W
Brastad, Sweden ........... 9 G14 58 23N 11 30 E
Bratislava, Slovak Rep. ...... 17 D9 48 10N 17 7 E
Bratsk, Russia ............. 29 D11 56 10N 101 30 E
Brattleboro, U.S.A. ......... 85 D12 42 51N 72 34W
Braunau, Austria ........... 16 D7 48 15N 13 3 E
Braunschweig, Germany ...... 16 B6 52 15N 10 31 E
Braunton, U.K. ............. 13 F3 51 7N 4 10W
Bravo del Norte, Rio = Grande,
    Rio →, U.S.A. ........... 81 N6 25 58N 97 9W
Brawley, U.S.A. ............ 79 N11 32 59N 115 31W
Bray, Ireland .............. 10 C5 53 13N 6 7W
Bray, Mt., Australia ......... 62 A1 14 0S 134 30 E
Bray, Pays de, France ....... 20 B4 49 46N 1 26 E
Brazeau →, Canada ......... 70 C5 52 55N 115 14W
Brazil, U.S.A. .............. 82 F2 39 32N 87 8W
Brazil ■, S. Amer. .......... 93 F9 12 0S 50 0W
Brazilian Highlands = Brasil,
    Planalto, Brazil ......... 90 E6 18 0S 46 30W
Brazo Sur →, S. Amer. ...... 94 B4 25 21S 57 42W
Brazos →, U.S.A. ........... 81 L7 28 53N 95 23W
Brazzaville, Congo .......... 52 E3 4 9S 15 12 E
Brčko, Bos.-H. ............. 23 B8 44 54N 18 46 E
Breaden, L., Australia ....... 61 E4 25 51S 125 28 E
Breaksea Sd., N.Z. .......... 59 L1 45 35S 166 35 E
Bream B., N.Z. ............. 59 F5 35 56S 174 28 E
Bream Hd., N.Z. ............ 59 F5 35 51S 174 36 E
Breas, Chile ............... 94 B1 25 29S 70 24W
Brebes, Indonesia .......... 37 G13 6 52S 109 3 E
Brechin, Canada ........... 84 B5 44 32N 79 10W
Brechin, U.K. .............. 11 E6 56 44N 2 39W
Brecht, Belgium ............ 15 C4 51 21N 4 38 E
Breckenridge, Colo., U.S.A. ... 76 G10 39 29N 106 3W
Breckenridge, Minn., U.S.A. ... 80 B6 46 16N 96 35W
Breckenridge, Tex., U.S.A. .... 81 J5 32 45N 98 54W
Breckland, U.K. ............ 13 E8 52 30N 0 40 E
Brecon, U.K. ............... 13 F4 51 57N 3 23W
Brecon Beacons, U.K. ........ 13 F4 51 53N 3 26W
Brecon Beacons △, U.K. ...... 13 F4 51 50N 3 30W
Breda, Neths. .............. 15 C4 51 35N 4 45 E
Bredasdorp, S. Africa ........ 56 E3 34 33S 20 2 E
Bree, Belgium .............. 15 C5 51 8N 5 35 E
Bregenz, Austria ........... 16 E5 47 30N 9 45 E
Breiðafjörður, Iceland ....... 8 D2 65 15N 23 15W
Brejo, Brazil ............... 93 D10 3 41S 42 47W
Bremen, Germany ........... 16 B5 53 4N 8 47 E
Bremer Bay, Australia ....... 61 F2 34 21S 119 20 E
Bremer I., Australia ......... 62 A2 12 5S 136 45 E
Bremerhaven, Germany ...... 16 B5 53 33N 8 36 E
Bremerton, U.S.A. ........... 78 C4 47 34N 122 38W
Brenham, U.S.A. ............ 81 K6 30 10N 96 24W
Brennerpass, Austria ........ 16 E6 47 2N 11 30 E
Brent, U.K. ................ 13 F7 51 33N 0 16W
Brentwood, U.K. ............ 13 F8 51 37N 0 19 E
Brentwood, Calif., U.S.A. ..... 78 H5 37 56N 121 42W
Brentwood, N.Y., U.S.A. ...... 85 F11 40 47N 73 15W
Bréscia, Italy .............. 20 D9 45 33N 10 15 E
Breskens, Neths. ........... 15 C3 51 23N 3 33 E
Breslau = Wrocław, Poland ... 17 C9 51 5N 17 5 E
Bressanone, Italy ........... 22 A4 46 43N 11 39 E
Bressay, U.K. .............. 11 A7 60 9N 1 6W
Brest, Belarus ............. 17 B12 52 10N 23 40 E
Brest, France .............. 20 B1 48 24N 4 31W
Brest-Litovsk = Brest, Belarus . 17 B12 52 10N 23 40 E
Bretagne □, France ......... 20 B2 48 10N 3 0W
Breton, Canada ............. 70 C6 53 7N 114 28W
Breton Sd., U.S.A. .......... 81 L10 29 35N 89 15W
Brett, C., N.Z. ............. 59 F5 35 10S 174 20 E
Brevard, U.S.A. ............ 83 H4 35 14N 82 44W
Breves, Brazil ............. 93 D8 1 40S 50 29W
Brewarrina, Australia ....... 63 D4 30 0S 146 51 E
Brewer, U.S.A. ............. 83 C11 44 48N 68 46W
Brewer, Mt., U.S.A. ......... 78 J8 36 44N 118 28W
Brewster, N.Y., U.S.A. ....... 85 E11 41 23N 73 37W
Brewster, Ohio, U.S.A. ....... 84 F3 40 43N 81 36W
Brewster, Wash., U.S.A. ...... 76 B4 48 6N 119 47W
Brewster, Kap = Kangikajik,
    Greenland .............. 4 B6 70 7N 22 0W
Brewton, U.S.A. ............ 83 K2 31 7N 87 4W
Breyten, S. Africa .......... 57 D5 26 16S 30 0 E
Briançon, France ........... 20 D7 44 54N 6 39 E
Bribie I., Australia ......... 63 D5 27 0S 153 10 E
Bribri, Costa Rica .......... 88 E3 9 38N 82 50W

| | | | |
|---|---|---|---|
| Bridgefield, Barbados | 89 g | 13 9N | 59 36W |
| Bridgehampton, U.S.A. | 85 F12 | 40 56N | 72 19W |
| Bridgend, U.K. | 13 F4 | 51 30N | 3 34W |
| Bridgend □, U.K. | 13 F4 | 51 36N | 3 36W |
| Bridgeport, Calif., U.S.A. | 78 G7 | 38 15N | 119 14W |
| Bridgeport, Conn., U.S.A. | 85 E11 | 41 11N | 73 12W |
| Bridgeport, Nebr., U.S.A. | 80 E3 | 41 40N | 103 6W |
| Bridgeport, Tex., U.S.A. | 81 J6 | 33 13N | 97 45W |
| Bridger, U.S.A. | 76 D9 | 45 18N | 108 55W |
| Bridgeton, U.S.A. | 82 F8 | 39 26N | 75 14W |
| Bridgetown, Australia | 61 F2 | 33 58S | 116 7 E |
| Bridgetown, Barbados | 89 g | 13 6N | 59 37W |
| Bridgewater, Canada | 73 D6 | 44 55N | 65 18W |
| Bridgewater, Canada | 73 D7 | 44 25N | 64 31W |
| Bridgewater, Mass., U.S.A. | 85 E14 | 41 59N | 70 58W |
| Bridgewater, N.Y., U.S.A. | 85 D9 | 42 53N | 75 15W |
| Bridgewater, C., Australia | 63 F3 | 38 23S | 141 23 E |
| Bridgewater-Gagebrook, Australia | 63 G4 | 42 44S | 147 14 E |
| Bridgnorth, U.K. | 13 E5 | 52 32N | 2 25W |
| Bridgton, U.S.A. | 85 B14 | 44 3N | 70 42W |
| Bridgwater, U.K. | 13 F5 | 51 8N | 2 59W |
| Bridgwater B., U.K. | 13 F4 | 51 15N | 3 15W |
| Bridlington, U.K. | 12 C7 | 54 5N | 0 12W |
| Bridlington B., U.K. | 12 C7 | 54 4N | 0 10W |
| Bridport, Australia | 63 G4 | 40 59S | 147 23 E |
| Bridport, U.K. | 13 G5 | 50 44N | 2 45W |
| Brig, Switz. | 20 C7 | 46 18N | 7 59 E |
| Brigg, U.K. | 12 D7 | 53 34N | 0 28W |
| Brigham City, U.S.A. | 76 F7 | 41 31N | 112 1W |
| Bright, Australia | 63 F4 | 36 42S | 146 56 E |
| Brighton, Australia | 63 F2 | 35 5S | 138 30 E |
| Brighton, Canada | 84 B7 | 44 2N | 77 44W |
| Brighton, Trin. & Tob. | 93 K15 | 10 13N | 61 39W |
| Brighton, U.K. | 13 G7 | 50 49N | 0 7W |
| Brighton, Colo., U.S.A. | 80 F2 | 39 59N | 104 49W |
| Brighton, N.Y., U.S.A. | 84 C7 | 43 8N | 77 34W |
| Brilliant, U.S.A. | 84 F4 | 40 15N | 80 39W |
| Brindisi, Italy | 23 D7 | 40 39N | 17 55 E |
| Brinkley, U.S.A. | 81 H9 | 34 53N | 91 12W |
| Brinnon, U.S.A. | 78 C4 | 47 41N | 122 54W |
| Brion, I., Canada | 73 C7 | 47 46N | 61 26W |
| Brisbane, Australia | 63 D5 | 27 25S | 153 2 E |
| Brisbane →, Australia | 63 D5 | 27 24S | 153 9 E |
| Bristol, U.K. | 13 F5 | 51 26N | 2 35W |
| Bristol, Conn., U.S.A. | 85 E12 | 41 40N | 72 57W |
| Bristol, Pa., U.S.A. | 85 F10 | 40 6N | 74 51W |
| Bristol, R.I., U.S.A. | 85 E13 | 41 40N | 71 16W |
| Bristol, Tenn., U.S.A. | 83 G4 | 36 36N | 82 11W |
| Bristol, City of □, U.K. | 13 F5 | 51 27N | 2 36W |
| Bristol B., U.S.A. | 68 C4 | 58 0N | 160 0W |
| Bristol Channel, U.K. | 13 F3 | 51 18N | 4 30W |
| Bristol I., Antarctica | 5 B1 | 58 45S | 28 0W |
| Bristol L., U.S.A. | 77 J5 | 34 23N | 116 50W |
| Bristow, U.S.A. | 81 H6 | 35 50N | 96 23W |
| Britain = Great Britain, Europe | 6 E5 | 54 0N | 2 15W |
| British Columbia □, Canada | 70 C3 | 55 0N | 125 15W |
| British Indian Ocean Terr. = Chagos Arch. ☒, Ind. Oc. | 27 K11 | 6 0S | 72 0 E |
| British Isles, Europe | 14 D5 | 54 0N | 4 0W |
| British Virgin Is. ☒, W. Indies | 89 e | 18 30N | 64 30W |
| Brits, S. Africa | 57 D4 | 25 37S | 27 48 E |
| Britstown, S. Africa | 56 E3 | 30 37S | 23 30 E |
| Britt, Canada | 84 A4 | 45 46N | 80 34W |
| Brittany = Bretagne □, France | 20 B2 | 48 10N | 3 0W |
| Britton, U.S.A. | 80 C6 | 45 48N | 97 45W |
| Brive-la-Gaillarde, France | 20 D4 | 45 10N | 1 32 E |
| Brixen = Bressanone, Italy | 22 A4 | 46 43N | 11 39 E |
| Brixham, U.K. | 13 G4 | 50 23N | 3 31W |
| Brno, Czech Rep. | 17 D9 | 49 10N | 16 35 E |
| Broach = Bharuch, India | 40 J8 | 21 47N | 73 0 E |
| Broad →, U.S.A. | 83 J5 | 34 1N | 81 4W |
| Broad Arrow, Australia | 61 F3 | 30 23S | 121 15 E |
| Broad B., U.K. | 11 C2 | 58 14N | 6 18W |
| Broad Haven, Ireland | 10 B2 | 54 20N | 9 55W |
| Broad Law, U.K. | 11 F5 | 55 30N | 3 21W |
| Broad Sd., Australia | 62 C4 | 22 0S | 149 45 E |
| Broadalbin, U.S.A. | 85 C10 | 43 4N | 74 12W |
| Broadback →, Canada | 72 B4 | 51 21N | 78 52W |
| Broadhurst Ra., Australia | 60 D3 | 22 30S | 122 30 E |
| Broads △, U.K. | 13 E9 | 52 45N | 1 30 E |
| Broads, The, U.K. | 12 E9 | 52 45N | 1 30 E |
| Broadus, U.S.A. | 80 C2 | 45 27N | 105 25W |
| Brochet, Canada | 71 B8 | 57 53N | 101 40W |
| Brochet, L., Canada | 71 B8 | 58 36N | 101 35W |
| Brocken, Germany | 16 C6 | 51 47N | 10 37 E |
| Brockport, U.S.A. | 84 C7 | 43 13N | 77 56W |
| Brockton, U.S.A. | 85 D13 | 42 5N | 71 1W |
| Brockville, Canada | 85 B9 | 44 35N | 75 41W |
| Brockway, Mont., U.S.A. | 80 B2 | 47 18N | 105 45W |
| Brockway, Pa., U.S.A. | 84 E6 | 41 15N | 78 47W |
| Brocton, U.S.A. | 84 D5 | 42 23N | 79 26W |
| Brodeur Pen., Canada | 69 A11 | 72 30N | 88 10W |
| Brodhead, Mt., U.S.A. | 84 E7 | 41 39N | 77 47W |
| Brodick, U.K. | 11 F5 | 55 35N | 5 9W |
| Brodnica, Poland | 17 B10 | 53 15N | 19 25 E |
| Brody, Ukraine | 17 C13 | 50 5N | 25 10 E |
| Brogan, U.S.A. | 76 D5 | 44 15N | 117 31W |
| Broken Arrow, U.S.A. | 81 G7 | 36 3N | 95 48W |
| Broken Bow, Nebr., U.S.A. | 80 E5 | 41 24N | 99 38W |
| Broken Bow, Okla., U.S.A. | 81 H7 | 34 2N | 94 44W |
| Broken Bow Lake, U.S.A. | 81 H7 | 34 9N | 94 40W |
| Broken Hill, Australia | 63 E3 | 31 58S | 141 29 E |
| Broken River Ra., Australia | 62 K6 | 21 0S | 148 22 E |
| Bromley □, U.K. | 13 F8 | 51 24N | 0 2 E |
| Bromo, Indonesia | 37 G15 | 7 55S | 112 55 E |
| Bromsgrove, U.K. | 13 E5 | 52 21N | 2 2W |
| Brønderslev, Denmark | 9 H13 | 57 16N | 9 57 E |
| Bronkhorstspruit, S. Africa | 57 D4 | 25 46S | 28 45 E |
| Brønnøysund, Norway | 8 D15 | 65 28N | 12 14 E |
| Brook Park, U.S.A. | 84 E4 | 41 24N | 81 51W |
| Brookhaven, U.S.A. | 81 K9 | 31 35N | 90 26W |
| Brookings, Oreg., U.S.A. | 76 E1 | 42 3N | 124 17W |
| Brookings, S. Dak., U.S.A. | 80 C6 | 44 19N | 96 48W |
| Brooklin, Canada | 84 C6 | 43 55N | 78 55W |
| Brooklyn Park, U.S.A. | 80 C8 | 45 6N | 93 23W |
| Brooks, Canada | 70 C6 | 50 35N | 111 55W |
| Brooks Range, U.S.A. | 68 B5 | 68 0N | 152 0W |
| Brooksville, U.S.A. | 83 L4 | 28 33N | 82 23W |
| Brookton, Australia | 61 F2 | 32 22S | 117 0 E |
| Brookville, U.S.A. | 84 E5 | 41 10N | 79 5W |
| Broom, L., U.K. | 11 D3 | 57 55N | 5 15W |
| Broome, Australia | 60 C3 | 18 0S | 122 15 E |
| Brora, U.K. | 11 C5 | 58 0N | 3 52W |
| Brora →, U.K. | 11 C5 | 58 0N | 3 51W |
| Brosna →, Ireland | 10 C4 | 53 14N | 7 58W |
| Brothers, U.S.A. | 76 E3 | 43 49N | 120 36W |
| Brough, U.K. | 12 C5 | 54 32N | 2 18W |
| Brough Hd., U.K. | 11 B5 | 59 8N | 3 20W |
| Broughton Island = Qikiqtarjuaq, Canada | 69 B13 | 67 33N | 63 0W |
| Brown, L., Australia | 61 F2 | 31 5S | 118 15 E |
| Brown, Pt., Australia | 63 E1 | 32 32S | 133 50 E |
| Brown City, U.S.A. | 84 C2 | 43 13N | 82 59W |
| Brown Willy, U.K. | 13 G3 | 50 35N | 4 37W |
| Brownfield, U.S.A. | 81 J3 | 33 11N | 102 17W |
| Browning, U.S.A. | 76 B7 | 48 34N | 113 1W |
| Brownsville, Oreg., U.S.A. | 76 D2 | 44 24N | 122 59W |
| Brownsville, Pa., U.S.A. | 84 F5 | 40 1N | 79 53W |
| Brownsville, Tenn., U.S.A. | 81 H10 | 35 36N | 89 16W |
| Brownsville, Tex., U.S.A. | 81 N6 | 25 54N | 97 30W |
| Brownville, U.S.A. | 85 C9 | 44 0N | 75 59W |
| Brownwood, U.S.A. | 81 K5 | 31 43N | 98 59W |
| Browse I., Australia | 60 B3 | 14 7S | 123 33 E |
| Bruas, Malaysia | 39 K3 | 4 30N | 100 47 E |
| Bruay-la-Buissière, France | 20 A5 | 50 29N | 2 33 E |
| Bruce, Mt., Australia | 60 D2 | 22 37S | 118 8 E |
| Bruce Pen., Canada | 84 B3 | 45 0N | 81 30W |
| Bruce Peninsula △, Canada | 84 A3 | 45 14N | 81 36W |
| Bruce Rock, Australia | 61 F2 | 31 52S | 118 8 E |
| Bruck an der Leitha, Austria | 17 D9 | 48 1N | 16 47 E |
| Bruck an der Mur, Austria | 16 E8 | 47 24N | 15 16 E |
| Brue →, U.K. | 13 F5 | 51 13N | 2 59W |
| Bruges = Brugge, Belgium | 15 C3 | 51 13N | 3 13 E |
| Brugge, Belgium | 15 C3 | 51 13N | 3 13 E |
| Bruin, U.S.A. | 84 E5 | 41 3N | 79 43W |
| Brûlé, Canada | 70 C5 | 53 15N | 117 58W |
| Brumado, Brazil | 93 F10 | 14 14S | 41 40W |
| Brumunddal, Norway | 9 F14 | 60 53N | 10 56 E |
| Bruneau, U.S.A. | 76 E6 | 42 53N | 115 48W |
| Bruneau →, U.S.A. | 76 E6 | 42 56N | 115 57W |
| Brunei = Bandar Seri Begawan, Brunei | 36 C4 | 4 52N | 115 0 E |
| Brunei ■, Asia | 36 D4 | 4 50N | 115 0 E |
| Brunner, L., N.Z. | 59 K3 | 42 37S | 171 27 E |
| Brunssum, Neths. | 15 D5 | 50 57N | 5 59 E |
| Brunswick = Braunschweig, Germany | 16 B6 | 52 15N | 10 31 E |
| Brunswick, Ga., U.S.A. | 83 K5 | 31 10N | 81 30W |
| Brunswick, Maine, U.S.A. | 83 D11 | 43 55N | 69 58W |
| Brunswick, Md., U.S.A. | 82 F7 | 39 19N | 77 38W |
| Brunswick, Mo., U.S.A. | 80 F8 | 39 26N | 93 8W |
| Brunswick, Ohio, U.S.A. | 84 E3 | 41 14N | 81 51W |
| Brunswick, Pen. de, Chile | 96 G2 | 53 30S | 71 30W |
| Brunswick B., Australia | 60 C3 | 15 15S | 124 50 E |
| Brunswick Junction, Australia | 61 F2 | 33 15S | 115 50 E |
| Bruny I., Australia | 63 G4 | 43 20S | 147 15 E |
| Brus Laguna, Honduras | 88 C3 | 15 47N | 84 35W |
| Brush, U.S.A. | 80 E3 | 40 15N | 103 37W |
| Brushton, U.S.A. | 85 B10 | 44 50N | 74 31W |
| Brusque, Brazil | 95 B6 | 27 5S | 49 0W |
| Brussel, Belgium | 15 D4 | 50 51N | 4 21 E |
| Brussel ✕ (BRU), Belgium | 15 D5 | 50 54N | 5 41 E |
| Brussels = Brussel, Belgium | 15 D4 | 50 51N | 4 21 E |
| Brussels, Canada | 84 C3 | 43 44N | 81 15W |
| Bruthen, Australia | 63 F4 | 37 42S | 147 50 E |
| Bruxelles = Brussel, Belgium | 15 D4 | 50 51N | 4 21 E |
| Bryan, Ohio, U.S.A. | 82 E3 | 41 28N | 84 33W |
| Bryan, Tex., U.S.A. | 81 K6 | 30 40N | 96 22W |
| Bryan, Mt., Australia | 63 E2 | 33 30S | 139 0 E |
| Bryansk, Russia | 18 D4 | 53 13N | 34 25 E |
| Bryce Canyon △, U.S.A. | 77 H7 | 37 30N | 112 10W |
| Bryne, Norway | 9 G11 | 58 44N | 5 38 E |
| Bryson City, U.S.A. | 83 H4 | 35 26N | 83 27W |
| Bsharri, Lebanon | 46 A5 | 34 15N | 36 0 E |
| Bū Baqarah, U.A.E. | 45 E8 | 25 35N | 56 25 E |
| Bu Craa, W. Sahara | 50 C3 | 26 45N | 12 50W |
| Bū Ḥasā, U.A.E. | 45 F7 | 23 30N | 53 20 E |
| Bua Yai, Thailand | 38 E4 | 15 33N | 102 26 E |
| Buapinang, Indonesia | 37 E6 | 4 40S | 121 30 E |
| Bubanza, Burundi | 54 C2 | 3 6S | 29 23 E |
| Būbiyān, Kuwait | 45 D6 | 29 45N | 48 15 E |
| Bucaramanga, Colombia | 92 B4 | 7 0N | 73 0W |
| Bucasia, Australia | 62 K7 | 21 2S | 149 10 E |
| Buccaneer Arch., Australia | 60 C3 | 16 7S | 123 20 E |
| Buccoo Reef, Trin. & Tob. | 93 J16 | 11 10N | 60 51W |
| Buchach, Ukraine | 17 D13 | 49 5N | 25 25 E |
| Buchan, U.K. | 11 D6 | 57 32N | 2 21W |
| Buchan Ness, U.K. | 11 D7 | 57 29N | 1 46W |
| Buchanan, Canada | 71 C8 | 51 40N | 102 45W |
| Buchanan, Liberia | 50 G3 | 5 57N | 10 2W |
| Buchanan, L., Queens., Australia | 62 C4 | 21 35S | 145 52 E |
| Buchanan, L., W. Austral., Australia | 61 E3 | 25 33S | 123 2 E |
| Buchanan, L., U.S.A. | 81 K5 | 30 45N | 98 25W |
| Buchanan Cr. →, Australia | 62 B2 | 19 13S | 136 33 E |
| Buchans, Canada | 73 C8 | 48 50N | 56 52W |
| Bucharest = București, Romania | 17 F14 | 44 27N | 26 10 E |
| Buchon, Pt., U.S.A. | 78 K6 | 35 15N | 120 54W |
| Buck Hill Falls, U.S.A. | 85 E9 | 41 11N | 75 16W |
| Buckeye, U.S.A. | 77 K7 | 33 22N | 112 35W |
| Buckeye Lake, U.S.A. | 84 G2 | 39 55N | 82 29W |
| Buckhannon, U.S.A. | 82 F5 | 39 0N | 80 8W |
| Buckhaven, U.K. | 11 E5 | 56 11N | 3 3W |
| Buckhorn L., Canada | 84 B6 | 44 29N | 78 23W |
| Buckie, U.K. | 11 D6 | 57 41N | 2 58W |
| Buckingham, Canada | 72 C4 | 45 37N | 75 24W |
| Buckingham, U.K. | 13 F7 | 51 59N | 0 57W |
| Buckingham B., Australia | 62 A2 | 12 10S | 135 40 E |
| Buckinghamshire □, U.K. | 13 F7 | 51 53N | 0 55W |
| Buckle Hd., Australia | 60 B4 | 14 26S | 127 52 E |
| Buckleboo, Australia | 63 E2 | 32 54S | 136 12 E |
| Buckley, U.S.A. | 12 D4 | 53 10N | 3 5W |
| Buckley →, Australia | 62 C2 | 20 10S | 138 49 E |
| Bucklin, U.S.A. | 81 G5 | 37 33N | 99 38W |
| Bucks L., U.S.A. | 78 F5 | 39 54N | 121 12W |
| Buctouche, Canada | 73 C7 | 46 30N | 64 45W |
| Bud, Norway | 8 E12 | 62 54N | 6 55 E |
| Budalin, Burma | 41 H19 | 22 20N | 95 10 E |
| Budapest, Hungary | 17 E10 | 47 29N | 19 5 E |
| Budaun, India | 43 E8 | 28 5N | 79 10 E |
| Budd Coast, Antarctica | 5 C8 | 68 0S | 112 0 E |
| Bude, U.K. | 13 G3 | 50 49N | 4 34W |
| Budennovsk, Russia | 19 F7 | 44 50N | 44 10 E |
| Budge Budge = Baj Baj, India | 43 H13 | 22 30N | 88 5 E |
| Budgewoi, Australia | 63 E5 | 33 13S | 151 34 E |
| Budjala, Dem. Rep. of the Congo | 52 D3 | 2 50N | 19 40 E |
| Buellton, U.S.A. | 79 L6 | 34 37N | 120 12W |
| Buena Esperanza, Argentina | 94 C2 | 34 45S | 65 15W |
| Buena Park, U.S.A. | 79 M9 | 33 52N | 117 59W |
| Buena Vista, Colo., U.S.A. | 77 G10 | 38 51N | 106 8W |
| Buena Vista, Va., U.S.A. | 82 G6 | 37 44N | 79 21W |
| Buena Vista Lake Bed, U.S.A. | 79 K7 | 35 12N | 119 18W |
| Buenaventura, Colombia | 92 C3 | 3 53N | 77 4W |
| Buenaventura, Mexico | 86 B3 | 29 50N | 107 30W |
| Buenos Aires, Argentina | 94 C4 | 34 30S | 58 20W |
| Buenos Aires, Costa Rica | 88 E3 | 9 10N | 83 20W |
| Buenos Aires □, Argentina | 94 D4 | 36 30S | 60 0W |
| Buenos Aires, L., Chile | 96 F2 | 46 35S | 72 30W |
| Buffalo, Mo., U.S.A. | 81 G8 | 37 39N | 93 6W |
| Buffalo, N.Y., U.S.A. | 84 D6 | 42 53N | 78 53W |
| Buffalo, Okla., U.S.A. | 81 G5 | 36 50N | 99 38W |
| Buffalo, S. Dak., U.S.A. | 80 C3 | 45 35N | 103 33W |
| Buffalo, Wyo., U.S.A. | 76 D10 | 44 21N | 106 42W |
| Buffalo →, Canada | 70 A5 | 60 5N | 115 5W |
| Buffalo →, Canada | 57 D5 | 28 43S | 30 37 E |
| Buffalo Head Hills, Canada | 70 B5 | 57 25N | 115 55W |
| Buffalo L., Alta., Canada | 70 C6 | 52 27N | 112 54W |
| Buffalo L., N.W.T., Canada | 70 A5 | 60 12N | 115 25W |
| Buffalo Springs △, Kenya | 54 B4 | 0 32N | 37 35 E |
| Buffels →, S. Africa | 56 D2 | 29 36S | 17 3 E |
| Buford, U.S.A. | 83 H4 | 34 10N | 84 0W |
| Bug = Buh →, Ukraine | 19 E5 | 46 59N | 31 58 E |
| Bug →, Poland | 17 B11 | 52 31N | 21 5 E |
| Buga, Colombia | 92 C3 | 4 0N | 76 15W |
| Bugala I., Uganda | 54 C3 | 0 40S | 32 20 E |
| Buganda, Uganda | 54 C3 | 0 0 | 31 30 E |
| Buganga, Uganda | 54 C3 | 0 3 | 32 0 E |
| Bugel, Tanjung, Indonesia | 37 G14 | 6 26S | 111 3 E |
| Bugibba, Malta | 25 D1 | 35 57N | 14 25 E |
| Bugsuk, Phil. | 36 C5 | 8 15N | 117 15 E |
| Bugulma, Russia | 18 D9 | 54 33N | 52 48 E |
| Bugun Shara, Mongolia | 32 B5 | 49 0N | 104 0 E |
| Bugungu △, Uganda | 54 B3 | 2 17N | 31 50 E |
| Buguruslan, Russia | 18 D9 | 53 39N | 52 26 E |
| Buh →, Ukraine | 19 E5 | 46 59N | 31 58 E |
| Buhera, Zimbabwe | 57 B5 | 19 18S | 31 29 E |
| Buhl, U.S.A. | 76 E6 | 42 36N | 114 46W |
| Buholyong, China | 33 F11 | 22 37N | 114 5 E |
| Bujumbura, Burundi | 54 C2 | 3 16S | 29 18 E |
| Bukachacha, Russia | 29 D12 | 52 55N | 116 50 E |
| Bukama, Dem. Rep. of the Congo | 55 D2 | 9 10S | 25 50 E |
| Bukavu, Dem. Rep. of the Congo | 54 C2 | 2 20S | 28 52 E |
| Bukene, Tanzania | 54 C3 | 4 15S | 32 48 E |
| Bukhara = Bukhoro, Uzbekistan | 28 F7 | 39 48N | 64 25 E |
| Bukhoro, Uzbekistan | 28 F7 | 39 48N | 64 25 E |
| Bukima, Tanzania | 54 C3 | 1 50S | 33 25 E |
| Bukit Badung, Indonesia | 37 K18 | 8 49S | 115 10 E |
| Bukit Kerajaan, Malaysia | 39 c | 5 25N | 100 15 E |
| Bukit Mertajam, Malaysia | 39 c | 5 22N | 100 28 E |
| Bukit Ni, Malaysia | 39 d | 1 22N | 104 12 E |
| Bukit Panjang, Singapore | 39 d | 1 23N | 103 46 E |
| Bukit Tengah, Malaysia | 39 c | 5 22N | 100 28 E |
| Bukittinggi, Indonesia | 36 E2 | 0 20S | 100 20 E |
| Bukoba, Tanzania | 54 C3 | 1 20S | 31 49 E |
| Bukum, Pulau, Singapore | 39 d | 1 14N | 103 46 E |
| Bukuya, Uganda | 54 B3 | 0 40N | 31 52 E |
| Bül, Kuh-e, Iran | 45 D7 | 30 48N | 52 45 E |
| Bula, Indonesia | 37 E8 | 3 6S | 130 30 E |
| Bulahdelah, Australia | 63 E5 | 32 23S | 152 13 E |
| Bulan, Phil. | 37 B6 | 12 40N | 123 52 E |
| Bulandshahr, India | 42 E7 | 28 28N | 77 51 E |
| Bulawayo, Zimbabwe | 55 G2 | 20 7S | 28 32 E |
| Buldan, Turkey | 23 E13 | 38 2N | 28 50 E |
| Bulgar, Russia | 18 D8 | 54 57N | 49 4 E |
| Bulgaria ■, Europe | 23 C11 | 42 35N | 25 30 E |
| Buli, Teluk, Indonesia | 37 D7 | 0 48N | 128 25 E |
| Buliluyan, C., Phil. | 36 C5 | 8 20N | 117 15 E |
| Bulim, Singapore | 39 d | 1 22N | 103 43 E |
| Bulkley →, Canada | 70 B3 | 55 15N | 127 40W |
| Bull Shoals L., U.S.A. | 81 G8 | 36 22N | 92 35W |
| Bullaring, Australia | 62 B3 | 17 39S | 143 56 E |
| Bullhead City, U.S.A. | 79 K12 | 35 8N | 114 32W |
| Büllingen, Belgium | 15 D6 | 50 25N | 6 16 E |
| Bullock Creek, Australia | 62 B3 | 17 43S | 144 31 E |
| Bulloo →, Australia | 63 D3 | 28 43S | 142 30 E |
| Bulloo L., Australia | 63 D3 | 28 43S | 142 25 E |
| Bulls, N.Z. | 59 J5 | 40 10S | 175 24 E |
| Bulnes, Chile | 94 D1 | 36 42S | 72 19W |
| Bulsar = Valsad, India | 40 J8 | 20 40N | 72 58 E |
| Bultfontein, S. Africa | 56 D4 | 28 18S | 26 10 E |
| Bulukumba, Indonesia | 37 F6 | 5 33S | 120 11 E |
| Bulun, Russia | 29 B13 | 70 37N | 127 30 E |
| Bumba, Dem. Rep. of the Congo | 52 D4 | 2 13N | 22 30 E |
| Bumbiri I., Tanzania | 54 C3 | 1 40S | 31 55 E |
| Bumhpa Bum, Burma | 41 F20 | 26 51N | 97 14 E |
| Bumi →, Zimbabwe | 55 F2 | 17 0S | 28 20 E |
| Buna, Kenya | 54 B4 | 2 58N | 39 30 E |
| Bunazi, Tanzania | 54 C3 | 1 3S | 31 23 E |
| Bunbury, Australia | 61 F2 | 33 20S | 115 35 E |
| Bunclody, Ireland | 10 D5 | 52 39N | 6 40W |
| Buncrana, Ireland | 10 A4 | 55 8N | 7 27W |
| Bundaberg, Australia | 63 C5 | 24 54S | 152 22 E |
| Bundey →, Australia | 62 C2 | 21 46S | 135 37 E |
| Bundi, India | 42 G6 | 25 30N | 75 35 E |
| Bundjalung △, Australia | 63 D5 | 29 16S | 153 21 E |
| Bundoran, Ireland | 10 B3 | 54 28N | 8 16W |
| Bung Kan, Thailand | 38 C4 | 18 23N | 103 37 E |
| Bungay, U.K. | 13 E9 | 52 27N | 1 28 E |
| Bungil Cr. →, Australia | 63 D4 | 27 5S | 149 5 E |
| Bungle Bungle = Purnululu Nat. Park △, Australia | 60 C4 | 17 20S | 128 20 E |
| Bungo-Suidō, Japan | 31 H6 | 33 0N | 132 15 E |
| Bungoma, Kenya | 54 B3 | 0 34N | 34 34 E |
| Bungotakada, Japan | 31 H5 | 33 35N | 131 25 E |
| Bungu, Tanzania | 54 D4 | 7 35S | 39 0 E |
| Bunia, Dem. Rep. of the Congo | 54 B3 | 1 35N | 30 20 E |
| Bunji, Pakistan | 43 B6 | 35 45N | 74 40 E |
| Bunkie, U.S.A. | 81 K8 | 30 57N | 92 11W |
| Bunnell, U.S.A. | 83 L5 | 29 28N | 81 16W |
| Buntok, Indonesia | 36 E4 | 1 40S | 114 58 E |
| Bunya Mts. △, Australia | 63 D5 | 26 51S | 151 34 E |
| Bunyu, Indonesia | 36 D5 | 3 35N | 117 50 E |
| Buol, Indonesia | 37 D6 | 1 15N | 121 32 E |
| Buon Brieng, Vietnam | 38 F7 | 13 9N | 108 12 E |
| Buon Ma Thuot, Vietnam | 38 F7 | 12 40N | 108 3 E |
| Buong Long, Cambodia | 38 F6 | 13 44N | 106 59 E |
| Buorkhaya, Mys, Russia | 29 B14 | 71 50N | 132 40 E |
| Buqayq, Si. Arabia | 45 E6 | 26 0N | 49 45 E |
| Bur Acaba, Somali Rep. | 47 G3 | 3 12N | 44 20 E |
| Bûr Safâga, Egypt | 44 E2 | 26 43N | 33 57 E |
| Bûr Sa'îd, Egypt | 51 B12 | 31 16N | 32 18 E |
| Bûr Sûdân, Sudan | 51 E13 | 19 32N | 37 9 E |
| Bura, Kenya | 54 C4 | 1 4S | 39 58 E |
| Burakin, Australia | 61 F2 | 30 31S | 117 10 E |
| Burao, Somali Rep. | 47 F4 | 9 32N | 45 32 E |
| Burāq, Syria | 46 B5 | 33 11N | 36 29 E |
| Buraydah, Si. Arabia | 44 E4 | 26 20N | 43 59 E |
| Burbank, U.S.A. | 79 L8 | 34 11N | 118 19W |
| Burda, India | 42 G6 | 25 50N | 77 35 E |
| Burdekin →, Australia | 62 B4 | 19 38S | 147 25 E |
| Burdur, Turkey | 19 G5 | 37 45N | 30 17 E |
| Burdwan = Barddhaman, India | 43 H12 | 23 14N | 87 39 E |
| Bure, Ethiopia | 47 E2 | 10 40N | 37 4 E |
| Bure →, U.K. | 12 E9 | 52 38N | 1 43 E |
| Bureya →, Russia | 29 E13 | 49 27N | 129 30 E |
| Burford, Canada | 84 C4 | 43 7N | 80 27W |
| Burgas, Bulgaria | 23 C12 | 42 33N | 27 29 E |
| Burgeo, Canada | 73 C8 | 47 37N | 57 38W |
| Burgersdorp, S. Africa | 56 E4 | 31 0S | 26 20 E |
| Burges, Mt., Australia | 61 F3 | 30 50S | 121 5 E |
| Burghead, U.K. | 11 D5 | 57 43N | 3 30W |
| Burgos, Spain | 21 A4 | 42 21N | 3 41W |
| Burgsvik, Sweden | 9 H18 | 57 3N | 18 19 E |
| Burgundy = Bourgogne □, France | 20 C6 | 47 0N | 4 50 E |
| Burhaniye, Turkey | 23 E12 | 39 30N | 26 58 E |
| Burhanpur, India | 40 J10 | 21 18N | 76 14 E |
| Burhi Gandak →, India | 43 G12 | 25 20N | 86 37 E |
| Burhner →, India | 43 H9 | 22 43N | 80 31 E |
| Burias I., Phil. | 37 B6 | 12 55N | 123 5 E |
| Burica, Pta., Costa Rica | 88 E3 | 8 3N | 82 51W |
| Burien, U.S.A. | 78 C4 | 47 28N | 122 21W |
| Burigi □, Tanzania | 54 C3 | 2 20S | 31 6 E |
| Burigi, L., Tanzania | 54 C3 | 2 2S | 31 22 E |
| Burin, Canada | 73 C8 | 47 1N | 55 14W |
| Buriram, Thailand | 38 E4 | 15 0N | 103 0 E |
| Burj Sāfiṭā, Syria | 44 C3 | 34 48N | 36 7 E |
| Burkburnett, U.S.A. | 81 H5 | 34 6N | 98 34W |
| Burke →, Australia | 62 C2 | 23 12S | 139 33 E |
| Burke Chan., Canada | 70 C3 | 52 10N | 127 30W |
| Burketown, Australia | 62 B2 | 17 45S | 139 33 E |
| Burkina Faso ■, Africa | 50 F5 | 12 0N | 1 0W |
| Burk's Falls, Canada | 72 C4 | 45 37N | 79 24W |
| Burleigh Falls, Canada | 84 B6 | 44 33N | 78 12W |
| Burley, U.S.A. | 76 E7 | 42 32N | 113 48W |
| Burlingame, U.S.A. | 78 H4 | 37 35N | 122 21W |
| Burlington, Canada | 84 C5 | 43 18N | 79 45W |
| Burlington, Colo., U.S.A. | 80 F3 | 39 18N | 102 16W |
| Burlington, Iowa, U.S.A. | 80 E9 | 40 49N | 91 14W |
| Burlington, Kans., U.S.A. | 80 F7 | 38 12N | 95 45W |
| Burlington, N.C., U.S.A. | 83 G6 | 36 6N | 79 26W |
| Burlington, N.J., U.S.A. | 85 F10 | 40 4N | 74 51W |
| Burlington, Vt., U.S.A. | 85 B11 | 44 29N | 73 12W |
| Burlington, Wash., U.S.A. | 78 B4 | 48 28N | 122 20W |
| Burlington, Wis., U.S.A. | 82 D1 | 42 41N | 88 17W |
| Burlyu-Tyube, Kazakhstan | 28 E8 | 46 30N | 79 10 E |
| Burma ■, Asia | 41 J20 | 21 0N | 96 30 E |
| Burnaby I., Canada | 70 C2 | 52 25N | 131 19W |
| Burnet, U.S.A. | 81 K5 | 30 45N | 98 14W |
| Burney, U.S.A. | 76 F3 | 40 53N | 121 40W |
| Burnham, U.S.A. | 84 F7 | 40 38N | 77 34W |
| Burnham-on-Sea, U.K. | 13 F5 | 51 14N | 3 0W |
| Burnie, Australia | 63 G4 | 41 4S | 145 56 E |
| Burnley, U.K. | 12 D5 | 53 47N | 2 14W |
| Burns, U.S.A. | 76 E4 | 43 35N | 119 3W |
| Burns Lake, Canada | 70 C3 | 54 20N | 125 45W |
| Burnside →, Canada | 68 B9 | 66 51N | 108 4W |
| Burnside, L., Australia | 61 E3 | 25 22S | 123 0 E |
| Burnsville, U.S.A. | 80 C8 | 44 47N | 93 17W |
| Burnt River, Canada | 84 B6 | 44 41N | 78 42W |
| Burntwood →, Canada | 71 B9 | 56 8N | 96 34W |
| Burntwood L., Canada | 71 B8 | 55 22N | 100 26W |
| Burqān, Kuwait | 44 D5 | 29 0N | 47 57 E |
| Burra, Australia | 63 E2 | 33 40S | 138 55 E |
| Burray, U.K. | 11 C6 | 58 51N | 2 54W |
| Burren →, Ireland | 10 C3 | 53 1N | 8 58W |
| Burren Junction, Australia | 63 E4 | 30 7S | 148 59 E |
| Burrinjuck Res., Australia | 63 F4 | 35 0S | 148 36 E |
| Burro, Serranías del, Mexico | 86 B4 | 29 0N | 102 0W |
| Burrow Hd., U.K. | 11 G4 | 54 41N | 4 24W |
| Burrum Coast △, Australia | 63 D5 | 25 13S | 152 36 E |
| Burruyacú, Argentina | 94 B3 | 26 30S | 64 40W |
| Burry Port, U.K. | 13 F3 | 51 41N | 4 15W |
| Bursa, Turkey | 23 D13 | 40 15N | 29 5 E |
| Burstall, Canada | 71 C7 | 50 39N | 109 54W |
| Burton, Ohio, U.S.A. | 84 E3 | 41 28N | 81 8W |
| Burton, S.C., U.S.A. | 83 J5 | 32 25N | 80 45W |
| Burton, L., Canada | 72 B4 | 54 45N | 78 20W |
| Burton upon Trent, U.K. | 12 E6 | 52 48N | 1 38W |
| Buru, Indonesia | 37 E7 | 3 30S | 126 30 E |
| Burûn, Râs, Egypt | 46 D2 | 31 14N | 33 7 E |
| Burundi ■, Africa | 54 C3 | 3 15S | 30 0 E |
| Bururi, Burundi | 54 C2 | 3 57S | 29 37 E |
| Burutu, Nigeria | 50 G7 | 5 20N | 5 29 E |
| Burwell, U.S.A. | 80 E5 | 41 47N | 99 8W |
| Burwick, U.K. | 11 C5 | 58 45N | 2 58W |
| Bury, U.K. | 12 D5 | 53 35N | 2 17W |
| Bury St. Edmunds, U.K. | 13 E8 | 52 15N | 0 43 E |
| Buryatia □, Russia | 29 D11 | 53 0N | 110 0 E |
| Busango Swamp, Zambia | 55 E2 | 14 15S | 25 45 E |
| Buşayrah, Syria | 44 C4 | 35 9N | 40 26 E |
| Büshehr, Iran | 45 D6 | 28 55N | 50 55 E |
| Büshehr □, Iran | 45 D6 | 28 20N | 51 45 E |
| Bushell, Canada | 71 B7 | 59 31N | 108 45W |
| Bushenyi, Uganda | 54 C3 | 0 35S | 30 10 E |
| Bushire = Büshehr, Iran | 45 D6 | 28 55N | 50 55 E |
| Businga, Dem. Rep. of the Congo | 52 D4 | 3 16N | 20 59 E |
| Buşra ash Shām, Syria | 46 C5 | 32 30N | 36 25 E |
| Busselton, Australia | 61 F2 | 33 42S | 115 15 E |
| Bussum, Neths. | 15 B5 | 52 16N | 5 10 E |
| Busto Arsízio, Italy | 20 D8 | 45 37N | 8 51 E |
| Busu Djanoa, Dem. Rep. of the Congo | 52 D4 | 1 43N | 21 23 E |
| Busuanga I., Phil. | 37 B5 | 12 10N | 120 0 E |
| Busungbiu, Indonesia | 37 J17 | 8 16S | 114 58 E |
| Buta, Dem. Rep. of the Congo | 54 B1 | 2 50N | 24 53 E |
| Butare, Rwanda | 54 C2 | 2 31S | 29 52 E |
| Butaritari, Kiribati | 64 G9 | 3 30N | 174 0 E |
| Bute, U.K. | 11 F3 | 55 48N | 5 2W |
| Bute Inlet, Canada | 70 C4 | 50 40N | 124 53W |
| Butemba, Uganda | 54 B3 | 1 9N | 31 37 E |
| Butembo, Dem. Rep. of the Congo | 54 B2 | 0 9N | 29 18 E |
| Butha Qi, China | 33 B7 | 48 0N | 122 32 E |
| Butiaba, Uganda | 54 B3 | 1 50N | 31 20 E |
| Butler, Mo., U.S.A. | 80 F7 | 38 16N | 94 20W |
| Butler, Pa., U.S.A. | 84 F5 | 40 52N | 79 54W |
| Buton, Indonesia | 37 E6 | 5 0S | 122 45 E |
| Butte, Mont., U.S.A. | 76 C7 | 46 0N | 112 32W |
| Butte, Nebr., U.S.A. | 80 D5 | 42 58N | 98 51W |
| Butte Creek →, U.S.A. | 78 F5 | 39 12N | 121 56W |
| Butterworth = Gcuwa, S. Africa | 57 E4 | 32 20S | 28 11 E |
| Butterworth, Malaysia | 39 c | 5 24N | 100 23 E |
| Buttevant, Ireland | 10 D3 | 52 14N | 8 40W |
| Buttfield, Mt., Australia | 61 D4 | 24 45S | 128 9 E |

Button B., *Canada* ............ 71 B10 58 45N 94 23W
Buttonwillow, *U.S.A.* .......... 79 K7 35 24N 119 28W
Butty Hd., *Australia* .......... 61 F3 33 54S 121 39 E
Butuan, *Phil.* ................ 37 C7 8 57N 125 33 E
Butung = Buton, *Indonesia* ..... 37 E6 5 0S 122 45 E
Buturlinovka, *Russia* ......... 19 D7 50 50N 40 35 E
Buur Hakaba = Bur Acaba,
  *Somali Rep.* ........... 47 G3 3 12N 44 20 E
Buxa Duar, *India* ............. 43 F13 27 45N 89 35 E
Buxar, *India* ................. 43 G10 25 34N 83 58 E
Buxtehude, *Germany* ........... 16 B5 53 28N 9 39 E
Buxton, *U.K.* ................. 12 D6 53 16N 1 54W
Buy, *Russia* .................. 18 C7 58 28N 41 28 E
Büyük Menderes →, *Turkey* ..... 23 F12 37 28N 27 11 E
Büyükçekmece, *Turkey* ......... 23 D13 41 2N 28 35 E
Buzău, *Romania* ............... 17 F14 45 10N 26 50 E
Buzău →, *Romania* ............. 17 F14 45 26N 27 44 E
Buzen, *Japan* ................. 31 H5 33 35N 131 5 E
Buzi →, *Mozam.* ............... 55 F3 19 50S 34 43 E
Buzuluk, *Russia* .............. 18 D9 52 48N 52 12 E
Buzzards B., *U.S.A.* .......... 85 E14 41 45N 70 37W
Buzzards Bay, *U.S.A.* ......... 85 E14 41 44N 70 37W
Bwana Mkubwe, *Dem. Rep. of*
  *the Congo* ............ 55 E2 13 8S 28 38 E
Bwindi ∆, *Uganda* ............. 54 C2 1 2S 29 42 E
Byarezina →, *Belarus* ......... 17 B16 52 33N 30 14 E
Bydgoszcz, *Poland* ............ 17 B9 53 10N 18 0 E
Byelarus = Belarus ■, *Europe* .. 17 B14 53 30N 27 0 E
Byelorussia = Belarus ■, *Europe* 17 B14 53 30N 27 0 E
Byers, *U.S.A.* ................ 80 F2 39 43N 104 14W
Byesville, *U.S.A.* ............ 84 G3 39 58N 81 32W
Byfield ∆, *Australia* ......... 62 C5 22 52S 150 45 E
Byford, *Australia* ............ 61 F2 32 15S 116 0 E
Bykhaw, *Belarus* .............. 17 B16 53 31N 30 14 E
Bykhov = Bykhaw, *Belarus* ..... 17 B16 53 31N 30 14 E
Bylas, *U.S.A.* ................ 77 K8 33 8N 110 7W
Bylot, *Canada* ................ 71 B10 58 25N 94 8W
Bylot I., *Canada* ............. 69 A12 73 13N 78 34W
Byrd, C., *Antarctica* ......... 5 C17 69 38S 76 7W
Byrock, *Australia* ............ 63 E4 30 40S 146 27 E
Byron, C., *Australia* ......... 63 D5 28 43S 153 38 E
Byron Bay, *Australia* ......... 63 D5 28 43S 153 37 E
Byrranga, Gory, *Russia* ....... 29 B11 75 0N 100 0 E
Byrranga Mts. = Byrranga, Gory,
  *Russia* ............... 29 B11 75 0N 100 0 E
Byske, *Sweden* ................ 8 D19 64 57N 21 11 E
Byskeälven →, *Sweden* ......... 8 D19 64 57N 21 13 E
Bytom, *Poland* ................ 17 C10 50 25N 18 54 E
Bytów, *Poland* ................ 17 A9 54 10N 17 30 E
Byumba, *Rwanda* ............... 54 C3 1 35S 30 4 E

## C

Ca →, *Vietnam* ................ 38 C5 18 45N 105 45 E
Ca Mau, *Vietnam* .............. 39 H5 9 7N 105 8 E
Ca Mau, Mui, *Vietnam* ......... 39 H5 8 38N 104 44 E
Ca Na, *Vietnam* ............... 39 G7 11 20N 108 54 E
Caacupé, *Paraguay* ............ 94 B4 25 23S 57 5W
Caaguazú ∆, *Paraguay* ......... 95 B4 26 5S 55 31W
Caála, *Angola* ................ 53 G3 12 46S 15 30 E
Caamaño Sd., *Canada* .......... 70 C3 52 55N 129 25W
Caazapá, *Paraguay* ............ 94 B4 26 8S 56 19W
Caazapá □, *Paraguay* .......... 95 B4 26 10S 56 0W
Caballeria, C. de, *Spain* ..... 24 A11 40 5N 4 5 E
Cabanatuan, *Phil.* ............ 37 A6 15 30N 120 58 E
Cabano, *Canada* ............... 73 C6 47 40N 68 56W
Cabazon, *U.S.A.* .............. 79 M10 33 55N 116 47W
Cabedelo, *Brazil* ............. 93 E12 7 0S 34 50W
Cabildo, *Chile* ............... 94 C1 32 30S 71 5W
Cabimas, *Venezuela* ........... 92 A4 10 23N 71 25W
Cabinda, *Angola* .............. 52 F2 5 33S 12 11 E
Cabinda □, *Angola* ............ 52 F2 5 0S 12 30 E
Cabinet Mts., *U.S.A.* ......... 76 C6 48 0N 115 30W
Cabo Blanco, *Argentina* ....... 96 F3 47 15S 65 47W
Cabo Frio, *Brazil* ............ 95 A7 22 51S 42 3W
Cabo Pantoja, *Peru* ........... 92 D3 1 0S 75 10W
Cabonga, Réservoir, *Canada* ... 72 C4 47 20N 76 40W
Cabool, *U.S.A.* ............... 81 G8 37 7N 92 6W
Caboolture, *Australia* ........ 63 D5 27 5S 152 58 E
Cabora Bassa Dam = Cahora
  Bassa, Reprêsa de, *Mozam.* . 55 F3 15 20S 32 50 E
Caborca, *Mexico* .............. 86 A2 30 40N 112 10W
Cabot, Mt., *U.S.A.* ........... 85 B13 44 30N 71 25W
Cabot Hd., *Canada* ............ 84 A3 45 14N 81 17W
Cabot Str., *Canada* ........... 73 C8 47 15N 59 40W
Cabra, *Spain* ................. 21 D3 37 30N 4 28W
Cabrera, *Spain* ............... 24 B9 39 8N 2 57 E
Cabri, *Canada* ................ 71 C7 50 35N 108 25W
Cabriel →, *Spain* ............. 21 C5 39 14N 1 3W
Caçador, *Brazil* .............. 95 B5 26 47S 51 0W
Čačak, *Serbia & M.* ........... 23 C9 43 54N 20 20 E
Caçapava do Sul, *Brazil* ...... 95 C5 30 30S 53 30W
Cáceres, *Brazil* .............. 92 G7 16 5S 57 40W
Cáceres, *Spain* ............... 21 C2 39 26N 6 23W
Cache Bay, *Canada* ............ 72 C4 46 22N 80 0W
Cache Cr. →, *U.S.A.* .......... 78 G5 38 42N 121 42W
Cache Creek, *Canada* .......... 70 C4 50 48N 121 19W
Cachi, *Argentina* ............. 94 B2 25 5S 66 10W
Cachimbo, Serra do, *Brazil* ... 93 E7 9 30S 55 30W
Cachinal de la Sierra, *Chile* . 94 A2 24 58S 69 32W
Cachoeira, *Brazil* ............ 93 F11 12 30S 39 0W
Cachoeira do Sul, *Brazil* ..... 95 C5 30 3S 52 53W
Cachoeiro de Itapemirim, *Brazil* 95 A7 20 51S 41 7W
Cacoal, *Brazil* ............... 92 F6 11 32S 61 18W
Cacólo, *Angola* ............... 52 G3 10 9S 19 21 E
Caconda, *Angola* .............. 53 G3 13 48S 15 8 E
Caddo, *U.S.A.* ................ 81 H6 34 7N 96 16W
Cader Idris, *U.K.* ............ 13 E4 52 42N 3 53W
Cadereyta, *Mexico* ............ 86 B5 25 36N 100 0W
Cadibarrawirracanna, L.,
  *Australia* ............ 63 D2 28 52S 135 27 E
Cadillac, *U.S.A.* ............. 82 C3 44 15N 85 24W
Cadiz, *U.S.A.* ................ 37 B6 10 57N 123 15 E
Cádiz, *Spain* ................. 21 D2 36 30N 6 20W
Cadiz, *Ohio, U.S.A.* .......... 84 F4 40 22N 81 0W
Cadiz, G. de, *Spain* .......... 21 D2 36 40N 7 0W
Cadiz L., *U.S.A.* ............. 77 J6 34 18N 115 24W
Cadney Park, *Australia* ....... 63 D1 27 55S 134 3 E
Cadomin, *Canada* .............. 70 C5 53 2N 117 20W
Cadotte Lake, *Canada* ......... 70 B5 56 26N 117 6W
Cadoux, *Australia* ............ 61 F2 30 46S 117 7 E
Caen, *France* ................. 20 B3 49 10N 0 22W
Caernarfon, *U.K.* ............. 12 D3 53 8N 4 16W
Caernarfon B., *U.K.* .......... 12 D3 53 4N 4 40W

Caernarvon = Caernarfon, *U.K.* . 12 D3 53 8N 4 16W
Caerphilly, *U.K.* ............. 13 F4 51 35N 3 13W
Caerphilly □, *U.K.* ........... 13 F4 51 37N 3 12W
Caesarea, *Israel* ............. 46 C3 32 30N 34 53 E
Cafayate, *Argentina* .......... 94 B2 26 2S 66 0W
Cafu, *Angola* ................. 56 B2 16 30S 15 8 E
Cagayan de Oro, *Phil.* ........ 37 C6 8 30N 124 40 E
Cagayan Is., *Phil.* ........... 37 C5 9 40N 121 16 E
Cágliari, *Italy* .............. 22 E3 39 13N 9 7 E
Cágliari, G. di, *Italy* ....... 22 E3 39 8N 9 11 E
Caguán →, *Colombia* ........... 92 D4 0 8S 74 18W
Caguas, *Puerto Rico* .......... 89 d 18 14N 66 2W
Caha Mts., *Ireland* ........... 10 E2 51 45N 9 40W
Cahama, *Angola* ............... 56 B1 16 17S 14 19 E
Caher, *Ireland* ............... 10 D4 52 22N 7 56W
Caherciveen, *Ireland* ......... 10 E1 51 56N 10 14W
Cahora Bassa, L. de, *Mozam.* .. 55 F3 15 35S 32 0 E
Cahora Bassa, Reprêsa de,
  *Mozam.* ............... 55 F3 15 20S 32 50 E
Cahore Pt., *Ireland* .......... 10 D5 52 33N 6 12W
Cahors, *France* ............... 20 D4 44 27N 1 27 E
Cahul, *Moldova* ............... 17 F15 45 50N 28 15 E
Cai Bau, Dao, *Vietnam* ........ 38 B6 21 10N 107 27 E
Cai Nuoc, *Vietnam* ............ 39 H5 8 56N 105 1 E
Caia, *Mozam.* ................. 55 F4 17 51S 35 24 E
Caianda, *Angola* .............. 55 E1 11 2S 23 31 E
Caibarién, *Cuba* .............. 88 B4 22 30N 79 30W
Caicara, *Venezuela* ........... 92 B5 7 38N 66 10W
Caicó, *Brazil* ................ 93 E11 6 20S 37 0W
Caicos Is., *Turks & Caicos* ... 89 B5 21 40N 71 40W
Caicos Passage, *W. Indies* .... 89 B5 22 45N 72 45W
Caird Coast, *Antarctica* ...... 5 D1 75 0S 25 0W
Cairn Gorm, *U.K.* ............. 11 D5 57 7N 3 39W
Cairngorm Mts., *U.K.* ......... 11 D5 57 6N 3 42W
Cairngorms ∆, *U.K.* ........... 11 D5 57 10N 3 50W
Cairnryan, *U.K.* .............. 11 G3 54 59N 5 1W
Cairns, *Australia* ............ 62 B4 16 57S 145 45 E
Cairns L., *Canada* ............ 71 C10 51 42N 94 30W
Cairo = El Qâhira, *Egypt* ..... 51 B12 30 1N 31 14 E
Cairo, *Ga., U.S.A.* ........... 83 K3 30 52N 84 13W
Cairo, *Ill., U.S.A.* .......... 81 G10 37 0N 89 11W
Cairo, *N.Y., U.S.A.* .......... 85 D11 42 18N 74 0W
Caithness, *U.K.* .............. 11 C5 58 25N 3 35W
Caithness, Ord of, *U.K.* ...... 11 C5 58 8N 3 36W
Caja de Muertos, I., *Puerto Rico* 89 d 17 54N 66 32W
Cajamarca, *Peru* .............. 92 E3 7 5S 78 28W
Cajàzeiras, *Brazil* ........... 93 E11 6 52S 38 30W
Cala d'Or, *Spain* ............. 24 B10 39 23N 3 14 E
Cala en Porter, *Spain* ........ 24 B11 39 52N 4 8 E
Cala Figuera, C. de, *Spain* ... 24 B9 39 27N 2 31 E
Cala Forcat, *Spain* ........... 24 B10 40 0N 3 47 E
Cala Major, *Spain* ............ 24 B9 39 33N 2 37 E
Cala Mezquida = Sa Mesquida,
  *Spain* ................ 24 B11 39 55N 4 16 E
Cala Millor, *Spain* ........... 24 B10 39 35N 3 22 E
Cala Ratjada, *Spain* .......... 24 B10 39 43N 3 27 E
Cala Santa Galdana, *Spain* .... 24 B10 39 56N 3 58 E
Calabar, *Nigeria* ............. 50 H7 4 57N 8 20 E
Calabogie, *Canada* ............ 85 A8 45 18N 76 43W
Calabozo, *Venezuela* .......... 92 B5 9 0N 67 28W
Calábria □, *Italy* ............ 22 E7 39 0N 16 30 E
Calafate, *Argentina* .......... 96 G2 50 19S 72 15W
Calahorra, *Spain* ............. 21 A5 42 18N 1 59W
Calais, *France* ............... 20 A4 50 57N 1 56 E
Calais, *U.S.A.* ............... 83 C12 45 11N 67 17W
Calakmul ◌, *Mexico* ........... 87 D7 18 14N 89 48W
Calalaste, Cord. de, *Argentina* 94 B2 25 0S 67 0W
Calama, *Brazil* ............... 92 E6 8 0S 62 50W
Calama, *Chile* ................ 94 A2 22 30S 68 55W
Calamar, *Colombia* ............ 92 A4 10 15N 74 55W
Calamian Group, *Phil.* ........ 37 B5 11 50N 119 55 E
Calamocha, *Spain* ............. 21 B5 40 50N 1 17W
Calang, *Indonesia* ............ 36 D1 4 37N 95 37 E
Calapan, *Phil.* ............... 37 B6 13 25N 121 7 E
Călărași, *Romania* ............ 17 F14 44 12N 27 20 E
Calatayud, *Spain* ............. 21 B5 41 20N 1 40W
Calauag, *Phil.* ............... 37 B6 13 55N 122 15 E
Calavite, C., *Phil.* .......... 37 B6 13 26N 120 20 E
Calbayog, *Phil.* .............. 37 B6 12 4N 124 38 E
Calca, *Peru* .................. 92 F4 13 22S 72 0W
Calcasieu L., *U.S.A.* ......... 81 L8 29 55N 93 18W
Calcutta = Kolkata, *India* .... 43 H13 22 36N 88 24 E
Calcutta, *U.S.A.* ............. 84 F4 40 40N 80 34W
Caldas da Rainha, *Portugal* ... 21 C1 39 24N 9 8W
Calder →, *U.K.* ............... 12 D6 53 44N 1 22W
Caldera, *Chile* ............... 94 B1 27 5S 70 55W
Caldera de Taburiente ∆,
  *Canary Is.* ........... 24 F2 28 43N 17 52W
Caldwell, *Idaho, U.S.A.* ...... 76 E5 43 40N 116 41W
Caldwell, *Kans., U.S.A.* ...... 81 G6 37 2N 97 37W
Caldwell, *Tex., U.S.A.* ....... 81 K6 30 32N 96 42W
Caledon, *S. Africa* ........... 56 E2 34 14S 19 26 E
Caledon →, *S. Africa* ......... 56 E4 30 31S 26 5 E
Caledon B., *Australia* ........ 62 A2 12 45S 137 0 E
Caledonia, *Canada* ............ 84 C5 43 7N 79 58W
Caledonia, *U.S.A.* ............ 84 D7 42 58N 77 51W
Calemba, *Angola* .............. 56 B2 16 0S 15 44 E
Calen, *Australia* ............. 62 J6 20 56S 148 48 E
Caletones, *Chile* ............. 94 C1 34 6S 70 27W
Calexico, *U.S.A.* ............. 79 N11 32 40N 115 30W
Calf of Man, *I. of Man* ....... 12 C3 54 3N 4 48W
Calgary, *Canada* .............. 70 C6 51 0N 114 10W
Calheta, *Madeira* ............. 24 D2 32 44N 17 11W
Calhoun, *U.S.A.* .............. 83 H3 34 30N 84 57W
Cali, *Colombia* ............... 92 C3 3 25N 76 35W
Calicut, *India* ............... 40 P9 11 15N 75 43 E
Caliente, *U.S.A.* ............. 77 H6 37 37N 114 31W
California, *Mo., U.S.A.* ....... 80 F8 38 38N 92 34W
California, *Pa., U.S.A.* ....... 84 F5 40 4N 79 54W
California □, *U.S.A.* .......... 78 H7 37 30N 119 30W
California, Baja, *Mexico* ...... 86 A1 32 10N 115 12W
California, Baja, T.N. = Baja
  California □, *Mexico* ...... 86 B2 30 0N 115 0W
California, Baja, T.S. = Baja
  California Sur □, *Mexico* ... 86 B2 25 50N 111 50W
California, G. de, *Mexico* ..... 86 B2 27 0N 111 0W
California City, *U.S.A.* ....... 79 K9 35 10N 117 55W
California Hot Springs, *U.S.A.* . 79 K8 35 51N 118 41W
Calingasta, *Argentina* ........ 94 C2 31 15S 69 30W
Calipatria, *U.S.A.* ........... 79 M11 33 8N 115 31W
Calistoga, *U.S.A.* ............ 78 G4 38 35N 122 35W
Calitzdorp, *S. Africa* ........ 56 E3 33 33S 21 42 E
Callabonna, L., *Australia* .... 63 D3 29 40S 140 5 E
Callan, *Ireland* .............. 10 D4 52 32N 7 24W
Callander, *U.K.* .............. 11 E4 56 15N 4 13W
Callao, *Peru* ................. 92 F3 12 0S 77 0W

Calles, *Mexico* ............... 87 C5 23 2N 98 42W
Callicoon, *U.S.A.* ............ 85 E9 41 46N 75 3W
Calling Lake, *Canada* ......... 70 B6 55 15N 113 12W
Calliope, *Australia* .......... 62 C5 24 0S 151 16 E
Calne, *U.K.* .................. 13 F6 51 26N 2 0W
Calola, *Angola* ............... 56 B2 16 25S 17 48 E
Caloundra, *Australia* ......... 63 D5 26 45S 153 10 E
Calpella, *U.S.A.* ............. 78 F3 39 14N 123 12W
Calpine, *U.S.A.* .............. 78 F6 39 40N 120 27W
Calstock, *Canada* ............. 72 C3 49 47N 84 9W
Caltagirone, *Italy* ........... 22 F6 37 14N 14 31 E
Caltanissetta, *Italy* ......... 22 F6 37 29N 14 4 E
Calulo, *Angola* ............... 52 G2 10 1S 14 56 E
Calvert →, *Australia* ......... 62 B2 16 17S 137 44 E
Calvert I., *Canada* ........... 70 C3 51 30N 128 0W
Calvert Ra., *Australia* ....... 60 D3 24 0S 122 30 E
Calvi, *France* ................ 20 E8 42 34N 8 45 E
Calviá, *Spain* ................ 21 C7 39 34N 2 31 E
Calvillo, *Mexico* ............. 86 C4 21 51N 102 43W
Calvinia, *S. Africa* .......... 56 E2 31 28S 19 45 E
Calwa, *U.S.A.* ................ 78 J7 36 42N 119 46W
Cam →, *U.K.* .................. 13 E8 52 21N 0 16 E
Cam Lam, *Vietnam* ............. 39 G7 11 54N 109 10 E
Cam Pha, *Vietnam* ............. 38 B6 21 7N 107 18 E
Cam Ranh, *Vietnam* ............ 39 G7 11 54N 109 12 E
Cam Xuyen, *Vietnam* ........... 38 C6 18 15N 106 0 E
Camabatela, *Angola* ........... 52 F3 8 20S 15 26 E
Camacha, *Madeira* ............. 24 D3 32 41N 16 49W
Camacho, *Mexico* .............. 86 C4 24 25N 102 18W
Camacupa, *Angola* ............. 53 G3 11 58S 17 22 E
Camagüey, *Cuba* ............... 88 B4 21 20N 77 55W
Camaná, *Peru* ................. 92 G4 16 30S 72 50W
Camanche Reservoir, *U.S.A.* ... 78 G6 38 14N 121 1W
Camaquã, *Brazil* .............. 95 C5 30 51S 51 49W
Camaquã →, *Brazil* ............ 95 C5 31 17S 51 47W
Câmara de Lobos, *Madeira* ..... 24 D3 32 39N 16 59W
Camargo, *Mexico* .............. 87 B5 26 19N 98 50W
Camarillo, *U.S.A.* ............ 79 L7 34 13N 119 2W
Camarón, C., *Honduras* ........ 88 C2 16 0N 85 5W
Camarones, *Argentina* ......... 96 E3 44 50S 65 40W
Camas, *U.S.A.* ................ 78 E4 45 35N 122 24W
Camas Valley, *U.S.A.* ......... 76 E2 43 2N 123 40W
Camballin, *Australia* ......... 60 C3 17 59S 124 12 E
Cambará, *Brazil* .............. 95 A5 23 2S 50 5W
Cambay = Khambhat, *India* ..... 42 H5 22 23N 72 33 E
Cambay, G. of = Khambhat, G.
  of, *India* ............ 40 J8 20 45N 72 30 E
Cambodia ■, *Asia* ............. 38 F5 12 15N 105 0 E
Camborne, *U.K.* ............... 13 G2 50 12N 5 19W
Cambrai, *France* .............. 20 A5 50 11N 3 14 E
Cambria, *U.S.A.* .............. 78 K5 35 34N 121 5W
Cambrian Mts., *U.K.* .......... 13 E4 52 3N 3 57W
Cambridge, *Canada* ............ 84 C4 43 23N 80 15W
Cambridge, *Jamaica* ........... 88 a 18 18N 77 54W
Cambridge, *N.Z.* .............. 59 G5 37 54S 175 29 E
Cambridge, *U.K.* .............. 13 E8 52 12N 0 8 E
Cambridge, *Mass., U.S.A.* ..... 85 D13 42 22N 71 6W
Cambridge, *Minn., U.S.A.* ..... 80 C8 45 34N 93 13W
Cambridge, *N.Y., U.S.A.* ...... 85 C11 43 2N 73 22W
Cambridge, *Nebr., U.S.A.* ..... 80 E4 40 17N 100 10W
Cambridge, *Ohio, U.S.A.* ...... 84 F3 40 2N 81 35W
Cambridge Bay = Ikaluktutiak,
  *Canada* ............... 68 B9 69 10N 105 0W
Cambridge G., *Australia* ...... 60 B4 14 55S 128 15 E
Cambridge Springs, *U.S.A.* .... 84 E4 41 48N 80 4W
Cambridgeshire □, *U.K.* ....... 13 E7 52 25N 0 7W
Cambuci, *Brazil* .............. 95 A7 21 35S 41 55W
Cambundi-Catembo, *Angola* ..... 52 G3 10 10S 17 35 E
Camden, *Ala., U.S.A.* ......... 83 K2 31 59N 87 17W
Camden, *Ark., U.S.A.* ......... 81 J8 33 35N 92 50W
Camden, *Maine, U.S.A.* ........ 83 C11 44 13N 69 4W
Camden, *N.J., U.S.A.* ......... 85 G9 39 56N 75 7W
Camden, *N.Y., U.S.A.* ......... 85 C9 43 20N 75 45W
Camden, *S.C., U.S.A.* ......... 83 H5 34 16N 80 36W
Camden Sd., *Australia* ........ 60 C3 15 27S 124 25 E
Camdenton, *U.S.A.* ............ 81 F8 38 1N 92 45W
Camelford, *U.K.* .............. 13 G3 50 37N 4 42W
Cameron, *Ariz., U.S.A.* ....... 77 J8 35 53N 111 25W
Cameron, *La., U.S.A.* ......... 81 L8 29 48N 93 20W
Cameron, *Mo., U.S.A.* ......... 80 F7 39 44N 94 14W
Cameron, *Tex., U.S.A.* ........ 81 K6 30 51N 96 59W
Cameron Highlands, *Malaysia* .. 39 K3 4 27N 101 22 E
Cameron Hills, *Canada* ........ 70 B5 59 48N 118 0W
Cameroon ■, *Africa* ........... 52 C2 6 0N 12 30 E
Cameroun, Mt., *Cameroon* ...... 52 D1 4 13N 9 10 E
Cametá, *Brazil* ............... 93 D9 2 12S 49 30W
Camiguin I., *Phil.* ........... 37 C6 18 56N 121 55 E
Camilla, *U.S.A.* .............. 83 K3 31 14N 84 12W
Caminha, *Portugal* ............ 21 B1 41 50N 8 50W
Camino, *U.S.A.* ............... 78 G6 38 44N 120 41W
Camira Creek, *Australia* ...... 63 D5 29 15S 152 58 E
Cammal, *U.S.A.* ............... 84 E7 41 24N 77 28W
Camocim, *Brazil* .............. 93 D10 2 55S 40 50W
Camooweal, *Australia* ......... 62 B2 19 56S 138 7 E
Camooweal Caves ∆, *Australia* . 62 C2 20 1S 138 11 E
Camopi, *Fr. Guiana* ........... 93 C8 3 12N 52 17W
Camp Borden, *Canada* .......... 84 B5 44 18N 79 56W
Camp Hill, *U.S.A.* ............ 84 F8 40 14N 76 55W
Camp Nelson, *U.S.A.* .......... 79 J8 36 8N 118 39W
Camp Pendleton, *U.S.A.* ....... 79 M9 33 16N 117 23W
Camp Verde, *U.S.A.* ........... 77 J8 34 34N 111 51W
Camp Wood, *U.S.A.* ............ 81 L5 29 40N 100 1W
Campana, *Argentina* ........... 94 C4 34 10S 58 55W
Campana, I., *Chile* ........... 96 F1 48 20S 75 20W
Campanário, *Madeira* .......... 24 D2 32 39N 17 2W
Campánia □, *Italy* ............ 22 D6 41 0N 14 30 E
Campbell, *S. Africa* .......... 56 D3 28 48S 23 44 E
Campbell, *Calif., U.S.A.* ..... 78 H5 37 17N 121 57W
Campbell, *Ohio, U.S.A.* ....... 84 E4 41 5N 80 37W
Campbell I., *Pac. Oc.* ........ 64 N8 52 30S 169 0 E
Campbell L., *Canada* .......... 71 A7 63 14N 106 55W
Campbell River, *Canada* ....... 70 C3 50 5N 125 20W
Campbell Town, *Australia* ..... 63 G4 41 52S 147 30 E
Campbellford, *Canada* ......... 84 B7 44 18N 77 48W
Campbellpur, *Pakistan* ........ 42 C5 33 46N 72 26 E
Campbellsville, *U.S.A.* ....... 82 G3 37 21N 85 20W
Campbellton, *Canada* .......... 73 C6 47 57N 66 43W
Campbelltown, *Australia* ...... 63 E5 34 4S 150 49 E
Campbeltown, *U.K.* ............ 11 F3 55 26N 5 36W
Campeche, *Mexico* ............. 87 D6 19 50N 90 32W
Campeche □, *Mexico* ........... 87 D6 19 50N 90 32W
Campeche, Golfo de, *Mexico* ... 87 D6 19 30N 93 0W
Camperdown, *Australia* ........ 63 F3 38 14S 143 9 E
Camperville, *Canada* .......... 71 C8 51 59N 100 9W
Câmpina, *Romania* ............. 17 F13 45 10N 25 45 E
Campina Grande, *Brazil* ....... 93 E11 7 20S 35 47W
Campinas, *Brazil* ............. 95 A6 22 50S 47 0W
Campo Grande, *Brazil* ......... 93 H8 20 25S 54 40W

Campo Maior, *Brazil* .......... 93 D10 4 50S 42 12W
Campo Mourão, *Brazil* ......... 95 A5 24 3S 52 22W
Campobasso, *Italy* ............ 22 D6 41 34N 14 39 E
Campos, *Brazil* ............... 95 A7 21 50S 41 20W
Campos Belos, *Brazil* ......... 93 F9 13 10S 47 3W
Campos del Port, *Spain* ....... 24 B10 39 26N 3 1 E
Campos Novos, *Brazil* ......... 95 B5 27 21S 51 50W
Camptonville, *U.S.A.* ......... 78 F5 39 27N 121 3W
Camptown, *U.S.A.* ............. 85 E8 41 44N 76 14W
Câmpulung, *Romania* ........... 17 F13 45 17N 25 3 E
Camrose, *Canada* .............. 70 C6 53 0N 112 50W
Camsell Portage, *Canada* ...... 71 B7 59 37N 109 15W
Çan, *Turkey* .................. 23 D12 40 2N 27 3 E
Can Clavo, *Spain* ............. 24 C7 38 57N 1 27 E
Can Creu, *Spain* .............. 24 C7 38 58N 1 28 E
Can Gio, *Vietnam* ............. 39 G6 10 25N 106 58 E
Can Tho, *Vietnam* ............. 39 G5 10 2N 105 46 E
Canaan, *U.S.A.* ............... 85 D11 42 2N 73 20W
Canada ■, *N. Amer.* ........... 68 C10 60 0N 100 0W
Canada Basin, *Arctic* ......... 4 B18 80 0N 145 0W
Cañada de Gómez, *Argentina* ... 94 C3 32 40S 61 30W
Canadian, *U.S.A.* ............. 81 H4 35 55N 100 23W
Canadian →, *U.S.A.* ........... 81 H7 35 28N 95 3W
Canajoharie, *U.S.A.* .......... 85 D10 42 54N 74 35W
Çanakkale, *Turkey* ............ 23 D12 40 8N 26 24 E
Çanakkale Boğazı, *Turkey* ..... 23 D12 40 17N 26 32 E
Canal Flats, *Canada* .......... 70 C5 50 10N 115 48W
Canalejas, *Argentina* ......... 94 D2 35 15S 66 34W
Canals, *Argentina* ............ 94 C3 33 35S 62 53W
Canandaigua, *U.S.A.* .......... 84 D7 42 54N 77 17W
Canandaigua L., *U.S.A.* ....... 84 D7 42 47N 77 19W
Cananea, *Mexico* .............. 86 A2 31 0N 110 20W
Canarias, Is., *Atl. Oc.* ...... 24 F4 28 30N 16 0W
Canaries, *St. Lucia* .......... 89 f 13 55N 61 4W
Canarreos, Arch. de los, *Cuba* . 88 B3 21 35N 81 40W
Canary Is. = Canarias, Is., *Atl. Oc.* 24 F4 28 30N 16 0W
Canaseraga, *U.S.A.* ........... 84 D7 42 27N 77 45W
Canatlán, *Mexico* ............. 86 C4 24 31N 104 47W
Canaveral, C., *U.S.A.* ........ 83 L5 28 27N 80 32W
Canavieiras, *Brazil* .......... 93 G11 15 39S 39 0W
Canberra, *Australia* .......... 63 F4 35 15S 149 8 E
Canby, *Calif., U.S.A.* ........ 76 F3 41 27N 120 52W
Canby, *Minn., U.S.A.* ......... 80 C6 44 43N 96 16W
Canby, *Oreg., U.S.A.* ......... 78 E4 45 16N 122 42W
Cancún, *Mexico* ............... 87 C7 21 8N 86 44W
Candelaria, *Argentina* ........ 95 B4 27 29S 55 44W
Candelaria, *Canary Is.* ....... 24 F3 28 22N 16 22W
Candelo, *Australia* ........... 63 F4 36 47S 149 43 E
Candi Dasa, *Indonesia* ........ 37 J18 8 30S 115 34 E
Candia = Iráklion, *Greece* .... 25 D7 35 20N 25 12 E
Candle L., *Canada* ............ 71 C7 53 50N 105 18W
Candlemas I., *Antarctica* ..... 5 B1 57 3S 26 40W
Cando, *U.S.A.* ................ 80 A5 48 32N 99 12W
Canea = Khaniá, *Greece* ....... 25 D6 35 30N 24 4 E
Canelones, *Uruguay* ........... 95 C4 34 32S 56 17W
Cañete, *Chile* ................ 94 D1 37 50S 73 30W
Cañete, *Peru* ................. 92 F3 13 8S 76 30W
Cangas de Narcea, *Spain* ...... 21 A2 43 10N 6 32W
Canguaretama, *Brazil* ......... 93 E11 6 20S 35 5W
Canguçu, *Brazil* .............. 95 C5 31 22S 52 43W
Canguçu, Serra do, *Brazil* .... 95 C5 31 20S 52 40W
Cangzhou, *China* .............. 34 E9 38 19N 116 52 E
Caniapiscau →, *Canada* ........ 73 A6 56 40N 69 30W
Caniapiscau, L. de, *Canada* ... 73 B6 54 10N 69 55W
Canicatti, *Italy* ............. 22 F5 37 21N 13 51 E
Canim Lake, *Canada* ........... 70 C4 51 47N 120 54W
Canindeyu □, *Paraguay* ........ 95 A5 24 10S 55 0W
Canisteo, *U.S.A.* ............. 84 D7 42 16N 77 36W
Canisteo →, *U.S.A.* ........... 84 D7 42 7N 77 8W
Cañitas, *Mexico* .............. 86 C4 23 36N 102 43W
Çankırı, *Turkey* .............. 19 F5 40 40N 33 37 E
Cankuzo, *Burundi* ............. 54 C3 3 10S 30 31 E
Canmore, *Canada* .............. 70 C5 51 7N 115 18W
Cann River, *Australia* ........ 63 F4 37 35S 149 7 E
Canna, *U.K.* .................. 11 D2 57 3N 6 33W
Cannanore, *India* ............. 40 P9 11 53N 75 27 E
Cannes, *France* ............... 20 E7 43 32N 7 1 E
Canning Town = Port Canning,
  *India* ................ 43 H13 22 23N 88 40 E
Cannington, *Canada* ........... 84 B5 44 20N 79 2W
Cannock, *U.K.* ................ 13 E5 52 41N 2 1W
Cannon Ball →, *U.S.A.* ........ 80 B4 46 20N 100 38W
Cannondale Mt., *Australia* .... 62 D4 25 13S 148 57 E
Cannonsville Reservoir, *U.S.A.* 85 D9 42 4N 75 22W
Cannonvale, *Australia* ........ 62 J6 20 17S 148 43 E
Canoas, *Brazil* ............... 95 B5 29 56S 51 11W
Canoe L., *Canada* ............. 71 B7 55 10N 108 15W
Canon City, *U.S.A.* ........... 80 F2 38 27N 105 14W
Cañón de Rio Blanco ◌, *Mexico* . 87 D5 18 43N 97 15W
Cañón del Sumidero ◌, *Mexico* . 87 D5 19 22N 96 24W
Canora, *Canada* ............... 71 C8 51 40N 102 30W
Canowindra, *Australia* ........ 63 E4 33 35S 148 38 E
Canso, *Canada* ................ 73 C7 45 20N 61 0W
Cantabria □, *Spain* ........... 21 A4 43 10N 4 0W
Cantabrian Mts. = Cantábrica,
  Cordillera, *Spain* ....... 21 A3 43 0N 5 10W
Cantábrica, Cordillera, *Spain* . 21 A3 43 0N 5 10W
Cantal, Plomb du, *France* ..... 20 D5 45 3N 2 45 E
Canterbury, *Australia* ........ 62 D3 25 23S 141 53 E
Canterbury, *U.K.* ............. 13 F9 51 16N 1 6 E
Canterbury Bight, *N.Z.* ....... 59 L3 44 16S 171 55 E
Canterbury Plains, *N.Z.* ...... 59 K3 43 55S 171 22 E
Cantil, *U.S.A.* ............... 79 K9 35 18N 117 58W
Canton = Guangzhou, *China* .... 33 D6 23 5N 113 10 E
Canton, *Ga., U.S.A.* .......... 83 H3 34 14N 84 29W
Canton, *Ill., U.S.A.* ......... 80 E9 40 33N 90 2W
Canton, *Miss., U.S.A.* ........ 81 J9 32 37N 90 2W
Canton, *Mo., U.S.A.* .......... 80 E9 40 8N 91 32W
Canton, *N.Y., U.S.A.* ......... 85 B9 44 36N 75 10W
Canton, *Ohio, U.S.A.* ......... 84 F3 40 48N 81 23W
Canton, *Pa., U.S.A.* .......... 84 E8 41 39N 76 51W
Canton, *S. Dak., U.S.A.* ...... 80 D6 43 18N 96 35W
Canton L., *U.S.A.* ............ 81 G5 36 6N 98 35W
Canudos, *Brazil* .............. 92 E7 7 13S 58 5W
Canumã →, *Brazil* ............. 92 D7 3 55S 59 10W
Canutama, *Brazil* ............. 92 E6 6 30S 64 20W
Canutillo, *U.S.A.* ............ 77 L10 31 55N 106 36W
Canvey, *U.K.* ................. 13 F8 51 31N 0 37 E
Canyon, *U.S.A.* ............... 81 H4 34 59N 101 55W
Canyon De Chelly ◌, *U.S.A.* ... 77 H9 36 10N 109 20W
Canyon of the Ancients ◌, *U.S.A.* 77 H9 37 30N 108 50W
Canyonlands ◌, *U.S.A.* ........ 77 G9 38 15N 110 0W
Canyonville, *U.S.A.* .......... 76 E2 42 56N 123 17W
Cao Bang, *Vietnam* ............ 38 A6 22 40N 106 15 E
Cao He →, *China* .............. 35 D13 40 10N 124 32 E
Cao Lanh, *Vietnam* ............ 39 G5 10 27N 105 38 E
Cao Xian, *China* .............. 34 G8 34 50N 115 35 E

Cap-aux-Meules, Canada ...... 73 C7 47 23N 61 52W
Cap-Chat, Canada ............. 73 C6 49 6N 66 40W
Cap-de-la-Madeleine, Canada .. 72 C5 46 22N 72 31W
Cap-Haïtien, Haiti ............ 89 C5 19 40N 72 20W
Cap Pt., St. Lucia ............. 89 f 14 7N 60 57W
Capac, U.S.A. ................ 84 C2 43 1N 82 56W
Capanaparo →, Venezuela .... 92 B5 7 1N 67 7W
Cape →, Australia ............ 62 C4 20 59S 146 51 E
Cape Arid △, Australia ....... 61 F3 33 58S 123 13 E
Cape Barren I., Australia ...... 63 G4 40 25S 148 15 E
Cape Breton Highlands △,
Canada ................... 73 C7 46 50N 60 40W
Cape Breton I., Canada ....... 73 C7 46 0N 60 30W
Cape Charles, U.S.A. ......... 82 G8 37 16N 76 1W
Cape Coast, Ghana ........... 50 G5 5 5N 1 15W
Cape Cod △, U.S.A. ......... 82 E10 41 56N 70 6W
Cape Coral, U.S.A. .......... 83 M5 26 33N 81 57W
Cape Dorset, Canada ......... 69 B12 64 14N 76 32W
Cape Fear →, U.S.A. ........ 83 H6 33 53N 78 1W
Cape Girardeau, U.S.A. ....... 81 G10 37 19N 89 32W
Cape Hatteras △, U.S.A. ..... 83 H8 35 30N 75 28W
Cape Lee △, Australia ........ 61 F3 33 54S 122 26 E
Cape Lookout △, U.S.A. ...... 83 H7 35 45N 76 25W
Cape May, U.S.A. ........... 82 F8 38 56N 74 56W
Cape May Point, U.S.A. ...... 82 F8 38 56N 74 58W
Cape Melville △, Australia .... 62 A3 14 26S 144 28 E
Cape Peninsula △, S. Africa ... 56 E2 34 20S 18 28 E
Cape Range △, Australia ...... 60 D1 22 3S 111 0 E
Cape Tormentine, Canada ..... 73 C7 46 8N 63 47W
Cape Town, S. Africa ......... 56 E2 33 55S 18 22 E
Cape Tribulation △, Australia .. 62 B4 16 5S 145 25 E
Cape Verde Is. ■, Atl. Oc. .... 49 E1 16 0N 24 0W
Cape Vincent, U.S.A. ........ 85 B8 44 8N 76 20W
Cape York Peninsula, Australia 62 A3 12 0S 142 30 E
Capela, Brazil ............... 93 F11 10 30S 37 0W
Capella, Australia ........... 62 C4 23 2S 148 1 E
Capesterre-Belle-Eau,
Guadeloupe .............. 88 b 16 4N 61 36W
Capesterre-de-Marie-Galante,
Guadeloupe .............. 88 b 15 53N 61 14W
Capim →, Brazil ............ 93 D9 1 40S 47 47W
Capitan, U.S.A. ............. 77 K11 33 35N 105 35W
Capitán Arturo Prat, Antarctica 5 C17 63 0S 61 0W
Capitol Reef △, U.S.A. ....... 77 G8 38 15N 111 10W
Capitola, U.S.A. ............. 78 J5 36 59N 121 57W
Capoche →, Mozam. ......... 55 F3 15 35S 33 0 E
Capraia, Italy ............... 20 E8 43 2N 9 50 E
Capreol, Canada ............ 72 C3 46 43N 80 56W
Capri, Italy ................. 22 D6 40 33N 14 14 E
Capricorn Group, Australia .... 62 C5 23 30S 151 55 E
Capricorn Ra., Australia ....... 60 D2 23 20S 116 50 E
Caprivi Game △, Namibia ..... 56 B3 17 55S 22 37 E
Caprivi Strip, Namibia ........ 56 B3 18 0S 23 0 E
Captain's Flat, Australia ...... 63 F4 35 35S 149 27 E
Capulin Volcano △, U.S.A. .... 81 G3 36 47N 103 58W
Caquetá →, Colombia ........ 92 D5 1 15S 69 15W
Caracal, Romania ............ 17 F13 44 8N 24 22 E
Caracas, Venezuela .......... 92 A5 10 30N 66 55W
Caracol, Mato Grosso do Sul,
Brazil ................... 94 A4 22 18S 57 1W
Caracol, Piauí, Brazil ......... 93 E10 9 15S 43 22W
Carajas, Brazil .............. 93 E8 6 5S 50 23W
Carajás, Serra dos, Brazil ..... 93 E8 6 0S 51 30W
Carangola, Brazil ............ 95 A7 20 44S 42 5W
Caransebeş, Romania ........ 17 F12 45 28N 22 18 E
Caraquet, Canada ........... 73 C6 47 48N 64 57W
Caras, Peru ................. 92 E3 9 3S 77 47W
Caratasca, L., Honduras ...... 88 C3 15 20N 83 40W
Caratinga, Brazil ............ 93 G10 19 50S 42 10W
Caraúbas, Brazil ............. 93 E11 5 43S 37 33W
Caravaca de la Cruz, Spain .... 21 C5 38 8N 1 52W
Caravelas, Brazil ............ 93 G11 17 45S 39 15W
Caraveli, Peru ............... 92 G4 15 45S 73 25W
Caravelle, Presqu'île de la,
Martinique ............... 88 c 14 46N 60 48W
Caràzinho, Brazil ............ 95 B5 28 16S 52 46W
Carballo, Spain ............. 21 A1 43 13N 8 41W
Carberry, Canada ........... 71 D9 49 50N 99 25W
Carbó, Mexico .............. 86 B2 29 42N 110 58W
Carbonara, C., Italy .......... 22 E3 39 6N 9 31 E
Carbondale, Colo., U.S.A. ..... 76 G10 39 24N 107 13W
Carbondale, Ill., U.S.A. ....... 81 G10 37 44N 89 13W
Carbondale, Pa., U.S.A. ....... 85 E9 41 35N 75 30W
Carbonear, Canada .......... 73 C9 47 42N 53 13W
Carbónia, Italy .............. 22 E3 39 10N 8 30 E
Carcajou, Canada ........... 70 B5 57 47N 117 6W
Carcarana →, Argentina ...... 94 C3 32 27S 60 48W
Carcasse, C., Haiti ........... 89 C5 18 30N 74 28W
Carcassonne, France ......... 20 E5 43 13N 2 20 E
Carcross, Canada ............ 70 A2 60 13N 134 45W
Cardamon Hills, India ........ 40 Q10 9 30N 77 15 E
Cárdenas, Cuba ............. 88 B3 23 0N 81 30W
Cárdenas, San Luis Potosí,
Mexico .................. 87 C5 22 0N 99 41W
Cárdenas, Tabasco, Mexico .... 87 D6 17 59N 93 21W
Cardiff, U.K. ................ 13 F4 51 29N 3 10W
Cardiff □, U.K. .............. 13 F4 51 31N 3 12W
Cardiff-by-the-Sea, U.S.A. ..... 79 M9 33 1N 117 17W
Cardigan, U.K. .............. 13 E3 52 5N 4 40W
Cardigan B., U.K. ............ 13 E3 52 30N 4 30W
Cardinal, Canada ............ 85 B9 44 47N 75 23W
Cardona, Uruguay ........... 94 C4 33 53S 57 18W
Cardoso, Ilha do, Brazil ....... 95 B5 25 8S 47 58W
Cardston, Canada ........... 70 D6 49 15N 113 20W
Cardwell, Australia .......... 62 B4 18 14S 146 2 E
Careen L., Canada ........... 71 B7 57 0N 108 11W
Carei, Romania ............. 17 E12 47 40N 22 29 E
Careme = Ciremay, Indonesia . 37 G13 6 55S 108 27 E
Carey, U.S.A. ............... 76 E7 43 19N 113 57W
Carey, L., Australia .......... 61 E3 29 0S 122 15 E
Carey L., Canada ............ 71 A8 62 12N 102 55W
Carhué, Argentina ........... 94 D3 37 10S 62 50W
Caria, Turkey ............... 23 F13 37 20N 28 10 E
Cariacica, Brazil ............. 93 H10 20 16S 40 25W
Caribbean Sea, W. Indies ..... 89 D5 15 0N 75 0W
Cariboo Mts., Canada ........ 70 C4 53 0N 121 0W
Caribou, U.S.A. ............. 83 B12 46 52N 68 1W
Caribou →, Man., Canada ..... 71 B10 59 20N 94 44W
Caribou →, N.W.T., Canada ... 70 A3 61 27N 125 45W
Caribou Is., Canada .......... 70 A6 61 55N 113 15W
Caribou L., Man., Canada ..... 71 B9 59 21N 96 10W
Caribou L., Ont., Canada ...... 72 B2 50 25N 89 5W
Caribou Mts., Canada ........ 70 B5 59 12N 115 40W
Caribou River △, Canada ...... 71 B9 59 35N 96 35W
Carichic, Mexico ............ 86 B3 27 56N 107 3W
Carillo, Mexico ............. 86 B4 26 50N 103 55W
Carinda, Australia ........... 63 E4 30 28S 147 41 E

Carinhanha, Brazil .......... 93 F10 14 15S 44 46W
Carinhanha →, Brazil ........ 93 F10 14 20S 43 47W
Carinthia = Kärnten □, Austria . 16 E8 46 52N 13 30 E
Caripito, Venezuela .......... 92 A6 10 8N 63 6W
Carleton, Mt., Canada ........ 73 C6 47 23N 66 53W
Carleton Place, Canada ....... 85 A8 45 8N 76 9W
Carletonville, S. Africa ....... 56 D4 26 23S 27 22 E
Carlin, U.S.A. ............... 76 F5 40 43N 116 7W
Carlingford L., U.K. .......... 10 B5 54 3N 6 9W
Carlinville, U.S.A. ........... 80 F10 39 17N 89 53W
Carlisle, U.K. ............... 12 C5 54 54N 2 56W
Carlisle, U.S.A. ............. 84 F7 40 12N 77 12W
Carlisle B., Barbados ......... 89 g 13 5N 59 37W
Carlisle I., Australia ......... 62 J7 20 49S 149 18 E
Carlos Casares, Argentina ..... 94 D3 35 32S 61 20W
Carlos Tejedor, Argentina ..... 94 D3 35 25S 62 25W
Carlow, Ireland ............. 10 D5 52 50N 6 56W
Carlow □, Ireland ........... 10 D5 52 43N 6 50W
Carlsbad, Calif., U.S.A. ....... 79 M9 33 10N 117 21W
Carlsbad, N. Mex., U.S.A. ..... 81 J2 32 25N 104 14W
Carlsbad Caverns △, U.S.A. ... 81 J2 32 10N 104 35W
Carluke, U.S.A. ............. 11 F5 55 45N 3 50W
Carlyle, Canada ............. 71 D8 49 40N 102 20W
Carmacks, Canada .......... 68 B6 62 5N 136 16W
Carman, Canada ............ 71 D9 49 30N 98 0W
Carmarthen, U.K. ........... 13 F3 51 52N 4 19W
Carmarthen B., U.K. ......... 13 F3 51 40N 4 30W
Carmarthenshire □, U.K. ...... 13 F3 51 55N 4 13W
Carmaux, France ............ 20 D5 44 3N 2 10 E
Carmel, U.S.A. ............. 85 E11 41 26N 73 41W
Carmel-by-the-Sea, U.S.A. .... 78 J5 36 33N 121 55W
Carmel Valley, U.S.A. ........ 78 J5 36 29N 121 43W
Carmelo, Uruguay ........... 94 C4 34 0S 58 20W
Carmen, Colombia ........... 92 B3 9 43N 75 8W
Carmen, Paraguay ........... 95 B4 27 13S 56 12W
Carmen →, Mexico .......... 86 A3 30 42N 106 29W
Carmen I., Mexico ........... 86 B2 26 0N 111 20W
Carmen de Patagones, Argentina 96 E4 40 50S 63 0W
Carmensa, Argentina ........ 94 D2 35 15S 67 40W
Carmi, Canada .............. 70 D5 49 36N 119 8W
Carmi, U.S.A. ............... 82 F1 38 5N 88 10W
Carmichael, U.S.A. .......... 78 G5 38 38N 121 19W
Carmila, Australia ........... 62 C4 21 55S 149 24 E
Carmona, Costa Rica ......... 88 E2 10 0N 85 15W
Carmona, Spain ............. 21 D3 37 28N 5 42W
Carn Ban, U.K. .............. 11 D4 57 7N 4 15W
Carn Eige, U.K. ............. 11 D3 57 17N 5 8W
Carnac, France ............. 20 C2 47 35N 3 6W
Carnamah, Australia ......... 61 E2 29 41S 115 53 E
Carnarvon, Australia ......... 61 D1 24 51S 113 42 E
Carnarvon, S. Africa ......... 56 E3 30 56S 22 8 E
Carnarvon △, Australia ....... 62 C4 24 54S 148 2 E
Carnarvon Ra., Queens.,
Australia ................. 62 D4 25 15S 148 30 E
Carnarvon Ra., W. Austral.,
Australia ................. 61 E3 25 20S 120 45 E
Carnation, U.S.A. ........... 78 C5 47 39N 121 55W
Carndonagh, Ireland ......... 10 A4 55 16N 7 15W
Carnduff, Canada ........... 71 D8 49 10N 101 50W
Carnegie, U.S.A. ............ 84 F4 40 24N 80 5W
Carnegie, L., Australia ....... 61 E3 26 5S 122 30 E
Carnic Alps = Karnische Alpen,
Europe .................. 16 E7 46 36N 13 0 E
Carniche Alpi = Karnische Alpen,
Europe .................. 16 E7 46 36N 13 0 E
Carnot, C.A.R. .............. 52 D3 4 59N 15 56 E
Carnot, C., Australia ......... 63 E2 34 57S 135 38 E
Carnot B., Australia ......... 60 C3 17 20S 122 15 E
Carnoustie, U.K. ............ 11 E6 56 30N 2 42W
Carnsore Pt., Ireland ........ 10 D5 52 10N 6 22W
Caro, U.S.A. ................ 82 D4 43 29N 83 24W
Carol City, U.S.A. ........... 83 N5 25 56N 80 16W
Carolina, Brazil ............. 93 E9 7 10S 47 30W
Carolina, Puerto Rico ........ 89 d 18 23N 65 58W
Carolina, S. Africa ........... 57 D5 26 5S 30 6 E
Caroline I., Kiribati .......... 65 H12 9 58S 150 13W
Caroline Is., Micronesia ....... 26 J17 8 0N 150 0 E
Caroni, Trin. & Tob. .......... 93 K15 10 34N 61 23W
Caroni →, Venezuela ........ 92 B6 8 21N 62 43W
Caronie = Nébrodi, Monti, Italy 22 F6 37 54N 14 35 E
Caroona, Australia .......... 63 E5 31 24S 150 26 E
Carpathians, Europe ......... 17 D11 49 30N 21 0 E
Carpaţii Meridionali, Romania . 17 F13 45 30N 25 0 E
Carpentaria, G. of, Australia ... 62 A2 14 0S 139 0 E
Carpentras, France .......... 20 D6 44 3N 5 2 E
Carpi, Italy ................. 22 B4 44 47N 10 53 E
Carpinteria, U.S.A. .......... 79 L7 34 24N 119 31W
Carr Boyd Ra., Australia ...... 60 C4 16 15S 128 35 E
Carrabelle, U.S.A. ........... 83 L3 29 51N 84 40W
Carranza, Presa V., Mexico .... 86 B4 27 20N 100 50W
Carrara, Italy ............... 20 D9 44 5N 10 6 E
Carrauntoohill, Ireland ....... 10 D2 52 0N 9 45W
Carrick-on-Shannon, Ireland .. 10 D4 52 21N 7 24W
Carrick-on-Suir, Ireland ...... 10 D4 52 21N 7 24W
Carrickfergus, U.K. .......... 10 B6 54 43N 5 49W
Carrickmacross, Ireland ...... 10 C5 53 59N 6 43W
Carrieton, Australia .......... 63 E2 32 25S 138 31 E
Carrington, U.S.A. .......... 80 B5 47 27N 99 8W
Carrizal Bajo, Chile .......... 94 B1 28 5S 71 20W
Carrizalillo, Chile ........... 94 B1 29 5S 71 30W
Carrizo Cr. →, U.S.A. ........ 81 G3 36 55N 103 55W
Carrizo Plain △, U.S.A. ....... 78 K7 35 12N 119 48W
Carrizo Springs, U.S.A. ....... 81 L5 28 31N 99 52W
Carrizozo, U.S.A. ........... 77 K11 33 38N 105 53W
Carroll, U.S.A. ............. 80 D7 42 4N 94 52W
Carrollton, Ga., U.S.A. ....... 83 J3 33 35N 85 5W
Carrollton, Ill., U.S.A. ....... 80 F9 39 18N 90 24W
Carrollton, Ky., U.S.A. ....... 82 F3 38 41N 85 11W
Carrollton, Mo., U.S.A. ....... 80 F8 39 22N 93 30W
Carrollton, Ohio, U.S.A. ...... 84 F3 40 34N 81 5W
Carron →, U.K. ............. 11 D4 57 53N 4 22W
Carron, L., U.K. ............. 11 D3 57 22N 5 35W
Carrot →, Canada ........... 71 C8 53 50N 101 17W
Carrot River, Canada ........ 71 C8 53 17N 103 35W
Carruthers, Canada ......... 71 C7 52 52N 109 16W
Carson, Calif., U.S.A. ........ 79 M8 33 48N 118 17W
Carson, N. Dak., U.S.A. ....... 80 B4 46 25N 101 34W
Carson →, U.S.A. ........... 78 F8 39 45N 118 40W
Carson City, U.S.A. .......... 78 F7 39 10N 119 46W
Carson Sink, U.S.A. .......... 76 G4 39 50N 118 25W
Cartagena, Colombia ........ 92 A3 10 25N 75 33W
Cartagena, Spain ........... 21 D5 37 38N 0 59W
Cartago, Colombia .......... 92 C3 4 45N 75 55W
Cartago, Costa Rica .......... 88 E3 9 50N 83 55W
Cartersville, U.S.A. .......... 83 H3 34 10N 84 48W
Carterton, N.Z. ............. 59 J5 41 2S 175 31 E
Carthage, Tunisia ........... 51 A8 36 50N 10 21 E
Carthage, Ill., U.S.A. ......... 80 E9 40 25N 91 8W

Carthage, Mo., U.S.A. ........ 81 G7 37 11N 94 19W
Carthage, N.Y., U.S.A. ........ 82 D8 43 59N 75 37W
Carthage, Tex., U.S.A. ........ 81 J7 32 9N 94 20W
Cartier I., Australia .......... 60 B3 12 31S 123 29 E
Cartwright, Canada .......... 73 B8 53 41N 56 58W
Caruaru, Brazil ............. 93 E11 8 15S 35 55W
Carúpano, Venezuela ........ 92 A6 10 39N 63 15W
Caruthersville, U.S.A. ........ 81 G10 36 11N 89 39W
Carvoeiro, Brazil ........... 92 D6 1 30S 61 59W
Carvoeiro, C., Portugal ....... 21 C1 39 21N 9 24W
Cary, U.S.A. ............... 83 H6 35 47N 78 46W
Casa Grande, U.S.A. ......... 77 K8 32 53N 111 45W
Casablanca, Chile ........... 94 C1 33 20S 71 25W
Casablanca, Morocco ........ 50 B4 33 36N 7 36W
Cascada de Basaseachic △,
Mexico .................. 86 B3 28 9N 108 15W
Cascade, Idaho, U.S.A. ....... 76 D5 44 31N 116 2W
Cascade, Mont., U.S.A. ....... 76 C8 47 16N 111 42W
Cascade Locks, U.S.A. ........ 78 E5 45 40N 121 54W
Cascade Ra., U.S.A. ......... 78 D5 47 0N 121 30W
Cascade Reservoir, U.S.A. ..... 76 D5 44 32N 116 3W
Cascais, Portugal ........... 21 C1 38 41N 9 25W
Cascavel, Brazil ............ 95 A5 24 57S 53 28W
Cáscina, Italy .............. 22 C4 43 41N 10 33 E
Casco B., U.S.A. ............ 83 D10 43 45N 70 0W
Caserta, Italy ............... 22 D6 41 4N 14 20 E
Casey, Antarctica ........... 5 C8 66 0S 76 0 E
Caseyr, Raas = Asir, Ras,
Somali Rep. ............. 47 E5 11 55N 51 10 E
Cashel, Ireland ............. 10 D4 52 30N 7 53W
Casiguran, Phil. ............ 37 A6 16 22N 122 7 E
Casilda, Argentina .......... 94 C3 33 10S 61 10W
Casino, Australia ........... 63 D5 28 52S 153 3 E
Casiquiare →, Venezuela ..... 92 C5 2 1N 67 7W
Casma, Peru ................ 92 E3 9 30S 78 20W
Casmalia, U.S.A. ........... 79 L6 34 50N 120 32W
Caspe, Spain ............... 21 B5 41 14N 0 1W
Casper, U.S.A. .............. 76 E10 42 51N 106 19W
Caspian Depression, Eurasia .. 19 E8 47 0N 48 0 E
Caspian Sea, Eurasia ........ 19 F9 43 0N 50 0 E
Cass Lake, U.S.A. ........... 80 B7 47 23N 94 37W
Cassadaga, U.S.A. .......... 84 D5 42 20N 79 19W
Casselman, Canada ......... 85 A9 45 19N 75 5W
Casselton, U.S.A. ........... 80 B6 46 54N 97 13W
Cassiar, Canada ............ 70 B2 59 30N 130 30W
Cassiar Mts., Canada ........ 70 B2 59 30N 130 30W
Cassino, Italy ............... 22 D5 41 30N 13 49 E
Cassville, U.S.A. ............ 81 G8 36 41N 93 52W
Castaic, U.S.A. ............. 79 L8 34 30N 118 38W
Castalia, U.S.A. ............ 84 E2 41 24N 82 49W
Castanhal, Brazil ........... 93 D9 1 18S 47 55W
Castara, Trin. & Tob. ........ 93 J16 11 17N 60 42W
Castellammare di Stábia, Italy .. 22 D6 40 42N 14 29 E
Castelli, Argentina .......... 94 D4 36 7S 57 47W
Castelló de la Plana, Spain .... 21 C5 39 58N 0 3W
Castelo, Brazil ............. 95 A7 20 33S 41 14W
Castelo Branco, Portugal ..... 21 C2 39 50N 7 31W
Castelsarrasin, France ....... 20 E4 44 2N 1 7 E
Castelvetrano, Italy ......... 22 F5 37 41N 12 47 E
Casterton, Australia ......... 63 F3 37 30S 141 30 E
Castile, U.S.A. ............. 84 D6 42 38N 78 3W
Castilla-La Mancha □, Spain ... 21 C4 39 30N 3 30W
Castilla y León □, Spain ...... 21 B3 42 0N 5 0W
Castillos, Uruguay .......... 95 C5 34 12S 53 52W
Castle Dale, U.S.A. .......... 76 G8 39 13N 111 1W
Castle Douglas, U.K. ......... 11 G5 54 56N 3 56W
Castle Rock, Colo., U.S.A. ..... 80 F2 39 22N 104 51W
Castle Rock, Wash., U.S.A. .... 78 D4 46 17N 122 54W
Castlebar, Ireland .......... 10 C2 53 52N 9 18W
Castleblayney, Ireland ....... 10 C5 54 7N 6 44W
Castleblaney, Ireland ........ 10 B5 54 7N 6 44W
Castlederg, U.K. ............ 10 B4 54 42N 7 35W
Castleford, U.K. ............ 12 D6 53 43N 1 21W
Castlegar, Canada .......... 70 D5 49 20N 117 40W
Castlemaine, Australia ....... 63 F3 37 2S 144 12 E
Castlepollard, Ireland ........ 10 C4 53 41N 7 19W
Castlerea, Ireland .......... 10 C3 53 46N 8 29W
Castlereagh →, Australia ..... 63 E4 30 12S 147 32 E
Castlereagh B., Australia ..... 62 A2 12 10S 135 10 E
Castleton, U.S.A. ........... 85 C11 43 37N 73 11W
Castletown, I. of Man ........ 12 C3 54 5N 4 38W
Castletown Bearhaven, Ireland . 10 E2 51 39N 9 56W
Castor, Canada ............. 70 C6 52 15N 111 50W
Castor →, Canada .......... 72 B4 53 24N 78 58W
Castorland, U.S.A. .......... 85 C9 43 53N 75 31W
Castres, France ............. 20 E5 43 37N 2 13 E
Castricum, Neths. .......... 15 B4 52 33N 4 40 E
Castries, St. Lucia .......... 89 f 14 2N 60 58W
Castro, Brazil .............. 95 A6 24 45S 50 0W
Castro, Chile .............. 96 E2 42 30S 73 50W
Castro Alves, Brazil ......... 93 F11 12 46S 39 33W
Castroville, U.S.A. .......... 78 J5 36 46N 121 45W
Castuera, Spain ............ 21 C3 38 43N 5 37W
Cat Ba △, Vietnam .......... 38 B6 20 47N 107 3 E
Cat Ba, Dao, Vietnam ........ 38 B6 20 50N 107 0 E
Cat I., Bahamas ............ 89 B4 24 30N 75 30W
Cat L., Canada ............. 72 B1 51 40N 91 50W
Cat Lake, Canada .......... 72 B1 51 40N 91 50W
Cat Tien △, Vietnam ......... 39 G6 11 25N 107 17 E
Catacamas, Honduras ....... 88 D2 14 54N 85 56W
Cataguases, Brazil .......... 95 A7 21 23S 42 39W
Catalão, Brazil ............. 93 G9 18 10S 47 57W
Çatalca, Turkey ............ 23 D13 41 8N 28 27 E
Catalina, Canada ........... 73 C9 48 31N 53 4W
Catalina, Chile ............. 94 B2 25 13S 69 43W
Catalina, U.S.A. ............ 77 K8 32 30N 110 50W
Catalonia = Cataluña □, Spain . 21 B6 41 40N 1 15 E
Cataluña □, Spain .......... 21 B6 41 40N 1 15 E
Catamarca, Argentina ....... 94 B2 28 30S 65 50W
Catamarca □, Argentina ...... 94 B2 27 0S 65 50W
Catanduanes □, Phil. ........ 37 B6 13 50N 124 20 E
Catanduva, Brazil .......... 95 A6 21 5S 48 58W
Catánia, Italy .............. 22 F6 37 30N 15 6 E
Catanzaro, Italy ............ 22 E7 38 54N 16 35 E
Catarman, Phil. ............ 37 B6 12 28N 124 35 E
Catatumbo-Barí △, Colombia .. 92 B4 9 0N 73 0W
Cateel, Phil. ............... 37 C7 7 47N 126 24 E
Catembe, Mozam. .......... 57 D5 26 0S 32 33 E
Caterham, U.K. ............. 13 F7 51 15N 0 4W
Cathcart, S. Africa .......... 56 E4 32 18S 27 10 E
Cathlamet, U.S.A. .......... 78 D3 46 12N 123 23W
Catlettsburg, U.S.A. ......... 82 F4 38 25N 82 36W
Catoche, C., Mexico ......... 87 C7 21 40N 87 8W
Catril, Argentina ........... 94 D3 36 26S 69 5W
Catrimani, Brazil ........... 92 C6 0 27N 61 41W
Catrimani →, Brazil ......... 92 C6 0 28N 61 44W
Catskill, U.S.A. ............. 85 D11 42 14N 73 52W
Catskill △, U.S.A. ........... 85 D10 42 7N 74 39W

Catskill Mts., U.S.A. ......... 85 D10 42 10N 74 25W
Catt, Mt., Australia .......... 62 A1 13 49S 134 23 E
Cattaraugus, U.S.A. ......... 84 D6 42 22N 78 52W
Catterick, U.K. ............. 12 C6 54 23N 1 37W
Catuala, Angola ............ 56 B2 16 25S 19 2 E
Catur, Mozam. ............. 55 E4 13 45S 35 30 E
Catwick Is., Vietnam ........ 39 G7 10 0N 109 0 E
Cauca →, Colombia ......... 92 B4 8 54N 74 28W
Caucaia, Brazil ............. 93 D11 3 40S 38 35W
Caucasus Mountains, Eurasia . 19 F7 42 50N 44 0 E
Caungula, Angola ........... 52 F3 8 26S 18 38 E
Cauquenes, Chile ........... 94 D1 36 0S 72 22W
Caura →, Venezuela ........ 92 B6 7 38N 64 53W
Cauresi →, Mozam. ........ 55 F3 17 8S 33 0 E
Causapscal, Canada ......... 73 C6 48 19N 67 12W
Cauvery →, India .......... 40 P11 11 9N 78 52 E
Caux, Pays de, France ....... 20 B4 49 38N 0 35 E
Cavalier, U.S.A. ............ 80 A6 48 48N 97 37W
Cavan, Ireland ............. 10 B4 54 0N 7 22W
Cavan □, Ireland ........... 10 C4 54 1N 7 16W
Cave Creek, U.S.A. ......... 77 K7 33 50N 111 57W
Cavenagh Ra., Australia ...... 61 E4 26 12S 127 55 E
Cavendish, Australia ........ 63 F3 37 31S 142 2 E
Caviana, I., Brazil .......... 93 C8 0 10N 50 10W
Cavite, Phil. ............... 37 B6 14 29N 120 55 E
Cawndilla L., Australia ....... 63 E3 32 30S 142 15 E
Cawnpore = Kanpur, India .... 43 F9 26 28N 80 20 E
Caxias, Brazil .............. 93 D10 4 55S 43 20W
Caxias do Sul, Brazil ........ 95 B5 29 10S 51 10W
Cay Sal Bank, Bahamas ...... 88 B4 23 45N 80 0W
Cayambe, Ecuador .......... 92 C3 0 3N 78 8W
Cayenne, Fr. Guiana ........ 93 B8 5 5N 52 18W
Cayey, Puerto Rico .......... 89 d 18 7N 66 10W
Cayman Brac, Cayman Is. ..... 88 C4 19 43N 79 49W
Cayman Is. □, W. Indies ...... 88 C3 19 40N 80 30W
Cayman Trough, Caribbean ... 66 H11 19 0N 81 0W
Cayuga, Canada ............ 84 D5 42 59N 79 50W
Cayuga, U.S.A. ............. 85 D8 42 54N 76 44W
Cayuga L., U.S.A. ........... 85 D8 42 41N 76 41W
Cazenovia, U.S.A. .......... 85 D9 42 56N 75 51W
Cazombo, Angola ........... 53 G4 11 54S 22 56 E
Ceanannus Mor, Ireland ..... 10 C5 53 44N 6 53W
Ceará = Fortaleza, Brazil ..... 93 D11 3 45S 38 35W
Ceará □, Brazil ............. 93 E11 5 0S 40 0W
Ceará Mirim, Brazil ......... 93 E11 5 38S 35 25W
Cebaco, I. de, Panama ....... 88 E3 7 33N 81 9W
Ceballos, Argentina ......... 94 B2 29 10S 66 35W
Cebu, Phil. ................ 37 B6 10 18N 123 54 E
Cecil Plains, Australia ....... 63 D5 27 30S 151 11 E
Cedar →, U.S.A. ........... 80 E9 41 17N 91 21W
Cedar City, U.S.A. ........... 77 H7 37 41N 113 4W
Cedar Creek Reservoir, U.S.A. . 81 J6 32 11N 96 4W
Cedar Falls, Iowa, U.S.A. ..... 80 D8 42 32N 92 27W
Cedar Falls, Wash., U.S.A. .... 78 C5 47 25N 121 45W
Cedar Key, U.S.A. .......... 83 L4 29 8N 83 2W
Cedar L., Canada ........... 71 C8 53 10N 100 0W
Cedar Rapids, U.S.A. ........ 80 E9 41 59N 91 40W
Cedartown, U.S.A. .......... 83 H3 34 1N 85 15W
Cedarvale, Canada .......... 70 B3 55 1N 128 22W
Cedarville, S. Africa ......... 57 E4 30 23S 29 3 E
Cedral, Mexico ............. 86 C4 23 50N 100 42W
Cedro, Brazil .............. 93 E11 6 34S 39 3W
Cedros, I. de, Mexico ........ 86 B1 28 10N 115 20W
Cedros B., Trin. & Tob. ....... 93 K15 10 16N 61 54W
Ceduna, Australia .......... 63 E1 32 7S 133 46 E
Ceerigaabo = Erigavo,
Somali Rep. ............. 47 E4 10 35N 47 20 E
Cefalù, Italy ............... 22 E6 38 2N 14 1 E
Cegléd, Hungary ........... 17 E10 47 11N 19 47 E
Cekik, Indonesia ........... 37 J17 8 12S 114 27 E
Celaque △, Honduras ........ 88 D2 14 30N 88 43W
Celaya, Mexico ............ 86 C4 20 31N 100 37W
Celebes Sea, Indonesia ...... 37 D6 3 0N 123 0 E
Celina, U.S.A. ............. 82 E3 40 33N 84 35W
Celje, Slovenia ............. 16 E8 46 16N 15 18 E
Celle, Germany ............ 16 B6 52 37N 10 4 E
Celtic Sea, Atl. Oc. ......... 14 F2 50 9N 9 34W
Cenderwasih, Teluk, Indonesia . 37 E9 3 0S 135 20 E
Center, N. Dak., U.S.A. ....... 80 B4 47 7N 101 18W
Center, Tex., U.S.A. ......... 81 K7 31 48N 94 11W
Centerburg, U.S.A. .......... 84 F2 40 18N 82 42W
Centerville, Calif., U.S.A. ..... 78 J7 36 44N 119 30W
Centerville, Iowa, U.S.A. ..... 80 E8 40 44N 92 52W
Centerville, Pa., U.S.A. ...... 84 F5 40 3N 79 59W
Centerville, Tenn., U.S.A. ..... 83 H2 35 47N 87 28W
Centerville, Tex., U.S.A. ...... 81 K7 31 16N 95 59W
Central = Tsentralnyy □, Russia 28 D4 53 0N 40 0 E
Central □, Kenya ........... 54 C4 0 30S 37 30 E
Central □, Malawi .......... 55 E3 13 30S 33 30 E
Central □, Zambia .......... 55 E2 14 25S 28 50 E
Central, Cordillera, Colombia .. 92 C4 5 0N 75 0W
Central, Cordillera, Costa Rica . 88 D3 10 10N 84 5W
Central, Cordillera, Dom. Rep. . 89 C5 19 15N 71 0W
Central, Cordillera, Puerto Rico . 89 d 18 8N 66 35W
Central African Rep. ■, Africa . 51 G9 7 0N 20 0 E
Central America, America ..... 66 H11 12 0N 85 0W
Central Butte, Canada ....... 71 C7 50 48N 106 31W
Central City, Colo., U.S.A. .... 76 G11 39 48N 105 31W
Central City, Ky., U.S.A. ...... 82 G2 37 18N 87 7W
Central City, Nebr., U.S.A. .... 80 E6 41 7N 98 0W
Central I., Kenya ........... 54 B4 3 30N 36 0 E
Central Island △, Kenya ...... 54 B4 2 33N 36 1 E
Central Kalahari △, Botswana . 56 C3 23 36S 23 58 E
Central Makran Range, Pakistan 40 F4 26 30N 64 15 E
Central Patricia, Canada ...... 72 B1 51 30N 90 9W
Central Point, U.S.A. ........ 76 E2 42 23N 122 55W
Central Russian Uplands, Europe 6 E13 54 0N 36 0 E
Central Siberian Plateau, Russia 26 C14 65 0N 105 0 E
Central Square, U.S.A. ....... 85 C8 43 17N 76 9W
Centralia, Ill., U.S.A. ........ 80 F10 38 32N 89 8W
Centralia, Mo., U.S.A. ....... 80 F8 39 13N 92 8W
Centralia, Wash., U.S.A. ...... 78 D4 46 43N 122 58W
Cephalonia = Kefalliniá, Greece 23 E9 38 15N 20 30 E
Cepu, Indonesia ............ 37 G14 7 9S 111 35 E
Ceram = Seram, Indonesia .... 37 E7 3 10S 129 0 E
Ceram Sea = Seram Sea,
Indonesia ............... 37 E7 2 30S 128 30 E
Ceredigion □, U.K. .......... 13 E3 52 16N 4 15W
Ceres, Argentina ........... 94 B3 29 55S 61 55W
Ceres, S. Africa ............ 56 E2 33 21S 19 18 E
Ceres, U.S.A. .............. 78 H6 37 35N 120 57W
Cerignola, Italy ............ 22 D6 41 17N 15 53 E
Cerigo = Kithira, Greece ...... 23 F10 36 8N 23 0 E
Çerkezköy, Turkey .......... 23 D12 41 17N 28 0 E
Cerralvo, I., Mexico ......... 86 C3 24 20N 109 45W
Cerritos, Mexico ........... 86 C4 22 27N 100 20W
Cerro Chato, Uruguay ....... 95 C4 33 6S 55 8W
Cerro Corá △, Paraguay ...... 95 A4 22 35S 56 2W

Cerro el Copey △, Venezuela ... **89 D7** 10 59N 63 53W
Cerro Hoya △, Panama ...... **88 E3** 7 17N 80 45W
Cerro Saroche △, Venezuela .. **89 D6** 10 8N 69 38W
Cerventes, Australia ........ **61 F2** 30 31S 115 3 E
Cervera, Spain ............. **21 B6** 41 40N 1 16 E
Cesena, Italy .............. **22 B5** 44 8N 12 15 E
Cēsis, Latvia .............. **9 H21** 57 18N 25 15 E
České Budějovice, Czech Rep. . **16 D8** 48 55N 14 25 E
Českomoravská Vrchovina,
　Czech Rep. .............. **16 D8** 49 30N 15 40 E
Çeşme, Turkey ............. **23 E12** 38 20N 26 23 E
Cessnock, Australia ........ **63 E5** 32 50S 151 21 E
Cetinje, Serbia & M. ....... **23 C8** 42 23N 18 59 E
Cetraro, Italy ............. **22 E6** 39 31N 15 55 E
Ceuta, N. Afr. ............ **21 E3** 35 52N 5 18W
Cévennes, France .......... **20 D5** 44 10N 3 50 E
Ceyhan, Turkey ........... **44 B2** 37 4N 35 47 E
Ceylon = Sri Lanka ■, Asia .. **40 R12** 7 30N 80 50 E
Cha-am, Thailand .......... **38 F2** 12 48N 99 58 E
Cha Pa, Vietnam .......... **38 A4** 22 20N 103 47 E
Chacabuco, Argentina ...... **94 C3** 34 40S 60 27W
Chachapoyas, Peru ......... **92 E3** 6 15S 77 50W
Chachoengsao, Thailand .... **38 F3** 13 42N 101 5 E
Chachran, Pakistan ........ **40 E7** 28 55N 70 30 E
Chachro, Pakistan ......... **42 G4** 25 5N 70 15 E
Chaco □, Argentina ........ **94 B4** 27 0S 59 30W
Chaco □, Argentina ........ **94 B3** 26 30S 61 0W
Chaco □, Paraguay ........ **94 B4** 26 0S 60 0W
Chaco →, U.S.A. .......... **77 H9** 36 46N 108 39W
Chaco Austral, S. Amer. .... **96 B4** 27 0S 61 30W
Chaco Boreal, S. Amer. ..... **92 H6** 22 0S 60 0W
Chaco Central, S. Amer. .... **96 A4** 24 0S 61 0W
Chaco Culture △, U.S.A. .... **77 H10** 36 3N 107 58W
Chacon, C., U.S.A. ........ **70 C2** 54 42N 132 0W
Chad ■, Africa ............ **51 F8** 15 0N 17 15 E
Chad, L. = Tchad, L., Chad .. **51 F8** 13 30N 14 30 E
Chadan, Russia ........... **29 D10** 51 17N 91 35 E
Chadileuvú →, Argentina .... **94 D2** 37 46S 66 0W
Chadiza, Zambia .......... **55 E3** 14 45S 32 27 E
Chadron, U.S.A. .......... **80 D3** 42 50N 103 0W
Chadyr-Lunga = Ciadâr-Lunga,
　Moldova ................ **17 E15** 46 3N 28 51 E
Chae Hom, Thailand ....... **38 C2** 18 43N 99 35 E
Chae Son △, Thailand ...... **38 C2** 18 42N 99 20 E
Chaem →, Thailand ........ **38 C2** 18 11N 98 38 E
Chaeryŏng, N. Korea ....... **35 E13** 38 24N 125 36 E
Chagai Hills = Chāh Gay Hills,
　Afghan. ................ **40 E3** 29 30N 64 0 E
Chagda, Russia ........... **29 D14** 58 45N 130 38 E
Chaghcharān, Afghan. ...... **40 B4** 34 31N 65 15 E
Chagos Arch. ☒, Ind. Oc. ... **27 K11** 6 0S 72 0 E
Chagres △, Panama ........ **88 E4** 9 33N 79 37W
Chagrin Falls, U.S.A. ...... **84 E3** 41 26N 81 24W
Chaguanas, Trin. & Tob. ... **93 K15** 10 30N 61 26W
Chāh Akhvor, Iran ........ **45 C8** 32 41N 59 40 E
Chāh Bahar, Iran ......... **45 E9** 25 20N 60 40 E
Chāh-e Kavīr, Iran ........ **45 C8** 34 29N 56 52 E
Chahar Burjak, Afghan. .... **40 D3** 30 15N 62 0 E
Chahār Mahāll va Bakhtīārī □,
　Iran ................... **45 C6** 32 0N 49 0 E
Chai Wan, China .......... **33 G11** 22 16N 114 14 E
Chaibasa, India .......... **41 H14** 22 42N 85 49 E
Chainat, Thailand ........ **38 E3** 15 11N 100 8 E
Chaiya, Thailand ......... **39 H2** 9 23N 99 14 E
Chaiyaphum, Thailand ..... **38 E4** 15 48N 102 2 E
Chaj Doab, Pakistan ...... **42 C5** 32 15N 73 0 E
Chajari, Argentina ....... **94 C4** 30 42S 58 0W
Chak Amru, Pakistan ...... **42 C6** 32 22N 75 11 E
Chakar →, Pakistan ....... **42 E3** 29 29N 68 2 E
Chakari, Zimbabwe ........ **57 B4** 18 5S 29 51 E
Chake Chake, Tanzania .... **54 D4** 5 15S 39 45 E
Chakhānsūr, Afghan. ...... **40 D3** 31 10N 62 0 E
Chakonipau, L., Canada ... **73 A6** 56 18N 68 30W
Chakradharpur, India ..... **43 H11** 22 45N 85 40 E
Chakrata, India .......... **42 D7** 30 42N 77 51 E
Chakwal, Pakistan ........ **42 C5** 32 56N 72 53 E
Chala, Peru ............. **92 G4** 15 48S 74 20W
Chalchihuites, Mexico ..... **86 C4** 23 29N 103 53W
Chalcis = Khalkís, Greece .. **23 E10** 38 27N 23 42 E
Chaleur B., Canada ....... **73 C6** 47 55N 65 30W
Chalfant, U.S.A. ......... **78 H8** 37 32N 118 21W
Chalhuanca, Peru ........ **92 F4** 14 15S 73 15W
Chalisgaon, India ........ **40 J9** 20 30N 75 10 E
Chalk River, Canada ...... **72 C4** 46 1N 77 27W
Chalky Inlet, N.Z. ........ **59 M1** 46 3S 166 31 E
Challapata, Bolivia ....... **92 G5** 18 53S 66 50W
Challis, U.S.A. ........... **76 D6** 44 30N 114 14W
Chalmette, U.S.A. ........ **81 L10** 29 56N 89 58W
Chalon-sur-Saône, France .. **20 C6** 46 48N 4 50 E
Châlons-en-Champagne, France **20 B6** 48 58N 4 20 E
Chālūs, Iran ............. **45 B6** 36 38N 51 26 E
Cham, Cu Lao, Vietnam .... **38 E7** 15 57N 108 30 E
Chama, U.S.A. ........... **77 H10** 36 54N 106 35W
Chamaicó, Argentina ...... **94 D3** 35 3S 64 58W
Chaman, Pakistan ........ **40 D5** 30 58N 66 25 E
Chamba, India ........... **42 C7** 32 35N 76 10 E
Chamba, Tanzania ........ **55 E4** 11 37S 37 0 E
Chambal →, India ........ **43 F8** 26 29N 79 15 E
Chamberlain, U.S.A. ...... **80 D5** 43 49N 99 20W
Chamberlain →, Australia .. **60 C4** 15 30S 127 54 E
Chamberlain L., U.S.A. .... **83 B11** 46 14N 69 19W
Chambers, U.S.A. ......... **77 J9** 35 11N 109 26W
Chambersburg, U.S.A. ..... **82 F7** 39 56N 77 40W
Chambéry, France ........ **20 D6** 45 34N 5 55 E
Chambeshi →, Zambia ..... **52 G6** 11 53S 29 48 E
Chambly, Canada ......... **85 A11** 45 27N 73 17W
Chambord, Canada ........ **73 C5** 48 25N 72 6W
Chamchamal, Iraq ........ **44 C5** 35 32N 44 50 E
Chamela, Mexico ......... **86 D3** 19 32N 105 5W
Chamical, Argentina ...... **94 C2** 30 22S 66 27W
Chamkar Luong, Cambodia . **39 G4** 11 0N 103 45 E
Chamoli, India .......... **43 D8** 30 24N 79 21 E
Chamonix-Mont Blanc, France **20 D7** 45 55N 6 51 E
Champa, India ........... **43 H10** 22 2N 82 43 E
Champagne, Canada ....... **70 A1** 60 49N 136 30W
Champagne, France ....... **20 B6** 48 40N 4 20 E
Champaign, U.S.A. ........ **82 E1** 40 7N 88 15W
Champassak, Laos ........ **38 E5** 14 53N 105 52 E
Champdoré, L., Canada .... **73 A6** 55 55N 65 49W
Champion, U.S.A. ........ **84 E4** 41 19N 80 51W
Champlain, U.S.A. ........ **85 B11** 44 59N 73 27W
Champlain, L., U.S.A. ..... **85 B11** 44 40N 73 20W
Champotón, Mexico ....... **87 D6** 19 20N 90 50W
Champua, India .......... **43 H12** 22 2N 85 43 E
Chana, Thailand ......... **39 J3** 6 55N 100 44 E
Chañaral, Chile .......... **94 B1** 26 23S 70 40W

Chanārān, Iran ........... **45 B8** 36 39N 59 6 E
Chanasma, India ......... **42 H5** 23 44N 72 5 E
Chancery Lane, Barbados .. **89 g** 13 3N 59 30W
Chanco, Chile ........... **94 D1** 35 44S 72 32W
Chand, India ............ **43 J8** 21 57N 79 7 E
Chandan, India .......... **43 G12** 24 38N 86 40 E
Chandan Chauki, India .... **43 E9** 28 33N 80 47 E
Chandannagar, India ..... **43 H13** 22 52N 88 24 E
Chandausi, India ........ **43 E8** 28 27N 78 49 E
Chandeleur Is., U.S.A. .... **81 L10** 29 55N 88 57W
Chandeleur Sd., U.S.A. .... **81 L10** 29 55N 89 0W
Chandigarh, India ....... **42 D7** 30 43N 76 47 E
Chandil, India .......... **43 H12** 22 58N 86 3 E
Chandler, Australia ...... **63 D1** 27 0S 133 19 E
Chandler, Canada ........ **73 C7** 48 18N 64 46W
Chandler, Ariz., U.S.A. ... **77 K8** 33 18N 111 50W
Chandler, Okla., U.S.A. ... **81 H6** 35 42N 96 53W
Chandod, India .......... **42 J5** 21 59N 73 28 E
Chandpur, Bangla. ....... **41 H17** 23 8N 90 45 E
Chandrapur, India ....... **40 K11** 19 57N 79 25 E
Chānf, Iran ............. **45 E9** 26 38N 60 29 E
Chang, Pakistan ......... **42 F3** 26 59N 68 30 E
Chang, Ko, Thailand ...... **39 F4** 12 0N 102 23 E
Ch'ang Chiang = Chang Jiang →,
　China ................. **33 C7** 31 48N 121 10 E
Chang Jiang →, China ..... **33 C7** 31 48N 121 10 E
Changa, India ........... **43 C7** 33 53N 77 35 E
Changan, China ......... **33 F10** 22 48N 113 48 E
Changanacheri, India ..... **40 Q10** 9 25N 76 31 E
Changane →, Mozam. ..... **57 C5** 24 30S 33 30 E
Changbai, China ......... **35 D15** 41 25N 128 5 E
Changbai Shan, China .... **35 C15** 42 20N 129 0 E
Changchiak'ou = Zhangjiakou,
　China ................. **34 D8** 40 48N 114 55 E
Changchun, China ....... **35 C13** 43 57N 125 17 E
Changchunling, China .... **35 B13** 45 18N 125 27 E
Changde, China ......... **33 D6** 29 4N 111 35 E
Changdo-ri, N. Korea ..... **35 E14** 38 30N 127 40 E
Changhai = Shanghai, China **33 C7** 31 15N 121 26 E
Changhua, Taiwan ....... **33 D7** 24 2N 120 30 E
Changhǔng, S. Korea ..... **35 G14** 34 41N 126 52 E
Changhǔngni, N. Korea ... **35 D15** 40 24N 128 19 E
Changi, Singapore ....... **39 d** 1 23N 103 59 E
Changi, Singapore ✈ (SIN),
　Singapore ............. **39 M4** 1 23N 103 59 E
Changjiang, China ....... **38 C7** 19 20N 108 55 E
Changjiang Shuiku, China . **33 G10** 22 29N 113 27 E
Changjin, N. Korea ....... **35 D14** 40 23N 127 15 E
Changjin-chŏsuji, N. Korea . **35 D14** 40 30N 127 15 E
Changli, China .......... **35 E10** 39 40N 119 19 E
Changling, China ........ **35 B12** 44 20N 123 58 E
Changlun, Malaysia ...... **39 J3** 6 25N 100 26 E
Changping, China ........ **34 D9** 40 14N 116 12 E
Changsha, China ........ **33 D6** 28 12N 113 0 E
Changwu, China ......... **34 G4** 35 10N 107 45 E
Changyi, China .......... **35 F10** 36 40N 119 30 E
Changyŏn, N. Korea ...... **35 E13** 38 15N 125 6 E
Changyuan, China ....... **34 G8** 35 15N 114 42 E
Changzhi, China ......... **34 F7** 36 10N 113 6 E
Changzhou, China ....... **33 C6** 31 47N 119 58 E
Chanhanga, Angola ...... **56 B1** 16 0S 14 8 E
Chania = Khaniá, Greece .. **25 D6** 35 30N 24 4 E
Channapatna, India ...... **40 N10** 12 40N 77 15 E
Channel Is., U.K. ........ **13 H5** 49 19N 2 24W
Channel Is., U.S.A. ...... **79 M7** 33 40N 119 15W
Channel Islands △, U.S.A. . **79 L7** 34 0N 119 24W
Channel-Port aux Basques,
　Canada ............... **73 C8** 47 30N 59 9W
Channing, U.S.A. ........ **81 H3** 35 41N 102 20W
Chantada, Spain ........ **21 A2** 42 36N 7 46W
Chanthaburi, Thailand ... **38 F4** 12 38N 102 12 E
Chantrey Inlet, Canada ... **68 B10** 67 48N 96 20W
Chanute, U.S.A. ......... **81 G7** 37 41N 95 27W
Chao Phraya →, Thailand .. **38 F3** 13 32N 100 36 E
Chao Phraya Lowlands, Thailand **38 E3** 15 30N 100 0 E
Chaocheng, China ....... **34 F8** 36 4N 115 37 E
Chaoyang, China ........ **35 D11** 41 35N 120 22 E
Chaozhou, China ........ **33 D6** 23 42N 116 32 E
Chapais, Canada ........ **72 C5** 49 47N 74 51W
Chapala, Mozam. ........ **55 F4** 15 50S 37 35 E
Chapala, L. de, Mexico .... **86 C4** 20 10N 103 20W
Chapayev, Kazakhstan .... **19 D9** 50 25N 51 10 E
Chapayevsk, Russia ...... **18 D8** 53 0N 49 40 E
Chapecó, Brazil ......... **95 B5** 27 14S 52 41W
Chapel Hill, U.S.A. ...... **83 H6** 35 55N 79 4W
Chapleau, Canada ....... **72 C3** 47 50N 83 24W
Chaplin, Canada ........ **71 C7** 50 28N 106 40W
Chaplin L., Canada ...... **71 C7** 50 22N 106 36W
Chappell, U.S.A. ........ **80 E3** 41 6N 102 28W
Chapra = Chhapra, India .. **43 G11** 25 48N 84 44 E
Chara, Russia .......... **29 D12** 56 54N 118 20 E
Charadai, Argentina ..... **94 B4** 27 35S 59 55W
Charagua, Bolivia ....... **92 G6** 19 45S 63 10W
Charaña, Bolivia ........ **92 G5** 17 30S 69 25W
Charanwala, India ....... **42 F5** 27 51N 72 10 E
Charata, Argentina ...... **94 B3** 27 13S 61 14W
Charcas, Mexico ........ **86 C4** 23 10N 101 20W
Charcot I., Antarctica .... **5 C17** 70 0S 70 0W
Chard, U.K. ............ **13 G5** 50 52N 2 58W
Chardon, U.S.A. ........ **84 E3** 41 35N 81 12W
Chardzhou = Chärjew,
　Turkmenistan .......... **28 F7** 39 6N 63 34 E
Charente →, France ...... **20 D3** 45 57N 1 5W
Chari →, Chad .......... **51 F8** 12 58N 14 31 E
Chārīkār, Afghan. ....... **40 B6** 35 0N 69 10 E
Chariton →, U.S.A. ...... **80 F8** 39 19N 92 58W
Chärjew, Turkmenistan ... **28 F7** 39 6N 63 34 E
Charkhari, India ........ **43 G8** 25 24N 79 45 E
Charkhi Dadri, India ..... **42 E7** 28 37N 76 17 E
Charleroi, Belgium ...... **15 D4** 50 24N 4 27 E
Charleroi, U.S.A. ....... **84 F5** 40 9N 79 57W
Charles, C., U.S.A. ...... **82 G8** 37 7N 75 58W
Charles City, U.S.A. ..... **80 D8** 43 4N 92 41W
Charles L., Canada ...... **71 B6** 59 50N 110 33W
Charles Town, U.S.A. .... **82 F7** 39 17N 77 52W
Charleston, Ill., U.S.A. ... **82 F1** 39 30N 88 10W
Charleston, Miss., U.S.A. . **81 H9** 34 1N 90 4W
Charleston, Mo., U.S.A. .. **81 G10** 36 55N 89 21W
Charleston, S.C., U.S.A. .. **83 J6** 32 46N 79 56W
Charleston, W. Va., U.S.A. **82 F5** 38 21N 81 38W
Charleston L., Canada .... **85 B9** 44 32N 76 0W
Charleston Peak, U.S.A. .. **79 J11** 36 16N 115 42W
Charlestown, Ireland .... **10 C3** 53 58N 8 48W
Charlestown, S. Africa ... **57 D4** 27 26S 29 53 E
Charlestown, Ind., U.S.A. . **82 F3** 38 27N 85 40W

Charlestown, N.H., U.S.A. .. **85 C12** 43 14N 72 25W
Charlestown of Aberlour, U.K. . **11 D5** 57 28N 3 14W
Charleville = Rath Luirc, Ireland **10 D3** 52 21N 8 40W
Charleville, Australia ..... **63 D4** 26 24S 146 15 E
Charleville-Mézières, France . **20 B6** 49 44N 4 40 E
Charlevoix, U.S.A. ....... **82 C3** 45 19N 85 16W
Charlotte, Mich., U.S.A. .. **82 D3** 42 34N 84 50W
Charlotte, N.C., U.S.A. ... **83 H5** 35 13N 80 51W
Charlotte, Vt., U.S.A. .... **85 B11** 44 19N 73 14W
Charlotte Amalie, U.S. Virgin Is. **89 e** 18 21N 64 56W
Charlotte Harbor, U.S.A. .. **83 M4** 26 50N 82 10W
Charlottesville, U.S.A. .... **82 F6** 38 2N 78 30W
Charlottetown, Nfld. & L.,
　Canada ................ **73 B8** 52 46N 56 7W
Charlottetown, P.E.I., Canada **73 C7** 46 14N 63 8W
Charlottteville, Trin. & Tob. . **93 J16** 11 20N 60 33W
Charlton, Australia ...... **63 F3** 36 16S 143 24 E
Charlton, U.S.A. ........ **80 E8** 40 59N 93 20W
Charlton I., Canada ...... **72 B4** 52 0N 79 20W
Charny, Canada ......... **73 C5** 46 43N 71 15W
Charolles, France ....... **20 C6** 46 27N 4 16 E
Charre, Mozam. ......... **55 F4** 17 13S 35 10 E
Charsadda, Pakistan ..... **42 B4** 34 7N 71 45 E
Charters Towers, Australia . **62 C4** 20 5S 146 13 E
Chartres, France ........ **20 B4** 48 29N 1 30 E
Chascomús, Argentina ... **94 D4** 35 30S 58 0W
Chasefu, Zambia ........ **55 E3** 11 55S 33 8 E
Chashma Barrage, Pakistan . **42 C4** 32 27N 71 20 E
Chāt, Iran ............. **45 B7** 37 59N 55 16 E
Châteaubriant, France .... **20 C3** 47 43N 1 23W
Chateaugay, U.S.A. ...... **85 B10** 44 56N 74 5W
Châteauguay, L., Canada .. **73 A5** 56 26N 70 3W
Châteaulin, France ...... **20 B1** 48 11N 4 8W
Châteauroux, France ..... **20 C4** 46 50N 1 40 E
Châteaux, Pte. des, Guadeloupe **88 b** 16 15N 61 10W
Châtellerault, France .... **20 C4** 46 50N 0 30 E
Chatham = Chatham-Kent,
　Canada ................ **84 D2** 42 24N 82 11W
Chatham = Miramichi, Canada **73 C6** 47 2N 65 28W
Chatham, U.K. .......... **13 F8** 51 22N 0 32 E
Chatham, U.S.A. ........ **85 D11** 42 21N 73 36W
Chatham Is., Pac. Oc. .... **64 M10** 44 0S 176 40W
Chatham-Kent, Canada ... **84 D2** 42 24N 82 11W
Chatmohar, Bangla. ...... **43 G13** 24 15N 89 15 E
Chatra, India ........... **43 G11** 24 12N 84 56 E
Chatrapur, India ........ **41 K14** 19 22N 85 2 E
Chats, L. des, Canada .... **85 A8** 45 30N 76 20W
Chatsu, India .......... **42 F6** 26 36N 75 57 E
Chatsworth, Canada ..... **84 B4** 44 27N 80 54W
Chatsworth, Zimbabwe ... **55 F3** 19 38S 31 13 E
Chāttagām = Chittagong, Bangla. **41 H17** 22 19N 91 48 E
Chattahoochee, U.S.A. ... **83 K3** 30 42N 84 51W
Chattahoochee →, U.S.A. . **83 K3** 30 54N 84 57W
Chattanooga, U.S.A. ..... **83 H3** 35 3N 85 19W
Chatteris, U.K. ......... **13 E8** 52 28N 0 2 E
Chaturat, Thailand ...... **38 E3** 15 40N 101 51 E
Chau Doc, Vietnam ...... **39 G5** 10 42N 105 7 E
Chaukan Pass, Burma .... **41 F20** 27 0N 97 15 E
Chaumont, France ....... **20 B6** 48 7N 5 8 E
Chaumont, U.S.A. ....... **85 B8** 44 4N 76 8W
Chaunskaya G., Russia ... **4 C16** 69 0N 169 0 E
Chautauqua L., U.S.A. .... **84 D5** 42 10N 79 24W
Chauvin, Canada ........ **71 C6** 52 45N 110 10W
Chaves, Brazil .......... **93 D9** 0 15S 49 55W
Chaves, Portugal ........ **21 B2** 41 45N 7 32W
Chawang, Thailand ...... **39 H2** 8 25N 99 30 E
Chaykovskiy, Russia ..... **18 C9** 56 47N 54 9 E
Chazy, U.S.A. .......... **85 B11** 44 53N 73 26W
Cheb, Czech Rep. ....... **16 C7** 50 9N 12 28 E
Cheboksary, Russia ...... **18 C8** 56 8N 47 12 E
Cheboygan, U.S.A. ...... **82 C3** 45 39N 84 29W
Chech, Erg, Africa ...... **50 D5** 25 0N 2 15W
Chechenia □, Russia ..... **19 F8** 43 30N 45 29 E
Checheno-Ingush Republic =
　Chechenia □, Russia .... **19 F8** 43 30N 45 29 E
Chechnya = Chechenia □, Russia **19 F8** 43 30N 45 29 E
Chech'ŏn, S. Korea ...... **35 F15** 37 8N 128 12 E
Checotah, U.S.A. ........ **81 H7** 35 28N 95 31W
Chedabucto B., Canada ... **73 C7** 45 25N 61 8W
Cheduba I., Burma ...... **41 K18** 18 45N 93 40 E
Cheepie, Australia ...... **63 D4** 26 33S 145 1 E
Chegdomyn, Russia ...... **29 D14** 51 7N 133 1 E
Chegga, Mauritania ...... **50 C4** 25 27N 5 40W
Chegutu, Zimbabwe ..... **55 F3** 18 10S 30 14 E
Chehalis, U.S.A. ........ **78 D4** 46 40N 122 58W
Chehalis →, U.S.A. ...... **78 D3** 46 57N 123 50W
Cheju do, S. Korea ...... **35 H14** 33 29N 126 34 E
Chekiang = Zhejiang □, China . **33 D7** 29 0N 120 0 E
Chela, Sa. da, Angola .... **56 B1** 16 20S 13 20 E
Chelan, U.S.A. ......... **76 C4** 47 51N 120 1W
Chelan, L., U.S.A. ...... **76 B3** 48 11N 120 30W
Cheleken, Turkmenistan .. **19 G9** 39 34N 53 16 E
Cheleken Yarymadasy,
　Turkmenistan .......... **45 B7** 39 30N 53 15 E
Chelforó, Argentina ..... **96 D3** 39 0S 66 33W
Chelkar = Shalqar, Kazakhstan . **28 E6** 47 48N 59 39 E
Chelkar Tengiz, Solonchak,
　Kazakhstan ............ **28 E7** 48 5N 63 7 E
Chełm, Poland ......... **17 C12** 51 8N 23 30 E
Chełmno, Poland ....... **17 B10** 53 20N 18 30 E
Chelmsford, U.K. ....... **13 F8** 51 44N 0 29 E
Chelsea, U.S.A. ......... **85 C12** 43 59N 72 27W
Cheltenham, U.K. ....... **13 F5** 51 54N 2 4W
Chelyabinsk, Russia ..... **28 D7** 55 10N 61 24 E
Chelyuskin, C. = Chelyuskin, Mys,
　Russia ................ **29 B11** 77 30N 103 0 E
Chelyuskin, Mys, Russia .. **29 B11** 77 30N 103 0 E
Chemainus, Canada ..... **78 B3** 48 55N 123 42W
Chemba, Mozam. ........ **53 H6** 17 9S 34 53 E
Chemnitz, Germany ..... **16 C7** 50 51N 12 54 E
Chemult, U.S.A. ........ **76 E3** 43 14N 121 47W
Chen, Gora, Russia ...... **29 C15** 65 16N 141 50 E
Chenab →, Pakistan ..... **42 D4** 30 23N 71 2 E
Chenango Forks, U.S.A. .. **85 D9** 42 15N 75 51W
Cheney, U.S.A. ......... **76 C5** 47 30N 117 35W
Cheng Xian, China ...... **34 H3** 33 43N 105 42 E
Chengcheng, China ...... **34 G5** 35 8N 109 56 E
Chengchou = Zhengzhou, China **34 G7** 34 45N 113 34 E
Chengde, China ........ **35 D9** 40 59N 117 58 E
Chengdu, China ........ **32 C5** 30 38N 104 2 E
Chengjiang, China ...... **32 D5** 24 39N 103 0 E
Ch'engtu = Chengdu, China . **32 C5** 30 38N 104 2 E
Chengwu, China ........ **34 G8** 34 58N 115 50 E
Chengyang, China ....... **35 F11** 36 18N 120 21 E
Chenjiagang, China ..... **35 G10** 34 23N 119 47 E

Chenkán, Mexico ......... **87 D6** 19 8N 90 58W
Chennai, India .......... **40 N12** 13 8N 80 19 E
Cheo Reo, Vietnam ...... **36 B3** 13 25N 108 28 E
Cheom Ksan, Cambodia ... **38 E5** 14 13N 104 56 E
Chepén, Peru ........... **92 E3** 7 15S 79 23W
Chepes, Argentina ....... **94 C2** 31 20S 66 35W
Chepo, Panama ......... **88 E4** 9 10N 79 6W
Chepstow, U.K. ......... **13 F5** 51 38N 2 41W
Chequamegon B., U.S.A. .. **80 B9** 46 40N 90 30W
Cher →, France ......... **20 C4** 47 21N 0 29 E
Cheraw, U.S.A. ......... **83 H6** 34 42N 79 53W
Cherbourg, France ...... **20 B3** 49 39N 1 40W
Cherdyn, Russia ........ **18 B10** 60 24N 56 29 E
Cheremkhovo, Russia .... **29 D11** 53 8N 103 1 E
Cherepanovo, Russia .... **28 D9** 54 15N 83 30 E
Cherepovets, Russia ..... **18 C6** 59 5N 37 55 E
Chergui, Chott ech, Algeria . **50 B6** 34 21N 0 25 E
Cherikov = Cherykaw, Belarus **17 B16** 53 32N 31 20 E
Cherkasy, Ukraine ....... **19 E5** 49 27N 32 4 E
Cherkessk, Russia ....... **19 F7** 44 15N 42 5 E
Cherlak, Russia ......... **28 D8** 54 15N 74 55 E
Chernaya, Russia ........ **29 B9** 70 30N 89 10 E
Chernigov = Chernihiv, Ukraine **18 D5** 51 28N 31 20 E
Chernihiv, Ukraine ...... **18 D5** 51 28N 31 20 E
Chernivtsi, Ukraine ...... **17 D13** 48 15N 25 52 E
Chernobyl = Chornobyl, Ukraine **17 C16** 51 20N 30 15 E
Chernogorsk, Russia ..... **29 D10** 53 49N 91 18 E
Chernovtsy = Chernivtsi, Ukraine **17 D13** 48 15N 25 52 E
Chernyakhovsk, Russia ... **9 J19** 54 36N 21 48 E
Chernysheyskiy, Russia ... **29 C12** 63 0N 112 30 E
Cherokee, Iowa, U.S.A. ... **80 D7** 42 45N 95 33W
Cherokee, Okla., U.S.A. .. **81 G5** 36 45N 98 21W
Cherokee Village, U.S.A. .. **81 G9** 36 17N 91 30W
Cherokees, Grand Lake O' The,
　U.S.A. ................ **81 G7** 36 28N 95 2W
Cherrapunji, India ...... **41 G17** 25 17N 91 47 E
Cherry Valley, Calif., U.S.A. **79 M10** 33 59N 116 57W
Cherry Valley, N.Y., U.S.A. . **85 D10** 42 48N 74 45W
Cherskiy, Russia ........ **29 C17** 68 45N 161 18 E
Cherskogo Khrebet, Russia . **29 C15** 65 0N 143 0 E
Cherven, Belarus ....... **17 B15** 53 45N 28 28 E
Chervonohrad, Ukraine ... **17 C13** 50 25N 24 10 E
Cherwell →, U.K. ........ **13 F6** 51 44N 1 14W
Cherykaw, Belarus ...... **17 B16** 53 32N 31 20 E
Chesapeake, U.S.A. ..... **82 G7** 36 50N 76 17W
Chesapeake B., U.S.A. ... **82 G7** 38 0N 76 10W
Cheshire □, U.K. ....... **12 D5** 53 14N 2 30W
Cheshskaya Guba, Russia . **18 A8** 67 20N 47 0 E
Cheshunt, U.K. ......... **13 F7** 51 43N 0 1W
Chesil Beach, U.K. ...... **13 G5** 50 37N 2 33W
Chesley, Canada ........ **84 B3** 44 17N 81 5W
Chester, U.K. .......... **12 D5** 53 12N 2 53W
Chester, Calif., U.S.A. .... **76 F3** 40 19N 121 14W
Chester, Ill., U.S.A. ..... **81 G10** 37 55N 89 49W
Chester, Mont., U.S.A. ... **76 B8** 48 31N 110 58W
Chester, Pa., U.S.A. ..... **82 F8** 39 51N 75 22W
Chester, S.C., U.S.A. .... **83 H5** 34 43N 81 12W
Chester, Vt., U.S.A. ..... **85 C12** 43 16N 72 36W
Chester, W. Va., U.S.A. .. **84 F4** 40 37N 80 34W
Chester-le-Street, U.K. ... **12 C6** 54 51N 1 34W
Chesterfield, U.K. ...... **12 D6** 53 15N 1 25W
Chesterfield, Is., N. Cal. .. **64 J7** 19 52S 158 15 E
Chesterfield Inlet, Canada . **68 B10** 63 30N 90 45W
Chesterton Ra., Australia .. **63 D4** 25 30S 147 27 E
Chesterton Range △, Australia **63 D4** 26 16S 147 22 E
Chestertown, U.S.A. ..... **85 C11** 43 40N 73 48W
Chesterville, Canada .... **85 A9** 45 6N 75 14W
Chestnut Ridge, U.S.A. ... **84 F5** 40 20N 79 10W
Chesuncook L., U.S.A. ... **83 C11** 46 0N 69 21W
Chéticamp, Canada ...... **73 C7** 46 37N 60 59W
Chetumal, Mexico ....... **87 D7** 18 30N 88 20W
Chetumal, B. de, Mexico .. **87 D7** 18 40N 88 10W
Chetwynd, Canada ...... **70 B4** 55 45N 121 36W
Cheviot, The, U.K. ...... **12 B5** 55 29N 2 9W
Cheviot Hills, U.K. ...... **12 B5** 55 20N 2 30W
Cheviot Ra., Australia ... **62 D3** 25 20S 143 45 E
Chew Bahir, Ethiopia .... **47 G2** 4 40N 36 50 E
Chewelah, U.S.A. ....... **76 B5** 48 17N 117 43W
Cheyenne, Okla., U.S.A. .. **81 H5** 35 37N 99 40W
Cheyenne, Wyo., U.S.A. .. **80 E2** 41 8N 104 49W
Cheyenne →, U.S.A. ..... **80 C4** 44 41N 101 18W
Cheyenne Wells, U.S.A. .. **80 F3** 38 49N 102 21W
Cheyne B., Australia ..... **61 F2** 34 35S 118 50 E
Chhabra, India ......... **42 G7** 24 40N 76 54 E
Chhaktala, India ....... **42 H6** 22 6N 74 11 E
Chhapra, India ......... **43 G11** 25 48N 84 44 E
Chhata, India .......... **42 F7** 27 42N 77 30 E
Chhatarpur, Jharkhand, India . **43 G11** 24 23N 84 11 E
Chhatarpur, Mad. P., India . **43 G8** 24 55N 79 35 E
Chhattisgarh □, India .... **43 J10** 22 0N 82 0 E
Chhep, Cambodia ....... **38 F5** 13 45N 105 24 E
Chhindwara, Mad. P., India **43 H8** 22 3N 79 29 E
Chhindwara, Mad. P., India **43 H8** 22 2N 78 59 E
Chhlong, Cambodia ..... **39 F5** 12 15N 105 58 E
Chhota Tawa →, India ... **42 H7** 22 14N 76 36 E
Chhoti Kali Sindh →, India **42 G6** 24 2N 75 31 E
Chhuikhadan, India ..... **43 J9** 21 32N 80 59 E
Chhuk, Cambodia ...... **39 G5** 10 46N 104 28 E
Chi →, Thailand ........ **38 E5** 15 11N 104 43 E
Chiai, Taiwan .......... **33 D7** 23 29N 120 25 E
Chiamboni, Somali Rep. .. **52 E8** 1 39S 41 35 E
Chiang Dao, Thailand .... **38 C2** 19 22N 98 58 E
Chiang Kham, Thailand .. **38 C3** 19 32N 100 18 E
Chiang Khan, Thailand .. **38 D3** 17 52N 101 36 E
Chiang Khong, Thailand .. **38 B3** 20 17N 100 24 E
Chiang Mai, Thailand ... **38 C2** 18 47N 98 59 E
Chiang Rai, Thailand .... **38 C2** 19 52N 99 50 E
Chiang Saen, Thailand ... **38 B3** 20 16N 100 5 E
Chiapa →, Mexico ...... **87 D6** 16 42N 93 0W
Chiapa de Corzo, Mexico . **87 D6** 16 42N 93 0W
Chiapas □, Mexico ...... **87 D5** 18 18N 98 34W
Chiautla, Mexico ....... **87 D5** 18 18N 98 34W
Chiávari, Italy ......... **20 D8** 44 19N 9 19 E
Chiavenna, Italy ....... **20 C8** 46 19N 9 24 E
Chiba, Japan .......... **31 G10** 35 30N 140 7 E
Chiba □, Japan ........ **31 G10** 35 30N 140 20 E
Chibabava, Mozam. ..... **57 C5** 20 17S 33 35 E
Chibemba, Cunene, Angola **53 H2** 15 48S 14 8 E
Chibemba, Huíla, Angola . **56 B2** 16 20S 15 20 E
Chibi, Zimbabwe ....... **57 C5** 20 18S 30 25 E
Chibia, Angola ........ **53 H2** 15 10S 13 42 E
Chibougamau, Canada ... **72 C5** 49 56N 74 24W
Chibougamau, L., Canada . **72 C5** 49 50N 74 20W
Chibuto, Mozam. ....... **57 C5** 24 40S 33 33 E
Chic-Chocs, Mts., Canada . **73 C6** 48 55N 66 0W
Chicacole = Srikakulam, India **41 K13** 18 14N 83 58 E
Chicago, U.S.A. ........ **82 E2** 41 53N 87 38W

Chicago Heights, U.S.A. ...... 82 E2 41 30N 87 38W
Chichagof I., U.S.A. ......... 68 C6 57 30N 135 30W
Chichén-Itzá, Mexico ....... 87 C7 20 40N 88 36W
Chicheng, China ........... 34 D8 40 55N 115 55 E
Chichester, U.K. ........... 13 G7 50 50N 0 47W
Chichester Ra., Australia .... 60 D2 22 12S 119 15 E
Chichibu, Japan ........... 31 F9 35 59N 139 10 E
Chichibu-Tama △, Japan .... 31 G9 35 52N 138 42 E
Ch'ich'ihaerh = Qiqihar, China . 29 E13 47 26N 124 0 E
Chicholi, India ........... 42 H8 22 1N 77 40 E
Chickasaw △, U.S.A. ....... 81 H6 34 26N 97 0W
Chickasha, U.S.A. ......... 81 H6 35 3N 97 58W
Chiclana de la Frontera, Spain . 21 D2 36 26N 6 9W
Chiclayo, Peru ........... 92 E3 6 42S 79 50W
Chico, U.S.A. ........... 78 F5 39 44N 121 50W
Chico →, Chubut, Argentina .. 96 E3 44 0S 67 0W
Chico →, Santa Cruz, Argentina 96 G3 50 0S 68 30W
Chicomo, Mozam. ......... 57 C5 24 31S 34 6 E
Chicomostoc, Mexico ....... 86 C4 22 28N 102 49W
Chicontepec, Mexico ....... 87 C5 20 58N 98 10W
Chicopee, U.S.A. ......... 85 D12 42 9N 72 37W
Chicoutimi, Canada ....... 73 C5 48 28N 71 5W
Chicualacuala, Mozam. ..... 57 C5 22 6S 31 42 E
Chidambaram, India ....... 40 P11 11 20N 79 45 E
Chidenguele, Mozam. ...... 57 C5 24 55S 34 11 E
Chidley, C., Canada ....... 69 B13 60 23N 64 26W
Chiducuane, Mozam. ...... 57 C5 24 35S 34 25 E
Chiede, Angola ........... 56 B2 17 15S 16 22 E
Chiefs Pt., Canada ....... 84 B3 44 41N 81 18W
Chiem Hoa, Vietnam ...... 38 A5 22 12N 105 17 E
Chiemsee, Germany ....... 16 E7 47 53N 12 28 E
Chiengi, Zambia ......... 55 D2 8 45S 29 10 E
Chiengmai = Chiang Mai,
  Thailand ........... 38 C2 18 47N 98 59 E
Chiese →, Italy ........... 20 D9 45 8N 10 25 E
Chieti, Italy ........... 22 C6 42 21N 14 10 E
Chifeng, China ........... 35 C10 42 18N 118 58 E
Chignecto B., Canada ...... 73 C7 45 30N 64 40W
Chiguana, Bolivia ......... 94 A2 21 0S 67 58W
Chigwell, U.K. ........... 13 F8 51 37N 0 5 E
Chiha-ri, N. Korea ....... 35 E14 38 40N 126 30 E
Chihli, G. of = Bo Hai, China . 35 E10 39 0N 119 0 E
Chihuahua, Mexico ....... 86 B3 28 40N 106 3W
Chihuahua □, Mexico ...... 86 B3 28 40N 106 3W
Chiili = Shieli, Kazakhstan ... 28 E7 44 20N 66 15 E
Chik Bollapur, India ...... 40 N10 13 25N 77 45 E
Chikmagalur, India ....... 40 N9 13 15N 75 45 E
Chikwawa, Malawi ....... 55 F3 16 2S 34 50 E
Chilac, Mexico ........... 87 D5 18 20N 97 24W
Chilam Chavki, Pakistan .... 43 B6 35 5N 75 5 E
Chilanga, Zambia ......... 55 F2 15 33S 28 16 E
Chilapa, Mexico ......... 87 D5 17 40N 99 11W
Chilas, Pakistan ......... 43 B6 35 25N 74 5 E
Chilaw, Sri Lanka ....... 40 R11 7 30N 79 50 E
Chilcotin →, Canada ...... 70 C4 51 44N 122 23W
Childers, Australia ....... 63 D5 25 15S 152 17 E
Childress, U.S.A. ........ 81 H4 34 25N 100 13W
Chile ■, S. Amer. ........ 96 D2 35 0S 72 0W
Chile Rise, Pac. Oc. ...... 65 L18 38 0S 92 0W
Chilecito, Argentina ...... 94 B2 29 10S 67 30W
Chilete, Peru ........... 92 E3 7 10S 78 50W
Chililabombwe, Zambia .... 55 E2 12 18S 27 43 E
Chilin = Jilin, China ...... 35 C14 43 44N 126 30 E
Chilka L., India ......... 41 K14 19 40N 85 25 E
Chilko →, Canada ....... 70 C4 52 0N 123 40W
Chilko L., Canada ....... 70 C4 51 20N 124 10W
Chillagoe, Australia ...... 62 B3 17 7S 144 33 E
Chillán, Chile ........... 94 D1 36 40S 72 10W
Chillicothe, Ill., U.S.A. .... 80 E10 40 55N 89 29W
Chillicothe, Mo., U.S.A. .... 80 F8 39 48N 93 33W
Chillicothe, Ohio, U.S.A. ... 82 F4 39 20N 82 59W
Chilliwack, Canada ....... 70 D4 49 10N 121 54W
Chilo, India ........... 42 F5 27 25N 73 32 E
Chiloane, I., Mozam. ...... 57 C5 20 40S 34 55 E
Chiloé, I. de, Chile ....... 96 E2 42 30S 73 50W
Chilpancingo, Mexico ...... 87 D5 17 30N 99 30W
Chiltern Hills, U.K. ....... 13 F7 51 40N 0 53W
Chilton, U.S.A. ......... 82 C1 44 2N 88 10W
Chilubi, Zambia ......... 55 E2 11 5S 29 58 E
Chilubula, Zambia ....... 55 E3 10 14S 30 51 E
Chilumba, Malawi ....... 55 E3 10 28S 34 12 E
Chilung, Taiwan ......... 33 D7 25 3N 121 45 E
Chilwa, L., Malawi ....... 55 F4 15 15S 35 40 E
Chimaltitán, Mexico ...... 86 C4 21 46N 103 50W
Chiman, Panama ......... 88 E4 8 45N 78 40W
Chimanimani, Zimbabwe ... 57 B5 19 48S 32 52 E
Chimanimani △, Zimbabwe .. 55 F3 19 48S 33 0 E
Chimay, Belgium ......... 15 D4 50 3N 4 20 E
Chimayo, U.S.A. ......... 77 H11 36 0N 105 56W
Chimbay, Uzbekistan ...... 28 E6 42 57N 59 47 E
Chimborazo, Ecuador ...... 92 D3 1 29S 78 55W
Chimbote, Peru ......... 92 E3 9 0S 78 35W
Chimkent = Shymkent,
  Kazakhstan ......... 28 E7 42 18N 69 36 E
Chimoio, Mozam. ....... 55 F3 19 4S 33 30 E
Chimpembe, Zambia ...... 55 D2 9 31S 29 33 E
Chin □, Burma ......... 41 J18 22 0N 93 0 E
Chin Ling Shan = Qinling Shandi,
  China ........... 34 H5 33 50N 108 10 E
China, Mexico ......... 87 B5 25 40N 99 20W
China ■, Asia ......... 33 C6 30 0N 110 0 E
China, Great Plain of, Asia ... 26 F15 35 0N 115 0 E
China Lake, U.S.A. ....... 79 K9 35 44N 117 37W
Chinan = Jinan, China ..... 34 F9 36 38N 117 1 E
Chinandega, Nic. ......... 88 D2 12 35N 87 12W
Chinati Peak, U.S.A. ...... 81 L2 29 57N 104 29W
Chincha Alta, Peru ....... 92 F3 13 25S 76 7W
Chinchaga →, Canada ..... 70 B5 58 53N 118 20W
Chinchilla, Australia ...... 63 D5 26 45S 150 38 E
Chinchorro, Banco, Mexico .. 87 D7 18 35N 87 20W
Chinchou = Jinzhou, China .. 35 D11 41 5N 121 3 E
Chincoteague, U.S.A. ...... 82 G8 37 56N 75 23W
Chinde, Mozam. ......... 55 F4 18 35S 36 30 E
Chindo, S. Korea ......... 35 G14 34 28N 126 15 E
Chindwin →, Burma ...... 41 J19 21 26N 95 15 E
Chineni, India ........... 43 C6 33 2N 75 15 E
Chinga, Mozam. ......... 55 F4 15 13S 38 35 E
Chingola, Zambia ........ 55 E2 12 31S 27 53 E
Chingole, Malawi ........ 55 E3 13 4S 34 17 E
Ch'ingtao = Qingdao, China .. 35 F11 36 5N 120 20 E
Chingune, Mozam. ....... 57 C5 20 33S 35 0 E
Chinhae, S. Korea ....... 35 G15 35 9N 128 47 E
Chinhanguanine, Mozam. ... 57 D5 25 21S 32 30 E
Chinhoyi, Zimbabwe ..... 55 F3 17 20S 30 8 E
Chini, India ........... 42 D8 31 32N 78 15 E
Chiniot, Pakistan ....... 42 D5 31 45N 73 0 E
Chínipas, Mexico ....... 86 B3 27 24N 108 32W

Chinji, Pakistan ......... 42 C5 32 42N 72 22 E
Chinju, S. Korea ......... 35 G15 35 12N 128 2 E
Chinnampo = Namp'o, N. Korea 35 E13 38 52N 125 10 E
Chino, Japan ........... 31 G9 35 59N 138 9 E
Chino, U.S.A. ........... 79 L9 34 1N 117 41W
Chino Valley, U.S.A. ...... 77 J7 34 45N 112 27W
Chinon, France ......... 20 C4 47 10N 0 15 E
Chinook, U.S.A. ......... 76 B9 48 35N 109 14W
Chinsali, Zambia ......... 55 E3 10 30S 32 2 E
Chióggia, Italy ........... 22 B5 45 13N 12 17 E
Chíos = Khíos, Greece ..... 23 E12 38 27N 26 9 E
Chipata, Zambia ......... 55 E3 13 38S 32 28 E
Chipinge, Zimbabwe ...... 55 G3 20 13S 32 28 E
Chipinge △, Zimbabwe .... 55 G3 20 14S 33 0 E
Chipley, U.S.A. ......... 83 K3 30 47N 85 32W
Chipman, Canada ......... 73 C6 46 6N 65 53W
Chipoka, Malawi ......... 55 E3 13 57S 34 28 E
Chippenham, U.K. ....... 13 F5 51 27N 2 6W
Chippewa →, U.S.A. ...... 80 C8 44 25N 92 5W
Chippewa Falls, U.S.A. .... 80 C9 44 56N 91 24W
Chipping Norton, U.K. .... 13 F6 51 56N 1 32W
Chiputneticook Lakes, U.S.A. . 83 C11 45 35N 67 35W
Chiquián, Peru ......... 92 F3 10 10S 77 0W
Chiquibul △, Belize ...... 88 C2 16 49N 88 52W
Chiquimula, Guatemala .... 88 D2 14 51N 89 37W
Chiquinquira, Colombia .... 92 B4 5 37N 73 50W
Chirala, India ........... 40 M12 15 50N 80 26 E
Chiramba, Mozam. ....... 55 F3 16 55S 34 39 E
Chirawa, India ......... 42 E6 28 14N 75 42 E
Chirchiq, Uzbekistan ...... 28 E7 41 29N 69 35 E
Chiredzi, Zimbabwe ...... 57 C5 21 0S 31 38 E
Chiricahua △, U.S.A. ...... 77 L9 32 0N 109 20W
Chiricahua Peak, U.S.A. .... 77 L9 31 51N 109 18W
Chiriquí, G. de, Panama .... 88 E3 8 0N 82 10W
Chiriquí, L. de, Panama .... 88 E3 9 10N 82 0W
Chirisa △, Zimbabwe ...... 55 F2 17 53S 28 15 E
Chirivira Falls, Zimbabwe ... 55 G3 21 10S 32 12 E
Chirmiri, India ......... 41 H13 23 15N 82 20 E
Chirripó Grande, Cerro,
  Costa Rica ......... 88 E3 9 29N 83 29W
Chirundu, Zimbabwe ...... 57 B4 16 3S 28 50 E
Chisamba, Zambia ....... 55 E2 14 55S 28 20 E
Chisapani Garhi, Nepal .... 41 F14 27 30N 84 2 E
Chisasibi, Canada ....... 72 B4 53 50N 79 0W
Chisholm, Canada ....... 70 C6 54 55N 114 10W
Chisholm, U.S.A. ......... 80 B8 47 29N 92 53W
Chishtian Mandi, Pakistan .. 42 E5 29 50N 72 55 E
Chisimaio, Somali Rep. ..... 49 G8 0 22S 42 32 E
Chisimba Falls, Zambia .... 55 E3 10 12S 30 56 E
Chişinău, Moldova ....... 17 E15 47 2N 28 50 E
Chisos Mts., U.S.A. ...... 81 L3 29 5N 103 15W
Chistopol, Russia ....... 18 C9 55 25N 50 38 E
Chita, Russia ........... 29 D12 52 0N 113 35 E
Chitipa, Malawi ......... 55 D3 9 41S 33 19 E
Chitose, Japan ......... 30 C10 42 49N 141 39 E
Chitral, Pakistan ....... 40 B7 35 50N 71 56 E
Chitré, Panama ......... 88 E3 7 59N 80 27W
Chittagong, Bangla. ...... 41 H17 22 19N 91 48 E
Chittagong □, Bangla. ..... 41 G17 24 5N 91 0 E
Chittaurgarh, India ...... 42 G6 24 52N 74 38 E
Chittoor, India ......... 40 N11 13 15N 79 5 E
Chitungwiza, Zimbabwe ... 55 F3 18 0S 31 6 E
Chiusi, Italy ........... 22 C4 43 1N 11 57 E
Chivasso, Italy ......... 20 D7 45 11N 7 53 E
Chivhu, Zimbabwe ....... 55 F3 19 2S 30 52 E
Chivilcoy, Argentina ...... 94 C4 34 55S 60 0W
Chiwanda, Tanzania ...... 55 E3 11 23S 34 55 E
Chizarira, Zimbabwe ...... 55 F2 17 36S 27 45 E
Chizarira △, Zimbabwe .... 55 F2 17 44S 27 52 E
Chizera, Zambia ......... 55 E2 13 10S 25 0 E
Chkalov = Orenburg, Russia .. 18 D10 51 45N 55 6 E
Chloride, U.S.A. ......... 79 K12 35 25N 114 12W
Cho Bo, Vietnam ....... 38 B5 20 46N 105 10 E
Cho-do, N. Korea ....... 35 E13 38 30N 124 40 E
Cho Phuoc Hai, Vietnam ... 39 G6 10 26N 107 18 E
Choa Chu Kang, Singapore .. 39 d 1 22N 103 41 E
Choba, Kenya ......... 54 B4 2 30N 38 5 E
Chobe △, Botswana ...... 56 B4 18 37S 24 23 E
Choch'iwŏn, S. Korea ..... 35 F14 36 37N 127 18 E
Chocolate Mts., U.S.A. .... 79 M11 33 15N 115 15W
Choctawhatchee →, U.S.A. .. 83 K3 30 25N 86 8W
Choele Choel, Argentina ... 96 D3 39 11S 65 40W
Choiseul, St. Lucia ...... 89 f 13 47N 61 3W
Choix, Mexico ......... 86 B3 26 40N 108 23W
Chojnice, Poland ......... 17 B9 53 42N 17 32 E
Chōkai-San, Japan ....... 30 E10 39 6N 140 3 E
Choke Canyon L., U.S.A. ... 81 L5 28 30N 98 20W
Chokurdakh, Russia ...... 29 B15 70 38N 147 55 E
Cholame, U.S.A. ......... 78 K6 35 44N 120 18W
Cholet, France ......... 20 C3 47 4N 0 52W
Cholguan, Chile ......... 94 D1 37 10S 72 3W
Choluteca, Honduras ..... 88 D2 13 20N 87 14W
Choluteca →, Honduras .... 88 D2 13 0N 87 20W
Chom Bung, Thailand ..... 38 F2 13 37N 99 36 E
Chom Thong, Thailand .... 38 C2 18 25N 98 41 E
Choma, Zambia ......... 55 F2 16 48S 26 59 E
Chomolungma = Everest, Mt.,
  Nepal ........... 43 E12 28 5N 86 58 E
Chomun, India ......... 42 F6 27 15N 75 40 E
Chomutov, Czech Rep. .... 16 C7 50 28N 13 23 E
Chon Buri, Thailand ...... 38 F3 13 21N 101 1 E
Chon Thanh, Vietnam .... 39 G6 11 24N 106 36 E
Ch'onan, S. Korea ....... 35 F14 36 48N 127 9 E
Chone, Ecuador ......... 92 D3 0 40S 80 0W
Chong Kai, Cambodia ..... 38 F4 13 57N 103 35 E
Chong Mek, Thailand ..... 38 E5 15 10N 105 27 E
Chong Phangan, Thailand .. 39 b 9 39N 100 0 E
Chong Samui, Thailand ... 39 b 9 21N 99 50 E
Chŏngdo, S. Korea ....... 35 G15 35 38N 128 42 E
Chŏngha, S. Korea ....... 35 F15 36 12N 129 21 E
Chŏngjin, N. Korea ....... 35 D15 41 47N 129 50 E
Chŏngju, S. Korea ....... 35 F14 36 39N 127 27 E
Chŏngju, N. Korea ....... 35 E13 39 40N 125 5 E
Chongli, China ......... 34 D8 40 58N 115 15 E
Chongqing, China ....... 35 C15 36 39N 126 53 E
Chongqing Shi □, China ... 32 C5 30 0N 108 0 E
Chonguene, Mozam. ...... 57 C5 25 3S 33 49 E
Chŏngup, S. Korea ....... 35 G14 35 35N 126 50 E
Chŏngju, S. Korea ....... 35 G14 35 35N 127 0 E
Chonos, Arch. de los, Chile .. 96 F2 45 0S 75 0W
Chop, Ukraine ......... 17 D12 48 26N 22 12 E
Chopim →, Brazil ....... 95 B5 25 35S 53 5W
Chor, Pakistan ......... 42 G3 25 31N 69 46 E
Chorbat La, India ....... 43 B7 34 42N 76 37 E
Chorley, U.K. ........... 12 D5 53 39N 2 38W
Chornobyl, Ukraine ...... 17 C16 51 20N 30 15 E
Chorolque, Cerro, Bolivia ... 94 A2 20 59S 66 5W

Chorregon, Australia ...... 62 C3 22 40S 143 32 E
Chorro el Indio △, Venezuela . 89 E5 7 43N 72 9W
Chortkiv, Ukraine ....... 17 D13 49 2N 25 46 E
Ch'ŏrwon, S. Korea ....... 35 E14 38 15N 127 10 E
Chorzów, Poland ......... 17 C10 50 18N 18 57 E
Chos-Malal, Argentina .... 94 D1 37 20S 70 15W
Ch'osan, N. Korea ....... 35 D13 40 50N 125 47 E
Choszczno, Poland ....... 16 B8 53 7N 15 25 E
Choteau, U.S.A. ......... 76 C7 47 49N 112 11W
Chotila, India ......... 42 H4 22 23N 71 15 E
Chotta Udepur, India ..... 42 H6 22 19N 74 1 E
Chowchilla, U.S.A. ....... 78 H6 37 7N 120 16W
Choybalsan, Mongolia .... 33 B6 48 4N 114 30 E
Christchurch, N.Z. ....... 59 K4 43 33S 172 47 E
Christchurch, U.K. ....... 13 G6 50 44N 1 47W
Christian I., Canada ...... 84 B4 44 50N 80 12W
Christiana, S. Africa ...... 56 D4 27 52S 25 8 E
Christiansted, U.S. Virgin Is. . 89 C7 17 45N 64 42W
Christie B., Canada ....... 71 A6 62 32N 111 10W
Christina →, Canada ...... 71 B6 56 40N 111 3W
Christmas Cr. →, Australia . 60 C4 18 29S 125 23 E
Christmas I. = Kiritimati, Kiribati 65 G12 1 58N 157 27W
Christmas I., Ind. Oc. ..... 64 J2 10 30S 105 40 E
Christopher L., Australia ... 61 D4 24 49S 127 42 E
Chtimba, Malawi ....... 55 E3 10 35S 34 13 E
Chū = Shū, Kazakhstan .... 28 E8 43 36N 73 42 E
Chū = Shū →, Kazakhstan .. 26 E10 45 0N 67 44 E
Chu →, Vietnam ....... 38 C5 19 53N 105 45 E
Chu Lai, Vietnam ....... 38 E7 15 28N 108 45 E
Chuak, Ko, Thailand ..... 39 b 9 28N 99 41 E
Ch'uanchou = Quanzhou, China 33 D6 24 55N 118 34 E
Chuankou, China ....... 34 G6 34 20N 110 59 E
Chubbuck, U.S.A. ....... 76 E7 42 55N 112 28W
Chūbu □, Japan ......... 31 F8 36 45N 137 30 E
Chubu-Sangaku △, Japan ... 31 F8 36 30N 137 40 E
Chubut →, Argentina ..... 96 E3 43 20S 65 5W
Chuchi L., Canada ....... 70 B4 55 12N 124 30W
Chuda, India ........... 42 H4 22 29N 71 41 E
Chudskoye, Ozero, Russia .. 9 G22 58 13N 27 30 E
Chūgoku □, Japan ....... 31 G6 35 0N 133 0 E
Chūgoku-Sanchi, Japan .... 31 G6 35 0N 133 0 E
Chugwater, U.S.A. ....... 80 E2 41 46N 104 50W
Chukchi Sea, Russia ...... 29 C19 68 0N 175 0W
Chukotskoye Nagorye, Russia 29 C18 68 0N 175 0 E
Chula Vista, U.S.A. ...... 79 N9 32 39N 117 5W
Chulucanas, Peru ....... 92 E2 5 8S 80 10W
Chulym →, Russia ....... 28 D9 57 43N 83 51 E
Chum Phae, Thailand ..... 38 D4 16 40N 102 6 E
Chum Saeng, Thailand .... 38 E3 15 55N 100 15 E
Chumar, India ......... 43 C8 32 40N 78 35 E
Chumbicha, Argentina .... 94 B2 29 0S 66 10W
Chumphon, Thailand ..... 39 G2 10 35N 99 14 E
Chumuare, Mozam. ...... 55 E3 14 31S 31 50 E
Chumunjin, S. Korea ..... 35 F15 37 55N 128 54 E
Chuna →, Russia ....... 29 D10 57 47N 94 37 E
Ch'unch'ŏn, S. Korea ..... 35 F14 37 58N 127 44 E
Chunchura, India ....... 43 H13 22 53N 88 27 E
Chunga, Zambia ....... 55 F2 15 0S 26 2 E
Chunggang-ŭp, N. Korea ... 35 D14 41 48N 126 48 E
Chunghwa, N. Korea ..... 35 E13 38 52N 125 47 E
Ch'ungju, S. Korea ....... 35 F14 36 58N 127 58 E
Chungking = Chongqing, China 32 D5 29 35N 106 25 E
Ch'ungmu, S. Korea ...... 35 G15 34 50N 128 20 E
Chungt'iaoshan = Zhongtiao
  Shan, China ....... 34 G6 35 0N 111 10 E
Chunian, Pakistan ....... 42 D6 30 57N 74 0 E
Chunya, Tanzania ....... 55 D3 8 30S 33 27 E
Chunyang, China ....... 35 C15 43 38N 129 23 E
Chupara Pt., Trin. & Tob. ... 93 K15 10 49N 61 22W
Chuquibamba, Peru ...... 92 G4 15 47S 72 44W
Chuquicamata, Chile ..... 94 A2 22 15S 69 0W
Chur, Switz. ........... 20 C8 46 52N 9 32 E
Churachandpur, India ..... 41 G18 24 20N 93 40 E
Church Stretton, U.K. .... 13 E5 52 32N 2 48W
Churchill, Canada ....... 71 B10 58 47N 94 11W
Churchill →, Man., Canada . 71 B10 58 47N 94 12W
Churchill →, Nfld. & L., Canada 73 B7 53 19N 60 10W
Churchill, C., Canada ..... 71 B10 58 46N 93 12W
Churchill Falls, Canada .... 73 B7 53 36N 64 19W
Churchill L., Canada ...... 71 B7 55 55N 108 20W
Churchill Pk., Canada .... 70 B3 58 10N 125 10W
Churki, India ........... 43 H10 23 50N 83 12 E
Churu, India ........... 42 E6 28 20N 74 50 E
Churún Merú = Angel Falls,
  Venezuela ......... 92 B6 5 57N 62 30W
Chushal, India ......... 43 C8 33 40N 78 40 E
Chuska Mts., U.S.A. ...... 77 H9 36 15N 108 50W
Chusovoy, Russia ....... 18 C10 58 22N 57 50 E
Chute-aux-Outardes, Canada . 73 C6 49 7N 68 24W
Chuuronjang, N. Korea .... 35 D15 41 35N 129 40 E
Chuvash Republic =
  Chuvashia □, Russia ... 18 C8 55 30N 47 0 E
Chuvashia □, Russia ..... 18 C8 55 30N 47 0 E
Chuwārtah, Iraq ....... 44 C5 35 43N 45 34 E
Chuy, Uruguay ......... 95 C5 33 41S 53 27W
Ci Xian, China ......... 34 F8 36 20N 114 25 E
Ciadâr-Lunga, Moldova .... 17 E15 46 3N 28 51 E
Ciamis, Indonesia ....... 37 G13 7 20S 108 21 E
Cianjur, Indonesia ....... 37 G12 6 49S 107 8 E
Cianorte, Brazil ......... 95 A5 23 37S 52 37W
Cibola, U.S.A. ......... 79 M12 33 17N 114 42W
Ciégas del Catumbo △,
  Venezuela ......... 89 E5 9 25N 71 54W
Ciechanów, Poland ...... 17 B11 52 52N 20 38 E
Ciego de Ávila, Cuba ..... 88 B4 21 50N 78 50W
Ciénaga, Colombia ...... 92 A4 11 1N 74 15W
Cienfuegos, Cuba ....... 88 B3 22 10N 80 30W
Cieszyn, Poland ......... 17 D10 49 45N 18 35 E
Cieza, Spain ........... 21 C5 38 17N 1 23W
Cihuatlán, Mexico ....... 86 D4 19 14N 104 35W
Cijara, Embalse de, Spain .. 21 C3 39 18N 4 52W
Cijulang, Indonesia ...... 37 G13 7 42S 108 27 E
Cilacap, Indonesia ....... 37 G13 7 43S 109 0 E
Cill Chainnigh = Kilkenny, Ireland 10 D4 52 39N 7 15W
Cilo Dağı, Turkey ....... 19 G7 37 28N 43 55 E
Cima, U.S.A. ........... 79 K11 35 14N 115 30W
Cimarron, Kans., U.S.A. ... 81 G4 37 48N 100 21W
Cimarron, N. Mex., U.S.A. .. 81 G2 36 31N 104 55W
Cimarron →, U.S.A. ..... 81 G6 36 10N 96 17W
Cimişlia, Moldova ....... 17 E15 46 34N 28 44 E
Cimone, Mte., Italy ...... 22 B4 44 12N 10 42 E
Cinca →, Spain ......... 21 B6 41 26N 0 21 E
Cincar, Bos.-H. ......... 22 C7 43 55N 17 5 E
Cincinnati, U.S.A. ....... 82 F3 39 6N 84 31W
Cincinnatus, U.S.A. ...... 85 D9 42 33N 75 54W
Çine, Turkey ........... 23 F13 37 37N 28 2 E

Ciney, Belgium ......... 15 D5 50 18N 5 5 E
Cinto, Mte., France ...... 20 E8 42 24N 8 54 E
Circle, Alaska, U.S.A. ..... 68 B5 65 50N 144 4W
Circle, Mont., U.S.A. ..... 80 B2 47 25N 105 35W
Circleville, U.S.A. ....... 82 F4 39 36N 82 57W
Cirebon, Indonesia ...... 36 F3 6 45S 108 32 E
Ciremay, Indonesia ...... 37 G13 6 55S 108 27 E
Cirencester, U.K. ....... 13 F6 51 43N 1 57W
Cirium, Cyprus ......... 25 E11 34 40N 32 53 E
Cisco, U.S.A. ........... 81 J5 32 23N 98 59W
Citlaltépetl = Orizaba, Pico de,
  Mexico ........... 87 D5 19 0N 97 20W
Citrus Heights, U.S.A. .... 78 G5 38 42N 121 17W
Citrusdal, S. Africa ...... 56 E2 32 35S 19 0 E
Città di Castello, Italy .... 22 C5 43 27N 12 14 E
Ciudad Altamirano, Mexico . 86 D4 18 20N 100 40W
Ciudad Bolívar, Venezuela .. 92 B6 8 5N 63 36W
Ciudad Camargo, Mexico ... 86 B3 27 41N 105 10W
Ciudad de Valles, Mexico .. 87 C5 22 0N 99 0W
Ciudad del Carmen, Mexico . 87 D6 18 38N 91 50W
Ciudad del Este, Paraguay .. 95 B5 25 30S 54 50W
Ciudad Delicias = Delicias,
  Mexico ........... 86 B3 28 10N 105 30W
Ciudad Guayana, Venezuela . 92 B6 8 0N 62 30W
Ciudad Guerrero, Mexico ... 86 B3 28 33N 107 28W
Ciudad Guzmán, Mexico ... 86 D4 19 40N 103 30W
Ciudad Juárez, Mexico .... 86 A3 31 40N 106 28W
Ciudad Madero, Mexico ... 87 C5 22 19N 97 50W
Ciudad Mante, Mexico .... 87 C5 22 50N 99 0W
Ciudad Obregón, Mexico ... 86 B3 27 28N 109 59W
Ciudad Real, Spain ...... 21 C4 38 59N 3 55W
Ciudad Rodrigo, Spain .... 21 B2 40 35N 6 32W
Ciudad Victoria, Mexico ... 87 C5 23 41N 99 9W
Ciudadela, Spain ....... 24 B10 40 0N 3 50 E
Civitanova Marche, Italy ... 22 C5 43 18N 13 44 E
Civitavécchia, Italy ...... 22 C4 42 6N 11 48 E
Cizre, Turkey ........... 19 G7 37 19N 42 10 E
Clackmannanshire □, U.K. .. 11 E5 56 10N 3 43W
Clacton-on-Sea, U.K. ..... 13 F9 51 47N 1 11 E
Claire, L., Canada ....... 70 B6 58 35N 112 5W
Clairton, U.S.A. ......... 84 F5 40 18N 79 53W
Clallam Bay, U.S.A. ...... 78 B2 48 16N 124 16W
Clanton, U.S.A. ......... 83 J2 32 51N 86 38W
Clanwilliam, S. Africa .... 56 E2 32 11S 18 52 E
Clara, Ireland ......... 10 C4 53 21N 7 37W
Claraville, U.S.A. ....... 79 K8 35 24N 118 20W
Clare, Australia ......... 63 E2 33 50S 138 37 E
Clare, U.S.A. ........... 82 D3 43 49N 84 46W
Clare □, Ireland ......... 10 D3 52 45N 9 0W
Clare →, Ireland ....... 10 C2 53 20N 9 2W
Clare I., Ireland ......... 10 C1 53 49N 10 0W
Claremont, Calif., U.S.A. ... 79 L9 34 6N 117 43W
Claremont, N.H., U.S.A. ... 85 C12 43 23N 72 20W
Claremont Pt., Australia ... 62 A3 14 1S 143 41 E
Claremore, U.S.A. ....... 81 G7 36 19N 95 36W
Claremorris, Ireland ..... 10 C3 53 45N 9 0W
Clarence →, Australia .... 63 D5 29 25S 153 22 E
Clarence →, N.Z. ....... 59 K4 42 10S 173 56 E
Clarence, I., Chile ....... 96 G2 54 0S 72 0W
Clarence I., Antarctica .... 5 C18 61 10S 54 0W
Clarence Str., Australia ... 60 B5 12 0S 131 0 E
Clarence Town, Bahamas ... 89 B5 23 6N 74 59W
Clarendon, Pa., U.S.A. .... 84 E5 41 47N 79 6W
Clarendon, Tex., U.S.A. ... 81 H4 34 56N 100 53W
Clarenville-Shoal Harbour,
  Canada ........... 73 C9 48 10N 54 1W
Claresholm, Canada ...... 70 D6 50 0N 113 33W
Clarie Coast, Antarctica ... 5 C9 68 0S 135 0 E
Clarinda, U.S.A. ......... 80 E7 40 44N 95 2W
Clarington, Canada ...... 84 C6 43 55N 78 41W
Clarion, Iowa, U.S.A. ..... 80 D8 42 44N 93 44W
Clarion, Pa., U.S.A. ...... 84 E5 41 13N 79 23W
Clarion →, U.S.A. ....... 84 E5 41 7N 79 41W
Clarion Fracture Zone, Pac. Oc. 66 H7 20 0N 120 0W
Clark, U.S.A. ........... 80 C6 44 53N 97 44W
Clark, Pt., Canada ....... 84 B3 44 4N 81 45W
Clark Fork, U.S.A. ....... 76 B5 48 9N 116 11W
Clark Fork →, U.S.A. ..... 76 B5 48 9N 116 15W
Clarkdale, U.S.A. ....... 77 J7 34 46N 112 3W
Clarke City, Canada ...... 73 B6 50 12N 66 38W
Clarke I., Australia ...... 63 G4 40 32S 148 10 E
Clarke Ra., Australia ..... 62 J6 20 40S 148 30 E
Clark's Fork →, U.S.A. .... 76 D9 45 39N 108 43W
Clark's Harbour, Canada ... 73 D6 43 25N 65 38W
Clarks Hill, U.S.A. ....... 83 J4 33 40N 82 12W
Clarks Summit, U.S.A. .... 85 E9 41 30N 75 42W
Clarksburg, U.S.A. ...... 82 F5 39 17N 80 30W
Clarksdale, U.S.A. ...... 81 H9 34 12N 90 35W
Clarksville, Ark., U.S.A. ... 81 H8 35 28N 93 28W
Clarksville, Tenn., U.S.A. .. 83 G2 36 32N 87 21W
Clarksville, Tex., U.S.A. ... 81 J7 33 37N 95 3W
Clatskanie, U.S.A. ...... 78 D3 46 6N 123 12W
Claude, U.S.A. ......... 81 H4 35 7N 101 22W
Claveria, Phil. ......... 37 A6 18 37N 121 4 E
Clay, U.S.A. ........... 78 G5 38 17N 121 10W
Clay Center, U.S.A. ...... 80 F6 39 23N 97 8W
Claypool, U.S.A. ....... 77 K8 33 25N 110 51W
Claysburg, U.S.A. ....... 84 F6 40 17N 78 27W
Claysville, U.S.A. ....... 84 F4 40 7N 80 25W
Clayton, N. Mex., U.S.A. ... 81 G3 36 27N 103 11W
Clayton, N.Y., U.S.A. ..... 85 B8 44 14N 76 5W
Clear, C., Ireland ....... 10 E2 51 25N 9 32W
Clear, L., Canada ....... 84 A7 45 26N 77 12W
Clear Hills, Canada ...... 70 B5 56 40N 119 30W
Clear I., Ireland ......... 10 E2 51 26N 9 30W
Clear Lake, Iowa, U.S.A. ... 80 D8 43 8N 93 23W
Clear Lake, S. Dak., U.S.A. . 80 C6 44 45N 96 41W
Clear Lake Reservoir, U.S.A. . 76 F3 41 56N 121 5W
Clearfield, Pa., U.S.A. .... 84 E6 41 2N 78 27W
Clearfield, Utah, U.S.A. ... 76 F8 41 7N 112 2W
Clearlake, U.S.A. ....... 76 G2 38 57N 122 38W
Clearlake Highlands, U.S.A. . 78 G4 38 57N 122 38W
Clearwater, Canada ...... 70 C4 51 38N 120 2W
Clearwater, U.S.A. ...... 83 M4 27 58N 82 48W
Clearwater →, Alta., Canada 70 B6 56 44N 111 23W
Clearwater →, Alta., Canada 71 B6 56 44N 111 23W
Clearwater L., Canada .... 71 C9 53 34N 99 49W
Clearwater Mts., U.S.A. ... 76 C6 46 5N 115 20W
Clearwater River △, Canada . 71 B7 56 55N 109 10W
Cleburne, U.S.A. ....... 81 J6 32 21N 97 23W
Clee Hills, U.K. ......... 13 E5 52 26N 2 35W
Cleethorpes, U.K. ....... 12 D7 53 33N 0 3W
Cleeve Cloud, U.K. ...... 13 F6 51 56N 2 0W
Clemson, U.S.A. ......... 83 H4 34 41N 82 50W
Clerke Reef, Australia .... 60 C2 17 22S 119 20 E
Clermont, Australia ...... 62 C4 22 49S 147 39 E

Clermont, *U.S.A.* .......... 83 L5 28 33N 81 46W
Clermont-Ferrand, *France* .... 20 D5 45 46N 3 4 E
Clervaux, *Lux.* ......... 15 D6 50 4N 6 2 E
Clevedon, *U.K.* ........ 13 F5 51 26N 2 52W
Cleveland, *Miss., U.S.A.* .... 81 J9 33 45N 90 43W
Cleveland, *Ohio, U.S.A.* ..... 84 E3 41 30N 81 42W
Cleveland, *Okla., U.S.A.* .... 81 G6 36 19N 96 28W
Cleveland, *Tenn., U.S.A.* .... 83 H3 35 10N 84 53W
Cleveland, *Tex., U.S.A.* ..... 81 K7 30 21N 95 5W
Cleveland, C., *Australia* ..... 62 B4 19 11S 147 1 E
Cleveland, Mt., *U.S.A.* ...... 76 B7 48 56N 113 51W
Cleveland Heights, *U.S.A.* ... 84 E3 41 30N 81 34W
Clevelândia, *Brazil* ........ 95 B5 26 24S 52 23W
Clew B., *Ireland* .......... 10 C2 53 50N 9 49W
Clewiston, *U.S.A.* ........ 83 M5 26 45N 80 56W
Clifden, *Ireland* ......... 10 C1 53 29N 10 1W
Clifden, *N.Z.* ........... 59 M1 46 1S 167 42 E
Cliffdell, *U.S.A.* ........ 78 D5 46 56N 121 5W
Cliffy Hd., *Australia* ...... 61 G2 35 1S 116 29 E
Clifton, *Australia* ......... 63 D5 27 59S 151 53 E
Clifton, *Ariz., U.S.A.* ...... 77 K9 33 3N 109 18W
Clifton, *Colo., U.S.A.* ...... 77 G9 39 7N 108 25W
Clifton, *Tex., U.S.A.* ....... 81 K6 31 47N 97 35W
Clifton Beach, *Australia* .... 62 B4 16 46S 145 39 E
Climax, *Canada* .......... 71 D7 49 10N 108 20W
Clinch →, *U.S.A.* ......... 83 H3 35 53N 84 29W
Clingmans Dome, *U.S.A.* .... 83 H4 35 34N 83 30W
Clint, *U.S.A.* ........... 77 L10 31 35N 106 14W
Clinton, *B.C., Canada* ...... 70 C4 51 6N 121 35W
Clinton, *Ont., Canada* ...... 84 C3 43 37N 81 32W
Clinton, *N.Z.* ........... 59 M2 46 12S 169 23 E
Clinton, *Ark., U.S.A.* ...... 81 H8 35 36N 92 28W
Clinton, *Conn., U.S.A.* ..... 85 E12 41 17N 72 32W
Clinton, *Ill., U.S.A.* ....... 80 E10 40 9N 88 57W
Clinton, *Ind., U.S.A.* ...... 82 F2 39 40N 87 24W
Clinton, *Iowa, U.S.A.* ...... 80 E9 41 51N 90 12W
Clinton, *Mass., U.S.A.* ..... 85 D13 42 25N 71 41W
Clinton, *Miss., U.S.A.* ..... 81 J9 32 20N 90 20W
Clinton, *Mo., U.S.A.* ...... 80 F8 38 22N 93 46W
Clinton, *N.C., U.S.A.* ...... 83 H6 35 0N 78 22W
Clinton, *Okla., U.S.A.* ..... 81 H5 35 31N 98 58W
Clinton, *S.C., U.S.A.* ...... 83 H5 34 29N 81 53W
Clinton, *Tenn., U.S.A.* ..... 83 G3 36 6N 84 8W
Clinton, *Wash., U.S.A.* ..... 78 C4 47 59N 122 21W
Clinton C., *Australia* ...... 62 C5 22 30S 150 45 E
Clinton Colden L., *Canada* ... 68 B9 63 58N 107 27W
Clintonville, *U.S.A.* ....... 80 C10 44 37N 88 46W
Clipperton, I., *Pac. Oc.* .... 65 F17 10 18N 109 13W
Clisham, *U.K.* ........... 11 D2 57 57N 6 49W
Clitheroe, *U.K.* .......... 12 D5 53 53N 2 22W
Clo-oose, *Canada* ........ 78 B2 48 39N 124 49W
Cloates, Pt., *Australia* ..... 60 D1 22 43S 113 40 E
Clocolan, *S. Africa* ....... 57 D4 28 55S 27 34 E
Clodomira, *Argentina* ...... 94 B3 27 35S 64 14W
Clogher Hd., *Ireland* ...... 10 C5 53 48N 6 14W
Clonakilty, *Ireland* ....... 10 E3 51 37N 8 53W
Clonakilty B., *Ireland* ...... 10 E3 51 35N 8 51W
Cloncurry, *Australia* ....... 62 C3 20 40S 140 28 E
Cloncurry →, *Australia* ..... 62 B3 18 37S 140 40 E
Clondalkin, *Ireland* ....... 10 C5 53 19N 6 25W
Clones, *Ireland* .......... 10 B4 54 11N 7 15W
Clonmel, *Ireland* ......... 10 D4 52 21N 7 42W
Cloquet, *U.S.A.* .......... 80 B8 46 43N 92 28W
Clorinda, *Argentina* ....... 94 B4 25 16S 57 45W
Cloud Bay, *Canada* ....... 72 C2 48 5N 89 26W
Cloud Peak, *U.S.A.* ....... 76 D10 44 23N 107 11W
Cloudcroft, *U.S.A.* ....... 77 K11 32 58N 105 45W
Cloverdale, *U.S.A.* ....... 78 G4 38 48N 123 1W
Clovis, *Calif., U.S.A.* ...... 78 J7 36 49N 119 42W
Clovis, *N. Mex., U.S.A.* .... 81 H3 34 24N 103 12W
Cloyne, *Canada* .......... 84 B7 44 49N 77 11W
Cluj-Napoca, *Romania* ..... 17 E12 46 47N 23 38 E
Clunes, *Australia* ......... 63 F3 37 20S 143 45 E
Clutha →, *N.Z.* .......... 59 M2 46 20S 169 49 E
Clwyd →, *U.K.* .......... 12 D4 53 19N 3 31W
Clyde, *Canada* .......... 70 C6 54 9N 113 39W
Clyde, *N.Z.* ............ 59 L2 45 12S 169 20 E
Clyde, *U.S.A.* ........... 84 C8 43 5N 76 52W
Clyde →, *U.K.* ........... 11 F4 55 55N 4 30W
Clyde, Firth of, *U.K.* ...... 11 F3 55 22N 5 1W
Clyde Muirshiel △, *U.K.* .... 11 F4 55 50N 4 40W
Clyde River, *Canada* ...... 69 A13 70 30N 68 30W
Clydebank, *U.K.* ......... 11 F4 55 54N 4 23W
Clymer, *N.Y., U.S.A.* ...... 84 D5 42 1N 79 37W
Clymer, *Pa., U.S.A.* ....... 84 D5 40 40N 79 1W
Coachella, *U.S.A.* ........ 79 M10 33 41N 116 10W
Coachella Canal, *U.S.A.* .... 79 N12 32 43N 114 57W
Coahoma, *U.S.A.* ........ 81 J4 32 18N 101 18W
Coahuayana →, *Mexico* .... 86 D4 18 41N 103 45W
Coahuila □, *Mexico* ....... 86 B4 27 0N 103 0W
Coal →, *Canada* ......... 70 B3 59 39N 126 57W
Coalane, *Mozam.* ........ 55 F4 17 48S 37 2 E
Coalcomán, *Mexico* ....... 86 D4 18 40N 103 10W
Coaldale, *Canada* ........ 70 D6 49 45N 112 35W
Coalgate, *U.S.A.* ......... 81 H6 34 32N 96 13W
Coalinga, *U.S.A.* ......... 78 J6 36 9N 120 21W
Coalisland, *U.K.* ......... 10 B5 54 33N 6 42W
Coalville, *U.K.* .......... 12 E6 52 44N 1 23W
Coalville, *U.S.A.* ......... 76 F8 40 55N 111 24W
Coamo, *Puerto Rico* ....... 89 d 18 5N 66 22W
Coari, *Brazil* ............ 92 D6 4 8S 63 7W
Coast □, *Kenya* .......... 54 C4 2 40S 39 45 E
Coast Mts., *Canada* ....... 70 C3 55 0N 129 20W
Coast Ranges, *U.S.A.* ...... 78 G4 39 0N 123 0W
Coatbridge, *U.K.* ......... 11 F4 55 52N 4 6W
Coatepec, *Mexico* ........ 87 D5 19 27N 96 58W
Coatepeque, *Guatemala* .... 88 D1 14 46N 91 55W
Coatesville, *U.S.A.* ....... 82 F8 39 59N 75 50W
Coaticook, *Canada* ....... 85 A13 45 10N 71 46W
Coats I., *Canada* ......... 69 B11 62 30N 83 0W
Coats Land, *Antarctica* .... 5 D17 77 0S 25 0W
Coatzacoalcos, *Mexico* .... 87 D6 18 7N 94 25W
Coba, *Mexico* ........... 87 C7 20 31N 87 39W
Cobalt, *Canada* .......... 72 C4 47 25N 79 42W
Cobán, *Guatemala* ........ 88 C1 15 30N 90 21W
Cobar, *Australia* ......... 63 E4 31 27S 145 48 E
Cóbh, *Ireland* ........... 10 E3 51 51N 8 17W
Cobija, *Bolivia* .......... 92 F5 11 0S 68 50W
Cobleskill, *U.S.A.* ........ 85 D10 42 41N 74 29W
Coboconk, *Canada* ....... 84 B6 44 39N 78 48W
Cobourg, *Canada* ........ 84 C6 43 58N 78 10W
Cobourg ○, *Canada* ...... 60 B5 11 20S 132 15 E
Cobourg Pen., *Australia* ... 60 B5 11 20S 132 15 E
Cobram, *Australia* ....... 63 F4 35 54S 145 40 E
Cóbué, *Mozam.* .......... 55 E3 12 0S 34 58 E
Coburg, *Germany* ........ 16 C6 50 15N 10 58 E
Cocanada = Kakinada, *India* .. 41 L13 16 57N 82 11 E
Cochabamba, *Bolivia* ...... 92 G5 17 26S 66 10W

Cochemane, *Mozam.* ........ 55 F3 17 0S 32 54 E
Cochin, *India* ............ 40 Q10 9 58N 76 20 E
Cochin China = Nam-Phan,
 *Vietnam* ............... 39 G6 10 30N 106 0 E
Cochran, *U.S.A.* .......... 83 J4 32 23N 83 21W
Cochrane, *Alta., Canada* .... 70 C6 51 11N 114 30W
Cochrane, *Ont., Canada* .... 72 C3 49 0N 81 0W
Cochrane, *Chile* .......... 96 F2 47 15S 72 33W
Cochrane →, *Canada* ...... 71 B8 59 0N 103 40W
Cochrane, L., *Chile* ....... 96 F2 47 10S 72 0W
Cochranton, *U.S.A.* ....... 84 E4 41 31N 80 3W
Cockburn, *Australia* ...... 63 E3 32 5S 141 0 E
Cockburn, Canal, *Chile* .... 96 G2 54 30S 72 0W
Cockburn I., *Canada* ...... 72 C3 45 55N 83 22W
Cockburn Ra., *Australia* .... 60 C4 15 46S 128 0 E
Cockermouth, *U.K.* ....... 12 C4 54 40N 3 22W
Cocklebiddy, *Australia* .... 61 F4 32 0S 126 3 E
Coco →, *Cent. Amer.* ...... 88 D3 15 0N 83 8W
Cocoa, *U.S.A.* ........... 83 L5 28 21N 80 44W
Cocobeach, *Gabon* ....... 52 D1 0 59N 9 34 E
Cocos B., *Trin. & Tob.* ..... 93 K15 10 25N 61 2W
Cocos Is., *Ind. Oc.* ....... 64 J1 12 10S 96 55 E
Cod, C., *U.S.A.* .......... 82 D10 42 5N 70 10W
Codajás, *Brazil* .......... 92 D6 3 55S 62 0W
Codó, *Brazil* ............ 93 D10 4 30S 43 55W
Cody, *U.S.A.* ........... 76 D9 44 32N 109 3W
Coe Hill, *Canada* ......... 84 B7 44 52N 77 50W
Coelemu, *Chile* .......... 94 D1 36 30S 72 48W
Coen, *Australia* .......... 62 A3 13 52S 143 12 E
Cœur d'Alene, *U.S.A.* ...... 76 C5 47 45N 116 51W
Cœur d'Alene L., *U.S.A.* .... 76 C5 47 32N 116 48W
Coevorden, *Neths.* ....... 15 B6 52 40N 6 44 E
Cofete, *Canary Is.* ....... 24 F5 28 6N 14 23W
Coffeyville, *U.S.A.* ....... 81 G7 37 2N 95 37W
Coffin B., *Australia* ....... 63 E2 34 38S 135 28 E
Coffin Bay, *Australia* ...... 63 E2 34 37S 135 29 E
Coffin Bay △, *Australia* .... 63 E2 34 34S 135 19 E
Coffin Bay Peninsula, *Australia* . 63 E2 34 32S 135 15 E
Coffs Harbour, *Australia* ... 63 E5 30 16S 153 5 E
Cofre de Perote △, *Mexico* .. 87 D5 19 29N 97 8W
Cognac, *France* .......... 20 D3 45 41N 0 20W
Cohocton, *U.S.A.* ........ 84 D7 42 30N 77 30W
Cohocton →, *U.S.A.* ...... 84 D7 42 9N 77 6W
Cohoes, *U.S.A.* .......... 85 D11 42 46N 73 42W
Cohuna, *Australia* ........ 63 F3 35 45S 144 15 E
Coiba, I., *Panama* ........ 88 E3 7 30N 81 40W
Coig →, *Argentina* ....... 96 G3 51 0S 69 10W
Coigeach, Rubha, *U.K.* ..... 11 C3 58 6N 5 26W
Coihaique, *Chile* ......... 96 F2 45 30S 71 45W
Coimbatore, *India* ........ 40 P10 11 2N 76 59 E
Coimbra, *Brazil* .......... 92 G7 19 55S 57 48W
Coimbra, *Portugal* ........ 21 B1 40 15N 8 27W
Coin, *Spain* ............. 21 D3 36 40N 4 48W
Coipasa, Salar de, *Bolivia* ... 92 G5 19 26S 68 9W
Cojimies, *Ecuador* ........ 92 C3 0 20N 80 0W
Cojutepeque, *El Salv.* ...... 88 D2 13 41N 88 54W
Cokeville, *U.S.A.* ......... 76 E8 42 5N 110 57W
Colac, *Australia* .......... 63 F3 38 21S 143 35 E
Colatina, *Brazil* .......... 93 G10 19 32S 40 37W
Colbeck, C., *Antarctica* .... 5 D13 77 6S 157 48W
Colborne, *Canada* ........ 84 C7 44 0N 77 53W
Colby, *U.S.A.* ........... 80 F4 39 24N 101 3W
Colchester, *U.K.* ......... 13 F8 51 54N 0 55 E
Cold L., *Canada* ......... 71 C7 54 33N 110 5W
Coldstream, *Canada* ...... 70 C5 50 13N 119 11W
Coldstream, *U.K.* ........ 11 F6 55 39N 2 15W
Coldwater, *Canada* ....... 84 B5 44 42N 79 40W
Coldwater, *Kans., U.S.A.* ... 81 G5 37 16N 99 20W
Coldwater, *Mich., U.S.A.* ... 82 E3 41 57N 85 0W
Colebrook, *U.S.A.* ........ 85 B13 44 54N 71 30W
Coleman, *U.S.A.* ......... 81 K5 31 50N 99 26W
Coleman →, *Australia* ..... 62 B3 15 6S 141 38 E
Colenso, *S. Africa* ........ 57 D4 28 44S 29 50 E
Coleraine, *Australia* ....... 63 F3 37 36S 141 40 E
Coleraine, *U.K.* .......... 10 A5 55 8N 6 41W
Coleridge, L., *N.Z.* ....... 59 K3 43 17S 171 30 E
Colesberg, *S. Africa* ...... 56 E4 30 45S 25 5 E
Coleville, *U.S.A.* ......... 78 G7 38 34N 119 30W
Colfax, *Calif., U.S.A.* ...... 78 F6 39 6N 120 57W
Colfax, *La., U.S.A.* ....... 81 K8 31 31N 92 42W
Colfax, *Wash., U.S.A.* ..... 76 C5 46 53N 117 22W
Colhué Huapi, L., *Argentina* .. 96 F3 45 30S 69 0W
Coligny, *S. Africa* ........ 57 D4 26 17S 26 15 E
Colima, *Mexico* .......... 86 D4 19 14N 103 43W
Colima □, *Mexico* ........ 86 D4 19 10N 103 40W
Colima, Nevado de, *Mexico* . 86 D4 19 35N 103 45W
Colina, *Chile* ........... 94 C1 33 13S 70 45W
Colinas, *Brazil* .......... 93 E10 6 0S 44 10W
Coll, *U.K.* ............. 11 E2 56 39N 6 34W
Collaguasi, *Chile* ........ 94 A2 21 5S 68 45W
Collarenebri, *Australia* .... 63 D4 29 33S 148 34 E
Colleen Bawn, *Zimbabwe* .. 55 G2 21 0S 29 12 E
College Park, *U.S.A.* ...... 83 J3 33 40N 84 27W
College Station, *U.S.A.* .... 81 K6 30 37N 96 21W
Collie, *Australia* ......... 61 F2 33 22S 116 8 E
Collier B., *Australia* ....... 60 C3 16 10S 124 15 E
Collier Ra., *Australia* ...... 61 D2 24 45S 119 10 E
Collier Range △, *Australia* .. 61 D2 24 39S 119 7 E
Collina, Passo di, *Italy* .... 22 B4 44 2N 10 56 E
Collingwood, *Canada* ..... 84 B4 44 29N 80 13W
Collingwood, *N.Z.* ....... 59 J4 40 41S 172 40 E
Collins, *Canada* .......... 72 B2 50 17N 89 27W
Collinsville, *Australia* ..... 62 C4 20 30S 147 56 E
Collipulli, *Chile* ......... 94 D1 37 55S 72 30W
Collooney, *Ireland* ....... 10 B3 54 11N 8 29W
Colmar, *France* .......... 20 B7 48 5N 7 20 E
Colo →, *Australia* ........ 63 E5 33 25S 150 52 E
Colom, I. d'en, *Spain* ..... 24 B11 39 58N 4 16 E
Coloma, *U.S.A.* ......... 78 G6 38 48N 120 53W
Colomb-Béchar = Béchar, *Algeria* . 50 B5 31 38N 2 18W
Colombia ■, *S. Amer.* ..... 92 C4 3 45N 73 0W
Colombian Basin, *S. Amer.* .. 66 H12 14 0N 76 0W
Colombo, *Sri Lanka* ....... 40 R11 6 56N 79 58 E
Colón, *Buenos Aires, Argentina* . 94 C3 33 53S 61 7W
Colón, *Entre Ríos, Argentina* . 94 C4 32 12S 58 10W
Colón, *Cuba* ............ 88 B3 22 42N 80 54W
Colón, *Panama* .......... 88 E4 9 20N 79 54W
Colón, Arch. de, *Ecuador* ... 90 D1 0 0 91 0W
Colònia de Sant Jordi, *Spain* . 24 B9 39 19N 2 59 E
Colonia del Sacramento,
 *Uruguay* .............. 94 C4 34 25S 57 50W
Colonia Dora, *Argentina* .... 94 B3 28 34S 62 59W
Colonial Beach, *U.S.A.* .... 82 F7 38 15N 76 58W
Colonie, *U.S.A.* ......... 85 D11 42 43N 73 50W
Colonsay, *Canada* ........ 71 C7 51 59N 105 52W

Colonsay, *U.K.* .......... 11 E2 56 5N 6 12W
Colorado □, *U.S.A.* ....... 77 G10 39 30N 105 30W
Colorado →, *Argentina* .... 96 D4 39 50S 62 8W
Colorado →, *N. Amer.* ..... 77 L6 31 45N 114 40W
Colorado →, *U.S.A.* ....... 81 L7 28 36N 95 59W
Colorado City, *U.S.A.* ..... 81 J4 32 24N 100 52W
Colorado Plateau, *U.S.A.* ... 77 H8 37 0N 111 0W
Colorado River Aqueduct, *U.S.A.* . 79 L12 34 17N 114 10W
Colorado Springs, *U.S.A.* ... 80 F2 38 50N 104 49W
Colotlán, *Mexico* ........ 86 C4 22 6N 103 16W
Colstrip, *U.S.A.* ......... 76 D10 45 53N 106 38W
Colton, *U.S.A.* .......... 85 B10 44 33N 74 56W
Columbia, *Ky., U.S.A.* ..... 82 G3 37 6N 85 18W
Columbia, *La., U.S.A.* ..... 81 J8 32 6N 92 5W
Columbia, *Miss., U.S.A.* .... 81 K10 31 15N 89 50W
Columbia, *Mo., U.S.A.* ..... 80 F8 38 57N 92 20W
Columbia, *Pa., U.S.A.* ..... 84 F8 40 2N 76 30W
Columbia, *S.C., U.S.A.* .... 83 J5 34 0N 81 2W
Columbia, *Tenn., U.S.A.* ... 83 H2 35 37N 87 2W
Columbia →, *N. Amer.* .... 78 D2 46 15N 124 5W
Columbia, C., *Canada* ..... 4 A4 83 6N 69 57W
Columbia, District of □, *U.S.A.* . 82 F7 38 55N 77 0W
Columbia, Mt., *Canada* .... 70 C5 52 8N 117 20W
Columbia Basin, *U.S.A.* .... 76 C4 46 45N 119 5W
Columbia Falls, *U.S.A.* .... 76 B6 48 23N 114 11W
Columbia Mts., *Canada* .... 70 C5 52 0N 119 0W
Columbia Plateau, *U.S.A.* ... 76 D5 44 0N 117 30W
Columbiana, *U.S.A.* ...... 84 F4 40 53N 80 42W
Columbretes, Is., *Spain* .... 21 C6 39 50N 0 50 E
Columbus, *Ga., U.S.A.* .... 83 J3 32 28N 84 59W
Columbus, *Ind., U.S.A.* .... 82 F3 39 13N 85 55W
Columbus, *Kans., U.S.A.* ... 81 G7 37 10N 94 50W
Columbus, *Miss., U.S.A.* ... 83 J1 33 30N 88 25W
Columbus, *Mont., U.S.A.* ... 76 D9 45 38N 109 15W
Columbus, *N. Mex., U.S.A.* .. 77 L10 31 50N 107 38W
Columbus, *Nebr., U.S.A.* ... 80 E6 41 26N 97 22W
Columbus, *Ohio, U.S.A.* ... 82 F4 39 58N 83 0W
Columbus, *Tex., U.S.A.* .... 81 L6 29 42N 96 33W
Colusa, *U.S.A.* .......... 78 F4 39 13N 122 1W
Colville, *U.S.A.* ......... 76 B5 48 33N 117 54W
Colville →, *U.S.A.* ....... 68 A4 70 25N 150 30W
Colville, C., *N.Z.* ........ 59 G5 36 29S 175 21 E
Colwood, *Canada* ........ 78 B3 48 26N 123 29W
Colwyn Bay, *U.K.* ........ 12 D4 53 18N 3 44W
Comácchio, *Italy* ........ 22 B5 44 42N 12 11 E
Comallo, *Argentina* ....... 96 E2 41 0S 70 5W
Comanche, *U.S.A.* ........ 81 K5 31 54N 98 36W
Comandante Ferraz, *Antarctica* . 5 C18 62 30S 58 0W
Comayagua, *Honduras* .... 88 D2 14 25N 87 37W
Combahee →, *U.S.A.* ...... 83 J5 32 30N 80 31W
Combarbalá, *Chile* ....... 94 C1 31 11S 71 2W
Combe Martin, *U.K.* ...... 13 F3 51 12N 4 3W
Comber, *Canada* ......... 84 D2 42 14N 82 33W
Comber, *U.K.* ........... 10 B6 54 33N 5 45W
Combermere, *Canada* ..... 84 A7 45 22N 77 37W
Comblain-au-Pont, *Belgium* . 15 D5 50 29N 5 35 E
Comeragh Mts., *Ireland* .... 10 D4 52 18N 7 34W
Comet, *Australia* ........ 62 C4 23 36S 148 38 E
Comilla, *Bangla.* ........ 41 H17 23 28N 91 10 E
Comino, *Malta* .......... 25 C1 36 1N 14 20 E
Comino, C., *Italy* ........ 22 D3 40 32N 9 49 E
Comitán, *Mexico* ........ 87 D6 16 18N 92 9W
Commerce, *Ga., U.S.A.* .... 83 H4 34 12N 83 28W
Commerce, *Tex., U.S.A.* ... 81 J7 33 15N 95 54W
Committee B., *Canada* ..... 69 B11 68 30N 86 30W
Commonwealth B., *Antarctica* . 5 C10 67 0S 144 0 E
Commoron Cr. →, *Australia* . 63 D5 28 22S 150 8 E
Communism Pk. = Kommunizma,
 Pik, *Tajikistan* ......... 28 F8 39 0N 72 2 E
Como, *Italy* ............ 20 D8 45 47N 9 5 E
Como, Lago di, *Italy* ...... 20 D8 46 0N 9 11 E
Comodoro Rivadavia, *Argentina* . 96 F3 45 50S 67 40W
Comorin, C., *India* ....... 40 Q10 8 3N 77 40 E
Comoro Is. = Comoros ■,
 *Ind. Oc.* .............. 49 H8 12 10S 44 15 E
Comoros ■, *Ind. Oc.* ...... 49 H8 12 10S 44 15 E
Comox, *Canada* ......... 70 D4 49 42N 124 55W
Compiègne, *France* ....... 20 B5 49 24N 2 50 E
Compostela, *Mexico* ...... 86 C4 21 15N 104 53W
Comprida, I., *Brazil* ....... 95 A6 24 50S 47 42W
Compton, *Canada* ........ 85 A13 45 14N 71 49W
Compton, *U.S.A.* ........ 79 M8 33 54N 118 13W
Comrat, *Moldova* ........ 17 E15 46 18N 28 40 E
Con Cuong, *Vietnam* ...... 38 C5 19 2N 104 54 E
Con Dao △, *Vietnam* ...... 39 H6 8 42N 106 35 E
Con Son, *Vietnam* ....... 39 H6 8 41N 106 37 E
Conakry, *Guinea* ........ 50 G3 9 29N 13 49W
Conara, *Australia* ........ 63 G4 41 50S 147 26 E
Concarneau, *France* ...... 20 C2 47 52N 3 56W
Conceição, *Mozam.* ...... 55 F4 18 47S 36 7 E
Conceição da Barra, *Brazil* .. 93 G11 18 35S 39 45W
Conceição do Araguaia, *Brazil* . 93 E9 8 0S 49 2W
Concepción, *Argentina* .... 94 B2 27 20S 65 35W
Concepción, *Bolivia* ...... 92 G6 16 15S 62 8W
Concepción, *Chile* ....... 94 D1 36 50S 73 0W
Concepción, *Mexico* ...... 87 D6 18 15N 90 5W
Concepción, *Paraguay* .... 94 A4 23 22S 57 26W
Concepción □, *Chile* ...... 94 D1 37 0S 72 30W
Concepción →, *Mexico* .... 86 A2 30 32N 113 2W
Concepción, Est. de, *Chile* .. 96 G2 50 30S 74 55W
Concepción, L., *Bolivia* .... 92 G6 17 20S 61 20W
Concepción, Punta, *Mexico* . 86 B2 26 55N 111 59W
Concepción del Oro, *Mexico* . 86 C4 24 40N 101 30W
Concepción del Uruguay,
 *Argentina* ............. 94 C4 32 35S 58 20W
Conception, Pt., *U.S.A.* .... 79 L6 34 27N 120 28W
Conception B., *Canada* .... 73 C9 47 45N 53 0W
Conception, *Namibia* ...... 56 C1 23 55S 14 22 E
Conception I., *Bahamas* .... 89 B4 23 52N 75 9W
Concession, *Zimbabwe* .... 55 F3 17 27S 30 56 E
Conchas Dam, *U.S.A.* ..... 81 H2 35 22N 104 11W
Concho, *U.S.A.* ......... 77 J9 34 28N 109 36W
Concho →, *U.S.A.* ....... 81 K5 31 34N 99 43W
Conchos →, *Chihuahua, Mexico* . 86 B4 29 32N 105 0W
Conchos →, *Tamaulipas, Mexico* . 87 B5 25 9N 98 35W
Concord, *Calif., U.S.A.* .... 78 H4 37 59N 122 2W
Concord, *N.C., U.S.A.* ..... 83 H5 35 25N 80 35W
Concord, *N.H., U.S.A.* ..... 85 C13 43 12N 71 32W
Concordia, *Argentina* ..... 94 C4 31 20S 58 2W
Concórdia, *Brazil* ........ 92 D5 4 36S 66 36W
Concordia, *Mexico* ....... 86 C3 23 18N 106 2W
Concordia, *U.S.A.* ....... 80 F6 39 34N 97 40W
Concrete, *U.S.A.* ........ 76 B3 48 32N 121 45W
Condamine, *Australia* ..... 63 D5 26 56S 150 9 E
Condeúba, *Brazil* ........ 93 F10 14 52S 42 0W
Condobolin, *Australia* ..... 63 E4 33 4S 147 6 E

Condon, *U.S.A.* ......... 76 D3 45 14N 120 11W
Conegliano, *Italy* ........ 22 B5 45 53N 12 18 E
Conejera, I. = Conills, I. des,
 *Spain* ................ 24 B9 39 11N 2 58 E
Conejos, *Mexico* ......... 86 B4 26 14N 103 53W
Confuso →, *Paraguay* ..... 94 B4 25 9S 57 34W
Congleton, *U.K.* ......... 12 D5 53 10N 2 13W
Congo (Kinshasa) = Congo, Dem.
 Rep. of the ■, *Africa* ..... 52 E4 3 0S 23 0 E
Congo ■, *Africa* ......... 52 E3 1 0S 16 0 E
Congo →, *Africa* ......... 52 F2 6 4S 12 24 E
Congo, Dem. Rep. of the ■,
 *Africa* ................ 52 E4 3 0S 23 0 E
Congo Basin, *Africa* ...... 52 E4 0 10S 24 30 E
Congonhas, *Brazil* ....... 95 A7 20 30S 43 52W
Congress, *U.S.A.* ........ 77 J7 34 9N 112 51W
Conills, I. des, *Spain* ...... 24 B9 39 11N 2 58 E
Coniston, *Canada* ........ 72 C3 46 29N 80 51W
Conjeeveram = Kanchipuram,
 *India* ................ 40 N11 12 52N 79 45 E
Conklin, *Canada* ......... 71 B6 55 38N 111 5W
Conklin, *U.S.A.* ......... 85 D9 42 2N 75 49W
Conn, L., *Ireland* ........ 10 C2 54 3N 9 15W
Connacht □, *Ireland* ...... 10 C2 53 43N 9 12W
Conneaut, *U.S.A.* ........ 84 E4 41 57N 80 34W
Connecticut □, *U.S.A.* .... 85 E12 41 30N 72 45W
Connecticut →, *U.S.A.* .... 85 E12 41 16N 72 20W
Connell, *U.S.A.* ......... 76 C4 46 40N 118 52W
Connellsville, *U.S.A.* ..... 84 F5 40 1N 79 35W
Connemara, *Ireland* ...... 10 C2 53 29N 9 45W
Connemara △, *Ireland* ..... 10 C2 53 32N 9 52W
Connersville, *U.S.A.* ...... 82 F3 39 39N 85 8W
Connors Ra., *Australia* .... 62 C4 21 40S 149 10 E
Conquest, *Canada* ....... 71 C7 51 32N 107 14W
Conrad, *U.S.A.* ......... 76 B8 48 10N 111 57W
Conran, C., *Australia* ..... 63 F4 37 49S 148 44 E
Conroe, *U.S.A.* ......... 81 K7 30 19N 95 27W
Consecon, *Canada* ....... 84 C7 44 0N 77 31W
Conselheiro Lafaiete, *Brazil* . 95 A7 20 40S 43 48W
Consett, *U.K.* .......... 12 C6 54 51N 1 50W
Consort, *Canada* ........ 71 C6 52 1N 110 46W
Constance = Konstanz, *Germany* . 16 E5 47 40N 9 10 E
Constance, L. = Bodensee,
 *Europe* ............... 20 C8 47 35N 9 25 E
Constanța, *Romania* ...... 17 F15 44 14N 28 38 E
Constantia, *U.S.A.* ....... 85 C8 43 15N 76 1W
Constantine, *Algeria* ...... 50 A7 36 25N 6 42 E
Constitución, *Chile* ....... 94 D1 35 20S 72 30W
Constitución, *Uruguay* .... 94 C4 31 0S 57 50W
Constitucion de 1857 △, *Mexico* . 86 A1 32 4N 115 55W
Consul, *Canada* ......... 71 D7 49 20N 109 30W
Contact, *U.S.A.* ......... 76 F6 41 46N 114 45W
Contai, *India* ........... 43 J12 21 54N 87 46 E
Contamana, *Peru* ........ 92 E4 7 19S 74 55W
Contas →, *Brazil* ........ 93 F11 14 17S 39 1W
Contoocook, *U.S.A.* ...... 85 C13 43 13N 71 45W
Contra Costa, *Mozam.* .... 57 D5 25 9S 33 30 E
Contwoyto L., *Canada* .... 68 B8 65 42N 110 50W
Conway = Conwy, *U.K.* .... 12 D4 53 17N 3 50W
Conway = Conwy →, *U.K.* .. 12 D4 53 17N 3 50W
Conway, *Australia* ........ 62 J6 20 24S 148 41 E
Conway, *Ark., U.S.A.* ..... 81 H8 35 5N 92 26W
Conway, *N.H., U.S.A.* ..... 85 C13 43 59N 71 7W
Conway, *S.C., U.S.A.* ..... 83 J6 33 51N 79 3W
Conway, C., *Australia* ..... 62 J6 20 34S 148 46 E
Conway, L., *Australia* ..... 63 D2 28 17S 135 35 E
Conwy, *U.K.* ........... 12 D4 53 17N 3 50W
Conwy □, *U.K.* .......... 12 D4 53 10N 3 44W
Conwy →, *U.K.* ......... 12 D4 53 17N 3 50W
Coober Pedy, *Australia* .... 63 D1 29 1S 134 43 E
Cooch Behar = Koch Bihar, *India* . 41 F16 26 22N 89 29 E
Cooinda, *Australia* ....... 60 B5 13 15S 130 5 E
Cook, *Australia* ......... 61 F5 30 37S 130 25 E
Cook, *U.S.A.* ........... 80 B8 47 49N 92 39W
Cook, B., *Chile* ......... 96 H3 55 10S 70 0W
Cook, C., *Canada* ........ 70 C3 50 8N 127 55W
Cook, Mt. = Aoraki Mount Cook,
 *N.Z.* ................ 59 K3 43 36S 170 9 E
Cook Inlet, *U.S.A.* ....... 68 C4 60 0N 152 0W
Cook Is., *Pac. Oc.* ....... 65 J12 17 0S 160 0W
Cook Strait, *N.Z.* ........ 59 J5 41 15S 174 29 E
Cookeville, *U.S.A.* ....... 83 G3 36 10N 85 30W
Cookhouse, *S. Africa* ..... 56 E4 32 44S 25 47 E
Cookshire, *Canada* ....... 85 A13 45 25N 71 38W
Cookstown, *U.K.* ........ 10 B5 54 39N 6 45W
Cooksville, *Canada* ....... 84 C5 43 36N 79 35W
Cooktown, *Australia* ...... 62 B4 15 30S 145 16 E
Coolabah, *Australia* ...... 63 E4 31 1S 146 43 E
Cooladdi, *Australia* ....... 63 D4 26 37S 145 23 E
Coolah, *Australia* ........ 63 E4 31 48S 149 41 E
Coolamon, *Australia* ...... 63 E4 34 46S 147 8 E
Coolgardie, *Australia* ..... 61 F3 30 55S 121 8 E
Coolidge, *U.S.A.* ........ 77 K8 32 59N 111 31W
Coolidge Dam, *U.S.A.* .... 77 K8 33 0N 110 20W
Cooloola △, *Australia* ..... 63 D5 26 13S 153 2 E
Cooma, *Australia* ........ 63 F4 36 12S 149 8 E
Coon Rapids, *U.S.A.* ...... 80 C8 45 9N 93 19W
Coonabarabran, *Australia* .. 63 E4 31 14S 149 18 E
Coonamble, *Australia* ..... 63 E4 30 56S 148 27 E
Coonana, *Australia* ....... 61 F3 31 0S 123 0 E
Coondapoor, *India* ....... 40 N9 13 42N 74 40 E
Cooninie, L., *Australia* ..... 63 D2 26 4S 139 59 E
Cooper, *U.S.A.* ......... 81 J7 33 23N 95 42W
Cooper Cr. →, *Australia* ... 63 D2 28 37S 137 46 E
Cooperstown, *N. Dak., U.S.A.* . 80 B5 47 27N 98 8W
Cooperstown, *N.Y., U.S.A.* .. 85 D10 42 42N 74 56W
Coorabie, *Australia* ...... 61 F5 31 54S 132 18 E
Coorong, The, *Australia* ... 63 F2 35 50S 139 20 E
Coorow, *Australia* ....... 61 E2 29 53S 116 2 E
Cooroy, *Australia* ........ 63 D5 26 22S 152 54 E
Coos Bay, *U.S.A.* ........ 76 E1 43 22N 124 13W
Coosa →, *U.S.A.* ........ 83 J2 32 30N 86 16W
Cootamundra, *Australia* ... 63 E4 34 36S 148 1 E
Cootehill, *Ireland* ....... 10 B4 54 4N 7 5W
Copahue Paso, *Argentina* .. 94 D1 37 49S 71 8W
Copainalá, *Mexico* ....... 87 D6 17 8N 93 11W
Copake Falls, *U.S.A.* ..... 85 D11 42 7N 73 31W
Copán, *Honduras* ........ 88 D2 14 50N 89 9W
Cope, *U.S.A.* ........... 80 F3 39 40N 102 51W
Copenhagen = København,
 *Denmark* ............. 9 J15 55 41N 12 34 E
Copenhagen, *U.S.A.* ...... 85 C9 43 54N 75 41W
Copiapó, *Chile* .......... 94 B1 27 30S 70 20W
Copiapó →, *Chile* ........ 94 B1 27 19S 70 56W
Coplay, *U.S.A.* ......... 85 F9 40 44N 75 29W
Copp L., *Canada* ........ 70 A6 60 14N 114 40W
Coppename →, *Suriname* ... 93 B7 5 48N 55 55W

| | | | |
|---|---|---|---|
| Copper Harbor, U.S.A. | 82 B2 | 47 28N | 87 53W |
| Copper Queen, Zimbabwe | 55 F2 | 17 29S | 29 18 E |
| Copperas Cove, U.S.A. | 81 K6 | 31 8N | 97 54W |
| Copperbelt □, Zambia | 55 E2 | 13 15S | 27 30 E |
| Coppermine →, Canada | 68 B8 | 67 50N | 115 5W |
| Coppermine = Kugluktuk, Canada | 68 B8 | 67 50N | 115 5W |
| Copperopolis, U.S.A. | 78 H6 | 37 58N | 120 38W |
| Coquet →, U.K. | 12 B6 | 55 20N | 1 32W |
| Coquille, U.S.A. | 76 E1 | 43 11N | 124 11W |
| Coquimbo, Chile | 94 C1 | 30 0S | 71 20W |
| Coquimbo □, Chile | 94 C1 | 31 0S | 71 0W |
| Corabia, Romania | 17 G13 | 43 48N | 24 30 E |
| Coracora, Peru | 92 G4 | 15 5S | 73 45W |
| Coraki, Australia | 63 D5 | 28 59S | 153 17 E |
| Coral, U.S.A. | 84 F5 | 40 29N | 79 10W |
| Coral Gables, U.S.A. | 83 N5 | 25 45N | 80 16W |
| Coral Harbour, Canada | 69 B11 | 64 8N | 83 10W |
| Coral Sea, Pac. Oc. | 64 J7 | 15 0S | 150 0 E |
| Coral Springs, U.S.A. | 83 M5 | 26 16N | 80 13W |
| Coraopolis, U.S.A. | 84 F4 | 40 31N | 80 10W |
| Corato, Italy | 22 D7 | 41 9N | 16 25 E |
| Corbin, U.S.A. | 82 G3 | 36 57N | 84 6W |
| Corby, U.K. | 13 E7 | 52 30N | 0 41W |
| Corcaigh = Cork, Ireland | 10 E3 | 51 54N | 8 29W |
| Corcoran, U.S.A. | 78 J7 | 36 6N | 119 33W |
| Corcovado △, Costa Rica | 88 E3 | 8 33N | 83 35W |
| Corcubión, Spain | 21 A1 | 42 56N | 9 12W |
| Cordele, U.S.A. | 83 K4 | 31 58N | 83 47W |
| Cordell, U.S.A. | 81 H5 | 35 17N | 98 59W |
| Córdoba, Argentina | 94 C3 | 31 20S | 64 10W |
| Córdoba, Mexico | 87 D5 | 18 50N | 97 0W |
| Córdoba, Spain | 21 D3 | 37 50N | 4 50W |
| Córdoba □, Argentina | 94 C3 | 31 22S | 64 15W |
| Córdoba, Sierra de, Argentina | 94 C3 | 31 10S | 64 25W |
| Cordova, U.S.A. | 68 B5 | 60 33N | 145 45W |
| Corella →, Australia | 62 B3 | 19 34S | 140 47 E |
| Corfield, Australia | 62 C3 | 21 40S | 143 21 E |
| Corfu = Kérkira, Greece | 25 A3 | 39 38N | 19 50 E |
| Corfu, Str. of, Greece | 25 A4 | 39 34N | 20 0 E |
| Coria, Spain | 21 C2 | 39 58N | 6 33W |
| Corigliano Cálabro, Italy | 22 E7 | 39 36N | 16 31 E |
| Coringa Is., Australia | 62 B4 | 16 58S | 149 58 E |
| Corinth = Kórinthos, Greece | 23 F10 | 37 56N | 22 55 E |
| Corinth, Miss., U.S.A. | 83 H1 | 34 56N | 88 31W |
| Corinth, N.Y., U.S.A. | 85 C11 | 43 15N | 73 49W |
| Corinth, G. of = Korinthiakós Kólpos, Greece | 23 E10 | 38 16N | 22 30 E |
| Corinto, Brazil | 93 G10 | 18 20S | 44 30W |
| Corinto, Nic. | 88 D2 | 12 30N | 87 10W |
| Cork, Ireland | 10 E3 | 51 54N | 8 29W |
| Cork □, Ireland | 10 E3 | 51 57N | 8 40W |
| Cork Harbour, Ireland | 10 E3 | 51 47N | 8 16W |
| Çorlu, Turkey | 23 D12 | 41 11N | 27 49 E |
| Cormack L., Canada | 70 A4 | 60 56N | 121 37W |
| Cormorant, Canada | 71 C8 | 54 14N | 100 35W |
| Cormorant L., Canada | 71 C8 | 54 15N | 100 50W |
| Corn Is. = Maíz, Is. del, Nic. | 88 D3 | 12 15N | 83 4W |
| Cornélio Procópio, Brazil | 95 A5 | 23 7S | 50 40W |
| Corner Brook, Canada | 73 C8 | 48 57N | 57 58W |
| Corneşti, Moldova | 17 E15 | 47 21N | 28 1 E |
| Corning, Ark., U.S.A. | 81 G9 | 36 25N | 90 35W |
| Corning, Calif., U.S.A. | 76 G2 | 39 56N | 122 11W |
| Corning, Iowa, U.S.A. | 80 E7 | 40 59N | 94 44W |
| Corning, N.Y., U.S.A. | 84 D7 | 42 9N | 77 3W |
| Cornwall, Canada | 85 A10 | 45 2N | 74 44W |
| Cornwall, U.S.A. | 85 F8 | 40 17N | 76 25W |
| Cornwall □, U.K. | 13 G3 | 50 26N | 4 40W |
| Corny Pt., Australia | 63 E2 | 34 55S | 137 0 E |
| Coro, Venezuela | 92 A5 | 11 25N | 69 41W |
| Coroatá, Brazil | 93 D10 | 4 8S | 44 0W |
| Corocoro, Bolivia | 92 G5 | 17 15S | 68 28W |
| Coroico, Bolivia | 92 G5 | 16 0S | 67 50W |
| Coromandel, N.Z. | 59 G5 | 36 45S | 175 31 E |
| Coromandel Coast, India | 40 N12 | 12 30N | 81 0 E |
| Corona, Calif., U.S.A. | 79 M9 | 33 53N | 117 34W |
| Corona, N. Mex., U.S.A. | 77 J11 | 34 15N | 105 36W |
| Coronach, Canada | 71 D7 | 49 7N | 105 31W |
| Coronado, U.S.A. | 79 N9 | 32 41N | 117 11W |
| Coronado, B. de, Costa Rica | 88 E3 | 9 0N | 83 40W |
| Coronados, Is. los, U.S.A. | 79 N9 | 32 25N | 117 15W |
| Coronation, Canada | 70 C6 | 52 5N | 111 27W |
| Coronation Gulf, Canada | 68 B8 | 68 25N | 110 0W |
| Coronation I., Antarctica | 5 C18 | 60 45S | 46 0W |
| Coronation Is., Australia | 60 B3 | 14 57S | 124 55 E |
| Coronda, Argentina | 94 C3 | 31 58S | 60 56W |
| Coronel, Chile | 94 D1 | 37 0S | 73 10W |
| Coronel Bogado, Paraguay | 94 B4 | 27 11S | 56 18W |
| Coronel Dorrego, Argentina | 94 D3 | 38 40S | 61 10W |
| Coronel Oviedo, Paraguay | 94 B4 | 25 24S | 56 30W |
| Coronel Pringles, Argentina | 94 D3 | 38 0S | 61 30W |
| Coronel Suárez, Argentina | 94 D3 | 37 30S | 61 52W |
| Coronel Vidal, Argentina | 94 D4 | 37 28S | 57 45W |
| Coropuna, Nevado, Peru | 92 G4 | 15 30S | 72 41W |
| Corowa, Australia | 63 F4 | 35 58S | 146 21 E |
| Corozal □, Belize | 87 D7 | 18 23N | 88 23W |
| Corozal Pt., Trin. & Tob. | 93 K15 | 10 45N | 61 37W |
| Corpus, Argentina | 95 B4 | 27 10S | 55 30W |
| Corpus Christi, U.S.A. | 81 M6 | 27 47N | 97 24W |
| Corpus Christi, L., U.S.A. | 81 L6 | 28 2N | 97 52W |
| Corralejo, Canary Is. | 24 F6 | 28 43N | 13 53W |
| Corraun Pen., Ireland | 10 C2 | 53 54N | 9 54W |
| Correntes, C. das, Mozam. | 57 C6 | 24 6S | 35 34 E |
| Corrib, L., Ireland | 10 C2 | 53 27N | 9 16W |
| Corrientes, Argentina | 94 B4 | 27 30S | 58 45W |
| Corrientes □, Argentina | 94 B4 | 28 0S | 57 0W |
| Corrientes →, Argentina | 94 C4 | 30 42S | 59 38W |
| Corrientes →, Peru | 92 D4 | 3 43S | 74 35W |
| Corrientes, C., Colombia | 92 B3 | 5 30N | 77 34W |
| Corrientes, C., Cuba | 88 B3 | 21 43N | 84 30W |
| Corrientes, C., Mexico | 86 C3 | 20 25N | 105 42W |
| Corrigan, U.S.A. | 81 K7 | 31 0N | 94 52W |
| Corrigin, Australia | 61 F2 | 32 20S | 117 53 E |
| Corry, U.S.A. | 84 E5 | 41 55N | 79 39W |
| Corse □, France | 20 F8 | 42 0N | 9 0 E |
| Corse, C., France | 20 F8 | 43 1N | 9 25 E |
| Corsica = Corse □, France | 20 F8 | 42 0N | 9 0 E |
| Corsicana, U.S.A. | 81 J6 | 32 6N | 96 28W |
| Corte, France | 20 E8 | 42 19N | 9 11 E |
| Cortés, Mar de = California, G. de, Mexico | 86 B2 | 27 0N | 111 0W |
| Cortez, U.S.A. | 77 H9 | 37 21N | 108 35W |
| Cortland, N.Y., U.S.A. | 85 D8 | 42 36N | 76 11W |
| Cortland, Ohio, U.S.A. | 84 E4 | 41 20N | 80 44W |
| Çorum, Turkey | 19 F5 | 40 30N | 34 57 E |
| Corumbá, Brazil | 92 G7 | 19 0S | 57 30W |
| Corunna = A Coruña, Spain | 21 A1 | 43 20N | 8 25W |
| Corvallis, U.S.A. | 76 D2 | 44 34N | 123 16W |
| Corvette, L. de la, Canada | 72 B5 | 53 25N | 74 3W |
| Corydon, U.S.A. | 80 E8 | 40 46N | 93 19W |
| Cosalá, Mexico | 86 C3 | 24 28N | 106 40W |
| Cosamaloapan, Mexico | 87 D5 | 18 23N | 95 50W |
| Cosenza, Italy | 22 E7 | 39 18N | 16 15 E |
| Coshocton, U.S.A. | 84 F3 | 40 16N | 81 51W |
| Cosmo Newberry, Australia | 61 E3 | 28 0S | 122 54 E |
| Coso Junction, U.S.A. | 79 J9 | 36 3N | 117 57W |
| Coso Pk., U.S.A. | 79 J9 | 36 13N | 117 44W |
| Cosquín, Argentina | 94 C3 | 31 15S | 64 30W |
| Costa Blanca, Spain | 21 C5 | 38 25N | 0 10W |
| Costa Brava, Spain | 21 B7 | 41 30N | 3 0 E |
| Costa del Sol, Spain | 21 D3 | 36 30N | 4 30W |
| Costa Dorada, Spain | 21 B6 | 41 12N | 1 15 E |
| Costa Mesa, U.S.A. | 79 M9 | 33 38N | 117 55W |
| Costa Rica ■, Cent. Amer. | 88 E3 | 10 0N | 84 0W |
| Cosumnes →, U.S.A. | 78 G5 | 38 16N | 121 26W |
| Cotabato, Phil. | 37 C6 | 7 14N | 124 15 E |
| Cotagaita, Bolivia | 94 A2 | 20 45S | 65 40W |
| Côte-d'Azur, France | 20 E7 | 43 25N | 7 10 E |
| Côte-d'Ivoire = Ivory Coast ■, Africa | 50 G4 | 7 30N | 5 0W |
| Coteau des Prairies, U.S.A. | 80 C6 | 45 20N | 97 50W |
| Coteau du Missouri, U.S.A. | 80 B4 | 47 0N | 100 0W |
| Cotentin, France | 20 B3 | 49 15N | 1 30W |
| Cotonou, Benin | 50 G6 | 6 20N | 2 25 E |
| Cotopaxi, Ecuador | 92 D3 | 0 40S | 78 30W |
| Cotswold Hills, U.K. | 13 F5 | 51 42N | 2 0W |
| Cottage Grove, U.S.A. | 76 E2 | 43 48N | 123 3W |
| Cottbus, Germany | 16 C8 | 51 45N | 14 20 E |
| Cottonwood, U.S.A. | 77 J7 | 34 45N | 112 1W |
| Cotulla, U.S.A. | 81 L5 | 28 26N | 99 14W |
| Coudersport, U.S.A. | 84 E6 | 41 46N | 78 1W |
| Couedic, C. du, Australia | 63 F2 | 36 5S | 136 40 E |
| Coulee City, U.S.A. | 76 C4 | 47 37N | 119 17W |
| Coulman I., Antarctica | 5 D11 | 73 35S | 170 0 E |
| Coulonge →, Canada | 72 C4 | 45 52N | 76 46W |
| Coulterville, U.S.A. | 78 H6 | 37 43N | 120 12W |
| Council, U.S.A. | 76 D5 | 44 44N | 116 26W |
| Council Bluffs, U.S.A. | 80 E7 | 41 16N | 95 52W |
| Council Grove, U.S.A. | 80 F6 | 38 40N | 96 29W |
| Coupeville, U.S.A. | 78 B4 | 48 13N | 122 41W |
| Courantyne →, S. Amer. | 92 B7 | 5 55N | 57 5W |
| Courcelles, Belgium | 15 D4 | 50 28N | 4 22 E |
| Courtenay, Canada | 70 D4 | 49 45N | 125 0W |
| Courtland, U.S.A. | 78 G5 | 38 20N | 121 34W |
| Courtrai = Kortrijk, Belgium | 15 D3 | 50 50N | 3 17 E |
| Courtright, Canada | 84 D2 | 42 49N | 82 28W |
| Coushatta, U.S.A. | 81 J8 | 32 1N | 93 21W |
| Coutts Crossing, Australia | 63 D5 | 29 49S | 152 55 E |
| Couva, Trin. & Tob. | 93 K15 | 10 25N | 61 27W |
| Couvin, Belgium | 15 D4 | 50 3N | 4 29 E |
| Cove I., Canada | 84 A3 | 45 17N | 81 44W |
| Coventry, U.K. | 13 E6 | 52 25N | 1 28W |
| Covilhã, Portugal | 21 B2 | 40 17N | 7 31W |
| Covington, Ga., U.S.A. | 83 J4 | 33 36N | 83 51W |
| Covington, Ky., U.S.A. | 82 F3 | 39 5N | 84 31W |
| Covington, Okla., U.S.A. | 81 G6 | 36 18N | 97 35W |
| Covington, Tenn., U.S.A. | 81 H10 | 35 34N | 89 39W |
| Covington, Va., U.S.A. | 82 G5 | 37 47N | 79 59W |
| Cowal, L., Australia | 63 E4 | 33 40S | 147 25 E |
| Cowan, L., Australia | 61 F3 | 31 45S | 121 45 E |
| Cowan, L., Canada | 71 C7 | 54 0N | 107 15W |
| Cowangie, Australia | 63 F3 | 35 12S | 141 26 E |
| Cowansville, Canada | 85 A12 | 45 14N | 72 46W |
| Coward Springs, Australia | 63 D2 | 29 24S | 136 49 E |
| Cowcowing Lakes, Australia | 61 F2 | 30 55S | 117 20 E |
| Cowdenbeath, U.K. | 11 E5 | 56 7N | 3 21W |
| Cowell, Australia | 63 E2 | 33 39S | 136 56 E |
| Cowes, U.K. | 13 G6 | 50 45N | 1 18W |
| Cowichan L., Canada | 78 B2 | 48 53N | 124 17W |
| Cowlitz →, U.S.A. | 78 D4 | 46 6N | 122 55W |
| Cowra, Australia | 63 E4 | 33 49S | 148 42 E |
| Coxilha Grande, Brazil | 95 B5 | 28 18S | 51 30W |
| Coxim, Brazil | 93 G8 | 18 30S | 54 55W |
| Cox's Bazar, Bangla. | 41 J17 | 21 26N | 91 59 E |
| Coyote Wells, U.S.A. | 79 N11 | 32 44N | 115 58W |
| Coyuca de Benítez, Mexico | 87 D4 | 17 1N | 100 8W |
| Coyuca de Catalan, Mexico | 86 D4 | 18 18N | 100 41W |
| Cozad, U.S.A. | 80 E5 | 40 52N | 99 59W |
| Cozumel, Mexico | 87 C7 | 20 31N | 86 55W |
| Cozumel, Isla, Mexico | 87 C7 | 20 30N | 86 40W |
| Crab Hill, Barbados | 89 g | 13 19N | 59 38W |
| Cracow = Kraków, Poland | 17 C10 | 50 4N | 19 57 E |
| Cracow, Australia | 63 D5 | 25 17S | 150 17 E |
| Cradle Mt.-Lake St. Clair △, Australia | 63 G4 | 41 49S | 147 56 E |
| Cradock, Australia | 63 E2 | 32 6S | 138 31 E |
| Cradock, S. Africa | 56 E4 | 32 8S | 25 36 E |
| Craig, U.S.A. | 76 F10 | 40 31N | 107 33W |
| Craigavon, U.K. | 10 B5 | 54 27N | 6 23W |
| Craigmore, Zimbabwe | 55 G3 | 20 28S | 32 50 E |
| Craik, Canada | 71 C7 | 51 3N | 105 49W |
| Crailsheim, Germany | 16 D6 | 49 8N | 10 5 E |
| Craiova, Romania | 17 F12 | 44 21N | 23 48 E |
| Cramsie, Australia | 62 C3 | 23 20S | 144 15 E |
| Cranberry L., U.S.A. | 85 B10 | 44 11N | 74 50W |
| Cranberry Portage, Canada | 71 C8 | 54 35N | 101 23W |
| Cranbrook, Australia | 61 F2 | 34 18S | 117 33 E |
| Cranbrook, Canada | 70 D5 | 49 30N | 115 46W |
| Crandon, U.S.A. | 80 C10 | 45 34N | 88 54W |
| Crane, Oreg., U.S.A. | 76 E4 | 43 25N | 118 35W |
| Crane, Tex., U.S.A. | 81 K3 | 31 24N | 102 21W |
| Cranston, U.S.A. | 85 E13 | 41 47N | 71 26W |
| Crater L., U.S.A. | 76 E2 | 42 56N | 122 6W |
| Crater Lake △, U.S.A. | 76 E2 | 42 55N | 122 10W |
| Craters of the Moon △, U.S.A. | 76 E7 | 43 25N | 113 30W |
| Crateús, Brazil | 93 E10 | 5 10S | 40 39W |
| Crato, Brazil | 93 E11 | 7 10S | 39 25W |
| Craven, L., Canada | 72 B4 | 54 20N | 76 56W |
| Crawford, U.S.A. | 80 D3 | 42 41N | 103 25W |
| Crawfordsville, U.S.A. | 82 E2 | 40 2N | 86 54W |
| Crawley, U.K. | 13 F7 | 51 7N | 0 11W |
| Crazy Mts., U.S.A. | 76 C8 | 46 12N | 110 20W |
| Crean L., Canada | 71 C7 | 54 5N | 106 9W |
| Crediton, Canada | 84 C3 | 43 17N | 81 33W |
| Crediton, U.K. | 13 G4 | 50 47N | 3 40W |
| Cree →, Canada | 71 B7 | 58 57N | 105 47W |
| Cree →, U.K. | 11 G4 | 54 55N | 4 25W |
| Cree L., Canada | 71 B7 | 57 30N | 106 30W |
| Creede, U.S.A. | 77 H10 | 37 51N | 106 56W |
| Creekside, U.S.A. | 84 F5 | 40 40N | 79 11W |
| Creel, Mexico | 86 B3 | 27 45N | 107 38W |
| Creemore, Canada | 84 B4 | 44 19N | 80 6W |
| Creighton, Canada | 71 C8 | 54 45N | 101 54W |
| Creighton, U.S.A. | 80 D6 | 42 28N | 97 54W |
| Crema, Italy | 20 D8 | 45 22N | 9 41 E |
| Cremona, Italy | 20 D9 | 45 7N | 10 2 E |
| Cres, Croatia | 16 F8 | 44 58N | 14 25 E |
| Crescent City, U.S.A. | 76 F1 | 41 45N | 124 12W |
| Crespo, Argentina | 94 C3 | 32 2S | 60 19W |
| Cresson, U.S.A. | 84 F6 | 40 28N | 78 36W |
| Crestline, Calif., U.S.A. | 79 L9 | 34 14N | 117 18W |
| Crestline, Ohio, U.S.A. | 84 F2 | 40 47N | 82 44W |
| Creston, Canada | 70 D5 | 49 10N | 116 31W |
| Creston, Calif., U.S.A. | 78 K6 | 35 32N | 120 33W |
| Creston, Iowa, U.S.A. | 80 E7 | 41 4N | 94 22W |
| Crestview, Calif., U.S.A. | 78 H8 | 37 46N | 118 58W |
| Crestview, Fla., U.S.A. | 83 K2 | 30 46N | 86 34W |
| Crete = Kríti, Greece | 25 D7 | 35 15N | 25 0 E |
| Crete, U.S.A. | 80 E6 | 40 38N | 96 58W |
| Créteil, France | 20 B5 | 48 47N | 2 28 E |
| Creus, C. de, Spain | 21 A7 | 42 20N | 3 19 E |
| Creuse →, France | 20 C4 | 47 0N | 0 34 E |
| Crewe, U.K. | 12 D5 | 53 6N | 2 26W |
| Crewkerne, U.K. | 13 G5 | 50 53N | 2 48W |
| Crianlarich, U.K. | 11 E4 | 56 24N | 4 37W |
| Criciúma, Brazil | 95 B6 | 28 40S | 49 23W |
| Crieff, U.K. | 11 E5 | 56 22N | 3 50W |
| Crimea □, Ukraine | 19 E5 | 45 30N | 33 10 E |
| Crimean Pen. = Krymskyy Pivostriv, Ukraine | 19 F5 | 45 0N | 34 0 E |
| Crişul Alb →, Romania | 17 E11 | 46 42N | 21 17 E |
| Crişul Negru →, Romania | 17 E11 | 46 42N | 21 16 E |
| Crna →, Macedonia | 23 D9 | 41 33N | 21 59 E |
| Crna Gora = Montenegro □, Serbia & M. | 23 C8 | 42 40N | 19 20 E |
| Crna Gora, Macedonia | 23 D9 | 42 10N | 21 30 E |
| Crna Reka = Crna →, Macedonia | 23 D9 | 41 33N | 21 59 E |
| Croagh Patrick, Ireland | 10 C2 | 53 46N | 9 40W |
| Croatia ■, Europe | 16 F9 | 45 20N | 16 0 E |
| Crocker, Banjaran, Malaysia | 36 C5 | 5 40N | 116 30 E |
| Crockett, U.S.A. | 81 K7 | 31 19N | 95 27W |
| Crocodile = Krokodil →, Mozam. | 57 D5 | 25 14S | 32 18 E |
| Crocodile Is., Australia | 62 A1 | 12 3S | 134 58 E |
| Crohy Hd., Ireland | 10 B3 | 54 55N | 8 26W |
| Croix, L. La, Canada | 72 C1 | 48 20N | 92 15W |
| Croker, C., Australia | 60 B5 | 10 58S | 132 35 E |
| Croker, C., Canada | 84 B4 | 44 58N | 80 59W |
| Croker I., Australia | 60 B5 | 11 12S | 132 32 E |
| Cromarty, U.K. | 11 D4 | 57 40N | 4 2W |
| Cromer, U.K. | 12 E9 | 52 56N | 1 17 E |
| Cromwell, N.Z. | 59 L2 | 45 3S | 169 14 E |
| Cromwell, U.S.A. | 85 E12 | 41 36N | 72 39W |
| Crook, U.K. | 12 C6 | 54 43N | 1 45W |
| Crooked →, Canada | 70 C4 | 54 50N | 122 54W |
| Crooked →, U.S.A. | 76 D3 | 44 32N | 121 16W |
| Crooked I., Bahamas | 89 B5 | 22 50N | 74 10W |
| Crooked Island Passage, Bahamas | 89 B5 | 22 55N | 74 35W |
| Crookston, Minn., U.S.A. | 80 B6 | 47 47N | 96 37W |
| Crookston, Nebr., U.S.A. | 80 D4 | 42 56N | 100 45W |
| Crookwell, Australia | 63 E4 | 34 28S | 149 24 E |
| Crosby, N. Dak., U.S.A. | 80 A3 | 48 55N | 103 18W |
| Crosby, Pa., U.S.A. | 84 E6 | 41 45N | 78 23W |
| Crosbyton, U.S.A. | 81 J4 | 33 40N | 101 14W |
| Cross City, U.S.A. | 83 L4 | 29 38N | 83 7W |
| Cross Fell, U.K. | 12 C5 | 54 43N | 2 28W |
| Cross L., Canada | 71 C9 | 54 45N | 97 30W |
| Cross Lake, Canada | 71 C9 | 54 37N | 97 47W |
| Cross Sound, U.S.A. | 68 C6 | 58 0N | 135 0W |
| Crossett, U.S.A. | 81 J9 | 33 8N | 91 58W |
| Crosshaven, Ireland | 10 E3 | 51 47N | 8 17W |
| Crossville, U.S.A. | 83 G3 | 35 57N | 85 2W |
| Croswell, U.S.A. | 84 C2 | 43 16N | 82 37W |
| Croton-on-Hudson, U.S.A. | 85 E11 | 41 12N | 73 55W |
| Crotone, Italy | 22 E7 | 39 5N | 17 8 E |
| Crow →, Canada | 70 B4 | 59 41N | 124 20W |
| Crow Agency, U.S.A. | 76 D10 | 45 36N | 107 28W |
| Crow Hd., Ireland | 10 E1 | 51 35N | 10 9W |
| Crowell, U.S.A. | 81 J5 | 33 59N | 99 43W |
| Crowley, U.S.A. | 81 K8 | 30 13N | 92 22W |
| Crowley, L., U.S.A. | 78 H8 | 37 35N | 118 42W |
| Crown Point, Ind., U.S.A. | 82 E2 | 41 25N | 87 22W |
| Crown Point, N.Y., U.S.A. | 85 C11 | 43 57N | 73 26W |
| Crown Pt., Trin. & Tob. | 93 J16 | 11 18N | 60 51W |
| Crownpoint, U.S.A. | 77 J9 | 35 41N | 108 9W |
| Crows Landing, U.S.A. | 78 H5 | 37 23N | 121 6W |
| Crows Nest, Australia | 63 D5 | 27 16S | 152 4 E |
| Crowsnest Pass, Canada | 70 D6 | 49 40N | 114 40W |
| Croydon, Australia | 62 B3 | 18 13S | 142 14 E |
| Croydon □, U.K. | 13 F7 | 51 22N | 0 5W |
| Crozet, I., Ind. Oc. | 3 G12 | 46 27S | 52 0 E |
| Cruz, C., Cuba | 88 C4 | 19 50N | 77 50W |
| Cruz Alta, Brazil | 95 B5 | 28 45S | 53 40W |
| Cruz Bay, U.S. Virgin Is. | 89 e | 18 20N | 64 48W |
| Cruz del Eje, Argentina | 94 C3 | 30 45S | 64 50W |
| Cruzeiro, Brazil | 95 A7 | 22 33S | 45 0W |
| Cruzeiro do Oeste, Brazil | 95 A5 | 23 46S | 53 4W |
| Cruzeiro do Sul, Brazil | 92 E4 | 7 35S | 72 35W |
| Cry L., Canada | 70 B3 | 58 45N | 129 0W |
| Crystal Bay, U.S.A. | 78 F7 | 39 15N | 120 0W |
| Crystal Brook, Australia | 63 E2 | 33 21S | 138 12 E |
| Crystal City, U.S.A. | 81 L5 | 28 41N | 99 50W |
| Crystal Falls, U.S.A. | 82 B1 | 46 5N | 88 20W |
| Crystal River, U.S.A. | 83 L4 | 28 54N | 82 35W |
| Crystal Springs, U.S.A. | 81 K9 | 31 59N | 90 21W |
| Csongrád, Hungary | 17 E11 | 46 43N | 20 12 E |
| Cu Lao Hon, Vietnam | 39 G7 | 10 54N | 108 18 E |
| Cua Rao, Vietnam | 38 C5 | 19 16N | 104 27 E |
| Cuácua →, Mozam. | 55 F4 | 17 54S | 37 0 E |
| Cuamato, Angola | 56 B2 | 17 2S | 15 7 E |
| Cuamba, Mozam. | 55 E4 | 14 45S | 36 22 E |
| Cuando →, Angola | 53 H4 | 17 30S | 23 15 E |
| Cuando Cubango □, Angola | 56 B2 | 16 25S | 20 0 E |
| Cuango = Kwango →, Dem. Rep. of the Congo | 52 E3 | 3 14S | 17 22 E |
| Cuanza →, Angola | 52 F2 | 9 21S | 13 9 E |
| Cuarto →, Argentina | 94 C3 | 33 25S | 63 2W |
| Cuatrociénegas, Mexico | 86 B4 | 26 59N | 102 5W |
| Cuauhtémoc, Mexico | 86 B3 | 28 25N | 106 52W |
| Cuba, N. Mex., U.S.A. | 77 J10 | 36 1N | 107 4W |
| Cuba, N.Y., U.S.A. | 84 D6 | 42 13N | 78 17W |
| Cuba ■, W. Indies | 88 B4 | 22 0N | 79 0W |
| Cubango →, Africa | 56 B3 | 18 50S | 22 25 E |
| Cuc Phuong △, Vietnam | 38 B5 | 20 17N | 105 38 E |
| Cuchumatanes, Sierra de los, Guatemala | 88 C1 | 15 35N | 91 25W |
| Cuckfield, U.K. | 13 F7 | 51 1N | 0 8W |
| Cucuí, Brazil | 92 C5 | 1 5N | 66 50W |
| Cucurpe, Mexico | 86 A2 | 30 20N | 110 43W |
| Cúcuta, Colombia | 92 B4 | 7 54N | 72 31W |
| Cuddalore, India | 40 P11 | 11 46N | 79 45 E |
| Cuddapah, India | 40 M11 | 14 30N | 78 47 E |
| Cuddapan, L., Australia | 62 D3 | 25 45S | 141 26 E |
| Cue, Australia | 61 E2 | 27 25S | 117 54 E |
| Cuenca, Ecuador | 92 D3 | 2 50S | 79 9W |
| Cuenca, Spain | 21 B4 | 40 5N | 2 10W |
| Cuenca, Serranía de, Spain | 21 C5 | 39 55N | 1 50W |
| Cuernavaca, Mexico | 87 D5 | 18 55N | 99 15W |
| Cuero, U.S.A. | 81 L6 | 29 6N | 97 17W |
| Cueva de la Quebrada del Toro △, Venezuela | 89 D6 | 10 46N | 69 3W |
| Cuevas del Almanzora, Spain | 21 D5 | 37 18N | 1 58W |
| Cuevo, Bolivia | 92 H6 | 20 15S | 63 30W |
| Cuiabá, Brazil | 93 G7 | 15 30S | 56 0W |
| Cuiabá →, Brazil | 93 G7 | 17 5S | 56 36W |
| Cuihangcun, China | 33 G10 | 22 27N | 113 32 E |
| Cuijk, Neths. | 15 C5 | 51 44N | 5 50 E |
| Cuilco, Guatemala | 88 C1 | 15 24N | 91 58W |
| Cuillin Hills, U.K. | 11 D2 | 57 13N | 6 15W |
| Cuillin Sd., U.K. | 11 D2 | 57 4N | 6 20W |
| Cuito →, Angola | 56 B3 | 18 1S | 20 48 E |
| Cuitzeo, L. de, Mexico | 86 D4 | 19 55N | 101 5W |
| Cukai, Malaysia | 39 K4 | 4 13N | 103 25 E |
| Culbertson, U.S.A. | 80 A2 | 48 9N | 104 31W |
| Culcairn, Australia | 63 F4 | 35 41S | 147 3 E |
| Culebra, Isla de, Puerto Rico | 89 d | 18 19N | 65 18W |
| Culgoa →, Australia | 63 D4 | 29 56S | 146 20 E |
| Culgoa Flood Plain △, Australia | 63 D4 | 28 58S | 147 5 E |
| Culiacán, Mexico | 86 C3 | 24 50N | 107 23W |
| Culiacán →, Mexico | 86 C3 | 24 30N | 107 42W |
| Culik, Indonesia | 37 J18 | 8 21S | 115 37 E |
| Culion, Phil. | 37 B6 | 11 54N | 119 58 E |
| Cullarin Ra., Australia | 63 E4 | 34 30S | 149 30 E |
| Cullen, U.K. | 11 D6 | 57 42N | 2 49W |
| Cullen Pt., Australia | 62 A3 | 11 57S | 141 54 E |
| Cullera, Spain | 21 C5 | 39 9N | 0 17W |
| Cullman, U.S.A. | 83 H2 | 34 11N | 86 51W |
| Cullompton, U.K. | 13 G4 | 50 51N | 3 24W |
| Culpeper, U.S.A. | 82 F7 | 38 30N | 78 0W |
| Culuene →, Brazil | 93 F8 | 12 56S | 52 51W |
| Culver, Pt., Australia | 61 F3 | 32 54S | 124 43 E |
| Culverden, N.Z. | 59 K4 | 42 47S | 172 49 E |
| Cumaná, Venezuela | 92 A6 | 10 30N | 64 5W |
| Cumberland, B.C., Canada | 70 D4 | 49 40N | 125 0W |
| Cumberland, Ont., Canada | 85 A9 | 45 29N | 75 24W |
| Cumberland, U.S.A. | 82 F6 | 39 39N | 78 46W |
| Cumberland →, U.S.A. | 83 G2 | 36 15N | 87 0W |
| Cumberland, L., U.S.A. | 83 G3 | 36 57N | 84 55W |
| Cumberland Gap △, U.S.A. | 83 G4 | 36 36N | 83 40W |
| Cumberland Is., Australia | 62 J7 | 20 35S | 149 10 E |
| Cumberland Island △, U.S.A. | 83 K5 | 30 12N | 81 24W |
| Cumberland L., Canada | 71 C8 | 54 3N | 102 18W |
| Cumberland Pen., Canada | 69 B13 | 67 0N | 64 0W |
| Cumberland Plateau, U.S.A. | 83 H3 | 36 0N | 85 0W |
| Cumberland Sd., Canada | 69 B13 | 65 30N | 66 0W |
| Cumbernauld, U.K. | 11 F5 | 55 57N | 3 58W |
| Cumborah, Australia | 63 D4 | 29 40S | 147 45 E |
| Cumbres de Majalca △, Mexico | 86 B3 | 28 52N | 106 24W |
| Cumbres de Monterrey △, Mexico | 86 B4 | 25 40N | 100 35W |
| Cumbria □, U.K. | 12 C5 | 54 42N | 2 52W |
| Cumbrian Mts., U.K. | 12 C5 | 54 30N | 3 0W |
| Cumbum, India | 40 M11 | 15 40N | 79 10 E |
| Cuminá →, Brazil | 93 D7 | 1 30S | 56 0W |
| Cummings Mt., U.S.A. | 79 K8 | 35 2N | 118 34W |
| Cummins, Australia | 63 E2 | 34 16S | 135 43 E |
| Cumnock, Australia | 63 E4 | 32 59S | 148 46 E |
| Cumnock, U.K. | 11 F4 | 55 28N | 4 17W |
| Cumpas, Mexico | 86 B3 | 30 0N | 109 48W |
| Cumplida, Pta., Canary Is. | 24 F2 | 28 50N | 17 48W |
| Cunco, Chile | 96 D2 | 38 55S | 72 2W |
| Cuncumén, Chile | 94 C1 | 31 53S | 70 38W |
| Cunderdin, Australia | 61 F2 | 31 37S | 117 12 E |
| Cunene →, Angola | 56 B1 | 17 20S | 11 50 E |
| Cúneo, Italy | 20 D7 | 44 23N | 7 32 E |
| Çüngüş, Turkey | 44 B3 | 38 13N | 39 17 E |
| Cunillera, I. = Sa Conillera, Spain | 24 C7 | 38 59N | 1 13 E |
| Cunnamulla, Australia | 63 D4 | 28 2S | 145 38 E |
| Cupar, Canada | 71 C8 | 50 57N | 104 10W |
| Cupar, U.K. | 11 E5 | 56 19N | 3 1W |
| Cupica, G. de, Colombia | 92 B3 | 6 25N | 77 30W |
| Curaçao, Neth. Ant. | 89 D6 | 12 10N | 69 0W |
| Curanilahue, Chile | 94 D1 | 37 29S | 73 28W |
| Curaray →, Peru | 92 D4 | 2 20S | 74 5W |
| Curepto, Chile | 94 D1 | 35 8S | 72 1W |
| Curiapo, Venezuela | 92 B6 | 8 33N | 61 5W |
| Curicó, Chile | 94 C1 | 34 55S | 71 20W |
| Curitiba, Brazil | 95 B6 | 25 20S | 49 10W |
| Curitibanos, Brazil | 95 B5 | 27 18S | 50 36W |
| Currabubula, Australia | 63 E5 | 31 16S | 150 44 E |
| Currais Novos, Brazil | 93 E11 | 6 13S | 36 30W |
| Curralinho, Brazil | 93 D9 | 1 45S | 49 46W |
| Currant, U.S.A. | 76 G6 | 38 51N | 115 32W |
| Currawinya △, Australia | 63 D3 | 28 55S | 144 27 E |
| Current →, U.S.A. | 81 G9 | 36 15N | 90 55W |
| Currie, U.S.A. | 76 F6 | 40 16N | 114 45W |
| Curtea de Argeş, Romania | 17 F13 | 45 12N | 24 42 E |
| Curtis, U.S.A. | 80 E4 | 40 38N | 100 31W |
| Curtis Group, Australia | 63 F4 | 39 30S | 146 37 E |
| Curtis I., Australia | 62 C5 | 23 35S | 151 10 E |
| Curuápanema →, Brazil | 93 D7 | 2 25S | 55 2W |
| Curuçá, Brazil | 93 D9 | 0 43S | 47 50W |
| Curuguaty, Paraguay | 94 A4 | 24 31S | 55 42W |
| Curup, Indonesia | 36 E2 | 4 26S | 102 13 E |
| Cururupu, Brazil | 93 D10 | 1 50S | 44 50W |
| Curuzú Cuatiá, Argentina | 94 B4 | 29 50S | 58 5W |
| Curvelo, Brazil | 93 G10 | 18 45S | 44 27W |
| Cushing, U.S.A. | 81 H6 | 35 59N | 96 46W |
| Cushing, Mt., Canada | 70 B3 | 57 35N | 126 57W |
| Cusihuiriáchic, Mexico | 86 B3 | 28 10N | 106 50W |
| Cut Bank, U.S.A. | 76 B7 | 48 38N | 112 20W |
| Cutchogue, U.S.A. | 85 E12 | 41 1N | 72 30W |
| Cuthbert, U.S.A. | 83 K3 | 31 46N | 84 48W |
| Cutler, U.S.A. | 78 J7 | 36 31N | 119 17W |
| Cuttaburra →, Australia | 63 D3 | 29 43S | 144 22 E |
| Cuttack, India | 41 J14 | 20 25N | 85 57 E |
| Cuvier, C., Australia | 61 D1 | 23 14S | 113 22 E |
| Cuvier I., N.Z. | 59 G5 | 36 27S | 175 50 E |
| Cuxhaven, Germany | 16 B5 | 53 51N | 8 41 E |
| Cuyahoga Falls, U.S.A. | 84 E3 | 41 8N | 81 29W |
| Cuyahoga Valley △, U.S.A. | 84 E3 | 41 18N | 81 33W |
| Cuyo, Phil. | 37 B6 | 10 50N | 121 5 E |
| Cuyuni →, Guyana | 92 B7 | 6 23N | 58 41W |
| Cuzco, Bolivia | 92 H5 | 20 0S | 66 50W |
| Cuzco, Peru | 92 F4 | 13 32S | 72 0W |
| Cwmbran, U.K. | 13 F4 | 51 39N | 3 2W |
| Cyangugu, Rwanda | 54 C2 | 2 29S | 28 54 E |

Cyclades = Kikládhes, Greece .. 23 F11 37 0N 24 30 E
Cygnet, Australia .. 63 G4 43 8S 147 1 E
Cynthiana, U.S.A. .. 82 F3 38 23N 84 18W
Cypress Hills, Canada .. 71 D7 49 40N 109 30W
Cypress Hills △, Canada .. 71 D7 49 40N 109 30W
Cyprus ■, Asia .. 25 E12 35 0N 33 0 E
Cyrenaica, Libya .. 51 C10 27 0N 23 0 E
Czar, Canada .. 71 C6 52 27N 110 50W
Czech Rep. ■, Europe .. 16 D8 50 0N 15 0 E
Częstochowa, Poland .. 17 C10 50 49N 19 7 E

### D

Da →, Vietnam .. 38 B5 21 15N 105 20 E
Da Hinggan Ling, China .. 33 B7 48 0N 121 0 E
Da Lat, Vietnam .. 39 G7 11 56N 108 25 E
Da Nang, Vietnam .. 38 D7 16 4N 108 13 E
Da Qaidam, China .. 32 C4 37 50N 95 15 E
Da Yunhe →, China .. 35 G11 34 25N 120 5 E
Da'an, China .. 35 B13 45 30N 124 7 E
Daan Viljoen △, Namibia .. 56 C2 22 2S 16 45 E
Daba Shan, China .. 33 C5 32 0N 109 0 E
Dabbagh, Jabal, Si. Arabia .. 44 E2 27 52N 35 45 E
Dabhoi, India .. 42 H5 22 10N 73 20 E
Dabo = Pasirkuning, Indonesia .. 36 E2 0 30S 104 33 E
Dabola, Guinea .. 50 F3 10 50N 11 5W
Dabung, Malaysia .. 39 K4 5 23N 102 1 E
Dacca = Dhaka, Bangla. .. 43 H14 23 43N 90 26 E
Dacca = Dhaka □, Bangla. .. 43 G14 24 25N 90 25 E
Dachau, Germany .. 16 D6 48 15N 11 26 E
Dadanawa, Guyana .. 92 C7 2 50N 59 30W
Dade City, U.S.A. .. 83 L4 28 22N 82 11W
Dadhar, Pakistan .. 42 E2 29 28N 67 39 E
Dadra & Nagar Haveli □, India .. 40 J8 20 5N 73 0 E
Dadri = Charkhi Dadri, India .. 42 E7 28 37N 76 17 E
Dadu, Pakistan .. 42 F2 26 45N 67 45 E
Daet, Phil. .. 37 B6 14 2N 122 55 E
Dagana, Senegal .. 50 E2 16 30N 15 35W
Dagestan □, Russia .. 19 F8 42 30N 47 0 E
Daggett, U.S.A. .. 79 L10 34 52N 116 52W
Daghestan Republic = Dagestan □, Russia .. 19 F8 42 30N 47 0 E
Dağlıq Qarabağ = Nagorno-Karabakh □, Azerbaijan .. 19 F8 39 55N 46 45 E
Dagö = Hiiumaa, Estonia .. 9 G20 58 50N 22 45 E
Dagu, China .. 35 E9 38 59N 117 40 E
Dagupan, Phil. .. 37 A6 16 3N 120 20 E
Daguragu, Australia .. 60 C5 17 33S 130 30 E
Dahlak Kebir, Eritrea .. 47 D3 15 50N 40 10 E
Dahlonega, U.S.A. .. 83 H4 34 32N 83 59W
Dahod, India .. 42 H6 22 50N 74 15 E
Dahūk, Iraq .. 44 B3 36 50N 43 1 E
Dai Hao, Vietnam .. 38 C6 18 1N 106 25 E
Dai-Sen, Japan .. 31 G6 35 22N 133 32 E
Dai Xian, China .. 34 E7 39 4N 112 58 E
Daicheng, China .. 34 E9 38 42N 116 38 E
Daingean, Ireland .. 10 C4 53 18N 7 17W
Daintree, Australia .. 62 B4 16 20S 145 20 E
Daintree △, Australia .. 62 B4 16 8S 145 2 E
Daiō-Misaki, Japan .. 31 G8 34 15N 136 45 E
Daisen-Oki △, Japan .. 31 G6 35 23N 133 34 E
Daisetsu-Zan, Japan .. 30 C11 43 30N 142 57 E
Daisetsu-Zan △, Japan .. 30 C11 43 30N 142 52 E
Dajarra, Australia .. 62 C2 21 42S 139 30 E
Dak Dam, Cambodia .. 38 F6 12 20N 107 21 E
Dak Nhe, Vietnam .. 38 E6 15 28N 107 48 E
Dak Pek, Vietnam .. 38 E6 15 4N 107 44 E
Dak Song, Vietnam .. 39 F6 12 19N 107 35 E
Dak Sui, Vietnam .. 38 E6 14 55N 107 43 E
Dakar, Senegal .. 50 F2 14 34N 17 29W
Dakhla, W. Sahara .. 50 D2 23 50N 15 53W
Dakhla, El Wâhât el-, Egypt .. 51 C11 25 30N 28 50 E
Dakor, India .. 42 H5 22 45N 73 11 E
Dakota City, U.S.A. .. 80 D6 42 25N 96 25W
Ðakovica, Serbia & M. .. 23 C9 42 22N 20 26 E
Dalachi, China .. 34 F3 36 48N 105 0 E
Dalai Nur, China .. 34 C9 43 20N 116 45 E
Dālakī, Iran .. 45 D6 29 26N 51 17 E
Dalälven →, Sweden .. 9 F17 60 12N 16 43 E
Dalaman →, Turkey .. 23 F13 36 41N 28 43 E
Dalandzadgad, Mongolia .. 34 C3 43 27N 104 30 E
Dalap-Uliga-Darrit, Marshall Is. .. 64 G9 7 7N 171 24 E
Dalarna, Sweden .. 9 F16 61 0N 14 0 E
Dālbandin, Pakistan .. 40 E4 29 0N 64 23 E
Dalbeattie, U.K. .. 11 G5 54 56N 3 50W
Dalbeg, Australia .. 62 C4 20 16S 147 18 E
Dalby, Australia .. 63 D5 27 10S 151 17 E
Dale City, U.S.A. .. 82 F7 38 38N 77 18W
Dale Hollow L., U.S.A. .. 83 G3 36 32N 85 27W
Dalgán, Iran .. 45 E8 27 31N 59 19 E
Dalhart, U.S.A. .. 81 G3 36 4N 102 31W
Dalhousie, Canada .. 73 C6 48 5N 66 26W
Dalhousie, India .. 42 C6 32 38N 75 58 E
Dali, Shaanxi, China .. 34 G5 34 48N 109 58 E
Dali, Yunnan, China .. 32 D5 25 40N 100 10 E
Dalian, China .. 35 E11 38 50N 121 40 E
Daliang Shan, China .. 32 D5 28 0N 102 45 E
Daling He →, China .. 35 D11 40 55N 121 40 E
Dāliyat el Karmel, Israel .. 46 C4 32 43N 35 2 E
Dalkeith, U.K. .. 11 F5 55 54N 3 4W
Dallas, Oreg., U.S.A. .. 76 D2 44 55N 123 19W
Dallas, Tex., U.S.A. .. 81 J6 32 47N 96 49W
Dalmā, U.A.E. .. 45 E7 24 30N 52 20 E
Dalmacija, Croatia .. 22 C7 43 20N 17 0 E
Dalmas, L., Canada .. 73 B5 53 30N 71 50W
Dalmatia = Dalmacija, Croatia .. 22 C7 43 20N 17 0 E
Dalmau, India .. 43 F9 26 4N 81 2 E
Dalmellington, U.K. .. 11 F4 55 19N 4 23W
Dalnegorsk, Russia .. 29 E14 44 32N 135 33 E
Dalnerechensk, Russia .. 29 E14 45 50N 133 40 E
Dalnevostochnyy □, Russia .. 29 C14 67 0N 140 0 E
Daloa, Ivory C. .. 50 G4 7 0N 6 30W
Dalry, U.K. .. 11 F4 55 42N 4 43W
Dalrymple, L., Australia .. 62 C4 20 40S 147 0 E
Dalrymple, Mt., Australia .. 62 K6 21 1S 148 39 E
Dalsland, Sweden .. 9 G14 58 50N 12 15 E
Daltenganj, India .. 43 H11 24 0N 84 4 E
Dalton, Ga., U.S.A. .. 83 H3 34 46N 84 58W
Dalton, Mass., U.S.A. .. 85 D11 42 28N 73 11W
Dalton, Nebr., U.S.A. .. 80 E3 41 25N 102 58W
Dalton-in-Furness, U.K. .. 12 C4 54 10N 3 11W
Dalvík, Iceland .. 8 D4 65 58N 18 32W
Dálvvadis = Jokkmokk, Sweden .. 8 C18 66 35N 19 50 E
Dalwallinu, Australia .. 61 F2 30 17S 116 40 E
Daly →, Australia .. 60 B5 13 35S 130 19 E

Daly City, U.S.A. .. 78 H4 37 42N 122 28W
Daly L., Canada .. 71 B7 56 32N 105 39W
Daly River, Australia .. 60 B5 13 46S 130 42 E
Daly Waters, Australia .. 62 B1 16 15S 133 24 E
Dam Doi, Vietnam .. 39 H5 8 50N 105 12 E
Dam Ha, Vietnam .. 38 B6 21 21N 107 36 E
Daman, India .. 40 J8 20 25N 72 57 E
Dāmaneh, Iran .. 45 C6 33 1N 50 29 E
Damanhûr, Egypt .. 51 B12 31 0N 30 30 E
Damant L., Canada .. 71 A7 61 45N 105 5W
Damanzhuang, China .. 34 E9 38 5N 116 35 E
Damar, Indonesia .. 37 F7 7 7S 128 40 E
Damaraland, Namibia .. 56 C2 20 0S 15 0 E
Damascus = Dimashq, Syria .. 46 B5 33 30N 36 18 E
Dāmāvand, Iran .. 45 C7 35 47N 52 0 E
Dāmāvand, Qolleh-ye, Iran .. 45 C7 35 56N 52 10 E
Damba, Angola .. 52 F3 6 44S 15 20 E
Dâmbovița →, Romania .. 17 F14 44 12N 26 26 E
Dame Marie, Haiti .. 89 C5 18 36N 74 26W
Dāmghān, Iran .. 45 B7 36 10N 54 17 E
Damiel, Spain .. 21 C4 39 4N 3 37W
Damietta = Dumyât, Egypt .. 51 B12 31 24N 31 48 E
Daming, China .. 34 F8 36 15N 115 6 E
Damir Qābū, Syria .. 44 B4 36 58N 41 51 E
Dammam = Ad Dammām, Si. Arabia .. 45 E6 26 20N 50 5 E
Damodar →, India .. 43 H12 23 17N 87 35 E
Damoh, India .. 43 H8 23 50N 79 28 E
Dampier, Australia .. 60 D2 20 41S 116 42 E
Dampier, Selat, Indonesia .. 37 E8 0 40S 131 0 E
Dampier Arch., Australia .. 60 D2 20 38S 116 32 E
Damrei, Chuor Phnum, Cambodia .. 39 G4 11 30N 103 0 E
Dan Xian, China .. 33 C7 19 31N 109 33 E
Dana, Indonesia .. 37 F6 11 0S 122 52 E
Dana, L., Canada .. 72 B4 50 53N 77 20W
Dana, Mt., U.S.A. .. 78 H7 37 54N 119 12W
Danakil Desert, Ethiopia .. 47 E3 12 45N 41 0 E
Danané, Ivory C. .. 50 G4 7 16N 8 9W
Danau Poso, Indonesia .. 37 E6 1 52S 120 35 E
Danbury, U.S.A. .. 85 E11 41 24N 73 28W
Danby L., U.S.A. .. 77 J6 34 13N 115 5W
Dand, Afghan. .. 42 D1 31 28N 65 32 E
Dande →, Zimbabwe .. 55 F3 15 56S 30 16 E
Dandeldhura, Nepal .. 43 E9 29 20N 80 35 E
Dandeli, India .. 40 M9 15 5N 74 30 E
Dandenong, Australia .. 63 F4 38 0S 145 15 E
Dandong, China .. 35 D13 40 10N 124 20 E
Danfeng, China .. 34 H6 33 45N 110 25 E
Danger Is. = Pukapuka, Cook Is. .. 65 J11 10 53S 165 49W
Danger Pt., S. Africa .. 56 E2 34 40S 19 17 E
Danginpuri, Indonesia .. 37 K18 8 40S 115 13 E
Dangla Shan = Tanggula Shan, China .. 32 C4 32 40N 92 10 E
Dangrek, Phnom, Thailand .. 38 E5 14 15N 105 0 E
Dangriga, Belize .. 87 D7 17 0N 88 13W
Dangshan, China .. 34 G9 34 27N 116 22 E
Daniel, U.S.A. .. 76 E8 42 52N 110 4W
Daniel's Harbour, Canada .. 73 B8 50 13N 57 35W
Danielskuil, S. Africa .. 56 D3 28 11S 23 33 E
Danielson, U.S.A. .. 85 E13 41 48N 71 53W
Danilov, Russia .. 18 C7 58 16N 40 13 E
Daning, China .. 34 F6 36 28N 110 45 E
Dankhar Gompa, India .. 40 C11 32 10N 78 10 E
Danlí, Honduras .. 88 D2 14 4N 86 35W
Dannemora, U.S.A. .. 85 B11 44 43N 73 44W
Dannevirke, N.Z. .. 59 J6 40 12S 176 8 E
Dannhauser, S. Africa .. 57 D5 28 0S 30 3 E
Dansville, U.S.A. .. 84 D7 42 34N 77 42W
Danta, India .. 42 G5 24 11N 72 46 E
Dantan, India .. 43 J12 21 57N 87 20 E
Danube = Dunărea →, Europe .. 17 F15 45 20N 29 40 E
Danvers, U.S.A. .. 85 D14 42 34N 70 56W
Danville, Ill., U.S.A. .. 82 E2 40 8N 87 37W
Danville, Ky., U.S.A. .. 82 G3 37 39N 84 46W
Danville, Pa., U.S.A. .. 85 F8 40 58N 76 37W
Danville, Va., U.S.A. .. 83 G6 36 36N 79 23W
Danville, Vt., U.S.A. .. 85 B12 44 25N 72 9W
Danzig = Gdańsk, Poland .. 17 A10 54 22N 18 40 E
Dapaong, Togo .. 50 F6 10 55N 0 16 E
Daqing Shan, China .. 34 D6 40 40N 111 0 E
Dar Banda, Africa .. 48 F6 8 0N 23 0 E
Dar el Beida = Casablanca, Morocco .. 50 B4 33 36N 7 36W
Dar es Salaam, Tanzania .. 54 D4 6 50S 39 12 E
Dar Mazār, Iran .. 45 D8 29 14N 57 20 E
Dar'ā, Syria .. 46 C5 32 36N 36 7 E
Dar'ā □, Syria .. 46 C5 32 55N 36 10 E
Dārāb, Iran .. 45 D7 28 50N 54 30 E
Daraban, Pakistan .. 42 D4 31 44N 70 20 E
Daraina, Madag. .. 57 A8 13 12S 49 40 E
Daraj, Libya .. 51 B8 30 10N 10 28 E
Dārān, Iran .. 45 C6 32 59N 50 24 E
Dārayyā, Syria .. 46 B5 33 28N 36 15 E
Darband, Pakistan .. 42 B5 34 20N 72 50 E
Darband, Kūh-e, Iran .. 45 D8 31 34N 57 8 E
Darbhanga, India .. 43 F11 26 15N 85 55 E
D'Arcy, Canada .. 70 C4 50 27N 122 35W
Dardanelle, Ark., U.S.A. .. 81 H8 35 13N 93 9W
Dardanelle, Calif., U.S.A. .. 78 G7 38 20N 119 50W
Dardanelles = Çanakkale Boğazı, Turkey .. 23 D12 40 17N 26 32 E
Dārestān, Iran .. 45 D8 29 9N 58 42 E
Dārfūr, Sudan .. 51 F10 13 40N 24 0 E
Dargai, Pakistan .. 42 B4 34 25N 71 55 E
Dargan Ata, Turkmenistan .. 28 E7 40 29N 62 10 E
Dargaville, N.Z. .. 59 F4 35 57S 173 52 E
Darhan, Mongolia .. 32 B5 49 37N 106 21 E
Darhan Muminggan Lianheqi, China .. 34 D6 41 40N 110 28 E
Darıca, Turkey .. 23 D13 40 45N 29 23 E
Darién □, Panama .. 88 E4 7 36N 77 57W
Darién, G. del, Colombia .. 92 B3 9 0N 77 0W
Dariganga = Ovoot, Mongolia .. 34 B7 45 21N 113 45 E
Darjeeling = Darjiling, India .. 43 F13 27 3N 88 18 E
Darjiling, India .. 43 F13 27 3N 88 18 E
Darkan, Australia .. 61 F2 33 20S 116 43 E
Darkhana, Pakistan .. 42 D5 30 39N 72 11 E
Darkhazineh, Iran .. 45 D6 31 54N 48 39 E
Darkot Pass, Pakistan .. 43 A5 36 45N 73 26 E
Darling →, Australia .. 63 E3 34 4S 141 54 E
Darling Downs, Australia .. 63 D5 27 30S 150 30 E
Darling Ra., Australia .. 61 F2 32 30S 116 0 E
Darlington, U.K. .. 12 C6 54 32N 1 33W
Darlington □, U.K. .. 12 C6 54 32N 1 33W
Darlington, S.C., U.S.A. .. 83 H6 34 18N 79 52W
Darlington, L., S. Africa .. 56 E4 33 10S 25 9 E

Darlot, L., Australia .. 61 E3 27 48S 121 35 E
Darłowo, Poland .. 16 A9 54 25N 16 25 E
Darmstadt, Germany .. 16 D5 49 51N 8 39 E
Darnah, Libya .. 51 B10 32 45N 22 45 E
Darnall, S. Africa .. 57 D5 29 23S 31 18 E
Darnley, C., Antarctica .. 5 C6 68 0S 69 0 E
Darnley B., Canada .. 68 B7 69 30N 123 30W
Darr →, Australia .. 62 C3 23 39S 143 50 E
Darra Pezu, Pakistan .. 42 C4 32 19N 70 44 E
Darrequeira, Argentina .. 94 D3 37 42S 63 10W
Darrington, U.S.A. .. 76 B3 48 15N 121 36W
Dart →, U.K. .. 13 G4 50 24N 3 39W
Dart, C., Antarctica .. 5 D14 73 6S 126 20W
Dartford, U.K. .. 13 F8 51 26N 0 13 E
Dartmoor, U.K. .. 13 G4 50 38N 3 57W
Dartmoor △, U.K. .. 13 G4 50 37N 3 59W
Dartmouth, Canada .. 73 D7 44 40N 63 30W
Dartmouth, U.K. .. 13 G4 50 21N 3 36W
Dartmouth Res., Australia .. 63 D4 26 4S 145 18 E
Dartuch, C. = Artrutx, C. de, Spain .. 24 B10 39 55N 3 49 E
Darvaza, Turkmenistan .. 28 E6 40 11N 58 24 E
Darvel, Teluk = Lahad Datu, Teluk, Malaysia .. 37 D5 4 50N 118 20 E
Darwen, U.K. .. 12 D5 53 42N 2 29W
Darwendale, Zimbabwe .. 57 B5 17 41S 30 33 E
Darwha, India .. 40 J10 20 15N 77 45 E
Darwin, Australia .. 60 B5 12 25S 130 51 E
Darwin, U.S.A. .. 79 J9 36 15N 117 35W
Darya Khan, Pakistan .. 42 D4 31 48N 71 6 E
Daryoi Amu = Amudarya →, Uzbekistan .. 28 E6 43 58N 59 34 E
Dashen, Ras, Ethiopia .. 47 E2 13 8N 38 26 E
Dashetai, China .. 34 D5 41 0N 109 5 E
Dashhowuz, Turkmenistan .. 28 E6 41 49N 59 58 E
Dashköpri, Turkmenistan .. 45 B9 36 16N 62 8 E
Dasht, Iran .. 45 B8 37 17N 56 7 E
Dasht →, Pakistan .. 40 G2 25 10N 61 40 E
Daska, Pakistan .. 42 C6 32 20N 74 20 E
Dasuya, India .. 42 D6 31 49N 75 38 E
Datça, Turkey .. 23 F12 36 46N 27 40 E
Datia, India .. 43 G8 25 39N 78 27 E
Datong, China .. 34 D7 40 6N 113 18 E
Dattakhel, Pakistan .. 42 C3 32 54N 69 46 E
Datu, Tanjung, Indonesia .. 36 D3 2 5N 109 39 E
Datu Piang, Phil. .. 37 C6 7 2N 124 30 E
Datuk, Tanjong = Datu, Tanjung, Indonesia .. 36 D3 2 5N 109 39 E
Daud Khel, Pakistan .. 42 C4 32 53N 71 34 E
Daudnagar, India .. 43 G11 25 2N 84 24 E
Daugava →, Latvia .. 9 H21 57 4N 24 3 E
Daugavpils, Latvia .. 9 J22 55 53N 26 32 E
Daulpur, India .. 42 F7 26 45N 77 59 E
Dauphin, Canada .. 71 C8 51 9N 100 5W
Dauphin, U.S.A. .. 84 F8 40 22N 76 56W
Dauphin L., Canada .. 71 C9 51 20N 99 45W
Dauphiné, France .. 20 D6 45 15N 5 25 E
Dausa, India .. 42 F7 26 52N 76 20 E
Davangere, India .. 40 M9 14 25N 75 55 E
Davao, Phil. .. 37 C7 7 0N 125 40 E
Davao G., Phil. .. 37 C7 6 30N 125 48 E
Dāvar Panāh = Sarāvān, Iran .. 45 E9 27 25N 62 15 E
Davenport, Calif., U.S.A. .. 78 H4 37 1N 122 12W
Davenport, Iowa, U.S.A. .. 80 E9 41 32N 90 35W
Davenport, Wash., U.S.A. .. 76 C4 47 39N 118 9W
Davenport Ra., Australia .. 62 C1 20 28S 134 0 E
Daventry, U.K. .. 13 E6 52 16N 1 10W
David, Panama .. 88 E3 8 30N 82 30W
David City, U.S.A. .. 80 E6 41 15N 97 8W
David Gorodok = Davyd Haradok, Belarus .. 17 B14 52 4N 27 8 E
Davidson, Canada .. 71 C7 51 16N 105 59W
Davis, Antarctica .. 5 C6 68 34S 77 55 E
Davis, U.S.A. .. 78 G5 38 33N 121 44W
Davis Dam, U.S.A. .. 79 K12 35 11N 114 34W
Davis Inlet, Canada .. 73 A7 55 50N 60 59W
Davis Mts., U.S.A. .. 81 K2 30 50N 103 55W
Davis Sea, Antarctica .. 5 C7 66 0S 92 0 E
Davis Str., N. Amer. .. 69 B14 65 0N 58 0W
Davos, Switz. .. 20 C8 46 48N 9 49 E
Davy L., Canada .. 71 B7 58 53N 108 18W
Davyd Haradok, Belarus .. 17 B14 52 4N 27 8 E
Dawei = Tavoy, Burma .. 38 E2 14 2N 98 12 E
Dawes Ra., Australia .. 62 C5 24 40S 150 40 E
Dawlish, U.K. .. 13 G4 50 35N 3 28W
Dawna Ra., Burma .. 38 D2 16 30N 98 30 E
Dawros Hd., Ireland .. 10 B3 54 50N 8 33W
Dawson, Canada .. 68 B6 64 10N 139 30W
Dawson, U.S.A. .. 83 K3 31 46N 84 27W
Dawson, I., Chile .. 96 G2 53 50S 70 50W
Dawson B., Canada .. 71 C8 52 53N 100 49W
Dawson Creek, Canada .. 70 B4 55 45N 120 15W
Dawson Inlet, Canada .. 71 A10 61 50N 93 25W
Dawson Ra., Australia .. 62 C4 24 30S 149 48 E
Dax, France .. 20 E3 43 44N 1 3W
Daxian, China .. 32 C5 31 15N 107 23 E
Daxindian, China .. 35 F11 37 30N 120 50 E
Daxinggou, China .. 35 C15 43 25N 129 40 E
Daxue Shan, China .. 32 C5 30 30N 101 30 E
Daylesford, Australia .. 63 F3 37 21S 144 9 E
Dayr az Zawr, Syria .. 44 C4 35 20N 40 5 E
Daysland, Canada .. 70 C6 52 50N 112 20W
Dayton, Nev., U.S.A. .. 78 F7 39 14N 119 36W
Dayton, Ohio, U.S.A. .. 82 F3 39 45N 84 12W
Dayton, Tenn., U.S.A. .. 83 H3 35 30N 85 1W
Dayton, Wash., U.S.A. .. 76 C4 46 19N 117 59W
Dayton, Wyo., U.S.A. .. 76 D10 44 53N 107 16W
Daytona Beach, U.S.A. .. 83 L5 29 13N 81 1W
Dayville, U.S.A. .. 76 D4 44 28N 119 32W
De Aar, S. Africa .. 56 E3 30 39S 24 0 E
De Biesbosch △, Neths. .. 15 C4 51 45N 4 48 E
De Funiak Springs, U.S.A. .. 83 K2 30 43N 86 7W
De Grey →, Australia .. 60 D2 20 12S 119 13 E
De Haan, Belgium .. 15 C3 51 16N 3 2 E
De Hoge Veluwe △, Neths. .. 15 B5 52 5N 5 46 E
De Hoop △, S. Africa .. 56 E3 34 30S 20 28 E
De Kalb, U.S.A. .. 80 E10 41 56N 88 46W
De Kennemerduinen △, Neths. .. 15 B4 52 27N 4 33 E
De Land, U.S.A. .. 83 L5 29 2N 81 18W
De Leon, U.S.A. .. 81 J5 32 7N 98 32W
De Panne, Belgium .. 15 C2 51 6N 2 34 E
De Pere, U.S.A. .. 82 C1 44 27N 88 4W
De Queen, U.S.A. .. 81 H7 34 2N 94 21W
De Quincy, U.S.A. .. 81 K8 30 27N 93 26W
De Ridder, U.S.A. .. 81 K8 30 51N 93 17W
De Smet, U.S.A. .. 80 C6 44 23N 97 33W

De Soto, U.S.A. .. 80 F9 38 8N 90 34W
De Tour Village, U.S.A. .. 82 C4 46 0N 83 56W
De Witt, U.S.A. .. 81 H9 34 18N 91 20W
Dead Sea, Asia .. 46 D4 31 30N 35 30 E
Deadwood, U.S.A. .. 80 C3 44 23N 103 44W
Deadwood L., Canada .. 70 B3 59 10N 128 30W
Deal, U.K. .. 13 F9 51 13N 1 25 E
Deal I., Australia .. 63 F4 39 30S 147 20 E
Dealesville, S. Africa .. 56 D4 28 41S 25 44 E
Dean →, Canada .. 70 C3 52 49N 126 58W
Dean, Forest of, U.K. .. 13 F5 51 45N 2 33W
Dean Chan., Canada .. 70 C3 52 30N 127 15W
Deán Funes, Argentina .. 94 C3 30 20S 64 20W
Dease →, Canada .. 70 B3 59 56N 128 32W
Dease L., Canada .. 70 B2 58 40N 130 5W
Dease Lake, Canada .. 70 B2 58 25N 130 6W
Death Valley, U.S.A. .. 79 J10 36 15N 116 50W
Death Valley △, U.S.A. .. 79 J10 36 45N 117 15W
Death Valley Junction, U.S.A. .. 79 J10 36 20N 116 25W
Debar, Macedonia .. 23 D9 41 31N 20 30 E
Debden, Canada .. 71 C7 53 30N 106 50W
Dębica, Poland .. 17 C11 50 2N 21 25 E
DeBolt, Canada .. 70 B5 55 12N 118 1W
Deborah East, L., Australia .. 61 F2 30 45S 119 0 E
Deborah West, L., Australia .. 61 F2 30 45S 118 50 E
Debre Markos, Ethiopia .. 47 E2 10 20N 37 40 E
Debre Tabor, Ethiopia .. 47 E2 11 50N 38 26 E
Debre Zebit, Ethiopia .. 47 E2 11 48N 38 30 E
Debrecen, Hungary .. 17 E11 47 33N 21 42 E
Decatur, Ala., U.S.A. .. 83 H2 34 36N 86 59W
Decatur, Ga., U.S.A. .. 83 J3 33 47N 84 18W
Decatur, Ill., U.S.A. .. 80 F10 39 51N 88 57W
Decatur, Ind., U.S.A. .. 82 E3 40 50N 84 56W
Decatur, Tex., U.S.A. .. 81 J6 33 14N 97 35W
Deccan, India .. 40 L11 18 0N 79 0 E
Deception Bay, Australia .. 63 D5 27 10S 153 5 E
Deception I., Antarctica .. 5 C17 63 0S 60 15W
Deception L., Canada .. 71 B8 56 33N 104 13W
Dechhu, India .. 42 F5 26 46N 72 20 E
Děčín, Czech Rep. .. 16 C8 50 47N 14 12 E
Deckerville, U.S.A. .. 84 C2 43 32N 82 44W
Decorah, U.S.A. .. 80 D9 43 18N 91 48W
Dedéagach = Alexandroúpolis, Greece .. 23 D11 40 50N 25 54 E
Dedham, U.S.A. .. 85 D13 42 15N 71 10W
Dedza, Malawi .. 55 E3 14 20S 34 20 E
Dee →, Dumf. & Gall., U.K. .. 11 G4 54 51N 4 3W
Dee →, Wales, U.K. .. 12 D4 53 22N 3 17W
Deep B., Canada .. 70 A5 61 15N 116 35W
Deep Bay = Shenzhen Wan, China .. 33 G10 22 27N 113 55 E
Deepwater, Australia .. 63 D5 29 25S 151 51 E
Deer →, Canada .. 71 B10 58 23N 94 13W
Deer Lake, Nfld. & L., Canada .. 73 C8 49 11N 57 27W
Deer Lake, Ont., Canada .. 71 C10 52 40N 94 20W
Deer Lodge, U.S.A. .. 76 C7 46 24N 112 44W
Deer Park, U.S.A. .. 76 C5 47 57N 117 28W
Deer River, U.S.A. .. 80 B8 47 20N 93 48W
Deeragun, Australia .. 62 B4 19 16S 146 33 E
Deerdepoort, S. Africa .. 56 C4 24 37S 26 27 E
Defiance, U.S.A. .. 82 E3 41 17N 84 22W
Degana, India .. 42 F6 26 50N 74 20 E
Dégelis, Canada .. 73 C6 47 30N 68 35W
Deggendorf, Germany .. 16 D7 48 50N 12 57 E
Deh Bid, Iran .. 45 D7 30 39N 53 11 E
Deh-e Shīr, Iran .. 45 D7 31 29N 53 45 E
Dehaj, Iran .. 45 D7 30 42N 54 53 E
Dehak, Iran .. 45 E9 27 11N 62 37 E
Dehdez, Iran .. 45 D6 31 43N 50 17 E
Dehej, India .. 42 J5 21 44N 72 40 E
Dehgolān, Iran .. 44 C5 35 17N 47 25 E
Dehibat, Tunisia .. 51 B8 32 0N 10 47 E
Dehlorān, Iran .. 44 C5 32 41N 47 16 E
Dehnow-e Kūhestān, Iran .. 45 E8 27 58N 58 32 E
Dehra Dun, India .. 42 D8 30 20N 78 4 E
Dehri, India .. 43 G11 24 50N 84 15 E
Dehui, China .. 35 B13 44 30N 125 40 E
Deinze, Belgium .. 15 D3 50 59N 3 32 E
Dej, Romania .. 17 E12 47 10N 23 52 E
Deka →, Zimbabwe .. 56 B4 18 4S 26 42 E
Dekese, Dem. Rep. of the Congo .. 52 E4 3 24S 21 24 E
Del Mar, U.S.A. .. 79 N9 32 58N 117 16W
Del Norte, U.S.A. .. 77 H10 37 41N 106 21W
Delambre I., Australia .. 60 D2 20 26S 117 5 E
Delano, U.S.A. .. 79 K7 35 46N 119 15W
Delano Peak, U.S.A. .. 77 G7 38 22N 112 22W
Delareyville, S. Africa .. 56 D4 26 41S 25 26 E
Delaronde L., Canada .. 71 C7 54 3N 107 3W
Delavan, U.S.A. .. 80 D10 42 38N 88 39W
Delaware, U.S.A. .. 82 E4 40 18N 83 4W
Delaware □, U.S.A. .. 85 F8 39 0N 75 20W
Delaware →, U.S.A. .. 85 G9 39 15N 75 20W
Delaware B., U.S.A. .. 81 F8 39 0N 75 10W
Delaware Water Gap △, U.S.A. .. 85 E10 41 10N 74 55W
Delay →, Canada .. 73 A5 56 56N 71 28W
Delegate, Australia .. 63 F4 37 4S 148 56 E
Delevan, U.S.A. .. 84 D6 42 29N 78 29W
Delft, Neths. .. 15 B4 52 1N 4 22 E
Delfzijl, Neths. .. 15 A6 53 20N 6 55 E
Delgado, C., Mozam. .. 55 E5 10 45S 40 40 E
Delgerhet, Mongolia .. 34 B6 45 50N 110 30 E
Delgo, Sudan .. 51 D12 20 6N 30 40 E
Delhi, Canada .. 84 D4 42 51N 80 30W
Delhi, India .. 42 E7 28 38N 77 17 E
Delhi, La., U.S.A. .. 81 J9 32 28N 91 30W
Delhi, N.Y., U.S.A. .. 85 D10 42 17N 74 55W
Delia, Canada .. 70 C6 51 38N 112 23W
Delice, Turkey .. 19 G5 39 54N 34 2 E
Delicias, Mexico .. 86 B3 28 10N 105 30W
Déline, Canada .. 68 B7 65 11N 123 25W
Delisle, Canada .. 71 C7 51 55N 107 8W
Dell City, U.S.A. .. 77 L11 31 56N 105 12W
Dell Rapids, U.S.A. .. 80 D6 43 50N 96 43W
Delmar, U.S.A. .. 85 D11 42 37N 73 47W
Delmenhorst, Germany .. 16 B5 53 3N 8 37 E
Delonga, Ostrova, Russia .. 29 B15 76 40N 149 20 E
Deloraine, Australia .. 63 G4 41 30S 146 40 E
Deloraine, Canada .. 71 D8 49 15N 100 29W
Delphi, U.S.A. .. 82 E2 40 36N 86 41W
Delphos, U.S.A. .. 82 E3 40 51N 84 21W
Delportshoop, S. Africa .. 56 D3 28 22S 24 20 E

Delray Beach, *U.S.A.* . . . . . . . . . 83 M5　26 28N　80　4W
Delta, *Colo., U.S.A.* . . . . . . . . 77 G9　38 44N 108　4W
Delta, *Utah, U.S.A.* . . . . . . . . 76 G7　39 21N 112 35W
Delta Junction, *U.S.A.* . . . . . . 68 B5　64　2N 145 44W
Deltona, *U.S.A.* . . . . . . . . . . 83 L5　28 54N　81 16W
Delungra, *Australia* . . . . . . . 63 D5　29 39S 150 51 E
Delvada, *India* . . . . . . . . . . 42 J4　20 46N　71　2 E
Delvinë, *Albania* . . . . . . . . . 23 E9　39 59N　20　6 E
Demak, *Indonesia* . . . . . . . . 37 G14　6 53S 110 38 E
Demanda, Sierra de la, *Spain* . . 21 A4　42 15N　3　0W
Demavend = Damāvand, Qolleh-
　ye, *Iran* . . . . . . . . . . . . . 45 C7　35 56N　52 10 E
Dembia, *Dem. Rep. of the Congo* 54 B2　3 33N　25 48 E
Dembidolo, *Ethiopia* . . . . . . . 47 F1　8 34N　34 50 E
Demchok, *India* . . . . . . . . . 43 C8　32 42N　79 29 E
Demer ➤, *Belgium* . . . . . . . . 15 D4　50 57N　4 42 E
Deming, *N. Mex., U.S.A.* . . . 77 K10　32 16N 107 46W
Deming, *Wash., U.S.A.* . . . . . 78 B4　48 50N 122 13W
Demini ➤, *Brazil* . . . . . . . . 92 D6　0 46S　62 56W
Demirci, *Turkey* . . . . . . . . 23 E13　39　2N　28 38 E
Demirköy, *Turkey* . . . . . . . 23 D12　41 49N　27 45 E
Demopolis, *U.S.A.* . . . . . . . . 83 J2　32 31N　87 50W
Dempo, *Indonesia* . . . . . . . . 36 E2　4　2S 103 15 E
Den Burg, *Neths.* . . . . . . . . 54 B2　3 33N　25 48 E
Den Chai, *Thailand* . . . . . . . 38 D3　17 59N 100　4 E
Den Haag = 's-Gravenhage,
　*Neths.* . . . . . . . . . . . . . . 15 B4　52　7N　4 17 E
Den Helder, *Neths.* . . . . . . . . 15 B4　52 57N　4 45 E
Den Oever, *Neths.* . . . . . . . . 15 B5　52 56N　5　2 E
Denair, *U.S.A.* . . . . . . . . . 78 H6　37 32N 120 48W
Denau, *Uzbekistan* . . . . . . . 28 F7　38 16N　67 54 E
Denbigh, *Canada* . . . . . . . . 84 A7　45　8N　77 15W
Denbigh, *U.K.* . . . . . . . . . . 12 D4　53 12N　3 25W
Denbighshire □, *U.K.* . . . . . . 12 D4　53　8N　3 22W
Dendang, *Indonesia* . . . . . . . 36 E3　3　7S 107 56 E
Dendermonde, *Belgium* . . . . . 15 C4　51　2N　4　5 E
Dengfeng, *China* . . . . . . . . 34 G7　34 25N 113　2 E
Dengkou, *China* . . . . . . . . . 34 D4　40 18N 106 55 E
Denham, *Australia* . . . . . . . 61 E1　25 56S 113 31 E
Denham, Mt., *Jamaica* . . . . . 88 a　18 13N　77 32W
Denham Ra., *Australia* . . . . . 62 C4　21 55S 147 46 E
Denham Sd., *Australia* . . . . . 61 E1　25 45S 113 15 E
Denholm, *Canada* . . . . . . . . 71 C7　52 39N 108　1W
Denia, *Spain* . . . . . . . . . . 21 C6　38 49N　0　8 E
Denial B., *Australia* . . . . . . 63 E1　32 14S 133 32 E
Deniliquin, *Australia* . . . . . . 63 F3　35 30S 144 58 E
Denison, *Iowa, U.S.A.* . . . . . 80 E7　42　1N　95 21W
Denison, *Tex., U.S.A.* . . . . . 81 J6　33 45N　96 33W
Denison Plains, *Australia* . . . 60 C4　18 35S 128　0 E
Denizli, *Turkey* . . . . . . . . 19 G4　37 42N　29　2 E
Denman Glacier, *Antarctica* . . 5 C7　66 45S　99 25 E
Denmark, *Australia* . . . . . . . 61 F2　34 59S 117 25 E
Denmark ■, *Europe* . . . . . . . 9 J13　55 45N　10　0 E
Denmark Str., *Atl. Oc.* . . . . . 4 C6　66　0N　30　0W
Dennery, *St. Lucia* . . . . . . . 89 f　13 55N　60 54W
Dennison, *U.S.A.* . . . . . . . . 84 F3　40 24N　81 19W
Denny, *U.K.* . . . . . . . . . . 11 E5　56　1N　3 55W
Denpasar, *Indonesia* . . . . . . 36 F5　8 39S 115 13 E
Denpasar ✈ (DPS), *Indonesia* . 37 K18　8 44S 115 10 E
Denton, *Mont., U.S.A.* . . . . . 76 C9　47 19N 109 57W
Denton, *Tex., U.S.A.* . . . . . . 81 J6　33 13N　97　8W
D'Entrecasteaux △, *Australia* . 61 F2　34 20S 115 33 E
D'Entrecasteaux, Pt., *Australia* 61 F2　34 50S 115 57 E
Denver, *Colo., U.S.A.* . . . . . 80 F2　39 44N 104 59W
Denver, *Pa., U.S.A.* . . . . . . 85 F8　40 14N　76　8W
Denver City, *U.S.A.* . . . . . . 81 J3　32 58N 102 50W
Deoband, *India* . . . . . . . . . 42 E7　29 42N　77 43 E
Deogarh, *India* . . . . . . . . . 42 G5　25 32N　73 54 E
Deoghar, *India* . . . . . . . . 43 G12　24 30N　86 42 E
Deolali, *India* . . . . . . . . . 40 K8　19 58N　73 50 E
Deoli = Devli, *India* . . . . . . 42 G6　25 50N　75 20 E
Deora, *India* . . . . . . . . . . 42 F4　26 22N　70 55 E
Deori, *India* . . . . . . . . . . 43 H8　23 24N　79　1 E
Deoria, *India* . . . . . . . . . 43 F10　26 31N　83 48 E
Deosai Mts., *Pakistan* . . . . . 43 B6　35 40N　75　0 E
Deosri, *India* . . . . . . . . . 43 F14　26 46N　90 29 E
Depalpur, *India* . . . . . . . . 42 H6　22 51N　75 33 E
Deping, *China* . . . . . . . . . 35 F9　37 25N 116 58 E
Deposit, *U.S.A.* . . . . . . . . 85 D9　42　4N　75 25W
Depuch I., *Australia* . . . . . . 60 D2　20 37S 117 44 E
Deputatskiy, *Russia* . . . . . 29 C14　69 18N 139 54 E
Dera Ghazi Khan, *Pakistan* . . 42 D4　30　5N　70 43 E
Dera Ismail Khan, *Pakistan* . . 42 D4　31 50N　70 50 E
Derabugti, *Pakistan* . . . . . . 42 E3　29　2N　69　9 E
Derawar Fort, *Pakistan* . . . . 42 E4　28 46N　71 20 E
Derbent, *Russia* . . . . . . . . 19 F8　42　5N　48 15 E
Derby, *Australia* . . . . . . . . 60 C3　17 18S 123 38 E
Derby, *U.K.* . . . . . . . . . . 12 E6　52 56N　1 28W
Derby, *Conn., U.S.A.* . . . . . 85 E11　41 19N　73　5W
Derby, *Kans., U.S.A.* . . . . . 81 G6　37 33N　97 16W
Derby, *N.Y., U.S.A.* . . . . . . 84 D6　42 41N　78 58W
Derby City □, *U.K.* . . . . . . 12 E6　52 56N　1 28W
Derby Line, *U.S.A.* . . . . . . 85 B12　45　0N　72　6W
Derbyshire □, *U.K.* . . . . . . 12 D6　53 11N　1 38W
Derdepoort, *S. Africa* . . . . . 56 C4　24 38S　26 24 E
Dereham, *U.K.* . . . . . . . . 13 E8　52 41N　0 57 E
Derg ➤, *U.K.* . . . . . . . . . 10 B4　54 44N　7 26W
Derg, L., *Ireland* . . . . . . . . 10 D3　53　0N　8 20W
Dergaon, *India* . . . . . . . . 41 F19　26 45N　94　0 E
Dermott, *U.S.A.* . . . . . . . . 81 J9　33 32N　91 26W
Derry = Londonderry, *U.K.* . . 10 B4　55　0N　7 20W
Derry = Londonderry □, *U.K.* . 10 B4　55　0N　7 20W
Derry, *N.H., U.S.A.* . . . . . 85 D13　42 53N　71 19W
Derry, *Pa., U.S.A.* . . . . . . 84 F5　40 20N　79 18W
Derryveagh Mts., *Ireland* . . . 10 B3　54 56N　8 11W
Derwent ➤, *Cumb., U.K.* . . . 12 C4　54 39N　3 33W
Derwent ➤, *Derby, U.K.* . . . 12 E6　52 57N　1 28W
Derwent ➤, *N. Yorks., U.K.* . 12 D7　53 45N　0 58W
Derwent Water, *U.K.* . . . . . 12 C4　54 35N　3　9W
Des Moines, *Iowa, U.S.A.* . . . 80 E8　41 35N　93 37W
Des Moines, *N. Mex., U.S.A.* . 81 G3　36 46N 103 50W
Des Moines ➤, *U.S.A.* . . . . 80 E9　40 23N　91 25W
Desaguadero ➤, *Argentina* . . 94 C2　34 30S　66 46W
Desaguadero ➤, *Bolivia* . . . 92 G5　16 35S　69　5W
Desar, *Malaysia* . . . . . . . . 39 d　1 31N 104 17 E
Descanso, Pta., *Mexico* . . . . 79 N9　32 21N 117　3W
Deschaillons-sur-St-Laurent,
　*Canada* . . . . . . . . . . . . 73 C5　46 32N　72　7W
Deschambault L., *Canada* . . . 71 C8　54 50N 103 30W
Deschutes ➤, *U.S.A.* . . . . . 76 D3　45 38N 120 55W
Dese, *Ethiopia* . . . . . . . . 47 E2　11　5N　39 40 E
Deseado ➤, *Argentina* . . . . 96 F3　47 45S　65 54W
Desert Center, *U.S.A.* . . . . 79 M11　33 43N 115 24W
Desert Hot Springs, *U.S.A.* . 79 M10　33 58N 116 30W
Deshnok, *India* . . . . . . . . 42 F5　27 48N　73 21 E
Desierto Central de Baja
　California △, *Mexico* . . . . . 86 B2　29 40N 114 43W
Desna ➤, *Ukraine* . . . . . . 17 C16　50 33N　30 32 E

Desolación, I., *Chile* . . . . . . 96 G2　53　0S　74　0W
Despeñaperros, Paso, *Spain* . . 21 C4　38 24N　3 30W
Dessau, *Germany* . . . . . . . 16 C7　51 51N　12 14 E
Dessye = Dese, *Ethiopia* . . . 47 E2　11　5N　39 40 E
D'Estrees B., *Australia* . . . . 63 F2　35 55S 137 45 E
Desuri, *India* . . . . . . . . . 42 G5　25 18N　73 35 E
Det Udom, *Thailand* . . . . . 38 E5　14 54N 105　5 E
Dete, *Zimbabwe* . . . . . . . . 56 B4　18 38S　26 50 E
Detmold, *Germany* . . . . . . 16 C5　51 56N　8 52 E
Detour, Pt., *U.S.A.* . . . . . . 82 C2　45 40N　86 40W
Detroit, *U.S.A.* . . . . . . . . 84 D1　42 20N　83　3W
Detroit Lakes, *U.S.A.* . . . . . 80 B7　46 49N　95 51W
Deurne, *Neths.* . . . . . . . . 15 C5　51 27N　5 49 E
Deutsche Bucht, *Germany* . . 16 A5　54 15N　8　0 E
Deva, *Romania* . . . . . . . . 17 F12　45 53N　22 55 E
Devakottai, *India* . . . . . . . 40 Q11　9 55N　78 45 E
Devaprayag, *India* . . . . . . 43 D8　30 13N　78 35 E
Deventer, *Neths.* . . . . . . . 15 B6　52 15N　6 10 E
Deveron ➤, *U.K.* . . . . . . . 11 D6　57 41N　2 32W
Devgadh Bariya, *India* . . . . 42 H5　22 40N　73 55 E
Devikot, *India* . . . . . . . . 42 F4　26 42N　71 12 E
Devils Den, *U.S.A.* . . . . . . 78 K7　35 46N 119 58W
Devils Lake, *U.S.A.* . . . . . . 80 A5　48　7N　98 52W
Devils Paw, *Canada* . . . . . 70 B2　58 47N 134　0W
Devils Postpile △, *U.S.A.* . . 78 H7　37 37N 119　5W
Devils Tower, *U.S.A.* . . . . . 80 C2　44 35N 104 43W
Devils Tower Junction, *U.S.A.* 80 C2　44 31N 104 57W
Devine, *U.S.A.* . . . . . . . . 81 L5　29　8N　98 54W
Devizes, *U.K.* . . . . . . . . . 13 F6　51 22N　1 58W
Devli, *India* . . . . . . . . . . 42 G6　25 50N　75 20 E
Devon, *Canada* . . . . . . . . 70 C6　53 24N 113 44W
Devon □, *U.K.* . . . . . . . . 13 G4　50 50N　3 40W
Devon I., *Canada* . . . . . . . 4 B3　75 10N　85　0W
Devonport, *Australia* . . . . . 63 G4　41 10S 146 22 E
Devonport, *N.Z.* . . . . . . . 59 G5　36 49S 174 49 E
Dewas, *India* . . . . . . . . . 42 H7　22 59N　76　3 E
Dewetsdorp, *S. Africa* . . . . 56 D4　29 33S　26 39 E
Dewey, *Puerto Rico* . . . . . . 89 d　18 18N　65 18W
Dexter, *Maine, U.S.A.* . . . 83 C11　45　1N　69 18W
Dexter, *Mo., U.S.A.* . . . . . 81 G10　36 48N　89 57W
Dexter, *N. Mex., U.S.A.* . . . 81 J2　33 12N 104 22W
Dey-Dey, L., *Australia* . . . . 61 E5　29 12S 131　4 E
Deyhūk, *Iran* . . . . . . . . . 45 C8　33 15N　57 30 E
Deyyer, *Iran* . . . . . . . . . 45 E6　27 55N　51 55 E
Dezadeash L., *Canada* . . . . 70 A1　60 28N 136 58W
Dezfūl, *Iran* . . . . . . . . . 45 C6　32 20N　48 30 E
Dezhneva, Mys, *Russia* . . . 29 C19　66　5N 169 40W
Dezhou, *China* . . . . . . . . 34 F9　37 26N 116 18 E
Dhādhar ➤, *India* . . . . . . 43 G11　24 56N　85 24 E
Dháfni, *Greece* . . . . . . . . 25 D7　35 13N　25　3 E
Dhahiriya = Az̧ Z̧āhirīyah,
　*West Bank* . . . . . . . . . . 46 D3　31 25N　34 58 E
Dhahran = Az̧ Z̧ahrān, *Si. Arabia* 45 E6　26 10N　50　7 E
Dhak, *Pakistan* . . . . . . . . 42 C5　32 25N　72 33 E
Dhaka, *Bangla.* . . . . . . . 43 H14　23 43N　90 26 E
Dhaka □, *Bangla.* . . . . . . 43 G14　24 25N　90 25 E
Dhali, *Cyprus* . . . . . . . . 25 D12　35　1N　33 25 E
Dhampur, *India* . . . . . . . 43 E8　29 19N　78 33 E
Dhamtari, *India* . . . . . . . 41 J12　20 42N　81 35 E
Dhanbad, *India* . . . . . . . 43 H12　23 50N　86 30 E
Dhangarhi, *Nepal* . . . . . . 41 E12　28 55N　80 40 E
Dhankuta, *Nepal* . . . . . . 43 F12　26 55N　87 40 E
Dhar, *India* . . . . . . . . . . 42 H6　22 35N　75 26 E
Dharampur, *India* . . . . . . 42 H6　22 13N　75 18 E
Dharamsala = Dharmsala, *India* 42 C7　32 16N　76 23 E
Dhariwal, *India* . . . . . . . 42 D6　31 57N　75 19 E
Dharla ➤, *Bangla.* . . . . . 43 G13　25 46N　89 42 E
Dharmapuri, *India* . . . . . 40 N11　12 10N　78 10 E
Dharmjaygarh, *India* . . . . 43 H10　22 28N　83 13 E
Dharmsala, *India* . . . . . . 42 C7　32 16N　76 23 E
Dharni, *India* . . . . . . . . 42 J7　21 33N　76 53 E
Dharwad, *India* . . . . . . . 40 M9　15 30N　75　4 E
Dhasan ➤, *India* . . . . . . 43 G8　25 48N　79 24 E
Dhaulagiri, *Nepal* . . . . . . 43 E10　28 39N　83 28 E
Dhebar, L., *India* . . . . . . 42 G6　24 10N　74　0 E
Dheftera, *Cyprus* . . . . . . 25 D12　35　5N　33 16 E
Dhenkanal, *India* . . . . . . 41 J14　20 45N　85 35 E
Dherinia, *Cyprus* . . . . . . 25 D12　35　3N　33 57 E
Dhī Qār □, *Iraq* . . . . . . . 44 D5　31　0N　46 15 E
Dhiarrizos ➤, *Cyprus* . . . 25 E11　34 41N　32 34 E
Dhībān, *Jordan* . . . . . . . 46 D4　31 30N　35 46 E
Dhíkti Óros, *Greece* . . . . . 25 D7　35　8N　25 30 E
Dhilwan, *India* . . . . . . . 42 D6　31 31N　75 21 E
Dhimarkhera, *India* . . . . . 43 H9　23 28N　80 22 E
Dhírfis Óros, *Greece* . . . . 23 E10　38 40N　23 54 E
Dhodhekánisos, *Greece* . . 23 F12　36 35N　27　0 E
Dholka, *India* . . . . . . . . 42 H5　22 44N　72 29 E
Dhoraji, *India* . . . . . . . . 42 J4　21 45N　70 37 E
Dhrángadhra, *India* . . . . . 42 H4　22 59N　71 31 E
Dhrápanon, Ákra, *Greece* . . 25 D6　35 28N　24 14 E
Dhrol, *India* . . . . . . . . . 42 H4　22 33N　70 25 E
Dhuburi, *India* . . . . . . . 41 F16　26　2N　89 59 E
Dhule, *India* . . . . . . . . . 40 J9　20 58N　74 50 E

Diekirch, *Lux.* . . . . . . . . 15 E6　49 52N　6 10 E
Dien Ban, *Vietnam* . . . . . . 38 E7　15 53N 108 16 E
Dien Bien, *Vietnam* . . . . . . 38 B4　21 20N 103　0 E
Dien Khanh, *Vietnam* . . . . . 39 F7　12 15N 109　6 E
Dieppe, *France* . . . . . . . . 20 B4　49 54N　1　4 E
Dierks, *U.S.A.* . . . . . . . . 84 H8　34　7N　94　1W
Diest, *Belgium* . . . . . . . . 15 D5　50 58N　5　4 E
Dif, *Somali Rep.* . . . . . . . 47 G3　0 59N　40 58 E
Differdange, *Lux.* . . . . . . . 15 E5　49 31N　5 54 E
Dig, *India* . . . . . . . . . . . 42 F7　27 28N　77 20 E
Digba, *Dem. Rep. of the Congo* 54 B2　4 25N　25 48 E
Digby, *Canada* . . . . . . . . 73 D6　44 38N　65 50W
Diggi, *India* . . . . . . . . . 42 F6　26 22N　75 26 E
Dighinala, *Bangla.* . . . . . 43 H18　23 15N　92　5 E
Dighton, *U.S.A.* . . . . . . . 80 F4　38 29N 100 28W
Digne-les-Bains, *France* . . . 20 D7　44　5N　6 12 E
Digos, *Phil.* . . . . . . . . . 37 C7　6 45N 125 20 E
Digranes, *Iceland* . . . . . . 8 C6　66　4N　14 44W
Digul ➤, *Indonesia* . . . . . 37 F9　7　7S 138 42 E
Dihang = Brahmaputra ➤, *Asia* 32 D3　23 40N　90 35 E
Dijlah, Nahr ➤, *Asia* . . . . 44 D5　31　0N　47 25 E
Dijon, *France* . . . . . . . . 20 C6　47 20N　5　3 E
Dikhil, *Djibouti* . . . . . . . 47 E3　11　8N　42 20 E
Dikkil = Dikhil, *Djibouti* . . . 47 E3　11　8N　42 20 E
Diksmuide, *Belgium* . . . . . 15 C2　51　2N　2 52 E
Dikson, *Russia* . . . . . . . 28 B9　73 40N　80　5 E
Dila, *Ethiopia* . . . . . . . . 47 F2　6 21N　38 22 E
Dili, *E. Timor* . . . . . . . . 37 F7　8 39S 125 34 E
Dilley, *U.S.A.* . . . . . . . . 81 L5　28 40N　99 10W
Dilli = Delhi, *India* . . . . . 42 E7　28 38N　77 17 E
Dillingham, *U.S.A.* . . . . . 68 C4　59　3N 158 28W
Dillon, *Canada* . . . . . . . 71 B7　55 56N 108 35W
Dillon, *Mont., U.S.A.* . . . . 76 D7　45 13N 112 38W
Dillon, *S.C., U.S.A.* . . . . . 83 H6　34 25N　79 22W
Dillon ➤, *Canada* . . . . . . 71 B7　55 56N 108 56W
Dillsburg, *U.S.A.* . . . . . . 84 F7　40　7N　77　2W
Dilolo, *Dem. Rep. of the Congo* 52 G4　10 28S　22 18 E
Dimas, *Mexico* . . . . . . . 86 C3　23 43N 106 47W
Dimashq, *Syria* . . . . . . . 46 B5　33 30N　36 18 E
Dimashq □, *Syria* . . . . . 46 B5　33 30N　36 15 E
Dimbaza, *S. Africa* . . . . . 57 E4　32 50S　27 14 E
Dimboola, *Australia* . . . . 63 F3　36 28S 142　7 E
Dîmboviţa = Dâmboviţa ➤,
　*Romania* . . . . . . . . . . 17 F14　44 12N　26 26 E
Dimbulah, *Australia* . . . . 62 B4　17　8S 145　4 E
Dimitrovgrad, *Bulgaria* . . 23 C11　42　5N　25 35 E
Dimitrovgrad, *Russia* . . . 18 D8　54 14N　49 39 E
Dimitrovo = Pernik, *Bulgaria* 23 C10　42 35N　23　2 E
Dimmitt, *U.S.A.* . . . . . . 81 H3　34 33N 102 19W
Dimona, *Israel* . . . . . . . 46 D4　31　2N　35　1 E
Dinagat, *Phil.* . . . . . . . 37 B7　10 10N 125 40 E
Dinajpur, *Bangla.* . . . . . 41 G16　25 33N　88 43 E
Dinan, *France* . . . . . . . 20 B2　48 28N　2　2W
Dīnān Āb, *Iran* . . . . . . . 45 C8　32　4N　56 49 E
Dinant, *Belgium* . . . . . . 15 D4　50 16N　4 55 E
Dinapur, *India* . . . . . . . 43 G11　25 38N　85　5 E
Dīnār, Kūh-e, *Iran* . . . . . 45 D6　30 42N　51 46 E
Dinara Planina, *Croatia* . . 22 C7　44　0N　16 30 E
Dinard, *France* . . . . . . . 20 B2　48 38N　2　6W
Dinaric Alps = Dinara Planina,
　*Croatia* . . . . . . . . . . . 22 C7　44　0N　16 30 E
Dindigul, *India* . . . . . . . 40 P11　10 25N　78　0 E
Dindori, *India* . . . . . . . 43 H9　22 57N　81　5 E
Ding Xian = Dingzhou, *China* 34 E8　38 30N 114 59 E
Dinga, *Pakistan* . . . . . . 42 G2　25 26N　67 10 E
Dingbian, *China* . . . . . . 34 F4　37 35N 107 32 E
Dingle, *Ireland* . . . . . . . 10 D1　52　9N　10 17W
Dingle B., *Ireland* . . . . . 10 D1　52　3N　10 20W
Dingmans Ferry, *U.S.A.* . . 85 E10　41 13N　74 55W
Dingo, *Australia* . . . . . . 62 C4　23 38S 149 19 E
Dingtao, *China* . . . . . . . 34 G8　35　5N 115 35 E
Dingwall, *U.K.* . . . . . . . 11 D4　57 36N　4 26W
Dingxi, *China* . . . . . . . 34 G3　35 30N 104 33 E
Dingxiang, *China* . . . . . 34 E7　38 30N 112 58 E
Dingzhou, *China* . . . . . . 34 E8　38 30N 114 59 E
Dinh, Mui, *Vietnam* . . . . 39 G7　11 22N 109　1 E
Dinh Lap, *Vietnam* . . . . . 38 B6　21 33N 107　6 E
Dinira ➤, *Venezuela* . . . . 89 E6　9 57N　70　6W
Dinokwe, *Botswana* . . . . 56 C4　23　29S　26 37 E
Dinorwic, *Canada* . . . . . 71 D10　49 41N　92 30W
Dinosaur △, *Canada* . . . . 70 C6　50 47N 111 30W
Dinosaur △, *U.S.A.* . . . . 76 F9　40 30N 108 45W
Dinuba, *U.S.A.* . . . . . . 78 J7　36 32N 119 23W
Dipalpur, *Pakistan* . . . . 42 D5　30 40N　73 39 E
Diplo, *Pakistan* . . . . . . 42 G3　24 35N　69 35 E
Dipolog, *Phil.* . . . . . . . 37 C6　8 36N 123 20 E
Dipperu △, *Australia* . . . 62 C4　21 56S 148 42 E
Dir, *Pakistan* . . . . . . . 40 B7　35　8N　71 59 E
Dire, *Mali* . . . . . . . . . 50 E5　16 20N　3 25W
Dire Dawa, *Ethiopia* . . . 47 F3　9 35N　41 45 E
Diriamba, *Nic.* . . . . . . 88 D2　11 51N　86 19W
Dirk Hartog I., *Australia* . 61 E1　25 50S 113　5 E
Dirranbandi, *Australia* . . 63 D4　28 33S 148 17 E
Disa, *India* . . . . . . . . 42 G5　24 18N　72 10 E
Disappointment, C., *U.S.A.* 76 C2　46 18N 124　5W
Disappointment, L., *Australia* 60 D3　23 20S 122 40 E
Disaster B., *Australia* . . . 63 F4　37 15S 149 58 E
Discovery B., *Australia* . . 63 F3　38 10S 140 40 E
Disko = Qeqertarsuaq, *Greenland* 69 B5　69 45N　53 30W
Diss, *U.K.* . . . . . . . . . 13 E9　52 23N　1　7 E
Disteghil Sar, *Pakistan* . . 43 A6　36 20N　75 12 E
Distrito Federal □, *Brazil* . 93 G9　15 45S　47 45W
Distrito Federal □, *Mexico* 87 D5　19 15N　99 10W
Diu, *India* . . . . . . . . . 42 J4　20 45N　70 58 E
Dīvāndarreh, *Iran* . . . . . 44 C5　35 55N　47　2 E
Divide, *U.S.A.* . . . . . . . 76 D7　45 45N 112 45W
Dividing Ra., *Australia* . . 61 E2　27 45S 116　0 E
Divinópolis, *Brazil* . . . . 93 H10　20 10S　44 54W
Divnoye, *Russia* . . . . . . 19 E7　45 55N　43 21 E
Divo, *Ivory C.* . . . . . . . 50 G4　5 48N　5 15W
Diwāl Kol, *Afghan.* . . . . 42 B2　34 23N　67 52 E
Dixie Mt., *U.S.A.* . . . . . 78 F6　39 55N 120 16W
Dixon, *Calif., U.S.A.* . . . 78 G5　38 27N 121 49W
Dixon, *Ill., U.S.A.* . . . . . 80 E10　41 50N　89 29W
Dixon Entrance, *U.S.A.* . . 68 C6　54 30N 132　0W
Dixville, *Canada* . . . . . 85 A13　45　4N　71 46W
Diyālā □, *Iraq* . . . . . . . 44 C5　33 45N　44 50 E
Diyālā ➤, *Iraq* . . . . . . 44 C5　33 14N　44 31 E
Diyarbakır, *Turkey* . . . . 19 G7　37 55N　40 18 E
Diyodar, *India* . . . . . . . 42 G4　24　8N　71 50 E
Djakarta = Jakarta, *Indonesia* 36 F3　6　9S 106 49 E
Djamba, *Angola* . . . . . 56 B1　16 45S 13 58 E
Djambala, *Congo* . . . . . 52 E2　2 32S　14 30 E
Djawa = Jawa, *Indonesia* 36 F3　7　0S 110　0 E
Djelfa, *Algeria* . . . . . . 50 B6　34 40N　3 15 E
Djema, *C.A.R.* . . . . . . 54 A2　6　3N　25 15 E
Djerba, I. de, *Tunisia* . . 51 B8　33 50N　10 48 E

Djerid, Chott, *Tunisia* . . . 50 B7　33 42N　8 30 E
Djibouti, *Djibouti* . . . . . . 47 E3　11 30N　43　5 E
Djibouti ■, *Africa* . . . . . . 47 E3　12　0N　43　0 E
Djolu, *Dem. Rep. of the Congo* 52 D4　0 35N　22　5 E
Djoum, *Cameroon* . . . . . . 52 D2　2 41N　12 35 E
Djourab, Erg du, *Chad* . . . 51 E9　16 40N　18 50 E
Djugu, *Dem. Rep. of the Congo* 54 B3　1 55N　30 35 E
Djúpivogur, *Iceland* . . . . . 8 D6　64 39N　14 17W
Dmitriya Lapteva, Proliv, *Russia* 29 B15　73　0N 140　0 E
Dnepr = Dnipro ➤, *Ukraine* . 19 E5　46 30N　32 18 E
Dneprodzerzhinsk =
　Dniprodzerzhynsk, *Ukraine* . 19 E5　48 32N　34 37 E
Dnepropetrovsk =
　Dnipropetrovsk, *Ukraine* . . 19 E6　48 30N　35　0 E
Dnestr = Dnister ➤, *Europe* . 17 E16　46 18N　30 17 E
Dnieper = Dnipro ➤, *Ukraine* 19 E5　46 30N　32 18 E
Dniester = Dnister ➤, *Europe* 17 E16　46 18N　30 17 E
Dnipro ➤, *Ukraine* . . . . . 19 E5　46 30N　32 18 E
Dniprodzerzhynsk, *Ukraine* . 19 E5　48 32N　34 37 E
Dnipropetrovsk, *Ukraine* . . 19 E6　48 30N　35　0 E
Dnister ➤, *Europe* . . . . . 17 E16　46 18N　30 17 E
Dno, *Russia* . . . . . . . . 18 C4　57 50N　29 58 E
Dnyapro = Dnipro ➤, *Ukraine* 19 E5　46 30N　32 18 E
Doaktown, *Canada* . . . . . 73 C6　46 33N　66　8W
Doan Hung, *Vietnam* . . . . 38 B5　21 30N 105 10 E
Doany, *Madag.* . . . . . . . 57 A8　14 21S　49 30 E
Doba, *Chad* . . . . . . . . 51 G9　8 40N　16 50 E
Dobandi, *Pakistan* . . . . . 42 D2　31 13N　66 50 E
Dobbyn, *Australia* . . . . . 62 B3　19 44S 140　2 E
Dobele, *Latvia* . . . . . . . 9 H20　56 37N　23 16 E
Doberai, Jazirah, *Indonesia* 37 E8　1 25S 133　0 E
Doblas, *Argentina* . . . . . 94 D3　37　5S　64　0W
Dobo, *Indonesia* . . . . . . 37 F8　5 45S 134 15 E
Doboj, Bos.-H. . . . . . . . 23 B8　44 46N　18　4 E
Dobrich, *Bulgaria* . . . . 23 C12　43 37N　27 49 E
Dobruja, *Europe* . . . . . 17 F15　44 30N　28 15 E
Dobrush, *Belarus* . . . . 17 B16　52 25N　31 22 E
Doc, Mui, *Vietnam* . . . . 38 D6　17 58N 106 30 E
Docker River, *Australia* . 61 D4　24 52S 129　5 E
Doctor Arroyo, *Mexico* . . 86 C4　23 40N 100 11W
Doda, *India* . . . . . . . . 43 C6　33　10N　75 34 E
Doda, L., *Canada* . . . . . 72 C4　49 25N　75 13W
Dodecanese = Dhodhekánisos,
　*Greece* . . . . . . . . . . 23 F12　36 35N　27　0 E
Dodge City, *U.S.A.* . . . . 81 G5　37 45N 100　1W
Dodge L., *Canada* . . . . . 71 B7　59 50N 105 36W
Dodgeville, *U.S.A.* . . . . 80 D9　42 58N　90　8W
Dodo, *Indonesia* . . . . . 37 F8　5 45S 134 15 E
Dodoma, *Tanzania* . . . . 54 D4　6　8S　35 45 E
Dodoma □, *Tanzania* . . . 54 D4　6　0S　36　0 E
Dodori △, *Kenya* . . . . . 54 C5　1 55S　41　7 E
Dodsland, *Canada* . . . . 71 C7　51 50N 108 45W
Dodson, *U.S.A.* . . . . . . 76 B9　48 24N 108 15W
Doesburg, *Neths.* . . . . 15 B6　52　1N　6　9 E
Doetinchem, *Neths.* . . . 15 C6　51 59N　6 18 E
Dog Creek, *Canada* . . . 70 C4　51 35N 122 14W
Dog L., Man., *Canada* . . 71 C9　51　2N　98 31W
Dog L., Ont., *Canada* . . 72 C2　48 48N　89 30W
Dogran, *Pakistan* . . . . 42 D5　31 48N　73 35 E
Doğubayazıt, *Turkey* . . 44 B5　39 31N　44　5 E
Doha = Ad Dawḩah, *Qatar* 45 E6　25 15N　51 35 E
Dohazari, *Bangla.* . . . 41 H18　22 10N　92　5 E
Dohrighat, *India* . . . . 43 F10　26 16N　83 31 E
Doi, *Indonesia* . . . . . 37 D7　2 14N 127 49 E
Doi Inthanon △, *Thailand* 38 C2　18 33N　98 34 E
Doi Khuntan △, *Thailand* 38 C2　18 33N　99 14 E
Doi Luang, *Thailand* . . 38 C3　18 30N 101　0 E
Doi Luang △, *Thailand* . 38 C2　19 22N　99 35 E
Doi Saket, *Thailand* . . 38 C2　18 52N　99　9 E
Doi Suthep △, *Thailand* 38 C2　18 49N　98 53 E
Dois Irmãos, Sa., *Brazil* 93 E10　9　0S　42 30W
Dokkum, *Neths.* . . . . 15 A5　53 20N　5 59 E
Dokri, *Pakistan* . . . . . 42 F3　27 25N　68　7 E
Dolak, Pulau, *Indonesia* 37 F9　8　0S 138 30 E
Dolbeau-Mistassini, *Canada* 73 C5　48 53N　72 14W
Dole, *France* . . . . . . 20 C6　47　7N　5 31 E
Dolgellau, *U.K.* . . . . . 12 E4　52 45N　3 53W
Dolgelley = Dolgellau, *U.K.* 12 E4　52 45N　3 53W
Dollard, *Neths.* . . . . . 15 A7　53 20N　7 10 E
Dolo, *Ethiopia* . . . . . . 47 G3　4 11N　42　3 E
Dolomites = Dolomiti, *Italy* 22 A4　46 23N　11 51 E
Dolomiti, *Italy* . . . . . . 22 A4　46 23N　11 51 E
Dolores, *Argentina* . . . 94 D4　36 20S　57 40W
Dolores, *Uruguay* . . . . 94 C4　33 34S　58 15W
Dolores, *U.S.A.* . . . . . 77 H9　37 28N 108 30W
Dolores ➤, *U.S.A.* . . . 77 G9　38 49N 109 17W
Dolphin, C., *Falk. Is.* . . 96 G5　51 10S　59 0W
Dolphin and Union Str., *Canada* 68 B8　69　5N 114 45W
Dom Pedrito, *Brazil* . . 95 C5　31　0S　54 40W
Doma, *Zimbabwe* . . . . 55 F3　16 28S　30 12 E
Domariaganj ➤, *India* . 43 F10　26 17N　83 44 E
Domasi, *Malawi* . . . . 55 F4　15 15S　35 22 E
Dombarovskiy, *Russia* . 28 D6　50 46N　59 32 E
Dombås, *Norway* . . . . 9 E13　62　4N　9　8 E
Dome Fuji, *Antarctica* . 5 D5　77 20S　39 45 E
Domel I. = Letsôk-aw Kyun,
　*Burma* . . . . . . . . . 39 G2　11 30N　98 25 E
Domeyko, *Chile* . . . . 94 B1　29　0S　71　0W
Domeyko, Cordillera, *Chile* 94 A2　24 30S　69　0W
Dominador, *Chile* . . . 94 A2　24 21S　69 20W
Dominica ■, *W. Indies* . 89 C7　15 20N　61 20W
Dominica Passage, *W. Indies* 89 C7　15 10N　61 20W
Dominican Rep. ■, *W. Indies* 89 C5　19　0N　70 30W
Domodóssola, *Italy* . . . 20 D8　46　7N　8 17 E
Domville, Mt., *Australia* 63 D5　28　1S 151 15 E
Don ➤, *Russia* . . . . . 19 E6　47　4N　39 18 E
Don ➤, *Aberds., U.K.* . 11 D6　57 11N　2　5W
Don ➤, *S. Yorks., U.K.* 12 D7　53 41N　0 52W
Don, C., *Australia* . . . 60 B5　11 18S 131 46 E
Don Benito, *Spain* . . . 21 C3　38 53S　5 51W
Don Figuereo Mts., *Jamaica* 88 a　18　5N　77 36W
Don Sak, *Thailand* . . . 39 b　9 18N　99 41 E
Dona Ana = Nhamaabué,
　*Mozam.* . . . . . . . . 55 F4　17 25S　35　5 E
Donaghadee, *U.K.* . . . 10 B6　54 39N　5 33W
Donald, *Australia* . . . 63 F3　36 23S 143　0 E
Donaldsonville, *U.S.A.* 81 K9　30　6N　90 59W
Donalsonville, *U.S.A.* . 83 K3　31　3N　84 53W
Donau = Dunărea ➤, *Europe* 17 F15　45 20N　29 40 E
Donauwörth, *Germany* 16 D6　48 43N　10 47 E
Doncaster, *U.K.* . . . . 12 D6　53 32N　1　6W
Dondo, *Mozam.* . . . . 55 F3　19 33S　34 46 E
Dondo, Teluk, *Indonesia* 37 D6　0 50N 120 30 E
Dondra Head, *Sri Lanka* 40 S12　5 55N　80 40 E
Donegal, *Ireland* . . . 10 B3　54 39N　8　5W
Donegal □, *Ireland* . . 10 B4　54 53N　8　0W
Donegal B., *Ireland* . . 10 B3　54 31N　8 49W
Donets ➤, *Russia* . . . 19 E7　47 33N　40 55 E
Donets Basin, *Ukraine* 6 F13　49　0N　38　0 E

Donetsk, *Ukraine* .......... **19 E6** 48 0N 37 45 E
Dong Ba Thin, *Vietnam* ......... **39 F7** 12 8N 109 13 E
Dong Dang, *Vietnam* ......... **38 B6** 21 54N 106 42 E
Dong Giam, *Vietnam* ......... **38 C5** 19 25N 105 31 E
Dong Ha, *Vietnam* ......... **38 D6** 16 55N 107 8 E
Dong Hoi, *Vietnam* ......... **38 D6** 17 29N 106 36 E
Dong Khe, *Vietnam* ......... **38 A6** 22 26N 106 27 E
Dong Ujimqin Qi, *China* ......... **34 B9** 45 32N 116 55 E
Dong Van, *Vietnam* ......... **38 A5** 23 16N 105 22 E
Dong Xoai, *Vietnam* ......... **39 G6** 11 32N 106 55 E
Dongara, *Australia* ......... **61 E1** 29 14S 114 57 E
Dongbei, *China* ......... **29 E13** 45 0N 125 0 E
Dongchuan, *China* ......... **32 D5** 26 8N 103 1 E
Dongfang, *China* ......... **38 C7** 18 50N 108 33 E
Dongfeng, *China* ......... **35 C13** 42 40N 125 34 E
Donggala, *Indonesia* ......... **37 E5** 0 30S 119 40 E
Donggou, *China* ......... **35 E13** 39 52N 124 10 E
Dongguang, *China* ......... **34 F9** 37 50N 116 30 E
Dongjingcheng, *China* ......... **35 B15** 44 5N 129 10 E
Dongning, *China* ......... **35 B16** 44 2N 131 5 E
Dongola, *Sudan* ......... **51 E12** 19 9N 30 22 E
Dongping, *China* ......... **34 G9** 35 55N 116 20 E
Dongsheng, *China* ......... **34 E6** 39 50N 110 0 E
Dongtai, *China* ......... **35 H11** 32 51N 120 21 E
Dongting Hu, *China* ......... **33 D6** 29 18N 112 45 E
Doniphan, *U.S.A.* ......... **81 G9** 36 37N 90 50W
Dønna, *Norway* ......... **8 C15** 66 6N 12 30 E
Donna, *U.S.A.* ......... **81 M5** 26 9N 98 4W
Donnacona, *Canada* ......... **73 C5** 46 41N 71 41W
Donnelly's Crossing, *N.Z.* ......... **59 F4** 35 42S 173 38 E
Donnybrook, *Australia* ......... **61 F2** 33 34S 115 48 E
Donnybrook, *S. Africa* ......... **57 D4** 29 59S 29 48 E
Donora, *U.S.A.* ......... **84 F5** 40 11N 79 52W
Donostia = Donostia-San
  Sebastián, *Spain* ......... **21 A5** 43 17N 1 58W
Donostia-San Sebastián, *Spain* ......... **21 A5** 43 17N 1 58W
Doon →, *U.K.* ......... **11 F4** 55 27N 4 39W
Dora, L., *Australia* ......... **60 D3** 22 0S 123 0 E
Dora Báltea →, *Italy* ......... **20 D8** 45 11N 8 3 E
Doran L., *Canada* ......... **71 A7** 61 13N 108 6 W
Dorchester, *U.K.* ......... **13 G5** 50 42N 2 27W
Dorchester, C., *Canada* ......... **69 B12** 65 27N 77 27W
Dordabis, *Namibia* ......... **56 C2** 22 52S 17 38 E
Dordogne →, *France* ......... **20 D3** 45 2N 0 36W
Dordrecht, *Neths.* ......... **15 C4** 51 48N 4 39 E
Dordrecht, *S. Africa* ......... **56 E4** 31 20S 27 3 E
Doré L., *Canada* ......... **71 C7** 54 46N 107 17W
Doré Lake, *Canada* ......... **71 C7** 54 38N 107 36W
Dori, *Burkina Faso* ......... **50 F5** 14 3N 0 2W
Doring →, *S. Africa* ......... **56 E2** 31 54S 18 39 E
Doringbos, *S. Africa* ......... **56 E2** 31 59S 19 16 E
Dorking, *U.K.* ......... **13 F7** 51 14N 0 19W
Dornbirn, *Austria* ......... **16 E5** 47 25N 9 45 E
Dornie, *U.K.* ......... **11 D3** 57 17N 5 31W
Dornoch, *U.K.* ......... **11 D4** 57 53N 4 2W
Dornoch Firth, *U.K.* ......... **11 D4** 57 51N 4 4W
Dornogovĭ □, *Mongolia* ......... **34 C6** 44 0N 110 0 E
Dorohoi, *Romania* ......... **17 E14** 47 56N 26 23 E
Döröö Nuur, *Mongolia* ......... **32 B4** 48 0N 93 0 E
Dorr, *Iran* ......... **45 C6** 33 17N 50 38 E
Dorre I., *Australia* ......... **61 E1** 25 13S 113 12 E
Dorrigo, *Australia* ......... **63 E5** 30 20S 152 44 E
Dorris, *U.S.A.* ......... **76 F3** 41 58N 121 55W
Dorset, *Canada* ......... **84 A6** 45 14N 78 54W
Dorset, *U.S.A.* ......... **84 E4** 41 40N 80 40W
Dorset □, *U.K.* ......... **13 G5** 50 45N 2 26W
Dortmund, *Germany* ......... **16 C4** 51 30N 7 28 E
Doruma, *Dem. Rep. of the Congo* **54 B2** 4 42N 27 33 E
Dorūneh, *Iran* ......... **45 C8** 35 10N 57 18 E
Dos Bahías, C., *Argentina* ......... **96 E3** 44 58S 65 32W
Dos Hermanas, *Spain* ......... **21 D3** 37 16N 5 55W
Dos Palos, *U.S.A.* ......... **78 J6** 36 59N 120 37W
Dosso, *Niger* ......... **50 F6** 13 0N 3 13 E
Dothan, *U.S.A.* ......... **83 K3** 31 13N 85 24W
Doty, *U.S.A.* ......... **78 D3** 46 38N 123 17W
Douai, *France* ......... **20 A5** 50 21N 3 4 E
Douala, *Cameroon* ......... **52 D1** 4 0N 9 45 E
Douarnenez, *France* ......... **20 B1** 48 6N 4 21W
Double Island Pt., *Australia* ......... **63 D5** 25 56S 153 11 E
Double Mountain Fork →, *U.S.A.* **81 J4** 33 16N 100 0W
Doubs →, *France* ......... **20 C6** 46 53N 5 1 E
Doubtful Sd., *N.Z.* ......... **59 L1** 45 20S 166 49 E
Doubtless B., *N.Z.* ......... **59 F4** 34 55S 173 26 E
Douglas, *I. of Man* ......... **12 C3** 54 10N 4 28W
Douglas, *S. Africa* ......... **56 D3** 29 4S 23 46 E
Douglas, *Ariz., U.S.A.* ......... **77 L9** 31 21N 109 33W
Douglas, *Ga., U.S.A.* ......... **83 K4** 31 31N 82 51W
Douglas, *Wyo., U.S.A.* ......... **80 D2** 42 45N 105 24W
Douglas Apsley △, *Australia* ......... **63 G4** 41 45S 148 11 E
Douglas Chan., *Canada* ......... **70 C3** 53 40N 129 20W
Douglas Pt., *Canada* ......... **84 B3** 44 19N 81 37W
Douglasville, *U.S.A.* ......... **83 J3** 33 45N 84 45W
Dounreay, *U.K.* ......... **11 C5** 58 35N 3 44W
Dourada, Serra, *Brazil* ......... **93 F9** 13 10S 48 45W
Dourados, *Brazil* ......... **95 A5** 22 9S 54 50W
Dourados →, *Brazil* ......... **95 A5** 21 58S 54 18W
Dourados, Serra dos, *Brazil* ......... **95 A5** 23 30S 53 30W
Douro →, *Europe* ......... **21 B1** 41 8N 8 40W
Dove →, *U.K.* ......... **12 E6** 52 51N 1 36W
Dove Creek, *U.S.A.* ......... **77 H9** 37 46N 108 54W
Dover, *Australia* ......... **63 G4** 43 18S 147 2 E
Dover, *U.K.* ......... **13 F9** 51 7N 1 19 E
Dover, *Del., U.S.A.* ......... **82 F8** 39 10N 75 32W
Dover, *N.H., U.S.A.* ......... **85 C14** 43 12N 70 56W
Dover, *N.J., U.S.A.* ......... **85 F10** 40 53N 74 34W
Dover, *Ohio, U.S.A.* ......... **84 F3** 40 32N 81 29W
Dover, Pt., *Australia* ......... **61 F4** 32 32S 125 32 E
Dover, Str. of, *Europe* ......... **13 G9** 51 0N 1 30 E
Dover-Foxcroft, *U.S.A.* ......... **83 C11** 45 11N 69 13W
Dover Plains, *U.S.A.* ......... **85 E11** 41 43N 73 35W
Dovey = Dyfi →, *U.K.* ......... **13 E3** 52 32N 4 3W
Dovrefjell, *Norway* ......... **9 E13** 62 15N 9 33 E
Dow Rūd, *Iran* ......... **45 C6** 33 28N 49 4 E
Dowa, *Malawi* ......... **55 E3** 13 38S 33 58 E
Dowagiac, *U.S.A.* ......... **82 E2** 41 59N 86 6W
Dowerin, *Australia* ......... **61 F2** 31 12S 117 2 E
Dowgha'i, *Iran* ......... **45 B8** 36 54N 58 32 E
Dowlatābād, *Iran* ......... **45 D8** 28 20N 56 40 E
Down □, *U.K.* ......... **10 B5** 54 23N 6 2W
Downey, *Calif., U.S.A.* ......... **79 M8** 33 56N 118 8W
Downey, *Idaho, U.S.A.* ......... **76 E7** 42 26N 112 7W
Downham Market, *U.K.* ......... **13 E8** 52 37N 0 23 E
Downieville, *U.S.A.* ......... **78 F6** 39 34N 120 50W
Downpatrick, *U.K.* ......... **10 B6** 54 20N 5 43W
Downpatrick Hd., *Ireland* ......... **10 B2** 54 20N 9 21W
Downsville, *U.S.A.* ......... **85 D10** 42 5N 74 50W

Downton, Mt., *Canada* ......... **70 C4** 52 42N 124 52W
Dowsāri, *Iran* ......... **45 D8** 28 25N 57 59 E
Doyle, *U.S.A.* ......... **78 E6** 40 2N 120 6W
Doylestown, *U.S.A.* ......... **85 F9** 40 21N 75 10W
Dozois, Rés., *Canada* ......... **72 C4** 47 30N 77 5W
Dra Khel, *Pakistan* ......... **42 F2** 27 58N 66 45 E
Drachten, *Neths.* ......... **15 A6** 53 7N 6 5 E
Drăgășani, *Romania* ......... **17 F13** 44 39N 24 17 E
Dragichyn, *Belarus* ......... **17 B13** 52 15N 25 8 E
Dragoman, Prokhod, *Bulgaria* ......... **23 C10** 42 58N 22 53 E
Dragon's Mouth = Boca de
  Drago, *Venezuela* ......... **93 K15** 11 0N 61 50W
Draguignan, *France* ......... **20 E7** 43 32N 6 27 E
Drain, *U.S.A.* ......... **76 E2** 43 40N 123 19W
Drake, *U.S.A.* ......... **80 B4** 47 55N 100 23W
Drake Passage, *S. Ocean* ......... **5 B17** 58 0S 68 0W
Drakensberg, *S. Africa* ......... **57 D4** 31 0S 28 0 E
Dráma, *Greece* ......... **23 D11** 41 9N 24 10 E
Drammen, *Norway* ......... **9 G14** 59 42N 10 12 E
Drangajökull, *Iceland* ......... **8 C2** 66 9N 22 15W
Dras, *India* ......... **43 B6** 34 25N 75 48 E
Drau = Drava →, *Croatia* ......... **23 B8** 45 33N 18 55 E
Drava →, *Croatia* ......... **23 B8** 45 33N 18 55 E
Drayton Valley, *Canada* ......... **70 C6** 53 12N 114 58W
Drenthe □, *Neths.* ......... **15 B6** 52 52N 6 40 E
Drepanum, C., *Cyprus* ......... **25 E11** 34 54N 32 19 E
Dresden, *Canada* ......... **84 D2** 42 35N 82 11W
Dresden, *Germany* ......... **16 C7** 51 3N 13 44 E
Dreux, *France* ......... **20 B4** 48 44N 1 23 E
Driffield, *U.K.* ......... **12 C7** 54 0N 0 26W
Driftwood, *U.S.A.* ......... **84 E6** 41 20N 78 8W
Driggs, *U.S.A.* ......... **76 E8** 43 44N 111 6W
Drin →, *Albania* ......... **23 C8** 42 1N 19 38 E
Drina →, *Bos.-H.* ......... **23 B8** 44 53N 19 21 E
Drøbak, *Norway* ......... **9 G14** 59 39N 10 39 E
Drobeta-Turnu Severin, *Romania* **17 F12** 44 39N 22 41 E
Drochia, *Moldova* ......... **17 D14** 48 2N 27 48 E
Drogheda, *Ireland* ......... **10 C5** 53 43N 6 22W
Drogichin = Dragichyn, *Belarus* **17 B13** 52 15N 25 8 E
Drogobych = Drohobych, *Ukraine* **17 D12** 49 20N 23 30 E
Drohobych, *Ukraine* ......... **17 D12** 49 20N 23 30 E
Droichead Atha = Drogheda,
  *Ireland* ......... **10 C5** 53 43N 6 22W
Droichead Nua, *Ireland* ......... **10 C5** 53 11N 6 48W
Droitwich, *U.K.* ......... **13 E5** 52 16N 2 8W
Dromedary, C., *Australia* ......... **63 F5** 36 17S 150 10 E
Dromore, *U.K.* ......... **10 B4** 54 31N 7 28W
Dromore West, *Ireland* ......... **10 B3** 54 15N 8 52W
Dronfield, *U.K.* ......... **12 D6** 53 19N 1 27W
Dronning Maud Land, *Antarctica* **5 D3** 72 30S 12 0 E
Dronten, *Neths.* ......... **15 B5** 52 32N 5 43 E
Drumbo, *Canada* ......... **84 C4** 43 16N 80 35W
Drumheller, *Canada* ......... **70 C6** 51 25N 112 40W
Drummond, *U.S.A.* ......... **76 C7** 46 40N 113 9W
Drummond I., *U.S.A.* ......... **82 C4** 46 1N 83 39W
Drummond Pt., *Australia* ......... **63 E2** 34 9S 135 16 E
Drummond Ra., *Australia* ......... **62 C4** 23 45S 147 10 E
Drummondville, *Canada* ......... **72 C5** 45 55N 72 25W
Drumright, *U.S.A.* ......... **81 H6** 35 59N 96 36W
Druskininkai, *Lithuania* ......... **9 J20** 54 3N 23 58 E
Drut →, *Belarus* ......... **17 B16** 53 8N 30 5 E
Druzhina, *Russia* ......... **29 C15** 68 14N 145 18 E
Dry Harbour Mts., *Jamaica* ......... **88 a** 18 19N 77 24W
Dry Tortugas, *U.S.A.* ......... **88 B3** 24 38N 82 55W
Dryden, *Canada* ......... **71 D10** 49 47N 92 50W
Dryden, *U.S.A.* ......... **85 D8** 42 30N 76 18W
Drygalski I., *Antarctica* ......... **5 C7** 66 0S 92 0 E
Drysdale →, *Australia* ......... **60 B4** 13 59S 126 51 E
Drysdale I., *Australia* ......... **62 A2** 11 41S 136 0 E
Drysdale River △, *Australia* ......... **60 B4** 14 56S 127 2 E
Du Bois, *U.S.A.* ......... **84 E6** 41 8N 78 46W
Du Gué →, *Canada* ......... **72 A5** 57 21N 70 45W
Du Quoin, *U.S.A.* ......... **80 G10** 38 1N 89 14W
Duanesburg, *U.S.A.* ......... **85 D10** 42 45N 74 11W
Duaringa, *Australia* ......... **62 C4** 23 42S 149 42 E
Duarte, Pico, *Dom. Rep.* ......... **89 D5** 19 2N 70 59W
Dubā, *Si. Arabia* ......... **44 E2** 27 10N 35 40 E
Dubai = Dubayy, *U.A.E.* ......... **45 E7** 25 18N 55 20 E
Dubāsari, *Moldova* ......... **17 E15** 47 15N 29 10 E
Dubāsari Vdkhr., *Moldova* ......... **17 E15** 47 30N 29 0 E
Dubawnt →, *Canada* ......... **71 A8** 64 33N 100 6W
Dubawnt L., *Canada* ......... **71 A8** 63 8N 101 28W
Dubayy, *U.A.E.* ......... **45 E7** 25 18N 55 20 E
Dubbo, *Australia* ......... **63 E4** 32 11S 148 35 E
Dubele, *Dem. Rep. of the Congo* **54 B2** 2 56N 29 35 E
Dublin, *Ireland* ......... **10 C5** 53 21N 6 15W
Dublin, *Ga., U.S.A.* ......... **83 J4** 32 32N 82 54W
Dublin, *Tex., U.S.A.* ......... **81 J5** 32 5N 98 21W
Dublin □, *Ireland* ......... **10 C5** 53 24N 6 20W
Dublin ✈ (DUB), *Ireland* ......... **10 C5** 53 26N 6 15W
Dubno, *Ukraine* ......... **17 C13** 50 25N 25 45 E
Dubois, *U.S.A.* ......... **76 D7** 44 10N 112 14W
Dubossary = Dubăsari, *Moldova* **17 E15** 47 15N 29 10 E
Dubossary Vdkhr. = Dubăsari
  Vdkhr., *Moldova* ......... **17 E15** 47 30N 29 0 E
Dubovka, *Russia* ......... **19 E7** 49 5N 44 50 E
Dubrajpur, *India* ......... **43 H12** 23 48N 87 25 E
Dubréka, *Guinea* ......... **50 G3** 9 46N 13 31W
Dubrovitsa = Dubrovytsya,
  *Ukraine* ......... **17 C14** 51 31N 26 35 E
Dubrovnik, *Croatia* ......... **23 C8** 42 39N 18 6 E
Dubrovytsya, *Ukraine* ......... **17 C14** 51 31N 26 35 E
Dubuque, *U.S.A.* ......... **80 D9** 42 30N 90 41W
Duchesne, *U.S.A.* ......... **76 F8** 40 10N 110 24W
Duchess, *Australia* ......... **62 C2** 21 20S 139 50 E
Ducie I., *Pac. Oc.* ......... **65 K15** 24 40S 124 48W
Duck →, *U.S.A.* ......... **83 G2** 36 2N 87 52W
Duck Cr. →, *Australia* ......... **60 D2** 22 37S 116 53 E
Duck Lake, *Canada* ......... **71 C7** 52 50N 106 16W
Duck Mountain △, *Canada* ......... **71 C8** 51 45N 101 0W
Duckwall, Mt., *U.S.A.* ......... **78 H6** 37 58N 120 7W
Dudhi, *India* ......... **41 G13** 24 15N 83 10 E
Dudinka, *Russia* ......... **29 C9** 69 30N 86 13 E
Dudley, *U.K.* ......... **13 E5** 52 31N 2 5W
Dudwa, *India* ......... **43 E9** 28 30N 80 41 E
Duero = Douro →, *Europe* ......... **21 B1** 41 8N 8 40W
Dufftown, *U.K.* ......... **11 D5** 57 27N 3 8W
Düghi Kalā, *Afghan.* ......... **40 C3** 32 20N 62 30 E
Dugi Otok, *Croatia* ......... **16 G8** 44 0N 15 3 E
Duifken Pt., *Australia* ......... **62 A3** 12 33S 141 38 E
Duisburg, *Germany* ......... **16 C4** 51 26N 6 45 E
Duiwelskloof, *S. Africa* ......... **57 C5** 23 42S 30 10 E
Dükdamin, *Iran* ......... **45 C8** 35 59N 57 43 E
Dukelský Průsmyk, *Slovak Rep.* **17 D11** 49 25N 21 42 E
Dukhān, *Qatar* ......... **45 E6** 25 25N 50 50 E
Duki, *Pakistan* ......... **40 D6** 30 14N 68 25 E
Duku, *Nigeria* ......... **51 F8** 10 43N 10 43 E
Dulce, *U.S.A.* ......... **77 H10** 36 56N 107 0W

Dulce →, *Argentina* ......... **94 C3** 30 32S 62 33W
Dulce, G., *Costa Rica* ......... **88 E3** 8 40N 83 20W
Dulf, *Iraq* ......... **44 C5** 35 7N 45 51 E
Dulit, Banjaran, *Malaysia* ......... **36 D4** 3 15N 114 30 E
Duliu, *China* ......... **34 E9** 39 2N 116 55 E
Dullewala, *Pakistan* ......... **42 D4** 31 50N 71 25 E
Dullstroom, *S. Africa* ......... **57 D5** 25 27S 30 7 E
Duluth, *U.S.A.* ......... **80 B8** 46 47N 92 6W
Dum Dum, *India* ......... **43 H13** 22 39N 88 33 E
Dum Duma, *India* ......... **41 F19** 27 40N 95 40 E
Dūmā, *Syria* ......... **46 B5** 33 34N 36 24 E
Dumaguete, *Phil.* ......... **37 C6** 9 17N 123 15 E
Dumai, *Indonesia* ......... **36 D2** 1 35N 101 28 E
Dumaran, *Phil.* ......... **37 B5** 10 33N 119 50 E
Dumas, *Ark., U.S.A.* ......... **81 J9** 33 53N 91 29W
Dumas, *Tex., U.S.A.* ......... **81 H4** 35 52N 101 58W
Dumayr, *Syria* ......... **46 B5** 33 39N 36 42 E
Dumbarton, *U.K.* ......... **11 F4** 55 57N 4 33W
Dumbleyung, *Australia* ......... **61 F2** 33 17S 117 42 E
Dumfries, *U.K.* ......... **11 F5** 55 4N 3 37W
Dumfries & Galloway □, *U.K.* ......... **11 F5** 55 9N 3 58W
Dumka, *India* ......... **43 G12** 24 12N 87 15 E
Dumoine →, *Canada* ......... **72 C4** 46 13N 77 51W
Dumoine, L., *Canada* ......... **72 C4** 46 55N 77 55W
Dumont d'Urville, *Antarctica* ......... **5 C10** 67 0S 110 0 E
Dumraon, *India* ......... **43 G11** 25 33N 84 8 E
Dumyât, *Egypt* ......... **51 B12** 31 24N 31 48 E
Dún Dealgan = Dundalk, *Ireland* **10 B5** 54 1N 6 24W
Dún Laoghaire, *Ireland* ......... **10 C5** 53 17N 6 8W
Duna = Dunărea →, *Europe* ......... **17 F15** 45 20N 29 40 E
Dunagiri, *India* ......... **43 D8** 30 31N 79 52 E
Dunaj = Dunărea →, *Europe* ......... **17 F15** 45 20N 29 40 E
Dunakeszi, *Hungary* ......... **17 E10** 47 37N 19 8 E
Dunărea →, *Europe* ......... **17 F15** 45 20N 29 40 E
Dunaújváros, *Hungary* ......... **17 E10** 46 58N 18 57 E
Dunav = Dunărea →, *Europe* ......... **17 F15** 45 20N 29 40 E
Dunay, *Russia* ......... **30 C6** 42 52N 132 22 E
Dunback, *N.Z.* ......... **59 L3** 45 23S 170 36 E
Dunbar, *U.K.* ......... **11 E6** 56 0N 2 31W
Dunblane, *U.K.* ......... **11 E5** 56 11N 3 58W
Duncan, *Ariz., U.S.A.* ......... **77 K9** 32 43N 109 6W
Duncan, *Okla., U.S.A.* ......... **81 H6** 34 30N 97 57W
Duncan, L., *Canada* ......... **72 B4** 53 29N 77 58W
Duncan L., *Canada* ......... **70 A6** 62 51N 113 58W
Duncannon, *U.S.A.* ......... **84 F7** 40 23N 77 2W
Duncansby Head, *U.K.* ......... **11 C5** 58 38N 3 1W
Duncansville, *U.S.A.* ......... **84 F6** 40 25N 78 26W
Dundalk, *Canada* ......... **84 B4** 44 10N 80 24W
Dundalk, *Ireland* ......... **10 B5** 54 1N 6 24W
Dundalk, *U.S.A.* ......... **82 F7** 39 16N 76 32W
Dundalk Bay, *Ireland* ......... **10 C5** 53 55N 6 15W
Dundas = Uummannaq,
  *Greenland* ......... **4 B4** 77 0N 69 0W
Dundas = Uummannaq,
  *Greenland* ......... **4 B5** 70 58N 52 0W
Dundas, *Canada* ......... **84 C5** 43 17N 79 59W
Dundas, L., *Australia* ......... **61 F3** 32 35S 121 50 E
Dundas I., *Canada* ......... **70 C2** 54 30N 130 50W
Dundas Str., *Australia* ......... **60 B5** 11 15S 131 35 E
Dundee, *S. Africa* ......... **57 D5** 28 11S 30 15 E
Dundee, *U.K.* ......... **11 E6** 56 28N 2 59W
Dundee, *U.S.A.* ......... **84 D8** 42 32N 76 59W
Dundee City □, *U.K.* ......... **11 E6** 56 30N 2 58W
Dundgovĭ □, *Mongolia* ......... **34 B4** 45 10N 106 0 E
Dundrum, *U.K.* ......... **10 B6** 54 16N 5 52W
Dundrum B., *U.K.* ......... **10 B6** 54 13N 5 47W
Dunedin, *N.Z.* ......... **59 L3** 45 50S 170 33 E
Dunedin, *U.S.A.* ......... **83 L4** 28 1N 82 47W
Dunfermline, *U.K.* ......... **11 E5** 56 5N 3 27W
Dungannon, *Canada* ......... **84 C3** 43 51N 81 36W
Dungannon, *U.K.* ......... **10 B5** 54 31N 6 46W
Dungarpur, *India* ......... **42 H5** 23 52N 73 45 E
Dungarvan, *Ireland* ......... **10 D4** 52 5N 7 37W
Dungarvan Harbour, *Ireland* ......... **10 D4** 52 4N 7 35W
Dungeness, *U.K.* ......... **13 G8** 50 54N 0 59 E
Dungo, L. do, *Angola* ......... **56 B2** 17 15S 19 0 E
Dungog, *Australia* ......... **63 E5** 32 22S 151 46 E
Dungu, *Dem. Rep. of the Congo* **54 B2** 3 40N 28 32 E
Dungun, *Malaysia* ......... **39 K4** 4 45N 103 25 E
Dunhua, *China* ......... **35 C15** 43 20N 128 14 E
Dunhuang, *China* ......... **32 B4** 40 8N 94 36 E
Dunk I., *Australia* ......... **62 B4** 17 59S 146 29 E
Dunkeld, *Australia* ......... **63 E4** 33 25S 149 29 E
Dunkeld, *U.K.* ......... **11 E5** 56 34N 3 35W
Dunkerque, *France* ......... **20 A5** 51 2N 2 20 E
Dunkery Beacon, *U.K.* ......... **13 F4** 51 9N 3 36W
Dunkirk = Dunkerque, *France* ......... **20 A5** 51 2N 2 20 E
Dunkirk, *U.S.A.* ......... **84 D5** 42 29N 79 20W
Dúnleary = Dún Laoghaire,
  *Ireland* ......... **10 C5** 53 17N 6 8W
Dunleer, *Ireland* ......... **10 C5** 53 50N 6 24W
Dunmanus B., *Ireland* ......... **10 E2** 51 31N 9 50W
Dunmanway, *Ireland* ......... **10 E2** 51 43N 9 6W
Dunmara, *Australia* ......... **62 B1** 16 42S 133 25 E
Dunmore, *U.S.A.* ......... **85 E9** 41 25N 75 38W
Dunmore Hd., *Ireland* ......... **10 D1** 52 10N 10 35W
Dunmore Town, *Bahamas* ......... **88 A4** 25 30N 76 39W
Dunn, *U.S.A.* ......... **83 H6** 35 19N 78 37W
Dunnellon, *U.S.A.* ......... **83 L4** 29 3N 82 28W
Dunnet Hd., *U.K.* ......... **11 C5** 58 40N 3 21W
Dunning, *U.S.A.* ......... **80 E4** 41 50N 100 6W
Dunnville, *Canada* ......... **84 D5** 42 54N 79 36W
Dunolly, *Australia* ......... **63 F3** 36 51S 143 44 E
Dunoon, *U.K.* ......... **11 F4** 55 57N 4 56W
Dunphy, *U.S.A.* ......... **76 F5** 40 42N 116 31W
Duns, *U.K.* ......... **11 F6** 55 47N 2 20W
Dunseith, *U.S.A.* ......... **80 A4** 48 50N 100 3W
Dunsmuir, *U.S.A.* ......... **76 F2** 41 13N 122 16W
Dunstable, *U.K.* ......... **13 F7** 51 53N 0 32W
Dunstan Mts., *N.Z.* ......... **59 L2** 44 53S 169 35 E
Dunster, *Canada* ......... **70 C5** 53 8N 119 50W
Dunvegan, *U.K.* ......... **11 D2** 57 27N 6 35W
Dunvegan L., *Canada* ......... **71 A7** 60 8N 107 10W
Duolun, *China* ......... **34 C9** 42 12N 116 28 E
Duong Dong, *Vietnam* ......... **39 G4** 10 13N 103 58 E
Dupree, *U.S.A.* ......... **80 C4** 45 4N 101 35W
Dupuyer, *U.S.A.* ......... **76 B7** 48 13N 112 30W
Duque de Caxias, *Brazil* ......... **95 A7** 22 45S 43 19W
Durack →, *Australia* ......... **60 C4** 15 33S 127 52 E
Durack Ra., *Australia* ......... **60 C4** 16 50S 127 40 E
Durance →, *France* ......... **20 E6** 43 55N 4 45 E
Durand, *U.S.A.* ......... **80 C9** 44 38N 91 58W
Durango, *Mexico* ......... **86 C4** 24 3N 104 39W
Durango □, *Mexico* ......... **86 C4** 25 0N 105 0W

Durant, *Miss., U.S.A.* ......... **81 J10** 33 4N 89 51W
Durant, *Okla., U.S.A.* ......... **81 J6** 33 59N 96 25W
Durazno, *Uruguay* ......... **94 C4** 33 25S 56 31W
Durazzo = Durrës, *Albania* ......... **23 D8** 41 19N 19 28 E
Durban, *S. Africa* ......... **57 D5** 29 49S 31 1 E
Durbuy, *Belgium* ......... **15 D5** 50 21N 5 28 E
Düren, *Germany* ......... **16 C4** 50 48N 6 29 E
Durg, *India* ......... **41 J12** 21 15N 81 22 E
Durgapur, *India* ......... **43 H12** 23 30N 87 20 E
Durham, *Canada* ......... **84 B4** 44 10N 80 49W
Durham, *U.K.* ......... **12 C6** 54 47N 1 34W
Durham, *Calif., U.S.A.* ......... **78 F5** 39 39N 121 48W
Durham, *N.C., U.S.A.* ......... **83 H6** 35 59N 78 54W
Durham, *N.H., U.S.A.* ......... **85 C14** 43 8N 70 56W
Durham □, *U.K.* ......... **12 C6** 54 42N 1 45W
Qurmā, *Si. Arabia* ......... **44 E5** 24 37N 46 8 E
Durmitor, *Serbia & M.* ......... **23 C8** 43 10N 19 0 E
Durness, *U.K.* ......... **11 C4** 58 34N 4 45W
Durrës, *Albania* ......... **23 D8** 41 19N 19 28 E
Durrow, *Ireland* ......... **10 D4** 52 51N 7 24W
Dursey I., *Ireland* ......... **10 E1** 51 36N 10 12W
Dursley, *U.K.* ......... **13 F5** 51 40N 2 21W
Dursunbey, *Turkey* ......... **23 E13** 39 35N 28 37 E
Duru, *Dem. Rep. of the Congo* ......... **54 B2** 4 14N 28 50 E
Durūz, Jabal ad, *Jordan* ......... **46 C5** 32 35N 36 40 E
D'Urville, Tanjung, *Indonesia* ......... **37 E9** 1 28S 137 54 E
D'Urville I., *N.Z.* ......... **59 J4** 40 50S 173 55 E
Duryea, *U.S.A.* ......... **85 E9** 41 20N 75 45W
Dushak, *Turkmenistan* ......... **28 F7** 37 13N 60 1 E
Dushanbe, *Tajikistan* ......... **28 F7** 38 33N 68 48 E
Dushore, *U.S.A.* ......... **85 E8** 41 31N 76 24W
Dusky Sd., *N.Z.* ......... **59 L1** 45 47S 166 30 E
Dussejour, C., *Australia* ......... **60 B4** 14 45S 128 13 E
Düsseldorf, *Germany* ......... **16 C4** 51 14N 6 47 E
Dutch Harbor, *U.S.A.* ......... **68 C3** 53 53N 166 32W
Dutlwe, *Botswana* ......... **56 C3** 23 58S 23 46 E
Dutton, *Canada* ......... **84 D3** 42 39N 81 30W
Dutton →, *Australia* ......... **62 C3** 20 44S 143 10 E
Duyun, *China* ......... **32 D5** 26 18N 107 29 E
Dvina, Severnaya →, *Russia* ......... **18 B7** 64 32N 40 30 E
Dvinsk = Daugavpils, *Latvia* ......... **9 J22** 55 53N 26 32 E
Dvinskaya Guba, *Russia* ......... **18 B6** 65 0N 39 0 E
Dwarka, *India* ......... **42 H3** 22 18N 69 8 E
Dwellingup, *Australia* ......... **61 F2** 32 43S 116 4 E
Dwight, *Canada* ......... **84 A5** 45 20N 79 1W
Dwight, *U.S.A.* ......... **82 E1** 41 5N 88 26W
Dyatlovo = Dzyatlava, *Belarus* **17 B13** 53 28N 25 28 E
Dyce, *U.K.* ......... **11 D6** 57 13N 2 12W
Dyer, C., *Canada* ......... **69 B13** 66 37N 61 16W
Dyer Bay, *Canada* ......... **84 A3** 45 10N 81 20W
Dyer Plateau, *Antarctica* ......... **5 D17** 70 45S 65 30W
Dyersburg, *U.S.A.* ......... **81 G10** 36 3N 89 23W
Dyfi →, *U.K.* ......... **13 E3** 52 32N 4 3W
Dymer, *Ukraine* ......... **17 C16** 50 47N 30 18 E
Dysart, *Australia* ......... **62 C4** 22 32S 148 23 E
Dzerzhinsk, *Russia* ......... **18 C7** 56 14N 43 30 E
Dzhambul = Taraz, *Kazakhstan* **28 E8** 42 54N 71 22 E
Dzhankoy, *Ukraine* ......... **19 E5** 45 40N 34 20 E
Dzhezkazgan = Zhezqazghan,
  *Kazakhstan* ......... **28 E7** 47 44N 67 40 E
Dzhizak = Jizzakh, *Uzbekistan* **28 E7** 40 6N 67 50 E
Dzhugdzur, Khrebet, *Russia* ......... **29 D14** 57 30N 138 0 E
Dzhungarskiye Vorota =
  Dzungarian Gates, *Asia* ......... **32 B3** 45 0N 82 0 E
Działdowo, *Poland* ......... **17 B11** 53 15N 20 15 E
Dzibilchaltún, *Mexico* ......... **87 C7** 21 5N 89 36W
Dzibilchaltún, *Yucatán, Mexico* **87 C7** 21 5N 89 36W
Dzierżoniów, *Poland* ......... **17 C9** 50 45N 16 39 E
Dzilam de Bravo, *Mexico* ......... **87 C7** 21 24N 88 53W
Dzungaria = Junggar Pendi,
  *China* ......... **32 B3** 44 30N 86 0 E
Dzungarian Basin = Junggar
  Pendi, *China* ......... **32 B3** 44 30N 86 0 E
Dzungarian Gates, *Asia* ......... **32 B3** 45 0N 82 0 E
Dzuumod, *Mongolia* ......... **32 B5** 47 45N 106 58 E
Dzyarzhynsk, *Belarus* ......... **17 B14** 53 40N 27 1 E
Dzyatlava, *Belarus* ......... **17 B13** 53 28N 25 28 E

# E

E.C. Manning △, *Canada* ......... **70 D4** 49 5N 120 45W
Eabamet L., *Canada* ......... **72 B2** 51 30N 87 46W
Eads, *U.S.A.* ......... **80 F3** 38 29N 102 47W
Eagar, *U.S.A.* ......... **77 J9** 34 6N 109 17W
Eagle, *Alaska, U.S.A.* ......... **68 B5** 64 47N 141 12W
Eagle, *Colo., U.S.A.* ......... **76 G10** 39 39N 106 50W
Eagle →, *Canada* ......... **73 B8** 53 36N 57 26W
Eagle Butte, *U.S.A.* ......... **80 C4** 45 0N 101 10W
Eagle Grove, *U.S.A.* ......... **80 D8** 42 40N 93 54W
Eagle L., *Canada* ......... **71 D10** 49 42N 93 13W
Eagle L., *Calif., U.S.A.* ......... **76 F3** 40 39N 120 45W
Eagle L., *Maine, U.S.A.* ......... **83 B11** 46 20N 69 22W
Eagle Lake, *Canada* ......... **84 A6** 45 8N 78 29W
Eagle Lake, *Maine, U.S.A.* ......... **83 B11** 47 3N 68 36W
Eagle Lake, *Tex., U.S.A.* ......... **81 L6** 29 35N 96 20W
Eagle Mountain, *U.S.A.* ......... **79 M11** 33 49N 115 27W
Eagle Nest, *U.S.A.* ......... **77 H11** 36 33N 105 16W
Eagle Pass, *U.S.A.* ......... **81 L4** 28 43N 100 30W
Eagle Pk., *U.S.A.* ......... **78 G7** 38 10N 119 25W
Eagle Pt., *U.S.A.* ......... **60 C3** 16 11S 124 23 E
Eagle River, *Mich., U.S.A.* ......... **82 B1** 47 24N 88 18W
Eagle River, *Wis., U.S.A.* ......... **80 C10** 45 55N 89 15W
Eaglehawk, *Australia* ......... **63 F3** 36 44S 144 15 E
Eagles Mere, *U.S.A.* ......... **85 E8** 41 25N 76 33W
Ealing □, *U.K.* ......... **13 F7** 51 31N 0 20W
Ear Falls, *Canada* ......... **71 C10** 50 38N 93 13W
Earle, *U.S.A.* ......... **81 H9** 35 16N 90 28W
Earlimart, *U.S.A.* ......... **79 K7** 35 53N 119 16W
Earn →, *U.K.* ......... **11 E5** 56 21N 3 18W
Earn, L., *U.K.* ......... **11 E4** 56 23N 4 13W
Earnslaw, Mt., *N.Z.* ......... **59 L2** 44 32S 168 27 E
Earth, *U.S.A.* ......... **81 H3** 34 14N 102 24W
Easley, *U.S.A.* ......... **83 H4** 34 50N 82 36W
East Anglia, *U.K.* ......... **12 E9** 52 30N 1 0 E
East Angus, *Canada* ......... **73 C5** 45 30N 71 40W
East Antarctica, *Antarctica* ......... **5 D7** 80 0S 90 0 E
East Aurora, *U.S.A.* ......... **84 D6** 42 46N 78 37W
East Ayrshire □, *U.K.* ......... **11 F4** 55 26N 4 11W
East Bengal, *Bangla.* ......... **41 H17** 24 0N 90 0 E
East Beskids = Vychodné
  Beskydy, *Europe* ......... **17 D11** 49 20N 22 0 E
East Brady, *U.S.A.* ......... **84 F5** 40 59N 79 36W
East C., *N.Z.* ......... **59 G7** 37 42S 178 35 E

East Chicago, *U.S.A.* . . . . . . . . . 82 E2　41 38N　87 27W
East China Sea, *Asia* . . . . . . . . . 33 D7　30　0N 126　0 E
East Coulee, *Canada* . . . . . . . . 70 C6　51 23N 112 27W
East Dereham, *U.K.* . . . . . . . . . 13 E8　52 41N　0 57 E
East Dunbartonshire □, *U.K.* . . 11 F4　55 57N　4 13W
East Falkland, *Falk. Is.* . . . . . . . 96 G5　51 30S　58 30W
East Grand Forks, *U.S.A.* . . . . . 80 B6　47 56N　97　1W
East Greenwich, *U.S.A.* . . . . . . 85 E13　41 40N　71 27W
East Grinstead, *U.K.* . . . . . . . . 13 F8　51　7N　0　0W
East Hartford, *U.S.A.* . . . . . . . . 85 E12　41 46N　72 39W
East Helena, *U.S.A.* . . . . . . . . . 76 C8　46 35N 111 56W
East Indies, *Asia* . . . . . . . . . . . 26 K15　0　0 120　0 E
East Kilbride, *U.K.* . . . . . . . . . 11 F4　55 47N　4 11W
East Lamma Channel, *China* . . 33 G11　22 14N 114　9 E
East Lansing, *U.S.A.* . . . . . . . . . 82 D3　42 44N　84 29W
East Liverpool, *U.S.A.* . . . . . . . 84 F4　40 37N　80 35W
East London, *S. Africa* . . . . . . . 57 E4　33　0S　27 55 E
East Lothian □, *U.K.* . . . . . . . . 11 F6　55 58N　2 44W
East Main = Eastmain, *Canada* . 72 B4　52 10N　78 30W
East Northport, *U.S.A.* . . . . . . . 85 F11　40 53N　73 20W
East Orange, *U.S.A.* . . . . . . . . . 85 F10　40 46N　74 13W
East Pacific Ridge, *Pac. Oc.* . . . 65 J17　15　0S 110　0W
East Palestine, *U.S.A.* . . . . . . . . 84 F4　40 50N　80 32W
East Pine, *Canada* . . . . . . . . . . 70 B4　55 48N 120 12W
East Point, *U.S.A.* . . . . . . . . . . 83 J3　33 41N　84 27W
East Providence, *U.S.A.* . . . . . . 85 E13　41 49N　71 23W
East Pt., *Br. Virgin Is.* . . . . . . . 89 e　18 40N　64 18W
East Pt., *Canada* . . . . . . . . . . . 73 C7　46 27N　61 58W
East Renfrewshire □, *U.K.* . . . . 11 F4　55 46N　4 21W
East Retford = Retford, *U.K.* . . 12 D7　53 19N　0 56W
East Riding of Yorkshire □, *U.K.* 12 D7　53 55N　0 30W
East Rochester, *U.S.A.* . . . . . . . 84 C7　43　7N　77 29W
East St. Louis, *U.S.A.* . . . . . . . . 80 F9　38 37N　90　9W
East Schelde = Oosterschelde →,
　*Neths.* . . . . . . . . . . . . . . . . . 15 C4　51 33N　4　0 E
East Sea = Japan, Sea of, *Asia* . 30 E7　40　0N 135　0 E
East Siberian Sea, *Russia* . . . . . 29 B17　73　0N 160　0 E
East Stroudsburg, *U.S.A.* . . . . . 85 E9　41　1N　75 11W
East Sussex □, *U.K.* . . . . . . . . . 13 G8　50 56N　0 19 E
East Tawas, *U.S.A.* . . . . . . . . . . 82 C4　44 17N　83 29W
East Timor ■, *Asia* . . . . . . . . . 37 F7　8 50S 126　0 E
East Toorale, *Australia* . . . . . . . 63 E4　30 27S 145 28 E
East Walker →, *U.S.A.* . . . . . . . 78 G7　38 52N 119 10W
East Windsor, *U.S.A.* . . . . . . . . 85 F10　40 17N　74 34W
Eastbourne, *N.Z.* . . . . . . . . . . . 59 J5　41 19S 174 55 E
Eastbourne, *U.K.* . . . . . . . . . . . 13 G8　50 46N　0 18 E
Eastend, *Canada* . . . . . . . . . . . 71 D7　49 32N 108 50W
Easter I. = Pascua, I. de, *Chile* . 65 K17　27　7S 109 23W
Eastern □, *Kenya* . . . . . . . . . . 54 C4　0　0　38 30 E
Eastern Cape □, *S. Africa* . . . . . 56 E4　32　0S　26　0 E
Eastern Cr. →, *Australia* . . . . . . 62 C3　20 40S 141 35 E
Eastern Ghats, *India* . . . . . . . . 40 N11　14　0N　78 50 E
Eastern Group = Lau Group, *Fiji* 59 C9　17　0S 178 30W
Eastern Group, *Australia* . . . . . 61 F3　33 30S 124 30 E
Eastern Transvaal =
　Mpumalanga □, *S. Africa* . . . 57 D5　26　0S　30　0 E
Easterville, *Canada* . . . . . . . . . 71 C9　53　8N　99 49W
Easthampton, *U.S.A.* . . . . . . . . 85 D12　42 16N　72 40W
Eastlake, *U.S.A.* . . . . . . . . . . . 84 E3　41 40N　81 26W
Eastland, *U.S.A.* . . . . . . . . . . . 81 J5　32 24N　98 49W
Eastleigh, *U.K.* . . . . . . . . . . . . 13 G6　50 58N　1 21W
Eastmain, *Canada* . . . . . . . . . . 72 B4　52 10N　78 30W
Eastmain →, *Canada* . . . . . . . . 72 B4　52 27N　78 26W
Eastman, *Canada* . . . . . . . . . . 85 A12　45 18N　72 19W
Eastman, *U.S.A.* . . . . . . . . . . . 83 J4　32 12N　83 11W
Easton, *Md., U.S.A.* . . . . . . . . . 82 F7　38 47N　76　5W
Easton, *Pa., U.S.A.* . . . . . . . . . . 85 F9　40 41N　75 13W
Easton, *Wash., U.S.A.* . . . . . . . 78 C5　47 14N 121 11W
Eastpointe, *U.S.A.* . . . . . . . . . . 84 D2　42 27N　82 56W
Eastport, *U.S.A.* . . . . . . . . . . . 83 C12　44 56N　67　0W
Eastsound, *U.S.A.* . . . . . . . . . . 78 B4　48 42N 122 55W
Eaton, *U.S.A.* . . . . . . . . . . . . . 80 E2　40 32N 104 42W
Eatonia, *Canada* . . . . . . . . . . . 71 C7　51 13N 109 25W
Eatonton, *U.S.A.* . . . . . . . . . . . 83 J4　33 20N　83 23W
Eatontown, *U.S.A.* . . . . . . . . . 85 F10　40 19N　74　4W
Eatonville, *U.S.A.* . . . . . . . . . . 78 D4　46 52N 122 16W
Eau Claire, *U.S.A.* . . . . . . . . . . 80 C9　44 49N　91 30W
Eau Claire, L. à l', *Canada* . . . . 72 A5　56 10N　74 25W
Ebbw Vale, *U.K.* . . . . . . . . . . . 13 F4　51 46N　3 12W
Ebeltoft, *Denmark* . . . . . . . . . . 9 H14　56 12N　10 41 E
Ebensburg, *U.S.A.* . . . . . . . . . . 84 F6　40 29N　78 44W
Eberswalde-Finow, *Germany* . . 16 B7　52 50N　13 49 E
Ebetsu, *Japan* . . . . . . . . . . . . . 30 C10　43　7N 141 34 E
Ebey's Landing →, *U.S.A.* . . . . . 78 B4　48 13N 122 41W
Ebolowa, *Cameroon* . . . . . . . . 52 D2　2 55N　11 10 E
Ebro →, *Spain* . . . . . . . . . . . . 21 B6　40 43N　0 54 E
Eceabat, *Turkey* . . . . . . . . . . . 23 D12　40 11N　26 21 E
Ech Chélif, *Algeria* . . . . . . . . . 50 A6　36 10N　1 20 E
Echigo-Sammyaku, *Japan* . . . . 31 F9　36 50N 139 50 E
Echizen-Misaki, *Japan* . . . . . . 31 G7　35 59N 135 57 E
Echo Bay, *N.W.T., Canada* . . . . 68 B8　66　5N 117 55W
Echo Bay, *Ont., Canada* . . . . . . 72 C3　46 29N　84　4W
Echoing →, *Canada* . . . . . . . . 72 B1　55 51N　92　5W
Echternach, *Lux.* . . . . . . . . . . . 15 E6　49 49N　6 25 E
Echuca, *Australia* . . . . . . . . . . 63 F3　36 10S 144 45 E
Ecija, *Spain* . . . . . . . . . . . . . . 21 D3　37 30N　5 10W
Eclipse I., *Australia* . . . . . . . . . 61 G2　35　5S 117 58 E
Eclipse Is., *Australia* . . . . . . . . 60 B4　13 54S 126 19 E
Eclipse Sd., *Canada* . . . . . . . . . 69 A11　72 38N　79　0W
Ecuador ■, *S. Amer.* . . . . . . . . 92 D3　2　0S　78　0W
Ed Damazin, *Sudan* . . . . . . . . 51 F12　11 46N　34 21 E
Ed Dar el Beida = Casablanca,
　*Morocco* . . . . . . . . . . . . . . 50 B4　33 36N　7 36W
Ed Debba, *Sudan* . . . . . . . . . . 51 E12　18　0N　30 51 E
Ed Dueim, *Sudan* . . . . . . . . . . 51 F12　14　0N　32 10 E
Edam, *Canada* . . . . . . . . . . . . 71 C7　53 11N 108 46W
Edam, *Neths.* . . . . . . . . . . . . . 15 B5　52 31N　5　3 E
Eday, *U.K.* . . . . . . . . . . . . . . . 11 B6　59 11N　2 47W
Eddrachillis B., *U.K.* . . . . . . . . 11 C3　58 17N　5 14W
Eddystone Pt., *Australia* . . . . . . 63 G4　40 59S 148 20 E
Ede, *Neths.* . . . . . . . . . . . . . . . 15 B5　52　4N　5 40 E
Edehon L., *Canada* . . . . . . . . . 71 A9　60 25N　97 15W
Eden, *Australia* . . . . . . . . . . . . 63 F4　37　3S 149 55 E
Eden, *N.C., U.S.A.* . . . . . . . . . . 83 G6　36 29N　79 53W
Eden, *N.Y., U.S.A.* . . . . . . . . . . 84 D6　42 39N　78 55W
Eden, *Tex., U.S.A.* . . . . . . . . . . 81 K5　31 13N　99 51W
Eden →, *U.K.* . . . . . . . . . . . . . 12 C4　54 57N　3　1W
Edenburg, *S. Africa* . . . . . . . . . 56 D4　29 43S　25 58 E
Edendale, *S. Africa* . . . . . . . . . 57 D5　29 39S　30 18 E
Edenderry, *Ireland* . . . . . . . . . 10 C4　53 21N　7　4W
Edenton, *U.S.A.* . . . . . . . . . . . 83 G7　36　4N　76 39W
Edenville, *S. Africa* . . . . . . . . . 57 D4　27 37S　27 34 E
Eder →, *Germany* . . . . . . . . . . 16 C5　51 12N　9 28 E
Edgar, *U.S.A.* . . . . . . . . . . . . . 80 E6　40 22N　97 58W
Edgartown, *U.S.A.* . . . . . . . . . 85 E14　41 23N　70 31W
Edge Hill, *U.K.* . . . . . . . . . . . . 13 E6　52　8N　1 26W
Edgefield, *U.S.A.* . . . . . . . . . . 83 J5　33 47N　81 56W

Edgeley, *U.S.A.* . . . . . . . . . . . . 80 B5　46 22N　98 43W
Edgemont, *U.S.A.* . . . . . . . . . . 80 D3　43 18N 103 50W
Edgeøya, *Svalbard* . . . . . . . . . . 4 B9　77 45N　22 30 E
Édhessa, *Greece* . . . . . . . . . . . 23 D10　40 48N　22　5 E
Edievale, *N.Z.* . . . . . . . . . . . . . 59 L2　45 49S 169 22 E
Edina, *U.S.A.* . . . . . . . . . . . . . 80 E8　40 10N　92 11W
Edinboro, *U.S.A.* . . . . . . . . . . . 84 E4　41 52N　80　8W
Edinburg, *U.S.A.* . . . . . . . . . . . 81 M5　26 18N　98 10W
Edinburgh, *U.K.* . . . . . . . . . . . 11 F5　55 57N　3 13W
Edinburgh ✈ (EDI), *U.K.* . . . . . 11 F5　55 54N　3 22W
Edinburgh, City of □, *U.K.* . . . 11 F5　55 57N　3 17W
Edineţ, *Moldova* . . . . . . . . . . . 17 D14　48　9N　27 18 E
Edirne, *Turkey* . . . . . . . . . . . . 23 D12　41 40N　26 34 E
Edison, *U.S.A.* . . . . . . . . . . . . . 78 B4　48 33N 122 27W
Edithburgh, *Australia* . . . . . . . 63 F2　35　5S 137 43 E
Edmeston, *U.S.A.* . . . . . . . . . . 85 D9　42 42N　75 15W
Edmond, *U.S.A.* . . . . . . . . . . . 81 H6　35 39N　97 29W
Edmonds, *U.S.A.* . . . . . . . . . . . 78 C4　47 49N 122 23W
Edmonton, *Australia* . . . . . . . . 62 B4　17　2S 145 46 E
Edmonton, *Canada* . . . . . . . . . 70 C6　53 30N 113 30W
Edmund L., *Canada* . . . . . . . . 71 B1　54 45N　93 17W
Edmundston, *Canada* . . . . . . . 73 C6　47 23N　68 20W
Edna, *U.S.A.* . . . . . . . . . . . . . . 81 L6　28 59N　96 39W
Edremit, *Turkey* . . . . . . . . . . . 23 E12　39 34N　27　0 E
Edremit Körfezi, *Turkey* . . . . . . 23 E12　39 30N　26 45 E
Edson, *Canada* . . . . . . . . . . . . 70 C5　53 35N 116 28W
Eduardo Castex, *Argentina* . . . 94 D3　35 50S　64 18W
Edward →, *Australia* . . . . . . . . 63 F3　35　5S 143 30 E
Edward, L., *Africa* . . . . . . . . . . 54 C2　0 25S　29 40 E
Edward River, *Australia* . . . . . . 62 A3　14 59S 141 26 E
Edward VII Land, *Antarctica* . . 5 E13　80　0S 150　0W
Edwards, *Calif., U.S.A.* . . . . . . . 79 L9　34 55N 117 51W
Edwards, *N.Y., U.S.A.* . . . . . . . . 85 B9　44 20N　75 15W
Edwards Air Force Base, *U.S.A.* 79 L9　34 50N 117 40W
Edwards Plateau, *U.S.A.* . . . . . 81 K4　30 45N 101 20W
Edwardsville, *U.S.A.* . . . . . . . . 85 E9　41 15N　75 56W
Edxná, *Mexico* . . . . . . . . . . . . 87 D6　19 35N　90 15W
Edzo, *Canada* . . . . . . . . . . . . . 70 A5　62 49N 116　4W
Eeklo, *Belgium* . . . . . . . . . . . . 15 C3　51 11N　3 33 E
Effigy Mounds △, *U.S.A.* . . . . . 80 D9　43　5N　91 11W
Effingham, *U.S.A.* . . . . . . . . . . 82 F1　39　7N　88 33W
Égadi, Ísole, *Italy* . . . . . . . . . . 22 F5　37 55N　12 16 E
Egan Range, *U.S.A.* . . . . . . . . . 76 G6　39 35N 114 55W
Eganville, *Canada* . . . . . . . . . . 84 A7　45 32N　77　5W
Eger = Cheb, *Czech Rep.* . . . . . 16 C7　50　9N　12 28 E
Eger, *Hungary* . . . . . . . . . . . . . 17 E11　47 53N　20 27 E
Egersund, *Norway* . . . . . . . . . . 9 G12　58 26N　6　1 E
Egg L., *Canada* . . . . . . . . . . . . 71 B7　55　5N 105 30W
Éghezée, *Belgium* . . . . . . . . . . 15 D4　50 35N　4 55 E
Egmont, *Canada* . . . . . . . . . . . 70 D4　49 45N 123 56W
Egmont △, *N.Z.* . . . . . . . . . . . . 59 H5　39 17S 174　4 E
Egmont, C., *N.Z.* . . . . . . . . . . . 59 H5　39 16S 173 45 E
Egmont, Mt. = Taranaki, Mt., *N.Z.* 59 H5　39 17S 174　5 E
Egra, *India* . . . . . . . . . . . . . . . 43 J12　21 54N　87 32 E
Eğridir, *Turkey* . . . . . . . . . . . . 19 G5　37 52N　30 51 E
Eğridir Gölü, *Turkey* . . . . . . . . 19 G5　37 53N　30 50 E
Egvekinot, *Russia* . . . . . . . . . . 29 C19　66 19N 179 50W
Egypt ■, *Africa* . . . . . . . . . . . . 51 C12　28　0N　31　0 E
Ehime □, *Japan* . . . . . . . . . . . 31 H6　33 30N 132 40 E
Ehrenberg, *U.S.A.* . . . . . . . . . . 79 M12　33 36N 114 31W
Eibar, *Spain* . . . . . . . . . . . . . . 21 A4　43 11N　2 28W
Eidsvold, *Australia* . . . . . . . . . 63 D5　25 25S 151 12 E
Eidsvoll, *Norway* . . . . . . . . . . . 9 F14　60 19N　11 14 E
Eifel, *Germany* . . . . . . . . . . . . 16 C4　50 15N　6 50 E
Eiffel Flats, *Zimbabwe* . . . . . . . 55 F3　18 20S　30　0 E
Eigg, *U.K.* . . . . . . . . . . . . . . . . 11 E2　56 54N　6 10W
Eighty Mile Beach, *Australia* . . 60 C3　19 30S 120 40 E
Eil, *Somali Rep.* . . . . . . . . . . . 47 F4　8　0N　49 50 E
Eil, L., *U.K.* . . . . . . . . . . . . . . . 11 E3　56 51N　5 16W
Eildon, L., *Australia* . . . . . . . . . 63 F4　37 10S 146　0 E
Einasleigh, *Australia* . . . . . . . . 62 B3　18 32S 144　5 E
Einasleigh →, *Australia* . . . . . . 62 B3　17 30S 142 17 E
Eindhoven, *Neths.* . . . . . . . . . . 15 C5　51 26N　5 28 E
Eire = Ireland ■, *Europe* . . . . . 10 C4　53 50N　7 52W
Eiriksjökull, *Iceland* . . . . . . . . 8 D3　64 46N　20 24W
Eirunepé, *Brazil* . . . . . . . . . . . 92 E5　6 35S　69 53W
Eiseb →, *Namibia* . . . . . . . . . . 56 C2　20 33S　20 59 E
Eisenach, *Germany* . . . . . . . . . 16 C6　50 58N　10 19 E
Eisenerz, *Austria* . . . . . . . . . . . 16 E8　47 32N　14 54 E
Eivissa, *Spain* . . . . . . . . . . . . . 24 C7　38 54N　1 26 E
Ejeda, *Madag.* . . . . . . . . . . . . . 57 C7　24 20S　44 31 E
Ejutla, *Mexico* . . . . . . . . . . . . . 87 D5　16 34N　96 44W
Ekalaka, *U.S.A.* . . . . . . . . . . . . 80 C2　45 53N 104 33W
Ekenäs = Tammisaari, *Finland* . 9 F20　60　0N　23 26 E
Eketahuna, *N.Z.* . . . . . . . . . . . 59 J5　40 38S 175 43 E
Ekibastuz, *Kazakhstan* . . . . . . . 28 D8　51 50N　75 10 E
Ekoli, *Dem. Rep. of the Congo* . 54 C1　0 23S　24 13 E
Eksjö, *Sweden* . . . . . . . . . . . . . 9 H16　57 40N　14 58 E
Ekuma →, *Namibia* . . . . . . . . . 56 B2　18 40S　16　2 E
Ekwan →, *Canada* . . . . . . . . . 72 B3　53 12N　82 15W
Ekwan Pt., *Canada* . . . . . . . . . 72 B3　53 16N　82　7W
El Aaiún, *W. Sahara* . . . . . . . . . 50 C3　27　9N 13 12W
El Abanico, *Chile* . . . . . . . . . . 94 D1　37 20S　71 31W
El 'Agrûd, *Egypt* . . . . . . . . . . . 46 E3　30 14N　34 24 E
El 'Alamein, *Egypt* . . . . . . . . . 51 B11　30 48N　28 58 E
El 'Aqaba, W. →, *Egypt* . . . . . . 46 E2　30　7N　33 54 E
El Ariha, *West Bank* . . . . . . . . . 46 D4　31 52N　35 27 E
El 'Arîsh, *Egypt* . . . . . . . . . . . . 46 D2　31　8N　33 50 E
El 'Arîsh, W. →, *Egypt* . . . . . . . 46 D2　31　8N　33 47 E
El Asnam = Ech Chélif, *Algeria* 50 A6　36 10N　1 20 E
El Bayadh, *Algeria* . . . . . . . . . 50 B6　33 40N　1　1 E
El Bluff, *Nic.* . . . . . . . . . . . . . . 88 D3　11 59N　83 40W
El Brûk, W. →, *Egypt* . . . . . . . . 46 E2　30 55N　32 59 E
El Cajon, *U.S.A.* . . . . . . . . . . . . 79 N10　32 48N 116 58W
El Campo, *U.S.A.* . . . . . . . . . . . 81 L6　29 12N　96 16W
El Centro, *U.S.A.* . . . . . . . . . . . 79 N11　32 48N 115 34W
El Cerro, *Bolivia* . . . . . . . . . . . 92 G6　17 30S　61 40W
El Compadre, *Mexico* . . . . . . . 79 N10　32 20N 116 14W
El Cuy, *Argentina* . . . . . . . . . . 96 D3　39 55S　68 25W
El Cuyo, *Mexico* . . . . . . . . . . . 87 C7　21 30N　87 40W
El Daheir, *Egypt* . . . . . . . . . . . 46 D3　31 13N　34 10 E
El Dátil, *Mexico* . . . . . . . . . . . 86 B2　30　7N 112 15W
El Dere, *Somali Rep.* . . . . . . . . 47 G4　3 50N　47　8 E
El Descanso, *Mexico* . . . . . . . . 79 N10　32 12N 116 58W
El Diviso, *Colombia* . . . . . . . . 92 C3　1 22N　78 14W
El Djouf, *Mauritania* . . . . . . . . 50 D4　20　0N　9　0W
El Dorado, *Ark., U.S.A.* . . . . . . . 81 J8　33 12N　92 40W
El Dorado, *Kans., U.S.A.* . . . . . 81 G6　37 49N　96 52W
El Dorado, *Venezuela* . . . . . . . 92 B6　6 55N　61 37W
El Escorial, *Spain* . . . . . . . . . . 21 B3　40 35N　4　7W
El Faiyûm, *Egypt* . . . . . . . . . . . 51 C12　29 19N　30 50 E
El Fâsher, *Sudan* . . . . . . . . . . . 51 F11　13 33N　25 26 E
El Ferrol = Ferrol, *Spain* . . . . . 21 A1　43 29N　8 15W
El Fuerte, *Mexico* . . . . . . . . . . 86 B3　26 30N 108 40W
El Gal, *Somali Rep.* . . . . . . . . . 47 E5　10 58N　50 20 E
El Geneina = Al Junaynah, *Sudan* 51 F10　13 27N　22 45 E
El Gîza, *Egypt* . . . . . . . . . . . . . 51 C12　30　0N　31 10 E

El Gogorron △, *Mexico* . . . . . . 86 C4　21 50N 100 50W
El Goléa, *Algeria* . . . . . . . . . . . 50 B6　30 30N　2 50 E
El Guácharo △, *Venezuela* . . . . 89 D7　10　8N　63 21W
El Guache △, *Venezuela* . . . . . . 89 E6　9 45N　69 30W
El Iskandarîya, *Egypt* . . . . . . . 51 B11　31 13N　29 58 E
El Istiwa'iya, *Sudan* . . . . . . . . . 51 G11　5　0N　28　0 E
El Jadida, *Morocco* . . . . . . . . . 50 B4　33 11N　8 17W
El Jardal, *Honduras* . . . . . . . . . 88 D2　14 54N　88 50W
El Kabrît, G., *Egypt* . . . . . . . . . 46 F2　29 42N　33 16 E
El Khârga, *Egypt* . . . . . . . . . . . 51 C12　25 30N　30 33 E
El Khartûm, *Sudan* . . . . . . . . . 51 E12　15 31N　32 35 E
El Kuntilla, *Egypt* . . . . . . . . . . 46 E3　30　1N　34 45 E
El Maestrazgo, *Spain* . . . . . . . . 21 B5　40 30N　0 25W
El Mahalla el Kubra, *Egypt* . . . 51 B12　31　0N　31　0 E
El Malpais △, *U.S.A.* . . . . . . . . 77 J10　34 53N 108　0W
El Mansûra, *Egypt* . . . . . . . . . 51 B12　31　0N　31 19 E
El Medano, *Canary Is.* . . . . . . . 24 F3　28　3N　16 32W
El Milagro, *Argentina* . . . . . . . 94 C2　30 59S　65 59W
El Minyâ, *Egypt* . . . . . . . . . . . 51 C12　28　7N　30 33 E
El Monte, *U.S.A.* . . . . . . . . . . . 79 L8　34　4N 118　1W
El Obeid, *Sudan* . . . . . . . . . . . 51 F12　13　8N　30 10 E
El Odaiya, *Sudan* . . . . . . . . . . 51 F11　12　8N　28 12 E
El Oro, *Mexico* . . . . . . . . . . . . 87 D4　19 48N 100　8W
El Oued, *Algeria* . . . . . . . . . . . 50 B7　33 20N　6 58 E
El Palmar, *Venezuela* . . . . . . . . 94 C4　32 10S　58 31W
El Palmito, Presa, *Mexico* . . . . 86 B3　25 40N 105 30W
El Paso, *U.S.A.* . . . . . . . . . . . . 77 L10　31 45N 106 29W
El Paso Robles, *U.S.A.* . . . . . . . 78 K6　35 38N 120 41W
El Pinacate y Gran Desierto de
　Altar = Gran Desierto del
　Pinacate △, *Mexico* . . . . . . 86 A2　31 51N 113 32W
El Portal, *U.S.A.* . . . . . . . . . . . 78 H7　37 41N 119 47W
El Porvenir, *Mexico* . . . . . . . . . 86 A3　31 15N 105 51W
El Prat de Llobregat, *Spain* . . . 21 B7　41 18N　2　3 E
El Progreso, *Honduras* . . . . . . 88 C2　15 26N　87 51W
El Pueblito, *Mexico* . . . . . . . . . 86 B3　29　3N 105　4W
El Puerto de Santa Maria, *Spain* 21 D2　36 36N　6 13W
El Qâhira, *Egypt* . . . . . . . . . . . 51 B12　30　1N　31 14 E
El Qantara, *Egypt* . . . . . . . . . . 46 E1　30 51N　32 20 E
El Quseima, *Egypt* . . . . . . . . . . 46 E3　30 40N　34 15 E
El Real, *Panama* . . . . . . . . . . . 92 B3　8　0N　77 40W
El Reno, *U.S.A.* . . . . . . . . . . . . 81 H6　35 32N　97 57W
El Rey △, *Argentina* . . . . . . . . 94 A3　24 40S　64 34W
El Rio, *U.S.A.* . . . . . . . . . . . . . 79 L7　34 14N 119 10W
El Roque, Pta., *Canary Is.* . . . . 24 F4　28 10N　15 25W
El Rosarito, *Mexico* . . . . . . . . . 86 B2　28 38N 114　4W
El Saheira, W. →, *Egypt* . . . . . . 46 E2　30　5N　33 25 E
El Salto, *Mexico* . . . . . . . . . . . 86 C3　23 47N 105 22W
El Salvador ■, *Cent. Amer.* . . . 88 D2　13 50N　89　0W
El Sauce, *Nic.* . . . . . . . . . . . . . 88 D2　13　0N　86 40W
El Sueco, *Mexico* . . . . . . . . . . 86 B3　29 54N 106 24W
El Suweis, *Egypt* . . . . . . . . . . . 51 C12　29 58N　32 31 E
El Tamarâni, W. →, *Egypt* . . . . 46 E3　30　7N　34 43 E
El Thamad, *Egypt* . . . . . . . . . . 46 F3　29 40N　34 28 E
El Tigre, *Venezuela* . . . . . . . . . 92 B6　8 44N　64 15W
El Tîh, *Egypt* . . . . . . . . . . . . . . 46 F2　29 40N　33 42 E
El Tina, Khalig, *Egypt* . . . . . . . 46 D1　31 10N　32 40 E
El Tofo, *Chile* . . . . . . . . . . . . . 94 B1　29 22S　71 18W
El Tránsito, *Chile* . . . . . . . . . . 94 B1　28 52S　70 17W
El Tûr, *Egypt* . . . . . . . . . . . . . . 46 F2　28 14N　33 36 E
El Turbio, *Argentina* . . . . . . . . 96 G2　51 45S　72　5W
El Uqsur, *Egypt* . . . . . . . . . . . . 51 C12　25 41N　32 38 E
El Venado, *Mexico* . . . . . . . . . 86 C4　22 56N 101 10W
El Vergel, *Mexico* . . . . . . . . . . 86 B3　26 28N 106 22W
El Vigía, *Venezuela* . . . . . . . . . 92 B4　8 38N　71 39W
El Wabeira, *Egypt* . . . . . . . . . . 46 F2　29 34N　33　6 E
El Wak, *Kenya* . . . . . . . . . . . . . 54 B5　2 49N　40 56 E
El Wuz, *Sudan* . . . . . . . . . . . . 51 E12　15　5N　30 7 E
Elat, *Israel* . . . . . . . . . . . . . . . 46 F3　29 30N　34 56 E
Elâziğ, *Turkey* . . . . . . . . . . . . . 19 G6　38 37N　39 14 E
Elba, *Italy* . . . . . . . . . . . . . . . . 22 C4　42 46N　10 17 E
Elba, *U.S.A.* . . . . . . . . . . . . . . 83 K2　31 25N　86　4W
Elbasan, *Albania* . . . . . . . . . . . 23 D9　41　9N　20　9 E
Elbe, *U.S.A.* . . . . . . . . . . . . . . 78 D4　46 45N 122 10W
Elbe →, *Europe* . . . . . . . . . . . . 16 B5　53 50N　9　0 E
Elbert, Mt., *U.S.A.* . . . . . . . . . . 77 G10　39　7N 106 27W
Elberton, *U.S.A.* . . . . . . . . . . . 83 H4　34　7N　82 52W
Elbeuf, *France* . . . . . . . . . . . . . 20 B4　49 17N　1　2 E
Elbidtan, *Turkey* . . . . . . . . . . . 44 B3　38 13N　37 12 E
Elbing = Elbląg, *Poland* . . . . . 17 A10　54 10N　19 25 E
Elbląg, *Poland* . . . . . . . . . . . . 17 A10　54 10N　19 25 E
Elbow, *Canada* . . . . . . . . . . . . 71 C7　51　7N 106 35W
Elbrus, *Asia* . . . . . . . . . . . . . . . 19 F7　43 21N　42 30 E
Elburz Mts. = Alborz, Reshteh-ye
　Kūhhā-ye, *Iran* . . . . . . . . . . 45 C7　36　0N　52　0 E
Elche, *Spain* . . . . . . . . . . . . . . 21 C5　38 15N　0 42W
Elcho I., *Australia* . . . . . . . . . . 62 A2　11 55S 135 45 E
Elda, *Spain* . . . . . . . . . . . . . . . 21 C5　38 29N　0 47W
Elde →, *Germany* . . . . . . . . . . 16 B6　53　7N　11 15 E
Eldon, *Mo., U.S.A.* . . . . . . . . . . 80 F8　38 21N　92 35W
Eldon, *Wash., U.S.A.* . . . . . . . . 78 C3　47 33N 123　3W
Eldora, *U.S.A.* . . . . . . . . . . . . . 80 D8　42 22N　93 5W
Eldorado, *Argentina* . . . . . . . . 95 B5　26 28S　54 43W
Eldorado, *Canada* . . . . . . . . . . 84 B7　44 35N　77 31W
Eldorado, *Mexico* . . . . . . . . . . 86 C3　24 20N 107 22W
Eldorado, *Ill., U.S.A.* . . . . . . . . 82 G1　37 49N　88 26W
Eldorado, *Tex., U.S.A.* . . . . . . . 81 K4　30 52N 100 36W
Eldorado Springs, *U.S.A.* . . . . . 81 G8　37 52N　94　1W
Eldoret, *Kenya* . . . . . . . . . . . . 54 B4　0 30N　35 17 E
Eldred, *U.S.A.* . . . . . . . . . . . . . 84 E6　41 58N　78 23W
Elea, C., *Cyprus* . . . . . . . . . . . . 25 D13　35 19N　34　4 E
Eleanora, Pk., *Australia* . . . . . . 61 F3　32 57S 121　9 E
Elefantes →, *Africa* . . . . . . . . . 57 C5　24 10S　32 40 E
Elektrostal, *Russia* . . . . . . . . . 18 C6　55 41N　38 32 E
Elephant Butte Reservoir, *U.S.A.* 77 K10　33　9N 107 11W
Elephant I., *Antarctica* . . . . . . . 5 C18　61　0S　55　0W
Eleuthera, *Bahamas* . . . . . . . . 88 B4　25　0N　76 20W
Elgin, *Canada* . . . . . . . . . . . . . 85 B8　44 36N　76 13W
Elgin, *U.K.* . . . . . . . . . . . . . . . 11 D5　57 39N　3 19W
Elgin, *Ill., U.S.A.* . . . . . . . . . . . 82 D1　42 2N　88 17W
Elgin, *N. Dak., U.S.A.* . . . . . . . 80 B4　46 24N 101 51W
Elgin, *Oreg., U.S.A.* . . . . . . . . . 76 D5　45 34N 117 55W
Elgin, *Tex., U.S.A.* . . . . . . . . . . 81 K6　30 21N　97 22W
Elgon, Mt., *Africa* . . . . . . . . . . 54 B3　1 10N　34 30 E
Eliase, *Indonesia* . . . . . . . . . . . 37 F8　8 21S 130 48 E
Elim, *Namibia* . . . . . . . . . . . . . 56 B2　17 48S　15 31 E
Elim, *S. Africa* . . . . . . . . . . . . . 56 E2　34 35S　19 45 E
Elista, *Russia* . . . . . . . . . . . . . 19 E7　46 16N　44 14 E
Elizabeth, *Australia* . . . . . . . . . 63 E2　34 42S 138 41 E
Elizabeth, *U.S.A.* . . . . . . . . . . . 85 F10　40 40N　74 13W
Elizabeth City, *U.S.A.* . . . . . . . 83 G7　36 18N　76 14W
Elizabethton, *U.S.A.* . . . . . . . . 83 G4　36 21N　82 13W
Elizabethtown, *Ky., U.S.A.* . . . . 82 G3　37 42N　85 52W
Elizabethtown, *N.Y., U.S.A.* . . . 85 B11　44 13N　73 36W
Elizabethtown, *Pa., U.S.A.* . . . . 85 F8　40 9N　76 36W
Elk, *Poland* . . . . . . . . . . . . . . . 17 B12　53 50N　22 21 E
Elk →, *Canada* . . . . . . . . . . . . . 70 C5　49 11N 115 14W

Elk →, *U.S.A.* . . . . . . . . . . . . . 83 H2　34 46N　87 16W
Elk City, *U.S.A.* . . . . . . . . . . . . 81 H5　35 25N　99 25W
Elk Creek, *U.S.A.* . . . . . . . . . . 78 F4　39 36N 122 32W
Elk Grove, *U.S.A.* . . . . . . . . . . 78 G5　38 25N 121 22W
Elk Island △, *Canada* . . . . . . . 70 C6　53 35N 112 59W
Elk Lake, *Canada* . . . . . . . . . . 72 C3　47 40N　80 25W
Elk Point, *Canada* . . . . . . . . . . 71 C6　53 54N 110 55W
Elk River, *Idaho, U.S.A.* . . . . . . 76 C5　46 47N 116 11W
Elk River, *Minn., U.S.A.* . . . . . . 80 C8　45 18N　93 35W
Elkedra →, *Australia* . . . . . . . . 62 C2　21　8S 136 22 E
Elkhart, *Ind., U.S.A.* . . . . . . . . 82 E3　41 41N　85 58W
Elkhart, *Kans., U.S.A.* . . . . . . . 81 G4　37　0N 101 54W
Elkhorn, *Canada* . . . . . . . . . . . 71 D8　49 59N 101 14W
Elkhorn →, *U.S.A.* . . . . . . . . . . 80 E6　41　8N　96 19W
Elkhovo, *Bulgaria* . . . . . . . . . . 23 C12　42 10N　26 35 E
Elkin, *U.S.A.* . . . . . . . . . . . . . . 83 G5　36 15N　80 51W
Elkins, *U.S.A.* . . . . . . . . . . . . . 82 F6　38 55N　79 51W
Elkland, *U.S.A.* . . . . . . . . . . . . 84 E7　41 59N　77 19W
Elko, *Canada* . . . . . . . . . . . . . 70 D5　49 20N 115 10W
Elko, *U.S.A.* . . . . . . . . . . . . . . 76 F6　40 50N 115 46W
Elkton, *U.S.A.* . . . . . . . . . . . . . 84 C1　43 49N　83 11W
Ell, L., *Australia* . . . . . . . . . . . . 61 E4　29 13S 127 46 E
Ellef Ringnes I., *Canada* . . . . . . 4 B2　78 30N 102　2W
Ellen, Mt., *U.S.A.* . . . . . . . . . . 85 B12　44　9N　72 56W
Ellenburg, *U.S.A.* . . . . . . . . . . 85 B11　44 54N　73 48W
Ellendale, *U.S.A.* . . . . . . . . . . . 80 B5　46　0N　98 32W
Ellensburg, *U.S.A.* . . . . . . . . . . 76 C3　46 59N 120 34W
Ellenville, *U.S.A.* . . . . . . . . . . . 85 E10　41 43N　74 24W
Ellerton, *Barbados* . . . . . . . . . 89 g　13　7N　59 33W
Ellery, Mt., *Australia* . . . . . . . . 63 F4　37 28S 148 47 E
Ellesmere, L., *N.Z.* . . . . . . . . . 59 M4　43 47S 172 28 E
Ellesmere I., *Canada* . . . . . . . . 4 B4　79 30N　80　0W
Ellesmere Port, *U.K.* . . . . . . . . 12 D5　53 17N　2 54W
Ellice Is. = Tuvalu ■, *Pac. Oc.* . . 64 H9　8　0S 178　0 E
Ellicottville, *U.S.A.* . . . . . . . . . 84 D6　42 17N　78 40W
Elliot, *Australia* . . . . . . . . . . . . 62 B1　17 33S 133 32 E
Elliot, *S. Africa* . . . . . . . . . . . . 57 E4　31 22S　27 48 E
Elliot Lake, *Canada* . . . . . . . . . 72 C3　46 25N　82 35W
Elliotdale = Xhora, *S. Africa* . . 57 E4　31 55S　28 38 E
Ellis, *U.S.A.* . . . . . . . . . . . . . . 80 F5　38 56N　99 34W
Elliston, *Australia* . . . . . . . . . . 63 E1　33 39S 134 53 E
Ellisville, *U.S.A.* . . . . . . . . . . . 81 K10　31 36N　89 12W
Ellon, *U.K.* . . . . . . . . . . . . . . . 11 D6　57 22N　2　4W
Ellore = Eluru, *India* . . . . . . . . 41 L12　16 48N　81　8 E
Ellsworth, *Kans., U.S.A.* . . . . . . 80 F5　38 44N　98 14W
Ellsworth, *Maine, U.S.A.* . . . . . 83 C11　44 33N　68 25W
Ellsworth Land, *Antarctica* . . . 5 D16　76　0S　89　0W
Ellsworth Mts., *Antarctica* . . . . 5 D16　78 30S　85　0W
Ellwood City, *U.S.A.* . . . . . . . . 84 F4　40 52N　80 17W
Elma, *Canada* . . . . . . . . . . . . . 71 D9　49 52N　95 55W
Elma, *U.S.A.* . . . . . . . . . . . . . . 78 D3　47　0N 123 25W
Elmalı, *Turkey* . . . . . . . . . . . . . 19 G4　36 44N　29 56 E
Elmhurst, *U.S.A.* . . . . . . . . . . . 82 E2　41 53N　87 56W
Elmira, *Canada* . . . . . . . . . . . . 84 C4　43 36N　80 33W
Elmira, *U.S.A.* . . . . . . . . . . . . . 84 D8　42　6N　76 48W
Elmira Heights, *U.S.A.* . . . . . . 84 D8　42　8N　76 50W
Elmore, *Australia* . . . . . . . . . . 63 F3　36 30S 144 37 E
Elmore, *U.S.A.* . . . . . . . . . . . . 79 M11　33　7N 115 49W
Elmshorn, *Germany* . . . . . . . . 16 B5　53 43N　9 40 E
Elmvale, *Canada* . . . . . . . . . . . 84 B5　44 35N　79 52W
Elora, *Canada* . . . . . . . . . . . . . 84 C4　43 41N　80 26W
Eloúnda, *Greece* . . . . . . . . . . . 25 D7　35 16N　25 42 E
Eloy, *U.S.A.* . . . . . . . . . . . . . . . 77 K8　32 45N 111 33W
Elrose, *Canada* . . . . . . . . . . . . 71 C7　51 12N 108　0W
Elsie, *U.S.A.* . . . . . . . . . . . . . . 78 E3　45 52N 123 36W
Elsinore = Helsingør, *Denmark* 9 H15　56　2N　12 35 E
Eltham, *N.Z.* . . . . . . . . . . . . . . 59 H5　39 26S 174 19 E
Eluru, *India* . . . . . . . . . . . . . . 41 L12　16 48N　81　8 E
Elvas, *Portugal* . . . . . . . . . . . . 21 C2　38 50N　7 10W
Elverum, *Norway* . . . . . . . . . . 9 F14　60 53N　11 34 E
Elvire →, *Australia* . . . . . . . . . . 60 C4　17 51S 128 11 E
Elvire, Mt., *Australia* . . . . . . . . 61 E2　29 22S 119 36 E
Elwell, L., *U.S.A.* . . . . . . . . . . . 76 B8　48 22N 111 17W
Elwood, *Ind., U.S.A.* . . . . . . . . 82 E3　40 17N　85 50W
Elwood, *Nebr., U.S.A.* . . . . . . . 80 E5　40 36N　99 52W
Elx = Elche, *Spain* . . . . . . . . . . 21 C5　38 15N　0 42W
Ely, *U.K.* . . . . . . . . . . . . . . . . . 13 E8　52 24N　0 16 E
Ely, *Minn., U.S.A.* . . . . . . . . . . 80 B9　47 55N　91 51W
Ely, *Nev., U.S.A.* . . . . . . . . . . . 76 G6　39 15N 114 54W
Elyria, *U.S.A.* . . . . . . . . . . . . . 84 E2　41 22N　82　7W
Emāmrūd, *Iran* . . . . . . . . . . . . 45 B7　36 30N　55　0 E
Emba, *Kazakhstan* . . . . . . . . . . 28 E6　48 50N　58　8 E
Emba →, *Kazakhstan* . . . . . . . . 19 E9　46 55N　53 28 E
Embarcación, *Argentina* . . . . . 94 A3　23 10S　64　0W
Embarras Portage, *Canada* . . . 71 B6　58 27N 111 28W
Embetsu, *Japan* . . . . . . . . . . . . 30 B10　44 44N 141 47 E
Embi = Emba, *Kazakhstan* . . . . 28 E6　48 50N　58　8 E
Embi = Emba →, *Kazakhstan* . . 19 E9　46 55N　53 28 E
Embóna, *Greece* . . . . . . . . . . . 25 C9　36 13N　27 51 E
Embrun, *France* . . . . . . . . . . . 20 D7　44 34N　6 30 E
Embu, *Kenya* . . . . . . . . . . . . . 54 C4　0 32S　37 38 E
Emden, *Germany* . . . . . . . . . . 16 B4　53 21N　7 12 E
Emerald, *Australia* . . . . . . . . . 62 C4　23 32S 148 10 E
Emerson, *Canada* . . . . . . . . . . 71 D9　49　0N　97 10W
Emet, *Turkey* . . . . . . . . . . . . . 23 E13　39 20N　29 15 E
Emi Koussi, *Chad* . . . . . . . . . . 51 E9　19 45N　18 55 E
Eminabad, *Pakistan* . . . . . . . . 42 C6　32　2N　74　8 E
Emine, Nos, *Bulgaria* . . . . . . . 23 C12　42 40N　27 56 E
Emissi, Tarso, *Chad* . . . . . . . . 51 D9　21 27N　18 36 E
Emlenton, *U.S.A.* . . . . . . . . . . 84 E5　41 11N　79 43W
Emmaus, *S. Africa* . . . . . . . . . 56 D4　29　2S　25 15 E
Emmaus, *U.S.A.* . . . . . . . . . . . 85 F9　40 32N　75 30W
Emmeloord, *Neths.* . . . . . . . . . 15 B5　52 44N　5 46 E
Emmen, *Neths.* . . . . . . . . . . . . 15 B6　52 48N　6 57 E
Emmet, *Australia* . . . . . . . . . . 62 C3　24 45S 144 30 E
Emmetsburg, *U.S.A.* . . . . . . . . 80 D7　43　7N　94 41W
Emmett, *Idaho, U.S.A.* . . . . . . . 76 E5　43 52N 116 30W
Emmett, *Mich., U.S.A.* . . . . . . 84 D2　42 59N　82 46W
Emmonak, *U.S.A.* . . . . . . . . . . 68 B3　62 46N 164 30W
Emo, *Canada* . . . . . . . . . . . . . 71 D10　48 38N　93 50W
Empalme, *Mexico* . . . . . . . . . . 86 B2　28　1N 110 49W
Empangeni, *S. Africa* . . . . . . . 57 D5　28 50S　31 52 E
Empedrado, *Argentina* . . . . . . 94 B4　28　0S　58 46W
Emperor Seamount Chain,
　*Pac. Oc.* . . . . . . . . . . . . . . . 64 D9　40　0N 170　0 E
Emporia, *Kans., U.S.A.* . . . . . . 80 F6　38 25N　96 11W
Emporia, *Va., U.S.A.* . . . . . . . . 83 G7　36 42N　77 32W
Emporium, *U.S.A.* . . . . . . . . . . 84 E6　41 31N　78 14W
Empress, *Canada* . . . . . . . . . . 71 C7　50 57N 110　0W
Empty Quarter = Rub' al Khālī,
　*Si. Arabia* . . . . . . . . . . . . . . 47 D4　19　0N　48　0 E
Ems →, *Germany* . . . . . . . . . . 16 B4　53 20N　7 12 E
Emsdale, *Canada* . . . . . . . . . . 84 A5　45 32N　79 19W
Emu, *China* . . . . . . . . . . . . . . . 35 C15　43 40N 128　6 E
Emu Park, *Australia* . . . . . . . . 62 C5　23 13S 150 50 E
'En 'Avrona, *Israel* . . . . . . . . . . 46 F4　29 43N　35　0 E
En Nahud, *Sudan* . . . . . . . . . . 51 F11　12 45N　28 25 E
Ena, *Japan* . . . . . . . . . . . . . . . 31 G8　35 25N 137 25 E

Enana, Namibia .......... 56 B2  17 30S  16 23 E
Enard B., U.K. .......... 11 C3  58  5N   5 20W
Enare = Inarijärvi, Finland ..... 8 B22 69  0N  28  0 E
Enarotali, Indonesia ........ 37 E9   3 55S 136 21 E
Encampment, U.S.A. ....... 76 F10 41 12N 106 47W
Encantadas, Serra, Brazil .... 95 C5  30 40S  53  0W
Encarnación, Paraguay ...... 95 B4  27 15S  55 50W
Encarnación de Diaz, Mexico . 86 C4  21 30N 102 13W
Encinitas, U.S.A. ......... 79 M9  33  3N 117 17W
Encino, U.S.A. .......... 77 J11 34 39N 105 28W
Encounter B., Australia ..... 63 F2  35 45S 138 45 E
Endako, Canada .......... 70 C3  54  6N 125  2W
Ende, Indonesia ......... 37 F6   8 45S 121 40 E
Endeavour Str., Australia .... 62 A3  10 45S 142  0 E
Enderbury I., Kiribati ...... 64 H10  3  8S 171  5W
Enderby, Canada ......... 70 C5  50 35N 119 10W
Enderby I., Australia ...... 60 D2  20 35S 116 30 E
Enderby Land, Antarctica .... 5 C5  66  0S  53  0 E
Enderlin, U.S.A. ......... 80 B6  46 38N  97 36W
Endicott, U.S.A. ......... 85 D8  42  6N  76  4W
Endwell, U.S.A. ......... 85 D8  42  6N  76  2W
Endyalgout I., Australia ..... 60 B5  11 40S 132 35 E
Eneabba, Australia ....... 61 E2  29 49S 115 16 E
Enewetak Atoll, Marshall Is. .. 64 F8  11 30N 162 15 E
Enez, Turkey ........... 23 D12 40 45N  26  5 E
Enfer, Pte. d', Martinique ... 88 c  14 22N  60 54W
Enfield, Canada ......... 73 D7  44 56N  63 32W
Enfield, Conn., U.S.A. ..... 85 E12 41 58N  72 36W
Enfield, N.H., U.S.A. ...... 85 C12 43 39N  72  9W
Engadin, Switz. ......... 20 C9  46 45N  10 10 E
Engaño, C., Dom. Rep. ..... 89 C6  18 30N  68 20W
Engaño, C., Phil. ........ 37 A6  18 35N 122 23 E
Engaru, Japan .......... 30 B11 44  3N 143 31 E
Engcobo, S. Africa ....... 57 E4  31 37S  28  0 E
Engels, Russia .......... 19 D8  51 28N  46  6 E
Engemann L., Canada ..... 71 B7  58  0N 106 55W
Enggano, Indonesia ....... 36 F2   5 20S 102 40 E
England, U.S.A. ......... 81 H9  34 33N  91 58W
England □, U.K. ......... 13 E5  53  0N   2  0W
Englee, Canada ......... 73 B8  50 45N  56  5W
Englehart, Canada ....... 72 C4  47 49N  79 52W
Englewood, U.S.A. ....... 80 F2  39 39N 104 59W
English →, Canada ....... 71 C10 49 12N  91  5W
English Bazar = Ingraj Bazar,
   India .............. 43 G13 24 58N  88 10 E
English Channel, Europe .... 13 G6  50  0N   2  0W
English Company's Is., The,
   Australia .......... 62 A2  11 50S 136 32 E
English River, Canada ..... 72 C1  49 14N  91  0W
Enid, U.S.A. ........... 81 G6  36 24N  97 53W
Enkhuizen, Neths. ....... 15 B5  52 42N   5 17 E
Enna, Italy ........... 22 F6  37 34N  14 16 E
Ennadai, Canada ........ 71 A8  61  8N 100 53W
Ennadai L., Canada ....... 71 A8  60 58N 101 20W
Ennedi, Chad .......... 51 E10 17 15N  22  0 E
Enngonia, Australia ...... 63 D4  29 21S 145 50 E
Ennis, Ireland .......... 10 D3  52 51N   8 59W
Ennis, Mont., U.S.A. ...... 76 D8  45 21N 111 44W
Ennis, Tex., U.S.A. ...... 81 J6  32 20N  96 38W
Enniscorthy, Ireland ...... 10 D5  52 30N   6 34W
Enniskillen, U.K. ........ 10 B4  54 21N   7 39W
Ennistimon, Ireland ...... 10 D2  52 57N   9 17W
Enns →, Austria ........ 16 D8  48 14N  14 32 E
Enontekiö, Finland ....... 8 B20 68 23N  23 37 E
Enosburg Falls, U.S.A. .... 85 B12 44 55N  72 48W
Enriquillo, L., Dom. Rep. ... 89 C5  18 20N  72  5W
Enschede, Neths. ....... 15 B6  52 13N   6 53 E
Ensenada, Argentina ..... 94 C4  34 55S  57 55W
Ensenada, Mexico ....... 86 A1  31 50N 116 50W
Ensenada de los Muertos,
   Mexico ............ 86 C2  23 59N 109 50W
Ensiola, Pta. de n', Spain ... 24 B9  39  7N   2 55 E
Entebbe, Uganda ....... 54 B3   0  4N  32 28 E
Enterprise, Canada ...... 70 A5  60 47N 115 45W
Enterprise, Ala., U.S.A. .... 83 K3  31 19N  85 51W
Enterprise, Oreg., U.S.A. ... 76 D5  45 25N 117 17W
Entre Rios, Bolivia ...... 94 A3  21 30S  64 25W
Entre Ríos □, Argentina ... 94 C4  30 30S  58 30W
Entroncamento, Portugal ... 21 C1  39 28N   8 28W
Enugu, Nigeria ........ 50 G7  6 30N   7 30 E
Enumclaw, U.S.A. ...... 78 C5  47 12N 121 59W
Eólie, Ís., Italy ........ 22 E6  38 30N  14 57 E
Epe, Neths. ........... 15 B5  52 21N   5 59 E
Épernay, France ........ 20 B5  49  3N   3 56 E
Ephesus, Turkey ........ 23 F12 37 55N  27 22 E
Ephraim, U.S.A. ........ 76 G8  39 22N 111 35W
Ephrata, Pa., U.S.A. ..... 85 F8  40 11N  76 11W
Ephrata, Wash., U.S.A. ... 76 C4  47 19N 119 33W
Épinal, France ......... 20 B7  48 10N   6 27 E
Episkopi, Cyprus ....... 25 E11 34 40N  32 54 E
Episkopi, Greece ....... 25 D6  35 20N  24 20 E
Episkopi Bay, Cyprus ..... 25 E11 34 35N  32 50 E
Epsom, U.K. .......... 13 F7  51 19N   0 16W
Epukiro, Namibia ....... 56 C2  21 40S  19  9 E
Equatoria = El Istiwa'iya, Sudan 51 G11  5  0N  28  0 E
Equatorial Guinea ■, Africa .. 52 D1  2  0N   8  0 E
Er Rachidia, Morocco ..... 50 B5  31 58N   4 20W
Er Rahad, Sudan ....... 51 F12 12 45N  30 32 E
Er Rif, Morocco ........ 50 A5  35  1N   4  1W
Erāwadī Myit = Irrawaddy →,
   Burma ............ 41 M19 15 50N  95  6 E
Erāwadī Myitwanya = Irrawaddy,
   Mouths of the, Burma ... 41 M19 15 30N  95  0 E
Erbil = Arbīl, Iraq ...... 44 B5  36 15N  44  5 E
Erçek, Turkey ......... 44 B4  38 39N  43 36 E
Erciyaş Dağı, Turkey ..... 44 B2  38 30N  35 30 E
Érd, Hungary ......... 17 E10 47 22N  18 56 E
Erdao Jiang →, China .... 35 C14 43  0N 127  0 E
Erdek, Turkey ......... 23 D12 40 23N  27 47 E
Erdene = Ulaan-Uul, Mongolia 34 B6  44 13N 111 10 E
Erdenet, Mongolia ...... 32 B5  49  2N 104  5 E
Erdenetsogt, Mongolia .... 34 C4  42 55N 106  5 E
Erebus, Mt., Antarctica ... 5 D11 77 35S 167  0 E
Erechim, Brazil ........ 95 B5  27 35S  52 15W
Ereğli, Konya, Turkey .... 19 G5  37 31N  34  4 E
Ereğli, Zonguldak, Turkey .. 19 F5  41 15N  31 24 E
Erenhot, China ........ 34 C7  43 48N 112  2 E
Eresma →, Spain ....... 21 B3  41 26N   4 45W
Erfenisdam, S. Africa .... 56 D4  28 30S  26 50 E
Erfurt, Germany ....... 16 C6  50 58N  11  2 E
Ergani, Turkey ........ 44 B3  38 17N  39 49 E
Ergel, Mongolia ........ 34 C5  43 8N 109  5 E
Ergeni Vozvyshennost, Russia 19 E7  47  0N  44  0 E
Érgli, Latvia .......... 9 H21 56 54N  25 38 E
Eriboll, L., U.K. ........ 11 C4  58 30N   4 42W
Érice, Italy ........... 22 E5  38  2N  12 35 E
Erie, U.S.A. .......... 84 D4  42  8N  80  5W
Erie, L., N. Amer. ...... 84 D4  42 15N  81  0W
Erie Canal, U.S.A. ...... 84 C7  43  5N  78 43W
Erieau, Canada ........ 84 D3  42 16N  81 57W
Erigavo, Somali Rep. .... 47 E4  10 35N  47 20 E
Erikoúsa, Greece ....... 25 A3  39 53N  19 34 E
Eriksdale, Canada ...... 71 C9  50 52N  98  7W
Erimanthos, Greece ..... 23 F9  37 57N  21 50 E
Erimo-misaki, Japan ..... 30 D11 41 50N 143 15 E
Erinpura, India ........ 42 G5  25  9N  73  3 E
Erin Pt., Trin. & Tob. .... 93 K15 10  3N  61 39W
Eriskay, U.K. ......... 11 D1  57  4N   7 18W
Eritrea ■, Africa ....... 47 D2  14  0N  38 30 E
Erlangen, Germany ..... 16 D6  49 36N  11  0 E
Erldunda, Australia ..... 62 D1  25 14S 133 12 E
Ermelo, Neths. ........ 15 B5  52 18N   5 35 E
Ermelo, S. Africa ...... 57 D4  26 31S  29 59 E
Ermenek, Turkey ....... 44 B2  36 38N  33  0 E
Ermones, Greece ....... 25 A3  39 37N  19 46 E
Ernakulam, India ....... 40 Q10  9 59N  76 22 E
Erne →, Ireland ....... 10 B3  54 30N   8 16W
Erne, Lower L., U.K. .... 10 B4  54 28N   7 47W
Erne, Upper L., U.K. .... 10 B4  54 14N   7 32W
Ernest Giles Ra., Australia . 61 E3  27  0S 123 45 E
Erode, India .......... 40 P10 11 24N  77 45 E
Eromanga, Australia .... 63 D3  26 40S 143 11 E
Erongo, Namibia ....... 56 C2  21 39S  15 58 E
Erramala Hills, India .... 40 M11 15 30N  78 15 E
Errigal, Ireland ....... 10 A3  55  2N   8  6W
Erris Hd., Ireland ...... 10 B1  54 19N  10  0W
Erskine, U.S.A. ........ 80 B7  47 40N  96  0W
Ertis = Irtysh →, Russia .. 28 C7  61  4N  68 52 E
Erwin, U.S.A. ......... 83 G4  36  9N  82 25W
Erzgebirge, Germany .... 16 C7  50 27N  12 55 E
Erzin, Russia ......... 29 D10 50 15N  95 10 E
Erzincan, Turkey ...... 19 G6  39 46N  39 30 E
Erzurum, Turkey ...... 19 G7  39 57N  41 15 E
Es Caló, Spain ........ 24 C8  38 40N   1 30 E
Es Canar, Spain ....... 24 B8  39  2N   1 36 E
Es Mercadal, Spain ..... 24 B11 39 59N   4  5 E
Es Migjorn Gran, Spain ... 24 B11 39 57N   4  3 E
Es Sahrâ' Esh Sharqîya, Egypt 51 C12 27 30N  32  0 E
Es Sînâ', Egypt ........ 46 F3  29  0N  34  0 E
Es Vedrà, Spain ....... 24 C7  38 52N   1 12 E
Esambo, Dem. Rep. of the Congo 54 C1  3 48S  23 30 E
Esan-Misaki, Japan ..... 30 D10 41 40N 141 10 E
Esashi, Hokkaidō, Japan .. 30 B11 44 56N 142 35 E
Esashi, Hokkaidō, Japan .. 30 D10 41 52N 140  7 E
Esbjerg, Denmark ...... 9 J13 55 29N   8 29 E
Esbo = Espoo, Finland ... 9 F21 60 12N  24 40 E
Escalante, U.S.A. ...... 77 H8  37 47N 111 36W
Escalante →, U.S.A. .... 77 H8  37 24N 110 57W
Escalón, Mexico ....... 86 B4  26 46N 104 20W
Escambia →, U.S.A. .... 83 K2  30 32N  87 11W
Escanaba, U.S.A. ...... 82 C2  45 45N  87  4W
Esch-sur-Alzette, Lux. ... 15 E6  49 32N   6  0 E
Escondido, U.S.A. ...... 79 M9  33  7N 117  5W
Escuinapa, Mexico ..... 86 C3  22 50N 105 50W
Escuintla, Guatemala ... 88 D1  14 20N  90 48W
Esenguly, Turkmenistan .. 28 F6  37 37N  53 59 E
Eşfahān, Iran ......... 45 C6  32 39N  51 43 E
Eşfahān □, Iran ....... 45 C6  32 50N  51 50 E
Esfarāyen, Iran ....... 45 B8  37  4N  57 30 E
Esfideh, Iran ......... 45 C8  33 39N  59 46 E
Esh Sham = Dimashq, Syria 46 B5  33 30N  36 18 E
Esha Ness, U.K. ....... 11 A7  60 29N   1 38W
Esher, U.K. .......... 13 F7  51 21N   0 20W
Eshkol △, Israel ....... 46 D3  31 20N  34 30 E
Eshowe, S. Africa ...... 57 D5  28 50S  31 30 E
Esigodini, Zimbabwe .... 57 C4  20 18S  28 56 E
Esil = Ishim →, Russia .. 28 D8  57 45N  71 10 E
Esira, Madag. ........ 57 C8  24 20S  46 42 E
Esk →, Cumb., U.K. .... 11 G5  54 58N   3  2W
Esk →, N. Yorks., U.K. .. 12 C7  54 30N   0 37W
Eskån, Iran .......... 45 E9  26 48N  63  9 E
Esker, Canada ........ 73 B6  53 53N  66 25W
Eskifjörður, Iceland .... 8 D7  65  3N  13 55W
Eskilstuna, Sweden .... 9 G17 59 22N  16 32 E
Eskimo Point = Arviat, Canada 71 A10 61  6N  93 59W
Eskişehir, Turkey ...... 19 G5  39 50N  30 30 E
Esla →, Spain ........ 21 B2  41 29N   6  3W
Eslāmābād-e Gharb, Iran .. 44 C5  34 10N  46 30 E
Eslāmshahr, Iran ...... 45 C6  35 40N  51 10 E
Eşme, Turkey ........ 23 E13 38 23N  28 58 E
Esmeraldas, Ecuador .... 92 C3  1  0N  79 40W
Esnagi L., Canada ..... 72 C3  48 36N  84 33W
Espanola, Canada ..... 72 C3  46 15N  81 46W
Espanola, U.S.A. ...... 77 H10 35 59N 106  5W
Esparta, Costa Rica .... 88 E3  9 59N  84 40W
Esperance, Australia ... 61 F3  33 45S 121 55 E
Esperance B., Australia .. 61 F3  33 48S 121 55 E
Esperance Harbour, St. Lucia 89 f  14  4N  60 55W
Esperanza, Antarctica ... 5 C18 65  0S  55  0W
Esperanza, Argentina ... 94 C3  3 29S  61  3W
Esperanza, Puerto Rico .. 89 d  18  6N  65 28W
Espichel, C., Portugal ... 21 C1  38 22N   9 16W
Espigão, Serra do, Brazil .. 95 B5  26 35S  50 30W
Espinazo, Sierra del = Espinhaço,
   Serra do, Brazil ..... 93 G10 17 30S  43 30W
Espinhaço, Serra do, Brazil . 93 G10 17 30S  43 30W
Espinilho, Serra do, Brazil . 95 B5  28 30S  55  0W
Espírito Santo □, Brazil ... 93 H10 20  0S  40 45W
Espíritu Santo, Vanuatu .. 64 J8  15 15S 166 50 E
Espíritu Santo, B. del, Mexico 87 D7  19 15N  87  0W
Espíritu Santo, I., Mexico .. 86 C2  24 30N 110 23W
Espita, Mexico ....... 87 C7  21  1N  88 19W
Espoo, Finland ....... 9 F21 60 12N  24 40 E
Espungabera, Mozam. ... 57 C5  20 29S  32 45 E
Esquel, Argentina ..... 96 E2  42 55S  71 20W
Esquimalt, Canada .... 70 D4  48 26N 123 25W
Esquina, Argentina ... 94 C4  30  0S  59 30W
Essaouira, Morocco ... 50 B4  31 32N   9 42W
Essebie, Dem. Rep. of the Congo 54 B3  2 58N  30 40 E
Essen, Belgium ....... 15 C4  51 28N   4 28 E
Essen, Germany ...... 16 C4  51 28N   7  2 E
Essendon, Mt., Australia . 61 E3  25  0S 120 29 E
Essequibo →, Guyana .. 92 B7  6 50N  58 30W
Essex, Canada ....... 84 D2  42 10N  82 49W
Essex, Calif., U.S.A. .... 79 L11 34 44N 115 15W
Essex, N.Y., U.S.A. .... 85 B11 44 19N  73 21W
Essex □, U.K. ........ 13 F8  51 54N   0 27 E
Essex Junction, U.S.A. .. 85 B11 44 29N  73  7W
Esslingen, Germany ... 16 D5  48 44N   9 18 E
Estados, I. de Los, Argentina 96 G4  54 40S  64 30W
Eştahbānāt, Iran ...... 45 D7  29  8N  54  4 E
Estancia, Brazil ...... 93 F11 11 16S  37 26W
Estancia, U.S.A. ...... 77 J10 34 46N 106  4W
Estārm, Iran ......... 45 D8  28 21N  58 21 E
Estcourt, S. Africa .... 57 D4  29  0S  29 53 E
Este △, Dom. Rep. .... 89 C6  18 14N  68 42W
Esteli, Nic. .......... 88 D2  13  9N  86 22W
Estellencs, Spain ..... 24 B9  39 39N   2 29 E
Esterhazy, Canada .... 71 C8  50 37N 102  5W
Estevan, Canada ...... 71 D8  49 10N 102 59W
Estevan Group, Canada . 70 C3  53  3N 129 38W
Estherville, U.S.A. .... 80 D7  43 24N  94 50W
Eston, Canada ....... 71 C7  51  8N 108 40W
Estonia ■, Europe .... 9 G21 58 30N  25 30 E
Estreito, Brazil ...... 93 E9  6 32S  47 25W
Estrela, Serra da, Portugal 21 B2  40 10N   7 45W
Estremoz, Portugal ... 21 C2  38 51N   7 39W
Estrondo, Serra do, Brazil . 93 E9  7 20S  48  0W
Esztergom, Hungary ... 17 E10 47 47N  18 44 E
Etah, India ......... 43 F8  27 35N  78 40 E
Étampes, France ..... 20 B5  48 26N   2 10 E
Etanga, Namibia ..... 56 B1  17 55S  13  0 E
Etawah, India ....... 43 F8  26 48N  79  6 E
Etawney L., Canada ... 71 B9  57 50N  96 50W
Ethel, U.S.A. ........ 78 D4  46 32N 122 46W
Ethelbert, Canada .... 71 C8  51 32N 100 25W
Ethiopia ■, Africa ... 47 F3  8  0N  40  0 E
Ethiopian Highlands, Ethiopia 26 J7  10  0N  37  0 E
Etive, L., U.K. ....... 11 E3  56 29N   5 10W
Etna, Italy .......... 22 F6  37 50N  14 55 E
Etoile, Dem. Rep. of the Congo 55 E2  11 33S  27 30 E
Etosha △, Namibia ... 56 B2  19  0S  16  0 E
Etosha Pan, Namibia .. 56 B2  18 40S  16 30 E
Etowah, U.S.A. ...... 83 H3  35 20N  84 32W
Ettelbruck, Lux. ..... 15 E6  49 51N   6  5 E
Ettrick Water →, U.K. .. 11 F6  55 31N   2 55W
Etuku, Dem. Rep. of the Congo 54 C2  3 42S  25 45 E
Etzatlán, Mexico ..... 86 C4  20 48N 104  5W
Etzná, Mexico ....... 87 D6  19 35N  90 15W
Etzná-Tixmucuy = Edxná, Mexico 87 D6  19 35N  90 15W
Eubenangee Swamp △, Australia 62 B4  16 25S 146  1 E
Euboea = Évvoia, Greece . 23 E11 38 30N  24  0 E
Eucla, Australia ...... 61 F4  31 41S 128 52 E
Eucumbene, L., Australia . 63 F4  36  2S 148 40 E
Eudora, U.S.A. ....... 81 J9  33  7N  91 16W
Eufaula, Ala., U.S.A. ... 83 K3  31 54N  85  9W
Eufaula, Okla., U.S.A. .. 81 H7  35 17N  95 35W
Eufaula L., U.S.A. .... 81 H7  35 18N  95 21W
Eugene, U.S.A. ...... 76 E2  44  5N 123  4W
Eugowra, Australia ... 63 E4  33 22S 148 24 E
Eulo, Australia ...... 63 D4  28 10S 145  3 E
Eungella △, Australia . 62 C4  20 57S 148 40 E
Eunice, La., U.S.A. ... 81 K8  30 30N  92 25W
Eunice, N. Mex., U.S.A. . 81 J3  32 26N 103 10W
Eupen, Belgium ..... 15 D6  50 37N   6  3 E
Euphrates = Furāt, Nahr al →,
   Asia ............ 44 D5  31  0N  47 25 E
Eureka, Canada ..... 4 B3  80  0N  85 56W
Eureka, Calif., U.S.A. .. 76 F1  40 47N 124 9W
Eureka, Kans., U.S.A. .. 81 G6  37 49N  96 17W
Eureka, Mont., U.S.A. .. 76 B6  48 53N 115  3W
Eureka, Nev., U.S.A. .. 76 G5  39 31N 115 58W
Eureka, S. Dak., U.S.A. . 80 C5  45 46N  99 38W
Eureka, Mt., Australia .. 61 E3  26 35S 121 35 E
Euroa, Australia ..... 63 F4  36 44S 145 35 E
Europa, Île, Ind. Oc. .. 53 J8  22 20S  40 22 E
Europa, Picos de, Spain . 21 A3  43 10N   4 49W
Europa, Pta. de, Gib. .. 21 D3  36  3N   5 21W
Europe ........... 6 E10 50  0N  20  0 E
Europoort, Neths. ... 15 C4  51 57N   4 10 E
Eustis, U.S.A. ...... 83 L5  28 51N  81 41W
Eutsuk L., Canada ... 70 C3  53 20N 126 45W
Evale, Angola ...... 56 B2  16 33S  15 44 E
Evans, U.S.A. ...... 80 E2  40 23N 104 41W
Evans, L., Canada ... 72 B4  50 50N  77  0W
Evans City, U.S.A. .. 84 F4  40 46N  80  4W
Evans Head, Australia . 63 D5  29  7S 153 27 E
Evans Mills, U.S.A. .. 85 B9  44  6N  75 48W
Evansburg, Canada .. 70 C5  53 36N 114 59W
Evanston, Ill., U.S.A. . 82 E2  42  3N  87 41W
Evanston, Wyo., U.S.A. 76 F8  41 16N 110 58W
Evansville, U.S.A. ... 82 G2  37 58N  87 35W
Évaz, Iran ......... 45 E7  27 46N  53 59 E
Eveleth, U.S.A. .... 80 B8  47 28N  92 32W
Evensk, Russia ..... 29 C16 62 12N 159 30 E
Everard, L., Australia . 63 E2  31 30S 135  0 E
Everard Ranges, Australia 61 E5  27  5S 132 28 E
Everest, Mt., Nepal .. 43 E12 28  5N  86 58 E
Everett, Pa., U.S.A. .. 84 F6  40  1N  78 23W
Everett, Wash., U.S.A. . 78 C4  47 59N 122 12W
Everglades △, U.S.A. . 83 N5  25 30N  81  0W
Everglades, The, U.S.A. . 83 N5  25 50N  81  0W
Everglades City, U.S.A. . 83 N5  25 52N  81 23W
Evergreen, Ala., U.S.A. . 83 K2  31 26N  86 57W
Evergreen, Mont., U.S.A. 76 B6  48  9N 114 13W
Evesham, U.K. ...... 13 E6  52  6N   1 56W
Evje, Norway ....... 9 G12 58 36N   7 51 E
Évora, Portugal ..... 21 C2  38 33N   7 57W
Evowghlī, Iran ...... 44 B5  38 43N  45 13 E
Évreux, France ..... 20 B4  49  3N   1  8 E
Évros →, Greece ... 23 D12 41 40N  26 34 E
Évry, France ....... 20 B5  48 38N   2 27 E
Évvoia, Greece ..... 23 E11 38 30N  24  0 E
Ewe, L., U.K. ...... 11 D3  57 49N   5 38W
Ewing, U.S.A. ...... 80 D5  42 16N  98 21W
Ewo, Congo ....... 52 E2  0 48S  14 45 E
Exaltación, Bolivia .. 92 F5  13 10S  65 20W
Excelsior Springs, U.S.A. 80 F7  39 20N  94 13W
Exe →, U.K. ...... 13 G4  50 41N   3 29W
Exeter, Canada ..... 84 C3  43 21N  81 29W
Exeter, U.K. ....... 13 G4  50 43N   3 31W
Exeter, Calif., U.S.A. . 78 J7  36 18N 119  9W
Exeter, N.H., U.S.A. . 85 D14 42 59N  70 57W
Exmoor, U.K. ...... 13 F4  51 12N   3 45W
Exmoor △, U.K. .... 13 F4  51  8N   3 42W
Exmouth, Australia .. 60 D1  21 54S 114 10 E
Exmouth, U.K. ..... 13 G4  50 37N   3 25W
Exmouth G., Australia . 60 D1  22 15S 114 15 E
Expedition △, Australia 63 D4  25 41S 149  7 E
Expedition Ra., Australia 62 C4  24 30S 149 12 E
Extremadura □, Spain . 21 C2  39 30N   6  5W
Exuma Sound, Bahamas 88 B4  24 30N  76 20W
Eyasi, L., Tanzania ... 54 C4  3 30S  35  0 E
Eye Pen., U.K. ..... 11 C2  58 13N   6 10W
Eyemouth, U.K. .... 11 F6  55 52N   2  5W
Eyjafjarðará →, Iceland 8 C4  66 15N  18 30W
Eyjafjörður, Iceland .. 8 C4  66  5N  18 30W
Eyre (North), L., Australia 63 D2  28 30S 137 20 E
Eyre (South), L., Australia 63 D2  29 18S 137 25 E
Eyre Mts., N.Z. ..... 59 L2  45 25S 168 25 E
Eyre Pen., Australia .. 63 E2  33 30S 136 17 E
Eysturoy, Færoe Is. .. 8 E9  62 13N   6 54W
Eyvānkī, Iran ...... 45 C6  35 24N  51 56 E
Ezine, Turkey ...... 23 E12 39 48N  26 20 E
Ezouza →, Cyprus .. 25 E11 34 44N  32 27 E

F.Y.R.O.M. = Macedonia ■,
   Europe .......... 23 D9  41 53N  21 40 E
Fabala, Guinea ..... 50 G4  9 44N   9  5W
Fabens, U.S.A. ..... 77 L10 31 30N 106 10W
Fabriano, Italy ..... 22 C5  43 20N  12 54 E
Fachi, Niger ....... 51 E8  18  6N  11 34 E
Fada, Chad ........ 51 E10 17 13N  21 34 E
Fada-n-Gourma, Burkina Faso 50 F6  12 10N   0 30 E
Faddeyevskiy, Ostrov, Russia 29 B15 76  0N 144  0 E
Fadghāmī, Syria .... 44 C4  35 53N  40 52 E
Faenza, Italy ...... 22 B4  44 17N  11 53 E
Færoe Is. = Føroyar, Atl. Oc. 8 F9  62  0N   7  0W
Făgăraş, Romania .. 17 F13 45 48N  24 58 E
Fagersta, Sweden .. 9 F16 60  1N  15 46 E
Fagnano, L., Argentina 96 G3  54 30S  68  0W
Fahlīān, Iran ...... 45 D6  30 11N  51 28 E
Fahraj, Kermān, Iran .. 45 D8  29  0N  59  0 E
Fahraj, Yazd, Iran .. 45 D7  31 46N  54 36 E
Faial, Madeira ..... 24 D3  32 47N  16 53W
Fair Haven, U.S.A. . 82 D9  43 36N  73 16W
Fair Hd., U.K. ..... 10 A5  55 14N   6  9W
Fair Isle, U.K. ..... 14 B6  59 30N   1 40W
Fair Oaks, U.S.A. .. 78 G5  38 39N 121 16W
Fairbanks, U.S.A. .. 68 B5  64 51N 147 43W
Fairbury, U.S.A. ... 80 E6  40  8N  97 11W
Fairfax, U.S.A. .... 85 B11 44 40N  73  1W
Fairfield, Ala., U.S.A. 83 J2  33 29N  86 55W
Fairfield, Calif., U.S.A. 78 G4  38 15N 122  3W
Fairfield, Conn., U.S.A. 85 E11 41  9N  73 16W
Fairfield, Idaho, U.S.A. 76 E6  43 21N 114 44W
Fairfield, Ill., U.S.A. . 82 F1  38 23N  88 22W
Fairfield, Iowa, U.S.A. 80 E9  40 56N  91 57W
Fairfield, Tex., U.S.A. 81 K7  31 44N  96 10W
Fairford, Canada ... 71 C9  51 37N  98 38W
Fairhope, U.S.A. ... 83 K2  30 31N  87 54W
Fairlie, N.Z. ...... 59 L3  44  5S 170 49 E
Fairmead, U.S.A. .. 78 H6  37  5N 120 10W
Fairmont, Minn., U.S.A. 80 D7  43 39N  94 28W
Fairmont, W. Va., U.S.A. 82 F5  39 29N  80  9W
Fairmount, Calif., U.S.A. 79 L8  34 45N 118 26W
Fairmount, N.Y., U.S.A. 85 C8  43  5N  76 12W
Fairplay, U.S.A. ... 77 G11 39 15N 106 2W
Fairport, U.S.A. ... 84 C7  43  6N  77 27W
Fairport Harbor, U.S.A. 84 E3  41 45N  81 17W
Fairview, Canada .. 70 B5  56  5N 118 25W
Fairview, Mont., U.S.A. 80 B2  47 51N 104  3W
Fairview, Okla., U.S.A. 81 G5  36 16N  98 29W
Fairweather, Mt., U.S.A. 70 B1  58 55N 137 32W
Faisalabad, Pakistan . 42 D5  31 30N  73  5 E
Faith, U.S.A. ...... 80 C3  45  2N 102  2W
Faizabad, India .... 43 F10 26 45N  82 10 E
Fajardo, Puerto Rico .. 89 d  18 20N  65 39W
Fajr, W. →, Si. Arabia 44 D3  29 10N  38 10 E
Fakenham, U.K. ... 12 E8  52 50N   0 51 E
Fakfak, Indonesia .. 37 E8  2 55S 132 18 E
Faku, China ...... 35 C12 42 32N 123 21 E
Falaise, France .... 20 B3  48 54N   0 12W
Falaise, Mui, Vietnam 38 C5  19  6N 105 45 E
Falam, Burma ..... 41 H18 23  0N  93 45 E
Falcó, C. des, Spain . 24 C7  38 50N   1 23 E
Falcón, Presa, Mexico 87 B5  26 35N  99 10W
Falcon Lake, Canada . 71 D9  49 42N  95 15W
Falcon Reservoir, U.S.A. 81 M5  26 34N  99 10W
Falconara Maríttima, Italy 22 C5  43 37N  13 24 E
Falcone, C. del, Italy . 22 D3  40 58N   8 12 E
Falconer, U.S.A. ... 84 D5  42  7N  79 13W
Faleshty = Fălești, Moldova 17 E14 47 32N  27 44 E
Fălești, Moldova ... 17 E14 47 32N  27 44 E
Falfurrias, U.S.A. .. 81 M5  27 14N  98  9W
Falher, Canada .... 70 B5  55 44N 117 15W
Faliraki, Greece ... 25 C10 36 20N  28 12 E
Falkenberg, Sweden . 9 H15 56 54N  12 30 E
Falkirk, U.K. ...... 11 F5  56  0N   3 47W
Falkirk □, U.K. .... 11 F5  55 58N   3 49W
Falkland, U.K. .... 11 E5  56 16N   3 12W
Falkland Is. ☑, Atl. Oc. 96 G5  51 30S  59  0W
Falkland Sd., Falk. Is. . 96 G5  52  0S  60  0W
Falköping, Sweden . 9 G15 58 12N  13 33 E
Fall River, U.S.A. .. 85 E13 41 43N  71 10W
Fallbrook, U.S.A. .. 79 M9  33 23N 117 15W
Fallon, U.S.A. ..... 76 G4  39 28N 118 47W
Falls City, U.S.A. .. 80 E7  40  3N  95 36W
Falls Creek, U.S.A. . 84 E6  41  9N  78 48W
Falmouth, Jamaica .. 88 a  18 30N  77 40W
Falmouth, U.K. .... 13 G2  50  9N   5  5W
Falmouth, U.S.A. .. 85 E14 41 33N  70 37W
Falsa, Pta., Mexico . 86 B1  27 51N 115  3W
False B., S. Africa .. 56 E2  34 15S  18 40 E
Falso, C., Honduras . 88 C3  15 12N  83 21W
Falster, Denmark .. 9 J14 54 45N  11 55 E
Falsterbo, Sweden . 9 J15 55 23N  12 50 E
Fălticeni, Romania . 17 E14 47 21N  26 20 E
Falun, Sweden .... 9 F16 60 37N  15 37 E
Famagusta, Cyprus . 25 D12 35  8N  33 55 E
Famagusta Bay, Cyprus 25 D13 35 15N  34  0 E
Famalé, Niger ..... 50 F6  14 33N   1  5 E
Famatina, Sierra de, Argentina 94 B2  27 30S  68  0W
Family L., Canada . 71 C9  51 54N  95 27W
Famoso, U.S.A. ... 79 K7  35 37N 119 12W
Fan Xian, China ... 34 G8  35 55N 115 38 E
Fanad Hd., Ireland . 10 A4  55 17N   7 38W
Fandriana, Madag. . 57 C8  20 14S  47 21 E
Fang, Thailand .... 38 C2  19 55N  99 13 E
Fangcheng, China .. 34 H7  33 18N 112 59 E
Fangshan, China .. 34 E6  38 3N 111 25 E
Fangzi, China ..... 35 F10 36 33N 119 12 E
Fanjakana, Madag. . 57 C8  21 10S  46 53 E
Fanjiatun, China ... 35 C13 43 40N 125 15 E
Fanling, China .... 33 F11 22 30N 114  8 E
Fannich, L., U.K. .. 11 D4  57 38N   4 59W
Fannūj, Iran ...... 45 E8  26 35N  59 38 E
Fano, Denmark .... 9 J13 55 25N   8 25 E
Fano, Italy ....... 22 C5  43 50N  13  1 E
Fanshi, China ..... 34 E7  39 12N 113 20 E
Fao = Al Fāw, Iraq . 45 D6  30  0N  48 30 E
Faqīrwali, Pakistan . 42 E5  29 27N  73  0 E
Far East = Dalnevostochnyy □,
   Russia .......... 29 C14 67  0N 140  0 E
Far East, Asia ..... 26 E16 40  0N 130  0 E
Faradje, Dem. Rep. of the Congo 54 B2  3 50N  29 45 E
Farafangana, Madag. 57 C8  22 49S  47 50 E
Farāh, Afghan. .... 40 C3  32 20N  62  7 E
Farāh □, Afghan. .. 40 C3  32 25N  62  0 E
Farahalana, Madag. . 57 A9  14 26S  50 10 E
Faranah, Guinea ... 50 F3  10  3N  10 45W

Farasān, Jazā'ir, Si. Arabia ..... 47 D3  16 45N  41 55 E
Farasan Is. = Farasān, Jazā'ir,
  Si. Arabia ................... 47 D3  16 45N  41 55 E
Faratsiho, Madag. ............. 57 B8  19 24S  46 57 E
Fareham, U.K. ................ 13 G6  50 51N   1 11W
Farewell, C., N.Z. ............. 59 J4  40 29S 172 43 E
Farewell C. = Nunap Isua,
  Greenland ................... 69 C15 59 48N  43 55W
Farghona, Uzbekistan ......... 28 E8  40 23N  71 19 E
Fargo, U.S.A. ................. 80 B6  46 53N  96 48W
Fär'iah, W. al →, West Bank ... 46 C4  32 12N  35 27 E
Faribault, U.S.A. .............. 80 C8  44 18N  93 16W
Faridabad, India .............. 42 E6  28 26N  77 19 E
Faridkot, India ............... 42 D6  30 44N  74 45 E
Faridpur, Bangla. ............. 43 H13 23 15N  89 55 E
Faridpur, India ............... 43 E8  28 13N  79 33 E
Farīmān, Iran ................ 45 C8  35 40N  59 49 E
Farina, Australia ............. 63 E2  30  3S 138 15 E
Fariones, Pta., Canary Is. ..... 24 E6  29 13N  13 28W
Farleigh, Australia ........... 62 K7  21  4S 149  8 E
Farmerville, U.S.A. ........... 81 J8  32 47N  92 24W
Farmingdale, U.S.A. .......... 85 F10 40 12N  74 10W
Farmington, Canada .......... 70 B4  55 54N 120 30W
Farmington, Calif., U.S.A. .... 78 H6  37 55N 120 59W
Farmington, Maine, U.S.A. ... 83 C10 44 40N  70  9W
Farmington, Mo., U.S.A. ...... 81 G9  37 47N  90 25W
Farmington, N.H., U.S.A. ..... 85 C13 43 24N  71  4W
Farmington, N. Mex., U.S.A. .. 77 H9  36 44N 108 12W
Farmington, Utah, U.S.A. ..... 76 F8  41  0N 111 12W
Farmington →, U.S.A. ........ 85 E12 41 51N  72 38W
Farmville, U.S.A. ............. 82 G6  37 18N  78 24W
Farne Is., U.K. ............... 12 B6  55 38N   1 37W
Farnham, Canada ............. 85 A12 45 17N  72 59W
Farnham, Mt., Canada ........ 70 C5  50 29N 116 30W
Faro, Brazil .................. 93 D7   2 10S  56 39W
Faro, Canada ................. 68 B6  62 11N 133 22W
Faro, Portugal ............... 21 D2  37  2N   7 55W
Fårö, Sweden ................. 9 H18  57 55N  19  5 E
Farquhar, C., Australia ....... 61 D1  23 50S 113 36 E
Farrars Cr. →, Australia ...... 62 D3  25 35S 140 43 E
Farrāshband, Iran ............ 45 D7  28 57N  52  5 E
Farrell, U.S.A. ............... 84 E4  41 13N  80 30W
Farrokhī, Iran ............... 45 C8  33 50N  59 31 E
Farruch, C. = Ferrutx, C., Spain 24 B10 39 47N   3 21 E
Fārs □, Iran ................. 45 D7  29 30N  55  0 E
Fársala, Greece .............. 23 E10 39 17N  22 23 E
Farson, U.S.A. ............... 76 E9  42  6N 109 27W
Farsund, Norway ............. 9 G12  58  5N   6 55 E
Fartak, Rās, Si. Arabia ....... 44 D2  28  5N  34 34 E
Fartak, Ra's, Yemen .......... 47 D5  15 38N  52 15 E
Fartura, Serra da, Brazil ...... 95 B5  26 21S  52 52W
Fārūj, Iran .................. 45 B8  37 14N  58 14 E
Farvel, Kap = Nunap Isua,
  Greenland ................... 69 C15 59 48N  43 55W
Farwell, U.S.A. ............... 81 H3  34 23N 103  2W
Fāryāb □, Afghan. ............ 40 B4  36  0N  65  0 E
Fasā, Iran ................... 45 D7  29  0N  53 39 E
Fasano, Italy ................ 22 D7  40 50N  17 22 E
Fastiv, Ukraine .............. 17 C15 50  7N  29 57 E
Fastnet Rock, Ireland ......... 10 E2  51 22N   9 37W
Fastov = Fastiv, Ukraine ...... 17 C15 50  7N  29 57 E
Fatagar, Tanjung, Indonesia ... 37 E8   2 46S 131 57 E
Fatehabad, Haryana, India .... 42 E6  29 31N  75 27 E
Fatehabad, Ut. P., India ...... 42 F8  27  1N  78 19 E
Fatehgarh, India ............. 43 F8  27 25N  79 35 E
Fatehpur, Bihar, India ........ 43 G11 24 38N  85 14 E
Fatehpur, Raj., India ......... 42 F6  28  0N  74 40 E
Fatehpur, Ut. P., India ....... 43 G9  25 56N  81 13 E
Fatehpur, Ut. P., India ....... 43 F9  27 10N  81 13 E
Fatehpur Sikri, India ......... 42 F6  27  6N  77 40 E
Fathom Five △, Canada ....... 84 A3  45 17N  81 40W
Fatima, Canada .............. 73 C7  47 24N  61 53W
Faulkton, U.S.A. ............. 80 C5  45  2N  99  8W
Faure I., Australia ............ 61 E1  25 52S 113 50 E
Fauresmith, S. Africa ......... 56 D4  29 44S  25 17 E
Fauske, Norway .............. 8 C16  67 17N  15 25 E
Favara, Italy ................ 22 F5  37 19N  13 39 E
Faváritx, C. de, Spain ........ 24 B11 40  0N   4 15 E
Favignana, Italy ............. 22 F5  37 56N  12 20 E
Fawcett, Pt., Australia ....... 60 B5  11 46S 130  2 E
Fawn →, Canada ............. 72 A2  55 20N  87 35W
Fawnskin, U.S.A. ............. 79 L10 34 16N 116 56W
Faxaflói, Iceland ............. 8 D2  64 29N  23  0W
Faya-Largeau, Chad .......... 51 E9  17 58N  19  6 E
Fayd, Si. Arabia .............. 44 E4  27  1N  42 52 E
Fayette, Ala., U.S.A. ......... 83 J2  33 41N  87 50W
Fayette, Mo., U.S.A. ......... 80 F8  39  9N  92 41W
Fayetteville, Ark., U.S.A. ..... 81 G7  36  4N  94 10W
Fayetteville, N.C., U.S.A. ..... 83 H6  35  3N  78 53W
Fayetteville, Tenn., U.S.A. .... 83 H2  35  9N  86 34W
Fazilka, India ............... 42 D6  30 27N  74  2 E
Fazilpur, Pakistan ............ 42 E4  29 18N  70 29 E
Fdérik, Mauritania ........... 50 D3  22 40N  12 45W
Feale →, Ireland ............. 10 D2  52 27N   9 37W
Fear, C., U.S.A. .............. 83 J7  33 50N  77 58W
Feather →, U.S.A. ............ 76 G3  38 47N 121 36W
Feather Falls, U.S.A. ......... 78 F5  39 36N 121 16W
Featherston, N.Z. ............ 59 J5  41  6S 175 20 E
Featherstone, Zimbabwe ...... 55 F3  18 42S  30 55 E
Fécamp, France .............. 20 B4  49 45N   0 22 E
Fedala = Mohammedia, Morocco 50 B4  33 44N   7 21W
Federación, Argentina ........ 94 C4  31  0S  57 55W
Féderal, Argentina ........... 96 C5  30 57S  58 48W
Federal Way, U.S.A. .......... 78 C4  47 18N 122 19W
Fedeshkūh, Iran ............. 45 D7  28 49N  53 50 E
Fehmarn, Germany ........... 16 A6  54 27N  11  7 E
Fehmarn Bælt, Europe ........ 9 J14  54 35N  11 20 E
Fehmarn Belt = Fehmarn Bælt,
  Europe ..................... 9 J14  54 35N  11 20 E
Fei Xian, China .............. 35 G9  35 18N 117 59 E
Feijó, Brazil ................. 92 E4   8  9S  70 21W
Feilding, N.Z. ............... 59 J5  40 13S 175 35 E
Feira de Santana, Brazil ...... 93 F11 12 15S  38 57W
Feixiang, China .............. 34 F8  36 30N 114 45 E
Felanitx, Spain .............. 24 B10 39 28N   3  9 E
Feldkirch, Austria ............ 16 E5  47 15N   9 37 E
Felipe Carrillo Puerto, Mexico . 87 D7  19 38N  88  3W
Felixburg, Zimbabwe ......... 57 B5  19 29S  30 51 E
Felixstowe, U.K. ............. 13 F9  51 58N   1 23 E
Felton, U.S.A. ............... 78 H4  37  3N 122  4W
Femer Bælt = Fehmarn Bælt,
  Europe ..................... 9 J14  54 35N  11 20 E
Femunden, Norway ........... 9 E14  62 10N  11 53 E
Fen →, China ................ 34 G6  35 36N 110 42 E
Fenelon Falls, Canada ........ 84 B6  44 32N  78 45W
Feng Xian, Jiangsu, China ..... 34 G9  34 43N 116 35 E
Feng Xian, Shaanxi, China .... 34 H4  33 54N 106 40 E
Fengcheng, China ............ 35 D13 40 28N 124  5 E

Fengfeng, China .............. 34 F8  36 28N 114  8 E
Fengning, China .............. 34 D9  41 10N 116 33 E
Fengqiu, China ............... 34 G8  35  2N 114 25 E
Fengrun, China ............... 35 E10 39 48N 118  8 E
Fengtai, China ............... 34 E9  39 50N 116 18 E
Fengxiang, China ............. 34 G4  34 29N 107 25 E
Fengyang, China ............. 35 H9  32 51N 117 29 E
Fengzhen, China ............. 34 D7  40 25N 113  2 E
Fenoarivo, Fianarantsoa, Madag. 57 C8  21 43S  46 24 E
Fenoarivo, Fianarantsoa, Madag. 57 C8  20 52S  46 53 E
Fenoarivo Afovoany, Madag. ... 57 B8  18 26S  46 34 E
Fenoarivo Atsinanana, Madag. . 57 B8  17 22S  49 25 E
Fens, The, U.K. .............. 12 E7  52 38N   0  2W
Fenton, U.S.A. ............... 82 D4  42 48N  83 42W
Fenxi, China ................. 34 F6  36 40N 111 31 E
Fenyang, China .............. 34 F6  37 18N 111 48 E
Feodosiya, Ukraine ........... 19 E6  45  2N  35 16 E
Ferdows, Iran ................ 45 C8  33 58N  58  2 E
Ferfer, Somali Rep. ........... 47 F4   5  4N  45  9 E
Fergana = Farghona, Uzbekistan 28 E8  40 23N  71 19 E
Fergus, Canada .............. 84 C4  43 43N  80 24W
Fergus Falls, U.S.A. .......... 80 B6  46 17N  96  4W
Ferkéssédougou, Ivory C. ..... 50 G4   9 35N   5  6W
Ferland, Canada ............. 72 B2  50 19N  88 27W
Fermanagh □, U.K. .......... 10 B4  54 21N   7 40W
Fermo, Italy ................. 22 C5  43  9N  13 43 E
Fermont, Canada ............ 73 B6  52 47N  67  5W
Fermoy, Ireland .............. 10 D3  52  9N   8 16W
Fernández, Argentina ......... 94 B3  27 55S  63 50W
Fernandina Beach, U.S.A. ..... 83 K5  30 40N  81 27W
Fernando de Noronha, Brazil .. 93 D12  4  0S  33 10W
Fernando Póo = Bioko, Eq. Guin. 52 D1  3 30N   8 40 E
Ferndale, U.S.A. ............. 78 B4  48 51N 122 36W
Fernie, Canada .............. 70 D5  49 30N 115  5W
Fernlees, Australia ........... 62 C4  23 51S 148  7 E
Fernley, U.S.A. .............. 76 G4  39 36N 119 15W
Ferozepore = Firozpur, India .. 42 D6  30 55N  74 40 E
Ferrara, Italy ................ 22 B4  44 50N  11 35 E
Ferreñafe, Peru .............. 92 E3   6 42S  79 50W
Ferrerías, Spain ............. 24 B11 39 59N   4  1 E
Ferret, C., France ............ 20 D3  44 38N   1 15W
Ferriday, U.S.A. ............. 81 K9  31 38N  91 33W
Ferrol, Spain ................ 21 A1  43 29N   8 15W
Ferron, U.S.A. ............... 77 G8  39  5N 111  8W
Ferrutx, C., Spain ............ 24 B10 39 47N   3 21 E
Ferryland, Canada ........... 73 C9  47  2N  52 53W
Fertile, U.S.A. ............... 80 B6  47 32N  96 17W
Fès, Morocco ................ 50 B5  34  0N   5  0W
Fessenden, U.S.A. ............ 80 B5  47 39N  99 38W
Festus, U.S.A. ............... 80 F9  38 13N  90 24W
Feteşti, Romania ............. 17 F14 44 22N  27 51 E
Fethiye, Turkey .............. 19 G4  36 36N  29  6 E
Fetlar, U.K. ................. 11 A8  60 36N   0 52W
Feuilles →, Canada .......... 69 C12 58 47N  70  4W
Fez = Fès, Morocco ........... 50 B5  34  0N   5  0W
Fezzan, Libya ................ 51 C8  27  0N  13  0 E
Fiambalá, Argentina .......... 94 B2  27 45S  67 37W
Fianarantsoa, Madag. ........ 57 C8  21 26S  47  5 E
Fianarantsoa □, Madag. ...... 57 B8  19 30S  47  0 E
Ficksburg, S. Africa .......... 57 D4  28 51S  27 53 E
Field →, Australia ........... 62 C2  23 48S 138  0 E
Field I., Australia ............ 60 B5  12  5S 132 23 E
Fier, Albania ................ 23 D8  40 43N  19 33 E
Fife □, U.K. ................. 11 E5  56 16N   3 15W
Fife Ness, U.K. .............. 11 E6  56 17N   2 35W
Fifth Cataract, Sudan ......... 51 E12 18 22N  33 50 E
Figeac, France ............... 20 D5  44 37N   2  2 E
Figtree, Zimbabwe ........... 55 G2  20 22S  28 20 E
Figueira da Foz, Portugal ..... 21 B1  40  7N   8 54W
Figueres, Spain .............. 21 A7  42 18N   2 58 E
Figuig, Morocco ............. 50 B5  32  5N   1 11W
Fihaonana, Madag. ........... 57 B8  18 36S  47 12 E
Fiherenana, Madag. .......... 57 B8  18 29S  48 24 E
Fiherenana →, Madag. ....... 57 C7  23 19S  43 37 E
Fiji ■, Pac. Oc. .............. 59 C8  17 20S 179  0 E
Filabusi, Zimbabwe .......... 55 G2  20 34S  29 20 E
Filey, U.K. .................. 12 C7  54 12N   0 18W
Filey B., U.K. ................ 12 C7  54 12N   0 15W
Fifla, Malta ................. 25 D1  35 47N  14 24 E
Filiatrá, Greece .............. 23 F9  37  9N  21 35 E
Filingué, Niger .............. 50 F6  14 21N   3 22 E
Filipstad, Sweden ............ 9 G16 59 43N  14  9 E
Fillmore, Calif., U.S.A. ....... 79 L8  34 24N 118 55W
Fillmore, Utah, U.S.A. ........ 77 G7  38 58N 112 20W
Finch, Canada ............... 85 A9  45 11N  75  7W
Finch Hatton, Australia ....... 62 K6  20 25S 148 39 E
Findhorn →, U.K. ........... 11 D5  57 38N   3 38W
Findlay, U.S.A. .............. 82 E4  41  2N  83 39W
Finger, U.S.A. ............... 72 B1  53 33N  93 30W
Finger Lakes, U.S.A. ......... 85 D8  42 40N  76 30W
Fingoè, Mozam. ............. 55 E3  14 55S  31 50 E
Finisterre, C. = Fisterra, C., Spain 21 A1  42 50N   9 19W
Finke, Australia ............. 62 D1  25 34S 134 35 E
Finke Gorge △, Australia ..... 60 D5  24  8S 132 49 E
Finland ■, Europe ........... 8 E22  63  0N  27  0 E
Finland, G. of, Europe ........ 9 G21 60  0N  26  0 E
Finlay →, Canada ........... 70 B3  57  0N 125 10W
Finley, Australia ............. 63 F4  35 38S 145 35 E
Finley, U.S.A. ............... 80 B6  47 31N  97 50W
Finn →, Ireland ............. 10 B4  54 51N   7 28W
Finnigan, Mt., Australia ...... 62 B4  15 49S 145 17 E
Finniss, C., Australia ......... 63 E1  33  8S 134 51 E
Finnmark, Norway ........... 8 B20  69 37N  23 57 E
Finnsnes, Norway ............ 8 B18  69 14N  18  0 E
Finspång, Sweden ........... 9 G16 58 43N  15 47 E
Fiora →, Italy ............... 22 C4  42 20N  11 34 E
Fiordland △, N.Z. ........... 59 L1  45 46S 167  0 E
Fiq, Syria ................... 46 C4  32 46N  35 41 E
Firat = Furāt, Nahr al →, Asia . 44 D5  31  0N  47 25 E
Fire Island △, U.S.A. ........ 85 F11 40 38N  73  8W
Firebag →, Canada .......... 71 B6  57 45N 111 21W
Firebaugh, U.S.A. ........... 78 J6  36 52N 120 27W
Firedrake L., Canada ......... 71 A8  61 25N 104 30W
Firenze, Italy ................ 22 C4  43 46N  11 15 E
Firk, Sha'īb →, Iraq ......... 44 D5  30 59N  44 34 E
Firozabad, India ............. 43 F8  27 10N  78 25 E
Firozpur, India .............. 42 D6  30 55N  74 40 E
Firozpur-Jhirka, India ........ 42 F7  27 48N  76 57 E
Firūzābād, Iran .............. 45 D7  28 52N  52 35 E
Firūzkūh, Iran ............... 45 C7  35 50N  52 50 E
Firvale, Canada ............. 70 C3  52 27N 126 13W
Fish →, Namibia ............. 56 D2  28  7S  17 10 E
Fish →, S. Africa ............ 56 E3  31 30S  20 16 E
Fish River Canyon, Namibia ... 56 D2  27 40S  17 35 E
Fisher, Australia ............. 61 F5  30 30S 131  0 E
Fisher B., Canada ............ 71 C9  51 35N  97 13W
Fishers I., U.S.A. ............ 85 E13 41 15N  72  0W

Fishguard, U.K. .............. 13 E3  52  0N   4 58W
Fishing L., Canada ........... 71 C9  52 10N  95 24W
Fishkill, U.S.A. .............. 85 E11 41 32N  73 53W
Fisterra, C., Spain ........... 21 A1  42 50N   9 19W
Fitchburg, U.S.A. ............ 85 D13 42 35N  71 48W
Fitz Roy, Argentina .......... 96 F3  47  0S  67  0W
Fitzgerald, Canada ........... 70 B6  59 51N 111 36W
Fitzgerald, U.S.A. ............ 83 K4  31 43N  83 15W
Fitzgerald River △, Australia .. 61 F3  33 53S 120  3 E
Fitzmaurice →, Australia ..... 60 B5  14 45S 130  5 E
Fitzroy →, Queens., Australia . 62 C5  23 32S 150 52 E
Fitzroy →, W. Austral., Australia 60 C3  17 31S 123 35 E
Fitzroy, Mte., Argentina ...... 96 F2  49 17S  73  5W
Fitzroy Crossing, Australia .... 60 C4  18  9S 125 38 E
Fitzwilliam I., Canada ........ 84 A3  45 30N  81 45W
Fiume = Rijeka, Croatia ...... 16 F8  45 20N  14 21 E
Five Points, U.S.A. ........... 78 J6  36 26N 120 6W
Fizi, Dem. Rep. of the Congo .. 54 C2   4 17S  28 55 E
Flagstaff, U.S.A. ............. 77 J8  35 12N 111 39W
Flagstaff L., U.S.A. .......... 83 C10 45 12N  70 18W
Flaherty I., Canada .......... 72 A4  56 15N  79 15W
Flåm, Norway ............... 9 F12 60 50N   7  7 E
Flambeau →, U.S.A. ......... 80 C9  45 18N  91 14W
Flamborough Hd., U.K. ....... 12 C7  54  7N   0  5W
Flaming Gorge △, U.S.A. ..... 76 F9  41  10N 109 25W
Flaming Gorge Reservoir, U.S.A. 76 F9  41 10N 109 25W
Flamingo, Teluk, Indonesia ... 37 F9   5 30S 138  0 E
Flanders = Flandre, Europe .... 14 F8  50 50N   2 30 E
Flandre, Europe .............. 14 F8  50 50N   2 30 E
Flandre-Occidentale = West-
  Vlaanderen □, Belgium ...... 15 D2  51  0N   3  0 E
Flandre-Orientale = Oost-
  Vlaanderen □, Belgium ...... 15 C3  51  0N   3 50 E
Flandreau, U.S.A. ............ 80 C6  44  3N  96 36W
Flanigan, U.S.A. ............. 78 E7  40 10N 119 53W
Flannan Is., U.K. ............ 11 C1  58  9N   7 52W
Flåsjön, Sweden ............. 8 D16 64  5N  15 40 E
Flat →, U.S.A. ............... 70 A3  61 33N 125 18W
Flathead L., U.S.A. .......... 76 C7  47 51N 114  8W
Flattery, C., Australia ......... 62 A4  14 58S 145 21 E
Flattery, C., U.S.A. .......... 78 B2  48 23N 124 29W
Flatwoods, U.S.A. ............ 82 F4  38 31N  82 43W
Fleetwood, Australia ......... 62 C4  23 30S 149 30 E
Fleetwood, U.K. ............. 12 D4  53 55N   3  1W
Fleetwood, U.S.A. ........... 85 F9  40 27N  75 49W
Flekkefjord, Norway .......... 9 G12 58 18N   6 39 E
Flemington, U.S.A. ........... 84 F7  41  7N  77 28W
Flensburg, Germany .......... 16 A5  54 47N   9 27 E
Flers, France ................ 20 B3  48 47N   0 33W
Flesherton, Canada .......... 84 B4  44 16N  80 33W
Flesko, Tanjung, Indonesia .... 37 D6   0 29N 124 30 E
Fleurieu Pen., Australia ....... 63 F2  35 40S 138  5 E
Flevoland □, Neths. ......... 15 B5  52 30N   5 30 E
Flin Flon, Canada ............ 71 C8  54 46N 101 53W
Flinders →, Australia ........ 62 B3  17 36S 140 36 E
Flinders B., Australia ........ 61 F2  34 19S 115 19 E
Flinders Group, Australia ..... 62 A3  14 11S 144 15 E
Flinders I., S. Austral., Australia 63 E1  33 44S 134 41 E
Flinders I., Tas., Australia .... 63 G4  40  0S 148  0 E
Flinders Ranges, Australia .... 63 E2  31 30S 138 30 E
Flinders Reefs, Australia ...... 62 B4  17 37S 148 31 E
Flint, U.K. .................. 12 D4  53 15N   3  8W
Flint, U.S.A. ................ 82 D4  43  1N  83 41W
Flint →, U.S.A. .............. 83 K3  30 57N  84 34W
Flint I., Kiribati ............. 65 J12 11 26S 151 48W
Flintshire □, U.K. ........... 12 D4  53 17N   3 17W
Flodden, U.K. ............... 12 B5  55 37N   2  8W
Floodwood, U.S.A. ........... 80 B8  46 55N  92 55W
Flora, U.S.A. ................ 82 F1  38 40N  88 29W
Florala, U.S.A. .............. 83 K2  31  0N  86 20W
Florence = Firenze, Italy ...... 22 C4  43 46N  11 15 E
Florence, Ala., U.S.A. ........ 83 H2  34 48N  87 41W
Florence, Ariz., U.S.A. ....... 77 K8  33  2N 111 23W
Florence, Colo., U.S.A. ....... 80 F2  38 23N 105  8W
Florence, Oreg., U.S.A. ....... 76 E1  43 58N 124  7W
Florence, S.C., U.S.A. ........ 83 H6  34 12N  79 46W
Florence, L., Australia ........ 63 D2  28 53S 138  9 E
Florencia, Colombia .......... 92 C3   1 36N  75 36W
Florennes, Belgium ........... 15 D4  50 15N   4 35 E
Florenville, Belgium .......... 15 E5  49 40N   5 19 E
Flores, Guatemala ........... 88 C2  16 59N  89 50W
Flores, Indonesia ............ 37 F6   8 35S 121  0 E
Flores I., Canada ............ 70 D3  49 20N 126 10W
Flores Sea, Indonesia ........ 37 F6   6 30S 120  0 E
Floreşti, Moldova ............ 17 E15 47 53N  28 17 E
Floresville, U.S.A. ........... 81 L5  29  8N  98 10W
Floriano, Brazil ............. 93 E10  6 50S  43  0W
Florianópolis, Brazil ......... 95 B6  27 30S  48 30W
Florida, Cuba ............... 88 B4  21 32N  78 14W
Florida, Uruguay ............ 95 C4  34  7S  56 10W
Florida □, U.S.A. ............ 83 L5  28  0N  82  0W
Florida, Straits of, U.S.A. ..... 88 B4  25  0N  80 45W
Florida B., U.S.A. ............ 83 N5  25  0N  81  0W
Florida Keys, U.S.A. ......... 83 N5  24 40N  81  0W
Flórina, Greece .............. 23 D9  40 48N  21 26 E
Florø, Norway ............... 9 F11 61 35N   5  1 E
Flower Station, Canada ....... 85 A8  45 10N  76 41W
Flowerpot I., Canada ......... 84 A3  45 18N  81 38W
Floydada, U.S.A. ............. 81 J4  33 59N 101 20W
Fluk, Indonesia ............. 37 E7   1 42S 127 44 E
Flushing = Vlissingen, Neths. .. 15 C3  51 26N   3 34 E
Flying Fish, C., Antarctica ..... 5 D15  72  6S 102 29W
Foam Lake, Canada .......... 71 C8  51 40N 103 32W
Foça, Turkey ................ 23 E12 38 39N  26 46 E
Fochabers, U.K. ............. 11 D5  57 37N   3  6W
Focşani, Romania ........... 17 F14 45 41N  27 15 E
Fóggia, Italy ................ 22 D6  41 27N  15 34 E
Fogo, Canada ............... 73 C9  49 43N  54 17W
Fogo I., Canada ............. 73 C9  49 40N  54  5W
Föhr, Germany .............. 16 A5  54 43N   8 30 E
Foix, France ................ 20 E4  42 58N   1 38 E
Folda, Nord-Trøndelag, Norway 8 D14 64 32N  10 30 E
Folda, Nordland, Norway ..... 8 C16 67 38N  14 50 E
Foley, Botswana ............. 56 C4  21 34S  27 21 E
Foley, U.S.A. ................ 83 K2  30 24N  87 41W
Foleyet, Canada ............. 72 C3  48 15N  82 25W
Folgefonni, Norway .......... 9 F12 60  3N   6 23 E
Foligno, Italy ............... 22 C5  42 57N  12 42 E
Folkestone, U.K. ............ 13 F9  51  5N   1 12 E
Folkston, U.S.A. ............. 83 K5  30 50N  82  0W
Follansbee, U.S.A. ........... 84 F4  40 19N  80 35W
Fond-du-Lac, Canada ........ 71 B7  59 19N 107 12W
Fond du Lac, U.S.A. .......... 80 D10 43 47N  88 27W
Fond-du-Lac →, Canada ...... 71 B7  59 17N 106  0W
Fonda, U.S.A. ............... 85 D10 42 57N  74 23W
Fondi, Italy ................. 22 D5  41 21N  13 25 E
Fonsagrada = A Fonsagrada,
  Spain ...................... 21 A2  43  8N   7  4W

Fonseca, G. de, Cent. Amer. ... 88 D2  13 10N  87 40W
Fontainebleau, France ........ 20 B5  48 24N   2 40 E
Fontana, U.S.A. ............. 79 L9  34  6N 117 26W
Fontas →, Canada ........... 70 B4  58 14N 121 48W
Fonte Boa, Brazil ............ 92 D5   2 33S  66  0W
Fontenay-le-Comte, France ... 20 C3  46 28N   0 48W
Fontenelle Reservoir, U.S.A. ... 76 E8  42  1N 110  3W
Fontur, Iceland .............. 8 C6  66 23N  14 32W
Foochow = Fuzhou, China .... 33 D6  26  5N 119 16 E
Foping, China ............... 34 H5  33 41N 108  0 E
Forbes, Australia ............ 63 E4  33 22S 148  5 E
Forbesganj, India ............ 43 F12 26 17N  87 18 E
Ford City, Calif., U.S.A. ...... 79 K7  35  9N 119 27W
Ford City, Pa., U.S.A. ........ 84 F5  40 46N  79 32W
Førde, Norway .............. 9 F11 61 27N   5 53 E
Ford's Bridge, Australia ...... 63 D4  29 41S 145 29 E
Fordyce, U.S.A. .............. 81 J8  33 49N  92 25W
Forel, Mt., Greenland ........ 4 C6  66 52N  36 55W
Foremost, Canada ........... 70 D6  49 26N 111 34W
Forest, Canada .............. 84 C3  43  6N  82  0W
Forest, U.S.A. ............... 81 J10 32 22N  89 29W
Forest City, Iowa, U.S.A. ..... 80 D8  43 16N  93 39W
Forest City, N.C., U.S.A. ..... 83 H5  35 20N  81 52W
Forest City, Pa., U.S.A. ...... 85 E9  41 39N  75 28W
Forest Grove, U.S.A. ......... 78 E3  45 31N 123  7W
Forestburg, Canada .......... 70 C6  52 35N 112  1W
Foresthill, U.S.A. ............ 78 F6  39  1N 120 49W
Forestier Pen., Australia ...... 63 G4  43  0S 148  0 E
Forestville, Canada .......... 73 C6  48 48N  69  2W
Forestville, Calif., U.S.A. ..... 78 G4  38 28N 122 54W
Forestville, N.Y., U.S.A. ...... 84 D5  42 28N  79 10W
Forfar, U.K. ................. 11 E6  56 39N   2 53W
Forillon △, Canada .......... 73 C7  48 46N  64 12W
Forks, U.S.A. ................ 78 C2  47 57N 124 23W
Forksville, U.S.A. ............ 85 E8  41 29N  76 35W
Forlì, Italy .................. 22 B5  44 13N  12  3 E
Forman, U.S.A. .............. 80 B6  46  7N  97 38W
Formby Pt., U.K. ............. 12 D4  53 33N   3  6W
Formentera, Spain ........... 24 C7  38 43N   1 27 E
Formentor, C. de, Spain ...... 24 B10 39 58N   3 13 E
Former Yugoslav Republic of
  Macedonia = Macedonia ■,
  Europe ..................... 23 D9  41 53N  21 40 E
Fórmia, Italy ................ 22 D5  41 15N  13 37 E
Formosa = Taiwan ■, Asia .... 33 D7  23 30N 121  0 E
Formosa, Argentina .......... 94 B4  26 15S  58 10W
Formosa, Brazil ............. 93 G9  15 32S  47 20W
Formosa □, Argentina ........ 94 B4  25  0S  60  0W
Formosa, Serra, Brazil ........ 93 F8  12  0S  55  0W
Formosa B. = Ungwana B., Kenya 54 C5   2 45S  40 20 E
Fornells, Spain .............. 24 A11 40  3N   4  7 E
Føroyar, Atl. Oc. ............ 8 F9  62  0N   7  0W
Forres, U.K. ................. 11 D5  57 37N   3 37W
Forrest, Australia ............ 61 F4  30 51S 128  6 E
Forrest, Mt., Australia ........ 61 D4  24 48S 127 45 E
Forrest City, U.S.A. .......... 81 H9  35  1N  90 47W
Forsayth, Australia ........... 62 B3  18 33S 143 34 E
Forssa, Finland .............. 9 F20 60 49N  23 38 E
Forst, Germany .............. 16 C8  51 45N  14 37 E
Forsyth, U.S.A. .............. 76 C10 46 16N 106 41W
Fort Abbas, Pakistan ......... 42 E5  29 12N  72 52 E
Fort Albany, Canada ......... 72 B3  52 15N  81 35W
Fort Ann, U.S.A. ............ 85 C11 43 25N  73 30W
Fort Assiniboine, Canada ..... 70 C6  54 20N 114 45W
Fort Augustus, U.K. .......... 11 D4  57  9N   4 42W
Fort Beaufort, S. Africa ....... 56 E4  32 46S  26 40 E
Fort Benton, U.S.A. .......... 76 C8  47 49N 110 40W
Fort Bragg, U.S.A. ........... 76 G2  39 26N 123 48W
Fort Bridger, U.S.A. .......... 76 F8  41 19N 110 23W
Fort Chipewyan, Canada ...... 71 B6  58 42N 111  8W
Fort Clatsop △, Canada ...... 78 D3  46  8N 123 53W
Fort Collins, U.S.A. .......... 80 E2  40 35N 105  5W
Fort-Coulonge, Canada ....... 72 C4  45 50N  76 45W
Fort Covington, U.S.A. ....... 85 B10 44 59N  74 29W
Fort Davis, U.S.A. ........... 81 K3  30 35N 103 54W
Fort-de-France, Martinique ... 88 c  14 36N  61  2W
Fort Defiance, U.S.A. ......... 77 J9  35 45N 109  5W
Fort Dodge, U.S.A. .......... 80 D7  42 30N  94 11W
Fort Edward, U.S.A. ......... 85 C11 43 16N  73 35W
Fort Erie, Canada ............ 84 D6  42 54N  78 56W
Fort Fairfield, U.S.A. ......... 83 B12 46 46N  67 50W
Fort Frances, Canada ......... 71 D10 48 36N  93 24W
Fort Franklin = Déline, Canada 68 B7  37 26N 105 26W
Fort Garland, U.S.A. ......... 77 H11 37 26N 105 26W
Fort George = Chisasibi, Canada 72 B4  53 50N  79  0W
Fort Good Hope, Canada ...... 68 B7  66 14N 128 40W
Fort Hancock, U.S.A. ........ 77 L11 31 18N 105 51W
Fort Hope, Canada ........... 72 B2  51 30N  88  0W
Fort Irwin, U.S.A. ........... 79 K10 35 16N 116 34W
Fort Kent, U.S.A. ............ 83 B11 47 15N  68 36W
Fort Klamath, U.S.A. ......... 76 E3  42 42N 122  0W
Fort Laramie, U.S.A. ......... 80 D2  42 13N 104 31W
Fort Lauderdale, U.S.A. ...... 83 M5  26  7N  80  8W
Fort Liard, Canada .......... 70 A4  60 14N 123 30W
Fort Liberté, Haiti ........... 89 C5  19 42N  71 51W
Fort Lupton, U.S.A. .......... 80 E2  40  5N 104 49W
Fort MacKay, Canada ........ 70 B6  57 12N 111 41W
Fort Macleod, Canada ........ 70 D6  49 45N 113 30W
Fort McMurray, Canada ...... 70 B6  56 44N 111  7W
Fort McPherson, Canada ...... 68 B6  67 30N 134 55W
Fort Madison, U.S.A. ........ 80 E9  40 38N  91 27W
Fort Meade, U.S.A. .......... 83 M5  27 45N  81 48W
Fort Morgan, U.S.A. ......... 80 E3  40 15N 103 48W
Fort Myers, U.S.A. ........... 83 M5  26 39N  81 52W
Fort Nelson, Canada ......... 70 B4  58 50N 122 44W
Fort Nelson →, Canada ....... 70 B4  59 32N 124 10W
Fort Norman = Tulita, Canada . 68 B7  64 57N 125 30W
Fort Payne, U.S.A. ........... 83 H3  34 26N  85 43W
Fort Peck, U.S.A. ............ 76 B10 48  1N 106 27W
Fort Peck Dam, U.S.A. ....... 76 C10 48  0N 106 26W
Fort Peck L., U.S.A. .......... 76 C10 48  0N 106 26W
Fort Pierce, U.S.A. ........... 83 M5  27 27N  80 20W
Fort Pierre, U.S.A. ........... 80 C4  44 21N 100 22W
Fort Plain, U.S.A. ............ 85 D10 42 56N  74 37W
Fort Portal, Uganda .......... 54 B3   0 40N  30 20 E
Fort Providence, Canada ...... 70 A5  61  3N 117 40W
Fort Qu'Appelle, Canada ..... 71 C8  50 45N 103 50W
Fort Resolution, Canada ...... 70 A6  61 10N 113 40W
Fort Rixon, Zimbabwe ........ 55 G2  20  2S  29 17 E
Fort Ross, U.S.A. ............ 78 G3  38 32N 123 13W
Fort Rupert = Waskaganish,
  Canada .................... 72 B4  51 30N  78 40W
Fort St. James, Canada ....... 70 C4  54 30N 124 10W
Fort St. John, Canada ........ 70 B4  56 15N 120 50W
Fort Saskatchewan, Canada ... 70 C6  53 40N 113 15W
Fort Scott, U.S.A. ............ 81 G7  37 50N  94 42W
Fort Severn, Canada ......... 72 A2  56  0N  87 40W
Fort Shevchenko, Kazakhstan .. 19 F9  44 35N  50 23 E

Fort Simpson, *Canada* . . . . . . . . **70 A4** 61 45N 121 15W
Fort Smith, *Canada* . . . . . . . . . . **70 B6** 60 0N 111 51W
Fort Smith, *U.S.A.* . . . . . . . . . . **81 H7** 35 23N 94 25W
Fort Stockton, *U.S.A.* . . . . . . . . **81 K3** 30 53N 102 53W
Fort Sumner, *U.S.A.* . . . . . . . . . **81 H2** 34 28N 104 15W
Fort Thompson, *U.S.A.* . . . . . . . **80 C5** 44 3N 99 26W
Fort Union △, *U.S.A.* . . . . . . . . **81 H2** 35 54N 105 1W
Fort Valley, *U.S.A.* . . . . . . . . . . **83 J4** 32 33N 83 53W
Fort Vermilion, *Canada* . . . . . . **70 B5** 58 24N 116 0W
Fort Walton Beach, *U.S.A.* . . . . . **83 K2** 30 25N 86 36W
Fort Wayne, *U.S.A.* . . . . . . . . . . **82 E3** 41 4N 85 9W
Fort William, *U.K.* . . . . . . . . . . **11 E3** 56 49N 5 7W
Fort Worth, *U.S.A.* . . . . . . . . . . **81 J6** 32 45N 97 18W
Fort Yates, *U.S.A.* . . . . . . . . . . **80 B4** 46 5N 100 38W
Fort Yukon, *U.S.A.* . . . . . . . . . . **68 B5** 66 34N 145 16W
Fortaleza, *Brazil* . . . . . . . . . . . **93 D11** 3 45S 38 35W
Forteau, *Canada* . . . . . . . . . . . **73 B8** 51 28N 56 58W
Fortescue →, *Australia* . . . . . . . **60 D2** 21 0S 116 4 E
Forth →, *U.K.* . . . . . . . . . . . . . **11 E5** 56 9N 3 50W
Forth, Firth of, *U.K.* . . . . . . . . **11 E6** 56 5N 2 55W
Fortrose, *U.K.* . . . . . . . . . . . . . **11 D4** 57 35N 4 9W
Fortuna, *Calif., U.S.A.* . . . . . . . **76 F1** 40 36N 124 9W
Fortuna, *N. Dak., U.S.A.* . . . . . . **80 A3** 48 55N 103 47W
Fortune, *Canada* . . . . . . . . . . . **73 C8** 47 4N 55 50W
Fortune B., *Canada* . . . . . . . . . **73 C8** 47 30N 55 22W
Forûr, *Iran* . . . . . . . . . . . . . . . **45 E7** 26 17N 54 32 E
Foshan, *China* . . . . . . . . . . . . . **33 D6** 23 4N 113 5 E
Fosna, *Norway* . . . . . . . . . . . . **8 E14** 63 50N 10 20 E
Fosnavåg, *Norway* . . . . . . . . . . **9 E11** 62 22N 5 38 E
Fossano, *Italy* . . . . . . . . . . . . . **20 D7** 44 33N 7 43 E
Fossil, *U.S.A.* . . . . . . . . . . . . . **76 D3** 45 0N 120 9W
Fossil Butte △, *U.S.A.* . . . . . . . . **76 F8** 41 50N 110 27W
Foster, *Canada* . . . . . . . . . . . . **85 A12** 45 17N 72 30W
Foster →, *Canada* . . . . . . . . . . **71 B7** 55 47N 105 49W
Fosters Ra., *Australia* . . . . . . . . **62 C1** 21 35S 133 48 E
Fostoria, *U.S.A.* . . . . . . . . . . . . **82 E4** 41 10N 83 25W
Fotadrevo, *Madag.* . . . . . . . . . . **57 C8** 24 3S 45 1 E
Fougères, *France* . . . . . . . . . . . **20 B3** 48 21N 1 14W
Foul Pt., *Sri Lanka* . . . . . . . . . . **40 Q12** 8 35N 81 18 E
Foula, *U.K.* . . . . . . . . . . . . . . . **11 A6** 60 10N 2 5W
Foulness I., *U.K.* . . . . . . . . . . . **13 F8** 51 36N 0 55 E
Foulpointe, *Madag.* . . . . . . . . . **57 B8** 17 41S 49 31 E
Foulweather, C., *U.S.A.* . . . . . . . **74 B2** 44 50N 124 5W
Foumban, *Cameroon* . . . . . . . . **52 C2** 5 45N 10 50 E
Fountain, *U.S.A.* . . . . . . . . . . . **80 F2** 38 41N 104 42W
Fountain Springs, *U.S.A.* . . . . . . **79 K8** 35 54N 118 51W
Fouriesburg, *S. Africa* . . . . . . . . **56 D4** 28 38S 28 14 E
Foúrnoi, *Greece* . . . . . . . . . . . **23 F12** 37 36N 26 32 E
Fourth Cataract, *Sudan* . . . . . . . **51 E12** 18 47N 32 3 E
Fouta Djallon, *Guinea* . . . . . . . . **50 F3** 11 20N 12 10W
Foux, Cap-à-, *Haiti* . . . . . . . . . . **89 C5** 19 43N 73 27W
Foveaux Str., *N.Z.* . . . . . . . . . . **59 M2** 46 42S 168 10 E
Fowey, *U.K.* . . . . . . . . . . . . . . **13 G3** 50 20N 4 39W
Fowler, *Calif., U.S.A.* . . . . . . . . **78 J7** 36 38N 119 41W
Fowler, *Colo., U.S.A.* . . . . . . . . **80 F3** 38 8N 104 2W
Fowlers B., *Australia* . . . . . . . . . **61 F5** 31 59S 132 34 E
Fowman, *Iran* . . . . . . . . . . . . . **45 B6** 37 13N 49 19 E
Fox →, *Canada* . . . . . . . . . . . . **71 B10** 56 3N 93 18W
Fox Creek, *Canada* . . . . . . . . . . **70 C5** 54 24N 116 48W
Fox Lake, *Canada* . . . . . . . . . . . **70 B6** 58 28N 114 31W
Fox Valley, *Canada* . . . . . . . . . . **71 C7** 50 30N 109 25W
Foxboro, *U.S.A.* . . . . . . . . . . . . **85 D13** 42 4N 71 16W
Foxdale, *Australia* . . . . . . . . . . **62 J6** 20 22S 148 35 E
Foxe Basin, *Canada* . . . . . . . . . **69 B12** 66 0N 77 0W
Foxe Chan., *Canada* . . . . . . . . . **69 B11** 65 0N 80 0W
Foxe Pen., *Canada* . . . . . . . . . . **69 B12** 65 0N 76 0W
Foxton, *N.Z.* . . . . . . . . . . . . . . **59 J5** 40 29S 175 18 E
Foyle, Lough, *U.K.* . . . . . . . . . . **10 A4** 55 7N 7 4W
Foynes, *Ireland* . . . . . . . . . . . . **10 D2** 52 37N 9 7W
Foz do Cunene, *Angola* . . . . . . . **56 B1** 17 15S 11 48 E
Foz do Iguaçu, *Brazil* . . . . . . . . **95 B5** 25 30S 54 30W
Frackville, *U.S.A.* . . . . . . . . . . . **85 F8** 40 47N 76 14W
Fraile Muerto, *Uruguay* . . . . . . . **95 C5** 32 31S 54 32W
Fram Basin, *Arctic* . . . . . . . . . . **4 A** 87 30N 80 0 E
Framingham, *U.S.A.* . . . . . . . . . **85 D13** 42 17N 71 25W
Franca, *Brazil* . . . . . . . . . . . . . **93 H9** 20 33S 47 30W
Francavilla Fontana, *Italy* . . . . . . **23 D7** 40 32N 17 35 E
France ■, *Europe* . . . . . . . . . . . **20 C5** 47 0N 3 0 E
Frances, *Australia* . . . . . . . . . . **63 F3** 36 41S 140 55 E
Frances →, *Canada* . . . . . . . . . **70 A3** 60 16N 129 10W
Frances L., *Canada* . . . . . . . . . . **70 A3** 61 23N 129 30W
Franceville, *Gabon* . . . . . . . . . . **52 E2** 1 40S 13 32 E
Franche-Comté □, *France* . . . . . . **20 C6** 46 50N 5 55 E
Francis Case, L., *U.S.A.* . . . . . . . **80 D5** 43 4N 98 34W
Francisco Beltrão, *Brazil* . . . . . . **95 B5** 26 5S 53 4W
Francisco I. Madero, Coahuila,
   *Mexico* . . . . . . . . . . . . . . . . **86 B4** 25 48N 103 18W
Francisco I. Madero, Durango,
   *Mexico* . . . . . . . . . . . . . . . . **86 C4** 24 32N 104 22W
Francistown, *Botswana* . . . . . . . **57 C4** 21 7S 27 33 E
François, *Canada* . . . . . . . . . . . **73 C8** 47 35N 56 45W
François L., *Canada* . . . . . . . . . . **70 C3** 54 0N 125 30W
François Peron △, *Australia* . . . . . **61 E1** 25 42S 113 33 E
Franeker, *Neths.* . . . . . . . . . . . **15 A5** 53 12N 5 33 E
Frank Hann △, *Australia* . . . . . . . **61 F3** 32 52S 120 19 E
Frankford, *Canada* . . . . . . . . . . **84 B7** 44 12N 77 36W
Frankfort, *S. Africa* . . . . . . . . . . **57 D4** 27 17S 28 30 E
Frankfort, *Ind., U.S.A.* . . . . . . . . **82 E2** 40 17N 86 31W
Frankfort, *Kans., U.S.A.* . . . . . . . **80 F6** 39 42N 96 25W
Frankfort, *Ky., U.S.A.* . . . . . . . . **82 F3** 38 12N 84 52W
Frankfort, *N.Y., U.S.A.* . . . . . . . . **85 C9** 43 2N 75 4W
Frankfurt, Brandenburg,
   *Germany* . . . . . . . . . . . . . . **16 B8** 52 20N 14 32 E
Frankfurt, Hessen, *Germany* . . . . **16 C5** 50 7N 8 41 E
Fränkische Alb, *Germany* . . . . . . **16 D6** 49 10N 11 23 E
Frankland →, *Australia* . . . . . . . **61 G2** 35 0S 116 48 E
Franklin, *Ky., U.S.A.* . . . . . . . . . **82 G2** 36 43N 86 35W
Franklin, *La., U.S.A.* . . . . . . . . . **81 L9** 29 48N 91 30W
Franklin, *Mass., U.S.A.* . . . . . . . **85 D13** 42 5N 71 24W
Franklin, *N.H., U.S.A.* . . . . . . . . **85 C13** 43 27N 71 39W
Franklin, *Nebr., U.S.A.* . . . . . . . **80 E5** 40 6N 98 57W
Franklin, *Pa., U.S.A.* . . . . . . . . . **84 E5** 41 24N 79 50W
Franklin, *Va., U.S.A.* . . . . . . . . . **83 G7** 36 41N 76 56W
Franklin, *W. Va., U.S.A.* . . . . . . . **82 F6** 38 39N 79 20W
Franklin B., *Canada* . . . . . . . . . **68 B7** 69 45N 126 0W
Franklin D. Roosevelt L., *U.S.A.* . . **76 B4** 48 18N 118 9W
Franklin-Gordon Wild Rivers △,
   *Australia* . . . . . . . . . . . . . . **63 G4** 42 19S 145 51 E
Franklin I., *Antarctica* . . . . . . . . **5 D11** 76 10S 168 30 E
Franklin L., *U.S.A.* . . . . . . . . . . **76 F6** 40 25N 115 22W
Franklin Mts., *Canada* . . . . . . . . **68 B7** 65 0N 125 0W
Franklin Str., *Canada* . . . . . . . . **68 A10** 72 0N 96 0W
Franklinton, *U.S.A.* . . . . . . . . . . **81 K9** 30 51N 90 9W
Franklinville, *U.S.A.* . . . . . . . . . **84 D6** 42 20N 78 27W
Franks Pk., *U.S.A.* . . . . . . . . . . . **76 E9** 43 58N 109 18W
Frankston, *Australia* . . . . . . . . . **63 F4** 38 8S 145 8 E
Fransfontein, *Namibia* . . . . . . . . **56 C2** 20 12S 15 1 E
Frantsa Iosifa, Zemlya, *Russia* . . . **28 A6** 82 0N 55 0 E

Franz, *Canada* . . . . . . . . . . . . . **72 C3** 48 25N 84 30W
Franz Josef Land = Frantsa Iosifa,
   Zemlya, *Russia* . . . . . . . . . . **28 A6** 82 0N 55 0 E
Fraser, *U.S.A.* . . . . . . . . . . . . . **84 D2** 42 32N 82 57W
Fraser →, *B.C., Canada* . . . . . . . **70 D4** 49 7N 123 11W
Fraser →, *Nfld. & L., Canada* . . . . **73 A7** 56 39N 62 10W
Fraser, Mt., *Australia* . . . . . . . . . **61 E2** 25 35S 118 20 E
Fraser I., *Australia* . . . . . . . . . . **63 D5** 25 15S 153 10 E
Fraser Lake, *Canada* . . . . . . . . . **70 C4** 54 0N 124 50W
Fraserburg, *S. Africa* . . . . . . . . . **56 E3** 31 55S 21 30 E
Fraserburgh, *U.K.* . . . . . . . . . . . **11 D6** 57 42N 2 1W
Fraserdale, *Canada* . . . . . . . . . . **72 C3** 49 55N 81 37W
Fray Bentos, *Uruguay* . . . . . . . . **94 C4** 33 10S 58 15W
Fray Jorge △, *Chile* . . . . . . . . . . **94 C1** 30 42S 71 40W
Fredericia, *Denmark* . . . . . . . . . **9 J13** 55 34N 9 45 E
Frederick, *Md., U.S.A.* . . . . . . . . **82 F7** 39 25N 77 25W
Frederick, *Okla., U.S.A.* . . . . . . . **81 H5** 34 23N 99 1W
Frederick, *S. Dak., U.S.A.* . . . . . . **80 C5** 45 50N 98 31W
Fredericksburg, *Pa., U.S.A.* . . . . . **85 F8** 40 27N 76 26W
Fredericksburg, *Tex., U.S.A.* . . . . **81 K5** 30 16N 98 52W
Fredericksburg, *Va., U.S.A.* . . . . . **82 F7** 38 18N 77 28W
Fredericktown, *Mo., U.S.A.* . . . . . **81 G9** 37 34N 90 18W
Fredericktown, *Ohio, U.S.A.* . . . . **84 F2** 40 29N 82 33W
Frederico I. Madero, Presa,
   *Mexico* . . . . . . . . . . . . . . . . **86 B3** 28 7N 105 40W
Frederico Westphalen, *Brazil* . . . . **95 B5** 27 22S 53 24W
Fredericton, *Canada* . . . . . . . . . **73 C6** 45 57N 66 40W
Fredericton Junction, *Canada* . . . **73 C6** 45 41N 66 40W
Frederikshåb = Paamiut,
   *Greenland* . . . . . . . . . . . . . . **69 B15** 62 0N 49 43W
Frederikshamn = Hamina,
   *Finland* . . . . . . . . . . . . . . . . **9 F22** 60 34N 27 12 E
Frederikshavn, *Denmark* . . . . . . **9 H14** 57 28N 10 31 E
Frederiksted, *U.S. Virgin Is.* . . . . **89 C7** 17 43N 64 53W
Fredonia, *Ariz., U.S.A.* . . . . . . . . **77 H7** 36 57N 112 32W
Fredonia, *Kans., U.S.A.* . . . . . . . **81 G7** 37 32N 95 49W
Fredonia, *N.Y., U.S.A.* . . . . . . . . **84 D5** 42 26N 79 20W
Fredrikstad, *Norway* . . . . . . . . . **9 G14** 59 13N 10 57 E
Free State □, *S. Africa* . . . . . . . . **56 D4** 28 30S 27 0 E
Freehold, *U.S.A.* . . . . . . . . . . . . **85 F10** 40 16N 74 17W
Freel Peak, *U.S.A.* . . . . . . . . . . . **78 G7** 38 52N 119 54W
Freeland, *U.S.A.* . . . . . . . . . . . . **85 E9** 41 1N 75 54W
Freels, C., *Canada* . . . . . . . . . . . **73 C9** 49 15N 53 30W
Freeman, *Calif., U.S.A.* . . . . . . . . **79 K9** 35 35N 117 53W
Freeman, *S. Dak., U.S.A.* . . . . . . **80 D6** 43 21N 97 26W
Freeport, *Bahamas* . . . . . . . . . . **88 A4** 26 30N 78 47W
Freeport, *Ill., U.S.A.* . . . . . . . . . **80 D10** 42 17N 89 36W
Freeport, *N.Y., U.S.A.* . . . . . . . . **85 F11** 40 39N 73 35W
Freeport, *Ohio, U.S.A.* . . . . . . . . **84 F3** 40 12N 81 15W
Freeport, *Pa., U.S.A.* . . . . . . . . . **84 F5** 40 41N 79 41W
Freeport, *Tex., U.S.A.* . . . . . . . . **81 L7** 28 57N 95 21W
Freetown, *S. Leone* . . . . . . . . . . **50 G3** 8 30N 13 17W
Frégate, L. de la, *Canada* . . . . . . **72 B5** 53 15N 74 45W
Fregenal de la Sierra, *Spain* . . . . **21 C2** 38 10N 6 39W
Freibourg = Fribourg, *Switz.* . . . . **20 C7** 46 49N 7 9 E
Freiburg, *Germany* . . . . . . . . . . **16 E4** 47 59N 7 51 E
Freire, *Chile* . . . . . . . . . . . . . . . **96 D2** 38 54S 72 38W
Freirina, *Chile* . . . . . . . . . . . . . **94 B1** 28 30S 71 10W
Freising, *Germany* . . . . . . . . . . . **16 D6** 48 24N 11 45 E
Freistadt, *Austria* . . . . . . . . . . . **16 D8** 48 30N 14 30 E
Fréjus, *France* . . . . . . . . . . . . . **20 E7** 43 25N 6 44 E
Fremantle, *Australia* . . . . . . . . . **61 F2** 32 7S 115 47 E
Fremont, *Calif., U.S.A.* . . . . . . . . **78 H4** 37 32N 121 57W
Fremont, *Mich., U.S.A.* . . . . . . . **82 D3** 43 28N 85 57W
Fremont, *Nebr., U.S.A.* . . . . . . . . **80 E6** 41 26N 96 30W
Fremont, *Ohio, U.S.A.* . . . . . . . . **82 E4** 41 21N 83 7W
Fremont →, *U.S.A.* . . . . . . . . . . **77 G8** 38 24N 110 42W
French Camp, *U.S.A.* . . . . . . . . . **78 H5** 37 53N 121 16W
French Cays = Plana Cays,
   *Bahamas* . . . . . . . . . . . . . . **89 B5** 22 38N 73 30W
French Creek →, *U.S.A.* . . . . . . . **84 E5** 41 24N 79 50W
French Guiana ☑, *S. Amer.* . . . . . **93 C8** 4 0N 53 0W
French Polynesia ☑, *Pac. Oc.* . . . **65 K13** 20 0S 145 0W
Frenchman Cr. →, *N. Amer.* . . . . **76 B10** 48 31N 107 10W
Frenchman Cr. →, *U.S.A.* . . . . . . **80 E4** 40 14N 100 50W
Fresco →, *Brazil* . . . . . . . . . . . . **93 E8** 7 15S 51 30W
Freshfield, C., *Antarctica* . . . . . . **5 C10** 68 25S 151 10 E
Fresnillo, *Mexico* . . . . . . . . . . . **86 C4** 23 10N 103 0W
Fresno, *U.S.A.* . . . . . . . . . . . . . **78 J7** 36 44N 119 47W
Fresno Reservoir, *U.S.A.* . . . . . . . **76 B9** 48 36N 109 57W
Frew →, *Australia* . . . . . . . . . . . **62 C2** 20 0S 135 38 E
Frewsburg, *U.S.A.* . . . . . . . . . . . **84 D5** 42 3N 79 10W
Freycinet △, *Australia* . . . . . . . . **63 G4** 42 11S 148 19 E
Freycinet Pen., *Australia* . . . . . . . **63 G4** 42 10S 148 25 E
Fria, C., *Namibia* . . . . . . . . . . . . **56 B1** 18 0S 12 0 E
Friant, *U.S.A.* . . . . . . . . . . . . . . **78 J7** 36 59N 119 43W
Frías, *Argentina* . . . . . . . . . . . . **94 B2** 28 40S 65 5W
Fribourg, *Switz.* . . . . . . . . . . . . **20 C7** 46 49N 7 9 E
Friday Harbor, *U.S.A.* . . . . . . . . . **78 B3** 48 32N 123 1W
Friedens, *U.S.A.* . . . . . . . . . . . . **84 F6** 40 3N 78 59W
Friedrichshafen, *Germany* . . . . . . **16 E5** 47 39N 9 30 E
Friendship, *U.S.A.* . . . . . . . . . . . **84 D6** 42 12N 78 8W
Friesland □, *Neths.* . . . . . . . . . . **15 A5** 53 5N 5 50 E
Frio →, *U.S.A.* . . . . . . . . . . . . . **81 L5** 28 26N 98 11W
Frio, C., *Brazil* . . . . . . . . . . . . . **90 F6** 22 50S 41 50W
Friona, *U.S.A.* . . . . . . . . . . . . . . **81 H3** 34 38N 102 43W
Fritch, *U.S.A.* . . . . . . . . . . . . . . **81 H4** 35 38N 101 36W
Frobisher B., *Canada* . . . . . . . . . **69 B13** 62 30N 66 0W
Frobisher Bay = Iqaluit, *Canada* . . **69 B13** 63 44N 68 31W
Frobisher L., *Canada* . . . . . . . . . **71 B7** 56 20N 108 15W
Frohavet, *Norway* . . . . . . . . . . . **8 E13** 64 0N 9 30 E
Frome, *U.K.* . . . . . . . . . . . . . . . **13 F5** 51 14N 2 19W
Frome →, *U.K.* . . . . . . . . . . . . . **13 G5** 50 41N 2 6W
Frome, L., *Australia* . . . . . . . . . . **63 E2** 30 45S 139 45 E
Frome, The →, *Australia* . . . . . . . **63 D2** 29 8S 137 54 E
Front Range, *U.S.A.* . . . . . . . . . . **74 C5** 40 25N 105 45W
Front Royal, *U.S.A.* . . . . . . . . . . **82 F6** 38 55N 78 12W
Frontera, *Canary Is.* . . . . . . . . . **24 G2** 27 47N 17 59W
Frontera, *Mexico* . . . . . . . . . . . **87 D6** 18 30N 92 40W
Fronteras, *Mexico* . . . . . . . . . . . **86 A3** 30 56N 109 31W
Frosinone, *Italy* . . . . . . . . . . . . **22 D5** 41 38N 13 19 E
Frostburg, *U.S.A.* . . . . . . . . . . . **82 F6** 39 39N 78 56W
Frostisen, *Norway* . . . . . . . . . . . **8 B17** 68 14N 17 10 E
Frøya, *Norway* . . . . . . . . . . . . . **8 E13** 63 43N 8 40 E
Frunze = Bishkek, *Kyrgyzstan* . . . **28 E8** 42 54N 74 46 E
Frutal, *Brazil* . . . . . . . . . . . . . . **93 H9** 20 0S 49 0W
Frýdek-Místek, *Czech Rep.* . . . . . **17 D10** 49 40N 18 20 E
Fryeburg, *U.S.A.* . . . . . . . . . . . . **85 B14** 44 1N 70 59W
Fu Xian = Wafangdian, *China* . . . **35 E11** 39 38N 121 58 E
Fu Xian, *China* . . . . . . . . . . . . . **34 G5** 36 0N 109 20 E
Fucheng, *China* . . . . . . . . . . . . . **34 F9** 37 50N 116 10 E
Fuchou = Fuzhou, *China* . . . . . . . **33 D6** 26 5N 119 16 E
Fuchü, *Japan* . . . . . . . . . . . . . . **31 G6** 34 34N 133 14 E
Fuencaliente, *Canary Is.* . . . . . . . **24 F2** 28 28N 17 50W
Fuencaliente, Pta., *Canary Is.* . . . **24 F2** 28 27N 17 51W
Fuengirola, *Spain* . . . . . . . . . . . **21 D3** 36 32N 4 41W
Fuentes de Oñoro, *Spain* . . . . . . **21 B2** 40 33N 6 52W
Fuerte →, *Mexico* . . . . . . . . . . . **86 B3** 25 50N 109 25W

Fuerte Olimpo, *Paraguay* . . . . . . **94 A4** 21 0S 57 51W
Fuerteventura, *Canary Is.* . . . . . . **24 F6** 28 30N 14 0W
Fuerteventura ✈ (FUE), *Canary Is.* **24 F6** 28 24N 13 52W
Fufeng, *China* . . . . . . . . . . . . . . **34 G5** 34 22N 108 0 E
Fugou, *China* . . . . . . . . . . . . . . **34 G8** 34 3N 114 25 E
Fugu, *China* . . . . . . . . . . . . . . . **34 E6** 39 2N 111 3 E
Fuhai, *China* . . . . . . . . . . . . . . . **32 B3** 47 2N 87 25 E
Fuḥaymī, *Iraq* . . . . . . . . . . . . . . **44 C4** 34 16N 42 10 E
Fuji, *Japan* . . . . . . . . . . . . . . . . **31 G9** 35 9N 138 39 E
Fuji-Hakone-Izu △, *Japan* . . . . . . **31 G9** 35 15N 138 45 E
Fuji-San, *Japan* . . . . . . . . . . . . . **31 G9** 35 22N 138 44 E
Fuji-Yoshida, *Japan* . . . . . . . . . . **31 G9** 35 30N 138 46 E
Fujian □, *China* . . . . . . . . . . . . . **33 D6** 26 0N 118 0 E
Fujinomiya, *Japan* . . . . . . . . . . . **31 G9** 35 10N 138 40 E
Fujisawa, *Japan* . . . . . . . . . . . . **31 G9** 35 22N 139 29 E
Fujiyama, Mt. = Fuji-San, *Japan* . . **31 G9** 35 22N 138 44 E
Fukagawa, *Japan* . . . . . . . . . . . **30 C11** 43 43N 142 2 E
Fukuchiyama, *Japan* . . . . . . . . . **31 G7** 35 19N 135 9 E
Fukue-Shima, *Japan* . . . . . . . . . **31 H4** 32 40N 128 45 E
Fukui, *Japan* . . . . . . . . . . . . . . . **31 F8** 36 5N 136 10 E
Fukui □, *Japan* . . . . . . . . . . . . . **31 G8** 36 0N 136 12 E
Fukuoka, *Japan* . . . . . . . . . . . . **31 H5** 33 39N 130 21 E
Fukuoka □, *Japan* . . . . . . . . . . . **31 H5** 33 30N 131 0 E
Fukushima, *Japan* . . . . . . . . . . . **30 F10** 37 44N 140 28 E
Fukushima □, *Japan* . . . . . . . . . **30 F10** 37 30N 140 15 E
Fukuyama, *Japan* . . . . . . . . . . . **31 G6** 34 35N 133 20 E
Fulda, *Germany* . . . . . . . . . . . . **16 C5** 50 32N 9 40 E
Fulda →, *Germany* . . . . . . . . . . **16 C5** 51 25N 9 39 E
Fulford Harbour, *Canada* . . . . . . **78 B3** 48 47N 123 27W
Fullerton, *Calif., U.S.A.* . . . . . . . . **79 M9** 33 53N 117 56W
Fullerton, *Nebr., U.S.A.* . . . . . . . **80 E6** 41 22N 97 58W
Fulongquan, *China* . . . . . . . . . . **35 B13** 44 20N 124 42 E
Fulton, *Mo., U.S.A.* . . . . . . . . . . **80 F9** 38 52N 91 57W
Fulton, *N.Y., U.S.A.* . . . . . . . . . . **85 C8** 43 19N 76 25W
Funabashi, *Japan* . . . . . . . . . . . **31 G10** 35 45N 140 0 E
Funafuti = Fongafale, *Tuvalu* . . . . **64 H9** 8 31S 179 13 E
Funchal, *Madeira* . . . . . . . . . . . **24 D3** 32 38N 16 54W
Funchal ✈ (FNC), *Madeira* . . . . . **24 D3** 32 42N 16 45W
Fundación, *Colombia* . . . . . . . . . **92 A4** 10 31N 74 11W
Fundão, *Portugal* . . . . . . . . . . . **21 B2** 40 8N 7 30W
Fundy, B. of, *Canada* . . . . . . . . . **73 C6** 45 0N 66 0W
Fundy △, *Canada* . . . . . . . . . . . **73 C6** 45 35N 65 10W
Funhalouro, *Mozam.* . . . . . . . . . **57 C5** 23 3S 34 25 E
Funing, *Hebei, China* . . . . . . . . . **35 E10** 39 53N 119 12 E
Funing, *Jiangsu, China* . . . . . . . . **35 H10** 33 45N 119 50 E
Funiu Shan, *China* . . . . . . . . . . . **34 H7** 33 30N 112 20 E
Funtua, *Nigeria* . . . . . . . . . . . . . **50 F7** 11 30N 7 18 E
Fuping, *Hebei, China* . . . . . . . . . **34 E8** 38 48N 114 12 E
Fuping, *Shaanxi, China* . . . . . . . . **34 G5** 34 42N 109 10 E
Furano, *Japan* . . . . . . . . . . . . . . **30 C11** 43 21N 142 23 E
Furāt, Nahr al →, *Asia* . . . . . . . . **44 D5** 31 0N 47 25 E
Fûrg, *Iran* . . . . . . . . . . . . . . . . . **45 D7** 28 18N 55 13 E
Furnás, *Spain* . . . . . . . . . . . . . . **24 B8** 39 3N 1 32 E
Furnas, Reprêsa de, *Brazil* . . . . . **95 A6** 20 50S 45 30W
Furneaux Group, *Australia* . . . . . **63 G4** 40 10S 147 50 E
Furqlus, *Syria* . . . . . . . . . . . . . . **46 A6** 34 36N 37 8 E
Fürstenwalde, *Germany* . . . . . . . **16 B8** 52 22N 14 3 E
Fürth, *Germany* . . . . . . . . . . . . . **16 D6** 49 28N 10 59 E
Furukawa, *Japan* . . . . . . . . . . . . **30 E10** 38 34N 140 58 E
Fury and Hecla Str., *Canada* . . . . **69 B11** 69 56N 84 0W
Fusagasuga, *Colombia* . . . . . . . . **92 C4** 4 21N 74 22W
Fushan, *Shandong, China* . . . . . . **35 F11** 37 30N 121 15 E
Fushan, *Shanxi, China* . . . . . . . . **34 G6** 35 58N 111 51 E
Fushun, *China* . . . . . . . . . . . . . . **35 D12** 41 50N 123 56 E
Fusong, *China* . . . . . . . . . . . . . . **35 C14** 42 20N 127 15 E
Fustic, *Barbados* . . . . . . . . . . . . **89 g** 13 16N 59 38W
Futian, *China* . . . . . . . . . . . . . . **33 F11** 22 32N 114 4 E
Futuna, Wall. & F. Is. . . . . . . . . . . **59 B8** 14 25S 178 20W
Fuxin, *China* . . . . . . . . . . . . . . . **35 C11** 42 5N 121 48 E
Fuyang, *China* . . . . . . . . . . . . . . **34 H8** 33 0N 115 48 E
Fuyang He →, *China* . . . . . . . . . **34 E9** 38 12N 117 0 E
Fuyong, *China* . . . . . . . . . . . . . . **33 F10** 22 40N 113 49 E
Fuyu, *China* . . . . . . . . . . . . . . . . **35 B13** 45 12N 124 43 E
Fuzhou, *China* . . . . . . . . . . . . . . **33 D6** 26 5N 119 16 E
Fylde, *U.K.* . . . . . . . . . . . . . . . . **12 D5** 53 50N 2 58W
Fyn, *Denmark* . . . . . . . . . . . . . . **9 J14** 55 20N 10 30 E
Fyne, L., *U.K.* . . . . . . . . . . . . . . **11 F3** 55 59N 5 23W

## G

Gabela, *Angola* . . . . . . . . . . . . . **52 G2** 11 0S 14 24 E
Gabès, *Tunisia* . . . . . . . . . . . . . **51 B8** 33 53N 10 2 E
Gabès, G. de, *Tunisia* . . . . . . . . . **51 B8** 34 0N 10 30 E
Gabon ■, *Africa* . . . . . . . . . . . . **52 E2** 0 10S 10 0 E
Gaborone, *Botswana* . . . . . . . . . **56 C4** 24 45S 25 57 E
Gabriels, *U.S.A.* . . . . . . . . . . . . . **85 B10** 44 26N 74 12W
Gäbrīk, *Iran* . . . . . . . . . . . . . . . **45 E8** 25 44N 58 28 E
Gabrovo, *Bulgaria* . . . . . . . . . . . **23 C11** 42 52N 25 19 E
Gāch Sār, *Iran* . . . . . . . . . . . . . **45 B6** 36 7N 51 19 E
Gachsārān, *Iran* . . . . . . . . . . . . **45 D6** 30 15N 50 45 E
Gadag, *India* . . . . . . . . . . . . . . . **40 M9** 15 30N 75 45 E
Gadap, *Pakistan* . . . . . . . . . . . . **42 G2** 25 5N 67 28 E
Gadarwara, *India* . . . . . . . . . . . . **43 H8** 22 50N 78 50 E
Gadhada, *India* . . . . . . . . . . . . . **42 J4** 22 0N 71 35 E
Gadra, *Pakistan* . . . . . . . . . . . . . **42 G4** 25 40N 70 38 E
Gadsden, *U.S.A.* . . . . . . . . . . . . **83 H3** 34 1N 86 1W
Gadwal, *India* . . . . . . . . . . . . . . **40 L10** 16 10N 77 50 E
Gaffney, *U.S.A.* . . . . . . . . . . . . . **83 H5** 35 5N 81 39W
Gafsa, *Tunisia* . . . . . . . . . . . . . . **50 B7** 34 24N 8 43 E
Gagaria, *India* . . . . . . . . . . . . . . **42 G4** 25 43N 70 46 E
Gagnoa, *Ivory C.* . . . . . . . . . . . . **50 G4** 6 56N 5 16W
Gagnon, *Canada* . . . . . . . . . . . . **73 B6** 51 50N 68 5W
Gagnon, L., *Canada* . . . . . . . . . . **71 A6** 62 3N 110 27W
Gahini, *Rwanda* . . . . . . . . . . . . . **54 C3** 1 50S 30 30 E
Gahmar, *India* . . . . . . . . . . . . . . **43 G10** 25 27N 83 49 E
Gai Xian = Gaizhou, *China* . . . . . **35 D12** 40 22N 122 20 E
Gaïdhouronísi, *Greece* . . . . . . . . **25 E7** 34 53N 25 41 E
Gail, *U.S.A.* . . . . . . . . . . . . . . . . **81 J4** 32 46N 101 27W
Gaillimh = Galway, *Ireland* . . . . . **10 C2** 53 17N 9 3W
Gaines, *U.S.A.* . . . . . . . . . . . . . . **84 E7** 41 46N 77 35W
Gainesville, *Fla., U.S.A.* . . . . . . . **83 L4** 29 40N 82 20W
Gainesville, *Ga., U.S.A.* . . . . . . . **83 H4** 34 18N 83 50W
Gainesville, *Mo., U.S.A.* . . . . . . . **81 G8** 36 36N 92 26W
Gainesville, *Tex., U.S.A.* . . . . . . . **81 J6** 33 38N 97 8W
Gainsborough, *U.K.* . . . . . . . . . . **12 D7** 53 24N 0 46W
Gairdner, L., *Australia* . . . . . . . . **63 E2** 31 30S 136 0 E
Gairloch, *U.K.* . . . . . . . . . . . . . . **11 D3** 57 43N 5 41W
Gairloch, L., *U.K.* . . . . . . . . . . . . **11 D3** 57 43N 5 45W
Gaizhou, *China* . . . . . . . . . . . . . **35 D12** 40 22N 122 20 E
Gaj →, *Pakistan* . . . . . . . . . . . . **42 F2** 26 26N 67 21 E
Gakuch, *Pakistan* . . . . . . . . . . . . **43 A5** 36 7N 73 45 E
Galán, Cerro, *Argentina* . . . . . . . **94 B2** 25 55S 66 52W
Galápagos = Colón, Arch. de,
   *Ecuador* . . . . . . . . . . . . . . . . **90 D1** 0 0 91 0W

Galashiels, *U.K.* . . . . . . . . . . . . . **11 F6** 55 37N 2 49W
Galaţi, *Romania* . . . . . . . . . . . . . **17 F15** 45 27N 28 2 E
Galatina, *Italy* . . . . . . . . . . . . . . **23 D8** 40 10N 18 10 E
Galax, *U.S.A.* . . . . . . . . . . . . . . . **83 G5** 36 40N 80 56W
Galcaio, *Somali Rep.* . . . . . . . . . **47 F4** 6 30N 47 30 E
Galdhøpiggen, *Norway* . . . . . . . . **9 F12** 61 38N 8 18 E
Galeana, Chihuahua, *Mexico* . . . . **86 A3** 30 7N 107 38W
Galeana, Nuevo León, *Mexico* . . . **86 A3** 24 50N 100 4W
Galela, *Indonesia* . . . . . . . . . . . **37 D7** 1 50N 127 49 E
Galena, *U.S.A.* . . . . . . . . . . . . . . **68 B4** 64 44N 156 56W
Galeota Pt., *Trin. & Tob.* . . . . . . . **93 K16** 10 8N 61 0W
Galera Pt., *Trin. & Tob.* . . . . . . . **89 D7** 10 49N 60 54W
Galesburg, *U.S.A.* . . . . . . . . . . . **80 E9** 40 57N 90 22W
Galeton, *U.S.A.* . . . . . . . . . . . . . **84 E7** 41 44N 77 39W
Galich, *Russia* . . . . . . . . . . . . . . **18 C7** 58 22N 42 24 E
Galicia □, *Spain* . . . . . . . . . . . . **21 A2** 42 43N 7 45W
Galilee = Hagalil, *Israel* . . . . . . . **46 C4** 32 53N 35 18 E
Galilee, L., *Australia* . . . . . . . . . . **62 C4** 22 20S 145 50 E
Galilee, Sea of = Yam Kinneret,
   *Israel* . . . . . . . . . . . . . . . . . . **46 C4** 32 45N 35 35 E
Galina Pt., *Jamaica* . . . . . . . . . . **88 a** 18 24N 76 58W
Galinoporni, *Cyprus* . . . . . . . . . . **25 D13** 35 31N 34 18 E
Galion, *U.S.A.* . . . . . . . . . . . . . . **84 F2** 40 44N 82 47W
Galiuro Mts., *U.S.A.* . . . . . . . . . . **77 K8** 32 30N 110 20W
Galiwinku, *Australia* . . . . . . . . . . **62 A2** 12 2S 135 34 E
Gallan Hd., *U.K.* . . . . . . . . . . . . . **11 C1** 58 15N 7 2W
Gallatin, *U.S.A.* . . . . . . . . . . . . . **83 G2** 36 24N 86 27W
Galle, *Sri Lanka* . . . . . . . . . . . . . **40 R12** 6 5N 80 10 E
Gállego →, *Spain* . . . . . . . . . . . **21 B5** 41 39N 0 51W
Gallegos →, *Argentina* . . . . . . . . **96 G3** 51 35S 69 0W
Galley Hd., *Ireland* . . . . . . . . . . . **10 E3** 51 32N 8 55W
Gallinas, Pta., *Colombia* . . . . . . . **92 A4** 12 28N 71 40W
Gallipoli = Gelibolu, *Turkey* . . . . **23 D12** 40 28N 26 43 E
Gallipoli, *Italy* . . . . . . . . . . . . . . **23 D8** 40 3N 17 58 E
Gallipolis, *U.S.A.* . . . . . . . . . . . . **82 F4** 38 49N 82 12W
Gällivare, *Sweden* . . . . . . . . . . . **8 C19** 67 9N 20 40 E
Galloo I., *U.S.A.* . . . . . . . . . . . . . **85 C8** 43 55N 76 25W
Galloway, *U.K.* . . . . . . . . . . . . . **11 F4** 55 1N 4 29W
Galloway □, *U.K.* . . . . . . . . . . . . **11 F4** 55 3N 4 20W
Galloway, Mull of, *U.K.* . . . . . . . **11 G4** 54 39N 4 52W
Gallup, *U.S.A.* . . . . . . . . . . . . . . **77 J9** 35 32N 108 45W
Galoya, *Sri Lanka* . . . . . . . . . . . **40 Q12** 8 10N 80 55 E
Galt, *U.S.A.* . . . . . . . . . . . . . . . . **78 G5** 38 15N 121 18W
Galty Mts., *Ireland* . . . . . . . . . . . **10 D3** 52 22N 8 10W
Galtymore, *Ireland* . . . . . . . . . . . **10 D3** 52 21N 8 11W
Galva, *U.S.A.* . . . . . . . . . . . . . . . **80 E9** 41 10N 90 3W
Galveston, *U.S.A.* . . . . . . . . . . . . **81 L7** 29 18N 94 48W
Galveston B., *U.S.A.* . . . . . . . . . . **81 L7** 29 36N 94 50W
Gálvez, *Argentina* . . . . . . . . . . . **94 C3** 32 0S 61 14W
Galway, *Ireland* . . . . . . . . . . . . . **10 C2** 53 17N 9 3W
Galway □, *Ireland* . . . . . . . . . . . **10 C2** 53 22N 9 1W
Galway B., *Ireland* . . . . . . . . . . . **10 C2** 53 13N 9 10W
Gam →, *Vietnam* . . . . . . . . . . . . **38 B5** 21 55N 105 12 E
Gamagōri, *Japan* . . . . . . . . . . . . **31 G8** 34 50N 137 14 E
Gambat, *Pakistan* . . . . . . . . . . . **42 F3** 27 17N 68 26 E
Gambhir →, *India* . . . . . . . . . . . **42 F6** 26 58N 77 27 E
Gambia ■, *W. Afr.* . . . . . . . . . . . **50 F2** 13 25N 16 0W
Gambia →, *W. Afr.* . . . . . . . . . . . **50 F2** 13 28N 16 34W
Gambier, *U.S.A.* . . . . . . . . . . . . . **84 F2** 40 22N 82 23W
Gambier, C., *Australia* . . . . . . . . **60 B5** 11 56S 130 57 E
Gambier Is., *Australia* . . . . . . . . . **63 F2** 35 3S 136 30 E
Gambo, *Canada* . . . . . . . . . . . . . **73 C9** 48 47N 54 13W
Gamboli, *Pakistan* . . . . . . . . . . . **42 E3** 29 53N 68 24 E
Gamboma, *Congo* . . . . . . . . . . . **52 E3** 1 55S 15 52 E
Gamka →, *S. Africa* . . . . . . . . . . **56 E3** 33 18S 21 39 E
Gamkab →, *Namibia* . . . . . . . . . **56 D2** 28 4S 17 54 E
Gamlakarleby = Kokkola, *Finland* . **8 E20** 63 50N 23 8 E
Gammon →, *Canada* . . . . . . . . . **71 C9** 51 24N 95 44W
Gammon Ranges △, *Australia* . . . **63 E2** 30 38S 139 8 E
Gamtoos →, *S. Africa* . . . . . . . . . **56 E4** 33 58S 25 1 E
Gan Jiang →, *China* . . . . . . . . . . **33 D6** 29 15N 116 0 E
Ganado, *U.S.A.* . . . . . . . . . . . . . **77 J9** 35 43N 109 33W
Gananoque, *Canada* . . . . . . . . . . **85 B8** 44 20N 76 10W
Ganāveh, *Iran* . . . . . . . . . . . . . . **45 D6** 29 35N 50 35 E
Gäncä, *Azerbaijan* . . . . . . . . . . . **19 F8** 40 45N 46 20 E
Gancheng, *China* . . . . . . . . . . . . **38 C7** 18 51N 108 37 E
Gand = Gent, *Belgium* . . . . . . . . **15 C3** 51 2N 3 42 E
Ganda, *Angola* . . . . . . . . . . . . . **53 G2** 13 3S 14 35 E
Gandajika, Dem. Rep. of
   the Congo . . . . . . . . . . . . . . . **52 F4** 6 45S 23 57 E
Gandak →, *India* . . . . . . . . . . . . **43 G11** 25 39N 85 13 E
Gandava, *Pakistan* . . . . . . . . . . . **42 E2** 28 32N 67 32 E
Gander, *Canada* . . . . . . . . . . . . . **73 C9** 48 58N 54 35W
Gander L., *Canada* . . . . . . . . . . . **73 C9** 48 58N 54 35W
Ganderowe Falls, *Zimbabwe* . . . . **55 F2** 17 20S 29 10 E
Gandhi Sagar, *India* . . . . . . . . . . **42 G6** 24 40N 75 40 E
Gandhinagar, *India* . . . . . . . . . . **42 H5** 23 15N 72 45 E
Gandía, *Spain* . . . . . . . . . . . . . . **21 C5** 38 58N 0 9W
Gando, Pta., *Canary Is.* . . . . . . . . **24 G4** 27 55N 15 22W
Ganedidalem = Gani, *Indonesia* . . **37 E7** 0 48S 128 14 E
Ganga →, *India* . . . . . . . . . . . . . **43 H14** 23 20N 90 30 E
Ganga Sagar, *India* . . . . . . . . . . **43 J13** 21 38N 88 5 E
Gangan →, *India* . . . . . . . . . . . . **43 E8** 28 38N 78 58 E
Ganganagar, *India* . . . . . . . . . . . **42 E5** 29 56N 73 56 E
Gangapur, *India* . . . . . . . . . . . . . **42 F7** 26 32N 76 49 E
Gangaw, *Burma* . . . . . . . . . . . . . **41 H19** 22 5N 94 5 E
Gangdisê Shan, *China* . . . . . . . . **41 D12** 31 20N 81 0 E
Ganges = Ganga →, *India* . . . . . **43 H14** 23 20N 90 30 E
Ganges, *Canada* . . . . . . . . . . . . **70 D4** 48 51N 123 31W
Ganges, Mouths of the, *India* . . . . **43 J14** 21 30N 90 0 E
Gangotri, *India* . . . . . . . . . . . . . **43 D8** 30 50N 79 10 E
Gangtok, *India* . . . . . . . . . . . . . **41 F16** 27 20N 88 37 E
Gangu, *China* . . . . . . . . . . . . . . . **34 G3** 34 40N 105 15 E
Gangyao, *China* . . . . . . . . . . . . . **35 B14** 44 12N 126 37 E
Gani, *Indonesia* . . . . . . . . . . . . . **37 E7** 0 48S 128 14 E
Ganj, *India* . . . . . . . . . . . . . . . . **43 F8** 27 45N 78 57 E
Gannett Peak, *U.S.A.* . . . . . . . . . **76 E9** 43 11N 109 39W
Ganquan, *China* . . . . . . . . . . . . . **34 F5** 36 20N 109 20 E
Gansu □, *China* . . . . . . . . . . . . . **34 G3** 36 0N 104 0 E
Gantheaume, C., *Australia* . . . . . . **63 F2** 36 4S 137 32 E
Gantheaume B., *Australia* . . . . . . **61 E1** 27 40S 114 10 E
Gantsevichi = Hantsavichy,
   *Belarus* . . . . . . . . . . . . . . . . **17 B14** 52 49N 26 30 E
Ganyem = Genyem, *Indonesia* . . . **37 E10** 2 46S 140 12 E
Ganyu, *China* . . . . . . . . . . . . . . . **35 G10** 34 50N 119 8 E
Ganzhou, *China* . . . . . . . . . . . . . **33 D6** 25 51N 114 56 E
Gao, *Mali* . . . . . . . . . . . . . . . . . **50 E5** 16 15N 0 5W
Gaoping, *China* . . . . . . . . . . . . . **34 G7** 35 45N 112 55 E
Gaotang, *China* . . . . . . . . . . . . . **34 F9** 36 50N 116 15 E
Gaoua, *Burkina Faso* . . . . . . . . . **50 F5** 10 20N 3 8W
Gaoual, *Guinea* . . . . . . . . . . . . . **50 F3** 11 45N 13 25W
Gaoxiong = Kaohsiung, *Taiwan* . . **33 D7** 22 35N 120 16 E
Gaoyou Hu, *China* . . . . . . . . . . . **35 H10** 32 45N 119 20 E
Gaoyuan, *China* . . . . . . . . . . . . . **35 F9** 37 8N 117 58 E

Gap, France .................. 20 D7 44 33N 6 5 E
Gapat, India ................. 43 G10 24 30N 82 28 E
Gapuwiyak, Australia ........ 62 A2 12 25 S 135 43 E
Gar, China .................. 32 C2 32 10N 79 58 E
Garabogazköl Aylagy,
  Turkmenistan .............. 19 F9 41 0N 53 30 E
Garachico, Canary Is. ....... 24 F3 28 22N 16 46W
Garachiné, Panama ........... 88 E4 8 0N 78 12W
Garafia, Canary Is. ......... 24 F2 28 48N 17 57W
Garah, Australia ............ 63 D4 29 5S 149 38 E
Garajonay, Canary Is. ....... 24 F2 28 7N 17 14W
Garamba △, Dem. Rep. of
  the Congo ................. 54 B2 4 10N 29 40 E
Garanhuns, Brazil ........... 93 E11 8 50S 36 30W
Garautha, India ............. 43 G8 25 34N 79 18 E
Garba Tula, Kenya ........... 54 B4 0 30N 38 32 E
Garberville, U.S.A. ......... 76 F2 40 6N 123 48W
Garbiyang, India ............ 43 D9 30 8N 80 54 E
Garda, L. di, Italy ......... 22 B4 45 40N 10 41 E
Garde L., Canada ............ 71 A7 62 50N 106 13W
Garden City, Ga., U.S.A. .... 83 J5 32 6N 81 9W
Garden City, Kans., U.S.A. .. 81 G4 37 58N 100 53W
Garden City, Tex., U.S.A. ... 81 K4 31 52N 101 29W
Garden Grove, U.S.A. ........ 79 M9 33 47N 117 55W
Gardēz, Afghan. ............. 42 C3 33 37N 69 9 E
Gardiner, Maine, U.S.A. ..... 83 C11 44 14N 69 47W
Gardiner, Mont., U.S.A. ..... 76 D8 45 2N 110 22W
Gardiners I., U.S.A. ........ 85 E12 41 6N 72 6W
Gardner, U.S.A. ............. 85 D13 42 34N 71 59W
Gardner Canal, Canada ....... 70 C3 53 27N 128 8W
Gardnerville, U.S.A. ........ 78 G7 38 56N 119 45W
Gardo, Somali Rep. .......... 47 F4 9 30N 49 6 E
Garey, U.S.A. ............... 79 L6 34 53N 120 19W
Garfield, U.S.A. ............ 76 C5 47 1N 117 9W
Garforth, U.K. .............. 12 D6 53 47N 1 24W
Gargett, Australia .......... 62 K6 21 9S 148 46 E
Garibaldi △, Canada ......... 70 D4 49 50N 122 40W
Gariep, L., S. Africa ....... 56 E4 30 40S 25 40 E
Garies, S. Africa ........... 56 E2 30 32S 17 59 E
Garigliano →, Italy ......... 22 D5 41 13N 13 45 E
Garissa, Kenya .............. 54 C4 0 25S 39 40 E
Garland, Tex., U.S.A. ....... 81 J6 32 55N 96 38W
Garland, Utah, U.S.A. ....... 76 F7 41 47N 112 10W
Garm, Tajikistan ............ 28 F8 39 0N 70 20 E
Garmāb, Iran ................ 45 C8 35 25N 56 45 E
Garmisch-Partenkirchen,
  Germany ................... 16 E6 47 30N 11 6 E
Garmo, Qullai = Kommunizma,
  Pik, Tajikistan ........... 28 F8 39 0N 72 2 E
Garmsār, Iran ............... 45 C7 35 20N 52 25 E
Garner, U.S.A. .............. 80 D8 43 6N 93 36W
Garnett, U.S.A. ............. 80 F7 38 17N 95 14W
Garo Hills, India ........... 43 G14 25 30N 90 30 E
Garonne →, France ........... 20 D3 45 2N 0 36W
Garoowe = Garoe, Somali Rep. 47 F4 8 25N 48 33 E
Garot, India ................ 42 G6 24 19N 75 41 E
Garoua, Cameroon ............ 51 G8 9 19N 13 21 E
Garrauli, India ............. 43 G8 25 5N 79 22 E
Garrison, Mont., U.S.A. ..... 76 C7 46 31N 112 49W
Garrison, N. Dak., U.S.A. ... 80 B4 47 40N 101 25W
Garrison Res. = Sakakawea, L.,
  U.S.A. .................... 80 B4 47 30N 101 25W
Garron Pt., U.K. ............ 10 A6 55 3N 5 59W
Garry →, U.K. ............... 11 E5 56 44N 3 47W
Garry, L., Canada ........... 68 B9 65 58N 100 18W
Garsen, Kenya ............... 54 C5 2 20S 40 5 E
Garson L., Canada ........... 71 B6 56 19N 110 2W
Garstang, U.K. .............. 12 D5 53 55N 2 46W
Garu, India ................. 43 H11 23 40N 84 14 E
Garub, Namibia .............. 56 D2 26 37S 16 0 E
Garut, Indonesia ............ 37 G12 7 14S 107 53 E
Garvie Mts., N.Z. ........... 59 L2 45 30S 168 50 E
Garwa = Garoua, Cameroon .... 51 G8 9 19N 13 21 E
Garwa, India ................ 43 G10 24 11N 83 47 E
Gary, U.S.A. ................ 82 E2 41 36N 87 20W
Garzê, China ................ 32 C5 31 38N 100 1 E
Garzón, Colombia ............ 92 C3 2 10N 75 40W
Gas-San, Japan .............. 30 E10 38 32N 140 1 E
Gasan Kuli = Esenguly,
  Turkmenistan .............. 28 F6 37 37N 53 59 E
Gascogne, France ............ 20 E4 43 45N 0 20 E
Gascogne, G. de, Europe ..... 20 D2 44 0N 2 0W
Gascony = Gascogne, France .. 20 E4 43 45N 0 20 E
Gascoyne →, Australia ....... 61 D1 24 52S 113 37 E
Gascoyne Junction, Australia  61 E2 25 2S 115 17 E
Gashaka, Nigeria ............ 51 G8 7 20N 11 29 E
Gasherbrum, Pakistan ........ 43 B7 35 40N 76 40 E
Gashua, Nigeria ............. 51 F8 12 54N 11 0 E
Gasparillo, Trin. & Tob. .... 93 K15 10 18N 61 26W
Gaspé, Canada ............... 73 C7 48 52N 64 30W
Gaspé, C., Canada ........... 73 C7 48 48N 64 7W
Gaspé Pen. = Gaspésie, Pén. de
  la, Canada ................ 73 C6 48 55N 66 10W
Gaspésie △, Canada .......... 73 C6 48 55N 66 10W
Gaspésie, Pén. de la, Canada  73 C6 48 55N 66 10W
Gasteiz = Vitoria-Gasteiz, Spain  21 A4 42 50N 2 41W
Gastonia, U.S.A. ............ 83 H5 35 16N 81 11W
Gastre, Argentina ........... 96 E3 42 20S 69 15W
Gata, C., Cyprus ............ 25 E12 34 34N 33 2 E
Gata, C. de, Spain .......... 21 D4 36 41N 2 13W
Gata, Sierra de, Spain ...... 21 B2 40 20N 6 45W
Gataga →, Canada ............ 70 B3 58 35N 126 59W
Gatehouse of Fleet, U.K. .... 11 G4 54 53N 4 12W
Gates, U.S.A. ............... 84 C7 43 9N 77 42W
Gateshead, U.K. ............. 12 C6 54 57N 1 35W
Gatesville, U.S.A. .......... 81 K6 31 26N 97 45W
Gateway △, U.S.A. ........... 85 F11 40 26N 73 59W
Gaths, Zimbabwe ............. 55 G3 20 2S 30 32 E
Gatico, Chile ............... 94 A1 22 29S 70 20W
Gatineau, Canada ............ 85 A9 45 29N 75 38W
Gatineau △, Canada .......... 72 C4 45 40N 76 0W
Gatineau →, Canada .......... 72 C4 45 27N 75 42W
Gatton, Australia ........... 63 D5 27 32S 152 17 E
Gatun, L., Panama ........... 88 E4 9 7N 79 56W
Gatwick, London ✈ (LGW), U.K.  13 F7 51 10N 0 11W
Gatyana, S. Africa .......... 57 E4 32 16S 28 31 E
Gau, Fiji ................... 59 D8 18 2S 179 18 E
Gauer L., Canada ............ 71 B9 57 0N 97 50W
Gauhati = Guwahati, India ... 41 F17 26 10N 91 45 E
Gauja →, Latvia ............. 9 H21 57 10N 24 16 E
Gaula →, Norway ............. 8 E14 63 21N 10 14 E
Gauri Phanta, India ......... 43 E9 28 41N 80 36 E
Gausta, Norway .............. 9 G13 59 48N 8 40 E
Gauteng □, S. Africa ........ 57 D4 26 0S 28 0 E
Gāv Koshī, Iran ............. 45 D8 28 38N 57 12 E
Gāvakān, Iran ............... 45 D7 29 37N 53 10 E
Gavāter, Iran ............... 45 E9 25 10N 61 31 E

Gāvbandī, Iran .............. 45 E7 27 12N 53 4 E
Gavdhopoúla, Greece ......... 25 E6 34 56N 24 0 E
Gávdhos, Greece ............. 25 E6 34 50N 24 5 E
Gaviota, U.S.A. ............. 79 L6 34 29N 120 13W
Gávkūnī, Bāţlāq-e, Iran ..... 45 C7 32 6N 52 52 E
Gävle, Sweden ............... 9 F17 60 40N 17 9 E
Gawachab, Namibia ........... 56 D2 27 4S 17 55 E
Gawilgarh Hills, India ...... 40 J10 21 15N 76 45 E
Gawler, Australia ........... 63 E2 34 30S 138 42 E
Gaxun Nur, China ............ 32 B5 42 22N 100 30 E
Gay, Russia ................. 18 D10 51 27N 58 27 E
Gaya, India ................. 43 G11 24 47N 85 4 E
Gaya, Niger ................. 50 F6 11 52N 3 28 E
Gaylord, U.S.A. ............. 82 C3 45 2N 84 41W
Gayndah, Australia .......... 63 D5 25 35S 151 32 E
Gaysin = Haysyn, Ukraine .... 17 D15 48 57N 29 25 E
Gayvoron = Hayvoron, Ukraine  17 D15 48 22N 29 52 E
Gaza, Gaza Strip ............ 46 D3 31 30N 34 28 E
Gaza □, Mozam. .............. 57 C5 23 10S 32 45 E
Gaza Strip ☒, Asia .......... 46 D3 31 29N 34 25 E
Gazanjyk, Turkmenistan ...... 45 B7 39 16N 55 32 E
Gāzbor, Iran ................ 45 D8 28 5N 58 51 E
Gazi, Dem. Rep. of the Congo  54 B1 1 3N 24 30 E
Gaziantep, Turkey ........... 19 G6 37 6N 37 23 E
Gazimağosa = Famagusta,
  Cyprus .................... 25 D12 35 8N 33 55 E
Gcoverega, Botswana ......... 56 B3 19 8S 24 18 E
Gcuwa, S. Africa ............ 57 E4 32 20S 28 11 E
Gdańsk, Poland .............. 17 A10 54 22N 18 40 E
Gdańska, Zatoka, Poland ..... 17 A10 54 30N 19 20 E
Gdov, Russia ................ 9 G22 58 48N 27 55 E
Gdynia, Poland .............. 17 A10 54 35N 18 33 E
Gebe, Indonesia ............. 37 D7 0 5N 129 25 E
Gebze, Turkey ............... 23 D13 40 47N 29 25 E
Gedaref, Sudan .............. 51 F13 14 2N 35 28 E
Gediz →, Turkey ............. 23 E12 38 35N 26 48 E
Gedser, Denmark ............. 9 J14 54 35N 11 55 E
Gedung, Pulau, Malaysia ..... 39 c 5 17N 100 23 E
Geegully Cr. →, Australia ... 60 C3 18 32S 123 41 E
Geel, Belgium ............... 15 C4 51 10N 4 59 E
Geelong, Australia .......... 63 F3 38 10S 144 22 E
Geelvink B. = Cenderawasih,
  Teluk, Indonesia .......... 37 E9 3 0S 135 20 E
Geelvink Chan., Australia ... 61 E1 28 30S 114 0 E
Geesthacht, Germany ......... 16 B6 53 26N 10 22 E
Geidam, Nigeria ............. 51 F8 12 57N 11 57 E
Geikie →, Canada ............ 71 B8 57 45N 103 52W
Geikie Gorge △, Australia ... 60 C4 18 3S 125 41 E
Geistown, U.S.A. ............ 84 F6 40 18N 78 52W
Geita, Tanzania ............. 54 C3 2 48S 32 12 E
Gejiu, China ................ 32 D5 23 20N 103 10 E
Gel, Meydān-e, Iran ......... 45 D7 29 4N 54 50 E
Gela, Italy ................. 22 F6 37 4N 14 15 E
Gelang Patah, Malaysia ...... 39 d 1 27N 103 35 E
Gelderland □, Neths. ........ 15 B6 52 5N 6 10 E
Geldrop, Neths. ............. 15 C5 51 25N 5 32 E
Geleen, Neths. .............. 15 D5 50 57N 5 49 E
Gelibolu, Turkey ............ 23 D12 40 28N 26 43 E
Gelsenkirchen, Germany ...... 16 C4 51 32N 7 6 E
Gelugur, Malaysia ........... 39 c 5 22N 100 18 E
Gemas, Malaysia ............. 39 L4 2 37N 102 36 E
Gembloux, Belgium ........... 15 D4 50 34N 4 43 E
Gemena, Dem. Rep. of
  the Congo ................. 52 D3 3 13N 19 48 E
Gemerek, Turkey ............. 44 B3 39 15N 36 10 E
Gemlik, Turkey .............. 23 D13 40 26N 29 9 E
Gemsbok △, Botswana ......... 56 D3 25 5S 21 1 E
Genale →, Ethiopia .......... 47 F2 6 2N 39 1 E
General Acha, Argentina ..... 94 D3 37 20S 64 38W
General Alvear, Buenos Aires,
  Argentina ................. 94 D4 36 0S 60 0W
General Alvear, Mendoza,
  Argentina ................. 94 D2 35 0S 67 40W
General Artigas, Paraguay ... 94 B4 26 52S 56 16W
General Belgrano, Argentina . 94 D4 36 35S 58 47W
General Bernardo O'Higgins,
  Antarctica ................ 5 C18 63 0S 58 3W
General Cabrera, Argentina .. 94 C3 32 53S 63 52W
General Cepeda, Mexico ...... 86 B4 25 23N 101 27W
General Guido, Argentina .... 94 D4 36 40S 57 50W
General Juan Madariaga,
  Argentina ................. 94 D4 37 0S 57 0W
General La Madrid, Argentina  94 D3 37 17S 61 20W
General MacArthur, Phil. .... 37 B7 11 18N 125 28 E
General Martín Miguel de
  Güemes, Argentina ......... 94 A3 24 50S 65 0W
General Paz, Argentina ...... 94 B4 27 45S 57 36W
General Pico, Argentina ..... 94 D3 35 45S 63 50W
General Pinedo, Argentina ... 94 B3 27 15S 61 20W
General Pinto, Argentina .... 94 C3 34 45S 61 50W
General Roca, Argentina ..... 96 D3 39 2S 67 35W
General Santos, Phil. ....... 37 C7 6 5N 125 14 E
General Trevino, Mexico ..... 87 B5 26 14N 99 29W
General Trías, Mexico ....... 86 B3 28 21N 106 22W
General Viamonte, Argentina . 94 D3 35 1S 61 3W
General Villegas, Argentina . 94 D3 35 5S 63 0W
Genesee, Idaho, U.S.A. ...... 76 C5 46 33N 116 56W
Genesee, Pa., U.S.A. ........ 84 E7 41 59N 77 54W
Genesee →, U.S.A. ........... 84 C7 43 16N 77 36W
Geneseo, Ill., U.S.A. ....... 80 E9 41 27N 90 9W
Geneseo, N.Y., U.S.A. ....... 84 D7 42 48N 77 49W
Geneva = Genève, Switz. ..... 20 C7 46 12N 6 9 E
Geneva, Ala., U.S.A. ........ 83 K3 31 2N 85 52W
Geneva, N.Y., U.S.A. ........ 84 D8 42 52N 76 59W
Geneva, Nebr., U.S.A. ....... 80 E6 40 32N 97 36W
Geneva, Ohio, U.S.A. ........ 84 E4 41 48N 80 57W
Geneva, L. = Léman, L., Europe  20 C7 46 26N 6 30 E
Genève, Switz. .............. 20 C7 46 12N 6 9 E
Genil →, Spain .............. 21 D3 37 42N 5 19W
Genk, Belgium ............... 15 D5 50 58N 5 32 E
Gennargentu, Mti. del, Italy  22 D3 40 1N 9 19 E
Genoa = Génova, Italy ....... 20 D8 44 25N 8 57 E
Genoa, Australia ............ 63 F4 37 29S 149 35 E
Genoa, N.Y., U.S.A. ......... 85 D8 42 40N 76 32W
Genoa, Nebr., U.S.A. ........ 80 E6 41 27N 97 44W
Genoa, Nev., U.S.A. ......... 78 F7 39 2N 119 50W
Génova, Italy ............... 20 D8 44 25N 8 57 E
Génova, G. di, Italy ........ 22 C3 44 0N 9 0 E
Genriyetty, Ostrov, Russia .. 29 B16 77 6N 156 30 E
Gent, Belgium ............... 15 C3 51 2N 3 42 E
Genteng, Bali, Indonesia .... 37 J17 8 22S 114 9 E
Genteng, Jawa, Indonesia .... 37 G12 7 22S 106 24 E
Genyem, Indonesia ........... 37 E10 2 46S 140 12 E
Geographe B., Australia ..... 61 F2 33 30S 115 15 E
Geographe Chan., Australia .. 61 D1 24 30S 113 0 E
Georg Forster, Antarctica ... 5 D3 71 0S 12 0 E
Georg von Neumayer, Antarctica  5 D17 71 0S 68 30W

Georga, Zemlya, Russia ...... 28 A5 80 30N 49 0 E
George, S. Africa ........... 56 E3 33 58S 22 29 E
George →, Canada ............ 73 A6 58 49N 66 10W
George, L., N.S.W., Australia  63 F4 35 10S 149 25 E
George, L., S. Austral., Australia  63 F3 37 25S 140 0 E
George, L., W. Austral., Australia  60 D3 22 45S 123 40 E
George, L., Uganda .......... 54 B3 0 5N 30 10 E
George, L., Fla., U.S.A. .... 83 L5 29 17N 81 36W
George, L., N.Y., U.S.A. .... 85 C11 43 37N 73 33W
George Gill Ra., Australia .. 60 D5 24 22S 131 45 E
George Pt., Australia ....... 62 J6 20 6S 148 36 E
George River =
  Kangiqsualujjuaq, Canada .. 69 C13 58 30N 65 59W
George Sound, N.Z. .......... 59 L1 44 52S 167 25 E
George Town, Australia ...... 62 B3 18 17S 143 33 E
George Town, Bahamas ........ 88 B4 23 33N 75 47W
George Town, Cayman Is. ..... 88 C3 19 20N 81 24W
George Town, Malaysia ....... 39 c 5 25N 100 20 E
George V Land, Antarctica ... 5 C10 69 0S 148 0 E
George VI Sound, Antarctica . 5 D17 71 0S 68 0W
George West, U.S.A. ......... 81 L5 28 20N 98 7W
Georgetown = Janjanbureh,
  Gambia .................... 50 F3 13 30N 14 47W
Georgetown, Australia ....... 62 B3 18 17S 143 33 E
Georgetown, Ont., Canada .... 84 C5 43 40N 79 56W
Georgetown, P.E.I., Canada .. 73 C7 46 13N 62 24W
Georgetown, Guyana .......... 92 B7 6 50N 58 12W
Georgetown, Calif., U.S.A. .. 78 G6 38 54N 120 50W
Georgetown, Colo., U.S.A. ... 76 G11 39 42N 105 42W
Georgetown, Ky., U.S.A. ..... 81 F3 38 13N 84 33W
Georgetown, N.Y., U.S.A. .... 85 D9 42 46N 75 44W
Georgetown, Ohio, U.S.A. .... 82 F4 38 52N 83 54W
Georgetown, S.C., U.S.A. .... 83 J6 33 23N 79 17W
Georgetown, Tex., U.S.A. .... 81 K6 30 38N 97 41W
Georgia □, U.S.A. ........... 83 K5 32 50N 83 15W
Georgia ■, Asia ............. 19 F7 42 0N 43 0 E
Georgia, Str. of, Canada .... 70 D4 49 25N 124 0W
Georgian B., Canada ......... 84 A4 45 15N 81 0W
Georgian Bay Islands △, Canada  84 B5 44 53N 79 52W
Georgina →, Australia ....... 62 C2 23 30S 139 47 E
Georgina I., Canada ......... 84 B5 44 22N 79 17W
Georgiyevsk, Russia ......... 19 F7 44 12N 43 28 E
Gera, Germany ............... 16 C7 50 53N 12 4 E
Geraardsbergen, Belgium ..... 15 D3 50 45N 3 53 E
Geral, Serra, Brazil ........ 95 B6 26 25S 50 0W
Geral de Goiás, Serra, Brazil  93 F9 12 0S 46 0W
Geraldine, U.S.A. ........... 76 C8 47 36N 110 16W
Geraldton, Australia ........ 61 E1 28 48S 114 32 E
Geraldton, Canada ........... 72 C2 49 44N 86 59W
Gereshk, Afghan. ............ 40 D4 31 47N 64 35 E
Gerik, Malaysia ............. 39 K3 5 50N 101 15 E
Gering, U.S.A. .............. 80 E3 41 50N 103 40W
Gerlach, U.S.A. ............. 76 F4 40 39N 119 21W
Germansen Landing, Canada ... 70 B4 55 43N 124 40W
Germantown, U.S.A. .......... 81 M10 35 5N 89 49W
Germany ■, Europe ........... 16 C6 51 0N 10 0 E
Germí, Iran ................. 45 B6 39 1N 48 3 E
Germiston, S. Africa ........ 57 D4 26 15S 28 10 E
Gernika-Lumo, Spain ......... 21 A4 43 19N 2 40W
Gero, Japan ................. 31 G8 35 48N 137 14 E
Gerokgak, Indonesia ......... 37 J17 8 15S 114 27 E
Gerona = Girona, Spain ...... 21 B7 41 58N 2 46 E
Gerrard, Canada ............. 70 C5 50 30N 117 17W
Gertak Sanggul, Malaysia .... 39 c 5 17N 100 12 E
Gertak Sanggul, Tanjung,
  Malaysia .................. 39 c 5 16N 100 11 E
Gerung, Indonesia ........... 37 K19 8 43S 116 7 E
Geser, Indonesia ............ 37 E8 3 50S 130 54 E
Getafe, Spain ............... 21 B4 40 18N 3 43W
Gettysburg, Pa., U.S.A. ..... 82 F7 39 50N 77 14W
Gettysburg, S. Dak., U.S.A. . 80 C5 45 1N 99 57W
Getxo, Spain ................ 21 A4 43 21N 2 59W
Getz Ice Shelf, Antarctica .. 5 D14 75 0S 130 0W
Geyser, U.S.A. .............. 76 C8 47 16N 110 30W
Geyserville, U.S.A. ......... 78 G4 38 42N 122 54W
Ghaggar →, India ............ 42 E6 29 30N 74 53 E
Ghaghara →, India ........... 43 G11 25 45N 84 40 E
Ghaghat →, Bangla. .......... 43 G13 25 19N 89 38 E
Ghagra, India ............... 43 H11 23 17N 84 33 E
Ghagra →, India ............. 43 F9 27 29N 81 9 E
Ghana ■, W. Afr. ............ 50 G5 8 0N 1 0W
Ghansor, India .............. 43 H9 22 39N 80 1 E
Ghanzi, Botswana ............ 56 C3 21 50S 21 34 E
Ghardaïa, Algeria ........... 50 B6 32 20N 3 37 E
Gharyān, Libya .............. 51 B8 32 10N 13 0 E
Ghat, Libya ................. 51 D8 24 59N 10 11 E
Ghatal, India ............... 43 H12 22 40N 87 46 E
Ghataprabha →, India ........ 40 L9 16 15N 75 20 E
Ghats, Eastern, India ....... 40 N11 14 0N 78 50 E
Ghats, Western, India ....... 40 N9 14 0N 75 0 E
Ghatsila, India ............. 43 H12 22 36N 86 29 E
Ghaţţī, Si. Arabia .......... 44 D3 31 16N 37 31 E
Ghawdex = Gozo, Malta ....... 25 C1 36 3N 14 15 E
Ghazal, Bahr el →, Chad ..... 51 F9 13 0N 15 47 E
Ghazāl, Bahr el →, Sudan .... 51 G12 9 31N 30 25 E
Ghaziabad, India ............ 42 E7 28 42N 77 26 E
Ghazipur, India ............. 43 G10 25 38N 83 35 E
Ghazni, Afghan. ............. 42 C3 33 30N 68 28 E
Ghazni □, Afghan. ........... 40 C6 32 10N 68 20 E
Ghent = Gent, Belgium ....... 15 C3 51 2N 3 42 E
Gheorghe Gheorghiu-Dej =
  Oneşti, Romania ........... 17 E14 46 17N 26 47 E
Ghinah, Wādī al →, Si. Arabia  44 D3 30 27N 38 14 E
Ghizao, Afghan. ............. 42 C1 33 20N 65 44 E
Ghizar →, Pakistan .......... 43 A5 36 15N 73 43 E
Ghotaru, India .............. 42 F4 27 20N 70 1 E
Ghotki, Pakistan ............ 42 E3 28 5N 69 21 E
Ghowr □, Afghan. ............ 40 C4 34 0N 64 20 E
Ghudāf, W. al →, Iraq ....... 44 C4 32 56N 43 30 E
Ghugus, India ............... 40 K11 19 58N 79 12 E
Ghulam Mohammad Barrage,
  Pakistan .................. 42 G3 25 30N 68 20 E
Ghūrīān, Afghan. ............ 40 B2 34 17N 61 25 E
Gia Dinh, Vietnam ........... 39 G6 10 49N 106 42 E
Gia Lai = Plei Ku, Vietnam .. 38 F7 13 57N 108 0 E
Gia Nghia, Vietnam .......... 39 G6 11 58N 107 42 E
Gia Vuc, Vietnam ............ 38 E7 14 42N 108 34 E
Giant Forest, U.S.A. ........ 78 J8 36 36N 118 43 E
Giant Sequoia △, U.S.A. ..... 78 K8 36 0N 118 32W
Giants Causeway, U.K. ....... 10 A5 55 16N 6 29W
Gianyar, Indonesia .......... 37 K18 8 32S 115 20 E
Giarabub = Al Jaghbūb, Libya  51 C10 29 42N 24 38 E
Giarre, Italy ............... 22 F6 37 43N 15 11 E
Gibara, Cuba ................ 88 B4 21 9N 76 11W

Gibb River, Australia ....... 60 C4 16 26S 126 26 E
Gibbon, U.S.A. .............. 80 E5 40 45N 98 51W
Gibeon, Namibia ............. 56 D2 25 9S 17 43 E
Gibraltar ☒, Europe ......... 21 E3 36 7N 5 22W
Gibraltar, Str. of, Medit. S.  21 E3 35 55N 5 40W
Gibraltar Range △, Australia  63 D5 29 31S 152 19 E
Gibson Desert, Australia .... 60 D4 24 0S 126 0 E
Gibsons, Canada ............. 70 D4 49 24N 123 32W
Gibsonville, U.S.A. ......... 78 F6 39 46N 120 54W
Giddings, U.S.A. ............ 81 K6 30 11N 96 56W
Giebnegáisi = Kebnekaise,
  Sweden .................... 8 C18 67 53N 18 33 E
Giessen, Germany ............ 16 C5 50 34N 8 41 E
Gīfān, Iran ................. 45 B8 37 54N 57 28 E
Gift Lake, Canada ........... 70 B5 55 53N 115 49W
Gifu, Japan ................. 31 G8 35 30N 136 45 E
Gifu □, Japan ............... 31 G8 35 40N 137 0 E
Giganta, Sa. de la, Mexico .. 86 B2 25 30N 111 30W
Gigha, U.K. ................. 11 F3 55 42N 5 44W
Giglio, Italy ............... 22 C4 42 20N 10 52 E
Gijón, Spain ................ 21 A3 43 32N 5 42W
Gil I., Canada .............. 70 C3 53 12N 129 15W
Gila →, U.S.A. .............. 77 K6 32 43N 114 33W
Gila Bend, U.S.A. ........... 77 K7 32 57N 112 43W
Gila Bend Mts., U.S.A. ...... 77 K7 33 10N 113 0W
Gila Cliff Dwellings △, U.S.A.  77 K9 33 2N 108 16W
Gīlān □, Iran ............... 45 B6 37 0N 50 0 E
Gilbert →, Australia ........ 62 B3 16 35S 141 15 E
Gilbert Is., Kiribati ....... 64 G9 1 0N 172 0 E
Gilbert River, Australia .... 62 B3 18 9S 142 52 E
Gilead, U.S.A. .............. 85 B14 44 24N 70 59W
Gilford I., Canada .......... 70 C3 50 40N 126 30W
Gilgandra, Australia ........ 63 E4 31 43S 148 39 E
Gilgil, Kenya ............... 54 C4 0 30S 36 20 E
Gilgit, India ............... 43 B6 35 50N 74 15 E
Gilgit →, Pakistan .......... 43 B6 35 44N 74 37 E
Gili △, Mozam. .............. 55 F4 16 39S 38 27 E
Gilimanuk, Indonesia ........ 37 J17 8 10S 114 26 E
Gillam, Canada .............. 71 B10 56 20N 94 40W
Gillen, L., Australia ....... 61 E3 26 11S 124 38 E
Gilles, L., Australia ....... 63 E2 32 50S 136 45 E
Gillette, U.S.A. ............ 80 C2 44 18N 105 30W
Gilliat, Australia .......... 62 C3 20 40S 141 28 E
Gillingham, U.K. ............ 13 F8 51 23N 0 33 E
Gilmer, U.S.A. .............. 81 J7 32 44N 94 57W
Gilmore, L., Australia ...... 61 F3 32 29S 121 37 E
Gilroy, U.S.A. .............. 78 H5 37 1N 121 34W
Gimie, Mt, St. Lucia ........ 89 f 13 54N 61 0W
Gimli, Canada ............... 71 C9 50 40N 97 0W
Gin Gin, Australia .......... 63 D5 25 0S 151 58 E
Gingin, Australia ........... 61 F2 31 22S 115 54 E
Gingindlovu, S. Africa ...... 57 D5 29 2S 31 30 E
Ginir, Ethiopia ............. 47 F3 7 6N 40 40 E
Gióna, Óros, Greece ......... 23 E10 38 38N 22 14 E
Gir Hills, India ............ 42 J4 21 0N 71 0 E
Girab, India ................ 42 F4 26 2N 70 38 E
Girāfi, W. →, Egypt ......... 46 F3 29 58N 34 39 E
Girard, Kans., U.S.A. ....... 81 G7 37 31N 94 51W
Girard, Ohio, U.S.A. ........ 84 E4 41 9N 80 42W
Girard, Pa., U.S.A. ......... 84 E4 42 0N 80 19W
Girdle Ness, U.K. ........... 11 D6 57 9N 2 3W
Giresun, Turkey ............. 19 F6 40 55N 38 30 E
Girga, Egypt ................ 51 C12 26 17N 31 55 E
Giri →, India ............... 42 D7 30 28N 77 41 E
Giridih, India .............. 43 G12 24 10N 86 21 E
Girne = Kyrenia, Cyprus ..... 25 D12 35 20N 33 20 E
Giron = Kiruna, Sweden ...... 8 C19 67 52N 20 15 E
Girona, Spain ............... 21 B7 41 58N 2 46 E
Gironde →, France ........... 20 D3 45 32N 1 7W
Girraween △, Australia ...... 63 D5 28 46S 151 54 E
Giru, Australia ............. 62 B4 19 30S 147 5 E
Girvan, U.K. ................ 11 F4 55 14N 4 51W
Gisborne, N.Z. .............. 59 H7 38 39S 178 5 E
Gisenyi, Rwanda ............. 54 C2 1 41S 29 15 E
Gislaved, Sweden ............ 9 H15 57 19N 13 32 E
Gitega, Burundi ............. 54 C2 3 26S 29 56 E
Giuba →, Somali Rep. ........ 47 G3 1 30N 42 35 E
Giurgiu, Romania ............ 17 G13 43 52N 25 57 E
Giza = El Gîza, Egypt ....... 51 C12 30 0N 31 10 E
Gizhiga, Russia ............. 29 C17 62 3N 160 30 E
Gizhiginskaya Guba, Russia .. 29 C16 61 0N 158 0 E
Giżycko, Poland ............. 17 A11 54 2N 21 48 E
Gizo, Solomon Is. ........... 58 a 8 6S 156 51 E
Gjoa Haven, Canada .......... 68 B10 68 38N 95 53W
Gjøvik, Norway .............. 9 F14 60 47N 10 43 E
Glace Bay, Canada ........... 73 C8 46 11N 59 58W
Glacier △, Canada ........... 70 C5 51 15N 117 30W
Glacier △, U.S.A. ........... 76 B7 48 30N 118 39 E
Glacier Bay △, U.S.A. ....... 70 B1 58 45N 136 30W
Glacier Peak, U.S.A. ........ 76 B3 48 7N 121 7W
Gladewater, U.S.A. .......... 81 J7 32 33N 94 56W
Gladstone, Queens., Australia  62 C5 23 52S 151 16 E
Gladstone, S. Austral., Australia  63 E2 33 15S 138 22 E
Gladstone, U.S.A. ........... 71 C9 50 13N 98 57W
Gladstone, U.S.A. ........... 82 C2 45 51N 87 1W
Gladwin, U.S.A. ............. 82 D3 43 59N 84 29W
Glagah, Indonesia ........... 37 J17 8 13S 114 18 E
Glåma = Glomma →, Norway .... 9 G14 59 12N 10 57 E
Gláma, Iceland .............. 8 D2 65 48N 23 0W
Glamis, U.S.A. .............. 79 N11 32 55N 115 5W
Glamorgan, Vale of □, U.K. .. 13 F4 51 28N 3 25W
Glasco, Kans., U.S.A. ....... 80 F6 39 22N 97 50W
Glasco, N.Y., U.S.A. ........ 85 D11 42 3N 73 57W
Glasgow, U.K. ............... 11 F4 55 51N 4 15W
Glasgow, Ky., U.S.A. ........ 82 G3 37 0N 85 55W
Glasgow, Mont., U.S.A. ...... 76 B10 48 12N 106 38W
Glasgow, City of □, U.K. .... 11 F4 55 51N 4 12W
Glasgow International ✈ (GLA),
  U.K. ...................... 11 F4 55 51N 4 21W
Glaslyn, Canada ............. 71 C7 53 22N 108 21W
Glastonbury, U.K. ........... 13 F5 51 9N 2 43W
Glastonbury, U.S.A. ......... 85 E12 41 43N 72 37W
Glazov, Russia .............. 18 C9 58 9N 52 40 E
Gleichen, Canada ............ 70 C6 50 52N 113 3W
Gleiwitz = Gliwice, Poland .. 17 C10 50 22N 18 41 E
Glen, U.S.A. ................ 85 B13 44 7N 71 11W
Glen Affric, U.K. ........... 11 D3 57 17N 5 1W
Glen Canyon △, U.S.A. ....... 77 H8 37 15N 111 0W
Glen Canyon Dam, U.S.A. ..... 77 H8 37 57N 111 0W
Glen Coe, U.K. .............. 11 E3 56 40N 5 0W
Glen Cove, U.S.A. ........... 85 F11 40 52N 73 38W
Glen Garry, U.K. ............ 11 D3 57 3N 5 7W
Glen Innes, Australia ....... 63 D5 29 44S 151 44 E
Glen Lyon, U.S.A. ........... 85 E8 41 10N 76 5W
Glen Mor, U.K. .............. 11 D4 57 9N 4 37W
Glen More, U.K. ............. 11 D5 57 8N 3 40W
Glen Moriston, U.K. ......... 11 D4 57 11N 4 52W

Glen Robertson, Canada ....... 85 A10 45 22N 74 30W
Glen Spean, U.K. ........... 11 E4 56 53N 4 40W
Glen Ullin, U.S.A. .......... 80 B4 46 49N 101 50W
Glencoe, Canada .......... 84 D3 42 45N 81 43W
Glencoe, S. Africa .......... 57 D5 28 11S 30 11 E
Glencoe, U.S.A. ........... 80 C7 44 46N 94 9W
Glendale, Ariz., U.S.A. ..... 77 K7 33 32N 112 11W
Glendale, Calif., U.S.A. ..... 79 L8 34 9N 118 15W
Glendale, Zimbabwe ....... 55 F3 17 22S 31 5 E
Glendive, U.S.A. .......... 80 B2 47 7N 104 43W
Glendo, U.S.A. ........... 80 D2 42 30N 105 2W
Glenelg ➡, Australia ...... 63 F3 38 4S 140 59 E
Glenfield, U.S.A. .......... 85 C9 43 43N 75 24W
Glengarriff, Ireland ....... 10 E2 51 45N 9 34W
Glenmont, U.S.A. ......... 84 F2 40 31N 82 6W
Glenmorgan, Australia ..... 63 D4 27 14S 149 42 E
Glenn, U.S.A. ............ 78 F4 39 31N 122 1W
Glennallen, U.S.A. ........ 68 B5 62 7N 145 33W
Glenns Ferry, U.S.A. ...... 76 E6 42 57N 115 18W
Glenore, Australia ........ 62 B3 17 50S 141 12 E
Glenreagh, Australia ...... 63 E5 30 2S 153 1 E
Glenrock, U.S.A. .......... 76 E11 42 52N 105 52W
Glenrothes, U.K. ......... 11 E5 56 12N 3 10W
Glens Falls, U.S.A. ........ 85 C11 43 19N 73 39W
Glenside, U.S.A. .......... 85 F9 40 6N 75 9W
Glenties, Ireland .......... 10 B3 54 49N 8 16W
Glenveagh △, Ireland ...... 10 A3 55 3N 8 1W
Glenville, U.S.A. .......... 82 F5 38 56N 80 50W
Glenwood, Canada ........ 73 C9 49 0N 54 58W
Glenwood, Ark., U.S.A. .... 81 H8 34 20N 93 33W
Glenwood, Iowa, U.S.A. .... 80 E7 41 3N 95 45W
Glenwood, Minn., U.S.A. ... 80 C7 45 39N 95 23W
Glenwood, Wash., U.S.A. ... 78 D5 46 1N 121 17W
Glenwood Springs, U.S.A. .. 76 G10 39 33N 107 19W
Glettinganes, Iceland ...... 8 D7 65 30N 13 37W
Gliwice, Poland .......... 17 C10 50 22N 18 41 E
Globe, U.S.A. ............ 77 K8 33 24N 110 47W
Głogów, Poland .......... 16 C9 51 37N 16 5 E
Glomma ➡, Norway ....... 9 G14 59 12N 10 57 E
Glorieuses, Is., Ind. Oc. .... 57 A8 11 30S 47 20 E
Glossop, U.K. ........... 12 D6 53 27N 1 56W
Gloucester, Australia ...... 63 E5 32 0S 151 59 E
Gloucester, U.K. ......... 13 F5 51 53N 2 15W
Gloucester, U.S.A. ........ 85 D14 42 37N 70 40W
Gloucester I., Australia ..... 62 J6 20 0S 148 30 E
Gloucester Island △, Australia . 62 J6 20 2S 148 30 E
Gloucester Point, U.S.A. .... 82 G7 37 15N 76 29W
Gloucestershire □, U.K. .... 13 F5 51 46N 2 15W
Gloversville, U.S.A. ....... 85 C10 43 3N 74 21W
Glovertown, Canada ....... 73 C9 48 40N 54 3W
Glusk, Belarus ........... 17 B15 52 53N 28 41 E
Gmünd, Austria .......... 16 D8 48 45N 15 0 E
Gmunden, Austria ........ 16 E7 47 55N 13 48 E
Gniezno, Poland ......... 17 B9 52 30N 17 35 E
Gnowangerup, Australia .... 61 F2 33 58S 118 0 E
Go Cong, Vietnam ........ 39 G6 10 22N 106 40 E
Gō-no-ura, Japan ........ 31 H4 33 44N 129 40 E
Goa, India .............. 40 M8 15 33N 73 59 E
Goa □, India ............ 40 M8 15 33N 73 59 E
Goalen Hd., Australia ...... 63 F5 36 33S 150 4 E
Goalpara, India .......... 41 F17 26 10N 90 40 E
Goaltor, India ........... 43 H12 22 43N 87 10 E
Goalundo Ghat, Bangla. .... 43 H13 23 50N 89 47 E
Goat Fell, U.K. .......... 11 F3 55 38N 5 11W
Goba, Ethiopia ........... 47 F2 7 1N 39 59 E
Goba, Mozam. ........... 57 D5 26 15S 32 13 E
Gobabis, Namibia ........ 56 C2 22 30S 19 0 E
Gobi, Asia .............. 34 C6 44 0N 110 0 E
Gobō, Japan ............ 31 H7 33 53N 135 10 E
Gochas, Namibia ......... 56 C2 24 59S 18 55 E
Godalming, U.K. ......... 13 F7 51 11N 0 36W
Godavari ➡, India ........ 41 L13 16 25N 82 18 E
Godavari Pt., India ....... 41 L13 17 0N 82 20 E
Godbout, Canada ......... 73 C6 49 20N 67 38W
Godda, India ............ 43 G12 24 50N 87 13 E
Goderich, Canada ........ 84 C3 43 45N 81 41W
Godfrey Ra., Australia ..... 61 D2 24 0S 117 0 E
Godhavn = Qeqertarsuaq,
  Greenland ............ 69 B14 69 15N 53 38W
Godhra, India ........... 42 H5 22 49N 73 40 E
Godoy Cruz, Argentina ..... 94 C2 32 56S 68 52W
Gods ➡, Canada .......... 72 A1 56 22N 92 51W
Gods L., Canada .......... 72 B1 54 40N 94 15W
Gods River, Canada ....... 71 C10 54 50N 94 5W
Godthåb = Nuuk, Greenland . 69 B14 64 10N 51 35W
Goeie Hoop, Kaap die = Good
  Hope, C. of, S. Africa .... 56 E2 34 24S 18 30 E
Goéland, L. au, Canada .... 72 C4 49 50N 76 48W
Goélands, L. aux, Canada ... 73 A7 55 27N 64 17W
Goeree, Neths. .......... 15 C3 51 50N 4 0 E
Goes, Neths. ............ 15 C3 51 30N 3 55 E
Goffstown, U.S.A. ........ 85 C13 43 1N 71 36W
Gogama, Canada ......... 72 C3 47 35N 81 43W
Gogebic, L., U.S.A. ....... 80 B10 46 30N 89 35W
Gogra = Ghaghara ➡, India . 43 G11 25 45N 84 40 E
Gogriâl, Sudan .......... 51 G11 8 30N 28 8 E
Gohana, India ........... 42 E7 29 8N 76 42 E
Goharganj, India ......... 42 H7 23 1N 77 41 E
Goi ➡, India ............ 42 H6 22 4N 74 46 E
Goiânia, Brazil .......... 93 G9 16 43S 49 20W
Goiás, Brazil ............ 93 G8 15 55S 50 10W
Goiás □, Brazil .......... 93 F9 12 10S 48 0W
Goio-Erê, Brazil ......... 95 A5 24 12S 53 1W
Gojō, Japan ............ 31 G7 34 21N 135 42 E
Gojra, Pakistan .......... 42 D5 31 10N 72 40 E
Gökçeada, Turkey ........ 23 D11 40 10N 25 50 E
Gökova Körfezi, Turkey .... 23 F12 36 55N 27 50 E
Gokteik, Burma .......... 41 H20 22 26N 97 0 E
Gokurt, Pakistan ......... 42 E2 29 40N 67 26 E
Gokwe, Zimbabwe ........ 57 B4 18 7S 28 58 E
Gola, India ............. 43 E9 28 3N 80 32 E
Golakganj, India ......... 43 F13 26 8N 89 52 E
Golan Heights = Hagolan, Syria . 46 C4 33 0N 35 45 E
Goláshkerd, Iran ........ 45 E8 27 59N 57 16 E
Golchikha, Russia ........ 4 B12 71 45N 83 30 E
Golconda, U.S.A. ........ 76 F5 40 58N 117 30W
Gold, U.S.A. ............ 84 E7 41 52N 77 50W
Gold Beach, U.S.A. ....... 76 E1 42 25N 124 25W
Gold Coast, W. Afr. ...... 50 H5 4 0N 1 40W
Gold Hill, U.S.A. ......... 76 E2 42 26N 123 3W
Gold River, Canada ....... 70 D3 49 46N 126 3W
Golden, Canada .......... 70 C5 51 20N 116 59W
Golden B., N.Z. .......... 59 J4 40 40S 172 50 E
Golden Gate, U.S.A. ...... 76 H2 37 54N 122 30W
Golden Gate Highlands △,
  S. Africa .............. 57 D4 28 40S 28 40 E

Golden Hinde, Canada ..... 70 D3 49 40N 125 44W
Golden Lake, Canada ...... 84 A7 45 34N 77 21W
Golden Spike △, U.S.A. .... 76 F7 41 37N 112 33W
Golden Vale, Ireland ...... 10 D3 52 33N 8 17W
Goldendale, U.S.A. ....... 76 D3 45 49N 120 50W
Goldfield, U.S.A. ......... 77 H5 37 42N 117 14W
Goldsand L., Canada ...... 71 B8 57 2N 101 8W
Goldsboro, U.S.A. ........ 83 H7 35 23N 77 59W
Goldsmith, U.S.A. ........ 81 K3 31 59N 102 37W
Goldsworthy, Australia .... 60 D2 20 21S 119 30 E
Goldthwaite, U.S.A. ...... 81 K5 31 27N 98 34W
Goleniów, Poland ........ 16 B8 53 35N 14 50 E
Golestan □, Iran ......... 45 B7 37 20N 55 25 E
Golestának, Iran ......... 45 D7 30 36N 54 14 E
Goleta, U.S.A. ........... 79 L7 34 27N 119 50W
Golfito, Costa Rica ....... 88 E3 8 41N 83 5W
Golfo Aranci, Italy ....... 22 D3 40 59N 9 38 E
Goliad, U.S.A. ........... 81 L6 28 40N 97 23W
Golpāyegān, Iran ........ 45 C6 33 27N 50 18 E
Golra, Pakistan .......... 42 C5 33 37N 72 56 E
Golspie, U.K. ........... 11 D5 57 58N 3 59W
Goma, Dem. Rep. of the Congo . 54 C2 1 37S 29 10 E
Gomal Pass, Pakistan ..... 42 D3 31 56N 69 20 E
Gomati ➡, India ......... 43 G10 25 32N 83 11 E
Gombari, Dem. Rep. of
  the Congo ............ 54 B2 2 45N 29 3 E
Gombe, Nigeria .......... 51 F8 10 19N 11 2 E
Gombe ➡, Tanzania ...... 54 C3 4 38S 31 40 E
Gomel = Homyel, Belarus ... 17 B16 52 28N 31 0 E
Gomera, Canary Is. ....... 24 F2 28 7N 17 14W
Gómez Palacio, Mexico .... 86 B4 25 40N 104 0W
Gomishān, Iran .......... 45 B7 37 4N 54 6 E
Gomogomo, Indonesia ..... 37 F8 6 39S 134 43 E
Gomoh, India ........... 41 H15 23 52N 86 10 E
Gompa = Ganta, Liberia .... 50 G4 7 15N 8 59W
Gonābād, Iran ........... 45 C8 34 15N 58 45 E
Gonaïves, Haiti .......... 89 C5 19 20N 72 42W
Gonarezhou △, Zimbabwe .. 55 G3 21 32S 31 55 E
Gonâve, G. de la, Haiti ..... 89 C5 19 29N 72 42W
Gonâve, Île de la, Haiti ..... 89 C5 18 51N 73 3W
Gonbad-e Kāvūs, Iran ..... 45 B7 37 20N 55 25 E
Gonda, India ............ 43 F9 27 9N 81 58 E
Gondal, India ........... 42 J4 21 58N 70 52 E
Gonder, Ethiopia ........ 47 E2 12 39N 37 30 E
Gondia, India ........... 40 J12 21 23N 80 10 E
Gondola, Mozam. ........ 55 F3 19 10S 33 37 E
Gönen, Turkey .......... 23 D12 40 6N 27 39 E
Gongbei, China .......... 33 G10 22 12N 113 32 E
Gonghe, China .......... 32 C5 36 18N 100 32 E
Gongming, China ........ 33 F10 22 47N 113 53 E
Gongolgon, Australia ..... 63 E4 30 21S 146 54 E
Gongzhuling, China ...... 35 C13 43 30N 124 40 E
Gonzales, Calif., U.S.A. .... 78 J5 36 30N 121 26W
Gonzales, Tex., U.S.A. ..... 81 L6 29 30N 97 27W
González Chaves, Argentina . 94 D3 38 2S 60 5W
Good Hope, C. of, S. Africa .. 56 E2 34 24S 18 30 E
Gooderham, Canada ...... 84 B6 44 54N 78 21W
Goodhouse, S. Africa ..... 56 D2 28 57S 18 13 E
Gooding, U.S.A. ......... 76 E6 42 56N 114 43W
Goodland, U.S.A. ........ 80 F4 39 21N 101 43W
Goodlow, Canada ........ 70 B4 56 20N 120 8W
Goodooga, Australia ..... 63 D4 29 3S 147 28 E
Goodsprings, U.S.A. ...... 79 K11 35 49N 115 27W
Goole, U.K. ............. 12 D7 53 42N 0 53W
Goolgowi, Australia ...... 63 E4 33 58S 145 41 E
Goomalling, Australia ..... 61 F2 31 15S 116 49 E
Goomeri, Australia ....... 63 D5 26 12S 152 6 E
Goonda, Mozam. ........ 55 F3 19 48S 33 57 E
Goondiwindi, Australia .... 63 D5 28 30S 150 21 E
Goongarrie △, Australia ... 61 F3 30 7S 121 30 E
Goongarrie, L., Australia ... 61 F3 30 3S 121 9 E
Goonyella, Australia ...... 62 C4 21 47S 147 58 E
Goose ➡, Canada ........ 73 B7 53 20N 60 35W
Goose Creek, U.S.A. ...... 83 J5 32 59N 80 2W
Goose L., U.S.A. ......... 76 F3 41 56N 120 26W
Gop, India ............. 40 H6 22 5N 69 50 E
Gopalganj, India ......... 43 F11 26 28N 84 30 E
Göppingen, Germany ...... 16 D5 48 42N 9 39 E
Gorakhpur, India ........ 43 F10 26 47N 83 23 E
Goražde, Bos.-H. ......... 23 C8 43 38N 18 58 E
Gorda, U.S.A. ........... 78 K5 35 53N 121 26W
Gorda, Pta., Canary Is. ..... 24 F2 28 45N 18 0W
Gorda, Pta., Nic. ......... 88 D3 14 20N 83 10W
Gordan B., Australia ...... 60 B5 11 35S 130 10 E
Gordon, U.S.A. .......... 80 D3 42 48N 102 12W
Gordon ➡, Australia ...... 63 G4 42 27S 145 30 E
Gordon L., Alta., Canada ... 71 B6 56 30N 110 25W
Gordon L., N.W.T., Canada .. 70 A6 63 5N 113 11W
Gordonvale, Australia .... 62 B4 17 5S 145 50 E
Gore, Ethiopia .......... 47 F2 8 12N 35 32 E
Gore, N.Z. ............. 59 M2 46 5S 168 58 E
Gore Bay, Canada ........ 72 C3 45 57N 82 28W
Gorey, Ireland .......... 10 D5 52 41N 6 18W
Gorg, Iran ............. 45 D8 29 29N 59 43 E
Gorgān, Iran ........... 45 B7 36 55N 54 30 E
Gorgona, I., Colombia ..... 92 C3 3 0N 78 10W
Gorham, U.S.A. ......... 85 B13 44 23N 71 10W
Goriganga ➡, India ....... 43 E9 29 45N 80 23 E
Gorinchem, Neths. ....... 15 C4 51 50N 4 59 E
Goris, Armenia .......... 19 G8 39 31N 46 22 E
Gorizia, Italy ........... 22 B5 45 56N 13 37 E
Gorki = Nizhniy Novgorod,
  Russia ............... 18 C7 56 20N 44 0 E
Gorkiy = Nizhniy Novgorod,
  Russia ............... 18 C7 56 20N 44 0 E
Gorkovskoye Vdkhr., Russia . 18 C7 57 2N 43 4 E
Gorleston, U.K. ......... 13 E9 52 35N 1 44 E
Görlitz, Germany ........ 16 C8 51 9N 14 58 E
Gorlovka = Horlivka, Ukraine . 19 E6 48 19N 38 5 E
Gorman, U.S.A. ......... 79 L8 34 47N 118 51W
Gorna Dzhumayo = Blagoevgrad,
  Bulgaria ............. 23 C10 42 2N 23 5 E
Gorna Oryakhovitsa, Bulgaria . 23 C11 43 7N 25 40 E
Gorno-Altay □, Russia ..... 28 D9 51 0N 86 0 E
Gorno-Altaysk, Russia ..... 28 D9 51 50N 86 5 E
Gornyatski, Russia ....... 18 A11 67 32N 64 3 E
Gornyy, Russia .......... 30 B6 44 57N 133 59 E
Gorodenka = Horodenka, Ukraine . 17 D13 48 41N 25 29 E
Gorodok = Horodok, Ukraine . 17 D12 49 46N 23 32 E
Gorokhov = Horokhiv, Ukraine . 17 C13 50 30N 24 45 E
Goromonzi, Zimbabwe ..... 55 F3 17 52S 31 22 E
Gorong, Kepulauan, Indonesia . 37 E8 3 59S 131 25 E
Gorongosa △, Mozam. ..... 57 B5 18 50S 34 29 E
Gorongoza, Mozam. ...... 55 F3 20 30S 34 40 E
Gorongoza, Mozam. ...... 55 F3 18 44S 34 2 E
Gorongoza, Sa. da, Mozam. . 55 F3 18 27S 34 2 E
Gorontalo, Indonesia ..... 37 D6 0 35N 123 5 E
Gorontalo □, Indonesia .... 37 D6 0 50N 122 20 E

Gort, Ireland ........... 10 C3 53 3N 8 49W
Gortis, Greece .......... 25 D6 35 4N 24 58 E
Gorzów Wielkopolski, Poland . 16 B8 52 43N 15 15 E
Gosford, Australia ....... 63 E5 33 23S 151 18 E
Goshen, Calif., U.S.A. ..... 78 J7 36 21N 119 25W
Goshen, Ind., U.S.A. ...... 82 E3 41 35N 85 50W
Goshen, N.Y., U.S.A. ...... 85 E10 41 24N 74 20W
Goshogawara, Japan ...... 30 D10 40 48N 140 27 E
Goslar, Germany ........ 16 C6 51 54N 10 25 E
Gospič, Croatia ......... 16 F8 44 35N 15 23 E
Gosport, U.K. ........... 13 G6 50 48N 1 9W
Gosse ➡, Australia ...... 62 B1 19 32S 134 37 E
Göta älv ➡, Sweden ...... 9 H14 57 42N 11 54 E
Göta kanal, Sweden ...... 9 G16 58 30N 15 58 E
Götaland, Sweden ....... 9 G15 57 30N 14 30 E
Göteborg, Sweden ....... 9 H14 57 43N 11 59 E
Gotha, Germany ......... 16 C6 50 56N 10 42 E
Gothenburg = Göteborg, Sweden . 9 H14 57 43N 11 59 E
Gothenburg, U.S.A. ...... 80 E4 40 56N 100 10W
Gotland, Sweden ........ 9 H18 57 30N 18 33 E
Gotō-Rettō, Japan ....... 31 H4 32 55N 129 5 E
Gotska Sandön, Sweden ... 9 G18 58 24N 19 15 E
Gōtsu, Japan ........... 31 G6 35 0N 132 14 E
Gott Pk., Canada ........ 70 C4 50 18N 122 16W
Göttingen, Germany ...... 16 C5 51 31N 9 55 E
Gottwaldov = Zlín, Czech Rep. . 17 D9 49 14N 17 40 E
Goubangzi, China ........ 35 D11 41 20N 121 52 E
Gouda, Neths. ........... 15 B4 52 1N 4 42 E
Goúdhoura, Ákra, Greece .. 25 E8 34 59N 26 6 E
Gough I., Atl. Oc. ........ 2 G9 40 10S 9 45W
Gouin, Rés., Canada ...... 72 C5 48 35N 74 40W
Goulburn, Australia ...... 63 E4 34 44S 149 44 E
Goulburn Is., Australia .... 62 A1 11 40S 133 20 E
Goulimine, Morocco ...... 50 C3 28 56N 10 0W
Gourits ➡, S. Africa ...... 56 E3 34 21S 21 52 E
Goúrnais, Greece ........ 25 D7 35 19N 25 16 E
Gourock, U.K. .......... 11 F4 55 57N 4 49W
Gouverneur, U.S.A. ...... 85 B9 44 20N 75 28W
Governador Valadares, Brazil . 93 G10 18 15S 41 57W
Governor's Harbour, Bahamas . 88 A4 25 10N 76 14W
Govindgarh, India ....... 43 G9 24 23N 81 18 E
Gowan Ra., Australia ..... 62 D4 25 0S 145 0 E
Gowanda, U.S.A. ........ 84 D6 42 28N 78 56W
Gower, U.K. ............ 13 F3 51 35N 4 10W
Gowna, L., Ireland ....... 10 C4 53 51N 7 34W
Goya, Argentina ........ 94 B4 29 10S 59 10W
Goyder Lagoon, Australia .. 63 D2 27 3S 138 58 E
Goyllarisquisga, Peru ..... 92 F3 10 31S 76 24W
Goz Beïda, Chad ......... 51 F10 12 10N 21 20 E
Gozo, Malta ............ 25 C1 36 3N 14 15 E
Graaff-Reinet, S. Africa .... 56 E3 32 13S 24 32 E
Gračac, Croatia ......... 16 F8 44 18N 15 57 E
Gracias a Dios, C., Honduras . 88 D3 15 0N 83 10W
Graciosa, I., Canary Is. .... 24 E6 29 15N 13 32W
Grado, Spain ........... 21 A2 43 23N 6 4W
Grady, U.S.A. ........... 81 H3 34 49N 103 19W
Grafham Water, U.K. ..... 13 E7 52 19N 0 18W
Grafton, Canada ......... 85 C8 43 59N 78 5W
Grafton, N. Dak., U.S.A. ... 80 A6 48 25N 97 25W
Grafton, W. Va., U.S.A. .... 82 F5 39 21N 80 2W
Graham, Canada ......... 72 C1 49 20N 90 30W
Graham, U.S.A. ......... 77 K9 32 42N 109 52W
Graham Bell, Ostrov = Greem-
  Bell, Ostrov, Russia ..... 28 A7 81 0N 62 0 E
Graham I., Canada ....... 70 C2 53 40N 132 30W
Graham Land, Antarctica ... 5 C17 65 0S 64 0W
Grahamstown, S. Africa .... 56 E4 33 19S 26 31 E
Grahamsville, U.S.A. ..... 85 E10 41 51N 74 33W
Grain Coast, W. Afr. ...... 50 H3 4 20N 10 0W
Grajagan, Indonesia ...... 37 K17 8 35S 114 13 E
Grajagan, Teluk, Indonesia . 37 K17 8 40S 114 18 E
Grajaú, Brazil ........... 93 E9 5 50S 46 4W
Grajaú ➡, Brazil ......... 93 D10 3 41S 44 48W
Grampian, U.S.A. ........ 84 F6 40 58N 78 37W
Grampian Highlands = Grampian
  Mts., U.K. ............ 11 E5 56 50N 4 0W
Grampian Mts., U.K. ...... 11 E5 56 50N 4 0W
Grampians, The, Australia .. 63 F3 37 0S 142 20 E
Gran Canaria, Canary Is. ... 24 G4 27 55N 15 35W
Gran Chaco, S. Amer. ..... 94 B3 25 0S 61 0W
Gran Desierto del Pinacate △,
  Mexico .............. 86 A2 31 51N 113 32W
Gran Paradiso, Italy ...... 20 D7 45 33N 7 17 E
Gran Sasso d'Itália, Italy ... 22 C5 42 27N 13 42 E
Granada, Nic. ........... 88 D2 11 58N 86 0W
Granada, Spain .......... 21 D4 37 10N 3 35W
Granada, U.S.A. ......... 81 F3 38 4N 102 19W
Granadilla de Abona, Canary Is. . 24 F3 28 7N 16 33W
Granard, Ireland ........ 10 C4 53 47N 7 30W
Granbury, U.S.A. ........ 81 J6 32 27N 97 47W
Granby, Canada ......... 85 A12 45 25N 72 45W
Granby, U.S.A. .......... 76 F11 40 5N 105 56W
Grand ➡, Canada ........ 84 D5 42 51N 79 34W
Grand ➡, Mo., U.S.A. ..... 80 F8 39 23N 93 7W
Grand ➡, S. Dak., U.S.A. ... 80 C4 45 40N 100 45W
Grand Bahama I., Bahamas .. 88 A4 26 40N 78 30W
Grand Bassam, Ivory C. .... 50 G5 5 10N 3 49W
Grand-Bourg, Guadeloupe .. 88 b 15 53N 61 19W
Grand Canal = Yun Ho ➡, China . 35 E9 39 10N 117 10 E
Grand Canyon, U.S.A. ..... 77 H7 36 3N 112 9W
Grand Canyon △, U.S.A. ... 77 H7 36 15N 112 30W
Grand Canyon-Parashant △,
  U.S.A. ............... 77 H7 36 30N 113 20W
Grand Cayman, Cayman Is. .. 88 C3 19 20N 81 20W
Grand Centre, Canada ..... 71 C6 54 25N 110 13W
Grand Coulee, U.S.A. ..... 76 C4 47 57N 119 0W
Grand Coulee Dam, U.S.A. .. 76 C4 47 57N 118 59W
Grand Falls, Canada ...... 73 C6 47 3N 67 44W
Grand Falls-Windsor, Canada . 73 C8 48 56N 55 40W
Grand Forks, Canada ...... 70 D5 49 0N 118 30W
Grand Forks, U.S.A. ...... 80 B6 47 55N 97 3W
Grand Gorge, U.S.A. ...... 85 D10 42 21N 74 29W
Grand Haven, U.S.A. ...... 82 D2 43 4N 86 13W
Grand I., Mich., U.S.A. ..... 82 B2 46 31N 86 40W
Grand I., N.Y., U.S.A. ...... 84 D6 43 0N 78 58W
Grand Island, U.S.A. ...... 80 E5 40 55N 98 21W
Grand Isle, La., U.S.A. ..... 81 L9 29 14N 90 0W
Grand Isle, Vt., U.S.A. ..... 85 B11 44 43N 73 18W
Grand Junction, U.S.A. .... 77 G9 39 4N 108 33W
Grand L., N.B., Canada .... 73 C6 45 57N 66 7W
Grand L., Nfld. & L., Canada . 73 B8 53 40N 60 30W
Grand L., Nfld. & L., Canada . 73 B7 49 0N 57 30W
Grand L., U.S.A. ......... 81 L8 29 55N 92 47W
Grand Lake, U.S.A. ....... 76 F11 40 15N 105 49W
Grand Manan I., Canada ... 73 D6 44 45N 66 52W

Grand Marais, Canada ..... 80 B9 47 45N 90 25W
Grand Marais, U.S.A. ..... 82 B3 46 40N 85 59W
Grand-Mère, Canada ...... 72 C5 46 36N 72 40W
Grand Portage, U.S.A. ..... 80 B10 47 58N 89 41W
Grand Prairie, U.S.A. ..... 81 J6 32 47N 97 0W
Grand Rapids, Canada ..... 71 C9 53 12N 99 19W
Grand Rapids, Mich., U.S.A. . 82 D2 42 58N 85 40W
Grand Rapids, Minn., U.S.A. . 80 B8 47 14N 93 31W
Grand St-Bernard, Col du,
  Europe .............. 20 D7 45 50N 7 10 E
Grand Staircase-Escalante △,
  U.S.A. ............... 77 H8 37 5N 112 0W
Grand Teton, U.S.A. ...... 76 E8 43 54N 111 50W
Grand Teton △, U.S.A. .... 76 D8 43 50N 110 50W
Grand Union Canal, U.K. ... 13 E7 52 7N 0 53W
Grand-Vigie, Pte. de la,
  Guadeloupe .......... 88 b 16 32N 61 27W
Grande ➡, Jujuy, Argentina . 94 A2 24 20S 65 2W
Grande ➡, Mendoza, Argentina . 94 D2 36 52S 69 45W
Grande ➡, Bolivia ....... 92 G6 15 51S 64 39W
Grande ➡, Bahia, Brazil ... 93 F10 11 30S 44 30W
Grande ➡, Minas Gerais, Brazil . 93 H8 20 6S 51 4W
Grande, B., Argentina ..... 96 G3 50 30S 68 20W
Grande, Rio ➡, U.S.A. .... 81 N6 25 58N 97 9W
Grande Baleine, R. de la ➡,
  Canada .............. 72 A4 55 16N 77 47W
Grande Cache, Canada .... 70 C5 53 53N 119 8W
Grande-Entrée, Canada .... 73 C7 47 30N 61 40W
Grande Prairie, Canada .... 70 B5 55 10N 118 50W
Grande-Rivière, Canada ... 73 C7 48 26N 64 30W
Grande-Terre, Guadeloupe . 88 b 16 20N 61 25W
Grande-Vallée, Canada .... 73 C6 49 14N 65 8W
Grandfalls, U.S.A. ....... 81 K3 31 20N 102 51W
Grands-Jardins △, Canada .. 73 C5 47 41N 70 51W
Grandview, Canada ....... 71 C8 51 10N 100 42W
Grandview, U.S.A. ....... 76 C4 46 15N 119 54W
Graneros, Chile ......... 94 C1 34 5S 70 45W
Grangemouth, U.K. ...... 11 E5 56 1N 3 42W
Granger, U.S.A. ......... 76 F9 41 35N 109 58W
Grangeville, U.S.A. ...... 76 D5 45 56N 116 7W
Granisle, Canada ........ 70 C3 54 53N 126 13W
Granite City, U.S.A. ...... 80 F9 38 42N 90 9W
Granite Falls, U.S.A. ...... 80 C7 44 49N 95 33W
Granite L., Canada ....... 73 C8 48 8N 57 5W
Granite Mt., U.S.A. ...... 79 M10 33 5N 116 28W
Granite Pk., U.S.A. ....... 76 D9 45 10N 109 48W
Graniteville, U.S.A. ...... 85 B12 44 8N 72 29W
Granity, N.Z. ........... 59 J3 41 39S 171 51 E
Granja, Brazil .......... 93 D10 3 7S 40 50W
Granollers, Spain ....... 21 B7 41 39N 2 18 E
Grant, U.S.A. .......... 80 E4 40 53N 101 42W
Grant, Mt., U.S.A. ....... 76 G4 38 34N 118 48W
Grant City, U.S.A. ....... 80 E7 40 29N 94 25W
Grant I., Australia ....... 60 B5 11 10S 132 52 E
Grant Range, U.S.A. ...... 77 G6 38 30N 115 25W
Grantham, U.K. ......... 12 E7 52 55N 0 38W
Grantown-on-Spey, U.K. ... 11 D5 57 20N 3 36W
Grants, U.S.A. .......... 77 J10 35 9N 107 52W
Grants Pass, U.S.A. ...... 76 E2 42 26N 123 19W
Grantsville, U.S.A. ...... 76 F7 40 36N 112 28W
Granville, France ........ 20 B3 48 50N 1 35W
Granville, N. Dak., U.S.A. ... 80 A4 48 16N 100 47W
Granville, N.Y., U.S.A. ..... 85 C11 43 24N 73 16W
Granville, Ohio, U.S.A. .... 84 F2 40 4N 82 31W
Granville L., Canada ...... 71 B8 56 18N 100 30W
Graskop, S. Africa ....... 57 C5 24 56S 30 49 E
Grass ➡, Canada ........ 71 B9 56 3N 96 33W
Grass Range, U.S.A. ...... 76 C9 47 0N 109 0W
Grass River △, Canada .... 71 C8 54 40N 100 50W
Grass Valley, Calif., U.S.A. .. 78 F6 39 13N 121 4W
Grass Valley, Oreg., U.S.A. .. 76 D3 45 22N 120 47W
Grasse, France .......... 20 E7 43 38N 6 56 E
Grassflat, U.S.A. ........ 84 F6 41 0N 78 6W
Grasslands △, Canada ..... 71 D7 49 11N 107 38W
Grassy, Australia ........ 63 G3 40 3S 144 5 E
Graulhet, France ........ 20 E4 43 45N 1 59 E
Gravelbourg, Canada ..... 71 D7 49 50N 106 35W
's-Gravenhage, Neths. .... 15 B4 52 7N 4 17 E
Gravenhurst, Canada ..... 84 B5 44 52N 79 20W
Gravesend, Australia ..... 63 D5 29 35S 150 20 E
Gravesend, U.K. ........ 13 F8 51 26N 0 22 E
Gravois, Pointe-à-, Haiti ... 89 C5 18 15N 73 56W
Grayling, U.S.A. ........ 82 C3 44 40N 84 43W
Grays, U.K. ............ 13 F8 51 28N 0 21 E
Grays Harbor, U.S.A. ..... 76 C1 46 59N 124 1W
Grays L., U.S.A. ........ 76 E8 43 4N 111 26W
Grays River, U.S.A. ...... 78 D3 46 21N 123 37W
Graz, Austria ........... 16 E8 47 4N 15 27 E
Greasy L., Canada ....... 70 A4 62 55N 122 12W
Great Abaco I. = Abaco I.,
  Bahamas ............. 88 A4 26 25N 77 10W
Great Artesian Basin, Australia . 62 C3 23 0S 144 0 E
Great Australian Bight, Australia . 61 F5 33 30S 130 0 E
Great Bahama Bank, Bahamas . 88 B4 23 15N 78 0W
Great Barrier I., N.Z. ...... 59 G5 36 11S 175 25 E
Great Barrier Reef, Australia . 62 B4 18 0S 146 50 E
Great Barrier Reef △, Australia . 62 B4 20 0S 150 0 E
Great Barrington, U.S.A. ... 85 D11 42 12N 73 22W
Great Basalt Wall △, Australia . 62 B4 19 52S 145 43 E
Great Basin, U.S.A. ...... 76 G5 40 0N 117 0W
Great Basin △, U.S.A. ..... 76 G6 38 56N 114 14W
Great Bear ➡, Canada .... 68 B7 65 0N 124 0W
Great Bear L., Canada ..... 68 B7 65 30N 120 0W
Great Belt = Store Bælt, Denmark . 9 J14 55 20N 11 0 E
Great Bend, Kans., U.S.A. .. 80 F5 38 22N 98 46W
Great Bend, Pa., U.S.A. .... 85 E9 41 58N 75 45W
Great Blasket I., Ireland ... 10 D1 52 6N 10 32W
Great Britain, Europe ..... 6 E5 54 0N 2 15W
Great Camanoe, Br. Virgin Is. . 89 e 18 30N 64 35W
Great Codroy, Canada .... 73 C8 47 51N 59 16W
Great Dividing Ra., Australia . 62 C4 23 0S 146 0 E
Great Driffield = Driffield, U.K. . 12 C7 54 0N 0 26W
Great Exuma I., Bahamas ... 88 B4 23 30N 75 50W
Great Falls, U.S.A. ....... 76 C8 47 30N 111 17W
Great Fish = Groot Vis ➡,
  S. Africa ............. 56 E4 33 28S 27 5 E
Great Guana Cay, Bahamas . 88 B4 24 0N 76 20W
Great Inagua I., Bahamas ... 89 B5 21 0N 73 20W
Great Indian Desert = Thar
  Desert, India ......... 42 F5 28 0N 72 0 E
Great Karoo, S. Africa .... 56 E3 31 55S 21 0 E
Great Khingan Mts. = Da
  Hinggan Ling, China .... 33 B7 48 0N 121 0 E
Great Lake, Australia ..... 63 G4 41 50S 146 40 E
Great Lakes, N. Amer. ..... 66 E11 46 0N 84 0W
Great Malvern, U.K. ...... 13 E5 52 7N 2 18W
Great Miami ➡, U.S.A. .... 82 F3 39 20N 84 40W
Great Ormes Head, U.K. ... 12 D4 53 20N 3 52W

Great Ouse →, U.K. ... 12 E8 52 48N 0 21 E
Great Palm I., Australia ... 62 B4 18 45S 146 40 E
Great Pedro Bluff, Jamaica .... 88 a 17 51N 77 44W
Great Plains, N. Amer. ... 66 E9 47 0N 105 0W
Great Ruaha →, Tanzania ... 54 D4 7 56S 37 52 E
Great Sacandaga L., U.S.A. ... 85 C10 43 6N 74 16W
Great Saint Bernard Pass =
  Grand St-Bernard, Col du,
  Europe ... 20 D7 45 50N 7 10 E
Great Salt L., U.S.A. ... 76 F7 41 15N 112 40W
Great Salt Lake Desert, U.S.A. .. 76 F7 40 50N 113 30W
Great Salt Plains L., U.S.A. ... 81 G5 36 45N 98 8W
Great Sand Dunes △, U.S.A. ... 77 H11 37 48N 105 45W
Great Sandy △, Australia ... 63 D5 26 13S 153 2 E
Great Sandy Desert, Australia .. 60 D3 21 0S 124 0 E
Great Sangi = Sangihe, Pulau,
  Indonesia ... 37 D7 3 35N 125 30 E
Great Skellig, Ireland ... 10 E1 51 47N 10 33W
Great Slave L., Canada ... 70 A5 61 23N 115 38W
Great Smoky Mts. △, U.S.A. ... 83 H4 35 40N 83 40W
Great Snow Mt., Canada ... 70 B4 57 26N 124 0W
Great Stour = Stour →, U.K. ... 13 F9 51 18N 1 22 E
Great Victoria Desert, Australia . 61 E4 29 30S 126 30 E
Great Wall, Antarctica ... 5 C18 62 30S 58 0W
Great Wall, China ... 34 E5 38 30N 109 30 E
Great Whernside, U.K. ... 12 C6 54 10N 1 58W
Great Yarmouth, U.K. ... 13 E9 52 37N 1 44 E
Great Zab = Zāb al Kabīr →, Iraq .. 44 C4 36 1N 43 24 E
Great Zimbabwe, Zimbabwe ... 55 G3 20 16S 30 54 E
Greater Antilles, W. Indies ... 89 C5 17 40N 74 0W
Greater London □, U.K. ... 13 F7 51 31N 0 6W
Greater Manchester □, U.K. ... 12 D5 53 30N 2 15W
Greater St. Lucia Wetlands △,
  S. Africa ... 57 D5 28 6S 32 27 E
Greater Sudbury = Sudbury,
  Canada ... 72 C3 46 30N 81 0W
Greater Sunda Is., Indonesia ... 36 F4 7 0S 112 0 E
Greco, C., Cyprus ... 25 E13 34 57N 34 5 E
Gredos, Sierra de, Spain ... 21 B3 40 20N 5 0W
Greece, U.S.A. ... 84 C7 43 13N 77 41W
Greece ■, Europe ... 23 E9 40 0N 23 0 E
Greeley, Colo., U.S.A. ... 80 E2 40 25N 104 42W
Greeley, Nebr., U.S.A. ... 80 E5 41 33N 98 32W
Greem-Bell, Ostrov, Russia ... 28 A7 81 0N 62 0 E
Green →, Ky., U.S.A. ... 76 E2 43 9N 123 22W
Green →, Utah, U.S.A. ... 82 G2 37 54N 87 30W
Green B., U.S.A. ... 77 G9 38 11N 109 53W
Green Bay, U.S.A. ... 82 C2 45 0N 87 30W
Green C., Australia ... 82 C2 44 31N 88 0W
Green Cove Springs, U.S.A. ... 63 F5 37 13S 150 1 E
Green Lake, Canada ... 83 L5 29 59N 81 42W
Green Mts., U.S.A. ... 71 C7 54 17N 107 47W
Green River, Utah, U.S.A. ... 85 C12 43 45N 72 45W
Green River, Wyo., U.S.A. ... 77 G8 38 59N 110 10W
Green Valley, U.S.A. ... 76 F9 41 32N 109 28W
Greenbank, U.S.A. ... 77 L8 31 52N 110 56W
Greenbush, Mich., U.S.A. ... 78 B4 48 6N 122 34W
Greenbush, Minn., U.S.A. ... 84 B1 44 35N 83 19W
Greencastle, U.S.A. ... 80 A6 48 42N 96 11W
Greene, U.S.A. ... 82 F2 39 38N 86 52W
Greenfield, Calif., U.S.A. ... 85 D9 42 20N 75 46W
Greenfield, Calif., U.S.A. ... 78 J5 36 19N 121 15W
Greenfield, Ind., U.S.A. ... 78 K8 35 15N 119 0W
Greenfield, Iowa, U.S.A. ... 82 F3 39 47N 85 46W
Greenfield, Mass., U.S.A. ... 80 E7 41 18N 94 28W
Greenfield, Mo., U.S.A. ... 85 D12 42 35N 72 36W
Greenfield Park, Canada ... 81 G8 37 25N 93 51W
Greenland □, N. Amer. ... 85 A11 45 29N 73 29W
Greenland Sea, Arctic ... 4 C5 66 0N 45 0W
Greenock, U.K. ... 4 B7 73 0N 10 0W
Greenore, Ireland ... 11 F4 55 57N 4 46W
Greenore Pt., Ireland ... 10 B5 54 2N 6 8W
Greenough, Australia ... 10 D5 52 14N 6 19W
Greenough →, Australia ... 61 E1 28 58S 114 43 E
Greenough Pt., Canada ... 61 E1 28 51S 114 38 E
Greenport, U.S.A. ... 84 B3 44 58N 81 26W
Greensboro, Ga., U.S.A. ... 85 E12 41 6N 72 22W
Greensboro, N.C., U.S.A. ... 83 J4 33 35N 83 11W
Greensboro, Vt., U.S.A. ... 83 G6 36 4N 79 48W
Greensburg, Ind., U.S.A. ... 85 B12 44 36N 72 18W
Greensburg, Kans., U.S.A. ... 82 F3 39 20N 85 29W
Greensburg, Pa., U.S.A. ... 81 G5 37 36N 99 18W
Greenstone Pt., U.K. ... 84 F5 40 18N 79 33W
Greenvale, Australia ... 11 D3 57 55N 5 37W
Greenville, Ala., U.S.A. ... 62 B4 18 59S 145 7 E
Greenville, Calif., U.S.A. ... 83 K2 31 50N 86 38W
Greenville, Calif., U.S.A. ... 78 E6 40 8N 120 57W
Greenville, Maine, U.S.A. ... 83 C11 45 28N 69 35W
Greenville, Mich., U.S.A. ... 82 D3 43 11N 85 15W
Greenville, Miss., U.S.A. ... 81 J9 33 24N 91 4W
Greenville, Mo., U.S.A. ... 81 G9 37 8N 90 27W
Greenville, N.C., U.S.A. ... 83 H7 35 37N 77 23W
Greenville, N.H., U.S.A. ... 85 D13 42 46N 71 49W
Greenville, N.Y., U.S.A. ... 85 D10 42 25N 74 1W
Greenville, Ohio, U.S.A. ... 82 E3 40 6N 84 38W
Greenville, Pa., U.S.A. ... 84 E4 41 24N 80 23W
Greenville, S.C., U.S.A. ... 83 H4 34 51N 82 24W
Greenville, Tenn., U.S.A. ... 83 G4 36 13N 82 51W
Greenville, Tex., U.S.A. ... 81 J6 33 8N 96 7W
Greenwater Lake △, Canada .. 71 C8 52 32N 103 30W
Greenwich, Conn., U.S.A. ... 85 E11 41 2N 73 38W
Greenwich, N.Y., U.S.A. ... 85 C11 43 5N 73 30W
Greenwich, Ohio, U.S.A. ... 84 E2 41 2N 82 31W
Greenwich □, U.K. ... 13 F8 51 29N 0 1 E
Greenwood, Canada ... 70 D5 49 10N 118 40W
Greenwood, Ark., U.S.A. ... 81 H7 35 13N 94 16W
Greenwood, Ind., U.S.A. ... 82 F2 39 37N 86 7W
Greenwood, Miss., U.S.A. ... 81 J9 33 31N 90 11W
Greenwood, S.C., U.S.A. ... 83 H4 34 12N 82 10W
Greenwood, Mt., Australia ... 60 B5 13 48S 130 4 E
Gregory, U.S.A. ... 80 D5 43 14N 99 20W
Gregory △, Australia ... 60 C5 15 38S 131 15 E
Gregory →, Australia ... 62 B2 17 53S 139 17 E
Gregory, L., S. Austral., Australia 63 D2 28 55S 139 0 E
Gregory, L., W. Austral.,
  Australia ... 61 E2 25 38S 119 58 E
Gregory Downs, Australia ... 62 B2 18 35S 138 45 E
Gregory L., Australia ... 60 D4 20 0S 127 40 E
Gregory Ra., Queens., Australia . 62 B3 19 30S 143 40 E
Gregory Ra., W. Austral.,
  Australia ... 60 D3 21 20S 121 12 E
Greifswald, Germany ... 16 A7 54 5N 13 23 E
Greiz, Germany ... 16 C7 50 39N 12 10 E
Gremikha, Russia ... 18 A6 67 59N 39 47 E
Grenå, Denmark ... 9 H14 56 25N 10 53 E
Grenada ■, W. Indies ... 81 J10 33 47N 89 48W
Grenada, U.S.A. ... 89 D7 12 10N 61 40W
Grenadier I., U.S.A. ... 85 B8 44 3N 76 22W

Grenadines, The, St. Vincent ... 89 D7 12 40N 61 20W
Grenen, Denmark ... 9 H14 57 44N 10 40 E
Grenfell, Australia ... 63 E4 33 52S 148 8 E
Grenfell, Canada ... 71 C8 50 30N 102 56W
Grenoble, France ... 20 D6 45 12N 5 42 E
Grenville, C., Australia ... 62 A3 12 0S 143 13 E
Grenville Chan., Canada ... 70 C3 53 40N 129 46W
Gresham, U.S.A. ... 78 E4 45 30N 122 26W
Gresik, Indonesia ... 37 G15 7 13S 112 38 E
Gretna, U.K. ... 11 F5 55 0N 3 3W
Grevenmacher, Lux. ... 15 E6 49 41N 6 26 E
Grey →, Canada ... 73 C8 47 34N 57 6W
Grey →, N.Z. ... 59 K3 42 27S 171 12 E
Grey, C., Australia ... 62 A2 13 0S 136 35 E
Grey Ra., Australia ... 63 D3 27 0S 143 30 E
Greybull, U.S.A. ... 76 D9 44 30N 108 3W
Greymouth, N.Z. ... 59 K3 42 29S 171 13 E
Greystones, Ireland ... 10 C5 53 9N 6 5W
Greytown, N.Z. ... 59 J5 41 5S 175 29 E
Greytown, S. Africa ... 57 D5 29 1S 30 36 E
Gribbell I., Canada ... 70 C3 53 23N 129 0W
Gridley, U.S.A. ... 78 F5 39 22N 121 42W
Griekwastad, S. Africa ... 56 D3 28 49S 23 15 E
Griffin, U.S.A. ... 83 J3 33 15N 84 16W
Griffith, Australia ... 63 E4 34 18S 146 2 E
Griffith, Canada ... 84 A7 45 15N 77 10W
Griffith I., Canada ... 84 B4 44 50N 80 55W
Grimaylov = Hrymayliv, Ukraine . 17 D14 49 20N 26 5 E
Grimes, U.S.A. ... 78 F5 39 4N 121 54W
Grimsay, U.K. ... 11 D1 57 29N 7 14W
Grimsby, Canada ... 84 C5 43 12N 79 34W
Grimsby, U.K. ... 12 D7 53 34N 0 5W
Grímsey, Iceland ... 8 C5 66 33N 17 58W
Grimshaw, Canada ... 70 B5 56 10N 117 40W
Grimstad, Norway ... 9 G13 58 20N 8 35 E
Grindstone I., Canada ... 85 B8 44 43N 76 14W
Grinnell, U.S.A. ... 80 E8 41 45N 92 43W
Gris-Nez, C., France ... 20 A4 50 52N 1 35 E
Groais I., Canada ... 73 B8 50 55N 55 35W
Groblersdal, S. Africa ... 57 D4 25 15S 29 25 E
Grodno = Hrodna, Belarus ... 17 B12 53 42N 23 52 E
Grodzyanka = Hrodzyanka,
  Belarus ... 17 B15 53 31N 28 42 E
Groesbeck, U.S.A. ... 81 K6 30 48N 96 31W
Grójec, Poland ... 17 C11 51 50N 20 58 E
Grong, Norway ... 8 D15 64 25N 12 8 E
Groningen, Neths. ... 15 A6 53 15N 6 35 E
Groningen □, Neths. ... 15 A6 53 16N 6 40 E
Groom, U.S.A. ... 81 H4 35 12N 101 6W
Groot →, S. Africa ... 56 E3 33 45S 24 36 E
Groot Berg →, S. Africa ... 56 E2 32 47S 18 8 E
Groot-Brakrivier, S. Africa ... 56 E3 34 2S 22 18 E
Groot Karasberge, Namibia ... 56 D2 27 20S 18 40 E
Groot-Kei →, S. Africa ... 57 E4 32 41S 28 22 E
Groot Vis →, S. Africa ... 56 E4 33 28S 27 5 E
Grootdrink, S. Africa ... 56 D3 28 33S 21 42 E
Groote Eylandt, Australia ... 62 A2 14 0S 136 40 E
Grootfontein, Namibia ... 56 B2 19 31S 18 6 E
Grootlaagte →, Africa ... 56 C3 20 55S 21 27 E
Grootvloer →, S. Africa ... 56 E3 30 0S 20 40 E
Gros C., Canada ... 70 A6 61 59N 113 32W
Gros Islet, St. Lucia ... 89 f 14 5N 60 58W
Gros Morne △, Canada ... 73 C8 49 40N 57 50W
Gros Piton, St. Lucia ... 89 f 13 49N 61 5W
Gros Piton Pt., St. Lucia ... 89 f 13 49N 61 5W
Grossa, Pta., Spain ... 24 B8 39 6N 1 36 E
Grosser Arber, Germany ... 16 D7 49 6N 13 8 E
Grosseto, Italy ... 22 C4 42 46N 11 8 E
Grossglockner, Austria ... 16 E7 47 5N 12 40 E
Groswater B., Canada ... 73 B8 54 20N 57 40W
Groton, Conn., U.S.A. ... 85 E12 41 21N 72 5W
Groton, N.Y., U.S.A. ... 85 D8 42 36N 76 22W
Groton, S. Dak., U.S.A. ... 80 C5 45 27N 98 6W
Grouard Mission, Canada ... 70 B5 55 33N 116 9W
Groundhog →, Canada ... 72 C3 48 45N 82 58W
Grouw, Neths. ... 15 A5 53 5N 5 51 E
Grove City, U.S.A. ... 84 E4 41 10N 80 5W
Grove Hill, U.S.A. ... 83 K2 31 42N 87 47W
Groveland, U.S.A. ... 78 H6 37 50N 120 14W
Grover City, U.S.A. ... 79 K6 35 7N 120 37W
Groves, U.S.A. ... 81 L8 29 57N 93 54W
Groveton, U.S.A. ... 85 B13 44 36N 71 31W
Groznyy, Russia ... 19 F8 43 20N 45 45 E
Grudziądz, Poland ... 17 B10 53 30N 18 47 E
Gruinard B., U.K. ... 11 D3 57 56N 5 35W
Grundy Center, U.S.A. ... 80 D8 42 22N 92 47W
Gruver, U.S.A. ... 81 G4 36 16N 101 24W
Gryazi, Russia ... 18 D6 52 30N 39 58 E
Gryazovets, Russia ... 18 C7 58 50N 40 10 E
Gua, India ... 41 H14 22 18N 85 20 E
Gua Musang, Malaysia ... 39 K3 4 53N 101 58 E
Guacanayabo, G. de, Cuba ... 88 B4 20 40N 77 20W
Guachipas →, Argentina ... 94 B2 25 40S 65 30W
Guadalajara, Mexico ... 86 C4 20 40N 103 20W
Guadalajara, Spain ... 21 B4 40 37N 3 12W
Guadalcanal, Solomon Is. ... 64 H8 9 32S 160 12 E
Guadales, Argentina ... 94 C2 34 30S 67 55W
Guadalete →, Spain ... 21 D2 36 35N 6 13W
Guadalquivir →, Spain ... 21 D2 36 47N 6 22W
Guadalupe = Guadeloupe □,
  W. Indies ... 88 b 16 20N 61 40W
Guadalupe, Mexico ... 79 N10 32 4N 116 32W
Guadalupe, U.S.A. ... 79 L6 34 59N 120 33W
Guadalupe →, Mexico ... 79 N10 32 6N 116 51W
Guadalupe →, U.S.A. ... 81 L6 28 27N 96 47W
Guadalupe, Sierra de, Spain ... 21 C3 39 28N 5 30W
Guadalupe Bravos, Mexico ... 86 A3 31 20N 106 10W
Guadalupe I., Pac. Oc. ... 66 G8 29 0N 118 50W
Guadalupe Mts. △, U.S.A. ... 81 K2 31 40N 104 30W
Guadalupe Peak, U.S.A. ... 81 K2 31 50N 104 52W
Guadalupe y Calvo, Mexico ... 86 B3 26 6N 106 58W
Guadarrama, Sierra de, Spain .. 21 B4 41 0N 4 0W
Guadeloupe □, W. Indies ... 88 b 16 20N 61 40W
Guadeloupe Passage, W. Indies . 89 C7 16 50N 62 15W
Guadiana →, Portugal ... 21 D2 37 14N 7 22W
Guadix, Spain ... 21 D4 37 18N 3 11W
Guafo, Boca del, Chile ... 96 E2 43 35S 74 0W
Guaico, Trin. & Tob. ... 93 K15 10 35N 61 9W
Guainía →, Colombia ... 92 C5 2 1N 67 7W
Guaíra, Brazil ... 95 A5 24 5S 54 10W
Guaíra □, Paraguay ... 94 B4 25 45S 56 30W
Guaitecas, Is., Chile ... 96 E2 44 0S 74 30W
Guajará-Mirim, Brazil ... 92 F5 10 50S 65 20W
Guajira, Pen. de la, Colombia .. 92 A4 12 0N 72 0W
Gualán, Guatemala ... 88 C2 15 8N 89 22W
Gualeguay, Argentina ... 94 C4 33 10S 59 14W
Gualeguaychú, Argentina ... 94 C4 33 3S 59 31W

Gualequay →, Argentina ... 94 C4 33 19S 59 39W
Guam ☒, Pac. Oc. ... 64 F6 13 27N 144 45 E
Guamini, Argentina ... 94 D3 37 1S 62 28W
Guamúchil, Mexico ... 86 B3 25 25N 108 3W
Guana I., Br. Virgin Is. ... 89 e 18 30N 64 30W
Guanabacoa, Cuba ... 88 B3 23 8N 82 18W
Guanacaste, Cordillera del,
  Costa Rica ... 88 D2 10 57N 85 30W
Guanacaste △, Costa Rica ... 88 D2 10 40N 85 4W
Guanahani = San Salvador I.,
  Bahamas ... 89 B5 24 0N 74 40W
Guanajay, Cuba ... 88 B3 22 56N 82 42W
Guanajuato, Mexico ... 86 C4 21 0N 101 20W
Guanajuato □, Mexico ... 86 C4 20 40N 101 20W
Guandacol, Argentina ... 94 B2 29 30S 68 40W
Guane, Cuba ... 88 B3 22 10N 84 7W
Guangdong □, China ... 33 D6 23 0N 113 0 E
Guangling, China ... 34 E8 39 47N 114 22 E
Guangrao, China ... 35 F10 37 5N 118 25 E
Guangwu, China ... 34 F3 37 48N 105 57 E
Guangxi Zhuangzu Zizhiqu □,
  China ... 33 D5 24 0N 109 0 E
Guangzhou, China ... 33 D6 23 0N 113 0 E
Guánica, Puerto Rico ... 89 d 17 58N 66 55W
Guanipa →, Venezuela ... 92 B6 9 56N 62 26W
Guannan, China ... 35 G10 34 8N 119 21 E
Guantánamo, Cuba ... 89 B4 20 10N 75 14W
Guantánamo B., Cuba ... 89 C4 19 59N 75 10W
Guantao, China ... 34 F8 36 42N 115 25 E
Guanyun, China ... 35 G10 34 20N 119 18 E
Guápiles, Costa Rica ... 88 D3 10 10N 83 46W
Guapo B., Trin. & Tob. ... 93 K15 10 12N 61 41W
Guaporé, Brazil ... 95 B5 28 51S 51 54W
Guaporé →, Brazil ... 92 F5 11 55S 65 4W
Guaqui, Bolivia ... 92 G5 16 41S 68 54W
Guaramacal △, Venezuela ... 89 E5 9 13N 70 12W
Guarapari, Brazil ... 95 A7 20 40S 40 30W
Guarapuava, Brazil ... 95 B5 25 20S 51 30W
Guaratinguetá, Brazil ... 95 A6 22 49S 45 9W
Guaratuba, Brazil ... 95 B6 25 53S 48 38W
Guarda, Portugal ... 21 B2 40 32N 7 20W
Guardafui, C. = Asir, Ras,
  Somali Rep. ... 47 E5 11 55N 51 10 E
Guárico □, Venezuela ... 92 B5 8 40N 66 35W
Guarujá, Brazil ... 95 A6 24 2S 46 25W
Guarulhos, Brazil ... 95 A6 23 29S 46 33W
Guarus, Brazil ... 95 A7 21 44S 41 20W
Guasave, Mexico ... 86 B3 25 34N 108 27W
Guasdualito, Venezuela ... 92 B4 7 15N 70 44W
Guatemala, Guatemala ... 88 D1 14 40N 90 22W
Guatemala ■, Cent. Amer. ... 88 C1 15 40N 90 30W
Guatemala Trench, Pac. Oc. ... 66 H10 15 0N 95 0W
Guatopo △, Venezuela ... 89 D6 10 5N 66 30W
Guatuaro Pt., Trin. & Tob. ... 93 K16 10 19N 60 59W
Guaviare →, Colombia ... 92 C5 4 3N 67 44W
Guaxupé, Brazil ... 95 A6 21 10S 47 5W
Guayaguayare, Trin. & Tob. ... 93 K15 10 8N 61 2W
Guayama, Puerto Rico ... 89 d 17 59N 66 7W
Guayaquil, Ecuador ... 92 D3 2 15S 79 52W
Guayaquil, G. de, Ecuador ... 92 D2 3 10S 81 0W
Guaymas, Mexico ... 86 B2 27 59N 110 54W
Guba, Dem. Rep. of the Congo . 55 E2 10 38S 26 27 E
Gubkin, Russia ... 19 D6 51 17N 37 32 E
Gudbrandsdalen, Norway ... 9 F14 61 33N 10 10 E
Guddu Barrage, Pakistan ... 40 E6 28 30N 69 50 E
Gudur, India ... 40 M11 14 12N 79 55 E
Guecho = Getxo, Spain ... 21 A4 43 21N 2 59W
Guelmine = Goulimine, Morocco 50 C3 28 56N 10 0W
Guelph, Canada ... 84 C4 43 35N 80 20W
Guéret, France ... 20 C4 46 11N 1 51 E
Guernsey, U.S.A. ... 80 D2 42 19N 104 45W
Guernsey, U.K. ... 13 H5 49 26N 2 35W
Guerrero □, Mexico ... 87 D5 17 30N 100 0W
Güğer, Iran ... 45 D8 29 28N 56 27 E
Guhakolak, Tanjung, Indonesia . 37 G11 6 50S 105 14 E
Guia, Canary Is. ... 24 F4 28 8N 15 38W
Guia de Isora, Canary Is. ... 24 F3 28 12N 16 46W
Guia Lopes da Laguna, Brazil ... 95 A4 21 26S 56 7W
Guiana Highlands, S. Amer. ... 90 C4 5 10N 60 40W
Guidónia-Montecélio, Italy ... 22 C5 42 1N 12 45 E
Guijá, Mozam. ... 57 C5 24 27S 33 0 E
Guildford, U.K. ... 13 F7 51 14N 0 34W
Guilford, U.S.A. ... 85 E12 41 17N 72 41W
Guilin, China ... 33 D6 25 18N 110 15 E
Guillaume-Delisle, L., Canada .. 72 A4 56 15N 76 17W
Güimar, Canary Is. ... 24 F3 28 18N 16 24W
Guimarães, Portugal ... 21 B1 41 28N 8 24W
Guimaras □, Phil. ... 37 B6 10 35N 122 37 E
Guinda, U.S.A. ... 78 G4 38 50N 122 12W
Guinea, Africa ... 48 F4 8 0N 8 0 E
Guinea ■, W. Afr. ... 50 F3 10 20N 11 30W
Guinea, Gulf of, Atl. Oc. ... 49 F4 3 0N 2 30 E
Guinea-Bissau ■, Africa ... 50 F3 12 0N 15 0W
Güines, Cuba ... 88 B3 22 50N 82 0W
Guingamp, France ... 20 B2 48 34N 3 10W
Güiria, Venezuela ... 92 A6 10 32N 62 18W
Guiuan, Phil. ... 37 B7 11 5N 125 55 E
Guiyang, China ... 32 D5 26 32N 106 40 E
Guizhou □, China ... 32 D5 27 0N 107 0 E
Gujar Khan, Pakistan ... 42 C5 33 16N 73 19 E
Gujarat □, India ... 42 H4 23 20N 71 0 E
Gujranwala, Pakistan ... 42 C6 32 10N 74 12 E
Gujrat, Pakistan ... 42 C6 32 40N 74 2 E
Gulbarga, India ... 40 L10 17 20N 76 50 E
Gulbene, Latvia ... 9 H22 57 8N 26 52 E
Gulf, The = Persian Gulf, Asia .. 45 E6 27 0N 50 0 E
Gulf Islands △, U.S.A. ... 83 E2 30 10N 87 10W
Gulfport, U.S.A. ... 81 K10 30 22N 89 6W
Gulgong, Australia ... 63 E4 32 20S 149 49 E
Gulistan, Pakistan ... 42 D2 30 30N 66 35 E
Gull Lake, Canada ... 71 C7 50 10N 108 29W
Güllük, Turkey ... 23 F12 37 14N 27 35 E
Gulmarg, India ... 43 B6 34 3N 74 25 E
Gulshad, Kazakhstan ... 28 E8 46 45N 74 25 E
Gulu, Uganda ... 54 B3 2 48N 32 17 E
Gulwe, Tanzania ... 54 D4 6 30S 36 25 E
Gumal →, Pakistan ... 42 D3 31 40N 71 50 E
Gumbaz, Pakistan ... 42 D3 30 2N 69 0 E
Gumel, Nigeria ... 50 F7 12 39N 9 22 E
Gumla, India ... 43 H11 23 3N 84 33 E
Gumlu, Australia ... 62 B4 19 53S 147 41 E
Gumma □, Japan ... 31 F9 36 30N 138 20 E
Gumzai, Indonesia ... 37 F8 5 28S 134 42 E
Guna, India ... 42 G7 24 40N 77 19 E
Gunisao →, Canada ... 71 C9 53 56N 97 53W

Gunisao L., Canada ... 71 C9 53 33N 96 15W
Gunjyal, Pakistan ... 42 C4 32 20N 71 55 E
Gunnbjørn Fjeld, Greenland ... 4 C6 68 55N 29 47W
Gunnedah, Australia ... 63 E5 30 59S 150 15 E
Gunnewin, Australia ... 63 D4 25 59S 148 33 E
Gunnison, Colo., U.S.A. ... 77 G10 38 33N 106 56W
Gunnison, Utah, U.S.A. ... 76 G8 39 9N 111 49W
Gunnison →, U.S.A. ... 77 G9 39 4N 108 35W
Guntakal, India ... 40 M10 15 11N 77 27 E
Guntersville, U.S.A. ... 83 H2 34 21N 86 18W
Guntong, Malaysia ... 39 K3 4 36N 101 3 E
Guntur, India ... 41 L12 16 23N 80 30 E
Gunungapi, Indonesia ... 37 F7 6 45S 126 30 E
Gunungsitoli, Indonesia ... 36 D1 1 15N 97 30 E
Gunza, Angola ... 52 G2 10 50S 13 50 E
Guo He →, China ... 35 H9 32 59N 117 10 E
Guoyang, China ... 34 H9 33 32N 116 12 E
Gupis, Pakistan ... 43 A5 36 15N 73 20 E
Gurdaspur, India ... 42 C6 32 5N 75 31 E
Gurdon, U.S.A. ... 81 J8 33 55N 93 9W
Gurgaon, India ... 42 E7 28 27N 77 1 E
Gurgueia →, Brazil ... 93 E10 6 50S 43 24W
Gurha, India ... 42 G4 25 12N 71 39 E
Guri, Embalse de, Venezuela ... 92 B6 7 50N 62 52W
Gurig △, Australia ... 60 B5 11 36S 132 7 E
Gurkha, Nepal ... 43 E11 28 5N 84 40 E
Gurley, Australia ... 63 D4 29 45S 149 48 E
Gurnet Point, U.S.A. ... 85 D14 42 1N 70 34W
Guro, Mozam. ... 55 F3 17 26S 32 30 E
Gurué, Mozam. ... 55 F4 15 25S 36 58 E
Gurun, Malaysia ... 39 K3 5 49N 100 27 E
Gürün, Turkey ... 19 G6 38 43N 37 15 E
Gurupá, Brazil ... 93 D8 1 25S 51 35W
Gurupá, I. Grande de, Brazil ... 93 D8 1 25S 51 45W
Gurupi, Brazil ... 93 F9 11 43S 49 4W
Gurupi →, Brazil ... 93 D9 1 13S 46 6W
Guruwe, Zimbabwe ... 57 B5 16 40S 30 42 E
Guryev = Atyraū, Kazakhstan .. 19 E9 47 5N 52 0 E
Gusau, Nigeria ... 50 F7 12 12N 6 40 E
Gusev, Russia ... 9 J20 54 35N 22 10 E
Gushan, China ... 35 E12 39 50N 123 35 E
Gushgy, Turkmenistan ... 28 F7 35 20N 62 18 E
Gusinoozersk, Russia ... 29 D11 51 16N 106 27 E
Gustavus, U.S.A. ... 70 B1 58 25N 135 44W
Gustine, U.S.A. ... 78 H6 37 16N 121 0W
Güstrow, Germany ... 16 B7 53 47N 12 10 E
Gütersloh, Germany ... 16 C5 51 54N 8 24 E
Gutha, Australia ... 61 E2 28 58S 115 55 E
Guthalungra, Australia ... 62 B4 19 52S 147 50 E
Guthrie, Okla., U.S.A. ... 81 H6 35 53N 97 25W
Guthrie, Tex., U.S.A. ... 81 J4 33 37N 100 19W
Guttenberg, U.S.A. ... 80 D9 42 47N 91 6W
Gutu, Zimbabwe ... 57 B5 19 41S 31 9 E
Guwahati, India ... 41 F17 26 10N 91 45 E
Guy Fawkes River △, Australia . 63 D5 30 15S 152 20 E
Guyana ■, S. Amer. ... 92 C7 5 0N 59 0W
Guyane française = French
  Guiana ☒, S. Amer. ... 93 C8 4 0N 53 0W
Guyang, China ... 34 D6 41 0N 110 5 E
Guyenne, France ... 20 D4 44 30N 0 40 E
Guymon, U.S.A. ... 81 G4 36 41N 101 29W
Guyra, Australia ... 63 E5 30 15S 151 40 E
Guyuan, Hebei, China ... 34 D8 41 37N 115 40 E
Guyuan, Ningxia Huizu, China .. 34 G4 36 0N 106 20 E
Güzelyurt = Morphou, Cyprus .. 25 D11 35 12N 32 59 E
Guzhen, China ... 35 H9 33 22N 117 18 E
Guzmán, L. de, Mexico ... 86 A3 31 25N 107 25W
Gvardeysk, Russia ... 9 J19 54 39N 21 5 E
Gwa, Burma ... 41 L19 17 36N 94 34 E
Gwaai, Zimbabwe ... 55 F2 19 15S 27 45 E
Gwaai →, Zimbabwe ... 55 F2 17 59S 26 52 E
Gwabegar, Australia ... 63 E4 30 31S 149 0 E
Gwädar, Pakistan ... 40 G3 25 10N 62 18 E
Gwaii Haanas △, Canada ... 70 C2 52 21N 131 26W
Gwalior, India ... 42 F8 26 12N 78 10 E
Gwanda, Zimbabwe ... 55 G2 20 55S 29 0 E
Gwane, Dem. Rep. of the Congo 54 B2 4 45N 25 48 E
Gweebarra B., Ireland ... 10 B3 54 51N 8 23W
Gweedore, Ireland ... 10 A3 55 3N 8 13W
Gweru, Zimbabwe ... 55 F2 19 28S 29 45 E
Gwinn, U.S.A. ... 82 B2 46 19N 87 27W
Gwydir →, Australia ... 63 D4 29 27S 149 48 E
Gwynedd □, U.K. ... 12 E3 52 52N 4 10W
Gyandzha = Gäncä, Azerbaijan . 19 F8 40 45N 46 20 E
Gyaring Hu, China ... 32 C4 34 50N 97 40 E
Gydanskiy Poluostrov, Russia .. 28 C8 70 0N 78 0 E
Gympie, Australia ... 63 D5 26 11S 152 38 E
Gyöngyös, Hungary ... 17 E10 47 48N 19 56 E
Győr, Hungary ... 17 E9 47 41N 17 40 E
Gypsum Pt., Canada ... 70 A6 61 53N 114 35W
Gypsumville, Canada ... 71 C9 51 45N 98 40W
Gyula, Hungary ... 17 E11 46 38N 21 17 E
Gyumri, Armenia ... 19 F7 40 47N 43 50 E
Gyzylarbat, Turkmenistan ... 28 F6 39 4N 56 23 E
Gyzyletrek, Turkmenistan ... 45 B7 37 36N 54 46 E

## H

Ha 'Arava →, Israel ... 46 E4 30 50N 35 20 E
Ha Coi, Vietnam ... 38 B6 21 26N 107 46 E
Ha Dong, Vietnam ... 38 B5 20 58N 105 46 E
Ha Giang, Vietnam ... 38 A5 22 50N 104 59 E
Ha Karmel △, Israel ... 46 C4 32 45N 35 5 E
Ha Tien, Vietnam ... 39 G5 10 23N 104 29 E
Ha Tinh, Vietnam ... 38 C5 18 20N 105 54 E
Ha Trung, Vietnam ... 38 C5 19 58N 105 50 E
Ha Yaek Chalong, Thailand ... 39 a 7 50N 98 22 E
Haaksbergen, Neths. ... 15 B6 52 9N 6 45 E
Haapsalu, Estonia ... 9 G20 58 56N 23 30 E
Haarlem, Neths. ... 15 B4 52 23N 4 39 E
Haast →, N.Z. ... 59 K2 43 50S 169 2 E
Haast Bluff, Australia ... 60 D5 23 22S 132 0 E
Hab →, Pakistan ... 42 G3 24 53N 66 41 E
Hab Nadi Chauki, Pakistan ... 42 G2 25 0N 66 50 E
Habaswein, Kenya ... 54 B4 1 2N 39 30 E
Habay, Canada ... 70 B5 58 50N 118 44W
Ḩabbānīyah, Iraq ... 44 C4 33 17N 43 29 E
Haboro, Japan ... 30 B10 44 22N 141 42 E
Ḩabshān, U.A.E. ... 45 F7 23 50N 53 37 E
Hachijō-Jima, Japan ... 31 H9 33 5N 139 45 E
Hachinohe, Japan ... 30 D10 40 30N 141 29 E
Hachiōji, Japan ... 31 G9 35 40N 139 20 E
Hachŏn, N. Korea ... 35 D15 41 29N 129 2 E

Hackensack, U.S.A. .......... 85 F10 40 53N 74 3W
Hackettstown, U.S.A. ...... 85 F10 40 51N 74 50W
Hadali, Pakistan ........... 42 C5 32 16N 72 11 E
Hadarba, Ras, Sudan ...... 51 D13 22 4N 36 51 E
Hadarom □, Israel ......... 46 E4 31 0N 35 0 E
Hadd, Ra's al, Oman ....... 47 C6 22 35N 59 50 E
Haddington, U.K. .......... 11 F6 55 57N 2 47W
Hadejia, Nigeria .......... 50 F7 12 30N 10 5 E
Hadera, Israel ............ 46 C3 32 27N 34 55 E
Hadera, N. →, Israel ...... 46 C3 32 28N 34 52 E
Haderslev, Denmark ....... 9 J13 55 15N 9 30 E
Hadhramaut = Hadramawt,
  Yemen .................. 47 D4 15 30N 49 30 E
Hadiboh, Yemen ........... 47 E5 12 39N 54 2 E
Hadong, S. Korea ......... 35 G14 35 5N 127 44 E
Hadramawt, Yemen ........ 47 D4 15 30N 49 30 E
Hadraniyah, Iraq ......... 44 C4 35 38N 43 14 E
Hadrian's Wall, U.K. ...... 12 B5 55 0N 2 30W
Haeju, N. Korea .......... 35 E13 38 3N 125 45 E
Haenam, S. Korea ........ 35 G14 34 34N 126 35 E
Haenertsburg, S. Africa ... 57 C4 24 0S 29 50 E
Haerhpin = Harbin, China . 35 B14 45 48N 126 40 E
Hafar al Bāṭin, Si. Arabia . 44 D5 28 32N 45 52 E
Ḥafirat al 'Aydā, Si. Arabia 44 E3 26 26N 39 12 E
Ḥafit, Oman ............. 45 F7 23 59N 55 49 E
Hafizabad, Pakistan ...... 42 C5 32 5N 73 40 E
Haflong, India ........... 41 G18 25 10N 93 5 E
Hafnarfjörður, Iceland ..... 8 D3 64 4N 21 57W
Hafun, Ras, Somali Rep. ... 47 E5 10 29N 51 30 E
Hagalil, Israel ........... 46 C4 32 53N 35 18 E
Hagen, Germany .......... 16 C4 51 21N 7 27 E
Hagerman, U.S.A. ........ 81 J2 33 7N 104 20W
Hagerman Fossil Beds △, U.S.A. 76 E6 42 48N 114 57W
Hagerstown, U.S.A. ...... 82 F7 39 39N 77 43W
Hagersville, Canada ...... 84 D4 42 58N 80 3W
Hagfors, Sweden ......... 9 F15 60 3N 13 45 E
Hagi, Japan ............. 31 G5 34 30N 131 22 E
Hagolan, Syria .......... 46 C4 33 0N 35 45 E
Hagondange, France ...... 20 B7 49 16N 6 11 E
Hags Hd., Ireland ........ 10 D2 52 57N 9 28W
Hague, C. de la, France ... 20 B3 49 44N 1 56W
Hague, The = 's-Gravenhage,
  Neths. ................. 15 B4 52 7N 4 17 E
Haguenau, France ........ 20 B7 48 49N 7 47 E
Hai Duong, Vietnam ...... 38 B6 20 56N 106 19 E
Haicheng, China ......... 35 D12 40 50N 122 45 E
Haidar Khel, Afghan. ..... 42 C3 33 58N 68 38 E
Haidarâbâd = Hyderabad, India 40 L11 17 22N 78 29 E
Haidargarh, India ........ 43 F9 26 37N 81 22 E
Haifa = Ḥefa, Israel ...... 46 C4 32 46N 35 0 E
Haikou, China ........... 33 D6 20 1N 110 16 E
Ḥā'il, Si. Arabia ......... 44 E4 27 28N 41 45 E
Hailar, China ........... 33 B6 49 10N 119 38 E
Hailey, U.S.A. .......... 76 E6 43 31N 114 19W
Haileybury, Canada ...... 72 C4 47 30N 79 38W
Hailin, China ........... 35 B15 44 37N 129 30 E
Hailong, China .......... 35 C13 42 32N 125 40 E
Hailuoto, Finland ........ 8 D21 65 3N 24 45 E
Hainan □, China ......... 33 E5 19 0N 109 30 E
Hainaut □, Belgium ...... 15 D4 50 30N 4 0 E
Haines, Alaska, U.S.A. ... 70 B1 59 14N 135 26W
Haines, Oreg., U.S.A. .... 76 D5 44 55N 117 56W
Haines City, U.S.A. ...... 83 L5 28 7N 81 38W
Haines Junction, Canada .. 70 A1 60 45N 137 30W
Haiphong, Vietnam ....... 32 D5 20 47N 106 41 E
Haiti ■, W. Indies ....... 89 C5 19 0N 72 30W
Haiya, Sudan ........... 51 E13 18 20N 36 21 E
Haiyang, China .......... 35 F11 36 47N 121 9 E
Haiyuan, China .......... 34 F3 36 35N 105 52 E
Haizhou, China .......... 35 G10 34 37N 119 7 E
Haizhou Wan, China ...... 35 G10 34 50N 119 20 E
Hajdúböszörmény, Hungary 17 E11 47 40N 21 30 E
Hajipur, India .......... 43 G11 25 45N 85 13 E
Ḥājjī Muḥsin, Iraq ....... 44 C5 32 35N 45 29 E
Ḥājjīābād, Iran ......... 45 D7 28 19N 55 55 E
Ḥājjīābād-e Zarrīn, Iran .. 45 C7 33 9N 54 51 E
Hajnówka, Poland ........ 17 B12 52 47N 23 35 E
Hakansson, Mts., Dem. Rep. of
  the Congo .............. 55 D2 8 40S 25 45 E
Hakkâri, Turkey ......... 44 B4 37 34N 43 44 E
Hakken-Zan, Japan ...... 31 G7 34 10N 135 54 E
Hakodate, Japan ........ 30 D10 41 45N 140 44 E
Hakos, Namibia ......... 56 C2 23 13S 16 21 E
Haku-San, Japan ........ 31 F8 36 9N 136 46 E
Haku-San △, Japan ...... 31 F8 36 15N 136 45 E
Hakui, Japan ........... 31 F8 36 53N 136 47 E
Hala, Pakistan .......... 40 G6 25 43N 68 20 E
Halab, Syria ............ 44 B3 36 10N 37 15 E
Halabjah, Iraq .......... 44 C5 35 10N 45 58 E
Halaib, Sudan ........... 51 D13 22 12N 36 30 E
Hālat 'Ammār, Si. Arabia . 44 D3 29 10N 36 4 E
Halbā, Lebanon ......... 46 A5 34 34N 36 6 E
Halberstadt, Germany .... 16 C6 51 54N 11 3 E
Halcombe, N.Z. ......... 59 J5 40 8S 175 30 E
Halcon, Phil. ........... 37 B6 13 0N 121 30 E
Halde Fjäll = Haltiatunturi,
  Finland ................ 8 B19 69 17N 21 18 E
Halden, Norway ......... 9 G14 59 9N 11 23 E
Haldia, India ........... 41 H16 22 5N 88 3 E
Haldimand, Canada ...... 84 D5 42 59N 79 52W
Haldwani, India ......... 43 E8 29 31N 79 30 E
Hale →, Australia ....... 62 C2 24 56S 135 53 E
Halesowen, U.K. ........ 13 E5 52 27N 2 3W
Halesworth, U.K. ....... 13 E9 52 20N 1 31 E
Haleyville, U.S.A. ....... 83 H2 34 14N 87 37W
Halfmoon Bay, N.Z. ..... 59 M2 46 50S 168 5 E
Halfway →, Canada ..... 70 B4 56 12N 121 32W
Halia, India ............ 43 G10 24 50N 82 19 E
Haliburton, Canada ...... 84 A6 45 3N 78 30W
Halifax, Australia ....... 62 B4 18 32S 146 22 E
Halifax, Canada ......... 73 D7 44 38N 63 35W
Halifax, U.K. ........... 12 D6 53 43N 1 52W
Halifax B., Australia ..... 62 B4 18 50S 147 0 E
Halifax I., Namibia ...... 56 D2 26 38S 15 4 E
Halīl →, Iran ........... 45 E8 27 40N 58 30 E
Halkirk, U.K. ........... 11 C5 58 30N 3 29W
Hall Beach = Sanirajak, Canada 69 B11 68 46N 81 12W
Hall Pen., Canada ....... 69 B13 63 30N 66 0W
Hall Pt., Australia ....... 60 C3 15 40S 124 23 E
Halland, Sweden ........ 9 H15 57 8N 12 47 E
Halle, Belgium .......... 15 D4 50 44N 4 13 E
Halle, Germany ......... 16 C6 51 30N 11 56 E
Hällefors, Sweden ....... 9 G16 59 47N 14 31 E
Hallett, Australia ....... 63 E2 33 25S 138 55 E
Hallettsville, U.S.A. ..... 81 L6 29 27N 96 57W
Hallim, S. Korea ........ 35 H14 33 24N 126 15 E

Hallingdalselvi →, Norway . 9 F13 60 23N 9 35 E
Hallock, U.S.A. ......... 80 A6 48 47N 96 57W
Halls Creek, Australia .... 60 C4 18 16S 127 38 E
Hallsberg, Sweden ....... 9 G16 59 5N 15 7 E
Hallstead, U.S.A. ....... 85 E9 41 58N 75 45W
Halmahera, Indonesia .... 37 D7 0 40N 128 0 E
Halmstad, Sweden ....... 9 H15 56 41N 12 52 E
Hälsingborg = Helsingborg,
  Sweden ................ 9 H15 56 3N 12 42 E
Hälsingland, Sweden ..... 9 F16 61 40N 16 5 E
Halstead, U.K. .......... 13 F8 51 57N 0 40 E
Halti, Australia ......... 12 D5 53 22N 2 45W
Haltiatunturi, Finland ..... 8 B19 69 17N 21 18 E
Halton □, U.K. .......... 12 D5 53 22N 2 45W
Haltwhistle, U.K. ....... 12 C5 54 58N 2 26W
Hālūl, Qatar ............ 45 E7 25 40N 52 40 E
Halvad, India ........... 42 H4 23 1N 71 11 E
Halvān, Iran ............ 45 C8 33 57N 56 15 E
Ham Tan, Vietnam ....... 39 G6 10 40N 107 45 E
Ham Yen, Vietnam ....... 38 A5 22 4N 105 3 E
Hamab, Namibia ........ 56 D2 28 7S 19 16 E
Hamada, Japan .......... 31 G6 34 56N 132 4 E
Hamadān, Iran .......... 45 C6 34 52N 48 32 E
Hamadān □, Iran ........ 45 C6 35 0N 49 0 E
Hamāh, Syria ........... 44 C3 35 5N 36 40 E
Hamamatsu, Japan ...... 31 G8 34 45N 137 45 E
Hamar, Norway ......... 9 F14 60 48N 11 7 E
Hamâta, Gebel, Egypt .... 44 E2 24 17N 35 0 E
Hambantota, Sri Lanka ... 40 R12 6 10N 81 10 E
Hamber △, Canada ...... 70 C5 52 20N 118 0W
Hamburg, Germany ...... 16 B5 53 33N 9 59 E
Hamburg, Ark., U.S.A. ... 81 J9 33 14N 91 48W
Hamburg, N.Y., U.S.A. ... 84 D6 42 43N 78 50W
Hamburg, Pa., U.S.A. .... 85 F9 40 33N 75 59W
Ḥamḍ, W. al →, Si. Arabia 44 E3 24 55N 36 20 E
Hamden, U.S.A. ......... 85 E12 41 23N 72 54W
Häme, Finland .......... 9 F20 61 38N 24 10 E
Hämeenlinna, Finland .... 9 F21 61 0N 24 28 E
Hamelin Pool, Australia .. 61 E1 26 22S 114 20 E
Hameln, Germany ....... 16 B5 52 6N 9 21 E
Hamerkaz □, Israel ...... 46 C3 32 15N 34 55 E
Hamersley Ra., Australia . 60 D2 22 0S 117 45 E
Hamhung, N. Korea ...... 35 E14 39 54N 127 30 E
Hami, China ............ 32 B4 42 55N 93 25 E
Hamilton, Australia ...... 63 F3 37 45S 142 2 E
Hamilton, Canada ....... 84 C5 43 15N 79 50W
Hamilton, N.Z. .......... 59 G5 37 47S 175 19 E
Hamilton, U.K. .......... 11 F4 55 46N 4 2W
Hamilton, Ala., U.S.A. ... 83 H1 34 9N 87 59W
Hamilton, Mont., U.S.A. . 76 C6 46 15N 114 10W
Hamilton, N.Y., U.S.A. ... 85 D9 42 50N 75 33W
Hamilton, Ohio, U.S.A. .. 82 F3 39 24N 84 34W
Hamilton, Tex., U.S.A. ... 81 K5 31 42N 98 7W
Hamilton →, Australia .... 62 C2 23 30S 139 47 E
Hamilton, The →, Australia 63 D2 26 40S 135 19 E
Hamilton City, U.S.A. .... 78 F4 39 45N 122 1W
Hamilton I., Australia .... 62 J6 20 21S 148 56 E
Hamilton Inlet, Canada ... 73 B8 54 0N 57 30W
Hamilton Mt., U.S.A. .... 85 C10 43 25N 74 22W
Hamina, Finland ........ 9 F22 60 34N 27 12 E
Hamirpur, H.P., India .... 42 D7 31 41N 76 31 E
Hamirpur, Ut. P., India ... 43 G9 25 57N 80 9 E
Hamley Bridge, Australia . 63 E2 34 17S 138 35 E
Hamlin, N.Y., U.S.A. ..... 84 C7 43 17N 77 55W
Hamlin, Tex., U.S.A. ..... 81 J4 32 53N 100 8W
Hamm, Germany ........ 16 C4 51 40N 7 50 E
Hammār, Hawr al, Iraq ... 44 D5 30 50N 47 10 E
Hammerfest, Norway ..... 8 A20 70 39N 23 41 E
Hammond, Ind., U.S.A. .. 82 E2 41 38N 87 30W
Hammond, La., U.S.A. ... 81 K9 30 30N 90 28W
Hammond, N.Y., U.S.A. .. 85 B9 44 27N 75 42W
Hammondsport, U.S.A. ... 84 D7 42 25N 77 13W
Hammonton, U.S.A. ..... 82 F8 39 39N 74 48W
Hampden, N.Z. ......... 59 L3 45 18S 170 50 E
Hampshire □, U.K. ...... 13 F6 51 7N 1 23W
Hampshire Downs, U.K. .. 13 F6 51 15N 1 10W
Hampton, N.B., Canada .. 73 C6 45 32N 65 51W
Hampton, Ont., Canada .. 84 C6 43 58N 78 45W
Hampton, Ark., U.S.A. ... 81 J8 33 32N 92 28W
Hampton, Iowa, U.S.A. .. 80 D8 42 45N 93 13W
Hampton, N.H., U.S.A. .. 85 D14 42 57N 70 50W
Hampton, S.C., U.S.A. ... 83 J5 32 52N 81 7W
Hampton, Va., U.S.A. .... 82 G7 37 2N 76 21W
Hampton Bays, U.S.A. ... 85 F12 40 53N 72 30W
Hampton Tableland, Australia 61 F4 32 0S 127 0 E
Hamyang, S. Korea ...... 35 G14 35 32N 127 42 E
Han Pijesak, Bos.-H. ..... 23 B8 44 5N 18 57 E
Hanak, S. Arabia ........ 44 E3 25 32N 37 0 E
Hanamaki, Japan ........ 30 E10 39 23N 141 7 E
Hanang, Tanzania ....... 54 C4 4 30S 35 25 E
Hanau, Germany ........ 16 C5 50 7N 8 56 E
Hanbogd = Ihbulag, Mongolia 34 C4 43 11N 107 10 E
Hancheng, China ........ 34 G6 35 31N 110 25 E
Hancock, Mich., U.S.A. .. 80 B10 47 8N 88 35W
Hancock, N.Y., U.S.A. ... 85 E9 41 57N 75 17W
Handa, Japan ........... 31 G8 34 53N 136 55 E
Handan, China .......... 34 F8 36 35N 114 28 E
Handeni, Tanzania ...... 54 D4 5 25S 38 2 E
Handwara, India ........ 43 B6 34 21N 74 20 E
Hanegev, Israel ......... 46 E4 30 50N 35 0 E
Hanford, U.S.A. ......... 78 J7 36 20N 119 39W
Hanford Reach △, U.S.A. . 76 C4 46 40N 119 28W
Hang Chat, Thailand ..... 38 C2 18 20N 99 21 E
Hang Dong, Thailand .... 38 C2 18 41N 98 55 E
Hangang →, S. Korea .... 35 F14 37 50N 126 30 E
Hangayn Nuruu, Mongolia 32 B4 47 30N 99 0 E
Hangchou = Hangzhou, China 33 C7 30 18N 120 11 E
Hanggin Houqi, China .... 34 D4 40 58N 107 4 E
Hanggin Qi, China ...... 34 E5 39 52N 108 50 E
Hangu, China ........... 35 E9 39 18N 117 53 E
Hangzhou, China ........ 33 C7 30 18N 120 11 E
Hangzhou Wan, China ... 33 C7 30 15N 120 45 E
Hanhongor, Mongolia .... 34 C3 43 55N 104 28 E
Ḥanīdh, Si. Arabia ....... 45 E6 26 35N 48 38 E
Hanish, Yemen ......... 47 E3 13 45N 42 46 E
Hankinson, U.S.A. ....... 80 B6 46 4N 96 54W
Hankö, Finland ......... 9 G20 59 50N 22 57 E
Hanksville, U.S.A. ....... 77 G8 38 22N 110 43W
Hanle, India ............ 43 C8 32 42N 79 4 E
Hanmer Springs, N.Z. .... 59 K4 42 32S 172 50 E
Hann →, Australia ....... 60 C4 17 26S 126 17 E
Hann, Mt., Australia ..... 60 C4 15 45S 126 0 E
Hanna, Canada ......... 70 C6 51 40N 111 54W
Hannah B., Canada ...... 72 B4 51 40N 80 0W
Hannibal, Mo., U.S.A. ... 80 F9 39 42N 91 22W
Hannibal, N.Y., U.S.A. ... 85 C8 43 19N 76 35W

Hannover, Germany ...... 16 B5 52 22N 9 46 E
Hanoi, Vietnam ......... 32 D5 21 5N 105 55 E
Hanover = Hannover, Germany 16 B5 52 22N 9 46 E
Hanover, Canada ........ 84 B3 44 9N 81 2W
Hanover, S. Africa ....... 56 E3 31 4S 24 29 E
Hanover, N.H., U.S.A. ... 85 C12 43 42N 72 17W
Hanover, Ohio, U.S.A. ... 84 F2 40 4N 82 16W
Hanover, Pa., U.S.A. .... 82 F7 39 48N 76 59W
Hanover, I., Chile ....... 96 G2 51 0S 74 50W
Hans Lollik I., U.S. Virgin Is. 89 e 18 24N 64 53W
Hansdiha, India ........ 43 G12 24 36N 87 5 E
Hansi, India ............ 42 E6 29 10N 75 57 E
Hanson, L., Australia .... 63 E2 31 0S 136 15 E
Hantsavichy, Belarus .... 17 B14 52 49N 26 30 E
Hanumangarh, India ..... 42 E6 29 35N 74 19 E
Hanzhong, China ....... 34 H4 33 10N 107 1 E
Hanzhuang, China ...... 35 G9 34 33N 117 23 E
Haora, India ........... 43 H13 22 37N 88 20 E
Happy, U.S.A. .......... 81 H4 34 45N 101 52W
Happy Camp, U.S.A. .... 76 F2 41 48N 123 23W
Happy Valley-Goose Bay, Canada 73 B7 53 15N 60 20W
Hapsu, N. Korea ........ 35 D15 41 13N 128 51 E
Hapur, India ........... 42 E7 28 45N 77 45 E
Ḥaql, Si. Arabia ........ 46 F3 29 10N 34 58 E
Har, Indonesia ......... 37 F8 5 16S 133 14 E
Har-Ayrag, Mongolia .... 34 B5 45 47N 109 16 E
Har Hu, China .......... 32 C4 38 20N 97 38 E
Har Us Nuur, Mongolia .. 32 B4 48 0N 92 0 E
Har Yehuda, Israel ...... 46 D3 31 35N 34 57 E
Ḥaraḍ, Si. Arabia ....... 47 C4 24 22N 49 0 E
Haranomachi, Japan ..... 30 F10 37 38N 140 58 E
Harare, Zimbabwe ...... 55 F3 17 43S 31 2 E
Harbin, China .......... 35 B14 45 48N 126 40 E
Harbor Beach, U.S.A. ... 84 C2 43 51N 82 39W
Harbour Breton, Canada . 73 C8 47 29N 55 50W
Harbour Deep, Canada .. 73 B8 50 25N 56 32W
Harda, India ........... 42 H7 22 27N 77 5 E
Hardangerfjorden, Norway 9 F12 60 5N 6 0 E
Hardangervidda, Norway . 9 F12 60 7N 7 20 E
Hardap △, Namibia ..... 56 C2 24 29S 17 45 E
Hardap Dam, Namibia ... 56 C2 24 32S 17 50 E
Hardenberg, Neths. ..... 15 B6 52 34N 6 37 E
Harderwijk, Neths. ...... 15 B5 52 21N 5 38 E
Hardey →, Australia ..... 60 D2 22 45S 116 8 E
Hardin, U.S.A. ......... 76 D10 45 44N 107 37W
Harding, S. Africa ...... 57 E4 30 35S 29 55 E
Harding Ra., Australia ... 60 C3 16 17S 124 55 E
Hardisty, Canada ....... 70 C6 52 40N 111 18W
Hardoi, India .......... 43 F9 27 26N 80 6 E
Hardwar = Haridwar, India 42 E8 29 58N 78 9 E
Hardwick, U.S.A. ....... 85 B12 44 30N 72 22W
Hardy, Pen., Chile ...... 96 H3 55 30S 68 20W
Hardy, Pte., St. Lucia ... 89 f 14 6N 60 56W
Hare B., Canada ....... 73 B8 51 15N 55 45W
Hareid, Norway ........ 9 E12 62 22N 6 1 E
Harer, Ethiopia ........ 47 F3 9 20N 42 8 E
Hargeisa, Somali Rep. ... 47 F3 9 30N 44 2 E
Hari →, Indonesia ...... 36 E2 1 16S 104 5 E
Haria, Canary Is. ....... 24 E6 29 8N 13 32W
Haridwar, India ........ 42 E8 29 58N 78 9 E
Harim, Jabal al, Oman ... 45 E8 25 58N 56 14 E
Haringhata →, Bangla. ... 41 J16 22 0N 89 58 E
Harirūd →, Asia ........ 40 A2 37 24N 60 38 E
Härjedalen, Sweden ..... 9 E15 62 22N 13 5 E
Harlan, Iowa, U.S.A. .... 80 E7 41 39N 95 19W
Harlan, Ky., U.S.A. ..... 83 G4 36 51N 83 19W
Harlech, U.K. .......... 12 E3 52 52N 4 6W
Harlem, U.S.A. ......... 76 B9 48 32N 108 47W
Harlingen, Neths. ...... 15 A5 53 11N 5 25 E
Harlingen, U.S.A. ...... 81 M6 26 12N 97 42W
Harlow, U.K. ........... 13 F8 51 46N 0 8 E
Harlowton, U.S.A. ...... 76 C9 46 26N 109 50W
Harnai, Pakistan ....... 42 D2 30 6N 67 56 E
Harney Basin, U.S.A. ... 76 E4 43 30N 119 0W
Harney L., U.S.A. ....... 76 E4 43 14N 119 8W
Harney Peak, U.S.A. .... 80 D3 43 52N 103 32W
Härnösand, Sweden ..... 9 E17 62 38N 17 55 E
Haroldswick, U.K. ...... 11 A8 60 48N 0 50W
Harp L., Canada ........ 73 A7 55 5N 61 50W
Harper, Liberia ........ 50 H4 4 25N 7 43W
Harrai, India .......... 43 H8 22 37N 79 13 E
Harrand, Pakistan ...... 42 E4 29 28N 70 3 E
Harricana →, Canada ... 72 B4 50 56N 79 32W
Harriman, U.S.A. ....... 83 H3 35 56N 84 33W
Harrington Harbour, Canada 73 B8 50 31N 59 30W
Harris, U.K. ........... 11 D2 57 50N 6 55W
Harris, L., Australia .... 63 E2 31 10S 135 10 E
Harris, Sd. of, U.K. ..... 11 D1 57 44N 7 6W
Harris Pt., Canada ...... 84 C2 43 6N 82 9W
Harrisburg, Ill., U.S.A. .. 81 G10 37 44N 88 32W
Harrisburg, Nebr., U.S.A. 80 E3 41 33N 103 44W
Harrisburg, Pa., U.S.A. . 84 F8 40 16N 76 53W
Harrismith, S. Africa .... 57 D4 28 15S 29 8 E
Harrison, Ark., U.S.A. ... 81 G8 36 14N 93 7W
Harrison, Maine, U.S.A. . 85 B14 44 7N 70 39W
Harrison, Nebr., U.S.A. .. 80 D3 42 41N 103 53W
Harrison, C., Canada .... 73 B8 54 55N 57 55W
Harrison L., Canada ..... 70 D4 49 33N 121 50W
Harrisonburg, U.S.A. .... 82 F6 38 27N 78 52W
Harrisonville, U.S.A. .... 80 F7 38 39N 94 21W
Harriston, Canada ...... 84 C4 43 57N 80 53W
Harrisville, Mich., U.S.A. 84 B1 44 39N 83 17W
Harrisville, N.Y., U.S.A. . 85 B9 44 9N 75 19W
Harrisville, Pa., U.S.A. .. 84 E5 41 8N 80 0W
Harrodsburg, U.S.A. .... 82 G3 37 46N 84 51W
Harrogate, U.K. ........ 12 C6 54 0N 1 33W
Harrow □, U.K. ........ 13 F7 51 35N 0 21W
Harrowsmith, Canada ... 85 B8 44 24N 76 40W
Harry S. Truman Reservoir,
  U.S.A. ................. 80 F7 38 16N 93 24W
Harsin, Iran ........... 44 C5 34 18N 47 33 E
Harstad, Norway ....... 8 B17 68 48N 16 30 E
Harsud, India .......... 42 H7 22 6N 76 44 E
Hart, U.S.A. ........... 82 D2 43 42N 86 22W
Hart, L., Australia ...... 63 E2 31 10S 136 25 E
Hartbees →, S. Africa ... 56 D3 28 45S 20 32 E
Hartford, Conn., U.S.A. .. 85 E12 41 46N 72 41W
Hartford, Ky., U.S.A. .... 82 G2 37 27N 86 55W
Hartford, S. Dak., U.S.A. 80 D6 43 38N 96 57W
Hartford, Wis., U.S.A. ... 80 D10 43 19N 88 22W
Hartford City, U.S.A. .... 82 E3 40 27N 85 22W
Hartland, Canada ....... 73 C6 46 20N 67 32W
Hartland Pt., U.K. ...... 13 F3 51 1N 4 32W
Hartlepool, U.K. ....... 12 C6 54 42N 1 13W
Hartley Bay, Canada .... 70 C3 53 25N 129 15W
Hartmannberge, Namibia 56 B1 17 0S 13 0 E

Hartney, Canada ........ 71 D8 49 30N 100 35W
Harts →, S. Africa ...... 56 D3 28 24S 24 17 E
Hartselle, U.S.A. ....... 83 H2 34 27N 86 56W
Hartshorne, U.S.A. ..... 81 H7 34 51N 95 34W
Hartstown, U.S.A. ...... 84 E4 41 33N 80 23W
Hartsville, U.S.A. ...... 83 H5 34 23N 80 4W
Hartswater, S. Africa ... 56 D3 27 34S 24 43 E
Hartwell, U.S.A. ....... 83 H4 34 21N 82 56W
Harunabad, Pakistan .... 42 E5 29 35N 73 8 E
Harvand, Iran .......... 45 D7 28 25N 55 43 E
Harvey, Australia ....... 61 F2 33 5S 115 54 E
Harvey, Ill., U.S.A. ..... 82 E2 41 36N 87 50W
Harvey, N. Dak., U.S.A. . 80 B5 47 47N 99 56W
Harwich, U.K. .......... 13 F9 51 56N 1 17 E
Haryana □, India ....... 42 E7 29 0N 76 10 E
Haryn →, Belarus ....... 17 B14 52 7N 27 17 E
Harz, Germany ......... 16 C6 51 38N 10 44 E
Hasa □, Si. Arabia ...... 45 E6 25 50N 49 0 E
Hasanābād, Iran ........ 45 C7 32 8N 52 44 E
Ḥasb, W. →, Iraq ....... 44 D5 31 45N 44 17 E
Hasdo →, India ......... 43 J10 21 44N 82 44 E
Hashimoto, Japan ...... 31 G7 34 19N 135 37 E
Hashtjerd, Iran ........ 45 C6 35 52N 50 40 E
Haskell, U.S.A. ........ 81 J5 33 10N 99 44W
Haslemere, U.K. ....... 13 F7 51 5N 0 43W
Hasselt, Belgium ....... 15 D5 50 56N 5 21 E
Hassi Messaoud, Algeria 50 B7 31 51N 6 1 E
Hässleholm, Sweden .... 9 H15 56 10N 13 46 E
Hastings, N.Z. ......... 59 H6 39 39S 176 52 E
Hastings, U.K. ......... 13 G8 50 51N 0 35 E
Hastings, Mich., U.S.A. . 82 D3 42 39N 85 17W
Hastings, Minn., U.S.A. . 80 C8 44 44N 92 51W
Hastings, Nebr., U.S.A. . 80 E5 40 35N 98 23W
Hastings Ra., Australia .. 63 E5 31 15S 152 14 E
Hat Yai, Thailand ...... 39 J3 7 1N 100 27 E
Hatanbulag = Ergel, Mongolia 34 C5 43 8N 109 5 E
Hatay = Antalya, Turkey . 19 G5 36 52N 30 45 E
Hatch, U.S.A. .......... 77 K10 32 40N 107 9W
Hatchet L., Canada ..... 71 B8 58 36N 103 40W
Hateruma-Shima, Japan . 31 M1 24 3N 123 47 E
Hatfield P.O., Australia .. 63 E3 33 54S 143 49 E
Hatgal, Mongolia ....... 32 A5 50 26N 100 9 E
Hathras, India ......... 42 F8 27 36N 78 6 E
Hatia, Bangla. ......... 41 H17 22 30N 91 5 E
Hato Mayor, Dom. Rep. . 89 C6 18 46N 69 15W
Hatta, India ........... 43 G8 24 7N 79 36 E
Hattah, Australia ....... 63 E3 34 48S 142 17 E
Hatteras, C., U.S.A. ..... 83 H8 35 14N 75 32W
Hattiesburg, U.S.A. ..... 81 K10 31 20N 89 17W
Hatvan, Hungary ....... 17 E10 47 40N 19 45 E
Hau Bon = Cheo Reo, Vietnam 36 B3 13 25N 108 28 E
Hau Duc, Vietnam ...... 38 E7 15 20N 108 13 E
Haugesund, Norway .... 9 G11 59 23N 5 13 E
Haukipudas, Finland .... 8 D21 65 12N 25 20 E
Haultain →, Canada .... 71 B7 55 51N 106 46W
Hauraki G., N.Z. ....... 59 G5 36 35S 175 5 E
Haut Atlas, Morocco .... 50 B4 32 30N 5 0W
Hautes Fagnes = Hohe Venn,
  Belgium ............... 15 D6 50 30N 6 5 E
Hauts Plateaux, Algeria . 48 C4 35 0N 1 0 E
Havana = La Habana, Cuba 88 B3 23 8N 82 22W
Havana, U.S.A. ........ 80 E9 40 18N 90 4W
Havant, U.K. .......... 13 G7 50 51N 0 58W
Havasor = Kiĝzi, Turkey . 44 B4 38 18N 43 25 E
Havasu, L., U.S.A. ..... 79 L12 34 18N 114 28W
Havel →, Germany ..... 16 B7 52 50N 12 3 E
Havelian, Pakistan ..... 42 B5 34 2N 73 10 E
Havelock, Canada ...... 84 B7 44 26N 77 53W
Havelock, N.Z. ........ 59 J4 41 17S 173 48 E
Havelock, U.S.A. ...... 83 H7 34 53N 76 54W
Haverfordwest, U.K. ... 13 F3 51 48N 4 58W
Haverhill, U.K. ........ 13 E8 52 5N 0 28 E
Haverhill, U.S.A. ...... 85 D13 42 47N 71 5W
Haverstraw, U.S.A. .... 85 E11 41 12N 73 58W
Havirga, Mongolia ..... 34 B7 45 41N 113 5 E
Havířov, Czech Rep. ... 17 D10 49 46N 18 20 E
Havlíčkův Brod, Czech Rep. 16 D8 49 36N 15 33 E
Havre, U.S.A. ......... 76 B9 48 33N 109 41W
Havre-Aubert, Canada .. 73 C7 47 12N 61 56W
Havre-St.-Pierre, Canada 73 B7 50 18N 63 33W
Haw →, U.S.A. ........ 83 H6 35 36N 79 3W
Hawaii □, U.S.A. ...... 74 H16 19 30N 156 30W
Hawaii I., Pac. Oc. ..... 74 H17 20 30N 156 0W
Hawaiian Is., Pac. Oc. .. 74 H17 20 30N 156 0W
Hawaiian Ridge, Pac. Oc. 65 E11 24 0N 165 0W
Hawarden, U.S.A. ...... 80 D6 43 0N 96 29W
Hawea, L., N.Z. ........ 59 L2 44 28S 169 19 E
Hawera, N.Z. .......... 59 H5 39 35S 174 19 E
Hawick, U.K. .......... 11 F6 55 26N 2 47W
Hawk Junction, Canada . 72 C3 48 5N 84 38W
Hawke B., N.Z. ........ 59 H6 39 25S 177 20 E
Hawker, Australia ...... 63 E2 31 59S 138 22 E
Hawkesbury, Canada ... 72 C5 45 37N 74 37W
Hawkesbury I., Canada . 70 C3 53 37N 129 3W
Hawkesbury Pt., Australia 62 A1 11 55S 134 5 E
Hawkinsville, U.S.A. .... 83 J4 32 17N 83 28W
Hawley, Minn., U.S.A. .. 80 B6 46 53N 96 19W
Hawley, Pa., U.S.A. .... 85 E9 41 28N 75 11W
Ḥawrān, W. →, Iraq .... 44 C4 33 58N 42 34 E
Hawsh Mūssá, Lebanon . 46 B4 33 45N 35 55 E
Hawthorne, U.S.A. ..... 76 G4 38 32N 118 38W
Hay, Australia ......... 63 E3 34 30S 144 51 E
Hay →, Australia ...... 62 C2 24 50S 138 0 E
Hay →, Canada ........ 70 A5 60 50N 116 26W
Hay, C., Canada ....... 60 B4 14 5S 129 29 E
Hay I., Canada ........ 84 B4 44 53N 80 58W
Hay L., Canada ........ 70 B5 58 50N 118 50W
Hay-on-Wye, U.K. ..... 13 E4 52 5N 3 8W
Hay River, Canada ..... 70 A5 60 51N 115 44W
Hay Springs, U.S.A. .... 80 D3 42 41N 102 41W
Haya = Tehoru, Indonesia 37 E7 3 23S 129 30 E
Hayachine-San, Japan .. 30 E10 39 34N 141 29 E
Hayden, U.S.A. ........ 76 F10 40 30N 107 16W
Hayes, U.S.A. ......... 80 C4 44 23N 101 1W
Hayes →, Canada ...... 72 A1 57 3N 92 12W
Hayes Creek, Australia .. 60 B5 13 43S 131 22 E
Hayle, U.K. ........... 13 G2 50 11N 5 26W
Hayling I., U.K. ........ 13 G7 50 48N 0 59W
Haymen I., Australia ... 62 J6 20 3S 148 52 E
Hayrabolu, Turkey ..... 23 D12 41 12N 27 5 E
Hays, Canada ......... 70 C6 50 6N 111 48W
Hays, U.S.A. .......... 80 F5 38 53N 99 20W
Haysyn, Ukraine ....... 17 D15 48 57N 29 25 E
Hayvoron, Ukraine ..... 17 D15 48 22N 29 52 E
Hayward, Calif., U.S.A. . 78 H4 37 40N 122 5W
Hayward, Wis., U.S.A. .. 80 B9 46 1N 91 29W
Haywards Heath, U.K. .. 13 G7 51 0N 0 5W

Hazafon □, *Israel* . . . . . . . . . . . . . . 46 C4  32 40N  35 20 E
Hazārān, Kūh-e, *Iran* . . . . . . . . . 45 D8  29 35N  57 20 E
Hazard, *U.S.A.* . . . . . . . . . . . . . . . 82 G4  37 15N  83 12W
Hazaribag, *India* . . . . . . . . . . . . . 43 H11  23 58N  85 26 E
Hazaribag Road, *India* . . . . . . . 43 G11  24 12N  85 57 E
Hazelton, *Canada* . . . . . . . . . . . . 70 B3  55 20N 127 42W
Hazelton, *U.S.A.* . . . . . . . . . . . . . 80 B4  46 29N 100 17W
Hazen, *U.S.A.* . . . . . . . . . . . . . . . . 80 B4  47 18N 101 38W
Hazlehurst, Ga., *U.S.A.* . . . . . . 83 K4  31 52N  82 36W
Hazlehurst, Miss., *U.S.A.* . . . . 81 K9  31 52N  90 24W
Hazlet, *U.S.A.* . . . . . . . . . . . . . . . 85 F10  40 25N  74 12W
Hazleton, *U.S.A.* . . . . . . . . . . . . . 85 F9  40 57N  75 59W
Hazlett, L., *Australia* . . . . . . . . 60 D4  21 30S 128 48 E
Hazro, *Turkey* . . . . . . . . . . . . . . . 44 B4  38 15N  40 47 E
Head of Bight, *Australia* . . . . . 61 F5  31 30S 131 25 E
Headlands, *Zimbabwe* . . . . . . . 55 F3  18 15S  32  2 E
Healdsburg, *U.S.A.* . . . . . . . . . . 78 G4  38 37N 122 52W
Healdton, *U.S.A.* . . . . . . . . . . . . 81 H6  34 14N  97 29W
Healesville, *Australia* . . . . . . . . 63 F4  37 35S 145 30 E
Heany Junction, *Zimbabwe* . . 55 C4  20 6S  28 54 E
Heard I., *Ind. Oc.* . . . . . . . . . . . . 3 G13  53 0S  74  0 E
Hearne, *U.S.A.* . . . . . . . . . . . . . . 81 K6  30 53N  96 36W
Hearst, *Canada* . . . . . . . . . . . . . . 72 C3  49 40N  83 41W
Heart →, *U.S.A.* . . . . . . . . . . . . . 80 B4  46 46N 100 50W
Heart's Content, *Canada* . . . . . 73 C9  47 54N  53 27W
Heath, Pte., *Canada* . . . . . . . . . 71 B9  49 8N  61 40W
Heathrow, London ✈ (LHR), *U.K.* 13 F7  51 28N  0 27W
Heavener, *U.S.A.* . . . . . . . . . . . . 81 H7  34 53N  94 36W
Hebbronville, *U.S.A.* . . . . . . . . 81 M5  27 18N  98 41W
Hebei □, *China* . . . . . . . . . . . . . . 34 E9  39  0N 116  0 E
Hebel, *Australia* . . . . . . . . . . . . . 63 D4  28 58S 147 47 E
Heber, *U.S.A.* . . . . . . . . . . . . . . . 79 N11  32 44N 115 32W
Heber City, *U.S.A.* . . . . . . . . . . 76 F8  40 31N 111 25W
Heber Springs, *U.S.A.* . . . . . . . 81 H9  35 30N  92  2W
Hebert, *Canada* . . . . . . . . . . . . . 71 C7  50 30N 107 10W
Hebgen L., *U.S.A.* . . . . . . . . . . . 76 D8  44 52N 111 20W
Hebi, *China* . . . . . . . . . . . . . . . . . 34 G8  35 57N 114  7 E
Hebrides, *U.K.* . . . . . . . . . . . . . . 6 D4  57 30N  7  0W
Hebrides, Sea of the, *U.K.* . . . 11 D2  57 5N  7  0W
Hebron = El Khalīl, *West Bank* . 46 D4  31 32N  35  6 E
Hebron, *Canada* . . . . . . . . . . . . . 69 C13  58  5N  62 30W
Hebron, N. Dak., *U.S.A.* . . . . . 80 B3  46 54N 102  3W
Hebron, Nebr., *U.S.A.* . . . . . . . 80 E6  40 10N  97 35W
Hecate Str., *Canada* . . . . . . . . . 70 C2  53 10N 130 30W
Heceta I., *U.S.A.* . . . . . . . . . . . . 70 B2  55 46N 133 40W
Hechi, *China* . . . . . . . . . . . . . . . . 32 D5  24 40N 108  2 E
Hechuan, *China* . . . . . . . . . . . . . 32 C6  30  2N 106 12 E
Hecla, *U.S.A.* . . . . . . . . . . . . . . . 80 C5  45 53N  98  9W
Hecla I., *Canada* . . . . . . . . . . . . 71 C9  51 10N  96 43W
Hede, *Sweden* . . . . . . . . . . . . . . . 9 E15  62 23N  13 30 E
Hedemora, *Sweden* . . . . . . . . . . 9 F16  60 18N  15 58 E
Heerde, *Neths.* . . . . . . . . . . . . . . 15 B6  52 24N  6  2 E
Heerenveen, *Neths.* . . . . . . . . . 15 B5  52 57N  5 55 E
Heerhugowaard, *Neths.* . . . . . . 15 B4  52 40N  4 51 E
Heerlen, *Neths.* . . . . . . . . . . . . . 15 D5  50 55N  5 58 E
Hefa, *Israel* . . . . . . . . . . . . . . . . 46 C4  32 46N  35  0 E
Hefa □, *Israel* . . . . . . . . . . . . . . 46 C4  32 40N  35  0 E
Hefei, *China* . . . . . . . . . . . . . . . . 33 C6  31 52N 117 18 E
Hegang, *China* . . . . . . . . . . . . . . 33 B8  47 20N 130 19 E
Hei Ling Chau, *China* . . . . . . . . 33 G11  22 15N 114  2 E
Heichengzhen, *China* . . . . . . . . 34 F4  36 24N 106  3 E
Heidelberg, *Germany* . . . . . . . . 16 D5  49 24N  8 42 E
Heidelberg, S. Africa . . . . . . . . . 56 E3  34  6S  20 59 E
Heilbron, S. Africa . . . . . . . . . . . 57 D4  27 16S  27 59 E
Heilbronn, *Germany* . . . . . . . . . 16 D5  49  9N  9 13 E
Heilongjiang □, *China* . . . . . . . 33 B7  48  0N 126  0 E
Heilunkiang = Heilongjiang □,
  *China* . . . . . . . . . . . . . . . . . . . . 33 B7  48  0N 126  0 E
Heimaey, *Iceland* . . . . . . . . . . . 8 E3  63 26N  20 17W
Heinola, *Finland* . . . . . . . . . . . . 9 F22  61 13N  26  2 E
Heinze Kyun, *Burma* . . . . . . . . 38 E1  14 25N  97 45 E
Heishan, *China* . . . . . . . . . . . . . 35 D12  41 40N 122  5 E
Heishui, *China* . . . . . . . . . . . . . . 35 C10  42 8N 119 30 E
Hejaz = Ḥijāz □, Si. Arabia . . . 44 E3  24  0N  40  0 E
Hejian, *China* . . . . . . . . . . . . . . . 34 E9  38 25N 116  5 E
Hejin, *China* . . . . . . . . . . . . . . . . 34 G6  35 35N 110 42 E
Hekimhan, *Turkey* . . . . . . . . . . 44 B3  38 50N  37 55 E
Hekla, *Iceland* . . . . . . . . . . . . . . 8 E4  63 56N  19 35W
Hekou, *China* . . . . . . . . . . . . . . . 32 D5  22 30N 103 59 E
Helan Shan, *China* . . . . . . . . . . 34 E3  38 30N 105 55 E
Helen Atoll, Pac. Oc. . . . . . . . . . 37 D8  2 40N 132  0 E
Helena, Ark., *U.S.A.* . . . . . . . . 81 H9  34 32N  90 36W
Helena, Mont., *U.S.A.* . . . . . . . 76 C7  46 36N 112  2W
Helendale, *U.S.A.* . . . . . . . . . . . 79 L9  34 44N 117 19W
Helensburgh, *U.K.* . . . . . . . . . . 11 E4  56  1N  4 43W
Helensville, *N.Z.* . . . . . . . . . . . . 59 G5  36 41S 174 29 E
Helenvale, *Australia* . . . . . . . . 62 B4  15 43S 145 14 E
Helgeland, *Norway* . . . . . . . . . . 8 C15  66  7N  13 29 E
Helgoland, *Germany* . . . . . . . . 16 A4  54 10N  7 53 E
Heligoland = Helgoland,
  *Germany* . . . . . . . . . . . . . . . . . 16 A4  54 10N  7 53 E
Heligoland B. = Deutsche Bucht,
  *Germany* . . . . . . . . . . . . . . . . . 16 A5  54 15N  8  0 E
Hella, *Iceland* . . . . . . . . . . . . . . 8 E3  63 50N  20 24W
Hellertown, *U.S.A.* . . . . . . . . . . 85 F9  40 35N  75 21W
Hellespont = Çanakkale Boğazı,
  *Turkey* . . . . . . . . . . . . . . . . . . 23 D12  40 17N  26 32 E
Hellevoetsluis, *Neths.* . . . . . . . 15 C4  51 50N  4  8 E
Hellhole Gorge △, *Australia* . . 62 D3  25 31S 144 12 E
Hellín, *Spain* . . . . . . . . . . . . . . . 21 C5  38 31N  1 40W
Hells Canyon, *U.S.A.* . . . . . . . 76 D5  45 30N 117 45W
Hell's Gate △, *Kenya* . . . . . . . 54 C4  0 54S  36 19 E
Helmand □, *Afghan.* . . . . . . . . . 40 D4  31 20N  64  0 E
Helmand →, *Afghan.* . . . . . . . . 40 D2  31 12N  61 34 E
Helmeringhausen, *Namibia* . . . 56 D2  25 54S  16 57 E
Helmond, *Neths.* . . . . . . . . . . . . 15 C5  51 29N  5 41 E
Helmsdale, *U.K.* . . . . . . . . . . . . 11 C5  58  7N  3 39W
Helmsdale →, *U.K.* . . . . . . . . . . 11 C5  58  7N  3 40W
Helong, *China* . . . . . . . . . . . . . . 35 C15  42 40N 129  0 E
Helper, *U.S.A.* . . . . . . . . . . . . . . 76 G8  39 41N 110 51W
Helsingborg, *Sweden* . . . . . . . . 9 H15  56  3N  12 42 E
Helsingfors = Helsinki, *Finland* . 9 F21  60 15N  25  3 E
Helsingør, *Denmark* . . . . . . . . . 9 H15  56  2N  12 35 E
Helsinki, *Finland* . . . . . . . . . . . 9 F21  60 15N  25  3 E
Helston, *U.K.* . . . . . . . . . . . . . . . 13 G2  50  6N  5 17W
Helvellyn, *U.K.* . . . . . . . . . . . . . 12 C4  54 32N  3  1W
Helwân, *Egypt* . . . . . . . . . . . . . . 51 C12  29 50N  31 20 E
Hemel Hempstead, *U.K.* . . . . . 13 F7  51 44N  0 28W
Hemet, *U.S.A.* . . . . . . . . . . . . . . 79 M10  33 45N 116 58W
Hemingford, *U.S.A.* . . . . . . . . . 80 D3  42 19N 103  4W
Hemmingford, *Canada* . . . . . . . 85 A11  45  3N  73 35W
Hempstead, *U.S.A.* . . . . . . . . . . 81 K6  30  6N  96  5W
Hemse, *Sweden* . . . . . . . . . . . . . 9 H18  57 15N  18 22 E
Henan □, *China* . . . . . . . . . . . . . 34 H8  34  0N 114  0 E
Henares →, *Spain* . . . . . . . . . . . 21 B4  40 24N  3 30W
Henashi-Misaki, *Japan* . . . . . . 30 D9  40 37N 139 51 E
Henderson, *Argentina* . . . . . . . 94 D3  36 18S  61 43W
Henderson, Ky., *U.S.A.* . . . . . . 82 G2  37 50N  87 35W

Henderson, N.C., *U.S.A.* . . . . . 83 G6  36 20N  78 25W
Henderson, Nev., *U.S.A.* . . . . . 79 J12  36  2N 114 59W
Henderson, Tenn., *U.S.A.* . . . . 83 H1  35 26N  88 38W
Henderson, Tex., *U.S.A.* . . . . . 81 J7  32  9N  94 48W
Hendersonville, N.C., *U.S.A.* . 83 H4  35 19N  82 28W
Hendersonville, Tenn., *U.S.A.* . 83 G2  36 18N  86 37W
Hendījān, *Iran* . . . . . . . . . . . . . 45 D6  30 14N  49 43 E
Hendorābī, *Iran* . . . . . . . . . . . . 45 E7  26 40N  53 37 E
Hengcheng, *China* . . . . . . . . . . 34 E4  38 18N 106 28 E
Hengdaohezi, *China* . . . . . . . . 35 B15  44 52N 129  0 E
Hengelo, *Neths.* . . . . . . . . . . . . 15 B6  52 16N  6 48 E
Henggang, *China* . . . . . . . . . . . 33 F11  22 39N 114 12 E
Hengqin Dao, *China* . . . . . . . . 33 F10  22 33N 113 35 E
Hengshan, *China* . . . . . . . . . . . 34 F5  37 58N 109  5 E
Hengshui, *China* . . . . . . . . . . . . 34 F8  37 41N 115 40 E
Hengyang, *China* . . . . . . . . . . . 33 D6  26 59N 112 22 E
Henley-on-Thames, *U.K.* . . . . . 13 F7  51 32N  0 54W
Henlopen, C., *U.S.A.* . . . . . . . . 82 F8  38 48N  75  6W
Hennenman, S. Africa . . . . . . . . 56 D4  27 59S  27  1 E
Hennessey, *U.S.A.* . . . . . . . . . . 81 G6  36  6N  97 54W
Henri Pittier △, *Venezuela* . . . 89 D6  10 26N  67 37W
Henrietta, *U.S.A.* . . . . . . . . . . . 81 J5  33 49N  98 12W
Henrietta, Ostrov = Genriyetty,
  Ostrov, *Russia* . . . . . . . . . . . . 29 B16  77  6N 156 30 E
Henrietta Maria, C., *Canada* . . 72 A3  55  9N  82 20W
Henry, *U.S.A.* . . . . . . . . . . . . . . 80 E10  41  7N  89 22W
Henryetta, *U.S.A.* . . . . . . . . . . . 81 H7  35 27N  95 59W
Henryville, *Canada* . . . . . . . . . 85 A11  45  8N  73 11W
Hensall, *Canada* . . . . . . . . . . . . 84 C3  43 26N  81 30W
Hentiesbaai, *Namibia* . . . . . . . 56 C1  22  8S  14 18 E
Hentiyn Nuruu, *Mongolia* . . . . 33 B5  48 30N 108 30 E
Henty, *Australia* . . . . . . . . . . . . 63 F4  35 30S 147  0 E
Henzada, *Burma* . . . . . . . . . . . . 41 L19  17 38N  95 26 E
Heppner, *U.S.A.* . . . . . . . . . . . . 84 B3  44 37N  81  9W
Hepworth, *Canada* . . . . . . . . . . 34 E6  39 21N 111 15 E
Hequ, *China* . . . . . . . . . . . . . . . . 8 D6  65 42N  14 12W
Heraðsflói, *Iceland* . . . . . . . . . 8 D6  65 45N  19 25W
Heraðsvötn →, *Iceland* . . . . . . 25 D7  35 20N  25 12 E
Heraklion = Iráklion, *Greece* . 62 B4  16 58S 149  9 E
Herald Cays, *Australia* . . . . . . 40 B3  34 20N  62  7 E
Herāt, *Afghan.* . . . . . . . . . . . . . 40 B3  35  0N  62  0 E
Herāt □, *Afghan.* . . . . . . . . . . . 62 B4  18 31S 146 17 E
Herbert →, *Australia* . . . . . . . . 62 B4  18 15S 145 32 E
Herbert River Falls △, *Australia* . 62 B4  17 20S 145 25 E
Herberton, *Australia* . . . . . . . . 56 E3  34  1S  21 46 E
Herbertsdale, S. Africa . . . . . . . 23 C8  42 30N  18 33 E
Herchmer, *Canada* . . . . . . . . . . 71 B10  57 22N  94 10W
Herceg-Novi, Serbia & M. . . . . . 8 D5  65 11N  16 21W
Herðubreið, *Iceland* . . . . . . . . . 13 E5  52  4N  2 43W
Hereford, *U.K.* . . . . . . . . . . . . . 81 H3  34 49N 102 24W
Hereford, *U.S.A.* . . . . . . . . . . . . 13 E5  52  8N  2 40W
Herefordshire □, *U.K.* . . . . . . . 15 C4  51 12N  4 51 E
Herentals, *Belgium* . . . . . . . . . 16 B5  52  7N  8 39 E
Herford, *Germany* . . . . . . . . . . 80 F6  38 40N  96 57W
Herington, *U.S.A.* . . . . . . . . . . 85 D10  43  0N  74 59W
Herkimer, *U.S.A.* . . . . . . . . . . . 78 E6  40  8N 120  8W
Herlong, *U.S.A.* . . . . . . . . . . . . 13 H5  49 30N  2 28W
Herm, *U.K.* . . . . . . . . . . . . . . . . 80 F9  38 42N 121  8W
Hermann, *U.S.A.* . . . . . . . . . . . 60 D5  23 57S 132 45 E
Hermannsburg, *Australia* . . . . 56 E2  34 27S  19 12 E
Hermanus, S. Africa . . . . . . . . . 63 E4  31 30S 146 42 E
Hermidale, *Australia* . . . . . . . . 76 D4  45 51N 119 17W
Hermiston, *U.S.A.* . . . . . . . . . . 96 H3  55 50S  68  0W
Hermite, I., Chile . . . . . . . . . . . . 85 B9  44 28N  75 14W
Hermon, Mt. = Shaykh, J. ash,
  Lebanon . . . . . . . . . . . . . . . . . . 46 B4  33 25N  35 50 E
Hermosillo, *Mexico* . . . . . . . . . 86 B2  29 10N 111  0W
Hernád →, *Hungary* . . . . . . . . . 17 D11  47 56N  21  8 E
Hernandarias, *Paraguay* . . . . . 95 B5  25 20S  54 40W
Hernandez, *U.S.A.* . . . . . . . . . . 78 J6  36 24N 120 46W
Hernando, *Argentina* . . . . . . . . 94 C3  32 28S  63 40W
Hernando, *U.S.A.* . . . . . . . . . . . 81 H10  34 50N  90  0W
Herndon, *U.S.A.* . . . . . . . . . . . . 84 F8  40 43N  76 51W
Herne, *Germany* . . . . . . . . . . . . 15 C7  51 32N  7 14 E
Herne Bay, *U.K.* . . . . . . . . . . . . 13 F9  51 21N  1  8 E
Herning, *Denmark* . . . . . . . . . . 9 H13  56  8N  8 58 E
Heroica = Caborca, *Mexico* . . 86 A2  30 40N 112 10W
Heroica Nogales = Nogales,
  *Mexico* . . . . . . . . . . . . . . . . . . 86 A2  31 20N 110 56W
Heron Bay, *Canada* . . . . . . . . . 72 C2  48 40N  86 25W
Herradura, Pta. de la, Canary Is. . 24 F5  28 26N  14  8W
Herreid, *U.S.A.* . . . . . . . . . . . . . 80 C4  45 50N 100  4W
Herrin, *U.S.A.* . . . . . . . . . . . . . . 81 G10  37 48N  89  2W
Herriot, *Canada* . . . . . . . . . . . . 71 B8  56 22N 101 16W
Herschel I., *Canada* . . . . . . . . . 4 C1  69 35N 139  5W
Hershey, *U.S.A.* . . . . . . . . . . . . 85 F8  40 17N  76 39W
Hersonissos, *Greece* . . . . . . . . 25 D7  35 18N  25 22 E
Herstal, *Belgium* . . . . . . . . . . . 15 D5  50 40N  5 38 E
Hertford, *U.K.* . . . . . . . . . . . . . . 13 F7  51 48N  0  4W
Hertfordshire □, *U.K.* . . . . . . . 13 F7  51 51N  0  5W
's-Hertogenbosch, *Neths.* . . . . 15 C5  51 42N  5 17 E
Hertzogville, S. Africa . . . . . . . . 56 D4  28  9S  25 30 E
Hervey B., *Australia* . . . . . . . . 62 C5  25  0S 152 52 E
Herzliyya, *Israel* . . . . . . . . . . . 46 C3  32 10N  34 50 E
Ḥeşār, Fārs, Iran . . . . . . . . . . . . 45 D6  29 52N  50 16 E
Ḥeşār, Markazī, Iran . . . . . . . . . 45 C6  35 50N  49 12 E
Heshui, *China* . . . . . . . . . . . . . . 34 G5  35 48N 108  0 E
Heshun, *China* . . . . . . . . . . . . . 34 F7  37 22N 113 32 E
Hesperia, *U.S.A.* . . . . . . . . . . . . 79 L9  34 25N 117 18W
Hesse = Hessen □, *Germany* . . 16 C5  50 30N  9  0 E
Hessen □, *Germany* . . . . . . . . . 16 C5  50 30N  9  0 E
Hetch Hetchy Aqueduct, *U.S.A.* . 78 H5  37 29N 122 19W
Hettinger, *U.S.A.* . . . . . . . . . . . 80 C3  46  0N 102 42W
Heuvelton, *U.S.A.* . . . . . . . . . . 85 B9  44 37N  75 25W
Hewitt, *U.S.A.* . . . . . . . . . . . . . . 81 K6  31 27N  97 11W
Hexham, *U.K.* . . . . . . . . . . . . . . 12 C5  54 58N  2  4W
Hexigten Qi, *China* . . . . . . . . . 35 C9  43 18N 117 30 E
Ḥeydarābād, *Iran* . . . . . . . . . . . 45 D7  30 33N  55 38 E
Heysham, *U.K.* . . . . . . . . . . . . . 12 C5  54  3N  2 53W
Heywood, *Australia* . . . . . . . . . 63 F3  38  8S 141 37 E
Heze, *China* . . . . . . . . . . . . . . . . 34 G8  35 14N 115 20 E
Hi, Thailand . . . . . . . . . . . . . . . . . 39 a  7 44N  98 22 E
Hi Vista, *U.S.A.* . . . . . . . . . . . . 79 L9  34 45N 117 46W
Hialeah, *U.S.A.* . . . . . . . . . . . . 83 N5  25 50N  80 17W
Hiawatha, *U.S.A.* . . . . . . . . . . . 80 F7  39 51N  95 32W
Hibbing, *U.S.A.* . . . . . . . . . . . . 80 B8  47 25N  92 56W
Hibbs B., *Australia* . . . . . . . . . 63 G4  42 35S 145 15 E
Hibernia Reef, *Australia* . . . . . 60 B3  12  0S 123 23 E
Hickman, *U.S.A.* . . . . . . . . . . . . 81 G10  36 34N  89 11W
Hickory, *U.S.A.* . . . . . . . . . . . . . 83 H5  35 44N  81 21W
Hicks, Pt., *Australia* . . . . . . . . 63 F4  37 49S 149 17 E
Hicks L., *Canada* . . . . . . . . . . . 71 A9  61 25N 100  0W
Hicksville, *U.S.A.* . . . . . . . . . . . 85 F11  40 46N  73 32W
Hida-Gawa →, *Japan* . . . . . . . 31 G8  35 26N 137  3 E
Hida-Sammyaku, *Japan* . . . . . 31 F8  36 30N 137 40 E
Hidaka-Sammyaku, *Japan* . . . 30 C11  42 35N 142 45 E

Hidalgo, *Mexico* . . . . . . . . . . . . 87 C5  24 15N  99 26W
Hidalgo □, *Mexico* . . . . . . . . . . 87 C5  20 30N  99 10W
Hidalgo, Presa M., *Mexico* . . . 86 B3  26 30N 108 35W
Hidalgo del Parral, *Mexico* . . . 86 B3  26 58N 105 40W
Hierro, Canary Is. . . . . . . . . . . . 24 G1  27 44N  18  0W
Higashiajima-San, *Japan* . . . . 30 F10  37 40N 140 10 E
Higashiōsaka, *Japan* . . . . . . . . 31 G7  34 40N 135 37 E
Higgins, *U.S.A.* . . . . . . . . . . . . . 81 G4  36  7N 100  2W
Higgins Corner, *U.S.A.* . . . . . . 78 F5  39  2N 121 5W
High Bridge, *U.S.A.* . . . . . . . . . 85 F10  40 40N  74 54W
High Island Res., *China* . . . . . . 33 G11  22 22N 114 21 E
High Level, *Canada* . . . . . . . . . 70 B5  58 31N 117  8W
High Point, *U.S.A.* . . . . . . . . . . 83 H6  35 57N  80  0W
High Prairie, *Canada* . . . . . . . . 70 B5  55 30N 116 30W
High River, *Canada* . . . . . . . . . 70 C6  50 30N 113 50W
High Tatra = Tatry, Slovak Rep. . 17 D11  49 20N  20  0 E
High Veld, *Africa* . . . . . . . . . . . 48 J6  27  0S  27  0 E
High Wycombe, *U.K.* . . . . . . . . 13 F7  51 37N  0 45W
Highland □, *U.K.* . . . . . . . . . . . 11 D4  57 17N  4 21W
Highland Park, *U.S.A.* . . . . . . . 82 D2  42 11N  87 48W
Highmore, *U.S.A.* . . . . . . . . . . . 80 C5  44 31N  99 27W
Highrock L., Man., *Canada* . . . 71 B8  55 45N 100 30W
Highrock L., Sask., *Canada* . . . 71 B7  57  5N 105 32W
Higüey, Dom. Rep. . . . . . . . . . . 89 C6  18 37N  68 42W
Hiiumaa, *Estonia* . . . . . . . . . . . 9 G20  58 50N  22 45 E
Ḥijāz □, Si. Arabia . . . . . . . . . . 44 E3  24  0N  40  0 E
Hijo = Tagum, Phil. . . . . . . . . . . 37 C7  7 33N 125 53 E
Hikari, *Japan* . . . . . . . . . . . . . . 31 H5  33 58N 131 58 E
Hiko, *U.S.A.* . . . . . . . . . . . . . . . . 78 H11  37 32N 115 14W
Hikone, *Japan* . . . . . . . . . . . . . . 31 G8  35 15N 136 10 E
Hikurangi, Gisborne, N.Z. . . . . 59 H6  37 55S 178  4 E
Hikurangi, Northland, N.Z. . . . . 59 F5  35 36S 174 17 E
Hildesheim, *Germany* . . . . . . . 16 B5  52  9N  9 56 E
Hill →, *Australia* . . . . . . . . . . . 61 F2  30 23S 115  3 E
Hill City, Idaho, *U.S.A.* . . . . . . 76 E6  43 18N 115  3W
Hill City, Kans., *U.S.A.* . . . . . . 80 F5  39 22N  99 51W
Hill City, S. Dak., *U.S.A.* . . . . . 80 D3  43 56N 103 35W
Hill Island L., *Canada* . . . . . . . 71 A7  60 30N 109 50W
Hillaby, Mt., Barbados . . . . . . . 89 g  13 12N  59 35W
Hillcrest, Barbados . . . . . . . . . . 89 g  13 13N  59 31W
Hillcrest Center, *U.S.A.* . . . . . . 79 K8  35 23N 118 57W
Hillegom, *Neths.* . . . . . . . . . . . 15 B4  52 18N  4 35 E
Hillerød, *Denmark* . . . . . . . . . . 9 J15  55 56N  12 31 E
Hillsboro, Kans., *U.S.A.* . . . . . 80 F6  38 21N  97 12W
Hillsboro, N. Dak., *U.S.A.* . . . . 80 B6  47 26N  97  3W
Hillsboro, Ohio, *U.S.A.* . . . . . . 82 F4  39 12N  83 37W
Hillsboro, Oreg., *U.S.A.* . . . . . 78 E4  45 31N 122 59W
Hillsboro, Tex., *U.S.A.* . . . . . . 81 J6  32  1N  97  8W
Hillsborough, Grenada . . . . . . . 89 D7  12 28N  61 28W
Hillsborough Channel, *Australia* . 85 C13  43  7N  71 54W
Hillsdale, Mich., *U.S.A.* . . . . . 82 E3  41 56N  84 38W
Hillsdale, N.Y., *U.S.A.* . . . . . . . 85 D11  42 11N  73 30W
Hillsport, *Canada* . . . . . . . . . . . 72 C2  49 27N  85 34W
Hillston, *Australia* . . . . . . . . . . 63 E4  33 30S 145 31 E
Hilo, *U.S.A.* . . . . . . . . . . . . . . . . 74 J17  19 44N 155  5W
Hilton, *U.S.A.* . . . . . . . . . . . . . . 84 C7  43 17N  77 48W
Hilton Head Island, *U.S.A.* . . . 83 J5  32 13N  80 45W
Hilversum, *Neths.* . . . . . . . . . . 15 B5  52 14N  5 10 E
Himachal Pradesh □, *India* . . . 42 D7  31 30N  77  0 E
Himalaya, *Asia* . . . . . . . . . . . . . 43 E11  29  0N  84  0 E
Himatnagar, *India* . . . . . . . . . . 40 H8  23 37N  72 57 E
Himeji, *Japan* . . . . . . . . . . . . . . 31 G7  34 50N 134 40 E
Himi, *Japan* . . . . . . . . . . . . . . . . 31 F8  36 50N 136 55 E
Ḥimş, Syria . . . . . . . . . . . . . . . . . 46 A5  34 40N  36 45 E
Ḥimş □, Syria . . . . . . . . . . . . . . . 46 A6  34 30N  37  0 E
Hinche, Haiti . . . . . . . . . . . . . . . . 89 C5  19  9N  72  1W
Hinchinbrook I., *Australia* . . . 62 B4  18 20N  20 20 E
Hinchinbrook Island △, *Australia* . 62 B4  18 14S 146  6 E
Hinckley, *U.K.* . . . . . . . . . . . . . . 13 E6  52 33N  1 22W
Hinckley, *U.S.A.* . . . . . . . . . . . . 80 B8  46  1N  92 56W
Hindaun, *India* . . . . . . . . . . . . . 42 F7  26 44N  77  5 E
Hindmarsh, L., *Australia* . . . . . 63 F3  36  5S 141 55 E
Hindu Bagh, *Pakistan* . . . . . . . 42 D2  30 56N  67 50 E
Hindu Kush, *Asia* . . . . . . . . . . . 40 B7  36  0N  71  0 E
Hindupur, *India* . . . . . . . . . . . . 40 N10  13 49N  77 32 E
Hines Creek, *Canada* . . . . . . . . 70 B5  56 20N 118 40W
Hinesville, *U.S.A.* . . . . . . . . . . 83 K5  31 51N  81 36W
Hinganghat, *India* . . . . . . . . . . 40 J11  20 30N  78 52 E
Hingham, *U.S.A.* . . . . . . . . . . . . 76 B8  48 33N 110 25W
Hingir, *India* . . . . . . . . . . . . . . . 43 J10  21 57N  83 41 E
Hingoli, *India* . . . . . . . . . . . . . . 40 K10  19 41N  77 15 E
Hinna = Imi, Ethiopia . . . . . . . . 47 F3  6 28N  42 10 E
Hinnøya, *Norway* . . . . . . . . . . . 8 B16  68 35N  15 50 E
Hinojosa del Duque, Spain . . . . 21 C3  38 30N  5  9W
Hinsdale, *U.S.A.* . . . . . . . . . . . . 85 D12  42 47N  72 29W
Hinton, *Canada* . . . . . . . . . . . . . 70 C5  53 26N 117 34W
Hinton, *U.S.A.* . . . . . . . . . . . . . . 82 G5  37 40N  80 54W
Hirado, *Japan* . . . . . . . . . . . . . . 31 H4  33 22N 129 33 E
Hirakud Dam, *India* . . . . . . . . . 41 J13  21 32N  83 45 E
Hiran →, *India* . . . . . . . . . . . . . 43 H8  23  6N  79 21 E
Hirapur, *India* . . . . . . . . . . . . . . 43 G8  24 22N  79 13 E
Hiratsuka, *Japan* . . . . . . . . . . . 31 G9  35 19N 139 21 E
Hiroo, *Japan* . . . . . . . . . . . . . . . 30 C11  42 17N 143 19 E
Hirosaki, *Japan* . . . . . . . . . . . . 30 D10  40 34N 140 28 E
Hiroshima, *Japan* . . . . . . . . . . . 31 G6  34 24N 132 30 E
Hiroshima □, Japan . . . . . . . . . . 31 G6  34 50N 133  0 E
Hisar, *India* . . . . . . . . . . . . . . . . 42 E6  29 12N  75 45 E
Hisb, Sha'ib →, Iraq . . . . . . . . . 44 D3  31 45N  44 17 E
Ḥismá, Si. Arabia . . . . . . . . . . . 44 D3  28 30N  36  0 E
Hispaniola, W. Indies . . . . . . . . 89 C5  19  0N  71  0W
Hīt, *Iraq* . . . . . . . . . . . . . . . . . . . 44 C4  33 38N  42 49 E
Hita, *Japan* . . . . . . . . . . . . . . . . 31 H5  33 20N 130 58 E
Hitachi, *Japan* . . . . . . . . . . . . . 31 F10  36 36N 140 39 E
Hitchin, *U.K.* . . . . . . . . . . . . . . . 13 F7  51 58N  0 16W
Hitoyoshi, *Japan* . . . . . . . . . . . 31 H5  32 13N 130 45 E
Hitra, *Norway* . . . . . . . . . . . . . . 8 E13  63 30N  8 45 E
Hixon, *Canada* . . . . . . . . . . . . . 70 C4  53 25N 122 35W
Ḥiyyon, N. →, *Israel* . . . . . . . . 46 E4  30 25N  35 10 E
Hjalmar L., *Canada* . . . . . . . . . 71 A7  61 33N 109 25W
Hjälmaren, *Sweden* . . . . . . . . . 9 G16  59 18N  15 40 E
Hjørring, *Denmark* . . . . . . . . . . 9 H13  57 29N  9 59 E
Hkakabo Razi, *Burma* . . . . . . . 41 E20  28 25N  97 23 E
Hlobane, S. Africa . . . . . . . . . . . 57 D5  27 42S  31  0 E
Hluhluwe, S. Africa . . . . . . . . . . 57 D5  28  1S  32 15 E
Hluhluwe △, S. Africa . . . . . . . . 57 C5  22  0S  31 15 E
Hlyboka, *Ukraine* . . . . . . . . . . . 17 D13  48  5N  25 56 E
Ho Chi Minh City = Thanh Pho
  Ho Chi Minh, *Vietnam* . . . . . 39 G6  10 58N 106 40 E
Ho Thuong, *Vietnam* . . . . . . . . 38 C5  20 50N 105 48 E
Hoa Binh, *Vietnam* . . . . . . . . . 38 B5  20 50N 105 20 E
Hoa Da, *Vietnam* . . . . . . . . . . . 39 G7  11 16N 108 40 E
Hoa Hiep, *Vietnam* . . . . . . . . . 39 G5  11 34N 105 51 E
Hoai Nhon, *Vietnam* . . . . . . . . 38 E7  14 28N 109  1 E
Hoang Lien Son, *Vietnam* . . . . 38 A4  22  0N 104  0 E
Hoanib →, Namibia . . . . . . . . . . 56 B2  19 27S  12 46 E
Hoare B., *Canada* . . . . . . . . . . . 69 B13  65 17N  62 30W
Hoarusib →, Namibia . . . . . . . . 56 B2  19  3S  12 36 E

Hobart, *Australia* . . . . . . . . . . . 63 G4  42 50S 147 21 E
Hobart, *U.S.A.* . . . . . . . . . . . . . 81 H5  35  1N  99  6W
Hobbs, *U.S.A.* . . . . . . . . . . . . . . 81 J3  32 42N 103  8W
Hobbs Coast, *Antarctica* . . . . . 5 D14  74 50S 131  0W
Hobe Sound, *U.S.A.* . . . . . . . . . 83 M5  27  4N  80  8W
Hoboken, *U.S.A.* . . . . . . . . . . . . 85 F10  40 45N  74  4W
Hobro, *Denmark* . . . . . . . . . . . . 9 H13  56 39N  9 46 E
Hoburgen, *Sweden* . . . . . . . . . . 9 H18  56 55N  18  7 E
Hochfeld, *Namibia* . . . . . . . . . . 56 C2  21 28S  17 58 E
Hodaka-Dake, *Japan* . . . . . . . . 31 F8  36 17N 137 39 E
Hodeida = Al Ḥudaydah, Yemen . 47 E3  14 50N  43  0 E
Hodgeville, *Canada* . . . . . . . . . 71 C7  50 7N 106 58W
Hodgson, *Canada* . . . . . . . . . . . 71 C9  51 13N  97 36W
Hódmezővásárhely, *Hungary* . 17 E11  46 28N  20 22 E
Hodna, Chott el, *Algeria* . . . . . 50 A6  35 26N  4 43 E
Hodonín, Czech Rep. . . . . . . . . . 17 D9  48 50N  17 10 E
Hoeamdong, N. Korea . . . . . . . . 35 C16  42 30N 130 16 E
Hoek van Holland, *Neths.* . . . . 15 C4  52  0N  4  7 E
Hoengsŏng, S. Korea . . . . . . . . . 35 F14  37 29N 127 59 E
Hoeryong, N. Korea . . . . . . . . . . 35 C15  42 30N 129 45 E
Hoeyang, N. Korea . . . . . . . . . . . 35 E14  38 43N 127 36 E
Hof, *Germany* . . . . . . . . . . . . . . 16 C6  50 19N  11 55 E
Hofmeyr, S. Africa . . . . . . . . . . . 56 E4  31 39S  25 50 E
Höfn, Iceland . . . . . . . . . . . . . . . 8 D6  64 15N  15 13W
Hofors, *Sweden* . . . . . . . . . . . . 9 F17  60 31N  16 15 E
Hofsjökull, Iceland . . . . . . . . . . 8 D4  64 49N  18 48W
Hōfu, *Japan* . . . . . . . . . . . . . . . . 31 G5  34  3N 131 34 E
Hogan Group, *Australia* . . . . . 63 F4  39 13S 147  1 E
Hogarth, Mt., *Australia* . . . . . . 62 C2  21 48S 136 58 E
Hoggar = Ahaggar, *Algeria* . . 50 D7  23  0N  6 30 E
Hogsty Reef, *Bahamas* . . . . . . 89 B5  21 41N  73 48W
Hoh →, *U.S.A.* . . . . . . . . . . . . . 78 C2  47 45N 124 29W
Hohe Venn, *Belgium* . . . . . . . . 15 D6  50 30N  6  5 E
Hohenwald, *U.S.A.* . . . . . . . . . . 83 H2  35 33N  87 33W
Hoher Rhön = Rhön, *Germany* . 16 C5  50 24N  9 58 E
Hohhot, *China* . . . . . . . . . . . . . . 34 D6  40 52N 111 40 E
Höhlakas, *Greece* . . . . . . . . . . . 25 D9  35 57N  27 53 E
Hoi An, *Vietnam* . . . . . . . . . . . . 38 E7  15 30N 108 19 E
Hoi Xuan, *Vietnam* . . . . . . . . . 38 B5  20 25N 105  9 E
Hoisington, *U.S.A.* . . . . . . . . . . 80 F5  38 31N  98 47W
Hōjō, *Japan* . . . . . . . . . . . . . . . . 31 H6  33 58N 132 46 E
Hokianga Harbour, *N.Z.* . . . . . 59 F4  35 31S 173 22 E
Hokitika, *N.Z.* . . . . . . . . . . . . . . 59 K3  42 42S 171  0 E
Hokkaidō □, *Japan* . . . . . . . . . . 30 C11  43 30N 143  0 E
Holbrook, *Australia* . . . . . . . . . 63 F4  35 42S 147 18 E
Holbrook, *U.S.A.* . . . . . . . . . . . 77 J8  34 54N 110 10W
Holden, *U.S.A.* . . . . . . . . . . . . . 76 G7  39  6N 112 16W
Holdenville, *U.S.A.* . . . . . . . . . 81 H6  35  5N  96 24W
Holdrege, *U.S.A.* . . . . . . . . . . . 80 E5  40 26N  99 23W
Holetown, Barbados . . . . . . . . . 89 g  13 11N  59 38W
Holguín, Cuba . . . . . . . . . . . . . . 88 B4  20 50N  76 20W
Hollams Bird I., Namibia . . . . . . 56 C1  24 40S  14 30 E
Holland, Mich., *U.S.A.* . . . . . . 82 D2  42 47N  86  7W
Holland, N.Y., *U.S.A.* . . . . . . . . 84 D6  42 38N  78 32W
Hollandale, *U.S.A.* . . . . . . . . . . 81 J9  33 10N  90 51W
Holley, *U.S.A.* . . . . . . . . . . . . . . 84 C6  43 14N  78  2W
Hollidaysburg, *U.S.A.* . . . . . . . 84 F6  40 26N  78 24W
Hollis, *U.S.A.* . . . . . . . . . . . . . . 81 H5  34 41N  99 55W
Hollister, Calif., *U.S.A.* . . . . . . 78 J5  36 51N 121 24W
Hollister, Idaho, *U.S.A.* . . . . . . 76 E6  42 21N 114 35W
Holly Hill, *U.S.A.* . . . . . . . . . . . 83 L5  29 16N  81  3W
Holly Springs, *U.S.A.* . . . . . . . 81 H10  34 46N  89 27W
Hollywood, *U.S.A.* . . . . . . . . . . 83 N5  26  1N  80  9W
Holman, *Canada* . . . . . . . . . . . . 68 A8  70 44N 117 44W
Hólmavík, Iceland . . . . . . . . . . . 8 D3  65 42N  21 40W
Holmen, *U.S.A.* . . . . . . . . . . . . . 80 D9  43 58N  91 15W
Holmes Reefs, *Australia* . . . . . 62 B4  16 27S 148  0 E
Holmsund, *Sweden* . . . . . . . . . 8 E19  63 41N  20 20 E
Holroyd →, Australia . . . . . . . . . 62 A3  14 10S 141 36 E
Holstebro, Denmark . . . . . . . . . 9 H13  56 22N  8 37 E
Holsworthy, *U.K.* . . . . . . . . . . . 13 G3  50 48N  4 22W
Holton, *Canada* . . . . . . . . . . . . . 73 B8  54 31N  57 12W
Holton, *U.S.A.* . . . . . . . . . . . . . . 80 F7  39 28N  95 44W
Holtville, *U.S.A.* . . . . . . . . . . . . 79 N11  32 49N 115 23W
Holwerd, *Neths.* . . . . . . . . . . . . 15 A5  53 22N  5 54 E
Holy I., Angl., *U.K.* . . . . . . . . . . 12 D3  53 17N  4 37W
Holy I., Northumberland, *U.K.* . 12 B6  55 40N  1 47W
Holyhead, *U.K.* . . . . . . . . . . . . . 12 D3  53 18N  4 38W
Holyoke, Colo., *U.S.A.* . . . . . . . 80 E3  40 35N 102 18W
Holyoke, Mass., *U.S.A.* . . . . . . 85 D12  42 12N  72 37W
Holyrood, *Canada* . . . . . . . . . . 73 C9  47 27N  53  8W
Homa Bay, *Kenya* . . . . . . . . . . . 54 C3  0 36S  34 30 E
Homalin, *Burma* . . . . . . . . . . . . 41 G19  24 55N  95  0 E
Homand, *Iran* . . . . . . . . . . . . . . 45 C8  32 28N  59 37 E
Homathko →, *Canada* . . . . . . . 70 C4  51  0N 124 56W
Hombori, *Mali* . . . . . . . . . . . . . . 50 E5  15 20N  1 38W
Home B., *Canada* . . . . . . . . . . . 69 B13  68 40N  67 10W
Home Hill, *Australia* . . . . . . . . 62 B4  19 43S 147 25 E
Homedale, *U.S.A.* . . . . . . . . . . . 76 E5  43 37N 116 56W
Homer, Alaska, *U.S.A.* . . . . . . . 68 C4  59 39N 151 33W
Homer, La., *U.S.A.* . . . . . . . . . . 81 J8  32 48N  93  4W
Homer City, *U.S.A.* . . . . . . . . . . 84 F5  40 32N  79 10W
Homestead, *Australia* . . . . . . . 62 C4  20 20S 145 40 E
Homestead, *U.S.A.* . . . . . . . . . . 83 N5  25 28N  80 29W
Homewood, △, U.S.A. . . . . . . . . . 80 E6  40 17N  96 50W
Homewood, *U.S.A.* . . . . . . . . . . 78 F6  39  4N 120  8W
Homoine, Mozam. . . . . . . . . . . . 57 C6  23 55S  35  8 E
Homs = Ḥimş, Syria . . . . . . . . . 46 A5  34 40N  36 45 E
Homyel, Belarus . . . . . . . . . . . . . 17 B16  52 28N  31  0 E
Hon Chong, *Vietnam* . . . . . . . . 39 G5  10 25N 104 30 E
Hon Me, *Vietnam* . . . . . . . . . . . 38 C5  19 23N 105 56 E
Honan = Henan □, *China* . . . . . 34 H8  34  0N 114  0 E
Honbetsu, *Japan* . . . . . . . . . . . . 30 C11  43  7N 143 37 E
Honcut, *U.S.A.* . . . . . . . . . . . . . 78 F5  39 20N 121 32W
Hondeklipbaai, S. Africa . . . . . . 56 E2  30 19S  17  17 E
Hondo, *Japan* . . . . . . . . . . . . . . 31 H5  32 27N 130 12 E
Hondo, *U.S.A.* . . . . . . . . . . . . . . 81 L5  29 21N  99  9W
Hondo, Río →, Belize . . . . . . . . 87 D7  18 25N  88 21W
Honduras ■, Cent. Amer. . . . . . 88 D2  14 40N  86 30W
Honduras, G. de, Caribbean . . . 88 C2  16 50N  87  0W
Hønefoss, *Norway* . . . . . . . . . . 9 F14  60 10N  10 18 E
Honesdale, *U.S.A.* . . . . . . . . . . 85 E9  41 34N  75 16W
Honey L., *U.S.A.* . . . . . . . . . . . . 78 E6  40 15N 120 19W
Honfleur, France . . . . . . . . . . . . 20 B4  49 25N  0 13 E
Hong →, Vietnam . . . . . . . . . . . . 32 D5  22  0N 104  0 E
Hong Gai, Vietnam . . . . . . . . . . 38 B6  20 57N 107  5 E
Hong He →, China . . . . . . . . . . . 34 H8  32 25N 115 35 E
Hong Kong □, China . . . . . . . . . 33 G11  22 11N 114 14 E
Hong Kong I., China . . . . . . . . . 33 G11  22 16N 114 12 E
Hong Kong International ✈
  (HKG), China . . . . . . . . . . . . . 33 G10  22 19N 113 57 E
Hongch'ŏn, S. Korea . . . . . . . . . 35 F14  37 44N 127 53 E
Hongjiang, China . . . . . . . . . . . . 33 D5  27  7N 109 59 E
Hongliu He →, China . . . . . . . . . 34 F5  38 0N 109 50 E
Hongor, Mongolia . . . . . . . . . . . 34 B7  45 45N 112 50 E
Hongsa, Laos . . . . . . . . . . . . . . . 38 C3  19 43N 101 20 E
Hongshui He →, China . . . . . . . 33 D5  23 48N 109 30 E
Hongsŏng, S. Korea . . . . . . . . . . 35 F14  36 37N 126 38 E

Hongtong, China . . . . . . . . . . . 34 F6   36 16N 111 40 E
Honguedo, Détroit d', Canada . 73 C7   49 15N  64  0W
Hongwon, N. Korea . . . . . . . . . 35 E14  40  0N 127 56 E
Hongze Hu, China . . . . . . . . . 35 H10  33 15N 118 35 E
Honiara, Solomon Is. . . . . . . . 64 H7    9 27S 159 57 E
Honiton, U.K. . . . . . . . . . . . . 13 G4   50 47N   3 11W
Honjō, Japan . . . . . . . . . . . . 30 E10  39 23N 140  3 E
Honningsvåg, Norway . . . . . . .  8 A21  70 59N  25 59 E
Honolulu, U.S.A. . . . . . . . . . . 74 H16  21 19N 157 52W
Honshū, Japan . . . . . . . . . . . 33 C8   36  0N 138  0 E
Hood, Mt., U.S.A. . . . . . . . . . 76 D3   45 23N 121 42W
Hood, Pt., Australia . . . . . . . . 61 F2   34 23S 119 34 E
Hood River, U.S.A. . . . . . . . . . 76 D3   45 43N 121 31W
Hoodsport, U.S.A. . . . . . . . . . 78 C3   47 24N 123  9W
Hoogeveen, Neths. . . . . . . . . 15 B6   52 44N   6 28 E
Hoogezand-Sappemeer, Neths. . 15 A6   53  9N   6 45 E
Hooghly = Hugli →, India . . . . 43 J13  21 56N  88  4 E
Hooghly-Chinsura = Chunchura,
    India . . . . . . . . . . . . . . . 43 H13  22 53N  88 27 E
Hook Hd., Ireland . . . . . . . . . 10 D5   52  7N   6 56W
Hook I., Australia . . . . . . . . . . 62 J6   20  4S 149  0 E
Hook of Holland = Hoek van
    Holland, Neths. . . . . . . . . . 15 C4   52  0N   4  7 E
Hooker, U.S.A. . . . . . . . . . . . 81 G4   36 52N 101 13W
Hooker Creek, Australia . . . . . 60 C5   18 23S 130 38 E
Hoonah, U.S.A. . . . . . . . . . . . 70 B1   58 7N 135 27W
Hooper Bay, U.S.A. . . . . . . . . 68 B3   61 32N 166 6W
Hoopeston, U.S.A. . . . . . . . . . 82 E2   40 28N  87 40W
Hoopstad, S. Africa . . . . . . . . 56 D4   27 50S  25 55 E
Hoorn, Neths. . . . . . . . . . . . . 15 B5   52 38N   5  4 E
Hoover, U.S.A. . . . . . . . . . . . 83 J2   33 20N  86 11W
Hoover Dam, U.S.A. . . . . . . . . 79 K12  36  1N 114 44W
Hooversville, U.S.A. . . . . . . . . 84 F6   40  9N  78 55W
Hop Bottom, U.S.A. . . . . . . . . 85 E9   41 42N  75 46W
Hope, Canada . . . . . . . . . . . . 70 D4   49 25N 121 25W
Hope, Ariz., U.S.A. . . . . . . . . 79 M13 33 43N 113 42W
Hope, Ark., U.S.A. . . . . . . . . . 81 J8   33 40N  93 36W
Hope, L., S. Austral., Australia . 63 D2   28 24S 139 18 E
Hope, L., W. Austral., Australia 61 F3   32 35S 120 15 E
Hope, Pt., U.S.A. . . . . . . . . . .  4 C17  68 20N 166 50W
Hope I., Canada . . . . . . . . . . 84 B4   44 55N  80 11W
Hope Town, Bahamas . . . . . . 88 A4   26 35N  76 57W
Hopedale, Canada . . . . . . . . . 73 A7   55 28N  60 13W
Hopedale, U.S.A. . . . . . . . . . . 85 D13  42  8N  71 33W
Hopefield, S. Africa . . . . . . . . 56 E2   33  3S  18 22 E
Hopei = Hebei □, China . . . . . 34 E9   39  0N 116  0 E
Hopelchén, Mexico . . . . . . . . . 87 D7   19 46N  89 50W
Hopetoun, Vic., Australia . . . . . 63 F3   35 42S 142 22 E
Hopetoun, W. Austral., Australia 61 F3   33 57S 120  7 E
Hopetown, S. Africa . . . . . . . . 56 D3   29 34S  24  3 E
Hopevale, Australia . . . . . . . . 62 B4   15 16S 145 20 E
Hopewell, U.S.A. . . . . . . . . . . 82 G7   37 18N  77 17W
Hopkins, L., Australia . . . . . . . 60 D4   24 15S 128 35 E
Hopkinsville, U.S.A. . . . . . . . . 83 G2   36 52N  87 29W
Hopland, U.S.A. . . . . . . . . . . . 78 G3   38 58N 123  7W
Hoquiam, U.S.A. . . . . . . . . . . 78 D3   46 59N 123 53W
Horden Hills, Australia . . . . . . 60 D5   20 15S 130  0 E
Horinger, China . . . . . . . . . . . 34 D6   40 28N 111 48 E
Horlick Mts., Antarctica . . . . . .  5 E15  84  0S 102  0W
Horlivka, Ukraine . . . . . . . . . . 19 E6   48 19N  38  5 E
Hormak, Iran . . . . . . . . . . . . . 45 D9   29 58N  60 51 E
Hormoz, Iran . . . . . . . . . . . . . 45 E7   27 35N  55  0 E
Hormoz, Jaz.-ye, Iran . . . . . . . 45 E8   27  8N  56 28 E
Hormozgān □, Iran . . . . . . . . . 45 E8   27 30N  56  0 E
Hormoz, Kūh-e, Iran . . . . . . . . 45 E7   27 27N  55 10 E
Hormuz, Str. of, The Gulf . . . . . 45 E8   26 30N  56 30 E
Horn, Austria . . . . . . . . . . . . . 16 D8   48 39N  15 40 E
Horn, Iceland . . . . . . . . . . . . .  8 C2   66 28N  22 28W
Horn →, Canada . . . . . . . . . . 70 A5   61 30N 118  1W
Horn, Cape = Hornos, C. de, Chile 96 H3  55 50S  67 30W
Horn Head, Ireland . . . . . . . . . 10 A3   55 14N   8  0W
Horn I., Australia . . . . . . . . . . 62 A3   10 37S 142 17 E
Horn Plateau, Canada . . . . . . 70 A5   62 15N 119 15W
Hornavan, Sweden . . . . . . . . .  8 C17  66 15N  17 30 E
Hornbeck, U.S.A. . . . . . . . . . . 81 K8   31 20N  93 24W
Hornbrook, U.S.A. . . . . . . . . . 76 F2   41 55N 122 33W
Horncastle, U.K. . . . . . . . . . . 12 D7   53 13N   0  7W
Hornell, U.S.A. . . . . . . . . . . . 84 D7   42 20N  77 40W
Hornell L., Canada . . . . . . . . . 70 A5   62 20N 119 25W
Hornepayne, Canada . . . . . . . 72 C3   49 14N  84 48W
Hornings Mills, Canada . . . . . . 84 B4   44  9N  80 12W
Hornitos, U.S.A. . . . . . . . . . . 78 H6   37 30N 120 14W
Hornos, C. de, Chile . . . . . . . . 96 H3   55 50S  67 30W
Hornsea, U.K. . . . . . . . . . . . . 12 D7   53 55N   0 11W
Horobetsu = Noboribetsu, Japan 30 C10 42 24N 141  6 E
Horodenka, Ukraine . . . . . . . . 17 D13  48 41N  25 29 E
Horodok, Khmelnytskyy, Ukraine 17 D14 49 10N  26 34 E
Horodok, Lviv, Ukraine . . . . . . 17 D12  49 46N  23 32 E
Horokhiv, Ukraine . . . . . . . . . 17 C13  50 30N  24 45 E
Horqin Youyi Qianqi, China . . . 35 A12  46  5N 122  3 E
Horqueta, Paraguay . . . . . . . . 94 A4   23 15S  56 55W
Horse Creek, U.S.A. . . . . . . . . 80 E3   41 57N 105 10W
Horse I., Canada . . . . . . . . . . 71 C9   53 20N  99  6W
Horse Is., Canada . . . . . . . . . 73 B8   50 15N  55 50W
Horsefly L., Canada . . . . . . . . 70 C4   52 25N 121  0W
Horseheads, U.S.A. . . . . . . . . 84 D8   42 10N  76 49W
Horsens, Denmark . . . . . . . . .  9 J13  55 52N   9 51 E
Horsham, Australia . . . . . . . . . 63 F3   36 44S 142 13 E
Horsham, U.K. . . . . . . . . . . . . 13 F7   51  4N   0 20W
Horten, Norway . . . . . . . . . . .  9 G14  59 25N  10 32 E
Horton, U.S.A. . . . . . . . . . . . . 80 F7   39 40N  95 32W
Horton →, Canada . . . . . . . . . 68 B7   69 56N 126 52W
Horwood L., Canada . . . . . . . . 72 C3   48  5N  82 20W
Hose, Gunung-Gunung, Malaysia 36 D4    2  5N 114  6 E
Ḥoseynābād, Khuzestān, Iran . 45 C6   32 45N  48 20 E
Ḥoseynābād, Kordestān, Iran . 44 C5   35 33N  47  8 E
Hoshangabad, India . . . . . . . . 42 H7   22 45N  77 45 E
Hoshiarpur, India . . . . . . . . . . 42 D6   31 30N  75 58 E
Hospet, India . . . . . . . . . . . . . 40 M10 15 15N  76 20 E
Hoste, I., Chile . . . . . . . . . . . 96 H3   55  0S  69  0W
Hot, Thailand . . . . . . . . . . . . . 38 C2   18  8N  98 29 E
Hot Creek Range, U.S.A. . . . . 76 G6   38 40N 116 20W
Hot Springs, Ark., U.S.A. . . . . 81 H8   34 31N  93  3W
Hot Springs, S. Dak., U.S.A. . . 80 D3   43 26N 103 29W
Hotagen, Sweden . . . . . . . . . .  8 E16  63 59N  14 12 E
Hotan, China . . . . . . . . . . . . . 32 C2   37 25N  79 55 E
Hotazel, S. Africa . . . . . . . . . 56 D3   27 17S  22 58 E
Hotchkiss, U.S.A. . . . . . . . . . 77 G10  38 48N 107 43W
Hotham, C., Australia . . . . . . . 60 B5   12 2S 131 18 E
Hoting, Sweden . . . . . . . . . . .  8 D17  64  8N  16 15 E
Hotte, Massif de la, Haiti . . . . . 89 C5   18 30N  73 45W
Hottentotsbaai, Namibia . . . . . 56 D1   26  8S  14 59 E
Hou Hai, China . . . . . . . . . . . 33 F10  22 32N 113 56 E
Houffalize, Belgium . . . . . . . . 15 D5   50  8N   5 48 E
Houghton, Mich., U.S.A. . . . . . 80 B10  47  7N  88 34W
Houghton, N.Y., U.S.A. . . . . . . 84 D6   42 25N  78 10W

Houghton L., U.S.A. . . . . . . . . 82 C3   44 21N  84 44W
Houghton-le-Spring, U.K. . . . . 12 C6   54 51N   1 28W
Houhora Heads, N.Z. . . . . . . . 59 F4   34 49S 173  9 E
Houlton, U.S.A. . . . . . . . . . . . 83 B12  46  8N  67 51W
Houma, U.S.A. . . . . . . . . . . . . 81 L9   29 36N  90 43W
Housatonic →, U.S.A. . . . . . . . 85 E11  41 10N  73  7W
Houston, Canada . . . . . . . . . . 70 C3   54 25N 126 39W
Houston, Mo., U.S.A. . . . . . . . 81 G9   37 22N  91 58W
Houston, Tex., U.S.A. . . . . . . . 81 L7   29 46N  95 22W
Hout →, S. Africa . . . . . . . . . 57 C4   23  4S  29 36 E
Houtkraal, S. Africa . . . . . . . . 56 E3   30 23S  24  5 E
Houtman Abrolhos, Australia . . 61 E1   28 43S 113 48 E
Hovd, Mongolia . . . . . . . . . . . 32 B4   48  2N  91 37 E
Hove, U.K. . . . . . . . . . . . . . . 13 G7   50 50N   0 10W
Hovenweep △, U.S.A. . . . . . . . 77 H9   37 20N 109  0W
Hoveyzeh, Iran . . . . . . . . . . . 45 D6   31 27N  48  4 E
Hövsgöl, Mongolia . . . . . . . . . 34 C5   43 37N 109 39 E
Hövsgöl Nuur, Mongolia . . . . . 32 A5   51  0N 100 30 E
Howard, Australia . . . . . . . . . . 63 D5   25 16S 152 32 E
Howard, Pa., U.S.A. . . . . . . . . 84 F7   41  1N  77 40W
Howard, S. Dak., U.S.A. . . . . . 80 C6   44  1N  97 32W
Howe, U.S.A. . . . . . . . . . . . . . 76 E7   43 48N 113  0W
Howe, C., Australia . . . . . . . . 63 F5   37 30S 150  0 E
Howe I., Canada . . . . . . . . . . 85 B8   44 16N  76 17W
Howell, U.S.A. . . . . . . . . . . . . 82 D4   42 36N  83 56W
Howick, Canada . . . . . . . . . . . 85 A11  45 11N  73 51W
Howick, S. Africa . . . . . . . . . . 57 D5   29 28S  30 14 E
Howick Group, Australia . . . . . 62 A4   14 20S 145 30 E
Howitt, L., Australia . . . . . . . . 63 D2   27 40S 138 40 E
Howland I., Pac. Oc. . . . . . . . 64 G10   0 48N 176 38W
Howrah = Haora, India . . . . . . 43 H13  22 37N  88 20 E
Howth Hd., Ireland . . . . . . . . . 10 C5   53 22N   6  3W
Höxter, Germany . . . . . . . . . . 16 C5   51 46N   9 22 E
Hoy, U.K. . . . . . . . . . . . . . . . 11 C5   58 50N   3 15W
Høyanger, Norway . . . . . . . . .  9 F12  61 13N   6  4 E
Hoyerswerda, Germany . . . . . . 16 C8   51 26N  14 14 E
Hoylake, U.K. . . . . . . . . . . . . 12 D4   53 24N   3 10W
Hpa-an = Pa-an, Burma . . . . . 41 L20  16 51N  97 40 E
Hpungan Pass, Burma . . . . . . 41 F20  27 30N  96 55 E
Hradec Králové, Czech Rep. . . 16 C8   50 15N  15 50 E
Hrodna, Belarus . . . . . . . . . . . 17 B12  53 42N  23 52 E
Hrodzyanka, Belarus . . . . . . . 17 B15  53 31N  28 42 E
Hron →, Slovak Rep. . . . . . . . 17 E10  47 49N  18 45 E
Hrvatska = Croatia ■, Europe . 16 F9   45 20N  16  0 E
Hrymayliv, Ukraine . . . . . . . . . 17 D14  49 20N  26  5 E
Hsenwi, Burma . . . . . . . . . . . . 41 H20  23 22N  97 55 E
Hsiamen = Xiamen, China . . . . 33 D6   24 25N 118 4 E
Hsian = Xi'an, China . . . . . . . . 34 G5   34 15N 109  0 E
Hsinchu, Taiwan . . . . . . . . . . 33 D7   24 48N 120 58 E
Hsinhailien = Lianyungang,
    China . . . . . . . . . . . . . . . . 35 G10  34 40N 119 11 E
Hsüchou = Xuzhou, China . . . . 35 G9   34 18N 117 10 E
Hu Xian, China . . . . . . . . . . . 34 G5   34  8N 108 42 E
Hua Hin, Thailand . . . . . . . . . 38 F2   12 34N  99 58 E
Hua Xian, Henan, China . . . . . 34 G8   35 30N 114 30 E
Hua Xian, Shaanxi, China . . . . 34 G5   34 30N 109 48 E
Huab →, Namibia . . . . . . . . . 56 B2   20 52S  13 25 E
Huachinera, Mexico . . . . . . . . 86 A3   30  9N 108 55W
Huacho, Peru . . . . . . . . . . . . 92 F3   11 10S  77 35W
Huade, China . . . . . . . . . . . . 34 D7   41 55N 113 59 E
Huadian, China . . . . . . . . . . . 35 C14  43  0N 126 40 E
Huai Had △, Thailand . . . . . . . 38 D5   16 52N 104 17 E
Huai He →, China . . . . . . . . . 33 C6   33  0N 118 30 E
Huai Yot, Thailand . . . . . . . . . 39 J2    7 45N  99 37 E
Huai'an, Hebei, China . . . . . . 34 D8   40 30N 114 20 E
Huai'an, Jiangsu, China . . . . . 35 H10  33 30N 119 10 E
Huaibei, China . . . . . . . . . . . 34 G9   34  0N 116 48 E
Huaide = Gongzhuling, China . 35 C13  43 30N 124 40 E
Huaidezhen, China . . . . . . . . 35 C13  43 48N 124 50 E
Huainan, China . . . . . . . . . . . 33 C6   32 38N 116 58 E
Huairen, China . . . . . . . . . . . 34 E7   39 48N 113 20 E
Huairou, China . . . . . . . . . . . 34 D9   40 20N 116 35 E
Huaiyang, China . . . . . . . . . . 34 H8   33 40N 114 52 E
Huaiyin, China . . . . . . . . . . . 35 H10  33 30N 119  2 E
Huaiyuan, China . . . . . . . . . . 35 H9   32 55N 117 10 E
Huajianzi, China . . . . . . . . . . 35 D13  41 23N 125 20 E
Huajuapan de Leon, Mexico . . 87 D5   17 50N  98  0W
Hualapai Peak, U.S.A. . . . . . . 77 J7   35  5N 113 54W
Huallaga →, Peru . . . . . . . . . 92 E3    5 15S  75 30W
Huambo, Angola . . . . . . . . . . 53 G3   12 42S  15 54 E
Huan Jiang →, China . . . . . . . 34 G5   34 28N 109  0 E
Huan Xian, China . . . . . . . . . 34 F4   36 33N 107  7 E
Huancabamba, Peru . . . . . . . . 92 E3    5 10S  79 15W
Huancane, Peru . . . . . . . . . . . 92 G5   15 10S  69 44W
Huancavelica, Peru . . . . . . . . 92 F3   12 50S  75  5W
Huancayo, Peru . . . . . . . . . . . 92 F3   12  5S  75 12W
Huanchaca, Bolivia . . . . . . . . 92 H5   20 15S  66 40W
Huang Hai = Yellow Sea, China 35 G12  35  0N 123  0 E
Huang He →, China . . . . . . . . 35 F10  37 55N 118 50 E
Huang Xian, China . . . . . . . . . 35 F11  37 38N 120 30 E
Huangling, China . . . . . . . . . . 34 G5   35 34N 109 15 E
Huanglong, China . . . . . . . . . 34 G5   35 30N 109 59 E
Huangshan, China . . . . . . . . . 33 D6   29 42N 118 25 E
Huangshi, China . . . . . . . . . . 33 C6   30 10N 115  3 E
Huangsongdian, China . . . . . . 35 C14  43 45N 127 25 E
Huantai, China . . . . . . . . . . . 35 F9   36 58N 117 56 E
Huánuco, Peru . . . . . . . . . . . 92 E3    9 55S  76 15W
Huaraz, Peru . . . . . . . . . . . . 92 E3    9 30S  77 32W
Huarmey, Peru . . . . . . . . . . . 92 F3   10  5S  78 5W
Huascarán, Peru . . . . . . . . . . 92 E3    9  8S  77 36W
Huasco, Chile . . . . . . . . . . . . 94 B1   28 30S  71 15W
Huasco →, Chile . . . . . . . . . . 94 B1   28 27S  71 13W
Huasna, U.S.A. . . . . . . . . . . . 79 K6   35  6N 120 24W
Huatabampo, Mexico . . . . . . . 86 B3   26 50N 109 50W
Huauchinango, Mexico . . . . . . 87 C5   20 11N  98  3W
Huautla de Jiménez, Mexico . . 87 D5   18 8N  96 51W
Huay Namota, Mexico . . . . . . 86 C4   21 56N 104 30W
Huayin, China . . . . . . . . . . . . 34 G6   34 35N 110  5 E
Hubbard, Ohio, U.S.A. . . . . . . 84 E4   41  9N  80 34W
Hubbard, Tex., U.S.A. . . . . . . 81 K6   31 51N  96 48W
Hubbart Pt., Canada . . . . . . . 71 B10  59 21N  94 41W
Hubei □, China . . . . . . . . . . . 33 C6   31  0N 112  0 E
Hubli, India . . . . . . . . . . . . . . 40 M9  15 22N  75 15 E
Huch'ang, N. Korea . . . . . . . . 35 D14  41 25N 127  2 E
Hucknall, U.K. . . . . . . . . . . . . 12 D6   53  3N   1 13W
Huddersfield, U.K. . . . . . . . . . 12 D6   53 39N   1 47W
Hudiksvall, Sweden . . . . . . . .  9 F17  61 43N  17 10 E
Hudson, Canada . . . . . . . . . . 72 B1   50  6N  92  9W
Hudson, Mass., U.S.A. . . . . . . 85 D13  42 23N  71 34W
Hudson, N.Y., U.S.A. . . . . . . . 85 D11  42 15N  73 46W
Hudson, Wis., U.S.A. . . . . . . . 80 C8   44 58N  92 45W
Hudson, Wyo., U.S.A. . . . . . . 76 E9   42 54N 108 35W
Hudson →, U.S.A. . . . . . . . . . 85 F10  40 42N  74  2W
Hudson Bay, Nunavut, Canada . 69 C11  60  0N  86  0W
Hudson Bay, Sask., Canada . . 71 C8   52 51N 102 23W
Hudson Falls, U.S.A. . . . . . . . 85 C11  43 18N  73 35W
Hudson Mts., Antarctica . . . . .  5 D16  74 32S  99 20W

Hudson Str., Canada . . . . . . . 69 B13  62  0N  70  0W
Hudson's Hope, Canada . . . . . 70 B4   56  0N 121 54W
Hue, Vietnam . . . . . . . . . . . . . 38 D6   16 30N 107 35 E
Huehuetenango, Guatemala . . 88 C1   15 20N  91 28W
Huejúcar, Mexico . . . . . . . . . . 86 C4   22 21N 103 13W
Huelva, Spain . . . . . . . . . . . . 21 D2   37 18N   6 57W
Huentelauquén, Chile . . . . . . . 94 C1   31 38S  71 33W
Huerta, Sa. de la, Argentina . . 94 C2   31 10S  67 30W
Huesca, Spain . . . . . . . . . . . . 21 A5   42  8N   0 25W
Huetamo, Mexico . . . . . . . . . . 86 D4   18 36N 100 54W
Hugh →, Australia . . . . . . . . . 62 D1   25  1S 134  1 E
Hughenden, Australia . . . . . . . 62 C3   20 52S 144 10 E
Hughes, Australia . . . . . . . . . 61 F4   30 42S 129 31 E
Hughesville, U.S.A. . . . . . . . . 85 E8   41 14N  76 44W
Hugli →, India . . . . . . . . . . . . 43 J13  21 56N  88  4 E
Hugo, Colo., U.S.A. . . . . . . . . 80 F3   39  8N 103 28W
Hugo, Okla., U.S.A. . . . . . . . . 81 H7   34  1N  95 31W
Hugoton, U.S.A. . . . . . . . . . . 81 G4   37 11N 101 21W
Hui Xian = Huixian, China . . . . 34 G7   35 27N 113 12 E
Hui Xian, China . . . . . . . . . . . 34 H4   33 50N 106  4 E
Hui'anbu, China . . . . . . . . . . . 34 F4   37 28N 106 38 E
Huichapán, Mexico . . . . . . . . . 87 C5   20 24N  99 40W
Huifa He →, China . . . . . . . . . 35 C14  43  0N 127 50 E
Huila, Nevado del, Colombia . . 92 C3    3  0N  76  0W
Huimin, China . . . . . . . . . . . . 35 F9   37 27N 117 28 E
Huinan, China . . . . . . . . . . . . 35 C14  42 40N 126  2 E
Huinca Renancó, Argentina . . 94 C3   34 51S  64 22W
Huining, China . . . . . . . . . . . 34 G3   35 38N 105  0 E
Huinong, China . . . . . . . . . . . 34 E4   39  5N 106 35 E
Huisache, Mexico . . . . . . . . . 86 C4   22 55N 100 25W
Huiting, China . . . . . . . . . . . . 34 G9   34  5N 116  5 E
Huixian, China . . . . . . . . . . . 34 G7   35 27N 113 12 E
Huixtla, Mexico . . . . . . . . . . . 87 D6   15  9N  92 28W
Huize, China . . . . . . . . . . . . . 32 D5   26 24N 103 15 E
Huizhou, China . . . . . . . . . . . 33 D6   23 0N 114 18 E
Hukawng Valley, Burma . . . . . 41 F20  26 30N  96 30 E
Hŭksan-chedo, S. Korea . . . . 35 G13  34 40N 125 30 E
Hukuntsi, Botswana . . . . . . . . 56 C3   23 58S  21 45 E
Hulayfā', Si. Arabia . . . . . . . . 44 E4   25 58N  40 45 E
Hulin He →, China . . . . . . . . . 35 B12  45  0N 122 10 E
Hull = Kingston upon Hull, U.K. 12 D7   53 45N   0 21W
Hull, Canada . . . . . . . . . . . . . 85 A9   45 25N  75 44W
Hull →, U.K. . . . . . . . . . . . . . 12 D7   53 44N   0 20W
Hulst, Neths. . . . . . . . . . . . . . 15 C4   51 17N   4  2 E
Hulun Nur, China . . . . . . . . . . 33 B6   49  0N 117 30 E
Huma, Tanjung, Malaysia . . . . 39 c    5 29N 100 16 E
Humacao, Puerto Rico . . . . . . 89 d   18  9N  65 50W
Humahuaca, Argentina . . . . . . 94 A2   23 10S  65 25W
Humaitá, Brazil . . . . . . . . . . . 92 E6    7 35S  63  1W
Humaitá, Paraguay . . . . . . . . 94 B4   27  2S  58 31W
Humansdorp, S. Africa . . . . . . 56 E3   34  2S  24 46 E
Humbe, Angola . . . . . . . . . . . 56 B1   16 40S  14 55 E
Humber →, U.K. . . . . . . . . . . 12 D7   53 42N   0 27W
Humboldt, Canada . . . . . . . . . 71 C7   52 15N 105 39W
Humboldt, Iowa, U.S.A. . . . . . 80 D7   42 44N  94 13W
Humboldt, Tenn., U.S.A. . . . . . 81 H10  35 50N  88 55W
Humboldt →, U.S.A. . . . . . . . . 76 F4   39 59N 118 36W
Humboldt Gletscher =
    Sermersuaq, Greenland . . . .  4 B4   79 30N  62  0W
Hume, U.S.A. . . . . . . . . . . . . 78 J8   36 48N 118 54W
Hume, L., Australia . . . . . . . . 63 F4   36  0S 147  5 E
Humen, China . . . . . . . . . . . . 33 F10  22 50N 113 40 E
Humenné, Slovak Rep. . . . . . . 17 D11  48 55N  21 50 E
Humphreys, Mt., U.S.A. . . . . . 78 H8   37 17N 118 40W
Humphreys Peak, U.S.A. . . . . 77 J8   35 21N 111 41W
Humptulips, U.S.A. . . . . . . . . 78 C3   47 14N 123 57W
Hūn, Libya . . . . . . . . . . . . . . 51 C9   29  2N  16  0 E
Hun Jiang →, China . . . . . . . . 35 D13  40 50N 125 38 E
Húnaflói, Iceland . . . . . . . . . .  8 D3   65 50N  20 50W
Hunan □, China . . . . . . . . . . . 33 D6   27 30N 112  0 E
Hunchun, China . . . . . . . . . . 35 C16  42 52N 130 28 E
Hundewali, Pakistan . . . . . . . 42 D5   31 55N  72 38 E
Hundred Mile House, Canada . 70 C4   51 38N 121 18W
Hunedoara, Romania . . . . . . . 17 F12  45 40N  22 50 E
Hung Yen, Vietnam . . . . . . . . 38 B6   20 39N 106  4 E
Hungary ■, Europe . . . . . . . . 17 E10  47 20N  19  0 E
Hungary, Plain of, Europe . . . .  6 F10  47  0N  20  0 E
Hungerford, Australia . . . . . . . 63 D3   28 58S 144 24 E
Hŭngnam, N. Korea . . . . . . . . 35 E14  39 49N 127 45 E
Hunsberge, Namibia . . . . . . . 56 D2   27 45S  17 12 E
Hunsrück, Germany . . . . . . . . 16 D4   49 56N   7 27 E
Hunstanton, U.K. . . . . . . . . . . 12 E8   52 56N   0 29 E
Hunter I., Australia . . . . . . . . 63 G3   40 30S 144 45 E
Hunter I., Canada . . . . . . . . . 70 C3   51 55N 128  0W
Hunter Ra., Australia . . . . . . . 63 E5   32 45S 150 15 E
Hunters Road, Zimbabwe . . . . 55 F2   19  9S  29 49 E
Hunterville, N.Z. . . . . . . . . . . 59 H5   39 56S 175 35 E
Huntingburg, U.S.A. . . . . . . . . 82 F2   38 18N  86 57W
Huntingdon, Canada . . . . . . . 72 C5   45  6N  74 10W
Huntingdon, U.K. . . . . . . . . . . 13 E7   52 20N   0 11W
Huntingdon, Pa., U.S.A. . . . . . 84 F6   40 30N  78  1W
Huntington, Ind., U.S.A. . . . . . 82 E3   40 53N  85 30W
Huntington, N.Y., U.S.A. . . . . . 85 F11  40 52N  73 26W
Huntington, Oreg., U.S.A. . . . . 76 D5   44 21N 117 16W
Huntington, Utah, U.S.A. . . . . 76 G8   39 20N 110 58W
Huntington, W. Va., U.S.A. . . . 82 F4   38 25N  82 27W
Huntington Beach, U.S.A. . . . . 79 M9  33 40N 118  5W
Huntly, N.Z. . . . . . . . . . . . . . . 59 G5   37 34S 175 11 E
Huntly, U.K. . . . . . . . . . . . . . 11 D6   57 27N   2 47W
Huntsville, Canada . . . . . . . . 84 A5   45 20N  79 14W
Huntsville, Ala., U.S.A. . . . . . . 83 H2   34 44N  86 35W
Huntsville, Tex., U.S.A. . . . . . 81 K7   30 43N  95 33W
Hunyani →, Zimbabwe . . . . . . 55 F3   15 57S  30 39 E
Hunyuan, China . . . . . . . . . . 34 E7   39 42N 113 42 E
Hunza →, India . . . . . . . . . . . 43 B6   35 54N  74 20 E
Huo Xian = Huozhou, China . . 34 F6   36 36N 111 42 E
Huong Khe, Vietnam . . . . . . . 38 C5   18 13N 105 41 E
Huonville, Australia . . . . . . . . 63 G4   43  0S 147  5 E
Huozhou, China . . . . . . . . . . 34 F6   36 36N 111 42 E
Hupeh = Hubei □, China . . . . . 33 C6   31  0N 112  0 E
Ḥūr, Iran . . . . . . . . . . . . . . . . 45 D8   30 50N  57  7 E
Hure Qi, China . . . . . . . . . . . 35 C11  42 45N 121 45 E
Hurghada, Egypt . . . . . . . . . . 51 C12  27 15N  33 50 E
Hurley, N. Mex., U.S.A. . . . . . 77 K9   32 42N 108  8W
Hurley, Wis., U.S.A. . . . . . . . . 80 B9   46 27N  90 11W
Huron, Calif., U.S.A. . . . . . . . 78 J6   36 12N 120  6W
Huron, Ohio, U.S.A. . . . . . . . . 84 E2   41 24N  82 33W
Huron, S. Dak., U.S.A. . . . . . . 80 C5   44 22N  98 13W
Huron, L., U.S.A. . . . . . . . . . . 84 B2   44 30N  82 40W
Huron East, Canada . . . . . . . 84 C3   43 37N  81 18W
Hurricane, U.S.A. . . . . . . . . . 77 H7   37 11N 113 17W
Hurungwe △, Zimbabwe . . . . . 55 F2   16  7S  29  5 E
Hurunui →, N.Z. . . . . . . . . . . 59 K4   42 54S 173 18 E
Húsavík, Iceland . . . . . . . . . .  8 C5   66  3N  17 21W
Huși, Romania . . . . . . . . . . . . 17 E15  46 41N  28  7 E
Huskvarna, Sweden . . . . . . . .  9 H16  57 47N  14 15 E
Hustadvika, Norway . . . . . . . .  8 E12  63  0N   7  0 E

Hustontown, U.S.A. . . . . . . . . 84 F6   40  3N  78  2W
Hutchinson, Kans., U.S.A. . . . 81 F6   38  5N  97 56W
Hutchinson, Minn., U.S.A. . . . 80 C7   44 54N  94 22W
Hutte Sauvage, L. de la, Canada 73 A7  56 15N  64 45W
Hutton, Mt., Australia . . . . . . . 63 D4   25 51S 148 20 E
Huy, Belgium . . . . . . . . . . . . . 15 D5   50 31N   5 15 E
Huzhou, China . . . . . . . . . . . 33 C7   30 51N 120  8 E
Hvammstangi, Iceland . . . . . . .  8 D3   65 24N  20 57W
Hvar, Croatia . . . . . . . . . . . . 22 C7   43 11N  16 28 E
Hvítá →, Iceland . . . . . . . . . .  8 D3   64 30N  21 58W
Hwachŏn-chŏsuji, S. Korea . . 35 E14  38  5N 127 50 E
Hwang Ho = Huang He →, China 35 F10 37 55N 118 50 E
Hwange, Zimbabwe . . . . . . . . 55 F2   18 18S  26 30 E
Hwange △, Zimbabwe . . . . . . 56 B4   19  0S  26 30 E
Hyannis, Mass., U.S.A. . . . . . 82 E10  41 39N  70 17W
Hyannis, Nebr., U.S.A. . . . . . . 80 E4   42  0N 101 46W
Hyargas Nuur, Mongolia . . . . . 32 B4   49  0N  93  0 E
Hydaburg, U.S.A. . . . . . . . . . 70 B2   55 15N 132 50W
Hyde Park, U.S.A. . . . . . . . . . 85 E11  41 47N  73 56W
Hyden, Australia . . . . . . . . . . 61 F2   32 24S 118 53 E
Hyder, U.S.A. . . . . . . . . . . . . 70 B2   55 55N 130  5W
Hyderabad, India . . . . . . . . . . 40 L11  17 22N  78 29 E
Hyderabad, Pakistan . . . . . . . 42 G3   25 23N  68 24 E
Hyères, France . . . . . . . . . . . 20 E7   43  8N   6  9 E
Hyères, Îs. d', France . . . . . . . 20 E7   43  0N   6 20 E
Hyesan, N. Korea . . . . . . . . . 35 D15 41 20N 128 10 E
Hyland →, Canada . . . . . . . . 70 B3   59 52N 128 12W
Hymia, India . . . . . . . . . . . . . 43 C8   33 40N  78  2 E
Hyndman Peak, U.S.A. . . . . . . 76 E6   43 45N 114  8W
Hyōgo □, Japan . . . . . . . . . . 31 G7   35 15N 134 50 E
Hyrum, U.S.A. . . . . . . . . . . . . 76 F8   41 38N 111 51W
Hysham, U.S.A. . . . . . . . . . . . 76 C10  46 18N 107 14W
Hythe, U.K. . . . . . . . . . . . . . 13 F9   51  4N   1  5 E
Hyūga, Japan . . . . . . . . . . . . 31 H5   32 25N 131 35 E
Hyvinge = Hyvinkää, Finland . .  9 F21  60 38N  24 50 E
Hyvinkää, Finland . . . . . . . . .  9 F21  60 38N  24 50 E

## I

I-n-Gall, Niger . . . . . . . . . . . . 50 E7   16 51N   7  1 E
Iaco →, Brazil . . . . . . . . . . . . 92 E5    9  3S  68 34W
Iakora, Madag. . . . . . . . . . . . 57 C8   23  6S  46 40 E
Ialomița →, Romania . . . . . . . 17 F14  44 42N  27 51 E
Iași, Romania . . . . . . . . . . . . 17 E14  47 10N  27 40 E
Ib →, India . . . . . . . . . . . . . . 43 J10  21 34N  83 48 E
Iba, Phil. . . . . . . . . . . . . . . . . 37 A6   15 22N 120  0 E
Ibadan, Nigeria . . . . . . . . . . . 50 G6    7 22N   3 58 E
Ibagué, Colombia . . . . . . . . . 92 C3    4 20N  75 20W
Ibar →, Serbia & M. . . . . . . . 23 C9   43 43N  20 45 E
Ibaraki □, Japan . . . . . . . . . . 31 F10  36 10N 140 10 E
Ibarra, Ecuador . . . . . . . . . . 92 C3    0 21N  78  7W
Ibembo, Dem. Rep. of the Congo 54 B1    2 35N  23 35 E
Ibera, L., Argentina . . . . . . . . 94 B4   28 30S  57  9W
Iberian Peninsula, Europe . . . .  6 H5   40  0N   5  0W
Iberville, Canada . . . . . . . . . . 85 A11  45 19N  73 17W
Iberville, Lac d', Canada . . . . 72 A5   55 55N  73 15W
Ibiá, Brazil . . . . . . . . . . . . . . 93 G9   19 30S  46 30W
Ibiapaba, Sa. da, Brazil . . . . . 93 D10   4  0S  41 30W
Ibicuí →, Brazil . . . . . . . . . . . 95 B4   29 25S  56 47W
Ibicuy, Argentina . . . . . . . . . . 94 C4   33 55S  59 10W
Ibiza = Eivissa, Spain . . . . . . 24 C7   38 54N   1 26 E
Ibo, Mozam. . . . . . . . . . . . . . 55 E5   12 22S  40 40 E
Ibonma, Indonesia . . . . . . . . 37 E8    3 29S 133 31 E
Ibotirama, Brazil . . . . . . . . . . 93 F10  12 13S  43 12W
Ibrāhīm →, Lebanon . . . . . . . 46 A4   34  4N  35 38 E
'Ibrī, Oman . . . . . . . . . . . . . . 45 F8   23 14N  56 30 E
Ibu, Indonesia . . . . . . . . . . . . 37 D7    1 35N 127 33 E
Ibusuki, Japan . . . . . . . . . . . 31 J5   31 12N 130 40 E
Ica, Peru . . . . . . . . . . . . . . . . 92 F3   14  0S  75 48W
Iça →, Brazil . . . . . . . . . . . . 92 D5    2 55S  67 58W
Icacos Pt., Trin. & Tob. . . . . . . 93 K15  10  3N  61 57W
Içana, Brazil . . . . . . . . . . . . . 92 C5    0 21N  67 19W
Içana →, Brazil . . . . . . . . . . . 92 C5    0 26N  67 19W
İçel = Mersin, Turkey . . . . . . . 19 G5   36 51N  34 36 E
Iceland ■, Europe . . . . . . . . .  8 D4   64 45N  19  0W
Iceland Plateau, Arctic . . . . . .  4 C7   64  0N  10  0W
Ich'ang = Yichang, China . . . . 33 C6   30 40N 111 20 E
Ichchapuram, India . . . . . . . . 41 K14  19 10N  84 40 E
Ichhawar, India . . . . . . . . . . . 42 H7   23  1N  77  1 E
Ichihara, Japan . . . . . . . . . . 31 G10  35 28N 140  5 E
Ichikawa, Japan . . . . . . . . . . 31 G9   35 44N 139 55 E
Ichilo →, Bolivia . . . . . . . . . . 92 G6   15 57S  64 50W
Ichinohe, Japan . . . . . . . . . . 30 D10  40 13N 141 17 E
Ichinomiya, Japan . . . . . . . . . 31 G8   35 18N 136 48 E
Ichinoseki, Japan . . . . . . . . . 30 E10  38 55N 141  8 E
Icod, Canary Is. . . . . . . . . . . 24 F3   28 22N  16 43W
Ida Grove, U.S.A. . . . . . . . . . 80 D7   42 21N  95 28W
Idabel, U.S.A. . . . . . . . . . . . . 81 J7   33 54N  94 50W
Idaho □, U.S.A. . . . . . . . . . . . 76 D7   45  0N 115  0W
Idaho City, U.S.A. . . . . . . . . . 76 E6   43 50N 115 50W
Idaho Falls, U.S.A. . . . . . . . . 76 E7   43 30N 112  2W
Idalia △, Australia . . . . . . . . . 62 C3   24 49S 144 36 E
Idar-Oberstein, Germany . . . . 16 D4   49 43N   7 16 E
Idensalmi = Iisalmi, Finland . .  8 E22  63 32N  27 10 E
Idfû, Egypt . . . . . . . . . . . . . . 51 D12  24 55N  32 49 E
Ídhi Óros, Greece . . . . . . . . . 25 D6   35 15N  24 45 E
Ídhra, Greece . . . . . . . . . . . . 23 F10  37 20N  23 28 E
Idi, Indonesia . . . . . . . . . . . . 36 C1    5  2N  97 37 E
Idiofa, Dem. Rep. of the Congo 52 E3    4 55S  19 42 E
Idlib, Syria . . . . . . . . . . . . . . 44 C3   35 55N  36 36 E
Idria, U.S.A. . . . . . . . . . . . . . 78 J6   36 25N 120 41W
Idutywa, S. Africa . . . . . . . . . 57 E4   32  8S  28 18 E
Ieper, Belgium . . . . . . . . . . . 15 D2   50 51N   2 53 E
Ierápetra, Greece . . . . . . . . . 25 E7   35  1N  25 44 E
Iesi, Italy . . . . . . . . . . . . . . . 22 C5   43 31N  13 14 E
Ifakara, Tanzania . . . . . . . . . 52 F7    8  8S  36 41 E
'Ifāl, W. al →, Si. Arabia . . . . 44 D2   28  7N  35  3 E
Ifanadiana, Madag. . . . . . . . . 57 C8   21 19S  47 39 E
Ife, Nigeria . . . . . . . . . . . . . . 50 G6    7 30N   4 31 E
Iffley, Australia . . . . . . . . . . . 62 B3   18 53S 141 12 E
Iforas, Adrar des, Africa . . . . . 50 E6   19 40N   1 40 E
Ifould, L., Australia . . . . . . . . 61 F5   30 52S 132  6 E
Iganga, Uganda . . . . . . . . . . 54 B3    0 37N  33 28 E
Igarapava, Brazil . . . . . . . . . . 93 H9   20  3S  47 47W
Igarka, Russia . . . . . . . . . . . 28 C9   67 30N  86 33 E
Igatimi, Paraguay . . . . . . . . . 95 A4   24  5S  55 40W
Iggesund, Sweden . . . . . . . . .  9 F17  61 39N  17  4 E
Iglésias, Italy . . . . . . . . . . . . 22 E3   39 19N   8 32 E
Igloolik, Canada . . . . . . . . . . 69 B11  69 20N  81 49W
Igluligaarjuk = Chesterfield Inlet,
    Canada . . . . . . . . . . . . . . 68 B10  63 30N  90 45W
Iglulik = Igloolik, Canada . . . . 69 B11  69 20N  81 49W
Ignace, Canada . . . . . . . . . . 72 C1   49 30N  91 40W
İğneada Burnu, Turkey . . . . . . 23 D13 41 53N  28  2 E
Igoumenítsa, Greece . . . . . . . 23 E9   39 32N  20 18 E

Iguaçu △, Brazil .......... 95 B5  25 30S  54  0W
Iguaçu ➤, Brazil .......... 95 B5  25 36S  54 36W
Iguaçu, Cat. del, Brazil ... 95 B5  25 41S  54 26W
Iguaçu Falls = Iguaçu, Cat. del,
  Brazil ................. 95 B5  25 41S  54 26W
Iguala, Mexico ........... 87 D5  18 20N  99 40W
Igualada, Spain .......... 21 B6  41 37N   1 37 E
Iguassu = Iguaçu ➤, Brazil . 95 B5  25 36S  54 36W
Iguatu, Brazil ........... 93 E11  6 20S  39 18W
Iguazú △, Argentina ...... 95 B5  25 42S  54 22W
Iguidi, Erg, Africa ....... 50 C4  27  0N   7  0 E
Iharana, Madag. ......... 57 A9  13 25S  50  0 E
Ihbulag, Mongolia ....... 34 C4  43 11N 107 10 E
Iheya-Shima, Japan ...... 31 L3  27  4N 127 58 E
Ihosy, Madag. ........... 57 C8  22 24S  46  8 E
Ihotry, Farihy, Madag. .... 57 C7  21 56S  43 41 E
Ii, Finland ............... 8 D21  65 19N  25 22 E
Ii-Shima, Japan .......... 31 L3  26 43N 127 47 E
Iida, Japan .............. 31 G8  35 35N 137 50 E
Iijoki ➤, Finland ......... 8 D21  65 20N  25 20 E
Iisalmi, Finland .......... 8 E22  63 32N  27 10 E
Iiyama, Japan ............ 31 F9  36 51N 138 22 E
Iizuka, Japan ............ 31 H5  33 38N 130 42 E
Ijebu-Ode, Nigeria ....... 50 G6   6 47N   3 58 E
IJmuiden, Neths. ......... 15 B4  52 28N   4 35 E
Ijo älv = Iijoki ➤, Finland .. 8 D21  65 20N  25 20 E
IJssel ➤, Neths. .......... 15 B5  52 35N   5 50 E
IJsselmeer, Neths. ........ 15 B5  52 45N   5 20 E
Ijui, Brazil .............. 95 B5  28 23S  53 55W
Ijuí ➤, Brazil ............ 95 B4  27 58S  55 20W
Ikalamavony, Madag. ..... 57 C8  21  9S  46 35 E
Ikaluktutiak, Canada ..... 68 B9  69 10N 105  0W
Ikare, Nigeria ........... 50 G7   7 32N   5 40 E
Ikaria, Greece ........... 23 F12  37 35N  26 10 E
Ikeda, Japan ............ 31 G6  34  1N 133 48 E
Ikela, Dem. Rep. of the Congo 52 E4   1  6S  23  6 E
Iki, Japan ............... 31 H4  33 45N 129 42 E
Ikimba L., Tanzania ...... 54 C3   1 30S  31 20 E
Ikongo, Madag. .......... 57 C8  21 52S  47 27 E
Ikopa ➤, Madag. ......... 57 B8  16 45S  46 40 E
Ikorongo △, Tanzania ..... 54 C3   1 50S  34 53 E
Ikparjuk = Arctic Bay, Canada 69 A11  73  1N  85  7W
Ikungu, Tanzania ......... 54 C3   1 33S  33 42 E
Ilagan, Phil. ............. 37 A6  17  7N 121 53 E
Ilaka, Madag. ............ 57 B8  19 33S  48 52 E
Ilâm, Iran ............... 44 C5  33 36N  46 36 E
Ilam, Nepal ............. 43 F12  26 58N  87 58 E
Ilam □, Iran ............. 44 C5  33  0N  47  0 E
Ilanskiy, Russia ......... 29 D10  56 14N  96  3 E
Iława, Poland ............ 17 B10  53 36N  19 34 E
Ile ➤, Kazakhstan ........ 28 E8  45 53N  77 10 E
Île-à-la-Crosse, Canada ... 71 B7  55 27N 107 53W
Île-à-la-Crosse, Lac, Canada 71 B7  55 40N 107 45W
Île-de-France □, France ... 20 B5  49  0N   2 20 E
Ilebo, Dem. Rep. of the Congo 52 E4   4 17S  20 55 E
Ilek, Russia ............. 28 D6  51 32N  53 21 E
Ilek ➤, Russia ........... 18 D9  51 30N  53 22 E
Ilesha, Nigeria .......... 50 G6   7 37N   4 40 E
Ilford, Canada ........... 71 B9  56  4N  95 35W
Ilfracombe, Australia ..... 62 C3  23 30S 144 30 E
Ilfracombe, U.K. ......... 13 F3  51 12N   4  8W
Ilha de Moçambique, Mozam. 55 F5  15  4S  40 52 E
Ilhéus, Brazil ............ 93 F11  14 49S  39  2W
Ili = Ile ➤, Kazakhstan ... 28 E8  45 53N  77 10 E
Iliamna L., U.S.A. ....... 68 C4  59 30N 155  0W
Iligan, Phil. ............. 37 C6   8 12N 124 13 E
Ilion, U.S.A. ............. 85 D9  43  1N  75  2W
Ilkeston, U.K. ........... 12 E6  52 58N   1 19W
Ilkley, U.K. ............. 12 D6  53 56N   1 48W
Illampu = Ancohuma, Nevado,
  Bolivia ................ 92 G5  16  0S  68 50W
Illana B., Phil. .......... 37 C6   7 35N 123 45 E
Illapel, Chile ............ 94 C1  32  0S  71 10W
Iller ➤, Germany ......... 16 D6  48 23N   9 58 E
Illetas, Spain ............ 24 B9  39 32N   2 35 E
Illimani, Nevado, Bolivia .. 92 G5  16 30S  67 50W
Illinois □, U.S.A. ........ 80 E10  40 15N  89 30W
Illinois ➤, U.S.A. ........ 80 F9  38 58N  90 28W
Illizi, Algeria ........... 50 C7  26 31N   8 32 E
Ilmajoki, Finland ........ 8 E20  62 44N  22 34 E
Ilmen, Ozero, Russia ..... 18 C5  58 15N  31 10 E
Ilo, Peru ................ 92 G4  17 40S  71 20W
Iloilo, Phil. ............. 37 B6  10 45N 122 33 E
Ilorin, Nigeria .......... 50 G6   8 30N   4 35 E
Ilwaco, U.S.A. ........... 78 D2  46 19N 124  3W
Ilwaki, Indonesia ........ 37 F7   7 55S 126 30 E
Imabari, Japan .......... 31 G6  34  4N 133  0 E
Imaloto ➤, Madag. ....... 57 C8  23 27S  45 13 E
Imandra, Ozero, Russia ... 18 A5  67 30N  33  0 E
Imanombo, Madag. ....... 57 C8  24 26S  45 49 E
Imari, Japan ............ 31 H4  33 15N 129 52 E
Imatra, Finland .......... 18 B4  61 12N  28 48 E
imeni 26 Bakinskikh
  Komissarov = Neftçala,
  Azerbaijan ............ 19 G8  39 19N  49 12 E
imeni 26 Bakinskikh Komissarov,
  Turkmenistan .......... 45 B7  39 22N  54 10 E
Imeri, Serra, Brazil ...... 92 C5   0 50N  65 25W
Imerimandroso, Madag. ... 57 B8  17 26S  48 35 E
Imi, Ethiopia ............ 47 F3   6 28N  42 10 E
Imlay, U.S.A. ........... 76 F4  40 40N 118  9W
Imlay City, U.S.A. ....... 84 D1  43  2N  83  5W
Immingham, U.K. ........ 12 D7  53 37N   0 13W
Immokalee, U.S.A. ....... 83 M5  26 25N  81 25W
Ímola, Italy ............. 22 B4  44 20N  11 42 E
Imperatriz, Brazil ....... 93 E9   5 30S  47 29W
Impéria, Italy ........... 20 E8  43 53N   8  3 E
Imperial, Canada ........ 71 C7  51 21N 105 28W
Imperial, Calif., U.S.A. ... 79 N11  32 51N 115 34W
Imperial, Nebr., U.S.A. ... 80 E4  40 31N 101 39W
Imperial Beach, U.S.A. ... 79 N9  32 35N 117  8W
Imperial Dam, U.S.A. .... 79 N12  32 55N 114 25W
Imperial Reservoir, U.S.A. . 79 N12  32 53N 114 28W
Imperial Valley, U.S.A. ... 79 N11  33  0N 115 30W
Imperieuse Reef, Australia . 60 C2  17 36S 118 50 E
Impfondo, Congo ......... 52 D3   1 40N  18  0 E
Imphal, India ........... 41 G18  24 48N  93 56 E
İmroz = Gökçeada, Turkey . 23 D11  40 10N  26  0 E
Imuris, Mexico .......... 86 A2  30 47N 110 52W
Imuruan B., Phil. ........ 37 B5  10 40N 119 10 E
In Salah, Algeria ........ 50 C6  27 10N   2 32 E
Ina, Japan .............. 31 G8  35 50N 137 55 E
Inagua □, Bahamas ...... 89 B5  21  5N  73 24W
Inangahua, N.Z. ......... 59 J3  41 52S 171 59 E
Inanwatan, Indonesia .... 37 E8   2  8S 132 10 E
Iñapari, Peru ............ 92 F5  11  0S  69 40W
Inari, Finland ........... 8 B22  68 54N  27  1 E
Inarijärvi, Finland ....... 8 B22  69  0N  28  0 E

Inawashiro-Ko, Japan ..... 30 F10  37 29N 140  6 E
Inca, Spain .............. 24 B9  39 43N   2 54 E
Inca de Oro, Chile ....... 94 B2  26 45S  69 54W
Incaguasi, Chile ......... 94 B1  29 12S  71  5W
İnce Burun, Turkey ....... 19 F5  42  7N  34 56 E
İncesu, Turkey ........... 44 B2  38 38N  35 11 E
Inch'ŏn, S. Korea ........ 35 F14  37 27N 126 40 E
İncirliova, Turkey ........ 23 F12  37 50N  27 41 E
Incline Village, U.S.A. .... 76 G4  39 10N 119 58W
Incomáti ➤, Mozam. ...... 57 D5  25 46S  32 43 E
Indalsälven ➤, Sweden ... 9 E17  62 36N  17 30 E
Indaw, Burma ........... 41 G20  24 15N  96  5 E
Independence, Calif., U.S.A. 78 J8  36 48N 118 12W
Independence, Iowa, U.S.A. 80 D9  42 28N  91 54W
Independence, Kans., U.S.A. 81 G7  37 14N  95 42W
Independence, Ky., U.S.A. . 82 F3  38 57N  84 33W
Independence, Mo., U.S.A. . 80 F7  39  6N  94 25W
Independence Fjord, Greenland 4 A6  82 10N  29  0W
Independence Mts., U.S.A. . 76 F5  41 20N 116  0W
Index, U.S.A. ........... 78 C5  47 50N 121 33W
India ■, Asia ............ 40 K11  20  0N  78  0 E
Indian ➤, U.S.A. ......... 83 M5  27 59N  80 34W
Indian Cabins, Canada ... 70 B5  59 52N 117 40W
Indian Harbour, Canada ... 73 B8  54 27N  57 13W
Indian Head, Canada ..... 71 C8  50 30N 103 41W
Indian Lake, U.S.A. ...... 85 C10  43 47N  74 16W
Indian Ocean ............ 26 K11  5  0S  75  0 E
Indian Springs, U.S.A. .... 79 J11  36 35N 115 40W
Indiana, U.S.A. .......... 84 F5  40 37N  79  9W
Indiana □, U.S.A. ........ 82 F3  40  0N  86  0W
Indianapolis, U.S.A. ...... 82 F2  39 46N  86  9W
Indianola, Iowa, U.S.A. ... 80 E8  41 22N  93 34W
Indianola, Miss., U.S.A. ... 81 J9  33 27N  90 39W
Indiga, Russia ........... 18 A8  67 38N  49  9 E
Indigirka ➤, Russia ...... 29 B15  70 48N 148 54 E
Indio, U.S.A. ............ 79 M10  33 43N 116 13W
Indira Gandhi Canal, India . 42 F5  28  0N  72  0 E
Indo-China, Asia ......... 26 H14  15  0N 102  0 E
Indonesia ■, Asia ........ 36 F5   5  0S 115  0 E
Indore, India ............ 42 H6  22 42N  75 53 E
Indramayu, Indonesia .... 37 G13  6 20S 108 19 E
Indravati ➤, India ....... 41 K12  19 20N  80 20 E
Indre ➤, France .......... 20 C4  47 16N   0 11 E
Indulkana, Australia ..... 63 D1  26 58S 133  5 E
Indus ➤, Pakistan ........ 42 G2  24 20N  67 47 E
Indus, Mouths of the, Pakistan 42 H3  24  0N  68  0 E
İnebolu, Turkey .......... 19 F5  41 55N  33 40 E
Infiernillo, Presa del, Mexico 86 D4  18  9N 102  0W
Ingenio, Canary Is. ....... 24 G4  27 55N  15 26W
Ingenio Santa Ana, Argentina 94 B2  27 25S  65 40W
Ingersoll, Canada ........ 84 C4  43  4N  80 55W
Ingham, Australia ........ 62 B4  18 43S 146 10 E
Ingleborough, U.K. ....... 12 C5  54 10N   2 22W
Inglewood, Queens., Australia 63 D5  28 25S 151  2 E
Inglewood, Vic., Australia . 63 F3  36 29S 143 53 E
Inglewood, N.Z. .......... 59 H5  39  9S 174 14 E
Inglewood, U.S.A. ........ 79 M8  33 58N 118 21W
Ingólfshöfði, Iceland ...... 8 E5  63 48N  16 39W
Ingolstadt, Germany ...... 16 D6  48 46N  11 26 E
Ingomar, U.S.A. .......... 76 C10  46 35N 107 23W
Ingonish, Canada ........ 73 C7  46 42N  60 18W
Ingraj Bazar, India ....... 43 G13  24 58N  88 10 E
Ingrid Christensen Coast,
  Antarctica ............. 5 C6  69 30S  76  0 E
Ingulec = Inhulec, Ukraine . 19 E5  47 42N  33 14 E
Ingushetia □, Russia ..... 19 F8  43 20N  44 50 E
Ingwavuma, S. Africa ..... 57 D5  27  9S  31 59 E
Inhaca, Mozam. ......... 57 D5  26  1S  32 57 E
Inhafenga, Mozam. ....... 57 C5  20 36S  33 53 E
Inhambane, Mozam. ...... 57 C6  23 54S  35 30 E
Inhambane □, Mozam. .... 57 C5  22 30S  34 20 E
Inhaminga, Mozam. ...... 57 F4  18 26S  35  0 E
Inharrime, Mozam. ....... 57 C6  24 30S  35  0 E
Inharrime ➤, Mozam. ..... 57 C6  24 30S  35  0 E
Inhulec, Ukraine ......... 19 E5  47 42N  33 14 E
Ining = Yining, China .... 28 E9  43 58N  81 10 E
Inírida ➤, Colombia ...... 92 C5   3 55N  67 52W
Inishbofin, Ireland ....... 10 C1  53 37N  10 13W
Inisheer, Ireland ......... 10 C2  53  3N   9 32W
Inishfree B., Ireland ...... 10 A3  55  4N   8 23W
Inishkea North, Ireland ... 10 B1  54  9N  10 11W
Inishkea South, Ireland ... 10 B1  54  7N  10 12W
Inishmaan, Ireland ....... 10 C2  53  5N   9 35W
Inishmore, Ireland ....... 10 C2  53  8N   9 45W
Inishowen Pen., Ireland ... 10 A4  55 14N   7 15W
Inishshark, Ireland ....... 10 C1  53 37N  10 16W
Inishturk, Ireland ........ 10 C1  53 42N  10  7W
Inishvickillane, Ireland .... 10 D1  52  3N  10 37W
Injune, Australia ......... 63 D4  25 53S 148 32 E
Inklin ➤, Canada ......... 70 B2  58 50N 133 10W
Inland Kaikoura Ra., N.Z. . 59 J4  41 59S 173 41 E
Inland Sea = Setonaikai, Japan 31 G6  34 20N 133 30 E
Inle L., Burma ........... 41 J20  20 30N  96 58 E
Inlet, U.S.A. ............. 85 C10  43 45N  74 48W
Inn ➤, Austria ........... 16 D7  48 35N  13 28 E
Innamincka, Australia .... 63 D3  27 44S 140 46 E
Inner Hebrides, U.K. ..... 11 E2  57  0N   6 30W
Inner Mongolia = Nei Monggol
  Zizhiqu □, China ....... 34 D7  42  0N 112  0 E
Inner Sound, U.K. ....... 11 D3  57 30N   5 55W
Innerkip, Canada ........ 84 C4  43 13N  80 42W
Innetalling I., Canada .... 72 A4  56  0N  79  0W
Innisfail, Australia ....... 62 B4  17 33S 146  5 E
Innisfail, Canada ........ 70 C6  52  2N 113 57W
In'noshima, Japan ....... 31 G6  34 19N 133 10 E
Innsbruck, Austria ....... 16 E6  47 16N  11 23 E
Inny ➤, Ireland .......... 10 C4  53 30N   7 50W
Inongo, Dem. Rep. of the Congo 52 E3   1 55S  18 30 E
Inoucdjouac = Inukjuak, Canada 69 C12  58 25N  78 15W
Inowrocław, Poland ....... 17 B10  52 50N  18 12 E
Inpundong, N. Korea ...... 35 D14  41 25N 126 34 E
Inscription, C., Australia .. 61 E1  25 29S 112 59 E
Insein, Burma ........... 41 L20  16 50N  96  5 E
Inta, Russia ............. 18 A11  66 5N  60  8 E
Intendente Alvear, Argentina 94 D3  35 12S  63 32W
Interior, U.S.A. .......... 80 D4  43 44N 101 59W
Interlaken, Switz. ........ 20 C7  46 41N   7 50 E
Interlaken, U.S.A. ........ 85 D8  42 37N  76 44W
International Falls, U.S.A. .. 80 A8  48 36N  93 25W
Intiyaco, Argentina ...... 94 B3  28 43S  60  5W
Inukjuak, Canada ........ 69 C12  58 25N  78 15W
Inútil, B., Chile .......... 96 G2  53 30N  70 15W
Inuvik, Canada .......... 68 B6  68 16N 133 40W
Inveraray, U.K. .......... 11 E3  56 14N   5  5W
Inverbervie, U.K. ......... 11 E6  56 51N   2 17W
Invercargill, N.Z. ........ 59 M2  46 24S 168 24 E
Inverclyde □, U.K. ....... 11 F4  55 55N   4 49W
Inverell, Australia ....... 63 D5  29 45S 151  8 E
Invergordon, U.K. ........ 11 D4  57 41N   4 10W

Inverloch, Australia ...... 63 F4  38 38S 145 45 E
Invermere, Canada ....... 70 C5  50 30N 116  2W
Inverness, Canada ........ 73 C7  46 15N  61 19W
Inverness, U.K. .......... 11 D4  57 29N   4 13W
Inverness, U.S.A. ........ 83 L4  28 50N  82 20W
Inverurie, U.K. .......... 11 D6  57 17N   2 23W
Investigator Group, Australia 63 E1  34 45S 134 20 E
Investigator Str., Australia . 63 F2  35 30S 137  0 E
Inya, Russia ............. 28 D9  50 28N  86 37 E
Inyanga, Zimbabwe ...... 55 F3  18 12S  32 40 E
Inyangani, Zimbabwe ..... 55 F3  18 5S  32 50 E
Inyantue, Zimbabwe ...... 56 B4  18 33S  26 39 E
Inyo Mts., U.S.A. ......... 78 J9  36 40N 118  0W
Inyokern, U.S.A. ......... 79 K9  35 39N 117 49W
Inza, Russia ............. 18 D8  53 55N  46 25 E
Iō-Jima, Japan ........... 31 J5  30 48N 130 18 E
Ioánnina, Greece ......... 23 E9  39 42N  20 47 E
Iola, U.S.A. ............. 81 G7  37 55N  95 24W
Iona, U.K. ............... 11 E2  56 20N   6 25W
Ione, U.S.A. ............. 78 G6  38 21N 120 56W
Ionia, U.S.A. ............ 82 D3  42 59N  85  4W
Ionian Is. = Iónioi Nísoi, Greece 23 E9  38 40N  20  0 E
Ionian Sea, Medit. S. ..... 23 E7  37 30N  17 30 E
Iónioi Nísoi, Greece ...... 23 E9  38 40N  20  0 E
Íos, Greece .............. 23 F11  36 41N  25 20 E
Iowa □, U.S.A. ........... 80 D8  42 18N  93 30W
Iowa ➤, U.S.A. ........... 80 E9  41 10N  91  1W
Iowa City, U.S.A. ........ 80 E9  41 40N  91 32W
Iowa Falls, U.S.A. ........ 80 D8  42 31N  93 16W
Iowa Park, U.S.A. ........ 81 J5  33 57N  98 40W
Ipala, Tanzania .......... 54 C3   4 30S  32 52 E
Ipameri, Brazil .......... 93 G9  17 44S  48  9W
Ipatinga, Brazil .......... 93 G10  19 32S  42 30W
Ipiales, Colombia ........ 92 C3   0 50N  77 37W
Ipin = Yibin, China ....... 32 D5  28 45N 104 32 E
Ipixuna, Brazil .......... 92 E4   7  0S  71 40W
Ipoh, Malaysia .......... 39 K3   4 35N 101  5 E
Ippy, C.A.R. ............. 52 C4   6  5N   7 E
Ipsala, Turkey ........... 23 D12  40 55N  26 23 E
Ipswich, Australia ....... 63 D5  27 35S 152 40 E
Ipswich, U.K. ............ 13 E9  52  4N   1 10 E
Ipswich, Mass., U.S.A. .... 85 D14  42 41N  70 50W
Ipswich, S. Dak., U.S.A. ... 80 C5  45 27N  99  2W
Ipu, Brazil .............. 93 D10  4 23S  40 44W
Iqaluit, Canada .......... 69 B13  63 44N  68 31W
Iquique, Chile ........... 92 H4  20 19S  70  5W
Iquitos, Peru ............ 92 D4   3 45S  73 10W
Irabu-Jima, Japan ........ 31 M2  24 50N 125 10 E
Iracoubo, Fr. Guiana ...... 93 B8   5 30N  53 10W
Irafshân, Iran ........... 45 E9  26 42N  61 56 E
Iráklion, Greece .......... 25 D7  35 20N  25 12 E
Iráklion □, Greece ........ 25 D7  35 10N  25 10 E
Irala, Paraguay .......... 95 B5  25 55S  54 35W
Iran ■, Asia ............. 45 C7  33  0N  53  0 E
Iran, Gunung-Gunung, Malaysia 36 D4  2  0N 114 50 E
Iran, Plateau of, Asia ..... 26 F9  32  0N  55  0 E
Iran Ra. = Iran, Gunung-Gunung,
  Malaysia .............. 36 D4   2 20N 114 50 E
Īrānshahr, Iran .......... 45 E9  27 15N  60 40 E
Irapuato, Mexico ........ 86 C4  20 40N 101 30W
Iraq ■, Asia ............. 44 C5  33  0N  44  0 E
Irati, Brazil ............. 95 B5  25 25S  50 38W
Irbid, Jordan ............ 46 C4  32 35N  35 48 E
Irbid □, Jordan .......... 46 C5  32 15N  36 35 E
Ireland ■, Europe ........ 10 C4  53 50N   7 52W
Irhyangdong, N. Korea .... 35 D15  41 15N 129 30 E
Iri, S. Korea ............. 35 G14  35 59N 127  0 E
Irian Jaya = Papua □, Indonesia 37 E9   4  0S 137  0 E
Iringa, Tanzania ......... 54 D4   7 48S  35 43 E
Iringa □, Tanzania ....... 54 D4   7 48S  35 43 E
Iriomote △, Japan ........ 31 M1  24 29N 123 53 E
Iriomote-Jima, Japan ..... 31 M1  24 19N 123 48 E
Iriona, Honduras ......... 88 C2  15 57N  85 11W
Iriri ➤, Brazil ........... 93 D8   3 52S  52 37W
Irish Republic ■, Europe .. 10 C4  53 50N   7 52W
Irish Sea, Europe ........ 12 D3  53 38N   4 48W
Irkutsk, Russia .......... 29 D11  52 18N 104 20 E
Irma, Canada ............ 71 C6  52 55N 111 14W
Irō-Zaki, Japan .......... 31 G9  34 36N 138 51 E
Iron Baron, Australia ..... 63 E2  32 58S 137 11 E
Iron Gate = Portile de Fier,
  Europe ................ 17 F12  44 44N  22 30 E
Iron Knob, Australia ...... 63 E2  32 46S 137  8 E
Iron Mountain, U.S.A. .... 82 C1  45 49N  88  4W
Iron Range △, Australia ... 62 A3  12 34S 143 18 E
Iron River, U.S.A. ........ 80 B10  46  6N  88 39W
Irondequoit, U.S.A. ....... 84 C7  43 13N  77 35W
Ironton, Mo., U.S.A. ...... 81 G9  37 36N  90 38W
Ironton, Ohio, U.S.A. ..... 82 F4  38 32N  82 41W
Ironwood, U.S.A. ........ 80 B9  46 27N  90  9W
Ironwood Forest △, U.S.A. . 77 K8  32 28N 111 36W
Iroquois, Canada ........ 85 B9  44 51N  75 19W
Iroquois Falls, Canada .... 72 C3  48 46N  80 41W
Irpin, Ukraine ........... 17 C16  50 30N  30 15 E
Irrara Cr. ➤, Australia .... 63 D4  29 35S 145 31 E
Irrawaddy □, Burma ...... 41 L19  17  0N  95  0 E
Irrawaddy ➤, Burma ...... 41 M19  15 50N  95  6 E
Irrawaddy, Mouths of the, Burma 41 M19  15 30N  95  0 E
Irricana, Canada ......... 70 C6  51 19N 113 37W
Irtysh ➤, Russia ......... 28 C7  61  4N  68 52 E
Irumu, Dem. Rep. of the Congo 54 B2  1 32N  29 53 E
Irún, Spain .............. 21 A5  43 20N   1 52W
Irunea = Pamplona, Spain . 21 A5  42 48N   1 38W
Irvine, U.K. ............. 11 F4  55 37N   4 41W
Irvine, Calif., U.S.A. ...... 79 M9  33 41N 117 46W
Irvine, Ky., U.S.A. ........ 82 G4  37 42N  83 58W
Irvinestown, U.K. ........ 10 B4  54 28N   7 39W
Irving, U.S.A. ............ 81 J6  32 49N  96 56W
Irvona, U.S.A. ........... 84 F6  40 46N  78 33W
Irwin ➤, Australia ........ 61 E1  29 15S 114 54 E
Irymple, Australia ........ 63 E3  34 14S 142  8 E
Isa Khel, Pakistan ....... 42 C4  32 41N  71 17 E
Isaac ➤, Australia ........ 62 C4  22 55S 149 20 E
Isabel, U.S.A. ........... 80 C4  45 24N 101 26W
Isabela, Phil. ............ 37 C6   6 40N 121 59 E
Isabela, Puerto Rico ...... 89 d  18 30N  67  2W
Isabela, I., Mexico ....... 86 C3  21 51N 105 55W
Isabella, Cord., Nic. ...... 88 D2  13 30N  85 25W
Isabella Ra., Australia .... 60 D3  21  0S 121  4 E
Ísafjarðardjúp, Iceland .... 8 C2  66  5N  23  0W
Ísafjörður, Iceland ....... 8 C2  66  5N  23  9W
Isagarh, India ........... 42 G7  24 48N  77 51 E
Isahaya, Japan .......... 31 H5  32 52N 130  2 E
Isaka, Tanzania .......... 54 C3   3 56S  32 59 E
Isalo △, Madag. ......... 57 C8  22 23S  45 16 E
Isan ➤, India ............ 43 F9  26 51N  80  7 E
Isana = Içana ➤, Brazil ... 92 C5   0 26N  67 19W
Isangano △, Zambia ...... 55 E3  11  8S  30 35 E

Isar ➤, Germany ......... 16 D7  48 48N  12 57 E
Ischia, Italy ............. 22 D5  40 44N  13 57 E
Isdell ➤, Australia ....... 60 C3  16 27S 124 51 E
Ise, Japan .............. 31 G8  34 25N 136 45 E
Ise-Shima △, Japan ...... 31 G8  34 25N 136 48 E
Ise-Wan, Japan .......... 31 G8  34 43N 136 43 E
Iseramagazi, Tanzania .... 54 C3   4 37S  32 10 E
Isère ➤, France .......... 20 D6  44 59N   4 51 E
Isérnia, Italy ............ 22 D6  41 36N  14 14 E
Isfahan = Eşfahān, Iran ... 45 C6  32 39N  51 43 E
Ishigaki-Shima, Japan .... 31 M2  24 20N 124 10 E
Ishikari-Gawa ➤, Japan ... 30 C10  43 15N 141 23 E
Ishikari-Sammyaku, Japan . 30 C11  43 30N 143  0 E
Ishikari-Wan, Japan ...... 30 C10  43 25N 141  1 E
Ishikawa □, Japan ....... 31 F8  36 30N 136 30 E
Ishim, Russia ........... 28 D7  56 10N  69 30 E
Ishim ➤, Russia ......... 28 D8  57 45N  71 10 E
Ishinomaki, Japan ....... 30 E10  38 32N 141 20 E
Ishioka, Japan .......... 31 F10  36 11N 140 16 E
Ishkuman, Pakistan ...... 43 A5  36 30N  73 50 E
Ishpeming, U.S.A. ....... 82 B2  46 29N  87 40W
Isil Kul, Russia .......... 28 D8  54 55N  71 16 E
Isiolo, Kenya ............ 54 B4   0 24N  37 33 E
Isiro, Dem. Rep. of the Congo 54 B2  2 53N  27 40 E
Isisford, Australia ....... 62 C3  24 15S 144 21 E
İskenderun, Turkey ....... 19 G6  36 32N  36 10 E
İskenderun Körfezi, Turkey . 19 G6  36 40N  35 50 E
Iskŭr ➤, Bulgaria ........ 23 C11  43 45N  24 25 E
Iskut ➤, Canada ......... 70 B2  56 45N 131 49W
Isla ➤, U.K. ............. 11 E5  56 32N   3 20W
Isla Coiba △, Panama ..... 88 E3   7 33N  81 36W
Isla de Salamanca △, Colombia 89 D5  10 59N  74 40W
Isla Gorge △, Australia ... 62 D4  25 10S 149 57 E
Isla Tiburón y San Estebán △,
  Mexico ................ 86 B2  29  0N 112 27W
Isla Vista, U.S.A. ........ 79 L7  34 25N 119 53W
Islam Headworks, Pakistan . 42 E5  29 49N  72 33 E
Islamabad, Pakistan ...... 42 C5  33 40N  73 10 E
Islamgarh, Pakistan ...... 42 F4  27 51N  70 48 E
Islamkot, Pakistan ....... 42 G4  24 42N  70 13 E
Islampur, India .......... 43 G11  25 9N  85 12 E
Island L., Canada ........ 71 C10  53 47N  94 25W
Island Lagoon, Australia .. 63 E2  31 30S 136 40 E
Island Pond, U.S.A. ...... 85 B13  44 49N  71 53W
Islands, B. of, Canada .... 73 C8  49 11N  58 15W
Islands, B. of, N.Z. ...... 59 F5  35 15S 174  6 E
Islay, U.K. ............... 11 F2  55 46N   6 10W
Isle ➤, France ........... 20 D3  44 55N   0 15W
Isle aux Morts, Canada ... 73 C8  47 35N  59  0W
Isle of Wight □, U.K. ..... 13 G6  50 41N   1 17W
Isle Royale △, U.S.A. ..... 82 B1  48  0N  88 55W
Isleton, U.S.A. .......... 78 G5  38 10N 121 37W
Ismail = Izmayil, Ukraine .. 17 F15  45 22N  28 46 E
Ismâ'ilîya, Egypt ........ 51 B12  30 37N  32 18 E
Isoanala, Madag. ........ 57 C8  23 50S  45 44 E
Isogstalo, India ......... 43 B8  34 15N  78 46 E
Isparta, Turkey .......... 19 G5  37 47N  30 30 E
İspica, Italy ............. 22 F6  36 47N  14 55 E
Israel ■, Asia ........... 46 D3  32  0N  34 50 E
Issoire, France .......... 20 D5  45 32N   3 15 E
Issyk-Kul, Ozero = Ysyk-Köl,
  Kyrgyzstan ............ 28 E8  42 25N  77 15 E
İstanbul, Turkey ......... 23 D13  41  0N  29  0 E
İstanbul Boğazı, Turkey ... 23 D13  41 10N  29 10 E
Istiaía, Greece .......... 23 E10  38 57N  23  9 E
Istokpoga, L., U.S.A. ..... 83 M5  27 23N  81 17W
Istra, Croatia ........... 16 F7  45 10N  14  0 E
Istres, France ........... 20 E6  43 31N   4 59 E
Istria = Istra, Croatia ..... 16 F7  45 10N  14  0 E
Itá, Paraguay ........... 94 B4  25  8S  57 21W
Itaberaba, Brazil ........ 93 F10  12 32S  40 18W
Itabira, Brazil ........... 93 G10  19 37S  43 13W
Itabirito, Brazil ......... 95 A7  20 15S  43 48W
Itabuna, Brazil .......... 93 F11  14 48S  39 16W
Itacaunas ➤, Brazil ...... 93 E9   5 21S  49  8W
Itacoatiara, Brazil ....... 92 D7   3 8S  58 25W
Itaipú, Reprêsa de, Brazil . 95 B5  25 30S  54 30W
Itaituba, Brazil .......... 93 D7   4 10S  55 50W
Itajaí, Brazil ............ 95 B6  27 50S  48 39W
Itajubá, Brazil ........... 95 A6  22 24S  45 30W
Itaka, Tanzania .......... 55 D3   8 50S  32 49 E
Itala △, S. Africa ........ 57 D5  27 30S  31  7 E
Itamaraju, Brazil ........ 93 G11  17 5S  39 31W
Itampolo, Madag. ........ 57 C7  24 41S  43 57 E
Itandrano, Madag. ....... 57 C8  21 47S  45 17 E
Itapecuru-Mirim, Brazil ... 93 D10  3 24S  44 20W
Itaperuna, Brazil ........ 95 A7  21 10S  41 54W
Itapetininga, Brazil ...... 95 A6  23 36S  48 7W
Itapeva, Brazil .......... 95 A6  23 59S  48 59W
Itapicuru ➤, Bahia, Brazil . 93 F11  11 47S  37 32W
Itapicuru ➤, Maranhão, Brazil 93 D10  2 52S  44 12W
Itapipoca, Brazil ......... 93 D11  3 30S  39 35W
Itapuá □, Paraguay ....... 95 B4  26 40S  55 40W
Itaquarí, Brazil .......... 95 A7  20 20S  40 25W
Itaquí, Brazil ........... 94 B4  29  8S  56 30W
Itararé, Brazil ........... 95 A6  24  6S  49 23W
Itarsi, India ............. 42 H7  22 36N  77 51 E
Itatí, Argentina .......... 94 B4  27 16S  58 15W
Itatiaia △, Brazil ........ 95 A7  22 22S  44 38W
Itchen ➤, U.K. ........... 13 G6  50 55N   1 22W
Itezhi Tezhi, L., Zambia ... 55 F2  15 30S  25 30 E
Ithaca = Itháki, Greece .... 23 E9  38 25N  20 40 E
Ithaca, U.S.A. ........... 85 D8  42 27N  76 30W
Itháki, Greece ........... 23 E9  38 25N  20 40 E
Itiquira ➤, Brazil ........ 93 G7  17 18S  56 44W
Itō, Japan .............. 31 G9  34 58N 139  5 E
Itoigawa, Japan ......... 31 F8  37  2N 137 51 E
Itonamas ➤, Bolivia ...... 92 F6  12 28S  64 24W
Ittoqqortoormiit, Greenland 4 B6  70 20N  23  0W
Itu, Brazil .............. 95 A6  23 17S  47 15W
Itu Aba I., S. China Sea ... 36 B4  10 23N 114 21 E
Ituiutaba, Brazil ......... 93 G9  19  0S  49 25W
Itumbiara, Brazil ........ 93 G9  18 20S  49 10W
Ituna, Canada ........... 71 C8  51 10N 103 24W
Itunge Port, Tanzania .... 55 D3   9 40S  33 55 E
Iturbe, Argentina ........ 94 A2  23  0S  65 25W
Ituri ➤, Dem. Rep. of the Congo 54 B2  1 40N  27  1 E
Iturup, Ostrov, Russia .... 29 E15  45  0N 148  0 E
Ituxi ➤, Brazil ........... 92 E6   7 18S  64 51W
Ituyuro ➤, Argentina ..... 94 A3  22 40S  63 50W
Itzehoe, Germany ........ 16 B5  53 55N   9 31 E
Ivahona, Madag. ......... 57 C8  23 27S  46 10 E
Ivaí ➤, Brazil ........... 95 A5  23 18S  53 42W
Ivalo, Finland ........... 8 B22  68 38N  27 35 E
Ivalojoki ➤, Finland ...... 8 B22  68 40N  27 40 E
Ivanava, Belarus ......... 17 B13  52  7N  25 29 E
Ivanhoe, Australia ....... 63 E3  32 56S 144 20 E

Ivanhoe, Calif., U.S.A. ...... 78 J7 36 23N 119 13W
Ivanhoe, Minn., U.S.A. ...... 80 C6 44 28N 96 15W
Ivano-Frankivsk, Ukraine ...... 17 D13 48 40N 24 40 E
Ivanovo = Ivanava, Belarus ...... 17 B13 52 7N 25 29 E
Ivanovo, Russia ...... 18 C7 57 5N 41 0 E
Ivato, Madag. ...... 57 C8 20 37S 47 10 E
Ivatsevichy, Belarus ...... 17 B13 52 43N 25 21 E
Ivdel, Russia ...... 18 B11 60 42N 60 24 E
Ivinheima →, Brazil ...... 95 A5 23 14S 53 42W
Ivinhema, Brazil ...... 95 A5 22 10S 53 37W
Ivohibe, Madag. ...... 57 C8 22 31S 46 57 E
Ivory Coast, W. Afr. ...... 50 H4 4 20N 5 0W
Ivory Coast ■, Africa ...... 50 G4 7 30N 5 0W
Ivrea, Italy ...... 20 D7 45 28N 7 52 E
Ivujivik, Canada ...... 69 B12 62 24N 77 55W
Ivybridge, U.K. ...... 13 G4 50 23N 3 56W
Iwaizumi, Japan ...... 30 E10 39 50N 141 45 E
Iwaki, Japan ...... 31 F10 37 3N 140 55 E
Iwakuni, Japan ...... 31 G6 34 15N 132 8 E
Iwamizawa, Japan ...... 30 C10 43 12N 141 46 E
Iwanai, Japan ...... 30 C10 42 58N 140 30 E
Iwata, Japan ...... 31 G8 34 42N 137 51 E
Iwate □, Japan ...... 30 E10 39 30N 141 30 E
Iwate-San, Japan ...... 30 E10 39 51N 141 0 E
Iwo, Nigeria ...... 50 G6 7 39N 4 9 E
Ixiamas, Bolivia ...... 92 F5 13 50S 68 5W
Ixopo, S. Africa ...... 57 E5 30 11S 30 5 E
Ixtepec, Mexico ...... 87 D5 16 32N 95 10W
Ixtlán del Río, Mexico ...... 86 C4 21 5N 104 21W
Iyo, Japan ...... 31 H6 33 45N 132 45 E
Izabal, L. de, Guatemala ...... 88 C2 15 30N 89 10W
Izamal, Mexico ...... 87 C7 20 56N 89 1W
Izena-Shima, Japan ...... 31 L3 26 56N 127 56 E
Izhevsk, Russia ...... 18 C9 56 51N 53 14 E
Izhma →, Russia ...... 18 A9 65 19N 52 54 E
Izmayil, Ukraine ...... 17 F15 45 22N 28 46 E
İzmir, Turkey ...... 23 E12 38 25N 27 8 E
İzmit = Kocaeli, Turkey ...... 19 F4 40 45N 29 50 E
İznik Gölü, Turkey ...... 23 D13 40 27N 29 30 E
Izra, Syria ...... 46 C5 32 51N 36 15 E
Izu-Shotō, Japan ...... 31 G10 34 30N 140 0 E
Izúcar de Matamoros, Mexico ...... 87 D5 18 36N 98 28W
Izumi-Sano, Japan ...... 31 G7 34 23N 135 18 E
Izumo, Japan ...... 31 G6 35 20N 132 46 E
Izyaslav, Ukraine ...... 17 C14 50 5N 26 50 E

J

Jabalpur, India ...... 43 H8 23 9N 79 58 E
Jabbūl, Syria ...... 44 B3 36 4N 37 30 E
Jabiru, Australia ...... 60 B5 12 40S 132 53 E
Jablah, Syria ...... 44 C3 35 20N 36 0 E
Jablonec nad Nisou, Czech Rep. ...... 16 C8 50 43N 15 10 E
Jaboatão, Brazil ...... 93 E11 8 7S 35 1W
Jaboticabal, Brazil ...... 95 A6 21 15S 48 17W
Jaca, Spain ...... 21 A5 42 35N 0 33W
Jacarei, Brazil ...... 95 A6 23 20S 46 0W
Jacarèzinho, Brazil ...... 95 A6 23 5S 49 58W
Jackman, U.S.A. ...... 83 C10 45 35N 70 17W
Jacksboro, U.S.A. ...... 81 J5 33 14N 98 15W
Jackson, Barbados ...... 89 g 13 7N 59 36W
Jackson, Ala., U.S.A. ...... 83 K2 31 31N 87 53W
Jackson, Calif., U.S.A. ...... 78 G6 38 21N 120 46W
Jackson, Ky., U.S.A. ...... 82 G4 37 33N 83 23W
Jackson, Mich., U.S.A. ...... 82 D3 42 15N 84 24W
Jackson, Minn., U.S.A. ...... 80 D7 43 37N 95 1W
Jackson, Miss., U.S.A. ...... 81 J9 32 18N 90 12W
Jackson, Mo., U.S.A. ...... 81 G10 37 23N 89 40W
Jackson, N.H., U.S.A. ...... 85 B13 44 10N 71 11W
Jackson, Ohio, U.S.A. ...... 82 F4 39 3N 82 39W
Jackson, Tenn., U.S.A. ...... 83 H1 35 37N 88 49W
Jackson, Wyo., U.S.A. ...... 76 E8 43 29N 110 46W
Jackson, B., N.Z. ...... 59 K2 43 58S 168 42 E
Jackson L., U.S.A. ...... 76 E8 43 52N 110 36W
Jacksons, N.Z. ...... 59 K3 42 46S 171 32 E
Jackson's Arm, Canada ...... 73 C8 49 52N 56 47W
Jacksonville, Ala., U.S.A. ...... 83 J3 33 49N 85 46W
Jacksonville, Ark., U.S.A. ...... 81 H8 34 52N 92 7W
Jacksonville, Calif., U.S.A. ...... 78 H6 37 52N 120 24W
Jacksonville, Fla., U.S.A. ...... 83 K5 30 20N 81 39W
Jacksonville, Ill., U.S.A. ...... 80 F9 39 44N 90 14W
Jacksonville, N.C., U.S.A. ...... 83 H7 34 45N 77 26W
Jacksonville, Tex., U.S.A. ...... 81 K7 31 58N 95 17W
Jacksonville Beach, U.S.A. ...... 83 K5 30 17N 81 24W
Jacmel, Haiti ...... 89 C5 18 14N 72 32W
Jacob Lake, U.S.A. ...... 77 H7 36 43N 112 13W
Jacobabad, Pakistan ...... 42 E3 28 20N 68 29 E
Jacobina, Brazil ...... 93 F10 11 11S 40 30W
Jacques-Cartier ≏, Canada ...... 73 C5 47 15N 71 33W
Jacques-Cartier, Dét. de, Canada ...... 73 C7 50 0N 63 30W
Jacques-Cartier, Mt., Canada ...... 73 C6 48 57N 66 0W
Jacuí →, Brazil ...... 95 C5 30 2S 51 15W
Jacumba, U.S.A. ...... 79 N10 32 37N 116 11W
Jacundá →, Brazil ...... 93 D8 1 57S 50 26W
Jaén, Peru ...... 92 E3 5 25S 78 40W
Jaén, Spain ...... 21 D4 37 44N 3 43W
Jafarabad, India ...... 42 J4 20 52N 71 22 E
Jaffa = Tel Aviv-Yafo, Israel ...... 46 C3 32 4N 34 48 E
Jaffa, C., Australia ...... 63 F2 36 58S 139 40 E
Jaffna, Sri Lanka ...... 40 Q12 9 45N 80 2 E
Jaffray, Canada ...... 71 D10 49 47N 94 26W
Jaffrey, U.S.A. ...... 85 D12 42 49N 72 2W
Jagadhri, India ...... 42 D7 30 10N 77 20 E
Jagadishpur, India ...... 43 G11 25 30N 84 21 E
Jagdalpur, India ...... 41 K13 19 3N 82 0 E
Jagersfontein, S. Africa ...... 56 D4 29 44S 25 27 E
Jaghin →, Iran ...... 45 E8 27 17N 57 13 E
Jagodina, Serbia & M. ...... 23 C9 44 5N 21 15 E
Jagraon, India ...... 40 D9 30 50N 75 25 E
Jagtial, India ...... 40 K11 18 50N 79 0 E
Jaguariaíva, Brazil ...... 95 A6 24 10S 49 50W
Jaguaribe →, Brazil ...... 93 D11 4 25S 37 45W
Jagüey Grande, Cuba ...... 88 B3 22 35N 81 7W
Jahanabad, India ...... 43 G11 25 13N 84 59 E
Jahazpur, India ...... 42 G6 25 37N 75 17 E
Jahrom, Iran ...... 45 D7 28 30N 53 31 E
Jaijon, India ...... 42 D7 31 21N 76 9 E
Jailolo, Indonesia ...... 37 D7 1 5N 127 30 E
Jailolo, Selat, Indonesia ...... 37 D7 0 5N 129 5 E
Jaipur, India ...... 42 F6 27 0N 75 50 E
Jais, India ...... 43 F9 26 15N 81 32 E
Jaisalmer, India ...... 42 F4 26 55N 70 54 E
Jaisinghnagar, India ...... 43 H8 23 38N 78 34 E
Jaitaran, India ...... 42 F5 26 12N 73 56 E
Jaithari, India ...... 43 H8 23 14N 78 37 E

Jäjarm, Iran ...... 45 B8 36 58N 56 27 E
Jakam →, India ...... 42 H6 23 54N 74 13 E
Jakarta, Indonesia ...... 36 F3 6 9S 106 49 E
Jakhal, India ...... 42 E6 29 48N 75 50 E
Jakhau, India ...... 42 H3 23 13N 68 43 E
Jakobstad = Pietarsaari, Finland ...... 8 E20 63 40N 22 43 E
Jal, U.S.A. ...... 81 J3 32 7N 103 12W
Jalālābād, Afghan. ...... 42 B4 34 30N 70 29 E
Jalalabad, India ...... 43 F8 27 41N 79 42 E
Jalalpur Jattan, Pakistan ...... 42 C6 32 38N 74 11 E
Jalama, U.S.A. ...... 79 L6 34 29N 120 29W
Jalapa, Guatemala ...... 88 D2 14 39N 89 59W
Jalapa Enríquez = Xalapa, Mexico ...... 87 D5 19 32N 96 55W
Jalasjärvi, Finland ...... 9 E20 62 29N 22 47 E
Jalaun, India ...... 43 F8 26 8N 79 25 E
Jalesar, India ...... 42 F8 27 29N 78 19 E
Jaleswar, Nepal ...... 43 F11 26 38N 85 48 E
Jalgaon, India ...... 40 J9 21 0N 75 42 E
Jalibah, Iraq ...... 44 D5 30 35N 46 32 E
Jalisco □, Mexico ...... 86 D4 20 0N 104 0W
Jalkot, Pakistan ...... 43 B5 35 14N 73 24 E
Jalna, India ...... 40 K9 19 48N 75 38 E
Jalón →, Spain ...... 21 B5 41 47N 1 4W
Jalor, India ...... 42 G5 25 21N 72 37 E
Jalpa, Mexico ...... 86 C4 21 38N 102 58W
Jalpaiguri, India ...... 41 F16 26 32N 88 46 E
Jaluit I., Marshall Is. ...... 64 G8 6 0N 169 30 E
Jalūlā, Iraq ...... 44 C5 34 16N 45 10 E
Jamaica ■, W. Indies ...... 88 a 18 10N 77 30W
Jamalpur, Bangla. ...... 41 G16 24 52N 89 56 E
Jamalpur, India ...... 43 G12 25 18N 86 28 E
Jamalpurganj, India ...... 43 H13 23 2N 87 59 E
Jamanxim →, Brazil ...... 93 D7 4 43S 56 18W
Jambewangi, Indonesia ...... 37 J17 8 17S 114 7 E
Jambi, Indonesia ...... 36 E2 1 38S 103 30 E
Jambi □, Indonesia ...... 36 E2 1 30S 102 30 E
Jambusar, India ...... 42 H5 22 3N 72 51 E
James →, S. Dak., U.S.A. ...... 80 D6 42 52N 97 18W
James →, Va., U.S.A. ...... 82 G7 36 56N 76 27W
James B., Canada ...... 72 B3 54 0N 80 0W
James Ranges, Australia ...... 60 D5 24 10S 132 30 E
James Ross I., Antarctica ...... 5 C18 63 58S 57 50W
Jamesabad, Pakistan ...... 42 G3 25 17N 69 15 E
Jamestown, Australia ...... 63 E2 33 10S 138 32 E
Jamestown, S. Africa ...... 56 E4 31 6S 26 45 E
Jamestown, N. Dak., U.S.A. ...... 80 B5 46 54N 98 42W
Jamestown, N.Y., U.S.A. ...... 84 D5 42 6N 79 14W
Jamestown, Pa., U.S.A. ...... 84 E4 41 29N 80 27W
Jamīlābād, Iran ...... 45 C6 34 24N 48 28 E
Jamiltepec, Mexico ...... 87 D5 16 17N 97 49W
Jamira →, India ...... 43 J13 21 35N 88 28 E
Jamkhandi, India ...... 40 L9 16 30N 75 15 E
Jammu, India ...... 42 C6 32 43N 74 54 E
Jammu & Kashmir □, India ...... 43 B7 34 25N 77 0 E
Jamnagar, India ...... 42 H4 22 30N 70 6 E
Jamni →, India ...... 43 G8 25 13N 78 35 E
Jampur, Pakistan ...... 42 E4 29 39N 70 40 E
Jamrud, Pakistan ...... 42 C4 33 59N 71 24 E
Jämsä, Finland ...... 9 F21 61 53N 25 10 E
Jamshedpur, India ...... 43 H12 22 44N 86 12 E
Jamtara, India ...... 43 H12 23 59N 86 49 E
Jämtland, Sweden ...... 8 E15 63 31N 14 0 E
Jan L., Canada ...... 71 C8 54 56N 102 55W
Jan Mayen, Arctic ...... 4 B7 71 0N 9 0W
Janakkala, Finland ...... 9 F21 60 54N 24 36 E
Janaúba, Brazil ...... 93 G10 15 48S 43 19W
Jand, Pakistan ...... 42 C5 33 30N 72 6 E
Jandaq, Iran ...... 45 C7 34 3N 54 22 E
Jandía, Canary Is. ...... 24 F5 28 6N 14 21W
Jandía, Pta. de, Canary Is. ...... 24 F5 28 3N 14 31W
Jandola, Pakistan ...... 42 C4 32 20N 70 9 E
Jandowae, Australia ...... 63 D5 26 45S 151 7 E
Janesville, U.S.A. ...... 80 D10 42 41N 89 1W
Jangamo, Mozam. ...... 57 C6 24 6S 35 21 E
Janghai, India ...... 43 G10 25 33N 82 19 E
Janjanbureh, Gambia ...... 50 F3 13 30N 14 47W
Janjgir, India ...... 43 J10 22 1N 82 34 E
Janjina, Madag. ...... 57 C8 20 30S 45 50 E
Janos, Mexico ...... 86 A3 30 45N 108 10W
Januária, Brazil ...... 93 G10 15 25S 44 25W
Janūb Sīnī □, Egypt ...... 46 F2 29 30N 33 50 E
Janubio, Canary Is. ...... 24 F6 28 56N 13 50W
Jaora, India ...... 42 H6 23 40N 75 10 E
Japan ■, Asia ...... 31 G8 36 0N 136 0 E
Japan, Sea of, Asia ...... 30 E7 40 0N 135 0 E
Japan Trench, Pac. Oc. ...... 26 F18 32 0N 142 0 E
Japen = Yapen, Indonesia ...... 37 E9 1 50S 136 0 E
Japla, India ...... 43 G11 24 33N 84 1 E
Japurá →, Brazil ...... 92 D5 3 8S 65 46W
Jaquarão, Brazil ...... 95 C5 32 34S 53 23W
Jaqué, Panama ...... 88 E4 7 27N 78 8W
Jarābulus, Syria ...... 44 B3 36 49N 38 1 E
Jarama →, Spain ...... 21 B4 40 24N 3 32W
Jaranwala, Pakistan ...... 42 D5 31 15N 73 26 E
Jarash, Jordan ...... 46 C4 32 17N 35 54 E
Jarash □, Jordan ...... 46 C4 32 17N 35 54 E
Jardim, Brazil ...... 94 A4 21 28S 56 2W
Jardine River ≏, Australia ...... 62 A3 11 9S 142 21 E
Jardines de la Reina, Arch. de los, Cuba ...... 88 B4 20 50N 78 50W
Jargalang, China ...... 35 C12 43 5N 122 55 E
Jari →, Brazil ...... 93 D8 1 9S 51 54W
Jarir, W. al →, Si. Arabia ...... 44 E4 25 38N 42 30 E
Jarosław, Poland ...... 17 C12 50 2N 22 42 E
Jarrahdale, Australia ...... 61 F2 32 24S 116 5 E
Jarrahi →, Iran ...... 45 D6 30 49N 48 48 E
Jarres, Plaine des, Laos ...... 38 C4 19 27N 103 10 E
Jartai, China ...... 34 E3 39 45N 105 48 E
Jarud Qi, China ...... 35 B11 44 28N 120 50 E
Järvenpää, Finland ...... 9 F21 60 29N 25 5 E
Jarvis, Canada ...... 84 D4 42 53N 80 6W
Jarvis I., Pac. Oc. ...... 65 H12 0 15S 160 5W
Jarwa, India ...... 43 F10 27 38N 82 30 E
Jasdan, India ...... 42 H4 22 2N 71 12 E
Jashpurnagar, India ...... 43 H11 22 54N 84 9 E
Jasidih, India ...... 43 G12 24 31N 86 39 E
Jāsimīyah, Iraq ...... 44 C5 33 45N 44 41 E
Jasin, Malaysia ...... 39 L4 2 20N 102 26 E
Jāsk, Iran ...... 45 E8 25 38N 57 45 E
Jasło, Poland ...... 17 D11 49 45N 21 30 E
Jaso, India ...... 43 G9 24 30N 80 29 E
Jasper, Alta., Canada ...... 70 C5 52 55N 118 5W
Jasper, Ont., Canada ...... 85 B9 44 52N 75 57W
Jasper, Ala., U.S.A. ...... 83 J2 33 50N 87 17W
Jasper, Fla., U.S.A. ...... 83 K4 30 31N 82 57W

Jasper, Ind., U.S.A. ...... 82 F2 38 24N 86 56W
Jasper, Tex., U.S.A. ...... 81 K8 30 56N 94 1W
Jasper ≏, Canada ...... 70 C5 52 50N 118 8W
Jasrasar, India ...... 42 F5 27 43N 73 49 E
Jászberény, Hungary ...... 17 E10 47 30N 19 55 E
Jataí, Brazil ...... 93 G8 17 58S 51 48W
Jati, Pakistan ...... 42 G3 24 20N 68 19 E
Jatibarang, Indonesia ...... 37 G13 6 28S 108 18 E
Jatiluwih, Indonesia ...... 37 J18 8 23S 115 8 E
Jatinegara, Indonesia ...... 37 G12 6 13S 106 52 E
Játiva = Xàtiva, Spain ...... 21 C5 38 59N 0 32W
Jaú, Brazil ...... 95 A6 22 10S 48 30W
Jauja, Peru ...... 92 F3 11 45S 75 15W
Jaunpur, India ...... 43 G10 25 46N 82 44 E
Java = Jawa, Indonesia ...... 36 F3 7 0S 110 0 E
Java Sea, Indonesia ...... 36 E3 4 35S 107 15 E
Java Trench, Ind. Oc. ...... 36 F3 9 0S 105 0 E
Jawa, Indonesia ...... 36 F3 7 0S 110 0 E
Jawa Barat □, Indonesia ...... 37 G12 7 0S 107 0 E
Jawa Tengah □, Indonesia ...... 37 G14 7 0S 110 0 E
Jawa Timur □, Indonesia ...... 37 G15 8 0S 113 0 E
Jawad, India ...... 42 G6 24 36N 74 51 E
Jay Peak, U.S.A. ...... 85 B12 44 55N 72 32W
Jaya, Puncak, Indonesia ...... 37 E9 3 57S 137 17 E
Jayanti, India ...... 41 F16 26 45N 89 40 E
Jayapura, Indonesia ...... 37 E10 2 28S 140 38 E
Jayawijaya, Pegunungan, Indonesia ...... 37 E9 5 0S 139 0 E
Jaynagar, India ...... 41 F15 26 43N 86 9 E
Jayrūd, Syria ...... 44 C3 33 49N 36 44 E
Jayton, U.S.A. ...... 81 J4 33 15N 100 34W
Jāz Mūrīān, Hāmūn-e, Iran ...... 45 E8 27 20N 58 55 E
Jazīreh-ye Shīf, Iran ...... 45 D6 29 4N 50 54 E
Jazminal, Mexico ...... 86 C4 24 56N 101 25W
Jazzin, Lebanon ...... 46 B4 33 31N 35 35 E
Jean, U.S.A. ...... 79 K11 35 47N 115 20W
Jean Marie River, Canada ...... 70 A4 61 32N 120 38W
Jean-Rabel, Haiti ...... 89 C5 19 50N 73 5W
Jeanerette, U.S.A. ...... 81 L9 29 55N 91 40W
Jeanette, Ostrov = Zhannetty, Ostrov, Russia ...... 29 B16 76 43N 158 0 E
Jeannette, U.S.A. ...... 84 F5 40 20N 79 36W
Jebāl Bārez, Kūh-e, Iran ...... 45 D8 28 30N 58 20 E
Jebel, Bahr el →, Sudan ...... 51 G12 9 30N 30 25 E
Jedburgh, U.K. ...... 11 F6 55 29N 2 33W
Jedda = Jiddah, Si. Arabia ...... 47 C2 21 29N 39 10 E
Jeddore L., Canada ...... 73 C8 48 3N 55 55W
Jędrzejów, Poland ...... 17 C11 50 35N 20 15 E
Jefferson, Iowa, U.S.A. ...... 80 D7 42 1N 94 23W
Jefferson, Ohio, U.S.A. ...... 84 E4 41 44N 80 46W
Jefferson, Tex., U.S.A. ...... 81 J7 32 46N 94 21W
Jefferson, Mt., Nev., U.S.A. ...... 76 G5 38 51N 117 0W
Jefferson, Mt., Oreg., U.S.A. ...... 76 D3 44 41N 121 48W
Jefferson City, Mo., U.S.A. ...... 80 F8 38 34N 92 10W
Jefferson City, Tenn., U.S.A. ...... 83 G4 36 7N 83 30W
Jeffersontown, U.S.A. ...... 82 F3 38 12N 85 35W
Jeffersonville, U.S.A. ...... 82 F3 38 17N 85 44W
Jeffrey City, U.S.A. ...... 76 E10 42 30N 107 49W
Jega, Nigeria ...... 50 F6 12 15N 4 23 E
Jeju = Cheju do, S. Korea ...... 35 H14 33 29N 126 34 E
Jēkabpils, Latvia ...... 9 H21 56 29N 25 57 E
Jekyll I., U.S.A. ...... 83 K5 31 4N 81 25W
Jelenia Góra, Poland ...... 16 C8 50 50N 15 45 E
Jelgava, Latvia ...... 9 H20 56 41N 23 49 E
Jemaja, Indonesia ...... 39 L5 3 5N 105 45 E
Jemaluang, Malaysia ...... 39 L4 2 16N 103 52 E
Jember, Indonesia ...... 37 H15 8 11S 113 41 E
Jembongan, Malaysia ...... 36 C5 6 45N 117 20 E
Jena, Germany ...... 16 C6 50 54N 11 35 E
Jena, U.S.A. ...... 81 K8 31 41N 92 8W
Jenin, West Bank ...... 46 C4 32 28N 35 18 E
Jenkins, U.S.A. ...... 82 G4 37 10N 82 38W
Jenner, U.S.A. ...... 78 G3 38 27N 123 7W
Jennings, U.S.A. ...... 81 K8 30 13N 92 40W
Jepara, Indonesia ...... 37 G14 7 40S 109 14 E
Jeparit, Australia ...... 63 F3 36 8S 142 1 E
Jequié, Brazil ...... 93 F10 13 51S 40 5W
Jequitinhonha, Brazil ...... 93 G10 16 30S 41 0W
Jequitinhonha →, Brazil ...... 93 G11 15 51S 38 53W
Jerantut, Malaysia ...... 39 L4 3 56N 102 22 E
Jerejak, Pulau, Malaysia ...... 39 c 5 19N 100 19 E
Jérémie, Haiti ...... 89 C5 18 40N 74 10W
Jerez, Punta, Mexico ...... 87 C5 22 58N 97 40W
Jerez de García Salinas, Mexico ...... 86 C4 22 39N 103 0W
Jerez de la Frontera, Spain ...... 21 D2 36 41N 6 7W
Jerez de los Caballeros, Spain ...... 21 C2 38 20N 6 45W
Jericho = El Arīḥā, West Bank ...... 46 D4 31 52N 35 27 E
Jericho, Australia ...... 62 C4 23 38S 146 6 E
Jerid, Chott el = Djerid, Chott, Tunisia ...... 50 B7 33 42N 8 30 E
Jerilderie, Australia ...... 63 F4 35 20S 145 41 E
Jermyn, U.S.A. ...... 85 E9 41 31N 75 31W
Jerome, U.S.A. ...... 76 E6 42 44N 114 31W
Jerramungup, Australia ...... 61 F2 33 55S 118 55 E
Jersey, U.K. ...... 13 H5 49 11N 2 7W
Jersey City, U.S.A. ...... 85 F10 40 44N 74 4W
Jersey Shore, U.S.A. ...... 84 E7 41 12N 77 15W
Jerseyville, U.S.A. ...... 80 F9 39 7N 90 20W
Jerusalem, Israel ...... 46 D4 31 47N 35 10 E
Jervis B., Australia ...... 63 F5 35 8S 150 46 E
Jervis Inlet, Canada ...... 70 C4 50 0N 123 57W
Jesi = Iesi, Italy ...... 22 C5 43 31N 13 14 E
Jessore, Bangla. ...... 41 H16 23 10N 89 10 E
Jesup, U.S.A. ...... 83 K5 31 36N 81 53W
Jesús Carranza, Mexico ...... 87 D5 17 28N 95 1W
Jesús María, Argentina ...... 94 C3 30 59S 64 5W
Jetmore, U.S.A. ...... 81 F5 38 4N 99 54W
Jetpur, India ...... 42 J4 21 45N 70 10 E
Jevnaker, Norway ...... 9 F14 60 15N 10 26 E
Jewett, U.S.A. ...... 84 F3 40 22N 81 2W
Jewett City, U.S.A. ...... 85 E13 41 36N 71 59W
Jeyhūnābād, Iran ...... 45 C6 34 58N 48 59 E
Jeypore, India ...... 41 K13 18 50N 82 38 E
Jha Jha, India ...... 43 G12 24 46N 86 22 E
Jhabua, India ...... 42 H6 22 46N 74 36 E
Jhajjar, India ...... 42 E7 28 37N 76 42 E
Jhal, Pakistan ...... 42 E2 28 17N 67 27 E
Jhal Jhao, Pakistan ...... 40 F4 26 20N 65 35 E
Jhalawar, India ...... 42 G7 24 40N 76 10 E
Jhalida, India ...... 43 H11 23 22N 85 58 E
Jhalrapatan, India ...... 42 G7 24 33N 76 10 E
Jhang Maghiana, Pakistan ...... 42 D5 31 15N 72 22 E
Jhansi, India ...... 43 G8 25 30N 78 36 E
Jhargram, India ...... 43 H12 22 27N 86 59 E
Jharia, India ...... 43 H12 23 45N 86 26 E
Jharkhand □, India ...... 43 H11 24 0N 85 50 E
Jharsuguda, India ...... 41 J14 21 56N 84 5 E

Jhelum, Pakistan ...... 42 C5 33 0N 73 45 E
Jhelum →, Pakistan ...... 42 D5 31 20N 72 10 E
Jhilmilli, India ...... 43 H10 23 24N 82 51 E
Jhudo, Pakistan ...... 42 G3 24 58N 69 18 E
Jhunjhunu, India ...... 42 E6 28 10N 75 30 E
Ji-Paraná, Brazil ...... 92 F6 10 52S 62 57W
Ji Xian, Hebei, China ...... 34 F8 37 35N 115 30 E
Ji Xian, Henan, China ...... 34 G8 35 22N 114 5 E
Ji Xian, Shanxi, China ...... 34 F6 36 7N 110 40 E
Jia Xian, Henan, China ...... 34 H7 33 59N 113 12 E
Jia Xian, Shaanxi, China ...... 33 F6 38 12N 110 28 E
Jiamusi, China ...... 33 B8 46 40N 130 26 E
Ji'an, Jiangxi, China ...... 35 D6 27 6N 114 59 E
Ji'an, Jilin, China ...... 35 D14 41 5N 126 10 E
Jianchang, China ...... 35 D11 40 55N 120 35 E
Jianchangying, China ...... 35 D10 40 10N 118 50 E
Jiangcheng, China ...... 32 D5 22 36N 101 52 E
Jiangmen, China ...... 33 D6 22 32N 113 0 E
Jiangsu □, China ...... 35 H11 33 0N 120 0 E
Jiangxi □, China ...... 33 D6 27 30N 116 0 E
Jiao Xian = Jiaozhou, China ...... 35 F11 36 18N 120 1 E
Jiaohe, Hebei, China ...... 34 E9 38 2N 116 20 E
Jiaohe, Jilin, China ...... 35 C14 43 40N 127 22 E
Jiaozhou, China ...... 35 F11 36 18N 120 1 E
Jiaozhou Wan, China ...... 35 F11 36 5N 120 10 E
Jiaozuo, China ...... 34 G7 35 16N 113 12 E
Jiawang, China ...... 35 G9 34 28N 117 26 E
Jiaxiang, China ...... 34 G9 35 25N 116 20 E
Jiaxing, China ...... 33 C7 30 49N 120 45 E
Jiayi = Chiai, Taiwan ...... 33 D7 23 29N 120 25 E
Jibuti = Djibouti ■, Africa ...... 47 E3 12 0N 43 0 E
Jicarón, I., Panama ...... 88 E3 7 10N 81 50W
Jiddah, Si. Arabia ...... 47 C2 21 29N 39 10 E
Jido, India ...... 41 E19 29 2N 94 58 E
Jieshou, China ...... 34 H8 33 18N 115 22 E
Jiexiu, China ...... 34 F6 37 2N 111 55 E
Jiggalong, Australia ...... 60 D3 23 21S 120 47 E
Jigni, India ...... 43 G8 25 45N 79 25 E
Jihlava, Czech Rep. ...... 16 D8 49 28N 15 35 E
Jihlava →, Czech Rep. ...... 17 D9 48 55N 16 36 E
Jijiga, Ethiopia ...... 47 F3 9 20N 42 50 E
Jilin, China ...... 35 C14 43 44N 126 30 E
Jilin □, China ...... 35 C14 44 0N 127 0 E
Jilong = Chilung, Taiwan ...... 33 D7 25 3N 121 45 E
Jim Thorpe, U.S.A. ...... 85 F9 40 52N 75 44W
Jima, Ethiopia ...... 47 F2 7 40N 36 47 E
Jimbaran, Teluk, Indonesia ...... 37 K18 8 46S 115 9 E
Jiménez, Mexico ...... 86 B4 27 10N 104 54W
Jimo, China ...... 35 F11 36 23N 120 30 E
Jin Xian = Jinzhou, China ...... 34 E8 38 2N 115 2 E
Jin Xian, China ...... 35 E11 39 7N 121 42 E
Jinan, China ...... 34 F9 36 38N 117 1 E
Jinchang, China ...... 32 C5 38 30N 102 10 E
Jincheng, China ...... 34 G7 35 29N 112 50 E
Jind, India ...... 42 E7 29 19N 76 22 E
Jindabyne, Australia ...... 63 F4 36 25S 148 35 E
Jinding, China ...... 33 G10 22 21N 113 33 E
Jindřichův Hradec, Czech Rep. ...... 16 D8 49 10N 15 2 E
Jing He →, China ...... 34 G5 34 27N 109 4 E
Jingbian, China ...... 34 F5 37 20N 108 30 E
Jingchuan, China ...... 34 G4 35 20N 107 20 E
Jingdezhen, China ...... 33 D6 29 20N 117 11 E
Jinggu, China ...... 32 D5 23 35N 100 41 E
Jinghai, China ...... 34 E9 38 55N 116 55 E
Jingle, China ...... 34 E6 38 20N 111 55 E
Jingning, China ...... 34 G3 35 30N 105 43 E
Jingpo Hu, China ...... 35 C15 43 55N 128 55 E
Jingtai, China ...... 34 F3 37 10N 104 6 E
Jingxing, China ...... 34 E8 38 2N 114 8 E
Jingyang, China ...... 34 G5 34 30N 108 50 E
Jingyu, China ...... 35 C14 42 25N 126 45 E
Jingyuan, China ...... 34 F3 36 30N 104 40 E
Jingziguan, China ...... 34 H6 33 15N 111 0 E
Jinhua, China ...... 33 D6 29 8N 119 38 E
Jining, Nei Monggol Zizhiqu, China ...... 34 D7 41 5N 113 0 E
Jining, Shandong, China ...... 34 G9 35 22N 116 34 E
Jinja, Uganda ...... 54 B3 0 25N 33 12 E
Jinjang, Malaysia ...... 39 L3 3 13N 101 39 E
Jinji, China ...... 34 F4 37 58N 106 8 E
Jinnah Barrage, Pakistan ...... 40 C7 32 58N 71 33 E
Jinotega, Nic. ...... 88 D2 13 6N 85 59W
Jinotepe, Nic. ...... 88 D2 11 50N 86 10W
Jinsha Jiang →, China ...... 32 D5 28 50N 104 36 E
Jinxi, China ...... 35 D11 40 52N 120 50 E
Jinxiang, China ...... 34 G9 35 5N 116 22 E
Jinzhou, Hebei, China ...... 34 E8 38 2N 115 2 E
Jinzhou, Liaoning, China ...... 35 D11 41 5N 121 3 E
Jiparaná →, Brazil ...... 92 E6 8 3S 62 52W
Jipijapa, Ecuador ...... 92 D2 1 0S 80 40W
Jiquilpan, Mexico ...... 86 D4 19 57N 102 42W
Jishan, China ...... 34 G6 35 34N 110 58 E
Jisr ash Shughūr, Syria ...... 44 C3 35 49N 36 18 E
Jitarning, Australia ...... 61 F2 32 48S 117 57 E
Jitra, Malaysia ...... 39 J3 6 16N 100 25 E
Jiu →, Romania ...... 17 F12 43 47N 23 48 E
Jiudengkou, China ...... 34 E4 39 56N 106 40 E
Jiujiang, China ...... 33 D6 29 42N 115 58 E
Jiulong = Kowloon, China ...... 33 G11 22 19N 114 11 E
Jiutai, China ...... 35 B13 44 10N 125 50 E
Jiuxincheng, China ...... 34 E8 39 17N 115 59 E
Jixi, China ...... 35 B16 45 20N 130 50 E
Jiyang, China ...... 35 F9 37 0N 117 12 E
Jiyuan, China ...... 34 G7 35 7N 112 57 E
Jīzān, Si. Arabia ...... 47 D3 17 0N 42 20 E
Jize, China ...... 34 F8 36 54N 114 56 E
Jizl, Wādī al →, Si. Arabia ...... 44 E3 25 39N 38 25 E
Jizō-Zaki, Japan ...... 31 G6 35 34N 133 20 E
Jizzakh, Uzbekistan ...... 28 E7 40 6N 67 50 E
Joaçaba, Brazil ...... 95 B5 27 5S 51 31W
João Pessoa, Brazil ...... 93 E12 7 10S 34 52W
Joaquín V. González, Argentina ...... 94 B3 25 10S 64 0W
Jobat, India ...... 42 H6 22 25N 74 34 E
Jodhpur, India ...... 42 F5 26 23N 73 8 E
Jodiya, India ...... 42 H4 22 42N 70 18 E
Joensuu, Finland ...... 8 E4 62 37N 29 49 E
Jōetsu, Japan ...... 31 F9 37 12N 138 10 E
Jofane, Mozam. ...... 57 C5 21 15S 34 18 E
Jogbani, India ...... 43 F12 26 25N 87 15 E
Jõgeva, Estonia ...... 9 G22 58 45N 26 24 E
Jogjakarta = Yogyakarta, Indonesia ...... 36 F4 7 49S 110 22 E
Johannesburg, S. Africa ...... 57 D4 26 10S 28 2 E
Johannesburg, U.S.A. ...... 79 K9 35 22N 117 38W
Johilla →, India ...... 43 H9 23 37N 81 14 E
John Crow Mts., Jamaica ...... 88 a 18 5N 76 25W
John Day, U.S.A. ...... 76 D4 44 25N 118 57W
John Day →, U.S.A. ...... 76 D3 45 44N 120 39W

John Day Fossil Beds △, U.S.A. .... 76 D4 44 33N 119 38W
John D'Or Prairie, Canada .... 70 B5 58 30N 115 8W
John F. Kennedy International,
New York ✈ (JFK), U.S.A. .. 85 F11 40 38N 73 47W
John H. Kerr Reservoir, U.S.A. .. 83 G6 36 36N 78 18W
Johnnie, U.S.A. .... 79 J10 36 25N 116 5W
John's Ra., Australia .... 62 C1 21 55S 133 23 E
Johnson, Kans., U.S.A. .... 81 G4 37 34N 101 45W
Johnson, Vt., U.S.A. .... 85 B12 44 38N 72 41W
Johnson City, N.Y., U.S.A. .... 85 D9 42 7N 75 58W
Johnson City, Tenn., U.S.A. .... 83 G4 36 19N 82 21W
Johnson City, Tex., U.S.A. .... 81 K5 30 17N 98 25W
Johnsonburg, U.S.A. .... 84 E6 41 29N 78 41W
Johnsondale, U.S.A. .... 79 K8 35 58N 118 32W
Johnsons Crossing, Canada .. 70 A2 60 29N 133 18W
Johnston, L., Australia .... 61 F3 32 25S 120 30 E
Johnston Falls = Mambilima
Falls, Zambia .... 55 E2 10 31S 28 45 E
Johnston I., Pac. Oc. .... 65 F11 17 10N 169 8W
Johnstone Str., Canada .... 70 C3 50 28N 126 0W
Johnstown, N.Y., U.S.A. .. 85 C10 43 0N 74 22W
Johnstown, Ohio, U.S.A. .. 84 F2 40 9N 82 41W
Johnstown, Pa., U.S.A. .... 84 F6 40 20N 78 55W
Johor, Selat, Asia .... 39 d 1 28N 103 47 E
Johor Bahru, Malaysia .... 39 d 1 28N 103 46 E
Jõhvi, Estonia .... 9 G22 59 22N 27 27 E
Joinville, Brazil .... 95 B6 26 15S 48 55W
Joinville I., Antarctica .... 5 C18 65 0S 55 30W
Jojutla, Mexico .... 87 D5 18 37N 99 11W
Jokkmokk, Sweden .... 8 C18 66 35N 19 50 E
Jökulsá á Bru ➤, Iceland .... 8 D6 65 40N 14 16W
Jökulsá á Fjöllum ➤, Iceland .. 8 C5 66 10N 16 30W
Jolfā, Āzarbājān-e Sharqi, Iran .. 44 B5 38 57N 45 38 E
Jolfā, Eşfahan, Iran .... 45 C6 32 58N 51 37 E
Joliet, U.S.A. .... 82 E1 41 32N 88 5W
Joliette, Canada .... 72 C5 46 3N 73 24W
Jolo, Phil. .... 37 C6 6 0N 121 0 E
Jolon, U.S.A. .... 78 K5 35 58N 121 9W
Jombang, Indonesia .... 37 G15 7 33S 112 14 E
Jonava, Lithuania .... 9 J21 55 8N 24 12 E
Jones Sound, Canada .... 4 B3 76 0N 85 0W
Jonesboro, Ark., U.S.A. .. 81 H9 35 50N 90 42W
Jonesboro, La., U.S.A. .. 81 J8 32 15N 92 43W
Joniškis, Lithuania .... 9 H20 56 13N 23 35 E
Jönköping, Sweden .... 9 H16 57 45N 14 8 E
Jonquière, Canada .... 73 C5 48 27N 71 14W
Joplin, U.S.A. .... 81 G7 37 6N 94 31W
Jora, India .... 42 F6 26 20N 77 49 E
Jordan, Mont., U.S.A. .. 76 C10 47 19N 106 55W
Jordan, N.Y., U.S.A. .... 85 C8 43 4N 76 29W
Jordan ■, Asia .... 46 E5 31 0N 36 0 E
Jordan ➤, Asia .... 46 D4 31 48N 35 32 E
Jordan Valley, U.S.A. .. 76 E5 42 59N 117 3W
Jorhat, India .... 41 F19 26 45N 94 12 E
Jörn, Sweden .... 8 D19 65 4N 20 1 E
Jorong, Indonesia .... 36 E4 3 58S 114 56 E
Jørpeland, Norway .... 9 G11 59 3N 6 1 E
Jorquera ➤, Chile .... 94 B2 28 3S 69 58W
Jos, Nigeria .... 50 G7 9 53N 8 51 E
José Batlle y Ordóñez, Uruguay 95 C4 33 20S 55 10W
Joseph, L., Nfld. & L., Canada .. 73 B6 52 45N 65 18W
Joseph, L., Ont., Canada .... 84 A5 45 10N 79 44W
Joseph Bonaparte G., Australia 60 B4 14 35S 128 50 E
Joshinath, India .... 43 D8 30 34N 79 34 E
Joshinetsu-Kōgen △, Japan .. 31 F9 36 42N 138 32 E
Joshua Tree, U.S.A. .... 79 L10 34 8N 116 19W
Joshua Tree △, U.S.A. .. 79 M10 33 55N 116 0W
Jost Van Dyke, Br. Virgin Is. .. 89 e 18 29N 64 47W
Jostedalsbreen, Norway .... 9 F12 61 40N 6 59 E
Jotunheimen, Norway .... 9 F13 61 35N 8 25 E
Joubertberge, Namibia .... 56 B1 18 30S 14 0 E
Jourdanton, U.S.A. .... 81 L5 28 55N 98 33W
Jovellanos, Cuba .... 88 B3 22 40N 81 10W
Ju Xian, China .... 35 F10 36 35N 118 20 E
Juan Aldama, Mexico .... 86 C4 24 20N 103 23W
Juan Bautista Alberdi, Argentina 94 C3 34 26S 61 48W
Juan de Fuca Str., Canada .. 78 B3 48 15N 124 0W
Juan de Nova, Ind. Oc. .... 57 B7 17 3S 43 45 E
Juan Fernández, Arch. de,
Pac. Oc. .... 90 G2 33 50S 80 0W
Juan José Castelli, Argentina .. 94 B3 25 27S 60 57W
Juan L. Lacaze, Uruguay .. 94 C4 34 26S 57 25W
Juankoski, Finland .... 8 E23 63 3N 28 19 E
Juárez, Argentina .... 94 D4 37 40S 59 43W
Juárez, Mexico .... 79 N11 32 20N 115 57W
Juárez, Sierra de, Mexico .. 86 A1 32 0N 116 0W
Juàzeiro, Brazil .... 93 E10 9 30S 40 30W
Juàzeiro do Norte, Brazil .. 93 E11 7 10S 39 18W
Juba = Giuba ➤, Somali Rep. .. 47 G3 1 30N 42 35 E
Juba, Sudan .... 51 H12 4 50N 31 35 E
Jubany, Antarctica .... 5 C18 62 30S 58 0W
Jubayl, Lebanon .... 46 A4 34 5N 35 39 E
Jubbah, Si. Arabia .... 44 D4 28 2N 40 56 E
Jubbal, India .... 42 D7 31 5N 77 40 E
Jubbulpore = Jabalpur, India .. 43 H8 23 9N 79 58 E
Jubilee L., Australia .... 61 E4 29 0S 126 50 E
Juby, C., Morocco .... 50 C3 28 0N 12 59W
Júcar = Xúquer ➤, Spain .. 21 C5 39 5N 0 10W
Júcaro, Cuba .... 88 B4 21 37N 78 51W
Juchitán, Mexico .... 87 D5 16 27N 95 5W
Judaea = Har Yehuda, Israel .. 46 D3 31 35N 34 57 E
Judith ➤, U.S.A. .... 76 C9 47 44N 109 39W
Judith, Pt., U.S.A. .... 85 E13 41 22N 71 29W
Judith Gap, U.S.A. .... 76 C9 46 41N 109 45W
Jugoslavia = Serbia &
Montenegro ■, Europe .... 23 B9 43 20N 20 0 E
Juigalpa, Nic. .... 88 D2 12 6N 85 26W
Juiz de Fora, Brazil .... 95 A7 21 43S 43 19W
Jujuy □, Argentina .... 94 A2 23 20S 65 40W
Julesburg, U.S.A. .... 80 E3 40 59N 102 16W
Juli, Peru .... 92 G5 16 10S 69 25W
Julia Cr. ➤, Australia .... 62 C3 20 0S 141 11 E
Julia Creek, Australia .... 62 C3 20 39S 141 44 E
Juliaca, Peru .... 92 G4 15 25S 70 10W
Julian, U.S.A. .... 79 M10 33 4N 116 38W
Julian, L., Canada .... 72 B4 54 25N 77 57W
Julianatop, Suriname .... 93 C7 3 40N 56 30W
Julianehåb = Qaqortoq,
Greenland .... 69 B6 60 43N 46 0W
Julimes, Mexico .... 86 B3 28 25N 105 27W
Jullundur, India .... 42 D6 31 20N 75 40 E
Julu, China .... 34 F8 37 15N 115 2 E
Jumbo, Zimbabwe .... 55 F3 17 30S 30 58 E
Jumbo Pk., U.S.A. .... 79 J12 36 12N 114 11W
Jumentos Cays, Bahamas .. 88 B4 23 0N 75 40W
Jumilla, Spain .... 21 C5 38 28N 1 19W
Jumla, Nepal .... 43 E10 29 15N 82 13 E

Jumna = Yamuna ➤, India .... 43 G9 25 30N 81 53 E
Junagadh, India .... 42 J4 21 30N 70 30 E
Junction, Tex., U.S.A. .. 81 K5 30 29N 99 46W
Junction, Utah, U.S.A. .. 77 G7 38 14N 112 13W
Junction B., Australia .... 62 A1 11 52S 133 55 E
Junction City, Kans., U.S.A. .. 80 F6 39 2N 96 50W
Junction City, Oreg., U.S.A. .. 76 D2 44 13N 123 12W
Junction Pt., Australia .... 62 A1 11 45S 133 50 E
Jundah, Australia .... 62 C3 24 46S 143 2 E
Jundiaí, Brazil .... 95 A6 24 30S 47 0W
Juneau, U.S.A. .... 70 B2 58 18N 134 25W
Junee, Australia .... 63 E4 34 53S 147 35 E
Jungfrau, Switz. .... 20 C7 46 32N 7 58 E
Junggar Pendi, China .... 32 B3 44 30N 86 0 E
Jungshahi, Pakistan .... 42 G2 24 52N 67 44 E
Juniata ➤, U.S.A. .... 84 F7 40 30N 77 40W
Junín, Argentina .... 94 C3 34 33S 60 57W
Junín de los Andes, Argentina . 96 D2 39 45S 71 0W
Jūniyah, Lebanon .... 46 B4 33 59N 35 38 E
Juntas, Chile .... 94 B2 28 24S 69 58W
Juntura, U.S.A. .... 76 E4 43 45N 118 5W
Jur, Nahr el ➤, Sudan .... 51 G11 8 45N 29 15 E
Jura = Jura, Mts. du, Europe .. 20 C7 46 40N 6 5 E
Jura = Schwäbische Alb,
Germany .... 16 D5 48 20N 9 30 E
Jura, U.K. .... 11 F3 56 0N 5 50W
Jura, Mts. du, Europe .... 20 C7 46 40N 6 5 E
Jura, Sd. of, U.K. .... 11 F3 55 57N 5 45W
Jurbarkas, Lithuania .... 9 J20 55 4N 22 46 E
Jurien, Australia .... 61 F2 30 18S 115 2 E
Jūrmala, Latvia .... 9 H20 56 58N 23 34 E
Jurong, Singapore .... 39 d 1 19N 103 42 E
Juruá ➤, Brazil .... 92 D5 2 37S 65 44W
Juruena ➤, Brazil .... 92 F7 13 0S 58 10W
Juruena ➤, Brazil .... 92 E7 7 20S 58 3W
Juruti, Brazil .... 93 D7 2 9S 56 4W
Justo Daract, Argentina .... 94 C2 33 52S 65 12W
Jutaí ➤, Brazil .... 92 D5 2 43S 66 57W
Juticalpa, Honduras .... 88 D2 14 40N 86 12W
Jutland = Jylland, Denmark .. 9 H13 56 25N 9 30 E
Juventud, I. de la, Cuba .... 88 B3 21 40N 82 40W
Jüy Zar, Iran .... 44 C5 33 50N 46 18 E
Juye, China .... 34 G9 35 22N 116 5 E
Jwaneng, Botswana .... 53 J4 24 45S 24 50 E
Jylland, Denmark .... 9 H13 56 25N 9 30 E
Jyväskylä, Finland .... 9 E21 62 14N 25 50 E

# K

K2, Pakistan .... 43 B7 35 58N 76 32 E
Kaap Plateau, S. Africa .... 56 D3 28 30S 24 0 E
Kaapkruis, Namibia .... 56 C1 21 55S 13 57 E
Kaapstad = Cape Town, S. Africa 56 E2 33 55S 18 22 E
Kabaena, Indonesia .... 37 F6 5 15S 122 0 E
Kabala, S. Leone .... 50 G3 9 38N 11 37W
Kabale, Uganda .... 54 C3 1 15S 30 0 E
Kabalo, Dem. Rep. of the Congo 54 D2 6 0S 27 0 E
Kabambare, Dem. Rep. of
the Congo .... 54 C2 4 41S 27 39 E
Kabango, Dem. Rep. of
the Congo .... 55 D2 8 35S 28 30 E
Kabanjahe, Indonesia .... 36 D1 3 6N 98 30 E
Kabardino-Balkar Republic =
Kabardino-Balkaria □, Russia 19 F7 43 30N 43 30 E
Kabardino-Balkaria □, Russia .. 19 F7 43 30N 43 30 E
Kabarega Falls = Murchison
Falls, Uganda .... 54 B3 2 15N 31 30 E
Kabasalan, Phil. .... 37 C6 7 47N 122 44 E
Kabat, Indonesia .... 37 J17 8 16S 114 19 E
Kabetogama, U.S.A. .... 80 A8 48 28N 92 59W
Kabin Buri, Thailand .... 38 F3 13 57N 101 43 E
Kabinakagami L., Canada .. 72 C3 48 54N 84 25W
Kabinda, Dem. Rep. of the Congo 52 F4 6 19S 24 20 E
Kabompo □, Zambia .... 55 E1 13 36S 24 14 E
Kabompo ➤, Zambia .... 53 G4 14 10S 23 11 E
Kabondo, Dem. Rep. of
the Congo .... 55 D2 8 58S 25 40 E
Kabongo, Dem. Rep. of
the Congo .... 54 D2 7 22S 25 33 E
Kabūd Gonbad, Iran .... 45 B8 37 5N 59 45 E
Kābul, Afghan. .... 42 B3 34 28N 69 11 E
Kābul □, Afghan. .... 40 B6 34 30N 69 0 E
Kābul ➤, Pakistan .... 42 C5 33 55N 72 14 E
Kabunga, Dem. Rep. of
the Congo .... 54 C2 1 38S 28 3 E
Kaburuang, Indonesia .... 37 D7 3 50N 126 30 E
Kabwe, Zambia .... 55 E2 14 30S 28 29 E
Kachchh, Gulf of, India .... 42 H3 22 50N 69 15 E
Kachchh, Rann of, India .. 42 H4 24 0N 70 0 E
Kachchhidhana, India .... 43 J8 21 44N 78 46 E
Kachebera, Zambia .... 55 E3 13 50S 32 50 E
Kachikau, Botswana .... 56 B3 18 8S 24 26 E
Kachin □, Burma .... 41 G20 26 0N 97 30 E
Kachira, L., Uganda .... 54 C3 0 40S 31 7 E
Kachiry, Kazakhstan .... 28 D8 53 10N 75 50 E
Kachnara, India .... 42 H6 23 50N 75 6 E
Kachot, Cambodia .... 39 G4 11 30N 103 3 E
Kaçkar, Turkey .... 19 F7 40 45N 41 10 E
Kadan Kyun, Burma .... 38 F2 12 30N 98 20 E
Kadanai ➤, Afghan. .... 42 D1 31 22N 65 45 E
Kadavu, Fiji .... 59 D8 19 0S 178 15 E
Kadhimain = Al Kāzimīyah, Iraq 44 C5 33 22N 44 18 E
Kadi, India .... 42 H5 23 18N 72 23 E
Kadina, Australia .... 63 E2 33 55S 137 43 E
Kadipur, India .... 43 F10 26 10N 82 23 E
Kadirli, Turkey .... 44 B3 37 23N 36 5 E
Kadiyevka = Stakhanov, Ukraine 19 E6 48 35N 38 40 E
Kadoka, U.S.A. .... 80 D4 43 50N 101 31W
Kadoma, Zimbabwe .... 55 F2 18 20N 29 52 E
Kādugli, Sudan .... 51 F11 11 0N 29 45 E
Kaduna, Nigeria .... 50 F7 10 30N 7 21 E
Kaédi, Mauritania .... 50 E3 16 9N 13 28W
Kaeng Khoï, Thailand .... 38 E3 14 35N 101 0 E
Kaeng Kra Chan △, Thailand .. 38 F2 12 57N 99 23 E
Kaeng Tana △, Thailand .. 38 E5 15 25N 105 32 E
Kaesŏng, N. Korea .... 35 F14 37 58N 126 35 E
Kāf, Si. Arabia .... 44 D3 31 25N 37 29 E
Kafan = Kapan, Armenia .. 19 G8 39 18N 46 27 E
Kafanchan, Nigeria .... 50 G7 9 40N 8 20 E
Kafinda, Zambia .... 55 E3 12 32S 30 20 E
Kafirévs, Ákra, Greece .... 23 E11 38 9N 24 38 E
Kafue, Zambia .... 55 F2 15 46S 28 9 E
Kafue ➤, Zambia .... 53 H5 15 30S 29 0 E
Kafue △, Zambia .... 55 E2 15 12S 25 38 E
Kafue Flats, Zambia .... 55 F2 15 40S 27 25 E

Kafulwe, Zambia .... 55 D2 9 0S 29 1 E
Kaga, Afghan. .... 42 B4 34 14N 70 10 E
Kaga Bandoro, C.A.R. .... 52 C3 7 0N 19 10 E
Kagan, Uzbekistan .... 28 F7 39 43N 64 33 E
Kagawa □, Japan .... 31 G7 34 15N 134 0 E
Kagera □, Tanzania .... 54 C3 2 0S 31 30 E
Kagera ➤, Uganda .... 54 C3 0 57S 31 47 E
Kağızman, Turkey .... 44 B4 40 5N 43 10 E
Kagoshima, Japan .... 31 J5 31 35N 130 33 E
Kagoshima □, Japan .... 31 J5 31 30N 130 30 E
Kagul = Cahul, Moldova .... 17 F15 45 50N 28 15 E
Kahak, Iran .... 45 B6 36 6N 49 46 E
Kahama, Tanzania .... 54 C3 4 8S 32 30 E
Kahan, Pakistan .... 42 E3 29 18N 68 54 E
Kahang, Malaysia .... 39 L4 2 12N 103 32 E
Kahayan ➤, Indonesia .... 36 E4 3 40S 114 0 E
Kahe, Tanzania .... 54 C4 3 30S 37 25 E
Kahnūj, Iran .... 45 E8 27 55N 57 40 E
Kahoka, U.S.A. .... 80 E9 40 25N 91 44W
Kahoolawe, U.S.A. .... 74 H16 20 33N 156 37W
Kahramanmaraş, Turkey .... 19 G6 37 37N 36 53 E
Kahurangi △, N.Z. .... 59 J4 41 10S 172 32 E
Kahuta, Pakistan .... 42 C5 33 35N 73 24 E
Kahuzi-Biega △, Dem. Rep. of
the Congo .... 54 C2 1 50S 27 55 E
Kai, Kepulauan, Indonesia .. 37 F8 5 55S 132 45 E
Kai Besar, Indonesia .... 37 F8 5 35S 133 0 E
Kai Is. = Kai, Kepulauan,
Indonesia .... 37 F8 5 55S 132 45 E
Kai Kecil, Indonesia .... 37 F8 5 45S 132 40 E
Kaiapoi, N.Z. .... 59 K4 43 24S 172 40 E
Kaieteur Falls, Guyana .... 92 B7 5 1N 59 10W
Kaifeng, China .... 34 G8 34 48N 114 21 E
Kaikohe, N.Z. .... 59 F4 35 25S 173 49 E
Kaikoura, N.Z. .... 59 K4 42 25S 173 43 E
Kailash = Kangrinboqe Feng,
China .... 43 D9 31 0N 81 25 E
Kailu, China .... 35 C11 43 38N 121 18 E
Kailua Kona, U.S.A. .... 74 J17 19 39N 155 59W
Kaimana, Indonesia .... 37 E8 3 39S 133 45 E
Kaimanawa Mts., N.Z. .... 59 H5 39 15S 175 56 E
Kaimganj, India .... 43 F8 27 33N 79 24 E
Kaimur Hills, India .... 43 G10 24 30N 82 0 E
Kainab ➤, Namibia .... 56 D2 28 32S 19 34 E
Kainji Res., Nigeria .... 50 F6 10 1N 4 40 E
Kainuu, Finland .... 8 D23 64 30N 29 7 E
Kaipara Harbour, N.Z. .... 59 G5 36 25S 174 14 E
Kaipokok B., Canada .... 73 B8 54 54N 59 47W
Kaira, India .... 42 H5 22 45N 72 50 E
Kairana, India .... 42 E7 29 24N 77 15 E
Kaironi, Indonesia .... 37 E8 0 47S 133 40 E
Kairouan, Tunisia .... 51 A8 35 45N 10 5 E
Kaiserslautern, Germany .... 16 D4 49 26N 7 45 E
Kaitaia, N.Z. .... 59 F4 35 8S 173 17 E
Kaitangata, N.Z. .... 59 M2 46 17S 169 51 E
Kaithal, India .... 42 E7 29 48N 76 26 E
Kaitu ➤, Pakistan .... 42 C4 33 10N 70 30 E
Kaiyuan, China .... 35 C13 42 28N 124 1 E
Kajaani, Finland .... 8 D22 64 17N 27 46 E
Kajabbi, Australia .... 62 C3 20 0S 140 1 E
Kajana = Kajaani, Finland .. 8 D22 64 17N 27 46 E
Kajang, Malaysia .... 39 L3 2 59N 101 48 E
Kajiado, Kenya .... 54 C4 1 53S 36 48 E
Kajo Kaji, Sudan .... 51 H12 3 58N 31 40 E
Kakabeka Falls, Canada .... 72 C2 48 24N 89 37W
Kakadu △, Australia .... 60 B5 12 0S 132 3 E
Kakamas, S. Africa .... 56 D3 28 45S 20 33 E
Kakamega, Kenya .... 54 B3 0 20N 34 46 E
Kakanui Mts., N.Z. .... 59 L3 45 10S 170 30 E
Kakdwip, India .... 43 J13 21 53N 88 11 E
Kake, Japan .... 31 G6 34 36N 132 19 E
Kake, U.S.A. .... 70 B2 56 59N 133 57W
Kakegawa, Japan .... 31 G9 34 45N 138 1 E
Kakeroma-Jima, Japan .... 31 K4 28 8N 129 14 E
Kakhovka, Ukraine .... 19 E5 46 45N 33 30 E
Kakhovske Vdskh., Ukraine .. 19 E5 47 5N 34 0 E
Kakinada, India .... 41 L13 16 57N 82 11 E
Kakisa ➤, Canada .... 70 A5 61 3N 118 10W
Kakisa L., Canada .... 70 A5 60 56N 117 43W
Kakogawa, Japan .... 31 G7 34 46N 134 51 E
Kakwa ➤, Canada .... 70 C5 54 37N 118 28W
Kāl Gūsheh, Iran .... 45 D8 30 59N 58 12 E
Kal Safid, Iran .... 44 C5 34 52N 47 23 E
Kalaallit Nunaat = Greenland ☒,
N. Amer. .... 4 C5 66 0N 45 0W
Kalabagh, Pakistan .... 42 C4 33 0N 71 28 E
Kalabahi, Indonesia .... 37 F6 8 13S 124 31 E
Kalach, Russia .... 19 D7 50 22N 41 0 E
Kaladan ➤, Burma .... 41 J18 20 20N 93 5 E
Kaladar, Canada .... 84 B7 44 37N 77 5W
Kalahari, Africa .... 56 C3 24 0S 21 30 E
Kalahari Gemsbok △, S. Africa . 56 D3 25 30S 20 30 E
Kalajoki, Finland .... 8 D20 64 12N 24 10 E
Kalakamati, Botswana .... 57 C4 20 40S 27 25 E
Kalakan, Russia .... 29 D12 55 15N 116 45 E
K'alak'unlun Shank'ou =
Karakoram Pass, Asia .... 43 B7 35 33N 77 50 E
Kalam, Pakistan .... 43 B5 35 34N 72 30 E
Kalama, Dem. Rep. of the Congo 54 C2 2 52S 28 35 E
Kalama, U.S.A. .... 78 E4 46 1N 122 51W
Kalámai, Greece .... 23 F10 37 3N 22 10 E
Kalamazoo, U.S.A. .... 82 D3 42 17N 85 35W
Kalamazoo ➤, U.S.A. .... 82 D2 42 40N 86 10W
Kalambo Falls, Tanzania .... 55 D3 8 37S 31 35 E
Kalan, Turkey .... 44 B3 39 7N 39 32 E
Kalannie, Australia .... 61 F2 30 22S 117 5 E
Kalāntari, Iran .... 45 C7 32 10N 54 8 E
Kalao, Indonesia .... 37 F6 7 21S 121 0 E
Kalaotoa, Indonesia .... 37 F6 7 20S 121 50 E
Kalasin, Thailand .... 38 D4 16 26N 103 30 E
Kalāt, Iran .... 45 E8 25 29N 59 22 E
Kalat, Pakistan .... 40 E5 29 8N 66 31 E
Kalāteh, Iran .... 45 B7 36 33N 55 41 E
Kalāteh-ye Ganj, Iran .... 45 E8 27 31N 57 55 E
Kalbarri, Australia .... 61 E1 27 40S 114 10 E
Kalbarri △, Australia .... 61 E1 27 55S 114 30 E
Kale, Turkey .... 23 F13 37 27N 28 49 E
Kalegauk Kyun, Burma .... 41 M20 15 33N 97 35 E
Kalehe, Dem. Rep. of the Congo 54 C2 2 6S 28 50 E
Kalema, Tanzania .... 54 C3 1 12S 31 55 E
Kalemie, Dem. Rep. of the Congo 54 D2 5 55S 29 9 E
Kalewa, Burma .... 41 H19 23 10N 94 15 E
Kaleybar, Iran .... 44 B5 38 47N 47 2 E
Kalgoorlie-Boulder, Australia .. 61 F3 30 40S 121 22 E
Kali ➤, India .... 43 F8 27 6N 79 55 E
Kali Sindh ➤, India .... 42 G6 25 32N 76 17 E
Kaliakra, Nos, Bulgaria .... 23 C13 43 21N 28 30 E

Kalianda, Indonesia .... 36 F3 5 50S 105 45 E
Kalibo, Phil. .... 37 B6 11 43N 122 22 E
Kalima, Dem. Rep. of the Congo 54 C2 2 33S 26 32 E
Kalimantan, Indonesia .... 36 E4 0 0 114 0 E
Kalimantan Barat □, Indonesia . 36 E4 0 0 110 30 E
Kalimantan Selatan □, Indonesia 36 E5 2 30S 115 30 E
Kalimantan Tengah □, Indonesia 36 E4 2 0S 113 30 E
Kalimantan Timur □, Indonesia 36 D5 1 30N 116 30 E
Kálimnos, Greece .... 23 F12 37 0N 27 0 E
Kalimpong, India .... 43 F13 27 4N 88 35 E
Kaliningrad, Russia .... 9 J19 54 42N 20 32 E
Kalinkavichy, Belarus .... 17 B15 52 12N 29 20 E
Kalinkovichi = Kalinkavichy,
Belarus .... 17 B15 52 12N 29 20 E
Kaliro, Uganda .... 54 B3 0 56N 33 30 E
Kalispell, U.S.A. .... 76 B6 48 12N 114 19W
Kalisz, Poland .... 17 C10 51 45N 18 8 E
Kaliua, Tanzania .... 54 D3 5 5S 31 48 E
Kalix = Kalixälven ➤, Sweden . 8 D20 65 50N 23 11 E
Kalix, Sweden .... 8 D20 65 53N 23 12 E
Kalixälven ➤, Sweden .... 8 D20 65 50N 23 11 E
Kalka, India .... 42 D7 30 46N 76 57 E
Kalkarindji, Australia .... 60 C5 17 30S 130 47 E
Kalkaska, U.S.A. .... 82 C3 44 44N 85 11W
Kalkfeld, Namibia .... 56 C2 20 57S 16 14 E
Kalkfontein, Botswana .... 56 C3 22 4S 20 57 E
Kalkrand, Namibia .... 56 C2 24 1S 17 35 E
Kallavesi, Finland .... 8 E22 62 58N 27 30 E
Kallsjön, Sweden .... 8 E15 63 38N 13 0 E
Kalmar, Sweden .... 9 H17 56 40N 16 20 E
Kalmyk Republic = Kalmykia □,
Russia .... 19 E8 46 5N 46 1 E
Kalmykia □, Russia .... 19 E8 46 5N 46 1 E
Kalmykovo, Kazakhstan .... 19 E9 49 0N 51 47 E
Kalna, India .... 43 H13 23 13N 88 25 E
Kalnai, India .... 43 H10 22 46N 83 30 E
Kalocsa, Hungary .... 17 E10 46 32N 19 0 E
Kalokhorio, Cyprus .... 25 E12 34 51N 33 2 E
Kaloko, Dem. Rep. of the Congo 54 D2 6 47S 25 48 E
Kalol, Gujarat, India .... 42 H5 22 37N 73 31 E
Kalol, Gujarat, India .... 42 H5 23 15N 72 33 E
Kalomo, Zambia .... 55 F2 17 0S 26 30 E
Kalpi, India .... 43 F8 26 8N 79 47 E
Kalu, Pakistan .... 42 G2 25 5N 67 39 E
Kaluga, Russia .... 18 D6 54 35N 36 10 E
Kalulushi, Zambia .... 55 E2 12 50S 28 3 E
Kalundborg, Denmark .... 9 J14 55 41N 11 5 E
Kalush, Ukraine .... 17 D13 49 3N 24 23 E
Kalutara, Sri Lanka .... 40 R12 6 35N 80 0 E
Kalya, Russia .... 18 B10 60 15N 59 59 E
Kalyan, India .... 40 K8 19 15N 73 9 E
Kama, Dem. Rep. of the Congo . 54 C2 3 30S 27 5 E
Kama ➤, Russia .... 18 C9 55 45N 52 0 E
Kamachumu, Tanzania .... 54 C3 1 37S 31 37 E
Kamaishi, Japan .... 30 E10 39 16N 141 53 E
Kamalia, Pakistan .... 42 D5 30 44N 72 42 E
Kaman, India .... 42 F6 27 39N 77 16 E
Kamanjab, Namibia .... 56 B2 19 35S 14 51 E
Kamapanda, Zambia .... 55 E1 12 5S 24 0 E
Kamarán, Yemen .... 47 D3 15 21N 42 35 E
Kamativi, Zimbabwe .... 56 B4 18 20S 27 6 E
Kambalda, Australia .... 61 F3 31 10S 121 37 E
Kambar, Pakistan .... 42 F3 27 37N 68 1 E
Kambarka, Russia .... 18 C9 56 15N 54 11 E
Kambolé, Zambia .... 55 D3 8 47S 30 48 E
Kambos, Cyprus .... 25 D11 35 2N 32 44 E
Kambove, Dem. Rep. of
the Congo .... 55 E2 10 51S 26 33 E
Kamchatka, Poluostrov, Russia . 29 D16 57 0N 160 0 E
Kamchatka Pen. = Kamchatka,
Poluostrov, Russia .... 29 D16 57 0N 160 0 E
Kamchiya ➤, Bulgaria .... 23 C12 43 4N 27 44 E
Kame Ruins, Zimbabwe .... 55 G2 20 7S 28 25 E
Kamen, Russia .... 28 D9 53 50N 81 30 E
Kamen-Rybolov, Russia .... 30 B6 44 46N 132 2 E
Kamenjak, Rt, Croatia .... 16 F7 44 47N 13 55 E
Kamenka, Russia .... 18 A7 65 58N 44 0 E
Kamenka Bugskaya = Kamyanka-
Buzka, Ukraine .... 17 C13 50 8N 24 16 E
Kamensk Uralskiy, Russia .. 28 D7 56 25N 62 2 E
Kamenskoye, Russia .... 29 C17 62 45N 165 30 E
Kameoka, Japan .... 31 G7 35 0N 135 35 E
Kamiah, U.S.A. .... 76 C5 46 14N 116 2W
Kamieskroon, S. Africa .... 56 E2 30 9S 17 56 E
Kamilukuak L., Canada .... 71 A8 62 22N 101 40W
Kamin-Kashyrskyy, Ukraine .. 17 C13 51 39N 24 56 E
Kamina, Dem. Rep. of the Congo 55 D2 8 45S 25 0 E
Kaminak L., Canada .... 71 A10 62 10N 95 0W
Kaministiquia, Canada .... 72 C1 48 32N 89 35W
Kaminoyama, Japan .... 30 E10 38 9N 140 17 E
Kamiros, Greece .... 25 C9 36 20N 27 56 E
Kamituga, Dem. Rep. of
the Congo .... 54 C2 3 2S 28 10 E
Kamla ➤, India .... 43 G12 25 35N 86 36 E
Kamloops, Canada .... 70 C4 50 40N 120 20W
Kamo, Japan .... 30 F9 37 39N 139 3 E
Kamoke, Pakistan .... 42 C6 32 4N 74 4 E
Kampala, Uganda .... 54 B3 0 20N 32 30 E
Kampar, Malaysia .... 39 K3 4 18N 101 9 E
Kampar ➤, Indonesia .... 36 D2 0 30N 103 8 E
Kampen, Neths. .... 15 B5 52 33N 5 53 E
Kampene, Dem. Rep. of
the Congo .... 54 C2 3 36S 26 40 E
Kamphaeng Phet, Thailand .. 38 D2 16 28N 99 30 E
Kampolombo, L., Zambia .... 55 E2 11 37S 29 42 E
Kampong Chhnang, Cambodia . 39 F5 12 20N 104 35 E
Kampong Pengerang, Malaysia . 39 d 1 22N 104 7 E
Kampong Punggai, Malaysia .. 39 d 1 27N 104 18 E
Kampong Saom, Cambodia .. 39 G4 10 38N 103 30 E
Kampong Saom, Chaak,
Cambodia .... 39 G4 10 50N 103 32 E
Kampong Tanjong Langsat,
Malaysia .... 39 d 1 28N 104 1 E
Kampong Telok Ramunia,
Malaysia .... 39 d 1 22N 104 15 E
Kampong To, Thailand .... 39 J3 6 3N 101 13 E
Kampot, Cambodia .... 39 G5 10 36N 104 10 E
Kampuchea = Cambodia ■, Asia 38 F5 12 15N 105 0 E
Kampung Air Putih, Malaysia .. 39 K4 4 15N 103 10 E
Kampung Jerangau, Malaysia .. 39 K4 4 50N 103 10 E
Kampung Raja, Malaysia .... 39 K4 5 45N 102 35 E
Kampungbaru = Tolitoli,
Indonesia .... 37 D6 1 5N 120 50 E
Kamrau, Teluk, Indonesia .. 37 E8 3 30S 133 36 E
Kamsack, Canada .... 71 C8 51 34N 101 54W
Kamskoye Vdkhr., Russia .. 18 C10 58 41N 56 7 E
Kamui-Misaki, Japan .... 30 C10 43 20N 140 21 E

Kamyanets-Podilskyy, *Ukraine* . 17 D14 48 45N 26 40 E
Kamyanka-Buzka, *Ukraine* ..... 17 C13 50 8N 24 16 E
Kāmyārān, *Iran* ............... 44 C5 34 47N 46 56 E
Kamyshin, *Russia* ............. 19 D8 50 10N 45 24 E
Kanaaupscow, *Canada* ........ 69 C12 53 39N 77 9W
Kanaaupscow ➤, *Canada* .... 72 B4 54 2N 76 30W
Kanab, *U.S.A.* ................ 77 H7 37 3N 112 32W
Kanab ➤, *U.S.A.* ............ 77 H7 36 24N 112 38W
Kanagi, *Japan* ............... 30 D10 40 54N 140 27 E
Kanairiktok ➤, *Canada* ...... 73 A7 55 2N 60 18W
Kananga, *Dem. Rep. of*
  *the Congo* ................. 52 F4 5 55S 22 18 E
Kanash, *Russia* .............. 18 C8 55 30N 47 32 E
Kanaskat, *U.S.A.* ............. 78 C5 47 19N 121 54W
Kanastraíon, Ákra = Palioúrion,
  *Ákra, Greece* ............... 23 E10 39 57N 23 45 E
Kanawha ➤, *U.S.A.* .......... 82 F4 38 50N 82 9W
Kanazawa, *Japan* ............ 31 F8 36 30N 136 38 E
Kanchanaburi, *Thailand* ...... 38 E2 14 2N 99 31 E
Kanchenjunga, *Nepal* ........ 43 F13 27 50N 88 10 E
Kanchipuram, *India* .......... 40 N11 12 52N 79 45 E
Kandaghat, *India* ............ 42 D7 30 59N 77 7 E
Kandahar = Qandahār, *Afghan.* . 40 D4 31 32N 65 43 E
Kandalaksha, *Russia* ........ 18 A5 67 9N 32 30 E
Kandalakshskiy Zaliv, *Russia* . 18 A6 66 0N 35 0 E
Kandangan, *Indonesia* ....... 36 E5 2 50S 115 20 E
Kandanghaur, *Indonesia* ..... 37 G13 6 21S 108 6 E
Kandanos, *Greece* ........... 25 D5 35 19N 23 44 E
Kandavu = Kadavu, *Fiji* ...... 59 D8 19 0S 178 15 E
Kandhkot, *Pakistan* .......... 42 E3 28 16N 69 8 E
Kandhla, *India* .............. 42 E7 29 18N 77 19 E
Kandi, *Benin* ................ 50 F6 11 7N 2 55 E
Kandi, *India* ................ 43 H13 23 58N 88 5 E
Kandiaro, *Pakistan* .......... 42 F3 27 4N 68 13 E
Kandla, *India* ............... 42 H4 23 0N 70 10 E
Kandos, *Australia* ........... 63 E4 32 45S 149 58 E
Kandreho, *Madag.* ........... 57 B8 17 29S 46 6 E
Kandy, *Sri Lanka* ............ 40 R12 7 18N 80 43 E
Kane, *U.S.A.* ................ 84 E6 41 40N 78 49W
Kane Basin, *Greenland* ....... 4 B4 79 1N 70 0W
Kaneohe, *U.S.A.* ............ 74 H16 21 25N 157 48W
Kang, *Botswana* ............. 56 C3 23 41S 22 50 E
Kang Krung △, *Thailand* ..... 39 H2 9 30N 98 50 E
Kangān, *Fārs, Iran* .......... 45 E7 27 50N 52 3 E
Kangān, *Hormozgān, Iran* .... 45 E8 25 48N 57 28 E
Kangar, *Malaysia* ........... 39 J3 6 27N 100 12 E
Kangaroo I., *Australia* ....... 63 F2 35 45S 137 0 E
Kangaroo Mts., *Australia* .... 62 C3 23 29S 141 51 E
Kangasala, *Finland* .......... 9 F21 61 28N 24 4 E
Kangāvar, *Iran* .............. 45 C6 34 40N 48 0 E
Kangdong, *N. Korea* ......... 35 E14 39 9N 126 5 E
Kangean, Kepulauan, *Indonesia* 36 F5 6 55S 115 23 E
Kangean Is. = Kangean,
  *Kepulauan, Indonesia* ....... 36 F5 6 55S 115 23 E
Kanggye, *N. Korea* .......... 35 D14 41 0N 126 35 E
Kanggyŏng, *S. Korea* ........ 35 F14 36 10N 127 0 E
Kanghwa, *S. Korea* .......... 35 F14 37 45N 126 30 E
Kangikajik, *Greenland* ....... 4 B6 70 7N 22 0W
Kangiqliniq = Rankin Inlet,
  *Canada* .................... 68 B10 62 30N 93 0W
Kangiqsualujjuaq, *Canada* ... 69 C13 58 30N 65 59W
Kangiqsujuaq, *Canada* ...... 69 B12 61 30N 72 0W
Kangiqtugaapik = Clyde River,
  *Canada* .................... 69 A13 70 30N 68 30W
Kangirsuk, *Canada* .......... 69 B13 60 0N 70 0W
Kangkar Chemaran, *Malaysia* . 39 d 1 34N 104 12 E
Kangkar Sungai Tiram, *Malaysia* 39 d 1 35N 103 55 E
Kangkar Teberau, *Malaysia* ... 39 d 1 32N 103 51 E
Kangnŭng, *S. Korea* ......... 35 F15 37 45N 128 54 E
Kangping, *China* ............ 35 C12 42 43N 123 18 E
Kangra, *India* ............... 42 C7 32 6N 76 16 E
Kangrinboqe Feng, *China* .... 43 D9 31 0N 81 25 E
Kangto, *India* ............... 41 F18 27 50N 92 35 E
Kanhar ➤, *India* ............ 43 G10 24 28N 83 8 E
Kaniama, *Dem. Rep. of*
  *the Congo* ................. 54 D1 7 30S 24 12 E
Kaniapiskau = Caniapiscau ➤,
  *Canada* .................... 73 A6 56 40N 69 30W
Kaniapiskau, L. = Caniapiscau, L.
  *de, Canada* ................. 73 B6 54 10N 69 55W
Kanin, Poluostrov, *Russia* .... 18 A8 68 0N 45 0 E
Kanin Nos, Mys, *Russia* ..... 18 A7 68 39N 43 32 E
Kanin Pen. = Kanin, Poluostrov,
  *Russia* .................... 18 A8 68 0N 45 0 E
Kaniva, *Australia* ........... 63 F3 36 22S 141 18 E
Kanjut Sar, *Pakistan* ........ 43 A6 36 7N 75 25 E
Kankaanpää, *Finland* ........ 9 F20 61 44N 22 50 E
Kankakee, *U.S.A.* ........... 82 E2 41 7N 87 52W
Kankakee ➤, *U.S.A.* ........ 82 E1 41 23N 88 15W
Kankan, *Guinea* ............. 50 F4 10 23N 9 15W
Kankendy = Xankändi,
  *Azerbaijan* ................. 19 G8 39 52N 46 49 E
Kanker, *India* ............... 41 J12 20 10N 81 40 E
Kankroli, *India* .............. 42 G5 25 4N 73 53 E
Kannapolis, *U.S.A.* .......... 83 H5 35 30N 80 37W
Kannauj, *India* .............. 43 F8 27 3N 79 56 E
Kannod, *India* ............... 40 H10 22 45N 76 40 E
Kano, *Nigeria* ............... 50 F7 12 2N 8 30 E
Kan'onji, *Japan* ............. 31 G6 34 7N 133 39 E
Kanowit, *Malaysia* .......... 36 D4 2 14N 112 20 E
Kanoya, *Japan* .............. 31 J5 31 25N 130 50 E
Kanpetlet, *Burma* ........... 41 J18 21 10N 93 59 E
Kanpur, *India* ............... 43 F9 26 28N 80 20 E
Kansas □, *U.S.A.* ........... 80 F6 38 30N 99 0W
Kansas ➤, *U.S.A.* .......... 80 F7 39 7N 94 37W
Kansas City, *Kans., U.S.A.* ... 80 F7 39 7N 94 38W
Kansas City, *Mo., U.S.A.* .... 80 F7 39 6N 94 35W
Kansenia, *Dem. Rep. of*
  *the Congo* ................. 55 E2 10 20S 26 0 E
Kansk, *Russia* ............... 29 D10 56 20N 95 37 E
Kansŏng, *S. Korea* .......... 35 E15 38 24N 128 30 E
Kansu = Gansu □, *China* .... 34 G3 36 0N 104 0 E
Kantang, *Thailand* .......... 39 J2 7 25N 99 31 E
Kantang, *Thailand* .......... 39 J2 7 25N 99 31 E
Kantharalak, *Thailand* ....... 38 E5 14 39N 104 39 E
Kantli ➤, *India* ............. 42 E6 28 20N 75 30 E
Kantō □, *Japan* ............. 31 F9 36 15N 139 30 E
Kantō-Sanchi, *Japan* ........ 31 G9 35 59N 138 50 E
Kanturk, *Ireland* ............ 10 D3 52 11N 8 54W
Kanuma, *Japan* ............. 31 F9 36 34N 139 42 E
Kanus, *Namibia* ............. 56 D2 27 50S 18 39 E
Kanye, *Botswana* ........... 56 C4 24 55S 25 28 E
Kanzenze, *Dem. Rep. of*
  *the Congo* ................. 55 E2 10 30S 25 12 E
Kanzi, Ras, *Tanzania* ........ 54 D4 7 1S 39 33 E
Kao Phara, *Thailand* ........ 39 a 8 3N 98 22 E
Kaohsiung, *Taiwan* .......... 33 D7 22 35N 120 16 E
Kaokoveld, *Namibia* ......... 56 B1 19 15S 14 30 E
Kaolack, *Senegal* ........... 50 F2 14 5N 16 8W
Kaoshan, *China* ............. 35 B13 44 38N 124 50 E

Kapaa, *U.S.A.* ............... 74 G15 22 5N 159 19W
Kapadvanj, *India* ............ 42 H5 23 5N 73 0 E
Kapan, *Armenia* ............. 19 G8 39 18N 46 27 E
Kapanga, *Dem. Rep. of*
  *the Congo* ................. 52 F4 8 30S 22 40 E
Kapchagai = Qapshaghay,
  *Kazakhstan* ................. 28 E8 43 51N 77 14 E
Kapela = Velika Kapela, *Croatia* . 16 F8 45 10N 15 5 E
Kapema, *Dem. Rep. of the Congo* 55 E2 10 45S 28 22 E
Kapfenberg, *Austria* ......... 16 E8 47 26N 15 18 E
Kapiri Mposhi, *Zambia* ....... 55 E2 13 59S 28 43 E
Kāpīsā □, *Afghan.* .......... 40 B6 35 0N 69 20 E
Kapiskau ➤, *Canada* ....... 72 B3 52 47N 81 55W
Kapit, *Malaysia* ............. 36 D4 2 0N 112 55 E
Kapoe, *Thailand* ............ 39 H2 9 34N 98 32 E
Kapoeta, *Sudan* ............ 51 H12 4 50N 33 35 E
Kaposvár, *Hungary* .......... 17 E9 46 25N 17 47 E
Kapowsin, *U.S.A.* ........... 78 D4 46 59N 122 13W
Kapps, *Namibia* ............. 56 C2 22 32S 17 18 E
Kapsan, *N. Korea* ........... 35 D15 41 4N 128 19 E
Kapsukas = Marijampolė,
  *Lithuania* .................. 9 J20 54 33N 23 19 E
Kaptai L., *Bangla.* ........... 41 H18 22 40N 92 20 E
Kapuas ➤, *Indonesia* ....... 36 E3 0 25S 109 20 E
Kapuas Hulu, Pegunungan,
  *Malaysia* ................... 36 D4 1 30N 113 30 E
Kapuas Hulu Ra. = Kapuas Hulu,
  *Pegunungan, Malaysia* ...... 36 D4 1 30N 113 30 E
Kapulo, *Dem. Rep. of the Congo* 55 D2 8 18S 29 15 E
Kapunda, *Australia* .......... 63 E2 34 20S 138 56 E
Kapuni, *N.Z.* ................ 59 H5 39 29S 174 8 E
Kapurthala, *India* ............ 42 D6 31 23N 75 25 E
Kapuskasing, *Canada* ........ 72 C3 49 25N 82 30W
Kapuskasing ➤, *Canada* .... 72 C3 49 49N 82 0W
Kaputar, *Australia* ........... 63 E5 30 15S 150 10 E
Kaputir, *Kenya* .............. 54 B4 2 5N 35 28 E
Kaputar, *Kenya* .............. 28 C7 69 10N 65 0 E
Kara Bogaz Gol, Zaliv =
  Garabogazköl Aylagy,
  *Turkmenistan* ............... 19 F9 41 0N 53 30 E
Kara Kalpak Republic =
  Qoraqalpoghistan □,
  *Uzbekistan* ................. 28 E6 43 0N 58 0 E
Kara Kum, *Turkmenistan* ..... 28 F6 39 30N 60 0 E
Kara Sea, *Russia* ........... 28 B7 75 0N 70 0 E
Karabiğa, *Turkey* ............ 23 D12 40 23N 27 17 E
Karabük, *Turkey* ............ 19 F5 41 12N 32 37 E
Karaburun, *Turkey* .......... 23 E12 38 41N 26 28 E
Karabutak = Qarabutaq,
  *Kazakhstan* ................. 28 E7 49 59N 60 14 E
Karacabey, *Turkey* .......... 23 D13 40 12N 28 21 E
Karacasu, *Turkey* ........... 23 F13 37 43N 28 35 E
Karachey-Cherkessia □, *Russia* . 19 F7 43 40N 41 30 E
Karachi, *Pakistan* ........... 42 G2 24 53N 67 0 E
Karad, *India* ................ 40 L9 17 15N 74 10 E
Karaganda = Qaraghandy,
  *Kazakhstan* ................. 28 E8 49 50N 73 10 E
Karagayly = Qaraghayly,
  *Kazakhstan* ................. 28 E8 49 26N 76 0 E
Karaginskiy, Ostrov, *Russia* .. 29 D17 58 45N 164 0 E
Karagiye, Vpadina, *Kazakhstan* . 19 F9 43 27N 51 45 E
Karagiye Depression = Karagiye,
  *Vpadina, Kazakhstan* ....... 19 F9 43 27N 51 45 E
Karagola Road, *India* ........ 43 G12 25 29N 87 23 E
Karaikal, *India* .............. 40 P11 10 59N 79 50 E
Karaikkudi, *India* ........... 40 P11 10 5N 78 45 E
Karaj, *Iran* ................. 45 C6 35 48N 51 0 E
Karak, *Malaysia* ............ 39 L4 3 25N 102 2 E
Karakalpakstan =
  Qoraqalpoghistan □,
  *Uzbekistan* ................. 28 E6 43 0N 58 0 E
Karakelong, *Indonesia* ....... 37 D7 4 35N 126 50 E
Karakitang, *Indonesia* ....... 37 D7 3 14N 125 28 E
Karakol, *Kyrgyzstan* ......... 28 E8 42 30N 78 20 E
Karakoram Pass, *Asia* ....... 43 B7 35 33N 77 50 E
Karakoram Ra., *Pakistan* .... 43 B7 35 30N 77 0 E
Karakuwisa, *Namibia* ........ 56 B2 18 56S 19 40 E
Karalon, *Russia* ............. 29 D12 57 5N 115 50 E
Karama, *Jordan* ............. 46 D4 31 57N 35 35 E
Karaman, *Turkey* ........... 19 G5 37 14N 33 13 E
Karamay, *China* ............. 32 B3 45 30N 84 58 E
Karambu, *Indonesia* ......... 36 E5 3 53S 116 6 E
Karamea Bight, *N.Z.* ........ 59 J3 41 22S 171 40 E
Karamnasa ➤, *India* ........ 43 G10 25 31N 83 52 E
Karand, *Iran* ............... 44 C5 34 16N 46 15 E
Karanganyar, *Indonesia* ...... 37 G13 7 38S 109 37 E
Karangasem, *Indonesia* ...... 37 J18 8 27S 115 37 E
Karanjia, *India* .............. 43 J11 21 47N 85 58 E
Karasburg, *Namibia* ......... 56 D2 28 0S 18 44 E
Karasino, *Russia* ............ 28 C9 66 50N 86 50 E
Karasjok, *Norway* ........... 8 B21 69 27N 25 30 E
Karasuk, *Russia* ............ 28 D8 53 44N 78 2 E
Karasuyama, *Japan* ......... 31 F10 36 39N 140 9 E
Karatau, Khrebet = Qarataū,
  *Kazakhstan* ................. 28 E7 43 30N 69 30 E
Karatsu, *Japan* ............. 31 H5 33 26N 129 58 E
Karaul, *Russia* .............. 28 B9 70 6N 82 15 E
Karauli, *India* ............... 42 F7 26 30N 77 4 E
Karavostasi, *Cyprus* ......... 25 D11 35 8N 32 50 E
Karawang, *Indonesia* ........ 37 G12 6 30S 107 15 E
Karawanken, *Europe* ........ 16 E8 46 30N 14 40 E
Karayazı, *Turkey* ............ 19 G7 39 41N 42 9 E
Karazhal, *Kazakhstan* ....... 28 E8 48 2N 70 49 E
Karbalā' *Iraq* ............... 44 C5 32 36N 44 3 E
Karcag, *Hungary* ............ 17 E11 47 19N 20 57 E
Karcha ➤, *Pakistan* ........ 43 B7 34 45N 76 10 E
Karchana, *India* ............. 43 G9 25 17N 81 56 E
Kardhitsa, *Greece* .......... 23 E9 39 23N 21 54 E
Kārdla, *Estonia* ............. 9 G20 59 0N 22 45 E
Kareeberge, *S. Africa* ....... 56 E3 30 59S 21 50 E
Kareha ➤, *India* ............ 43 G12 25 44N 86 21 E
Kareima, *Sudan* ............ 51 E12 18 30N 31 49 E
Karelia □, *Russia* ........... 18 A5 65 30N 32 30 E
Karelian Republic = Karelia □,
  *Russia* .................... 18 A5 65 30N 32 30 E
Karera, *India* ............... 42 G8 25 32N 78 9 E
Kārevāndar, *Iran* ........... 45 E9 27 53N 60 44 E
Kargasok, *Russia* ........... 28 D9 59 3N 80 53 E
Kargat, *Russia* ............. 28 D9 55 10N 80 15 E
Kargil, *India* ............... 43 B7 34 32N 76 12 E
Kargopol, *Russia* ........... 18 B6 61 30N 38 58 E
Karhal, *India* ............... 43 F8 27 1N 78 57 E
Kariān, *Iran* ................ 45 E8 26 57N 57 14 E
Karianga, *Madag.* ........... 57 C8 22 25S 47 22 E
Kariba, *Zimbabwe* ........... 55 F2 16 28S 28 50 E
Kariba, L., *Zimbabwe* ........ 55 F2 16 40S 28 25 E

Kariba Dam, *Zimbabwe* ...... 55 F2 16 30S 28 35 E
Kariba Gorge, *Zambia* ....... 55 F2 16 30S 28 50 E
Karibib, *Namibia* ............ 56 C2 22 0S 15 56 E
Karijini △, *Australia* ......... 60 D2 23 8S 118 15 E
Karimata, Kepulauan, *Indonesia* 36 E3 1 25S 109 0 E
Karimata, Selat, *Indonesia* ... 36 E3 2 0S 108 40 E
Karimata Is. = Karimata,
  *Kepulauan, Indonesia* ....... 36 E3 1 25S 109 0 E
Karimnagar, *India* ........... 40 K11 18 26N 79 10 E
Karimun Kecil, Pulau, *Indonesia* 39 d 1 8N 103 22 E
Karimunjawa, Kepulauan,
  *Indonesia* .................. 36 F4 5 50S 110 30 E
Karin, *Somali Rep.* .......... 47 E4 10 50N 45 52 E
Karit, *Iran* ................. 45 C8 33 29N 56 55 E
Kariya, *Japan* ............... 31 G8 34 58N 137 1 E
Kariyangwe, *Zimbabwe* ...... 57 B4 18 0S 27 38 E
Karkaralinsk = Qarqaraly,
  *Kazakhstan* ................. 28 E8 49 26N 75 30 E
Karkheh ➤, *Iran* ........... 44 D5 31 2N 47 29 E
Karkinitska Zatoka, *Ukraine* .. 19 E5 45 56N 33 0 E
Karkinitskiy Zaliv = Karkinitska
  *Zatoka, Ukraine* ............ 19 E5 45 56N 33 0 E
Karkuk = Kirkūk, *Iraq* ....... 44 C5 35 30N 44 21 E
Karleby = Kokkola, *Finland* ... 8 E20 63 50N 23 8 E
Karlovac, *Croatia* ........... 16 F8 45 31N 15 36 E
Karlovo, *Bulgaria* ........... 23 C11 42 38N 24 47 E
Karlovy Vary, *Czech Rep.* .... 16 C7 50 13N 12 51 E
Karlsbad = Karlovy Vary,
  *Czech Rep.* ................. 16 C7 50 13N 12 51 E
Karlsborg, *Sweden* .......... 9 G16 58 33N 14 33 E
Karlshamn, *Sweden* ......... 9 H16 56 10N 14 51 E
Karlskoga, *Sweden* ......... 9 G16 59 28N 14 33 E
Karlskrona, *Sweden* ......... 9 H16 56 10N 15 35 E
Karlsruhe, *Germany* ......... 16 D5 49 0N 8 23 E
Karlstad, *Sweden* ........... 9 G15 59 23N 13 30 E
Karlstad, *U.S.A.* ............ 80 A6 48 35N 96 31W
Karmi'el, *Israel* ............. 46 C4 32 55N 35 18 E
Karnak, *Egypt* .............. 51 C12 25 43N 32 39 E
Karnal, *India* ............... 42 E7 29 42N 77 2 E
Karnali ➤, *Nepal* ........... 43 E9 28 45N 81 16 E
Karnaphuli Res. = Kaptai L.,
  *Bangla.* .................... 41 H18 22 40N 92 20 E
Karnaprayag, *India* .......... 43 D8 30 16N 79 15 E
Karnataka □, *India* .......... 40 N10 13 15N 77 0 E
Karnes City, *U.S.A.* ......... 81 L6 28 53N 97 54W
Karnische Alpen, *Europe* .... 16 E7 46 36N 13 0 E
Kärnten □, *Austria* .......... 16 E8 46 52N 13 30 E
Karoi, *Zimbabwe* ............ 55 F2 16 48S 29 45 E
Karon, Ao, *Thailand* ......... 39 a 7 51N 98 17 E
Karonga, *Malawi* ............ 55 D3 9 57S 33 55 E
Karoo △, *S. Africa* .......... 56 E3 32 18S 22 27 E
Karoonda, *Australia* ......... 63 F2 35 1S 139 59 E
Karor, *Pakistan* ............. 42 D4 31 15N 70 59 E
Karora, *Sudan* .............. 51 E13 17 44N 38 15 E
Karpasia, *Cyprus* ........... 25 D13 35 32N 34 15 E
Kárpathos, *Greece* .......... 23 G12 35 37N 27 10 E
Karpinsk, *Russia* ........... 18 C11 59 45N 60 1 E
Karpogory, *Russia* .......... 18 B7 64 0N 44 27 E
Karpuz Burnu = Apostolos
  *Andreas, C., Cyprus* ........ 25 D13 35 42N 34 35 E
Karratha, *Australia* .......... 60 D2 20 53S 116 40 E
Kars, *Turkey* ................ 19 F7 40 40N 43 5 E
Karsakpay, *Kazakhstan* ...... 28 E7 47 55N 66 40 E
Karsiyang, *India* ............ 43 F13 26 56N 88 18 E
Karsog, *India* ............... 42 D7 31 23N 77 12 E
Kartaly, *Russia* ............. 28 D7 53 3N 60 40 E
Kartapur, *India* ............. 42 D6 31 27N 75 32 E
Karthaus, *U.S.A.* ........... 84 E6 41 8N 78 9W
Karufa, *Indonesia* ........... 37 E8 3 50S 133 20 E
Karuma △, *Uganda* .......... 54 B3 2 5N 32 15 E
Karumba, *Australia* .......... 62 B3 17 31S 140 50 E
Karumo, *Tanzania* .......... 54 C3 2 25S 32 50 E
Karumwa, *Tanzania* ......... 54 C3 3 12S 32 38 E
Kārūn ➤, *Iran* .............. 45 D6 30 26N 48 10 E
Karungu, *Kenya* ............. 54 C3 0 50S 34 10 E
Karviná, *Czech Rep.* ......... 17 D10 49 53N 18 31 E
Karwan ➤, *India* ........... 42 F8 27 26N 78 4 E
Karwar, *India* ............... 40 M9 14 55N 74 13 E
Karwi, *India* ................ 43 G9 25 12N 80 57 E
Kasache, *Malawi* ............ 55 E3 13 25S 34 20 E
Kasai ➤, *Dem. Rep. of*
  *the Congo* ................. 52 E3 3 30S 16 10 E
Kasai-Oriental □, *Dem. Rep. of*
  *the Congo* ................. 54 D1 5 0S 24 30 E
Kasaji, *Dem. Rep. of the Congo* . 55 E1 10 25S 23 27 E
Kasama, *Zambia* ............ 55 E3 10 16S 31 9 E
Kasan-dong, *N. Korea* ....... 35 D14 41 18N 126 55 E
Kasanga, *Tanzania* .......... 55 D3 8 30S 31 10 E
Kasane, *Namibia* ............ 56 B3 17 34S 24 50 E
Kasanga □, *Zambia* ......... 55 E3 11 34S 30 15 E
Kasaragod, *India* ........... 40 N9 12 30N 74 58 E
Kasba L., *Canada* ........... 71 A8 60 20N 102 10W
Kāseh Garān, *Iran* .......... 44 C5 34 5N 46 2 E
Kasempa, *Zambia* ........... 55 E2 13 30S 25 44 E
Kasenga, *Dem. Rep. of*
  *the Congo* ................. 55 E2 10 20S 28 45 E
Kasese, *Uganda* ............ 54 B3 0 13N 30 3 E
Kasewa, *Zambia* ............ 55 E2 14 28S 28 53 E
Kasganj, *India* .............. 43 F8 27 48N 78 42 E
Kashabowie, *Canada* ........ 72 C1 48 40N 90 26W
Kashaf, *Iran* ................ 45 C9 35 58N 61 7 E
Kāshān, *Iran* ............... 45 C6 34 5N 51 30 E
Kashechewan, *Canada* ...... 72 B3 52 18N 81 37W
Kashgar = Kashi, *China* ..... 32 C2 39 30N 76 2 E
Kashi, *China* ............... 32 C2 39 30N 76 2 E
Kashimbo, *Dem. Rep. of*
  *the Congo* ................. 55 E2 11 12S 26 19 E
Kashipur, *India* ............. 43 E8 29 15N 79 0 E
Kashk-e Kohneh, *Afghan.* .... 40 B3 34 55N 62 30 E
Kashkū'īyeh, *Iran* ........... 45 D7 30 31N 55 40 E
Kashmar, *Iran* .............. 45 C8 35 16N 58 0 E
Kashmir, *Asia* ............... 43 C7 34 0N 76 0 E
Kashun Noerh = Gaxun Nur,
  *China* ..................... 32 B5 42 22N 100 30 E
Kasiari, *India* ............... 43 H12 22 8N 87 14 E
Kasimov, *Russia* ............ 18 D7 54 55N 41 20 E
Kasinge, *Dem. Rep. of Congo* . 54 D2 6 15S 26 58 E
Kasiruta, *Indonesia* ......... 37 E7 0 25S 127 12 E
Kaskaskia ➤, *U.S.A.* ....... 80 G10 37 58N 89 57W
Kaskattama ➤, *Canada* .... 71 B10 57 3N 90 4W
Kaskinen, *Finland* ........... 9 E19 62 22N 21 15 E
Kaskö = Kaskinen, *Finland* ... 9 E19 62 22N 21 15 E
Kaslo, *Canada* .............. 70 D5 49 55N 116 55W
Kasmere L., *Canada* ......... 71 B8 59 34N 101 10W
Kasongo, *Dem. Rep. of*
  *the Congo* ................. 54 C2 4 30S 26 33 E

Kasongo Lunda, *Dem. Rep. of*
  *the Congo* ................. 52 F3 6 35S 16 49 E
Kásos, *Greece* .............. 23 G12 35 20N 26 55 E
Kassalâ, *Sudan* ............. 51 E13 15 30N 36 0 E
Kassel, *Germany* ........... 16 C5 51 18N 9 26 E
Kassiópi, *Greece* ........... 25 A3 39 48N 19 53 E
Kasson, *U.S.A.* ............. 80 C8 44 2N 92 45W
Kastamonu, *Turkey* ......... 19 F5 41 25N 33 43 E
Kastélli, *Greece* ............ 25 D5 35 12N 25 20 E
Kastéllion, *Greece* .......... 25 D7 35 12N 25 20 E
Kasterlee, *Belgium* .......... 15 C4 51 15N 4 59 E
Kastoría, *Greece* ........... 23 D9 40 30N 21 19 E
Kasulu, *Tanzania* ........... 54 C3 4 37S 30 5 E
Kasumi, *Japan* .............. 31 G7 35 38N 134 38 E
Kasungu, *Malawi* ........... 55 E3 13 0S 33 29 E
Kasungu △, *Malawi* ......... 55 E3 12 53S 33 9 E
Kasur, *Pakistan* ............. 42 D6 31 5N 74 25 E
Kata Tjuta = Olga, Mt., *Australia* 61 E5 25 20S 130 50 E
Katahdin, Mt., *U.S.A.* ....... 83 C11 45 54N 68 56W
Katako Kombe, *Dem. Rep. of*
  *the Congo* ................. 54 C1 3 25S 24 20 E
Katale, *Tanzania* ............ 54 C3 4 52S 31 7 E
Katanda, *Katanga, Dem. Rep. of*
  *the Congo* ................. 54 D1 7 52S 24 13 E
Katanda, *Nord-Kivu, Dem. Rep.*
  *of the Congo* .............. 54 C2 0 55S 29 21 E
Katanga □, *Dem. Rep. of*
  *the Congo* ................. 54 D2 8 0S 25 0 E
Katangi, *India* .............. 40 J11 21 56N 79 50 E
Katanning, *Australia* ........ 61 F2 33 40S 117 33 E
Katavi △, *Tanzania* ......... 54 D3 6 51S 31 3 E
Katavi Swamp, *Tanzania* ..... 54 D3 6 50S 31 10 E
Katerini, *Greece* ............ 23 D10 40 18N 22 37 E
Katghora, *India* ............. 43 H10 22 30N 82 33 E
Katha, *Burma* ............... 41 G20 24 10N 96 30 E
Katherîna, Gebel, *Egypt* ..... 44 D2 28 30N 33 57 E
Katherine, *Australia* ......... 60 B5 14 27S 132 20 E
Katherine Gorge, *Australia* ... 60 B5 14 18S 132 24 E
Kathi, *India* ................. 42 J6 21 47N 74 3 E
Kathiawar, *India* ............ 42 H4 22 20N 71 0 E
Kathikas, *Cyprus* ........... 25 E11 34 55N 32 25 E
Kathmandu = Katmandu, *Nepal* . 43 F11 27 45N 85 20 E
Kathua, *India* ............... 42 C6 32 23N 75 34 E
Katihar, *India* .............. 43 G12 25 34N 87 36 E
Katima Mulilo, *Zambia* ....... 56 B3 17 28S 24 13 E
Katimbira, *Malawi* .......... 55 E3 12 40S 34 0 E
Katingan = Mendawai ➤,
  *Indonesia* .................. 36 E4 3 30S 113 0 E
Katiola, *Ivory C.* ............ 50 G4 8 10N 5 10W
Katmandu, *Nepal* ........... 43 F11 27 45N 85 20 E
Katni, *India* ................ 43 H9 23 51N 80 24 E
Káto Arkhánai, *Greece* ...... 25 D7 35 15N 25 10 E
Káto Khorió, *Greece* ........ 25 D7 35 3N 25 47 E
Káto Pyrgos, *Cyprus* ........ 25 D11 35 11N 32 41 E
Katompe, *Dem. Rep. of*
  *the Congo* ................. 54 D2 6 2S 26 23 E
Katong, *Singapore* .......... 39 d 1 18N 103 53 E
Katonga ➤, *Uganda* ........ 54 B3 0 34N 31 50 E
Katoomba, *Australia* ........ 63 E5 33 41S 150 19 E
Katowice, *Poland* ........... 17 C10 50 17N 19 5 E
Katrine, L., *U.K.* ............ 11 E4 56 15N 4 30W
Katrineholm, *Sweden* ....... 9 G17 59 9N 16 12 E
Katsepe, *Madag.* ........... 57 B8 15 45S 46 15 E
Katsina, *Nigeria* ............ 50 F7 13 0N 7 32 E
Katsumoto, *Japan* .......... 31 H4 33 51N 129 42 E
Katsuura, *Japan* ............ 31 G10 35 10N 140 20 E
Katsuyama, *Japan* .......... 31 F8 36 3N 136 30 E
Kattaviá, *Greece* ........... 25 D9 35 57N 27 46 E
Kattegat, *Denmark* ......... 9 H14 56 40N 11 20 E
Katumba, *Dem. Rep. of*
  *the Congo* ................. 54 D2 7 40S 25 17 E
Katwa, *India* ............... 43 H13 23 30N 88 5 E
Katwijk, *Neths.* ............. 15 B4 52 12N 4 24 E
Kauai, *U.S.A.* ............... 74 H15 22 3N 159 30W
Kauai Channel, *U.S.A.* ....... 74 H15 21 45N 158 50W
Kaudom △, *Namibia* ........ 56 B3 18 45S 20 51 E
Kaufman, *U.S.A.* ........... 81 J6 32 35N 96 19W
Kauhajoki, *Finland* .......... 9 E20 62 25N 22 10 E
Kaukauna, *U.S.A.* .......... 82 C1 44 17N 88 17W
Kaukauveld, *Namibia* ....... 56 C3 20 0S 20 15 E
Kaunakakai, *U.S.A.* ......... 74 H16 21 6N 157 1W
Kaunas, *Lithuania* .......... 9 J20 54 54N 23 54 E
Kaunia, *Bangla.* ............ 43 G13 25 46N 89 26 E
Kautokeino, *Norway* ........ 8 B20 69 0N 23 4 E
Kauwapur, *India* ............ 43 F10 27 31N 82 18 E
Kavacha, *Russia* ............ 29 C17 60 16N 169 51 E
Kavali, *India* ............... 40 M12 14 55N 80 1 E
Kaválla, *Greece* ............ 23 D11 40 57N 24 28 E
Kavār, *Iran* ................ 45 D7 29 11N 52 44 E
Kavi, *India* ................. 42 H5 22 12N 72 38 E
Kavimba, *Botswana* ......... 56 B3 18 2S 24 38 E
Kavīr, Dasht-e, *Iran* ......... 45 C7 34 30N 55 0 E
Kavos, *Greece* .............. 25 B4 39 23N 20 3 E
Kaw, *Fr. Guiana* ............ 93 C8 4 30N 52 15W
Kawagama L., *Canada* ....... 84 A6 45 18N 78 45W
Kawagoe, *Japan* ............ 31 G9 35 55N 139 29 E
Kawaguchi, *Japan* .......... 31 G9 35 52N 139 45 E
Kawambwa, *Zambia* ......... 55 D2 9 48S 29 3 E
Kawanoe, *Japan* ............ 31 G6 34 1N 133 34 E
Kawardha, *India* ............ 43 J9 22 0N 81 17 E
Kawasaki, *Japan* ........... 31 G9 35 31N 139 43 E
Kawasi, *Indonesia* .......... 37 E7 1 38S 127 28 E
Kawerau, *N.Z.* .............. 59 H6 38 7S 176 42 E
Kawhia, *N.Z.* ............... 59 H5 38 5S 174 51 E
Kawhia Harbour, *N.Z.* ....... 59 H5 38 5S 174 51 E
Kawio, Kepulauan, *Indonesia* . 37 D7 4 30N 125 30 E
Kawthaung, *Burma* .......... 39 H2 10 5N 98 36 E
Kawthoolei = Kayin □, *Burma* . 41 L20 18 0N 97 30 E
Kawthule = Kayin □, *Burma* .. 41 L20 18 0N 97 30 E
Kaya, *Burkina Faso* ......... 50 F5 13 4N 1 10W
Kayah □, *Burma* ............ 41 K20 19 15N 97 15 E
Kayan ➤, *Indonesia* ........ 36 D5 2 55N 117 35 E
Kaycee, *U.S.A.* ............. 76 E10 43 43N 106 38W
Kayeli, *Indonesia* ........... 37 E7 3 20S 127 10 E
Kayenta, *U.S.A.* ............ 77 H8 36 44N 110 15W
Kayes, *Mali* ................ 50 F3 14 25N 11 30W
Kayin □, *Burma* ............ 41 L20 18 0N 97 30 E
Kayoa, *Indonesia* ........... 37 D7 0 1N 127 28 E
Kayomba, *Zambia* .......... 55 E1 13 11S 24 2 E
Kayseri, *Turkey* ............ 19 G6 38 45N 35 30 E
Kaysville, *U.S.A.* ........... 76 F8 41 2N 111 56W
Kazachye, *Russia* .......... 29 B14 70 52N 135 58 E
Kazakhstan ■, *Asia* ......... 28 E7 50 0N 70 0 E
Kazan, *Russia* .............. 18 C8 55 50N 49 10 E
Kazan ➤, *Canada* .......... 71 A9 64 2N 95 29W

Kazan-Rettō, *Pac. Oc.* ......... 64 E6 25 0N 141 0 E
Kazanlŭk, *Bulgaria* ......... 23 C11 42 38N 25 20 E
Kazatin = Kozyatyn, *Ukraine* ... 17 D15 49 45N 28 50 E
Kāzerūn, *Iran* ......... 45 D6 29 38N 51 40 E
Kazi Magomed = Qazimämmäd,
   *Azerbaijan* ......... 45 A6 40 3N 49 0 E
Kazuma Pan △, *Zimbabwe* ... 55 F2 18 20S 25 48 E
Kazuno, *Japan* ......... 30 D10 40 10N 140 45 E
Kazym ➤, *Russia* ......... 28 C7 63 54N 65 50 E
Kéa, *Greece* ......... 23 F11 37 35N 24 22 E
Keady, *U.K.* ......... 10 B5 54 15N 6 42W
Kearney, *U.S.A.* ......... 80 E5 40 42N 99 5W
Kearny, *U.S.A.* ......... 77 K8 33 3N 110 55W
Kearsarge, Mt., *U.S.A.* ... 85 C13 43 22N 71 50W
Keban, *Turkey* ......... 19 G6 38 50N 38 50 E
Keban Baraji, *Turkey* ... 19 G6 38 41N 38 33 E
Kebnekaise, *Sweden* ...... 8 C18 67 53N 18 33 E
Kebri Dehar, *Ethiopia* ... 47 F3 6 45N 44 17 E
Kebumen, *Indonesia* ... 37 G13 7 42S 109 40 E
Kechika ➤, *Canada* ... 70 B3 59 41N 127 12W
Kecskemét, *Hungary* ... 17 E10 46 57N 19 42 E
Kėdainiai, *Lithuania* ... 9 J21 55 15N 24 2 E
Kedarnath, *India* ...... 43 D8 30 44N 79 4 E
Kedgwick, *Canada* ... 73 C6 47 40N 67 20W
Kédhros Óros, *Greece* ... 25 D6 35 11N 24 37 E
Kediri, *Indonesia* ...... 36 F4 7 51S 112 1 E
Keeler, *U.S.A.* ...... 78 J9 36 29N 117 52W
Keeley L., *Canada* ... 71 C7 54 54N 108 8W
Keeling Is. = Cocos Is., *Ind. Oc.* 64 J1 12 10S 96 55 E
Keelung = Chilung, *Taiwan* ... 33 D7 25 3N 121 45 E
Keene, *Canada* ...... 84 B6 44 15N 78 10W
Keene, *Calif., U.S.A.* ... 79 K8 35 13N 118 33W
Keene, *N.H., U.S.A.* ... 85 D12 42 56N 72 17W
Keene, *N.Y., U.S.A.* ... 85 B11 44 16N 73 46W
Keep River △, *Australia* ... 60 C4 15 49S 129 8 E
Keeper Hill, *Ireland* ... 10 D3 52 45N 8 16W
Keer-Weer, C., *Australia* ... 62 A3 14 0S 141 32 E
Keeseville, *U.S.A.* ...... 85 B11 44 29N 73 30W
Keetmanshoop, *Namibia* ... 56 D2 26 35S 18 8 E
Keewatin, *Canada* ... 71 D10 49 46N 94 34W
Keewatin ➤, *Canada* ... 71 B8 56 29N 100 46W
Kefallinía, *Greece* ... 23 E9 38 15N 20 30 E
Kefamenanu, *Indonesia* ... 37 F6 9 28S 124 29 E
Kefar Sava, *Israel* ... 46 C3 32 11N 34 54 E
Keffi, *Nigeria* ...... 50 G7 8 55N 7 43 E
Keflavík, *Iceland* ... 8 D2 64 2N 22 35W
Keg River, *Canada* ... 70 B5 57 54N 117 55W
Kegaska, *Canada* ... 73 B7 50 9N 61 18W
Keighley, *U.K.* ...... 12 D6 53 52N 1 54W
Keila, *Estonia* ...... 9 G21 59 18N 24 25 E
Keimoes, *S. Africa* ... 56 D3 28 41N 20 59 E
Keitele, *Finland* ...... 8 E22 63 10N 26 20 E
Keith, *Australia* ...... 63 F3 36 6S 140 20 E
Keith, *U.K.* ...... 11 D6 57 32N 2 57W
Keizer, *U.S.A.* ...... 76 D2 44 57N 123 1W
Kejimkujik △, *Canada* ... 73 D6 44 25N 65 25W
Kejserr Franz Joseph Fd.,
   *Greenland* ...... 4 B6 73 30N 24 30W
Kekri, *India* ...... 42 G6 26 0N 75 10 E
Kelan, *China* ...... 34 E6 38 43N 111 31 E
Kelang = Klang, *Malaysia* ... 39 L3 3 2N 101 26 E
Kelantan ➤, *Malaysia* ... 39 J4 6 13N 102 14 E
Kelkit ➤, *Turkey* ... 19 F6 40 45N 36 32 E
Kellerberrin, *Australia* ... 61 F2 31 36S 117 38 E
Kellett, C., *Canada* ... 4 B1 72 0N 126 0W
Kelleys I., *U.S.A.* ... 84 E2 41 36N 82 42W
Kellogg, *U.S.A.* ...... 76 C5 47 32N 116 7W
Kells = Ceanannus Mor, *Ireland* 10 C5 53 44N 6 53W
Kelokedhara, *Cyprus* ... 25 E11 34 48N 32 39 E
Kelowna, *Canada* ... 70 D5 49 50N 119 25W
Kelsey Creek, *Australia* ... 62 J6 20 26S 148 31 E
Kelseyville, *U.S.A.* ... 78 G4 38 59N 122 50W
Kelso, *N.Z.* ...... 59 L2 45 54S 169 15 E
Kelso, *U.K.* ...... 11 F6 55 36N 2 26W
Kelso, *U.S.A.* ...... 78 D4 46 9N 122 54W
Keluang, *Malaysia* ... 39 L4 2 3N 103 18 E
Kelvington, *Canada* ... 71 C8 52 10N 103 30W
Kem, *Russia* ...... 18 B5 65 0N 34 38 E
Kem ➤, *Russia* ...... 18 B5 64 57N 34 41 E
Kema, *Indonesia* ...... 37 D7 1 22N 125 8 E
Kemah, *Turkey* ...... 44 B3 39 32N 39 5 E
Kemaman, *Malaysia* ... 36 D2 4 12N 103 18 E
Kemano, *Canada* ... 70 C3 53 35N 128 0W
Kemasik, *Malaysia* ... 39 K4 4 25N 103 27 E
Kemerovo, *Russia* ... 28 D9 55 20N 86 5 E
Kemi, *Finland* ...... 8 D21 65 44N 24 34 E
Kemi älv = Kemijoki ➤, *Finland* 8 D21 65 47N 24 32 E
Kemi träsk = Kemijärvi, *Finland* 8 C22 66 43N 27 22 E
Kemijärvi, *Finland* ... 8 C22 66 43N 27 22 E
Kemijoki ➤, *Finland* ... 8 D21 65 47N 24 32 E
Kemmerer, *U.S.A.* ... 76 F8 41 48N 110 32W
Kemmuna = Comino, *Malta* ... 25 C1 36 1N 14 20 E
Kemp, L., *U.S.A.* ... 81 J5 33 46N 99 9W
Kemp Land, *Antarctica* ... 5 C5 69 0S 55 0 E
Kempas, *Malaysia* ...... 39 d 1 33N 103 42 E
Kempsey, *Australia* ... 63 E5 31 1S 152 50 E
Kempt, L., *Canada* ... 72 C5 47 25N 74 22W
Kempten, *Germany* ... 16 E6 47 45N 10 17 E
Kempton, *Australia* ... 63 G4 42 31S 147 12 E
Kemptville, *Canada* ... 85 B9 45 0N 75 38W
Ken ➤, *India* ...... 43 G9 25 13N 80 27 E
Kenai, *U.S.A.* ...... 68 B4 60 33N 151 16W
Kendai, *India* ...... 43 H10 22 45N 82 37 E
Kendal, *Indonesia* ... 37 G14 6 56S 110 14 E
Kendal, *U.K.* ...... 12 C5 54 20N 2 44W
Kendall, *Australia* ... 63 E5 31 35S 152 44 E
Kendall, *U.S.A.* ...... 83 N5 25 41N 80 19W
Kendall ➤, *Australia* ... 62 A3 14 4S 141 35 E
Kendallville, *U.S.A.* ... 82 E3 41 27N 85 16W
Kendari, *Indonesia* ... 37 E6 3 50S 122 30 E
Kendawangan, *Indonesia* ... 36 E4 2 32S 110 17 E
Kendi, Pulau, *Malaysia* ... 39 c 5 13N 100 11 E
Kendrapara, *India* ... 41 J15 20 35N 86 30 E
Kendrew, *S. Africa* ... 56 E3 32 32S 24 30 E
Kene Thao, *Laos* ...... 38 D3 17 44N 101 10 E
Kenedy, *U.S.A.* ...... 81 L6 28 49N 97 51W
Kenema, *S. Leone* ... 50 G3 7 50N 11 14W
Keng Kok, *Laos* ...... 38 D5 16 26N 105 12 E
Keng Tawng, *Burma* ... 41 J21 20 45N 98 18 E
Keng Tung, *Burma* ... 41 J21 21 0N 99 30 E
Kengeja, *Tanzania* ... 54 D4 5 26S 39 45 E
Kenhardt, *S. Africa* ... 56 D3 29 19S 21 12 E
Kenitra, *Morocco* ... 50 B4 34 15N 6 40W
Kenli, *China* ...... 35 F10 37 30N 118 20 E
Kenmare, *Ireland* ... 10 E2 51 53N 9 36W
Kenmare, *U.S.A.* ... 80 A3 48 41N 102 5W
Kenmare River, *Ireland* ... 10 E2 51 48N 9 51W
Kennebago Lake, *U.S.A.* ... 85 A14 45 4N 70 40W

Kennebec, *U.S.A.* ...... 80 D5 43 54N 99 52W
Kennebec ➤, *U.S.A.* ... 83 D11 43 45N 69 46W
Kennebunk, *U.S.A.* ... 85 C14 43 23N 70 33W
Kennedy, *Zimbabwe* ... 56 B4 18 52S 27 10 E
Kennedy Ra., *Australia* ... 61 D2 24 45S 115 10 E
Kennedy Range △, *Australia* ... 61 D2 24 34S 115 2 E
Kenner, *U.S.A.* ...... 81 L9 29 59N 90 15W
Kennet ➤, *U.K.* ...... 13 F7 51 27N 0 57W
Kenneth Ra., *Australia* ... 61 D2 23 50S 117 8 E
Kennett, *U.S.A.* ...... 81 G9 36 14N 90 3W
Kennewick, *U.S.A.* ... 76 C4 46 12N 119 7W
Kenogami ➤, *Canada* ... 72 B3 51 6N 84 28W
Kenora, *Canada* ...... 71 D10 49 47N 94 29W
Kenosha, *U.S.A.* ...... 82 D2 42 35N 87 49W
Kensington, *Canada* ... 73 C7 46 28N 63 34W
Kent, *Ohio, U.S.A.* ... 84 E3 41 9N 81 22W
Kent, *Tex., U.S.A.* ... 81 K2 31 4N 104 13W
Kent, *Wash., U.S.A.* ... 78 C4 47 23N 122 14W
Kent □, *U.K.* ...... 13 F8 51 12N 0 40 E
Kent Group, *Australia* ... 63 F4 39 30S 147 20 E
Kent Pen., *Canada* ... 68 B9 68 30N 107 0W
Kentaū, *Kazakhstan* ... 28 E7 43 32N 68 36 E
Kentland, *U.S.A.* ...... 82 E2 40 46N 87 27W
Kenton, *U.S.A.* ...... 82 E4 40 39N 83 37W
Kentucky □, *U.S.A.* ... 82 G3 37 0N 84 0W
Kentucky ➤, *U.S.A.* ... 82 F3 38 41N 85 11W
Kentucky L., *U.S.A.* ... 83 G2 37 1N 88 16W
Kentville, *Canada* ... 73 C7 45 6N 64 29W
Kentwood, *U.S.A.* ... 81 K9 30 56N 90 31W
Kenya ■, *Africa* ...... 54 B4 1 0N 38 0 E
Kenya, Mt., *Kenya* ... 54 C4 0 10S 37 18 E
Keo Neua, Deo, *Vietnam* ... 38 C5 18 23N 105 10 E
Keokuk, *U.S.A.* ...... 80 E9 40 24N 91 24W
Keonjhargarh, *India* ... 43 J11 21 28N 85 35 E
Kep, *Cambodia* ...... 39 G5 10 29N 104 19 E
Kep, *Vietnam* ...... 38 B6 21 24N 106 16 E
Kepala Batas, *Malaysia* ... 39 c 5 31N 100 26 E
Kepi, *Indonesia* ...... 37 F9 6 32S 139 19 E
Kerala □, *India* ...... 40 P10 11 0N 76 15 E
Kerama-Rettō, *Japan* ... 31 L3 26 5N 127 15 E
Keran, *Pakistan* ...... 43 B5 34 35N 73 59 E
Kerang, *Australia* ... 63 F3 35 40S 143 55 E
Keraudren, C., *Australia* ... 60 C2 19 58S 119 45 E
Kerava, *Finland* ...... 9 F21 60 25N 25 5 E
Kerch, *Ukraine* ...... 19 E6 45 20N 36 20 E
Kerguelen, *Ind. Oc.* ... 3 G13 49 15S 69 10 E
Kericho, *Kenya* ...... 54 C4 0 22S 35 15 E
Kerinci, *Indonesia* ... 36 E2 1 40S 101 15 E
Kerki, *Turkmenistan* ... 28 F7 37 50N 65 12 E
Kérkira, *Greece* ...... 25 A3 39 38N 19 50 E
Kerkrade, *Neths.* ...... 15 D6 50 53N 6 4 E
Kermadec Is., *Pac. Oc.* ... 64 L10 30 0S 178 15W
Kermadec Trench, *Pac. Oc.* ... 64 L10 30 30S 176 0W
Kermān, *Iran* ...... 45 D8 30 15N 57 1 E
Kerman, *U.S.A.* ...... 78 J6 36 43N 120 4W
Kermān □, *Iran* ...... 45 D8 30 0N 57 0 E
Kermān, Bīābān-e, *Iran* ... 45 D8 28 45N 59 45 E
Kermānshāh = Bākhtarān, *Iran* 44 C5 34 23N 47 0 E
Kermit, *U.S.A.* ...... 81 K3 31 52N 103 6W
Kern ➤, *U.S.A.* ...... 79 K7 35 16N 119 18W
Kernow = Cornwall □, *U.K.* ... 13 G3 50 26N 4 40W
Kernville, *U.S.A.* ...... 79 K8 35 45N 118 26W
Keroh, *Malaysia* ...... 39 K3 5 43N 101 1 E
Kerrera, *U.K.* ...... 11 E3 56 24N 5 33W
Kerrobert, *Canada* ... 71 C7 51 56N 109 8W
Kerrville, *U.S.A.* ...... 81 K5 30 3N 99 8W
Kerry □, *Ireland* ...... 10 D2 52 7N 9 35W
Kerry Hd., *Ireland* ... 10 D2 52 25N 9 56W
Kerulen ➤, *Asia* ...... 33 B6 48 48N 117 0 E
Kervo = Kerava, *Finland* ... 9 F21 60 25N 25 5 E
Kerzaz, *Algeria* ...... 50 C5 29 29N 1 37W
Kesagami ➤, *Canada* ... 72 B4 51 40N 79 45W
Kesagami L., *Canada* ... 72 B3 50 23N 80 15W
Keşan, *Turkey* ...... 23 D12 40 49N 26 38 E
Kesennuma, *Japan* ... 30 E10 38 54N 141 35 E
Keshit, *Iran* ...... 45 D8 29 43N 58 17 E
Kestell, *S. Africa* ... 57 D4 28 17S 28 42 E
Kestenga, *Russia* ... 18 A5 65 50N 31 45 E
Keswick, *U.K.* ...... 12 C4 54 36N 3 8W
Ket ➤, *Russia* ...... 28 D9 58 55N 81 32 E
Ketapang, *Bali, Indonesia* ... 37 J17 8 9S 114 23 E
Ketapang, *Kalimantan, Indonesia* 36 E4 1 55S 110 0 E
Ketchikan, *U.S.A.* ... 70 B2 55 21N 131 39W
Ketchum, *U.S.A.* ... 76 E6 43 41N 114 22W
Ketef, Khalîg Umm el, *Egypt* ... 44 F2 23 40N 35 35 E
Keti Bandar, *Pakistan* ... 42 G2 24 8N 67 27 E
Ketri, *India* ...... 42 E6 28 1N 75 50 E
Ketrzyn, *Poland* ...... 17 A11 54 7N 21 22 E
Kettering, *U.K.* ...... 13 E7 52 24N 0 43W
Kettering, *U.S.A.* ... 82 F3 39 41N 84 10W
Kettle ➤, *Canada* ... 71 B11 56 40N 89 34W
Kettle Falls, *U.S.A.* ... 76 B4 48 37N 118 3W
Kettle Pt., *Canada* ... 84 C2 43 13N 82 1W
Kettleman City, *U.S.A.* ... 78 J7 36 1N 119 58W
Keuka L., *U.S.A.* ...... 84 D7 42 30N 77 9W
Keuruu, *Finland* ...... 9 E21 62 16N 24 41 E
Kewanee, *U.S.A.* ...... 80 E10 41 14N 89 56W
Kewaunee, *U.S.A.* ... 82 C2 44 27N 87 31W
Keweenaw B., *U.S.A.* ... 82 B1 47 0N 88 15W
Keweenaw Pen., *U.S.A.* ... 82 B2 47 30N 88 0W
Keweenaw Pt., *U.S.A.* ... 82 B2 47 25N 87 43W
Key Largo, *U.S.A.* ... 83 N5 25 5N 80 27W
Key West, *U.S.A.* ... 75 F10 24 33N 81 48W
Keynsham, *U.K.* ...... 13 F5 51 24N 2 29W
Keyser, *U.S.A.* ...... 82 F6 39 26N 78 59W
Kezhma, *Russia* ...... 29 D11 58 59N 101 9 E
Kezi, *Zimbabwe* ...... 57 C4 20 58S 28 32 E
Kgalagadi Transfrontier △, *Africa* 56 D3 25 10S 21 0 E
Khabarovsk, *Russia* ... 29 E14 48 30N 135 5 E
Khabr, *Iran* ...... 45 D8 28 51N 56 22 E
Khābūr ➤, *Syria* ...... 44 C4 35 17N 40 35 E
Khachmas = Xaçmaz, *Azerbaijan* 19 F8 41 31N 48 42 E
Khachrod, *India* ...... 42 H6 23 25N 75 20 E
Khadro, *India* ...... 42 F3 26 11N 68 50 E
Khadzhilyangar, *China* ... 43 B8 35 45N 79 20 E
Khaga, *India* ...... 43 G9 25 47N 81 7 E
Khagaria, *India* ...... 43 G12 25 30N 86 32 E
Khaipur, *Pakistan* ... 42 E5 29 34N 72 17 E
Khair, *India* ...... 42 F7 27 57N 77 46 E
Khairabad, *India* ...... 43 F9 27 33N 80 47 E
Khairagarh, *India* ... 43 J9 21 27N 81 2 E
Khairpur, *Pakistan* ... 42 F3 27 32N 68 49 E
Khairpur Nathan Shah, *Pakistan* 42 F2 27 6N 67 44 E
Khairwara, *India* ...... 42 H5 23 58N 73 38 E
Khaisor ➤, *Pakistan* ... 42 D3 31 17N 68 59 E
Khajuri Kach, *Pakistan* ... 42 C3 32 4N 69 51 E
Khakhea, *Botswana* ... 56 C3 24 48S 23 22 E

Khalafābād, *Iran* ...... 45 D6 30 54N 49 24 E
Khalilabad, *India* ... 43 F10 26 48N 83 5 E
Khalīlī, *Iran* ...... 45 E7 27 38N 53 17 E
Khalkhāl, *Iran* ...... 45 B6 37 37N 48 32 E
Khalkis, *Greece* ...... 23 E10 38 27N 23 42 E
Khalmer Yu, *Russia* ... 28 C7 67 58N 65 1 E
Khalturin, *Russia* ... 18 C8 58 40N 48 50 E
Khalūf, *Oman* ...... 47 C6 20 30N 58 13 E
Kham Keut, *Laos* ...... 38 C5 18 15N 104 43 E
Khamaria, *India* ...... 43 H9 23 5N 80 48 E
Khambhaliya, *India* ... 42 H3 22 14N 69 41 E
Khambhat, *India* ...... 42 H5 22 23N 72 33 E
Khambhat, G. of, *India* ... 40 J8 20 45N 72 30 E
Khamir, *Iran* ...... 45 E7 26 57N 55 36 E
Khamir, *Yemen* ...... 47 D3 16 2N 44 0 E
Khamsa, *Egypt* ...... 46 E1 30 27N 32 23 E
Khān ➤, *Namibia* ...... 56 C2 22 37S 14 56 E
Khān Abū Shāmat, *Syria* ... 46 B5 33 39N 36 53 E
Khān Āzād, *Iraq* ...... 44 C5 33 7N 44 22 E
Khān Mujiddah, *Iraq* ... 44 C4 32 21N 43 48 E
Khān Shaykhūn, *Syria* ... 44 C3 35 26N 36 38 E
Khān Yūnis, *Gaza Strip* ... 46 D3 31 21N 34 18 E
Khanai, *Pakistan* ...... 42 D2 30 30N 67 8 E
Khānaqīn, *Iraq* ...... 44 C5 34 23N 45 25 E
Khānbāghī, *Iran* ...... 45 B7 36 10N 55 25 E
Khandwa, *India* ...... 40 J10 21 49N 76 22 E
Khandyga, *Russia* ... 29 C14 62 42N 135 35 E
Khāneh, *Iran* ...... 44 B5 36 41N 45 8 E
Khanewal, *Pakistan* ... 42 D4 30 20N 71 55 E
Khangah Dogran, *Pakistan* ... 42 D5 31 50N 73 37 E
Khanh Duong, *Vietnam* ... 38 F7 12 44N 108 44 E
Khaniá, *Greece* ...... 25 D6 35 30N 24 4 E
Khaniá □, *Greece* ...... 25 D6 35 30N 24 0 E
Khaniadhana, *India* ... 42 G8 25 1N 78 8 E
Khanion, Kólpos, *Greece* ... 25 D5 35 33N 23 55 E
Khanka, L., *Asia* ...... 29 E14 45 0N 132 24 E
Khankendy = Xankändi,
   *Azerbaijan* ...... 19 G8 39 52N 46 49 E
Khanna, *India* ...... 42 D7 30 42N 76 16 E
Khanozai, *Pakistan* ... 42 D2 30 37N 67 19 E
Khanpur, *Pakistan* ... 42 E4 28 42N 70 35 E
Khanty-Mansiysk, *Russia* ... 28 C7 61 0N 69 0 E
Khao Laem △, *Thailand* ... 38 E2 14 56N 98 31 E
Khao Laem Res., *Thailand* ... 38 E2 14 50N 98 30 E
Khao Luang △, *Thailand* ... 39 H2 8 34N 99 42 E
Khao Phlu, *Thailand* ... 39 b 9 29N 99 59 E
Khao Pu-Khao Ya △, *Thailand* ... 39 J2 7 26N 99 57 E
Khao Sam Roi Yot △, *Thailand* ... 39 F2 12 13N 99 57 E
Khao Sok △, *Thailand* ... 39 H2 8 55N 98 38 E
Khao Yai △, *Thailand* ... 38 E3 14 21N 101 29 E
Khaoen Si Nakarin △, *Thailand* ... 38 E2 14 47N 99 0 E
Khapalu, *Pakistan* ... 43 B7 35 10N 76 20 E
Khapcheranga, *Russia* ... 29 E12 49 42N 112 24 E
Kharaghoda, *India* ... 42 H4 23 11N 71 46 E
Kharagpur, *India* ... 43 H12 22 20N 87 25 E
Khárakas, *Greece* ... 25 D7 35 1N 25 7 E
Kharan Kalat, *Pakistan* ... 40 E4 28 34N 65 21 E
Kharānaq, *Iran* ...... 45 C7 32 20N 54 45 E
Kharda, *India* ...... 40 K9 18 40N 75 34 E
Khardung La, *India* ... 43 B7 34 20N 77 43 E
Kharg = Khārk, Jazireh-ye, *Iran* 45 D6 29 15N 50 28 E
Khārga, El Wâhât-el, *Egypt* ... 51 C12 25 10N 30 35 E
Khargon, *India* ...... 40 J9 21 45N 75 40 E
Khari ➤, *India* ...... 42 G6 25 54N 74 31 E
Kharian, *Pakistan* ... 42 C5 32 49N 73 52 E
Khārk, Jazireh-ye, *Iran* ... 45 D6 29 15N 50 28 E
Kharkiv, *Ukraine* ... 19 E6 49 58N 36 20 E
Kharkov = Kharkiv, *Ukraine* ... 19 E6 49 58N 36 20 E
Kharovsk, *Russia* ... 18 C7 59 56N 40 13 E
Kharsawangarh, *India* ... 43 H11 22 48N 85 50 E
Kharta, *Turkey* ...... 23 D13 40 55N 29 7 E
Khartoum = El Khartûm, *Sudan* 51 E12 15 31N 32 35 E
Khasan, *Russia* ...... 30 C5 42 25N 130 40 E
Khāsh, *Iran* ...... 40 E2 28 15N 61 15 E
Khashm el Girba, *Sudan* ... 51 F13 14 59N 35 58 E
Khaskovo, *Bulgaria* ... 23 D11 41 56N 25 30 E
Khatanga, *Russia* ... 29 B11 72 0N 102 20 E
Khatanga ➤, *Russia* ... 29 B11 72 55N 106 0 E
Khatauli, *India* ...... 42 E7 29 17N 77 43 E
Khatra, *India* ...... 43 H12 22 59N 86 51 E
Khātūnābād, *Iran* ... 45 D7 30 1N 55 25 E
Khavda, *India* ...... 42 H3 23 51N 69 43 E
Khaybar, Harrat, *Si. Arabia* ... 44 E4 25 45N 40 0 E
Khayelitsha, *S. Africa* ... 53 L3 34 5S 18 42 E
Khāzimiyah, *Iraq* ...... 44 C4 34 46N 43 37 E
Khe Bo, *Vietnam* ...... 38 C5 19 8N 104 41 E
Khe Long, *Vietnam* ... 38 B5 21 29N 104 46 E
Khe Sanh, *Vietnam* ... 38 D6 16 37N 106 45 E
Khed Brahma, *India* ... 40 G8 24 7N 73 5 E
Kheda, *India* ...... 42 E7 22 45N 72 30 E
Khemarak Phouminville,
   *Cambodia* ...... 39 G4 11 37N 102 59 E
Khemisset, *Morocco* ... 50 B4 33 50N 6 1W
Khemmarat, *Thailand* ... 38 D5 16 10N 105 15 E
Khenāmān, *Iran* ...... 45 D8 30 27N 56 29 E
Khenchela, *Algeria* ... 50 A7 35 28N 7 11 E
Khenchela, *Algeria* ... 50 A7 35 28N 7 11 E
Khersān ➤, *Iran* ...... 45 D6 31 33N 50 22 E
Kherson, *Ukraine* ... 19 E5 46 35N 32 35 E
Khersónisos Akrotíri, *Greece* ... 25 D6 35 30N 24 10 E
Kheta ➤, *Russia* ...... 29 B11 71 54N 102 6 E
Khewari, *Pakistan* ... 42 F3 26 36N 68 52 E
Khilchipur, *India* ... 42 G7 24 2N 76 34 E
Khilok, *Russia* ...... 29 D12 51 30N 110 45 E
Khíos, *Greece* ...... 23 E12 38 27N 26 9 E
Khirsadoh, *India* ... 43 H8 22 11N 78 47 E
Khiuma = Hiiumaa, *Estonia* ... 9 G20 58 50N 22 45 E
Khiva, *Uzbekistan* ... 28 E7 41 30N 60 18 E
Khiyāv, *Iran* ...... 44 B5 38 30N 47 45 E
Khlong Khlung, *Thailand* ... 38 D2 16 12N 99 43 E
Khlong, *India* ...... 42 E7 28 12N 78 57 E
Khmelnik, *Ukraine* ... 17 D14 49 33N 27 58 E
Khmelnitskiy = Khmelnytskyy,
   *Ukraine* ...... 17 D14 49 23N 27 0 E
Khmelnytskyy, *Ukraine* ... 17 D14 49 23N 27 0 E
Khmer Rep. = Cambodia ■, *Asia* 38 F5 12 15N 105 0 E
Khoai, Hon, *Vietnam* ... 39 H5 8 26N 104 50 E
Khodoriv, *Ukraine* ... 17 D13 49 24N 24 19 E
Khodzent = Khŭjand, *Tajikistan* 28 E7 40 17N 69 37 E
Khojak Pass, *Afghan.* ... 42 D2 30 51N 66 34 E
Khok Kloi, *Thailand* ... 39 a 8 17N 98 19 E
Khok Pho, *Thailand* ... 39 J3 6 43N 101 6 E
Kholm, *Russia* ...... 18 C5 57 10N 31 15 E
Kholmsk, *Russia* ... 29 E15 47 40N 142 5 E
Khomas Hochland, *Namibia* ... 56 C2 22 40S 16 0 E
Khomeyn, *Iran* ...... 45 C6 33 40N 50 7 E
Khomeyni Shahr, *Iran* ... 45 C6 32 41N 51 31 E
Khomodino, *Botswana* ... 56 C3 22 46S 23 52 E
Khon Kaen, *Thailand* ... 38 D4 16 30N 102 47 E

Khong ➤, *Cambodia* ... 38 F5 13 32N 105 58 E
Khong Sedone, *Laos* ... 38 E5 15 34N 105 49 E
Khonuu, *Russia* ...... 29 C15 66 30N 143 12 E
Khoper ➤, *Russia* ... 19 D6 49 30N 42 20 E
Khóra Sfakíon, *Greece* ... 25 D6 35 15N 24 9 E
Khorāsān □, *Iran* ...... 45 C8 34 0N 58 0 E
Khorat = Nakhon Ratchasima,
   *Thailand* ...... 38 E4 14 59N 102 12 E
Khorat, Cao Nguyen, *Thailand* ... 38 E4 15 30N 102 50 E
Khorixas, *Namibia* ... 56 C1 20 16S 14 59 E
Khorramābād, *Khorāsān, Iran* ... 45 C8 35 6N 57 57 E
Khorramābād, *Lorestān, Iran* ... 45 C6 33 30N 48 25 E
Khorrāmshahr, *Iran* ... 45 D6 30 29N 48 15 E
Khorugh, *Tajikistan* ... 28 F8 37 30N 71 36 E
Khosravi, *Iran* ...... 45 D6 30 48N 51 28 E
Khosrowābād, *Khuzestān, Iran* ... 45 D6 30 10N 48 25 E
Khosrowābād, *Kordestān, Iran* ... 44 C5 35 31N 47 38 E
Khost, *Pakistan* ...... 42 D2 30 13N 67 35 E
Khosūyeh, *Iran* ...... 45 D7 28 32N 54 26 E
Khotyn, *Ukraine* ... 17 D14 48 31N 26 27 E
Khouribga, *Morocco* ... 50 B4 32 58N 6 57W
Khowst, *Afghan.* ...... 42 C3 33 22N 69 58 E
Khowst □, *Afghan.* ... 40 C6 33 20N 70 0 E
Khoyniki, *Belarus* ... 17 C15 51 54N 29 55 E
Khrysokhou B., *Cyprus* ... 25 D11 35 6N 32 25 E
Khu Khan, *Thailand* ... 38 E5 14 42N 104 12 E
Khuan Wa, *Thailand* ... 39 a 7 53N 98 17 E
Khudzhand = Khŭjand, *Tajikistan* 28 E7 40 17N 69 37 E
Khuff, *Si. Arabia* ...... 44 E5 24 55N 44 53 E
Khūgiānī, *Afghan.* ... 42 D2 31 34N 66 32 E
Khuis, *Botswana* ...... 56 D3 26 40S 21 49 E
Khuiyala, *India* ...... 42 F4 27 9N 70 25 E
Khŭjand, *Tajikistan* ... 28 E7 40 17N 69 37 E
Khujner, *India* ...... 42 H7 23 47N 76 36 E
Khulna, *Bangla.* ...... 41 H16 22 45N 89 34 E
Khulna □, *Bangla.* ... 41 H16 22 25N 89 35 E
Khumago, *Botswana* ... 56 C3 20 26S 24 32 E
Khūnsorkh, *Iran* ...... 45 E8 27 9N 56 7 E
Khunti, *India* ...... 43 H11 23 5N 85 17 E
Khurai, *India* ...... 42 G8 24 3N 78 23 E
Khurayş, *Si. Arabia* ... 45 E6 25 6N 48 2 E
Khuriyā Muriyā, Jazā'ir, *Oman* 47 D6 17 30N 55 58 E
Khurja, *India* ...... 42 E7 28 15N 77 58 E
Khūrmāl, *Iraq* ...... 44 C5 35 18N 46 2 E
Khurr, Wādī al, *Iraq* ... 44 C4 32 3N 43 52 E
Khūsf, *Iran* ...... 45 C8 32 46N 58 53 E
Khush, *Afghan.* ...... 40 C3 32 55N 62 10 E
Khushab, *Pakistan* ... 42 C5 32 20N 72 20 E
Khust, *Ukraine* ...... 17 D12 48 10N 23 18 E
Khutse △, *Botswana* ... 56 C3 23 31S 24 12 E
Khuzdar, *Pakistan* ... 42 F2 27 52N 66 30 E
Khūzestān □, *Iran* ... 45 D6 31 0N 49 0 E
Khvāf, *Iran* ...... 45 C9 34 33N 60 8 E
Khvājeh, *Iran* ...... 44 B5 38 9N 46 35 E
Khvānsār, *Iran* ...... 45 D7 29 56N 54 8 E
Khvor, *Iran* ...... 45 C7 33 45N 55 0 E
Khvorgū, *Iran* ...... 45 E8 27 34N 56 27 E
Khvormūj, *Iran* ...... 45 D6 28 40N 51 30 E
Khvoy, *Iran* ...... 44 B5 38 35N 45 0 E
Khyber Pass, *Afghan.* ... 42 B4 34 10N 71 8 E
Kiabukwa, *Dem. Rep. of
   the Congo* ...... 55 D1 8 40S 24 48 E
Kiama, *Australia* ...... 63 E5 34 40S 150 50 E
Kiamba, *Phil.* ...... 37 C6 6 2N 124 46 E
Kiambi, *Dem. Rep. of the Congo* 54 D2 7 15S 28 0 E
Kiambu, *Kenya* ...... 54 C4 1 8S 36 50 E
Kiangara, *Madag.* ... 57 B8 17 58S 47 2 E
Kiangsi = Jiangxi □, *China* ... 33 D6 27 30N 116 0 E
Kiangsu = Jiangsu □, *China* ... 35 H11 33 0N 120 0 E
Kibale △, *Uganda* ...... 54 B3 0 16N 30 18 E
Kibanga Port, *Uganda* ... 54 B3 0 10N 32 58 E
Kibara, *Tanzania* ...... 54 C3 2 8S 33 30 E
Kibare, Mts., *Dem. Rep. of
   the Congo* ...... 54 D2 8 25S 27 10 E
Kibira △, *Burundi* ... 54 C3 3 6S 30 24 E
Kibombo, *Dem. Rep. of
   the Congo* ...... 54 C2 3 57S 25 53 E
Kibondo, *Tanzania* ... 54 C3 3 35S 30 45 E
Kibre Mengist, *Ethiopia* ... 47 F2 5 54N 38 59 E
Kibumbu, *Burundi* ... 54 C2 3 32S 29 45 E
Kibungo, *Rwanda* ... 54 C3 2 10S 30 32 E
Kibuye, *Burundi* ...... 54 C2 3 39S 29 59 E
Kibuye, *Rwanda* ...... 54 C2 2 3S 29 21 E
Kibwesa, *Tanzania* ... 54 D2 6 30S 29 58 E
Kibwezi, *Kenya* ...... 54 C4 2 27S 37 57 E
Kichha, *India* ...... 43 E8 28 53N 79 30 E
Kichha ➤, *India* ...... 43 E8 28 41N 79 18 E
Kichmengskiy Gorodok, *Russia* 18 B8 59 59N 45 48 E
Kicking Horse Pass, *Canada* ... 70 C5 51 28N 116 16W
Kidal, *Mali* ...... 50 E6 18 26N 1 22 E
Kidderminster, *U.K.* ... 13 E5 52 24N 2 15W
Kidepo Valley △, *Uganda* ... 54 B3 3 52N 33 50 E
Kidete, *Tanzania* ...... 54 D4 6 25S 37 17 E
Kidnappers, C., *N.Z.* ... 59 H6 39 38S 177 5 E
Kidsgrove, *U.K.* ...... 12 D5 53 5N 2 14W
Kidston, *Australia* ... 62 B3 18 52S 144 8 E
Kidugallo, *Tanzania* ... 54 D4 6 49S 38 15 E
Kiel, *Germany* ...... 16 A6 54 19N 10 8 E
Kiel Canal = Nord-Ostsee-Kanal,
   *Germany* ...... 16 A5 54 12N 9 32 E
Kielce, *Poland* ...... 17 C11 50 52N 20 42 E
Kielder Water, *U.K.* ... 12 B5 55 11N 2 31W
Kieler Bucht, *Germany* ... 16 A6 54 35N 10 25 E
Kien Binh, *Vietnam* ... 39 H5 9 55N 105 19 E
Kien Tan, *Vietnam* ... 39 G5 10 7N 105 17 E
Kienge, *Dem. Rep. of the Congo* 55 E2 10 30S 27 30 E
Kiev = Kyyiv, *Ukraine* ... 17 C16 50 30N 30 28 E
Kiffa, *Mauritania* ...... 50 E3 16 37N 11 24W
Kifrī, *Iraq* ...... 44 C5 34 45N 45 0 E
Kigali, *Rwanda* ...... 54 C3 1 59S 30 4 E
Kigarama, *Tanzania* ... 54 C3 1 1S 31 50 E
Kigezi △, *Uganda* ...... 54 C2 0 34S 29 55 E
Kigoma □, *Tanzania* ... 54 D3 5 0S 30 0 E
Kigoma-Ujiji, *Tanzania* ... 54 C2 4 55S 29 36 E
Kigomasha, Ras, *Tanzania* ... 54 C4 4 58S 38 58 E
Kiğzı, *Turkey* ...... 44 B4 38 18N 43 25 E
Kihei, *U.S.A.* ...... 74 H16 20 47N 156 28W
Kihnu, *Estonia* ...... 9 G21 58 9N 24 1 E
Kii-Sanchi, *Japan* ... 31 G8 34 20N 136 0 E
Kii-Suidō, *Japan* ...... 31 H7 33 40N 134 45 E
Kikaiga-Shima, *Japan* ... 31 K4 28 19N 129 59 E
Kikinda, *Serbia & M.* ... 23 B9 45 50N 20 30 E
Kikládhes, *Greece* ... 23 F11 37 0N 24 30 E
Kikwit, *Dem. Rep. of the Congo* 52 E3 5 0S 18 45 E
Kilar, *India* ...... 42 C7 33 6N 76 25 E
Kilauea Crater, *U.S.A.* ... 74 J17 19 25N 155 17W
Kilbrannan Sd., *U.K.* ... 11 F3 55 37N 5 26W

Kilchu, N. Korea □ 35 D15 40 57N 129 25 E
Kilcoy, Australia 63 D5 26 59S 152 30 E
Kildare, Ireland 10 C5 53 9N 6 55W
Kildare □, Ireland 10 C5 53 10N 6 50W
Kilfinnane, Ireland 10 D3 52 21N 8 28W
Kilgore, U.S.A. 81 J7 32 23N 94 53W
Kilifi, Kenya 54 C4 3 40S 39 48 E
Kilimanjaro, Tanzania 54 C4 3 7S 37 20 E
Kilimanjaro □, Tanzania 54 C4 4 0S 38 0 E
Kilindini, Kenya 54 C4 4 4S 39 40 E
Kilis, Turkey 44 B3 36 42N 37 6 E
Kiliya, Ukraine 17 F15 45 28N 29 16 E
Kilkee, Ireland 10 D2 52 41N 9 39W
Kilkenny, Ireland 10 D4 52 39N 7 15W
Kilkenny □, Ireland 10 D4 52 35N 7 15W
Kilkieran B., Ireland 10 C2 53 20N 9 41W
Kilkis, Greece 23 D10 40 58N 22 57 E
Killala, Ireland 10 B2 54 13N 9 12W
Killala B., Ireland 10 B2 54 16N 9 8W
Killaloe, Canada 84 A7 45 33N 77 25W
Killaloe, Ireland 10 D3 52 48N 8 28W
Killarney, Australia 63 D5 28 20S 152 18 E
Killarney, Canada 71 D9 49 10N 99 40W
Killarney, Ireland 10 D2 52 4N 9 30W
Killarney △, Ireland 10 D2 52 0N 9 33W
Killary Harbour, Ireland 10 C2 53 38N 9 52W
Killdeer, U.S.A. 80 B3 47 26N 102 48W
Killeen, U.S.A. 81 K6 31 7N 97 44W
Killin, U.K. 11 E4 56 28N 4 19W
Killini, Greece 23 F10 37 54N 22 25 E
Killorglin, Ireland 10 D2 52 6N 9 47W
Killybegs, Ireland 10 B3 54 38N 8 26W
Kilmarnock, U.K. 11 F4 55 37N 4 29W
Kilmore, Australia 63 F3 37 25S 144 53 E
Kilondo, Tanzania 55 D3 9 45S 34 20 E
Kilosa, Tanzania 54 D4 6 48S 37 0 E
Kilrush, Ireland 10 D2 52 38N 9 29W
Kilwa Kisiwani, Tanzania 55 D4 8 58S 39 32 E
Kilwa Kivinje, Tanzania 55 D4 8 45S 39 25 E
Kilwa Masoko, Tanzania 55 D4 8 55S 39 30 E
Kilwinning, U.K. 11 F4 55 39N 4 43W
Kim, U.S.A. 81 G3 37 15N 103 21W
Kimaam, Indonesia 37 F9 7 58S 138 53 E
Kimamba, Tanzania 54 D4 6 45S 37 10 E
Kimba, Australia 63 E2 33 8S 136 23 E
Kimball, Nebr., U.S.A. 80 E3 41 14N 103 40W
Kimball, S. Dak., U.S.A. 80 D5 43 45N 98 57W
Kimberley, Australia 60 C4 16 20S 127 0 E
Kimberley, Canada 70 D5 49 40N 115 59W
Kimberley, S. Africa 56 D3 28 43S 24 46 E
Kimberly, U.S.A. 76 E6 42 32N 114 22W
Kimch'aek, N. Korea 35 D15 40 40N 129 10 E
Kimch'ŏn, S. Korea 35 F15 36 11N 128 4 E
Kimje, S. Korea 35 G14 35 48N 126 45 E
Kimmirut, Canada 69 B13 62 50N 69 50W
Kimpese, Dem. Rep. of
  the Congo 52 F2 5 35S 14 26 E
Kimry, Russia 18 C6 56 55N 37 15 E
Kinabalu, Gunung, Malaysia 36 C5 6 3N 116 14 E
Kinaskan L., Canada 70 B2 57 38N 130 8W
Kinbasket L., Canada 70 C5 52 0N 118 10W
Kincardine, Canada 84 B3 44 10N 81 40W
Kincolith, Canada 70 C3 55 0N 129 57W
Kinda, Dem. Rep. of the Congo 55 D2 9 18S 25 4 E
Kinde, U.S.A. 84 C2 43 56N 83 0W
Kinder Scout, U.K. 12 D6 53 24N 1 52W
Kindersley, Canada 71 C7 51 30N 109 10W
Kindia, Guinea 50 F3 10 0N 12 52W
Kindu, Dem. Rep. of the Congo 54 C2 2 55S 25 50 E
Kineshma, Russia 18 C7 57 30N 42 5 E
Kinesi, Tanzania 54 C3 1 25S 33 50 E
King, L., Australia 61 F2 33 10S 119 35 E
King, Mt., Australia 62 D4 25 10S 147 30 E
King City, U.S.A. 78 J5 36 13N 121 8W
King Cr. →, Australia 62 C2 24 35S 139 30 E
King Edward →, Australia 60 B4 14 14S 126 35 E
King Frederik VI Land = Kong
  Frederik VI Kyst, Greenland 69 B15 63 0N 43 0W
King George B., Falk. Is. 96 G4 51 30S 60 30W
King George I., Antarctica 5 C18 60 0S 60 0W
King George Is., Canada 69 C11 57 20N 80 30W
King I. = Kadan Kyun, Burma 38 F2 12 30N 98 20 E
King I., Australia 63 F3 39 50S 144 0 E
King I., Canada 70 C3 52 10N 127 40W
King Leopold Ranges, Australia 60 C4 17 30S 125 45 E
King of Prussia, U.S.A. 85 F9 40 5N 75 23W
King Sd., Australia 60 C3 16 50S 123 20 E
King Sejong, Antarctica 5 C18 62 30S 58 0W
King William I., Canada 68 B10 69 10N 97 25W
King William's Town, S. Africa 56 E4 32 51S 27 22 E
Kingait = Cape Dorset, Canada 69 B12 64 14N 76 32W
Kingaok = Bathurst Inlet, Canada 68 B9 66 50N 108 1W
Kingaroy, Australia 63 D5 26 32S 151 51 E
Kingfisher, U.S.A. 81 H6 35 52N 97 56W
Kingirbān, Iraq 44 C5 34 40N 44 54 E
Kingisepp = Kuressaare, Estonia 9 G20 58 15N 22 30 E
Kingman, Ariz., U.S.A. 79 K12 35 12N 114 4W
Kingman, Kans., U.S.A. 81 G5 37 39N 98 7W
Kingoonya, Australia 63 E2 30 55S 135 19 E
Kingri, Pakistan 42 D3 30 27N 69 49 E
Kings →, U.S.A. 78 J7 36 3N 119 50W
Kings Canyon △, U.S.A. 78 J8 36 50N 118 40W
King's Lynn, U.K. 12 E8 52 45N 0 24 E
Kings Mountain, U.S.A. 83 H5 35 15N 81 20W
King's Peak, U.S.A. 76 F8 40 46N 110 27W
Kingsbridge, U.K. 13 G4 50 17N 3 47W
Kingsburg, U.S.A. 78 J7 36 31N 119 33W
Kingscote, Australia 63 F2 35 40S 137 38 E
Kingscourt, Ireland 10 C5 53 55N 6 48W
Kingsford, U.S.A. 82 C1 45 48N 88 4W
Kingsland, U.S.A. 83 K5 30 48N 81 41W
Kingsley, U.S.A. 80 D7 42 35N 95 58W
Kingsport, U.S.A. 83 G4 36 33N 82 33W
Kingston, Canada 85 B8 44 14N 76 30W
Kingston, Jamaica 88 a 18 0N 76 50W
Kingston, N.Z. 59 L2 45 20S 168 43 E
Kingston, N.H., U.S.A. 85 D13 42 56N 71 3W
Kingston, N.Y., U.S.A. 85 E11 41 56N 73 59W
Kingston, Pa., U.S.A. 85 E9 41 16N 75 54W
Kingston, R.I., U.S.A. 85 E13 41 29N 71 30W
Kingston Pk., U.S.A. 79 K11 35 45N 115 54W
Kingston South East, Australia 63 F2 36 51S 139 55 E
Kingston upon Hull, U.K. 12 D7 53 45N 0 21W
Kingston upon Hull □, U.K. 12 D7 53 45N 0 21W
Kingston-upon-Thames □, U.K. 13 F7 51 24N 0 17W
Kingstown, St. Vincent 89 D7 13 10N 61 10W

Kingstree, U.S.A. 83 J6 33 40N 79 50W
Kingsville, Canada 84 D2 42 2N 82 45W
Kingsville, U.S.A. 81 M6 27 31N 97 52W
Kingussie, U.K. 11 D4 57 6N 4 2W
Kingwood, U.S.A. 81 K7 29 54N 95 18W
Kınık, Turkey 23 E12 39 6N 27 24 E
Kinistino, Canada 71 C7 52 57N 105 2W
Kinkala, Congo 52 E2 4 18S 14 49 E
Kinki □, Japan 31 H8 33 45N 136 0 E
Kinleith, N.Z. 59 H5 38 20S 175 56 E
Kinlochleven, U.K. 11 E4 56 43N 5 0W
Kinmount, Canada 84 B6 44 48N 78 45W
Kinna, Sweden 9 H15 57 32N 12 42 E
Kinnairds Hd., U.K. 11 D6 57 43N 2 1W
Kino, Mexico 86 B2 28 45N 111 59W
Kinoje →, Canada 72 B3 52 8N 81 25W
Kinomoto, Japan 31 G8 35 30N 136 13 E
Kinoni, Uganda 54 C3 0 41S 30 28 E
Kinoosao, Canada 71 B8 57 5N 102 1W
Kinross, U.K. 11 E5 56 13N 3 25W
Kinsale, Ireland 10 E3 51 42N 8 31W
Kinsale, Old Hd. of, Ireland 10 E3 51 37N 8 33W
Kinsha = Chang Jiang →, China 33 C7 31 48N 121 10 E
Kinshasa, Dem. Rep. of
  the Congo 52 E3 4 20S 15 15 E
Kinsley, U.S.A. 81 G5 37 55N 99 25W
Kinsman, U.S.A. 84 E4 41 26N 80 35W
Kinston, U.S.A. 83 H7 35 16N 77 35W
Kintamani, Indonesia 37 J18 8 14S 115 19 E
Kintore, U.S.A. 11 D6 57 14N 2 20W
Kintore Ra., Australia 60 D4 23 15S 128 47 E
Kintyre, U.K. 11 F3 55 30N 5 35W
Kintyre, Mull of, U.K. 11 F3 55 17N 5 47W
Kinushseo →, Canada 72 A3 55 15N 83 45W
Kinuso, Canada 70 B5 55 20N 115 25W
Kinyangiri, Tanzania 54 C3 4 25S 34 37 E
Kinzua, U.S.A. 84 E6 41 52N 78 58W
Kinzua Dam, U.S.A. 84 E6 41 53N 79 0W
Kiosk, Canada 72 C4 46 6N 78 53W
Kiowa, Kans., U.S.A. 81 G5 37 1N 98 29W
Kiowa, Okla., U.S.A. 81 H7 34 43N 95 54W
Kipahigan L., Canada 71 B8 55 20N 101 55W
Kipanga, Tanzania 54 D4 6 15S 35 20 E
Kiparissia, Greece 23 F9 37 15N 21 40 E
Kiparissiakós Kólpos, Greece 23 F9 37 25N 21 25 E
Kipawa, L., Canada 72 C4 46 50N 79 0W
Kipembawe, Tanzania 54 D3 7 38S 33 27 E
Kipengere Ra., Tanzania 55 D3 9 12S 34 15 E
Kipili, Tanzania 54 D3 7 28S 30 32 E
Kipini, Kenya 54 C5 2 30S 40 32 E
Kippure, Ireland 10 C5 53 11N 6 21W
Kipushi, Dem. Rep. of the Congo 55 E2 11 48S 27 12 E
Kiranomena, Madag. 57 B8 18 17S 46 2 E
Kirensk, Russia 29 D11 57 50N 107 55 E
Kirghizia = Kyrgyzstan ■, Asia 28 E8 42 0N 75 0 E
Kirghizstan = Kyrgyzstan ■, Asia 28 E8 42 0N 75 0 E
Kirgiziya Steppe, Eurasia 19 E10 50 0N 55 0 E
Kiribati ■, Pac. Oc. 64 H10 5 0S 180 0 E
Kırıkkale, Turkey 19 G5 39 51N 33 32 E
Kirillov, Russia 18 C6 59 49N 38 24 E
Kirin = Jilin, China 35 C14 43 44N 126 30 E
Kirinyaga = Kenya, Mt., Kenya 54 C4 0 10S 37 18 E
Kirishima Yaku △, Japan 31 J5 31 24N 130 50 E
Kiritimati, Kiribati 65 G12 1 58N 157 27W
Kirkby, U.K. 12 D5 53 30N 2 54W
Kirkby-in-Ashfield, U.K. 12 D6 53 6N 1 14W
Kirkby Lonsdale, U.K. 12 C5 54 12N 2 36W
Kirkby Stephen, U.K. 12 C5 54 29N 2 21W
Kirkcaldy, U.K. 11 E5 56 7N 3 9W
Kirkcudbright, U.K. 11 G4 54 50N 4 2W
Kirkee, India 40 K8 18 34N 73 56 E
Kirkenes, Norway 8 B23 69 40N 30 5 E
Kirkfield, Canada 84 B6 44 34N 78 59W
Kirkintilloch, U.K. 11 F4 55 56N 4 8W
Kirkjubæjarklaustur, Iceland 8 E4 63 47N 18 4W
Kirkkonummi, Finland 9 F21 60 8N 24 26 E
Kirkland Lake, Canada 72 C3 48 9N 80 2W
Kırklareli, Turkey 23 D12 41 44N 27 15 E
Kirksville, U.S.A. 80 E8 40 12N 92 35W
Kirkūk, Iraq 44 C5 35 30N 44 21 E
Kirkwall, U.K. 11 C6 58 59N 2 58W
Kirkwood, S. Africa 56 E4 33 22S 25 15 E
Kirov, Russia 18 C8 58 35N 49 40 E
Kirovabad = Gäncä, Azerbaijan 19 F8 40 45N 46 20 E
Kirovograd = Kirovohrad,
  Ukraine 19 E5 48 35N 32 20 E
Kirovohrad, Ukraine 19 E5 48 35N 32 20 E
Kirovsk, Russia 18 A5 67 32N 33 41 E
Kirovskiy, Kamchatka, Russia 29 D16 54 27N 155 42 E
Kirovskiy, Primorsk, Russia 30 B6 45 7N 133 30 E
Kirriemuir, U.K. 11 E5 56 41N 3 1W
Kirsanov, Russia 18 D7 52 35N 42 40 E
Kırşehir, Turkey 19 G5 39 14N 34 5 E
Kirthar Range, Pakistan 42 F2 27 0N 67 0 E
Kirtland, U.S.A. 77 H9 36 44N 108 21W
Kiruna, Sweden 8 C19 67 52N 20 15 E
Kirundu, Dem. Rep. of the Congo 54 C2 0 50S 25 35 E
Kiryū, Japan 31 F9 36 24N 139 20 E
Kisaga, Tanzania 54 C3 4 30S 34 23 E
Kisalaya, Nic. 88 D3 14 40N 84 3W
Kisámou, Kólpos, Greece 25 D5 35 30N 23 38 E
Kisanga, Dem. Rep. of the Congo 54 B2 2 30N 26 35 E
Kisangani, Dem. Rep. of
  the Congo 54 B2 0 35N 25 15 E
Kisar, Indonesia 37 F7 8 5S 127 10 E
Kisarazu, Japan 31 G9 35 23N 139 55 E
Kishanganj, India 43 F13 26 3N 88 14 E
Kishangarh, Raj., India 42 F6 26 34N 74 52 E
Kishangarh, Raj., India 42 F4 27 50N 70 30 E
Kishinev = Chişinău, Moldova 17 E15 47 2N 28 50 E
Kishiwada, Japan 31 G7 34 28N 135 22 E
Kishtwar, India 43 C6 33 20N 75 48 E
Kisigo →, Tanzania 54 D3 6 27S 34 17 E
Kisii, Kenya 54 C3 0 40S 34 45 E
Kisiju, Tanzania 54 D4 7 23S 39 19 E
Kisizi, Uganda 54 C2 1 0S 29 58 E
Kiskőrös, Hungary 17 E10 46 37N 19 20 E
Kiskunfélegyháza, Hungary 17 E10 46 42N 19 53 E
Kiskunhalas, Hungary 17 E10 46 28N 19 37 E
Kislovodsk, Russia 19 F7 43 50N 42 45 E
Kismayu = Chisimaio,
  Somali Rep. 49 G8 0 22S 42 32 E
Kiso-Gawa →, Japan 31 G8 35 20N 136 45 E
Kiso-Sammyaku, Japan 31 G8 35 45N 137 45 E
Kisofukushima, Japan 31 G8 35 52N 137 43 E

Kisoro, Uganda 54 C2 1 17S 29 48 E
Kissidougou, Guinea 50 G3 9 5N 10 5W
Kissimmee, U.S.A. 83 L5 28 18N 81 24W
Kissimmee →, U.S.A. 83 M5 27 9N 80 52W
Kississing L., Canada 71 B8 55 10N 101 20W
Kissónerga, Cyprus 25 E11 34 49N 32 24 E
Kisumu, Kenya 54 C3 0 3S 34 45 E
Kiswani, Tanzania 54 C4 4 5S 37 57 E
Kiswere, Tanzania 55 D4 9 27S 39 30 E
Kit Carson, U.S.A. 80 F3 38 46N 102 48W
Kita, Mali 50 F4 13 5N 9 25W
Kitaibaraki, Japan 31 F10 36 50N 140 45 E
Kitakami, Japan 30 E10 39 20N 141 10 E
Kitakami-Gawa →, Japan 30 E10 38 25N 141 19 E
Kitakami-Sammyaku, Japan 30 E10 39 30N 141 30 E
Kitakata, Japan 30 F9 37 39N 139 52 E
Kitakyūshū, Japan 31 H5 33 50N 130 50 E
Kitale, Kenya 54 B4 1 0N 35 0 E
Kitami, Japan 30 C11 43 48N 143 54 E
Kitami-Sammyaku, Japan 30 B11 44 22N 142 43 E
Kitangiri, L., Tanzania 54 C3 4 5S 34 20 E
Kitaya, Tanzania 55 E5 10 38S 40 8 E
Kitchener, Canada 84 C4 43 27N 80 29W
Kitega = Gitega, Burundi 54 C2 3 26S 29 56 E
Kitengo, Dem. Rep. of the Congo 54 D1 7 26S 24 8 E
Kitgum, Uganda 54 B3 3 17N 32 52 E
Kithira, Greece 23 F10 36 8N 23 0 E
Kithnos, Greece 23 F11 37 26N 24 27 E
Kiti, Cyprus 25 E12 34 50N 33 34 E
Kiti, C., Cyprus 25 E12 34 48N 33 36 E
Kitimat, Canada 70 C3 54 3N 128 38W
Kitinen →, Finland 8 C22 67 14N 27 27 E
Kitsuki, Japan 31 H5 33 25N 131 37 E
Kittakittaooloo, L., Australia 63 D2 28 3S 138 14 E
Kittanning, U.S.A. 84 F5 40 49N 79 31W
Kittatinny Mts., U.S.A. 85 F10 41 0N 75 0W
Kittery, U.S.A. 83 D10 43 5N 70 45W
Kittilä, Finland 8 C21 67 40N 24 51 E
Kitui, Kenya 54 C4 1 17S 38 0 E
Kitwanga, Canada 70 B3 55 6N 128 4W
Kitwe, Zambia 55 E2 12 54S 28 13 E
Kivarli, India 42 G5 24 33N 72 46 E
Kivertsi, Ukraine 17 C13 50 50N 25 28 E
Kividhes, Cyprus 25 E11 34 46N 32 51 E
Kivu, L., Dem. Rep. of the Congo 54 C2 1 48S 29 0 E
Kiyev = Kyyiv, Ukraine 17 C16 50 30N 30 28 E
Kiyevskoye Vdkhr. = Kyyivske
  Vdskh., Ukraine 17 C16 51 0N 30 25 E
Kizel, Russia 18 C10 59 3N 57 40 E
Kiziguru, Rwanda 54 C3 1 46S 30 23 E
Kızıl Irmak →, Turkey 19 F6 41 44N 35 58 E
Kizil Jilga, China 43 B8 35 26N 78 50 E
Kızıltepe, Turkey 44 B4 37 12N 40 35 E
Kizimkazi, Tanzania 54 D4 6 28S 39 30 E
Kizlyar, Russia 19 F8 43 51N 46 40 E
Kizyl-Arvat = Gyzylarbat,
  Turkmenistan 28 F6 39 4N 56 23 E
Kjölur, Iceland 8 D4 64 50N 19 25W
Kladno, Czech Rep. 16 C8 50 10N 14 7 E
Klaeng, Thailand 38 F3 12 47N 101 39 E
Klagenfurt, Austria 16 E8 46 38N 14 20 E
Klaipėda, Lithuania 9 J19 55 43N 21 10 E
Klaksvík, Færoe Is. 8 E9 62 14N 6 35W
Klamath →, U.S.A. 76 F1 41 33N 124 5W
Klamath Falls, U.S.A. 76 E3 42 13N 121 46W
Klamath Mts., U.S.A. 76 F2 41 20N 123 0W
Klamono, Indonesia 37 E8 1 8S 131 30 E
Klang, Malaysia 39 L3 3 2N 101 26 E
Klappan →, Canada 70 B3 58 0N 129 43 E
Klarälven →, Sweden 9 G15 59 23N 13 32 E
Klatovy, Czech Rep. 16 D7 49 23N 13 18 E
Klawer, S. Africa 56 E2 31 44S 18 36 E
Klazienaveen, Neths. 15 B6 52 44N 7 0 E
Kleena Kleene, Canada 70 C4 52 0N 124 59W
Klein-Karas, Namibia 56 D2 27 33S 18 7 E
Klerksdorp, S. Africa 56 D4 26 53S 26 38 E
Kletsk = Klyetsk, Belarus 17 B14 53 5N 26 45 E
Kletskiy, Russia 19 E7 49 16N 43 11 E
Klickitat, U.S.A. 76 D3 45 49N 121 9W
Klickitat →, U.S.A. 78 E5 45 42N 121 17W
Klidhes, Cyprus 25 D13 35 42N 34 36 E
Klinaklini →, Canada 70 C3 51 21N 125 40W
Klip →, S. Africa 57 D4 27 3S 29 3 E
Klipdale, S. Africa 56 E2 34 19S 19 57 E
Klipplaat, S. Africa 56 E3 33 1S 24 22 E
Kłodzko, Poland 17 C9 50 28N 16 38 E
Klong Wang Chao △, Thailand 38 D2 16 20N 99 9 E
Klouto, Togo 50 G6 6 57N 0 44 E
Kluane △, Canada 70 A1 60 45N 139 30W
Kluane L., Canada 68 B6 61 15N 138 40W
Kluczbork, Poland 17 C10 50 58N 18 12 E
Klukwan, U.S.A. 70 B1 59 24N 135 54W
Klungkung, Indonesia 37 K18 8 32S 115 24 E
Klyetsk, Belarus 17 B14 53 5N 26 45 E
Klyuchevskaya, Gora, Russia 29 D17 55 50N 160 30 E
Knaresborough, U.K. 12 C6 54 1N 1 28W
Knee L., Man., Canada 72 A1 55 3N 94 45W
Knee L., Sask., Canada 71 B7 55 51N 107 0W
Knight Inlet, Canada 70 C3 50 45N 125 40W
Knighton, U.K. 13 E4 52 21N 3 3W
Knights Ferry, U.S.A. 78 H6 37 50N 120 40W
Knights Landing, U.S.A. 78 G5 38 48N 121 43W
Knob, C., Australia 61 F2 34 32S 119 16 E
Knock, Ireland 10 C3 53 48N 8 55W
Knockmealdown Mts., Ireland 10 D4 52 14N 7 56W
Knokke-Heist, Belgium 15 C3 51 21N 3 17 E
Knossós, Greece 25 D7 35 16N 25 10 E
Knowlton, Canada 85 A12 45 13N 72 31W
Knox, U.S.A. 82 E2 41 18N 86 37W
Knox Coast, Antarctica 5 C8 66 30S 108 0 E
Knoxville, Iowa, U.S.A. 80 E8 41 19N 93 6W
Knoxville, Tenn., U.S.A. 83 H4 35 58N 83 55W
Knud Rasmussen Land,
  Greenland 4 A5 79 0N 60 0W
Knysna, S. Africa 56 E3 34 2S 23 2 E
Ko Kha, Thailand 38 C2 18 11N 99 24 E
Ko Tarutao △, Thailand 39 J2 6 31N 99 26 E
Ko Yao, Thailand 39 a 8 7N 98 35 E
Koartac = Quaqtaq, Canada 69 B13 60 55N 69 40W
Koba, Indonesia 37 F8 6 37S 134 37 E
Kobarid, Slovenia 16 E7 46 15N 13 30 E
Kobayashi, Japan 31 J5 31 56N 130 59 E
København, Denmark 9 J15 55 41N 12 34 E
Kōbi-Sho, Japan 31 M1 25 56N 123 41 E
Koblenz, Germany 16 C4 50 21N 7 36 E
Kobryn, Belarus 17 B13 52 15N 24 22 E

Kocaeli, Turkey 19 F4 40 45N 29 50 E
Kočani, Macedonia 23 D10 41 55N 22 25 E
Koch Bihar, India 41 F16 26 22N 89 29 E
Kochang, S. Korea 35 G14 35 41N 127 55 E
Kochas, India 43 G10 25 15N 83 56 E
Kochi = Cochin, India 40 Q10 9 58N 76 20 E
Kōchi, Japan 31 H6 33 30N 133 35 E
Kōchi □, Japan 31 H6 33 40N 133 30 E
Kochiu = Gejiu, China 32 D5 23 20N 103 10 E
Kodarma, India 43 G11 24 28N 85 36 E
Kodiak, U.S.A. 68 C4 57 47N 152 24W
Kodiak I., U.S.A. 68 C4 57 30N 152 45W
Kodinar, India 42 J4 20 46N 70 46 E
Koedoesberg, S. Africa 56 E3 32 40S 20 11 E
Koes, Namibia 56 D2 26 0S 19 15 E
Koffiefontein, S. Africa 56 D4 29 30S 25 0 E
Kofiau, Indonesia 37 E7 1 11S 129 50 E
Koforidua, Ghana 50 G5 6 3N 0 17W
Kōfu, Japan 31 G9 35 40N 138 30 E
Koga, Japan 31 F9 36 11N 139 43 E
Kogaluc →, Canada 73 A7 56 12N 61 44W
Køge, Denmark 9 J15 55 27N 12 11 E
Koh-i-Khurd, Afghan. 42 C1 33 30N 65 59 E
Koh-i-Maran, Pakistan 42 E2 29 18N 66 50 E
Kohat, Pakistan 42 C4 33 40N 71 29 E
Kohima, India 41 G19 25 35N 94 10 E
Kohkilūyeh va Būyer Ahmadi □,
  Iran 45 D6 31 30N 50 30 E
Kohler Ra., Antarctica 5 D15 77 0S 110 0W
Kohlu, Pakistan 42 E3 29 54N 69 15 E
Kohtla-Järve, Estonia 9 G22 59 20N 27 20 E
Koi Sanjaq, Iraq 44 B5 36 5N 44 38 E
Koillismaa, Finland 8 D23 65 44N 28 36 E
Koin-dong, N. Korea 35 D14 40 28N 126 18 E
Kojō, N. Korea 35 E14 38 58N 127 58 E
Kojonup, Australia 61 F2 33 48S 117 10 E
Kojūr, Iran 45 B6 36 23N 51 43 E
Kokand = Qŭqon, Uzbekistan 28 E8 40 30N 70 57 E
Kokas, Indonesia 37 E8 2 42S 132 26 E
Kokchetav = Kökshetaū,
  Kazakhstan 28 D7 53 20N 69 25 E
Kokemäenjoki →, Finland 9 F19 61 32N 21 44 E
Kokkola, Finland 8 E20 63 50N 23 8 E
Koko Kyunzu, Burma 41 M18 14 10N 93 25 E
Kokomo, U.S.A. 82 E2 40 29N 86 8W
Koksan, N. Korea 35 E14 38 46N 126 40 E
Kökshetaū, Kazakhstan 28 D7 53 20N 69 25 E
Koksoak →, Canada 69 C13 58 30N 68 10W
Kokstad, S. Africa 57 E4 30 32S 29 29 E
Kokubu, Japan 31 J5 31 44N 130 46 E
Kola, Indonesia 37 F8 5 35S 134 30 E
Kola, Russia 18 A5 68 45N 33 8 E
Kola Pen. = Kolskiy Poluostrov,
  Russia 18 A6 67 30N 38 0 E
Kolachi →, Pakistan 42 F2 27 8N 67 2 E
Kolahoi, India 43 B6 34 12N 75 22 E
Kolaka, Indonesia 37 E6 4 3S 121 46 E
Kolar, India 40 N11 13 12N 78 15 E
Kolar Gold Fields, India 40 N11 12 58N 78 16 E
Kolaras, India 42 G6 25 14N 77 36 E
Kolari, Finland 8 C20 67 20N 23 48 E
Kolayat, India 40 F8 27 50N 72 50 E
Kolding, Denmark 9 J13 55 30N 9 29 E
Kolepom = Dolak, Pulau,
  Indonesia 37 F9 8 0S 138 30 E
Kolguyev, Ostrov, Russia 18 A8 69 20N 48 30 E
Kolhapur, India 40 L9 16 43N 74 15 E
Kolín, Czech Rep. 16 C8 50 2N 15 9 E
Kolkas rags, Latvia 9 H20 57 46N 22 37 E
Kolkata, India 43 H13 22 36N 88 24 E
Kollam = Quilon, India 40 Q10 8 50N 76 38 E
Kollum, Neths. 15 A6 53 17N 6 10 E
Kolmanskop, Namibia 56 D2 26 45S 15 14 E
Köln, Germany 16 C4 50 56N 6 57 E
Koło, Poland 17 B10 52 14N 18 40 E
Kołobrzeg, Poland 16 A8 54 10N 15 35 E
Kolomna, Russia 18 C6 55 8N 38 45 E
Kolomyya, Ukraine 17 D13 48 31N 25 2 E
Kolonodale, Indonesia 37 E6 2 0S 121 19 E
Kolosib, India 41 G18 24 15N 92 45 E
Kolpashevo, Russia 28 D9 58 20N 83 5 E
Kolpino, Russia 18 C5 59 44N 30 39 E
Kolskiy Poluostrov, Russia 18 A6 67 30N 38 0 E
Kolskiy Zaliv, Russia 18 A5 69 23N 33 0 E
Kolwezi, Dem. Rep. of the Congo 55 E2 10 40S 25 25 E
Kolyma →, Russia 29 C17 69 30N 161 0 E
Kolymskoye Nagorye, Russia 29 C16 63 0N 157 0 E
Kôm Ombo, Egypt 51 D12 24 25N 32 52 E
Komandorskiye Is. =
  Komandorskiye Ostrova,
  Russia 29 D17 55 0N 167 0 E
Komandorskiye Ostrova, Russia 29 D17 55 0N 167 0 E
Komárno, Slovak Rep. 17 E10 47 49N 18 5 E
Komatipoort, S. Africa 57 D5 25 25S 31 55 E
Komatou Yialou, Cyprus 25 D13 35 25N 34 8 E
Komatsu, Japan 31 F8 36 25N 136 30 E
Komatsushima, Japan 31 H7 34 0N 134 35 E
Komi □, Russia 18 B10 64 0N 55 0 E
Kommunarsk = Alchevsk,
  Ukraine 19 E6 48 30N 38 45 E
Kommunizma, Pik, Tajikistan 28 F8 39 0N 72 2 E
Komodo, Indonesia 37 F5 8 37S 119 20 E
Komoran, Pulau, Indonesia 37 F9 8 18S 138 45 E
Komoro, Japan 31 F9 36 19N 138 26 E
Komotini, Greece 23 D11 41 9N 25 26 E
Kompasberg, S. Africa 56 E3 31 45S 24 32 E
Kompong Bang, Cambodia 39 F5 12 24N 104 40 E
Kompong Chhnang = Kampong
  Chhnang, Cambodia 39 F5 12 20N 104 35 E
Kompong Chikreng, Cambodia 38 F5 13 5N 104 18 E
Kompong Kleang, Cambodia 38 F5 13 6N 104 8 E
Kompong Luong, Cambodia 39 G5 11 49N 104 48 E
Kompong Pranak, Cambodia 38 F5 13 35N 104 55 E
Kompong Som = Kampong
  Saom, Cambodia 39 G4 10 38N 103 30 E
Kompong Som, Chhung =
  Kampong Saom, Chaak,
  Cambodia 39 G4 10 50N 103 32 E
Kompong Speu, Cambodia 39 G5 11 26N 104 32 E
Kompong Sralau, Cambodia 38 E5 14 5N 105 46 E
Kompong Thom, Cambodia 38 F5 12 35N 104 51 E
Kompong Trabeck, Cambodia 38 F5 13 6N 105 14 E
Kompong Trabeck, Cambodia 39 G5 11 25N 105 48 E
Kompong Trach, Cambodia 39 G5 11 25N 105 48 E
Komrat = Comrat, Moldova 17 E15 46 18N 28 40 E
Komsberg, S. Africa 56 E3 32 40S 20 45 E

Komsomolets, Ostrov, Russia .. 29 A10 80 30N 95 0 E
Komsomolsk, Russia .......... 29 D14 50 30N 137 0 E
Kon Tum, Vietnam ........... 38 E7 14 24N 108 0 E
Kon Tum, Plateau du, Vietnam . 38 E7 14 30N 108 30 E
Konarhā □, Afghan. .......... 40 B7 34 30N 71 3 E
Konāri, Iran ................ 45 D6 28 13N 51 36 E
Konch, India ............... 43 G8 26 0N 79 10 E
Konde, Tanzania ............ 54 C4 4 57S 39 45 E
Kondinin, Australia .......... 61 F2 32 34S 118 8 E
Kondoa, Tanzania ........... 54 C4 4 55S 35 50 E
Kondókali, Greece ........... 25 A3 39 38N 19 51 E
Kondopaga, Russia ........... 18 B5 62 12N 34 17 E
Kondratyevo, Russia .......... 29 D10 57 22N 98 15 E
Köneürgench, Turkmenistan ... 28 E6 42 19N 59 10 E
Konevo, Russia .............. 18 B6 62 8N 39 20 E
Kong = Khong →, Cambodia .. 38 F5 13 32N 105 58 E
Kong, Ivory C. .............. 50 G5 8 54N 4 36W
Kong, Koh, Cambodia ........ 39 G4 11 20N 103 0 E
Kong Christian IX Land,
  Greenland ................ 4 C6 68 0N 36 0W
Kong Christian X Land,
  Greenland ................ 4 B6 74 0N 29 0W
Kong Frederik IX Land,
  Greenland ................ 4 C5 67 0N 52 0W
Kong Frederik VI Kyst, Greenland 69 B15 63 0N 43 0W
Kong Frederik VIII Land,
  Greenland ................ 4 B6 78 30N 26 0W
Kong Oscar Fjord, Greenland . 4 B6 72 20N 24 0W
Kongju, S. Korea ............ 35 F14 36 30N 127 0 E
Konglu, Burma .............. 41 F20 27 13N 97 57 E
Kongola, Namibia ........... 56 B3 17 45S 23 20 E
Kongolo, Kasai-Or., Dem. Rep. of
  the Congo ............. 54 D1 5 26S 24 49 E
Kongolo, Katanga, Dem. Rep. of
  the Congo ............. 54 D2 5 22S 27 0 E
Kongsberg, Norway .......... 9 G13 59 39N 9 39 E
Kongsvinger, Norway ........ 9 F15 60 12N 12 2 E
Kongwa, Tanzania ........... 54 D4 6 11S 36 26 E
Koni, Dem. Rep. of the Congo . 55 E2 10 40S 27 11 E
Koni, Mts., Dem. Rep. of
  the Congo ............. 55 E2 10 36S 27 10 E
Konin, Poland .............. 17 B10 52 12N 18 15 E
Konjic, Bos.-H. ............. 23 C7 43 42N 17 58 E
Konkiep, Namibia ........... 56 D2 26 49S 17 15 E
Konosha, Russia ............ 18 B7 61 0N 40 5 E
Kōnosu, Japan .............. 31 F9 36 3N 139 31 E
Konotop, Ukraine ........... 19 D5 51 12N 33 7 E
Końskie, Poland ............ 17 C11 51 10N 20 23 E
Konstanz, Germany .......... 16 E5 47 40N 9 10 E
Kont, Iran ................. 45 E9 26 55N 61 50 E
Kontagora, Nigeria .......... 50 F7 10 23N 5 27 E
Konya, Turkey .............. 19 G5 37 52N 32 35 E
Konza, Kenya .............. 54 C4 1 45S 37 7 E
Koocanusa, L., Canada ....... 76 B6 49 20N 115 15W
Kookynie, Australia .......... 61 E3 29 17S 121 22 E
Koolyanobbing, Australia ..... 61 F2 30 48S 119 36 E
Koonibba, Australia .......... 63 E1 31 54S 133 25 E
Koorawatha, Australia ........ 63 E4 34 2S 148 33 E
Koorda, Australia ........... 61 F2 30 48S 117 35 E
Kooskia, U.S.A. ............ 76 C6 46 9N 115 59W
Kootenay →, Canada ........ 70 C5 51 0N 116 0W
Kootenay →, U.S.A. ......... 70 D5 49 19N 117 39W
Kootenay L., Canada ........ 70 D5 49 45N 116 50W
Kootjieskolk, S. Africa ....... 56 E3 31 15S 20 21 E
Kopaonik, Serbia & M. ....... 23 C9 43 10N 20 50 E
Kópavogur, Iceland .......... 8 D3 64 6N 21 55W
Koper, Slovenia ............ 16 F7 45 31N 13 44 E
Kopervik, Norway ........... 9 G11 59 17N 5 17 E
Kopet Dagh, Asia ........... 45 B8 38 0N 58 0 E
Kopi, Australia ............. 63 E2 33 24S 135 40 E
Köping, Sweden ............ 9 G17 59 31N 16 3 E
Koppeh Dāgh = Kopet Dagh, Asia 45 B8 38 0N 58 0 E
Koppies, S. Africa ........... 57 D4 27 20S 27 30 E
Koprivnica, Croatia .......... 22 A7 46 12N 16 45 E
Kopychyntsi, Ukraine ........ 17 D13 49 7N 25 58 E
Kora △, Kenya ............. 54 C4 0 14S 38 44 E
Korab, Macedonia ........... 23 D9 41 44N 20 40 E
Korakiána, Greece ........... 25 A3 39 42N 19 45 E
Koral, India ............... 42 J5 21 50N 73 12 E
Korba, India ............... 43 H10 22 20N 82 45 E
Korbu, G., Malaysia ......... 39 K3 4 41N 101 18 E
Korçë, Albania ............. 23 D9 40 37N 20 50 E
Korčula, Croatia ............ 22 C7 42 56N 16 57 E
Kord Kūy, Iran ............. 45 B7 36 48N 54 7 E
Kord Sheykh, Iran .......... 45 D7 28 31N 52 53 E
Kordestān □, Iran .......... 44 C5 36 0N 47 0 E
Kordofân, Sudan ........... 51 F11 13 0N 29 0 E
Korea, North ■, Asia ........ 35 E14 40 0N 127 0 E
Korea, South ■, Asia ........ 35 G15 36 0N 128 0 E
Korea Bay, Korea ........... 35 E13 39 0N 124 0 E
Korea Strait, Asia .......... 35 H15 34 0N 129 30 E
Korets, Ukraine ............ 17 C14 50 40N 27 5 E
Korhogo, Ivory C. ........... 50 G4 9 29N 5 28W
Korinthiakós Kólpos, Greece .. 23 E10 38 16N 22 30 E
Kórinthos, Greece .......... 23 F10 37 56N 22 55 E
Kórissa, Límni, Greece ....... 25 B3 39 27N 19 53 E
Kōriyama, Japan ............ 30 F10 37 24N 140 23 E
Korla, China ............... 32 B3 41 45N 86 4 E
Kormakiti, C., Cyprus ........ 25 D11 35 23N 32 56 E
Korneshty = Corneşti, Moldova . 17 E15 47 21N 28 1 E
Koro, Fiji ................. 59 C8 17 19S 179 23 E
Koro, Ivory C. ............. 50 G4 8 32N 7 30W
Koro Sea, Fiji ............. 59 C9 17 30S 179 45W
Korogwe, Tanzania .......... 54 D4 5 5S 38 25 E
Koronadal, Phil. ............ 37 C6 6 12N 125 1 E
Koror, Palau ............... 64 G5 7 20N 134 28 E
Körös →, Hungary .......... 17 E11 46 43N 20 12 E
Korosten, Ukraine .......... 17 C15 50 54N 28 36 E
Korostyshev, Ukraine ........ 17 C15 50 19N 29 4 E
Korraraika, Helodranon' i,
  Madag. ................ 57 B7 17 45S 43 57 E
Korsakov, Russia ........... 29 E15 46 36N 142 42 E
Korshunovo, Russia ......... 29 D12 58 37N 110 10 E
Korsør, Denmark ........... 9 J14 55 20N 11 9 E
Kortrijk, Belgium ........... 15 D3 50 50N 3 17 E
Korwai, India .............. 42 G8 24 7N 78 5 E
Koryakskoye Nagorye, Russia . 29 C18 61 0N 171 0 E
Koryŏng, S. Korea .......... 35 G15 35 44N 128 15 E
Kos, Greece ............... 23 F12 36 50N 27 15 E
Koschagyl, Kazakhstan ....... 19 E9 46 40N 54 0 E
Kościan, Poland ............ 17 B9 52 5N 16 40 E
Kosciusko, U.S.A. .......... 81 J10 33 4N 89 35W
Kosciuszko, Mt., Australia .... 63 F4 36 27S 148 16 E
Kosha, Sudan .............. 51 D12 20 50N 30 30 E
K'oshih = Kashi, China ....... 32 C2 39 30N 76 2 E
Koshiki-Rettō, Japan ........ 31 J4 31 45N 129 49 E
Kosi, India ................ 42 F7 27 48N 77 29 E
Kosi →, India .............. 43 E8 28 41N 78 57 E

Košice, Slovak Rep. .......... 17 D11 48 42N 21 15 E
Koskinoú, Greece ........... 25 C10 36 23N 28 13 E
Koslan, Russia ............. 18 B8 63 34N 49 14 E
Kosŏng, N. Korea ........... 35 E15 38 40N 128 22 E
Kosovo □, Serbia & M. ....... 23 C9 42 30N 21 0 E
Kosovska Mitrovica, Serbia & M. 23 C9 42 54N 20 52 E
Kossou, L. de, Ivory C. ....... 50 G4 6 59N 5 31W
Koster, S. Africa ............ 56 D4 25 52S 26 54 E
Kôstî, Sudan ............... 51 F12 13 8N 32 43 E
Kostopil, Ukraine ........... 17 C14 50 51N 26 22 E
Kostroma, Russia ........... 18 C7 57 50N 40 58 E
Kostrzyn, Poland ........... 16 B8 52 35N 14 39 E
Koszalin, Poland ........... 16 A9 54 11N 16 8 E
Kot Addu, Pakistan .......... 42 D4 30 30N 71 0 E
Kot Kapura, India .......... 42 D6 30 35N 74 50 E
Kot Moman, Pakistan ........ 42 C5 32 13N 73 0 E
Kot Sultan, Pakistan ........ 42 D4 30 46N 70 56 E
Kota, India ................ 42 G6 25 14N 75 49 E
Kota Barrage, India ......... 42 G6 25 6N 75 51 E
Kota Belud, Malaysia ........ 36 C5 6 21N 116 26 E
Kota Bharu, Malaysia ........ 39 J4 6 7N 102 14 E
Kota Kinabalu, Malaysia ...... 36 C5 6 0N 116 4 E
Kota Kubu Bharu, Malaysia ... 39 L3 3 34N 101 39 E
Kota Tinggi, Malaysia ....... 39 M4 1 44N 103 53 E
Kotaagung, Indonesia ....... 36 F2 5 38S 104 29 E
Kotabaru, Indonesia ........ 36 E5 3 20S 116 20 E
Kotabumi, Indonesia ........ 36 E2 4 49S 104 54 E
Kotamobagu, Indonesia ...... 37 D6 0 57N 124 31 E
Kotcho L., Canada .......... 70 B4 59 7N 121 12W
Kotdwara, India ............ 43 E8 29 45N 78 32 E
Kotelnich, Russia ........... 18 C8 58 22N 48 24 E
Kotelnikovo, Russia ......... 19 E7 47 38N 43 8 E
Kotelnyy, Ostrov, Russia ..... 29 B14 75 10N 139 0 E
Kothari →, India ........... 42 G6 25 20N 75 4 E
Kothi, Chhattisgarh, India .... 43 H10 23 21N 82 3 E
Kothi, Mad. P., India ........ 43 G9 24 45N 80 40 E
Kotiro, Pakistan ............ 42 F2 26 17N 67 13 E
Kotka, Finland ............. 9 F22 60 28N 26 58 E
Kotlas, Russia ............. 18 B8 61 17N 46 43 E
Kotli, Pakistan ............. 42 C5 33 30N 73 55 E
Kotma, India ............... 43 H9 23 12N 81 58 E
Kotmul, Pakistan ........... 43 B6 35 32N 75 10 E
Kotor, Serbia & M. .......... 23 C8 42 25N 18 47 E
Kotovsk, Ukraine ........... 17 E15 47 45N 29 35 E
Kotputli, India ............. 42 F7 27 43N 76 12 E
Kotri, Pakistan ............. 42 G3 25 22N 68 22 E
Kotturu, India ............. 40 M10 14 45N 76 10 E
Kotuy →, Russia ........... 29 B11 71 54N 102 6 E
Kotzebue, U.S.A. ........... 68 B3 66 53N 162 39W
Kouchibouguac △, Canada .. 73 C6 46 50N 65 0W
Koudougou, Burkina Faso .... 50 F5 12 10N 2 20W
Koufonísi, Greece ........... 25 E8 34 56N 26 8 E
Kougaberge, S. Africa ........ 56 E3 33 48S 23 50 E
Kouilou →, Congo .......... 52 E2 4 10S 12 5 E
Koula Moutou, Gabon ....... 52 E2 1 15S 12 25 E
Koulen = Kulen, Cambodia ... 38 F5 13 50N 104 40 E
Kouloúra, Greece ........... 25 A3 39 42N 19 54 E
Koúm-bournoú, Ákra, Greece . 25 C10 36 15N 28 11 E
Koumala, Australia .......... 62 C4 21 38S 149 15 E
Koumra, Chad .............. 51 G9 8 50N 17 35 E
Kounradskiy, Kazakhstan ..... 28 E8 46 59N 75 0 E
Kountze, U.S.A. ............ 81 K7 30 22N 94 19W
Kouris →, Cyprus .......... 25 E11 34 38N 32 54 E
Kourou, Fr. Guiana ......... 93 B8 5 9N 52 39W
Kousséri, Cameroon ........ 51 F8 12 0N 14 55 E
Kouvola, Finland ........... 9 F22 60 52N 26 43 E
Kovdor, Russia ............. 18 A5 67 34N 30 24 E
Kovel, Ukraine ............. 17 C13 51 11N 24 38 E
Kovrov, Russia ............. 18 C7 56 25N 41 25 E
Kowanyama, Australia ....... 62 B3 15 29S 141 44 E
Kowloon, China ............ 33 G11 22 19N 114 11 E
Kowŏn, N. Korea ........... 35 E14 39 26N 127 14 E
Koyampattur = Coimbatore, India 40 P10 11 2N 76 59 E
Köyceğiz, Turkey ........... 23 F13 36 57N 28 40 E
Koza, Japan ............... 31 L3 26 19N 127 46 E
Kozan, Turkey ............. 44 B2 37 26N 35 50 E
Kozáni, Greece ............. 23 D9 40 19N 21 47 E
Kozhikode = Calicut, India .... 40 P9 11 15N 75 43 E
Kozhva, Russia ............. 18 A10 65 10N 57 0 E
Kozyatyn, Ukraine .......... 17 D15 49 45N 28 50 E
Kra, Isthmus of = Kra, Kho Khot,
  Thailand ............... 39 G2 10 15N 99 30 E
Kra, Kho Khot, Thailand ..... 39 G2 10 15N 99 30 E
Kra Buri, Thailand .......... 39 G2 10 22N 98 46 E
Kraai →, S. Africa .......... 56 E4 30 40S 26 45 E
Krabi, Thailand ............ 39 H2 8 4N 98 55 E
Krachen, Cambodia ......... 38 F6 12 32N 106 10 E
Kragan, Indonesia .......... 37 G14 6 43S 111 38 E
Kragerø, Norway ........... 9 G13 58 52N 9 25 E
Kragujevac, Serbia & M. ..... 23 B9 44 2N 20 56 E
Krakatau = Rakata, Pulau,
  Indonesia ............... 36 F3 6 10S 105 20 E
Krakatoa = Rakata, Pulau,
  Indonesia ............... 36 F3 6 10S 105 20 E
Krakor, Cambodia .......... 38 F5 12 32N 104 12 E
Kraków, Poland ............ 17 C10 50 4N 19 57 E
Kralanh, Cambodia ......... 38 F4 13 35N 103 25 E
Kraljevo, Serbia & M. ....... 23 C9 43 44N 20 41 E
Kramatorsk, Ukraine ........ 19 E6 48 50N 37 30 E
Kramfors, Sweden .......... 9 E17 62 55N 17 48 E
Kranj, Slovenia ............ 16 E8 46 16N 14 22 E
Krankskop, S. Africa ........ 57 D5 28 0S 30 47 E
Krasavino, Russia ........... 18 B8 60 58N 46 29 E
Kraskino, Russia ........... 29 E14 42 44N 130 48 E
Kraśnik, Poland ............ 17 C12 50 55N 22 15 E
Krasnoarmeysk, Russia ...... 28 D5 51 0N 45 42 E
Krasnodar, Russia .......... 19 E6 45 5N 39 0 E
Krasnokamsk, Russia ........ 18 C10 58 4N 55 48 E
Krasnoperekopsk, Ukraine .... 19 E5 46 0N 33 54 E
Krasnorechenskiy, Russia .... 30 B7 44 41N 135 14 E
Krasnoselkup, Russia ........ 28 C9 65 20N 82 10 E
Krasnoturinsk, Russia ....... 18 C11 59 46N 60 12 E
Krasnoufimsk, Russia ....... 18 C10 56 57N 57 38 E
Krasnouralsk, Russia ........ 18 C11 58 21N 60 3 E
Krasnovishersk, Russia ...... 18 B10 60 23N 57 3 E
Krasnyy Kut, Russia ........ 19 D8 50 50N 47 0 E
Krasnyy Luch, Ukraine ...... 19 E6 48 13N 39 0 E
Krasnyy Yar, Russia ........ 19 E8 46 43N 48 23 E
Kratie = Kracheh, Cambodia .. 38 F6 12 32N 106 10 E
Krau, Indonesia ............ 37 E10 3 19S 140 5 E
Kravanh, Chuor Phnum,
  Cambodia ............... 39 G4 12 0N 103 32 E
Krefeld, Germany ........... 16 C4 51 20N 6 34 E
Kremen, Croatia ............ 16 F8 44 28N 15 53 E
Kremenchuk, Ukraine ........ 19 E5 49 5N 33 25 E
Kremenchuksk Vdskh., Ukraine 19 E5 49 20N 32 30 E
Kremenets, Ukraine ......... 17 C13 50 8N 25 43 E
Kremmling, U.S.A. .......... 76 F10 40 4N 106 24W

Krems, Austria ............. 16 D8 48 25N 15 36 E
Kretinga, Lithuania ......... 9 J19 55 53N 21 15 E
Kribi, Cameroon ............ 52 D1 2 57N 9 56 E
Krichev = Krychaw, Belarus ... 17 B16 53 40N 31 41 E
Kriós, Ákra, Greece ......... 25 D5 35 13N 23 34 E
Krishna →, India ........... 41 M12 15 57N 80 59 E
Krishnanagar, India ......... 43 H13 23 24N 88 33 E
Kristiansand, Norway ........ 9 G13 58 8N 8 1 E
Kristianstad, Sweden ........ 9 H16 56 2N 14 9 E
Kristiansund, Norway ........ 8 E12 63 7N 7 45 E
Kristiinankaupunki, Finland ... 9 E19 62 16N 21 21 E
Kristinehamn, Sweden ....... 9 G16 59 18N 14 7 E
Kristinestad = Kristiinankaupunki,
  Finland ................ 9 E19 62 16N 21 21 E
Kríti, Greece .............. 25 D7 35 15N 25 0 E
Kritsá, Greece ............. 25 D7 35 10N 25 41 E
Krivoy Rog = Kryvyy Rih, Ukraine 19 E5 47 51N 33 20 E
Krk, Croatia ............... 16 F8 45 8N 14 40 E
Krokodil →, Mozam. ........ 57 D5 25 14S 32 18 E
Krong Kaoh Kong, Cambodia . 36 B2 11 35N 103 0 E
Kronprins Olav Kyst, Antarctica 5 C5 69 0S 42 0 E
Kronprinsesse Märtha Kyst,
  Antarctica .............. 5 D2 73 30S 10 0W
Kronshtadt, Russia .......... 18 B4 59 57N 29 51 E
Kroonstad, S. Africa ........ 56 D4 27 43S 27 19 E
Kropotkin, Russia .......... 19 E7 45 28N 40 28 E
Krosno, Poland ............ 17 D11 49 42N 21 46 E
Krotoszyn, Poland .......... 17 C9 51 42N 17 23 E
Kroussón, Greece .......... 25 D6 35 13N 24 59 E
Kruger △, S. Africa ......... 57 C5 24 50S 26 10 E
Krugersdorp, S. Africa ....... 57 D4 26 5S 27 46 E
Kruisfontein, S. Africa ....... 56 E3 33 59S 24 43 E
Krung Thep = Bangkok, Thailand 38 F3 13 45N 100 35 E
Krupki, Belarus ............ 17 A15 54 19N 29 8 E
Kruševac, Serbia & M. ....... 23 C9 43 35N 21 28 E
Krychaw, Belarus ........... 17 B16 53 40N 31 41 E
Krymskiy Poluostrov = Krymskyy
  Pivostriv, Ukraine ....... 19 F5 45 0N 34 0 E
Krymskyy Pivostriv, Ukraine .. 19 F5 45 0N 34 0 E
Kryvyy Rih, Ukraine ........ 19 E5 47 51N 33 20 E
Ksar el Kebir, Morocco ...... 50 B4 35 0N 6 0W
Ksar es Souk = Er Rachidia,
  Morocco ............... 50 B5 31 58N 4 20W
Kuah, Malaysia ............ 39 J2 6 19N 99 51 E
Kuala Belait, Malaysia ....... 36 D4 4 35N 114 11 E
Kuala Berang, Malaysia ...... 39 K4 5 5N 103 1 E
Kuala Dungun = Dungun,
  Malaysia ............... 39 K4 4 45N 103 25 E
Kuala Kangsar, Malaysia ..... 39 K3 4 46N 100 56 E
Kuala Kelawang, Malaysia .... 39 L4 2 56N 102 5 E
Kuala Kerai, Malaysia ....... 39 K4 5 30N 102 12 E
Kuala Kerian, Malaysia ...... 39 c 5 10N 100 25 E
Kuala Lipis, Malaysia ....... 39 K4 4 10N 102 3 E
Kuala Lumpur, Malaysia ..... 39 L3 3 9N 101 41 E
Kuala Nerang, Malaysia ...... 39 J3 6 16N 100 37 E
Kuala Pilah, Malaysia ....... 39 L4 2 45N 102 15 E
Kuala Rompin, Malaysia ..... 39 L4 2 49N 103 29 E
Kuala Selangor, Malaysia ..... 39 L3 3 20N 101 15 E
Kuala Sepetang, Malaysia .... 39 K3 4 49N 100 28 E
Kuala Terengganu, Malaysia .. 39 K4 5 20N 103 8 E
Kualajelai, Indonesia ........ 36 E4 2 58S 110 46 E
Kualakapuas, Indonesia ...... 36 E4 2 55S 114 20 E
Kualakurun, Indonesia ....... 36 E4 1 10S 113 50 E
Kualapembuang, Indonesia ... 36 E4 3 14S 112 38 E
Kualasimpang, Indonesia ..... 36 D1 4 17N 98 3 E
Kuancheng, China .......... 35 D10 40 37N 118 30 E
Kuandang, Indonesia ........ 37 D6 0 56N 123 1 E
Kuandian, China ........... 35 D13 40 45N 124 45 E
Kuangchou = Guangzhou, China 33 D6 23 5N 113 10 E
Kuantan, Malaysia .......... 39 L4 3 49N 103 20 E
Kuba = Quba, Azerbaijan .... 19 F8 41 21N 48 32 E
Kuban →, Russia ........... 19 E6 45 20N 37 30 E
Kubokawa, Japan ........... 31 H6 33 12N 133 8 E
Kubu, Indonesia ........... 37 J18 8 16S 115 35 E
Kubutambahan, Indonesia ... 37 J18 8 5S 115 10 E
Kucar, Tanjung, Indonesia ... 37 K18 8 39S 114 34 E
Kucha Gompa, India ........ 43 B7 34 25N 76 56 E
Kuchaman, India ........... 42 F6 27 13N 74 47 E
Kuchinda, India ............ 43 J11 21 44N 84 21 E
Kuching, Malaysia .......... 36 D4 1 33N 110 25 E
Kuchino-eruba-jima, Japan ... 31 J5 30 28N 130 12 E
Kuchino-Shima, Japan ....... 31 K4 29 57N 129 55 E
Kuchinotsu, Japan .......... 31 H5 32 36N 130 11 E
Kuda, India ............... 40 H7 23 10N 71 15 E
Kudat, Malaysia ............ 36 C5 6 55N 116 55 E
Kudus, Indonesia ........... 37 G14 6 48S 110 51 E
Kudymkar, Russia .......... 18 C9 59 1N 54 39 E
Kueiyang = Guiyang, China .. 32 D5 26 32N 106 40 E
Kufra Oasis = Al Kufrah, Libya . 51 D10 24 17N 23 15 E
Kufstein, Austria ........... 16 E7 47 35N 12 11 E
Kugaaruk = Pelly Bay, Canada . 69 B11 68 38N 89 50W
Kugong I., Canada .......... 72 A4 56 18N 79 50W
Kūhak, Iran ............... 45 E9 27 12N 63 10 E
Kūhbonān, Iran ............ 45 D8 31 23N 56 19 E
Kühestak, Iran ............. 45 E8 26 47N 57 2 E
Kuhin, Iran ............... 45 B6 36 22N 49 40 E
Kūhīrī, Iran ............... 45 E9 26 55N 61 2 E
Kühpāyeh, Eşfahan, Iran ..... 45 C7 32 44N 52 20 E
Kühpāyeh, Kermān, Iran ..... 45 D8 30 35N 57 15 E
Kührān, Küh-e, Iran ........ 45 E8 26 46N 58 12 E
Kui Buri, Thailand .......... 39 F2 12 3N 99 52 E
Kuichong, China ........... 33 F11 22 38N 114 25 E
Kuiseb →, Namibia ......... 56 C1 22 59S 14 31 E
Kuito, Angola .............. 53 G3 12 22S 16 55 E
Kuiu I., U.S.A. ............. 70 B2 57 45N 134 10W
Kujang, N. Korea ........... 35 E14 39 57N 126 1 E
Kuji, Japan ............... 30 D10 40 11N 141 46 E
Kujū-San, Japan ........... 31 H5 33 5N 131 15 E
Kukës, Albania ............. 23 C9 42 5N 20 27 E
Kukup, Malaysia ........... 39 d 1 20N 103 27 E
Kukup, Pulau, Malaysia ...... 39 d 1 18N 103 25 E
Kula, Turkey .............. 23 E13 38 32N 28 40 E
Kulachi, Pakistan .......... 42 D4 31 56N 70 27 E
Kulai, Malaysia ............ 39 M4 1 44N 103 35 E
Kulasekarappattinam, India .. 40 Q11 8 20N 78 5 E
Kuldiga, Latvia ............ 9 H19 56 58N 21 59 E
Kulen, Cambodia .......... 38 F5 13 50N 104 40 E
Kulgam, India ............. 43 C6 33 36N 75 2 E
Kulgera, Australia .......... 62 D1 25 50S 133 18 E
Kulim, Malaysia ............ 39 K3 5 22N 100 34 E
Kulin, Australia ............ 61 F2 32 40S 118 2 E
Kulkayu = Hartley Bay, Canada 70 C3 53 25N 129 15W
Kulm, U.S.A. .............. 80 B5 46 18N 98 57W
Kulsary, Kazakhstan ........ 19 E9 46 59N 54 1 E
Kulti, India ............... 43 H12 23 43N 86 50 E

Kulu, India ............... 42 D7 31 58N 77 6 E
Kulumbura, Australia ........ 60 B4 13 55S 126 35 E
Kulunda, Russia ........... 28 D8 52 35N 78 57 E
Kulungar, Afghan. .......... 42 C3 34 0N 69 2 E
Kulwin, Australia ........... 63 F3 35 0S 142 42 E
Kulyab = Kŭlob, Tajikistan ... 28 F7 37 55N 69 50 E
Kuma →, Russia ........... 19 F8 44 55N 47 0 E
Kumagaya, Japan .......... 31 F9 36 9N 139 22 E
Kumai, Indonesia .......... 36 E4 2 44S 111 43 E
Kumamba, Kepulauan, Indonesia 37 E9 1 36S 138 45 E
Kumamoto, Japan .......... 31 H5 32 45N 130 45 E
Kumamoto □, Japan ........ 31 H5 32 55N 130 55 E
Kumanovo, Macedonia ...... 23 C9 42 9N 21 42 E
Kumara, N.Z. .............. 59 K3 42 37S 171 12 E
Kumarina, Australia ........ 61 D2 24 41S 119 32 E
Kumasi, Ghana ............ 50 G5 6 41N 1 38W
Kumba, Cameroon ......... 52 D1 4 36N 9 24 E
Kumbakonam, India ........ 40 P11 10 58N 79 25 E
Kumbarilla, Australia ....... 63 D5 27 15S 150 55 E
Kumbhraj, India ........... 42 G7 24 22N 77 3 E
Kumbia, Australia .......... 63 D5 26 41S 151 39 E
Kŭmch'ŏn, N. Korea ........ 35 E14 38 10N 126 29 E
Kumdok, India ............ 43 C8 33 32N 78 10 E
Kume-Shima, Japan ........ 31 L3 26 20N 126 47 E
Kumertau, Russia .......... 18 D10 52 45N 55 57 E
Kumharsain, India ......... 42 D7 31 19N 77 27 E
Kŭmhwa, S. Korea ......... 35 E14 38 17N 127 28 E
Kumi, Uganda ............. 54 B3 1 30N 33 58 E
Kumla, Sweden ............ 9 G16 59 8N 15 10 E
Kumo, Nigeria ............. 51 F8 10 1N 11 12 E
Kumo älv = Kokemäenjoki →,
  Finland ................ 9 F19 61 32N 21 44 E
Kumon Bum, Burma ........ 41 F20 26 30N 97 15 E
Kunashir, Ostrov, Russia ..... 29 E15 44 0N 146 0 E
Kunda, Estonia ............ 9 G22 59 30N 26 34 E
Kunda, India .............. 43 G9 25 43N 81 31 E
Kundar →, Pakistan ........ 42 D3 31 56N 69 19 E
Kundelungu △, Dem. Rep. of
  the Congo ............. 55 E2 10 30S 27 40 E
Kundelungu Ouest △, Dem. Rep.
  of the Congo ........ 55 D2 9 55S 27 17 E
Kundian, Pakistan .......... 42 C4 32 27N 71 28 E
Kundla, India ............. 42 J4 21 21N 71 25 E
Kunga →, Bangla. ......... 43 J13 21 46N 89 30 E
Kunghit I., Canada ......... 70 C2 52 6N 131 3W
Kungrad = Qŭnghirot, Uzbekistan 28 E6 43 6N 58 54 E
Kungsbacka, Sweden ....... 9 H15 57 30N 12 5 E
Kungur, Russia ............ 18 C10 57 25N 56 57 E
Kungurri, Australia ......... 62 K6 21 4S 148 45 E
Kunhar →, Pakistan ........ 43 B5 34 20N 73 30 E
Kuningan, Indonesia ........ 37 G13 6 59S 108 29 E
Kunlong, Burma ........... 41 H21 23 20N 98 50 E
Kunlun Shan, Asia ......... 32 C3 36 0N 86 30 E
Kunming, China ........... 32 D5 25 1N 102 41 E
Kunsan, S. Korea .......... 35 G14 35 59N 126 45 E
Kununurra, Australia ....... 60 C4 15 40S 128 50 E
Kunwari →, India .......... 43 F8 26 26N 79 11 E
Kunya-Urgench = Köneürgench,
  Turkmenistan .......... 28 E6 42 19N 59 10 E
Kuopio, Finland ........... 8 E22 62 53N 27 35 E
Kupa →, Croatia ........... 16 F9 45 28N 16 24 E
Kupang, Indonesia ......... 37 F6 10 19S 123 39 E
Kupreanof I., U.S.A. ........ 70 B2 56 50N 133 30W
Kupyansk-Uzlovoi, Ukraine ... 19 E6 49 40N 37 43 E
Kuqa, China .............. 32 B3 41 35N 82 30 E
Kūr →, Azerbaijan ......... 19 G8 39 29N 49 15 E
Kür Dili, Azerbaijan ........ 45 B6 39 3N 49 13 E
Kura = Kür →, Azerbaijan ... 19 G8 39 29N 49 15 E
Kuranda, Australia ......... 62 B4 16 48S 145 35 E
Kuranga, India ............ 42 H3 22 4N 69 10 E
Kurashiki, Japan ........... 31 G6 34 40N 133 50 E
Kurayoshi, Japan .......... 31 G6 35 26N 133 50 E
Kürdzhali, Bulgaria ......... 23 D11 41 38N 25 21 E
Kure, Japan .............. 31 G6 34 14N 132 32 E
Kuressaare, Estonia ........ 9 G20 58 15N 22 30 E
Kurgan, Russia ............ 28 D7 55 26N 65 18 E
Kuri, India ............... 42 F4 26 37N 70 43 E
Kuria Maria Is. = Khuriyā Muriyā,
  Jazā'ir, Oman ....... 47 D6 17 30N 55 58 E
Kuridala, Australia ......... 62 C3 21 16S 140 29 E
Kurigram, Bangla. ......... 41 G16 25 49N 89 39 E
Kurikka, Finland ........... 9 E20 62 36N 22 24 E
Kuril Is. = Kurilskiye Ostrova,
  Russia ................ 29 E15 45 0N 150 0 E
Kuril Trench, Pac. Oc. ...... 26 E19 44 0N 153 0 E
Kurilsk, Russia ............ 29 E15 45 14N 147 53 E
Kurilskiye Ostrova, Russia ... 29 E15 45 0N 150 0 E
Kurino, Japan ............. 31 J5 31 57N 130 43 E
Kurinskaya Kosa = Kür Dili,
  Azerbaijan ............. 45 B6 39 3N 49 13 E
Kurnool, India ............ 40 M11 15 45N 78 0 E
Kuro-Shima, Kagoshima, Japan 31 J4 30 50N 129 57 E
Kuro-Shima, Okinawa, Japan . 31 M2 24 14N 124 1 E
Kurow, N.Z. ............... 59 L3 44 44S 170 29 E
Kurram →, Pakistan ........ 42 C4 32 36N 71 20 E
Kurri Kurri, Australia ....... 63 E5 32 50S 151 28 E
Kurrimine, Australia ........ 62 B4 17 47S 146 6 E
Kurshskiy Zaliv, Russia ...... 9 J19 55 9N 21 6 E
Kursk, Russia ............. 18 D6 51 42N 36 11 E
Kuruçay, Turkey ........... 44 B3 39 39N 38 29 E
Kuruktag, China ........... 32 B3 41 0N 89 0 E
Kuruman, S. Africa ......... 56 D3 27 28S 23 28 E
Kuruman →, S. Africa ...... 56 D3 26 56S 20 39 E
Kurume, Japan ............ 31 H5 33 15N 130 30 E
Kurunegala, Sri Lanka ...... 40 R12 7 30N 80 23 E
Kurya, Russia ............. 18 B10 61 42N 57 9 E
Kus Gölü, Turkey .......... 23 D12 40 10N 27 55 E
Kuşadası, Turkey .......... 23 F12 37 52N 27 15 E
Kusamba, Indonesia ........ 37 K18 8 34S 115 27 E
Kusatsu, Japan ............ 31 G9 35 3N 135 57 E
Kusawa L., Canada ......... 70 A1 60 20N 136 13W
Kushalgarh, India .......... 42 H6 23 10N 74 27 E
Kushikino, Japan .......... 31 J5 31 44N 130 16 E
Kushima, Japan ........... 31 J5 31 29N 131 14 E
Kushimoto, Japan .......... 31 H7 33 28N 135 47 E
Kushiro, Japan ............ 30 C12 43 0N 144 25 E
Kushiro-Gawa →, Japan .... 30 C12 42 59N 144 23 E
Kushiro Shitsugen △, Japan .. 30 C12 43 9N 144 26 E
Kūshk, Iran ............... 45 D8 28 46N 56 51 E
Kushka = Gushgy, Turkmenistan 28 F7 35 20N 62 18 E
Kūshkī, Iran .............. 44 C5 33 31N 47 13 E
Kushol, India ............. 43 C7 33 40N 76 36 E
Kushtia, Bangla. ........... 41 H16 23 55N 89 5 E
Kushva, Russia ............ 18 C10 58 18N 59 45 E
Kuskokwim B., U.S.A. ....... 68 C3 59 45N 162 25W
Kusmi, India .............. 43 H10 23 17N 83 55 E
Kussharo-Ko, Japan ........ 30 C12 43 38N 144 21 E

Kustanay = Qostanay, Kazakhstan ... 28 D7 53 10N 63 35 E
Kut, Ko, Thailand ... 39 G4 11 40N 102 35 E
Kuta, Indonesia ... 37 K18 8 43S 115 11 E
Kütahya, Turkey ... 19 G5 39 30N 30 2 E
Kutaisi, Georgia ... 19 F7 42 19N 42 40 E
Kutaraja = Banda Aceh, Indonesia ... 36 C1 5 35N 95 20 E
Kutch, Gulf of = Kachchh, Gulf of, India ... 42 H3 22 50N 69 15 E
Kutch, Rann of = Kachchh, Rann of, India ... 42 H4 24 0N 70 0 E
Kutiyana, India ... 42 J4 21 36N 70 2 E
Kutno, Poland ... 17 B10 52 15N 19 23 E
Kutse, Botswana ... 56 C3 21 7S 22 16 E
Kuttabul, Australia ... 62 K6 21 1S 148 54 E
Kutu, Dem. Rep. of the Congo ... 52 E3 2 40S 18 11 E
Kutum, Sudan ... 51 F10 14 10N 24 40 E
Kuujjuaq, Canada ... 69 C13 58 6N 68 15W
Kuujjuarapik, Canada ... 72 A4 55 20N 77 35W
Kuŭp-tong, N. Korea ... 35 D14 40 45N 126 1 E
Kuusamo, Finland ... 8 D23 65 57N 29 8 E
Kuusankoski, Finland ... 9 F22 60 55N 26 38 E
Kuwait = Al Kuwayt, Kuwait ... 44 D5 29 30N 48 0 E
Kuwait ■, Asia ... 44 D5 29 30N 47 30 E
Kuwana, Japan ... 31 G8 35 5N 136 43 E
Kuwana →, India ... 43 F10 26 25N 83 15 E
Kuybyshev = Samara, Russia ... 18 D9 53 8N 50 6 E
Kuybyshev, Russia ... 18 D9 55 27N 78 19 E
Kuybyshevskoye Vdkhr., Russia ... 18 C8 55 2N 49 30 E
Kuye He →, China ... 34 E6 38 23N 110 46 E
Kuyeh, Iran ... 44 B5 38 45N 47 57 E
Kuyto, Ozero, Russia ... 18 B5 65 6N 31 20 E
Kuyumba, Russia ... 29 C10 60 58N 96 59 E
Kuzey Anadolu Dağları, Turkey ... 19 F6 41 30N 35 0 E
Kuznetsk, Russia ... 18 D8 53 12N 46 40 E
Kuzomen, Russia ... 18 A6 66 22N 36 50 E
Kvænangen, Norway ... 8 A19 70 5N 21 15 E
Kvaløy, Norway ... 8 B18 69 40N 18 30 E
Kvarner, Croatia ... 16 F8 44 50N 14 10 E
Kvarnerič, Croatia ... 16 F8 44 43N 14 37 E
Kwa-Nobuhle, S. Africa ... 53 L5 33 50S 25 22 E
Kwabhaca, S. Africa ... 57 E4 30 51S 29 0 E
Kwakhanai, Botswana ... 56 C3 21 39S 21 16 E
Kwakoegron, Suriname ... 93 B7 5 12N 55 25W
Kwale, Kenya ... 54 C4 4 15S 39 31 E
KwaMashu, S. Africa ... 57 D5 29 45S 30 58 E
Kwando →, Africa ... 56 B3 18 27S 23 32 E
Kwangchow = Guangzhou, China 33 D6 23 5N 113 10 E
Kwangdaeri, N. Korea ... 35 D14 40 31N 127 32 E
Kwangju, S. Korea ... 35 G14 35 9N 126 54 E
Kwango →, Dem. Rep. of the Congo ... 52 E3 3 14S 17 22 E
Kwangsi-Chuang = Guangxi Zhuangzu Zizhiqu □, China 33 D5 24 0N 109 0 E
Kwangtung = Guangdong □, China ... 33 D6 23 0N 113 0 E
Kwataboahegan →, Canada ... 72 B3 51 9N 80 50W
Kwatisore, Indonesia ... 37 E8 3 18S 134 50 E
KwaZulu Natal □, S. Africa ... 57 D5 29 0S 30 0 E
Kweichow = Guizhou □, China ... 32 D5 27 0N 107 0 E
Kwekwe, Zimbabwe ... 55 F2 18 58S 29 48 E
Kwidzyn, Poland ... 17 B10 53 44N 18 55 E
Kwinana New Town, Australia ... 61 F2 32 15S 115 47 E
Kwoka, Indonesia ... 37 E8 0 31S 132 27 E
Kwun Tong, China ... 33 G11 22 19N 114 13 E
Kyabra Cr. →, Australia ... 63 D3 25 36S 142 55 E
Kyabram, Australia ... 63 F4 36 19S 145 4 E
Kyaikto, Burma ... 38 D1 17 20N 97 3 E
Kyakhta, Russia ... 29 D11 50 30N 106 25 E
Kyambura ∩, Uganda ... 54 C3 0 7S 30 9 E
Kyancutta, Australia ... 63 E2 33 8S 135 33 E
Kyaukpadaung, Burma ... 41 J19 20 52N 95 8 E
Kyaukpyu, Burma ... 41 K18 19 28N 93 30 E
Kyaukse, Burma ... 41 J20 21 36N 96 10 E
Kyburz, U.S.A. ... 78 G6 38 47N 120 18W
Kyelang, India ... 42 C7 32 35N 77 2 E
Kyenjojo, Uganda ... 54 B3 0 40N 30 37 E
Kyle, Canada ... 71 C7 50 50N 108 2W
Kyle Dam, Zimbabwe ... 55 G3 20 15S 31 0 E
Kyle of Lochalsh, U.K. ... 11 D3 57 17N 5 44W
Kymijoki →, Finland ... 9 F22 60 30N 26 55 E
Kymmene älv = Kymijoki →, Finland ... 9 F22 60 30N 26 55 E
Kyneton, Australia ... 63 F3 37 10S 144 29 E
Kynuna, Australia ... 62 C3 21 37S 141 55 E
Kyō-ga-Saki, Japan ... 31 G7 35 45N 135 15 E
Kyoga, L., Uganda ... 54 B3 1 35N 33 0 E
Kyogle, Australia ... 63 D5 28 40S 153 0 E
Kyongju, S. Korea ... 35 G15 35 51N 129 14 E
Kyongpyaw, Burma ... 41 L19 17 12N 95 10 E
Kyŏngsŏng, N. Korea ... 35 D15 41 35N 129 36 E
Kyōto, Japan ... 31 G7 35 0N 135 45 E
Kyōto □, Japan ... 31 G7 35 15N 135 45 E
Kyparissovouno, Cyprus ... 25 D12 35 19N 33 10 E
Kyperounda, Cyprus ... 25 E11 34 56N 32 58 E
Kyrenia, Cyprus ... 25 D12 35 20N 33 20 E
Kyrgyzstan ■, Asia ... 28 E8 42 0N 75 0 E
Kyro älv = Kyrönjoki →, Finland ... 8 E19 63 14N 21 45 E
Kyrönjoki →, Finland ... 8 E19 63 14N 21 45 E
Kystatyam, Russia ... 29 C13 67 20N 123 10 E
Kythréa, Cyprus ... 25 D12 35 15N 33 29 E
Kyunhla, Burma ... 41 H19 23 25N 95 15 E
Kyuquot Sound, Canada ... 70 D3 50 2N 127 22W
Kyūshū, Japan ... 31 H5 33 0N 131 0 E
Kyūshū □, Japan ... 31 H5 33 0N 131 0 E
Kyūshū-Sanchi, Japan ... 31 H5 32 35N 131 17 E
Kyustendil, Bulgaria ... 23 C10 42 16N 22 41 E
Kyusyur, Russia ... 29 B13 70 19N 127 30 E
Kyyiv, Ukraine ... 17 C16 50 30N 30 28 E
Kyyivske Vdskh., Ukraine ... 17 C16 51 0N 30 25 E
Kyzyl, Russia ... 29 D10 51 50N 94 30 E
Kyzyl Kum, Uzbekistan ... 28 E7 42 30N 65 0 E
Kyzyl-Kyya, Kyrgyzstan ... 28 E8 40 16N 72 8 E
Kyzyl-Orda = Qyzylorda, Kazakhstan ... 28 E7 44 48N 65 28 E

## L

La Alcarria, Spain ... 21 B4 40 31N 2 45W
La Amistad ∩, Cent. Amer. ... 88 E3 9 28N 83 18W
La Asunción, Venezuela ... 92 A6 11 2N 63 53W
La Baie, Canada ... 73 C5 48 19N 70 53W
La Banda, Argentina ... 94 B3 27 45S 64 10W
La Barca, Mexico ... 86 C4 20 20N 102 40W

La Barge, U.S.A. ... 76 E8 42 16N 110 12W
La Belle, U.S.A. ... 83 M5 26 46N 81 26W
La Biche →, Canada ... 70 B4 59 57N 123 50W
La Biche, L., Canada ... 70 C6 54 50N 112 5W
La Blanquilla, Venezuela ... 89 D7 11 51N 64 37W
La Bomba, Mexico ... 86 A1 31 53N 115 2W
La Brea, Trin. & Tob. ... 93 K15 10 15N 61 37W
La Calera, Chile ... 94 C1 32 50S 71 10W
La Campana ∩, Chile ... 94 C1 32 58S 71 14W
La Canal = Sa Canal, Spain ... 24 C7 38 51N 1 23 E
La Carlota, Argentina ... 94 C3 33 30S 63 20W
La Ceiba, Honduras ... 88 C2 15 40N 86 50W
La Chorrera, Panama ... 88 E4 8 53N 79 47W
La Chaux-de-Fonds, Switz. ... 20 C7 47 7N 6 50 E
La Cocha, Argentina ... 94 B2 27 50S 65 40W
La Concepción, Panama ... 88 E3 8 31N 82 37W
La Concordia, Mexico ... 87 D6 16 8N 92 38W
La Coruña = A Coruña, Spain ... 21 A1 43 20N 8 25W
La Crescent, U.S.A. ... 80 D9 43 50N 91 18W
La Crete, Canada ... 70 B5 58 11N 116 24W
La Crosse, Kans., U.S.A. ... 80 F5 38 32N 99 18W
La Crosse, Wis., U.S.A. ... 80 D9 43 48N 91 15W
La Cruz, Costa Rica ... 88 D2 11 4N 85 39W
La Cruz, Mexico ... 86 C3 23 55N 106 54W
La Désirade, Guadeloupe ... 88 b 16 18N 61 3W
La Escondida, Mexico ... 86 C5 24 6N 99 55W
La Esmeralda, Paraguay ... 94 A3 22 16S 62 33W
La Esperanza, Cuba ... 88 B3 22 46N 83 44W
La Esperanza, Honduras ... 88 D2 14 15N 88 10W
La Estrada = A Estrada, Spain ... 21 A1 42 43N 8 27W
La Fayette, U.S.A. ... 83 H3 34 42N 85 17W
La Fé, Cuba ... 88 B3 22 2N 84 15W
La Follette, U.S.A. ... 83 G3 36 23N 84 7W
La Grande, U.S.A. ... 76 D4 45 20N 118 5W
La Grande →, Canada ... 72 B5 53 50N 79 0W
La Grande Deux, Rés., Canada ... 72 B4 53 40N 76 55W
La Grande Quatre, Rés., Canada ... 72 B5 54 0N 73 15W
La Grande Trois, Rés., Canada ... 72 B4 53 40N 75 10W
La Grange, Calif., U.S.A. ... 78 H6 37 42N 120 27W
La Grange, Ga., U.S.A. ... 83 J3 33 2N 85 2W
La Grange, Ky., U.S.A. ... 82 F3 38 25N 85 23W
La Grange, Tex., U.S.A. ... 81 L6 29 54N 96 52W
La Guaira, Venezuela ... 92 A5 10 36N 66 56W
La Habana, Cuba ... 88 B3 23 8N 82 22W
La Independencia, Mexico ... 87 D6 16 31N 91 47W
La Isabela, Dom. Rep. ... 89 C5 19 58N 71 2W
La Junta, U.S.A. ... 81 F3 37 59N 103 33W
La Laguna, Canary Is. ... 24 F3 28 28N 16 18W
La Libertad, Guatemala ... 88 C1 16 47N 90 7W
La Libertad, Mexico ... 86 B2 29 55N 112 41W
La Ligua, Chile ... 94 C1 32 30S 71 16W
La Línea de la Concepción, Spain 21 D3 36 15N 5 23W
La Loche, Canada ... 71 B7 56 29N 109 26W
La Louvière, Belgium ... 15 D4 50 27N 4 10 E
La Lune, Trin. & Tob. ... 93 K15 10 3N 61 22W
La Malbaie, Canada ... 73 C5 47 40N 70 10W
La Malinche ∩, Mexico ... 87 D5 19 15N 98 3W
La Mancha, Spain ... 21 C4 39 10N 2 54W
La Martre, L., Canada ... 70 A5 63 15N 117 55W
La Mesa, U.S.A. ... 79 N9 32 46N 117 3W
La Misión, Mexico ... 86 A1 32 5N 116 50W
La Moure, U.S.A. ... 80 B5 46 21N 98 18W
La Negra, Chile ... 94 A1 23 46S 70 18W
La Oliva, Canary Is. ... 24 F6 28 36N 13 57W
La Orotava, Canary Is. ... 24 F3 28 22N 16 31W
La Oroya, Peru ... 92 F3 11 32S 75 54W
La Palma, Canary Is. ... 24 F2 28 40N 17 50W
La Palma, Panama ... 88 E4 8 15N 78 0W
La Palma del Condado, Spain ... 21 D2 37 21N 6 38W
La Paloma, Chile ... 94 C1 30 35S 71 0W
La Pampa □, Argentina ... 94 D2 36 50S 66 0W
La Paragua, Venezuela ... 92 B6 6 50N 63 20W
La Paz, Entre Ríos, Argentina ... 94 C4 30 50S 59 45W
La Paz, San Luis, Argentina ... 94 C2 33 30S 67 20W
La Paz, Bolivia ... 92 G5 16 20S 68 10W
La Paz, Honduras ... 88 D2 14 20N 87 47W
La Paz, Mexico ... 86 C2 24 10N 110 20W
La Paz Centro, Nic. ... 88 D2 12 20N 86 41W
La Pedrera, Colombia ... 92 D5 1 18S 69 43W
La Pérade, Canada ... 73 C5 46 35N 72 12W
La Perouse Str., Asia ... 30 B11 45 40N 142 0 E
La Pesca, Mexico ... 87 C5 23 46N 97 47W
La Piedad, Mexico ... 86 C4 20 20N 102 1W
La Pine, U.S.A. ... 76 E3 43 40N 121 30W
La Plata, Argentina ... 94 D4 35 0S 57 55W
La Pocatière, Canada ... 73 C5 47 22N 70 2W
La Porte, Ind., U.S.A. ... 82 E2 41 36N 86 43W
La Porte, Tex., U.S.A. ... 81 L7 29 39N 95 1W
La Purísima, Mexico ... 86 B2 26 10N 112 4W
La Push, U.S.A. ... 78 C2 47 55N 124 38W
La Quiaca, Argentina ... 94 A2 22 5S 65 35W
La Restinga, Canary Is. ... 24 G2 27 38N 17 59W
La Rioja, Argentina ... 94 B2 29 20S 67 0W
La Rioja □, Argentina ... 94 B2 29 30S 67 0W
La Rioja □, Spain ... 21 A4 42 20N 2 20W
La Robla, Spain ... 21 A3 42 50N 5 41W
La Roche-en-Ardenne, Belgium ... 15 D5 50 11N 5 35 E
La Roche-sur-Yon, France ... 20 C3 46 40N 1 25W
La Rochelle, France ... 20 C3 46 10N 1 9W
La Roda, Spain ... 21 C4 39 13N 2 15W
La Romana, Dom. Rep. ... 89 C6 18 27N 68 57W
La Ronge, Canada ... 71 B7 55 5N 105 20W
La Rumorosa, Mexico ... 79 N10 32 33N 116 4W
La Sabina = Sa Savina, Spain ... 24 C7 38 44N 1 25 E
La Salle, U.S.A. ... 80 E10 41 20N 89 6W
La Santa, Canary Is. ... 24 E6 29 5N 13 40W
La Sarre, Canada ... 72 C4 48 45N 79 15W
La Scie, Canada ... 73 C8 49 57N 55 36W
La Selva Beach, U.S.A. ... 78 J5 36 56N 121 51W
La Serena, Chile ... 94 B1 29 55S 71 10W
La Seu d'Urgell, Spain ... 21 A6 42 22N 1 23 E
La Seyne-sur-Mer, France ... 20 E6 43 7N 5 52 E
La Soufrière, St. Vincent ... 89 D7 13 20N 61 11W
La Spézia, Italy ... 20 D8 44 7N 9 50 E
La Tagua, Colombia ... 92 C4 0 3N 74 40W
La Tortuga, Venezuela ... 89 D6 11 0N 65 22W
La Trinité, Martinique ... 88 c 14 43N 60 58W
La Tuque, Canada ... 72 C5 47 30N 72 50W
La Unión, Chile ... 96 E2 40 10S 73 0W
La Unión, El Salv. ... 88 D2 13 20N 87 50W
La Unión, Mexico ... 86 D4 17 58N 101 49W
La Urbana, Venezuela ... 92 B5 7 8N 66 56W
La Vache Pt., Trin. & Tob. ... 93 K15 10 47N 61 28W
La Vall d'Uixó, Spain ... 21 C5 39 49N 0 15W
La Vega, Dom. Rep. ... 89 C5 19 20N 70 30W
La Vela de Coro, Venezuela ... 92 A5 11 27N 69 34W
La Venta, Mexico ... 87 D6 18 8N 94 3W
La Ventura, Mexico ... 86 C4 24 38N 100 54W

Laas Caanood = Las Anod, Somali Rep. ... 47 F4 8 26N 47 19 E
Labasa, Fiji ... 59 C8 16 30S 179 27 E
Labe = Elbe →, Europe ... 16 B5 53 50N 9 0 E
Labé, Guinea ... 50 F3 11 24N 12 16W
Laberge, L., Canada ... 70 A1 61 11N 135 12W
Labinsk, Russia ... 19 F7 44 40N 40 48 E
Labis, Malaysia ... 39 L4 2 22N 103 2 E
Laborie, St. Lucia ... 89 f 13 45N 61 2W
Laboulaye, Argentina ... 94 C3 34 10S 63 30W
Labrador, Canada ... 73 B7 53 20N 61 0W
Labrador City, Canada ... 73 B6 52 57N 66 55W
Labrador Sea, Atl. Oc. ... 69 C14 57 0N 54 0W
Lábrea, Brazil ... 92 E6 7 15S 64 51W
Labuan, Indonesia ... 37 G11 6 22S 105 50 E
Labuan, Pulau, Malaysia ... 36 C5 5 21N 115 13 E
Labuha, Indonesia ... 37 E7 0 30S 127 30 E
Labuhan, Indonesia ... 37 G11 6 22S 105 50 E
Labuhanbajo, Indonesia ... 37 F6 8 28S 119 54 E
Labuk, Telok, Malaysia ... 36 C5 6 10N 117 50 E
Labyrinth, L., Australia ... 63 E2 30 40S 135 11 E
Labytnangi, Russia ... 28 C7 66 39N 66 21 E
Lac-Bouchette, Canada ... 73 C5 48 16N 72 11W
Lac Édouard, Canada ... 72 C5 47 40N 72 16W
Lac La Biche, Canada ... 70 C6 54 45N 111 58W
Lac la Martre = Wha Ti, Canada ... 68 B8 63 8N 117 16W
Lac La Ronge ∩, Canada ... 71 B7 55 9N 104 41W
Lac-Mégantic, Canada ... 73 C5 45 35N 70 53W
Lac Thien, Vietnam ... 38 F7 12 25N 108 11 E
Lacanau, France ... 20 D3 44 58N 1 5W
Lacantúm →, Mexico ... 87 D6 16 36N 90 40W
Laccadive Is. = Lakshadweep Is., India ... 27 H11 10 0N 72 30 E
Lacepede B., Australia ... 63 F2 36 40S 139 40 E
Lacepede Is., Australia ... 60 C3 16 55S 122 0 E
Lacerdónia, Mozam. ... 55 F4 18 3S 35 35 E
Lacey, U.S.A. ... 78 C4 47 7N 122 49W
Lachhmangarh, India ... 42 F6 27 50N 75 4 E
Lachine, Canada ... 72 C5 45 30N 73 40W
Lachlan →, Australia ... 63 E3 34 22S 143 55 E
Lachute, Canada ... 72 C5 45 39N 74 21W
Lackawanna, U.S.A. ... 84 D6 42 50N 78 50W
Lackawaxen, U.S.A. ... 85 E10 41 29N 74 59W
Lacolle, Canada ... 85 A11 45 5N 73 22W
Lacombe, Canada ... 70 C6 52 30N 113 44W
Lacona, U.S.A. ... 85 C8 43 39N 76 10W
Laconia, U.S.A. ... 85 C13 43 32N 71 28W
Ladakh Ra., India ... 43 C8 34 0N 78 0 E
Ladismith, S. Africa ... 56 E3 33 28S 21 15 E
Lādiz, Iran ... 45 D9 28 55N 61 15 E
Ladnun, India ... 42 F6 27 38N 74 25 E
Ladoga, L. = Ladozhskoye Ozero, Russia ... 18 B5 61 15N 30 30 E
Ladozhskoye Ozero, Russia ... 18 B5 61 15N 30 30 E
Lady Elliott I., Australia ... 62 C5 24 7S 152 42 E
Lady Grey, S. Africa ... 56 E4 30 43S 27 13 E
Ladybrand, S. Africa ... 56 D4 29 9S 27 29 E
Ladysmith, Canada ... 70 D4 49 0N 123 49W
Ladysmith, S. Africa ... 57 D4 28 32S 29 46 E
Ladysmith, U.S.A. ... 80 C9 45 28N 91 12W
Lae, Papua N. G. ... 64 H6 6 40S 147 2 E
Laem Hin Khom, Thailand ... 39 b 9 25N 99 56 E
Laem Khat, Thailand ... 39 a 8 6N 98 26 E
Laem Nga, Thailand ... 39 a 7 55N 98 27 E
Laem Ngop, Thailand ... 39 F4 12 10N 102 26 E
Laem Phan Wa, Thailand ... 39 a 7 47N 98 25 E
Laem Pho, Thailand ... 39 J3 6 55N 101 19 E
Laem Phrom Thep, Thailand ... 39 a 7 45N 98 19 E
Laem Riang, Thailand ... 39 a 8 7N 98 19 E
Laem Sam Rong, Thailand ... 39 a 9 35N 100 4 E
Laem Son, Thailand ... 39 a 7 59N 98 16 E
Laem Yamu, Thailand ... 39 a 7 59N 98 18 E
Læsø, Denmark ... 9 H14 57 15N 11 5 E
Lafayette, Colo., U.S.A. ... 80 F2 39 58N 105 12W
Lafayette, Ind., U.S.A. ... 82 E2 40 25N 86 54W
Lafayette, La., U.S.A. ... 81 K9 30 14N 92 1W
Lafayette, Tenn., U.S.A. ... 83 G2 36 31N 86 2W
Laferte →, Canada ... 70 A5 61 53N 117 44W
Lafia, Nigeria ... 50 G7 8 30N 8 34 E
Lafleche, Canada ... 71 D7 49 45N 106 40W
Lagan →, U.K. ... 10 B6 54 36N 5 55W
Lagarfljót →, Iceland ... 8 D6 65 40N 14 18W
Lågen →, Oppland, Norway ... 9 F14 61 8N 10 25 E
Lågen →, Vestfold, Norway ... 9 G14 59 3N 10 3 E
Laghouat, Algeria ... 50 B6 33 50N 2 59 E
Lagoa do Peixe ∩, Brazil ... 95 C5 31 12S 50 55W
Lagoa Vermelha, Brazil ... 95 B5 28 13S 51 32W
Lagonoy G., Phil. ... 37 B6 13 35N 123 50 E
Lagos, Nigeria ... 50 G6 6 25N 3 27 E
Lagos, Portugal ... 21 D1 37 5N 8 41W
Lagos de Moreno, Mexico ... 86 C4 21 21N 101 55W
Lagrange, Australia ... 60 C3 18 45S 121 43 E
Lagrange B., Australia ... 60 C3 18 38S 121 42 E
Laguna, Brazil ... 95 B6 28 30S 48 50W
Laguna, U.S.A. ... 77 J10 35 2N 107 25W
Laguna Beach, U.S.A. ... 79 M9 33 33N 117 47W
Laguna de la Restinga ∩, Venezuela ... 89 D6 10 58N 64 0W
Laguna del Laja ∩, Chile ... 94 D1 37 27S 71 20W
Laguna del Tigre ∩, Guatemala ... 88 C1 17 32N 90 56W
Laguna Limpia, Argentina ... 94 B4 26 32S 59 45W
Lagunas, Chile ... 94 A2 21 0S 69 45W
Lagunas, Peru ... 92 E3 5 10S 75 35W
Lagunas de Chacahua ∩, Mexico ... 87 D5 16 0N 97 43W
Lagunas de Montebello ∩, Mexico ... 87 D6 16 6N 91 41W
Lahad Datu, Malaysia ... 37 C5 5 0N 118 20 E
Lahad Datu, Teluk, Malaysia ... 37 D5 4 50N 118 20 E
Lahan Sai, Thailand ... 38 E4 14 25N 102 52 E
Lahanam, Laos ... 38 D5 16 16N 105 16 E
Lahar, India ... 43 F8 26 12N 78 57 E
Laharpur, India ... 43 F9 27 43N 80 56 E
Lahat, Indonesia ... 36 E2 3 45S 103 30 E
Lahewa, Indonesia ... 36 D1 1 22N 97 12 E
Lähījän, Iran ... 45 B6 37 10N 50 6 E
Lahn →, Germany ... 16 C4 50 19N 7 37 E
Laholm, Sweden ... 9 H15 56 30N 13 2 E
Lahore, Pakistan ... 42 D6 31 32N 74 22 E
Lahri, Pakistan ... 42 E3 29 11N 68 13 E
Lahti, Finland ... 9 F21 60 58N 25 40 E
Lahtis = Lahti, Finland ... 9 F21 60 58N 25 40 E
Laï, Chad ... 51 G9 9 25N 16 18 E
Lai Chau, Vietnam ... 38 A4 22 5N 103 3 E
Laila = Layla, Si. Arabia ... 46 C4 22 10N 46 40 E
Laingsburg, S. Africa ... 56 E3 33 9S 20 52 E
Lainioälven →, Sweden ... 8 C20 67 35N 22 40 E
Lairg, U.K. ... 11 C4 58 2N 4 24W

Laishui, China ... 34 E8 39 23N 115 45 E
Laiwu, China ... 35 F9 36 15N 117 40 E
Laixi, China ... 35 F11 36 50N 120 31 E
Laiyang, China ... 35 F11 36 59N 120 45 E
Laiyuan, China ... 34 E8 39 20N 114 40 E
Laizhou, China ... 35 F10 37 8N 119 57 E
Laizhou Wan, China ... 35 F10 37 30N 119 30 E
Laja →, Mexico ... 86 C4 20 55N 100 46W
Lajes, Brazil ... 95 B5 27 48S 50 20W
Lak Sao, Laos ... 38 C5 18 11N 104 59 E
Lakaband, Pakistan ... 42 D3 31 2N 69 15 E
Lake Alpine, U.S.A. ... 78 G7 38 29N 120 0W
Lake Andes, U.S.A. ... 80 D5 43 9N 98 32W
Lake Arthur, U.S.A. ... 81 K8 30 5N 92 41W
Lake Cargelligo, Australia ... 63 E4 33 15S 146 22 E
Lake Charles, U.S.A. ... 81 K8 30 14N 93 13W
Lake City, Colo., U.S.A. ... 77 G10 38 2N 107 19W
Lake City, Fla., U.S.A. ... 83 K4 30 11N 82 38W
Lake City, Mich., U.S.A. ... 82 C3 44 20N 85 13W
Lake City, Minn., U.S.A. ... 80 C8 44 27N 92 16W
Lake City, Pa., U.S.A. ... 84 D4 42 1N 80 21W
Lake City, S.C., U.S.A. ... 83 J6 33 52N 79 45W
Lake Cowichan, Canada ... 70 D4 48 49N 124 3W
Lake District ∩, U.K. ... 12 C4 54 30N 3 21W
Lake Elsinore, U.S.A. ... 79 M9 33 38N 117 20W
Lake Eyre ∩, Australia ... 63 D2 28 40S 137 10 E
Lake Gairdner ∩, Australia ... 63 E2 31 41S 135 51 E
Lake George, U.S.A. ... 85 C11 43 26N 73 43W
Lake Grace, Australia ... 61 F2 33 7S 118 28 E
Lake Harbour = Kimmirut, Canada ... 69 B13 62 50N 69 50W
Lake Havasu City, U.S.A. ... 79 L12 34 27N 114 22W
Lake Hughes, U.S.A. ... 79 L8 34 41N 118 26W
Lake Isabella, U.S.A. ... 79 K8 35 38N 118 28W
Lake Jackson, U.S.A. ... 81 L7 29 3N 95 27W
Lake Junction, U.S.A. ... 76 D8 44 35N 110 28W
Lake King, Australia ... 61 F2 33 5S 119 45 E
Lake Lenore, Canada ... 71 C8 52 24N 104 59W
Lake Louise, Canada ... 70 C5 51 30N 116 10W
Lake Malawi ∩, Malawi ... 55 E3 14 2S 34 53 E
Lake Mburo ∩, Uganda ... 54 C3 0 33S 30 56 E
Lake Mead ∩, U.S.A. ... 79 K12 36 15N 114 30W
Lake Meredith ∩, U.S.A. ... 81 H4 35 50N 101 50W
Lake Mills, U.S.A. ... 80 D8 43 25N 93 32W
Lake Nakuru ∩, Kenya ... 54 C4 0 21S 36 8 E
Lake Placid, U.S.A. ... 85 B11 44 17N 73 59W
Lake Pleasant, U.S.A. ... 85 C10 43 28N 74 25W
Lake Providence, U.S.A. ... 81 J9 32 48N 91 10W
Lake Roosevelt ∩, U.S.A. ... 76 C4 47 57N 118 59W
Lake St. Peter, Canada ... 84 A6 45 18N 78 2W
Lake Superior ∩, Canada ... 72 C3 47 45N 84 45W
Lake Torrens ∩, Australia ... 63 E2 30 55S 137 40 E
Lake Village, U.S.A. ... 81 J9 33 20N 91 17W
Lake Wales, U.S.A. ... 83 M5 27 54N 81 35W
Lake Worth, U.S.A. ... 83 M5 26 37N 80 3W
Lakeba, Fiji ... 59 D9 18 13S 178 47W
Lakefield, Canada ... 84 B6 44 25N 78 16W
Lakefield ∩, Australia ... 62 B3 15 24S 144 26 E
Lakehurst, U.S.A. ... 85 F10 40 1N 74 19W
Lakeland, Australia ... 62 B3 15 49S 144 57 E
Lakeland, U.S.A. ... 83 M5 28 3N 81 57W
Lakemba = Lakeba, Fiji ... 59 D9 18 13S 178 47W
Lakeport, Calif., U.S.A. ... 78 F4 39 3N 122 55W
Lakeport, Mich., U.S.A. ... 84 C2 43 7N 82 30W
Lakes Entrance, Australia ... 63 F4 37 50S 148 0 E
Lakeside, Ariz., U.S.A. ... 77 J9 34 9N 109 58W
Lakeside, Calif., U.S.A. ... 79 N10 32 52N 116 55W
Lakeside, Nebr., U.S.A. ... 80 D3 42 3N 102 26W
Lakeside, Ohio, U.S.A. ... 84 E2 41 32N 82 46W
Lakeview, U.S.A. ... 76 E3 42 11N 120 21W
Lakeville, U.S.A. ... 80 C8 44 39N 93 14W
Lakewood, Colo., U.S.A. ... 80 F2 39 44N 105 5W
Lakewood, N.J., U.S.A. ... 85 F10 40 6N 74 13W
Lakewood, N.Y., U.S.A. ... 84 D5 42 6N 79 19W
Lakewood, Ohio, U.S.A. ... 84 E3 41 29N 81 48W
Lakewood, Wash., U.S.A. ... 78 C4 47 11N 122 32W
Lakha, India ... 42 F4 26 9N 70 54 E
Lakhaniá, Greece ... 25 D9 35 58N 27 54 E
Lakhnadon, India ... 43 H8 22 36N 79 36 E
Lakhnau = Lucknow, India ... 43 F9 26 50N 81 0 E
Lakhonpheng, Laos ... 38 E5 15 54N 105 34 E
Lakhpat, India ... 42 H3 23 48N 68 47 E
Lakin, U.S.A. ... 81 G4 37 57N 101 15W
Lakitusaki →, Canada ... 72 B3 54 21N 82 25W
Lakki, Pakistan ... 42 C4 32 36N 70 55 E
Lákkoi, Greece ... 25 D5 35 24N 23 57 E
Lakonikós Kólpos, Greece ... 23 F10 36 40N 22 40 E
Lakor, Indonesia ... 37 F7 8 15S 128 17 E
Lakota, Ivory C. ... 50 G4 5 50N 5 30W
Lakota, U.S.A. ... 80 A5 48 2N 98 21W
Laksar, India ... 42 E8 29 46N 78 3 E
Laksefjorden, Norway ... 8 A22 70 45N 26 50 E
Lakselv, Norway ... 8 A21 70 2N 25 0 E
Lakshadweep Is., India ... 27 H11 10 0N 72 30 E
Lakshmanpur, India ... 43 H10 22 58N 83 3 E
Lakshmikantapur, India ... 43 H13 22 5N 88 20 E
Lala Musa, Pakistan ... 42 C5 32 40N 73 57 E
Lalaghat, India ... 41 G18 24 30N 92 40 E
Lalago, Tanzania ... 54 C3 3 28S 33 58 E
Lalapanzi, Zimbabwe ... 55 F3 19 20S 30 15 E
L'Albufera, Spain ... 21 C5 39 20N 0 27W
Lalganj, India ... 43 G11 25 52N 85 13 E
Lalgola, India ... 43 G13 24 25N 88 15 E
Lālī, Iran ... 45 C6 32 21N 49 6 E
Lalibela, Ethiopia ... 47 E2 12 3N 39 0 E
Lalin, China ... 35 B14 45 12N 127 0 E
Lalín, Spain ... 21 A1 42 40N 8 5W
Lalin He →, China ... 35 B13 45 32N 125 40 E
Lalitapur, Nepal ... 43 F11 27 40N 85 20 E
Lalitpur, India ... 43 G8 24 42N 78 28 E
Lalkua, India ... 43 E8 29 5N 79 31 E
Lalsot, India ... 42 F7 26 34N 76 20 E
Lam, Vietnam ... 38 B6 21 21N 106 31 E
Lam Pao Res., Thailand ... 38 D4 16 50N 103 15 E
Lamaing, Burma ... 41 M20 15 25N 97 53 E
Lamar, Colo., U.S.A. ... 80 F3 38 5N 102 37W
Lamar, Mo., U.S.A. ... 81 G7 37 30N 94 16W
Lamas, Peru ... 92 E3 6 28S 76 31W
Lambaréné, Gabon ... 52 E2 0 41S 10 12 E
Lambasa = Labasa, Fiji ... 59 C8 16 30S 179 27 E
Lambay I., Ireland ... 10 C5 53 29N 6 1W
Lambert Glacier, Antarctica ... 5 D6 71 0S 70 0 E
Lambert's Bay, S. Africa ... 56 E2 32 5S 18 17 E
Lambeth, Canada ... 84 D3 42 54N 81 18W
Lambomakondro, Madag. ... 57 C7 22 41S 44 44 E
Lambton Shores, Canada ... 84 C3 43 10N 81 56W

Lame Deer, U.S.A. . . . . . . . . . . **76 D10** 45 37N 106 40W
Lamego, Portugal . . . . . . . . . . **21 B2** 41 5N 7 52W
Lamèque, Canada . . . . . . . . . . **73 C7** 47 45N 64 38W
Lameroo, Australia . . . . . . . . . . **63 F3** 35 19S 140 33 E
Lamesa, U.S.A. . . . . . . . . . . **81 J4** 32 44N 101 58W
Lamia, Greece . . . . . . . . . . **23 E10** 38 55N 22 26 E
Lamington △, Australia . . . . . . **63 D5** 28 13S 153 12 E
Lamma I., China . . . . . . . . . . **33 G11** 22 12N 114 8 E
Lammermuir Hills, U.K. . . . . . . **11 F6** 55 50N 2 40W
Lamon B., Phil. . . . . . . . . . . **37 B6** 14 30N 122 20 E
Lamont, Canada . . . . . . . . . . **70 C6** 53 46N 112 50W
Lamont, Calif., U.S.A. . . . . . . **79 K8** 35 15N 118 55W
Lamont, Wyo., U.S.A. . . . . . . **76 E10** 42 13N 107 29W
Lampa, Peru . . . . . . . . . . **92 G4** 15 22S 70 22W
Lampang, Thailand . . . . . . . . **38 C2** 18 16N 99 32 E
Lampasas, U.S.A. . . . . . . . . **81 K5** 31 4N 98 11W
Lampazos de Naranjo, Mexico . **86 B4** 27 2N 100 32W
Lampedusa, Medit. S. . . . . . . **22 G5** 35 36N 12 40 E
Lampeter, U.K. . . . . . . . . . . **13 E3** 52 7N 4 4W
Lampione, Medit. S. . . . . . . . **22 G5** 35 33N 12 20 E
Lampman, Canada . . . . . . . . **71 D8** 49 25N 102 50W
Lampung □, Indonesia . . . . . . **36 F2** 5 30S 104 30 E
Lamta, India . . . . . . . . . . **43 H9** 22 8N 80 7 E
Lamu, Kenya . . . . . . . . . . **54 C5** 2 16S 40 55 E
Lamy, U.S.A. . . . . . . . . . . **77 J11** 35 29N 105 53W
Lan Xian, China . . . . . . . . . **34 E6** 38 15N 111 35 E
Lanak La, China . . . . . . . . . **43 B8** 34 27N 79 32 E
Lanak'o Shank'ou = Lanak La,
    China . . . . . . . . . . **43 B8** 34 27N 79 32 E
Lanark, Canada . . . . . . . . . **85 A8** 45 1N 76 22W
Lanark, U.K. . . . . . . . . . . **11 F5** 55 40N 3 47W
Lanbi Kyun, Burma . . . . . . . **39 G2** 10 50N 98 20 E
Lancang Jiang ➤, China . . . . **32 D5** 21 40N 101 10 E
Lancashire □, U.K. . . . . . . . **12 D5** 53 50N 2 48W
Lancaster, Canada . . . . . . . **85 A10** 45 10N 74 30W
Lancaster, U.K. . . . . . . . . . **12 C5** 54 3N 2 48W
Lancaster, Calif., U.S.A. . . . . **79 L8** 34 42N 118 8W
Lancaster, Ky., U.S.A. . . . . . **82 G3** 37 37N 84 35W
Lancaster, N.H., U.S.A. . . . . **85 B13** 44 29N 71 34W
Lancaster, N.Y., U.S.A. . . . . **84 D6** 42 54N 78 40W
Lancaster, Ohio, U.S.A. . . . . **82 F4** 39 43N 82 36W
Lancaster, Pa., U.S.A. . . . . . **85 F8** 40 2N 76 19W
Lancaster, S.C., U.S.A. . . . . **83 H5** 34 43N 80 46W
Lancaster, Wis., U.S.A. . . . . **80 D9** 42 51N 90 43W
Lancaster Sd., Canada . . . . . **69 A11** 74 13N 84 0W
Lancelin, Australia . . . . . . . **61 F2** 31 0S 115 18 E
Lanchow = Lanzhou, China . . **34 F2** 36 1N 103 52 E
Lanciano, Italy . . . . . . . . . . **22 C6** 42 14N 14 23 E
Lancun, China . . . . . . . . . . **35 F11** 36 25N 120 10 E
Land Between the Lakes △,
    U.S.A. . . . . . . . . . . **83 G1** 36 55N 88 7W
Landeck, Austria . . . . . . . . **16 E6** 47 9N 10 34 E
Lander, U.S.A. . . . . . . . . . . **76 E9** 42 50N 108 44W
Lander ➤, Australia . . . . . . **60 D5** 22 0S 132 0 E
Landes, France . . . . . . . . . **20 D3** 44 0N 1 0W
Landi Kotal, Pakistan . . . . . . **42 B4** 34 7N 71 6 E
Landisburg, U.S.A. . . . . . . . **84 F7** 40 21N 77 19W
Land's End, U.K. . . . . . . . . **13 G2** 50 4N 5 44W
Landsborough Cr. ➤, Australia **62 C3** 22 28S 144 35 E
Landshut, Germany . . . . . . . **16 D7** 48 34N 12 8 E
Landskrona, Sweden . . . . . . **9 J15** 55 53N 12 50 E
Lanesboro, U.S.A. . . . . . . . **85 E9** 41 57N 75 34W
Lanett, U.S.A. . . . . . . . . . . **83 J3** 32 52N 85 12W
Lang Qua, Vietnam . . . . . . . **38 A5** 22 16N 104 27 E
Lang Shan, China . . . . . . . . **34 D4** 41 0N 106 30 E
Lang Son, Vietnam . . . . . . . **38 B6** 21 52N 106 42 E
Lang Suan, Thailand . . . . . . **39 H2** 9 57N 99 4 E
La'nga Co, China . . . . . . . . **41 D12** 30 45N 81 15 E
Langar, Iran . . . . . . . . . . . **45 C9** 35 23N 60 25 E
Langara I., Canada . . . . . . . **70 C2** 54 14N 133 1W
Langdon, U.S.A. . . . . . . . . **80 A5** 48 45N 98 22W
Langeberg, S. Africa . . . . . . **56 E3** 33 55S 21 0 E
Langeberge, S. Africa . . . . . . **56 D3** 28 15S 22 33 E
Langeland, Denmark . . . . . . **9 J14** 54 56N 10 48 E
Langenburg, Canada . . . . . . **71 C8** 50 51N 101 43W
Langholm, U.K. . . . . . . . . . **11 F5** 55 9N 3 0W
Langjökull, Iceland . . . . . . . **8 D3** 64 39N 20 12W
Langkawi, Pulau, Malaysia . . **39 J2** 6 25N 99 45 E
Langklip, S. Africa . . . . . . . **56 D3** 28 12S 20 20 E
Langkon, Malaysia . . . . . . . **36 C5** 6 30N 116 40 E
Langlade, St-P. & M. . . . . . . **73 C8** 46 50N 56 20W
Langley, Canada . . . . . . . . **78 A4** 49 7N 122 39W
Langøya, Norway . . . . . . . . **8 B16** 68 45N 14 50 E
Langreo, Spain . . . . . . . . . **21 A3** 43 18N 5 40W
Langres, France . . . . . . . . . **20 C6** 47 52N 5 20 E
Langres, Plateau de, France . . **20 C6** 47 45N 5 3 E
Langsa, Indonesia . . . . . . . **36 D1** 4 30N 97 57 E
Langtry, U.S.A. . . . . . . . . . **81 L4** 29 49N 101 34W
Langu, Thailand . . . . . . . . . **39 J2** 6 53N 99 47 E
Languedoc, France . . . . . . . **20 E5** 43 58N 3 55 E
Langwang, China . . . . . . . . **33 F9** 22 38N 115 22 E
Langxiangzhen, China . . . . . **34 E9** 39 43N 116 8 E
Lanigan, Canada . . . . . . . . **71 C7** 51 51N 105 2W
Lankao, China . . . . . . . . . . **34 G8** 34 48N 114 50 E
Länkäran, Azerbaijan . . . . . . **19 G8** 38 48N 48 52 E
Lannion, France . . . . . . . . . **20 B2** 48 46N 3 29W
L'Annonciation, Canada . . . . **72 C5** 46 25N 74 55W
Lansdale, U.S.A. . . . . . . . . **85 F9** 40 14N 75 17W
Lansdowne, Australia . . . . . . **63 E5** 31 48S 152 30 E
Lansdowne, Canada . . . . . . **85 B8** 44 24N 76 1W
Lansdowne, India . . . . . . . . **43 E8** 29 50N 78 41 E
Lansdowne House, Canada . . **72 B2** 52 14N 87 53W
L'Anse, U.S.A. . . . . . . . . . . **82 B1** 46 45N 88 27W
L'Anse au Loup, Canada . . . . **73 B8** 51 32N 56 50W
L'Anse aux Meadows, Canada . **73 B8** 51 36N 55 32W
Lansford, U.S.A. . . . . . . . . **85 F9** 40 50N 75 53W
Lansing, U.S.A. . . . . . . . . . **82 D3** 42 44N 84 33W
Lanta Yai, Ko, Thailand . . . . **39 J2** 7 35N 99 3 E
Lantau I., China . . . . . . . . . **33 G10** 22 15N 113 56 E
Lantian, China . . . . . . . . . . **34 G5** 34 11N 109 20 E
Lanus, Argentina . . . . . . . . **94 C4** 34 44S 58 27W
Lanusei, Italy . . . . . . . . . . **22 E3** 39 52N 9 34 E
Lanzarote, Canary Is. . . . . . . **24 F6** 29 0N 13 40W
Lanzarote ✈ (ACE), Canary Is. . **24 F6** 29 0N 13 30W
Lanzhou, China . . . . . . . . . **34 F2** 36 1N 103 52 E
Lao Bao, Laos . . . . . . . . . . **38 D6** 16 35N 106 30 E
Lao Cai, Vietnam . . . . . . . . **38 A4** 22 30N 103 57 E
Laoag, Phil. . . . . . . . . . . . **37 A6** 18 7N 120 34 E
Laoang, Phil. . . . . . . . . . . . **37 B7** 12 32N 125 8 E
Laoha He ➤, China . . . . . . **35 C11** 43 25N 120 35 E
Laois □, Ireland . . . . . . . . . **10 D4** 52 57N 7 36W
Laon, France . . . . . . . . . . . **20 B5** 49 33N 3 35 E
Laona, U.S.A. . . . . . . . . . . **82 C1** 45 34N 88 40W
Laos ■, Asia . . . . . . . . . . . **38 D5** 17 45N 105 0 E
Lapa, Brazil . . . . . . . . . . . **95 B6** 25 46S 49 44W
Lapeer, U.S.A. . . . . . . . . . . **82 D4** 43 3N 83 19W
Lapithos, Cyprus . . . . . . . . **25 D12** 35 21N 33 11 E

Lapland = Lappland, Europe . . . **8 B21** 68 7N 24 0 E
Laporte, U.S.A. . . . . . . . . . . **85 E8** 41 25N 76 30W
Lappeenranta, Finland . . . . . . **9 F23** 61 3N 28 12 E
Lappland, Europe . . . . . . . . . **8 B21** 68 7N 24 0 E
Lappo = Lapua, Finland . . . . . . **8 E20** 62 58N 23 0 E
Laprida, Argentina . . . . . . . . **94 D3** 37 34S 60 45W
Lapseki, Turkey . . . . . . . . . . **23 D12** 40 20N 26 41 E
Laptev Sea, Russia . . . . . . . . **29 B13** 76 0N 125 0 E
Lapua, Finland . . . . . . . . . . **8 E20** 62 58N 23 0 E
L'Aquila, Italy . . . . . . . . . . . **22 C5** 42 22N 13 22 E
Lār, Āzarbājān-e Sharqī, Iran . . **44 B5** 38 30N 47 52 E
Lār, Fārs, Iran . . . . . . . . . . . **45 E7** 27 40N 54 14 E
Laramie, U.S.A. . . . . . . . . . . **80 E2** 41 19N 105 35W
Laramie ➤, U.S.A. . . . . . . . . **76 F11** 42 13N 104 33W
Laramie Mts., U.S.A. . . . . . . . **80 E2** 42 0N 105 30W
Laranjeiras do Sul, Brazil . . . . **95 B5** 25 23S 52 23W
Larantuka, Indonesia . . . . . . . **37 F6** 8 21S 122 55 E
Larat, Indonesia . . . . . . . . . **37 F8** 7 0S 132 0 E
Larde, Mozam. . . . . . . . . . . **55 F4** 16 28S 39 43 E
Larder Lake, Canada . . . . . . . **72 C4** 48 5N 79 40W
Lárdhos, Ákra = Líndhos, Ákra,
    Greece . . . . . . . . . . . . **25 C10** 36 4N 28 10 E
Lárdhos, Órmos, Greece . . . . **25 C10** 36 4N 28 2 E
Laredo, U.S.A. . . . . . . . . . . **81 M5** 27 30N 99 30W
Laredo Sd., Canada . . . . . . . **70 C3** 52 30N 128 53W
Largo, U.S.A. . . . . . . . . . . . **83 M4** 27 55N 82 47W
Largs, U.K. . . . . . . . . . . . . **11 F4** 55 47N 4 52W
Lariang, Indonesia . . . . . . . . **37 E5** 1 26S 119 17 E
Larimore, U.S.A. . . . . . . . . . **80 B6** 47 54N 97 38W
Lárisa, Greece . . . . . . . . . . **23 E10** 39 36N 22 27 E
Larkana, Pakistan . . . . . . . . **42 F3** 27 32N 68 18 E
Larnaca, Cyprus . . . . . . . . . **25 E12** 34 55N 33 38 E
Larnaca Bay, Cyprus . . . . . . . **25 E12** 34 53N 33 45 E
Larne, U.K. . . . . . . . . . . . . **10 B6** 54 51N 5 51W
Larned, U.S.A. . . . . . . . . . . **80 F5** 38 11N 99 6W
Larose, U.S.A. . . . . . . . . . . **81 L9** 29 34N 90 23W
Larrimah, Australia . . . . . . . . **60 C5** 15 35S 133 12 E
Larsen Ice Shelf, Antarctica . . . **5 C17** 67 0S 62 0W
Larvik, Norway . . . . . . . . . . **9 G14** 59 4N 10 2 E
Las Animas, U.S.A. . . . . . . . . **80 F3** 38 4N 103 13W
Las Anod, Somali Rep. . . . . . . **47 F4** 8 26N 47 19 E
Las Brenãs, Argentina . . . . . . **94 B3** 27 5S 61 7W
Las Cañadas del Teide △,
    Canary Is. . . . . . . . . . . **24 F3** 28 15N 16 37W
Las Cejas, Argentina . . . . . . . **96 B4** 26 53S 64 44W
Las Chimeneas, Mexico . . . . . **79 N10** 32 8N 116 5W
Las Cruces, U.S.A. . . . . . . . . **77 K10** 32 19N 106 47W
Las Flores, Argentina . . . . . . . **94 D4** 36 10S 59 7W
Las Heras, Argentina . . . . . . . **94 C2** 32 51S 68 49W
Las Lajas, Argentina . . . . . . . **96 D2** 38 30S 70 25W
Las Lomitas, Argentina . . . . . . **94 A3** 24 43S 60 35W
Las Palmas, Argentina . . . . . . **94 B4** 27 8S 58 45W
Las Palmas, Canary Is. . . . . . **24 F4** 28 7N 15 26W
Las Palmas ➤, Mexico . . . . . . **79 N10** 32 26N 116 54W
Las Palmas ✈ (LPA), Canary Is. . **24 G4** 27 55N 15 25W
Las Piedras, Uruguay . . . . . . . **95 C4** 34 44S 56 14W
Las Pipinas, Argentina . . . . . . **94 D4** 35 30S 57 19W
Las Plumas, Argentina . . . . . . **96 E3** 43 40S 67 15W
Las Rosas, Argentina . . . . . . . **94 C3** 32 30S 61 35W
Las Tablas, Panama . . . . . . . **88 E3** 7 49N 80 14W
Las Termas, Argentina . . . . . . **94 B3** 27 29S 64 52W
Las Toscas, Argentina . . . . . . **94 B4** 28 21S 59 18W
Las Truchas, Mexico . . . . . . . **86 D4** 17 57N 102 13W
Las Varillas, Argentina . . . . . . **94 C3** 31 50S 62 50W
Las Vegas, N. Mex., U.S.A. . . . **77 J11** 35 36N 105 13W
Las Vegas, Nev., U.S.A. . . . . . **79 J11** 36 10N 115 9W
Las Vegas McCarran
    International ✈ (LAS), U.S.A. . **79 J11** 36 5N 115 9W
Lascano, Uruguay . . . . . . . . **95 C5** 33 35S 54 12W
Lash-e Joveyn, Afghan. . . . . . **40 D2** 31 45N 61 30 E
Lashburn, Canada . . . . . . . . **71 C7** 53 10N 109 40W
Lashio, Burma . . . . . . . . . . **41 H20** 22 56N 97 45 E
Lashkar, India . . . . . . . . . . . **42 F8** 26 10N 78 10 E
Lasithi, Greece . . . . . . . . . . **25 D7** 35 11N 25 31 E
Lasithi □, Greece . . . . . . . . . **25 D7** 35 5N 25 50 E
Lāsjerd, Iran . . . . . . . . . . . . **45 C7** 35 24N 53 4 E
Lassen Pk., U.S.A. . . . . . . . . **76 F3** 40 29N 121 31W
Lassen Volcanic △, U.S.A. . . . **76 F3** 40 30N 121 20W
Last Mountain L., Canada . . . . **71 C7** 51 5N 105 14W
Lastchance Cr. ➤, U.S.A. . . . . **78 E5** 40 2N 121 15W
Lastoursville, Gabon . . . . . . . **52 E2** 0 55S 12 38 E
Lastovo, Croatia . . . . . . . . . **22 C7** 42 46N 16 55 E
Lat Yao, Thailand . . . . . . . . **38 E2** 15 45N 99 48 E
Latacunga, Ecuador . . . . . . . **92 D3** 0 50S 78 35W
Latakia = Al Lādhiqīyah, Syria . . **44 C2** 35 30N 35 45 E
Latchford, Canada . . . . . . . . **72 C4** 47 20N 79 50W
Latehar, India . . . . . . . . . . . **43 H11** 23 45N 84 30 E
Latham, Australia . . . . . . . . . **61 E2** 29 44S 116 20 E
Lathi, India . . . . . . . . . . . . **42 F4** 27 43N 71 23 E
Lathrop Wells, U.S.A. . . . . . . . **79 J10** 36 39N 116 24W
Latina, Italy . . . . . . . . . . . . **22 D5** 41 28N 12 52 E
Latium = Lazio □, Italy . . . . . . **22 C5** 42 10N 12 30 E
Laton, U.S.A. . . . . . . . . . . . **78 J7** 36 26N 119 41W
Latouche Treville, C., Australia . **60 C3** 18 27S 121 49 E
Latrobe, Australia . . . . . . . . . **63 G4** 41 14S 146 30 E
Latrobe, U.S.A. . . . . . . . . . . **84 F5** 40 19N 79 23W
Latvia ■, Europe . . . . . . . . . **9 H20** 56 50N 24 0 E
Lau Fau Shan, China . . . . . . . **33 G10** 22 28N 113 59 E
Lau Group, Fiji . . . . . . . . . . **59 C9** 17 0S 178 30W
Lauchhammer, Germany . . . . . **16 C7** 51 29N 13 47 E
Laughlin, U.S.A. . . . . . . . . . **77 J6** 35 8N 114 35W
Laukaa, Finland . . . . . . . . . **9 E21** 62 24N 25 56 E
Launceston, Australia . . . . . . **63 G4** 41 24S 147 8 E
Launceston, U.K. . . . . . . . . . **13 G3** 50 38N 4 22W
Laune ➤, Ireland . . . . . . . . . **10 D2** 52 7N 9 47W
Launglon Bok, Burma . . . . . . **38 F1** 13 50N 97 54 E
Laura, Australia . . . . . . . . . . **62 B3** 15 32S 144 32 E
Laurel, Miss., U.S.A. . . . . . . . **81 K10** 31 41N 89 8W
Laurel, Mont., U.S.A. . . . . . . . **76 D9** 45 40N 108 46W
Laurencekirk, U.K. . . . . . . . . **11 E6** 56 50N 2 28W
Laurens, U.S.A. . . . . . . . . . . **83 H4** 34 30N 82 1W
Laurentian Plateau, Canada . . **73 B6** 52 0N 70 0W
Lauria, Italy . . . . . . . . . . . . **22 E6** 40 2N 15 50 E
Laurie L., Canada . . . . . . . . . **71 B8** 56 35N 101 57W
Laurinburg, U.S.A. . . . . . . . . **83 H6** 34 47N 79 28W
Laurium, U.S.A. . . . . . . . . . . **82 B1** 47 14N 88 27W
Lausanne, Switz. . . . . . . . . . **20 C7** 46 32N 6 38 E
Laut, Indonesia . . . . . . . . . . **36 D3** 4 45N 108 0 E
Laut, Pulau, Indonesia . . . . . . **36 E5** 3 40S 116 10 E
Laut Kecil, Kepulauan, Indonesia **36 E5** 4 45S 115 40 E
Lautoka, Fiji . . . . . . . . . . . . **59 C7** 17 37S 177 27 E
Lava Beds △, U.S.A. . . . . . . . **76 F3** 41 40N 121 30W
Lavagh More, Ireland . . . . . . **10 B3** 54 46N 8 6W
Laval, France . . . . . . . . . . . **20 B3** 48 4N 0 48W
Lavalle, Argentina . . . . . . . . **94 B2** 28 15S 65 15W
Lavant Station, Canada . . . . . **85 A8** 45 3N 76 42W
Lāvar Meydān, Iran . . . . . . . . **45 D7** 30 20N 54 30 E

Laverton, Australia . . . . . . . . **61 E3** 28 44S 122 29 E
Lavras, Brazil . . . . . . . . . . . **95 A7** 21 20S 45 0W
Lávrion, Greece . . . . . . . . . . **23 F11** 37 40N 24 4 E
Lávris, Greece . . . . . . . . . . . **25 D6** 35 25N 24 40 E
Lavumisa, Swaziland . . . . . . . **57 D5** 27 20S 31 55 E
Lavushi Manda △, Zambia . . . **55 E3** 12 46S 31 0 E
Lawas, Malaysia . . . . . . . . . **36 D5** 4 55N 115 25 E
Lawele, Indonesia . . . . . . . . **37 F6** 5 13S 122 57 E
Lawn Hill △, Australia . . . . . . **62 B2** 18 15S 138 6 E
Lawng Pit, Burma . . . . . . . . . **41 G20** 25 30N 97 25 E
Lawqah, Si. Arabia . . . . . . . . **44 D4** 29 49N 42 45 E
Lawrence, N.Z. . . . . . . . . . . **59 L2** 45 55S 169 41 E
Lawrence, Kans., U.S.A. . . . . . **80 F7** 38 58N 95 14W
Lawrence, Mass., U.S.A. . . . . **85 D13** 42 43N 71 10W
Lawrenceburg, Ind., U.S.A. . . . **82 F3** 39 6N 84 52W
Lawrenceburg, Tenn., U.S.A. . . **83 H2** 35 14N 87 20W
Lawrenceville, Ga., U.S.A. . . . **83 J4** 33 57N 83 59W
Lawrenceville, Pa., U.S.A. . . . **84 E7** 41 59N 77 8W
Laws, U.S.A. . . . . . . . . . . . **78 H8** 37 24N 118 20W
Lawton, U.S.A. . . . . . . . . . . **81 H5** 34 37N 98 25W
Lawu, Indonesia . . . . . . . . . **37 G14** 7 40S 111 13 E
Laxford, L., U.K. . . . . . . . . . **11 C3** 58 24N 5 6W
Layla, Si. Arabia . . . . . . . . . **47 C4** 22 10N 46 40 E
Laylān, Iraq . . . . . . . . . . . . **44 C5** 35 18N 44 31 E
Layton, U.S.A. . . . . . . . . . . **76 F7** 41 4N 111 58W
Laytonville, U.S.A. . . . . . . . . **76 G2** 39 41N 123 29W
Lazarivo, Madag. . . . . . . . . . **57 C8** 23 54S 44 59 E
Lazio □, Italy . . . . . . . . . . . **22 C5** 42 10N 12 30 E
Lazo, Russia . . . . . . . . . . . **30 C6** 43 25N 133 55 E
Le Bic, Canada . . . . . . . . . . **73 C6** 48 20N 68 41W
Le Creusot, France . . . . . . . . **20 C6** 46 48N 4 24 E
Le François, Martinique . . . . . **88 c** 14 38N 60 57W
Le Gosier, Guadeloupe . . . . . **88 b** 16 14N 61 29W
Le Havre, France . . . . . . . . . **20 B4** 49 30N 0 5 E
Le Lamentin, Martinique . . . . . **88 c** 14 35N 61 2W
Le Mans, France . . . . . . . . . **20 C4** 48 0N 0 10 E
Le Marin, Martinique . . . . . . . **88 c** 14 27N 60 55W
Le Mars, U.S.A. . . . . . . . . . . **80 D6** 42 47N 96 10W
Le Mont-St-Michel, France . . . **20 B3** 48 40N 1 30W
Le Moule, Guadeloupe . . . . . . **88 b** 16 20N 61 22W
Le Prêcheur, Martinique . . . . . **88 c** 14 50N 61 12W
Le Puy-en-Velay, France . . . . **20 D5** 45 3N 3 52 E
Le Robert, Martinique . . . . . . **88 c** 14 40N 60 56W
Le St-Esprit, Martinique . . . . . **88 c** 14 28N 60 53W
Le Sueur, U.S.A. . . . . . . . . . **80 C8** 44 28N 93 55W
Le Thuy, Vietnam . . . . . . . . . **38 D6** 17 14N 106 49 E
Le Touquet-Paris-Plage, France **20 A4** 50 30N 1 36 E
Le Tréport, France . . . . . . . . **20 A4** 50 3N 1 20 E
Le Verdon-sur-Mer, France . . . **20 D3** 45 33N 1 4W
Lea ➤, U.K. . . . . . . . . . . . . **13 F8** 51 31N 0 1 E
Leach, Cambodia . . . . . . . . . **39 F4** 12 21N 103 46 E
Lead, U.S.A. . . . . . . . . . . . . **80 C3** 44 21N 103 46W
Leader, Canada . . . . . . . . . . **71 C7** 50 50N 109 30W
Leadville, U.S.A. . . . . . . . . . **77 G10** 39 15N 106 18W
Leaf ➤, U.S.A. . . . . . . . . . . **81 K10** 30 59N 88 44W
Leaf Rapids, Canada . . . . . . . **71 B9** 56 30N 99 59W
Leamington, Canada . . . . . . . **84 D2** 42 3N 82 36W
Leamington, U.S.A. . . . . . . . **76 G7** 39 32N 112 17W
Leamington Spa = Royal
    Leamington Spa, U.K. . . . . **13 E6** 52 18N 1 31W
Leandro Norte Alem, Argentina **95 B4** 27 34S 55 15W
Leane, L., Ireland . . . . . . . . . **10 D2** 52 2N 9 32W
Learmonth, Australia . . . . . . . **60 D1** 22 13S 114 10 E
Leask, Canada . . . . . . . . . . **71 C7** 53 5N 106 45W
Leatherhead, U.K. . . . . . . . . **13 F7** 51 18N 0 20W
Leavenworth, Kans., U.S.A. . . . **80 F7** 39 19N 94 55W
Leavenworth, Wash., U.S.A. . . . **76 C3** 47 36N 120 40W
Lebak, Phil. . . . . . . . . . . . . **37 C6** 6 32N 124 5 E
Lebam, U.S.A. . . . . . . . . . . . **78 D3** 46 34N 123 33W
Lebanon, Ind., U.S.A. . . . . . . **82 E2** 40 3N 86 28W
Lebanon, Kans., U.S.A. . . . . . **80 F5** 39 49N 98 33W
Lebanon, Ky., U.S.A. . . . . . . **82 G3** 37 34N 85 15W
Lebanon, Mo., U.S.A. . . . . . . **81 G8** 37 41N 92 40W
Lebanon, N.H., U.S.A. . . . . . . **85 C12** 43 39N 72 15W
Lebanon, Oreg., U.S.A. . . . . . **76 D2** 44 32N 122 55W
Lebanon, Pa., U.S.A. . . . . . . **85 F8** 40 20N 76 26W
Lebanon, Tenn., U.S.A. . . . . . **83 G2** 36 12N 86 18W
Lebanon ■, Asia . . . . . . . . . **46 B5** 34 0N 36 0 E
Lebec, U.S.A. . . . . . . . . . . . **79 L8** 34 50N 118 52W
Lebel-sur-Quévillon, Canada . . **72 C4** 49 3N 76 59W
Lebomboberge, S. Africa . . . . **57 C5** 24 30S 32 0 E
Lębork, Poland . . . . . . . . . . **17 A9** 54 33N 17 46 E
Lebrija, Spain . . . . . . . . . . . **21 D2** 36 53N 6 5W
Lebu, Chile . . . . . . . . . . . . **94 D1** 37 40S 73 47W
Lecce, Italy . . . . . . . . . . . . **23 D8** 40 23N 18 11 E
Lecco, Italy . . . . . . . . . . . . **20 D8** 45 51N 9 23 E
Lech ➤, Germany . . . . . . . . **16 D6** 48 43N 10 56 E
Lecontes Mills, U.S.A. . . . . . . **84 E6** 41 5N 78 17W
Ledong, China . . . . . . . . . . **38 C7** 18 41N 109 5 E
Leduc, Canada . . . . . . . . . . **70 C6** 53 15N 113 30W
Lee ➤, Ireland . . . . . . . . . . **10 E3** 51 53N 8 56W
Lee Vining, U.S.A. . . . . . . . . **78 H7** 37 58N 119 7W
Leech L., U.S.A. . . . . . . . . . **80 B7** 47 10N 94 24W
Leechburg, U.S.A. . . . . . . . . **84 F5** 40 37N 79 36W
Leeds, U.K. . . . . . . . . . . . . **12 D6** 53 48N 1 33W
Leeds, U.S.A. . . . . . . . . . . . **83 J2** 33 33N 86 33W
Leek, Neths. . . . . . . . . . . . **15 A6** 53 10N 6 24 E
Leek, U.K. . . . . . . . . . . . . . **12 D5** 53 7N 2 1W
Leeman, Australia . . . . . . . . **61 E1** 29 57S 114 58 E
Leeper, U.S.A. . . . . . . . . . . **84 E5** 41 22N 79 18W
Leer, Germany . . . . . . . . . . **16 B4** 53 13N 7 26 E
Leesburg, U.S.A. . . . . . . . . . **83 L5** 28 49N 81 53W
Leeton, Australia . . . . . . . . . **63 E4** 34 33S 146 23 E
Leetonia, U.S.A. . . . . . . . . . **84 F4** 40 53N 80 45W
Leeu Gamka, S. Africa . . . . . **56 E3** 32 47S 21 59 E
Leeuwarden, Neths. . . . . . . . **15 A5** 53 15N 5 48 E
Leeuwin, C., Australia . . . . . . **61 F2** 34 20S 115 9 E
Leeuwin-Naturaliste △, Australia **61 F2** 34 6S 115 3 E
Leeward Is., Atl. Oc. . . . . . . . **89 C7** 16 30N 63 30W
Lefka, Cyprus . . . . . . . . . . . **25 D11** 35 6N 32 51 E
Lefkoniko, Cyprus . . . . . . . . **25 D12** 35 18N 33 44 E
Lefroy, L., Australia . . . . . . . . **61 F3** 31 21S 121 40 E
Lefroy, Canada . . . . . . . . . . **84 B5** 44 16N 79 34W
Leganés, Spain . . . . . . . . . . **21 B4** 40 19N 3 45W
Legazpi, Phil. . . . . . . . . . . . **37 B6** 13 10N 123 45 E
Legendre I., Australia . . . . . . **60 D2** 20 22S 116 55 E
Leghorn = Livorno, Italy . . . . . **22 C4** 43 33N 10 19 E
Legionowo, Poland . . . . . . . . **17 B11** 52 25N 20 50 E
Legnago, Italy . . . . . . . . . . . **22 B4** 45 11N 11 18 E
Legnica, Poland . . . . . . . . . **16 C9** 51 12N 16 10 E
Legume, Australia . . . . . . . . **63 D5** 28 20S 152 19 E
Leh, India . . . . . . . . . . . . . **43 B7** 34 9N 77 35 E
Lehigh Acres, U.S.A. . . . . . . . **83 M5** 26 36N 81 39W
Lehighton, U.S.A. . . . . . . . . . **85 F9** 40 50N 75 43W
Lehututu, Botswana . . . . . . . **56 C3** 23 54S 21 55 E
Leiah, Pakistan . . . . . . . . . . **42 D4** 30 58N 70 58 E

Leicester, U.K. . . . . . . . . . . . **13 E6** 52 38N 1 8W
Leicester City □, U.K. . . . . . . . **13 E6** 41 20S 45 0W
Leicestershire □, U.K. . . . . . . . **13 E6** 52 41N 1 17W
Leichhardt ➤, Australia . . . . . **62 B2** 17 35S 139 48 E
Leichhardt Ra., Australia . . . . . **62 C4** 20 46S 147 40 E
Leiden, Neths. . . . . . . . . . . . **15 B4** 52 9N 4 30 E
Leie ➤, Belgium . . . . . . . . . **15 C3** 51 2N 3 45 E
Leine ➤, Germany . . . . . . . . **16 B5** 52 43N 9 36 E
Leinster, Australia . . . . . . . . . **61 E3** 27 51S 120 36 E
Leinster □, Ireland . . . . . . . . . **10 C4** 53 3N 7 8W
Leinster, Mt., Ireland . . . . . . . **10 D5** 52 37N 6 46W
Leipzig, Germany . . . . . . . . . **16 C7** 51 18N 12 22 E
Leiria, Portugal . . . . . . . . . . **21 C1** 39 46N 8 53W
Leirvik, Norway . . . . . . . . . . **9 G11** 59 47N 5 28 E
Leisler, Mt., Australia . . . . . . . **60 D4** 23 23S 129 20 E
Leith, U.K. . . . . . . . . . . . . . **11 F5** 55 59N 3 11W
Leith Hill, U.K. . . . . . . . . . . . **13 F7** 51 11N 0 22W
Leitrim, Ireland . . . . . . . . . . . **10 B3** 54 0N 8 5W
Leitrim □, Ireland . . . . . . . . . **10 B4** 54 8N 8 0W
Leizhou Bandao, China . . . . . . **33 D6** 21 0N 110 0 E
Lek ➤, Neths. . . . . . . . . . . . **15 C4** 51 54N 4 35 E
Leka, Norway . . . . . . . . . . . **8 D14** 65 5N 11 35 E
Lékva Óros, Greece . . . . . . . . **25 D6** 35 18N 24 3 E
Leland, Mich., U.S.A. . . . . . . . **82 C3** 45 1N 85 45W
Leland, Miss., U.S.A. . . . . . . . **81 J9** 33 24N 90 54W
Leleque, Argentina . . . . . . . . **96 E2** 42 28S 71 0W
Lelystad, Neths. . . . . . . . . . . **15 B5** 52 30N 5 25 E
Léman, L., Europe . . . . . . . . . **20 C7** 46 26N 6 30 E
Lembar, Indonesia . . . . . . . . **37 K19** 8 45S 116 4 E
Lembuak, Indonesia . . . . . . . **37 K19** 8 36S 116 11 E
Lemera, Dem. Rep. of the Congo **54 C2** 3 0S 28 55 E
Lemhi Ra., U.S.A. . . . . . . . . . **76 D7** 44 30N 113 30W
Lemmer, Neths. . . . . . . . . . . **15 B5** 52 51N 5 43 E
Lemmon, U.S.A. . . . . . . . . . . **80 C3** 45 57N 102 10W
Lemon Grove, U.S.A. . . . . . . . **79 N9** 32 45N 117 2W
Lemoore, U.S.A. . . . . . . . . . . **78 J7** 36 18N 119 46W
Lemvig, Denmark . . . . . . . . . **9 H13** 56 33N 8 20 E
Lena ➤, Russia . . . . . . . . . . **29 B13** 72 52N 126 40 E
Léndas, Greece . . . . . . . . . . **25 E6** 34 56N 24 56 E
Lendeh, Iran . . . . . . . . . . . . **45 D6** 30 58N 50 25 E
Lenggong, Malaysia . . . . . . . **39 K3** 5 6N 100 58 E
Lengua de Vaca, Pta., Chile . . . **94 C1** 30 14S 71 38W
Lengwe △, Malawi . . . . . . . . **55 F3** 16 14S 34 45 E
Leninogorsk, Kazakhstan . . . . **28 D9** 50 20N 83 30 E
Leninsk, Russia . . . . . . . . . . **19 E8** 48 40N 45 15 E
Leninsk-Kuznetskiy, Russia . . . **28 D9** 54 44N 86 10 E
Lenmalu, Indonesia . . . . . . . . **37 E8** 1 45S 130 15 E
Lennox, U.S.A. . . . . . . . . . . . **80 D6** 43 21N 96 53W
Lennoxville, Canada . . . . . . . **85 A13** 45 22N 71 51W
Lenoir, U.S.A. . . . . . . . . . . . **83 H5** 35 55N 81 32W
Lenoir City, U.S.A. . . . . . . . . **83 H3** 35 48N 84 16W
Lenore L., Canada . . . . . . . . **71 C8** 52 30N 104 59W
Lenox, U.S.A. . . . . . . . . . . . **85 D11** 42 22N 73 17W
Lens, France . . . . . . . . . . . . **20 A5** 50 26N 2 50 E
Lensk, Russia . . . . . . . . . . . **29 C12** 60 48N 114 55 E
Lentini, Italy . . . . . . . . . . . . **22 F6** 37 17N 15 0 E
Lenwood, U.S.A. . . . . . . . . . **79 L9** 34 53N 117 7W
Lenya, Burma . . . . . . . . . . . **36 B1** 11 33N 98 57 E
Leoben, Austria . . . . . . . . . . **16 E8** 47 22N 15 5 E
Leodhas = Lewis, U.K. . . . . . . **11 C2** 58 9N 6 40W
Leola, U.S.A. . . . . . . . . . . . **80 C5** 45 43N 98 56W
Leominster, U.K. . . . . . . . . . **13 E5** 52 14N 2 43W
Leominster, U.S.A. . . . . . . . . **85 D13** 42 32N 71 46W
León, Mexico . . . . . . . . . . . **86 C4** 21 7N 101 40W
León, Nic. . . . . . . . . . . . . . **88 D2** 12 20N 86 51W
León, Spain . . . . . . . . . . . . **21 A3** 42 38N 5 34W
León, U.S.A. . . . . . . . . . . . . **80 E8** 40 44N 93 45W
León □, Spain . . . . . . . . . . . **21 K6** 31 14N 97 28W
León, Montes de, Spain . . . . . **21 A2** 42 30N 6 18W
Leonardtown, U.S.A. . . . . . . . **82 F7** 38 17N 76 38W
Leonardville, Namibia . . . . . . **56 C2** 23 29S 18 49 E
Leongatha, Australia . . . . . . . **63 F4** 38 30S 145 58 E
Leonora, Australia . . . . . . . . . **61 E3** 28 49S 121 19 E
Leopoldina, Brazil . . . . . . . . . **95 A7** 21 28S 42 40W
Leopoldsburg, Belgium . . . . . **15 C5** 51 7N 5 13 E
Leoti, U.S.A. . . . . . . . . . . . . **80 F4** 38 29N 101 21W
Leova, Moldova . . . . . . . . . . **17 E15** 46 28N 28 15 E
Leoville, Canada . . . . . . . . . **71 C7** 53 39N 107 33W
Lepel = Lyepyel, Belarus . . . . **18 D4** 54 50N 28 40 E
Lépo, L. do, Angola . . . . . . . . **56 B2** 17 0S 19 0 E
Leppävirta, Finland . . . . . . . . **9 E22** 62 29N 27 46 E
Lerdo, Mexico . . . . . . . . . . . **86 B4** 25 32N 103 32W
Léribe, Lesotho . . . . . . . . . . **57 D4** 28 51S 28 3 E
Lérida = Lleida, Spain . . . . . . **21 B6** 41 37N 0 39 E
Lerwick, U.K. . . . . . . . . . . . **11 A7** 60 9N 1 9W
Les Cayes, Haiti . . . . . . . . . . **89 C5** 18 15N 73 46W
Les Coteaux, Canada . . . . . . **85 A10** 45 15N 74 13W
Les Sables-d'Olonne, France . . **20 C3** 46 30N 1 45W
Lesbos = Lésvos, Greece . . . . **23 E12** 39 10N 26 20 E
Leshan, China . . . . . . . . . . . **32 D5** 29 33N 103 41 E
Leshukonskoye, Russia . . . . . **18 B8** 64 54N 45 46 E
Leshwe △, Dem. Rep. of
    the Congo . . . . . . . . . . . **55 E2** 12 45S 29 30 E
Leskov I., Antarctica . . . . . . . **5 B1** 56 0S 28 0W
Leskovac, Serbia & M. . . . . . . **23 C9** 43 0N 21 58 E
Lesopilnoye, Russia . . . . . . . **30 A7** 46 44N 134 20 E
Lesotho ■, Africa . . . . . . . . . **57 D4** 29 40S 28 0 E
Lesozavodsk, Russia . . . . . . . **29 E14** 45 30N 133 29 E
Lesse ➤, Belgium . . . . . . . . **15 D4** 50 15N 4 54 E
Lesse et Lomme ○, Belgium . . **15 D5** 50 8N 5 9 E
Lesser Antilles, W. Indies . . . . **89 D7** 15 0N 61 0W
Lesser Slave L., Canada . . . . **70 B5** 55 30N 115 25W
Lesser Sunda Is., Indonesia . . **37 F6** 8 0S 120 0 E
Lessines, Belgium . . . . . . . . **15 D3** 50 42N 3 50 E
Lester, U.S.A. . . . . . . . . . . . **78 C5** 47 12N 121 29W
Lester B. Pearson International,
    Toronto ✈ (YYZ), Canada . . **84 C5** 43 40N 79 34W
Lestock, Canada . . . . . . . . . **71 C8** 51 19N 103 59W
Lesueur I., Australia . . . . . . . **60 B4** 13 50S 127 17 E
Lesueur ○, Australia . . . . . . . **61 F2** 30 11S 115 10 E
Lésvos, Greece . . . . . . . . . . **23 E12** 39 10N 26 20 E
Leszno, Poland . . . . . . . . . . **17 C9** 51 50N 16 30 E
Letaba, S. Africa . . . . . . . . . **57 C5** 23 59S 31 50 E
Letchworth, U.K. . . . . . . . . . **13 F7** 51 59N 0 13W
Lethbridge, Canada . . . . . . . **70 D6** 49 45N 112 45W
Lethem, Guyana . . . . . . . . . **92 C7** 3 20N 59 50W
Leti, Kepulauan, Indonesia . . . **37 F7** 8 10S 128 0 E
Leti Is. = Leti, Kepulauan,
    Indonesia . . . . . . . . . . . **37 F7** 8 10S 128 0 E
Letiahau ➤, Botswana . . . . . **56 C3** 21 16S 24 0 E
Leticia, Colombia . . . . . . . . . **92 D5** 4 9S 70 0W
Leting, China . . . . . . . . . . . **35 E10** 39 23N 118 55 E
Letjiesbos, S. Africa . . . . . . . **56 E3** 32 34S 22 16 E
Letlhakane, Botswana . . . . . . **56 C4** 21 27S 25 30 E
Letlhakeng, Botswana . . . . . . **56 C4** 24 0S 24 59 E
Letong, Indonesia . . . . . . . . **36 D3** 2 58N 105 42 E
Letpadan, Burma . . . . . . . . . **41 L19** 17 45N 95 45 E

Letpan, Burma ............. 41 K19 19 28N 94 10 E
Letsôk-aw Kyun, Burma ...... 39 G2 11 30N 98 25 E
Letterkenny, Ireland ........ 10 B4 54 57N 7 45W
Leucadia, U.S.A. .......... 79 M9 33 4N 117 18W
Leuchars, U.K. ............ 11 E6 56 24N 2 53W
Leuser, G., Indonesia ....... 36 D1 3 46N 97 12 E
Leuven, Belgium ........... 15 D4 50 52N 4 42 E
Leuze-en-Hainaut, Belgium ... 15 D3 50 36N 3 37 E
Levádhia, Greece ........... 23 E10 38 27N 22 54 E
Levanger, Norway .......... 8 E14 63 45N 11 19 E
Levelland, U.S.A. .......... 81 J3 33 35N 102 23W
Leven, U.K. ............... 11 E6 56 12N 3 0W
Leven, L., U.K. ............ 11 E5 56 12N 3 22W
Leven, Toraka, Madag. ...... 57 A8 12 30S 47 45 E
Leveque C., Australia ....... 60 C3 16 20S 123 0 E
Levice, Slovak Rep. ......... 17 D10 48 13N 18 35 E
Levin, N.Z. ............... 59 J5 40 37S 175 18 E
Lévis, Canada ............. 73 C5 46 48N 71 9W
Levis, L., Canada .......... 70 A5 62 37N 117 58W
Levittown, N.Y., U.S.A. ...... 85 F11 40 44N 73 31W
Levittown, Pa., U.S.A. ...... 85 F10 40 9N 74 51W
Levkás, Greece ............ 23 E9 38 40N 20 43 E
Levkímmi, Greece .......... 25 B4 39 25N 20 3 E
Levkímmi, Ákra, Greece ..... 25 B4 39 29N 20 4 E
Levkôsia = Nicosia, Cyprus ... 25 D12 35 10N 33 25 E
Levskigrad = Karlovo, Bulgaria . 23 C11 42 38N 24 47 E
Lewes, U.K. ............... 13 G8 50 52N 0 1 E
Lewes, U.S.A. ............. 82 F8 38 46N 75 9W
Lewis, U.K. ............... 11 C2 58 9N 6 40W
Lewis →, U.S.A. ............ 78 E4 45 51N 122 48W
Lewis, Butt of, U.K. ........ 11 C2 58 31N 6 16W
Lewis Ra., Australia ........ 60 D4 20 3S 128 50 E
Lewis Range, U.S.A. ........ 76 C7 48 5N 113 5W
Lewis Run, U.S.A. .......... 84 E6 41 52N 78 40W
Lewisburg, Pa., U.S.A. ...... 84 F8 40 58N 76 54W
Lewisburg, Tenn., U.S.A. .... 83 H2 35 27N 86 48W
Lewisburg, W. Va., U.S.A. .... 82 G5 37 48N 80 27W
Lewisporte, Canada ........ 73 C8 49 15N 55 3W
Lewiston, Idaho, U.S.A. ..... 76 C5 46 25N 117 1W
Lewiston, Maine, U.S.A. ..... 83 C11 44 6N 70 13W
Lewiston, N.Y., U.S.A. ...... 84 C5 43 11N 79 3W
Lewistown, Mont., U.S.A. .... 76 C9 47 4N 109 26W
Lewistown, Pa., U.S.A. ...... 84 F7 40 36N 77 34W
Lexington, Ill., U.S.A. ...... 80 E10 40 39N 88 47W
Lexington, Ky., U.S.A. ...... 82 F3 38 3N 84 30W
Lexington, Mich., U.S.A. .... 84 C2 43 16N 82 32W
Lexington, Mo., U.S.A. ...... 80 F8 39 11N 93 52W
Lexington, N.C., U.S.A. ..... 83 H5 35 49N 80 15W
Lexington, N.Y., U.S.A. ..... 85 D10 42 15N 74 22W
Lexington, Nebr., U.S.A. .... 80 E5 40 47N 99 45W
Lexington, Ohio, U.S.A. ..... 84 F2 40 41N 82 35W
Lexington, Tenn., U.S.A. .... 83 H1 35 39N 88 24W
Lexington, Va., U.S.A. ...... 82 G6 37 47N 79 27W
Lexington Park, U.S.A. ...... 82 F7 38 16N 76 27W
Leyburn, U.K. ............. 12 C6 54 19N 1 48W
Leyland, U.K. ............. 12 D5 53 42N 2 43W
Leyte □, Phil. ............. 37 B6 11 0N 125 0 E
Lezhë, Albania ............ 23 D8 41 47N 19 39 E
Lhasa, China .............. 32 D4 29 25N 90 58 E
Lhazê, China .............. 32 D3 29 5N 87 38 E
Lhokkruet, Indonesia ....... 36 D1 4 55N 95 24 E
Lhokseumawe, Indonesia .... 36 C1 5 10N 97 10 E
L'Hospitalet de Llobregat, Spain . 21 B7 41 21N 2 6 E
Li, Thailand .............. 38 D2 17 48N 98 57 E
Li Xian, Gansu, China ....... 34 G3 34 10N 105 5 E
Li Xian, Hebei, China ....... 34 E8 38 30N 115 35 E
Liancourt Rocks = Tok-do, Asia . 31 F5 37 15N 131 52 E
Lianga, Phil. .............. 37 C7 8 38N 126 6 E
Liangcheng,
  Nei Monggol Zizhiqu, China . 34 D7 40 28N 112 25 E
Liangcheng, Shandong, China . 35 G10 35 32N 119 37 E
Liangdang, China .......... 34 H4 33 56N 106 18 E
Liangpran, Indonesia ....... 36 D4 1 4N 114 23 E
Lianshanguan, China ....... 35 D12 40 53N 123 43 E
Lianshui, China ........... 35 H10 33 42N 119 20 E
Lianyungang, China ........ 35 G10 34 40N 119 11 E
Liao He →, China .......... 35 D11 41 0N 121 50 E
Liaocheng, China .......... 34 F8 36 28N 115 58 E
Liaodong Bandao, China .... 35 E12 40 0N 122 30 E
Liaodong Wan, China ....... 35 D11 40 20N 121 10 E
Liaoning □, China ......... 35 D12 41 40N 122 30 E
Liaotung, G. of = Liaodong Wan,
  China ................. 35 D11 40 20N 121 10 E
Liaoyang, China ........... 35 D12 41 15N 122 58 E
Liaoyuan, China ........... 35 C13 42 58N 125 2 E
Liaozhong, China .......... 35 D12 41 23N 122 50 E
Liard →, Canada .......... 70 A4 61 51N 121 18W
Liard River, Canada ........ 70 B3 59 25N 126 5W
Liari, Pakistan ............ 42 G2 25 37N 66 30 E
Libau = Liepāja, Latvia ...... 9 H19 56 30N 21 0 E
Libby, U.S.A. ............. 76 B6 48 23N 115 33W
Libenge, Dem. Rep. of the Congo 52 D3 3 40N 18 55 E
Liberal, U.S.A. ............ 81 G4 37 3N 100 55W
Liberec, Czech Rep. ........ 16 C8 50 47N 15 7 E
Liberia, Costa Rica ........ 88 D2 10 40N 85 30W
Liberia ■, W. Afr. .......... 50 G4 6 30N 9 30W
Liberty, Mo., U.S.A. ........ 80 F7 39 15N 94 25W
Liberty, N.Y., U.S.A. ........ 85 E10 41 48N 74 45W
Liberty, Pa., U.S.A. ........ 84 E7 41 34N 77 6W
Liberty, Tex., U.S.A. ........ 81 K7 30 3N 94 48W
Lîbîya, Sahrâ', Africa ....... 51 C10 25 0N 25 0 E
Libobo, Tanjung, Indonesia ... 37 E7 0 54S 128 28 E
Libode, S. Africa ........... 57 E4 31 33S 29 2 E
Libourne, France .......... 20 D3 44 55N 0 14W
Libramont, Belgium ........ 15 E5 49 55N 5 23 E
Libreville, Gabon .......... 52 D1 0 25N 9 26 E
Libya ■, N. Afr. ........... 51 C9 27 0N 17 0 E
Libyan Desert = Lîbîya, Sahrâ',
  Africa ................. 51 C10 25 0N 25 0 E
Licantén, Chile ............ 94 D1 35 55S 72 0W
Licata, Italy .............. 22 F5 37 6N 13 56 E
Licheng, China ............ 34 F7 36 28N 113 20 E
Lichfield, U.K. ............ 13 E6 52 41N 1 49W
Lichinga, Mozam. .......... 55 E4 13 13S 35 11 E
Lichtenburg, S. Africa ....... 56 D4 26 8S 26 8 E
Licking →, U.S.A. .......... 82 F3 39 6N 84 30W
Licungo →, Mozam. ........ 55 F4 17 40S 37 15 E
Lida, Belarus ............. 9 K21 53 53N 25 15 E
Lidköping, Sweden ......... 9 G15 58 31N 13 14 E
Liebig, Mt., Australia ....... 60 D5 23 18S 131 22 E
Liechtenstein ■, Europe ..... 18 E5 47 8N 9 35 E
Liège, Belgium ............ 15 D5 50 38N 5 35 E
Liège □, Belgium .......... 15 D5 50 32N 5 35 E
Liegnitz = Legnica, Poland ... 16 C9 51 12N 16 10 E
Lienart, Dem. Rep. of the Congo 54 B2 3 3N 25 31 E
Lienyünchiangshih =
  Lianyungang, China ...... 35 G10 34 40N 119 11 E
Lienz, Austria ............ 16 E7 46 50N 12 46 E

Liepāja, Latvia ............ 9 H19 56 30N 21 0 E
Lier, Belgium ............. 15 C4 51 7N 4 34 E
Lièvre →, Canada ......... 72 C4 45 31N 75 26W
Liffey →, Ireland .......... 10 C5 53 21N 6 13W
Lifford, Ireland ........... 10 B4 54 51N 7 29W
Lifudzin, Russia ........... 30 B7 44 21N 134 58 E
Lightning Ridge, Australia ... 63 D4 29 22S 148 0 E
Ligonha →, Mozam. ........ 55 F4 16 54S 39 9 E
Ligonier, U.S.A. ........... 84 F5 40 15N 79 14W
Liguria □, Italy ........... 20 D8 44 30N 8 50 E
Ligurian Sea, Medit. S. ...... 22 C3 43 20N 9 0 E
Lihou Reefs and Cays, Australia 62 B5 17 25S 151 40 E
Lihue, U.S.A. ............. 74 H15 21 59N 159 23W
Lihué Calel △, Argentina .... 94 D2 38 0S 65 10W
Lijiang, China ............ 32 D5 26 55N 100 20 E
Likasi, Dem. Rep. of the Congo 55 E2 10 55S 26 48 E
Likoma I., Malawi .......... 55 E3 12 3S 34 45 E
Likumburu, Tanzania ....... 55 D4 9 43S 35 8 E
Lille, France .............. 20 A5 50 38N 3 3 E
Lille Bælt, Denmark ........ 9 J13 55 20N 9 45 E
Lillehammer, Norway ....... 9 F14 61 8N 10 30 E
Lillesand, Norway ......... 9 G13 58 15N 8 23 E
Lillian Pt., Australia ........ 61 E4 27 40S 126 6 E
Lillooet, Canada ........... 70 C4 50 44N 121 57W
Lillooet →, Canada ........ 70 D4 49 15N 121 57W
Lilongwe, Malawi .......... 55 E3 14 0S 33 48 E
Liloy, Phil. ............... 37 C6 8 4N 122 39 E
Lim →, Bos.-H. ........... 23 C8 43 45N 19 15 E
Lim Chu Kang, Singapore .... 39 d 1 26N 103 43 E
Lima, Indonesia ........... 37 E7 3 39S 127 58 E
Lima, Peru ............... 92 F3 12 0S 77 0W
Lima, Mont., U.S.A. ........ 76 D7 44 38N 112 36W
Lima, Ohio, U.S.A. ......... 82 E3 40 44N 84 6W
Lima →, Portugal .......... 21 B1 41 41N 8 50W
Liman, Indonesia .......... 37 G14 7 48S 111 45 E
Limassol, Cyprus .......... 25 E12 34 42N 33 1 E
Limavady, U.K. ............ 10 A5 55 3N 6 56W
Limay →, Argentina ........ 96 D3 39 0S 68 0W
Limay Mahuida, Argentina ... 94 D2 37 10S 66 45W
Limbang, Brunei ........... 36 D5 4 42N 115 6 E
Limbaži, Latvia ........... 9 H21 57 31N 24 42 E
Limbdi, India ............. 42 H4 22 34N 71 51 E
Limbe, Cameroon .......... 52 D1 4 1N 9 10 E
Limburg, Germany ......... 16 C5 50 22N 8 4 E
Limburg □, Belgium ........ 15 C5 51 2N 5 25 E
Limburg □, Neths. ......... 15 C5 51 20N 5 55 E
Limeira, Brazil ............ 95 A6 22 35S 47 28W
Limerick, Ireland .......... 10 D3 52 40N 8 37W
Limerick, U.S.A. ........... 85 C14 43 41N 70 48W
Limerick □, Ireland ........ 10 D3 52 30N 8 50W
Limestone →, Canada ...... 84 D6 42 2N 78 38W
Limestone →, Canada ...... 71 B10 56 31N 94 7W
Limfjorden, Denmark ....... 9 H13 56 55N 9 0 E
Limia = Lima →, Portugal ... 21 B1 41 41N 8 50W
Limingen, Norway ......... 8 D15 64 48N 13 35 E
Limmen Bight, Australia ..... 62 A2 14 40S 135 35 E
Limmen Bight →, Australia .. 62 B2 15 7S 135 44 E
Límnos, Greece ........... 23 E11 39 50N 25 5 E
Limoges, Canada .......... 85 A9 45 20N 75 16W
Limoges, France ........... 20 D4 45 50N 1 15 E
Limón, Costa Rica ......... 88 E3 10 0N 83 2W
Limon, U.S.A. ............. 80 F3 39 16N 103 41W
Limousin □, France ........ 20 D4 45 30N 1 30 E
Limoux, France ........... 20 E5 43 4N 2 12 E
Limpopo □, S. Africa ....... 57 C4 24 5S 29 0 E
Limpopo →, Africa ........ 57 D5 25 5S 33 30 E
Limuru, Kenya ............ 54 C4 1 2S 36 35 E
Lin Xian, China ........... 34 F6 37 57N 110 58 E
Linares, Chile ............ 94 D1 35 50S 71 40W
Linares, Mexico ........... 87 C5 24 50N 99 40W
Linares, Spain ............ 21 C4 38 10N 3 40W
Lincheng, China ........... 34 F8 37 25N 114 30 E
Lincoln = Beamsville, Canada . 84 C5 43 12N 79 28W
Lincoln, Argentina ......... 94 C3 34 55S 61 30W
Lincoln, N.Z. ............. 59 K4 43 38S 172 30 E
Lincoln, U.K. ............. 12 D7 53 14N 0 32W
Lincoln, Calif., U.S.A. ....... 78 G5 38 54N 121 17W
Lincoln, Ill., U.S.A. ........ 80 E10 40 9N 89 22W
Lincoln, Kans., U.S.A. ...... 80 F5 39 3N 98 9W
Lincoln, Maine, U.S.A. ...... 83 C11 45 22N 68 30W
Lincoln, N.H., U.S.A. ....... 85 B13 44 3N 71 40W
Lincoln, N. Mex., U.S.A. ..... 77 K11 33 30N 105 23W
Lincoln, Nebr., U.S.A. ...... 80 E6 40 49N 96 41W
Lincoln City, U.S.A. ........ 76 D1 44 57N 124 1W
Lincoln Hav = Lincoln Sea, Arctic 4 A5 84 0N 55 0W
Lincoln Sea, Arctic ........ 4 A5 84 0N 55 0W
Lincolnshire □, U.K. ....... 12 D7 53 14N 0 32W
Lincolnshire Wolds, U.K. .... 12 D7 53 26N 0 13W
Lincolnton, U.S.A. ......... 83 H5 35 29N 81 16W
Lind, U.S.A. .............. 76 C4 46 58N 118 37W
Linda, U.S.A. ............. 78 F5 39 8N 121 34W
Lindeman I., Australia ...... 62 J7 20 27S 149 3 E
Linden, Guyana ........... 92 B7 6 0N 58 10W
Linden, Ala., U.S.A. ........ 83 J2 32 18N 87 48W
Linden, Calif., U.S.A. ....... 78 G5 38 1N 121 5W
Linden, Tex., U.S.A. ........ 81 J7 33 1N 94 22W
Lindenhurst, U.S.A. ........ 85 F11 40 41N 73 23W
Lindesnes, Norway ........ 9 H12 57 58N 7 3 E
Líndhos, Greece ........... 25 C10 36 6N 28 4 E
Líndhos, Ákra, Greece ...... 25 C10 36 4N 28 10 E
Lindi, Tanzania ........... 55 D4 9 58S 39 38 E
Lindi □, Tanzania .......... 55 D4 9 40S 38 30 E
Lindi →, Dem. Rep. of the Congo 54 B2 0 33N 25 5 E
Lindsay, Canada ........... 84 B6 44 22N 78 43W
Lindsay, Calif., U.S.A. ...... 78 J7 36 12N 119 5W
Lindsay, Okla., U.S.A. ...... 81 H6 34 50N 97 38W
Lindsborg, U.S.A. ......... 80 F6 38 35N 97 40W
Line Islands, Pac. Oc. ...... 65 H12 7 0N 160 0W
Linesville, U.S.A. .......... 84 E4 41 39N 80 26W
Linfen, China ............. 34 F6 36 3N 111 30 E
Ling Xian, China .......... 34 F9 37 22N 116 30 E
Lingao, China ............. 38 C7 19 56N 109 42 E
Lingayen, Phil. ........... 37 A6 16 1N 120 14 E
Lingayen G., Phil. ......... 37 A6 16 10N 120 15 E
Lingbi, China ............. 35 H9 33 33N 117 33 E
Lingchuan, China ......... 34 G7 35 45N 113 12 E
Lingding Yang, China ....... 33 G10 22 25N 113 45 E
Lingen, Germany .......... 16 B4 52 31N 7 19 E
Lingga, Indonesia ......... 36 E2 0 10S 104 37 E
Lingga, Kepulauan, Indonesia . 36 E2 0 10S 104 30 E
Lingga Arch. = Lingga,
  Kepulauan, Indonesia ..... 36 E2 0 10S 104 30 E
Lingle, U.S.A. ............. 80 D2 42 8N 104 21W
Lingqiu, China ............ 34 E8 39 28N 114 22 E
Lingshi, China ............ 34 F6 36 48N 111 48 E
Lingshou, China .......... 34 E8 38 20N 114 20 E
Lingtai, China ............ 34 G4 35 0N 107 40 E

Linguère, Senegal ......... 50 E2 15 25N 15 5W
Lingwu, China ............ 34 E4 38 6N 106 20 E
Lingyuan, China .......... 35 D10 41 10N 119 15 E
Linhai, China ............. 33 D7 28 50N 121 8 E
Linhares, Brazil ........... 93 G10 19 25S 40 4W
Linhe, China ............. 34 D4 40 48N 107 20 E
Linjiang, China ........... 35 D14 41 50N 127 0 E
Linköping, Sweden ........ 9 G16 58 28N 15 36 E
Linkou, China ............ 35 B16 45 15N 130 18 E
Linnhe, L., U.K. ........... 11 E3 56 36N 5 25W
Linqi, China .............. 34 G7 35 45N 113 52 E
Linqing, China ............ 34 F8 36 50N 115 42 E
Linqu, China ............. 35 F10 36 25N 118 30 E
Linru, China ............. 34 G7 34 11N 112 52 E
Lins, Brazil .............. 95 A6 21 40S 49 44W
Linstead, Jamaica ......... 88 a 18 8N 77 2W
Linta →, Madag. .......... 57 D7 25 2S 44 5 E
Linton, Ind., U.S.A. ........ 82 F2 39 2N 87 10W
Linton, N. Dak., U.S.A. ..... 80 B4 46 16N 100 14W
Lintong, China ............ 34 G5 34 20N 109 10 E
Linwood, Canada .......... 84 C4 43 35N 80 43W
Linxi, China .............. 35 C10 43 36N 118 2 E
Linxia, China ............. 32 C5 35 36N 103 10 E
Linyanti →, Africa ......... 56 B4 17 50S 25 5 E
Linyi, China .............. 35 G10 35 5N 118 21 E
Linz, Austria ............. 16 D8 48 18N 14 18 E
Linzhenzhen, China ........ 34 F5 36 30N 109 59 E
Linzi, China .............. 35 F10 36 50N 118 20 E
Lion, G. du, France ........ 20 E6 43 10N 4 0 E
Lionárisso, Cyprus ........ 25 D13 35 28N 34 8 E
Lions, G. of = Lion, G. du, France 20 E6 43 10N 4 0 E
Lion's Den, Zimbabwe ...... 55 F3 17 15S 30 5 E
Lion's Head, Canada ....... 84 B3 44 58N 81 15W
Lipa, Phil. ............... 37 B6 13 57N 121 10 E
Lipali, Mozam. ............ 55 F4 15 50S 35 50 E
Lipari, Italy .............. 22 E6 38 26N 14 58 E
Lipari, Is. = Éólie, Ís., Italy .... 22 E6 38 30N 14 57 E
Lipcani, Moldova .......... 17 D14 48 14N 26 48 E
Lipetsk, Russia ........... 18 D6 52 37N 39 35 E
Lipkany = Lipcani, Moldova .. 17 D14 48 14N 26 48 E
Lipovcy Manzovka, Russia ... 30 B5 44 12N 132 26 E
Lipovets, Ukraine ......... 17 D15 49 12N 29 1 E
Lippe →, Germany ......... 16 C4 51 39N 6 36 E
Lipscomb, U.S.A. .......... 81 G4 36 14N 100 16W
Liptrap, C., Australia ....... 63 F4 38 50S 145 55 E
Liria = Lliria, Spain ........ 21 C5 39 37N 0 35W
Lisala, Dem. Rep. of the Congo . 52 D4 2 12N 21 38 E
Lisboa, Portugal .......... 21 C1 38 42N 9 10W
Lisbon = Lisboa, Portugal ... 21 C1 38 42N 9 10W
Lisbon, N. Dak., U.S.A. ..... 80 B6 46 27N 97 41W
Lisbon, N.H., U.S.A. ....... 85 B13 44 13N 71 55W
Lisbon, Ohio, U.S.A. ....... 84 F4 40 46N 80 46W
Lisbon Falls, U.S.A. ........ 83 D10 44 0N 70 4W
Lisburn, U.K. ............. 10 B5 54 31N 6 3W
Lisburne, C., U.S.A. ........ 4 C17 68 53N 166 13W
Liscannor B., Ireland ....... 10 D2 52 55N 9 24W
Lishi, China .............. 34 F6 37 31N 111 8 E
Lishu, China ............. 35 C13 43 20N 124 18 E
Lisianski I., Pac. Oc. ....... 64 E10 26 2N 174 0W
Lisichansk = Lysychansk, Ukraine 19 E6 48 55N 38 30 E
Lisieux, France ........... 20 B4 49 10N 0 12 E
Liski, Russia ............. 19 D6 51 3N 39 30 E
Lismore, Australia ......... 63 D5 28 44S 153 21 E
Lismore, Ireland .......... 10 D4 52 8N 7 55W
Lista, Norway ............ 9 G12 58 7N 6 39 E
Lister, Mt., Antarctica ...... 5 D11 78 0S 162 0 E
Liston, Australia .......... 63 D5 28 39S 152 6 E
Listowel, Canada .......... 84 C4 43 44N 80 58W
Listowel, Ireland .......... 10 D2 52 27N 9 29W
Litani →, Lebanon ......... 46 B4 33 20N 35 15 E
Litchfield, Calif., U.S.A. ..... 78 E6 40 24N 120 23W
Litchfield, Conn., U.S.A. .... 85 E11 41 45N 73 11W
Litchfield, Ill., U.S.A. ...... 80 F10 39 11N 89 39W
Litchfield, Minn., U.S.A. .... 80 C7 45 8N 94 32W
Litchfield △, Australia ...... 60 B5 13 14S 131 1 E
Lithgow, Australia ......... 63 E5 33 25S 150 8 E
Lithínon, Ákra, Greece ..... 25 E6 34 55N 24 44 E
Lithuania ■, Europe ....... 9 J20 55 30N 24 0 E
Lititz, U.S.A. ............. 85 F8 40 9N 76 18W
Litoměřice, Czech Rep. ..... 16 C8 50 33N 14 10 E
Little Abaco, Bahamas ...... 88 A4 26 50N 77 30W
Little Barrier I., N.Z. ........ 59 G5 36 12S 175 8 E
Little Belt Mts., U.S.A. ...... 76 C8 46 40N 110 45W
Little Bighorn Battlefield △,
  U.S.A. ................. 76 D10 45 34N 107 26W
Little Blue →, U.S.A. ....... 80 F6 39 42N 96 41W
Little Buffalo →, Canada .... 70 A6 61 0N 113 46W
Little Cayman, Cayman Is. ... 88 C3 19 41N 80 3W
Little Churchill →, Canada .. 71 B9 57 30N 95 22W
Little Colorado →, U.S.A. ... 77 H8 36 12N 111 48W
Little Current, Canada ...... 72 C3 45 55N 82 0W
Little Current →, Canada ... 72 B3 50 57N 84 36W
Little Falls, Minn., U.S.A. ... 80 C7 45 59N 94 22W
Little Falls, N.Y., U.S.A. ..... 85 C10 43 3N 74 51W
Little Fork →, U.S.A. ....... 80 A8 48 31N 93 35W
Little Grand Rapids, Canada . 71 C9 52 0N 95 29W
Little Humboldt →, U.S.A. .. 76 F5 41 1N 117 43W
Little Inagua I., Bahamas .... 89 B5 21 40N 73 50W
Little Karoo, S. Africa ...... 56 E3 33 45S 21 0 E
Little Khingan Mts. = Xiao
  Hinggan Ling, China ...... 33 B7 49 0N 127 0 E
Little Lake, U.S.A. ......... 79 K9 35 56N 117 55W
Little Laut Is. = Laut Kecil,
  Kepulauan, Indonesia ..... 36 E5 4 45S 115 40 E
Little Mecatina = Petit-
  Mécatina →, Canada ..... 73 B8 50 40N 59 30W
Little Minch, U.K. ......... 11 D2 57 35N 6 45W
Little Missouri →, U.S.A. ... 80 B3 47 36N 102 25W
Little Ouse →, U.K. ........ 13 E9 52 22N 1 12 E
Little Rann, India ......... 42 H4 23 25N 71 25 E
Little Red →, U.S.A. ....... 81 H9 35 11N 91 27W
Little River, N.Z. .......... 59 K4 43 45S 172 49 E
Little Rock, U.S.A. ......... 81 H8 34 45N 92 17W
Little Ruaha →, Tanzania ... 54 D4 7 57S 37 53 E
Little Sable Pt., U.S.A. ...... 82 D2 43 38N 86 33W
Little Sioux →, U.S.A. ...... 80 E6 41 48N 96 4W
Little Smoky →, Canada .... 70 C5 54 44N 117 11W
Little Snake →, U.S.A. ...... 76 F9 40 27N 108 26W
Little Tobago, Trin. & Tob. ... 93 J16 11 18N 60 30W
Little Valley, U.S.A. ........ 84 D6 42 15N 78 48W
Little Wabash →, U.S.A. .... 82 G1 37 55N 88 5W
Little White →, U.S.A. ...... 80 D4 43 40N 100 40W
Little Zab = Zāb aş Şaghīr →,
  Iraq ................... 44 C4 35 17N 43 29 E
Littlefield, U.S.A. ......... 81 J3 33 55N 102 20W

Littlehampton, U.K. ....... 13 G7 50 49N 0 32W
Littleton, U.S.A. .......... 85 B13 44 18N 71 46W
Liu He →, China .......... 35 D11 40 55N 121 35 E
Liuba, China ............. 34 H4 33 38N 106 55 E
Liugou, China ............ 35 D10 40 57N 118 15 E
Liuhe, China ............. 35 C13 42 17N 125 43 E
Liukang Tenggaja = Sabalana,
  Kepulauan, Indonesia .... 37 F5 6 45S 118 50 E
Liuli, Tanzania ........... 55 E3 11 3S 34 38 E
Liuwa Plain, Zambia ....... 53 G4 14 20S 22 30 E
Liuzhou, China ........... 33 D5 24 22N 109 22 E
Liuzhuang, China ......... 35 H11 33 12N 120 18 E
Livadhia, Cyprus .......... 25 E12 34 57N 33 38 E
Live Oak, Calif., U.S.A. ..... 78 F5 39 17N 121 40W
Live Oak, Fla., U.S.A. ....... 83 K4 30 18N 82 59W
Liveras, Cyprus ........... 25 D11 35 23N 32 57 E
Livermore, U.S.A. ......... 78 H5 37 41N 121 47W
Livermore, Mt., U.S.A. ..... 81 K2 30 38N 104 11W
Livermore Falls, U.S.A. ..... 83 C11 44 29N 70 11W
Liverpool, Canada ......... 73 D7 44 5N 64 41W
Liverpool, U.K. ........... 12 D4 53 25N 3 0W
Liverpool, U.S.A. ......... 85 C8 43 6N 76 13W
Liverpool Bay, U.K. ........ 12 D4 53 30N 3 20W
Liverpool Ra., Australia ..... 63 E5 31 50S 150 30 E
Livingston, Guatemala ..... 88 C2 15 50N 88 50W
Livingston, U.K. .......... 11 F5 55 54N 3 30W
Livingston, Ala., U.S.A. ..... 83 J1 32 35N 88 11W
Livingston, Calif., U.S.A. .... 78 H6 37 23N 120 43W
Livingston, Mont., U.S.A. ... 76 D8 45 40N 110 34W
Livingston, S.C., U.S.A. ..... 83 J5 33 32N 80 53W
Livingston, Tenn., U.S.A. .... 83 G3 36 23N 85 19W
Livingston, Tex., U.S.A. ..... 81 K7 30 43N 94 56W
Livingston, L., U.S.A. ....... 81 K7 30 50N 95 10W
Livingston Manor, U.S.A. ... 85 E10 41 54N 74 50W
Livingstone, Zambia ....... 55 F2 17 46S 25 52 E
Livingstone Mts., Tanzania .. 55 D3 9 40S 34 20 E
Livingstonia, Malawi ....... 55 E3 10 38S 34 5 E
Livny, Russia ............. 18 D6 52 30N 37 30 E
Livonia, Mich., U.S.A. ...... 82 D4 42 23N 83 23W
Livonia, N.Y., U.S.A. ....... 84 D7 42 49N 77 40W
Livorno, Italy ............. 22 C4 43 33N 10 19 E
Livramento, Brazil ........ 95 C4 30 55S 55 30W
Liwale, Tanzania .......... 55 D4 9 48S 37 58 E
Liwonde △, Malawi ........ 55 E4 14 48S 35 20 E
Lizard I., Australia ......... 62 A4 14 42S 145 30 E
Lizard Pt., U.K. ........... 13 H2 49 57N 5 13W
Ljubljana, Slovenia ........ 16 E8 46 4N 14 33 E
Ljungan →, Sweden ........ 9 E17 62 18N 17 23 E
Ljungby, Sweden .......... 9 H15 56 49N 13 55 E
Ljusdal, Sweden .......... 9 F17 61 46N 16 3 E
Ljusnan →, Sweden ........ 9 F17 61 12N 17 8 E
Ljusne, Sweden ........... 9 F17 61 13N 17 7 E
Llancanelo, Salina, Argentina . 94 D2 35 40S 69 8W
Llandeilo, U.K. ........... 13 F4 51 53N 3 59W
Llandovery, U.K. .......... 13 F4 51 59N 3 48W
Llandrindod Wells, U.K. .... 13 E4 52 14N 3 22W
Llandudno, U.K. .......... 12 D4 53 19N 3 50W
Llanelli, U.K. ............. 13 F3 51 41N 4 10W
Llanes, Spain ............ 21 A3 43 25N 4 50W
Llangollen, U.K. .......... 12 E4 52 58N 3 11W
Llanidloes, U.K. .......... 13 E4 52 27N 3 31W
Llano, U.S.A. ............. 81 K5 30 45N 98 41W
Llano →, U.S.A. .......... 81 K5 30 39N 98 26W
Llano Estacado, U.S.A. ..... 81 J3 33 30N 103 0W
Llanos, S. Amer. .......... 92 C4 5 0N 71 0W
Llanos de Challe △, Chile ... 94 B1 28 8S 71 1W
Llanquihue, L., Chile ....... 96 E1 41 10S 72 50W
Llanwrtyd Wells, U.K. ...... 13 E4 52 7N 3 38W
Llebeig, C. des, Spain ...... 24 B9 39 33N 2 18 E
Lleida, Spain ............. 21 B6 41 37N 0 39 E
Llentrisca, C., Spain ....... 24 C7 38 52N 1 15 E
Llera, Mexico ............ 87 C5 23 19N 99 1W
Lleyn Peninsula, U.K. ...... 12 E3 52 51N 4 36W
Llico, Chile .............. 94 C1 34 46S 72 5W
Lliria, Spain ............. 21 C5 39 37N 0 35W
Llobregat →, Spain ........ 21 B7 41 19N 2 9 E
Lloret de Mar, Spain ....... 21 B7 41 41N 2 53 E
Lloyd B., Australia ......... 62 A3 12 45S 143 27 E
Lloyd L., Canada .......... 71 B7 57 22N 108 57W
Lloydminster, Canada ...... 71 C7 53 17N 110 0W
Llucmajor, Spain .......... 24 B9 39 29N 2 53 E
Llullaillaco △, Chile ........ 94 A2 24 50S 68 51W
Llullaillaco, Volcán, S. Amer. . 94 A2 24 43S 68 30W
Lo →, Vietnam ........... 38 B5 21 18N 105 25 E
Loa, U.S.A. .............. 77 G8 38 24N 111 39W
Loa →, Chile ............. 94 A1 21 26S 70 41W
Loaita I., S. China Sea ...... 36 B4 10 41N 114 25 E
Loange →, Dem. Rep. of
  the Congo .............. 52 E4 4 17S 20 2 E
Lobatse, Botswana ........ 56 D4 25 12S 25 40 E
Loberia, Argentina ........ 94 D4 38 10S 58 40W
Lobito, Angola ........... 53 G2 12 18S 13 35 E
Lobos, Argentina ......... 94 D4 35 10S 59 0W
Lobos, I., Mexico ......... 86 B2 27 15N 110 30W
Lobos, I. de, Canary Is. ..... 24 F6 28 45N 13 50W
Loc Binh, Vietnam ........ 38 B6 21 46N 106 54 E
Loc Ninh, Vietnam ........ 39 G6 11 50N 106 34 E
Locarno, Switz. ........... 20 C8 46 10N 8 47 E
Loch Baghasdail = Lochboisdale,
  U.K. ................... 11 D1 57 9N 7 20W
Loch Garman = Wexford, Ireland 10 D5 52 20N 6 28W
Loch Lomond and the
  Trossachs △, U.K. ........ 11 E4 56 10N 4 40W
Loch Nam Madadh =
  Lochmaddy, U.K. ........ 11 D1 57 36N 7 10W
Lochaber, U.K. ........... 11 E3 56 59N 5 1W
Locharbriggs, U.K. ........ 11 F5 57 7N 3 35W
Lochboisdale, U.K. ........ 11 D1 57 9N 7 20W
Loche, L. La, Canada ....... 71 B7 56 30N 109 30W
Lochem, Neths. .......... 15 B6 52 9N 6 26 E
Loches, France ........... 20 C4 47 7N 1 0 E
Lochgilphead, U.K. ........ 11 E3 56 2N 5 26W
Lochinvar △, Zambia ....... 55 F2 15 55S 27 15 E
Lochinver, U.K. ........... 11 C3 58 9N 5 14W
Lochmaddy, U.K. ......... 11 D1 57 36N 7 10W
Lochnagar, Australia ....... 62 C4 23 33S 145 38 E
Lochnagar, U.K. .......... 11 E5 56 57N 3 15W
Lochy, L., U.K. ............ 11 E4 56 59N 4 53W
Lock, Australia ........... 63 E2 33 34S 135 46 E
Lock Haven, U.S.A. ........ 84 E7 41 8N 77 28W
Lockeford, U.S.A. ......... 78 G5 38 10N 121 9W
Lockeport, Canada ........ 73 D6 43 47N 65 4W
Lockerbie, U.K. ........... 11 F5 55 7N 3 21W
Lockhart, U.S.A. .......... 81 L6 29 53N 97 40W
Lockhart, L., Australia ...... 61 F2 33 15S 119 3 E
Lockhart River, Australia ... 62 A3 12 58S 143 30 E
Lockney, U.S.A. .......... 81 H4 34 7N 101 27W
Lockport, U.S.A. .......... 84 C6 43 10N 78 42W

Lod, Israel ................ 46 D3   31 57N   34 54 E
Lodeinoye Pole, Russia .... 18 B5   60 44N   33 33 E
Lodge Bay, Canada ....... 73 B8   52 14N   55 51W
Lodge Grass, U.S.A. ...... 76 D10  45 19N  107 22W
Lodgepole Cr. ➻, U.S.A. .. 80 E2   41 20N  104 30W
Lodhran, Pakistan ........ 42 E4   29 32N   71 30 E
Lodi, Italy .............. 20 D8   45 19N    9 30 E
Lodi, Calif., U.S.A. ...... 78 G5   38  8N  121 16W
Lodi, Ohio, U.S.A. ....... 84 E3   41  2N   82  0W
Lodja, Dem. Rep. of the Congo  54 C1   3 30S   23 23 E
Lodwar, Kenya .......... 54 B4    3 10N   35 40 E
Łódź, Poland ........... 17 C10  51 45N   19 27 E
Loei, Thailand .......... 38 D3   17 29N  101 35 E
Loeng, Dem. Rep. of the Congo  54 C2   4 48S   26 30 E
Loeriesfontein, S. Africa .. 56 E2   31  0S   19 26 E
Lofoten, Norway ......... 8 B15   68 30N   14  0 E
Logan, Iowa, U.S.A. ...... 80 E7   41 39N   95 47W
Logan, Ohio, U.S.A. ...... 82 F4   39 32N   82 25W
Logan, Utah, U.S.A. ...... 76 F8   41 44N  111 50W
Logan, W. Va., U.S.A. .... 82 G5   37 51N   81 59W
Logan, Mt., Canada ...... 68 B5   60 34N  140 23W
Logandale, U.S.A. ....... 79 J12  36 36N  114 29W
Logansport, Ind., U.S.A. .. 82 E2   40 45N   86 22W
Logansport, La., U.S.A. ... 81 K8   31 58N   94  0W
Logone ➻, Chad ......... 51 F9   12  6N   15  2 E
Logroño, Spain .......... 21 A4   42 28N    2 27W
Lohardaga, India ......... 43 H11  23 27N   84 45 E
Loharia, India ........... 42 H6   23 45N   74 14 E
Loharu, India ........... 42 E6   28 27N   75 49 E
Lohja, Finland ........... 9 F21   60 12N   24  5 E
Lohri Wah ➻, Pakistan .... 42 F2   27 27N   67 37 E
Loi-kaw, Burma .......... 41 K20  19 40N   97 17 E
Loimaa, Finland ......... 9 F20   60 50N   23  5 E
Loir ➻, France .......... 20 C3   47 33N    0 32W
Loire ➻, France ......... 20 C2   47 16N    2  0W
Loja, Ecuador ........... 92 D3    3 59S   79 16W
Loja, Spain ............. 21 D3   37 10N    4 10W
Loji = Kawasi, Indonesia .. 37 E7    1 38S  127 28 E
Lojo = Lohja, Finland ..... 9 F21   60 12N   24  5 E
Lokandu, Dem. Rep. of the Congo  54 C2   2 30S   25 45 E
Lokeren, Belgium ........ 15 C3   51  6N    3 59 E
Lokgwabe, Botswana ...... 56 C3   24 10S   21 50 E
Lokichokio, Kenya ....... 54 B3    4 19N   34 13 E
Lokitaung, Kenya ........ 54 B4    4 12N   35 48 E
Lokkan tekojärvi, Finland .. 8 C22   67 55N   27 35 E
Lokoja, Nigeria .......... 50 G7    7 47N    6 45 E
Lola, Mt., U.S.A. ........ 78 F6   39 26N  120 22W
Loliondo, Tanzania ....... 54 C4    2  2S   35 39 E
Lolland, Denmark ........ 9 J14   54 45N   11 30 E
Lolo, U.S.A. ........... 76 C6   46 45N  114  5W
Lom, Bulgaria .......... 23 C10  43 48N   23 12 E
Lom Kao, Thailand ....... 38 D3   16 53N  101 14 E
Lom Sak, Thailand ....... 38 D3   16 47N  101 15 E
Loma, U.S.A. ........... 76 C8   47 56N  110 30W
Loma Linda, U.S.A. ...... 79 L9   34  3N  117 16W
Lomami ➻, Dem. Rep. of the Congo  54 B1   0 46N   24 16 E
Lomas de Zamóra, Argentina 94 C4   34 45S   58 25W
Lombadina, Australia ..... 60 C3   16 31S  122 54 E
Lombárdia □, Italy ....... 20 D8   45 40N    9 30 E
Lombardy = Lombárdia □, Italy  20 D8   45 40N    9 30 E
Lomblen, Indonesia ...... 37 F6    8 30S  123 32 E
Lombok, Indonesia ....... 36 F5    8 45S  116 30 E
Lombok, Selat, Indonesia .. 37 K18   8 30S  115 50 E
Lomé, Togo ............ 50 G6    6  9N    1 20 E
Lomela, Dem. Rep. of the Congo  52 E4   2 19S   23 15 E
Lomela ➻, Dem. Rep. of the Congo  52 E4   0 15S   20 40 E
Lommel, Belgium ........ 15 C5   51 14N    5 19 E
Lomond, Canada ........ 70 C6   50 24N  112 36W
Lomond, L., U.K. ........ 11 E4   56  8N    4 38W
Lomonosov Ridge, Arctic .. 4 A    88  0N    0  0 E
Lomphat, Cambodia ...... 38 F6   13 30N  106 59 E
Lompobatang, Indonesia .. 37 F5    5 24S  119 56 E
Lompoc, U.S.A. ......... 79 L6   34 38N  120 28W
Łomża, Poland ......... 17 B12  53 10N   22  2 E
Lon, Ko, Thailand ....... 39 a    7 47N   98 23 E
Loncoche, Chile ......... 96 D2   39 20S   72 50W
Londa, India ........... 40 M9   15 30N   74 30 E
Londiani, Kenya ......... 54 C4    0 10S   35 33 E
London, Canada ......... 84 D3   42 59N   81 15W
London, U.K. ........... 13 F7   51 30N    0  3W
London, Ky., U.S.A. ...... 82 G3   37  8N   84  5W
London, Ohio, U.S.A. ..... 82 F4   39 53N   83 27W
London, Greater □, U.K. ... 13 F7   51 36N    0  5W
London Gatwick ✈ (LGW), U.K.  13 F7   51 10N    0 11W
London Heathrow ✈ (LHR), U.K.  13 F7   51 28N    0 27W
London Stansted ✈ (STN), U.K.  13 F8   51 54N    0 14 E
Londonderry □, U.K. ..... 10 B4   55  0N    7 20W
Londonderry, C., Australia .. 60 B4   13 45S  126 55 E
Londonderry, I., Chile ..... 96 H2   55  0S   71  0W
Londres, Argentina ...... 96 B3   27 43S   67  7W
Londrina, Brazil ......... 95 A5   23 18S   51 10W
Lone Pine, U.S.A. ....... 78 J8   36 36N  118  4W
Lonely Mine, Zimbabwe ... 57 B4   19 30S   28 49 E
Long B., U.S.A. ......... 83 J6   33 35N   78 45W
Long Beach, Calif., U.S.A. .. 79 M8   33 47N  118 11W
Long Beach, N.Y., U.S.A. .. 85 F11  40 35N   73 39W
Long Beach, Wash., U.S.A. .. 78 D2   46 21N  124  3W
Long Branch, U.S.A. ...... 85 F11  40 18N   74  0W
Long Creek, U.S.A. ...... 76 D4   44 43N  119  6W
Long Eaton, U.K. ........ 12 E6   52 53N    1 15W
Long I., Australia ........ 62 J6   20 22S  148 51 E
Long I., Bahamas ........ 89 B4   23 20N   75 10W
Long I., Canada ......... 72 B4   54 50N   79 20W
Long I., Ireland .......... 10 E2   51 30N    9 34W
Long I., U.S.A. .......... 85 F11  40 45N   73 30W
Long Island Sd., U.S.A. ... 85 E12  41 10N   73  0W
Long L., Canada ......... 72 C2   49 30N   86 50W
Long Lake, U.S.A. ....... 85 C10  43 58N   74 25W
Long Point B., Canada .... 84 D4   42 40N   80 10W
Long Prairie ➻, U.S.A. ... 80 C7   46 20N   94 36W
Long Pt., Canada ....... 84 D4   42 35N   80  2W
Long Range Mts., Canada .. 73 C8   49 30N   57 30W
Long Reef, Australia ..... 60 B4   14  1S  125 48 E
Long Spruce, Canada ..... 71 B10  56 24N   94 21W
Long Str. = Longa, Proliv, Russia  4 C13   70  0N  178  0 E
Long Thanh, Vietnam ..... 39 G6   10 47N  106 57 E
Long Xian, China ........ 34 G4   34 55N  106 55 E
Long Xuyen, Vietnam ..... 39 G5   10 19N  105 28 E
Longa, Proliv, Russia ..... 4 C16   70  0N  178  0 E
Longbenton, U.K. ....... 12 B6   55  1N    1 31W
Longboat Key, U.S.A. .... 83 M4   27 23N   82 39W
Longde, China .......... 34 G4   35 30N  106 20 E
Longford, Australia ...... 63 G4   41 32S  147  3 E
Longford, Ireland ........ 10 C4   53 43N    7 49W

Longford □, Ireland ...... 10 C4   53 42N    7 45W
Longhua, Guangdong, China  33 F11  22 39N  114  0 E
Longhua, Hebei, China .... 35 D9   41 18N  117 45 E
Longido, Tanzania ....... 54 C4    2 43S   36 42 E
Longiram, Indonesia ...... 36 E5    0  5S  115 45 E
Longkou, China ......... 35 F11  37 40N  120 18 E
Longlac, Canada ........ 72 C2   49 45N   86 25W
Longmeadow, U.S.A. ..... 85 D12  42  3N   72 34W
Longmont, U.S.A. ....... 80 E2   40 10N  105  6W
Longnawan, Indonesia .... 36 D4    1 51N  114 55 E
Longreach, Australia ..... 62 C3   23 28S  144 14 E
Longueuil, Canada ....... 85 A11  45 32N   73 28W
Longview, Tex., U.S.A. ... 81 J7   32 30N   94 44W
Longview, Wash., U.S.A. .. 78 D4   46  8N  122 57W
Longxi, China .......... 34 G3   34 53N  104 40 E
Longxue Dao, China ...... 33 F10  22 41N  113 38 E
Longyearbyen, Svalbard ... 4 B8   78 13N   15 40 E
Lonoke, U.S.A. ......... 81 H9   34 47N   91 54W
Lonquimay, Chile ........ 96 D2   38 26S   71 14W
Lons-le-Saunier, France ... 20 C6   46 40N    5 31 E
Looe, U.K. ............. 13 G3   50 22N    4 28W
Lookout, C., Canada ...... 72 A3   55 18N   83 56W
Lookout, C., U.S.A. ...... 83 H7   34 35N   76 32W
Loolmalasin, Tanzania .... 54 C4    3  0S   35 53 E
Loon ➻, Alta., Canada .... 70 B5   57  8N  115  3W
Loon ➻, Man., Canada .... 71 B8   55 53N  101 59W
Loon Lake, Canada ....... 71 C7   54 2N  109 10W
Loongana, Australia ...... 61 F4   30 52S  127  5 E
Loop Hd., Ireland ........ 10 D2   52 34N    9 56W
Lop Buri, Thailand ....... 38 E3   14 48N  100 37 E
Lop Nor = Lop Nur, China .. 32 B4   40 20N   90 10 E
Lop Nur, China ......... 32 B4   40 20N   90 10 E
Lopatina, Gora, Russia .... 29 D15  50 47N  143 10 E
Lopez, U.S.A. .......... 85 E8   41 27N   76 20W
Lopez, C., Gabon ........ 52 E1    0 47S    8 40 E
Lopphavet, Norway ...... 8 A19   70 27N   21 15 E
Lora ➻, Afghan. ........ 40 D4   31 35N   66 32 E
Lora, Hämún-i-, Pakistan .. 40 E4   29 38N   64 58 E
Lora Cr. ➻, Australia ..... 63 D2   28 10S  135 22 E
Lora del Río, Spain ...... 21 D3   37 39N    5 33W
Lorain, U.S.A. .......... 84 E2   41 28N   82 11W
Loralai, Pakistan ........ 42 D3   30 20N   68 41 E
Lorca, Spain ........... 21 D5   37 41N    1 42W
Lord Howe I., Pac. Oc. .... 64 L7   31 33S  159  6 E
Lord Howe Ridge, Pac. Oc. .. 64 L8   30  0S  162 30 E
Lordsburg, U.S.A. ....... 77 K9   32 21N  108 43W
Lorestan □, Iran ........ 45 C6   33 30N   48 40 E
Loreto, Brazil .......... 93 E9    7  5S   45 10W
Loreto, Mexico ......... 86 B2   26  1N  111 21W
Lorient, France ......... 20 C2   47 45N    3 23W
Lormi, India ........... 43 H9   22 17N   81 41 E
Lorn, U.K. ............. 11 E3   56 26N    5 10W
Lorn, Firth of, U.K. ...... 11 E3   56 20N    5 40W
Lorne, Australia ........ 63 F3   38 33S  143 59 E
Lorovouno, Cyprus ....... 25 D11   35  8N   32 36 E
Lorraine □, France ....... 20 B7   48 53N    6  0 E
Los Alamos, Calif., U.S.A. .. 79 L6   34 44N  120 17W
Los Alamos, N. Mex., U.S.A.  77 J10  35 53N  106 19W
Los Altos, U.S.A. ....... 78 H4   37 23N  122  7W
Los Andes, Chile ........ 94 C1   32 50S   70 40W
Los Angeles, Chile ....... 94 D1   37 28S   72 23W
Los Angeles, U.S.A. ...... 79 M8   34  4N  118 15W
Los Angeles, Bahía de, Mexico  86 B2   28 56N  113 34W
Los Angeles Aqueduct, U.S.A. 79 K9   35 22N  118  5W
Los Angeles International ✈
 (LAX), U.S.A. ......... 79 M8   33 57N  118 25W
Los Banos, U.S.A. ....... 78 H6   37  4N  120 51W
Los Blancos, Argentina ... 94 A3   23 40S   62 30W
Los Cardones △, Argentina  94 B2   25  8S   65 55W
Los Chiles, Costa Rica .... 88 D3   11  2N   84 43W
Los Cristianos, Canary Is. .. 24 F3   28  3N   16 42W
Los Gatos, U.S.A. ....... 78 H5   37 14N  121 59W
Los Haïtises △, Dom. Rep. .. 89 C6   19  4N   69 36W
Los Hermanos △, Venezuela  89 D7   11 45N   64 25W
Los Islotes, Canary Is. .... 24 E6   29  4N   13 44W
Los Llanos de Aridane, Canary Is. 24 F2  28 38N   17 54W
Los Loros, Chile ........ 94 B1   27 50S   70  6W
Los Lunas, U.S.A. ....... 77 J10  34 48N  106 44W
Los Mochis, Mexico ...... 86 B3   25 45N  108 57W
Los Olivos, U.S.A. ....... 79 L6   34 40N  120  7W
Los Palacios, Cuba ....... 88 B3   22 35N   83 15W
Los Reyes, Mexico ....... 86 D4   19 34N  102 30W
Los Roques Is., Venezuela .. 89 D6   11 50N   66 45W
Los Teques, Venezuela .... 92 A5   10 21N   67  2W
Los Testigos, Is., Venezuela  92 A6   11 23N   63  6W
Los Vilos, Chile ........ 94 C1   32 10S   71 30W
Lošinj, Croatia ......... 16 F8   44 30N   14 30 E
Loskop Dam, S. Africa .... 57 D4   25 23S   29 20 E
Lossiemouth, U.K. ....... 11 D5   57 42N    3 17W
Lossiemouth, U.K. ....... 13 G3   50 24N    4 41W
Lot ➻, France .......... 20 D4   44 18N    0 20 E
Lota, Chile ............ 94 D1   37  5S   73 10W
Lotfābād, Iran .......... 45 B8   37 32N   59 20 E
Lothair, S. Africa ....... 57 D5   26 22S   30 27 E
Loubomo, Congo ........ 52 E2    4  9S   12 47 E
Loudonville, U.S.A. ...... 84 F2   40 38N   82 14W
Louga, Senegal ......... 50 E2   15 45N   16  5W
Loughborough, U.K. ...... 12 E6   52 47N    1 11W
Loughrea, Ireland ....... 10 C3   53 12N    8 33W
Loughros More B., Ireland .. 10 B3   54 48N    8 32W
Louis Trichardt, S. Africa .. 57 C4   23  1S   29 43 E
Louis XIV, Pte., Canada ... 72 B4   54 37N   79 45W
Louisa, U.S.A. ......... 82 F4   38  7N   82 36W
Louisbourg, Canada ...... 73 C8   45 55N   60  0W
Louise I., Canada ....... 70 C2   52 55N  131 50W
Louiseville, Canada ...... 72 C5   46 20N   72 56W
Louisiade Arch., Papua N. G.  64 J7   11 10S  153  0 E
Louisiana, U.S.A. ....... 80 F9   39 27N   91  3W
Louisiana □, U.S.A. ...... 81 K9   30 50N   92  0W
Louisville, Ky., U.S.A. .... 82 F3   38 15N   85 46W
Louisville, Miss., U.S.A. ... 81 J10  33  7N   89  3W
Louisville, Ohio, U.S.A. .... 84 F3   40 50N   81 16W
Loulé, Portugal ......... 21 D1   37  9N    8  0W
Loup City, U.S.A. ....... 80 E5   41 17N   98 58W
Loups Marins, Lacs des, Canada  72 A5  56 30N   73 45W
Lourdes, France ......... 20 E3   43  6N    0  3W
Louth, Australia ........ 63 E4   30 30S  145  8 E
Louth, Ireland ......... 10 C5   53 58N    6 32W
Louth, U.K. ............ 12 D7   53 22N    0  1W
Louth □, Ireland ........ 10 C5   53 56N    6 34W
Louvain = Leuven, Belgium .. 15 D4   50 52N    4 42 E
Louwsburg, S. Africa ..... 57 D5   27 37S   31  7 E
Lovech, Bulgaria ........ 23 C11  43 8N   24 42 E
Loveland, U.S.A. ........ 80 E2   40 24N  105  5W
Lovell, U.S.A. .......... 76 D9   44 50N  108 24W
Lovelock, U.S.A. ........ 76 F4   40 11N  118 28W
Loviisa, Finland ........ 9 F22   60 28N   26 12 E
Loving, U.S.A. ......... 81 J2   32 17N  104  6W

Lovington, U.S.A. ....... 81 J3   32 57N  103 21W
Lovisa = Loviisa, Finland ... 9 F22   60 28N   26 12 E
Low, L., Canada ........ 72 B4   52 29N   76 17W
Low Pt., Australia ....... 61 F4   32 25S  127 25 E
Low Tatra = Nízké Tatry,
 Slovak Rep. ........... 17 D10  48 55N   19 30 E
Lowa, Dem. Rep. of the Congo  54 C2   1 25S   25 47 E
Lowa ➻, Dem. Rep. of the Congo  54 C2  1 24S   25 51 E
Lowell, U.S.A. ......... 85 D13  42 38N   71 19W
Lowellville, U.S.A. ...... 84 E4   41  2N   80 32W
Löwen ➻, Namibia ...... 56 D2   26 51S   18 17 E
Lower Alkali L., U.S.A. .... 76 F3   41 16N  120  2W
Lower Arrow L., Canada ... 70 D5   49 40N  118  5W
Lower California = Baja
 California, Mexico ...... 86 A1   31 10N  115 12W
Lower Hutt, N.Z. ........ 59 J5   41 10S  174 55 E
Lower Lake, U.S.A. ...... 78 G4   38 55N  122 37W
Lower Manitou L., Canada .. 71 D10  49 15N   93  0W
Lower Post, Canada ...... 70 B3   59 58N  128 30W
Lower Red L., U.S.A. ..... 80 B7   47 58N   95  0W
Lower Saxony =
 Niedersachsen □, Germany  16 B5   52 50N    9  0 E
Lower Tunguska = Tunguska,
 Nizhnyaya ➻, Russia .... 29 C9   65 48N   88  4 E
Lower Zambezi △, Zambia .. 55 F2   15 25S   29 40 E
Lowestoft, U.K. ........ 13 E9   52 29N    1 45 E
Lowgar □, Afghan. ....... 40 B6   34  0N   69  0 E
Łowicz, Poland ......... 17 B10  52  6N   19 55 E
Lowville, U.S.A. ........ 85 C9   43 47N   75 29W
Loxton, Australia ....... 63 E3   34 28S  140 31 E
Loxton, S. Africa ....... 56 E3   31 30S   22 22 E
Loyalton, U.S.A. ....... 78 F6   39 41N  120 14W
Loyalty Is. = Loyauté, Îs., N. Cal.  64 K8  20 50S  166 30 E
Loyang = Luoyang, China .. 34 G7   34 40N  112 26 E
Loyauté, Îs., N. Cal. ..... 64 K8   20 50S  166 30 E
Loyev = Loyew, Belarus .... 17 C16  51 56N   30 46 E
Loyew, Belarus ......... 17 C16  51 56N   30 46 E
Loyoro, Uganda ......... 54 B3    3 22N   34 14 E
Lu Wo, China .......... 33 F11  22 33N  114  6 E
Luachimo, Angola ....... 52 F4    7 23S   20 48 E
Luajan ➻, India ......... 43 G11  24 44N   85  1 E
Lualaba ➻, Dem. Rep. of the Congo  54 B2   0 26N   25 20 E
Luampa, Zambia ........ 55 F1   15  4S   24 20 E
Luan Chau, Vietnam ..... 38 B4   21 38N  103 24 E
Luan He ➻, China ....... 35 E10  39 20N  119  5 E
Luan Xian, China ....... 35 E10  39 40N  118 40 E
Luancheng, China ....... 34 F8   37 53N  114 40 E
Luanda, Angola ........ 52 F2    8 50S   13 15 E
Luang, Thale, Thailand .... 39 J3    7 30N  100 15 E
Luang Prabang, Laos ..... 38 C4   19 52N  102 10 E
Luangwa, Zambia ....... 55 F3   15 35S   30 16 E
Luangwa ➻, Zambia ...... 55 E3   14 25S   30 25 E
Luangwa Valley, Zambia .. 55 E3   13 30S   31 30 E
Luanne, China ......... 35 D9   40 55N  117 40 E
Luanping, China ........ 35 D9   40 53N  117 23 E
Luanshya, Zambia ....... 55 E2   13  3S   28 28 E
Luapula □, Zambia ...... 55 E2   11  0S   29  0 E
Luapula ➻, Africa ....... 55 D2    9 26S   28 33 E
Luarca, Spain .......... 21 A2   43 32N    6 32W
Luashi, Dem. Rep. of the Congo  55 E1   10 50S   23 36 E
Luau, Angola .......... 52 G4   10 40S   22 10 E
Lubana, Ozero = Lubānas Ezers,
 Latvia ............... 9 H22   56 45N   27  0 E
Lubānas Ezers, Latvia ..... 9 H22   56 45N   27  0 E
Lubang Is., Phil. ........ 37 B6   13 50N  120 12 E
Lubango, Angola ........ 53 G2   14 55S   13 30 E
Lubao, Dem. Rep. of the Congo  54 D2   5 17S   25 42 E
Lubbock, U.S.A. ........ 81 J4   33 35N  101 51W
Lübeck, Germany ....... 16 B6   53 52N   10 40 E
Lubefu, Dem. Rep. of the Congo  54 C1   4 47S   24 27 E
Lubefu ➻, Dem. Rep. of the Congo  54 C1  4 10S   23  0 E
Lubero = Luofu, Dem. Rep. of the Congo  54 C2  0 10S   29 15 E
Lubicon L., Canada ...... 70 B5   56 23N  115 56W
Lubilash ➻, Dem. Rep. of the Congo  54 D1  6 2S   23 45 E
Lubin, Poland .......... 16 C9   51 24N   16 11 E
Lublin, Poland ......... 17 C12  51 12N   22 38 E
Lubnān, Jabal, Lebanon ... 46 B4   33 45N   35 40 E
Lubny, Ukraine ......... 28 D4   50  3N   32 58 E
Lubongola, Dem. Rep. of the Congo  54 C2  2 35S   27 50 E
Lubudi, Dem. Rep. of the Congo  52 F5   9 57S   25 58 E
Lubudi ➻, Dem. Rep. of the Congo  55 D2  9 0S   25 35 E
Lubuklinggau, Indonesia ... 36 E2    3 15S  102 55 E
Lubuksikaping, Indonesia .. 36 D2    0 10N  100 15 E
Lubumbashi, Dem. Rep. of the Congo  55 E2  11 40S   27 28 E
Lubunda, Dem. Rep. of the Congo  54 D2   5 12S   26 41 E
Lubungu, Zambia ....... 55 E2   14 35S   26 24 E
Lubutu, Dem. Rep. of the Congo  54 C2   0 45S   26 30 E
Luc An Chau, Vietnam .... 38 A5   22  6N  104 43 E
Lucan, Canada ......... 84 C3   43 11N   81 24W
Lucania, Mt., Canada .... 68 B5   61  1N  140 27W
Lucas Channel, Canada ... 84 A3   45 21N   81 45W
Lucca, Italy ........... 22 C4   43 50N   10 29 E
Luce Bay, U.K. ......... 11 G4   54 45N    4 48W
Lucea, Jamaica ......... 88 a   18 27N   78 10W
Lucedale, U.S.A. ........ 83 K1   30 56N   88 35W
Lucena, Phil. .......... 37 B6   13 56N  121 37 E
Lucena, Spain .......... 21 D3   37 27N    4 31W
Lučenec, Slovak Rep. ..... 17 D10  48 18N   19 42 E
Lucerne = Luzern, Switz. .. 20 C8   47  3N    8 18 E
Lucerne, U.S.A. ........ 78 F4   39  6N  122 48W
Lucerne Valley, U.S.A. .... 79 L10  34 27N  116 57W
Lucero, Mexico ......... 86 A3   30 49N  106 30W
Lucheng, China ........ 34 F7   36 20N  113 11 E
Lucheringo ➻, Mozam. .... 55 E4   11 43S   36 17 E
Lucia, U.S.A. .......... 78 J5   36  2N  121 33W
Lucinda, Australia ...... 62 B4   18 32S  146 20 E
Luckenwalde, Germany ... 16 B7   52  5N   13 10 E
Luckhoff, S. Africa ...... 56 D3   29 44S   24 43 E
Lucknow, Canada ....... 84 C3   43 57N   81 31W
Lucknow, India ......... 43 F9   26 50N   81  0 E
Lüda = Dalian, China ..... 35 E11  38 50N  121 40 E
Lüderitz, Namibia ....... 56 D2   26 41S   15  8 E
Lüderitzbaai, Namibia .... 56 D2   26 36S   15  8 E
Ludhiana, India ........ 42 D6   30 57N   75 56 E
Ludington, U.S.A. ....... 82 D2   43 57N   86 27W
Ludlow, U.K. ........... 13 E5   52 22N    2 42W
Ludlow, Calif., U.S.A. .... 79 L10  34 43N  116 10W
Ludlow, Pa., U.S.A. ...... 84 E6   41 43N   78 56W
Ludlow, Vt., U.S.A. ...... 85 C12  43 24N   72 42W

Ludvika, Sweden ....... 9 F16   60  8N   15 14 E
Ludwigsburg, Germany ... 16 D5   48 53N    9 11 E
Ludwigshafen, Germany .. 16 D5   49 29N    8 26 E
Lueki, Dem. Rep. of the Congo  54 C2   3 20S   25 48 E
Luena, Dem. Rep. of the Congo  55 D2   9 28S   25 43 E
Luena, Zambia ......... 55 E3   10 40S   30 25 E
Luenha = Ruenya ➻, Africa  55 F3   16 24S   33 48 E
Lüeyang, China ........ 34 H4   33 22N  106 10 E
Lufira ➻, Dem. Rep. of the Congo  55 D2  9 30S   27  0 E
Lufkin, U.S.A. ......... 81 K7   31 21N   94 44W
Lufupa, Dem. Rep. of the Congo  55 E1   10 37S   24 56 E
Luga, Russia .......... 18 C4   58 40N   29 55 E
Lugano, Switz. ......... 20 C8   46  1N    8 57 E
Lugansk = Luhansk, Ukraine  19 E6   48 38N   39 15 E
Lugard's Falls, Kenya ..... 54 C4    3  6S   38 41 E
Lugela, Mozam. ........ 55 F4   16 25S   36 43 E
Lugenda ➻, Mozam. ..... 55 E4   11 25S   38 33 E
Lugh Ganana, Somali Rep. .. 47 G3    3 48N   42 34 E
Lugnaquillia, Ireland ..... 10 D5   52 58N    6 28W
Lugo, Italy ............ 22 B4   44 25N   11 54 E
Lugo, Spain ........... 21 A2   43  2N    7 35W
Lugoj, Romania ........ 17 F11  45 42N   21 57 E
Lugovoy = Qulan, Kazakhstan  28 E8  42 55N   72 43 E
Luhansk, Ukraine ....... 19 E6   48 38N   39 15 E
Luiana, Angola ........ 56 B3   17 25S   22 59 E
Luichow Pen. = Leizhou Bandao,
 China ............... 33 D6   21  0N  110  0 E
Luimneach = Limerick, Ireland  10 D3  52 40N    8 37W
Luing, U.K. ........... 11 E3   56 14N    5 39W
Luís Correia, Brazil ...... 93 D10   3  0S   41 35W
Luitpold Coast, Antarctica .. 5 D1   78 30S   32  0W
Luiza, Dem. Rep. of the Congo  52 F4   7 40S   22 30 E
Luizi, Dem. Rep. of the Congo  54 D2   6 0S   27 25 E
Luján, Argentina ....... 94 C4   34 45S   59  5W
Lukanga Swamp, Zambia ... 55 E2   14 30S   27 40 E
Lukenie ➻, Dem. Rep. of the Congo  52 E3   3 0S   18 50 E
Lukhisaral, India ....... 43 G12  25 11N   86  5 E
Lukolela, Dem. Rep. of the Congo  54 D1   5 23S   24 32 E
Lukosi, Zimbabwe ...... 55 F2   18 30S   26 30 E
Łuków, Poland ......... 17 C12  51 55N   22 23 E
Lukusuzi △, Zambia ..... 55 E3   12 43S   32 36 E
Luleå, Sweden ......... 8 D20   65 35N   22 10 E
Luleälven ➻, Sweden .... 8 D19   65 35N   22 10 E
Lüleburgaz, Turkey ...... 23 D12  41 23N   27 22 E
Luling, U.S.A. ......... 81 L6   29 41N   97 39W
Lulong, China ......... 35 E10  39 53N  118 51 E
Lulonga ➻, Dem. Rep. of the Congo  52 D3   1 0N   18 10 E
Lulua ➻, Dem. Rep. of the Congo  52 E4   4 30S   20 30 E
Lumajang, Indonesia ..... 37 H15   8  8S  113 13 E
Lumbala N'guimbo, Angola  53 G4   14  18S   21 18 E
Lumberton, U.S.A. ...... 83 H6   34 37N   79  0W
Lumsden, Canada ....... 71 C8   50 39N  104 52W
Lumsden, N.Z. ......... 59 L2   45 44S  168 27 E
Lumut, Malaysia ....... 39 K3    4 13N  100 37 E
Lumut, Tanjung, Indonesia .. 36 E3   3 50S  105 58 E
Luna, India ........... 42 H3   23 43N   69 16 E
Lunavada, India ........ 42 H5   23  8N   73 37 E
Lund, Sweden ......... 9 J15   55 44N   13 12 E
Lundazi, Zambia ....... 55 E3   12 20S   33  7 E
Lundi ➻, Zimbabwe ..... 55 G3   21 43S   32 34 E
Lundu, Malaysia ....... 36 D3    1 40N  109 50 E
Lundy, U.K. ........... 13 F3   51 10N    4 41W
Lune ➻, U.K. .......... 12 C5   54  0N    2 51W
Lüneburg, Germany ..... 16 B6   53 15N   10 24 E
Lüneburg Heath = Lüneburger
 Heide, Germany ....... 16 B6   53 10N   10 12 E
Lüneburger Heide, Germany  16 B6   53 10N   10 12 E
Lunenburg, Canada ...... 73 D7   44 22N   64 18W
Lunéville, France ....... 20 B7   48 36N    6 30 E
Lunga ➻, Zambia ....... 55 E2   14 34S   26 25 E
Lunglei, India ......... 41 H18  22 55N   92 45 E
Luni, India ........... 42 G5   26  0N   73  6 E
Luni ➻, India .......... 42 G4   24 41N   71 14 E
Luninets = Luninyets, Belarus  17 B14  52 15N   26 50 E
Luning, U.S.A. ......... 76 G4   38 30N  118 11W
Lunkaransar, India ...... 42 E5   28 29N   73 44 E
Luninyets, Belarus ...... 17 B14  52 15N   26 50 E
Lunsemfwa ➻, Zambia ... 55 E3   14 54S   30 12 E
Lunsemfwa Falls, Zambia .. 55 E2   14 30S   29  6 E
Luo He ➻, China ....... 34 G6   34 35N  110 20 E
Luochuan, China ....... 34 G5   35 45N  109 26 E
Luofu, Dem. Rep. of the Congo  54 C2   0 10S   29 15 E
Luohe, China .......... 34 H8   33 32N  114  2 E
Luonan, China ......... 34 G6   34 5N  110 10 E
Luoning, China ........ 34 G6   34 35N  111 40 E
Luoyang, China ........ 34 G7   34 40N  112 26 E
Luozigou, China ....... 35 C16  43 42N  130 18 E
Lupanshui, China ...... 32 D5   26 38N  104 48 E
Lupilichi, Mozam. ...... 55 E4   11 47S   35 13 E
Luque, Paraguay ....... 94 B4   25 19S   57 25W
Luray, U.S.A. ......... 82 F6   38 40N   78 28W
Lurgan, U.K. .......... 10 B5   54 28N    6 19W
Lusaka, Zambia ........ 55 F2   15 28S   28 16 E
Lusaka □, Zambia ...... 55 F2   15 30S   29  0 E
Lusambo, Dem. Rep. of the Congo  54 C1   4 58S   23 28 E
Lusangaye, Dem. Rep. of the Congo  54 C2   4 54S   26  0 E
Luseland, Canada ....... 71 C7   52  5N  109 24W
Lusenga Plain △, Zambia .. 55 D2    9 23S  114 55 E
Lushan, China ......... 34 H7   33 45N  112 55 E
Lushi, China .......... 34 G6   34  3N  111 3 E
Lushnjë, Albania ....... 23 D8   40 55N   19 41 E
Lushoto, Tanzania ...... 54 C4    4 47S   38 20 E
Lüshun, China ......... 35 E11  38 45N  121 15 E
Lusk, U.S.A. .......... 80 D2   42 46N  104 27W
Lüt, Dasht-e, Iran ....... 45 D8   31 30N   58  0 E
Luta = Dalian, China ..... 35 E11  38 50N  121 40 E
Lutherstadt Wittenberg,
 Germany ............. 16 C7   51 53N   12 39 E
Luton, U.K. ........... 13 F7   51 53N    0 24W
Luton □, U.K. ......... 13 F7   51 53N    0 24W
Łutselk'e, Canada ....... 71 A6   62 24N  110 44W
Lutsk, Ukraine ......... 17 C13  50 50N   25 15 E
Lützow Holmbukta, Antarctica  5 C4  69 10S   37 30 E
Lutzputs, S. Africa ...... 56 D3   28  3S   20 40 E
Luuq = Lugh Ganana,
 Somali Rep. .......... 47 G3    3 48N   42 34 E
Luverne, Ala., U.S.A. .... 83 K2   31 43N   86 16W
Luverne, Minn., U.S.A. ... 80 D6   43 39N   96 13W
Luvua, Dem. Rep. of the Congo  55 D2   8 48S   25 17 E
Luvua ➻, Dem. Rep. of the Congo  54 D2   6 50S   27 30 E
Luvuvhu ➻, S. Africa ..... 57 C5   22 25S   31 18 E

Luwegu →, Tanzania .......... 55 D4　8 31S 37 23 E
Luwuk, Indonesia ............. 37 E6　0 56S 122 47 E
Luxembourg, Lux. ............ 15 E6　49 37N　6 9 E
Luxembourg □, Belgium ..... 15 E5　49 58N　5 30 E
Luxembourg ■, Europe ...... 20 B7　49 45N　6 0 E
Luxi, China ................... 32 D4　24 27N 98 36 E
Luxor = El Uqsur, Egypt ..... 51 C12　25 41N 32 38 E
Luyi, China ................... 34 H8　33 50N 115 35 E
Luza, Russia .................. 18 B8　60 39N 47 10 E
Luzern, Switz. ................ 20 C8　47 3N　8 18 E
Luzhou, China ................ 32 D5　28 52N 105 20 E
Luziânia, Brazil .............. 93 G9　16 20S 48　0W
Luzon, Phil. .................. 37 A6　16　0N 121　0 E
Lviv, Ukraine ................. 17 D13　49 50N 24　0 E
Lvov = Lviv, Ukraine ......... 17 D13　49 50N 24　0 E
Lyakhavichy, Belarus ......... 17 B14　53　2N 26 32 E
Lyakhovskiye, Ostrova, Russia . 29 B15　73 40N 141　0 E
Lyal I., Canada ............... 84 B3　44 57N 81 24W
Lybster, U.K. ................. 11 C5　58 18N　3 15W
Lycksele, Sweden ............. 8 D18　64 38N 18 40 E
Lydda = Lod, Israel .......... 46 D3　31 57N 34 54 E
Lydenburg, S. Africa ......... 57 D5　25 10S 30 29 E
Lydia, Turkey ................ 23 E13　38 48N 28 19 E
Lyell, N.Z. ................... 59 J4　41 48S 172　4 E
Lyell I., Canada ............. 70 C2　52 40N 131 35W
Lyepyel, Belarus ............. 18 D4　54 50N 28 40 E
Lykens, U.S.A. ............... 85 F8　40 34N 76 42W
Lyman, U.S.A. ................ 76 F8　41 20N 110 18W
Lyme B., U.K. ................ 13 G4　50 42N　2 53W
Lyme Regis, U.K. ............ 13 G5　50 43N　2 57W
Lymington, U.K. .............. 13 G6　50 45N　1 32W
Łyna →, Poland .............. 9 J19　54 37N 21 14 E
Lynchburg, U.S.A. ........... 82 G6　37 25N 79　9W
Lynd →, Australia ........... 62 B3　16 28S 143 18 E
Lynd Ra., Australia .......... 63 D4　25 30S 149 20 E
Lynden, Canada .............. 84 C4　43 14N 80　9W
Lynden, U.S.A. .............. 78 B4　48 57N 122 27W
Lyndhurst, Australia ......... 63 E2　30 15S 138 18 E
Lyndon →, Australia ......... 61 D1　23 29S 114　6 E
Lyndonville, N.Y., U.S.A. .... 84 C6　43 20N 78 23W
Lyndonville, Vt., U.S.A. ..... 85 B12　44 31N 72　1W
Lyngen, Norway .............. 8 B19　69 45N 20 30 E
Lynher Reef, Australia ....... 60 C3　15 27S 121 55 E
Lynn, U.S.A. ................. 85 D14　42 28N 70 57W
Lynn Lake, Canada .......... 71 B8　56 51N 101　3W
Lynnwood, U.S.A. ........... 78 C4　47 49N 122 19W
Lynton, U.K. ................. 13 F4　51 13N　3 50W
Lyntupy, Belarus ............. 9 J22　55　4N 26 23 E
Lynx L., Canada ............. 71 A7　62 25N 106 15W
Lyon, France ................. 20 D6　45 46N　4 50 E
Lyonnais, France ............. 20 D6　45 45N　4 15 E
Lyons = Lyon, France ........ 20 D6　45 46N　4 50 E
Lyons, Ga., U.S.A. ........... 83 J4　32 12N 82 19W
Lyons, Kans., U.S.A. ......... 80 F5　38 21N 98 12W
Lyons, N.Y., U.S.A. .......... 84 C8　43　5N 77　0W
Lyons →, Australia .......... 61 E2　25　2S 115　9 E
Lyons Falls, U.S.A. .......... 85 C9　43 37N 75 22W
Lys = Leie →, Belgium ...... 15 C3　51　2N　3 45 E
Lysva, Russia ................ 18 C10　58　7N 57 49 E
Lysychansk, Ukraine ......... 19 E6　48 55N 38 30 E
Lytham St. Anne's, U.K. ..... 12 D4　53 45N　3　0W
Lyttelton, N.Z. .............. 59 K4　43 35S 172 44 E
Lytton, Canada .............. 70 C4　50 13N 121 31W
Lyubertsy, Russia ............ 18 C6　55 39N 37 50 E
Lyuboml, Ukraine ............ 17 C13　51 11N 24　4 E

## M

M.R. Gomez, Presa, Mexico .... 87 B5　26 10N 99　0W
Ma →, Vietnam .............. 38 C5　19 47N 105 56 E
Ma'adaba, Jordan ............ 46 E4　30 43N 35 47 E
Maamba, Zambia ............ 56 B4　17 17S 26 28 E
Ma'ān, Jordan ............... 46 E4　30 12N 35 44 E
Ma'ān □, Jordan ............. 46 F5　30　0N 36　0 E
Maanselkä, Finland .......... 8 C23　63 52N 28 32 E
Ma'anshan, China ........... 33 C6　31 44N 118 29 E
Maarianhamina, Finland ..... 9 F18　60　5N 19 55 E
Ma'arrat an Nu'mān, Syria .. 44 C3　35 43N 36 43 E
Maas →, Neths. ............. 15 C4　51 45N　4 32 E
Maaseik, Belgium ............ 15 C5　51　6N　5 45 E
Maasin, Phil. ................ 37 B6　10　8N 124 50 E
Maastricht, Neths. ........... 15 D5　50 50N　5 40 E
Maave, Mozam. .............. 57 C5　21　4S 34 47 E
Mababe Depression, Botswana . 56 B3　18 50S 24 15 E
Mabalane, Mozam. ........... 57 C5　23 37S 32 31 E
Mabel L., Canada ............ 70 C5　50 35N 118 43W
Mabenge, Dem. Rep. of
　the Congo ................. 54 B1　4 15N 24 12 E
Maberly, Canada ............. 85 B8　44 50N 76 32W
Mablethorpe, U.K. ........... 12 D8　53 20N　0 15 E
Maboma, Dem. Rep. of
　the Congo ................. 54 B2　2 30N 28 10 E
Mabuasehube △, Botswana ... 56 D3　25　5S 21 10 E
Mac Bac, Vietnam ........... 39 H6　9 46N 106　7 E
Macachin, Argentina ......... 94 D3　37 10S 63 43W
Macaé, Brazil ................ 95 A7　22 20S 41 43W
McAlester, U.S.A. ............ 81 H7　34 56N 95 46W
McAllen, U.S.A. .............. 81 M5　26 12N 98 14W
MacAlpine L., Canada ....... 68 B9　66 32N 102 45W
Macamic, Canada ............ 72 C4　48 45N 79　0W
Macao = Macau, China ...... 33 G10　22 12N 113 33 E
Macapá, Brazil ............... 93 C8　0　5N 51　4W
Macarao △, Venezuela ....... 89 D6　10 20N 67　0W
McArthur →, Australia ...... 62 B2　15 54S 136 40 E
McArthur, Port, Australia ... 62 B2　16　4S 136 23 E
Macau, Brazil ................ 93 E11　5　0S 36 40W
Macau, China ................ 33 G10　22 12N 113 33 E
McBride, Canada ............ 70 C4　53 20N 120 19W
McCall, U.S.A. ............... 76 D5　44 55N 116　6W
McCamey, U.S.A. ............ 81 K3　31　8N 102 14W
McCammon, U.S.A. .......... 76 E7　42 39N 112 12W
McCauley I., Canada ........ 70 C2　53 40N 130 15W
McCleary, U.S.A. ............ 78 C3　47　3N 123 16W
Macclenny, U.S.A. ........... 83 K4　30 17N 82　7W
Macclesfield, U.K. ........... 12 D5　53 15N　2　8W
M'Clintock Chan., Canada ... 68 A9　72　0N 102　0W
McClintock Ra., Australia .... 60 C4　18 44S 127 38 E
McCloud, U.S.A. ............. 76 F2　41 15N 122 8W
McCluer I., Australia ........ 60 B5　11　5S 133　0 E
McClure, U.S.A. ............. 84 F7　40 42N 77 19W
McClure, L., U.S.A. .......... 78 H6　37 35N 120 16W
M'Clure Str., Canada ........ 4 B2　75　0N 119　0W
McClusky, U.S.A. ............ 80 B4　47 29N 100 27W
McComb, U.S.A. ............. 81 K9　31 15N 90 27W

McConaughy, L., U.S.A. ...... 80 E4　41 14N 101 40W
McCook, U.S.A. .............. 80 E4　40 12N 100 38W
McCreary, Canada ........... 71 C9　50 47N 99 29W
McCullough Mt., U.S.A. ...... 79 K11　35 35N 115 13W
McCusker →, Canada ........ 71 B7　55 32N 108 39W
McDame, Canada ............ 70 B3　59 44N 128 59W
McDermitt, U.S.A. ........... 76 F5　41 59N 117 43W
McDonald, U.S.A. ............ 84 F4　40 22N 80 14W
Macdonald, L., Australia ..... 60 D4　23 30S 129　0 E
McDonald Is., Ind. Oc. ...... 3 G13　53　0S 73　0 E
MacDonnell Ranges, Australia . 60 D5　23 40S 133　0 E
McDowell L., Canada ........ 72 B1　52 15N 92 45W
Macduff, U.K. ................ 11 D6　57 40N　2 31W
Macedonia = Makedhonía □,
　Greece ..................... 23 D10　40 39N 22　0 E
Macedonia, U.S.A. ........... 84 E3　41 19N 81 31W
Macedonia ■, Europe ....... 23 D9　41 53N 21 40 E
Maceió, Brazil ............... 93 E11　9 40S 35 41W
Macerata, Italy .............. 22 C5　43 18N 13 27 E
McFarland, U.S.A. ........... 79 K7　35 41N 119 14W
McFarlane →, Canada ....... 71 B7　59 12N 107 58W
Macfarlane, L., Australia .... 63 E2　32　0S 136 40 E
McGehee, U.S.A. ............ 81 J9　33 38N 91 24W
McGill, U.S.A. ............... 76 G6　39 23N 114 47W
Macgillycuddy's Reeks, Ireland . 10 E2　51 58N　9 45W
McGraw, U.S.A. .............. 85 D8　42 36N 76　8W
McGregor, U.S.A. ............ 80 D9　43　1N 91 11W
McGregor Ra., Australia ..... 63 D3　27　0S 142 45 E
McGuire, Mt., U.S.A. ........ 62 J6　20 18S 148 23 E
Mach, Pakistan .............. 40 E5　29 50N 67 20 E
Māch Kowr, Iran ............ 45 E9　25 48N 61 28 E
Machado = Jiparaná →, Brazil . 92 E6　8　3S 62 52W
Machagai, Argentina ......... 94 B3　26 56S 60　2W
Machakos, Kenya ............ 54 C4　1 30S 37 15 E
Machala, Ecuador ............ 92 D3　3 20S 79 57W
Machanga, Mozam. .......... 57 C6　20 59S 35　0 E
Machattie, L., Australia ..... 62 C2　24 50S 139 48 E
Machava, Mozam. ............ 57 D5　25 54S 32 28 E
Machece, Mozam. ........... 55 F4　19 15S 35 32 E
Macheke, Zimbabwe ......... 57 B5　18　5S 31 51 E
Machhu →, India ........... 42 H4　23　6N 70 46 E
Machias, Maine, U.S.A. ...... 83 C14　44 43N 67 28W
Machias, N.Y., U.S.A. ....... 84 D6　42 25N 78 30W
Machichi →, Canada ........ 71 B10　57　3N 92　6W
Machico, Madeira ............ 24 D3　32 43N 16 44W
Machilipatnam, India ........ 41 L12　16 12N 81　8 E
Machiques, Venezuela ....... 92 A4　10　4N 72 34W
Machupicchu, Peru .......... 92 F4　13　8S 72 30W
Machynlleth, U.K. ........... 13 E4　52 35N　3 50W
Macia, Mozam. ............... 57 D5　25　2S 33　8 E
McIlwraith Ra., Australia .... 62 A3　13 50S 143 20 E
McInnes L., Canada ......... 71 C10　52 13N 93 45W
McIntosh, U.S.A. ............ 80 C4　45 55N 101 21W
McIntosh L., Canada ........ 71 B8　55 45N 105　0W
Macintosh Ra., Australia ..... 61 E4　27 39S 125 32 E
Macintyre →, Australia ...... 63 D5　28 37S 150 47 E
Mackay, Australia ............ 62 K7　21　8S 149 11 E
MacKay →, Canada ......... 70 B6　57 10N 111 38W
Mackay, L., Australia ........ 60 D4　22 30S 129　0 E
McKay Ra., Australia ........ 60 D3　23　0S 122 30 E
McKeesport, U.S.A. .......... 84 F5　40 21N 79 52W
McKellar, Canada ........... 84 A5　45 30N 79 55W
McKenna, U.S.A. ............ 78 D4　46 56N 122 33W
Mackenzie, Canada .......... 70 B4　55 20N 123　5W
Mackenzie →, Australia ..... 62 C4　23 38S 149 46 E
Mackenzie →, Canada ....... 68 B6　69 10N 134 20W
McKenzie →, U.S.A. ........ 76 D2　44 7N 123　6W
Mackenzie Bay, Canada ...... 4 B1　69　0N 137 30W
Mackenzie City = Linden, Guyana . 92 B7　6　0N 58 10W
Mackenzie Mts., Canada ..... 68 B6　64　0N 130　0W
Mackinaw City, U.S.A. ....... 82 C3　45 47N 84 44W
McKinlay, Australia .......... 62 C3　21 16S 141 18 E
McKinlay →, Australia ...... 62 C3　20 50S 141 28 E
McKinley, Mt., U.S.A. ....... 68 B4　63　4N 151　0W
McKinley Sea, Arctic ........ 4 A7　82　0N　0　0 E
McKinney, U.S.A. ........... 81 J6　33 12N 96 37W
Mackinnon Road, Kenya ..... 54 C4　3 40S 39　1 E
McKittrick, U.S.A. ........... 79 K7　35 18N 119 37W
Macklin, Canada ............. 71 C7　52 20N 109 56W
Macksville, Australia ......... 63 E5　30 40S 152 56 E
McLaughlin, U.S.A. .......... 80 C4　45 49N 100 49W
Maclean, Australia ........... 63 D5　29 26S 153 16 E
McLean, U.S.A. .............. 81 H4　35 14N 100 36W
McLeansboro, U.S.A. ........ 80 F10　38　6N 88 32W
Maclear, S. Africa ........... 57 E4　31　2S 28 23 E
Maclear, L., Malawi ......... 55 E3　13 58S 34 49 E
Macleay →, Australia ....... 63 E5　30 56S 153　0 E
McLennan, Canada .......... 70 B5　55 42N 116 50W
McLeod →, Canada ......... 70 C5　54　9N 115 44W
MacLeod, B., Canada ....... 71 A7　62 53N 110　0W
MacLeod, L., Australia ....... 61 D1　24　9S 113 47 E
MacLeod Lake, Canada ...... 70 C4　54 58N 123　0W
McLoughlin, Mt., U.S.A. ..... 76 E2　42 27N 122 19W
McMechen, U.S.A. ........... 84 G4　39 57N 80 44W
McMinnville, Oreg., U.S.A. ... 76 D2　45 13N 123 12W
McMinnville, Tenn., U.S.A. .. 83 H3　35 41N 85 46W
McMurdo Sd., Antarctica .... 5 D11　77　0S 170　0 E
McMurray = Fort McMurray,
　Canada .................... 70 B6　56 44N 111　7W
McMurray, U.S.A. ........... 78 B4　48 19N 122 14W
Macodoene, Mozam. ......... 57 C6　23 32S 35　5 E
Macomb, U.S.A. ............. 80 E9　40 27N 90 40W
Mâcon, France ............... 20 C6　46 19N　4 50 E
Macon, Ga., U.S.A. .......... 83 J4　32 51N 83 38W
Macon, Miss., U.S.A. ........ 83 J1　33 7N 88 34W
Macon, Mo., U.S.A. ......... 80 F8　39 44N 92 28W
Macossa, Mozam. ............ 55 F3　17 55S 33 56 E
Macoun L., Canada .......... 71 B8　56 32N 103 40W
Macovane, Mozam. .......... 57 C6　21 30S 35　2 E
McPherson, U.S.A. ........... 80 F6　38 22N 97 40W
McPherson Pk., U.S.A. ....... 79 L7　34 53N 119 53W
McPherson Ra., Australia .... 63 D5　28 15S 153 15 E
Macquarie →, Australia ...... 63 E4　30　5S 147 24 E
Macquarie Harbour, Australia . 63 G4　42 15S 145 23 E
Macquarie Is., Pac. Oc. ...... 64 N7　54 36S 158 55 E
MacRobertson Land, Antarctica . 5 D6　71　0S 64　0 E
Macroom, Ireland ........... 10 E3　51 54N　8 57W
MacTier, Canada ............. 84 A5　45　9N 79 46W
Macubela, Mozam. .......... 55 F4　16 53S 37 49 E
Macuira △, Colombia ........ 89 D5　12　9N 71 21W
Macuiza, Mozam. ............ 55 F3　18 7S 34 29 E
Macumba, The →, Australia . 63 D2　27 52S 137 12 E
Macuro, Venezuela .......... 93 K15　10 42N 61 55W
Macusani, Peru .............. 92 F4　14　4S 70 29W
Macuse, Mozam. ............. 55 F4　17 45S 37 10 E
Macuspana, Mexico .......... 87 D6　17 46N 92 36W

Macusse, Angola ............ 56 B3　17 48S 20 23 E
Ma'dabā, Jordan ............ 46 D4　31 43N 35 47 E
Madadeni, S. Africa .......... 57 D5　27 43S 30　3 E
Madagascar ■, Africa ........ 57 C8　20　0S 47　0 E
Madā'in Sālih, Si. Arabia .... 44 E3　26 46N 37 57 E
Madama, Niger .............. 51 D8　22　0N 13 40 E
Madame, I., Canada ......... 73 C7　45 30N 60 58W
Madaripur, Bangla. .......... 41 H17　23 19N 90 15 E
Madauk, Burma ............. 41 L20　17 56N 96 52 E
Madawaska, Canada ......... 84 A7　45 30N 78　0W
Madawaska →, Canada ...... 84 A8　45 27N 76 21W
Madaya, Burma ............. 41 H20　22 12N 96 10 E
Madbar, Sudan .............. 51 G12　6 17N 30 45 E
Maddalena, Italy ............ 22 D3　41 16N　9 23 E
Madeira, Atl. Oc. ............ 24 D3　32 50N 17　0W
Madeira →, Brazil .......... 92 D7　3 22S 58 45W
Madeleine, Îs. de la, Canada . 73 C7　47 30N 61 40W
Madera, Mexico ............. 86 B3　29 12N 108 7W
Madera, Calif., U.S.A. ....... 78 J6　36 57N 120 3W
Madera, Pa., U.S.A. ......... 84 F6　40 49N 78 26W
Madha, India ................ 40 L9　18　0N 75 30 E
Madhavpur, India ........... 42 J3　21 15N 69 58 E
Madhepura, India ........... 43 F12　26 11N 86 23 E
Madhubani, India ........... 43 F12　26 21N 86　7 E
Madhupur, India ............ 43 G12　24 16N 86 39 E
Madhya Pradesh □, India ... 42 J8　22 50N 78　0 E
Madidi →, Bolivia .......... 92 F5　12 32S 66 52W
Madikeri, India .............. 40 N9　12 30N 75 45 E
Madikwe △, S. Africa ....... 57 D5　27 38S 32 15 E
Madill, U.S.A. ............... 81 H6　34　6N 96 46W
Madimba, Dem. Rep. of
　the Congo ................. 52 E3　4 58S 15　5 E
Ma'din, Syria ................ 44 C3　35 45N 39 36 E
Madingou, Congo ........... 52 E2　4 10S 13 33 E
Madirovalo, Madag. .......... 57 B8　16 26S 46 32 E
Madison, Calif., U.S.A. ...... 78 G5　38 41N 121 59W
Madison, Fla., U.S.A. ........ 83 K4　30 28N 83 25W
Madison, Ind., U.S.A. ....... 82 F3　38 44N 85 23W
Madison, Nebr., U.S.A. ...... 80 E6　41 50N 97 27W
Madison, Ohio, U.S.A. ....... 84 E3　41 46N 81　3W
Madison, S. Dak., U.S.A. .... 80 D6　44　0N 97 7W
Madison, Wis., U.S.A. ....... 80 D10　43　4N 89 24W
Madison →, U.S.A. ......... 76 D8　45 56N 111 31W
Madison Heights, U.S.A. ..... 82 G6　37 25N 79 8W
Madisonville, Ky., U.S.A. .... 82 G2　37 20N 87 30W
Madisonville, Tex., U.S.A. ... 81 K7　30 57N 95 55W
Madista, Botswana .......... 56 C4　21 15S 25　6 E
Madiun, Indonesia ........... 36 F4　7 38S 111 32 E
Madoc, Canada .............. 84 B7　44 30N 77 28W
Madona, Latvia .............. 9 H22　56 53N 26　5 E
Madrakah, Ra's al, Oman .... 47 D6　19　0N 57 50 E
Madras = Chennai, India .... 40 N12　13　8N 80 19 E
Madras = Tamil Nadu □, India . 40 P10　11　0N 77　0 E
Madras, U.S.A. .............. 76 D3　44 38N 121　8W
Madre, Laguna, U.S.A. ...... 81 M6　27　0N 97 30W
Madre, Sierra, Phil. ......... 37 A6　17　0N 122　0 E
Madre de Dios →, Bolivia ... 92 F5　10 59S 66　8W
Madre de Dios, I., Chile ..... 96 G1　50 20S 75 10W
Madre del Sur, Sierra, Mexico . 87 D5　17 30N 100　0W
Madre Occidental, Sierra, Mexico . 86 B3　27　0N 107　0W
Madre Oriental, Sierra, Mexico . 86 C5　25　0N 100　0W
Madri, India ................. 42 G5　24 16N 73 32 E
Madrid, Spain ............... 21 B4　40 25N　3 45W
Madrid, U.S.A. .............. 85 B9　44 45N 75　8W
Madura, Australia ........... 61 F4　31 55S 127　0 E
Madura, Indonesia ........... 37 G15　7 30S 114　0 E
Madura, Selat, Indonesia .... 37 G15　7 30S 113 20 E
Madurai, India .............. 40 Q11　9 55N 78 10 E
Madurantakam, India ........ 40 N11　12 30N 79 50 E
Mae Chan, Thailand ......... 38 B2　20　9N 99 52 E
Mae Hong Son, Thailand .... 38 C2　19 16N 97 56 E
Mae Khlong →, Thailand .... 38 F3　13 24N 100　0 E
Mae Phrik, Thailand ........ 38 D2　17 27N 99　7 E
Mae Ping △, Thailand ....... 38 D2　17 37N 98 51 E
Mae Ramat, Thailand ....... 38 D2　16 58N 98 31 E
Mae Rim, Thailand ......... 38 C2　18 54N 98 57 E
Mae Sot, Thailand .......... 38 D2　16 43N 98 34 E
Mae Suai, Thailand ......... 38 C2　19 39N 99 33 E
Mae Tha, Thailand ......... 38 C2　18 28N 99　8 E
Mae Wong △, Thailand ..... 38 E2　15 54N 99 12 E
Mae Yom △, Thailand ...... 38 C3　18 43N 100 15 E
Maebashi, Japan ............ 31 F9　36 24N 139　4 E
Maesteg, U.K. ............... 13 F4　51 36N　3 40W
Maestra, Sierra, Cuba ....... 88 B4　20 15N 77　0W
Maevatanana, Madag. ....... 57 B8　16 56S 46 49 E
Mafeking = Mafikeng, S. Africa . 56 D4　25 50S 25 38 E
Mafeking, Canada ........... 71 C8　52 40N 101 10W
Mafeteng, Lesotho .......... 56 D4　29 51S 27 15 E
Maffra, Australia ............ 63 F4　37 53S 146 58 E
Mafia I., Tanzania ........... 54 D4　7 45S 39 50 E
Mafikeng, S. Africa ......... 56 D4　25 50S 25 38 E
Mafra, Brazil ................ 95 B6　26 10S 49 55W
Mafra, Portugal ............. 21 C1　38 55N　9 20W
Mafungabusi Plateau, Zimbabwe . 55 F2　18 30S 29　8 E
Magadan, Russia ............ 29 D16　59 38N 150 50 E
Magadi, Kenya .............. 54 C4　1 54S 36 19 E
Magadi, L., Kenya ........... 54 C4　1 54S 36 19 E
Magaliesburg, S. Africa ...... 57 D4　26　0S 27 32 E
Magallanes, Estrecho de, Chile . 96 G2　52 30S 75　0W
Magangué, Colombia ........ 92 B4　9 14N 74 45W
Magdalen Is. = Madeleine, Îs. de
　la, Canada ................. 73 C7　47 30N 61 40W
Magdalena, Argentina ....... 94 D4　35　5S 57 30W
Magdalena, Bolivia .......... 92 F6　13 13S 63 57W
Magdalena, Mexico .......... 86 A2　30 50N 112　0W
Magdalena, U.S.A. ........... 77 J10　34 7N 107 15W
Magdalena →, Colombia .... 92 A4　11　6N 74 51W
Magdalena →, Mexico ...... 86 A2　30 40N 112 25W
Magdalena, B., Mexico ...... 86 C2　24 30N 112 10W
Magdalena, Llano de la, Mexico . 86 C2　25　0N 111 30W
Magdeburg, Germany ........ 16 B6　52　7N 11 38 E
Magdelaine Cays, Australia .. 62 B5　16 33S 150 18 E
Magee, U.S.A. ............... 81 K10　31 52N 89 44W
Magelang, Indonesia ........ 36 F4　7 29S 110 13 E
Magellan's Str. = Magallanes,
　Estrecho de, Chile ......... 96 G2　52 30S 75　0W
Magenta, L., Australia ....... 61 F2　33 30S 119　2 E
Magerøya, Norway .......... 8 A21　71　3N 25 40 E
Maggiore, Lago, Italy ........ 20 D8　45 57N　8 39 E
Maggotty, Jamaica ........... 88 a　18　9N 77 46W
Maghāgha, Egypt ............ 51 C12　28 38N 30 50 E
Magherafelt, U.K. ........... 10 B5　54 45N　6 37W
Maghreb, N. Afr. ............ 50 B5　32　0N　4　0W
Magistralnyy, Russia ......... 29 D11　56 16N 107 36 E
Magnetic Pole (North), Canada . 4 A2　88 30N 107　0 W
Magnetic Pole (South),
　Antarctica ................. 5 C9　64　8S 138　8 E
Magnitogorsk, Russia ........ 18 D10　53 27N 59　4 E
Magnolia, Ark., U.S.A. ....... 81 J8　33 16N 93 14W

Magnolia, Miss., U.S.A. ...... 81 K9　31　9N 90 28W
Magog, Canada .............. 85 A12　45 18N 72　9W
Magoro, Uganda ............ 54 B3　1 45N 34 12 E
Magoša = Famagusta, Cyprus . 25 D12　35　8N 33 55 E
Magouládhes, Greece ....... 25 A3　39 45N 19 42 E
Magoye, Zambia ............ 55 F2　16　1S 27 30 E
Magozal, Mexico ............ 87 C5　21 34N 97 59W
Magpie, L., Canada .......... 73 B7　51　0N 64 41W
Magrath, Canada ............ 70 D6　49 25N 112 50W
Maguarinho, C., Brazil ...... 93 D9　0 15S 48 30W
Magude, Mozam. ............ 57 D5　25　2S 32 40 E
Maguse L., Canada .......... 71 A9　61 37N 95 10W
Maguse Pt., Canada ......... 71 A10　61 20N 93 50W
Magvana, India .............. 42 H3　23 13N 69 22 E
Magwe, Burma .............. 41 J19　20 10N 95　0 E
Maha Sarakham, Thailand ... 38 D4　16 12N 103 16 E
Mahābād, Iran .............. 44 B5　36 50N 45 45 E
Mahabharat Lekh, Nepal .... 43 E10　28 30N 82　0 E
Mahabo, Madag. ............ 57 C7　20 23S 44 40 E
Mahadeo Hills, India ........ 43 H8　22 20N 78 30 E
Mahaffey, U.S.A. ............ 84 F6　40 53N 78 44W
Mahagi, Dem. Rep. of the Congo . 54 B3　2　20N 31　0 E
Mahajamba →, Madag. ...... 57 B8　15 33S 47　8 E
Mahajamba, Helodranon' i,
　Madag. .................... 57 B8　15 24S 47　5 E
Mahajan, India .............. 42 E5　28 48N 73 56 E
Mahajanga, Madag. ......... 57 B8　15 40S 46 25 E
Mahajanga □, Madag. ....... 57 B8　17　0S 47　0 E
Mahajilo →, Madag. ........ 57 B8　19 42S 45 22 E
Mahakam →, Indonesia ..... 36 E5　0 35S 117 17 E
Mahalapye, Botswana ....... 56 C4　23　1S 26 51 E
Mahale Mts., Tanzania ...... 54 D3　6 20S 30　0 E
Mahale Mts. △, Tanzania .... 54 D2　6 10S 29 50 E
Mahallāt, Iran .............. 45 C6　33 55N 50 30 E
Māhān, Iran ................ 45 D8　30　5N 57 18 E
Mahan →, India ............ 43 H10　23 30N 82 50 E
Mahanadi →, India ......... 41 J15　20 20N 86 25 E
Mahananda →, India ....... 43 G12　25 12N 87 52 E
Mahanoro, Madag. .......... 57 B8　19 54S 48 48 E
Mahanoy City, U.S.A. ....... 85 F8　40 49N 76　9W
Maharashtra □, India ....... 40 J9　20 30N 75 30 E
Mahasham, W. →, Egypt .... 46 E3　30 15N 34 10 E
Mahasoa, Madag. ........... 57 C8　23 46S 47 41 E
Mahasolo, Madag. .......... 57 B8　19 7S 46 22 E
Mahattat 'Unayzah, Jordan .. 46 E4　30 30N 35 47 E
Mahavavy →, Madag. ....... 57 B8　15 57S 45 54 E
Mahaxay, Laos .............. 38 D5　17 22N 105 12 E
Mahbubnagar, India ......... 40 L10　16 45N 77 59 E
Mahdah, Oman .............. 45 E7　24 24N 55 59 E
Mahdia, Tunisia ............. 51 A8　35 28N 11　0 E
Mahe, India ................. 43 C8　33 10N 78 32 E
Mahendragarh, India ........ 42 E7　28 17N 76 14 E
Mahenge, Tanzania .......... 55 D4　8 45S 36 41 E
Maheno, N.Z. ................ 59 L3　45 10S 170 50 E
Mahesana, India ............ 42 H5　23 39N 72 26 E
Maheshwar, India ........... 42 H6　22 11N 75 35 E
Mahgawan, India ............ 43 F8　26 29N 78 37 E
Mahi →, India .............. 42 H5　22 15N 72 55 E
Mahia Pen., N.Z. ............ 59 H6　39　9S 177 55 E
Mahilyow, Belarus .......... 17 B16　53 55N 30 18 E
Mahinerangi, L., N.Z. ....... 59 L2　45 50S 169 56 E
Mahmud Kot, Pakistan ...... 42 D4　30 16N 71　0 E
Mahnomen, U.S.A. .......... 80 B7　47 19N 95 58W
Mahoba, India .............. 43 G8　25 15N 79 55 E
Mahón = Maó, Spain ........ 24 B11　39 53N　4 16 E
Mahone Bay, Canada ........ 73 D7　44 30N 64 20W
Mahopac, U.S.A. ............ 85 E11　41 22N 73 45W
Mahuva, India .............. 42 J4　21　5N 71 48 E
Mai-Ndombe, L., Dem. Rep. of
　the Congo ................. 52 E3　2　0S 18 20 E
Mai-Sai, Thailand ........... 38 B2　20 20N 99 55 E
Mai Thon, Ko, Thailand ..... 39 a　7 40N 98 28 E
Maicurú →, Brazil .......... 93 D8　2　14S 54 17W
Maidan Khula, Afghan. ...... 42 C3　33 36N 69 50 E
Maidenhead, U.K. ........... 13 F7　51 31N　0 42W
Maidstone, Canada .......... 71 C7　53 5N 109 20W
Maidstone, U.K. ............. 13 F8　51 16N　0 32 E
Maiduguri, Nigeria .......... 51 F8　12　0N 13　0 E
Maihar, India ............... 43 G9　24 16N 80 45 E
Maijdi, Bangla. .............. 41 H17　22 48N 91 10 E
Maikala Ra., India .......... 41 J12　22　0N 81　0 E
Maiko △, Dem. Rep. of
　the Congo ................. 54 C2　0 30S 27 50 E
Mailani, India ............... 43 E9　28 17N 80 21 E
Mailsi, Pakistan ............. 42 E5　29 48N 72 15 E
Main →, Germany ........... 16 C5　50　0N　8 18 E
Main →, U.K. ............... 10 B5　54 48N　6 18W
Main Range △, Australia .... 63 D5　28 11S 152 27 E
Main Ridge, Trin. & Tob. .... 93 J16　11 16N 60 40W
Maine, France ............... 20 C3　48 20N　0 15W
Maine □, U.S.A. ............. 83 C11　45 20N 69　0W
Maine →, Ireland ........... 10 D2　52　9N　9 45W
Maingkwan, Burma .......... 41 F20　26 15N 96 37 E
Mainit, L., Phil. ............. 37 C7　9 31N 125 30 E
Mainland, Orkney, U.K. ..... 11 C5　58 59N　3　8W
Mainland, Shet., U.K. ....... 11 A6　60 15N　1 22W
Mainoru, Australia .......... 62 A1　14　0S 134　6 E
Mainpuri, India ............. 43 F8　27 18N 79　4 E
Maintirano, Madag. ......... 57 B7　18　3S 44　1 E
Mainz, Germany ............. 16 C5　50　1N　8 14 E
Maipú, Argentina ........... 94 D4　36 52S 57 50W
Maiquetía, Venezuela ........ 92 A5　10 36N 66 57W
Mairabari, India ............. 41 F18　26 30N 92 22 E
Maisí, Cuba ................. 89 B5　20 17N 74　9W
Maisí, Pta. de, Cuba ........ 89 B5　20 10N 74 10W
Maitland, N.S.W., Australia .. 63 E5　32 33S 151 36 E
Maitland, S. Austral., Australia . 63 E2　34 23S 137 40 E
Maitland →, Canada ........ 84 C3　43 45N 81 43W
Maitri, Antarctica ........... 5 D3　70　0S　3　0W
Maiz, Is. del, Nic. ........... 88 D3　12 15N 83　4W
Maizuru, Japan .............. 31 G7　35 25N 135 22 E
Majalengka, Indonesia ....... 37 G13　6 50S 108 13 E
Majene, Indonesia ........... 37 E5　3 38S 118 57 E
Majete △, Malawi ........... 55 F3　15 54S 34 34 E
Majorca = Mallorca, Spain ... 24 B10　39 30N　3　0 E
Makaha, Zimbabwe .......... 57 B5　17 20S 32 39 E
Makalamabedi, Botswana .... 56 C3　20 19S 23 51 E
Makale, Indonesia .......... 37 E5　3　6S 119 51 E
Makari, Burundi ............ 54 C2　4　8S 29 49 E
Makarikari = Makgadikgadi Salt
　Pans, Botswana ............ 56 C4　20 40S 25 45 E
Makarov Basin, Arctic ....... 4 A　87　0N 150　0W
Makarovo, Russia ........... 29 D11　57 40N 107 45 E
Makasar = Ujung Pandang,
　Indonesia ................. 37 F5　5 10S 119 20 E
Makasar, Selat, Indonesia .... 37 E5　1　0S 118 20 E

Makasar, Str. of = Makasar, Selat,
  Indonesia . . . . . . . . . . . . . . . **37 E5** 1 0S 118 20 E
Makat, Kazakhstan . . . . . . . . . . **19 E9** 47 39N 53 19 E
Makedhonía, Greece . . . . . **23 D10** 40 39N 22 0 E
Makedonija = Macedonia ■,
  Europe . . . . . . . . . . . . . . . **23 D9** 41 53N 21 40 E
Makeyevka = Makiyivka, Ukraine **19 E6** 48 0N 38 0 E
Makgadikgadi △, Botswana . . . . **56 C3** 20 27S 24 47 E
Makgadikgadi Salt Pans,
  Botswana . . . . . . . . . . . . . . **56 C4** 20 40S 25 45 E
Makhachkala, Russia . . . . . **19 F8** 43 0N 47 30 E
Makhado = Louis Trichardt,
  S. Africa . . . . . . . . . . . . . . **57 C4** 23 1S 29 43 E
Makhfar al Buşayyah, Iraq . . . . **44 D5** 30 0N 46 10 E
Makhmūr, Iraq . . . . . . . . . . **44 C4** 35 46N 43 35 E
Makian, Indonesia . . . . . . . . **37 D7** 0 20N 127 20 E
Makindu, Kenya . . . . . . . . . **54 C4** 2 18S 37 50 E
Makinsk, Kazakhstan . . . . . **28 D8** 52 37N 70 26 E
Makiyivka, Ukraine . . . . . **19 E6** 48 0N 38 0 E
Makkah, Si. Arabia . . . . . . **47 C2** 21 30N 39 54 E
Makkovik, Canada . . . . . . **73 A8** 55 10N 59 10W
Makó, Hungary . . . . . . . **17 E11** 46 14N 20 33 E
Makokou, Gabon . . . . . . . **52 D2** 0 40N 12 50 E
Makongo, Dem. Rep. of
  the Congo . . . . . . . . . . . . . **54 B2** 3 25N 26 17 E
Makoro, Dem. Rep. of Congo **54 B2** 3 10N 29 59 E
Makrai, India . . . . . . . . **40 H10** 22 2N 77 0 E
Makran Coast Range, Pakistan . **40 G4** 25 40N 64 0 E
Makrana, India . . . . . . . . **42 F6** 27 2N 74 46 E
Makriyialos, Greece . . . . . **25 D7** 35 2N 25 59 E
Mākū, Iran . . . . . . . . . . . **44 B5** 39 15N 44 31 E
Makunda, Botswana . . . . . **56 C3** 22 30S 20 7 E
Makurazaki, Japan . . . . . . **31 J5** 31 15N 130 20 E
Makurdi, Nigeria . . . . . . . **50 G7** 7 43N 8 35 E
Makūyeh, Iran . . . . . . . . . **45 D7** 28 7N 53 9 E
Makwassie, S. Africa . . . . . **56 D4** 27 17S 26 0 E
Makwiro, Zimbabwe . . . . . **57 B5** 17 58S 30 25 E
Mal B., Ireland . . . . . . . . **10 D2** 52 50N 9 30W
Mala, Pta., Panama . . . . . . **88 E3** 7 28N 80 2W
Malabar Coast, India . . . . . **40 P9** 11 0N 75 0 E
Malacca, Straits of, Indonesia . **39 L3** 3 0N 101 0 E
Malad City, U.S.A. . . . . . . **76 E7** 42 12N 112 15W
Maladzyechna, Belarus . . . **17 A14** 54 20N 26 50 E
Málaga, Spain . . . . . . . . **21 D3** 36 43N 4 23W
Malagarasi, Tanzania . . . . . **54 D3** 5 5S 30 50 E
Malagarasi →, Tanzania . . . . **54 D2** 5 12S 29 47 E
Malagasy Rep. = Madagascar ■,
  Africa . . . . . . . . . . . . . . . **57 C8** 20 0S 47 0 E
Malahide, Ireland . . . . . . **10 C5** 53 26N 6 9W
Malaimbandy, Madag. . . . . **57 C8** 20 20S 45 36 E
Malakâl, Sudan . . . . . . . **51 G12** 9 33N 31 40 E
Malakand, Pakistan . . . . . **42 B4** 34 40N 71 55 E
Malakwal, Pakistan . . . . . **42 C5** 32 34N 73 13 E
Malamala, Indonesia . . . . . **37 E6** 3 21S 120 55 E
Malanda, Australia . . . . . . **62 B4** 17 22S 145 35 E
Malang, Indonesia . . . . . . **36 F4** 7 59S 112 45 E
Malangen, Norway . . . . . . **8 B18** 69 24N 18 37 E
Malanje, Angola . . . . . . . **52 F3** 9 36S 16 17 E
Mälaren, Sweden . . . . . . **9 G17** 59 30N 17 10 E
Malargüe, Argentina . . . . . **94 D2** 35 32S 69 30W
Malartic, Canada . . . . . . **72 C4** 48 9N 78 9W
Malaryta, Belarus . . . . . **17 C13** 51 50N 24 3 E
Malatya, Turkey . . . . . . . **19 G6** 38 25N 38 20 E
Malawi ■, Africa . . . . . . . **55 E3** 11 55S 34 0 E
Malawi, L. = Nyasa, L., Africa . **55 E3** 12 30S 34 30 E
Malay Pen., Asia . . . . . . . **39 J3** 7 25N 100 0 E
Malaya Vishera, Russia . . . **18 C5** 58 55N 32 25 E
Malaybalay, Phil. . . . . . . . **37 C7** 8 5N 125 7 E
Malâyer, Iran . . . . . . . . . **45 C6** 34 19N 48 51 E
Malaysia ■, Asia . . . . . . . **39 K4** 5 0N 110 0 E
Malazgirt, Turkey . . . . . . . **19 G7** 39 10N 42 33 E
Malbon, Australia . . . . . . **62 C3** 21 5S 140 17 E
Malbooma, Australia . . . . . **63 E1** 30 41S 134 11 E
Malbork, Poland . . . . . . . **17 B10** 54 3N 19 1 E
Malcolm, Australia . . . . . . **61 E3** 28 51S 121 25 E
Malcolm, Pt., Australia . . . . **61 F3** 33 48S 123 45 E
Maldah, India . . . . . . . . **43 G13** 25 2N 88 9 E
Maldegem, Belgium . . . . . **15 C3** 51 14N 3 26 E
Malden, Mass., U.S.A. . . . . **85 D13** 42 26N 71 4W
Malden, Mo., U.S.A. . . . . . **81 G10** 36 34N 89 57W
Malden I., Kiribati . . . . . . **65 H12** 4 3S 155 1W
Maldives ■, Ind. Oc. . . . . . **27 J11** 5 0N 73 0 E
Maldon, U.K. . . . . . . . . **13 F8** 51 44N 0 42 E
Maldonado, Uruguay . . . . **95 C5** 34 59S 55 0W
Maldonado, Punta, Mexico . . **87 D5** 16 19N 98 35W
Male, Maldives . . . . . . . **27 J11** 4 0N 73 28 E
Malé Karpaty, Slovak Rep. . . **17 D9** 48 30N 17 20 E
Maléa, Ákra, Greece . . . . . **23 F10** 36 28N 23 7 E
Malegaon, India . . . . . . . **40 J9** 20 30N 74 38 E
Malei, Mozam. . . . . . . . **55 F4** 17 12S 36 58 E
Malek Kandi, Iran . . . . . . **44 B5** 37 9N 46 6 E
Malela, Dem. Rep. of the Congo **54 C2** 4 22S 26 8 E
Malema, Mozam. . . . . . . **55 E4** 14 57S 37 20 E
Máleme, Greece . . . . . . . **25 D5** 35 31N 23 49 E
Malerkotla, India . . . . . . **42 D6** 30 32N 75 58 E
Máles, Greece . . . . . . . . **25 D7** 35 6N 25 35 E
Malgomaj, Sweden . . . . . **8 D17** 64 40N 16 30 E
Malha, Sudan . . . . . . . **51 E11** 15 8N 25 10 E
Malhargarh, India . . . . . . **42 G6** 24 17N 74 59 E
Malheur →, U.S.A. . . . . . . **76 D5** 44 4N 116 59W
Malheur L., U.S.A. . . . . . . **76 E4** 43 20N 118 48W
Mali ■, Africa . . . . . . . . **50 E5** 17 0N 3 0W
Mali →, Burma . . . . . . . **41 G20** 25 40N 97 40 E
Mali Kyun, Burma . . . . . . **38 F2** 13 0N 98 20 E
Malibu, U.S.A. . . . . . . . **79 L8** 34 2N 118 41W
Maliku, Indonesia . . . . . . **37 E6** 0 39S 123 16 E
Malili, Indonesia . . . . . . . **37 E6** 2 42S 121 6 E
Malimba, Mts., Dem. Rep. of
  the Congo . . . . . . . . . . . . . **54 D2** 7 30S 29 30 E
Malin Hd., Ireland . . . . . **10 A4** 55 23N 7 23W
Malin Pen., Ireland . . . . . **10 A4** 55 20N 7 17W
Malindi, Kenya . . . . . . . **54 C5** 3 12S 40 5 E
Malines = Mechelen, Belgium . **15 C4** 51 2N 4 29 E
Malino, Indonesia . . . . . . **37 D6** 1 0N 121 0 E
Malinyi, Tanzania . . . . . . **55 D4** 8 56S 36 0 E
Malita, Phil. . . . . . . . . . **37 C7** 6 19N 125 39 E
Maliwun, Burma . . . . . . . **36 B1** 10 17N 98 40 E
Maliya, India . . . . . . . . **42 H4** 23 5N 70 46 E
Malka Mari △, Kenya . . . . **54 B5** 4 10N 40 57 E
Malkara, Turkey . . . . . . . **23 D12** 40 53N 26 53 E
Mallacoota Inlet, Australia . . **63 F4** 37 34S 149 40 E
Mallaig, U.K. . . . . . . . . **11 D3** 57 0N 5 50W
Mallawan, India . . . . . . . **43 F9** 27 4N 80 12 E
Mallawi, Egypt . . . . . . . **51 C12** 27 44N 30 44 E
Mállia, Greece . . . . . . . . **25 D7** 35 17N 25 32 E
Mallión, Kólpos, Greece . . . **25 D7** 35 19N 25 27 E
Mallorca, Spain . . . . . . . **24 B10** 39 30N 3 0 E
Mallorytown, Canada . . . . . **85 B9** 44 29N 75 53W

Mallow, Ireland . . . . . . . **10 D3** 52 8N 8 39W
Malmberget, Sweden . . . . **8 C19** 67 11N 20 40 E
Malmédy, Belgium . . . . . . **15 D6** 50 25N 6 2 E
Malmesbury, S. Africa . . . . **56 E2** 33 28S 18 41 E
Malmivaara = Malmberget,
  Sweden . . . . . . . . . . . . . **8 C19** 67 11N 20 40 E
Malmö, Sweden . . . . . . . **9 J15** 55 36N 12 59 E
Malolos, Phil. . . . . . . . . **37 B6** 14 50N 120 49 E
Malolotja △, Swaziland . . . **57 D5** 26 4S 31 6 E
Malombe L., Malawi . . . . . **55 E4** 14 40S 35 15 E
Malone, U.S.A. . . . . . . . **85 B10** 44 51N 74 18W
Måløy, Norway . . . . . . . . **9 F11** 61 57N 5 6 E
Malpaso, Canary Is. . . . . . **24 G1** 27 43N 18 3W
Malpelo, I. de, Colombia . . . **92 C2** 4 3N 81 35W
Malpur, India . . . . . . . . **42 H5** 23 21N 73 27 E
Malpura, India . . . . . . . . **42 F6** 26 17N 75 23 E
Malta, Idaho, U.S.A. . . . . . **76 E7** 42 18N 113 22W
Malta, Mont., U.S.A. . . . . . **76 B10** 48 21N 107 52W
Malta ■, Europe . . . . . . . **25 D2** 35 55N 14 26 E
Maltahöhe, Namibia . . . . . **56 C2** 24 55S 17 0 E
Malton, Canada . . . . . . . **84 C5** 43 42N 79 38W
Malton, U.K. . . . . . . . . **12 C7** 54 8N 0 49W
Maluku, Indonesia . . . . . . **37 E7** 1 0S 127 0 E
Maluku □, Indonesia . . . . . **37 E7** 3 0S 128 0 E
Maluku Sea = Molucca Sea,
  Indonesia . . . . . . . . . . . . . **37 E6** 0 0 125 0 E
Maluku Utara □, Indonesia . . **37 D7** 1 0N 129 0 E
Malvan, India . . . . . . . . **40 L8** 16 2N 73 30 E
Malvern, U.S.A. . . . . . . . **81 H8** 34 22N 92 49W
Malvern Hills, U.K. . . . . . **13 E5** 52 0N 2 19W
Malvinas, Is. = Falkland Is. ☑,
  Atl. Oc. . . . . . . . . . . . . . **96 G5** 51 30S 59 0W
Malya, Tanzania . . . . . . . **54 C3** 3 5S 33 38 E
Malyn, Ukraine . . . . . . . **17 C15** 50 46N 29 3 E
Malyy Lyakhovskiy, Ostrov,
  Russia . . . . . . . . . . . . . **29 B15** 74 7N 140 36 E
Mama, Russia . . . . . . . . **29 D12** 58 18N 112 54 E
Mamanguape, Brazil . . . . . **93 E11** 6 50S 35 4W
Mamarr Mitlâ, Egypt . . . . . **46 E1** 30 2N 32 54 E
Mamasa, Indonesia . . . . . **37 E5** 2 55S 119 20 E
Mambasa, Dem. Rep. of
  the Congo . . . . . . . . . . . . . **54 B2** 1 22N 29 3 E
Mamberamo →, Indonesia . . **37 E9** 2 0S 137 50 E
Mambilima Falls, Zambia . . **55 E2** 10 31S 28 45 E
Mambirima, Dem. Rep. of
  the Congo . . . . . . . . . . . . . **55 E2** 11 25S 27 33 E
Mambo, Tanzania . . . . . . **54 C4** 4 52S 38 22 E
Mambrui, Kenya . . . . . . . **54 C5** 3 5S 40 5 E
Mamburao, Phil. . . . . . . . **37 B6** 13 13N 120 39 E
Mameigwess L., Canada . . . **72 B2** 52 35N 87 50W
Mammoth, U.S.A. . . . . . . **77 K8** 32 43N 110 39W
Mammoth Cave △, U.S.A. . . **82 G3** 37 8N 86 13W
Mamoré →, Bolivia . . . . . **92 F5** 10 23S 65 53W
Mamou, Guinea . . . . . . . **50 F3** 10 15N 12 0W
Mamoudzou, Mayotte . . . . **49 H8** 12 48S 45 14 E
Mampikony, Madag. . . . . . **57 B8** 16 6S 47 38 E
Mamuju, Indonesia . . . . . **37 E5** 2 41S 118 50 E
Mamuno, Botswana . . . . . **56 C3** 22 16S 20 1 E
Man, Ivory C. . . . . . . . . **50 G4** 7 30N 7 40W
Man, I. of, U.K. . . . . . . . **12 C3** 54 15N 4 30W
Man-Bazar, India . . . . . . **43 H12** 23 4N 86 39 E
Man Na, Burma . . . . . . . **41 H20** 23 27N 97 19 E
Mana →, Fr. Guiana . . . . . **93 B8** 5 45N 53 55W
Mana Pools △, Zimbabwe . . **55 F2** 15 56S 29 25 E
Manaar, G. of = Mannar, G. of,
  Asia . . . . . . . . . . . . . . . **40 Q11** 8 30N 79 0 E
Manacapuru, Brazil . . . . . **92 D6** 3 16S 60 37W
Manacor, Spain . . . . . . . **24 B10** 39 34N 3 13 E
Manado, Indonesia . . . . . **37 D6** 1 29N 124 51 E
Managua, Nic. . . . . . . . . **88 D2** 12 6N 86 20W
Managua, L. de, Nic. . . . . . **88 D2** 12 20N 86 30W
Manakara, Madag. . . . . . . **57 C8** 22 8S 48 1 E
Manali, India . . . . . . . . **42 C7** 32 16N 77 10 E
Manama = Al Manāmah, Bahrain **45 E6** 26 10N 50 30 E
Manambao →, Madag. . . . . **57 B7** 17 35S 44 0 E
Manambato, Madag. . . . . . **57 A8** 13 43S 49 7 E
Manambolo →, Madag. . . . **57 B7** 19 18S 44 22 E
Manambolosy, Madag. . . . . **57 B8** 16 2S 49 40 E
Mananara →, Madag. . . . . **57 B8** 16 10S 49 46 E
Mananara △, Madag. . . . . **57 B8** 16 14S 49 45 E
Mananjary →, Madag. . . . . **57 C8** 23 21S 47 42 E
Mananjary, Madag. . . . . . **57 C8** 21 13S 48 20 E
Manantenina, Madag. . . . . **57 C8** 24 17S 47 19 E
Manaos = Manaus, Brazil . . **92 D7** 3 0S 60 0W
Manapire →, Venezuela . . . **92 B5** 7 42N 66 7W
Manapouri, N.Z. . . . . . . . **59 L1** 45 34S 167 39 E
Manapouri, L., N.Z. . . . . . **59 L1** 45 32S 167 32 E
Manār, Jabal, Yemen . . . . . **47 E3** 14 2N 44 17 E
Manaravolo, Madag. . . . . . **57 C8** 23 59S 45 39 E
Manas, China . . . . . . . . **32 B3** 44 17N 85 56 E
Manas →, India . . . . . . . **41 F17** 26 12N 90 40 E
Manaslu, Nepal . . . . . . . **43 E11** 28 33N 84 33 E
Manasquan, U.S.A. . . . . . **85 F10** 40 8N 74 3W
Manassa, U.S.A. . . . . . . . **77 H11** 37 11N 105 56W
Manati, Puerto Rico . . . . . **89 d** 18 26N 66 29W
Manaung, Burma . . . . . . **41 K18** 18 45N 93 40 E
Manaus, Brazil . . . . . . . **92 D7** 3 0S 60 0W
Manawan L., Canada . . . . . **71 B8** 55 24N 103 14W
Manbij, Syria . . . . . . . . **44 B3** 36 31N 37 57 E
Manchegorsk, Russia . . . . **28 C4** 67 54N 32 58 E
Manchester, U.K. . . . . . . **12 D5** 53 29N 2 12W
Manchester, Calif., U.S.A. . . **78 G3** 38 58N 123 41W
Manchester, Conn., U.S.A. . . **85 E12** 41 47N 72 31W
Manchester, Ga., U.S.A. . . . **83 J3** 32 51N 84 37W
Manchester, Iowa, U.S.A. . . **80 D9** 42 29N 91 27W
Manchester, Ky., U.S.A. . . . **82 G4** 37 9N 83 46W
Manchester, N.H., U.S.A. . . **85 D13** 42 59N 71 28W
Manchester, N.Y., U.S.A. . . . **84 D7** 42 56N 77 16W
Manchester, Pa., U.S.A. . . . **85 F8** 40 4N 76 43W
Manchester, Tenn., U.S.A. . . **83 H2** 35 29N 86 5W
Manchester, Vt., U.S.A. . . . **85 C11** 43 10N 73 5W
Manchester International ✈
  (MAN), U.K. . . . . . . . . . **12 D5** 53 21N 2 17W
Manchhar L., Canada . . . . **71 A7** 61 28N 107 29W
Manchhar L., Pakistan . . . . **42 F2** 26 25N 67 39 E
Manchuria = Dongbei, China . **29 E13** 45 0N 125 0 E
Manchurian Plain, China . . . **26 E16** 47 0N 124 0 E
Mand →, India . . . . . . . **43 J10** 21 42N 83 15 E
Mand →, Iran . . . . . . . . **45 D7** 28 20N 52 30 E
Manda, Ludewe, Tanzania . . **55 E3** 10 30S 34 40 E
Manda, Mbeya, Tanzania . . **54 D3** 7 58S 32 29 E
Manda, Mbeya, Tanzania . . **55 D3** 8 30S 32 49 E
Mandabé, Madag. . . . . . . **57 C7** 21 0S 44 55 E
Mandaguari, Brazil . . . . . **95 A5** 23 32S 51 42W
Mandah = Töhöm, Mongolia . **34 B5** 44 27N 108 2 E
Mandal, Norway . . . . . . . **9 G12** 58 2N 7 25 E
Mandala, Puncak, Indonesia . **37 E10** 4 44S 140 20 E
Mandalay, Burma . . . . . . **41 J20** 22 0N 96 4 E

Mandale = Mandalay, Burma . **41 J20** 22 0N 96 4 E
Mandalgarh, India . . . . . . **42 G6** 25 12N 75 6 E
Mandalgovi, Mongolia . . . . **34 B4** 45 45N 106 10 E
Mandali, Iraq . . . . . . . . **44 C5** 33 43N 45 28 E
Mandan, U.S.A. . . . . . . . **80 B4** 46 50N 100 54W
Mandar, Teluk, Indonesia . . **37 E5** 3 35S 119 15 E
Mandaue, Phil. . . . . . . . **37 B6** 10 20N 123 56 E
Mandera, Kenya . . . . . . . **54 B5** 3 55N 41 53 E
Mandeville, Jamaica . . . . . **88 a** 18 2N 77 31W
Mandi, India . . . . . . . . **42 D7** 31 39N 76 58 E
Mandi Dabwali, India . . . . **42 E6** 29 58N 74 42 E
Mandimba, Mozam. . . . . . **55 E4** 14 20S 35 40 E
Mandioli, Indonesia . . . . . **37 E7** 0 40S 127 20 E
Mandla, India . . . . . . . . **43 H9** 22 39N 80 30 E
Mandorah, Australia . . . . . **60 B5** 12 32S 130 42 E
Mandra, Pakistan . . . . . . **42 C5** 33 23N 73 12 E
Mandrare →, Madag. . . . . **57 D8** 25 10S 46 30 E
Mandritsara, Madag. . . . . . **57 B8** 15 50S 48 49 E
Mandsaur, India . . . . . . . **42 G6** 24 3N 75 8 E
Mandurah, Australia . . . . . **61 F2** 32 36S 115 48 E
Mandvi, India . . . . . . . . **42 H3** 22 51N 69 22 E
Mandya, India . . . . . . . **40 N10** 12 30N 77 0 E
Mandzai, Pakistan . . . . . . **42 D2** 30 55N 67 6 E
Maneh, Iran . . . . . . . . . **45 B8** 37 39N 57 7 E
Manera, Madag. . . . . . . . **57 C7** 22 55S 44 20 E
Maneroo Cr. →, Australia . . **62 C3** 23 21S 143 53 E
Manfalût, Egypt . . . . . . . **51 C12** 27 20N 30 52 E
Manfredónia, Italy . . . . . . **22 D6** 41 38N 15 55 E
Mangabeiras, Chapada das,
  Brazil . . . . . . . . . . . . . . **93 F9** 10 0S 46 30W
Mangalia, Romania . . . . . **17 G15** 43 50N 28 35 E
Mangalore, India . . . . . . **40 N9** 12 55N 74 47 E
Mangan, India . . . . . . . **43 F13** 27 31N 88 32 E
Mangaung, S. Africa . . . . . **53 K5** 29 10S 26 25 E
Mangawan, India . . . . . . **43 G9** 24 41N 81 33 E
Mangaweka, N.Z. . . . . . . **59 H5** 39 48S 175 47 E
Manggar, Indonesia . . . . . **36 E3** 2 50S 108 10 E
Manggawitu, Indonesia . . . **37 E8** 4 8S 133 32 E
Manggis, Indonesia . . . . . **37 J18** 8 29S 115 31 E
Mangindrano, Madag. . . . . **57 A8** 14 17S 48 58 E
Mangla, Pakistan . . . . . . **42 C5** 33 7N 73 39 E
Mangla Dam, Pakistan . . . . **43 C5** 33 9N 73 44 E
Manglaur, India . . . . . . . **42 E7** 29 44N 77 49 E
Mangnai, China . . . . . . . **32 C4** 37 52N 91 43 E
Mango, Togo . . . . . . . . **50 F6** 10 20N 0 30 E
Mangoche, Malawi . . . . . . **55 E4** 14 25S 35 16 E
Mangoky →, Madag. . . . . . **57 C7** 21 29S 43 41 E
Mangole, Indonesia . . . . . **37 E6** 1 50S 125 55 E
Mangombe, Dem. Rep. of
  the Congo . . . . . . . . . . . . . **54 C2** 1 20S 26 48 E
Mangonui, N.Z. . . . . . . . **59 F4** 35 1S 173 32 E
Mangoro →, Madag. . . . . . **57 B8** 20 0S 48 45 E
Mangrol, Mad. P., India . . . **42 J4** 21 7N 70 7 E
Mangrol, Raj., India . . . . . **42 G6** 25 20N 76 31 E
Mangueira, L. da, Brazil . . . **95 C5** 33 0S 52 50W
Mangum, U.S.A. . . . . . . . **81 H5** 34 53N 99 30W
Mangyshlak, Poluostrov,
  Kazakhstan . . . . . . . . . . . . **19 E8** 44 30N 52 30 E
Manhattan, U.S.A. . . . . . . **80 F6** 39 11N 96 35W
Manhiça, Mozam. . . . . . . **57 D5** 25 23S 32 49 E
Mania →, Madag. . . . . . . **57 B8** 19 42S 45 22 E
Manica, Mozam. . . . . . . . **57 B5** 18 58S 32 59 E
Manica □, Mozam. . . . . . . **57 B5** 19 10S 33 45 E
Manicaland □, Zimbabwe . . **55 F3** 19 0S 32 30 E
Manicoré, Brazil . . . . . . . **92 E6** 5 48S 61 16W
Manicouagan →, Canada . . **73 C6** 49 30N 68 30W
Manicouagan, Rés., Canada . **73 B6** 51 5N 68 40W
Maniema □, Dem. Rep. of
  the Congo . . . . . . . . . . . . . **54 C2** 3 0S 26 0 E
Manifah, Si. Arabia . . . . . **45 E6** 27 44N 49 0 E
Manifold, C., Australia . . . . **62 C5** 22 41S 150 50 E
Manigotagan, Canada . . . . **71 C9** 51 6N 96 18W
Manigotagan →, Canada . . . **71 C9** 51 7N 96 20W
Manihari, India . . . . . . . **43 G12** 25 21N 87 38 E
Manihiki, Cook Is. . . . . . . **65 J11** 10 24S 161 1W
Manika, Plateau de la, Dem. Rep.
  of the Congo . . . . . . . . . . . **55 E2** 10 0S 25 5 E
Manikpur, India . . . . . . . **43 G9** 25 4N 81 7 E
Manila, Phil. . . . . . . . . **37 B6** 14 40N 121 3 E
Manila, U.S.A. . . . . . . . . **76 F9** 40 59N 109 43W
Manila B., Phil. . . . . . . . **37 B6** 14 40N 120 35 E
Manilla, Australia . . . . . . **63 E5** 30 45S 150 43 E
Maningrida, Australia . . . . **62 A1** 12 3S 134 13 E
Manipur □, India . . . . . . **41 G19** 25 0N 94 0 E
Manipur →, Burma . . . . . . **41 H19** 23 45N 94 20 E
Manisa, Turkey . . . . . . . **23 E12** 38 38N 27 30 E
Manistee, U.S.A. . . . . . . . **82 C2** 44 15N 86 19W
Manistee →, U.S.A. . . . . . **82 C2** 44 15N 86 21W
Manistique, U.S.A. . . . . . . **82 C2** 45 57N 86 15W
Manito L., Canada . . . . . . **71 C7** 52 43N 109 43W
Manitoba □, Canada . . . . . **71 B9** 53 30N 97 0W
Manitoba, L., Canada . . . . **71 C9** 51 0N 98 45W
Manitou, Canada . . . . . . **71 D9** 49 15N 98 32W
Manitou, L., Canada . . . . . **73 B6** 50 55N 65 17W
Manitou Is., U.S.A. . . . . . **82 C3** 45 8N 86 0W
Manitou L., Canada . . . . . **71 C7** 52 43N 109 43W
Manitou Springs, U.S.A. . . . **80 F2** 38 52N 104 55W
Manitoulin I., Canada . . . . **72 C3** 45 40N 82 30W
Manitouwadge, Canada . . . **72 C2** 49 8N 85 48W
Manitowoc, U.S.A. . . . . . . **82 C2** 44 5N 87 40W
Manizales, Colombia . . . . . **92 B3** 5 5N 75 32W
Manja, Madag. . . . . . . . **57 C7** 21 26S 44 20 E
Manjacaze, Mozam. . . . . . **57 C5** 24 45S 34 0 E
Manjakandriana, Madag. . . . **57 B8** 18 55S 47 47 E
Manjhand, Pakistan . . . . . **42 G3** 25 50N 68 10 E
Manjil, Iran . . . . . . . . . **45 B6** 36 46N 49 30 E
Manjimup, Australia . . . . . **61 F2** 34 15S 116 6 E
Manjra →, India . . . . . . . **40 K10** 18 49N 77 52 E
Mankato, Kans., U.S.A. . . . **80 F5** 39 47N 98 13W
Mankato, Minn., U.S.A. . . . **80 C8** 44 10N 94 0W
Mankayane, Swaziland . . . **57 D5** 26 40S 31 4 E
Mankera, Pakistan . . . . . . **42 D4** 31 23N 71 26 E
Mankono, Ivory C. . . . . . . **50 G4** 8 1N 6 10W
Mankota, Canada . . . . . . **71 D7** 49 25N 107 5W
Manlay = Üydzin, Mongolia . **34 B4** 44 9N 107 0 E
Manmad, India . . . . . . . **40 J9** 20 18N 74 28 E
Mann Ranges, Australia . . . **61 E5** 26 6S 130 5 E
Manna, Indonesia . . . . . . **36 E2** 4 25S 102 55 E
Mannahill, Australia . . . . . **63 E3** 32 25S 140 0 E
Mannar, Sri Lanka . . . . . . **40 Q11** 9 1N 79 54 E
Mannar, G. of, Asia . . . . . **40 Q11** 8 30N 79 0 E
Mannar I., Sri Lanka . . . . . **40 Q11** 9 5N 79 45 E
Mannheim, Germany . . . . . **16 D5** 49 29N 8 29 E
Manning, Canada . . . . . . **70 B5** 56 53N 117 39W
Manning, Oreg., U.S.A. . . . **78 E3** 45 45N 123 13W
Manning, S.C., U.S.A. . . . . **83 J5** 33 42N 80 13W
Mannum, Australia . . . . . **63 E2** 34 50S 139 20 E

Manoharpur, India . . . . . . **43 H11** 22 23N 85 12 E
Manokwari, Indonesia . . . . **37 E8** 0 54S 134 0 E
Manombo, Madag. . . . . . . **57 C7** 22 57S 43 28 E
Manono, Dem. Rep. of the Congo **54 D2** 7 15S 27 25 E
Manosque, France . . . . . . **20 E6** 43 49N 5 47 E
Manotick, Canada . . . . . . **85 A9** 45 13N 75 41W
Manouane →, Canada . . . . **73 C5** 49 30N 71 10W
Manouane, L., Canada . . . . **73 B5** 50 45N 70 45W
Manp'o, N. Korea . . . . . . **35 D14** 41 6N 126 24 E
Manpojin = Manp'o, N. Korea **35 D14** 41 6N 126 24 E
Manpur, Chhattisgarh, India . **43 H10** 23 17N 83 35 E
Manpur, Mad. P., India . . . **42 H6** 22 26N 75 37 E
Manresa, Spain . . . . . . . **21 B6** 41 48N 1 50 E
Mansa, Gujarat, India . . . . **42 H5** 23 27N 72 45 E
Mansa, Punjab, India . . . . **42 E6** 30 0N 75 27 E
Mansa, Zambia . . . . . . . **55 E2** 11 13S 28 55 E
Mansehra, Pakistan . . . . . **42 B5** 34 20N 73 15 E
Mansel I., Canada . . . . . . **69 B11** 62 0N 80 0W
Mansfield, Australia . . . . . **63 F4** 37 4S 146 6 E
Mansfield, U.K. . . . . . . . **12 D6** 53 9N 1 11W
Mansfield, La., U.S.A. . . . . **81 J8** 32 2N 93 43W
Mansfield, Mass., U.S.A. . . **85 D13** 42 2N 71 13W
Mansfield, Ohio, U.S.A. . . . **84 F2** 40 45N 82 31W
Mansfield, Pa., U.S.A. . . . . **84 E7** 41 48N 77 5W
Mansfield, Mt., U.S.A. . . . **85 B12** 44 33N 72 49W
Manson Creek, Canada . . . **70 B4** 55 37N 124 32W
Manta, Ecuador . . . . . . . **92 D2** 1 0S 80 40W
Mantadia △, Madag. . . . . . **57 B8** 18 54S 48 21 E
Mantalingajan, Mt., Phil. . . . **36 C5** 8 55N 117 45 E
Mantare, Tanzania . . . . . . **54 C3** 2 42S 33 13 E
Manteca, U.S.A. . . . . . . . **78 H5** 37 48N 121 13W
Manteo, U.S.A. . . . . . . . **83 H8** 35 55N 75 40W
Mantes-la-Jolie, France . . . **20 B4** 48 58N 1 41 E
Manthani, India . . . . . . . **40 K11** 18 40N 79 35 E
Manton, U.S.A. . . . . . . . **76 G8** 39 16N 111 38W
Mantiqueira, Serra da, Brazil . **95 A7** 22 0S 44 0W
Manton, U.S.A. . . . . . . . **82 C3** 44 25N 85 24W
Mántova, Italy . . . . . . . . **22 B4** 45 9N 10 48 E
Mänttä, Finland . . . . . . . **9 E21** 62 3N 24 40 E
Mantua = Mántova, Italy . . . **22 B4** 45 9N 10 48 E
Manu, Peru . . . . . . . . . **92 F4** 12 10S 70 51W
Manu →, Peru . . . . . . . . **92 F4** 12 16S 70 55W
Manu'a Is., Amer. Samoa . . **59 B14** 14 13S 169 35W
Manuel Alves →, Brazil . . . **93 F9** 11 19S 48 28W
Manui, Indonesia . . . . . . **37 E6** 3 35S 123 5 E
Manukau, N.Z. . . . . . . . **59 G5** 37 0S 174 52 E
Manuripi →, Bolivia . . . . . **92 F5** 11 6S 67 36W
Many, U.S.A. . . . . . . . . **81 K8** 31 34N 93 29W
Manyara, L., Tanzania . . . . **54 C4** 3 40S 35 50 E
Manych-Gudilo, Ozero, Russia **19 E7** 46 24N 42 38 E
Manyonga →, Tanzania . . . **54 C3** 4 10S 34 15 E
Manyoni, Tanzania . . . . . **54 D3** 5 45S 34 55 E
Manzai, Pakistan . . . . . . **42 C4** 32 12N 70 15 E
Manzanar △, U.S.A. . . . . . **78 J7** 36 44N 118 9W . . . 5W
Manzanares, Spain . . . . . **21 C4** 39 2N 3 22W
Manzanillo, Cuba . . . . . . **88 B4** 20 20N 77 31W
Manzanillo, Mexico . . . . . **86 D4** 19 0N 104 20W
Manzanillo, Pta., Panama . . **88 E4** 9 30N 79 40W
Manzano Mts., U.S.A. . . . . **77 J10** 34 40N 106 20W
Manzariyeh, Iran . . . . . . **45 C6** 34 53N 50 50 E
Manzhouli, China . . . . . . **33 B6** 49 35N 117 25 E
Manzini, Swaziland . . . . . **57 D5** 26 30S 31 25 E
Mao, Chad . . . . . . . . . . **51 F9** 14 4N 15 19 E
Maó, Spain . . . . . . . . . **24 B11** 39 53N 4 16 E
Maoke, Pegunungan, Indonesia **37 E9** 3 40S 137 30 E
Maolin, China . . . . . . . . **35 C12** 43 58N 123 30 E
Maoming, China . . . . . . . **33 D6** 21 50N 110 54 E
Maoxing, China . . . . . . . **35 B13** 45 28N 124 40 E
Mapam Yumco, China . . . . **32 C3** 30 45N 81 28 E
Mapastepec, Mexico . . . . . **87 D6** 15 26N 92 54W
Maphrao, Ko, Thailand . . . . **39 a** 7 56N 98 26 E
Mapia, Kepulauan, Indonesia . **37 D8** 0 50N 134 20 E
Mapimí, Mexico . . . . . . . **86 B4** 25 50N 103 50W
Mapimí, Bolsón de, Mexico . **86 B4** 27 30N 104 15W
Mapinga, Tanzania . . . . . **54 D4** 6 40S 39 12 E
Mapinhane, Mozam. . . . . . **57 C6** 22 20S 35 0 E
Maple Creek, Canada . . . . **71 D7** 49 55N 109 29W
Maple Valley, U.S.A. . . . . . **78 C4** 47 25N 122 3W
Mapleton, U.S.A. . . . . . . **76 D2** 44 2N 123 52W
Mapuera →, Brazil . . . . . . **92 D7** 1 5S 57 2W
Mapulanguene, Mozam. . . . **57 C5** 24 29S 32 6 E
Maputo, Mozam. . . . . . . . **57 D5** 25 58S 32 32 E
Maputo □, Mozam. . . . . . **57 D5** 26 0S 32 25 E
Maputo, B. de, Mozam. . . . **57 D5** 25 50S 32 45 E
Maqiaohe, China . . . . . . . **35 B16** 44 40N 130 30 E
Maqnā, Si. Arabia . . . . . . **44 D2** 28 25N 34 50 E
Maquan He = Brahmaputra →,
  Asia . . . . . . . . . . . . . . . **32 D3** 23 40N 90 35 E
Maquela do Zombo, Angola . **52 F3** 6 0S 15 15 E
Maquinchao, Argentina . . . **96 E3** 41 15S 68 50W
Maquoketa, U.S.A. . . . . . . **80 D9** 42 4N 90 40W
Mar, Serra do, Brazil . . . . . **95 B6** 25 30S 49 0W
Mar Chiquita, L., Argentina . **94 C3** 30 40S 62 50W
Mar del Plata, Argentina . . . **94 D4** 38 0S 57 30W
Mar Menor, Spain . . . . . . **21 D5** 37 40N 0 45W
Mara, Tanzania . . . . . . . **54 C3** 1 30S 34 32 E
Mara □, Tanzania . . . . . . **54 C3** 1 45S 34 20 E
Maraã, Brazil . . . . . . . . **92 D5** 1 52S 65 25W
Marabá, Brazil . . . . . . . **93 E9** 5 20S 49 5W
Maracá, I. de, Brazil . . . . . **93 C8** 2 10N 50 30W
Maracaibo, Venezuela . . . . **92 A4** 10 40N 71 37W
Maracaibo, L. de, Venezuela . **92 B4** 9 40N 71 30W
Maracaju, Brazil . . . . . . . **95 A4** 21 38S 55 9W
Maracás Bay Village, Trin. & Tob. **93 K15** 10 46N 61 28W
Maradi, Niger . . . . . . . . **50 F7** 13 29N 7 20 E
Marägheh, Iran . . . . . . . **44 B5** 37 30N 46 12 E
Marāh, Si. Arabia . . . . . . **44 E5** 25 0N 45 35 E
Marajó, I. de, Brazil . . . . . **93 D9** 1 0S 49 30W
Marākand, Iran . . . . . . . **44 B5** 38 51N 45 16 E
Marakele △, S. Africa . . . . **57 E4** 32 14S 25 27 E
Maralal, Kenya . . . . . . . **54 B4** 1 0N 36 38 E
Maralinga, Australia . . . . . **61 F5** 30 13S 131 32 E
Marambio, Antarctica . . . . **5 C18** 64 0S 56 0W
Maran, Malaysia . . . . . . . **39 L4** 3 35N 102 45 E
Marand, Iran . . . . . . . . **44 B5** 38 30N 45 45 E
Maranboy, Australia . . . . . **60 B5** 14 40S 132 39 E
Marand, Iran . . . . . . . . **44 B5** 38 30N 45 45 E
Maranguape, Brazil . . . . . **93 D11** 3 55S 38 50W
Maranhão = São Luís, Brazil . **93 D10** 2 39S 44 15W
Maranhão □, Brazil . . . . . **93 E9** 5 0S 46 0W
Maranoa →, Australia . . . . **63 D4** 27 50S 148 37 E
Marañón →, Peru . . . . . . **92 D4** 4 30S 73 35W
Marão, Mozam. . . . . . . . **57 C5** 24 18S 34 2 E
Maraş = Kahramanmaraş, Turkey **19 G6** 37 37N 36 53 E
Marathasa, Cyprus . . . . . **25 E11** 34 59N 32 51 E

| | | | |
|---|---|---|---|
| Marathon, Australia | 62 C3 | 20 51S | 143 32 E |
| Marathon, Canada | 72 C2 | 48 44N | 86 23W |
| Marathon, N.Y., U.S.A. | 85 D8 | 42 27N | 76 2W |
| Marathon, Tex., U.S.A. | 81 K3 | 30 12N | 103 15W |
| Maratua, Indonesia | 37 D5 | 2 10N | 118 35 E |
| Maraval, Trin. & Tob. | 93 K15 | 10 42N | 61 31W |
| Maravatío, Mexico | 86 D4 | 19 51N | 100 25W |
| Marāwih, U.A.E. | 45 E7 | 24 18N | 53 18 E |
| Marbella, Spain | 21 D3 | 36 30N | 4 57W |
| Marble Bar, Australia | 60 D2 | 21 9S | 119 44 E |
| Marble Falls, U.S.A. | 81 K5 | 30 35N | 98 16W |
| Marblehead, U.S.A. | 85 D14 | 42 30N | 70 51W |
| Marburg, Germany | 16 C5 | 50 47N | 8 46 E |
| March, U.K. | 13 E8 | 52 33N | 0 5 E |
| Marche, France | 20 C4 | 46 5N | 1 20 E |
| Marche-en-Famenne, Belgium | 15 D5 | 50 14N | 5 19 E |
| Marchena, Spain | 21 D3 | 37 18N | 5 23W |
| Marco, U.S.A. | 83 N5 | 25 58N | 81 44W |
| Marcos Juárez, Argentina | 94 C3 | 32 42S | 62 5W |
| Marcus I. = Minami-Tori-Shima, Pac. Oc. | 64 E7 | 24 20N | 153 58 E |
| Marcus Necker Ridge, Pac. Oc. | 64 F9 | 20 0N | 175 0 E |
| Marcy, Mt., U.S.A. | 85 B11 | 44 7N | 73 56W |
| Mardan, Pakistan | 42 B5 | 34 20N | 72 0 E |
| Mardin, Turkey | 19 G7 | 37 20N | 40 43 E |
| Maree, L., U.K. | 11 D3 | 57 40N | 5 26W |
| Mareeba, Australia | 62 B4 | 16 59S | 145 28 E |
| Mareetsane, S. Africa | 56 D4 | 26 9S | 25 25 E |
| Marek = Stanke Dimitrov, Bulgaria | 23 C10 | 42 17N | 23 9 E |
| Marengo, U.S.A. | 80 E8 | 41 48N | 92 4W |
| Marerano, Madag. | 57 C7 | 21 23S | 44 52 E |
| Marfa, U.S.A. | 81 K2 | 30 19N | 104 1W |
| Marfa Pt., Malta | 25 D1 | 35 59N | 14 19 E |
| Margaret →, Australia | 60 C4 | 18 9S | 125 41 E |
| Margaret Bay, Canada | 70 C3 | 51 20N | 127 35W |
| Margaret L., Canada | 70 B5 | 58 56N | 115 25W |
| Margaret River, Australia | 61 F2 | 33 57S | 115 4 E |
| Margarita, I. de, Venezuela | 92 A6 | 11 0N | 64 0W |
| Margaritovo, Russia | 30 C7 | 43 25N | 134 45 E |
| Margate, S. Africa | 57 E5 | 30 50S | 30 20 E |
| Margate, U.K. | 13 F9 | 51 23N | 1 23 E |
| Margherita Pk., Uganda | 54 B3 | 0 22N | 29 51 E |
| Mārgow, Dasht-e, Afghan. | 40 D3 | 30 40N | 62 30 E |
| Marguerite, Canada | 70 C4 | 52 30N | 122 25W |
| Mari El □, Russia | 18 C8 | 56 30N | 48 0 E |
| Mari Indus, Pakistan | 42 C4 | 32 57N | 71 34 E |
| Mari Republic = Mari El □, Russia | 18 C8 | 56 30N | 48 0 E |
| María Elena, Chile | 94 A2 | 22 18S | 69 40W |
| María Grande, Argentina | 94 C4 | 31 45S | 59 55W |
| Maria I., N. Terr., Australia | 62 A2 | 14 52S | 135 45 E |
| Maria I., Tas., Australia | 63 G4 | 42 35S | 148 0 E |
| Maria Island △, Australia | 63 G4 | 42 38S | 148 5 E |
| Maria van Diemen, C., N.Z. | 59 F4 | 34 29S | 172 40 E |
| Mariakani, Kenya | 54 C4 | 3 50S | 39 27 E |
| Mariala △, Australia | 63 D4 | 25 57S | 145 2 E |
| Marian, Australia | 62 K6 | 21 9S | 148 57 E |
| Marian L., Canada | 70 A5 | 63 0N | 116 15W |
| Mariana Trench, Pac. Oc. | 26 H18 | 13 0N | 145 0 E |
| Marianao, Cuba | 88 B3 | 23 8N | 82 24W |
| Marianna, Ark., U.S.A. | 81 H9 | 34 46N | 90 46W |
| Marianna, Fla., U.S.A. | 83 K3 | 30 46N | 85 14W |
| Marias →, U.S.A. | 76 C8 | 47 56N | 110 30W |
| Mariato, Punta, Panama | 88 E3 | 7 12N | 80 52W |
| Maribor, Slovenia | 16 E8 | 46 36N | 15 40 E |
| Marico →, Africa | 56 C4 | 23 35S | 26 57 E |
| Maricopa, Ariz., U.S.A. | 77 K7 | 33 4N | 112 3W |
| Maricopa, Calif., U.S.A. | 79 K7 | 35 4N | 119 24W |
| Marié →, Brazil | 92 D5 | 0 27S | 66 26W |
| Marie Byrd Land, Antarctica | 5 D14 | 79 30S | 125 0W |
| Marie-Galante, Guadeloupe | 88 b | 15 56N | 61 16W |
| Mariecourt = Kangiqsujuaq, Canada | 69 B12 | 61 30N | 72 0W |
| Mariehamn = Maarianhamina, Finland | 9 F18 | 60 5N | 19 55 E |
| Mariembourg, Belgium | 15 D4 | 50 6N | 4 31 E |
| Mariental, Namibia | 56 C2 | 24 36S | 18 0 E |
| Marienville, U.S.A. | 84 E5 | 41 28N | 79 8W |
| Mariestad, Sweden | 9 G15 | 58 43N | 13 50 E |
| Marietta, Ga., U.S.A. | 83 J3 | 33 57N | 84 33W |
| Marietta, Ohio, U.S.A. | 82 F5 | 39 25N | 81 27W |
| Marieville, Canada | 85 A11 | 45 26N | 73 10W |
| Mariinsk, Russia | 28 D9 | 56 10N | 87 20 E |
| Marijampolė, Lithuania | 9 J20 | 54 33N | 23 19 E |
| Marília, Brazil | 95 A6 | 22 13S | 50 0W |
| Marín, Spain | 21 A1 | 42 23N | 8 42W |
| Marina, U.S.A. | 78 J5 | 36 41N | 121 48W |
| Marinduque, Phil. | 37 B6 | 13 25N | 122 0 E |
| Marine City, U.S.A. | 84 D2 | 42 43N | 82 30W |
| Marinette, U.S.A. | 82 C2 | 45 6N | 87 38W |
| Maringá, Brazil | 95 A5 | 23 26S | 52 2W |
| Marion, Ala., U.S.A. | 83 J2 | 32 38N | 87 19W |
| Marion, Ill., U.S.A. | 81 G10 | 37 44N | 88 56W |
| Marion, Ind., U.S.A. | 82 E3 | 40 32N | 85 40W |
| Marion, Iowa, U.S.A. | 80 D9 | 42 2N | 91 36W |
| Marion, Kans., U.S.A. | 80 F6 | 38 21N | 97 1W |
| Marion, N.C., U.S.A. | 83 H5 | 35 41N | 82 1W |
| Marion, Ohio, U.S.A. | 82 E4 | 40 35N | 83 8W |
| Marion, S.C., U.S.A. | 83 H6 | 34 11N | 79 24W |
| Marion, Va., U.S.A. | 83 G5 | 36 50N | 81 31W |
| Marion, L., U.S.A. | 83 J5 | 33 28N | 80 10W |
| Mariposa, U.S.A. | 78 H7 | 37 29N | 119 58W |
| Mariscal Estigarribia, Paraguay | 94 A3 | 22 3S | 60 40W |
| Maritime Alps = Maritimes, Alpes, Europe | 20 D7 | 44 10N | 7 10 E |
| Maritimes, Alpes, Europe | 20 D7 | 44 10N | 7 10 E |
| Maritsa = Évros →, Greece | 23 D12 | 41 40N | 26 34 E |
| Maritsá, Greece | 25 C10 | 36 22N | 28 8 E |
| Mariupol, Ukraine | 19 E6 | 47 5N | 37 31 E |
| Mariusa △, Venezuela | 89 E7 | 9 24N | 61 27W |
| Marivān, Iran | 44 C5 | 35 30N | 46 25 E |
| Marj 'Uyūn, Lebanon | 46 B4 | 33 20N | 35 35 E |
| Marka = Merca, Somali Rep. | 47 G3 | 1 48N | 44 50 E |
| Markdale, Canada | 84 B4 | 44 19N | 80 39W |
| Marked Tree, U.S.A. | 81 H9 | 35 32N | 90 25W |
| Market Drayton, U.K. | 12 E5 | 52 54N | 2 29W |
| Market Harborough, U.K. | 13 E7 | 52 29N | 0 55W |
| Market Rasen, U.K. | 12 D7 | 53 24N | 0 20W |
| Markham, Canada | 84 C5 | 43 52N | 79 16W |
| Markham, Mt., Antarctica | 5 E11 | 83 0S | 164 0 E |
| Markleeville, U.S.A. | 78 G7 | 38 42N | 119 47W |
| Markovo, Russia | 29 C17 | 64 40N | 170 24 E |
| Marks, Russia | 18 D8 | 51 45N | 46 50 E |
| Marksville, U.S.A. | 81 K8 | 31 8N | 92 4W |
| Marla, Australia | 63 D1 | 27 19S | 133 33 E |
| Marlbank, Canada | 84 B7 | 44 26N | 77 6W |
| Marlboro, Mass., U.S.A. | 85 D13 | 42 19N | 71 33W |
| Marlboro, N.Y., U.S.A. | 85 E11 | 41 36N | 73 59W |
| Marlborough, Australia | 62 C4 | 22 46S | 149 52 E |
| Marlborough, U.K. | 13 F6 | 51 25N | 1 43W |
| Marlborough Downs, U.K. | 13 F6 | 51 27N | 1 53W |
| Marlin, U.S.A. | 81 K6 | 31 18N | 96 54W |
| Marlow, U.K. | 13 F7 | 51 34N | 0 46W |
| Marlow, U.S.A. | 81 H6 | 34 39N | 97 58W |
| Marmagao, India | 40 M8 | 15 25N | 73 56 E |
| Marmara, Turkey | 23 D12 | 40 35N | 27 34 E |
| Marmara, Sea of = Marmara Denizi, Turkey | 23 D13 | 40 45N | 28 15 E |
| Marmara Denizi, Turkey | 23 D13 | 40 45N | 28 15 E |
| Marmaris, Turkey | 23 F13 | 36 50N | 28 14 E |
| Marmion, Mt., Australia | 61 E2 | 29 16S | 119 50 E |
| Marmion L., Canada | 72 C1 | 48 55N | 91 20W |
| Marmolada, Mte., Italy | 22 A4 | 46 26N | 11 51 E |
| Marmora, Canada | 84 B7 | 44 28N | 77 41W |
| Marne →, France | 20 B5 | 48 48N | 2 24 E |
| Maroala, Madag. | 57 B8 | 15 23S | 47 59 E |
| Maroantsetra, Madag. | 57 B8 | 15 26S | 49 44 E |
| Maroelaboom, Namibia | 56 B2 | 19 15S | 18 53 E |
| Marofandilia, Madag. | 57 C7 | 20 7S | 44 34 E |
| Marojejy △, Madag. | 57 A8 | 14 26S | 49 21 E |
| Marolambo, Madag. | 57 C8 | 20 2S | 48 7 E |
| Maromandia, Madag. | 57 A8 | 14 13S | 48 5 E |
| Maromokotro, Madag. | 57 A8 | 14 0S | 49 0 E |
| Marondera, Zimbabwe | 55 F3 | 18 5S | 31 42 E |
| Maroni →, Fr. Guiana | 93 B8 | 5 30N | 54 0W |
| Maroochydore, Australia | 63 D5 | 26 29S | 153 5 E |
| Maroona, Australia | 63 F3 | 37 27S | 142 54 E |
| Marosakoa, Madag. | 57 B8 | 15 26S | 46 38 E |
| Maroseranana, Madag. | 57 B8 | 18 32S | 48 51 E |
| Marotandrano, Madag. | 57 B8 | 16 10S | 48 50 E |
| Marotaolano, Madag. | 57 A8 | 12 47S | 49 15 E |
| Maroua, Cameroon | 51 F8 | 10 40N | 14 20 E |
| Marovato, Madag. | 57 B8 | 15 48S | 48 5 E |
| Marovoay, Madag. | 57 B8 | 16 6S | 46 39 E |
| Marquard, S. Africa | 56 D4 | 28 40S | 27 28 E |
| Marquesas Is. = Marquises, Îs., French Polynesia | 65 H14 | 9 30S | 140 0W |
| Marquette, U.S.A. | 82 B2 | 46 33N | 87 24W |
| Marquis, St. Lucia | 89 f | 14 2N | 60 54W |
| Marquises, Îs., French Polynesia | 65 H14 | 9 30S | 140 0W |
| Marra, Djebel, Sudan | 51 F10 | 13 10N | 24 22 E |
| Marracuene, Mozam. | 57 D5 | 25 45S | 32 35 E |
| Marrakech, Morocco | 50 B4 | 31 9N | 8 0W |
| Marrawah, Australia | 63 G3 | 40 55S | 144 42 E |
| Marree, Australia | 63 D2 | 29 39S | 138 1 E |
| Marrero, U.S.A. | 81 L9 | 29 54N | 90 6W |
| Marrimane, Mozam. | 57 C5 | 22 58S | 33 34 E |
| Marromeu, Mozam. | 57 B6 | 18 15S | 36 25 E |
| Marromeu △, Mozam. | 57 B6 | 19 0S | 36 0 E |
| Marrowie Cr. →, Australia | 63 E4 | 33 23S | 145 40 E |
| Marrubane, Mozam. | 55 F4 | 18 0S | 37 0 E |
| Marrupa, Mozam. | 55 E4 | 13 8S | 37 30 E |
| Mars Hill, U.S.A. | 83 B12 | 46 31N | 67 52W |
| Marsá Matrûh, Egypt | 51 B11 | 31 19N | 27 9 E |
| Marsabit, Kenya | 54 B4 | 2 18N | 38 0 E |
| Marsabit △, Kenya | 54 B4 | 2 23N | 37 56 E |
| Marsala, Italy | 22 F5 | 37 48N | 12 26 E |
| Marsalforn, Malta | 25 C1 | 36 4N | 14 16 E |
| Marsden, Australia | 63 E4 | 33 47S | 147 32 E |
| Marseille, France | 20 E6 | 43 18N | 5 23 E |
| Marseilles = Marseille, France | 20 E6 | 43 18N | 5 23 E |
| Marsh I., U.S.A. | 81 L9 | 29 34N | 91 53W |
| Marshall, Ark., U.S.A. | 81 H8 | 35 55N | 92 38W |
| Marshall, Mich., U.S.A. | 82 D3 | 42 16N | 84 58W |
| Marshall, Minn., U.S.A. | 80 C7 | 44 25N | 95 45W |
| Marshall, Mo., U.S.A. | 80 F8 | 39 7N | 93 12W |
| Marshall, Tex., U.S.A. | 81 J7 | 32 33N | 94 23W |
| Marshall →, Australia | 62 C2 | 22 59S | 136 59 E |
| Marshall Is. ■, Pac. Oc. | 64 G9 | 9 0N | 171 0 E |
| Marshalltown, U.S.A. | 80 D8 | 42 3N | 92 55W |
| Marshbrook, Zimbabwe | 57 B5 | 18 33S | 31 9 E |
| Marshfield, Mo., U.S.A. | 81 G8 | 37 15N | 92 54W |
| Marshfield, Vt., U.S.A. | 85 B12 | 44 20N | 72 20W |
| Marshfield, Wis., U.S.A. | 80 C9 | 44 40N | 90 10W |
| Marshūn, Iran | 45 B6 | 36 19N | 49 23 E |
| Märsta, Sweden | 9 G17 | 59 37N | 17 52 E |
| Mart, U.S.A. | 81 K6 | 31 33N | 96 50W |
| Martaban, Burma | 41 L20 | 16 30N | 97 35 E |
| Martaban, G. of, Burma | 41 L20 | 16 5N | 96 30 E |
| Martapura, Kalimantan, Indonesia | 36 E4 | 3 22S | 114 47 E |
| Martapura, Sumatera, Indonesia | 36 E2 | 4 19S | 104 22 E |
| Martelange, Belgium | 15 E5 | 49 49N | 5 43 E |
| Martha's Vineyard, U.S.A. | 85 E14 | 41 25N | 70 38W |
| Martigny, Switz. | 20 C7 | 46 6N | 7 3 E |
| Martigues, France | 20 E6 | 43 24N | 5 4 E |
| Martin, Slovak Rep. | 17 D10 | 49 6N | 18 58 E |
| Martin, S. Dak., U.S.A. | 80 D4 | 43 11N | 101 44W |
| Martin, Tenn., U.S.A. | 81 G10 | 36 21N | 88 51W |
| Martin, L., U.S.A. | 83 J3 | 32 41N | 85 55W |
| Martina Franca, Italy | 22 D7 | 40 42N | 17 20 E |
| Martinborough, N.Z. | 59 J5 | 41 14S | 175 29 E |
| Martinez, Calif., U.S.A. | 78 G4 | 38 1N | 122 8W |
| Martinez, Ga., U.S.A. | 83 J4 | 33 31N | 82 4W |
| Martinique ☑, W. Indies | 88 c | 14 40N | 61 0W |
| Martinique Passage, W. Indies | 89 C7 | 15 15N | 61 0W |
| Martinópolis, Brazil | 95 A5 | 22 11S | 51 12W |
| Martin's Bay, Barbados | 89 g | 13 12N | 59 29W |
| Martins Ferry, U.S.A. | 84 F4 | 40 6N | 80 44W |
| Martinsburg, Pa., U.S.A. | 84 F6 | 40 19N | 78 20W |
| Martinsburg, W. Va., U.S.A. | 82 F7 | 39 27N | 77 58W |
| Martinsville, Ind., U.S.A. | 82 F2 | 39 26N | 86 25W |
| Martinsville, Va., U.S.A. | 83 G6 | 36 41N | 79 52W |
| Marton, N.Z. | 59 J5 | 40 4S | 175 23 E |
| Martos, Spain | 21 D4 | 37 44N | 3 58W |
| Marudi, Malaysia | 36 D4 | 4 11N | 114 19 E |
| Maruf, Afghan. | 40 D5 | 31 30N | 67 6 E |
| Marugame, Japan | 31 G6 | 34 15N | 133 40 E |
| Marunga, Angola | 56 B3 | 17 28S | 20 2 E |
| Marungu, Mts., Dem. Rep. of the Congo | 54 D3 | 7 30S | 30 0 E |
| Marv Dasht, Iran | 45 D7 | 29 50N | 52 40 E |
| Marvast, Iran | 45 D7 | 30 30N | 54 15 E |
| Marvel Loch, Australia | 61 F2 | 31 28S | 119 29 E |
| Marwar, India | 42 G5 | 25 43S | 73 45 E |
| Mary, Turkmenistan | 28 F7 | 37 40N | 61 50 E |
| Maryborough = Port Laoise, Ireland | 10 C4 | 53 2N | 7 18W |
| Maryborough, Queens., Australia | 63 D5 | 25 31S | 152 37 E |
| Maryborough, Vic., Australia | 63 F3 | 37 0S | 143 44 E |
| Maryfield, Canada | 71 D8 | 49 50N | 101 35W |
| Maryland □, U.S.A. | 82 F7 | 39 0N | 76 30W |
| Maryland Junction, Zimbabwe | 55 F3 | 17 45S | 30 31 E |
| Maryport, U.K. | 12 C4 | 54 44N | 3 28W |
| Mary's Harbour, Canada | 73 B8 | 52 18N | 55 51W |
| Marystown, Canada | 73 C8 | 47 10N | 55 10W |
| Marysville, Canada | 70 D5 | 49 35N | 116 0W |
| Marysville, Calif., U.S.A. | 78 F5 | 39 9N | 121 35W |
| Marysville, Kans., U.S.A. | 80 F6 | 39 51N | 96 39W |
| Marysville, Mich., U.S.A. | 84 D2 | 42 54N | 82 29W |
| Marysville, Ohio, U.S.A. | 82 E4 | 40 14N | 83 22W |
| Marysville, Wash., U.S.A. | 78 B4 | 48 3N | 122 11W |
| Maryville, Mo., U.S.A. | 80 E7 | 40 21N | 94 52W |
| Maryville, Tenn., U.S.A. | 83 H4 | 35 46N | 83 58W |
| Marzūq, Libya | 51 C8 | 25 53N | 13 57 E |
| Masahunga, Tanzania | 54 C3 | 2 6S | 33 18 E |
| Masai, Malaysia | 39 d | 1 29N | 103 53 E |
| Masai Mara △, Kenya | 54 C4 | 1 25S | 35 5 E |
| Masai Steppe, Tanzania | 54 C4 | 4 30S | 36 30 E |
| Masaka, Uganda | 54 C3 | 0 21S | 31 45 E |
| Masalembo, Kepulauan, Indonesia | 36 F4 | 5 35S | 114 30 E |
| Masalima, Kepulauan, Indonesia | 36 F5 | 5 4S | 117 5 E |
| Masamba, Indonesia | 37 E6 | 2 30S | 120 15 E |
| Masan, S. Korea | 35 G15 | 35 11N | 128 32 E |
| Masandam, Ra's, Oman | 45 E8 | 26 30N | 56 30 E |
| Masasi, Tanzania | 55 E4 | 10 45S | 38 52 E |
| Masaya, Nic. | 88 D2 | 12 0N | 86 7W |
| Masbate, Phil. | 37 B6 | 12 21N | 123 36 E |
| Mascara, Algeria | 50 A6 | 35 26N | 0 6 E |
| Mascota, Mexico | 86 C4 | 20 30N | 104 50W |
| Masela, Indonesia | 37 F7 | 8 9S | 129 51 E |
| Maseru, Lesotho | 56 D4 | 29 18S | 27 30 E |
| Mashaba, Zimbabwe | 55 G3 | 20 2S | 30 29 E |
| Mashābih, Si. Arabia | 44 E3 | 25 35N | 36 30 E |
| Mashatu △, Botswana | 57 C4 | 22 5S | 29 5 E |
| Masherbrum, Pakistan | 43 B7 | 35 38N | 76 18 E |
| Mashhad, Iran | 45 B8 | 36 20N | 59 35 E |
| Mashīz, Iran | 45 D8 | 29 56N | 56 37 E |
| Māshkel, Hāmūn-i-, Pakistan | 40 E3 | 28 20N | 62 56 E |
| Mashki Chāh, Pakistan | 40 E3 | 29 5N | 62 30 E |
| Mashonaland, Zimbabwe | 53 H6 | 16 30S | 31 0 E |
| Mashonaland Central □, Zimbabwe | 57 B5 | 17 30S | 31 0 E |
| Mashonaland East □, Zimbabwe | 57 B5 | 18 0S | 32 0 E |
| Mashonaland West □, Zimbabwe | 57 B4 | 17 30S | 29 30 E |
| Mashrakh, India | 43 F11 | 26 7N | 84 48 E |
| Masindi, Uganda | 54 B3 | 1 40N | 31 43 E |
| Masindi Port, Uganda | 54 B3 | 1 43N | 32 2 E |
| Maşīrah, Oman | 47 C6 | 21 0N | 58 50 E |
| Maşīrah, Khalīj, Oman | 47 C6 | 20 10N | 58 10 E |
| Masisi, Dem. Rep. of the Congo | 54 C2 | 1 23S | 28 49 E |
| Masjed Soleyman, Iran | 45 D6 | 31 55N | 49 18 E |
| Mask, L., Ireland | 10 C2 | 53 36N | 9 22W |
| Maskin, Oman | 45 F8 | 23 30N | 56 50 E |
| Masoala, △, Madag. | 57 B9 | 15 30S | 50 12 E |
| Masoala, Tanjon' i, Madag. | 57 B9 | 15 59S | 50 13 E |
| Masoarivo, Madag. | 57 B7 | 19 3S | 44 19 E |
| Masohi = Amahai, Indonesia | 37 E7 | 3 20S | 128 55 E |
| Masomeloka, Madag. | 57 C8 | 20 17S | 48 37 E |
| Mason, Nev., U.S.A. | 78 G7 | 38 56N | 119 8W |
| Mason, Tex., U.S.A. | 81 K5 | 30 45N | 99 14W |
| Mason City, U.S.A. | 80 D8 | 43 9N | 93 12W |
| Maspalomas, Canary Is. | 24 G4 | 27 46N | 15 35W |
| Maspalomas, Pta., Canary Is. | 24 G4 | 27 43N | 15 36W |
| Masqat, Oman | 47 C6 | 23 37N | 58 36 E |
| Massa, Italy | 20 D9 | 44 1N | 10 9 E |
| Massachusetts □, U.S.A. | 85 D13 | 42 30N | 72 0W |
| Massachusetts B., U.S.A. | 85 D14 | 42 20N | 70 50W |
| Massakory, Chad | 51 F9 | 13 0N | 15 49 E |
| Massanella, Spain | 24 B9 | 39 48N | 2 51 E |
| Massangena, Mozam. | 57 C5 | 21 34S | 33 0 E |
| Massango, Angola | 52 F3 | 8 2S | 16 21 E |
| Massawa = Mitsiwa, Eritrea | 47 D2 | 15 35N | 39 25 E |
| Massena, U.S.A. | 85 B10 | 44 56N | 74 54W |
| Massénya, Chad | 51 F9 | 11 21N | 16 9 E |
| Masset, Canada | 70 C2 | 54 2N | 132 10W |
| Massiah Street, Barbados | 89 g | 13 9N | 59 29W |
| Massif Central, France | 20 D5 | 44 55N | 3 0 E |
| Massillon, U.S.A. | 84 F3 | 40 48N | 81 32W |
| Massinga, Mozam. | 57 C6 | 23 15S | 35 22 E |
| Massingir, Mozam. | 57 C5 | 23 51S | 32 4 E |
| Masson-Angers, Canada | 85 A9 | 45 32N | 75 25W |
| Masson I., Antarctica | 5 C7 | 66 10S | 93 20 E |
| Mastanli = Momchilgrad, Bulgaria | 23 D11 | 41 33N | 25 23 E |
| Masterton, N.Z. | 59 J5 | 40 56S | 175 39 E |
| Mastic, U.S.A. | 85 F12 | 40 47N | 72 54W |
| Mastuj, Pakistan | 43 A5 | 36 20N | 72 36 E |
| Mastung, Pakistan | 40 E5 | 29 50N | 66 56 E |
| Masty, Belarus | 17 B13 | 53 27N | 24 38 E |
| Masuda, Japan | 31 G5 | 34 40N | 131 51 E |
| Masvingo, Zimbabwe | 55 G3 | 20 8S | 30 49 E |
| Masvingo □, Zimbabwe | 55 G3 | 21 0S | 31 30 E |
| Maswa △, Tanzania | 54 C3 | 2 58S | 34 19 E |
| Masyaf, Syria | 44 C3 | 35 4N | 36 20 E |
| Matabeleland, Zimbabwe | 53 H5 | 18 0S | 27 0 E |
| Matabeleland North □, Zimbabwe | 55 F2 | 19 0S | 28 0 E |
| Matabeleland South □, Zimbabwe | 55 G2 | 21 0S | 29 0 E |
| Matachewan, Canada | 72 C3 | 47 56N | 80 39W |
| Matadi, Dem. Rep. of the Congo | 52 F2 | 5 52S | 13 31 E |
| Matagalpa, Nic. | 88 D2 | 13 0N | 85 58W |
| Matagami, Canada | 72 C4 | 49 45N | 77 34W |
| Matagami, L., Canada | 72 C4 | 49 50N | 77 40W |
| Matagorda B., U.S.A. | 81 L6 | 28 40N | 96 0W |
| Matagorda I., U.S.A. | 81 L6 | 28 15N | 96 30W |
| Matak, Indonesia | 36 D3 | 3 18N | 106 16 E |
| Matam, Senegal | 50 E3 | 15 34N | 13 17W |
| Matamoros, Campeche, Mexico | 87 D6 | 18 50N | 90 50W |
| Matamoros, Coahuila, Mexico | 86 B4 | 25 33N | 103 15W |
| Matamoros, Tamaulipas, Mexico | 87 B5 | 25 50N | 97 30W |
| Ma'ţan as Sarra, Libya | 51 D10 | 21 45N | 22 0 E |
| Matandu →, Tanzania | 55 D3 | 8 45S | 34 19 E |
| Matane, Canada | 73 C6 | 48 50N | 67 33W |
| Matanomadh, India | 42 H3 | 23 33N | 68 57 E |
| Matanzas, Cuba | 88 B3 | 23 0N | 81 40W |
| Matapa, Botswana | 56 C3 | 23 11S | 24 39 E |
| Matapan, C. = Taínaron, Ákra, Greece | 23 F10 | 36 22N | 22 27 E |
| Matapédia, Canada | 73 C6 | 48 0N | 66 59W |
| Matapo △, Zimbabwe | 55 G2 | 20 30S | 29 40 E |
| Mataram, Indonesia | 36 F5 | 8 35S | 116 7 E |
| Matarani, Peru | 92 G4 | 17 0S | 72 10W |
| Mataranka, Australia | 60 B5 | 14 55S | 133 4 E |
| Matarma, Râs, Egypt | 46 E1 | 30 27N | 32 44 E |
| Mataró, Spain | 21 B7 | 41 32N | 2 29 E |
| Matatiele, S. Africa | 57 E4 | 30 20S | 28 49 E |
| Mataura, N.Z. | 59 M2 | 46 11S | 168 51 E |
| Matehuala, Mexico | 86 C4 | 23 40N | 100 40W |
| Mateke Hills, Zimbabwe | 55 G3 | 21 48S | 31 0 E |
| Matelot, Trin. & Tob. | 93 K15 | 10 50N | 61 7W |
| Matera, Italy | 22 D7 | 40 40N | 16 36 E |
| Matetsi, Zimbabwe | 55 F2 | 18 12S | 26 0 E |
| Matheniko △, Uganda | 54 B3 | 2 49N | 34 27 E |
| Mathis, U.S.A. | 81 L6 | 28 6N | 97 50W |
| Mathráki, Greece | 25 A3 | 39 48N | 19 31 E |
| Mathura, India | 42 F7 | 27 30N | 77 40 E |
| Mati, Phil. | 37 C7 | 6 55N | 126 15 E |
| Matiali, India | 43 F13 | 26 56N | 88 49 E |
| Matías Romero, Mexico | 87 D5 | 16 53N | 95 2W |
| Matibane, Mozam. | 55 E5 | 14 49S | 40 45 E |
| Matiri Ra., N.Z. | 59 J4 | 41 38S | 172 20 E |
| Matjiesfontein, S. Africa | 56 E3 | 33 14S | 20 35 E |
| Matla →, India | 43 J13 | 21 40N | 88 40 E |
| Matlamanyane, Botswana | 56 B4 | 19 33S | 25 57 E |
| Matli, Pakistan | 42 G3 | 25 2N | 68 39 E |
| Matlock, U.K. | 12 D6 | 53 9N | 1 33W |
| Mato Grosso □, Brazil | 93 F8 | 14 0S | 55 0W |
| Mato Grosso, Planalto do, Brazil | 93 G8 | 15 0S | 55 0W |
| Mato Grosso do Sul □, Brazil | 93 G8 | 18 0S | 55 0W |
| Matobo = Matapo △, Zimbabwe | 55 G2 | 20 36S | 28 20 E |
| Matochkin Shar, Russia | 28 B6 | 73 10N | 56 40 E |
| Matopo Hills, Zimbabwe | 55 G2 | 20 36S | 28 29 E |
| Matopos, Zimbabwe | 55 G2 | 20 20S | 28 29 E |
| Matosinhos, Portugal | 21 B1 | 41 11N | 8 42W |
| Matroosberg, S. Africa | 56 E2 | 33 23S | 19 40 E |
| Matruḥ, Oman | 47 C6 | 23 37N | 58 30 E |
| Matsue, Japan | 31 G6 | 35 25N | 133 10 E |
| Matsum, Ko, Thailand | 39 b | 9 22N | 99 59 E |
| Matsumae, Japan | 30 D10 | 41 26N | 140 7 E |
| Matsumoto, Japan | 31 F9 | 36 15N | 138 0 E |
| Matsusaka, Japan | 31 G8 | 34 34N | 136 32 E |
| Matsuura, Japan | 31 H4 | 33 20N | 129 49 E |
| Matsuyama, Japan | 31 H6 | 33 45N | 132 45 E |
| Mattagami →, Canada | 72 B3 | 50 43N | 81 29W |
| Mattancheri, India | 40 Q10 | 9 50N | 76 15 E |
| Mattawa, Canada | 72 C4 | 46 20N | 78 45W |
| Matterhorn, Switz. | 20 D7 | 45 58N | 7 39 E |
| Matthew Town, Bahamas | 89 B5 | 20 57N | 73 40W |
| Matthews Ridge, Guyana | 92 B6 | 7 37N | 60 10W |
| Mattice, Canada | 72 C3 | 49 40N | 83 20W |
| Mattituck, U.S.A. | 85 F12 | 40 59N | 72 32W |
| Mattō, Japan | 31 F8 | 36 31N | 136 34 E |
| Mattoon, U.S.A. | 82 F1 | 39 29N | 88 23W |
| Matuba, Mozam. | 57 C5 | 24 28S | 32 49 E |
| Matucana, Peru | 92 F3 | 11 55S | 76 25W |
| Matún = Khowst, Afghan. | 42 C3 | 33 22N | 69 58 E |
| Matura B., Trin. & Tob. | 93 K15 | 10 39N | 61 1W |
| Maturín, Venezuela | 92 B6 | 9 45N | 63 11W |
| Matusadona △, Zimbabwe | 55 F2 | 16 58S | 28 42 E |
| Mau, Mad. P., India | 43 F8 | 26 17N | 78 41 E |
| Mau, Ut. P., India | 43 G10 | 25 56N | 83 33 E |
| Mau, Ut. P., India | 43 G9 | 25 17N | 81 23 E |
| Mau Escarpment, Kenya | 54 C4 | 0 40S | 36 0 E |
| Mau Ranipur, India | 43 G8 | 25 16N | 79 8 E |
| Maubeuge, France | 20 A6 | 50 17N | 3 57 E |
| Maud, Pt., Australia | 60 D1 | 23 6S | 113 45 E |
| Maude, Australia | 63 E3 | 34 29S | 144 18 E |
| Maudin Sun, Burma | 41 M19 | 16 0N | 94 30 E |
| Maués, Brazil | 92 D7 | 3 20S | 57 45W |
| Mauganj, India | 41 G12 | 24 50N | 81 55 E |
| Maughold Hd., I. of Man | 12 C3 | 54 18N | 4 18W |
| Maui, U.S.A. | 74 H16 | 20 48N | 156 20W |
| Maulamyaing = Moulmein, Burma | 41 L20 | 16 30N | 97 40 E |
| Maule □, Chile | 94 D1 | 36 5S | 72 30W |
| Maumee, U.S.A. | 82 E4 | 41 34N | 83 39W |
| Maumee →, U.S.A. | 82 E4 | 41 42N | 83 28W |
| Maumere, Indonesia | 37 F6 | 8 38S | 122 13 E |
| Maun, Botswana | 56 C3 | 20 0S | 23 26 E |
| Mauna Kea, U.S.A. | 74 J17 | 19 50N | 155 28W |
| Mauna Loa, U.S.A. | 74 J17 | 19 30N | 155 35W |
| Maungmagan Kyunzu, Burma | 38 E1 | 14 0N | 97 48 E |
| Maupin, U.S.A. | 76 D3 | 45 11N | 121 5W |
| Maurepas, L., U.S.A. | 81 K9 | 30 15N | 90 30W |
| Maurice, L., Australia | 61 E5 | 29 30S | 131 0 E |
| Mauricie △, Canada | 72 C5 | 46 45N | 73 0W |
| Mauritania ■, Africa | 50 E3 | 20 50N | 10 0W |
| Mauritius ■, Ind. Oc. | 49 J9 | 20 0S | 57 0 E |
| Mauston, U.S.A. | 80 D9 | 43 48N | 90 5W |
| Mavli, India | 42 G5 | 24 45N | 73 55 E |
| Mavuradonha Mts., Zimbabwe | 55 F3 | 16 30S | 31 30 E |
| Mawa, Dem. Rep. of the Congo | 54 B2 | 2 45S | 26 40 E |
| Mawai, India | 43 H9 | 22 30N | 81 4 E |
| Mawana, India | 42 E7 | 29 6N | 77 58 E |
| Mawand, Pakistan | 42 E3 | 29 33N | 68 38 E |
| Mawk Mai, Burma | 41 J20 | 20 14N | 97 37 E |
| Mawlaik, Burma | 41 H19 | 23 40N | 94 26 E |
| Mawlamyine = Moulmein, Burma | 41 L20 | 16 30N | 97 40 E |
| Mawqaq, Si. Arabia | 44 E4 | 27 25N | 41 8 E |
| Mawson Base, Antarctica | 5 C6 | 67 30S | 62 53 E |
| Mawson Coast, Antarctica | 5 C6 | 68 30S | 63 0 E |
| Max, U.S.A. | 80 B4 | 47 49N | 101 18W |
| Maxcanú, Mexico | 87 C6 | 20 40N | 90 10W |
| Maxesibeni, S. Africa | 57 E4 | 30 49S | 29 23 E |
| Maxhamish L., Canada | 70 B4 | 59 50N | 123 17W |
| Maxixe, Mozam. | 57 C6 | 23 54S | 35 17 E |
| Maxville, Canada | 85 A10 | 45 17N | 74 51W |
| Maxwell, U.S.A. | 78 F4 | 39 17N | 122 11W |
| Maxwelton, Australia | 62 C3 | 20 43S | 142 41 E |
| May, U.S.A. | 82 F8 | 38 56N | 78 56W |
| May Pen, Jamaica | 88 a | 17 58N | 77 15W |
| Maya →, Russia | 29 D14 | 60 28N | 134 28 E |
| Maya Mts., Belize | 87 D7 | 16 30N | 89 0W |
| Mayaguana, Bahamas | 89 B5 | 22 30N | 72 44W |
| Mayagüez, Puerto Rico | 89 d | 18 12N | 67 9W |
| Mayamey, Iran | 45 B7 | 36 24N | 55 42 E |
| Mayanup, Australia | 61 F2 | 33 57S | 116 27 E |
| Mayapan, Mexico | 87 C7 | 20 30N | 89 25W |
| Mayari, Cuba | 89 B4 | 20 40N | 75 41W |
| Mayaro B., Trin. & Tob. | 93 K16 | 10 14N | 60 59W |
| Maybell, U.S.A. | 76 F9 | 40 31N | 108 5W |
| Maybole, U.K. | 11 F4 | 55 21N | 4 42W |
| Maydān, Iraq | 44 C5 | 34 55N | 45 37 E |
| Maydena, Australia | 63 G4 | 42 45S | 146 30 E |
| Mayenne →, France | 20 C3 | 47 30N | 0 32W |
| Mayer, U.S.A. | 77 J7 | 34 24N | 112 14W |
| Mayerthorpe, Canada | 70 C5 | 53 57N | 115 8W |
| Mayfield, Ky., U.S.A. | 83 G1 | 36 44N | 88 38W |
| Mayfield, N.Y., U.S.A. | 85 C10 | 43 6N | 74 16W |
| Mayhill, U.S.A. | 77 K11 | 32 53N | 105 29W |
| Maykop, Russia | 19 F7 | 44 35N | 40 10 E |
| Maymyo, Burma | 38 A1 | 22 2N | 96 28 E |
| Maynard, Mass., U.S.A. | 85 D13 | 42 26N | 71 27W |
| Maynard, Wash., U.S.A. | 78 C4 | 47 59N | 122 55W |
| Maynard Hills, Australia | 61 E2 | 28 28S | 119 49 E |

Mayne →, Australia ........... 62 C3 23 40S 141 55 E
Maynooth, Ireland .......... 10 C5 53 23N 6 34W
Mayo, Canada .............. 68 B6 63 38N 135 57W
Mayo □, Ireland ........... 10 C2 53 53N 9 3W
Mayon Volcano, Phil. ...... 37 B6 13 15N 123 41 E
Mayor I., N.Z. .............. 59 G6 37 16S 176 17 E
Mayotte ☑, Ind. Oc. ....... 53 G9 12 50S 45 10 E
Maysān □, Iraq ............ 44 D5 31 55N 47 15 E
Maysville, U.S.A. .......... 82 F4 38 39N 83 46W
Mayu, Indonesia ........... 37 D7 1 30N 126 30 E
Mayville, N. Dak., U.S.A. .. 80 B6 47 30N 97 20W
Mayville, N.Y., U.S.A. ..... 84 D5 42 15N 79 30W
Mayya, Russia ............. 29 C14 61 44N 130 18 E
Mazabuka, Zambia ......... 55 F2 15 52S 27 44 E
Mazagán = El Jadida, Morocco 50 B4 33 11N 8 17W
Mazagão, Brazil ........... 93 D8 0 7S 51 16W
Mazán, Peru .............. 92 D4 3 30S 73 0W
Māzandarān □, Iran ....... 45 B7 36 30N 52 0 E
Mazapil, Mexico .......... 86 C4 24 38N 101 34W
Mazara del Vallo, Italy .... 22 F5 37 39N 12 35 E
Mazarrón, Spain .......... 21 D5 37 38N 1 19W
Mazaruni →, Guyana ....... 92 B7 6 25N 58 35W
Mazatán, Mexico .......... 86 B2 29 0N 110 8W
Mazatenango, Guatemala ... 88 D1 14 35N 91 30W
Mazatlán, Mexico ......... 86 C3 23 13N 106 25W
Mažeikiai, Lithuania ...... 9 H20 56 20N 22 20 E
Māzhān, Iran ............. 45 C8 32 30N 59 0 E
Mazinān, Iran ............ 45 B8 36 19N 56 56 E
Mazoe, Mozam. ........... 55 F3 16 42S 33 7 E
Mazoe →, Mozam. ........ 55 F3 16 20S 33 30 E
Mazowe, Zimbabwe ....... 55 F3 17 28S 30 58 E
Mazurian Lakes = Mazurski,
　Pojezierze, Poland ....... 17 B11 53 50N 21 0 E
Mazurski, Pojezierze, Poland ... 17 B11 53 50N 21 0 E
Mazyr, Belarus ........... 17 B15 51 59N 29 15 E
Mbaïki, C.A.R. ............ 52 D3 3 53N 18 1 E
Mbala, Zambia ........... 55 D3 8 46S 31 24 E
Mbalabala, Zimbabwe ..... 57 C4 20 27S 29 3 E
Mbale, Uganda ........... 54 B3 1 8N 34 12 E
Mbalmayo, Cameroon ..... 52 D2 3 33N 11 33 E
Mbamba Bay, Tanzania .... 55 E3 11 13S 34 49 E
Mbandaka, Dem. Rep. of
　the Congo ............... 52 D3 0 1N 18 18 E
Mbanza Congo, Angola .... 52 F2 6 18S 14 16 E
Mbanza Ngungu, Dem. Rep. of
　the Congo ............... 52 F2 5 12S 14 53 E
Mbarangandu, Tanzania ... 55 D4 10 11S 36 48 E
Mbarara, Uganda ......... 54 C3 0 35S 30 40 E
Mbashe →, S. Africa ...... 57 E4 32 15S 28 54 E
Mbenkuru →, Tanzania .... 55 D4 9 25S 39 50 E
Mberengwa, Zimbabwe .... 55 G2 20 29S 29 57 E
Mberengwa, Mt., Zimbabwe . 55 G2 20 37S 29 55 E
Mbesuma, Zambia ........ 55 E3 10 0S 32 2 E
Mbeya, Tanzania ......... 55 D3 8 54S 33 29 E
Mbeya □, Tanzania ....... 54 D3 8 15S 33 30 E
Mbinga, Tanzania ........ 55 E4 10 50S 35 0 E
Mbini = Rio Muni □, Eq. Guin. . 52 D2 1 30N 10 0 E
Mbour, Senegal .......... 50 F2 14 22N 16 54W
Mbuji-Mayi, Dem. Rep. of
　the Congo ............... 54 D1 6 9S 23 40 E
Mbulu, Tanzania ......... 54 C4 3 45S 35 30 E
Mburucuyá, Argentina .... 94 B4 28 1S 58 14W
McCarran International, Las
　Vegas ✈ (LAS), U.S.A. ... 79 J11 36 5N 115 9W
Mchinja, Tanzania ........ 55 D4 9 44S 39 45 E
Mchinji, Malawi .......... 55 E3 13 47S 32 58 E
McMurdo, Antarctica ..... 5 D11 77 0S 170 0 E
Mdantsane, S. Africa ..... 53 L5 32 56S 27 46 E
Mead, L., U.S.A. .......... 79 J12 36 1N 114 44W
Meade, U.S.A. ............ 81 G4 37 17N 100 20W
Meadow Lake, Canada .... 71 C7 54 10N 108 26W
Meadow Lake ❄, Canada .. 71 C7 54 27N 109 0W
Meadow Valley Wash →, U.S.A. 79 J12 36 40N 114 34W
Meadville, U.S.A. ......... 84 E4 41 39N 80 9W
Meaford, Canada ......... 84 B4 44 36N 80 35W
Mealy Mts., Canada ...... 73 B8 53 10N 58 0W
Meander River, Canada ... 70 B5 59 2N 117 42W
Meares, C., U.S.A. ........ 76 D2 45 37N 124 0W
Mearim →, Brazil ........ 93 D10 3 4S 44 35W
Meath □, Ireland ......... 10 C5 53 40N 6 57W
Meath Park, Canada ...... 71 C7 53 27N 105 22W
Meaux, France ........... 20 B5 48 58N 2 50 E
Mebechi-Gawa →, Japan .. 30 D10 40 31N 141 31 E
Mebulu, Tanjung, Indonesia . 37 K18 8 50S 115 5 E
Mecca = Makkah, Si. Arabia . 47 C2 21 30N 39 54 E
Mecca, U.S.A. ............ 84 F8 40 13N 77 1W
Mechanicsburg, U.S.A. ... 84 F8 40 13N 77 1W
Mechanicville, U.S.A. ..... 85 D11 42 54N 73 41W
Mechelen, Belgium ....... 15 C4 51 2N 4 29 E
Mecheria, Algeria ........ 50 B5 33 35N 0 18W
Mecklenburg, Germany ... 16 B6 53 33N 11 40 E
Mecklenburger Bucht, Germany 16 A6 54 20N 11 40 E
Meconta, Mozam. ........ 55 E4 14 59S 39 50 E
Medan, Indonesia ........ 36 D1 3 40N 98 38 E
Médanos de Coro △, Venezuela 92 A5 11 35N 69 44W
Medanosa, Pta., Argentina . 96 F3 48 8S 66 0W
Médéa, Algeria .......... 50 A6 36 12N 2 50 E
Medellín, Colombia ...... 92 B3 6 15N 75 35W
Medelpad, Sweden ....... 9 E17 62 33N 16 30 E
Medemblik, Neths. ....... 15 B5 52 46N 5 8 E
Medford, Mass., U.S.A. ... 85 D13 42 25N 71 7W
Medford, Oreg., U.S.A. ... 76 E2 42 19N 122 52W
Medford, Wis., U.S.A. .... 80 C9 45 9N 90 20W
Medgidia, Romania ....... 17 F15 44 15N 28 19 E
Media Agua, Argentina ... 94 C2 31 58S 68 25W
Media Luna, Argentina ... 94 C2 34 45S 66 44W
Medianeira, Brazil ....... 95 B5 25 17S 54 5W
Mediaș, Romania ........ 17 E13 46 9N 24 22 E
Medicine Bow, U.S.A. .... 76 F10 41 54N 106 12W
Medicine Bow Pk., U.S.A. . 76 F10 41 21N 106 19W
Medicine Bow Ra., U.S.A. . 76 F10 41 10N 106 25W
Medicine Hat, Canada .... 71 D6 50 0N 110 45W
Medicine Lake, U.S.A. .... 80 A2 48 30N 104 30W
Medicine Lodge, U.S.A. ... 81 G5 37 17N 98 35W
Medina = Al Madīnah, Si. Arabia 44 E3 24 35N 39 52 E
Medina, N. Dak., U.S.A. ... 80 B5 46 54N 99 18W
Medina, N.Y., U.S.A. ..... 84 C6 43 13N 78 23W
Medina, Ohio, U.S.A. ..... 84 E3 41 8N 81 52W
Medina →, U.S.A. ........ 81 L5 29 16N 98 29W
Medina del Campo, Spain .. 21 B3 41 18N 4 55W
Medina L., U.S.A. ........ 81 L5 29 32N 98 56W
Medina Sidonia, Spain .... 21 D3 36 28N 5 57W
Medinipur, India ......... 43 H12 22 25N 87 21 E
Mediterranean Sea, Europe . 49 C5 35 0N 15 0 E
Médoc, France ........... 20 D3 45 10N 0 50W
Medveditsa →, Russia .... 19 E7 49 35N 42 41 E

Medvezhi, Ostrava, Russia . 29 B17 71 0N 161 0 E
Medvezhyegorsk, Russia .. 18 B5 63 0N 34 25 E
Medway □, U.K. .......... 13 F8 51 25N 0 32 E
Medway →, U.K. ......... 13 F8 51 27N 0 46 E
Meekatharra, Australia ... 61 E2 26 32S 118 29 E
Meeker, U.S.A. ........... 76 F10 40 2N 107 55W
Meelpaeg Res., Canada ... 73 C8 48 15N 56 33W
Meerut, India ............ 42 E7 29 1N 77 42 E
Meeteetse, U.S.A. ........ 76 D9 44 9N 108 52W
Mega, Ethiopia ........... 47 G2 3 57N 38 19 E
Mégara, Greece .......... 23 F10 37 58N 23 22 E
Megasini, India .......... 43 J12 21 38N 86 21 E
Meghalaya □, India ...... 41 G17 25 50N 91 0 E
Meghna →, Bangla. ....... 41 H17 22 50N 90 50 E
Mégiscane, L., Canada ... 72 C4 48 35N 75 55W
Meharry, Mt., Australia ... 60 D2 22 59S 118 35 E
Mehlville, U.S.A. ......... 80 F9 38 30N 90 19W
Mehndawal, India ........ 43 F10 26 58N 83 5 E
Mehr Jān, Iran ........... 45 C7 33 50N 55 6 E
Mehrābād, Iran .......... 44 B5 36 53N 47 55 E
Mehrān, Iran ............ 44 C5 33 7N 46 10 E
Mehriz, Iran ............. 45 D7 31 35N 54 28 E
Mei Xian, China .......... 34 G4 34 18N 107 55 E
Meiktila, Burma .......... 41 J19 20 53N 95 54 E
Meissen, Germany ........ 16 C7 51 9N 13 29 E
Meizhou, China .......... 33 D6 24 16N 116 6 E
Meja, India .............. 43 G10 25 9N 82 7 E
Mejillones, Chile ........ 94 A1 23 10S 70 30W
Mekele, Ethiopia ......... 47 E2 13 33N 39 30 E
Mekhtar, Pakistan ....... 40 D6 30 30N 69 15 E
Meknès, Morocco ........ 50 B4 33 57N 5 33W
Mekong →, Asia ......... 39 H6 9 30N 106 15 E
Mekongga, Indonesia ..... 37 E6 3 39S 121 15 E
Mekvari = Kür →, Azerbaijan 19 G8 39 29N 49 15 E
Melagiri Hills, India ...... 40 N10 12 20N 77 30 E
Melaka, Malaysia ........ 39 L4 2 15N 102 15 E
Melalap, Malaysia ....... 36 C5 5 10N 116 5 E
Mélambes, Greece ....... 25 D6 35 8N 24 40 E
Melanesia, Pac. Oc. ...... 64 H7 4 0S 155 0 E
Melaya, Indonesia ....... 37 J17 8 17S 114 30 E
Melbourne, Australia ..... 63 F4 37 50S 145 0 E
Melbourne, U.S.A. ....... 83 L5 28 5N 80 37W
Melchor Múzquiz, Mexico . 86 B4 27 50N 101 30W
Melchor Ocampo, Mexico . 86 C4 24 52N 101 40W
Mélèzes →, Canada ...... 72 A5 57 40N 69 29W
Melfort, Canada ......... 71 C8 52 50N 104 37W
Melfort, Zimbabwe ....... 55 F3 18 0S 31 25 E
Melhus, Norway ......... 8 E14 63 17N 10 18 E
Melilla, N. Afr. .......... 21 E4 35 21N 2 57W
Melipilla, Chile ......... 94 C1 33 42S 71 15W
Mélissa, Ákra, Greece .... 25 D6 35 6N 24 33 E
Melita, Canada .......... 71 D8 49 15N 101 0W
Melitopol, Ukraine ....... 19 E6 46 50N 35 22 E
Melk, Austria ............ 16 D8 48 13N 15 20 E
Mellansel, Sweden ....... 8 E18 63 26N 18 19 E
Mellen, U.S.A. .......... 80 B9 46 20N 90 40W
Mellerud, Sweden ....... 9 G15 58 41N 12 28 E
Mellette, U.S.A. ......... 80 C5 45 9N 98 30W
Mellieha, Malta ......... 25 D1 35 57N 14 22 E
Melo, Uruguay .......... 95 C5 32 20S 54 10W
Melolo, Indonesia ....... 37 F6 9 53S 120 40 E
Melouprey, Cambodia .... 38 F5 13 48N 105 16 E
Melrose, Australia ....... 63 E4 32 42S 146 57 E
Melrose, U.K. ............ 11 F6 55 36N 2 43W
Melrose, Minn., U.S.A. ... 80 C7 45 40N 94 49W
Melrose, N. Mex., U.S.A. .. 81 H3 34 26N 103 38W
Melstone, U.S.A. ........ 76 C10 46 36N 107 52W
Melton Mowbray, U.K. .... 12 E7 52 47N 0 54W
Melun, France ........... 20 B5 48 32N 2 39 E
Melville, Canada ........ 71 C8 50 55N 102 50W
Melville, C., Australia .... 62 A3 14 11S 144 30 E
Melville, L., Canada ...... 73 B8 53 30N 60 0W
Melville B., Australia ..... 62 A2 12 0S 136 45 E
Melville I., Australia ..... 60 B5 11 30S 131 0 E
Melville I., Canada ....... 4 B2 75 30N 112 0W
Melville Pen., Canada .... 69 B11 68 0N 84 0W
Memba, Mozam. ......... 55 E5 14 11S 40 30 E
Memboro, Indonesia ..... 37 F5 9 30S 119 30 E
Memel = Klaipėda, Lithuania 9 J19 55 43N 21 10 E
Memel, S. Africa ......... 57 D4 27 38S 29 36 E
Memmingen, Germany .... 16 E6 47 58N 10 10 E
Mempawah, Indonesia ... 36 D3 0 30N 109 5 E
Memphis, Mich., U.S.A. ... 84 D2 42 54N 82 46W
Memphis, Tenn., U.S.A. ... 81 H10 35 8N 90 3W
Memphis, Tex., U.S.A. .... 81 H4 34 44N 100 33W
Memphremagog, L., U.S.A. . 85 B12 45 0N 72 12W
Mena, U.S.A. ............ 81 H7 34 35N 94 15W
Ménaka, Mali ........... 50 E6 15 5N 2 14 E
Menan = Chao Phraya →,
　Thailand ............... 38 F3 13 32N 100 36 E
Menarandra →, Madag. ... 57 D7 25 17S 44 30 E
Menard, U.S.A. .......... 81 K5 30 55N 99 47W
Mendawai →, Indonesia .. 36 E4 3 30S 113 0 E
Mende, France ........... 20 D5 44 31N 3 30 E
Mendeleyev Ridge, Arctic . 4 B17 80 0N 178 0 E
Mendez, Mexico ......... 87 B5 25 7N 98 34W
Mendhar, India .......... 43 C6 33 35N 74 10 E
Mendip Hills, U.K. ....... 13 F5 51 17N 2 40W
Mendocino, U.S.A. ....... 76 G2 39 19N 123 48W
Mendocino, C., U.S.A. .... 76 F1 40 26N 124 25W
Mendota, Calif., U.S.A. ... 78 J6 36 45N 120 23W
Mendota, Ill., U.S.A. ..... 80 E10 41 33N 89 7W
Mendoyo, Indonesia ..... 37 J17 8 23S 114 42 E
Mendoza, Argentina ..... 94 C2 32 50S 68 52W
Mendoza □, Argentina .... 94 C2 33 0S 69 0W
Mene Grande, Venezuela . 92 B4 9 49N 70 56W
Menemen, Turkey ........ 23 E12 38 34N 27 3 E
Menen, Belgium ......... 15 D3 50 47N 3 7 E
Menggala, Indonesia ..... 36 E3 4 30S 105 15 E
Mengjin, China .......... 34 G7 34 55N 112 45 E
Mengyin, China ......... 35 G9 35 40N 117 58 E
Mengzi, China ........... 32 D5 23 20N 103 22 E
Menihek, Canada ........ 73 B6 54 28N 56 36W
Menihek L., Canada ...... 73 B6 54 0N 67 0W
Menin = Menen, Belgium . 15 D3 50 47N 3 7 E
Menindee, Australia ..... 63 E3 32 20S 142 25 E
Menindee L., Australia ... 63 E3 32 20S 142 25 E
Meningie, Australia ...... 63 F2 35 50S 139 18 E
Menjangan, Pulau, Indonesia 37 J17 8 7S 114 31 E
Menlo Park, U.S.A. ....... 78 H4 37 27N 122 12W
Menominee, U.S.A. ....... 82 C2 45 6N 87 37W
Menominee →, U.S.A. .... 82 C2 45 6N 87 36W
Menomonie, U.S.A. ...... 80 C9 44 53N 91 55W
Menongue, Angola ....... 53 G3 14 48S 17 52 E
Menorca, Spain .......... 24 B11 40 0N 4 0 E
Mentakab, Malaysia ...... 39 L4 3 29N 102 21 E
Mentawai, Kepulauan, Indonesia 36 E1 2 0S 99 0 E

Menton, France .......... 20 E7 43 50N 7 29 E
Mentor, U.S.A. ........... 84 E3 41 40N 81 21W
Menzelinsk, Russia ...... 18 C9 55 47N 53 11 E
Menzies, Australia ....... 61 E3 29 40S 121 2 E
Meob B., Namibia ........ 56 C1 24 25S 14 34 E
Me'ona, Israel ........... 46 B4 33 1N 35 15 E
Meoqui, Mexico ......... 86 B3 28 17N 105 29W
Mepaco, Mozam. ........ 55 F3 15 57S 30 48 E
Meppel, Neths. .......... 15 B6 52 42N 6 12 E
Merabéllou, Kólpos, Greece . 25 D7 35 10N 25 50 E
Merak, Indonesia ........ 37 F12 6 10N 106 26 E
Meramangye, L., Australia . 61 E5 28 25S 132 13 E
Meran = Merano, Italy .... 22 A4 46 40N 11 9 E
Merano, Italy ............ 22 A4 46 40N 11 9 E
Merauke, Indonesia ...... 37 F10 8 29S 140 24 E
Merbein, Australia ....... 63 E3 34 10S 142 2 E
Merbuk, Gunung, Indonesia 37 J17 8 13S 114 39 E
Merca, Somali Rep. ....... 47 G3 1 48N 44 50 E
Merced, U.S.A. .......... 78 H6 37 18N 120 29W
Merced →, U.S.A. ....... 78 H6 37 21N 120 59W
Merced Pk., U.S.A. ....... 78 H7 37 36N 119 24W
Mercedes, Buenos Aires,
　Argentina .............. 94 C4 34 40S 59 30W
Mercedes, Corrientes, Argentina 94 B4 29 10S 58 5W
Mercedes, San Luis, Argentina 94 C2 33 40S 65 21W
Mercedes, Uruguay ...... 94 C4 33 12S 58 0W
Merceditas, Chile ........ 94 B1 28 20S 70 35W
Mercer, N.Z. ............ 59 G5 37 16S 175 5 E
Mercer, U.S.A. .......... 84 E4 41 14N 80 15W
Mercer Island, U.S.A. .... 78 C4 47 35N 122 15W
Mercury, U.S.A. ......... 79 J11 36 40N 115 58W
Mercy, C., Canada ....... 69 B13 65 0N 63 30W
Mere, U.K. .............. 13 F5 51 6N 2 16W
Meredith, C., Falk. Is. .... 96 G4 52 15S 60 40W
Meredith, L., U.S.A. ...... 81 H4 35 43N 101 33W
Mergui, Burma .......... 38 F2 12 26N 98 34 E
Mergui Arch. = Myeik Kyunzu,
　Burma ................. 39 G1 11 30N 97 30 E
Mérida, Mexico ......... 87 C7 20 58N 89 37W
Mérida, Spain ........... 21 C2 38 55N 6 25W
Mérida, Venezuela ....... 92 B4 8 24N 71 8W
Mérida, Cord. de, Venezuela 92 B4 9 0N 71 0W
Meriden, U.K. ........... 13 E6 52 26N 1 38W
Meriden, U.S.A. ......... 85 E12 41 32N 72 48W
Meridian, Calif., U.S.A. ... 78 F5 39 9N 121 55W
Meridian, Idaho, U.S.A. ... 76 E5 43 37N 116 24W
Meridian, Miss., U.S.A. ... 83 J1 32 22N 88 42W
Merinda, Australia ....... 62 C4 20 2S 148 11 E
Merir, Pac. Oc. .......... 37 D8 4 10N 132 30 E
Merirumã, Brazil ........ 93 C8 1 15N 54 50W
Merkel, U.S.A. ........... 81 J5 32 28N 100 1W
Merksem, Belgium ....... 15 C4 51 16N 4 25 E
Mermaid Reef, Australia .. 60 C2 17 6S 119 36 E
Merredin, Australia ...... 61 F2 31 28S 118 18 E
Merrick, U.K. ............ 11 F4 55 8N 4 28W
Merrickville, Canada ..... 85 B9 44 55N 75 50W
Merrill, Oreg., U.S.A. ..... 76 E3 42 1N 121 36W
Merrill, Wis., U.S.A. ...... 80 C10 45 11N 89 41W
Merriman, U.S.A. ........ 80 D4 42 55N 101 42W
Merritt, Canada ......... 70 C4 50 10N 120 45W
Merritt Island, U.S.A. .... 83 L5 28 21N 80 42W
Merriwa, Australia ....... 63 E5 32 6S 150 22 E
Merry I., Canada ......... 72 A4 55 29N 77 31W
Merryville, U.S.A. ....... 81 K8 30 45N 93 33W
Mersch, Lux. ............ 15 E6 49 44N 6 7 E
Mersea I., U.K. .......... 13 F8 51 47N 0 58 E
Merseburg, Germany ..... 16 C6 51 22N 11 59 E
Mersey →, U.K. ......... 12 D4 53 25N 3 1W
Merseyside □, U.K. ...... 12 D4 53 31N 3 2W
Mersin, Turkey .......... 19 G5 36 51N 34 36 E
Mersing, Malaysia ....... 39 L4 2 25N 103 50 E
Merta, India ............. 42 F6 26 39N 74 4 E
Merta Road, India ....... 42 F5 26 43N 73 55 E
Merthyr Tydfil, U.K. ...... 13 F4 51 45N 3 22W
Merthyr Tydfil □, U.K. .... 13 F4 51 46N 3 21W
Mértola, Portugal ....... 21 D2 37 40N 7 40W
Mertzon, U.S.A. ......... 81 K4 31 16N 100 49W
Meru, Kenya ............ 54 B4 0 3N 37 40 E
Meru, Tanzania .......... 54 C4 3 15S 36 46 E
Meru △, Kenya ......... 54 B4 0 5N 38 10 E
Mesa, U.S.A. ............ 77 K8 33 25N 111 50W
Mesa Verde △, U.S.A. ... 77 H9 37 11N 108 29W
Mesanagrós, Greece ..... 25 C9 36 1N 27 49 E
Mesaras, Kólpos, Greece .. 25 D12 35 12N 33 14 E
Mesgouez, L., Canada .... 72 B5 51 20N 75 0W
Meshed = Mashhad, Iran .. 45 B8 36 20N 59 35 E
Meshoppen, U.S.A. ...... 85 E8 41 36N 76 3W
Mesilinka →, Canada ..... 70 B4 56 6N 124 30W
Mesilla, U.S.A. .......... 77 K10 32 16N 106 48W
Mesolóngion, Greece .... 23 E3 38 21N 21 28 E
Mesopotamia = Al Jazirah, Iraq 44 C5 33 30N 44 0 E
Mesquite, U.S.A. ........ 77 H6 36 47N 114 6W
Messaad, Algeria ........ 50 B6 34 8N 3 30 E
Messalo →, Mozam. ..... 55 E4 12 25S 39 15 E
Messina = Musina, S. Africa 57 C5 22 20S 30 5 E
Messina, Italy ........... 22 E6 38 11N 15 34 E
Messina, Str. di, Italy ..... 22 F6 38 15N 15 35 E
Messíni, Greece ......... 23 F10 37 4N 22 1 E
Messiniakós Kólpos, Greece 23 F10 36 45N 22 5 E
Messonghi, Greece ...... 25 B3 39 29N 19 56 E
Mesta →, S. Amer. ....... 92 B5 6 12N 67 28W
Meta Incognita Pen., Canada 69 B13 62 45S 68 30W
Metabetchouan, Canada .. 73 C5 48 26N 71 52W
Metairie, U.S.A. ......... 81 L9 29 58N 90 10W
Metaline Falls, U.S.A. .... 76 B5 48 52N 117 22W
Metán, Argentina ........ 94 B3 25 30S 65 0W
Metangula, Mozam. ...... 55 E3 12 40S 34 50 E
Metengobalame, Mozam. . 55 E3 14 49S 34 30 E
Methven, N.Z. ........... 59 K3 43 38S 171 40 E
Metil, Mozam. .......... 55 F4 16 24S 39 0 E
Metlakatla, U.S.A. ....... 68 C6 55 8N 131 35W
Metropolis, U.S.A. ....... 81 G10 37 9N 88 44W
Metu, Ethiopia .......... 47 F2 8 18N 35 35 E
Metz, France ............ 20 B7 49 8N 6 10 E
Meulaboh, Indonesia .... 36 D1 4 11N 96 3 E
Meureudu, Indonesia .... 36 C1 5 19N 96 10 E
Meuse →, Europe ....... 15 D5 50 45N 5 41 E
Mexia, U.S.A. ........... 81 K6 31 41N 96 29W
Mexiana, I., Brazil ....... 93 D9 0 0 49 30W
Mexicali, Mexico ........ 79 N11 32 40N 115 30W
Mexican Plateau, Mexico . 66 G9 25 0N 105 0W
Mexican Water, U.S.A. ... 77 H9 36 57N 109 32W
México, Mexico ......... 87 D5 19 20N 99 10W
Mexico, Maine, U.S.A. ... 85 B14 44 34N 70 33W

Mexico, Mo., U.S.A. ...... 80 F9 39 10N 91 53W
Mexico, N.Y., U.S.A. ...... 85 C8 43 28N 76 18W
México □, Mexico ........ 87 D5 19 20N 99 10W
Mexico ■, Cent. Amer. .... 86 C4 25 0N 105 0W
Mexico, G. of, Cent. Amer. . 87 C7 25 0N 90 0W
Mexico B., U.S.A. ........ 85 C8 43 35N 76 20W
Meydān-e Naftūn, Iran ... 45 D6 31 56N 49 18 E
Meydani, Ra's-e, Iran ..... 45 E8 25 24N 59 6 E
Meymaneh, Afghan. ...... 40 B4 35 53N 64 38 E
Mezen, Russia ........... 18 A7 65 50N 44 20 E
Mezen →, Russia ........ 18 A7 66 44N 44 22 E
Mézenc, Mt., France ...... 20 D6 44 54N 4 11 E
Mezhdurechenskiy, Russia . 28 D7 59 36N 65 56 E
Mezőkövesd, Hungary .... 17 E11 47 49N 20 35 E
Mezőtúr, Hungary ........ 17 E11 47 1N 20 41 E
Mezquital, Mexico ....... 86 C4 23 29N 104 23W
Mfolozi →, S. Africa ..... 57 D5 28 25S 32 26 E
Mgeta, Tanzania ......... 55 D4 8 22S 36 6 E
Mhlaba Hills, Zimbabwe .. 55 F3 18 30S 30 30 E
Mhow, India ............ 42 H6 22 33N 75 50 E
Miahuatlán, Mexico ...... 87 D5 16 21N 96 36W
Miami, Fla., U.S.A. ....... 83 N5 25 47N 80 11W
Miami, Okla., U.S.A. ...... 81 G7 36 53N 94 53W
Miami, Tex., U.S.A. ....... 81 H4 35 42N 100 38W
Miami Beach, U.S.A. ..... 83 N5 25 47N 80 8W
Mian Xian, China ........ 34 H4 33 10N 106 32 E
Mianchi, China .......... 34 G6 34 48N 111 48 E
Miāndarreh, Iran ........ 45 C7 35 37N 53 39 E
Miāndowāb, Iran ........ 44 B5 37 0N 46 5 E
Miandrivazo, Madag. ..... 57 B8 19 31S 45 29 E
Miāneh, Iran ............ 44 B5 37 30N 47 40 E
Mianwali, Pakistan ...... 42 C4 32 38N 71 28 E
Miarinarivo, Antananarivo,
　Madag. ................ 57 B8 18 57S 46 55 E
Miarinarivo, Toamasina, Madag. 57 B8 16 38S 48 15 E
Miariravaratra, Madag. ... 57 C8 20 13S 47 31 E
Miass, Russia ........... 18 D11 54 59N 60 6 E
Mica, S. Africa .......... 57 C5 24 10S 30 48 E
Michalovce, Slovak Rep. .. 17 D11 48 47N 21 58 E
Michigan □, U.S.A. ....... 82 C3 44 0N 85 0W
Michigan, L., U.S.A. ...... 82 D2 44 0N 87 0W
Michigan City, U.S.A. ..... 82 E2 41 43N 86 54W
Michipicoten I., Canada .. 72 C2 47 40N 85 40W
Michoacan □, Mexico .... 86 D4 19 0N 102 0W
Michurin, Bulgaria ....... 23 C12 42 9N 27 51 E
Michurinsk, Russia ....... 18 D7 52 58N 40 27 E
Mico, Pta., Nic. .......... 88 D3 12 0N 83 30W
Micoud, St. Lucia ....... 89 f 13 49N 60 54W
Micronesia, Pac. Oc. ..... 64 G7 11 0N 160 0 E
Micronesia, Federated States
　of ■, Pac. Oc. .......... 64 G7 9 0N 150 0 E
Mid-Oceanic Ridge, Ind. Oc. 64 M1 42 0S 90 0 E
Midai, Indonesia ......... 36 D3 3 0N 107 47 E
Midale, Canada ......... 71 D8 49 25N 103 20W
Middelburg, Neths. ...... 15 C3 51 30N 3 36 E
Middelburg, Eastern Cape,
　S. Africa ............... 56 E4 31 30S 25 0 E
Middelburg, Mpumalanga,
　S. Africa ............... 57 D4 25 49S 29 28 E
Middelpos, S. Africa ..... 56 E3 31 55S 20 13 E
Middelwit, S. Africa ..... 56 C4 24 51S 27 3 E
Middle Alkali L., U.S.A. ... 76 F3 41 27N 120 5W
Middle Bass I., U.S.A. .... 84 E2 41 41N 82 49W
Middle East, Asia ....... 26 F7 38 0N 40 0 E
Middle Fork Feather →, U.S.A. 78 F5 38 33N 121 30W
Middle I., Australia ...... 61 F3 34 6S 123 11 E
Middle Loup →, U.S.A. ... 80 E5 41 17N 98 24W
Middle Sackville, Canada . 73 D7 44 47N 63 42W
Middleboro, U.S.A. ...... 85 E14 41 54N 70 55W
Middleburg, Fla., U.S.A. .. 83 K5 30 4N 81 52W
Middleburg, Pa., U.S.A. .. 84 F7 40 47N 77 3W
Middleburgh, U.S.A. ..... 85 D10 42 36N 74 20W
Middlebury, U.S.A. ....... 85 B11 44 1N 73 10W
Middlemount, Australia .. 62 C4 22 50S 148 40 E
Middleport, N.Y., U.S.A. .. 84 C6 43 13N 78 29W
Middleport, Ohio, U.S.A. . 82 F4 39 0N 82 3W
Middlesboro, U.S.A. ..... 83 G4 36 36N 83 43W
Middlesbrough, U.K. ..... 12 C6 54 35N 1 13W
Middlesbrough □, U.K. ... 12 C6 54 28N 1 13W
Middlesex, Belize ........ 88 C2 17 2N 88 31W
Middlesex, N.J., U.S.A. ... 85 F10 40 36N 74 30W
Middlesex, N.Y., U.S.A. ... 84 D7 42 42N 77 16W
Middleton, Australia ..... 62 C3 22 22S 141 32 E
Middleton, Canada ...... 73 D6 44 57N 65 4W
Middleton Cr. →, Australia 62 C3 22 35S 141 51 E
Middletown, U.K. ........ 10 B5 54 17N 6 51W
Middletown, Calif., U.S.A. . 78 G4 38 45N 122 37W
Middletown, Conn., U.S.A. 85 E12 41 34N 72 39W
Middletown, N.Y., U.S.A. . 85 E10 41 27N 74 25W
Middletown, Ohio, U.S.A. . 82 F3 39 31N 84 24W
Middletown, Pa., U.S.A. .. 84 F8 40 12N 76 44W
Midge Point, Australia ... 62 J6 20 39S 148 43 E
Midhurst, U.K. .......... 13 G7 50 59N 0 44W
Midi, Canal du →, France . 20 E4 43 45N 1 21 E
Midland, Australia ....... 61 F2 31 54S 116 1 E
Midland, Canada ........ 84 B5 44 45N 79 50W
Midland, Calif., U.S.A. .... 79 M12 33 52N 114 48W
Midland, Mich., U.S.A. ... 82 D3 43 37N 84 14W
Midland, Pa., U.S.A. ..... 84 F4 40 39N 80 27W
Midland, Tex., U.S.A. ..... 81 K3 32 0N 102 3W
Midlands □, Zimbabwe ... 55 F2 19 40S 29 0 E
Midleton, Ireland ........ 10 E3 51 55N 8 10W
Midlothian, U.S.A. ....... 81 J6 32 30N 97 0W
Midlothian □, U.K. ....... 11 F5 55 51N 3 5W
Midongy, Tangorombohitr' i,
　Madag. ................ 57 C8 23 30S 47 0 E
Midongy Atsimo, Madag. . 57 C8 23 35S 47 1 E
Midway Is., Pac. Oc. ...... 64 E10 28 13N 177 22W
Midway Wells, U.S.A. .... 79 N11 32 41N 115 7W
Midwest, Wyo., U.S.A. ... 76 E10 43 25N 106 16W
Midwest City, U.S.A. ..... 81 H6 35 27N 97 24W
Midyat, Turkey .......... 44 B4 37 25N 41 23 E
Midzŏr, Bulgaria ........ 23 C10 43 24N 22 40 E
Mie □, Japan ............ 31 G8 34 30N 136 10 E
Międzychód, Poland ..... 16 B8 52 35N 15 53 E
Międzyrzec Podlaski, Poland 17 C12 51 58N 22 45 E
Mielec, Poland .......... 17 C11 50 15N 21 25 E
Mienga, Angola ......... 56 B2 17 12S 19 48 E
Miercurea-Ciuc, Romania . 17 E13 46 21N 25 48 E
Mieres, Spain ........... 21 A3 43 18N 5 48W
Mifflintown, U.S.A. ...... 84 F7 40 34N 77 24W
Mifraz Ḥefa, Israel ....... 46 C4 32 52N 35 0 E
Miguel Alemán, Presa, Mexico 87 D5 18 15N 96 40W
Mihara, Japan .......... 31 G6 34 24N 133 5 E
Mikese, Tanzania ........ 54 D4 6 48S 37 55 E
Mikhaylovgrad = Montana,
　Bulgaria ............... 23 C10 43 27N 23 16 E

Mikhaylovka, Russia ........... 19 D7 50 3N 43 5 E
Mikkeli, Finland ............. 9 F22 61 43N 27 15 E
Mikkwa →, Canada ......... 70 B6 58 25N 114 46W
Mikonos, Greece ........... 23 F11 37 30N 25 25 E
Mikumi, Tanzania ............ 54 D4 7 26S 37 0 E
Mikumi △, Tanzania .......... 54 D4 7 35S 37 15 E
Mikun, Russia ............... 18 B9 62 20N 50 0 E
Milaca, U.S.A. .............. 80 C8 45 45N 93 39W
Milagro, Ecuador ............ 92 D3 2 11S 79 36W
Milan = Milano, Italy ......... 20 D8 45 28N 9 12 E
Milan, Mo., U.S.A. ........... 80 E8 40 12N 93 7W
Milan, Tenn., U.S.A. ......... 83 H1 35 55N 88 46W
Milange, Mozam. ............ 55 F4 16 3S 35 45 E
Milano, Italy ............... 20 D8 45 28N 9 12 E
Milanoa, Madag. ............ 57 A8 13 35S 49 47 E
Milâs, Turkey ............... 23 F12 37 20N 27 50 E
Milatos, Greece ............. 25 D7 35 18N 25 34 E
Milazzo, Italy .............. 22 E6 38 13N 15 15 E
Milbank, U.S.A. ............. 80 C6 45 13N 96 38W
Milbanke Sd., Canada ........ 70 C3 52 15N 128 35W
Milden, Canada ............. 71 C7 51 29N 107 32W
Mildenhall, U.K. ............ 13 E8 52 21N 0 32 E
Mildmay, Canada ............ 84 B3 44 3N 81 7W
Mildura, Australia ........... 63 E3 34 13S 142 9 E
Miles, Australia ............. 63 D5 26 40S 150 9 E
Miles City, U.S.A. ........... 80 B2 46 25N 105 51W
Milestone, Canada ........... 71 D8 49 59N 104 31W
Miletus, Turkey ............. 23 F12 37 30N 27 18 E
Milford, Calif., U.S.A. ........ 78 E6 40 10N 120 22W
Milford, Conn., U.S.A. ....... 85 E11 41 14N 73 3W
Milford, Del., U.S.A. ......... 82 F8 38 55N 75 26W
Milford, Mass., U.S.A. ....... 85 D13 42 8N 71 31W
Milford, N.H., U.S.A. ........ 85 D13 42 50N 71 39W
Milford, Pa., U.S.A. ......... 85 E10 41 19N 74 48W
Milford, Utah, U.S.A. ........ 77 G7 38 24N 113 1W
Milford Sd., N.Z. ........... 59 L1 44 41S 167 47 E
Milford Haven, U.K. ......... 13 F2 51 42N 5 7W
Milford Sd., N.Z. ........... 59 L1 44 41S 167 55 E
Milford Sound, N.Z. ......... 59 L1 44 41S 167 55 E
Milh, Baḥr al = Razāzah, Buḥayrat
ar, Iraq ................ 44 C4 32 40N 43 35 E
Milikapiti, Australia .......... 60 B5 11 26S 130 40 E
Miling, Australia ............ 61 F2 30 30S 116 17 E
Milk →, U.S.A. ............. 76 B10 48 4N 106 19W
Milk River, Canada .......... 70 D6 49 10N 112 5W
Mill I., Antarctica .......... 5 C8 66 0S 101 30 E
Mill Valley, U.S.A. .......... 78 H4 37 54N 122 32W
Millau, France ............. 20 D5 44 8N 3 4 E
Millbridge, Canada .......... 84 B7 44 41N 77 36W
Millbrook, Canada .......... 84 B6 44 10N 78 29W
Millbrook, U.S.A. ........... 85 E11 41 47N 73 42W
Mille Lacs, L. des, Canada .... 72 C1 48 45N 90 35W
Mille Lacs L., U.S.A. ......... 80 B8 46 15N 93 39W
Milledgeville, U.S.A. ........ 83 J4 33 5N 83 14W
Millen, U.S.A. ............. 83 J5 32 48N 81 57W
Millennium I. = Caroline I.,
Kiribati ................ 65 H12 9 58S 150 13W
Miller, U.S.A. ............. 80 C5 44 31N 98 59W
Millersburg, Ohio, U.S.A. ..... 84 F3 40 33N 81 55W
Millersburg, Pa., U.S.A. ...... 84 F8 40 32N 76 58W
Millerton, U.S.A. ........... 85 E11 41 57N 73 31W
Millerton L., U.S.A. ......... 78 J7 37 1N 119 41W
Millet, St. Lucia ............ 89 f 13 55N 60 59W
Millheim, U.S.A. ........... 84 F7 40 54N 77 29W
Millicent, Australia .......... 63 F3 37 34S 140 21 E
Millington, U.S.A. .......... 81 H10 35 20N 89 53W
Millinocket, U.S.A. ......... 83 C11 45 39N 68 43W
Millmerran, Australia ........ 63 D5 27 53S 151 16 E
Millom, U.K. .............. 12 C4 54 13N 3 16W
Mills L., Canada ........... 70 A5 61 30N 118 20W
Millsboro, U.S.A. .......... 84 G5 40 0N 80 0W
Millstream-Chichester △,
Australia ............... 60 D2 21 35S 117 6 E
Milltown Malbay, Ireland ..... 10 D2 52 52N 9 24W
Millville, N.J., U.S.A. ........ 82 F8 39 24N 75 2W
Millville, Pa., U.S.A. ........ 85 E8 41 7N 76 32W
Millwood L., U.S.A. ......... 81 J8 33 42N 93 58W
Milne →, Australia ......... 62 C2 21 10S 137 33 E
Milo, U.S.A. .............. 83 C11 45 15N 68 59W
Milos, Greece ............. 23 F11 36 44N 24 25 E
Milparinka, Australia ........ 63 D3 29 46S 141 57 E
Milton, N.S., Canada ........ 73 D7 44 4N 64 45W
Milton, Ont., Canada ........ 84 C5 43 31N 79 53W
Milton, N.Z. .............. 59 M2 46 7S 169 59 E
Milton, Calif., U.S.A. ........ 78 G6 38 3N 120 51W
Milton, Fla., U.S.A. ......... 83 K2 30 38N 87 3W
Milton, Pa., U.S.A. ......... 84 F8 41 1N 76 51W
Milton, Vt., U.S.A. .......... 85 B11 44 38N 73 7W
Milton-Freewater, U.S.A. ..... 76 D4 45 56N 118 23W
Milton Keynes, U.K. ......... 13 E7 52 1N 0 44W
Milton Keynes □, U.K. ....... 13 E7 52 1N 0 44W
Milverton, Canada .......... 84 C4 43 34N 80 55W
Milwaukee, U.S.A. .......... 82 D2 43 2N 87 55W
Milwaukee Deep, Atl. Oc. .... 89 C6 19 50N 68 0W
Milwaukie, U.S.A. .......... 78 E4 45 27N 122 38W
Min Jiang →, Fujian, China ... 33 D6 26 0N 119 35 E
Min Jiang →, Sichuan, China .. 32 D5 28 45N 104 40 E
Min Xian, China ........... 34 G3 34 25N 104 5 E
Mina Pirquitas, Argentina .... 94 A2 22 40S 66 30W
Minā Su'ud, Si. Arabia ....... 45 D6 28 45N 48 28 E
Minā'al Aḥmadi, Kuwait ...... 45 D6 29 5N 48 10 E
Minago →, Canada ......... 71 C9 54 33N 98 59W
Minaki, Canada ............ 71 D10 49 59N 94 40W
Minamata, Japan ........... 31 H5 32 10N 130 30 E
Minami-Arapusa △, Japan .... 31 G9 35 30N 138 9 E
Minami-Tori-Shima, Pac. Oc. .. 64 E7 24 20N 153 58 E
Minas, Uruguay ............ 95 C4 34 20S 55 10W
Minas, Sierra de las, Guatemala 88 C2 15 9N 89 31W
Minas Basin, Canada ........ 73 C7 45 20N 64 12W
Minas Gerais □, Brazil ....... 93 G9 18 50S 46 0W
Minatitlán, Mexico .......... 87 D6 17 59N 94 31W
Minbu, Burma ............. 41 J19 20 10N 94 52 E
Minchinabad, Pakistan ...... 42 D5 30 10N 73 34 E
Mindanao, Phil. ........... 37 C6 8 0N 125 0 E
Mindanao Sea = Bohol Sea, Phil. 37 C6 9 0N 124 0 E
Mindanao Trench, Pac. Oc. ... 37 B7 12 0N 126 6 E
Minden, Canada ............ 84 B6 44 55N 78 43W
Minden, Germany .......... 16 B5 52 17N 8 55 E
Minden, La., U.S.A. ......... 81 J8 32 37N 93 17W
Minden, Nev., U.S.A. ........ 78 G7 38 57N 119 46W
Mindiptana, Indonesia ....... 37 F10 5 55S 140 22 E
Mindoro, Phil. ............ 37 B6 13 0N 121 0 E
Mindoro Str., Phil. ......... 37 B6 12 30N 120 30 E
Mine, Japan .............. 31 G5 34 12N 131 7 E
Minehead, U.K. ............ 13 F4 51 12N 3 29W
Mineola, N.Y., U.S.A. ....... 85 F11 40 45N 73 39W
Mineola, Tex., U.S.A. ....... 81 J7 32 40N 95 29W
Mineral King, U.S.A. ........ 78 J8 36 27N 118 36W
Mineral Wells, U.S.A. ....... 81 J5 32 48N 98 7W

Minersville, U.S.A. ......... 85 F8 40 41N 76 16W
Minerva, U.S.A. ........... 84 F3 40 44N 81 6W
Minetto, U.S.A. ........... 85 C8 43 24N 76 28W
Mingāçevir Su Anbarı,
Azerbaijan ............. 19 F8 40 57N 46 50 E
Mingan, Canada ........... 73 B7 50 20N 64 0W
Mingechaurskoye Vdkhr. =
Mingāçevir Su Anbarı,
Azerbaijan ............. 19 F8 40 57N 46 50 E
Mingela, Australia .......... 62 B4 19 52S 146 38 E
Mingenew, Australia ........ 61 E2 29 12S 115 21 E
Mingera Cr. →, Australia ..... 62 C2 20 38S 137 45 E
Mingin, Burma ............ 41 H19 22 50N 94 30 E
Mingo Junction, U.S.A. ...... 84 F4 40 19N 80 37W
Mingteke Daban = Mintaka Pass,
Pakistan ............... 43 A6 37 0N 74 58 E
Mingyuegue, China ......... 35 C15 43 2N 128 50 E
Minho = Miño →, Spain ...... 21 A2 41 52N 8 40W
Minho, Portugal ........... 21 B1 41 25N 8 20W
Minidoka, U.S.A. ........... 76 E7 42 45N 113 29W
Minigwal, L., Australia ....... 61 E3 29 31S 123 14 E
Minilya →, Australia ........ 61 D1 23 45S 114 0 E
Minilya Roadhouse, Australia .. 61 D1 23 55S 114 0 E
Minipi L., Canada .......... 73 B7 52 25N 60 45W
Mink L., Canada ........... 70 A5 61 54N 117 40W
Minna, Nigeria ............ 50 G7 9 37N 6 30 E
Minneapolis, Kans., U.S.A. .... 80 F6 39 8N 97 42W
Minneapolis, Minn., U.S.A. ... 80 C8 44 59N 93 16W
Minnedosa, Canada ........ 71 C9 50 14N 99 50W
Minnesota □, U.S.A. ........ 80 B8 46 0N 94 15W
Minnesota →, U.S.A. ....... 80 C8 44 54N 93 9W
Minnewaukan, U.S.A. ....... 80 A5 48 4N 99 15W
Minnipa, Australia ......... 63 E2 32 51S 135 9 E
Minnitaki L., Canada ........ 72 C1 49 57N 92 10W
Mino, Japan .............. 31 G8 35 32N 136 55 E
Miño →, Spain ............ 21 A2 41 52N 8 40W
Minorca = Menorca, Spain .... 24 B11 40 0N 4 0 E
Minot, U.S.A. ............. 80 A4 48 14N 101 18W
Minqin, China ............ 34 E2 38 38N 103 20 E
Minsk, Belarus ............ 17 B14 53 52N 27 30 E
Mińsk Mazowiecki, Poland .... 17 B11 52 10N 21 33 E
Mintabie, Australia ......... 63 D1 27 15S 133 7 E
Mintaka Pass, Pakistan ...... 43 A6 37 0N 74 58 E
Minto, Canada ............ 73 C6 46 5N 66 5W
Minto, L., Canada .......... 72 A5 57 13N 75 0W
Minton, Canada ........... 71 D8 49 10N 104 35W
Minturn, U.S.A. ........... 76 G10 39 35N 106 26W
Minusinsk, Russia .......... 29 D10 53 43N 91 20 E
Minutang, India ........... 41 E20 28 15N 96 30 E
Minzhong, China .......... 33 F10 22 37N 113 30 E
Miquelon, Canada .......... 72 C4 49 25N 76 27W
Miquelon, St-P. & M. ....... 73 C8 47 8N 56 22W
Mir Kūh, Iran ............. 45 E8 26 22N 58 55 E
Mir Shahdād, Iran ......... 45 E8 26 15N 58 29 E
Mira, Italy ............... 22 B5 45 26N 12 8 E
Mira por vos Cay, Bahamas ... 89 B5 22 9N 74 30W
Mirador-Río Azul △, Guatemala 88 C2 17 45N 89 50W
Miraj, India .............. 40 L9 16 50N 74 45 E
Miram Shah, Pakistan ....... 42 C4 33 0N 70 2 E
Miramar, Argentina ......... 94 D4 38 15S 57 50W
Miramar, Mozam. .......... 57 C6 23 50S 35 35 E
Miramichi, Canada ......... 73 C6 47 2N 65 28W
Miramichi B., Canada ....... 73 C7 47 15N 65 0W
Miranda, Brazil ........... 93 H7 20 10S 56 15W
Miranda →, Brazil ......... 92 G7 19 25S 57 20W
Miranda de Ebro, Spain ...... 21 A4 42 41N 2 57W
Miranda do Douro, Portugal .. 21 B2 41 30N 6 16W
Mirandópolis, Brazil ........ 95 A5 21 9S 51 6W
Mirango, Malawi .......... 55 E3 13 32S 34 58 E
Mirani, Australia .......... 62 K6 21 8S 148 53 E
Mirassol, Brazil ........... 95 A6 20 46S 49 28W
Mirbāṭ, Oman ............ 47 D5 17 0N 54 45 E
Miri, Malaysia ............ 36 D4 4 23N 113 59 E
Miriam Vale, Australia ....... 62 C5 24 20S 151 33 E
Mirim, L., S. Amer. ......... 95 C5 32 45S 52 50W
Mirnyy, Russia ............ 29 C12 62 33N 113 53 E
Mirokhan, Pakistan ........ 42 F3 27 46N 68 6 E
Mirond L., Canada ......... 71 B8 55 6N 102 47W
Mirpur, Pakistan .......... 43 C5 33 32N 73 56 E
Mirpur Batoro, Pakistan ..... 42 G3 24 44N 68 16 E
Mirpur Bibiwari, Pakistan .... 42 E2 28 33N 67 44 E
Mirpur Khas, Pakistan ...... 42 G3 25 30N 69 0 E
Mirpur Sakro, Pakistan ...... 42 G2 24 33N 67 41 E
Mirs Bay = Tai Pang Wan, H.K. 33 F11 22 33N 114 24 E
Mirtağ, Turkey ............ 44 B4 38 23N 41 56 E
Miryang, S. Korea ......... 35 G15 35 31N 128 44 E
Mirzapur, India ........... 43 G10 25 10N 82 34 E
Mirzapur-cum-Vindhyachal =
Mirzapur, India .......... 43 G10 25 10N 82 34 E
Misantla, Mexico .......... 87 D5 19 56N 96 50W
Misawa, Japan ............ 30 D10 40 41N 141 24 E
Miscou I., Canada ......... 73 C7 47 57N 64 31W
Mish'āb, Ra's al, Si. Arabia ... 45 D6 28 15N 48 43 E
Mishan, China ............ 33 B8 45 37N 131 48 E
Mishawaka, U.S.A. ......... 82 E2 41 40N 86 11W
Mishima, Japan ........... 31 G9 35 10N 138 52 E
Misión, Mexico ........... 79 N10 32 6N 116 53W
Misiones □, Argentina ....... 95 B5 27 0S 55 0W
Misiones □, Paraguay ....... 94 B4 27 0S 56 0W
Miskah, Si. Arabia ......... 44 E4 24 49N 42 56 E
Miskitos, Cayos, Nic. ....... 88 D3 14 26N 82 50W
Miskolc, Hungary .......... 17 D11 48 7N 20 50 E
Misoke, Dem. Rep. of the Congo 54 C2 0 42S 28 2 E
Misool, Indonesia ......... 37 E8 1 52S 130 10 E
Miṣrātah, Libya ........... 51 B9 32 24N 15 3 E
Missanabie, Canada ........ 72 C3 48 20N 84 6W
Missinaibi →, Canada ....... 72 B3 50 43N 81 29W
Missinaibi L., Canada ....... 72 C3 48 23N 83 40W
Mission, Canada .......... 70 D4 49 10N 122 15W
Mission, S. Dak., U.S.A. ..... 80 D4 43 18N 100 39W
Mission, Tex., U.S.A. ....... 81 M5 26 13N 98 20W
Mission Beach, Australia .... 62 B4 17 53S 146 6 E
Mission Viejo, U.S.A. ....... 79 M9 33 36N 117 40W
Missisa L., Canada ........ 72 B2 52 20N 85 7W
Missisicabi →, Canada ...... 72 B4 51 14N 79 31W
Mississagi →, Canada ...... 72 C3 46 15N 83 9W
Mississauga, Canada ....... 84 C5 43 32N 79 35W
Mississippi □, U.S.A. ....... 81 J10 33 0N 90 0W
Mississippi →, U.S.A. ...... 81 L10 29 9N 89 15W
Mississippi L., Canada ...... 85 A8 45 5N 76 10W
Mississippi River Delta, U.S.A. . 81 L10 29 10N 89 15W
Mississippi Sd., U.S.A. ...... 81 K10 30 20N 89 0W
Missoula, U.S.A. .......... 76 C7 46 52N 114 1W
Missouri □, U.S.A. ......... 80 F8 38 25N 92 30W
Missouri →, U.S.A. ........ 80 F9 38 49N 90 7W
Missouri City, U.S.A. ....... 81 L7 29 37N 95 32W
Missouri Valley, U.S.A. ...... 80 E7 41 34N 95 53W
Mist, U.S.A. ............. 78 E3 45 59N 123 15W

Mistassibi →, Canada ....... 73 B5 48 53N 72 13W
Mistassini →, Canada ....... 73 C5 48 42N 72 20W
Mistassini, L., Canada ...... 72 B5 51 0N 73 30W
Mistastin L., Canada ....... 73 A7 55 57N 63 20W
Mistinibi, L., Canada ....... 73 A7 55 56N 64 17W
Mistissini, Canada ......... 73 C5 48 53N 72 12W
Misty L., Canada .......... 71 B8 58 53N 101 40W
Misurata = Miṣrātah, Libya ... 51 B9 32 24N 15 3 E
Mitchell, Australia ......... 63 D4 26 29S 147 58 E
Mitchell, Canada .......... 84 C3 43 28N 81 12W
Mitchell, Nebr., U.S.A. ...... 80 E3 41 57N 103 49W
Mitchell, Oreg., U.S.A. ...... 76 D3 44 34N 120 9W
Mitchell, S. Dak., U.S.A. ..... 80 D6 43 43N 98 2W
Mitchell →, Australia ....... 62 B3 15 12S 141 35 E
Mitchell, Mt., U.S.A. ....... 83 H4 35 46N 82 16W
Mitchell and Alice Rivers △,
Australia ............... 62 B3 15 28S 142 5 E
Mitchell Ranges, Australia ... 62 A2 12 49S 135 36 E
Mitha Tiwana, Pakistan ..... 42 C5 32 13N 72 6 E
Mithi, Pakistan ........... 42 G3 24 44N 69 48 E
Mithrao, Pakistan ......... 42 F3 27 28N 69 40 E
Mitilini, Greece ........... 23 E12 39 6N 26 35 E
Mito, Japan .............. 31 F10 36 20N 140 30 E
Mitrovica = Kosovska Mitrovica,
Serbia & M. ............. 23 C9 42 54N 20 52 E
Mitsinjo, Madag. .......... 57 B8 16 1S 45 52 E
Mitsiwa, Eritrea ........... 47 D2 15 35N 39 25 E
Mitsukaidō, Japan ......... 31 F9 36 1N 139 59 E
Mittagong, Australia ....... 63 E5 34 28S 150 29 E
Mittimatalik = Pond Inlet, Canada 69 A12 72 40N 77 0W
Mitú, Colombia ........... 92 C4 1 15N 70 13W
Mitumba, Tanzania ........ 54 D3 7 8S 31 2 E
Mitumba, Mts., Dem. Rep. of
the Congo ............. 54 D2 7 0S 27 30 E
Mitwaba, Dem. Rep. of
the Congo ............. 55 D2 8 2S 27 17 E
Mityana, Uganda .......... 54 B3 0 23N 32 2 E
Mixteco →, Mexico ........ 87 D5 18 11N 98 30W
Miyagi □, Japan .......... 30 E10 38 15N 140 45 E
Miyah, W. el →, Syria ...... 44 C3 34 44N 39 57 E
Miyake-Jima, Japan ........ 31 G9 34 5N 139 30 E
Miyako, Japan ............ 30 E10 39 40N 141 59 E
Miyako-Jima, Japan ........ 31 M2 24 45N 125 20 E
Miyako-Rettō, Japan ....... 31 M2 24 24N 125 0 E
Miyakonojō, Japan ......... 31 J5 31 40N 131 5 E
Miyani, India ............. 42 J3 21 50N 69 26 E
Miyanoura-Dake, Japan ..... 31 J5 30 20N 130 31 E
Miyazaki, Japan ........... 31 J5 31 56N 131 30 E
Miyazaki □, Japan ......... 31 H5 32 30N 131 30 E
Miyazu, Japan ............ 31 G7 35 35N 135 10 E
Miyet, Bahr el = Dead Sea, Asia 46 D4 31 30N 35 30 E
Miyoshi, Japan ........... 31 G6 34 48N 132 51 E
Miyun, China ............. 34 D9 40 28N 116 50 E
Miyun Shuiku, China ....... 35 D9 40 30N 117 0 E
Mizdah, Libya ............ 51 B8 31 30N 13 0 E
Mizen Hd., Cork, Ireland .... 10 E2 51 27N 9 50W
Mizen Hd., Wicklow, Ireland .. 10 D5 52 51N 6 4W
Mizhi, China ............. 34 F6 37 47N 110 12 E
Mizoram □, India .......... 41 H18 23 30N 92 40 E
Mizpe Ramon, Israel ....... 46 E3 30 34N 34 49 E
Mizuho, Antarctica ........ 5 D5 70 30S 41 0 E
Mizusawa, Japan .......... 30 E10 39 8N 141 8 E
Mjölby, Sweden ........... 9 G16 58 20N 15 10 E
Mjøsa, Norway ............ 9 F14 60 40N 11 0 E
Mkata, Tanzania .......... 54 D4 5 45S 38 20 E
Mkhaya △, Swaziland ...... 57 D5 26 34S 31 45 E
Mkokotoni, Tanzania ....... 54 D4 5 55S 39 15 E
Mkomazi, Tanzania ........ 54 C4 4 40S 38 7 E
Mkomazi →, S. Africa ...... 57 E5 30 12S 30 50 E
Mkulwe, Tanzania ......... 55 D3 8 37S 32 20 E
Mkumbi, Ras, Tanzania ..... 54 D4 7 38S 39 55 E
Mkushi, Zambia ........... 55 E2 14 25S 29 15 E
Mkushi River, Zambia ...... 55 E2 13 32S 29 45 E
Mkuze, S. Africa .......... 57 D5 27 10S 32 0 E
Mladá Boleslav, Czech Rep. .. 16 C8 50 27N 14 53 E
Mlala Hills, Tanzania ....... 54 D3 6 50S 31 40 E
Mlange = Mulanje, Malawi ... 55 F4 16 2S 35 33 E
Mlanje, Pic, Malawi ....... 53 H7 15 57S 35 38 E
Mława, Poland ............ 17 B11 53 9N 20 25 E
Mlawula △, Swaziland ...... 57 D5 26 12S 32 2 E
Mljet, Croatia ............ 22 C7 42 43N 17 30 E
Mmabatho, S. Africa ....... 56 D4 25 49S 25 30 E
Mo i Rana, Norway ........ 8 C16 66 20N 14 7 E
Moa, Cuba .............. 88 B4 20 40N 74 56W
Moa, Indonesia ........... 37 F7 8 0S 128 0 E
Moab, U.S.A. ............ 77 G9 38 35N 109 33W
Moala, Fiji .............. 59 D8 18 36S 179 53 E
Moama, Australia ......... 63 F3 36 7S 144 46 E
Moamba, Mozam. ......... 57 D5 25 36S 32 15 E
Moapa, U.S.A. ........... 79 J12 36 40N 114 37W
Moate, Ireland ........... 10 C4 53 24N 7 44W
Moba, Dem. Rep. of the Congo 54 D2 7 0S 29 48 E
Mobārakābād, Iran ........ 45 D7 28 24N 53 20 E
Mobaye, C.A.R. ........... 52 D4 4 25N 21 5 E
Mobayi, Dem. Rep. of the Congo 52 D4 4 15N 21 8 E
Moberley Lake, Canada ..... 70 B4 55 50N 121 44W
Moberly, U.S.A. .......... 80 F8 39 25N 92 26W
Mobile, U.S.A. ........... 83 K1 30 41N 88 3W
Mobile B., U.S.A. ......... 83 K2 30 30N 88 0W
Mobridge, U.S.A. ......... 80 C4 45 32N 100 26W
Moc Chau, Vietnam ....... 38 B5 20 50N 104 38 E
Moc Hoa, Vietnam ........ 39 G5 10 46N 105 56 E
Mocabe Kasari, Dem. Rep. of
the Congo ............. 55 D2 9 58S 26 12 E
Moçambique, Mozam. ...... 55 F5 15 3S 40 42 E
Mocanaqua, U.S.A. ........ 85 E8 41 9N 76 8W
Mochima, Venezuela ....... 89 D6 10 27N 64 5W
Mochudi, Botswana ....... 56 C4 24 27S 26 7 E
Mocimboa da Praia, Mozam. .. 55 E5 11 25S 40 20 E
Mociu, Colombia ......... 78 C2 1 7N 76 35W
Mococa, Brazil ........... 95 A6 21 28S 47 0W
Mocorito, Mexico ......... 86 B3 25 30N 107 53W
Moctezuma, Mexico ....... 86 B3 29 50N 109 0W
Moctezuma →, Mexico ..... 87 C5 21 59N 98 34W
Mocuba, Mozam. ......... 55 F4 16 54S 36 57 E
Mocúzari, Presa, Mexico .... 86 B3 27 10N 109 10W
Modane, France .......... 20 D7 45 12N 6 40 E
Modasa, India ............ 42 H5 23 30N 73 21 E
Modder →, S. Africa ...... 56 D3 29 2S 24 37 E
Modderrivier, S. Africa ..... 56 D3 29 2S 24 38 E
Módena, Italy ............ 22 B4 44 40N 10 55 E
Modena, U.S.A. .......... 77 H7 37 48N 113 56W
Modesto, U.S.A. .......... 78 H6 37 39N 121 0W
Módica, Italy ............ 22 F6 36 52N 14 46 E

Modimolle, S. Africa ....... 57 C4 24 42S 28 22 E
Moe, Australia ........... 63 F4 38 12S 146 19 E
Moebase, Mozam. ......... 55 F4 17 3S 38 41 E
Moengo, Suriname ........ 93 B8 5 45N 54 20W
Moffat, U.K. ............. 11 F5 55 21N 3 27W
Moga, India ............. 42 D6 30 48N 75 8 E
Mogadishu = Muqdisho,
Somali Rep. ............ 47 G4 2 2N 45 25 E
Mogador = Essaouira, Morocco 50 B4 31 32N 9 42W
Mogalakwena →, S. Africa .. 57 C4 22 38S 28 40 E
Mogami-Gawa →, Japan .... 30 E10 38 45N 140 0 E
Mogán, Canary Is. ........ 24 G4 27 53N 15 43W
Mogaung, Burma ......... 41 G20 25 20N 97 0 E
Mogi das Cruzes, Brazil ..... 95 A6 23 31S 46 11W
Mogi-Guaçu →, Brazil ...... 95 A6 20 53S 48 10W
Mogi-Mirim, Brazil ........ 95 A6 22 29S 47 0W
Mogilev = Mahilyow, Belarus . 17 B16 53 55N 30 18 E
Mogilev-Podolskiy = Mohyliv-
Podilskyy, Ukraine ....... 17 D14 48 26N 27 48 E
Mogincual, Mozam. ....... 55 F5 15 35S 40 25 E
Mogocha, Russia .......... 29 D12 53 40N 119 50 E
Mogok, Burma ........... 41 H20 23 0N 96 40 E
Mogollon Rim, U.S.A. ...... 77 J8 34 10N 110 50W
Mogumber, Australia ...... 61 F2 31 2S 116 3 E
Mohács, Hungary ......... 17 F10 45 58N 18 41 E
Mohales Hoek, Lesotho ..... 56 E4 30 7S 27 26 E
Mohall, U.S.A. ........... 80 A4 48 46N 101 31W
Mohammadābād, Iran ...... 45 B8 37 52N 59 5 E
Mohammedia, Morocco ..... 50 B4 33 44N 7 21W
Mohana →, India ......... 43 G11 24 43N 85 0 E
Mohanlalganj, India ....... 43 F9 26 41N 80 58 E
Mohave, L., U.S.A. ........ 79 K12 35 12N 114 34W
Mohawk →, U.S.A. ........ 85 D11 42 47N 73 41W
Mohenjodaro, Pakistan ..... 42 F3 27 19N 68 7 E
Moher, Cliffs of, Ireland .... 10 D2 52 58N 9 27W
Mohicanville Reservoir, U.S.A. . 84 F3 40 45N 82 0W
Mohoro, Tanzania ........ 54 D4 8 6S 39 8 E
Mohyliv-Podilskyy, Ukraine .. 17 D14 48 26N 27 48 E
Moidart, L., U.K. ......... 11 E3 56 47N 5 52W
Moira →, Canada ......... 84 B7 44 21N 77 24W
Moires, Greece ........... 25 D6 35 4N 24 56 E
Moisaküla, Estonia ........ 9 G21 58 3N 25 12 E
Moisie, Canada ........... 73 B6 50 12N 66 1W
Moisie →, Canada ........ 73 B6 50 14N 66 5W
Mojave, U.S.A. ........... 79 K8 35 3N 118 10W
Mojave →, U.S.A. ........ 79 K11 35 7N 115 30W
Mojave Desert, U.S.A. ..... 79 L10 35 0N 116 30W
Mojo, Bolivia ............ 94 A2 21 48S 65 33W
Mojokerto, Indonesia ...... 37 G15 7 28S 112 26 E
Mokai, N.Z. ............. 59 H5 38 32S 175 56 E
Mokambo, Dem. Rep. of
the Congo ............. 55 E2 12 25S 28 20 E
Mokameh, India .......... 43 G11 25 24N 85 55 E
Mokau, N.Z. ............. 59 H5 38 42S 174 39 E
Mokelumne →, U.S.A. ..... 78 G5 38 13N 121 28W
Mokelumne Hill, U.S.A. ..... 78 G6 38 18N 120 43W
Mokhós, Greece .......... 25 D7 35 16N 25 27 E
Mokhotlong, Lesotho ...... 57 D4 29 22S 29 2 E
Mokokchung, India ........ 41 F19 26 15N 94 30 E
Mokolo →, S. Africa ....... 57 C4 23 14S 27 43 E
Mokopane, S. Africa ....... 57 C4 24 10S 28 55 E
Mokp'o, S. Korea ......... 35 G14 34 50N 126 25 E
Mokra Gora, Serbia & M. .... 23 C9 42 50N 20 30 E
Mol, Belgium ............ 15 C5 51 11N 5 5 E
Molchanovo, Russia ....... 28 D9 57 40N 83 50 E
Mold, U.K. .............. 12 D4 53 9N 3 8W
Moldavia = Moldova ■, Europe 17 E15 47 0N 28 0 E
Molde, Norway ........... 8 E12 62 45N 7 9 E
Moldova ■, Europe ........ 17 E15 47 0N 28 0 E
Moldoveanu, Vf., Romania ... 17 F13 45 36N 24 45 E
Mole →, U.K. ........... 13 F7 51 24N 0 21W
Mole Creek, Australia ...... 63 G4 41 34S 146 24 E
Molepolole, Botswana ..... 56 C4 24 28S 25 28 E
Molfetta, Italy ........... 22 D7 41 12N 16 36 E
Moline, U.S.A. ........... 80 E9 41 30N 90 31W
Molinos, Argentina ........ 94 B2 25 28S 66 15W
Moliro, Dem. Rep. of the Congo 54 D3 8 12S 30 30 E
Mollendo, Peru ........... 92 G4 17 0S 72 0W
Mollerin, L., Australia ...... 61 F2 30 30S 117 35 E
Molodechno = Maladzyechna,
Belarus ............... 17 A14 54 20N 26 50 E
Molokai, U.S.A. .......... 74 H16 21 8N 157 0W
Molong, Australia ......... 63 E4 33 5S 148 54 E
Molopo →, Africa ......... 56 D3 28 30S 20 12 E
Molson L., Canada ........ 71 C9 54 22N 96 40W
Molteno, S. Africa ........ 56 E4 31 22S 26 22 E
Molu, Indonesia .......... 37 F8 6 45S 131 40 E
Molucca Sea, Indonesia .... 37 E6 0 0 125 0 E
Moluccas = Maluku, Indonesia 37 E7 1 0S 127 0 E
Moma, Dem. Rep. of the Congo 54 C1 1 35S 23 52 E
Moma, Mozam. ........... 55 F4 16 47S 39 4 E
Mombasa, Kenya ......... 54 C4 4 2S 39 43 E
Mombetsu, Japan ......... 30 B11 44 21N 143 22 E
Momchilgrad, Bulgaria ..... 23 D11 41 33N 25 23 E
Momi, Dem. Rep. of the Congo 54 C2 1 42S 27 0 E
Mompós, Colombia ........ 92 B4 9 14N 74 26W
Møn, Denmark ........... 9 J15 54 57N 12 20 E
Mon □, Burma ........... 41 L20 16 0N 97 30 E
Mona, Canal de la = Mona
Passage, W. Indies ....... 89 C6 18 30N 67 45W
Mona, Isla, Puerto Rico ..... 89 C6 18 5N 67 54W
Mona, Pta., Costa Rica ..... 88 E3 9 37N 82 36W
Mona Passage, W. Indies .... 89 C6 18 30N 67 45W
Monaca, U.S.A. .......... 84 F4 40 41N 80 17W
Monaco ■, Europe ........ 20 E7 43 46N 7 23 E
Monadhliath Mts., U.K. ..... 11 D4 57 10N 4 4W
Monadnock, Mt., U.S.A. .... 85 D12 42 52N 72 7W
Monaghan, Ireland ........ 10 B5 54 15N 6 57W
Monaghan □, Ireland ...... 10 B5 54 11N 6 56W
Monahans, U.S.A. ......... 81 K3 31 36N 102 54W
Monapo, Mozam. ......... 55 E5 14 56S 40 19 E
Monar, L., U.K. .......... 11 D3 57 26N 5 8W
Monarch Mt., Canada ...... 70 C3 51 55N 125 57W
Monashee Mts., Canada .... 70 C5 51 0N 118 43W
Monasterevin, Ireland ...... 10 C4 53 8N 7 4W
Monastir = Bitola, Macedonia . 23 D9 41 1N 21 20 E
Moncayo, Sierra del, Spain ... 21 B5 41 48N 1 50W
Monchegorsk, Russia ...... 18 A5 67 54N 32 58 E
Mönchengladbach, Germany . 16 C4 51 11N 6 27 E
Monchique, Portugal ...... 21 D1 37 19N 8 38W
Moncks Corner, U.S.A. ..... 83 J5 33 12N 80 1W
Monclova, Mexico ........ 86 B4 26 50N 101 30W
Moncton, Canada ......... 73 C7 46 7N 64 51W
Mondego →, Portugal ..... 21 B1 40 9N 8 52W
Mondeodo, Indonesia ...... 37 E6 3 34S 122 9 E
Mondoví, Italy ........... 20 D7 44 23N 7 49 E
Mondrain I., Australia ...... 61 F3 34 9S 122 14 E
Moneague, Jamaica ....... 88 a 18 16N 77 7W

Monessen, U.S.A. ............ 84 F5   40  9N  79 54W
Monett, U.S.A. .............. 81 G8   36 55N  93 55W
Moneymore, U.K. ............ 10 B5   54 41N   6 40W
Monforte de Lemos, Spain .... 21 A2   42 31N   7 33W
Mong Cai, Vietnam .......... 38 B6   21 27N 107 54 E
Mong Hsu, Burma ........... 41 J21  21 54N  98 30 E
Mong Kung, Burma .......... 41 J20  21 35N  97 35 E
Mong Nai, Burma ........... 41 J20  20 32N  97 46 E
Mong Pawk, Burma .......... 41 H21  22  4N  99 16 E
Mong Ton, Burma ........... 41 J21  20 17N  98 45 E
Mong Wa, Burma ............ 41 J22  21 26N 100 27 E
Mong Yai, Burma ........... 41 H21  22 21N  98  3 E
Mongalla, Sudan ............ 51 G12   5  8N  31 42 E
Mongers, L., Australia ....... 61 E2   29 25S 117  5 E
Monghyr = Munger, India .... 43 G12  25 23N  86 30 E
Mongibello = Etna, Italy ..... 22 F6   37 50N  14 55 E
Mongo, Chad ............... 51 F9   12 14N  18 43 E
Mongolia ■, Asia ........... 29 E10  47  0N 103  0 E
Mongolia, Plateau of, Asia ... 26 E14  45  0N 105  0 E
Mongu, Zambia ............. 53 H4   15 16S  23 12 E
Mõngua, Angola ............ 56 B2   16 43S  15 20 E
Monifieth, U.K. ............. 11 E6   56 30N   2 48W
Monkey Bay, Malawi ........ 55 E4   14  7S  35  1 E
Monkey Mia, Australia ...... 61 E1   25 48S 113 43 E
Monkey River Town, Belize ... 87 D7   16 22N  88 29W
Monkoto, Dem. Rep. of
  the Congo ................ 52 E4    1 38S  20 35 E
Monkton, Canada ........... 84 C3   43 35N  81  5W
Monmouth, U.K. ............ 13 F5   51 48N   2 42W
Monmouth, Ill., U.S.A. ...... 80 E9   40 55N  90 39W
Monmouth, Oreg., U.S.A. .... 76 D2   44 51N 123 14W
Monmouthshire □, U.K. ..... 13 F5   51 48N   2 54W
Mono L., U.S.A. ............ 78 H7   38  1N 119  1W
Monolith, U.S.A. ........... 79 K8   35  7N 118 22W
Monólithos, Greece ......... 25 C9   36  7N  27 45 E
Monongahela, U.S.A. ....... 84 F5   40 12N  79 56W
Monópoli, Italy ............. 22 D7   40 57N  17 18 E
Monos I., Trin. & Tob. ...... 93 K15  10 42N  61 44W
Monroe, Ga., U.S.A. ........ 83 J4   33 47N  83 43W
Monroe, La., U.S.A. ........ 81 J8   32 30N  92  7W
Monroe, Mich., U.S.A. ...... 82 E4   41 55N  83 24W
Monroe, N.C., U.S.A. ....... 83 H5   34 59N  80 33W
Monroe, N.Y., U.S.A. ....... 85 E10  41 20N  74 11W
Monroe, Utah, U.S.A. ....... 77 G7   38 38N 112  7W
Monroe, Wash., U.S.A. ...... 78 C5   47 51N 121 58W
Monroe, Wis., U.S.A. ....... 80 D10  42 36N  89 38W
Monroe City, U.S.A. ........ 80 F9   39 39N  91 44W
Monroeton, U.S.A. ......... 85 E8   41 43N  76 29W
Monroeville, Ala., U.S.A. .... 83 K2   31 31N  87 20W
Monroeville, Pa., U.S.A. ..... 84 F5   40 26N  79 45W
Monrovia, Liberia .......... 50 G3    6 18N  10 47W
Mons, Belgium ............. 15 D3   50 27N   3 58 E
Monse, Indonesia ........... 37 E6    4  7S 123 15 E
Mont-de-Marsan, France ..... 20 E3   43 54N   0 31W
Mont-Joli, Canada .......... 73 C6   48 37N  68 10W
Mont-Laurier, Canada ....... 72 C4   46 35N  75 30W
Mont-Louis, Canada ........ 73 C6   49 15N  65 44W
Mont-St-Michel, Le, France ... 20 B3   48 40N   1 30W
Mont-Tremblant △, Canada ... 72 C5   46 30N  74 30W
Montagne d'Ambre △, Madag. . 57 A8   12 37 S  49 8 E
Montagu, S. Africa ......... 56 E3   33 45S  20  8 E
Montagu I., Antarctica ...... 5 B1   58 25S  26 20W
Montague, Canada .......... 73 C7   46 10N  62 39W
Montague, I., Mexico ....... 86 A2   31 40N 114 56W
Montague Ra., Australia ..... 61 E2   27 15S 119 30 E
Montague Sd., Australia ..... 60 B4   14 28S 125 20 E
Montalbán, Spain .......... 21 B5   40 50N   0 45W
Montalvo, U.S.A. ........... 79 L7   34 15N 119 12W
Montana, Bulgaria ......... 23 C10  43 27N  23 16 E
Montaña, Peru ............. 92 E4    6  0S  73  0W
Montana □, U.S.A. ......... 76 C9   47  0N 110  0W
Montaña Clara, I., Canary Is. . 24 E6   29 17N  13 33W
Montargis, France .......... 20 C5   47 59N   2 43 E
Montauban, France ......... 20 D4   44  2N   1 21 E
Montauk, U.S.A. ........... 85 E13  41  3N  71 57W
Montauk Pt., U.S.A. ........ 85 E13  41  4N  71 52W
Montbéliard, France ........ 20 C7   47 31N   6 48 E
Montceau-les-Mines, France .. 20 C6   46 40N   4 23 E
Montclair, U.S.A. .......... 85 F10  40 49N  74 13W
Monte Albán, Mexico ....... 87 D5   17  2N  96 45W
Monte Alegre, Brazil ........ 93 D8    2  0S  54  0W
Monte Azul, Brazil ......... 93 G10  15  9S  42 53W
Monte-Carlo, Monaco ....... 20 E7   43 44N   7 25 E
Monte Caseros, Argentina ... 94 C4   30 10S  57 50W
Monte Comán, Argentina .... 94 C2   34 40S  67 53W
Monte Cristi, Dom. Rep. .... 89 C5   19 52N  71 39W
Monte Lindo →, Paraguay ... 94 A4   23 56S  57 12W
Monte Patria, Chile ........ 94 C1   30 42S  70 58W
Monte Quemado, Argentina .. 94 B3   25 53S  62 41W
Monte Rio, U.S.A. .......... 78 G4   38 28N 123  0W
Monte Santu, C. di, Italy .... 22 D3   40 5N    9 44 E
Monte Vista, U.S.A. ........ 77 H10  37 35N 106  9W
Monteagudo, Argentina ..... 95 B5   27 14S  54  8W
Montebello, Canada ........ 72 C5   45 40N  74 55W
Montebello Is., Australia .... 60 D2   20 30S 115 45 E
Montecito, U.S.A. .......... 79 L7   34 26N 119 40W
Montecristo, Italy .......... 22 C4   42 20N  10 19 E
Montego Bay, Jamaica ...... 88 a    18 28N  77 55W
Montélimar, France ........ 20 D6   44 33N   4 45 E
Montello, U.S.A. ........... 80 D10  43 48N  89 20W
Montemorelos, Mexico ...... 87 B5   25 11N  99 42W
Montenegro, Brazil ......... 95 B5   29 39S  51 29W
Montenegro □, Serbia & M. .. 23 C8   42 40N  19 20 E
Montepuez, Mozam. ........ 55 E4   13  8S  38 59 E
Montepuez →, Mozam. ..... 55 E5   12 32S  40 27 E
Monterey, U.S.A. ........... 78 J5   36 37N 121 55W
Monterey B., U.S.A. ........ 78 J5   36 45N 122  0W
Monteria, Colombia ........ 92 B3    8 46N  75 53W
Monteros, Argentina ....... 94 B2   27 11S  65 30W
Monterrey, Mexico ......... 86 B4   25 40N 100 30W
Montes Azules △, Mexico ... 87 D6   16 21N  91  3W
Montes Claros, Brazil ....... 93 G10  16 30S  43 50W
Montesano, U.S.A. ......... 78 D3   46 59N 123 36W
Montesilvano, Italy ......... 22 C6   42 29N  14  8 E
Montevideo, Uruguay ....... 95 C4   34 50S  56 11W
Montevideo, U.S.A. ........ 80 C7   44 57N  95 43W
Montezuma, U.S.A. ........ 80 E8   41 35N  92 32W
Montezuma Castle △, U.S.A. . 77 J8   34 34N 111 45W
Montgomery, U.K. .......... 13 E4   52 34N   3  8W
Montgomery, Ala., U.S.A. ... 83 J2   32 23N  86 19W
Montgomery, W. Va., U.S.A. .. 82 F5   38 11N  81 19W
Montgomery City, U.S.A. .... 80 F9   38 59N  91 30W
Monticello, Ark., U.S.A. ..... 81 J9   33 38N  91 47W
Monticello, Fla., U.S.A. ..... 83 K4   30 33N  83 52W
Monticello, Ind., U.S.A. ..... 82 E2   40 45N  86 46W
Monticello, Iowa, U.S.A. .... 80 D9   42 15N  91 12W
Monticello, Ky., U.S.A. ..... 83 G3   36 50N  84 51W

Monticello, Minn., U.S.A. .... 80 C8   45 18N  93 48W
Monticello, Miss., U.S.A. .... 81 K9   31 33N  90  7W
Monticello, N.Y., U.S.A. ..... 85 E10  41 39N  74 42W
Monticello, Utah, U.S.A. .... 77 H9   37 52N 109 21W
Montijo, Portugal .......... 21 C1   38 41N   8 54W
Montilla, Spain ............ 21 D3   37 36N   4 40W
Montluçon, France ......... 20 C5   46 58N   2 34 E
Montmagny, Canada ........ 71 C8   50 14N 103 27W
Montmartre, Canada ........ 71 C8   50 14N 103 27W
Montmorillon, France ....... 20 C4   46 26N   0 50 E
Monto, Australia ........... 62 C5   24 52S 151  6 E
Montongbuwoh, Indonesia ... 37 K19   8 33S 116  4 E
Montoro, Spain ............ 21 C3   38  1N   4 27W
Montour Falls, U.S.A. ....... 84 D8   42 21N  76 51W
Montoursville, U.S.A. ....... 84 E8   41 15N  76 55W
Montpelier, Idaho, U.S.A. .... 76 E8   42 19N 111 18W
Montpelier, Vt., U.S.A. ...... 85 B12  44 16N  72 35W
Montpellier, France ........ 20 E5   43 37N   3 52 E
Montréal, Canada .......... 85 A11  45 31N  73 34W
Montreal →, Canada ........ 72 C3   47 14N  84 39W
Montreal L., Canada ........ 71 C7   54 20N 105 45W
Montreal Lake, Canada ...... 71 C7   54 3N  105 46W
Montreux, Switz. ........... 20 C7   46 26N   6 55 E
Montrose, U.K. ............ 11 E6   56 44N   2 27W
Montrose, Colo., U.S.A. ..... 77 G10  38 29N 107 53W
Montrose, Pa., U.S.A. ...... 85 E9   41 50N  75 53W
Monts, Pte. des, Canada ..... 73 C6   49 20N  67 12W
Montserrat ☑, W. Indies .... 89 C7   16 40N  62 10W
Montuiri, Spain ............ 24 B9   39 34N   2 59 E
Monywa, Burma ............ 41 H19  22  7N  95 11 E
Monza, Italy ............... 20 D8   45 35N   9  16 E
Monze, Zambia ............ 55 F2   16 17S  27 29 E
Monze, C., Pakistan ........ 42 G2   24 47N  66 37 E
Monzón, Spain ............ 21 B6   41 52N   0 10 E
Mooers, U.S.A. ............ 85 B11  44 58N  73 35W
Mooi →, S. Africa .......... 57 D5   28 45S  30 34 E
Mooi River, S. Africa ....... 57 D4   29 13S  29 50 E
Moonah →, Australia ....... 62 C2   22  3S 138 33 E
Moonda, L., Australia ....... 62 D3   25 52S 140 25 E
Moonie, Australia .......... 63 D5   27 46S 150 20 E
Moonie →, Australia ....... 63 D4   29 19S 148 43 E
Moonta, Australia .......... 63 E2   34  6S 137 32 E
Moora, Australia ........... 61 F2   30 37S 115 58 E
Moorcroft, U.S.A. .......... 80 C2   44 16N 104 57W
Moore →, Australia ........ 61 E1   31 22S 115 30 E
Moore, L., Australia ........ 61 E2   29 50S 117 35 E
Moore Park, Australia ...... 62 C5   24 43S 152 17 E
Moore River △, Australia ... 61 F2   31  7S 115 39 E
Moorefield, U.S.A. ......... 82 F6   39  5N  78 59W
Moores Res., U.S.A. ........ 85 B13  44 45N  71 50W
Moorfoot Hills, U.K. ........ 11 F5   55 44N   3  8W
Moorhead, U.S.A. .......... 80 B6   46 53N  96 45W
Moorpark, U.S.A. .......... 79 L8   34 17N 118 53W
Moorreesburg, S. Africa ..... 56 E2   33  6S  18 38 E
Moorrinya △, Australia ..... 62 C3   21 42S 144 58 E
Moose →, Canada .......... 72 B3   51 20N  80 25W
Moose →, U.S.A. .......... 85 C9   43 38N  75 24W
Moose Creek, Canada ....... 85 A10  45 15N  74 58W
Moose Factory, Canada ..... 72 B3   51 16N  80 32W
Moose Jaw, Canada ........ 71 C7   50 24N 105 30W
Moose Jaw →, Canada ...... 71 C7   50 34N 105 18W
Moose Lake, U.S.A. ........ 80 B8   46 27N  92 46W
Moose Mountain △, Canada . 71 D8   49 48N 102 25W
Moosehead L., U.S.A. ....... 83 C11  45 38N  69 40W
Mooselookmeguntic L., U.S.A. 83 C10  44 55N  70 49W
Moosilauke, Mt., U.S.A. ..... 85 B13  44  3N  71 40W
Moosomin, Canada ......... 71 C8   50  9N 101 40W
Moosonee, Canada ......... 72 B3   51 17N  80 39W
Moosup, U.S.A. ............ 85 E13  41 43N  71 53W
Mopane, S. Africa .......... 57 C4   22 37S  29 52 E
Mopeia Velha, Mozam. ...... 55 F4   17 30S  35 40 E
Mopipi, Botswana .......... 56 C3   21  6S  24 55 E
Mopoi, C.A.R. ............. 54 A2    5  6N  26 54 E
Mopti, Mali ............... 50 F5   14 30N   4  0W
Moqor, Afghan. ............ 42 C2   32 50N  67 42 E
Moquegua, Peru ........... 92 G4   17 15S  70 46W
Mora, Sweden ............. 9 F16   61  2N  14 38 E
Mora, Minn., U.S.A. ........ 80 C8   45 53N  93 18W
Mora, N. Mex., U.S.A. ...... 77 J11  35 58N 105 20W
Mora →, U.S.A. ........... 81 H2   35 35N 104 25W
Moradabad, India .......... 43 E8   28 50N  78 50 E
Morafenobe, Madag. ........ 57 B7   17 50S  44 53 E
Moramanga, Madag. ........ 57 B8   18 56S  48 12 E
Moran, Kans., U.S.A. ....... 81 G7   37 55N  95 10W
Moran, Wyo., U.S.A. ....... 76 E8   43 53N 110 37W
Moranbah, Australia ....... 62 C4   22  1S 148  6 E
Morant Bay, Jamaica ....... 88 a    17 53N  76 25W
Morant Cays, Jamaica ...... 88 C4   17 22N  76  0W
Morant Pt., Jamaica ........ 88 a    17 55N  76 12W
Morar, India .............. 42 F8   26 14N  78 14 E
Morar, L., U.K. ............ 11 E3   56 57N   5 40W
Moratuwa, Sri Lanka ....... 40 R11   6 45N  79 55 E
Morava →, Serbia & M. ..... 23 B9   44 36N  21  4 E
Morava →, Slovak Rep. ..... 17 D9   48 10N  16 59 E
Moravian Hts. = Českomoravská
  Vrchovina, Czech Rep. .... 16 D8   49 30N  15 40 E
Morawa, Australia ......... 61 E2   29 13S 116  0 E
Morawhanna, Guyana ...... 92 B7    8 30N  59 40W
Moray □, U.K. ............. 11 D5   57 31N   3 18W
Moray Firth, U.K. .......... 11 D5   57 40N   3 52W
Morbi, India .............. 42 H4   22 50N  70 42 E
Morden, Canada ........... 71 D9   49 15N  98 10W
Mordovian Republic =
  Mordvinia □, Russia ...... 18 D7   54 20N  44 30 E
Mordvinia □, Russia ....... 18 D7   54 20N  44 30 E
Morea, Greece ............. 6 H10   37 45N  22 10 E
Moreau →, U.S.A. ......... 80 C4   45 18N 100 43W
Morecambe, U.K. .......... 12 C5   54  5N   2 52W
Morecambe B., U.K. ........ 12 C5   54  7N   3  0W
Moree, Australia ........... 63 D4   29 28S 149 54 E
Morehead, U.S.A. .......... 82 F4   38 11N  83 26W
Morehead City, U.S.A. ...... 83 H7   34 43N  76 43W
Morel →, India ............ 42 F7   26 13N  76 36 E
Morelia, Mexico ........... 86 D4   19 42N 101  7W
Morella, Australia ......... 62 C3   23  0S 143 52 E
Morella, Spain ............ 21 B5   40 35N   0  5W
Morelos, Mexico ........... 86 B3   26 42N 107 40W
Morelos □, Mexico ......... 87 D5   18 40N  99 10W
Moremi △, Botswana ....... 56 B3   19 18S  23 10 E
Morena, India ............. 42 F8   26 30N  78  4 E
Morena, Sierra, Spain ...... 21 C3   38 20N   4  0W
Moreno Valley, U.S.A. ...... 79 M10 33 56N 117 15W
Moresby I., Canada ........ 70 C2   52 30N 131 40W
Moreton I., Australia ....... 63 D5   27 10S 153 25 E
Moreton Island △, Australia . 63 D5   27  2S 153 24 E
Morey, Spain ............. 24 B10  39 44N   3 20 E
Morgan, U.S.A. ............ 76 F8   41  2N 111 41W

Morgan City, U.S.A. ........ 81 L9   29 42N  91 12W
Morgan Hill, U.S.A. ........ 78 H5   37  8N 121 39W
Morganfield, U.S.A. ........ 82 G2   37 41N  87 55W
Morganton, U.S.A. ......... 83 H5   35 45N  81 41W
Morgantown, U.S.A. ........ 82 F6   39 38N  79 57W
Morgenzon, S. Africa ....... 57 D4   26 45S  29 36 E
Morghak, Iran ............. 45 D8   29  7N  57 54 E
Morhar →, India ........... 43 G11  25 29N  85 11 E
Mori, Japan ............... 30 C10  42  6N 140 35 E
Moriarty, U.S.A. ........... 77 J10  34 59N 106  3W
Morice L., Canada .......... 70 C3   53 50N 127 40W
Morinville, Canada ......... 70 C6   53 49N 113 41W
Morioka, Japan ............ 30 E10  39 45N 141  8 E
Moris, Mexico ............. 86 B3   28  8N 108 32W
Morlaix, France ............ 20 B2   48 36N   3 52W
Mornington, Australia ...... 63 F4   38 15S 145  5 E
Mornington, I., Chile ....... 96 F1   49 50S  75 30W
Mornington I., Australia ..... 62 B2   16 30S 139 30 E
Moro, Pakistan ............ 42 F2   26 40N  68  0 E
Moro →, Pakistan .......... 42 E2   29 42N  67 22 E
Moro G., Phil. ............. 37 C6    6 30N 123  0 E
Morocco ■, N. Afr. ......... 50 B4   32  0N   5 50W
Morogoro, Tanzania ........ 54 D4    6 50S  37 40 E
Morogoro □, Tanzania ...... 54 D4    8  0S  37  0 E
Moroleón, Mexico .......... 86 C4   20  8N 101 32W
Morombe, Madag. .......... 57 C7   21 45S  43 22 E
Moron, Argentina .......... 94 C4   34 39S  58 37W
Morón, Cuba .............. 88 B4   22  8N  78 39W
Morón de la Frontera, Spain . 21 D3   37  6N   5 28W
Morona →, Peru ........... 92 D3    4 40S  77 10W
Morondava, Madag. ........ 57 C7   20 17S  44 17 E
Morongo Valley, U.S.A. ..... 79 L10  34  3N 116 37W
Moroni, Comoros Is. ........ 49 H8   11 40S  43 16 E
Moroni, U.S.A. ............ 76 G8   39 32N 111 35W
Morotai, Indonesia ......... 37 D7    2 10N 128 30 E
Moroto, Uganda ........... 54 B3    2 28N  34 42 E
Moroto, Mt., Uganda ....... 54 B3    2 30N  34 43 E
Morpeth, U.K. ............. 12 B6   55 10N   1 41W
Morphou, Cyprus .......... 25 D11  35 12N  32 59 E
Morphou Bay, Cyprus ...... 25 D11  35 15N  32 50 E
Morrilton, U.S.A. .......... 81 H8   35  9N  92 44W
Morrinhos, Brazil .......... 93 G9   17 45S  49 10W
Morrinsville, N.Z. .......... 59 G5   37 40S 175 32 E
Morris, Canada ............ 71 D9   49 25N  97 22W
Morris, Ill., U.S.A. ......... 80 E10  41 22N  88 26W
Morris, Minn., U.S.A. ....... 80 C7   45 35N  95 55W
Morris, N.Y., U.S.A. ........ 85 D9   42 33N  75 15W
Morris, Mt., Australia ...... 61 E5   26  9S 131  4 E
Morris Jesup, Kap, Greenland  4 A5   83 40N  34  0W
Morrisburg, Canada ........ 85 B9   44 55N  75  7W
Morristown, Ariz., U.S.A. .... 77 K7   33 51N 112 37W
Morristown, N.J., U.S.A. .... 85 F10  40 48N  74 29W
Morristown, N.Y., U.S.A. .... 85 B9   44 35N  75 39W
Morristown, Tenn., U.S.A. ... 83 G4   36 13N  83 18W
Morrisville, N.Y., U.S.A. ..... 85 D9   42 53N  75 35W
Morrisville, Pa., U.S.A. ..... 85 F10  40 13N  74 47W
Morrisville, Vt., U.S.A. ...... 85 B12  44 34N  72 36W
Morro, Pta., Chile .......... 94 B1   27  6S  71  0W
Morro Bay, U.S.A. .......... 78 K6   35 22N 120 51W
Morro del Jable, Canary Is. .. 24 F5   28  3N  14 23W
Morro Jable, Pta. de, Canary Is. 24 F5   28  2N  14 20W
Morrocoy △, Venezuela ..... 89 D6   10 48N  68 13W
Morrosquillo, G. de, Colombia  88 E4    9 35N  75 40W
Morrumbene, Mozam. ...... 57 C6   23 31S  35 16 E
Morshansk, Russia ......... 18 D7   53 28N  41 50 E
Morteros, Argentina ....... 94 C3   30 50S  62  0W
Mortlach, Canada .......... 71 C7   50 27N 106  4W
Mortlake, Australia ........ 63 F3   38  5S 142 50 E
Morton, Tex., U.S.A. ....... 81 J3   33 44N 102 46W
Morton, Wash., U.S.A. ..... 78 D4   46 34N 122 17W
Moruga, Trin. & Tob. ....... 93 K15  10  4N  61 16W
Morundah, Australia ....... 63 E4   34 57S 146 19 E
Moruya, Australia ......... 63 F5   35 58S 150  3 E
Morvan, France ............ 20 C6   47  5N   4  3 E
Morven, Australia .......... 63 D4   26 22S 147  5 E
Morvern, U.K. ............. 11 E3   56 38N   5 44W
Morwell, Australia ......... 63 F4   38 10S 146 22 E
Morzhovets, Ostrov, Russia .. 18 A7   66 44N  42 35 E
Moscos Is., Burma ......... 38 E1   14  0N  97 30 E
Moscow = Moskva, Russia ... 18 C6   55 45N  37 35 E
Moscow, Idaho, U.S.A. ...... 76 C5   46 44N 117  0W
Moscow, Pa., U.S.A. ........ 85 E9   41 20N  75 31W
Mosel →, Europe .......... 20 A7   50 22N   7 36 E
Moselle = Mosel →, Europe .. 20 A7   50 22N   7 36 E
Moses Lake, U.S.A. ........ 76 C4   47  8N 119 17W
Mosgiel, N.Z. ............. 59 L3   45 53S 170 21 E
Moshaweng →, S. Africa .... 56 D3   26 35S  22 50 E
Moshi, Tanzania ........... 54 C4    3 22S  37 18 E
Moshupa, Botswana ........ 56 C4   24 46S  25 29 E
Mosjøen, Norway .......... 8 D15   65 51N  13 12 E
Moskenesøya, Norway ...... 8 C15   67 58N  13  0 E
Moskenstraumen, Norway ... 8 C15   67 47N  12 45 E
Moskva, Russia ............ 18 C6   55 45N  37 35 E
Mosomane, Botswana ....... 56 C4   24  2S  26 19 E
Mosonmagyaróvár, Hungary . 17 E9   47 52N  17 18 E
Mosquera, Colombia ....... 92 C3    2 35N  78 24W
Mosquero, U.S.A. .......... 81 H3   35 47N 103 58W
Mosquitia, Honduras ....... 88 C3   15 20N  84 10W
Mosquito Coast = Mosquitia,
  Honduras ............... 88 C3   15 20N  84 10W
Mosquito Creek L., U.S.A. ... 84 E4   41 18N  80 46W
Mosquito L., Canada ........ 71 A8   62 35N 103 20W
Mosquitos, G. de los, Panama  88 E3    9 15N  81 10W
Moss, Norway ............. 9 G14   59 27N  10 40 E
Moss Vale, Australia ....... 63 E5   34 32S 150 25 E
Mossbank, Canada ......... 71 D7   49 56N 105 56W
Mossburn, N.Z. ............ 59 L2   45 41S 168 15 E
Mosselbaai, S. Africa ....... 56 E3   34 11S  22  8 E
Mossendjo, Congo ......... 52 E2    2 55S  12 42 E
Mossgiel, Australia ........ 63 E3   33 15S 144  5 E
Mossman, Australia ........ 62 B4   16 21S 145 15 E
Mossoró, Brazil ............ 93 E11   5 10S  37 15W
Mossuril, Mozam. .......... 55 E5   14 58S  40 42 E
Most, Czech Rep. .......... 16 C7   50 31N  13 38 E
Mosta, Malta .............. 25 D1   35 55N  14 26 E
Mostaganem, Algeria ....... 50 A6   35 54N   0  5 E
Mostar, Bos.-H. ........... 23 C7   43 22N  17 50 E
Mostardas, Brazil .......... 95 C5   31  2S  50 51W
Mostiska = Mostyska, Ukraine 17 D12  49 48N  23  4 E
Mosty = Masty, Belarus ..... 17 B13  53 27N  24 38 E
Mostyska, Ukraine ......... 17 D12  49 48N  23  4 E
Mosul = Al Mawşil, Iraq .... 44 B4   36 15N  43  5 E
Mosúlpo, S. Korea ......... 35 H14  33 20N 126 17 E
Motagua →, Guatemala ..... 88 C2   15 44N  88 14W
Motala, Sweden ........... 9 G16   58 32N  15  1 E
Motaze, Mozam. ........... 57 C5   24 48S  32 52 E
Moth, India ............... 43 G8   25 43N  78 57 E

Motherwell, U.K. ........... 11 F5   55 47N   3 58W
Motihari, India ............ 43 F11  26 30N  84 55 E
Motozintla de Mendoza, Mexico 87 D6   15 21N  92 14W
Motril, Spain .............. 21 D4   36 31N   3 37W
Mott, U.S.A. .............. 80 B3   46 23N 102 20W
Motueka, N.Z. ............. 59 J4   41  7S 173  1 E
Motueka →, N.Z. .......... 59 J4   41  5S 173  1 E
Motul, Mexico ............. 87 C7   21  0N  89 20W
Mouchalagane →, Canada ... 73 B6   50 56N  68 41W
Moúdhros, Greece ......... 23 E11  39 50N  25 18 E
Mouila, Gabon ............. 52 E2    1 50S  11  0 E
Moulamein, Australia ....... 63 F3   35  3S 144  1 E
Moule à Chique, C., St. Lucia . 89 f   13 43N  60 57W
Moulianá, Greece .......... 25 D7   35 10N  25 59 E
Moulins, France ........... 20 C5   46 35N   3 19 E
Moulmein, Burma .......... 41 L20  16 30N  97 40 E
Moulouya, O. →, Morocco ... 50 B5   35  5N   2 25W
Moultrie, U.S.A. ........... 83 K4   31 11N  83 47W
Moultrie, L., U.S.A. ........ 83 J5   33 20N  80  5W
Mound City, Mo., U.S.A. .... 80 E7   40  7N  95 14W
Mound City, S. Dak., U.S.A. . 80 C4   45 44N 100  4W
Moundou, Chad ............ 51 G9   8 40N   16 10 E
Moundsville, U.S.A. ........ 84 G4   39 55N  80 44W
Moung, Cambodia .......... 38 F4   12 46N 103 27 E
Mount Airy, U.S.A. ......... 83 G5   36 31N  80 37W
Mount Albert, Canada ...... 84 B5   44 8N   79 19W
Mount Aspiring △, N.Z. ..... 59 L2   44 19S 168 47 E
Mount Barker, S. Austral.,
  Australia ................ 63 F2   35  5S 138 52 E
Mount Barker, W. Austral.,
  Australia ................ 61 F2   34 38S 117 40 E
Mount Brydges, Canada ..... 84 D3   42 54N  81 29W
Mount Burr, Australia ...... 63 F3   37 34S 140 26 E
Mount Carmel = Ha Karmel △,
  Israel ................... 46 C4   32 45N  35  5 E
Mount Carmel, Ill., U.S.A. ... 82 F2   38 25N  87 46W
Mount Carmel, Pa., U.S.A. .. 85 F8   40 47N  76 24W
Mount Charleston, U.S.A. ... 79 J11  36 16N 115 37W
Mount Clemens, U.S.A. ..... 84 D2   42 35N  82 53W
Mount Coolon, Australia .... 62 C4   21 25S 147 25 E
Mount Darwin, Zimbabwe ... 55 F3   16 47S  31 38 E
Mount Desert I., U.S.A. ..... 83 C11  44 21N  68 20W
Mount Dora, U.S.A. ........ 83 L5   28 48N  81 38W
Mount Edziza △, Canada .... 70 B2   57 30N 130 45W
Mount Elgon △, E. Afr. ..... 54 B3    1  4N  34 42 E
Mount Field △, Australia .... 63 G4   42 39S 146 35 E
Mount Fletcher, S. Africa .... 57 E4   30 40S  28 30 E
Mount Forest, Canada ...... 84 C4   43 59N  80 43W
Mount Gambier, Australia ... 63 F3   37 50S 140 46 E
Mount Garnet, Australia .... 62 B4   17 37S 145  6 E
Mount Holly, U.S.A. ........ 85 G10  39 59N  74 47W
Mount Holly Springs, U.S.A. . 84 F7   40  7N  77 12W
Mount Hope, N.S.W., Australia 63 E4   32 51S 145 51 E
Mount Hope, S. Austral.,
  Australia ................ 63 E2   34  7S 135 23 E
Mount Isa, Australia ....... 62 C2   20 42S 139 26 E
Mount Jewett, U.S.A. ....... 84 E6   41 44N  78 39W
Mount Kaputar △, Australia . 63 E5   30 16S 150 10 E
Mount Kenya △, Kenya ..... 54 C4    0  7S  37 19 E
Mount Kilimanjaro △, Tanzania 54 C4    3  2S  37 19 E
Mount Kisco, U.S.A. ........ 85 E11  41 12N  73 44W
Mount Laguna, U.S.A. ...... 79 N10  32 52N 116 25W
Mount Larcom, Australia ... 62 C5   23 48S 150 59 E
Mount Lofty Ra., Australia .. 63 E2   34 35S 139  5 E
Mount Magnet, Australia ... 61 E2   28  2S 117 47 E
Mount Maunganui, N.Z. .... 59 G6   37 40S 176 14 E
Mount Molloy, Australia .... 62 B4   16 42S 145 20 E
Mount Morgan, Australia ... 62 C5   23 40S 150 25 E
Mount Morris, U.S.A. ....... 84 D7   42 44N  77 52W
Mount Pearl, Canada ....... 73 C9   47 31N  52 47W
Mount Penn, U.S.A. ........ 85 F9   40 20N  75 54W
Mount Perry, Australia ..... 63 D5   25 13S 151 42 E
Mount Pleasant, Iowa, U.S.A. . 80 E9   40 58N  91 33W
Mount Pleasant, Mich., U.S.A. 82 D3   43 36N  84 46W
Mount Pleasant, Pa., U.S.A. . 84 F5   40  9N  79 33W
Mount Pleasant, S.C., U.S.A. . 83 J6   32 47N  79 52W
Mount Pleasant, Tenn., U.S.A. 83 H2   35 32N  87 12W
Mount Pleasant, Tex., U.S.A. . 81 J7   33  9N  94 58W
Mount Pleasant, Utah, U.S.A. 76 G8   39 33N 111 27W
Mount Pocono, U.S.A. ...... 85 E9   41  7N  75 22W
Mount Rainier △, U.S.A. .... 78 D5   46 55N 121 50W
Mount Revelstoke △, Canada  70 C5   51  5N 118 30W
Mount Robson △, Canada ... 70 C5   53  0N 119  0W
Mount St. Helens △, U.S.A. .. 78 D4   46 14N 122 11W
Mount Selinda, Zimbabwe ... 57 C5   20 24S  32 43 E
Mount Shasta, U.S.A. ....... 76 F2   41 19N 122 19W
Mount Signal, U.S.A. ....... 79 N11  32 39N 115 37W
Mount Sterling, Ill., U.S.A. ... 80 F9   39 59N  90 45W
Mount Sterling, Ky., U.S.A. .. 82 F4   38  4N  83 56W
Mount Surprise, Australia ... 62 B3   18 10S 144 17 E
Mount Union, U.S.A. ....... 84 F7   40 23N  77 53W
Mount Upton, U.S.A. ....... 85 D9   42 26N  75 23W
Mount Vernon, Australia .... 62 F11  18 19N  88 55W
Mount Vernon, Ind., U.S.A. .. 80 F10  38 17N  88 57W
Mount Vernon, N.Y., U.S.A. .. 85 F11  40 55N  73 50W
Mount Vernon, Ohio, U.S.A. . 84 F2   40 23N  82 29W
Mount Vernon, Wash., U.S.A. 78 B4   48 25N 122 20W
Mount William △, Australia . 63 G4   40 56S 148 14 E
Mountain Ash, U.K. ........ 13 F4   51 40N   3 23W
Mountain Center, U.S.A. .... 79 M10 33 42N 116 44W
Mountain City, Nev., U.S.A. .. 76 F6   41 50N 115 58W
Mountain City, Tenn., U.S.A. . 83 G5   36 29N  81 48W
Mountain Dale, U.S.A. ...... 85 E10  41 41N  74 32W
Mountain Grove, U.S.A. ..... 81 G8   37  8N  92 16W
Mountain Home, Ark., U.S.A. 81 G8   36 20N  92 23W
Mountain Home, Idaho, U.S.A. 76 E6   43  8N 115 41W
Mountain Iron, U.S.A. ...... 80 B8   47 32N  92 37W
Mountain Pass, U.S.A. ...... 79 K11  35 29N 115 35W
Mountain View, Ark., U.S.A. . 81 H8   35 52N  92  7W
Mountain View, Calif., U.S.A. 78 H4   37 23N 122 5W
Mountain View, Hawaii, U.S.A. 74 J17  19 33N 155  7W
Mountain Zebra △, S. Africa  56 E4   32 14S  25 27 E
Mountainair, U.S.A. ........ 77 J10  34 31N 106 15W
Mountlake Terrace, U.S.A. ... 78 C4   47 47N 122 19W
Mountmellick, Ireland ...... 10 C4   53  7N   7 20W
Mountrath, Ireland ........ 10 D4   53  0N   7 28W
Moura, Australia .......... 62 C4   24 35S 149 58 E
Moura, Brazil ............. 92 D6    1 32S  61 38W
Moura, Portugal ........... 21 C2   38  7N   7 30W
Mourdi, Dépression du, Chad . 51 E10  18 10N  23  0 E
Mourilyan, Australia ....... 62 B4   17 35S 146  3 E
Mourne →, U.K. ........... 10 B4   54 52N   7 26W
Mourne Mts., U.K. ......... 10 B5   54 10N   6  0W
Mourniaí, Greece .......... 25 D6   35 29N  24  1 E
Mournies = Mourniaí, Greece  25 D6   35 29N  24  1 E
Mouscron, Belgium ........ 15 D3   50 45N   3 12 E
Moussoro, Chad ........... 51 F9   13 41N  16 35 E
Moutohara, Indonesia ...... 37 D6    0 28N 121 13 E

Movas, Mexico .............. 86 B3   28 10N 109 25W
Moville, Ireland .............. 10 A4   55 11N    7  3W
Mowandjum, Australia ...... 60 C3   17 22S 123 40 E
Moy →, Ireland .............. 10 B2   54  8N    9  8W
Moyale, Kenya .............. 54 B4   3 30N   39  0 E
Moyen Atlas, Morocco ...... 50 B4   33  0N    5  0W
Moyne, L. le, Canada ...... 73 A6   56 45N  68 47W
Moyobamba, Peru .......... 92 E3    6  0S   77  0W
Moyyero →, Russia ........ 29 C11 68 44N 103 42 E
Moyynty, Kazakhstan ...... 28 E8   47 10N  73 18 E
Mozambique = Moçambique,
  Mozam. .................. 55 F5   15  3S  40 42 E
Mozambique ■, Africa ...... 55 F4   19  0S  35  0 E
Mozambique Chan., Africa .. 57 B7   17 30S  42 30 E
Mozdok, Russia ............ 19 F7   43 45N  44 48 E
Mozdūrān, Iran ............ 45 B9   36  9N  60 35 E
Mozhnābād, Iran .......... 45 C9   34  7N  60  6 E
Mozyr = Mazyr, Belarus .... 17 B15 51 59N  29 15 E
Mpanda, Tanzania .......... 54 D3    6 23S  31 1 E
Mphoengs, Zimbabwe ...... 57 C4   21 10S  27 51 E
Mpika, Zambia ............ 55 E3   11 51S  31 25 E
Mpulungu, Zambia .......... 55 D3    8 51S  31  5 E
Mpumalanga, S. Africa .... 57 D5   29 50S  30 33 E
Mpumalanga □, S. Africa .. 57 D5   26  0S  30  0 E
Mpwapwa, Tanzania ........ 54 D4    6 23S  36 30 E
Mqanduli, S. Africa ........ 57 E4   31 49S  28 45 E
Msambansovu, Zimbabwe .. 55 F3   15 50S   30  3 E
M'sila →, Algeria .......... 50 A6   35 30N   4 29 E
Msoro, Zambia ............ 55 E3   13 35S  31 50 E
Mstislavl = Mstsislaw, Belarus  17 A16 54  0N  31 50 E
Mstsislaw, Belarus ........ 17 A16 54  0N  31 50 E
Mtama, Tanzania .......... 55 E4   10 17S  39 21 E
Mtamvuna →, S. Africa .... 57 E5   31  6S  30 12 E
Mtilikwe →, Zimbabwe .... 55 G3   21  9S  31 30 E
Mtubatuba, S. Africa ...... 57 D5   28 30S  32  8 E
Mtwalume, S. Africa ...... 57 E5   30 30S  30 38 E
Mtwara-Mikindani, Tanzania  55 E5   10 20S  40 20 E
Mu Gia, Deo, Vietnam ...... 38 D5   17 40N 105 47 E
Mu Ko Chang △, Thailand .. 39 G4   11 59N 102 22 E
Mu Us Shamo, China ...... 34 E5   39  0N 109  0 E
Muang Chiang Rai = Chiang Rai,
  Thailand ................ 38 C2   19 52N  99 50 E
Muang Khong, Laos ........ 38 E5   14  7N 105 51 E
Muang Lamphun, Thailand .. 38 C2   18 40N  99  2 E
Muang Mai, Thailand ...... 39 a     8  5N  98 21 E
Muang Pak Beng, Laos .... 38 C3   19 54N 101  8 E
Muar, Malaysia ............ 39 L4    2  3N 102 34 E
Muarabungo, Indonesia .... 36 E2    1 28S 102 52 E
Muaraenim, Indonesia ...... 36 E2    3 40S 103 50 E
Muarajuloi, Indonesia ...... 36 E4    0 12S 114  3 E
Muarakaman, Indonesia .... 36 E5    0  2S 116 45 E
Muaratebo, Indonesia ...... 36 E2    1 30S 102 26 E
Muaratembesi, Indonesia .. 36 E2    1 42S 103  8 E
Muaratewe, Indonesia ...... 36 E4    0 58S 114 52 E
Mubarakpur, India .......... 43 F10  26  6N  83 18 E
Mubarraz = Al Mubarraz,
  Si. Arabia ................ 45 E6   25 30N  49 40 E
Mubende, Uganda .......... 54 B3    0 33N  31 22 E
Mubi, Nigeria .............. 51 F8   10 18N  13 16 E
Mucajaí →, Brazil .......... 92 C6    2 25N  60 52W
Muchachos, Roque de los,
  Canary Is. ................ 24 F2   28 44N  17 52W
Muchinga Mts., Zambia .... 55 E3   11 30S  31 30 E
Muck, U.K. ................ 11 E2   56 50N   6 15W
Muckadilla, Australia ...... 63 D4   26 35S 148 23 E
Muckle Flugga, U.K. ...... 11 A8   60 51N   0 54W
Mucuri, Brazil ............ 93 G11  18  0S  39 36W
Mucusso, Angola .......... 56 B3   18  1S  21 25 E
Muda, Canary Is. .......... 24 F6   28 34N  13 57W
Mudanjiang, China ........ 35 B15  44 38N 129 30 E
Mudanya, Turkey .......... 23 D13  40 25N  28 50 E
Muddy Cr. →, U.S.A. ...... 77 H8   38 24N 110 42W
Mudgee, Australia ........ 63 E4   32 32S 149 31 E
Mudjatik →, Canada ...... 71 B7   56  1N 107 36W
Muecate, Mozam. .......... 55 E4   14 55S  39 40 E
Mueda, Mozam. ............ 55 E4   11 36S  39 28 E
Mueller Ra., Australia ...... 60 C4   18 18S 126 46 E
Muende, Mozam. .......... 55 E3   14 28S  33  0 E
Muerto, Mar, Mexico ...... 87 D6   16 10N  94 10W
Mufulira, Zambia .......... 55 E2   12 32S  28 15 E
Mufumbiro Range, Africa .. 54 C2    1 25S  29 30 E
Mughal Sarai, India ........ 43 G10  25 18N  83  7 E
Mughayrā', Si. Arabia ...... 44 D3   29 17N  37 41 E
Mugi, Japan ................ 31 H7   33 40N 134 25 E
Mugila, Mts., Dem. Rep. of
  the Congo ................ 54 D2    7  0S  28 50 E
Muğla, Turkey ............ 23 F13  37 15N  28 22 E
Mugu, Nepal .............. 43 E10  29 45N  82 30 E
Muhammad, Râs, Egypt .... 44 E2   27 44N  34 16 E
Muhammad Qol, Sudan .... 51 D13  20 53N  37  9 E
Muhammadabad, India .... 43 F10  26  4N  83 25 E
Muhesi →, Tanzania ...... 54 D4    7  0S  35 20 E
Mühlhausen, Germany .... 16 C6   51 12N  10 27 E
Mühlig Hofmann fjell, Antarctica  5 D3   72 30S   5  0 E
Muhos, Finland ............ 8 D22  64 47N  25 59 E
Muhu, Estonia ............ 9 G20  58 36N  23 11 E
Muhutwe, Tanzania ........ 54 C3    1 35S  31 45 E
Mui Wo, China ............ 33 G10  22 16N 113 59 E
Muine Bheag, Ireland ...... 10 D5   52 42N   6 58W
Muir, L., Australia ........ 61 F2   34 30S 116  0 E
Muir of Ord, U.K. .......... 11 D4   57 32N   4 28W
Mujnak = Muynak, Uzbekistan  28 E6   43 44N  59 10 E
Muka, Tanjung, Malaysia .. 39 c     5 28N 100 11 E
Mukacheve, Ukraine ...... 17 D12  48 27N  22 45 E
Mukachevo = Mukacheve,
  Ukraine .................. 17 D12  48 27N  22 45 E
Mukah, Malaysia .......... 36 D4    2 55N 112  5 E
Mukandwara, India ........ 42 G6   24 49N  75 59 E
Mukdahan, Thailand ...... 38 D5   16 32N 104 43 E
Mukden = Shenyang, China  35 D12  41 48N 123 27 E
Mukerian, India ............ 42 D6   31 57N  75 37 E
Mukinbudin, Australia ...... 61 F2   30 55S 118  5 E
Mukishi, Dem. Rep. of the Congo  55 D1   8 30S  24 44 E
Mukomuko, Indonesia ...... 36 E2    2 30S 101 10 E
Mukomwenze, Dem. Rep. of
  the Congo ................ 54 D2    6  49S  27 15 E
Muktsar, India ............ 42 D6   30 30N  74 30 E
Mukur = Moqor, Afghan. .. 42 C2   32 50N  67 42 E
Mukutawa →, Canada .... 71 C9   53 10N  97 24W
Mukwela, Zambia .......... 55 F2   17  0S  26 40 E
Mula, Spain ................ 21 C5   38  3N   1 33W
Mula →, Pakistan .......... 42 F2   27 57N  67 36 E
Mulange, Dem. Rep. of
  the Congo ................ 54 C2    3 40S  27 10 E
Mulanje, Malawi .......... 55 F4   16  2S  35 33 E
Mulanje, Mt., Malawi ...... 55 F4   16  0S  35 30 E
Mulchén, Chile ............ 94 D1   37 45S  72 20W

Mulde →, Germany ........ 16 C7   51 53N  12 15 E
Mule Creek Junction, U.S.A. .. 80 D2  43 19N 104  8W
Muleba, Tanzania .......... 54 C3    1 50S  31 37 E
Mulejé, Mexico ............ 86 B2   26 53N 112  1W
Muleshoe, U.S.A. .......... 81 H3   34 13N 102 43W
Mulgrave, Canada .......... 73 C7   45 38N  61 31W
Mulhacén, Spain .......... 21 D4   37  4N   3 20W
Mülheim, Germany ........ 33 C6   51 25N   6 54 E
Mulhouse, France .......... 20 C7   47 40N   7 20 E
Muling, China .............. 35 B16  44 35N 130 10 E
Mull, U.K. ................ 11 E3   56 25N   5 56W
Mull, Sound of, U.K. ...... 11 E3   56 30N   5 50W
Mullaittivu, Sri Lanka ...... 40 Q12   9 15N  80 49 E
Mullen, U.S.A. ............ 80 D4   42  3N 101  1W
Mullens, U.S.A. ............ 82 G5   37 35N  81 23W
Mullet Pen., Ireland ...... 10 B1   54 13N  10  2W
Mullewa, Australia ........ 61 E2   28 29S 115 30 E
Mulligan →, Australia .... 62 D2   25  0S 139  0 E
Mullingar, Ireland .......... 10 C4   53 31N   7 21W
Mullins, U.S.A. ............ 83 H6   34 12N  79 15W
Mullumbimby, Australia .... 63 D5   28 30S 153 30 E
Mulobezi, Zambia .......... 55 F2   16 45S  25  7 E
Mulroy B., Ireland ........ 10 A4   55 15N   7 46W
Multan, Pakistan .......... 42 D4   30 15N  71 36 E
Mulumbe, Mts., Dem. Rep. of
  the Congo ................ 55 D2    8 40S  27 30 E
Mulungushi Dam, Zambia .. 55 E2   14 48S  28 48 E
Mulvane, U.S.A. .......... 81 G6   37 29N  97 15W
Mumbai, India ............ 40 K8   18 55N  72 50 E
Mumbwa, Zambia .......... 55 F2   15  0S  27  0 E
Mun →, Thailand .......... 38 E5   15 19N 105 30 E
Muna, Indonesia .......... 37 F6    5  0S 122 30 E
Munabao, India ............ 42 G4   25 45N  70 17 E
Munamagi, Estonia ........ 9 H22  57 43N  27  4 E
Muncan, Indonesia ........ 37 K18   8 34S 115 11 E
Muncar, Indonesia ........ 37 J17   8 26S 114 20 E
München, Germany ........ 16 D6   48  8N  11 34 E
Munchen-Gladbach =
  Mönchengladbach, Germany  16 C4  51 11N   6 27 E
Muncho Lake, Canada .... 70 B3   59  0N 125 50W
Munch'ŏn, N. Korea ...... 35 E14  39 14N 127 19 E
Muncie, U.S.A. ............ 82 E3   40 12N  85 23W
Muncoonie, L., Australia .. 62 D2   25 12S 138 40 E
Mundabbera, Australia .... 63 D5   25 36S 151 18 E
Munday, U.S.A. ............ 81 J5   33 27N  99 38W
Münden, Germany ........ 16 C5   51 25N   9 38 E
Mundiwindi, Australia ...... 60 D3   23 47S 120  9 E
Mundo Novo, Brazil ...... 93 F10  11 50S  40 29W
Mundra, India ............ 42 H3   22 54N  69 48 E
Mundrabilla, Australia .... 61 F4   31 52S 127 51 E
Mungallala, Australia ...... 63 D4   26 28S 147 34 E
Mungallala Cr. →, Australia  63 D4  28 53S 147  5 E
Mungana, Australia ........ 62 B3   17  8S 144 27 E
Mungaoli, India ............ 42 G8   24 24N  78  7 E
Mungari, Mozam. .......... 55 F3   17 12S  33 30 E
Mungbere, Dem. Rep. of
  the Congo ................ 54 B2    2 36N  28 28 E
Mungeli, India ............ 43 H9   22  4N  81 41 E
Munger, India ............ 43 G12  25 23N  86 30 E
Mungkan Kandju △, Australia  62 A3  13 35S 142 52 E
Munich = München, Germany  16 D6  48  8N  11 34 E
Munising, U.S.A. .......... 82 B2   46 25N  86 40W
Munku-Sardyk, Russia .... 29 D11  51 45N 100 20 E
Muñoz Gamero, Pen., Chile  96 G2  52 30S  73  5W
Munroe L., Canada ........ 71 B9   59 13N  98 35W
Munsan, S. Korea .......... 35 F14  37 51N 126 48 E
Münster, Germany ........ 16 C4   51 58N   7 37 E
Munster □, Ireland ........ 10 D3   52 18N   8 44W
Muntadgin, Australia ...... 61 F2   31 45S 118 33 E
Muntok, Indonesia ........ 36 E3    2  5S 105 10 E
Munyama, Zambia .......... 55 F2   16  5S  28 31 E
Muong Beng, Laos ........ 38 B3   20 23N 101 46 E
Muong Boum, Vietnam .... 38 A4   22 24N 102 49 E
Muong Et, Laos ............ 38 B5   20 49N 104  1 E
Muong Hai, Laos .......... 38 B3   21 3N 101 49 E
Muong Hiem, Laos ........ 38 B4   20 5N 103 22 E
Muong Houn, Laos ........ 38 B3   20 8N 101 23 E
Muong Hung, Vietnam .... 38 B4   20 56N 103 53 E
Muong Kau, Laos .......... 38 E5   15  6N 105 47 E
Muong Khao, Laos ........ 38 C4   19 38N 103 32 E
Muong Khoua, Laos ...... 38 B4   21  5N 102 31 E
Muong Liep, Laos .......... 38 C3   18 29N 101 40 E
Muong May, Laos .......... 38 E6   14 49N 106 56 E
Muong Ngeun, Laos ...... 38 B3   20 36N 101  3 E
Muong Ngoi, Laos ........ 38 B4   20 43N 102 41 E
Muong Nhie, Vietnam .... 38 A4   22 12N 102 28 E
Muong Nong, Laos ........ 38 D6   16 22N 106 30 E
Muong Ou Tay, Laos ...... 38 A3   22  7N 101 48 E
Muong Oua, Laos .......... 38 C3   18 18N 101 20 E
Muong Peun, Laos ........ 38 B4   20 13N 103 52 E
Muong Phalane, Laos .... 38 D5   16 39N 105 34 E
Muong Phieng, Laos ...... 38 C3   19  6N 101 32 E
Muong Phine, Laos ........ 38 D6   16 32N 106  2 E
Muong Sai, Laos .......... 38 B3   20 42N 101 59 E
Muong Saiapoun, Laos .... 38 C3   18 24N 101 31 E
Muong Sen, Vietnam ...... 38 C5   19 24N 104  8 E
Muong Sing, Laos .......... 38 B3   21 11N 101  9 E
Muong Son, Laos .......... 38 B4   20 27N 103 19 E
Muong Soui, Laos ........ 38 C4   19 33N 102 52 E
Muong Va, Laos .......... 38 B4   21 53N 102 19 E
Muong Xia, Vietnam ...... 38 B5   20 19N 104 50 E
Muonio, Finland .......... 8 C20   67 57N  23 40 E
Muonio älv = Muonionjoki →,
  Finland .................. 8 C20   67 11N  23 34 E
Muonioälven = Muonionjoki →,
  Finland .................. 8 C20   67 11N  23 34 E
Muonionjoki →, Finland .. 8 C20   67 11N  23 34 E
Muping, China ............ 35 F11  37 22N 121 36 E
Muqdisho, Somali Rep. .... 47 G4    2  2N  45 25 E
Mur →, Austria ............ 17 E9   46 18N  16 52 E
Murakami, Japan .......... 30 E9   38 14N 139 29 E
Murallón, Cerro, Chile .... 96 F2   49 48S  73 30W
Muranda, Rwanda .......... 54 C2    1 52S  29 20 E
Murang'a, Kenya .......... 54 C4    0 45S  37  9 E
Murashi, Russia .......... 18 C8   59 30N  49  0 E
Murat →, Turkey .......... 19 G7   38 46N  40  0 E
Muratli, Turkey ............ 23 D12  41 10N  27 29 E
Murayama, Japan .......... 30 E10  38 30N 140 25 E
Murchison →, Australia .. 61 E1   27 45S 114  0 E
Murchison, Mt., Antarctica  5 D11  73  0S 168  0 E
Murchison Falls, Uganda .. 54 B3   2 15N  31 30 E
Murchison Falls △, Uganda  54 B3   2 17N  31 48 E
Murchison Rapids, Malawi .. 55 F3  15 55S  34 35 E
Murcia, Spain ............ 21 D5   38  5N   1 10W
Murcia □, Spain .......... 21 D5   37 50N   1 30W
Murdo, U.S.A. ............ 80 D4   43 53N 100 43W

Murdoch Pt., Australia .... 62 A3   14 37S 144 55 E
Mureş →, Romania ........ 17 E11  46 15N  20 13 E
Mureşul = Mureş →, Romania  17 E11  46 15N  20 13 E
Murewa, Zimbabwe ........ 57 B5   17 39S  31 47 E
Murfreesboro, N.C., U.S.A. .. 83 G7  36 27N  77  6W
Murfreesboro, Tenn., U.S.A. .. 83 H2  35 51N  86 24W
Murgab = Murghob, Tajikistan  28 F8  38 10N  74  2 E
Murgab →, Turkmenistan .. 45 B9   38 18N  61 12 E
Murgenella, Australia ...... 60 B5   11 34S 132 56 E
Murgha Kibzai, Pakistan .. 42 D3   30 44N  69 25 E
Murghob, Tajikistan ...... 28 F8   38 10N  74  2 E
Murgon, Australia ........ 63 D5   26 15S 151 54 E
Muri, India ................ 43 H11  23 22N  85 52 E
Muria, Indonesia .......... 37 G14   6 36S 110 53 E
Muriaé, Brazil ............ 95 A7   21  8S  42 23W
Muriel Mine, Zimbabwe .. 55 F3   17 14S  30 40 E
Müritz, Germany .......... 16 B7   53 25N  12 42 E
Murliganj, India .......... 43 G12  25 54N  86 59 E
Murmansk, Russia ........ 18 A5   68 57N  33 10 E
Muro, Spain .............. 24 B10  39 44N   3  3 E
Murom, Russia ............ 18 C7   55 35N  42  3 E
Muroran, Japan .......... 30 C10  42 25N 141  0 E
Muroto, Japan ............ 31 H7   33 18N 134  9 E
Muroto-Misaki, Japan .... 31 H7   33 15N 134 10 E
Murphy, U.S.A. ............ 76 E5   43 13N 116 33W
Murphys, U.S.A. .......... 78 G6   38  8N 120 28W
Murray, Ky., U.S.A. ...... 83 G1   36 37N  88 19W
Murray, Utah, U.S.A. ...... 76 F8   40 40N 111 53W
Murray →, Australia ...... 63 F2   35 20S 139 22 E
Murray, L., U.S.A. ........ 83 H5   34  3N  81 13W
Murray Bridge, Australia .. 63 F2   35  6S 139 14 E
Murray Harbour, Canada .. 73 C7   46  0N  62 28W
Murray River △, Australia  63 F3  34 23S 140 32 E
Murraysburg, S. Africa .... 56 E3   31 58S  23 47 E
Murree, Pakistan .......... 42 C5   33 56N  73 28 E
Murrieta, U.S.A. .......... 79 M9  33 33N 117 13W
Murrumbidgee →, Australia  63 E3  34 43S 143 12 E
Murrumburrah, Australia .. 63 E4   34 32S 148 22 E
Murrurundi, Australia ...... 63 E5   31 42S 150 51 E
Murshidabad, India ........ 43 G13  24 11N  88 19 E
Murtle L., Canada ........ 70 C5   52  8N 119 38W
Murtoa, Australia ........ 63 F3   36 35S 142 28 E
Murungu, Tanzania ........ 54 C3    4 12S  31 10 E
Mururoa, French Polynesia  65 K14  21 52S 138 55W
Murwara, India ............ 43 H9   23 46N  80 28 E
Murwillumbah, Australia .. 63 D5   28 18S 153 27 E
Mürzzuschlag, Austria .... 16 E8   47 36N  15 41 E
Muş, Turkey .............. 19 G7   38 45N  41 30 E
Mûsa, Gebel, Egypt ...... 44 D2   28 33N  33 59 E
Musa Khel, Pakistan ...... 42 D3   30 59N  69 52 E
Mûsa Qal'eh, Afghan. .... 40 C4   32 20N  64 50 E
Musafirkhana, India ...... 43 F9   26 22N  81 48 E
Musala, Bulgaria .......... 23 C10  42 13N  23 37 E
Musala, Indonesia ........ 36 D1    1 41N  98 28 E
Musan, N. Korea .......... 35 C15  42 12N 129 12 E
Musangu, Dem. Rep. of
  the Congo ................ 55 E1   10 28S  23 55 E
Musasa, Tanzania ........ 54 C3    3 25S  31 30 E
Musay'īd, Qatar .......... 45 E6   25  0N  51 33 E
Muscat = Masqaṭ, Oman .. 47 C6   23 37N  58 36 E
Muscatine, U.S.A. ........ 80 E9   41 25N  91  3W
Musengezi = Unsengedsi →,
  Zimbabwe ................ 55 F3   15 43S  31 14 E
Musgrave Harbour, Canada  73 C9  49 27N  53 58W
Musgrave Ranges, Australia  61 E5  26  0S 132  0 E
Mushie, Dem. Rep. of the Congo  52 E3   2 56S  16 55 E
Musi →, Indonesia ........ 36 E2    2 20S 104 56 E
Musina, S. Africa .......... 57 C5   22 20S  30  5 E
Muskeg →, Canada ...... 70 A4   60 20N 123 20W
Muskegon, U.S.A. ........ 82 D2   43 14N  86 16W
Muskegon →, U.S.A. .... 82 D2   43 14N  86 21W
Muskegon Heights, U.S.A. .. 82 D2  43 12N  86 16W
Muskogee, U.S.A. ........ 81 H7   35 45N  95 22W
Muskoka, L., Canada .... 84 B5   45  0N  79 25W
Muskwa →, Canada ...... 70 B4   58 47N 122 48W
Muslimiyah, Syria ........ 44 B3   36 19N  37 12 E
Musoma, Tanzania ........ 54 C3    1 30S  33 48 E
Musquaro, L., Canada .... 73 B7   50 38N  61  5W
Musquodoboit Harbour, Canada  73 D7  44 50N  63  9W
Musselburgh, U.K. ........ 11 F5   55 57N   3  2W
Musselshell →, U.S.A. .... 76 C10  47 21N 107 57W
Mussoorie, India .......... 42 D8   30 27N  78  6 E
Mussuco, Angola .......... 56 B2   17  2S  19  3 E
Mustang, Nepal ............ 43 E10  29 10N  83 55 E
Musters, L., Argentina .... 96 F3   45 20S  69 25W
Musudan, N. Korea ...... 35 D15  40 50N 129 43 E
Muswellbrook, Australia .. 63 E5   32 16S 150 56 E
Mût, Egypt ................ 51 C11  25 28N  28 58 E
Mut, Turkey .............. 44 B2   36 40N  33 28 E
Mutanda, Mozam. .......... 57 C5   21  0S  33 34 E
Mutanda, Zambia .......... 55 E2   12 24S  26 13 E
Mutare, Zimbabwe ........ 55 F3   18 58S  32 38 E
Muting, Indonesia ........ 37 F10   7 23S 140 20 E
Mutki = Mirtağ, Turkey .. 44 B4   38 23N  41 56 E
Mutoko, Zimbabwe ........ 57 B5   17 24S  32 13 E
Mutoray, Russia .......... 29 C11  60 56N 101  0 E
Mutshatsha, Dem. Rep. of
  the Congo ................ 55 E1   10 35S  24 20 E
Mutsu, Japan ............ 30 D10  41 5N 140 55 E
Mutsu-Wan, Japan ........ 30 D10  41  5N 140 55 E
Muttaburra, Australia .... 62 C3   22 38S 144 29 E
Mutton I., Ireland ........ 10 D2   52 49N   9 32W
Mutuáli, Mozam. .......... 55 E4   14 55S  37  0 E
Muweilih, Egypt .......... 46 E3   30 42N  34 19 E
Muy Muy, Nic. ............ 88 D2   12 39N  85 36W
Muyinga, Burundi ........ 54 C3    3 14S  30 33 E
Muynak, Uzbekistan ...... 28 E6   43 44N  59 10 E
Muzaffarabad, Pakistan .. 43 B5   34 25N  73 30 E
Muzaffargarh, Pakistan .. 42 D4   30  5N  71 14 E
Muzaffarnagar, India ...... 42 E7   29 26N  77 40 E
Muzaffarpur, India ........ 43 F11  26  7N  85 23 E
Muzafirpur, Pakistan .... 42 G3   24 28N  70 46 E
Muzhi, Russia ............ 18 A11  65 25N  64 40 E
Mvurwi, Zimbabwe ........ 55 F3   17  0S  30 57 E
Mwabvi, Malawi .......... 55 F3   16 42S  35  0 E
Mwambo, Tanzania ........ 55 E5   10 30S  40 22 E
Mwandi, Zambia .......... 55 F1   17 30S  24 51 E
Mwanza, Dem. Rep. of the Congo  54 D2   7 55S  26 43 E
Mwanza, Tanzania ........ 54 C3    2 30S  32 58 E
Mwanza, Zambia .......... 55 F1    2  0S  30  0 E
Mwanza □, Tanzania ...... 54 C3    2  0S  33  0 E
Mweelrea, Ireland ........ 10 C2   53 39N   9 49W
Mweka, Dem. Rep. of Congo  52 E4    4 50S  21 34 E

Mwenezi, Zimbabwe ...... 55 G3   21 15S  30 48 E
Mwenezi →, Mozam. ...... 55 G3   22 40S  31 50 E
Mwenga, Dem. Rep. of
  the Congo ................ 54 C2    3  1S  28 28 E
Mweru, L., Zambia ........ 55 D2    9  0S  28 40 E
Mweru Wantipa △, Zambia  55 D2   8 39S  29 25 E
Mweza Range, Zimbabwe .. 55 G3   21  0S  30  0 E
Mwilambwe, Dem. Rep. of
  the Congo ................ 54 D2    8  7S  25  5 E
Mwimbi, Tanzania ........ 55 D3    8 38S  31 39 E
Mwinilunga, Zambia ...... 55 E1   11 43S  24 25 E
My Tho, Vietnam .......... 39 G6   10 29N 106 23 E
Myajlar, India ............ 42 F4   26 15N  70 20 E
Myanaung, Burma ........ 41 K19  18 18N  95 22 E
Myanmar = Burma ■, Asia  41 J20  21  0N  96 30 E
Myaungmya, Burma ...... 41 L19  16 30N  94 40 E
Mycenæ, Greece .......... 23 F10  37 39N  22 52 E
Myeik Kyunzu, Burma .... 39 G1   11 30N  97 30 E
Myers Chuck, U.S.A. ...... 70 B2   55 44N 132 11W
Myerstown, U.S.A. ........ 85 F8   40 22N  76 19W
Myingyan, Burma .......... 41 J19  21 30N  95 20 E
Myitkyina, Burma ........ 41 G20  25 24N  97 26 E
Mykines, Færoe Is. ...... 8 E9   62  7N   7 35W
Mykolayiv, Ukraine ...... 19 E5   46 58N  32  0 E
Mymensingh, Bangla. .... 41 G17  24 45N  90 24 E
Mynydd Du, U.K. .......... 13 F4   51 52N   3 50W
Mýrdalsjökull, Iceland .... 8 E4   63 40N  19  6W
Myrtle Beach, U.S.A. ...... 83 J6   33 42N  78 53W
Myrtle Creek, U.S.A. ...... 76 E2   43  1N 123 17W
Myrtle Point, U.S.A. ...... 76 E1   43  4N 124  8W
Myrtou, Cyprus .......... 25 D12  35 18N  33  4 E
Mysia, Turkey ............ 23 E12  39 50N  27  0 E
Mysore = Karnataka □, India  40 N10  13 15N  77  0 E
Mysore, India ............ 40 N10  12 17N  76 41 E
Mystic, U.S.A. ............ 85 E13  41 21N  71 58W
Myszków, Poland .......... 17 C10  50 45N  19 22 E
Mytishchi, Russia ........ 18 C6   55 50N  37 50 E
Mývatn, Iceland .......... 8 D5   65 36N  17  0W
Mzimba, Malawi .......... 55 E3   11 55S  33 39 E
Mzimkulu →, S. Africa .... 57 E5   30 44S  30 28 E
Mzimvubu →, S. Africa .. 57 E4   31 38S  29 33 E
Mzuzu, Malawi ............ 55 E3   11 30S  33 55 E

**N**

Na Hearadh = Harris, U.K. .. 11 D2  57 50N   6 55W
Na Noi, Thailand .......... 38 C3   18 19N 100 43 E
Na Phao, Laos ............ 38 D5   17 35N 105 44 E
Na Sam, Vietnam .......... 38 A6   22  3N 106 37 E
Na San, Vietnam .......... 38 B5   21 12N 104  2 E
Na Thon, Thailand ........ 39 b     9 32N  99 56 E
Naab →, Germany ........ 16 D6   49  1N  12  2 E
Naantali, Finland .......... 9 F19  60 29N  22  2 E
Naas, Ireland ............ 10 C5   53 12N   6 40W
Nababeep, S. Africa ...... 56 D2   29 36S  17 46 E
Nabadwip = Navadwip, India  43 H13  23 34N  88 20 E
Nabawa, Australia ........ 61 E1   28 30S 114 48 E
Nabberu, L., Australia .... 61 E3   25 50S 120 30 E
Naberezhnyye Chelny, Russia  18 C9  55 42N  52 19 E
Nabeul, Tunisia .......... 51 A8   36 30N  10 44 E
Nabha, India .............. 42 D7   30 26N  76 14 E
Nabid, Iran .............. 45 D8   29 40N  57 38 E
Nabire, Indonesia ........ 37 E9    3 15S 135 26 E
Nabisar, Pakistan ........ 42 G3   25  8N  69 40 E
Nabisipi →, Canada ...... 73 B7   50 14N  62 13W
Nabiswera, Uganda ...... 54 B3    1 27N  32 15 E
Nāblus = Nābulus, West Bank  46 C4  32 14N  35 15 E
Naboomspruit, S. Africa .. 57 C4   24 32S  28 40 E
Nābulus, West Bank ...... 46 C4   32 14N  35 15 E
Nacala, Mozam. .......... 55 E5   14 31S  40 34 E
Nacala-Velha, Mozam. .... 55 E5   14 32S  40 34 E
Nacaome, Honduras ...... 88 D2   13 31N  87 30W
Nacaroa, Mozam. .......... 55 E4   14 22S  39 56 E
Naches, U.S.A. ............ 76 C3   46 44N 120 42W
Naches →, U.S.A. ........ 78 D6   46 38N 120 31W
Nachicapau, L., Canada .. 73 A6   56 40N  68  5W
Nachingwea, Tanzania .... 55 E4   10 23S  38 49 E
Nachna, India ............ 42 F4   27 34N  71 41 E
Nacimiento L., U.S.A. .... 78 K6   35 46N 120 53W
Naco, Mexico ............ 86 A3   31 20N 109 56W
Nacogdoches, U.S.A. ...... 81 K7   31 36N  94 39W
Nácori Chico, Mexico .... 86 B3   29 39N 109  1W
Nacozari, Mexico .......... 86 A3   30 25N 109 39W
Nādendal = Naantali, Finland  9 F19  60 29N  22  2 E
Nadi, Fiji ................ 59 C7   17 42S 177 20 E
Nadiad, India ............ 42 H5   22 41N  72 56 E
Nador, Morocco .......... 50 B5   35 14N   2 58W
Nadur, Malta ............ 25 C1   36  2N  14 18 E
Nadūshan, Iran .......... 45 C7   32  2N  53 35 E
Nadvirna, Ukraine ........ 17 D13  48 37N  24 30 E
Nadvornaya = Nadvirna, Ukraine  17 D13  48 37N  24 30 E
Nadym, Russia ............ 28 C8   65 35N  72 42 E
Nadym →, Russia ........ 28 C8   66 12N  72  0 E
Nærbø, Norway .......... 9 G11  58 40N   5 39 E
Næstved, Denmark ...... 9 J14  55 13N  11 44 E
Naft-e Safīd, Iran ........ 45 D6   31 40N  49 17 E
Naftshahr, Iran .......... 44 C5   34  0N  45 30 E
Nafud Desert = An Nafūd,
  Si. Arabia ................ 44 D4   28 15N  41  0 E
Naga, Phil. .............. 37 B6   13 38N 123 15 E
Nagahama, Japan ........ 31 G8   35 23N 136 16 E
Nagai, Japan ............ 30 E10  38  6N 140  2 E
Nagaland □, India ........ 41 G19  26  0N  94 30 E
Nagano, Japan ............ 31 F9   36 40N 138 10 E
Nagano □, Japan .......... 31 F9   36 15N 138  0 E
Nagaoka, Japan .......... 31 F9   37 27N 138 51 E
Nagappattinam, India .... 40 P11  10 46N  79 51 E
Nagar →, Bangla. ........ 43 G13  24 27N  89 12 E
Nagar Parkar, Pakistan .. 42 G4   24 28N  70 46 E
Nagasaki, Japan .......... 31 H4   32 47N 129 50 E
Nagasaki □, Japan ...... 31 H4   32 50N 129 40 E
Nagaur, India ............ 42 F5   27 15N  73 45 E
Nagda, India ............ 42 H6   23 27N  75 25 E
Nagercoil, India .......... 40 Q10   8 12N  77 26 E
Nagina, India ............ 43 E8   29 30N  78 30 E
Nagineh, Iran ............ 45 C8   34 20N  57 15 E
Nagir, Pakistan .......... 43 A6   36  0N  74 40 E
Nagod, India ............ 43 G9   24 34N  80 36 E
Nagoorin, Australia ...... 62 C5   24 17S 151 15 E
Nagorno-Karabakh □, Azerbaijan  19 F8  39 55N  46 45 E
Nagornyy, Russia ........ 29 D13  55 58N 124 57 E
Nagoya, Japan ............ 31 G8   35 10N 136 50 E
Nagpur, India ............ 40 J11  21  8N  79 10 E

Nagua, _Dom. Rep._ ............ **89 C6**   19 23N  69 50W
Naguabo, _Puerto Rico_ ........ **89 d**    18 13N  65 44W
Nagykanizsa, _Hungary_ ........ **17 E9**   46 28N  17  0 E
Nagykőrös, _Hungary_ .......... **17 E10**  47  5N  19 48 E
Naha, _Japan_ ................. **31 L3**   26 13N 127 42 E
Nahan, _India_ ................ **42 D7**   30 33N  77 18 E
Nahanni △, _Canada_ ........... **70 A4**   61 36N 125 41W
Nahanni Butte, _Canada_ ....... **70 A4**   61  2N 123 31W
Nahargarh, _Mad. P., India_ ... **42 G6**   24 10N  75 14 E
Nahargarh, _Raj., India_ ...... **42 G7**   24 55N  76 50 E
Nahariyya, _Israel_ ........... **44 C2**   33  1N  35  5 E
Nahāvand, _Iran_ .............. **45 C6**   34 10N  48 22 E
Nahuelbuta △, _Chile_ ......... **94 D1**   37 44S  72 57W
Nai Yong, _Thailand_ .......... **39 a**     8 14N  98 22 E
Naicá, _Mexico_ ............... **86 B3**   27 53N 105 31W
Naicam, _Canada_ .............. **71 C8**   52 30N 104 30W
Naikoon △, _Canada_ ........... **70 C2**   53 55N 131 55W
Naimisharanya, _India_ ........ **43 F9**   27 21N  80 30 E
Nain, _Canada_ ................ **73 A7**   56 34N  61 40W
Nā'īn, _Iran_ ................. **45 C7**   32 54N  53  0 E
Naini Tal, _India_ ............ **43 E8**   29 30N  79 30 E
Nainpur, _India_ .............. **40 H12**  22 30N  80 10 E
Nainwa, _India_ ............... **42 G6**   25 46N  75 51 E
Nairn, _U.K._ ................. **11 D5**   57 35N   3 53W
Nairobi, _Kenya_ .............. **54 C4**    1 17S  36 48 E
Nairobi △, _Kenya_ ............ **54 C4**    1 22S  36 50 E
Naissaar, _Estonia_ ........... **9 G21**   59 34N  24 29 E
Naivasha, _Kenya_ ............. **54 C4**    0 40S  36 30 E
Naivasha, L., _Kenya_ ......... **54 C4**    0 48S  36 20 E
Najaf = An Najaf, _Iraq_ ...... **44 C5**   32  3N  44 15 E
Najafābād, _Iran_ ............. **45 C6**   32 40N  51 15 E
Najd, _Si. Arabia_ ............ **47 B3**   26 30N  42  0 E
Najibabad, _India_ ............ **42 E8**   29 40N  78 20 E
Najin, _N. Korea_ ............. **35 C16**  42 12N 130 15 E
Najmah, _Si. Arabia_ .......... **45 E6**   26 42N  50  6 E
Najrān, _Si. Arabia_ .......... **47 D3**   17 34N  44 18 E
Naju, _S. Korea_ .............. **35 G14**  35  3N 126 43 E
Nakadōri-Shima, _Japan_ ....... **31 H4**   32 57N 129  4 E
Nakalagba, _Dem. Rep. of
  the Congo_ .................. **54 B2**    2 50N  27 58 E
Nakaminato, _Japan_ ........... **31 F10**  36 21N 140 36 E
Nakamura, _Japan_ ............. **31 H6**   32 59N 132 56 E
Nakano, _Japan_ ............... **31 F9**   36 45N 138 22 E
Nakano-Shima, _Japan_ ......... **31 K4**   29 51N 129 52 E
Nakashibetsu, _Japan_ ......... **30 C12**  43 33N 144 59 E
Nakfa, _Eritrea_ .............. **47 D2**   16 40N  38 32 E
Nakha Yai, Ko, _Thailand_ ..... **39 a**     8  3N  98 28 E
Nakhichevan =
  Naxçıvan, _Azerbaijan_ ...... **19 G8**   39 12N  45 15 E
Nakhichevan Rep. = Naxçıvan □,
  _Azerbaijan_ ................ **19 G8**   39 25N  45 26 E
Nakhl, _Egypt_ ................ **46 F2**   29 55N  33 43 E
Nakhl-e Taqī, _Iran_ .......... **45 E7**   27 28N  52 36 E
Nakhodka, _Russia_ ............ **29 E14**  42 53N 132 54 E
Nakhon Nayok, _Thailand_ ...... **38 E3**   14 12N 101 13 E
Nakhon Pathom, _Thailand_ ..... **38 F3**   13 49N 100  3 E
Nakhon Phanom, _Thailand_ ..... **38 D5**   17 23N 104 43 E
Nakhon Ratchasima, _Thailand_ . **38 E4**   14 59N 102 12 E
Nakhon Sawan, _Thailand_ ...... **38 E3**   15 35N 100 10 E
Nakhon Si Thammarat, _Thailand_ **39 H3**    8 29N 100  0 E
Nakhon Thai, _Thailand_ ....... **38 D3**   17  5N 100 44 E
Nakhtarana, _India_ ........... **42 H3**   23 20N  69 15 E
Nakina, _Canada_ .............. **72 B2**   50 10N  86 40W
Nakodar, _India_ .............. **42 D6**   31  8N  75 31 E
Nakskov, _Denmark_ ............ **9 J14**   54 50N  11  8 E
Naktong →, _S. Korea_ ......... **35 G15**  35  7N 128 57 E
Nakuru, _Kenya_ ............... **54 C4**    0 15S  36  4 E
Nakuru, L., _Kenya_ ........... **54 C4**    0 23S  36  5 E
Nakusp, _Canada_ .............. **70 C5**   50 20N 117 45W
Nal, _Pakistan_ ............... **42 F2**   27 40N  66 12 E
Nal →, _Pakistan_ ............. **42 G1**   25 20N  65 30 E
Nalázi, _Mozam._ .............. **57 C5**   24  3S  33 20 E
Nalchik, _Russia_ ............. **19 F7**   43 30N  43 33 E
Nalgonda, _India_ ............. **40 L11**  17  6N  79 15 E
Nalhati, _India_ .............. **43 G12**  24 17N  87 52 E
Naliya, _India_ ............... **42 H3**   23  16N  68 50 E
Nallamalai Hills, _India_ ..... **40 M11**  15 30N  78 50 E
Nam Can, _Vietnam_ ............ **39 H5**    8 46N 104 59 E
Nam-ch'on, _N. Korea_ ......... **35 E14**  38 15N 126 26 E
Nam Co, _China_ ............... **32 C4**   30 30N  90 45 E
Nam Dinh, _Vietnam_ ........... **38 B6**   20 25N 106  5 E
Nam Du, Hon, _Vietnam_ ........ **39 H5**    9 41N 104 21 E
Nam Nao △, _Thailand_ ......... **38 D3**   16 44N 101 32 E
Nam Ngum Dam, _Laos_ .......... **38 C4**   18 35N 102 34 E
Nam-Phan, _Vietnam_ ........... **39 G6**   10 30N 106  0 E
Nam Phong, _Thailand_ ......... **38 D4**   16 42N 102 52 E
Nam Tha, _Laos_ ............... **38 B3**   20 58N 101 30 E
Nam Tok, _Thailand_ ........... **38 E2**   14 21N  99  4 E
Namacunde, _Angola_ ........... **56 B2**   17 18S  15 50 E
Namacurra, _Mozam._ ........... **57 B6**   17 30S  36 50 E
Namak, Daryācheh-ye, _Iran_ ... **45 C7**   34 30N  52  0 E
Namak, Kavir-e, _Iran_ ........ **45 C8**   34 30N  57 30 E
Namakzār, Daryācheh-ye, _Iran_  **45 C9**   34  0N  60 30 E
Namaland, _Namibia_ ........... **56 C2**   26  0S  17  0 E
Namangan, _Uzbekistan_ ........ **28 E8**   41  0N  71 40 E
Namapa, _Mozam._ .............. **55 E4**   13 43S  39 50 E
Namaqualand, _S. Africa_ ...... **56 E2**   30  0S  17 25 E
Namasagali, _Uganda_ .......... **54 B3**    1  2N  33  0 E
Namber, _Indonesia_ ........... **37 E8**    1  2S 134 49 E
Nambour, _Australia_ .......... **63 D5**   26 32S 152 58 E
Nambucca Heads, _Australia_ ... **63 E5**   30 37S 153  0 E
Nambung △, _Australia_ ........ **61 F2**   30 30S 115  5 E
Namcha Barwa, _China_ ......... **32 D4**   29 40N  95 10 E
Namche Bazar, _Nepal_ ......... **43 F12**  27 51N  86 47 E
Namchonjŏm = Nam-ch'on,
  _N. Korea_ .................. **35 E14**  38 15N 126 26 E
Namecunda, _Mozam._ ........... **55 E4**   14 54S  37 37 E
Nameponda, _Mozam._ ........... **55 F4**   15 50S  39 50 E
Nametil, _Mozam._ ............. **55 F4**   15 40S  39 21 E
Namew L., _Canada_ ............ **71 C8**   54 14N 101 56W
Namgia, _India_ ............... **43 D8**   31 48N  78 40 E
Namib Desert, _Namibia_ ....... **56 C2**   22 30S  15  0 E
Namib-Naukluft △, _Namibia_ ... **56 C2**   24 15S  15 16 E
Namibe, _Angola_ .............. **53 H2**   15  7S  12 11 E
Namibe □, _Angola_ ............ **56 B1**   16 35S  12 30 E
Namibia ■, _Africa_ ........... **56 C2**   22  0S  18  9 E
Namibwoestyn = Namib Desert,
  _Namibia_ ................... **56 C2**   22 30S  15  0 E
Namlea, _Indonesia_ ........... **37 E7**    3 18S 127  5 E
Namoi →, _Australia_ .......... **63 E4**   30 12S 149 30 E
Nampa, _U.S.A._ ............... **76 E5**   43 34N 116 34W
Namp'o, _N. Korea_ ............ **35 E13**  38 52N 125 10 E
Nampō-Shotō, _Japan_ .......... **31 J10**  32  0N 140  0 E
Nampula, _Mozam._ ............. **55 F4**   15  6S  39 15 E
Namrole, _Indonesia_ .......... **37 E7**    3 46S 126 46 E
Namse Shankou, _China_ ........ **41 E13**  30  0N  82 25 E
Namsen →, _Norway_ ............ **8 D14**   64 28N  11 37 E
Namsos, _Norway_ .............. **8 D14**   64 29N  11 30 E

Namtok Chat Trakan △, _Thailand_ **38 D3**  17 17N 100 40 E
Namtok Mae Surin △, _Thailand_ . **38 C2**  18 55N  98  2 E
Namtsy, _Russia_ .............. **29 C13**  62 43N 129 37 E
Namtu, _Burma_ ................ **41 H20**  23  5N  97 28 E
Namtumbo, _Tanzania_ .......... **55 E4**   10 30S  36  4 E
Namu, _Canada_ ................ **70 C3**   51 52N 127 50W
Namur, _Belgium_ .............. **15 D4**   50 27N   4 52 E
Namur □, _Belgium_ ............ **15 D4**   50 17N   5  0 E
Namutoni, _Namibia_ ........... **56 B2**   18 49S  16 55 E
Namwala, _Zambia_ ............. **55 F2**   15 44S  26 30 E
Namwŏn, _S. Korea_ ............ **35 G14**  35 23N 127 23 E
Nan, _Thailand_ ............... **38 C3**   18 48N 100 46 E
Nan →, _Thailand_ ............. **38 E3**   15 42N 100  9 E
Nan-ch'ang = Nanchang, _China_  **33 D6**   28 42N 115 55 E
Nanaimo, _Canada_ ............. **70 D4**   49  10N 124  0W
Nanam, _N. Korea_ ............. **35 D15**  41 44N 129 40 E
Nanango, _Australia_ .......... **63 D5**   26 40S 152  0 E
Nanao, _Japan_ ................ **31 F8**   37  0N 137  0 E
Nanchang, _China_ ............. **33 D6**   28 42N 115 55 E
Nanching = Nanjing, _China_ ... **33 C6**   32  2N 118 47 E
Nanchong, _China_ ............. **32 C5**   30 43N 106  2 E
Nancy, _France_ ............... **20 B7**   48 42N   6 12 E
Nanda Devi, _India_ ........... **43 D8**   30 23N  79 59 E
Nanda Kot, _India_ ............ **43 D9**   30 17N  80  5 E
Nandan, _Japan_ ............... **31 G7**   34 10N 134 42 E
Nanded, _India_ ............... **40 K10**  19 10N  77 20 E
Nandewar Ra., _Australia_ ..... **63 E5**   30 15S 150 35 E
Nandi = Nadi, _Fiji_ .......... **59 C7**   17 42S 177 20 E
Nandigram, _India_ ............ **43 H12**  22  1N  87 58 E
Nandurbar, _India_ ............ **40 J9**   21 20N  74 15 E
Nandyal, _India_ .............. **40 M11**  15 30N  78 30 E
Nanga-Eboko, _Cameroon_ ....... **52 D2**    4 41N  12 22 E
Nanga Parbat, _India_ ......... **43 B6**   35 10N  74 35 E
Nangade, _Mozam._ ............. **55 E4**   11  5S  39 36 E
Nangapinoh, _Indonesia_ ....... **36 E4**    0 20S 111 44 E
Nangarhār □, _Afghan._ ........ **40 B7**   34 20N  70  0 E
Nangatayap, _Indonesia_ ....... **36 E4**    1 32S 110 34 E
Nangeya Mts., _Uganda_ ........ **54 B3**    3 30N  33 30 E
Nangong, _China_ .............. **34 F8**   37 23N 115 22 E
Nanhuang, _China_ ............. **35 F11**  36 58N 121 48 E
Nanjeko, _Zambia_ ............. **55 F1**   15 31S  23 30 E
Nanjing, _China_ .............. **33 C6**   32  2N 118 47 E
Nanjirinji, _Tanzania_ ........ **55 D4**    9 41S  39  5 E
Nankana Sahib, _Pakistan_ ..... **42 D5**   31 27N  73 38 E
Nanking = Nanjing, _China_ .... **33 C6**   32  2N 118 47 E
Nankoku, _Japan_ .............. **31 H6**   33 39N 133 44 E
Nanlang, _China_ ............... **33 G10**  22 30N 113 32 E
Nanning, _China_ .............. **32 D5**   22 48N 108 20 E
Nannup, _Australia_ ........... **61 F2**   33 59S 115 48 E
Nanpara, _India_ .............. **43 F9**   27 52N  81 33 E
Nanpi, _China_ ................ **34 E9**   38  2N 116 45 E
Nanping, _China_ .............. **33 D6**   26 38N 118 10 E
Nanripe, _Mozam._ ............. **55 E4**   13 52S  38 52 E
Nansei-Shotō = Ryūkyū-rettō,
  _Japan_ ..................... **31 M3**   26  0N 126  0 E
Nansen Basin, _Arctic_ ........ **4 A10**   84  0N  50  0 E
Nansen Cordillera, _Arctic_ ... **4 A**     80  0N  90  0 E
Nansen Sd., _Canada_ .......... **4 A3**    81  0N  91  0W
Nansha, _China_ ............... **33 F10**  22 45N 113 34 E
Nanshan I., _S. China Sea_ .... **36 B5**   10 45N 115 49 E
Nansio, _Tanzania_ ............ **54 C3**    2  3S  33  4 E
Nantes, _France_ .............. **20 C3**   47 12N   1 33W
Nanticoke, _U.S.A._ ........... **85 E8**   41 12N  76  0W
Nanton, _Canada_ .............. **70 C6**   50 21N 113 46W
Nantong, _China_ .............. **33 C7**   32  1N 120 52 E
Nantou, _China_ ............... **33 F10**  22 32N 113 55 E
Nantucket I., _U.S.A._ ........ **82 E10**  41 16N  70  5W
Nantwich, _U.K._ .............. **12 D5**   53  4N   2 31W
Nanty Glo, _U.S.A._ ........... **84 F6**   40 28N  78 50W
Nanuque, _Brazil_ ............. **93 G10**  17 50S  40 21W
Nanusa, Kepulauan, _Indonesia_  **37 D7**    4 45N 127  1 E
Nanutarra Roadhouse, _Australia_ **60 D2**  22 32S 115 30 E
Nanyang, _China_ .............. **34 H7**   33 11N 112 30 E
Nanyuki, _Kenya_ .............. **54 B4**    0  2N   37  4 E
Nao, C. de la, _Spain_ ........ **21 C6**   38 44N   0 14 E
Naococane, L., _Canada_ ....... **73 B5**   52 50N  70 45W
Napa, _U.S.A._ ................ **78 G4**   38 18N 122 17W
Napa →, _U.S.A._ .............. **78 G4**   38 10N 122 19W
Napanee, _Canada_ ............. **84 B8**   44 15N  77  0W
Napanoch, _U.S.A._ ............ **85 E10**  41 44N  74 22W
Nape, _Laos_ .................. **38 C5**   18 18N 105  6 E
Nape Pass = Keo Neua, Deo,
  _Vietnam_ ................... **38 C5**   18 23N 105 10 E
Napier, _N.Z._ ................ **59 H6**   39 30S 176 56 E
Napier Broome B., _Australia_ . **60 B4**   14  2S 126 37 E
Napier Pen., _Australia_ ...... **62 A2**   12 4S 135 43 E
Napierville, _Canada_ ......... **85 A11**  45 11N  73 25W
Naples = Nápoli, _Italy_ ...... **22 D6**   40 50N  14 15 E
Naples, _U.S.A._ .............. **83 M5**   26  8N  81 48W
Napo →, _Peru_ ................ **92 D4**   3 20S  72 40W
Napoleon, N. Dak., _U.S.A._ ... **80 B5**   46 30N  99 46W
Napoleon, Ohio, _U.S.A._ ...... **82 E3**   41 23N  84  8W
Nápoli, _Italy_ ............... **22 D6**   40 50N  14 15 E
Napopo, _Dem. Rep. of the Congo_ **54 B2**   4 15N  28  0 E
Naqb, Ra's an, _Jordan_ ....... **46 F4**   30  0N  35 29 E
Naqqāsh, _Iran_ ............... **45 C6**   35 40N  49  6 E
Nara, _Japan_ ................. **31 G7**   34 40N 135 49 E
Nara, _Mali_ .................. **50 E4**   15 10N   7 20W
Nara □, _Japan_ ............... **31 G8**   34 30N 136  0 E
Nara Canal, _Pakistan_ ........ **42 G3**   24 30N  69 20 E
Nara Visa, _U.S.A._ ........... **81 H3**   35 37N 103  6W
Naracoorte, _Australia_ ....... **63 F3**   36 58S 140 45 E
Naradhan, _Australia_ ......... **63 E4**   33 34S 146 17 E
Naraini, _India_ .............. **43 G9**   25 11N  80 29 E
Narasapur, _India_ ............ **41 L12**  16 26N  81 40 E
Narathiwat, _Thailand_ ........ **39 J3**    6 30N 101 48 E
Narayanganj, _Bangla._ ........ **41 H17**  23 40N  90 33 E
Narayanpet, _India_ ........... **40 L10**  16 45N  77 30 E
Narberth, _U.K._ .............. **13 F3**   51 47N   4 44W
Narbonne, _France_ ............ **20 E5**   43 11N   3  0 E
Nardīn, _Iran_ ................ **45 B7**   37  3N  55 59 E
Nardò, _Italy_ ................ **23 D8**   40 11N  18  2 E
Narembeen, _Australia_ ........ **61 F2**   32  7S 118 24 E
Narendranagar, _India_ ........ **42 D8**   30 10N  78 18 E
Nares Str., _Arctic_ .......... **66 A13**  80  0N  70  0W
Naretha, _Australia_ .......... **61 F3**   31  0S 124 45 E
Narew →, _Poland_ ............. **17 B11**  52 26N  20 41 E
Nari →, _Pakistan_ ............ **42 E2**   29  0N  67 40 E
Narin, _Afghan._ ............. **40 A6**   36  5N  69  0 E
Narindra, Helodranon' i, _Madag._ **57 A8**  14 55S  47 30 E
Narita, _Japan_ ............... **31 G10**  35 47N 140 19 E
Nariva Swamp, _Trin. & Tob._ .. **93 K15**  10 26N  61  4W
Narmada →, _India_ ............ **42 J5**   21 38N  72 36 E
Narman, _Sweden_ .............. **9 F15**  60  0N  13 30 E
Narnaul, _India_ .............. **42 E7**   28  5N  76 11 E
Narodnaya, _Russia_ ........... **18 A10**  65  5N  59 58 E
Narok, _Kenya_ ................ **54 C4**    1 55S  35 52 E
Narooma, _Australia_ .......... **63 F5**   36 14S 150  4 E

Narowal, _Pakistan_ ........... **42 C6**   32  6N  74 52 E
Narrabri, _Australia_ ......... **63 E4**   30 19S 149 46 E
Narran →, _Australia_ ......... **63 D4**   28 37S 148 12 E
Narrandera, _Australia_ ....... **63 E4**   34 42S 146 31 E
Narrogin, _Australia_ ......... **61 F2**   32 58S 117 14 E
Narromine, _Australia_ ........ **63 E4**   32 12S 148 12 E
Narrow Hills △, _Canada_ ...... **71 C8**   54  0N 104 37W
Narsimhapur, _India_ .......... **43 H8**   22 54N  79 14 E
Narsinghgarh, _India_ ......... **42 H7**   23 45N  76 40 E
Naruto, _Japan_ ............... **31 G7**   34 11N 134 37 E
Narva, _Estonia_ .............. **18 C4**   59 23N  28 12 E
Narva →, _Russia_ ............. **9 G22**  59 27N  28  2 E
Narva Bay = Narva Laht, _Estonia_ **9 G19**  59 35N  27 35 E
Narva Laht, _Estonia_ ......... **9 G19**  59 35N  27 35 E
Narvik, _Norway_ .............. **8 B17**   68 28N  17 26 E
Narwana, _India_ .............. **42 E7**   29 39N  76  6 E
Naryan-Mar, _Russia_ .......... **18 A9**   67 42N  53 12 E
Narym, _Russia_ ............... **28 D9**   59  0N  81 30 E
Naryn, _Kyrgyzstan_ ........... **28 E8**   41 26N  75 58 E
Nasa, _Norway_ ................ **8 C16**  66 29N  15 23 E
Naseby, _N.Z._ ................ **59 L3**   45  1S 170 10 E
Naselle, _U.S.A._ ............. **78 D3**   46 22N 123 49W
Naser, Buheirat en, _Egypt_ ... **51 D12**  23  0N  32 30 E
Nashua, Mont., _U.S.A._ ....... **76 B10**  48  8N 106 22W
Nashua, N.H., _U.S.A._ ........ **85 D13**  42 45N  71 28W
Nashville, Ga., _U.S.A._ ...... **83 K4**   31 12N  83 15W
Nashville, Tenn., _U.S.A._ .... **83 G2**   36 10N  86 47W
Nasik, _India_ ................ **40 K8**   19 58N  73 50 E
Nasirabad, _India_ ............ **42 F6**   26 15N  74 45 E
Nasirabad, _Pakistan_ ......... **42 E3**   28 23N  68 24 E
Nasiriyah = An Nāşiriyah, _Iraq_ **44 D5**  31  0N  46 15 E
Naskaupi →, _Canada_ .......... **73 B7**   53 47N  60 51W
Naşrābād, _Iran_ .............. **45 C6**   34  8N  51 26 E
Naşrīān-e Pā'īn, _Iran_ ....... **44 C5**   32 52N  46 52 E
Nass →, _Canada_ .............. **70 C3**   55  0N 129 40W
Nassau, _Bahamas_ ............. **88 A4**   25  5N  77 20W
Nassau, _U.S.A._ .............. **85 D11**  42 31N  73 37W
Nassau, B., _Chile_ ........... **96 H3**   55 20S  68  0W
Nasser, L. = Naser, Buheirat en,
  _Egypt_ ..................... **51 D12**  23  0N  32 30 E
Nässjö, _Sweden_ .............. **9 H16**  57 39N  14 42 E
Nastapoka →, _Canada_ ......... **72 A4**   56 55N  76 33W
Nastapoka, Is., _Canada_ ...... **72 A4**   56 55N  76 50W
Nata, _Botswana_ .............. **56 C4**   20 12S  26 12 E
Nata →, _Botswana_ ............ **56 C4**   20 14S  26 10 E
Natal, _Brazil_ ............... **93 E11**   5 47S  35 13W
Natal, _Indonesia_ ............ **36 D1**    0 35N  99  7 E
Natal, _S. Africa_ ............ **53 K6**   28 30S  30 30 E
Natal Drakensberg △, _S. Africa_ **57 D4**   29 27S  29 30 E
Naţanz, _Iran_ ................ **45 C6**   33 30N  51 55 E
Natashquan, _Canada_ .......... **73 B7**   50 14N  61 46W
Natashquan →, _Canada_ ........ **73 B7**   50  7N  61 50W
Natchez, _U.S.A._ ............. **81 K9**   31 34N  91 24W
Natchitoches, _U.S.A._ ........ **81 K8**   31 46N  93  5W
Nathalia, _Australia_ ......... **63 F4**   36  1S 145 13 E
Nathdwara, _India_ ............ **42 G5**   24 55N  73 50 E
Nati, Pta., _Spain_ ........... **24 A10**  40  3N   3 50 E
Natimuk, _Australia_ .......... **63 F3**   36 42S 142  0 E
Nation →, _Canada_ ............ **70 B4**   55 30N 123 32W
National City, _U.S.A._ ....... **79 N9**   32 41N 117  6W
Natitingou, _Benin_ ........... **50 F6**   10 20N   1 26 E
Natividad, I., _Mexico_ ....... **86 B1**   27 50N 115 10W
Natkyizin, _Burma_ ............ **38 E1**   14 57N  97 59 E
Natron, L., _Tanzania_ ........ **54 C4**    2 20S  36  0 E
Natrona Heights, _U.S.A._ ..... **84 F5**   40 37N  79 44W
Natukanaoka Pan, _Namibia_ .... **56 B2**   18 40S  15 45 E
Natuna Besar, Kepulauan,
  _Indonesia_ ................. **36 D3**    4  0N 108 15 E
Natuna Is. = Natuna Besar,
  Kepulauan, _Indonesia_ ...... **36 D3**    4  0N 108 15 E
Natuna Selatan, Kepulauan,
  _Indonesia_ ................. **36 D3**    2 45N 109  0 E
Natural Bridge, _U.S.A._ ...... **85 B9**   44 5N  75 30W
Natural Bridges △, _U.S.A._ ... **77 H8**   37 36N 110  1W
Naturaliste, C., _Australia_ .. **63 G4**   40 50S 148 15 E
Nau Qala, _Afghan._ ........... **42 B3**   34  5N  68  5 E
Naugatuck, _U.S.A._ ........... **85 E11**  41 30N  73  3W
Naujaat = Repulse Bay, _Canada_ **69 B11**  66 30N  86 30W
Naumburg, _Germany_ ........... **16 C6**   51  9N  11 47 E
Nā'ūr at Tunayb, _Jordan_ ..... **46 D4**   31 48N  35 57 E
Nauru ■, _Pac. Oc._ ........... **64 H8**    1  0S 166  0 E
Naushahra = Nowshera, _Pakistan_ **40 C8**   34  0N  72  0 E
Naushahro, _Pakistan_ ......... **42 F3**   26 50N  68  7 E
Naushon I., _U.S.A._ .......... **85 E14**  41 29N  70 45W
Nauta, _Peru_ ................. **92 D4**    4 31S  73 35W
Nautanwa, _India_ ............. **41 F13**  27 20N  83 25 E
Naute △, _Namibia_ ............ **56 D2**   26 55S  17 57 E
Nautla, _Mexico_ .............. **87 C5**   20  20N  96 50W
Nava, _Mexico_ ................ **86 B4**   28 25N 100 46W
Navadwip, _India_ ............. **43 H13**  23 34N  88 20 E
Navahrudak, _Belarus_ ......... **17 B13**  53 40N  25 50 E
Navajo Reservoir, _U.S.A._ .... **77 H10**  36 48N 107 36W
Navalmoral de la Mata, _Spain_  **21 C3**   39 52N   5 33W
Navan = An Uaimh, _Ireland_ ... **10 C5**   53 39N   6 41W
Navarino, I., _Chile_ ......... **96 H3**   55  0S  67 40W
Navarra □, _Spain_ ............ **21 A5**   42 40N   1 40W
Navarro →, _U.S.A._ ........... **78 F3**   39 11N 123 45W
Navassa I., _W. Indies_ ....... **89 C5**   18 30N  75  0W
Naver →, _U.K._ ............... **11 C4**   58 32N   4  14W
Navibandar, _India_ ........... **42 J3**   21 26N  69 48 E
Navidad, _Chile_ .............. **94 C1**   33 57S  71 50W
Navirai, _Brazil_ ............. **95 A5**   23  8S  54 13W
Navlakhi, _India_ ............. **42 H4**   22 58N  70 28 E
Năvodari, _Romania_ ........... **17 F15**  44 19N  28 36 E
Navoi = Nawoiy, _Uzbekistan_ .. **28 E7**   40  9N  65 22 E
Navojoa, _Mexico_ ............. **86 B3**   27  0N 109 30W
Navolato, _Mexico_ ............ **86 C3**   24 47N 107 42W
Năvpaktos, _Greece_ ........... **23 E9**   38 24N  21 50 E
Năvplion, _Greece_ ............ **23 F10**  37 33N  22 50 E
Navsari, _India_ .............. **40 J8**   20 57N  72 59 E
Nawa Kot, _Pakistan_ .......... **42 E4**   28 21N  71 24 E
Nawab Khan, _Pakistan_ ........ **42 D3**   30 17N  69 12 E
Nawabganj, Ut. P., _India_ .... **43 F9**   26 56N  81 14 E
Nawabganj, Ut. P., _India_ .... **43 E8**   28 32N  79 40 E
Nawabshah, _Pakistan_ ......... **42 F3**   26 15N  68 25 E
Nawada, _India_ ............... **43 G11**  24 50N  85 33 E
Nawakot, _Nepal_ .............. **43 F11**  27 55N  85 10 E
Nawalgarh, _India_ ............ **42 F6**   27 50N  75 15 E
Nawanshahr, _India_ ........... **43 C6**   32 33N  74 48 E
Nawar, Dasht-i-, _Afghan._ .... **40 C6**   33 52N  67 53 E
Nawoiy, _Uzbekistan_ .......... **28 E7**   40  9N  65 22 E
Naxçıvan, _Azerbaijan_ ........ **19 G8**   39 12N  45 15 E
Naxçıvan □, _Azerbaijan_ ...... **19 G8**   39 25N  45 26 E
Náxos, _Greece_ ............... **23 F11**  37  8N  25 25 E

Nay, Mui, _Vietnam_ ........... **36 B3**   12 55N 109 23 E
Nāy Band, Būshehr, _Iran_ ..... **45 E7**   27 20N  52 40 E
Nāy Band, Khorāsān, _Iran_ .... **45 C8**   32 20N  57 34 E
Nayakhan, _Russia_ ............ **29 C16**  61 56N 159  0 E
Nayarit □, _Mexico_ ........... **86 C4**   22  0N 105  0W
Nayoro, _Japan_ ............... **30 B11**  44 21N 142 28 E
Nayyāl, W. →, _Si. Arabia_ .... **44 D3**   28 35N  39  4 E
Nazaré, _Brazil_ .............. **93 F11**  13  2S  39  0W
Nazareth = Nazerat, _Israel_ .. **46 C4**   32 42N  35 17 E
Nazareth, _U.S.A._ ............ **85 F9**   40 44N  75 19W
Nazas, _Mexico_ ............... **86 B4**   25 10N 104  6W
Nazas →, _Mexico_ ............. **86 B4**   25 35N 103 25W
Nazca, _Peru_ ................. **92 F4**   14 50S  74 57W
Naze, The, _U.K._ ............. **13 F9**   51 53N   1 18 E
Nazerat, _Israel_ ............. **46 C4**   32 42N  35 17 E
Nāzik, _Iran_ ................. **44 B5**   39  1N  45  4 E
Nazilli, _Turkey_ ............. **23 F13**  37 55N  28 15 E
Nazko, _Canada_ ............... **70 C4**   53  1N 123 37W
Nazko →, _Canada_ ............. **70 C4**   53  7N 123 34W
Nazret, _Ethiopia_ ............ **47 F2**    8 32N  39 22 E
Nazwa, _Oman_ ................. **47 C6**   22 56N  57 32 E
Nchanga, _Zambia_ ............. **55 E2**   12 30S  27 49 E
Ncheu, _Malawi_ ............... **55 E3**   14 50S  34 47 E
Ndala, _Tanzania_ ............. **54 C3**    4 45S  33 15 E
Ndalatando, _Angola_ .......... **52 F2**    9 12S  14 48 E
Ndareda, _Tanzania_ ........... **54 C4**    4 12S  35 30 E
Ndélé, _C.A.R._ ............... **52 C4**    8 25N  20 36 E
Ndjamena, _Chad_ .............. **51 F8**   12 10N  14 59 E
Ndola, _Zambia_ ............... **55 E2**   13  0S  28 34 E
Ndoto Mts., _Kenya_ ........... **54 B4**    2  0N  37  0 E
Nduguti, _Tanzania_ ........... **54 C3**    4 18S  34 41 E
Ndumu □, S. Africa_ ........... **57 D5**   26 52S  32 15 E
Neagh, Lough, _U.K._ .......... **10 B5**   54 37N   6 25W
Neah Bay, _U.S.A._ ............ **78 B2**   48 22N 124 37W
Neale, L., _Australia_ ........ **60 D5**   24 15S 130  0 E
Neales, The →, _Australia_ .... **63 D2**   28  8S 136 47 E
Neápolis, _Greece_ ............ **25 D7**   35 15N  25 37 E
Near Is., _U.S.A._ ............ **68 C1**   52 30N 174  0 E
Neath, _U.K._ ................. **13 F4**   51 39N   3 48W
Neath Port Talbot □, _U.K._ ... **13 F4**   51 42N   3 45W
Nebine Cr. →, _Australia_ ..... **63 D4**   29 27S 146 56 E
Nebitdag, _Turkmenistan_ ...... **19 G9**   39 30N  54 22 E
Nebo, _Australia_ ............. **62 C4**   21 42S 148 42 E
Nebraska □, _U.S.A._ .......... **80 E5**   41 30N  99 30W
Nebraska City, _U.S.A._ ....... **80 E7**   40 41N  95 52W
Nébrodi, Monti, _Italy_ ....... **22 F6**   37 54N  14 35 E
Necedah, _U.S.A._ ............. **80 C9**   44  2N  90  4W
Nechako →, _Canada_ ........... **70 C4**   53 55N 122 42W
Neches →, _U.S.A._ ............ **81 L8**   29 58N  93 51W
Neckar →, _Germany_ ........... **16 D5**   49 27N   8 29 E
Necochea, _Argentina_ ......... **94 D4**   38 30S  58 50W
Needles, _Canada_ ............. **70 D5**   49 53N 118  7W
Needles, _U.S.A._ ............. **79 L12**  34 51N 114 37W
Needles, The, _U.K._ .......... **13 G6**   50 39N   1 35W
Ñeembucú □, _Paraguay_ ........ **94 B4**   27  0S  58  0W
Neemuch = Nimach, _India_ ..... **42 G6**   24 30N  74 56 E
Neenah, _U.S.A._ .............. **82 C1**   44 11N  88 28W
Neepawa, _Canada_ ............. **71 C9**   50 15N  99 30W
Neftçala, _Azerbaijan_ ........ **19 G8**   39 19N  49 12 E
Neftekumsk, _Russia_ .......... **19 F7**   44 46N  44 50 E
Nefyn, _U.K._ ................. **12 E3**   52 56N   4 31W
Negapatam = Nagappattinam,
  _India_ ..................... **40 P11**  10 46N  79 51 E
Negara, _Indonesia_ ........... **37 J17**   8 22S 114 37 E
Negaunee, _U.S.A._ ............ **82 B2**   46 30N  87 36W
Negele, _Ethiopia_ ............ **47 F2**    5 20N  39 36 E
Negev Desert = Hanegev, _Israel_ **46 E4**  30 50N  35  0 E
Negombo, _Sri Lanka_ .......... **40 R11**   7 12N  79 50 E
Negotin, _Serbia & M._ ........ **23 B10**  44 16N  22 37 E
Negra, Pta., _Peru_ ........... **92 E2**    6  6S  81 10W
Negrais, C. = Maudin Sun, _Burma_ **41 M19** 16  0N  94 30 E
Negril, _Jamaica_ ............. **88 a**    18 22N  78 20W
Negro →, _Argentina_ .......... **96 E4**   41  2S  62 47W
Negro →, _Brazil_ ............. **92 D7**    3  0S  60  0W
Negro →, _Uruguay_ ............ **95 C4**   33 24S  58 22W
Negros, _Phil._ ............... **37 C6**    9 30N 122 40 E
Neguac, _Canada_ ............. **73 C6**   47 15N  65  5W
Nehalem →, _U.S.A._ ........... **78 E3**   45 40N 123 56W
Nehāvand, _Iran_ .............. **45 C6**   35 56N  49 31 E
Nehbandān, _Iran_ ............. **45 D9**   31 35N  60  5 E
Nei Monggol Zizhiqu □, _China_  **34 D7**   42  0N 112  0 E
Neijiang, _China_ ............. **32 D5**   29 35N 104 55 E
Neilingding Dao, _China_ ...... **33 G10**  22 25N 113 48 E
Neillsville, _U.S.A._ ......... **80 C9**   44 34N  90 36W
Neilton, _U.S.A._ ............. **78 C2**   47 25N 123 53W
Neiqiu, _China_ ............... **34 F8**   37 15N 114 30 E
Neiva, _Colombia_ ............. **92 C3**    2 56N  75 18W
Neixiang, _China_ ............. **34 H6**   33 10N 111 52 E
Nejanilini L., _Canada_ ....... **71 B9**   59 33N  97 48W
Nejd = Najd, _Si. Arabia_ ..... **47 B3**   26 30N  42  0 E
Nekā, _Iran_ .................. **45 B7**   36 39N  53 19 E
Nekemte, _Ethiopia_ ........... **47 F2**    9  4N  36 30 E
Neksø, _Denmark_ .............. **9 J16**  55  4N  15  8 E
Nelia, _Australia_ ............ **62 C3**   20 39S 142 12 E
Neligh, _U.S.A._ .............. **80 D5**   42 8N  98  2W
Nelkan, _Russia_ .............. **29 D14**  57 40N 136  4 E
Nellore, _India_ .............. **40 M11**  14 27N  79 59 E
Nelson, _Canada_ .............. **70 D5**   49 30N 117 20W
Nelson, _N.Z._ ................ **59 J4**   41 18S 173 16 E
Nelson, _U.K._ ................ **12 D5**   53 50N   2 13W
Nelson, Ariz., _U.S.A._ ....... **77 J7**   35 31N 113 19W
Nelson, Nev., _U.S.A._ ........ **79 K12**  35 42N 114 50W
Nelson →, _Canada_ ............ **71 C9**   54 33N  98  2W
Nelson, C., _Australia_ ....... **63 F3**   38 26S 141 32 E
Nelson, Estrecho, _Chile_ ..... **96 G2**   51 30S  75  0W
Nelson Forks, _Canada_ ........ **70 B4**   59 30N 124  0W
Nelson House, _Canada_ ........ **71 B9**   55 47N  98 51W
Nelson L., _Canada_ ........... **71 B8**   55 48N 100  7W
Nelson Lakes △, _N.Z._ ........ **59 J4**   41 55S 172 44 E
Nelspoort, _S. Africa_ ........ **56 E3**   32  7S  23  0 E
Nelspruit, _S. Africa_ ........ **57 D5**   25 29S  30 59 E
Néma, _Mauritania_ ............ **50 E4**   16 40N   7 15W
Neman = Nemunas →, _Lithuania_ **9 J19**  55 25N  21 10 E
Neman, _Russia_ .............. **9 J20**  55 2N  22 2 E
Nemeiben L., _Canada_ ......... **71 B7**   55 20N 105 20W
Nemiscau, _Canada_ ............ **72 B4**   51 25N  76 54W
Nemiscau, L., _Canada_ ........ **72 B4**   51 25N  76 40W
Nemunas →, _Lithuania_ ........ **9 J19**  55 25N  21 10 E
Nemuro, _Japan_ ............... **30 C12**  43 20N 145 35 E
Nemuro-Kaikyō, _Japan_ ........ **30 C12**  43 30N 145 30 E
Nen Jiang →, _China_ .......... **35 B13**  45 28N 124 30 E
Nenagh, _Ireland_ ............. **10 D3**   52 52N   8 11W
Nenasi, _Malaysia_ ............ **39 L4**    3  9N 103 23 E
Nene →, _U.K._ ................ **13 E8**   52 49N   0 11 E
Nenjiang, _China_ ............. **33 B7**   49 10N 125 10 E
Neno, _Malawi_ ................ **55 F3**   15 25S  34 40 E
Neodesha, _U.S.A._ ............ **81 G7**   37 25N  95 41W
Neosho, _U.S.A._ .............. **81 G7**   36 52N  94 22W

Neosho →, U.S.A. 81 H7 36 48N 95 18W
Nepal ■, Asia 43 F11 28 0N 84 30 E
Nepalganj, Nepal 43 E9 28 5N 81 40 E
Nepalganj Road, India 43 E9 28 1N 81 41 E
Nephi, U.S.A. 76 G8 39 43N 111 50W
Nephin, Ireland 10 B2 54 1N 9 22W
Neptune, U.S.A. 85 F10 40 13N 74 2W
Nerang, Australia 63 D5 27 58S 153 20 E
Nerchinsk, Russia 29 D12 52 0N 116 39 E
Néret, L., Canada 73 B5 54 45N 70 44W
Neretva →, Croatia 23 C7 43 1N 17 27 E
Neringa, Lithuania 9 J19 55 20N 21 5 E
Neris →, Lithuania 9 J21 55 8N 24 16 E
Neryungri, Russia 29 D13 57 38N 124 28 E
Nescopeck, U.S.A. 85 E8 41 3N 76 12W
Ness, L., U.K. 11 D4 57 15N 4 32W
Ness City, U.S.A. 80 F5 38 27N 99 54W
Nesterov, Ukraine 17 C12 50 4N 23 58 E
Nesvizh = Nyasvizh, Belarus 17 B14 53 14N 26 38 E
Netanya, Israel 46 C3 32 20N 34 51 E
Netarhat, India 43 H11 23 29N 84 16 E
Nete →, Belgium 15 C4 51 7N 4 14 E
Netherdale, Australia 62 K6 21 10S 148 33 E
Netherlands ■, Europe 15 C5 52 0N 5 30 E
Netherlands Antilles ☑, W. Indies 92 A5 12 15N 69 0W
Netrang, India 42 J5 21 39N 73 21 E
Nettilling L., Canada 69 B12 66 30N 71 0W
Netzahualcoyotl, Presa, Mexico 87 D6 17 10N 93 30W
Neubrandenburg, Germany 16 B7 53 33N 13 15 E
Neuchâtel, Switz. 20 C7 47 0N 6 55 E
Neuchâtel, Lac de, Switz. 20 C7 46 53N 6 50 E
Neufchâteau, Belgium 15 E5 49 50N 5 25 E
Neumünster, Germany 16 A5 54 4N 9 58 E
Neunkirchen, Germany 16 D4 49 20N 7 9 E
Neuquén, Argentina 96 D3 38 55S 68 0W
Neuquén □, Argentina 94 D2 38 0S 69 50W
Neuruppin, Germany 16 B7 52 55N 12 48 E
Neuse →, U.S.A. 83 H7 35 6N 76 29W
Neusiedler See, Austria 17 E9 47 50N 16 47 E
Neustrelitz, Germany 16 B7 53 21N 13 4 E
Neva →, Russia 18 C5 59 50N 30 30 E
Nevada, Iowa, U.S.A. 80 D8 42 1N 93 27W
Nevada, Mo., U.S.A. 81 G7 37 51N 94 22W
Nevada □, U.S.A. 76 G5 39 0N 117 0W
Nevada City, U.S.A. 78 F6 39 16N 121 1W
Nevado, Cerro, Argentina 94 D2 35 30S 68 32W
Nevado de Colima = Volcán de Colima △, Mexico 86 D4 19 30N 103 40W
Nevado de Tres Cruces △, Chile 94 B2 27 13S 69 5W
Nevel, Russia 18 C4 56 0N 29 55 E
Nevers, France 20 C5 47 0N 3 9 E
Nevertire, Australia 63 E4 31 50S 147 44 E
Neville, Canada 71 D7 49 58N 107 39W
Nevinnomyssk, Russia 19 F7 44 40N 42 0 E
Nevis, St. Kitts & Nevis 89 C7 17 0N 62 30W
Nevşehir, Turkey 44 B2 38 33N 34 40 E
Nevyansk, Russia 18 C11 57 30N 60 13 E
New →, U.S.A. 82 F5 38 10N 81 12W
New Aiyansh, Canada 70 B3 55 12N 129 4W
New Albany, Ind., U.S.A. 82 F3 38 18N 85 49W
New Albany, Miss., U.S.A. 81 H10 34 29N 89 0W
New Albany, Pa., U.S.A. 85 E8 41 36N 76 27W
New Amsterdam, Guyana 92 B7 6 15N 57 36W
New Angledool, Australia 63 D4 29 5S 147 55 E
New Baltimore, U.S.A. 84 D2 42 41N 82 44W
New Bedford, U.S.A. 85 E14 41 38N 70 56W
New Berlin, N.Y., U.S.A. 85 D9 42 37N 75 20W
New Berlin, Pa., U.S.A. 84 F8 40 50N 76 57W
New Bern, U.S.A. 83 H7 35 7N 77 3W
New Bethlehem, U.S.A. 84 F5 41 0N 79 20W
New Bloomfield, U.S.A. 84 F7 40 25N 77 11W
New Boston, U.S.A. 81 J7 33 28N 94 25W
New Braunfels, U.S.A. 81 L5 29 42N 98 8W
New Brighton, N.Z. 59 K4 43 29S 172 43 E
New Brighton, U.S.A. 84 F4 40 42N 80 19W
New Britain, Papua N. G. 64 H7 5 50S 150 20 E
New Britain, U.S.A. 85 E12 41 40N 72 47W
New Brunswick, U.S.A. 85 F10 40 30N 74 27W
New Brunswick □, Canada 73 C6 46 50N 66 30W
New Caledonia ☑, Pac. Oc. 64 K8 21 0S 165 0 E
New Castile = Castilla-La Mancha □, Spain 21 C4 39 30N 3 30W
New Castle, Ind., U.S.A. 82 F3 39 55N 85 22W
New Castle, Pa., U.S.A. 84 F4 41 0N 80 21W
New City, U.S.A. 85 E11 41 9N 73 59W
New Concord, U.S.A. 84 G3 39 59N 81 54W
New Cumberland, U.S.A. 84 F4 40 30N 80 36W
New Cuyama, U.S.A. 79 L7 34 57N 119 38W
New Delhi, India 42 E7 28 37N 77 13 E
New Denver, Canada 70 D5 50 0N 117 25W
New Don Pedro Reservoir, U.S.A. 78 H6 37 43N 120 24W
New England, U.S.A. 75 B12 43 0N 71 0W
New England, N. Dak., U.S.A. 80 B3 46 32N 102 52W
New England Ra., Australia 63 E5 30 20S 151 45 E
New Forest, U.K. 13 G6 50 53N 1 34W
New Galloway, U.K. 11 F4 55 5N 4 9W
New Glasgow, Canada 73 C7 45 35N 62 36W
New Guinea, Oceania 26 K17 4 0S 136 0 E
New Hamburg, Canada 84 C4 43 23N 80 42W
New Hampshire □, U.S.A. 85 C13 44 0N 71 30W
New Hampton, U.S.A. 80 D8 43 3N 92 19W
New Hanover, S. Africa 57 D5 29 22S 30 31 E
New Hartford, U.S.A. 85 C9 43 4N 75 18W
New Haven, Conn., U.S.A. 85 E12 41 18N 72 55W
New Haven, Mich., U.S.A. 84 D2 42 44N 82 48W
New Hazelton, Canada 70 B3 55 20N 127 30W
New Hebrides = Vanuatu ■, Pac. Oc. 64 J8 15 0S 168 0 E
New Holland, U.S.A. 85 F8 40 6N 76 5W
New Iberia, U.S.A. 81 K9 30 1N 91 49W
New Ireland, Papua N. G. 64 H7 3 20S 151 50 E
New Jersey □, U.S.A. 82 E8 40 0N 74 30W
New Kensington, U.S.A. 84 F5 40 34N 79 46W
New Lexington, U.S.A. 82 F4 39 43N 82 13W
New Liskeard, Canada 72 C4 47 31N 79 41W
New London, Conn., U.S.A. 85 E12 41 22N 72 6W
New London, Ohio, U.S.A. 84 E2 41 5N 82 24W
New London, Wis., U.S.A. 80 C10 44 23N 88 45W
New Madrid, U.S.A. 81 G10 36 36N 89 32W
New Martinsville, U.S.A. 84 F5 39 39N 80 52W
New Meadows, U.S.A. 76 D5 44 58N 116 18W
New Melones, U.S.A. 78 H6 37 57N 120 31W
New Mexico □, U.S.A. 77 J10 34 30N 106 0W
New Milford, Conn., U.S.A. 85 E11 41 35N 73 25W
New Milford, Pa., U.S.A. 85 E9 41 52N 75 44W
New Norcia, Australia 61 F2 30 57S 116 13 E
New Norfolk, Australia 63 G4 42 46S 147 2 E
New Orleans, U.S.A. 81 L9 29 58N 90 4W

New Philadelphia, U.S.A. 84 F3 40 30N 81 27W
New Plymouth, N.Z. 59 H5 39 4S 174 5 E
New Plymouth, U.S.A. 76 E5 43 58N 116 49W
New Port Richey, U.S.A. 83 L4 28 16N 82 43W
New Providence, Bahamas 88 A4 25 25N 78 35W
New Quay, U.K. 13 E3 52 13N 4 21W
New Radnor, U.K. 13 E4 52 15N 3 9W
New Richmond, Canada 73 C6 48 15N 65 45W
New Richmond, U.S.A. 80 C8 45 7N 92 32W
New River Gorge △, U.S.A. 82 G5 37 53N 81 5W
New Roads, U.S.A. 81 K9 30 42N 91 26W
New Rochelle, U.S.A. 85 F11 40 55N 73 47W
New Rockford, U.S.A. 80 B5 47 41N 99 8W
New Romney, U.K. 13 G8 50 59N 0 57 E
New Ross, Ireland 10 D5 52 23N 6 57W
New Scone = Scone, U.K. 11 E5 56 25N 3 24W
New Siberian I. = Novaya Sibir, Ostrov, Russia 29 B16 75 10N 150 0 E
New Siberian Is. = Novosibirskiye Ostrova, Russia 29 B15 75 0N 142 0 E
New Smyrna Beach, U.S.A. 83 L5 29 1N 80 56W
New South Wales □, Australia 63 E4 33 0S 146 0 E
New Tecumseh, Canada 84 B5 44 9N 79 52W
New Town, U.S.A. 80 B3 47 59N 102 30W
New Tredegar, U.K. 13 F4 51 44N 3 16W
New Ulm, U.S.A. 80 C7 44 19N 94 28W
New Waterford, Canada 73 C7 46 13N 60 4W
New-Wes-Valley, Canada 73 C9 49 8N 53 36W
New Westminster, Canada 78 A4 49 13N 122 55W
New York, U.S.A. 85 F11 40 45N 74 0W
New York □, U.S.A. 85 D9 43 0N 75 0W
New York J.F. Kennedy International ✕ (JFK), U.S.A. 85 F11 40 38N 73 47W
New York Mts., U.S.A. 77 J6 35 0N 115 20W
New Zealand ■, Oceania 59 J6 40 0S 176 0 E
Newaj →, India 42 G7 24 24N 76 49 E
Newala, Tanzania 55 E4 10 58S 39 18 E
Newark, Del., U.S.A. 82 F8 39 41N 75 46W
Newark, N.J., U.S.A. 85 F10 40 44N 74 10W
Newark, N.Y., U.S.A. 84 C7 43 3N 77 6W
Newark, Ohio, U.S.A. 84 F2 40 3N 82 24W
Newark International ✕ (EWR), U.S.A. 85 F10 40 42N 74 10W
Newark-on-Trent, U.K. 12 D7 53 5N 0 48W
Newark Valley, U.S.A. 85 D8 42 14N 76 11W
Newberg, U.S.A. 76 D2 45 18N 122 58W
Newberry, Mich., U.S.A. 82 B3 46 21N 85 30W
Newberry, S.C., U.S.A. 83 H5 34 17N 81 37W
Newberry △, U.S.A. 76 E2 43 42N 122 43W
Newberry Springs, U.S.A. 79 L10 34 50N 116 41W
Newboro L., Canada 85 B8 44 38N 76 20W
Newbridge = Droichead Nua, Ireland 10 C5 53 11N 6 48W
Newburgh, Canada 84 B8 44 19N 76 52W
Newburgh, U.S.A. 85 E10 41 30N 74 1W
Newbury, U.K. 13 F6 51 24N 1 20W
Newbury, N.H., U.S.A. 85 B12 43 19N 72 3W
Newbury, Vt., U.S.A. 85 B12 44 5N 72 4W
Newburyport, U.S.A. 83 D10 42 49N 70 53W
Newcastle, Australia 63 E5 33 0S 151 46 E
Newcastle, N.B., Canada 73 C6 47 1N 65 38W
Newcastle, Ont., Canada 72 D4 43 55N 78 35W
Newcastle, S. Africa 57 D4 27 45S 29 58 E
Newcastle, U.K. 10 B6 54 13N 5 54W
Newcastle, Calif., U.S.A. 78 G5 38 53N 121 8W
Newcastle, Wyo., U.S.A. 80 D2 43 50N 104 11W
Newcastle Emlyn, U.K. 13 E3 52 2N 4 28W
Newcastle Ra., Australia 60 C5 15 45S 130 15 E
Newcastle-under-Lyme, U.K. 12 D5 53 1N 2 14W
Newcastle-upon-Tyne, U.K. 12 C6 54 58N 1 36W
Newcastle Waters, Australia 62 B1 17 30S 133 28 E
Newcastle West, Ireland 10 D2 52 27N 9 3W
Newcomb, U.S.A. 85 C10 43 58N 74 10W
Newcomerstown, U.S.A. 84 F3 40 16N 81 36W
Newdegate, Australia 61 F2 33 6S 119 0 E
Newell, Australia 62 B4 16 20S 145 16 E
Newell, U.S.A. 80 C3 44 43N 103 25W
Newfane, U.S.A. 84 C6 43 17N 78 43W
Newfield, U.S.A. 85 D8 42 18N 76 33W
Newfound L., U.S.A. 85 C13 43 40N 71 47W
Newfoundland, Canada 73 C8 49 0N 55 0W
Newfoundland, U.S.A. 85 E9 41 18N 75 19W
Newfoundland & Labrador □, Canada 73 B8 53 0N 58 0W
Newhall, U.S.A. 79 L8 34 23N 118 32W
Newhaven, U.K. 13 G8 50 47N 0 3 E
Newkirk, U.S.A. 81 G6 36 53N 97 3W
Newlyn, U.K. 13 G2 50 6N 5 34W
Newman, Australia 60 D2 23 18S 119 45 E
Newman, U.S.A. 78 H5 37 19N 121 1W
Newmarket, Canada 84 B5 44 3N 79 28W
Newmarket, Ireland 10 D2 52 13N 9 0W
Newmarket, U.K. 13 E8 52 15N 0 25 E
Newmarket, U.S.A. 85 C14 43 4N 70 56W
Newnan, U.S.A. 83 J3 33 23N 84 48W
Newport, Ireland 10 C2 53 53N 9 33W
Newport, I. of W., U.K. 13 G6 50 42N 1 17W
Newport, Newp., U.K. 13 F5 51 35N 3 0W
Newport, Ark., U.S.A. 81 H9 35 37N 91 16W
Newport, Ky., U.S.A. 82 F3 39 5N 84 30W
Newport, N.H., U.S.A. 85 C12 43 22N 72 10W
Newport, N.Y., U.S.A. 85 C9 43 11N 75 1W
Newport, Oreg., U.S.A. 76 D1 44 39N 124 3W
Newport, Pa., U.S.A. 84 F7 40 29N 77 8W
Newport, R.I., U.S.A. 85 E13 41 29N 71 19W
Newport, Tenn., U.S.A. 83 H4 35 58N 83 11W
Newport, Vt., U.S.A. 85 B12 44 56N 72 13W
Newport, Wash., U.S.A. 76 B5 48 11N 117 3W
Newport □, U.K. 13 F4 51 33N 3 1W
Newport Beach, U.S.A. 79 M9 33 37N 117 56W
Newport News, U.S.A. 82 G7 36 59N 76 25W
Newport Pagnell, U.K. 13 E7 52 5N 0 43W
Newquay, U.K. 13 G2 50 25N 5 6W
Newry, U.K. 10 B5 54 11N 6 21W
Newton, Ill., U.S.A. 80 F10 38 59N 88 10W
Newton, Iowa, U.S.A. 80 E8 41 42N 93 3W
Newton, Kans., U.S.A. 81 F6 38 3N 97 21W
Newton, Mass., U.S.A. 85 D13 42 21N 71 12W
Newton, Miss., U.S.A. 81 J10 32 19N 89 10W
Newton, N.C., U.S.A. 83 H5 35 40N 81 13W
Newton, N.J., U.S.A. 85 E10 41 3N 74 45W
Newton, Tex., U.S.A. 81 K8 30 51N 93 46W
Newton Abbot, U.K. 13 G4 50 32N 3 37W
Newton Aycliffe, U.K. 12 C6 54 37N 1 34W
Newton Falls, U.S.A. 84 E4 41 11N 80 59W
Newton Stewart, U.K. 11 G4 54 57N 4 30W
Newtonmore, U.K. 11 D4 57 4N 4 8W

Newtown, U.K. 13 E4 52 31N 3 19W
Newtownabbey, U.K. 10 B6 54 40N 5 56W
Newtownards, U.K. 10 B6 54 36N 5 42W
Newtownbarry = Bunclody, Ireland 10 D5 52 39N 6 40W
Newtownstewart, U.K. 10 B4 54 43N 7 23W
Newville, U.S.A. 84 F7 40 10N 77 24W
Neya, Russia 18 C7 58 21N 43 49 E
Neyrīz, Iran 45 D7 29 15N 54 19 E
Neyshābūr, Iran 45 B8 36 10N 58 50 E
Nezhin = Nizhyn, Ukraine 19 D5 51 5N 31 55 E
Nezperce, U.S.A. 76 C5 46 14N 116 14W
Ngabang, Indonesia 36 D3 0 23N 109 55 E
Ngabordamlu, Tanjung, Indonesia 37 F8 6 56S 134 11 E
N'Gage, Angola 52 F3 7 46S 15 16 E
Ngami Depression, Botswana 56 C3 20 30S 22 46 E
Ngamo, Zimbabwe 55 F2 19 3S 27 32 E
Nganglong Kangri, China 41 C12 33 0N 81 0 E
Ngao, Thailand 38 C2 18 46N 99 59 E
Ngaoundéré, Cameroon 52 C2 7 15N 13 35 E
Ngapara, N.Z. 59 L3 44 57S 170 46 E
Ngara, Tanzania 54 C3 2 29S 30 40 E
Ngawi, Indonesia 37 G14 7 24S 111 26 E
Nghia Lo, Vietnam 38 B5 21 33N 104 28 E
Ngoma, Malawi 55 E3 13 8S 33 45 E
Ngomahura, Zimbabwe 55 G3 20 26S 30 43 E
Ngomba, Tanzania 55 D3 8 20S 32 53 E
Ngoring Hu, China 32 C4 34 55N 97 5 E
Ngorongoro, Tanzania 54 C4 3 11S 35 32 E
Ngorongoro △, Tanzania 54 C4 2 40S 35 30 E
Ngozi, Burundi 54 C2 2 54S 29 50 E
Ngudu, Tanzania 54 C3 2 58S 33 25 E
Nguigmi, Niger 51 F8 14 20N 13 20 E
Nguiu, Australia 60 B5 11 46S 130 38 E
Ngukurr, Australia 62 A1 14 44S 134 44 E
Ngunga, Tanzania 54 C3 3 37S 33 37 E
Nguru, Nigeria 51 F8 12 56N 10 29 E
Nguru Mts., Tanzania 54 D4 6 0S 37 30 E
Ngusi, Malawi 55 E3 14 0S 34 50 E
Nguyen Binh, Vietnam 38 A5 22 39N 105 56 E
Nha Trang, Vietnam 39 F7 12 16N 109 10 E
Nhacoongo, Mozam. 57 C6 24 18S 35 14 E
Nhamaabué, Mozam. 55 F4 17 25S 35 5 E
Nhamundá →, Brazil 93 D7 2 12S 56 41W
Nhangulaze, L., Mozam. 57 C5 24 0S 34 30 E
Nhill, Australia 63 F3 36 18S 141 40 E
Nho Quan, Vietnam 38 B5 20 18N 105 45 E
Nhulunbuy, Australia 62 A2 12 10S 137 20 E
Nia-nia, Dem. Rep. of the Congo 54 B2 1 30N 27 40 E
Niagara Falls, Canada 84 C5 43 7N 79 5W
Niagara Falls, U.S.A. 84 C6 43 5N 79 4W
Niagara-on-the-Lake, Canada 84 C5 43 15N 79 4W
Niah, Malaysia 36 D4 3 58N 113 46 E
Niamey, Niger 50 F6 13 27N 2 6 E
Niangara, Dem. Rep. of the Congo 54 B2 3 42N 27 50 E
Niantic, U.S.A. 85 E12 41 20N 72 11W
Nias, Indonesia 36 D1 1 0N 97 30 E
Niassa □, Mozam. 55 E4 12 4S 36 57 E
Niassa △, Mozam. 55 E4 13 30S 36 0 E
Nibāk, Si. Arabia 45 E7 24 25N 50 50 E
Nicaragua ■, Cent. Amer. 88 D2 11 40N 85 30W
Nicaragua, L. de, Nic. 88 D2 12 0N 85 30W
Nicastro, Italy 22 E7 38 59N 16 19 E
Nice, France 20 E7 43 42N 7 14 E
Niceville, U.S.A. 83 K2 30 31N 86 30W
Nichicun, L., Canada 73 B5 53 5N 71 0W
Nichinan, Japan 31 J5 31 38N 131 23 E
Nicholasville, U.S.A. 82 G3 37 53N 84 34W
Nichols, U.S.A. 85 D8 42 1N 76 22W
Nicholson, Australia 60 C4 18 2S 128 54 E
Nicholson, U.S.A. 85 E9 41 37N 75 47W
Nicholson →, Australia 62 B2 17 31S 139 36 E
Nicholson L., Canada 71 A8 62 40N 102 40W
Nicholson Ra., Australia 61 E2 27 15S 116 45 E
Nicholville, U.S.A. 85 B10 44 41N 74 39W
Nicobar Is., Ind. Oc. 27 J13 9 0N 93 30 E
Nicola, Canada 70 C4 50 12N 120 40W
Nicolls Town, Bahamas 88 A4 25 8N 78 0W
Nicosia, Cyprus 25 D12 35 10N 33 25 E
Nicoya, Costa Rica 88 D2 10 9N 85 27W
Nicoya, G. de, Costa Rica 88 E3 10 0N 85 0W
Nicoya, Pen. de, Costa Rica 88 E2 9 45N 85 40W
Nidd →, U.K. 12 D6 53 59N 1 23W
Niedersachsen □, Germany 16 B5 52 50N 9 0 E
Niekerkshoop, S. Africa 56 D3 29 19S 22 51 E
Niemba, Dem. Rep. of the Congo 54 D2 5 58S 28 24 E
Niemen = Nemunas →, Lithuania 9 J19 55 25N 21 10 E
Nienburg, Germany 16 B5 52 39N 9 13 E
Nieu Bethesda, S. Africa 56 E3 31 51S 24 34 E
Nieuw Amsterdam, Suriname 93 B7 5 53N 55 5W
Nieuw Nickerie, Suriname 93 B7 6 0N 56 59W
Nieuwoudtville, S. Africa 56 E2 31 23S 19 7 E
Nieuwpoort, Belgium 15 C2 51 8N 2 45 E
Nieves, Pico de las, Canary Is. 24 G4 27 57N 15 35W
Niğde, Turkey 19 G5 37 58N 34 40 E
Nigel, S. Africa 57 D4 26 27S 28 25 E
Niger ■, W. Afr. 50 E7 17 30N 10 0 E
Niger →, W. Afr. 50 G7 5 33N 6 33 E
Nigeria ■, W. Afr. 50 G7 8 30N 8 0 E
Nighasin, India 43 E9 28 14N 80 52 E
Nightcaps, N.Z. 59 L2 45 57S 168 2 E
Niigata, Japan 31 G9 34 20N 139 15 E
Niigata □, Japan 31 F9 37 15N 138 45 E
Niihama, Japan 31 H6 33 55N 133 16 E
Niihau, U.S.A. 74 H14 21 54N 160 9W
Niimi, Japan 31 G6 34 59N 133 28 E
Niitsu, Japan 30 F9 37 48N 139 7 E
Nijil, Jordan 46 E4 30 32N 35 33 E
Nijkerk, Neths. 15 B5 52 13N 5 30 E
Nijmegen, Neths. 15 C5 51 50N 5 52 E
Nijverdal, Neths. 15 B6 52 22N 6 28 E
Nik Pey, Iran 45 B6 36 50N 48 10 E
Nikiniki, Indonesia 37 F6 9 49S 124 30 E
Nikkō, Japan 31 F9 36 45N 139 35 E
Nikkō △, Japan 31 F9 36 45N 139 35 E
Nikolayev = Mykolayiv, Ukraine 19 E5 46 58N 32 0 E
Nikolayevsk, Russia 19 E8 50 0N 45 35 E
Nikolayevsk-na-Amur, Russia 29 D15 53 8N 140 44 E
Nikolskoye, Russia 29 D17 55 12N 166 0 E
Nikopol, Ukraine 19 E5 47 35N 34 25 E
Nikshahr, Iran 45 E9 26 15N 60 10 E
Nikšić, Serbia & M. 23 C8 42 50N 18 57 E
Nîl, Nahr en →, Africa 51 B12 30 10N 31 6 E

Nîl el Abyad →, Sudan 51 E12 15 38N 32 31 E
Nîl el Azraq →, Sudan 51 E12 15 38N 32 31 E
Nila, Indonesia 37 F7 6 44S 129 31 E
Niland, U.S.A. 79 M11 33 14N 115 31W
Nile = Nîl, Nahr en →, Africa 51 B12 30 10N 31 6 E
Niles, Mich., U.S.A. 82 E2 41 50N 86 15W
Niles, Ohio, U.S.A. 84 E4 41 11N 80 46W
Nim Ka Thana, India 42 F6 27 44N 75 48 E
Nimach, India 42 G6 24 30N 74 56 E
Nimbahera, India 42 G6 24 37N 74 45 E
Nîmes, France 20 E6 43 50N 4 23 E
Nimfaíon, Ákra = Pínnes, Ákra, Greece 23 D11 40 5N 24 20 E
Nimmitabel, Australia 63 F4 36 29S 149 15 E
Ninawá, Iraq 44 B4 36 25N 43 10 E
Ninawá □, Iraq 44 B4 36 15N 43 0 E
Nindigully, Australia 63 D4 28 21S 148 50 E
Ninepin Group, China 33 G11 22 16N 114 21 E
Nineveh = Ninawá, Iraq 44 B4 36 25N 43 10 E
Ning Xian, China 34 G4 35 30N 107 58 E
Ningaloo △, Australia 60 D1 22 23S 113 32 E
Ning'an, China 35 B15 44 22N 129 20 E
Ningbo, China 33 D7 29 51N 121 28 E
Ningcheng, China 35 D10 41 32N 119 53 E
Ningjin, China 34 F8 37 35N 114 57 E
Ningjing Shan, China 32 D4 30 0N 98 20 E
Ningling, China 34 G8 34 25N 115 22 E
Ningpo = Ningbo, China 33 D7 29 51N 121 28 E
Ningqiang, China 34 H4 32 47N 106 15 E
Ningshan, China 34 H5 33 21N 108 21 E
Ningsia Hui A.R. = Ningxia Huizu Zizhiqu □, China 34 F4 38 0N 106 0 E
Ningwu, China 34 E7 39 0N 112 18 E
Ningxia Huizu Zizhiqu □, China 34 F4 38 0N 106 0 E
Ningyang, China 34 G9 35 47N 116 45 E
Ninh Binh, Vietnam 38 B5 20 15N 105 55 E
Ninh Giang, Vietnam 38 B6 20 44N 106 24 E
Ninh Hoa, Vietnam 38 F7 12 30N 109 7 E
Ninh Ma, Vietnam 38 F7 12 48N 109 21 E
Ninove, Belgium 15 D4 50 51N 4 2 E
Nioaque, Brazil 95 A4 21 5S 55 50W
Niobrara, U.S.A. 80 D6 42 45N 98 2W
Niobrara →, U.S.A. 80 D6 42 46N 98 3W
Nioro du Sahel, Mali 50 E4 15 15N 9 30W
Niort, France 20 C3 46 19N 0 29W
Nipawin, Canada 71 C8 53 20N 104 0W
Nipigon, Canada 72 C2 49 0N 88 17W
Nipigon, L., Canada 72 C2 49 50N 88 30W
Nipishish L., Canada 73 B7 54 12N 60 45W
Nipissing, L., Canada 72 C4 46 20N 80 0W
Nipomo, U.S.A. 79 K6 35 3N 120 29W
Nipton, U.S.A. 79 K11 35 28N 115 16W
Niquelândia, Brazil 93 F9 14 33S 48 23W
Nir, Iran 44 B5 38 2N 47 59 E
Nirasaki, Japan 31 G9 35 42N 138 27 E
Nirmal, India 40 K11 19 3N 78 20 E
Nirmali, India 43 F12 26 20N 86 35 E
Niš, Serbia & M. 23 C9 43 19N 21 58 E
Niṣāb, Si. Arabia 44 D5 29 11N 44 43 E
Niṣāb, Yemen 47 E4 14 25N 46 29 E
Nishinomiya, Japan 31 G7 34 45N 135 20 E
Nishino'omote, Japan 31 J5 30 43N 130 59 E
Nishiwaki, Japan 31 G7 34 59N 134 58 E
Niskibi →, Canada 72 A2 56 29N 88 9W
Nisqually →, U.S.A. 78 C4 47 6N 122 42W
Nissáki, Greece 25 A3 39 43N 19 52 E
Nissum Bredning, Denmark 9 H13 56 40N 8 20 E
Nistru = Dnister →, Europe 17 E16 46 18N 30 17 E
Nisutlin →, Canada 70 A2 60 14N 132 34W
Nitchequon, Canada 73 B5 53 10N 70 58W
Niterói, Brazil 95 A7 22 52S 43 0W
Nith →, Canada 84 C4 43 12N 80 23W
Nith →, U.K. 11 F5 55 14N 3 33W
Nitmiluk △, Australia 60 B5 14 6S 132 15 E
Nitra, Slovak Rep. 17 D10 48 19N 18 4 E
Nitra →, Slovak Rep. 17 E10 47 46N 18 10 E
Niuafo'ou, Tonga 59 B11 15 30S 175 58W
Niue, Cook Is. 65 J11 19 2S 169 54W
Niut, Indonesia 36 D4 0 55N 110 6 E
Niuzhuang, China 35 D12 40 58N 122 28 E
Nivala, Finland 8 E21 63 56N 24 57 E
Nivelles, Belgium 15 D4 50 35N 4 20 E
Nivernais, France 20 C5 47 15N 3 30 E
Niwas, India 43 H9 23 3N 80 26 E
Nixon, U.S.A. 81 L6 29 16N 97 46W
Nizamabad, India 40 K11 18 45N 78 7 E
Nizamghat, India 41 E19 28 20N 95 45 E
Nizhne Kolymsk, Russia 29 C17 68 34N 160 55 E
Nizhneangarsk, Russia 29 D11 55 47N 109 30 E
Nizhnekamsk, Russia 18 C9 55 38N 51 49 E
Nizhneudinsk, Russia 29 D10 54 54N 99 3 E
Nizhnevartovsk, Russia 28 C8 60 56N 76 38 E
Nizhniy Novgorod, Russia 18 C7 56 20N 44 0 E
Nizhniy Tagil, Russia 18 C10 57 55N 59 57 E
Nizhyn, Ukraine 19 D5 51 5N 31 55 E
Nizip, Turkey 44 B3 37 1N 37 50 E
Nízké Tatry, Slovak Rep. 17 D10 48 55N 19 30 E
Njakwa, Malawi 55 E3 11 1S 33 56 E
Njanji, Zambia 55 E3 14 25S 31 46 E
Njinjo, Tanzania 55 D4 8 48S 38 54 E
Njombe, Tanzania 55 D3 9 20S 34 50 E
Njombe →, Tanzania 54 D4 6 56S 35 6 E
Nkana, Zambia 55 E2 12 50S 28 8 E
Nkandla, S. Africa 57 D5 28 37S 31 5 E
Nkayi, Zimbabwe 55 F2 19 41S 29 20 E
Nkhata Bay, Malawi 54 E3 11 33S 34 16 E
Nkhotakota, Malawi 55 E3 12 56S 34 15 E
Nkhotakota △, Malawi 55 E3 12 50S 34 0 E
Nkongsamba, Cameroon 52 D1 4 55N 9 55 E
Nkurenkuru, Namibia 56 B2 17 42S 18 32 E
Nmai →, Burma 41 G20 25 30N 97 25 E
Noakhali = Maijdi, Bangla. 41 H17 22 48N 91 10 E
Nobel, Canada 84 A4 45 25N 80 6W
Nobeoka, Japan 31 H5 32 36N 131 41 E
Noblesville, U.S.A. 82 E3 40 3N 86 1W
Noboribetsu, Japan 30 C10 42 24N 141 6 E
Nocera Inferiore, Italy 22 D6 40 44N 14 38 E
Nocona, U.S.A. 81 J6 33 47N 97 44W
Noda, Japan 31 G9 35 56N 139 52 E
Nogales, Mexico 86 A2 31 20N 110 56W
Nogales, U.S.A. 77 L8 31 20N 110 56W
Nōgata, Japan 31 H5 33 48N 130 44 E
Nogerup, Australia 61 F2 33 32S 116 5 E
Noginsk, Russia 29 C10 64 30N 90 50 E
Nogoa →, Australia 62 C4 23 40S 147 55 E
Nogoyá, Argentina 94 C4 32 24S 59 48W
Nohar, India 42 E6 29 11N 74 49 E
Nohta, India 43 H8 23 40N 79 34 E
Noires, Mts., France 20 B2 48 11N 3 40W

Noirmoutier, Î. de, France . . . . . 20 C2  46 58N   2  0W
Nojane, Botswana . . . . . . . . . . 56 C3  23 15S  20 14 E
Nojima-Zaki, Japan . . . . . . . . . 31 G9  34 54N 139 53 E
Nok Kundi, Pakistan . . . . . . . . 40 E3  28 50N  62 45 E
Nok Ta Phao, Ko, Thailand . . . . 39 b     9 23N  99 40 E
Nokaneng, Botswana . . . . . . . . 56 B3  19 40S  22 17 E
Nokia, Finland . . . . . . . . . . . . 9 F20 61 30N  23 30 E
Nokomis, Canada . . . . . . . . . . 71 C8  51 35N 105  0W
Nokomis L., Canada . . . . . . . . . 71 B8  57  0N 103  0W
Nola, C.A.R. . . . . . . . . . . . . . 52 D3   3 35N  16  4 E
Noma Omuramba →, Namibia . 56 B3  18 52S  20 53 E
Nombre de Dios, Panama . . . . . 88 E4   9 34N  79 28W
Nome, U.S.A. . . . . . . . . . . . . . 68 B3  64 30N 165 25W
Nomo-Zaki, Japan . . . . . . . . . . 31 H4  32 35N 129 44 E
Nonacho L., Canada . . . . . . . . 71 A7  61 42N 109 40W
Nonda, Australia . . . . . . . . . . . 62 C3  20 40S 142 28 E
Nong Chang, Thailand . . . . . . . 38 E2  15 23N  99 51 E
Nong Het, Laos . . . . . . . . . . . 38 C4  19 29N 103 59 E
Nong Khai, Thailand . . . . . . . . 38 D4  17 50N 102 46 E
Nong'an, China . . . . . . . . . . . 35 B13 44 25N 125  5 E
Nongoma, S. Africa . . . . . . . . . 57 D5  27 58S  31 35 E
Nongsa, Indonesia . . . . . . . . . 39 d    1 11N 104  8 E
Nonoava, Mexico . . . . . . . . . . 86 B3  27 28N 106 44W
Nonoava →, Mexico . . . . . . . . 86 B3  27 29N 106 45W
Nonthaburi, Thailand . . . . . . . . 38 F3  13 51N 100 34 E
Noonamah, Australia . . . . . . . . 60 B5  12 40S 131  4 E
Noondie, L., Australia . . . . . . . 61 E2  28 30S 119 30 E
Noord Brabant □, Neths. . . . . . 15 C5  51 40N   5  0 E
Noord Holland □, Neths. . . . . . 15 B4  52 30N   4 45 E
Noordbeveland, Neths. . . . . . . . 15 C3  51 35N   3 50 E
Noordoostpolder, Neths. . . . . . . 15 B5  52 45N   5 45 E
Noordwijk, Neths. . . . . . . . . . . 15 B4  52 14N   4 26 E
Noosa Heads, Australia . . . . . . 63 D5  26 25S 153  6 E
Nootka I., Canada . . . . . . . . . . 70 D3  49 32N 126 42W
Nopiming □, Canada . . . . . . . . 71 C9  50 30N  95 37W
Noralee, Canada . . . . . . . . . . . 70 C3  53 59N 126 26W
Noranda = Rouyn-Noranda,
    Canada . . . . . . . . . . . . . . 72 C4  48 20N  79  0W
Norco, U.S.A. . . . . . . . . . . . . 79 M9  33 56N 117 33W
Nord-Kivu □, Dem. Rep. of
    the Congo . . . . . . . . . . . . 54 C2   1  0S  29  0 E
Nord-Ostsee-Kanal, Germany . . 16 A5  54 12N   9 32 E
Nordaustlandet, Svalbard . . . . . 4 B9  79 14N  23  0 E
Nordegg, Canada . . . . . . . . . . 70 C5  52 29N 116  5W
Norderney, Germany . . . . . . . . 16 B4  53 42N   7  9 E
Norderstedt, Germany . . . . . . . 16 B5  53 42N  10  1 E
Nordfjord, Norway . . . . . . . . . . 9 F11 61 55N   5 30 E
Nordfriesische Inseln, Germany . 16 A5  54 40N   8 20 E
Nordhausen, Germany . . . . . . . 16 C6  51 30N  10 47 E
Norðoyar, Færoe Is. . . . . . . . . 8 E9  62 17N   6 35W
Nordkapp, Norway . . . . . . . . . 8 A21 71 10N  25 50 E
Nordkapp, Svalbard . . . . . . . . 4 A9  80 31N  20  0 E
Nordkinnhalvøya, Norway . . . . 8 A22 70 55N  27 40 E
Nordrhein-Westfalen □,
    Germany . . . . . . . . . . . . . 16 C4  51 45N   7  0 E
Nordvik, Russia . . . . . . . . . . . 29 B12 74  2N 111 32 E
Nore →, Ireland . . . . . . . . . . . 10 D4  52 25N   6 58W
Norfolk, Canada . . . . . . . . . . . 84 D4  42 50N  80 23W
Norfolk, Nebr., U.S.A. . . . . . . . 80 D6  42  2N  97 25W
Norfolk, Va., U.S.A. . . . . . . . . 82 G7  36 51N  76 17W
Norfolk □, U.K. . . . . . . . . . . . 13 E8  52 39N   1  0 E
Norfolk I., Pac. Oc. . . . . . . . . . 64 K8  28 58S 168  3 E
Norfork L., U.S.A. . . . . . . . . . . 81 G8  36 15N  92 14W
Norilsk, Russia . . . . . . . . . . . 29 C9  69 20N  88  6 E
Norma, Mt., Australia . . . . . . . 62 C3  20 55S 140 42 E
Normal, U.S.A. . . . . . . . . . . . . 80 E10 40 31N  88 59W
Norman, U.S.A. . . . . . . . . . . . 81 H6  35 13N  97 26W
Norman →, Australia . . . . . . . 62 B3  19 18S 141 51 E
Norman Wells, Canada . . . . . . 68 B7  65 17N 126 51W
Normanby →, Australia . . . . . . 62 A3  14 23S 144 10 E
Normandie, France . . . . . . . . . 20 B4  48 45N   0 10 E
Normandin, Canada . . . . . . . . 72 C5  48 49N  72 31W
Normandy = Normandie, France 20 B4  48 45N   0 10 E
Normanhurst, Mt., Australia . . . 61 E3  25  4S 122 30 E
Normanton, Australia . . . . . . . 62 B3  17 40S 141 10 E
Normétal, Canada . . . . . . . . . 72 C4  49  0N  79 22W
Norquay, Canada . . . . . . . . . . 71 C8  51 53N 102  5W
Norquinco, Argentina . . . . . . . 96 E2  41 51S  70 55W
Norrbottens län □, Sweden . . . 8 C19 66 50N  20  0 E
Norris Point, Canada . . . . . . . . 73 C8  49 31N  57 53W
Norristown, U.S.A. . . . . . . . . . 85 F9  40  7N  75 21W
Norrköping, Sweden . . . . . . . . 9 G17 58 37N  16 11 E
Norrland, Sweden . . . . . . . . . . 9 E16 62 15N  15 45 E
Norrtälje, Sweden . . . . . . . . . . 9 G18 59 46N  18 42 E
Norseman, Australia . . . . . . . . 61 F3  32  8S 121 43 E
Norsk, Russia . . . . . . . . . . . . 29 D14 52 30N 130  5 E
Norte, Pta. del, Canary Is. . . . . 24 G2  27 51N  17 57W
Norte, Serra do, Brazil . . . . . . 92 F7  11 20S  59  0W
North, C., Canada . . . . . . . . . 73 C7  47  2N  60 20W
North, C., U.S.A. . . . . . . . . . . 59 F4  34 23S 173  4 E
North Adams, U.S.A. . . . . . . . . 85 D11 42 42N  73  7W
North America . . . . . . . . . . . . 66 F10 40  0N 100  0W
North Arm, Canada . . . . . . . . . 70 A5  62  0N 114 30W
North Atlantic Ocean, Atl. Oc. . . 2 C7  30  0N  50  0W
North Augusta, U.S.A. . . . . . . . 83 J5  33 30N  81 59W
North Ayrshire □, U.K. . . . . . . 11 F4  55 45N   4 44W
North Bass I., U.S.A. . . . . . . . 84 E2  41 44N  82 53W
North Battleford, Canada . . . . . 71 C7  52 50N 108 17W
North Bay, Canada . . . . . . . . . 72 C4  46 20N  79 30W
North Belcher Is., Canada . . . . 72 A4  56 50N  79 50W
North Bend, Oreg., U.S.A. . . . . 76 E1  43 24N 124 14W
North Bend, Pa., U.S.A. . . . . . . 84 E7  41 20N  77 42W
North Bend, Wash., U.S.A. . . . . 78 C5  47 30N 121 47W
North Bennington, U.S.A. . . . . . 85 D11 42 56N  73 15W
North Berwick, U.K. . . . . . . . . 11 E6  56  4N   2 42W
North Berwick, U.S.A. . . . . . . . 85 C14 43 18N  70 44W
North C., Canada . . . . . . . . . . 73 C7  47  5N  64  0W
North C., N.Z. . . . . . . . . . . . . 59 F4  34 23S 173  4 E
North Canadian →, U.S.A. . . . . 81 H7  35 16N  95 31W
North Canton, U.S.A. . . . . . . . . 84 F3  40 53N  81 24W
North Cape = Nordkapp, Norway 8 A21 71 10N  25 50 E
North Cape = Nordkapp,
    Svalbard . . . . . . . . . . . . . 4 A9  80 31N  20  0 E
North Caribou L., Canada . . . . 72 B1  52 50N  90 40W
North Carolina □, U.S.A. . . . . . 83 H6  35 30N  80  0W
North Cascades △, U.S.A. . . . . 76 B3  48 45N 121 10W
North Channel, Canada . . . . . . 72 C3  46  0N  83  0W
North Channel, U.K. . . . . . . . . 11 F3  55 13N   5 52W
North Charleston, U.S.A. . . . . . 83 J6  32 53N  79 58W
North Creek, U.S.A. . . . . . . . . 85 C11 43 41N  73 59W
North Dakota □, U.S.A. . . . . . . 80 B5  47 30N 100 15W
North Downs, U.K. . . . . . . . . . 13 F8  51 19N   0 21 E
North East, U.S.A. . . . . . . . . . 84 D5  42 13N  79 50W
North East Frontier Agency =
    Arunachal Pradesh □, India . 41 F19 28  0N  95  0 E
North East Lincolnshire □, U.K. . 12 D7  53 34N   0  2W
North Eastern □, Kenya . . . . . . 54 B5   1 30N  40  0 E
North Esk →, U.K. . . . . . . . . . 11 E6  56 46N   2 24W

North European Plain, Europe . . 6 E10 55  0N  25  0 E
North Foreland, U.K. . . . . . . . . 13 F9  51 22N   1 28 E
North Fork, U.S.A. . . . . . . . . . 78 H7  37 14N 119 21W
North Fork American →, U.S.A. . 78 G5  38 57N 120 59W
North Fork Feather →, U.S.A. . . 78 F5  38 33N 121 30W
North Fork Grand →, U.S.A. . . . 80 C3  45 47N 102 16W
North Fork Red →, U.S.A. . . . . 81 H5  34 24N  99 14W
North Frisian Is. = Nordfriesische
    Inseln, Germany . . . . . . . . 16 A5  54 40N   8 20 E
North Gower, Canada . . . . . . . 85 A9  45  8N  75 43W
North Hd., Australia . . . . . . . . 61 F1  30 14S 114 59 E
North Henik L., Canada . . . . . . 71 A9  61 45N  97 40W
North Highlands, U.S.A. . . . . . . 78 G5  38 40N 121 23W
North Horr, Kenya . . . . . . . . . . 54 B4   3 20N  37  8 E
North I., Kenya . . . . . . . . . . . . 54 B4   4  5N  36  5 E
North I., N.Z. . . . . . . . . . . . . . 59 H5  38  0S 175  0 E
North Kingsville, U.S.A. . . . . . . 84 E4  41 54N  80 42W
North Kitui △, Kenya . . . . . . . 54 C4   0 15S  38 29 E
North Knife →, Canada . . . . . . 71 B10 58 53N  94 45W
North Koel →, India . . . . . . . . 43 G10 24 45N  83 50 E
North Korea ■, Asia . . . . . . . . 35 E14 40  0N 127  0 E
North Lakhimpur, India . . . . . . 41 F19 27 14N  94  7 E
North Lanarkshire □, U.K. . . . . 11 F5  55 52N   3 56W
North Las Vegas, U.S.A. . . . . . 79 J11 36 12N 115  7W
North Lincolnshire □, U.K. . . . . 12 D7  53 36N   0 30W
North Little Rock, U.S.A. . . . . . 81 H8  34 45N  92 16W
North Loup →, U.S.A. . . . . . . . 80 E5  41 17N  98 24W
North Luangwa △, Zambia . . . . 55 E3  11 49S  32  9 E
North Magnetic Pole, Canada . . 4 A2  88 30N 107  0W
North Minch, U.K. . . . . . . . . . . 11 C3  58  5N   5 55W
North Moose L., Canada . . . . . 71 C8  54 11N 100  6W
North Moose L., Man., Canada . 71 C8  54  4N 100 12W
North Myrtle Beach, U.S.A. . . . 83 J6  33 48N  78 42W
North Nahanni →, Canada . . . . 70 A4  62 15N 123 20W
North Olmsted, U.S.A. . . . . . . . 84 E3  41 25N  81 56W
North Ossetia □, Russia . . . . . 19 F7  43 30N  44 30 E
North Pagai, I. = Pagai Utara,
    Pulau, Indonesia . . . . . . . . 36 E2   2 35S 100  0 E
North Palisade, U.S.A. . . . . . . . 78 H8  37  6N 118 31W
North Platte, U.S.A. . . . . . . . . 80 E4  41  8N 100 46W
North Platte →, U.S.A. . . . . . . 80 E4  41  7N 100 42W
North Pole, Arctic . . . . . . . . . . 4 A   90  0N   0  0W
North Portal, Canada . . . . . . . . 71 D8  49  0N 102 33W
North Powder, U.S.A. . . . . . . . 76 D5  45  2N 117 55W
North Pt., U.S.A. . . . . . . . . . . . 89 g   13 20N  59 37W
North Pt., Trin. & Tob. . . . . . . . 93 J16 11 21N  60 31W
North Pt., U.S.A. . . . . . . . . . . . 84 A1  45  2N  83 16W
North Rhine Westphalia =
    Nordrhein-Westfalen □,
    Germany . . . . . . . . . . . . . 16 C4  51 45N   7 30 E
North River, Canada . . . . . . . . 73 B8  53 49N  57 6W
North Ronaldsay, U.K. . . . . . . . 11 B6  59 22N   2 26W
North Saskatchewan →, Canada 71 C7  53 15N 105  5W
North Sea, Europe . . . . . . . . . 14 C7  56  0N   4  0 E
North Seal →, Canada . . . . . . 71 B9  58 50N  98  7W
North Somerset □, U.K. . . . . . . 13 F5  51 24N   2 45W
North Sporades = Vóriai
    Sporádhes, Greece . . . . . . 23 E10 39 15N  23 30 E
North Sydney, Canada . . . . . . 73 C7  46 12N  60 15W
North Syracuse, U.S.A. . . . . . . 85 C8  43  8N  76  7W
North Taranaki Bight, N.Z. . . . . 59 H5  38 50S 174 15 E
North Thompson →, Canada . . 70 C4  50 40N 120 20W
North Tonawanda, U.S.A. . . . . . 84 C6  43  2N  78 53W
North Troy, U.S.A. . . . . . . . . . 85 B12 45  0N  72 24W
North Truchas Pk., U.S.A. . . . . 77 J11 36  0N 105 30W
North Twin I., Canada . . . . . . . 72 B4  53 20N  80  0W
North Tyne →, U.K. . . . . . . . . 12 B5  55  0N   2  8W
North Uist, U.K. . . . . . . . . . . . 11 D1  57 40N   7 15W
North Vancouver, Canada . . . . 70 D4  49 19N 123  4W
North Vernon, U.S.A. . . . . . . . . 82 F3  39  0N  85 38W
North Wabasca L., Canada . . . 70 B6  56  0N 113 55W
North Walsham, U.K. . . . . . . . . 12 E9  52 50N   1 22 E
North West = Severo-
    Zapadnyy □, Russia . . . . . . 28 C4  65  0N  40  0 E
North-West □, S. Africa . . . . . . 56 D4  27  0S  25  0 E
North West □, Australia . . . . . . 60 D1  21 45S 114  9 E
North West Christmas I. Ridge,
    Pac. Oc. . . . . . . . . . . . . . 65 G11 6 30N 165  0 W
North West Frontier □, Pakistan 42 C4  34  0N  72  0 E
North West Highlands, U.K. . . . 11 D4  57 33N   4 58W
North West River, Canada . . . . 73 B7  53 30N  60 10W
North Western □, Zambia . . . . 55 E2  13 30S  25 30 E
North Wildwood, U.S.A. . . . . . . 82 F8  39  0N  74 48W
North York Moors, U.K. . . . . . . 12 C7  54 23N   0 53W
North York Moors △, U.K. . . . . 12 C7  54 27N   0 51W
North Yorkshire □, U.K. . . . . . 12 C6  54 15N   1 25W
Northallerton, U.K. . . . . . . . . . 12 C6  54 20N   1 26W
Northam, Australia . . . . . . . . . 61 F2  31 35S 116 42 E
Northam, S. Africa . . . . . . . . . 56 C4  24 56S  27 18 E
Northampton, Australia . . . . . . 61 E1  28 27S 114 33 E
Northampton, U.K. . . . . . . . . . 13 E7  52 15N   0 53W
Northampton, Mass., U.S.A. . . . 85 D12 42 19N  72 38W
Northampton, Pa., U.S.A. . . . . . 85 F9  40 41N  75 30W
Northamptonshire □, U.K. . . . . 13 E7  52 16N   0 55W
Northbridge, U.S.A. . . . . . . . . . 85 D13 42  9N  71 39W
Northcliffe, Australia . . . . . . . . 61 F2  34 39S 116  7 E
Northeast Providence Chan.,
    W. Indies . . . . . . . . . . . . . 88 A4  26  0N  76  0W
Northern □, Malawi . . . . . . . . . 55 E3  11  0S  34  0 E
Northern □, Zambia . . . . . . . . 55 E3  10 30S  31  0 E
Northern Areas □, Pakistan . . . 43 A5  36 30N  73  0 E
Northern Cape □, S. Africa . . . 56 D3  30  0S  20  0 E
Northern Circars, India . . . . . . 41 L13 17 30N  82 30 E
Northern Indian L., Canada . . . 71 B9  57 20N  97 20W
Northern Ireland □, U.K. . . . . . 10 B5  54 45N   7  0W
Northern Lights, Canada . . . . . 72 C1  48 15N  90 39W
Northern Marianas ☑, Pac. Oc. 64 F6  17  0N 145  0 E
Northern Mid-Atlantic Ridge,
    Atl. Oc. . . . . . . . . . . . . . . 4 D6  35  0N  35  0W
Northern Province □, S. Africa . 57 C4  24  0S  29  0 E
Northern Range, Trin. & Tob. . . 93 K15 10 46N  61 15W
Northern Territory □, Australia . 60 D5  20  0S 133  0 E
Northfield, Minn., U.S.A. . . . . . 80 C8  44 27N  93  9W
Northfield, Vt., U.S.A. . . . . . . . 85 B12 44  9N  72 40W
Northland □, N.Z. . . . . . . . . . . 59 F4  35 30S 173 30 E
Northome, U.S.A. . . . . . . . . . . 80 B7  47 52N  94 17W
Northport, Ala., U.S.A. . . . . . . . 83 J2  33  9N  87 35W
Northport, Wash., U.S.A. . . . . . 76 B5  48 55N 117 48W
Northumberland □, U.K. . . . . . . 12 B6  55 12N   2  0W
Northumberland, C., Australia . . 63 F3  38  5S 140 40 E
Northumberland Is., Australia . . 62 C4  21 30S 149 50 E
Northumberland Str., Canada . . 73 C7  46 20N  64  0W
Northville, U.S.A. . . . . . . . . . . 85 C10 43 13N  74 11W
Northwest Providence Channel,
    W. Indies . . . . . . . . . . . . . 88 A4  26  0N  78  0W
Northwest Territories □, Canada 68 B9  63  0N 118  0W
Northwich, U.K. . . . . . . . . . . . 12 D5  53 15N   2 31W

Northwood, Iowa, U.S.A. . . . . . 80 D8  43 27N  93 13W
Northwood, N. Dak., U.S.A. . . . 80 B6  47 44N  97 34W
Norton, U.S.A. . . . . . . . . . . . . 80 F5  39 50N  99 53W
Norton, Zimbabwe . . . . . . . . . 55 F3  17 52S  30 40 E
Norton Sd., U.S.A. . . . . . . . . . 68 B3  63 50N 164  0W
Norwalk, Calif., U.S.A. . . . . . . 79 M8  33 54N 118  5W
Norwalk, Conn., U.S.A. . . . . . . 85 E11 41  7N  73 22W
Norwalk, Iowa, U.S.A. . . . . . . . 80 E8  41 29N  93 41W
Norwalk, Ohio, U.S.A. . . . . . . . 84 E2  41 15N  82 37W
Norway, Maine, U.S.A. . . . . . . . 83 C10 44 13N  70 32W
Norway, Mich., U.S.A. . . . . . . . 82 C2  45 47N  87 55W
Norway ■, Europe . . . . . . . . . 8 E14 63  0N  11  0 E
Norway House, Canada . . . . . . 71 C9  53 59N  97 50W
Norwegian Sea, Atl. Oc. . . . . . 4 C8  66  0N   1  0 E
Norwich, Canada . . . . . . . . . . 84 D4  42 59N  80 36W
Norwich, U.K. . . . . . . . . . . . . 13 E9  52 38N   1 18 E
Norwich, Conn., U.S.A. . . . . . . 85 E12 41 31N  72  5W
Norwich, N.Y., U.S.A. . . . . . . . 85 D9  42 32N  75 32W
Norwood, Canada . . . . . . . . . . 84 B7  44 23N  77 59W
Norwood, U.S.A. . . . . . . . . . . . 85 B10 44 45N  75  0W
Noshiro, Japan . . . . . . . . . . . . 30 D10 40 12N 140  0 E
Noşratābād, Iran . . . . . . . . . . 45 D8  29 55N  60  0 E
Noss Hd., U.K. . . . . . . . . . . . . 11 C5  58 28N   3  3W
Nossob →, S. Africa . . . . . . . . 56 D3  26 55S  20 45 E
Nosy Barren, Madag. . . . . . . . . 53 H8  18 25S  43 40 E
Nosy Be, Madag. . . . . . . . . . . 53 G9  13 25S  48 15 E
Nosy Boraha, Madag. . . . . . . . 57 B8  16 50S  49 55 E
Nosy Lava, Madag. . . . . . . . . . 57 A8  14 33S  47 36 E
Nosy Varika, Madag. . . . . . . . . 57 C8  20 35S  48 32 E
Noteć →, Poland . . . . . . . . . . 16 B8  52 44N  15 26 E
Notikewin →, Canada . . . . . . . 70 B5  57  2N 117 38W
Notodden, Norway . . . . . . . . . 9 G13 59 35N   9 17 E
Notre Dame B., Canada . . . . . 73 C8  49 45N  55 30W
Notre-Dame-de-Koartac =
    Quaqtaq, Canada . . . . . . . 69 B13 60 55N  69 40W
Notre-Dame-des-Bois, Canada . 85 A13 45 24N  71  4W
Notre-Dame-d'Ivugivic = Ivujivik,
    Canada . . . . . . . . . . . . . . 69 B12 62 24N  77 55W
Notre-Dame-du-Nord, Canada . 72 C4  47 36N  79 30W
Nottawasaga B., Canada . . . . . 84 B4  44 35N  80 15W
Nottaway →, Canada . . . . . . . 72 B4  51 22N  78 55W
Nottingham, U.K. . . . . . . . . . . 12 E6  52 58N   1 10W
Nottingham, City of □, U.K. . . . 12 E6  52 58N   1 10W
Nottingham I., Canada . . . . . . 69 B12 63 20N  77 55W
Nottinghamshire □, U.K. . . . . . 12 D6  53 10N   1  3W
Nottoway →, U.S.A. . . . . . . . . 82 G7  36 33N  76 55W
Notwane →, Botswana . . . . . . 56 C4  23 35S  26 58 E
Nouâdhibou, Mauritania . . . . . 50 D2  20 54N  17  0W
Nouâdhibou, Ras, Mauritania . . 50 D2  20 50N  17  0W
Nouakchott, Mauritania . . . . . . 50 E2  18  9N  15 58W
Nouméa, N. Cal. . . . . . . . . . . 64 K8  22 17S 166 30 E
Noupoort, S. Africa . . . . . . . . . 56 E3  31 10S  24 57 E
Nouveau Comptoir = Wemindji,
    Canada . . . . . . . . . . . . . . 72 B4  53  0N  78 49W
Nouvelle-Amsterdam, Î., Ind. Oc. 3 F13 38 30S  77 30 E
Nouvelle-Calédonie = New
    Caledonia ☑, Pac. Oc. . . . . 64 K8  21  0S 165  0 E
Nova Casa Nova, Brazil . . . . . 93 E10 9 25S  41  5W
Nova Esperança, Brazil . . . . . . 95 A5  23  8S  52 24W
Nova Friburgo, Brazil . . . . . . . 95 A7  22 16S  42 30W
Nova Iguaçu, Brazil . . . . . . . . 95 A7  22 45S  43 28W
Nova Iorque, Brazil . . . . . . . . . 93 E10 7  0S  44  5W
Nova Lima, Brazil . . . . . . . . . . 95 A7  19 59S  43 51W
Nova Lisbon = Huambo, Angola 53 G3  12 42S  15 54 E
Nova Lusitânia, Mozam. . . . . . 55 F3  19 50S  34 34 E
Nova Mambone, Mozam. . . . . . 57 C6  21  0S  35  3 E
Nova Scotia □, Canada . . . . . . 73 C7  45 10N  63  0W
Nova Sofala, Mozam. . . . . . . . 57 C5  20  7S  34 42 E
Nova Venécia, Brazil . . . . . . . 93 G10 18 45S  40 24W
Nova Zagora, Bulgaria . . . . . . 23 C11 42 32N  26  1 E
Novara, Italy . . . . . . . . . . . . . 20 D8  45 28N   8 38 E
Novato, U.S.A. . . . . . . . . . . . . 78 G4  38  6N 122 35W
Novaya Ladoga, Russia . . . . . . 18 B5  60  7N  32 16 E
Novaya Lyalya, Russia . . . . . . 28 C11 59  4N  60 45 E
Novaya Sibir, Ostrov, Russia . . 29 B16 75 10N 150  0 E
Novaya Zemlya, Russia . . . . . . 28 B6  75  0N  56  0 E
Nové Zámky, Slovak Rep. . . . . 17 D10 48  2N  18  8 E
Novgorod, Russia . . . . . . . . . . 18 C5  58 30N  31 25 E
Novgorod-Severskiy =
    Novhorod-Siverskyy, Ukraine 17 C14 52  2N  33 10 E
Novhorod-Siverskyy, Ukraine . . 18 D5  52  2N  33 10 E
Novi Ligure, Italy . . . . . . . . . . 20 D8  44 46N   8 47 E
Novi Pazar, Serbia & M. . . . . . 23 C9  43 12N  20 28 E
Novi Sad, Serbia & M. . . . . . . 23 B8  45 18N  19 52 E
Novo Hamburgo, Brazil . . . . . . 95 B5  29 37S  51  7W
Novo Mesto, Slovenia . . . . . . . 22 B6  45 47N  15 12 E
Novo Remanso, Brazil . . . . . . 93 E10 9 41S  42  4W
Novoaltaysk, Russia . . . . . . . . 28 D9  53 30N  84  0 E
Novocherkassk, Russia . . . . . . 19 E7  47 27N  40 15 E
Novogrudok = Navahrudak,
    Belarus . . . . . . . . . . . . . . 17 B13 53 40N  25 50 E
Novohrad-Volynskyy, Ukraine . . 17 C14 50 34N  27 35 E
Novokachalinsk, Russia . . . . . . 30 B6  45 5N 132  0 E
Novokuybyshevsk, Russia . . . . 18 D8  53  7N  49 58 E
Novokuznetsk, Russia . . . . . . . 28 D9  53 45N  87 10 E
Novomoskovsk, Russia . . . . . . 18 D6  54  5N  38 15 E
Novorossiysk, Russia . . . . . . . 19 F6  44 43N  37 46 E
Novorybnoye, Russia . . . . . . . 29 B11 72 50N 105 50 E
Novoselytsya, Ukraine . . . . . . 17 D14 48 14N  26 15 E
Novoshakhtinsk, Russia . . . . . . 19 E6  47 46N  39 58 E
Novosibirsk, Russia . . . . . . . . 28 D9  55  0N  83  5 E
Novosibirskiye Ostrova, Russia . 29 B15 75  0N 142  0 E
Novotroitsk, Russia . . . . . . . . . 18 D10 51 10N  58 15 E
Novouzensk, Russia . . . . . . . . 19 D8  50 32N  48 17 E
Novovolynsk, Ukraine . . . . . . . 17 C13 50 45N  24  4 E
Novska, Croatia . . . . . . . . . . . 22 B7  45 19N  17  0 E
Novvy Urengoy, Russia . . . . . . 28 C8  66 48N  76 52 E
Novyy Bor, Russia . . . . . . . . . 18 A9  66 43N  52 19 E
Novyy Port, Russia . . . . . . . . . 28 C8  67 40N  72 30 E
Now Shahr, Iran . . . . . . . . . . 45 B6  36 40N  51 30 E
Nowa Sól, Poland . . . . . . . . . . 16 C8  51 48N  15 44 E
Nowata, U.S.A. . . . . . . . . . . . 81 G7  36 42N  95 38W
Nowbarān, Iran . . . . . . . . . . . 45 C6  35 8N  49 42 E
Nowghāb, Iran . . . . . . . . . . . . 45 C8  33 53N  59  4 E
Nowgong, Assam, India . . . . . 41 F18 26 20N  92 50 E
Nowgong, Mad. P., India . . . . . 43 G8  25  4N  79 27 E
Nowra, Australia . . . . . . . . . . . 63 E5  34 53S 150 35 E
Nowrangapur = Nabarangpur,
    India . . . . . . . . . . . . . . . . 41 K13 19 14N  82 33 E
Nowshera, Pakistan . . . . . . . . 40 C8  34  0N  72  0 E
Nowy Sącz, Poland . . . . . . . . . 17 D11 49 40N  20 41 E
Nowy Targ, Poland . . . . . . . . . 17 D11 49 29N  20  2 E
Nowy Tomyśl, Poland . . . . . . . 16 B9  52 19N  16 10 E
Noxen, U.S.A. . . . . . . . . . . . . 85 E9  41 25N  76  4W
Noxon, U.S.A. . . . . . . . . . . . . 76 C6  48  0N 115 43W
Noyabr'sk, Russia . . . . . . . . . . 28 C8  64 34N  76 21 E
Noyon, France . . . . . . . . . . . . 20 B5  49 34N   2 59 E
Noyon, Mongolia . . . . . . . . . . 34 C2  43  2N 102  4 E
Nqutu, S. Africa . . . . . . . . . . . 57 D5  28 13S  30 32 E
Nsanje, Malawi . . . . . . . . . . . 55 F4  16 55S  35 12 E

Nsomba, Zambia . . . . . . . . . . 55 E2  10 45S  29 51 E
Nu Jiang →, China . . . . . . . . . 32 D4  29 58N  97 25 E
Nu Shan, China . . . . . . . . . . . 32 D4  26  0N  99 20 E
Nubia, Africa . . . . . . . . . . . . . 48 D7  21  0N  32  0 E
Nubian Desert = Nûbîya, Es
    Sahrâ en, Sudan . . . . . . . . 51 D12 21 30N  33 30 E
Nûbîya, Es Sahrâ en, Sudan . . 51 D12 21 30N  33 30 E
Nuboai, Indonesia . . . . . . . . . 37 E9   2 10S 136 30 E
Nubra →, India . . . . . . . . . . . 43 B7  34 35N  77 35 E
Nueces →, U.S.A. . . . . . . . . . 81 M6  27 51N  97 30W
Nueltin L., Canada . . . . . . . . . 71 A9  60 30N  99 30W
Nueva Gerona, Cuba . . . . . . . 88 B3  21 53N  82 49W
Nueva Palmira, Uruguay . . . . . 94 C4  33 52S  58 20W
Nueva Rosita, Mexico . . . . . . . 86 B4  28  0N 101 11W
Nueva San Salvador, El Salv. . 88 D2  13 40N  89 18W
Nuéve de Julio, Argentina . . . . 94 D3  35 30S  61  0W
Nuevitas, Cuba . . . . . . . . . . . 88 B4  21 30N  77 20W
Nuevo, G., Argentina . . . . . . . 96 E4  43  0S  64 30W
Nuevo Casas Grandes, Mexico . 86 A3  30 22N 108  0W
Nuevo Guerrero, Mexico . . . . . 87 B5  26 34N  99 15W
Nuevo Laredo, Mexico . . . . . . 87 B5  27 30N  99 30W
Nuevo León □, Mexico . . . . . . 86 C5  25  0N 100  0W
Nuevo Rocafuerte, Ecuador . . . 92 D3   0 55S  75 27W
Nugget Pt., N.Z. . . . . . . . . . . . 59 M2  46 27S 169 50 E
Nuhaka, N.Z. . . . . . . . . . . . . . 59 H6  39  3S 177 45 E
Nukey Bluff, Australia . . . . . . . 63 E2  32 26S 135 29 E
Nukhayb, Iraq . . . . . . . . . . . . 44 C4  32  4N  42  3 E
Nuku'alofa, Tonga . . . . . . . . . . 59 E12 21 10S 174  0W
Nukus, Uzbekistan . . . . . . . . . 28 E6  42 27N  59 41 E
Nullagine, Australia . . . . . . . . 60 D3  21 53S 120  7 E
Nullagine →, Australia . . . . . . 60 D3  21 20S 120 20 E
Nullarbor, Australia . . . . . . . . . 61 F5  31 28S 130 55 E
Nullarbor, △, Australia . . . . . . 61 F2  32 35S 115 37 E
Nullarbor Plain, Australia . . . . . 61 F4  31 10S 129  0 E
Numalla, L., Australia . . . . . . . 63 D3  28 43S 144 20 E
Numan, Nigeria . . . . . . . . . . . 51 G8   9 29N  12  3 E
Numata, Japan . . . . . . . . . . . 31 F9  36 45N 139  4 E
Numazu, Japan . . . . . . . . . . . 31 G9  35  7N 138 51 E
Numbulwar, Australia . . . . . . . 62 A2  14 15S 135 45 E
Numfoor, Indonesia . . . . . . . . 37 E8   1  0S 134 50 E
Numurkah, Australia . . . . . . . . 63 F4  36  5S 145 26 E
Nunaksaluk I., Canada . . . . . . 73 A7  55 49N  60 20W
Nunap Isua, Greenland . . . . . . 69 C15 59 48N  43 55W
Nunavut □, Canada . . . . . . . . 69 D8  66  0N  85  0W
Nunda, U.S.A. . . . . . . . . . . . . 84 D7  42 35N  77 56W
Nungarin, Australia . . . . . . . . . 61 F2  31 12S 118  6 E
Nungo, Mozam. . . . . . . . . . . . 55 E4  13 23S  37 43 E
Nungwe, Tanzania . . . . . . . . . 54 C3   2 48S  32  2 E
Nunivak I., U.S.A. . . . . . . . . . . 68 B3  60 10N 166 30W
Nunkun, India . . . . . . . . . . . . 43 C7  33 57N  76  2 E
Núoro, Italy . . . . . . . . . . . . . . 22 D3  40 20N   9 20 E
Nūrābād, Iran . . . . . . . . . . . . 45 E8  27 47N  57 12 E
Nuremberg = Nürnberg,
    Germany . . . . . . . . . . . . . 16 D6  49 27N  11  3 E
Nuri, Mexico . . . . . . . . . . . . . 86 B3  28 2N 109 22W
Nuriootpa, Australia . . . . . . . . 63 E2  34 27S 139  0 E
Nuristān □, Afghan. . . . . . . . . 40 B7  35 20N  71  0 E
Nurmes, Finland . . . . . . . . . . . 8 E23 63 33N  29 10 E
Nürnberg, Germany . . . . . . . . 16 D6  49 27N  11  3 E
Nurpur, Pakistan . . . . . . . . . . 42 D4  31 53N  71 54 E
Nurran, L. = Terewah, L.,
    Australia . . . . . . . . . . . . . 63 D4  29 52S 147 35 E
Nurrari Lakes, Australia . . . . . . 61 E5  29  1S 130  5 E
Nusa Barung, Indonesia . . . . . 37 H15  8 30S 113 30 E
Nusa Dua, Indonesia . . . . . . . 37 K18  8 48S 115 14 E
Nusa Kambangan, Indonesia . . 37 G13  7 40S 108 10 E
Nusa Tenggara Barat □,
    Indonesia . . . . . . . . . . . . . 36 F5   8 50S 117 30 E
Nusa Tenggara Timur □,
    Indonesia . . . . . . . . . . . . . 37 F6   9 30S 122  0 E
Nusaybin, Turkey . . . . . . . . . . 19 G7  37  3N  41 10 E
Nushki, Pakistan . . . . . . . . . . 42 E2  29 35N  66  0 E
Nuuk, Greenland . . . . . . . . . . 69 B14 64 10N  51 35W
Nuwakot, Nepal . . . . . . . . . . . 43 E10 28 10N  83 55 E
Nuweiba', Egypt . . . . . . . . . . . 44 D2  28 59N  34 39 E
Nuwerus, S. Africa . . . . . . . . . 56 E2  31  8S  18 24 E
Nuweveldberge, S. Africa . . . . 56 E3  32 10S  21 45 E
Nuyts, C., Australia . . . . . . . . 61 F5  32 2S 132 21 E
Nuyts, Pt., Australia . . . . . . . . 61 G2  35  4S 116 38 E
Nuyts Arch., Australia . . . . . . . 63 E1  32 35S 133 20 E
Nxai Pan △, Botswana . . . . . . 56 B3  19 50S  24 46 E
Nxau-Nxau, Botswana . . . . . . 56 B3  18 57S  21  4 E
Nyabing, Australia . . . . . . . . . 61 F2  33 33S 118  9 E
Nyack, U.S.A. . . . . . . . . . . . . 85 E11 41  5N  73 55W
Nyagan, Russia . . . . . . . . . . . 28 C7  62 30N  65 38 E
Nyahanga, Tanzania . . . . . . . . 54 C3   2 20S  33 37 E
Nyahua, Tanzania . . . . . . . . . 54 D3   5 25S  33 23 E
Nyahururu, Kenya . . . . . . . . . 54 B4   0 2N  36 27 E
Nyainqentanglha Shan, China . 32 D4  30  0N  90  0 E
Nyakanazi, Tanzania . . . . . . . 54 C3   3  2S  31 10 E
Nyâlâ, Sudan . . . . . . . . . . . . 51 F10 12  2N  24 58 E
Nyamandhlovu, Zimbabwe . . . 55 F2  19 55S  28 16 E
Nyambiti, Tanzania . . . . . . . . . 54 C3   2 48S  33 27 E
Nyamwaga, Tanzania . . . . . . . 54 C3   1 27S  34 33 E
Nyandekwa, Tanzania . . . . . . . 54 C3   3 57S  32 32 E
Nyandoma, Russia . . . . . . . . . 18 B7  61 40N  40 12 E
Nyanga △, Zimbabwe . . . . . . 55 F3  18 17S  32 44 E
Nyangana, Namibia . . . . . . . . 56 B3  18  0S  20 40 E
Nyanguge, Tanzania . . . . . . . . 54 C3   2 30S  33 12 E
Nyanza, Rwanda . . . . . . . . . . 54 C2   2 20S  29 42 E
Nyanza □, Kenya . . . . . . . . . 54 C3   0 10S  34 15 E
Nyanza-Lac, Burundi . . . . . . . 54 C2   4 21S  29 36 E
Nyasa, L., Africa . . . . . . . . . . 55 E3  12 30S  34 30 E
Nyasvizh, Belarus . . . . . . . . . 17 B14 53 14N  26 38 E
Nyazepetrovsk, Russia . . . . . . 18 C10 56  3N  59 36 E
Nyazura, Zimbabwe . . . . . . . . 55 F3  18 40S  32 16 E
Nyazwidzi →, Zimbabwe . . . . 55 G3  20  0S  31 17 E
Nybro, Sweden . . . . . . . . . . . 9 H16 56 44N  15 55 E
Nyda, Russia . . . . . . . . . . . . . 28 C8  66 40N  72 58 E
Nyeri, Kenya . . . . . . . . . . . . . 54 C4   0 23S  36 56 E
Nyika △, Malawi . . . . . . . . . . 55 E3  10 30S  33 57 E
Nyíregyháza, Hungary . . . . . . 17 E11 47 58N  21 47 E
Nykarleby = Uusikaarlepyy,
    Finland . . . . . . . . . . . . . . 8 E20 63 32N  22 31 E
Nykøbing, Storstrøm, Denmark . 9 J14 54 56N  11 52 E
Nykøbing, Vestsjælland,
    Denmark . . . . . . . . . . . . . 9 J14 55 55N  11 40 E
Nykøbing, Viborg, Denmark . . . 9 H13 56 48N   8 51 E
Nyköping, Sweden . . . . . . . . . 9 G17 58 45N  17  1 E
Nylstroom = Modimolle, S. Africa 57 C4  24 42S  28 22 E
Nymagee, Australia . . . . . . . . 63 E4  32  7S 146 20 E
Nymboida →, Australia . . . . . . 63 D5  29 38S 152 26 E
Nynäshamn, Sweden . . . . . . . 9 G17 58 54N  17 57 E
Nyngan, Australia . . . . . . . . . . 63 E4  31 30S 147  8 E
Nyoma Rap, India . . . . . . . . . 43 C8  33 10N  78 40 E
Nyoman = Nemunas →,
    Lithuania . . . . . . . . . . . . . 9 J19 55 25N  21 10 E

| | | | |
|---|---|---|---|
| Nysa, Poland | 17 C9 | 50 30N | 17 22 E |
| Nysa →, Europe | 16 B8 | 52 4N | 14 46 E |
| Nyslott = Savonlinna, Finland | 8 B4 | 61 52N | 28 53 E |
| Nyssa, U.S.A. | 76 E5 | 43 53N | 117 0W |
| Nystad = Uusikaupunki, Finland | 9 F19 | 60 47N | 21 25 E |
| Nyunzu, Dem. Rep. of the Congo | 54 D2 | 5 57S | 27 58 E |
| Nyurba, Russia | 29 C12 | 63 17N | 118 28 E |
| Nzega, Tanzania | 54 C3 | 4 10S | 33 12 E |
| Nzérékoré, Guinea | 50 G4 | 7 49N | 8 48W |
| Nzeto, Angola | 52 F2 | 7 10S | 12 52 E |
| Nzilo, Chutes de, Dem. Rep. of the Congo | 55 E2 | 10 18S | 25 27 E |
| Nzubuka, Tanzania | 54 C3 | 4 45S | 32 50 E |

## O

| | | | |
|---|---|---|---|
| Ô-Shima, Japan | 31 G9 | 34 44N | 139 24 E |
| Oa, Mull of, U.K. | 11 F2 | 55 35N | 6 20W |
| Oacoma, U.S.A. | 80 D5 | 43 48N | 99 24W |
| Oahe, L., U.S.A. | 80 C4 | 44 27N | 100 24W |
| Oahe Dam, U.S.A. | 80 C4 | 44 27N | 100 24W |
| Oahu, U.S.A. | 74 H16 | 21 28N | 157 58W |
| Oak Harbor, U.S.A. | 78 B4 | 48 18N | 122 39W |
| Oak Hill, U.S.A. | 82 G5 | 37 59N | 81 9W |
| Oak Ridge, U.S.A. | 83 G3 | 36 1N | 84 16W |
| Oak View, U.S.A. | 79 L7 | 34 24N | 119 18W |
| Oakan-Dake, Japan | 30 C12 | 43 27N | 144 10 E |
| Oakdale, Calif., U.S.A. | 78 H6 | 37 46N | 120 51W |
| Oakdale, La., U.S.A. | 81 K8 | 30 49N | 92 40W |
| Oakes, U.S.A. | 80 B5 | 46 8N | 98 6W |
| Oakesdale, U.S.A. | 76 C5 | 47 8N | 117 15W |
| Oakey, Australia | 63 D5 | 27 25S | 151 43 E |
| Oakfield, U.S.A. | 84 C6 | 43 4N | 78 16W |
| Oakham, U.K. | 13 E7 | 52 40N | 0 43W |
| Oakhurst, U.S.A. | 78 H7 | 37 19N | 119 40W |
| Oakland, U.S.A. | 78 H4 | 37 49N | 122 16W |
| Oakley, Idaho, U.S.A. | 76 E7 | 42 15N | 113 53W |
| Oakley, Kans., U.S.A. | 80 F4 | 39 8N | 100 51W |
| Oakover →, Australia | 60 D3 | 21 0S | 120 40 E |
| Oakridge, U.S.A. | 76 E2 | 43 45N | 122 28W |
| Oakville, Canada | 84 C5 | 43 27N | 79 41W |
| Oakville, U.S.A. | 78 D3 | 46 51N | 123 14W |
| Oamaru, N.Z. | 59 L3 | 45 5S | 170 59 E |
| Oasis, Calif., U.S.A. | 79 M10 | 33 28N | 116 6W |
| Oasis, Nev., U.S.A. | 78 H9 | 37 29N | 117 55W |
| Oates Land, Antarctica | 5 C11 | 69 0S | 160 0 E |
| Oatlands, Australia | 63 G4 | 42 17S | 147 21 E |
| Oatman, U.S.A. | 79 K12 | 35 1N | 114 19W |
| Oaxaca, Mexico | 87 D5 | 17 2N | 96 40W |
| Oaxaca □, Mexico | 87 D5 | 17 0N | 97 0W |
| Ob →, Russia | 28 C7 | 66 45N | 69 30 E |
| Oba, Canada | 72 C3 | 49 4N | 84 7W |
| Obama, Japan | 31 G7 | 35 30N | 135 45 E |
| Oban, U.K. | 11 E3 | 56 25N | 5 29W |
| Obbia, Somali Rep. | 47 F4 | 5 25N | 48 30 E |
| Obera, Argentina | 95 B4 | 27 21S | 55 2W |
| Oberhausen, Germany | 16 C4 | 51 28N | 6 51 E |
| Oberlin, Kans., U.S.A. | 80 F4 | 39 49N | 100 32W |
| Oberlin, La., U.S.A. | 81 K8 | 30 37N | 92 46W |
| Oberlin, Ohio, U.S.A. | 84 E2 | 41 18N | 82 13W |
| Oberon, Australia | 63 E4 | 33 45S | 149 52 E |
| Obi, Indonesia | 37 E7 | 1 23S | 127 45 E |
| Óbidos, Brazil | 93 D7 | 1 50S | 55 30W |
| Obihiro, Japan | 30 C11 | 42 56N | 143 12 E |
| Obilatu, Indonesia | 37 E7 | 1 25S | 127 20 E |
| Obluchye, Russia | 29 E14 | 49 1N | 131 4 E |
| Obo, C.A.R. | 54 A2 | 5 20N | 26 32 E |
| Oboa, Mt., Uganda | 54 B3 | 1 45N | 34 45 E |
| Oboyan, Russia | 28 D4 | 51 15N | 36 21 E |
| Obozerskaya = Obozerskiy, Russia | 18 B7 | 63 34N | 40 21 E |
| Obozerskiy, Russia | 18 B7 | 63 34N | 40 21 E |
| Observatory Inlet, Canada | 70 B3 | 55 10N | 129 54W |
| Obshchi Syrt, Russia | 6 E16 | 52 0N | 53 0 E |
| Obskaya Guba, Russia | 28 C8 | 69 0N | 73 0 E |
| Obuasi, Ghana | 50 G5 | 6 17N | 1 40W |
| Ocala, U.S.A. | 83 L4 | 29 11N | 82 8W |
| Ocampo, Chihuahua, Mexico | 86 B3 | 28 9N | 108 24W |
| Ocampo, Tamaulipas, Mexico | 87 C5 | 22 50N | 99 20W |
| Ocaña, Spain | 21 C4 | 39 55N | 3 30W |
| Ocanomowoc, U.S.A. | 80 D10 | 43 7N | 88 30W |
| Occidental, Cordillera, Colombia | 92 C3 | 5 0N | 76 0W |
| Occidental, Grand Erg, Algeria | 50 B6 | 30 20N | 1 0 E |
| Ocean City, Md., U.S.A. | 82 F8 | 38 20N | 75 5W |
| Ocean City, N.J., U.S.A. | 82 F8 | 39 17N | 74 35W |
| Ocean City, Wash., U.S.A. | 78 C2 | 47 4N | 124 10W |
| Ocean Falls, Canada | 70 C3 | 52 18N | 127 48W |
| Ocean I. = Banaba, Kiribati | 64 H8 | 0 45S | 169 50 E |
| Ocean Park, U.S.A. | 78 D2 | 46 30N | 124 3W |
| Oceano, U.S.A. | 79 K6 | 35 6N | 120 37W |
| Oceanport, U.S.A. | 85 F10 | 40 19N | 74 3W |
| Oceanside, U.S.A. | 79 M9 | 33 12N | 117 23W |
| Ochil Hills, U.K. | 11 E5 | 56 14N | 3 40W |
| Ocho Rios, Jamaica | 88 a | 18 24N | 77 6W |
| Ocilla, U.S.A. | 83 K4 | 31 36N | 83 15W |
| Ocmulgee →, U.S.A. | 83 K4 | 31 58N | 82 33W |
| Ocniţa, Moldova | 17 D14 | 48 25N | 27 30 E |
| Oconee →, U.S.A. | 83 K4 | 31 58N | 82 33W |
| Oconto, U.S.A. | 82 C2 | 44 53N | 87 52W |
| Oconto Falls, U.S.A. | 82 C1 | 44 52N | 88 9W |
| Ocosingo, Mexico | 87 D6 | 17 10N | 92 15W |
| Ocotal, Nic. | 88 D2 | 13 41N | 86 31W |
| Ocotlán, Mexico | 86 C4 | 20 21N | 102 42W |
| Ocotlán de Morelos, Mexico | 87 D5 | 16 48N | 96 40W |
| Ōda, Japan | 31 G6 | 35 11N | 132 30 E |
| Óðáðahraun, Iceland | 8 D5 | 65 5N | 17 0W |
| Odate, Japan | 30 D10 | 40 16N | 140 34 E |
| Odawara, Japan | 31 G9 | 35 20N | 139 6 E |
| Odda, Norway | 9 F12 | 60 3N | 6 35 E |
| Odei →, Canada | 71 B9 | 56 6N | 96 54W |
| Ödemiş, Turkey | 23 E13 | 38 15N | 28 0 E |
| Odendaalsrus, S. Africa | 56 D4 | 27 48S | 26 45 E |
| Odense, Denmark | 9 J14 | 55 22N | 10 23 E |
| Oder →, Europe | 16 B8 | 53 33N | 14 38 E |
| Odesa, Ukraine | 19 E5 | 46 30N | 30 45 E |
| Odessa = Odesa, Ukraine | 19 E5 | 46 30N | 30 45 E |
| Odessa, Canada | 85 B8 | 44 17N | 76 43W |
| Odessa, Tex., U.S.A. | 81 K3 | 31 52N | 102 23W |
| Odessa, Wash., U.S.A. | 76 C4 | 47 20N | 118 41W |
| Odiakwe, Botswana | 56 C4 | 20 12S | 25 17 E |
| Odienné, Ivory C. | 50 G4 | 9 30N | 7 34W |
| Odintsovo, Russia | 18 C6 | 55 39N | 37 15 E |
| O'Donnell, U.S.A. | 81 J4 | 32 58N | 101 50W |
| Odorheiu Secuiesc, Romania | 17 E13 | 46 21N | 25 21 E |
| Odra = Oder →, Europe | 16 B8 | 53 33N | 14 38 E |
| Odzi, Zimbabwe | 57 B5 | 19 0S | 32 20 E |
| Odzi →, Zimbabwe | 57 B5 | 19 45S | 32 23 E |
| Oeiras, Brazil | 93 E10 | 7 0S | 42 8W |
| Oelrichs, U.S.A. | 80 D3 | 43 11N | 103 14W |
| Oelwein, U.S.A. | 80 D9 | 42 41N | 91 55W |
| Oenpelli, Australia | 60 B5 | 12 20S | 133 4 E |
| Ofanto →, Italy | 22 D7 | 41 22N | 16 13 E |
| Offa, Nigeria | 50 G6 | 8 13N | 4 42 E |
| Offaly □, Ireland | 10 C4 | 53 15N | 7 30W |
| Offenbach, Germany | 16 C5 | 50 6N | 8 44 E |
| Offenburg, Germany | 16 D4 | 48 28N | 7 56 E |
| Officer, The →, Australia | 61 E5 | 27 46S | 132 30 E |
| Ofotfjorden, Norway | 8 B17 | 68 27N | 17 0 E |
| Ōfunato, Japan | 30 E10 | 39 4N | 141 43 E |
| Oga, Japan | 30 E9 | 39 55N | 139 50 E |
| Oga-Hantō, Japan | 30 E9 | 39 58N | 139 47 E |
| Ogaden, Ethiopia | 47 F3 | 7 30N | 45 30 E |
| Ōgaki, Japan | 31 G8 | 35 21N | 136 37 E |
| Ogallala, U.S.A. | 80 E4 | 41 8N | 101 43W |
| Ogasawara Gunto, Pac. Oc. | 26 G18 | 27 0N | 142 0 E |
| Ogbomosho, Nigeria | 50 G6 | 8 1N | 4 11 E |
| Ogden, U.S.A. | 76 F7 | 41 13N | 111 58W |
| Ogdensburg, U.S.A. | 85 B9 | 44 42N | 75 30W |
| Ogeechee →, U.S.A. | 83 K5 | 31 50N | 81 3W |
| Ogilby, U.S.A. | 79 N12 | 32 49N | 114 50W |
| Oglio →, Italy | 22 B4 | 45 2N | 10 39 E |
| Ogmore, Australia | 62 C4 | 22 37S | 149 35 E |
| Ogoki, Canada | 72 B2 | 51 38N | 85 58W |
| Ogoki →, Canada | 72 B2 | 51 38N | 85 57W |
| Ogoki L., Canada | 72 B2 | 50 50N | 87 10W |
| Ogoki Res., Canada | 72 B2 | 50 45N | 88 15W |
| Ogooué →, Gabon | 52 E1 | 1 0S | 9 0 E |
| Ogowe = Ogooué →, Gabon | 52 E1 | 1 0S | 9 0 E |
| Ogre, Latvia | 9 H21 | 56 49N | 24 36 E |
| Ogurchinskiy, Ostrov, Turkmenistan | 45 B7 | 38 55N | 53 2 E |
| Ohai, N.Z. | 59 L2 | 45 55S | 168 0 E |
| Ohakune, N.Z. | 59 H5 | 39 24S | 175 24 E |
| Ohata, Japan | 30 D10 | 41 24N | 141 10 E |
| Ohau, L., N.Z. | 59 L2 | 44 15S | 169 53 E |
| Ohio □, U.S.A. | 84 F2 | 40 15N | 82 45W |
| Ohio →, U.S.A. | 82 G1 | 36 59N | 89 8W |
| Ohře →, Czech Rep. | 16 C8 | 50 30N | 14 10 E |
| Ohrid, Macedonia | 23 D9 | 41 8N | 20 52 E |
| Ohridsko Jezero, Macedonia | 23 D9 | 41 8N | 20 52 E |
| Ohrigstad, S. Africa | 57 C5 | 24 39S | 30 36 E |
| Oiapoque, Brazil | 93 | 3 50N | 51 50W |
| Oikou, China | 35 E9 | 38 35N | 117 42 E |
| Oil City, U.S.A. | 84 E5 | 41 26N | 79 42W |
| Oil Springs, Canada | 84 D2 | 42 47N | 82 7W |
| Oildale, U.S.A. | 79 K7 | 35 25N | 119 1W |
| Oise →, France | 20 B5 | 49 0N | 2 4 E |
| Oistins, Barbados | 89 g | 13 4N | 59 33W |
| Oistins B., Barbados | 89 g | 13 4N | 59 33W |
| Ōita, Japan | 31 H5 | 33 14N | 131 36 E |
| Ōita □, Japan | 31 H5 | 33 15N | 131 30 E |
| Oiticica, Brazil | 93 E10 | 5 3S | 41 5W |
| Ojacaliente, Mexico | 86 C4 | 22 34N | 102 15W |
| Ojai, U.S.A. | 79 L7 | 34 27N | 119 15W |
| Ojinaga, Mexico | 86 B4 | 29 34N | 104 25W |
| Ojiya, Japan | 31 F9 | 37 18N | 138 48 E |
| Ojo de Liebre △, Mexico | 86 B2 | 27 50N | 114 0W |
| Ojos del Salado, Cerro, Argentina | 94 B2 | 27 0S | 68 40W |
| Oka →, Russia | 18 C7 | 56 20N | 43 59 E |
| Okaba, Indonesia | 37 F9 | 8 6S | 139 42 E |
| Okahandja, Namibia | 56 C2 | 22 0S | 16 59 E |
| Okanagan L., Canada | 70 D5 | 50 0N | 119 30W |
| Okanogan, U.S.A. | 76 B4 | 48 22N | 119 35W |
| Okanogan →, U.S.A. | 76 B4 | 48 6N | 119 44W |
| Okapi △, Dem. Rep. of the Congo | 54 B2 | 2 30N | 27 20 E |
| Okaputa, Namibia | 56 C2 | 20 5S | 17 0 E |
| Okara, Pakistan | 42 D5 | 30 50N | 73 31 E |
| Okaukuejo, Namibia | 56 B2 | 19 10S | 16 0 E |
| Okavango Delta, Botswana | 56 B3 | 18 45S | 22 45 E |
| Okavango Swamp = Okavango Delta, Botswana | 56 B3 | 18 45S | 22 45 E |
| Okaya, Japan | 31 F9 | 36 5N | 138 10 E |
| Okayama, Japan | 31 G6 | 34 40N | 133 54 E |
| Okayama □, Japan | 31 G6 | 35 0N | 133 50 E |
| Okazaki, Japan | 31 G8 | 34 57N | 137 10 E |
| Okeechobee, U.S.A. | 83 M5 | 27 15N | 80 50W |
| Okeechobee, L., U.S.A. | 83 M5 | 27 0N | 80 50W |
| Okefenokee △, U.S.A. | 83 K4 | 30 44N | 82 7W |
| Okefenokee Swamp, U.S.A. | 83 K4 | 30 40N | 82 20W |
| Okehampton, U.K. | 13 G4 | 50 44N | 4 0W |
| Okha, India | 42 H3 | 22 27N | 69 4 E |
| Okha, Russia | 29 D15 | 53 40N | 143 0 E |
| Okhotsk, Russia | 29 D15 | 59 20N | 143 10 E |
| Okhotsk, Sea of, Asia | 29 D15 | 55 0N | 145 0 E |
| Okhotskiy Perevoz, Russia | 29 C14 | 61 52N | 135 35 E |
| Okhtyrka, Ukraine | 19 D5 | 50 25N | 35 0 E |
| Oki-Shotō, Japan | 31 F6 | 36 5N | 133 15 E |
| Okiep, S. Africa | 56 D2 | 29 39S | 17 53 E |
| Okinawa □, Japan | 31 L4 | 26 40N | 128 0 E |
| Okinawa-Guntō, Japan | 31 L4 | 26 40N | 128 0 E |
| Okinawa-Jima, Japan | 31 L4 | 26 32N | 128 0 E |
| Okino-erabu-Shima, Japan | 31 L4 | 27 21N | 128 33 E |
| Oklahoma □, U.S.A. | 81 H6 | 35 20N | 97 30W |
| Oklahoma City, U.S.A. | 81 H6 | 35 30N | 97 30W |
| Okmulgee, U.S.A. | 81 H7 | 35 37N | 95 58W |
| Oknitsa = Ocniţa, Moldova | 17 D14 | 48 25N | 27 30 E |
| Okolo, Uganda | 54 B3 | 2 37N | 31 8 E |
| Okolona, U.S.A. | 81 J10 | 34 0N | 88 45W |
| Okombahe, Namibia | 56 C2 | 21 23S | 15 22 E |
| Okotoks, Canada | 70 C6 | 50 43N | 113 58W |
| Oksibil, Indonesia | 37 E10 | 4 59S | 140 35 E |
| Oksovskiy, Russia | 18 B6 | 62 33N | 39 57 E |
| Oktabrsk = Oktyabrsk, Kazakhstan | 19 E10 | 49 28N | 57 25 E |
| Oktyabrsk, Kazakhstan | 19 E10 | 49 28N | 57 25 E |
| Oktyabrskiy = Aktsyabrski, Belarus | 17 B15 | 52 38N | 28 53 E |
| Oktyabrskiy, Russia | 18 D9 | 54 28N | 53 28 E |
| Oktyabrskoy Revolyutsii, Ostrov, Russia | 29 B10 | 78 30N | 97 0 E |
| Okuru, N.Z. | 59 K2 | 43 55S | 168 55 E |
| Okushiri-Tō, Japan | 30 C9 | 42 15N | 139 30 E |
| Okwa →, Botswana | 56 C3 | 22 30S | 23 0 E |
| Ola, U.S.A. | 81 H8 | 35 2N | 93 13W |
| Ólafsfjörður, Iceland | 8 C4 | 66 4N | 18 39W |
| Ólafsvík, Iceland | 8 D2 | 64 53N | 23 43W |
| Olancha, U.S.A. | 79 J8 | 36 17N | 118 1W |
| Olancha Pk., U.S.A. | 79 J8 | 36 15N | 118 7W |
| Olanchito, Honduras | 88 C2 | 15 30N | 86 30W |
| Öland, Sweden | 9 H17 | 56 45N | 16 38 E |
| Olary, Australia | 63 E3 | 32 18S | 140 19 E |
| Olascoaga, Argentina | 94 D3 | 35 15S | 60 39W |
| Olathe, U.S.A. | 80 F7 | 38 53N | 94 49W |
| Olavarría, Argentina | 94 D3 | 36 55S | 60 20W |
| Oława, Poland | 17 C9 | 50 57N | 17 20 E |
| Ólbia, Italy | 22 D3 | 40 55N | 9 31 E |
| Olcott, U.S.A. | 84 C6 | 43 20N | 78 42W |
| Old Bahama Chan. = Bahama, Canal Viejo de, W. Indies | 88 B4 | 22 10N | 77 30W |
| Old Baldy Pk. = San Antonio, Mt., U.S.A. | 79 L9 | 34 17N | 117 38W |
| Old Castile = Castilla y Leon □, Spain | 21 B3 | 42 0N | 5 0W |
| Old Crow, Canada | 68 B6 | 67 30N | 139 55W |
| Old Dale, U.S.A. | 79 L11 | 34 8N | 115 47W |
| Old Forge, N.Y., U.S.A. | 85 C10 | 43 43N | 74 58W |
| Old Forge, Pa., U.S.A. | 85 E9 | 41 22N | 75 45W |
| Old Perlican, Canada | 73 C9 | 48 5N | 53 1W |
| Old Shinyanga, Tanzania | 54 C3 | 3 33S | 33 27 E |
| Old Speck Mt., U.S.A. | 85 B14 | 44 34N | 70 57W |
| Old Town, U.S.A. | 83 C11 | 44 56N | 68 39W |
| Old Washington, U.S.A. | 84 F3 | 40 2N | 81 27W |
| Old Wives L., Canada | 71 C7 | 50 5N | 106 0W |
| Oldbury, U.K. | 13 F5 | 51 38N | 2 33W |
| Oldcastle, Ireland | 10 C4 | 53 46N | 7 10W |
| Oldeani, Tanzania | 54 C4 | 3 22S | 35 35 E |
| Oldenburg, Germany | 16 B5 | 53 9N | 8 13 E |
| Oldenzaal, Neths. | 15 B6 | 52 19N | 6 53 E |
| Oldham, U.K. | 12 D5 | 53 33N | 2 7W |
| Oldman →, Canada | 70 D6 | 49 57N | 111 42W |
| Oldmeldrum, U.K. | 11 D6 | 57 20N | 2 19W |
| Olds, Canada | 70 C6 | 51 50N | 114 10W |
| Olduvai Gorge, Tanzania | 54 C4 | 2 57S | 35 23 E |
| Oldziyt, Mongolia | 34 B5 | 44 40N | 109 1 E |
| Olean, U.S.A. | 84 D6 | 42 5N | 78 26W |
| Olekma →, Russia | 29 C13 | 60 22N | 120 42 E |
| Olekminsk, Russia | 29 C13 | 60 25N | 120 30 E |
| Oleksandriya, Ukraine | 17 C14 | 50 37N | 26 19 E |
| Olema, U.S.A. | 78 G4 | 38 3N | 122 47W |
| Olenegorsk, Russia | 18 A5 | 68 9N | 33 18 E |
| Olenek, Russia | 29 C12 | 68 28N | 112 18 E |
| Olenek →, Russia | 29 B13 | 73 0N | 120 10 E |
| Oléron, Î. d', France | 20 D3 | 45 55N | 1 15W |
| Oleśnica, Poland | 17 C9 | 51 13N | 17 22 E |
| Olevsk, Ukraine | 17 C14 | 51 12N | 27 39 E |
| Olga, Russia | 29 E14 | 43 50N | 135 14 E |
| Olga, L., Canada | 72 C4 | 49 47N | 77 15W |
| Olga, Mt., Australia | 61 E5 | 25 20S | 130 50 E |
| Ölgiy, Mongolia | 32 B3 | 48 56N | 89 57 E |
| Olhão, Portugal | 21 D2 | 37 3N | 7 48W |
| Olifants = Elefantes →, Africa | 57 C5 | 24 10S | 32 40 E |
| Olifants →, Namibia | 56 C2 | 25 30S | 19 30 E |
| Olifantshoek, S. Africa | 56 D3 | 27 57S | 22 42 E |
| Ólimbos, Óros, Greece | 23 D10 | 40 6N | 22 23 E |
| Olímpia, Brazil | 95 A6 | 20 44S | 48 54W |
| Olinda, Brazil | 93 E12 | 8 1S | 34 51W |
| Oliva, Argentina | 94 C3 | 32 0S | 63 38W |
| Olivehurst, U.S.A. | 78 F5 | 39 6N | 121 34W |
| Olivenza, Spain | 21 C2 | 38 41N | 7 9W |
| Oliver, Canada | 70 D5 | 49 13N | 119 37W |
| Oliver L., Canada | 71 B8 | 56 56N | 103 22W |
| Ollagüe, Chile | 94 A2 | 21 15S | 68 10W |
| Olney, Ill., U.S.A. | 82 F1 | 38 44N | 88 5W |
| Olney, Tex., U.S.A. | 81 J5 | 33 22N | 98 45W |
| Olomane →, Canada | 73 B7 | 50 14N | 60 37W |
| Olomouc, Czech Rep. | 17 D9 | 49 38N | 17 12 E |
| Olonets, Russia | 18 B5 | 61 0N | 32 54 E |
| Olongapo, Phil. | 37 B6 | 14 50N | 120 18 E |
| Olot, Spain | 21 A7 | 42 11N | 2 30 E |
| Olovyannaya, Russia | 29 D12 | 50 58N | 115 35 E |
| Oloy →, Russia | 29 C16 | 66 29N | 159 29 E |
| Olsztyn, Poland | 17 B11 | 53 48N | 20 29 E |
| Olt →, Romania | 17 G13 | 43 43N | 24 51 E |
| Olteniţa, Romania | 17 F14 | 44 7N | 26 42 E |
| Olton, U.S.A. | 81 H3 | 34 11N | 102 8W |
| Olymbos, Cyprus | 25 D12 | 35 21N | 33 45 E |
| Olympia, Greece | 23 F9 | 37 39N | 21 39 E |
| Olympia, U.S.A. | 78 D4 | 47 3N | 122 53W |
| Olympic Dam, Australia | 63 E2 | 30 30S | 136 55 E |
| Olympic Mts., U.S.A. | 78 C3 | 47 55N | 123 45W |
| Olympus, Cyprus | 25 E11 | 34 56N | 32 52 E |
| Olympus, Mt. = Ólimbos, Óros, Greece | 23 D10 | 40 6N | 22 23 E |
| Olympus, Mt. = Uludağ, Turkey | 23 D13 | 40 4N | 29 13 E |
| Olympus, Mt., U.S.A. | 78 C3 | 47 48N | 123 43W |
| Olyphant, U.S.A. | 85 E9 | 41 27N | 75 36W |
| Om →, Russia | 28 D8 | 54 59N | 73 22 E |
| Om Koi, Thailand | 38 D2 | 17 48N | 98 22 E |
| Ōma, Japan | 30 D10 | 41 45N | 141 5 E |
| Ōmachi, Japan | 31 F8 | 36 30N | 137 50 E |
| Ōmae-Zaki, Japan | 31 G9 | 34 36N | 138 14 E |
| Ōmagari, Japan | 30 E10 | 39 27N | 140 29 E |
| Omagh, U.K. | 10 B4 | 54 36N | 7 19W |
| Omagh □, U.K. | 10 B4 | 54 35N | 7 15W |
| Omaha, U.S.A. | 80 E7 | 41 17N | 95 58W |
| Omak, U.S.A. | 76 B4 | 48 25N | 119 31W |
| Omalos, Greece | 25 D5 | 35 19N | 23 55 E |
| Oman ■, Asia | 47 C6 | 23 0N | 58 0 E |
| Oman, G. of, Asia | 45 E8 | 24 30N | 58 30 E |
| Omaruru, Namibia | 56 C2 | 21 26S | 16 0 E |
| Omaruru →, Namibia | 56 C1 | 22 7S | 14 15 E |
| Omate, Peru | 92 G4 | 16 45S | 71 0W |
| Ombai, Selat, Indonesia | 37 F6 | 8 30S | 124 50 E |
| Omboué, Gabon | 52 E1 | 1 35S | 9 15 E |
| Ombrone →, Italy | 22 C4 | 42 42N | 11 5 E |
| Omdurmân, Sudan | 51 E12 | 15 40N | 32 28 E |
| Omemee, Canada | 84 B6 | 44 18N | 78 33W |
| Omeonga, Dem. Rep. of the Congo | 54 C1 | 3 40S | 24 22 E |
| Ometepe, I. de, Nic. | 88 D2 | 11 32N | 85 35W |
| Ometepec, Mexico | 87 D5 | 16 39N | 98 23W |
| Ominato, Japan | 30 D10 | 41 17N | 141 10 E |
| Omineca →, Canada | 70 B4 | 56 3N | 124 16W |
| Omitara, Namibia | 56 C2 | 22 16S | 18 2 E |
| Ōmiya, Japan | 31 G9 | 35 54N | 139 38 E |
| Ommen, Neths. | 15 B6 | 52 31N | 6 26 E |
| Ömnögovĭ □, Mongolia | 34 C3 | 43 15N | 104 0 E |
| Omo →, Ethiopia | 47 F2 | 6 25N | 36 10 E |
| Omodhos, Cyprus | 25 E11 | 34 51N | 32 48 E |
| Omolon →, Russia | 29 C16 | 68 42N | 158 36 E |
| Omono-Gawa →, Japan | 30 E10 | 39 46N | 140 3 E |
| Omsk, Russia | 28 D8 | 55 0N | 73 12 E |
| Omsukchan, Russia | 29 C16 | 62 32N | 155 48 E |
| Ōmu, Japan | 30 B11 | 44 34N | 142 58 E |
| Omul, Vf., Romania | 17 F13 | 45 27N | 25 29 E |
| Ōmura, Japan | 31 H4 | 32 56N | 129 57 E |
| Omuramba Omatako →, Namibia | 56 B2 | 17 45S | 20 25 E |
| Omuramba Ovambo →, Namibia | 56 B2 | 18 45S | 16 59 E |
| Ōmuta, Japan | 31 H5 | 33 5N | 130 26 E |
| Onaga, U.S.A. | 80 F6 | 39 29N | 96 10W |
| Onalaska, U.S.A. | 80 D9 | 43 53N | 91 14W |
| Onancock, U.S.A. | 82 G8 | 37 43N | 75 45W |
| Onang, Indonesia | 37 E5 | 3 2S | 118 49 E |
| Onaping L., Canada | 72 C3 | 47 3N | 81 30W |
| Onavas, Mexico | 86 B3 | 28 28N | 109 30W |
| Onawa, U.S.A. | 80 D6 | 42 2N | 96 6W |
| Oncócua, Angola | 56 B1 | 16 30S | 13 25 E |
| Onda, Spain | 21 C5 | 39 55N | 0 17W |
| Ondaejin, N. Korea | 35 D15 | 41 34N | 129 40 E |
| Ondangwa, Namibia | 56 B2 | 17 57S | 16 4 E |
| Ondjiva, Angola | 56 B2 | 16 48S | 15 50 E |
| Öndörshil, Mongolia | 34 B5 | 45 13N | 108 5 E |
| Öndverðarnes, Iceland | 8 D1 | 64 52N | 24 0W |
| One Tree, Australia | 63 E3 | 34 11S | 144 43 E |
| Onega, Russia | 18 B6 | 64 0N | 38 10 E |
| Onega →, Russia | 18 B6 | 63 58N | 38 2 E |
| Onega, G. of = Onezhskaya Guba, Russia | 18 B6 | 64 24N | 36 38 E |
| Onega, L. = Onezhskoye Ozero, Russia | 18 B6 | 61 44N | 35 22 E |
| Oneida, U.S.A. | 85 C9 | 43 6N | 75 39W |
| Oneida L., U.S.A. | 85 C9 | 43 12N | 75 54W |
| O'Neill, U.S.A. | 80 D5 | 42 27N | 98 39W |
| Onekotan, Ostrov, Russia | 29 E16 | 49 25N | 154 45 E |
| Onema, Dem. Rep. of the Congo | 54 C1 | 4 35S | 24 30 E |
| Oneonta, U.S.A. | 85 D9 | 42 27N | 75 4W |
| Oneşti, Romania | 17 E14 | 46 17N | 26 47 E |
| Onezhskaya Guba, Russia | 18 B6 | 64 24N | 36 38 E |
| Onezhskoye Ozero, Russia | 18 B6 | 61 44N | 35 22 E |
| Ongarue, N.Z. | 59 H5 | 38 42S | 175 19 E |
| Ongers →, S. Africa | 56 E3 | 31 4S | 23 13 E |
| Ongerup, Australia | 61 F2 | 33 58S | 118 28 E |
| Ongjin, N. Korea | 35 F13 | 37 56N | 125 21 E |
| Ongkharak, Thailand | 38 E3 | 14 8N | 101 1 E |
| Ongniud Qi, China | 35 C10 | 43 0N | 118 38 E |
| Ongoka, Dem. Rep. of the Congo | 54 C2 | 1 20S | 26 0 E |
| Ongole, India | 40 M12 | 15 33N | 80 2 E |
| Ongon = Havirga, Mongolia | 34 B7 | 45 41N | 113 5 E |
| Onida, U.S.A. | 80 C4 | 44 42N | 100 4W |
| Onilahy →, Madag. | 57 C7 | 23 34S | 43 45 E |
| Onitsha, Nigeria | 50 G7 | 6 6N | 6 42 E |
| Onoda, Japan | 31 G5 | 33 59N | 131 11 E |
| Onpyŏng-ni, S. Korea | 35 H14 | 33 25N | 126 45 E |
| Onslow, Australia | 60 D2 | 21 40S | 115 12 E |
| Onslow B., U.S.A. | 83 H7 | 34 20N | 77 15W |
| Ontake-San, Japan | 31 G8 | 35 53N | 137 29 E |
| Ontario, Calif., U.S.A. | 79 L9 | 34 4N | 117 39W |
| Ontario, Oreg., U.S.A. | 76 D5 | 44 2N | 116 58W |
| Ontario □, Canada | 72 B2 | 48 0N | 83 0W |
| Ontario, L., N. Amer. | 84 C7 | 43 20N | 78 0W |
| Ontonagon, U.S.A. | 80 B10 | 46 52N | 89 19W |
| Onyx, U.S.A. | 79 K8 | 35 41N | 118 14W |
| Oodnadatta, Australia | 63 D2 | 27 33S | 135 30 E |
| Ooldea, Australia | 61 F5 | 30 27S | 131 50 E |
| Oombulgurri, Australia | 60 C4 | 15 15S | 127 45 E |
| Oorindi, Australia | 62 C3 | 20 40S | 141 1 E |
| Oost-Vlaanderen □, Belgium | 15 C3 | 51 5N | 3 50 E |
| Oostende, Belgium | 15 C2 | 51 15N | 2 54 E |
| Oosterhout, Neths. | 15 C4 | 51 39N | 4 47 E |
| Oosterschelde →, Neths. | 15 C4 | 51 33N | 4 0 E |
| Oosterwolde, Neths. | 15 B6 | 53 0N | 6 17 E |
| Ootacamund = Udagamandalam, India | 40 P10 | 11 30N | 76 44 E |
| Ootsa L., Canada | 70 C3 | 53 50N | 126 2W |
| Op Luang △, Thailand | 38 C2 | 18 12N | 98 32 E |
| Opala, Dem. Rep. of the Congo | 54 C1 | 0 40S | 24 20 E |
| Opanake, Sri Lanka | 40 R12 | 6 35N | 80 40 E |
| Opasatika, Canada | 72 C3 | 49 30N | 82 50W |
| Opasquia △, Canada | 72 B1 | 53 33N | 93 5W |
| Opava, Czech Rep. | 17 D9 | 49 57N | 17 58 E |
| Opelika, U.S.A. | 83 J3 | 32 39N | 85 23W |
| Opelousas, U.S.A. | 81 K8 | 30 32N | 92 5W |
| Opémisca, L., Canada | 72 C5 | 49 56N | 74 52W |
| Opheim, U.S.A. | 76 B10 | 48 51N | 106 24W |
| Ophthalmia Ra., Australia | 60 D2 | 23 15S | 119 30 E |
| Opinaca →, Canada | 72 B4 | 52 15N | 78 2W |
| Opinaca, Rés., Canada | 72 B4 | 52 39N | 76 20W |
| Opinnagau →, Canada | 72 B3 | 54 12N | 82 25W |
| Opiscotéo, L., Canada | 73 B6 | 53 10N | 68 10W |
| Opole, Poland | 17 C9 | 50 42N | 17 58 E |
| Oponono L., Namibia | 56 B2 | 18 8S | 15 45 E |
| Oporto = Porto, Portugal | 21 B1 | 41 8N | 8 40W |
| Opotiki, N.Z. | 59 H6 | 38 1S | 177 19 E |
| Opp, U.S.A. | 83 K2 | 31 17N | 86 16W |
| Oppdal, Norway | 9 E13 | 62 35N | 9 41 E |
| Opportunity, U.S.A. | 76 C5 | 47 39N | 117 15W |
| Opua, N.Z. | 59 F5 | 35 19S | 174 9 E |
| Opunake, N.Z. | 59 H4 | 39 26S | 173 52 E |
| Opuwo, Namibia | 56 B1 | 18 3S | 13 45 E |
| Ora, Cyprus | 25 E12 | 34 51N | 33 12 E |
| Oracle, U.S.A. | 77 K8 | 32 37N | 110 46W |
| Oradea, Romania | 17 E11 | 47 2N | 21 58 E |
| Öræfajökull, Iceland | 8 D5 | 64 2N | 16 39W |
| Orai, India | 43 G8 | 25 58N | 79 30 E |
| Oral = Zhayyq →, Kazakhstan | 19 E9 | 47 0N | 51 48 E |
| Oral, Kazakhstan | 19 D9 | 51 20N | 51 20 E |
| Oran, Algeria | 50 A5 | 35 45N | 0 39W |
| Orange, Australia | 63 E4 | 33 15S | 149 7 E |
| Orange, France | 20 D6 | 44 8N | 4 47 E |
| Orange, Calif., U.S.A. | 79 M9 | 33 47N | 117 51W |
| Orange, Mass., U.S.A. | 85 D12 | 42 35N | 72 19W |
| Orange, Tex., U.S.A. | 81 K8 | 30 6N | 93 44W |
| Orange, Va., U.S.A. | 82 F6 | 38 15N | 78 7W |
| Orange →, S. Africa | 56 D2 | 28 41S | 16 28 E |
| Orange, C., Brazil | 93 C8 | 4 20N | 51 30W |
| Orange Cove, U.S.A. | 78 J7 | 36 38N | 119 19W |
| Orange Free State = Free State □, S. Africa | 56 D4 | 28 30S | 27 0 E |
| Orange Grove, U.S.A. | 81 M6 | 27 58N | 97 56W |
| Orange Walk, Belize | 87 D7 | 18 6N | 88 33W |
| Orangeburg, U.S.A. | 83 J5 | 33 30N | 80 52W |
| Orangeville, Canada | 84 C4 | 43 55N | 80 5W |
| Oranienburg, Germany | 16 B7 | 52 45N | 13 14 E |
| Oranje = Orange →, S. Africa | 56 D2 | 28 41S | 16 28 E |
| Oranjemund, Namibia | 56 D2 | 28 38S | 16 29 E |
| Oranjerivier, S. Africa | 56 D3 | 29 40S | 24 12 E |
| Oranjestad, Aruba | 89 D5 | 12 32N | 70 2W |
| Orapa, Botswana | 53 J5 | 21 15S | 25 30 E |
| Oras, Phil. | 37 B7 | 12 9N | 125 28 E |
| Orbetello, Italy | 22 C4 | 42 27N | 11 13 E |
| Orbisonia, U.S.A. | 84 F7 | 40 15N | 77 54W |
| Orbost, Australia | 63 F4 | 37 40S | 148 29 E |
| Orcas I., U.S.A. | 78 B4 | 48 42N | 122 56W |
| Orchard City, U.S.A. | 77 G10 | 38 50N | 107 58W |
| Orchila, I., Venezuela | 89 D6 | 11 48N | 66 10W |

Orchilla, Pta., Canary Is. ........ 24 G1 27 42N 18 10W
Orcutt, U.S.A. ........ 79 L6 34 52N 120 27W
Ord, U.S.A. ........ 80 E5 41 36N 98 56W
Ord ➤, Australia ........ 60 C4 15 33S 128 15 E
Ord, Mt., Australia ........ 60 C4 17 20S 125 34 E
Orderville, U.S.A. ........ 77 H7 37 17N 112 38W
Ordos = Mu Us Shamo, China .... 34 E5 39 0N 109 0 E
Ordu, Turkey ........ 19 F6 40 55N 37 53 E
Ordway, U.S.A. ........ 80 F3 38 13N 103 46W
Ore, Dem. Rep. of the Congo .... 54 B2 3 17N 29 30 E
Ore Mts. = Erzgebirge, Germany 16 C7 50 27N 12 55 E
Örebro, Sweden ........ 9 G16 59 20N 15 18 E
Oregon, U.S.A. ........ 80 D10 42 1N 89 20W
Oregon □, U.S.A. ........ 76 E3 44 0N 121 0W
Oregon City, U.S.A. ........ 78 E4 45 21N 122 36W
Oregon Dunes △, U.S.A. ........ 76 E1 42 3N 123 26W
Orekhovo-Zuyevo, Russia ........ 18 C6 55 50N 38 55 E
Orel, Russia ........ 18 D6 52 57N 36 3 E
Orem, U.S.A. ........ 76 F8 40 19N 111 42W
Ören, Turkey ........ 23 F12 37 3N 27 57 E
Orenburg, Russia ........ 18 D10 51 45N 55 6 E
Orense = Ourense, Spain ........ 21 A2 42 19N 7 55W
Orepuki, N.Z. ........ 59 M1 46 19S 167 46 E
Orestiás, Greece ........ 23 D12 41 30N 26 33 E
Orestos Pereyra, Mexico ........ 86 B3 26 31N 105 40W
Orford Ness, U.K. ........ 13 E9 52 5N 1 35 E
Organ Pipe Cactus △, U.S.A. .... 77 K7 32 0N 113 10W
Organos, Pta. de los, Canary Is. 24 F2 28 12N 17 17W
Orgaz, Spain ........ 21 C4 39 39N 3 53W
Orgeyev = Orhei, Moldova ........ 17 E15 47 24N 28 50 E
Orhaneli, Turkey ........ 23 E13 39 54N 28 59 E
Orhangazi, Turkey ........ 23 D13 40 29N 29 18 E
Orhei, Moldova ........ 17 E15 47 24N 28 50 E
Orhon Gol ➤, Mongolia ........ 32 A5 50 21N 106 0 E
Oriental, Cordillera, Colombia .. 92 B4 6 0N 73 0W
Oriental, Grand Erg, Algeria .... 50 B7 30 0N 6 30 E
Orientale □, Dem. Rep. of
the Congo ........ 54 B2 2 20N 26 0 E
Oriente, Argentina ........ 94 D3 38 44S 60 37W
Orihuela, Spain ........ 21 C5 38 7N 0 55W
Orillia, Canada ........ 84 B5 44 40N 79 24W
Orinoco ➤, Venezuela ........ 92 B6 9 15N 61 30W
Orion, Canada ........ 71 D6 49 27N 110 49W
Oriskany, U.S.A. ........ 85 C9 43 10N 75 20W
Orissa □, India ........ 41 K14 20 0N 84 0 E
Orissaare, Estonia ........ 9 G20 58 34N 23 5 E
Oristano, Italy ........ 22 E3 39 54N 8 36 E
Oristano, G. di, Italy ........ 22 E3 39 50N 8 29 E
Orizaba, Mexico ........ 87 D5 18 51N 97 6W
Orizaba, Pico de, Mexico ........ 87 D5 19 0N 97 20W
Orkanger, Norway ........ 8 E13 63 18N 9 52 E
Orkla ➤, Norway ........ 8 E13 63 18N 9 51 E
Orkney, S. Africa ........ 56 D4 26 58S 26 40 E
Orkney □, U.K. ........ 11 B5 59 2N 3 13W
Orkney Is., U.K. ........ 11 B6 59 0N 3 0W
Orland, U.S.A. ........ 78 F4 39 45N 122 12W
Orlando, U.S.A. ........ 83 L5 28 33N 81 23W
Orléanais, France ........ 20 C5 48 0N 2 0 E
Orléans, France ........ 20 C4 47 54N 1 52 E
Orléans, U.S.A. ........ 85 B12 44 49N 72 12W
Orléans, Î. d', Canada ........ 73 C5 46 54N 70 58W
Ormara, Pakistan ........ 40 G4 25 16N 64 33 E
Ormoc, Phil. ........ 37 B6 11 0N 124 37 E
Ormond, N.Z. ........ 59 H6 38 33S 177 56 E
Ormond Beach, U.S.A. ........ 83 L5 29 17N 81 3W
Ormskirk, U.K. ........ 12 D5 53 35N 2 54W
Ormstown, Canada ........ 85 A11 45 8N 74 0W
Örnsköldsvik, Sweden ........ 8 E18 63 17N 18 40 E
Oro, N. Korea ........ 35 D14 40 1N 127 27 E
Oro ➤, Mexico ........ 86 B3 25 35N 105 2W
Oro Grande, U.S.A. ........ 79 L9 34 36N 117 20W
Oro Valley, U.S.A. ........ 77 K8 32 26N 110 58W
Orocué, Colombia ........ 92 C4 4 48N 71 20W
Orofino, U.S.A. ........ 76 C5 46 29N 116 15W
Orol Dengizi = Aral Sea, Asia .. 28 E7 44 30N 60 0 E
Oromocto, Canada ........ 73 C6 45 54N 66 29W
Orono, Canada ........ 84 C6 43 59N 78 37W
Orono, U.S.A. ........ 83 C11 44 53N 68 40W
Oronsay, U.K. ........ 11 E2 56 1N 6 15W
Oroqen Zizhiqi, China ........ 33 A7 50 34N 123 43 E
Oroquieta, Phil. ........ 37 C6 8 32N 123 44 E
Orosháza, Hungary ........ 17 E11 46 32N 20 42 E
Orotukan, Russia ........ 29 C16 62 16N 151 42 E
Oroville, Calif., U.S.A. ........ 78 F5 39 31N 121 33W
Oroville, Wash., U.S.A. ........ 76 B4 48 56N 119 26W
Oroville, L., U.S.A. ........ 78 F5 39 33N 121 29W
Orroroo, Australia ........ 63 E2 32 43S 138 38 E
Orrville, U.S.A. ........ 84 F3 40 50N 81 46W
Orsha, Belarus ........ 18 D5 54 30N 30 25 E
Orsk, Russia ........ 18 D10 51 12N 58 34 E
Orșova, Romania ........ 17 F12 44 41N 22 25 E
Ortaca, Turkey ........ 23 F13 36 49N 28 45 E
Ortegal, C., Spain ........ 21 A2 43 43N 7 52W
Orthez, France ........ 20 E3 43 29N 0 48W
Ortigueira, Spain ........ 21 A2 43 40N 7 50W
Orting, U.S.A. ........ 78 C4 47 6N 122 12W
Ortles, Italy ........ 20 C9 46 31N 10 33 E
Ortón ➤, Bolivia ........ 92 F5 10 50S 67 0W
Ortonville, U.S.A. ........ 80 C6 45 19N 96 27W
Orümïyeh, Iran ........ 44 B5 37 40N 45 0 E
Orümïyeh, Daryācheh-ye, Iran .. 44 B5 37 50N 45 30 E
Oruro, Bolivia ........ 92 G5 18 0S 67 9W
Orust, Sweden ........ 9 G14 58 10N 11 40 E
Oruzgān □, Afghan. ........ 40 C5 33 30N 66 0 E
Orvieto, Italy ........ 22 C5 42 43N 12 7 E
Orwell, N.Y., U.S.A. ........ 85 C9 43 35N 75 50W
Orwell, Ohio, U.S.A. ........ 84 E4 41 32N 80 52W
Orwell ➤, U.K. ........ 13 F9 51 59N 1 18 E
Orwigsburg, U.S.A. ........ 85 F8 40 38N 76 6W
Oryakhovo, Bulgaria ........ 23 C10 43 40N 23 57 E
Osa, Russia ........ 18 C10 57 17N 55 26 E
Osa, Pen. de, Costa Rica ........ 88 E3 8 0N 84 0W
Osage, U.S.A. ........ 80 D8 43 17N 92 49W
Osage ➤, U.S.A. ........ 80 F9 38 35N 91 57W
Osage City, U.S.A. ........ 80 F7 38 38N 95 50W
Osaka, Japan ........ 31 G7 34 40N 135 30 E
Osan, S. Korea ........ 35 F14 37 11N 127 4 E
Osawatomie, U.S.A. ........ 80 F7 38 31N 94 57W
Osborne, U.S.A. ........ 80 F5 39 26N 98 42W
Osceola, Ark., U.S.A. ........ 81 H10 35 42N 89 58W
Osceola, Iowa, U.S.A. ........ 80 E8 41 2N 93 46W
Oscoda, U.S.A. ........ 84 B1 44 26N 83 20W
Ösel = Saaremaa, Estonia ........ 9 G20 58 30N 22 30 E
Osgoode, Canada ........ 85 A9 45 8N 75 36W
Osh, Kyrgyzstan ........ 28 E8 40 37N 72 49 E
Oshakati, Namibia ........ 53 H3 17 45S 15 40 E
Oshawa, Canada ........ 84 C6 43 50N 78 50W
Oshigambo, Namibia ........ 56 B2 17 45S 16 5 E

Oshkosh, Nebr., U.S.A. ........ 80 E3 41 24N 102 21W
Oshkosh, Wis., U.S.A. ........ 80 C10 44 1N 88 33W
Oshmyany = Ashmyany, Belarus 9 J21 54 26N 25 52 E
Oshnovïyeh, Iran ........ 44 B5 37 2N 45 6 E
Oshogbo, Nigeria ........ 50 G6 7 48N 4 37 E
Oshtorïnān, Iran ........ 45 C6 34 1N 48 38 E
Oshwe, Dem. Rep. of the Congo 52 E3 3 25S 19 28 E
Osijek, Croatia ........ 23 B8 45 34N 18 41 E
Osipovichi = Asipovichy, Belarus 17 B15 53 19N 28 33 E
Osiyan, India ........ 42 F5 26 43N 72 55 E
Osizweni, S. Africa ........ 57 D5 27 49S 30 7 E
Oskaloosa, U.S.A. ........ 80 E8 41 18N 92 39W
Oskarshamn, Sweden ........ 9 H17 57 15N 16 27 E
Oskélanéo, Canada ........ 72 C4 48 5N 75 15W
Öskemen, Kazakhstan ........ 28 E9 50 0N 82 36 E
Oslo, Norway ........ 9 G14 59 55N 10 45 E
Oslofjorden, Norway ........ 9 G14 59 20N 10 35 E
Osmanabad, India ........ 40 K10 18 5N 76 10 E
Osmaniye, Turkey ........ 19 G6 37 5N 36 10 E
Osnabrück, Germany ........ 16 B5 52 17N 8 3 E
Osorio, Brazil ........ 95 B5 29 53S 50 17W
Osorno, Chile ........ 96 E2 40 25S 73 0W
Osoyoos, Canada ........ 70 D5 49 0N 119 30W
Osøyro, Norway ........ 9 F11 60 9N 5 30 E
Ospika ➤, Canada ........ 70 B4 56 20N 124 0W
Osprey Reef, Australia ........ 62 A4 13 52S 146 36 E
Oss, Neths. ........ 15 C5 51 46N 5 32 E
Ossa, Mt., Australia ........ 63 G4 41 52S 146 3 E
Óssa, Óros, Greece ........ 23 E10 39 47N 22 42 E
Ossabaw I., U.S.A. ........ 83 K5 31 50N 81 5W
Ossining, U.S.A. ........ 85 E11 41 10N 73 55W
Ossipee, U.S.A. ........ 85 C13 43 41N 71 7W
Ossokmanuan L., Canada ........ 73 B7 53 25N 65 0W
Ossora, Russia ........ 29 D17 59 20N 163 13 E
Ostend = Oostende, Belgium .... 15 C2 51 15N 2 54 E
Oster, Ukraine ........ 17 C16 50 57N 30 53 E
Österbotten = Pohjanmaa,
Finland ........ 8 E20 62 58N 22 50 E
Osterburg, U.S.A. ........ 84 F6 40 16N 78 31W
Österdalälven, Sweden ........ 9 F16 61 30N 13 45 E
Österdalen, Norway ........ 9 F14 61 40N 10 50 E
Östermyra = Seinäjoki, Finland . 9 E20 62 40N 22 51 E
Östersund, Sweden ........ 8 E16 63 10N 14 38 E
Ostfriesische Inseln, Germany .. 16 B4 53 42N 7 0 E
Ostrava, Czech Rep. ........ 17 D10 49 51N 18 18 E
Ostróda, Poland ........ 17 B10 53 42N 19 58 E
Ostroh, Ukraine ........ 17 C14 50 20N 26 30 E
Ostrołęka, Poland ........ 17 B11 53 4N 21 32 E
Ostrów Mazowiecka, Poland .... 17 B11 52 50N 21 51 E
Ostrów Wielkopolski, Poland .... 17 C9 51 36N 17 44 E
Ostrowiec-Świętokrzyski, Poland 17 C11 50 55N 21 22 E
Ostuni, Italy ........ 23 D7 40 44N 17 35 E
Ōsumi-Kaikyō, Japan ........ 31 J5 30 55N 131 0 E
Ōsumi-Shotō, Japan ........ 31 J5 30 30N 130 0 E
Osuna, Spain ........ 21 D3 37 14N 5 8W
Oswegatchie ➤, U.S.A. ........ 85 B9 44 42N 75 30W
Oswego, U.S.A. ........ 85 C8 43 27N 76 31W
Oswego ➤, U.S.A. ........ 85 C8 43 27N 76 30W
Oswestry, U.K. ........ 12 E4 52 52N 3 3W
Oświęcim, Poland ........ 17 C10 50 2N 19 11 E
Otago □, N.Z. ........ 59 L2 45 15S 170 0 E
Otago Harbour, N.Z. ........ 59 L3 45 47S 170 42 E
Ōtake, Japan ........ 31 G6 34 12N 132 13 E
Otaki, N.Z. ........ 59 J5 40 45S 175 10 E
Otaru, Japan ........ 30 C10 43 10N 141 0 E
Otaru-Wan = Ishikari-Wan, Japan 30 C10 43 25N 141 1 E
Otavalo, Ecuador ........ 92 C3 0 13N 78 20W
Otavi, Namibia ........ 56 B2 19 40S 17 24 E
Otchinjau, Angola ........ 56 B1 16 30S 13 56 E
Otelnuk, L., Canada ........ 73 A6 56 9N 68 12W
Othello, U.S.A. ........ 76 C4 46 50N 119 10W
Otjiwarongo, Namibia ........ 56 C2 20 30S 16 33 E
Otoineppu, Japan ........ 30 B11 44 44N 142 16 E
Otorohanga, N.Z. ........ 59 H5 38 12S 175 14 E
Otoskwin ➤, Canada ........ 72 B2 52 13N 88 6W
Otra ➤, Norway ........ 9 G13 58 9N 8 1 E
Otranto, Italy ........ 23 D8 40 9N 18 28 E
Otranto, C. d', Italy ........ 23 D8 40 7N 18 30 E
Otranto, Str. of, Italy ........ 23 D8 40 15N 18 40 E
Otse, S. Africa ........ 56 D4 25 2S 25 45 E
Ōtsu, Japan ........ 31 G7 35 0N 135 50 E
Ōtsuki, Japan ........ 31 G9 35 36N 138 57 E
Ottawa = Outaouais ➤, Canada 72 C5 45 27N 74 8W
Ottawa, Canada ........ 85 A9 45 27N 75 42W
Ottawa, Ill., U.S.A. ........ 80 E10 41 21N 88 51W
Ottawa, Kans., U.S.A. ........ 80 F7 38 37N 95 16W
Ottawa Is., Canada ........ 69 C11 59 35N 80 10W
Otter Cr. ➤, U.S.A. ........ 85 B11 44 13N 73 17W
Otter L., Canada ........ 71 B8 55 35N 104 39W
Otterville, Canada ........ 84 D4 42 55N 80 36W
Ottery St. Mary, U.K. ........ 13 G4 50 44N 3 17W
Otto Beit Bridge, Zimbabwe .... 55 F2 15 59S 28 56 E
Ottosdal, S. Africa ........ 56 D4 26 46S 25 59 E
Ottumwa, U.S.A. ........ 80 E8 41 1N 92 25W
Oturkpo, Nigeria ........ 50 G7 7 16N 8 8 E
Otway, B., Chile ........ 96 G2 53 30S 74 0W
Otway, C., Australia ........ 63 F3 38 52S 143 30 E
Otwock, Poland ........ 17 B11 52 5N 21 20 E
Ou ➤, Laos ........ 38 B4 20 4N 102 13 E
Ou Neua, Laos ........ 38 A3 22 18N 101 48 E
Ou-Sammyaku, Japan ........ 30 E10 39 20N 140 35 E
Ouachita ➤, U.S.A. ........ 81 K9 31 38N 91 49W
Ouachita, L., U.S.A. ........ 81 H8 34 34N 93 12W
Ouachita Mts., U.S.A. ........ 81 H7 34 40N 94 25W
Ouagadougou, Burkina Faso .... 50 F5 12 25N 1 30W
Ouahran = Oran, Algeria ........ 50 A5 35 45N 0 39W
Ouallene, Algeria ........ 50 D6 24 41N 1 11 E
Ouargla, Algeria ........ 50 B7 31 59N 5 16 E
Ouarzazate, Morocco ........ 50 B4 30 55N 6 50W
Oubangi ➤, Dem. Rep. of
the Congo ........ 52 E3 0 30S 17 50 E
Ouddorp, Neths. ........ 15 C3 51 50N 3 57 E
Oude Rijn ➤, Neths. ........ 15 B4 52 12N 4 24 E
Oudenaarde, Belgium ........ 15 D3 50 50N 3 37 E
Oudtshoorn, S. Africa ........ 56 E3 33 35S 22 14 E
Ouessant, Î. d', France ........ 20 B1 48 28N 5 6W
Ouesso, Congo ........ 52 D3 1 37N 16 5 E
Ouest, Pte. de l', Canada ........ 73 C7 49 52N 64 40W
Ouezzane, Morocco ........ 50 B4 34 51N 5 35W
Oughterard, Ireland ........ 10 C2 53 26N 9 18W
Oujda, Morocco ........ 50 B5 34 41N 1 55W
Oulainen, Finland ........ 8 D21 64 17N 24 47 E
Oulu, Finland ........ 8 D21 65 1N 25 29 E
Oulujärvi, Finland ........ 8 D22 64 25N 27 15 E
Oulujoki ➤, Finland ........ 8 D21 65 1N 25 30 E
Oum Chalouba, Chad ........ 51 E10 15 48N 20 46 E
Oum Hadjer, Chad ........ 51 F9 13 18N 19 41 E

Ounasjoki ➤, Finland ........ 8 C21 66 31N 25 40 E
Ounguati, Namibia ........ 56 C2 22 0S 15 46 E
Ounianga Sérir, Chad ........ 51 E10 18 54N 20 51 E
Our ➤, Lux. ........ 15 E6 49 55N 6 5 E
Ouray, U.S.A. ........ 77 G10 38 1N 107 40W
Ourense, Spain ........ 21 A2 42 19N 7 55W
Ouricuri, Brazil ........ 93 E10 7 53S 40 5W
Ourinhos, Brazil ........ 95 A6 23 0S 49 54W
Ouro Fino, Brazil ........ 95 A6 22 16S 46 25W
Ouro Prêto, Brazil ........ 95 A7 20 20S 43 30W
Ourthe ➤, Belgium ........ 15 D5 50 29N 5 35 E
Ouse ➤, E. Susx., U.K. ........ 13 G8 50 47N 0 4 E
Ouse ➤, N. Yorks., U.K. ........ 12 D7 53 44N 0 6 E
Outaouais ➤, Canada ........ 72 C5 45 27N 74 8W
Outardes ➤, Canada ........ 73 C6 49 24N 69 30W
Outer Hebrides, U.K. ........ 11 D1 57 30N 7 40W
Outjo, Namibia ........ 56 C2 20 5S 16 7 E
Outlook, Canada ........ 71 C7 51 30N 107 0W
Outokumpu, Finland ........ 8 E23 62 43N 29 1 E
Ouyen, Australia ........ 63 F3 35 1S 142 22 E
Ovalau, Fiji ........ 59 C8 17 40S 178 48 E
Ovalle, Chile ........ 94 C1 30 33S 71 18W
Ovamboland, Namibia ........ 56 B2 18 30S 16 0 E
Overflakkee, Neths. ........ 15 C4 51 44N 4 10 E
Overijssel □, Neths. ........ 15 B6 52 25N 6 35 E
Overland Park, U.S.A. ........ 80 F7 38 55N 94 50W
Overton, U.S.A. ........ 79 J12 36 33N 114 27W
Övertorneå, Sweden ........ 8 C20 66 23N 23 38 E
Ovid, U.S.A. ........ 85 D8 42 41N 76 49W
Oviedo, Spain ........ 21 A3 43 25N 5 50W
Oviši, Latvia ........ 9 H19 57 33N 21 44 E
Ovoot, Mongolia ........ 34 B7 45 21N 113 45 E
Övör Hangay □, Mongolia ........ 34 B2 45 0N 102 30 E
Øvre Ärdal, Norway ........ 9 F12 61 19N 7 48 E
Ovruch, Ukraine ........ 17 C15 51 25N 28 45 E
Owaka, N.Z. ........ 59 M2 46 27S 169 40 E
Owambo = Ovamboland,
Namibia ........ 56 B2 18 30S 16 0 E
Owasco L., U.S.A. ........ 85 D8 42 50N 76 31W
Owase, Japan ........ 31 G8 34 7N 136 12 E
Owatonna, U.S.A. ........ 80 C8 44 5N 93 14W
Owbeh, Afghan. ........ 40 B3 34 28N 63 10 E
Owego, U.S.A. ........ 85 D8 42 6N 76 16W
Owen Falls Dam, Uganda ........ 54 B3 0 30N 33 5 E
Owen Sound, Canada ........ 84 B4 44 35N 80 55W
Owens ➤, U.S.A. ........ 78 J9 36 32N 117 59W
Owens L., U.S.A. ........ 79 J9 36 26N 117 57W
Owensboro, U.S.A. ........ 82 G2 37 46N 87 7W
Owl ➤, Canada ........ 71 B10 57 51N 92 44W
Owo, Nigeria ........ 50 G7 7 10N 5 39 E
Owosso, U.S.A. ........ 82 D3 43 0N 84 10W
Owyhee, U.S.A. ........ 76 F5 41 57N 116 6W
Owyhee ➤, U.S.A. ........ 76 E5 43 49N 117 2W
Owyhee, L., U.S.A. ........ 76 E5 43 38N 117 14W
Ox Mts. = Slieve Gamph, Ireland 10 B3 54 6N 9 0W
Öxarfjörður, Iceland ........ 8 C5 66 15N 16 45W
Oxbow, Canada ........ 71 D8 49 14N 102 10W
Oxelösund, Sweden ........ 9 G17 58 43N 17 5 E
Oxford, N.Z. ........ 59 K4 43 18S 172 11 E
Oxford, U.K. ........ 13 F6 51 46N 1 15W
Oxford, Mass., U.S.A. ........ 85 D13 42 7N 71 52W
Oxford, Miss., U.S.A. ........ 81 H10 34 22N 89 31W
Oxford, N.C., U.S.A. ........ 83 G6 36 19N 78 35W
Oxford, N.Y., U.S.A. ........ 85 D9 42 27N 75 36W
Oxford, Ohio, U.S.A. ........ 82 F3 39 31N 84 45W
Oxford, L., Canada ........ 71 C9 54 51N 95 37W
Oxfordshire □, U.K. ........ 13 F6 51 48N 1 16W
Oxnard, U.S.A. ........ 79 L7 34 12N 119 11W
Oxus = Amudarya ➤, Uzbekistan 28 E6 43 58N 59 34 E
Oya, Malaysia ........ 36 D4 2 55N 111 55 E
Oyama, Japan ........ 31 F9 36 18N 139 48 E
Oyem, Gabon ........ 52 D2 1 34N 11 31 E
Oyen, Canada ........ 71 C6 51 22N 110 28W
Oykel ➤, U.K. ........ 11 D4 57 56N 4 26W
Oymyakon, Russia ........ 29 C15 63 25N 142 44 E
Oyo, Nigeria ........ 50 G6 7 46N 3 56 E
Oyster Bay, U.S.A. ........ 85 F11 40 52N 73 32W
Öyübari, Japan ........ 30 C11 43 1N 142 5 E
Ozamiz, Phil. ........ 37 C6 8 15N 123 50 E
Ozark, Ala., U.S.A. ........ 83 K3 31 28N 85 39W
Ozark, Ark., U.S.A. ........ 81 H8 35 29N 93 50W
Ozark, Mo., U.S.A. ........ 81 G8 37 1N 93 12W
Ozark Plateau, U.S.A. ........ 81 G9 37 20N 91 40W
Ozarks, L. of the, U.S.A. ........ 80 F8 38 12N 92 38W
Özd, Hungary ........ 17 D11 48 14N 20 15 E
Ozette L., U.S.A. ........ 78 B2 48 6N 124 38W
Ozona, U.S.A. ........ 81 K4 30 43N 101 12W
Ozuluama, Mexico ........ 87 C5 21 40N 97 50W

# P

Pa-an, Burma ........ 41 L20 16 51N 97 40 E
Pa Mong Dam, Thailand ........ 38 D4 18 0N 102 22 E
Pa Sak ➤, Thailand ........ 38 E3 15 30N 101 0 E
Paamiut, Greenland ........ 69 B15 62 0N 49 43W
Paarl, S. Africa ........ 56 E2 33 45S 18 56 E
Pabbay, U.K. ........ 11 D1 57 46N 7 14W
Pabianice, Poland ........ 17 C10 51 40N 19 20 E
Pabna, Bangla. ........ 41 G16 24 1N 89 18 E
Pabo, Uganda ........ 54 B3 3 1N 32 10 E
Pacaja ➤, Brazil ........ 93 D8 1 56S 50 50W
Pacaraima, Sa., S. Amer. ........ 92 C6 4 0N 62 30W
Pacasmayo, Peru ........ 92 E3 7 20S 79 35W
Pachhar, India ........ 42 G7 24 40N 77 42 E
Pachitea ➤, Peru ........ 92 E4 8 46S 74 33W
Pachpadra, India ........ 40 G8 25 58N 72 10 E
Pachmarhi, India ........ 43 H8 22 28N 78 26 E
Pachuca, Mexico ........ 87 C5 20 10N 98 40W
Pacific, Canada ........ 70 C3 54 48N 128 28W
Pacific-Antarctic Ridge, Pac. Oc. 5 B13 43 0S 115 0W
Pacific Grove, U.S.A. ........ 78 J5 36 38N 121 56W
Pacific Ocean ........ 65 G14 10 0N 140 0W
Pacific Rim △, Canada ........ 70 D4 48 40N 124 45W
Pacitan, Indonesia ........ 37 H14 8 12S 111 7 E
Packwood, U.S.A. ........ 78 D5 46 36N 121 40W
Padaido, Kepulauan, Indonesia . 37 E9 1 15S 136 30 E
Padang Endau, Malaysia ........ 39 L4 2 40N 103 38 E
Padangpanjang, Indonesia ........ 36 E2 0 40S 100 20 E
Padangsidempuan, Indonesia .... 36 D1 1 30N 99 15 E
Paddle Prairie, Canada ........ 70 B5 57 57N 117 29W
Paddockwood, Canada ........ 71 C7 53 30N 105 30W
Paderborn, Germany ........ 16 C5 51 42N 8 45 E

Padma, India ........ 43 G11 24 12N 85 22 E
Pádova, Italy ........ 22 B4 45 25N 11 53 E
Padra, India ........ 42 H5 22 15N 73 7 E
Padrauna, India ........ 43 F10 26 54N 83 59 E
Padre I., U.S.A. ........ 81 M6 27 10N 97 25W
Padre Island △, U.S.A. ........ 81 M6 26 36N 97 17W
Padstow, U.K. ........ 13 G3 50 33N 4 58W
Padua = Pádova, Italy ........ 22 B4 45 25N 11 53 E
Paducah, Ky., U.S.A. ........ 82 G1 37 5N 88 37W
Paducah, Tex., U.S.A. ........ 81 H4 34 1N 100 18W
Paengnyŏng-do, S. Korea ........ 35 F13 37 57N 124 40 E
Paeroa, N.Z. ........ 59 G5 37 23S 175 41 E
Pafúri, Mozam. ........ 57 C5 22 28S 31 17 E
Pag, Croatia ........ 16 F8 44 25N 15 3 E
Pagadian, Phil. ........ 37 C6 7 55N 123 30 E
Pagai Selatan, Pulau, Indonesia 36 E2 3 0S 100 15 E
Pagai Utara, Pulau, Indonesia .. 36 E2 2 35S 100 0 E
Pagalu = Annobón, Atl. Oc. .... 49 G4 1 25S 5 36 E
Pagara, India ........ 43 G9 24 22N 80 1 E
Pagastikós Kólpos, Greece ........ 23 E10 39 15N 23 0 E
Pagatan, Indonesia ........ 36 E5 3 33S 115 59 E
Page, U.S.A. ........ 77 H8 36 57N 111 27W
Pago Pago, Amer. Samoa ........ 59 B13 14 16S 170 43W
Pagosa Springs, U.S.A. ........ 77 H10 37 16N 107 1W
Pagwa River, Canada ........ 72 B2 50 2N 85 14W
Pahala, U.S.A. ........ 74 J17 19 12S 155 29W
Pahang ➤, Malaysia ........ 39 L4 3 30N 103 9 E
Pahiatua, N.Z. ........ 59 J5 40 27S 175 50 E
Pahokee, U.S.A. ........ 83 M5 26 50N 80 40W
Pahrump, U.S.A. ........ 79 J11 36 12N 115 59W
Pahute Mesa, U.S.A. ........ 78 H10 37 20N 116 45W
Pai, Thailand ........ 38 C2 19 19N 98 27 E
Paicines, U.S.A. ........ 78 J5 36 44N 121 17W
Paide, Estonia ........ 9 G21 58 53N 25 33 E
Päijänne, Finland ........ 9 F21 61 30N 25 30 E
Pailani, India ........ 43 G9 25 45N 80 26 E
Pailin, Cambodia ........ 38 F4 12 46N 102 36 E
Painan, Indonesia ........ 36 E2 1 21S 100 34 E
Painesville, U.S.A. ........ 84 E3 41 43N 81 15W
Paint Hills = Wemindji, Canada . 72 B4 53 0N 78 49W
Paint L., Canada ........ 71 B9 55 28N 97 57W
Painted Desert, U.S.A. ........ 77 J8 36 0N 111 0W
Paintsville, U.S.A. ........ 82 G4 37 49N 82 48W
País Vasco □, Spain ........ 21 A4 42 50N 2 45W
Paisley, Canada ........ 84 B3 44 18N 81 16W
Paisley, U.K. ........ 11 F4 55 50N 4 25W
Paisley, U.S.A. ........ 76 E3 42 42N 120 32W
Paita, Peru ........ 92 E2 5 11S 81 9W
Pajares, Puerto de, Spain ........ 21 A3 42 58N 5 46W
Pak Lay, Laos ........ 38 C3 18 15N 101 27 E
Pak Phanang, Thailand ........ 39 H3 8 21N 100 12 E
Pak Sane, Laos ........ 38 C4 18 22N 103 39 E
Pak Song, Laos ........ 38 E6 15 11N 106 14 E
Pak Suong, Laos ........ 38 C4 19 58N 102 15 E
Pak Tam Chung, China ........ 33 G11 22 24N 114 19 E
Pakaur, India ........ 43 G12 24 38N 87 51 E
Pakenham, Canada ........ 85 A8 45 18N 76 18W
Pákhnes, Greece ........ 25 D6 35 16N 24 4 E
Pakhuis, S. Africa ........ 56 E2 32 9S 19 5 E
Pakistan ■, Asia ........ 42 E4 30 0N 70 0 E
Pakkading, Laos ........ 38 C4 18 19N 103 59 E
Pakokku, Burma ........ 41 J19 21 20N 95 0 E
Pakowki L., Canada ........ 71 D6 49 20N 111 0W
Pakpattan, Pakistan ........ 42 D5 30 25N 73 27 E
Paktīā □, Afghan. ........ 40 C6 33 0N 69 15 E
Paktīkā □, Afghan. ........ 40 C6 32 30N 69 0 E
Pakwach, Uganda ........ 54 B3 2 28N 31 27 E
Pakxe, Laos ........ 38 E5 15 5N 105 52 E
Pal Lahara, India ........ 43 J11 21 27N 85 11 E
Pala, Chad ........ 51 G9 9 25N 15 5 E
Pala, Dem. Rep. of the Congo .. 54 D2 6 45S 29 30 E
Pala, U.S.A. ........ 79 M9 33 22N 117 5W
Palabek, Uganda ........ 54 B3 3 22N 32 33 E
Palacios, U.S.A. ........ 81 L6 28 42N 96 13W
Palagruža, Croatia ........ 22 C7 42 24N 16 15 E
Palaiókastron, Greece ........ 25 D8 35 12N 26 15 E
Palaiokhóra, Greece ........ 25 D5 35 16N 23 39 E
Palam, India ........ 40 K10 19 0N 77 0 E
Palampur, India ........ 42 C7 32 10N 76 30 E
Palana, Australia ........ 63 F4 39 45S 147 55 E
Palana, Russia ........ 29 D16 59 10N 159 59 E
Palanan, Phil. ........ 37 A6 17 17N 122 30 E
Palanan Pt., Phil. ........ 37 A6 17 17N 122 30 E
Palandri, Pakistan ........ 43 C5 33 42N 73 40 E
Palanga, Lithuania ........ 9 J19 55 58N 21 3 E
Palangkaraya, Indonesia ........ 36 E4 2 16S 113 56 E
Palani Hills, India ........ 40 P10 10 14N 77 33 E
Palanpur, India ........ 42 G5 24 10N 72 25 E
Palapye, Botswana ........ 56 C4 22 30S 27 7 E
Palas, Pakistan ........ 43 B5 35 4N 73 14 E
Palashi, India ........ 43 H13 23 47N 88 15 E
Palasponga, India ........ 43 J11 21 47N 85 34 E
Palatka, Russia ........ 29 C16 60 6N 150 54 E
Palatka, U.S.A. ........ 83 L5 29 39N 81 38W
Palau ■, Pac. Oc. ........ 26 J17 7 30N 134 30 E
Palauk, Burma ........ 38 F2 13 10N 98 40 E
Palawan, Phil. ........ 36 C5 9 30N 118 30 E
Palayankottai, India ........ 40 Q10 8 45N 77 45 E
Paldiski, Estonia ........ 9 G21 59 23N 24 9 E
Paleleh, Indonesia ........ 37 D6 1 10N 121 50 E
Palembang, Indonesia ........ 36 E2 3 0S 104 50 E
Palencia, Spain ........ 21 A3 42 1N 4 34W
Palenque, Mexico ........ 87 D6 17 31N 91 58W
Paleokastrítsa, Greece ........ 25 A3 39 40N 19 41 E
Paleometokho, Cyprus ........ 25 D12 35 7N 33 11 E
Palermo, Italy ........ 22 E5 38 7N 13 22 E
Palermo, U.S.A. ........ 76 G3 39 26N 121 33W
Palestina, Chile ........ 96 A3 23 50S 69 47W
Palestine, Asia ........ 46 D4 32 0N 35 0 E
Palestine, U.S.A. ........ 81 K7 31 46N 95 38W
Paletwa, Burma ........ 41 J18 21 10N 92 50 E
Palghat, India ........ 40 P10 10 46N 76 42 E
Palgrave, Mt., Australia ........ 60 D2 23 22S 115 58 E
Pali, India ........ 42 G5 25 50N 73 20 E
Palikir, Micronesia ........ 64 G7 6 55N 158 9 E
Paliouri, Ákra, Greece ........ 23 E10 39 57N 23 45 E
Palisades Reservoir, U.S.A. ........ 76 E8 43 20N 111 12W
Paliseul, Belgium ........ 15 E5 49 54N 5 8 E
Palitana, India ........ 42 J4 21 32N 71 49 E
Palizada, Mexico ........ 87 D6 18 18N 92 8W
Palk Bay, Asia ........ 40 Q11 9 30N 79 15 E
Palk Strait, Asia ........ 40 Q11 10 0N 79 45 E
Palkot, India ........ 43 H11 22 53N 84 39 E
Pallanza = Verbánia, Italy ........ 20 D8 45 56N 8 33 E
Pallarenda, Australia ........ 62 B4 19 12S 146 46 E
Pallinup ➤, Australia ........ 61 F2 34 27S 118 50 E

Pallisa, Uganda .............. 54 B3    1 12N  33 43 E
Pallu, India ................. 42 E6   28 59N  74 14 E
Palm Bay, U.S.A. ............ 83 L5   28  2N  80 35W
Palm Coast, U.S.A. .......... 83 L5   29 32N  81 10W
Palm Desert, U.S.A. ......... 79 M10  33 43N 116 22W
Palm Is., Australia .......... 62 B4   18 40S 146 35 E
Palm Springs, U.S.A. ........ 79 M10  33 50N 116 33W
Palma, Mozam. .............. 55 E5   10 46S  40 29 E
Palma, B. de, Spain ......... 24 B9   39 30N   2 39 E
Palma de Mallorca, Spain .... 24 B9   39 35N   2 39 E
Palma Soriano, Cuba ......... 88 B4   20 15N  76  0W
Palmares, Brazil ............ 93 E11   8 41S  35 28W
Palmas, Brazil .............. 95 B5   26 29S  52  0W
Palmas, C., Liberia ......... 50 H4    4 27N   7 46W
Pálmas, G. di, Italy ......... 22 E3   39  0N   8 30 E
Palmdale, U.S.A. ............ 79 L8   34 35N 118  7W
Palmeira das Missões, Brazil . 95 B5   27 55S  53 17W
Palmeira dos Índios, Brazil .. 93 E11   9 25S  36 37W
Palmer, Antarctica .......... 5 C17  64 35S  60  0W
Palmer, U.S.A. .............. 68 B5   61 36N 149  7W
Palmer →, Australia ......... 62 B3   16  0S 142 26 E
Palmer Arch., Antarctica .... 5 C17  64 15S  65  0W
Palmer Lake, U.S.A. ......... 80 F2   39  7N 104 55W
Palmer Land, Antarctica ..... 5 D18  73  0S  63  0W
Palmerston, Australia ....... 60 B5   12 31S 130 59 E
Palmerston, Canada ......... 84 C4   43 50N  80 51W
Palmerston, N.Z. ............ 59 L3   45 29S 170 43 E
Palmerston North, N.Z. ...... 59 J5   40 21S 175 39 E
Palmerton, U.S.A. ........... 85 F9   40 48N  75 37W
Palmetto, U.S.A. ............ 83 M4   27 31N  82 34W
Palmi, Italy ................. 22 E6   38 21N  15 51 E
Palmira, Argentina .......... 94 C2   32 59S  68 34W
Palmira, Colombia ........... 92 C3    3 32N  76 16W
Palmyra = Tudmur, Syria .... 44 C3   34 36N  38 15 E
Palmyra, Mo., U.S.A. ........ 80 F9   39 48N  91 32W
Palmyra, N.J., U.S.A. ........ 85 F9   40  1N  75  1W
Palmyra, N.Y., U.S.A. ........ 84 C7   43  5N  77 18W
Palmyra, Pa., U.S.A. ......... 85 F8   40 18N  76 36W
Palmyra Is., Pac. Oc. ........ 65 G11   5 52N 162  5W
Palo Alto, U.S.A. ............ 78 H4   37 27N 122 10W
Palo Seco, Trin. & Tob. ...... 93 K15  10  4N  61 36W
Palo Verde, U.S.A. ........... 79 M12  33 26N 114 44W
Palo Verde △, Costa Rica .... 88 D2   10 21N  85 21W
Palomar Mt., U.S.A. ......... 79 M10  33 22N 116 50W
Palopo, Indonesia ........... 37 E6    3  0S 120 16 E
Palos, C. de, Spain .......... 21 D5   37 38N   0 40W
Palos Verdes, U.S.A. ......... 79 M8   33 48N 118 23W
Palos Verdes, Pt., U.S.A. ..... 79 M8   33 43N 118 26W
Palu, Indonesia ............. 37 E5    1  0S 119 52 E
Palu, Turkey ................ 19 G7   38 45N  40  0 E
Palwal, India ............... 42 E7   28  8N  77 19 E
Pamanukan, Indonesia ....... 37 G12   6 16S 107 49 E
Pamekasan, Indonesia ....... 37 G15   7 10S 113 28 E
Pamenang, Indonesia ........ 37 J19   8 24S 116  6 E
Pamiers, France ............. 20 E4   43  7N   1 39 E
Pamir, Tajikistan ............ 28 F8   37 40N  73  0 E
Pamlico →, U.S.A. .......... 83 H7   35 20N  76 28W
Pamlico Sd., U.S.A. .......... 83 H8   35 20N  76  0W
Pampa, U.S.A. ............... 81 H4   35 32N 100 58W
Pampa de las Salinas, Argentina . 94 C2   32  1S  66 58W
Pampanua, Indonesia ........ 37 E6    4 16S 120  8 E
Pampas, Argentina .......... 94 D3   35  0S  63  0W
Pampas, Peru ............... 92 F4   12 20S  74 50W
Pamplona, Colombia ......... 92 B4    7 23N  72 39W
Pamplona, Spain ............ 21 A5   42 48N   1 38W
Pampoenpoort, S. Africa ..... 56 E3   31  3S  22 40 E
Pan de Azúcar △, Chile ..... 94 B1   26  0S  70 40W
Pana, U.S.A. ................ 80 F10  39 23N  89  5W
Panaca, U.S.A. .............. 77 H6   37 47N 114 23W
Panaitan, Indonesia ......... 37 G11   6 36S 105 12 E
Panaji, India ............... 40 M8   15 25N  73 50 E
Panamá, Panama ............ 88 E4    9  0N  79 25W
Panama ■, Cent. Amer. ...... 88 E4    8 48N  79 55W
Panamá, G. of, Panama ...... 88 E4    8 40N  79 20W
Panama Canal, Panama ...... 88 E4    9 10N  79 37W
Panama City, U.S.A. ......... 83 K3   30 10N  85 40W
Panamint Range, U.S.A. ..... 79 J9   36 20N 117 20W
Panamint Springs, U.S.A. .... 79 J9   36 20N 117 28W
Panão, Peru ................ 92 E3    9 55S  75 55W
Panare, Thailand ........... 39 J3    6 51N 101 30 E
Panay, Phil. ................ 37 B6   11 10N 122 30 E
Panay, G., Phil. ............. 37 B6   11  0N 122 30 E
Pančevo, Serbia & M. ........ 23 B9   44 52N  20 41 E
Panda, Mozam. .............. 57 C5   24  2S  34 45 E
Pandan, Malaysia ........... 39 d    1 32N 103 46 E
Pandan, Phil. ............... 37 B6   11 45N 122 10 E
Pandan, Selat, Singapore .... 39 d    1 15N 103 44 E
Pandan Tampoi = Tampoi,
 Malaysia ................. 39 d    1 30N 103 39 E
Pandegelang, Indonesia ...... 37 G12   6 25S 106  5 E
Pandhana, India ............ 42 J7   21 42N  76 13 E
Pandharpur, India .......... 40 L9   17 41N  75 20 E
Pando, Uruguay ............. 95 C4   34 44S  56  0W
Pando, L. = Hope, L., Australia . 63 D2   28 24S 139 18 E
Pandokrátor, Greece ......... 25 A3   39 45N  19 50 E
Pandora, Costa Rica ......... 88 E3    9 43N  83  3W
Panevėžys, Lithuania ........ 9 J21   55 42N  24 25 E
Panfilov, Kazakhstan ........ 28 E8   44 10N  80  0 E
Pang-Long, Burma .......... 41 H21  23 11N  98 45 E
Pang Sida △, Thailand ...... 38 E4   14  5N 102 17 E
Pang-Yang, Burma .......... 41 H21  22  7N  98 48 E
Panga, Dem. Rep. of the Congo . 54 B2    1 52N  26 18 E
Pangalanes, Canal des =
 Ampangalana, Lakandranon',
 Madag. .................. 57 C8   22 48S  47 50 E
Pangani, Tanzania .......... 54 D4    5 25S  38 58 E
Pangani →, Tanzania ........ 54 D4    5 26S  38 58 E
Pangfou = Bengbu, China .... 35 H9   32 58N 117 20 E
Pangil, Dem. Rep. of the Congo . 54 C2    3 10S  26 35 E
Pangkah, Tanjung, Indonesia . 37 G15   6 51S 112 33 E
Pangkajene, Indonesia ....... 37 E5    4 46S 119 34 E
Pangkalanbrandan, Indonesia . 36 D1    4  1N  98 20 E
Pangkalanbuun, Indonesia ... 36 E4    2 41S 111 37 E
Pangkalpinang, Indonesia .... 36 E3    2  0S 106  0 E
Pangnirtung, Canada ........ 69 B13  66  8N  65 43W
Pangong Tso, India .......... 42 B8   34 40N  78 40 E
Panguitch, U.S.A. ........... 77 H7   37 50N 112 26W
Pangutaran Group, Phil. ..... 37 C6    6 18N 120 34 E
Panhandle, U.S.A. ........... 81 H4   35 21N 101 23W
Pani Mines, India .......... 42 H5   22 29N  73 50 E
Pania-Mutombo, Dem. Rep. of
 the Congo ................ 54 D1    5 11S  23 51 E
Panikota I., India ........... 42 J4   20 46N  71 21 E
Panipat, India .............. 42 E7   29 25N  77  2 E
Panjal Range = Pir Panjal Range,
 India .................... 42 C7   32 30N  76 50 E
Panjang, Hon, Vietnam ...... 39 H4    9 20N 103 28 E

Panjgur, Pakistan ........... 40 F4   27  0N  64  5 E
Panjim = Panaji, India ....... 40 M8   15 25N  73 50 E
Panjin, China ............... 35 D12  41  3N 122  2 E
Panjinad Barrage, Pakistan ... 40 E7   29 22N  71 15 E
Panjnad →, Pakistan ........ 42 E4   28 57N  70 30 E
Panjwai, Afghan. ............ 42 D1   31 26N  65 27 E
Panmunjŏm, N. Korea ....... 35 F14  37 59N 126 38 E
Panna, India ................ 43 G9   24 40N  80 15 E
Panna Hills, India ........... 43 G9   24 40N  81 15 E
Pannawonica, Australia ...... 60 D2   21 39S 116 19 E
Pannga, Tanjung, Indonesia .. 37 K19   8 54S 116  2 E
Pano Akil, Pakistan .......... 42 F3   27 51N  69  7 E
Pano Lefkara, Cyprus ........ 25 E12  34 53N  33 20 E
Pano Panayia, Cyprus ........ 25 E11  34 55N  32 38 E
Panorama, Brazil ............ 95 A5   21 21S  51 51W
Pánormon, Greece ........... 25 D6   35 25N  24 41 E
Pansemal, India ............. 42 J6   21 39N  74 42 E
Panshan = Panjin, China ..... 35 D12  41  3N 122  2 E
Panshi, China ............... 35 C14  42 58N 126  5 E
Pantanal, Brazil ............. 92 H7   17 30S  57 40W
Pantanos de Centla ◊, Mexico . 87 D6   18 25N  92 25W
Pantar, Indonesia ........... 37 F6    8 28S 124 10 E
Pante Macassar, E. Timor .... 37 F6    9 30S 123 58 E
Pante Makasar = Pante Macassar,
 E. Timor ................. 37 F6    9 30S 123 58 E
Pantelleria, Italy ............ 22 F4   36 50N  11 57 E
Pánuco, Mexico ............. 87 C5   22  0N  98 15W
Paola, Malta ................ 25 D2   35 52N  14 30 E
Paola, U.S.A. ............... 80 F7   38 35N  94 53W
Paonia, U.S.A. .............. 77 G10  38 52N 107 36W
Paoting = Baoding, China .... 34 E8   38 50N 115 28 E
Paot'ou = Baotou, China ..... 34 D6   40 32N 110  2 E
Paoua, C.A.R. ............... 52 C3    7  9N  16 20 E
Pápa, Hungary .............. 17 E9   47 22N  17 30 E
Papa Stour, U.K. ............ 11 A7   60 20N   1 42W
Papa Westray, U.K. .......... 11 B6   59 20N   2 55W
Papagayo →, Mexico ........ 87 D5   16 36N  99 43W
Papagayo, G. de, Costa Rica .. 88 D2   10 30N  85 50W
Papakura, N.Z. .............. 59 G5   37  4S 174 59 E
Papantla, Mexico ........... 87 C5   20 30N  97 30W
Papar, Malaysia ............. 36 C5    5 45N 116  0 E
Paparoa △, N.Z. ............ 59 K3   42  7S 171 26 E
Papeete, Tahiti .............. 65 J13  17 32S 149 34W
Paphos, Cyprus ............. 25 E11  34 46N  32 25 E
Papigochic →, Mexico ....... 86 B3   29  9N 109 40W
Paposo, Chile ............... 25 E12  34 54N  33  4 E
Papoutsa, Cyprus ........... 25 E12  34 54N  33  4 E
Papua □, Indonesia ......... 37 E9    4  0S 137  0 E
Papua New Guinea ■, Oceania . 64 H6    8  0S 145  0 E
Papudo, Chile ............... 94 C1   32 29S  71 27W
Papun, Burma .............. 41 K20  18  2N  97 30 E
Papunya, Australia .......... 60 D5   23 15S 131 54 E
Pará = Belém, Brazil ........ 93 D9    1 20S  48 30W
Pará □, Brazil .............. 93 D8    3 20S  52  0W
Paraburdoo, Australia ....... 60 D2   23 14S 117 32 E
Paracatu, Brazil ............. 93 G9   17 10S  46 50W
Paracel Is., S. China Sea ..... 36 A4   15 50N 112  0 E
Parachilna, Australia ........ 63 E2   31 10S 138 21 E
Parachinar, Pakistan ........ 42 C4   33 55N  70  5 E
Paradhísi, Greece ........... 25 C10  36 18N  28  7 E
Paradip, India .............. 41 J15  20 15N  86 35 E
Paradise, Calif., U.S.A. ...... 78 F5   39 46N 121 37W
Paradise, Nev., U.S.A. ....... 79 J11  36  9N 115 10W
Paradise →, Canada ......... 73 B8   53 27N  57 19W
Paradise Hill, Canada ....... 71 C7   53 32N 109 28W
Paradise River, Canada ...... 73 B8   53 27N  57 17W
Paradise Valley, U.S.A. ...... 76 F5   41 30N 117 32W
Parado, Indonesia ........... 37 F5    8 42S 118 30 E
Paragould, U.S.A. ........... 81 G9   36  3N  90 29W
Paragua →, Venezuela ...... 92 B6    6 55N  62 55W
Paraguaçu →, Brazil ........ 93 F11  12 45S  38 54W
Paraguaçu Paulista, Brazil ... 95 A5   22 22S  50 35W
Paraguaná, Pen. de, Venezuela . 92 A5   12  0N  70  0W
Paraguarí, Paraguay ........ 94 B4   25 36S  57  0W
Paraguarí □, Paraguay ...... 94 B4   26  0S  57 10W
Paraguay ■, S. Amer. ....... 94 A4   23  0S  57  0W
Paraguay →, Paraguay ...... 94 B4   27 18S  58 38W
Paraíba = João Pessoa, Brazil . 93 E12   7 10S  34 52W
Paraíba □, Brazil ........... 93 E11   7  0S  36  0W
Paraíba do Sul →, Brazil .... 95 A7   21 37S  41  3W
Parainen, Finland ........... 9 F20   60 18N  22 18 E
Paraíso, Mexico ............. 87 D6   18 24N  93 14W
Parak, Iran ................. 45 E7   27 38N  52 25 E
Parakou, Benin ............. 50 G6    9 25N   2 40 E
Paralimni, Cyprus .......... 25 D12  35  2N  33 58 E
Paramaribo, Suriname ....... 93 B7    5 50N  55 10W
Páramos del Batallón y La
 Negra △, Venezuela ...... 89 E5    8  2N  71 55W
Paramushir, Ostrov, Russia ... 29 D16  50 24N 156  0 E
Paran →, Israel ............ 46 E4   30 20N  35 10 E
Paraná, Argentina .......... 94 C3   31 45S  60 30W
Paraná, Brazil .............. 93 F9   12 30S  47 48W
Paraná □, Brazil ............ 95 A5   24 30S  51  0W
Paraná →, Argentina ........ 94 C4   33 43S  59 15W
Paranaguá, Brazil ........... 95 B6   25 30S  48 30W
Paranaíba, Brazil ........... 93 G8   19 40S  51 11W
Paranaíba →, Brazil ......... 93 H8   20  6S  51  4W
Paranapanema →, Brazil .... 95 A5   22 40S  53  9W
Paranapiacaba, Serra do, Brazil . 95 A6   24 31S  48 35W
Paranavaí, Brazil ........... 95 A5   23  4S  52 56W
Parang, Maguindanao, Phil. .. 37 C6   7 23N 124  1 E
Parang, Sulu, Phil. .......... 37 C6    5 55N 120 54 E
Parângul Mare, Vf., Romania . 17 F12  45 20N  23 37 E
Paraparaumu, N.Z. .......... 59 J5   40 57S 175  3 E
Parbati →, M.P., India ...... 42 G7   25 50N  76 30 E
Parbati →, Raj., India ....... 42 F7   26 54N  77 53 E
Parbhani, India ............. 40 K10  19  8N  76 52 E
Parchim, Germany .......... 16 B6   53 26N  11 52 E
Pardes Hanna-Karkur, Israel . 46 C3   32 28N  34 57 E
Pardo →, Bahia, Brazil ...... 93 G11  15 40S  39  0W
Pardo →, Mato Grosso, Brazil . 95 A5   21 46S  52  9W
Pardubice, Czech Rep. ....... 16 C8   50  3N  15 45 E
Pare, Indonesia ............. 37 G15   7 43S 112 12 E
Pare Mts., Tanzania ......... 54 C4    4  0S  37 45 E
Parecis, Serra dos, Brazil .... 92 F7   13  0S  60  0W
Paren, Russia ............... 29 C17  62 30N 163 15 E
Parent, Canada ............. 72 C5   47 55N  74 35W
Parent, L., Canada .......... 72 C4   48 31N  77  1W
Parepare, Indonesia ......... 37 E5    4  0S 119 40 E
Párga, Greece .............. 23 E9   39 15N  20 29 E
Pargas = Parainen, Finland ... 9 F20   60 18N  22 18 E
Pargo, Pta. do, Madeira ...... 24 D2   32 49N  17 17W
Paria, G. de, Venezuela ...... 93 K14  10 20N  62  0W
Pariaguán, Venezuela ....... 92 B6    8 51N  64 34W
Paricutín, Cerro, Mexico ..... 86 D4   19 28N 102 15W
Parigi, Indonesia ............ 37 E6    0 50S 120  5 E

Parika, Guyana ............. 92 B7    6 50N  58 20W
Parima, Serra, Brazil ........ 92 C6    2 30N  64  0W
Parinari, Peru .............. 92 D4    4 35S  74 25W
Pariñas, Pta., S. Amer. ...... 90 D2    4 30S  82  0W
Parintins, Brazil ............ 92 D7    2 40S  56 50W
Pariparit Kyun, Burma ....... 41 M18  14 55N  93 45 E
Paris, Canada .............. 84 C4   43 12N  80 25W
Paris, France ............... 20 B5   48 50N   2 20 E
Paris, Idaho, U.S.A. ......... 76 E8   42 14N 111 24W
Paris, Ky., U.S.A. ........... 82 F3   38 13N  84 15W
Paris, Tenn., U.S.A. ......... 83 G1   36 18N  88 19W
Paris, Tex., U.S.A. .......... 81 J7   33 40N  95 33W
Park, U.S.A. ................ 85 C8   43 25N  76  8W
Parishville, U.S.A. .......... 85 B10  44 38N  74 49W
Park, U.S.A. ................ 78 B4   48 45N 122 18W
Park City, U.S.A. ........... 81 G6   37 48N  97 20W
Park Falls, U.S.A. ........... 80 C9   45 56N  90 27W
Park Head, Canada .......... 84 B3   44 36N  81  9W
Park Hills, U.S.A. ........... 81 G9   37 53N  90 28W
Park Range, U.S.A. .......... 76 G10  40  0N 106 30W
Park Rapids, U.S.A. ......... 80 B7   46 55N  95  4W
Park River, U.S.A. .......... 80 A6   48 24N  97 45W
Park Rynie, S. Africa ........ 57 E5   30 25S  30 45 E
Parkā Bandar, Iran ......... 45 E8   25 55N  59 35 E
Parkano, Finland ........... 9 E20   62  1N  23  0 E
Parker, Ariz., U.S.A. ........ 79 L12  34  9N 114 17W
Parker, Pa., U.S.A. .......... 84 E5   41  5N  79 41W
Parker Dam, U.S.A. ......... 79 L12  34 18N 114 11W
Parkersburg, U.S.A. ......... 82 F5   39 16N  81 34W
Parkes, Australia ........... 63 E4   33  9S 148 11 E
Parkfield, U.S.A. ............ 78 K6   35 54N 120 26W
Parkhill, Canada ............ 84 C3   43 15N  81 38W
Parkland, U.S.A. ............ 78 C4   47  9N 122 26W
Parkston, U.S.A. ............ 80 D6   43 24N  97 59W
Parksville, Canada .......... 70 D4   49 20N 124 21W
Parla, Spain ................ 21 B4   40 14N   3 46W
Parma, Italy ................ 20 D9   44 48N  10 20 E
Parma, Idaho, U.S.A. ........ 76 E5   43 47N 116 57W
Parma, Ohio, U.S.A. ......... 84 E3   41 23N  81 43W
Parnaguá, Brazil ............ 93 F10  10 10S  44 38W
Parnaíba, Brazil ............ 93 D10   2 54S  41 47W
Parnaíba →, Brazil ......... 93 D10   3  0S  41 50W
Parnassós, Greece .......... 23 E10  38 35N  22 30 E
Pärnu, Estonia .............. 9 G21   58 28N  24 33 E
Paroo →, Australia .......... 63 E3   31 28S 143 32 E
Páros, Greece .............. 23 F11  37  5N  25 12 E
Parowan, U.S.A. ............ 77 H7   37 51N 112 50W
Parral, Chile ............... 94 D1   36 10S  71 52W
Parras, Mexico ............. 86 B4   25 30N 102 20W
Parrett →, U.K. ............ 13 F4   51 12N   3  1W
Parris I., U.S.A. ............ 83 J5   32 20N  80 41W
Parrsboro, Canada .......... 73 C7   45 30N  64 25W
Parry I., Canada ............ 84 A5   45 18N  80 10W
Parry Is., Canada ........... 4 B2   77  0N 110  0W
Parry Sound, Canada ....... 84 A5   45 20N  80  0W
Parsnip →, Canada ......... 70 B4   55 10N 123  2W
Parsons, U.S.A. ............. 81 G7   37 20N  95 16W
Parsons Ra., Australia ...... 62 A2   13 30S 135 15 E
Partinico, Italy ............. 22 E5   38  3N  13  7 E
Partridge I., Canada ......... 72 A2   55 59N  87 37W
Paru →, Brazil .............. 93 D8    1 33S  52 38W
Parvān □, Afghan. .......... 40 B6   35  0N  69  0 E
Parvatipuram, India ........ 41 K13  18 50N  83 25 E
Parvatsar, India ............ 42 F6   26 52N  74 49 E
Parys, S. Africa ............. 56 D4   26 52S  27 29 E
Pas, Pta. des, Spain ......... 24 C7   38 46N   1 26 E
Pasadena, Canada .......... 73 C8   49  1N  57 36W
Pasadena, Calif., U.S.A. ..... 79 L8   34  9N 118  9W
Pasadena, Tex., U.S.A. ....... 81 L7   29 43N  95 13W
Pasaje →, Argentina ........ 94 B3   25 39S  63 56W
Pasar, Indonesia ............ 37 J17   8 27S 114 54 E
Pascagoula, U.S.A. ......... 81 K10  30 21N  88 33W
Pascagoula →, U.S.A. ....... 81 K10  30 23N  88 37W
Pașcani, Romania ........... 17 E14  47 14N  26 45 E
Pasco, U.S.A. ............... 76 C4   46 14N 119  6W
Pasco, Cerro de, Peru ....... 92 F3   10 45S  76 10W
Pasco I., Australia .......... 60 D2   20 57S 115 20 E
Pascoag, U.S.A. ............. 85 E13  41 57N  71 42W
Pascua, I. de, Chile ......... 65 K17   7  7S 109 23W
Pasfield L., Canada ......... 71 B7   58 24N 105 20W
Pasir Mas, Malaysia ......... 39 J4    6  2N 102  8 E
Pasir Panjang, Singapore .... 39 d    1 18N 103 46 E
Pasir Putih, Malaysia ....... 39 K4    5 50N 102 24 E
Pasirian, Indonesia ......... 37 H15   8 13S 113  8 E
Pasirkuning, Indonesia ...... 36 E2    0 30S 104 33 E
Paskůh, Iran ............... 45 E9   27 34N  63 58 E
Pasley, C., Australia ........ 61 F3   33 52S 123 35 E
Pašman, Croatia ............ 16 G8   43 58N  15 20 E
Pasni, Pakistan ............. 40 G3   25 15N  63 27 E
Paso Cantinela, Mexico ...... 79 N11  32 33N 115 47W
Paso de Indios, Argentina .... 96 E3   43 55S  69  0W
Paso de los Libres, Argentina . 94 B4   29 44S  57 10W
Paso de los Toros, Uruguay ... 94 C4   32 45S  56 30W
Paso Robles, U.S.A. ......... 77 J3   35 38N 120 41W
Paspébiac, Canada ......... 73 C6   48  3N  65 17W
Passage West, Ireland ....... 10 E3   51 52N   8 21W
Passaic, U.S.A. ............. 85 F10  40 51N  74  7W
Passau, Germany ........... 16 D7   48 34N  13 28 E
Passero, C., Italy ........... 22 F6   36 41N  15 10 E
Passo Fundo, Brazil ......... 95 B5   28 10S  52 20W
Passos, Brazil .............. 93 H9   20 45S  46 37W
Pastavy, Belarus ............ 9 J22   55  4N  26 50 E
Pastaza →, Peru ............ 92 D3    4 50S  76 52W
Pasto, Colombia ............ 92 C3    1 13N  77 17W
Pasuruan, Indonesia ........ 37 G15   7 40S 112 44 E
Patagonia, Argentina ....... 96 F3   45  0S  69  0W
Patagonia, U.S.A. ........... 77 L8   31 33N 110 45W
Patambar, Iran ............. 45 D9   29 45N  60 17 E
Patan = Lalitapur, Nepal .... 43 F11  27 40N  85 20 E
Patan, Gujarat, India ....... 40 H8   23 54N  72 14 E
Patan, Maharashtra, India ... 42 H5   23 54N  72 14 E
Patani, Indonesia .......... 37 D7    0 20N 128 50 E
Pataudi, India ............. 42 E7   28 18N  76 48 E
Patchewollock, Australia .... 63 F3   35 22S 142 12 E
Patchogue, U.S.A. .......... 85 F11  40 46N  73  1W
Pate, Kenya ................ 54 C5    2 10S  41  0 E
Patensie, S. Africa .......... 56 E3   33 46S  24 49 E
Paternò, Italy .............. 22 F6   37 34N  14 54 E
Paterson, U.S.A. ............ 85 F10  40 54N  74 10W
Paterson Ra., Australia ...... 60 D3   21 45S 122 10 E
Pathankot, India ............ 42 C6   32 18N  75 45 E
Pathein = Bassein, Burma ... 41 L19  16 45N  94 30 E
Pathfinder Reservoir, U.S.A. .. 76 E10  42 28N 106 51W
Pathiu, Thailand ........... 39 G2   10 42N  99 19 E
Pathum Thani, Thailand .... 38 E3   14  1N 100 32 E

Pati, Indonesia ............. 37 G14   6 45S 111  1 E
Patía →, Colombia ......... 92 C3    2 13N  78 40W
Patiala, Punjab, India ....... 42 D7   30 23N  76 26 E
Patiala, Ut. P., India ........ 43 F8   27 43N  79  1 E
Patkai Bum, India .......... 41 F19  27  0N  95 30 E
Pátmos, Greece ............. 23 F12  37 21N  26 36 E
Patna, India ................ 43 G11  25 35N  85 12 E
Pato Branco, Brazil ......... 95 B5   26 13S  52 40W
Patong, Ao, Thailand ........ 39 a    7 54N  98 17 E
Patonga, Uganda ........... 54 B3    2 45N  33 15 E
Patos, Brazil ............... 93 E11   6 55S  37 16W
Patos, L. dos, Brazil ........ 95 C5   31 20S  51  0W
Patos, Río de los →, Argentina . 94 C2   31 18S  69 25W
Patos de Minas, Brazil ...... 93 G9   18 35S  46 32W
Patquía, Argentina .......... 94 C2   30  2S  66 55W
Pátrai, Greece .............. 23 E9   38 14N  21 47 E
Pátraikós Kólpos, Greece .... 23 E9   38 17N  21 30 E
Patras = Pátrai, Greece ...... 23 E9   38 14N  21 47 E
Patrocínio, Brazil ........... 93 G9   18 57S  47  0W
Pattani, Thailand ........... 39 J3    6 48N 101 15 E
Pattaya, Thailand ........... 38 B2   12 52N 100 55 E
Patten, U.S.A. .............. 83 C11  46  0N  68 38W
Patterson, Calif., U.S.A. ..... 78 H5   37 28N 121  8W
Patterson, La., U.S.A. ....... 81 L9   29 42N  91 18W
Patterson, Mt., U.S.A. ....... 78 G7   38 29N 119 20W
Patti, Punjab, India ......... 42 D6   31 17N  74 54 E
Patti, Ut. P., India .......... 43 G10  25 55N  82 12 E
Pattoki, Pakistan ........... 42 D5   31  5N  73 52 E
Patton, U.S.A. .............. 84 F6   40 38N  78 39W
Patuakhali, Bangla. ......... 41 H17  22 20N  90 25 E
Patuanak, Canada .......... 71 B7   55 55N 107 43W
Patuca →, Honduras ........ 88 C3   15 50N  84 18W
Patuca, Punta, Honduras .... 88 C3   15 49N  84 14W
Pátzcuaro, Mexico .......... 86 D4   19 30N 101 40W
Pau, France ................ 20 E3   43 19N   0 25W
Pauk, Burma ............... 41 J19  21 27N  94 30 E
Paul I., Canada ............. 73 A7   56 30N  61 20W
Paul Smiths, U.S.A. ......... 85 B10  44 26N  74 15W
Paulatuk, Canada .......... 68 B7   69 25N 124  0W
Paulistana, Brazil .......... 93 E10   8  9S  41  9W
Paulo Afonso, Brazil ........ 93 E11   9 21S  38 15W
Paulpietersburg, S. Africa ... 57 D5   27 23S  30 50 E
Pauls Valley, U.S.A. ......... 81 H6   34 44N  97 13W
Pauma Valley, U.S.A. ........ 79 M10  33 16N 116 58W
Pauri, India ................ 43 D8   30  9N  78 47 E
Pāveh, Iran ................ 44 C5   35  3N  46 22 E
Pavia, Italy ................ 20 D8   45  7N   9 18 E
Pavilion, U.S.A. ............ 84 D6   42 52N  78  1W
Pāvilosta, Latvia ........... 9 H19   56 53N  21 14 E
Pavlodar, Kazakhstan ....... 28 D8   52 33N  77  0 E
Pavlograd = Pavlohrad, Ukraine . 19 E6   48 30N  35 52 E
Pavlohrad, Ukraine ......... 19 E6   48 30N  35 52 E
Pavlovo, Russia ............. 18 C7   55 58N  43  5 E
Pavlovsk, Russia ............ 19 D7   50 26N  40  5 E
Pavlovskaya, Russia ........ 19 E6   46 17N  39 47 E
Pawai, Pulau, Singapore .... 39 d    1 11N 103 44 E
Pawayan, India ............. 43 E9   28  4N  80  6 E
Pawhuska, U.S.A. .......... 81 G6   36 40N  96 20W
Pawling, U.S.A. ............. 85 E11  41 34N  73 36W
Pawnee, U.S.A. ............. 81 G6   36 20N  96 48W
Pawnee City, U.S.A. ......... 80 E6   40  7N  96  9W
Pawtucket, U.S.A. .......... 85 E13  41 53N  71 23W
Paximádhia, Greece ........ 25 E6   35  0N  24 35 E
Paxoí, Greece .............. 23 E9   39 14N  20 12 E
Paxton, Ill., U.S.A. .......... 82 E1   40 27N  88  6W
Paxton, Nebr., U.S.A. ....... 80 E4   41  7N 101 21W
Payakumbuh, Indonesia ..... 36 E2    0 20S 100 35 E
Payette, U.S.A. ............. 76 D5   44  5N 116 56W
Payne Bay = Kangirsuk, Canada . 69 B13  60  0N  70  0W
Payne L., Canada ........... 69 C12  59 30N  74 30W
Paynes Find, Australia ....... 61 E2   29 15S 117 42 E
Paynesville, U.S.A. ......... 80 C7   45 23N  94 43W
Paysandú, Uruguay ......... 94 C4   32 19S  58  8W
Payson, U.S.A. ............. 77 J8   34 14N 111 20W
Paz →, Guatemala .......... 88 D1   13 44N  90 10W
Paz, B. de la, Mexico ........ 86 C2   24 15N 110 25W
Pāzanān, Iran .............. 45 D6   30 35N  49 59 E
Pazardzhik, Bulgaria ....... 23 C11  42 12N  24 20 E
Pe Ell, U.S.A. .............. 78 D3   46 34N 123 18W
Peabody, U.S.A. ............ 85 D14  42 31N  70 56W
Peace →, Canada ........... 70 B6   59  0N 111 25W
Peace Point, Canada ........ 70 B6   59  7N 112 27W
Peace River, Canada ........ 70 B5   56 15N 117 18W
Peach Springs, U.S.A. ....... 77 J7   35 32N 113 25W
Peachland, Canada ......... 70 D5   49 47N 119 45W
Peachtree City, U.S.A. ....... 83 J3   33 25N  84 35W
Peak, The = Kinder Scout, U.K. . 12 D6   53 24N   1 52W
Peak Charles △, Australia ... 61 F3   32 42S 121 10 E
Peak District △, U.K. ....... 12 D6   53 24N   1 46W
Peak Hill, N.S.W., Australia .. 63 E4   32 47S 148 11 E
Peak Hill, W. Austral., Australia . 61 E2   25 35S 118 43 E
Peak Ra., Australia ......... 62 C4   22 50S 148 20 E
Peake Cr. →, Australia ...... 63 D2   28  2S 136  7 E
Peale, Mt., U.S.A. .......... 77 G9   38 26N 109 14W
Pearblossom, U.S.A. ........ 79 L9   34 30N 117 55W
Pearl →, U.S.A. ............ 81 K10  30 11N  89 32W
Pearl City, U.S.A. ........... 74 H16  21 24N 157 59W
Pearl Harbor, U.S.A. ........ 74 H16  21 21N 157 57W
Pearl River, U.S.A. .......... 85 E10  41  4N  74  2W
Pearsall, U.S.A. ............ 81 L5   28 54N  99  6W
Peary Land, Greenland ...... 4 A6   82 40N  33  0W
Pease →, U.S.A. ............ 81 H5   34 12N  99  2W
Peawanuck, Canada ........ 69 C11  55  5N  85 12W
Pebane, Mozam. ............ 55 F4   17 10S  38  8 E
Pebas, Peru ................ 92 D4    3 10S  71 46W
Pebble Beach, U.S.A. ........ 78 J5   36 34N 121 57W
Peć, Serbia & M. ........... 23 C9   42 40N  20 17 E
Pechenga, Russia ........... 8 A5   69 29N  31  4 E
Pechenizhyn, Ukraine ....... 17 D13  48 30N  24 48 E
Pechiguera, Pta., Canary Is. .. 24 F6   28 51N  13 53W
Pechora, Russia ............ 18 A10  65 10N  57 11 E
Pechora →, Russia .......... 18 A9   68 13N  54 15 E
Pechorskaya Guba, Russia ... 18 A9   68 40N  54  0 E
Pechory, Russia ............ 9 H22   57 48N  27 40 E
Pecos, U.S.A. .............. 81 K3   31  6N 103 30W
Pecos →, U.S.A. ............ 81 L3   29 42N 101 22W
Pécs, Hungary .............. 17 E10  46  5N  18 15 E
Pedder, L., Australia ........ 63 G4   42 55S 146 10 E
Peddie, S. Africa ........... 57 E4   33 14S  27  7 E
Pedernales, Dom. Rep. ...... 89 C5   18  2N  71 44W
Pedieos →, Cyprus ......... 25 D12  35 10N  33 54 E
Pedirka, Australia .......... 63 D2   26 40S 135 14 E
Pedra Azul, Brazil .......... 93 G10  16  2S  41 17W
Pedreiras, Brazil ........... 93 D10   4 32S  44 40W
Pedro Afonso, Brazil ........ 93 E9    9  0S  48 10W
Pedro Cays, Jamaica ........ 88 C4   17  5N  77 48W
Pedro de Valdivia, Chile ..... 94 A2   22 55S  69 38W

Pedro Juan Caballero, Paraguay 95 A4 22 30S 55 40W
Pee Dee ➤, U.S.A. 83 J6 33 22N 79 16W
Peebinga, Australia 63 E3 34 52S 140 57 E
Peebles, U.K. 11 F5 55 40N 3 11W
Peekskill, U.S.A. 85 E11 41 17N 73 55W
Peel, I. of Man 12 C3 54 13N 4 40W
Peel ➤, Australia 63 E5 30 50S 150 29 E
Peel ➤, Canada 68 B6 67 0N 135 0W
Peel Sd., Canada 68 A10 73 0N 96 0W
Peera Peera Poolanna L.,
  Australia 63 D2 26 30S 138 0 E
Peerless Lake, Canada 70 B6 56 37N 114 40W
Peers, Canada 70 C5 53 40N 116 0W
Pegasus Bay, N.Z. 59 K4 43 20S 173 10 E
Pegu, Burma 41 L20 17 20N 96 29 E
Pegu Yoma, Burma 41 K20 19 0N 96 0 E
Pehuajó, Argentina 94 D3 35 45S 62 0W
Pei Xian = Pizhou, China 34 G9 34 44N 116 55 E
Peine, Chile 94 A2 23 45S 68 8W
Peine, Germany 16 B6 52 19N 10 14 E
Peip'ing = Beijing, China 34 E9 39 55N 116 20 E
Peipus, L. = Chudskoye, Ozero,
  Russia 9 G22 58 13N 27 30 E
Peixe, Brazil 93 F9 12 0S 48 40W
Peixe ➤, Brazil 93 H8 21 31S 51 58W
Pekalongan, Indonesia 36 F3 6 53S 109 40 E
Pekan, Malaysia 39 L4 3 30N 103 25 E
Pekan Nenas, Malaysia 39 d 1 31N 103 31 E
Pekanbaru, Indonesia 36 D2 0 30N 101 15 E
Pekin, U.S.A. 80 E10 40 35N 89 40W
Peking = Beijing, China 34 E9 39 55N 116 20 E
Pekutatan, Indonesia 37 J17 8 25S 114 49 E
Pelabuhan Klang, Malaysia 39 L3 3 0N 101 23 E
Pelabuhan Ratu, Teluk, Indonesia 37 G12 7 5S 106 30 E
Pelabuhanratu, Indonesia 37 G12 7 0S 106 32 E
Pelagie, Is., Italy 22 G5 35 39N 12 33 E
Pelaihari, Indonesia 36 E4 3 55S 114 45 E
Peleaga, Vf., Romania 17 F12 45 22N 22 55 E
Pelée, Mt., Martinique 88 c 14 48N 61 10W
Pelee, Pt., Canada 72 D3 41 54N 82 31W
Pelee I., Canada 84 E2 41 47N 82 40W
Pelekech, Kenya 54 B4 3 52N 35 8 E
Peleng, Indonesia 37 E6 1 20S 123 30 E
Pelentong, Malaysia 39 d 1 32N 103 49 E
Pelican, U.S.A. 70 B1 57 58N 136 14W
Pelican L., Canada 71 C8 52 28N 100 20W
Pelican Narrows, Canada 71 B8 55 10N 102 56W
Peljesac, Croatia 22 C7 42 55N 17 25 E
Pelkosenniemi, Finland 8 C22 67 6N 27 28 E
Pella, S. Africa 56 D2 29 1S 19 6 E
Pella, U.S.A. 80 E8 41 25N 92 55W
Pello, Finland 8 C21 66 47N 23 59 E
Pelly ➤, Canada 68 B6 62 47N 137 19W
Pelly Bay, Canada 69 B11 68 38N 89 50W
Peloponnese = Pelopónnisos □,
  Greece 23 F10 37 10N 22 0 E
Pelopónnisos □, Greece 23 F10 37 10N 22 0 E
Pelorus Sd., N.Z. 59 J4 40 59S 173 59 E
Pelotas, Brazil 95 C5 31 42S 52 23W
Pelotas ➤, Brazil 95 B5 27 28S 51 55W
Pelvoux, Massif du, France 20 D7 44 52N 6 20 E
Pemalang, Indonesia 37 G13 6 53S 109 23 E
Pemanggil, Pulau, Malaysia 39 L5 2 37N 104 21 E
Pematangsiantar, Indonesia 36 D1 2 57N 99 5 E
Pemba, Mozam. 55 E5 12 58S 40 30 E
Pemba, Zambia 55 F2 16 30S 27 28 E
Pemba Channel, Tanzania 54 D4 5 0S 39 37 E
Pemba I., Tanzania 54 D4 5 0S 39 45 E
Pemberton, Australia 61 F2 34 30S 116 0 E
Pemberton, Canada 70 C4 50 25N 122 50W
Pembina, U.S.A. 80 A6 48 58N 97 15W
Pembroke, Canada 72 C4 45 50N 77 7W
Pembroke, U.K. 13 F3 51 41N 4 55W
Pembrokeshire □, U.K. 13 F3 51 52N 4 56W
Pembrokeshire Coast △, U.K. 13 F2 51 50N 5 2W
Pen-y-Ghent, U.K. 12 C5 54 10N 2 14W
Penal, Trin. & Tob. 93 K15 10 9N 61 29W
Penang = Pinang, Malaysia 39 c 5 25N 100 15 E
Penápolis, Brazil 95 A6 21 30S 50 0W
Peñarroya-Pueblonuevo, Spain 21 C3 38 19N 5 16W
Penarth, U.K. 13 F4 51 26N 3 11W
Peñas, C. de, Spain 21 A3 43 42N 5 52W
Peñas, G. de, Chile 96 F2 47 0S 75 0W
Peñas del Chache, Canary Is. 24 E6 29 6N 13 33W
Pench'i = Benxi, China 35 D12 41 20N 123 48 E
Pend Oreille ➤, U.S.A. 76 B5 49 4N 117 37W
Pend Oreille, L., U.S.A. 76 C5 48 10N 116 21W
Pendembu, S. Leone 50 G3 9 7N 11 14W
Pender B., Australia 60 C3 16 45S 122 42 E
Pendleton, U.S.A. 76 D4 45 40N 118 47W
Pendra, India 43 H9 22 46N 81 57 E
Penedo, Brazil 93 F11 10 15S 36 36W
Penelokan, Indonesia 37 J18 8 17S 115 22 E
Penetanguishene, Canada 84 B5 44 50N 79 55W
Penfield, U.S.A. 84 E6 41 13N 78 35W
Peng Chau, China 33 G11 22 17N 114 2 E
Pengalengan, Indonesia 37 G12 7 9S 107 30 E
Penge, Kasai-Or., Dem. Rep. of
  the Congo 54 D1 5 30S 24 33 E
Penge, Sud-Kivu, Dem. Rep. of
  the Congo 54 C2 4 27S 28 25 E
Penglai, China 35 F11 37 48N 120 42 E
Penguin, Australia 63 G4 41 8S 146 6 E
Penhalonga, Zimbabwe 55 F3 18 52S 32 40 E
Peniche, Portugal 21 C1 39 19N 9 22W
Penicuik, U.K. 11 F5 55 50N 3 13W
Penida, Nusa, Indonesia 37 K18 8 45S 115 30 E
Peninsular Malaysia □, Malaysia 39 L4 4 0N 102 0 E
Penitente, Serra do, Brazil 93 E9 8 45S 36 0W
Penkridge, U.K. 12 E5 52 44N 2 6W
Penmarch, Pte. de, France 20 C1 47 48N 4 22W
Penn Hills, U.S.A. 84 F5 40 28N 79 52W
Penn Yan, U.S.A. 84 D7 42 40N 77 3W
Pennant, Canada 71 C7 50 32N 108 14W
Penner ➤, India 40 M12 14 35N 80 10 E
Pennines, U.K. 12 C5 54 45N 2 27W
Pennington, U.S.A. 78 F5 39 15N 121 47W
Pennsburg, U.S.A. 85 F9 40 23N 75 29W
Pennsylvania □, U.S.A. 82 E7 40 45N 77 30W
Penny, Canada 70 C4 53 51N 121 20W
Penobscot ➤, U.S.A. 83 C11 44 30N 68 48W
Penobscot B., U.S.A. 83 C11 44 35N 68 50W
Penola, Australia 63 F3 37 25S 140 48 E
Penong, Australia 61 F5 31 56S 133 1 E
Penonomé, Panama 88 E3 8 31N 80 21W
Penrith, Australia 63 E5 33 43S 150 38 E
Penrith, U.K. 12 C5 54 40N 2 45W
Penryn, U.K. 13 G2 50 9N 5 7W

Pensacola, U.S.A. 83 K2 30 25N 87 13W
Pensacola Mts., Antarctica 5 E1 84 0S 40 0W
Pense, Canada 71 C8 50 25N 104 59W
Penshurst, Australia 63 F3 37 49S 142 20 E
Penticton, Canada 70 D5 49 30N 119 38W
Pentland, Australia 62 C4 20 32S 145 25 E
Pentland Firth, U.K. 11 C5 58 43N 3 10W
Pentland Hills, U.K. 11 F5 55 48N 3 25W
Pentland Hills △, U.K. 11 F5 55 50N 3 20W
Penza, Russia 18 D8 53 15N 45 5 E
Penzance, U.K. 13 G2 50 7N 5 33W
Penzhino, Russia 29 C17 63 30N 167 55 E
Penzhinskaya Guba, Russia 29 C17 61 30N 163 0 E
Peoria, Ariz., U.S.A. 77 K7 33 35N 112 14W
Peoria, Ill., U.S.A. 80 E10 40 42N 89 36W
Pepacton Reservoir, U.S.A. 85 D10 42 5N 74 58W
Pepani ➤, S. Africa 56 D3 25 49S 22 47 E
Pera Hd., Australia 62 A3 12 55S 141 37 E
Perabumulih, Indonesia 36 E2 3 27S 104 15 E
Perak ➤, Malaysia 39 K3 4 0N 100 50 E
Pérama, Kérkira, Greece 25 A3 39 34N 19 54 E
Pérama, Kríti, Greece 25 D6 35 20N 24 40 E
Perancak, Indonesia 37 J17 8 24S 114 37 E
Peräpohjola, Finland 8 C22 66 16N 26 10 E
Percé, Canada 73 C7 48 31N 64 13W
Perche, Collines du, France 20 B4 48 30N 0 40 E
Percival Lakes, Australia 60 D4 21 25S 125 0 E
Percy Is., Australia 62 C5 21 39S 150 16 E
Perdido, Mte., Spain 21 A6 42 40N 0 5 E
Perdu, Mt. = Perdido, Mte., Spain 21 A6 42 40N 0 5 E
Pereira, Colombia 92 C3 4 49N 75 43W
Perenjori, Australia 61 E2 29 26S 116 16 E
Pereyaslav-Khmelnytskyy,
  Ukraine 19 D5 50 3N 31 28 E
Pérez, I., Mexico 87 C7 22 24N 89 42W
Pergamino, Argentina 94 C3 33 52S 60 30W
Pergau ➤, Malaysia 39 K3 5 23N 102 2 E
Perham, U.S.A. 80 B7 46 36N 95 34W
Perhentian, Kepulauan, Malaysia 39 K4 5 54N 102 42 E
Péribonka ➤, Canada 73 C5 48 45N 72 5W
Péribonka, L., Canada 73 B5 50 1N 71 10W
Perico, Argentina 94 A2 24 20S 65 5W
Pericos, Mexico 86 B3 25 3N 107 42W
Périgueux, France 20 D4 45 10N 0 42 E
Perijá, Venezuela 89 E5 9 30N 72 55W
Perijá, Sierra de, Colombia 92 B4 9 30N 73 3W
Peristerona ➤, Cyprus 25 D12 35 8N 33 5 E
Perito Moreno, Argentina 96 F2 46 36S 70 56W
Perkasie, U.S.A. 85 F9 40 22N 75 18W
Perlas, Arch. de las, Panama 88 E4 8 41N 79 7W
Perlas, Punta de, Nic. 88 D3 12 30N 83 30W
Perm, Russia 18 C10 58 0N 56 10 E
Pernambuco = Recife, Brazil 93 E12 8 0S 35 0W
Pernambuco □, Brazil 93 E11 8 0S 37 0W
Pernatty Lagoon, Australia 63 E2 31 30S 137 12 E
Pernik, Bulgaria 23 C10 42 35N 23 2 E
Peron Is., Australia 60 B5 13 9S 130 4 E
Peron Pen., Australia 61 E1 26 0S 113 10 E
Perow, Canada 70 C3 54 35N 126 10W
Perpignan, France 20 E5 42 42N 2 53 E
Perris, U.S.A. 79 M9 33 47N 117 14W
Perry, Fla., U.S.A. 83 K4 30 7N 83 35W
Perry, Ga., U.S.A. 83 J4 32 28N 83 44W
Perry, Iowa, U.S.A. 80 E7 41 51N 94 6W
Perry, Okla., U.S.A. 81 G6 36 17N 97 14W
Perryton, U.S.A. 81 G4 36 24N 100 48W
Perryville, U.S.A. 81 G10 37 43N 89 52W
Persepolis, Iran 45 D7 29 55N 52 50 E
Pershotravensk, Ukraine 17 C14 50 13N 27 40 E
Persia = Iran ■, Asia 45 C7 33 0N 53 0 E
Persian Gulf, Asia 45 E6 27 0N 50 0 E
Perth, Australia 61 F2 31 57S 115 52 E
Perth, Canada 85 B8 44 55N 76 15W
Perth, U.K. 11 E5 56 24N 3 26W
Perth & Kinross □, U.K. 11 E5 56 45N 3 55W
Perth Amboy, U.S.A. 85 F10 40 31N 74 16W
Perth-Andover, Canada 73 C6 46 44N 67 42W
Peru, Ind., U.S.A. 82 E2 40 45N 86 4W
Peru, N.Y., U.S.A. 85 B11 44 35N 73 32W
Peru ■, S. Amer. 92 D4 4 0S 75 0W
Peru Basin, Pac. Oc. 65 J18 20 0S 95 0W
Peru-Chile Trench, Pac. Oc. 92 G3 20 0S 72 0W
Perúgia, Italy 22 C5 43 7N 12 23 E
Pervomaysk, Ukraine 19 E5 48 10N 30 46 E
Pervouralsk, Russia 18 C10 56 59N 59 59 E
Pésaro, Italy 22 C5 43 54N 12 55 E
Pescara, Italy 22 C6 42 28N 14 13 E
Peshawar, Pakistan 42 B4 34 2N 71 37 E
Peshkopi, Albania 23 D9 41 41N 20 25 E
Peshtigo, U.S.A. 82 C2 45 4N 87 46W
Pesqueira, Brazil 93 E11 8 20S 36 42W
Petah Tiqwa, Israel 46 C3 32 6N 34 53 E
Petaling Jaya, Malaysia 39 L3 3 4N 101 42 E
Petaloudhes, Greece 25 C10 36 18N 28 5 E
Petaluma, U.S.A. 78 G4 38 14N 122 39W
Pétange, Lux. 15 E5 49 33N 5 55 E
Petaro, Pakistan 42 G3 25 31N 68 18 E
Petatlán, Mexico 86 D4 17 31N 101 16W
Petauke, Zambia 55 E3 14 14S 31 20 E
Petawawa, Canada 72 C4 45 54N 77 17W
Petén Itzá, L., Guatemala 88 C2 16 58N 89 50W
Peter I., Br. Virgin Is. 89 e 18 22N 64 35W
Peter I. Øy, Antarctica 5 C16 69 0S 91 0W
Peter Pond L., Canada 71 B7 55 55N 108 44W
Peterbell, Canada 72 C3 48 36N 83 21W
Peterborough, Australia 63 E2 32 58S 138 51 E
Peterborough, Canada 84 B6 44 20N 78 20W
Peterborough, U.K. 13 E7 52 35N 0 15W
Peterborough, U.S.A. 85 D13 42 53N 71 57W
Peterborough □, U.K. 13 E7 52 35N 0 15W
Peterculter, U.K. 11 D6 57 6N 2 16W
Peterhead, U.K. 11 D7 57 31N 1 48W
Peterlee, U.K. 12 C6 54 47N 1 20W
Petermann Ranges, Australia 60 E5 26 0S 130 30 E
Petersburg, Alaska, U.S.A. 68 C6 56 48N 132 58W
Petersburg, Pa., U.S.A. 84 F6 40 34N 78 3W
Petersburg, Va., U.S.A. 82 G7 37 14N 77 24W
Petersburg, W. Va., U.S.A. 82 F6 39 1N 79 5W
Petersfield, U.K. 13 F7 51 1N 0 56W
Petit Goâve, Haiti 89 C5 18 27N 72 51W
Petit Jardin, Canada 73 C8 48 28N 59 14W
Petit Lac Manicouagan, Canada 73 B6 51 25N 67 40W
Petit-Mécatina ➤, Canada 73 B8 50 40N 59 30W
Petit-Mécatina, Î. du, Canada 73 B8 50 30N 59 25W
Petit Piton, St. Lucia 89 f 13 51N 61 5W
Petit-Saguenay, Canada 73 C5 48 15N 70 4W
Petitcodiac, Canada 73 C6 45 57N 65 11W

Petite Terre, Îles de la,
  Guadeloupe 88 b 16 13N 61 9W
Petitot ➤, Canada 70 A4 60 14N 123 29W
Petitsikapau L., Canada 73 B6 54 37N 66 25W
Petlad, India 42 H5 22 30N 72 45 E
Peto, Mexico 87 C7 20 10N 88 53W
Petone, N.Z. 59 J5 41 13S 174 53 E
Petorca, Chile 94 C1 32 15S 70 56W
Petoskey, U.S.A. 82 C3 45 22N 84 57W
Petra, Jordan 46 E4 30 20N 35 22 E
Petra, Spain 24 B10 39 37N 3 6 E
Petra, Ostrova, Russia 4 B13 76 15N 118 30 E
Petra Velikogo, Zaliv, Russia 30 C6 42 40N 132 0 E
Petrich, Bulgaria 23 D10 41 24N 23 13 E
Petrified Forest △, U.S.A. 77 J9 35 0N 109 30W
Petrikov = Pyetrikaw, Belarus 17 B15 52 11N 28 29 E
Petrolândia, Brazil 93 E11 9 5S 38 20W
Petrolia, Canada 84 D2 42 54N 82 9W
Petrolina, Brazil 93 E10 9 24S 40 30W
Petropavl, Kazakhstan 28 D7 54 53N 69 13 E
Petropavlovsk = Petropavl,
  Kazakhstan 28 D7 54 53N 69 13 E
Petropavlovsk-Kamchatskiy,
  Russia 29 D16 53 3N 158 43 E
Petrópolis, Brazil 95 A7 22 33S 43 9W
Petroşani, Romania 17 F12 45 28N 23 20 E
Petrovaradin, Serbia & M. 23 B8 45 16N 19 55 E
Petrovsk, Russia 18 D8 52 22N 45 19 E
Petrovsk-Zabaykalskiy, Russia 29 D11 51 20N 108 55 E
Petrozavodsk, Russia 18 B5 61 41N 34 20 E
Petrus Steyn, S. Africa 57 D4 27 38S 28 8 E
Petrusburg, S. Africa 56 D4 29 4S 25 26 E
Peumo, Chile 94 C1 34 21S 71 12W
Peureulak, Indonesia 36 D1 4 48N 97 45 E
Pevek, Russia 29 C18 69 41N 171 19 E
Pforzheim, Germany 16 D5 48 52N 8 41 E
Pha Taem △, Thailand 38 E5 15 32N 105 30 E
Phagwara, India 40 D9 31 10N 75 40 E
Phaistós, Greece 25 D6 35 2N 24 50 E
Phala, Botswana 56 C4 23 45S 26 50 E
Phalera = Phulera, India 42 F6 26 52N 75 16 E
Phalodi, India 42 F5 27 12N 72 24 E
Phaluai, Ko, Thailand 39 b 9 32N 99 41 E
Phan, Thailand 38 C2 19 28N 99 43 E
Phan Rang, Vietnam 39 G7 11 34N 109 0 E
Phan Ri = Hoa Da, Vietnam 39 G7 11 16N 108 40 E
Phan Thiet, Vietnam 39 G7 11 1N 108 9 E
Phanat Nikhom, Thailand 38 F3 13 27N 101 11 E
Phangan, Ko, Thailand 39 H3 9 45N 100 0 E
Phangnga, Thailand 39 H2 8 28N 98 30 E
Phangnga, Ao, Thailand 39 a 8 16N 98 23 E
Phanom Sarakham, Thailand 38 F3 13 45N 101 21 E
Phaphund, India 43 F8 26 36N 79 28 E
Pharenda, India 43 F10 27 5N 83 17 E
Pharr, U.S.A. 81 M5 26 12N 98 11W
Phatthalung, Thailand 39 J3 7 39N 100 6 E
Phayao, Thailand 38 C2 19 11N 99 55 E
Phelps, U.S.A. 84 D7 42 58N 77 3W
Phelps L., Canada 71 B8 59 15N 103 15W
Phenix City, U.S.A. 83 J3 32 28N 85 0W
Phet Buri, Thailand 38 F2 13 1N 99 55 E
Phetchabun, Thailand 38 D3 16 25N 101 8 E
Phetchabun, Thiu Khao, Thailand 38 E3 16 0N 101 20 E
Phetchaburi = Phet Buri, Thailand 38 F2 13 1N 99 55 E
Phi Phi, Ko, Thailand 39 J2 7 45N 98 46 E
Phiafay, Laos 38 E6 14 48N 106 0 E
Phibun Mangsahan, Thailand 38 E5 15 14N 105 14 E
Phichai, Thailand 38 D3 17 22N 100 10 E
Phichit, Thailand 38 D3 16 26N 100 22 E
Philadelphia, Miss., U.S.A. 81 J10 32 46N 89 7W
Philadelphia, N.Y., U.S.A. 85 B9 44 9N 75 43W
Philadelphia, Pa., U.S.A. 85 G9 39 57N 75 10W
Philip, U.S.A. 80 C4 44 2N 101 40W
Philippeville, Belgium 15 D4 50 12N 4 33 E
Philippi, U.S.A. 82 F5 39 9N 80 3W
Philippi L., Australia 62 C2 24 20S 138 55 E
Philippine Sea, Pac. Oc. 26 H16 18 0N 125 0 E
Philippines ■, Asia 37 B6 12 0N 123 0 E
Philippolis, S. Africa 56 E4 30 15S 25 16 E
Philippopolis = Plovdiv, Bulgaria 23 C11 42 8N 24 44 E
Philipsburg, Canada 85 A11 45 2N 73 5W
Philipsburg, Mont., U.S.A. 76 C7 46 20N 113 18W
Philipsburg, Pa., U.S.A. 84 F6 40 54N 78 13W
Philipstown = Daingean, Ireland 10 C4 53 18N 7 17W
Philipstown, S. Africa 56 E3 30 28S 24 30 E
Phillip I., Australia 63 F4 38 30S 145 12 E
Phillips, U.S.A. 80 C9 45 42N 90 24W
Phillipsburg, Kans., U.S.A. 80 F5 39 45N 99 19W
Phillipsburg, N.J., U.S.A. 85 F9 40 42N 75 12W
Philmont, U.S.A. 85 D11 42 15N 73 39W
Philomath, U.S.A. 76 D2 44 32N 123 22W
Phimai, Thailand 38 E4 15 13N 102 30 E
Phitsanulok, Thailand 38 D3 16 50N 100 12 E
Phnom Dangrek, Thailand 36 B2 14 20N 104 0 E
Phnom Penh, Cambodia 39 G5 11 33N 104 55 E
Phnum Penh = Phnom Penh,
  Cambodia 39 G5 11 33N 104 55 E
Phoenicia, U.S.A. 85 D10 42 5N 74 14W
Phoenix, Ariz., U.S.A. 77 K7 33 27N 112 4W
Phoenix, N.Y., U.S.A. 85 C8 43 14N 76 18W
Phoenix Is., Kiribati 64 H10 3 30S 172 0W
Phoenixville, U.S.A. 85 F9 40 8N 75 31W
Phon, Thailand 38 E4 15 49N 102 36 E
Phon Tiou, Laos 38 D5 17 53N 104 37 E
Phong ➤, Thailand 38 D4 16 23N 102 56 E
Phong Saly, Laos 38 B4 21 42N 102 9 E
Phong Tho, Vietnam 38 A4 22 32N 103 21 E
Phonhong, Laos 38 C4 18 30N 102 25 E
Phonum, Thailand 39 H2 8 49N 98 48 E
Phosphate Hill, Australia 62 C2 21 53S 139 58 E
Photharam, Thailand 38 F2 13 41N 99 51 E
Phra Nakhon Si Ayutthaya,
  Thailand 38 E3 14 25N 100 30 E
Phra Thong, Ko, Thailand 39 H2 9 5N 98 17 E
Phrae, Thailand 38 C3 18 7N 100 9 E
Phrom Phiram, Thailand 38 D3 17 2N 100 12 E
Phu Chong-Na Yoi △, Thailand 38 E5 14 25N 105 30 E
Phu Hin Rang Kla △, Thailand 38 D3 17 0N 100 59 E
Phu Kradung △, Thailand 38 D3 16 58N 101 32 E
Phu Loi, Laos 38 B4 20 14N 103 14 E
Phu Luang, Thailand 38 D3 17 35N 101 29 E
Phu Ly, Vietnam 38 B5 20 35N 105 50 E
Phu Quoc, Dao, Vietnam 39 G4 10 20N 104 0 E
Phu Yen, Vietnam 38 B5 21 16N 105 45 E
Phuc Yen, Vietnam 38 B5 21 16N 105 45 E
Phuket, Thailand 39 a 7 53N 98 24 E

Phuket, Ko, Thailand 39 a 8 0N 98 22 E
Phul, India 42 D6 30 19N 75 14 E
Phulad, India 42 G5 25 38N 73 49 E
Phulchari, Bangla. 43 G13 25 11N 89 37 E
Phulera, India 42 F6 26 52N 75 16 E
Phulpur, India 43 G10 25 31N 82 49 E
Phun Phin, Thailand 39 H2 9 7N 99 12 E
Piacenza, Italy 20 D8 45 1N 9 40 E
Piai, Tanjung, Malaysia 39 d 1 17N 103 30 E
Pian Cr. ➤, Australia 63 E4 30 2S 148 12 E
Pian-Upe △, Uganda 54 B3 1 44N 34 20 E
Pianosa, Italy 22 C4 42 35N 10 5 E
Piapot, Canada 71 D7 49 59N 109 8W
Piatra Neamţ, Romania 17 E14 46 56N 26 21 E
Piauí □, Brazil 93 E10 7 0S 43 0W
Piauí ➤, Brazil 93 E10 6 38S 42 42W
Piave ➤, Italy 22 B5 45 32N 12 44 E
Pibor Post, Sudan 51 G12 6 47N 33 3 E
Picardie □, France 20 B5 49 50N 3 0 E
Picardy = Picardie □, France 20 B5 49 50N 3 0 E
Picayune, U.S.A. 81 K10 30 32N 89 41W
Pichhor, India 43 G8 25 58N 78 20 E
Pichilemu, Chile 94 C1 34 22S 72 0W
Pichor, India 42 G8 25 11N 78 11 E
Pickerel L., Canada 72 C1 48 40N 91 25W
Pickering, U.K. 12 C7 54 15N 0 46W
Pickering, Vale of, U.K. 12 C7 54 14N 0 45W
Pickle Lake, Canada 72 B1 51 30N 90 12W
Pickwick L., U.S.A. 83 H1 35 4N 88 15W
Pico Bonito △, Honduras 88 C2 15 34N 86 48W
Pico Truncado, Argentina 96 F3 46 40S 68 0W
Picos, Brazil 93 E10 7 5S 41 28W
Picton, Australia 63 E5 34 12S 150 34 E
Picton, Canada 84 B7 44 1N 77 9W
Picton, N.Z. 59 J5 41 18S 174 3 E
Pictou, Canada 73 C7 45 41N 62 42W
Picture Butte, Canada 70 D6 49 55N 112 45W
Pictured Rocks △, U.S.A. 82 B2 46 30N 86 30W
Picún Leufú, Argentina 96 D3 39 30S 69 5W
Pidurutalagala, Sri Lanka 40 R12 7 10N 80 50 E
Piedmont = Piemonte □, Italy 20 D7 45 0N 8 0 E
Piedmont, Ala., U.S.A. 83 J3 33 55N 85 37W
Piedmont, S.C., U.S.A. 75 D10 34 0N 81 30W
Piedras Negras, Mexico 86 B4 28 42N 100 31W
Pieksämäki, Finland 9 E22 62 18N 27 10 E
Piemonte □, Italy 20 D7 45 0N 8 0 E
Pienaarsrivier, S. Africa 57 D4 25 15S 28 18 E
Piercefield, U.S.A. 85 B10 44 13N 74 35W
Pierceland, Canada 71 C7 54 20N 109 46W
Pierpont, U.S.A. 84 E4 41 45N 80 34W
Pierre, U.S.A. 80 C4 44 22N 100 21W
Pierreville, Trin. & Tob. 93 K16 10 16N 61 0W
Piet Retief, S. Africa 57 D5 27 1S 30 50 E
Pietarsaari, Finland 8 E20 63 40N 22 43 E
Pietermaritzburg, S. Africa 57 D5 29 35S 30 25 E
Pietersburg = Polokwane,
  S. Africa 57 C4 23 54S 29 25 E
Pietrosul, Vf., Maramures,
  Romania 17 E13 47 35N 24 43 E
Pietrosul, Vf., Suceava, Romania 17 E13 47 12N 25 18 E
Pigeon L., Canada 84 B6 44 27N 78 30W
Piggott, U.S.A. 81 G9 36 23N 90 11W
Pigüe, Argentina 94 D3 37 36S 62 25W
Pihani, India 43 F9 27 36N 80 15 E
Pihlajavesi, Finland 9 F23 61 45N 28 45 E
Pijijiapan, Mexico 87 D6 15 42N 93 14W
Pikangikum Berens, Canada 71 C10 51 49N 94 0W
Pikes Peak, U.S.A. 80 F2 38 50N 105 3W
Piketberg, S. Africa 56 E2 32 55S 18 40 E
Pikeville, U.S.A. 82 G4 37 29N 82 31W
Pikou, China 35 E12 39 18N 122 22 E
Pikwitonei, Canada 71 B9 55 35N 97 9W
Piła, Poland 17 B9 53 10N 16 48 E
Pilanesberg △, S. Africa 56 D4 25 15S 27 4 E
Pilani, India 42 E6 28 22N 75 33 E
Pilar, Paraguay 94 B4 26 50S 58 20W
Pilaya ➤, Bolivia 92 H6 20 55S 64 4W
Pilbara, Australia 60 D2 23 35S 117 25 E
Pilcomayo ➤, Paraguay 94 B4 25 21S 57 42W
Pilgrim's Rest, S. Africa 57 C5 24 55S 30 44 E
Pilibhit, India 43 E8 28 40N 79 50 E
Pilica ➤, Poland 17 C11 51 52N 21 17 E
Pilkhawa, India 42 E7 28 43N 77 42 E
Pilliga, Australia 63 E4 30 21S 148 54 E
Pílos, Greece 23 F9 36 55N 21 42 E
Pilot Mound, Canada 71 D9 49 15N 98 54W
Pilot Point, U.S.A. 81 J6 33 24N 96 58W
Pilot Rock, U.S.A. 76 D4 45 29N 118 50W
Pima, U.S.A. 77 K9 32 54N 109 50W
Pimba, Australia 63 E2 31 18S 136 46 E
Pimenta Bueno, Brazil 92 F6 11 35S 61 10W
Pimentel, Peru 92 E3 6 45S 79 55W
Pinang, Malaysia 39 c 5 25N 100 15 E
Pinar, C. des, Spain 24 B10 39 53N 3 12 E
Pinar del Río, Cuba 88 B3 22 26N 83 40W
Pınarhisar, Turkey 23 D12 41 37N 27 30 E
Pinatubo, Mt., Phil. 37 A6 15 8N 120 21 E
Pincher Creek, Canada 70 D6 49 30N 113 57W
Pinchi L., Canada 70 C4 54 38N 124 30W
Pinckneyville, U.S.A. 80 F10 38 5N 89 23W
Pińczów, Poland 17 C11 50 32N 20 32 E
Pindar, Australia 61 E2 28 30S 115 47 E
Pindi Gheb, Pakistan 42 C5 33 14N 72 21 E
Pindos Óros, Greece 23 E9 40 0N 21 0 E
Pindus Mts. = Pindos Óros,
  Greece 23 E9 40 0N 21 0 E
Pine ➤, B.C., Canada 70 B4 56 8N 120 43W
Pine ➤, Sask., Canada 71 B7 58 50N 105 38W
Pine, C., Canada 73 C9 46 37N 53 32W
Pine Bluff, U.S.A. 81 H9 34 13N 92 1W
Pine Bluffs, U.S.A. 76 E2 41 11N 104 4W
Pine City, U.S.A. 80 C8 45 50N 92 59W
Pine Cr. ➤, U.S.A. 84 E7 41 10N 77 16W
Pine Creek, Australia 60 B5 13 50S 131 50 E
Pine Falls, Canada 71 C9 50 34N 96 11W
Pine Flat Res., U.S.A. 78 J7 36 50N 119 20W
Pine Grove, U.S.A. 85 F8 40 33N 76 23W
Pine Pass, Canada 70 B4 55 25N 122 42W
Pine Point, Canada 70 A6 60 50N 114 28W
Pine Ridge, U.S.A. 80 D3 43 2N 102 33W
Pine River, Canada 71 C8 51 45N 100 30W
Pine Valley, U.S.A. 79 N10 32 50N 116 32W
Pinecrest, U.S.A. 78 G6 38 12N 120 1W
Pinedale, Calif., U.S.A. 78 J7 36 50N 119 48W
Pinedale, Wyo., U.S.A. 76 E9 42 52N 109 52W
Pinega ➤, Russia 18 B8 64 30N 44 19 E
Pinehill, Australia 62 C4 23 38S 146 57 E

Pinehouse L., Canada .......... 71 B7　55 32N 106 35W
Pineimuta →, Canada .......... 72 B1　52 8N 88 33W
Pinerolo, Italy .......... 20 D7　44 53N 7 21 E
Pinetop, U.S.A. .......... 77 J9　34 8N 109 56W
Pinetown, S. Africa .......... 57 D5　29 48S 30 54 E
Pineville, U.S.A. .......... 81 K8　31 19N 92 26W
Ping →, Thailand .......... 38 E3　15 42N 100 9 E
Pingaring, Australia .......... 61 F2　32 40S 118 32 E
Pingding, China .......... 34 F7　37 47N 113 38 E
Pingdingshan, China .......... 34 H7　33 43N 113 27 E
Pingdong, Taiwan .......... 33 D7　22 39N 120 30 E
Pingdu, China .......... 35 F10　36 42N 119 59 E
Pingelly, Australia .......... 61 F2　32 32S 117 5 E
Pingliang, China .......... 34 G4　35 35N 106 31 E
Pinglu, China .......... 34 E7　39 31N 112 30 E
Pingluo, China .......... 34 E4　38 52N 106 30 E
Pingquan, China .......... 35 D10　41 1N 118 37 E
Pingrup, Australia .......... 61 F2　33 32S 118 29 E
P'ingtung, Taiwan .......... 33 D7　22 38N 120 30 E
Pingwu, China .......... 32 D5　22 6N 106 46 E
Pingxiang, China .......... 34 F7　37 12N 112 10 E
Pingyao, China .......... 34 F7　37 12N 112 10 E
Pingyi, China .......... 35 G9　35 30N 117 35 E
Pingyin, China .......... 34 F9　36 20N 116 25 E
Pingyuan, China .......... 34 F9　37 10N 116 22 E
Pinhal, Brazil .......... 95 A6　22 10S 46 46W
Pinheiro, Brazil .......... 93 D9　2 31S 45 5W
Pinheiro Machado, Brazil .......... 95 C5　31 34S 53 23W
Pinhel, Portugal .......... 21 B2　40 50N 7 1W
Pini, Indonesia .......... 36 D1　0 10N 98 40 E
Piniós →, Greece .......... 23 E10　39 55N 22 41 E
Pinjarra, Australia .......... 61 F2　32 37S 115 52 E
Pink Mountain, Canada .......... 70 B4　57 3N 122 52W
Pinnacles, U.S.A. .......... 78 J5　36 33N 121 19W
Pinnacles △, U.S.A. .......... 78 J5　36 25N 121 12W
Pinnaroo, Australia .......... 63 F3　35 17S 140 53 E
Pinnes, Ákra, Greece .......... 23 D11　40 5N 24 20 E
Pinon Hills, U.S.A. .......... 79 L9　34 26N 117 39W
Pinos, Mexico .......... 86 C4　22 20N 101 40W
Pinos, Mt., U.S.A. .......... 79 L7　34 49N 119 8W
Pinos Pt., U.S.A. .......... 77 H3　36 38N 121 57W
Pinotepa Nacional, Mexico .......... 87 D5　16 19N 98 3W
Pinrang, Indonesia .......... 37 E5　3 46S 119 41 E
Pins, Pte. aux, Canada .......... 84 D3　42 15N 81 51W
Pinsk, Belarus .......... 17 B14　52 10N 26 1 E
Pintados, Chile .......... 92 H5　20 35S 69 40W
Pinyug, Russia .......... 18 B8　60 5N 48 0 E
Pioche, U.S.A. .......... 77 H6　37 56N 114 27W
Piombino, Italy .......... 22 C4　42 55N 10 32 E
Pioner, Ostrov, Russia .......... 29 B10　79 50N 92 0 E
Piorini, L., Brazil .......... 92 D6　3 15S 62 35W
Piotrków Trybunalski, Poland .......... 17 C10　51 23N 19 43 E
Pip, Iran .......... 45 E9　26 45N 60 10 E
Pipar, India .......... 42 F5　26 25N 73 31 E
Pipar Road, India .......... 42 F5　26 25N 73 27 E
Piparia, Mad. P., India .......... 42 H8　22 45N 78 23 E
Piparia, Mad. P., India .......... 42 J7　21 49N 77 37 E
Pipestone, U.S.A. .......... 80 D6　44 0N 96 19W
Pipestone →, Canada .......... 72 B2　52 53N 89 23W
Pipestone Cr. →, Canada .......... 71 D8　49 38N 100 15W
Piplan, Pakistan .......... 42 C4　32 17N 71 21 E
Piploda, India .......... 42 H6　23 37N 74 56 E
Pipmuacan, Rés., Canada .......... 73 C5　49 45N 70 30W
Pippingarra, Australia .......... 60 D2　20 27S 118 42 E
Piqua, U.S.A. .......... 82 E3　40 9N 84 15W
Piquiri →, Brazil .......... 95 A5　24 3S 54 14W
Pir Panjal Range, India .......... 42 C7　32 30N 76 50 E
Pîr Sohrâb, Iran .......... 45 E9　25 44N 60 54 E
Piracicaba, Brazil .......... 95 A6　22 45S 47 40 E
Piracicaba, Brazil .......... 93 D10　3 50S 41 50W
Piracuruca, Brazil .......... 93 D10　3 50S 41 50W
Piræus = Piraiévs, Greece .......... 23 F10　37 57N 23 42 E
Piraiévs, Greece .......... 23 F10　37 57N 23 42 E
Pirajuí, Brazil .......... 95 A6　21 59S 49 29W
Piram I., India .......... 42 J5　21 36N 72 21 E
Pirané, Argentina .......... 94 B4　25 42S 59 6W
Pirapora, Brazil .......... 93 G10　17 20S 44 56W
Pirawa, India .......... 42 G7　24 10N 76 2 E
Pirgos, Greece .......... 23 F9　37 40N 21 27 E
Piribebuy, Paraguay .......... 94 B4　25 26S 57 2W
Pirimapun, Indonesia .......... 37 F9　6 20S 138 24 E
Pirin Planina, Bulgaria .......... 23 D10　41 40N 23 30 E
Pírineos = Pyrénées, Europe .......... 20 E4　42 45N 0 18 E
Piripiri, Brazil .......... 93 D10　4 15S 41 46W
Pirmasens, Germany .......... 16 D4　49 12N 7 36 E
Pirot, Serbia & M. .......... 23 C10　43 9N 22 33 E
Piru, Indonesia .......... 37 E7　3 4S 128 12 E
Piru, U.S.A. .......... 79 L8　34 25N 118 48W
Pisa, Italy .......... 22 C4　43 43N 10 23 E
Pisagua, Chile .......... 92 G4　19 40S 70 15W
Pisco, Peru .......... 92 F3　13 50S 76 12W
Pisek, Czech Rep. .......... 16 D8　49 19N 14 10 E
Pishan, China .......... 32 C2　37 30N 78 33 E
Pishin, Iran .......... 45 E9　26 6N 61 47 E
Pishin, Pakistan .......... 42 D2　30 35N 67 0 E
Pishin Lora →, Pakistan .......... 42 E1　29 9N 64 5 E
Pising, Indonesia .......... 37 F6　5 8S 121 53 E
Pismo Beach, U.S.A. .......... 79 K6　35 9N 120 38W
Pissis, Cerro, Argentina .......... 94 B2　27 45S 68 48W
Pissouri, Cyprus .......... 25 E11　34 40N 32 42 E
Pistóia, Italy .......... 22 C4　43 55N 10 54 E
Pistol B., Canada .......... 71 A10　62 25N 92 37W
Pisuerga →, Spain .......... 21 B3　41 33N 4 52W
Pit →, U.S.A. .......... 76 F2　40 47N 122 6W
Pitarpunga, L., Australia .......... 63 E3　34 24S 143 30 E
Pitcairn I., Pac. Oc. .......... 65 K14　25 5S 130 5W
Pitch L., Trin. & Tob. .......... 93 K15　10 12N 61 39W
Piteå, Sweden .......... 8 D19　65 20N 21 25 E
Piteälven →, Sweden .......... 8 D19　65 20N 21 25 E
Pitești, Romania .......... 17 F13　44 52N 24 54 E
Pithapuram, India .......... 41 L13　17 10N 82 15 E
Pithara, Australia .......... 61 F2　30 20S 116 35 E
Pithoragarh, India .......... 43 E9　29 35N 80 13 E
Pithoro, Pakistan .......... 42 G3　25 31N 69 23 E
Pitlochry, U.K. .......... 11 E5　56 42N 3 44W
Pitsilia, Cyprus .......... 25 E12　34 55N 33 0 E
Pitt I., Canada .......... 70 C3　53 30N 129 50W
Pittsburg, Calif., U.S.A. .......... 78 G5　38 2N 121 53W
Pittsburg, Kans., U.S.A. .......... 81 G7　37 25N 94 42W
Pittsburg, Tex., U.S.A. .......... 81 J7　33 0N 94 59W
Pittsburgh, U.S.A. .......... 84 F5　40 26N 80 1W
Pittsfield, Ill., U.S.A. .......... 80 F9　39 36N 90 49W
Pittsfield, Maine, U.S.A. .......... 83 C11　44 47N 69 23W
Pittsfield, Mass., U.S.A. .......... 85 D11　42 27N 73 15W
Pittsfield, N.H., U.S.A. .......... 85 C13　43 18N 71 20W
Pittston, U.S.A. .......... 85 E9　41 19N 75 47W
Pittsworth, Australia .......... 63 D5　27 41S 151 37 E
Pituri →, Australia .......... 62 C2　22 35S 138 30 E
Piura, Peru .......... 92 E2　5 15S 80 38W

Pixley, U.S.A. .......... 78 K7　35 58N 119 18W
Pizhou, China .......... 34 G9　34 44N 116 55 E
Placentia, Canada .......... 73 C9　47 20N 54 0W
Placentia B., Canada .......... 73 C9　47 0N 54 40W
Placerville, U.S.A. .......... 78 G6　38 44N 120 48W
Placetas, Cuba .......... 88 B4　22 15N 79 44W
Plainfield, N.J., U.S.A. .......... 85 F10　40 37N 74 25W
Plainfield, Ohio, U.S.A. .......... 84 F3　40 13N 81 43W
Plainfield, Vt., U.S.A. .......... 85 B12　44 17N 72 26W
Plains, Mont., U.S.A. .......... 76 C6　47 28N 114 53W
Plains, Tex., U.S.A. .......... 81 J3　33 11N 102 50W
Plainview, Nebr., U.S.A. .......... 80 D6　42 21N 97 47W
Plainview, Tex., U.S.A. .......... 81 H4　34 11N 101 43W
Plainwell, U.S.A. .......... 82 D3　42 27N 85 38W
Plaistow, U.S.A. .......... 85 D13　42 50N 71 6W
Pláka, Ákra, Greece .......... 25 D8　35 11N 26 19 E
Plana Cays, Bahamas .......... 89 B5　22 38N 73 30W
Planada, U.S.A. .......... 78 H6　37 16N 120 19W
Plano, U.S.A. .......... 81 J6　33 1N 96 42W
Plant City, U.S.A. .......... 83 M4　28 1N 82 7W
Plaquemine, U.S.A. .......... 81 K9　30 17N 91 14W
Plasencia, Spain .......... 21 B2　40 3N 6 8W
Plaster City, U.S.A. .......... 79 N11　32 47N 115 51W
Plaster Rock, Canada .......... 73 C6　46 53N 67 22W
Plastun, Russia .......... 30 B8　44 45N 136 19 E
Plata, Río de la, S. Amer. .......... 94 C4　34 45S 57 30W
Plátani →, Italy .......... 22 F5　37 23N 13 16 E
Plátanos, Greece .......... 25 D5　35 28N 23 33 E
Platte, U.S.A. .......... 80 D5　43 23N 98 51W
Platte →, Mo., U.S.A. .......... 80 F7　39 16N 94 50W
Platte →, Nebr., U.S.A. .......... 80 E7　41 4N 95 53W
Platteville, U.S.A. .......... 80 D9　42 44N 90 29W
Plattsburgh, U.S.A. .......... 85 B11　44 42N 73 28W
Plattsmouth, U.S.A. .......... 80 E7　41 1N 95 53W
Plauen, Germany .......... 16 C7　50 30N 12 8 E
Plavinas, Latvia .......... 9 H21　56 35N 25 46 E
Playa Blanca, Canary Is. .......... 24 F6　28 55N 13 37W
Playa Blanca Sur, Canary Is. .......... 24 F6　28 51N 13 50W
Playa de las Americas, Canary Is. .......... 24 F3　28 5N 16 43W
Playa de Mogán, Canary Is. .......... 24 G4　27 48N 15 47W
Playa del Inglés, Canary Is. .......... 24 G4　27 45N 15 33W
Playa Esmeralda, Canary Is. .......... 24 F5　28 8N 14 16W
Playgreen L., Canada .......... 71 C9　54 0N 98 15W
Pleasant Bay, Canada .......... 73 C7　46 51N 60 48W
Pleasant Hill, U.S.A. .......... 78 H4　37 57N 122 4W
Pleasant Mount, U.S.A. .......... 85 E9　41 44N 75 26W
Pleasanton, Calif., U.S.A. .......... 78 H5　37 39N 121 52W
Pleasanton, Tex., U.S.A. .......... 81 L5　28 58N 98 29W
Pleasantville, N.J., U.S.A. .......... 82 F8　39 24N 74 32W
Pleasantville, Pa., U.S.A. .......... 84 E5　41 35N 79 34W
Plei Ku, Vietnam .......... 38 F7　13 57N 108 0 E
Plenty →, Australia .......... 62 C2　23 25S 136 31 E
Plenty, B. of, N.Z. .......... 59 G6　37 45S 177 0 E
Plentywood, U.S.A. .......... 80 A2　48 47N 104 34W
Plesetsk, Russia .......... 18 B7　62 43N 40 20 E
Plessisville, Canada .......... 73 C5　46 14N 71 47W
Plétipi, L., Canada .......... 73 B5　51 44N 70 6W
Pleven, Bulgaria .......... 23 C11　43 26N 24 37 E
Plevlja, Serbia & M. .......... 23 C8　43 21N 19 21 E
Plevna, Canada .......... 84 B8　44 58N 76 59W
Płock, Poland .......... 17 B10　52 32N 19 40 E
Plöckenstein, Germany .......... 16 D7　48 46N 13 51 E
Ploiești, Romania .......... 17 F14　44 57N 26 5 E
Plonge, Lac la, Canada .......... 71 B7　55 8N 107 20W
Plovdiv, Bulgaria .......... 23 C11　42 8N 24 44 E
Plover Cove Res., China .......... 33 G11　22 28N 114 15 E
Plum, U.S.A. .......... 84 F5　40 29N 79 47W
Plum I., U.S.A. .......... 85 E12　41 11N 72 12W
Plumas, U.S.A. .......... 78 F7　39 45N 120 4W
Plummer, U.S.A. .......... 76 C5　47 20N 116 53W
Plumtree, Zimbabwe .......... 55 G2　20 27S 27 55 E
Plungė, Lithuania .......... 9 J19　55 53N 21 59 E
Plymouth, Trin. & Tob. .......... 93 J16　11 14N 60 48W
Plymouth, U.K. .......... 13 G3　50 22N 4 10W
Plymouth, Calif., U.S.A. .......... 78 G6　38 29N 120 51W
Plymouth, Ind., U.S.A. .......... 82 E2　41 21N 86 19W
Plymouth, Mass., U.S.A. .......... 85 E14　41 57N 70 40W
Plymouth, N.C., U.S.A. .......... 83 H7　35 52N 76 43W
Plymouth, N.H., U.S.A. .......... 85 C13　43 46N 71 41W
Plymouth, Pa., U.S.A. .......... 85 E9　41 14N 75 57W
Plymouth, Wis., U.S.A. .......... 82 D2　43 45N 87 59W
Plympton-Wyoming, Canada .......... 84 D2　42 57N 82 7W
Plynlimon = Pumlumon Fawr, U.K. .......... 13 E4　52 28N 3 46W
Plzeň, Czech Rep. .......... 16 D7　49 45N 13 22 E
Po →, Italy .......... 22 B5　44 57N 12 4 E
Po Hai = Bo Hai, China .......... 35 E10　39 0N 119 0 E
Po Toi, China .......... 33 G11　22 10N 114 16 E
Pobeda, Russia .......... 29 C15　65 12N 146 12 E
Pobedy, Pik, Kyrgyzstan .......... 28 E8　42 0N 79 58 E
Pocahontas, Ark., U.S.A. .......... 81 G9　36 16N 90 58W
Pocahontas, Iowa, U.S.A. .......... 80 D7　42 44N 94 40W
Pocatello, U.S.A. .......... 76 E7　42 52N 112 27W
Pochutla, Mexico .......... 87 D5　15 50N 96 31W
Pocito Casas, Mexico .......... 86 B2　28 32N 111 6W
Pocomoke City, U.S.A. .......... 82 F8　38 5N 75 34W
Poços de Caldas, Brazil .......... 95 A6　21 50S 46 33W
Podgorica, Serbia & M. .......... 23 C8　42 30N 19 19 E
Podilska Vysochyna, Ukraine .......... 17 D14　49 0N 28 0 E
Podolsk, Russia .......... 18 C6　55 25N 37 30 E
Podporozhye, Russia .......... 18 B5　60 55N 34 2 E
Pofadder, S. Africa .......... 56 D2　29 10S 19 22 E
Pogranichnyy, Russia .......... 30 B5　44 25N 131 24 E
Poh, Indonesia .......... 37 E6　0 46S 122 51 E
P'ohang, S. Korea .......... 35 F15　36 1N 129 23 E
Pohjanmaa, Finland .......... 8 E20　62 58N 22 50 E
Pohnpei, Micronesia .......... 64 G7　6 55N 158 10 E
Pohri, India .......... 42 G6　25 32N 77 22 E
Poinsett, C., Antarctica .......... 5 C8　65 42S 113 18 E
Point Arena, U.S.A. .......... 78 G3　38 55N 123 41W
Point Baker, U.S.A. .......... 70 B2　56 21N 133 37W
Point Edward, Canada .......... 72 D3　43 0N 82 30W
Point Fortin, Trin. & Tob. .......... 93 K15　10 10N 61 42W
Point Hope, U.S.A. .......... 68 B3　68 21N 166 47W
Point L., Canada .......... 68 B8　65 15N 113 4W
Point Lisas, Trin. & Tob. .......... 93 K15　10 32N 61 30W
Point Pedro, Sri Lanka .......... 40 Q12　9 50N 80 15 E
Point Pelee △, Canada .......... 84 E2　41 57N 82 1W
Point Pleasant, N.J., U.S.A. .......... 85 F10　40 5N 74 4W
Point Pleasant, W. Va., U.S.A. .......... 82 F4　38 51N 82 8W
Point Reyes △, U.S.A. .......... 78 G2　38 10N 122 55W
Pointe-au-Pic = La Malbaie, Canada .......... 73 C5　47 40N 70 10W
Pointe-Claire, Canada .......... 85 A11　45 26N 73 50W
Pointe-Gatineau, Canada .......... 85 A9　45 28N 75 42W
Pointe-Noire, Congo .......... 52 E2　4 48S 11 53 E
Pointe Noire, Guadeloupe .......... 88 b　16 14N 61 47W

Poisonbush Ra., Australia .......... 60 D3　22 30S 121 30 E
Poissonnier Pt., Australia .......... 60 C2　19 57S 119 10 E
Poitiers, France .......... 20 C4　46 35N 0 20 E
Poitou, France .......... 20 C3　46 40N 0 10W
Pojoaque, U.S.A. .......... 77 J11　35 54N 106 1W
Pokaran, India .......... 40 F7　27 0N 71 50 E
Pokataroo, Australia .......... 63 D4　29 30S 148 36 E
Pokhara, Nepal .......... 43 E10　28 14N 83 58 E
Poko, Dem. Rep. of the Congo .......... 54 B2　3 7N 26 52 E
Pokrovsk, Russia .......... 29 C13　61 29N 129 0 E
Pola = Pula, Croatia .......... 16 F7　44 54N 13 57 E
Polacca, U.S.A. .......... 77 J8　35 50N 110 23W
Polan, Iran .......... 45 E9　25 30N 61 10 E
Poland ■, Europe .......... 17 C10　52 0N 20 0 E
Polar Bear △, Canada .......... 72 A2　55 0N 83 45W
Polcura, Chile .......... 94 D1　37 17S 71 43W
Polessk, Russia .......... 9 J19　54 50N 21 8 E
Polesye = Pripet Marshes, Europe .......... 17 B15　52 10N 28 10 E
Polevskoy, Russia .......... 18 C11　56 26N 60 11 E
Põlgyo-ri, S. Korea .......... 35 G14　34 51N 127 21 E
Police, Poland .......... 16 B8　53 33N 14 33 E
Polillo Is., Phil. .......... 37 B6　14 56N 122 0 E
Polis, Cyprus .......... 25 D11　35 2N 32 26 E
Políyiros, Greece .......... 23 D10　40 23N 23 25 E
Polk, U.S.A. .......... 84 E5　41 22N 79 56W
Pollachi, India .......... 40 P10　10 35N 77 0 E
Pollença, Spain .......... 24 B10　39 54N 3 1 E
Pollença, B. de, Spain .......... 24 B10　39 53N 3 8 E
Polnovat, Russia .......... 28 C7　63 50N 65 54 E
Polokwane, S. Africa .......... 57 C4　23 54S 29 25 E
Polonne, Ukraine .......... 17 C14　50 6N 27 30 E
Polonnoye = Polonne, Ukraine .......... 17 C14　50 6N 27 30 E
Polson, U.S.A. .......... 76 C6　47 41N 114 9W
Poltava, Ukraine .......... 19 E5　49 35N 34 35 E
Põltsamaa, Estonia .......... 9 G21　58 39N 25 58 E
Polunochnoye, Russia .......... 28 C7　60 52N 60 25 E
Põlva, Estonia .......... 9 G22　58 3N 27 3 E
Polyarny, Russia .......... 18 A5　69 8N 33 20 E
Polynesia, Pac. Oc. .......... 65 F11　10 0S 162 0W
Polynésie française = French Polynesia ☑, Pac. Oc. .......... 65 K13　20 0S 145 0W
Pomaro, Mexico .......... 86 D4　18 20N 103 18W
Pombal, Portugal .......... 21 C1　39 55N 8 40W
Pómbia, Greece .......... 25 E6　35 0N 24 51 E
Pomene, Mozam. .......... 57 C6　22 53S 35 33 E
Pomeroy, Ohio, U.S.A. .......... 82 F4　39 2N 82 2W
Pomeroy, Wash., U.S.A. .......... 76 C5　46 28N 117 36W
Pomézia, Italy .......... 22 D5　41 40N 12 30 E
Pomona, Australia .......... 63 D5　26 22S 152 52 E
Pomona, U.S.A. .......... 79 L9　34 4N 117 45W
Pomorskie, Pojezierze, Poland .......... 17 B9　53 40N 16 37 E
Pomos, Cyprus .......... 25 D11　35 9N 32 33 E
Pomos, C., Cyprus .......... 25 D11　35 10N 32 33 E
Pompano Beach, U.S.A. .......... 83 M5　26 14N 80 8W
Pompeys Pillar, U.S.A. .......... 76 D10　45 59N 107 57W
Pompeys Pillar △, U.S.A. .......... 76 D10　46 0N 108 0W
Pompton Lakes, U.S.A. .......... 85 F10　41 0N 74 17W
Ponape = Pohnpei, Micronesia .......... 64 G7　6 55N 158 10 E
Ponask L., Canada .......... 72 B1　54 0N 92 41W
Ponca, U.S.A. .......... 80 D6　42 34N 96 43W
Ponca City, U.S.A. .......... 81 G6　36 42N 97 5W
Ponce, Puerto Rico .......... 89 d　18 1N 66 37W
Ponchatoula, U.S.A. .......... 81 K9　30 26N 90 26W
Poncheville, L., Canada .......... 72 B4　50 10N 76 55W
Pond, U.S.A. .......... 79 K7　35 43N 119 20W
Pond Inlet, Canada .......... 69 A12　72 40N 77 0W
Pondicherry, India .......... 40 P11　11 59N 79 50 E
Ponds, I. of, Canada .......... 73 B8　53 27N 55 52W
Ponferrada, Spain .......... 21 A2　42 32N 6 35W
Ponnani, India .......... 40 P9　10 45N 75 59 E
Ponoka, Canada .......... 70 C6　52 42N 113 40W
Ponorogo, Indonesia .......... 37 G14　7 52S 111 27 E
Ponoy, Russia .......... 18 A7　67 0N 41 13 E
Ponoy →, Russia .......... 18 A7　66 59N 41 17 E
Ponta do Sol, Madeira .......... 24 D2　32 42N 17 7W
Ponta Grossa, Brazil .......... 95 B5　25 7S 50 10W
Ponta Pora, Brazil .......... 95 A4　22 20S 55 35W
Pontarlier, France .......... 20 C7　46 54N 6 20 E
Pontchartrain L., U.S.A. .......... 81 K10　30 5N 90 5W
Ponte do Pungué, Mozam. .......... 55 F3　19 30S 34 33 E
Ponte Nova, Brazil .......... 95 A7　20 25S 42 54W
Ponteix, Canada .......... 71 D7　49 46N 107 29W
Pontevedra, Spain .......... 21 A1　42 26N 8 40W
Pontiac, Ill., U.S.A. .......... 80 E10　40 53N 88 38W
Pontiac, Mich., U.S.A. .......... 82 D4　42 38N 83 18W
Pontian Kechil, Malaysia .......... 39 d　1 29N 103 23 E
Pontianak, Indonesia .......... 36 E3　0 3S 109 15 E
Pontine Is. = Ponziane, Ísole, Italy .......... 22 D5　40 55N 12 57 E
Pontine Mts. = Kuzey Anadolu Dağları, Turkey .......... 19 F6　41 30N 35 0 E
Pontivy, France .......... 20 B2　48 5N 2 58W
Pontoise, France .......... 20 B5　49 3N 2 5 E
Ponton →, Canada .......... 70 B5　58 27N 116 11W
Pontypool, Canada .......... 84 B6　44 6N 78 38W
Pontypool, U.K. .......... 13 F4　51 42N 3 2W
Ponziane, Ísole, Italy .......... 22 D5　40 55N 12 57 E
Poochera, Australia .......... 63 E1　32 43S 134 51 E
Poole, U.K. .......... 13 G6　50 43N 1 59W
Poole □, U.K. .......... 13 G6　50 43N 1 59W
Poona = Pune, India .......... 40 K8　18 29N 73 57 E
Pooncarie, Australia .......... 63 E3　33 22S 142 31 E
Poopelloe L., Australia .......... 63 E3　31 40S 144 0 E
Poopó, L. de, Bolivia .......... 92 G5　18 30S 67 35W
Popayán, Colombia .......... 92 C3　2 27N 76 36W
Poperinge, Belgium .......... 15 D2　50 51N 2 42 E
Popilta L., Australia .......... 63 E3　33 10S 141 42 E
Popio L., Australia .......... 63 E3　33 10S 141 52 E
Poplar, U.S.A. .......... 80 A2　48 7N 105 12W
Poplar →, Canada .......... 71 C9　53 0N 97 19W
Poplar Bluff, U.S.A. .......... 81 G9　36 46N 90 24W
Poplarville, U.S.A. .......... 81 K10　30 51N 89 32W
Popocatépetl, Volcán, Mexico .......... 87 D5　19 2N 98 38W
Popokabaka, Dem. Rep. of the Congo .......... 52 F3　5 41S 16 40 E
Poprad, Slovak Rep. .......... 17 D11　49 3N 20 18 E
Porali →, Pakistan .......... 42 G2　25 58N 66 26 E
Porbandar, India .......... 42 J3　21 44N 69 43 E
Porcher I., Canada .......... 70 C2　53 50N 130 30W
Porcupine →, Canada .......... 71 B8　59 11N 104 46W
Porcupine →, U.S.A. .......... 68 B5　66 34N 145 19W
Porcupine Gorge △, Australia .......... 62 C3　20 22S 144 26 E
Pordenone, Italy .......... 22 B5　45 57N 12 39 E
Pori, Finland .......... 9 F19　61 29N 21 48 E
Porlamar, Venezuela .......... 92 A6　10 57N 63 51W
Poronaysk, Russia .......... 29 E15　49 13N 143 0 E
Poroshiri-Dake, Japan .......... 30 C11　42 41N 142 52 E

Poroto Mts., Tanzania .......... 55 D3　9 0S 33 30 E
Porpoise B., Antarctica .......... 5 C9　66 0S 127 0 E
Porreres, Spain .......... 24 B10　39 31N 3 2 E
Porsangen, Norway .......... 8 A21　70 40N 25 40 E
Porsgrunn, Norway .......... 9 G13　59 10N 9 40 E
Port Alberni, Canada .......... 70 D4　49 14N 124 50W
Port Alfred, S. Africa .......... 56 E4　33 36S 26 55 E
Port Alice, Canada .......... 70 C3　50 20N 127 25W
Port Allegany, U.S.A. .......... 84 E6　41 48N 78 17W
Port Allen, U.S.A. .......... 81 K9　30 27N 91 12W
Port Alma, Australia .......... 62 C5　23 38S 150 53 E
Port Angeles, U.S.A. .......... 78 B3　48 7N 123 27W
Port Antonio, Jamaica .......... 88 a　18 10N 76 26W
Port Aransas, U.S.A. .......... 81 M6　27 50N 97 4W
Port Arthur, Australia .......... 63 G4　43 7S 147 50 E
Port Arthur, U.S.A. .......... 81 L8　29 54N 93 56W
Port au Choix, Canada .......... 73 B8　50 43N 57 22W
Port au Port B., Canada .......... 73 C8　48 40N 58 50W
Port-au-Prince, Haiti .......... 89 C5　18 40N 72 20W
Port Augusta, Australia .......... 63 E2　32 30S 137 50 E
Port Austin, U.S.A. .......... 84 B2　44 3N 83 1W
Port Bell, Uganda .......... 54 B3　0 18N 32 35 E
Port Bergé Vaovao, Madag. .......... 57 B8　15 33S 47 40 E
Port Blandford, Canada .......... 73 C9　48 20N 54 10W
Port Bradshaw, Australia .......... 62 A2　12 30S 137 20 E
Port Broughton, Australia .......... 63 E2　33 37S 137 56 E
Port Burwell, Canada .......... 84 D4　42 40N 80 48W
Port Canning, India .......... 43 H13　22 23N 88 40 E
Port-Cartier, Canada .......... 73 B6　50 2N 66 50W
Port Chalmers, N.Z. .......... 59 L3　45 49S 170 30 E
Port Charlotte, U.S.A. .......... 83 M4　26 59N 82 6W
Port Chester, U.S.A. .......... 85 F11　41 0N 73 40W
Port Clements, Canada .......... 70 C2　53 40N 132 10W
Port Clinton, U.S.A. .......... 82 E4　41 31N 82 56W
Port Colborne, Canada .......... 84 D5　42 50N 79 10W
Port Coquitlam, Canada .......... 78 A4　49 15N 122 45W
Port Credit, Canada .......... 84 C5　43 33N 79 35W
Port Curtis, Australia .......... 62 C5　23 57S 151 20 E
Port d'Alcúdia, Spain .......... 24 B10　39 50N 3 7 E
Port Dalhousie, Canada .......... 84 C5　43 13N 79 16W
Port d'Andratx, Spain .......... 24 B9　39 32N 2 23 E
Port Darwin, Australia .......... 60 B5　12 24S 130 45 E
Port Darwin, Falk. Is. .......... 96 G5　51 50S 59 0W
Port Davey, Australia .......... 63 G4　43 16S 145 55 E
Port-de-Paix, Haiti .......... 89 C5　19 50N 72 50W
Port de Pollença, Spain .......... 24 B10　39 54N 3 4 E
Port de Sóller, Spain .......... 24 B9　39 48N 2 42 E
Port Dickson, Malaysia .......... 39 L3　2 30N 101 49 E
Port Douglas, Australia .......... 62 B4　16 30S 145 30 E
Port Dover, Canada .......... 84 D4　42 47N 80 12W
Port Edward, Canada .......... 70 C2　54 12N 130 10W
Port Elgin, Canada .......... 84 B3　44 25N 81 25W
Port Elizabeth, S. Africa .......... 56 E4　33 58S 25 40 E
Port Ellen, U.K. .......... 11 F2　55 38N 6 11W
Port Erin, I. of Man .......... 12 C3　54 5N 4 45W
Port Essington, Australia .......... 60 B5　11 15S 132 10 E
Port Ewen, U.S.A. .......... 85 E11　41 54N 73 59W
Port Fairy, Australia .......... 63 F3　38 22S 142 12 E
Port Gamble, U.S.A. .......... 78 C4　47 51N 122 35W
Port-Gentil, Gabon .......... 52 E1　0 40S 8 50 E
Port Germein, Australia .......... 63 E2　33 1S 138 1 E
Port Gibson, U.S.A. .......... 81 K9　31 58N 90 59W
Port Glasgow, U.K. .......... 11 F4　55 56N 4 41W
Port Harcourt, Nigeria .......... 50 H7　4 40N 7 10 E
Port Hardy, Canada .......... 70 C3　50 41N 127 30W
Port Harrison = Inukjuak, Canada .......... 69 C12　58 25N 78 15W
Port Hawkesbury, Canada .......... 73 C7　45 36N 61 22W
Port Hedland, Australia .......... 60 D2　20 25S 118 35 E
Port Henry, U.S.A. .......... 85 B11　44 3N 73 28W
Port Hood, Canada .......... 73 C7　46 0N 61 32W
Port Hope, Canada .......... 84 C6　43 56N 78 20W
Port Hope, U.S.A. .......... 84 C2　43 57N 82 43W
Port Hope Simpson, Canada .......... 73 B8　52 33N 56 18W
Port Hueneme, U.S.A. .......... 79 L7　34 7N 119 12W
Port Huron, U.S.A. .......... 84 D2　42 58N 82 26W
Port Jefferson, U.S.A. .......... 85 F11　40 57N 73 3W
Port Jervis, U.S.A. .......... 85 E10　41 22N 74 41W
Port Kelang = Pelabuhan Klang, Malaysia .......... 39 L3　3 0N 101 23 E
Port Kenny, Australia .......... 63 E1　33 10S 134 41 E
Port Lairge = Waterford, Ireland .......... 10 D4　52 15N 7 8W
Port Laoise, Ireland .......... 10 C4　53 2N 7 18W
Port Lavaca, U.S.A. .......... 81 L6　28 37N 96 38W
Port Leyden, U.S.A. .......... 85 C9　43 35N 75 21W
Port Lincoln, Australia .......... 63 E2　34 42S 135 52 E
Port Loko, S. Leone .......... 50 G3　8 48N 12 46W
Port-Louis, Guadeloupe .......... 88 b　16 28N 61 32W
Port Louis, Mauritius .......... 49 H9　20 10S 57 30 E
Port MacDonnell, Australia .......... 63 F3　38 5S 140 48 E
Port McNeill, Canada .......... 70 C3　50 35N 127 6W
Port Macquarie, Australia .......... 63 E5　31 25S 152 25 E
Port Maria, Jamaica .......... 88 a　18 22N 76 54W
Port Matilda, U.S.A. .......... 84 F6　40 48N 78 3W
Port Mellon, Canada .......... 70 D4　49 32N 123 31W
Port-Menier, Canada .......... 73 C7　49 51N 64 15W
Port Moody, Canada .......... 78 A4　49 17N 122 51W
Port Morant, Jamaica .......... 88 a　17 54N 76 19W
Port Moresby, Papua N. G. .......... 64 H6　9 24S 147 8 E
Port Musgrave, Australia .......... 62 A3　11 55S 141 50 E
Port Neches, U.S.A. .......... 81 L8　30 0N 93 59W
Port Nolloth, S. Africa .......... 56 D2　29 17S 16 52 E
Port Nouveau-Québec = Kangiqsualujjuaq, Canada .......... 69 C13　58 30N 65 59W
Port of Spain, Trin. & Tob. .......... 89 D7　10 40N 61 31W
Port Orange, U.S.A. .......... 83 L5　29 9N 80 59W
Port Orchard, U.S.A. .......... 78 C4　47 32N 122 38W
Port Orford, U.S.A. .......... 76 E1　42 45N 124 30W
Port Pegasus, N.Z. .......... 59 M1　47 12S 167 41 E
Port Perry, Canada .......... 84 B6　44 6N 78 56W
Port Phillip B., Australia .......... 63 F3　38 10S 144 50 E
Port Pirie, Australia .......... 63 E2　33 10S 138 1 E
Port Renfrew, Canada .......... 70 D4　48 30N 124 20W
Port Roper, Australia .......... 62 A2　14 45S 135 25 E
Port Rowan, Canada .......... 84 D4　42 40N 80 30W
Port Safaga = Bûr Safâga, Egypt .......... 44 E2　26 43N 33 57 E
Port Said = Bûr Sa'îd, Egypt .......... 51 B12　31 16N 32 18 E
Port St. Johns = Umzimvubu, S. Africa .......... 57 E4　31 38S 29 33 E
Port St. Lucie, U.S.A. .......... 83 M5　27 18N 80 21W
Port Sanilac, U.S.A. .......... 84 C2　43 26N 82 33W
Port Severn, Canada .......... 84 B5　44 48N 79 43W
Port Shepstone, S. Africa .......... 57 E5　30 44S 30 28 E
Port Simpson, Canada .......... 70 C2　54 30N 130 20W
Port Stanley = Stanley, Falk. Is. .......... 96 G5　51 40S 59 51W
Port Stanley, Canada .......... 84 D3　42 40N 81 10W
Port Sudan = Bûr Sûdân, Sudan .......... 51 E13　19 32N 37 9 E
Port Sulphur, U.S.A. .......... 81 L10　29 29N 89 42W

Port Talbot, U.K. ............ 13 F4 51 35N 3 47W
Port Townsend, U.S.A. ....... 78 B4 48 7N 122 45W
Port-Vendres, France ....... 20 E5 42 32N 3 8 E
Port Vila, Vanuatu ......... 64 J8 17 45S 168 18 E
Port Vladimir, Russia ...... 18 A5 69 25N 33 6 E
Port Wakefield, Australia ... 63 E2 34 12S 138 10 E
Port Washington, U.S.A. .... 82 D2 43 23N 87 53W
Porta Orientalis, Romania ... 17 F12 45 6N 22 18 E
Portadown, U.K. ............ 10 B5 54 25N 6 27W
Portaferry, U.K. ........... 10 B6 54 23N 5 33W
Portage, U.S.A. ............ 84 F6 46 23N 78 41W
Portage, Wis., U.S.A. ...... 80 D10 43 33N 89 28W
Portage la Prairie, Canada .. 71 D9 49 58N 98 18W
Portageville, U.S.A. ....... 81 G10 36 26N 89 42W
Portalegre, Portugal ....... 21 C2 39 19N 7 25W
Portales, U.S.A. ........... 81 H3 34 11N 103 20W
Portarlington, Ireland ..... 10 C4 53 9N 7 14W
Portbou, Spain ............. 21 A7 42 25N 3 9 E
Porter L., N.W.T., Canada ... 71 A7 61 41N 108 5W
Porter L., Sask., Canada .... 71 B7 56 20N 107 20W
Porterville, S. Africa ..... 56 E2 33 0S 19 0 E
Porterville, U.S.A. ........ 78 J8 36 4N 119 1W
Porthcawl, U.K. ............ 13 F4 51 29N 3 42W
Porthill, U.S.A. ........... 76 B5 48 59N 116 30W
Porthmadog, U.K. ........... 12 E3 52 55N 4 8W
Portile de Fier, Europe .... 17 F12 44 44N 22 30 E
Portimão, Portugal ......... 21 D1 37 8N 8 32W
Portishead, U.K. ........... 13 F5 51 29N 2 46W
Portknockie, U.K. .......... 11 D6 57 42N 2 51W
Portland, N.S.W., Australia . 63 E5 33 20S 150 0 E
Portland, Vic., Australia ... 63 F3 38 20S 141 35 E
Portland, Canada ........... 85 B8 44 42N 76 12W
Portland, Conn., U.S.A. .... 85 E12 41 34N 72 38W
Portland, Maine, U.S.A. .... 69 D12 43 39N 70 16W
Portland, Mich., U.S.A. .... 82 D3 42 52N 84 54W
Portland, Oreg., U.S.A. .... 78 E4 45 32N 122 37W
Portland, Pa., U.S.A. ...... 85 F9 40 55N 75 6W
Portland, Tex., U.S.A. ..... 81 M6 27 53N 97 20W
Portland ✈ (PDX), U.S.A. ... 78 E4 45 35N 122 36W
Portland, I. of, U.K. ...... 13 G5 50 33N 2 26W
Portland B., Australia ..... 63 F3 38 15S 141 45 E
Portland Bight, Jamaica .... 88 a 17 52N 77 5W
Portland Bill, U.K. ........ 13 G5 50 31N 2 28W
Portland Canal, U.S.A. ..... 70 B2 55 56N 130 0W
Portland Pt., Jamaica ...... 88 a 17 42N 77 11W
Portmadoc = Porthmadog, U.K. 12 E3 52 55N 4 8W
Portmore, Jamaica .......... 88 a 17 53N 77 53W
Porto, Portugal ............ 21 B1 41 8N 8 40W
Pôrto Alegre, Brazil ....... 95 C5 30 5S 51 10W
Porto Cristo, Spain ........ 24 B10 39 33N 3 20 E
Pôrto de Móz, Brazil ....... 93 D8 1 41S 52 13W
Porto Empédocle, Italy ..... 22 F5 37 17N 13 32 E
Pôrto Esperança, Brazil .... 92 G7 19 37S 57 29W
Pôrto Franco, Brazil ....... 93 E9 6 20S 47 24W
Pôrto Mendes, Brazil ....... 95 A5 24 30S 54 15W
Pôrto Moniz, Madeira ....... 24 D2 32 52N 17 11W
Pôrto Murtinho, Brazil ..... 92 H7 21 45S 57 55W
Pôrto Nacional, Brazil ..... 93 F9 10 40S 48 30W
Porto-Novo, Benin .......... 50 G6 6 23N 2 42 E
Porto Petro, Spain ......... 24 B10 39 22N 3 13 E
Porto Santo, I. de, Madeira . 50 B2 33 45N 16 25W
Pôrto São José, Brazil ..... 95 A5 22 43S 53 10W
Pôrto Seguro, Brazil ....... 93 G11 16 26S 39 5W
Porto Tórres, Italy ........ 22 D3 40 50N 8 24 E
Pôrto União, Brazil ........ 95 B5 26 10S 51 10W
Pôrto Válter, Brazil ....... 92 E4 8 15S 72 40W
Porto-Vecchio, France ...... 20 F8 41 35N 9 16 E
Pôrto Velho, Brazil ........ 92 E6 8 46S 63 54W
Portobelo, Panama .......... 88 E4 9 35N 79 42W
Portoferráio, Italy ........ 22 C4 42 48N 10 20 E
Portola, U.S.A. ............ 78 F6 39 49N 120 28W
Portoscuso, Italy .......... 22 E3 39 12N 8 24 E
Portoviejo, Ecuador ........ 92 D2 1 7S 80 28W
Portpatrick, U.K. .......... 11 G3 54 51N 5 7W
Portree, U.K. .............. 11 D2 57 25N 6 12W
Portrush, U.K. ............. 10 A5 55 12N 6 40W
Portsmouth, Dominica ....... 89 C7 15 34N 61 27W
Portsmouth, U.K. ........... 13 G6 50 48N 1 6W
Portsmouth, N.H., U.S.A. ... 83 D10 43 5N 70 45W
Portsmouth, Ohio, U.S.A. ... 82 F4 38 44N 82 57W
Portsmouth, R.I., U.S.A. ... 85 E13 41 36N 71 15W
Portsmouth, Va., U.S.A. .... 82 G7 36 50N 76 18W
Portsmouth □, U.K. ......... 13 G6 50 48N 1 6W
Portsoy, U.K. .............. 11 D6 57 41N 2 41W
Portstewart, U.K. .......... 10 A5 55 11N 6 43W
Porttipahdan tekojärvi, Finland . 8 B22 68 5N 26 40 E
Portugal ■, Europe ......... 21 C1 40 0N 8 0W
Portumna, Ireland .......... 10 C3 53 6N 8 14W
Portville, U.S.A. .......... 84 D6 42 3N 78 20W
Porvenir, Chile ............ 96 G2 53 10S 70 16W
Porvoo, Finland ............ 9 F21 60 24N 25 40 E
Posadas, Argentina ......... 95 B4 27 30S 55 50W
Posht-e Badam, Iran ........ 45 C7 33 2N 55 23 E
Poso, Indonesia ............ 37 E6 1 20S 120 55 E
Posong, S. Korea ........... 35 G14 34 46N 127 5 E
Posse, Brazil .............. 93 F9 14 4S 46 18W
Possession I., Antarctica .. 5 D11 72 4S 172 0 E
Possum Kingdom L., U.S.A. .. 81 J5 32 52N 98 26W
Post, U.S.A. ............... 81 J4 33 12N 101 23W
Post Falls, U.S.A. ......... 76 C5 47 43N 116 57W
Postavy = Pastavy, Belarus . 9 J22 55 4N 26 50 E
Poste-de-la-Baleine =
  Kuujjuarapik, Canada ..... 72 A4 55 20N 77 35W
Postmasburg, S. Africa ..... 56 D3 28 18S 23 5 E
Postojna, Slovenia ......... 16 F8 45 46N 14 12 E
Poston, U.S.A. ............. 79 M12 34 0N 114 24W
Postville, Canada .......... 73 B8 54 54N 59 47W
Potchefstroom, S. Africa ... 56 D4 26 41S 27 7 E
Poteau, U.S.A. ............. 81 H7 35 3N 94 37W
Poteet, U.S.A. ............. 81 L5 29 2N 98 35W
Potenza, Italy ............. 22 D6 40 38N 15 48 E
Poteriteri, L., N.Z. ....... 59 M1 46 5S 167 10 E
Potgietersrus = Mokopane,
  S. Africa ................ 57 C4 24 10S 28 55 E
Poti, Georgia .............. 19 F7 42 10N 41 38 E
Potiskum, Nigeria .......... 51 F8 11 39N 11 2 E
Potomac →, U.S.A. .......... 82 G7 38 0N 76 23W
Potosí, Bolivia ............ 92 G5 19 38S 65 50W
Potosi Mt., U.S.A. ......... 79 K11 35 57N 115 29W
Pototan, Phil. ............. 37 B6 10 54N 122 38 E
Potrerillos, Chile ......... 94 B2 26 30S 69 30W
Potsdam, Germany ........... 16 B7 52 25N 13 4 E
Potsdam, U.S.A. ............ 85 B10 44 40N 74 59W
Pottersville, U.S.A. ....... 85 C11 43 43N 73 50W
Pottstown, U.S.A. .......... 85 F9 40 15N 75 39W
Pottsville, U.S.A. ......... 85 F8 40 41N 76 12W
Pottuvil, Sri Lanka ........ 40 R12 6 55N 81 50 E
Pouce Coupé, Canada ........ 70 B4 55 40N 120 10W

Poughkeepsie, U.S.A. ....... 85 E11 41 42N 73 56W
Poulaphouca Res., Ireland .. 10 C5 53 8N 6 30W
Poulsbo, U.S.A. ............ 78 C4 47 44N 122 39W
Poultney, U.S.A. ........... 85 C11 43 31N 73 14W
Poulton-le-Fylde, U.K. ..... 12 D5 53 51N 2 58W
Pouso Alegre, Brazil ....... 95 A6 22 14S 45 57W
Pouthisat, Cambodia ........ 38 F4 12 34N 103 50 E
Považská Bystrica, Slovak Rep. . 17 D10 49 8N 18 27 E
Povenets, Russia ........... 18 B5 62 50N 34 50 E
Poverty B., N.Z. ........... 59 H7 38 43S 178 2 E
Póvoa de Varzim, Portugal .. 21 B1 41 25N 8 46W
Povungnituk = Puvirnituq,
  Canada ................... 69 B12 60 2N 77 10W
Powassan, Canada ........... 72 C4 46 5N 79 25W
Poway, U.S.A. .............. 79 N9 32 58N 117 2W
Powder →, U.S.A. ........... 80 B2 46 45N 105 26W
Powder River, U.S.A. ....... 76 E10 43 2N 106 59W
Powell, U.S.A. ............. 76 D9 44 45N 108 46W
Powell, L., U.S.A. ......... 77 H8 36 57N 111 29W
Powell River, Canada ....... 70 D4 49 50N 124 35W
Powers, U.S.A. ............. 82 C2 45 41N 87 32W
Powys □, U.K. .............. 13 E4 52 20N 3 20W
Poyang Hu, China ........... 33 D6 29 5N 116 20 E
Poyarkovo, Russia .......... 29 E13 49 36N 128 41 E
Poza Rica, Mexico .......... 87 C5 20 33N 97 27W
Požarevac, Serbia & M. ..... 23 B9 44 35N 21 18 E
Poznań, Poland ............. 17 B9 52 25N 16 55 E
Pozo, U.S.A. ............... 79 K6 35 20N 120 24W
Pozo Almonte, Chile ........ 92 H5 20 10S 69 50W
Pozo Colorado, Paraguay .... 94 A4 23 30S 58 45W
Pozoblanco, Spain .......... 21 C3 38 23N 4 51W
Pozzuoli, Italy ............ 22 D6 40 49N 14 7 E
Prachin Buri, Thailand ..... 38 E3 14 0N 101 25 E
Prachuap Khiri Khan, Thailand . 39 G2 11 49N 99 48 E
Prado, Brazil .............. 93 G11 17 20S 39 13W
Prague = Praha, Czech Rep. . 16 C8 50 5N 14 22 E
Praha, Czech Rep. .......... 16 C8 50 5N 14 22 E
Praia, C. Verde Is. ........ 49 E1 15 2N 23 34W
Prainha, Amazonas, Brazil .. 92 E6 7 10S 60 30W
Prainha, Pará, Brazil ...... 93 D8 1 45S 53 30W
Prairie, Australia ......... 62 C3 20 50S 144 35 E
Prairie City, U.S.A. ....... 76 D4 44 28N 118 43W
Prairie Dog Town Fork →, U.S.A. . 81 H5 34 30N 99 23W
Prairie du Chien, U.S.A. ... 80 D9 43 3N 91 9W
Prairies, L. of the, Canada . 71 C8 51 16N 101 32W
Pran Buri, Thailand ........ 38 F2 12 23N 99 55 E
Prapat, Indonesia .......... 36 D1 2 41N 98 58 E
Prasonisi, Ákra, Greece .... 25 D9 35 42N 27 46 E
Prata, Brazil .............. 93 G9 19 25S 48 54W
Pratabpur, India ........... 43 H10 23 28N 83 15 E
Pratapgarh, Raj., India .... 42 G6 24 2N 74 40 E
Pratapgarh, Ut. P., India .. 43 G9 25 56N 81 59 E
Prato, Italy ............... 22 C4 43 53N 11 6 E
Pratt, U.S.A. .............. 81 G5 37 39N 98 44W
Prattville, U.S.A. ......... 83 J2 32 28N 86 29W
Pravia, Spain .............. 21 A2 43 30N 6 12W
Praya, Indonesia ........... 36 F5 8 39S 116 17 E
Precipice △, Australia ..... 63 D5 25 18S 150 5 E
Precordillera, Argentina ... 94 C2 30 0S 69 1W
Preeceville, Canada ........ 71 C8 51 57N 102 40W
Preiļi, Latvia ............. 9 H22 56 18N 26 43 E
Premont, U.S.A. ............ 81 M5 27 22N 98 7W
Prentice, U.S.A. ........... 80 C9 45 33N 90 17W
Preobrazheniye, Russia ..... 30 C6 42 54N 133 54 E
Preparis North Channel, Ind. Oc. . 41 M18 15 12N 93 40 E
Preparis South Channel, Ind. Oc. . 41 M18 14 36N 93 40 E
Přerov, Czech Rep. ......... 17 D9 49 28N 17 27 E
Prescott, Canada ........... 85 B9 44 45N 75 30W
Prescott, Ariz., U.S.A. .... 77 J7 34 33N 112 28W
Prescott, Ark., U.S.A. ..... 81 J8 33 48N 93 23W
Prescott Valley, U.S.A. .... 77 J7 34 40N 112 18W
Preservation Inlet, N.Z. ... 59 M1 46 8S 166 35 E
Presho, U.S.A. ............. 80 D4 43 54N 100 3W
Presidencia de la Plaza,
  Argentina ................ 94 B4 27 0S 59 50W
Presidencia Roque Saenz Peña,
  Argentina ................ 94 B3 26 45S 60 30W
Presidente Epitácio, Brazil . 93 H8 21 56S 52 6W
Presidente Hayes □, Paraguay . 94 A4 24 0S 59 0W
Presidente Prudente, Brazil . 95 A5 22 5S 51 25W
Presidio, Mexico ........... 86 B4 29 29N 104 23W
Presidio, U.S.A. ........... 81 L2 29 34N 104 22W
Prešov, Slovak Rep. ........ 17 D11 49 0N 21 15 E
Prespa, L. = Prespansko Jezero,
  Macedonia ................ 23 D9 40 55N 21 0 E
Prespansko Jezero, Macedonia . 23 D9 40 55N 21 0 E
Presque I., U.S.A. ......... 84 D4 42 9N 80 6W
Presque Isle, U.S.A. ....... 83 B12 46 41N 68 1W
Prestatyn, U.K. ............ 12 D4 53 20N 3 24W
Presteigne, U.K. ........... 13 E4 52 17N 3 0W
Preston, Canada ............ 84 C4 43 23N 80 21W
Preston, U.K. .............. 12 D5 53 46N 2 42W
Preston, Idaho, U.S.A. ..... 76 E8 42 6N 111 53W
Preston, Minn., U.S.A. ..... 80 D8 43 40N 92 5W
Preston, C., Australia ..... 60 D2 20 51S 116 12 E
Prestonburg, U.S.A. ........ 82 G4 37 39N 82 46W
Prestwick, U.K. ............ 11 F4 55 29N 4 37W
Pretoria, S. Africa ........ 57 D4 25 44S 28 12 E
Préveza, Greece ............ 23 E9 38 57N 20 45 E
Prey Veng, Cambodia ........ 39 G5 11 35N 105 29 E
Pribilof Is., U.S.A. ....... 68 C2 57 0N 170 0W
Příbram, Czech Rep. ........ 16 D8 49 41N 14 2 E
Price, U.S.A. .............. 76 G8 39 36N 110 49W
Price I., Canada ........... 70 C3 52 23N 128 41W
Prichard, U.S.A. ........... 83 K1 30 44N 88 5W
Priekule, Latvia ........... 9 H19 56 26N 21 35 E
Prienai, Lithuania ......... 9 J20 54 38N 23 57 E
Prieska, S. Africa ......... 56 D3 29 40S 22 42 E
Priest L., U.S.A. .......... 76 B5 48 35N 116 52W
Priest River, U.S.A. ....... 76 B5 48 10N 116 54W
Priest Valley, U.S.A. ...... 78 J6 36 10N 120 39W
Prievidza, Slovak Rep. ..... 17 D10 48 46N 18 36 E
Prikaspiyskaya Nizmennost =
  Caspian Depression, Eurasia . 19 E8 47 0N 48 0 E
Prilep, Macedonia .......... 23 D9 41 21N 21 32 E
Priluki = Pryluky, Ukraine . 19 D5 50 30N 32 24 E
Prime Seal I., Australia ... 63 G4 40 3S 147 43 E
Primrose L., Canada ........ 71 C7 54 55N 109 45W
Prince Albert, Canada ...... 71 C7 53 15N 105 50W
Prince Albert, S. Africa ... 56 E3 33 12S 22 2 E
Prince Albert △, Canada .... 71 C7 54 0N 106 25W
Prince Albert Mts., Antarctica . 5 D11 76 0S 161 30 E
Prince Albert Pen., Canada . 68 A8 72 30N 116 0W
Prince Albert Sd., Canada .. 68 A8 70 25N 115 0W
Prince Alfred, C., Canada .. 4 B1 74 20N 124 40W
Prince Charles I., Canada .. 69 B12 67 47N 76 12W
Prince Charles Mts., Antarctica . 5 D6 72 0S 67 0 E
Prince Edward I. □, Canada . 73 C7 46 20N 63 20W

Prince Edward Is., Ind. Oc. . 3 G11 46 35S 38 0 E
Prince Edward Pt., Canada .. 84 C8 43 56N 76 52W
Prince George, Canada ...... 70 C4 53 55N 122 50W
Prince of Wales, C., U.S.A. . 66 C3 65 36N 168 5W
Prince of Wales I., Australia . 62 A3 10 40S 142 10 E
Prince of Wales I., Canada . 68 A10 73 0N 99 0W
Prince of Wales I., U.S.A. . 68 C6 55 47N 132 50W
Prince Patrick I., Canada .. 4 B2 77 0N 120 0W
Prince Regent Inlet, Canada . 4 B3 73 0N 90 0W
Prince Rupert, Canada ...... 70 C2 54 20N 130 20W
Princes Town, Trin. & Tob. . 93 K15 10 16N 61 23W
Princess Charlotte B., Australia . 62 A3 14 25S 144 0 E
Princess May Ranges, Australia . 60 C4 15 30S 125 30 E
Princess Royal I., Canada .. 70 C3 53 0N 128 40W
Princeton, Canada .......... 70 D4 49 27N 120 30W
Princeton, Calif., U.S.A. .. 78 F4 39 24N 122 1W
Princeton, Ill., U.S.A. .... 80 E10 41 23N 89 28W
Princeton, Ind., U.S.A. .... 82 F2 38 21N 87 34W
Princeton, Ky., U.S.A. ..... 82 G2 37 7N 87 53W
Princeton, Mo., U.S.A. ..... 80 E8 40 24N 93 35W
Princeton, N.J., U.S.A. .... 85 F10 40 21N 74 39W
Princeton, W. Va., U.S.A. .. 82 G5 37 22N 81 6W
Principe, I. de, Atl. Oc. .. 48 F4 1 37N 7 27 E
Principe da Beira, Brazil .. 92 F6 12 20S 64 30W
Prineville, U.S.A. ......... 76 D3 44 18N 120 51W
Prins Harald Kyst, Antarctica . 5 D4 70 0S 35 1 E
Prinsesse Astrid Kyst, Antarctica . 5 D3 70 45S 12 30 E
Prinsesse Ragnhild Kyst,
  Antarctica ............... 5 D4 70 15S 27 30 E
Prinzapolca, Nic. .......... 88 D3 13 20N 83 35W
Priozersk, Russia .......... 18 B5 61 2N 30 7 E
Pripet = Prypyat →, Europe . 17 C16 51 20N 30 15 E
Pripet Marshes, Europe ..... 17 B15 52 10N 28 10 E
Pripyat Marshes = Pripet
  Marshes, Europe .......... 17 B15 52 10N 28 10 E
Pripyats = Prypyat →, Europe . 17 C16 51 20N 30 15 E
Priština, Serbia & M. ...... 23 C9 42 40N 21 13 E
Privas, France ............. 20 D6 44 45N 4 37 E
Privolzhskaya Vozvyshennost,
  Russia ................... 19 D8 51 0N 46 0 E
Privolzhskiy □, Russia ..... 28 D6 56 0N 50 0 E
Prizren, Serbia & M. ....... 23 C9 42 13N 20 45 E
Probolinggo, Indonesia ..... 37 G15 7 46S 113 13 E
Proctor, U.S.A. ............ 85 C11 43 40N 73 2W
Proddatur, India ........... 40 M11 14 45N 78 30 E
Prodhromos, Cyprus ......... 25 E11 34 57N 32 50 E
Profitis Ilías, Greece ..... 25 C9 36 17N 27 56 E
Profondeville, Belgium ..... 15 D4 50 23N 4 52 E
Progreso, Coahuila, Mexico . 86 B4 27 28N 101 4W
Progreso, Yucatán, Mexico .. 87 C7 21 20N 89 40W
Prokopyevsk, Russia ........ 28 D9 54 0N 86 45 E
Prokuplje, Serbia & M. ..... 23 C9 43 16N 21 36 E
Prome, Burma ............... 41 K19 18 49N 95 13 E
Prophet →, Canada .......... 70 B4 58 48N 122 40W
Prophet River, Canada ...... 70 B4 58 6N 122 43W
Propriá, Brazil ............ 93 F11 10 13S 36 51W
Proserpine, Australia ...... 62 J6 20 21S 148 36 E
Prosna →, Poland ........... 17 B9 52 6N 17 44 E
Prospect, U.S.A. ........... 85 C9 43 18N 75 9W
Prosser, U.S.A. ............ 76 C4 46 12N 119 46W
Prostějov, Czech Rep. ...... 17 D9 49 30N 17 9 E
Proston, Australia ......... 63 D5 26 8S 151 32 E
Provence, France ........... 20 E6 43 40N 5 46 E
Providence, Ky., U.S.A. .... 82 G2 37 24N 87 46W
Providence, R.I., U.S.A. ... 85 E13 41 49N 71 24W
Providence Bay, Canada ..... 72 C3 45 41N 82 15W
Providence Mts., U.S.A. .... 79 K11 35 10N 115 15W
Providencia, I. de, Colombia . 88 D3 13 25N 81 26W
Provideniya, Russia ........ 29 C19 64 23N 173 18W
Provins, France ............ 20 B5 48 33N 3 15 E
Provo, U.S.A. .............. 76 F8 40 14N 111 39W
Provost, Canada ............ 71 C6 52 25N 110 20W
Prudhoe Bay, U.S.A. ........ 68 A5 70 18N 148 22W
Prudhoe I., Australia ...... 62 C4 21 19S 149 41 E
Prud'homme, Canada ......... 71 C7 52 20N 105 54W
Pruszków, Poland ........... 17 B11 52 9N 20 49 E
Prut →, Romania ............ 17 F15 45 28N 28 10 E
Pruzhany, Belarus .......... 17 B13 52 33N 24 28 E
Prydz B., Antarctica ....... 5 C6 69 0S 74 0 E
Pryluky, Ukraine ........... 19 D5 50 30N 32 24 E
Pryor, U.S.A. .............. 81 G7 36 19N 95 19W
Prypyat →, Europe .......... 17 C16 51 20N 30 15 E
Przemyśl, Poland ........... 17 D12 49 50N 22 45 E
Przhevalsk = Karakol, Kyrgyzstan . 28 E8 42 30N 78 20 E
Psará, Greece .............. 23 E11 38 37N 25 38 E
Psíra, Greece .............. 25 D7 35 12N 25 52 E
Pskov, Russia .............. 18 C4 57 50N 28 25 E
Ptich = Ptsich →, Belarus .. 17 B15 52 9N 28 52 E
Ptolemaís, Greece .......... 23 D9 40 30N 21 43 E
Ptsich →, Belarus .......... 17 B15 52 9N 28 52 E
Pu Xian, China ............. 34 F6 36 24N 111 6 E
Pua, Thailand .............. 38 C3 19 11N 100 55 E
Puán, Argentina ............ 94 D3 37 30S 62 45W
Puan, S. Korea ............. 35 G14 35 44N 126 44 E
Pucallpa, Peru ............. 92 E4 8 25S 74 30W
Pudasjärvi, Finland ........ 8 D22 65 23N 26 53 E
Pudozh, Russia ............. 18 B6 61 48N 36 32 E
Puduchcheri = Pondicherry, India . 40 P11 11 59N 79 50 E
Pudukkottai, India ......... 40 P11 10 28N 78 47 E
Puebla, Mexico ............. 87 D5 19 3N 98 12W
Puebla □, Mexico ........... 87 D5 18 30N 98 0W
Pueblo, U.S.A. ............. 80 F2 38 16N 104 37W
Pueblo Hundido, Chile ...... 94 B1 26 20S 70 5W
Puelches, Argentina ........ 94 D2 38 5S 65 51W
Puelén, Argentina .......... 94 D2 37 32S 67 38W
Puente Alto, Chile ......... 94 C1 33 32S 70 35W
Puente-Genil, Spain ........ 21 D3 37 22N 4 47W
Puerca, Pta., Puerto Rico .. 89 d 18 13N 65 36W
Puerco →, U.S.A. ........... 77 J10 34 22N 107 50W
Puerto Aisén, Chile ........ 96 F2 45 27S 73 0W
Puerto Ángel, Mexico ....... 87 D5 15 40N 96 29W
Puerto Arista, Mexico ...... 87 D6 15 56N 93 48W
Puerto Armuelles, Panama ... 88 E3 8 20N 82 51W
Puerto Ayacucho, Venezuela . 92 B5 5 40N 67 35W
Puerto Barrios, Guatemala .. 88 C2 15 40N 88 32W
Puerto Bermejo, Argentina .. 94 B4 26 55S 58 34W
Puerto Bermúdez, Peru ...... 92 F4 10 20S 74 58W
Puerto Bolívar, Ecuador .... 92 D3 3 19S 79 55W
Puerto Cabello, Venezuela .. 92 A5 10 28N 68 1W
Puerto Cabezas, Nic. ....... 88 D3 14 0N 83 30W
Puerto Cabo Gracias á Dios, Nic. . 88 D3 15 0N 83 10W
Puerto Carreño, Colombia ... 92 B5 6 12N 67 22W
Puerto Castilla, Honduras .. 88 C2 16 0N 86 0W
Puerto Chicama, Peru ....... 92 E3 7 45S 79 20W
Puerto Coig, Argentina ..... 96 G3 50 54S 69 15W
Puerto Cortés, Costa Rica .. 88 E3 8 55N 84 0W
Puerto Cortés, Honduras .... 88 C2 15 51N 88 0W
Puerto Cumarebo, Venezuela . 92 A5 11 29N 69 30W

Puerto de Alcudia = Port
  d'Alcúdia, Spain ......... 24 B10 39 50N 3 7 E
Puerto de Cabrera, Spain ... 24 B9 39 8N 2 56 E
Puerto de Gran Tarajal,
  Canary Is. ............... 24 F5 28 13N 14 1W
Puerto de la Cruz, Canary Is. . 24 F3 28 24N 16 32W
Puerto de los Angeles △, Mexico . 86 C3 23 39N 105 45W
Puerto de Pozo Negro, Canary Is. . 24 F6 28 19N 13 55W
Puerto de Sóller = Port de Sóller,
  Spain .................... 24 B9 39 48N 2 42 E
Puerto del Carmen, Canary Is. . 24 F6 28 55N 13 38W
Puerto del Rosario, Canary Is. . 24 F6 28 30N 13 52W
Puerto Deseado, Argentina .. 96 F3 47 55S 66 0W
Puerto Escondido, Mexico ... 87 D5 15 50N 97 3W
Puerto Heath, Bolivia ...... 92 F5 12 34S 68 39W
Puerto Inírida, Colombia ... 92 C5 3 53N 67 52W
Puerto Juárez, Mexico ...... 87 C7 21 11N 86 49W
Puerto La Cruz, Venezuela .. 92 A6 10 13N 64 38W
Puerto Leguízamo, Colombia . 92 D4 0 12S 74 46W
Puerto Limón, Colombia ..... 92 C4 3 23N 73 30W
Puerto Lobos, Argentina .... 96 E3 42 0S 65 3W
Puerto Madryn, Argentina ... 96 E3 42 48S 65 4W
Puerto Maldonado, Peru ..... 92 F5 12 30S 69 10W
Puerto Manatí, Cuba ........ 88 B4 21 22N 76 50W
Puerto Montt, Chile ........ 96 E2 41 28S 73 0W
Puerto Morazán, Nic. ....... 88 D2 12 51N 87 11W
Puerto Morelos, Mexico ..... 87 C7 20 49N 86 52W
Puerto Natales, Chile ...... 96 G2 51 45S 72 15W
Puerto Padre, Cuba ......... 88 B4 21 13N 76 35W
Puerto Páez, Venezuela ..... 92 B5 6 13N 67 28W
Puerto Peñasco, Mexico ..... 86 A2 31 20N 113 33W
Puerto Pinasco, Paraguay ... 94 A4 22 36S 57 50W
Puerto Plata, Dom. Rep. .... 89 C5 19 48N 70 45W
Puerto Pollensa = Port de
  Pollença, Spain .......... 24 B10 39 54N 3 4 E
Puerto Princesa, Phil. ..... 37 C5 9 46N 118 45 E
Puerto Quepos, Costa Rica .. 88 E3 9 29N 84 6W
Puerto Rico, Canary Is. .... 24 G4 27 47N 15 42W
Puerto Rico ☑, W. Indies ... 89 d 18 15N 66 45W
Puerto Rico Trench, Atl. Oc. . 89 C6 19 50N 66 0W
Puerto San Julián, Argentina . 96 F3 49 18S 67 43W
Puerto Sastre, Paraguay .... 94 A4 22 2S 57 55W
Puerto Suárez, Bolivia ..... 92 G7 18 58S 57 52W
Puerto Vallarta, Mexico .... 86 C3 20 36N 105 15W
Puerto Wilches, Colombia ... 92 B4 7 21N 73 54W
Puertollano, Spain ......... 21 C3 38 43N 4 7W
Pueyrredón, L., Argentina .. 96 F2 47 20S 72 0W
Puffin I., Ireland ......... 10 E1 51 50N 10 24W
Pugachev, Russia ........... 18 D8 52 0N 48 49 E
Pugal, India ............... 42 E5 28 30N 72 48 E
Puge, Tanzania ............. 54 C3 4 45S 33 11 E
Puget Sound, U.S.A. ........ 76 C2 47 50N 122 30W
Pugŏdong, N. Korea ......... 35 C16 42 5N 130 0 E
Pugu, Tanzania ............. 54 D4 6 55S 39 4 E
Pūgūnzi, Iran .............. 45 E8 25 49N 59 10 E
Puig Major, Spain .......... 24 B9 39 48N 2 47 E
Puigcerdà, Spain ........... 21 A6 42 24N 1 50 E
Puigpunyent, Spain ......... 24 B9 39 38N 2 32 E
Pujon-chŏsuji, N. Korea .... 35 D14 40 35N 127 35 E
Pukaki, L., N.Z. ........... 59 L3 44 4S 170 1 E
Pukapuka, Cook Is. ......... 65 J11 10 53S 165 49W
Pukaskwa △, Canada ......... 72 C2 48 20N 86 0W
Pukatawagan, Canada ........ 71 B8 55 45N 101 20W
Pukchin, N. Korea .......... 35 D13 40 12N 125 45 E
Pukch'ŏng, N. Korea ........ 35 D15 40 14N 128 10 E
Pukekohe, N.Z. ............. 59 G5 37 12S 174 55 E
Pukhrayan, India ........... 43 F8 26 14N 79 51 E
Pula, Croatia .............. 16 F7 44 54N 13 57 E
Pulacayo, Bolivia .......... 92 H5 20 25S 66 41W
Pulai, Malaysia ............ 39 d 1 20N 103 31 E
Pulandian, China ........... 35 E11 39 25N 121 58 E
Pularumpi, Australia ....... 60 B5 11 24S 130 26 E
Pulaski, N.Y., U.S.A. ...... 85 C8 43 34N 76 8W
Pulaski, Tenn., U.S.A. ..... 83 H2 35 12N 87 2W
Pulaski, Va., U.S.A. ....... 82 G5 37 3N 80 47W
Pulau →, Indonesia ......... 37 F9 5 50S 138 15 E
Puławy, Poland ............. 17 C11 51 23N 21 59 E
Pulga, U.S.A. .............. 78 F5 39 48N 121 29W
Pulicat L., India .......... 40 N12 13 40N 80 15 E
Pullman, U.S.A. ............ 76 C5 46 44N 117 10W
Pulog, Mt., Phil. .......... 37 A6 16 40N 120 50 E
Pułtusk, Poland ............ 17 B11 52 43N 21 6 E
Pumlumon Fawr, U.K. ........ 13 E4 52 28N 3 46W
Puná, I., Ecuador .......... 92 D2 2 55S 80 5W
Punakaiki, N.Z. ............ 59 K3 42 7S 171 20 E
Punakha, Bhutan ............ 41 F16 27 42N 89 52 E
Punasar, India ............. 42 F5 27 6N 73 6 E
Punata, Bolivia ............ 92 G5 17 32S 65 50W
Punch, India ............... 43 C6 33 48N 74 4 E
Punch →, Pakistan .......... 42 C5 33 12N 73 40 E
Punda Maria, S. Africa ..... 57 C5 22 40S 31 5 E
Pune, India ................ 40 K8 18 29N 73 57 E
P'ungsan, N. Korea ......... 35 D15 40 50N 128 9 E
Pungue, Ponte de, Mozam. ... 55 F3 19 0S 34 0 E
Punjab □, India ............ 42 D7 31 0N 76 0 E
Punjab □, Pakistan ......... 42 E6 32 0N 72 30 E
Puno, Peru ................. 92 G4 15 55S 70 3W
Punpun →, India ............ 43 G11 25 31N 85 18 E
Punta, Cerro de, Puerto Rico . 89 d 18 10N 66 37W
Punta Alta, Argentina ...... 96 D4 38 53S 62 4W
Punta Arenas, Chile ........ 96 G2 53 10S 71 0W
Punta de Díaz, Chile ....... 94 B1 28 0S 70 45W
Punta del Hidalgo, Canary Is. . 24 F3 28 33N 16 19W
Punta Gorda, Belize ........ 87 D7 16 10N 88 45W
Punta Gorda, U.S.A. ........ 83 M5 26 56N 82 3W
Punta Prieta, Mexico ....... 86 B2 28 58N 114 17W
Punta Prima, Spain ......... 24 B11 39 48N 4 16 E
Puntarenas, Costa Rica ..... 88 E3 10 0N 84 50W
Punto Fijo, Venezuela ...... 92 A4 11 50N 70 13W
Punxsatawney, U.S.A. ....... 84 F6 40 57N 78 59W
Pupuan, Indonesia .......... 37 J18 8 19S 115 0 E
Puquio, Peru ............... 92 F4 14 45S 74 10W
Pur →, Russia .............. 28 C8 67 31N 77 55 E
Puracé, Vol., Colombia ..... 92 C3 2 21N 76 23W
Puralia = Puruliya, India .. 43 H12 23 17N 86 24 E
Puranpur, India ............ 43 E9 28 31N 80 9 E
Purbeck, Isle of, U.K. ..... 13 G5 50 39N 1 59W
Purcell, U.S.A. ............ 81 H6 35 1N 97 22W
Purcell Mts., Canada ....... 70 D5 49 55N 116 15W
Puri, India ................ 41 K14 19 50N 85 58 E
Purmerend, Neths. .......... 15 B4 52 32N 4 58 E
Purnia, India .............. 43 G12 25 45N 87 31 E
Purnululu Nat. Park △, Australia . 60 C4 17 20S 128 20 E
Pursat = Pouthisat, Cambodia . 38 F4 12 34N 103 50 E
Purukcahu, Indonesia ....... 36 E4 0 35S 114 35 E
Puruliya, India ............ 43 H12 23 17N 86 24 E
Purus →, Brazil ............ 92 D6 3 42S 61 28W
Purvis, U.S.A. ............. 81 K10 31 9N 89 25W

Purwa, India . . . . . . . . . . . . . . . . 43 F9 26 28N 80 47 E
Purwakarta, Indonesia . . . . . . . 37 G12 6 35S 107 29 E
Purwo, Tanjung, Indonesia . . . . . 37 K18 8 44S 114 21 E
Purwokerto, Indonesia . . . . . . . 37 G13 7 25S 109 14 E
Purwodadi, Indonesia . . . . . . . 37 G14 7 7S 110 55 E
Puryŏng, N. Korea . . . . . . . . . . 35 C15 42 5N 129 43 E
Pusa, India . . . . . . . . . . . . . . . 43 G11 25 59N 85 41 E
Pushkino, Russia . . . . . . . . . . . 19 D8 51 16N 47 0 E
Putahow L., Canada . . . . . . . . . 71 B8 59 54N 100 40W
Putao, Burma . . . . . . . . . . . . . 41 F20 27 28N 97 30 E
Putaruru, N.Z. . . . . . . . . . . . . . 59 H5 38 2S 175 50 E
Putignano, Italy . . . . . . . . . . . . 22 D7 40 51N 17 7 E
Puting, Tanjung, Indonesia . . . . . 36 E4 3 31S 111 46 E
Putnam, U.S.A. . . . . . . . . . . . . 85 E13 41 55N 71 55W
Putorana, Gory, Russia . . . . . . . 29 C10 69 0N 95 0 E
Putrajaya, Malaysia . . . . . . . . . 39 L3 2 55N 101 40 E
Puttalam, Sri Lanka . . . . . . . . . 40 Q11 8 1N 79 55 E
Puttgarden, Germany . . . . . . . . 16 A6 54 30N 11 10 E
Putumayo →, S. Amer. . . . . . . 92 D5 3 7S 67 58W
Putussibau, Indonesia . . . . . . . 36 D4 0 50N 112 56 E
Puvirnituq, Canada . . . . . . . . . 69 B12 60 2N 77 10W
Puy-de-Dôme, France . . . . . . . 20 D5 45 46N 2 57 E
Puyallup, U.S.A. . . . . . . . . . . . 78 C4 47 12N 122 18W
Puyang, China . . . . . . . . . . . . 34 G8 35 40N 115 1 E
Püzeh Rīg, Iran . . . . . . . . . . . . 45 E8 27 20N 58 40 E
Pwani □, Tanzania . . . . . . . . . 54 D4 7 0S 39 0 E
Pweto, Dem. Rep. of the Congo . 55 D2 8 25S 28 51 E
Pwllheli, U.K. . . . . . . . . . . . . . 12 E3 52 53N 4 25W
Pya-ozero, Russia . . . . . . . . . . 18 A5 66 5N 30 58 E
Pyapon, Burma . . . . . . . . . . . . 41 L19 16 20N 95 40 E
Pyasina →, Russia . . . . . . . . . 29 B9 73 30N 87 0 E
Pyatigorsk, Russia . . . . . . . . . . 19 F7 44 2N 43 6 E
Pyè = Prome, Burma . . . . . . . . 41 K19 18 49N 95 13 E
Pyetrikaw, Belarus . . . . . . . . . 17 B15 52 11N 28 29 E
Pyhäjoki, Finland . . . . . . . . . . . 8 D21 64 28N 24 14 E
Pyinmana, Burma . . . . . . . . . . 41 K20 19 45N 96 12 E
Pyla, C., Cyprus . . . . . . . . . . . 25 E12 34 56N 33 51 E
Pymatuning Reservoir, U.S.A. . . . 84 E4 41 30N 80 28W
Pyŏktong, N. Korea . . . . . . . . . 35 D13 40 50N 125 50 E
Pyŏnggang, N. Korea . . . . . . . . 35 E14 38 24N 127 17 E
P'yŏngt'aek, S. Korea . . . . . . . . 35 F14 37 1N 127 4 E
P'yŏngyang, N. Korea . . . . . . . . 35 E13 39 0N 125 30 E
Pyote, U.S.A. . . . . . . . . . . . . . 81 K3 31 32N 103 8W
Pyramid L., U.S.A. . . . . . . . . . . 76 G4 40 1N 119 35W
Pyramid Pk., U.S.A. . . . . . . . . . 79 J10 36 25N 116 37W
Pyrénées, Europe . . . . . . . . . . 20 E4 42 45N 0 18 E
Pyu, Burma . . . . . . . . . . . . . . 41 K20 18 30N 96 28 E

Q

Qaanaaq, Greenland . . . . . . . . 4 B4 77 40N 69 0W
Qachasnek, S. Africa . . . . . . . . 57 E4 30 6S 28 42 E
Qa'el Jafr, Jordan . . . . . . . . . . 46 E5 30 20N 36 25 E
Qa'emābād, Iran . . . . . . . . . . . 45 D9 31 44N 60 2 E
Qa'emshahr, Iran . . . . . . . . . . 45 B7 36 30N 52 53 E
Qagan Nur, China . . . . . . . . . . 34 C8 43 30N 114 55 E
Qahar Youyi Zhongqi, China . . . 34 D7 41 12N 112 40 E
Qahremānshahr = Bākhtarān,
Iran . . . . . . . . . . . . . . . . . . . 44 C5 34 23N 47 0 E
Qaidam Pendi, China . . . . . . . . 32 C4 37 0N 95 0 E
Qajarīyeh, Iran . . . . . . . . . . . . 45 D6 31 1N 48 22 E
Qala, Ras il, Malta . . . . . . . . . 25 C1 36 2N 14 20 E
Qala-i-Jadid = Spīn Būldak,
Afghan. . . . . . . . . . . . . . . . . 42 D2 31 1N 66 25 E
Qala Point = Qala, Ras il, Malta . 25 C1 36 2N 14 20 E
Qala Viala, Pakistan . . . . . . . . 42 D2 30 49N 67 17 E
Qala Yangi, Afghan. . . . . . . . . . 42 B2 34 20N 66 30 E
Qal'at al Akhḍar, Si. Arabia . . . . 44 E3 28 0N 37 10 E
Qal'at Dīzah, Iraq . . . . . . . . . . 44 B5 36 11N 45 7 E
Qal'at Şāliḥ, Iraq . . . . . . . . . . . 44 D5 31 31N 47 16 E
Qal'at Sukkar, Iraq . . . . . . . . . 44 D5 31 51N 46 5 E
Qamani'tuaq = Baker Lake,
Canada . . . . . . . . . . . . . . . . 68 B10 64 20N 96 3W
Qamdo, China . . . . . . . . . . . . 32 C4 31 15N 97 6 E
Qamruddin Karez, Pakistan . . . . 42 D3 31 45N 68 20 E
Qandahār, Afghan. . . . . . . . . . . 40 D4 31 32N 65 43 E
Qandahār □, Afghan. . . . . . . . . 40 D4 31 0N 65 0 E
Qapān, Iran . . . . . . . . . . . . . . 45 B7 37 40N 55 47 E
Qapshaghay, Kazakhstan . . . . . 28 E8 43 51N 77 14 E
Qaqortoq, Greenland . . . . . . . . 69 B6 60 43N 46 0W
Qara Qash →, China . . . . . . . . 43 B8 35 0N 78 30 E
Qarabutaq, Kazakhstan . . . . . . 28 E7 49 59N 60 14 E
Qaraghandy, Kazakhstan . . . . . 28 E8 49 50N 73 10 E
Qaraghayly, Kazakhstan . . . . . . 28 E8 49 26N 76 0 E
Qārah, Si. Arabia . . . . . . . . . . 44 D4 29 55N 40 3 E
Qaratau, Kazakhstan . . . . . . . . 28 E8 43 10N 70 28 E
Qarataū, Kazakhstan . . . . . . . . 28 E8 43 30N 69 30 E
Qardho = Gardo, Somali Rep. . . 47 F4 9 30N 49 6 E
Qareh →, Iran . . . . . . . . . . . . 44 B5 39 25N 47 22 E
Qareh Tekān, Iran . . . . . . . . . . 45 B6 36 38N 49 29 E
Qarqan He →, China . . . . . . . . 32 C3 39 30N 88 30 E
Qarqaraly, Kazakhstan . . . . . . . 28 E8 49 26N 75 30 E
Qarshi, Uzbekistan . . . . . . . . . 28 F7 38 53N 65 48 E
Qartabā, Lebanon . . . . . . . . . . 46 A4 34 4N 35 50 E
Qaryat al Gharab, Iraq . . . . . . . 44 D5 31 27N 44 48 E
Qaryat al 'Ulyā, Si. Arabia . . . . . 44 E5 27 33N 47 42 E
Qasr 'Amra, Jordan . . . . . . . . . 44 D3 31 48N 36 35 E
Qasr-e Qand, Iran . . . . . . . . . . 45 E9 26 15N 60 45 E
Qasr Farâfra, Egypt . . . . . . . . . 51 C11 27 0N 28 1 E
Qatanā, Syria . . . . . . . . . . . . . 46 B5 33 26N 36 4 E
Qatar ■, Asia . . . . . . . . . . . . . 45 E6 25 30N 51 15 E
Qatlish, Iran . . . . . . . . . . . . . . 45 B8 37 50N 57 19 E
Qattâra, Munkhafed el, Egypt . . . 51 C11 29 30N 27 30 E
Qattâra Depression = Qattâra,
Munkhafed el, Egypt . . . . . . . 51 C11 29 30N 27 30 E
Qawām al Ḥamzah = Al Ḥamzah,
Iraq . . . . . . . . . . . . . . . . . . . 44 D5 31 43N 44 58 E
Qāyen, Iran . . . . . . . . . . . . . . 45 C8 33 40N 59 10 E
Qazaqstan = Kazakhstan ■, Asia 28 E7 50 0N 70 0 E
Qazimämmäd, Azerbaijan . . . . . 45 A6 40 3N 49 0 E
Qazvin, Iran . . . . . . . . . . . . . . 45 B6 36 15N 50 0 E
Qazvin □, Iran . . . . . . . . . . . . 45 B6 36 20N 50 0 E
Qena, Egypt . . . . . . . . . . . . . . 51 C12 26 10N 32 43 E
Qeqertarsuaq, Greenland . . . . . 69 B5 69 45N 53 30W
Qeqertarsuaq, Greenland . . . . . 69 B14 69 15N 53 38W
Qeshlāq, Iran . . . . . . . . . . . . . 44 C5 34 55N 46 28 E
Qeshm, Iran . . . . . . . . . . . . . . 45 E8 26 55N 56 10 E
Qeys, Iran . . . . . . . . . . . . . . . 45 E7 26 32N 53 58 E
Qezel Owzen →, Iran . . . . . . . 45 B6 36 45N 49 22 E
Qezi'ot, Israel . . . . . . . . . . . . . 46 E3 30 52N 34 26 E
Qi Xian, China . . . . . . . . . . . . 34 G8 34 40N 114 48 E
Qian Gorlos, China . . . . . . . . . 35 B13 45 5N 124 42 E
Qian Xian, China . . . . . . . . . . . 34 G5 34 31N 108 15 E

Qianshan, China . . . . . . . . . . . 33 G10 22 15N 113 31 E
Qianyang, China . . . . . . . . . . . 34 G4 34 40N 107 8 E
Qi'ao, China . . . . . . . . . . . . . . 33 G10 22 25N 113 39 E
Qi'ao Dao, China . . . . . . . . . . 33 G10 22 25N 113 38 E
Qikiqtarjuaq, Canada . . . . . . . . 69 B13 67 33N 63 0W
Qila Safed, Pakistan . . . . . . . . 40 E2 29 0N 61 30 E
Qila Saifullāh, Pakistan . . . . . . 42 D3 30 45N 68 17 E
Qilian Shan, China . . . . . . . . . 32 C4 38 30N 96 0 E
Qin He →, China . . . . . . . . . . 34 G7 35 1N 113 22 E
Qin Ling = Qinling Shandi, China 34 H5 33 50N 108 10 E
Qin'an, China . . . . . . . . . . . . . 34 G3 34 48N 105 40 E
Qing Xian, China . . . . . . . . . . . 34 E9 38 35N 116 45 E
Qingcheng, China . . . . . . . . . . 35 F9 37 15N 117 40 E
Qingdao, China . . . . . . . . . . . . 35 F11 36 5N 120 20 E
Qingfeng, China . . . . . . . . . . . 34 G8 35 52N 115 8 E
Qinghai □, China . . . . . . . . . . 32 C4 36 0N 98 0 E
Qinghai Hu, China . . . . . . . . . . 32 C5 36 40N 100 10 E
Qinghecheng, China . . . . . . . . 35 D13 41 28N 124 15 E
Qinghemen, China . . . . . . . . . . 35 D11 41 48N 121 25 E
Qingjian, China . . . . . . . . . . . . 34 F6 37 8N 110 8 E
Qingjiang = Huaiyin, China . . . . 35 H10 33 30N 119 2 E
Qingshui, China . . . . . . . . . . . 34 G4 34 48N 106 8 E
Qingshuihe, China . . . . . . . . . . 34 E6 39 55N 111 35 E
Qingtongxia Shuiku, China . . . . 34 F3 37 50N 105 58 E
Qingxu, China . . . . . . . . . . . . . 34 F7 37 34N 112 22 E
Qingyang, China . . . . . . . . . . . 34 F4 36 2N 107 55 E
Qingyuan, China . . . . . . . . . . . 35 C13 42 10N 124 55 E
Qingyun, China . . . . . . . . . . . . 35 F9 37 45N 117 20 E
Qinhuangdao, China . . . . . . . . 35 E10 39 56N 119 30 E
Qinling Shandi, China . . . . . . . . 34 H5 33 50N 108 10 E
Qinshui, China . . . . . . . . . . . . 34 G7 35 40N 112 8 E
Qinyang, China . . . . . . . . . . . . 34 G7 35 7N 112 57 E
Qinyuan, China . . . . . . . . . . . . 34 F7 36 29N 112 20 E
Qinzhou, China . . . . . . . . . . . . 32 D5 21 58N 108 38 E
Qionghai, China . . . . . . . . . . . 38 C8 19 15N 110 26 E
Qiongzhou Haixia, China . . . . . . 38 B8 20 10N 110 15 E
Qiqihar, China . . . . . . . . . . . . . 29 E13 47 26N 124 0 E
Qiraîya, W. →, Egypt . . . . . . . . 46 E3 30 27N 34 0 E
Qiryat Ata, Israel . . . . . . . . . . . 46 C4 32 47N 35 6 E
Qiryat Gat, Israel . . . . . . . . . . . 46 D3 31 32N 34 46 E
Qiryat Mal'akhi, Israel . . . . . . . 46 D3 31 44N 34 44 E
Qiryat Shemona, Israel . . . . . . . 46 B4 33 13N 35 35 E
Qiryat Yam, Israel . . . . . . . . . . 46 C4 32 51N 35 4 E
Qishan, China . . . . . . . . . . . . . 34 G4 34 25N 107 38 E
Qitai, China . . . . . . . . . . . . . . 32 B3 44 2N 89 35 E
Qixia, China . . . . . . . . . . . . . . 35 F11 37 17N 120 52 E
Qızılağac Körfäzi, Azerbaijan . . . 45 B6 39 9N 49 0 E
Qom, Iran . . . . . . . . . . . . . . . . 45 C6 34 40N 51 0 E
Qom □, Iran . . . . . . . . . . . . . . 45 C6 34 40N 51 0 E
Qomolangma Feng = Everest,
Mt., Nepal . . . . . . . . . . . . . . 43 E12 28 5N 86 58 E
Qomsheh, Iran . . . . . . . . . . . . 45 D6 32 0N 51 55 E
Qoraqalpoghistan □, Uzbekistan 28 E6 43 0N 58 0 E
Qostanay, Kazakhstan . . . . . . . 28 D7 53 10N 63 35 E
Quabbin Reservoir, U.S.A. . . . . . 85 D12 42 20N 72 20W
Quairading, Australia . . . . . . . . 61 F2 32 0S 117 21 E
Quakertown, U.S.A. . . . . . . . . . 85 F9 40 26N 75 21W
Qualicum Beach, Canada . . . . . 70 D4 49 22N 124 26W
Quambatook, Australia . . . . . . . 63 F3 35 49S 143 34 E
Quambone, Australia . . . . . . . . 63 E4 30 57S 147 53 E
Quamby, Australia . . . . . . . . . . 62 C3 20 22S 140 17 E
Quan Long = Ca Mau, Vietnam . 39 H5 9 7N 105 8 E
Quanah, U.S.A. . . . . . . . . . . . . 81 H5 34 18N 99 44W
Quang Ngai, Vietnam . . . . . . . . 38 E7 15 13N 108 58 E
Quang Tri, Vietnam . . . . . . . . . 38 D6 16 45N 107 13 E
Quang Yen, Vietnam . . . . . . . . 38 B6 20 56N 106 52 E
Quantock Hills, U.K. . . . . . . . . . 13 F4 51 8N 3 10W
Quanzhou, China . . . . . . . . . . . 33 D6 24 55N 118 34 E
Qu'Appelle, Canada . . . . . . . . . 71 C8 50 33N 103 53W
Quaqtaq, Canada . . . . . . . . . . 69 B13 60 55N 69 40W
Quarai, Brazil . . . . . . . . . . . . . 94 C4 30 15S 56 20W
Quartu Sant'Élena, Italy . . . . . . 22 E3 39 15N 9 10 E
Quartzsite, U.S.A. . . . . . . . . . . 79 M12 33 40N 114 13W
Quatsino Sd., Canada . . . . . . . 70 C3 50 25N 127 58W
Qüchān, Iran . . . . . . . . . . . . . 45 B8 37 10N 58 27 E
Queanbeyan, Australia . . . . . . . 63 F4 35 17S 149 14 E
Québec, Canada . . . . . . . . . . . 73 C5 46 52N 71 13W
Québec □, Canada . . . . . . . . . 73 C6 48 0N 74 0W
Quebrada del Condorito △,
Argentina . . . . . . . . . . . . . . . 94 C3 31 49S 64 40W
Queen Alexandra Ra., Antarctica 5 E11 85 0S 170 0 E
Queen Charlotte City, Canada . . 70 C2 53 15N 132 2W
Queen Charlotte Is., Canada . . . 70 C2 53 20N 132 10W
Queen Charlotte Sd., Canada . . 70 C3 51 0N 128 0W
Queen Charlotte Strait, Canada . 70 C3 50 45N 127 10W
Queen Elizabeth △, U.K. . . . . . . 11 E4 56 7N 4 30W
Queen Elizabeth △, Uganda . . . 54 C3 0 0 30 0 E
Queen Elizabeth Is., Canada . . . 66 B10 76 0N 95 0W
Queen Mary Land, Antarctica . . 5 D7 70 0S 95 0 E
Queen Maud G., Canada . . . . . 68 B9 68 15N 102 30W
Queen Maud Land = Dronning
Maud Land, Antarctica . . . . . . 5 D3 72 30S 12 0 E
Queen Maud Mts., Antarctica . . 5 E13 86 0S 160 0W
Queens Chan., Australia . . . . . . 60 C4 15 0S 129 30 E
Queenscliff, Australia . . . . . . . . 63 F3 38 16S 144 39 E
Queensland □, Australia . . . . . . 62 C3 22 0S 142 0 E
Queenstown, Australia . . . . . . . 63 G4 42 4S 145 35 E
Queenstown, N.Z. . . . . . . . . . . 59 L2 45 1S 168 40 E
Queenstown, Singapore . . . . . . 39 d 1 18N 103 48 E
Queenstown, S. Africa . . . . . . . 56 E4 31 52S 26 52 E
Queets, U.S.A. . . . . . . . . . . . . 78 C2 47 32N 124 20W
Queguay Grande →, Uruguay . . 94 C4 32 9S 58 9W
Queimadas, Brazil . . . . . . . . . . 93 F11 11 0S 39 38W
Quelimane, Mozam. . . . . . . . . . 55 F4 17 53S 36 58 E
Quellón, Chile . . . . . . . . . . . . . 96 E2 43 7S 73 37W
Quelpart = Cheju do, S. Korea . . 35 H14 33 29N 126 34 E
Quemado, N. Mex., U.S.A. . . . . 77 J9 34 20N 108 30W
Quemado, Tex., U.S.A. . . . . . . . 81 L4 28 58N 100 35W
Quemú-Quemú, Argentina . . . . 94 D3 36 3S 63 36W
Quequén, Argentina . . . . . . . . . 94 D4 38 30S 58 30W
Querétaro, Mexico . . . . . . . . . . 86 C4 20 36N 100 23W
Querétaro □, Mexico . . . . . . . . 86 C5 20 50N 100 0W
Queshan, China . . . . . . . . . . . 34 H8 32 55N 114 2 E
Quesnel, Canada . . . . . . . . . . 70 C4 53 0N 122 30W
Quesnel →, Canada . . . . . . . . 70 C4 52 58N 122 29W
Quesnel L., Canada . . . . . . . . . 70 C4 52 30N 121 20W
Questa, U.S.A. . . . . . . . . . . . . 77 H11 36 42N 105 36W
Quetico △, Canada . . . . . . . . . 72 C1 48 30N 91 45W
Quetta, Pakistan . . . . . . . . . . . 42 D2 30 15N 66 55 E
Quezaltenango, Guatemala . . . . 88 D1 14 50N 91 30W
Quezon City, Phil. . . . . . . . . . . 37 B6 14 38N 121 0 E
Qufār, Si. Arabia . . . . . . . . . . . 44 E4 27 26N 41 37 E
Qui Nhon, Vietnam . . . . . . . . . 38 F7 13 40N 109 13 E
Quiaca, Angola . . . . . . . . . . . . 52 F2 12 34S 14 27 E
Quibdo, Colombia . . . . . . . . . . 92 B3 5 42N 76 40W
Quiberon, France . . . . . . . . . . . 20 C2 47 29N 3 9W

Quiet L., Canada . . . . . . . . . . . 70 A2 61 5N 133 5W
Quiindy, Paraguay . . . . . . . . . . 94 B4 25 58S 57 14W
Quila, Mexico . . . . . . . . . . . . . 86 C3 24 23N 107 13W
Quilán, C., Chile . . . . . . . . . . . 96 E2 43 15S 74 30W
Quilcene, U.S.A. . . . . . . . . . . . 78 C4 47 49N 122 53W
Quilimarí, Chile . . . . . . . . . . . . 94 C1 32 5S 71 30W
Quilino, Argentina . . . . . . . . . . 94 C3 30 14S 64 29W
Quillabamba, Peru . . . . . . . . . . 92 F4 12 50S 72 50W
Quillaicillo, Chile . . . . . . . . . . . 94 C1 31 17S 71 40W
Quillota, Chile . . . . . . . . . . . . . 94 C1 32 54S 71 16W
Quilmes, Argentina . . . . . . . . . 94 C4 34 43S 58 15W
Quilon, India . . . . . . . . . . . . . . 40 Q10 8 50N 76 38 E
Quilpie, Australia . . . . . . . . . . . 63 D3 26 35S 144 11 E
Quilpué, Chile . . . . . . . . . . . . . 94 C1 33 5S 71 33W
Quilua, Mozam. . . . . . . . . . . . . 55 F4 16 17S 39 54 E
Quimilí, Argentina . . . . . . . . . . 94 B3 27 40S 62 30W
Quimper, France . . . . . . . . . . . 20 B1 48 0N 4 9W
Quimperlé, France . . . . . . . . . . 20 C2 47 53N 3 33W
Quinault →, U.S.A. . . . . . . . . . 78 C2 47 21N 124 18W
Quincy, Calif., U.S.A. . . . . . . . . 78 F6 39 56N 120 57W
Quincy, Fla., U.S.A. . . . . . . . . . 83 K3 30 35N 84 34W
Quincy, Ill., U.S.A. . . . . . . . . . . 80 F9 39 56N 91 23W
Quincy, Mass., U.S.A. . . . . . . . 85 D14 42 15N 71 0W
Quincy, Wash., U.S.A. . . . . . . . 76 C4 47 22N 119 56W
Quines, Argentina . . . . . . . . . . 94 C2 32 13S 65 48W
Quinga, Mozam. . . . . . . . . . . . 55 F5 15 49S 40 15 E
Quintana Roo □, Mexico . . . . . 87 D7 19 0N 88 0W
Quintanar de la Orden, Spain . . 21 C4 39 36N 3 5W
Quinte West, Canada . . . . . . . . 84 B7 44 10N 77 34W
Quintero, Chile . . . . . . . . . . . . 94 C1 32 45S 71 30W
Quirihue, Chile . . . . . . . . . . . . 94 D1 36 15S 72 35W
Quirindi, Australia . . . . . . . . . . 63 E5 31 28S 150 40 E
Quirinópolis, Brazil . . . . . . . . . 93 G8 18 32S 50 30W
Quissanga, Mozam. . . . . . . . . . 55 E5 12 24S 40 28 E
Quissico, Mozam. . . . . . . . . . . 57 C5 24 42S 34 44 E
Quitilipi, Argentina . . . . . . . . . . 94 B3 26 50S 60 13W
Quitman, U.S.A. . . . . . . . . . . . 83 K4 30 47N 83 34W
Quito, Ecuador . . . . . . . . . . . . 92 D3 0 15S 78 35W
Quixadá, Brazil . . . . . . . . . . . . 93 D11 4 55S 39 0W
Quixaxe, Mozam. . . . . . . . . . . . 55 F5 15 17S 40 4 E
Qulan, Kazakhstan . . . . . . . . . 28 E8 42 55N 72 43 E
Qul'ān, Jazā'ir, Egypt . . . . . . . . 44 E2 24 22N 35 31 E
Qumbu, S. Africa . . . . . . . . . . . 57 E4 31 10S 28 48 E
Quneitra, Syria . . . . . . . . . . . . 46 B4 33 7N 35 48 E
Qünghirot, Uzbekistan . . . . . . . 28 E6 43 6N 58 54 E
Quoin I., Australia . . . . . . . . . . 60 B4 14 54S 129 32 E
Quoin Pt., S. Africa . . . . . . . . . 56 E2 34 46S 19 37 E
Quorn, Australia . . . . . . . . . . . 63 E2 32 25S 138 5 E
Qŭqon, Uzbekistan . . . . . . . . . 28 E8 40 30N 70 57 E
Qurnat as Sawdā', Lebanon . . . 46 A5 34 18N 36 6 E
Quşaybā', Si. Arabia . . . . . . . . 44 E4 26 53N 43 35 E
Quşaybah, Iraq . . . . . . . . . . . . 44 C4 34 24N 40 59 E
Quseir, Egypt . . . . . . . . . . . . . 44 E2 26 7N 34 16 E
Qüshchī, Iran . . . . . . . . . . . . . 44 B5 37 59N 45 3 E
Quthing, Lesotho . . . . . . . . . . . 57 E4 30 25S 27 36 E
Qūţīābād, Iran . . . . . . . . . . . . . 45 C6 35 47N 48 30 E
Quwo, China . . . . . . . . . . . . . . 34 G6 35 38N 111 25 E
Quyang, China . . . . . . . . . . . . 34 E8 38 35N 114 40 E
Quynh Nhai, Vietnam . . . . . . . . 38 B4 21 49N 103 33 E
Quyon, Canada . . . . . . . . . . . . 85 A8 45 31N 76 14W
Quzhou, China . . . . . . . . . . . . 33 D6 28 57N 118 54 E
Quzi, China . . . . . . . . . . . . . . 34 F4 36 20N 107 20 E
Qyzylorda, Kazakhstan . . . . . . . 28 E7 44 48N 65 28 E

R

Ra, Ko, Thailand . . . . . . . . . . . 39 H2 9 13N 98 16 E
Raahe, Finland . . . . . . . . . . . . 8 D21 64 40N 24 28 E
Raalte, Neths. . . . . . . . . . . . . . 15 B6 52 23N 6 16 E
Raasay, U.K. . . . . . . . . . . . . . . 11 D2 57 25N 6 4W
Raasay, Sd. of, U.K. . . . . . . . . . 11 D2 57 30N 6 8W
Raba, Indonesia . . . . . . . . . . . 37 F5 8 36S 118 55 E
Rába →, Hungary . . . . . . . . . . 17 E9 47 38N 17 38 E
Rabai, Kenya . . . . . . . . . . . . . 54 C4 3 50S 39 31 E
Rabat = Victoria, Malta . . . . . . 25 C1 36 3N 14 14 E
Rabat, Malta . . . . . . . . . . . . . . 25 D1 35 53N 14 24 E
Rabat, Morocco . . . . . . . . . . . . 50 B4 34 2N 6 48W
Rabaul, Papua N. G. . . . . . . . . 64 H7 4 24S 152 18 E
Rābigh, Si. Arabia . . . . . . . . . . 47 C2 22 50N 39 5 E
Râbniţa, Moldova . . . . . . . . . . . 17 E15 47 45N 29 0 E
Rābor, Iran . . . . . . . . . . . . . . . 45 D8 29 17N 56 55 E
Race, C., Canada . . . . . . . . . . 73 C9 46 40N 53 5W
Rach Gia, Vietnam . . . . . . . . . . 39 G5 10 5N 105 5 E
Rachid, Mauritania . . . . . . . . . . 50 E3 18 45N 11 35W
Racibórz, Poland . . . . . . . . . . . 17 C10 50 7N 18 18 E
Racine, U.S.A. . . . . . . . . . . . . . 82 D2 42 41N 87 51W
Rackerby, U.S.A. . . . . . . . . . . . 78 F5 39 26N 121 22W
Radama, Nosy, Madag. . . . . . . . 57 A8 14 0S 47 47 E
Radama, Saikanosy, Madag. . . . 57 A8 14 16S 47 53 E
Rădăuţi, Romania . . . . . . . . . . 17 E13 47 50N 25 59 E
Radcliff, U.S.A. . . . . . . . . . . . . 82 G3 37 51N 85 57W
Radekhiv, Ukraine . . . . . . . . . . 17 C13 50 25N 24 32 E
Radekhov = Radekhiv, Ukraine . 17 C13 50 25N 24 32 E
Radford, U.S.A. . . . . . . . . . . . . 82 G5 37 8N 80 34W
Radhanpur, India . . . . . . . . . . . 42 H4 23 50N 71 38 E
Radhwa, Jabal, Si. Arabia . . . . . 44 E3 24 34N 38 18 E
Radisson, Qué., Canada . . . . . . 72 B4 53 47N 77 37W
Radisson, Sask., Canada . . . . . 71 C7 52 30N 107 20W
Radium Hot Springs, Canada . . . 70 C5 50 35N 116 2W
Radnor Forest, U.K. . . . . . . . . . 13 E4 52 17N 3 10W
Radom, Poland . . . . . . . . . . . . 17 C11 51 23N 21 12 E
Radomsko, Poland . . . . . . . . . . 17 C10 51 5N 19 28 E
Radomyshl, Ukraine . . . . . . . . . 17 C15 50 30N 29 12 E
Radstock, C., Australia . . . . . . . 63 E1 33 12S 134 20 E
Radviliškis, Lithuania . . . . . . . . 9 J20 55 49N 23 33 E
Radville, Canada . . . . . . . . . . . 71 D8 49 30N 104 15W
Rae, Canada . . . . . . . . . . . . . . 70 A5 62 50N 116 3W
Rae Bareli, India . . . . . . . . . . . 43 F9 26 18N 81 20 E
Rae Isthmus, Canada . . . . . . . . 69 B11 66 40N 87 30W
Raeren, Belgium . . . . . . . . . . . 15 D6 50 41N 6 7 E
Raeside, L., Australia . . . . . . . . 61 E3 29 20S 122 0 E
Raetihi, N.Z. . . . . . . . . . . . . . . 59 H5 39 25S 175 17 E
Rafaela, Argentina . . . . . . . . . . 94 C3 31 10S 61 30W
Rafah, Gaza Strip . . . . . . . . . . 46 D3 31 18N 34 14 E
Rafai, C.A.R. . . . . . . . . . . . . . . 54 B1 4 59N 23 58 E
Raffadali, Si. Arabia . . . . . . . . . 44 D4 29 35N 43 35 E
Rafsanjān, Iran . . . . . . . . . . . . 45 D8 30 30N 56 5 E
Raft Pt., Australia . . . . . . . . . . 60 C3 16 4S 124 26 E
Râga, Sudan . . . . . . . . . . . . . . 51 G11 8 28N 25 41 E
Ragachow, Belarus . . . . . . . . . 17 B16 53 8N 30 5 E
Ragama, Sri Lanka . . . . . . . . . 40 R11 7 0N 79 50 E
Ragged, Mt., Australia . . . . . . . 61 F3 33 27S 123 25 E
Ragged Pt., Barbados . . . . . . . 89 g 13 10N 59 26W

Raghunathpalli, India . . . . . . . . 43 H11 22 14N 84 48 E
Raghunathpur, India . . . . . . . . . 43 H12 23 33N 86 40 E
Raglan, N.Z. . . . . . . . . . . . . . . 59 G5 37 55S 174 55 E
Ragusa, Italy . . . . . . . . . . . . . . 22 F6 36 55N 14 44 E
Raha, Indonesia . . . . . . . . . . . 37 E6 4 55S 123 0 E
Rahaeng = Tak, Thailand . . . . . 38 D2 16 52N 99 8 E
Rahatgarh, India . . . . . . . . . . . 43 H8 23 47N 78 22 E
Rahimyar Khan, Pakistan . . . . . 42 E4 28 30N 70 25 E
Rāhjerd, Iran . . . . . . . . . . . . . . 45 C6 34 22N 50 22 E
Rahole △, Kenya . . . . . . . . . . . 54 B4 0 5N 38 57 E
Rahon, India . . . . . . . . . . . . . . 42 D7 31 3N 76 7 E
Raichur, India . . . . . . . . . . . . . 40 L10 16 10N 77 20 E
Raiganj, India . . . . . . . . . . . . . 43 G13 25 37N 88 10 E
Raigarh, India . . . . . . . . . . . . . 41 J13 21 56N 83 25 E
Raijua, Indonesia . . . . . . . . . . . 37 F6 10 37S 121 36 E
Raikot, India . . . . . . . . . . . . . . 42 D6 30 41N 75 42 E
Railton, Australia . . . . . . . . . . . 63 G4 41 25S 146 28 E
Rainbow Bridge △, U.S.A. . . . . . 77 H8 37 5N 110 58W
Rainbow Lake, Canada . . . . . . . 70 B5 58 30N 119 23W
Rainier, U.S.A. . . . . . . . . . . . . . 78 D4 46 53N 122 41W
Rainier, Mt., U.S.A. . . . . . . . . . 78 D5 46 52N 121 46W
Rainy L., Canada . . . . . . . . . . . 71 D10 48 42N 93 10W
Rainy River, Canada . . . . . . . . 71 D10 48 43N 94 29W
Raippaluoto, Finland . . . . . . . . . 8 E19 63 13N 21 14 E
Raipur, India . . . . . . . . . . . . . . 41 J12 21 17N 81 45 E
Raisen, India . . . . . . . . . . . . . . 42 H8 23 20N 77 48 E
Raisio, Finland . . . . . . . . . . . . 9 F20 60 28N 22 11 E
Raj Nandgaon, India . . . . . . . . 41 J12 21 5N 81 5 E
Raj Nilgiri, India . . . . . . . . . . . . 43 J12 21 28N 86 46 E
Raja, Ujung, Indonesia . . . . . . . 36 D1 3 40N 96 25 E
Raja Ampat, Kepulauan,
Indonesia . . . . . . . . . . . . . . . 37 E7 0 30S 130 0 E
Rajahmundry, India . . . . . . . . . 41 L12 17 1N 81 48 E
Rajang →, Malaysia . . . . . . . . . 36 D4 2 30N 112 0 E
Rajanpur, Pakistan . . . . . . . . . . 42 E4 29 6N 70 19 E
Rajapalaiyam, India . . . . . . . . . 40 Q10 9 25N 77 35 E
Rajasthan □, India . . . . . . . . . . 42 F5 26 45N 73 30 E
Rajasthan Canal = Indira Gandhi
Canal, India . . . . . . . . . . . . . 42 F5 28 0N 72 0 E
Rajauri, India . . . . . . . . . . . . . 43 C6 33 25N 74 21 E
Rajgarh, Mad. P., India . . . . . . . 42 G7 24 2N 76 45 E
Rajgarh, Raj., India . . . . . . . . . 42 F7 27 14N 76 38 E
Rajgarh, Raj., India . . . . . . . . . 42 E6 28 40N 75 25 E
Rajgir, India . . . . . . . . . . . . . . 43 G11 25 2N 85 25 E
Rajkot, India . . . . . . . . . . . . . . 42 H4 22 15N 70 56 E
Rajmahal Hills, India . . . . . . . . 43 G12 24 30N 87 30 E
Rajpipla, India . . . . . . . . . . . . . 40 J8 21 50N 73 30 E
Rajpur, India . . . . . . . . . . . . . . 42 H6 22 18N 74 21 E
Rajpura, India . . . . . . . . . . . . . 42 D7 30 25N 76 32 E
Rajshahi, Bangla. . . . . . . . . . . 41 G16 24 22N 88 39 E
Rajshahi □, Bangla. . . . . . . . . . 43 G13 25 0N 89 0 E
Rajula, India . . . . . . . . . . . . . . 42 J4 21 3N 71 26 E
Rakaia, N.Z. . . . . . . . . . . . . . . 59 K4 43 45S 172 1 E
Rakaia →, N.Z. . . . . . . . . . . . . 59 K4 43 36S 172 15 E
Rakan, Ra's, Qatar . . . . . . . . . 45 E6 26 10N 51 20 E
Rakaposhi, Pakistan . . . . . . . . . 43 A6 36 10N 74 25 E
Rakata, Pulau, Indonesia . . . . . 36 F3 6 10S 105 20 E
Rakhiv, Ukraine . . . . . . . . . . . . 17 D13 48 3N 24 12 E
Rakhni, Pakistan . . . . . . . . . . . 42 D3 30 4N 69 56 E
Rakhni →, Pakistan . . . . . . . . . 42 E3 29 31N 69 36 E
Rakitnoye, Russia . . . . . . . . . . 30 B7 45 36N 134 17 E
Rakiura △, N.Z. . . . . . . . . . . . . 59 M1 47 0S 167 50 E
Rakops, Botswana . . . . . . . . . . 56 C3 21 1S 24 28 E
Rakvere, Estonia . . . . . . . . . . . 9 G22 59 20N 26 25 E
Raleigh, U.S.A. . . . . . . . . . . . . 83 H6 35 47N 78 39W
Ralls, U.S.A. . . . . . . . . . . . . . . 81 J4 33 41N 101 24W
Ralston, U.S.A. . . . . . . . . . . . . 84 E8 41 30N 76 57W
Ram →, Canada . . . . . . . . . . . 70 A4 62 1N 123 41W
Rām Allāh, West Bank . . . . . . . 46 D4 31 55N 35 10 E
Rama, Nic. . . . . . . . . . . . . . . . 88 D3 12 9N 84 15W
Ramakona, India . . . . . . . . . . . 43 J8 21 43N 78 50 E
Rāmallāh = Rām Allāh,
West Bank . . . . . . . . . . . . . . 46 D4 31 55N 35 10 E
Raman, Thailand . . . . . . . . . . . 39 J3 6 29N 101 18 E
Ramanathapuram, India . . . . . . 40 Q11 9 25N 78 55 E
Ramanetaka, B. de, Madag. . . . 57 A8 14 13S 47 52 E
Ramanujganj, India . . . . . . . . . 43 H10 23 48N 83 42 E
Ramat Gan, Israel . . . . . . . . . . 46 C3 32 4N 34 48 E
Ramatlhabama, S. Africa . . . . . 56 D4 25 37S 25 33 E
Ramban, India . . . . . . . . . . . . 43 C6 33 14N 75 12 E
Rambipuji, Indonesia . . . . . . . . 37 H15 8 12S 113 37 E
Rame Hd., Australia . . . . . . . . . 63 F4 37 47S 149 30 E
Ramechhap, Nepal . . . . . . . . . 43 F12 27 25N 86 10 E
Ramganga →, India . . . . . . . . . 43 F8 27 5N 79 58 E
Ramgarh, Jharkhand, India . . . . 43 H11 23 40N 85 35 E
Ramgarh, Raj., India . . . . . . . . 42 F6 27 16N 75 14 E
Ramgarh, Raj., India . . . . . . . . 42 F4 27 30N 70 36 E
Rāmhormoz, Iran . . . . . . . . . . . 45 D6 31 15N 49 35 E
Ramīān, Iran . . . . . . . . . . . . . . 45 B7 37 3N 55 16 E
Ramingining, Australia . . . . . . . 62 A2 12 19S 135 3 E
Ramla, Israel . . . . . . . . . . . . . . 46 D3 31 55N 34 52 E
Ramm = Rum, Jordan . . . . . . . 46 F4 29 39N 35 26 E
Ramm, Jabal, Jordan . . . . . . . . 46 F4 29 35N 35 24 E
Ramnad = Ramanathapuram,
India . . . . . . . . . . . . . . . . . . . 40 Q11 9 25N 78 55 E
Ramnagar, Jammu & Kashmir,
India . . . . . . . . . . . . . . . . . . . 43 C6 32 47N 75 18 E
Ramnagar, Uttaranchal, India . . 43 E8 29 24N 79 7 E
Râmnicu Sărat, Romania . . . . . 17 F14 45 26N 27 3 E
Râmnicu Vâlcea, Romania . . . . 17 F13 45 9N 24 21 E
Ramona, U.S.A. . . . . . . . . . . . . 79 M10 33 2N 116 52W
Ramore, Canada . . . . . . . . . . . 72 C3 48 30N 80 25W
Ramotswa, Botswana . . . . . . . . 56 C4 24 50S 25 52 E
Rampur, H.P., India . . . . . . . . . 42 D7 31 26N 77 43 E
Rampur, Mad. P., India . . . . . . . 42 H5 23 25N 73 53 E
Rampur, Ut. P., India . . . . . . . . 43 E8 28 50N 79 5 E
Rampur Hat, India . . . . . . . . . . 43 G12 24 10N 87 50 E
Rampura, India . . . . . . . . . . . . 42 G6 24 30N 75 27 E
Ramrama Tola, India . . . . . . . . 43 J8 21 52N 79 55 E
Ramree I., Burma . . . . . . . . . . 41 K19 19 0N 93 40 E
Râmsar, Iran . . . . . . . . . . . . . . 45 B6 36 53N 50 41 E
Ramsey, I. of Man . . . . . . . . . . 12 C3 54 20N 4 22W
Ramsey, U.S.A. . . . . . . . . . . . . 85 E10 41 4N 74 9W
Ramsey L., Canada . . . . . . . . . 72 C3 47 13N 82 15W
Ramsgate, U.K. . . . . . . . . . . . . 13 F9 51 20N 1 25 E
Ramtek, India . . . . . . . . . . . . . 40 J11 21 20N 79 15 E
Rana Pratap Sagar Dam, India . 42 G6 24 58N 75 38 E
Ranaghat, India . . . . . . . . . . . . 43 H13 23 15N 88 35 E
Ranahu, Pakistan . . . . . . . . . . 42 G3 25 55N 69 45 E
Ranau, Malaysia . . . . . . . . . . . 36 C5 6 2N 116 40 E
Rancagua, Chile . . . . . . . . . . . 94 C1 34 10S 70 50W
Rancheria →, Canada . . . . . . . 70 A3 60 13N 129 7W
Ranchester, U.S.A. . . . . . . . . . . 76 D10 44 54N 107 10W
Ranchi, India . . . . . . . . . . . . . . 43 H11 23 19N 85 27 E
Rancho Cucamonga, U.S.A. . . . 79 L9 34 10N 117 30W
Randalstown, U.K. . . . . . . . . . . 10 B5 54 45N 6 19W
Randers, Denmark . . . . . . . . . . 9 H14 56 29N 10 1 E
Randfontein, S. Africa . . . . . . . 57 D4 26 8S 27 45 E

Randle, U.S.A. . . . . . . . . . . . . . 78 D5　46 32N 121 57W
Randolph, Mass., U.S.A. . . . . . 85 D13　42 10N　71　2W
Randolph, N.Y., U.S.A. . . . . . . 84 D6　42 10N　78 59W
Randolph, Utah, U.S.A. . . . . . . 76 F8　41 40N 111 11W
Randolph, Vt., U.S.A. . . . . . . . 85 C12　43 55N　72 40W
Randsburg, U.S.A. . . . . . . . . . . 79 K9　35 22N 117 39W
Råneälven →, Sweden . . . . . . . 8 D20　65 50N　22 20 E
Rangaunu B., N.Z. . . . . . . . . . . 59 F4　34 51S 173 15 E
Rangeley, U.S.A. . . . . . . . . . . . 85 B14　44 58N　70 39W
Rangeley L., U.S.A. . . . . . . . . . 85 B14　44 55N　70 43W
Rangely, U.S.A. . . . . . . . . . . . . 76 F9　40　5N 108 48W
Ranger, U.S.A. . . . . . . . . . . . . . 81 J5　32 28N　98 41W
Rangia, India . . . . . . . . . . . . . . 41 F17　26 28N　91 38 E
Rangiora, N.Z. . . . . . . . . . . . . . 59 K4　43 19S 172 36 E
Rangitaiki →, N.Z. . . . . . . . . . . 59 G6　37 54S 176 49 E
Rangitata →, N.Z. . . . . . . . . . . 59 K3　43 45S 171 15 E
Rangitoto ke te tonga = D'Urville
I., N.Z. . . . . . . . . . . . . . . . . . 59 J4　40 50S 173 55 E
Rangkasbitung, Indonesia . . . . 37 G12　6 21S 106 15 E
Rangon →, Burma . . . . . . . . . . 41 L20　16 28N　96 40 E
Rangoon, Burma . . . . . . . . . . . 41 L20　16 45N　96 20 E
Rangpur, Bangla. . . . . . . . . . . . 41 G16　25 42N　89 22 E
Rangsit, Thailand . . . . . . . . . . 38 F3　13 59N 100 37 E
Ranibennur, India . . . . . . . . . . 40 M9　14 35N　75 30 E
Raniganj, Ut. P., India . . . . . . . 43 F9　27 3N　82　4 E
Raniganj, W. Bengal, India . . . 41 H15　23 40N　87　5 E
Ranikhet, India . . . . . . . . . . . . 43 E8　29 39N　79 25 E
Raniwara, India . . . . . . . . . . . . 40 G8　24 50N　72 10 E
Rāniyah, Iraq . . . . . . . . . . . . . . 44 B5　36 15N　44 53 E
Ranka, India . . . . . . . . . . . . . . . 43 H10　23 59N　83 47 E
Ranken →, Australia . . . . . . . . 62 C2　20 31S 137 36 E
Rankin, U.S.A. . . . . . . . . . . . . . 81 K4　31 13N 101 56W
Rankin Inlet, Canada . . . . . . . . 68 B10　62 30N　93　0W
Rankins Springs, Australia . . . 63 E4　33 49S 146 14 E
Rannoch, L., U.K. . . . . . . . . . . . 11 E4　56 41N　4 20W
Rannoch Moor, U.K. . . . . . . . . . 11 E4　56 38N　4 48W
Ranobe, Helodranon' i, Madag. . 57 C7　23 3S　43 33 E
Ranohira, Madag. . . . . . . . . . . . 57 C8　22 29S　45 24 E
Ranomafana, Toamasina,
Madag. . . . . . . . . . . . . . . . . . 57 B8　18 57S　48 50 E
Ranomafana, Toliara, Madag. . . 57 C8　24 34S　47　0 E
Ranomafana △, Madag. . . . . . . 57 C8　21 16S　47 25 E
Ranomena, Madag. . . . . . . . . . . 57 C8　23 25S　47 17 E
Ranong, Thailand . . . . . . . . . . . 39 H2　9 56N　98 40 E
Ranotsara Nord, Madag. . . . . . 57 C8　22 48S　46 36 E
Ränsa, Iran . . . . . . . . . . . . . . . . 45 C6　33 39N　48 18 E
Ransiki, Indonesia . . . . . . . . . . 37 E8　1 30S 134 10 E
Rantabe, Madag. . . . . . . . . . . . 57 B8　15 42S　49 39 E
Rantauprapat, Indonesia . . . . . 36 D1　2 15N　99 50 E
Rantemario, Indonesia . . . . . . 37 E5　3 15S 119 57 E
Rantoul, U.S.A. . . . . . . . . . . . . 82 E1　40 19N　88　9W
Raoyang, China . . . . . . . . . . . . . 34 E8　38 15N 115 45 E
Rap, Ko, Thailand . . . . . . . . . . . 39 b　9 19N　99 58 E
Rapa, French Polynesia . . . . . . 65 K13　27 35S 144 20W
Rapa Nui = Pascua, I. de, Chile . 65 K17　27　7S 109 23W
Rapallo, Italy . . . . . . . . . . . . . . 20 D8　44 21N　9 14 E
Rapar, India . . . . . . . . . . . . . . . 42 H4　23 34N　70 38 E
Rāpch, Iran . . . . . . . . . . . . . . . . 45 E8　25 40N　59 15 E
Raper, C., Canada . . . . . . . . . . 69 B13　69 44N　67　6W
Rapid City, U.S.A. . . . . . . . . . . 80 D3　44　5N 103 14W
Rapid River, U.S.A. . . . . . . . . . 82 C2　45 55N　86 58W
Rapla, Estonia . . . . . . . . . . . . . 9 G21　59　1N　24 52 E
Rapti →, India . . . . . . . . . . . . . 43 F10　26 18N　83 41 E
Raquette →, U.S.A. . . . . . . . . . 85 B10　45　0N　74 42W
Raquette Lake, U.S.A. . . . . . . . 85 C10　43 49N　74 40W
Rarotonga, Cook Is. . . . . . . . . . 65 K12　21 30S 160　0W
Ra's al 'Ayn, Syria . . . . . . . . . . 44 B4　36 45N　40 12 E
Ra's al Khaymah, U.A.E. . . . . . 45 E7　25 50N　55 59 E
Rasca, Pta. de la, Canary Is. . . . 24 G3　27 59N　16 41W
Raseiniai, Lithuania . . . . . . . . . 9 J20　55 25N　23　5 E
Rashmi, India . . . . . . . . . . . . . . 42 G6　25　4N　74 22 E
Rasht, Iran . . . . . . . . . . . . . . . . 45 B6　37 20N　49 40 E
Rasi Salai, Thailand . . . . . . . . . 38 E5　15 20N 104　9 E
Rason L., Australia . . . . . . . . . . 61 E3　28 45S 124 25 E
Rasra, India . . . . . . . . . . . . . . . 43 G10　25 50N　83 50 E
Rasul, Pakistan . . . . . . . . . . . . 42 C5　32 42N　73 34 E
Rat →, Thailand . . . . . . . . . . . . 38 F2　13 30N　99 54 E
Rat Islands, U.S.A. . . . . . . . . . . 68 C1　52　0N 178　0 E
Rat L., Canada . . . . . . . . . . . . . 71 B9　56 10N　99 40W
Ratangarh, India . . . . . . . . . . . 42 E6　28　5N　74 35 E
Raţāwi, Iraq . . . . . . . . . . . . . . . 44 D5　30 38N　47 13 E
Rath, India . . . . . . . . . . . . . . . . 43 G8　25 36N　79 37 E
Rath Luirc, Ireland . . . . . . . . . . 10 D3　52 21N　8 40W
Rathdrum, Ireland . . . . . . . . . . 10 D5　52 56N　6 14W
Rathenow, Germany . . . . . . . . 16 B7　52 37N　12 19 E
Rathkeale, Ireland . . . . . . . . . . 10 D3　52 32N　8 56W
Rathlin I., U.K. . . . . . . . . . . . . . 10 A5　55 18N　6 14W
Rathmelton, Ireland . . . . . . . . . 10 A4　55　2N　7 38W
Ratibor = Racibórz, Poland . . . 17 C10　50 7N　18 18 E
Ratlam, India . . . . . . . . . . . . . . 42 H6　23 20N　75　0 E
Ratnagiri, India . . . . . . . . . . . . 40 L8　16 57N　73 18 E
Ratodero, Pakistan . . . . . . . . . 42 F3　27 48N　68 18 E
Raton, U.S.A. . . . . . . . . . . . . . . 81 G2　36 54N 104 24W
Rattaphum, Thailand . . . . . . . . 39 J3　7 8N 100 16 E
Rattray Hd., U.K. . . . . . . . . . . . 11 D7　57 38N　1 50W
Ratz, Mt., Canada . . . . . . . . . . 70 B2　57 23N 132 12W
Raub, Malaysia . . . . . . . . . . . . 39 L3　3 47N 101 52 E
Rauch, Argentina . . . . . . . . . . . 94 D4　36 45S　59　5W
Raudales de Malpaso, Mexico . 87 D6　17 30N　23 30W
Raufarhöfn, Iceland . . . . . . . . . 8 C6　66 27N　15 57W
Raufoss, Norway . . . . . . . . . . . 9 F14　60 44N　10 37 E
Raukumara Ra., N.Z. . . . . . . . . 59 H6　38　5S 177 55 E
Rauma, Finland . . . . . . . . . . . . 9 F19　61 10N　21 30 E
Raumo = Rauma, Finland . . . . 9 F19　61 10N　21 30 E
Raung, Gunung, Indonesia . . . 37 J17　8　8S 114　3 E
Raurkela, India . . . . . . . . . . . . . 43 H11　22 14N　84 50 E
Rausu-Dake, Japan . . . . . . . . . 30 B12　44　4N 145　7 E
Rava-Ruska, Ukraine . . . . . . . . 17 C12　50 15N　23 42 E
Rava Russkaya = Rava-Ruska,
Ukraine . . . . . . . . . . . . . . . . 17 C12　50 15N　23 42 E
Ravalli, U.S.A. . . . . . . . . . . . . . 76 C6　47 17N 114 11W
Rävansar, Iran . . . . . . . . . . . . . 44 C5　34 43N　46 40 E
Rāvar, Iran . . . . . . . . . . . . . . . . 45 D8　31 20N　56 51 E
Ravena, U.S.A. . . . . . . . . . . . . . 85 D11　42 28N　73 49W
Ravenna, Italy . . . . . . . . . . . . . 22 B5　44 25N　12 12 E
Ravenna, Nebr., U.S.A. . . . . . . 80 E5　41　1N　98 55W
Ravenna, Ohio, U.S.A. . . . . . . . 84 E3　41　9N　81 15W
Ravensburg, Germany . . . . . . . 16 E5　47 46N　9 36 E
Ravenshoe, Australia . . . . . . . 62 B4　17 37S 145 29 E
Ravensthorpe, Australia . . . . . 61 F3　33 35S 120　2 E
Ravenswood, Australia . . . . . . 62 C4　20　6S 146 54 E
Ravenswood, U.S.A. . . . . . . . . 82 F5　38 57N　81 46W
Ravi →, Pakistan . . . . . . . . . . . 42 D4　30 35N　71 49 E
Rawalpindi, Pakistan . . . . . . . . 42 C5　33 38N　73　8 E
Rawāndūz, Iraq . . . . . . . . . . . . 44 B5　36 40N　44 30 E
Rawang, Malaysia . . . . . . . . . . 39 L3　3 20N 101 35 E
Rawene, N.Z. . . . . . . . . . . . . . . 59 F4　35 25S 173 32 E

Rawlinna, Australia . . . . . . . . . 61 F4　30 58S 125 28 E
Rawlins, U.S.A. . . . . . . . . . . . . 76 F10　41 47N 107 14W
Rawlinson Ra., Australia . . . . . 61 D4　24 40S 128 30 E
Rawson, Argentina . . . . . . . . . 96 E3　43 15S　65　5W
Raxaul, India . . . . . . . . . . . . . . 43 F11　26 59N　84 51 E
Ray, U.S.A. . . . . . . . . . . . . . . . . 80 A3　48 21N 103 10W
Ray, C., Canada . . . . . . . . . . . . 73 C8　47 33N　59 15W
Raya Ring, Ko, Thailand . . . . . 39 a　8 18N　98 29 E
Rayadurg, India . . . . . . . . . . . . 40 M10　14 40N　76 50 E
Rayagada, India . . . . . . . . . . . . 41 K13　19 15N　83 20 E
Raychikhinsk, Russia . . . . . . . . 29 E13　49 46N 129 25 E
Räyen, Iran . . . . . . . . . . . . . . . . 45 D8　29 34N　57 26 E
Rayleigh, U.K. . . . . . . . . . . . . . 13 F8　51 36N　0 37 E
Raymond, Canada . . . . . . . . . . 70 D6　49 30N 112 35W
Raymond, Calif., U.S.A. . . . . . 78 H7　37 13N 119 54W
Raymond, N.H., U.S.A. . . . . . . 85 C13　43　2N　71 11W
Raymond, Wash., U.S.A. . . . . . 78 D3　46 41N 123 44W
Raymondville, U.S.A. . . . . . . . . 81 M6　26 29N　97 47W
Raymore, Canada . . . . . . . . . . 71 C8　51 25N 104 31W
Rayón, Mexico . . . . . . . . . . . . . 86 B2　29 43N 110 35W
Rayong, Thailand . . . . . . . . . . . 38 F3　12 40N 101 20 E
Rayville, U.S.A. . . . . . . . . . . . . 81 J9　32 29N　91 46W
Raz, Pte. du, France . . . . . . . . . 20 C1　48　2N　4 47W
Razan, Iran . . . . . . . . . . . . . . . . 45 C6　35 23N　49　2 E
Razāzah, Buḩayrat ar, Iraq . . . . 44 C4　32 40N　43 35 E
Razāzah, L. = Razāzah, Buḩayrat
ar, Iraq . . . . . . . . . . . . . . . . . 44 C4　32 40N　43 35 E
Razdel'naya = Rozdilna, Ukraine . 17 E16　46 50N　30　2 E
Razdolnoye, Russia . . . . . . . . . 30 C5　43 30N 131 52 E
Razeh, Iran . . . . . . . . . . . . . . . . 45 C6　32 47N　48　9 E
Razgrad, Bulgaria . . . . . . . . . . 23 C12　43 33N　26 34 E
Razim, Lacul, Romania . . . . . . 17 F15　44 50N　29　0 E
Razmak, Pakistan . . . . . . . . . . 42 C3　32 45N　69 50 E
Ré, Î. de, France . . . . . . . . . . . . 20 C3　46 12N　1 30W
Reading, U.K. . . . . . . . . . . . . . . 13 F7　51 27N　0 58W
Reading, U.S.A. . . . . . . . . . . . . 85 F9　40 20N　75 56W
Reading □, U.K. . . . . . . . . . . . . 13 F7　51 27N　0 58W
Realicó, Argentina . . . . . . . . . . 94 D3　35　0S　64 15W
Ream, Cambodia . . . . . . . . . . . 39 G4　10 34N 103 39 E
Reata, Mexico . . . . . . . . . . . . . 86 B4　26 8N 101　5W
Reay Forest, U.K. . . . . . . . . . . . 11 C4　58 22N　4 55W
Rebi, Indonesia . . . . . . . . . . . . 37 F8　6 23S 134　7 E
Rebiana, Libya . . . . . . . . . . . . . 51 D10　24 12N　22 10 E
Rebiana, Sahrâ', Libya . . . . . . 51 D10　24 30N　21　0 E
Rebun-Tō, Japan . . . . . . . . . . . 30 B10　45 23N 141　2 E
Recherche, Arch. of the, Australia . 61 F3　34 15S 122 50 E
Rechna Doab, Pakistan . . . . . . 42 D5　31 35N　73 30 E
Rechytsa, Belarus . . . . . . . . . . 17 B16　52 21N　30 24 E
Recife, Brazil . . . . . . . . . . . . . . 93 E12　8　0S　35　0W
Recklinghausen, Germany . . . 15 C7　51 37N　7 12 E
Reconquista, Argentina . . . . . . 94 B4　29 10S　59 45W
Recreo, Argentina . . . . . . . . . . 94 B2　29 25S　65 10W
Red →, La., U.S.A. . . . . . . . . . . 81 K9　31　1N　91 45W
Red →, N. Dak., U.S.A. . . . . . . 68 C10　49　0N　97 15W
Red Bank, U.S.A. . . . . . . . . . . . 85 F10　40 21N　74　5W
Red Bay, Canada . . . . . . . . . . . 73 B8　51 44N　56 25W
Red Bluff, U.S.A. . . . . . . . . . . . 76 F2　40 11N 122 15W
Red Bluff L., U.S.A. . . . . . . . . . 81 K3　31 54N 103 55W
Red Cliffs, Australia . . . . . . . . . 63 E3　34 19S 142 11 E
Red Cloud, U.S.A. . . . . . . . . . . 80 E5　40　5N　98 32W
Red Creek, U.S.A. . . . . . . . . . . 85 C8　43 14N　76 45W
Red Deer, Canada . . . . . . . . . . 70 C6　52 20N 113 50W
Red Deer →, Alta., Canada . . . 71 C7　50 58N 110　0W
Red Deer →, Man., Canada . . . 71 C8　52 53N 101　1W
Red Deer L., Canada . . . . . . . . 71 C8　52 55N 101 20W
Red Hook, U.S.A. . . . . . . . . . . . 85 E11　41 55N　73 53W
Red Indian L., Canada . . . . . . . 73 C8　48 35N　57　0W
Red L., Canada . . . . . . . . . . . . . 71 C10　51　3N　93 49W
Red Lake, Canada . . . . . . . . . . 71 C10　51　3N　93 49W
Red Lake Falls, U.S.A. . . . . . . . 80 B6　47 53N　96 16W
Red Lake Road, Canada . . . . . . 71 C10　49 59N　93 25W
Red Lodge, U.S.A. . . . . . . . . . . 76 D9　45 11N 109 15W
Red Mountain, U.S.A. . . . . . . . 79 K9　35 37N 117 38W
Red Oak, U.S.A. . . . . . . . . . . . . 80 E7　41　1N　95 14W
Red Rock, Canada . . . . . . . . . . 72 C2　48 55N　88 15W
Red Rock, L., U.S.A. . . . . . . . . . 80 E8　41 22N　92 59W
Red Rocks Pt., Australia . . . . . 61 F4　32 13S 127 32 E
Red Sea, Asia . . . . . . . . . . . . . . 47 C2　25 0N　36　0 E
Red Slate Mt., U.S.A. . . . . . . . 78 H8　37 31N 118 52W
Red Sucker L., Canada . . . . . . 72 B1　54　9N　93 40W
Red Tower Pass = Turnu Roşu,
P., Romania . . . . . . . . . . . . . 17 F13　45 33N　24 17 E
Red Wing, U.S.A. . . . . . . . . . . . 80 C8　44 34N　92 31W
Redang, Malaysia . . . . . . . . . . 39 K4　5 49N 103　2 E
Redange, Lux. . . . . . . . . . . . . . . 15 E5　49 46N　5 52 E
Redcar, U.K. . . . . . . . . . . . . . . . 12 C6　54 37N　1　4W
Redcar & Cleveland □, U.K. . . . 12 C7　54 29N　1　0W
Redcliff, Canada . . . . . . . . . . . 71 C6　50 10N 110 50W
Redcliffe, Australia . . . . . . . . . 63 D5　27 12S 153　0 E
Redcliffe, Mt., Australia . . . . . . 61 E3　28 30S 121 30 E
Reddersburg, S. Africa . . . . . . 56 D4　29 41S　26 10 E
Redding, U.S.A. . . . . . . . . . . . . 76 F2　40 35N 122 24W
Redditch, U.K. . . . . . . . . . . . . . 13 E6　52 18N　1 55W
Redfield, U.S.A. . . . . . . . . . . . . 80 C5　44 53N　98 31W
Redford, U.S.A. . . . . . . . . . . . . 85 B11　44 38N　73 48W
Redhead, Trin. & Tob. . . . . . . . 93 K16　10 44N　60 58W
Redlands, U.S.A. . . . . . . . . . . . 79 M9　34　4N 117 11W
Redmond, Oreg., U.S.A. . . . . . 76 D3　44 17N 121 11W
Redmond, Wash., U.S.A. . . . . . 78 C4　47 41N 122　7W
Redon, France . . . . . . . . . . . . . 20 C2　47 40N　2　6W
Redonda, Antigua & B. . . . . . . 89 C7　16 58N　62 19W
Redondela, Spain . . . . . . . . . . . 21 A1　42 15N　8 38W
Redondo Beach, U.S.A. . . . . . . 79 M8　33 50N 118 23W
Redruth, U.K. . . . . . . . . . . . . . . 13 G2　50 14N　5 14W
Redvers, Canada . . . . . . . . . . . 71 D8　49 35N 101 40W
Redwater, Canada . . . . . . . . . . 70 C6　53 55N 113　6W
Redwood, U.S.A. . . . . . . . . . . . 85 B9　44 18N　75 48W
Redwood City, U.S.A. . . . . . . . 78 H4　37 30N 122 15W
Redwood Falls, U.S.A. . . . . . . . 80 C7　44 32N　95　7W
Ree, L., Ireland . . . . . . . . . . . . . 10 C3　53 35N　8　0W
Reed, L., Canada . . . . . . . . . . . 71 C8　54 38N 100 30W
Reed City, U.S.A. . . . . . . . . . . . 82 D3　43 53N　85 31W
Reedley, U.S.A. . . . . . . . . . . . . 78 J7　36 36N 119 27W
Reedsburg, U.S.A. . . . . . . . . . . 80 D9　43 32N　90　0W
Reedsport, U.S.A. . . . . . . . . . . 76 E1　43 42N 124　6W
Reedsville, U.S.A. . . . . . . . . . . 84 F7　40 39N　77 35W
Reefton, N.Z. . . . . . . . . . . . . . . 59 K3　42　6S 171 51 E
Reese →, U.S.A. . . . . . . . . . . . 76 F5　40 48N 117　4W
Refugio, U.S.A. . . . . . . . . . . . . . 81 L6　28 18N　97 17W
Regensburg, Germany . . . . . . . 16 D7　49　1N　12　6 E
Réggio di Calábria, Italy . . . . . 22 E6　38　6N　15 39 E
Réggio nell'Emília, Italy . . . . . 22 B4　44 43N　10 36 E
Reghin, Romania . . . . . . . . . . . 17 E13　46 46N　24 42 E
Regina, Canada . . . . . . . . . . . . 71 C8　50 27N 104 35W
Regina Beach, Canada . . . . . . 71 C8　50 47N 105　0W

Registro, Brazil . . . . . . . . . . . . 95 A6　24 29S　47 49W
Rehar →, India . . . . . . . . . . . . . 43 H10　23 55N　82 40 E
Rehli, India . . . . . . . . . . . . . . . . 43 H8　23 38N　79　5 E
Rehoboth, Namibia . . . . . . . . . 56 C2　23 15S　17　4 E
Rehovot, Israel . . . . . . . . . . . . . 46 D3　31 54N　34 48 E
Reichenbach, Germany . . . . . . 16 C7　50 37N　12 17 E
Reid, Australia . . . . . . . . . . . . . 61 F4　30 49S 128 26 E
Reidsville, U.S.A. . . . . . . . . . . . 83 G6　36 21N　79 40W
Reigate, U.K. . . . . . . . . . . . . . . 13 F7　51 14N　0 12W
Reims, France . . . . . . . . . . . . . . 20 B6　49 15N　4　1 E
Reina Adelaida, Arch., Chile . . 96 G2　52 20S　74　0W
Reina Sofía, Tenerife ✈ (TFS),
Canary Is. . . . . . . . . . . . . . . 24 F3　28　3N　16 33W
Reindeer →, Canada . . . . . . . . 71 B8　55 36N 103 11W
Reindeer I., Canada . . . . . . . . . 71 C9　52 30N　98　0W
Reindeer L., Canada . . . . . . . . 71 B8　57 15N 102 15W
Reinga, C., N.Z. . . . . . . . . . . . . 59 F4　34 25S 172 43 E
Reinosa, Spain . . . . . . . . . . . . . 21 A3　43　2N　4 15W
Reitz, S. Africa . . . . . . . . . . . . . 57 D4　27 48S　28 29 E
Reivilo, S. Africa . . . . . . . . . . . 56 D3　27 36S　24　8 E
Reliance, Canada . . . . . . . . . . . 71 A7　63　0N 109 20W
Remarkable, Mt., Australia . . . 63 E2　32 48S 138 10 E
Rembang, Indonesia . . . . . . . . 37 G14　6 42S 111 21 E
Remedios, Panama . . . . . . . . . 88 E3　8 15N　81 50W
Remeshk, Iran . . . . . . . . . . . . . 45 E8　26 55N　58 50 E
Remich, Lux. . . . . . . . . . . . . . . . 15 E6　49 32N　6 22 E
Remscheid, Germany . . . . . . . 15 C7　51 11N　7 12 E
Ren Xian, China . . . . . . . . . . . . 34 F8　37　8N 114 40 E
Rendang, Indonesia . . . . . . . . . 37 J18　8 26S 115 25 E
Rendsburg, Germany . . . . . . . . 16 A5　54 17N　9 39 E
Renfrew, Canada . . . . . . . . . . . 85 A8　45 30N　76 40W
Renfrewshire □, U.K. . . . . . . . . 11 F4　55 49N　4 38W
Rengat, Indonesia . . . . . . . . . . 36 E2　0 30S 102 45 E
Rengo, Chile . . . . . . . . . . . . . . . 94 C1　34 24S　70 50W
Reni, Ukraine . . . . . . . . . . . . . . 17 F15　45 28N　28 15 E
Renmark, Australia . . . . . . . . . 63 E3　34 11S 140 43 E
Rennell Sd., Canada . . . . . . . . 70 C2　53 23N 132 35W
Renner Springs, Australia . . . . 62 B1　18 20S 133 47 E
Rennes, France . . . . . . . . . . . . . 20 B3　48　7N　1 41W
Rennie L., Canada . . . . . . . . . . 71 A7　61 32N 105 35W
Reno, U.S.A. . . . . . . . . . . . . . . . 78 F7　39 31N 119 48W
Reno →, Italy . . . . . . . . . . . . . . 22 B5　44 38N　12 16 E
Renovo, U.S.A. . . . . . . . . . . . . . 84 E7　41 20N　77 45W
Renqiu, China . . . . . . . . . . . . . . 34 E9　38 43N 116　5 E
Rensselaer, Ind., U.S.A. . . . . . 82 E2　40 57N　87　9W
Rensselaer, N.Y., U.S.A. . . . . . 85 D11　42 38N　73 45W
Rentería, Spain . . . . . . . . . . . . 21 A5　43 19N　1 54W
Renton, U.S.A. . . . . . . . . . . . . . 78 C4　47 29N 122 12W
Reotipur, India . . . . . . . . . . . . . 43 G10　25 33N　83 45 E
Republic, Mo., U.S.A. . . . . . . . 81 G8　37　7N　93 29W
Republic, Wash., U.S.A. . . . . . 76 B4　48 39N 118 44W
Republican →, U.S.A. . . . . . . . 80 F6　39　4N　96 48W
Repulse B., Australia . . . . . . . . 62 J6　20 35S 148 46 E
Repulse Bay, Canada . . . . . . . 69 B11　66 30N　86 30W
Requena, Peru . . . . . . . . . . . . . 92 E4　5　5S　73 52W
Requena, Spain . . . . . . . . . . . . 21 C5　39 30N　1　4W
Reşadiye = Datça, Turkey . . . . 23 F12　36 46N　27 40 E
Reserve, U.S.A. . . . . . . . . . . . . 77 K9　33 43N 108 45W
Resht = Rasht, Iran . . . . . . . . . 45 B6　37 20N　49 40 E
Resistencia, Argentina . . . . . . 94 B4　27 30S　59　0W
Reşiţa, Romania . . . . . . . . . . . 17 F11　45 18N　21 53 E
Reso = Raisio, Finland . . . . . . . 9 F20　60 28N　22 11 E
Resolution I., Canada . . . . . . . 69 B13　61 30N　65　0W
Resolution I., N.Z. . . . . . . . . . . 59 L1　45 40S 166 40 E
Ressano Garcia, Mozam. . . . . . 57 D5　25 25S　32　0 E
Reston, Canada . . . . . . . . . . . . 71 D8　49 33N 101　6W
Retalhuleu, Guatemala . . . . . . 88 D1　14 33N　91 46W
Retenue, L. de, Dem. Rep. of
the Congo . . . . . . . . . . . . . . 55 E2　11　0S　27　0 E
Retford, U.K. . . . . . . . . . . . . . . 12 D7　53 19N　0 56W
Réthímnon, Greece . . . . . . . . . 25 D6　35 18N　24 30 E
Réthímnon □, Greece . . . . . . . 25 D6　35 23N　24 28 E
Reti, Pakistan . . . . . . . . . . . . . . 42 E3　28　5N　69 48 E
Réunion ☑, Ind. Oc. . . . . . . . . 49 J9　21　0S　56　0 E
Reus, Spain . . . . . . . . . . . . . . . 21 B6　41 10N　1　5 E
Reutlingen, Germany . . . . . . . 16 D5　48 29N　9 12 E
Reval = Tallinn, Estonia . . . . . . 9 G21　59 22N　24 48 E
Revda, Russia . . . . . . . . . . . . . 18 C10　56 48N　59 57 E
Revelganj, India . . . . . . . . . . . . 43 G11　25 50N　84 40 E
Revelstoke, Canada . . . . . . . . . 70 C5　51　0N 118 10W
Reventazón, Peru . . . . . . . . . . . 92 E2　6 10S　80 58W
Revilla Gigedo, Is. de, Pac. Oc. . 86 D2　18 40N 112　0W
Revuè →, Mozam. . . . . . . . . . . 55 F3　19 50S　34　0 E
Rewa, India . . . . . . . . . . . . . . . . 43 G9　24 33N　81 25 E
Rewari, India . . . . . . . . . . . . . . 42 E7　28 15N　76 40 E
Rexburg, U.S.A. . . . . . . . . . . . . 76 E8　43 49N 111 47W
Rey, Iran . . . . . . . . . . . . . . . . . . 45 C6　35 35N　51 25 E
Rey, I. del, Panama . . . . . . . . . 88 E4　8 20N　78 30W
Rey Malabo, Eq. Guin. . . . . . . . 52 D1　3 45N　8 50 E
Reyðarfjörður, Iceland . . . . . . 8 D6　65　2N　14 13W
Reyes, Pt., U.S.A. . . . . . . . . . . . 78 H3　38　0N 123　0W
Reykjahlíð, Iceland . . . . . . . . . 8 D5　65 40N　16 55W
Reykjanes, Iceland . . . . . . . . . 8 E2　63 48N　22 40W
Reykjavík, Iceland . . . . . . . . . . 8 D3　64 10N　21 57W
Reynolds Ra., Australia . . . . . . 60 D5　22 30S 133　0 E
Reynoldsville, U.S.A. . . . . . . . . 84 E6　41　5N　78 58W
Reynosa, Mexico . . . . . . . . . . . 87 B5　26　5N　98 18W
Rēzekne, Latvia . . . . . . . . . . . . 9 H22　56 30N　27 17 E
Rezvān, Iran . . . . . . . . . . . . . . . 45 E8　27 34N　56　6 E
Rhayader, U.K. . . . . . . . . . . . . . 13 E4　52 18N　3 29W
Rhein →, Europe . . . . . . . . . . . 15 C6　51 52N　6　2 E
Rhein-Main-Donau-Kanal,
Germany . . . . . . . . . . . . . . . 16 D6　49　1N　11 27 E
Rheine, Germany . . . . . . . . . . . 16 B4　52 17N　7 26 E
Rheinland-Pfalz □, Germany . . 16 C4　50　0N　7　0 E
Rhine = Rhein →, Europe . . . . 15 C6　51 52N　6　2 E
Rhinebeck, U.S.A. . . . . . . . . . . 85 E11　41 56N　73 55W
Rhineland-Palatinate =
Rheinland-Pfalz □, Germany . . 16 C4　50　0N　7　0 E
Rhinelander, U.S.A. . . . . . . . . . 80 C10　45 38N　89 25W
Rhinns Pt., U.K. . . . . . . . . . . . . 11 F2　55 40N　6 29W
Rhino Camp, Uganda . . . . . . . 54 B3　3　0N　31 22 E
Rhir, Cap, Morocco . . . . . . . . . 50 B4　30 38N　9 54W
Rhode Island □, U.S.A. . . . . . . 85 E13　41 40N　71 30W
Rhodes = Ródhos, Greece . . . 25 C10　36 15N　28 10 E
Rhodope Mts. = Rhodopi Planina,
Bulgaria . . . . . . . . . . . . . . . . 23 D11　41 40N　24 20 E
Rhodopi Planina, Bulgaria . . . 23 D11　41 40N　24 20 E
Rhön, Germany . . . . . . . . . . . . 16 C5　50 24N　9 58 E
Rhondda, U.K. . . . . . . . . . . . . . 13 F4　51 39N　3 31W
Rhondda Cynon Taff □, U.K. . . 13 F4　51 42N　3 27W
Rhône →, France . . . . . . . . . . . 20 E6　43 28N　4 42 E
Rhum, U.K. . . . . . . . . . . . . . . . . 11 E2　57　0N　6 20W
Rhyl, U.K. . . . . . . . . . . . . . . . . . 12 D4　53 20N　3 29W
Riachão, Brazil . . . . . . . . . . . . . 93 E9　7 20S　46 37W
Riasi, India . . . . . . . . . . . . . . . . 43 C6　33 10N　74 50 E
Riau □, Indonesia . . . . . . . . . . 36 D2　0　0 102 35 E

Riau, Kepulauan, Indonesia . . . 36 D2　0 30N 104 20 E
Riau Arch. = Riau, Kepulauan,
Indonesia . . . . . . . . . . . . . . . 36 D2　0 30N 104 20 E
Ribadeo, Spain . . . . . . . . . . . . 21 A2　43 35N　7　5W
Ribas do Rio Pardo, Brazil . . . . 93 H8　20 27S　53 46W
Ribauè, Mozam. . . . . . . . . . . . . 55 E4　14 57S　38 17 E
Ribble →, U.K. . . . . . . . . . . . . . 12 D5　53 52N　2 25W
Ribe, Denmark . . . . . . . . . . . . . 9 J13　55 19N　8 44 E
Ribeira Brava, Madeira . . . . . . 24 D2　32 41N　17　4W
Ribeirão Prêto, Brazil . . . . . . . . 95 A6　21 10S　47 50W
Riberalta, Bolivia . . . . . . . . . . . 92 F5　11　0S　66　0W
Riccarton, N.Z. . . . . . . . . . . . . . 59 K4　43 32S 172 37 E
Rice, U.S.A. . . . . . . . . . . . . . . . . 79 L12　34　5N 114 51W
Rice L., Canada . . . . . . . . . . . . 84 B6　44 12N　78 10W
Rice Lake, U.S.A. . . . . . . . . . . . 80 C9　45 30N　91 44W
Rich, C., Canada . . . . . . . . . . . 84 B4　44 43N　80 38W
Richards Bay, S. Africa . . . . . . 57 D5　28 48S　32　6 E
Richardson →, Canada . . . . . . 71 B6　58 25N 111 14W
Richardson Lakes, U.S.A. . . . . 82 C10　44 46N　70 58W
Richardson Springs, U.S.A. . . . 78 F5　39 51N 121 46W
Riche, C., Australia . . . . . . . . . 61 F2　34 36S 118 47 E
Richey, U.S.A. . . . . . . . . . . . . . 80 B2　47 39N 105　4W
Richfield, U.S.A. . . . . . . . . . . . . 77 G8　38 46N 112　5W
Richfield Springs, U.S.A. . . . . . 85 D10　42 51N　74 59W
Richford, U.S.A. . . . . . . . . . . . . 85 B12　45　0N　72 40W
Richibucto, Canada . . . . . . . . . 73 C7　46 42N　64 54W
Richland, Ga., U.S.A. . . . . . . . . 83 J3　32　5N　84 40W
Richland, Wash., U.S.A. . . . . . 76 C4　46 17N 119 18W
Richland Center, U.S.A. . . . . . . 80 D9　43 21N　90 23W
Richlands, U.S.A. . . . . . . . . . . . 82 G5　37　6N　81 48W
Richmond, Australia . . . . . . . . 62 C3　20 43S 143　8 E
Richmond, N.Z. . . . . . . . . . . . . 59 J4　41 20S 173 12 E
Richmond, U.K. . . . . . . . . . . . . 12 C6　54 25N　1 43W
Richmond, Calif., U.S.A. . . . . . 78 H4　37 56N 122 21W
Richmond, Ind., U.S.A. . . . . . . 82 F3　39 50N　84 53W
Richmond, Ky., U.S.A. . . . . . . . 82 G3　37 45N　84 18W
Richmond, Mich., U.S.A. . . . . . 84 D2　42 49N　82 45W
Richmond, Mo., U.S.A. . . . . . . 80 F8　39 17N　93 58W
Richmond, Tex., U.S.A. . . . . . . 81 L7　29 35N　95 46W
Richmond, Utah, U.S.A. . . . . . . 76 F8　41 56N 111 48W
Richmond, Va., U.S.A. . . . . . . . 82 G7　37 33N　77 27W
Richmond, Vt., U.S.A. . . . . . . . 85 B12　44 24N　72 59W
Richmond Hill, Canada . . . . . . 84 C5　43 52N　79 27W
Richmond Ra., Australia . . . . . 63 D5　29　0S 152 45 E
Richtersveld △, S. Africa . . . . . 56 D2　28 15S　17 10 E
Richwood, U.S.A. . . . . . . . . . . . 82 F5　38 14N　80 32W
Ridder = Leninogorsk,
Kazakhstan . . . . . . . . . . . . . 28 D9　50 20N　83 30 E
Riddlesburg, U.S.A. . . . . . . . . . 84 F6　40 9N　78 15W
Ridgecrest, U.S.A. . . . . . . . . . . 79 K9　35 38N 117 40W
Ridgefield, Conn., U.S.A. . . . . . 85 E11　41 17N　73 30W
Ridgefield, Wash., U.S.A. . . . . 78 E4　45 49N 122 45W
Ridgeland, U.S.A. . . . . . . . . . . 83 J5　32 29N　80 59W
Ridgetown, Canada . . . . . . . . . 84 D3　42 26N　81 52W
Ridgewood, U.S.A. . . . . . . . . . . 85 F10　40 59N　74　7W
Ridgway, U.S.A. . . . . . . . . . . . . 84 E6　41 25N　78 44W
Riding Mountain △, Canada . . 71 C9　50 50N 100 02W
Ridley, Mt., Australia . . . . . . . . 61 F3　33 12S 122　7 E
Riebeek-Oos, S. Africa . . . . . . 56 E4　33 10S　26 10 E
Ried, Austria . . . . . . . . . . . . . . 16 D7　48 14N　13 30 E
Riesa, Germany . . . . . . . . . . . . 16 C7　51 17N　13 17 E
Riet →, S. Africa . . . . . . . . . . . 56 D3　29　0S　23 54 E
Rietbron, S. Africa . . . . . . . . . . 56 E3　32 54S　23 10 E
Rietfontein, Namibia . . . . . . . . 56 C3　21 58S　20 58 E
Rieti, Italy . . . . . . . . . . . . . . . . 22 C5　42 24N　12 51 E
Rif = Er Rif, Morocco . . . . . . . . 50 A5　35　1N　4　1W
Riffe L., U.S.A. . . . . . . . . . . . . . 78 D4　46 32N 122 26W
Rifle, U.S.A. . . . . . . . . . . . . . . . 76 G10　39 32N 107 47W
Rift Valley, Africa . . . . . . . . . . . 48 G7　7　0N　30　0 E
Rift Valley □, Kenya . . . . . . . . . 54 B4　0 20N　36　0 E
Riga, Latvia . . . . . . . . . . . . . . . 9 H21　56 53N　24　8 E
Riga, G. of, Latvia . . . . . . . . . . 9 H20　57 40N　23 45 E
Rīgān, Iran . . . . . . . . . . . . . . . . 45 D8　28 37N　58 58 E
Rīgas Jūras Līcis = Riga, G. of,
Latvia . . . . . . . . . . . . . . . . . . 9 H20　57 40N　23 45 E
Rigaud, Canada . . . . . . . . . . . . 85 A10　45 29N　74 18W
Rigby, U.S.A. . . . . . . . . . . . . . . 76 E8　43 40N 111 55W
Rīgestān, Afghan. . . . . . . . . . . 40 D4　30 15S　65　0 E
Riggins, U.S.A. . . . . . . . . . . . . . 76 D5　45 25N 116 19W
Rigolet, Canada . . . . . . . . . . . . 73 B8　54 10N　58 23W
Rihand Dam, India . . . . . . . . . . 43 G10　24　9N　83　2 E
Riihimäki, Finland . . . . . . . . . . 9 F21　60 45N　24 48 E
Riiser-Larsen-halvøya, Antarctica . 5 C4　68　0S　35　0 E
Rijeka, Croatia . . . . . . . . . . . . . 16 F8　45 20N　14 21 E
Rijssen, Neths. . . . . . . . . . . . . . 15 B6　52 19N　6 31 E
Rikuchū-Kaigan △, Japan . . . . 30 E11　39 20N 142　0 E
Rikuzentakada, Japan . . . . . . . 30 E10　39　0N 141 40 E
Riley, U.S.A. . . . . . . . . . . . . . . . 76 E4　43 32N 119 28W
Rimah, Wadi ar →, Si. Arabia . . 44 E4　26　5N　41 30 E
Rimau, Pulau, Malaysia . . . . . 39 c　5 15N 100 16 E
Rimbey, Canada . . . . . . . . . . . . 70 C6　52 35N 114 15W
Rimersburg, U.S.A. . . . . . . . . . 84 E5　41　3N　79 30W
Rímini, Italy . . . . . . . . . . . . . . . 22 B5　44　3N　12 33 E
Rimouski, Canada . . . . . . . . . . 73 C6　48 27N　68 30W
Rimrock, U.S.A. . . . . . . . . . . . . 78 D5　46 38N 121 10W
Rinca, Indonesia . . . . . . . . . . . 37 F5　8 45S 119 35 E
Rincón de Romos, Mexico . . . . 86 C4　22 14N 102 18W
Rinconada, Argentina . . . . . . . 94 A2　22 26S　66 10W
Rind →, India . . . . . . . . . . . . . . 43 G9　25 53N　80 33 E
Ringas, India . . . . . . . . . . . . . . 42 F6　27 21N　75 34 E
Ringkøbing, Denmark . . . . . . . 9 H13　56　5N　8 15 E
Ringvassøy, Norway . . . . . . . . 8 B18　69 56N　19 15 E
Ringwood, U.S.A. . . . . . . . . . . . 85 E10　41　7N　74 15W
Rinjani, Indonesia . . . . . . . . . . 36 F5　8 24S 116 28 E
Rio Branco, Brazil . . . . . . . . . . 92 E5　9 58S　67 49W
Río Branco, Uruguay . . . . . . . . 95 C5　32 40S　53 40W
Río Bravo →, N. Amer. . . . . . . 86 B4　29 21N 102 45W
Río Bravo del Norte →, Mexico . 87 B5　25 57N　97　9W
Rio Brilhante, Brazil . . . . . . . . 95 A5　21 48S　54 33W
Rio de Janeiro, Brazil . . . . . . . 95 A7　23　0S　43 12W
Rio de Janeiro □, Brazil . . . . . . 95 A7　22 50S　43　0W
Rio do Sul, Brazil . . . . . . . . . . . 95 B6　27 13S　49 37W
Río Dulce △, Guatemala . . . . . 15 43N　88 50W
Río Gallegos, Argentina . . . . . 96 G3　51 35S　69 15W
Rio Grande, Brazil . . . . . . . . . . 95 C5　32　0S　52 20W
Río Grande, Mexico . . . . . . . . . 86 C4　23 50N 103　2W
Río Grande, Nic. . . . . . . . . . . . . 88 D3　12 54N　83 33W
Río Grande, Puerto Rico . . . . . 89 d　18 23N　65 50W
Rio Grande →, U.S.A. . . . . . . . 81 N6　25 58N　97　9W
Rio Grande →, U.S.A. . . . . . . . 81 M5　26 23N　98 49W
Rio Grande de Santiago →,
Mexico . . . . . . . . . . . . . . . . . 86 C3　21 36N 105 26W

Rio Grande do Norte □, *Brazil* . . **93 E11** 5 40S 36 0W
Rio Grande do Sul □, *Brazil* . . **95 C5** 30 0S 53 0W
Río Hato, *Panama* . . . . . . . . . . . **88 E3** 8 22N 80 10W
Rio Lagartos, *Mexico* . . . . . . . . **87 C7** 21 36N 88 10W
Rio Largo, *Brazil* . . . . . . . . . . . **93 E11** 9 28S 35 50W
Río Muni □, *Eq. Guin.* . . . . . . . **52 D2** 1 30N 10 0 E
Rio Negro, *Brazil* . . . . . . . . . . **95 B6** 26 0S 49 55W
Rio Pardo, *Brazil* . . . . . . . . . . . **95 C5** 30 0S 52 30W
Río Pilcomayo △, *Argentina* . . **94 B4** 25 5S 58 5W
Río Platano △, *Honduras* . . . . . **88 C3** 15 45N 85 0W
Rio Rancho, *U.S.A.* . . . . . . . . . . **77 J10** 35 14N 106 38W
Rio Segundo, *Argentina* . . . . . . **94 C3** 31 40S 63 59W
Rio Tercero, *Argentina* . . . . . . . **94 C3** 32 15S 64 8W
Rio Verde, *Brazil* . . . . . . . . . . . **93 G8** 17 50S 51 0W
Rio Verde, *Mexico* . . . . . . . . . . **87 C5** 21 56N 99 59W
Rio Vista, *U.S.A.* . . . . . . . . . . . **78 G5** 38 10N 121 42W
Ríobamba, *Ecuador* . . . . . . . . . **92 D3** 1 50S 78 45W
Ríohacha, *Colombia* . . . . . . . . . **92 A4** 11 33N 72 55W
Ríosucio, *Colombia* . . . . . . . . . **92 B3** 7 27N 77 7W
Riou L., *Canada* . . . . . . . . . . . . **71 B7** 59 7N 106 25W
Ripley, *Canada* . . . . . . . . . . . . . **84 B3** 44 4N 81 35W
Ripley, *Calif., U.S.A.* . . . . . . . **79 M12** 33 32N 114 39W
Ripley, *N.Y., U.S.A.* . . . . . . . . . **84 D5** 42 16N 79 43W
Ripley, *Tenn., U.S.A.* . . . . . . . . **81 H10** 35 45N 89 32W
Ripley, *W. Va., U.S.A.* . . . . . . . **82 F5** 38 49N 81 43W
Ripon, *U.K.* . . . . . . . . . . . . . . . . **12 C6** 54 9N 1 31W
Ripon, *Calif., U.S.A.* . . . . . . . . **78 H5** 37 44N 121 7W
Ripon, *Wis., U.S.A.* . . . . . . . . . **82 D1** 43 51N 88 50W
Rishā', *W. ar* →, *Si. Arabia* . . . **44 E5** 25 33N 44 5 E
Rishiri-Rebun-Sarobetsu △,
  *Japan* . . . . . . . . . . . . . . . . . . . **30 B10** 45 26N 141 30 E
Rishiri-Tō, *Japan* . . . . . . . . . . **30 B10** 45 11N 141 15 E
Rishon le Ziyyon, *Israel* . . . . . . **46 D3** 31 58N 34 48 E
Rison, *U.S.A.* . . . . . . . . . . . . . . **81 J8** 33 58N 92 11W
Risør, *Norway* . . . . . . . . . . . . . **9 G13** 58 43N 9 13 E
Rita Blanca Cr. →, *U.S.A.* . . . . **81 H3** 35 40N 102 29W
Ritter, Mt., *U.S.A.* . . . . . . . . . . **78 H7** 37 41N 119 12W
Rittman, *U.S.A.* . . . . . . . . . . . . **84 F3** 40 58N 81 47W
Ritzville, *U.S.A.* . . . . . . . . . . . . **76 C4** 47 8N 118 23W
Riva del Garda, *Italy* . . . . . . . . **22 B4** 45 53N 10 50 E
Rivadavia, *Buenos Aires,
  Argentina* . . . . . . . . . . . . . . . **94 D3** 35 29S 62 59W
Rivadavia, *Mendoza, Argentina* **94 C2** 33 13S 68 30W
Rivadavia, *Salta, Argentina* . . . **94 A3** 24 5S 62 54W
Rivadavia, *Chile* . . . . . . . . . . . **94 B1** 29 57S 70 35W
Rivas, *Nic.* . . . . . . . . . . . . . . . . **88 D2** 11 30N 85 50W
River Cess, *Liberia* . . . . . . . . . . **50 G4** 5 30N 9 32W
River Jordan, *Canada* . . . . . . . . **78 B2** 48 26N 124 3W
Rivera, *Argentina* . . . . . . . . . . . **94 D3** 37 12S 63 14W
Rivera, *Uruguay* . . . . . . . . . . . . **95 C4** 31 0S 55 50W
Riverbank, *U.S.A.* . . . . . . . . . . . **78 H6** 37 44N 120 56W
Riverdale, *U.S.A.* . . . . . . . . . . . **78 J7** 36 26N 119 52W
Riverhead, *U.S.A.* . . . . . . . . . . **85 F12** 40 55N 72 40W
Riverhurst, *Canada* . . . . . . . . . **71 C7** 50 55N 106 50W
Rivers, *Canada* . . . . . . . . . . . . . **71 C8** 50 2N 100 14W
Rivers Inlet, *Canada* . . . . . . . . . **70 C3** 51 42N 127 15W
Riverside, *S. Africa* . . . . . . . . . **56 E3** 34 7S 21 15 E
Riverside, *U.S.A.* . . . . . . . . . . . **79 M9** 33 59N 117 22W
Riverton, *Australia* . . . . . . . . . . **63 E2** 34 10S 138 46 E
Riverton, *Canada* . . . . . . . . . . . **71 C9** 51 1N 97 0W
Riverton, *N.Z.* . . . . . . . . . . . . . **59 M2** 46 21S 168 0 E
Riverton, *U.S.A.* . . . . . . . . . . . . **76 E9** 43 2N 108 23W
Riverton Heights, *U.S.A.* . . . . . **78 C4** 47 28N 122 17W
Riviera, *U.S.A.* . . . . . . . . . . . . **79 K12** 35 4N 114 35W
Riviera di Levante, *Italy* . . . . . . **20 D8** 44 15N 9 30 E
Riviera di Ponente, *Italy* . . . . . **20 D8** 44 10N 8 20 E
Rivière-au-Renard, *Canada* . . . . **73 C7** 48 59N 64 23W
Rivière-du-Loup, *Canada* . . . . . **73 C6** 47 50N 69 30W
Rivière-Pentecôte, *Canada* . . . . **73 C6** 49 57N 67 1W
Rivière-Pilote, *Martinique* . . . . . **88 c** 14 26N 60 53W
Rivière St-Paul, *Canada* . . . . . . **73 B8** 51 28N 57 45W
Rivière-Salée, *Martinique* . . . . . **88 c** 14 31N 61 0W
Rivne, *Ukraine* . . . . . . . . . . . . **17 C14** 50 40N 26 10 E
Rívoli, *Italy* . . . . . . . . . . . . . . . . **20 D7** 45 3N 7 31 E
Rívoli B., *Australia* . . . . . . . . . . **63 F3** 37 32S 140 3 E
Riyadh = Ar Riyāḑ, *Si. Arabia* . **44 E5** 24 41N 46 42 E
Rize, *Turkey* . . . . . . . . . . . . . . . **19 F7** 41 0N 40 30 E
Rizhao, *China* . . . . . . . . . . . . . **35 G10** 35 25N 119 30 E
Rizokarpaso, *Cyprus* . . . . . . . . **25 D13** 35 36N 34 23 E
Rizzuto, C., *Italy* . . . . . . . . . . . **22 E7** 38 53N 17 5 E
Rjukan, *Norway* . . . . . . . . . . . . **9 G13** 59 54N 8 33 E
Road Town, *Br. Virgin Is.* . . . . . **89 e** 18 27N 64 37W
Roan Plateau, *U.S.A.* . . . . . . . . **76 G9** 39 20N 109 20W
Roanne, *France* . . . . . . . . . . . . **20 C6** 46 3N 4 4 E
Roanoke, *Ala., U.S.A.* . . . . . . . **83 J3** 33 9N 85 22W
Roanoke, *Va., U.S.A.* . . . . . . . . **82 G6** 37 16N 79 56W
Roanoke →, *U.S.A.* . . . . . . . . . **83 H7** 35 57N 76 42W
Roanoke I., *U.S.A.* . . . . . . . . . . **83 H8** 35 55N 75 40W
Roanoke Rapids, *U.S.A.* . . . . . . **83 G7** 36 28N 77 40W
Roatán, *Honduras* . . . . . . . . . . **88 C2** 16 18N 86 35W
Robāt Sang, *Iran* . . . . . . . . . . . **45 C8** 35 35N 59 10 E
Robāţkarīm, *Iran* . . . . . . . . . . . **45 C6** 35 25N 50 59 E
Robāţkarīm □, *Iran* . . . . . . . . . **45 B6** 35 26N 50 59 E
Robbins I., *Australia* . . . . . . . . . **63 G4** 40 42S 145 0 E
Robe →, *Australia* . . . . . . . . . . **60 D2** 21 42S 116 15 E
Robert Lee, *U.S.A.* . . . . . . . . . . **81 K4** 31 54N 100 29W
Robertsdale, *U.S.A.* . . . . . . . . . **84 F6** 40 11N 78 6W
Robertsganj, *India* . . . . . . . . . **43 G10** 24 44N 83 4 E
Robertson, *S. Africa* . . . . . . . . **56 E2** 33 46S 19 50 E
Robertson I., *Antarctica* . . . . . . **5 C18** 65 15S 59 30W
Robertson Ra., *Australia* . . . . . **60 D3** 23 15S 121 0 E
Robertstown, *Australia* . . . . . . . **63 E2** 33 58S 139 5 E
Roberval, *Canada* . . . . . . . . . . **73 C5** 48 32N 72 15W
Robeson Chan., *N. Amer.* . . . . . **4 A4** 82 0N 61 30W
Robesonia, *U.S.A.* . . . . . . . . . . **85 F8** 40 21N 76 8W
Robinson, *U.S.A.* . . . . . . . . . . . **82 F2** 39 0N 87 44W
Robinson →, *Australia* . . . . . . . **62 B2** 16 3S 137 16 E
Robinson Ra., *Australia* . . . . . . **61 E2** 25 40S 119 0 E
Robinvale, *Australia* . . . . . . . . . **63 E3** 34 40S 142 45 E
Roblin, *Canada* . . . . . . . . . . . . **71 C8** 51 14N 101 21W
Roboré, *Bolivia* . . . . . . . . . . . . **92 G7** 18 10S 59 45W
Robson, *Canada* . . . . . . . . . . . **70 D5** 49 20N 117 41W
Robson, Mt., *Canada* . . . . . . . . **70 C5** 53 10N 119 10W
Robstown, *U.S.A.* . . . . . . . . . . . **81 M6** 27 47N 97 40W
Roca, C. da, *Portugal* . . . . . . . . **21 C1** 38 40N 9 31W
Roca Partida, I., *Mexico* . . . . . . **86 D2** 19 1N 112 2W
Rocas, I., *Brazil* . . . . . . . . . . . . **93 D12** 4 0S 34 1W
Rocha, *Uruguay* . . . . . . . . . . . . **95 C5** 34 30S 54 25W
Rochdale, *U.K.* . . . . . . . . . . . . **12 D5** 53 38N 2 9W
Rochefort, *Belgium* . . . . . . . . . **15 D5** 50 9N 5 12 E
Rochefort, *France* . . . . . . . . . . . **20 D3** 45 56N 0 57W
Rochelle, *U.S.A.* . . . . . . . . . . . **80 E10** 41 56N 89 4W
Rocher River, *Canada* . . . . . . . **70 A6** 61 23N 112 44W
Rochester, *U.K.* . . . . . . . . . . . . **13 F8** 51 23N 0 31 E
Rochester, *Ind., U.S.A.* . . . . . . . **82 E2** 41 4N 86 13W
Rochester, *Minn., U.S.A.* . . . . . **80 C8** 44 1N 92 28W
Rochester, *N.H., U.S.A.* . . . . . . **85 C14** 43 18N 70 59W

Rochester, *N.Y., U.S.A.* . . . . . . **84 C7** 43 10N 77 37W
Rock →, *Canada* . . . . . . . . . . . **70 A3** 60 7N 127 7W
Rock Creek, *U.S.A.* . . . . . . . . . **84 E4** 41 40N 80 52W
Rock Falls, *U.S.A.* . . . . . . . . . . **80 E10** 41 47N 89 41W
Rock Hill, *U.S.A.* . . . . . . . . . . . **83 H5** 34 56N 81 1W
Rock Island, *U.S.A.* . . . . . . . . . **80 E9** 41 30N 90 34W
Rock Rapids, *U.S.A.* . . . . . . . . . **80 D6** 43 26N 96 10W
Rock Sound, *Bahamas* . . . . . . . **88 B4** 24 54N 76 12W
Rock Springs, *Mont., U.S.A.* . . . **76 C10** 46 49N 106 15W
Rock Springs, *Wyo., U.S.A.* . . . **76 F9** 41 35N 109 14W
Rock Valley, *U.S.A.* . . . . . . . . . **80 D6** 43 12N 96 18W
Rockall, *Atl. Oc.* . . . . . . . . . . . . **6 D3** 57 37N 13 42W
Rockdale, *Tex., U.S.A.* . . . . . . . **81 K6** 30 39N 97 0W
Rockdale, *Wash., U.S.A.* . . . . . . **78 C5** 47 22N 121 28W
Rockeby = Mungkan Kandju △,
  *Australia* . . . . . . . . . . . . . . . . **62 A3** 13 35S 142 52 E
Rockefeller Plateau, *Antarctica* . **5 E14** 80 0S 140 0W
Rockford, *U.S.A.* . . . . . . . . . . . **80 D10** 42 16N 89 6W
Rockglen, *Canada* . . . . . . . . . . **71 D7** 49 11N 105 57W
Rockhampton, *Australia* . . . . . . **62 C5** 23 22S 150 32 E
Rockingham, *Australia* . . . . . . . **61 F2** 32 15S 115 38 E
Rockingham, *U.S.A.* . . . . . . . . . **83 H6** 34 57N 79 46W
Rockingham B., *Australia* . . . . . **62 B4** 18 5S 146 10 E
Rocklake, *U.S.A.* . . . . . . . . . . . **80 A5** 48 47N 99 15W
Rockland, *Canada* . . . . . . . . . . **85 A9** 45 33N 75 17W
Rockland, *Idaho, U.S.A.* . . . . . . **76 E7** 42 34N 112 53W
Rockland, *Maine, U.S.A.* . . . . . . **83 C11** 44 6N 69 7W
Rockland, *Mich., U.S.A.* . . . . . . **80 B10** 46 44N 89 11W
Rocklin, *U.S.A.* . . . . . . . . . . . . **78 G5** 38 48N 121 14W
Rockly B., *Trin. & Tob.* . . . . . . . **93 J16** 11 9N 60 46W
Rockmart, *U.S.A.* . . . . . . . . . . . **83 H3** 34 0N 85 3W
Rockport, *Mass., U.S.A.* . . . . . . **85 D14** 42 39N 70 37W
Rockport, *Mo., U.S.A.* . . . . . . . **80 E7** 40 25N 95 31W
Rockport, *Tex., U.S.A.* . . . . . . . **81 L6** 28 2N 97 3W
Rocksprings, *U.S.A.* . . . . . . . . . **81 K4** 30 1N 100 13W
Rockville, *Conn., U.S.A.* . . . . . . **85 E12** 41 52N 72 28W
Rockville, *Md., U.S.A.* . . . . . . . . **82 F7** 39 5N 77 9W
Rockwall, *U.S.A.* . . . . . . . . . . . **81 J6** 32 56N 96 28W
Rockwell City, *U.S.A.* . . . . . . . . **80 D7** 42 24N 94 38W
Rockwood, *Canada* . . . . . . . . . **84 C4** 43 37N 80 8W
Rockwood, *Maine, U.S.A.* . . . . . **83 C11** 45 41N 69 45W
Rockwood, *Tenn., U.S.A.* . . . . . **83 H3** 35 52N 84 41W
Rocky Ford, *U.S.A.* . . . . . . . . . **80 F3** 38 3N 103 43W
Rocky Gully, *Australia* . . . . . . . . **61 F2** 34 30S 116 57 E
Rocky Harbour, *Canada* . . . . . . **73 C8** 49 36N 57 55W
Rocky Island L., *Canada* . . . . . . **72 C3** 46 55N 83 0W
Rocky Lane, *Canada* . . . . . . . . . **70 B5** 58 31N 116 22W
Rocky Mount, *U.S.A.* . . . . . . . . **83 H7** 35 57N 77 48W
Rocky Mountain △, *U.S.A.* . . . . **76 F11** 40 25N 105 45W
Rocky Mountain House, *Canada* **70 C6** 52 22N 114 55W
Rocky Mts., *N. Amer.* . . . . . . . . **76 G10** 49 0N 115 0W
Rocky Point, *Namibia* . . . . . . . . **56 B2** 19 3S 12 30 E
Rod, *Pakistan* . . . . . . . . . . . . . . **40 E3** 28 10N 63 5 E
Rødbyhavn, *Denmark* . . . . . . . . **9 J14** 54 39N 11 22 E
Roddickton, *Canada* . . . . . . . . . **73 B8** 50 51N 56 8W
Rodez, *France* . . . . . . . . . . . . . **20 D5** 44 21N 2 33 E
Rodhopoú, *Greece* . . . . . . . . . . **25 D5** 35 34N 23 45 E
Ródhos, *Greece* . . . . . . . . . . . . **25 C10** 36 15N 28 10 E
Rodney, *Canada* . . . . . . . . . . . **84 D3** 42 34N 81 41W
Rodney, C., *N.Z.* . . . . . . . . . . . **59 G5** 36 17S 174 50 E
Rodriguez, *Ind. Oc.* . . . . . . . . . **3 E13** 19 45S 63 20 E
Roe →, *U.K.* . . . . . . . . . . . . . . . **10 A5** 55 6N 6 59W
Roebling, *U.S.A.* . . . . . . . . . . . **85 F10** 40 7N 74 47W
Roebourne, *Australia* . . . . . . . . **60 D2** 20 44S 117 9 E
Roebuck B., *Australia* . . . . . . . . **60 C3** 18 5S 122 20 E
Roermond, *Neths.* . . . . . . . . . . **15 C6** 51 12N 6 0 E
Roes Welcome Sd., *Canada* . . . **69 B11** 65 0N 87 0W
Roeselare, *Belgium* . . . . . . . . . **15 D3** 50 57N 3 7 E
Rogachev = Ragachow, *Belarus* **17 B16** 53 8N 30 5 E
Rogagua, L., *Bolivia* . . . . . . . . . **92 F5** 13 43S 66 50W
Rogatyn, *Ukraine* . . . . . . . . . . **17 D13** 49 24N 24 36 E
Rogdhia, *Greece* . . . . . . . . . . . **25 D7** 35 22N 25 1 E
Rogers, *U.S.A.* . . . . . . . . . . . . . **81 G7** 36 20N 94 7W
Rogers City, *U.S.A.* . . . . . . . . . **82 C4** 45 25N 83 49W
Rogersville, *Canada* . . . . . . . . . **73 C6** 46 44N 65 26W
Roggan →, *Canada* . . . . . . . . . **72 B4** 54 24N 79 25W
Roggan L., *Canada* . . . . . . . . . **72 B4** 54 8N 77 50W
Roggeveldberge, *S. Africa* . . . . **56 E3** 32 10S 20 10 E
Rogoaguado, L., *Bolivia* . . . . . . **92 F5** 13 0S 65 30W
Rogojampi, *Indonesia* . . . . . . . **37 J17** 8 19S 114 17 E
Rogue →, *U.S.A.* . . . . . . . . . . . **76 E1** 42 26N 124 26W
Róhda, *Greece* . . . . . . . . . . . . . **25 A3** 39 48N 19 46 E
Rohnert Park, *U.S.A.* . . . . . . . . **78 G4** 38 16N 122 40W
Rohri, *Pakistan* . . . . . . . . . . . . . **42 F3** 27 45N 68 51 E
Rohri Canal, *Pakistan* . . . . . . . . **42 F3** 26 15N 68 27 E
Rohtak, *India* . . . . . . . . . . . . . . **42 E7** 28 55N 76 43 E
Roi Et, *Thailand* . . . . . . . . . . . . **38 D4** 16 4N 103 40 E
Roja, *Latvia* . . . . . . . . . . . . . . . . **9 H20** 57 29N 22 43 E
Rojas, *Argentina* . . . . . . . . . . . **94 C3** 34 10S 60 45W
Rojo, C., *Mexico* . . . . . . . . . . . . **87 C5** 21 33N 97 20W
Rokan →, *Indonesia* . . . . . . . . **36 D2** 2 0N 100 50 E
Rokiškis, *Lithuania* . . . . . . . . . . **9 J21** 55 55N 25 35 E
Rolândia, *Brazil* . . . . . . . . . . . . **95 A5** 23 18S 51 23W
Rolla, *U.S.A.* . . . . . . . . . . . . . . . **81 G9** 37 57N 91 46W
Rolleston, *Australia* . . . . . . . . . **62 C4** 24 28S 148 35 E
Rollingstone, *Australia* . . . . . . . **62 B4** 19 2S 146 24 E
Roma, *Australia* . . . . . . . . . . . . **63 D5** 26 32S 148 49 E
Roma, *Italy* . . . . . . . . . . . . . . . . **22 D5** 41 54N 12 29 E
Roma, *Sweden* . . . . . . . . . . . . . **9 H18** 57 32N 18 26 E
Romain C., *U.S.A.* . . . . . . . . . . . **83 J6** 33 0N 79 22W
Romaine, *Canada* . . . . . . . . . . **73 B7** 50 13N 60 40W
Romaine →, *Canada* . . . . . . . . **73 B7** 50 18N 63 47W
Roman, *Romania* . . . . . . . . . . . **17 E14** 46 57N 26 55 E
Romang, *Indonesia* . . . . . . . . . **37 F7** 7 30S 127 20 E
Rômani, *Egypt* . . . . . . . . . . . . . **46 E1** 30 59N 32 38 E
Romania ■, *Europe* . . . . . . . . . **17 F12** 46 0N 25 0 E
Romano, Cayo, *Cuba* . . . . . . . . **88 B4** 22 0N 77 30W
Romans-sur-Isère, *France* . . . . **20 D6** 45 3N 5 3 E
Romblon, *Phil.* . . . . . . . . . . . . . **37 B6** 12 33N 122 17 E
Rome = Roma, *Italy* . . . . . . . . . **22 D5** 41 54N 12 29 E
Rome, *Ga., U.S.A.* . . . . . . . . . . **83 H3** 34 15N 85 10W
Rome, *N.Y., U.S.A.* . . . . . . . . . . **85 C9** 43 13N 75 27W
Rome, *Pa., U.S.A.* . . . . . . . . . . . **85 E8** 41 51N 76 21W
Romney, *U.S.A.* . . . . . . . . . . . . **82 F6** 39 21N 78 45W
Romney Marsh, *U.K.* . . . . . . . . **13 F8** 51 2N 0 54 E
Rømø, *Denmark* . . . . . . . . . . . . **9 J13** 55 10N 8 30 E
Romorantin-Lanthenay, *France* . **20 C4** 47 21N 1 45 E
Romsdalen, *Norway* . . . . . . . . . **9 E12** 62 25N 7 52 E
Ron, *Vietnam* . . . . . . . . . . . . . . **38 D6** 17 53N 106 27 E
Rona, *U.K.* . . . . . . . . . . . . . . . . **11 D3** 57 34N 5 59W
Ronan, *U.S.A.* . . . . . . . . . . . . . **76 C6** 47 32N 114 6W
Roncador, Cayos, *Colombia* . . . **88 D3** 13 32N 80 4W
Roncador, Serra do, *Brazil* . . . . **93 F8** 12 30S 52 30W
Ronda, *Spain* . . . . . . . . . . . . . . **21 D3** 36 46N 5 12W
Rondane, *Norway* . . . . . . . . . . **9 F13** 61 57N 9 50 E
Rondônia □, *Brazil* . . . . . . . . . . **92 F6** 11 0S 63 0W

Rondonópolis, *Brazil* . . . . . . . . **93 G8** 16 28S 54 38W
Rong, Koh, *Cambodia* . . . . . . . **39 G4** 10 45N 103 15 E
Ronge, L. la, *Canada* . . . . . . . . **71 B7** 55 6N 105 17W
Rønne, *Denmark* . . . . . . . . . . . **9 J16** 55 6N 14 43 E
Ronne Ice Shelf, *Antarctica* . . . **5 D18** 78 0S 60 0W
Ronsard, C., *Australia* . . . . . . . . **61 D1** 24 46S 113 10 E
Ronse, *Belgium* . . . . . . . . . . . . **15 D3** 50 45N 3 35 E
Roodepoort, *S. Africa* . . . . . . . . **57 D4** 26 11S 27 54 E
Roof Butte, *U.S.A.* . . . . . . . . . . **77 H9** 36 28N 109 5W
Rooiboklaagte →, *Namibia* . . . **56 C3** 20 50S 21 0 E
Roorkee, *India* . . . . . . . . . . . . . **42 E7** 29 52N 77 59 E
Roosendaal, *Neths.* . . . . . . . . . **15 C4** 51 32N 4 29 E
Roosevelt, *U.S.A.* . . . . . . . . . . . **76 F8** 40 18N 109 59W
Roosevelt →, *Brazil* . . . . . . . . . **92 E6** 7 35S 60 20W
Roosevelt, Mt., *Canada* . . . . . . **70 B3** 58 26N 125 20W
Roosevelt I., *Antarctica* . . . . . . . **5 D12** 79 30S 162 0W
Roper →, *Australia* . . . . . . . . . . **62 A2** 14 43S 135 27 E
Roper Bar, *Australia* . . . . . . . . . **62 A1** 14 44S 134 44 E
Roque Pérez, *Argentina* . . . . . . **94 D4** 35 25S 59 24W
Roquetas de Mar, *Spain* . . . . . . **21 D4** 36 46N 2 36W
Roraima □, *Brazil* . . . . . . . . . . . **92 C6** 2 0N 61 30W
Roraima, Mt., *Venezuela* . . . . . . **92 B6** 5 10N 60 40W
Røros, *Norway* . . . . . . . . . . . . . **9 E14** 62 35N 11 23 E
Rosa, *Zambia* . . . . . . . . . . . . . . **55 D3** 9 33S 31 15 E
Rosa, L., *Bahamas* . . . . . . . . . . **89 B5** 21 0N 73 30W
Rosa, Monte, *Europe* . . . . . . . . **20 D7** 45 57N 7 53 E
Rosalia, *U.S.A.* . . . . . . . . . . . . . **76 C5** 47 14N 117 22W
Rosamond, *U.S.A.* . . . . . . . . . . **79 L8** 34 52N 118 10W
Rosario, *Argentina* . . . . . . . . . . **94 C3** 33 0S 60 40W
Rosário, *Brazil* . . . . . . . . . . . . . **93 D10** 3 0S 44 15W
Rosario, *Baja Calif., Mexico* . . . **86 B1** 30 0N 115 50W
Rosario, *Sinaloa, Mexico* . . . . . **86 C3** 23 0N 105 52W
Rosario, *Paraguay* . . . . . . . . . . **94 A4** 24 30S 65 0W
Rosario de la Frontera, *Argentina* **94 B3** 25 50S 65 0W
Rosario de Lerma, *Argentina* . . **94 A2** 24 59S 65 35W
Rosario del Tala, *Argentina* . . . . **94 C4** 32 20S 59 10W
Rosário do Sul, *Brazil* . . . . . . . . **95 C5** 30 15S 54 55W
Rosarito, *Mexico* . . . . . . . . . . . **79 N9** 32 18N 117 4W
Roscoe, *U.S.A.* . . . . . . . . . . . . . **85 E10** 41 56N 74 55W
Roscommon, *Ireland* . . . . . . . . **10 C3** 53 38N 8 11W
Roscommon □, *Ireland* . . . . . . . **10 C3** 53 49N 8 23W
Roscrea, *Ireland* . . . . . . . . . . . **10 D4** 52 57N 7 49W
Rose →, *Australia* . . . . . . . . . . **62 A2** 14 16S 135 45 E
Rose Blanche-Harbour Le Cou,
  *Canada* . . . . . . . . . . . . . . . . . **73 C8** 47 38N 58 45W
Rose Pt., *Canada* . . . . . . . . . . . **70 C2** 54 11N 131 39W
Rose Valley, *Canada* . . . . . . . . **71 C8** 52 19N 103 49W
Roseau, *Dominica* . . . . . . . . . . **89 C7** 15 17N 61 24W
Roseau, *U.S.A.* . . . . . . . . . . . . **80 A7** 48 51N 95 46W
Rosebery, *Australia* . . . . . . . . . **63 G4** 41 46S 145 33 E
Rosebud, *S. Dak., U.S.A.* . . . . . **80 D4** 43 14N 100 51W
Rosebud, *Tex., U.S.A.* . . . . . . . **81 K6** 31 4N 96 59W
Roseburg, *U.S.A.* . . . . . . . . . . . **76 E2** 43 13N 123 20W
Rosedale, *U.S.A.* . . . . . . . . . . . **81 J9** 33 51N 91 2W
Rosehearty, *U.K.* . . . . . . . . . . . **11 D6** 57 42N 2 7W
Roseland, *U.S.A.* . . . . . . . . . . . **78 G4** 38 25N 122 43W
Rosemary, *Canada* . . . . . . . . . . **70 C6** 50 46N 112 5W
Rosenberg, *U.S.A.* . . . . . . . . . . **81 L7** 29 34N 95 49W
Rosenheim, *Germany* . . . . . . . . **16 E7** 47 51N 12 7 E
Roses, G. de, *Spain* . . . . . . . . . **21 A7** 42 10N 3 15 E
Rosetown, *Canada* . . . . . . . . . . **71 C7** 51 35N 107 59W
Roseville, *Calif., U.S.A.* . . . . . . . **78 G5** 38 45N 121 17W
Roseville, *Mich., U.S.A.* . . . . . . **84 D2** 42 30N 82 56W
Rosewood, *Australia* . . . . . . . . **63 D5** 27 38S 152 36 E
Roshkhvār, *Iran* . . . . . . . . . . . . **45 C8** 34 58N 59 37 E
Rosignano Marittimo, *Italy* . . . . **22 C4** 43 24N 10 28 E
Rosignol, *Guyana* . . . . . . . . . . **92 B7** 6 15N 57 30W
Roşiori de Vede, *Romania* . . . . . **17 F13** 44 9N 25 0 E
Roskilde, *Denmark* . . . . . . . . . . **9 J15** 55 38N 12 3 E
Roslavl, *Russia* . . . . . . . . . . . . . **18 D5** 53 57N 32 55 E
Rosmead, *S. Africa* . . . . . . . . . . **56 E4** 31 29S 25 8 E
Ross, *Australia* . . . . . . . . . . . . . **63 G4** 42 2S 147 30 E
Ross, *N.Z.* . . . . . . . . . . . . . . . . . **59 K3** 42 53S 170 49 E
Ross Dependency, *Antarctica* . . **5 D12** 76 0S 170 0W
Ross I., *Antarctica* . . . . . . . . . . . **5 D11** 77 30S 168 0 E
Ross Ice Shelf, *Antarctica* . . . . . **5 E12** 80 0S 180 0 E
Ross L., *U.S.A.* . . . . . . . . . . . . . **76 B3** 48 44N 121 4W
Ross-on-Wye, *U.K.* . . . . . . . . . . **13 F5** 51 54N 2 34W
Ross River, *Australia* . . . . . . . . **62 C1** 23 44S 134 30 E
Ross River, *Canada* . . . . . . . . . **70 A2** 62 30N 131 30W
Ross Sea, *Antarctica* . . . . . . . . **5 D11** 74 0S 178 0 E
Rossall Pt., *U.K.* . . . . . . . . . . . . **12 D4** 53 55N 3 3W
Rossan Pt., *Ireland* . . . . . . . . . . **10 B3** 54 42N 8 47W
Rossano, *Italy* . . . . . . . . . . . . . **22 E7** 39 36N 16 39 E
Rossburn, *Canada* . . . . . . . . . . **71 C8** 50 40N 100 49W
Rosseau, *Canada* . . . . . . . . . . . **84 A5** 45 16N 79 39W
Rosseau, L., *Canada* . . . . . . . . **84 A5** 45 10N 79 35W
Rosses, The, *Ireland* . . . . . . . . . **10 A3** 55 2N 8 20W
Rossignol, L., *Canada* . . . . . . . **72 B5** 52 43N 73 40W
Rossignol L., *Canada* . . . . . . . . **73 D6** 44 12N 65 10W
Rossland, *Canada* . . . . . . . . . . **70 D5** 49 6N 117 50W
Rosslare, *Ireland* . . . . . . . . . . . **10 D5** 52 17N 6 24W
Rosslare Harbour, *Ireland* . . . . . **10 D5** 52 15N 6 20W
Rosso, *Mauritania* . . . . . . . . . . **50 E2** 16 40N 15 45W
Rossosh, *Russia* . . . . . . . . . . . **19 D6** 50 15N 39 28 E
Røssvatnet, *Norway* . . . . . . . . . **8 D16** 65 45N 14 5 E
Røst, *Norway* . . . . . . . . . . . . . . **8 C15** 67 32N 12 0 E
Rosthern, *Canada* . . . . . . . . . . **71 C7** 52 40N 106 20W
Rostock, *Germany* . . . . . . . . . . **16 A7** 54 5N 12 8 E
Rostov, *Don, Russia* . . . . . . . . . **19 E6** 47 15N 39 45 E
Rostov, *Yaroslavl, Russia* . . . . . **18 C6** 57 14N 39 25 E
Roswell, *Ga., U.S.A.* . . . . . . . . . **83 H3** 34 2N 84 22W
Roswell, *N. Mex., U.S.A.* . . . . . **81 J2** 33 24N 104 32W
Rotan, *U.S.A.* . . . . . . . . . . . . . . **81 J4** 32 51N 100 28W
Rother →, *U.K.* . . . . . . . . . . . . **13 G8** 50 59N 0 45 E
Rothera, *Antarctica* . . . . . . . . . **5 C17** 67 20S 63 0W
Rotherham, *U.K.* . . . . . . . . . . . **12 D6** 53 26N 1 20W
Rothes, *U.K.* . . . . . . . . . . . . . . . **11 D5** 57 32N 3 13W
Rothesay, *Canada* . . . . . . . . . . **73 C6** 45 23N 66 0W
Rothesay, *U.K.* . . . . . . . . . . . . . **11 F3** 55 50N 5 3W
Roti, *Indonesia* . . . . . . . . . . . . . **37 F6** 10 50S 123 0 E
Roto, *Australia* . . . . . . . . . . . . . **63 E4** 33 0S 145 30 E
Rotondo, Mte., *France* . . . . . . . **20 E8** 42 14N 9 8 E
Rotorua, *N.Z.* . . . . . . . . . . . . . . **59 H6** 38 9S 176 16 E
Rotorua, L., *N.Z.* . . . . . . . . . . . **59 H6** 38 5S 176 18 E
Rotterdam, *Neths.* . . . . . . . . . . **15 C4** 51 55N 4 30 E
Rottnest I., *Australia* . . . . . . . . . **61 F2** 32 0S 115 27 E
Rottumeroog, *Neths.* . . . . . . . . **15 A6** 53 33N 6 34 E
Rottweil, *Germany* . . . . . . . . . . **16 D5** 48 9N 8 37 E
Rotuma, *Fiji* . . . . . . . . . . . . . . . **64 J9** 12 25S 177 5 E
Roubaix, *France* . . . . . . . . . . . . **20 A5** 50 40N 3 10 E
Rouen, *France* . . . . . . . . . . . . . **20 B4** 49 27N 1 4 E
Rouleau, *Canada* . . . . . . . . . . . **71 C8** 50 10N 104 56W
Round Mountain, *U.S.A.* . . . . . . **76 G5** 38 43N 117 4W
Round Mt., *Australia* . . . . . . . . . **63 E5** 30 26S 152 16 E
Round Rock, *U.S.A.* . . . . . . . . . **81 K6** 30 31N 97 41W

Roundup, *U.S.A.* . . . . . . . . . . . **76 C9** 46 27N 108 33W
Rousay, *U.K.* . . . . . . . . . . . . . . **11 B5** 59 10N 3 2W
Rouses Point, *U.S.A.* . . . . . . . . **85 B11** 44 59N 73 22W
Rouseville, *U.S.A.* . . . . . . . . . . **84 E5** 41 28N 79 42W
Roussillon, *France* . . . . . . . . . . **20 E5** 42 30N 2 35 E
Rouxville, *S. Africa* . . . . . . . . . . **56 E4** 30 25S 26 50 E
Rouyn-Noranda, *Canada* . . . . . . **72 C4** 48 20N 79 0W
Rovaniemi, *Finland* . . . . . . . . . . **8 C21** 66 29N 25 41 E
Rovereto, *Italy* . . . . . . . . . . . . . **22 B4** 45 53N 11 3 E
Rovigo, *Italy* . . . . . . . . . . . . . . . **22 B4** 45 4N 11 47 E
Rovinj, *Croatia* . . . . . . . . . . . . . **16 F7** 45 5N 13 40 E
Rovno = Rivne, *Ukraine* . . . . . . **17 C14** 50 40N 26 10 E
Rovuma = Ruvuma →, *Tanzania* **55 E5** 10 29S 40 28 E
Row'ān, *Iran* . . . . . . . . . . . . . . . **45 C6** 35 8N 48 51 E
Rowena, *Australia* . . . . . . . . . . **63 D4** 29 48S 148 55 E
Rowley Shoals, *Australia* . . . . . **60 C2** 17 30S 119 0 E
Roxas, *Phil.* . . . . . . . . . . . . . . . **37 B6** 11 36N 122 49 E
Roxboro, *U.S.A.* . . . . . . . . . . . . **83 G6** 36 24N 78 59W
Roxborough, *Trin. & Tob.* . . . . . **93 J16** 11 15N 60 35W
Roxburgh, *N.Z.* . . . . . . . . . . . . **59 L2** 45 33S 169 19 E
Roxbury, *U.S.A.* . . . . . . . . . . . . **84 F7** 40 6N 77 39W
Roy, *Mont., U.S.A.* . . . . . . . . . . **76 C9** 47 20N 108 58W
Roy, *N. Mex., U.S.A.* . . . . . . . . **81 H2** 35 57N 104 12W
Roy, *Utah, U.S.A.* . . . . . . . . . . . **76 F7** 41 10N 112 2W
Royal Canal, *Ireland* . . . . . . . . . **10 C4** 53 30N 7 13W
Royal Leamington Spa, *U.K.* . . . **13 E6** 52 18N 1 31W
Royal Natal △, *S. Africa* . . . . . . **57 D4** 28 43S 28 51 E
Royal Tunbridge Wells, *U.K.* . . . **13 F8** 51 7N 0 16 E
Royale, Isle, *U.S.A.* . . . . . . . . . **80 B10** 48 0N 88 54W
Royan, *France* . . . . . . . . . . . . . **20 D3** 45 37N 1 2W
Royston, *U.K.* . . . . . . . . . . . . . . **13 E7** 52 3N 0 0W
Rozdilna, *Ukraine* . . . . . . . . . . **17 E16** 46 50N 30 2 E
Rozhyshche, *Ukraine* . . . . . . . . **17 C13** 50 54N 25 15 E
Rtishchevo, *Russia* . . . . . . . . . . **18 D7** 52 18N 43 46 E
Ruacaná, *Namibia* . . . . . . . . . . **56 B1** 17 27S 14 21 E
Ruaha △, *Tanzania* . . . . . . . . . . **54 D3** 7 41S 34 30 E
Ruahine Ra., *N.Z.* . . . . . . . . . . . **59 H6** 39 55S 176 2 E
Ruapehu, *N.Z.* . . . . . . . . . . . . . **59 H5** 39 17S 175 35 E
Ruapuke I., *N.Z.* . . . . . . . . . . . . **59 M2** 46 46S 168 31 E
Ruâq, W. →, *Egypt* . . . . . . . . . **46 F2** 30 0N 33 49 E
Rub' al Khālī, *Si. Arabia* . . . . . . **47 D4** 19 0N 48 0 E
Rubeho Mts., *Tanzania* . . . . . . . **54 D4** 6 50S 36 25 E
Rubh a' Mhail, *U.K.* . . . . . . . . . **11 F2** 55 56N 6 8W
Rubha Hunish, *U.K.* . . . . . . . . . **11 D2** 57 42N 6 20W
Rubha Robhanais = Lewis, Butt
  of, *U.K.* . . . . . . . . . . . . . . . . . **11 C2** 58 31N 6 16W
Rubicon →, *U.S.A.* . . . . . . . . . . **78 G5** 38 53N 121 4W
Rubio, *Venezuela* . . . . . . . . . . . **92 B4** 7 43N 72 22W
Rubondo △, *Tanzania* . . . . . . . . **54 C3** 2 18S 31 58 E
Rubtsovsk, *Russia* . . . . . . . . . . **28 D9** 51 30N 81 10 E
Ruby L., *U.S.A.* . . . . . . . . . . . . . **76 F6** 40 10N 115 28W
Ruby Mts., *U.S.A.* . . . . . . . . . . . **76 F6** 40 30N 115 20W
Rubyvale, *Australia* . . . . . . . . . **62 C4** 23 25S 147 42 E
Rūd Sar, *Iran* . . . . . . . . . . . . . . **45 B6** 37 8N 50 18 E
Rudall, *Australia* . . . . . . . . . . . . **63 E2** 33 43S 136 17 E
Rudall →, *Australia* . . . . . . . . . **60 D3** 22 34S 122 13 E
Rudall River △, *Australia* . . . . . . **60 D3** 22 38S 122 30 E
Rudewa, *Tanzania* . . . . . . . . . . **55 E3** 10 7S 34 40 E
Rudnyy, *Kazakhstan* . . . . . . . . . **28 D7** 52 57N 63 7 E
Rudolfa, Ostrov, *Russia* . . . . . . **28 A6** 81 45N 58 30 E
Rudyard, *U.S.A.* . . . . . . . . . . . . **82 B3** 46 14N 84 36W
Ruenya →, *Africa* . . . . . . . . . . . **55 F3** 16 24S 33 48 E
Rufiji →, *Tanzania* . . . . . . . . . . **54 D4** 7 50S 39 15 E
Rufino, *Argentina* . . . . . . . . . . . **94 C3** 34 20S 62 50W
Rufunsa, *Zambia* . . . . . . . . . . . **55 F2** 15 4S 29 34 E
Rugby, *U.K.* . . . . . . . . . . . . . . . **13 E6** 52 23N 1 16W
Rugby, *U.S.A.* . . . . . . . . . . . . . . **80 A5** 48 22N 100 0W
Rügen, *Germany* . . . . . . . . . . . **16 A7** 54 22N 13 24 E
Ruhengeri, *Rwanda* . . . . . . . . . **54 C2** 1 30S 29 36 E
Ruhnu, *Estonia* . . . . . . . . . . . . . **9 H20** 57 48N 23 15 E
Ruhr →, *Germany* . . . . . . . . . . **16 C4** 51 27N 6 43 E
Ruhuhu →, *Tanzania* . . . . . . . . **55 E3** 10 31S 34 34 E
Ruidoso, *U.S.A.* . . . . . . . . . . . . **77 K11** 33 20N 105 41W
Rujm Tal'at al Jamā'ah, *Jordan* . **46 E4** 30 24N 35 30 E
Ruk, *Pakistan* . . . . . . . . . . . . . . **42 F3** 27 50N 68 42 E
Rukhla, *Pakistan* . . . . . . . . . . . **42 C4** 32 27N 71 57 E
Ruki →, *Dem. Rep. of the Congo* **52 E3** 0 5N 18 17 E
Rukwa □, *Tanzania* . . . . . . . . . . **54 D3** 7 0S 31 30 E
Rukwa, L., *Tanzania* . . . . . . . . . **54 D3** 8 0S 32 20 E
Rulhieres, C., *Australia* . . . . . . . **60 B4** 13 56S 127 22 E
Rum = Rhum, *U.K.* . . . . . . . . . . **11 E2** 57 0N 6 20W
Rum, *Jordan* . . . . . . . . . . . . . . . **46 F4** 29 39N 35 26 E
Rum Cay, *Bahamas* . . . . . . . . . **89 B5** 23 40N 74 58W
Rum Jungle, *Australia* . . . . . . . . **60 B5** 13 0S 130 59 E
Ruma, *Kenya* . . . . . . . . . . . . . . **54 C3** 0 39S 34 18 E
Rumāh, *Si. Arabia* . . . . . . . . . . **44 E5** 25 29N 47 10 E
Rumania ■, *Europe* . . . . . . . . . **17 F12** 46 0N 25 0 E
Rumaylah, *Iraq* . . . . . . . . . . . . . **44 D5** 30 47N 47 37 E
Rumbêk, *Sudan* . . . . . . . . . . . . **51 G11** 6 54N 29 37 E
Rumford, *U.S.A.* . . . . . . . . . . . . **83 C10** 44 33N 70 33W
Rumia, *Poland* . . . . . . . . . . . . . **17 A10** 54 37N 18 25 E
Rumoi, *Japan* . . . . . . . . . . . . . . **30 C10** 43 56N 141 39 E
Rumonge, *Burundi* . . . . . . . . . . **54 C2** 3 59S 29 26 E
Rumson, *U.S.A.* . . . . . . . . . . . . **85 F11** 40 23N 74 0W
Rumuruti, *Kenya* . . . . . . . . . . . **54 B4** 0 17N 36 32 E
Runan, *China* . . . . . . . . . . . . . . **34 H8** 33 0N 114 30 E
Runanga, *N.Z.* . . . . . . . . . . . . . **59 K3** 42 25S 171 15 E
Runaway, C., *N.Z.* . . . . . . . . . . **59 G6** 37 32S 177 59 E
Runaway Bay, *Jamaica* . . . . . . . **88 a** 18 27N 77 20W
Runcorn, *U.K.* . . . . . . . . . . . . . . **12 D5** 53 21N 2 44W
Rundu, *Namibia* . . . . . . . . . . . . **56 B2** 17 52S 19 43 E
Rungwa, *Tanzania* . . . . . . . . . . **54 D3** 6 55S 33 32 E
Rungwa →, *Tanzania* . . . . . . . . **54 D3** 7 36S 31 50 E
Rungwa △, *Tanzania* . . . . . . . . **54 D3** 7 36S 31 50 E
Rungwe, *Tanzania* . . . . . . . . . . **55 D3** 9 11S 33 32 E
Rungwe, Mt., *Tanzania* . . . . . . . **52 F6** 9 8S 33 40 E
Runton Ra., *Australia* . . . . . . . . **60 D3** 23 31S 123 6 E
Ruoqiang, *China* . . . . . . . . . . . **32 C3** 38 55N 88 10 E
Rupa, *India* . . . . . . . . . . . . . . . . **41 F18** 27 15N 92 21 E
Rupar, *India* . . . . . . . . . . . . . . . . **42 D7** 31 2N 76 38 E
Rupat, *Indonesia* . . . . . . . . . . . **36 D2** 1 45N 101 40 E
Rupen →, *India* . . . . . . . . . . . . **42 H4** 23 28N 71 31 E
Rupert, *U.S.A.* . . . . . . . . . . . . . **76 E7** 42 37N 113 41W
Rupert →, *Canada* . . . . . . . . . . **72 B4** 51 29N 78 45W
Rupert B., *Canada* . . . . . . . . . . **72 B4** 51 35N 79 0W
Rupert House = Waskaganish,
  *Canada* . . . . . . . . . . . . . . . . . **72 B4** 51 30N 78 40W
Rupsa, *India* . . . . . . . . . . . . . . . **43 J12** 21 37N 87 1 E
Rurrenabaque, *Bolivia* . . . . . . . **92 F5** 14 30S 67 32W
Rusambo, *Zimbabwe* . . . . . . . . **55 F3** 16 30S 32 4 E
Rusape, *Zimbabwe* . . . . . . . . . . **55 F3** 18 35S 32 8 E
Ruschuk = Ruse, *Bulgaria* . . . . **23 C12** 43 48N 25 59 E
Ruse, *Bulgaria* . . . . . . . . . . . . . **23 C12** 43 48N 25 59 E
Rush, *Ireland* . . . . . . . . . . . . . . **10 C5** 53 31N 6 6W
Rushan, *China* . . . . . . . . . . . . . **35 F11** 36 56N 121 30 E
Rushden, *U.K.* . . . . . . . . . . . . . **13 E7** 52 18N 0 35W

Rushmore, Mt., *U.S.A.* **80 D3** 43 53N 103 28W
Rushville, *Ill., U.S.A.* **80 E9** 40 7N 90 34W
Rushville, *Ind., U.S.A.* **82 F3** 39 37N 85 27W
Rushville, *Nebr., U.S.A.* **80 D3** 42 43N 102 28W
Russas, *Brazil* **93 D11** 4 55S 37 50W
Russell, *Canada* **71 C8** 50 50N 101 20W
Russell, *Kans., U.S.A.* **80 F5** 38 54N 98 52W
Russell, *N.Y., U.S.A.* **85 B9** 44 27N 75 9W
Russell, *Pa., U.S.A.* **84 E5** 41 56N 79 8W
Russell Cave ⌓, *U.S.A.* **83 H3** 34 59N 85 49W
Russell L., *Man., Canada* **71 B8** 56 15N 101 30W
Russell L., *N.W.T., Canada* **70 A5** 63 5N 115 44W
Russellkonda, *India* **41 K14** 19 57N 84 42 E
Russellville, *Ala., U.S.A.* **83 H2** 34 30N 87 44W
Russellville, *Ark., U.S.A.* **81 H8** 35 17N 93 8W
Russellville, *Ky., U.S.A.* **83 G2** 36 51N 86 53W
Russia ■, *Eurasia* **29 C11** 62 0N 105 0 E
Russian →, *U.S.A.* **78 G3** 38 27N 123 8W
Russkoye Ustie, *Russia* **4 B15** 71 0N 149 0 E
Rustam, *Pakistan* **42 B5** 34 25N 72 13 E
Rustam Shahr, *Pakistan* **42 F2** 26 58N 66 6 E
Rustavi, *Georgia* **19 F8** 41 30N 45 0 E
Rustenburg, *S. Africa* **56 D4** 25 41S 27 14 E
Ruston, *U.S.A.* **81 J8** 32 32N 92 38W
Rutana, *Burundi* **54 C3** 3 55S 30 0 E
Ruteng, *Indonesia* **37 F6** 8 35S 120 30 E
Ruth, *U.S.A.* **84 C2** 43 42N 82 45W
Rutherford, *U.S.A.* **78 G4** 38 26N 122 24W
Rutland, *U.S.A.* **85 C12** 43 37N 72 58W
Rutland □, *U.K.* **13 E7** 52 38N 0 40W
Rutland Water, *U.K.* **13 E7** 52 39N 0 38W
Rutledge →, *Canada* **71 A6** 61 4N 112 0W
Rutledge L., *Canada* **71 A6** 61 33N 110 47W
Rutshuru, *Dem. Rep. of the Congo* **54 C2** 1 13S 29 25 E
Ruvu, *Tanzania* **54 D4** 6 49S 38 43 E
Ruvu →, *Tanzania* **54 D4** 6 23S 38 52 E
Ruvuba △, *Burundi* **54 C2** 3 3S 29 33 E
Ruvuma □, *Tanzania* **55 E4** 10 20S 36 0 E
Ruvuma →, *Tanzania* **55 E5** 10 29S 40 28 E
Ruwais, *U.A.E.* **45 E7** 24 5N 52 50 E
Ruwenzori, *Africa* **54 B2** 0 30N 29 55 E
Ruwenzori △, *Uganda* **54 B2** 0 20S 30 0 E
Ruya →, *Zimbabwe* **57 B5** 16 27S 32 5 E
Ruyigi, *Burundi* **54 C3** 3 29S 30 15 E
Ružomberok, *Slovak Rep.* **17 D10** 49 3N 19 17 E
Rwanda ■, *Africa* **54 C3** 2 0S 30 0 E
Ryan, L., *U.K.* **11 G3** 55 0N 5 2W
Ryazan, *Russia* **18 D6** 54 40N 39 40 E
Ryazhsk, *Russia* **18 D7** 53 45N 40 3 E
Rybache = Rybachye, *Kazakhstan* **28 E9** 46 40N 81 20 E
Rybachiy Poluostrov, *Russia* **18 A5** 69 43N 32 0 E
Rybachye, *Kazakhstan* **28 E9** 46 40N 81 20 E
Rybinsk, *Russia* **18 C6** 58 5N 38 50 E
Rybinskoye Vdkhr., *Russia* **18 C6** 58 30N 38 25 E
Rybnitsa = Râbniţa, *Moldova* **17 E15** 47 45N 29 0 E
Rycroft, *Canada* **70 B5** 55 45N 118 40W
Ryde, *U.K.* **13 G6** 50 43N 1 9W
Ryderwood, *U.S.A.* **78 D3** 46 23N 123 3W
Rye, *U.K.* **13 G8** 50 57N 0 45 E
Rye →, *U.K.* **12 C7** 54 11N 0 44W
Rye Bay, *U.K.* **13 G8** 50 52N 0 49 E
Rye Patch Reservoir, *U.S.A.* **76 F4** 40 28N 118 19W
Ryegate, *U.S.A.* **76 C9** 46 18N 109 15W
Ryley, *Canada* **70 C6** 53 17N 112 26W
Rylstone, *Australia* **63 E4** 32 46S 149 58 E
Ryōtsu, *Japan* **30 E9** 38 5N 138 26 E
Rypin, *Poland* **17 B10** 53 3N 19 25 E
Ryūgasaki, *Japan* **31 G10** 35 54N 140 11 E
Ryūkyū Is. = Ryūkyū-rettō, *Japan* **31 M3** 26 0N 126 0 E
Ryūkyū-rettō, *Japan* **31 M3** 26 0N 126 0 E
Rzeszów, *Poland* **17 C11** 50 5N 21 58 E
Rzhev, *Russia* **18 C5** 56 20N 34 20 E


# S


Sa, *Thailand* **38 C3** 18 34N 100 45 E
Sa Canal, *Spain* **24 C7** 38 51N 1 23 E
Sa Conillera, *Spain* **24 C7** 38 59N 1 13 E
Sa Dec, *Vietnam* **39 G5** 10 20N 105 46 E
Sa Dragonera, *Spain* **24 B9** 39 35N 2 19 E
Sa Mesquida, *Spain* **24 B11** 39 55N 4 16 E
Sa Savina, *Spain* **24 C7** 38 44N 1 25 E
Sa'ādatābād, *Fārs, Iran* **45 D7** 30 10N 53 5 E
Sa'ādatābād, *Hormozgān, Iran* **45 D7** 28 3N 55 53 E
Sa'ādatābād, *Kermān, Iran* **45 D7** 29 40N 55 51 E
Saale →, *Germany* **16 C6** 51 56N 11 54 E
Saalfeld, *Germany* **16 C6** 50 38N 11 21 E
Saanich, *Canada* **78 B3** 48 29N 123 26W
Saar →, *Europe* **15 E6** 49 41N 6 32 E
Saarbrücken, *Germany* **16 D4** 49 14N 6 59 E
Saaremaa, *Estonia* **9 G20** 58 30N 22 30 E
Saarijärvi, *Finland* **9 E21** 62 43N 25 16 E
Saariselkä, *Finland* **8 B23** 68 16N 28 15 E
Sab 'Ābar, *Syria* **44 C3** 33 46N 37 41 E
Saba, *W. Indies* **89 C7** 17 38N 63 14W
Šabac, *Serbia & M.* **23 B8** 44 48N 19 42 E
Sabadell, *Spain* **21 B7** 41 28N 2 7 E
Sabah □, *Malaysia* **36 C5** 6 0N 117 0 E
Sabak Bernam, *Malaysia* **39 L3** 3 46N 100 58 E
Sabalān, Kūhhā-ye, *Iran* **44 B5** 38 15N 47 45 E
Sabalana, Kepulauan, *Indonesia* **37 F5** 6 45S 118 50 E
Sábana de la Mar, *Dom. Rep.* **89 C6** 19 7N 69 24W
Sábanalarga, *Colombia* **92 A4** 10 38N 74 55W
Sabang, *Indonesia* **36 C1** 5 50N 95 15 E
Sabará, *Brazil* **93 G10** 19 55S 43 46W
Sabarmati →, *India* **42 H5** 22 18N 72 22 E
Sabattis, *U.S.A.* **85 B10** 44 6N 74 40W
Saberania, *Indonesia* **37 E9** 2 5S 138 18 E
Sabhah, *Libya* **51 C8** 27 9N 14 29 E
Sabi →, *India* **42 E7** 28 29N 76 44 E
Sabie, *S. Africa* **57 D5** 25 10S 30 48 E
Sabinal, *Mexico* **86 A3** 30 58N 107 25W
Sabinal, *U.S.A.* **81 L5** 29 19N 99 28W
Sabinas, *Mexico* **86 B4** 27 50N 101 10W
Sabinas →, *Mexico* **86 B4** 27 37N 100 42W
Sabinas Hidalgo, *Mexico* **86 B4** 26 33N 100 10W
Sabine →, *U.S.A.* **81 L8** 29 59N 93 47W
Sabine L., *U.S.A.* **81 L8** 29 53N 93 51W
Sabine Pass, *U.S.A.* **81 L8** 29 44N 93 54W
Sabinsville, *U.S.A.* **84 E7** 41 52N 77 31W
Sablayan, *Phil.* **37 B6** 12 50N 120 50 E
Sable, *Canada* **73 A6** 55 30N 68 21W
Sable, C., *Canada* **73 D6** 43 29N 65 38W
Sable, C., *U.S.A.* **75 E10** 25 9N 81 8W
Sable I., *Canada* **73 D8** 44 0N 60 0W
Sabrina Coast, *Antarctica* **5 C9** 68 0S 120 0 E
Sabulubbek, *Indonesia* **36 E1** 1 36S 98 40 E
Sabzevār, *Iran* **45 B8** 36 15N 57 40 E
Sabzvārān, *Iran* **45 D8** 28 45N 57 50 E
Sac City, *U.S.A.* **80 D7** 42 25N 95 0W
Săcele, *Romania* **17 F13** 45 37N 25 41 E
Sachigo →, *Canada* **72 A2** 55 6N 88 58W
Sachigo, L., *Canada* **72 B1** 53 50N 92 12W
Sachsen □, *Germany* **16 C7** 50 55N 13 10 E
Sachsen-Anhalt □, *Germany* **16 C7** 52 0N 12 0 E
Sackets Harbor, *U.S.A.* **85 C8** 43 57N 76 7W
Sackville, *Canada* **73 C7** 45 54N 64 22W
Saco, *Maine, U.S.A.* **83 D10** 43 30N 70 27W
Saco, *Mont., U.S.A.* **76 B10** 48 28N 107 21W
Sacramento, *U.S.A.* **78 G5** 38 35N 121 29W
Sacramento →, *U.S.A.* **78 G5** 38 3N 121 56W
Sacramento Mts., *U.S.A.* **77 K11** 32 30N 105 30W
Sacramento Valley, *U.S.A.* **78 G5** 39 30N 122 0W
Sada-Misaki, *Japan* **31 H6** 33 20N 132 1 E
Sadabad, *India* **42 F8** 27 27N 78 3 E
Sadani, *Tanzania* **54 D4** 5 58S 38 35 E
Sadao, *Thailand* **39 J3** 6 38N 100 26 E
Sadd el Aali, *Egypt* **51 D12** 23 54N 32 54 E
Saddle Mt., *U.S.A.* **78 E3** 45 58N 123 41W
Sadimi, *Dem. Rep. of the Congo* **55 D1** 9 25S 23 32 E
Sado, *Japan* **30 F9** 38 0N 138 25 E
Sadon, *Burma* **41 G20** 25 28N 97 55 E
Sadra, *India* **42 H5** 23 21N 72 43 E
Sadri, *India* **42 G5** 25 11N 73 26 E
Sæby, *Denmark* **9 H14** 57 21N 10 30 E
Saegertown, *U.S.A.* **84 E4** 41 43N 80 9W
Şafājah, *Si. Arabia* **44 E3** 26 25N 39 0 E
Säffle, *Sweden* **9 G15** 59 8N 12 55 E
Safford, *U.S.A.* **77 K9** 32 50N 109 43W
Saffron Walden, *U.K.* **13 E8** 52 1N 0 16 E
Safi, *Morocco* **50 B4** 32 18N 9 20W
Şafīābād, *Iran* **45 B8** 36 45N 57 58 E
Safid Dasht, *Iran* **45 C6** 33 27N 48 11 E
Safid Kūh, *Afghan.* **40 B3** 34 45N 63 0 E
Safid Rūd →, *Iran* **45 B6** 37 23N 50 11 E
Safipur, *India* **43 F9** 26 44N 80 21 E
Şafwān, *Iraq* **44 D5** 30 7N 47 43 E
Sag Harbor, *U.S.A.* **85 F12** 41 0N 72 18W
Saga, *Japan* **31 H5** 33 15N 130 16 E
Saga □, *Japan* **31 H5** 33 15N 130 20 E
Sagae, *Japan* **30 E10** 38 22N 140 17 E
Sagamartha = Everest, Mt., *Nepal* **43 E12** 28 5N 86 58 E
Sagamore, *U.S.A.* **84 F5** 40 46N 79 14W
Sagar, *Karnataka, India* **40 M9** 14 14N 75 6 E
Sagar, *Mad. P., India* **43 H8** 23 50N 78 44 E
Sagara, L., *Tanzania* **54 D3** 5 20S 31 0 E
Saginaw, *U.S.A.* **82 D4** 43 26N 83 56W
Saginaw →, *U.S.A.* **82 D4** 43 39N 83 51W
Saginaw B., *U.S.A.* **82 D4** 43 50N 83 40W
Saglouc = Salluit, *Canada* **69 B12** 62 14N 75 38W
Sagō-ri, *S. Korea* **35 G14** 35 25N 126 49 E
Sagua la Grande, *Cuba* **88 B3** 22 50N 80 10W
Saguache, *U.S.A.* **77 G10** 38 5N 106 8W
Saguaro △, *U.S.A.* **77 K8** 32 12N 110 38W
Saguenay →, *Canada* **73 C5** 48 22N 71 0W
Sagunt, *Spain* **21 C5** 39 42N 0 18W
Sagunto = Sagunt, *Spain* **21 C5** 39 42N 0 18W
Sagwara, *India* **42 H6** 23 41N 74 1 E
Sahagún, *Spain* **21 A3** 42 18N 5 2W
Saḩam al Jawlān, *Syria* **46 C4** 32 45N 35 55 E
Sahamandrevo, *Madag.* **57 C8** 23 15S 45 35 E
Sahand, Kūh-e, *Iran* **44 B5** 37 44N 46 27 E
Sahara, *Africa* **50 D6** 23 0N 5 0 E
Saharan Atlas = Saharien, Atlas, *Algeria* **50 B6** 33 30N 1 0 E
Saharanpur, *India* **42 E7** 29 58N 77 33 E
Saharien, Atlas, *Algeria* **50 B6** 33 30N 1 0 E
Saharsa, *India* **43 G12** 25 53N 86 36 E
Sahasinaka, *Madag.* **57 C8** 21 49S 47 49 E
Sahaswan, *India* **43 E8** 28 5N 78 45 E
Sahel, *Africa* **50 E5** 16 0N 5 0 E
Sahibganj, *India* **43 G12** 25 12N 87 40 E
Şāḩilīyah, *Iraq* **44 C4** 33 43N 42 42 E
Sahiwal, *Pakistan* **42 D5** 30 45N 73 8 E
Şaḩneh, *Iran* **44 C5** 34 29N 47 41 E
Sahrawi = Western Sahara ■, *Africa* **50 D3** 25 0N 13 0W
Sahuaripa, *Mexico* **86 B3** 29 0N 109 13W
Sahuarita, *U.S.A.* **77 L8** 31 57N 110 58W
Sahuayo, *Mexico* **86 C4** 20 4N 102 43W
Sai →, *India* **43 G10** 25 39N 82 47 E
Sai Buri, *Thailand* **39 J3** 6 43N 101 45 E
Sai Kung, *China* **33 G11** 22 23N 114 16 E
Sa'id Bundas, *Sudan* **51 G10** 8 24N 24 48 E
Sa'īdābād = Sīrjān, *Iran* **45 D7** 29 30N 55 45 E
Sa'īdābād, *Iran* **45 B7** 36 8N 54 11 E
Sa'īdīyeh, *Iran* **45 B6** 36 20N 48 55 E
Saidpur, *Bangla.* **41 G16** 25 48N 89 0 E
Saidpur, *India* **43 G10** 25 33N 83 11 E
Saidu, *Pakistan* **43 B5** 34 43N 72 24 E
Saigon = Thanh Pho Ho Chi Minh, *Vietnam* **39 G6** 10 58N 106 40 E
Saijō, *Japan* **31 H6** 33 55N 133 11 E
Saikai △, *Japan* **31 H4** 33 12N 129 36 E
Saikanosy Masoala, *Madag.* **57 B9** 15 45S 50 10 E
Saikhoa Ghat, *India* **41 F19** 27 50N 95 40 E
Saiki, *Japan* **31 H5** 32 58N 131 51 E
Sailana, *India* **42 H6** 23 28N 74 55 E
Sailolof, *Indonesia* **37 E8** 1 15S 130 46 E
Saimaa, *Finland* **9 F23** 61 15N 28 15 E
Saimen = Saimaa, *Finland* **9 F23** 61 15N 28 15 E
Şa'in Dezh, *Iran* **44 B5** 36 40N 46 25 E
St. Abb's Head, *U.K.* **11 F6** 55 55N 2 8W
St. Alban's, *Canada* **73 C8** 47 51N 55 50W
St. Albans, *U.K.* **13 F7** 51 45N 0 19W
St. Albans, *Vt., U.S.A.* **85 B11** 44 49N 73 5W
St. Albans, *W. Va., U.S.A.* **82 F5** 38 23N 81 50W
St. Alban's Head, *U.K.* **13 G5** 50 34N 2 4W
St. Albert, *Canada* **70 C6** 53 37N 113 32W
St. Andrew's, *Canada* **73 C8** 47 45N 59 15W
St. Andrews, *U.K.* **11 E6** 56 20N 2 47W
St-Anicet, *Canada* **85 A10** 45 8N 74 22W
St. Anns B., *Canada* **73 C7** 46 22N 60 25W
St. Ann's Bay, *Jamaica* **88 a** 18 26N 77 12W
St. Anthony, *Canada* **73 B8** 51 22N 55 35W
St. Anthony, *U.S.A.* **76 E8** 43 58N 111 41W
St-Antoine, *Canada* **73 C7** 46 22N 64 45W
St. Arnaud, *Australia* **63 F3** 36 40S 143 16 E
St-Augustin, *Canada* **73 B8** 51 13N 58 38W
St-Augustin →, *Canada* **73 B8** 51 16N 58 40W
St. Augustine, *U.S.A.* **83 L5** 29 54N 81 19W
St. Austell, *U.K.* **13 G3** 50 20N 4 47W
St. Barbe, *Canada* **73 B8** 51 12N 56 46W
St-Barthélemy, *W. Indies* **89 C7** 17 50N 62 50W
St. Bees Hd., *U.K.* **12 C4** 54 31N 3 38W
St. Bees I., *Australia* **62 J7** 20 56S 149 26 E
St. Bride's, *Canada* **73 C9** 46 56N 54 10W
St. Brides B., *U.K.* **13 F2** 51 49N 5 9W
St-Brieuc, *France* **20 B2** 48 30N 2 46W
St. Catharines, *Canada* **84 C5** 43 10N 79 15W
St. Catherines I., *U.S.A.* **83 K5** 31 40N 81 10W
St. Catherine's Pt., *U.K.* **13 G6** 50 34N 1 18W
St-Chamond, *France* **20 D6** 45 28N 4 31 E
St. Charles, *Ill., U.S.A.* **82 E1** 41 54N 88 19W
St. Charles, *Mo., U.S.A.* **80 F9** 38 47N 90 29W
St. Charles, *Va., U.S.A.* **82 F7** 36 48N 83 4W
St. Christopher-Nevis = St. Kitts & Nevis ■, *W. Indies* **89 C7** 17 20N 62 40W
St. Clair, *Mich., U.S.A.* **84 D2** 42 50N 82 30W
St. Clair, *Pa., U.S.A.* **85 F8** 40 43N 76 12W
St. Clair →, *U.S.A.* **84 D2** 42 38N 82 31W
St. Clair, L., *Canada* **72 D3** 42 30N 82 45W
St. Clair, L., *U.S.A.* **84 D2** 42 27N 82 39W
St. Clairsville, *U.S.A.* **84 F4** 40 5N 80 54W
St. Claude, *Canada* **71 D9** 49 40N 98 20W
St. Clears, *U.K.* **13 F3** 51 49N 4 31W
St-Clet, *Canada* **85 A10** 45 21N 74 13W
St. Cloud, *Fla., U.S.A.* **83 L5** 28 15N 81 17W
St. Cloud, *Minn., U.S.A.* **80 C7** 45 34N 94 10W
St. Cricq, C., *Australia* **61 E1** 25 17S 113 6 E
St. Croix, *U.S. Virgin Is.* **89 C7** 17 45N 64 45W
St. Croix →, *U.S.A.* **80 C8** 44 45N 92 48W
St. Croix Falls, *U.S.A.* **80 C8** 45 24N 92 38W
St. David's, *Canada* **73 C8** 48 12N 58 52W
St. David's, *U.K.* **13 F2** 51 53N 5 16W
St. David's Head, *U.K.* **13 F2** 51 54N 5 19W
St-Denis, *France* **20 B5** 48 56N 2 22 E
St-Dizier, *France* **20 B6** 48 38N 4 56 E
St. Elias, Mt., *U.S.A.* **68 B5** 60 18N 140 56W
St. Elias Mts., *N. Amer.* **70 A1** 60 33N 139 28W
St-Étienne, *France* **20 D6** 45 27N 4 22 E
St. Eugène, *Canada* **85 A10** 45 30N 74 28W
St. Eustatius, *W. Indies* **89 C7** 17 20N 63 0W
St-Félicien, *Canada* **72 C5** 48 40N 72 25W
St-Flour, *France* **20 D5** 45 2N 3 6 E
St. Francis, *U.S.A.* **80 F4** 39 47N 101 48W
St. Francis →, *U.S.A.* **81 H9** 34 38N 90 36W
St. Francis, C., *S. Africa* **56 E3** 34 14S 24 49 E
St. Francisville, *U.S.A.* **81 K9** 30 47N 91 23W
St-François, L., *Canada* **85 A10** 45 10N 74 22W
St-Gabriel, *Canada* **72 C5** 46 17N 73 24W
St. Gallen = Sankt Gallen, *Switz.* **20 C8** 47 26N 9 22 E
St-Gaudens, *France* **20 E4** 43 6N 0 44 E
St. George, *Australia* **63 D4** 28 1S 148 30 E
St. George, *Canada* **73 C6** 45 11N 66 50W
St. George, *S.C., U.S.A.* **83 J5** 33 11N 80 35W
St. George, *Utah, U.S.A.* **77 H7** 37 6N 113 35W
St. George, C., *Canada* **73 C8** 48 30N 59 16W
St. George, C., *U.S.A.* **83 L3** 29 40N 85 5W
St. George Ra., *Australia* **60 C4** 18 40S 125 0 E
St. George's, *Canada* **73 C8** 48 26N 58 31W
St-Georges, *Canada* **73 C5** 46 8N 70 40W
St. George's, *Grenada* **89 D7** 12 5N 61 43W
St. George's B., *Canada* **73 C8** 48 24N 58 53W
St. Georges Basin, *N.S.W., Australia* **63 F5** 35 7S 150 36 E
St. Georges Basin, *W. Austral., Australia* **60 C4** 15 23S 125 2 E
St. George's Channel, *Europe* **10 E6** 52 0N 6 0W
St. Georges Hd., *Australia* **63 F5** 35 12S 150 42 E
St. Gotthard P. = San Gottardo, P. del, *Switz.* **20 C8** 46 33N 8 33 E
St. Helena, *Atl. Oc.* **48 H3** 15 58S 5 42W
St. Helena, *U.S.A.* **76 G2** 38 30N 122 28W
St. Helena, Mt., *U.S.A.* **78 G4** 38 40N 122 36W
St. Helena B., *S. Africa* **56 E2** 32 40S 18 10 E
St. Helens, *Australia* **63 G4** 41 20S 148 15 E
St. Helens, *U.K.* **12 D5** 53 27N 2 44W
St. Helens, *U.S.A.* **78 E4** 45 52N 122 48W
St. Helens, Mt., *U.S.A.* **78 D4** 46 12N 122 12W
St. Helier, *U.K.* **13 H5** 49 10N 2 7W
St-Hubert, *Belgium* **15 D5** 50 2N 5 23 E
St-Hyacinthe, *Canada* **72 C5** 45 40N 72 58W
St. Ignace, *U.S.A.* **82 C3** 45 52N 84 44W
St. Ignace I., *Canada* **72 C2** 48 45N 88 0W
St. Ignatius, *U.S.A.* **76 C6** 47 19N 114 6W
St. Ives, *Cambs., U.K.* **13 E7** 52 20N 0 4W
St. Ives, *Corn., U.K.* **13 G2** 50 12N 5 30W
St. James, *U.S.A.* **80 D7** 43 59N 94 38W
St-Jean →, *Canada* **73 B7** 50 17N 64 20W
St-Jean, L., *Canada* **73 C5** 48 40N 72 0W
St-Jean-Port-Joli, *Canada* **73 C5** 47 15N 70 13W
St-Jean-sur-Richelieu, *Canada* **85 A11** 45 20N 73 20W
St-Jérôme, *Canada* **72 C5** 45 47N 74 0W
St. John, *Canada* **73 C6** 45 20N 66 8W
St. John, *U.S.A.* **81 G5** 38 0N 98 46W
St. John →, *U.S.A.* **83 C12** 45 12N 66 5W
St. John, C., *Canada* **73 C8** 50 0N 55 32W
St. John I., *U.S. Virgin Is.* **89 e** 18 20N 64 42W
St. John's, *Antigua & B.* **89 C7** 17 6N 61 51W
St. John's, *Canada* **73 C9** 47 35N 52 40W
St. Johns, *Ariz., U.S.A.* **77 J9** 34 30N 109 22W
St. Johns, *Mich., U.S.A.* **82 D3** 43 0N 84 33W
St. Johns →, *U.S.A.* **83 K5** 30 24N 81 24W
St. John's Pt., *Ireland* **10 B3** 54 34N 8 27W
St. Johnsbury, *U.S.A.* **85 B12** 44 25N 72 1W
St. Johnsville, *U.S.A.* **85 D10** 43 0N 74 43W
St-Joseph, *Martinique* **88 c** 14 39N 61 4W
St. Joseph, *La., U.S.A.* **81 K9** 31 55N 91 14W
St. Joseph, *Mo., U.S.A.* **80 F7** 39 46N 94 50W
St. Joseph →, *U.S.A.* **82 D2** 42 7N 86 29W
St. Joseph, I., *Canada* **72 C3** 46 12N 83 58W
St. Joseph, L., *Canada* **72 B1** 51 10N 90 35W
St-Jovite, *Canada* **72 C5** 46 8N 74 38W
St. Kilda, *U.K.* **14 C2** 57 49N 8 34W
St. Kitts & Nevis ■, *W. Indies* **89 C7** 17 20N 62 40W
St. Laurent, *Canada* **71 C9** 50 25N 97 58W
St. Lawrence, *Australia* **62 C4** 22 16S 149 31 E
St. Lawrence, *Canada* **73 C8** 46 54N 55 23W
St. Lawrence →, *Canada* **73 C6** 49 30N 66 0W
St. Lawrence, Gulf of, *Canada* **73 C7** 48 25N 62 0W
St. Lawrence I., *U.S.A.* **68 B3** 63 30N 170 30W
St. Lawrence Islands △, *Canada* **85 B9** 44 27N 75 52W
St. Leonard, *Canada* **73 C6** 47 12N 67 58W
St. Lewis →, *Canada* **73 B8** 52 26N 56 11W
St-Lô, *France* **20 B3** 49 7N 1 5W
St-Louis, *Guadeloupe* **88 b** 15 56N 61 19W
St. Louis, *Senegal* **50 E2** 16 8N 16 27W
St. Louis, *U.S.A.* **80 F9** 38 37N 90 12W
St. Louis →, *U.S.A.* **80 B8** 47 15N 92 45W
St. Lucia ■, *W. Indies* **89 f** 14 0N 60 57W
St. Lucia, L., *S. Africa* **57 D5** 28 5S 32 30 E
St. Lucia Channel, *W. Indies* **89 D7** 14 15N 61 0W
St. Maarten ⊠, *W. Indies* **89 C7** 18 0N 63 5W
St. Magnus B., *U.K.* **11 A7** 60 25N 1 35W
St-Malo, *France* **20 B2** 48 39N 2 1W
St-Marc, *Haiti* **89 C5** 19 10N 72 41W
St. Maries, *U.S.A.* **76 C5** 47 19N 116 35W
St-Martin ⊠, *W. Indies* **89 C7** 18 0N 63 0W
St-Martin, C., *Martinique* **88 c** 14 52N 61 14W
St. Martin, L., *Canada* **71 C9** 51 40N 98 30W
St. Martins, *Barbados* **89 g** 13 5N 59 28W
St. Mary Pk., *Australia* **63 E2** 31 32S 138 34 E
St. Marys, *Australia* **63 G4** 41 35S 148 11 E
St. Marys, *Canada* **84 C3** 43 20N 81 10W
St. Mary's, *Corn., U.K.* **13 H1** 49 55N 6 18W
St. Mary's, *Orkney, U.K.* **11 C6** 58 54N 2 54W
St. Marys, *Ga., U.S.A.* **83 K5** 30 44N 81 33W
St. Marys, *Pa., U.S.A.* **84 E6** 41 26N 78 34W
St. Mary's, C., *Canada* **73 C9** 46 50N 54 12W
St. Mary's B., *Canada* **73 C9** 46 50N 53 50W
St. Marys Bay, *Canada* **73 D6** 44 25N 66 10W
St-Mathieu, Pte., *France* **20 B1** 48 20N 4 45W
St. Matthew I., *U.S.A.* **68 B2** 60 24N 172 42W
St-Maurice →, *Canada* **72 C5** 46 21N 72 31W
St. Mawes, *U.K.* **13 G2** 50 10N 5 2W
St-Nazaire, *France* **20 C2** 47 17N 2 12W
St. Neots, *U.K.* **13 E7** 52 14N 0 15W
St-Niklaas, *Belgium* **15 C4** 51 10N 4 8 E
St-Omer, *France* **20 A5** 50 45N 2 15 E
St-Pamphile, *Canada* **73 C6** 46 58N 69 48W
St-Pascal, *Canada* **73 C6** 47 32N 69 48W
St. Paul, *Canada* **70 C6** 54 0N 111 17W
St. Paul, *Minn., U.S.A.* **80 C8** 44 57N 93 6W
St. Paul, *Nebr., U.S.A.* **80 E5** 41 13N 98 27W
St-Paul →, *Canada* **73 B8** 51 27N 57 42W
St. Paul, I., *Ind. Oc.* **3 F13** 38 55S 77 34 E
St. Paul I., *Canada* **73 C7** 47 12N 60 9W
St. Peter, *U.S.A.* **80 C8** 44 20N 93 57W
St. Peter Port, *U.K.* **13 H5** 49 26N 2 33W
St. Peters, *N.S., Canada* **73 C7** 45 40N 60 53W
St. Peters, *P.E.I., Canada* **73 C7** 46 25N 62 35W
St. Petersburg = Sankt-Peterburg, *Russia* **18 C5** 59 55N 30 20 E
St. Petersburg, *U.S.A.* **83 M4** 27 46N 82 39W
St-Pie, *Canada* **85 A12** 45 30N 72 54W
St-Pierre, *Martinique* **88 c** 14 45N 61 10W
St-Pierre, *St-P. & M.* **73 C8** 46 46N 56 12W
St-Pierre, L., *Canada* **72 C5** 46 12N 72 52W
St-Pierre-et-Miquelon ⊠, *N. Amer.* **73 C8** 46 55N 56 10W
St-Quentin, *Canada* **73 C6** 47 30N 67 23W
St-Quentin, *France* **20 B5** 49 50N 3 16 E
St. Regis, *U.S.A.* **76 C6** 47 18N 115 6W
St. Sebastien, Tanjon' i, *Madag.* **57 A8** 12 26S 48 44 E
St-Siméon, *Canada* **73 C6** 47 51N 69 54W
St. Simons I., *U.S.A.* **83 K5** 31 12N 81 15W
St. Simons Island, *U.S.A.* **83 K5** 31 9N 81 22W
St. Stephen, *Canada* **73 C6** 45 16N 67 17W
St. Thomas, *Canada* **84 D3** 42 45N 81 10W
St. Thomas I., *U.S. Virgin Is.* **89 e** 18 20N 64 55W
St-Tite, *Canada* **72 C5** 46 45N 72 34W
St-Tropez, *France* **20 E7** 43 17N 6 38 E
St-Troud = St. Truiden, *Belgium* **15 D5** 50 48N 5 10 E
St. Truiden, *Belgium* **15 D5** 50 48N 5 10 E
St. Vincent, G., *Australia* **63 F2** 35 0S 138 0 E
St. Vincent & the Grenadines ■, *W. Indies* **89 D7** 13 0N 61 10W
St. Vincent Passage, *W. Indies* **89 D7** 13 30N 61 0W
St-Vith, *Belgium* **15 D6** 50 17N 6 9 E
St. Walburg, *Canada* **71 C7** 53 39N 109 12W
Ste-Agathe-des-Monts, *Canada* **72 C5** 46 3N 74 17W
Ste-Anne, *Guadeloupe* **88 b** 16 13N 61 24W
Ste-Anne, L., *Canada* **73 B6** 50 0N 67 42W
Ste-Anne-des-Monts-Tourelle, *Canada* **73 C6** 49 8N 66 30W
Ste. Genevieve, *U.S.A.* **80 G9** 37 59N 90 2W
Ste-Marguerite →, *Canada* **73 B6** 50 9N 66 36W
Ste-Marie, *Canada* **73 C5** 46 26N 71 0W
Ste-Marie, *Martinique* **88 c** 14 48N 61 1W
Ste-Rose, *Guadeloupe* **88 b** 16 20N 61 45W
Ste. Rose du Lac, *Canada* **71 C9** 51 4N 99 30W
Saintes, *France* **20 D3** 45 45N 0 37W
Saintes, Îs. des, *Guadeloupe* **88 b** 15 50N 61 35W
Saintfield, *U.K.* **10 B6** 54 28N 5 49W
Saintonge, *France* **20 D3** 45 40N 0 50W
Saipan, *Pac. Oc.* **64 F6** 15 12N 145 45 E
Sairang, *India* **41 H18** 23 50N 92 45 E
Sairecábur, Cerro, *Bolivia* **94 A2** 22 43S 67 54W
Saitama □, *Japan* **31 F9** 36 25N 139 30 E
Saiyid, *Pakistan* **42 C5** 33 7N 73 2 E
Sajama, *Bolivia* **92 G5** 18 7S 69 0W
Sajószentpéter, *Hungary* **17 D11** 48 12N 20 44 E
Sajum, *India* **43 C8** 33 20N 79 0 E
Sak →, *S. Africa* **56 E3** 30 52S 20 25 E
Sakai, *Japan* **31 G7** 34 30N 135 30 E
Sakaide, *Japan* **31 G6** 34 19N 133 50 E
Sakaiminato, *Japan* **31 G6** 35 38N 133 11 E
Sakākah, *Si. Arabia* **44 D4** 30 0N 40 8 E
Sakakawea, L., *U.S.A.* **80 B4** 47 30N 101 25W
Sakami →, *Canada* **72 B4** 53 40N 76 40W
Sakami, L., *Canada* **72 B4** 53 15N 77 0W
Sakania, *Dem. Rep. of the Congo* **55 E2** 12 43S 28 30 E
Sakarraha, *Madag.* **57 C7** 22 55S 44 32 E
Sakarya, *Turkey* **19 F5** 40 48N 30 25 E
Sakashima-Guntō, *Japan* **31 M2** 24 46N 124 0 E
Sakata, *Japan* **30 E9** 38 55N 139 50 E
Sakchu, *N. Korea* **35 D13** 40 23N 125 2 E
Sakeny →, *Madag.* **57 C8** 20 0S 45 25 E
Sakha □, *Russia* **29 C13** 66 0N 130 0 E
Sakhalin, *Russia* **29 D15** 51 0N 143 0 E
Sakhalinskiy Zaliv, *Russia* **29 D15** 54 0N 141 0 E
Šakiai, *Lithuania* **9 J20** 54 59N 23 2 E
Sakon Nakhon, *Thailand* **38 D5** 17 10N 104 9 E
Sakrand, *Pakistan* **42 F3** 26 10N 68 15 E
Sakri, *India* **43 F12** 26 13N 86 5 E
Sakrivier, *S. Africa* **56 E3** 30 54S 20 28 E
Sakti, *India* **43 H10** 22 2N 82 58 E
Sakuma, *Japan* **31 G8** 35 3N 137 49 E
Sakurai, *Japan* **31 G7** 34 30N 135 51 E
Sala, *Sweden* **9 G17** 59 58N 16 35 E
Sala Consilina, *Italy* **22 D6** 40 23N 15 36 E
Sala-y-Gómez, *Pac. Oc.* **65 K17** 26 28S 105 28W
Salaberry-de-Valleyfield, *Canada* **85 A10** 45 15N 74 8W
Salada, L., *Mexico* **77 K6** 32 20N 115 40W
Saladas, *Argentina* **94 B4** 28 15S 58 40W
Saladillo, *Argentina* **94 D4** 35 40S 59 55W

Salado →, Buenos Aires,
  Argentina .............. 94 D4  35 44S  57 22W
Salado →, La Pampa, Argentina 96 D3  37 30S  67  0W
Salado →, Santa Fe, Argentina . 94 C3  31 40S  60 41W
Salado →, Mexico ........... 81 M5  26 52N  99 19W
Salaga, Ghana ............. 50 G5  8 31N   0 31W
Sãlah, Syria ............... 46 C5  32 40N  36 45 E
Ŝalāt ad Dīn □, Iraq ........ 44 C4  34 35N  43 35 E
Sálakhos, Greece .......... 25 C9  36 17N  27 57 E
Salālah, Oman ............. 47 D5  16 56N  53 59 E
Salamanca, Chile ........... 94 C1  31 46S  70 59W
Salamanca, Spain .......... 21 B3  40 58N   5 39W
Salamanca, U.S.A. .......... 84 D6  42 10N  78 43W
Salāmatābād, Iran .......... 44 C5  35 39N  47 50 E
Salamis, Cyprus ............ 25 D12 35 11N  33 54 E
Salamís, Greece ........... 23 F10 37 56N  23 30 E
Salar de Atacama, Chile ..... 94 A2  23 30S  68 25W
Salar de Uyuni, Bolivia ...... 92 H5  20 30S  67 45W
Salatiga, Indonesia ......... 37 G14  7 19S 110 30 E
Salavat, Russia ............ 18 D10 53 21N  55 55 E
Salaverry, Peru ............ 92 E3  8 15S  79  0W
Salawati, Indonesia ......... 37 E8  1 7S 130 52 E
Salaya, India ............. 42 H3  22 19N  69 35 E
Salayar, Indonesia ......... 37 F6  6 7S 120 30 E
Salcombe, U.K. ............ 13 G4  50 14N   3 47W
Saldanha, S. Africa ........ 56 E2  33  0S  17 58 E
Saldanha B., S. Africa ...... 56 E2  33  6S  18  0 E
Saldus, Latvia ............ 9 H20 56 38N  22 30 E
Sale, Australia ............ 63 F4  38  6S 147  6 E
Salé, Morocco ............ 50 B4  34  3N   6 48W
Sale, U.K. ............... 12 D5  53 26N   2 19W
Salekhard, Russia ......... 28 C7  66 30N  66 35 E
Salem, India ............. 40 P11 11 40N  78 11 E
Salem, Ill., U.S.A. ......... 82 F1  38 38N  88 57W
Salem, Ind., U.S.A. ........ 82 F2  38 36N  86  6W
Salem, Mass., U.S.A. ....... 85 D14 42 31N  70 53W
Salem, Mo., U.S.A. ......... 81 G9  37 39N  91 32W
Salem, N.H., U.S.A. ........ 85 D13 42 45N  71 12W
Salem, N.J., U.S.A. ........ 82 F8  39 34N  75 28W
Salem, N.Y., U.S.A. ........ 85 C11 43 10N  73 20W
Salem, Ohio, U.S.A. ........ 84 F4  40 54N  80 52W
Salem, Oreg., U.S.A. ....... 76 D2  44 56N 123  2W
Salem, S. Dak., U.S.A. ...... 80 D6  43 44N  97 23W
Salem, Va., U.S.A. ......... 82 G5  37 18N  80  3W
Salerno, Italy ............. 22 D6  40 41N  14 47 E
Salford, U.K. ............. 12 D5  53 30N   2 18W
Salgótarján, Hungary ....... 17 D10 48  5N  19 47 E
Salgueiro, Brazil .......... 93 E11  8  4S  39  6W
Salibabu, Indonesia ........ 37 D7  3 51N 126 40 E
Salibea = Salybia, Trin. & Tob. . 93 K15 10 43N  61  2W
Salida, U.S.A. ............ 74 C5  38 32N 106  0W
Salihli, Turkey ............ 23 E13 38 28N  28  8 E
Salihorsk, Belarus ......... 17 B14 52 51N  27 27 E
Salima, Malawi ............ 53 G6  13 47S  34 28 E
Salina, Italy .............. 22 E6  38 34N  14 50 E
Salina, Kans., U.S.A. ....... 80 F6  38 50N  97 37W
Salina, Utah, U.S.A. ........ 77 G8  38 58N 111 51W
Salina Cruz, Mexico ........ 87 D5  16 10N  95 10W
Salinas, Brazil ............ 93 G10 16 10S  42 10W
Salinas, Chile ............. 94 A2  23 31S  69 29W
Salinas, Ecuador .......... 92 D2  2 10S  80 58W
Salinas, U.S.A. ............ 78 J5  36 40N 121 39W
Salinas →, Guatemala ...... 87 D6  16 28N  90 31W
Salinas →, U.S.A. .......... 78 J5  36 45N 121 48W
Salinas, B. de, Nic. ........ 88 D2  11 4S  85 45W
Salinas, Pampa de las, Argentina 94 C2  31 58S  66 42W
Salinas Ambargasta, Argentina 94 B3  29  0S  65  0W
Salinas de Hidalgo, Mexico .. 86 C4  22 30N 101 40W
Salinas Grandes, Argentina .. 94 C3  30  0S  65  0W
Salinas Pueblo Missions △,
  U.S.A. ................ 77 J10 34 16N 106  5W
Saline →, Ark., U.S.A. ...... 81 J8  33 10N  92  8W
Saline →, Kans., U.S.A. ..... 80 F6  38 52N  97 30W
Salines, C. de ses, Spain .... 24 B10 39 16N   3  4 E
Salinópolis, Brazil ......... 93 D9  0 40S  47 20W
Salisbury, U.K. ............ 13 F6  51  4N   1 47W
Salisbury, Md., U.S.A. ...... 82 F8  38 22N  75 36W
Salisbury, N.C., U.S.A. ...... 83 H5  35 40N  80 29W
Salisbury I., Canada ........ 69 B12 63 30N  77  0W
Salisbury Plain, U.K. ........ 13 F6  51 14N   1 55W
Şalkhad, Syria ............ 46 C5  32 29N  36 43 E
Salla, Finland ............. 8 C23 66 50N  28 49 E
Sallíq = Coral Harbour, Canada . 69 B11 64  8N  83 10W
Sallisaw, U.S.A. ........... 81 H7  35 28N  94 47W
Salluit, Canada ............ 69 B12 62 14N  75 38W
Salmās, Iran .............. 44 B5  38 11N  44 47 E
Salmo, Canada ............ 70 D5  49 10N 117 20W
Salmon, U.S.A. ............ 76 D7  45 11N 113 54W
Salmon →, Canada ......... 70 C4  54  3N 122 40W
Salmon →, U.S.A. .......... 76 D5  45 51N 116 47W
Salmon Arm, Canada ....... 70 C5  50 40N 119 15W
Salmon Gums, Australia ..... 61 F3  32 59S 121 38 E
Salmon River Mts., U.S.A. ... 76 D6  45  0N 114 30W
Salo, Finland ............. 9 F20 60 22N  23 10 E
Salome, U.S.A. ............ 79 M13 33 47N 113 37W
Salon, India .............. 43 F9  26  2N  81 27 E
Salon-de-Provence, France .. 20 E6  43 39N   5  6 E
Salonica = Thessaloníki, Greece . 23 D10 40 38N  22 58 E
Salonta, Romania .......... 17 E11 46 49N  21 42 E
Salpausselkä, Finland ....... 9 F22 61  3N  26 15 E
Salsacate, Argentina ....... 94 C2  31 20S  65  5W
Salso →, Italy ............ 22 F5  37  6N  13 57 E
Salt →, Canada ............ 70 B6  60  0N 112 25W
Salt →, U.S.A. ............ 77 K7  33 23N 112 19W
Salt L., The, Australia ....... 63 E3  30  6S 142  8 E
Salt Lake City, U.S.A. ....... 76 F8  40 45N 111 53W
Salt Range, Pakistan ....... 42 C5  32 30N  72 25 E
Salta, Argentina ........... 94 A2  24 57S  65 25W
Salta □, Argentina ......... 94 A2  24 48S  65 30W
Saltash, U.K. ............. 13 G3  50 24N   4 14W
Saltburn by the Sea, U.K. .... 12 C7  54 35N   0 58W
Saltcoats, U.K. ............ 11 F4  55 38N   4 47W
Saltee Is., Ireland ......... 10 D5  52  7N   6 37W
Saltfjellet, Norway ......... 8 C16 66 40N  15 15 E
Saltfjorden, Norway ........ 8 C16 67 15N  14 10 E
Saltillo, Mexico ........... 86 B4  25 25N 101  0W
Salto, Argentina ........... 94 C3  34  20S  60 15W
Salto, Uruguay ............ 94 C4  31 27S  57 50W
Salto →, Italy ............. 22 C5  42  26N  12 25 E
Salto del Guairá, Paraguay ... 95 A5  24  3S  54 17W
Salton City, U.S.A. ......... 79 M11 33 29N 115 51W
Salton Sea, U.S.A. ......... 79 M11 33 15N 115 45W
Saltsburg, U.S.A. .......... 84 F5  40 29N  79 27W
Saluda →, U.S.A. .......... 83 J5  34  1N  81  4W
Salūm, Egypt ............. 51 B11 31 31N  25  7 E
Salur, India .............. 41 K13 18 27N  83 18 E
Salvador, Brazil ........... 93 F11 13  0S  38 30W

Salvador, Canada .......... 71 C7  52 10N 109 32W
Salvador, El ■, Cent. Amer. ... 88 D2  13 50N  89  0W
Salvador, L., U.S.A. ........ 81 L9  29 43N  90 15W
Salween →, Burma ......... 41 L20 16 31N  97 37 E
Salyan, Azerbaijan ......... 19 G8  39 33N  48 59 E
Salybia, Trin. & Tob. ....... 93 K15 10 43N  61  2W
Salzach →, Austria ......... 16 D7  48 12N  12 56 E
Salzburg, Austria .......... 16 E7  47 48N  13  2 E
Salzgitter, Germany ........ 16 B6  52  9N  10 19 E
Salzwedel, Germany ........ 16 B6  52 52N  11 10 E
Sam, India ............... 42 F4  26 50N  70 31 E
Sam Neua, Laos ........... 38 B5  20 29N 104  5 E
Sam Ngao, Thailand ........ 38 D2  17 18N  99  0 E
Sam Rayburn Reservoir, U.S.A. 81 K7  31  4N  94  5W
Sam Son, Vietnam ......... 38 C5  19 44N 105 54 E
Sam Teu, Laos ............ 38 C5  19 59N 104 38 E
Sama de Langreo = Langreo,
  Spain ................. 21 A3  43 18N   5 40W
Samagaltay, Russia ......... 29 D10 50 36N  95  3 E
Samales Group, Phil. ....... 37 C6  6  0N 122  0 E
Samana, India ............ 42 D7  30 10N  76 13 E
Samana Cay, Bahamas ...... 89 B5  23  3N  73 45W
Samanga, Tanzania ......... 55 D4  8 20S  39 13 E
Samangān □, Afghan. ...... 40 B5  36 15N  68  3 E
Samangwa, Dem. Rep. of
  the Congo ............. 54 C1  4 23S  24 10 E
Samani, Japan ............ 30 C11 42  7N 142 56 E
Samar, Phil. ............. 37 B7  12  0N 125  0 E
Samara, Russia ........... 18 D9  53  8N  50  6 E
Samaria = Shomron, West Bank 46 C4  32 15N  35 13 E
Samariá, Greece .......... 25 D5  35 17N  23 58 E
Samarinda, Indonesia ....... 36 E5  0 30S 117  9 E
Samarkand = Samarqand,
  Uzbekistan ............ 28 F7  39 40N  66 55 E
Samarqand, Uzbekistan ..... 28 F7  39 40N  66 55 E
Sāmarrā', Iraq ............ 44 C4  34 12N  43 52 E
Samastipur, India ......... 43 G11 25 50N  85 50 E
Samba, Dem. Rep. of the Congo 54 C2  4 38S  26 22 E
Samba, India ............. 43 C6  32 32N  75 10 E
Sambalpur, India .......... 41 J14 21 28N  84  4 E
Sambar, Tanjung, Indonesia .. 36 E4  2 59S 110 19 E
Sambas, Indonesia ......... 36 D3  1 20N 109 20 E
Sambava, Madag. .......... 57 A9  14 16S  50 10 E
Sambawizi, Zimbabwe ....... 55 F2  18 24S  26 13 E
Sambhal, India ............ 43 E8  28 35N  78 37 E
Sambhar, India ........... 42 F6  26 52N  75 6 E
Sambhar L., India ......... 42 F6  26 55N  75 12 E
Sambiase, Italy ........... 22 E7  38 58N  16 17 E
Sambir, Ukraine ........... 17 D12 49 30N  23 10 E
Sambor, Cambodia ......... 38 F6  12 46N 106  0 E
Samborombón, B., Argentina . 94 D4  36  5S  57 20W
Samburu □, Kenya ......... 54 B4  0 37N  37 31 E
Samch'ŏk, S. Korea ........ 35 F15 37 30N 129 10 E
Samch'onp'o, S. Korea ...... 35 G15 35  0N 128  6 E
Same, Tanzania ........... 54 C4  4  2S  37 38 E
Samfya, Zambia ........... 55 E2  11 22S  29 31 E
Samnah, Si. Arabia ......... 44 E3  25 10N  37 15 E
Samo Alto, Chile .......... 94 C1  30 22S  71  0W
Samoa ■, Pac. Oc. ......... 59 B13 14  0S 172  0W
Samoan Is., Pac. Oc. ....... 59 A13 14  0S 171  0W
Samokov, Bulgaria ......... 23 C10 42 18N  23 35 E
Sámos, Greece ........... 23 F12 37 45N  26 50 E
Samothráki = Mathráki, Greece . 25 A3  39 48N  19 31 E
Samothráki, Greece ........ 23 D11 40 28N  25 28 E
Sampacho, Argentina ....... 94 C3  33 20S  64 50W
Sampalan, Indonesia ....... 37 K18  8 41S 115 34 E
Sampang, Indonesia ........ 37 G15  7 11S 113 13 E
Sampit, Indonesia .......... 36 E4  2 34S 113  0 E
Sampit, Teluk, Indonesia .... 36 E4  3  5S 113  3 E
Samrong, Cambodia ........ 38 E4  14 15N 103 30 E
Samrong, Thailand ......... 38 E3  15 10N 100 40 E
Samsø, Denmark .......... 9 J14 55 50N  10 35 E
Samsun, Turkey ........... 19 F6  41 15N  36 22 E
Samui, Ko, Thailand ........ 39 b  9 30N  99 55 E
Samusole, Dem. Rep. of
  the Congo ............. 55 E1  10  2S  24  0 E
Samut Prakan, Thailand ..... 38 F3  13 32N 100 40 E
Samut Songkhram →, Thailand 36 B1  13 24N 100  1 E
Samwari, Pakistan ......... 42 E2  28 30N  66 46 E
San, Mali ................ 50 F5  13 15N   4 57W
San →, Cambodia ......... 38 F5  13 32N 105 57 E
San →, Poland ............ 17 C11 50 45N  21 51 E
San Agustin →, Phil. ....... 37 C7  6 20N 126 13 E
San Agustín de Valle Fértil,
  Argentina ............. 94 C2  30 35S  67 30W
San Ambrosio, Pac. Oc. ..... 90 F3  26 28S  79 53W
San Andreas, U.S.A. ........ 78 G6  38 12N 120 41W
San Andrés, I. de, Caribbean .. 88 D3  12 42N  81 46W
San Andrés Mts., U.S.A. ..... 77 K10 33  0N 106 30W
San Andrés Tuxtla, Mexico ... 87 D5  18 30N  95 20W
San Angelo, U.S.A. ......... 81 K4  31 28N 100 26W
San Anselmo, U.S.A. ........ 78 H4  37 59N 122 34W
San Antonio, Belize ........ 87 D7  16 15N  89  2W
San Antonio, Chile ......... 94 C1  33 40S  71 40W
San Antonio, N. Mex., U.S.A. .. 77 K10 33 55N 106 52W
San Antonio, Tex., U.S.A. .... 81 L5  29 25N  98 30W
San Antonio →, U.S.A. ...... 81 L6  28 30N  96 54W
San Antonio, C. de, Argentina . 94 D4  36 15S  56 40W
San Antonio, C. de, Cuba .... 88 B3  21 50N  84 57W
San Antonio, Mt., U.S.A. .... 79 L9  34 17N 117 38W
San Antonio de los Baños, Cuba 88 B3  22 54N  82 31W
San Antonio de los Cobres,
  Argentina ............. 94 A2  24 10S  66 17W
San Antonio Oeste, Argentina . 96 E4  40 40S  65  0W
San Ardo, U.S.A. .......... 78 J6  36  1N 120 54W
San Augustín, Canary Is. .... 24 G4  27 47N  15 32W
San Agustine, U.S.A. ....... 81 K7  31 30N  94  7W
San Jose, Nueva Ecija, Phil. .. 37 A6  15 45N 120 55 E
San Bartolomé, Canary Is. ... 24 F6  28 59N  13 37W
San Bartolomé de Tirajana,
  Canary Is. ............. 24 G4  27 54N  15 34W
San Benedetto del Tronto, Italy . 22 C5  42 57N  13 53 E
San Benedicto, I., Mexico .... 86 D2  19 18N 110 49W
San Benito, U.S.A. ......... 81 M6  26  8N  97 38W
San Benito →, U.S.A. ....... 78 J5  36 53N 121 34W
San Benito Mt., U.S.A. ...... 78 J6  36 22N 120 37W
San Bernardino, U.S.A. ..... 79 L9  34 7N 117 19W
San Bernardino Mts., U.S.A. .. 79 L10 34 10N 116 45W
San Bernardino Str., Phil. ... 37 B6  13  0N 125  0 E
San Bernardo, Chile ........ 94 C1  33 40S  70 50W
San Bernardo, I. de, Colombia . 92 B3  9 45N  75 50W
San Blas, Mexico .......... 86 B3  26  4N 108 46W
San Blas, Arch. de, Panama .. 88 E4  9 50N  78 31W
San Blas, Cord. de, Panama .. 88 E4  9 15N  78 30W
San Borja, Bolivia ......... 92 F5  14 50S  66 52W
San Buenaventura = Ventura,
  U.S.A. ................ 79 L7  34 17N 119 18W
San Buenaventura, Mexico ... 86 B4  27  5N 101 32W
San Carlos = Sant Carles, Spain 24 B8  39  3N   1 34 E

San Carlos, Argentina ...... 94 C2  33 50S  69  0W
San Carlos, Chile .......... 94 D1  36 10S  72  0W
San Carlos, Baja Calif. S., Mexico 86 C2  24 47N 112  6W
San Carlos, Coahuila, Mexico . 86 B4  29  0N 100 54W
San Carlos, Nic. ........... 88 D3  11 12N  84 50W
San Carlos, Phil. .......... 37 B6  10 29N 123 25 E
San Carlos, Uruguay ........ 95 C5  34 46S  54 58W
San Carlos, Venezuela ...... 92 B5  9 40N  68 36W
San Carlos de Bariloche,
  Argentina ............. 96 E2  41 10S  71 25W
San Carlos de Bolívar, Argentina 94 D4  36 15S  61  6W
San Carlos del Zulia, Venezuela 92 B4  9  1N  71 55W
San Carlos L., U.S.A. ....... 77 K8  33 11N 110 32W
San Clemente, Chile ........ 94 C1  35 30S  71 29W
San Clemente, U.S.A. ....... 79 M9  33 26N 117 37W
San Clemente I., U.S.A. ..... 79 N8  32 53N 118 29W
San Cristóbal = Es Migjorn Gran,
  Spain ................. 24 B11 39 57N   4  3 E
San Cristóbal, Argentina .... 94 C3  30 20S  61 10W
San Cristóbal, Dom. Rep. .... 89 C5  18 25N  70  6W
San Cristóbal, Venezuela .... 92 B4  7 46N  72 14W
San Cristóbal de la Casas,
  Mexico ............... 87 D6  16 50N  92 33W
San Diego, Calif., U.S.A. .... 79 N9  32 43N 117  9W
San Diego, Tex., U.S.A. ..... 81 M5  27 46N  98 14W
San Diego, C., Argentina .... 96 G3  54 40S  65 10W
San Diego de la Unión, Mexico 86 C4  21 28N 100 52W
San Diego International ✈ (SAN),
  U.S.A. ................ 79 N9  32 44N 117 11W
San Dimitri, Ras, Malta ..... 25 C1  36  4N  14 11 E
San Dimitri Point = San Dimitri,
  Ras, Malta ............ 25 C1  36  4N  14 11 E
San Estanislao, Paraguay .... 94 A4  24 39S  56 26W
San Felipe, Chile .......... 94 C1  32 43S  70 42W
San Felipe, Mexico ........ 86 A2  31  0N 114 52W
San Felipe, Venezuela ...... 92 A5  10 20N  68 44W
San Felipe →, U.S.A. ....... 79 M11 33 12N 115 49W
San Félix, Chile ........... 94 B1  28 56S  70 28W
San Félix, Pac. Oc. ......... 90 F2  26 23S  80  0W
San Fernando = Sant Ferran,
  Spain ................. 24 C7  38 42N   1 28 E
San Fernando, Chile ........ 94 C1  34 30S  71  0W
San Fernando, Baja Calif.,
  Mexico ............... 86 B1  29 55N 115 10W
San Fernando, Tamaulipas,
  Mexico ............... 87 C5  24 51N  98 10W
San Fernando, La Union, Phil. . 37 A6  16 40N 120 23 E
San Fernando, Pampanga, Phil. 37 A6  15  5N 120 37 E
San Fernando, Spain ........ 21 D2  36 28N   6 17W
San Fernando, Trin. & Tob. ... 89 D7  10 16N  61 28W
San Fernando, U.S.A. ....... 79 L8  34 17N 118 26W
San Fernando de Apure,
  Venezuela ............. 92 B5  7 54N  67 15W
San Fernando de Atabapo,
  Venezuela ............. 92 C5  4  3N  67 42W
San Francisco, Argentina .... 94 C3  31 30S  62  5W
San Francisco, U.S.A. ....... 78 H4  37 47N 122 25W
San Francisco →, U.S.A. .... 77 K9  32 59N 109 22W
San Francisco, C. de, Colombia 90 C3  6 18N  77 29W
San Francisco, Paso de, S. Amer. 94 B2  27  0S  68  0W
San Francisco de Macorís,
  Dom. Rep. ............ 89 C5  19 19N  70 15W
San Francisco del Monte de Oro,
  Argentina ............. 94 C2  32 36S  66  8W
San Francisco del Oro, Mexico 86 B3  26 52N 105 50W
San Francisco International ✈
  (SFO), U.S.A. .......... 78 H4  37 37N 122 22W
San Francisco Javier = Sant
  Francesc de Formentera, Spain 24 C7  38 42N   1 26 E
San Gabriel, Chile ......... 94 C1  33 47S  70 15W
San Gabriel Mts., U.S.A. ..... 79 L9  34 20N 118  0W
San German, Puerto Rico .... 89 d  18  4N  67  4W
San Gorgonio Mt., U.S.A. .... 79 L10 34  7N 116 51W
San Gottardo, P. del, Switz. .. 20 C8  46 33N   8 33 E
San Gregorio, Uruguay ...... 95 C4  32 37S  55 40W
San Gregorio, U.S.A. ....... 78 H4  37 20N 122 23W
San Ignacio, Belize ........ 87 D7  17 10N  89  5W
San Ignacio, Bolivia ........ 92 G6  16 20S  60 55W
San Ignacio, Mexico ........ 86 B2  27 27N 113  0W
San Ignacio, Paraguay ...... 88 C2  26 52S  57  3W
San Ignacio □, Mexico ...... 86 B2  27  0N 113 10W
San Ignacio, L., Mexico ..... 86 B2  26 50N 113 11W
San Ildefonso, C., Phil. ...... 37 A6  16  0N 122  1 E
San Isidro, Argentina ....... 94 C4  34 29S  58 31W
San Jacinto, U.S.A. ........ 79 M10 33 47N 116 57W
San Jaime = Sant Jaume, Spain 24 B11 39 54N   4  4 E
San Javier, Misiones, Argentina 95 B4  27 55S  55  5W
San Javier, Santa Fe, Argentina 94 C4  30 40S  59 55W
San Javier, Bolivia ......... 92 G6  16 18S  62 30W
San Javier, Chile .......... 94 D1  35 40S  71 45W
San Jeronimo Taviche, Mexico . 87 D5  16 38N  96 32W
San Joaquin, U.S.A. ........ 78 J6  36 36N 120 11W
San Joaquin →, U.S.A. ...... 78 G5  38  4N 121 51W
San Joaquin Valley, U.S.A. ... 78 J6  37 20N 121  0W
San Jon, U.S.A. ........... 81 H3  35 6N 103 20W
San Jordi = Sant Jordi, Spain . 24 B9  39 33N   2 46 E
San Jorge, Argentina ....... 94 C3  31 54S  61 50W
San Jorge, B. de, Mexico .... 86 A2  31 20N 113 20W
San Jorge, G., Argentina .... 96 F3  46  0S  66  0W
San José = San Josep, Spain . 24 C7  38 55N   1 18 E
San José, Costa Rica ....... 88 E3  9 55N  84  2W
San José, Guatemala ....... 88 D1  14  0N  90 50W
San José, Mexico .......... 86 C2  25  0N 110 50W
San Jose, Mind. Occ., Phil. ... 37 B6  12 27N 121  4 E
San Jose →, U.S.A. ........ 77 J10 34 25N 106 45W
San Jose de Buenavista, Phil. . 37 B6  10 45N 121 56 E
San José de Chiquitos, Bolivia . 92 G6  17 53S  60 50W
San José de Feliciano, Argentina 94 C4  30 26S  58 46W
San José de Jáchal, Argentina . 94 C2  30 15S  68 46W
San José de Mayo, Uruguay .. 94 C4  34 27S  56 40W
San José del Cabo, Mexico ... 86 C3  23  0N 109 40W
San José del Guaviare, Colombia 92 C4  2 35N  72 38W
San Josep, Spain .......... 24 C7  38 55N   1 18 E
San Juan, Argentina ........ 94 C2  31 30S  68 30W
San Juan, Puerto Rico ....... 89 d  18 28N  66  7W
San Juan, Trin. & Tob. ...... 93 K15 10 39N  61 29W
San Juan □, Argentina ...... 94 C2  31  9S  69  0W
San Juan →, Argentina ...... 94 C2  32 20S  67 25W
San Juan →, Nic. .......... 88 D3  10 56N  83 42W
San Juan →, U.S.A. ........ 77 H8  37 16N 110 26W
San Juan Bautista = Sant Joan
  Baptista, Spain ......... 24 B8  39  5N   1 31 E
San Juan Bautista, Paraguay .. 94 B4  26 37S  57  6W
San Juan Bautista, U.S.A. .... 78 J5  36 51N 121 32W

San Juan Bautista Valle
  Nacional, Mexico ....... 87 D5  17 47N  96 19W
San Juan Capistrano, U.S.A. .. 79 M9  33 30N 117 40W
San Juan Cr. →, U.S.A. ..... 78 J5  35 40N 120 22W
San Juan de Guadalupe, Mexico 86 C4  24 38N 102 44W
San Juan de la Costa, Mexico . 86 C2  24 23N 110 45W
San Juan de los Morros,
  Venezuela ............. 92 B5  9 55N  67 21W
San Juan del Norte, Nic. ..... 88 D3  10 58N  83 40W
San Juan del Norte, B. de, Nic. . 88 D3  11  0N  83 40W
San Juan del Río, Mexico .... 87 C5  20 25N 100  0W
San Juan del Sur, Nic. ...... 88 D2  11 20N  85 51W
San Juan I., U.S.A. ......... 78 B3  48 32N 123  5W
San Juan Island △, U.S.A. ... 78 B4  48 27N 123  0W
San Juan Mts., U.S.A. ...... 77 H10 37 30N 107  0W
San Justo, Argentina ....... 94 C3  30 47S  60 30W
San Kamphaeng, Thailand ... 38 C2  18 45N  99  8 E
San Lázaro, C., Mexico ...... 86 C2  24 50N 112 18W
San Lázaro, Sa., Mexico ..... 86 C3  23 25N 110  0W
San Leandro, U.S.A. ........ 78 H4  37 44N 122  9W
San Lorenzo = Sant Llorenç des
  Cardassar, Spain ....... 24 B10 39 37N   3 17 E
San Lorenzo, Argentina ..... 94 C3  32 45S  60 45W
San Lorenzo, Ecuador ....... 92 C3  1 15N  78 50W
San Lorenzo, Paraguay ...... 94 B4  25 20S  57 32W
San Lorenzo →, Mexico ..... 86 C3  24 15N 107 24W
San Lorenzo, I., Mexico ...... 86 B2  28 35N 112 50W
San Lorenzo, Mte., Argentina . 96 F2  47 40S  72 20W
San Lucas, Bolivia ......... 92 H5  20 5S  65  7W
San Lucas, Baja Calif. S., Mexico 86 C3  22 53N 109 54W
San Lucas, Baja Calif. S., Mexico 86 B2  27 10N 112 14W
San Lucas, U.S.A. ......... 78 J5  36 8N 121  1W
San Lucas, C., Mexico ...... 86 C3  22 50N 110  0W
San Luis, Argentina ........ 94 C2  33 20S  66 20W
San Luis, Cuba ............ 88 B3  22 17N  83 46W
San Luis, Guatemala ........ 88 C2  16 14N  89 27W
San Luis, Ariz., U.S.A. ...... 77 K6  32 29N 114 47W
San Luis, Colo., U.S.A. ...... 77 H11 37 12N 105 25W
San Luis □, Argentina ...... 94 C2  34  0S  66  0W
San Luis, I., Mexico ........ 86 B2  29 58N 114 26W
San Luis, Sierra de, Argentina . 94 C2  32 30S  66 10W
San Luis de la Paz, Mexico ... 86 C4  21 19N 100 32W
San Luis Obispo, U.S.A. ..... 79 K6  35 17N 120 40W
San Luis Potosí, Mexico ..... 86 C4  22  9N 100 59W
San Luis Potosí □, Mexico ... 86 C4  22 10N 101  0W
San Luis Reservoir, U.S.A. ... 78 H5  37  4N 121  5W
San Luis Río Colorado, Mexico 86 A2  32 29N 114 58W
San Manuel, U.S.A. ........ 77 K8  32 36N 110 38W
San Marcos, Guatemala ..... 88 D1  14 59N  91 52W
San Marcos, Mexico ........ 86 D2  18 13N 112  6W
San Marcos, Calif., U.S.A. ... 79 M9  33  9N 117 10W
San Marcos, Tex., U.S.A. .... 81 L6  29 53N  97 56W
San Marino, San Marino ..... 16 G7  43 55N  12 28 E
San Marino ■, Europe ...... 22 C5  43 56N  12 25 E
San Martín, Antarctica ...... 5 C17 68 11S  67  0W
San Martín, Argentina ...... 94 C2  33  5S  68 28W
San Martín →, Bolivia ...... 92 F6  13  8S  63 43W
San Martín, L., Argentina .... 96 F2  48 50S  72 50W
San Martín de los Andes,
  Argentina ............. 96 E2  40 10S  71 20W
San Mateo = Sant Mateu, Spain 24 B7  39  3N   1 23 E
San Mateo, U.S.A. ......... 78 H4  37 34N 122 19W
San Matías, Bolivia ........ 92 G7  16 25S  58 20W
San Matías, G., Argentina .... 96 E4  41 30S  64  0W
San Miguel = Sant Miguel, Spain 24 B7  39  3N   1 26 E
San Miguel, El Salv. ....... 88 D2  13 30N  88 12W
San Miguel, Panama ........ 88 E4  8 27N  78 55W
San Miguel, U.S.A. ........ 78 K6  35 45N 120 42W
San Miguel →, Bolivia ...... 92 F6  13 52S  63 56W
San Miguel de Tucumán,
  Argentina ............. 94 B2  26 50S  65 20W
San Miguel del Monte, Argentina 94 D4  35 23S  58 50W
San Miguel I., U.S.A. ....... 79 L6  34  2N 120 23W
San Nicolás, Canary Is. ..... 24 G4  27 58N  15 47W
San Nicolás de los Arroyas,
  Argentina ............. 94 C3  33  6S  60 35W
San Nicolas I., U.S.A. ....... 79 M7  33 15N 119 30W
San Onofre, U.S.A. ......... 79 M9  33 22N 117 34W
San Pablo, Bolivia ......... 94 A2  21 43S  66 38W
San Pablo, U.S.A. .......... 78 H4  37 58N 122 21W
San Pedro, Buenos Aires,
  Argentina ............. 94 C4  33 40S  59 40W
San Pedro, Misiones, Argentina 95 B5  26 30S  54 10W
San Pédro, Ivory C. ........ 50 H4  4 50N   6 33W
San Pedro □, Paraguay ...... 94 A4  24  0S  57  0W
San Pedro →, Chihuahua,
  Mexico ............... 86 B3  28 20N 106 10W
San Pedro →, Nayarit, Mexico 86 C3  21 45N 105 30W
San Pedro →, U.S.A. ....... 77 K8  32 59N 110 47W
San Pedro, Pta., Chile ...... 94 B1  25 30S  70 38W
San Pedro Channel, U.S.A. ... 79 M8  33 30N 118 25W
San Pedro de Atacama, Chile . 94 A2  22 55S  68 15W
San Pedro de Jujuy, Argentina 94 A3  24 12S  64 55W
San Pedro de las Colonias,
  Mexico ............... 86 B4  25 50N 102 59W
San Pedro de Macorís,
  Dom. Rep. ............ 89 C6  18 30N  69 18W
San Pedro del Norte, Nic. .... 88 D3  13  4N  84 33W
San Pedro del Paraná, Paraguay 94 B4  26 43S  56 13W
San Pedro Mártir △, Mexico .. 86 A1  31  0N 115 21W
San Pedro Mártir, Sierra, Mexico 86 A1  31  0N 115 30W
San Pedro Mixtepec, Mexico .. 87 D5  16  2N  97  7W
San Pedro Ocampo = Melchor
  Ocampo, Mexico ....... 86 C4  24 52N 101 40W
San Pedro Sula, Honduras ... 88 C2  15 30N  88  0W
San Pietro, Italy ........... 22 E3  39  8N   8 17 E
San Quintín, Mexico ........ 86 A1  30 29N 115 57W
San Rafael, Argentina ...... 94 C2  34 40S  68 21W
San Rafael, Calif., U.S.A. .... 78 H4  37 58N 122 32W
San Rafael, N. Mex., U.S.A. .. 77 J10 35  7N 107 53W
San Rafael Mt., U.S.A. ...... 79 L7  34 41N 119 52W
San Rafael Mts., U.S.A. ..... 79 L7  34 40N 119 50W
San Ramón de la Nueva Orán,
  Argentina ............. 94 A3  23 10S  64 20W
San Remo, Italy ........... 20 E7  43 49N   7 46 E
San Roque, Argentina ....... 94 B4  28 25S  58 45W
San Roque, Spain .......... 21 D3  36 17N   5 21W
San Rosendo, Chile ........ 94 D1  37 16S  72 43W
San Saba, U.S.A. .......... 81 K5  31 12N  98 43W
San Salvador, El Salv. ....... 88 D2  13 40N  89 10W
San Salvador, Spain ........ 24 B10 39 27N   3 11 E
San Salvador de Jujuy,
  Argentina ............. 94 A3  24 10S  64 48W
San Salvador I., Bahamas .... 89 B5  24  0N  74 40W
San Sebastián = Donostia-San
  Sebastián, Spain ....... 21 A5  43 17N   1 58W

San Sebastián, Argentina ..... 96 G3 53 10S 68 30W
San Sebastian, Puerto Rico ... 89 d 18 20N 66 59W
San Sebastián de la Gomera,
Canary Is. ................ 24 F2 28 5N 17 7W
San Serra = Son Serra, Spain . 24 B10 39 43N 3 13 E
San Severo, Italy .......... 22 D6 41 41N 15 23 E
San Simeon, U.S.A. ......... 78 K5 35 39N 121 11W
San Simon, U.S.A. .......... 77 K9 32 16N 109 14W
San Telmo = Sant Telm, Spain . 24 B9 39 35N 2 21 E
San Telmo, Mexico .......... 86 A1 30 58N 116 6W
San Tiburcio, Mexico ........ 86 C4 24 8N 101 32W
San Valentin, Mte., Chile ..... 96 F2 46 30S 73 30W
San Vicente de la Barquera,
Spain ................... 21 A3 43 23N 4 29W
San Vito, Costa Rica ........ 88 E3 8 50N 82 58W
Sana', Yemen .............. 47 D3 15 27N 44 12 E
Sana →, Bos.-H. ........... 16 F9 45 3N 16 23 E
Sanaga →, Cameroon ........ 52 D1 3 35N 9 38 E
Sanaloa, Presa, Mexico ...... 86 C3 24 50N 107 20W
Sanana, Indonesia .......... 37 E7 2 4S 125 58 E
Sanand, India ............. 42 H5 22 59N 72 25 E
Sanandaj, Iran ............ 44 C5 35 18N 47 1 E
Sanandita, Bolivia .......... 94 A3 21 40S 63 45W
Sanawad, India ............ 42 H7 22 11N 76 5 E
Sancellas = Sencelles, Spain .. 24 B9 39 39N 2 54 E
Sanchahe, China ........... 35 B14 44 50N 126 2 E
Sánchez, Dom. Rep. ........ 89 C6 19 15N 69 36W
Sanchor, India ............ 42 G4 24 45N 71 55 E
Sancti Spíritus, Cuba ....... 88 B4 21 52N 79 33W
Sancy, Puy de, France ...... 20 D5 45 32N 2 50 E
Sand →, S. Africa .......... 57 C5 22 25S 30 5 E
Sand Hills, U.S.A. .......... 80 D4 42 10N 101 30W
Sand Lakes △, Canada ...... 71 B9 57 51N 98 32W
Sand Springs, U.S.A. ....... 81 G6 36 9N 96 7W
Sanda, Japan ............. 31 G7 34 53N 135 14 E
Sandakan, Malaysia ........ 36 C5 5 53N 118 4 E
Sandan = Sambor, Cambodia .. 38 F6 12 46N 106 0 E
Sandanski, Bulgaria ........ 23 D10 41 35N 23 16 E
Sanday, U.K. ............. 11 B6 59 16N 2 31W
Sandefjord, Norway ........ 9 G14 59 10N 10 15 E
Sanders, U.S.A. ........... 77 J9 35 13N 109 20W
Sanderson, U.S.A. ......... 81 K3 30 9N 102 24W
Sandersville, U.S.A. ........ 83 J4 32 59N 82 48W
Sandfire Roadhouse, Australia . 60 C3 19 45S 121 15 E
Sandfly L., Canada ......... 71 B7 55 43N 106 6W
Sandfontein, Namibia ....... 56 C2 23 48S 29 1 E
Sandheads, The, India ...... 43 J13 21 10N 88 20 E
Sandía, Peru ............. 92 F5 14 10S 69 30W
Sandila, India ............ 43 F9 27 5N 80 31 E
Sandnes, Norway .......... 9 G11 58 50N 5 45 E
Sandnessjøen, Norway ...... 8 C15 66 2N 12 38 E
Sandoa, Dem. Rep. of the Congo 52 F4 9 41S 23 0 E
Sandomierz, Poland ........ 17 C11 50 40N 21 43 E
Sandover →, Australia ...... 62 C2 21 43S 136 32 E
Sandoway, Burma .......... 41 K19 18 20N 94 30 E
Sandoy, Faeroe Is. ......... 8 F9 61 52N 6 46W
Sandpoint, U.S.A. .......... 76 B5 48 17N 116 33W
Sandray, U.K. ............ 11 E1 56 53N 7 31W
Sandringham, U.K. ......... 12 E8 52 51N 0 31 E
Sandstone, Australia ....... 61 E2 27 59S 119 16 E
Sandusky, Mich., U.S.A. ..... 84 C2 43 25N 82 50W
Sandusky, Ohio, U.S.A. ..... 84 E2 41 27N 82 42W
Sandviken, Sweden ........ 9 F17 60 38N 16 46 E
Sandwich, C., Australia ..... 62 B4 18 14S 146 18 E
Sandwich B., Canada ....... 73 B8 53 40N 57 15W
Sandwich B., Namibia ....... 56 C1 23 25S 14 20 E
Sandy, Oreg., U.S.A. ....... 78 E4 45 24N 122 16W
Sandy, Pa., U.S.A. ......... 84 E6 41 6N 78 46W
Sandy, Utah, U.S.A. ........ 76 F8 40 35N 111 50W
Sandy Bay, Canada ........ 71 B8 55 31N 102 19W
Sandy Bight, Australia ...... 61 F3 33 50S 123 20 E
Sandy C., Queens., Australia .. 62 C5 24 42S 153 15 E
Sandy C., Tas., Australia .... 63 G3 41 25S 144 45 E
Sandy Cay, Bahamas ....... 89 B4 23 13N 75 18W
Sandy Cr. →, U.S.A. ....... 76 F9 41 51N 109 47W
Sandy L., Canada .......... 72 B1 53 2N 93 0W
Sandy Lake, Canada ........ 72 B1 53 0N 93 0W
Sandy Valley, U.S.A. ....... 79 K11 35 49N 115 36W
Sanford, Fla., U.S.A. ....... 83 L5 28 48N 81 16W
Sanford, Maine, U.S.A. ..... 83 D10 43 27N 70 47W
Sanford, N.C., U.S.A. ....... 83 H6 35 29N 79 10W
Sanford →, Australia ....... 61 E2 27 22S 115 53 E
Sanford, Mt., U.S.A. ....... 68 B5 62 13N 144 8W
Sang-i-Masha, Afghan. ...... 42 C2 33 8N 67 27 E
Sanga, Mozam. ............ 55 E4 12 22S 35 21 E
Sanga →, Congo ........... 52 E3 1 5S 17 0 E
Sangamner, India .......... 40 K9 19 37N 74 15 E
Sangar, Afghan. ........... 42 C1 32 56N 65 30 E
Sangar, Russia ............ 29 C13 64 2N 127 31 E
Sangar Sarai, Afghan. ...... 42 B4 34 27N 70 35 E
Sangarh →, Pakistan ....... 42 D4 30 43N 70 44 E
Sangay, Ecuador .......... 92 D3 2 0S 78 20W
Sange, Dem. Rep. of the Congo 54 D2 6 58S 28 21 E
Sangeang, Indonesia ....... 37 F5 8 12S 119 6 E
Sanger, U.S.A. ............ 78 J7 36 42N 119 33W
Sangerhausen, Germany ..... 16 C6 51 28N 11 18 E
Sanggan He →, China ...... 34 E9 38 12N 117 15 E
Sanggau, Indonesia ........ 36 D4 0 5N 110 30 E
Sanghar, Pakistan ......... 42 F3 26 2N 68 57 E
Sangihe, Kepulauan, Indonesia . 37 D7 3 0N 125 30 E
Sangihe, Pulau, Indonesia .... 37 D7 3 35N 125 30 E
Sangju, S. Korea .......... 35 F15 36 25N 128 10 E
Sangkapura, Indonesia ...... 36 F4 5 52S 112 40 E
Sangkhla, Thailand ......... 38 E2 14 57N 98 28 E
Sangkulirang, Indonesia ..... 36 D5 0 59N 117 58 E
Sangla, Pakistan .......... 42 D5 31 43N 73 23 E
Sangli, India ............. 40 L9 16 55N 74 33 E
Sangmélima, Cameroon ..... 52 D2 2 57N 12 1 E
Sangod, India ............ 42 G7 24 55N 76 17 E
Sangre de Cristo Mts., U.S.A. . 81 G2 37 30N 105 20W
Sangre Grande, Trin. & Tob. .. 93 K15 10 35N 61 8W
Sangrur, India ............ 42 D6 30 14N 75 50 E
Sangudo, Canada .......... 70 C6 53 50N 114 54W
Sangue →, Brazil .......... 92 F7 11 1S 58 39W
Sanibel, U.S.A. ........... 83 M4 26 26N 82 1W
Sanikiluaq, Canada ........ 69 C12 56 32N 79 14W
Sanin-Kaigan △, Japan ..... 31 G7 35 39N 134 37 E
Sanirajak, Canada ......... 69 B11 68 46N 81 12W
Sanjawi, Pakistan ......... 42 D3 30 17N 68 21 E
Sanje, Uganda ............ 54 C3 0 49S 31 30 E
Sanjo, Japan ............. 30 F9 37 37N 138 57 E
Sankh →, India ........... 43 H11 22 15N 84 48 E
Sankt Gallen, Switz. ....... 20 C8 47 26N 9 22 E
Sankt Michel = Mikkeli, Finland . 9 F22 61 43N 27 15 E
Sankt Moritz, Switz. ....... 20 C8 46 30N 9 50 E
Sankt-Peterburg, Russia .... 18 C5 59 55N 30 20 E
Sankt Pölten, Austria ...... 16 D8 48 12N 15 38 E
Sankuru →, Dem. Rep. of
the Congo ............... 52 E4 4 17S 20 25 E

Sanliurfa, Turkey .......... 19 G6 37 12N 38 50 E
Sanlúcar de Barrameda, Spain . 21 D2 36 46N 6 21W
Sanmenxia, China ......... 34 G6 34 47N 111 12 E
Sanming, China ........... 33 D6 26 15N 117 40 E
Sannaspos, S. Africa ....... 56 D4 29 6S 26 34 E
Sannicandro Gargánico, Italy .. 22 D6 41 50N 15 34 E
Sânnicolau Mare, Romania ... 17 E11 46 5N 20 39 E
Sannieshof, S. Africa ....... 56 D4 26 30S 25 47 E
Sannin, J., Lebanon ........ 46 B4 33 57N 35 52 E
Sanniquellie, Liberia ....... 50 G4 7 19N 8 38W
Sanoe, Antarctica ......... 5 D2 70 20S 9 0W
Sanok, Poland ............ 17 D12 49 35N 22 10 E
Sanquhar, U.K. ........... 11 F5 55 22N 3 54W
Sans Souci, Trin. & Tob. .... 93 K16 10 50N 61 0W
Sant Antoni Abat, Spain .... 24 C7 38 59N 1 19 E
Sant Carles, Spain ........ 24 B8 39 3N 1 34 E
Sant Feliu de Guíxols, Spain .. 21 B7 41 45N 3 1 E
Sant Ferran, Spain ........ 24 C7 38 42N 1 28 E
Sant Francesc de Formentera,
Spain ................... 24 C7 38 42N 1 26 E
Sant Jaume, Spain ........ 24 B11 39 54N 4 4 E
Sant Joan Baptista, Spain ... 24 B8 39 5N 1 31 E
Sant Jordi, Ibiza, Spain .... 24 C7 38 53N 1 24 E
Sant Jordi, Mallorca, Spain .. 24 B9 39 33N 2 46 E
Sant Jordi, G. de, Spain .... 21 B6 40 53N 1 2 E
Sant Llorenç des Cardassar,
Spain ................... 24 B10 39 37N 3 17 E
Sant Mateu, Spain ........ 24 B7 39 3N 1 23 E
Sant Miquel, Spain ........ 24 B7 39 3N 1 26 E
Sant Telm, Spain ......... 24 B9 39 35N 2 21 E
Santa Agnés, Spain ....... 24 B7 39 3N 1 21 E
Santa Ana, Bolivia ........ 92 F5 13 50S 65 40W
Santa Ana, El Salv. ........ 88 D2 14 0N 89 31W
Santa Ana, Mexico ........ 86 A2 30 31N 111 8W
Santa Ana, U.S.A. ......... 79 M9 33 46N 117 52W
Sant' Antíoco, Italy ........ 22 E3 39 4N 8 27 E
Santa Bárbara, Chile ....... 94 D1 37 40S 72 1W
Santa Barbara, Honduras .... 88 D2 14 53N 88 14W
Santa Bárbara, Mexico ..... 86 B3 26 48N 105 50W
Santa Barbara, U.S.A. ...... 79 L7 34 25N 119 42W
Santa Barbara Channel, U.S.A. . 79 L7 34 15N 120 0W
Santa Barbara I., U.S.A. .... 79 M7 33 29N 119 2W
Santa Catalina, Gulf of, U.S.A. . 79 N9 33 10N 117 50W
Santa Catalina I., Mexico .... 86 B2 25 40N 110 50W
Santa Catalina I., U.S.A. .... 79 M8 33 23N 118 25W
Santa Catarina □, Brazil .... 95 B6 27 25S 48 30W
Santa Catarina, I. de, Brazil .. 95 B6 27 30S 48 40W
Santa Cecília, Brazil ....... 95 B5 26 56S 50 18W
Santa Clara, Cuba ......... 88 B4 22 20N 80 0W
Santa Clara, Calif., U.S.A. ... 78 H5 37 21N 121 57W
Santa Clara, Utah, U.S.A. ... 77 H7 37 8N 113 39W
Santa Clara, El Golfo de, Mexico 86 A2 31 42N 114 30W
Santa Clara de Olimar, Uruguay 95 C5 32 54S 54 54W
Santa Clarita, U.S.A. ....... 79 L8 34 24N 118 30W
Santa Clotilde, Peru ....... 92 D4 2 33S 73 45W
Santa Coloma de Gramenet,
Spain ................... 21 B7 41 27N 2 13 E
Santa Cruz, Argentina ...... 96 G3 50 0S 68 32W
Santa Cruz, Bolivia ........ 92 G6 17 43S 63 10W
Santa Cruz, Chile ......... 94 C1 34 38S 71 27W
Santa Cruz, Costa Rica ..... 88 D2 10 15N 85 35W
Santa Cruz, Madeira ....... 24 D3 32 42N 16 46W
Santa Cruz, Phil. .......... 37 B6 14 20N 121 24 E
Santa Cruz, U.S.A. ........ 78 J4 36 58N 122 1W
Santa Cruz →, Argentina ... 96 G3 50 10S 68 20W
Santa Cruz de la Palma,
Canary Is. ............... 24 F2 28 41N 17 46W
Santa Cruz de la Palma ✈ (SPC),
Canary Is. ............... 24 F2 28 40N 17 45W
Santa Cruz de Tenerife,
Canary Is. ............... 24 F3 28 28N 16 15W
Santa Cruz del Norte, Cuba .. 88 B3 23 9N 81 55W
Santa Cruz del Sur, Cuba ... 88 B4 20 44N 78 0W
Santa Cruz do Rio Pardo, Brazil . 95 A6 22 54S 49 37W
Santa Cruz do Sul, Brazil ... 95 B5 29 42S 52 25W
Santa Cruz I., U.S.A. ....... 79 M7 34 1N 119 43W
Santa Cruz Is., Solomon Is. .. 64 J8 10 30S 166 0 E
Santa Cruz Mts., Jamaica ... 88 a 17 58N 77 43W
Santa Domingo, Cay, Bahamas . 88 B4 21 25N 75 15W
Santa Elena, Argentina ..... 94 C4 30 58S 59 47W
Santa Elena, C., Costa Rica .. 88 D2 10 54N 85 56W
Santa Eulàlia des Riu, Spain .. 24 C8 38 59N 1 32 E
Santa Fe, Argentina ....... 94 C3 31 35S 60 41W
Santa Fe, U.S.A. .......... 77 J11 35 41N 105 57W
Santa Fé □, Argentina ..... 94 C3 31 50S 60 55W
Santa Fé do Sul, Brazil ..... 93 H8 20 13S 50 56W
Santa Filomena, Brazil ..... 93 E9 9 6S 45 50W
Santa Gertrudis, Spain ..... 24 C7 39 0N 1 26 E
Santa Inés, Brazil ......... 93 F11 3 17S 39 48W
Santa Inés, I., Chile ....... 96 G2 54 0S 73 0W
Santa Isabel, Argentina ..... 94 D2 36 10S 66 54W
Santa Isabel do Morro, Brazil . 93 F8 11 34S 50 40W
Santa Lucía, Corrientes,
Argentina ............... 94 B4 28 58S 59 5W
Santa Lucia, San Juan, Argentina 94 C2 31 30S 68 30W
Santa Lucía, Uruguay ...... 94 C4 34 27S 56 24W
Santa Lucia Range, U.S.A. .. 78 K5 36 0N 121 20W
Santa Magdalena, I., Mexico .. 86 C2 24 40N 112 15W
Santa Margarita, Argentina .. 94 D3 38 28S 61 35W
Santa Margarita, Spain ..... 24 B10 39 42N 3 6 E
Santa Margarita →, U.S.A. .. 79 M9 33 13N 117 23W
Santa Margarita, I., Mexico .. 86 C2 24 30N 111 50W
Santa María, Argentina ..... 94 B2 26 40S 66 0W
Santa Maria, Brazil ........ 95 B5 29 40S 53 48W
Santa Maria, U.S.A. ....... 79 L6 34 57N 120 26W
Santa María →, Mexico ..... 86 A3 31 0N 107 14W
Santa María, B. de, Mexico .. 86 B3 25 10N 108 40W
Santa Maria da Vitória, Brazil . 93 F10 13 24S 44 12W
Santa Maria del Camí, Spain . 24 B9 39 38N 2 47 E
Santa Maria di Léuca, C., Italy . 23 E8 39 47N 18 22 E
Santa Marta, Colombia ..... 92 A4 11 15N 74 13W
Santa Marta, Sierra Nevada de,
Colombia ................ 92 A4 10 55N 73 50W
Santa Marta Grande, C., Brazil . 95 B6 28 43S 48 50W
Santa Maura = Levkás, Greece . 23 E9 38 40N 20 43 E
Santa Monica, U.S.A. ...... 79 M8 34 1N 118 29W
Santa Monica Mts. △, U.S.A. . 79 L8 34 4N 118 44W
Santa Paula, U.S.A. ....... 79 L7 34 21N 119 4W
Santa Ponça, Spain ....... 24 B9 39 30N 2 31 E
Santa Rita, U.S.A. ........ 77 K10 32 48N 108 4W
Santa Rosa, La Pampa, Argentina 94 D3 36 40S 64 17W
Santa Rosa, San Luis, Argentina 94 C2 32 21S 65 10W
Santa Rosa, Brazil ........ 95 B5 27 52S 54 29W
Santa Rosa, Calif., U.S.A. ... 78 G4 38 26N 122 43W
Santa Rosa, N. Mex., U.S.A. . 81 H2 34 57N 104 41W
Santa Rosa and San Jacinto
Mts. △, U.S.A. ........... 79 M10 33 28N 116 20W

Santa Rosa de Copán, Honduras 88 D2 14 47N 88 46W
Santa Rosa de Río Primero,
Argentina ............... 94 C3 31 8S 63 20W
Santa Rosa del Sara, Bolivia .. 92 G6 17 7S 63 35W
Santa Rosa I., Calif., U.S.A. .. 79 M6 33 58N 120 6W
Santa Rosa I., Fla., U.S.A. ... 83 K2 30 20N 86 50W
Santa Rosa Range, U.S.A. ... 76 F5 41 45N 117 40W
Santa Rosalía, Mexico ...... 86 B2 27 20N 112 20W
Santa Sylvina, Argentina .... 94 B3 27 50S 61 10W
Santa Tecla = Nueva San
Salvador, El Salv. ......... 88 D2 13 40N 89 18W
Santa Teresa, Argentina .... 94 C3 33 25S 60 47W
Santa Teresa, Australia ..... 62 C1 24 8S 134 22 E
Santa Teresa, Mexico ...... 87 B5 25 17N 97 51W
Santa Teresa △, Uruguay ... 95 C5 33 57S 53 31W
Santa Vitória do Palmar, Brazil . 95 C5 33 32S 53 25W
Santa Ynez →, U.S.A. ...... 79 L6 35 41N 120 36W
Santa Ynez Mts., U.S.A. .... 79 L6 34 30N 120 0W
Santa Ysabel, U.S.A. ...... 79 M10 33 7N 116 40W
Santai, China ............ 32 C5 31 5N 104 58 E
Santana, Madeira ......... 24 D3 32 48N 16 52W
Santana, Coxilha de, Brazil .. 95 C4 30 50S 55 35W
Santana do Livramento, Brazil . 95 C4 30 55S 55 30W
Santander, Spain ......... 21 A4 43 27N 3 51W
Santander Jiménez, Mexico .. 87 C5 24 11N 98 29W
Santanilla, Is., Honduras .... 88 C3 17 22N 83 57W
Santanyí, Spain ........... 24 B10 39 20N 3 5 E
Santaquin, U.S.A. ......... 76 G8 39 59N 111 47W
Santarém, Brazil .......... 93 D8 2 25S 54 42W
Santarém, Portugal ........ 21 C1 39 12N 8 42W
Santaren Channel, W. Indies .. 88 B4 24 0N 79 30W
Santee, U.S.A. ........... 79 N10 32 50N 116 58W
Santee →, U.S.A. ......... 83 J6 33 7N 79 17W
Santiago, Brazil .......... 95 B5 29 11S 54 52W
Santiago, Canary Is. ....... 24 F2 28 2N 17 12W
Santiago, Chile ........... 94 C1 33 24S 70 40W
Santiago, Panama ......... 88 E3 8 0N 81 0W
Santiago □, Chile ......... 94 C1 33 30S 70 50W
Santiago →, Mexico ....... 66 G9 25 11N 105 26W
Santiago →, Peru ......... 92 D3 4 27S 77 38W
Santiago de Compostela, Spain . 21 A1 42 52N 8 37W
Santiago de Cuba, Cuba .... 88 C4 20 0N 75 49W
Santiago de los Cabelleros,
Dom. Rep. ............... 89 C5 19 30N 70 40W
Santiago del Estero, Argentina . 94 B3 27 50S 64 15W
Santiago del Estero □, Argentina 94 B3 27 40S 63 15W
Santiago del Teide, Canary Is. . 24 F3 28 17N 16 48W
Santiago Ixcuintla, Mexico ... 86 C3 21 50N 105 11W
Santiago Papasquiaro, Mexico . 86 C3 25 0N 105 20W
Santiaguillo, L. de, Mexico ... 86 C4 24 50N 104 50W
Santo Amaro, Brazil ....... 93 F11 12 30S 38 43W
Santo Anastácio, Brazil ..... 95 A5 21 58S 51 39W
Santo André, Brazil ........ 95 A6 23 39S 46 29W
Santo Ângelo, Brazil ....... 95 B5 28 15S 54 15W
Santo Antônio do Içá, Brazil .. 92 D5 3 5S 67 57W
Santo Antônio do Leverger,
Brazil ................... 93 G7 15 52S 56 5W
Santo Domingo, Dom. Rep. .. 89 C6 18 30N 69 59W
Santo Domingo, Baja Calif.,
Mexico .................. 86 A1 30 43N 116 2W
Santo Domingo, Baja Calif. S.,
Mexico .................. 86 B2 25 32N 112 2W
Santo Domingo, Nic. ....... 88 D3 12 14N 84 59W
Santo Domingo de los
Colorados, Ecuador ....... 92 D3 0 15S 79 9W
Santo Domingo Pueblo, U.S.A. . 77 J10 35 31N 106 22W
Santo Tomás, Mexico ...... 86 A1 31 33N 116 24W
Santo Tomás →, Peru ...... 92 F4 14 26S 72 8W
Santo Tomé, Argentina ..... 95 B4 28 40S 56 5W
Santo Tomé de Guayana =
Ciudad Guayana, Venezuela . 92 B6 8 0N 62 30W
Santoña, Spain ........... 21 A4 43 29N 3 27W
Santorini = Thíra, Greece ... 23 F11 36 23N 25 27 E
Santos, Brazil ............ 95 A6 24 0S 46 20W
Santos Dumont, Brazil ..... 95 A7 22 55S 43 10W
Sanur, Indonesia .......... 37 K18 8 41S 115 15 E
Sanwer, India ............ 42 H6 22 59N 75 50 E
Sanxiang, China .......... 33 G9 22 21N 113 25 E
Sanyuan, China .......... 34 G5 34 35N 108 58 E
São Bernardo do Campo, Brazil . 95 A6 23 45S 46 34W
São Borja, Brazil ......... 95 B4 28 39S 56 0W
São Carlos, Brazil ........ 95 A6 22 0S 47 50W
São Cristóvão, Brazil ...... 93 F11 11 1S 37 15W
São Domingos, Brazil ...... 93 F9 13 25S 46 19W
São Francisco, Brazil ...... 93 G10 16 0S 44 50W
São Francisco →, Brazil .... 93 F11 10 30S 36 24W
São Francisco do Sul, Brazil .. 95 B6 26 15S 48 36W
São Gabriel, Brazil ........ 95 C5 30 20S 54 20W
São Gonçalo, Brazil ....... 95 A7 22 48S 43 5W
Sao Hill, Tanzania ........ 55 D4 8 20S 35 12 E
São João da Boa Vista, Brazil . 95 A6 22 0S 46 52W
São João da Madeira, Portugal . 21 B1 40 54N 8 30W
São João del Rei, Brazil .... 95 A7 21 8S 44 15W
São João do Araguaia, Brazil . 93 E9 5 23S 48 46W
São João do Piauí, Brazil ... 93 E10 8 21S 42 15W
São Joaquim, Brazil ....... 95 B6 28 18S 49 56W
São Jorge, Pta. de, Madeira .. 24 D3 32 50N 16 53W
São José, Brazil .......... 95 B5 27 38S 48 39W
São José do Norte, Brazil ... 95 C5 32 1S 52 3W
São José do Rio Prêto, Brazil . 95 A6 20 50S 49 20W
São José dos Campos, Brazil . 95 A6 23 7S 45 52W
São Leopoldo, Brazil ...... 95 B5 29 50S 51 10W
São Lourenço, Brazil ...... 95 A6 22 7S 45 3W
São Lourenço →, Brazil .... 93 G7 17 53S 57 27W
São Lourenço, Pta. de, Madeira . 24 D3 32 44N 16 39W
São Lourenço do Sul, Brazil . 95 C5 31 22S 51 58W
São Luís, Brazil .......... 93 D10 2 39S 44 15W
São Marcos →, Brazil ...... 93 G9 18 15S 47 37W
São Marcos, B. de, Brazil ... 93 D10 2 0S 44 0W
São Mateus, Brazil ........ 93 G11 18 44S 39 50W
São Mateus do Sul, Brazil .. 95 B5 25 52S 50 23W
São Miguel do Oeste, Brazil .. 95 B5 26 45S 53 34W
São Paulo, Brazil ......... 95 A6 23 32S 46 37W
São Paulo □, Brazil ....... 95 A6 22 0S 49 0W
São Paulo, I., Atl. Oc. ...... 2 D8 0 50N 31 40W
São Pedro do Sul, Portugal .. 21 B1 40 46N 8 4W
São Roque, Madeira ....... 24 D3 32 46N 16 48W
São Roque, C. de, Brazil .... 93 E12 5 30S 35 16W
São Sebastião, I. de, Brazil .. 95 A6 23 50S 45 18W
São Sebastião do Paraíso, Brazil . 95 A6 20 54S 46 59W
São Tomé, São Tomé & Príncipe 48 F4 0 10N 6 39 E
São Tomé, C. de, Brazil .... 95 A7 22 0S 40 59W
São Tomé & Príncipe ■, Africa . 49 F4 0 12N 6 39 E
São Vicente, Brazil ........ 95 A6 23 57S 46 23W
São Vicente, Madeira ...... 24 D2 32 48N 17 3W
São Vicente, C. de, Portugal . 21 D1 37 0N 9 0W

Saona, I., Dom. Rep. ....... 89 C6 18 10N 68 40W
Saône →, France .......... 20 D6 45 44N 4 50 E
Saonek, Indonesia ........ 37 E8 0 22S 130 55 E
Sapam, Ao, Thailand ...... 39 a 8 0N 98 26 E
Saparua, Indonesia ........ 37 E7 3 33S 128 40 E
Sapele, Nigeria ........... 50 G7 5 50N 5 40 E
Sapelo I., U.S.A. .......... 83 K5 31 25N 81 12W
Sapi △, Zimbabwe ........ 55 F2 15 48S 29 42 E
Saposoa, Peru ............ 92 E3 6 55S 76 45W
Sapphire, Australia ........ 62 C4 23 28S 147 43 E
Sappho, U.S.A. ........... 78 B2 48 4N 124 16W
Sapporo, Japan ........... 30 C10 43 0N 141 21 E
Sapulpa, U.S.A. .......... 81 H6 35 59N 96 5W
Saqqez, Iran ............. 44 B5 36 15N 46 20 E
Sar Dasht, Iran ........... 45 C6 32 32N 48 52 E
Sar-e Pol □, Afghan. ....... 40 B4 36 20N 65 50 E
Sar Gachîneh = Yâsûj, Iran .. 45 D6 30 31N 51 31 E
Sar Planina, Macedonia ..... 23 C9 42 0N 21 0 E
Sara Buri = Saraburi, Thailand . 38 E3 14 30N 100 55 E
Sarāb, Iran .............. 44 B5 37 55N 47 40 E
Sarabadi, Iraq ............ 44 C5 33 1N 44 48 E
Saraburi, Thailand ........ 38 E3 14 30N 100 55 E
Saradiya, India ........... 42 J4 21 34N 70 2 E
Saragossa = Zaragoza, Spain . 21 B5 41 39N 0 53W
Saraguro, Ecuador ........ 92 D3 3 35S 79 16W
Sarai Naurang, Pakistan .... 42 C4 32 50N 70 47 E
Saraikela, India .......... 43 H11 22 42N 85 56 E
Sarajevo, Bos.-H. ......... 23 C8 43 52N 18 26 E
Sarakhs, Turkmenistan ..... 45 B9 36 32N 61 13 E
Saran, Gunung, Indonesia ... 36 E4 0 30S 111 25 E
Saranac L., U.S.A. ........ 85 B10 44 20N 74 10W
Saranac Lake, U.S.A. ...... 85 B10 44 20N 74 8W
Saranda, Tanzania ........ 54 D3 5 45S 34 59 E
Sarandí del Yi, Uruguay ..... 95 C4 33 18S 55 38W
Sarandí Grande, Uruguay ... 94 C4 33 44S 56 20W
Sarangani B., Phil. ........ 37 C7 6 0N 125 13 E
Sarangani Is., Phil. ....... 37 C7 5 25N 125 25 E
Sarangarh, India ......... 41 J13 21 30N 83 5 E
Saransk, Russia .......... 18 D8 54 10N 45 10 E
Sarapul, Russia .......... 18 C9 56 28N 53 48 E
Sarasota, U.S.A. ......... 83 M4 27 20N 82 32W
Saratoga, Calif., U.S.A. .... 78 H4 37 16N 122 2W
Saratoga, Wyo., U.S.A. .... 76 F10 41 27N 106 49W
Saratoga △, U.S.A. ....... 85 D11 43 0N 73 37W
Saratoga Springs, U.S.A. ... 85 C11 43 5N 73 47W
Saratok, Malaysia ........ 36 D4 1 55N 111 17 E
Saratov, Russia .......... 19 D8 51 30N 46 2 E
Saravan, Laos ............ 38 E6 15 43N 106 25 E
Sarawak □, Malaysia ...... 36 D4 2 0N 113 0 E
Saray, Turkey ............ 23 D12 41 26N 27 55 E
Sarayköy, Turkey ......... 23 F13 37 55N 28 54 E
Sarbāz, Iran ............. 45 E9 26 38N 61 19 E
Sarbīsheh, Iran .......... 45 C8 32 30N 59 40 E
Sarda →, India ........... 41 F12 27 21N 81 23 E
Sardarshahr, India ........ 42 E6 28 30N 74 29 E
Sardegna □, Italy ......... 22 D3 40 0N 9 0 E
Sardhana, India .......... 42 E7 29 9N 77 39 E
Sardina, Pta., Canary Is. .... 24 F4 28 9N 15 44W
Sardinia = Sardegna □, Italy . 22 D3 40 0N 9 0 E
Sardis, Turkey ........... 23 E12 38 28N 28 2 E
Sārdūïyeh = Dar Mazār, Iran . 45 D8 29 14N 57 20 E
Saren, Indonesia ......... 37 J18 8 26S 115 34 E
Sargasso Sea, Atl. Oc. ..... 66 G13 27 0N 72 0W
Sargodha, Pakistan ....... 42 C5 32 10N 72 40 E
Sarh, Chad .............. 51 G9 9 5N 18 23 E
Sārī, Iran ............... 45 B7 36 30N 53 4 E
Saria, India ............. 43 J10 21 38N 83 22 E
Sariab, Pakistan .......... 42 D2 30 6N 66 59 E
Sarıgöl, Turkey .......... 23 E13 38 14N 28 41 E
Sarikei, Malaysia ......... 36 D4 2 8N 111 30 E
Sarila, India ............ 43 G8 25 46N 79 41 E
Sarina, Australia ......... 62 C4 21 22S 149 13 E
Sarita, U.S.A. ............ 81 M6 27 13N 97 47W
Sariwŏn, N. Korea ........ 35 E13 38 31N 125 46 E
Sarju →, India ........... 43 F9 27 21N 81 23 E
Sark, U.K. .............. 13 H5 49 25N 2 22W
Sarkari Tala, India ........ 42 F4 27 39N 70 52 E
Şarköy, Turkey ........... 23 D12 40 36N 27 6 E
Sarlat-la-Canéda, France ... 20 D4 44 54N 1 13 E
Sarmi, Indonesia ......... 37 E9 1 49S 138 44 E
Sarmiento, Argentina ...... 96 F3 45 35S 69 5W
Särna, Sweden ........... 9 F15 61 41N 13 8 E
Sarnia, Canada ........... 84 D2 42 58N 82 23W
Sarolangun, Indonesia ..... 36 E2 2 19S 102 42 E
Saronikós Kólpos, Greece ... 23 F10 37 45N 23 45 E
Saros Körfezi, Turkey ...... 23 D12 40 30N 26 15 E
Sarpsborg, Norway ....... 9 G14 59 16N 11 7 E
Sarre = Saar →, Europe .... 15 E6 49 41N 6 32 E
Sarreguemines, France .... 20 B7 49 5N 7 4 E
Sarthe →, France ......... 20 C3 47 33N 0 31W
Saruna →, Pakistan ....... 42 F2 26 31N 67 7 E
Sarvar, India ............ 42 F6 26 4N 75 0 E
Sarvestān, Iran .......... 45 D7 29 20N 53 10 E
Sary-Tash, Kyrgyzstan ..... 28 F8 39 44N 73 15 E
Saryshagan, Kazakhstan .... 28 E8 46 12N 73 38 E
Sasan Gir, India .......... 42 J4 21 10N 70 36 E
Sasaram, India .......... 43 G11 24 57N 84 5 E
Sasebo, Japan ........... 31 H4 33 10N 129 43 E
Saser, India ............. 43 B7 34 50N 77 50 E
Saskatchewan □, Canada ... 71 C7 54 40N 106 0W
Saskatchewan →, Canada .. 71 C8 53 37N 100 40W
Saskatoon, Canada ....... 71 C7 52 10N 106 38W
Saskylakh, Russia ........ 29 B12 71 55N 114 1 E
Saslaya △, Nic. .......... 88 D2 13 45N 85 4W
Sasolburg, S. Africa ....... 57 D4 26 46S 27 49 E
Sasovo, Russia ........... 18 D7 54 25N 41 55 E
Sassandra, Ivory C. ....... 50 H4 4 58N 6 5W
Sassandra →, Ivory C. ..... 50 H4 4 58N 6 5W
Sássari, Italy ............ 22 D3 40 43N 8 34 E
Sassnitz, Germany ........ 16 A7 54 29N 13 39 E
Sassuolo, Italy ........... 22 B4 44 33N 10 47 E
Sasyk, Ozero, Ukraine ..... 17 F15 45 45N 29 20 E
Sata-Misaki, Japan ....... 31 J5 31 0N 130 40 E
Satadougou, Mali ......... 50 F3 12 25N 11 25W
Satakunda = Satakunta, Finland . 9 F20 61 45N 23 0 E
Satakunta, Finland ........ 9 F20 61 45N 23 0 E
Satara, India ............ 40 L8 17 44N 73 58 E
Satara, S. Africa ......... 57 C5 24 35S 31 45 E
Satarwala, India ......... 43 H11 23 55N 84 16 E
Satevó, Mexico ........... 86 B3 27 57N 106 7W
Satilla →, U.S.A. ......... 83 K5 30 59N 81 29W
Satmala Hills, India ....... 40 J9 20 15N 74 40 E
Satna, India ............. 43 G9 24 35N 80 50 E
Sátoraljaújhely, Hungary ... 17 D11 48 25N 21 41 E
Satpura Ra., India ........ 40 J10 21 25N 76 10 E

Satsuna-Shotō, *Japan* ......... **31 K5** 30 0N 130 0 E
Sattahip, *Thailand* ......... **38 F3** 12 41N 100 54 E
Satu Mare, *Romania* ......... **17 E12** 47 46N 22 55 E
Satui, *Indonesia* ......... **36 E5** 3 50S 115 27 E
Satun, *Thailand* ......... **39 J3** 6 43N 100 2 E
Saturnina →, *Brazil* ......... **92 F7** 12 15S 58 10W
Sauce, *Argentina* ......... **94 C4** 30 5S 58 46W
Sauceda, *Mexico* ......... **86 B4** 25 55N 101 18W
Saucillo, *Mexico* ......... **86 B3** 28 1N 105 17W
Sauda, *Norway* ......... **9 G12** 59 40N 6 20 E
Sauðarkrókur, *Iceland* ......... **8 D4** 65 45N 19 40W
Saudi Arabia ■, *Asia* ......... **44 B3** 26 0N 44 0 E
Sauerland, *Germany* ......... **16 C4** 51 12N 7 59 E
Saugeen →, *Canada* ......... **84 B3** 44 30N 81 22W
Saugerties, *U.S.A.* ......... **85 D11** 42 5N 73 57W
Saugus, *U.S.A.* ......... **79 L8** 34 25N 118 32W
Sauk Centre, *U.S.A.* ......... **80 C7** 45 44N 94 57W
Sauk Rapids, *U.S.A.* ......... **80 C7** 45 35N 94 10W
Sault Ste. Marie, *Canada* ......... **72 C3** 46 30N 84 20W
Sault Ste. Marie, *U.S.A.* ......... **69 D11** 46 30N 84 21W
Saumlaki, *Indonesia* ......... **37 F8** 7 55S 131 20 E
Saumur, *France* ......... **20 C3** 47 15N 0 5W
Saunders, C., *N.Z.* ......... **59 L3** 45 53S 170 45 E
Saunders I., *Antarctica* ......... **5 B1** 57 48S 26 28W
Saunders Point, *Australia* ......... **61 E4** 27 52S 125 38 E
Saurimo, *Angola* ......... **52 F4** 9 40S 20 12 E
Sausalito, *U.S.A.* ......... **78 H4** 37 51N 122 29W
Savá, *Honduras* ......... **88 C2** 15 32N 86 15W
Sava →, *Serbia & M.* ......... **23 B9** 44 50N 20 26 E
Savage, *U.S.A.* ......... **80 B2** 47 27N 104 21W
Savage I. = Niue, *Cook Is.* ......... **65 J11** 19 2S 169 54W
Savage River, *Australia* ......... **63 G4** 41 31S 145 14 E
Savai'i, *Samoa* ......... **59 A12** 13 28S 172 24W
Savalou, *Benin* ......... **50 G6** 7 57N 1 58 E
Savane, *Mozam.* ......... **55 F4** 19 37S 35 8 E
Savanna, *U.S.A.* ......... **80 D9** 42 5N 90 8W
Savanna-la-Mar, *Jamaica* ......... **88 a** 18 10N 78 10W
Savannah, *Ga., U.S.A.* ......... **83 J5** 32 5N 81 6W
Savannah, *Mo., U.S.A.* ......... **80 F7** 39 56N 94 50W
Savannah, *Tenn., U.S.A.* ......... **83 H1** 35 14N 88 15W
Savannah →, *U.S.A.* ......... **83 J5** 32 2N 80 53W
Savannakhet, *Laos* ......... **38 D5** 16 30N 104 49 E
Savant L., *Canada* ......... **72 B1** 50 16N 90 44W
Savant Lake, *Canada* ......... **72 B1** 50 14N 90 40W
Save →, *Mozam.* ......... **57 C5** 21 16S 34 0 E
Sāveh, *Iran* ......... **45 C6** 35 2N 50 20 E
Savelugu, *Ghana* ......... **50 G5** 9 38N 0 54W
Savo, *Finland* ......... **8 E22** 62 45N 27 30 E
Savoie □, *France* ......... **20 D7** 45 26N 6 25 E
Savolax = Savo, *Finland* ......... **8 E22** 62 45N 27 30 E
Savona, *Italy* ......... **20 D8** 44 17N 8 30 E
Savona, *U.S.A.* ......... **84 D7** 42 17N 77 13W
Savonlinna, *Finland* ......... **18 B4** 61 52N 28 53 E
Savoy = Savoie □, *France* ......... **20 D7** 45 26N 6 25 E
Savur, *Turkey* ......... **44 B4** 37 34N 40 53 E
Sawahlunto, *Indonesia* ......... **36 E2** 0 40S 100 52 E
Sawai, *Indonesia* ......... **37 E7** 3 0S 129 5 E
Sawai Madhopur, *India* ......... **42 G7** 26 0N 76 25 E
Sawang Daen Din, *Thailand* ......... **38 D4** 17 28N 103 28 E
Sawankhalok, *Thailand* ......... **38 D2** 17 19N 99 50 E
Sawara, *Japan* ......... **31 G10** 35 55N 140 30 E
Sawatch Range, *U.S.A.* ......... **77 G10** 38 30N 106 30W
Sawel Mt., *U.K.* ......... **10 B4** 54 50N 7 2W
Sawi, *Thailand* ......... **39 G2** 10 14N 99 5 E
Sawmills, *Zimbabwe* ......... **55 F2** 19 30S 28 2 E
Sawtooth △, *U.S.A.* ......... **76 D6** 44 0N 114 50W
Sawtooth Range, *U.S.A.* ......... **76 E6** 44 3N 114 58W
Sawu, *Indonesia* ......... **37 F6** 10 35S 121 50 E
Sawu Sea, *Indonesia* ......... **37 F6** 9 30S 121 50 E
Saxby →, *Australia* ......... **62 B3** 18 25S 140 53 E
Saxmundham, *U.K.* ......... **13 E9** 52 13N 1 30 E
Saxony = Sachsen □, *Germany* ......... **16 C7** 50 55N 13 10 E
Saxony, Lower =
  Niedersachsen □, *Germany* ......... **16 B5** 52 50N 9 0 E
Saxton, *U.S.A.* ......... **84 F6** 40 13N 78 15W
Sayabec, *Canada* ......... **73 C6** 48 35N 67 41W
Sayaboury, *Laos* ......... **38 C3** 19 15N 101 45 E
Sayán, *Peru* ......... **92 F3** 11 8S 77 12W
Sayan, Vostochnyy, *Russia* ......... **29 D10** 54 0N 96 0 E
Sayan, Zapadnyy, *Russia* ......... **29 D10** 52 30N 94 0 E
Saydā, *Lebanon* ......... **46 B4** 33 35N 35 25 E
Sayhandulaan = Oldziyt,
  *Mongolia* ......... **34 B5** 44 40N 109 1 E
Sayhūt, *Yemen* ......... **47 D5** 15 12N 51 10 E
Saylac = Zeila, *Somali Rep.* ......... **47 E3** 11 21N 43 30 E
Saynshand, *Mongolia* ......... **33 B6** 44 55N 110 11 E
Sayre, *Okla., U.S.A.* ......... **81 H5** 35 18N 99 38W
Sayre, *Pa., U.S.A.* ......... **85 E8** 41 59N 76 32W
Sayreville, *U.S.A.* ......... **85 F10** 40 28N 74 22W
Sayula, *Mexico* ......... **86 D4** 19 50N 103 40W
Sayward, *Canada* ......... **70 C3** 50 21N 125 55W
Sazanit, *Albania* ......... **23 D8** 40 30N 19 20 E
Sázava →, *Czech Rep.* ......... **16 D8** 49 53N 14 24 E
Sazin, *Pakistan* ......... **43 B5** 35 35N 73 30 E
Scafell Pike, *U.K.* ......... **12 C4** 54 27N 3 14W
Scalloway, *U.K.* ......... **11 A7** 60 9N 1 17W
Scalpay, *U.K.* ......... **11 D3** 57 18N 6 0W
Scandia, *Canada* ......... **70 C6** 50 20N 112 2W
Scandicci, *Italy* ......... **22 C4** 43 45N 11 11 E
Scandinavia, *Europe* ......... **8 E16** 64 0N 12 0 E
Scapa Flow, *U.K.* ......... **11 C5** 58 53N 3 3W
Scappoose, *U.S.A.* ......... **78 E4** 45 45N 122 53W
Scarba, *U.K.* ......... **11 E3** 56 11N 5 43W
Scarborough, *Trin. & Tob.* ......... **89 D7** 11 11N 60 42W
Scarborough, *U.K.* ......... **12 C7** 54 17N 0 24W
Scariff I., *Ireland* ......... **10 E1** 51 44N 10 15W
Scarp, *U.K.* ......... **11 C1** 58 1N 7 8W
Scebeli, Wabi →, *Somali Rep.* ......... **47 G3** 2 0N 44 0 E
Schaffhausen, *Switz.* ......... **20 C8** 47 42N 8 39 E
Schagen, *Neths.* ......... **15 B4** 52 49N 4 48 E
Schaghticoke, *U.S.A.* ......... **85 D11** 42 54N 73 35W
Schefferville, *Canada* ......... **73 B6** 54 48N 66 50W
Schelde →, *Belgium* ......... **15 C4** 51 15N 4 16 E
Schell Creek Ra., *U.S.A.* ......... **76 G6** 39 15N 114 30W
Schellsburg, *U.S.A.* ......... **84 F6** 40 3N 78 39W
Schenectady, *U.S.A.* ......... **85 D11** 42 49N 73 57W
Schenevus, *U.S.A.* ......... **85 D10** 42 33N 74 50W
Schiedam, *Neths.* ......... **15 C4** 51 55N 4 25 E
Schiermonnikoog, *Neths.* ......... **15 A6** 53 30N 6 15 E
Schio, *Italy* ......... **22 B4** 45 43N 11 21 E
Schiphol, Amsterdam ✈ (AMS),
  *Neths.* ......... **15 B4** 52 18N 4 45 E
Schleswig, *Germany* ......... **16 A5** 54 31N 9 34 E
Schleswig-Holstein □, *Germany* ......... **16 A5** 54 30N 9 30 E
Schœlcher, *Martinique* ......... **88 c** 14 36N 61 7W
Schoharie, *U.S.A.* ......... **85 D10** 42 40N 74 18W
Schoharie Cr. →, *U.S.A.* ......... **85 D10** 42 57N 74 18W
Scholls, *U.S.A.* ......... **78 E4** 45 24N 122 56W

Schouten I., *Australia* ......... **63 G4** 42 20S 148 20 E
Schouten Is. = Supiori, *Indonesia* **37 E9** 1 0S 136 0 E
Schouwen, *Neths.* ......... **15 C3** 51 43N 3 45 E
Schreiber, *Canada* ......... **72 C2** 48 45N 87 20W
Schroffenstein, *Namibia* ......... **56 D2** 27 11S 18 42 E
Schroon Lake, *U.S.A.* ......... **85 C11** 43 50N 73 46W
Schuler, *Canada* ......... **71 C6** 50 20N 110 6W
Schumacher, *Canada* ......... **72 C3** 48 30N 81 16W
Schurz, *U.S.A.* ......... **76 G4** 38 57N 118 49W
Schuyler, *U.S.A.* ......... **80 E6** 41 27N 97 4W
Schuylerville, *U.S.A.* ......... **85 C11** 43 6N 73 35W
Schuylkill →, *U.S.A.* ......... **85 G9** 39 53N 75 12W
Schuylkill Haven, *U.S.A.* ......... **85 F8** 40 37N 76 11W
Schwäbische Alb, *Germany* ......... **16 D5** 48 20N 9 30 E
Schwaner, Pegunungan,
  *Indonesia* ......... **36 E4** 1 0S 112 30 E
Schwarzrand, *Namibia* ......... **56 D2** 25 37S 16 50 E
Schwarzwald, *Germany* ......... **16 D5** 48 30N 8 20 E
Schwedt, *Germany* ......... **16 B8** 53 3N 14 16 E
Schweinfurt, *Germany* ......... **16 C6** 50 3N 10 14 E
Schweizer-Reneke, *S. Africa* ......... **56 D4** 27 11S 25 18 E
Schwenningen = Villingen-
  Schwenningen, *Germany* ......... **16 D5** 48 3N 8 26 E
Schwerin, *Germany* ......... **16 B6** 53 36N 11 22 E
Schwyz, *Switz.* ......... **20 C8** 47 2N 8 39 E
Sciacca, *Italy* ......... **22 F5** 37 31N 13 3 E
Scilla, *Italy* ......... **22 E6** 38 15N 15 43 E
Scilly, Isles of, *U.K.* ......... **13 H1** 49 56N 6 22W
Scioto →, *U.S.A.* ......... **82 F4** 38 44N 83 1W
Scituate, *U.S.A.* ......... **85 D14** 42 12N 70 44W
Scobey, *U.S.A.* ......... **80 A2** 48 47N 105 25W
Scone, *Australia* ......... **63 E5** 32 5S 150 52 E
Scone, *U.K.* ......... **11 E5** 56 25N 3 24W
Scoresbysund = Ittoqqortoormiit,
  *Greenland* ......... **4 B6** 70 20N 23 0W
Scotia, *Calif., U.S.A.* ......... **76 F1** 40 29N 124 6W
Scotia, *N.Y., U.S.A.* ......... **85 D11** 42 50N 73 58W
Scotia Sea, *Antarctica* ......... **5 B18** 56 5S 56 0W
Scotland, *Canada* ......... **84 C4** 43 1N 80 22W
Scotland □, *U.K.* ......... **11 E5** 57 0N 4 0W
Scott, *Antarctica* ......... **5 D11** 77 0S 165 0 E
Scott, C., *Australia* ......... **60 B4** 13 30S 129 49 E
Scott City, *U.S.A.* ......... **80 F4** 38 29N 100 54W
Scott Glacier, *Antarctica* ......... **5 C8** 66 15S 100 5 E
Scott I., *Antarctica* ......... **5 C11** 67 0S 179 0 E
Scott I., *Canada* ......... **70 C3** 50 48N 128 40W
Scott L., *Canada* ......... **71 B7** 59 55N 106 18W
Scott Reef, *Australia* ......... **60 B3** 14 0S 121 50 E
Scottburgh, *S. Africa* ......... **57 E5** 30 15S 30 47 E
Scottdale, *U.S.A.* ......... **84 F5** 40 6N 79 35W
Scottish Borders □, *U.K.* ......... **11 F6** 55 35N 2 50W
Scottsboro, *U.S.A.* ......... **83 H3** 34 40N 86 2W
Scottsburg, *U.S.A.* ......... **82 F3** 38 41N 85 47W
Scottsdale, *Australia* ......... **63 G4** 41 9S 147 31 E
Scottsdale, *U.S.A.* ......... **77 K7** 33 29N 111 56W
Scottsville, *Ky., U.S.A.* ......... **83 G2** 36 45N 86 11W
Scottsville, *N.Y., U.S.A.* ......... **84 C7** 43 2N 77 47W
Scottville, *U.S.A.* ......... **82 D2** 43 58N 86 17W
Scranton, *U.S.A.* ......... **85 E9** 41 25N 75 40W
Scugog, L., *Canada* ......... **84 B6** 44 10N 78 55W
Scunthorpe, *U.K.* ......... **12 D7** 53 36N 0 39W
Scutari = Shkodër, *Albania* ......... **23 C8** 42 4N 19 32 E
Seabrook, L., *Australia* ......... **61 F2** 30 55S 119 40 E
Seaford, *U.K.* ......... **13 G8** 50 47N 0 7 E
Seaford, *U.S.A.* ......... **82 F8** 38 39N 75 37W
Seaforth, *Australia* ......... **62 J6** 20 55S 148 57 E
Seaforth, *Canada* ......... **84 C3** 43 35N 81 25W
Seaforth, L., *U.K.* ......... **11 D2** 57 52N 6 36W
Seagraves, *U.S.A.* ......... **81 J3** 32 57N 102 34W
Seaham, *U.K.* ......... **12 C6** 54 50N 1 20W
Seal →, *Canada* ......... **71 B10** 59 4N 94 48W
Seal L., *Canada* ......... **73 B7** 54 20N 61 30W
Sealy, *U.S.A.* ......... **81 L6** 29 47N 96 9W
Searchlight, *U.S.A.* ......... **79 K12** 35 28N 114 55W
Searcy, *U.S.A.* ......... **81 H9** 35 15N 91 44W
Searles L., *U.S.A.* ......... **79 K9** 35 44N 117 21W
Seascale, *U.K.* ......... **12 C4** 54 24N 3 29W
Seaside, *Calif., U.S.A.* ......... **78 J5** 36 37N 121 50W
Seaside, *Oreg., U.S.A.* ......... **78 E3** 46 0N 123 56W
Seaspray, *Australia* ......... **63 F4** 38 25S 147 15 E
Seattle, *U.S.A.* ......... **78 C4** 47 36N 122 20W
Seattle-Tacoma International ✈
  (SEA), *U.S.A.* ......... **78 C4** 47 27N 122 18W
Seaview Ra., *Australia* ......... **62 B4** 18 40S 145 45 E
Sebago, L., *U.S.A.* ......... **85 C14** 43 52N 70 34W
Sebago Lake, *U.S.A.* ......... **85 C14** 43 51N 70 34W
Sebastián Vizcaíno, B., *Mexico* **86 B2** 28 0N 114 30W
Sebastopol = Sevastopol,
  *Ukraine* ......... **19 F5** 44 35N 33 30 E
Sebastopol, *U.S.A.* ......... **78 G4** 38 24N 122 49W
Sebewaing, *U.S.A.* ......... **82 D4** 43 44N 83 27W
Sebha = Sabhah, *Libya* ......... **51 C8** 27 9N 14 29 E
Şebinkarahisar, *Turkey* ......... **19 F6** 40 22N 38 28 E
Sebring, *Fla., U.S.A.* ......... **83 M5** 27 30N 81 27W
Sebring, *Ohio, U.S.A.* ......... **84 F3** 40 55N 81 2W
Sebringville, *Canada* ......... **84 C3** 43 24N 81 4W
Sebta = Ceuta, *N. Afr.* ......... **21 E3** 35 52N 5 18W
Sebuku, *Indonesia* ......... **36 E5** 3 30S 116 25 E
Sebuku, Teluk, *Malaysia* ......... **36 D5** 4 0N 118 10 E
Sechelt, *Canada* ......... **70 D4** 49 25N 123 42W
Sechura, Desierto de, *Peru* ......... **92 E2** 6 0S 80 30W
Secretary I., *N.Z.* ......... **59 L1** 45 15S 166 56 E
Secunderabad, *India* ......... **40 L11** 17 28N 78 30 E
Security-Widefield, *U.S.A.* ......... **80 F2** 38 45N 104 45W
Sedalia, *U.S.A.* ......... **80 F8** 38 42N 93 14W
Sedan, *France* ......... **20 B6** 49 43N 4 57 E
Sedan, *U.S.A.* ......... **81 G6** 37 8N 96 11W
Sedbergh, *U.K.* ......... **12 C5** 54 20N 2 31W
Seddon, *N.Z.* ......... **59 J5** 41 40S 174 7 E
Seddonville, *N.Z.* ......... **59 J4** 41 33S 172 1 E
Sedé Boqér, *Israel* ......... **46 E3** 30 52N 34 47 E
Sedeh, *Fārs, Iran* ......... **45 D7** 30 45N 52 11 E
Sedeh, *Khorāsān, Iran* ......... **45 C8** 33 20N 59 14 E
Sederot, *Israel* ......... **46 D3** 31 32N 34 37 E
Sédhiou, *Senegal* ......... **50 F2** 12 44N 15 30W
Sedley, *Canada* ......... **71 C8** 50 10N 104 0W
Sedona, *U.S.A.* ......... **77 J8** 34 52N 111 46W
Sedova, Pik, *Russia* ......... **28 B6** 73 29N 54 58 E
Sedro Woolley, *U.S.A.* ......... **78 B4** 48 30N 122 14W
Seeheim, *Namibia* ......... **56 D2** 26 50S 17 45 E
Seeis, *Namibia* ......... **56 C2** 22 29S 17 39 E
Seekoei →, *S. Africa* ......... **56 E4** 30 18S 25 1 E
Seeley's Bay, *Canada* ......... **85 B8** 44 29N 76 14W
Seferihisar, *Turkey* ......... **23 E12** 38 10N 26 50 E
Seg-ozero, *Russia* ......... **18 B5** 63 20N 33 46 E
Segamat, *Malaysia* ......... **39 L4** 2 30N 102 50 E
Segesta, *Italy* ......... **22 F5** 37 56N 12 50 E

Seget, *Indonesia* ......... **37 E8** 1 24S 130 58 E
Segezha, *Russia* ......... **18 B5** 63 44N 34 19 E
Ségou, *Mali* ......... **50 F4** 13 30N 6 16W
Segovia = Coco →, *Cent. Amer.* **88 D3** 15 0N 83 8W
Segovia, *Spain* ......... **21 B3** 40 57N 4 10W
Segre →, *Spain* ......... **21 B6** 41 40N 0 43 E
Séguéla, *Ivory C.* ......... **50 G4** 7 55N 6 40W
Seguin, *U.S.A.* ......... **81 L6** 29 34N 97 58W
Segundo →, *Argentina* ......... **94 C3** 30 53S 62 44W
Segura →, *Spain* ......... **21 C5** 38 3N 0 44W
Seh Konj, Kūh-e, *Iran* ......... **45 C8** 33 40N 58 24 E
Seh Qal'eh, *Iran* ......... **45 C8** 33 40N 58 24 E
Sehitwa, *Botswana* ......... **56 C3** 20 30S 22 30 E
Sehlabathebe △, *Lesotho* ......... **57 D4** 29 53S 29 7 E
Sehore, *India* ......... **42 H7** 23 10N 77 5 E
Sehwan, *Pakistan* ......... **42 F2** 26 28N 67 53 E
Seil, *U.K.* ......... **11 E3** 56 18N 5 38W
Seiland, *Norway* ......... **8 A20** 70 25N 23 15 E
Seiling, *U.S.A.* ......... **81 G5** 36 9N 98 56W
Seinäjoki, *Finland* ......... **9 E20** 62 40N 22 51 E
Seine →, *France* ......... **20 B4** 49 26N 0 26 E
Seistan = Sīstān, *Asia* ......... **45 D9** 30 50N 61 0 E
Seistan, Daryācheh-ye = Sīstān,
  Daryācheh-ye, *Iran* ......... **45 D9** 31 0N 61 0 E
Sekayu, *Indonesia* ......... **36 E2** 2 51S 103 51 E
Seke, *Tanzania* ......... **54 C3** 3 20S 33 31 E
Sekenke, *Tanzania* ......... **54 C3** 4 18S 34 11 E
Sekondi-Takoradi, *Ghana* ......... **50 H5** 4 58N 1 45W
Sekudai, *Malaysia* ......... **39 d** 1 32N 103 39 E
Sekuma, *Botswana* ......... **56 C3** 24 36S 23 50 E
Selah, *U.S.A.* ......... **76 C3** 46 39N 120 32W
Selama, *Malaysia* ......... **39 K3** 5 12N 100 42 E
Selaru, *Indonesia* ......... **37 F8** 8 9S 131 0 E
Selatan, Selat, *Malaysia* ......... **39 c** 5 15N 100 20 E
Selby, *U.K.* ......... **12 D6** 53 47N 1 5W
Selby, *U.S.A.* ......... **80 C4** 45 31N 100 2W
Selçuk, *Turkey* ......... **23 F12** 37 56N 27 22 E
Selden, *U.S.A.* ......... **80 F4** 39 33N 100 34W
Sele →, *Italy* ......... **22 D6** 40 29N 14 56 E
Selebi-Pikwe, *Botswana* ......... **57 C4** 21 58S 27 48 E
Selemdzha →, *Russia* ......... **29 D13** 51 42N 128 53 E
Selenga = Selenge Mörön →,
  *Asia* ......... **32 A5** 52 16N 106 16 E
Selenge Mörön →, *Asia* ......... **32 A5** 52 16N 106 16 E
Seletan, Tanjung, *Indonesia* ......... **36 E4** 4 10S 114 40 E
Sélibabi, *Mauritania* ......... **50 E3** 15 10N 12 15W
Seligman, *U.S.A.* ......... **77 J7** 35 20N 112 53W
Selīma, El Wâhât el, *Sudan* ......... **51 D11** 21 22N 29 19 E
Selinda Spillway →, *Botswana* ......... **56 B3** 18 35S 23 10 E
Selinsgrove, *U.S.A.* ......... **84 F8** 40 48N 76 52W
Selkirk, *Canada* ......... **71 C9** 50 10N 96 55W
Selkirk, *U.K.* ......... **11 F6** 55 33N 2 50W
Selkirk I. = Horse I., *Canada* ......... **71 C9** 53 20N 99 6W
Selkirk Mts., *Canada* ......... **68 C8** 51 15N 117 40W
Sellafield, *U.K.* ......... **12 C4** 54 25N 3 29W
Selliá, *Greece* ......... **25 D6** 35 12N 24 23 E
Sells, *U.S.A.* ......... **77 L8** 31 55N 111 53W
Selma, *Ala., U.S.A.* ......... **83 J2** 32 25N 87 1W
Selma, *Calif., U.S.A.* ......... **78 J7** 36 34N 119 37W
Selma, *N.C., U.S.A.* ......... **83 H6** 35 32N 78 17W
Selmer, *U.S.A.* ......... **83 H1** 35 10N 88 36W
Selous △, *Tanzania* ......... **55 D4** 8 37S 37 42 E
Selowandoma Falls, *Zimbabwe* ......... **37 E8** 0 1S 130 5 E
Selpele, *Indonesia* ......... **37 E8** 0 1S 130 5 E
Selsey Bill, *U.K.* ......... **13 G7** 50 43N 0 47W
Seltso, *Russia* ......... **18 D5** 53 22N 34 4 E
Selu, *Indonesia* ......... **37 F8** 7 32S 130 55 E
Selva, *Argentina* ......... **94 B3** 29 50S 62 0W
Selva Lancandona = Montes
  Azules △, *Mexico* ......... **87 D6** 16 21N 91 3W
Selvas, *Brazil* ......... **92 E5** 6 30S 67 0W
Selwyn L., *Canada* ......... **71 B8** 60 0N 104 30W
Selwyn Mts., *Canada* ......... **68 B6** 63 0N 130 0W
Selwyn Ra., *Australia* ......... **62 C3** 21 10S 140 0 E
Seman →, *Albania* ......... **23 D8** 40 47N 19 30 E
Semarang, *Indonesia* ......... **37 G14** 7 0S 110 26 E
Sembabule, *Uganda* ......... **54 C3** 0 4S 31 25 E
Sembawang, *Singapore* ......... **39 d** 1 27N 103 49 E
Sembung, *Indonesia* ......... **37 J18** 8 28S 115 11 E
Semenanjung Blambangan,
  *Indonesia* ......... **37 K17** 8 42S 114 29 E
Semeru, *Indonesia* ......... **37 H15** 8 4S 112 55 E
Semey, *Kazakhstan* ......... **28 D9** 50 30N 80 10 E
Seminoe Reservoir, *U.S.A.* ......... **76 F10** 42 9N 106 55W
Seminole, *Okla., U.S.A.* ......... **81 H6** 35 14N 96 41W
Seminole, *Tex., U.S.A.* ......... **81 J3** 32 43N 102 39W
Seminole Draw →, *U.S.A.* ......... **81 J3** 32 27N 102 20W
Semipalatinsk = Semey,
  *Kazakhstan* ......... **28 D9** 50 30N 80 10 E
Semirara Is., *Phil.* ......... **37 B6** 12 0N 121 20 E
Semitau, *Indonesia* ......... **36 D4** 0 29N 111 57 E
Semiyarka, *Kazakhstan* ......... **28 D8** 50 55N 78 23 E
Semiyarskoye = Semiyarka,
  *Kazakhstan* ......... **28 D8** 50 55N 78 23 E
Semmering P., *Austria* ......... **16 E8** 47 41N 15 45 E
Semnān, *Iran* ......... **45 C7** 35 40N 53 23 E
Semnān □, *Iran* ......... **45 C7** 36 0N 54 0 E
Semporna, *Malaysia* ......... **37 D5** 4 30N 118 33 E
Semuda, *Indonesia* ......... **36 E4** 2 51S 112 58 E
Sen →, *Cambodia* ......... **38 B3** 13 45N 105 12 E
Sena, *Iran* ......... **44 D5** 28 27N 51 36 E
Sena, *Mozam.* ......... **55 F4** 17 25S 35 0 E
Sena Madureira, *Brazil* ......... **92 E5** 9 5S 68 45W
Senador Pompeu, *Brazil* ......... **93 E11** 5 40S 39 20W
Senang, Pulau, *Singapore* ......... **39 d** 1 10N 103 44 E
Senanga, *Zambia* ......... **53 H4** 16 7S 23 16 E
Senatobia, *U.S.A.* ......... **81 H10** 34 37N 89 58W
Sencelles, *Spain* ......... **24 B9** 39 39N 2 54 E
Sendai, *Kagoshima, Japan* ......... **31 J5** 31 50N 130 20 E
Sendai, *Miyagi, Japan* ......... **30 E10** 38 15N 140 53 E
Sendai-Wan, *Japan* ......... **30 E10** 38 15N 141 0 E
Sendhwa, *India* ......... **42 J6** 21 41N 75 6 E
Seneca, *U.S.A.* ......... **83 H4** 34 41N 82 57W
Seneca Falls, *U.S.A.* ......... **85 D8** 42 55N 76 48W
Seneca L., *U.S.A.* ......... **84 D8** 42 40N 76 54W
Senecaville L., *U.S.A.* ......... **84 G3** 39 55N 81 25W
Senegal ■, *W. Afr.* ......... **50 F3** 14 30N 14 30W
Senegal →, *W. Afr.* ......... **50 E2** 15 48N 16 32W
Senegambia, *Africa* ......... **48 E2** 12 45N 12 0W
Senekal, *S. Africa* ......... **57 D4** 28 20S 27 36 E
Senga Hill, *Zambia* ......... **55 D3** 9 19S 31 11 E
Senge Khambab = Indus →,
  *Pakistan* ......... **42 G2** 24 20N 67 47 E
Sengua →, *Zimbabwe* ......... **55 F2** 17 7S 28 5 E
Senhor-do-Bonfim, *Brazil* ......... **93 F10** 10 30S 40 10W
Senigállia, *Italy* ......... **22 C5** 43 43N 13 13 E
Senj, *Croatia* ......... **16 F8** 45 0N 14 58 E
Senja, *Norway* ......... **8 B17** 69 25N 17 30 E

Senkaku-Shotō, *Japan* ......... **31 L1** 25 45N 124 0 E
Senkuang, *Indonesia* ......... **39 d** 1 11N 104 2 E
Senlis, *France* ......... **20 B5** 49 13N 2 35 E
Senmonorom, *Cambodia* ......... **38 F6** 12 27N 107 12 E
Senneterre, *Canada* ......... **72 C4** 48 25N 77 15W
Seno, *Laos* ......... **38 D5** 16 35N 104 50 E
Sens, *France* ......... **20 B5** 48 11N 3 15 E
Senta, *Serbia & M.* ......... **23 B9** 45 55N 20 3 E
Sentani, *Indonesia* ......... **37 E10** 2 36S 140 37 E
Sentery = Lubao, *Dem. Rep. of
  the Congo* ......... **54 D2** 5 17S 25 42 E
Sentinel, *U.S.A.* ......... **77 K7** 32 52N 113 13W
Sentosa, *Singapore* ......... **39 d** 1 15N 103 50 E
Seo de Urgel = La Seu d'Urgell,
  *Spain* ......... **21 A6** 42 22N 1 23 E
Seohara, *India* ......... **43 E8** 29 15N 78 33 E
Seonath →, *India* ......... **43 J10** 21 44N 82 28 E
Seondha, *India* ......... **43 F8** 26 9N 78 48 E
Seoni, *India* ......... **43 H8** 22 5N 79 30 E
Seoni Malwa, *India* ......... **42 H8** 22 27N 77 28 E
Seoul = Sŏul, *S. Korea* ......... **35 F14** 37 31N 126 58 E
Sepīdān, *Iran* ......... **45 D7** 30 20N 52 5 E
Sepo-ri, *N. Korea* ......... **35 E14** 38 57N 127 25 E
Sepone, *Laos* ......... **38 D6** 16 45N 106 13 E
Sept-Îles, *Canada* ......... **73 B6** 50 13N 66 22W
Sequim, *U.S.A.* ......... **78 B3** 48 5N 123 6W
Sequoia △, *U.S.A.* ......... **78 J8** 36 30N 118 30W
Seraing, *Belgium* ......... **15 D5** 50 35N 5 32 E
Serakhis →, *Cyprus* ......... **25 D11** 35 13N 32 55 E
Seram, *Indonesia* ......... **37 E7** 3 10S 129 0 E
Seram Sea, *Indonesia* ......... **37 E7** 2 30S 128 30 E
Seranantsara, *Madag.* ......... **57 B8** 18 30S 49 5 E
Serang, *Indonesia* ......... **37 G12** 6 8S 106 10 E
Serangoon, *Singapore* ......... **39 d** 1 23N 103 54 E
Serasan, *Indonesia* ......... **36 D3** 2 29N 109 4 E
Serbia ■, *Serbia & M.* ......... **23 C9** 43 30N 21 0 E
Serbia & Montenegro ■, *Europe* **23 B9** 43 20N 20 0 E
Serdobsk, *Russia* ......... **18 D7** 52 28N 44 10 E
Seremban, *Malaysia* ......... **39 L3** 2 43N 101 53 E
Serengeti △, *Tanzania* ......... **54 C3** 2 11S 35 0 E
Serengeti Plain, *Tanzania* ......... **54 C4** 2 40S 35 0 E
Serenje, *Zambia* ......... **55 E3** 13 14S 30 15 E
Sereth = Siret →, *Romania* ......... **17 F14** 45 24N 28 1 E
Sergino, *Russia* ......... **28 C7** 62 25N 65 12 E
Sergipe □, *Brazil* ......... **93 F11** 10 30S 37 30W
Sergiyev Posad, *Russia* ......... **18 C6** 56 20N 38 10 E
Seria, *Brunei* ......... **36 D4** 4 37N 114 23 E
Serian, *Malaysia* ......... **36 D4** 1 10N 110 31 E
Seribu, Kepulauan, *Indonesia* ......... **36 F3** 5 36S 106 33 E
Sérifos, *Greece* ......... **23 F11** 37 9N 24 30 E
Sérigny →, *Canada* ......... **73 A6** 56 47N 66 0W
Seringapatam Reef, *Australia* ......... **60 B3** 13 38S 122 5 E
Seririt, *Indonesia* ......... **37 J17** 8 12S 114 56 E
Sermata, *Indonesia* ......... **37 F7** 8 15S 128 50 E
Sermersuaq, *Greenland* ......... **4 B4** 79 30N 62 0W
Serov, *Russia* ......... **18 C11** 59 29N 60 35 E
Serowe, *Botswana* ......... **56 C4** 22 25S 26 43 E
Serpentine Lakes, *Australia* ......... **61 E4** 28 30S 129 10 E
Serpent's Mouth = Sierpe, Bocas
  de la, *Venezuela* ......... **93 L15** 10 0N 61 30W
Serpukhov, *Russia* ......... **18 D6** 54 55N 37 28 E
Serra do Navio, *Brazil* ......... **93 C8** 0 59N 52 3W
Sérrai, *Greece* ......... **23 D10** 41 5N 23 31 E
Serranía San Luis △, *Paraguay* ......... **94 A4** 22 35S 57 22W
Serrezuela, *Argentina* ......... **94 C2** 30 40S 65 20W
Serrinha, *Brazil* ......... **93 F11** 11 39S 39 0W
Sertanópolis, *Brazil* ......... **95 A5** 23 4S 51 2W
Serua, *Indonesia* ......... **37 F8** 6 18S 130 1 E
Serui, *Indonesia* ......... **37 E9** 1 53S 136 10 E
Serule, *Botswana* ......... **56 C4** 21 57S 27 20 E
Ses Salines, *Spain* ......... **24 B10** 39 21N 3 3 E
Sese Is., *Uganda* ......... **54 C3** 0 30S 32 30 E
Sesepe, *Indonesia* ......... **37 E7** 1 30S 127 59 E
Sesfontein, *Namibia* ......... **56 B1** 19 7S 13 39 E
Sesheke, *Zambia* ......... **56 B3** 17 29S 24 13 E
S'Espalmador, *Spain* ......... **24 C7** 38 47N 1 26 E
S'Espardell, *Spain* ......... **24 C7** 38 48N 1 29 E
S'Estanyol, *Spain* ......... **24 B9** 39 22N 2 54 E
Setana, *Japan* ......... **30 C9** 42 26N 139 51 E
Sète, *France* ......... **20 E5** 43 25N 3 42 E
Sete Lagôas, *Brazil* ......... **93 G10** 19 27S 44 16W
Sétif, *Algeria* ......... **50 A7** 36 9N 5 26 E
Seto, *Japan* ......... **31 G8** 35 14N 137 6 E
Setonaikai, *Japan* ......... **31 G6** 34 20N 133 30 E
Setonaikai △, *Japan* ......... **31 G6** 34 15N 133 15 E
Settat, *Morocco* ......... **50 B4** 33 0N 7 40W
Setting L., *Canada* ......... **71 C9** 55 0N 98 38W
Settle, *U.K.* ......... **12 C5** 54 5N 2 16W
Settlement Pt., *Bahamas* ......... **83 M6** 26 40N 79 0W
Settlers, *S. Africa* ......... **57 C4** 25 2S 28 30 E
Setúbal, *Portugal* ......... **21 C1** 38 30N 8 58W
Setúbal, B. de, *Portugal* ......... **21 C1** 38 40N 8 56W
Seul, Lac, *Canada* ......... **72 B1** 50 20N 92 30W
Sevan, Ozero = Sevana Lich,
  *Armenia* ......... **19 F8** 40 30N 45 20 E
Sevana Lich, *Armenia* ......... **19 F8** 40 30N 45 20 E
Sevastopol, *Ukraine* ......... **19 F5** 44 35N 33 30 E
Seven Sisters, *Canada* ......... **70 C3** 54 56N 128 10W
Severn →, *Canada* ......... **72 A2** 56 2N 87 36W
Severn →, *U.K.* ......... **13 F5** 51 35N 2 40W
Severn L., *Canada* ......... **72 B1** 53 54N 90 48W
Severnaya Zemlya, *Russia* ......... **29 B10** 79 0N 100 0 E
Severnyye Uvaly, *Russia* ......... **18 C8** 60 0N 50 0 E
Severo-Kurilsk, *Russia* ......... **29 D16** 50 40N 156 8 E
Severo-Yeniseyskiy, *Russia* ......... **29 C10** 60 22N 93 1 E
Severo-Zapadnyy □, *Russia* ......... **28 C5** 65 0N 40 0 E
Severodvinsk, *Russia* ......... **18 B6** 64 27N 39 58 E
Severomorsk, *Russia* ......... **18 A5** 69 5N 33 27 E
Severouralsk, *Russia* ......... **18 B11** 60 9N 59 57 E
Sevier, *U.S.A.* ......... **77 G7** 38 39N 112 11W
Sevier →, *U.S.A.* ......... **77 G7** 39 4N 113 6W
Sevier Desert, *U.S.A.* ......... **76 G7** 39 40N 112 45W
Sevier L., *U.S.A.* ......... **76 G7** 38 54N 113 9W
Sevilla, *Spain* ......... **21 D2** 37 23N 5 58W
Seville = Sevilla, *Spain* ......... **21 D2** 37 23N 5 58W
Sevlievo, *Bulgaria* ......... **23 C11** 43 2N 25 6 E
Sewani, *India* ......... **42 E6** 28 58N 75 39 E
Seward, *Alaska, U.S.A.* ......... **68 B5** 60 7N 149 27W
Seward, *Nebr., U.S.A.* ......... **80 E6** 40 55N 97 6W
Seward Peninsula, *U.S.A.* ......... **68 B3** 65 30N 166 0W
Sewell, *Chile* ......... **94 C1** 34 10S 70 23W
Sewer, *Indonesia* ......... **37 F8** 5 53S 134 40 E
Sewickley, *U.S.A.* ......... **84 F4** 40 32N 80 12W
Sexsmith, *Canada* ......... **70 B5** 55 21N 118 47W
Seychelles ■, *Ind. Oc.* ......... **27 K9** 5 0S 56 0 E
Seyðisfjörður, *Iceland* ......... **8 D7** 65 16N 13 57W
Seydişehir, *Turkey* ......... **19 G5** 37 25N 31 51 E

Seydvān, Iran ............ 44 B5  38 34N  45  2 E
Seyhan →, Turkey ........ 44 B2  36 43N  34 53 E
Seym →, Ukraine ........ 19 D5  51 27N  32 34 E
Seymour, Australia ...... 63 F4  37  0S 145 10 E
Seymour, S. Africa ...... 57 E4  32 33S  26 46 E
Seymour, Conn., U.S.A. .. 85 E11 41 24N  73  4W
Seymour, Ind., U.S.A. ... 82 F3  38 58N  85 53W
Seymour, Tex., U.S.A. ... 81 J5  33 35N  99 16W
Sfântu Gheorghe, Romania .. 17 F13 45 52N  25 48 E
Sfax, Tunisia ........... 51 B8  34 49N  10 48 E
Sha Tau Kok, China ...... 33 F11 22 33N 114 13 E
Sha Tin, China ......... 33 G11 22 23N 114 12 E
Shaanxi □, China ........ 34 G5  35  0N 109  0 E
Shaba = Katanga □, Dem. Rep. of
  the Congo ............ 54 D2   8  0S  25  0 E
Shaba △, Kenya ......... 54 B4   0 38N  37 48 E
Shaballe = Scebeli, Wabi →,
  Somali Rep. .......... 47 G3   2  0N  44  0 E
Shabogamo L., Canada ... 73 B6  53 15N  66 30W
Shabunda, Dem. Rep. of
  the Congo ............ 54 C2   2 40S  27 16 E
Shache, China .......... 32 C2  38 20N  77 10 E
Shackleton Ice Shelf, Antarctica .. 5 C8  66  0S 100  0 E
Shackleton Inlet, Antarctica .. 5 E11 83  0S 160  0 E
Shādegān, Iran ......... 45 D6  30 40N  48 38 E
Shadi, China .......... 43 C7  33 24N  77 14 E
Shadrinsk, Russia ...... 28 D7  56  5N  63 32 E
Shadyside, U.S.A. ...... 84 G4  39 58N  80 45W
Shafter, U.S.A. ........ 79 K7  35 30N 119 16W
Shaftesbury, U.K. ...... 13 F5  51  0N   2 11W
Shagram, Pakistan ...... 43 A5  36 24N  72 20 E
Shah Alizai, Pakistan ... 42 E2  29 25N  66 33 E
Shah Bunder, Pakistan .. 42 G2  24 13N  67 56 E
Shahabad, Punjab, India . 42 D7  30 10N  76 55 E
Shahabad, Raj., India ... 42 G7  25 15N  77 11 E
Shahabad, Ut. P., India . 43 F8  27 36N  79 56 E
Shahadpur, Pakistan .... 42 G3  25 55N  68 35 E
Shahba, Syria .......... 46 C5  32 52N  36 38 E
Shahdād, Iran .......... 45 D8  30 30N  57 40 E
Shahdād, Namakzār-e, Iran .. 45 D8  30 20N  58 20 E
Shahdadkot, Pakistan ... 42 F2  27 50N  67 55 E
Shahdol, India ......... 43 H9  23 19N  81 26 E
Shahe, China .......... 34 F8  37  0N 114 32 E
Shahganj, India ........ 43 F10 26  3N  82 44 E
Shahgarh, India ........ 40 F6  27 15N  69 50 E
Shahjahanpur, India .... 43 F8  27 54N  79 57 E
Shahpur, India ......... 42 H7  22 12N  77 58 E
Shahpur, Baluchistan, Pakistan .. 42 E3  28 46N  68 27 E
Shahpur, Punjab, Pakistan .. 42 C5  32 17N  72 26 E
Shahpur Chakar, Pakistan .. 42 F3  26 9N  68 39 E
Shahpura, Mad. P., India . 43 H9  23 10N  80 45 E
Shahpura, Raj., India ... 42 G6  25 38N  74 56 E
Shahr-e Bābak, Iran .... 45 D7  30  7N  55  9 E
Shahr-e Kord, Iran ..... 45 C6  32 15N  50 55 E
Shāhrakht, Iran ........ 45 C9  33 38N  60 16 E
Shahrig, Pakistan ...... 42 D2  30 15N  67 40 E
Shahukou, China ....... 34 D7  40 20N 112 18 E
Shaikhabad, Afghan. .... 42 B3  34  2N  68 45 E
Shajapur, India ........ 42 H7  23 27N  76 21 E
Shajing, China ........ 33 F10 22 44N 113 48 E
Shakargarh, Pakistan ... 42 C6  32 17N  75 10 E
Shakawe, Botswana ..... 56 B3  18 28S  21 49 E
Shaker Heights, U.S.A. .. 84 E3  41 29N  81 32W
Shakhty, Russia ........ 19 E7  47 40N  40 16 E
Shakhunya, Russia ...... 18 C8  57 40N  46 46 E
Shaki, Nigeria ......... 50 G6   8 41N   3 21 E
Shaksam Valley, Asia ... 43 A7  36  0N  76 20 E
Shallow Lake, Canada ... 84 B3  44 36N  81  5W
Shalqar, Kazakhstan .... 28 E6  47 48N  59 39 E
Shaluli Shan, China .... 32 C4  30 40N  99 55 E
Shām, Iran ............ 45 E8  26 39N  57 21 E
Shām, Bādiyat ash, Asia . 44 C3  32 0N  40 0 E
Shamāl Sīnī □, Egypt ... 46 E2  30 30N  33 30 E
Shamattawa, Canada .... 72 A1  55 51N  92  5W
Shamattawa →, Canada .. 72 A2  55 1N  85 23W
Shamil, Iran .......... 45 E8  27 30N  56 55 E
Shāmkūh, Iran ......... 45 C8  35 47N  57 50 E
Shamli, India ......... 42 E7  29 32N  77 18 E
Shammar, Jabal, Si. Arabia .. 44 E4  27 40N  41  0 E
Shamo = Gobi, Asia .... 34 C6  44  0N 110  0 E
Shamo, L., Ethiopia .... 47 F2   5 45N  37 30 E
Shamokin, U.S.A. ...... 85 F8  40 47N  76 34W
Shamrock, U.S.A. ...... 81 H4  35 13N 100 15W
Shamva, Zimbabwe ..... 55 F3  17 20S  31 32 E
Shan □, Burma ........ 41 J21 21 30N  98 30 E
Shan Xian, China ...... 34 G9  34 50N 116  5 E
Shanchengzhen, China .. 35 C13 42 20N 125 20 E
Shāndak, Iran ......... 45 D9  28 28N  60 27 E
Shandon, U.S.A. ....... 78 K6  35 39N 120 23W
Shandong □, China ..... 35 G10 36  0N 118  0 E
Shandong Bandao, China . 35 F11 37  0N 121  0 E
Shang Xian = Shangzhou, China .. 34 H5  33 50N 109 58 E
Shanga, Nigeria ....... 50 F6  11 12N   4 33 E
Shangalowe, Dem. Rep. of
  the Congo ........... 55 E2  10 50S  26 30 E
Shangani, Zimbabwe .... 57 B4  19 41S  29 20 E
Shangani →, Zimbabwe .. 55 F2  18 41S  27 10 E
Shangbancheng, China .. 35 D10 40 50N 118  1 E
Shangdu, China ........ 34 D7  41 30N 113 30 E
Shanghai, China ....... 33 C7  31 15N 121 26 E
Shanghe, China ........ 35 F9  37 20N 117 10 E
Shangnan, China ....... 34 H6  33 32N 110 50 E
Shangqiu, China ....... 34 G8  34 26N 115 36 E
Shangrao, China ....... 33 D6  28 25N 117 59 E
Shangshui, China ...... 33 C6  33 42N 114 35 E
Shangzhi, China ....... 35 B14 45 22N 127 56 E
Shangzhou, China ...... 34 H5  33 50N 109 58 E
Shanhetun, China ...... 35 B14 44 33N 127 15 E
Shanklin, U.K. ........ 13 G6  50 38N   1 11W
Shannon, N.Z. ......... 59 J5  40 33S 175 25 E
Shannon △, Australia ... 61 F2  31 55S 117 51 E
Shannon →, Ireland .... 10 D2  52 35N   9 30W
Shannon, Mouth of the, Ireland .. 10 D2  52 30N   9 55W
Shannon Airport, Ireland .. 10 D3  52 42N   8 57W
Shansi = Shanxi □, China .. 34 F7  37  0N 112  0 E
Shantar, Ostrov Bolshoy, Russia .. 29 D14 55  9N 137 40 E
Shantipur, India ...... 43 H13 23 17N  88 25 E
Shantou, China ........ 33 D6  23 18N 116 40 E
Shantung = Shandong □, China .. 35 G10 36  0N 118  0 E
Shanxi □, China ....... 34 F7  37  0N 112  0 E
Shanyang, China ....... 34 H5  33 31N 109 55 E
Shanyin, China ........ 34 E7  39 25N 112 56 E
Shaoguan, China ....... 33 D6  24 48N 113 35 E
Shaoxing, China ....... 33 C7  30  0N 120 35 E
Shaoyang, China ....... 33 D6  27 14N 111 25 E
Shap, U.K. ........... 12 C5  54 32N   2 40W
Shapinsay, U.K. ....... 11 B6  59  3N   2 51W
Shaqra', Si. Arabia .... 44 E5  25 15N  45 16 E

Shaqrā', Yemen ......... 47 E4  13 22N  45 44 E
Sharafkhāneh, Iran ..... 44 B5  38 11N  45 29 E
Sharbot Lake, Canada ... 84 B8  44 46N  76 41W
Shari, Japan .......... 30 C12 43 55N 144 40 E
Sharjah = Ash Shāriqah, U.A.E. .. 45 E7  25 23N  55 26 E
Shark B., Australia .... 61 E1  25 30S 113 32 E
Shark Bay △, Australia .. 61 F2  32 49S 118 49 E
Sharon, Mass., U.S.A. .. 85 D13 42  7N  71 11W
Sharon, Pa., U.S.A. .... 84 E4  41 14N  80 31W
Sharon Springs, Kans., U.S.A. .. 80 F4  38 54N 101 45W
Sharon Springs, N.Y., U.S.A. .. 85 D10 42 48N  74 37W
Sharp Pt., Australia ... 62 A3  10 58S 142 43 E
Sharpe L., Canada ..... 72 B1  54 24N  93 40W
Sharpsville, U.S.A. .... 84 E4  41 15N  80 29W
Sharya, Russia ........ 18 C8  58 22N  45 20 E
Shashemene, Ethiopia ... 47 F2   7 13N  38 33 E
Shashi, Botswana ...... 57 C4  21 15S  27 27 E
Shashi, China ......... 33 C6  30 25N 112 14 E
Shashi →, Africa ...... 55 G2  21 14S  29 20 E
Shasta, Mt., U.S.A. .... 76 F2  41 25N 122 12W
Shasta L., U.S.A. ...... 76 F2  40 43N 122 25W
Shatt al Arab, Asia .... 45 D6  30  0N  48 31 E
Shaunavon, Canada .... 71 D7  49 35N 108 25W
Shaver L., U.S.A. ...... 78 H7  37  9N 119 18W
Shaw →, Australia ..... 60 D2  20 21S 119 17 E
Shaw I., Australia ..... 62 J7  20 30S 149  2 E
Shawanaga, Canada .... 84 A4  45 31N  80 17W
Shawangunk Mts., U.S.A. .. 85 E10 41 35N  74 30W
Shawano, U.S.A. ....... 82 C1  44 47N  88 36W
Shawinigan, Canada .... 72 C5  46 35N  72 50W
Shawnee, U.S.A. ....... 81 H6  35 20N  96 55W
Shay Gap, Australia .... 60 D3  20 30S 120 10 E
Shaybārā, Si. Arabia ... 44 E3  25 26N  36 47 E
Shaykh, J. ash, Lebanon . 46 B4  33 25N  35 50 E
Shaykh Miskin, Syria ... 46 C5  32 49N  36  9 E
Shaykh Sa'īd, Iraq ..... 44 C5  32 34N  46 17 E
Shchuchinsk, Kazakhstan . 28 D8  52 56N  70 12 E
She Xian, China ....... 34 F7  36 30N 113 40 E
Shebele = Scebeli, Wabi →,
  Somali Rep. .......... 47 G3   2  0N  44  0 E
Sheboygan, U.S.A. ..... 82 D2  43 46N  87 45W
Shediac, Canada ...... 73 C7  46 14N  64 32W
Sheelin, L., Ireland .... 10 C4  53 48N   7 20W
Sheep Haven, Ireland ... 10 A4  55 11N   7 52W
Sheerness, U.K. ....... 13 F8  51 26N   0 47 E
Sheet Harbour, Canada . 73 D7  44 56N  62 31W
Sheffield, U.K. ........ 12 D6  53 23N   1 28W
Sheffield, Ala., U.S.A. .. 83 H2  34 46N  87 41W
Sheffield, Mass., U.S.A. . 85 D11 42  5N  73 21W
Sheffield, Pa., U.S.A. ... 84 E5  41 42N  79  3W
Sheikhpura, India ...... 43 G11 25  9N  85 53 E
Shekhupura, Pakistan ... 42 D5  31 42N  73 58 E
Shekou, China ......... 33 G10 22 30N 113 55 E
Shelburne, N.S., Canada . 73 D6  43 47N  65 20W
Shelburne, Ont., Canada . 84 B4  44  4N  80 15W
Shelburne, U.S.A. ...... 85 B11 44 23N  73 14W
Shelburne B., Australia .. 62 A3  11 50S 143 0 E
Shelburne Falls, U.S.A. . 85 D12 42 36N  72 45W
Shelby, Mich., U.S.A. ... 82 D2  43 37N  86 22W
Shelby, Miss., U.S.A. ... 81 J9  33 57N  90 46W
Shelby, Mont., U.S.A. .. 76 B8  48 30N 111 51W
Shelby, N.C., U.S.A. ... 83 H5  35 17N  81 32W
Shelby, Ohio, U.S.A. ... 84 F2  40 53N  82 40W
Shelbyville, Ill., U.S.A. . 80 F10 39 24N  88 48W
Shelbyville, Ind., U.S.A. . 82 F3  39 31N  85 47W
Shelbyville, Ky., U.S.A. . 82 F3  38 13N  85 14W
Shelbyville, Tenn., U.S.A. .. 83 H2  35 29N  86 28W
Sheldon, U.S.A. ....... 80 D7  43 11N  95 51W
Sheldrake, Canada ..... 73 B7  50 20N  64 51W
Shelikhova, Zaliv, Russia . 29 D16 59 30N 157  0 E
Shell Lakes, Australia .. 61 E4  29 20S 127 30 E
Shellbrook, Canada .... 71 C7  53 13N 106 24W
Shellharbour, Australia . 63 E5  34 31S 150 51 E
Shelter I., U.S.A. ...... 85 E12 41  5N  72 21W
Shelton, Conn., U.S.A. .. 85 E11 41 19N  73  5W
Shelton, Wash., U.S.A. .. 78 C3  47 13N 123  6W
Shen Xian, China ...... 34 F8  36 15N 115 40 E
Shenandoah, Iowa, U.S.A. .. 80 E7  40 46N  95 22W
Shenandoah, Pa., U.S.A. .. 85 F8  40 49N  76 12W
Shenandoah, Va., U.S.A. .. 82 F6  38 29N  78 37W
Shenandoah △, U.S.A. ... 82 F6  38 35N  78 22W
Shenandoah →, U.S.A. .. 82 F7  39 19N  77 44W
Shenchi, China ........ 34 E7  39  8N 112 10 E
Shendam, Nigeria ...... 50 G7   8 49N   9 30 E
Shendī, Sudan ........ 51 E12 16 46N  33 22 E
Shengfang, China ...... 34 E9  39  3N 116 42 E
Shenjingzi, China ...... 35 B13 44 40N 124 30 E
Shenmu, China ........ 34 E6  38 50N 110 29 E
Shenqiu, China ........ 34 H8  33 25N 115  5 E
Shensi = Shaanxi □, China .. 34 G5  35  0N 109  0 E
Shenyang, China ....... 35 D12 41 48N 123 27 E
Shenzhen, China ....... 33 F10 22 32N 114  5 E
Shenzhen ✕ (SZX), China .. 33 F10 22 41N 113 49 E
Shenzhen Shuiku, China . 33 F11 22 34N 114  8 E
Shenzhen Wan, China .. 33 G10 22 27N 113 55 E
Sheo, India .......... 42 F4  26 11N  71 15 E
Sheopur Kalan, India ... 42 G10 25 40N  76 40 E
Shepetivka, Ukraine .... 17 C14 50 10N  27 10 E
Shepetovka = Shepetivka,
  Ukraine ............. 17 C14 50 10N  27 10 E
Shepparton, Australia ... 63 F4  36 23S 145 26 E
Sheppey, I. of, U.K. .... 13 F8  51 25N   0 48 E
Shepton Mallet, U.K. ... 13 F5  51 11N   2 33W
Sheqi, China .......... 34 H7  33 12N 112 57 E
Sher Qila, Pakistan .... 43 A6  36  7N  74  2 E
Sherborne, U.K. ....... 13 G5  50 57N   2 31W
Sherbro I., S. Leone ... 50 G3   7 30N  12 40W
Sherbrooke, N.S., Canada . 73 C7  45  8N  61 59W
Sherbrooke, Qué., Canada .. 85 A13 45 28N  71 57W
Sherburne, U.S.A. ..... 85 D9  42 41N  75 30W
Shergarh, India ....... 42 F5  26 20N  72 18 E
Sherghati, India ....... 43 G11 24 34N  84 47 E
Sheridan, Ark., U.S.A. .. 81 H8  34 19N  92 24W
Sheridan, Wyo., U.S.A. .. 76 D10 44 48N 106 58W
Sheringham, U.K. ...... 12 E9  52 56N   1 13 E
Sherkin I., Ireland ..... 10 E2  51 28N   9 26W
Sherkot, India ........ 43 E8  29 22N  78 35 E
Sherman, U.S.A. ....... 81 J6  33 40N  96 35W
Sherpur, India ........ 43 G10 25 34N  83 47 E
Sherridon, Canada ..... 71 B8  55  8N 101  5W
Sherwood Forest, U.K. .. 12 D6  53  6N   1  7W
Sherwood Park, Canada . 70 C6  53 31N 113 19W
Sheslay →, Canada ..... 70 B2  58 48N 132  5W
Shethanei L., Canada ... 71 B9  58 48N  97 50W
Shetland □, U.K. ...... 11 A7  60 30N   1 30W
Shetland Is., U.K. ..... 11 A7  60 30N   1 30W
Shetrunji →, India .... 42 J5  21 19N  72  7 E
Sheung Shui, China .... 33 F11 22 31N 114  7 E

Sheyenne →, U.S.A. .... 80 B6  47  2N  96 50W
Shibām, Yemen ........ 47 D4  15 59N  48 36 E
Shibata, Japan ........ 30 F9  37 57N 139 20 E
Shibecha, Japan ....... 30 C12 43 17N 144 36 E
Shibetsu, Japan ....... 30 B11 44 10N 142 23 E
Shibogama L., Canada .. 72 B2  53 35N  88 15W
Shibushi, Japan ....... 31 J5  31 25N 131  8 E
Shickshinny, U.S.A. .... 85 E8  41  9N  76  9W
Shickshock Mts. = Chic-Chocs,
  Mts., Canada ........ 73 C6  48.55N  66  0W
Shidao, China ........ 35 F12 36 50N 122 25 E
Shido, Japan .......... 31 G7  34 19N 134 10 E
Shiel, L., U.K. ........ 11 E3  56 48N   5 34W
Shield, C., Australia ... 62 A2  13 20S 136 20 E
Shieli, Kazakhstan ..... 28 E7  44 20N  66 15 E
Shiga □, Japan ........ 31 G8  35 20N 136  0 E
Shiguaigou, China ..... 34 D6  40 52N 110 15 E
Shihchiachuangi = Shijiazhuang,
  China ............... 34 E8  38  2N 114 28 E
Shihezi, China ........ 32 B3  44 15N  86  2 E
Shijiazhuang, China .... 34 E8  38  2N 114 28 E
Shikarpur, India ...... 42 E8  28 17N  78  7 E
Shikarpur, Pakistan .... 42 F3  27 57N  68 39 E
Shikohabad, India ..... 43 F8  27  6N  78 36 E
Shikoku □, Japan ...... 31 H6  33 30N 133 30 E
Shikoku-Sanchi, Japan .. 31 H6  33 30N 133 30 E
Shikotsu-Ko, Japan .... 30 C10 42 45N 141 25 E
Shikotsu-Tōya △, Japan . 30 C10 42 44N 141  8 E
Shiliguri, India ....... 41 F16 26 45N  88 25 E
Shilka, Russia ........ 29 D12 52  0N 115 55 E
Shilka →, Russia ...... 29 D13 53 20N 121 26 E
Shillelagh, Ireland .... 10 D5  52 45N   6 32W
Shillington, U.S.A. .... 85 F9  40 18N  75 58W
Shillong, India ....... 41 G17 25 35N  91 53 E
Shilo, West Bank ...... 46 C4  32  4N  35 18 E
Shilou, China ........ 34 F6  37  0N 110 48 E
Shimabara, Japan ..... 31 H5  32 48N 130 20 E
Shimada, Japan ....... 31 G9  34 49N 138 19 E
Shimane □, Japan ..... 31 G6  35  0N 132 30 E
Shimanovsk, Russia .... 29 D13 52 15N 127 30 E
Shimba Hills △, Kenya .. 54 C4   4 14S  39 25 E
Shimizu, Japan ....... 31 G9  35  0N 138 30 E
Shimodate, Japan ..... 31 F9  36 20N 139 55 E
Shimoga, India ....... 40 N9  13 57N  75 32 E
Shimoni, Kenya ....... 54 C4   4 38S  39 20 E
Shimonoseki, Japan ... 31 H5  33 58N 130 55 E
Shimpuru Rapids, Namibia .. 56 B2  17 45S  19 55 E
Shin, L., U.K. ........ 11 C4  58  5N   4 30W
Shinano-Gawa →, Japan . 31 F9  36 50N 138 30 E
Shināş, Oman ........ 45 E8  24 46N  56 28 E
Shindand, Afghan. .... 40 C3  33 12N  62  8 E
Shinglehouse, U.S.A. .. 84 E6  41 58N  78 12W
Shingū, Japan ........ 31 H7  33 40N 135 55 E
Shingwidzi, S. Africa ... 57 C5  23 5S  31 25 E
Shinjō, Japan ......... 30 E10 38 46N 140 18 E
Shinshār, Syria ....... 46 A5  34 36N  36 43 E
Shinyanga, Tanzania ... 54 C3   3 45S  33 27 E
Shinyanga □, Tanzania .. 54 C3   3 50S  34  0 E
Shio-no-Misaki, Japan .. 31 H7  33 25N 135 45 E
Shiogama, Japan ...... 30 E10 38 19N 141  1 E
Shiojiri, Japan ....... 31 F8  36  6N 137 58 E
Shipchenski Prokhod, Bulgaria .. 23 C11 42 45N  25 15 E
Shiping, China ........ 32 D5  23 45N 102 23 E
Shippagan, Canada .... 73 C7  47 45N  64 45W
Shippensburg, U.S.A. .. 84 F7  40  3N  77 31W
Shippenville, U.S.A. ... 84 E5  41 15N  79 28W
Shiprock, U.S.A. ...... 77 H9  36 47N 108 41W
Shiqian, N. →, Israel ... 46 D3  31 37N  34 30 E
Shiqian, China ........ 34 H5  33  5N 108 15 E
Shiquan He = Indus →, Pakistan .. 42 G2  24 20N  67 47 E
Shir Kūh, Iran ....... 45 D7  31 39N  54  3 E
Shiragami-Misaki, Japan .. 30 D10 41 24N 140 12 E
Shirakawa, Fukushima, Japan .. 31 F10 37  7N 140 13 E
Shirakawa, Gifu, Japan . 31 F8  36 17N 136 56 E
Shirane-San, Gumma, Japan .. 31 F9  36 48N 139 22 E
Shirane-San, Yamanashi, Japan .. 31 G9  35 42N 138  9 E
Shiraoi, Japan ........ 30 C10 42 33N 141 21 E
Shīrāz, Iran .......... 45 D7  29 42N  52 30 E
Shire →, Africa ....... 55 F4  17 42S  35 19 E
Shiretoko-Misaki, Japan . 30 B12 44 21N 145 20 E
Shirinab →, Pakistan ... 42 D2  30 15N  66 28 E
Shiriya-Zaki, Japan .... 30 D10 41 25N 141 30 E
Shiroishi, Japan ...... 30 F10 38  0N 140 37 E
Shīrvān, Iran ........ 45 B8  37 30N  57 50 E
Shirwa, L. = Chilwa, L., Malawi .. 55 F4  15 15S  35 40 E
Shivpuri, India ....... 42 G7  25 26N  77 42 E
Shixian, China ........ 35 C15 43  5N 129 50 E
Shiyan, China ........ 33 F10 32 42N 110 56 E
Shiyan Shuiku, China .. 33 F10 22 42N 113 54 E
Shizuishan, China ..... 34 E4  39 15N 106 50 E
Shizuoka, Japan ....... 31 G9  34 57N 138 24 E
Shizuoka □, Japan ..... 31 G9  35  0N 138 40 E
Shklov = Shklow, Belarus . 17 A16 54 16N  30 15 E
Shklow, Belarus ...... 17 A16 54 16N  30 15 E
Shkodër, Albania ..... 23 C8  42  4N  19 32 E
Shkumbini →, Albania .. 23 D8  41  2N  19 31 E
Shmidta, Ostrov, Russia . 29 A10 81  0N  91  0 E
Shō-Gawa →, Japan .... 31 F8  36 47N 137  4 E
Shoal L., Canada ...... 71 D9  49 33N  95  1W
Shoal Lake, Canada .... 71 C8  50 30N 100 35W
Shōdo-Shima, Japan ... 31 G7  34 30N 134 15 E
Sholapur = Solapur, India .. 40 L9  17 43N  75 56 E
Shōmrōn, West Bank ... 46 C4  32 15N  35 13 E
Shoreham by Sea, U.K. .. 13 G7  50 50N   0 16W
Shori →, Pakistan ..... 42 E3  28 29N  69 44 E
Shorkot Road, Pakistan . 42 D5  30 47N  72 15 E
Shoshone, Calif., U.S.A. . 79 K10 35 58N 116 16W
Shoshone, Idaho, U.S.A. . 76 E6  42 56N 114 25W
Shoshone L., U.S.A. ... 76 D8  44 22N 110 43W
Shoshone Mts., U.S.A. .. 76 G5  39 20N 117 25W
Shoshong, Botswana ... 56 C4  22 56S  26 31 E
Shoshoni, U.S.A. ...... 76 E9  43 14N 108  7W
Shouguang, China ..... 35 F10 37 54N 118 45 E
Shouyang, China ...... 34 F7  37 54N 113  8 E
Show Low, U.S.A. ...... 77 J9  34 15N 110  2W
Shreveport, U.S.A. .... 81 J8  32 31N  93 45W
Shrewsbury, U.K. ...... 13 E5  52 43N   2 45W
Shri Mohangarh, India .. 42 F4  27 17N  71 18 E
Shrirampur, India ..... 43 H13 22 44N  88 21 E
Shropshire □, U.K. .... 13 E5  52 36N   2 45W
Shū, Kazakhstan ...... 28 E8  43 36N  73 42 E
Shū →, Kazakhstan .... 26 E10 45 0N  67 44 E
Shuangcheng, China ... 35 B14 45 20N 126 15 E
Shuanggou, China ..... 35 G9  34 2N 117 30 E
Shuangliao, China ..... 35 C12 43 29N 123 30 E
Shuangshanzi, China ... 35 D10 40 20N 119 30 E
Shuangyang, China .... 35 C13 43 28N 125 40 E
Shuangyashan, China .. 33 B8  46 28N 131  5 E

Shuguri Falls, Tanzania .. 55 D4   8 33S  37 22 E
Shuiye, China ........ 34 F8  36  7N 114  8 E
Shujalpur, India ...... 42 H7  23 18N  76 46 E
Shukpa Kunzang, India .. 43 B8  34 22N  78 22 E
Shulan, China ........ 35 B14 44 28N 127  0 E
Shule, China ......... 32 C2  39  5N  76  3 E
Shumagin Is., U.S.A. .. 68 C4  55  7N 160 30W
Shumen, Bulgaria ..... 23 C12 43 18N  26 55 E
Shumikha, Russia ..... 28 D7  55 10N  63 15 E
Shuo Xian = Shuozhou, China .. 34 E7  39 20N 112 33 E
Shuozhou, China ...... 34 E7  39 20N 112 33 E
Shūr →, Fārs, Iran .... 45 D7  28 30N  55  0 E
Shūr →, Kermān, Iran .. 45 D8  30 52N  57 37 E
Shūr →, Yazd, Iran .... 45 D7  31 45N  55 15 E
Shūr Āb, Iran ........ 45 C6  34 23N  51 11 E
Shūr Gaz, Iran ....... 45 D8  34 23N  59 20 E
Shūrāb, Iran ......... 45 C8  33 43N  56 29 E
Shūrjestān, Iran ...... 45 D7  31 24N  52 25 E
Shurugwi, Zimbabwe ... 55 F3  19 40S  30  0 E
Shūsf, Iran .......... 45 D9  31 50N  60  5 E
Shūshtar, Iran ....... 45 D6  32  0N  48 50 E
Shuswap L., Canada ... 70 C5  50 55N 119  3W
Shuyang, China ....... 35 G10 34 10N 118 42 E
Shūzū, Iran .......... 45 D7  29 52N  54 30 E
Shwebo, Burma ....... 41 H19 22 30N  95 45 E
Shwegu, Burma ....... 41 G20 24 15N  96 26 E
Shweli →, Burma ...... 41 H20 23 45N  96 45 E
Shymkent, Kazakhstan .. 28 E7  42 18N  69 36 E
Shyok, India ......... 43 B8  34 13N  78 12 E
Shyok →, Pakistan .... 43 B6  35 13N  75 53 E
Si Chon, Thailand ..... 39 H2   9  0N  99 54 E
Si Kiang = Xi Jiang →, China .. 33 D6  22  5N 113 20 E
Si Lanna △, Thailand .. 38 C2  19 17N  99 12 E
Si-ngan = Xi'an, China . 34 G5  34 15N 109  0 E
Si Prachan, Thailand ... 38 E3  14 37N 100  9 E
Si Racha, Thailand .... 38 F3  13 10N 100 48 E
Si Xian, China ........ 35 H9  33 30N 117 50 E
Siachen Glacier, Asia .. 43 B7  35 20N  77 30 E
Siahaf →, Pakistan .... 42 E3  29  3N  68 57 E
Siahan Range, Pakistan . 40 F4  27 30N  64 40 E
Siaksriindrapura, Indonesia .. 36 D2   0 51N 102  0 E
Sialkot, Pakistan ..... 42 C6  32 32N  74 30 E
Siam = Thailand ■, Asia . 38 E4  16  0N 102  0 E
Sian = Xi'an, China .... 34 G5  34 15N 109  0 E
Sian Ka'an △, Mexico .. 87 D7  19 35N  87 40W
Siantan, Indonesia .... 36 D3   3 10N 106 15 E
Siāreh, Iran ......... 45 D9  28  5N  60 14 E
Siargao I., Phil. ...... 37 C7   9 52N 126  3 E
Siari, Pakistan ....... 43 B7  34 55N  76 40 E
Siasi, Phil. ......... 37 C6   5 34N 120 50 E
Siau, Indonesia ...... 37 D7   2 50N 125 25 E
Šiauliai, Lithuania .... 9 J20  55 56N  23 15 E
Sibā', Gebel el, Egypt .. 44 E2  25 45N  34 10 E
Sibang, China ........ 37 K18  8 34S 115 13 E
Sibay, Russia ........ 18 D10 52 42N  58 39 E
Sibayi, L., S. Africa ... 57 D5  27 20S  32 45 E
Šibenik, Croatia ...... 22 C6  43 48N  15 54 E
Siberia = Sibirskiy □, Russia .. 29 D10 58  0N  90  0 E
Siberia, Russia ....... 4 D13  60  0N 100  0 E
Siberut, Indonesia .... 36 E1   1 30S  99  0 E
Sibi, Pakistan ........ 42 E2  29 30N  67 54 E
Sibil = Oksibil, Indonesia .. 37 E10  4 59S 140 35 E
Sibiloi △, Kenya ...... 54 B4   4  0N  36 20 E
Sibirskiy □, Russia .... 29 D10 58  0N  90  0 E
Sibiti, Congo ......... 52 E2   3 38S  13 19 E
Sibiu, Romania ....... 17 F13 45 45N  24  9 E
Sibley, U.S.A. ........ 80 D7  43 24N  95 45W
Sibolga, Indonesia .... 36 D1   1 42N  98 45 E
Sibsagar, India ....... 41 F19 27  0N  94 36 E
Sibu, Malaysia ....... 36 D4   2 18N 111 49 E
Sibuco, Phil. ........ 37 C6   7 20N 122 10 E
Sibuguey B., Phil. .... 37 C6   7 50N 122 45 E
Sibut, C.A.R. ........ 52 C3   5 46N  19 10 E
Sibutu, Phil. ........ 37 D5   4 45N 119 30 E
Sibutu Passage, E. Indies . 37 D5   4 50N 120  0 E
Sibuyan I., Phil. ..... 37 B6  12 25N 122 40 E
Sibuyan Sea, Phil. .... 37 B6  12 30N 122 20 E
Sicamous, Canada ..... 70 C5  50 49N 119  0W
Siccus →, Australia ... 63 E2  31 55S 139 17 E
Sichuan □, China ..... 32 C5  30 30N 103  0 E
Sicilia, Italy ........ 22 F6  37 30N  14 30 E
Sicily = Sicilia, Italy .. 22 F6  37 30N  14 30 E
Sicuani, Peru ........ 92 F4  14 21S  71 10W
Sidári, Greece ....... 25 A3  39 47N  19 41 E
Siddhapur, India ...... 42 H5  23 56N  72 25 E
Siddipet, India ....... 40 K11 18  5N  78 51 E
Sidhauli, India ....... 43 F9  27 17N  80 50 E
Sidheros, Ákra, Greece . 25 D8  35 19N  26 19 E
Sidhi, India ......... 43 G9  24 25N  81 53 E
Sidi-bel-Abbès, Algeria . 50 A5  35 13N   0 39W
Sidi Ifni, Morocco .... 50 C3  29 29N  10 12W
Sidlaw Hills, U.K. .... 11 E5  56 32N   3  2W
Sidley, Mt., Antarctica . 5 D14 77  2S 126  2W
Sidmouth, U.K. ....... 13 G4  50 40N   3 15W
Sidmouth, C., Australia . 62 A3  13 25S 143 36 E
Sidney, Canada ....... 70 D4  48 39N 123 24W
Sidney, Mont., U.S.A. . 80 B2  47 43N 104  9W
Sidney, N.Y., U.S.A. .. 85 D9  42 19N  75 24W
Sidney, Nebr., U.S.A. . 80 E3  41  8N 102 59W
Sidney, Ohio, U.S.A. .. 82 E3  40 17N  84  9W
Sidney Lanier, L., U.S.A. .. 83 H4  34 10N  84  4W
Sidoarjo, Indonesia ... 37 G15  7 27S 112 43 E
Sidon = Saydā, Lebanon . 46 B4  33 35N  35 25 E
Sidra, G. of = Surt, Khalīj, Libya .. 51 B9  31 40N  18 30 E
Siedlce, Poland ....... 17 B12 52 10N  22 20 E
Sieg →, Germany ...... 16 C4  50 46N   7  6 E
Siegen, Germany ...... 16 C5  50 51N   8  0 E
Siem Pang, Cambodia .. 38 E6  14  7N 106 23 E
Siem Reap = Siemreab,
  Cambodia ........... 38 F4  13 20N 103 52 E
Siemreab, Cambodia .. 38 F4  13 20N 103 52 E
Siena, Italy ......... 22 C4  43 19N  11 21 E
Sieradz, Poland ...... 17 C10 51 37N  18 41 E
Sierpe, Bocas de la, Venezuela .. 93 L15 10  0N  61 30W
Sierra Blanca, U.S.A. .. 77 L11 31 11N 105 22W
Sierra Blanca Peak, U.S.A. .. 77 K11 33 23N 105 49W
Sierra City, U.S.A. ... 78 F6  39 34N 120 38W
Sierra Colorada, Argentina .. 96 E3  40 35S  67 50W
Sierra de Bahoruco △, Dom. Rep. .. 89 C5  18 10N  71 25W
Sierra de la Culata △, Venezuela .. 89 E5   8 45N  71 10W
Sierra de Lancandón △,
  Guatemala .......... 88 C1  16 59N  90 23W
Sierra de las Quijadas △,
  Argentina .......... 94 C2  32 29S  67  5W
Sierra de San Luis △, Venezuela .. 89 D6  11 20N  69 43W
Sierra Gorda, Chile .... 94 A2  22 50S  69 15W
Sierra Leone ■, W. Afr. .. 50 G3   9  0N  12  0W
Sierra Madre, Mexico .. 87 D6  16  0N  93  0W

Sierra Mojada, Mexico . . . . . . . 86 B4 27 19N 103 42W
Sierra Nevada, Spain . . . . . . . . 21 D4 37 3N 3 15W
Sierra Nevada, U.S.A. . . . . . . . . 78 H8 39 0N 120 30W
Sierra Nevada △, Venezuela . . . 89 E5 8 35N 70 45W
Sierra Nevada de Santa Marta △,
  Colombia . . . . . . . . . . . . . . 89 D5 10 56N 73 36W
Sierra Vista, U.S.A. . . . . . . . . . 77 L8 31 33N 110 18W
Sierraville, U.S.A. . . . . . . . . . . 78 F6 39 36N 120 22W
Sífnos, Greece . . . . . . . . . . . . 23 F11 37 0N 24 45 E
Sifton, Canada . . . . . . . . . . . . 71 C8 51 21N 100 8W
Sifton Pass, Canada . . . . . . . . 70 B3 57 52N 126 15W
Sighetu-Marmaţiei, Romania . . 17 E12 47 57N 23 52 E
Sighişoara, Romania . . . . . . . . 17 E13 46 12N 24 50 E
Sigli, Indonesia . . . . . . . . . . . 36 C1 5 25N 96 0 E
Siglufjörður, Iceland . . . . . . . . 8 C4 66 12N 18 55W
Signal, U.S.A. . . . . . . . . . . . . . 79 L13 34 30N 113 38W
Signal de Botrang, Belgium . . . 15 D6 50 29N 6 4 E
Signal Pk., U.S.A. . . . . . . . . . . 79 M12 33 20N 114 2W
Signy I., Antarctica . . . . . . . . . 5 C18 60 45S 45 56W
Sigsig, Ecuador . . . . . . . . . . . 92 D3 3 0S 78 50W
Sigüenza, Spain . . . . . . . . . . . 21 B4 41 3N 2 40W
Siguiri, Guinea . . . . . . . . . . . . 50 F4 11 31N 9 10W
Sigulda, Latvia . . . . . . . . . . . . 9 H21 57 10N 24 55 E
Sihora, India . . . . . . . . . . . . . 43 H9 23 29N 80 6 E
Siikajoki →, Finland . . . . . . . . 8 D21 64 50N 24 43 E
Siilinjärvi, Finland . . . . . . . . . 8 E22 63 4N 27 39 E
Sijarira Ra. = Chizarira,
  Zimbabwe . . . . . . . . . . . . . 55 F2 17 36S 27 45 E
Sika, India . . . . . . . . . . . . . . . 42 H3 22 26N 69 47 E
Sikani Chief →, Canada . . . . . 70 B4 57 47N 122 15W
Sikao, Thailand . . . . . . . . . . . 39 J2 7 34N 99 21 E
Sikar, India . . . . . . . . . . . . . . 42 F6 27 33N 75 10 E
Sikasso, Mali . . . . . . . . . . . . . 50 F4 11 18N 5 35W
Sikeston, U.S.A. . . . . . . . . . . . 81 G10 36 53N 89 35W
Sikhote Alin, Khrebet, Russia . . 29 E14 45 0N 136 0 E
Sikhote Alin Ra. = Sikhote Alin,
  Khrebet, Russia . . . . . . . . . 29 E14 45 0N 136 0 E
Síkinos, Greece . . . . . . . . . . . 23 F11 36 40N 25 8 E
Sikkim □, India . . . . . . . . . . . 41 F16 27 50N 88 30 E
Sil →, Spain . . . . . . . . . . . . . 21 A2 42 27N 7 43W
Silacayoapan, Mexico . . . . . . . 87 D5 17 30N 98 9W
Silawad, India . . . . . . . . . . . . 42 J6 21 54N 74 54 E
Silchar, India . . . . . . . . . . . . . 41 G18 24 49N 92 48 E
Siler City, U.S.A. . . . . . . . . . . 83 H6 35 44N 79 28W
Silesia = Śląsk, Poland . . . . . . 16 C9 51 0N 16 30 E
Silgarhi Doti, Nepal . . . . . . . . 43 E9 29 15N 81 0 E
Silghat, India . . . . . . . . . . . . . 41 F18 26 35N 93 0 E
Silifke, Turkey . . . . . . . . . . . . 19 G5 36 22N 33 58 E
Siliguri = Shiliguri, India . . . . . 41 F16 26 45N 88 25 E
Siling Co, China . . . . . . . . . . . 32 C3 31 50N 89 20 E
Silistra, Bulgaria . . . . . . . . . . 23 B12 44 6N 27 19 E
Silivri, Turkey . . . . . . . . . . . . 23 D13 41 4N 28 14 E
Siljan, Sweden . . . . . . . . . . . . 9 F16 60 55N 14 45 E
Silkeborg, Denmark . . . . . . . . 9 H13 56 10N 9 32 E
Silkwood, Australia . . . . . . . . 62 B4 17 45S 146 2 E
Sillajhuay, Cordillera, Chile . . . 92 G5 19 46S 68 40W
Sillamäe, Estonia . . . . . . . . . . 9 G22 59 24N 27 45 E
Silloth, U.K. . . . . . . . . . . . . . . 12 C4 54 52N 3 23W
Siloam Springs, U.S.A. . . . . . . 81 G7 36 11N 94 32W
Silsbee, U.S.A. . . . . . . . . . . . . 81 K7 30 21N 94 11W
Šilutė, Lithuania . . . . . . . . . . . 9 J19 55 21N 21 33 E
Silvani, India . . . . . . . . . . . . . 43 H8 23 18N 78 25 E
Silver City, U.S.A. . . . . . . . . . . 77 K9 32 46N 108 17W
Silver Cr. →, U.S.A. . . . . . . . . 76 E4 43 16N 119 13W
Silver Creek, U.S.A. . . . . . . . . 84 D5 42 33N 79 10W
Silver L., U.S.A. . . . . . . . . . . . 78 G6 38 39N 120 6W
Silver Lake, Calif., U.S.A. . . . . 79 K10 35 21N 116 7W
Silver Lake, Oreg., U.S.A. . . . . 76 E3 43 8N 121 3W
Silverton, Colo., U.S.A. . . . . . . 77 H10 37 49N 107 40W
Silverton, Tex., U.S.A. . . . . . . . 81 H4 34 28N 101 19W
Silvies →, U.S.A. . . . . . . . . . . 76 E4 43 34N 119 2W
Simaltala, India . . . . . . . . . . . 43 G12 24 43N 86 33 E
Simanggang = Bandar Sri Aman,
  Malaysia . . . . . . . . . . . . . . 36 D4 1 15N 111 32 E
Simard, L., Canada . . . . . . . . . 72 C4 47 40N 78 40W
Simav, Turkey . . . . . . . . . . . . 23 E13 39 4N 28 58 E
Simba, Tanzania . . . . . . . . . . . 54 C4 2 10S 37 36 E
Simbirsk, Russia . . . . . . . . . . 18 D8 54 20N 48 25 E
Simbo, Tanzania . . . . . . . . . . . 54 C2 4 51S 29 41 E
Simcoe, Canada . . . . . . . . . . . 84 D4 42 50N 80 20W
Simcoe, L., Canada . . . . . . . . . 84 B5 44 25N 79 20W
Simdega, India . . . . . . . . . . . . 43 H11 22 37N 84 31 E
Simeria, Romania . . . . . . . . . . 17 F12 45 51N 23 1 E
Simeulue, Indonesia . . . . . . . . 36 D1 2 45N 95 45 E
Simferopol, Ukraine . . . . . . . . 19 F5 44 55N 34 3 E
Sími, Greece . . . . . . . . . . . . . 23 F12 36 35N 27 50 E
Simi Valley, U.S.A. . . . . . . . . . 79 L8 34 16N 118 47W
Simikot, Nepal . . . . . . . . . . . . 43 E9 30 0N 81 50 E
Simla, India . . . . . . . . . . . . . . 42 D7 31 2N 77 9 E
Simmie, Canada . . . . . . . . . . . 71 D7 49 56N 108 6W
Simmler, U.S.A. . . . . . . . . . . . 79 K7 35 21N 119 59W
Simo älv = Simojoki →, Finland 8 D21 65 35N 25 1 E
Simojoki →, Finland . . . . . . . . 8 D21 65 35N 25 1 E
Simojovel, Mexico . . . . . . . . . 87 D6 17 12N 92 38W
Simonette →, Canada . . . . . . . 70 B5 55 9N 118 15W
Simonstown, S. Africa . . . . . . . 56 E2 34 14S 18 26 E
Simpang Empat, Malaysia . . . . 39 c 5 27N 100 29 E
Simplonpass, Switz. . . . . . . . . 20 C8 46 15N 8 3 E
Simpson Desert, Australia . . . . 62 D2 25 0S 137 0 E
Simpson Desert △, Australia . . 62 C2 24 59S 138 21 E
Simpson Pen., Canada . . . . . . 69 B11 68 34N 88 45W
Simpungdong, N. Korea . . . . . . 35 D15 40 56N 129 29 E
Simrishamn, Sweden . . . . . . . . 9 J16 55 33N 14 22 E
Simsbury, U.S.A. . . . . . . . . . . 85 E12 41 53N 72 48W
Simushir, Ostrov, Russia . . . . . 29 E16 46 50N 152 30 E
Sin Cowe I., S. China Sea . . . . 36 C4 9 53N 114 19 E
Sinabang, Indonesia . . . . . . . . 36 D1 2 30N 96 24 E
Sinadogo, Somali Rep. . . . . . . 47 F4 5 50N 47 0 E
Sinai = Es Sînâ', Egypt . . . . . . 44 F3 29 0N 34 0 E
Sinai, Mt. = Mûsa, Gebel, Egypt 44 D2 28 33N 33 59 E
Sinai Peninsula, Egypt . . . . . . 26 G7 29 30N 34 0 E
Sinaloa □, Mexico . . . . . . . . . 86 C3 25 0N 107 30W
Sinaloa de Leyva, Mexico . . . . 86 B3 25 50N 108 20W
Sinarádhes, Greece . . . . . . . . 25 A3 39 34N 19 51 E
Sincelejo, Colombia . . . . . . . . 92 B3 9 18N 75 24W
Sinch'ang, N. Korea . . . . . . . . 35 D15 40 7N 128 28 E
Sinchang-ni, N. Korea . . . . . . . 35 E14 39 24N 126 8 E
Sinclair, U.S.A. . . . . . . . . . . . . 76 F10 41 47N 107 7W
Sinclair Mills, Canada . . . . . . . 70 C4 54 5N 121 40W
Sinclair's B., U.K. . . . . . . . . . . 11 C5 58 31N 3 5W
Sinclairville, U.S.A. . . . . . . . . . 84 D5 42 16N 79 16W
Sincorá, Serra do, Brazil . . . . . 93 F10 13 30S 41 0W
Sind, Pakistan . . . . . . . . . . . . 42 G3 26 0N 68 30 E
Sind □, Pakistan . . . . . . . . . . 42 G3 26 0N 69 0 E
Sind →, Jammu & Kashmir,
  India . . . . . . . . . . . . . . . . . 43 B6 34 18N 74 45 E
Sind →, Mad. P., India . . . . . . 43 F8 26 26N 79 13 E
Sind Sagar Doab, Pakistan . . . 42 D4 32 0N 71 30 E

Sindangan, Phil. . . . . . . . . . . . 37 C6 8 10N 123 5 E
Sindangbarang, Indonesia . . . . 37 G12 7 27S 107 1 E
Sinde, Zambia . . . . . . . . . . . . 55 F2 17 28S 25 51 E
Sindh = Sind □, Pakistan . . . . 42 G3 26 0N 69 0 E
Sindri, India . . . . . . . . . . . . . . 43 H12 23 45N 86 42 E
Sines, Portugal . . . . . . . . . . . . 21 D1 37 56N 8 51W
Sines, C. de, Portugal . . . . . . . 21 D1 37 58N 8 53W
Sineu, Spain . . . . . . . . . . . . . . 24 B10 39 38N 3 1 E
Sing Buri, Thailand . . . . . . . . . 38 E3 14 53N 100 25 E
Singa, Sudan . . . . . . . . . . . . . 51 F12 13 10N 33 57 E
Singapore ■, Asia . . . . . . . . . . 39 d 1 17N 103 51 E
Singapore, Straits of, Asia . . . . 39 d 1 15N 104 0 E
Singapore Changi ✈ (SIN),
  Singapore . . . . . . . . . . . . . 39 M4 1 23N 103 59 E
Singaraja, Indonesia . . . . . . . . 36 F5 8 7S 115 6 E
Singida, Tanzania . . . . . . . . . . 54 C3 4 49S 34 48 E
Singida □, Tanzania . . . . . . . . 54 D3 6 0S 34 30 E
Singitikós Kólpos, Greece . . . . 23 D11 40 6N 24 0 E
Singkaling Hkamti, Burma . . . . 41 G19 26 0N 95 39 E
Singkang, Indonesia . . . . . . . . 37 E6 4 8S 120 1 E
Singkawang, Indonesia . . . . . . 36 D3 1 0N 108 57 E
Singkep, Indonesia . . . . . . . . . 36 E2 0 30S 104 25 E
Singleton, Australia . . . . . . . . 63 E5 32 33S 151 0 E
Singleton, Mt., N. Terr., Australia 60 D5 22 0S 130 46 E
Singleton, Mt., W. Austral.,
  Australia . . . . . . . . . . . . . . 61 E2 29 27S 117 15 E
Singoli, India . . . . . . . . . . . . . 42 G6 25 0N 75 22 E
Singora = Songkhla, Thailand . . 39 J3 7 13N 100 37 E
Singosan, N. Korea . . . . . . . . . 35 E14 38 52N 127 25 E
Sinhung, N. Korea . . . . . . . . . 35 D14 40 11N 127 34 E
Sinjai, Indonesia . . . . . . . . . . 37 F6 5 7S 120 20 E
Sinjär, Iraq . . . . . . . . . . . . . . . 44 B4 36 19N 41 52 E
Sinkat, Sudan . . . . . . . . . . . . 51 E13 18 55N 36 49 E
Sinkiang Uighur = Xinjiang
  Uygur Zizhiqu □, China . . . . 32 C3 42 0N 86 0 E
Sinmak, N. Korea . . . . . . . . . . 35 E14 38 25N 126 14 E
Sinnamary, Fr. Guiana . . . . . . . 93 B8 5 25N 53 0W
Sinni →, Italy . . . . . . . . . . . . . 22 D7 40 8N 16 41 E
Sinop, Turkey . . . . . . . . . . . . . 19 F6 42 1N 35 11 E
Sinor, India . . . . . . . . . . . . . . 42 J5 21 55N 73 20 E
Sinp'o, N. Korea . . . . . . . . . . . 35 E15 40 0N 128 13 E
Sinsk, Russia . . . . . . . . . . . . . 29 C13 61 8N 126 48 E
Sintang, Indonesia . . . . . . . . . 36 D4 0 5N 111 35 E
Sinton, U.S.A. . . . . . . . . . . . . . 81 L6 28 2N 97 31W
Sintra, Portugal . . . . . . . . . . . 21 C1 38 47N 9 25W
Sinŭiju, N. Korea . . . . . . . . . . 35 D13 40 5N 124 24 E
Siocon, Phil. . . . . . . . . . . . . . . 37 C6 7 40N 122 10 E
Siófok, Hungary . . . . . . . . . . . 17 E10 46 54N 18 3 E
Sion, Switz. . . . . . . . . . . . . . . 20 C7 46 14N 7 20 E
Sion Mills, U.K. . . . . . . . . . . . 10 B4 54 48N 7 29W
Sioux City, U.S.A. . . . . . . . . . . 80 D6 42 30N 96 24W
Sioux Falls, U.S.A. . . . . . . . . . 80 D6 43 33N 96 44W
Sioux Lookout, Canada . . . . . . 72 B1 50 10N 91 50W
Sioux Narrows, Canada . . . . . . 71 D10 49 25N 94 10W
Siparia, Trin. & Tob. . . . . . . . . 93 K15 10 8N 61 31W
Siping, China . . . . . . . . . . . . . 35 C13 43 8N 124 21 E
Sipiwesk L., Canada . . . . . . . . 71 B9 55 5N 97 35W
Siple, Antarctica . . . . . . . . . . . 5 D7 75 0S 74 0 E
Sipra →, India . . . . . . . . . . . . 42 H6 23 55N 75 28 E
Sipura, Indonesia . . . . . . . . . . 36 E1 2 18S 99 40 E
Siquia →, Nic. . . . . . . . . . . . . 88 D3 12 10N 84 20W
Siquijor, Phil. . . . . . . . . . . . . . 37 C6 9 12N 123 35 E
Siquirres, Costa Rica . . . . . . . . 88 D3 10 6N 83 30W
Şir Abū Nu'ayr, U.A.E. . . . . . . 45 E7 25 20N 54 20 E
Şīr Banī Yās, U.A.E. . . . . . . . . 45 E7 24 19N 52 37 E
Sir Edward Pellew Group,
  Australia . . . . . . . . . . . . . . 62 B2 15 40S 137 10 E
Sir Graham Moore Is., Australia 60 B4 13 53S 126 34 E
Sir James MacBrien, Mt., Canada 68 B7 62 7N 127 41W
Sira →, Norway . . . . . . . . . . . 9 G12 58 23N 6 34 E
Siracusa, Italy . . . . . . . . . . . . 22 F6 37 4N 15 17 E
Sirajganj, Bangla. . . . . . . . . . . 43 G13 24 25N 89 47 E
Sirathu, India . . . . . . . . . . . . . 43 G9 25 39N 81 19 E
Sīrdān, Iran . . . . . . . . . . . . . . 45 B6 36 39N 49 12 E
Sirdaryo = Syrdarya →,
  Kazakhstan . . . . . . . . . . . . 28 E7 46 3N 61 0 E
Siren, U.S.A. . . . . . . . . . . . . . 80 C8 45 47N 92 24W
Sirer, Spain . . . . . . . . . . . . . . 24 C7 38 56N 1 22 E
Siret →, Romania . . . . . . . . . . 17 F14 45 24N 28 1 E
Sirghāyā, Syria . . . . . . . . . . . 46 B5 33 51N 36 8 E
Sirinat △, Thailand . . . . . . . . . 39 a 8 6N 98 17 E
Sirjān, Iran . . . . . . . . . . . . . . . 45 D7 29 30N 55 45 E
Sirmaur, India . . . . . . . . . . . . 43 G9 24 51N 81 23 E
Sirohi, India . . . . . . . . . . . . . . 42 G5 24 52N 72 53 E
Sironj, India . . . . . . . . . . . . . . 42 G7 24 5N 77 39 E
Síros, Greece . . . . . . . . . . . . . 23 F11 37 28N 24 57 E
Sirretta Pk., U.S.A. . . . . . . . . . 79 K8 35 56N 118 19W
Sirri, Iran . . . . . . . . . . . . . . . . 45 E7 25 55N 54 32 E
Sirsa, India . . . . . . . . . . . . . . 42 E6 29 33N 75 4 E
Sirsa →, India . . . . . . . . . . . . 43 F8 26 51N 79 4 E
Sisak, Croatia . . . . . . . . . . . . . 16 F9 45 30N 16 21 E
Sisaket, Thailand . . . . . . . . . . 38 E5 15 8N 104 23 E
Sishen, S. Africa . . . . . . . . . . . 56 D3 27 47S 22 59 E
Sishui, Henan, China . . . . . . . . 34 G7 34 48N 113 15 E
Sishui, Shandong, China . . . . . 35 G9 35 42N 117 18 E
Sisipuk L., Canada . . . . . . . . . 71 B8 55 45N 101 50W
Sisophon, Cambodia . . . . . . . . 38 F4 13 38N 102 59 E
Sisseton, U.S.A. . . . . . . . . . . . 80 C6 45 40N 97 3W
Sīstān, Asia . . . . . . . . . . . . . . 45 D9 30 50N 61 0 E
Sīstān, Daryācheh-ye, Iran . . . 45 D9 31 0N 61 0 E
Sīstān va Balūchestān □, Iran . 45 E9 27 0N 62 0 E
Sisters, U.S.A. . . . . . . . . . . . . 76 D3 44 18N 121 33W
Siswa Bazar, India . . . . . . . . . 43 F10 27 9N 83 46 E
Sitamarhi, India . . . . . . . . . . . 43 F11 26 37N 85 30 E
Sitampiky, Madag. . . . . . . . . . 57 B8 16 41S 46 6 E
Sitapur, India . . . . . . . . . . . . . 43 F9 27 38N 80 45 E
Siteki, Swaziland . . . . . . . . . . 57 D5 26 32S 31 58 E
Sitges, Spain . . . . . . . . . . . . . 21 B6 41 17N 1 47 E
Sitía, Greece . . . . . . . . . . . . . 25 D8 35 13N 26 6 E
Sitka, U.S.A. . . . . . . . . . . . . . . 70 B1 57 3N 135 20W
Sitoti, Botswana . . . . . . . . . . . 56 C3 23 15S 23 40 E
Sittang Myit →, Burma . . . . . . 41 L20 17 20N 96 45 E
Sittard, Neths. . . . . . . . . . . . . 15 C5 51 0N 5 52 E
Sittingbourne, U.K. . . . . . . . . . 13 F8 51 21N 0 45 E
Sittoung = Sittang Myit →,
  Burma . . . . . . . . . . . . . . . . 41 L20 17 20N 96 45 E
Sittwe, Burma . . . . . . . . . . . . 41 J18 20 18N 92 45 E
Situbondo, Indonesia . . . . . . . 37 G16 7 42S 114 0 E
Siuna, Nic. . . . . . . . . . . . . . . . 88 D3 13 37N 84 45W
Siuri, India . . . . . . . . . . . . . . . 43 H12 23 50N 87 34 E
Sivand, India . . . . . . . . . . . . . 44 D7 30 5N 52 55 E
Sivas, Turkey . . . . . . . . . . . . . 19 G6 39 43N 36 58 E
Siverek, Turkey . . . . . . . . . . . . 44 B3 37 50N 39 19 E
Sivomaskinskiy, Russia . . . . . . 18 A11 66 40N 62 35 E
Sivrihisar, Turkey . . . . . . . . . . 19 G5 39 30N 31 35 E
Siwa, Egypt . . . . . . . . . . . . . . 51 C11 29 11N 25 31 E
Siwa, El Wâhât es, Egypt . . . . 48 D6 29 10N 25 30 E
Siwa Oasis = Sīwa, El Wâhât es,
  Egypt . . . . . . . . . . . . . . . . . 48 D6 29 10N 25 30 E

Siwalik Range, Nepal . . . . . . . 43 F10 28 0N 83 0 E
Siwan, India . . . . . . . . . . . . . . 43 F11 26 13N 84 21 E
Siwana, India . . . . . . . . . . . . . 42 G5 25 38N 72 25 E
Six Cross Roads, Barbados . . . 89 g 13 7N 59 28W
Sixmilebridge, Ireland . . . . . . . 10 D3 52 44N 8 46W
Sixth Cataract, Sudan . . . . . . . 51 E12 16 20N 32 42 E
Siziwang Qi, China . . . . . . . . . 34 D6 41 25N 111 40 E
Sjælland, Denmark . . . . . . . . . 9 J14 55 30N 11 30 E
Sjumen = Shumen, Bulgaria . . . 23 C12 43 18N 26 55 E
Skadarsko Jezero, Serbia & M. . 23 C8 42 10N 19 20 E
Skaftafell, Iceland . . . . . . . . . 8 D5 64 1N 17 0W
Skagafjörður, Iceland . . . . . . . 8 D4 65 54N 19 35W
Skagastølstindane, Norway . . . 9 F12 61 28N 7 52 E
Skagaströnd, Iceland . . . . . . . 8 D3 65 50N 20 19W
Skagen, Denmark . . . . . . . . . . 9 H14 57 43N 10 35 E
Skagerrak, Denmark . . . . . . . . 9 H13 57 30N 9 0 E
Skagit →, U.S.A. . . . . . . . . . . 78 B4 48 23N 122 22W
Skagway, U.S.A. . . . . . . . . . . . 68 C6 59 28N 135 19W
Skala-Podilska, Ukraine . . . . . 17 D14 48 50N 26 15 E
Skala Podolskaya = Skala-
  Podilska, Ukraine . . . . . . . . 17 D14 48 50N 26 15 E
Skalat, Ukraine . . . . . . . . . . . 17 D13 49 23N 25 55 E
Skåne, Sweden . . . . . . . . . . . . 9 J15 55 59N 13 30 E
Skaneateles, U.S.A. . . . . . . . . 85 D8 42 57N 76 26W
Skaneateles L., U.S.A. . . . . . . 85 D8 42 51N 76 22W
Skara, Sweden . . . . . . . . . . . . 9 G15 58 25N 13 30 E
Skardu, Pakistan . . . . . . . . . . 43 B6 35 20N 75 44 E
Skarżysko-Kamienna, Poland . . 17 C11 51 7N 20 52 E
Skeena →, Canada . . . . . . . . . 70 C2 54 9N 130 5W
Skeena Mts., Canada . . . . . . . 70 B3 56 40N 128 30W
Skegness, U.K. . . . . . . . . . . . . 12 D8 53 9N 0 20 E
Skeldon, Guyana . . . . . . . . . . 92 B7 5 55N 57 20W
Skeleton Coast, Namibia . . . . . 53 H2 20 0S 13 0 E
Skeleton Coast △, Namibia . . . 56 C1 20 0S 13 20 E
Skellefteå, Sweden . . . . . . . . . 8 D19 64 45N 20 50 E
Skellefteälven →, Sweden . . . . 8 D19 64 45N 21 10 E
Skelleftehamn, Sweden . . . . . . 8 D19 64 40N 21 9 E
Skerries, The, U.K. . . . . . . . . . 12 D3 53 25N 4 36W
Ski, Norway . . . . . . . . . . . . . . 9 G14 59 43N 10 52 E
Skíathos, Greece . . . . . . . . . . 23 E10 39 12N 23 30 E
Skibbereen, Ireland . . . . . . . . 10 E2 51 33N 9 16W
Skiddaw, U.K. . . . . . . . . . . . . 12 C4 54 39N 3 9W
Skidegate, Canada . . . . . . . . . 70 C2 53 15N 132 1W
Skien, Norway . . . . . . . . . . . . 9 G13 59 12N 9 35 E
Skierniewice, Poland . . . . . . . 17 C11 51 58N 20 10 E
Skikda, Algeria . . . . . . . . . . . . 50 A7 36 50N 6 58 E
Skilloura, Cyprus . . . . . . . . . . 25 D12 35 14N 33 10 E
Skipton, U.K. . . . . . . . . . . . . . 12 D5 53 58N 2 3W
Skirmish Pt., Australia . . . . . . . 62 A1 11 59S 134 17 E
Skíros, Greece . . . . . . . . . . . . 23 E11 38 55N 24 34 E
Skive, Denmark . . . . . . . . . . . 9 H13 56 33N 9 2 E
Skjálfandafljót →, Iceland . . . . 8 D5 65 59N 17 25W
Skjálfandi, Iceland . . . . . . . . . 8 C5 66 5N 17 30W
Skoghall, Sweden . . . . . . . . . . 9 G15 59 20N 13 30 E
Skole, Ukraine . . . . . . . . . . . . 17 D12 49 3N 23 30 E
Skópelos, Greece . . . . . . . . . . 23 E10 39 9N 23 47 E
Skopi, Greece . . . . . . . . . . . . 25 D8 35 11N 26 2 E
Skopje, Macedonia . . . . . . . . . 23 C9 42 1N 21 26 E
Skövde, Sweden . . . . . . . . . . . 9 G15 58 24N 13 50 E
Skovorodino, Russia . . . . . . . . 29 D13 54 0N 124 0 E
Skowhegan, U.S.A. . . . . . . . . . 83 C11 44 46N 69 43W
Skull, Ireland . . . . . . . . . . . . . 10 E2 51 32N 9 34W
Skunk →, U.S.A. . . . . . . . . . . 80 E9 40 42N 91 7W
Skuodas, Lithuania . . . . . . . . . 9 H19 56 16N 21 33 E
Skvyra, Ukraine . . . . . . . . . . . 17 D15 49 44N 29 40 E
Skye, U.K. . . . . . . . . . . . . . . . 11 D2 57 15N 6 10W
Skykomish, U.S.A. . . . . . . . . . 76 C3 47 42N 121 22W
Skyros = Skíros, Greece . . . . . 23 E11 38 55N 24 34 E
Slade Pt., Australia . . . . . . . . . 62 K7 21 5S 149 13 E
Slættaratindur, Færoe Is. . . . . 8 E9 62 18N 7 1W
Slagelse, Denmark . . . . . . . . . 9 J14 55 23N 11 19 E
Slamet, Indonesia . . . . . . . . . . 37 G13 7 16S 109 8 E
Slaney →, Ireland . . . . . . . . . 10 D5 52 26N 6 33W
Slangberge, S. Africa . . . . . . . 56 E3 31 32S 20 48 E
Śląsk, Poland . . . . . . . . . . . . . 16 C9 51 0N 16 30 E
Slate Is., Canada . . . . . . . . . . 72 C2 48 40N 87 0W
Slatina, Romania . . . . . . . . . . 17 F13 44 28N 24 22 E
Slatington, U.S.A. . . . . . . . . . . 85 F9 40 45N 75 37W
Slaton, U.S.A. . . . . . . . . . . . . . 81 J4 33 26N 101 39W
Slave →, Canada . . . . . . . . . . 70 A6 61 18N 113 39W
Slave Coast, W. Afr. . . . . . . . . 50 G6 6 0N 2 30 E
Slave Lake, Canada . . . . . . . . 70 B6 55 17N 114 43W
Slave Pt., Canada . . . . . . . . . . 70 A5 61 11N 115 56W
Slavgorod, Russia . . . . . . . . . . 28 D8 53 1N 78 37 E
Slavonski Brod, Croatia . . . . . . 23 B8 45 11N 18 1 E
Slavuta, Ukraine . . . . . . . . . . . 17 C14 50 15N 27 2 E
Slavyanka, Russia . . . . . . . . . . 30 C5 42 53N 131 21 E
Slavyansk = Slovyansk, Ukraine 19 E6 48 55N 37 36 E
Slawharad, Belarus . . . . . . . . . 17 B16 53 27N 31 0 E
Sleaford, U.K. . . . . . . . . . . . . . 12 D7 53 0N 0 24W
Sleaford B., Australia . . . . . . . 63 E2 34 55S 135 45 E
Sleat, Sd. of, U.K. . . . . . . . . . . 11 D3 57 5N 5 47W
Sleeper Is., Canada . . . . . . . . 69 C11 58 30N 81 0W
Sleeping Bear Dunes △, U.S.A. 82 C2 44 50N 86 5W
Sleepy Eye, U.S.A. . . . . . . . . . 80 C7 44 18N 94 43W
Slemon L., Canada . . . . . . . . . 70 A5 63 13N 116 4W
Slide Mt., U.S.A. . . . . . . . . . . . 81 K10 30 17N 89 47W
Slidell, U.S.A. . . . . . . . . . . . . . 81 K10 30 17N 89 47W
Sliema, Malta . . . . . . . . . . . . . 25 D2 35 55N 14 30 E
Slieve Aughty, Ireland . . . . . . . 10 C3 53 4N 8 30W
Slieve Bloom, Ireland . . . . . . . 10 C4 53 4N 7 40W
Slieve Donard, U.K. . . . . . . . . 10 B6 54 11N 5 55W
Slieve Gamph, Ireland . . . . . . . 10 B3 54 6N 9 0W
Slieve Gullion, U.K. . . . . . . . . 10 B5 54 7N 6 26W
Slieve League, Ireland . . . . . . . 10 B3 54 40N 8 42W
Slieve Mish, Ireland . . . . . . . . 10 D2 52 12N 9 50W
Slievenamon, Ireland . . . . . . . 10 D4 52 25N 7 34W
Sligeach = Sligo, Ireland . . . . 10 B3 54 16N 8 28W
Sligo, Ireland . . . . . . . . . . . . . 10 B3 54 16N 8 28W
Sligo, U.S.A. . . . . . . . . . . . . . 84 E5 41 6N 79 29W
Sligo □, Ireland . . . . . . . . . . . 10 B3 54 8N 8 42W
Sligo B., Ireland . . . . . . . . . . . 10 B3 54 18N 8 40W
Slippery Rock, U.S.A. . . . . . . . 84 E4 41 3N 80 3W
Slite, Sweden . . . . . . . . . . . . . 9 H18 57 42N 18 48 E
Sliven, Bulgaria . . . . . . . . . . . 23 C12 42 42N 26 19 E
Sloan, U.S.A. . . . . . . . . . . . . . 79 K11 35 57N 115 13W
Sloansville, U.S.A. . . . . . . . . . 85 D10 42 45N 74 22W
Slobodskoy, Russia . . . . . . . . 18 C9 58 40N 50 6 E
Slobozia, Romania . . . . . . . . . 17 F14 44 34N 27 23 E
Slocan, Canada . . . . . . . . . . . 70 D5 49 48N 117 28W
Slonim, Belarus . . . . . . . . . . . 17 B13 53 4N 25 19 E
Slough, U.K. . . . . . . . . . . . . . . 13 F7 51 30N 0 36W
Slough □, U.K. . . . . . . . . . . . . 13 F7 51 30N 0 36W
Sloughhouse, U.S.A. . . . . . . . . 78 G5 38 26N 121 12W
Slovak Rep. ■, Europe . . . . . . 17 D10 48 30N 20 0 E
Slovakia = Slovak Rep. ■, Europe 17 D10 48 30N 20 0 E
Slovakian Ore Mts. = Slovenské
  Rudohorie, Slovak Rep. . . . . 17 D10 48 45N 20 0 E

Slovenia ■, Europe . . . . . . . . . 16 F8 45 58N 14 30 E
Slovenija = Slovenia ■, Europe 16 F8 45 58N 14 30 E
Slovenské Rudohorie,
  Slovak Rep. . . . . . . . . . . . . 17 D10 48 45N 20 0 E
Slovyansk, Ukraine . . . . . . . . . 19 E6 48 55N 37 36 E
Sluch →, Ukraine . . . . . . . . . . 17 C14 51 37N 26 38 E
Sluis, Neths. . . . . . . . . . . . . . . 15 C3 51 18N 3 23 E
Słupsk, Poland . . . . . . . . . . . . 17 A9 54 30N 17 3 E
Slurry, S. Africa . . . . . . . . . . . 56 D4 25 49S 25 42 E
Slutsk, Belarus . . . . . . . . . . . . 17 B14 53 2N 27 31 E
Slyne Hd., Ireland . . . . . . . . . . 10 C1 53 25N 10 10W
Slyudyanka, Russia . . . . . . . . . 29 D11 51 40N 103 40 E
Småland, Sweden . . . . . . . . . . 9 H16 57 15N 15 25 E
Smalltree L., Canada . . . . . . . . 71 A8 61 0N 105 0W
Smallwood Res., Canada . . . . 73 B7 54 5N 64 30W
Smarhon, Belarus . . . . . . . . . . 17 A14 54 20N 26 24 E
Smartt Syndicate Dam, S. Africa 56 E3 30 45S 23 10 E
Smartville, U.S.A. . . . . . . . . . . 78 F5 39 13N 121 18W
Smeaton, Canada . . . . . . . . . . 71 C8 53 30N 104 49W
Smederevo, Serbia & M. . . . . . 23 B9 44 40N 20 57 E
Smerwick Harbour, Ireland . . . 10 D1 52 12N 10 23W
Smethport, U.S.A. . . . . . . . . . . 84 E6 41 49N 78 27W
Smidovich, Russia . . . . . . . . . . 29 E14 48 36N 133 49 E
Smith, Canada . . . . . . . . . . . . 70 B6 55 10N 114 0W
Smith Center, U.S.A. . . . . . . . . 80 F5 39 47N 98 47W
Smith River △, U.S.A. . . . . . . . 76 F2 41 55N 124 0W
Smith Sd., N. Amer. . . . . . . . . 4 B4 78 25N 74 0W
Smithburne →, Australia . . . . . 62 B3 17 3S 140 57 E
Smithers, Canada . . . . . . . . . . 70 C3 54 45N 127 10W
Smithfield, S. Africa . . . . . . . . 57 E4 30 9S 26 30 E
Smithfield, N.C., U.S.A. . . . . . . 83 H6 35 31N 78 21W
Smithfield, Utah, U.S.A. . . . . . . 76 F8 41 50N 111 50W
Smiths Falls, Canada . . . . . . . 85 B9 44 55N 76 0W
Smithton, Australia . . . . . . . . . 63 G4 40 53S 145 6 E
Smithville, Canada . . . . . . . . . 84 C5 43 6N 79 33W
Smithville, U.S.A. . . . . . . . . . . 81 K6 30 1N 97 10W
Smoky →, Canada . . . . . . . . . 70 B5 56 10N 117 21W
Smoky Bay, Australia . . . . . . . 63 E1 32 22S 134 13 E
Smoky Hill →, U.S.A. . . . . . . . 80 F5 39 4N 96 48W
Smoky Hills, U.S.A. . . . . . . . . . 80 F5 39 15N 99 30W
Smoky Lake, Canada . . . . . . . 70 C6 54 10N 112 30W
Smøla, Norway . . . . . . . . . . . . 8 E13 63 23N 8 3 E
Smolensk, Russia . . . . . . . . . . 18 D5 54 45N 32 5 E
Smolikas, Óros, Greece . . . . . . 23 D9 40 9N 20 58 E
Smolyan, Bulgaria . . . . . . . . . 23 D11 41 36N 24 38 E
Smooth Rock Falls, Canada . . . 72 C3 49 17N 81 37W
Smoothstone L., Canada . . . . . 71 C7 54 40N 106 50W
Smorgon = Smarhon, Belarus . . 17 A14 54 20N 26 24 E
Smyrna = İzmir, Turkey . . . . . . 23 E12 38 25N 27 8 E
Smyrna, U.S.A. . . . . . . . . . . . . 82 F8 39 18N 75 36W
Snæfell, Iceland . . . . . . . . . . . 8 D6 64 48N 15 34W
Snaefell, I. of Man . . . . . . . . . 12 C3 54 16N 4 27W
Snæfellsjökull, Iceland . . . . . . 8 D2 64 49N 23 46W
Snake →, U.S.A. . . . . . . . . . . 76 C4 46 12N 119 2W
Snake I., Australia . . . . . . . . . 63 F4 38 47S 146 33 E
Snake Range, U.S.A. . . . . . . . . 76 G6 39 0N 114 20W
Snake River Plain, U.S.A. . . . . 76 E7 42 50N 114 0W
Snåsavatnet, Norway . . . . . . . 8 D14 64 12N 12 0 E
Sneek, Neths. . . . . . . . . . . . . . 15 A5 53 2N 5 40 E
Sneeuberge, S. Africa . . . . . . . 56 E3 31 46S 24 20 E
Snelling, U.S.A. . . . . . . . . . . . 78 H6 37 31N 120 26W
Snežka, Europe . . . . . . . . . . . 16 C8 50 41N 15 50 E
Snizort, L., U.K. . . . . . . . . . . . 11 D2 57 33N 6 28W
Snøhetta, Norway . . . . . . . . . . 9 E13 62 19N 9 16 E
Snohomish, U.S.A. . . . . . . . . . 78 C4 47 55N 122 6W
Snoul, Cambodia . . . . . . . . . . 39 F6 12 4N 106 26 E
Snow Hill, U.S.A. . . . . . . . . . . 82 F8 38 11N 75 24W
Snow Lake, Canada . . . . . . . . 71 C8 54 52N 100 3W
Snow Mt., Calif., U.S.A. . . . . . 78 F4 39 23N 122 45W
Snow Mt., Maine, U.S.A. . . . . . 85 A14 45 18N 70 48W
Snow Shoe, U.S.A. . . . . . . . . . 84 E7 41 2N 77 57W
Snowbird L., Canada . . . . . . . 71 A8 60 45N 103 0W
Snowdon, U.K. . . . . . . . . . . . . 12 D3 53 4N 4 5W
Snowdonia △, U.K. . . . . . . . . . 12 D3 53 7N 3 59W
Snowdrift = Łutselk'e, Canada . 71 A6 62 24N 110 44W
Snowdrift →, Canada . . . . . . . 71 A6 62 24N 110 44W
Snowflake, U.S.A. . . . . . . . . . . 77 J8 34 30N 110 5W
Snowshoe Pk., U.S.A. . . . . . . . 76 B6 48 13N 115 41W
Snowtown, Australia . . . . . . . . 63 E2 33 46S 138 14 E
Snowville, U.S.A. . . . . . . . . . . 76 F7 41 58N 112 43W
Snowy →, Australia . . . . . . . . 63 F4 37 46S 148 30 E
Snowy Mt., U.S.A. . . . . . . . . . 85 C10 43 42N 74 23W
Snowy Mts., Australia . . . . . . . 63 F4 36 30S 148 20 E
Snug Corner, Bahamas . . . . . . 89 B5 22 33N 73 52W
Snyatyn, Ukraine . . . . . . . . . . 17 D13 48 27N 25 38 E
Snyder, Okla., U.S.A. . . . . . . . 81 H5 34 40N 98 57W
Snyder, Tex., U.S.A. . . . . . . . . 81 J4 32 44N 100 55W
Soahanina, Madag. . . . . . . . . . 57 B7 18 42S 44 13 E
Soalala, Madag. . . . . . . . . . . . 57 B8 16 6S 45 20 E
Soaloka, Madag. . . . . . . . . . . . 57 B8 18 32S 45 15 E
Soan →, Pakistan . . . . . . . . . . 42 C4 33 1N 71 44 E
Soanierana-Ivongo, Madag. . . . 57 B8 16 55S 49 35 E
Soavina, Madag. . . . . . . . . . . . 57 C8 20 23S 46 56 E
Soavinandriana, Madag. . . . . . 57 B8 19 9S 46 45 E
Sobat, Nahr →, Sudan . . . . . . 51 G12 9 22N 31 33 E
Sobhapur, India . . . . . . . . . . . 42 H8 22 47N 78 17 E
Sobradinho, Reprêsa de, Brazil 93 E10 9 30S 42 0W
Sobral, Brazil . . . . . . . . . . . . . 93 D10 3 50S 40 20W
Soc Giang, Vietnam . . . . . . . . 38 A6 22 54N 106 1 E
Soc Trang, Vietnam . . . . . . . . 39 H5 9 37N 105 50 E
Socastee, U.S.A. . . . . . . . . . . . 83 J6 33 41N 79 1W
Soch'e = Shache, China . . . . . 32 C2 38 20N 77 10 E
Sochi, Russia . . . . . . . . . . . . . 19 F6 43 35N 39 40 E
Société, Is. de la,
  French Polynesia . . . . . . . . 65 J12 17 0S 151 0W
Society Is. = Société, Is. de la,
  French Polynesia . . . . . . . . 65 J12 17 0S 151 0W
Socompa, Portezuelo de, Chile . 94 A2 24 27S 68 18W
Socorro, N. Mex., U.S.A. . . . . . 77 J10 34 4N 106 54W
Socorro, Tex., U.S.A. . . . . . . . 77 L10 31 39N 106 18W
Socorro, I., Mexico . . . . . . . . . 86 D2 18 45N 110 58W
Socotra, Yemen . . . . . . . . . . . 47 E5 12 30N 54 0 E
Soda L., U.S.A. . . . . . . . . . . . . 77 J5 35 10N 116 4W
Soda Plains, India . . . . . . . . . . 43 B8 35 30N 79 0 E
Soda Springs, U.S.A. . . . . . . . 76 E8 42 39N 111 36W
Sodankylä, Finland . . . . . . . . . 8 C22 67 29N 26 40 E
Soddy-Daisy, U.S.A. . . . . . . . . 83 H3 35 17N 85 10W
Söderhamn, Sweden . . . . . . . . 9 F17 61 18N 17 10 E
Söderköping, Sweden . . . . . . . 9 G17 58 31N 16 20 E
Södermanland, Sweden . . . . . . 9 G17 59 12N 17 39 E
Sodiri, Sudan . . . . . . . . . . . . . 51 F11 14 27N 29 0 E
Sodus, U.S.A. . . . . . . . . . . . . . 84 C7 43 14N 77 4W
Sodwana Bay △, S. Africa . . . . 57 C5 27 30S 32 30 E
Soekmekaar, S. Africa . . . . . . . 57 C4 23 30S 29 55 E
Soest, Neths. . . . . . . . . . . . . . 15 B5 52 9N 5 19 E

Sofala □, *Mozam.* ............ 57 **B5**   19 30S  34 30 E
Sofia = Sofiya, *Bulgaria* ...... 23 **C10**  42 45N  23 20 E
Sofia ➤, *Madag.* ............ 57 **B8**   15 27S  47 23 E
Sofiya, *Bulgaria* ............ 23 **C10**  42 45N  23 20 E
Sōfu-Gan, *Japan* ........ 31 **K10**  29 49N 140 21 E
Sogamoso, *Colombia* ...... 92 **B4**    5 43N  72 56W
Sogār, *Iran* ................ 45 **E8**   25 53N  58  6 E
Sogndalsfjøra, *Norway* ...... 9 **F12**  61 14N   7  5 E
Søgne, *Norway* ............ 9 **G12**  58  5N   7 48 E
Sognefjorden, *Norway* ...... 9 **F11**  61 10N   5 50 E
Sŏgwipo, *S. Korea* ...... 35 **H14**  33 13N 126 34 E
Soh, *Iran* ................ 45 **C6**   33 26N  51 27 E
Sohāg, *Egypt* ............ 51 **C12**  26 33N  31 43 E
Sohagpur, *India* ............ 42 **H8**   22 42N  78 12 E
Sohori, *N. Korea* ...... 35 **D15**  40  7N 128 23 E
Soignies, *Belgium* ...... 15 **D4**   50 35N   4  5 E
Soissons, *France* ...... 20 **B5**   49 25N   3 19 E
Sōja, *Japan* ............ 31 **G6**   34 40N 133 45 E
Sojat, *India* ............ 42 **G5**   25 55N  73 45 E
Sokal, *Ukraine* ............ 17 **C13**  50 31N  24 15 E
Sōke, *Turkey* ............ 23 **F12**  37 48N  27 28 E
Sokelo, *Dem. Rep. of the Congo* 55 **D1**    9 55S  24 36 E
Sokhumi, *Georgia* ...... 19 **F7**   43  0N  41  0 E
Soko Islands, *China* ...... 33 **G10**  22 10N 113 54 E
Sokodé, *Togo* ............ 50 **G6**    9  0N   1 11 E
Sokol, *Russia* ............ 18 **C7**   59 30N  40  5 E
Sokółka, *Poland* ...... 17 **B12**  53 25N  23 30 E
Sokołów Podlaski, *Poland* .. 17 **B12**  52 25N  22 15 E
Sokoto, *Nigeria* ...... 50 **F7**   13  2N   5 16 E
Sol Iletsk, *Russia* ...... 18 **D10**  51 10N  55  0 E
Solai, *Kenya* ............ 54 **B4**    0  2N  36 12 E
Solan, *India* ............ 42 **D7**   30 55N  77  7 E
Solander I., *N.Z.* ...... 59 **M1**   46 34S 166 54 E
Solano, *Phil.* ............ 37 **A6**   16 31N 121 15 E
Solapur, *India* ............ 40 **L9**   17 43N  75 56 E
Soldotna, *U.S.A.* ...... 68 **B4**   60 29N 151  3W
Soléa, *Cyprus* ............ 25 **D12**  35  5N  33  4 E
Soledad, *Colombia* ...... 92 **A4**   10 55N  74 46W
Soledad, *U.S.A.* ...... 78 **J5**   36 26N 121 20W
Soledad, *Venezuela* ...... 92 **B6**    8 10N  63 34W
Solent, The, *U.K.* ...... 13 **G6**   50 45N   1 25W
Solfonn, *Norway* ...... 9 **F12**  60  2N   6 57 E
Solhan, *Turkey* ...... 44 **B4**   38 57N  41  3 E
Soligalich, *Russia* ...... 18 **C7**   59  5N  42 10 E
Soligorsk = Salihorsk, *Belarus* 17 **B14**  52 51N  27 27 E
Solihull, *U.K.* ............ 13 **E6**   52 26N   1 47W
Solikamsk, *Russia* ...... 18 **C10**  59 38N  56 50 E
Solila, *Madag.* ............ 57 **C8**   21 25S  46 37 E
Solimões = Amazonas ➤,
   *S. Amer.* ............ 93 **D9**    0  5S  50  0W
Solingen, *Germany* ...... 16 **C4**   51 10N   7  5 E
Sollefteå, *Sweden* ...... 8 **E17**  63 12N  17 20 E
Sóller, *Spain* ............ 24 **B9**   39 46N   2 43 E
Solo ➤, *Indonesia* ...... 37 **G15**   6 47S 112 22 E
Sologne, *France* ...... 20 **C4**   47 40N   1 45 E
Solok, *Indonesia* ...... 36 **E2**    0 45S 100 40 E
Sololá, *Guatemala* ...... 88 **D1**   14 49N  91 10W
Solomon, N. Fork ➤, *U.S.A.* 80 **F5**   39 29N  98 26W
Solomon, S. Fork ➤, *U.S.A.* 80 **F5**   39 25N  99 12W
Solomon Is. ■, *Pac. Oc.* .. 64 **H7**    6  0S 155  0 E
Solon, *China* ............ 33 **B7**   46 32N 121 10 E
Solon Springs, *U.S.A.* .. 80 **B9**   46 22N  91 49W
Solor, *Indonesia* ...... 37 **F6**    8 27S 123  0 E
Solothurn, *Switz.* ...... 20 **C7**   47 13N   7 32 E
Šolta, *Croatia* ............ 22 **C7**   43 24N  16 15 E
Solţānābād, Khorāsān, *Iran* .. 45 **C8**   34 13N  59 58 E
Solţānābād, Khorāsān, *Iran* .. 45 **B8**   36 29N  58  5 E
Solunska Glava, *Macedonia* .. 23 **D9**   41 44N  21 31 E
Solvang, *U.S.A.* ...... 79 **L6**   34 36N 120  8W
Solvay, *U.S.A.* ...... 85 **C8**   43  3N  76 13W
Sölvesborg, *Sweden* ...... 9 **H16**  56  5N  14 35 E
Solvychegodsk, *Russia* .. 18 **B8**   61  5N  46 56 E
Solway Firth, *U.K.* ...... 12 **C4**   54 49N   3 35W
Solwezi, *Zambia* ...... 55 **E2**   12 11S  26 21 E
Sōma, *Japan* ............ 30 **F10**  37 40N 140 50 E
Soma, *Turkey* ............ 23 **E12**  39 10N  27 35 E
Somabhula, *Zimbabwe* .. 57 **B4**   19 42S  29 40 E
Somali Pen., *Africa* ...... 48 **F8**    7  0N  46  0 E
Somali Rep. ■, *Africa* .... 47 **F4**    7  0N  47  0 E
Somalia = Somali Rep. ■, *Africa* 47 **F4**    7  0N  47  0 E
Sombor, *Serbia & M.* ...... 23 **B8**   45 46N  19  9 E
Sombra, *Canada* ...... 84 **D2**   42 43N  82 29W
Sombrerete, *Mexico* ...... 86 **C4**   23 40N 103 40W
Sombrero, *Anguilla* ...... 89 **C7**   18 37N  63 30W
Somdari, *India* ............ 42 **G5**   25 47N  72 38 E
Somers, *U.S.A.* ...... 76 **B6**   48  5N 114 13W
Somerset, Ky., *U.S.A.* ...... 82 **G3**   37  5N  84 36W
Somerset, Mass., *U.S.A.* .. 85 **E13**  41 47N  71  8W
Somerset, Pa., *U.S.A.* .. 84 **F5**   40  1N  79  5W
Somerset □, *U.K.* ...... 13 **F5**   51  9N   3  0W
Somerset East, *S. Africa* .. 56 **E4**   32 42S  25 35 E
Somerset I., *Canada* ...... 68 **A10**  73 30N  93  0W
Somerset West, *S. Africa* .. 56 **E2**   34  8S  18 50 E
Somersworth, *U.S.A.* .. 85 **C14**  43 16N  70 52W
Somerton, *U.S.A.* ...... 77 **K6**   32 36N 114 43W
Somerville, *U.S.A.* .. 85 **F10**  40 35N  74 38W
Someş ➤, *Romania* .. 17 **D12**  47 49N  22 43 E
Somme ➤, *France* ...... 20 **A4**   50 11N   1 38 E
Somnath, *India* ............ 42 **J4**   20 53N  70 22 E
Somosierra, Puerto de, *Spain* 21 **B4**   41  4N   3 35W
Somoto, *Nic.* ............ 88 **D2**   13  8N  86 37W
Somport, Puerto de, *Spain* .. 20 **E3**   42 48N   0 31W
Son ➤, *India* ............ 43 **G11**  25 42N  84 52 E
Son Ha, *Vietnam* ...... 38 **E7**   15  3N 108 34 E
Son Hoa, *Vietnam* ...... 38 **F7**   13  2N 108 58 E
Son La, *Vietnam* ...... 38 **B4**   21 20N 103 50 E
Son Serra, *Spain* ...... 24 **B10**  39 43N   3 13 E
Son Tay, *Vietnam* ...... 38 **B5**   21  8N 105 30 E
Soná, *Panama* ............ 88 **E3**    8  0N  81 20W
Sonamarg, *India* ...... 43 **B6**   34 18N  75 21 E
Sonamukhi, *India* ...... 43 **H12**  23 18N  87 27 E
Sonar ➤, *India* ............ 43 **G8**   24 24N  79 56 E
Sŏnch'ŏn, *N. Korea* .. 35 **E13**  39 48N 124 55 E
Sondags ➤, *S. Africa* .. 56 **E4**   33 44S  25 51 E
Sondar, *India* ............ 43 **C6**   33 28N  75 56 E
Sønderborg, *Denmark* .. 9 **J13**  54 55N   9 49 E
Sóndrio, *Italy* ............ 20 **C8**   46 10N   9 52 E
Sone, *Mozam.* ............ 55 **F3**   17 23S  34 55 E
Sonepur, *India* ............ 41 **J13**  20 55N  83 50 E
Song, *Thailand* ............ 38 **C3**   18 28N 100 11 E
Song Cau, *Vietnam* ...... 38 **F7**   13 27N 109 18 E
Song Xian, *China* ...... 34 **G7**   34 12N 112  8 E
Songan, *Indonesia* .. 37 **J18**   8 13S 115 24 E
Songch'ŏn, *N. Korea* .. 35 **E14**  39 12N 126 15 E
Songea, *Tanzania* ...... 55 **E4**   10 40S  35 40 E
Songgang, *China* ...... 33 **F10**  22 46N 113 50 E
Songhua Hu, *China* ...... 35 **C14**  43 35N 126 50 E
Songhua Jiang ➤, *China* .. 33 **B8**   47 45N 132 30 E

Songimvelo △, *S. Africa* .. 57 **D5**   25 50S  31  2 E
Songjin, *N. Korea* ...... 35 **D15**  40 40N 129 10 E
Songjŏng-ni, *S. Korea* .. 35 **G14**  35  8N 126 47 E
Songkhla, *Thailand* ...... 39 **J3**    7 13N 100 37 E
Songnim, *N. Korea* .. 35 **E13**  38 45N 125 39 E
Songo, *Mozam.* ...... 53 **H6**   15 34S  32 38 E
Songo, *Sudan* ............ 51 **G10**   9 47N  24 21 E
Songpan, *China* ...... 32 **C5**   32 40N 103 30 E
Songwe, Dem. Rep. of the Congo 54 **C2**    3 20S  26 16 E
Songwe ➤, *Africa* ...... 55 **D3**    9 44S  33 58 E
Sonhat, *India* ............ 43 **H10**  23 29N  82 31 E
Sonid Youqi, *China* ...... 34 **C7**   42 45N 112 48 E
Sonipat, *India* ............ 42 **E7**   29  0N  77  5 E
Sonkach, *India* ............ 42 **H7**   22 59N  76 21 E
Sonmiani, *Pakistan* ...... 42 **G2**   25 25N  66 40 E
Sonmiani B., *Pakistan* .. 42 **G2**   25 15N  66 30 E
Sono ➤, *Brazil* ............ 93 **E9**    9 58S  48 11W
Sonoma, *U.S.A.* ...... 78 **G4**   38 18N 122 28W
Sonora, Calif., *U.S.A.* .. 78 **H6**   37 59N 120 23W
Sonora, Tex., *U.S.A.* .. 81 **K4**   30 34N 100 39W
Sonora □, *Mexico* ...... 86 **B2**   29  0N 111  0W
Sonora ➤, *Mexico* ...... 86 **B2**   28 50N 111 33W
Sonoran Desert, *U.S.A.* .. 79 **L12**  33 40N 114 15W
Sonoyta, *Mexico* ...... 86 **A2**   31 51N 112 50W
Sŏnsan, *S. Korea* ...... 35 **F15**  36 14N 128 17 E
Sonsonate, *El Salv.* ...... 88 **D2**   13 43N  89 44W
Soochow = Suzhou, *China* .. 33 **C7**   31 19N 120 38 E
Sooke, *Canada* ...... 78 **B3**   48 13N 123 43W
Sop Hao, *Laos* ...... 38 **B5**   20 33N 104 27 E
Sop Prap, *Thailand* ...... 38 **D2**   17 53N  99 20 E
Sopi, *Indonesia* ............ 37 **D7**    2 34N 128 28 E
Sopot, *Poland* ............ 17 **A10**  54 27N  18 31 E
Sopron, *Hungary* ...... 17 **E9**   47 45N  16 32 E
Sopur, *India* ............ 43 **B6**   34 18N  74 27 E
Sør-Rondane, *Antarctica* .. 5 **D4**   72  0S  25  0 E
Sorah, *Pakistan* ...... 42 **F3**   27 13N  68 56 E
Soraon, *India* ............ 43 **G9**   25 37N  81 51 E
Sorel-Tracy, *Canada* .. 72 **C5**   46  0N  73 10W
Sórgono, *Italy* ............ 22 **D3**   40  1N   9  6 E
Soria, *Spain* ............ 21 **B4**   41 43N   2 32W
Soriano, *Uruguay* ...... 94 **C4**   33 24S  58 19W
Sorkh, Kuh-e, *Iran* ...... 45 **C8**   35 40N  58 30 E
Soroca, *Moldova* ...... 17 **D15**  48  8N  28 12 E
Sorocaba, *Brazil* ...... 95 **A6**   23 31S  47 27W
Sorochinsk, *Russia* ...... 18 **D9**   52 26N  53 10 E
Soroki = Soroca, *Moldova* .. 17 **D15**  48  8N  28 12 E
Sorong, *Indonesia* ...... 37 **E8**    0 55S 131 15 E
Soroni, *Greece* ...... 25 **C10**  36 21N  28  1 E
Soroti, *Uganda* ............ 54 **B3**    1 43N  33 35 E
Sørøya, *Norway* ...... 8 **A20**  70 40N  22 30 E
Sørøysundet, *Norway* .. 8 **A20**  70 25N  23  0 E
Sorrell, *Australia* ...... 63 **G4**   42 47S 147 34 E
Sorsele, *Sweden* ...... 8 **D17**  65 31N  17 30 E
Sorsogon, *Phil.* ...... 37 **B6**   13  0N 124  0 E
Sortavala, *Russia* ...... 18 **B5**   61 42N  30 41 E
Sortland, *Norway* ...... 8 **B16**  68 42N  15 25 E
Sŏsan, *S. Korea* ...... 35 **F14**  36 47N 126 27 E
Soscumica, L., *Canada* .. 72 **B4**   50 15N  77 27W
Sosnogorsk, *Russia* .. 18 **B9**   63 37N  53 51 E
Sosnowiec, *Poland* ...... 17 **C10**  50 20N  19 10 E
Sossus Vlei, *Namibia* .. 56 **C2**   24 40S  15 23 E
Sŏsura, *N. Korea* ...... 35 **C16**  42 16N 130 36 E
Sot ➤, *India* ............ 43 **F8**   27 27N  79 37 E
Sotkamo, *Finland* ...... 8 **D23**  64  8N  28 23 E
Soto la Marina ➤, *Mexico* .. 87 **C5**   23 40N  97 40W
Sotuta, *Mexico* ...... 87 **C7**   20 29N  89 43W
Souanké, *Congo* ...... 52 **D2**    2 10N   14  3 E
Souderton, *U.S.A.* ...... 85 **F9**   40 19N  75 19W
Soúdha, *Greece* ...... 25 **D6**   35 29N  24  4 E
Soúdhas, Kólpos, *Greece* .. 25 **D6**   35 25N  24 10 E
Soufrière, *Guadeloupe* ...... 88 **b**   16  5N  61 40W
Soufrière, *St. Lucia* ...... 89 **f**   13 51N  61  3W
Soufrière Bay, *Dominica* .. 89 **f**   13 53N  61  6W
Soukhouma, *Laos* ...... 38 **E5**   14 38N 105 48 E
Sŏul, *S. Korea* ...... 35 **F14**  37 31N 126 58 E
Sound, The, *U.K.* ...... 13 **G3**   50 20N   4  10W
Sources, Mt. aux, *Lesotho* .. 57 **D4**   28 45S  28 50 E
Soure, *Brazil* ............ 93 **D9**    0 35S  48 30W
Souris, Man., *Canada* .. 71 **D8**   49 40N 100 20W
Souris, P.E.I., *Canada* .. 73 **C7**   46 21N  62 15W
Souris ➤, *Canada* ...... 80 **A5**   49 40N  99 34W
Sousa, *Brazil* ............ 93 **E11**   6 45S  38 10W
Sousse, *Tunisia* ...... 51 **A8**   35 50N  10 38 E
Sout ➤, *S. Africa* ...... 56 **E2**   31 35S  18 24 E
South Africa ■, *Africa* .. 56 **E3**   32  0S  23  0 E
South America ........ 90 **E5**   10  0S  60  0W
South Atlantic Ocean ...... 2 **F8**   20  0S  10  0W
South Aulatsivik I., *Canada* .. 73 **A7**   56 45N  61 30W
South Australia □, *Australia* .. 63 **E2**   32  0S 139  0 E
South Ayrshire □, *U.K.* .. 11 **F4**   55  5N   4 40W
South Baldy, *U.S.A.* ...... 77 **J10**  33 59N 107 11W
South Bass I., *U.S.A.* .. 84 **E2**   41 38N  82 53W
South Bend, Ind., *U.S.A.* .. 82 **E2**   41 41N  86 15W
South Bend, Wash., *U.S.A.* .. 78 **D3**   46 40N 123 48W
South Boston, *U.S.A.* .. 83 **G6**   36 42N  78 54W
South Branch, *Canada* .. 73 **C8**   47 55N  59  2W
South Brook, *Canada* .. 73 **C8**   49 26N  56  5W
South Carolina □, *U.S.A.* .. 83 **J5**   34  0N  81  0W
South Charleston, *U.S.A.* .. 82 **F5**   38 22N  81 44W
South China Sea, *Asia* .. 36 **C4**   10  0N 113  0 E
South Cumberland Is. △,
   *Australia* ............ 62 **J7**   20 42S 149 11 E
South Dakota □, *U.S.A.* .. 80 **C5**   44 15N 100  0W
South Deerfield, *U.S.A.* .. 85 **D12**  42 29N  72 37W
South Downs, *U.K.* ...... 13 **G7**   50 52N   0 25 E
South East C., *Australia* .. 63 **G4**   43 40S 146 50 E
South-East Indian Rise, Ind. Oc. 5 **B10**  43  0S  80  0 E
South East Is., *Australia* .. 61 **F3**   34 17S 123 30 E
South Esk ➤, *U.K.* ...... 11 **E6**   56 43N   2 31W
South Foreland, *U.K.* .. 13 **F9**   51  8N   1 24 E
South Fork American ➤, *U.S.A.* 78 **G5**   38 45N 121  5W
South Fork Feather ➤, *U.S.A.* 78 **F5**   39 17N 121 36W
South Fork Grand ➤, *U.S.A.* 80 **C3**   45 43N 102 17W
South Fork Republican ➤, *U.S.A.* 80 **E4**   40  3N 101 31W
South Georgia, *Antarctica* .. 96 **G9**   54 30S  37  0W
South Gloucestershire □, *U.K.* .. 13 **F5**   51 32N   2 28W
South Hadley, *U.S.A.* .. 85 **D12**  42 16N  72 35W
South Haven, *U.S.A.* .. 82 **D2**   42 24N  86 16W
South Henik L., *Canada* .. 71 **A9**   61 30N  97 20W
South Honshu Ridge, Pac. Oc. .. 64 **E6**   23  0N 143  0 E
South Horr, *Kenya* ...... 54 **B4**    2 12N  36 56 E
South I., *Kenya* ............ 54 **B4**    2 35N  36 35 E
South I., *N.Z.* ............ 59 **L3**   44  0S 170  0 E
South Indian Lake, *Canada* .. 71 **B9**   56 47N  98 56W
South Invercargill, *N.Z.* .. 59 **M2**   46 26S 168 23 E
South Knife ➤, *Canada* .. 71 **B10**  58 55N  94 37W

South Koel ➤, *India* ...... 43 **H11**  22 32N  85 14 E
South Korea ■, *Asia* .. 35 **G15**  36  0N 128  0 E
South Lake Tahoe, *U.S.A.* .. 78 **G6**   38 57N 119 59W
South Lanarkshire □, *U.K.* .. 11 **F5**   55 37N   3 53W
South Loup ➤, *U.S.A.* .. 80 **E5**   41  4N  98 39W
South Luangwa △, *Zambia* .. 55 **E3**   13  0S  31 20 E
South Magnetic Pole, Antarctica .. 5 **C9**   64  8S 138  8 E
South Milwaukee, *U.S.A.* .. 82 **D2**   42 55N  87 52W
South Molton, *U.K.* ...... 13 **F4**   51  1N   3 51W
South Moose L., *Canada* .. 71 **C8**   53 46N 100  8W
South Nahanni ➤, *Canada* .. 70 **A4**   61  3N 123 21W
South Nation ➤, *Canada* .. 85 **A9**   45 34N  75  6W
South Natuna Is. = Natuna
   Selatan, Kepulauan, *Indonesia* 36 **D3**    2 45N 109  0 E
South Negril Pt., *Jamaica* .. 88 **a**   18 16N  78 22W
South Orkney Is., *Antarctica* .. 5 **C18**  63  0S  45  0W
South Ossetia □, *Georgia* .. 19 **F7**   42 21N  44  2 E
South Pagai, I. = Pagai Selatan,
   Pulau, *Indonesia* ...... 36 **E2**    3  0S 100 15 E
South Paris, *U.S.A.* .. 85 **B14**  44 14N  70 31W
South Pittsburg, *U.S.A.* .. 83 **H3**   35  1N  85 42W
South Platte ➤, *U.S.A.* .. 80 **E4**   41  7N 100 42W
South Pole, Antarctica ...... 5 **E**   90  0S   0  0W
South Porcupine, *Canada* .. 72 **C3**   48 30N  81 12W
South Portland, *U.S.A.* .. 83 **D10**  43 38N  70 15W
South Pt. = Barbados ...... 89 **g**   13  2N  59 32W
South Pt., *U.S.A.* ...... 84 **B1**   44 52N  83 19W
South River, *Canada* .. 72 **C4**   45 52N  79 23W
South River, *U.S.A.* .. 85 **F10**  40 27N  74 23W
South Ronaldsay, *U.K.* .. 11 **C6**   58 48N   2 58W
South Sandwich Is., *Antarctica* .. 5 **B1**   57  0S  27  0W
South Saskatchewan ➤, *Canada* 71 **C7**   53 15N 105  5W
South Seal ➤, *Canada* .. 71 **B9**   58 48N  98  8W
South Shetland Is., *Antarctica* .. 5 **C18**  62  0S  59  0W
South Shields, *U.K.* .. 12 **C6**   55  0N   1 25W
South Sioux City, *U.S.A.* .. 80 **D6**   42 28N  96 24W
South Taranaki Bight, *N.Z.* .. 59 **H5**   39 40S 174  5 E
South Thompson ➤, *Canada* .. 70 **C4**   50 40N 120 20W
South Twin I., *Canada* .. 72 **B4**   53  7N  79 52W
South Tyne ➤, *U.K.* ...... 12 **C5**   54 59N   2  8W
South Uist, *U.K.* ...... 11 **D1**   57 20N   7 15W
South West C., *Australia* .. 63 **G4**   43 34S 146  3 E
South West C., *N.Z.* .. 59 **M1**   47 17S 167 28 E
South Williamsport, *U.S.A.* .. 84 **E8**   41 13N  77  0W
South Yorkshire □, *U.K.* .. 12 **D6**   53 27N   1 36W
Southampton, *Canada* .. 84 **B3**   44 30N  81 25W
Southampton, *U.K.* .. 13 **G6**   50 54N   1 23W
Southampton, *U.S.A.* .. 85 **F12**  40 53N  72 23W
Southampton □, *U.K.* .. 13 **G6**   50 54N   1 23W
Southampton I., *Canada* .. 69 **B11**  64 30N  84  0W
Southaven, *U.S.A.* ...... 81 **H9**   34 59N  90  2W
Southbank, *Canada* .. 70 **C3**   54  2N 125 46W
Southbridge, *N.Z.* ...... 59 **K4**   43 48S 172 16 E
Southbridge, *U.S.A.* .. 85 **D12**  42  5N  72  2W
Southeast Pacific Basin, Pac. Oc. .. 5 **C15**  16 30S  92  0W
Southend, *Canada* ...... 71 **B8**   56 19N 103 22W
Southend-on-Sea, *U.K.* .. 13 **F8**   51 32N   0 44 E
Southend-on-Sea □, *U.K.* .. 13 **F8**   51 32N   0 44 E
Southern □, *Malawi* ...... 55 **F4**   15  0S  35  0 E
Southern □, *Zambia* ...... 55 **F2**   16 20S  26 20 E
Southern Alps, *N.Z.* ...... 59 **K3**   43 41S 170 11 E
Southern Cross, *Australia* .. 61 **F2**   31 12S 119 15 E
Southern Indian L., *Canada* .. 71 **B9**   57 10N  98 30W
Southern Ocean, *Antarctica* .. 5 **C6**   62  0S  60  0 E
Southern Pines, *U.S.A.* .. 83 **H6**   35 11N  79 24W
Southern Uplands, *U.K.* .. 11 **F5**   55 28N   3 52W
Southington, *U.S.A.* .. 85 **E12**  41 36N  72 53W
Southland □, *N.Z.* ...... 59 **L1**   45 30S 168  0 E
Southold, *U.S.A.* ...... 85 **E12**  41  4N  72 26W
Southport, *Australia* .. 63 **D5**   27 58S 153 25 E
Southport, *U.K.* ...... 12 **D4**   53 39N   3  0W
Southport, Fla., *U.S.A.* .. 83 **K3**   30 17N  85 38W
Southport, N.Y., *U.S.A.* .. 84 **D8**   42  3N  76 49W
Southwest △, *Australia* .. 63 **G4**   43  8S 146  5 E
Southwestern Pacific Basin,
   Pac. Oc. ............ 5 **A12**  42  0S 170  0W
Southwold, *U.K.* ...... 13 **E9**   52 20N   1 41 E
Southwood △, *Australia* .. 63 **D5**   27 48S 150  8 E
Soutpansberg, *S. Africa* .. 57 **C4**   23  0S  29 30 E
Sovetsk, Kaliningrad, *Russia* .. 9 **J19**  55  6N  21 50 E
Sovetsk, Kirov, *Russia* .. 18 **C8**   57 38N  48 53 E
Sovetskaya Gavan = Vanino,
   *Russia* ............ 29 **E15**  48 50N 140  5 E
Soweto, *S. Africa* ...... 57 **D4**   26 14S  27 54 E
Sōya-Kaikyō = La Perouse Str.,
   *Asia* ............ 30 **B11**  45 40N 142  0 E
Sōya-Misaki, *Japan* .. 30 **B10**  45 30N 141 55 E
Sozh ➤, *Belarus* ...... 17 **B16**  51 57N  30 48 E
Spa, *Belgium* ............ 15 **D5**   50 29N   5 53 E
Spain ■, *Europe* ...... 21 **B4**   39  0N   4  0W
Spalding, *Australia* ...... 63 **E2**   33 30S 138 37 E
Spalding, *U.K.* ............ 12 **E7**   52 48N   0  9W
Spangler, *U.S.A.* ...... 84 **F6**   40 39N  78 48W
Spanish, *Canada* ...... 72 **C3**   46 12N  82 20W
Spanish Fork, *U.S.A.* .. 76 **F8**   40  7N 111 39W
Spanish Town, Br. Virgin Is. .. 89 **a**   17 43N  64 26W
Spanish Town, *Jamaica* .. 88 **a**   18  0N  76 57W
Sparks, *U.S.A.* ...... 78 **F7**   39 32N 119 45W
Sparta = Spárti, *Greece* .. 23 **F10**  37  5N  22 25 E
Sparta, N.J., *U.S.A.* .. 85 **E10**  41  2N  74 38W
Sparta, Wis., *U.S.A.* .. 80 **D9**   43 56N  90 49W
Spartanburg, *U.S.A.* .. 83 **H5**   34 56N  81 57W
Spartansburg, *U.S.A.* .. 84 **E5**   41 49N  79 41W
Spárti, *Greece* ............ 23 **F10**  37  5N  22 25 E
Spartivento, C., Calabria, Italy .. 22 **F7**   37 55N  16  4 E
Spartivento, C., Sard., Italy .. 22 **E3**   38 53N   8 50 E
Sparwood, *Canada* ...... 70 **D6**   49 44N 114 53W
Spassk Dalniy, *Russia* .. 29 **E14**  44 40N 132 48 E
Spátha, Ákra, *Greece* .. 25 **D5**   35 42N  23 43 E
Spatsizi ➤, *Canada* .. 70 **B3**   57 42N 128  7W
Spatsizi Plateau Wilderness △,
   *Canada* ............ 70 **B3**   57 40N 128  0W
Spean ➤, *U.K.* ...... 11 **E4**   56 55N   4 59W
Spearfish, *U.S.A.* ...... 80 **C3**   44 30N 103 52W
Spearman, *U.S.A.* ...... 81 **G4**   36 12N 101 12W
Speculator, *U.S.A.* .. 85 **C10**  43 30N  74 23W
Speightstown, Barbados .. 89 **g**   13 15N  59 39W
Speke Gulf, *Tanzania* .. 54 **C3**    2 20S  32 50 E
Spence Bay = Taloyoak, *Canada* 68 **B10**  69 32N  93 32W
Spencer, Idaho, *U.S.A.* .. 76 **D7**   44 22N 112 11W
Spencer, Iowa, *U.S.A.* .. 80 **D7**   43  9N  95  9W
Spencer, N.Y., *U.S.A.* .. 85 **D8**   42 13N  76 30W
Spencer, Nebr., *U.S.A.* .. 80 **D5**   42 53N  98 42W
Spencer B., *Namibia* .. 56 **D1**   25 30S  14 47 E
Spencer G., *Australia* .. 63 **E2**   34  0S 137 20 E

Spencerville, *Canada* .. 85 **B9**   44 51N  75 33W
Spences Bridge, *Canada* .. 70 **C4**   50 25N 121 20W
Spennymoor, *U.K.* ...... 12 **C6**   54 42N   1 36W
Spenser Mts., *N.Z.* ...... 59 **K4**   42 15S 172 45 E
Sperrin Mts., *U.K.* ...... 10 **B5**   54 50N   7  0W
Spey ➤, *U.K.* ............ 11 **D5**   57 40N   3  6W
Speyer, *Germany* ...... 16 **D5**   49 29N   8 25 E
Spezand, *Pakistan* ...... 42 **E2**   29 59N  67  0 E
Spili, *Greece* ............ 25 **D6**   35 13N  24 31 E
Spin Búldak, *Afghan.* .. 42 **D2**   31  1N  66 25 E
Spinalónga, *Greece* .. 25 **D7**   35 18N  25 44 E
Spirit Lake, *U.S.A.* .. 78 **D4**   46 15N 122  9W
Spirit River, *Canada* .. 70 **B5**   55 45N 118 50W
Spiritwood, *Canada* .. 71 **C7**   53 24N 107 33W
Spithead, *U.K.* ...... 13 **G6**   50 45N   1 10W
Spitzbergen = Svalbard, Arctic .. 4 **B8**   78  0N  17  0 E
Spjelkavik, *Norway* ...... 9 **E12**  62 28N   6 22 E
Split, *Croatia* ............ 22 **C7**   43 31N  16 26 E
Split L., *Canada* ...... 71 **B9**   56  8N  96 15W
Split Lake, *Canada* ...... 71 **B9**   56  8N  96 15W
Spofford, *U.S.A.* ...... 81 **L4**   29 10N 100 25W
Spokane, *U.S.A.* ...... 76 **C5**   47 40N 117 24W
Spoleto, *Italy* ............ 22 **C5**   42 44N  12 44 E
Spooner, *U.S.A.* ...... 80 **C9**   45 50N  91 53W
Sporyy Navolok, Mys, *Russia* .. 28 **B7**   75 50N  68 40 E
Sprague, *U.S.A.* ...... 76 **C5**   47 18N 117 59W
Spratly I., S. China Sea .. 36 **C4**    8 38N 111 55 E
Spratly Is., S. China Sea .. 36 **C4**    8 20N 112  0 E
Spray, *U.S.A.* ............ 76 **D4**   44 50N 119 48W
Spree ➤, *Germany* ...... 16 **B7**   52 32N  13 13 E
Sprengisandur, Iceland .. 8 **D5**   64 52N  18  7W
Spring City, *U.S.A.* .. 85 **F9**   40 11N  75 33W
Spring Creek, *U.S.A.* .. 76 **F6**   40 45N 115 38W
Spring Garden, *U.S.A.* .. 78 **F6**   39 52N 120 47W
Spring Hall, Barbados .. 89 **g**   13 18N  59 36W
Spring Hill, *U.S.A.* .. 83 **L4**   28 27N  82 41W
Spring Mts., *U.S.A.* .. 77 **H6**   36  0N 115 45W
Spring Valley, *U.S.A.* .. 79 **N10**  32 45N 117  5W
Springbok, S. Africa .. 56 **D2**   29 42S  17 54 E
Springboro, *U.S.A.* .. 84 **E4**   41 48N  80 22W
Springdale, *Canada* .. 73 **C8**   49 30N  56  6W
Springdale, *U.S.A.* .. 81 **G7**   36 11N  94 8W
Springer, *U.S.A.* ...... 81 **G2**   36 22N 104 36W
Springerville, *U.S.A.* .. 77 **J9**   34  8N 109 17W
Springfield, *Canada* .. 84 **D4**   42 50N  80 56W
Springfield, *N.Z.* ...... 59 **K3**   43 19S 171 56 E
Springfield, Colo., *U.S.A.* .. 81 **G3**   37 24N 102 37W
Springfield, Ill., *U.S.A.* .. 80 **F10**  39 48N  89 39W
Springfield, Mass., *U.S.A.* .. 85 **D12**  42  6N  72 35W
Springfield, Mo., *U.S.A.* .. 81 **G8**   37 13N  93 17W
Springfield, Ohio, *U.S.A.* .. 82 **F4**   39 55N  83 49W
Springfield, Oreg., *U.S.A.* .. 76 **D2**   44  3N 123  1W
Springfield, Tenn., *U.S.A.* .. 83 **G2**   36 31N  86 53W
Springfield, Vt., *U.S.A.* .. 85 **C12**  43 18N  72 29W
Springfontein, S. Africa .. 56 **E4**   30 15S  25 40 E
Springhill, *Canada* ...... 73 **C7**   45 40N  64  4W
Springhill, *U.S.A.* ...... 81 **J8**   33  0N  93 28W
Springhouse, *Canada* .. 70 **C4**   51 56N 122  7W
Springs, S. Africa ...... 57 **D4**   26 13S  28 25 E
Springsure, *Australia* .. 62 **C4**   24  8S 148  6 E
Springvale, *U.S.A.* .. 85 **C14**  43 28N  70 48W
Springville, Calif., *U.S.A.* .. 78 **J8**   36  8N 118 49W
Springville, N.Y., *U.S.A.* .. 84 **D6**   42 31N  78 40W
Springville, Utah, *U.S.A.* .. 76 **F8**   40 10N 111 37W
Springwater, *U.S.A.* .. 84 **D7**   42 38N  77 35W
Spruce-Creek, *U.S.A.* .. 84 **F6**   40 36N  78  9W
Spruce Knob-Seneca Rocks △,
   *U.S.A.* ............ 82 **F6**   38 50N  79 30W
Spruce Mt., *U.S.A.* .. 85 **D12**  44 12N  72 19W
Spur, *U.S.A.* ............ 81 **J4**   33 28N 100 52W
Spurn Hd., *U.K.* ...... 12 **D8**   53 35N   0  8 E
Spuzzum, *Canada* ...... 70 **D4**   49 37N 121 23W
Squam L., *U.S.A.* ...... 85 **C13**  43 45N  71 32W
Squamish, *Canada* ...... 70 **D4**   49 45N 123 10W
Square Islands, *Canada* .. 73 **B8**   52 47N  55 47W
Squires, Mt., *Australia* .. 61 **E4**   26 14S 127 28 E
Srbija = Serbia □, Serbia & M. .. 23 **C9**   43 30N  21  0 E
Sre Ambel, *Cambodia* .. 39 **G4**   11  8N 103 46 E
Sre Khtum, *Cambodia* .. 39 **F6**   12 10N 106 52 E
Sre Umbel = Sre Ambel,
   *Cambodia* ............ 39 **G4**   11  8N 103 46 E
Srebrenica, Bos.-H. ...... 23 **B8**   44  6N  19 18 E
Sredinny Ra. = Sredinnyy
   Khrebet, *Russia* .. 29 **D16**  57  0N 160  0 E
Sredinnyy Khrebet, *Russia* .. 29 **D16**  57  0N 160  0 E
Srednekolymsk, *Russia* .. 29 **C16**  67 27N 153 40 E
Śrem, *Poland* ............ 17 **B9**   52  6N  17  2 E
Sremska Mitrovica, Serbia & M. .. 23 **B8**   44 59N  19 38 E
Srepok ➤, *Cambodia* .. 38 **F6**   13 33N 106 16 E
Sretensk, *Russia* ...... 29 **D12**  52 10N 117 40 E
Sri Lanka ■, *Asia* ...... 40 **R12**   7 30N  80 50 E
Srikakulam, *India* ...... 41 **K13**  18 14N  83 58 E
Srinagar, *India* ...... 43 **B6**   34  5N  74 50 E
Srinagarind Res., *Thailand* .. 38 **E2**   14 35N  99  0 E
Srono, *Indonesia* ...... 37 **J17**   8 24S 114 16 E
Staaten ➤, *Australia* .. 62 **B3**   16 24S 141 17 E
Staaten River △, *Australia* .. 62 **B3**   16 15S 142 40 E
Stade, *Germany* ...... 16 **B5**   53 35N   9 29 E
Stadskanaal, Neths. ...... 15 **A6**   53  4N   6 55 E
Staffa, *U.K.* ............ 11 **E2**   56 27N   6 21W
Stafford, *U.K.* ............ 12 **E5**   52 49N   2  7W
Stafford, *U.S.A.* ...... 81 **G5**   37 58N  98 36W
Stafford Springs, *U.S.A.* .. 85 **E12**  41 57N  72 18W
Staffordshire □, *U.K.* .. 12 **E5**   52 53N   2 10W
Staines, *U.K.* ............ 13 **F7**   51 26N   0 29W
Stakhanov, Ukraine ...... 19 **E6**   48 35N  38 40 E
Stalis, *Greece* ............ 25 **D7**   35 17N  25 25 E
Stalowa Wola, Poland .. 17 **C12**  50 34N  22  3 E
Stalybridge, *U.K.* ...... 12 **D5**   53 28N   2  3W
Stamford, *Australia* .. 62 **C3**   21 15S 143 46 E
Stamford, *U.K.* ...... 12 **E7**   52 39N   0 29W
Stamford, Conn., *U.S.A.* .. 85 **E11**  41  3N  73 32W
Stamford, N.Y., *U.S.A.* .. 85 **D10**  42 25N  74 38W
Stamford, Tex., *U.S.A.* .. 81 **J5**   32 57N  99 48W
Stampriet, Namibia ...... 56 **C2**   24 20S  18 28 E
Stamps, *U.S.A.* ...... 81 **J8**   33 22N  93 30W
Standerton, S. Africa .. 57 **D4**   26 55S  29  7 E
Standerton, S. Africa .. 82 **D4**   43 59N  83 57W
Stanford, *U.S.A.* ...... 76 **C8**   47  9N 110 13W
Stanger, S. Africa ...... 57 **D5**   29 27S  31 14 E
Stängelsön = Salpausselkä,
   *Finland* ............ 9 **F22**  61  3N  26 15 E
Stanislaus ➤, *U.S.A.* .. 78 **H5**   37 40N 121 14W
Stanke Dimitrov, *Bulgaria* .. 23 **C10**  42 17N  23  9 E
Stanley, *Australia* ...... 63 **G4**   40 46S 145 19 E
Stanley, *China* ...... 33 **G11**  22 13N 114 12 E
Stanley, Falk. Is. ...... 96 **G5**   51 40S  59 51W

Stanley, *U.K.* ............... 12 C6  54 53N   1 41W
Stanley, *Idaho, U.S.A.* ...... 76 D6  44 13N 114 56W
Stanley, *N. Dak., U.S.A.* .... 80 A3  48 19N 102 23W
Stanley, *N.Y., U.S.A.* ....... 84 D7  42 48N  77  6W
Stanley Mission, *Canada* .... 71 B8  55 25N 104 33W
Stanovoy Khrebet, *Russia* ... 29 D13 55  0N 130  0 E
Stanovoy Ra. = Stanovoy
  Khrebet, *Russia* .......... 29 D13 55  0N 130  0 E
Stansmore Ra., *Australia* .... 60 D4  21 23S 128 33 E
Stansted, London ✕ (STN), *U.K.* 13 F8  51 54N  0 14 E
Stanthorpe, *Australia* ....... 63 D5  28 36S 151 59 E
Stanton, *U.S.A.* ............. 81 J4  32  8N 101 48W
Stanwood, *U.S.A.* ........... 78 B4  48 15N 122 23W
Staples, *U.S.A.* ............. 80 B7  46 21N  94 48W
Star City, *Canada* .......... 71 C8  52 50N 104 20W
Star Lake, *U.S.A.* ........... 85 B9  44 10N  75  2W
Stara Planina, *Bulgaria* ..... 23 C10 43 15N  23  0 E
Stara Zagora, *Bulgaria* ...... 23 C11 42 26N  25 39 E
Starachowice, *Poland* ....... 17 C11 51  3N  21  2 E
Staraya Russa, *Russia* ...... 18 C5  57 58N  31 23 E
Starbuck I., *Kiribati* ........ 65 H12  5 37S 155 55W
Starcke △, *Australia* ........ 62 A4  14 56S 145  2 E
Stargard Szczeciński, *Poland* . 16 B8  53 20N  15  0 E
Staritsa, *Russia* ............ 18 C5  56 33N  34 55 E
Starke, *U.S.A.* ............. 83 L4  29 57N  82  7W
Starogard Gdański, *Poland* ... 17 B10 53 59N  18 30 E
Starokonstantinov =
  Starokonstyantyniv, *Ukraine* 17 D14 49 48N  27 10 E
Starokonstyantyniv, *Ukraine* . 17 D14 49 48N  27 10 E
Start Pt., *U.K.* ............. 13 G4  50 13N   3 39W
Staryy Chartoriysk, *Ukraine* . 17 C13 51 15N  25 54 E
Staryy Oskol, *Russia* ....... 19 D6  51 19N  37 55 E
State College, *U.S.A.* ....... 84 F7  40 48N  77 52W
Stateline, *U.S.A.* ........... 78 G2  38 57N 119 56W
Staten, I. = Estados, I. de Los,
  *Argentina* ............... 96 G4  54 40S  64 30W
Staten I., *U.S.A.* ........... 85 F10 40 35N  74  9W
Statesboro, *U.S.A.* ......... 83 J5  32 27N  81 47W
Statesville, *U.S.A.* ......... 83 H5  35 47N  80 53W
Statia = St. Eustatius, *W. Indies* 89 C7  17 20N  63  0W
Stauffer, *U.S.A.* ........... 79 L7  34 45N 119  3W
Staunton, *Ill., U.S.A.* ....... 80 F10 39  1N  89 47W
Staunton, *Va., U.S.A.* ....... 82 F6  38  9N  79  4W
Stavanger, *Norway* ......... 9 G11 58 57N   5 40 E
Staveley, *N.Z.* ............. 59 K3  43 40S 171 32 E
Stavelot, *Belgium* .......... 15 D5  50 23N   5 55 E
Stavern, *Norway* ........... 9 G14 59  0N  10  1 E
Stavoren, *Neths.* ........... 15 B5  52 53N   5 22 E
Stavropol, *Russia* .......... 19 E7  45  5N  42  0 E
Stavros, *Cyprus* ........... 25 D11 35  1N  32 38 E
Stavrós, *Greece* ............ 25 D6  35 12N  24 45 E
Stavrós, Ákra, *Greece* ...... 25 D6  35 26N  24 58 E
Stawell, *Australia* .......... 63 F3  37  5S 142 47 E
Stawell �, *Australia* ....... 62 C3  20 20S 142 55 E
Stayner, *Canada* ........... 84 B4  44 25N  80  5W
Stayton, *U.S.A.* ............ 76 D2  44 48N 122 48W
Steamboat Springs, *U.S.A.* .. 76 F10 40 29N 106 50W
Steele, *U.S.A.* ............. 80 B5  46 51N  99 55W
Steelton, *U.S.A.* ........... 84 F8  40 14N  76 50W
Steen River, *Canada* ........ 70 B5  59 40N 117 12W
Steens Mt., *U.S.A.* ......... 76 E4  42 35N 118 40W
Steenwijk, *Neths.* .......... 15 B6  52 47N   6  7 E
Steep Pt., *Australia* ........ 61 E1  26  8S 113  8 E
Steep Rock, *Canada* ........ 71 C9  51 30N  98 48W
Stefanie L. = Chew Bahir,
  *Ethiopia* ................. 47 G2   4 40N  36 50 E
Stefansson Bay, *Antarctica* .. 5 C5  67 20S  59  8 E
Steiermark □, *Austria* ....... 16 E8  47 26N  15  0 E
Steilacoom, *U.S.A.* ......... 78 C4  47 10N 122 36W
Steilrandberge, *Namibia* .... 56 B1  17 45S 113  0 E
Steinbach, *Canada* ......... 71 D9  49 32N  96 40W
Steinhausen, *Namibia* ....... 56 C2  21 49S  18 20 E
Steinkjer, *Norway* .......... 8 D14 64  1N  11 31 E
Steinkopf, *S. Africa* ........ 56 D2  29 18S  17 43 E
Stellarton, *Canada* ......... 73 C7  45 32N  62 30W
Stellenbosch, *S. Africa* ..... 56 E2  33 58S  18 50 E
Stendal, *Germany* .......... 16 B6  52 36N  11 53 E
Steornabhaigh = Stornoway,
  *U.K.* ................... 11 C2  58 13N   6 23W
Stepanakert = Xankändi,
  *Azerbaijan* ............... 19 G8  39 52N  46 49 E
Stephens Creek, *Australia* ... 63 E3  31 50S 141 30 E
Stephens I., *Canada* ........ 70 C2  54 10N 130 45W
Stephens L., *Canada* ........ 71 B9  56 32N  95  0W
Stephenville, *Canada* ....... 73 C8  48 31N  58 35W
Stephenville, *U.S.A.* ........ 81 J5  32 13N  98 12W
Steppe, *Asia* .............. 26 D9  50  0N  50  0 E
Sterkstroom, *S. Africa* ...... 56 E4  31 32S  26 32 E
Sterling, *Colo., U.S.A.* ...... 80 E3  40 37N 103 13W
Sterling, *Ill., U.S.A.* ........ 80 E10 41 48N  89 42W
Sterling, *Kans., U.S.A.* ...... 80 F5  38 13N  98 12W
Sterling City, *U.S.A.* ........ 81 K4  31 51N 101  0W
Sterling Heights, *U.S.A.* ..... 82 D4  42 35N  83  0W
Sterling Run, *U.S.A.* ........ 84 E6  41 25N  78 12W
Sterlitamak, *Russia* ........ 18 D10 53 40N  56  0 E
Stérnes, *Greece* ........... 25 D6  35 30N  24  9 E
Stettin = Szczecin, *Poland* ... 16 B8  53 27N  14 27 E
Stettiner Haff, *Germany* ..... 16 B8  53 47N  14 15 E
Stettler, *Canada* ........... 70 C6  52 19N 112 40W
Steubenville, *U.S.A.* ........ 84 F4  40 22N  80 37W
Stevenage, *U.K.* ........... 13 F7  51 55N   0 13W
Stevens Point, *U.S.A.* ....... 80 C10 44 31N  89 34W
Stevenson, *U.S.A.* ......... 78 E5  45 42N 121 53W
Stevenson ➤, *Australia* ..... 63 D2  27  6S 135 33 E
Stevenson L., *Canada* ....... 71 C9  53 55N  96  0W
Stevensville, *U.S.A.* ........ 76 C6  46 30N 114  5W
Stewart, *Canada* ........... 70 B3  55 56N 129 57W
Stewart, *U.S.A.* ........... 78 G4  38 51N 119 23W
Stewart ➤, *Canada* ......... 68 B6  63 19N 139 26W
Stewart, C., *Australia* ....... 62 A1  11 57S 134 56 E
Stewart, I., *Chile* .......... 96 G2  54 50S  71 15W
Stewart I., *N.Z.* ........... 59 M1  46 58S 167 54 E
Stewarts Point, *U.S.A.* ...... 78 G3  38 39N 123 24W
Stewartville, *U.S.A.* ........ 80 D8  43 51N  92  9W
Stewiacke, *Canada* ......... 73 C7  45  9N  63 22W
Steynsburg, *S. Africa* ....... 56 E4  31 15S  25 49 E
Steyr, *Austria* ............ 16 D8  48  3N  14 25 E
Steytlerville, *S. Africa* ...... 56 E3  33 17S  24 19 E
Stigler, *U.S.A.* ............ 81 H7  35 15N  95 8W
Stikine ➤, *Canada* .......... 70 B2  56 40N 132 30W
Stilfontein, *S. Africa* ....... 56 D4  26 51S  26 50 E
Stillwater, *N.Z.* ........... 59 K3  42 27S 171 20 E
Stillwater, *Minn., U.S.A.* .... 80 C8  45 3N  92 49W
Stillwater, *N.Y., U.S.A.* ..... 85 D11 42 55N  73 41W
Stillwater, *Okla., U.S.A.* .... 81 G6  36 7N  97  4W
Stillwater Range, *U.S.A.* .... 76 G4  39 50N 118  5W
Stillwater Reservoir, *U.S.A.* . 85 C9  43 54N  75  3W
Stilwell, *U.S.A.* ........... 81 H7  35 49N  94 38W

Štip, *Macedonia* ........... 23 D10 41 42N  22 10 E
Stirling, *Canada* ........... 84 B7  44 18N  77 33W
Stirling, *U.K.* ............. 11 E5  56  8N   3 57W
Stirling □, *U.K.* ........... 11 E4  56 12N   4 18W
Stirling Ra., *Australia* ...... 61 F2  34 23S 118  0 E
Stirling Range △, *Australia* .. 61 F2  34 26S 118 20 E
Stittsville, *Canada* ......... 85 A9  45 15N  75 55W
Stjernøya, *Norway* ......... 8 A20 70 20N  22 40 E
Stjørdalshalsen, *Norway* .... 8 E14 63 29N  10 51 E
Stockerau, *Austria* ......... 16 D9  48 24N  16 12 E
Stockholm, *Sweden* ........ 9 G18 59 20N  18  3 E
Stockport, *U.K.* ........... 12 D5  53 25N   2  9W
Stocksbridge, *U.K.* ........ 12 D6  53 29N   1 35W
Stockton, *Calif., U.S.A.* ..... 78 H5  37 58N 121 17W
Stockton, *Kans., U.S.A.* ..... 80 F5  39 26N  99 16W
Stockton, *Mo., U.S.A.* ...... 81 G8  37 42N  93 48W
Stockton-on-Tees, *U.K.* ..... 12 C6  54 35N   1 19W
Stockton-on-Tees □, *U.K.* ... 12 C6  54 35N   1 19W
Stockton Plateau, *U.S.A.* .... 81 K3  30 30N 102 30W
Stoeng Treng, *Cambodia* .... 38 F5  13 31N 105 58 E
Stoer, Pt. of, *U.K.* ......... 11 C3  58 16N   5 23W
Stoke-on-Trent, *U.K.* ....... 12 D5  53  1N   2 11W
Stoke-on-Trent □, *U.K.* ..... 12 D5  53  1N   2 11W
Stokes △, *Australia* ........ 61 E2  29 55S 115  6 E
Stokes Pt., *Australia* ....... 63 G3  40 10S 143 56 E
Stokes Ra., *Australia* ....... 60 C5  15 50S 130 50 E
Stokksnes, *Iceland* ........ 8 D6  64 14N  14 58W
Stokmarknes, *Norway* ...... 8 B16 68 34N  14 54 E
Stolac, *Bos.-H.* ........... 23 C7  43  5N  17 59 E
Stolbovoy, Ostrov, *Russia* ... 29 B14 74 44N 135 14 E
Stolbtsy = Stowbtsy, *Belarus* . 17 B14 53 30N  26 43 E
Stolin, *Belarus* ........... 17 C14 51 53N  26 50 E
Stómion, *Greece* .......... 25 D5  35 21N  23 32 E
Stone, *U.K.* .............. 12 E5  52 55N   2  9W
Stoneboro, *U.S.A.* ......... 84 E4  41 20N  80  7W
Stonehaven, *U.K.* ......... 11 E6  56 59N   2 12W
Stonehenge, *Australia* ...... 62 C3  24 22S 143 17 E
Stonehenge, *U.K.* ......... 13 F6  51  9N   1 45W
Stonewall, *Canada* ......... 71 C9  50 10N  97 19W
Stony L., *Man., Canada* ..... 71 B9  58 51N  98 40W
Stony L., *Ont., Canada* ..... 84 B6  44 30N  78  5W
Stony Point, *U.S.A.* ........ 85 E11 41 14N  73 59W
Stony Pt., *U.S.A.* .......... 85 C8  43 50N  76 18W
Stony Rapids, *Canada* ...... 71 B7  59 16N 105 50W
Stony Tunguska = Tunguska,
  Podkamennaya ➤, *Russia* . 29 C10 61 50N  90 13 E
Stonyford, *U.S.A.* .......... 78 F4  39 23N 122 33W
Stora Lulevatten, *Sweden* ... 8 C18 67 10N  19 30 E
Storavan, *Sweden* ......... 8 D18 65 45N  18 10 E
Stord, *Norway* ............ 9 G11 59 52N   5 23 E
Store Bælt, *Denmark* ....... 9 J14 55 20N  11  0 E
Storm B., *Australia* ........ 63 G4  43 10S 147 30 E
Storm Lake, *U.S.A.* ........ 80 D7  42 39N  95 13W
Stormberge, *S. Africa* ...... 56 E4  31 16S  26 17 E
Stormsrivier, *S. Africa* ...... 56 E3  33 59S  23 52 E
Stornoway, *U.K.* .......... 11 C2  58 13N   6 23W
Storozhinets = Storozhynets,
  *Ukraine* ................. 17 D13 48 14N  25 45 E
Storozhynets, *Ukraine* ...... 17 D13 48 14N  25 45 E
Storrs, *U.S.A.* ............ 85 E12 41 49N  72 15W
Storsjön, *Sweden* ......... 8 E16 63  9N  14 30 E
Storuman, *Sweden* ........ 8 D17 65  5N  17 10 E
Storuman, *Sweden* ........ 8 D17 65 13N  16 50 E
Stouffville, *Canada* ........ 84 C5  43 58N  79 15W
Stoughton, *Canada* ........ 71 D8  49 40N 103  0W
Stour ➤, *Dorset, U.K.* ...... 13 G6  50 43N   1 47W
Stour ➤, *Kent, U.K.* ....... 13 F9  51 18N   1 22 E
Stour ➤, *Suffolk, U.K.* ..... 13 F9  51 57N   1  4 E
Stourbridge, *U.K.* ......... 13 E5  52 28N   2  8W
Stout L., *Canada* .......... 71 C10 52  0N  94 40W
Stove Pipe Wells Village, *U.S.A.* 79 J9  36 35N 117 11W
Stow, *U.S.A.* ............. 84 E3  41 10N  81 27W
Stowbtsy, *Belarus* ......... 17 B14 53 30N  26 43 E
Stowmarket, *U.K.* ......... 13 E9  52 12N   1  0 E
Strabane, *U.K.* ........... 10 B4  54 50N   7 27W
Strahan, *Australia* ......... 63 G4  42  9S 145 20 E
Stralsund, *Germany* ....... 16 A7  54 18N  13  4 E
Strand, *S. Africa* .......... 56 E2  34  9S  18 48 E
Stranda, Møre og Romsdal,
  *Norway* ................. 9 E12 62 19N   6 58 E
Stranda, Nord-Trøndelag,
  *Norway* ................. 8 E14 63 33N  10 14 E
Strangford L., *U.K.* ........ 10 B6  54 30N   5 37W
Stranraer, *U.K.* ........... 11 G3  54 54N   5  1W
Strasbourg, *Canada* ....... 71 C8  51  4N 104 55W
Strasbourg, *France* ........ 20 B7  48 35N   7 42 E
Stratford, *Canada* ......... 84 C4  43 23N  81  0W
Stratford, *N.Z.* ........... 59 H5  39 20S 174 19 E
Stratford, *Calif., U.S.A.* ..... 78 J7  36 11N 119 49W
Stratford, *Conn., U.S.A.* .... 85 E11 41 12N  73  8W
Stratford, *Tex., U.S.A.* ..... 81 G3  36 20N 102  4W
Stratford-upon-Avon, *U.K.* .. 13 E6  52 12N   1 42W
Strath Spey, *U.K.* ......... 11 D5  57  9N   3 49W
Strathalbyn, *Australia* ...... 63 F2  35 13S 138 53 E
Strathaven, *U.K.* .......... 11 F4  55 40N   4  5W
Strathcona △, *Canada* ...... 70 D3  49 38N 125 40W
Strathmore, *Canada* ....... 70 C6  51  5N 113 18W
Strathmore, *U.K.* .......... 11 E5  56 37N   3  7W
Strathmore, *U.S.A.* ........ 78 J7  36  9N 119  4W
Strathnaver, *Canada* ....... 70 C4  53 20N 122 33W
Strathpeffer, *U.K.* ......... 11 D4  57 35N   4 32W
Strathroy, *Canada* ......... 84 D3  42 58N  81 38W
Strathy Pt., *U.K.* .......... 11 C4  58 36N   4  1W
Strattanville, *U.S.A.* ....... 84 E5  41 12N  79 19W
Stratton, *U.S.A.* .......... 85 A14 45  8N  70 26W
Stratton Mt., *U.S.A.* ....... 85 C12 43  4N  72 55W
Straubing, *Germany* ....... 16 D7  48 52N  12 34 E
Straumnes, *Iceland* ........ 8 C2  66 26N  23  8W
Strawberry ➤, *U.S.A.* ...... 76 F8  40 10N 110 24W
Streaky B., *Australia* ....... 63 E1  32 48S 134 13 E
Streaky Bay, *Australia* ...... 63 E1  32 51S 134 18 E
Streator, *U.S.A.* ........... 80 E10 41  8N  88 50W
Streetsboro, *U.S.A.* ........ 84 E3  41 14N  81 21W
Streetsville, *Canada* ....... 84 C5  43 35N  79 42W
Strelka, *Russia* ........... 29 D10 58  5N  93  3 E
Streng ➤, *Cambodia* ....... 38 F4  13 12N 103 37 E
Streymoy, *Færoe Is.* ....... 8 E9  62  8N   7  5W
Strezhevoy, *Russia* ........ 28 C8  60 42N  77 34 E
Strimón ➤, *Greece* ........ 23 D10 40 46N  23 51 E
Strimonikós Kólpos, *Greece* . 23 D11 40 33N  24  0 E
Stroma, *U.K.* ............. 11 C5  58 41N   3  7W
Strómboli, *Italy* ........... 22 E6  38 47N  15 13 E
Stromeferry, *U.K.* ......... 11 D3  57 21N   5 33W
Stromness, *U.K.* .......... 11 C5  58 58N   3 17W
Stromsburg, *U.S.A.* ........ 80 E6  41  7N  97 36W
Strömstad, *Sweden* ........ 9 G14 58 56N  11 10 E
Strömsund, *Sweden* ....... 8 E16 63 51N  15 33 E
Strongsville, *U.S.A.* ........ 84 E3  41 19N  81 50W

Stronsay, *U.K.* ............ 11 B6  59  7N   2 35W
Stroud, *U.K.* ............. 13 F5  51 45N   2 13W
Stroud Road, *Australia* ..... 63 E5  32 18S 151 57 E
Stroudsburg, *U.S.A.* ....... 85 F9  40 59N  75 12W
Stroumbi, *Cyprus* ......... 25 E11 34 53N  32 29 E
Struer, *Denmark* .......... 9 H13 56 30N   8 35 E
Strumica, *Macedonia* ...... 23 D10 41 28N  22 41 E
Struthers, *Canada* ......... 72 C2  48 41N  85 51W
Struthers, *U.S.A.* .......... 84 E4  41  4N  80 39W
Stryker, *U.S.A.* ........... 76 B6  48 41N 114 46W
Stryy, *Ukraine* ............ 17 D12 49 16N  23 48 E
Strzelecki Cr. ➤, *Australia* .. 63 D2  29 37S 139 59 E
Stuart, *Fla., U.S.A.* ........ 83 M5  27 12N  80 15W
Stuart, *Nebr., U.S.A.* ...... 80 D5  42 36N  99  8W
Stuart ➤, *Canada* .......... 70 C4  54  0N 123 35W
Stuart Bluff Ra., *Australia* ... 60 D5  22 50S 131 52 E
Stuart L., *Canada* ......... 70 C4  54 30N 124 30W
Stuart Ra., *Australia* ....... 63 D1  29 10S 134 56 E
Stull L., *Canada* ........... 72 B1  54 24N  92 34W
Stung Treng = Stoeng Treng,
  *Cambodia* ............... 38 F5  13 31N 105 58 E
Stupart ➤, *Canada* ......... 72 A1  56  0N  93 25W
Sturgeon B., *Canada* ....... 71 C9  52  0N  97 50W
Sturgeon Bay, *U.S.A.* ...... 82 C2  44 50N  87 23W
Sturgeon Falls, *Canada* ..... 72 C4  46 25N  79 57W
Sturgeon L., *Alta., Canada* .. 70 B5  55  6N 117 32W
Sturgeon L., *Ont., Canada* .. 72 C1  50  0N  90 45W
Sturgeon L., *Ont., Canada* .. 84 B6  44 28N  78 43W
Sturgis, *Canada* ........... 71 C8  51 56N 102 36W
Sturgis, *Mich., U.S.A.* ...... 82 E3  41 48N  85 25W
Sturgis, *S. Dak., U.S.A.* .... 80 C3  44 25N 103 31W
Sturt △, *Australia* ......... 62 A3  17 17S 141 37 E
Sturt Cr. ➤, *Australia* ...... 60 C4  19  8S 127 50 E
Sturt Stony Desert, *Australia* . 63 D2  28 30S 141  0 E
Stutterheim, *S. Africa* ...... 56 E4  32 33S  27 28 E
Stuttgart, *Germany* ........ 16 D5  48 48N   9 11 E
Stuttgart, *U.S.A.* .......... 81 H9  34 30N  91 33W
Stuyvesant, *U.S.A.* ........ 85 D11 42 23N  73 45W
Stykkishólmur, *Iceland* ..... 8 D2  65  2N  22 40W
Styria = Steiermark □, *Austria* 16 E8  47 26N  15  0 E
Su Xian = Suzhou, *China* ... 34 H9  33 41N 116 59 E
Suakin, *Sudan* ............ 51 E13 19  8N  37 20 E
Suan, *N. Korea* ........... 35 E14 38 42N 126 22 E
Suaqui, *Mexico* ........... 86 B3  29 12N 109 41W
Suar, *India* ............... 43 E8  29  2N  79  3 E
Subang, *Indonesia* ......... 37 G12  6 34S 107 45 E
Subansiri ➤, *India* ......... 41 F18 26 48N  93 50 E
Subarnarekha ➤, *India* ..... 43 H12 22 34N  87 24 E
Subayhah, *Si. Arabia* ....... 44 D3  30  2N  38 50 E
Subi, *Indonesia* ........... 36 D3  2 58N 108 50 E
Subotica, *Serbia & M.* ...... 23 A8  46  6N  19 39 E
Suceava, *Romania* ......... 17 E14 47 38N  26 16 E
Suchan, *Russia* ........... 30 C6  43  8N 133  9 E
Suchitoto, *El Salv.* ........ 88 D2  13 56N  89  0W
Suchou = Suzhou, *China* .... 33 C7  31 19N 120 38 E
Süchow = Xuzhou, *China* ... 35 G9  34 18N 117 10 E
Suck ➤, *Ireland* ........... 10 C3  53 17N   8  3W
Sucre, *Bolivia* ............. 92 G5  19  0S  65 15W
Sucuriú ➤, *Brazil* .......... 93 H8  20 47S  51 38W
Sud, Pte. du, *Canada* ....... 73 C7  49  3N  62 14W
Sud-Kivu □, *Dem. Rep. of
  the Congo* ............... 54 C2   3  0S  28 30 E
Sud-Ouest, Pte., *Canada* .... 73 C7  49 23N  63 36W
Sudan ■, *Africa* .......... 51 E11 15  0N  30  0 E
Sudbury, *Canada* .......... 72 C3  46 30N  81  0W
Sudbury, *U.K.* ............ 13 E8  52  2N   0 45 E
Sûdd, *Sudan* ............. 51 G12  8 20N  30  0 E
Sudeten Mts. = Sudety, *Europe* 17 C9  50 20N  16 45 E
Sudety, *Europe* ........... 17 C9  50 20N  16 45 E
Suðuroy, *Færoe Is.* ........ 8 F9  61 32N   6 50W
Sudi, *Tanzania* ........... 55 E4  10 11S  39 57 E
Sudirman, Pegunungan,
  *Indonesia* ............... 37 E9   4 30S 137  0 E
Sudong, Pulau, *Singapore* ... 39 d   1 12N 103 43 E
Sueca, *Spain* ............. 21 C5  39 12N   0 21W
Suemez I., *U.S.A.* ......... 70 B2  55 15N 133 20W
Suez = El Suweis, *Egypt* .... 51 C12 29 58N  32 31 E
Suez, G. of = Suweis, Khalîg el,
  *Egypt* .................. 51 C12 28 40N  33  0 E
Suez Canal = Suweis, Qanâ es,
  *Egypt* .................. 51 B12 31  0N  32 20 E
Suffield, *Canada* .......... 70 C6  50 12N 111 10W
Suffolk, *U.S.A.* ........... 82 G7  36 44N  76 35W
Suffolk □, *U.K.* ........... 13 E9  52 16N   1  0 E
Sugargrove, *U.S.A.* ........ 84 E5  41 59N  79 21W
Sugarive ➤, *India* ......... 43 F12 26 16N  86 24 E
Sugluk = Salluit, *Canada* .... 69 B12 62 14N  75 38W
Şuḩār, *Oman* ............. 45 E8  24 20N  56 40 E
Sühbaatar □, *Mongolia* ..... 34 B8  45 30N 114  0 E
Suhl, *Germany* ........... 16 C6  50 36N  10 42 E
Sui, *Pakistan* ............. 42 E3  28 37N  69 19 E
Sui Xian, *China* ........... 34 G8  34 25N 115  2 E
Suide, *China* ............. 34 F6  37 30N 110 12 E
Suifenhe, *China* ........... 35 B16 44 25N 131  2 E
Suihua, *China* ............ 33 B7  46 32N 126 55 E
Suining, *China* ........... 35 H9  33 56N 117 58 E
Suiping, *China* ............ 34 H7  33 10N 113 59 E
Suir ➤, *Ireland* ........... 10 D4  52 16N   7  9W
Suisun City, *U.S.A.* ........ 78 G4  38 15N 122  2W
Suiyang, *China* ........... 35 B16 44 30N 130 56 E
Suizhong, *China* .......... 35 D11 40 21N 120 20 E
Sujangarh, *India* .......... 42 F6  27 42N  74 31 E
Sukabumi, *Indonesia* ...... 37 G12  6 56S 106 50 E
Sukadana, *Indonesia* ....... 36 E3  1 10S 110  0 E
Sukagawa, *Japan* ......... 31 F10 37 17N 140 23 E
Sukaraja, *Indonesia* ....... 36 E4   2 28S 110 25 E
Sukarnapura = Jayapura,
  *Indonesia* ............... 37 E10  2 28S 140 38 E
Sukawati, *Indonesia* ....... 37 K18  8 35S 115 17 E
Sukch'ŏn, *N. Korea* ........ 35 E13 39 22N 125 35 E
Sukhna ➤, *Russia* ......... 18 C6  61 15N  46 39 E
Sukhothai, *Thailand* ....... 38 D2  17  1N  99 49 E
Sukhumi = Sokhumi, *Georgia* 19 F7  43  0N  41  0 E
Sukkur, *Pakistan* .......... 42 F3  27 42N  68 54 E
Sukkur Barrage, *Pakistan* ... 42 F3  27 40N  68 50 E
Sukri ➤, *India* ............ 42 G4  25  4N  71 43 E
Sukumo, *Japan* ........... 31 H6  32 56N 132 44 E
Sukunka ➤, *Canada* ........ 70 B4  55 45N 121 15W
Sula, Kepulauan, *Indonesia* . 37 E7   1 45S 125  0 E
Sulaco ➤, *Honduras* ....... 88 C2  15  2N  87 44W
Sulaiman Range, *Pakistan* .. 42 D3  30 30N  69 50 E
Sūlār, *Iran* ............... 45 D6  31 53N  51 54 E
Sulawesi Sea = Celebes Sea,
  *Indonesia* ............... 37 D6   3  0N 123  0 E
Sulawesi Selatan □, *Indonesia* 37 E6   3 50S 120  0 E
Sulawesi Tengah □, *Indonesia* 37 E6   1 30S 121  0 E
Sulawesi Utara □, *Indonesia* . 37 D6   1  0N 124  0 E
Sulima, *S. Leone* .......... 50 G3   6 58N  11 32W

Sulina, *Romania* .......... 17 F15 45 10N  29 40 E
Sulitjelma, *Norway* ........ 8 C17 67  9N  16  3 E
Sullana, *Peru* ............. 92 D2   4 52S  80 39W
Sullivan, *Ill., U.S.A.* ........ 80 F10 39 36N  88 37W
Sullivan, *Ind., U.S.A.* ...... 82 F2  39  6N  87 24W
Sullivan, *Mo., U.S.A.* ...... 80 F9  38 13N  91 10W
Sullivan Bay, *Canada* ...... 70 C3  50 55N 126 50W
Sullivan I. = Lanbi Kyun, *Burma* 39 G2  10 50N  98 20 E
Sullom Voe, *U.K.* ......... 11 A7  60 27N   1 20W
Sulphur, *La., U.S.A.* ....... 81 K8  30 14N  93 23W
Sulphur, *Okla., U.S.A.* ...... 81 H6  34 31N  96 58W
Sulphur Pt., *Canada* ....... 70 A6  60 56N 114 48W
Sulphur Springs, *U.S.A.* .... 81 J7  33  8N  95 36W
Sultan, *Canada* ........... 72 C3  47 36N  82 47W
Sultan, *U.S.A.* ........... 78 C5  47 52N 121 49W
Sultanpur, *Mad. P., India* ... 42 H8  23  9N  77 56 E
Sultanpur, *Punjab, India* .... 42 D6  31 13N  75 11 E
Sultanpur, *Ut. P., India* ..... 43 F10 26 18N  82  4 E
Sulu Arch., *Phil.* .......... 37 C6   6  0N 121  0 E
Sulu Sea, *E. Indies* ........ 37 C6   8  0N 120  0 E
Suluq, *Libya* ............. 51 B10 31 44N  20 14 E
Sulzberger Ice Shelf, *Antarctica* 5 D16  78  0S 150  0W
Sumalata, *Indonesia* ....... 37 D6   1  0N 122 31 E
Sumampa, *Argentina* ....... 94 B3  29 25S  63 29W
Sumatera, *Indonesia* ....... 36 D2   0 40N 100 20 E
Sumatera Barat □, *Indonesia* 36 E2   1  0S 101  0 E
Sumatera Utara □, *Indonesia* 36 D1   2 30N  98  0 E
Sumatra = Sumatera, *Indonesia* 36 D2   0 40N 100 20 E
Sumba, *Indonesia* ......... 37 F5   9 45S 119 35 E
Sumba, Selat, *Indonesia* .... 37 F5   9  0S 118 40 E
Sumbawa, *Indonesia* ....... 36 F5   8 26S 117 30 E
Sumbawa Besar, *Indonesia* . 36 F5   8 30S 117 26 E
Sumbawanga □, *Tanzania* ... 52 F6   8  0S  31 30 E
Sumbe, *Angola* ........... 52 G2  11 10S  13 48 E
Sumburgh Hd., *U.K.* ....... 11 B7  59 52N   1 17W
Sumdeo, *India* ............ 43 D8  31 26N  78 44 E
Sumdo, *China* ............ 43 B8  35  6N  78 41 E
Sumedang, *Indonesia* ...... 37 G12  6 52S 107 55 E
Sumen = Shumen, *Bulgaria* . 23 C12 43 18N  26 55 E
Sumenep, *Indonesia* ....... 37 G15  7  1S 113 52 E
Sumgait = Sumqayıt, *Azerbaijan* 19 F8  40 34N  49 38 E
Summer L., *U.S.A.* ........ 76 E3  42 50N 120 45W
Summerland, *Canada* ...... 70 D5  49 32N 119 41W
Summerside, *Canada* ....... 73 C7  46 24N  63 47W
Summersville, *U.S.A.* ....... 82 F5  38 17N  80 51W
Summerville, *Ga., U.S.A.* ... 83 H3  34 29N  85 21W
Summerville, *S.C., U.S.A.* .. 83 J5  33  1N  80 11W
Summit Lake, *Canada* ...... 70 C4  54 20N 122 40W
Summit Peak, *U.S.A.* ...... 77 H10 37 21N 106 42W
Sumner, *Iowa, U.S.A.* ...... 80 D8  42 51N  92  6W
Sumner, *Wash., U.S.A.* ..... 78 C4  47 12N 122 14W
Sumoto, *Japan* ........... 31 G7  34 21N 134 54 E
Šumperk, *Czech Rep.* ...... 17 D9  49 59N  16 59 E
Sumqayıt, *Azerbaijan* ...... 19 F8  40 34N  49 38 E
Sumter, *U.S.A.* ........... 83 J5  33 55N  80 21W
Sumy, *Ukraine* ........... 19 D5  50 57N  34 50 E
Sun City, *S. Africa* ........ 56 D4  25 17S  27  3 E
Sun City, *Ariz., U.S.A.* ..... 77 K7  33 36N 112 17W
Sun City, *Calif., U.S.A.* ..... 79 M9  33 42N 117 11W
Sun City Center, *U.S.A.* .... 83 M4  27 43N  82 18W
Sun Lakes, *U.S.A.* ........ 77 K8  33 10N 111 52W
Sun Valley, *U.S.A.* ........ 76 E6  43 42N 114 21W
Sunagawa, *Japan* ......... 30 C10 43 29N 141 55 E
Sunan, *N. Korea* .......... 35 E13 39 15N 125 40 E
Sunart, L., *U.K.* .......... 11 E3  56 42N   5 43W
Sunburst, *U.S.A.* ......... 76 B8  48 53N 111 55W
Sunbury, *Australia* ........ 63 F3  37 35S 144 44 E
Sunbury, *U.S.A.* .......... 85 F8  40 52N  76 48W
Sunchales, *Argentina* ...... 94 C3  30 58S 101 35W
Suncho Corral, *Argentina* ... 94 B3  27 55S  63 27W
Sunch'ŏn, *S. Korea* ........ 35 G14 34 52N 127 31 E
Suncook, *U.S.A.* .......... 85 C13 43  8N  71 27W
Sunda, Selat, *Indonesia* .... 36 F3   6 20S 105 30 E
Sunda Is., *Indonesia* ....... 26 K14  5  0S 105  0 E
Sunda Str. = Sunda, Selat,
  *Indonesia* ............... 36 F3   6 20S 105 30 E
Sundance, *Canada* ......... 71 B10 56 32N  94 4W
Sundance, *U.S.A.* ......... 80 C2  44 24N 104 23W
Sundar Nagar, *India* ....... 42 D7  31 32N  76 53 E
Sundarbans, *Asia* ......... 41 J16 22  0N  89  0 E
Sundargarh, *India* ......... 41 H14 22  4N  84  5 E
Sundays = Sondags ➤, *S. Africa* 56 E4  33 44S  25 51 E
Sunderland, *Canada* ....... 84 B5  44 16N  79  4W
Sunderland, *U.K.* ......... 12 C6  54 55N   1 23W
Sundown △, *Australia* ...... 63 D5  28 49S 151 38 E
Sundre, *Canada* .......... 70 C6  51 49N 114 38W
Sundsvall, *Sweden* ........ 9 E17 62 23N  17 17 E
Sung Hei, *Vietnam* ........ 39 G6  10 20N 106  2 E
Sungai Acheh, *Malaysia* .... 39 c   5  8N 100 30 E
Sungai Kolok, *Thailand* ..... 39 J3   6  2N 101 58 E
Sungai Lembing, *Malaysia* .. 39 L4   3 55N 103  3 E
Sungai Petani, *Malaysia* .... 39 K3   5 37N 100 30 E
Sungaigerong, *Indonesia* ... 36 E2   2 59S 104 52 E
Sungailiat, *Indonesia* ...... 36 E3   1 51S 106  8 E
Sungaipenuh, *Indonesia* .... 36 E2   2  1S 101 20 E
Sungari = Songhua Jiang ➤,
  *China* .................. 33 B8  47 45N 132 30 E
Sunghua Chiang = Songhua
  Jiang ➤, *China* .......... 33 B8  47 45N 132 30 E
Sunland Park, *U.S.A.* ...... 77 L10 31 50N 106 40W
Sunndalsøra, *Norway* ...... 9 E13 62 40N   3 33 E
Sunnyside, *U.S.A.* ......... 76 C3  46 20N 120  0W
Sunnyvale, *U.S.A.* ......... 78 H4  37 23N 122  2W
Suntar, *Russia* ........... 29 C12 62 15N 117 30 E
Suomenselkä, *Finland* ...... 8 D23 64 54N  29 10 E
Suomussalmi, *Finland* ..... 8 D23 64 54N  29 10 E
Suoyarvi, *Russia* .......... 18 B5  62 3N   32 20 E
Supai, *U.S.A.* ............ 77 H7  36 15N 112 41W
Supaul, *India* ............. 43 F12 26 10N  86 40 E
Superior, *Ariz., U.S.A.* ..... 77 K8  33 18N 111  6W
Superior, *Mont., U.S.A.* .... 76 C6  47 12N 114 53W
Superior, *Nebr., U.S.A.* ..... 80 E5  40  1N  98  4W
Superior, *Wis., U.S.A.* ...... 80 B8  46 44N  92  6W
Superior, L., *N. Amer.* ...... 72 C2  47  0N  87  0W
Suphan Buri, *Thailand* ..... 38 E3  14 14N 100 10 E
Suphan Daği, *Turkey* ....... 44 B4  38 54N  42 48 E
Supiori, *Indonesia* ......... 37 E9   1  0S 136  0 E
Supung Shuiku, *China* ...... 35 D13 40 35N 124 50 E
Sûq Suwayq, *Si. Arabia* .... 44 E3  24 23N  38 27 E
Suqian, *China* ............ 35 H10 33 54N 118  8 E
Suqutra = Socotra, *Yemen* .. 47 E5  12 30N  54  0 E
Şür, *Lebanon* ............. 46 B4  33 19N  35 16 E
Şür, *Oman* ............... 47 C6  22 34N  59 32 E
Sur, Pt., *U.S.A.* ........... 78 J5  36 18N 121 54W
Sura ➤, *Russia* ............ 18 C8  56  6N  46  0 E
Surab, *Pakistan* ........... 42 E2  28 25N  66 15 E
Surabaja = Surabaya, *Indonesia* 36 F4   7 17S 112 45 E

Surabaya, Indonesia . . . . . . . . . . 36 F4    7 17S 112 45 E
Surakarta, Indonesia . . . . . . . . . 36 F4    7 35S 110 48 E
Surat, Australia . . . . . . . . . . . . . 63 D4   27 10S 149  6 E
Surat, India . . . . . . . . . . . . . . . . 40 J8   21 12N  72 55 E
Surat Thani, Thailand . . . . . . . . 39 H2    9  6N  99 20 E
Suratgarh, India . . . . . . . . . . . . 42 E5   29 18N  73 55 E
Surendranagar, India . . . . . . . . 42 H4   22 45N  71 40 E
Surf, U.S.A. . . . . . . . . . . . . . . . . 79 L6   34 41N 120 36W
Surfers Paradise, Australia . . . 63 D5   28  0S 153 25 E
Surgut, Russia . . . . . . . . . . . . . 28 C8   61 14N  73 20 E
Suriapet, India . . . . . . . . . . . . . 40 L11  17 10N  79 40 E
Surigao, Phil. . . . . . . . . . . . . . . 38 C7    9 47N 125 29 E
Surin, Thailand . . . . . . . . . . . . 38 E4   14 50N 103 34 E
Surin Nua, Ko, Thailand . . . . . 39 H1    9 30N  97 55 E
Surinam = Suriname ■, S. Amer. 93 C7    4  0N  56  0W
Suriname ■, S. Amer. . . . . . . . 93 C7    4  0N  56  0W
Suriname →, Suriname . . . . . . 93 B7    5 50N  55 15W
Sürmaq, Iran . . . . . . . . . . . . . . 45 D7   31  3N  52 48 E
Surrey, Canada . . . . . . . . . . . . 78 A4   49 10N 122 54W
Surrey □, U.K. . . . . . . . . . . . . 13 F7   51 15N   0 31W
Sursand, India . . . . . . . . . . . . . 43 F11  26 39N  85 43 E
Sursar →, India . . . . . . . . . . . . 43 F12  26 14N  87  3 E
Surt, Libya . . . . . . . . . . . . . . . . 51 B9   31 11N  16 39 E
Surt, Khalīj, Libya . . . . . . . . . 51 B9   31 40N  18 30 E
Surtanahu, Pakistan . . . . . . . . 42 F4   26 22N  70  0 E
Surtsey, Iceland . . . . . . . . . . . . 8 E3   63 20N  20 30W
Suruga-Wan, Japan . . . . . . . . . 31 G9   34 45N 138 30 E
Susaki, Japan . . . . . . . . . . . . . . 31 H6   33 22N 133 17 E
Süsangerd, Iran . . . . . . . . . . . . 45 D6   31 35N  48  6 E
Susanville, U.S.A. . . . . . . . . . . 76 F3   40 25N 120 39W
Susner, India . . . . . . . . . . . . . . 42 H7   23 57N  76  5 E
Susquehanna, U.S.A. . . . . . . . . 85 E9   41 57N  75 36W
Susquehanna →, U.S.A. . . . . . . 94 A2   23 35S  66 25W
Susques, Argentina . . . . . . . . . 94 A2   23 35S  66 25W
Sussex, Canada . . . . . . . . . . . . 73 C6   45 45N  65 37W
Sussex, U.S.A. . . . . . . . . . . . . . 85 E10  41 13N  74 37W
Sussex, E. □, U.K. . . . . . . . . . 13 G8   51  0N   0 20 E
Sussex, W. □, U.K. . . . . . . . . . 13 G7   51  0N   0 30W
Sustut →, Canada . . . . . . . . . . 70 B3   56 20N 127 30W
Susuman, Russia . . . . . . . . . . . 29 C15  62 47N 148 10 E
Susunu, Indonesia . . . . . . . . . . 37 E8    3  7S 133 39 E
Susurluk, Turkey . . . . . . . . . . . 23 E13  39 54N  28  8 E
Sutherland, S. Africa . . . . . . . . 56 E3   32 24S  20 40 E
Sutherland, U.K. . . . . . . . . . . . 11 C4   58 12N   4 50W
Sutherland, U.S.A. . . . . . . . . . . 80 E4   41 10N 101  8W
Sutherland Falls, N.Z. . . . . . . . 59 L1   44 48S 167 46 E
Sutherlin, U.S.A. . . . . . . . . . . . 76 E2   43 23N 123 19W
Suthrì, India . . . . . . . . . . . . . . 42 H3   23  3N  68 55 E
Sutlej →, Pakistan . . . . . . . . . 42 E4   29 23N  71  3 E
Sutter, U.S.A. . . . . . . . . . . . . . 78 F5   39 10N 121 45W
Sutter Creek, U.S.A. . . . . . . . . 78 G6   38 24N 120 48W
Sutton, Canada . . . . . . . . . . . . 85 A12  45  6N  72 37W
Sutton, Nebr., U.S.A. . . . . . . . . 80 E6   40 36N  97 52W
Sutton, W. Va., U.S.A. . . . . . . . 82 F5   38 40N  80 43W
Sutton →, Canada . . . . . . . . . . 72 A3   55 15N  83 45W
Sutton Coldfield, U.K. . . . . . . . 13 E6   52 35N   1 49W
Sutton in Ashfield, U.K. . . . . . . 12 D6   53  8N   1 16W
Sutton L., Canada . . . . . . . . . . 72 B3   54 15N  84 42W
Suttor →, Australia . . . . . . . . . 62 C4   21 36S 147  2 E
Suttsu, Japan . . . . . . . . . . . . . . 30 C10  42 48N 140 14 E
Suva, Fiji . . . . . . . . . . . . . . . . . 59 D8   18  6S 178 30 E
Suva Planina, Serbia & M. . . . 23 C10  43 10N  22  5 E
Suvorov Is. = Suwarrow Is.,
   Cook Is. . . . . . . . . . . . . . . . . 65 J11  15  0S 163  0W
Suwałki, Poland . . . . . . . . . . . . 17 A12  54  8N  22 59 E
Suwana, Indonesia . . . . . . . . . . 37 K18  8 44S 115 36 E
Suwannaphum, Thailand . . . . . 38 E4   15 33N 103 47 E
Suwannee →, U.S.A. . . . . . . . . 83 L4   29 17N  83 10W
Suwanose-Jima, Japan . . . . . . 31 K4   29 38N 129 43 E
Suwarrow Is., Cook Is. . . . . . . . 65 J11  15  0S 163  0W
Suwayq aş Şuqban, Iraq . . . . . 44 D5   31 32N  46  7 E
Suweis, Khalîg el, Egypt . . . . . 51 C12  28 40N  33  0 E
Suweis, Qanâ es, Egypt . . . . . . 51 B12  31  0N  32 20 E
Suwŏn, S. Korea . . . . . . . . . . . . 35 F14  37 17N 127  1 E
Suzdal, Russia . . . . . . . . . . . . . 18 C7   56 29N  40 26 E
Suzhou, Anhui, China . . . . . . . 34 H9   33 41N 116 59 E
Suzhou, Jiangsu, China . . . . . . 33 C7   31 19N 120 38 E
Suzu, Japan . . . . . . . . . . . . . . . 31 F8   37 25N 137 17 E
Suzu-Misaki, Japan . . . . . . . . . 31 F8   37 31N 137 21 E
Suzuka, Japan . . . . . . . . . . . . . 31 G8   34 55N 136 36 E
Svalbard, Arctic . . . . . . . . . . . . 4 B8   78  0N  17  0 E
Svalbard Radio = Longyearbyen,
   Svalbard . . . . . . . . . . . . . . . 4 B8   78 13N  15 40 E
Svappavaara, Sweden . . . . . . . . 8 C19  67 40N  21  3 E
Svartisen, Norway . . . . . . . . . . 8 C15  66 40N  13 59 E
Svay Chek, Cambodia . . . . . . . 38 F4   13 48N 102 58 E
Svay Rieng, Cambodia . . . . . . 39 G5   11  9N 105 45 E
Svealand □, Sweden . . . . . . . . 9 G16  60 20N  15  0 E
Sveg, Sweden . . . . . . . . . . . . . . 9 E16  62  2N  14 21 E
Svendborg, Denmark . . . . . . . . 9 J14  55  4N  10 35 E
Sverdrup Is., Canada . . . . . . . . 4 B3   79  0N  97  0W
Svetlaya, Russia . . . . . . . . . . . . 30 A9   46 33N 138 18 E
Svetlogorsk = Svyetlahorsk,
   Belarus . . . . . . . . . . . . . . . . 17 B15  52 38N  29 46 E
Svir →, Russia . . . . . . . . . . . . . 18 B5   60 30N  32 48 E
Svishtov, Bulgaria . . . . . . . . . . 23 C11  43 36N  25 23 E
Svislach, Belarus . . . . . . . . . . . 17 B13  53 3N   24  2 E
Svobodnyy, Russia . . . . . . . . . . 29 D13  51 20N 128  0 E
Svolvær, Norway . . . . . . . . . . . 8 B16  68 15N  14 34 E
Svyetlahorsk, Belarus . . . . . . . 17 B15  52 38N  29 46 E
Swabian Alps = Schwäbische
   Alb, Germany . . . . . . . . . . . 16 D5   48 20N   9 30 E
Swaffham, U.K. . . . . . . . . . . . . 13 E8   52 39N   0 42 E
Swainsboro, U.S.A. . . . . . . . . . 83 J4   32 36N  82 20W
Swakop →, Namibia . . . . . . . . 56 C2   22 38S  14 36 E
Swakopmund, Namibia . . . . . . 56 C1   22 37S  14 30 E
Swale →, U.K. . . . . . . . . . . . . . 12 C6   54  5N   1 20W
Swan →, Australia . . . . . . . . . . 61 F2   32  3S 115 45 E
Swan →, Canada . . . . . . . . . . . 71 C8   52 30N 100 45W
Swan Hill, Australia . . . . . . . . 63 F3   35 20S 143 33 E
Swan Hills, Canada . . . . . . . . . 70 C5   54 43N 115 24W
Swan Is. = Santanilla, Is.,
   Honduras . . . . . . . . . . . . . . 88 C3   17 22N  83 57W
Swan L., Canada . . . . . . . . . . . 71 C8   52 30N 100 40W
Swan Peak, U.S.A. . . . . . . . . . . 76 C7   47 43N 113 38W
Swan Ra., U.S.A. . . . . . . . . . . . 76 C7   48  0N 113 45W
Swan River, Canada . . . . . . . . 71 C8   52 10N 101 16W
Swanage, U.K. . . . . . . . . . . . . . 13 G6   50 36N   1 58W
Swansea, Australia . . . . . . . . . 63 G4   42  8S 148  4 E
Swansea, Canada . . . . . . . . . . 84 C4   43 38N  79 28W
Swansea, U.K. . . . . . . . . . . . . . 13 F4   51 37N   3 57W
Swansea □, U.K. . . . . . . . . . . . 13 F3   51 38N   4  3W
Swar →, Pakistan . . . . . . . . . . 43 B5   34 40N  72  5 E
Swartberge, S. Africa . . . . . . . . 56 E3   33 20S  22  0 E
Swartmodder, S. Africa . . . . . . 56 D3   28  1S  20 32 E
Swartnossob →, Namibia . . . . 56 C2   23  8S  18 42 E
Swartruggens, S. Africa . . . . . . 56 D4   25 39S  26 42 E
Swastika, Canada . . . . . . . . . . 72 C3   48  7N  80  6W

Swatow = Shantou, China . . . 33 D6   23 18N 116 40 E
Swaziland ■, Africa . . . . . . . . 57 D5   26 30S  31 30 E
Sweden ■, Europe . . . . . . . . . 9 G16  57  0N  15  0 E
Sweet Home, U.S.A. . . . . . . . . 76 D2   44 24N 122 44W
Sweetgrass, U.S.A. . . . . . . . . . 76 B8   48 59N 111 58W
Sweetwater, Nev., U.S.A. . . . . 78 G7   38 27N 119  9W
Sweetwater, Tenn., U.S.A. . . . 83 H3   35 36N  84 28W
Sweetwater, Tex., U.S.A. . . . . 81 J4   32 28N 100 25W
Sweetwater →, U.S.A. . . . . . . 76 E10  42 31N 107  2W
Swellendam, S. Africa . . . . . . 56 E3   34  1S  20 26 E
Świdnica, Poland . . . . . . . . . . 17 C9   50 50N  16 30 E
Świdnik, Poland . . . . . . . . . . . 17 C12  51 13N  22 39 E
Świebodzin, Poland . . . . . . . . 16 B8   52 15N  15 31 E
Świecie, Poland . . . . . . . . . . . 17 B10  53 25N  18 30 E
Swift Current, Canada . . . . . . 71 C7   50 20N 107 45W
Swift Current →, Canada . . . . 71 C7   50 38N 107 44W
Swilly, L., Ireland . . . . . . . . . . 10 A4   55 12N   7 33W
Swindon, U.K. . . . . . . . . . . . . 13 F6   51 34N   1 46W
Swindon □, U.K. . . . . . . . . . . 13 F6   51 34N   1 46W
Swinemünde = Świnoujście,
   Poland . . . . . . . . . . . . . . . 16 B8   53 54N  14 16 E
Swinford, Ireland . . . . . . . . . . 10 C3   53 57N   8 58W
Świnoujście, Poland . . . . . . . . 16 B8   53 54N  14 16 E
Switzerland ■, Europe . . . . . . 20 C8   46 30N   8  0 E
Swords, Ireland . . . . . . . . . . . 10 C5   53 28N   6 13W
Swoyerville, U.S.A. . . . . . . . . . 85 E9   41 18N  75 53W
Sydenham →, Canada . . . . . . 84 D2   42 33N  82 25W
Sydney, Australia . . . . . . . . . . 63 E5   33 53S 151 10 E
Sydney, Canada . . . . . . . . . . . 73 C7   46  7N  60  7W
Sydney L., Canada . . . . . . . . . 71 C10  50 41N  94 25W
Sydney Mines, Canada . . . . . . 73 C7   46 18N  60 15W
Sydprøven = Alluitsup Paa,
   Greenland . . . . . . . . . . . . . 69 B15  60 30N  45 35W
Sydra, G. of = Surt, Khalīj, Libya  51 B9   31 40N  18 30 E
Sykesville, U.S.A. . . . . . . . . . . 84 E6   41  3N  78 50W
Syktyvkar, Russia . . . . . . . . . . 18 B9   61 45N  50 40 E
Sylacauga, U.S.A. . . . . . . . . . . 83 J2   33 10N  86 15W
Sylarna, Sweden . . . . . . . . . . . 8 E15  63  2N  12 13 E
Sylhet, Bangla. . . . . . . . . . . . . 41 G17  24 54N  91 52 E
Sylhet □, Bangla. . . . . . . . . . . 41 G17  24 50N  91 50 E
Sylt, Germany . . . . . . . . . . . . . 16 A5   54 54N   8 22 E
Sylvan Beach, U.S.A. . . . . . . . 85 C9   43 12N  75 44W
Sylvan Lake, Canada . . . . . . . 70 C6   52 20N 114  3W
Sylvania, U.S.A. . . . . . . . . . . . 83 J5   32 45N  81 38W
Sylvester, U.S.A. . . . . . . . . . . . 83 K4   31 32N  83 50W
Sym, Russia . . . . . . . . . . . . . . 28 C9   60 20N  88 18 E
Symón, Mexico . . . . . . . . . . . . 86 C4   24 42N 102 35W
Synnott Ra., Australia . . . . . . 60 C4   16 30S 125 20 E
Syowa, Antarctica . . . . . . . . . . 5 C5   68 50S  12  0 E
Syracuse, Kans., U.S.A. . . . . . 81 G4   37 59N 101 45W
Syracuse, N.Y., U.S.A. . . . . . . 85 C8   43  3N  76  9W
Syracuse, Nebr., U.S.A. . . . . . 80 E6   40 39N  96 11W
Syrdarya →, Kazakhstan . . . . 28 E7   46  3N  61  0 E
Syria ■, Asia . . . . . . . . . . . . . . 44 C3   35  0N  38  0 E
Syrian Desert = Shām, Bādiyat
   ash, Asia . . . . . . . . . . . . . . 44 C3   32  0N  40  0 E
Syzran, Russia . . . . . . . . . . . . 18 D8   53 12N  48 30 E
Szczecin, Poland . . . . . . . . . . 16 B8   53 27N  14 27 E
Szczecinek, Poland . . . . . . . . 17 B9   53 43N  16 41 E
Szczeciński, Zalew = Stettiner
   Haff, Germany . . . . . . . . . . 16 B8   53 47N  14 15 E
Szczytno, Poland . . . . . . . . . . 17 B11  53 33N  21  0 E
Szechwan = Sichuan □, China  32 C5   30 30N 103  0 E
Szeged, Hungary . . . . . . . . . . 17 E11  46 16N  20 10 E
Székesfehérvár, Hungary . . . . 17 E10  47 15N  18 25 E
Szekszárd, Hungary . . . . . . . . 17 E10  46 22N  18 42 E
Szentes, Hungary . . . . . . . . . . 17 E11  46 39N  20 21 E
Szolnok, Hungary . . . . . . . . . 17 E11  47 10N  20 15 E
Szombathely, Hungary . . . . . . 17 E9   47 14N  16 38 E

T

Ta Khli Khok, Thailand . . . . . 38 E3   15 18N 100 20 E
Ta Lai, Vietnam . . . . . . . . . . . 39 G6   11 24N 107 23 E
Tabacal, Argentina . . . . . . . . . 94 A3   23 15S  64 15W
Tabaco, Phil. . . . . . . . . . . . . . 37 B6   13 22N 123 44 E
Ṭābah, Si. Arabia . . . . . . . . . . 44 E4   26 55N  42 38 E
Tabanan, Indonesia . . . . . . . . 37 K18  8 32S 115  8 E
Ṭabas, Khorāsān, Iran . . . . . . 45 C9   32 48N  60 12 E
Ṭabas, Khorāsān, Iran . . . . . . 45 C8   33 35N  56 55 E
Tabasará, Serranía de, Panama  88 E3   8 35N  81 40W
Tabasco □, Mexico . . . . . . . . 87 D6   17 45N  93 30W
Tabāsīn, Iran . . . . . . . . . . . . . 45 D8   31 12N  57 54 E
Tabatinga, Serra da, Brazil . . 93 F10  10 30S  44  0W
Taber, Canada . . . . . . . . . . . . 70 D6   49 47N 112  8W
Taberg, U.S.A. . . . . . . . . . . . . 85 C9   43 18N  75 37W
Tablas I., Phil. . . . . . . . . . . . . 37 B6   12 25N 122  2 E
Table B., S. Africa . . . . . . . . . 56 E2   33 35S  18  2 E
Table Mt., S. Africa . . . . . . . . 56 E2   34  0S  18 22 E
Table Rock L., U.S.A. . . . . . . . 81 G8   36 36N  93 19W
Tabletop, Mt., Australia . . . . . 62 C4   23 24S 147 11 E
Tábor, Czech Rep. . . . . . . . . . 16 D8   49 25N  14 39 E
Tabora, Tanzania . . . . . . . . . . 54 D3    5  2S  32 50 E
Tabora □, Tanzania . . . . . . . . 54 D3    5  0S  33  0 E
Tabou, Ivory C. . . . . . . . . . . . 50 H4    4 30N   7 20W
Tabrīz, Iran . . . . . . . . . . . . . . 44 B5   38  7N  46 20 E
Tabuaeran, Kiribati . . . . . . . . 65 G12  3 51N 159 22W
Tabūk, Si. Arabia . . . . . . . . . . 44 D3   28 23N  36 36 E
Tacámbaro de Codallos, Mexico  86 D4   19 14N 101 28W
Tacheng, China . . . . . . . . . . . 32 B3   46 40N  82 58 E
Tach'ing Shan = Daqing Shan,
   China . . . . . . . . . . . . . . . . 34 D6   40 40N 111  0 E
Tacloban, Phil. . . . . . . . . . . . . 37 B6   11 15N 124 58 E
Tacna, Peru . . . . . . . . . . . . . . 92 G4   18  0S  70 20W
Tacoma, U.S.A. . . . . . . . . . . . 78 C4   47 14N 122 26W
Tacuarembó, Uruguay . . . . . . 95 C4   31 45S  56  0W
Tademaït, Plateau du, Algeria  50 C6   28 30N   2 30 E
Tadjoura, Djibouti . . . . . . . . . 47 E3   11 50N  42 55 E
Tadmor, N.Z. . . . . . . . . . . . . . 59 J4   41 27S 172 45 E
Tadoule L., Canada . . . . . . . . 71 B9   58 36N  98 20W
Tadoussac, Canada . . . . . . . . 73 C6   48 11N  69 42W
Tadzhikistan = Tajikistan ■, Asia  28 F8   38 30N  70  0 E
Taechŏn-ni, S. Korea . . . . . . . 35 F14  36 21N 126 36 E
Taegu, S. Korea . . . . . . . . . . . 35 G15  35 50N 128 37 E
Taegwan, N. Korea . . . . . . . . 35 D13  40 13N 125 12 E
Taejŏn, S. Korea . . . . . . . . . . 35 F14  36 20N 127 28 E
Taen, Ko, Thailand . . . . . . . . 39 b    9 22N  99 57 E
Tafalla, Spain . . . . . . . . . . . . . 21 A5   42  3N   1 41W
Tafelbaai = Table B., S. Africa  56 E2   33 35S  18 25 E
Tafermaar, Indonesia . . . . . . . 37 F8    6 47S 134 10 E
Tafi Viejo, Argentina . . . . . . . 94 B2   26 43S  65 17W
Tafīhān, Iran . . . . . . . . . . . . . 45 D7   29 25N  52 39 E
Tafresh, Iran . . . . . . . . . . . . . 45 C6   34 45N  49 57 E
Taft, Iran . . . . . . . . . . . . . . . . 45 D7   31 45N  54 14 E

Taft, Phil. . . . . . . . . . . . . . . . . 37 B7   11 57N 125 30 E
Taft, U.S.A. . . . . . . . . . . . . . . 79 K7   35  8N 119 28W
Taftān, Kūh-e, Iran . . . . . . . . 45 D9   28 40N  61  0 E
Taga Dzong, Bhutan . . . . . . . 41 F16  27  5N  89 55 E
Tagbilaran, Phil. . . . . . . . . . . 37 C6    9 39N 123 51 E
Tagish, Canada . . . . . . . . . . . 70 A2   60 19N 134 16W
Tagish L., Canada . . . . . . . . . 70 A2   60 10N 134 20W
Tagliamento →, Italy . . . . . . . 22 B5   45 38N  13  6 E
Tagomago, Spain . . . . . . . . . . 24 B8   39  2N   1 39 E
Taguatinga, Brazil . . . . . . . . . 93 F10  12 16S  42 26W
Tagum, Phil. . . . . . . . . . . . . . 37 C7    7 33N 125 53 E
Tagus = Tejo →, Europe . . . . 21 C1   38 40N   9 24W
Tahakopa, N.Z. . . . . . . . . . . . 59 M2   46 30S 169 23 E
Tahan, Gunung, Malaysia . . . 39 K4    4 34N 102 17 E
Tahat, Algeria . . . . . . . . . . . . 50 D7   23 18N   5 33 E
Tāherī, Iran . . . . . . . . . . . . . . 45 E7   27 43N  52 20 E
Tahiti, French Polynesia . . . . 65 J13  17 37S 149 27W
Tahlequah, U.S.A. . . . . . . . . . 81 H7   35 55N  94 58W
Tahoe, L., U.S.A. . . . . . . . . . . 78 G6   39  6N 120  2W
Tahoe City, U.S.A. . . . . . . . . . 78 F6   39 10N 120  9W
Tahoka, U.S.A. . . . . . . . . . . . 81 J4   33 10N 101 48W
Taholah, U.S.A. . . . . . . . . . . . 78 C2   47 21N 124 17W
Tahoua, Niger . . . . . . . . . . . . 50 F7   14 57N   5 16 E
Tahrūd, Iran . . . . . . . . . . . . . 45 D8   29 26N  57 49 E
Tahsis, Canada . . . . . . . . . . . 70 D3   49 55N 126 40W
Tahta, Egypt . . . . . . . . . . . . . 51 C12  26 44N  31 32 E
Tahulandang, Indonesia . . . . 37 D7    2 27N 125 23 E
Tahuna, Indonesia . . . . . . . . . 37 D7    3 38N 125 30 E
Tai Au Mun, China . . . . . . . . 33 G11  22 18N 114 14 E
Tai Mo Shan, China . . . . . . . 33 G11  22 25N 114  7 E
Tai O, China . . . . . . . . . . . . . 33 G10  22 15N 113 52 E
Tai Pang Wan, H.K. . . . . . . . . 33 F11  22 33N 114 24 E
Tai Po, China . . . . . . . . . . . . 33 G11  22 27N 114 10 E
Tai Rom Yen △, Thailand . . . 39 H2    8 45N  99 30 E
Tai Shan, China . . . . . . . . . . 35 F9   36 25N 117 20 E
Tai Yue Shan = Lantau I., China  33 G10  22 15N 113 56 E
Tai'an, China . . . . . . . . . . . . . 35 F9   36 12N 117  8 E
Taibei = T'aipei, Taiwan . . . . 33 D7   25  2N 121 30 E
Taibique, Canary Is. . . . . . . . 24 G2   27 42N  17 58W
Taibus Qi, China . . . . . . . . . . 34 D8   41 54N 115 22 E
T'aichung, Taiwan . . . . . . . . . 33 D7   24  9N 120 37 E
Taieri →, N.Z. . . . . . . . . . . . . 59 M3   46  3S 170 12 E
Taigu, China . . . . . . . . . . . . . 34 F7   37 28N 112 30 E
Taihang Shan, China . . . . . . . 34 G7   36  0N 113 30 E
Taihape, N.Z. . . . . . . . . . . . . . 59 H5   39 41S 175 48 E
Taihe, China . . . . . . . . . . . . . 34 H8   33 20N 115 42 E
Taikang, China . . . . . . . . . . . 34 G8   34  5N 114 50 E
Tailem Bend, Australia . . . . . 63 F2   35 12S 139 29 E
Taimyr Peninsula = Taymyr,
   Poluostrov, Russia . . . . . . 29 B11  75  0N 100  0 E
Tain, U.K. . . . . . . . . . . . . . . . 11 D4   57 49N   4  4W
T'ainan, Taiwan . . . . . . . . . . . 33 D7   23  0N 120 10 E
Tainaron, Ákra, Greece . . . . . 23 F10  36 22N  22 27 E
Taipa, China . . . . . . . . . . . . . 33 G12  22 10N 113 35 E
T'aipei, Taiwan . . . . . . . . . . . 33 D7   25  2N 121 30 E
Taiping, Malaysia . . . . . . . . . 39 K3    4 51N 100 44 E
Taipingzhen, China . . . . . . . . 34 H6   33 35N 111 42 E
Tairbeart = Tarbert, U.K. . . . . 11 D2   57 54N   6 49W
Taita Hills, Kenya . . . . . . . . . 54 C4    3 25S  38 15 E
Taitao, Pen. de, Chile . . . . . . 96 F2   46 30S  75  0W
T'aitung, Taiwan . . . . . . . . . . 33 D7   22 43N 121  4 E
Taivalkoski, Finland . . . . . . . 8 D23  65 33N  28 12 E
Taiwan ■, Asia . . . . . . . . . . . 33 D7   23 30N 121  0 E
Taïyetos Óros, Greece . . . . . . 23 F10  37  0N  22 23 E
Taiyiba, Israel . . . . . . . . . . . . 46 C4   32 36N  35 27 E
Taiyuan, China . . . . . . . . . . . 34 F7   37 52N 112 33 E
Taizhong = T'aichung, Taiwan  33 D7   24  9N 120 37 E
Ta'izz, Yemen . . . . . . . . . . . . 47 E3   13 35N  44  2 E
Tājābād, Iran . . . . . . . . . . . . . 45 D7   30  2N  54 24 E
Tajikistan ■, Asia . . . . . . . . . 28 F8   38 30N  70  0 E
Tajima, Japan . . . . . . . . . . . . 31 F9   37 12N 139 46 E
Tajo = Tejo →, Europe . . . . . 21 C1   38 40N   9 24W
Tajrīsh, Iran . . . . . . . . . . . . . 45 C6   35 48N  51 25 E
Tak, Thailand . . . . . . . . . . . . 38 D2   16 52N  99  8 E
Takāb, Iran . . . . . . . . . . . . . . 44 B5   36 24N  47  7 E
Takachiho, Japan . . . . . . . . . 31 H5   32 42N 131 18 E
Takachu, Botswana . . . . . . . . 56 C3   22 37S  21 58 E
Takada, Japan . . . . . . . . . . . . 31 F9   37  7N 138 15 E
Takahagi, Japan . . . . . . . . . . 31 F10  36 43N 140 45 E
Takaka, N.Z. . . . . . . . . . . . . . 59 J4   40 51S 172 50 E
Takamatsu, Japan . . . . . . . . . 31 G7   34 20N 134  5 E
Takaoka, Japan . . . . . . . . . . . 31 F8   36 47N 137  0 E
Takapuna, N.Z. . . . . . . . . . . . 59 G5   36 47S 174 47 E
Takasaki, Japan . . . . . . . . . . 31 F9   36 20N 139  0 E
Takatsuki, Japan . . . . . . . . . . 31 G7   34 51N 135 37 E
Takaungu, Kenya . . . . . . . . . . 54 C4    3 38S  39 52 E
Takayama, Japan . . . . . . . . . 31 F8   36 18N 137 11 E
Take-Shima, Japan . . . . . . . . 31 J5   30 49N 130 26 E
Takefu, Japan . . . . . . . . . . . . 31 G8   35 50N 136 10 E
Takengon, Indonesia . . . . . . . 36 D1    4 45N  96 50 E
Takeo, Japan . . . . . . . . . . . . . 31 H5   33 12N 130  1 E
Takeshima = Tok-do, Asia . . 31 F5   37 15N 131 52 E
Taketa, Japan . . . . . . . . . . . . 31 H5   32 58N 131 24 E
Takev, Cambodia . . . . . . . . . . 39 G5   10 59N 104 47 E
Takh, India . . . . . . . . . . . . . . 43 C7   33 6N   77 32 E
Takht-Sulaiman, Pakistan . . . 42 D3   31 40N  69 58 E
Takikawa, Japan . . . . . . . . . . 30 C10  43 33N 141 54 E
Takla L., Canada . . . . . . . . . . 70 B3   55 15N 125 45W
Takla Landing, Canada . . . . . 70 B3   55 30N 125 50W
Takla Makan = Taklamakan
   Shamo, China . . . . . . . . . . 32 C3   38  0N  83  0 E
Taklamakan Shamo, China . . 32 C3   38  0N  83  0 E
Taku →, Canada . . . . . . . . . . 70 B2   58 30N 133 50W
Takua Thung, Thailand . . . . . 39 a    8 24N  98 27 E
Tal Halāl, Iran . . . . . . . . . . . . 45 D7   34 54N  55  1 E
Tala, Uruguay . . . . . . . . . . . . 95 C4   34 21S  55 46W
Talagang, Pakistan . . . . . . . . 42 C5   32 55N  72 25 E
Talagante, Chile . . . . . . . . . . 94 C1   33 40S  70 50W
Talamanca, Cordillera de,
   Cent. Amer. . . . . . . . . . . . . 88 E3    9 20N  83 20W
Talara, Peru . . . . . . . . . . . . . . 92 D2    4 38S  81 18W
Talas, Kyrgyzstan . . . . . . . . . 28 E8   42 30N  72 13 E
Talāta, Egypt . . . . . . . . . . . . . 46 E1   30 36N  32 20 E
Talaud, Kepulauan, Indonesia  37 D7    4 30N 126 50 E
Talaud Is. = Talaud, Kepulauan,
   Indonesia . . . . . . . . . . . . . 37 D7    4 30N 126 50 E
Talavera de la Reina, Spain . . 21 C3   39 55N   4 46W
Talayan, Phil. . . . . . . . . . . . . 37 C6    6 52N 124 24 E
Talbandh, India . . . . . . . . . . . 43 H12  22  3N  86 20 E
Talbot, C., Australia . . . . . . . . 60 B4   13 48S 126 43 E
Talbragar →, Australia . . . . . 63 E4   32 12S 148 37 E
Talca, Chile . . . . . . . . . . . . . . 94 D1   35 28S  71 40W
Talcahuano, Chile . . . . . . . . . 94 D1   36 40S  73 10W
Talcher, India . . . . . . . . . . . . 41 J14  21  0N  85 18 E
Taldy Kurgan = Taldyqorghan,
   Kazakhstan . . . . . . . . . . . . 28 E8   45 10N  78 45 E

Taldyqorghan, Kazakhstan . . . 28 E8   45 10N  78 45 E
Tālesh, Iran . . . . . . . . . . . . . . 45 B6   37 58N  48 58 E
Tālesh, Kūhhā-ye, Iran . . . . . 45 B6   37 42N  48 55 E
Taliabu, Indonesia . . . . . . . . 37 E6    1 50S 125  0 E
Talibon, Phil. . . . . . . . . . . . . 37 B6   10  9N 124 20 E
Talibong, Ko, Thailand . . . . . 39 J2    7 15N  99 23 E
Talihina, U.S.A. . . . . . . . . . . 81 H7   34 45N  95  3W
Taliwang, Indonesia . . . . . . . 36 F5    8 50S 116 55 E
Tall 'Afar, Iraq . . . . . . . . . . . 44 B4   36 22N  42 27 E
Tall Kalakh, Syria . . . . . . . . . 46 A5   34 41N  36 15 E
Talladega, U.S.A. . . . . . . . . . 83 J2   33 26N  86  6W
Tallahassee, U.S.A. . . . . . . . . 83 K3   30 27N  84 17W
Tallangatta, Australia . . . . . . 63 F4   36 15S 147 19 E
Tallering Pk., Australia . . . . . 61 E2   28  6S 115 37 E
Talli, Pakistan . . . . . . . . . . . . 42 E3   29 32N  68  8 E
Tallinn, Estonia . . . . . . . . . . . 9 G21  59 22N  24 48 E
Tallmadge, U.S.A. . . . . . . . . . 84 E3   41  6N  81 27W
Tallulah, U.S.A. . . . . . . . . . . . 81 J9   32 25N  91 11W
Taloyoak, Canada . . . . . . . . . 68 B10  69 32N  93 32W
Talpa de Allende, Mexico . . . 86 C4   20 23N 104 51W
Talparo, Trin. & Tob. . . . . . . . 93 K15  10 30N  61 17W
Talsi, Latvia . . . . . . . . . . . . . 9 H20  57 10N  22 30 E
Taltal, Chile . . . . . . . . . . . . . 94 B1   25 23S  70 33W
Taltson →, Canada . . . . . . . . 70 A6   61 24N 112 46W
Talwood, Australia . . . . . . . . 63 D4   28 29S 149 29 E
Talyawalka Cr. →, Australia . . 63 E3   32 28S 142 22 E
Tam Ky, Vietnam . . . . . . . . . 38 E7   15 34N 108 12 E
Tam Quan, Vietnam . . . . . . . 38 E7   14 35N 109  3 E
Tama, U.S.A. . . . . . . . . . . . . . 80 E8   41 58N  92 35W
Tamale, Ghana . . . . . . . . . . . 50 G5    9 22N   0 50W
Taman Negara △, Malaysia . . 39 K4    4 38N 102 26 E
Tamano, Japan . . . . . . . . . . . 31 G6   34 29N 133 59 E
Tamanrasset, Algeria . . . . . . 50 D7   22 50N   5 30 E
Tamaqua, U.S.A. . . . . . . . . . . 85 F9   40 48N  75 58W
Tamar →, U.K. . . . . . . . . . . . 13 G3   50 27N   4 15W
Tamarinda, Spain . . . . . . . . . 24 B10  39 55N   3 49 E
Tamashima, Japan . . . . . . . . 31 G6   34 32N 133 40 E
Tamaulipas □, Mexico . . . . . 87 C5   24  0N  99  0W
Tamaulipas, Sierra de, Mexico  87 C5   23 30N  98 20W
Tamazula, Mexico . . . . . . . . . 86 C3   24 55N 106 58W
Tamazunchale, Mexico . . . . . 87 C5   21 16N  98 47W
Tambacounda, Senegal . . . . . 50 F3   13 45N  13 40W
Tambelan, Kepulauan, Indonesia  36 D3   1  0N 107 30 E
Tambellup, Australia . . . . . . . 61 F2   34  4S 117 37 E
Tambo, Australia . . . . . . . . . . 62 C4   24 54S 146 14 E
Tambo de Mora, Peru . . . . . . 92 F3   13 30S  76  8W
Tambohorano, Madag. . . . . . . 57 B7   17 30S  43 58 E
Tambora, Indonesia . . . . . . . 36 F5    8 12S 118  5 E
Tambov, Russia . . . . . . . . . . . 18 D7   52 45N  41 28 E
Tambuku, Indonesia . . . . . . . 37 G15  7  8S 113 40 E
Tâmega →, Portugal . . . . . . . 21 B1   41  5N   8 21W
Tamenglong, India . . . . . . . . 41 G18  25  0N  93 35 E
Tamiahua, L. de, Mexico . . . . 87 C5   21 30N  97 30W
Tamil Nadu □, India . . . . . . . 40 P10  11  0N  77  0 E
Tamluk, India . . . . . . . . . . . . 43 H12  22 18N  87 58 E
Tammerfors = Tampere, Finland  9 F20  61 30N  23 50 E
Tammisaari, Finland . . . . . . . 9 F20  60  0N  23 26 E
Tamo Abu, Pegunungan,
   Malaysia . . . . . . . . . . . . . 36 D5    3 10N 115  5 E
Tampa, U.S.A. . . . . . . . . . . . . 83 M4   27 57N  82 27W
Tampa, Tanjung, Indonesia . . 37 K19  8 55S 116 12 E
Tampa B., U.S.A. . . . . . . . . . . 83 M4   27 50N  82 30W
Tampere, Finland . . . . . . . . . 9 F20  61 30N  23 50 E
Tampico, Mexico . . . . . . . . . . 87 C5   22 20N  97 50W
Tampin, Malaysia . . . . . . . . . 39 L4    2 28N 102 13 E
Tampoi, Malaysia . . . . . . . . . 39 d    1 30N 103 39 E
Tamu, Burma . . . . . . . . . . . . 41 G19  24 13N  94 12 E
Tamworth, Australia . . . . . . . 63 E5   31  7S 150 58 E
Tamworth, Canada . . . . . . . . 84 B8   44 29N  77  0W
Tamworth, U.K. . . . . . . . . . . 13 E6   52 39N   1 41W
Tamyang, S. Korea . . . . . . . . 35 G14  35 19N 126 59 E
Tan An, Vietnam . . . . . . . . . . 39 G6   10 32N 106 25 E
Tan Chau, Vietnam . . . . . . . . 39 G5   10 48N 105 12 E
Tan-Tan, Morocco . . . . . . . . . 50 C3   28 29N  11  1W
Tana →, Kenya . . . . . . . . . . . 54 C5    2 32S  40 31 E
Tana →, Norway . . . . . . . . . . 8 A23  70 30N  28 14 E
Tana, L., Ethiopia . . . . . . . . . 47 E2   13  5N  37 30 E
Tana River Primate △, Kenya . . 54 C5    1 55S  40  7 E
Tanabe, Japan . . . . . . . . . . . 31 H7   33 44N 135 22 E
Tanafjorden, Norway . . . . . . . 8 A23  70 45N  28 25 E
Tanahbala, Indonesia . . . . . . 36 E1    0 30S  98 30 E
Tanahgrogot, Indonesia . . . . 36 E5    1 55S 116 15 E
Tanahjampea, Indonesia . . . . 37 F6    7 10S 120 35 E
Tanahmasa, Indonesia . . . . . 36 E1    0 12S  98 39 E
Tanahmerah, Indonesia . . . . . 37 F10   6  5S 140 16 E
Tanakpur, India . . . . . . . . . . . 43 E9   29  5N  80  7 E
Tanakura, Japan . . . . . . . . . . 31 F10  37 10N 140 20 E
Tanami, Australia . . . . . . . . . 60 C4   19 59S 129 43 E
Tanami Desert, Australia . . . . 60 C5   18 50S 132  0 E
Tanana →, U.S.A. . . . . . . . . . 68 B4   65 10N 151 58W
Tananarive = Antananarivo,
   Madag. . . . . . . . . . . . . . . . 57 B8   18 55S  47 31 E
Tánaro →, Italy . . . . . . . . . . . 20 D8   44 55N   8 40 E
Tancheng, China . . . . . . . . . . 35 G10  34 25N 118 20 E
Tanch'ŏn, N. Korea . . . . . . . . 35 D15  40 27N 128 54 E
Tanda, Ut. P., India . . . . . . . . 43 F10  26 33N  82 35 E
Tanda, Ut. P., India . . . . . . . . 43 E8   28 57N  78 56 E
Tandag, Phil. . . . . . . . . . . . . 37 C7    9  4N 126  9 E
Tandaia, Tanzania . . . . . . . . 55 D3    9 25S  34  5 E
Tandaué, Angola . . . . . . . . . . 56 B2   16 58S  18  5 E
Tandil, Argentina . . . . . . . . . 94 D4   37 15S  59  6W
Tandil, Sa. del, Argentina . . . 94 D4   37 30S  59  0W
Tandlianwala, Pakistan . . . . . 42 D5   31  3N  73  9 E
Tando Adam, Pakistan . . . . . 42 G3   25 45N  68 40 E
Tando Allahyar, Pakistan . . . 42 G3   25 28N  68 43 E
Tando Bago, Pakistan . . . . . . 42 G3   24 47N  68 58 E
Tando Mohommed Khan,
   Pakistan . . . . . . . . . . . . . . 42 G3   25  8N  68 32 E
Tandou L., Australia . . . . . . . 63 E3   32 40S 142  5 E
Tandragee, U.K. . . . . . . . . . . 10 B5   54 21N   6 24W
Tane-ga-Shima, Japan . . . . . . 31 J5   30 30N 131  0 E
Taneatua, N.Z. . . . . . . . . . . . 59 H6   38  4S 177  1 E
Tanen Tong Dan = Dawna Ra.,
   Burma . . . . . . . . . . . . . . . . 38 D2   16 30N  98 30 E
Tanezrouft, Algeria . . . . . . . . 50 D6   23  9N   0 11 E
Tang, Koh, Cambodia . . . . . . 39 G4   10 16N 103  7 E
Tang, Ra's-e, Iran . . . . . . . . . 45 E8   25 21N  59 52 E
Tang Krasang, Cambodia . . . 38 F5   12 34N 105  3 E
Tanga, Tanzania . . . . . . . . . . 54 D4    5  5S  39  2 E
Tanga □, Tanzania . . . . . . . . 54 D4    5 20S  38  0 E
Tanganyika, L., Africa . . . . . . 54 D3    6 40S  30  0 E
Tanger, Morocco . . . . . . . . . . 50 A4   35 50N   5 49W
Tangerang, Indonesia . . . . . . 37 G12  6 11S 106 37 E
Tanggu, China . . . . . . . . . . . . 35 E9   39  2N 117 40 E
Tanggula Shan, China . . . . . . 32 C4   32 40N  92 10 E
Tanghla Range = Tanggula Shan,
   China . . . . . . . . . . . . . . . . 32 C4   32 40N  92 10 E

Tangier = Tanger, Morocco .... 50 A4  35 50N   5 49W
Tangjia, China ............ 33 G10 22 22N 113 35 E
Tangjia Wan, China ........ 33 G10 22 21N 113 36 E
Tangorin, Australia .......... 62 C3  21 47S 144 12 E
Tangorombohitr'i Makay,
  Madag. ................... 57 C8  21  0S  45 15 E
Tangshan, China ............ 35 E10 39 38N 118 10 E
Tangtou, China ............ 35 G10 35 28N 118 30 E
Tanimbar, Kepulauan, Indonesia 37 F8   7 30S 131 30 E
Tanimbar Is. = Tanimbar,
  Kepulauan, Indonesia ...... 37 F8   7 30S 131 30 E
Taninthari = Tenasserim, Burma 39 F2  12  6N  99  3 E
Tanjay, Phil. ............... 37 C6   9 30N 123  5 E
Tanjong Malim, Malaysia ...... 39 L3   3 42N 101 31 E
Tanjong Pelapas, Malaysia ..... 39 d   1 21N 103 33 E
Tanjore = Thanjavur, India .... 40 P11 10 48N  79 12 E
Tanjung, Indonesia .......... 37 J19  8 21S 116  9 E
Tanjung, Phil. ............. 36 E5   2 10S 115 25 E
Tanjung Tokong, Malaysia ..... 39 c   5 28N 100 18 E
Tanjungbalai, Indonesia ...... 36 D1   2 55N  99 44 E
Tanjungbatu, Indonesia ....... 36 D5   2 23N 118  3 E
Tanjungkarang Telukbetung,
  Indonesia ................ 36 F3   5 20S 105 10 E
Tanjungpandan, Indonesia ..... 36 E3   2 43S 107 38 E
Tanjungpinang, Indonesia ..... 36 D2   1  5N 104 30 E
Tanjungredeb, Indonesia ...... 36 D5   2  9N 117 29 E
Tanjungselor, Indonesia ...... 36 D5   2 55N 117 25 E
Tank, Pakistan ............. 42 C4  32 14N  70 25 E
Tankhala, India ............ 42 J5  21 58N  73 47 E
Tankwa-Karoo △., S. Africa .... 56 E2  32 14S  19 50 E
Tannersville, U.S.A. ......... 85 E9  41  3N  75 18W
Tannu-Ola, Russia .......... 29 D10 51  0N  94  0 E
Tannum Sands, Australia ...... 62 C5  23 57S 151 22 E
Tanout, Niger .............. 50 F7  14 50N   8 55 E
Tanta, Egypt ............... 51 B12 30 45N  30 57 E
Tantoyuca, Mexico .......... 87 C5  21 21N  98 10W
Tantung = Dandong, China .... 35 D13 40 10N 124 20 E
Tanunda, Australia .......... 63 E2  34 30S 139  0 E
Tanzania ■, Africa .......... 54 D3   6  0S  34  0 E
Tanzhou, China ............ 33 G9  22 16N 113 28 E
Tanzilla →, Canada .......... 70 B2  58  8N 130 43W
Tao, Ko, Thailand .......... 39 G2  10  5N  99 52 E
Tao'an = Taonan, China ...... 35 B12 45 22N 122 40 E
Tao'er He →, China ......... 35 B13 45 45N 124  5 E
Taolanaro, Madag. .......... 57 D8  25  2S  47  0 E
Taonan, China ............. 35 B12 45 22N 122 40 E
Taos, U.S.A. .............. 77 H11 36 24N 105 35W
Taoudenni, Mali ........... 50 D5  22 40N   3 55W
Tapa, Estonia ............. 9 G21  59 15N  25 50 E
Tapa Shan = Daba Shan, China . 33 C5  31 50N 109  0 E
Tapachula, Mexico .......... 87 E6  14 54N  92 17W
Tapah, Malaysia ............ 39 K3   4 12N 101 15 E
Tapajós →, Brazil .......... 93 D8   2 24S  54 41W
Tapaktuan, Indonesia ........ 36 D1   3 15N  97 10 E
Tapanahoni →, Suriname ..... 93 C8   4 20N  54 25W
Tapanui, N.Z. .............. 59 L2  45 56S 169 18 E
Tapauá →, Brazil ........... 92 E6   5 40S  64 21W
Tapes, Brazil .............. 95 C5  30 40S  51 23W
Tapeta, Liberia ............ 50 G4   6 29N   8 52W
Taphan Hin, Thailand ........ 38 D3  16 13N 100 26 E
Tapi →, India ............. 40 J8  21  8N  72 41 E
Tapirapecó, Serra, Venezuela .. 92 C6   1 10N  65  0W
Tapo-Capara △., Venezuela ... 89 E5   7 55N  71 15W
Tapuae-o-Uenuku, N.Z. ....... 59 K4  42  0S 173 39 E
Tapul Group, Phil. .......... 37 C6   5 35N 120 50 E
Tapurucuará, Brazil ......... 92 D5   0 24S  65  2W
Taqtaq, Iraq .............. 44 C5  35 53N  44 35 E
Taquara, Brazil ............ 95 B5  29 36S  50 46W
Taquari →, Brazil .......... 92 G7  19 15S  57 17W
Tara, Australia ............ 63 D5  27 17S 150 31 E
Tara, Canada .............. 84 B3  44 28N  81  9W
Tara, Russia .............. 28 D8  56 55N  74 24 E
Tara, Zambia .............. 55 F2  16 58S  26 45 E
Tara →, Serbia & M. ........ 23 C8  43 21N  18 51 E
Tarābulus, Lebanon ......... 46 A4  34 31N  35 50 E
Tarābulus, Libya ........... 51 B8  32 49N  13  7 E
Taradehi, India ............ 43 H8  23 18N  79 36 E
Tarajalejo, Canary Is. ....... 24 F5  28 12N  14  7W
Tarakan, Indonesia ......... 36 D5   3 20N 117 35 E
Tarakit, Mt., Kenya ......... 54 B4   2  2N  35 10 E
Tarama-Jima, Japan ......... 31 M2  24 39N 124 42 E
Taran, Mys, Russia ......... 9 J18  54 56N  19 59 E
Taranagar, India ........... 42 E6  28 43N  74 50 E
Taranaki □, N.Z. ........... 59 H5  39 25S 174 30 E
Taranaki, Mt., N.Z. ......... 59 H5  39 17S 174  5 E
Tarancón, Spain ............ 21 B4  40  1N   3  0W
Tarangire △, Tanzania ....... 54 C4   4 21S  36  7 E
Taransay, U.K. ............. 11 D1  57 54N   7  0W
Táranto, Italy ............. 22 D7  40 28N  17 14 E
Táranto, G. di, Italy ........ 22 D7  40  8N  17 20 E
Tarapacá, Colombia ......... 92 D5   2 56S  69 46W
Tarapacá □, Chile .......... 94 A2  20 45S  69 30W
Tarapoto, Peru ............ 92 E3   6 30S  76 20W
Tararua Ra., N.Z. .......... 59 J5  40 45S 175 25 E
Tarashcha, Ukraine ......... 17 D16 49 30N  30 31 E
Tarauacá, Brazil ........... 92 E4   8  6S  70 48W
Tarauacá →, Brazil ......... 92 E5   6 42S  69 48W
Tarawa, Kiribati ........... 64 G9   1 30N 173  0 E
Tarawera, N.Z. ............ 59 H6   9  2S 176 36 E
Tarawera, L., N.Z. .......... 59 H6  38 13S 176 27 E
Taraz, Kazakhstan .......... 28 E8  42 54N  71 22 E
Tarazona, Spain ........... 21 B5  41 55N   1 43W
Tarbagatay, Khrebet, Kazakhstan 28 E9  48  0N  83  0 E
Tarbat Ness, U.K. .......... 11 D5  57 52N   3 47W
Tarbela Dam, Pakistan ....... 42 B5  34  8N  72 52 E
Tarbert, Arg. & Bute, U.K. .... 11 F3  55 52N   5 25W
Tarbert, W. Isles, U.K. ...... 11 D2  57 54N   6 49W
Tarbes, France ............ 20 E4  43 15N   0  3 E
Tarboro, U.S.A. ............ 83 H7  35 54N  77 32W
Tarcoola, Australia ......... 63 E1  30 44S 134 36 E
Tarcoon, Australia .......... 63 E4  30 15S 146 43 E
Taree, Australia ........... 63 E5  31 50S 152 30 E
Tarfaya, Morocco ........... 50 C3  27 55N  12 55W
Tărgoviște, Romania ......... 17 F13 44 55N  25 27 E
Târgu-Jiu, Romania ......... 17 F12 45  5N  23 19 E
Târgu Mureș, Romania ....... 17 E13 46 31N  24 38 E
Ṭarīf, U.A.E. .............. 45 E7  24  3N  53 46 E
Tarifa, Spain .............. 21 D3  36  1N   5 36W
Tarija, Bolivia ............. 94 A3  21 30S  64 40W
Tarija □, Bolivia ........... 94 A3  21 30S  63 30W
Tariku →, Indonesia ........ 37 E9   2 55S 138 26 E
Tarim Basin = Tarim Pendi, China 32 B3  40  0N  84  0 E
Tarim He →, China ......... 32 C3  39 30N  88 30 E
Tarim Pendi, China ......... 32 B3  40  0N  84  0 E
Taritatu →, Indonesia ....... 37 E9   2 54S 138 27 E
Tarka →, S. Africa ......... 56 E4  32 10S  26  0 E
Tarkastad, S. Africa ........ 56 E4  32  0S  26 16 E

Tarkhankut, Mys, Ukraine ..... 19 E5  45 25N  32 30 E
Tarko Sale, Russia ......... 28 C8  64 55N  77 50 E
Tarkwa, Ghana ............ 50 G5   5 20N   2  0W
Tarlac, Phil. .............. 37 A6  15 29N 120 35 E
Tarma, Peru .............. 92 F3  11 25S  75 45W
Tarn →, France ............ 20 E4  44  5N   1  6 E
Târnăveni, Romania ......... 17 E13 46 19N  24 13 E
Tarnobrzeg, Poland ......... 17 C11 50 35N  21 41 E
Tarnów, Poland ............ 17 C11 50  3N  21  0 E
Tarnowskie Góry, Poland ..... 17 C10 50 27N  18 54 E
Ṭārom, Iran .............. 45 D7  28 11N  55 46 E
Taroom, Australia .......... 63 D4  25 36S 149 48 E
Taroudannt, Morocco ........ 50 B4  30 30N   8 52W
Tarpon Springs, U.S.A. ...... 83 L4  28  9N  82 45W
Tarragona, Spain ........... 21 B6  41  5N   1 17 E
Tarraleah, Australia ........ 63 G4  42 17S 146 26 E
Tarrasa = Terrassa, Spain .... 21 B7  41 34N   2  1 E
Tarrytown, U.S.A. .......... 85 E11 41  4N  73 52W
Tarshiha = Me'ona, Israel .... 46 B4  33  1N  35 15 E
Tarsus, Turkey ............ 19 G5  36 58N  34 55 E
Tartagal, Argentina ......... 94 A3  22 30S  63 50W
Tartu, Estonia ............. 9 G22  58 20N  26 44 E
Ṭarṭūs, Syria ............. 44 C2  34 55N  35 55 E
Tarumizu, Japan ........... 31 J5  31 29N 130 42 E
Tarutao = Ko Tarutao △., Thailand 39 J2   6 31N  99 26 E
Tarutao, Ko, Thailand ....... 39 J2   6 33N  99 40 E
Tarutung, Indonesia ........ 36 D1   2  0N  98 54 E
Taseko →, Canada .......... 70 C4  52  8N 123 45W
Tash-Kömür, Kyrgyzstan ..... 28 E8  41 40N  72 10 E
Tash-Kumyr = Tash-Kömür,
  Kyrgyzstan .............. 28 E8  41 40N  72 10 E
Tashauz = Dashhowuz,
  Turkmenistan ............ 28 E6  41 49N  59 58 E
Tashi Chho Dzong = Thimphu,
  Bhutan ................. 41 F16  27 31N  89 45 E
Ṭashk, Daryācheh-ye, Iran .... 45 D7  29 45N  53 35 E
Tashkent = Toshkent, Uzbekistan 28 E7  41 20N  69 10 E
Tashtagol, Russia .......... 28 D9  52 47N  87 53 E
Tasiilaq, Greenland ......... 4 C6  65 40N  37 20W
Tasikmalaya, Indonesia ...... 37 G13  7 18S 108 12 E
Tåsjön, Sweden ............ 8 D16  64 15N  15 40 E
Taskan, Russia ............ 29 C16 62 59N 150 20 E
Tasman B., N.Z. ........... 59 J4  40 59S 173 25 E
Tasman Mts., N.Z. .......... 59 J4  41  3S 172 25 E
Tasman Pen., Australia ...... 63 G4  43 10S 148  0 E
Tasman Plateau, S. Ocean .... 5 A10  48  0S 146  0 E
Tasman Sea, Pac. Oc. ....... 64 L8  36  0S 160  0 E
Tasmania □, Australia ....... 63 G4  42  0S 146 30 E
Tassili n'Ajjer, Algeria ...... 50 C7  25 47N   8  1 E
Tatabánya, Hungary ........ 17 E10 47 32N  18 25 E
Tatahouine, Tunisia ......... 51 B8  32 56N  10 27 E
Tataouine, Tunisia ......... 51 B8  32 57N  10 29 E
Tatar Republic = Tatarstan □,
  Russia .................. 18 C9  55 30N  51 30 E
Tatarbunary, Ukraine ........ 17 F15 45 50N  29 39 E
Tatarsk, Russia ............ 28 D8  55 14N  76  0 E
Tatarstan □, Russia ........ 18 C9  55 30N  51 30 E
Tateyama, Japan ........... 31 G9  35  0N 139 50 E
Tathlina L., Canada ......... 70 A5  60 33N 117 39W
Tathra, Australia ........... 63 F4  36 44S 149 59 E
Tatinnai L., Canada ......... 71 A9  60 55N  97 40W
Tatla L., Canada ........... 70 C4  52  0N 124 20W
Tatnam, C., Canada ......... 71 B10  57 16N  91  0W
Tatra = Tatry, Slovak Rep. .... 17 D11 49 20N  20  0 E
Tatry, Slovak Rep. .......... 17 D11 49 20N  20  0 E
Tatshenshini →, Canada ..... 70 B1  59 28N 137 45W
Tatsuno, Japan ............ 31 G7  34 52N 134 33 E
Tatta, Pakistan ............ 42 G2  24 42N  67 55 E
Tatuī, Brazil .............. 95 A6  23 25S  47 53W
Tatum, U.S.A. ............. 81 J3  33 16N 103 19W
Tat'ung = Datong, China ..... 34 D7  40  6N 113 18 E
Tatvan, Turkey ............ 19 G7  38 31N  42 15 E
Taubaté, Brazil ........... 95 A6  23  0S  45 36W
Tauern, Austria ............ 16 E7  47 15N  12 40 E
Taumarunui, N.Z. .......... 59 H5  38 53S 175 15 E
Taumaturgo, Brazil ........ 92 E4   8 54S  72 51W
Taung, S. Africa ........... 56 D3  27 33S  24 47 E
Taungdwingyi, Burma ....... 41 J19 20  1N  95 40 E
Taunggyi, Burma ........... 41 J20 20 50N  97  0 E
Taungup, Burma ........... 41 K19 18 51N  94 14 E
Taungup Taunggya, Burma .... 41 K18 18 20N  93 40 E
Taunsa, Pakistan .......... 42 D4  30 42N  70 39 E
Taunsa Barrage, Pakistan .... 42 D4  30 42N  70 50 E
Taunton, U.K. ............. 13 F4  51  1N   3  5W
Taunton, U.S.A. ........... 85 E13 41 54N  71  6W
Taunus, Germany .......... 16 C5  50 13N   8 34 E
Taupo, N.Z. ............... 59 H6  38 41S 176  7 E
Taupo, L., N.Z. ............ 59 H5  38 46S 175 55 E
Tauragė, Lithuania ......... 9 J20  55 14N  22 16 E
Tauranga, N.Z. ............ 59 G6  37 42S 176 11 E
Tauranga Harb., N.Z. ........ 59 G6  37 30S 176  5 E
Taureau, Rés., Canada ...... 72 C5  46 46N  73 50W
Taurianova, Italy .......... 22 E7  38 21N  16  1 E
Taurus Mts. = Toros Dağları,
  Turkey ................. 19 G5  37  0N  32 30 E
Tavastehus = Hämeenlinna,
  Finland ................ 9 F21  61  0N  24 28 E
Tavda, Russia ............. 28 D7  58  7N  65  8 E
Tavda →, Russia .......... 28 D7  57 47N  67 18 E
Taveta, Tanzania .......... 54 C4   3 23S  37 37 E
Taveuni, Fiji .............. 59 C9  16 51S 179 58W
Tavira, Portugal ........... 21 D2  37  8N   7 40W
Tavistock, Canada .......... 84 C4  43 19N  80 50W
Tavistock, U.K. ............ 13 G3  50 33N   4  9W
Tavoy, Burma ............. 38 E2  14  2N  98 12 E
Taw →, U.K. .............. 13 F3  51  4N   4  4W
Tawa →, India ............ 42 H8  22 48N  77 48 E
Tawas City, U.S.A. ......... 82 C4  44 16N  83 31W
Tawau, Malaysia ........... 36 D5   4 20N 117 55 E
Tawitawi, Phil. ............ 37 B6   5 10N 120  0 E
Taxco de Alarcón, Mexico .... 87 D5  18 33N  99 36W
Taxila, Pakistan ........... 42 C5  33 42N  72 52 E
Tay →, U.K. .............. 11 E5  56 43N   3 59W
Tay, Firth of, U.K. ......... 11 E5  56 25N   3  8W
Tay, L., Australia .......... 61 F3  32 55S 120 48 E
Tay, L., U.K. .............. 11 E4  56 32N   4  8W
Tay Ninh, Vietnam ......... 39 G6  11 20N 106  5 E
Tayabamba, Peru .......... 92 E3   8 15S  77 16W
Taylakova, Russia .......... 28 D8  59 13N  74  0 E
Taylakovy = Taylakova, Russia . 28 D8  59 13N  74  0 E
Taylor, Canada ............ 70 B4  56 13N 120 40W
Taylor, Nebr., U.S.A. ........ 80 E5  41 46N  99 23W
Taylor, Pa., U.S.A. ......... 85 E9  41 23N  75 43W
Taylor, Tex., U.S.A. ........ 81 K6  30 34N  97 25W
Taylor, Mt., U.S.A. ......... 77 J10  35 14N 107 37W
Taylorville, U.S.A. ......... 80 F10  39 33N  89 18W
Taymā, Si. Arabia .......... 44 E3  27 35N  38 45 E

Taymyr, Oz., Russia ........ 29 B11  74 20N 102  0 E
Taymyr, Poluostrov, Russia ... 29 B11  75  0N 100  0 E
Tayport, U.K. ............. 11 E6  56 27N   2 52W
Tayrona △, Colombia ........ 89 D5  11 20N  74  2W
Tayshet, Russia ........... 29 D10  55 58N  98  1 E
Taytay, Phil. ............. 37 B5  10 45N 119 30 E
Tāyyebād, Iran ............ 45 C9  34 45N  60 45 E
Tāyyebād □, Iran .......... 45 C9  34 44N  60 44 E
Taz →, Russia ............ 28 C8  67 32N  78 40 E
Taza, Morocco ............ 50 B5  34 16N   4  6W
Tāza Khurmātū, Iraq ........ 44 C5  35 18N  44 20 E
Tazawa-Ko, Japan .......... 30 E10  39 43N 140 40 E
Tazin, Canada ............ 71 B7  59 48N 109 55W
Tazin L., Canada .......... 71 B7  59 44N 108 42W
Tazovskiy, Russia .......... 28 C8  67 30N  78 44 E
Tbilisi, Georgia ........... 19 F7  41 43N  44 50 E
Tchad = Chad ■, Africa ..... 51 F8  15  0N  17 15 E
Tchad, L., Chad ........... 51 F8  13 30N  14 30 E
Tch'eng-tou = Chengdu, China . 32 C5  30 38N 104  2 E
Tchentlo L., Canada ........ 70 B4  55 15N 125  0W
Tchibanga, Gabon ......... 52 E2   2 45S  11  0 E
Tch'ong-k'ing = Chongqing,
  China .................. 32 D5  29 35N 106 25 E
Tczew, Poland ............. 17 A10  54  8N  18 50 E
Te Anau, L., N.Z. .......... 59 L1  45 15S 167 45 E
Te Aroha, N.Z. ............ 59 G5  37 32S 175 44 E
Te Awamutu, N.Z. .......... 59 H5  38  1S 175 20 E
Te Ika a Maui = North I., N.Z. . 59 H5  38  0S 175  0 E
Te Kuiti, N.Z. ............. 59 H5  38 20S 175 11 E
Te Puke, N.Z. ............. 59 G6  37 46S 176 22 E
Te Waewae B., N.Z. ......... 59 M1  46 13S 167 33 E
Te Wai Pounamu = South I., N.Z. 59 L3  44  0S 170  0 E
Teague, U.S.A. ............ 81 K6  31 38N  96 17W
Teapa, Mexico ............ 87 D6  18 35N  92 56W
Tebakang, Malaysia ........ 36 D4   1  6N 110 30 E
Teberu, Malaysia .......... 39 d   1 30N 103 42 E
Tébessa, Algeria ........... 50 A7  35 22N   8  8 E
Tebicuary →, Paraguay ...... 94 B4  26 36S  58 16W
Tebingtinggi, Riau, Indonesia .. 36 E2   1  0N 102 45 E
Tebingtinggi, Sumatera Utara,
  Indonesia ............... 36 D1   3 20N  99  9 E
Tecate, Mexico ............ 79 N10  32 34N 116 38W
Tecka, Argentina .......... 96 E2  43 29S  70 48W
Tecomán, Mexico .......... 86 D4  18 55N 103 53W
Tecopa, U.S.A. ............ 79 K10  35 51N 116 13W
Tecoripa, Mexico .......... 86 B3  28 37N 109 57W
Tecuala, Mexico ........... 86 C3  22 23N 105 27W
Tecuci, Romania ........... 17 F14  45 51N  27 27 E
Tecumseh, Canada ......... 84 D2  42 19N  82 54W
Tecumseh, Mich., U.S.A. ..... 82 D4  42  0N  83 57W
Tecumseh, Okla., U.S.A. ..... 81 H6  35 15N  96 56W
Tedzhen = Tejen, Turkmenistan 28 F7  37 23N  60 31 E
Tees →, U.K. ............. 12 C6  54 37N   1 10W
Tees B., U.K. ............. 12 C6  54 40N   1  9W
Teeswater, Canada ......... 84 C3  43 59N  81 17W
Tefé, Brazil .............. 92 D6   3 25S  64 50W
Tegal, Indonesia .......... 37 G13  6 52S 109  8 E
Tegallalang, Indonesia ...... 37 J18  8 27S 115 17 E
Tegalsari, Indonesia ........ 37 J17  8 25S 114  8 E
Tegid, L. = Bala, L., U.K. ..... 12 E4  52 53N   3 37W
Tegucigalpa, Honduras ...... 88 D2  14  5N  87 14W
Tehachapi, U.S.A. ......... 79 K8  35  8N 118 27W
Tehachapi Mts., U.S.A. ...... 79 L8  35  0N 118 30W
Teheran = Tehrān, Iran ...... 45 C6  35 44N  51 30 E
Tehoru, Indonesia ......... 37 E7   3 23S 129 30 E
Tehrān, Iran .............. 45 C6  35 44N  51 30 E
Tehrān □, Iran ............ 45 C6  35 30N  51 30 E
Tehri, India .............. 43 D8  30 23N  78 29 E
Tehuacán, Mexico .......... 87 D5  18 30N  97 30W
Tehuantepec, Mexico ....... 87 D5  16 21N  95 13W
Tehuantepec, G. de, Mexico .. 87 D5  15 50N  95 12W
Tehuantepec, Istmo de, Mexico 87 D6  17  0N  94 30W
Teide, Pico de, Canary Is. .... 24 F3  28 15N  16 38W
Teifi →, U.K. ............. 13 E3  52  5N   4 41W
Teign →, U.K. ............ 13 G4  50 32N   3 32W
Teignmouth, U.K. ......... 13 G4  50 33N   3 31W
Tejakula, Indonesia ........ 37 J18  8  8S 115 20 E
Tejam, India ............. 43 E9  29 57N  80 11 E
Tejen, Turkmenistan ....... 28 F7  37 23N  60 31 E
Tejen →, Turkmenistan ...... 45 B9  37 24N  60 38 E
Tejo →, Europe ........... 21 C1  38 40N   9 24W
Tejon Pass, U.S.A. ......... 79 L8  34 49N 118 53W
Tekamah, U.S.A. ........... 80 E6  41 47N  96 13W
Tekapo, L., N.Z. ........... 59 K3  43 53S 170 33 E
Tekax, Mexico ............ 87 C7  20 11N  89 18W
Tekeli, Kazakhstan ......... 28 E8  44 50N  79  0 E
Tekirdağ, Turkey .......... 23 D12  40 58N  27 30 E
Tekkali, India ............ 41 K14  18 37N  84 15 E
Tekoa, U.S.A. ............. 76 C5  47 14N 117  4W
Tekong Besar, Pulau, Singapore 39 d   1 25N 104  3 E
Tel Aviv ✈ (TLV), Israel ..... 46 C3  32  5N  34 49 E
Tel Aviv-Yafo, Israel ....... 46 C3  32  4N  34 48 E
Tel Lakhish, Israel ......... 46 D3  31 34N  34 51 E
Tel Megiddo, Israel ........ 46 C4  32 35N  35 11 E
Tela, Honduras ............ 88 C2  15 40N  87 28W
Telanaipura = Jambi, Indonesia 36 E2   1 38S 103 30 E
Telavi, Georgia ........... 19 F8  42  0N  45 30 E
Telde, Canary Is. .......... 24 G4  27 59N  15 25W
Telegraph Creek, Canada .... 70 B2  58  0N 131 10W
Telekhany = Tsyelyakhany,
  Belarus ................. 17 B13  52 30N  25 46 E
Telemark, Norway ......... 9 G12  59 15N   7 40 E
Telén, Argentina .......... 94 D2  36 15S  65 31W
Teles Pires →, Brazil ....... 92 E7   7 21S  58  3W
Telescope Pk., U.S.A. ....... 79 J9  36 10N 117  5W
Telfer Mine, Australia ...... 60 C3  21 40S 122 12 E
Telford, U.K. ............. 13 E5  52 40N   2 27W
Telford and Wrekin □, U.K. ... 12 E5  52 45N   2 27W
Telkwa, Canada ........... 70 C3  54 41N 127  5W
Tell City, U.S.A. ........... 82 G2  37 57N  86 46W
Tellicherry, India .......... 40 P9  11 45N  75 30 E
Telluride, U.S.A. .......... 77 H10  37 56N 107 49W
Teloloapán, Mexico ........ 87 D5  18 21N  99 51W
Telpos Iz, Russia .......... 18 B10  63 16N  59 13 E
Telsen, Argentina ......... 96 E3  42 30S  66 50W
Telšiai, Lithuania ......... 9 H20  55 59N  22 14 E
Teluk Anson = Teluk Intan,
  Malaysia ............... 39 K3   4  3N 101  0 E
Teluk Bahang, Malaysia ..... 39 c   5 28N 100 13 E
Teluk Betung = Tanjungkarang
  Telukbetung, Indonesia .... 36 F3   5 20S 105 10 E
Teluk Intan, Malaysia ...... 39 K3   4  3N 101  0 E
Teluk Kumbar, Malaysia ..... 39 c   5 18N 100 12 E
Telukbutun, Indonesia ...... 36 D3   4 13N 108 12 E
Telukdalam, Indonesia ...... 36 D1   0 33S  97 50 E
Tema, Ghana ............. 50 G5   5 41N   0  0 E
Temax, Mexico ............ 87 C7  21 10N  88 50W

Temba, S. Africa .......... 57 D4  25 20S  28 17 E
Tembagapura, Indonesia ..... 37 E9   4 20S 137  0 E
Tembe, Dem. Rep. of the Congo 54 C2   0 16S  28 14 E
Tembe △, S. Africa ......... 57 D5  26 51S  32 24 E
Temblor Range, U.S.A. ...... 79 K7  35 20N 119 50W
Teme →, U.K. ............ 13 E5  52 11N   2 13W
Temecula, U.S.A. .......... 79 M9  33 30N 117  9W
Temerloh, Malaysia ........ 36 D2   3 27N 102 25 E
Teminabuan, Indonesia ..... 37 E8   1 26S 132  1 E
Temir, Kazakhstan ......... 19 E10  49  1N  57 14 E
Temirtau, Kazakhstan ....... 28 D8  50  5N  72 56 E
Temirtau, Russia .......... 28 D9  53 10N  87 30 E
Temiscamie →, Canada ..... 73 B5  50 59N  73  5W
Témiscaming, Canada ....... 72 C4  46 44N  79  5W
Témiscamingue, L., Canada ... 72 C4  47 10N  79 25W
Temosachic, Mexico ........ 86 B3  28 58N 107 50W
Tempe, U.S.A. ............ 77 K8  33 25N 111 56W
Tempiute, U.S.A. .......... 78 H11  37 39N 115 38W
Temple, U.S.A. ............ 81 K6  31  6N  97 21W
Temple B., Australia ........ 62 A3  12 15S 143  3 E
Templemore, Ireland ....... 10 D4  52 47N   7 51W
Templeton, U.S.A. ......... 78 K6  35 33N 120 42W
Templeton →, Australia ..... 62 C2  21  0S 138 40 E
Tempoal, Mexico .......... 87 C5  21 31N  98 23W
Temuco, Chile ............ 96 D2  38 45S  72 40W
Temuka, N.Z. ............. 59 L3  44 14S 171 17 E
Tenabo, Mexico ........... 87 C6  20  2N  90 12W
Tenaha, U.S.A. ........... 81 K7  31 57N  94 15W
Tenakee Springs, U.S.A. ..... 70 B1  57 47N 135 13W
Tenali, India ............. 41 L12  16 15N  80 35 E
Tenancingo, Mexico ........ 87 D5  19  0N  99 33W
Tenango, Mexico .......... 87 D5  19  7N  99 33W
Tenasserim, Burma ........ 39 F2  12  6N  99  3 E
Tenasserim □, Burma ....... 38 F2  14  0N  98 30 E
Tenby, U.K. .............. 13 F3  51 40N   4 42W
Tenda, Colle di, France ...... 20 D7  44  7N   7 36 E
Tendaho, Ethiopia ......... 47 E3  11 48N  40 54 E
Tendukhera, India ......... 43 H8  23 24N  79 33 E
Teneguía, Volcanes de,
  Canary Is. .............. 24 F2  28 28N  17 51W
Tenerife, Canary Is. ....... 24 F3  28 15N  16 35W
Tenerife, Pico, Canary Is. .... 24 G1  27 43N  18  1W
Tenerife Norte ✈ (TFN),
  Canary Is. .............. 24 F3  28 28N  16 17W
Tenerife Sur ✈ (TFS), Canary Is. 24 F3  28 15N  16 34W
Teng Xian, China .......... 35 G9  35  5N 117 10 E
Tengah, Kepulauan, Indonesia . 32 D4  7  5S 118 15 E
Tengchong, China ......... 32 D4  25  0N  98 28 E
Tengchow = Penglai, China ... 35 F11  37 48N 120 42 E
Tenggarong, Indonesia ...... 36 E5   0 24S 116 58 E
Tenggol, Pulau, Malaysia .... 39 K4   4 48N 103 41 E
Tengiz, Ozero, Kazakhstan ... 28 D7  50 30N  69  0 E
Teniente Enciso △, Paraguay .. 94 A3  21  5S  61  8W
Teniente Rodolfo Marsh,
  Antarctica .............. 5 C18  62 30S  58  0W
Tenino, U.S.A. ............ 78 D4  46 51N 122 51W
Tenkasi, India ............ 40 Q10  8 55N  77 20 E
Tenke, Katanga, Dem. Rep. of
  the Congo .............. 55 E2  11 22S  26 40 E
Tenke, Katanga, Dem. Rep. of
  the Congo .............. 55 E2  10 32S  26  7 E
Tennant Creek, Australia .... 62 B1  19 30S 134 15 E
Tennessee □, U.S.A. ........ 83 H2  36  0N  86 30W
Tennessee →, U.S.A. ....... 82 G1  37  4N  88 34W
Teno, Pta. de, Canary Is. .... 24 F3  28 21N  16 55W
Tenom, Malaysia .......... 36 C5   5  4N 115 57 E
Tenosique, Mexico ......... 87 D6  17 30N  91 24W
Tenryū-Gawa →, Japan ...... 31 G8  35 39N 137 48 E
Tenterden, U.K. ........... 13 F8  51  4N   0 42 E
Tenterfield, Australia ....... 63 D5  29  0S 152  0 E
Teófilo Otoni, Brazil ........ 93 G10  17 50S  41 30W
Tepa, Indonesia ........... 37 F7   7 52S 129 31 E
Tepalcatepec →, Mexico ..... 86 D4  18 35N 101 59W
Tepehuanes, Mexico ........ 86 B3  25 21N 105 44W
Tepetongo, Mexico ......... 86 C4  22 28N 103  9W
Tepic, Mexico ............ 86 C4  21 30N 104 54W
Teplice, Czech Rep. ........ 16 C7  50 40N  13 48 E
Tepoca, C., Mexico ......... 86 A2  30 20N 112 25W
Tequila, Mexico ........... 86 C4  20 54N 103 47W
Ter →, Spain ............. 21 A7  42  2N   3 12 E
Ter Apel, Neths. ........... 15 B7  52 53N   7  5 E
Teraina, Kiribati .......... 65 G11  4 43N 160 25W
Téramo, Italy ............ 22 C5  42 39N  13 42 E
Terang, Australia .......... 63 F3  38 15S 142 55 E
Terang, Teluk, Indonesia ..... 37 K19  8 44S 116  0 E
Tercero →, Argentina ....... 94 C3  32 58S  61 47W
Terebovlya, Ukraine ........ 17 D13  49 18N  25 44 E
Terek →, Russia .......... 19 F8  44  0N  47 30 E
Terepaima △, Venezuela ..... 89 E6   9 58N  69 17W
Teresina, Brazil ........... 93 E10   5  9S  42 45W
Terewah, L., Australia ...... 63 D4  29 52S 147 35 E
Teridgerie Cr. →, Australia ... 63 E4  30 25S 148 50 E
Termez = Termiz, Uzbekistan . 28 F7  37 15N  67 15 E
Términi Imerese, Italy ...... 22 F5  37 59N  13 42 E
Términos, L. de, Mexico ..... 87 D6  18 35N  91 30W
Termiz, Uzbekistan ........ 28 F7  37 15N  67 15 E
Térmoli, Italy ............ 22 C6  42  0N  15  0 E
Ternate, Indonesia ........ 37 D7   0 45N 127 25 E
Terneuzen, Neths. ......... 15 C3  51 20N   3 50 E
Terney, Russia ........... 29 E14  45  3N 136 37 E
Terni, Italy .............. 22 C5  42 34N  12 37 E
Ternopil, Ukraine ......... 17 D13  49 30N  25 40 E
Ternopol = Ternopil, Ukraine . 17 D13  49 30N  25 40 E
Terowie, Australia ......... 63 E2  33  8S 138 55 E
Terra Bella, U.S.A. ......... 79 K7  35 58N 119  3W
Terra Nova △, Canada ...... 73 C9  48 33N  53 55W
Terrace, Canada ........... 70 C3  54 30N 128 35W
Terrace Bay, Canada ........ 72 C2  48 47N  87  5W
Terracina, Italy ........... 22 D5  41 17N  13 15 E
Terralba, Italy ............ 22 E3  39 43N   8 39 E
Terrassa, Spain ........... 21 B7  41 34N   2  1 E
Terre Haute, U.S.A. ........ 82 F2  39 28N  87 25W
Terrebonne B., U.S.A. ....... 81 L9  29  5N  90 35W
Terrell, U.S.A. ............ 81 J6  32 44N  96 17W
Terrenceville, Canada ....... 73 C9  47 40N  54 44W
Terry, U.S.A. ............. 80 B2  46 47N 105 19W
Terryville, U.S.A. .......... 85 E11  41 41N  73  3W
Terschelling, Neths. ........ 15 A5  53 25N   5 20 E
Teruel, Spain ............ 21 B5  40 22N   1  8W
Tervola, Finland .......... 8 C21  66 6N  24 49 E
Teryaweyna L., Australia .... 63 E3  32 18S 143 22 E
Teshio, Japan ............ 30 B10  44 53N 141 44 E
Teshio-Gawa →, Japan ...... 30 B10  44 53N 141 45 E
Tesiyn Gol →, Mongolia ..... 32 A4  50 40N  93 20 E
Teslin, Canada ........... 70 A2  60 10N 132 43W
Teslin →, Canada ......... 70 A2  61 34N 134 35W
Teslin L., Canada ......... 70 A2  60 15N 132 57W
Tessalit, Mali ............ 50 D6  20 12N   1  0 E

Test →, U.K. .............. 13 G6 50 56N 1 29W
Testigos, Is. Las, Venezuela . 89 D7 11 23N 63 7W
Tetachuck L., Canada ..... 70 C3 53 18N 125 55W
Tetas, Pta., Chile ......... 94 A1 23 31S 70 38W
Tete, Mozam. ............ 55 F3 16 13S 33 33 E
Tete □, Mozam. .......... 55 F3 15 15S 32 40 E
Teterev →, Ukraine ....... 17 C16 51 1N 30 5 E
Teteven, Bulgaria ........ 23 C11 42 58N 24 17 E
Tethul →, Canada ........ 70 A6 60 35N 112 12W
Tetiyev, Ukraine ......... 17 D15 49 22N 29 38 E
Teton →, U.S.A. ......... 76 C8 47 56N 110 31W
Tétouan, Morocco ........ 50 A4 35 35N 5 21W
Tetovo, Macedonia ....... 23 C9 42 1N 20 59 E
Teuco →, Argentina ...... 94 B3 25 35S 60 11W
Teulon, Canada .......... 71 C9 50 23N 97 16W
Teun, Indonesia ......... 37 F7 6 59S 129 8 E
Teutoburger Wald, Germany . 16 B5 52 5N 8 22 E
Tevere →, Italy .......... 22 D5 41 44N 12 14 E
Teverya, Israel .......... 46 C4 32 47N 35 32 E
Teviot →, U.K. .......... 11 F6 55 29N 2 38W
Tewantin, Australia ...... 63 D5 26 27S 153 3 E
Tewkesbury, U.K. ........ 13 F5 51 59N 2 9W
Texada I., Canada ....... 70 D4 49 40N 124 25W
Texarkana, Ark., U.S.A. ... 81 J8 33 26N 94 2W
Texarkana, Tex., U.S.A. ... 81 J7 33 26N 94 3W
Texas, Australia ......... 63 D5 28 49S 151 9 E
Texas □, U.S.A. ......... 81 K5 31 40N 98 30W
Texas City, U.S.A. ....... 81 L7 29 24N 94 54W
Texel, Neths. ........... 15 A4 53 5N 4 50 E
Texline, U.S.A. ......... 81 G3 36 23N 103 2W
Texoma, L., U.S.A. ...... 81 J6 33 50N 96 34W
Tezin, Afghan. .......... 42 B3 34 24N 69 30 E
Teziutlán, Mexico ....... 87 D5 19 50N 97 22W
Tezpur, India ........... 41 F18 26 40N 92 45 E
Tezzeron L., Canada ..... 70 C4 54 43N 124 30W
Tha-anne →, Canada ..... 71 A10 60 31N 94 37W
Tha Deua, Laos ......... 38 D4 17 57N 102 53 E
Tha Deua, Laos ......... 38 C3 19 26N 101 50 E
Tha Pla, Thailand ....... 38 D3 17 48N 100 32 E
Tha Rua, Thailand ...... 38 E3 14 34N 100 44 E
Tha Sala, Thailand ...... 39 H2 8 40N 99 56 E
Tha Song Yang, Thailand . 38 D1 17 34N 97 55 E
Thaba Putsoa, Lesotho ... 57 D4 29 45S 28 0 E
Thabana Ntlenyana, Lesotho . 57 D4 29 30S 29 16 E
Thabazimbi, S. Africa .... 57 C4 24 40S 27 21 E
Thādiq, Si. Arabia ...... 44 E5 25 18N 45 52 E
Thai Binh, Vietnam ...... 38 B6 20 35N 106 1 E
Thai Muang, Thailand .... 39 H2 8 24N 98 16 E
Thai Nguyen, Vietnam .... 38 B5 21 35N 105 55 E
Thailand ■, Asia ........ 38 E4 16 0N 102 0 E
Thailand, G. of, Asia .... 39 G3 11 30N 101 0 E
Thakhek, Laos .......... 38 D5 17 25N 104 45 E
Thal, Pakistan .......... 42 C4 33 28N 70 33 E
Thal Desert, Pakistan .... 42 D4 31 10N 71 30 E
Thala La = Hkakabo Razi, Burma 41 E20 28 25N 97 23 E
Thalabarivat, Cambodia ... 38 F5 13 33N 105 57 E
Thallon, Australia ....... 63 D4 28 39S 148 49 E
Thalu, Ko, Thailand ..... 39 b 9 26N 99 54 E
Thames →, N.Z. ........ 59 G5 37 7S 175 34 E
Thames →, Canada ...... 84 D2 42 20N 82 25W
Thames →, U.K. ........ 13 F8 51 29N 0 34 E
Thames →, U.S.A. ...... 85 E12 41 18N 72 5W
Thames Estuary, U.K. .... 13 F8 51 29N 0 52 E
Thamesford, Canada ..... 84 C4 43 4N 81 0W
Thamesville, Canada ..... 84 D3 42 33N 81 59W
Than, India ............ 42 H4 22 34N 71 11 E
Than Uyen, Vietnam ..... 38 B4 22 0N 103 54 E
Thana Gazi, India ....... 42 F7 27 25N 76 19 E
Thandla, India .......... 42 H6 23 0N 74 34 E
Thane, India ........... 40 K8 19 12N 72 59 E
Thanesar, India ......... 42 D7 30 1N 76 52 E
Thanet, I. of, U.K. ...... 13 F9 51 21N 1 20 E
Thangool, Australia ..... 62 C5 24 38S 150 42 E
Thanh Hoa, Vietnam ..... 38 C5 19 48N 105 46 E
Thanh Hung, Vietnam .... 39 H5 9 55N 105 43 E
Thanh Pho Ho Chi Minh, Vietnam 39 G6 10 58N 106 40 E
Thanh Thuy, Vietnam .... 38 A5 22 55N 104 51 E
Thanjavur, India ........ 40 P11 10 48N 79 12 E
Thano Bula Khan, Pakistan . 42 G2 25 22N 67 50 E
Thaolinta L., Canada .... 71 A9 61 30N 96 25W
Thap Lan △, Thailand ... 38 E4 14 15N 102 16 E
Thap Sakae, Thailand ... 39 G2 11 30N 99 37 E
Thap Than, Thailand .... 38 E2 15 27N 99 54 E
Thar Desert, India ...... 42 F5 28 0N 72 0 E
Tharad, India .......... 42 G4 24 30N 71 44 E
Thargomindah, Australia .. 63 D3 27 58S 143 46 E
Tharrawaddy, Burma ..... 41 L19 17 38N 95 48 E
Tharthar, L. = Tharthar, Buḩayrat ath, Iraq 44 C4 34 0N 43 15 E
Tharthar, W. ath →, Iraq . 44 C4 33 59N 43 12 E
Thásos, Greece ......... 23 D11 40 40N 24 40 E
That Khe, Vietnam ...... 38 A6 22 16N 106 28 E
Thatcher, Ariz., U.S.A. ... 77 K9 32 51N 109 46W
Thatcher, Colo., U.S.A. .. 81 G2 37 33N 104 7W
Thaton, Burma ......... 41 L20 16 55N 97 22 E
Thaungdut, Burma ...... 41 G19 24 30N 94 40 E
Thayer, U.S.A. ......... 81 G9 36 31N 91 33W
Thayetmyo, Burma ...... 41 K19 19 20N 95 10 E
Thazi, Burma .......... 41 J20 21 0N 96 5 E
The Bight, Bahamas ..... 89 B4 24 19N 75 24W
The Crane, Barbados .... 89 g 13 6N 59 27W
The Dalles, U.S.A. ...... 76 D3 45 36N 121 10W
The Great Divide = Great Dividing Ra., Australia . 62 C4 23 0S 146 0 E
The Hague = 's-Gravenhage, Neths. 15 B4 52 7N 4 17 E
The Pas, Canada ........ 71 C8 53 45N 101 15W
The Range, Zimbabwe .... 55 F3 19 2S 31 2 E
The Rock, Australia ..... 63 F4 35 15S 147 2 E
The Settlement, Br. Virgin Is. 89 e 18 43N 64 22W
The Woodlands, U.S.A. .. 81 K7 30 9N 95 27W
Thebes = Thívai, Greece .. 23 E10 38 19N 23 19 E
Thebes, Egypt .......... 51 C12 25 40N 32 35 E
Thedford, U.S.A. ....... 80 E4 41 59N 100 35W
Theebine, Australia ..... 63 D5 25 57S 152 34 E
Thekulthili L., Canada ... 71 A7 61 3N 110 0W
Thelon →, Canada ...... 71 A8 64 16N 96 4W
Theodore, Australia ..... 62 C5 24 55S 150 3 E
Theodore, Canada ...... 71 C8 51 26N 102 55W
Theodore, U.S.A. ....... 83 K1 30 33N 88 10W
Theodore Roosevelt △, U.S.A. 80 B3 47 0N 103 25W
Theodore Roosevelt L., U.S.A. 77 K8 33 40N 111 10W
Thepha, Thailand ....... 39 J3 6 52N 100 58 E
Theresa, U.S.A. ........ 85 B9 44 13N 75 48W
Thermaïkós Kólpos, Greece . 23 D10 40 15N 22 45 E
Thermopolis, U.S.A. .... 76 E9 43 39N 108 13W
Thermopylae P., Greece .. 23 E10 38 48N 22 35 E

Thessalon, Canada ...... 72 C3 46 20N 83 30W
Thessaloníki, Greece .... 23 D10 40 38N 22 58 E
Thessaloníki, Gulf of = Thermaïkós Kólpos, Greece . 23 D10 40 15N 22 45 E
Thetford, U.K. ......... 13 E8 52 25N 0 45 E
Thetford Mines, Canada . 73 C5 46 8N 71 18W
Theun →, Laos ........ 38 C5 18 19N 104 0 E
Theunissen, S. Africa ... 56 D4 28 26S 26 43 E
Thevenard, Australia .... 63 E1 32 9S 133 38 E
Thibodaux, U.S.A. ...... 81 L9 29 48N 90 49W
Thicket Portage, Canada . 71 B9 55 19N 97 42W
Thief River Falls, U.S.A. . 80 A6 48 7N 96 10W
Thiel Mts., Antarctica ... 5 E16 85 15S 91 0W
Thiers, France ......... 20 D5 45 52N 3 33 E
Thiès, Senegal ......... 50 F2 14 50N 16 51W
Thika, Kenya .......... 54 C4 1 1S 37 5 E
Thikombia, Fiji ......... 59 B9 15 44S 179 55W
Thimphu, Bhutan ....... 41 F16 27 31N 89 45 E
Þingvallavatn, Iceland .. 8 D3 64 11N 21 9W
Thionville, France ...... 20 B7 49 20N 6 10 E
Thíra, Greece .......... 23 F11 36 23N 25 27 E
Third Cataract, Sudan ... 51 E12 19 42N 30 20 E
Thirsk, U.K. ........... 12 C6 54 14N 1 19W
Thiruvananthapuram = Trivandrum, India ... 40 Q10 8 41N 77 0 E
Thisted, Denmark ...... 9 H13 56 58N 8 40 E
Thistle I., Australia ..... 63 F2 35 0S 136 8 E
Thívai, Greece ......... 23 E10 38 19N 23 19 E
Þjórsá →, Iceland ...... 8 E3 63 47N 20 48W
Thlewiaza →, Canada ... 71 A10 60 29N 94 40W
Thmar Puok, Cambodia .. 38 F4 13 57N 103 4 E
Tho Vinh, Vietnam ...... 38 C5 19 16N 105 42 E
Thoa →, Canada ....... 71 A7 60 31N 109 47W
Thoen, Thailand ....... 38 D2 17 43N 99 12 E
Thoeng, Thailand ...... 38 C3 19 41N 100 12 E
Thohoyandou, S. Africa .. 53 J6 22 58S 30 29 E
Tholdi, Pakistan ....... 43 B7 35 5N 76 6 E
Thomas, U.S.A. ........ 81 H5 35 45N 98 45W
Thomas, L., Australia ... 63 D2 26 4S 137 58 E
Thomaston, U.S.A. ..... 83 J3 32 53N 84 20W
Thomasville, Ala., U.S.A. 83 K2 31 55N 87 44W
Thomasville, Ga., U.S.A. 83 K4 30 50N 83 59W
Thomasville, N.C., U.S.A. 83 H5 35 53N 80 5W
Thompson, Canada ..... 71 B9 55 45N 97 52W
Thompson, U.S.A. ...... 85 E9 41 52N 75 31W
Thompson →, Canada .. 70 C4 50 15N 121 24W
Thompson →, U.S.A. ... 80 F8 39 46N 93 37W
Thompson Falls, U.S.A. . 76 C6 47 36N 115 21W
Thompson Pk., U.S.A. .. 76 F2 41 0N 123 0W
Thompson Springs, U.S.A. 77 G9 38 58N 109 43W
Thompsontown, U.S.A. .. 84 F7 40 33N 77 14W
Thomson, U.S.A. ....... 83 J4 33 28N 82 30W
Thomson →, Australia .. 62 C3 25 11S 142 53 E
Thong Yang, Thailand ... 39 b 9 28N 99 56 E
Þórisvatn, Iceland ...... 8 D4 64 20N 18 55W
Thornaby on Tees, U.K. . 12 C6 54 33N 1 18W
Thornbury, Canada ..... 84 B4 44 34N 80 26W
Thorne, U.K. .......... 12 D7 53 37N 0 57W
Thornhill, Canada ...... 70 C3 54 31N 128 32W
Thorold, Canada ....... 84 C5 43 7N 79 12W
Þórshöfn, Iceland ...... 8 C6 66 12N 15 20W
Thouin, C., Australia .... 60 D2 20 20S 118 10 E
Thousand Oaks, U.S.A. .. 79 L8 34 10N 118 50W
Thrace, Turkey ........ 23 D12 41 0N 27 0 E
Three Forks, U.S.A. .... 76 D8 45 54N 111 33W
Three Hills, Canada .... 70 C6 51 43N 113 15W
Three Hummock I., Australia 63 G3 40 25S 144 55 E
Three Pagodas Pass, Asia 38 E2 15 20N 98 30 E
Three Points, C., Ghana . 50 H5 4 42N 2 6W
Three Rivers, Calif., U.S.A. 78 J8 36 26N 118 54W
Three Rivers, Tex., U.S.A. 81 L5 28 28N 98 11W
Three Sisters, U.S.A. ... 76 D3 44 4N 121 51W
Three Springs, Australia . 61 E2 29 32S 115 45 E
Throssell, L., Australia .. 61 E3 27 33S 124 10 E
Throssell Ra., Australia . 60 D3 22 3S 121 43 E
Thruxton △, Australia ... 60 D3 24 47S 147 40 E
Thuan Hoa, Vietnam .... 39 H5 8 58N 105 30 E
Thubun Lakes, Canada .. 71 A6 61 30N 112 0W
Thuin, Belgium ........ 15 D4 50 20N 4 17 E
Thule = Qaanaaq, Greenland . 4 B4 77 40N 69 0W
Thule Air Base = Uummannaq, Greenland 4 B5 70 58N 52 0W
Thun, Switz. .......... 20 C7 46 45N 7 38 E
Thunder B., U.S.A. ..... 84 B1 45 0N 83 20W
Thunder Bay, Canada ... 72 C2 48 20N 89 15W
Thung Salaeng Luang △, Thailand 38 D3 16 43N 100 50 E
Thung Song, Thailand ... 39 H2 8 10N 99 40 E
Thunkar, Bhutan ....... 41 F17 27 55N 91 0 E
Thüringer Wald, Germany . 16 C6 50 35N 11 0 E
Thurles, Ireland ....... 10 D4 52 41N 7 49W
Thurrock □, U.K. ....... 13 F8 51 31N 0 23 E
Thursday I., Australia ... 62 A3 10 30S 142 3 E
Thurso, Canada ........ 72 C4 45 36N 75 15W
Thurso, U.K. .......... 11 C5 58 36N 3 32W
Thurso →, U.K. ........ 11 C5 58 36N 3 32W
Thurston I., Antarctica .. 5 D16 72 0S 100 0W
Thutade L., Canada ..... 70 B3 57 0N 126 55W
Thyolo, Malawi ........ 55 F4 16 7S 35 5 E
Ti Tree, Australia ...... 62 C1 22 5S 133 22 E
Tian Shan, Asia ....... 32 B3 40 30N 76 0 E
Tianjin, China ......... 35 E9 39 8N 117 10 E
Tianshui, China ....... 34 G3 34 32N 105 40 E
Tianyar, Indonesia ..... 37 J18 8 12S 115 30 E
Tianzhen, China ....... 34 D8 40 24N 114 5 E
Tianzhuangtai, China ... 35 D12 40 43N 122 5 E
Tiaret, Algeria ........ 50 A6 35 20N 1 21 E
Tibagi, Brazil ......... 95 A5 24 30S 50 24W
Tibagi →, Brazil ....... 95 A5 22 47S 51 1W
Tiber = Tevere →, Italy . 22 D5 41 44N 12 14 E
Tiberias = Teverya, Israel . 46 C4 32 47N 35 32 E
Tiberias, L. = Yam Kinneret, Israel 46 C4 32 45N 35 35 E
Tibesti, Chad ......... 51 D9 21 0N 17 30 E
Tibet = Xizang Zizhiqu □, China 32 C3 32 0N 88 0 E
Tibet, Plateau of, Asia .. 26 F12 32 0N 86 0 E
Tibooburra, Australia ... 63 D3 29 26S 142 1 E
Tiburón, I., Mexico ..... 86 B2 29 0N 112 30W
Ticino →, Italy ........ 20 D8 45 9N 9 14 E
Ticonderoga, U.S.A. .... 85 C11 43 51N 73 26W
Ticul, Mexico ......... 87 C7 20 20N 89 31W
Tidaholm, Sweden ..... 9 G15 58 12N 13 58 E
Tiddim, Burma ........ 41 H18 23 28N 93 45 E
Tidioute, U.S.A. ....... 84 E5 41 41N 79 24W
Tidjikja, Mauritania .... 50 E3 18 29N 11 35W
Tidore, Indonesia ...... 37 D7 0 40N 127 25 E

Tiegang Shuiku, China ... 33 F10 22 37N 113 53 E
Tiel, Neths. ........... 15 C5 51 53N 5 26 E
Tieling, China ......... 35 C12 42 20N 123 55 E
Tielt, Belgium ......... 15 C3 51 0N 3 20 E
Tien Shan = Tian Shan, Asia 32 B3 40 30N 76 0 E
Tien-tsin = Tianjin, China 35 E9 39 8N 117 10 E
Tien Yen, Vietnam ...... 38 B6 21 20N 107 24 E
T'ienching = Tianjin, China 35 E9 39 8N 117 10 E
Tienen, Belgium ....... 15 D4 50 48N 4 57 E
Tientsin = Tianjin, China . 35 E9 39 8N 117 10 E
Tieri, Australia ........ 62 C4 23 2S 148 21 E
Tierra Amarilla, Chile ... 94 B1 27 28S 70 18W
Tierra Amarilla, U.S.A. .. 77 H10 36 42N 106 33W
Tierra Colorada, Mexico . 87 D5 17 10N 99 35W
Tierra de Campos, Spain . 21 A3 42 10N 4 50W
Tierra del Fuego, I. Gr. de, Argentina 96 G3 54 0S 69 0W
Tiétar →, Spain ....... 21 C3 39 50N 6 1W
Tieté →, Brazil ........ 95 A5 20 40S 51 35W
Tiffin, U.S.A. ......... 82 E4 41 7N 83 11W
Tifton, U.S.A. ......... 83 K4 31 27N 83 31W
Tifu, Indonesia ....... 37 E7 3 39S 126 24 E
Tighina, Moldova ...... 17 E15 46 50N 29 30 E
Tigil, Russia .......... 29 D16 57 49N 158 40 E
Tignish, Canada ....... 73 C7 46 58N 64 2W
Tigre →, Peru ......... 92 D4 4 30S 74 10W
Tigre →, Venezuela .... 92 B6 9 20N 62 30W
Tigris = Dijlah, Nahr →, Asia 44 D5 31 0N 47 25 E
Tigyaing, Burma ....... 41 H20 23 45N 96 10 E
Tijara, India .......... 42 F7 27 56N 76 31 E
Tijuana, Mexico ....... 79 N9 32 30N 117 10W
Tikal, Guatemala ...... 88 C2 17 13N 89 24W
Tikal △, Guatemala .... 88 C2 17 23N 89 34W
Tikamgarh, India ...... 43 G8 24 44N 78 50 E
Tikhoretsk, Russia ..... 19 E7 45 56N 40 5 E
Tikhvin, Russia ....... 18 C5 59 35N 33 30 E
Tikiraqjuaq = Whale Cove, Canada 71 A10 62 10N 92 34W
Tikrit, Iraq ........... 44 C4 34 35N 43 37 E
Tiksi, Russia ......... 29 B13 71 40N 128 45 E
Tilamuta, Indonesia .... 37 D6 0 32N 122 23 E
Tilburg, Neths. ........ 15 C5 51 31N 5 6 E
Tilbury, Canada ....... 84 D2 42 17N 82 23W
Tilbury, U.K. ......... 13 F8 51 27N 0 22 E
Tilcara, Argentina ..... 94 A2 23 36S 65 23W
Tilden, U.S.A. ........ 80 D6 42 3N 97 50W
Tilhar, India .......... 43 F8 28 0N 79 45 E
Tilichiki, Russia ...... 29 C17 60 27N 166 5 E
Tílissos, Greece ...... 25 D7 35 20N 25 1 E
Till →, U.K. .......... 12 B5 55 41N 2 13W
Tillamook, U.S.A. ..... 76 D2 45 27N 123 51W
Tillsonburg, Canada ... 84 D4 42 53N 80 44W
Tillyeria, Cyprus ...... 25 D11 35 6N 32 40 E
Tilos, Greece ......... 23 F12 36 27N 27 27 E
Tilpa, Australia ....... 63 E3 30 57S 144 24 E
Tilt →, U.K. .......... 11 E5 56 46N 3 51W
Tilton, U.S.A. ........ 85 C13 43 27N 71 36W
Tiltonsville, U.S.A. .... 84 F4 40 10N 80 41W
Timagami, L., Canada .. 72 C3 47 0N 80 10W
Timanfaya △, Canary Is. . 24 F6 29 0N 13 46W
Timanskiy Kryazh, Russia 18 A9 65 58N 50 5 E
Timaru, N.Z. .......... 59 L3 44 23S 171 14 E
Timau, Kenya ......... 54 B4 0 4N 37 15 E
Timbákion, Greece ..... 25 D6 35 4N 24 45 E
Timber Creek, Australia . 60 C5 15 40S 130 29 E
Timber Lake, U.S.A. .... 80 C4 45 26N 101 5W
Timber Mt., U.S.A. ..... 78 H10 37 6N 116 28W
Timbuktu = Tombouctou, Mali 50 E5 16 50N 3 0W
Timi, Cyprus ......... 25 E11 34 44N 32 31 E
Timimoun, Algeria .... 50 C6 29 14N 0 17 E
Timirist, Râs, Mauritania 50 E2 19 21N 16 30W
Timișkaming = Témiscamingue, L., Canada 72 C4 47 10N 79 25W
Timișoara, Romania ... 17 F11 45 43N 21 15 E
Timmins, Canada ..... 72 C3 48 28N 81 25W
Timok →, Serbia & M. .. 23 B10 44 10N 22 40 E
Timor, Asia .......... 37 F7 9 0S 125 0 E
Timor Leste = East Timor ■, Asia 37 F7 8 50S 126 0 E
Timor Sea, Ind. Oc. .... 60 B4 12 0S 127 0 E
Tin Can Bay, Australia . 63 D5 25 56S 153 0 E
Tin Mt., U.S.A. ....... 78 J9 36 50N 117 10W
Tina →, S. Africa ..... 57 E4 31 18S 29 13 E
Tinaca Pt., Phil. ...... 37 C7 5 30N 125 25 E
Tinajo, Canary Is. ..... 24 E6 29 4N 13 42W
Tindal, Australia ...... 60 B5 14 31S 132 22 E
Tindouf, Algeria ...... 50 C4 27 42N 8 10W
Tinfunque △, Paraguay . 94 A3 23 55S 60 17W
Tinggi, Pulau, Malaysia . 39 L5 2 18N 104 7 E
Tingo Maria, Peru ..... 92 E3 9 10S 75 54W
Tingrela, Ivory C. ..... 50 F4 10 27N 6 25W
Tinh Bien, Vietnam .... 39 G5 10 36N 104 57 E
Tinnevelly = Tirunelveli, India 40 Q10 8 45N 77 45 E
Tinogasta, Argentina ... 94 B2 28 5S 67 32W
Tinos, Greece ........ 23 F11 37 33N 25 8 E
Tinpahar, India ....... 43 G12 24 59N 87 44 E
Tintina, Argentina ..... 94 B3 27 2S 62 45W
Tintinara, Australia ... 63 F3 35 48S 140 2 E
Tioga, N. Dak., U.S.A. . 80 A3 48 23N 102 56W
Tioga, Pa., U.S.A. ..... 84 E7 41 55N 77 8W
Tioman, Pulau, Malaysia . 39 L5 2 50N 104 10 E
Tionesta, U.S.A. ...... 84 E5 41 30N 79 28W
Tipongpani, India ..... 41 F19 27 20N 95 55 E
Tipperary, Ireland .... 10 D3 52 28N 8 10W
Tipperary □, Ireland ... 10 D4 52 37N 7 55W
Tipton, Calif., U.S.A. .. 78 J7 36 4N 119 19W
Tipton, Iowa, U.S.A. ... 80 E9 41 46N 91 8W
Tipton, Mt., U.S.A. .... 79 K12 35 32N 114 12W
Tiptonville, U.S.A. .... 81 G10 36 23N 89 29W
Tīrān, Iran .......... 45 C6 32 45N 51 8 E
Tiranë, Albania ....... 23 D8 41 18N 19 49 E
Tiraspol, Moldova ..... 17 E15 46 55N 29 35 E
Tire, Turkey ......... 23 E12 38 5N 27 50 E
Tirebolu, Turkey ...... 19 F6 40 58N 38 45 E
Tiree, U.K. .......... 11 E2 56 31N 6 55W
Tiree, Passage of, U.K. . 11 E2 56 30N 6 30W
Tîrgovişte = Târgovişte, Romania 17 F13 44 55N 25 27 E
Tîrgu-Jiu = Târgu-Jiu, Romania 17 F12 45 5N 23 19 E
Tîrgu Mureş = Târgu Mureş, Romania 17 E13 46 31N 24 38 E
Tirich Mir, Pakistan .... 40 A7 36 15N 71 55 E
Tírnavos, Greece ...... 23 E10 39 45N 22 18 E
Tirodi, India ......... 40 J11 21 40N 79 44 E
Tirol □, Austria ....... 16 E6 47 3N 10 43 E
Tirso →, Italy ........ 22 D3 39 53N 8 32 E
Tiruchchirappalli, India . 40 P11 10 45N 78 45 E
Tirunelveli, India ..... 40 Q10 8 45N 77 45 E

Tirupati, India ........ 40 N11 13 39N 79 25 E
Tiruppur, India ........ 40 P10 11 5N 77 22 E
Tiruvannamalai, India .. 40 N11 12 15N 79 5 E
Tisa, India ........... 42 C7 32 50N 76 9 E
Tisa →, Serbia & M. .... 23 B9 45 15N 20 17 E
Tisdale, Canada ....... 71 C8 52 50N 104 0W
Tishomingo, U.S.A. .... 81 H6 34 14N 96 41W
Tisza = Tisa →, Serbia & M. 23 B9 45 15N 20 17 E
Tit-Ary, Russia ....... 29 B13 71 55N 127 2 E
Tithwal, Pakistan ..... 43 B5 34 21N 73 50 E
Titicaca, L., S. Amer. .. 92 G5 15 30S 69 30W
Titule, Dem. Rep. of the Congo 54 B2 3 15N 25 31 E
Titusville, Fla., U.S.A. .. 83 L5 28 37N 80 49W
Titusville, Pa., U.S.A. .. 84 E5 41 38N 79 41W
Tivaouane, Senegal .... 50 F2 14 56N 16 45W
Tiverton, U.K. ........ 13 G4 50 54N 3 29W
Tívoli, Italy .......... 22 D5 41 58N 12 45 E
Tizi-Ouzou, Algeria .... 50 A6 36 42N 4 3 E
Tizimín, Mexico ....... 87 C7 21 0N 88 1W
Tjeggelvas, Sweden ... 8 C17 66 37N 17 45 E
Tjeggelvas = Tjeggelvas, Sweden 8 C17 66 37N 17 45 E
Tjirebon = Cirebon, Indonesia 36 F3 6 45S 108 32 E
Tjluring, Indonesia .... 37 J17 8 25S 114 13 E
Tjörn, Sweden ....... 9 G14 58 0N 11 35 E
Tlacotalpan, Mexico ... 87 D5 18 37N 95 40W
Tlahualilo, Mexico .... 86 B4 26 20N 103 30W
Tlaquepaque, Mexico ... 86 C4 20 39N 103 19W
Tlaxcala, Mexico ...... 87 D5 19 20N 98 14W
Tlaxcala □, Mexico .... 87 D5 19 30N 98 20W
Tlaxiaco, Mexico ...... 87 D5 17 18N 97 40W
Tlemcen, Algeria ...... 50 B5 34 52N 1 21W
To Bong, Vietnam ..... 38 F7 12 45N 109 16 E
Toa Payoh, Singapore .. 39 d 1 20N 103 51 E
Toad →, Canada ...... 70 B4 59 25N 124 57W
Toad River, Canada .... 70 B3 58 51S 125 14W
Toamasina, Madag. .... 57 B8 18 10S 49 25 E
Toamasina □, Madag. .. 57 B8 18 0S 49 0 E
Toay, Argentina ....... 94 D3 36 43S 64 38W
Toba, Japan .......... 31 G8 34 30N 136 51 E
Toba, Danau, Indonesia . 36 D1 2 30N 97 30 E
Toba Kakar, Pakistan ... 42 D3 31 30N 69 0 E
Toba Tek Singh, Pakistan 42 D5 30 55N 72 25 E
Tobago, Trin. & Tob. ... 89 D7 11 10N 60 30W
Tobelo, Indonesia ..... 37 D7 1 45N 127 56 E
Tobermory, Canada .... 84 A3 45 12N 81 40W
Tobermory, U.K. ...... 11 E2 56 38N 6 5W
Tobi, Pac. Oc. ........ 37 D8 2 40N 131 10 E
Tobin, U.S.A. ........ 78 F5 39 55N 121 19W
Tobin, L., Australia .... 60 D4 21 45S 125 49 E
Tobin, L., Canada ..... 71 C8 53 35N 103 30W
Toboali, Indonesia .... 36 E3 3 0S 106 25 E
Tobol →, Russia ...... 28 D7 58 10N 68 12 E
Toboli, Indonesia ..... 37 E6 0 38S 120 5 E
Tobolsk, Russia ...... 28 D7 58 15N 68 10 E
Tobruk = Tubruq, Libya . 51 B10 32 7N 23 55 E
Tobyhanna, U.S.A. .... 85 E9 41 11N 75 25W
Tobyl = Tobol →, Russia 28 D7 58 10N 68 12 E
Tocantinópolis, Brazil .. 93 E9 6 20S 47 25W
Tocantins □, Brazil .... 93 F9 10 0S 48 0W
Tocantins →, Brazil .... 93 D9 1 45S 49 10W
Toccoa, U.S.A. ....... 83 H4 34 35N 83 19W
Tochi →, Pakistan ..... 42 C4 32 49N 70 41 E
Tochigi, Japan ....... 31 F9 36 25N 139 45 E
Tochigi □, Japan ...... 31 F9 36 45N 139 45 E
Toco, Trin. & Tob. ..... 93 K16 10 49N 60 57W
Toconao, Chile ....... 94 A2 23 11S 68 1W
Tocopilla, Chile ...... 94 A1 22 5S 70 10W
Tocumwal, Australia ... 63 F4 35 51S 145 31 E
Tocuyo →, Venezuela .. 92 A5 11 3N 68 23W
Todd →, Australia ..... 62 C2 24 52S 135 48 E
Todeli, Indonesia ..... 37 E6 1 40S 124 29 E
Todenyang, Kenya ..... 54 B4 4 35N 35 56 E
Todgarh, India ....... 42 G5 25 42N 73 58 E
Todos os Santos, B. de, Brazil 93 F11 12 48S 38 38W
Todos Santos, Mexico .. 86 C2 23 27N 110 13W
Toe Hd., U.K. ........ 11 D1 57 50N 7 8W
Tofield, Canada ...... 70 C6 53 25N 112 40W
Tofino, Canada ....... 70 D3 49 11N 125 55W
Tofua, Tonga ......... 59 D11 19 45S 175 5W
Tōgane, Japan ........ 31 G10 35 33N 140 22 E
Togian, Kepulauan, Indonesia 37 E6 0 20S 121 50 E
Togliatti, Russia ...... 18 D8 53 32N 49 24 E
Togo ■, W. Afr. ....... 50 G6 8 30N 1 35 E
Togtoh, China ........ 34 D6 40 15N 111 10 E
Tōhoku □, Japan ...... 30 E10 39 50N 141 45 E
Tōhom, Mongolia ..... 34 B5 44 27N 108 2 E
Toinya, Sudan ........ 51 G11 6 17N 29 46 E
Toiyabe Range, U.S.A. . 76 G5 39 30N 117 0W
Tojikiston = Tajikistan ■, Asia 28 F8 38 30N 70 0 E
Tojo, Indonesia ....... 37 E6 1 20S 121 15 E
Tōjō, Japan .......... 31 G6 34 53N 133 16 E
Tok, U.S.A. .......... 68 B5 63 20N 142 59W
Tok-do, Asia ......... 31 F5 37 15N 131 52 E
Tokachi-Dake, Japan ... 30 C11 43 17N 142 5 E
Tokachi-Gawa →, Japan 30 C11 42 44N 143 42 E
Tokala, Indonesia ..... 37 E6 1 30N 121 40 E
Tōkamachi, Japan ..... 31 F9 37 8N 138 43 E
Tokanui, N.Z. ........ 59 M2 46 34S 168 56 E
Tokara-Rettō, Japan ... 31 K4 29 37N 129 43 E
Tokarahi, N.Z. ........ 59 L3 44 56S 170 39 E
Tokashiki-Shima, Japan . 31 L3 26 11N 127 21 E
Tokat, Turkey ........ 19 F6 40 22N 36 35 E
Tŏkch'ŏn, N. Korea .... 35 E14 39 45N 126 18 E
Tokeland, U.S.A. ...... 78 D3 46 42N 123 59W
Tokelau Is., Pac. Oc. ... 64 H10 9 0S 171 45W
Tokmak, Kyrgyzstan ... 28 E8 42 49N 75 15 E
Toko Ra., Australia .... 62 C2 23 5S 138 20 E
Tokoro-Gawa →, Japan 30 B12 44 7N 144 5 E
Tokuno-Shima, Japan .. 31 L4 27 56N 128 55 E
Tokushima, Japan ..... 31 G7 34 4N 134 34 E
Tokushima □, Japan ... 31 H7 33 55N 134 0 E
Tokuyama, Japan ...... 31 G5 34 3N 131 50 E
Tōkyō, Japan ........ 31 G9 35 45N 139 45 E
Tolaga Bay, N.Z. ...... 59 H7 38 21S 178 20 E
Tolbukhin = Dobrich, Bulgaria 23 C12 43 37N 27 49 E
Toledo, Brazil ........ 95 A5 24 44S 53 45W
Toledo, Spain ........ 21 C3 39 50N 4 2W
Toledo, Ohio, U.S.A. ... 82 E4 41 39N 83 33W
Toledo, Oreg., U.S.A. .. 76 D2 44 37N 123 56W
Toledo, Wash., U.S.A. .. 76 C2 46 26N 122 51W
Toledo, Montes de, Spain 21 C3 39 33N 4 20W
Toledo Bend Reservoir, U.S.A. 81 K8 31 11N 93 34W
Tolga, Australia ....... 62 B4 17 15S 145 29 E
Toliara, Madag. ....... 57 C7 23 21S 43 40 E
Toliara □, Madag. ..... 57 C8 21 0S 45 0 E
Tolima, Colombia ..... 92 C3 4 40N 75 19W
Tolitoli, Indonesia .... 37 D6 1 5N 120 50 E

Tollhouse, U.S.A. ........... 78 H7 37 1N 119 24W
Tolo, Teluk, Indonesia ...... 37 E6 2 0S 122 10 E
Tolo Harbour, China ........ 33 G11 22 27N 114 12 E
Toluca, Mexico ............. 87 D5 19 20N 99 40W
Tom Burke, S. Africa ....... 57 C4 23 5S 28 0 E
Tom Price, Australia ........ 60 D2 22 40S 117 48 E
Tomah, U.S.A. ............. 80 D9 43 59N 90 30W
Tomahawk, U.S.A. ......... 80 C10 45 28N 89 44W
Tomakomai, Japan ......... 30 C10 42 38N 141 36 E
Tomales, U.S.A. ........... 78 G4 38 15N 122 53W
Tomales B., U.S.A. ......... 78 G3 38 15N 123 58W
Tomar, Portugal ........... 21 C1 39 36N 8 25W
Tomaszów Mazowiecki, Poland 17 C10 51 30N 20 2 E
Tomatlán, Mexico .......... 86 D3 19 56N 105 15W
Tombador, Serra do, Brazil . 92 F7 12 0S 58 0W
Tombigbee →, U.S.A. ...... 83 K2 31 8N 87 57W
Tombouctou, Mali ......... 50 E5 16 50N 3 0W
Tombstone, U.S.A. ......... 77 L8 31 43N 110 4W
Tombua, Angola ........... 56 B1 15 55S 11 55 E
Tomé, Chile ............... 94 D1 36 36S 72 57W
Tomelloso, Spain .......... 21 C4 39 10N 3 2W
Tomini, Indonesia ......... 37 D6 0 30N 120 30 E
Tomini, Teluk, Indonesia ... 37 E6 0 10S 121 0 E
Tomintoul, U.K. ........... 11 D5 57 15N 3 23W
Tomkinson Ranges, Australia 61 E4 26 11S 129 5 E
Tommot, Russia ........... 29 D13 59 4N 126 20 E
Tomnop Ta Suos, Cambodia . 39 G5 11 20N 104 15 E
Tomo →, Colombia ........ 92 B5 5 20N 67 48W
Toms Place, U.S.A. ........ 78 H8 37 34N 118 41W
Toms River, U.S.A. ........ 85 G10 39 58N 74 12W
Tomsk, Russia ............ 28 D9 56 30N 85 5 E
Tonalá, Mexico ............ 87 D6 16 8N 93 41W
Tonantins, Brazil .......... 92 D5 2 45S 67 45W
Tonasket, U.S.A. .......... 76 B4 48 42N 119 26W
Tonawanda, U.S.A. ........ 84 D6 43 1N 78 53W
Tonb, Iran ................ 45 E7 26 15N 55 15 E
Tonbridge, U.K. ........... 13 F8 51 11N 0 17 E
Tondano, Indonesia ....... 37 D6 1 35N 124 54 E
Tondoro, Namibia ......... 56 B2 17 45S 18 50 E
Tone →, Australia ......... 61 F2 34 25S 116 25 E
Tone-Gawa →, Japan ...... 31 F9 35 44N 140 51 E
Tonekābon, Iran .......... 45 B6 36 45N 51 12 E
Tong Xian, China ......... 34 E9 39 55N 116 35 E
Tonga ■, Pac. Oc. ........ 59 D11 19 50S 174 30W
Tonga Trench, Pac. Oc. .... 64 J10 18 0S 173 0W
Tongaat, S. Africa ........ 57 D5 29 33S 31 9 E
Tongareva, Cook Is. ....... 65 H12 9 0S 158 0W
Tongariro △, N.Z. ......... 59 H5 39 8S 175 33 E
Tongatapu Group, Tonga ... 59 E12 21 0S 175 0W
Tongchŏn-ni, N. Korea .... 35 E14 39 50N 127 25 E
Tongchuan, China ......... 34 G5 35 6N 109 3 E
Tongeren, Belgium ........ 15 D5 50 47N 5 28 E
Tonggu Jiao, China ....... 33 G10 22 22N 113 37 E
Tongguan, China ......... 34 G6 34 40N 110 25 E
Tonghae, S. Korea ........ 35 F15 37 29N 129 7 E
Tonghua, China .......... 35 D13 41 42N 125 58 E
Tongjosŏn Man, N. Korea . 35 E15 39 30N 128 0 E
Tongking, G. of = Tonkin, G. of,
  Asia .................. 32 E5 20 0N 108 0 E
Tongliao, China .......... 35 C12 43 38N 122 18 E
Tongling, China .......... 33 C6 30 55N 117 48 E
Tongnae, S. Korea ........ 35 G15 35 12N 129 5 E
Tongobory, Madag. ....... 57 C7 23 32S 44 20 E
Tongoy, Chile ............ 94 C1 30 16S 71 31W
Tongres = Tongeren, Belgium 15 D5 50 47N 5 28 E
Tongsa Dzong, Bhutan .... 41 F17 27 31N 90 31 E
Tongue, U.K. ............. 11 C4 58 29N 4 25W
Tongue →, U.S.A. ........ 80 B2 46 25N 105 52W
Tongwei, China .......... 34 G3 35 0N 105 5 E
Tongxin, China .......... 34 F3 36 59N 105 58 E
Tongyang, N. Korea ...... 35 E14 39 9N 126 53 E
Tongyu, China ........... 35 B12 44 45N 123 4 E
Tonj, Sudan ............. 51 G11 7 20N 28 44 E
Tonk, India .............. 42 F6 26 6N 75 54 E
Tonkawa, U.S.A. ......... 81 G6 36 41N 97 18W
Tonkin = Bac Phan, Vietnam 38 B5 22 0N 105 0 E
Tonkin, G. of, Asia ....... 32 E5 20 0N 108 0 E
Tonle Sap, Cambodia ..... 38 F4 13 0N 104 0 E
Tono, Japan ............. 30 E10 39 19N 141 32 E
Tonopah, U.S.A. ......... 77 G5 38 4N 117 14W
Tonosí, Panama ......... 88 E3 7 20N 80 20W
Tons →, Haryana, India .. 42 D7 30 30N 77 39 E
Tons →, Ut. P., India .... 43 F10 24 1N 83 33 E
Tønsberg, Norway ........ 9 G14 59 19N 10 25 E
Tonto →, U.S.A. ......... 77 K8 33 39N 111 7W
Toobanna, Australia ...... 62 B4 18 42S 146 9 E
Toodyay, Australia ....... 61 F2 31 34S 116 28 E
Tooele, U.S.A. ........... 76 F7 40 32N 112 18W
Toompine, Australia ...... 63 D3 27 15S 144 19 E
Toora, Australia ......... 63 F4 38 39S 146 23 E
Toora-Khem, Russia ...... 29 D10 52 28N 96 17 E
Toowoomba, Australia .... 63 D5 27 32S 151 56 E
Top-ozero, Russia ........ 18 A5 65 35N 32 0 E
Top Springs, Australia .... 60 C5 16 37S 131 51 E
Topaz, U.S.A. ........... 78 G7 38 41N 119 30W
Topeka, U.S.A. ........... 80 F7 39 3N 95 40W
Topley, Canada .......... 70 C3 54 49N 126 18W
Topocalma, Pta., Chile ... 94 C1 34 10S 72 2W
Topock, U.S.A. .......... 79 L12 34 46N 114 29W
Topol'čany, Slovak Rep. .. 17 D10 48 35N 18 12 E
Topolobampo, Mexico .... 86 B3 25 40N 109 4W
Toppenish, U.S.A. ....... 76 C3 46 23N 120 19W
Toraka Vestale, Madag. .. 57 B7 16 20S 43 58 E
Torata, Peru ............ 92 G4 17 23S 70 1W
Torbalı, Turkey .......... 23 E12 38 10N 27 21 E
Torbat-e Heydārīyeh, Iran . 45 C8 35 15N 59 12 E
Torbat-e Jām, Iran ....... 45 C9 35 16N 60 35 E
Torbay, Canada ......... 73 C9 47 40N 52 42W
Torbay □, U.K. .......... 13 G4 50 26N 3 31W
Tordesillas, Spain ....... 21 B3 41 30N 5 0W
Torfaen □, U.K. ......... 13 F4 51 43N 3 3W
Torgau, Germany ........ 16 C7 51 34N 13 0 E
Torhout, Belgium ........ 15 C3 51 5N 3 7 E
Tori-Shima, Japan ....... 31 J10 30 29N 140 19 E
Torin, Mexico ........... 86 B2 27 33N 110 15W
Torino, Italy ............ 20 D7 45 3N 7 40 E
Torit, Sudan ............ 51 H12 4 27N 32 31 E
Torkamān, Iran ......... 44 B5 37 35N 47 23 E
Tormes →, Spain ........ 21 B2 41 18N 6 29W
Tornado Mt., Canada .... 70 D6 49 55N 114 40W
Torneå = Tornio, Finland . 8 D21 65 50N 24 12 E
Torneälven →, Europe ... 8 D21 65 50N 24 12 E
Torneträsk, Sweden ..... 8 B18 68 24N 19 15 E
Tornio, Finland ......... 8 D21 65 50N 24 12 E
Tornionjoki = Torneälven →,
  Europe ............... 8 D21 65 50N 24 12 E
Tornquist, Argentina .... 94 D3 38 8S 62 15W
Toro, Spain ............. 24 B11 39 59N 4 8 E

Toro △, Uganda .......... 54 C3 0 5S 30 22 E
Toro, Cerro del, Chile .... 94 B2 29 10S 69 50W
Toro Pk., U.S.A. ......... 79 M10 33 34N 116 24W
Toroníios Kólpos, Greece . 23 D10 40 5N 23 30 E
Toronto, Canada ........ 84 C5 43 39N 79 20W
Toronto, U.S.A. ......... 84 F4 40 28N 80 36W
Toronto Lester B. Pearson
  International ✈ (YYZ), Canada 84 C5 43 40N 79 34W
Toropets, Russia ........ 18 C5 56 30N 31 40 E
Tororo, Uganda ......... 54 B3 0 45N 34 12 E
Toros Dağları, Turkey .... 19 G5 37 0N 32 30 E
Torpa, India ............ 43 H11 22 57N 85 6 E
Torquay, U.K. ........... 13 G4 50 27N 3 32W
Torrance, U.S.A. ......... 79 M8 33 50N 118 19W
Torre de Moncorvo, Portugal 21 B2 41 12N 7 8W
Torre del Greco, Italy .... 22 D6 40 47N 14 22 E
Torrejón de Ardoz, Spain . 21 B4 40 27N 3 29W
Torrelavega, Spain ...... 21 A3 43 20N 4 5W
Torremolinos, Spain ..... 21 D3 36 38N 4 30W
Torrens, L., Australia .... 63 E2 31 0S 137 50 E
Torrens Cr. →, Australia . 62 C4 22 23S 145 9 E
Torrens Creek, Australia . 62 C4 20 48S 145 3 E
Torrent, Spain .......... 21 C5 39 27N 0 28W
Torreón, Mexico ........ 86 B4 25 33N 103 26W
Torres, Brazil ........... 95 B5 29 21S 49 44W
Torres, Mexico .......... 86 B2 28 46N 110 47W
Torres Strait, Australia ... 64 H6 9 50S 142 20 E
Torres Vedras, Portugal .. 21 C1 39 5N 9 15W
Torrevieja, Spain ....... 21 D5 37 59N 0 42W
Torrey, U.S.A. ........... 77 G8 38 18N 111 25W
Torridge →, U.K. ........ 13 G3 51 0N 4 13W
Torridon, L., U.K. ....... 11 D3 57 35N 5 50W
Torrington, Conn., U.S.A. . 85 E11 41 48N 73 7W
Torrington, Wyo., U.S.A. . 80 D2 42 4N 104 11W
Tórshavn, Færoe Is. ..... 8 E9 62 5N 6 56W
Tortola, Br. Virgin Is. .... 89 e 18 19N 64 45W
Tortosa, Spain .......... 21 B6 40 49N 0 31 E
Tortosa, C., Spain ....... 21 B6 40 41N 0 52 E
Tortue, I. de la, Haiti .... 89 B5 20 5N 72 57W
Tortuguero △, Costa Rica . 88 D3 10 31N 83 29W
Torūd, Iran ............. 45 C7 35 25N 55 5 E
Toruń, Poland .......... 17 B10 53 2N 18 39 E
Tory I., Ireland ......... 10 A3 55 16N 8 14W
Tosa, Japan ............ 31 H6 33 24N 133 23 E
Tosa-Shimizu, Japan .... 31 H6 32 52N 132 58 E
Tosa-Wan, Japan ....... 31 H6 33 15N 133 30 E
Toscana □, Italy ........ 22 C4 43 25N 11 0 E
Toshkent, Uzbekistan ... 28 E7 41 20N 69 10 E
Tostado, Argentina ..... 94 B3 29 15S 61 50W
Tostón, Pta. de, Canary Is. 24 F5 28 42N 14 2W
Tosu, Japan ............ 31 H5 33 22N 130 31 E
Toteng, Botswana ...... 56 C3 20 22S 22 58 E
Totma, Russia .......... 18 C7 60 0N 42 40 E
Totnes, U.K. ............ 13 G4 50 26N 3 42W
Totness, Suriname ...... 93 B7 5 53N 56 19W
Totonicapán, Guatemala . 88 D1 14 58N 91 12W
Totten Glacier, Antarctica 5 C8 66 45S 116 10 E
Tottenham, Australia .... 63 E4 32 14S 147 21 E
Tottenham, Canada ..... 84 B5 44 1N 79 49W
Tottori, Japan .......... 31 G7 35 30N 134 15 E
Tottori □, Japan ........ 31 G7 35 30N 134 12 E
Toubkal, Djebel, Morocco 50 B4 31 0N 8 0W
Tougan, Burkina Faso ... 50 F5 13 11N 2 58W
Touggourt, Algeria ...... 50 B7 33 6N 6 4 E
Toul, France ............ 20 B6 48 40N 5 53 E
Toulon, France .......... 20 E6 43 10N 5 55 E
Toulouse, France ....... 20 E4 43 37N 1 27 E
Toummo, Niger ......... 51 D8 22 45N 14 8 E
Toungoo, Burma ........ 41 K20 19 0N 96 30 E
Touraine, France ....... 20 C4 47 20N 0 30 E
Tourcoing, France ....... 20 A5 50 42N 3 10 E
Touriñán, C., Spain ..... 21 A1 43 3N 9 18W
Tournai, Belgium ....... 15 D3 50 35N 3 25 E
Tournon-sur-Rhône, France 20 D6 45 4N 4 50 E
Tours, France ........... 20 C4 47 22N 0 40 E
Toussora, Mt., C.A.R. ... 52 C4 9 7N 23 14 E
Touws →, S. Africa ...... 56 E3 33 45S 21 11 E
Touwsrivier, S. Africa .... 56 E3 33 20S 20 2 E
Towada, Japan ......... 30 D10 40 37N 141 13 E
Towada-Hachimantai △, Japan 30 D10 40 28N 140 55 E
Towada-Ko, Japan ...... 30 D10 40 28N 140 55 E
Towanda, U.S.A. ........ 85 E8 41 46N 76 27W
Towang, India .......... 41 F17 27 37N 91 50 E
Tower, U.S.A. ........... 80 B8 47 48N 92 17W
Towerhill Cr. →, Australia 62 C3 22 28S 144 35 E
Towner, U.S.A. .......... 80 A4 48 21N 100 25W
Townsend, U.S.A. ....... 76 C8 46 19N 111 31W
Townshend I., Australia .. 62 C5 22 10S 150 31 E
Townsville, Australia .... 62 B4 19 15S 146 45 E
Towraghondi, Afghan. ... 40 B3 35 13N 62 16 E
Towson, U.S.A. ......... 82 F7 39 24N 76 36W
Towuti, Danau, Indonesia 37 E6 2 45S 121 32 E
Toya-Ko, Japan ........ 30 C10 42 35N 140 51 E
Toyama, Japan ......... 31 F8 36 40N 137 15 E
Toyama □, Japan ....... 31 F8 36 45N 137 30 E
Toyama-Wan, Japan .... 31 F8 37 0N 137 30 E
Toyapakeh, Indonesia ... 37 K18 8 41S 115 29 E
Toyohashi, Japan ....... 31 G8 34 45N 137 25 E
Toyokawa, Japan ....... 31 G8 34 48N 137 27 E
Toyonaka, Japan ....... 31 G7 34 50N 135 28 E
Toyooka, Japan ......... 31 G7 35 35N 134 48 E
Toyota, Japan .......... 31 G8 35 3N 137 7 E
Tozeur, Tunisia ......... 50 B7 33 56N 8 0 E
Tozkhurmato, Iraq ...... 44 C5 34 56N 44 38 E
Trá Li = Tralee, Ireland .. 10 D2 52 16N 9 42W
Tra On, Vietnam ........ 39 H5 9 58N 105 55 E
Trabzon, Turkey ........ 19 F6 41 0N 39 45 E
Tracadie-Sheila, Canada . 73 C7 47 30N 64 55W
Tracy, Calif., U.S.A. ..... 78 H5 37 44N 121 26W
Tracy, Minn., U.S.A. ..... 80 C7 44 14N 95 37W
Trafalgar, C., Spain ..... 21 D2 36 10N 6 2W
Trail, Canada ........... 70 D5 49 5N 117 40W
Trainor L., Canada ...... 70 A4 60 24N 120 17W
Trákhonas, Cyprus ...... 25 D12 35 12N 33 21 E
Tralee, Ireland ......... 10 D2 52 16N 9 42W
Tralee B., Ireland ....... 10 D2 52 17N 9 55W
Tramore, Ireland ....... 10 D4 52 10N 7 10W
Tramore B., Ireland ..... 10 D4 52 9N 7 10W
Tran Ninh, Cao Nguyen, Laos 38 C4 19 30N 103 10 E
Tranås, Sweden ........ 9 G16 58 3N 14 59 E
Trancas, Argentina ..... 94 B2 26 11S 65 20W
Trang, Thailand ........ 39 J2 7 33N 99 38 E
Trangahy, Madag. ...... 57 B7 19 7S 44 31 E
Trangan, Indonesia ..... 37 F8 6 40S 134 20 E
Trangie, Australia ...... 63 E4 32 4S 148 0 E
Trani, Italy ............. 22 D7 41 17N 16 25 E
Tranoroa, Madag. ...... 57 C8 24 42S 45 4 E
Tranqueras, Uruguay ... 95 C4 31 13S 55 45W

Transantarctic Mts., Antarctica 5 E12 85 0S 170 0W
Transilvania, Romania .. 17 E12 46 30N 24 0 E
Transilvanian Alps = Carpații
  Meridionali, Romania .. 17 F13 45 30N 25 0 E
Transylvania = Transilvania,
  Romania .............. 17 E12 46 30N 24 0 E
Trápani, Italy ........... 22 E5 38 1N 12 29 E
Trapper Pk., U.S.A. ..... 76 D6 45 54N 114 18W
Traralgon, Australia .... 63 F4 38 12S 146 34 E
Trasimeno, L., Italy ..... 22 C5 43 8N 12 6 E
Trat, Thailand .......... 39 F4 12 14N 102 33 E
Tratani →, Pakistan .... 42 E3 29 19N 68 20 E
Traun, Austria .......... 16 D8 48 14N 14 15 E
Traveller's L., Australia .. 63 E3 33 20S 142 0 E
Travemünde, Germany .. 16 B6 53 57N 10 52 E
Travers, Mt., N.Z. ....... 59 K4 42 1S 172 45 E
Traverse City, U.S.A. .... 82 C3 44 46N 85 38W
Travis, L., U.S.A. ........ 81 K5 30 24N 97 55W
Travnik, Bos.-H. ........ 23 B7 44 17N 17 39 E
Trébbia →, Italy ........ 20 D8 45 4N 9 41 E
Trebič, Czech Rep. ...... 16 D8 49 14N 15 55 E
Trebinje, Bos.-H. ........ 23 C8 42 44N 18 22 E
Trebonne, Australia ..... 62 B4 18 37S 146 5 E
Tregaron, U.K. ......... 13 E4 52 14N 3 56W
Tregrosse Is., Australia .. 62 B5 17 41S 150 43 E
Treherne, Canada ...... 71 D9 49 38N 98 42W
Treinta y Tres, Uruguay . 95 C5 33 16S 54 17W
Trelawney, Zimbabwe ... 57 B5 17 30S 30 30 E
Trelew, Argentina ...... 96 E3 43 10S 65 20W
Trelleborg, Sweden ..... 9 J15 55 20N 13 10 E
Tremadog Bay, U.K. .... 12 E3 52 51N 4 18W
Tremonton, U.S.A. ..... 76 F7 41 43N 112 10W
Tremp, Spain ........... 21 A6 42 10N 0 52 E
Trenche →, Canada .... 72 C5 47 46N 72 53W
Trenčín, Slovak Rep. ... 17 D10 48 52N 18 4 E
Trenggalek, Indonesia .. 37 H14 8 3S 111 43 E
Trenque Lauquen, Argentina 94 D3 36 5S 62 45W
Trent →, Canada ....... 84 B7 44 6N 77 34W
Trent →, U.K. .......... 12 D7 53 41N 0 42W
Trento, Italy ............ 22 A4 46 4N 11 8 E
Trenton = Quinte West, Canada 84 B7 44 10N 77 34W
Trenton, Mo., U.S.A. .... 80 E8 40 5N 93 37W
Trenton, N.J., U.S.A. .... 85 F10 40 14N 74 46W
Trenton, Nebr., U.S.A. .. 80 E4 40 11N 101 1W
Trepassey, Canada ..... 73 C9 46 43N 53 25W
Tres Arroyos, Argentina . 94 D3 38 26S 60 20W
Três Corações, Brazil ... 95 A6 21 44S 45 15W
Tres Lagoas, Brazil ..... 93 H8 20 50S 51 43W
Tres Lomas, Argentina .. 94 D3 36 27S 62 51W
Tres Marías, Islas, Mexico 86 C3 21 25N 106 28W
Tres Montes, C., Chile ... 96 F1 46 50S 75 30W
Tres Pinos, U.S.A. ...... 78 J5 36 48N 121 19W
Três Pontas, Brazil ..... 95 A6 21 23S 45 29W
Tres Puentes, Chile ..... 94 B1 27 50S 70 15W
Tres Puntas, C., Argentina 96 F3 47 0S 66 0W
Três Rios, Brazil ........ 95 A7 22 6S 43 15W
Tres Valles, Mexico ..... 87 D5 18 15N 96 8W
Tresco, U.K. ............ 13 H1 49 57N 6 20W
Treviso, Italy ........... 22 B5 45 40N 12 15 E
Triabunna, Australia .... 63 G4 42 30S 147 55 E
Triánda, Greece ........ 25 C10 36 25N 28 10 E
Triangle, Zimbabwe .... 57 C5 21 2S 31 28 E
Tribal Areas □, Pakistan 42 C4 33 0N 70 0 E
Tribulation, C., Australia . 62 B4 16 5S 145 29 E
Tribune, U.S.A. ......... 80 F4 38 28N 101 45W
Trichinopoly = Tiruchchirappalli,
  India ................. 40 P11 10 45N 78 45 E
Trichur, India .......... 40 P10 10 30N 76 18 E
Trida, Australia ........ 63 E4 33 1S 145 1 E
Trier, Germany ......... 16 D4 49 45N 6 38 E
Trieste, Italy ........... 22 C6 45 40N 13 46 E
Triglav, Slovenia ....... 16 E7 46 21N 13 50 E
Trikala, Greece ......... 23 E9 39 34N 21 47 E
Trikomo, Cyprus ....... 25 D12 35 17N 33 52 E
Trikora, Puncak, Indonesia 37 E9 4 15S 138 45 E
Trim, Ireland ........... 10 C5 53 33N 6 48W
Trincomalee, Sri Lanka . 40 Q12 8 38N 81 15 E
Trindade, Brazil ........ 93 G9 16 40S 49 30W
Trindade, I., Atl. Oc. .... 2 F8 20 20S 29 50W
Trinidad, Bolivia ....... 92 F6 14 46S 64 50W
Trinidad, Cuba ......... 88 B4 21 48N 80 0W
Trinidad, Trin. & Tob. ... 89 D7 10 30N 61 15W
Trinidad, Uruguay ...... 94 C4 33 30S 56 50W
Trinidad, U.S.A. ........ 81 G2 37 10N 104 31W
Trinidad →, Mexico .... 87 D5 17 49N 95 9W
Trinidad & Tobago ■, W. Indies 89 D7 10 30N 61 20W
Trinity, Canada ......... 73 C9 48 59N 53 55W
Trinity, U.S.A. .......... 81 K7 30 57N 95 22W
Trinity →, Calif., U.S.A. . 76 F2 41 11N 123 42W
Trinity →, Tex., U.S.A. .. 81 L7 29 45N 94 43W
Trinity B., Canada ...... 73 C9 48 20N 53 10W
Trinity Hills, Trin. & Tob. . 93 K15 10 7N 61 7W
Trinity Is., U.S.A. ....... 68 C4 56 33N 154 25W
Trinity Range, U.S.A. ... 76 F4 40 15N 118 45W
Trinkitat, Sudan ........ 51 E13 18 45N 37 51 E
Trinway, U.S.A. ......... 84 F2 40 9N 82 1W
Tripoli = Tarābulus, Lebanon 46 A4 34 31N 35 50 E
Tripoli = Tarābulus, Libya 51 B8 32 49N 13 7 E
Tripolis, Greece ........ 23 F10 37 31N 22 25 E
Tripolitania, N. Afr. ..... 51 B8 31 0N 13 0 E
Tripura □, India ........ 41 H18 24 0N 92 0 E
Tripylos, Cyprus ........ 25 E11 34 59N 32 41 E
Tristan da Cunha, Atl. Oc. 49 K2 37 6S 12 20W
Trisul, India ............ 43 D8 30 19N 79 47 E
Trivandrum, India ...... 40 Q10 8 41N 77 0 E
Trnava, Slovak Rep. .... 17 D9 48 23N 17 35 E
Trochu, Canada ........ 70 C6 51 50N 113 13W
Trodely I., Canada ...... 72 B4 52 15N 79 26W
Troglav, Croatia ........ 22 C7 43 56N 16 36 E
Troilus, L., Canada ..... 72 B5 50 50N 74 35W
Trois-Pistoles, Canada .. 73 C6 48 5N 69 10W
Trois-Rivières, Canada .. 72 C5 46 25N 72 34W
Trois-Rivières, Guadeloupe 88 b 15 57N 61 40W
Troitsk, Russia ......... 28 D7 54 10N 61 35 E
Troitsko Pechorsk, Russia 18 B10 62 40N 56 10 E
Trölladyngja, Iceland ... 8 D5 64 54N 17 16W
Trollhättan, Sweden .... 9 G15 58 17N 12 20 E
Trollheimen, Norway .... 8 E13 62 46N 9 1 E
Trombetas →, Brazil ... 93 D7 1 55S 55 35W
Tromsø, Norway ........ 8 B18 69 40N 18 56 E
Trona, U.S.A. ........... 79 K9 35 46N 117 23W
Tronador, Mte., Argentina 96 E2 41 10S 71 50W
Trøndelag, Norway ..... 8 D14 64 17N 11 50 E
Trondheim, Norway .... 8 E14 63 36N 10 25 E
Trondheimsfjorden, Norway 8 E14 63 35N 10 30 E
Troodos, Cyprus ....... 25 E11 34 55N 32 52 E
Troon, U.K. ............ 11 F4 55 33N 4 39W
Tropic, U.S.A. .......... 77 H7 37 37N 112 5W

Trostan, U.K. ........... 10 A5 55 3N 6 10W
Trou Gras Pt., St. Lucia . 89 f 13 51N 60 53W
Trout →, Canada ....... 70 A5 61 19N 119 51W
Trout L., N.W.T., Canada . 70 A4 60 40N 121 14W
Trout L., Ont., Canada .. 71 C10 51 20N 93 15W
Trout Lake, Canada ..... 70 B6 56 30N 114 32W
Trout Lake, U.S.A. ...... 78 E5 46 0N 121 32W
Trout River, Canada .... 73 C8 49 29N 58 8W
Trout Run, U.S.A. ....... 84 E7 41 23N 77 3W
Trouville-sur-Mer, France 20 B4 49 21N 0 5 E
Trowbridge, U.K. ....... 13 F5 51 18N 2 12W
Troy, Turkey ........... 23 E12 39 57N 26 12 E
Troy, Ala., U.S.A. ....... 83 K3 31 48N 85 58W
Troy, Kans., U.S.A. ..... 80 F7 39 47N 95 5W
Troy, Mo., U.S.A. ....... 80 F9 38 59N 90 59W
Troy, Mont., U.S.A. ..... 76 B6 48 28N 115 53W
Troy, N.Y., U.S.A. ....... 85 D11 42 44N 73 41W
Troy, Ohio, U.S.A. ...... 82 E3 40 2N 84 12W
Troy, Pa., U.S.A. ........ 85 E8 41 47N 76 47W
Troyes, France ......... 20 B6 48 19N 4 3 E
Truchas Peak, U.S.A. ... 81 H2 35 58N 105 39W
Trucial States = United Arab
  Emirates ■, Asia ...... 45 F7 23 50N 54 0 E
Truckee, U.S.A. ........ 78 F6 39 20N 120 11W
Trudovoye, Russia ..... 30 C6 43 17N 132 5 E
Trujillo, Honduras ...... 88 C2 16 0N 86 0W
Trujillo, Peru ........... 92 E3 8 6S 79 0W
Trujillo, Spain .......... 21 C3 39 28N 5 55W
Trujillo, U.S.A. ......... 81 H2 35 32N 104 42W
Trujillo, Venezuela ..... 92 B4 9 22N 70 38W
Truk, Micronesia ....... 64 G7 7 25N 151 46 E
Trumann, U.S.A. ....... 81 H9 35 41N 90 31W
Trumansburg, U.S.A. ... 85 D8 42 33N 76 40W
Trumbull, Mt., U.S.A. ... 77 H7 36 25N 113 8W
Trundle, Australia ...... 63 E4 32 53S 147 35 E
Trung-Phan = Annam, Vietnam 38 E7 16 0N 108 0 E
Truro, Canada ......... 73 C7 45 21N 63 14W
Truro, U.K. ............. 13 G2 50 16N 5 4W
Truskavets, Ukraine .... 17 D12 49 17N 23 30 E
Trutch, Canada ........ 70 B4 57 44N 122 57W
Truth or Consequences, U.S.A. 77 K10 33 8N 107 15W
Trutnov, Czech Rep. .... 16 C8 50 37N 15 54 E
Truxton, U.S.A. ........ 84 E5 42 45N 76 2W
Tryonville, U.S.A. ...... 84 E5 41 42N 79 48W
Tsandi, Namibia ....... 56 B1 17 42S 14 50 E
Tsaratanana, Madag. .. 57 B8 16 47S 47 39 E
Tsaratanana, Mt. de =
  Maromokotro, Madag. . 57 A8 14 0S 49 0 E
Tsau, Botswana ........ 56 C3 20 8S 22 22 E
Tsavo East △, Kenya ... 54 C4 2 44S 38 47 E
Tsavo West △, Kenya ... 54 C4 3 19S 37 57 E
Tsentralnyy □, Russia .. 28 D4 52 0N 63 0 E
Tses, Namibia ......... 56 D2 25 58S 18 8 E
Tsetserleg, Mongolia ... 32 B5 47 36N 101 32 E
Tshabong, Botswana ... 56 D3 26 2S 22 29 E
Tshane, Botswana ..... 56 C3 24 5S 21 54 E
Tshela, Dem. Rep. of the Congo 52 E2 4 57S 13 4 E
Tshesebe, Botswana ... 57 C4 21 51S 27 32 E
Tshibeke, Dem. Rep. of
  the Congo ............ 54 C2 2 40S 28 35 E
Tshibinda, Dem. Rep. of
  the Congo ............ 54 C2 2 23S 28 43 E
Tshikapa, Dem. Rep. of
  the Congo ............ 52 F4 6 17S 20 48 E
Tshilenge, Dem. Rep. of
  the Congo ............ 54 D1 6 17S 23 48 E
Tshinsenda, Dem. Rep. of
  the Congo ............ 55 E2 12 20S 28 0 E
Tshofa, Dem. Rep. of the Congo 54 D2 5 13S 25 16 E
Tshwane, Botswana .... 56 C3 22 24S 22 1 E
Tsigara, Botswana ..... 56 C4 20 22S 25 54 E
Tsihombe, Madag. ..... 57 D8 25 10S 45 41 E
Tsiigehtchic, Canada ... 68 B6 67 15N 134 0W
Tsimlyansk Res. = Tsimlyanskoye
  Vdkhr., Russia ........ 19 E7 48 0N 43 0 E
Tsimlyanskoye Vdkhr., Russia 19 E7 48 0N 43 0 E
Tsinan = Jinan, China .. 34 F9 36 38N 117 1 E
Tsineng, S. Africa ...... 56 D3 27 5S 23 5 E
Tsing Yi, China ........ 33 G11 22 21N 114 6 E
Tsinghai = Qinghai □, China 32 C4 36 0N 98 0 E
Tsingtao = Qingdao, China 35 F11 36 5N 120 20 E
Tsingy de Bemaraha △, Madag. 57 B8 18 35S 45 25 E
Tsingy de Namoraka △, Madag. 57 B8 16 29S 45 25 E
Tsinjoarivo, Madag. .... 57 B8 19 37S 47 40 E
Tsinjomitondraka, Madag. 57 B8 15 40S 47 8 E
Tsiroanomandidy, Madag. 57 B8 18 46S 46 2 E
Tsitondroina, Madag. ... 57 C8 21 19S 46 0 E
Tsitsikamma △, S. Africa 56 E3 34 3S 23 40 E
Tsivory, Madag. ........ 57 C8 24 4S 46 5 E
Tskhinvali, Georgia ..... 19 F7 42 14N 44 1 E
Tsna →, Russia ........ 18 D7 54 55N 41 58 E
Tso Moriri, L., India .... 43 C8 32 50N 78 20 E
Tsobis, Namibia ....... 56 B2 19 27S 17 30 E
Tsodilo Hill, Botswana .. 56 B3 18 49S 21 43 E
Tsogttsetsiy = Baruunsuu,
  Mongolia ............. 34 C3 43 43N 105 35 E
Tsolo, S. Africa ........ 57 E4 31 18S 28 37 E
Tsomo, S. Africa ....... 57 E4 32 0S 27 42 E
Tsu, Japan ............ 31 G8 34 45N 136 25 E
Tsu L., Canada ........ 70 A6 60 40N 111 52W
Tsuchiura, Japan ...... 31 F10 36 5N 140 15 E
Tsuen Wan, China ..... 33 G11 22 22N 114 6 E
Tsugaru-Kaikyō, Japan . 30 D10 41 35N 141 0 E
Tsumeb, Namibia ...... 56 B2 19 9S 17 44 E
Tsumis, Namibia ....... 56 C2 23 39S 17 29 E
Tsuruga, Japan ........ 31 G8 35 45N 136 2 E
Tsurugi-San, Japan .... 31 H7 33 51N 134 6 E
Tsuruoka, Japan ....... 30 E9 38 44N 139 50 E
Tsushima, Gifu, Japan .. 31 G8 35 10N 136 43 E
Tsushima, Nagasaki, Japan 31 G4 34 20N 129 20 E
Tsuyama, Japan ....... 31 G7 35 3N 134 0 E
Tsyelyakhany, Belarus .. 17 B13 52 30N 25 46 E
Tual, Indonesia ........ 37 F8 5 38S 132 44 E
Tuam, Ireland ......... 10 C3 53 31N 8 51W
Tuamotu Arch. = Tuamotu Is.,
  French Polynesia ..... 65 J13 17 0S 144 0W
Tuamotu Is., French Polynesia 65 J13 17 0S 144 0W
Tuamotu Ridge, Pac. Oc. 65 K14 20 0S 138 0W
Tuao, Phil. ............ 37 A6 17 55N 121 22 E
Tuapse, Russia ........ 19 F6 44 5N 39 10 E
Tuas, Singapore ....... 39 d 1 19N 103 39 E
Tuatapere, N.Z. ........ 59 M1 46 8S 167 41 E
Tuba City, U.S.A. ...... 77 H8 36 8N 111 14W
Tuban, Indonesia ...... 37 G15 6 54S 112 3 E
Tubani, Botswana ...... 56 C3 24 46S 24 18 E
Tubarão, Brazil ........ 95 B6 28 30S 49 0W
Tūbās, West Bank ...... 46 C4 32 20N 35 22 E

Tubas →, Namibia ... 56 C2 22 54S 14 35 E
Tübingen, Germany ... 16 D5 48 31N 9 4 E
Tubruq, Libya ... 51 B10 32 7N 23 55 E
Tubuai Is., French Polynesia ... 65 K13 25 0S 150 0W
Tuc Trung, Vietnam ... 39 G6 11 1N 107 12 E
Tucacas, Venezuela ... 92 A5 10 48N 68 19W
Tuchodi →, Canada ... 70 B4 58 17N 123 42W
Tuckanarra, Australia ... 61 E2 27 7S 118 5 E
Tucson, U.S.A. ... 77 K8 32 13N 110 58W
Tucumán □, Argentina ... 94 B2 26 48S 66 2W
Tucumcari, U.S.A. ... 81 H3 35 10N 103 44W
Tucupita, Venezuela ... 92 B6 9 2N 62 3W
Tucuruí, Brazil ... 93 D9 3 42S 49 44W
Tucuruí, Reprêsa de, Brazil ... 93 D9 4 0S 49 30W
Tudela, Spain ... 21 A5 42 4N 1 39W
Tudmur, Syria ... 44 C3 34 36N 38 15 E
Tudor, L., Canada ... 73 A6 55 50N 65 25W
Tuen Mun, China ... 33 G10 22 24N 113 59 E
Tugela →, S. Africa ... 57 D5 29 14S 31 30 E
Tuguegarao, Phil. ... 37 A6 17 35N 121 42 E
Tugur, Russia ... 29 D14 53 44N 136 45 E
Tui, Spain ... 21 A1 42 3N 8 39W
Tuineje, Canary Is. ... 24 F5 28 19N 14 3W
Tukangbesi, Kepulauan, Indonesia ... 37 F6 6 0S 124 0 E
Tukarak I., Canada ... 72 A4 56 15N 78 45W
Tukayyid, Iraq ... 44 D5 29 47N 45 36 E
Tukkae, Ao, Thailand ... 39 a 7 51N 98 25 E
Tuktoyaktuk, Canada ... 68 B6 69 27N 133 2W
Tukums, Latvia ... 9 H20 56 58N 23 10 E
Tukuyu, Tanzania ... 55 D3 9 17S 33 35 E
Tula, Hidalgo, Mexico ... 87 C5 20 5N 99 20W
Tula, Tamaulipas, Mexico ... 87 C5 23 0N 99 40W
Tula, Russia ... 18 D6 54 13N 37 38 E
Tulancingo, Mexico ... 87 C5 20 5N 99 22W
Tulare, U.S.A. ... 78 J7 36 13N 119 21W
Tulare Lake Bed, U.S.A. ... 78 K7 36 0N 119 48W
Tularosa, U.S.A. ... 77 K10 33 5N 106 1W
Tulbagh, S. Africa ... 56 E2 33 16S 19 6 E
Tulcán, Ecuador ... 92 C3 0 48N 77 43W
Tulcea, Romania ... 17 F15 45 13N 28 46 E
Tulchyn, Ukraine ... 17 D15 48 41N 28 49 E
Tüleh, Iran ... 45 C7 34 35N 52 33 E
Tulemalu L., Canada ... 71 A9 62 58N 99 25W
Tuli, Zimbabwe ... 55 G2 21 58S 29 13 E
Tulia, U.S.A. ... 81 H4 34 32N 101 46W
Tulita, Canada ... 68 B7 64 57N 125 30W
Țülkarm, West Bank ... 46 C4 32 19N 35 2 E
Tulla, Ireland ... 10 D3 52 53N 8 46W
Tullahoma, U.S.A. ... 83 H2 35 22N 86 13W
Tullamore, Australia ... 63 E4 32 39S 147 36 E
Tullamore, Ireland ... 10 C4 53 16N 7 31W
Tulle, France ... 20 D4 45 16N 1 46 E
Tullow, Ireland ... 10 D5 52 49N 6 45W
Tully, Australia ... 62 B4 17 56S 145 55 E
Tully, U.S.A. ... 85 D8 42 48N 76 7W
Tulsa, U.S.A. ... 81 G7 36 10N 95 55W
Tulsequah, Canada ... 70 B2 58 39N 133 35W
Tulua, Colombia ... 92 C3 4 6N 76 11W
Tulun, Russia ... 29 D11 54 32N 100 35 E
Tulungagung, Indonesia ... 37 H14 8 5S 111 54 E
Tuma →, Nic. ... 88 D3 13 6N 84 35W
Tumacacori, U.S.A. ... 77 L8 31 34N 111 3W
Tumaco, Colombia ... 92 C3 1 50N 78 45W
Tumatumari, Guyana ... 92 B7 5 20N 58 55W
Tumba, Sweden ... 9 G17 59 12N 17 48 E
Tumba, L., Dem. Rep. of the Congo ... 52 E3 0 50S 18 0 E
Tumbarumba, Australia ... 63 F4 35 44S 148 0 E
Tumbaya, Argentina ... 94 A2 23 50S 65 26W
Tumbes, Peru ... 92 D2 3 37S 80 27W
Tumbwe, Dem. Rep. of the Congo ... 55 E2 11 25S 27 15 E
Tumby Bay, Australia ... 63 E2 34 21S 136 8 E
Tumd Youqi, China ... 34 D6 40 30N 110 30 E
Tumen, China ... 35 C15 43 0N 129 50 E
Tumen Jiang →, China ... 35 C16 42 20N 130 35 E
Tumeremo, Venezuela ... 92 B6 7 18N 61 30W
Tumkur, India ... 40 N10 13 18N 77 6 E
Tump, Pakistan ... 40 F3 26 7N 62 16 E
Tumpat, Malaysia ... 39 J4 6 11N 102 10 E
Tumu, Ghana ... 50 C5 10 56N 1 56W
Tumucumaque, Serra, Brazil ... 93 C8 2 0N 55 0W
Tumut, Australia ... 63 F4 35 16S 148 13 E
Tumwater, U.S.A. ... 78 C4 47 1N 122 54W
Tuna, India ... 42 H4 22 59N 70 5 E
Tunapuna, Trin. & Tob. ... 93 K15 10 38N 61 24W
Tunas de Zaza, Cuba ... 88 B4 21 39N 79 34W
Tunbridge Wells = Royal Tunbridge Wells, U.K. ... 13 F8 51 7N 0 16 E
Tuncurry, Australia ... 63 E5 32 17S 152 29 E
Tundla, India ... 42 F8 27 12N 78 17 E
Tunduru, Tanzania ... 55 E4 11 8S 37 25 E
Tundzha →, Bulgaria ... 23 C11 41 40N 26 35 E
Tung Chung, China ... 33 G10 22 17N 113 57 E
Tung Lung Chau, China ... 33 G11 22 15N 114 17 E
Tungabhadra →, India ... 40 M11 15 57N 78 15 E
Tungla, Nic. ... 88 D3 13 24N 84 21W
Tungsten, Canada ... 70 A3 61 57N 128 16W
Tunguska, Nizhnyaya →, Russia ... 29 C9 65 48N 88 4 E
Tunguska, Podkamennaya →, Russia ... 29 C10 61 50N 90 13 E
Tunica, U.S.A. ... 81 H9 34 41N 90 23W
Tunis, Tunisia ... 50 A7 36 50N 10 11 E
Tunisia ■, Africa ... 50 B6 33 30N 9 10 E
Tunja, Colombia ... 92 B4 5 33N 73 25W
Tunkhannock, U.S.A. ... 85 E9 41 32N 75 57W
Tunliu, China ... 34 F7 36 13N 112 52 E
Tunnel Creek △, Australia ... 60 C4 17 41S 125 18 E
Tunnsjøen, Norway ... 8 D15 64 45N 13 25 E
Tunungayualok I., Canada ... 73 A7 56 0N 61 0W
Tunuyán, Argentina ... 94 C2 33 35S 69 0W
Tunuyán →, Argentina ... 94 C2 33 33S 67 30W
Tuolumne, U.S.A. ... 78 H6 37 58N 120 15W
Tuolumne →, U.S.A. ... 78 H5 37 36N 121 13W
Tüp Ăghăj, Iran ... 44 B5 36 3N 47 50 E
Tupã, Brazil ... 95 A5 21 57S 50 28W
Tupelo, U.S.A. ... 83 H1 34 16N 88 43W
Tupinambaranas, Brazil ... 92 D7 3 0S 58 0W
Tupiza, Bolivia ... 94 A2 21 30S 65 40W
Tupman, U.S.A. ... 79 K7 35 18N 119 21W
Tupper, Canada ... 70 B4 55 32N 120 1W
Tupper Lake, U.S.A. ... 85 B10 44 14N 74 28W
Tupungato, Cerro, S. Amer. ... 94 C2 33 15S 69 50W
Tuquan, China ... 35 B11 45 18N 121 38 E
Túquerres, Colombia ... 92 C3 1 5N 77 37W
Tura, Russia ... 29 C11 64 20N 100 17 E
Turabah, Si. Arabia ... 44 D4 28 20N 43 15 E

Türän, Iran ... 45 C8 35 39N 56 42 E
Turan, Russia ... 29 D10 51 55N 95 0 E
Țurayf, Si. Arabia ... 44 D3 31 41N 38 39 E
Turda, Romania ... 17 E12 46 34N 23 47 E
Turek, Poland ... 17 B10 52 3N 18 30 E
Turen, Venezuela ... 92 B5 9 17N 69 6W
Turfan = Turpan, China ... 32 B3 43 58N 89 10 E
Turfan Basin = Turpan Hami, China ... 26 E12 42 40N 89 25 E
Turfan Depression = Turpan Hami, China ... 26 E12 42 40N 89 25 E
Turgeon →, Canada ... 72 C4 50 0N 78 56W
Türgovishte, Bulgaria ... 23 C12 43 17N 26 38 E
Turgutlu, Turkey ... 23 E12 38 30N 27 43 E
Turgwe →, Zimbabwe ... 57 C5 21 31S 32 15 E
Turia →, Spain ... 21 C5 39 27N 0 19W
Turiaçu, Brazil ... 93 D9 1 40S 45 19W
Turiaçu →, Brazil ... 93 D9 1 36S 45 19W
Turin = Torino, Italy ... 20 D7 45 3N 7 40 E
Turkana, L., Africa ... 54 B4 3 30N 36 5 E
Turkestan = Türkistan, Kazakhstan ... 28 E7 43 17N 68 16 E
Turkey ■, Eurasia ... 19 G6 39 0N 36 0 E
Turkey Creek, Australia ... 60 C4 17 2S 128 12 E
Türkistan, Kazakhstan ... 28 E7 43 17N 68 16 E
Türkmenbashi, Turkmenistan ... 19 G9 40 5N 53 5 E
Turkmenistan ■, Asia ... 28 F6 39 0N 59 0 E
Turks & Caicos Is. ☑, W. Indies ... 89 B5 21 20N 71 20W
Turks Island Passage, W. Indies ... 89 B5 21 30N 71 30W
Turku, Finland ... 9 F20 60 30N 22 19 E
Turkwel →, Kenya ... 54 B4 3 6N 36 6 E
Turlock, U.S.A. ... 78 H6 37 30N 120 51W
Turnagain →, Canada ... 70 B3 59 12N 127 35W
Turnagain, C., N.Z. ... 59 J6 40 28S 176 38 E
Turneffe Is., Belize ... 87 D7 17 20N 87 50W
Turner, U.S.A. ... 76 B9 48 51N 108 24W
Turner Pt., Australia ... 62 A1 11 47S 133 32 E
Turner Valley, Canada ... 70 C6 50 40N 114 17W
Turners Falls, U.S.A. ... 85 D12 42 36N 72 33W
Turnhout, Belgium ... 15 C4 51 19N 4 57 E
Turnor L., Canada ... 71 B7 56 35N 108 35W
Türnovo = Veliko Türnovo, Bulgaria ... 23 C11 43 5N 25 41 E
Turnu Măgurele, Romania ... 17 G13 43 46N 24 56 E
Turnu Roşu, P., Romania ... 17 F13 45 33N 24 17 E
Turpan, China ... 32 B3 43 58N 89 10 E
Turpan Hami, China ... 26 E12 42 40N 89 25 E
Turriff, U.K. ... 11 D6 57 32N 2 27W
Tursãq, Iraq ... 44 C5 33 27N 45 47 E
Turtle Head I., Australia ... 62 A3 10 56S 142 37 E
Turtle L., Canada ... 71 C7 53 36N 108 38W
Turtle Lake, U.S.A. ... 80 B4 47 31N 100 53W
Turtleford, Canada ... 71 C7 53 23N 108 57W
Turuépano △, Venezuela ... 89 D7 10 34N 62 43W
Turukhansk, Russia ... 29 C9 65 21N 88 5 E
Tuscaloosa, U.S.A. ... 83 J2 33 12N 87 34W
Tuscany = Toscana □, Italy ... 22 C4 43 25N 11 0 E
Tuscarawas →, U.S.A. ... 84 F3 40 24N 81 25W
Tuscarora Mt., U.S.A. ... 84 F7 40 55N 77 55W
Tuscola, Ill., U.S.A. ... 82 F1 39 48N 88 17W
Tuscola, Tex., U.S.A. ... 81 J5 32 12N 99 48W
Tuscumbia, U.S.A. ... 83 H2 34 44N 87 42W
Tuskegee, U.S.A. ... 83 J3 32 25N 85 42W
Tustin, U.S.A. ... 79 M9 33 44N 117 49W
Tuticorin, India ... 40 Q11 8 50N 78 12 E
Tutóia, Brazil ... 93 D10 2 45S 42 20W
Tutong, Brunei ... 36 D4 4 47N 114 40 E
Tutrakan, Bulgaria ... 23 B12 44 2N 26 40 E
Tuttle Creek L., U.S.A. ... 80 F6 39 22N 96 40W
Tuttlingen, Germany ... 16 E5 47 58N 8 48 E
Tutuala, E. Timor ... 37 F7 8 25S 127 15 E
Tutuila, Amer. Samoa ... 59 B13 14 19S 170 50W
Tutume, Botswana ... 53 J5 20 30S 27 5 E
Tututepec, Mexico ... 87 D5 16 9N 97 38W
Tuva □, Russia ... 29 D10 51 30N 95 0 E
Tuvalu ■, Pac. Oc. ... 64 H9 8 0S 178 0 E
Tuxpan, Mexico ... 87 C5 20 58N 97 23W
Tuxtla Gutiérrez, Mexico ... 87 D6 16 50N 93 10W
Tuy = Tui, Spain ... 21 A1 42 3N 8 39W
Tuy An, Vietnam ... 38 F7 13 17N 109 16 E
Tuy Duc, Vietnam ... 39 F6 12 15N 107 27 E
Tuy Hoa, Vietnam ... 38 F7 13 5N 109 10 E
Tuy Phong, Vietnam ... 39 G7 11 14N 108 43 E
Tuya →, Canada ... 70 B2 59 7N 130 35W
Tuyen Hoa, Vietnam ... 38 D6 17 50N 106 10 E
Tuyen Quang, Vietnam ... 38 B5 21 50N 105 10 E
Tüysärkän, Iran ... 45 C6 34 33N 48 27 E
Tüz Gölü, Turkey ... 19 G5 38 42N 33 18 E
Țüz Khurmātü = Tozkhurmato, Iraq ... 44 C5 34 56N 44 38 E
Tuzigoot △, U.S.A. ... 77 J7 34 46N 112 2W
Tuzla, Bos.-H. ... 23 B8 44 34N 18 41 E
Tver, Russia ... 18 C6 56 55N 35 55 E
Twain, U.S.A. ... 78 E5 40 1N 121 3W
Twain Harte, U.S.A. ... 78 G6 38 2N 120 14W
Tweed, Canada ... 84 B7 44 29N 77 19W
Tweed →, U.K. ... 11 F6 55 45N 2 0W
Tweed Heads, Australia ... 63 D5 28 10S 153 31 E
Tweedsmuir △, Canada ... 70 C3 53 0N 126 20W
Twentynine Palms, U.S.A. ... 79 L10 34 8N 116 3W
Twillingate, Canada ... 73 C9 49 42N 54 45W
Twin Bridges, U.S.A. ... 76 D7 45 33N 112 20W
Twin Falls, Canada ... 73 B7 53 30N 64 32W
Twin Falls, U.S.A. ... 76 E6 42 34N 114 28W
Twin Valley, U.S.A. ... 80 B6 47 16N 96 16W
Twinsburg, U.S.A. ... 84 E3 41 18N 81 26W
Twitchell Reservoir, U.S.A. ... 79 L6 34 59N 120 19W
Two Harbors, U.S.A. ... 80 B9 47 2N 91 40W
Two Hills, Canada ... 70 C6 53 43N 111 52W
Two Rivers, U.S.A. ... 82 C2 44 9N 87 34W
Two Rocks, Australia ... 61 F2 31 30S 115 35 E
Twofold B., Australia ... 63 F4 37 8S 149 59 E
Tyachiv, Ukraine ... 17 D12 48 1N 23 35 E
Tychy, Poland ... 17 C10 50 9N 18 59 E
Tyler, Minn., U.S.A. ... 80 C6 44 18N 96 8W
Tyler, Tex., U.S.A. ... 81 J7 32 21N 95 18W
Tynda, Russia ... 29 D13 55 10N 124 43 E
Tyndall, U.S.A. ... 80 D6 43 0N 97 50W
Tyne →, U.K. ... 12 C6 54 59N 1 32W
Tyne & Wear □, U.K. ... 12 B6 55 6N 1 17W
Tynemouth, U.K. ... 12 B6 55 1N 1 26W
Tyre = Sür, Lebanon ... 46 B4 33 19N 35 16 E
Tyrifjorden, Norway ... 9 F14 60 2N 10 8 E
Tyrol = Tirol □, Austria ... 16 E6 47 3N 10 43 E
Tyrone □, U.K. ... 10 B4 54 38N 7 11W
Tyrrell →, Australia ... 63 F3 35 26S 142 51 E
Tyrrell, L., Australia ... 63 F3 35 20S 142 50 E

Tyrrell L., Canada ... 71 A7 63 7N 105 27W
Tyrrhenian Sea, Medit. S. ... 22 E5 40 0N 12 30 E
Tysfjorden, Norway ... 8 B17 68 7N 16 25 E
Tyulgan, Russia ... 18 D10 52 22N 56 12 E
Tyumen, Russia ... 28 D7 57 11N 65 29 E
Tywi →, U.K. ... 13 F3 51 48N 4 21W
Tywyn, U.K. ... 13 E3 52 35N 4 5W
Tzaneen, S. Africa ... 57 C5 23 47S 30 9 E
Tzermiádhes, Greece ... 25 D7 35 12N 25 29 E
Tzukong = Zigong, China ... 32 D5 29 15N 104 48 E

## U

U Taphao, Thailand ... 38 F3 12 35N 101 0 E
U.S.A. = United States of America ■, N. Amer. ... 74 C7 37 0N 96 0W
U.S. Virgin Is. ☑, W. Indies ... 89 e 18 20N 65 0W
Uatumã →, Brazil ... 92 D7 2 26S 57 37W
Uaupés, Brazil ... 92 D5 0 8S 67 5W
Uaupés →, Brazil ... 92 C5 0 2N 67 16W
Uaxactún, Guatemala ... 88 C2 17 25N 89 29W
Ubá, Brazil ... 95 A7 21 8S 43 0W
Ubaitaba, Brazil ... 93 F11 14 18S 39 20W
Ubangi = Oubangui →, Dem. Rep. of the Congo ... 52 E3 0 30S 17 50 E
Ubauro, Pakistan ... 42 E3 28 15N 69 45 E
Ubayyiq, W. al →, Iraq ... 44 C4 32 34N 43 48 E
Ube, Japan ... 31 H5 33 56N 131 15 E
Úbeda, Spain ... 21 C4 38 3N 3 23W
Uberaba, Brazil ... 93 G9 19 50S 47 55W
Uberlândia, Brazil ... 93 G9 19 0S 48 20W
Ubin, Pulau, Singapore ... 39 d 1 25N 103 56 E
Ubolratna Res., Thailand ... 38 D4 16 45N 102 30 E
Ubombo, S. Africa ... 57 D5 27 31S 32 4 E
Ubon Ratchathani, Thailand ... 38 E5 15 15N 104 50 E
Ubondo, Dem. Rep. of the Congo ... 54 C2 0 55S 25 42 E
Ubort →, Belarus ... 17 B15 52 6N 28 30 E
Ubud, Indonesia ... 37 J18 8 30S 115 16 E
Ubundu, Dem. Rep. of the Congo ... 54 C2 0 22S 25 30 E
Ucayali →, Peru ... 92 D4 4 30S 73 30W
Uchab, Namibia ... 56 B2 19 47S 17 42 E
Uchiura-Wan, Japan ... 30 C10 42 25N 140 40 E
Uchquduq, Uzbekistan ... 28 E7 41 50N 62 50 E
Uchur →, Russia ... 29 D14 58 48N 130 35 E
Ucluelet, Canada ... 70 D3 48 57N 125 32W
Uda →, Russia ... 29 D14 54 42N 135 14 E
Udagamandalam, India ... 40 P10 11 30N 76 44 E
Udainagar, India ... 42 H7 22 33N 76 13 E
Udaipur, India ... 42 G5 24 36N 73 44 E
Udaipur Garhi, Nepal ... 43 F12 27 0N 86 35 E
Udala, India ... 43 J12 21 35N 86 34 E
Uddevalla, Sweden ... 9 G14 58 21N 11 55 E
Uddjaure, Sweden ... 8 D17 65 56N 17 49 E
Uden, Neths. ... 15 C5 51 40N 5 37 E
Udgir, India ... 40 K10 18 25N 77 5 E
Udhampur, India ... 43 C6 33 0N 75 5 E
Údine, Italy ... 22 A5 46 3N 13 14 E
Udmurtia □, Russia ... 18 C9 57 30N 52 30 E
Udon Thani, Thailand ... 38 D4 17 29N 102 46 E
Udupi, India ... 40 N9 13 25N 74 42 E
Udzungwa △, Tanzania ... 54 D4 7 52S 36 35 E
Udzungwa Range, Tanzania ... 55 D4 9 30S 35 10 E
Ueda, Japan ... 31 F9 36 24N 138 16 E
Uedineniya, Os., Russia ... 4 B12 78 0N 85 0 E
Uele →, Dem. Rep. of the Congo ... 52 D4 3 45N 24 45 E
Uelen, Russia ... 29 C19 66 10N 170 0W
Uelzen, Germany ... 16 B6 52 57N 10 32 E
Ufa, Russia ... 18 D10 54 45N 55 55 E
Ufa →, Russia ... 18 D10 54 40N 56 0 E
Ugab →, Namibia ... 56 C1 20 55S 13 30 E
Ugalla →, Tanzania ... 54 D3 5 8S 30 42 E
Ugalla River △, Tanzania ... 54 D3 5 50S 31 54 E
Uganda ■, Africa ... 54 B3 2 0N 32 0 E
Ugie, S. Africa ... 57 E4 31 10S 28 13 E
Uglegorsk, Russia ... 29 E15 49 5N 142 2 E
Ugljan, Croatia ... 16 F8 44 12N 15 10 E
Uhlenhorst, Namibia ... 56 C2 23 45S 17 55 E
Uhrichsville, U.S.A. ... 84 F3 40 24N 81 21W
Uibhist a Deas = South Uist, U.K. ... 11 D1 57 20N 7 15W
Uibhist a Tuath = North Uist, U.K. ... 11 D1 57 40N 7 15W
Uig, U.K. ... 11 D2 57 35N 6 21W
Uíge, Angola ... 52 F2 7 30S 14 40 E
Uijŏngbu, S. Korea ... 35 F14 37 48N 127 0 E
Ŭiju, N. Korea ... 35 D13 40 15N 124 35 E
Uinta Mts., U.S.A. ... 76 F8 40 45N 110 30W
Uis, Namibia ... 56 C1 21 8S 14 49 E
Uitenhage, S. Africa ... 56 E4 33 40S 25 28 E
Uithuizen, Neths. ... 15 A6 53 24N 6 41 E
Ujh →, India ... 42 C6 32 10N 75 18 E
Ujhani, India ... 43 F8 28 0N 79 6 E
Uji-guntō, Japan ... 31 J4 31 15N 129 25 E
Ujjain, India ... 42 H6 23 9N 75 43 E
Ujung Pandang, Indonesia ... 37 F5 5 10S 119 20 E
Uka, Russia ... 29 D17 57 50N 162 0 E
Ukara I., Tanzania ... 54 C3 1 50S 33 0 E
Uke-Shima, Japan ... 31 K4 28 2N 129 14 E
Ukerewe I., Tanzania ... 54 C3 2 0S 33 0 E
Ukhrul, India ... 41 G19 25 10N 94 25 E
Ukhta, Russia ... 18 B9 63 34N 53 41 E
Ukiah, U.S.A. ... 78 F3 39 9N 123 13W
Ukmergė, Lithuania ... 9 J21 55 15N 24 45 E
Ukraine ■, Europe ... 19 E5 49 0N 32 0 E
Ukwi, Botswana ... 56 C3 23 29S 20 30 E
Ulaan-Uul, Mongolia ... 34 B6 44 13N 111 10 E
Ulaanbaatar, Mongolia ... 29 E11 47 55N 106 53 E
Ulaangom, Mongolia ... 32 A4 50 5N 92 10 E
Ulaanjirem, Mongolia ... 34 B3 45 5N 105 30 E
Ulamba, Dem. Rep. of the Congo ... 55 D1 9 3S 23 38 E
Ulan Bator = Ulaanbaatar, Mongolia ... 29 E11 47 55N 106 53 E
Ulan Ude, Russia ... 29 D11 51 45N 107 40 E
Ulaya, Morogoro, Tanzania ... 54 D4 7 3S 36 55 E
Ulaya, Tabora, Tanzania ... 54 C3 4 25S 33 30 E
Ulcinj, Serbia & M. ... 23 D8 41 58N 19 10 E
Ulco, S. Africa ... 56 D3 28 21S 24 15 E
Ule älv = Oulujoki →, Finland ... 8 D21 65 1N 25 30 E
Ule träsk = Oulujärvi, Finland ... 8 D22 64 25N 27 15 E
Uleåborg = Oulu, Finland ... 8 D21 65 1N 25 29 E
Ulefoss, Norway ... 9 G13 59 17N 9 16 E
Ulhasnagar, India ... 40 K8 19 15N 73 10 E
Uliastay, Mongolia ... 32 B4 47 56N 97 28 E
Ulladulla, Australia ... 63 F5 35 21S 150 29 E
Ullapool, U.K. ... 11 D3 57 54N 5 9W
Ullswater, U.K. ... 12 C5 54 34N 2 52W
Ullŭng-do, S. Korea ... 31 F5 37 30N 130 30 E

Ulm, Germany ... 16 D5 48 23N 9 58 E
Ulmarra, Australia ... 63 D5 29 37S 153 4 E
Ulonguè, Mozam. ... 55 E3 14 37S 34 19 E
Ulricehamn, Sweden ... 9 H15 57 46N 13 26 E
Ulsan, S. Korea ... 35 G15 35 20N 129 15 E
Ulsta, U.K. ... 11 A7 60 30N 1 9W
Ulster □, U.K. ... 10 B5 54 35N 6 30W
Ulubat Gölü, Turkey ... 23 D13 40 9N 28 35 E
Uludağ, Turkey ... 23 D13 40 4N 29 13 E
Uluguru Mts., Tanzania ... 54 D4 7 15S 37 40 E
Ulungur He →, China ... 32 B3 47 1N 87 24 E
Uluru = Ayers Rock, Australia ... 61 E5 25 23S 131 5 E
Uluru-Kata Tjuta △, Australia ... 61 E5 25 19S 131 1 E
Ulutau, Kazakhstan ... 28 E7 48 39N 67 1 E
Uluwatu, Indonesia ... 37 K18 8 50S 115 5 E
Ulva, U.K. ... 11 E2 56 29N 6 13W
Ulverston, U.K. ... 12 C4 54 13N 3 5W
Ulverstone, Australia ... 63 G4 41 11S 146 11 E
Ulya, Russia ... 29 D15 59 10N 142 0 E
Ulyanovsk = Simbirsk, Russia ... 18 D8 54 20N 48 25 E
Ulyasutay = Uliastay, Mongolia ... 32 B4 47 56N 97 28 E
Ulysses, U.S.A. ... 81 G4 37 35N 101 22W
Umala, Bolivia ... 92 G5 17 25S 68 5W
Uman, Ukraine ... 17 D16 48 40N 30 12 E
Umaria, India ... 41 H12 23 35N 80 50 E
Umarkot, Pakistan ... 40 G6 25 15N 69 40 E
Umarpada, India ... 42 J5 21 27N 73 30 E
Umatilla, U.S.A. ... 76 D4 45 55N 119 21W
Umba, Russia ... 18 A5 66 42N 34 11 E
Umbagog L., U.S.A. ... 85 B13 44 46N 71 3W
Umbakumba, Australia ... 62 A2 13 47S 136 50 E
Umbrella Mts., N.Z. ... 59 L2 45 35S 169 5 E
Umeå, Sweden ... 8 E19 63 45N 20 20 E
Umeälven →, Sweden ... 8 E19 63 45N 20 20 E
Umera, Indonesia ... 37 E7 0 12S 129 37 E
Umfolozi △, S. Africa ... 57 D5 28 18S 31 50 E
Umfuli →, Zimbabwe ... 55 F2 17 30S 29 23 E
Umfurudzi △, Zimbabwe ... 55 F3 17 6S 31 40 E
Umgusa, Zimbabwe ... 55 F2 19 29S 27 52 E
Umkomaas, S. Africa ... 57 E5 30 13S 30 48 E
Umlazi, S. Africa ... 53 L6 29 59S 30 54 E
Umm ad Daraj, J., Jordan ... 46 C4 32 18N 35 48 E
Umm al Qaywayn, U.A.E. ... 45 E7 25 30N 55 35 E
Umm al Qittayn, Jordan ... 46 C5 32 18N 36 40 E
Umm Bāb, Qatar ... 45 E6 25 12N 50 48 E
Umm Durman = Omdurmân, Sudan ... 51 E12 15 40N 32 28 E
Umm el Fahm, Israel ... 46 C4 32 31N 35 9 E
Umm Keddada, Sudan ... 51 F11 13 33N 26 35 E
Umm Lajj, Si. Arabia ... 44 E3 25 0N 37 23 E
Umm Ruwaba, Sudan ... 51 F12 12 50N 31 20 E
Umnak I., U.S.A. ... 68 C3 53 15N 168 20W
Umniati →, Zimbabwe ... 55 F2 16 49S 28 45 E
Umpqua →, U.S.A. ... 76 E1 43 40N 124 12W
Umreth, India ... 42 H5 22 41N 73 4 E
Umtata, S. Africa ... 57 E4 31 36S 28 49 E
Umuarama, Brazil ... 95 A5 23 45S 53 20W
Umvukwe Ra., Zimbabwe ... 55 F3 16 45S 30 45 E
Umzimvubu, S. Africa ... 57 E4 31 38S 29 33 E
Umzingwane →, Zimbabwe ... 55 G2 22 12S 29 56 E
Umzinto, S. Africa ... 57 E5 30 15S 30 45 E
Una, India ... 42 J4 20 46N 71 8 E
Una →, Bos.-H. ... 16 F9 45 0N 16 20 E
Unadilla, U.S.A. ... 85 D9 42 20N 75 19W
Unalakleet, U.S.A. ... 68 B3 63 53N 160 47W
Unalaska, U.S.A. ... 68 C3 53 53N 166 32W
Unalaska I., U.S.A. ... 68 C3 53 35N 166 50W
'Unayzah, Si. Arabia ... 44 E4 26 6N 43 58 E
'Unayzah, J., Asia ... 44 C3 32 12N 39 18 E
Uncía, Bolivia ... 92 G5 18 25S 66 40W
Uncompahgre Peak, U.S.A. ... 77 G10 38 4N 107 28W
Uncompahgre Plateau, U.S.A. ... 77 G9 38 20N 108 15W
Undara Volcanic △, Australia ... 62 B3 18 14S 144 41 E
Underbool, Australia ... 63 F3 35 10S 141 51 E
Ungarie, Australia ... 63 E4 33 38S 146 56 E
Ungarra, Australia ... 63 E2 34 12S 136 2 E
Ungava, Pén. d', Canada ... 69 C12 60 0N 74 0W
Ungava B., Canada ... 69 C13 59 30N 67 30W
Ungeny = Ungheni, Moldova ... 17 E14 47 11N 27 51 E
Unggi, N. Korea ... 35 C16 42 16N 130 28 E
Ungheni, Moldova ... 17 E14 47 11N 27 51 E
Ungwana B., Kenya ... 54 C5 2 40S 40 20 E
União da Vitória, Brazil ... 95 B5 26 13S 51 5W
Unimak I., U.S.A. ... 68 C3 54 45N 164 0W
Union, Miss., U.S.A. ... 81 J10 32 34N 89 7W
Union, Mo., U.S.A. ... 80 F9 38 27N 91 0W
Union, S.C., U.S.A. ... 83 H5 34 43N 81 37W
Union, Calif., U.S.A. ... 78 H4 37 36N 122 1W
Union City, N.J., U.S.A. ... 85 F10 40 45N 74 2W
Union City, Pa., U.S.A. ... 84 E5 41 54N 79 51W
Union City, Tenn., U.S.A. ... 81 G10 36 26N 89 3W
Union Gap, U.S.A. ... 76 C3 46 33N 120 28W
Union Springs, U.S.A. ... 83 J3 32 9N 85 43W
Uniondale, S. Africa ... 56 E3 33 39S 23 7 E
Uniontown, U.S.A. ... 82 F6 39 54N 79 44W
Unionville, U.S.A. ... 80 E8 40 29N 93 1W
United Arab Emirates ■, Asia ... 45 F7 23 50N 54 0 E
United Kingdom ■, Europe ... 14 E6 53 0N 2 0W
United States of America ■, N. Amer. ... 74 C7 37 0N 96 0W
Unity, Canada ... 71 C7 52 30N 109 5W
University Park, U.S.A. ... 77 K10 32 17N 106 45W
Unjha, India ... 42 H5 23 46N 72 24 E
Unnao, India ... 43 F9 26 35N 80 30 E
Unsengedsi →, Zimbabwe ... 55 F3 15 43S 31 14 E
Unst, U.K. ... 11 A8 60 44N 0 53W
Unuk →, Canada ... 70 B2 56 5N 131 3W
Unzen-Amakusa △, Japan ... 31 H5 32 15N 130 10 E
Uozu, Japan ... 31 F8 36 48N 137 24 E
Upata, Venezuela ... 92 B6 8 1N 62 24W
Upemba, L., Dem. Rep. of the Congo ... 55 D2 9 0S 26 35 E
Upemba, L., Dem. Rep. of the Congo ... 55 D2 8 30S 26 20 E
Upernavik, Greenland ... 4 B5 72 49N 56 20W
Upington, S. Africa ... 56 D3 28 25S 21 15 E
Upleta, India ... 42 J4 21 46N 70 16 E
'Upolu, Samoa ... 59 A13 13 58S 172 0W
Upper Alkali L., U.S.A. ... 76 F3 41 47N 120 8W
Upper Arrow L., Canada ... 70 C5 50 30N 117 50W
Upper Foster L., Canada ... 71 B7 56 47N 105 20W
Upper Hutt, N.Z. ... 59 J5 41 8S 175 5 E
Upper Klamath L., U.S.A. ... 76 E3 42 25N 121 55W
Upper Lake, U.S.A. ... 78 F4 39 10N 122 54W
Upper Missouri River Breaks △, U.S.A. ... 76 C9 47 50N 108 55W
Upper Musquodoboit, Canada ... 73 C7 45 10N 62 58W

Upper Red L., U.S.A. . . . . . . . . **80 A7** 48 8N 94 45W
Upper Sandusky, U.S.A. . . . . . **82 E4** 40 50N 83 17W
Upper Volta = Burkina Faso ■,
  Africa . . . . . . . . . . . . . . . . **50 F5** 12 0N 1 0W
Uppland, Sweden . . . . . . . . . **9 F17** 59 59N 17 48 E
Uppsala, Sweden . . . . . . . . . **9 G17** 59 53N 17 38 E
Upshi, India . . . . . . . . . . . . . . **43 C7** 33 48N 77 52 E
Upstart, C., Australia . . . . . . **62 B4** 19 41S 147 45 E
Upton, U.S.A. . . . . . . . . . . . . **80 C2** 44 6N 104 38W
Uqsuqtuuq = Gjoa Haven,
  Canada . . . . . . . . . . . . . . **68 B10** 68 38N 95 53W
Ur, Iraq . . . . . . . . . . . . . . . . . **44 D5** 30 55N 46 25 E
Urad Qianqi, China . . . . . . . . **34 D5** 40 40N 108 30 E
Urakawa, Japan . . . . . . . . . **30 C11** 42 9N 142 47 E
Ural = Uralskiy □, Russia . . . **28 C7** 64 0N 70 0 E
Ural = Zhayyq ➤, Kazakhstan . **19 E9** 47 0N 51 48 E
Ural, Australia . . . . . . . . . . . **63 E4** 33 21S 146 12 E
Ural Mts. = Uralskie Gory,
  Eurasia . . . . . . . . . . . . . . **18 C10** 60 0N 59 0 E
Uralla, Australia . . . . . . . . . . **63 E5** 30 37S 151 29 E
Uralsk = Oral, Kazakhstan . . . **19 D9** 51 20N 51 20 E
Uralskie Gory, Eurasia . . . . . **18 C10** 60 0N 59 0 E
Uralskiy □, Russia . . . . . . . . **28 C7** 64 0N 70 0 E
Urambo, Tanzania . . . . . . . . . **54 D3** 5 4S 32 0 E
Urandangi, Australia . . . . . . . **62 C2** 21 32S 138 14 E
Uranium City, Canada . . . . . . **71 B7** 59 34N 108 37W
Uraricoera ➤, Brazil . . . . . . . **92 C6** 3 2N 60 30W
Urawa, Japan . . . . . . . . . . . . **31 G9** 35 50N 139 40 E
Uray, Russia . . . . . . . . . . . . . **28 C7** 60 5N 65 15 E
'Uray'irah, Si. Arabia . . . . . . **45 E6** 25 57N 48 53 E
Urbana, Ill., U.S.A. . . . . . . . . **82 E1** 40 7N 88 12W
Urbana, Ohio, U.S.A. . . . . . . **82 E4** 40 7N 83 45W
Urbino, Italy . . . . . . . . . . . . . **22 C5** 43 43N 12 38 E
Urbión, Picos de, Spain . . . . **21 A4** 42 1N 2 52W
Urcos, Peru . . . . . . . . . . . . . . **92 F4** 13 40S 71 38W
Urdinarrain, Argentina . . . . . **94 C4** 32 37S 58 52W
Urdzhar, Kazakhstan . . . . . . **28 E9** 47 5N 81 38 E
Ure ➤, U.K. . . . . . . . . . . . . . . **12 C6** 54 5N 1 20W
Ures, Mexico . . . . . . . . . . . . **86 B2** 29 30N 110 30W
Urewera △, N.Z. . . . . . . . . . . **59 H6** 38 29S 177 7 E
Urfa = Sanliurfa, Turkey . . . . **19 G6** 37 12N 38 50 E
Urganch, Uzbekistan . . . . . . **28 E7** 41 40N 60 41 E
Urgench = Urganch, Uzbekistan **28 E7** 41 40N 60 41 E
Ürgüp, Turkey . . . . . . . . . . . **44 B2** 38 38N 34 56 E
Uri, India . . . . . . . . . . . . . . . . **43 B6** 34 8N 74 2 E
Uribia, Colombia . . . . . . . . . . **92 A4** 11 43N 72 16W
Uriondo, Bolivia . . . . . . . . . . **94 A3** 21 41S 64 41W
Urique, Mexico . . . . . . . . . . . **86 B3** 27 13N 107 55W
Urique ➤, Mexico . . . . . . . . . **86 B3** 26 29N 107 58W
Urk, Neths. . . . . . . . . . . . . . . **15 B5** 52 39N 5 36 E
Urla, Turkey . . . . . . . . . . . . **23 E12** 38 20N 26 47 E
Urmia = Orümiyeh, Iran . . . . **44 B5** 37 40N 45 0 E
Uroševac, Serbia & M. . . . . . **23 C9** 42 23N 21 10 E
Uroyan, Montanas de,
  Puerto Rico . . . . . . . . . . . **89 d** 18 12N 67 0W
Uruaçu, Brazil . . . . . . . . . . . **93 F9** 14 30S 49 10W
Uruapan, Mexico . . . . . . . . . **86 D4** 19 30N 102 0W
Urubamba ➤, Peru . . . . . . . . **92 F4** 10 43S 73 48W
Uruçara, Brazil . . . . . . . . . . . **92 D7** 2 32S 57 45W
Uruçuí, Brazil . . . . . . . . . . . **93 E10** 7 20S 44 28W
Uruguai ➤, Brazil . . . . . . . . . **95 B5** 26 0S 53 30W
Uruguaiana, Brazil . . . . . . . . **94 B4** 29 50S 57 0W
Uruguay ■, S. Amer. . . . . . . . **94 C4** 32 30S 56 30W
Uruguay ➤, S. Amer. . . . . . . . **94 C4** 34 12S 58 18W
Urumchi = Ürümqi, China . . . **28 E9** 43 45N 87 45 E
Ürümqi, China . . . . . . . . . . . **28 E9** 43 45N 87 45 E
Urup, Ostrov, Russia . . . . . **29 E16** 46 0N 151 0 E
Usa ➤, Russia . . . . . . . . . . . **18 A10** 66 16N 59 49 E
Uşak, Turkey . . . . . . . . . . . . **19 G4** 38 43N 29 28 E
Usakos, Namibia . . . . . . . . . **56 C2** 21 54S 15 31 E
Usedom, Germany . . . . . . . . **16 B8** 53 55N 14 2 E
Useless Loop, Australia . . . . **61 E1** 26 8S 113 23 E
Ush-Tobe, Kazakhstan . . . . . **28 E8** 45 16N 78 0 E
Ushakova, Ostrov, Russia . . **4 A12** 82 0N 80 0 E
Ushant = Ouessant, Î. d', France **20 B1** 48 28N 5 6W
Ushashi, Tanzania . . . . . . . . **54 C3** 1 59S 33 57 E
Ushibuka, Japan . . . . . . . . . **31 H5** 32 11N 130 1 E
Ushuaia, Argentina . . . . . . . . **96 G3** 54 50S 68 23W
Ushumun, Russia . . . . . . . . **29 D13** 52 47N 126 32 E
Usk, Canada . . . . . . . . . . . . . **70 C3** 54 38N 128 26W
Usk ➤, U.K. . . . . . . . . . . . . . . **13 F5** 51 33N 2 58W
Uska, India . . . . . . . . . . . . . **43 F10** 27 12N 83 7 E
Usman, Russia . . . . . . . . . . . **18 D6** 52 5N 39 48 E
Usoke, Tanzania . . . . . . . . . . **54 D3** 5 8S 32 24 E
Usolye Sibirskoye, Russia . . **29 D11** 52 48N 103 40 E
Uspallata, P. de, Argentina . . **94 C2** 32 37S 69 22W
Uspenskiy, Kazakhstan . . . . . **28 E8** 48 41N 72 43 E
Ussuri ➤, Asia . . . . . . . . . . . **30 A7** 48 27N 135 0 E
Ussuriysk, Russia . . . . . . . **29 E14** 43 48N 131 59 E
Ussurka, Russia . . . . . . . . . **30 B6** 45 12N 133 31 E
Ust-Bolsheretsk, Russia . . . **29 D16** 52 50N 156 15 E
Ust-Chaun, Russia . . . . . . . **29 C18** 68 47N 170 30 E
Ust-Ilimsk, Russia . . . . . . . **29 D11** 58 3N 102 39 E
Ust-Ishim, Russia . . . . . . . . **28 D8** 57 45N 71 10 E
Ust-Kamchatsk, Russia . . . . **29 D17** 56 10N 162 28 E
Ust-Kamenogorsk = Öskemen,
  Kazakhstan . . . . . . . . . . . **28 E9** 50 0N 82 36 E
Ust-Khayryuzovo, Russia . . **29 D16** 57 15N 156 45 E
Ust-Kut, Russia . . . . . . . . . **29 D11** 56 50N 105 42 E
Ust-Kuyga, Russia . . . . . . . **29 B14** 70 1N 135 43 E
Ust-Maya, Russia . . . . . . . . **29 C14** 60 30N 134 28 E
Ust-Mil, Russia . . . . . . . . . **29 D14** 59 40N 133 11 E
Ust-Nera, Russia . . . . . . . . **29 C15** 64 35N 143 15 E
Ust-Nyukzha, Russia . . . . . **29 D13** 56 34N 121 37 E
Ust-Olenek, Russia . . . . . . **29 B12** 73 0N 120 5 E
Ust-Omchug, Russia . . . . . **29 C15** 61 9N 149 38 E
Ust-Port, Russia . . . . . . . . . **28 C9** 69 40N 84 26 E
Ust-Tsilma, Russia . . . . . . . **18 A9** 65 28N 52 11 E
Ust Urt = Ustyurt Plateau, Asia **28 E6** 44 0N 55 0 E
Ust-Usa, Russia . . . . . . . . . **18 A10** 66 2N 56 57 E
Ust-Vorkuta, Russia . . . . . . **18 A11** 67 24N 64 0 E
Ústí nad Labem, Czech Rep. . **16 C8** 50 41N 14 3 E
Ústica, Italy . . . . . . . . . . . . . **22 E5** 38 42N 13 11 E
Ustinov = Izhevsk, Russia . . **18 C9** 56 51N 53 14 E
Ustyurt Plateau, Asia . . . . . . **28 E6** 44 0N 55 0 E
Usu, China . . . . . . . . . . . . . . **32 B3** 44 27N 84 40 E
Usuki, Japan . . . . . . . . . . . . **31 H5** 33 8N 131 49 E
Usulután, El Salv. . . . . . . . . . **88 D2** 13 25N 88 28W
Usumacinta ➤, Mexico . . . . . **87 D6** 17 0N 91 0W
Usumbura = Bujumbura, Burundi **54 C2** 3 16S 29 18 E
Usure, Tanzania . . . . . . . . . . **54 C3** 4 40S 34 22 E
Usutuo ➤, Mozam. . . . . . . . . **57 D5** 26 48S 32 7 E
Uta, Indonesia . . . . . . . . . . . **37 E9** 4 33S 136 0 E
Utah □, U.S.A. . . . . . . . . . . . **76 G8** 39 20N 111 30W
Utah L., U.S.A. . . . . . . . . . . . **76 F8** 40 10N 111 58W
Utara, Selat, Malaysia . . . . . . **39 c** 5 28N 100 20 E
Utarni, India . . . . . . . . . . . . . **42 F4** 26 5N 71 58 E
Utatlan, Guatemala . . . . . . . . **88 C1** 15 2N 91 11W

Ute Creek ➤, U.S.A. . . . . . . . **81 H3** 35 21N 103 50W
Utena, Lithuania . . . . . . . . . **9 J21** 55 27N 25 40 E
Utete, Tanzania . . . . . . . . . . **54 D4** 8 0S 38 45 E
Uthai Thani, Thailand . . . . . . **38 E3** 15 22N 100 3 E
Uthal, Pakistan . . . . . . . . . . **42 G2** 25 44N 66 40 E
Utiariti, Brazil . . . . . . . . . . . **92 F7** 13 0S 58 10W
Utica, N.Y., U.S.A. . . . . . . . . **85 C9** 43 6N 75 14W
Utica, Ohio, U.S.A. . . . . . . . **84 F2** 40 14N 82 27W
Utikuma L., Canada . . . . . . . **70 B5** 55 50N 115 30W
Utopia, Australia . . . . . . . . . **62 C1** 22 14S 134 33 E
Utraula, India . . . . . . . . . . . **43 F10** 27 19N 82 25 E
Utrecht, Neths. . . . . . . . . . . **15 B5** 52 5N 5 8 E
Utrecht, S. Africa . . . . . . . . . **57 D5** 27 38S 30 20 E
Utrecht □, Neths. . . . . . . . . **15 B5** 52 6N 5 7 E
Utrera, Spain . . . . . . . . . . . . **21 D3** 37 12N 5 48W
Utsjoki ➤, Finland . . . . . . . . **8 B22** 69 51N 26 59 E
Utsunomiya, Japan . . . . . . . **31 F9** 36 30N 139 50 E
Uttar Pradesh □, India . . . . . **43 F9** 27 0N 80 0 E
Uttaradit, Thailand . . . . . . . . **38 D3** 17 36N 100 5 E
Uttaranchal □, India . . . . . . **43 D8** 30 0N 79 30 E
Uttoxeter, U.K. . . . . . . . . . . **12 E6** 52 54N 1 52W
Utuado, Puerto Rico . . . . . . **89 d** 18 16N 66 42W
Uummannaq, Greenland . . . . **4 B4** 77 0N 69 0W
Uummannaq, Greenland . . . . **4 B5** 70 58N 52 0W
Uummannarsuaq = Nunap Isua,
  Greenland . . . . . . . . . . . . **69 C15** 59 48N 43 55W
Uusikaarlepyy, Finland . . . . . **8 E20** 63 32N 22 31 E
Uusikaupunki, Finland . . . . . **9 F19** 60 47N 21 25 E
Uva, Russia . . . . . . . . . . . . . **18 C9** 56 59N 52 13 E
Uvalde, U.S.A. . . . . . . . . . . . **81 L5** 29 13N 99 47W
Uvat, Russia . . . . . . . . . . . . **28 D7** 59 5N 68 50 E
Uvinza, Tanzania . . . . . . . . . **54 D3** 5 5S 30 24 E
Uvira, Dem. Rep. of the Congo **54 C2** 3 22S 29 3 E
Uvs Nuur, Mongolia . . . . . . **32 A4** 50 20N 92 30 E
'Uwairidh, Ḥarrat al, Si. Arabia **44 E3** 26 50N 38 0 E
Uwajima, Japan . . . . . . . . . . **31 H6** 33 10N 132 35 E
Uwanda △, Tanzania . . . . . . **54 D3** 7 46S 32 0 E
Uweinat, Jebel, Sudan . . . . **51 D10** 21 54N 24 58 E
Uxbridge, Canada . . . . . . . . **84 B5** 44 6N 79 7W
Uxin Qi, China . . . . . . . . . . . **34 E5** 38 50N 109 5 E
Uxmal, Mexico . . . . . . . . . . **87 C7** 20 22N 89 46W
Üydzin, Mongolia . . . . . . . . **34 B4** 44 9N 107 0 E
Uyo, Nigeria . . . . . . . . . . . . **50 G7** 5 1N 7 53 E
Uyûn Mûsa, Egypt . . . . . . . . **46 F1** 29 53N 32 40 E
Uyuni, Bolivia . . . . . . . . . . . **92 H5** 20 28S 66 47W
Uzbekistan ■, Asia . . . . . . . **28 E7** 41 30N 65 0 E
Uzen, Kazakhstan . . . . . . . . **19 F9** 43 29N 52 54 E
Uzen, Mal ➤, Kazakhstan . . . **19 E8** 49 4N 49 44 E
Uzerche, France . . . . . . . . . **20 D4** 45 25N 1 34 E
Uzh ➤, Ukraine . . . . . . . . . **17 C16** 51 15N 30 12 E
Uzhgorod = Uzhhorod, Ukraine **17 D12** 48 36N 22 18 E
Uzhhorod, Ukraine . . . . . . . **17 D12** 48 36N 22 18 E
Užice, Serbia & M. . . . . . . . . **23 C8** 43 55N 19 50 E
Uzunköprü, Turkey . . . . . . . **23 D12** 41 16N 26 43 E

**V**

Vaal ➤, S. Africa . . . . . . . . . **56 D3** 29 4S 23 38 E
Vaal Dam, S. Africa . . . . . . . **57 D4** 27 0S 28 14 E
Vaalbos △, S. Africa . . . . . . **56 D3** 28 22S 24 20 E
Vaalwater, S. Africa . . . . . . **57 C4** 24 15S 28 8 E
Vaasa, Finland . . . . . . . . . . **8 E19** 63 6N 21 38 E
Vác, Hungary . . . . . . . . . . **17 E10** 47 49N 19 10 E
Vacaria, Brazil . . . . . . . . . . **95 B5** 28 31S 50 52W
Vacaville, U.S.A. . . . . . . . . . **78 G5** 38 21N 121 59W
Vach = Vakh ➤, Russia . . . . **28 C8** 60 45N 76 45 E
Vache, Î. à, Haiti . . . . . . . . . **89 C5** 18 2N 73 35W
Vadnagar, India . . . . . . . . . **42 H5** 23 47N 72 40 E
Vadodara, India . . . . . . . . . **42 H5** 22 20N 73 10 E
Vadsø, Norway . . . . . . . . . . **8 A23** 70 3N 29 50 E
Vaduz, Liech. . . . . . . . . . . . **20 C8** 47 8N 9 31 E
Værøy, Norway . . . . . . . . . . **8 C15** 67 40N 12 40 E
Vágar, Færoe Is. . . . . . . . . . **8 E9** 62 5N 7 15W
Vågsfjorden, Norway . . . . . . **8 B17** 68 50N 16 50 E
Váh ➤, Slovak Rep. . . . . . . **17 D9** 47 43N 18 7 E
Vahsel B., Antarctica . . . . . . **5 D1** 75 0S 35 0W
Váhtjer = Gällivare, Sweden . **8 C19** 67 9N 20 40 E
Vái, Greece . . . . . . . . . . . . . **25 D8** 35 15N 26 18 E
Vaigach, Russia . . . . . . . . . **28 B6** 70 10N 59 0 E
Vail, U.S.A. . . . . . . . . . . . . . **74 C5** 39 40N 106 20W
Vaisali ➤, India . . . . . . . . . . **43 F8** 26 28N 78 53 E
Vakh ➤, Russia . . . . . . . . . **28 C8** 60 45N 76 45 E
Val-d'Or, Canada . . . . . . . . . **72 C4** 48 7N 77 47W
Val Marie, Canada . . . . . . . . **71 D7** 49 15N 107 45W
Valahia, Romania . . . . . . . . **17 F13** 44 35N 25 0 E
Valandovo, Macedonia . . . . **23 D10** 41 19N 22 34 E
Valcheta, Argentina . . . . . . . **96 E3** 40 40S 66 8W
Valdai Hills = Valdayskaya
  Vozvyshennost, Russia . . . . **18 C5** 57 0N 33 30 E
Valdayskaya Vozvyshennost,
  Russia . . . . . . . . . . . . . . . **18 C5** 57 0N 33 30 E
Valdepeñas, Spain . . . . . . . . **21 C4** 38 43N 3 25W
Valdés, Pen., Argentina . . . . **96 E4** 42 30S 63 45W
Valdez, U.S.A. . . . . . . . . . . . **68 B5** 61 7N 146 16W
Valdivia, Chile . . . . . . . . . . . **96 D2** 39 50S 73 14W
Valdosta, U.S.A. . . . . . . . . . **83 K4** 30 50N 83 17W
Valdres, Norway . . . . . . . . . **9 F13** 61 5N 9 5 E
Vale, U.S.A. . . . . . . . . . . . . . **76 E5** 43 59N 117 15W
Vale of Glamorgan □, U.K. . . **13 F4** 51 28N 3 25W
Valemount, Canada . . . . . . . **70 C5** 52 50N 119 15W
Valença, Brazil . . . . . . . . . . **93 F11** 13 20S 39 5W
Valença do Piauí, Brazil . . . **93 E10** 6 20S 41 45W
Valence, France . . . . . . . . . **20 D6** 44 57N 4 54 E
Valencia, Spain . . . . . . . . . . **21 C5** 39 27N 0 23W
Valencia, Trin. & Tob. . . . . . **93 K15** 10 39N 61 11W
Valencia, U.S.A. . . . . . . . . . **77 J10** 34 48N 106 43W
Valencia, Venezuela . . . . . . **92 A5** 10 11N 68 0W
Valencia □, Spain . . . . . . . . **21 C5** 39 20N 0 40W
Valencia, G. de, Spain . . . . . **21 C6** 39 30N 0 20 E
Valencia de Alcántara, Spain . **21 C2** 39 25N 7 14W
Valencia I., Ireland . . . . . . . **10 E1** 51 54N 10 22W
Valenciennes, France . . . . . **20 A5** 50 20N 3 34 E
Valentim, Sa. do, Brazil . . . **93 E10** 6 0S 43 30W
Valentin, Russia . . . . . . . . . **30 C7** 43 8N 134 17 E
Valentine, U.S.A. . . . . . . . . . **81 K2** 30 35N 104 30W
Valera, Venezuela . . . . . . . . **92 B4** 9 19N 70 37W
Valga, Estonia . . . . . . . . . . **9 H22** 57 47N 26 3 E
Valier, U.S.A. . . . . . . . . . . . **76 B7** 48 18N 112 16W
Valjevo, Serbia & M. . . . . . . **23 B8** 44 18N 19 53 E
Valka, Latvia . . . . . . . . . . . . **9 H21** 57 46N 26 3 E
Valkeakoski, Finland . . . . . . **9 F20** 61 16N 24 2 E
Valkenswaard, Neths. . . . . . **15 C5** 51 21N 5 29 E
Vall de Uxó = La Vall d'Uixó,
  Spain . . . . . . . . . . . . . . . **21 C5** 39 49N 0 15W
Valladolid, Mexico . . . . . . . **87 C7** 20 41N 88 11W

Valladolid, Spain . . . . . . . . . **21 B3** 41 38N 4 43W
Valldemossa, Spain . . . . . . . **24 B9** 39 43N 2 37 E
Valle de la Pascua, Venezuela **92 B5** 9 13N 66 0W
Valle de las Palmas, Mexico . **79 N10** 32 20N 116 43W
Valle de Santiago, Mexico . . **86 C4** 20 25N 101 15W
Valle de Suchil, Mexico . . . . **86 C4** 23 38N 103 55W
Valle de Zaragoza, Mexico . . **86 B3** 27 28N 105 49W
Valle Fértil, Sierra del, Argentina **94 C2** 30 20S 68 0W
Valle Gran Rey, Canary Is. . . **24 F2** 28 5N 17 20W
Valle Hermoso, Mexico . . . . **87 B5** 25 35N 97 40W
Valledupar, Colombia . . . . . . **92 A4** 10 29N 73 15W
Vallehermoso, Canary Is. . . . **24 F2** 28 10N 17 15W
Vallejo, U.S.A. . . . . . . . . . . **78 G4** 38 7N 122 14W
Vallenar, Chile . . . . . . . . . . **94 B1** 28 30S 70 50W
Valletta, Malta . . . . . . . . . . **25 D2** 35 54N 14 31 E
Valley Center, U.S.A. . . . . . . **79 M9** 33 13N 117 2W
Valley City, U.S.A. . . . . . . . . **80 B6** 46 55N 98 0W
Valley Falls, Oreg., U.S.A. . . **76 E3** 42 29N 120 17W
Valley Falls, R.I., U.S.A. . . . **85 E13** 41 54N 71 24W
Valley Springs, U.S.A. . . . . . **78 G6** 38 12N 120 50W
Valley View, U.S.A. . . . . . . . **85 F8** 40 39N 76 33W
Valley Wells, U.S.A. . . . . . . **79 K11** 35 27N 115 46W
Valleyview, Canada . . . . . . . **70 B5** 55 5N 117 17W
Vallimanca, Arroyo, Argentina **94 D4** 35 40S 59 10W
Valls, Spain . . . . . . . . . . . . **21 B6** 41 18N 1 15 E
Valmiera, Latvia . . . . . . . . . **9 H21** 57 37N 25 29 E
Valognes, France . . . . . . . . **20 B3** 49 30N 1 28W
Valona = Vlorë, Albania . . . . **23 D8** 40 32N 19 28 E
Valozhyn, Belarus . . . . . . . **17 A14** 54 3N 26 30 E
Valparaíso, Chile . . . . . . . . **94 C1** 33 2S 71 40W
Valparaíso, Mexico . . . . . . . **86 C4** 22 50N 103 32W
Valparaiso, U.S.A. . . . . . . . **82 E2** 41 28N 87 4W
Valparaíso □, Chile . . . . . . **94 C1** 33 2S 71 40W
Vals ➤, S. Africa . . . . . . . . . **56 D4** 27 23S 26 30 E
Vals, Tanjung, Indonesia . . . **37 F9** 8 26S 137 25 E
Valsad, India . . . . . . . . . . . **40 J8** 20 40N 72 58 E
Valverde, Canary Is. . . . . . . **24 G2** 27 48N 17 55W
Valverde del Camino, Spain . **21 D2** 37 35N 6 47W
Vammala, Finland . . . . . . . . **9 F20** 61 20N 22 54 E
Vámos, Greece . . . . . . . . . . **25 D6** 35 24N 24 13 E
Van, Turkey . . . . . . . . . . . . **19 G7** 38 30N 43 20 E
Van, L. = Van Gölü, Turkey . **19 G7** 38 30N 43 0 E
Van Alstyne, U.S.A. . . . . . . . **81 J6** 33 25N 96 35W
Van Blommestein Meer,
  Suriname . . . . . . . . . . . . . **93 C7** 4 45N 55 5W
Van Buren, Canada . . . . . . . **73 C6** 47 10N 67 55W
Van Buren, Ark., U.S.A. . . . . **81 H7** 35 26N 94 21W
Van Buren, Maine, U.S.A. . . **83 B11** 47 10N 67 58W
Van Buren, Mo., U.S.A. . . . . **81 G9** 37 0N 91 1W
Van Canh, Vietnam . . . . . . . **38 F7** 13 37N 109 0 E
Van Diemen, C., N. Terr.,
  Australia . . . . . . . . . . . . . . **60 B5** 11 9S 130 24 E
Van Diemen, C., Queens.,
  Australia . . . . . . . . . . . . . . **62 B2** 16 30S 139 46 E
Van Diemen G., Australia . . . **60 B5** 11 45S 132 0 E
Van Gölü, Turkey . . . . . . . . **19 G7** 38 30N 43 0 E
Van Horn, U.S.A. . . . . . . . . **81 K2** 31 3N 104 50W
Van Ninh, Vietnam . . . . . . . . **38 F7** 12 42N 109 14 E
Van Rees, Pegunungan,
  Indonesia . . . . . . . . . . . . . **37 E9** 2 35S 138 15 E
Van Wert, U.S.A. . . . . . . . . . **82 E3** 40 52N 84 35W
Van Yen, Vietnam . . . . . . . . **38 B5** 21 4N 104 42 E
Vanadzor, Armenia . . . . . . . **19 F7** 40 48N 44 30 E
Vanavara, Russia . . . . . . . **29 C11** 60 22N 102 16 E
Vancouver, Canada . . . . . . . **70 D4** 49 15N 123 10W
Vancouver, U.S.A. . . . . . . . . **78 E4** 45 38N 122 40W
Vancouver, C., Australia . . . . **61 G2** 35 2S 118 11 E
Vancouver I., Canada . . . . . **70 D3** 49 50N 126 0W
Vancouver International ✈ (YVR),
  U.S.A. . . . . . . . . . . . . . . . **78 A3** 49 10N 123 10W
Vanda = Vantaa, Finland . . . . **9 F21** 60 18N 24 58 E
Vandalia, Ill., U.S.A. . . . . . . **80 F10** 38 58N 89 6W
Vandalia, Mo., U.S.A. . . . . . **80 F9** 39 19N 91 29W
Vandenburg, U.S.A. . . . . . . **79 L6** 34 35N 120 33W
Vanderbijlpark, S. Africa . . . **57 D4** 26 42S 27 54 E
Vandergrift, U.S.A. . . . . . . . **84 F5** 40 36N 79 34W
Vanderhoof, Canada . . . . . . **70 C4** 54 0N 124 0W
Vanderkloof Dam, S. Africa . **56 E3** 30 4S 24 40 E
Vanderlin I., Australia . . . . . **62 B2** 15 44S 137 2 E
Vänern, Sweden . . . . . . . . . **9 G15** 58 47N 13 30 E
Vänersborg, Sweden . . . . . . **9 G15** 58 26N 12 19 E
Vang Vieng, Laos . . . . . . . . **38 C4** 18 58N 102 32 E
Vanga, Kenya . . . . . . . . . . . **54 C4** 4 35S 39 12 E
Vangaindrano, Madag. . . . . . **57 C8** 23 21S 47 36 E
Vanguard, Canada . . . . . . . . **71 D7** 49 55N 107 20W
Vanino, Russia . . . . . . . . . **29 E15** 48 50N 140 5 E
Vanna, Norway . . . . . . . . . . **8 A18** 70 6N 19 50 E
Vännäs, Sweden . . . . . . . . . **8 E18** 63 58N 19 48 E
Vannes, France . . . . . . . . . . **20 C2** 47 40N 2 47W
Vanrhynsdorp, S. Africa . . . . **56 E2** 31 36S 18 44 E
Vansbro, Sweden . . . . . . . . **9 F16** 60 32N 14 15 E
Vantaa, Finland . . . . . . . . . **9 F21** 60 18N 24 58 E
Vanua Balavu, Fiji . . . . . . . **59 C9** 17 40S 178 57W
Vanua Levu, Fiji . . . . . . . . . **59 C8** 16 33S 179 15 E
Vanuatu ■, Pac. Oc. . . . . . . **64 J8** 15 0S 168 0 E
Vanwyksvlei, S. Africa . . . . . **56 E3** 30 18S 21 49 E
Vanzylsrus, S. Africa . . . . . **56 D3** 26 52S 22 4 E
Vapnyarka, Ukraine . . . . . . **17 D15** 48 32N 28 45 E
Varāmīn, Iran . . . . . . . . . . . **45 C6** 35 20N 51 39 E
Varāmīn □, Iran . . . . . . . . . **45 C6** 35 18N 51 35 E
Varanasi, India . . . . . . . . . **43 G10** 25 22N 83 0 E
Varangerfjorden, Norway . . . **8 A23** 70 3N 29 25 E
Varangerhalvøya, Norway . . **8 A23** 70 25N 29 30 E
Varaždin, Croatia . . . . . . . . **16 E9** 46 20N 16 20 E
Varberg, Sweden . . . . . . . . **9 H15** 57 6N 12 20 E
Vardak □, Afghan. . . . . . . . . **40 B6** 34 0N 68 0 E
Vardar = Axiós ➤, Greece . . **23 D10** 40 57N 22 35 E
Varde, Denmark . . . . . . . . . **9 J13** 55 38N 8 29 E
Varde ➤, Norway . . . . . . . . **8 A24** 70 23N 31 5 E
Varella, Mui, Vietnam . . . . . . **38 F7** 12 54N 109 26 E
Varéna, Lithuania . . . . . . . . **9 J21** 54 12N 24 30 E
Varese, Italy . . . . . . . . . . . **20 D8** 45 48N 8 50 E
Vargas □, Venezuela . . . . . . **89 D7** 10 30N 66 55W
Varginha, Brazil . . . . . . . . . **95 A6** 21 33S 45 25W
Varillas, Chile . . . . . . . . . . **94 A1** 24 0S 70 10W
Varkaus, Finland . . . . . . . . . **9 E22** 62 19N 27 50 E
Varna, Bulgaria . . . . . . . . **23 C12** 43 13N 27 50 E
Värnamo, Sweden . . . . . . . . **9 H16** 57 10N 14 3 E
Vars, Canada . . . . . . . . . . . **85 A9** 45 21N 75 21W
Varysburg, U.S.A. . . . . . . . . **84 D6** 42 46N 78 18W
Varzaneh, Iran . . . . . . . . . . **45 C7** 32 25N 52 40 E
Vasa = Vaasa, Finland . . . . . **8 E19** 63 6N 21 38 E
Vasa Barris ➤, Brazil . . . . **93 F11** 11 10S 37 10W
Vascongadas = País Vasco □,
  Spain . . . . . . . . . . . . . . . **21 A4** 42 50N 2 45W
Vasht = Khāsh, Iran . . . . . . **40 E2** 28 15N 61 15 E
Vasilevichi, Belarus . . . . . **17 B15** 52 15N 29 50 E
Vasilkov = Vasylkiv, Ukraine . **17 C16** 50 7N 30 15 E

Vaslui, Romania . . . . . . . . **17 E14** 46 38N 27 42 E
Vassar, Canada . . . . . . . . . . **71 D9** 49 10N 95 55W
Vassar, U.S.A. . . . . . . . . . . **82 D4** 43 22N 83 35W
Västerås, Sweden . . . . . . . **9 G17** 59 37N 16 38 E
Västerbotten, Sweden . . . . **8 D18** 64 36N 20 4 E
Västerdalälven ➤, Sweden . . **9 F16** 60 30N 14 7 E
Västervik, Sweden . . . . . . . **9 H17** 57 43N 16 33 E
Västmanland, Sweden . . . . **9 G16** 59 45N 16 20 E
Vasto, Italy . . . . . . . . . . . . **22 C6** 42 8N 14 40 E
Vasylkiv, Ukraine . . . . . . . **17 C16** 50 7N 30 15 E
Vatersay, U.K. . . . . . . . . . . **11 E1** 56 55N 7 32W
Vatican City ■, Europe . . . . **22 D5** 41 54N 12 27 E
Vatili, Cyprus . . . . . . . . . . **25 D12** 35 6N 33 40 E
Vatnajökull, Iceland . . . . . . . **8 D5** 64 30N 16 48W
Vatoa, Fiji . . . . . . . . . . . . . . **59 D9** 19 50S 178 13W
Vatólakkos, Greece . . . . . . **25 D5** 35 27N 23 53 E
Vatoloha, Madag. . . . . . . . . **57 B8** 17 52S 47 48 E
Vatomandry, Madag. . . . . . . **57 B8** 19 20S 48 59 E
Vatra-Dornei, Romania . . . . **17 E13** 47 22N 25 22 E
Vatrak ➤, India . . . . . . . . . . **42 H5** 23 9N 73 2 E
Vättern, Sweden . . . . . . . . . **9 G16** 58 25N 14 30 E
Vaudreuil-Dorion, Canada . . **85 A10** 45 23N 74 3W
Vaughn, Mont., U.S.A. . . . . . **76 C8** 47 33N 111 33W
Vaughn, N. Mex., U.S.A. . . . **77 J11** 34 36N 105 13W
Vaujours L., Canada . . . . . . **72 A5** 55 27N 74 15W
Vaupés = Uaupés ➤, Brazil . **92 C5** 0 2N 67 16W
Vaupés □, Colombia . . . . . . **92 C4** 1 0N 71 0W
Vauxhall, Canada . . . . . . . . **70 C6** 50 5N 112 9W
Vav, India . . . . . . . . . . . . . **42 G4** 24 22N 71 31 E
Vavatenina, Madag. . . . . . . **57 B8** 17 28S 49 12 E
Vava'u, Tonga . . . . . . . . . . **59 D12** 18 36S 174 0W
Vawkavysk, Belarus . . . . . . **17 B13** 53 9N 24 30 E
Växjö, Sweden . . . . . . . . . . **9 H16** 56 52N 14 50 E
Vaygach, Ostrov, Russia . . . **28 C6** 70 0N 60 0 E
Váyia, Ákra, Greece . . . . . . **25 C10** 36 15N 28 11 E
Veaikevárri = Svappavaara,
  Sweden . . . . . . . . . . . . . . **8 C19** 67 40N 21 3 E
Vechte ➤, Neths. . . . . . . . . **15 B6** 52 34N 6 6 E
Vedea ➤, Romania . . . . . . **17 G13** 43 42N 25 41 E
Vedia, Argentina . . . . . . . . **94 C3** 34 30S 61 31W
Veendam, Neths. . . . . . . . . **15 A6** 53 5N 6 52 E
Veenendaal, Neths. . . . . . . **15 B5** 52 2N 5 34 E
Vefsna ➤, Norway . . . . . . . **8 D15** 65 48N 13 10 E
Vega, Norway . . . . . . . . . . **8 D14** 65 40N 11 55 E
Vega, U.S.A. . . . . . . . . . . . **81 H3** 35 15N 102 26W
Vega Baja, Puerto Rico . . . . **89 d** 18 27N 66 23W
Vegreville, Canada . . . . . . . **70 C6** 53 30N 112 5W
Vejer de la Frontera, Spain . . **21 D3** 36 15N 5 59W
Vejle, Denmark . . . . . . . . . . **9 J13** 55 43N 9 30 E
Velas, C., Costa Rica . . . . . . **88 D2** 10 21N 85 52W
Velasco, Sierra de, Argentina **94 B2** 29 20S 67 10W
Velddrif, S. Africa . . . . . . . . **56 E2** 32 42S 18 11 E
Velebit Planina, Croatia . . . . **16 F8** 44 50N 15 20 E
Veles, Macedonia . . . . . . . **23 D9** 41 46N 21 47 E
Vélez-Málaga, Spain . . . . . . **21 D3** 36 48N 4 5W
Vélez Rubio, Spain . . . . . . . **21 D4** 37 41N 2 5W
Velhas ➤, Brazil . . . . . . . **93 G10** 17 13S 44 49W
Velika Kapela, Croatia . . . . . **16 F8** 45 10N 15 5 E
Velikaya ➤, Russia . . . . . . **18 C4** 57 48N 28 10 E
Velikaya Kema, Russia . . . . **30 B8** 45 30N 137 12 E
Veliki Ustyug, Russia . . . . . **18 B8** 60 47N 46 20 E
Velikiye Luki, Russia . . . . . **18 C5** 56 25N 30 32 E
Veliko Türnovo, Bulgaria . . **23 C11** 43 5N 25 41 E
Velikonda Range, India . . . **40 M11** 14 45N 79 10 E
Velletri, Italy . . . . . . . . . . . **22 D5** 41 41N 12 47 E
Vellore, India . . . . . . . . . . **40 N11** 12 57N 79 10 E
Velsk, Russia . . . . . . . . . . **18 B7** 61 10N 42 5 E
Veluwezoom △, Neths. . . . . **15 B6** 52 5N 6 0 E
Velva, U.S.A. . . . . . . . . . . . **80 A4** 48 4N 100 56W
Venado Tuerto, Argentina . . **94 C3** 33 50S 62 0W
Vendée □, France . . . . . . . **20 C3** 46 50N 1 35W
Vendôme, France . . . . . . . . **20 C4** 47 47N 1 3 E
Venézia, Italy . . . . . . . . . . . **22 B5** 45 27N 12 21 E
Venézia, G. di, Italy . . . . . . **22 B5** 45 15N 13 0 E
Venezuela ■, S. Amer. . . . . **92 B5** 8 0N 66 0W
Venezuela, G. de, Venezuela **92 A4** 11 30N 71 0W
Vengurla, India . . . . . . . . . **40 M8** 15 53N 73 45 E
Venice = Venézia, Italy . . . . **22 B5** 45 27N 12 21 E
Venice, U.S.A. . . . . . . . . . . **83 M4** 27 6N 82 27W
Venkatapuram, India . . . . . **41 K12** 18 20N 80 30 E
Venlo, Neths. . . . . . . . . . . . **15 C6** 51 22N 6 11 E
Vennesla, Norway . . . . . . . **9 G12** 58 15N 7 59 E
Venraij, Neths. . . . . . . . . . . **15 C6** 51 31N 6 0 E
Ventana, Punta de la, Mexico **86 C3** 24 4N 109 48W
Ventana, Sa. de la, Argentina **94 D3** 38 0S 62 30W
Ventersburg, S. Africa . . . . . **56 D4** 28 7S 27 9 E
Venterstad, S. Africa . . . . . . **56 E4** 30 47S 25 48 E
Ventnor, U.K. . . . . . . . . . . . **13 G6** 50 36N 1 12W
Ventotène, Italy . . . . . . . . . **22 D5** 40 47N 13 25 E
Ventoux, Mt., France . . . . . . **20 D6** 44 10N 5 17 E
Ventspils, Latvia . . . . . . . . . **9 H19** 57 25N 21 32 E
Ventuarí ➤, Venezuela . . . . **92 C5** 3 58N 67 2W
Ventucopa, U.S.A. . . . . . . . **79 L7** 34 50N 119 29W
Ventura, U.S.A. . . . . . . . . . **79 L7** 34 17N 119 18W
Venus B., Australia . . . . . . . **63 F4** 38 40S 145 42 E
Vera, Argentina . . . . . . . . . **94 B3** 29 30S 60 20W
Vera, Spain . . . . . . . . . . . . **21 D5** 37 15N 1 51W
Veracruz, Mexico . . . . . . . . **87 D5** 19 10N 96 10W
Veracruz □, Mexico . . . . . . **87 D5** 19 0N 96 15W
Veraval, India . . . . . . . . . . **42 J4** 20 53N 70 27 E
Verbánia, Italy . . . . . . . . . . **20 D8** 45 56N 8 33 E
Vercelli, Italy . . . . . . . . . . . **20 D8** 45 19N 8 25 E
Verdalsøra, Norway . . . . . . **8 E14** 63 48N 11 30 E
Verde ➤, Argentina . . . . . . **96 E3** 41 56S 65 5W
Verde ➤, Goiás, Brazil . . . . **93 G8** 18 1S 50 14W
Verde ➤, Mato Grosso do Sul,
  Brazil . . . . . . . . . . . . . . . **93 H8** 21 25S 52 20W
Verde ➤, Chihuahua, Mexico **86 B3** 26 29N 107 58W
Verde ➤, Oaxaca, Mexico . . **87 D5** 15 59N 97 50W
Verde ➤, Veracruz, Mexico . **86 C4** 21 10N 102 50W
Verde ➤, Paraguay . . . . . . . **94 A4** 23 9S 57 37W
Verde, Cay, Bahamas . . . . . **88 B4** 23 0N 75 5W
Verden, Germany . . . . . . . . **16 B5** 52 55N 9 14 E
Verdi, U.S.A. . . . . . . . . . . . **78 F7** 39 31N 119 59W
Verdun, France . . . . . . . . . . **20 B6** 49 9N 5 24 E
Vereeniging, S. Africa . . . . . **57 D4** 26 38S 27 57 E
Verga, C., Guinea . . . . . . . . **50 F3** 10 30N 14 10W
Vergara, Uruguay . . . . . . . . **95 C5** 32 56S 53 57W
Vergemont Cr. ➤, Australia . . **62 C3** 24 16S 143 16 E
Vergennes, U.S.A. . . . . . . **85 B11** 44 10N 73 15W
Verín, Spain . . . . . . . . . . . . **21 B2** 41 57N 7 27W
Verkhnevilyuysk, Russia . . **29 C13** 63 27N 120 18 E
Verkhniy Baskunchak, Russia **19 E8** 48 14N 46 44 E
Verkhoyansk, Russia . . . . **29 C14** 67 35N 133 25 E
Verkhoyansk Ra. =
  Verkhoyanskiy Khrebet, Russia **29 C13** 66 0N 129 0 E
Verkhoyanskiy Khrebet, Russia **29 C13** 66 0N 129 0 E

Vermilion, Canada ..... 71 C6 53 20N 110 50W
Vermilion, U.S.A. ..... 84 E2 41 25N 82 22W
Vermilion →, Canada ..... 71 C6 53 22N 110 51W
Vermilion, B., U.S.A. ..... 81 L9 29 45N 91 55W
Vermilion Bay, Canada ..... 71 D10 49 51N 93 34W
Vermilion L., U.S.A. ..... 80 B8 47 53N 92 26W
Vermillon →, Canada ..... 80 D6 42 47N 96 56W
Vermillion →, Canada ..... 72 C5 47 38N 72 56W
Vermont □, U.S.A. ..... 85 C12 44 0N 73 0W
Vernadsky, Antarctica ..... 5 C17 65 0S 64 0W
Vernal, U.S.A. ..... 76 F9 40 27N 109 32W
Vernalis, U.S.A. ..... 78 H5 37 36N 121 17W
Verner, Canada ..... 72 C3 46 25N 80 8W
Verneukpan, S. Africa ..... 56 E3 30 0S 21 0 E
Vernon, Canada ..... 70 C5 50 20N 119 15W
Vernon, U.S.A. ..... 81 H5 34 9N 99 17W
Vernonia, U.S.A. ..... 78 E3 45 52N 123 11W
Vero Beach, U.S.A. ..... 83 M5 27 38N 80 24W
Véroia, Greece ..... 23 D10 40 34N 22 12 E
Verona, Canada ..... 85 B8 44 29N 76 42W
Verona, Italy ..... 22 B4 45 27N 10 59 E
Verona, U.S.A. ..... 80 D10 42 59N 89 32W
Versailles, France ..... 20 B5 48 48N 2 8 E
Vert, C., Senegal ..... 50 F2 14 45N 17 30W
Verulam, S. Africa ..... 57 D5 29 38S 31 2 E
Verviers, Belgium ..... 15 D5 50 37N 5 52 E
Veselovskoye Vdkhr., Russia ..... 19 E7 46 58N 41 25 E
Vesoul, France ..... 20 C7 47 40N 6 11 E
Vesterålen, Norway ..... 8 B16 68 45N 15 0 E
Vestfjorden, Norway ..... 8 C15 67 55N 14 0 E
Vestmannaeyjar, Iceland ..... 8 E3 63 27N 20 15W
Vestspitsbergen, Svalbard ..... 4 B8 78 40N 17 0 E
Vestvågøy, Norway ..... 8 B15 68 18N 13 50 E
Vesuvio, Italy ..... 22 D6 40 49N 14 26 E
Vesuvius, Mt. = Vesuvio, Italy ..... 22 D6 40 49N 14 26 E
Veszprém, Hungary ..... 17 E9 47 8N 17 57 E
Vetlanda, Sweden ..... 9 H16 57 24N 15 3 E
Vetlugu →, Russia ..... 18 C8 56 36N 46 4 E
Vettore, Mte., Italy ..... 22 C5 42 49N 13 16 E
Veurne, Belgium ..... 15 C2 51 5N 2 40 E
Veys, Iran ..... 45 D6 31 30N 49 0 E
Vezhen, Bulgaria ..... 23 C11 42 50N 24 20 E
Vi Thanh, Vietnam ..... 39 H5 9 42N 105 26 E
Viacha, Bolivia ..... 92 G5 16 39S 68 18W
Viamão, Brazil ..... 95 C5 30 5S 51 0W
Viana, Brazil ..... 93 D10 3 13S 44 55W
Viana do Alentejo, Portugal ..... 21 C2 38 17N 7 59W
Viana do Castelo, Portugal ..... 21 B1 41 42N 8 50W
Vianden, Lux. ..... 15 E6 49 56N 6 12 E
Viangchan = Vientiane, Laos ..... 38 D4 17 58N 102 36 E
Vianópolis, Brazil ..... 93 G9 16 40S 48 35W
Viaréggio, Italy ..... 22 C4 43 52N 10 14 E
Vibo Valéntia, Italy ..... 22 E7 38 40N 16 6 E
Viborg, Denmark ..... 9 H13 56 27N 9 23 E
Vic, Spain ..... 21 B7 41 58N 2 19 E
Vicenza, Italy ..... 22 B4 45 33N 11 33 E
Vich = Vic, Spain ..... 21 B7 41 58N 2 19 E
Vichada →, Colombia ..... 92 C5 4 55N 67 50W
Vichy, France ..... 20 C5 46 9N 3 26 E
Vicksburg, Ariz., U.S.A. ..... 79 M13 33 45N 113 45W
Vicksburg, Miss., U.S.A. ..... 81 J9 32 21N 90 53W
Victor, India ..... 42 J4 21 0N 71 30 E
Victor, U.S.A. ..... 84 D7 42 58N 77 24W
Victor Harbor, Australia ..... 63 F2 35 30S 138 37 E
Victoria, Argentina ..... 94 C3 32 40S 60 10W
Victoria, Canada ..... 70 D4 48 30N 123 25W
Victoria, Chile ..... 96 D2 38 13S 72 20W
Victoria, China ..... 33 G1 22 17N 114 9 E
Victoria, Malta ..... 25 C1 36 3N 14 14 E
Victoria, Kans., U.S.A. ..... 80 F5 38 52N 99 9W
Victoria, Tex., U.S.A. ..... 81 L6 28 48N 97 0W
Victoria □, Australia ..... 63 F3 37 0S 144 0 E
Victoria →, Australia ..... 60 C4 15 10S 129 40 E
Victoria, Grand L., Canada ..... 72 C4 47 31N 77 30W
Victoria, L., Africa ..... 54 C3 1 0S 33 0 E
Victoria, L., Australia ..... 63 E3 33 57S 141 15 E
Victoria, Mt., Burma ..... 41 J18 21 15N 93 55 E
Victoria Beach, Canada ..... 71 C9 50 40N 96 35W
Victoria de Durango = Durango, Mexico ..... 86 C4 24 3N 104 39W
Victoria de las Tunas, Cuba ..... 88 B4 20 58N 76 59W
Victoria Falls, Zimbabwe ..... 55 F2 17 58S 25 52 E
Victoria Harbour, Canada ..... 84 B5 44 45N 79 45W
Victoria I., Canada ..... 68 A8 71 0N 111 0W
Victoria L., Canada ..... 73 C8 48 20N 57 27W
Victoria Ld., Antarctica ..... 5 D11 75 0S 160 0 E
Victoria Nile →, Uganda ..... 54 B3 2 14N 31 26 E
Victoria River, Australia ..... 60 C5 16 25S 131 0 E
Victoria Str., Canada ..... 68 B9 69 31N 100 30W
Victoria West, S. Africa ..... 56 E3 31 25S 23 4 E
Victoriaville, Canada ..... 73 C5 46 4N 71 56W
Victorica, Argentina ..... 94 D2 36 20S 65 30W
Victorville, U.S.A. ..... 79 L9 34 32N 117 18W
Vicuña, Chile ..... 94 C1 30 0S 70 50W
Vicuña Mackenna, Argentina ..... 94 C3 33 53S 64 25W
Vidal, U.S.A. ..... 79 L12 34 7N 114 31W
Vidal Junction, U.S.A. ..... 79 L12 34 11N 114 34W
Vidalia, U.S.A. ..... 83 J4 32 13N 82 25W
Vídho, Greece ..... 25 A3 39 38N 19 55 E
Vidin, Bulgaria ..... 23 C10 43 59N 22 50 E
Vidisha, India ..... 42 H7 23 28N 77 53 E
Vidzy, Belarus ..... 9 J22 55 23N 26 37 E
Viedma, Argentina ..... 96 E4 40 50S 63 0W
Viedma, L., Argentina ..... 96 F2 49 30S 72 30W
Vielsalm, Belgium ..... 15 D5 50 17N 5 54 E
Vieng Pou Kha, Laos ..... 38 B3 20 41N 101 4 E
Vienna = Wien, Austria ..... 16 D9 48 12N 16 22 E
Vienna, Ill., U.S.A. ..... 81 G10 37 25N 88 54W
Vienna, Mo., U.S.A. ..... 80 F9 38 11N 91 57W
Vienne, France ..... 20 D6 45 31N 4 53 E
Vienne →, France ..... 20 C4 47 13N 0 5 E
Vientiane, Laos ..... 38 D4 17 58N 102 36 E
Vientos, Paso de los, Caribbean ..... 89 C5 20 0N 74 0W
Vieques, Isla de, Puerto Rico ..... 89 d 18 8N 65 30W
Vierge Pt., St. Lucia ..... 89 f 13 49N 60 53W
Vierzon, France ..... 20 C5 47 13N 2 5 E
Vietnam ■, Asia ..... 38 C6 19 0N 106 0 E
Vieux Fort, St. Lucia ..... 89 f 13 46N 60 58W
Vigan, Phil. ..... 37 A6 17 35N 120 28 E
Vigévano, Italy ..... 20 D8 45 19N 8 51 E
Vigia, Brazil ..... 93 D9 0 50S 48 5W
Vigia Chico, Mexico ..... 87 D7 19 46N 87 35W
Víglas, Ákra, Greece ..... 25 D9 35 54N 27 51 E
Vigo, Spain ..... 21 A1 42 12N 8 41W
Vihowa, Pakistan ..... 42 D4 31 8N 70 30 E
Vihowa →, Pakistan ..... 42 D4 31 8N 70 41 E
Vijayawada, India ..... 41 L12 16 31N 80 39 E
Vijosë →, Albania ..... 23 D8 40 37N 19 24 E

Vik, Iceland ..... 8 E4 63 25N 19 1W
Vikeke = Viqueque, E. Timor ..... 37 F7 8 52S 126 23 E
Viking, Canada ..... 70 C6 53 7N 111 50W
Vikna, Norway ..... 8 D14 64 55N 10 58 E
Vila da Maganja, Mozam. ..... 55 F4 17 18S 37 30 E
Vila do Bispo, Portugal ..... 21 D1 37 5N 8 53W
Vila Franca de Xira, Portugal ..... 21 C1 38 57N 8 59W
Vila Gamito, Mozam. ..... 55 E3 14 12S 33 0 E
Vila Gomes da Costa, Mozam. ..... 57 C5 24 20S 33 37 E
Vila Machado, Mozam. ..... 55 F3 19 15S 34 14 E
Vila Mouzinho, Mozam. ..... 55 E3 14 48S 34 25 E
Vila Nova de Gaia, Portugal ..... 21 B1 41 8N 8 37W
Vila Real, Portugal ..... 21 B2 41 17N 7 48W
Vila-real de los Infantes, Spain ..... 21 C5 39 55N 0 3W
Vila Real de Santo António, Portugal ..... 21 D2 37 10N 7 28W
Vila Vasco da Gama, Mozam. ..... 55 E3 14 54S 32 14 E
Vila Velha, Brazil ..... 95 A7 20 20S 40 17W
Vilagarcía de Arousa, Spain ..... 21 A1 42 34N 8 46W
Vilaine →, France ..... 20 C2 47 30N 2 27W
Vilanandro, Tanjona, Madag. ..... 57 B7 16 11S 44 27 E
Vilanculos, Mozam. ..... 57 C6 22 1S 35 17 E
Vilanova i la Geltrú, Spain ..... 21 B6 41 13N 1 40 E
Vilcheka, Zemlya, Russia ..... 4 A11 80 30N 60 30 E
Vileyka, Belarus ..... 17 A14 54 30N 26 53 E
Vilhelmina, Sweden ..... 8 D17 64 35N 16 39 E
Vilhena, Brazil ..... 92 F6 12 40S 60 5W
Viliya = Neris →, Lithuania ..... 9 J21 55 8N 24 16 E
Viljandi, Estonia ..... 9 G21 58 28N 25 30 E
Vilkitskogo, Proliv, Russia ..... 29 B11 78 0N 103 0 E
Vilkovo = Vylkove, Ukraine ..... 17 F15 45 28N 29 32 E
Villa Abecia, Bolivia ..... 94 A2 21 0S 68 18W
Villa Ahumada, Mexico ..... 86 A3 30 38N 106 30W
Villa Ana, Argentina ..... 94 B4 28 28S 59 40W
Villa Ángela, Argentina ..... 94 B3 27 34S 60 45W
Villa Bella, Bolivia ..... 92 F5 10 25S 65 22W
Villa Cañás, Argentina ..... 94 C3 34 0S 61 35W
Villa Colón, Argentina ..... 94 C2 31 38S 68 20W
Villa Constitución, Argentina ..... 94 C3 33 15S 60 20W
Villa de María, Argentina ..... 94 B3 29 55S 63 43W
Villa Dolores, Argentina ..... 94 C2 31 58S 65 15W
Villa Frontera, Mexico ..... 86 B4 26 56N 101 27W
Villa Guillermina, Argentina ..... 94 B4 28 15S 59 29W
Villa Hayes, Paraguay ..... 94 B4 25 5S 57 20W
Villa Iris, Argentina ..... 94 D3 38 12S 63 12W
Villa Juárez, Mexico ..... 86 B4 27 37N 100 44W
Villa María, Argentina ..... 94 C3 32 20S 63 10W
Villa Mazán, Argentina ..... 94 B2 28 40S 66 30W
Villa Montes, Argentina ..... 94 A3 21 10S 63 30W
Villa Ocampo, Argentina ..... 94 B4 28 30S 59 20W
Villa Ocampo, Mexico ..... 86 B3 26 29N 105 30W
Villa Ojo de Agua, Argentina ..... 94 B3 29 30S 63 44W
Villa San José, Argentina ..... 94 C4 32 12S 58 15W
Villa San Martín, Argentina ..... 94 B3 28 15S 64 9W
Villa Unión, Mexico ..... 86 C3 23 12N 106 14W
Villacarlos, Spain ..... 24 B11 39 53N 4 17 E
Villacarrillo, Spain ..... 21 C4 38 7N 3 3W
Villach, Austria ..... 16 E7 46 37N 13 51 E
Villafranca de los Caballeros, Spain ..... 24 B10 39 34N 3 25 E
Villagrán, Mexico ..... 87 C5 24 29N 99 29W
Villaguay, Argentina ..... 94 C4 32 0S 59 0W
Villahermosa, Mexico ..... 87 D6 17 59N 92 55W
Villajoyosa, Spain ..... 21 C5 38 30N 0 12W
Villalba, Spain ..... 21 A2 43 26N 7 40W
Villanueva, U.S.A. ..... 81 H2 35 16N 105 22W
Villanueva de la Serena, Spain ..... 21 C3 38 59N 5 50W
Villanueva y Geltrú = Vilanova i la Geltrú, Spain ..... 21 B6 41 13N 1 40 E
Villarreal = Vila-real de los Infantes, Spain ..... 21 C5 39 55N 0 3W
Villarrica, Chile ..... 96 D2 39 15S 72 15W
Villarrica, Paraguay ..... 94 B4 25 40S 56 30W
Villarrobledo, Spain ..... 21 C4 39 18N 2 36W
Villavicencio, Argentina ..... 94 C2 32 28S 69 0W
Villavicencio, Colombia ..... 92 C4 4 9N 73 37W
Villaviciosa, Spain ..... 21 A3 43 32N 5 27W
Villazón, Bolivia ..... 94 A2 22 0S 65 35W
Ville-Marie, Canada ..... 72 C4 47 20N 79 30W
Ville Platte, U.S.A. ..... 81 K8 30 41N 92 17W
Villena, Spain ..... 21 C5 38 39N 0 52W
Villeneuve-d'Ascq, France ..... 20 A5 50 38N 3 9 E
Villeneuve-sur-Lot, France ..... 20 D4 44 24N 0 42 E
Villiers, S. Africa ..... 57 D4 27 2S 28 36 E
Villingen-Schwenningen, Germany ..... 16 D5 48 3N 8 26 E
Villmanstrand = Lappeenranta, Finland ..... 9 F23 61 3N 28 12 E
Vilnius, Lithuania ..... 9 J21 54 38N 25 19 E
Vilvoorde, Belgium ..... 15 D4 50 56N 4 26 E
Vilyuy →, Russia ..... 29 C13 64 24N 126 26 E
Vilyuysk, Russia ..... 29 C13 63 40N 121 35 E
Viña del Mar, Chile ..... 94 C1 33 0S 71 30W
Vinaròs, Spain ..... 21 B6 40 30N 0 27 E
Vincennes, U.S.A. ..... 82 F2 38 41N 87 32W
Vincent, U.S.A. ..... 79 L8 34 33N 118 11W
Vinchina, Argentina ..... 94 B2 28 45S 68 15W
Vindelälven →, Sweden ..... 8 E18 63 55N 19 50 E
Vindeln, Sweden ..... 8 D18 64 12N 19 43 E
Vindhya Ra., India ..... 42 H7 22 50N 77 0 E
Vineland, U.S.A. ..... 82 F8 39 29N 75 2W
Vinh, Vietnam ..... 38 C5 18 45N 105 38 E
Vinh Linh, Vietnam ..... 38 D6 17 4N 107 2 E
Vinh Long, Vietnam ..... 39 G5 10 16N 105 57 E
Vinh Yen, Vietnam ..... 38 B5 21 21N 105 35 E
Vinita, U.S.A. ..... 81 G7 36 39N 95 9W
Vinkovci, Croatia ..... 23 B8 45 19N 18 48 E
Vinnitsa = Vinnytsya, Ukraine ..... 17 D15 49 15N 28 30 E
Vinnytsya, Ukraine ..... 17 D15 49 15N 28 30 E
Vinson Massif, Antarctica ..... 5 D16 78 35S 85 25W
Vinton, Calif., U.S.A. ..... 78 F6 39 48N 120 10W
Vinton, Iowa, U.S.A. ..... 80 D8 42 10N 92 1W
Vinton, La., U.S.A. ..... 81 K8 30 11N 93 35W
Viqueque, E. Timor ..... 37 F7 8 52S 126 23 E
Virac, Phil. ..... 37 B6 13 30N 124 20 E
Virachey, Cambodia ..... 38 F6 13 59N 106 49 E
Virachei y, Cambodia ..... 38 E6 14 0N 106 50 E
Virago Sd., Canada ..... 70 C2 54 0N 132 30W
Viramgam, India ..... 42 H5 23 5N 72 0 E
Viranşehir, Turkey ..... 44 B3 37 13N 39 45 E
Virawah, Pakistan ..... 42 G4 24 31N 70 46 E
Virden, Canada ..... 71 D8 49 50N 100 56W
Vire, France ..... 20 B3 48 50N 0 53W
Vírgenes, C., Argentina ..... 96 G3 52 19S 68 21W
Virgin →, U.S.A. ..... 77 H6 36 28N 114 21W
Virgin Gorda, Br. Virgin Is. ..... 89 e 18 30N 64 26W
Virgin Is. (British) ☑, W. Indies ..... 89 e 18 30N 64 30W

Virgin Is. (U.S.) ☑, W. Indies ..... 89 e 18 20N 65 0W
Virgin Islands △, U.S. Virgin Is. ..... 89 C7 18 21N 64 43W
Virginia, S. Africa ..... 56 D4 28 8S 26 55 E
Virginia, U.S.A. ..... 80 B8 47 31N 92 32W
Virginia □, U.S.A. ..... 82 G7 37 30N 78 45W
Virginia Beach, U.S.A. ..... 82 G8 36 51N 75 59W
Virginia City, Mont., U.S.A. ..... 76 D8 45 18N 111 56W
Virginia City, Nev., U.S.A. ..... 78 F7 39 19N 119 39W
Virginia Falls, Canada ..... 70 A3 61 38N 125 42W
Virginiatown, Canada ..... 72 C4 48 9N 79 36W
Viroqua, U.S.A. ..... 80 D9 43 34N 90 53W
Virovitica, Croatia ..... 22 B7 45 51N 17 21 E
Virpur, India ..... 42 J4 21 51N 70 42 E
Virton, Belgium ..... 15 E5 49 35N 5 32 E
Virudunagar, India ..... 40 Q10 9 30N 77 58 E
Virunga △, Dem. Rep. of the Congo ..... 54 B2 0 5N 29 38 E
Vis, Croatia ..... 22 C7 43 4N 16 10 E
Visalia, U.S.A. ..... 78 J7 36 20N 119 18W
Visayan Sea, Phil. ..... 37 B6 11 30N 123 30 E
Visby, Sweden ..... 9 H18 57 37N 18 18 E
Viscount Melville Sd., Canada ..... 4 B2 74 10N 108 0W
Visé, Belgium ..... 15 D5 50 44N 5 41 E
Višegrad, Bos.-H. ..... 23 C8 43 47N 19 17 E
Viseu, Brazil ..... 93 D9 1 10S 46 5W
Viseu, Portugal ..... 21 B2 40 40N 7 55W
Vishakhapatnam, India ..... 41 L13 17 45N 83 20 E
Visnagar, India ..... 42 H5 23 45N 72 32 E
Viso, Mte., Italy ..... 20 D7 44 38N 7 5 E
Visokoi I., Antarctica ..... 5 B1 56 43S 27 15W
Vista, U.S.A. ..... 79 M9 33 12N 117 14W
Vistula = Wisła →, Poland ..... 17 A10 54 22N 18 55 E
Vitebsk = Vitsyebsk, Belarus ..... 18 C5 55 10N 30 15 E
Viterbo, Italy ..... 22 C5 42 25N 12 6 E
Viti Levu, Fiji ..... 59 C7 17 30S 177 30 E
Vitigudino, Spain ..... 21 B2 41 1N 6 26W
Vitim, Russia ..... 29 D12 59 28N 112 35 E
Vitim →, Russia ..... 29 D12 59 26N 112 34 E
Vitória, Brazil ..... 93 H10 20 20S 40 22W
Vitória da Conquista, Brazil ..... 93 F10 14 51S 40 51W
Vitória de São Antão, Brazil ..... 93 E11 8 10S 35 20W
Vitoria-Gasteiz, Spain ..... 21 A4 42 50N 2 41W
Vitsyebsk, Belarus ..... 18 C5 55 10N 30 15 E
Vittória, Italy ..... 22 F6 36 57N 14 32 E
Vittório Véneto, Italy ..... 22 B5 45 59N 12 18 E
Viveiro, Spain ..... 21 A2 43 39N 7 38W
Vivian, U.S.A. ..... 81 J8 32 53N 93 59W
Vizcaíno, Desierto de, Mexico ..... 86 B2 27 40N 113 50W
Vizcaíno, Sierra, Mexico ..... 86 B2 27 40N 114 0W
Vize, Turkey ..... 23 D12 41 34N 27 45 E
Vizianagaram, India ..... 41 K13 18 6N 83 30 E
Vlaardingen, Neths. ..... 15 C4 51 55N 4 21 E
Vladikavkaz, Russia ..... 19 F7 43 0N 44 35 E
Vladimir, Russia ..... 18 C7 56 15N 40 30 E
Vladimir Volynskiy = Volodymyr-Volynskyy, Ukraine ..... 17 C13 50 50N 24 18 E
Vladivostok, Russia ..... 29 E14 43 10N 131 53 E
Vlieland, Neths. ..... 15 A4 53 16N 4 55 E
Vlissingen, Neths. ..... 15 C3 51 26N 3 34 E
Vlorë, Albania ..... 23 D8 40 32N 19 28 E
Vltava →, Czech Rep. ..... 16 D8 50 21N 14 30 E
Vo Dat, Vietnam ..... 39 G6 11 9N 107 31 E
Voe, U.K. ..... 11 A7 60 21N 1 16W
Vogelkop = Doberai, Jazirah, Indonesia ..... 37 E8 1 25S 133 0 E
Vogelsberg, Germany ..... 16 C5 50 31N 9 12 E
Voghera, Italy ..... 20 D8 44 59N 9 1 E
Vohibinany, Madag. ..... 57 B8 18 49S 49 4 E
Vohilava, Madag. ..... 57 C8 21 4S 48 0 E
Vohimarina = Iharana, Madag. ..... 57 A9 13 25S 50 0 E
Vohimena, Tanjon' i, Madag. ..... 57 D8 25 36S 45 8 E
Vohipeno, Madag. ..... 57 C8 22 22S 47 51 E
Voi, Kenya ..... 54 C4 3 25S 38 32 E
Voiron, France ..... 20 D6 45 22N 5 35 E
Voisey B., Canada ..... 73 A7 56 15N 61 50W
Vojmsjön, Sweden ..... 8 D17 65 0N 16 24 E
Vojvodina □, Serbia & M. ..... 23 B9 45 20N 20 0 E
Volborg, U.S.A. ..... 80 C2 45 51N 105 41W
Volcán de Colima △, Mexico ..... 86 D4 19 30N 103 40W
Volcano Is. = Kazan-Rettō, Pac. Oc. ..... 64 E6 25 0N 141 0 E
Volcans △, Rwanda ..... 54 C2 1 30S 29 26 E
Volda, Norway ..... 9 E12 62 9N 6 5 E
Volga = Privolzhskiy □, Russia ..... 28 D6 56 0N 50 0 E
Volga →, Russia ..... 19 E8 46 0N 48 30 E
Volga Hts. = Privolzhskaya Vozvyshennost, Russia ..... 19 D8 51 0N 46 0 E
Volgodonsk, Russia ..... 19 E7 47 33N 42 5 E
Volgograd, Russia ..... 19 E7 48 40N 44 25 E
Volgogradskoye Vdkhr., Russia ..... 19 D8 50 0N 45 20 E
Volkhov →, Russia ..... 18 B5 60 8N 32 20 E
Volkovysk = Vawkavysk, Belarus ..... 17 B13 53 9N 24 30 E
Volksrust, S. Africa ..... 57 D4 27 24S 29 53 E
Volochanka, Russia ..... 29 B10 71 0N 94 28 E
Volodymyr-Volynskyy, Ukraine ..... 17 C13 50 50N 24 18 E
Vologda, Russia ..... 18 C6 59 10N 39 45 E
Vólos, Greece ..... 23 E10 39 24N 22 59 E
Volozhin = Valozhyn, Belarus ..... 17 A14 54 3N 26 30 E
Volsk, Russia ..... 18 D8 52 5N 47 22 E
Volta →, Ghana ..... 50 G6 5 46N 0 41 E
Volta, L., Ghana ..... 50 G6 7 30N 0 0
Volta Redonda, Brazil ..... 95 A7 22 31S 44 5W
Voltaire, C., Australia ..... 60 B4 14 16S 125 35 E
Volterra, Italy ..... 22 C4 43 24N 10 51 E
Volturno →, Italy ..... 22 D5 41 1N 13 55 E
Volzhskiy, Russia ..... 19 E7 48 56N 44 46 E
Vondrozo, Madag. ..... 57 C8 22 49S 47 20 E
Vopnafjörður, Iceland ..... 8 D6 65 45N 14 50W
Vóriai Sporádhes, Greece ..... 23 E10 39 15S 23 30 E
Vorkuta, Russia ..... 18 A11 67 48N 64 20 E
Vormsi, Estonia ..... 9 G20 59 1N 23 13 E
Voronezh, Russia ..... 19 D6 51 40N 39 10 E
Võrts Järv, Estonia ..... 9 G22 58 16N 26 3 E
Võru, Estonia ..... 9 H22 57 48N 26 54 E
Vosges, France ..... 20 B7 48 20N 7 10 E
Voss, Norway ..... 9 F12 60 38N 6 26 E
Vostok I., Kiribati ..... 65 J12 10 5S 152 23W
Votkinsk, Russia ..... 18 C9 57 22N 55 12 E
Votkinskoye Vdkhr., Russia ..... 18 C10 57 22N 55 0 E
Votsuri-Shima, Japan ..... 31 M1 25 45N 123 29 E
Vouga →, Portugal ..... 21 B1 40 41N 8 40W
Voúxa, Ákra, Greece ..... 25 D5 35 37N 23 32 E
Voyageurs △, U.S.A. ..... 80 A8 48 32N 93 0W
Vozhe, Ozero, Russia ..... 18 B6 60 45N 39 0 E

Vrangelya, Ostrov, Russia ..... 29 B19 71 0N 180 0 E
Vranje, Serbia & M. ..... 23 C9 42 34N 21 54 E
Vratsa, Bulgaria ..... 23 C10 43 15N 23 30 E
Vrbas →, Bos.-H. ..... 22 B7 45 8N 17 29 E
Vrede, S. Africa ..... 57 D4 27 24S 29 6 E
Vredefort, S. Africa ..... 56 D4 27 0S 27 22 E
Vredenburg, S. Africa ..... 56 E2 32 56S 18 0 E
Vredendal, S. Africa ..... 56 E2 31 41S 18 35 E
Vrindavan, India ..... 42 F7 27 37N 77 40 E
Vríses, Greece ..... 25 D6 35 23N 24 13 E
Vršac, Serbia & M. ..... 23 B9 45 8N 21 20 E
Vryburg, S. Africa ..... 56 D3 26 55S 24 45 E
Vryheid, S. Africa ..... 57 D5 27 45S 30 47 E
Vu Liet, Vietnam ..... 38 C5 18 43N 105 23 E
Vukovar, Croatia ..... 23 B8 45 21N 18 59 E
Vulcan, Canada ..... 70 C6 50 25N 113 15W
Vulcan, Romania ..... 17 F12 45 23N 23 17 E
Vulcaneşti, Moldova ..... 17 F15 45 41N 28 18 E
Vulcano, Italy ..... 22 E6 38 24N 14 58 E
Vulkaneshty = Vulcaneşti, Moldova ..... 17 F15 45 41N 28 18 E
Vunduzi →, Mozam. ..... 55 F3 18 56S 34 1 E
Vung Tau, Vietnam ..... 39 G6 10 21N 107 4 E
Vwaza △, Malawi ..... 55 E3 10 58S 33 25 E
Vyatka = Kirov, Russia ..... 18 C8 58 35N 49 40 E
Vyatka →, Russia ..... 18 C9 55 37N 51 28 E
Vyatskiye Polyany, Russia ..... 18 C9 56 14N 51 5 E
Vyazemskiy, Russia ..... 29 E14 47 32N 134 45 E
Vyazma, Russia ..... 18 C5 55 10N 34 15 E
Vyborg, Russia ..... 18 B5 60 43N 28 47 E
Vychegda →, Russia ..... 18 B8 61 18N 46 36 E
Vychodné Beskydy, Europe ..... 17 D11 49 20N 22 0 E
Vyg-ozero, Russia ..... 18 B5 63 47N 34 29 E
Vylkove, Ukraine ..... 17 F15 45 28N 29 32 E
Vynohradiv, Ukraine ..... 17 D12 48 9N 23 2 E
Vyrnwy, L., U.K. ..... 12 E4 52 48N 3 31W
Vyshniy Volochek, Russia ..... 18 C5 57 30N 34 30 E
Vyshzha = imeni 26 Bakinskikh Komissarov, Turkmenistan ..... 45 B7 39 22N 54 10 E
Výškov, Czech Rep. ..... 17 D9 49 17N 17 0 E
Vytegra, Russia ..... 18 B6 61 0N 36 27 E

## W

W.A.C. Bennett Dam, Canada ..... 70 B4 56 2N 122 6W
Waal →, Neths. ..... 15 C5 51 37N 5 0 E
Waalwijk, Neths. ..... 15 C5 51 42N 5 4 E
Wabakimi △, Canada ..... 72 B2 50 43N 89 29W
Wabana, Canada ..... 73 C9 47 40N 53 0W
Wabasca →, Canada ..... 70 B5 58 22N 115 20W
Wabasca-Desmarais, Canada ..... 70 B6 55 57N 113 56W
Wabash, U.S.A. ..... 82 E3 40 48N 85 49W
Wabash →, U.S.A. ..... 82 G1 37 48N 88 2W
Wabigoon L., Canada ..... 71 D10 49 44N 92 44W
Wabowden, Canada ..... 71 C9 54 55N 98 38W
Wabuk Pt., Canada ..... 72 A2 55 20N 85 5W
Wabush, Canada ..... 73 B6 52 55N 66 52W
Waco, U.S.A. ..... 81 K6 31 33N 97 9W
Waconichi, L., Canada ..... 72 B5 50 8N 74 0W
Wad Hamid, Sudan ..... 51 E12 16 30N 32 45 E
Wad Medanî, Sudan ..... 51 F12 14 28N 33 30 E
Wad Thana, Pakistan ..... 42 F2 27 22N 66 23 E
Wadai, Africa ..... 48 E5 12 0N 19 0 E
Wadayama, Japan ..... 31 G7 35 19N 134 52 E
Waddeneilanden, Neths. ..... 15 A5 53 25N 5 10 E
Waddenzee, Neths. ..... 15 A5 53 6N 5 10 E
Waddington, U.S.A. ..... 85 B9 44 52N 75 12W
Waddington, Mt., Canada ..... 70 C3 51 23N 125 15W
Waddy Pt., Australia ..... 63 C5 24 58S 153 21 E
Wadebridge, U.K. ..... 13 G3 50 31N 4 51W
Wadena, Canada ..... 71 C8 51 57N 103 47W
Wadena, U.S.A. ..... 80 B7 46 26N 95 8W
Wadeye, Australia ..... 60 B4 14 28S 129 52 E
Wadhams, Canada ..... 70 C3 51 30N 127 30W
Wādī as Sīr, Jordan ..... 46 D4 31 56N 35 49 E
Wadi Halfa, Sudan ..... 51 D12 21 53N 31 19 E
Wadi Rum △, Jordan ..... 46 F4 29 30N 35 20 E
Wadsworth, Nev., U.S.A. ..... 76 G4 39 38N 119 17W
Wadsworth, Ohio, U.S.A. ..... 84 E3 41 2N 81 44W
Waegwan, S. Korea ..... 35 G15 35 59N 128 23 E
Wafangdian, China ..... 35 E11 39 59N 121 58 E
Wafrah, Si. Arabia ..... 44 D5 28 33N 47 56 E
Wageningen, Neths. ..... 15 C5 51 58N 5 40 E
Wager B., Canada ..... 69 B11 65 26N 88 40W
Wagga Wagga, Australia ..... 63 F4 35 7S 147 24 E
Waghete, Indonesia ..... 37 E9 4 10S 135 50 E
Wagin, Australia ..... 61 F2 33 17S 117 25 E
Wagner, U.S.A. ..... 80 D5 43 5N 98 18W
Wagon Mound, U.S.A. ..... 81 G2 36 1N 104 42W
Wagoner, U.S.A. ..... 81 H7 35 58N 95 22W
Wah, Pakistan ..... 42 C5 33 45N 72 40 E
Wahai, Indonesia ..... 37 E7 2 48S 129 35 E
Wahiawa, U.S.A. ..... 74 H15 21 30N 158 2W
Wâhid, Egypt ..... 46 E1 30 48N 32 21 E
Wahnai, Afghan. ..... 42 C1 32 40N 65 50 E
Wahoo, U.S.A. ..... 80 E6 41 13N 96 37W
Wahpeton, U.S.A. ..... 80 B6 46 16N 96 36W
Waiau →, N.Z. ..... 59 K4 42 47S 173 22 E
Waibeem, Indonesia ..... 37 E8 0 30S 132 59 E
Waigeo, Indonesia ..... 37 E8 0 20S 130 40 E
Waihi, N.Z. ..... 59 G5 37 15S 175 52 E
Waihou →, N.Z. ..... 59 G5 37 15S 175 40 E
Waika, Dem. Rep. of the Congo ..... 54 C2 2 22S 25 42 E
Waikabubak, Indonesia ..... 37 F5 9 45S 119 25 E
Waikaremoana, L., N.Z. ..... 59 H6 38 49S 177 9 E
Waikari, N.Z. ..... 59 K4 42 58S 172 41 E
Waikato →, N.Z. ..... 59 G5 37 23S 174 43 E
Waikerie, Australia ..... 63 E3 34 9S 140 0 E
Waikokopu, N.Z. ..... 59 H6 39 3S 177 52 E
Waikouaiti, N.Z. ..... 59 L3 45 36S 170 41 E
Wailingding Dao, China ..... 33 G11 22 6N 113 50 E
Wailuku, U.S.A. ..... 74 H16 20 53N 156 30W
Waimakariri →, N.Z. ..... 59 K4 43 24S 172 42 E
Waimate, N.Z. ..... 59 L3 44 45S 171 3 E
Wainganga →, India ..... 40 K11 18 50N 79 55 E
Waingapu, Indonesia ..... 37 F6 9 35S 120 11 E
Waini →, Guyana ..... 92 B7 8 20N 59 50W
Wainwright, Canada ..... 71 C6 52 50N 110 50W
Waiouru, N.Z. ..... 59 H5 39 28S 175 41 E
Waipara, N.Z. ..... 59 K4 43 3S 172 46 E
Waipawa, N.Z. ..... 59 H6 39 56S 176 38 E
Waipiro, N.Z. ..... 59 G7 38 2S 178 22 E
Waipoua Forest, N.Z. ..... 59 F4 35 39S 173 33 E
Waipu, N.Z. ..... 59 F5 35 59S 174 29 E
Waipukurau, N.Z. ..... 59 J6 40 1S 176 33 E

Wairakei, N.Z. 59 H6 38 37S 176 6 E
Wairarapa, L., N.Z. 59 J5 41 14S 175 15 E
Wairoa, N.Z. 59 H6 39 3S 177 25 E
Waitaki →, N.Z. 59 L3 44 56S 171 7 E
Waitangi, N.Z. 59 F5 35 16S 174 5 E
Waitara, N.Z. 59 H5 38 59S 174 15 E
Waitomo Caves, N.Z. 59 G5 38 16S 175 7 E
Waitsburg, U.S.A. 76 C5 46 16N 118 9W
Waiuku, N.Z. 59 G5 37 15S 174 45 E
Wajima, Japan 31 F8 37 30N 137 0 E
Wajir, Kenya 54 B5 1 42N 40 5 E
Wakasa, Japan 31 G7 35 20N 134 24 E
Wakasa-Wan, Japan 31 G7 35 40N 135 30 E
Wakatipu, L., N.Z. 59 L2 45 5S 168 33 E
Wakaw, Canada 71 C7 52 39N 105 44W
Wakayama, Japan 31 G7 34 15N 135 15 E
Wakayama □, Japan 31 H7 33 50N 135 30 E
Wake Forest, U.S.A. 83 H6 35 59N 78 30W
Wake I., Pac. Oc. 64 F8 19 18N 166 36 E
WaKeeney, U.S.A. 80 F5 39 1N 99 53W
Wakefield, Jamaica 88 a 18 26N 77 42W
Wakefield, N.Z. 59 J4 41 24S 173 5 E
Wakefield, U.K. 12 D6 53 41N 1 29W
Wakefield, Mass., U.S.A. 85 D13 42 30N 71 4W
Wakefield, Mich., U.S.A. 80 B10 46 29N 89 56W
Wakkanai, Japan 30 B10 45 28N 141 35 E
Wakool, Australia 63 F3 35 28S 144 23 E
Wakool →, Australia 63 F3 35 5S 143 33 E
Wakre, Indonesia 37 E8 0 19S 131 5 E
Wakuach, L., Canada 73 A6 55 34N 67 32W
Walamba, Zambia 55 E2 13 30S 28 42 E
Wałbrzych, Poland 16 C9 50 45N 16 18 E
Walbury Hill, U.K. 13 F6 51 21N 1 28W
Walcha, Australia 63 E5 30 55S 151 31 E
Walcheren, Neths. 15 C3 51 30N 3 35 E
Walcott, U.S.A. 76 F10 41 46N 106 51W
Wałcz, Poland 16 B9 53 17N 16 27 E
Waldburg Ra., Australia 61 D2 24 40S 117 35 E
Walden, Colo., U.S.A. 76 F10 40 44N 106 17W
Walden, N.Y., U.S.A. 85 E10 41 34N 74 11W
Waldport, U.S.A. 76 D1 44 26N 124 4W
Waldron, U.S.A. 81 H7 34 54N 94 5W
Walebing, Australia 61 F2 30 41S 116 13 E
Wales □, U.K. 13 E3 52 19N 4 43W
Walgett, Australia 63 E4 30 0S 148 5 E
Walgreen Coast, Antarctica 5 D15 75 15S 105 0W
Walhalla, U.S.A. 80 B7 47 6N 94 35W
Walker, L., U.S.A. 73 B6 50 20N 67 11W
Walker L., Canada 71 C9 54 42N 95 57W
Walker L., U.S.A. 76 G4 38 42N 118 43W
Walkerston, Australia 62 K7 21 11S 149 8 E
Walkerton, Canada 84 B3 44 10N 81 10W
Wall, U.S.A. 80 D3 44 0N 102 8W
Walla Walla, U.S.A. 76 C4 46 4N 118 20W
Wallace, Idaho, U.S.A. 76 C6 47 28N 115 56W
Wallace, N.C., U.S.A. 83 H7 34 44N 77 59W
Wallaceburg, Canada 84 D2 42 34N 82 23W
Wallachia = Valahia, Romania 17 F13 44 35N 24 0 E
Wallal, Australia 63 D4 26 32S 146 7 E
Wallam Cr. →, Australia 63 D4 28 40S 147 20 E
Wallambin, L., Australia 61 F2 30 57S 117 35 E
Wallangarra, Australia 63 D5 28 56S 151 58 E
Wallaroo, Australia 63 E2 33 56S 137 39 E
Wallenpaupack, L., U.S.A. 85 E9 41 25N 75 15W
Wallingford, U.S.A. 85 E12 41 27N 72 50W
Wallis & Futuna, Is., Pac. Oc. 64 J10 13 18S 176 10W
Wallowa, U.S.A. 76 D5 45 34N 117 32W
Wallowa Mts., U.S.A. 76 D5 45 20N 117 30W
Walls, U.K. 11 A7 60 14N 1 33W
Walls of Jerusalem △, Australia 63 G4 41 56S 146 15 E
Wallula, U.S.A. 76 C4 46 5N 118 54W
Wallumbilla, Australia 63 D4 26 33S 149 9 E
Walmsley, L., Canada 71 A7 63 25N 108 36W
Walney, I. of, U.K. 12 C4 54 6N 3 15W
Walnut Canyon △, U.S.A. 77 J8 35 15N 111 20W
Walnut Creek, U.S.A. 78 H4 37 54N 122 4W
Walnut Ridge, U.S.A. 81 G9 36 4N 90 57W
Walpole, Australia 61 F2 34 58S 116 44 E
Walpole, U.S.A. 85 D13 42 9N 71 15W
Walsall, U.K. 13 E6 52 35N 1 58W
Walsenburg, U.S.A. 81 G2 37 38N 104 47W
Walsh, U.S.A. 81 G3 37 23N 102 17W
Walsh →, Australia 62 B3 16 31S 143 42 E
Walterboro, U.S.A. 83 J5 32 55N 80 40W
Walters, U.S.A. 81 H5 34 22N 98 19W
Waltham, U.S.A. 85 D13 42 23N 71 14W
Waltman, U.S.A. 76 E10 43 4N 107 12W
Walton, U.S.A. 85 D9 42 10N 75 8W
Walton-on-the-Naze, U.K. 13 F9 51 51N 1 17 E
Walvis Bay, Namibia 56 C1 23 0S 14 28 E
Walvisbaai = Walvis Bay, Namibia 56 C1 23 0S 14 28 E
Wamba, Dem. Rep. of the Congo 54 B2 2 10N 27 57 E
Wamba, Kenya 54 B4 0 58N 37 19 E
Wamego, U.S.A. 80 F6 39 12N 96 18W
Wamena, Indonesia 37 E9 4 4S 138 57 E
Wamsutter, U.S.A. 76 F9 41 40N 107 58W
Wamulan, Indonesia 37 E7 3 27S 126 7 E
Wan Xian, China 34 E8 38 47N 115 7 E
Wana, Pakistan 42 C3 32 20N 69 32 E
Wanaaring, Australia 63 D3 29 38S 144 9 E
Wanaka, N.Z. 59 L2 44 42S 169 9 E
Wanaka, L., N.Z. 59 L2 44 33S 169 7 E
Wanapitei L., Canada 72 C3 46 45N 80 40W
Wandel Sea = McKinley Sea, Arctic 4 A7 82 0N 0 0W
Wanderer, Zimbabwe 55 F3 19 36S 30 1 E
Wandhari, Pakistan 42 F2 27 42N 66 48 E
Wandoan, Australia 63 D4 26 5S 149 55 E
Wanfu, China 35 D12 40 8N 122 38 E
Wang →, Thailand 38 D2 17 8N 99 2 E
Wang Noi, Thailand 38 E3 14 13N 100 44 E
Wang Saphung, Thailand 38 D3 17 18N 101 46 E
Wang Thong, Thailand 38 D3 16 50N 100 26 E
Wanga, Dem. Rep. of the Congo 54 B2 2 58N 29 12 E
Wangal, Indonesia 37 F8 6 8S 134 9 E
Wanganella, Australia 63 F3 35 6S 144 49 E
Wanganui, N.Z. 59 H5 39 56S 175 3 E
Wangaratta, Australia 63 F4 36 21S 146 19 E
Wangary, Australia 63 E2 34 35S 135 29 E
Wangdu, China 34 E8 38 40N 115 7 E
Wangerooge, Germany 16 B4 53 47N 7 54 E
Wangiwangi, Indonesia 37 F6 5 22S 123 37 E
Wangqing, China 35 C15 43 12N 129 42 E
Wankaner, India 42 H4 22 35N 71 0 E
Wanless, Canada 71 C8 54 11N 101 21W
Wanneroo, Australia 61 F2 31 42S 115 46 E

Wanning, China 38 C8 18 48N 110 22 E
Wanon Niwat, Thailand 38 D4 17 38N 103 46 E
Wanqinsha, China 33 F10 22 43N 113 33 E
Wanquan, China 34 D8 40 50N 114 40 E
Wanrong, China 34 G6 35 25N 110 50 E
Wanshan Qundao, China 33 G10 21 57N 113 45 E
Wantage, U.K. 13 F6 51 35N 1 25W
Wanzai, China 33 G10 22 12N 113 31 E
Wapakoneta, U.S.A. 82 E3 40 34N 84 12W
Wapato, U.S.A. 76 C3 46 27N 120 25W
Wapawekka L., Canada 71 C8 54 55N 104 40W
Wapikopa L., Canada 72 B2 52 56N 87 53W
Wapiti →, Canada 70 B5 55 5N 118 18W
Wappingers Falls, U.S.A. 85 E11 41 36N 73 55W
Wapsipinicon →, U.S.A. 80 E9 41 44N 90 19W
Wapusk △, Canada 71 B10 57 46N 93 22W
Warangal, India 40 L11 17 58N 79 35 E
Waraseoni, India 43 J9 21 45N 80 2 E
Waratah, Australia 63 G4 41 30S 145 30 E
Waratah B., Australia 63 F4 38 54S 146 5 E
Warburton, Vic., Australia 63 F4 37 47S 145 42 E
Warburton, W. Austral., Australia 61 E4 26 8S 126 35 E
Warburton, The →, Australia 63 D2 28 4S 137 28 E
Warburton Ra., Australia 61 E4 25 55S 126 28 E
Ward, N.Z. 59 J5 41 49S 174 11 E
Ward →, Australia 63 D4 26 28S 146 6 E
Ward Mt., U.S.A. 78 H8 37 12N 118 54W
Warden, S. Africa 57 D4 27 50S 29 0 E
Wardha, India 40 J11 20 45N 78 39 E
Wardha →, India 40 K11 19 57N 79 11 E
Ware, Canada 70 B3 57 26N 125 41W
Ware, U.K. 13 F8 51 49N 0 0W
Ware, U.S.A. 85 D12 42 16N 72 14W
Waregem, Belgium 15 D3 50 53N 3 27 E
Wareham, U.S.A. 85 E14 41 46N 70 43W
Waremme, Belgium 15 D5 50 43N 5 15 E
Warialda, Australia 63 D5 29 29S 150 33 E
Wariap, Indonesia 37 E8 1 30S 134 5 E
Warin Chamrap, Thailand 38 E5 15 12N 104 53 E
Warkopi, Indonesia 37 E8 1 12S 134 9 E
Warm Springs, U.S.A. 77 G5 38 10N 116 20W
Warman, Canada 71 C7 52 19N 106 30W
Warmbad = Bela Bela, S. Africa 57 C4 24 51S 28 19 E
Warmbad, Namibia 56 D2 28 25S 18 42 E
Warminster, U.K. 13 F5 51 12N 2 10W
Warminster, U.S.A. 85 F9 40 12N 75 6W
Warner Mts., U.S.A. 76 F3 41 40N 120 15W
Warner Robins, U.S.A. 83 J4 32 37N 83 36W
Waroona, Australia 61 F2 32 50S 115 58 E
Warracknabeal, Australia 63 F3 36 9S 142 26 E
Warragul, Australia 63 F4 38 10S 145 58 E
Warrego →, Australia 63 E4 30 24S 145 21 E
Warrego Ra., Australia 62 C4 24 58S 146 0 E
Warren, Australia 63 E4 31 42S 147 51 E
Warren, Ark., U.S.A. 81 J8 33 37N 92 4W
Warren, Mich., U.S.A. 82 D4 42 30N 83 0W
Warren, Minn., U.S.A. 80 A6 48 12N 96 46W
Warren, Ohio, U.S.A. 84 E4 41 14N 80 49W
Warren, Pa., U.S.A. 84 E5 41 51N 79 9W
Warrenpoint, U.K. 10 B5 54 6N 6 15W
Warrensburg, Mo., U.S.A. 80 F8 38 46N 93 44W
Warrensburg, N.Y., U.S.A. 85 C11 43 29N 73 46W
Warrenton, S. Africa 56 D3 28 9S 24 47 E
Warrenton, U.S.A. 78 D3 46 10N 123 56W
Warri, Nigeria 50 G7 5 30N 5 41 E
Warrina, Australia 63 D2 28 12S 135 50 E
Warrington, U.K. 12 D5 53 24N 2 35W
Warrington, U.S.A. 83 K2 30 23N 87 17W
Warrington □, U.K. 12 D5 53 24N 2 35W
Warrnambool, Australia 63 F3 38 25S 142 30 E
Warroad, U.S.A. 80 A7 48 54N 95 19W
Warruwi, Australia 62 A1 11 36S 133 20 E
Warsa, Indonesia 37 E9 0 47S 135 55 E
Warsak Dam, Pakistan 42 B4 34 11N 71 19 E
Warsaw = Warszawa, Poland 17 B11 52 13N 21 0 E
Warsaw, Ind., U.S.A. 82 E3 41 14N 85 51W
Warsaw, N.Y., U.S.A. 84 D6 42 45N 78 8W
Warsaw, Ohio, U.S.A. 84 F3 40 20N 82 0W
Warszawa, Poland 17 B11 52 13N 21 0 E
Warta →, Poland 16 B8 52 35N 14 39 E
Warthe = Warta →, Poland 16 B8 52 35N 14 39 E
Waru, Indonesia 37 E8 3 30S 130 36 E
Warwick, Australia 63 D5 28 10S 152 1 E
Warwick, U.K. 13 E6 52 18N 1 35W
Warwick, N.Y., U.S.A. 85 E10 41 16N 74 22W
Warwick, R.I., U.S.A. 85 E13 41 42N 71 28W
Warwickshire □, U.K. 13 E6 52 14N 1 38W
Wasaga Beach, Canada 84 B4 44 31N 80 1W
Wasagaming, Canada 71 C9 50 39N 99 58W
Wasatch Ra., U.S.A. 76 F8 40 30N 111 15W
Wasbank, S. Africa 57 D5 28 15S 30 9 E
Wasco, Calif., U.S.A. 79 K7 35 36N 119 20W
Wasco, Oreg., U.S.A. 76 D3 45 36N 120 42W
Waseca, U.S.A. 80 C8 44 5N 93 30W
Wasekamio L., Canada 71 B7 56 45N 108 45W
Wash, The, U.K. 12 E8 52 58N 0 20 E
Washago, Canada 84 B5 44 45N 79 20W
Washburn, N. Dak., U.S.A. 80 B4 47 17N 101 2W
Washburn, Wis., U.S.A. 80 B9 46 40N 90 54W
Washim, India 40 J10 20 3N 77 0 E
Washington, U.K. 12 C6 54 55N 1 30W
Washington, D.C., U.S.A. 82 F7 38 54N 77 2W
Washington, Ga., U.S.A. 83 J4 33 44N 82 44W
Washington, Ind., U.S.A. 82 F2 38 40N 87 10W
Washington, Iowa, U.S.A. 80 E9 41 18N 91 42W
Washington, Mo., U.S.A. 80 F9 38 33N 91 1W
Washington, N.C., U.S.A. 83 H7 35 33N 77 3W
Washington, N.J., U.S.A. 85 F10 40 46N 74 59W
Washington, Pa., U.S.A. 84 F4 40 10N 80 15W
Washington, Utah, U.S.A. 77 H7 37 8N 113 31W
Washington □, U.S.A. 76 C3 47 30N 120 30W
Washington, Mt., U.S.A. 85 B13 44 16N 71 18W
Washington Court House, U.S.A. 82 F4 39 32N 83 26W
Washington I., U.S.A. 82 C2 45 23N 86 54W
Washougal, U.S.A. 78 E4 45 35N 122 21W
Washpool △, Australia 63 D5 29 22S 152 20 E
Wasian, Indonesia 37 E8 1 47S 133 19 E
Wasilla, U.S.A. 68 B5 61 35N 149 26W
Wasim, Indonesia 37 E8 1 42S 134 30 E
Wāsiṭ □, Iraq 44 C5 32 30N 46 0 E
Waskaganish, Canada 72 B4 51 30N 78 40W
Waskaiowaka, L., Canada 71 B9 56 33N 96 23W
Waskesiu Lake, Canada 71 C7 53 55N 106 5W
Wasserkuppe, Germany 16 C5 50 29N 9 55 E
Waswanipi, Canada 72 C4 49 40N 76 29W
Waswanipi, L., Canada 72 C4 49 35N 76 40W
Watampone, Indonesia 37 E6 4 29S 120 25 E
Watamu, Kenya 54 C5 3 23S 40 0 E
Watarrka △, Australia 60 D5 24 20S 131 30 E

Water Park Pt., Australia 62 C5 22 56S 150 47 E
Water Valley, U.S.A. 81 H10 34 10N 89 38W
Waterberg Plateau △, Namibia 56 C2 20 25S 17 18 E
Waterberge, S. Africa 57 C4 24 10S 28 0 E
Waterbury, Conn., U.S.A. 85 E11 41 33N 73 3W
Waterbury, Vt., U.S.A. 85 B12 44 20N 72 46W
Waterbury L., Canada 71 B8 58 10N 104 22W
Waterdown, Canada 84 C5 43 20N 79 53W
Waterford, Canada 84 D4 42 56N 80 17W
Waterford, Ireland 10 D4 52 15N 7 8W
Waterford, Calif., U.S.A. 78 H6 37 38N 120 46W
Waterford, Pa., U.S.A. 84 E5 41 57N 79 59W
Waterford □, Ireland 10 D4 52 10N 7 40W
Waterford Harbour, Ireland 10 D5 52 8N 6 58W
Waterhen L., Canada 71 C9 52 10N 99 40W
Waterloo, Belgium 15 D4 50 43N 4 25 E
Waterloo, Ont., Canada 84 C4 43 30N 80 32W
Waterloo, Qué., Canada 85 A12 45 22N 72 32W
Waterloo, Ill., U.S.A. 80 F9 38 20N 90 9W
Waterloo, Iowa, U.S.A. 80 D8 42 30N 92 21W
Waterloo, N.Y., U.S.A. 84 D8 42 54N 76 52W
Watersmeet, U.S.A. 80 B10 46 16N 89 11W
Waterton Lakes △, Canada 70 D6 48 45N 115 0W
Watertown, Conn., U.S.A. 85 E11 41 36N 73 7W
Watertown, N.Y., U.S.A. 85 C9 43 59N 75 55W
Watertown, S. Dak., U.S.A. 80 C6 44 54N 97 7W
Watertown, Wis., U.S.A. 80 D10 43 12N 88 43W
Waterval-Boven, S. Africa 57 D5 25 40S 30 18 E
Waterville, Canada 85 A13 45 16N 71 54W
Waterville, Maine, U.S.A. 83 C11 44 33N 69 38W
Waterville, N.Y., U.S.A. 85 D9 42 56N 75 23W
Waterville, Pa., U.S.A. 84 E7 41 19N 77 21W
Waterviet, U.S.A. 85 D11 42 44N 73 42W
Wates, Indonesia 37 G14 7 51S 110 10 E
Watford, Canada 84 D3 42 57N 81 53W
Watford, U.K. 13 F7 51 40N 0 24W
Watford City, U.S.A. 80 B3 47 48N 103 17W
Watham →, Canada 71 B8 57 16N 102 59W
Wathaman L., Canada 71 B8 56 58N 103 44W
Watheroo, Australia 61 F2 30 15S 116 0 E
Watheroo △, Australia 61 F2 30 19S 115 48 E
Wating, China 34 G4 35 40N 106 38 E
Watkins Glen, U.S.A. 84 D8 42 23N 76 52W
Watling I. = San Salvador I., Bahamas 89 B5 24 0N 74 40W
Watonga, U.S.A. 81 H5 35 51N 98 25W
Watrous, Canada 71 C7 51 40N 105 25W
Watrous, U.S.A. 81 H2 35 48N 104 59W
Watsa, Dem. Rep. of the Congo 54 B2 3 4N 29 30 E
Watseka, U.S.A. 82 E2 40 47N 87 44W
Watson, Australia 61 F5 30 29S 131 31 E
Watson, Canada 71 C8 52 10N 104 30W
Watson Lake, Canada 70 A3 60 6N 128 49W
Watsontown, U.S.A. 84 E8 41 5N 76 52W
Watsonville, U.S.A. 78 J5 36 55N 121 45W
Wattiwarriganna Cr. →, Australia 63 D2 28 57S 136 10 E
Watuata = Batuata, Indonesia 37 F6 6 12S 122 42 E
Watubela, Kepulauan, Indonesia 37 E8 4 28S 131 35 E
Watubela Is. = Watubela, Kepulauan, Indonesia 37 E8 4 28S 131 35 E
Wau = Wâw, Sudan 51 G11 7 45N 28 1 E
Waubamik, Canada 84 A4 45 27N 80 1W
Waubay, U.S.A. 80 C6 45 20N 97 18W
Wauchope, N.S.W., Australia 63 E5 31 28S 152 45 E
Wauchope, N. Terr., Australia 62 C1 20 36S 134 15 E
Wauchula, U.S.A. 83 M5 27 33N 81 49W
Waukarlycarly, L., Australia 60 D3 21 18S 121 56 E
Waukegan, U.S.A. 82 D2 42 22N 87 50W
Waukesha, U.S.A. 82 D1 43 1N 88 14W
Waukon, U.S.A. 80 D9 43 16N 91 29W
Waupaca, U.S.A. 80 C10 44 21N 89 5W
Waupun, U.S.A. 80 D10 43 38N 88 44W
Waurika, U.S.A. 81 H6 34 10N 98 0W
Wausau, U.S.A. 80 C10 44 58N 89 38W
Wautoma, U.S.A. 80 C10 44 4N 89 18W
Wauwatosa, U.S.A. 82 D1 43 3N 88 0W
Waveney →, U.K. 13 E9 52 35N 1 39 E
Waverley, N.Z. 59 H5 39 46S 174 37 E
Waverly, Iowa, U.S.A. 80 D8 42 44N 92 29W
Waverly, N.Y., U.S.A. 85 E8 42 1N 76 32W
Wavre, Belgium 15 D4 50 43N 4 38 E
Wâw, Sudan 51 G11 7 45N 28 1 E
Wāw al Kabīr, Libya 51 C9 25 20N 16 43 E
Wawa, Canada 72 C3 47 59N 84 47W
Wawanesa, Canada 71 D9 49 36N 99 40W
Wawona, U.S.A. 78 H7 37 32N 119 39W
Waxahachie, U.S.A. 81 J6 32 24N 96 51W
Way, L., Australia 61 E3 26 45S 120 16 E
Waycross, U.S.A. 83 K4 31 13N 82 21W
Wayland, U.S.A. 84 D7 42 34N 77 35W
Wayne, Nebr., U.S.A. 80 D6 42 14N 97 1W
Wayne, W. Va., U.S.A. 82 F4 38 13N 82 27W
Waynesboro, Ga., U.S.A. 83 J4 33 6N 82 1W
Waynesboro, Miss., U.S.A. 83 K1 31 40N 88 39W
Waynesboro, Pa., U.S.A. 82 F7 39 45N 77 35W
Waynesboro, Va., U.S.A. 82 F6 38 4N 78 53W
Waynesburg, U.S.A. 82 F5 39 54N 80 11W
Waynesville, U.S.A. 83 H4 35 28N 82 58W
Waynoka, U.S.A. 81 G5 36 35N 98 53W
Wazirabad, Pakistan 42 C6 32 30N 74 8 E
We, Indonesia 36 C1 5 51N 95 18 E
Weald, The, U.K. 13 F8 51 4N 0 20 E
Wear →, U.K. 12 C6 54 55N 1 23W
Weatherford, Okla., U.S.A. 81 H5 35 32N 98 43W
Weatherford, Tex., U.S.A. 81 J6 32 46N 97 48W
Weaverville, U.S.A. 76 F2 40 44N 122 56W
Webb City, U.S.A. 81 G7 37 9N 94 28W
Webequie, Canada 72 B2 52 59N 87 21W
Webster, Mass., U.S.A. 85 D13 42 3N 71 53W
Webster, N.Y., U.S.A. 84 C7 43 13N 77 26W
Webster, S. Dak., U.S.A. 80 C6 45 20N 97 31W
Webster City, U.S.A. 80 D8 42 28N 93 49W
Webster Springs, U.S.A. 82 F5 38 29N 80 25W
Weda, Indonesia 37 D7 0 21N 127 50 E
Weda, Teluk, Indonesia 37 D7 0 20N 128 0 E
Weddell I., Falk. Is. 96 G4 51 50S 61 0W
Weddell Sea, Antarctica 5 D1 72 30S 40 0W
Wedderburn, Australia 63 F3 36 26S 143 33 E
Wedgeport, Canada 73 D6 43 44N 65 59W
Wedza, Zimbabwe 55 F3 18 40S 31 33 E
Wee Waa, Australia 63 E4 30 11S 149 26 E
Weed, U.S.A. 76 F2 41 25N 122 23W
Weed Heights, U.S.A. 78 G7 38 59N 119 13W
Weedsport, U.S.A. 85 C8 43 3N 76 35W
Weedville, U.S.A. 84 E6 41 17N 78 30W
Weenen, S. Africa 57 D5 28 48S 30 7 E
Weert, Neths. 15 C5 51 15N 5 43 E
Wei He →, Hebei, China 34 F8 36 10N 115 45 E

Wei He →, Shaanxi, China 34 G6 34 38N 110 15 E
Weichang, China 35 D9 41 58N 117 49 E
Weichuan, China 34 G7 34 20N 113 59 E
Weiden, Germany 16 D7 49 41N 12 10 E
Weifang, China 35 F10 36 44N 119 7 E
Weihai, China 35 F12 37 30N 122 6 E
Weimar, Germany 16 C6 50 58N 11 19 E
Weinan, China 34 G5 34 31N 109 29 E
Weipa, Australia 62 A3 12 40S 141 50 E
Weir →, Australia 63 D4 28 20S 149 50 E
Weir →, Canada 71 B10 56 54N 93 21W
Weir River, Canada 71 B10 56 49N 94 6W
Weirton, U.S.A. 84 F4 40 24N 80 35W
Weiser, U.S.A. 76 D5 44 10N 117 0W
Weishan, China 35 G9 34 47N 117 5 E
Weiyuan, China 34 G3 35 7N 104 10 E
Wejherowo, Poland 17 A10 54 35N 18 12 E
Wekusko L., Canada 71 C9 54 40N 99 50W
Welch, U.S.A. 82 G5 37 26N 81 35W
Welford △, U.S.A. 62 D3 25 5S 143 16 E
Welkom, S. Africa 56 D4 28 0S 26 46 E
Welland, Canada 84 D5 43 0N 79 15W
Welland →, U.K. 13 E7 52 51N 0 5W
Wellesley Is., Australia 62 B2 16 42S 139 30 E
Wellingborough, U.K. 13 E7 52 19N 0 41W
Wellington, Australia 63 E4 32 35S 148 59 E
Wellington, Canada 84 C7 43 57N 77 20W
Wellington, N.Z. 59 J5 41 19S 174 46 E
Wellington, S. Africa 56 E2 33 38S 19 1 E
Wellington, Somst., U.K. 13 G4 50 58N 3 13W
Wellington, Telford & Wrekin, U.K. 13 E5 52 42N 2 30W
Wellington, Colo., U.S.A. 80 E2 40 42N 105 0W
Wellington, Kans., U.S.A. 81 G6 37 16N 97 24W
Wellington, Nev., U.S.A. 78 G7 38 45N 119 23W
Wellington, Ohio, U.S.A. 84 E2 41 10N 82 13W
Wellington, Tex., U.S.A. 81 H4 34 51N 100 13W
Wellington, I., Chile 96 F2 49 30S 75 0W
Wellington, L., Australia 63 F4 38 6S 147 20 E
Wells, U.K. 13 F5 51 13N 2 39W
Wells, Maine, U.S.A. 85 C14 43 20N 70 35W
Wells, N.Y., U.S.A. 85 C10 43 24N 74 17W
Wells, Nev., U.S.A. 76 F6 41 7N 114 58W
Wells, L., Australia 61 E3 26 44S 123 15 E
Wells, Mt., Australia 60 C4 17 25S 127 8 E
Wells Gray △, Canada 70 C4 52 30N 120 15W
Wells-next-the-Sea, U.K. 12 E8 52 57N 0 51 E
Wells River, U.S.A. 85 B12 44 9N 72 4W
Wellsboro, U.S.A. 84 E7 41 45N 77 18W
Wellsburg, U.S.A. 84 F4 40 16N 80 37W
Wellsville, N.Y., U.S.A. 84 D7 42 7N 77 57W
Wellsville, Ohio, U.S.A. 84 F4 40 36N 80 39W
Wellsville, Utah, U.S.A. 76 F8 41 38N 111 56W
Wellton, U.S.A. 77 K6 32 40N 114 8W
Wels, Austria 16 D8 48 9N 14 1 E
Welshpool, U.K. 13 E4 52 39N 3 8W
Welwyn Garden City, U.K. 13 F7 51 48N 0 12W
Wem, U.K. 12 E5 52 52N 2 44W
Wembere →, Tanzania 54 C3 4 10S 34 15 E
Wemindji, Canada 72 B4 53 0N 78 49W
Wen Xian, China 34 G7 34 55N 113 5 E
Wenatchee, U.S.A. 76 C3 47 25N 120 19W
Wenchang, China 38 C8 19 38N 110 42 E
Wenchi, Ghana 50 G5 7 46N 2 8W
Wenchow = Wenzhou, China 33 D7 28 0N 120 38 E
Wenden, U.S.A. 79 M13 33 49N 113 33W
Wendeng, China 35 F12 37 15N 122 5 E
Wendesi, Indonesia 37 E8 2 30S 134 17 E
Wendover, U.S.A. 76 F6 40 44N 114 2W
Wenlock →, Australia 62 A3 12 2S 141 55 E
Wenshan, China 32 D5 23 20N 104 18 E
Wenshang, China 34 G9 35 45N 116 30 E
Wenshui, China 34 F7 37 26N 112 1 E
Wensleydale, U.K. 12 C6 54 17N 2 0W
Wensu, China 32 B3 41 15N 80 10 E
Wensum →, U.K. 12 E8 52 40N 1 15 E
Wentworth, Australia 63 E3 34 2S 141 54 E
Wentzel L., Canada 70 B6 59 2N 114 28W
Wenut, Indonesia 37 E8 3 11S 133 19 E
Wenxi, China 34 G6 35 20N 111 10 E
Wenxian, China 34 H3 32 43N 104 36 E
Wenzhou, China 33 D7 28 0N 120 38 E
Weott, U.S.A. 76 F2 40 20N 123 55W
Wepener, S. Africa 56 D4 29 42S 27 3 E
Werda, Botswana 56 D3 25 24S 23 15 E
Weri, Indonesia 37 E8 3 10S 132 38 E
Werra →, Germany 16 C5 51 24N 9 39 E
Werrimull, Australia 63 E3 34 25S 141 38 E
Werris Creek, Australia 63 E5 31 18S 150 38 E
Weser →, Germany 16 B5 53 36N 8 28 E
Wesiri, Indonesia 37 F7 7 30S 126 30 E
Weslemkoon L., Canada 84 A7 45 2N 77 25W
Wesley ville, U.S.A. 84 D4 42 9N 80 0W
Wessel, C., Australia 62 A2 10 59S 136 46 E
Wessel Is., Australia 62 A2 11 10S 136 45 E
Wessington Springs, U.S.A. 80 C5 44 5N 98 34W
West, U.S.A. 81 K6 31 48N 97 6W
West →, U.S.A. 85 D12 42 52N 72 33W
West Antarctica, Antarctica 5 D15 80 0S 90 0W
West Baines →, Australia 60 C4 15 38S 129 59 E
West Bank ⊠, Asia 46 C4 32 6N 35 13 E
West Bend, U.S.A. 82 D1 43 25N 88 11W
West Bengal □, India 43 H13 23 0N 88 0 E
West Berkshire □, U.K. 13 F6 51 25N 1 17W
West Beskids = Západné Beskydy, Europe 17 D10 49 30N 19 0 E
West Branch Susquehanna →, U.S.A. 85 F8 40 53N 76 48W
West Bromwich, U.K. 13 E6 52 32N 1 59W
West Burra, U.K. 11 A7 60 5N 1 21W
West Canada Cr. →, U.S.A. 85 C10 43 1N 74 58W
West Cape Howe, Australia 61 G2 35 8S 117 36 E
West Chazy, U.S.A. 85 B11 44 49N 73 28W
West Chester, U.S.A. 85 G9 39 58N 75 36W
West Coast △, Namibia 56 C1 21 53S 14 14 E
West Coast △, S. Africa 56 E2 33 13S 18 0 E
West Columbia, U.S.A. 81 L7 29 9N 95 39W
West Covina, U.S.A. 79 L9 34 4N 117 54W
West Des Moines, U.S.A. 80 E8 41 35N 93 43W
West Dunbartonshire □, U.K. 11 F8 55 59N 4 30W
West End, Bahamas 88 A4 26 41N 78 58W
West Falkland, Falk. Is. 96 G5 51 40S 60 0W
West Fargo, U.S.A. 80 B6 46 52N 96 54W
West Farmington, U.S.A. 84 E4 41 23N 80 58W
West Fjord = Vestfjorden, Norway 8 C15 67 55N 14 0 E
West Fork Trinity →, U.S.A. 81 J6 32 48N 96 54W
West Frankfort, U.S.A. 80 G10 37 54N 88 55W

West Hartford, U.S.A. . . . . . . . . 85 E12 41 45N 72 44W
West Haven, U.S.A. . . . . . . . . . . 85 E12 41 17N 72 57W
West Hazleton, U.S.A. . . . . . . . . 85 F9 40 58N 76 0W
West Helena, U.S.A. . . . . . . . . . 81 H9 34 33N 90 38W
West Hurley, U.S.A. . . . . . . . . . 85 E10 41 59N 74 7W
West Ice Shelf, Antarctica . . . . . 5 C7 67 0S 85 0 E
West Indies, Cent. Amer. . . . . . . 89 D7 15 0N 65 0W
West Jordan, U.S.A. . . . . . . . . . 76 F8 40 36N 111 56W
West Lamma Channel, China . . . 33 G11 22 13N 114 4 E
West Lorne, Canada . . . . . . . . . 84 D3 42 36N 81 36W
West Lothian □, U.K. . . . . . . . . 11 F5 55 54N 3 36W
West Lunga →, Zambia . . . . . . . 55 E1 13 6S 24 39 E
West MacDonnell △, Australia . . 60 D5 23 38S 132 59 E
West Memphis, U.S.A. . . . . . . . 81 H9 35 9N 90 11W
West Midlands □, U.K. . . . . . . . 13 E6 52 26N 2 0W
West Mifflin, U.S.A. . . . . . . . . . 84 F5 40 22N 79 52W
West Milton, U.S.A. . . . . . . . . . 84 E8 41 1N 76 50W
West Monroe, U.S.A. . . . . . . . . 81 J8 32 31N 92 9W
West Newton, U.S.A. . . . . . . . . 84 F5 40 14N 79 46W
West Nicholson, Zimbabwe . . . . 55 G2 21 2S 29 20 E
West Palm Beach, U.S.A. . . . . . 83 M5 26 43N 80 3W
West Plains, U.S.A. . . . . . . . . . . 81 G9 36 44N 91 51W
West Point, N.Y., U.S.A. . . . . . . 85 E11 41 24N 73 58W
West Point, Nebr., U.S.A. . . . . . 80 E6 41 51N 96 43W
West Point, Va., U.S.A. . . . . . . . 82 G7 37 32N 76 48W
West Pt. = Ouest, Pte. de l',
 Canada . . . . . . . . . . . . . . . . . 73 C7 49 52N 64 40W
West Pt., Australia . . . . . . . . . . 63 F2 35 1S 135 56 E
West Road →, Canada . . . . . . . 70 C4 53 18N 122 53W
West Rutland, U.S.A. . . . . . . . . 85 C11 43 38N 73 5W
West Schelde =
 Westerschelde →, Neths. . . . . 15 C3 51 25N 3 25 E
West Seneca, U.S.A. . . . . . . . . . 84 D6 42 51N 78 48W
West Siberian Plain, Russia . . . . 26 C11 62 0N 75 0 E
West Sussex □, U.K. . . . . . . . . . 13 G7 50 55N 0 30W
West-Terschelling, Neths. . . . . . 15 A5 53 22N 5 13 E
West Valley City, U.S.A. . . . . . . 76 F8 40 42N 111 57W
West Virginia □, U.S.A. . . . . . . 82 F5 38 45N 80 30W
West-Vlaanderen □, Belgium . . 15 D2 51 0N 3 0 E
West Walker →, U.S.A. . . . . . . . 78 G7 38 54N 119 9W
West Wyalong, Australia . . . . . . 63 E4 33 56S 147 10 E
West Yellowstone, U.S.A. . . . . . 76 D8 44 40N 111 6W
West Yorkshire □, U.K. . . . . . . . 12 D6 53 45N 1 40W
Westall, Pt., Australia . . . . . . . . 63 E1 32 55S 134 4 E
Westbrook, U.S.A. . . . . . . . . . . 83 D10 43 41N 70 22W
Westbury, Australia . . . . . . . . . 63 G4 41 30S 146 51 E
Westby, U.S.A. . . . . . . . . . . . . . 80 A2 48 52N 104 3W
Westend, U.S.A. . . . . . . . . . . . . 79 K9 35 42N 117 24W
Westerland, Germany . . . . . . . . 9 J13 54 54N 8 17 E
Westerly, U.S.A. . . . . . . . . . . . . 85 E13 41 22N 71 50W
Western □, Kenya . . . . . . . . . . . 54 B3 0 30N 34 30 E
Western □, Zambia . . . . . . . . . . 55 F1 15 0S 24 4 E
Western Australia □, Australia . . 61 E2 25 0S 118 0 E
Western Cape □, S. Africa . . . . . 56 E3 34 0S 20 0 E
Western Dvina = Daugava →,
 Latvia . . . . . . . . . . . . . . . . . . 9 H21 57 4N 24 3 E
Western Ghats, India . . . . . . . . 40 N9 14 0N 75 0 E
Western Isles □, U.K. . . . . . . . . 11 D1 57 30N 7 10W
Western Sahara ■, Africa . . . . . 50 D3 25 0N 13 0W
Western Samoa = Samoa ■,
 Pac. Oc. . . . . . . . . . . . . . . . . . 59 B13 14 0S 172 0W
Westernport, U.S.A. . . . . . . . . . 82 F6 39 29N 79 3W
Westerschelde →, Neths. . . . . . 15 C3 51 25N 3 25 E
Westerwald, Germany . . . . . . . . 16 C4 50 38N 7 56 E
Westfield, Mass., U.S.A. . . . . . . 85 D12 42 7N 72 45W
Westfield, N.Y., U.S.A. . . . . . . . 84 D5 42 20N 79 35W
Westfield, Pa., U.S.A. . . . . . . . . 84 E7 41 55N 77 32W
Westhill, U.K. . . . . . . . . . . . . . . 11 D6 57 9N 2 19W
Westhope, U.S.A. . . . . . . . . . . . 80 A4 48 55N 101 1W
Westland △, N.Z. . . . . . . . . . . . 59 K2 43 16S 170 16 E
Westland Bight, N.Z. . . . . . . . . . 59 K3 42 55S 170 5 E
Westlock, Canada . . . . . . . . . . . 70 C6 54 9N 113 55W
Westmar, Australia . . . . . . . . . . 63 D4 27 55S 149 44 E
Westmeath □, Ireland . . . . . . . . 10 C4 53 33N 7 34W
Westminster, U.S.A. . . . . . . . . . 82 F7 39 34N 76 59W
Westmont, U.S.A. . . . . . . . . . . . 84 F6 40 19N 78 58W
Westmoreland, Barbados . . . . . 89 g 13 13N 59 37W
Westmorland, U.S.A. . . . . . . . . 79 M11 33 2N 115 37W
Weston, Oreg., U.S.A. . . . . . . . . 76 D4 45 49N 118 26W
Weston, W. Va., U.S.A. . . . . . . . 82 F5 39 2N 80 28W
Weston I., Canada . . . . . . . . . . . 72 B4 52 33N 79 36W
Weston-super-Mare, U.K. . . . . . 13 F5 51 21N 2 58W
Westover, Canada . . . . . . . . . . . 84 F6 40 45N 78 40W
Westport, Canada . . . . . . . . . . . 85 B8 44 40N 76 25W
Westport, Ireland . . . . . . . . . . . 10 C2 53 48N 9 31W
Westport, N.Z. . . . . . . . . . . . . . . 59 J3 41 46S 171 37 E
Westport, N.Y., U.S.A. . . . . . . . 85 B11 44 11N 73 26W
Westport, Oreg., U.S.A. . . . . . . 78 D3 46 8N 123 23W
Westport, Wash., U.S.A. . . . . . . 78 D2 46 53N 124 6W
Westray, Canada . . . . . . . . . . . . 71 C8 53 36N 101 24W
Westray, U.K. . . . . . . . . . . . . . . 11 B5 59 18N 3 0W
Westree, Canada . . . . . . . . . . . . 72 C3 47 26N 81 34W
Westville, U.S.A. . . . . . . . . . . . . 78 F6 39 8N 120 42W
Westwood, U.S.A. . . . . . . . . . . . 76 F3 40 18N 121 0W
Wetar, Indonesia . . . . . . . . . . . . 37 F7 7 48S 126 30 E
Wetaskiwin, Canada . . . . . . . . . 70 C6 52 55N 113 24W
Wete, Tanzania . . . . . . . . . . . . . 52 F7 5 4S 39 43 E
Wetherby, U.K. . . . . . . . . . . . . . 12 D6 53 56N 1 23W
Wethersfield, U.S.A. . . . . . . . . . 85 E12 41 42N 72 40W
Wetteren, Belgium . . . . . . . . . . 15 D3 51 0N 3 53 E
Wetzlar, Germany . . . . . . . . . . . 16 C5 50 32N 8 31 E
Wewoka, U.S.A. . . . . . . . . . . . . 81 H6 35 9N 96 30W
Wexford, Ireland . . . . . . . . . . . . 10 D5 52 20N 6 25W
Wexford □, Ireland . . . . . . . . . . 10 D5 52 20N 6 25W
Wexford Harbour, Ireland . . . . . 10 D5 52 20N 6 25W
Weyburn, Canada . . . . . . . . . . . 71 D8 49 40N 103 50W
Weymouth, Canada . . . . . . . . . . 73 D6 44 30N 66 1W
Weymouth, U.K. . . . . . . . . . . . . 13 G5 50 37N 2 28W
Weymouth, U.S.A. . . . . . . . . . . 85 D14 42 13N 70 58W
Weymouth, C., Australia . . . . . . 62 A3 12 37S 143 27 E
Wha Ti, Canada . . . . . . . . . . . . . 68 B8 63 8N 117 16W
Whakaari = White I., N.Z. . . . . . 59 G6 37 30S 177 13 E
Whakatane, N.Z. . . . . . . . . . . . . 59 G6 37 57S 177 1 E
Whale →, Canada . . . . . . . . . . . 73 A6 58 15N 67 40W
Whale Cove, Canada . . . . . . . . . 71 A10 62 10N 92 34W
Whales, B. of, Antarctica . . . . . 5 D12 78 0S 165 0W
Whalsay, U.K. . . . . . . . . . . . . . . 11 A8 60 22N 0 59W
Whangamata, N.Z. . . . . . . . . . . 59 G5 37 12S 175 53 E
Whangamomona, N.Z. . . . . . . . 59 H5 39 8S 174 44 E
Whanganui △, N.Z. . . . . . . . . . . 59 H5 39 17S 174 53 E
Whangarei, N.Z. . . . . . . . . . . . . 59 F5 35 43S 174 21 E
Whangarei Harb., N.Z. . . . . . . . 59 F5 35 45S 174 28 E
Wharfe →, U.K. . . . . . . . . . . . . . 12 D6 53 51N 1 9W
Wharfedale, U.K. . . . . . . . . . . . . 12 C5 54 6N 2 1W
Wharton, N.J., U.S.A. . . . . . . . . 85 F10 40 54N 74 35W
Wharton, Pa., U.S.A. . . . . . . . . 84 E6 41 31N 78 1W
Wharton, Tex., U.S.A. . . . . . . . . 81 L6 29 19N 96 6W
Wheatland, Calif., U.S.A. . . . . . 78 F5 39 1N 121 25W
Wheatland, Wyo., U.S.A. . . . . . 80 D2 42 3N 104 58W

Wheatley, Canada . . . . . . . . . . . 84 D2 42 6N 82 27W
Wheaton, Md., U.S.A. . . . . . . . . 82 F7 39 3N 77 3W
Wheaton, Minn., U.S.A. . . . . . . 80 C6 45 48N 96 30W
Wheelbarrow Pk., U.S.A. . . . . . 78 H10 37 26N 116 5W
Wheeler, Oreg., U.S.A. . . . . . . . 76 D2 45 41N 123 53W
Wheeler, Tex., U.S.A. . . . . . . . . 81 H4 35 27N 100 16W
Wheeler →, Canada . . . . . . . . . 73 A6 57 2N 67 13W
Wheeler L., U.S.A. . . . . . . . . . . . 83 H2 34 48N 87 23W
Wheeler Pk., N. Mex., U.S.A. . . 77 H11 36 34N 105 25W
Wheeler Pk., Nev., U.S.A. . . . . . 77 G6 38 57N 114 15W
Wheeler Ridge, U.S.A. . . . . . . . 79 L8 35 0N 118 57W
Wheeling, U.S.A. . . . . . . . . . . . . 84 F4 40 4N 80 43W
Whernside, U.K. . . . . . . . . . . . . 12 C5 54 14N 2 24W
Whiskey Jack L., Canada . . . . . 71 B8 58 23N 101 55W
Whiskeytown-Shasta-Trinity △,
 U.S.A. . . . . . . . . . . . . . . . . . . 76 F2 40 45N 122 15W
Whistleduck Cr. →, Australia . . 62 C2 20 15S 135 18 E
Whistler, Canada . . . . . . . . . . . . 70 C4 50 7N 122 58W
Whitby, Canada . . . . . . . . . . . . . 84 C6 43 52N 78 56W
Whitby, U.K. . . . . . . . . . . . . . . . 12 C7 54 29N 0 37W
White →, Ark., U.S.A. . . . . . . . . 81 J9 33 57N 91 5W
White →, Ind., U.S.A. . . . . . . . . 82 F2 38 25N 87 45W
White →, S. Dak., U.S.A. . . . . . 80 D5 43 42N 99 27W
White →, Tex., U.S.A. . . . . . . . . 81 J4 33 14N 100 56W
White →, Utah, U.S.A. . . . . . . . 76 F9 40 4N 109 41W
White →, Vt., U.S.A. . . . . . . . . . 85 C12 43 37N 72 20W
White →, Wash., U.S.A. . . . . . . 78 C4 47 12N 122 15W
White, L., Australia . . . . . . . . . . 60 D4 21 9S 128 56 E
White B., Canada . . . . . . . . . . . 73 C8 50 0N 56 35W
White Bird, U.S.A. . . . . . . . . . . 76 D5 45 46N 116 18W
White Butte, U.S.A. . . . . . . . . . . 80 B3 46 23N 103 18W
White City, U.S.A. . . . . . . . . . . . 78 E2 42 26N 122 51W
White Cliffs, Australia . . . . . . . . 63 E3 30 50S 143 10 E
White Hall, U.S.A. . . . . . . . . . . . 80 F9 39 26N 90 24W
White Haven, U.S.A. . . . . . . . . . 85 E9 41 4N 75 47W
White Horse, Vale of, U.K. . . . . 13 F6 51 37N 1 30W
White I., N.Z. . . . . . . . . . . . . . . . 59 G6 37 30S 177 13 E
White L., U.S.A. . . . . . . . . . . . . 85 A8 46 18N 76 31W
White L., Canada . . . . . . . . . . . 81 L8 29 44N 92 30W
White Mountain Peak, U.S.A. . . 77 G4 37 38N 118 15W
White Mts., Calif., U.S.A. . . . . . 78 H8 37 30N 118 15W
White Mts., N.H., U.S.A. . . . . . . 85 B13 44 15N 71 15W
White Mts. △, Australia . . . . . . 62 C4 20 43S 145 12 E
White Nile = Nîl el Abyad →,
 Sudan . . . . . . . . . . . . . . . . . . . 51 E12 15 38N 32 31 E
White Otter L., Canada . . . . . . . 72 C1 49 5N 91 55W
White Pass, U.S.A. . . . . . . . . . . 78 D5 46 38N 121 24W
White Plains, U.S.A. . . . . . . . . . 85 E11 41 2N 73 46W
White River, Canada . . . . . . . . . 72 C2 48 35N 85 20W
White River, S. Africa . . . . . . . . 57 D5 25 20S 31 0 E
White River, U.S.A. . . . . . . . . . . 80 D4 43 34N 100 45W
White Rock, Canada . . . . . . . . . 78 A4 49 2N 122 48W
White Russia = Belarus ■,
 Europe . . . . . . . . . . . . . . . . . . 17 B14 53 30N 27 0 E
White Sands △, U.S.A. . . . . . . . 77 K10 32 46N 106 20W
White Sea = Beloye More, Russia 18 A6 66 30N 38 0 E
White Sulphur Springs, Mont.,
 U.S.A. . . . . . . . . . . . . . . . . . . 76 C8 46 33N 110 54W
White Sulphur Springs, W. Va.,
 U.S.A. . . . . . . . . . . . . . . . . . . 82 G5 37 48N 80 18W
White Swan, U.S.A. . . . . . . . . . 78 D6 46 23N 120 44W
Whitecliffs, N.Z. . . . . . . . . . . . . 59 K3 43 26S 171 55 E
Whitecourt, Canada . . . . . . . . . 70 C5 54 10N 115 45W
Whiteface Mt., U.S.A. . . . . . . . . 85 B11 44 22N 73 54W
Whitefield, U.S.A. . . . . . . . . . . . 85 B13 44 23N 71 37W
Whitefish, U.S.A. . . . . . . . . . . . 76 B6 48 25N 114 20W
Whitefish L., Canada . . . . . . . . . 71 A7 62 41N 106 48W
Whitefish Point, U.S.A. . . . . . . . 82 B3 46 45N 84 59W
Whitegull, L. = Goélands, L. aux,
 Canada . . . . . . . . . . . . . . . . . 73 A7 55 27N 64 17W
Whitehall, Mich., U.S.A. . . . . . . 82 D2 43 24N 86 21W
Whitehall, Mont., U.S.A. . . . . . . 76 D7 45 52N 112 6W
Whitehall, N.Y., U.S.A. . . . . . . . 85 C11 43 33N 73 24W
Whitehall, Wis., U.S.A. . . . . . . . 80 C9 44 22N 91 19W
Whitehaven, U.K. . . . . . . . . . . . 12 C4 54 33N 3 35W
Whitehorse, Canada . . . . . . . . . 70 A1 60 43N 135 3W
Whitemark, Australia . . . . . . . . 63 G4 40 7S 148 3 E
Whiteriver, U.S.A. . . . . . . . . . . . 77 K9 33 50N 109 58W
Whitesand →, Canada . . . . . . . 70 A5 60 9N 115 45W
Whitesands, S. Africa . . . . . . . . 56 E3 34 23S 20 50 E
Whitesboro, N.Y., U.S.A. . . . . . 85 C9 43 7N 75 18W
Whitesboro, Tex., U.S.A. . . . . . 81 J6 33 39N 96 54W
Whiteshell △, Canada . . . . . . . . 71 D9 50 0N 95 40W
Whitesville, U.S.A. . . . . . . . . . . 84 D7 42 2N 77 46W
Whiteville, U.S.A. . . . . . . . . . . . 83 H6 34 20N 78 42W
Whitewater, U.S.A. . . . . . . . . . . 82 D1 42 50N 88 44W
Whitewater Baldy, U.S.A. . . . . . 77 K9 33 20N 108 39W
Whitewater L., Canada . . . . . . . 72 B2 50 50N 89 10W
Whitewood, Australia . . . . . . . . 62 C3 21 28S 143 30 E
Whitewood, Canada . . . . . . . . . 71 C8 50 20N 102 20W
Whithorn, U.K. . . . . . . . . . . . . . 11 G4 54 44N 4 26W
Whitianga, N.Z. . . . . . . . . . . . . . 59 G5 36 47S 175 41 E
Whitman, U.S.A. . . . . . . . . . . . . 85 D14 42 5N 70 56W
Whitney, Canada . . . . . . . . . . . . 84 A6 45 31N 78 14W
Whitney, Mt., U.S.A. . . . . . . . . . 78 J8 36 35N 118 18W
Whitney Point, U.S.A. . . . . . . . . 85 D9 42 20N 75 58W
Whitstable, U.K. . . . . . . . . . . . . 13 F9 51 21N 1 3 E
Whitsunday I., Australia . . . . . . 62 J7 20 15S 149 4 E
Whitsunday Islands △, Australia 62 J7 20 15S 149 0 E
Whitsunday Passage, Australia . 62 J6 20 12S 148 51 E
Whittier, U.S.A. . . . . . . . . . . . . . 79 M8 33 58N 118 3W
Whittlesea, Australia . . . . . . . . . 63 F4 37 27S 145 9 E
Wholdaia L., Canada . . . . . . . . . 71 A8 60 43N 104 20W
Whyalla, Australia . . . . . . . . . . . 63 E2 33 2S 137 30 E
Wiang Kosai △, Thailand . . . . . 38 D2 17 54N 99 29 E
Wiarton, Canada . . . . . . . . . . . . 84 B3 44 40N 81 10W
Wiay, U.K. . . . . . . . . . . . . . . . . . 11 D1 57 24N 7 13W
Wibaux, U.S.A. . . . . . . . . . . . . . 80 B2 46 59N 104 11W
Wichian Buri, Thailand . . . . . . . 38 E3 15 39N 101 7 E
Wichita, U.S.A. . . . . . . . . . . . . . 81 G6 37 42N 97 20W
Wichita Falls, U.S.A. . . . . . . . . . 81 J5 33 54N 98 30W
Wick, U.K. . . . . . . . . . . . . . . . . . 11 C5 58 26N 3 5W
Wicked Pt., Canada . . . . . . . . . . 84 C7 43 52N 77 15W
Wickenburg, U.S.A. . . . . . . . . . 77 K7 33 58N 112 44W
Wickepin, Australia . . . . . . . . . . 61 F2 32 50S 117 30 E
Wickham, Australia . . . . . . . . . . 60 D2 20 42S 117 11 E
Wickham, C., Australia . . . . . . . 63 F3 39 35S 143 57 E
Wickliffe, Australia . . . . . . . . . . 84 E3 41 36N 81 28W
Wicklow, Ireland . . . . . . . . . . . . 10 D5 52 59N 6 3W
Wicklow □, Ireland . . . . . . . . . . 10 D5 52 57N 6 25W
Wicklow Hd., Ireland . . . . . . . . 10 D6 52 58N 6 0W
Wicklow Mts., Ireland . . . . . . . . 10 C5 52 58N 6 26W
Widgeegoara Cr. →, Australia . . 63 D4 28 51S 146 34 E
Widgiemooltha, Australia . . . . . 61 F3 30 51S 121 34 E
Widnes, U.K. . . . . . . . . . . . . . . . 12 D5 53 23N 2 45W
Wieluń, Poland . . . . . . . . . . . . . 17 C10 51 15N 18 34 E
Wien, Austria . . . . . . . . . . . . . . . 16 D9 48 12N 16 22 E
Wiener Neustadt, Austria . . . . . 16 E9 47 49N 16 16 E

Wiesbaden, Germany . . . . . . . . 16 C5 50 4N 8 14 E
Wigan, U.K. . . . . . . . . . . . . . . . . 12 D5 53 33N 2 38W
Wiggins, Colo., U.S.A. . . . . . . . 80 E2 40 14N 104 4W
Wiggins, Miss., U.S.A. . . . . . . . 81 K10 30 51N 89 8W
Wight, I. of □, U.K. . . . . . . . . . . 13 G6 50 40N 1 20W
Wigston, U.K. . . . . . . . . . . . . . . 13 E6 52 35N 1 6W
Wigton, U.K. . . . . . . . . . . . . . . . 12 C4 54 50N 3 10W
Wigtown, U.K. . . . . . . . . . . . . . . 11 G4 54 53N 4 27W
Wigtown B., U.K. . . . . . . . . . . . 11 G4 54 46N 4 15W
Wilber, U.S.A. . . . . . . . . . . . . . . 80 E6 40 29N 96 58W
Wilberforce, Canada . . . . . . . . . 84 A6 45 2N 78 13W
Wilberforce, C., Australia . . . . . 62 A2 11 54S 136 35 E
Wilburton, U.S.A. . . . . . . . . . . . 81 H7 34 55N 95 19W
Wilcannia, Australia . . . . . . . . . 63 E3 31 30S 143 26 E
Wilcox, U.S.A. . . . . . . . . . . . . . . 84 E6 41 35N 78 41W
Wildrose, U.S.A. . . . . . . . . . . . . 79 J9 36 14N 117 11W
Wildspitze, Austria . . . . . . . . . . 16 E6 46 53N 10 53 E
Wilge →, S. Africa . . . . . . . . . . 57 D4 27 3S 28 20 E
Wilhelm II Coast, Antarctica . . . 5 C7 68 0S 90 0 E
Wilhelmshaven, Germany . . . . . 16 B5 53 31N 8 7 E
Wilhelmstal, Namibia . . . . . . . . 56 C2 21 58S 16 21 E
Wilkes-Barre, U.S.A. . . . . . . . . . 85 E9 41 15N 75 53W
Wilkes Land, Antarctica . . . . . . 5 D9 69 0S 120 0 E
Wilkie, Canada . . . . . . . . . . . . . 71 C7 52 27N 108 42W
Wilkinsburg, U.S.A. . . . . . . . . . . 84 F5 40 26N 79 53W
Wilkinson Lakes, Australia . . . . 61 E5 29 40S 132 39 E
Willandra Creek →, Australia . . 63 E4 33 22S 145 52 E
Willapa B., U.S.A. . . . . . . . . . . . 76 C2 46 40N 124 0W
Willapa Hills, U.S.A. . . . . . . . . . 78 D3 46 35N 123 25W
Willard, N.Y., U.S.A. . . . . . . . . . 84 D7 42 40N 76 50W
Willard, Ohio, U.S.A. . . . . . . . . 84 E2 41 3N 82 44W
Willcox, U.S.A. . . . . . . . . . . . . . 77 K9 32 15N 109 50W
Willemstad, Neth. Ant. . . . . . . . 89 D6 12 5N 69 0W
Willet, U.S.A. . . . . . . . . . . . . . . 85 D9 42 28N 75 55W
William →, Canada . . . . . . . . . . 71 B7 59 8N 109 19W
William 'Bill' Dannely Res.,
 U.S.A. . . . . . . . . . . . . . . . . . . 83 J2 32 10N 87 10W
William Creek, Australia . . . . . . 63 D2 28 58S 136 22 E
Williams, Australia . . . . . . . . . . 61 F2 33 2S 116 52 E
Williams, Ariz., U.S.A. . . . . . . . 77 J7 35 15N 112 11W
Williams, Calif., U.S.A. . . . . . . . 78 F4 39 9N 122 9W
Williams Harbour, Canada . . . . 73 B8 52 33S 55 47W
Williams Lake, Canada . . . . . . . 70 C4 52 10N 122 10W
Williamsburg, Ky., U.S.A. . . . . . 83 G3 36 44N 84 10W
Williamsburg, Pa., U.S.A. . . . . . 84 F6 40 28N 78 12W
Williamsburg, Va., U.S.A. . . . . . 82 G7 37 17N 76 44W
Williamson, N.Y., U.S.A. . . . . . 84 C7 43 14N 77 11W
Williamson, W. Va., U.S.A. . . . . 82 G4 37 41N 82 17W
Williamsport, U.S.A. . . . . . . . . . 84 E7 41 15N 77 0W
Williamston, U.S.A. . . . . . . . . . 83 H7 35 51N 77 4W
Williamstown, Australia . . . . . . 63 F3 37 51S 144 52 E
Williamstown, Ky., U.S.A. . . . . . 82 F3 38 38N 84 34W
Williamstown, Mass., U.S.A. . . 85 D11 42 41N 73 12W
Williamstown, N.Y., U.S.A. . . . . 85 C9 43 26N 75 53W
Willimantic, U.S.A. . . . . . . . . . . 85 E12 41 43N 72 13W
Willingboro, U.S.A. . . . . . . . . . . 82 E8 40 3N 74 54W
Williston, S. Africa . . . . . . . . . . 56 E3 31 20S 20 53 E
Williston, Fla., U.S.A. . . . . . . . . 83 L4 29 23N 82 27W
Williston, N. Dak., U.S.A. . . . . . 80 A3 48 9N 103 37W
Williston L., Canada . . . . . . . . . 70 B4 56 0N 124 0W
Willits, U.S.A. . . . . . . . . . . . . . . 76 G2 39 25N 123 21W
Willmar, U.S.A. . . . . . . . . . . . . . 80 C7 45 7N 95 3W
Willmore Wilderness △, Canada 70 C5 53 45N 119 30W
Willoughby, U.S.A. . . . . . . . . . . 84 E3 41 39N 81 24W
Willow Bunch, Canada . . . . . . . 71 D7 49 20N 105 35W
Willow L. →, Canada . . . . . . . . 70 A5 62 10N 119 8W
Willow Wall, The, China . . . . . . 35 C12 42 10N 122 0 E
Willowick, U.S.A. . . . . . . . . . . . 84 E3 41 38N 81 28W
Willowlake →, Canada . . . . . . . 70 A4 62 42N 123 8W
Willowmore, S. Africa . . . . . . . . 56 E3 33 15S 23 30 E
Willows, U.S.A. . . . . . . . . . . . . . 78 F4 39 31N 122 12W
Willowvale = Gatyana, S. Africa 57 E4 32 16S 28 31 E
Wills, L., Australia . . . . . . . . . . . 60 D4 21 25S 128 51 E
Wills Cr. →, Australia . . . . . . . . 62 C3 22 43S 140 2 E
Willsboro, U.S.A. . . . . . . . . . . . . 85 B11 44 21N 73 24W
Willunga, Australia . . . . . . . . . . 63 F2 35 15S 138 30 E
Wilmette, U.S.A. . . . . . . . . . . . . 82 D2 42 5N 87 42W
Wilmington, Australia . . . . . . . . 63 E2 32 39S 138 7 E
Wilmington, Del., U.S.A. . . . . . . 82 F8 39 45N 75 33W
Wilmington, N.C., U.S.A. . . . . . 83 H7 34 14N 77 55W
Wilmington, Ohio, U.S.A. . . . . . 81 F4 39 27N 83 50W
Wilmington, Vt., U.S.A. . . . . . . . 85 D12 42 52N 72 52W
Wilmslow, U.K. . . . . . . . . . . . . . 12 D5 53 19N 2 13W
Wilpena Cr. →, Australia . . . . . 63 E2 31 25S 139 29 E
Wilsall, U.S.A. . . . . . . . . . . . . . . 76 D8 45 59N 110 38W
Wilson, Australia . . . . . . . . . . . . 63 D3 27 38S 141 24 E
Wilson, N.C., U.S.A. . . . . . . . . . 83 H7 35 44N 77 55W
Wilson, N.Y., U.S.A. . . . . . . . . . 84 C6 43 19N 78 50W
Wilson, Pa., U.S.A. . . . . . . . . . . 85 F9 40 41N 75 15W
Wilson →, Australia . . . . . . . . . 60 C4 16 48S 128 16 E
Wilson Bluff, Australia . . . . . . . 61 F4 31 41S 129 0 E
Wilson Inlet, Australia . . . . . . . . 61 G2 35 0S 117 22 E
Wilsons Promontory, Australia . 63 F4 38 55S 146 25 E
Wilton, U.S.A. . . . . . . . . . . . . . . 80 B4 47 10N 100 47W
Wilton →, Australia . . . . . . . . . 62 A1 14 45S 134 33 E
Wiltshire □, U.K. . . . . . . . . . . . . 13 F6 51 18N 1 53W
Wiltz, Lux. . . . . . . . . . . . . . . . . . 15 E5 49 57N 5 55 E
Wiluna, Australia . . . . . . . . . . . . 61 E3 26 36S 120 14 E
Wimborne Minster, U.K. . . . . . . 13 G6 50 48N 1 59W
Wimmera →, Australia . . . . . . . 63 F3 36 8S 141 56 E
Winam G., Kenya . . . . . . . . . . . 54 C3 0 20S 34 15 E
Winburg, S. Africa . . . . . . . . . . . 56 D4 28 30S 27 2 E
Winchendon, U.S.A. . . . . . . . . . 85 D12 42 41N 72 3W
Winchester, U.K. . . . . . . . . . . . . 13 F6 51 4N 1 18W
Winchester, Conn., U.S.A. . . . . 85 E11 41 53N 73 9W
Winchester, Idaho, U.S.A. . . . . . 76 C5 46 14N 116 38W
Winchester, Ind., U.S.A. . . . . . . 82 E3 40 10N 84 59W
Winchester, Ky., U.S.A. . . . . . . 82 G3 38 0N 84 11W
Winchester, N.H., U.S.A. . . . . . 85 D12 42 46N 72 23W
Winchester, Nev., U.S.A. . . . . . 79 J11 36 6N 115 10W
Winchester, Tenn., U.S.A. . . . . 83 H2 35 11N 86 7W
Winchester, Va., U.S.A. . . . . . . 82 F6 39 11N 78 10W
Wind →, U.S.A. . . . . . . . . . . . . . 76 E9 43 12N 108 12W
Wind River Range, U.S.A. . . . . . 76 E9 43 0N 109 30W
Windau = Ventspils, Latvia . . . . 9 H19 57 25N 21 32 E
Windber, U.S.A. . . . . . . . . . . . . . 84 F6 40 14N 78 50W
Winder, U.S.A. . . . . . . . . . . . . . . 83 J4 34 0N 83 45W
Windermere, U.K. . . . . . . . . . . . 12 C5 54 23N 2 55W
Windhoek, Namibia . . . . . . . . . . 56 C2 22 35S 17 4 E
Windom, U.S.A. . . . . . . . . . . . . . 80 D7 43 52N 95 7W
Window Rock, U.S.A. . . . . . . . . 77 J9 35 41N 109 3W
Windrush →, U.K. . . . . . . . . . . . 13 F6 51 43N 1 24W
Windsor, Australia . . . . . . . . . . . 63 E5 33 37S 150 50 E
Windsor, N.S., Canada . . . . . . . 73 D7 44 59N 64 5W
Windsor, Ont., Canada . . . . . . . 84 D2 42 18N 83 0W
Windsor, U.K. . . . . . . . . . . . . . . 13 F7 51 29N 0 36W
Windsor, Colo., U.S.A. . . . . . . . 80 E2 40 29N 104 54W
Windsor, Conn., U.S.A. . . . . . . 85 E12 41 50N 72 39W

Windsor, Mo., U.S.A. . . . . . . . . 80 F8 38 32N 93 31W
Windsor, N.Y., U.S.A. . . . . . . . . 85 D9 42 5N 75 37W
Windsor, Vt., U.S.A. . . . . . . . . . 85 C12 43 29N 72 24W
Windsor & Maidenhead □, U.K. 13 F7 51 29N 0 40W
Windsorton, S. Africa . . . . . . . . 56 D3 28 16S 24 44 E
Windward Is., W. Indies . . . . . . 89 D7 13 0N 61 0W
Windward Passage = Vientos,
 Paso de los, Caribbean . . . . . . 89 C5 20 0N 74 0W
Winefred L., Canada . . . . . . . . . 71 B6 55 30N 110 30W
Winfield, U.S.A. . . . . . . . . . . . . . 81 G6 37 15N 96 59W
Wingate Mts., Australia . . . . . . 60 B5 14 25S 130 40 E
Wingham, Australia . . . . . . . . . . 63 E5 31 48S 152 22 E
Wingham, Canada . . . . . . . . . . . 84 C3 43 55N 81 20W
Winisk, Canada . . . . . . . . . . . . . 72 A2 55 20N 85 15W
Winisk →, Canada . . . . . . . . . . 72 A2 55 17N 85 5W
Winisk L., Canada . . . . . . . . . . . 72 B2 52 55N 87 22W
Wink, U.S.A. . . . . . . . . . . . . . . . 81 K3 31 45N 103 9W
Winkler, Canada . . . . . . . . . . . . 71 D9 49 10N 97 56W
Winlock, U.S.A. . . . . . . . . . . . . . 78 D4 46 30N 122 56W
Winnebago, L., U.S.A. . . . . . . . 82 D1 44 0N 88 26W
Winnecke Cr. →, Australia . . . . 60 C5 18 35S 131 34 E
Winnemucca, U.S.A. . . . . . . . . . 76 F5 40 58N 117 44W
Winnemucca L., U.S.A. . . . . . . . 76 F4 40 7N 119 21W
Winnett, U.S.A. . . . . . . . . . . . . . 76 C9 47 0N 108 21W
Winnfield, U.S.A. . . . . . . . . . . . . 81 K8 31 56N 92 38W
Winnibigoshish, L., U.S.A. . . . . 80 B7 47 27N 94 13W
Winnipeg, Canada . . . . . . . . . . . 71 D9 49 54N 97 9W
Winnipeg →, Canada . . . . . . . . 71 C9 50 38N 96 19W
Winnipeg, L., Canada . . . . . . . . 71 C9 52 0N 97 0W
Winnipeg Beach, Canada . . . . . 71 C9 50 30N 96 58W
Winnipegosis, Canada . . . . . . . 71 C9 51 39N 99 55W
Winnipegosis L., Canada . . . . . 71 C9 52 30N 100 0W
Winnipesaukee, L., U.S.A. . . . . 85 C13 43 38N 71 21W
Winnisquam L., U.S.A. . . . . . . . 85 C13 43 33N 71 31W
Winnsboro, La., U.S.A. . . . . . . . 81 J9 32 10N 91 43W
Winnsboro, S.C., U.S.A. . . . . . . 83 H5 34 23N 81 5W
Winnsboro, Tex., U.S.A. . . . . . . 81 J7 32 58N 95 17W
Winokapau, L., Canada . . . . . . . 73 B7 53 15N 62 50W
Winona, Minn., U.S.A. . . . . . . . 80 C9 44 3N 91 39W
Winona, Miss., U.S.A. . . . . . . . . 81 J10 33 29N 89 44W
Winooski, U.S.A. . . . . . . . . . . . . 85 B11 44 29N 73 11W
Winooski →, U.S.A. . . . . . . . . . 85 B11 44 32N 73 17W
Winschoten, Neths. . . . . . . . . . . 15 A7 53 9N 7 3 E
Winsford, U.K. . . . . . . . . . . . . . . 12 D5 53 12N 2 31W
Winslow, Ariz., U.S.A. . . . . . . . 77 J8 35 2N 110 42W
Winslow, Wash., U.S.A. . . . . . . 78 C4 47 38N 122 31W
Winsted, U.S.A. . . . . . . . . . . . . . 85 E11 41 55N 73 4W
Winston-Salem, U.S.A. . . . . . . . 83 G5 36 6N 80 15W
Winter Garden, U.S.A. . . . . . . . 83 L5 28 34N 81 35W
Winter Haven, U.S.A. . . . . . . . . 83 M5 28 1N 81 44W
Winter Park, U.S.A. . . . . . . . . . . 83 L5 28 36N 81 20W
Winterhaven, U.S.A. . . . . . . . . . 79 N12 32 47N 114 39W
Winters, U.S.A. . . . . . . . . . . . . . 78 G5 38 32N 121 58W
Wintersville, U.S.A. . . . . . . . . . 84 F4 40 23N 80 42W
Winterswijk, Neths. . . . . . . . . . . 15 C6 51 58N 6 43 E
Winterthur, Switz. . . . . . . . . . . . 20 C8 47 30N 8 44 E
Winthrop, U.S.A. . . . . . . . . . . . . 76 B3 48 28N 120 10W
Winton, Australia . . . . . . . . . . . . 62 C3 22 24S 143 3 E
Winton, N.Z. . . . . . . . . . . . . . . . 59 M2 46 8S 168 20 E
Wirrulla, Australia . . . . . . . . . . . 63 E1 32 24S 134 31 E
Wisbech, U.K. . . . . . . . . . . . . . . 13 E8 52 41N 0 9 E
Wisconsin □, U.S.A. . . . . . . . . . 80 C10 44 45N 89 30W
Wisconsin →, U.S.A. . . . . . . . . 80 D9 43 0N 91 15W
Wisconsin Rapids, U.S.A. . . . . . 80 C10 44 23N 89 49W
Wisdom, U.S.A. . . . . . . . . . . . . . 76 D7 45 37N 113 27W
Wishaw, U.K. . . . . . . . . . . . . . . 11 F5 55 46N 3 54W
Wishek, U.S.A. . . . . . . . . . . . . . 80 B5 46 16N 99 33W
Wisła →, Poland . . . . . . . . . . . . 17 A10 54 22N 18 55 E
Wismar, Germany . . . . . . . . . . . 16 B6 53 54N 11 29 E
Wisner, U.S.A. . . . . . . . . . . . . . . 80 E6 41 59N 96 55W
Witbank, S. Africa . . . . . . . . . . . 57 D4 25 51S 29 14 E
Witdraai, S. Africa . . . . . . . . . . . 56 D3 26 58S 20 48 E
Witham, U.K. . . . . . . . . . . . . . . . 13 F8 51 48N 0 40 E
Witham →, U.K. . . . . . . . . . . . . 12 E7 52 59N 0 2W
Withernsea, U.K. . . . . . . . . . . . . 12 D8 53 44N 0 1 E
Witjira △, Australia . . . . . . . . . . 63 D2 26 22S 135 37 E
Witney, U.K. . . . . . . . . . . . . . . . 13 F6 51 48N 1 28W
Witnossob →, Namibia . . . . . . . 56 D3 23 55S 18 45 E
Wittenberge, Germany . . . . . . . 16 B6 53 0N 11 45 E
Wittenoom, Australia . . . . . . . . 60 D2 22 15S 118 20 E
Witvlei, Namibia . . . . . . . . . . . . 56 C2 22 23S 18 32 E
Wkra →, Poland . . . . . . . . . . . . 17 B11 52 27N 20 44 E
Wlingi, Indonesia . . . . . . . . . . . . 37 H15 8 5S 112 25 E
Włocławek, Poland . . . . . . . . . . 17 B10 52 40N 19 3 E
Włodawa, Poland . . . . . . . . . . . 17 C12 51 33N 23 31 E
Woburn, U.S.A. . . . . . . . . . . . . . 85 D13 42 29N 71 9W
Wodian, China . . . . . . . . . . . . . . 34 H7 32 50N 112 35 E
Wodonga = Albury-Wodonga,
 Australia . . . . . . . . . . . . . . . . . 63 F4 36 3S 146 56 E
Wokam, Indonesia . . . . . . . . . . 37 F8 5 45S 134 28 E
Woking, U.K. . . . . . . . . . . . . . . . 13 F7 51 19N 0 34W
Wokingham, U.K. . . . . . . . . . . . 13 F7 51 24N 0 49W
Wokingham □, U.K. . . . . . . . . . 13 F7 51 25N 0 51W
Wolf →, U.S.A. . . . . . . . . . . . . . 70 A2 60 17N 132 33W
Wolf Creek, U.S.A. . . . . . . . . . . 76 C7 47 0N 112 4W
Wolf L., Canada . . . . . . . . . . . . . 70 A2 60 24N 131 40W
Wolf Point, U.S.A. . . . . . . . . . . . 80 A2 48 5N 105 39W
Wolfe I., Canada . . . . . . . . . . . . 85 B8 44 7N 76 20W
Wolfeboro, U.S.A. . . . . . . . . . . . 85 C13 43 35N 71 13W
Wolfsberg, Austria . . . . . . . . . . 16 E8 46 50N 14 52 E
Wolfsburg, Germany . . . . . . . . . 16 B6 52 25N 10 48 E
Wolin, Poland . . . . . . . . . . . . . . 16 B8 53 50N 14 37 E
Wollaston, Is., Chile . . . . . . . . . 96 H3 55 40S 67 30W
Wollaston, U.S.A. . . . . . . . . . . . 84 D5 42 15N 109 54 E
Wollaston Lake, Canada . . . . . . 71 B8 58 3N 103 33W
Wollaston Pen., Canada . . . . . . 68 B8 69 30N 115 0W
Wollongong, Australia . . . . . . . . 63 E5 34 25S 150 54 E
Wolmaransstad, S. Africa . . . . . 56 D4 27 12S 25 59 E
Wolseley, S. Africa . . . . . . . . . . 56 E2 33 26S 19 7 E
Wolsey, U.S.A. . . . . . . . . . . . . . 80 C5 44 24N 98 28W
Wolstenholme, C., Canada . . . . 66 C12 62 35N 77 30W
Wolvega, Neths. . . . . . . . . . . . . 15 B6 52 52N 6 0 E
Wolverhampton, U.K. . . . . . . . . 13 E5 52 35N 2 7W
Wondai, Australia . . . . . . . . . . . 63 D5 26 20S 151 49 E
Wongalarroo L., Australia . . . . . 63 E3 31 32S 144 0 E
Wongan Hills, Australia . . . . . . 61 F2 30 51S 116 37 E
Wŏnju, S. Korea . . . . . . . . . . . . 35 F14 37 22N 127 58 E
Wonosari, Indonesia . . . . . . . . . 37 G14 7 58S 110 36 E
Wonosobo, Indonesia . . . . . . . . 37 G13 7 22S 109 54 E
Wonowon, Canada . . . . . . . . . . 70 B4 56 44N 121 48W
Wŏnsan, N. Korea . . . . . . . . . . . 35 E14 39 11N 127 27 E
Wonthaggi, Australia . . . . . . . . 63 F4 38 37S 145 37 E
Wood Buffalo △, Canada . . . . . 70 B6 59 0N 113 41W
Wood Is., Australia . . . . . . . . . . 60 C3 16 24S 123 19 E
Wood L., Canada . . . . . . . . . . . . 71 B8 55 17N 103 17W
Woodah I., Australia . . . . . . . . . 62 A2 13 27S 136 10 E
Woodbourne, U.S.A. . . . . . . . . . 85 E10 41 46N 74 34W
Woodbridge, Canada . . . . . . . . 84 C5 43 47N 79 36W
Woodbridge, U.K. . . . . . . . . . . . 13 E9 52 6N 1 20 E

Woodburn, U.S.A. ............ 76 D2   45  9N 122 51W
Woodenbong, Australia ...... 63 D5   28 24S 152 39 E
Woodend, Australia .......... 63 F3   37 20S 144 33 E
Woodford, Australia ......... 63 D5   26 58S 152 47 E
Woodlake, U.S.A. ............ 78 J7   36 25N 119  6W
Woodland, Calif., U.S.A. .... 78 G5   38 41N 121 46W
Woodland, Maine, U.S.A. .... 83 C12  45  9N  67 25W
Woodland, Pa., U.S.A. ....... 84 F6   40 59N  78 21W
Woodland, Wash., U.S.A. .... 78 E4   45 54N 122 45W
Woodland Caribou △, Canada  71 C10  51  0N  94 45W
Woodlands, Singapore ........ 39 d     1 27N 103 47 E
Woodridge, Canada .......... 71 D9   49 20N  96  9W
Woodroffe, Mt., Australia .... 61 E5   26 20S 131 45 E
Woods, L., Australia ......... 62 B1   17 50S 133 30 E
Woods, L. of the, Canada .... 71 D10  49 15N  94 45W
Woodstock, Australia ........ 62 B4   19 35S 146 50 E
Woodstock, N.B., Canada .... 73 C6   46 11N  67 37W
Woodstock, Ont., Canada .... 84 C4   43 10N  80 45W
Woodstock, U.K. ............ 13 F6   51 51N   1 20W
Woodstock, Ill., U.S.A. ...... 80 D10  42 19N  88 27W
Woodstock, Vt., U.S.A. ...... 85 C12  43 37N  72 31W
Woodsville, U.S.A. .......... 85 B13  44  9N  72  2W
Woodville, N.Z. ............. 59 J5   40 20S 175 53 E
Woodville, Miss., U.S.A. ..... 81 K9   31  6N  91 18W
Woodville, Tex., U.S.A. ...... 81 K7   30 47N  94 25W
Woodward, U.S.A. ........... 81 G5   36  6N  99 24W
Woody, U.S.A. .............. 79 K8   35 42N 118 50W
Woody →, Canada ........... 71 C8   52 31N 100 51W
Woolacombe, U.K. ........... 13 F3   51 10N   4 13W
Woolamai, C., Australia ...... 63 F4   38 30S 145 23 E
Wooler, U.K. ............... 12 B5   55 33N   2  1W
Woolgoolga, Australia ....... 63 E5   30  6S 153 11 E
Woomera, Australia .......... 63 E2   31  5S 136 50 E
Woonsocket, R.I., U.S.A. ..... 85 E13  42  0N  71 31W
Woonsocket, S. Dak., U.S.A. . 80 C5   44  3N  98 17W
Wooramel →, Australia ....... 61 E1   25 47S 114 10 E
Wooramel Roadhouse, Australia 61 E1   25 45S 114 17 E
Wooster, U.S.A. ............ 84 F3   40 48N  81 56W
Worcester, S. Africa ......... 56 E2   33 39S  19 27 E
Worcester, U.K. ............. 13 E5   52 11N   2 12W
Worcester, Mass., U.S.A. ..... 85 D13  42 16N  71 48W
Worcester, N.Y., U.S.A. ...... 85 D10  42 36N  74 45W
Worcestershire □, U.K. ....... 13 E5   52 13N   2 10W
Workington, U.K. ........... 12 C4   54 39N   3 33W
Worksop, U.K. .............. 12 D6   53 18N   1  7W
Worland, U.S.A. ............ 76 D10  44 1N 107 57W
Worms, Germany ............ 16 D5   49 37N   8 21 E
Worsley, Canada ............ 70 B5   56 31N 119 8W
Wortham, U.S.A. ............ 81 K6   31 47N  96 28W
Worthing, Barbados .......... 89 g    13  5N  59 35W
Worthing, U.K. ............. 13 G7   50 49N   0 21W
Worthington, Minn., U.S.A. .. 80 D7   43 37N  95 36W
Worthington, Pa., U.S.A. ..... 84 F5   40 50N  79 38W
Wosi, Indonesia ............. 37 E7   0 15S 128  0 E
Wou-han = Wuhan, China .... 33 C6   30 31N 114 18 E
Wousi = Wuxi, China ........ 33 C7   31 33N 120 18 E
Wowoni, Indonesia .......... 37 E6    4  5S 123  5 E
Wrangel I. = Vrangelya, Ostrov,
  Russia .................. 29 B19  71  0N 180  0 E
Wrangell, U.S.A. ........... 70 B2   56 28N 132 23W
Wrangell Mts., U.S.A. ....... 68 B5   61 30N 142  0W
Wrath, C., U.K. ............ 11 C3   58 38N   5  1W
Wray, U.S.A. .............. 80 E3   40  5N 102 13W
Wrekin, The, U.K. .......... 13 E5   52 41N   2 32W
Wrens, U.S.A. ............. 83 J4   33 12N  82 23W
Wrexham, U.K. ............. 12 D4   53  3N   3  0W
Wrexham □, U.K. ........... 12 D5   53  1N   2 58W
Wright, U.S.A. ............. 80 D2   43 47N 105 30W
Wright Pt., Canada .......... 84 C3   43 48N  81 44W
Wrightson, Mt., U.S.A. ...... 77 L8   31 42N 110 51W
Wrightwood, U.S.A. ......... 79 L9   34 21N 117 38W
Wrigley, Canada ............ 68 B7   63 16N 123 37W
Wrocław, Poland ............ 17 C9   51  5N  17  5 E
Września, Poland ........... 17 B9   52 21N  17 36 E
Wu Jiang →, China ......... 32 D5   29 40N 107 20 E
Wu Kau Tang, China ........ 33 F11  22 30N 114 14 E
Wu'an, China .............. 34 F8   36 40N 114 15 E
Wubin, Australia ............ 61 F2   30  6S 116 37 E
Wubu, China ............... 34 F6   37 28N 110 42 E
Wuchang, China ............ 35 B14  44 55N 127  5 E
Wucheng, China ............ 34 F9   37 12N 116 20 E
Wuchuan, China ............ 34 D6   41  5N 111 28 E
Wudi, China ............... 35 F9   37 40N 117 35 E
Wuding He →, China ........ 34 F6   37  2N 110 23 E
Wudinna, Australia .......... 63 E2   33  0S 135 22 E
Wudu, China ............... 34 H3   33 22N 104 54 E
Wuguishan, China ........... 33 G9   22 25N 113 25 E
Wuhan, China .............. 33 C6   30 31N 114 18 E
Wuhe, China ............... 35 H9   33 10N 117 50 E
Wuhsi = Wuxi, China ........ 33 C7   31 33N 120 18 E
Wuhu, China ............... 33 C6   31 22N 118 21 E
Wukari, Nigeria ............. 50 G7    7 51N   9 42 E
Wulajie, China ............. 35 B14  44  6N 126 33 E
Wulanbulang, China ......... 34 D6   41  5N 110 55 E
Wular L., India ............. 43 B6   34 20N  74 30 E
Wulian, China .............. 35 G10  35 40N 119 12 E
Wuliaru, Indonesia .......... 37 F8    7 27S 131  0 E
Wuluk'omushih Ling, China .. 32 C3   36 25N  87 25 E
Wulumuchi = Ürümqi, China  28 E9   43 45N  87 45 E
Wunnummin L., Canada ...... 72 B2   52 55N  89 10W
Wuntho, Burma ............. 41 H19  23 55N  95 45 E
Wupatki △, U.S.A. .......... 77 J8   35 35N 111 20W
Wuppertal, Germany ......... 16 C4   51 16N   7 12 E
Wuppertal, S. Africa ......... 56 E2   32 13S  19 12 E
Wuqing, China ............. 35 E9   39 23N 117  4 E
Wurtsboro, U.S.A. .......... 85 E10  41 35N  74 29W
Würzburg, Germany ......... 16 D5   49 46N   9 55 E
Wushan, China ............. 34 G3   34 43N 104 53 E
Wusuli Jiang = Ussuri →, Asia 30 A7   48 27N 135  0 E
Wutai, China .............. 34 E7   38 40N 113 12 E
Wuting = Huimin, China ..... 35 F9   37 27N 117 28 E
Wutongqiao, China .......... 32 C5   29 22N 103 50 E
Wuwei, China .............. 32 C5   37 57N 102 34 E
Wuxi, China ............... 33 C7   31 33N 120 18 E
Wuxiang, China ............ 34 F7   36 49N 112 50 E
Wuyang, China ............. 34 H7   33 25N 113 35 E
Wuyi, China ............... 34 F8   37 46N 115 56 E
Wuyi Shan, China ........... 33 D6   27  0N 117  0 E
Wuyuan, China ............. 34 D5   41  2N 108 20 E
Wuzhai, China ............. 34 E6   38 54N 111 48 E
Wuzhi Shan, China .......... 38 C7   18 45N 109 45 E
Wuzhong, China ............ 34 E4   38  2N 106 12 E
Wuzhou, China ............. 33 D6   23 30N 111 18 E
Wyaaba →, Australia ........ 62 B3   16 27S 141 35 S
Wyalkatchem, Australia ...... 61 F2   31  8S 117 22 E
Wyalusing, U.S.A. .......... 85 E8   41 40N  76 16W
Wyandotte, U.S.A. .......... 82 D4   42 12N  83  9W
Wyandra, Australia .......... 63 D4   27 12S 145 56 E
Wyangala, L., Australia ...... 63 E4   33 54S 149  0 E
Wyara, L., Australia ......... 63 D3   28 42S 144 14 E
Wycheproof, Australia ....... 63 F3   36  5S 143 17 E
Wye →, U.K. ............... 13 F5   51 38N   2 40W
Wyemandoo, Australia ....... 61 E2   28 28S 118 29 E
Wymondham, U.K. .......... 13 E9   52 35N   1  7 E
Wymore, U.S.A. ............ 80 E6   40  7N  96 40W
Wyndham, Australia ......... 60 C4   15 33S 128  3 E
Wyndham, N.Z. ............ 59 M2   46 20S 168 51 E
Wynne, U.S.A. ............. 81 H9   35 14N  90 47W
Wynyard, Australia .......... 63 G4   41  5S 145 44 E
Wynyard, Canada ........... 71 C8   51 45N 104 10W
Wyola, L., Australia ......... 61 E5   29  8S 130 17 E
Wyoming = Plympton-Wyoming,
  Canada ................. 84 D2   42 57N  82  7W
Wyoming □, U.S.A. ......... 76 E10  43  0N 107 30W
Wyomissing, U.S.A. ......... 85 F9   40 20N  75 59W
Wyong, Australia ........... 63 E5   33 14S 151 24 E
Wytheville, U.S.A. .......... 82 G5   36 57N  81  5W

X

Xaafuun, Somali Rep. ....... 47 E5   10 25N  51 16 E
Xaçmaz, Azerbaijan ......... 19 F8   41 31N  48 42 E
Xai-Xai, Mozam. ........... 57 D5   25  6S  33 31 E
Xainza, China ............. 32 C3   30 58N  88 35 E
Xalapa, Mexico ............ 87 D5   19 32N  96 55W
Xangongo, Angola .......... 56 B2   16 45S  15  5 E
Xankändi, Azerbaijan ....... 19 G8   39 52N  46 49 E
Xánthi, Greece ............. 23 D11  41 10N  24 58 E
Xanxerê, Brazil ............ 95 B5   26 53S  52 23W
Xapuri, Brazil ............. 92 F5   10 35S  68 35W
Xar Moron He →, China .... 35 C11  43 25N 120 35 E
Xátiva, Spain .............. 21 C5   38 59N   0 32W
Xau, L., Botswana .......... 56 C3   21 15S  24 44 E
Xavantina, Brazil ........... 95 A5   21 15S  52 48W
Xenia, U.S.A. ............. 82 F4   39 41N  83 56W
Xeropotamos →, Cyprus ..... 25 E11  34 42N  32 33 E
Xhora, S. Africa ........... 57 E4   31 55S  28 38 E
Xhumo, Botswana .......... 56 C3   21  7S  24 35 E
Xi Jiang →, China ......... 33 D6   22  5N 113 20 E
Xia Xian, China ........... 34 G6   35  8N 111 12 E
Xiachengzi, China .......... 35 B16  44 40N 130 18 E
Xiaguan, China ............ 32 D5   25 32N 100 16 E
Xiajin, China .............. 34 F9   36 56N 116  0 E
Xiamen, China ............. 33 D6   24 25N 118  4 E
Xi'an, China .............. 34 G5   34 15N 109  0 E
Xian Xian, China .......... 34 E9   38 12N 116  6 E
Xiang Jiang →, China ...... 33 D6   28 55N 112 50 E
Xiangcheng, Henan, China .. 34 H8   33 29N 114 52 E
Xiangcheng, Henan, China .. 34 H7   33 50N 113 27 E
Xiangfan, China ........... 33 C6   32  2N 112  8 E
Xianggang = Hong Kong □,
  China ................. 33 G11  22 11N 114 14 E
Xianghuang Qi, China ...... 34 C7   42  2N 113 50 E
Xiangning, China .......... 34 G6   35 58N 110 50 E
Xiangquan, China .......... 34 F7   36 30N 113  1 E
Xiangquan He = Sutlej →,
  Pakistan ............... 42 E4   29 23N  71  3 E
Xiangshui, China .......... 35 G10  34 12N 119 33 E
Xiangtan, China ........... 33 D6   27 51N 112 54 E
Xianyang, China ........... 34 G5   34 20N 108 40 E
Xiao Hinggan Ling, China .. 33 B7   49  0N 127  0 E
Xiao Xian, China .......... 34 G9   34 15N 116 55 E
Xiaoyi, China ............. 34 F6   37  8N 111 48 E
Xiawa, China ............. 35 C11  42 35N 120 38 E
Xiayi, China .............. 34 G9   34 15N 116 10 E
Xichang, China ............ 32 D5   27 51N 102 19 E
Xichuan, China ............ 34 H6   33  0N 111 30 E
Xieng Khouang, Laos ....... 38 C4   19 17N 103 25 E
Xifei He →, China ......... 34 H9   32 45N 116 40 E
Xifeng, Gansu, China ...... 34 G4   35 40N 107 40 E
Xifeng, Liaoning, China .... 35 C13  42 42N 124 45 E
Xifengzhen = Xifeng, China  34 G4   35 40N 107 40 E
Xigazê, China ............. 32 D3   29  5N  88 45 E
Xihe, China .............. 34 G3   34  2N 105 20 E
Xihua, China ............. 34 H8   33 45N 114 30 E
Xili Shuiku, China ......... 33 F10  22 36N 113 57 E
Xiliao He →, China ........ 35 C12  43 32N 123 35 E
Ximana, Mozam. .......... 55 F3   19 24S  33 58 E
Xin Xian = Xinzhou, China . 34 E7   38 22N 112 46 E
Xinavane, Mozam. ......... 57 D5   25  2S  32 47 E
Xinbin, China ............. 35 D13  41 40N 125  2 E
Xing Xian, China .......... 34 E6   38 27N 111  7 E
Xing'an, China ............ 33 D6   25 38N 110 40 E
Xingcheng, China .......... 35 D11  40 40N 120 45 E
Xinghe, China ............. 34 D7   40 55N 113 55 E
Xinghua, China ............ 35 H10  32 58N 119 48 E
Xinglong, China ........... 35 D9   40 25N 117 30 E
Xingping, China ........... 34 G5   34 20N 108 28 E
Xingtai, China ............ 34 F8   37  3N 114 32 E
Xingu →, Brazil ........... 93 D8    1 30S  51 53W
Xingyang, China ........... 34 G7   34 45N 112 52 E
Xinhe, China ............. 34 F8   37 30N 115 15 E
Xining, China ............. 32 C5   36 34N 101 40 E
Xinjiang, China ........... 34 G6   35 34N 111 11 E
Xinjiang Uygur Zizhiqu □, China 32 C3   42  0N  86  0 E
Xinjin = Pulandian, China .. 35 E11  39 25N 121 58 E
Xinkai He →, China ........ 35 C12  43 32N 123 35 E
Xinken, China ............. 33 F10  22 39N 113 36 E
Xinle, China .............. 34 E8   38 25N 114 40 E
Xinlitun, China ........... 35 D12  42  0N 122  8 E
Xinmin, China ............. 35 D12  41 59N 122 50 E
Xintai, China ............. 35 G9   35 55N 117 45 E
Xinwan, China ............ 33 F10  22 47N 113 40 E
Xinxiang, China ........... 34 G7   35 18N 113 50 E
Xinzhan, China ............ 35 C14  43 50N 127 18 E
Xinzheng, China ........... 34 G7   34 20N 113 45 E
Xinzhou, China ............ 34 E7   38 22N 112 46 E
Xiongyuecheng, China ...... 35 D12  40 12N 122  5 E
Xiping, Henan, China ....... 34 H8   33 22N 114  5 E
Xiping, Henan, China ....... 34 H6   33 25N 111  8 E
Xique-Xique, Brazil ........ 93 F10  10 50S  42 40W
Xisha Qundao = Paracel Is.,
  S. China Sea ........... 36 A4   15 50N 112  0 E
Xiuyan, China ............ 35 D12  40 18N 123 11 E
Xixabangma Feng, China .... 41 E14  28 20N  85 40 E
Xixia, China ............. 34 H6   33 25N 111 29 E
Xixiang, China ............ 34 H4   33  0N 107 44 E
Xiyang, China ............. 34 F7   37 38N 113 38 E
Xizang Zizhiqu □, China .... 32 C3   32  0N  88  0 E
Xlendi, Malta ............. 25 C1   36  1N  14 12 E
Xochob, Mexico ........... 87 D7   19 28N  89 45W

Xuan Loc, Vietnam ......... 39 G6   10 56N 107 14 E
Xuanhua, China ........... 34 D8   40 40N 115  2 E
Xuchang, China ........... 34 G7   34  2N 113 48 E
Xun Xian, China ........... 34 G8   35 42N 114 33 E
Xunyang, China ........... 34 H5   32 48N 109 22 E
Xunyi, China ............. 34 G5   35  8N 108 20 E
Xúquer →, Spain ........... 21 C5   39  5N   0 10W
Xushui, China ............. 34 E8   39  2N 115 40 E
Xuyen Moc, Vietnam ....... 39 G6   10 34N 107 25 E
Xuzhou, China ............ 35 G9   34 18N 117 10 E
Xylophagou, Cyprus ........ 25 E12  34 54N  33 51 E

Y

Ya Xian, China ............ 38 C7   18 14N 109 29 E
Yaamba, Australia ......... 62 C5   23  8S 150 22 E
Yaapeet, Australia ......... 63 F3   35 45S 142  3 E
Yablonovy Ra. = Yablonovyy
  Khrebet, Russia ........ 29 D12  53  0N 114  0 E
Yablonovyy Khrebet, Russia . 29 D12  53  0N 114  0 E
Yabrai Shan, China ........ 34 E2   39 40N 103  0 E
Yabrūd, Syria ............. 46 B5   33 58N  36 39 E
Yabucoa, Puerto Rico ....... 89 d   18  3N  65 53W
Yacambú △, Venezuela ...... 89 E6    9 42N  69 27W
Yacheng, China ........... 33 E5   18 22N 109  6 E
Yacuiba, Bolivia ........... 94 A3   22  0S  63 43W
Yacuma →, Bolivia ......... 92 F5   13 38S  65 23W
Yadgir, India ............. 40 L10  16 45N  77  5 E
Yadkin →, U.S.A. .......... 83 H5   35 29N  80  9W
Yaeyama-Rettō, Japan ...... 31 M1   24 30N 123 40 E
Yagodnoye, Russia ......... 29 C15  62 33N 149 40 E
Yahila, Dem. Rep. of the Congo 54 B1    0 13N  24 28 E
Yahk, Canada ............. 70 D5   49  6N 116 10W
Yahuma, Dem. Rep. of the Congo 52 D4    1  0N  23 10 E
Yaita, Japan .............. 31 F9   36 48N 139 56 E
Yaiza, Canary Is. .......... 24 F6   28 57N  13 46W
Yakima, U.S.A. ............ 76 C3   46 36N 120 31W
Yakima →, U.S.A. .......... 76 C3   47  0N 120 30W
Yakobi I., U.S.A. .......... 70 C6   58  0N 136 30W
Yakovlevka, Russia ......... 30 B6   44 26N 133 28 E
Yaku-Shima, Japan ......... 31 J5   30 20N 130 30 E
Yakumo, Japan ............ 30 C10  42 15N 140 16 E
Yakutat, U.S.A. ........... 68 C6   59 33N 139 44W
Yakutia = Sakha □, Russia .. 29 C13  66  0N 130  0 E
Yakutsk, Russia ........... 29 C13  62  5N 129 50 E
Yala, Thailand ............ 39 J3    6 33N 101 18 E
Yalboroo, Australia ........ 62 J6   20 50S 148 40 E
Yale, U.S.A. .............. 84 C2   43  8N  82 48W
Yalgoo, Australia .......... 61 E2   28 16S 116 39 E
Yalgorup △, Australia ...... 61 D2   24 34S 115  2 E
Yalinga, C.A.R. ........... 52 C4    6 33N  23 10 E
Yalkubul, Punta, Mexico .... 87 C7   21 32N  88 37W
Yalleroi, Australia ......... 62 C4   24  3S 145 42 E
Yalobusha →, U.S.A. ....... 81 J9   33 33N  90 10W
Yalong Jiang →, China ..... 32 D5   26 40N 101 55 E
Yalova, Turkey ............ 23 D13  40 41N  29 15 E
Yalta, Ukraine ............. 19 F5   44 30N  34 10 E
Yalu Jiang →, China ....... 35 E13  40  0N 124 22 E
Yam Ha Melah = Dead Sea, Asia 46 D4  31 30N  35 30 E
Yam Kinneret, Israel ....... 46 C4   32 45N  35 35 E
Yamada, Japan ............ 31 H5   33 33N 130 49 E
Yamagata, Japan .......... 30 E10  38 15N 140 15 E
Yamagata □, Japan ........ 30 E10  38 30N 140  0 E
Yamaguchi, Japan ......... 31 G5   34 10N 131 32 E
Yamaguchi □, Japan ....... 31 G5   34 20N 131 40 E
Yamal, Poluostrov, Russia .. 28 B8   71  0N  70  0 E
Yamal Pen. = Yamal, Poluostrov,
  Russia ................. 28 B8   71  0N  70  0 E
Yamanashi □, Japan ....... 31 G9   35 40N 138 40 E
Yamanie Falls △, Australia .. 62 B4   18 29S 146  9 E
Yamantau, Gora, Russia .... 18 D10  54 15N  58  6 E
Yamba, Australia .......... 63 D5   29 26S 153 23 E
Yambarran Ra., Australia ... 60 C5   15 10S 130 25 E
Yâmbio, Sudan ........... 51 H11  4 35N  28 16 E
Yambol, Bulgaria .......... 23 C12  42 30N  26 30 E
Yamdena, Indonesia ....... 37 F8    7 45S 131 20 E
Yame, Japan ............. 31 H5   33 13N 130 35 E
Yamethin, Burma ......... 41 J20  20 29N  96 18 E
Yamma-Yamma, L., Australia 63 D3  26 16S 141 20 E
Yamoussoukro, Ivory C. .... 50 G4    6 49N   5 17W
Yampa →, U.S.A. ......... 76 F9   40 32N 108 59W
Yampi Sd., Australia ....... 60 C3   16  8S 123 38 E
Yampil, Moldova .......... 17 D15  48 15N  28 15 E
Yampol = Yampil, Moldova . 17 D15  48 15N  28 15 E
Yamuna →, India .......... 43 G9   25 30N  81 53 E
Yamunanagar, India ....... 42 D7   30  7N  77 17 E
Yamzho Yumco, China ..... 32 D4   28 48N  90 35 E
Yana →, Russia ........... 29 B14  71 30N 136  0 E
Yanagawa, Japan ......... 31 H5   33 10N 130 24 E
Yanai, Japan ............. 31 H6   33 58N 132  7 E
Yan'an, China ............ 34 F5   36 35N 109 26 E
Yanaul, Russia ........... 18 C10  56 25N  55  0 E
Yanbu 'al Baḥr, Si. Arabia .. 44 F3   24  0N  38  5 E
Yanchang, China .......... 34 F6   36 43N 110  1 E
Yancheng, Henan, China ... 34 H8   33 35N 114  0 E
Yancheng, Jiangsu, China .. 35 H11  33 23N 120  8 E
Yanchep Beach, Australia .. 61 F2   31 33S 115 37 E
Yanchi, China ............ 34 F4   37 48N 107 20 E
Yanchuan, China .......... 34 F6   36 51N 110 10 E
Yanco Cr. →, Australia ..... 63 F4   35 14S 145 35 E
Yandicoogina, Australia .... 60 D2   22 49S 119 12 E
Yandoon, Burma .......... 41 L19  17  0N  95 40 E
Yang Xian, China ......... 34 H4   33  15N 107 30 E
Yangambi, Dem. Rep. of
  the Congo .............. 54 B1    0 47N  24 24 E
Yangcheng, China ......... 34 G7   35 28N 112 22 E
Yangch'ü = Taiyuan, China . 34 F7   37 52N 112 33 E
Yanggao, China ........... 34 D7   40 21N 113 55 E
Yanggu, China ............ 34 F8   36  8N 115 43 E
Yangliuqing, China ........ 35 E9   39  2N 117  5 E
Yangon = Rangoon, Burma . 41 L20  16 45N  96 20 E
Yangpingguan, China ...... 34 H4   32 58N 106  5 E
Yangquan, China .......... 34 F7   37 58N 113 31 E
Yangtse = Chang Jiang →,
  China ................. 33 C7   31 48N 121 10 E
Yangtze Kiang = Chang Jiang →,
  China ................. 33 C7   31 48N 121 10 E
Yangyang, S. Korea ........ 35 E15  38  4N 128 38 E
Yangyuan, China .......... 34 D8   40  1N 114 10 E
Yangzhou, China .......... 33 C6   32 21N 119 26 E
Yanji, China ............. 35 C15  42 59N 129 30 E
Yankton, U.S.A. .......... 80 D6   42 53N  97 23W
Yanonge, Dem. Rep. of
  the Congo .............. 54 B1    0 35N  24 38 E
Yanqi, China ............. 32 B3   42  5N  86 35 E
Yanqing, China ........... 34 D8   40 30N 115 58 E
Yanshan, China ........... 35 E9   38  4N 117 22 E

Yanshou, China ........... 35 B15  45 28N 128 22 E
Yantabulla, Australia ....... 63 D4   29 21S 145  0 E
Yantai, China ............ 35 F11  37 34N 121 22 E
Yantian, China ........... 33 F11  22 35N 114 16 E
Yanzhou, China ........... 34 G9   35 35N 116 49 E
Yao Noi, Ko, Thailand ..... 39 a     8  7N  98 37 E
Yao Xian, China .......... 34 G5   34 55N 108 59 E
Yao Yai, Ko, Thailand ..... 39 a     8  0N  98 35 E
Yaoundé, Cameroon ....... 52 D2    3 50N  11 35 E
Yaowan, China ........... 35 G10  34 15N 118  3 E
Yap, Pac. Oc. ............ 64 G5    9 30N 138 10 E
Yapen, Indonesia ......... 37 E9    1 50S 136  0 E
Yapen, Selat, Indonesia .... 37 E9    1 20S 136 10 E
Yapero, Indonesia ........ 37 E9    4 59S 137 11 E
Yappar →, Australia ....... 62 B3   18 22S 141 16 E
Yaqui →, Mexico .......... 86 B2   27 37N 110 39W
Yar-Sale, Russia .......... 28 C8   66 50N  70 50 E
Yaraka, Australia ......... 62 C3   24 53S 144  3 E
Yaransk, Russia ........... 18 C8   57 22N  47 49 E
Yare →, U.K. ............. 13 E9   52 35N   1 38 E
Yaremcha, Ukraine ........ 17 D13  48 27N  24 33 E
Yarensk, Russia .......... 18 B8   62 11N  49 15 E
Yari →, Colombia ......... 92 D4   0 20S  72 20W
Yarkand = Shache, China .. 32 C2   38 20N  77 10 E
Yarker, Canada ........... 85 B8   44 23N  76 46W
Yarkhun →, Pakistan ...... 43 A5   36 17N  72 30 E
Yarlung Ziangbo Jiang =
  Brahmaputra →, Asia ... 43 J13  23 40N  90 35 E
Yarmouth, Canada ........ 73 D6   43 50N  66  7W
Yarmūk →, Syria ......... 46 C4   32 42N  35 40 E
Yaroslavl, Russia ......... 18 C6   57 35N  39 55 E
Yarqa, W. →, Egypt ....... 46 F2   30  0N 33 49 E
Yarra Yarra Lakes, Australia 61 E2  29 40S 115 45 E
Yarram, Australia ......... 63 F4   38 29S 146 39 E
Yarraman, Australia ....... 63 D5   26 50S 152  0 E
Yarras, Australia ......... 63 E5   31 25S 152 20 E
Yartsevo, Russia ......... 29 C10  60 20N  90  0 E
Yarumal, Colombia ........ 92 B3    6 58N  75 24W
Yasawa Group, Fiji ........ 59 C7   17  0S 177 23 E
Yaselda, Belarus .......... 17 B14  52  7N  26 28 E
Yasin, Pakistan ........... 43 A5   36 24N  73 23 E
Yasinski, L., Canada ....... 72 B4   53 16N  77 35W
Yasinya, Ukraine .......... 17 D13  48 16N  24 21 E
Yasothon, Thailand ....... 38 E5   15 50N 104 10 E
Yass, Australia ........... 63 E4   34 49S 148 54 E
Yāsūj, Iran .............. 45 D6   30 31N  51 31 E
Yatağan, Turkey .......... 23 F13  37 20N  28 10 E
Yates Center, U.S.A. ...... 81 G7   37 53N  95 44W
Yathkyed L., Canada ...... 71 A9   62 40N  98  0W
Yatsushiro, Japan ......... 31 H5   32 30N 130 40 E
Yatta Plateau, Kenya ...... 54 C4    2  0S  38  0 E
Yauco, Puerto Rico ....... 89 d   18  2N  66 51W
Yavari →, Peru ........... 92 D4    4 21S  70  2W
Yávaros, Mexico .......... 86 B3   26 42N 109 31W
Yavatmal, India .......... 40 J11  20 20N  78 15 E
Yavne, Israel ............. 46 D3   31 52N  34 45 E
Yavoriv, Ukraine ......... 17 D12  49 55N  23 20 E
Yavorov = Yavoriv, Ukraine  17 D12  49 55N  23 20 E
Yawatahama, Japan ....... 31 H6   33 27N 132 24 E
Yazd, Iran ............... 45 D7   31 55N  54 27 E
Yazd □, Iran ............. 45 D7   32  0N  55  0 E
Yazd-e Khvāst, Iran ....... 45 D7   31 31N  52  7 E
Yazman, Pakistan ......... 42 E4   29  8N  71 45 E
Yazoo →, U.S.A. .......... 81 J9   32 22N  90 54W
Yazoo City, U.S.A. ........ 81 J9   32 51N  90 25W
Ybycuí △, Paraguay ....... 94 B4   26  5S  56 46W
Ybytyruzú △, Paraguay ..... 95 B4   25 51S  56 11W
Yding Skovhøj, Denmark ... 9 J13   55 59N   9 46 E
Ye, Burma ............... 38 E1   15 15N  97 51 E
Ye Xian, China ........... 34 H7   33 35N 113 25 E
Yebyu, Burma ............ 38 E2   14 15N  98 13 E
Yechŏn, S. Korea ......... 35 F15  36 39N 128 27 E
Yecla, Spain ............. 21 C5   38 35N   1  5W
Yécora, Mexico ........... 86 B3   28 20N 108 58W
Yedintsy = Edineţ, Moldova  17 D14  48  9N  27 18 E
Yegros, Paraguay ......... 94 B4   26 20S  56 25W
Yehbuah, Indonesia ....... 37 J17   8 23S 114 45 E
Yehuda, Midbar, Israel .... 46 D4   31 35N  35 15 E
Yei, Sudan .............. 51 H12   4 9N  30 40 E
Yekaterinburg, Russia ..... 28 D7   56 50N  60 30 E
Yelarbon, Australia ....... 63 D5   28 33S 150 38 E
Yelets, Russia ........... 18 D6   52 40N  38 30 E
Yelizavetgrad = Kirovohrad,
  Ukraine ................ 19 E5   48 35N  32 20 E
Yell, U.K. ............... 11 A7   60 35N   1  5W
Yell Sd., U.K. ............ 11 A7   60 33N   1 15W
Yellow Sea, China ........ 35 G12  35  0N 123  0 E
Yellowhead Pass, Canada .. 70 C5   52 53N 118 25W
Yellowknife, Canada ...... 70 A6   62 27N 114 29W
Yellowknife →, Canada .... 70 A6   62 31N 114 19W
Yellowstone △, U.S.A. ..... 76 D9   44 40N 110 30W
Yellowstone →, U.S.A. ..... 80 B3   47 59N 103 59W
Yellowstone L., U.S.A. ..... 76 D8   44 27N 110 22W
Yelsk, Belarus ........... 17 C15  51 50N  29 10 E
Yemen ■, Asia ........... 47 E3   15  0N  44  0 E
Yen Bai, Vietnam ......... 38 B5   21 42N 104 52 E
Yenangyaung, Burma ...... 41 J19  20 30N  95  0 E
Yenbo = Yanbu 'al Baḥr,
  Si. Arabia .............. 44 F3   24  0N  38  5 E
Yenda, Australia ......... 63 E4   34 13S 146 14 E
Yenice, Turkey ........... 23 E12  39 27N  27 17 E
Yenisey →, Russia ........ 28 B9   71 50N  82 40 E
Yeniseysk, Russia ........ 29 D10  58 27N  92 13 E
Yeniseyskiy Zaliv, Russia .. 28 B9   72 20N  81  0 E
Yennádhi, Greece ......... 25 C9   36  2N  27 56 E
Yenyuka, Russia .......... 29 D13  57 57N 121 15 E
Yeo →, U.K. ............. 13 G5   51  2N   2 49W
Yeo, L., Australia ......... 61 E3   28  0S 124 30 E
Yeo I., Canada ........... 84 A3   45 24N  81 48W
Yeola, India ............. 40 J9   20  2N  74 30 E
Yeoryioúpolis, Greece ..... 25 D6   35 20N  24 15 E
Yeovil, U.K. ............. 13 G5   50 57N   2 38W
Yeppoon, Australia ....... 62 C5   23  5S 150 47 E
Yerbent, Turkmenistan .... 28 F6   39 30N  58 50 E
Yerbogachen, Russia ...... 29 C11  61 16N 108  0 E
Yerevan, Armenia ........ 19 F7   40 10N  44 31 E
Yerington, U.S.A. ........ 76 G4   38 59N 119 10W
Yermak, Kazakhstan ...... 28 D8   52  2N  76 55 E
Yermo, U.S.A. ........... 79 L10  34 54N 116 50W
Yerólakkos, Cyprus ....... 25 D12  35 11N  33 15 E
Yeropol, Russia .......... 29 C17  65 15N 168 40 E
Yeropótamos →, Greece ... 25 D6   35  3N  24 50 E
Yeroskipos, Cyprus ....... 25 E11  34 46N  32 28 E
Yershov, Russia .......... 19 D8   51 23N  48 27 E
Yerushalayim = Jerusalem, Israel 46 D4  31 47N  35 10 E
Yesan, S. Korea .......... 35 F14  36 41N 126 51 E
Yeso, U.S.A. ............. 81 H2   34 26N 104 37W
Yessey, Russia ........... 29 C11  68 29N 102 10 E

Yetman, Australia .......... 63 D5 28 56S 150 48 E
Yeu, Î. d', France ........ 20 C2 46 42N 2 20W
Yevpatoriya, Ukraine ...... 19 E5 45 15N 33 20 E
Yeysk, Russia ............. 19 E6 46 40N 38 12 E
Yezd = Yazd, Iran ......... 45 D7 31 55N 54 27 E
Yhati, Paraguay ........... 94 B4 25 45S 56 35W
Yhú, Paraguay ............. 95 B4 25 0S 56 0W
Yi →, Uruguay ............. 94 C4 33 7S 57 8W
Yi 'Allaq, G., Egypt ...... 46 E2 30 22N 33 32 E
Yi He →, China ............ 35 G10 34 10N 118 8 E
Yi Xian, Hebei, China ..... 34 E8 39 20N 115 30 E
Yi Xian, Liaoning, China .. 35 D11 41 30N 121 22 E
Yialiás →, Cyprus ......... 25 D12 35 9N 33 44 E
Yialousa, Cyprus .......... 25 D13 35 32N 34 10 E
Yianisádhes, Greece ....... 25 D8 35 20N 26 10 E
Yiannitsa, Greece ......... 23 D10 40 46N 22 24 E
Yibin, China .............. 32 D5 28 45N 104 32 E
Yichang, China ............ 33 C6 30 40N 111 20 E
Yicheng, China ............ 34 G5 35 42N 111 40 E
Yichuan, China ............ 34 F6 36 2N 110 10 E
Yichun, China ............. 33 D7 47 44N 128 52 E
Yidu, China ............... 35 F10 36 43N 118 28 E
Yijun, China .............. 34 G5 35 28N 109 8 E
Yıldız Dağları, Turkey .... 23 D12 41 48N 27 36 E
Yilehuli Shan, China ...... 33 A7 51 20N 124 20 E
Yimianpo, China ........... 35 B15 45 7N 128 2 E
Yinchuan, China ........... 34 E4 38 30N 106 15 E
Yindarlgooda, L., Australia .. 61 F3 30 40S 121 52 E
Ying He →, China .......... 34 H9 32 30N 116 30 E
Ying Xian, China .......... 34 E7 39 32N 113 10 E
Yingkou, China ............ 35 D12 40 37N 122 18 E
Yining, China ............. 28 E9 43 58N 81 10 E
Yinmabin, Burma ........... 41 H19 22 10N 94 55 E
Yiofiros →, Greece ........ 25 D7 35 20N 25 6 E
Yirga Alem, Ethiopia ...... 47 F2 6 48N 38 22 E
Yirrkala, Australia ....... 62 A2 12 14S 136 56 E
Yishan, China ............. 32 D5 24 28N 108 38 E
Yishui, China ............. 35 G10 35 47N 118 30 E
Yishun, Singapore ......... 39 d 1 26N 103 50 E
Yithion, Greece ........... 23 F10 36 46N 22 34 E
Yitong, China ............. 35 C13 43 13N 125 20 E
Yiyang, Henan, China ...... 34 G7 34 27N 112 10 E
Yiyang, Hunan, China ...... 33 D6 28 35N 112 18 E
Yli-Kitka, Finland ........ 8 C23 66 8N 28 30 E
Ylitornio, Finland ........ 8 C20 66 19N 23 39 E
Ylivieska, Finland ........ 8 D21 64 4N 24 28 E
Yoakum, U.S.A. ............ 81 L6 29 17N 97 9W
Yog Pt., Phil. ............ 37 B6 14 6N 124 12 E
Yogyakarta, Indonesia ..... 36 F4 7 49S 110 22 E
Yogyakarta □, Indonesia ... 37 G14 7 48S 110 22 E
Yoho △, Canada ............ 70 C5 51 25N 116 30W
Yôju, S. Korea ............ 35 F14 37 20N 127 35 E
Yok Don △, Vietnam ........ 38 F6 12 50N 107 40 E
Yokadouma, Cameroon ....... 52 D2 3 26N 14 55 E
Yokkaichi, Japan .......... 31 G8 34 55N 136 38 E
Yoko, Cameroon ............ 52 C2 5 32N 12 20 E
Yokohama, Japan ........... 31 G9 35 27N 139 28 E
Yokosuka, Japan ........... 31 G9 35 20N 139 40 E
Yokote, Japan ............. 30 E10 39 20N 140 30 E
Yola, Nigeria ............. 51 G8 9 10N 12 29 E
Yolaina, Cordillera de, Nic. .. 88 D3 11 30N 84 0W
Yoloten, Turkmenistan ..... 45 B9 37 18N 62 21 E
Yom →, Thailand ........... 36 A2 15 35N 100 1 E
Yonago, Japan ............. 31 G6 35 25N 133 19 E
Yonaguni-Jima, Japan ...... 31 M1 24 27N 123 0 E
Yōnan, N. Korea ........... 35 F14 37 55N 126 11 E
Yonezawa, Japan ........... 30 F10 37 57N 140 4 E
Yong Peng, Malaysia ....... 39 L4 2 0N 103 3 E
Yong Sata, Thailand ....... 39 J2 7 8N 99 41 E
Yongamp'o, N. Korea ....... 35 E13 39 56N 124 23 E
Yongcheng, China .......... 34 H9 33 55N 116 20 E
Yŏngch'ŏn, S. Korea ....... 35 G15 35 58N 128 56 E
Yongding, China ........... 34 F2 36 38N 103 25 E
Yŏngdŏk, S. Korea ......... 35 F15 36 24N 129 22 E
Yŏngdŭngpo, S. Korea ...... 35 F14 37 31N 126 54 E
Yonghe, China ............. 34 F6 36 46N 110 38 E
Yŏnghŭng, N. Korea ........ 35 E14 39 31N 127 18 E
Yongji, China ............. 34 G6 34 52N 110 28 E
Yŏngju, S. Korea .......... 35 F15 36 50N 128 40 E
Yongnian, China ........... 34 F8 36 47N 114 29 E
Yongning, China ........... 34 E4 38 15N 106 14 E
Yongqing, China ........... 34 E9 39 25N 116 28 E
Yŏngwŏl, S. Korea ......... 35 F15 37 11N 128 28 E
Yonibana, S. Leone ........ 50 G3 8 30N 12 19W
Yonkers, U.S.A. ........... 85 F11 40 56N 73 54W
Yonne →, France ........... 20 B5 48 23N 2 58 E
York, Australia ........... 61 F2 31 52S 116 47 E
York, U.K. ................ 12 D6 53 58N 1 6W
York, Ala., U.S.A. ........ 81 J10 32 29N 88 18W
York, Nebr., U.S.A. ....... 80 E6 40 52N 97 36W
York, Pa., U.S.A. ......... 82 F7 39 58N 76 44W
York, C., Australia ....... 62 A3 10 42S 142 31 E
York, City of □, U.K. ..... 12 D6 53 58N 1 6W
York, Kap, Greenland ...... 4 B4 75 55N 66 25W
York, Vale of, U.K. ....... 12 C6 54 15N 1 25W
York Haven, U.S.A. ........ 84 F8 40 7N 76 46W
York Sd., Australia ....... 60 C4 15 0S 125 5 E
Yorke Pen., Australia ..... 63 E2 34 50S 137 40 E
Yorkshire Dales △, U.K. ... 12 C5 54 12N 2 10W
Yorkshire Wolds, U.K. ..... 12 C7 54 8N 0 31W
Yorkton, Canada ........... 71 C8 51 11N 102 28W
Yorkville, U.S.A. ......... 78 G3 38 52N 123 13W
Yoro, Honduras ............ 88 C2 15 9N 87 7W
Yoron-Jima, Japan ......... 31 L4 27 2N 128 26 E
Yos Sudarso, Pulau = Dolak,
  Pulau, Indonesia ........ 37 F9 8 0S 138 30 E
Yosemite, U.S.A. .......... 78 H7 37 45N 119 40W
Yosemite Village, U.S.A. .. 78 H7 37 45N 119 35W
Yoshino-Kumano △, Japan ... 31 H8 34 12N 135 55 E
Yoshkar Ola, Russia ....... 18 C8 56 38N 47 55 E
Yŏsu, S. Korea ............ 35 G14 34 47N 127 45 E
Yotvata, Israel ........... 46 F4 29 55N 35 2 E
Youbou, Canada ............ 78 B2 48 53N 124 13W
Youghal, Ireland .......... 10 E4 51 56N 7 52W
Youghal B., Ireland ....... 10 E4 51 55N 7 49W
Young, Australia .......... 63 E4 34 19S 148 18 E
Young, Canada ............. 71 C7 51 47N 105 45W
Young, Uruguay ............ 94 C4 32 44S 57 36W
Younghusband, L., Australia .. 63 E2 30 50S 136 5 E
Younghusband Pen., Australia .. 63 F2 36 0S 139 25 E
Youngstown, Canada ........ 71 C6 51 35N 111 10W
Youngstown, N.Y., U.S.A. .. 84 C5 43 15N 79 3W
Youngstown, Ohio, U.S.A. .. 84 E4 41 6N 80 39W
Youngsville, U.S.A. ....... 84 E5 41 51N 79 19W
Youngwood, U.S.A. ......... 84 F5 40 14N 79 34W
Youyu, China .............. 34 D7 40 10N 112 20 E
Yozgat, Turkey ............ 19 G5 39 51N 34 47 E
Ypacaraí △, Paraguay ...... 94 B4 25 18S 57 19W

Ypané →, Paraguay ......... 94 A4 23 29S 57 19W
Ypres = Ieper, Belgium .... 15 D2 50 51N 2 53 E
Yreka, U.S.A. ............. 76 F2 41 44N 122 38W
Ystad, Sweden ............. 9 J15 55 26N 13 50 E
Ysyk-Köl, Kyrgyzstan ...... 28 E8 42 25N 77 15 E
Ythan →, U.K. ............. 11 D7 57 19N 1 59W
Ytyk-Kyuyel, Russia ....... 29 C14 62 30N 133 45 E
Yu Jiang →, China ......... 33 D6 23 22N 110 3 E
Yu Xian = Yuzhou, China ... 34 G7 34 10N 113 28 E
Yu Xian, Hebei, China ..... 34 E8 39 50N 114 35 E
Yu Xian, Shanxi, China .... 34 E7 38 5N 113 20 E
Yuan Jiang →, China ....... 33 D6 28 55N 111 50 E
Yuanqu, China ............. 34 G6 35 18N 111 40 E
Yuanyang, China ........... 34 G7 35 3N 113 58 E
Yuba →, U.S.A. ............ 78 F5 39 8N 121 36W
Yuba City, U.S.A. ......... 78 F5 39 8N 121 37W
Yūbari, Japan ............. 30 C10 43 4N 141 59 E
Yūbetsu, Japan ............ 30 B11 44 13N 143 50 E
Yucatán □, Mexico ......... 87 C7 21 30N 86 30W
Yucatán, Canal de, Caribbean .. 88 B2 22 0N 86 30W
Yucatán, Península de, Mexico .. 66 H11 19 30N 89 0W
Yucatan Basin, Cent. Amer. .. 66 H11 19 0N 86 0W
Yucatan Channel = Yucatán,
  Canal de, Caribbean ..... 88 B2 22 0N 86 30W
Yucca, U.S.A. ............. 79 L12 34 52N 114 9W
Yucca Valley, U.S.A. ...... 79 L10 34 8N 116 27W
Yucheng, China ............ 34 F9 36 55N 116 32 E
Yuci, China ............... 34 F7 37 42N 112 46 E
Yuen Long, China .......... 33 G11 22 26N 114 2 E
Yuendumu, Australia ....... 60 D5 22 16S 131 49 E
Yugoslavia = Serbia &
  Montenegro ■, Europe .... 23 B9 43 20N 20 0 E
Yukon →, U.S.A. ........... 68 B3 62 32N 163 54W
Yukon Territory □, Canada . 68 B6 63 0N 135 0W
Yukta, Russia ............. 29 C11 63 26N 105 42 E
Yukuhashi, Japan .......... 31 H5 33 44N 130 59 E
Yulara, Australia ......... 61 E5 25 10S 130 55 E
Yule →, Australia ......... 60 D2 20 41S 118 17 E
Yuleba, Australia ......... 63 D4 26 37S 149 24 E
Yülin, Hainan, China ...... 39 C7 18 10N 109 31 E
Yulin, Shaanxi, China ..... 34 E5 38 20N 109 30 E
Yuma, Ariz., U.S.A. ....... 79 N12 32 43N 114 37W
Yuma, Colo., U.S.A. ....... 80 E3 40 8N 102 43W
Yuma, B. de, Dom. Rep. .... 89 C6 18 20N 68 35W
Yumbe, Uganda ............. 54 B3 3 28N 31 15 E
Yumbi, Dem. Rep. of the Congo .. 54 C2 1 12S 26 15 E
Yumen, China .............. 32 C4 39 50N 97 30 E
Yun Ho →, China ........... 35 E9 39 10N 117 10 E
Yuna, Australia ........... 61 E2 28 20S 115 0 E
Yuncheng, Henan, China .... 34 G8 35 36N 115 57 E
Yuncheng, Shanxi, China ... 34 G6 35 2N 111 0 E
Yungas, Bolivia ........... 92 G5 17 0S 66 0W
Yungay, Chile ............. 94 D1 37 10S 72 5W
Yunnan □, China ........... 32 D5 25 0N 102 0 E
Yunta, Australia .......... 63 E2 32 34S 139 36 E
Yunxi, China .............. 34 H6 33 0N 110 22 E
Yupyongdong, N. Korea ..... 35 D15 41 49N 128 53 E
Yuraygir △, Australia ..... 63 D5 29 45S 153 15 E
Yurga, Russia ............. 28 D9 55 42N 84 51 E
Yurimaguas, Peru .......... 92 E3 5 55S 76 7W
Yurubí △, Venezuela ....... 89 D6 10 26N 68 42W
Yuscarán, Honduras ........ 88 D2 13 58N 86 45W
Yushe, China .............. 34 F7 37 4N 112 58 E
Yushu, Jilin, China ....... 35 B14 44 43N 126 38 E
Yushu, Qinghai, China ..... 32 C4 33 5N 96 55 E
Yutai, China .............. 34 G9 35 0N 116 45 E
Yutian, China ............. 35 E9 39 53N 117 45 E
Yuxarı Qarabağ = Nagorno-
  Karabakh □, Azerbaijan .. 19 F8 39 55N 46 45 E
Yuxi, China ............... 32 D5 24 30N 102 35 E
Yuzawa, Japan ............. 30 E10 39 10N 140 30 E
Yuzhno-Sakhalinsk, Russia . 29 E15 46 58N 142 45 E
Yuzhnyy □, Russia ......... 28 E5 44 0N 40 0 E
Yuzhou, China ............. 34 G7 34 10N 113 28 E
Yvetot, France ............ 20 B4 49 37N 0 44 E

Z

Zaanstad, Neths. .......... 15 B4 52 27N 4 50 E
Zāb al Kabīr →, Iraq ...... 44 C4 36 1N 43 24 E
Zāb aş Şaghīr →, Iraq ..... 44 C4 35 17N 43 29 E
Zabaykalsk, Russia ........ 29 E12 49 40N 117 25 E
Zābol, Iran ............... 45 D9 31 0N 61 32 E
Zābol □, Afghan. .......... 40 D5 32 0N 67 0 E
Zābolī, Iran .............. 45 E9 27 10N 61 35 E
Zabrze, Poland ............ 17 C10 50 18N 18 50 E
Zacapa, Guatemala ......... 88 D2 14 59N 89 31W
Zacapu, Mexico ............ 86 D4 19 50N 101 43W
Zacatecas, Mexico ......... 86 C4 22 49N 102 34W
Zacatecas □, Mexico ....... 86 C4 23 30N 103 0W
Zacatecoluca, El Salv. .... 88 D2 13 29N 88 51W
Zachary, U.S.A. ........... 81 K9 30 39N 91 9W
Zacoalco, Mexico .......... 86 C4 20 14N 103 33W
Zacualtipán, Mexico ....... 87 C5 20 39N 98 36W
Zadar, Croatia ............ 16 F8 44 8N 15 14 E
Zadetkyi Kyun, Burma ...... 39 G2 10 0N 98 25 E
Zafarqand, Iran ........... 45 C7 33 11N 52 29 E
Zafra, Spain .............. 21 C2 38 26N 6 30W
Żagań, Poland ............. 16 C8 51 39N 15 22 E
Zagaoua, Chad ............. 51 E10 15 30N 22 24 E
Zagazig, Egypt ............ 51 B12 30 40N 31 30 E
Zāgheh, Iran .............. 45 C6 33 30N 48 42 E
Zagreb, Croatia ........... 16 F9 45 50N 15 58 E
Zagros, Kūhhā-ye, Iran .... 45 C6 33 45N 48 5 E
Zagros Mts. = Zāgros, Kūhhā-ye,
  Iran .................... 45 C6 33 45N 48 5 E
Zahamena, Madag. .......... 57 B8 17 37S 48 49 E
Zāhedān, Fārs, Iran ....... 45 D7 28 46N 53 52 E
Zāhedān, Sīstān va Balūchestān,
  Iran .................... 45 D9 29 30N 60 50 E
Zahlah, Lebanon ........... 46 B4 33 52N 35 50 E
Zaïre = Congo →, Africa ... 52 F2 6 4S 12 24 E
Zaječar, Serbia & M. ...... 23 C10 43 53N 22 18 E
Zaka, Zimbabwe ............ 57 C5 20 20S 31 29 E
Zakamensk, Russia ......... 29 D11 50 23N 103 17 E
Zakhodnaya Dzvina =
  Daugava →, Latvia ....... 9 H21 57 4N 24 3 E
Zākhū, Iraq ............... 44 B4 37 10N 42 50 E
Zákinthos, Greece ......... 23 F9 37 47N 20 54 E
Zakopane, Poland .......... 17 D10 49 18N 19 57 E
Zákros, Greece ............ 25 D8 35 6N 26 10 E
Zalaegerszeg, Hungary ..... 17 E9 46 53N 16 47 E
Zalău, Romania ............ 17 E12 47 12N 23 3 E
Zaleshchiki = Zalishchyky,
  Ukraine ................. 17 D13 48 45N 25 45 E
Zalew Wiślany, Poland ..... 17 A10 54 20N 19 50 E

Zalingei, Sudan ........... 51 F10 12 51N 23 29 E
Zalishchyky, Ukraine ...... 17 D13 48 45N 25 45 E
Zama L., Canada ........... 70 B5 58 45N 119 5W
Zambeke, Dem. Rep. of
  the Congo ............... 54 B2 2 8N 25 17 E
Zambeze →, Africa ......... 55 F4 18 35S 36 20 E
Zambezi = Zambeze →, Africa .. 55 F4 18 35S 36 20 E
Zambezi, Zambia ........... 53 G4 13 30S 23 15 E
Zambezi □, Zimbabwe ....... 55 F2 17 54S 25 41 E
Zambezia □, Mozam. ........ 55 F4 16 15S 37 30 E
Zambia ■, Africa .......... 55 F2 15 0S 28 0 E
Zamboanga, Phil. .......... 37 C6 6 59N 122 3 E
Zamora, Mexico ............ 86 D4 20 0N 102 21W
Zamora, Spain ............. 21 B3 41 30N 5 45W
Zamość, Poland ............ 17 C12 50 43N 23 15 E
Zandvoort, Neths. ......... 15 B4 52 22N 4 32 E
Zanesville, U.S.A. ........ 84 G2 39 56N 82 1W
Zangābād, Iran ............ 44 B5 38 26N 46 44 E
Zangue →, Mozam. .......... 55 F4 17 50S 35 21 E
Zanjān, Iran .............. 45 B6 36 40N 48 35 E
Zanjān □, Iran ............ 45 B6 37 20N 49 30 E
Zanjān →, Iran ............ 45 B6 37 8N 47 47 E
Zante = Zákinthos, Greece . 23 F9 37 47N 20 54 E
Zanthus, Australia ........ 61 F3 31 2S 123 34 E
Zanzibar, Tanzania ........ 54 D4 6 12S 39 12 E
Zaouiet El-Kala = Bordj Omar
  Driss, Algeria .......... 50 C7 28 10N 6 40 E
Zaouiet Reggâne, Algeria .. 50 C6 26 32N 0 3 E
Zaozhuang, China .......... 35 G9 34 50N 117 35 E
Zap Suyu = Zāb al Kabīr →, Iraq .. 44 C4 36 1N 43 24 E
Zapadnaya Dvina = Daugava →,
  Latvia .................. 9 H21 57 4N 24 3 E
Západné Beskydy, Europe ... 17 D10 49 30N 19 0 E
Zapala, Argentina ......... 96 D2 39 0S 70 5W
Zapaleri, Cerro, Bolivia .. 94 A2 22 49S 67 11W
Zapata, U.S.A. ............ 81 M5 26 55N 99 16W
Zapolyarnyy, Russia ....... 18 A5 69 26N 30 51 E
Zaporizhzhya, Ukraine ..... 19 E6 47 50N 35 10 E
Zaporozhye = Zaporizhzhya,
  Ukraine ................. 19 E6 47 50N 35 10 E
Zara, Turkey .............. 44 B3 39 58N 37 43 E
Zaragoza, Coahuila, Mexico .. 86 B4 28 30N 101 0W
Zaragoza, Nuevo León, Mexico .. 87 C5 24 0N 99 46W
Zaragoza, Spain ........... 21 B5 41 39N 0 53W
Zarand, Kermān, Iran ...... 45 D8 30 46N 56 34 E
Zarand, Markazī, Iran ..... 45 C6 35 18N 50 25 E
Zaranj, Afghan. ........... 40 D2 30 55N 61 55 E
Zarasai, Lithuania ........ 9 J22 55 40N 26 20 E
Zárate, Argentina ......... 94 C4 34 7S 59 0W
Zard, Kūh-e, Iran ......... 45 C6 32 22N 50 4 E
Zāreh, Iran ............... 45 C6 35 7N 49 9 E
Zaria, Nigeria ............ 50 F7 11 0N 7 40 E
Zarneh, Iran .............. 44 C5 33 55N 46 10 E
Zarós, Greece ............. 25 D6 35 8N 24 54 E
Zarqā', Nahr az →, Jordan . 46 C4 32 10N 35 37 E
Zarrīn, Iran .............. 45 C7 32 46N 54 37 E
Zaruma, Ecuador ........... 92 D3 3 40S 79 38W
Żary, Poland .............. 16 C8 51 37N 15 10 E
Zarzis, Tunisia ........... 51 B8 33 31N 11 2 E
Zaskar →, India ........... 43 B7 34 13N 77 20 E
Zaskar Mts., India ........ 43 C7 33 15N 77 30 E
Zastron, S. Africa ........ 56 E4 30 18S 27 7 E
Zavāreh, Iran ............. 45 C7 33 29N 52 28 E
Zave, Zimbabwe ............ 57 B5 17 6S 30 1 E
Zavitinsk, Russia ......... 29 D13 50 10N 129 20 E
Zavodovski, I., Antarctica .. 5 B1 56 0S 27 45W
Zawiercie, Poland ......... 17 C10 50 30N 19 24 E
Zāwiyat al Bayḍā = Al Bayḍā,
  Libya ................... 51 B10 32 50N 21 44 E
Zāyā, Iraq ................ 44 C5 33 33N 44 13 E
Zāyandeh →, Iran .......... 45 C7 32 35N 52 0 E
Zayarsk, Russia ........... 29 D11 56 12N 102 55 E
Zaysan, Kazakhstan ........ 28 E9 47 28N 84 52 E
Zaysan, Oz., Kazakhstan ... 28 E9 48 0N 83 0 E
Zayü, China ............... 32 D4 28 48N 97 27 E
Zazafotsy, Madag. ......... 57 C8 21 11S 46 21 E
Zbarazh, Ukraine .......... 17 D13 49 43N 25 44 E
Zdolbuniv, Ukraine ........ 17 C14 50 30N 26 15 E
Zduńska Wola, Poland ...... 17 C10 51 37N 18 59 E
Zeballos, Canada .......... 70 D3 49 59N 126 50W
Zebediela, S. Africa ...... 57 C4 24 20S 29 17 E
Zeebrugge, Belgium ........ 15 C3 51 19N 3 12 E
Zeehan, Australia ......... 63 G4 41 52S 145 25 E
Zeeland □, Neths. ......... 15 C3 51 30N 3 50 E
Zeerust, S. Africa ........ 56 D4 25 31S 26 4 E
Zefat, Israel ............. 46 C4 32 58N 35 29 E
Zeil, Mt., Australia ...... 60 D5 23 30S 132 23 E
Zeila, Somali Rep. ........ 47 E3 11 21N 43 30 E
Zeist, Neths. ............. 15 B5 52 5N 5 15 E
Zeitz, Germany ............ 16 C7 51 2N 12 7 E
Zelenograd, Russia ........ 18 C6 56 1N 37 12 E
Zelenogradsk, Russia ...... 9 J19 54 53N 20 29 E
Zelienople, U.S.A. ........ 84 F4 40 48N 80 8W
Zémio, C.A.R. ............. 54 A2 5 2N 25 5 E
Zempoala, Mexico .......... 87 D5 19 22N 96 24W
Zemun, Serbia & M. ........ 23 B9 44 51N 20 25 E
Zenica, Bos.-H. ........... 23 B7 44 10N 17 57 E
Žepče, Bos.-H. ............ 23 B8 44 28N 18 2 E
Zevenaar, Neths. .......... 15 C6 51 56N 6 5 E
Zeya, Russia .............. 29 D13 53 48N 127 14 E
Zeya →, Russia ............ 29 D13 51 42N 128 53 E
Zêzere →, Portugal ........ 21 C1 39 28N 8 20W
Zghartā, Lebanon .......... 46 A4 34 21N 35 53 E
Zgorzelec, Poland ......... 16 C8 51 10N 15 0 E
Zhabinka, Belarus ......... 17 B13 52 13N 24 2 E
Zhailma, Kazakhstan ....... 28 D7 51 37N 61 33 E
Zhambyl = Taraz, Kazakhstan .. 28 E8 42 54N 71 22 E
Zhangagazaly, Kazakhstan .. 28 E7 45 48N 62 6 E
Zhangbei, China ........... 34 D8 41 10N 114 45 E
Zhangguangcai Ling, China . 35 B15 45 0N 129 0 E
Zhangjiabian, China ....... 33 F9 22 33N 113 28 E
Zhangjiakou, China ........ 34 D8 40 48N 114 55 E
Zhangwu, China ............ 35 C12 42 43N 123 52 E
Zhangye, China ............ 32 C5 38 50N 100 23 E
Zhangzhou, China .......... 33 D6 24 30N 117 35 E
Zhanhua, China ............ 35 F10 37 40N 118 8 E
Zhanjiang, China .......... 33 D6 21 15N 110 20 E
Zhannetty, Ostrov, Russia . 29 B16 76 43N 158 0 E
Zhanyi, China ............. 35 B12 44 30N 122 30 E
Zhao Xian, China .......... 34 F8 37 43N 114 45 E
Zhaocheng, China .......... 34 F6 36 22N 111 38 E
Zhaotong, China ........... 32 D5 27 20N 103 44 E
Zhaoyuan, Heilongjiang, China .. 35 B13 45 27N 125 0 E
Zhaoyuan, Shandong, China .. 35 F11 37 20N 120 23 E
Zhashkiv, Ukraine ......... 17 D16 49 15N 30 5 E
Zhashui, China ............ 34 H5 33 40N 109 8 E
Zhayyq →, Kazakhstan ...... 19 E9 47 0N 51 48 E
Zhdanov = Mariupol, Ukraine .. 19 E6 47 5N 37 31 E

Zhecheng, China ........... 34 G8 34 7N 115 20 E
Zhejiang □, China ......... 33 D7 29 0N 120 0 E
Zheleznodorozhnyy, Russia . 18 B9 62 35N 50 55 E
Zheleznogorsk-Ilimskiy, Russia .. 29 D11 56 34N 104 8 E
Zhen'an, China ............ 34 H5 33 27N 109 9 E
Zhengding, China .......... 34 E8 38 8N 114 42 E
Zhengzhou, China .......... 34 G7 34 45N 113 34 E
Zhenlai, China ............ 35 B12 45 50N 123 5 E
Zhenping, China ........... 34 G4 33 10N 112 16 E
Zhenyuan, China ........... 34 G4 35 35N 107 30 E
Zhetiqara, Kazakhstan ..... 28 D7 52 11N 61 12 E
Zhezqazghan, Kazakhstan ... 28 E7 47 44N 67 40 E
Zhidan, China ............. 34 F5 36 48N 108 48 E
Zhigansk, Russia .......... 29 C13 66 48N 123 27 E
Zhilinda, Russia .......... 29 C12 70 0N 114 20 E
Zhitomir = Zhytomyr, Ukraine .. 17 C15 50 20N 28 40 E
Zhlobin, Belarus .......... 17 B16 52 55N 30 0 E
Zhmerinka = Zhmerynka, Ukraine .. 17 D15 49 2N 28 2 E
Zhmerynka, Ukraine ........ 17 D15 49 2N 28 2 E
Zhob, Pakistan ............ 42 D3 31 20N 69 31 E
Zhob →, Pakistan .......... 42 C3 32 4N 69 50 E
Zhodino = Zhodzina, Belarus .. 17 A15 54 5N 28 17 E
Zhodzina, Belarus ......... 17 A15 54 5N 28 17 E
Zhokhova, Ostrov, Russia .. 29 B16 76 4N 152 40 E
Zhongdian, China .......... 32 D4 27 48N 99 42 E
Zhongning, China .......... 34 F3 37 29N 105 40 E
Zhongshan, Antarctica ..... 5 C6 69 0S 39 50 E
Zhongshan, China .......... 33 G9 22 26N 113 20 E
Zhongshankong, China ...... 33 F9 22 35N 113 29 E
Zhongtiao Shan, China ..... 34 G6 35 0N 111 10 E
Zhongwei, China ........... 34 F3 37 30N 105 12 E
Zhongyang, China .......... 34 F6 37 20N 111 11 E
Zhoucun, China ............ 35 F9 36 47N 117 48 E
Zhouzhi, China ............ 34 G5 34 10N 108 12 E
Zhuanghe, China ........... 35 E12 39 40N 123 0 E
Zhucheng, China ........... 35 G10 36 0N 119 27 E
Zhugqu, China ............. 34 H3 33 40N 104 30 E
Zhuhai, China ............. 33 G10 22 17N 113 34 E
Zhujiang Kou, China ....... 33 G10 22 20N 113 45 E
Zhumadian, China .......... 34 H8 32 59N 114 2 E
Zhuo Xian = Zhuozhou, China .. 34 E8 39 28N 115 58 E
Zhuolu, China ............. 34 D8 40 20N 115 12 E
Zhuozhou, China ........... 34 E8 39 28N 115 58 E
Zhuozi, China ............. 34 D7 41 0N 112 25 E
Zhytomyr, Ukraine ......... 17 C15 50 20N 28 40 E
Ziārān, Iran .............. 45 B6 36 7N 50 32 E
Ziarat, Pakistan .......... 42 D2 30 25N 67 49 E
Zibo, China ............... 35 F10 36 47N 118 3 E
Zichang, China ............ 34 F5 37 18N 109 40 E
Zidi = Wandhari, Pakistan . 42 F2 27 42N 66 48 E
Zielona Góra, Poland ...... 16 C8 51 57N 15 31 E
Zierikzee, Neths. ......... 15 C3 51 40N 3 55 E
Zigey, Chad ............... 51 F9 14 43N 15 50 E
Zigong, China ............. 32 D5 29 15N 104 48 E
Ziguinchor, Senegal ....... 50 F2 12 35N 16 20W
Zihuatanejo, Mexico ....... 86 D4 17 38N 101 33W
Žilina, Slovak Rep. ....... 17 D10 49 12N 18 42 E
Zillah, Libya ............. 51 C9 28 30N 17 33 E
Zima, Russia .............. 29 D11 54 0N 102 5 E
Zimapán, Mexico ........... 87 C5 20 54N 99 20W
Zimba, Zambia ............. 55 F2 17 20S 26 11 E
Zimbabwe, Zimbabwe ........ 55 G3 20 16S 30 54 E
Zimbabwe ■, Africa ........ 55 F3 19 0S 30 0 E
Zimnicea, Romania ......... 17 G13 43 40N 25 22 E
Zinave △, Mozam. .......... 57 C5 21 35S 33 40 E
Zinder, Niger ............. 50 F7 13 48N 9 0 E
Zinga, Tanzania ........... 55 D4 9 16S 38 49 E
Zion △, U.S.A. ............ 77 H7 37 15N 113 5W
Ziros, Greece ............. 25 D8 35 5N 26 8 E
Zirreh, Gowd-e, Afghan. ... 40 E3 29 45N 62 0 E
Zitácuaro, Mexico ......... 86 D4 19 28N 100 21W
Zitundo, Mozam. ........... 57 D5 26 48S 32 47 E
Ziwa Maghariba = Kagera □,
  Tanzania ................ 54 C3 2 0S 31 30 E
Ziway, L., Ethiopia ....... 47 F2 8 0N 38 50 E
Ziyang, China ............. 34 H5 32 32N 108 31 E
Zlatograd, Bulgaria ....... 23 D11 41 22N 25 7 E
Zlatoust, Russia .......... 18 C10 55 10N 59 40 E
Zlín, Czech Rep. .......... 17 D9 49 14N 17 40 E
Zmeinogorsk, Kazakhstan ... 28 D9 51 10N 82 13 E
Znojmo, Czech Rep. ........ 16 D9 48 50N 16 2 E
Zobeyrī, Iran ............. 44 C5 34 10N 46 40 E
Zobia, Dem. Rep. of the Congo .. 54 B2 3 0N 25 59 E
Zoetermeer, Neths. ........ 15 B4 52 3N 4 30 E
Zolochiv = Zolochiv, Ukraine .. 17 D13 49 45N 24 51 E
Zolochiv, Ukraine ......... 17 D13 49 45N 24 51 E
Zomba, Malawi ............. 55 F4 15 22S 35 19 E
Zongo, Dem. Rep. of the Congo .. 52 D3 4 20N 18 35 E
Zonguldak, Turkey ......... 19 F5 41 28N 31 50 E
Zonqor Pt., Malta ......... 25 D2 35 52N 14 34 E
Zorritos, Peru ............ 92 D2 3 43S 80 40W
Zou Xiang, China .......... 34 G9 35 30N 116 58 E
Zouar, Chad ............... 51 D9 20 30N 16 32 E
Zouérate = Zouîrât, Mauritania .. 50 D3 22 44N 12 21W
Zouîrât, Mauritania ....... 50 D3 22 44N 12 21W
Zoutkamp, Neths. .......... 15 A6 53 20N 6 18 E
Zrenjanin, Serbia & M. .... 23 B9 45 22N 20 23 E
Zufar, Oman ............... 47 D5 17 40N 54 0 E
Zug, Switz. ............... 20 C8 47 10N 8 31 E
Zugspitze, Germany ........ 16 E6 47 25N 10 59 E
Zuid-Holland □, Neths. .... 15 C4 52 0N 4 35 E
Zuidbeveland, Neths. ...... 15 C3 51 30N 3 50 E
Zuidhorn, Neths. .......... 15 A6 53 15N 6 23 E
Zula, Eritrea ............. 47 D2 15 17N 39 40 E
Zumbo, Mozam. ............. 55 F3 15 35S 30 26 E
Zumpango, Mexico .......... 87 D5 19 48N 99 6W
Zunhua, China ............. 35 D9 40 18N 117 58 E
Zuni, U.S.A. .............. 77 J9 35 4N 108 51W
Zunyi, China .............. 32 D5 27 42N 106 53 E
Zurbātīyah, Iraq .......... 44 C5 33 9N 46 3 E
Zürich, Switz. ............ 20 C8 47 22N 8 32 E
Zutphen, Neths. ........... 15 B6 52 9N 6 12 E
Zuurberg △, S. Africa ..... 56 E4 33 12S 25 32 E
Zuwārah, Libya ............ 51 B8 32 58N 12 1 E
Zūzan, Iran ............... 45 C8 34 22N 59 53 E
Zverinogolovskoye, Russia . 28 D7 54 26N 64 50 E
Zvishavane, Zimbabwe ...... 55 G3 20 17S 30 2 E
Zvolen, Slovak Rep. ....... 17 D10 48 33N 19 10 E
Zwelitsha, S. Africa ...... 53 L5 32 55S 27 22 E
Zwettl, Austria ........... 16 D8 48 35N 15 9 E
Zwickau, Germany .......... 16 C7 50 44N 12 30 E
Zwolle, Neths. ............ 15 B6 52 31N 6 6 E
Zwolle, U.S.A. ............ 81 K8 31 38N 93 39W
Żyrardów, Poland .......... 17 B11 52 3N 20 28 E
Zyryan, Kazakhstan ........ 28 E9 49 43N 84 20 E
Zyryanka, Russia .......... 29 C16 65 45N 150 51 E
Zyryanovsk = Zyryan, Kazakhstan .. 28 E9 49 43N 84 20 E
Żywiec, Poland ............ 17 D10 49 42N 19 10 E
Zyyi, Cyprus .............. 25 E12 34 43N 33 20 E

# World: Regions in the News

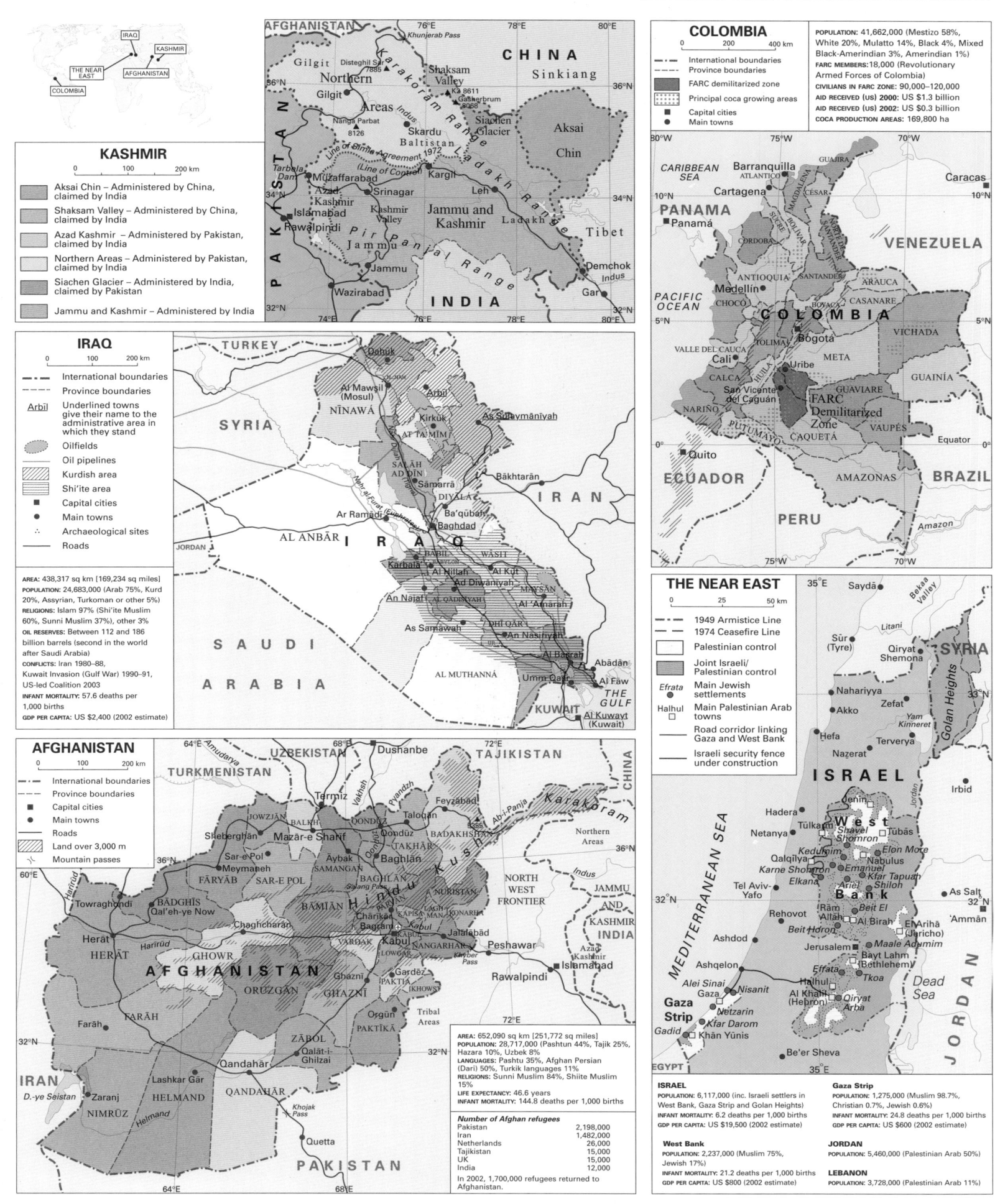

## KASHMIR

- Aksai Chin – Administered by China, claimed by India
- Shaksam Valley – Administered by China, claimed by India
- Azad Kashmir – Administered by Pakistan, claimed by India
- Northern Areas – Administered by Pakistan, claimed by India
- Siachen Glacier – Administered by India, claimed by Pakistan
- Jammu and Kashmir – Administered by India

## IRAQ

- International boundaries
- Province boundaries
- Arbīl  Underlined towns give their name to the administrative area in which they stand
- Oilfields
- Oil pipelines
- Kurdish area
- Shi'ite area
- Capital cities
- Main towns
- Archaeological sites
- Roads

AREA: 438,317 sq km [169,234 sq miles]
POPULATION: 24,683,000 (Arab 75%, Kurd 20%, Assyrian, Turkoman or other 5%)
RELIGIONS: Islam 97% (Shi'ite Muslim 60%, Sunni Muslim 37%), other 3%
OIL RESERVES: Between 112 and 186 billion barrels (second in the world after Saudi Arabia)
CONFLICTS: Iran 1980–88, Kuwait Invasion (Gulf War) 1990–91, US-led Coalition 2003
INFANT MORTALITY: 57.6 deaths per 1,000 births
GDP PER CAPITA: US $2,400 (2002 estimate)

## AFGHANISTAN

- International boundaries
- Province boundaries
- Capital cities
- Main towns
- Roads
- Land over 3,000 m
- Mountain passes

AREA: 652,090 sq km [251,772 sq miles]
POPULATION: 28,717,000 (Pashtun 44%, Tajik 25%, Hazara 10%, Uzbek 8%)
LANGUAGES: Pashtu 35%, Afghan Persian (Dari) 50%, Turkik languages 11%
RELIGIONS: Sunni Muslim 84%, Shiite Muslim 15%
LIFE EXPECTANCY: 46.6 years
INFANT MORTALITY: 144.8 deaths per 1,000 births

### Number of Afghan refugees

| | |
|---|---|
| Pakistan | 2,198,000 |
| Iran | 1,482,000 |
| Netherlands | 26,000 |
| Tajikistan | 15,000 |
| UK | 15,000 |
| India | 12,000 |

In 2002, 1,700,000 refugees returned to Afghanistan.

## COLOMBIA

- International boundaries
- Province boundaries
- FARC demilitarized zone
- Principal coca growing areas
- Capital cities
- Main towns

POPULATION: 41,662,000 (Mestizo 58%, White 20%, Mulatto 14%, Black 4%, Mixed Black-Amerindian 3%, Amerindian 1%)
FARC MEMBERS: 18,000 (Revolutionary Armed Forces of Colombia)
CIVILIANS IN FARC ZONE: 90,000–120,000
AID RECEIVED (US) 2000: US $1.3 billion
AID RECEIVED (US) 2002: US $0.3 billion
COCA PRODUCTION AREAS: 169,800 ha

## THE NEAR EAST

- 1949 Armistice Line
- 1974 Ceasefire Line
- Palestinian control
- Joint Israeli/Palestinian control
- Efrata  Main Jewish settlements
- Halhul  Main Palestinian Arab towns
- Road corridor linking Gaza and West Bank
- Israeli security fence under construction

### ISRAEL
POPULATION: 6,117,000 (inc. Israeli settlers in West Bank, Gaza Strip and Golan Heights)
INFANT MORTALITY: 6.2 deaths per 1,000 births
GDP PER CAPITA: US $19,500 (2002 estimate)

### West Bank
POPULATION: 2,237,000 (Muslim 75%, Jewish 17%)
INFANT MORTALITY: 21.2 deaths per 1,000 births
GDP PER CAPITA: US $800 (2002 estimate)

### Gaza Strip
POPULATION: 1,275,000 (Muslim 98.7%, Christian 0.7%, Jewish 0.6%)
INFANT MORTALITY: 24.8 deaths per 1,000 births
GDP PER CAPITA: US $600 (2002 estimate)

### JORDAN
POPULATION: 5,460,000 (Palestinian Arab 50%)

### LEBANON
POPULATION: 3,728,000 (Palestinian Arab 11%)

# KEY TO EUROPEAN MAP PAGES

 **Large scale maps**
(>1:2 500 000)

 **Medium scale maps**
(1:2 800 000 – 1:9 900 000)

 **Small scale maps**
(<1:10 000 000)

8

ICELAND

Arctic Circle

8

14

11

11

12

10

16

15

IRELAND

UNITED KINGDOM

N

20

B

21

FRANCE

ANDORRA

PORTUGAL

SPAIN

24

MOROCCO

ALG

# WORLD COUNTRY INDEX

| | | | | | |
|---|---|---|---|---|---|
| **A**fghanistan | 40 | Ghana | 50 | **P**akistan | 40, 42 |
| Albania | 23 | Greece | 23 | Panama | 88 |
| Algeria | 50 | Greenland | 4 | Papua New Guinea | 64 |
| Angola | 52–53 | Guadeloupe | 88 | Paraguay | 94–95 |
| Argentina | 94, 96 | Guatemala | 88 | Peru | 92 |
| Armenia | 19 | Guinea | 50 | Philippines | 37 |
| Australia | 60–63 | Guinea-Bissau | 50 | Poland | 16–17 |
| Austria | 16–17 | Guyana | 92 | Portugal | 21 |
| Azerbaijan | 19 | | | Puerto Rico | 89 |
| | | **H**aiti | 89 | | |
| **B**ahamas | 88–89 | Honduras | 88 | **Q**atar | 45 |
| Bahrain | 45 | Hungary | 17 | | |
| Bangladesh | 41 | | | **R**omania | 17 |
| Barbados | 89 | **I**celand | 8 | Russia | 18–19, 28–29 |
| Belarus | 17, 18–19 | India | 40–43 | Rwanda | 54 |
| Belgium | 15 | Indonesia | 36–37 | | |
| Belize | 88 | Iran | 44–45 | **S**t. Lucia | 89 |
| Benin | 50 | Iraq | 44–45 | Samoa | 59 |
| Bhutan | 41 | Irish Republic | 10 | Saudi Arabia | 44–45, 47 |
| Bolivia | 92 | Israel | 46 | Scotland | 11 |
| Bosnia-Herzegovina | 22–23 | Italy | 22–23 | Senegal | 50 |
| Botswana | 56 | Ivory Coast | 50 | Serbia and Montenegro | 23 |
| Brazil | 92–93, 95 | | | Sierra Leone | 50 |
| Brunei | 36 | **J**amaica | 88 | Singapore | 39 |
| Bulgaria | 23 | Japan | 30–31 | Slovak Republic | 17 |
| Burkina Faso | 50 | Jordan | 46 | Slovenia | 22 |
| Burma (Myanmar) | 41 | | | Solomon Is. | 64 |
| Burundi | 54 | **K**azakhstan | 28 | Somali Republic | 47 |
| | | Kenya | 54 | South Africa | 56–57 |
| **C**ambodia | 38–39 | Korea, North | 35 | Spain | 21 |
| Canary Is. | 24 | Korea, South | 35 | Sri Lanka | 40 |
| Cameroon | 52 | Kuwait | 44–45 | Sudan | 51 |
| Canada | 68–73 | Kyrgyzstan | 28 | Suriname | 92–93 |
| Central African Republic | 52 | | | Swaziland | 57 |
| Chad | 51 | **L**aos | 38 | Sweden | 8–9 |
| Chile | 94, 96–97 | Latvia | 9 | Switzerland | 16 |
| China | 32–35 | Lebanon | 46 | Syria | 44, 46 |
| Colombia | 92 | Lesotho | 57 | | |
| Congo | 52 | Liberia | 50 | **T**aiwan | 33 |
| Congo, Dem. Rep. | | Libya | 51 | Tajikistan | 28 |
| of the | 52–53, 54–55 | Lithuania | 9 | Tanzania | 54–55 |
| Costa Rica | 88 | Luxembourg | 15 | Thailand | 38–39 |
| Croatia | 22–23 | | | Togo | 50 |
| Cuba | 88–89 | **M**acedonia | 23 | Tonga | 59 |
| Cyprus | 25 | Madagascar | 57 | Trinidad and Tobago | 93 |
| Czech Republic | 16–17 | Malawi | 55 | Tunisia | 50–51 |
| | | Malaysia | 36–37, 39 | Turkey | 19 |
| **D**enmark | 9 | Mali | 50 | Turkmenistan | 28 |
| Djibouti | 47 | Malta | 25 | | |
| Dominican Republic | 89 | Martinique | 88 | **U**ganda | 54 |
| | | Mauritania | 50 | Ukraine | 18–19 |
| **E**cuador | 92 | Mexico | 86–87 | United Arab Emirates | 47 |
| Egypt | 51 | Moldova | 17 | United Kingdom | 10–13 |
| El Salvador | 88 | Mongolia | 32 | USA | 74–85 |
| England | 12–13 | Morocco | 50 | Uruguay | 94–95 |
| Equatorial Guinea | 52 | Mozambique | 55, 57 | Uzbekistan | 28 |
| Eritrea | 47 | | | | |
| Estonia | 9 | **N**amibia | 56 | **V**anuatu | 64 |
| Ethiopia | 47, 52 | Nepal | 43 | Venezuela | 92–93 |
| | | Netherlands | 15 | Vietnam | 38–39 |
| **F**iji | 59 | New Zealand | 59 | | |
| Finland | 8–9 | Nicaragua | 88 | **W**ales | 12–13 |
| France | 20–21 | Niger | 50–51 | | |
| French Guiana | 93 | Nigeria | 50–51 | **Y**emen | 47 |
| | | Northern Ireland | 10 | | |
| **G**abon | 52 | Norway | 8–9 | **Z**ambia | 55, 56–57 |
| Gambia | 50 | | | Zimbabwe | 55 |
| Georgia | 19 | **O**man | 47 | | |
| Germany | 16 | | | | |